Department of Economic and Social Affairs
Département des affaires économiques et sociales

2006
Demographic Yearbook
Annuaire démographique

Fifty-eighth issue/Cinquante-huitième édition

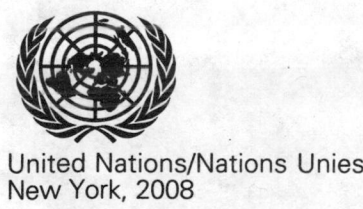

United Nations/Nations Unies
New York, 2008

The Department of Economic and Social Affairs of the United Nations Secretariat is a vital interface between global policies in the economic, social and environmental spheres and national action. The Department works in three main interlinked areas: (i) it compiles, generates and analyses a wide range of economic, social and environmental data and information on which States Members of the United Nations draw to review common problems and to take stock of policy options; (ii) it facilitates the negotiations of Member States in many intergovernmental bodies on joint courses of action to address ongoing or emerging global challenges; and (iii) it advises interested Governments on the ways and means of translating policy frameworks developed in United Nations conferences and summits into programmes at the country level and, through technical assistance, helps build national capacities.

Le Département des affaires économiques et sociales du Secrétariat de l'Organisation des Nations Unies sert de relais entre les orientations arrêtées au niveau international dans les domaines économiques, sociaux et environnementaux et les politiques exécutées à l'échelon national. Il intervient dans trois grands domaines liés les uns aux autres : i) il compile, produit et analyse une vaste gamme de données et d'éléments d'information sur des questions économiques, sociales et environnementales dont les États Membres de l'Organisation se servent pour examiner des problèmes communs et évaluer les options qui s'offrent à eux; ii) il facilite les négociations entre les États Membres dans de nombreux organes intergouvernementaux sur les orientations à suivre de façon collective afin de faire face aux problèmes mondiaux existants ou en voie d'apparition; iii) il conseille les gouvernements intéressés sur la façon de transposer les orientations politiques arrêtées à l'occasion des conférences et sommets des Nations Unies en programmes exécutables au niveau national et aide à renforcer les capacités nationales au moyen de programmes d'assistance technique.

NOTE

Symbols of United Nations documents are composed of capital letters combined with figures. Mention of such a symbol indicates reference to a United Nations document.

The designations employed and the presentation of material in this publication do not imply the expression of any opinion whatsoever on the part of the Secretariat of the United Nations concerning the legal status of any country, territory, city or area, or of its authorities, or concerning the delimitation of its frontiers or boundaries.

Where the designation "country or area" appears in the headings of tables, it covers countries, territories, cities or areas. In prior issues of this publication, where the designation "country" appears in the headings of tables, it should be interpreted to cover countries, territories, cities or areas.

NOTE

Les cotes des documents de l'Organisation des Nations Unies se composent de lettres majuscules et de chiffres. La simple mention d'une cote dans un texte signifie qu'il s'agit d'un document de l'Organisation.

Les appellations employées dans cette publication et la présentation des données qui y figurent n'impliquent de la part du Secrétariat de l'Organisation des Nations Unies aucune prise de position quant au statut juridique des pays, territoires, villes ou zones, ou de leurs autorités, ni quant au tracé de leurs frontières ou limites.

L'appellation "pays ou zone" figurant dans les titres des rubriques des tableaux désigne des pays, des territoires, des villes ou des zones. L'appellation "pays" figurant dans certaines rubriques des tableaux de numéros antérieurs de cette publication doit être interprétée comme désignant des pays, des territoires, des villes ou des zones.

ST/ESA/STAT/SER.R/37

UNITED NATIONS PUBLICATION
Sales number: E/F.09.XIII.1

PUBLICATION DES NATIONS UNIES
Numéro de vente: E/F.09.XIII.1

ISBN 978-92-1-051101-8
ISSN 0082-8041

Topics of the Demographic Yearbook series: 1948 - 2006

Sujets des diverses éditions de l'Annuaire démographique: 1948 - 2006

Year Année	Sales No. - Numéro de vente	Issue - Edition	Special topic - Sujet spécial
1948	49.XIII.1	First-Première	General demography-Démographie générale
1949-50	51.XIII.1	Second-Deuxième	Natality statistics-Statistiques de la natalité
1951	52.XIII.1	Third-Trosième	Mortality statistics-Statistiques de la mortalité
1952	53.XIII.1	Fourth-Quatrième	Population distribution-Répartition de la population
1953	54.XIII.1	Fifth-Cinquième	General demography-Démographie générale
1954	55.XIII.1	Sixth-Sixième	Natality statistics -Statistiques de la natalité
1955	56.XIII.1	Seventh-Septième	Population censuses-Recensement de population
1956	57.XIII.1	Eighth-Huitième	Ethnic and economic characteristics of population- Caractéristiques ethniques et économiques de la population
1957	58.XIII.1	Ninth-Neuvième	Mortality statistics- Statistiques de la mortalité
1958	59.XIII.1	Tenth-Dixième	Marriage and divorce statistics- Statistiques de la nuptialitè et de la divortialité
1959	60.XIII.1	Eleventh-Onzième	Natality statistics- Statistiques de la natalité
1960	61.XIII.1	Twelfth-Douzième	Population trends- l' évolution de la population
1961	62.XIII.1	Thirteenth-Treizième	Mortality Statistics- Statistiques de la mortalité
1962	63.XIII.1	Fourteenth-Quatorzième	Population census statistics I- Statistiques des recensements de population I
1963	64.XIII.1	Fifteenth-Quinzième	Population census statistics II- Statistiques des recensements de population II
1964	65.XIII.1	Sixteenth-Seizième	Population census statistics III- Statistiques des recensements de population III
1965	66.XIII.1	Seventeenth-Dix-septième	Natality statistics- Statistiques de la natalité
1966	67.XIII.1	Eighteenth-Dix-huitième	Mortality statistics I- Statistiques de la mortalité I
1967	E/F.68.XIII.1	Nineteenth-Dix-neuvième	Mortality statistics II - Statistiques de la mortalité II
1968	E/F.69.XIII.1	Twentieth-Vingtième	Marriage and divorce statistics-Statistiques de la nuptialité et de la divortialité
1969	E/F.70.XIII.1	Twenty-first-Vingt et unième	Natality statistics-Statistiques de la natalité
1970	E/F.71.XIII.1	Twenty-second-Vingt-deuxième	Population trends-l' évolution de la population
1971	E/F.72.XIII.1	Twenty-third-Vingh-troisième	Population census statistics I- Statistiques de recensements de population I
1972	E/F.73.XIII.1	Twenty-fourth-Vingt-quatrième	Population census statistics II- Statistiques des recensements de population II
1973	E/F.74.XIII.1	Twenty-fifth-Vingt-cinquième	Population census statistics III- Statistiques des recensements de population III
1974	E/F.75.XIII.1	Twenty-sixth-Vingt-sixième	Mortality statistics - Statistiques de la mortalité
1975	E/F.76.XIII.1	Twenty-seventh-Vingt-septième	Natality statistics- Statistiques de la natalité
1976	E/F.77.XIII.1	Twenty-eighth-Vingt-huitième	Marriage and divorce statistics- Statistiques de la nuptialité et de la divortialité
1977	E/F.78.XIII.1	Twenty-ninth-Vingt-neuvième	International Migration Statistics- internationales
1978	E/F.79.XIII.1	Thirtieth-Trentième	General tables- Tableaux de caractère général
1978	E/F.79.XIII.8	Special issue-Edition spéciale	Historical supplement-Supplément rétrospectif
1979	E/F.80.XIII.1	Thirty-first-Trente et unième	Population census statistics- Statistiques des recensements de population
1980	E/F.81.XIII.1	Thirty-second-Trente-deuxième	Mortality statistics- Statistiques de la mortalité
1981	E/F.82.XIII.1	Thirty-third-Trente-troisième	Natality statistics- Statistiques de la natalité
1982	E/F.83.XIII.1	Thirty-fourth-	Marriage and divorce statistics-

Topics of the Demographic Yearbook series: 1948 - 2006

Sujets des diverses éditions de l'Annuaire démographique: 1948 - 2006

Year Année	Sales No. - Numéro de vente	Issue - Edition	Special topic - Sujet spécial
		Trente-quatrième	Statistiques de la nuptialité et de la divortialité
1983	E/F.84.XIII.1	Thirty fifth- Trente-cinquième	Population census statistics I- Statistiques des recensements de population I
1984	E/F.85.XIII.1	Thirty-sixth- Trente-sixième	Population census statistics II- Statistiques des recensements de population II
1985	E/F.86.XIII.1	Thirty-seventh- Trente-septième	Mortality statistics- Statistiques de la mortalité
1986	E/F.87.XIII.1	Thirty-eightth- Trente-Hiutième	Natality statistics- Statistiques de la natalité
1987	E/F.88.XIII.1	Thirty-ninth- Trente-neuvième	Household composition- Les éléments du ménage
1988	E/F.89.XIII.1	Fortieth- Quarantième	Population census statistics- Statistiques des recensements de population
1989	E/F.90.XIII.1	Forty-first- Quarante-et-unième	International Migration Statistics- Statistiques des migration internationales
1990	E/F.91.XIII.1	Forty-second- Quarante-deuxième	Marriage and divorce statistics- Statistiques de la nuptialité et de la divortialité
1991	E/F.92.XIII.1	Forty-third- Quarante-troisième	General tables- Tableaux de caractère général
1991	E/F.92.XIII.8	Special issue- Edition spéciale	Population ageing and the situation of elderly persons- Vieillissement de la population et situation des personnes agées
1992	E/F.94.XIII.1	Forty-fourth- Quarante-quatrième	Fertility and mortality statistics- Statistiques de la fecondité et de la mortalité
1993	E/F.95.XIII.1	Forty-fifth- Quarante-cinquième	Population census statistics I- Statistiques des recensements de population I
1994	E/F.96.XIII.1	Forty-sixth- Quarante-sixième	Population census statistics II- Statistiques des recensements de population II
1995	E/F.97.XIII.1	Forty-seventh- Quarante-septième	Household composition-Les éléments du ménage
1996	E/F.98.XIII.1	Forty-eighth- Quarante-hutième	Mortality statistics- Statistiques de la mortalité
1997	E/F.99.XIII.1	Forty-ninth- Quarante-neuvième	General tables- Tableaux de caractère général
1997	E/F.99.XIII.12	Special issue- Edition spéciale (CD)	Historical supplement- Supplément rétrospectif
1998	E/F.00.XIII.1	Fiftieth- Cinquantième	General tables- Tableaux de caractère général
1999	E/F.01.XIII.1	Fifty-first- Cinquante-et-unième	General tables- Tableaux de caractère général
1999	E/F.02.XIII.6	Special issue- Edition spéciale (CD)	Natality Statistics- Statistiques de la natalité
2000	E/F.02.XIII.1	Fifty-second- Cinquante-deuxième	General tables- Tableaux de caractère général
2001	E/F.03.XIII.1	Fifty-third- Cinquante- troisième	General tables- Tableaux de caractère général
2002	E/F.05.XIII.1	Fifty-fourth- Cinquante-quatrième	General tables- Tableaux de caractère général
2003	E/F.06.XIII.1	Fifty-fifth- Cinquante-cinquième	General tables- Tableaux de caractère général
2004	E/F.07.XIII.1	Fifty-sixth- Cinquante- sixième	General tables- Tableaux de caractère général
2005	E/F.08.XIII.1	Fifty-seventh- Cinquante- septième	General tables- Tableaux de caractère général
2006	E/F.09.XIII.1	Fifty-eighth- Cinquante-hutième	General tables- Tableaux de caractère général

CONTENTS - TABLE DES MATIERES

TEXT   TEXTE

TABLES PUBLISHED ANNUALLY   TABLEAUX PUBLIES CHAQUE ANNEE

WORLD SUMMARY   APERCU MONDIAL

POPULATION   POPULATION

vi

EXPLANATIONS OF SYMBOLS

Category not applicable ....

Data not available.. ...

Magnitude zero or less than half of unit employed .... -

Provisional .... *

Data tabulated by year of registration rather than occurrence .... +

Based on less than specified minimum .... ◆

Relatively reliable data .... Roman type

Data of lesser reliability .... *Italics*

EXPLICATION DES SIGNES

Sans objet ....

Données non disponibles ....

Néant ou chiffre inférieur à la moitié de l'unité employée .... -

Données provisoires .... *

Donnée exploitées selon l'année de l'enregistrement et non l'année de l'événement +

Rapport fondé sur un nombre inférieur à celui spécifié.. ◆

Données relativement sûres.. Caractères romains

Données dont l'exactitude est moindre .... *Italiques*

INTRODUCTION

The *Demographic Yearbook* is an international compendium of national demographic statistics, provided by national statistical authorities to the Statistics Division of the United Nations Department of Economic and Social Affairs. The *Yearbook* is part of the set of coordinated and interrelated publications issued by the United Nations and its specialized agencies,[1] designed to supply basic statistical data for such users as demographers, economists, public-health workers and sociologists. Through the co-operation of national statistical services, official demographic statistics are compiled in the *Yearbook*, as available, for more than 230 countries or areas throughout the world.

The *Demographic Yearbook 2006* is the fifty-eighth in a series published by the United Nations since 1948. It contains general tables including a world summary of selected demographic statistics, statistics on the size, distribution and trends in national populations, natality, foetal mortality, infant and maternal mortality, general mortality, nuptiality and divorce. Data are shown by urban/rural residence, as available. In addition, the volume provides Technical Notes, a synoptic table, a historical index and a listing of the issues of the *Yearbook* published to date.

The Technical Notes on the Statistical Tables are provided to assist the reader in using the tables. Table A, the synoptic table, provides a glance of the completeness of data coverage of the current *Yearbook*. The cumulative historical index is a guide on content and coverage of all fifty-eight issues, and indicates for each of the topics that have been published, the issues in which they are presented and the years covered. A list of the *Demographic Yearbook* issues, with their corresponding sales number and the special topics featured in each issue are shown on pages iii and iv.

Until the 48th issue (1996), each issue consisted of two parts, the general tables and special topic tables, published in the same volume.[2] Beginning with the 49th issue (1997), the special topic tables were being disseminated on CD-ROMs as supplements to the regular issues. Two CD-ROMs have so far been issued: the *Demographic Yearbook Historical Supplement*, which presents a wide panorama of basic demographic statistics for the period 1948 to 1997, and the *Demographic Yearbook: Natality Statistics*, which contains a series of detailed tables dedicated to natality and covering the period from 1980 to 1998. Three volumes of a new Demographic Yearbook Special Census Topics have now been prepared and are presented at: http://unstats.un.org/unsd/demographic/products/dyb/default.htm

Population statistics are not available for all countries or areas, for a variety of reasons. In an effort to provide estimates of mid-year population and of selected vital statistics for all countries and areas, two annexes have been introduced since the 53rd issue of the *Demographic Yearbook*. Annex 1 presents United Nations population estimates for the period 1997-2006 and the second presents the medium variant estimates of crude birth and death rates, infant mortality and total fertility rates, as well as expectation of life at birth over the period 2005-2010. These data were produced by the United Nations Population Division and are published in the *World Population Prospects - The 2006 Revision*.[3]

Demographic statistics shown in this issue of the *Yearbook* are available online at the *Demographic Yearbook* website http://unstats.un.org/unsd/demographic/products/dyb/default.htm. Information about the Statistics Division's data collection and dissemination programme is also available on the same website. Additional information can be made available by contacting the Statistics Division of the United Nations Secretariat, at demostat@un.org.

TECHNICAL NOTES ON THE STATISTICAL TABLES

1. GENERAL REMARKS

1.1 Arrangement of Technical Notes

These Technical Notes are designed to provide the reader with relevant information for using the statistical tables. Information pertaining to the *Yearbook* in general is presented in the sections dealing with geographical aspects, population and vital statistics. In addition, preceding each table are notes describing the variables, remarks on the reliability and limitation of the data, countries and areas covered, and information on the presentation of earlier data. When appropriate, details on computation of rates, ratios or percentages are presented.

1.2 Arrangement of tables

This issue contains general tables only. Since the numbering of the tables does not correspond exactly to those in previous issues, the reader is advised to use the historical index that appears at the end of this book to find the reference to data in earlier issues.

1.3 Source of data

The statistics presented in the *Demographic Yearbook* are national data provided by official statistical authorities unless otherwise indicated. The primary source of data for the *Yearbook* is a set of questionnaires sent annually by the United Nations Statistics Division to over 230 national statistical services and other appropriate government offices. Data reported on these questionnaires are supplemented, to the extent possible, with data taken from official national publications, official websites and through correspondence with national statistical services. In the interest of comparability, rates, ratios and percentages have been calculated by the Statistics Division of the United Nations, except for the life table functions, the total fertility rate, and also crude birth rate and crude death rate for some countries or areas as appropriately noted. The methods used by the Statistics Division to calculate these rates and ratios are described in the Technical Notes for each table. The population figures used for these computations are those pertaining to the corresponding years published in this or previous issues of the *Yearbook*.

In cases when data in this issue of the *Demographic Yearbook* differ from those published in earlier issues or related publications, statistics in this issue may be assumed to reflect revisions to these data received by June 2008.

2. GEOGRAPHICAL ASPECTS

2.1 Coverage

Data are shown for all individual countries or areas that provided information. Table 3 is the most comprehensive in geographical coverage, presenting data on population and surface area for all countries or areas with a population of at least 50 persons. Not all of these countries or areas appear in subsequent tables. In many cases the data required for a particular table are not available. In general, the more detailed the data required for a table, the fewer the number of countries or areas that can provide them.

In addition, rates and ratios are presented only for countries or areas reporting at least a minimum number of relevant events. The minimums are stated in the Technical Notes to individual tables.

Except for summary data shown for the world and by major areas and regions in tables 1 and 2 and data shown for capital city and cities with a population of 100 000 or more in table 8, all data are presented at the national level. The number of countries shown in each table is provided in table A, the synoptic table.

2.2 Territorial composition

To the extent possible, all data, including time series data, relate to the territory within 2006 boundaries, when the data were requested from the countries or areas. Exceptions are footnoted in individual tables. Relevant clarifications are specified below.

Data relating to the **People's Republic of China** generally do not include those for Taiwan Province except in tables 1 and 2.

Data relating to **France** exclude Overseas Departments, namely, French Guiana, Guadeloupe, Martinique and Reunion, which are shown separately.

Data relating to **Denmark** exclude Faeroe Islands and Greenland, which are shown separately.

Data relating to **Western Sahara** comprise the Northern Region (former Saguia el Hamra) and Southern Region (former Rio de Oro).

Data relating to **United Kingdom** exclude the Channel Islands and Isle of Man, which are shown separately.

Data relating to **Norway** exclude Svalbard and Jan Mayen Island shown separately, if available.

Data relating to **Finland** include Aland Islands.

Data relating to **Aland Islands** are also included in Finland.

2.3 Nomenclature

Because of space limitations, the country or area names listed in the tables are generally the commonly employed short titles in use in the United Nations as of June 2008[4], the full titles being used only when a short form is not available. The latest version of the *Standard Country or Area Codes for Statistics Use* can be accessed at http://unstats.un.org/unsd/methods/m49/m49.htm.

2.3.1 Order of presentation

Countries or areas are listed in English alphabetical order within the following continents: Africa, North America, South America, Asia, Europe and Oceania.

The designations and presentation of the material in this publication were adopted solely for the purpose of providing a convenient geographical basis for the accompanying statistical series. The same qualification applies to all notes and explanations concerning the geographical units for which data are presented.

2.4 Surface area data

Surface area data, shown in tables 1 and 3, represent the total surface area, comprising land area and inland waters (assumed to consist of major rivers and lakes) and excluding only Polar Regions and uninhabited islands. The surface area given is the most recent estimate available. They are presented in square kilometres, a conversion factor of 2.589988 having been applied to surface areas originally reported in square miles.

2.4.1 Comparability over time

Comparability over time in surface area estimates for any given country or area may be affected by changes in the surface area estimation procedures, increases in actual land surface by reclamation, boundary changes, changes in the concept of "land surface area" used or a change in the unit of measurement used. In most cases it was possible to ascertain the reason for a revision; otherwise, the latest figures have generally been accepted as correct and substituted for those previously on file.

2.4.2 International comparability

Lack of international comparability between surface area estimates arises primarily from differences in definition. In particular, there is considerable variation in the treatment of coastal bays, inlets and gulfs, rivers and lakes. International comparability is also impaired by the variation in methods employed to estimate surface area. These range from surveys based on modern scientific methods to conjectures based on diverse types of information. Some estimates are recent while others may not be. Since neither the exact method of determining the surface area nor the precise definition of its composition and time reference is known for all countries or areas, the estimates in table 3 should not be considered strictly comparable from one country or area to another.

3. POPULATION

Population statistics, that is, those pertaining to the size, geographical distribution and demographic characteristics of the population, are presented in a number of tables of the *Demographic Yearbook*.

Data for countries or areas include population census figures, estimates based on results of sample surveys (in the absence of a census), postcensal or intercensal estimates and those derived from continuous population registers. In the present issue of the *Yearbook*, the latest available census figure of the total population of each country or area and mid-year estimates for 2000 and 2006 are presented in table 3. Mid-year estimates of total population for 10 years (1997-2006) are shown in table 5 and mid-year estimates of urban and total population by sex for 10 years (1997-2006) are shown in table 6. The latest available data on population by age, sex and urban/rural residence are given in table 7. The latest available figures on the population of capital cities and of cities or urban agglomerations of 100 000 or more inhabitants are presented in table 8.

Summary estimates of the mid-year population of the world, major areas and regions for selected years and of its age and sex distribution in 2006 are set forth in tables 1 and 2, respectively.

The statistics on total population, population by age, sex and urban/rural distribution are used in the calculation of rates in the *Yearbook*. Vital rates by age and sex were calculated using data that appear in table 7 in this issue or the corresponding tables of previous issues of the *Demographic Yearbook*.

3.1 Sources of variation of data

The comparability of data is affected by several factors, including (1) the definition of total population; (2) the definition used to classify the population into its urban/rural components; (3) the accuracy of age reporting; (4) the extent of over-enumeration or under-enumeration in the most recent census or other source of benchmark population statistics; and (5) the quality of population estimates. These five factors will be discussed in some detail in sections 3.1.1 to 3.2.2 below. Other relevant problems are discussed in the technical notes to the individual tables. Readers interested in more detail, relating in particular to the basic concepts of population size, distribution and characteristics as elaborated by the United Nations, should consult the *Principles and Recommendations for Population and Housing Censuses, Revision 2*.[5]

3.1.1 Total population

The most important impediment to comparability of total populations is the difference between the concept of a de facto and de jure population. A de facto population should include all persons physically present in the country or area at the reference date. The de jure population, by contrast, should include all usual residents of the given country or area, whether or not they were physically present in the area at the reference date. By definition, therefore, a de facto total and a de jure total are not entirely comparable.

Comparability of even two de facto or de jure totals is often affected by the fact that strict conformity to either of these concepts is rare. For example, some so-called de facto counts do not include foreign military, naval and diplomatic personnel present in the country or area on official duty, and their accompanying family members and servants; some do not include foreign visitors in transit through the country or area or transients on ships in the harbour. On the other hand, they may include such persons as merchant seamen and fishermen who are temporarily out of the country or area working at their trade.

The de jure population figure presents even greater variations in comparability, in part because it depends in the first place on the concept of "usual residence", which varies from one country or area to another and is difficult to apply consistently in a census or survey enumeration. For example, non-national civilians temporarily in a country or area as short-term workers may officially be considered residents after a stay of a specified period of time or they may be considered as non-residents throughout the duration of their stay; at the same time, these individuals may be officially considered as residents or non-residents of the country or area from which they came, depending on the duration and/or purpose of their absence. Furthermore, regardless of the official treatment, individual respondents may apply their own interpretation

4

of residence in responding to the inquiry. In addition, there may be considerable differences in the accuracy with which countries or areas are informed about the number of their residents temporarily out of the country or area.

As far as possible, the population statistics presented in the tables of the *Yearbook* refer to the de facto population. Those reported to have been based on the de jure concept are identified as such. Figures not otherwise qualified may, therefore, be assumed to have been reported by countries or areas as being based on a de facto definition of the population. In an effort to overcome, to the extent possible, the effect of the lack of strict conformity to either the de facto or the de jure concept given above, significant exceptions with respect to inclusions and exclusions of specific population groups, are footnoted when they are known.

It should be remembered, however, that the necessary detailed information has not been available in many cases. It cannot, therefore, be assumed that figures not thus qualified reflect strict de facto or de jure definitions.

A possible source of variation within the statistics of a single country or area may arise from the fact that some countries or areas collect information on both the de facto and the de jure population in, for example, a census, but prepare detailed tabulations for only the de jure population. Hence, even though the total population shown in table 3 is de facto, the figures shown in the tables presenting various characteristics of the population, for example, urban/rural distribution, age and sex distribution, may be de jure.

3.1.2 Urban/rural classification

International comparability of urban/rural distributions is seriously impaired by the wide variation among national definitions of the concept of "urban". The definitions used by individual countries or areas and their implications are shown at the end of technical notes for table 6.

3.1.3 Age distribution

The classification of population by age is a core element of most analyses, estimation and projection of population statistics. Unfortunately, age data are subject to a number of sources of error and non-comparability. Accordingly, the reliability of age data should be of concern to users of these statistics.

3.1.3.1 Collection and compilation of age data

Age is the estimated or calculated interval of time between the date of birth and the date of the census or survey, expressed in completed solar years.[6] There are two methods of collecting information on age. The first is to obtain the date of birth for each member of the population in a census or survey and then to calculate the completed age of the individual by subtracting the date of birth from the date of enumeration.[7] The second method is to record the individual's completed age at the time of the census or survey, that is to say, age at last birthday.

The recommended method is to calculate age at last birthday by subtracting the exact date of birth from the date of the census. Some practices, however, do not use this method but instead calculate the difference between the year of birth and the year of the census. Classifications of this type are footnoted whenever possible. They can be identified to a certain extent by a smaller than expected population under one year of age. However, an irregular number of births from one year to the next or age selective omission of infants may also obscure the expected population under one year of age.

3.1.3.2 Errors in age data

Errors in age data may be due to a variety of causes, including ignorance of the correct age; reporting years of age in terms of a calendar concept other than completed solar years since birth,[8] carelessness in reporting and recording age; a general tendency to state age in figures ending in certain digits (such as zero, two, five and eight); a tendency to exaggerate length of life at advanced ages; a subconscious aversion to certain numbers; and wilful misrepresentations.

These reasons for errors in reported age data are common to most investigations of age and to most countries or areas, and they may significantly impair comparability of the data.

As a result of the above-mentioned difficulties, the age-sex distribution of population in many countries or areas shows irregularities which may be summarized as follows: (1) a deficiency in the number of infants and young children; (2) a concentration at ages ending with zero and five (that is, 5, 10, 15, 20...); (3)

heaping at even ages (for example, 10, 12, 14...) relative to odd ages (for example, 11, 13, 15...); (4) unexpectedly large differences between the frequency of males and females at certain ages; and (5) unaccountably large differences between the frequencies in adjacent age groups. Comparing of identical age-sex cohorts from successive censuses, as well as studying the age-sex composition of each census, may reveal these and other inconsistencies, some of which in varying degree are characteristic of even the most modern censuses.

3.1.3.3 Evaluation of accuracy

To measure the accuracy of data by age, based on the evidence of irregularities in 5-year groups, an index was devised for presentation in the *Demographic Yearbook 1949-1950*[9]. Although this index was sensitive to various sources of inaccuracy in the data, it could also be affected considerably by real fluctuations in past demographic processes. It could not, therefore, be applied indiscriminately to all types of statistics, unless certain adjustments were made and caution used in the interpretation of results.

The publication of population statistics by single years of age in the *Demographic Yearbook 1955* made it possible to apply a simple, yet highly sensitive, index known as Whipple's Index, or the Index of Concentration[10], the interpretation of which is relatively free from consideration of factors not connected with the accuracy of age reporting. More refined methods for the measurement of accuracy of distributions by single year of age have been devised, but this particular index was selected for presentation in the *Demographic Yearbook* for its simplicity and the wide use it has already found in other sources.

Whipple's Index is obtained by summing the age returns between 23 and 62 years inclusive and finding what percentage is borne by the sum of the returns of years ending with 5 and 0 to one-fifth of the total sum.

The results would vary between a minimum of 0, if no returns were recorded ending with 0 or 5, and a maximum of 500, if no returns were recorded ending with any digits other than 0 or 5. If there is no age heaping at ages ending 0 or 5, the Whipple's index is 100.[11]

The index is applicable to all age distributions for which single years are given at least to the age of 62, with the following exceptions: (1) where the data presented are the result of graduation, no irregularity is scored by Whipple's Index, even though the graduated data may still be affected by inaccuracies of a different type; and (2) where statistics on age have been derived by reference to the year of birth, and tendencies to round off the birth year would result in an excessive number of ages ending in odd numbers, the frequency of age reporting with terminal digits 5 and 0 is not an adequate measure of their accuracy.

Most recently, the index has been computed for all the single-year age distributions from censuses held between 1985 and 2003, with the exception of those excluded on the criteria set forth above. Such data are published in the special issue of the *Demographic Yearbook* special topic on population censuses, Volume 1, which is available online at http://unstats.un.org/unsd/demographic/products/dyb/dybcens.htm.

Although Whipple's Index measures only the effects of preferences for ages ending in 5 and 0, it can be assumed that such digit preference is usually connected with other sources of inaccuracy in age statements and the index can be accepted as a fair measure of the general reliability of the age distribution.

3.2 Methods used to indicate quality of published statistics

To the extent possible, efforts have been made to give the reader an indication of reliability of the statistics published in the *Demographic Yearbook*. This has been approached in several ways. Any information regarding a possible under-enumeration or over-enumeration, coming from a postcensal survey, for example, has been noted in the footnotes to table 3. Any deviation from full national coverage, as explained in section 2.1 under Geographical Aspects, has also been noted. In addition, national statistical offices have been asked to evaluate the estimates of total population they submit to the Statistics Division of the United Nations.

3.2.1 Treatment of time series of population estimates

When a series of mid-year population estimates are presented, the same indication of quality is shown for the entire series as was determined for the latest estimate. The quality is indicated by the type face employed.

No attempt has been made to split the series even though it is evident that in cases where the data are now considered reliable, in earlier years, many may have been considerably less reliable than the current classification implies. Thus it will be evident that this method overstates the probable reliability of the time series in many cases. It may also understate the reliability of estimates for years immediately preceding or following a census enumeration.

3.2.2 Treatment of estimated distributions by age and other demographic characteristics

Estimates of the age-sex distribution of population may be constructed by two major methods: (1) by applying the specific components of population change to each age-sex group of the population as enumerated at the time of the census, and (2) by distributing the total estimated for a postcensal year proportionately according to the age-sex structure at the time of the census. Estimates constructed by the latter method are not published in the *Demographic Yearbook*.

Estimated age-sex distributions are categorized as "reliable" or otherwise, according to the method of construction established for the latest estimate of total mid-year population. Hence, the quality designation of the total figure, as indicated by the code, is considered to apply also to the whole distribution by age and sex, and the data are set in *italic* or roman type, as appropriate, on this basis alone. Further evaluation of detailed age structure data has not been undertaken to date.

4. VITAL STATISTICS

For purposes of the *Demographic Yearbook*, vital statistics have been defined as statistics of live birth, death, foetal death, marriage and divorce.

This volume of the *Yearbook* presents general tables on natality, nuptiality and divorce as well as tables on mortality referring to: foetal mortality, infant and maternal mortality and general mortality.

4.1 Sources of variation of data

Most of the vital statistics data published in this *Yearbook* come from national civil registration systems. The completeness and the accuracy of the data that these systems produce vary from one country or area to another.

The provision for a national civil registration system is not universal, and in some cases, the registration system covers only certain vital events. For example, in some countries or areas only births and deaths are registered. There are also differences in the effectiveness with which national laws pertaining to civil registration operate in the various countries or areas. The manner in which the law is implemented and the degree to which the public complies with the legislation determine the reliability of the vital statistics obtained from the civil registers.

It should be noted that some statistics on marriage and divorce are obtained from sources other than civil registers. For example, in some countries or areas, the only source for data on marriages is church registers. Divorce statistics, on the other hand, are obtained from court records and/or civil registers according to national practice. The actual compilation of these statistics may be the responsibility of the civil registrar, the national statistical office or other government offices.

Other factors affecting international comparability of vital statistics are much the same as those that must be considered in evaluating the variations in other population statistics. Differences in statistical definitions of vital events, differences in geographical and ethnic coverage of the data and diverse tabulation procedures may also influence comparability.

In addition to vital statistics from civil registers, some vital statistics published in the *Yearbook* are official estimates. These estimates are frequently from population censuses and sample surveys. As such, their comparability may be affected by the national completeness of reporting in population censuses and household surveys, whether a de facto or de jure based census, non-sampling and sampling errors and other sources of bias.

Readers interested in more detailed information on standards for vital statistics should consult the *Principles and Recommendations for a Vital Statistics System Revision 2* [12]; *Handbook on Civil Registration and Vital Statistics Systems: Preparation of a Legal Framework* [13]; *Handbook on Civil Registration and Vital*

Statistics Systems: Management, Operation and Maintenance;[14] *Handbook on Civil Registration and Vital Statistics Systems: Developing Information, Education and Communication* [15]; *Handbook on Civil Registration and Vital Statistics Systems: Policies and Protocols for the Release and Archiving of Individual Records* [16]; and *Handbook on Civil Registration and Vital Statistics Systems: Computerization* [17]. The *Handbook on the Collection of Fertility and Mortality Data* [18] provides information in collection and evaluation of data on fertility and mortality collected in population censuses and household surveys. These publications are also available on the website at
http://unstats.un.org/unsd/demographic/standmeth/handbooks/default.htm.

4.1.1 Statistical definition of events

An important source of variation lies in the statistical definition of each vital event. The *Demographic Yearbook* attempts to collect data on vital events, using the standard definitions put forth in paragraph 57 of *Principles and Recommendations for a Vital Statistics System Revision 2.*[12] These are as follows:

LIVE BIRTH is the complete expulsion or extraction from its mother of a product of conception, irrespective of the duration of pregnancy, which after such separation breathes or shows any other evidence of life such as beating of the heart, pulsation of the umbilical cord, or definite movement of voluntary muscles, whether or not the umbilical cord has been cut or the placenta is attached; each product of such a birth is considered live-born regardless of gestational age.

DEATH is the permanent disappearance of all evidence of life at any time after live birth has taken place (postnatal cessation of vital functions without capability of resuscitation). This definition therefore excludes foetal deaths.

FOETAL DEATH is death prior to the complete expulsion or extraction from its mother of a product of conception, irrespective of the duration of pregnancy; the death is indicated by the fact that after such separation the foetus does not breathe or show any other evidence of life, such as beating of the heart, pulsation of the umbilical cord, or definite movement of voluntary muscles. Late foetal deaths are those of twenty-eight or more completed weeks of gestation. These are synonymous with the events reported under the pre-1950 term stillbirth [19].

MARRIAGE is an act, ceremony or process by which the legal relationship of husband and wife is constituted. The legality of the union may be established by civil, religious or other means as recognized by the laws of each country or area.

DIVORCE is a final legal dissolution of a marriage, that is, that separation of husband and wife which confers on the parties the right to remarriage under civil, religious and/or other provisions, according to the laws of each country.

In addition to these recommended definitions, the *Demographic Yearbook* collects and presents data on abortions, defined as:

ABORTION is defined, with reference to the woman, as any interruption of pregnancy before 28 weeks of gestation with a dead foetus. There are two major categories of abortion: spontaneous and induced. Induced abortions are those initiated by deliberate action undertaken with the intention of terminating pregnancy; all other abortions are considered spontaneous.

4.1.2 Problems relating to standard definitions

A basic problem affecting international comparability of vital statistics is deviations from the standard definitions of vital events. An example of this can be seen in the cases of live births and foetal deaths.[20] In some countries or areas, an infant must survive for at least 24 hours, to be inscribed in the live-birth register. Infants who die before the expiration of the 24-hour period are classified as late foetal deaths and, barring special tabulation procedures, they would not be counted either as live births or as deaths. Similarly, in several other countries or areas, those infants who are born alive but die before registration of their birth, are also considered late foetal deaths.

Unless special tabulation procedures are adopted in such cases, the live-birth and death statistics will both be deficient by the number of these infants, while the incidence of late foetal deaths will be increased by the same amount. Hence the infant mortality rate is underestimated. Although both components (infant deaths and live births) are deficient by the same absolute amount, the deficiency is proportionately greater in relation to the infant deaths, causing greater errors in the infant mortality rate than in the birth rate.

Moreover, the practice exaggerates the late foetal death ratios. Some countries or areas make provision for correcting this deficiency (at least in the total frequencies) at the tabulation stage. Data for which the correction has not been made are indicated by footnote whenever possible.

The definitions used for marriage and divorce also present problems for international comparability. Unlike birth and death, which are biological events, marriage and divorce are defined only in terms of law and custom and as such are less amenable to universally applicable statistical definitions. They have therefore been defined for statistical purposes in general terms referring to the laws of individual countries or areas. Laws pertaining to marriage and particularly to divorce, vary from one country or area to another. With respect to marriage, the most widespread requirement relates to the minimum age at which persons may marry but frequently other requirements are specified.

When known the minimum legal age of men and women at which marriage can occur with (or in some cases without) parental consent is presented in table 24-1. Laws and regulations relating to the dissolution of marriage by divorce range from total prohibition, through a wide range of grounds upon which divorces may be granted, to the granting of divorce in response to a simple statement of desire or intention by husbands.

4.1.3 Fragmentary geographical or ethnic coverage

Ideally, vital statistics for any given country or area should cover the entire geographical area and include all ethnic groups. Fragmentary coverage is, however, not uncommon. In some countries or areas, registration is compulsory for only a small part of the population, limited to certain ethnic groups, for example. In other places there is no national provision for compulsory registration, but only municipal or state ordinances that do not cover the entire geographical area. Still others have developed a registration area that comprises only a part of the country or area, the remainder being excluded because of inaccessibility or for economic and cultural considerations that make regular registration practically impossible.

4.1.4 Tabulation procedures

4.1.4.1 By place of occurrence

Vital statistics presented at the national level relate to the de facto, that is, the present-in-area population. Thus, unless otherwise noted, vital statistics for a given country or area cover all the events that occur within its present boundaries and among all segments of the population therein. They may be presumed to include events among nomadic tribes and indigenous peoples, and among nationals and foreigners. When known, deviations from the de facto concept are footnoted.

Urban/rural differentials in vital rates for some countries may vary considerably depending on whether the relevant vital events were tabulated on the basis of place of occurrence or place of usual residence. For example, if a substantial number of women residing in rural areas near major urban centres travel to hospitals or maternity homes located in a city to give birth, urban fertility and neo-natal and infant mortality rates will usually be higher (and the corresponding rural rates will usually be lower) if the events are tabulated on the basis of place of occurrence rather than on the basis of place of usual residence. A similar process will affect general mortality differentials if substantial numbers of persons residing in rural areas use urban health facilities when seriously ill.

4.1.4.2 By date of occurrence versus by date of registration

To the extent possible, the vital statistics presented in the *Demographic Yearbook* refer to events that occurred during the specified year, rather than to those that were registered during that period. However, a considerable number of countries or areas tabulate their vital statistics not by date of occurrence, but by date of registration. Because such statistics can be very misleading, the countries or areas known to tabulate vital statistics by date of registration are identified in the tables by a plus sign (+). Since information on the method of tabulating vital statistics is not available for all countries and areas, tabulation by date of registration may be more prevalent than the symbols on the vital statistics tables would indicate.

Because quality of data is inextricably related to the timeliness of registration, this must always be considered in conjunction with the quality code description in section 4.2.1 below. If registration of births is complete and timely (code C), the ill effects of tabulating by date of registration, are, for all practical purposes, nullified. Similarly, with respect to death statistics, the effect of tabulating events by date of registration may be minimized in many countries or areas in which the sanitary code requires that a death must be registered before a burial permit can be issued, and this regulation tends to make registration prompt. With respect to foetal death, registration is usually done right away or not at all. Therefore, if registration is prompt, the difference between statistics tabulated by date of occurrence and those tabulated by date of registration may be negligible. In many cases, the length of the statutory time period allowed for registering various vital events plays an important part in determining the effects of tabulation by date of registration on comparability of data.

With respect to marriage and divorce, the practice of tabulating data by date of registration does not generally pose serious problems. In many countries or areas marriage is a civil legal contract which, to establish its legality, must be celebrated before a civil officer. It follows that for these countries or areas registration would tend to be almost automatic at the time of, or immediately following, the marriage ceremony. Because the registration of a divorce in many countries or areas is the responsibility solely of the court or the authority which granted it, and since the registration record in such cases is part of the records of the court proceedings, it follows that divorces are likely to be registered soon after the decree is granted.

On the other hand, if registration is not prompt, vital statistics by date of registration will not produce internationally comparable data. Under the best circumstances, statistics by date of registration will include primarily events that occurred in the immediately preceding year; in countries or areas with less developed systems, tabulations will include some events that occurred many years in the past. Examination of available information reveals that delays of many years are not uncommon for birth registration, though the majority is recorded between two to four years after birth.

As long as registration is not prompt, statistics by date of registration will not be internationally comparable either among themselves or with statistics by date of occurrence.

It should also be mentioned that lack of international comparability is not the only limitation introduced by date-of-registration tabulation. Even within the same country or area, comparability over time may be lost by the practice of counting registrations rather than occurrences. If the number of events registered from year to year fluctuates because of ad hoc incentives to stimulate registration, or to the sudden need, for example, for proof of (unregistered) birth or death to meet certain requirements, vital statistics tabulated by date of registration are not useful in measuring and analyzing demographic levels and trends. All they can give is an indication of the fluctuations in the need for a birth, death or marriage certificate and the work-load of the registrars. Therefore, statistics tabulated by date of registration may be of very limited use for either national or international studies.

4.2 Methods used to indicate quality of published vital statistics

The quality of vital statistics can be assessed in terms of a number of factors. Most fundamental is the completeness of the civil registration system on which the statistics are based. In some cases, the incompleteness of the data obtained from civil registration systems is revealed when these events are used to compute rates. However, this technique applies only where the data are markedly deficient, where they are tabulated by date of occurrence and where the population base is correctly estimated. Tabulation by date of registration will often produce rates which appear correct, simply because the numerator is artificially inflated by the inclusion of delayed registrations and, conversely, rates may be of credible magnitude because the population at risk has been underestimated. Moreover, it should be remembered that knowledge of what is credible in regard to levels of fertility, mortality and nuptiality is extremely scanty for many parts of the world, and borderline cases, which are the most difficult to appraise, are frequent.

4.2.1 Quality code for vital statistics from registers.

In the *Demographic Yearbook* annual "Questionnaire on Vital Statistics" national statistical offices are asked to provide their own estimates of the completeness of the births, deaths, late foetal deaths, marriages and divorces recorded in their civil registers.

On the basis of information from the questionnaires, from direct correspondence and from relevant official publications, it has been possible to classify current national statistics from civil registers of birth, death, infant death, late foetal death, marriage and divorce into three broad quality categories, as follows:

C: Data estimated to be virtually complete, that is, representing at least 90 per cent of the events occurring each year.

U: Data estimated to be incomplete, that is representing less than 90 per cent of the events occurring each year.

|: Data not derived from civil registration systems but considered reliable, such as estimates derived from projections, other estimation techniques or population and housing census.

...: Data for which no specific information is available regarding completeness.

These quality codes appear in the first column of the tables which show total frequencies and crude rates (or ratios) over a period of years for all tables on live births, late foetal deaths, infant deaths, deaths, marriages, and divorces. Reliability of maternal mortality statistics is provided by the World Health Organisation and instead of indicating data quality in the first column, reliable data are shown in roman type while unreliable data are shown in italics.

The classification of countries and areas in terms of these quality codes may not be uniform. Nevertheless, it was felt that national statistical offices were in the best position to judge the quality of their data. It was considered that even the very broad categories that could be established on the basis of the available information would provide useful indicators of the quality of the vital statistics presented in this *Yearbook.*

In the past, the bases of the national estimates of completeness were usually not available. In connection with the *Demographic Yearbook 1077,* countries were asked, for the first time, to provide some indication of the basis of their completeness estimates. They were requested to indicate whether the completeness estimates reported for registered live births, deaths, and infant deaths were prepared on the basis of demographic analysis, dual record checks or some other specified method. Relatively few countries or areas have responded to this new question; therefore, no attempt has been made to revise the system of quality codes used in connection with the vital statistics data presented in the *Yearbook*. It is hoped that, in the future, more countries will be able to provide this information so that the system of quality codes used in connection with the vital statistics data presented in the *Yearbook* may be revised.

Among the countries or areas indicating that the registration of live births was estimated to be 90 per cent or more complete (and hence classified as C in table 9), the following countries or areas provided information on the basis of this completeness estimate:

(a) Demographic analysis -- Argentina, Australia, Canada, Chile, Croatia, Cuba, Czech Republic, Egypt, French Guiana, Guadeloupe, Guernsey, Iceland, Ireland, Israel, Republic of Korea, Kuwait, Latvia, Mauritius, Puerto Rico, Romania, San Marino, Singapore, Sweden, Switzerland and United States.

(b) Dual record check -- Barbados, Belgium, Bulgaria, Cook Islands, Cuba, Cyprus, Denmark, Estonia, Fiji, Finland, France, French Guiana, Greece, Guam, Guadeloupe, Guernsey, Hungary, Iceland, Isle of Man, Japan, Kyrgyzstan, Lithuania, Maldives, New Zealand, Malaysia, Romania, Saint Kitts and Nevis, Saint Lucia, Singapore, Sri Lanka, Sweden, Switzerland, Uruguay and Venezuela.

(c) Other specified methods -- Belgium, Bermuda, Cayman Islands, China Hong Kong SAR, China Macao SAR, Germany, Greenland, Iceland, Japan, Luxembourg, Netherlands, Norway, Poland, Singapore and Slovenia.

Among the countries or areas indicating that the registration of deaths was estimated to be 90 per cent or more complete (and hence classified as C in table 18), the following countries or areas provided information on the basis of this completeness estimate:

(a) Demographic analysis -- Argentina, Australia, Canada, Chile, Cuba, Egypt, French Guiana, Guadeloupe, Guernsey, Iceland, Ireland, Israel, Kuwait, Latvia, Mauritius, Puerto Rico, Romania, San Marino, Singapore, Switzerland and United States.

(b) Dual record check -- Bahamas, Bulgaria, Cook Islands, Cuba, Denmark, Fiji, Finland, France, Greece, Greenland, Guam, Guernsey, Iceland, Isle of Man, Maldives, New Zealand, Romania, Saint Kitts and Nevis, Saint Lucia, Singapore, Sri Lanka, Sweden, Switzerland and Uruguay.

(c) Other specified methods -- Belgium, Bermuda, Cayman Islands, Germany, Hong Kong SAR, Iceland, Ireland, Japan, Luxembourg, Netherlands, Norway, Poland, Singapore and Slovenia.

Among the countries or areas indicating that the registration of infant deaths was estimated to be 90 per cent or more complete (and hence classified as C in table 15), the following countries or areas provided information on the basis of this completeness estimate:

(a) Demographic analysis -- Argentina, Australia, Canada, Chile, Cuba, Egypt, Iceland, Ireland, Israel, Kuwait, Latvia, Mauritius, Puerto Rico, Romania, San Marino, Singapore, Sri Lanka, Switzerland and United States.

(b) Dual record check -- Bahamas, Bulgaria, Cook Islands, Cuba, Denmark, Fiji, Finland, France, Greece, Greenland, Guam, Guernsey, Iceland, Isle of Man, Japan, Maldives, New Zealand, Romania, Saint Kitts and Nevis, Saint Lucia, Singapore, Sweden, Switzerland and Uruguay.

(c) Other specified methods -- Belgium, Bermuda, Cayman Islands, Germany, Hong Kong SAR, Iceland, Japan, Luxembourg, Netherlands, Norway, Poland, Singapore and Slovenia.

4.2.2 Treatment of vital statistics from registers

On the basis of the quality code described above, the vital statistics shown in all tables of the *Yearbook* are treated as either reliable or unreliable. Data coded C are considered reliable and appear in roman type. Data coded U or ... are considered unreliable and appear in *italics*. Although the quality code itself appears only in certain tables, the indication of reliability (that is, the use of *italics* to indicate unreliable data) is shown in all tables presenting vital statistics data.

In general, the quality code for deaths shown in table 18 is used to determine whether data on deaths in other tables appear in roman or *italic* type. However, for some of the maternal deaths data shown in *italics* in table 17, the known quality code differs from that ascribed on the basis of the completeness of registration of the total number of deaths. In cases where the quality code in table 18 does not correspond with the quality level implied by the typeface used in table 17, relevant information regarding the completeness of maternal mortality is given in a footnote.

The same indication of reliability used in connection with tables showing the frequencies of vital events is also used in connection with tables showing the corresponding vital rates. For example, death rates computed using deaths from a register that is incomplete or of unknown completeness are considered unreliable and appear in *italics*. Strictly speaking, to evaluate vital rates more precisely, one would have to also take into account the accuracy of population data used in the denominator of these rates. The quality of population data is discussed in section 3.2 of the Technical Notes.

It should be noted that the indications of reliability used for infant mortality rates, maternal mortality rates and late foetal death ratios (all of which are calculated using the number of live births in the denominator) are determined on the basis of the quality codes for infant deaths, deaths and late foetal deaths respectively. To evaluate these rates and ratios more precisely, one would have to take into account the quality of the live-birth data used in the denominator of these rates and ratios. The quality codes for live births are shown in table 9 and described more fully in the text of the technical notes for that table.

4.2.3 Treatment of time series of vital statistics from registers

The quality of a time series of vital statistics is more difficult to determine than the quality of data for a single year. Since a time series of vital statistics is usually generated only by a system of continuous civil registration, it was assumed that the quality of the entire series was the same as that for the latest year's data obtained from the civil register. The entire series is treated as described in section 4.2.2 above. That is, if the quality code for the latest registered data is C, the frequencies and rates for earlier years are also considered reliable and appear in roman type. Conversely, if the latest registered data are coded as U or ...

then data for earlier years are considered unreliable and appear in *italics*. It is recognized that this method is not entirely satisfactory because it is known that data from earlier years in many of the series were considerably less reliable than the current code implies.

4.2.4 Treatment of estimated vital statistics

In addition to data from vital registration systems, estimated frequencies and rates of the events, usually ad hoc official estimates that have been derived either from the results of a sample survey or by demographic analyses, also appear in the *Demographic Yearbook*. Estimated frequencies and rates have been included in the tables because it is assumed that they provide information that is more accurate than that from existing civil registration systems. By implication, they are assumed to be reliable and as such they are set in roman type. Estimated frequencies and rates continue to be treated in this manner even when they are interspersed in a time series with data from civil registers.

In tables showing the quality code, the code applies only to data from civil registers. If a series of data for a country or area contains both data from a civil register and estimated data, the code applies only to the registered data; if only estimated data are shown, the symbol (|) is shown.

4.3 Cause of death

World Health Organization (WHO) Member States are bound by the International Nomenclature Regulations to provide the Organization with cause of death data coded in accordance with the current revision of the International Statistical Classification of Diseases and Related Health Problems (ICD) as adopted from time to time by the World Health Assembly [21]. The data are collected by the WHO using the ICD. In order to promote international comparability of cause of death statistics, the World Health Organization organizes and conducts an international Conference for the revision of the ICD on a regular basis in order to ensure that the Classification is kept current with the most recent clinical and statistical concepts. The data are now usually submitted to WHO at the full four-character level of detail provided by the ICD and are stored in the WHO Mortality Database at the level of detail as provided by the country. For earlier versions, however, the data are only available according to the ICD's list of 150 causes. Data from the WHO Mortality Database are available in electronic format at http://www3.who.int/whosis/menu.cfm.

Although revisions provide an up-to-date version of the ICD, such revisions create several problems related to the comparability of cause of death statistics. The first is the lack of comparability over time that inevitably accompanies the use of a new classification. The second problem affects comparability between countries and areas because they may adopt a new classification at different times. The more refined the classification becomes the greater is the need for expert clinical diagnosis of cause of death. In many countries or areas, few of the deaths occur in the presence of an attendant, who is medically trained, i.e., most deaths are certified by a lay attendant. Because the ICD contains many diagnoses that cannot be identified by a non-medical person, the ICD does not always promote international comparability particularly between countries and areas where the level of medical services differ widely.

The chapters of the tenth revision [22], the latest revision of the ICD, consist of an alphanumeric coding scheme of one letter followed by three numbers at the four-character level. Chapter one contains infectious and parasitic diseases, chapter two refers to all neoplasms, chapter three to disorders of the immune mechanism including diseases of the blood and blood-forming organs; and chapter four to endocrine, nutritional and metabolic diseases. The remaining chapters group diseases according to the anatomical site affected, except for chapters that refer to mental disorders; complications of pregnancy, childbirth and the puerperium; congenital malformations; and conditions originating in the perinatal period. Finally, an entire chapter is devoted to symptoms, signs, and abnormal findings.

4.3.1 Maternal mortality

According to the tenth revision of the ICD, "Maternal death" is defined as the death of a woman while pregnant or within 42 days of termination of pregnancy, irrespective of the duration and the site of the pregnancy, from any cause related to or aggravated by the pregnancy or its management but not from accidental or incidental causes.

"Maternal deaths should be subdivided into direct and indirect obstetric deaths. Direct obstetric deaths are those resulting from obstetric complications of the pregnant state (pregnancy, labour and puerperium), from interventions, omissions, incorrect treatment, or from a chain of events resulting from any of the above. Indirect obstetric deaths are those resulting from previous existing disease or disease that developed during pregnancy and which was not due to direct obstetric causes, but which was aggravated by physiologic effects of pregnancy".

While the denominator maternal rate should be the number of pregnant women, it is impossible to determine the number of pregnant women. A further recommendation by the tenth revision conference is therefore that maternal mortality rates be expressed per 100,000 live births or per 100,000 total births (live births and foetal deaths). [23] The maternal mortality rate calculated here is expressed per 100,000 live births. Although live births do not represent an unbiased estimate of pregnant women, this figure is more reliable than other estimates in particular, live births are more accurately registered than live births plus foetal deaths.

NOTES

[1] The data on maternal mortality are from the World Health Organization, and are available at http://www3.who.int/whosis/menu.cfm, as one cause of death.

[2] There are two exceptions – the 1978 and 1991 issues, which were disseminated in separate volumes from the respective regular issues.

[3] *World Population Prospects - The 2006 Revision*, Sales No. E.07.XIII.7,. United Nations, New York. Highlights and selected output are available by following links at www.unpopulation.org,.

[4] ST/ESA/STAT/SER.M/49/Rev.4/WWW ; http://unstats.un.org/unsd/methods/m49/m49.htm; see also Standard Country or Area Codes for Statistical Use, Sales No. M.98.XVII.9, United Nations, New York, 1999.

[5] Forthcoming, Sales No. E.07.XVII.8, United Nations, New York, 2007. Until this is published, the publication is available online at http://unstats.un.org/unsd/demographic/sources/census/docs/P&R_%20Rev2.pdf

[6] Ibid, para. 2.135.

[7] Alternatively, if a population register is used, completed ages are calculated by subtracting the date of birth of individuals listed in the register from a reference date to which the age data pertain.

[8] A source of non-comparability may result from differences in the method of reckoning age, is for example, the Western versus the Eastern or, as it is usually known, the English versus the Chinese system. By the latter, a child is considered one year old at birth and advances an additional year at each Chinese New Year. The effect of this system is most obvious at the beginning of the age span, where the frequencies in the under-one-year category are markedly understated. The effect on higher age groups is not so apparent. Distributions constructed on this basis are often adjusted before publication, but the possibility of such aberrations should not be excluded when census data by age are compared.

[9] In this index, differences were scored from expected values of ratios between numbers of either sex in the same age group, and numbers of the same sex in adjoining age group. In compounding the score, allowance had to be made for certain factors such as the effects of past fluctuations in birth rates, of heavy war casualties, and of the smallness of the population itself. A detailed description of the index, with results from its application to the data presented in the 1949-1950 and 1951 issues of the *Demographic Yearbook*, is furnished in *Population Bulletin, No. 2* (United Nations publication, Sales No. 52.XIII.4), pp. 59-79. The scores obtained from statistics presented in *Demographic Yearbook 1952* are presented in that issue, and the index has also been briefly explained in that issue, as well as those of 1953 and 1954.

[10] United States, Bureau of the Census, Thirteenth Census, Vol. I (Washington, D.C., U.S. Government Printing Office), pp. 291-292.

[11] J. T. Marten, Census of India, 1921, vol. I, part I (Calcutta, 1924), pp. 126-127.

[12] Sales No. E. 01.XVII.10, United Nations, New York, 2001.

[13] Sales No. E. 98.XVII.7, United Nations, New York, 1998.

[14] Sales No. E.98.XVII.11, United Nations, New York, 1998.

[15] Sales No. E.98.XVII.4, United Nations, New York, 1998.

[16] Sales No. E.98.XVII.6, United Nations, New York, 1998;

[17] Sales No. E.98.XVII.10, United Nations, New York, 1998.

[18] *Handbook on the Collection of Fertility and Mortality data*, Sales No. 03.XVII.11, United Nations, New York, 2003.

[19] For more detailed discussion on this issue, refer to *Principles and Recommendations for a Vital Statistics System Revision 2*, Sales No. E. 01.XVII.10, United Nations, New York, 2001, para 57.

[20] For more information on historical and legal background on the use of differing definitions of live births and foetal deaths, comparisons of definitions used as of 1 January 1950, and evaluation of the effects of these differences on the calculation of various rates, see *Handbook of Vital Statistics Systems and Methods Volume 2, Review of National Practices*, Sales No. E.84.XVII.11, United Nations, New York, 1985, Chapter IV.

[21] The World Health Assembly is the annual meeting of the Member States of the World Health Organization and its highest governing body.

[22] *International Statistical Classification of Diseases and Related Health Problems*, Tenth Revision, Volume 2, World Health Organization, Geneva, 1992.

[23] *International Statistical Classification of Diseases and Related Health Problems*, Tenth Revision, Volume 2, World Health Organization, Geneva, 1992, pp. 129-136.

INTRODUCTION

L'Annuaire démographique est un recueil de statistiques démographiques internationales qui est établi par la Division de statistique du Département des affaires économiques et sociales de l'Organisation des Nations Unies. Il fait partie d'un ensemble de publications complémentaires publiées par l'Organisation des Nations Unies et les institutions spécialisées[1], qui ont pour objet de fournir des statistiques de base aux démographes, aux économistes, aux spécialistes de la santé publique et aux sociologues. Grâce à la coopération des services nationaux de statistique, il a été possible de faire figurer dans la présente édition des statistiques démographiques officielles pour plus de 230 pays ou zones du monde entier.

L'Annuaire démographique 2006 est le cinquante-huitième d'une série que publie l'ONU depuis 1948. Le présent volume contient des tableaux à caractère général, y compris un aperçu mondial des statistiques démographiques de base et des tableaux qui regroupent des statistiques sur la dimension, la répartition et les tendances de la population, la natalité, la mortalité fœtale, la mortalité infantile et la mortalité liée à la maternité, la mortalité générale, la nuptialité et la divortialité. Des données classées selon le lieu de résidence (zone urbaine ou rurale) sont présentées dans un grand nombre de tableaux. En outre, l'*Annuaire* contient des notes techniques, un tableau synoptique, un index historique et une liste des éditions de l'*Annuaire* publiées jusqu'à présent.

Les notes techniques sur les tableaux statistiques sont destinées à aider le lecteur. Le tableau A, qui correspond au tableau synoptique, permet de se rendre compte en un coup d'oeil du niveau d'exhaustivité des données publiées dans le présent *Annuaire* et l'index thématique facilite le repérage des sujets abordés. Un index cumulatif donne des renseignements sur les matières traitées dans chacune des 58 éditions et sur les années sur lesquelles portent les données. Les numéros de vente des éditions antérieures et une liste des sujets spéciaux traités dans les différentes éditions sont indiqués aux pages iii et iv.

Jusqu'à la 48ème édition (1996), chaque édition se composait de deux parties : les tableaux de caractère général et ceux sur des sujets spéciaux[2]. À partir de 49ème édition (1997), les tableaux sur les sujets spéciaux ont été publiés sur CD-ROM sous forme de suppléments à l'*Annuaire*. Deux CD-ROM ont été produits jusqu'à présent : l'*Annuaire démographique : Supplément historique*, qui présente un grand nombre de statistiques démographiques pour la période allant de 1948 à 1997, et l'*Annuaire démographique : Statistiques de la natalité*, qui contient des tableaux détaillés sur la natalité pour la période allant de 1980 à 1998. Trois volumes concernant un nouvel Annuaire démographique consacré à des thèmes de recensement spéciaux ont été produits et sont présentés à l'adresse suivante : http://unstats.un.org/unsd/demographic/products/dyb/default.htm.

Les statistiques sur la population ne sont pas disponibles pour tous les pays et zones pour plusieurs raisons. Deux annexes ont été ajoutées à partir de la 53ème édition afin d'offrir des estimations sur la population en milieu d'année et un aperçu des statistiques de l'état civil. La première porte sur des estimations concernant la population pour chaque pays ou zone pour la période 1997-2006. La seconde présente les estimations des variantes moyennes concernant les taux bruts de natalité et de mortalité, la mortalité infantile, les indicateurs synthétiques de fécondité et l'espérance de vie à la naissance pour la période 2005-2010. Ces données ont été établies par la Division de la population de l'ONU et publiées dans *World Population Prospects - The 2006 Revision*[3].

Les statistiques démographiques figurant dans la présente édition de l'*Annuaire* sont disponibles en ligne sur les pages Web consacrées à l'Annuaire : http://unstats.un.org/unsd/demographic/products/dyb/default.htm. On trouvera également des renseignements sur le programme de collecte et de diffusion des données de la Division de statistique sur le même site. Il est possible de se procurer d'autres données en contactant la Division de statistique de l'Organisation des Nations Unies à l'adresse suivante : demostat@un.org.

NOTES TECHNIQUES SUR LES TABLEAUX STATISTIQUES

1. REMARQUES D'ORDRE GÉNÉRAL

1.1 Notes techniques

Les notes techniques ont pour but de donner au lecteur tous les renseignements dont il a besoin pour se servir des tableaux statistiques. Les renseignements qui concernent l'*Annuaire* en général sont présentés dans des sections portant sur diverses considérations géographiques, sur la population et sur les statistiques de natalité et de mortalité. Les tableaux sont ensuite commentés séparément et l'on trouvera pour chacun une description des variables et des observations sur la fiabilité et les lacunes des données ainsi que sur les pays et zones visés et sur les données publiées antérieurement. Des détails sont également donnés, le cas échéant, sur le mode de calcul des taux, quotients et pourcentages.

1.2 Tableaux

La présente édition contient seulement des tableaux de caractère général. Comme la numérotation des tableaux ne correspond pas exactement à celle des éditions précédentes, il est recommandé de se reporter à l'index qui figure à la fin du présent ouvrage pour trouver les données publiées dans les précédentes éditions.

1.3 Origine des données

Sauf indication contraire, les statistiques présentées dans *l'Annuaire démographique* sont des données nationales fournies par les organismes de statistique officiels. Elles sont recueillies essentiellement au moyen de questionnaires qui sont envoyés tous les ans à plus de 230 services nationaux de statistique et autres services gouvernementaux compétents. Les données communiquées en réponse à ces questionnaires sont complétées, dans toute la mesure possible, par des données tirées de publications nationales officielles et des sites web d'organismes officiels et des renseignements communiqués par les services nationaux de statistique à la demande de l'ONU. Pour que les données soient comparables, les taux, rapports et pourcentages ont été calculés par la Division de statistique de l'ONU, à l'exception des paramètres des tables de mortalité et des indicateurs synthétiques de fécondité ainsi que des taux bruts de natalité et de mortalité pour certains pays et zones, qui ont été dûment signalés en note. Les méthodes suivies par la Division pour le calcul des taux et rapports sont décrites dans les notes techniques relatives à chaque tableau. Les chiffres de population utilisés pour ces calculs sont ceux qui figurent dans la présente édition de l'*Annuaire* ou qui ont paru dans des éditions antérieures.

Chaque fois que l'on constatera des différences entre les données du présent volume et celles des éditions antérieures de *l'Annuaire démographique*, ou de certaines publications apparentées, on pourra en conclure que les statistiques publiées cette année sont des chiffres révisés communiqués à la Division de statistique avant juin 2008.

2. CONSIDÉRATIONS GÉOGRAPHIQUES

2.1 Portée

La portée géographique des tableaux du présent *Annuaire* est aussi complète que possible. Des données sont présentées sur tous les pays ou zones qui en ont communiquées. Le tableau 3, le plus complet, contient des données sur la population et la superficie de chaque pays ou zone ayant une population d'au moins 50 habitants. Ces pays ou zones ne figurent pas tous dans les tableaux qui suivent. Dans bien des cas, les données requises pour un tableau particulier n'étaient pas disponibles. En général, les pays ou zones qui peuvent fournir des données sont d'autant moins nombreux que les données demandées sont plus détaillées.

De plus les taux et rapports ne sont présentés que pour les pays ou zones ayant communiqué des chiffres correspondant à un nombre minimal de faits considérés. Les minimums sont indiqués dans les notes techniques relatives à chacun des tableaux.

À l'exception des données récapitulatives présentées dans les tableaux 1 et 2 pour l'ensemble du monde et les grandes zones et régions et des données relatives aux capitales et aux villes de 100 000 habitants ou plus dans le tableau 8, toutes les données se rapportent aux pays. Le nombre de pays sur lequel porte chacun des tableaux est indiqué dans le tableau A.

2.2 Composition territoriale

Autant que possible, toutes les données, y compris les séries chronologiques, se rapportent au territoire de 2005. Les exceptions à cette règle sont signalées en note à la fin des tableaux. On trouve dans le tableau 3 des renseignements concernant les changements intervenus récemment et d'autres précisions intéressantes. Des clarifications importantes sont présentées ci-dessous.

Les données relatives à la République populaire de Chine ne comprennent généralement pas celles de la province de Taiwan ; à l'exception de celles des tableaux 1 et 2.

Les données relatives à la France ne comprennent pas les départements d'outre mer, c'est- à -dire la Guyane française, la Martinique et La Réunion, qui font l'objet de rubriques distinctes.

Les données relatives au Danemark ne comprennent pas les Iles Féroé et le Gröenland, qui font l'objet de rubriques distinctes.

Les données relatives au Sahara Occidental comprennent la région septentrionale (ancien Saguia-el-Hamra) et la région méridionale (ancien Rio de Oro).

Les données relatives au Royaume-Uni ne comprennent pas les îles Anglo-Normandes et l'île de Man, qui font l'objet de rubriques distinctes.

Les données relatives à la Norvège ne comprennent pas Svalbard et Jan Mayen qui font l'objet de rubriques distinctes, si disponible.

Les données relatives à la Finlande comprennent les Îles d'Åland.

Les données relatives aux Îles d'Åland sont aussi comprises dans celles relatives à la Finlande.

2.3 Nomenclature

En règle générale, pour gagner de la place, on a jugé commode de désigner dans les tableaux les pays ou zones par les noms abrégés couramment utilisés par l'Organisation des Nations Unies en juin 2008[4], les désignations complètes n'étant utilisées que lorsqu'il n'existait pas de forme abrégée. La liste des désignations des pays ou zones est disponible à l'adresse suivante : http://unstats.un.org/unsd/methods/m49/m49alphaf.htm.

2.3.1 Ordre de présentation

Les pays ou zones sont classés dans l'ordre alphabétique anglais et regroupés par continent comme ci-après : Afrique, Amérique du Nord, Amérique du Sud, Asie, Europe et Océanie.

Les appellations employées dans la présente édition et la présentation des données qui y figurent n'ont d'autre objet que de donner un cadre géographique commode aux séries statistiques. La même observation vaut pour toutes les notes et précisions concernant les unités géographiques pour lesquelles des données sont présentées.

2.4 Superficie

Les données relatives à la superficie qui figurent dans les tableaux 1 et 3 représentent la superficie totale, c'est-à-dire qu'elles englobent les terres émergées et les eaux intérieures (qui sont censées comprendre les principaux lacs et cours d'eau) mais excluent les régions polaires et les îles inhabitées. Les données relatives à la superficie correspondent aux chiffres estimatifs les plus récents. Les superficies sont toutes exprimées en kilomètres carrés ; les chiffres qui avaient été communiqués en miles carrés ont été convertis au moyen d'un coefficient de 2,589988.

2.4.1 Comparabilité dans le temps

La révision des estimations antérieures de la superficie, des augmentations effectives de la superficie terrestre due par exemple à des travaux d'assèchement, à des rectifications de frontières, à des changements d'interprétation du concept de « terres émergées » ou à l'utilisation de nouvelles unités de mesure peut avoir des incidences sur la comparabilité dans le temps des estimations relatives à la superficie d'un pays ou d'une zone donnés. Dans la plupart des cas, il a été possible de déterminer la raison de ces révisions; toutefois, même lorsque la raison n'était pas connue, on a remplacé les anciens chiffres par les nouveaux et on a généralement admis que ce sont ces derniers qui sont exacts.

2.4.2 Comparabilité internationale

Le manque de comparabilité internationale entre les données relatives à la superficie est dû principalement à des différences de définition. En particulier, la définition des golfes, baies et criques, lacs et cours d'eau varie sensiblement d'un pays à l'autre. La diversité des méthodes employées pour estimer les superficies nuit elle aussi à la comparabilité internationale. Certaines données proviennent de levés effectués selon des méthodes scientifiques modernes ; d'autres ne représentent que des conjectures reposant sur diverses catégories de renseignements. Certains chiffres sont récents, d'autres pas. Étant donné que ni la méthode de calcul de la superficie ni la composition du territoire et la date à laquelle se rapportent les données ne sont connues avec précision pour tous les pays ou zones, les estimations figurant dans le tableau 3 ne doivent pas être considérées comme rigoureusement comparables d'un pays ou d'une zone à une autre.

3. POPULATION

Les statistiques de la population, c'est-à-dire celles qui se rapportent à la dimension, à la répartition géographique et aux caractéristiques démographiques de la population, sont présentées dans un certain nombre de tableaux de l'Annuaire démographique.

Les données concernant les pays ou les zones représentent les résultats de recensements de population, des estimations fondées sur les résultats d'enquêtes par sondage (s'il n'y a pas eu recensement), des estimations postcensitaires ou intercensitaires, ou des estimations établies à partir de données provenant des registres permanents de population. Dans la présente édition, le tableau 3 indique pour chaque pays ou zone le chiffre le plus récent de la population totale issu du dernier recensement et des estimations établies au milieu de l'année 2000 et de l'année 2006. Le tableau 5 contient des estimations de la population totale au milieu de chaque année pendant 10 ans (1997-2006), et le tableau 6 des estimations de la population urbaine et de la population totale, par sexe, au milieu de chaque année pendant 10 ans (1997-2006). Les dernières données disponibles sur la répartition de la population selon l'âge, le sexe et le lieu de résidence (zone urbaine ou rurale) sont présentées dans le tableau 7. Les derniers chiffres disponibles sur la population des capitales et des villes de 100 000 habitants ou plus sont regroupés dans le tableau 8.

Les tableaux 1 et 2 présentent respectivement des estimations récapitulatives de la population du monde, des grandes zones et des régions en milieu d'année, pour certaines années, ainsi que des estimations récapitulatives pour 2006, concernant la population répartie selon l'âge et le sexe.

On a utilisé pour le calcul des taux les statistiques de la population totale et de la population répartie selon l'âge, le sexe et le lieu de résidence (zone urbaine ou rurale). Les taux démographiques selon l'âge et le sexe ont été calculés à partir des données qui figurent dans le tableau 7 de la présente édition ou dans les tableaux correspondants d'éditions précédentes de l'Annuaire démographique.

3.1 Sources de variation des données

Plusieurs facteurs influent sur la comparabilité des données : 1) la définition de la population totale ; 2) les définitions utilisées pour faire la distinction entre population urbaine et population rurale ; 3) les difficultés liées aux déclarations d'âge ; 4) l'étendue du sur-dénombrement ou du sous-dénombrement dans le recensement le plus récent ou dans une autre source de statistiques de référence sur la population ; 5) la qualité des estimations relatives à la population. Ces cinq facteurs sont analysés en détail aux sections 3.1.1 à 3.2.2 ci-après. D'autres questions seront traitées dans les notes techniques relatives à chaque tableau. Pour plus de précisions concernant, notamment, les notions fondamentales de dimension, de répartition et de caractéristiques de la population qui ont été élaborées par l'Organisation des Nations Unies, le lecteur est invité à se reporter aux *Principes et recommandations concernant les recensements de la population et de l'habitat. Révision 2*[5].

3.1.1 Population totale

Le principal obstacle à la comparabilité des données relatives à la population totale est la différence qui existe entre population de fait et population de droit. La population de fait comprend toutes les personnes présentes dans le pays ou la zone à la date de référence, tandis que la population de droit comprend toutes celles qui résident habituellement dans le pays ou la zone, qu'elles y aient été ou non présentes à la date de référence. Par définition, la population totale de fait et la population totale de droit ne sont donc pas rigoureusement comparables entre elles.

Même lorsque l'on veut comparer deux totaux qui se rapportent à des populations de fait ou deux totaux qui se rapportent à des populations de droit, on risque souvent de faire des erreurs pour cette raison qu'il est rare que l'une et l'autre notions soient appliquées strictement. Pour citer quelques exemples, certains chiffres qui sont censés porter sur la population de fait ne tiennent pas compte du personnel militaire, naval et diplomatique étranger en fonction dans le pays ou la zone, ni des membres de leurs familles et de leurs domestiques les accompagnant; d'autres ne comprennent pas les visiteurs étrangers de passage dans le pays ou la zone ni les personnes à bord de navires ancrés dans les ports. En revanche, il arrive que l'on compte des personnes, inscrits maritimes et marins pêcheurs par exemple, qui, en raison de leur activité professionnelle, se trouvent hors du pays ou de la zone de recensement.

Les risques de disparités sont encore plus grands quand il s'agit de comparer des populations de droit, car les comparaisons dépendent au premier chef de la définition que l'on donne à l'expression « lieu de résidence habituel », qui varie d'un pays ou d'une zone à l'autre et qu'il est, de toute façon, difficile d'appliquer uniformément pour le dénombrement lors d'un recensement ou d'une enquête. Par exemple, les civils étrangers qui se trouvent temporairement dans un pays ou une zone comme travailleurs à court terme peuvent officiellement être considérés comme résidents après un séjour d'une durée déterminée, mais ils peuvent aussi être considérés comme non-résidents pendant toute la durée de leur séjour ; ailleurs, ces mêmes personnes peuvent être considérées officiellement comme résidents ou comme non-résidents du pays ou de la zone d'où elles viennent, selon la durée et, éventuellement, la raison de leur absence. Qui plus est, quel que soit son statut officiel, chacun des recensés peut, au moment de l'enquête, interpréter à sa façon la notion de résidence. De plus, les autorités nationales ou les entités responsables des zones ne savent pas toutes avec la même précision combien de leurs résidents se trouvent temporairement à l'étranger.

Les chiffres de population présentés dans les tableaux de l'*Annuaire* représentent, autant qu'il a été possible, la population de fait. Sauf indication contraire, on peut supposer que les chiffres présentés ont été communiqués par les pays ou les zones comme se rapportant à la population de fait. Les chiffres qui ont été communiqués comme se rapportant à la population de droit sont indiqués comme tels. Lorsque l'on savait que les données avaient été recueillies selon une définition de la population de fait ou de la population de droit qui s'écartait sensiblement de celle exposée plus haut, on l'a signalé en note, de manière à compenser dans toute la mesure possible les conséquences des divergences.

Il ne faut pas oublier néanmoins que l'on ne disposait pas toujours de renseignements détaillés à ce sujet. On ne peut donc partir du principe que les chiffres qui ne sont pas accompagnés d'une note signalant une divergence correspondent exactement aux définitions de la population de fait ou de la population de droit.

Il peut y avoir hétérogénéité dans les statistiques d'un même pays ou d'une même zone dans le cas des pays ou zones qui ne font une exploitation statistique détaillée des données que pour la population de droit alors qu'ils recueillent des données sur la population de droit et sur la population de fait à l'occasion d'un recensement, par exemple. Ainsi, tandis que les chiffres relatifs à la population totale qui figurent au tableau 3 se rapportent à la population de fait, ceux des tableaux qui présentent des données sur diverses caractéristiques de la population, par exemple le lieu de résidence (zone urbaine ou rurale), l'âge et le sexe, peuvent n'avoir trait qu'à la population de droit.

3.1.2 Lieu de résidence (zone urbaine ou rurale)

L'hétérogénéité des définitions nationales du terme « urbain » nuit considérablement à la comparabilité internationale des données concernant la répartition selon le lieu de résidence. Les définitions utilisées par les différents pays ou zones et leurs implications sont exposées à la fin des notes techniques correspondant au tableau 6.

3.1.3 Répartition par âge

La répartition de la population selon l'âge est un paramètre fondamental de la plupart des analyses, estimations et projections relatives aux statistiques de la population. Malheureusement, ces données sont sujettes à un certain nombre d'erreurs et difficilement comparables. C'est pourquoi pratiquement tous les utilisateurs de ces statistiques doivent considérer ces répartitions avec la plus grande circonspection.

3.1.3.1 *Collecte et exploitation des données sur l'âge*

L'âge est l'intervalle de temps déterminé par calcul ou par estimation qui sépare la date de naissance de la date du recensement et qui est exprimé en années solaires révolues.[6] Les données sur l'âge peuvent être recueillies selon deux méthodes : la première consiste à obtenir la date de naissance de chaque personne à l'occasion d'un recensement ou d'un sondage, puis à calculer l'âge en années révolues en soustrayant la date de naissance de celle du dénombrement[7]. La seconde consiste à enregistrer l'âge en années révolues au moment du recensement, c'est-à-dire l'âge au dernier anniversaire.

La méthode recommandée consiste à calculer l'âge au dernier anniversaire en soustrayant la date exacte de la naissance de la date du recensement. Toutefois, on n'a pas toujours recours à cette méthode ; certains pays ou zones calculent l'âge en faisant la différence entre l'année du recensement et l'année de la naissance. Lorsque les données sur l'âge ont été établies de cette façon, on l'a signalé chaque fois que possible par une note. On peut d'ailleurs s'en rendre compte dans une certaine mesure, car les chiffres dans la catégorie des moins d'un an sont plus faibles qu'ils ne devraient l'être. Cependant, un nombre irrégulier de naissances d'une année à l'autre ou l'omission de certains âges parmi les moins d'un an peut aussi fausser les chiffres de la population de moins d'un an.

3.1.3.2 *Erreurs dans les données sur l'âge*

Les causes d'erreurs dans les données sur l'âge sont diverses : on peut citer notamment l'ignorance de l'âge exact, la déclaration d'années d'âge correspondant à un calendrier différent de celui des années solaires révolues depuis la naissance[8], la négligence dans les déclarations et dans la façon dont elles sont consignées, la tendance générale à déclarer des âges se terminant par certains chiffres tels que 0, 2, 5 ou 8, la tendance pour les personnes âgées à exagérer leur âge, une aversion subconsciente pour certains nombres, et les fausses déclarations faites délibérément.

Les causes d'erreurs mentionnées ci-dessus, communes à la plupart des enquêtes sur l'âge et à la plupart des pays ou zones, peuvent nuire sensiblement à la comparabilité.

À cause des difficultés indiquées ci-dessus, les répartitions par âge et par sexe de la population d'un grand nombre de pays ou de zones font apparaître les irrégularités suivantes : 1) sous-estimation des groupes d'âge correspondant aux enfants de moins d'un an et aux jeunes enfants ; 2) polarisation des déclarations sur les âges se terminant par les chiffres 0 ou 5 (c'est-à-dire 5, 10,15, 20...) ; 3) prépondérance des âges pairs (par exemple 10, 12, 14...) au détriment des âges impairs (par exemple 11, 13, 15...) ; 4) écart considérable et surprenant entre le rapport masculin/féminin à certains âges ; 5) différences importantes et difficilement explicables entre les données concernant des groupes d'âge voisins. En comparant les statistiques provenant de recensements successifs pour des cohortes identiques sur le plan de l'âge et de la répartition par sexe et en étudiant la répartition par âge et par sexe de la population à chaque recensement, on peut déceler l'existence de ces incohérences et de quelques autres, un certain nombre d'entre elles se retrouvant à des degrés divers même dans les recensements les plus modernes.

3.1.3.3 *Évaluation de l'exactitude*

Pour déterminer, sur la base des anomalies relevées dans les groupes d'âge quinquennaux, le degré d'exactitude des statistiques par âge, on avait mis au point un indice spécial[9] pour l'*Annuaire démographique 1949-1950*. Cet indice était sensible à l'influence des différents facteurs qui limitent l'exactitude des données et il n'échappait pas non plus à celle des véritables fluctuations démographiques du passé. On ne pouvait donc l'appliquer indistinctement à tous les types de données à moins d'effectuer les ajustements nécessaires et de faire preuve de prudence dans l'interprétation des résultats.

La publication dans *l'Annuaire démographique 1955* de statistiques de la population par année d'âge a permis d'utiliser un indice simple, mais très sensible, connu sous le nom d'indice de Whipple ou indice de concentration[10], dont l'interprétation échappe pratiquement à l'influence des facteurs sans rapport avec l'exactitude des déclarations d'âge. Il existe des méthodes plus perfectionnées pour évaluer l'exactitude des répartitions de population par année d'âge, mais on a décidé de se servir ici de l'indice de Whipple à cause de sa simplicité et de la large utilisation dont il a déjà fait l'objet dans d'autres publications.

L'indice de Whipple s'obtient en additionnant les déclarations d'âge comprises entre 23 et 62 ans inclusivement et en calculant le pourcentage des âges déclarés se terminant par 0 ou 5 par rapport au cinquième du nombre total de déclarations.

Les résultats varient entre 0, si aucun âge déclaré ne se termine par 0 ou 5, et un maximum de 500, si aucun âge déclaré ne se termine par un chiffre autre que 0 ou 5. S'il n'y a pas de concentration sur les âges se terminant par 0 et 5, l'indice de Whipple est de 100[11].

Cet indice est applicable à toutes les répartitions par âge pour lesquelles les années d'âge sont données au moins jusqu'à 62 ans, sauf dans les cas suivants : 1) lorsque les données présentées ont déjà fait l'objet d'un ajustement, l'indice de Whipple ne révèle aucune irrégularité bien que des inexactitudes d'un type différent puissent fausser ces données ; 2) lorsque les statistiques relatives à l'âge sont établies sur la base de l'année de naissance et que la tendance à arrondir l'année de naissance se traduit par une fréquence excessive des âges impairs, on ne peut utiliser la méthode reposant sur les déclarations d'âge se terminant par 5 et 0 pour évaluer l'exactitude des données recueillies.

L'indice a dernièrement été calculé pour toutes les distributions par année d'âge des recensements effectués entre 1985 et 2003, à l'exception de celles que l'on a écartées pour les motifs indiqués plus haut. Ces données sont publiées dans l 'édition spéciale de l'*Annuaire démographique* consacrée aux recensements de la population, volume I , que l'on peut consulter en ligne à l'adresse http://unstats.un.org/unsd/demographic/products/dyb/dybcens.htm .

Bien que l'indice de Whipple ne mesure que les effets de la préférence pour les âges se terminant par 5 et 0, il semble que l'on puisse admettre qu'il existe généralement certains liens entre cette préférence et d'autres sources d'inexactitudes dans les déclarations d'âge, de telle sorte que l'on peut dire qu'il donne une assez bonne idée de l'exactitude de la répartition par âge en général.

3.2 Méthodes utilisées pour indiquer la qualité des statistiques publiées

On a cherché dans toute la mesure possible à donner au lecteur une indication du degré de fiabilité des statistiques publiées dans *l'Annuaire démographique*. Pour ce faire, on a procédé de diverses façons. Chaque fois que l'on savait, grâce par exemple à une enquête post censitaire, qu'il y avait eu sous-dénombrement ou surdénombrement, on l'a signalé dans les notes qui accompagnent le tableau 3. Comme on l'a indiqué à la section 2.1 sous la rubrique « Considérations géographiques », chaque fois que les données ne portaient pas sur la totalité du pays, on l'a également signalé en note. De plus, les services nationaux de statistique ont été invités à fournir une évaluation des estimations de la population totale qu'ils communiquaient à la Division de statistique de l'ONU.

3.2.1 Traitement des séries chronologiques d'estimations de la population

En ce qui concerne les séries d'estimations de la population en milieu d'année, on considère que la qualité de la série tout entière est la même que celle de la dernière estimation. La qualité de la série est indiquée par le caractère d'imprimerie utilisé.

On n'a pas cherché à subdiviser les séries, mais il est évident que les données qui sont jugées sûres actuellement n'ont pas toutes le même degré de fiabilité et que, pour les premières années, nombre d'entre elles étaient peut-être bien moins sûres que la classification actuelle ne le laisse supposer. Ainsi, il apparaît clairement que cette méthode tend, dans bien des cas, à surestimer la fiabilité probable des séries chronologiques. Elle peut aussi inciter à sous-estimer la fiabilité des estimations pour les années qui précèdent ou qui suivent immédiatement un recensement.

3.2.2 Traitement des séries estimatives selon l'âge et d'autres caractéristiques démographiques

Des estimations de la répartition de la population par âge et par sexe peuvent être obtenues selon deux grandes méthodes : 1) en appliquant les composantes spécifiques du mouvement de la population, pour chaque groupe d'âge et pour chaque sexe, à la population dénombrée lors du recensement ; 2) en répartissant proportionnellement le chiffre total estimé pour une année postcensitaire d'après la composition par âge et par sexe au moment du recensement. Les estimations obtenues par la seconde méthode ne sont pas publiées dans l'*Annuaire démographique*.

Les séries estimatives selon l'âge et le sexe qui sont publiées sont classées en deux catégories, « sûres » ou « moins sûres », selon la méthode retenue pour le plus récent calcul estimatif de la population totale en milieu d'année. Ainsi, l'appréciation de la qualité du chiffre total, telle qu'elle ressort des signes de code, est censée s'appliquer aussi à l'ensemble de la répartition par âge et par sexe, et c'est sur cette seule base que l'on décide si les données figureront en caractères italiques ou romains. On n'a pas encore procédé à une évaluation plus poussée des données détaillées concernant la composition par âge.

4. STATISTIQUES DE L'ÉTAT CIVIL

Aux fins de l'*Annuaire démographique*, on entend par statistiques de l'état civil les statistiques des naissances vivantes.

Dans le présent volume de l'*Annuaire*, on n'a présenté que les tableaux de caractère général sur la natalité, la mortalité, la nuptialité et la divortialité. Les tableaux consacrés à la mortalité sont groupés sous les rubriques suivantes : mortalité fœtale, mortalité infantile, mortalité liée à la maternité et mortalité générale, y compris des tableaux portant sur la cause des décès.

4.1 Sources de variations des données

La plupart des statistiques de l'état civil publiées dans le présent *Annuaire* émanent des systèmes nationaux d'enregistrement des faits d'état civil. Le degré d'exhaustivité et d'exactitude de ces données varie d'un pays ou d'une zone à l'autre.

Il n'existe pas partout de système national d'enregistrement des faits d'état civil et, dans quelques cas, seuls certains faits sont enregistrés. Par exemple, dans certains pays ou zones, seuls les naissances et les décès sont enregistrés. Il existe également des différences quant au degré d'efficacité avec lequel les lois relatives à l'enregistrement des faits d'état civil sont appliquées dans les divers pays ou zones. La fiabilité des statistiques provenant des registres d'état civil dépend des modalités d'application de la loi et de la mesure dans laquelle le public s'y soumet.

Il est à signaler que dans certains cas les statistiques de la nuptialité et de la divortialité sont tirées d'autres sources que les registres d'état civil. Dans certains pays ou zones, par exemple, les seules données disponibles sur la nuptialité proviennent des registres des églises. Selon la pratique suivie par chaque pays, les statistiques de la divortialité sont tirées des actes des tribunaux et/ou des registres d'état civil. L'officier de l'état civil, le service national de statistique ou d'autres services administratifs peuvent être chargés d'établir ces statistiques.

Les autres facteurs qui influent sur la comparabilité internationale des statistiques de l'état civil sont à peu près les mêmes que ceux qu'il convient de prendre en considération pour interpréter les variations observées dans les statistiques de la population. La définition des faits d'état civil aux fins de statistique, la portée des données du point de vue géographique et ethnique ainsi que les méthodes d'exploitation des données sont autant d'éléments qui peuvent influer sur la comparabilité.

En plus des statistiques tirées des registres d'état civil, l'*Annuaire* présente des statistiques de l'état civil qui sont des estimations officielles nationales, fondées souvent sur les résultats de sondages. Aussi leur comparabilité varie-t-elle en fonction du degré d'exhaustivité des déclarations recueillies lors d'enquêtes sur les ménages, des erreurs d'échantillonnage ou autres, et des distorsions d'origines diverses.

Pour plus de détails au sujet des pratiques nationales relatives au rassemblement des statistiques d'état civil, le lecteur pourra se reporter aux : *Principes et recommandations pour un système de statistiques de l'état civil, deuxième révision*[12] ; *Manuel des systèmes d'enregistrement des faits d'état civil et de statistiques de l'état civil : Élaboration d'un cadre juridique*[13] ; *Manuel des systèmes d'enregistrement des faits d'état civil et de statistiques de l'état civil : Gestion, fonctionnement et tenue*[14]; *Manuel des systèmes* d'enregistrement des faits d'état civil et de statistiques de l'état civil. Élaboration de programmes d'information, d'éducation et de communication[15] ; *Manuel des systèmes d'enregistrement des faits d'état civil et de statistiques de l'état civil : Principes et protocoles concernant la communication et l'archivage des documents individuels*[16]; *Manuel des systèmes d'enregistrement des faits d'état civil et de statistiques de l'état civil : Informatisation*[17]. Le *Manuel de collecte de données sur la fécondité et la mortalité*[18] fournit des informations ayant trait à la collecte et à l'évaluation des données sur la fécondité, sur la mortalité et sur d'autres faits d'état civil, qui ont été recueillies au cours des enquêtes sur les ménages. Ces publications sont également disponibles sur le Web à partir de l'adresse suivante : http://unstats.un.org/unsd/demographic/sources/civilreg/default.htm.

4.1.1 Définition des faits d'état civil aux fins de la statistique

Une cause importante d'hétérogénéité dans les données est le manque d'uniformité des définitions des différents faits d'état civil. Aux fins de *l'Annuaire démographique*, il est recommandé de recueillir les données relatives aux faits d'état civil en utilisant les définitions établies au paragraphe 57 des *Principes et recommandations pour un système de statistiques de l'état civil, deuxième révision*[12]. Ces définitions sont les suivantes :

La *NAISSANCE VIVANTE est l'expulsion ou l'extraction complète du corps de la mère, indépendamment de la durée de la gestation, d'un produit de la conception qui, après cette séparation, respire ou manifeste tout autre signe de vie, tel que battement de cœur, pulsation du cordon ombilical ou contraction effective d'un muscle soumis à l'action de la volonté, que le cordon ombilical ait été coupé ou non et que le placenta soit ou non demeuré attaché; tout produit d'une telle naissance est considéré comme « enfant né vivant ».*

Le *DÉCÈS est la disparition permanente de tout signe de vie à un moment quelconque postérieur à la naissance vivante (cessation des fonctions vitales après la naissance sans possibilité de réanimation). Cette définition ne comprend donc pas les morts fœtales.*

La *MORT FŒTALE est le décès d'un produit de la conception lorsque ce décès est survenu avant l'expulsion ou l'extraction complète du corps de la mère, indépendamment de la durée de la gestation; le décès est indiqué par le fait qu'après cette séparation le fœtus ne respire ni ne manifeste aucun signe de vie, tel que battement de cœur, pulsation du cordon ombilical ou contraction effective d'un muscle soumis à l'action de la volonté. Les morts fœtales tardives sont celles qui sont survenues après 28 semaines de gestation ou plus. Il n'y a aucune différence entre ces « morts fœtales tardives » et les faits désignés, avant 1950, par le terme « mortinatalité*[19] *».*

Le *MARIAGE est l'acte, la cérémonie ou la procédure qui établit un rapport légal entre mari et femme. L'union peut être rendue légale par une procédure civile ou religieuse, ou par toute autre procédure, conformément à la législation du pays.*

Le *DIVORCE est la dissolution légale et définitive des liens du mariage, c'est-à-dire la séparation de l'époux et de l'épouse qui confère aux parties le droit de se remarier civilement ou religieusement, ou selon toute autre procédure, conformément à la législation du pays.*

Des données concernant les avortements sont également recueillies et présentées dans l'*Annuaire démographique*, la définition retenue étant la suivante :

Par référence à la femme, l'*AVORTEMENT se définit comme toute interruption de grossesse qui est survenue avant 28 semaines de gestation et dont le produit est un fœtus mort. Il existe deux grandes catégories d'avortement : l'avortement spontané et l'avortement provoqué. L'avortement provoqué a pour origine une action délibérée entreprise en vue d'interrompre une grossesse. Tout autre avortement est considéré comme spontané.*

4.1.2 Problèmes posés par les définitions établies

Les variations par rapport aux définitions établies des faits d'état civil sont le principal obstacle à la comparabilité internationale des statistiques de l'état civil. Un exemple en est fourni par le cas des naissances vivantes et celui des morts fœtales[20]. Dans certains pays ou zones, il faut que le nouveau-né ait vécu 24 heures pour pouvoir être inscrit sur le registre des naissances vivantes. Les décès d'enfants qui surviennent avant l'expiration du délai de 24 heures sont classés parmi les morts fœtales tardives et, en l'absence de méthodes spéciales d'exploitation des données, ne sont comptés ni dans les naissances vivantes ni dans les décès. De même, dans plusieurs autres pays ou zones, les décès d'enfants nés vivants et décédés avant l'enregistrement de leur naissance sont également comptés parmi les morts fœtales tardives.

À moins que des méthodes spéciales n'aient été adoptées pour l'exploitation de ces données, les statistiques des naissances vivantes et des décès ne tiendront pas compte de ces cas, qui viendront en revanche accroître d'autant le nombre des morts fœtales tardives. Le taux de mortalité infantile sera donc sous-estimé. Bien que les éléments constitutifs du taux (décès d'enfants de moins d'un an et naissances vivantes) accusent exactement la même insuffisance en valeur absolue, les lacunes sont proportionnellement plus fortes pour les décès de moins d'un an, ce qui cause des erreurs plus importantes dans les taux de mortalité infantile.

De plus, cette pratique augmente les rapports de mortinatalité. Quelques pays ou zones effectuent les ajustements nécessaires pour corriger cette anomalie (du moins dans les fréquences totales) au moment de l'établissement des tableaux. Si aucun ajustement n'a été effectué, cela est indiqué dans les notes chaque fois que possible.

Les définitions du mariage et du divorce posent aussi un problème du point de vue de la comparabilité internationale. Contrairement à la naissance et au décès, qui sont des faits biologiques, le mariage et le divorce sont uniquement déterminés par la législation et la coutume et, de ce fait, il est moins facile d'en donner une définition statistique qui ait une application universelle. À des fins statistiques, ces notions ont donc été définies de manière générale par référence à la législation de chaque pays ou zone. La législation relative au mariage et plus particulièrement au divorce varie d'un pays ou d'une zone à l'autre. En ce qui concerne le mariage, l'âge de nubilité est la condition la plus fréquemment requise mais il arrive souvent que d'autres conditions soient exigées.

Lorsqu'il est connu, l'âge minimum auquel le mariage peut avoir lieu avec le consentement des parents (et dans certains cas sans le consentement des parents) est indiqué au tableau 24-1 as part of the technical notes for table 24. Les lois et règlements relatifs à la dissolution du mariage par le divorce vont de l'interdiction absolue, en passant par diverses conditions requises pour l'obtention du divorce, jusqu'à la simple déclaration, par l'époux, de son désir ou de son intention de divorcer.

4.1.3 Portée géographique ou ethnique restreinte

En principe, les statistiques de l'état civil devraient s'étendre à l'ensemble du pays ou de la zone auxquels elles se rapportent et englober tous les groupes ethniques. En fait, il n'est pas rare que les données soient fragmentaires. Dans certains pays ou zones, l'enregistrement n'est obligatoire que pour une petite partie de la population, par exemple pour certains groupes ethniques. Dans d'autres, il n'existe pas de disposition qui prescrive l'enregistrement obligatoire sur le plan national, mais seulement des règlements ou décrets des municipalités ou des États, qui ne s'appliquent pas à l'ensemble du territoire. Il en est encore autrement dans d'autres pays ou zones où les autorités ont institué une zone d'enregistrement comprenant seulement une partie du territoire, le reste étant exclu en raison des difficultés d'accès ou parce qu'il est pratiquement impossible, pour des raisons d'ordre économique ou culturel, d'y procéder à un enregistrement régulier.

4.1.4 Exploitation des données

4.1.4.1 Selon le lieu de l'événement

Les statistiques de l'état civil qui sont présentées pour l'ensemble du territoire national se rapportent à la population de fait ou population présente. En conséquence, sauf indication contraire, les statistiques de l'état civil relatives à une zone ou à un pays donné portent sur tous les faits survenus dans l'ensemble de la population, à l'intérieur des frontières actuelles de la zone ou du pays considéré. On peut donc estimer qu'elles englobent les faits d'état civil survenus dans les tribus nomades et parmi les populations autochtones ainsi que parmi les ressortissants du pays et les étrangers. Des notes signalent les exceptions lorsque celles-ci sont connues.

Pour certains pays, les écarts entre les taux démographiques pour les zones urbaines et pour les zones rurales peuvent varier notablement selon que les faits d'état civil ont été exploités sur la base du lieu de l'événement ou du lieu de résidence habituel. Par exemple, si un nombre appréciable de femmes résidant dans des zones rurales proches de grands centres urbains accouchent dans les hôpitaux ou maternités d'une ville, les taux de fécondité ainsi que les taux de mortalité néo-natale et infantile seront généralement plus élevés dans les zones urbaines (et par conséquent plus faibles dans les zones rurales) si les faits sont exploités en se fondant sur le lieu de l'événement et non sur le lieu de résidence habituel. Le phénomène sera le même dans le cas de la mortalité générale si un bon nombre de personnes résidant dans des zones rurales font appel aux services de santé des villes lorsqu'elles sont gravement malades.

4.1.4.2 Selon la date de l'événement ou la date de l'enregistrement

Autant que possible, les statistiques de l'état civil figurant dans *l'Annuaire démographique* se rapportent aux faits survenus pendant l'année considérée et non aux faits enregistrés au cours de ladite année. Bon nombre de pays ou zones, toutefois, exploitent leurs statistiques de l'état civil selon la date de l'enregistrement et non selon la date de l'événement. Comme ces statistiques risquent d'induire gravement en erreur, les pays ou zones dont on sait qu'ils établissent leurs statistiques d'après la date de l'enregistrement sont signalés dans les tableaux par un signe plus (+). On ne dispose toutefois pas pour tous les pays ou zones de renseignements complets sur la méthode d'exploitation des statistiques de l'état civil et les données sont peut-être exploitées selon la date de l'enregistrement plus souvent que ne le laisserait supposer l'emploi des signes.

Étant donné que la qualité des données est inextricablement liée aux retards dans l'enregistrement, il faudra toujours considérer en même temps le code de qualité qui est décrit à la section 4.2.1 ci-après. Évidemment, si l'enregistrement des naissances est complet et effectué en temps voulu (code 'C'), les effets perturbateurs de la méthode consistant à exploiter les données selon la date de l'enregistrement seront pratiquement annulés. De même, s'agissant des statistiques des décès, les effets pourront bien souvent être réduits au minimum dans les pays ou zones où le code sanitaire subordonne la délivrance du permis d'inhumer à l'enregistrement du décès, ce qui tend à hâter l'enregistrement. Quant aux morts fœtales, elles sont généralement déclarées immédiatement ou ne sont pas déclarées du tout. En conséquence, si l'enregistrement se fait dans un délai très court, la différence entre les statistiques établies selon la date de l'événement et celles qui sont établies selon la date de l'enregistrement peut être négligeable. Dans bien des cas, la durée des délais légaux accordés pour l'enregistrement des faits d'état civil est un facteur dont dépend dans une large mesure l'incidence sur la comparabilité de l'exploitation des données selon la date de l'enregistrement.

En ce qui concerne le mariage et le divorce, la pratique consistant à exploiter les statistiques selon la date de l'enregistrement ne pose généralement pas de graves problèmes. Le mariage étant, dans de nombreux pays ou zones, un contrat juridique civil qui, pour être légal, doit être conclu devant un officier de l'état civil, il s'ensuit que dans ces pays ou zones l'enregistrement a lieu presque systématiquement au moment de la cérémonie ou immédiatement après. De même, dans de nombreux pays ou zones, le tribunal ou l'autorité qui a prononcé le divorce est seul habilité à enregistrer cet acte, et comme l'acte d'enregistrement figure alors sur les registres du tribunal l'enregistrement suit généralement de peu le jugement.

En revanche, si l'enregistrement n'a lieu qu'avec un certain retard, les statistiques de l'état civil établies selon la date de l'enregistrement ne sont pas comparables sur le plan international. Au mieux, les statistiques par date de l'enregistrement prendront surtout en considération des faits survenus au cours de l'année précédente ; dans les pays ou zones où le système d'enregistrement n'est pas très développé, il y entrera des faits datant de plusieurs années. Il ressort des documents dont on dispose que des retards de plusieurs années dans l'enregistrement des naissances ne sont pas rares, encore que, dans la majorité des cas, les retards ne dépassent pas deux à quatre ans.

Tant que l'enregistrement se fera avec retard, les statistiques fondées sur la date d'enregistrement ne seront comparables sur le plan international ni entre elles ni avec les statistiques établies selon la date de fait d'état civil.

Il convient également de noter que l'exploitation des données selon la date de l'enregistrement ne nuit pas seulement à la comparabilité internationale des statistiques. Même à l'intérieur d'un pays ou d'une zone, le procédé qui consiste à compter les enregistrements et non les faits peut compromettre la comparabilité des chiffres sur une longue période. Si le nombre des faits d'état civil enregistrés varie d'une année à l'autre (par suite de l'application de mesures visant tout particulièrement à encourager l'enregistrement ou parce qu'il est subitement devenu nécessaire de produire le certificat d'une naissance ou d'un décès non enregistré pour l'accomplissement de certaines formalités), les statistiques de l'état civil établies d'après la date de l'enregistrement ne permettent pas de quantifier ni d'analyser l'état et l'évolution de la population. Tout au plus peuvent-elles révéler l'évolution des conditions d'exigibilité du certificat de naissance, de décès ou de mariage et les fluctuations du volume de travail des bureaux d'état civil. Les statistiques établies selon

En général, le code de qualité pour les décès utilisé au tableau 18 sert à déterminer si, dans les autres tableaux, les données relatives aux décès apparaissent en caractères romains ou en italique. Toutefois, le code associé à certaines données sur les décès liés à la maternité dans le tableau 17 diffère de celui employé dans le tableau 18 lorsque l'on sait que le degré d'exhaustivité des données diffère grandement de celui du nombre total des décès. Dans les cas où le code de qualité du tableau 18 ne correspond pas aux caractères utilisés dans le tableau 17, les renseignements concernant l'exhaustivité des statistiques des décès selon la cause sont indiqués en note à la fin du tableau.

On a utilisé la même indication de fiabilité dans les tableaux des taux démographiques et dans ceux des fréquences correspondantes. Par exemple, les taux de mortalité calculés d'après les décès figurant sur un registre incomplet ou d'exhaustivité indéterminée sont jugés douteux et apparaissent en italique. Au sens strict, pour évaluer de façon plus précise les taux démographiques, il faudrait tenir compte de la précision des données sur la population figurant au dénominateur dans les taux. La qualité des données sur la population est étudiée à la section 3.2 des notes techniques.

Il convient de noter que, pour les taux de mortalité infantile, les taux de mortalité liée à la maternité et les rapports de morts fœtales tardives (calculées en utilisant au dénominateur le nombre de naissances vivantes), les indications relatives à la fiabilité sont déterminées sur la base des codes de qualité utilisés pour les décès d'enfants de moins d'un an, les décès totaux et les morts fœtales tardives, respectivement. Pour évaluer ces taux et rapports de façon plus précise, il faudrait tenir compte de la qualité des données relatives aux naissances vivantes, utilisées au dénominateur dans leur calcul. Les codes de qualité pour les naissances vivantes figurent au tableau 9 et sont décrits plus en détail dans les notes techniques se rapportant à ce tableau.

4.2.3 Traitement des séries chronologiques de statistiques tirées des registres d'état civil

Il est plus difficile de déterminer la qualité des séries chronologiques de statistiques de l'état civil que celle des données pour une seule année. Étant donné qu'une série chronologique de statistiques de l'état civil ne peut généralement avoir pour source qu'un système permanent d'enregistrement des faits d'état civil, on a arbitrairement supposé que le degré d'exactitude de la série tout entière était le même que celui de la dernière tranche annuelle de données tirées du registre d'état civil. La série tout entière est traitée de la manière décrite à la section 4.2.2 ci-dessus : lorsque le code de qualité relatif aux données d'enregistrement les plus récentes est 'C', les fréquences et les taux relatifs aux années antérieures sont eux aussi considérés comme sûrs et figurent en caractères romains. Inversement, si les données d'enregistrement les plus récentes sont codées 'U' ou '...', les données des années antérieures sont jugées douteuses et figurent en italique. Cette méthode n'est certes pas entièrement satisfaisante, car les données des premières années de la série sont souvent beaucoup moins sûres que le code actuel ne le laisse supposer.

4.2.4 Traitement des estimations fondées sur les statistiques de l'état civil

En plus des données provenant des systèmes d'enregistrement des faits d'état civil, l'*Annuaire démographique* contient aussi des estimations relatives aux fréquences et aux taux. Il s'agit d'estimations officielles, généralement calculées à partir des résultats d'un sondage ou par analyse démographique. Si des estimations concernant les fréquences et les taux figurent dans les tableaux, c'est parce que l'on considère qu'elles fournissent des renseignements plus exacts que les systèmes existants d'enregistrement des faits d'état civil. En conséquence, elles sont également jugées sûres et sont donc imprimées en caractères romains, même si elles sont entrecoupées dans une série chronologique de données tirées des registres d'état civil.

Dans les tableaux qui indiquent le code de qualité, ce code ne s'applique qu'aux données tirées des registres d'état civil. Si une série pour un pays ou une zone comprend à la fois des données tirées d'un registre d'état civil et des données estimatives, le code ne s'applique qu'aux données d'enregistrement. Si seules des données estimatives apparaissent, le symbole '|' est utilisé.

4.3 Causes de décès

Les États membres de l'Organisation mondiale de la santé (OMS) sont tenus de communiquer à celle-ci les données sur les causes de décès codifiées selon la révision en vigueur de la Classification internationale des maladies et des problèmes de santé connexes (CIM) adoptée par l'Assemblé mondiale de la santé[21]. Les données sont collectées par l'OMS sur la base de la CIM. Pour assurer la comparabilité internationale des statistiques des causes de décès, l'OMS organise régulièrement des conférences internationales de révision de la Classification internationale des maladies afin de suivre, au fur et à mesure, les progrès les plus récents de la médecine clinique et de la statistique. Les données sont généralement envoyées à l'OMS selon la classification à 4 caractères prévue par la CIM et sont archivées dans la base de données sur la mortalité de l'OMS telles qu'elles ont été présentées par le pays. Pour les versions antérieures, par contre, les données sont disponibles seulement selon la liste A de 150 causes de la CIM. Les données de l'OMS sont disponibles sur le site Internet suivant: http://www3.who.int/whosis/menu.cfm.

Les révisions de la CIM permettent certes de disposer d'une version actualisée, mais elles posent plusieurs problèmes de comparabilité des statistiques des causes de décès. Le premier tient au manque de comparabilité dans le temps, qui accompagne inévitablement la mise en oeuvre d'une classification nouvelle. Le deuxième est celui de la comparabilité entre pays ou zones, car les différents pays peuvent adopter la nouvelle classification à des époques différentes. Établir la cause des décès exige des compétences de plus en plus poussées à mesure que la classification devient plus précise. Or, dans beaucoup de pays ou zones, il est rare que les décès se produisent en présence d'un témoin possédant une formation médicale et le certificat de décès est le plus souvent établi par quelqu'un qui n'est pas qualifié sur le plan médical. Étant donné que la CIM répertorie de nombreux diagnostics qu'il est impossible d'établir si l'on n'a pas de formation en médecine, elle ne favorise pas toujours la comparabilité internationale, notamment entre pays ou zones où la qualité des services médicaux est très disparate.

La dixième révision[22] est la dernière qu'ait connue la CIM. Les chapitres de la dixième révision se fondent sur un système de codification alphanumérique à une lettre suivie de trois chiffres pour les catégories à quatre caractères. Le chapitre 1 concerne les maladies infectieuses et parasitaires et le chapitre 2 l'ensemble des néoplasmes. Le chapitre 3 a trait aux troubles du système immunitaire, aux maladies du sang et aux organes hématopoïétiques. Le chapitre 4 porte sur les maladies du système endocrinien, de la nutrition et du métabolisme. Les autres chapitres groupent les maladies selon leur site anatomique, à l'exception de ceux qui concernent les affections mentales, les complications de la grossesse, de l'accouchement et des suites de couches, les malformations congénitales et les affections de la période périnatale. Enfin, un chapitre entier est consacré aux symptômes, manifestations et résultats anormaux.

4.3.1 Mortalité liée à la maternité

D'après la dixième révision de la CIM, la « mortalité liée à la maternité » est définie comme le décès d'une femme survenu au cours de la grossesse ou dans un délai de 42 jours après sa terminaison, quelle qu'en soit la durée et la localisation, pour une cause quelconque déterminée ou aggravée par la grossesse ou les soins qu'elle a motivés, mais ni accidentelle ni fortuite.

Les décès liés à la maternité se répartissent en deux groupes :

1) Décès par cause obstétricale directe qui résultent de complications obstétricales (grossesse, travail et suites de couches), d'interventions, d'omissions, d'un traitement incorrect ou d'un enchaînement d'événements de l'un quelconque des facteurs ci-dessus ;
2) Décès par cause obstétricale indirecte qui résultent d'une maladie préexistante ou d'une affection apparue au cours de la grossesse, sans qu'elle soit due à des causes obstétricales directes, mais qui a été aggravée par les effets physiologiques de la grossesse.

Il est recommandé dans la dixième révision d'exprimer les taux de mortalité liée à la maternité sur la base de 100 000 naissances vivantes ou 100 000 naissances totales (naissances vivantes et morts fœtales)[23]. Le nombre de femmes enceintes aurait dû être pris comme dénominateur, mais étant donné qu'il est impossible de le déterminer, le taux de mortalité liée à la maternité est ici calculé par 100 000 naissances vivantes. Bien que les naissances vivantes ne permettent pas d'évaluer sans distorsion le nombre des femmes enceintes, leur nombre est plus fiable que d'autres estimations car le nombre des naissances vivantes est plus exactement enregistré que celui des naissances vivantes et des morts fœtales.

NOTES

[1] Les données relatives à la mortalité liée à la maternité et aux taux de mortalité selon la cause émanent de l'Organisation mondiale de la santé et sont disponibles à l'adresse suivante : http://www3.who.int/whosis/menu.cfm.

[2] Les éditions de 1978 et de 1991 font exception à la règle, puisque les tableaux sur des sujets spéciaux ont été publiés séparément.

[3] *World Population Prospects: The 2006 Revision*. Nations Unies, New York, numéro de vente: E.07.XIII.7, 2007. Dans l'intervalle, on peut consulter des extraits et certaines données sur le site www.unpopulation.org.

[4] ST/ESA/STAT/SER.M/49/Rev.4/WWW ; http://unstats.un.org/unsd/methods/m49/m49.htm; voir également *Code standard des pays et des zones à usage statistique*, numéro de vente : M.98.XVII.9, Nations Unies, New York, 1999.

[5] À paraître, F.07.XVII.8, Nations Unies, New York, 2007. Avant d'être publiée, cette publication est disponible en ligne à l'adresse suivante : http://unstats.un.org/unsd/demographic/sources/census/docs/P&R_%20Rev2.pdf

[6] Ibid., par. 2.135

[7] Lorsque l'on utilise un registre de la population, on peut également calculer l'âge en années révolues en soustrayant la date de naissance de chaque personne inscrite sur le registre de la date de référence à laquelle se rapportent les données sur l'âge.

[8] L'emploi de méthodes différentes de calcul de l'âge, par exemple la méthode occidentale et la méthode orientale, ou, comme on les désigne plus communément, la méthode anglaise et la méthode chinoise, représente une cause de non-comparabilité. Selon la méthode chinoise, on considère que l'enfant est âgé d'un an à sa naissance et qu'il avance d'un an à chaque nouvelle année chinoise. Les répercussions de cette méthode sont particulièrement apparentes dans les données pour le premier âge : les données concernant les enfants de moins d'un an sont nettement inférieures à la réalité. Les effets sur les chiffres relatifs aux groupes d'âge suivants sont moins visibles. Les séries ainsi établies sont souvent ajustées avant d'être publiées, mais il ne faut pas exclure la possibilité d'aberrations de ce genre lorsque l'on compare des données censitaires sur l'âge.

[9] Dans cet indice, on déterminait les différences à partir des rapports prévus de masculinité dans un groupe d'âge et dans les groupes d'âge adjacents. Il fallait pour cela tenir compte de l'influence de facteurs tels que les mouvements passés des taux de natalité, les pertes de guerre élevées et, le cas échéant, le faible effectif de la population. On trouvera dans le *Bulletin démographique*, no 2 (publication des Nations Unies, numéro de vente : 52.XIII.4), p. 64 à 87, un exposé détaillé sur cet indice ainsi que les résultats de son application aux données présentées dans les éditions de 1949-1950 et de 1951 de l'*Annuaire démographique*. On a fait les mêmes calculs sur les statistiques publiées dans l'*Annuaire démographique 1952* et les résultats obtenus sont indiqués dans l'édition correspondante de l'*Annuaire*, qui, comme celles de 1953 et de 1954, donne de brèves explications sur l'indice en question.

[10] United States Bureau of the Census, Thirteenth Census, vol. I (Washington, D.C., U.S. Government Printing Office), p. 291 et 292.

[11] J.T. Marten, Census of India, 1921, vol. I, partie I (Calcutta, 1924), p. 126 et 127.

[12] Numéro de vente : F.01.XVII.10, publication des Nations Unies, New York, 2003.

[13] Numéro de vente : F. 98.XVII.7, publication des Nations Unies, New York, 1998.

[14] Numéro de vente : F.98.XVII.11, publication des Nations Unies, New York, 1998.

[15] Numéro de vente : F.98.XVII.4, publication des Nations Unies, New York, 1998.

[16] Numéro de vente : F.98.XVII.6, publication des Nations Unies, New York, 1998.

[17] Numéro de vente : F.98.XVII.10, publication des Nations Unies, New York, 1998.

[18] *Manuel de Collecte de données sur la fécondité et la mortalité*, Numéro de vente 03.XVII.11, United Nations, New York, 2003.

[19] Pour plus de précisions, voir *Principes et recommandations pour un système de statistiques de l'état civil, deuxième révision*, numéro de vente : F.01.XVII.10, publication des Nations Unies, New York, 2001, par. 57.

[20] Pour plus de précisions au sujet des considérations historiques et juridiques auxquelles se rattachent les différentes définitions correspondant aux naissances vivantes et aux morts fœtales, pour une comparaison des définitions utilisées depuis le 1er janvier 1950 et pour une évaluation des effets de ces différences de définition sur le calcul de divers taux, voir le *Manuel de statistique de l'état civil, Volume II, Étude des pratiques nationales*, numéro de vente : *F*.84.XVII.11, publication des Nations Unies, New York, 1985, chap. IV.

[21] Les États membres de l'Organisation mondiale de la santé se réunissent annuellement dans le cadre de l'Assemblée mondiale de la santé, qui est l'organe directeur de l'Organisation.

[22] Organisation mondiale de la santé, *Classification statistique internationale des maladies et problèmes de santé connexes*, dixième révision, vol. 2, Genève, 1992.

[23] Organisation mondiale de la santé, *Classification statistique internationale des maladies et problèmes de santé connexes*, dixième révision, vol. 2, Genève, 1992, pp. 129-136.

Table A. *Demographic Yearbook 2006* synoptic table: Availability of data by country/area, table and sex, where applicable
Tableau A. Tableau synoptique de l'*Annuaire démographique 2006:* Disponibilité des données par pays ou zone, tableau et le sexe , si disponible

General topic and table number- Suject général et numéro de tableau

Continent, country or area / Continent, pays ou zone	Table totals	Summary - Apercu 3 Total	3 M/F	4	5	Population 6 Total	6 M/F	7 Total	7 M/F	8 Total	8 M/F	Natality 9	10 Total	10 M/F	11	12	13	14
Total number of countries or areas - Total des pays ou zones	..	235	218	178	215	219	218	198	195	217	120	168	141	103	108	93	62	47
AFRICA — AFRIQUE																		
Algeria - Algérie	16	•	…		•	•		•	•	…		•	•		…	•	…	…
Angola	3	•	…		•	•		…		…		•				…	…	…
Benin - Bénin	9	•	•		•	•		•		•		•					…	…
Botswana	14	•	•	•	•	•	•	•	•			•	•				…	…
Burkina Faso	9	•	•	•	•	•	•	•		…		•					…	…
Burundi	7	•	•		•	•		•		…		•					…	…
Cameroon - Cameroun	4	•	…		•	•		…		…		•					…	…
Cape Verde - Cap-Vert	10	•	•		•	•		•		•		•					…	…
Central African Republic - République centrafricaine	6	•	…		•	•		…		…		•					…	…
Chad - Tchad	3	•	…		•	•		…		…		•					…	…
Comoros - Comores	3	•	…		•	•		…		…		•					…	…
Congo	7	•	•		•	•		•		…		•					…	…
Côte d'Ivoire	6	•	•		•	•		•		…		•					…	…
Democratic Republic of the Congo - République démocratique du Congo	2	•	•					•		…							…	…
Djibouti	4	•	•			•		•		…		•					…	…
Egypt - Égypte	28	•	•	•	•	•	•	•	•	•		•	•	•	•	•	…	…
Equatorial Guinea - Guinée équatoriale	4	•	•			•		•		…		•					…	…
Eritrea - Érythrée	3	•	•			•		•		…		•					…	…
Ethiopia - Éthiopie	9	•	•		•	•		•		•		•					…	…
Gabon	4	•	…			•		•		…		•					…	…
Gambia - Gambie	7	•	•		•	•		•		…		•					…	…
Ghana	12	•	•	•	•	•	•	•		•		•					…	…
Guinea - Guinée	4	•	•		•	•		•		…		•					…	…
Guinea-Bissau - Guinée-Bissau	4	•	•		•	•		•		…		•					…	…
Kenya	16	•	•	•	•	•	•	•	•	•		•	•				…	…
Lesotho	8	•	•		•	•		•		•		•					…	…
Liberia - Libéria	4	•	•			•		•		…		•					…	…
Libyan Arab Jamahiriya - Jamahiriya arabe libyenne	15	•	•	•	•	•		•		•		•	•	•			…	…
Madagascar	8	•	•		•	•		•		•		•					…	…
Malawi	17	•	•		•	•		•	•	•		•	•				…	…
Mali	9	•	•		•	•		•		•		•					…	…
Mauritania - Mauritanie	8	•	•		•	•		•		•		•					…	…
Mauritius - Maurice	29	•	•	•	•	•	•	•	•	•		•	•	•	•	•	…	…
Mayotte	9	•	•		•	•		•		•		•					…	…
Morocco - Maroc	15	•	•	…	•	•		•		•		•	•				…	…
Mozambique	13	•	•		•	•		•		•		•					…	…
Namibia - Namibie	15	•	•		•	•		•		•		•	•				…	…
Niger	9	•	•		•	•		•		•		•					…	…
Nigeria - Nigéria	8	•	•		•	•		•		•		•					…	…
Réunion	30	•	•	•	•	•	•	•	•	•		•	•	•	•	•	•	…
Rwanda	8	•	•		…	•		•		•		•					…	…
Saint Helena ex. dep. - Sainte-Hélène sans dép.	21	•	•	•	…	•		•		•		•	•				…	…
Saint Helena: Ascension - Sainte-Hélène: Ascension	6	•	•			•		•									…	…
Saint Helena: Tristan da Cunha - Sainte-Hélène: Tristan da Cunha	3	•	•		•	•		•									…	…
Sao Tome and Principe - Sao Tomé-et-Principe	8	•	•		•	•		•		•		•					…	…
Senegal - Sénégal	8	•	•		•	•		•		•		•					…	…
Seychelles	24	•	•	•	•	•		•	•	•		•	•		•	•	…	…
Sierra Leone	7	•	•		…	•		•		•		•					…	…
Somalia - Somalie	7	•	•		•	•		•		•		•					…	…
South Africa - Afrique du Sud	21	•	•	•	•	•		•		•		•	•				•	…
Sudan - Soudan	6	•	•		•	•		•				•					…	…

Table A. *Demographic Yearbook 2006* synoptic table: Availability of data by country/area, table and sex, where applicable

Tableau A. Tableau synoptique de l'*Annuaire démographique 2006:* Disponibilité des données par pays ou zone, tableau et le sexe , si disponible (continued — suite)

| Continent, country or area / Continent, pays ou zone | General topic and table number- Suject général et numéro de tableau ||||||||||||||
| | Infant and maternal mortality - Mortalité infantile et mortalité liée à la maternité |||| General mortality - Mortalité générale ||||||| Nuptiality and divorces - Nuptialité et divortialité |||
	15	16 Total	16 M/F	17	18	19 Total	19 M/F	20 Total	20 M/F	21	22	23	24	25
Total number of countries or areas - Total des pays ou zones	140	105	103	108	169	154	150	94	94	96	131	130	103	118
AFRICA — AFRIQUE														
Algeria - Algérie	•	...	...	...	•	...	•	...	...	...	•	•	...	...
Angola	...	...	...	...	...	...	...	...	...	...	...	...	...	...
Benin - Bénin	...	...	...	...	...	...	...	...	...	...	...	...	...	...
Botswana	...	...	...	...	•	•	•	•	...	...	•	...	...	...
Burkina Faso	...	...	...	...	...	...	...	...	...	...	...	...	...	...
Burundi	...	...	...	...	...	...	...	...	...	...	...	...	...	...
Cameroon - Cameroun	...	...	...	...	...	...	...	...	...	...	...	...	...	...
Cape Verde - Cap-Vert	...	...	...	...	...	...	...	...	...	...	...	...	...	...
Central African Republic - République centrafricaine	...	...	...	...	...	...	...	...	...	...	...	...	...	...
Chad - Tchad	...	...	...	...	...	...	...	...	...	...	...	...	...	...
Comoros - Comores	...	...	...	...	...	...	...	...	...	...	...	...	...	...
Congo	...	...	...	...	...	...	...	...	...	...	...	...	...	...
Côte d'Ivoire	...	...	...	...	...	...	...	...	...	...	...	...	...	...
Democratic Republic of the Congo - République démocratique du Congo	...	...	...	...	...	...	...	...	...	...	...	...	...	...
Djibouti	...	...	...	...	...	...	...	...	...	...	•	...	...	...
Egypt - Égypte	•	•	•	...	•	•	•	...	...	...	•	•	•	•
Equatorial Guinea - Guinée équatoriale	...	...	...	...	...	...	...	...	...	...	...	...	...	...
Eritrea - Érythrée	...	...	...	...	...	...	...	...	...	...	...	...	...	...
Ethiopia - Éthiopie	...	...	...	...	...	...	...	...	...	...	...	...	...	...
Gabon	...	...	...	...	...	...	...	...	...	...	...	...	...	...
Gambia - Gambie	...	...	...	...	...	...	...	...	...	...	...	...	...	...
Ghana	•	...	...	...	•	...	...	...	...	...	...	...	...	...
Guinea - Guinée	...	...	...	...	...	...	...	...	...	...	...	...	...	...
Guinea-Bissau - Guinée-Bissau	...	...	...	...	...	...	...	...	...	...	...	...	...	...
Kenya	•	...	...	...	•	...	...	...	...	...	•	...	...	...
Lesotho	...	...	...	...	...	...	...	...	...	...	•	...	...	...
Liberia - Libéria	...	...	...	...	...	...	...	...	...	...	...	...	...	...
Libyan Arab Jamahiriya - Jamahiriya arabe libyenne	...	...	...	...	•	•	...	...	...	...	...	•	...	•
Madagascar	...	...	...	...	...	...	...	...	...	...	...	...	...	...
Malawi	...	...	...	...	•	•	•	...	...	...	•	...	...	...
Mali	...	...	...	...	...	...	...	...	...	...	...	...	...	...
Mauritania - Mauritanie	...	...	...	...	...	...	...	...	...	...	...	...	...	...
Mauritius - Maurice	•	•	•	...	•	•	•	•	•	•	•	•	•	•
Mayotte	...	...	...	...	•	...	...	...	...	...	...	...	...	...
Morocco - Maroc	...	•	•	...	•	•	...	...	...	...	...	...	...	...
Mozambique	...	...	...	...	...	•	•	•	•	...	...	...	...	...
Namibia - Namibie	...	...	...	...	•	•	...	...	...	...	...	...	...	...
Niger	...	...	...	...	...	...	...	...	...	...	...	...	...	...
Nigeria - Nigéria	...	...	...	...	...	...	...	...	...	...	...	...	...	...
Réunion	•	•	•	...	•	•	•	...	...	...	•	•	•	•
Rwanda	...	...	...	...	...	...	...	...	...	...	...	...	...	...
Saint Helena ex. dep. - Sainte-Hélène sans dép.	•	•	•	...	•	...	...	...	...	...	•	•	•	•
Saint Helena: Ascension - Sainte-Hélène: Ascension	...	...	...	...	...	...	...	...	...	...	...	...	...	...
Saint Helena: Tristan da Cunha - Sainte-Hélène: Tristan da Cunha	...	...	...	...	...	...	...	...	...	...	...	...	...	...
São Tomé and Príncipe - São Tomé-et-Principe	...	...	...	...	...	...	...	...	...	...	...	...	...	...
Senegal - Sénégal	...	...	...	...	...	...	...	...	...	...	...	...	...	...
Seychelles	•	...	...	...	•	...	...	...	...	...	•	•	•	...
Sierra Leone	...	...	...	...	...	...	...	...	...	...	...	...	...	...
Somalia - Somalie	...	...	...	...	...	...	...	...	...	...	...	...	...	...
South Africa - Afrique du Sud	...	...	•	...	•	•	...	...	...	...	•	•	•	•
Sudan - Soudan	...	...	...	...	...	...	...	...	...	...	...	...	...	...

Table A. *Demographic Yearbook 2006* synoptic table: Availability of data by country/area, table and sex, where applicable

Tableau A. Tableau synoptique de l'*Annuaire démographique 2006:* Disponibilité des données par pays ou zone, tableau et le sexe , si disponible (continued — suite)

Continent, country or area / Continent, pays ou zone	Table totals	Summary - Apercu 3 Total	3 M/F	4	5	Population 6 Total	6 M/F	7 Total	7 M/F	8 Total	8 M/F	9	Natality 10 Total	10 M/F	11	Foetal mortality 12	13	14
AFRICA — AFRIQUE																		
Swaziland	15	•	•	…	•	•	…	•	•	•	…	…	•	…	•	…	…	…
Togo	4	•	•	…	•	…	…	…	…	•	…	…	…	…	…	…	…	…
Tunisia - Tunisie	15	•	•	…	•	•	…	•	•	•	…	…	•	…	•	…	…	…
Uganda - Ouganda	9	•	•	…	•	•	•	•	•	•	•	…	…	…	…	…	…	…
United Republic of Tanzania - République Unie de Tanzanie	9	•	•	…	•	•	•	•	•	•	•	…	…	…	…	…	…	…
Western Sahara - Sahara occidental	3	•	•	…	…	…	…	…	…	…	…	…	…	…	…	…	…	…
Zambia - Zambie	12	•	•	•	•	•	•	•	•	•	•	…	•	…	…	…	…	…
Zimbabwe	16	•	•	•	•	•	•	•	•	•	•	…	•	…	…	…	…	…
AMERICA, NORTH — AMERIQUE DU NORD																		
Anguilla	23	•	•	•	•	•	•	•	•	•	•	…	•	•	•	•	•	…
Antigua and Barbuda - Antigua-et-Barbuda	14	•	•	…	•	•	•	•	•	•	…	…	•	•	•	…	…	…
Aruba	23	•	•	•	•	•	•	•	•	•	•	…	•	•	•	•	…	…
Bahamas	22	•	•	•	•	•	•	•	•	•	…	…	•	•	•	•	…	…
Barbados - Barbade	14	•	•	…	•	•	•	•	•	…	…	…	•	…	•	…	…	…
Belize	21	•	•	•	•	•	•	•	•	•	•	…	•	•	•	•	…	…
Bermuda - Bermudes	22	•	•	•	•	•	•	•	•	•	•	…	•	•	•	•	…	…
British Virgin Islands - Îles Vierges britanniques	18	•	•	•	•	•	•	•	•	•	•	…	•	•	•	•	…	…
Canada	30	•	•	•	•	•	•	•	•	•	•	…	•	•	•	•	•	•
Cayman Islands - Îles Caïmanes	21	•	•	•	•	•	•	•	•	•	•	…	•	•	…	•	…	…
Costa Rica	28	•	•	•	•	•	•	•	•	•	•	…	•	•	•	•	…	…
Cuba	29	•	•	•	•	•	•	•	•	•	•	…	•	•	•	•	•	…
Dominica - Dominique	15	•	•	•	•	•	•	•	•	…	…	…	•	•	•	…	…	…
Dominican Republic - République dominicaine	23	•	•	•	•	•	•	•	•	•	•	…	•	•	•	•	•	…
El Salvador	28	•	•	•	•	•	•	•	•	•	•	…	•	•	•	•	…	…
Greenland - Groenland	22	•	•	•	•	•	•	•	•	•	•	…	•	•	•	•	…	…
Grenada - Grenade	14	•	•	…	•	•	•	•	•	…	…	…	•	•	•	…	…	…
Guadeloupe	27	•	…	•	•	•	•	•	•	•	•	…	•	•	•	•	…	…
Guatemala	28	•	•	•	•	•	•	•	•	•	•	…	•	•	•	•	…	…
Haiti - Haïti	13	•	…	•	•	•	…	•	•	•	…	…	…	…	…	…	…	…
Honduras	13	•	…	•	•	•	•	•	•	•	…	…	•	…	…	…	…	…
Jamaica - Jamaïque	22	•	•	•	•	•	•	•	•	•	•	…	•	•	•	•	…	…
Martinique	27	•	…	•	•	•	•	•	•	•	•	…	•	•	•	•	…	…
Mexico - Mexique	29	•	•	•	•	•	•	•	•	•	•	…	•	•	•	•	•	•
Montserrat	13	•	•	•	•	•	•	•	•	…	…	…	•	…	…	…	…	…
Netherlands Antilles - Antilles néerlandaises	24	•	•	•	•	•	•	•	•	•	•	…	•	•	•	•	…	…
Nicaragua	23	•	•	•	•	•	•	•	•	•	•	…	•	•	•	•	…	…
Panama	28	•	•	•	•	•	•	•	•	•	•	…	•	•	•	•	…	…
Puerto Rico - Porto Rico	30	•	•	•	•	•	•	•	•	•	•	…	•	•	•	•	•	•
Saint Kitts and Nevis - Saint-Kitts-et-Nevis	15	•	•	…	•	•	•	•	•	•	…	…	•	…	•	…	…	…
Saint Lucia - Sainte-Lucie	28	•	•	•	•	•	•	•	•	•	•	…	•	•	•	•	…	…
Saint Pierre and Miquelon - Saint Pierre-et-Miquelon	6	•	…	…	•	…	…	…	…	…	…	…	…	…	…	…	…	…
Saint Vincent and the Grenadines - Saint Vincent-et-les Grenadines	25	•	•	•	•	•	•	•	•	•	•	…	•	•	•	•	…	…
Trinidad and Tobago - Trinité-et-Tobago	27	•	•	•	•	•	•	•	•	•	•	…	•	•	•	•	…	…
Turks Caicos Islands - Îles Turques et Caïques	27	•	•	•	•	•	•	•	•	•	•	…	•	•	•	•	…	•
United States - États-Unis	25	•	•	•	•	•	•	•	•	•	•	…	•	•	•	•	…	…
United States Virgin Islands - Îles Vierges américaines	16	•	•	•	•	•	•	•	•	•	•	…	•	•	•	•	…	…
AMERICA, SOUTH — AMERIQUE DU SUD																		
Argentina - Argentine	25	•	•	•	•	•	•	•	•	•	•	…	•	•	•	•	…	…
Bolivia - Bolivie	13	•	…	•	•	•	•	•	•	•	…	…	…	…	…	…	…	…
Brazil - Brésil	25	•	•	•	•	•	•	•	•	•	…	…	•	•	•	…	…	…

Table A. *Demographic Yearbook 2006* synoptic table: Availability of data by country/area, table and sex, where applicable

Tableau A. Tableau synoptique de l'*Annuaire démographique 2006:* Disponibilité des données par pays ou zone, tableau et le sexe , si disponible (continued — suite)

Continent, country or area / Continent, pays ou zone	General topic and table number- Suject général et numéro de tableau													
	Infant and maternal mortality - Mortalité infantile et mortalité liée à la maternité				General mortality - Mortalité générale						Nuptiality and divorces - Nuptialité et divortialité		
	15	16 Total	16 M/F	17	18	19 Total	19 M/F	20 Total	20 M/F	21	22	23	24	25
AFRICA — AFRIQUE														
Swaziland	...	...	...	...	•	...	...	•	•	...	•	...	...	...
Togo	...	...	...	...	...	...	...	...	...	...	...	...	...	...
Tunisia - Tunisie	...	•	•	...	•	•	•	...	...	...	...	...	...	...
Uganda - Ouganda	...	...	...	...	...	...	...	...	...	...	...	...	...	...
United Republic of Tanzania - République Unie de Tanzanie	...	...	...	...	...	...	...	...	...	...	...	...	...	...
Western Sahara - Sahara occidental	...	...	...	...	...	...	...	...	...	...	...	...	...	...
Zambia - Zambie	...	...	...	...	•	...	...	...	...	...	...	...	...	...
Zimbabwe	...	...	...	...	•	...	...	•	•	...	•	...	...	...
AMERICA, NORTH — AMERIQUE DU NORD														
Anguilla	•	...	...	•	•	...	...	•	•	...	•	•	•	•
Antigua and Barbuda - Antigua-et-Barbuda	•	...	...	...	•	...	...	...	...	...	...	...	...	•
Aruba	•	•	•	...	•	•	•	...	...	...	...	...	•	•
Bahamas	•	•	•	...	•	•	•	...	...	...	...	...	•	•
Barbados - Barbade	•	...	...	•	•	...	...	...	...	...	...	•	•	•
Belize	•	...	...	•	•	...	...	...	...	...	...	•	•	•
Bermuda - Bermudes	•	...	...	•	•	...	...	•	•	...	•	...	...	...
British Virgin Islands - Îles Vierges britanniques	...	...	...	•	•	...	...	•	•	...	•	...	...	...
Canada	•	•	•	•	•	•	•	•	•	•	•	•	•	•
Cayman Islands - Îles Caïmanes	•	•	•	•	•	•	...	•	•	...	•	•	•	•
Costa Rica	•	•	•	•	•	•	•	•	•	•	•	•	•	•
Cuba	•	•	•	•	•	•	•	...	...	•	•	•	•	•
Dominica - Dominique	...	...	...	•	•	...	...	...	...	...	•	...	•	•
Dominican Republic - République dominicaine	•	...	...	•	•	...	...	...	...	...	•	•	•	•
El Salvador	•	...	...	•	•	...	...	•	•	...	•	•	...	•
Greenland - Groenland	•	...	...	...	•	...	...	...	...	...	•	...	...	...
Grenada - Grenade	...	...	...	•	•	...	...	...	...	...	•	...	...	...
Guadeloupe	...	...	...	•	•	...	...	•	•	...	•	•	•	•
Guatemala	•	...	...	•	•	•	•	•	•	...	•	•	•	•
Haiti - Haïti	•	...	...	...	•	...	...	...	...	...	...	...	...	...
Honduras	•	...	...	...	•	...	...	...	...	...	...	...	...	...
Jamaica - Jamaïque	•	•	•	...	•	...	...	•	•	...	•	...	...	...
Martinique	...	...	...	•	•	...	...	•	•	...	•	•	•	...
Mexico - Mexique	•	•	•	•	•	•	•	•	•	...	•	•	•	•
Montserrat	...	...	...	•	•	...	...	...	...	...	•	...	...	...
Netherlands Antilles - Antilles néerlandaises	•	...	...	•	•	...	...	...	...	...	•	...	•	•
Nicaragua	•	...	...	•	•	...	...	•	•	...	•	•	•	•
Panama	•	...	...	•	•	•	•	•	•	...	•	•	•	•
Puerto Rico - Porto Rico	•	...	...	•	•	...	...	•	•	...	•	•	•	•
Saint Kitts and Nevis - Saint-Kitts-et-Nevis	•	...	...	•	•	...	...	...	...	...	•	...	•	•
Saint Lucia - Sainte-Lucie	•	•	•	...	•	•	•	...	...	...	•	•	•	•
Saint Pierre and Miquelon - Saint Pierre-et-Miquelon	...	...	...	•	•	...	...	...	...	...	...	...	...	...
Saint Vincent and the Grenadines - Saint Vincent-et-les Grenadines	•	•	•	...	•	•	•	...	...	...	•	•	...	...
Trinidad and Tobago - Trinité-et-Tobago	•	•	•	•	•	•	•	...	...	...	•	•	•	•
Turks Caicos Islands - Îles Turques et Caïques	•	...	...	•	•	...	...	...	...	...	•	...	...	...
United States - États-Unis	•	•	•	•	•	•	•	•	•	...	•	•	•	•
United States Virgin Islands - Îles Vierges américaines	•	...	...	...	•	...	...	...	...	...	•	...	...	...
AMERICA, SOUTH — AMERIQUE DU SUD														
Argentina - Argentine	•	•	•	...	•	•	•	•	•	...	•	•	...	...
Bolivia - Bolivie	•	...	...	...	•	...	...	...	...	...	...	•	•	...
Brazil - Brésil	•	•	•	•	•	•	•	•	•	...	•	•	•	•

Table A. *Demographic Yearbook 2006* synoptic table: Availability of data by country/area, table and sex, where applicable

Tableau A. Tableau synoptique de l'*Annuaire démographique 2006*: Disponibilité des données par pays ou zone, tableau et le sexe , si disponible (continued — suite)

Général topic and table number- Suject général et numéro de tableau

Continent, country or area / Continent, pays ou zone	Table totals	Summary - Apercu 3 Total	3 M/F	4	5	Population 6 Total	6 M/F	7 Total	7 M/F	8 Total	8 M/F	9	Natality 10 Total	10 M/F	11	Foetal mortality 12	13	14
AMERICA, SOUTH — AMERIQUE DU SUD																		
Chile - Chili	29	•	•	•	•	•	•	•	•	•	•	•	•	•	•	•	...	...
Colombia - Colombie	22	•	•	•	•	•	•	•	...	•	•	...	•	•	...	•	...	...
Ecuador - Équateur	25	•	•	•	•	•	•	•	...	•	•	...	•	•	•	•	...	...
Falkland Islands (Malvinas) - Îles Falkland (Malvinas)	10	•	•	•	...	•	•	•	•	•	•	...	•	•	...	...	...	...
French Guiana - Guyane française	25	•	...	•	•	•	•	•	•	•	•	•	•	•	•	•	...	...
Guyana	14	•	•	•	•	•	•	•	•	•	•	...	...	•	...	•	...	...
Paraguay	19	•	•	•	•	•	•	•	•	•	•	...	•	•	...	•	...	...
Peru - Pérou	19	•	...	•	•	•	•	•	•	•	•	...	•	•	...	•	...	...
Suriname	23	•	•	•	•	•	•	•	•	•	•	...	•	•	•	•	•	...
Uruguay	28	•	•	•	•	•	•	•	•	•	•	•	•	•	...	•	...	...
Venezuela (Bolivarian Republic of) - Venezuela (République bolivarienne du)	28	•	•	•	•	•	•	•	•	•	•	...	•	•	...	•	...	...
ASIA — ASIE																		
Afghanistan	8	•	•	•	•	•	•	...	...	...	•	...	...	•	...	...	...	...
Armenia - Arménie	30	•	•	•	•	•	•	•	•	•	•	•	•	•	•	•	•	...
Azerbaijan - Azerbaïdjan	31	•	•	•	•	•	•	•	•	•	•	•	•	•	•	•	•	•
Bahrain - Bahreïn	27	•	•	•	•	•	•	•	•	•	•	•	•	•	...	•	•	...
Bangladesh	11	•	•	•	•	•	•	•	•	•	•	...	...	•	...	...	...	...
Bhutan - Bhoutan	21	•	•	•	•	•	•	•	•	•	•	...	•	•	...	•	...	...
Brunei Darussalam - Brunéi Darussalam	23	•	•	•	•	•	•	•	•	•	•	•	•	•	...	•	...	...
Cambodia - Cambodge	15	•	•	•	•	•	•	•	•	•	•	•	•	•	...	...	...	...
China - Chine[1]	17	•	•	•	•	•	•	•	•	•	•	...	•	•	...	•	...	...
China: Hong Kong SAR - Chine: Hong Kong RAS	31	•	•	•	•	•	•	•	•	•	•	•	•	•	•	•	•	•
China: Macao SAR - Chine: Macao RAS	27	•	•	•	•	•	•	•	•	•	•	•	•	•	•	•	•	...
Cyprus - Chypre	27	•	•	•	•	•	•	•	•	•	•	•	•	•	•	•	•	...
Georgia - Géorgie	27	•	•	•	•	•	•	•	•	•	•	•	•	•	•	•	•	...
India - Inde[2]	14	•	•	•	•	•	•	•	•	•	•	...	•	•	...	•	...	...
Indonesia - Indonésie	8	•	•	...	•	•	•	•	•	...	•	...	•	•	...	...	...	...
Iran (Islamic Republic of) - Iran (République islamique d')	14	•	•	•	•	•	•	•	•	•	•	...	•	•	...	...	...	...
Iraq	15	•	•	•	•	•	•	•	•	•	•	...	•	•	...	...	...	...
Israel - Israël[3]	31	•	•	•	•	•	•	•	•	•	•	•	•	•	•	•	•	•
Japan - Japon	31	•	•	•	•	•	•	•	•	•	•	•	•	•	•	•	•	•
Jordan - Jordanie	16	•	•	•	•	•	•	•	•	•	•	•	•	•	...	•	...	...
Kazakhstan	31	•	•	•	•	•	•	•	•	•	•	•	•	•	•	•	•	•
Korea (Dem. People's Republic of) - Corée (Rép. populaire dém. de)	4	•	•	...	•	...	•	...	...	...	•	...	...	...	...	...	...	...
Korea (Republic of) - Corée (République de)	28	•	•	•	•	•	•	•	•	•	•	•	•	•	...	•	...	...
Kuwait - Koweït	28	•	•	•	•	•	•	•	•	•	•	•	•	•	...	•	...	...
Kyrgyzstan - Kirghizistan	31	•	•	•	•	•	•	•	•	•	•	•	•	•	•	•	•	•
Lao People's Democratic Republic - République démocratique populaire lao	10	•	•	•	•	•	•	•	•	...	...	...	...	•	...	...	...	...
Lebanon - Liban	10	•	•	•	•	•	•	...	...	•	•	...	•	•	...	...	...	...
Malaysia - Malaisie	23	•	•	•	•	•	•	•	•	•	•	...	•	•	...	•	...	...
Maldives	28	•	•	•	•	•	•	•	•	•	•	•	•	•	...	•	...	...
Mongolia - Mongolie	25	•	•	•	•	•	•	•	•	•	•	•	•	•	...	•	...	...
Myanmar	13	•	•	•	•	•	•	•	•	•	•	...	•	•	...	•	...	...
Nepal - Népal	15	•	•	•	•	•	•	•	•	•	•	...	•	•	...	...	...	...
Occupied Palestinian Territory - Territoire palestinien occupé	20	•	•	•	•	•	•	•	•	•	•	...	•	•	...	...	...	...
Oman	17	•	•	•	•	•	•	•	•	•	•	...	•	•	...	•	...	...
Pakistan[4]	23	•	•	•	•	•	•	•	•	•	•	...	•	•	...	•	...	...
Philippines	26	•	•	•	•	•	•	•	•	•	•	•	•	•	...	•	...	...

Table A. *Demographic Yearbook 2006* synoptic table: Availability of data by country/area, table and sex, where applicable
Tableau A. Tableau synoptique de l'*Annuaire démographique 2006*: Disponibilité des données par pays ou zone, tableau et le sexe , si disponible (continued — suite)

Continent, country or area / Continent, pays ou zone	General topic and table number- Suject général et numéro de tableau													
	Infant and maternal mortality - Mortalité infantile et mortalité liée à la maternité				General mortality - Mortalité générale							Nuptiality and divorces - Nuptialité et divortialité		
	15	16 Total	16 M/F	17	18	19 Total	19 M/F	20 Total	20 M/F	21	22	23	24	25
AMERICA, SOUTH — AMERIQUE DU SUD														
Chile - Chili	•	•	•	•	•	•	•	•	•	•	•	•	•	•
Colombia - Colombie	•	•	•	•	•	•	•	...	...	•	•	•	...	...
Ecuador - Équateur	•	•	•	•	•	•	•	...	...	•	•	•	...	...
Falkland Islands (Malvinas) - Îles Falkland (Malvinas)	•	...	...	...	•	...	...	...	...	...	...	•	...	...
French Guiana - Guyane française	•	•	...	•	•	•	•	...	...	•	•	•	•	...
Guyana	•	...	...	•	•	•	•	...	...	•	•	•	...	...
Paraguay	•	•	...	•	•	•	•	...	...	•	•	•	...	...
Peru - Pérou	•	•	•	•	•	•	...	...	•	•	•	...	...	...
Suriname	•	•	•	•	•	•	•	...	...	•	•	•	...	...
Uruguay	•	•	•	•	•	•	•	...	...	•	•	•	...	...
Venezuela (Bolivarian Republic of) - Venezuela (République bolivarienne du)	•	•	•	•	•	•	•	...	...	•	•	•	...	...
ASIA — ASIE														
Afghanistan	...	...	...	...	...	...	...	...	...	•	•	•	...	...
Armenia - Arménie	•	•	•	•	•	•	•	•	•	•	•	•	•	•
Azerbaijan - Azerbaïdjan	•	•	•	•	•	•	•	•	•	•	•	•	•	•
Bahrain - Bahreïn	•	•	•	•	•	•	•	•	•	•	•	•	•	•
Bangladesh	•	...	...	•	•	•	...	...	...	•	•	•	...	...
Bhutan - Bhoutan	•	...	...	...	•	•	...	...	...	•	•	•	...	...
Brunei Darussalam - Brunéi Darussalam	•	...	...	•	•	•	...	...	...	•	•	•	...	...
Cambodia - Cambodge	•	...	...	•	•	•	...	...	...	•	•	•	...	...
China - Chine[1]	•	...	...	•	•	•	...	...	...	•	•	•	...	...
China: Hong Kong SAR - Chine: Hong Kong RAS	•	•	•	•	•	•	•	•	•	•	•	•	•	•
China: Macao SAR - Chine: Macao RAS	•	•	•	...	•	•	•	•	•	•	•	•	•	•
Cyprus - Chypre	•	•	•	•	•	•	•	•	•	•	•	•	•	•
Georgia - Géorgie	•	•	•	•	•	•	•	•	...	•	•	•	•	...
India - Inde[2]	•	...	...	•	•	•	•	...	...	•	•	•	...	...
Indonesia - Indonésie	...	...	...	•	•	•	...	...	...	•	•	•	...	...
Iran (Islamic Republic of) - Iran (République islamique d')	•	•	•	•	•	•	•	...	...	•	•	•	...	...
Iraq	•	...	...	•	•	•	•	...	...	•	•	•	...	...
Israel - Israël[3]	•	•	•	•	•	•	•	•	•	•	•	•	•	•
Japan - Japon	•	•	•	•	•	•	•	•	•	•	•	•	•	•
Jordan - Jordanie	•	•	...	•	•	•	•	...	...	•	•	•	•	•
Kazakhstan	•	•	•	•	•	•	•	•	•	•	•	•	•	•
Korea (Dem. People's Republic of) - Corée (Rép. populaire dém. de)	...	...	...	...	...	...	...	...	...	...	...	•	...	...
Korea (Republic of) - Corée (République de)	•	•	•	•	•	•	•	•	•	•	•	•	•	•
Kuwait - Koweït	•	•	•	•	•	•	•	•	...	•	•	•	•	...
Kyrgyzstan - Kirghizistan	•	•	•	•	•	•	•	•	•	•	•	•	•	•
Lao People's Democratic Republic - République démocratique populaire lao	...	...	...	...	...	...	...	...	...	...	...	•	...	...
Lebanon - Liban	•	...	...	•	•	•	...	...	...	•	•	•	...	...
Malaysia - Malaisie	•	•	•	•	•	•	•	...	...	•	•	•	...	...
Maldives	•	•	•	•	•	•	•	...	...	•	•	•	...	...
Mongolia - Mongolie	•	...	...	•	•	•	•	...	...	•	•	•	...	...
Myanmar	•	...	...	•	•	•	...	...	...	•	•	•	...	...
Nepal - Népal	•	...	...	•	•	•	•	...	...	•	•	•	...	...
Occupied Palestinian Territory - Territoire palestinien occupé	•	•	•	•	•	•	•	...	...	•	•	•	•	...
Oman	•	•	...	•	•	•	•	...	...	•	•	•	•	...
Pakistan[4]	•	•	...	•	•	•	•	...	...	•	•	•	...	...
Philippines	•	•	•	•	•	•	•	...	...	•	•	•	•	•

Table A. *Demographic Yearbook 2006* synoptic table: Availability of data by country/area, table and sex, where applicable

Tableau A. Tableau synoptique de l'*Annuaire démographique 2006:* Disponibilité des données par pays ou zone, tableau et le sexe , si disponible (continued — suite)

General topic and table number   Sujet général et numéro de tableau

Continent, country or area / Continent, pays ou zone	Table totals	Summary - Apercu				Population							Natality - Natalité			Foetal mortality - Mortalité foetale		
		3		4	5	6		7		8		9	10		11	12	13	14
		Total	M/F			Total	M/F	Total	M/F	Total	M/F		Total	M/F				
ASIA — ASIE																		
Qatar	27	•	•	•	•	•	•	•	•	•	...	•	•	•	•	•	•	...
Saudi Arabia - Arabie saoudite	22	•	•	•	•	•	•	•	•	•	•	•	•	•	•	...	...	...
Singapore - Singapour	30	•	•	•	•	•	•	•	•	•	•	•	•	•	•	•	•	•
Sri Lanka	16	•	•	...	•	•	•	•	•	•	•	•	•	•	•	...	...	...
Syrian Arab Republic - République arabe syrienne	14	•	•	•	•	•	•	•	•	•	•	•	•	•	•	...	...	...
Tajikistan - Tadjikistan	21	•	•	•	•	•	•	•	•	•	•	•	•	•	•	•	•	...
Thailand - Thaïlande	20	•	•	•	•	•	•	•	•	•	•	•	•	•	•	...	...	...
Timor-Leste	5	•	•	...	...	•	•	...	...	...	...	...	...	...	...	...	...	...
Turkey - Turquie	20	•	•	•	•	•	•	•	•	•	•	•	•	•	•	...	...	...
Turkmenistan - Turkménistan	6	•	•	...	•	...	•	•	...	...	...	•	...	...	...	...	...	...
United Arab Emirates - Émirats arabes unis	18	•	•	•	•	•	•	•	•	•	•	•	•	•	•	...	...	...
Uzbekistan - Ouzbékistan	20	•	•	...	•	•	•	•	•	•	•	•	•	•	•	...	...	...
Viet Nam	10	•	•	...	•	•	•	•	•	•	•	•	•	•	•	...	...	...
Yemen - Yémen	14	•	•	•	•	•	•	•	•	•	•	•	•	•	...	...	...	...
EUROPE																		
Åland Islands - Îles d'Åland	20	•	...	•	•	•	•	•	•	•	...	•	•	•	•	•	•	•
Albania - Albanie	28	•	•	•	•	•	•	•	•	•	•	•	•	•	•	•	•	•
Andorra - Andorre	21	•	•	•	•	•	•	•	•	•	•	•	•	•	•	•	•	•
Austria - Autriche	29	•	•	•	•	•	•	•	•	•	•	•	•	•	•	•	•	•
Belarus - Bélarus	31	•	•	•	•	•	•	•	•	•	•	•	•	•	•	•	•	•
Belgium - Belgique	27	•	•	•	•	•	•	•	•	•	•	•	•	...	•	•	•	•
Bosnia and Herzegovina - Bosnie-Herzégovine	20	•	•	•	•	•	•	•	...	•	•	•	•	•	•	...	...	...
Bulgaria - Bulgarie	31	•	•	•	•	•	•	•	•	•	•	•	•	•	•	•	•	•
Channel Islands: Guernsey - Îles Anglo-Normandes: Guernesey	17	•	•	•	•	•	•	•	•	•	•	•	•	•	•	...	...	...
Channel Islands: Jersey - Îles Anglo-Normandes: Jersey	10	•	•	•	•	•	•	...	...	•	•	•	•	...	...	...	...	...
Croatia - Croatie	30	•	•	•	•	•	•	•	•	•	•	•	•	•	•	•	•	•
Czech Republic - République tchèque	31	•	•	•	•	•	•	•	•	•	•	•	•	•	•	•	•	•
Denmark - Danemark	30	•	•	•	•	•	•	•	•	•	•	•	•	•	•	•	•	•
Estonia - Estonie	31	•	•	•	•	•	•	•	•	•	•	•	•	•	•	•	•	•
Faeroe Islands - Îles Féroé	12	•	•	•	•	•	•	•	•	•	•	•	•	•	•	...	...	...
Finland - Finlande	31	•	•	•	•	•	•	•	•	•	•	•	•	•	•	•	•	•
France	31	•	•	•	•	•	•	•	•	•	•	•	•	•	•	•	•	•
Germany - Allemagne	31	•	•	•	•	•	•	•	•	•	•	•	•	•	•	•	•	•
Gibraltar	19	•	•	•	•	•	•	•	•	•	•	•	•	•	...	•	•	...
Greece - Grèce	31	•	•	•	•	•	•	•	•	•	•	•	•	•	•	•	•	•
Holy See - Saint-Siège	6	•	•	...	•	•	•	...	...	...	...	...	...	...	...	...	...	...
Hungary - Hongrie	31	•	•	•	•	•	•	•	•	•	•	•	•	•	•	•	•	•
Iceland - Islande	31	•	•	•	•	•	•	•	•	•	•	•	•	•	•	•	•	•
Ireland - Irlande	28	•	•	•	•	•	•	•	•	•	•	•	•	•	•	•	•	•
Isle of Man - Îles de Man	19	•	•	•	•	•	•	•	•	•	•	•	•	•	•	...	...	...
Italy - Italie	31	•	•	•	•	•	•	•	•	•	•	•	•	•	•	•	•	•
Latvia - Lettonie	31	•	•	•	•	•	•	•	•	•	•	•	•	•	•	•	•	•
Liechtenstein	20	•	•	•	•	•	•	•	•	•	•	•	•	•	•	...	...	...
Lithuania - Lituanie	31	•	•	•	•	•	•	•	•	•	•	•	•	•	•	•	•	•
Luxembourg	28	•	•	•	•	•	•	•	•	•	•	•	•	•	•	•	•	•
Malta - Malte	29	•	•	•	•	•	•	•	•	•	•	•	•	•	•	•	•	•
Moldova	29	•	•	•	•	•	•	•	•	•	•	•	•	•	•	•	•	•
Monaco	13	•	•	•	•	•	•	•	•	•	•	•	•	•	•	...	...	...
Montenegro	26	•	•	•	•	•	•	•	•	•	...	•	•	•	•	...	...	...
Netherlands - Pays-Bas	30	•	•	•	•	•	•	•	•	•	•	•	•	•	•	•	•	•
Norway - Norvège	31	•	•	•	•	•	•	•	•	•	•	•	•	•	•	•	•	•
Poland - Pologne	31	•	•	•	•	•	•	•	•	•	•	•	•	•	•	•	•	•

Table A. *Demographic Yearbook 2006* synoptic table: Availability of data by country/area, table and sex, where applicable
Tableau A. Tableau synoptique de l'*Annuaire démographique 2006:* Disponibilité des données par pays ou zone, tableau et le sexe , si disponible (continued — suite)

Continent, country or area / Continent, pays ou zone	General topic and table number- Suject général et numéro de tableau													
	Infant and maternal mortality - Mortalité infantile et mortalité liée à la maternité				General mortality - Mortalité générale							Nuptiality and divorces - Nuptialité et divortialité		
	15	16 Total	16 M/F	17	18	19 Total	19 M/F	20 Total	20 M/F	21	22	23	24	25
ASIA — ASIE														
Qatar	•	•	•	...	•	•	•	•	•	...	•	•	•	•
Saudi Arabia - Arabie saoudite	•	...	...	...	•	•	•	•	...	...	•	•	...	•
Singapore - Singapour	•	•	•	•	•	•	•	•	•	•	•	•	•	•
Sri Lanka	•	•	•	...	•	•	•	•	...	...	•	...	...	•
Syrian Arab Republic - République arabe syrienne	...	...	...	...	•	...	...	•	...	...	...	•	...	•
Tajikistan - Tadjikistan	•	•	•	•	•	•	•	•	•	...	•	•	...	•
Thailand - Thaïlande	•	•	•	•	•	•	•	•	•	...	•	•	•	•
Timor-Leste	...	...	...	...	...	...	...	...	...	...	...	...	...	...
Turkey - Turquie	...	...	...	...	...	...	...	...	...	...	•	•	•	•
Turkmenistan - Turkménistan	...	...	...	...	•	...	...	...	...	...	...	...	...	...
United Arab Emirates - Émirats arabes unis	...	...	...	...	•	...	...	...	...	...	•	•	•	•
Uzbekistan - Ouzbékistan	...	•	•	•	•	•	•	•	...	...	•	•	...	•
Viet Nam	...	...	...	...	•	...	...	...	...	...	•	•	...	•
Yemen - Yémen	...	...	...	...	•	...	...	...	...	...	•	•	...	•
EUROPE														
Åland Islands - Îles d'Åland	•	...	...	...	•	•	•	...	...	...	•	•	...	•
Albania - Albanie	•	•	•	•	•	•	•	•	•	...	•	•	...	...
Andorra - Andorre	•	•	•	•	•	•	•	•	•	...	•	•	...	...
Austria - Autriche	•	•	•	•	•	•	•	•	•	•	•	•	•	•
Belarus - Bélarus	•	•	•	•	•	•	•	•	•	•	•	•	•	•
Belgium - Belgique	•	•	•	•	•	•	•	•	•	•	•	•	•	•
Bosnia and Herzegovina - Bosnie-Herzégovine	•	•	•	•	•	•	•	•	•	•	•	•	•	•
Bulgaria - Bulgarie	•	•	•	•	•	•	•	•	•	•	•	•	•	•
Channel Islands: Guernsey - Îles Anglo-Normandes: Guernesey	...	...	...	...	•	...	...	...	...	...	...	...	...	...
Channel Islands: Jersey - Îles Anglo-Normandes: Jersey	...	...	...	...	•	...	...	...	...	...	...	...	...	...
Croatia - Croatie	•	•	•	•	•	•	•	•	•	•	•	•	•	•
Czech Republic - République tchèque	•	•	•	•	•	•	•	•	•	•	•	•	•	•
Denmark - Danemark	•	•	•	•	•	•	•	•	•	•	•	•	•	•
Estonia - Estonie	•	•	•	•	•	•	•	•	•	•	•	•	•	•
Faeroe Islands - Îles Féroé	•	...	...	...	•	...	...	...	...	...	•	•	...	•
Finland - Finlande	•	•	•	•	•	•	•	•	•	•	•	•	•	•
France	•	•	•	•	•	•	•	•	•	•	•	•	•	•
Germany - Allemagne	•	•	•	•	•	•	•	•	•	•	•	•	•	•
Gibraltar	•	•	•	•	•	•	•	•	•	•	•	•	•	•
Greece - Grèce	•	•	•	•	•	•	•	•	•	•	•	•	•	•
Holy See - Saint-Siège	...	...	...	...	...	...	...	...	...	...	...	...	...	...
Hungary - Hongrie	•	•	•	•	•	•	•	•	•	•	•	•	•	•
Iceland - Islande	•	•	•	•	•	•	•	•	•	•	•	•	•	•
Ireland - Irlande	•	•	•	•	•	•	•	•	•	•	•	•	•	•
Isle of Man - Îles de Man	•	•	•	...	•	•	•	•	•	...	•	•	...	•
Italy - Italie	•	•	•	•	•	•	•	•	•	•	•	•	•	•
Latvia - Lettonie	•	•	•	•	•	•	•	•	•	•	•	•	•	•
Liechtenstein	•	•	•	•	•	•	•	•	•	•	•	•	•	•
Lithuania - Lituanie	•	•	•	•	•	•	•	•	•	•	•	•	•	•
Luxembourg	•	•	•	•	•	•	•	•	•	•	•	•	•	•
Malta - Malte	•	•	•	•	•	•	•	•	•	•	•	•	•	•
Moldova	•	•	•	•	•	•	•	•	•	•	•	•	•	•
Monaco	...	...	...	...	•	•	•	...	...	...	•	•	...	•
Montenegro	•	•	•	•	•	•	•	•	•	•	•	•	•	•
Netherlands - Pays-Bas	•	•	•	•	•	•	•	•	•	•	•	•	•	•
Norway - Norvège	•	•	•	•	•	•	•	•	•	•	•	•	•	•
Poland - Pologne	•	•	•	•	•	•	•	•	•	•	•	•	•	•

Table A. *Demographic Yearbook 2006* synoptic table: Availability of data by country/area, table and sex, where applicable
Tableau A. Tableau synoptique de l'*Annuaire démographique 2006*: Disponibilité des données par pays ou zone, tableau et le sexe , si disponible (continued — suite)

General topic and table number   Sujet général et numéro de tableau

Continent, country or area / Continent, pays ou zone	Table totals	Summary - Aperçu 3 Total	M/F	4	5	Population 6 Total	M/F	7 Total	M/F	8 Total	M/F	Natality - Natalité 9	10 Total	M/F	11	Foetal mortality - Mortalité foetale 12	13	14
EUROPE																		
Portugal	29	•	•	•	•	•	•	•	•	•	•	•	•	•	•	•	...	...
Romania - Roumanie	31	•	•	•	•	•	•	•	•	•	•	•	•	•	•	•	•	•
Russian Federation - Fédération de Russie	29	•	•	•	•	•	•	•	•	•	•	•	...	•	•	•	•	•
San Marino - Saint-Marin	26	•	•	•	•	•	•	•	•	•	•	•	...	•	•	•	...	...
Serbia	31	•	•	•	•	•	•	•	•	•	•	•	•	•	•	•	•	•
Slovakia - Slovaquie	31	•	•	•	•	•	•	•	•	•	•	•	•	•	•	•	•	•
Slovenia - Slovénie	31	•	•	•	•	•	•	•	•	•	•	•	•	•	•	•	•	•
Spain - Espagne	31	•	•	•	•	•	•	•	•	•	•	•	•	•	•	•	•	•
Sweden - Suède	31	•	•	•	•	•	•	•	•	•	•	•	•	•	•	•	•	•
Switzerland - Suisse	29	•	•	•	•	•	•	•	•	•	•	•	•	•	•	•	...	...
The Former Yugoslav Rep. of Macedonia - L'ex-République yougoslave de Macédoine	30	•	•	•	•	•	•	•	•	•	•	•	•	•	•	•	•	...
Ukraine	31	•	•	•	•	•	•	•	•	•	•	•	•	•	•	•	•	•
United Kingdom - Royaume-Uni	29	•	•	•	•	•	•	•	•	•	•	•	•	•	•	•	•	•
OCEANIA — OCEANIE																		
American Samoa - Samoas américaines	18	•	•	•	•	•	•	•	•	•	•	•	•	•	...	...	...	...
Australia - Australie	29	•	•	•	•	•	•	•	•	•	•	•	•	•	•	...	...	...
Cook Islands - Îles Cook	13	•	•	•	•	•	•	•	...	•	...	•	•	...	...	...	...	...
Fiji - Fidji	16	•	...	•	•	•	...	•	...	•	...	•	•	...	...	...	...	...
French Polynesia - Polynésie française	13	•	...	•	•	•	•	•	...	•	...	•	•	...	...	•	...	...
Guam	21	•	•	•	•	•	•	•	...	•	•	•	•	...	...	...	...	...
Kiribati	10	•	•	...	•	•	•	•	...	•	...	•	...	...	...	...	...	...
Marshall Islands - Îles Marshall	16	•	•	•	•	•	•	•	•	•	•	•	•	•	...	...	...	...
Micronesia, Federated States of - Micronésie (États fédérés de)	13	•	•	•	•	•	•	•	•	•	•	•	•	...	...	...	...	...
Nauru	10	•	•	•	•	•	•	...	•	...	•	•	•	...	...	...	...	...
New Caledonia - Nouvelle-Calédonie	26	•	•	•	•	•	•	•	•	•	•	•	•	•	•	•	•	...
New Zealand - Nouvelle-Zélande	30	•	•	•	•	•	•	•	...	•	...	•	•	•	•	•	•	•
Niue - Nioué	14	•	•	•	•	•	•	•	•	•	•	•	•	...	...	...	...	...
Norfolk Island - Île Norfolk	7	•	•	...	...	•	•	•	...	...	...	•	...	...	...	...	...	...
Northern Mariana Islands - Îles Mariannes septentrionales	16	•	•	•	•	•	•	•	•	•	•	•	•	•	...	...	...	...
Palau - Palaos	19	•	•	•	•	•	•	•	•	•	•	•	•	•	•	•	•	...
Papua New Guinea - Papouasie-Nouvelle-Guinée	15	•	•	•	•	•	•	•	...	•	...	•	•	•	•	...	...	...
Pitcairn	3	•	•	...	...	...	...	...	...	...	...	...	...	...	...	...	...	...
Samoa	13	•	•	...	•	•	•	•	...	•	...	•	...	...	...	...	...	...
Solomon Islands - Îles Salomon	6	•	•	...	•	•	•	•	...	•	...	•	...	...	...	...	...	...
Tokelau - Tokélaou	8	•	•	...	•	•	•	•	...	•	...	•	...	...	...	...	...	...
Tonga	22	•	•	•	•	•	•	•	•	•	•	•	•	•	•	...	...	...
Tuvalu	17	•	•	•	•	•	•	•	•	•	•	•	•	...	...	...	...	...
Vanuatu	9	•	•	...	•	•	•	•	...	•	...	•	...	...	...	...	...	...
Wallis and Futuna Islands - Îles Wallis et Futuna	11	•	•	...	•	•	•	•	...	•	...	•	•	...	...	...	...	...

Table A. *Demographic Yearbook 2006* synoptic table: Availability of data by country/area, table and sex, where applicable
Tableau A. Tableau synoptique de l'*Annuaire démographique 2006:* Disponibilité des données par pays ou zone, tableau et le sexe , si disponible (continued — suite)

Continent, country or area / Continent, pays ou zone	General topic and table number- Suject général et numéro de tableau													
	Infant and maternal mortality - Mortalité infantile et mortalité liée à la maternité			General mortality - Mortalité générale							Nuptiality and divorces - Nuptialité et divortialité		
	15	16 Total	16 M/F	17	18	19 Total	19 M/F	20 Total	20 M/F	21	22	23	24	25

EUROPE

	15	16T	16MF	17	18	19T	19MF	20T	20MF	21	22	23	24	25
Portugal	•	•	•	•	•	•	•	•	•	•	•	•	•	•
Romania - Roumanie	•	•	•	•	•	•	•	•	•	•	•	•	•	•
Russian Federation - Fédération de Russie	•	•	•	•	•	•	•	•	•	•	•	...	•	•
San Marino - Saint-Marin	•	•	•	•	•	•	•	•	•	•	•	...	•	•
Serbia	•	•	•	•	•	•	•	•	•	•	•	•	•	•
Slovakia - Slovaquie	•	•	•	•	•	•	•	•	•	•	•	•	•	•
Slovenia - Slovénie	•	•	•	•	•	•	•	•	•	•	•	•	•	•
Spain - Espagne	•	•	•	•	•	•	•	•	•	•	•	•	•	•
Sweden - Suède	•	•	•	•	•	•	•	•	•	•	•	•	•	•
Switzerland - Suisse	•	•	•	•	•	•	•	•	•	•	•	•	•	•
The Former Yugoslav Rep. of Macedonia - L'ex-République yougoslave de Macédoine	•	•	•	•	•	•	•	•	•	•	•	•	•	•
Ukraine	•	•	•	•	•	•	•	•	•	•	•	•	•	•
United Kingdom - Royaume-Uni	•	•	•	•	•	•	•	•	•	•	•	•	•	•

OCEANIA — OCEANIE

	15	16T	16MF	17	18	19T	19MF	20T	20MF	21	22	23	24	25
American Samoa - Samoas américaines	•	...	...	...	•	•	...	•	...	•	...	•	...	...
Australia - Australie	•	•	•	•	•	•	•	•	•	•	•	•	•	•
Cook Islands - Îles Cook	•	...	...	...	•	•	...	•	...	•	...	•	...	...
Fiji - Fidji	•	...	...	...	•	•	...	•	...	•	...	•	...	•
French Polynesia - Polynésie française	•	...	...	...	•	•	...	•	...	•	...	•	•	•
Guam	•	...	...	...	•	•	...	•	...	•	...	•	•	•
Kiribati	...	...	...	•	...	...	...	...	...	•	...	...	...	...
Marshall Islands - Îles Marshall	...	...	...	...	•	•	...	...	...	•	...	...	...	...
Micronesia, Federated States of - Micronésie (États fédérés de)	...	...	...	...	...	...	...	...	...	...	...	...	...	...
Nauru	...	...	...	...	•	•	...	...	...	...	...	...	...	...
New Caledonia - Nouvelle-Calédonie	•	•	•	•	•	•	...	•	...	•	...	•	•	•
New Zealand - Nouvelle-Zélande	•	•	•	•	•	•	•	•	•	•	•	•	•	•
Niue - Nioué	...	...	...	...	•	...	...	...	...	•	...	...	•	...
Norfolk Island - Île Norfolk	...	...	...	...	...	...	...	...	...	...	...	...	...	...
Northern Mariana Islands - Îles Mariannes septentrionales	•	...	...	...	•	•	...	...	...	•	...	...	...	...
Palau - Palaos	•	...	...	...	•	•	...	•	...	•	...	...	...	...
Papua New Guinea - Papouasie-Nouvelle-Guinée	•	...	...	...	•	...	...	•	...	...	...	...	...	...
Pitcairn	...	...	...	...	...	...	...	...	...	...	...	...	...	...
Samoa	...	...	...	...	•	...	...	...	...	...	...	...	•	•
Solomon Islands - Îles Salomon	...	...	...	...	...	...	...	...	...	...	...	...	...	...
Tokelau - Tokélaou	...	...	...	...	...	...	...	...	...	...	...	...	...	...
Tonga	•	...	...	...	•	•	...	•	...	•	...	•	•	•
Tuvalu	•	...	...	...	•	•	...	•	...	...	...	...	...	...
Vanuatu	•	...	...	...	...	...	...	...	...	...	•	...	...	...
Wallis and Futuna Islands - Îles Wallis et Futuna	...	...	...	...	•	...	•	...	...	...	...	...	...	...

FOOTNOTES - NOTES

• Data presented in the table - Les données présentées dans le tableau.

··· Data not available - Données pas disponibles.

[1] For statistical purposes, the data for China do not include those for the Hong Kong Special Administrative Region (Hong Kong SAR), Macao special Administrative Region (Macao SAR) and Taiwan province of China. - Pour la présentation des statistiques, les données pour Chine ne comprend pas la Région Administrative Spéciale de Hong Kong (Hong Kong RAS), la Région Administrative Spéciale de Macao (Macao RAS) et Taïwan province de Chine.

[2] Including data for the Indian-held part of Jammu and Kashmir, the final status of which has not yet been determined. - Y compris les données pour la partie du Jammu et du Cachemire occupée par l'Inde dont le statut définitif n'a pas encore été déterminé.

[3] Including data for East Jerusalem and Israeli residents in certain other territories under occupation by Israeli military forces since June 1967. - Y compris les données pour Jérusalem-Est et les résidents israéliens dans certains autres territoires occupés depuis 1967 par les forces armées israéliennes.

[4] Excluding data for the Pakistan-held part of Jammu and Kashmir, the final status of which has not yet been determined. - Non compris les

données concernant la partie du Jammu et Cachemire occupée par le Pakistan dont le statut définitif n'a pas été déterminé.

Table 1

Table 1 presents for the world, major areas and regions estimates of the order of magnitude of population size, rates of population increase, crude birth and death rates, surface area as well as population density.

Description of variables: Estimates of world population by major areas and by regions are presented for 1950, 1960, 1970, 1980, 1990, 2000 and 2006. The average annual percentage rates of population growth, the crude birth and crude death rates are shown for the period from 2005 to 2010. Surface area in square kilometers and population density estimates relate to 2006.

All population estimates and rates presented in this table were prepared by the Population Division of the United Nations, Department of Economic and Social Affairs, and have been published in *World Population Prospects: The 2006 Revision, CD Rom Edition – Extended Dataset*[1].

The scheme of regionalization used for these estimates is described below. Although some continental totals are given, and all can be derived, the basic scheme presents six major areas that are so drawn as to obtain greater homogeneity in sizes of population, types of demographic circumstances and accuracy of demographic statistics. Five of the major areas are subdivided into a total of 20 regions, which are arranged within the major areas; these regions together with Northern America, which is not subdivided, make a total of 21 regions.

The major areas of Northern America and Latin America are distinguished, rather than the conventional continents of North America and South America, because population trends in the middle American mainland and the Caribbean region more closely resemble those of South America than those of America north of Mexico. Data for the traditional continents of North and South America can be obtained by adding Central America and Caribbean region to Northern America and deducting from Latin America. Latin America, as defined here, has somewhat wider limits than it would be if defined only to include the Spanish-speaking, French-speaking and Portuguese-speaking countries.

The average annual percentage rates of population growth are calculated by the Population Division, United Nations Department of Economic and Social Affairs, using an exponential rate of increase.

Crude birth and crude death rates are expressed in terms of the average annual number of births and deaths, respectively, per 1 000 mid-year population. These rates are estimated.

Surface area totals are estimated by Population Division, United Nations Department of Economic and Social Affairs.

Computation: Density, calculated by the Statistics Division of the United Nations Department of Social and Economic Affairs, is the number of persons in the 2005 total population per square kilometer of total surface area.

Reliability of data: With the exception of surface area, all data are set in *italic* type to indicate their conjectural quality.

Limitations: The estimated orders of magnitude of population and surface area are subject to all the basic limitations set forth in connection with table 3, and to the same qualifications set forth for population and surface area statistics in sections 3 and 2.4 of the Technical Notes, respectively.

Likewise, the rates of population increase and the density index are affected by the limitations of the original figures. However, it may be noted that, in compiling data for regional and major areas totals, errors in the components may tend to compensate each other and the resulting aggregates may be more reliable than the quality of the individual components would imply.

Because of their estimated character, many of the birth and death rates shown should also be considered only as orders of magnitude, and not as measures of the true level of natality or mortality.

In interpreting the population densities, one should consider that some of the regions include large segments of land that are uninhabitable or barely habitable, and density values calculated as described make no allowance for this, nor for differences in patterns of land settlement.

Composition of macro geographical regions and sub-regions

AFRICA

Eastern Africa
Burundi
Comoros
Djibouti
Eritrea
Ethiopia
Kenya
Madagascar
Malawi
Mauritius
Mozambique
Réunion
Rwanda
Seychelles
Somalia
Uganda
United Republic of Tanzania
Zambia
Zimbabwe

Middle Africa
Angola
Cameroon
Central African Republic
Chad
Congo
Democratic Republic of the
  Congo
Equatorial Guinea
Gabon
Sao Tome and Principe

Northern Africa
Algeria
Egypt
Libyan Arab Jamahiriya
Morocco
Sudan
Tunisia
Western Sahara

Southern Africa
Botswana
Lesotho
Namibia
South Africa
Swaziland

Western Africa
Benin
Burkina Faso
Cape Verde
Côte d'Ivoire
Gambia
Ghana

Guinea
Guinea-Bissau
Liberia
Mali
Mauritania
Niger
Nigeria
Saint Helena
Senegal
Sierra Leone
Togo

ASIA

Eastern Asia
China
China - Hong Kong SAR
China - Macao SAR
Japan
Korea, Democratic People's
  Republic of
Korea, Republic of
Mongolia

South-central Asia
Afghanistan
Bangladesh
Bhutan
India
Iran (Islamic Republic of)
Kazakhstan
Kyrgyzstan
Maldives
Nepal
Pakistan
Sri Lanka
Tajikistan
Turkmenistan
Uzbekistan

South-eastern Asia
Brunei Darussalam
Cambodia
Indonesia
Lao People's Democratic
  Republic
Malaysia
Myanmar
Philippines
Singapore
Thailand
Timor Leste
Viet Nam

Western Asia
Armenia
Azerbaijan
Bahrain

Cyprus
Georgia
Iraq
Israel
Jordan
Kuwait
Lebanon
Occupied Palestinian Territory
Oman
Qatar
Saudi Arabia
Syrian Arab Republic
Turkey
United Arab Emirates
Yemen

EUROPE

Eastern Europe
Belarus
Bulgaria
Czech Republic
Hungary
Poland
Republic of Moldova
Romania
Russian Federation
Slovakia
Ukraine

Northern Europe
Channel Islands
Denmark
Estonia
Faeroe Islands
Finland
Iceland
Ireland
Isle of Man
Latvia
Lithuania
Norway
Sweden
United Kingdom of Great Britain
  and Northern Ireland

Southern Europe
Albania
Andorra
Bosnia and Herzegovina
Croatia
Gibraltar
Greece
Holy See
Italy
Malta
Portugal

San Marino
Serbia and Montenegro
Slovenia
Spain
The Former Yugoslav Republic
of Macedonia

Western Europe
Austria
Belgium
France
Germany
Liechtenstein
Luxembourg
Monaco
Netherlands
Switzerland

LATIN AMERICA
and the CARIBBEAN

Caribbean
Anguilla
Antigua and Barbuda
Aruba
Bahamas
Barbados
British Virgin Islands
Cayman Islands
Cuba
Dominica
Dominican Republic
Grenada
Guadaloupe
Haiti
Jamaica
Martinique
Montserrat
Netherlands Antilles
Puerto Rico

Saint Kitts and Nevis
Saint Lucia
Saint Vincent and the
Grenadines
Trinidad and Tobago
Turks and Caicos Islands
United States Virgin
Islands

Central America
Belize
Costa Rica
El Salvador
Guatemala
Honduras
Mexico
Nicaragua
Panama

South America
Argentina
Bolivia
Brazil
Chile
Colombia
Ecuador
Falkland Islands (Malvinas)
French Guiana
Guyana
Paraguay
Peru
Suriname
Uruguay
Venezuela (Bolivarian Republic
of)

NORTHERN AMERICA

Bermuda

Canada
Greenland
Saint Pierre and Miquelon
United States of America

OCEANIA

Australia and New Zealand
Australia
New Zealand
Norfolk Island

Melanesia
Fiji
New Caledonia
Papua New Guinea
Solomon Islands
Vanuatu

Micronesia
Guam
Kiribati
Marshall Islands
Micronesia (Federated States of)
Nauru
Northern Mariana Islands
Palau

Polynesia
American Samoa
Cook Islands
French Polynesia
Niue
Pitcairn
Samoa
Tokelau
Tonga
Tuvalu
Wallis and Futuna Islands

NOTES

[1] *World Population Prospects: The 2006 Revision, CD Rom Edition – Extended Dataset in Excel and ASCII formats* (United Nations publication, Sales No. E.07.XIII.7), New York 2007.

Tableau 1

Le tableau 1 présente, pour l'ensemble du monde et les grandes zones et régions, des estimations concernant l'ordre de grandeur de la population, les taux d'accroissement démographique, les taux bruts de natalité et de mortalité, la superficie et la densité de peuplement.

Description des variables : des estimations de la population mondiale par grandes zones et régions sont présentées pour 1950, 1960, 1970, 1980, 1990 et 2000 ainsi que pour 2006. Les taux annuels moyens d'accroissement de la population et les taux bruts de natalité et de mortalité portent sur la période allant de 2005 à 2010. Les indications concernant la superficie exprimée en kilomètres carrés et les estimations de la densité de population se rapportent à 2006.

Toutes les estimations de population et les taux de natalité, taux de mortalité et taux annuels d'accroissement de la population qui sont présentés dans le tableau 1 ont été établis par la Division de la population du Département des affaires économiques et sociales (Secrétariat de l'Organisation des Nations Unies), et ont été publiés dans *World Population Prospects: The 2006 Revision, CD Rom Edition – Extended Dataset*[1].

Bien que l'on ait donné certains totaux pour les continents (tous les autres pouvant être calculés), on a réparti le monde en huit grandes zones qui ont été découpées de manière à obtenir une plus grande homogénéité du point de vue des dimensions de population, des types de situations démographiques et de l'exactitude des statistiques démographiques.

Cinq de ces huit grandes zones ont été subdivisées en 20 régions. Avec l'Amérique septentrionale, qui n'est pas subdivisée, on arrive à un total de 21 régions.

Au lieu de faire la distinction classique entre l'Amérique du Nord et l'Amérique du Sud, on a choisi d'opérer une comparaison entre l'Amérique septentrionale et l'Amérique latine, parce que les tendances démographiques dans la partie continentale de l'Amérique centrale et dans la région des Caraïbes se rapprochent davantage de celles de l'Amérique du Sud que de celles de l'Amérique au nord du Mexique. On obtient les données pour les continents traditionnels de l'Amérique du Nord et de l'Amérique du Sud en extrayant les données concernant l'Amérique centrale et les Caraïbes de celles relatives à l'Amérique latine et en les regroupant avec celles relatives à l'Amérique septentrionale. L'Amérique latine ainsi définie a par conséquent des limites plus larges que celles des pays ou zones de langues espagnole, portugaise et française qui constituent l'Amérique latine au sens le plus strict du terme.

La Division de la population a calculé les taux annuels moyens d'accroissement de la population en appliquant un taux d'accroissement exponentiel.

Les taux bruts de natalité et de mortalité représentent respectivement le nombre annuel moyen de naissances et de décès par millier d'habitants en milieu d'année. Ces taux sont estimatifs.

La superficie totale a été estimée par la Division de la population du Département des affaires économiques et sociales.

Calculs : la densité, calculée par la Division de statistique du Département des affaires économiques et sociales, est égale au rapport entre l'effectif total de la population en 2004 et la superficie totale exprimée en kilomètres carrés.

Fiabilité des données : á l'exception des données concernant la superficie, toutes les données sont reproduites en *italique* pour en faire ressortir le caractère conjectural.

Insuffisance des données : les estimations concernant l'ordre de grandeur de la population et la superficie reposent en partie sur les données du tableau 3 ; elles appellent donc toutes les réserves fondamentales formulées à propos de ce tableau, et celles qui ont été respectivement formulées aux sections 3 et 2.4 des Notes techniques en ce qui concerne les statistiques relatives à la population et à la superficie.

Les taux d'accroissement et les indices de densité de la population se ressentent eux aussi des insuffisances inhérentes aux données de base. Toutefois, il est à noter que, lorsque l'on additionne des données par territoire pour obtenir des totaux régionaux et par grandes zones, les erreurs qu'elles comportent arrivent parfois à s'équilibrer, de sorte que les agrégats obtenus peuvent être un peu plus exacts que chacun des éléments dont on est parti.

Vu leur caractère estimatif, nombre des taux de natalité et de mortalité du tableau 1 doivent être considérés uniquement comme des ordres de grandeur et ne sont pas censés mesurer exactement le niveau de la natalité ou de la mortalité.

Parce que les totaux des superficies ont été obtenus en additionnant les chiffres pour chaque pays ou zones, qui apparaissent dans le tableau 3, ils ne comprennent pas les lieux où la population est inférieure à 50 personnes, tels que les régions polaires inhabitées.

Pour interpréter les valeurs de la densité de population, on se souviendra qu'il existe dans certaines des régions de vastes étendues de terres inhabitables ou à peine habitables et que les chiffres calculés selon la méthode indiquée ne tiennent compte ni de ce fait ni des différences de dispersion de la population selon le mode d'habitat.

Composition des grandes zones et régions

AFRIQUE

Afrique orientale
Burundi
Comores
Djibouti
Érythrée
Éthiopie
Kenya
Madagascar
Malawi
Maurice
Mozambique
Ouganda
République-Unie de Tanzanie
Réunion
Rwanda
Seychelles
Somalie
Zambie
Zimbabwe

Afrique centrale
Angola
Cameroun
Congo
Gabon
Guinée équatoriale
République centrafricaine
République démocratique du Congo
Sao Tomé-et-Principe
Tchad

Afrique septentrionale
Algérie
Égypte
Jamahiriya arabe libyenne
Maroc
Sahara occidental
Soudan
Tunisie

Afrique australe
Afrique du Sud
Botswana
Lesotho
Namibie
Swaziland

Afrique occidentale
Bénin
Burkina Faso
Cap-Vert
Côte d'Ivoire
Gambie
Ghana
Guinée
Guinée-Bissau
Libéria
Mali
Mauritanie
Niger
Nigéria
Sainte-Hélène
Sénégal
Sierra Leone
Togo

AMÉRIQUE LATINE ET CARAÏBES

Caraïbes
Anguilla
Antigua-et-Barbuda
Antilles néerlandaises
Aruba
Bahamas
Barbade
Cuba
Dominique
Grenade
Guadeloupe

Haïti
Îles Caïmanes
Îles Turques et Caïques
Îles Vierges américaines
Îles Vierges britanniques
Jamaïque
Martinique
Montserrat
Porto Rico
République dominicaine
Saint-Kitts-et-Nevis
Sainte-Lucie
Saint-Vincent-et-les Grenadines
Trinité-et-Tobago

Amérique centrale
Belize
Costa Rica
El Salvador
Guatemala
Honduras
Mexique
Nicaragua
Panama

Amérique du Sud
Argentine
Bolivie
Brésil
Chili
Colombie
Équateur
Guyana
Guyane française
Îles Falkland (Malvinas)
Paraguay
Pérou
Suriname
Uruguay
Venezuela (République bolivarienne du)

AMÉRIQUE SEPTENTRIONALE

Bermudes
Canada
États-Unis d'Amérique
Groenland
Saint-Pierre-et-Miquelon

ASIE

Asie orientale
Chine
Chine - Région administrative spéciale de Hong Kong
Chine - Région administrative spéciale de Macao
Japon
Mongolie
République de Corée
République populaire démocratique de Corée

Asie centrale et Asie du Sud
Afghanistan
Bangladesh
Bhoutan
Inde
Iran (République Islamique d')
Kazakhstan
Kirghizistan
Maldives
Népal
Ouzbékistan
Pakistan
Sri Lanka
Tadjikistan
Turkménistan

Asie du Sud-Est
Brunéi Darussalam
Cambodge
Indonésie
Malaisie
Myanmar
Philippines
République démocratique populaire lao
Singapour
Thaïlande
Timor-Leste
Viet Nam

Asie occidentale
Arabie saoudite
Arménie
Azerbaïdjan

Bahreïn
Chypre
Émirats arabes unis
Géorgie
Iraq
Israël
Jordanie
Koweït
Liban
Oman
Qatar
République arabe syrienne
Territoire palestinien occupé
Turquie
Yémen

EUROPE

Europe orientale
Bélarus
Bulgarie
Fédération de Russie
Hongrie
Pologne
République de Moldova
République tchèque
Roumanie
Slovaquie
Ukraine

Europe septentrionale
Danemark
Estonie
Finlande
Île de Man
Îles Anglo-Normandes
Îles Féroé
Îles Svalbard et Jan Mayen
Irlande
Islande
Lettonie
Lituanie
Norvège
Royaume-Uni de Grande-Bretagne et d'Irlande du Nord
Suède

Europe méridionale
Albanie
Andorre
Bosnie-Herzégovine
Croatie
Espagne
Ex-République yougoslave de Macédoine
Gibraltar

Grèce
Italie
Malte
Portugal
Saint-Marin
Saint-Siège
Serbie-et-Monténégro
Slovénie

Europe occidentale
Allemagne
Autriche
Belgique
France
Liechtenstein
Luxembourg
Monaco
Pays-Bas
Suisse

OCÉANIE

Australie et Nouvelle-Zélande
Australie
Île Norfolk
Nouvelle-Zélande

Mélanésie
Fidji
Îles Salomon
Nouvelle-Calédonie
Papouasie-Nouvelle-Guinée
Vanuatu

Micronésie
Guam
Îles Mariannes septentrionales
Îles Marshall
Kiribati
Micronésie (États fédérés de)
Nauru
Palaos

Polynésie
Îles Cook
Îles Wallis et Futuna
Nioué
Pitcairn
Polynésie française
Samoa
Samoa américaines
Tokélaou
Tonga
Tuvalu

---

[1] *World Population Prospects, The 2006 Revision, CD Rom Edition – Extended Dataset in Excel and ASCII formats* (numéro de vente : E.07.XIII.7, publication des Nations Unies, New York, 2007).

1. Population, rate of increase, birth and death rates, surface area and density for the world, major areas and regions: selected years
Population, taux d'accroissement, taux de natalité et taux de mortalité, superficie et densité pour l'ensemble du monde, les régions macro géographiques et les composantes géographiques: diverses années

Major areas and regions / Régions macro géographiques et composantes	Mid-year population estimates - Estimations de population au milieu de l'année (millions)							Annual rate of increase - Taux d'accroiss-ement annuel (%)	Crude birth rate - Taux bruts de natali-té	Crude death rate - Taux bruts de morta-lité	Surface area (km2) - Superfic-ie (km2) (000s)	Density - Densité[1]
	1950	1960	1970	1980	1990	2000	2006	2005 - 2010			2006	
WORLD TOTAL - ENSEMBLE DU MONDE	2 520	3 024	3 697	4 442	5 280	6 086	6 593	1.2	20	9	136 127	48
AFRICA - AFRIQUE	224	282	364	479	636	812	943	2.2	39	13	30 312	31
Eastern Africa - Afrique orientale	65	82	109	146	198	256	300	2.5	39	14	6 361	47
Middle Africa - Afrique centrale	26	32	41	54	73	96	116	2.8	45	17	6 613	18
Northern Africa - Afrique septentrionale	53	67	86	112	144	175	193	1.7	24	6	8 525	23
Southern Africa - Afrique méridionale	16	20	26	33	42	52	55	0.6	23	17	2 675	21
Western Africa - Afrique occidentale	64	80	102	134	178	234	279	2.4	40	15	6 138	46
LATIN AMERICA AND CARIBBEAN - AMERIQUE LATINE ET CARAIBES	167	219	285	362	444	523	565	1.2	20	6	20 546	27
Caribbean - Caraïbes	17	20	25	29	34	38	41	0.9	19	8	234	175
Central America - Amérique centrale	37	50	68	91	113	136	146	1.3	21	5	2 480	59
South America - Amérique du Sud	113	148	192	242	297	349	379	1.2	19	6	17 832	21
NORTHERN AMERICA - AMERIQUE SEPTENTRIONALE[2]	172	204	232	256	283	315	336	1.0	14	8	21 776	15
ASIA - ASIE[3]	1 396	1 699	2 140	2 630	3 169	3 676	3 984	1.1	19	7	31 880	125
Eastern Asia - Asie orientale	671	792	987	1 178	1 350	1 479	1 531	0.5	13	7	11 763	130
South Central Asia - Asie centrale méridionale	496	617	780	978	1 226	1 485	1 672	1.5	24	8	10 791	155
South Eastern Asia - Asie méridionale orientale	178	223	286	358	440	519	565	1.2	20	6	4 495	126
Western Asia - Asie occidentale[3]	51	67	88	116	154	193	216	1.8	24	6	4 831	45
EUROPE[3]	547	604	656	692	721	728	731	0.0	10	12	23 049	32
Eastern Europe - Europe orientale	220	254	276	295	311	305	296	-0.5	10	15	18 814	16
Northern Europe - Europe septentrionale	77	81	86	89	92	94	97	0.4	12	10	1 810	53
Southern Europe - Europe méridionale	109	118	127	138	143	146	151	0.3	10	10	1 317	115
Western Europe - Europe occidentale	141	152	166	170	176	184	187	0.2	10	10	1 108	169
OCEANIA - OCEANIE[2]	12.8	15.9	19.6	22.9	26.7	30.9	33.8	1.2	17	7	8 564	4
Australia and New Zealand - Australie et Nouvelle-Zélande	10.1	12.6	15.5	17.8	20.3	22.9	24.7	1.0	13	7	8 012	3
Melanesia - Melanésie	2.3	2.7	3.4	4.4	5.5	6.9	8.0	1.9	28	9	541	15
Micronesia - Micronésie	0.1	0.2	0.2	0.3	0.4	0.5	0.5	1.3	22	5	3	167
Polynesia - Polynésie	0.2	0.3	0.4	0.5	0.5	0.6	0.7	1.0	22	5	8	88

FOOTNOTES - NOTES

[1] Population per square kilometre of surface area. Figures are estimates of population divided by surface area and are not to be considered as either reflecting density in the urban sense or as indicating the supporting power of a territory's land and resources. — Habitants par kilomètre carré. Il s'agit simplement du quotient calculé en divisant la population par la superficie et n'est par considéré comme indiquant la densité au sens urbain du terme ni l'effectif de population que les terres et les ressources du territoire sont capables de nourrir.

[2] Hawaii, a state of the United States of America, is included in Northern America rather than in Oceania. — Hawaii, un Etat des Etats-Unis d'Amérique, est compris en Amérique septentrionale plutôt qu'en Océanie.

[3] The European part of Turkey is included in Western Asia rather than Europe. — La partie européenne de la Turquie est comprise en Asie Occidentale plutôt qu'en Europe.

Table 2

Table 2 presents estimates of population and the percentage distribution by age and sex as well as the sex ratio for all ages; data are presented for the world, the six major areas and the 20 regions for 2006.

Description of variables: All population estimates presented in this table are prepared by the Population Division of the United Nations Department of Economic and Social Affairs. These estimates were published (using more detailed age groups) in the *World Population Prospects: The 2006 Revision, CD Rom Edition – Extended Dataset*[1].

The scheme of regionalization used for these estimates is discussed in detail in the technical notes for table 1. Age groups presented in this table are: under 15 years, 15-64 years and 65 years and over. Sex ratio refers to the number of males per 100 females of all ages.

The percentage distributions and the sex ratios that appear in this table were calculated by the Statistics Division of the United Nations Department of Economic and Social Affairs using the Population Division estimates.

Reliability of data: All data are set in *italic* type to indicate their conjectural quality.

Limitations: The data presented in this table are from the same series of estimates, prepared by the Population Division, presented in table 1. The estimated orders of magnitude of population are subject to all the basic limitations set forth for population statistics in section 3 of the Technical Notes. In brief, because they are estimates, these distributions by broad age groups and sex should be considered only as orders of magnitude. However, in compiling data for regional and macro region totals, errors in the components tend to compensate each other and the resulting aggregates may be somewhat more reliable than the quality of the individual components would imply.

In addition, data in this table are limited by factors affecting data by age. These factors are described in the technical notes for table 7. Because the age groups presented in this table are so broad, these problems are minimized.

NOTES

[1] *World Population Prospects: The 2006 Revision, CD Rom Edition – Extended Dataset in Excel and ASCII formats* (United Nations publication, Sales No. E.07.XIII.7), New York 2007

Tableau 2

Le tableau 2 présente, pour l'ensemble du monde, les six grandes zones et les 20 régions, des estimations concernant la population en 2006 ainsi que sa répartition en pourcentage selon l'âge et le sexe, et le rapport de masculinité pour tous les âges.

Description des variables : toutes les données figurant dans le tableau 2 ont été établies par la Division de la population du Département des affaires économiques et sociales (Secrétariat de l'Organisation des Nations Unies) et ont été publiées dans l'ouvrage intitulé *World Population Prospects: The 2006 Revision, CD Rom Edition – Extended Dataset* [1].

La classification géographique utilisée pour établir ces estimations est exposée en détail dans les notes techniques relatives au tableau 1. Les groupes d'âge présentés dans ce tableau sont définis comme suit : moins de 15 ans, de 15 à 64 ans et 65 ans et plus. Le rapport de masculinité correspond au nombre d'individus de sexe masculin pour 100 individus de sexe féminin sans considération d'âge.

Les pourcentages et les rapports de masculinité qui sont présentés dans le tableau 2 ont été calculés par la Division de statistique de l'ONU à partir des estimations établies par la Division de la population.

Fiabilité des données : toutes les données figurant dans ce tableau sont reproduites en *italique* pour en faire ressortir le caractère conjectural.

Insuffisance des données : les données de ce tableau appartiennent à la même série d'estimations, établie par la Division de la population, que celles qui figurent au tableau 1. Les estimations concernant l'ordre de grandeur de la population appellent donc toutes les réserves fondamentales qui ont été formulées à la section 3 des Notes techniques à propos des statistiques relatives à la population. Sans entrer dans le détail, il convient de préciser que les données relatives à la répartition par grand groupe d'âge et par sexe doivent être considérées uniquement comme des ordres de grandeur en raison de leur caractère estimatif. Toutefois, il est à noter que, lorsque l'on additionne des données par territoire pour obtenir des totaux régionaux et par grandes zones, les erreurs qu'elles comportent arrivent parfois à s'équilibrer, de sorte que les agrégats obtenus peuvent être un peu plus exacts que chacun des éléments dont on est parti.

En outre, les donnés figurant dans le tableau 2 comportent certaines imprécisions en raison des facteurs influant sur les données par âge (voir à ce propos les notes techniques relatives au tableau 7). Ces imprécisions sont cependant atténuées du fait de l'étendue des groupes d'âge présentés dans le tableau 2.

NOTE

[1] *World Population Prospects: The 2006 Revision, CD Rom Edition – Extended Dataset in Excel and ASCII formats* (United Nations publication, Sales No. E.07.XIII.7), New York 2007

2. Estimates of population and its percentage distribution, by age and sex and sex ratio for all ages for the world, major areas and regions: 2006
Estimations de la population et pourcentage de répartition selon l'âge et le sexe et rapport de masculinité pour l'ensemble du monde, les grandes régions et les régions géographiques: 2006

Major areas and regions / Grandes régions et régions	Population (millions)												Sex ratio - Rapport de masculinité[1]
	Both sexes - Les deux sexes				Male - Masculin				Female - Féminin				
	All ages - Tous âges	-15	15-64	65+	All ages - Tous âges	-15	15-64	65+	All ages - Tous âges	-15	15-64	65+	
WORLD TOTAL - ENSEMBLE DU MONDE													
Number - Nombre	6 593	1 846	4 260	487	3 322	951	2 156	214	3 271	894	2 104	273	
Percent - Pourcentage	100.0	28.0	64.6	7.4	100.0	28.6	64.9	6.5	100.0	27.3	64.3	8.3	101.5
AFRICA - AFRIQUE													
Number - Nombre	943	389	522	32	470	196	259	14	474	193	263	18	
Percent - Pourcentage	100.0	41.2	55.4	3.4	100.0	41.8	55.2	3.0	100.0	40.7	55.6	3.8	99.2
Eastern Africa - Afrique orientale													
Number - Nombre	300	133	159	9	149	67	78	4	151	66	80	5	
Percent - Pourcentage	100.0	44.2	52.9	2.9	100.0	44.8	52.6	2.6	100.0	43.7	53.1	3.2	98.4
Middle Africa - Afrique centrale													
Number - Nombre	116	53	60	3	57	26	29	1	58	26	30	2	
Percent - Pourcentage	100.0	45.6	51.5	2.8	100.0	46.1	51.4	2.5	100.0	45.1	51.7	3.2	98.2
Northern Africa - Afrique septentrionale													
Number - Nombre	193	63	121	9	97	32	60	4	96	31	60	5	
Percent - Pourcentage	100.0	32.7	62.6	4.7	100.0	33.3	62.5	4.2	100.0	32.1	62.7	5.1	100.5
Southern Africa - Afrique méridionale													
Number - Nombre	55	18	35	2	27	9	17	1	28	9	18	1	
Percent - Pourcentage	100.0	32.7	63.0	4.3	100.0	33.6	63.0	3.4	100.0	31.9	62.9	5.2	96.4
Western Africa - Afrique occidentale													
Number - Nombre	279	122	148	9	140	62	74	4	140	60	74	5	
Percent - Pourcentage	100.0	43.7	53.2	3.1	100.0	44.2	52.9	2.9	100.0	43.2	53.4	3.4	100.2
LATIN AMERICA AND CARIBBEAN - AMÉRIQUE LATIN ET CARAÏBES													
Number - Nombre	565	166	363	36	279	85	178	16	286	82	184	20	
Percent - Pourcentage	100.0	29.5	64.2	6.4	100.0	30.4	63.9	5.7	100.0	28.6	64.4	7.1	97.4
Caribbean - Caraïbes													
Number - Nombre	41	11	26	3	20	6	13	1	21	6	13	2	
Percent - Pourcentage	100.0	28.1	64.0	8.0	100.0	28.9	63.8	7.4	100.0	27.2	64.2	8.5	98.2
Central America - Amérique centrale													
Number - Nombre	146	47	91	8	71	24	44	4	74	23	47	5	
Percent - Pourcentage	100.0	32.2	62.2	5.7	100.0	33.2	61.5	5.2	100.0	31.1	62.8	6.1	96.0
South America - Amérique méridionale													
Number - Nombre	379	108	246	25	187	55	121	11	191	53	124	14	
Percent - Pourcentage	100.0	28.6	64.9	6.5	100.0	29.4	64.9	5.7	100.0	27.7	65.0	7.3	97.8
NORTHERN AMERICA - AMÉRIQUE SEPTENTRIONALE[2]													
Number - Nombre	336	68	226	42	165	35	113	18	170	33	113	24	
Percent - Pourcentage	100.0	20.3	67.3	12.4	100.0	21.2	68.2	10.6	100.0	19.5	66.4	14.1	97.0
ASIA - ASIE[3]													
Number - Nombre	3 984	1 099	2 628	257	2 039	572	1 347	119	1 945	527	1 280	138	
Percent - Pourcentage	100.0	27.6	66.0	6.5	100.0	28.1	66.1	5.8	100.0	27.1	65.8	7.1	104.8
Eastern Asia - Asie orientale													
Number - Nombre	1 531	312	1 082	137	785	166	556	63	745	146	526	73	
Percent - Pourcentage	100.0	20.4	70.7	8.9	100.0	21.1	70.8	8.1	100.0	19.6	70.5	9.8	105.4
South Central Asia - Asie centrale méridionale													
Number - Nombre	1 672	553	1 040	79	861	287	536	38	811	266	504	42	
Percent - Pourcentage	100.0	33.1	62.2	4.8	100.0	33.3	62.3	4.4	100.0	32.8	62.1	5.2	106.1
South Eastern Asia - Asie méridionale orientale													
Number - Nombre	565	163	371	31	282	83	185	14	283	80	186	17	
Percent - Pourcentage	100.0	28.9	65.6	5.5	100.0	29.6	65.5	4.9	100.0	28.2	65.7	6.1	99.4
Western Asia - Asie occidentale													
Number - Nombre	216	71	135	10	111	36	71	4	105	35	65	6	
Percent - Pourcentage	100.0	32.7	62.7	4.6	100.0	32.4	63.5	4.0	100.0	33.0	61.8	5.3	105.7
EUROPE[3]													
Number - Nombre	731	115	500	117	352	59	247	46	379	56	252	71	
Percent - Pourcentage	100.0	15.7	68.3	16.0	100.0	16.7	70.3	13.0	100.0	14.7	66.5	18.8	92.8
Eastern Europe - Europe orientale													
Number - Nombre	296	44	210	42	139	23	102	15	157	22	108	28	
Percent - Pourcentage	100.0	15.0	70.7	14.2	100.0	16.4	73.1	10.5	100.0	13.8	68.6	17.6	88.6
Northern Europe - Europe septentrionale													
Number - Nombre	97	17	64	15	47	9	32	6	49	8	32	9	
Percent - Pourcentage	100.0	17.8	66.3	15.9	100.0	18.6	67.7	13.7	100.0	17.0	65.0	18.0	95.8
Southern Europe - Europe méridionale													
Number - Nombre	151	23	102	27	74	12	51	11	77	11	51	15	
Percent - Pourcentage	100.0	15.0	67.3	17.7	100.0	15.8	69.0	15.2	100.0	14.2	65.7	20.1	95.8

2. Estimates of population and its percentage distribution, by age and sex and sex ratio for all ages for the world, major areas and regions: 2006
Estimations de la population et pourcentage de répartition selon l'âge et le sexe et rapport de masculinité pour l'ensemble du monde, les grandes régions et les régions géographiques: 2006 (continued - suite)

Major areas and regions	Population (millions)												Sex ratio - Rapport de masculinité[1]
	Both sexes - Les deux sexes				Male - Masculin				Female - Féminin				
Grandes régions et régions	All ages - Tous âges	-15	15-64	65+	All ages - Tous âges	-15	15-64	65+	All ages - Tous âges	-15	15-64	65+	
Western Europe - Europe occidentale													
Number - Nombre	187	30	124	33	91	16	63	13	96	15	62	19	
Percent - Pourcentage	100.0	16.2	66.3	17.5	100.0	17.0	68.3	14.7	100.0	15.4	64.4	20.1	95.7
OCEANIA - OCÉANIA[2]													
Number - Nombre	33.85	8.35	21.99	3.51	16.91	4.29	11.03	1.59	16.93	4.05	10.95	1.93	
Percent - Pourcentage	100.0	24.7	65.0	10.4	100.0	25.4	65.2	9.4	100.0	23.9	64.7	11.4	99.9
Australia and New Zealand - Australie et Nouvelle Zélande													
Number - Nombre	24.67	4.84	16.60	3.23	12.25	2.48	8.31	1.46	12.42	2.35	8.29	1.78	
Percent - Pourcentage	100.0	19.6	67.3	13.1	100.0	20.3	67.9	11.9	100.0	19.0	66.7	14.3	98.7
Melanesia - Melanésie													
Number - Nombre	7.98	3.12	4.64	0.22	4.05	1.61	2.34	0.11	3.92	1.51	2.30	0.11	
Percent - Pourcentage	100.0	39.1	58.2	2.8	100.0	39.6	57.8	2.6	100.0	38.5	58.6	2.9	103.3
Micronesia													
Number - Nombre	0.55	0.17	0.35	0.02	0.27	0.09	0.17	0.01	0.28	0.08	0.18	0.01	
Percent - Pourcentage	100.0	31.7	64.0	4.3	100.0	32.9	63.2	3.9	100.0	30.6	64.8	4.7	98.4
Polynesia - Polynésie													
Number - Nombre	0.65	0.22	0.40	0.03	0.33	0.11	0.21	0.02	0.32	0.11	0.19	0.02	
Percent - Pourcentage	100.0	33.7	61.0	5.3	100.0	34.0	61.3	4.8	100.0	33.4	60.8	5.8	105.3

FOOTNOTES - NOTES

[1] Males per 100 females of all ages - Hommes pour 100 femmes de tous âges

[2] Hawaii, a state of the United States of America, is included in Northern America rather than in Oceania. - Hawaii, un Etat des Etats-Unis d'Amérique, est compris en Amérique septentrionale plutôt qu'en Océanie.

[3] The European part of Turkey is included in Western Asia rather than Europe. - La partie européenne de la Turquie est comprise en Asie Occidentale plutôt qu'en Europe.

Table 3

Table 3 presents for each country or area of the world the total, male and female population enumerated at the latest population census, estimates of the mid-year total population for 2000 and 2006, the average annual exponential rate of increase (or decrease) for the period 2000 to 2006 the surface area and the population density for 2006.

Description of variables: The total, male and female population is, unless otherwise indicated, the *de facto* (present-in-area) population enumerated at the most recent census for which data are available. The date of this census is given. Population census data are usually the results of a nation-wide enumeration (traditional census). Alternatively other approaches for generating reliable statistics on population and housing can be used by countries, such as the use of population registers. Data that are the result of such an alternative approach are also coded as census and are footnoted accordingly. Also, the results of sample surveys, essentially national in character, may be presented showing the appropriate code. However, results of surveys referring to less than 50 percent of the total territory or population are not included.

Mid-year population estimates refer to the population on 1 July. Otherwise, a footnote is appended. Mid-year estimates of the total population are those provided by national statistical offices.

Surface area, expressed in square kilometres, refers to the total surface area, comprising land area and inland waters (assumed to consist of major rivers and lakes) and excluding Polar Regions as well as uninhabited islands. Exceptions to this are noted. Surface areas, originally reported in square miles by the country or area, have been converted to square kilometres using a conversion factor of 2.589988.

Computation: The annual rate of increase is the average annual percentage rate of population growth between 2000 and 2006, computed by the Statistics Division of the United Nations Department of Economic and Social Affairs using the unrounded mid-year estimates as presented in this table.

Density is the number of persons in the 2006 total population per square kilometre of total surface area.

Reliability of data: Reliable mid-year population estimates are those that are based on a complete census (or a sample survey) and have been adjusted by a continuous population register or on the basis of the calculated balance of births, deaths and migration. Mid-year estimates of this type are considered reliable and appear in roman type. Mid-year estimates not calculated on this basis are considered less reliable and are shown in italics. Estimates for years prior to 2006 are considered reliable or less reliable on the basis of the 2006 code and appear in roman type or in *italics*, accordingly.

Census data and sample survey results are considered reliable and, therefore, appear in roman type.

Rates of population increase that were calculated using population estimates considered less reliable, as described above, are set in italics rather than roman type.

All surface area data are assumed to be reliable and therefore appear in roman type.

Population density data, however, are considered reliable or less reliable on the basis of the reliability of the 2006 population estimates used as the numerator.

Limitations: Statistics on the total population enumerated at the time of the census, estimates of the mid-year total population and surface area data are subject to the same qualifications as have been set forth for population and surface area statistics in sections 3 and 2.4 of the Technical Notes, respectively.

Regarding the limitations of census data, it should be noted that although census data are considered reliable, and therefore appear in roman type, the actual quality of census data varies widely from one country or area to another. When known, an estimate of the extent of over-enumeration or under-enumeration is given in footnotes. In the case of sample surveys, a description of the population covered is provided.

Because the reliability of the population estimates for any given country or area is based on the quality of the 2006 estimate, the reliability of estimates prior to 2006 may be overstated.

Rates of population increase are subject to all the qualifications of the population estimates mentioned above. In some cases, they simply reflect the rate calculated or assumed in constructing the estimates themselves when adequate measures of natural increase and net migration were not available. Despite their shortcomings, these rates provide a useful index for studying population change and can be also useful in evaluating the accuracy of vital and migration statistics.

Population density data as shown in this table give only an indication of actual population density as they do not take account of the dispersion or concentration of population within countries or areas nor the proportion of habitable land. They should not be interpreted as reflecting density in the urban sense or as indicating the supporting power of a territory's land and resources.

Tableau 3

Le tableau 3 indique pour chaque pays ou zone du monde la population totale selon le sexe d'après les derniers recensements effectués, les estimations concernant la population totale au milieu de l'année 2000 et de l'année 2006, le taux moyen d'accroissement annuel exponentiel positif ou négatif pour la période allant de 2000 à 2006, ainsi que la superficie et la densité de population en 2006.

Description des variables : la population masculine et féminine totale est, sauf indication contraire, la population de fait (c'est-à-dire présente) enregistrée lors du recensement le plus récent sur lequel on dispose de données. La date de ce recensement est indiquée. Les données des recensements de la population sont habituellement obtenues au moyen d'un enregistrement à l'échelle nationale (recensement traditionnel). Les pays peuvent recourir à d'autres moyens pour établir des statistiques fiables sur la population et le logement, tels que des registres de la population. Les données obtenues par ce moyen sont présentées comme celles d'un recensement et sont annotées en conséquence. Par ailleurs, les résultats des enquêtes par sondage, réalisées habituellement à l'échelle nationale, peuvent être présentés à l'aide du code correspondant. En revanche, les résultats des enquêtes portant sur moins de 50 % du territoire total ou de la population ne sont pas indiqués.

Les estimations de la population en milieu d'année sont celles de la population au 1er juillet. Lorsque la date est différente, cela est signalé par une note. Les estimations de la population totale en milieu d'année sont celles qui ont été communiquées par les services nationaux de statistique.

La superficie - exprimée en kilomètres carrés - représente la superficie totale, c'est-à-dire qu'elle englobe les terres émergées et les eaux intérieures (qui sont censées comprendre les principaux lacs et cours d'eau) mais exclut les régions polaires et certaines îles inhabitées. Les exceptions à cette règle sont signalées en note. Les superficies initialement exprimées en miles carrés par les pays ou les zones ont été transformées en kilomètres carrés au moyen d'un coefficient de conversion de 2,589988.

Calculs : le taux d'accroissement annuel est le taux annuel moyen de variation (en pourcentage) de la population entre 2000 et 2006, calculé par la Division de statistique du Département des affaires économiques et sociales (Secrétariat de l'Organisation des Nations Unies) à partir des estimations en milieu d'année non arrondies qui figurent dans le tableau.

La densité est égale au rapport de l'effectif total de la population en 2006 à la superficie totale, exprimée en kilomètres carrés.

Fiabilité des données : les estimations en milieu d'année qui sont considérées sûres sont fondées sur un recensement complet (ou sur une enquête par sondage) et ont été ajustées en fonction des données provenant d'un registre permanent de population ou en fonction de la balance établie par le calcul des naissances, des décès et des migrations. Les estimations de ce type sont considérées comme sûres et apparaissent en caractères romains. Les estimations en milieu d'année dont le calcul n'a pas été effectué sur cette base sont considérées comme moins sûres et apparaissent en italique. Les estimations relatives aux années antérieures à 2006 sont jugées plus ou moins sûres en fonction du codage de 2006 et indiquées, selon le cas, en caractères romains ou en italique.

Les données de recensements ou les résultats d'enquêtes par sondage sont considérés comme sûrs et apparaissent par conséquent en caractères romains.

Les taux d'accroissement de la population, calculés à partir d'estimations jugées moins sûres d'après les normes décrites ci-dessus, sont indiqués en italique plutôt qu'en caractères romains.

Toutes les données de superficie sont présumées sûres et apparaissent par conséquent en caractères romains. En revanche, les données relatives à la densité de la population sont considérées plus ou moins sûres en fonction de la fiabilité des estimations de la population en 2006 ayant servi de numérateur.

Insuffisance des données : les statistiques portant sur la population totale dénombrée lors d'un recensement, les estimations de la population totale en milieu d'année et les données de superficie appellent les mêmes réserves que celles formulées aux sections 3 et 2.4 des Notes techniques à propos des statistiques relatives à la population et à la superficie.

S'agissant de l'insuffisance des données obtenues par recensement, il convient d'indiquer que, bien que ces données soient considérées comme sûres et apparaissent par conséquent en caractères romains, leur qualité réelle varie considérablement d'un pays ou d'une région à l'autre. Lorsque l'on possédait les renseignements voulus, on a donné une estimation du degré de sur-dénombrement ou de sous-dénombrement. Dans le cas des enquêtes par sondage, une description de la population considérée est fournie.

La fiabilité des estimations de la population d'un pays ou zone quelconque reposant sur la qualité des estimations de 2006, il se peut que la fiabilité des estimations antérieures à 2006 soit surévaluée.

Les taux d'accroissement appellent toutes les réserves formulées plus haut à propos des estimations concernant la population. Dans certains cas, ils représentent seulement le taux calculé ou que l'on a pris pour base pour établir les estimations elles-mêmes lorsque l'on ne disposait pas de mesures appropriées de l'accroissement naturel et des migrations nettes. Malgré leurs imperfections, ces taux fournissent des indications intéressantes pour l'étude du mouvement de la population et, utilisés avec les précautions nécessaires, ils peuvent également servir à évaluer l'exactitude des statistiques de l'état civil et des migrations.

Les données relatives à la densité de population figurant dans le tableau 3 n'ont qu'une valeur indicative en ce qui concerne la densité de population effective, car elles ne tiennent compte ni de la dispersion ou de la concentration de la population à l'intérieur des pays ou zones, ni de la proportion du territoire qui est habitable. Il ne faut donc y voir d'indication ni de la densité au sens urbain du terme ni du nombre d'habitants qui pourraient vivre sur les terres et avec les ressources naturelles du territoire considéré.

3. Population by sex, rate of population increase, surface area and density
Population selon le sexe, taux d'accroissement de la population, superficie et densité

Continent, country or area and census date / Continent, pays ou zone et date du recensement	Census type[a]	Latest available census — Dernier recensement disponible (in units — en unités)			Estimate type[a]	Mid-year estimates — Estimations au milieu de l'année (in thousands — en milliers)		Annual rate of increase Taux d'accrois sement annuel 2000-06	Surface area Superficie (km²) 2006	Density Densité 2006[b]
		Both sexes Les deux sexes	Male Masculin	Female Feminin		2000	2006			
AFRICA - AFRIQUE										
Algeria - Algérie										
16 IV 2008	DJ	*34 760 000	...	...	DJ	30 416	33 481	1.6	2 381 741	14
Angola										
15 XII 1970..............	DF	5 646 166	2 943 974	2 702 192		...	...	...	1 246 700	...
Benin - Bénin										
11 II 2002	DJ	6 769 914	3 284 119	3 485 795	DF	6 169	...	...	112 622	...
Botswana										
17 VIII 2001	DF	1 680 863	813 488	867 375	DF	1 653	1 720	0.7	582 000	3
Burkina Faso										
9 XII 2006	DJ	*13 730 258	*6 635 318	*7 094 940	DJ	11 347	...	...	274 222	...
Burundi										
16 VIII 1990	DF	5 139 073	2 473 599	2 665 474		...	...	...	27 834	...
Cameroon - Cameroun										
10 IV 1987	DF	10 493 655	...	...	DF	15 292[1]	...	...	475 442	...
Cape Verde - Cap-Vert										
16 VI 2000	DF	436 863	211 479	225 384	DF	435	483	1.8	4 033	120
Central African Republic - République centrafricaine										
8 XII 2003	DF	3 151 072	1 569 446	1 581 626		...	...	...	622 984	...
Chad - Tchad										
8 IV 1993	DF	6 279 931[2]	...	...		...	...	...	1 284 000	...
Comoros - Comores										
1 IX 2003..............	DF	575 660[3]	...	...		...	...	...	2 235	...
Congo										
6 VI 1996..............	DF	*2 600 000	...	...	DF	2 893	...	...	342 000	...
Côte d'Ivoire										
21 XI 1998	DF	15 366 672	7 844 621	7 522 050	DF	16 402	19 658	3.0	322 463	61
Democratic Republic of the Congo - République démocratique du Congo										
1 VII 1984	DF	29 916 800	14 543 800	15 373 000		...	...	...	2 344 858	...
Djibouti										
11 XII 1960	DF	81 200	...	...		...	...	...	23 200	...
Egypt - Égypte										
11 XI 2006..............	DF	72 798 031[4]	37 219 056[4]	35 578 975[4]	DF	63 975	72 009	2.0	1 002 000	72
Equatorial Guinea - Guinée équatoriale										
1 II 2002..............	DF	1 014 999	501 387	513 612		...	...	...	28 051	...
Eritrea - Érythrée										
9 V 1984	DF	2 748 304	1 374 452	1 373 852		...	...	...	117 600	...
Ethiopia - Éthiopie										
11 X 1994	DF	53 477 265	26 910 698	26 566 567	DF	63 495	75 067	2.8	1 104 300	68
Gabon										
1 XII 2003	DF	*1 269 000	...	...	DF	1 206	...	...	267 668	...
Gambia - Gambie										
15 IV 2003	DF	*1 364 507	*676 726	*687 781	DF	1 393	1 510	1.3	11 295	134
Ghana										
26 III 2000..............	DF	18 912 079	9 357 382	9 554 697	DF	18 412	...	...	238 533	...
Guinea - Guinée										
1 XII 1996	DF	7 156 406	3 497 979	3 658 427		...	...	...	245 857	...
Guinea-Bissau - Guinée-Bissau										
1 XII 1991	DF	983 367	476 210	507 157	DF	...	1 357[1]	...	36 125	38
Kenya										
24 VIII 1999	DF	28 686 607	14 205 589	14 481 018	DF	30 150	36 433	3.2	580 367	63
Lesotho										
9 IV 2006..............	DJ	*1 880 661	*916 281	*964 380	DF	2 144	...	...	30 355	...
Liberia - Libéria										
21 III 2008..............	DF	*3 489 072	*1 764 555	*1 724 517		...	...	...	111 369	...
Libyan Arab Jamahiriya - Jamahiriya arabe libyenne										
11 VIII 1995	DF	4 404 986[5]	2 236 943[5]	2 168 043[5]	DF	5 125[5]	...	...	1 759 540	...
Madagascar										
1 VIII 1993	DF	12 238 914	6 088 116	6 150 798	DF	15 085	...	...	587 041	...

3. Population by sex, rate of population increase, surface area and density
Population selon le sexe, taux d'accroissement de la population, superficie et densité (continued - suite)

Continent, country or area and census date / Continent, pays ou zone et date du recensement	Census type[a]	Latest available census Dernier recensement disponible (in units — en unités) Both sexes Les deux sexes	Male Masculin	Female Feminin	Estimate type[a]	Mid-year estimates Estimations au milieu de l'année (in thousands — en milliers) 2000	2006	Annual rate of increase Taux d' accrois sement annuel 2000-06	Surface area Superficie (km²) 2006	Density Densité 2006[b]

AFRICA - AFRIQUE

Malawi										
1 IX 1998	DF	9 933 868	4 867 563	5 066 305	DF	*10 475[1]	*12 758[1]	3.3	118 484	108
Mali										
1 IV 1998	DF	9 926 219[6]	4 905 510[6]	5 020 709[6]	DF	10 384	12 214	2.7	1 240 192	10
Mauritania - Mauritanie										
1 XI 2000	DF	2 548 157	1 240 414	1 307 743	DF	2 645	...	...	1 025 520	...
Mauritius - Maurice										
2 VII 2000	DJ	1 178 848	583 756	595 092	DJ	1 187	1 253	0.9	2 040	614
Mayotte										
31 VII 2007	DJ	186 337	91 379	94 958		...	...	...	...	...
Morocco - Maroc										
1 IX 2004	DF	29 680 069	14 640 662	15 039 407	DF	28 705	*30 506	1.0	446 550	68
Mozambique										
1 VIII 2007	DF	*20 530 714	*9 787 135	*10 743 579	DF	17 691[7]	...	...	801 590	...
Namibia - Namibie										
27 VIII 2001	DF	1 830 330	887 721[8]	942 572[8]	DF	*1 817	...	...	824 292	...
Niger										
20 V 2001	DF	*10 790 352	*5 380 287	*5 410 065	DJ	10 493	13 045	3.6	1 267 000	10
Nigeria - Nigéria										
21 III 2006	DF	*140 003 542	*71 709 859	*68 293 683	DF	115 224[1]	140 004[1]	3.2	923 768	152
Réunion										
1 I 2006	DJ	*784 000	...	...	DF	722	...	...	2 510	...
Rwanda										
16 VIII 2002	DJ	8 128 553	3 879 448	4 249 105		...	...	...	26 338	...
Saint Helena ex. dep. - Sainte-Hélène sans dép.										
8 III 1998	DF	5 157	2 612	2 545		...	...	...	122	...
Saint Helena: Ascension - Sainte-Hélène: Ascension										
8 III 1998	DJ	712	458	254		...	...	...	88	...
Saint Helena: Tristan da Cunha - Sainte-Hélène: Tristan da Cunha										
31 XII 1988	DF	296	139	157		...	...	...	98	...
Sao Tome and Principe - Sao Tomé-et-Principe										
25 VIII 2001	DJ	137 599	68 236	69 363	DF	135	152	1.9	964	158
Senegal - Sénégal										
8 XII 2002	DJ	9 552 442	4 665 730	4 886 712	DJ	9 427	*11 000	2.6	196 722	56
Seychelles										
26 VIII 2002	DJ	81 755[9]	40 751[9]	41 004[9]	DF	81	85	0.7	455	186
Sierra Leone										
4 XII 2004	DF	4 976 871	2 420 218	2 556 653	DF	4 944	...	...	71 740	...
Somalia - Somalie										
15 II 1987	DF	7 114 431	3 741 664	3 372 767		...	...	...	637 657	...
South Africa - Afrique du Sud										
10 X 2001	DF	*44 819 778	*21 434 041	*23 385 737	DF	43 686[7]	47 391[7]	1.4	1 221 037	39
Sudan - Soudan										
15 IV 1993	DF	24 940 683	12 518 638	12 422 045	DF	31 081	36 297	2.6	2 505 813	14
Swaziland										
11 V 2007	DF	*953 524	*460 498	*493 026	DF	1 003	1 146	2.2	17 364	66
Togo										
22 XI 1981	DF	2 719 567	1 325 641	1 393 926	DF	4 629	5 337	2.4	56 785	94
Tunisia - Tunisie										
28 IV 2004	DF	9 932 400	...	...	DF	9 564	10 126	1.0	163 610	62
Uganda - Ouganda										
12 IX 2002	DF	24 442 084	11 929 803	12 512 281	DF	22 575	27 357	3.2	241 038	113
United Republic of Tanzania - République Unie de Tanzanie										
24 VIII 2002	DF	*34 443 603	*16 829 861	*17 613 742	DF	...	38 251	...	945 087	40

3. Population by sex, rate of population increase, surface area and density
Population selon le sexe, taux d'accroissement de la population, superficie et densité (continued - suite)

Continent, country or area and census date / Continent, pays ou zone et date du recensement	Census type[a]	Latest available census — Dernier recensement disponible (in units — en unités)			Estimate type[a]	Mid-year estimates Estimations au milieu de l'année (in thousands — en milliers)		Annual rate of increase Taux d'accrois sement annuel 2000-06	Surface area Superficie (km²) 2006	Density Densité 2006[b]
		Both sexes Les deux sexes	Male Masculin	Female Feminin		2000	2006			
AFRICA - AFRIQUE										
Western Sahara - Sahara occidental[10]										
31 XII 1970	DF	76 425	43 981	32 444		...	...	...	266 000	...
Zambia - Zambie										
25 X 2000	DF	9 337 425	4 594 290	4 743 135	DF	...	11 799	...	752 618	16
Zimbabwe										
17 VIII 2002	DF	11 631 657	5 634 180	5 997 477	DF	...	12 225[11]	...	390 757	31
AMERICA, NORTH - AMÉRIQUE DU NORD										
Anguilla										
9 V 2001	DF	11 430	5 628	5 802	DF	11	*14	3.9	91	157
Antigua and Barbuda - Antigua-et-Barbuda										
28 V 2001	DF	77 426	37 002	40 424	DF	72	...		442	...
Aruba										
14 X 2000	DJ	90 508	43 435	47 073	DJ	91	103	2.1	180	571
Bahamas										
1 V 2000	DF	303 611	147 715	155 896	DF	...	330	...	13 943	24
Barbados - Barbade										
1 V 2000	DF	250 010	119 926	130 084	DF	269	274[12]	0.3	430	637
Belize										
12 V 2000	DF	240 204	121 278	118 926	DF	250	301	3.1	22 966	13
Bermuda - Bermudes										
20 V 2000	DJ	62 059[13]	29 802[13]	32 257[13]	DJ	63	64	0.2	54	1 181
British Virgin Islands - Îles Vierges britanniques										
21 V 2001	DF	20 647	10 627	10 020	DF	20	...	...	151	...
Canada										
16 V 2006	DJ	31 612 895	15 475 970	16 136 925	DJ	30 689[14]	32 649[15]	1.0	9 984 670	3
Cayman Islands - Îles Caïmanes										
10 X 1999	DJ	39 020[16]	19 033[16]	19 987[16]	DJ	40	52	4.3	264	197
Costa Rica										
26 VI 2000	DJ	3 810 179	1 902 614	1 907 565	DJ	3 810	4 354	2.2	51 100	85
Cuba										
6 IX 2002	DJ	11 177 743	5 597 233	5 580 510	DJ	11 130	11 241	0.2	109 886	102
Dominica - Dominique										
12 V 2001	DF	69 625[17]	35 073[17]	34 552[17]	DF	72	...	...	751	...
Dominican Republic - République dominicaine										
20 X 2002	DJ	8 562 541	4 265 215	4 297 326	DF	8 554	9 354	1.5	48 310	194
El Salvador										
12 V 2007	DJ	5 744 113	2 719 371	3 024 742	DF	6 276	6 991	1.8	21 041	332
Greenland - Groenland										
1 VII 2000	DJ	56 124[18]	29 989[18]	26 135[18]	DJ	56[18]	57[18]	0.2	2 166 086	
Grenada - Grenade										
25 V 2001	DF	102 632	50 481	52 151	DF	101	...	...	344	...
Guadeloupe										
1 I 2006	DJ	*447 000	...	...	DJ	428	*458	1.1	1 705	269
Guatemala										
24 XI 2002	DJ	11 237 196	...	...	DF	11 385[7]	13 019[7]	2.2	108 889	120
Haiti - Haïti										
11 I 2003	DJ	8 373 750	...	...	DJ	7 959	...	...	27 750	...
Honduras										
28 VII 2001	DF	6 071 200	3 000 530	3 070 670	DF	6 369	7 367	2.4	112 492	65
Jamaica - Jamaïque										
10 IX 2001	DJ	2 607 632	1 283 548	1 324 084	DJ	2 589	2 663	0.5	10 991	242
Martinique										
1 I 2006	DJ	*399 000	...	...	DJ	385	400	0.7	1 102	363

3. Population by sex, rate of population increase, surface area and density
Population selon le sexe, taux d'accroissement de la population, superficie et densité (continued - suite)

Continent, country or area and census date / Continent, pays ou zone et date du recensement	Census type[a]	Latest available census Dernier recensement disponible (in units — en unités) Both sexes Les deux sexes	Male Masculin	Female Feminin	Estimate type[a]	Mid-year estimates Estimations au milieu de l'année (in thousands — en milliers) 2000	2006	Annual rate of increase Taux d' accrois sement annuel 2000-06	Surface area Superficie (km²) 2006	Density Densité 2006[b]
AMERICA, NORTH - AMÉRIQUE DU NORD										
Mexico - Mexique										
17 X 2005	DJ	103 263 388	50 249 955	53 013 433	DJ	98 439	104 874	1.1	1 964 375	53
Montserrat										
12 V 2001	DF	4 491	2 418	2 073	DF	5	...	...	102	...
Netherlands Antilles - Antilles néerlandaises										
29 I 2001	DJ	175 653	82 521	93 132	DJ	179	190	0.9	800	237
Nicaragua										
4 VI 2005	DJ	5 144 553	2 535 461	2 609 092	DJ	5 106	5 530	1.3	120 340	46
Panama										
14 V 2000	DF	2 839 177	1 432 566	1 406 611	DF	2 856	3 284	2.3	75 517	43
Puerto Rico - Porto Rico										
1 IV 2000	DJ	3 808 610[19]	1 833 577[19]	1 975 033[19]	DJ	3 816[19]	3 928[19]	0.5	8 870	443
Saint Kitts and Nevis - Saint-Kitts-et-Nevis										
14 V 2001	DF	45 841	22 784	23 057	DF	40	...	...	261	...
Saint Lucia - Sainte-Lucie										
22 V 2001	DF	157 164	76 741	80 423	DF	156	*167	1.1	539	310
Saint Pierre and Miquelon - Saint Pierre-et-Miquelon										
19 I 2006	DF	6 125	...	...					242	...
Saint Vincent and the Grenadines - Saint Vincent-et-les Grenadines										
14 V 2001	DF	109 022[17]	55 456[17]	53 566[17]	DF	110	...	...	389	...
Trinidad and Tobago - Trinité-et-Tobago										
15 V 2000	DF	1 262 366	633 051	629 315	DF	1 290	...	...	5 130	...
Turks Caicos Islands - Îles Turques et Caïques										
20 VIII 2001	DF	19 886	9 897	9 989	DJ	18	33	9.8	948	35
United States - États-Unis										
1 IV 2000	DJ	281 421 906[20]	138 053 563[20]	143 368 343[20]	DJ	282 193[20]	299 398[20]	1.0	9 629 091	31
United States Virgin Islands - Îles Vierges américaines										
1 IV 2000	DJ	108 612[19]	51 864[19]	56 748[19]	DJ	109[19]	109[19]	0.1	347	314
AMERICA, SOUTH - AMÉRIQUE DU SUD										
Argentina - Argentine										
18 XI 2001	DF	36 260 130	17 659 072	18 601 058	DF	36 784	38 971	1.0	2 780 400	14
Bolivia - Bolivie										
5 IX 2001	DF	8 274 325	4 123 850	4 150 475	DF	8 428	9 627	2.2	1 098 581	9
Brazil - Brésil										
1 VIII 2000	DJ	169 799 170[21]	83 576 015[21]	86 223 155[21]	DJ	171 280[21]	186 771[21]	1.4	8 514 877[22]	22
Chile - Chili										
24 IV 2002	DF	15 116 435	7 447 695	7 668 740	DF	15 211	16 433	1.3	756 102	22
Colombia - Colombie										
22 V 2005	DF	41 468 384	20 336 117	21 132 267	DF	40 282[23]	43 405[23]	1.2	1 138 914	38
Ecuador - Équateur[24]										
25 XI 2001	DF	12 156 608	6 018 353	6 138 255	DF	12 299	13 408	1.4	283 561	47
Falkland Islands (Malvinas) - Îles Falkland (Malvinas)[25]										
8 X 2006	DF	2 955	1 569	1 386		...	...	...	12 173	...
French Guiana - Guyane française										
1 I 2006	DJ	*202 000	...	...	DJ	164	*197	3.1	90 000	2
Guyana										
15 IX 2002	DF	751 223	376 034	375 189	DF	742	760	0.4	214 969	4

Continent, country or area and census date Continent, pays ou zone et date du recensement	Census type[a]	Latest available census Dernier recensement disponible (in units — en unités)			Estimate type[a]	Mid-year estimates Estimations au milieu de l'année (in thousands — en milliers)		Annual rate of increase Taux d' accrois sement annuel 2000-06	Surface area Superficie (km²) 2006	Density Densité 2006[b]
		Both sexes Les deux sexes	Male Masculin	Female Feminin		2000	2006			
AMERICA, SOUTH - AMÉRIQUE DU SUD										
Paraguay										
28 VIII 2002 .... DF		5 163 198	2 603 242	2 559 956	DF	5 346	6 009	1.9	406 752	15
Peru - Pérou										
21 X 2007 .... DF		*27 419 294[26]	...	...	DF	25 982[7]	27 377[7]	0.9	1 285 216	21
Suriname										
2 VIII 2004 .... DJ		492 829[27]	247 846[28]	244 618[28]	DJ	464	*504	1.4	163 820	3
Uruguay										
1 VI 2004................ DF		3 241 003[29]	1 565 533[29]	1 675 470[29]	DF	3 301[7]	3 314[7]	0.1	176 215	19
Venezuela (Bolivarian Republic of) - Venezuela (République bolivarienne du)[30]										
30 X 2001 .... DF		23 054 210	11 402 869	11 651 341	DF	24 311	27 031	1.8	912 050	30
ASIA - ASIE										
Afghanistan										
23 VI 1979 .... DF		13 051 358[31]	6 712 377[31]	6 338 981[31]	DF	21 770	22 576[32]	0.6	652 090	35
Armenia - Arménie										
10 X 2001 .... DF		3 002 594[33]	1 407 220[33]	1 595 374[33]	DJ	3 221	3 221	0.0	29 743	108
Azerbaijan - Azerbaïdjan										
27 I 1999 .... DJ		7 953 438	3 883 155	4 070 283	DF	8 049	*8 485	0.9	86 600	98
Bahrain - Bahreïn										
7 IV 2001................ DJ		650 604	373 649	276 955	DF	638	743	2.5	741	1 002
Bangladesh										
22 I 2001 .... DF		130 522 598[34]	67 731 320[34]	62 791 278[34]	DF	129 300	140 600	1.4	143 998	976
Bhutan - Bhoutan										
30 V 2005 .... DF		634 982	333 595	301 387	DF	580	647	1.8	38 394	17
Brunei Darussalam - Brunéi Darussalam										
21 VIII 2001 .... DF		*332 844	*168 974	*163 870	DF	325	*383	2.7	5 765	66
Cambodia - Cambodge										
3 III 1998 .... DF		11 437 656[35]	5 511 408[35]	5 926 248[35]	DF	12 688[36]	...	...	181 035	...
China - Chine										
1 XI 2000................ DJ		1 242 612 226[38]	640 275 969[38]	602 336 257[38]	DF	1 262 645[39]	1 311 020[40]	0.6	9 596 961	137
China: Hong Kong SAR - Chine: Hong Kong RAS										
14 VII 2006 .... DJ		6 864 346	3 272 956	3 591 390	DJ	6 665	6 857	0.5	1 104	6 211
China: Macao SAR - Chine: Macao RAS										
19 VIII 2006 .... DJ		502 113[37]	245 167[37]	256 946[37]	DJ	431	499	2.5	29	17 202
Cyprus - Chypre										
1 X 2001 .... DJ		689 565[41]	338 497[41]	351 068[41]	DJ	694[42]	771[42]	1.8	9 251	83
Georgia - Géorgie										
17 I 2002 .... DJ		4 371 535	2 061 753	2 309 782	DF	4 418	4 398	-0.1	69 700	63
India - Inde										
1 III 2001 .... DF		1 028 610 328[43]	532 156 772[43]	496 453 556[43]	DF	1 016 210[44]	1 117 734[44]	1.6	3 287 263	340
Indonesia - Indonésie										
30 VI 2000 .... DF		206 264 595[45]	103 417 180[45]	102 847 415[45]	DJ	...	*222 051	...	1 904 569	117
Iran (Islamic Republic of) - Iran (République islamique d')										
28 X 2006 .... DJ		*70 495 782	*35 866 362	*34 629 420	DJ	63 664[46]	*70 603[46]	1.7	1 648 195	43
Iraq										
16 X 1997 .... DF		19 184 543[47]	9 536 570[47]	9 647 973[47]	DF	24 086	28 810	3.0	438 317	66
Israel - Israël										
4 XI 1995................ DJ		5 548 523[48]	2 738 175[48]	2 810 348[48]	DJ	6 289[48]	7 054[48]	1.9	22 072	320
Japan - Japon										
1 X 2005 .... DJ		127 767 994	62 348 977	65 419 017	DF	126 843[49]	127 756[49]	0.1	377 915	338
Jordan - Jordanie										
1 X 2004 .... DF		5 103 639[50]	2 626 287[50]	2 477 352[50]	DF	4 798[50]	5 537[50]	2.4	89 342	62

3. Population by sex, rate of population increase, surface area and density
Population selon le sexe, taux d'accroissement de la population, superficie et densité (continued - suite)

Continent, country or area and census date / Continent, pays ou zone et date du recensement	Census type[a]	Latest available census — Dernier recensement disponible (in units — en unités) Both sexes Les deux sexes	Male Masculin	Female Feminin	Estimate type[a]	Mid-year estimates Estimations au milieu de l'année (in thousands — en milliers) 2000	2006	Annual rate of increase Taux d'accrois sement annuel 2000-06	Surface area Superficie (km²) 2006	Density Densité 2006[b]
ASIA - ASIE										
Kazakhstan										
26 II 1999	DJ	14 953 126	7 201 785	7 751 341	DF	14 884	15 308	0.5	2 724 900	6
Korea (Dem. People's Republic of) - Corée (Rép. populaire dém. de)										
31 XII 1993	DF	21 213 378	10 329 699	10 883 679	DF	22 963	...	...	120 538	...
Korea (Republic of) - Corée (République de)										
1 XI 2005	DJ	47 278 951[51]	23 623 954[51]	23 654 997[51]	DJ	47 008	48 297	0.5	99 678	485
Kuwait - Koweït										
20 IV 2005	DF	*2 213 403	*1 310 067	*903 336	DF	2 138	...	...	17 818	...
Kyrgyzstan - Kirghizistan										
24 III 1999	DF	4 850 734	2 392 579	2 458 155	DF	4 915	5 192	0.9	199 951	26
Lao People's Democratic Republic - République démocratique populaire lao										
1 III 2005	DJ	5 621 982	2 800 551	2 821 431	DF	5 218[52]	5 747[53]	1.6	236 800	24
Lebanon - Liban										
15 XI 1970	SDF	2 126 325[54]	1 080 015[54]	1 046 310[54]		...	...	...	10 400	...
Malaysia - Malaisie										
5 VII 2000	DJ	23 274 690[55]	11 853 432[55]	11 421 258[55]	DF	23 495	26 640	2.1	329 847	81
Maldives										
21 III 2006	DF	298 968	151 459	147 509	DF	271	298	1.6	298	1 001
Mongolia - Mongolie										
5 I 2000	DF	2 373 493	1 177 981	1 195 512	DF	2 390	2 579	1.3	1 564 100	2
Myanmar										
31 III 1983	DF	35 307 913	17 518 255	17 789 658	DF	50 125	...	...	676 578	...
Nepal - Népal										
22 VI 2001	DJ	23 151 423[56]	11 563 921[56]	11 587 502[56]	DJ	*22 904	25 887	2.0	147 181	176
Occupied Palestinian Territory - Territoire palestinien occupé										
1 XII 2007	DF	*3 761 646[57]	*1 908 432[57]	*1 853 214[57]	DF	3 149	3 888	3.5	6 020	646
Oman										
7 XII 2003	DF	2 340 815	1 313 239	1 027 576	DF	2 401	2 577	1.2	309 500	8
Pakistan										
2 III 1998	DF	130 579 571[58]	67 840 137[58]	62 739 434[58]	DF	138 945[58]	*156 770[58]	2.0	796 095	197
Philippines										
1 VIII 2007	DJ	*88 574 614	...	...	DJ	76 348	*86 973	2.2	300 000	290
Qatar										
16 III 2004	DF	744 029	496 382	247 647	DF	617	936	7.0	11 586	81
Saudi Arabia - Arabie saoudite										
15 IX 2004	DF	22 678 262	12 557 240	10 121 022	DF	20 476	23 679	2.4	2 000 000	12
Singapore - Singapour										
1 VII 2000	DF	4 017 700[59]	2 061 800[59]	1 955 900[59]	DF	4 028	4 484	1.8	699	6 411
Sri Lanka										
17 VII 2001	DF	*16 864 544[60]	*8 343 964[60]	*8 520 580[60]	DF	19 359	*19 886	0.4	65 610	303
Syrian Arab Republic - République arabe syrienne										
3 IX 1994	DF	13 782 315[61]	7 048 906[61]	6 733 409[61]	DF	16 320[61]	18 717[61]	2.3	185 180	101
Tajikistan - Tadjikistan										
20 I 2000	DF	6 127 493	3 069 100	3 058 393	DF	6 188	6 992	2.0	143 100	49
Thailand - Thaïlande										
1 IV 2000	DJ	60 617 200	29 850 100	30 767 100	DJ	62 406[1]	65 306[1]	0.8	513 120	127
Timor-Leste										
11 VII 2004	DF	*924 642	*467 757	*456 885		...	...	...	14 874	...
Turkey - Turquie										
22 X 2000	DF	67 803 927	34 346 735	33 457 192	DF	67 420	72 974	1.3	783 562	93
Turkmenistan - Turkménistan										
10 I 1995	DF	4 483 251	2 225 331	2 257 920	DF	4 892	...	...	488 100	...

3. Population by sex, rate of population increase, surface area and density
Population selon le sexe, taux d'accroissement de la population, superficie et densité (continued - suite)

Continent, country or area and census date / Continent, pays ou zone et date du recensement	Census type[a]	Latest available census / Dernier recensement disponible (in units — en unités)			Estimate type[a]	Mid-year estimates Estimations au milieu de l'année (in thousands — en milliers)		Annual rate of increase Taux d' accrois sement annuel 2000-06	Surface area Superficie (km²) 2006	Density Densité 2006[b]
		Both sexes Les deux sexes	Male Masculin	Female Feminin		2000	2006			
ASIA - ASIE										
United Arab Emirates - Émirats arabes unis										
5 XII 2005	DF	4 106 427	2 806 141	1 300 286	DF	*2 995*	*4 229*	*5.8*	83 600	*51*
Uzbekistan - Ouzbékistan										
12 I 1989	DJ	19 810 077	9 784 156	10 025 921	DF	24 650	...	...	447 400	...
Viet Nam										
1 IV 1999	DF	76 323 173	37 469 117	38 854 056	DF	*77 635*	*84 156	*1.3*	331 689	254
Yemen - Yémen										
16 XII 2004	DF	19 685 161	10 036 953	9 648 208	DF	*18 261*	20 592	*2.0*	527 968	39
EUROPE										
Åland Islands - Îles d'Åland[62]										
		...	...		DF	26	27	0.7	1 552	17
Albania - Albanie										
1 IV 2001	DF	3 069 300	1 530 500	1 538 800	DF	3 061	3 151	0.5	28 748	110
Andorra - Andorre										
1 VII 2000	DF	66 089[18]	34 344[18]	31 745[18]	DF	66[18]	82[18]	3.6	468	176
Austria - Autriche										
15 V 2001	DJ	8 032 926	3 889 189	4 143 737	DJ	8 012	8 282	0.6	83 871	99
Belarus - Bélarus										
16 II 1999	DJ	10 045 237	4 717 621	5 327 616	DF	10 005	9 733	-0.5	208 000	47
Belgium - Belgique										
1 X 2001	DJ	10 296 350	5 035 446	5 260 904	DJ	10 251	10 542	0.5	30 528	345
Bosnia and Herzegovina - Bosnie-Herzégovine										
31 III 1991	DJ	4 377 033	2 183 795	2 193 238	DF	3 781	3 843	0.3	51 197	75
Bulgaria - Bulgarie										
1 III 2001	DF	7 928 901	3 862 465	4 066 436	DF	8 170	7 699	-1.0	110 879	69
Channel Islands: Guernsey - Îles Anglo-Normandes: Guernesey										
29 IV 2001	DJ	59 807	29 138	30 669	DF	60	61[63]	0.2	78	782
Channel Islands: Jersey - Îles Anglo-Normandes: Jersey										
11 III 2001	DJ	87 186	42 485	44 701	DF	...	89	...	116	766
Croatia - Croatie										
31 III 2001	DJ	4 437 460	2 135 900	2 301 560	DJ	4 381	4 440	0.2	56 594	78
Czech Republic - République tchèque										
1 III 2001	DJ	10 230 060	4 982 071	5 247 989	DJ	10 273	10 287	0.0	78 867	130
Denmark - Danemark[64]										
1 I 2001	DJ	5 349 212[18]	2 644 319[18]	2 704 893[18]	DJ	5 337[18]	5 435[18]	0.3	43 094	126
Estonia - Estonie										
31 III 2000	DJ	1 370 052	631 851	738 201	DF	1 370	1 344	-0.3	45 228	30
Faeroe Islands - Îles Féroé										
1 VII 2002	DJ	47 350[18]	...	...	DJ	46	48	0.9	1 393	35
Finland - Finlande[65]										
31 XII 2000	DJ	5 181 115[18]	2 529 341[18]	2 651 774[18]	DJ	5 176[18]	5 266[18]	0.3	338 145	16
France[66]										
1 I 2006	DJ	*61 166 822[67]	*29 722 384[67]	*31 444 438[67]	DJ	59 049[67]	*61 353[67]	0.6	551 500	111
Germany - Allemagne										
28 III 2004	SDJ	82 491 000[68]	40 330 000[68]	42 161 000[68]	DJ	82 188	82 366	0.0	357 022	231
Gibraltar										
12 XI 2001	DF	27 495[69]	13 644[69]	13 851[69]	DF	27[69]	29[69]	1.2	6	4 844
Greece - Grèce										
18 III 2001	DF	10 964 020[70]	5 431 816[70]	5 532 204[70]	DF	10 917[71]	11 149[71]	0.3	131 957	84
Holy See - Saint-Siège										
1 VII 2000	DF	*798[72]	*529[72]	*269[72]		...	...	...	[73]	...

3. Population by sex, rate of population increase, surface area and density
Population selon le sexe, taux d'accroissement de la population, superficie et densité (continued - suite)

Continent, country or area and census date / Continent, pays ou zone et date du recensement	Census type[a]	Latest available census / Dernier recensement disponible (in units — en unités)			Estimate type[a]	Mid-year estimates / Estimations au milieu de l'année (in thousands — en milliers)		Annual rate of increase / Taux d'accrois sement annuel 2000-06	Surface area / Superficie (km²) 2006	Density / Densité 2006[b]
		Both sexes / Les deux sexes	Male / Masculin	Female / Feminin		2000	2006			
EUROPE										
Hungary - Hongrie										
1 II 2001	DF	10 198 315	4 850 650	5 347 665	DF	10 024	10 071	0.1	93 028	108
Iceland - Islande										
1 VII 2000	DJ	281 154[18]	140 718[18]	140 436[18]	DJ	281[18]	304[18]	1.3	103 000	3
Ireland - Irlande										
23 IV 2006	DF	4 239 848	2 121 171	2 118 677	DF	3 790[74]	4 235[74]	1.9	70 273	60
Isle of Man - Îles de Man										
23 IV 2006	DJ	80 058	39 523	40 535	DJ	75	...	...	572	...
Italy - Italie										
21 X 2001	DF	57 110 144	27 617 335	29 492 809	DJ	56 942	58 941	0.6	301 318	196
Latvia - Lettonie										
31 III 2000	DJ	2 377 383	1 094 964	1 282 419	DJ	2 373	2 288	-0.6	64 589	35
Liechtenstein										
5 XII 2000	DF	33 307	16 420	16 887	DF	33	35	1.2	160	219
Lithuania - Lituanie										
6 IV 2001	DJ	3 483 972	1 629 148	1 854 824	DJ	3 500	3 394	-0.5	65 300	52
Luxembourg										
15 II 2001	DJ	439 539	216 541	222 998	DJ	436	473	1.3	2 586	183
Malta - Malte										
21 XI 2005	DJ	404 962[75]	200 819[75]	204 143[75]	DJ	383[75]	406[75]	1.0	316	1 286
Moldova										
5 X 2004	DF	*3 388 071[76]	*1 632 519[76]	*1 755 549[76]	DJ	3 640[76]	3 585[76]	-0.3	33 851	106
Monaco										
21 VI 2000	DJ	32 020	15 544	16 476		...	...	...	2	...
Montenegro										
31 III 2003	DJ	620 145	305 225	314 920	DF	654	...	...	13 812	
Netherlands - Pays-Bas										
1 I 2002	DJ	16 105 285[77]	7 971 967[77]	8 133 318[77]	DJ	15 926	16 346	0.4	41 543	393
Norway - Norvège[78]										
3 XI 2001	DJ	4 520 947[79]	2 240 281[79]	2 280 666[79]	DJ	4 491[80]	4 661[80]	0.6	323 802	14
Poland - Pologne										
20 V 2002	DF	38 230 080[81]	18 516 403[81]	19 713 677[81]	DF	38 256[81]	38 132[81]	-0.1	312 685[82]	122
Portugal										
12 III 2001	DF	*10 148 259	*4 862 699	*5 285 560	DJ	10 226	10 584	0.6	92 090	115
Romania - Roumanie										
18 III 2002	DJ	21 680 974	10 568 741	11 112 233	DJ	22 435	21 584	-0.6	238 391	91
Russian Federation - Fédération de Russie										
9 X 2002	DJ	145 166 731[83]	67 605 133[83]	77 561 598[83]	DJ	146 597	142 487	-0.5	17 098 242	8
San Marino - Saint-Marin										
1 VII 2000	DF	26 941[18]	13 185[18]	13 756[18]	DF	27[18]	31[18]	2.5	61	514
Serbia - Serbie										
31 III 2002	DJ	7 498 001[84]	3 645 930[84]	3 852 071[84]	DJ	7 516[84]	7 412[84]	-0.2	88 361	84
Slovakia - Slovaquie										
25 V 2001	DJ	5 379 455	2 612 515	2 766 940	DJ	5 401	5 391	0.0	49 035	110
Slovenia - Slovénie										
31 III 2002	DJ	*1 964 036	*958 576	*1 005 460	DJ	1 990	2 009	0.2	20 273	99
Spain - Espagne										
1 XI 2001	DF	40 847 371	20 012 882	20 834 489	DJ	40 264	44 068	1.5	505 992	87
Svalbard and Jan Mayen Islands - Îles Svalbard et Jan Mayen										
1 XI 1960	DF	3 431[85]	2 545[85]	886[85]		...	...	...	62 422	...
Sweden - Suède										
1 VII 2000	DJ	8 872 110[18]	4 386 436[18]	4 485 674[18]	DJ	8 872[18]	9 081[18]	0.4	531 796	17
Switzerland - Suisse										
5 XII 2000	DJ	7 204 055	3 519 698	3 684 357	DJ	7 184	7 484	0.7	41 277[86]	181
The Former Yugoslav Rep. of Macedonia - L'ex-République yougoslave de Macédoine										
1 XI 2002	DJ	2 022 547	1 015 377	1 007 170	DF	2 024	2 040	0.1	25 713	79

| Continent, country or area and census date — Continent, pays ou zone et date du recensement | Census type[a] | Latest available census — Dernier recensement disponible (in units — en unités) | | | Estimate type[a] | Mid-year estimates — Estimations au milieu de l'année (in thousands — en milliers) | | Annual rate of increase — Taux d'accrois sement annuel 2000-06 | Surface area — Superficie (km²) 2006 | Density — Densité 2006[b] |
		Both sexes — Les deux sexes	Male — Masculin	Female — Feminin		2000	2006			
EUROPE										
Ukraine										
5 XII 2001	DF	48 240 902	22 316 317	25 924 585	DJ	49 177[87]	*46 757	-0.8	603 500	77
United Kingdom - Royaume-Uni[88]										
29 IV 2001	DF	58 789 187[89]	28 579 867[89]	30 209 320[89]	DF	58 886[89]	60 587	0.5	242 900	249
OCEANIA - OCÉANIE										
American Samoa - Samoas américaines										
1 IV 2000	DJ	57 291[19]	29 264[19]	28 027[19]	DJ	58[19]	67[19]	2.5	199	336
Australia - Australie										
8 VIII 2006	DF	20 061 646	9 896 500	10 165 146	DJ	19 153[7]	*20 701[7]	1.3	7 692 024	3
Cook Islands - Îles Cook[90]										
1 XII 2006	DF	*19 569	*9 932	*9 637	DF	18	*21	2.4	236	88
Fiji - Fidji										
16 IX 2007	DJ	*835 230	...	...	DF	807	830	0.5	18 274	45
French Polynesia - Polynésie française										
20 VIII 2007	DJ	*259 596	...	...	DF	235	256	1.4	4 000	64
Guam										
1 IV 2000	DJ	154 805[19]	79 181[19]	75 624[19]	DJ	...	*171[19]	...	549	312
Kiribati										
7 XII 2005	DF	92 533	45 612	46 921		...	...	...	726	...
Marshall Islands - Îles Marshall										
1 VI 1999	DF	50 848	26 034	24 814	DF	...	52	...	181	288
Micronesia, Federated States of - Micronésie, États Fédérés de La										
1 IV 2000	DJ	107 008	54 191	52 817	DJ	119	...	...	702	...
Nauru										
17 IV 1992	DF	9 919	5 079	4 840	DF	12	...	...	21	...
New Caledonia - Nouvelle-Calédonie										
31 VIII 2004	DF	*230 789	*116 485	*114 304	DF	213	...	...	18 575	...
New Zealand - Nouvelle-Zélande										
7 III 2006	DF	4 143 282	2 021 277	2 122 005	DJ	3 858	4 185	1.4	270 467	15
Niue - Nioué										
7 IX 2006	DF	1 625	802	823	DJ	...	2	...	260	6
Norfolk Island - Île Norfolk										
8 VIII 2006	DF	2 523	1 218	1 305		...	...	...	36	...
Northern Mariana Islands - Îles Mariannes septentrionales										
1 IV 2000	DF	69 221	31 984	37 237	DF	72	82	2.1	464	177
Palau - Palaos										
1 IV 2005	DJ	19 907	10 699	9 208	DF	19	22	2.0	459	47
Papua New Guinea - Papouasie-Nouvelle-Guinée										
9 VII 2000	DF	5 190 786	2 691 744	2 499 042	DF	5 100	...	...	462 840	...
Pitcairn										
31 XII 1991	DF	66	...	...		...	...	...	5	...
Samoa										
5 XI 2006	DF	*179 186	*92 961	*86 225	DF	171	185	1.3	2 831	65
Solomon Islands - Îles Salomon										
21 XI 1999	DF	409 042	211 381	197 661	DF	415	483	2.5	28 896	17
Tokelau - Tokélaou										
19 X 2006	DF	1 151	583	568		...	...	...	12	...

3. Population by sex, rate of population increase, surface area and density
Population selon le sexe, taux d'accroissement de la population, superficie et densité (continued - suite)

Continent, country or area and census date — Continent, pays ou zone et date du recensement	Census type[a]	Latest available census — Dernier recensement disponible (in units — en unités)			Estimate type[a]	Mid-year estimates Estimations au milieu de l'année (in thousands — en milliers)		Annual rate of increase Taux d'accroissement annuel 2000-06	Surface area Superficie (km²) 2006	Density Densité 2006[b]
		Both sexes Les deux sexes	Male Masculin	Female Feminin		2000	2006			
OCEANIA - OCÉANIE										
Tonga										
30 XI 2006	DF	*101 134	*51 197	*49 937	DF	_100_[91]	...	...	747	...
Tuvalu										
1 XI 2002................	DF	9 561	4 729	4 832	DF	_9_	...	...	26	...
Vanuatu										
16 XI 1999	DJ	186 678	95 682	90 996	DF	...	221[1]	...	12 189	_18_
Wallis and Futuna Islands - Îles Wallis et Futuna										
22 VII 2003..............	DF	14 944	7 494	7 450		...	...	...	142	...

FOOTNOTES - NOTES

Italics: estimates which are less reliable. - Italiques: estimations moins sûres.

* Provisional. - Données provisoires.

a 'Code' indicates the source of data, as follows:
DF - De facto
DJ - De jure
SDF - Sample survey, de facto
SDJ - Sample survey, de jure

Le 'Code' indique la source des données, comme suit:
DF - Population de fait
DJ - Population de droit
SDF - Enquête par sondage, population de fait
SDJ - Enquête par sondage, Population de droit

b Population per square kilometre of surface area. Figures are estimates of population divided by surface area and are not to be considered either as reflecting density in the urban sense or as indicating the supporting power of a territory's land and resources. - Nombre d'habitants au kilomètre carré. Il s'agit simplement d'éstimations de la population divisé par celui de la superficie: il ne faut pas y voir d'indication de la densité au sens urbain du terme ni de l'effectif de population que les terres et les ressources du territoire sont capables de nourrir.

1 Data refer to national projections. - Les données se réfèrent aux projections nationales.
2 Census results have been adjusted for underenumeration, estimated at 1.4 per cent. - Les résultat du recensement ont été ajustées pour compenser les lacunes du dénombrement, estimées à 1,4 p. 100.
3 Excluding Mayotte. - Non compris Mayotte.
4 Exclude border population. - À l'exception de la population frontalière.
5 Data refer to Libyan nationals only. - Les données se raportent aux nationaux libyens seulement.
6 Including residents outside the country. - Y compris les résidents hors du pays.
7 Mid-year estimates have been adjusted for underenumeration, at latest census. - Les estimations au milieu de l'année tiennent compte d'un ajustement destiné à compenser les lacunes du dénombrement lors du dernier recensement.
8 The number of males and/or females excludes persons whose sex is not stated (18 urban, 19 rural). - Il n'est pas tenu compte dans le nombre d'hommes et de femmes des personnes dont le sexe n'est pas indiqué (18 en zone urbaine et 19 en zone rurale).
9 Data exclude adjustment for underenumeration, estimated at 2.4 per cent. - Les données n'ont pas été ajustées pour compenser les lacunes du dénombrement, estimées à 2,4 p. 100.
10 Comprising the Northern Region (former Saguia el Hamra) and Southern Region (former Rio de Oro). - Comprend la région septentrionale (ancien Saguia-el-Hamra) et la région méridionale (ancien Rio de Oro).

11 Based on the results of the population census of 2002 - D'après les résultats du recensement de la population de 2002.
12 Data refer to 31 December. - Données se rapportent au 31 Décembre.
13 Excluding the institutional population. - Non compris la population dans les institutions.
14 Final intercensal estimates. - Estimations inter censitaires finales.
15 Updated postcensal estimates. - Estimations post censitaires mises à jour.
16 Excluding 390 residents of institutions. - À l'exclusion de 390 personnes en établissements de soins.
17 Excluding persons residing in institutions. - Non compris les personnes dans les institutions.
18 Population statistics are compiled from registers. - Les statistiques de la population sont compilées à partir des registres.
19 Including armed forces stationed in the area. - Y compris les militaires en garnison sur le territoire.
20 Excluding armed forces overseas and civilian citizens absent from country for an extended period of time. - Non compris les militaires à l'étranger, et les civils hors du pays pendant une période prolongée.
21 Data include persons in remote areas, military personnel outside the country, merchant seamen at sea, civilian seasonal workers outside the country, and other civilians outside the country, and exclude nomads, foreign military, civilian aliens temporarily in the country, transients on ships and Indian jungle population. - Y compris les personnes vivant dans des régions éloignées, le personel militaire en dehors du pays, les marins marchands, les ouvriers saisonniers en dehors du pays, et autres civils en dehors du pays, et non compris les nomades, les militaires étrangers, les étrangers civils temporairement dans le pays, les transiteurs sur des bateaux et les Indiens de la jungle.
22 Exact reference date unknown. - La date de référence exacte n'est pas connue.
23 Data have been adjusted on the basis of the Population Census of 2005. - Données ajustées sur la base du recensement de la population de 2005.
24 Excluding nomadic Indian tribes. - Non compris les tribus d'Indiens nomades.
25 A dispute exists between the governments of Argentina and the United Kingdom of Great Britain and Northern Ireland concerning sovereignty over the Falkland Islands (Malvinas). - La souveraineté sur les îles Falkland (Malvinas) fait l'objet d'un différend entre le Gouvernement argentin et le Gouvernement du Royaume-Uni de Grande-Bretagne et d'Irlande du Nord.
26 Excluding population in the Carmen Alto district, Huamanga province and Ayacucho department. - À l'exclusion de la population du district de Carmen Alto, de la province de Huamanga et du département d'Ayacucho.
27 The previous census was conducted only 16 months earlier (on 31 Mar 2003) but it was repeated because all of its data were destroyed in a fire before they could be fully processed, analyzed, and reported. - Le recensement précédent a eu lieu seulement 16 mois auparavant (le 31 mars 2003), mais a dû être refait parce que toutes les données ont été détruites dans un incendie avant que l'on n'ait pu les traiter et les analyser.
28 The previous census was conducted only 16 months earlier (on 31 Mar 2003) but it was repeated because all of its data were destroyed in a fire before they could be fully processed, analyzed, and reported. Figures for male and female population do not add up to the figure for total population, because they exclude 365 persons of unknown sex (265 urban and 100 rural). - Le recensement précédent a eu lieu seulement 16 mois auparavant (le 31 mars 2003), mais a dû

être refait parce que toutes les données ont été détruites dans un incendie avant que l'on n'ait pu les traiter et les analyser. Les chiffres relatifs à la population masculine et féminine ne correspondent pas au chiffre de la population totale, parce que l'on en a exclu 365 personnes de sexe inconnu (265 en zones urbaines et 100 en zones rurales).

[29] Data refer to resident population in Uruguay according to Census Phase 1, carried out between the months of June and July 2004. - Les données se rapportent à la population résidente en Uruguay d'après la phase 1 du recensement, qui a eu lieu entre juin et juillet 2004.

[30] Excluding Indian jungle population. - Non compris les Indiens de la jungle.

[31] Excluding nomad population. - Non compris les nomades.

[32] Data refer to the settled population based on the 1979 Population Census and the latest household prelisting. The refugees of Afghanistan in Iran, Pakistan and estimated 1.5 million nomads are not included. The so adjusted total population of the country for 2006 is 24.1 million of which 12.3 million males and 11.8 million females. - Les données se rapportent à la population stationnaire sur la base du recensement de 1979 et du recensement préliminaire des logements le plus récent. Sont exclus les réfugiés d'Afghanistan en Iran et au Pakistan et les nomades estimés à 1,5 million. La population totale du pays ainsi ajustée pour 2006 comprend 24,1 millions de personnes (12,3 millions d'hommes et 11,8 millions de femmes).

[33] The methodology used for calculating the number of the de facto and de jure population in the 2001 census data differs as follows from the methodology used in previous censuses: the duration that defines a person as being ' temporary present ' or 'temporary absent' is now 'under one year'. The previously applied definition was for '6 months'. - La méthode utilisée pour dénombrer la population de fait et la population de droit dans le contexte du recensement de 2001 diffère de celle qui a été appliquée lors des recensements antérieurs en ce que la durée considérée pour définir la ' présence temporaire 'ou' l'absence temporaire' était dorénavant fixée à 'moins d'un an' alors qu'elle était de '6 mois' auparavant.

[34] Census results have been adjusted for underenumeration, estimated at 4.96 per cent. - Les données ont été ajustées pour compenser les lacunes du dénombrement, estimées à 4,96 %.

[35] Excluding foreign diplomatic personnel and their dependants. - Non compris le personnel diplomatique étranger et les membres de leur famille les accompagnant.

[36] Excluding foreign diplomatic personnel and their dependants. From 1998 based on census result. - Non compris le personnel diplomatique étranger et les membres de leur famille les accompagnant. Depuis 1998, à partir des résultats de recensement.

[37] Data derived from the By-Census 2006 held during 19 to 31 of August 2006. - Donnes dérivées du recensement partiel de 2006 organisé entre les 19 et 31 août 2006.

[38] For the civilian population of 31 provinces, municipalities and autonomous regions. For statistical purposes, the data for China do not include those for the Hong Kong Special Administrative Region (Hong Kong SAR), Macao Special Administrative Region (Macao SAR) and Taiwan province of China. - Pour la population civile seulement de 31 provinces, municipalités et régions autonomes. Pour la présentation des statistiques, les données pour la Chine ne comprennent pas la Région Administrative Spéciale de Hong Kong (Hong Kong RAS), la Région Administrative Spéciale de Macao (Macao RAS) et Taïwan province de Chine.

[39] For statistical purposes, the data for China do not include those for the Hong Kong Special Administrative Region (Hong Kong SAR), Macao Special Administrative Region (Macao SAR) and Taiwan province of China. Data for the period 1990 to 2000 have been adjusted on the basis of the Population Census of 2000. - Pour la présentation des statistiques, les données pour la Chine ne comprennent pas la Région Administrative Spéciale de Hong Kong (Hong Kong RAS), la Région Administrative Spéciale de Macao (Macao RAS) et Taïwan province de Chine. Les données pour la période allant de 1990 à 2000 ont été ajustées à partir des résultats du recensement de la population de 2000.

[40] Data have been estimated on the basis of the annual National Sample Surveys on Population Changes. For statistical purposes, the data for China do not include those for the Hong Kong Special Administrative Region (Hong Kong SAR), Macao Special Administrative Region (Macao SAR) and Taiwan province of China. - Les données ont été estimées sur la base de l'enquête annuelle "National Sample Survey on Population Changes". Pour la présentation des statistiques, les données pour la Chine ne comprennent pas la Région Administrative Spéciale de Hong Kong (Hong Kong RAS), la Région Administrative Spéciale de Macao (Macao RAS) et Taïwan province de Chine.

[41] Data refer to government controlled areas. Data include all population irrespective of citizenship, who at the time of the census resided in the country or intended to reside for a period of at least one year. It does not distinguish between those present or absent at the time of census. - Les données se rapportent aux zones contrôlées par le Gouvernement. Les chiffres comprennent toute la population, quelle que soit la nationalité, qui à l'époque de recensement avait résidé dans le pays, ou avait l'intention de résider, pendant une période d'au

moins un an. Il n'y a pas de distinction entre les personnes présentes ou absentes au moment du recensement.

[42] Data refer to government controlled areas. - Les données se rapportent aux zones contrôlées par le Gouvernement.

[43] Including data for the Indian-held part of Jammu and Kashmir, the final status of which has not yet been determined. Data exclude Mao-Maram, Paomata and Purul sub-divisions of Senapati district of Manipur. The population of Manipur including the estimated population of the three sub-divisions of Senapati district is 2,291,125 (Males 1,161,173 and females 1,129,952). - Y compris les données pour la partie du Jammu et du Cachemire occupée par l'Inde dont le statut définitif n'a pas encore été déterminé. Non compris les subdivisions Mao-Maram Paomata et Purul du district de Senapati dans l'État du Manipur. Cet État compte 2 291 125 habitants (1 161 173 hommes et 1 129 952 femmes), y compris la population estimative des trois subdivisions du district de Senapati.

[44] Including data for the Indian-held part of Jammu and Kashmir, the final status of which has not yet been determined. - Y compris les données pour la partie du Jammu et du Cachemire occupée par l'Inde dont le statut définitif n'a pas encore été déterminé.

[45] The figure includes an estimated population of 459 557 persons in urban and 1 857 659 persons in rural areas that were not directly enumerated, and a population of 566 403 persons in urban and 1 717 578 persons in rural areas that decline the participation. Also included are 421 399 non permanent residents (the homeless, the crew of ships carrying national flag, boat/floating house people, remote located tribesmen and refugees.) - Y compris la population estimée a 459 557 personnes dans les zones urbaines et de 1 857 659 personnes dans les zones rurales qui n'ont pas été énumérées directement, aussi que 566 403 personnes qui non pas répondu dans les zones urbaines et de 1 717 578 personnes dans les zones rurales. Y compris 421 399 résidants non permanents (les sans abri, l'équipage des bateaux portant le pavillon national, les habitants des embarcations ou des maisons flottantes, les habitants des tribus isolées et les réfugiés.)

[46] Data relate to the Iranian Year which begins on 21 March and ends on 20 March of the following year. - Les données concernent l'année iranienne, qui commence le 21 mars et se termine le 20 mars de l'année suivante.

[47] For the 1997 population census, data exclude population in three autonomous provinces in the north of the country. - Pour le recensement de 1997, la population des trois provinces autonomes dans le nord du pays est exclue.

[48] Including data for East Jerusalem and Israeli residents in certain other territories under occupation by Israeli military forces since June 1967. - Y compris les données pour Jérusalem-Est et les résidents israéliens dans certains autres territoires occupés depuis 1967 par les forces armées israéliennes.

[49] Excluding diplomatic personnel outside the country and foreign military and civilian personnel and their dependants stationed in the area. - Non compris le personnel diplomatique hors du pays ni les militaires et agents civils étrangers en poste sur le territoire et les membres de leur famille les accompagnant.

[50] Excluding data for Jordanian territory under occupation since June 1967 by Israeli military forces. Excluding foreigners, including registered Palestinian refugees. - Non compris les données pour le territoire jordanien occupé depuis juin 1967 par les forces armées israéliennes. Non compris les étrangers, mais y compris les réfugiés de Palestine enregistrés.

[51] Excluding usual residents not in country at time of census. - À l'exclusion des résidents habituels qui ne sont pas dans le pays au moment du recensement.

[52] From year 2000-2004, calculated based on Population census 1995 structure and growth rate at year 2000. - Pour les années 2000 à 2004, on a pris pour base la structure issue du recensement de population de 1995 et le taux de croissance de 2000.

[53] Data based on the results of the 2005 Population and Housing Census. - Données fondées sur les résultats du recensement de la population et de l'habitat de 2005.

[54] Excluding Palestinian refugees in camps. - Non compris les réfugiés de Palestine dans les camps.

[55] Excluding Malaysian citizens and permanent residents who were away or intended to be away from the country for more than six months. Excluding Malaysian military, naval and diplomatic personnel and their families outside the country, and tourists, businessman who intended to be in Malaysia for less than six months. Census results have been adjusted for underenumeration. - Non compris les citoyens malaisiens et les résidents permanents qui étaient ou qui ont prévu d'être hors du pays pour six mois ou plus. Non compris le personnel militaire Malaisien, le personnel naval ou diplomatique et leurs familles hors du pays, et les touristes et les hommes d'affaires qui avaient l'intention de rester en Malaisie moins de six mois. Les résultats du recensement ont été ajustées pour compenser les lacunes du dénombrement

[56] Data including estimated population from household listing from Village Development Committees and Wards which could not be enumerated at the time of census. - Les données incluent la population estimée par les listes des ménages des comités de développement des villages et des circonscriptions qui n'ont pas pu être énumérée au moment du recensement.

⁵⁷ Census results have been adjusted for underenumeration, estimated at 2.70 per cent. - Les données ont été ajustées pour compenser les lacunes du dénombrement, estimées à 2,70 %.

⁵⁸ Excluding data for the Pakistan-held part of Jammu and Kashmir, the final status of which has not yet been determined. - Non compris les données concernant la partie du Jammu et Cachemire occupée par le Pakistan dont le statut définitif n'a pas été déterminé.

⁵⁹ Excluding transients afloat and non-locally domiciled military and civilian services personnel and their dependants and visitors. - Non compris les personnes de passage à bord de navires ni les militaires et agents civils non-résidents et les membres de leur famille les accompagnants et visiteurs.

⁶⁰ The Population and Housing Census 2001 did not cover the whole area of the country due to the security problems; the Census was complete in 18 districts only; in three districts it was not possible to conduct it; and in four districts it was partially conducted. - Le recensement de la population et de l'habitat en 2001 n'a pas couvert la totalité du pays pour des problèmes de sécurité ; le recensement a été complété seulement en 18 districts ; dans 3 districts ça n'a pas été possible de conduire le recensement et dans 4 districts il a été partiellement conduit.

⁶¹ Including Palestinian refugees. - Y compris les réfugiés de Palestine.

⁶² Also included in Finland. - Comprise aussi dans Finlande.

⁶³ Data refer to 1st March. - Données se rapportent au 1er Mars.

⁶⁴ Excluding Faeroe Islands and Greenland shown separately, if available. - Non compris les Iles Féroé et le Gröenland, qui font l'objet de rubriques distinctes, si disponible.

⁶⁵ Including Aland Islands. - Y compris les Îles d'Åland.

⁶⁶ Excluding Overseas Departments, namely, French Guiana, Guadeloupe, Martinique and Reunion, shown separately, if available. - Non compris les départements d'outre mer, c'est-à-dire la Guyane française, la Guadeloupe, la Martinique et la Réunion, qui font l'objet de rubriques distinctes, si disponible.

⁶⁷ Excluding diplomatic personnel outside the country and including members of alien armed forces not living in military camps and foreign diplomatic personnel not living in embassies or consulates. - Non compris le personnel diplomatique hors du pays et y compris les militaires étrangers ne vivant pas dans des camps militaires et le personnel diplomatique étranger ne vivant pas dans les ambassades ou les consulats.

⁶⁸ Data of the microcensus - a 1% household sample survey - refer to a single reference week in spring (usually last week in April). Excluding homeless persons. Excluding foreign military personnel and foreign diplomatic and consular personnel and their family members in the country. - Les données du microrecensement (enquête sur les ménages, réalisée sur un échantillon de 1 %) concernent une seule semaine de référence au printemps (habituellement la dernière semaine d'avril). Non compris les personnes sans domicile fixe. Non compris le personnel militaire étranger, le personnel diplomatique et consulaire étranger et les membres de leur famille se trouvant dans le pays.

⁶⁹ Excluding families of military personnel, visitors and transients. - Non compris les familles des militaires, ni les visiteurs et transients.

⁷⁰ Census data including armed forces stationed outside the country, but excluding alien armed forces stationed in the area. - Les données de recensement comprennent les militaires se trouvant hors du pays, mais ne comprennent pas les militaires étrangers en poste sur le territoire.

⁷¹ Excluding armed forces stationed outside the country, but including alien armed forces stationed in the area. - Non compris les militaires en garnison hors du pays, mais y compris les militaires étrangers en garnison sur le territoire.

⁷² Data refer to the Vatican City State. Population statistics are compiled from registers. - Les données se rapportent à l'Etat de la Cité du Vatican. Les statistiques de la population sont compilées à partir des registres.

⁷³ Surface area is 0.44 Km2. - Superficie: 0,44 Km2.

⁷⁴ Data refer to 15th of April. - Données se rapportent au 15 Avril.

⁷⁵ Including civilian nationals temporarily outside the country. - Y compris les civils nationaux temporairement hors du pays.

⁷⁶ Data do not include information for Transnistria and the municipality of Bender. - Les données ne tiennent pas compte de l'information sur la Transnistria et la municipalité de Bender.

⁷⁷ Census result, based on compilation of continuous accounting and sample surveys. - Les résultat du recensement, d'après les résultats des dénombrements et enquêtes par sondage continue.

⁷⁸ Excluding Svalbard and Jan Mayen Island shown separately, if available. - Non compris Svalbard et Jan Mayen qui font l'objet de rubriques distinctes, si disponible.

⁷⁹ Population statistics are compiled from registers. Including residents temporarily outside the country. - Les statistiques de la population sont compilées à partir des registres. Y compris les résidents se trouvant temporairement hors du pays.

⁸⁰ Including residents temporarily outside the country. - Y compris les résidents se trouvant temporairement hors du pays.

⁸¹ Excluding civilian aliens within country, but including civilian nationals temporarily outside country. - Non compris les civils étrangers dans le pays, mais y compris les civils nationaux temporairement hors du pays.

⁸² Includes inland waters as well as part of internal waters. - Comprend les eaux intérieures et une partie des eaux situées en deçà de la ligne de base de la mer territoriale.

⁸³ Figures were updated taking into account the results of the 2002 All-Russian population census. - Les chiffres ont été calculés compte tenu des résultats du recensement de la population de la Fédération de Russie de 2002.

⁸⁴ Without data for Kosovo and Metohia. - Sans les données pour le Kosovo and Metohie.

⁸⁵ Inhabited only during the winter season. Census data are for total population while estimates refer to Norwegian population only. Included also in the de jure population of Norway. - N'est habitée pendant la saison d'hiver. Les données de recensement se rapportent à la population totale, mais les estimations ne concernent que la population norvégienne, comprise également dans la population de droit de la Norvège.

⁸⁶ Data do not include state forests and communanzas (7.15 km2). - Forêts domaniales et communanzas (7,15 km2) non comprises.

⁸⁷ Starting from 1997 until 1999 data is de facto and from 2000 and later data is de jure. - De 1997 à 1999, les données sont de fait, à partir de 2000 elles sont de jure.

⁸⁸ Excluding Channel Islands and Isle of Man, shown separately, if available. - Non compris les îles Anglo-Normandes et l'île de Man, qui font l'objet de rubriques distinctes, si disponible.

⁸⁹ Population estimates for 1994 to 2002 were revised in light of the local studies. - Les estimations de la population pour les années 1994 à 2002 ont été révisées en fonction d'études locales.

⁹⁰ Excluding Niue, shown separately, which is part of Cook Islands, but because of remoteness is administered separately. - Non compris Nioué, qui fait l'objet d'une rubrique distincte et qui fait partie des îles Cook, mais qui, en raison de son éloignement, est administrée séparément.

⁹¹ Based on the results of the 1996 population census not necessarily mid year estimated. - À partir des résultats du recensement de la population de 1996, pas nécessairement des estimations en milieu d'année.

Table 4

Table 4 presents, for each country or area of the world, basic vital statistics including: live births, crude birth rate, deaths, crude death rate, rate of natural increase, infant deaths, infant death rate, expectation of life at birth by sex and total fertility rate.

Description of variables: The vital events and rates shown in this table are defined as follows[1]:

Live birth is the complete expulsion or extraction from its mother of a product of conception, irrespective of the duration of pregnancy, which after such separation breathes or shows any other evidence of life such as beating of the heart, pulsation of the umbilical cord, of definite movement of voluntary muscles, whether or not the umbilical cord has been cut or the placenta is attached. Each product of such a birth is considered live-born regardless of gestational age.

Death is the permanent disappearance of all evidence of life at any time after live birth has taken place (post-natal cessation of vital functions without capability of resuscitation).

Infant deaths are deaths of live-born infants under one year of age.

Expectation of life at birth is defined as the average number of years of life for males and females if they continued to be subject to the same mortality experienced in the year(s) to which these life expectancies refer.

The total fertility rate is the average number of children that would be born alive to a hypothetical cohort of women if, throughout their reproductive years, the age-specific fertility rates remained unchanged. The standard method of calculating the total fertility rate is the sum of the age-specific fertility rates.

Crude birth rates and crude death rates presented in this table are calculated using the number of live births and the number of deaths obtained from civil registers. These civil registration data are used only if they are considered reliable (estimated completeness of 90 per cent or more).

Similarly, infant mortality rates presented in this table are calculated using the number of live births and the number of infant deaths obtained from civil registers. If, however, the registration of births or infant deaths for any given country or area is estimated to be less than 90 per cent complete, the rates are not calculated.

Rate computation: The crude birth and death rates are the annual number of each of these vital events per 1 000 mid-year population.

Infant mortality rate is the annual number of deaths of infants under one year of age per 1 000 live births in the same year.

Rates of natural increase are the difference between the crude birth rate and the crude death rate. It should be noted that the rates of natural increase presented here may differ from the population growth rates presented in table 3 as rates of natural increase do not take net international migration into account while the population growth rates do.

Rates that appear in this table have been calculated by the Statistics Division of the United Nations Department of Economic and Social Affairs, unless otherwise noted. Exceptions include official estimated rates for Bangladesh and India, which were based on sample registration systems in these countries.

Rates calculated by the Statistics Division of the United Nations presented in this table have been limited to those countries or areas having a minimum number of 30 events (for life births and deaths) or 100 events (for infant deaths) in a given year.

Reliability of data: Rates calculated on the basis of registered vital statistics which are considered unreliable (estimated to be less than 90 per cent complete) are not calculated. Estimated rates, prepared by individual countries or areas, are presented whenever applicable.

The designation of vital statistics as being either reliable or unreliable is discussed in general in section 4.2 of the Technical Notes. The technical notes for tables 9, 15 and 18 provide specific information on reliability of statistics on live births, infant deaths and deaths, respectively.

The values shown for life expectancy in this table come from official life tables. It is assumed that, if necessary, the basic data (population and deaths classified by age and sex) have been adjusted for deficiencies before their use in constructing the life tables.

Limitations: Statistics on births, deaths and infant deaths are subject to the same qualifications as have been set forth for vital statistics, in general, in section 4 of the Technical Notes and in the technical notes for individual tables presenting detailed data on these events (table 9, live births; table 15, infant deaths; table 18, deaths).

In assessing comparability it is important to take into account the reliability of the data used to calculate the rates, as discussed above.

The problem of obtaining precise correspondence between numerator (births and deaths) and denominator (population for crude birth and death rates) as regards the inclusion or exclusion of armed forces, refugees, displaced persons and other special groups is particularly difficult where vital rates are concerned. This is the case for Japan, where births and deaths refer to Japanese nationals only while the population include foreigners except foreign military and civilian personnel and their dependants stationed in the area.

It should also be noted that crude rates are particularly affected by the age-sex structure of the population. Infant mortality rates, and to a much lesser extent crude birth rates and crude death rates, are affected by the variation in the definition of a live birth and tabulation procedures.

NOTES

[1] *Principles and Recommendations for a Vital Statistics System, Revision 2,* United Nations publication, Sales No. E.01.XVII.10, United Nations, New York, 2001.

71

Tableau 4

Le tableau 4 présente, pour chaque pays ou zone du monde, des statistiques de base de l'état civil comprenant, dans l'ordre, les naissances vivantes, le taux brut de natalité, les décès, le taux brut de mortalité et le taux d'accroissement naturel de la population, les décès d'enfants de moins d'un an et le taux de mortalité infantile, l'espérance de vie à la naissance par sexe et l'indice synthétique de fécondité.

Description des variables : les faits d'état civil utilisés aux fins du calcul des taux présentés dans le tableau 4 sont définis comme suit[1] :

La naissance vivante est l'expulsion ou l'extraction complète du corps de la mère, indépendamment de la durée de la gestation, d'un produit de la conception qui après cette séparation, respire ou manifeste tout autre signe de vie, tel que battement de cœur, pulsation du cordon ombilical ou contraction effective d'un muscle soumis à l'action de la volonté, que le cordon ombilical ait été coupé ou non et que le placenta soit ou non demeuré attaché ; tout produit d'une telle naissance est considéré comme « enfant né vivant ».

Le décès est la disparition permanente de tout signe de vie à un moment quelconque postérieur à la naissance vivante (cessation des fonctions vitales après la naissance sans possibilité de réanimation).

Il convient de préciser que les chiffres relatifs aux décès d'enfants de moins d'un an se rapportent aux naissances vivantes.

L'espérance de vie à la naissance est le nombre moyen d'années que vivraient les individus de sexe masculin et de sexe féminin s'ils continuaient d'être soumis aux mêmes conditions de mortalité que celles qui existaient pendant les années auxquelles se rapportent les valeurs indiquées.

L'indice synthétique de fécondité représente le nombre moyen d'enfants que mettrait au monde une cohorte hypothétique de femmes qui seraient soumises, tout au long de leur vie, aux mêmes conditions de fécondité par âge que celles auxquelles sont soumises les femmes, dans chaque groupe d'âge, au cours d'une année ou d'une période donnée. La méthode standard pour calculer l'indice synthétique de fécondité consiste à additionner les taux de fécondité par âge simple.

Les taux bruts de natalité et de mortalité ont été établis sur la base du nombre de naissances vivantes et du nombre de décès inscrits sur les registres de l'état civil. Ces données n'ont été utilisées que lorsqu'elles étaient considérées comme sûres (degré estimatif de complétude égal ou supérieur à 90 p. 100).

De même, les taux de mortalité infantile présentés dans le tableau 4 ont été établis à partir du nombre de naissances vivantes et du nombre de décès d'enfants de moins d'un an inscrits sur les registres de l'état civil. Toutefois, lorsque les données relatives aux naissances ou aux décès d'enfants de moins d'un an pour un pays ou zone quelconque n'étaient pas considérées complètes à 90 p. 100 au moins, les indices n'ont pas été calculés.

Calcul des taux : les taux bruts de natalité et de mortalité, représentent le nombre annuel de chacun de ces faits d'état civil pour 1 000 habitants au milieu de l'année considérée.

Les taux de mortalité infantile correspondent au nombre annuel de décès d'enfants de moins d'un an pour 1 000 naissances vivantes survenues pendant la même année.

Le taux d'accroissement naturel est égal à la différence entre le taux brut de natalité et le taux brut de mortalité. Il y a lieu de noter que les taux d'accroissement naturel indiqués dans le tableau 4 peuvent différer des taux d'accroissement de la population figurant dans le tableau 3, les taux d'accroissement naturel ne tenant pas compte des taux nets de migration internationale, alors que ceux-ci sont inclus dans les taux d'accroissement de la population.

Sauf indication contraire, les taux figurant dans le tableau 4 ont été calculés par la Division de statistique du Département des affaires économiques et sociales (Secrétariat de l'Organisation des Nations Unies). Les exceptions comprennent le Bangladesh et l'Inde, pour lesquels les taux estimatifs officiels ont été fournis sur la base d'un système d'enregistrement par échantillonnage.

Les taux calculés par la Division de statistique de l'ONU qui sont présentés dans le tableau 4 se rapportent aux seuls pays ou zones où l'on a enregistré au moins 30 événements (pour les naissances vivantes et les décès) ou 100 événements (pour les décès d'enfants de moins d'un an) au cours d'une année donnée.

Fiabilité des données : les taux n'ont pas été calculés lorsque les statistiques de l'état civil issues de systèmes d'enregistrement d'état civil étaient jugées douteuses (degré estimatif de complétude inférieur à 90 p.100) et des taux estimatifs, calculés par les pays ou zones, ont été présentés lorsqu'ils étaient disponibles.

On trouve à la section 4.2 des Notes techniques des explications générales concernant la façon dont les statistiques de l'état civil ont été classées selon leur degré de fiabilité. Les notes techniques relatives aux tableaux 9, 15 et 18 ont trait respectivement à la fiabilité des statistiques des naissances vivantes, des décès d'enfants de moins d'un an et des décès.

Les valeurs relatives à l'espérance de vie figurant dans le tableau 4 proviennent de tables officielles de mortalité. On présume que les données de base (population t décès par sexe et âge) ont été rectifiées d'éventuelles insuffisances avant d'être utilisées pour construire les tables de mortalité.

Insuffisance des données : les statistiques des naissances, décès et décès d'enfants de moins d'un an appellent toutes les réserves qui ont été formulées à propos des statistiques de l'état civil en général à la section 4 des Notes techniques et dans les notes techniques relatives aux différents tableaux présentant des données détaillées sur ces événements [tableau 9 (naissances vivantes), tableau 15 (décès d'enfants de moins d'un an) et tableau 18 (décès)].

Pour évaluer la comparabilité des divers taux, il importe de tenir compte de la fiabilité des données utilisées pour calculer ces taux, comme il a été indiqué précédemment.

Le calcul des taux est particulièrement affecté par la difficulté à obtenir une correspondance parfaite entre le numérateur (naissances et décès) et le dénominateur (population, pour les taux bruts de natalité et de mortalité) en raison de l'inclusion ou non dans la population des forces armées, des réfugiés, des personnes déplacées ou d'autres groupes sociaux. C'est le cas pour le Japon, où les naissances et les décès se réfèrent aux seuls nationaux japonais tandis que la population inclus les étrangers, à l'exception toutefois des militaires étrangers ainsi que des personnels civils et leurs familles stationnés sur le territoire.

Il y a lieu de noter que la structure par âge et par sexe de la population influe de façon particulière sur les taux bruts. Le manque d'uniformité dans la définition des naissances vivantes et dans les procédures de mise en tableaux a une incidence sur les taux de mortalité infantile et, à un moindre degré, sur les taux bruts de natalité et les taux bruts de mortalité.

NOTE

[1] *Principes et recommandations pour un système de statistiques de l'état civil, deuxième révision*, numéro de vente : F.01.XVII.10, publication des Nations Unies, New York, 2001.

4. Vital statistics summary and expectation of life at birth: 2002 - 2006
Aperçu des statistiques de l'état civil et espérance de vie à la naissance: 2002 - 2006

Continent, country or area and year / Continent, pays ou zone et année	Code[a]	Live births / Naissances vivantes Number Nombre	Crude birth rate Taux brut de natalité	Code[a]	Deaths / Décès Number Nombre	Crude death rate Taux brut de mortalité	Rate of natural increase Taux d'accrois-sement naturel	Code[a]	Infant deaths / Décès d'enfants de moins d'un an Number Nombre	Rate (per 1000 births) Taux (par 1000 naiss-ances)	Expectation of life at birth / Espérance de vie à la naissance Male[b] Masculin[b]	Female[b] Féminin[b]	Total fertility rate L'indice synthétique de fécondité
AFRICA - AFRIQUE													
Algeria - Algérie[1]													
2002	C	616 963	19.7	U	126 557	...	...	U	19 850	...	...	...	...
2003	C	649 000	20.4	U	145 000	...	...		...	...	...	...	...
2004	C	669 000	20.7	U	141 000	...	...		...	...	...	...	...
2005	C	703 000	21.4	U	147 000	...	...		...	...	...	...	...
2006	C	739 000	22.1	U	144 000	...	...		...	...	...	...	...
Cape Verde - Cap-Vert													
2002	C	13 123	29.0		...	...	...		...	...	...	...	...
2003	C	13 334	28.9		...	...	...		...	...	...	...	...
Congo[2]													
2002	+U	40 708	...		...	...	...		...	...	...	...	...
2003	+U	44 132	...		...	...	...		...	...	...	...	...
2004	+U	44 473	...		...	...	...		...	...	...	...	...
Egypt - Égypte													
2002	C	1 766 589	26.5	C	424 034	6.4	20.2	C	37 904	21.5	67.5	71.9	...
2003	C	1 777 418	26.2	C	440 149	6.5	19.7	C	38 859	21.9	67.9	72.3	3.200
2004	C	1 779 500	25.7	C	440 790	6.4	19.3	C	40 177	22.6	...	...	...
2005	C	1 800 972	25.5	C	450 646	6.4	19.1	C	36 146	20.1	...	...	3.100
2006	C	1 853 746	25.7	C	451 863	6.3	19.0	C	35 952	19.4	...	...	...
Ghana													
2002		...	...	...	34 682	...	...		34 293	...	...	...	...
2003		...	...		...	...	...		...	...	...	...	4.400
Kenya													
2002	U	494 941	...	U	171 800	...	...	U	35 940	...	...	...	4.896
2003	U	495 433	...	U	174 950	...	...	U	35 515	...	...	...	4.900
2004		...	...	U	178 051	...	...	U	35 321	...	...	...	...
2005		...	...	U	168 919	...	...	U	35 252	...	...	...	...
2006		...	...	U	174 856	...	...	U	35 786	...	...	...	...
Libyan Arab Jamahiriya - Jamahiriya arabe libyenne													
2002	C	111 053	20.2	U	19 362	...	...		...	...	...	...	...
Madagascar													
2003		...	...		...	...	...		...	...	...	...	5.200
2004		...	...		...	...	...		...	...	...	...	5.200
Malawi													
2002	I	567 241[3]	50.8	I	217 205[3]	19.4	31.3		...	...	42.8[4]	45.5[4]	...
2003	I	578 978[3]	50.1	I	213 705[3]	18.5	31.6		...	...	43.4[4]	46.0[4]	...
2006	U	614 410	...	U	207 641	...	...		...	...	...	...	...
Mauritius - Maurice													
2002	+C	19 983	16.5	+C	8 310	6.9	9.6	+C	297	14.9	...	...	1.940
2003	+C	19 343	15.8	+C	8 520	7.0	8.9	+C	250	12.9	68.6	75.3	1.870
2004	+C	19 230	15.6	+C	8 475	6.9	8.7	+C	277	14.4	III68.4	75.3	1.870
2005	+C	18 820	15.1	+C	8 646	7.0	8.2	+C	248	13.2	68.9	75.6	1.820
2006	+C	17 604	14.1	+C	9 162	7.3	6.7	+C	249	14.1	...	...	1.700
Mayotte													
2002	C	7 128	44.5		...	...	...		...	...	...	...	...
2003	C	7 197	...		...	...	...		...	...	...	...	...
2004	C	7 452	...	C	513	...	...		...	...	...	...	...
Mozambique													
2002		...	...		...	...	...		...	...	...	...	5.500
Réunion													
2002	C	14 789[5]	19.8	C	4 004[5]	5.4	14.4	C	91	...	...	...	2.500
2003	C	14 427[5]	18.9	C*	4 022[5]	5.3	13.6	C*	107	7.4	71.3	79.8	2.430
2004	C	14 545[5]	18.9	C	3 884[5]	5.1	13.9		...	...	...	...	...
2005	C*	14 799[5]	19.0	C	4 357[5]	5.6	13.4		...	...	...	...	...
2006	C*	14 495[5]	18.5	C*	4 323[5]	5.5	13.0		...	...	...	...	...
Saint Helena ex. dep. - Sainte-Hélène sans dép.													
2002	C	39	...	C	52	...	...		...	...	...	...	...
2003	C	37	...	C	44	...	...	C	1	...	...	...	...

Continent, country or area and year — Continent, pays ou zone et année	Live births — Naissances vivantes			Deaths — Décès			Rate of natural increase — Taux d'accrois-sement naturel	Infant deaths — Décès d'enfants de moins d'un an			Expectation of life at birth — Espérance de vie à la naissance		Total fertility rate — L'indice synthétique de fécondité
	Code[a]	Number Nombre	Crude birth rate Taux brut de natalité	Code[a]	Number Nombre	Crude death rate Taux brut de mortalité		Code[a]	Number Nombre	Rate (per 1000 births) Taux (par 1000 naissances)	Male[b] Masculin[b]	Female[b] Féminin[b]	
AFRICA - AFRIQUE													
Saint Helena ex. dep. - Sainte-Hélène sans dép.													
2004	C	34	...	C	33	...	...		...	...	[x]71.9	79.1	...
2005	C	34	...	C	39	...	...	C	1	...	...	...	...
Seychelles													
2002	+C	1 481	17.7	+C	647	7.7	10.0	+C	26	...	...	...	...
2003	+C	1 498	18.1	+C	668	8.1	10.0	+C	24	...	...	...	...
2004	+C	1 435	17.4	+C	611	7.4	10.0	+C	17	...	...	...	2.200
2005	+C	1 536	18.5	+C	673	8.1	10.4	+C	16	...	...	...	2.200
2006	+C	1 467	17.3	+C	664	7.8	9.5	+C	14	...	...	...	2.200
South Africa - Afrique du Sud													
2002	U	899 286	...	U	499 925	...	...		...	...	...	...	...
2003	U	875 748	...	U	553 718	...	...		...	...	...	...	2.820
2004	U	897 514	...	U	572 350	...	...		...	...	49.9	52.9	2.800
2005	U	848 043	...	U	591 213	...	...		...	...	...	...	2.780
Zambia - Zambie[3]													
2006	I	509 766	43.2	I	152 549	12.9	30.3		...	...	...	...	...
Zimbabwe													
2002		...	...	I	200 294[6]	17.2	...		...	...	[II]42.7	45.9	...
2005		...	...		...	...	...		...	...	...	...	3.800
AMERICA, NORTH - AMÉRIQUE DU NORD													
Anguilla													
2002	+C	169	14.2	+C	52	4.4	9.8	+C	2	...	[III]76.5	81.1	...
2003	+C	139	11.4	+C	65	5.3	6.1	+C	2	...	...	...	...
2004	+C	164	13.1	+C	53	4.2	8.9	+C	-	...	...	...	2.910
2005	+C	167	12.2	+C	62	4.5	7.7	+C	3	...	...	...	1.840
2006	+C*	183	12.8	+C*	59	4.1	8.7	+C*	1	...	...	...	2.000
Antigua and Barbuda - Antigua-et-Barbuda[7]													
2002		...	...	+C	444	5.7	...		...	...	...	...	...
Aruba													
2002	C	1 228	13.2	C	492	5.3	7.9	+U	3	...	...	...	2.990
2003	C	1 244	13.1	C	501	5.3	7.8	+U	3	...	...	...	1.627
2004	C	1 193	12.2	C	502	5.1	7.1	+U	3	...	...	...	1.749
2005	C	1 234	12.3	C	482	4.8	7.5	+U	6	...	...	...	1.739
2006	C	1 227	11.9	C	537	5.2	6.7	+U	8	...	...	...	...
Bahamas													
2003	U	5 054	...	C	1 649	5.2	...	C	87	...	...	...	...
Barbados - Barbade													
2002	+C*	3 812	14.1	+C*	2 285	8.4	5.6	+C*	54	...	...	...	...
Belize													
2002	U	7 553	...	U	1 284	...	...	U	145	...	...	...	...
2003	U	7 440	...	U	1 277	...	...		...	...	...	...	...
2004	U	8 083	...	U	1 298	...	...	U	112	...	...	...	...
2005	U	8 396	...	U	1 369	...	...	U	137	...	...	...	...
Bermuda - Bermudes													
2002	C	830[8]	13.2	C	404[8]	6.4	6.8	C	-	...	...	...	...
2003	C	834[8]	13.2	C	434[8]	6.9	6.3	C	2	...	...	...	...
2004	C	831[8]	13.1	C	406[8]	6.4	6.7	C	-	...	...	...	...
2005	C	835[8]	13.1	C	437[8]	6.9	6.3	C	2	...	...	...	...
2006	C	798[8]	12.5	C	461[8]	7.2	5.3	C	6	...	...	...	...

Continent, country or area and year / Continent, pays ou zone et année	Code[a]	Live births - Naissances vivantes Number Nombre	Crude birth rate Taux brut de natalité	Code[a]	Deaths - Décès Number Nombre	Crude death rate Taux brut de mortalité	Rate of natural increase Taux d'accrois-sement naturel	Code[a]	Infant deaths - Décès d'enfants de moins d'un an Number Nombre	Rate (per 1000 births) Taux (par 1000 naiss-ances)	Expectation of life at birth - Espérance de vie à la naissance Male[b] Masculin[b]	Female[b] Féminin[b]	Total fertility rate L'indice synthétique de fécondité
AMERICA, NORTH - AMÉRIQUE DU NORD													
British Virgin Islands - Îles Vierges britanniques													
2002	C	253	12.1	C	97	4.6	7.4		...	...	76.6	75.4	1.620
2003	C	269	12.6	C	104	4.9	7.7		...	...	73.8	78.9	1.700
2004	C	318	14.7	C	120	5.5	9.1		...	...	69.9	78.5	1.990
Canada													
2002	C	328 802[9]	10.5	C	223 603[9]	7.1	3.4	C	1 762[9]	5.4	77.2	82.1	1.501
2003	C	335 202[9]	10.6	C	226 169[9]	7.1	3.4	C	1 765[9]	5.3	77.4	82.4	1.525
2004	C	337 422[9]	10.5	C	226 584[9]	7.1	3.5	C	1 775[9]	5.3	77.8	82.6	1.526
2005	C	342 176[9]	10.6	C	230 132[9]	7.1	3.5	C	1 863[9]	5.4	...	...	1.543
2006	C*	350 181[9]	10.7	C*	233 415[9]	7.1	3.6		...	...	...	...	...
Cayman Islands - Îles Caïmanes													
2002	C	583	13.7	C	120	2.8	10.9		...	...	...	...	...
2003	C	623	14.3	C	153	3.5	10.8		...	...	...	...	...
2004	C	611	13.8	C	165	3.7	10.1		...	...	...	...	...
2005	C	699	14.5	C	170	3.5	10.9	C	4	...	...	...	...
2006	C	710	13.7	C	182	3.5	10.2	C	7	...	...	...	...
Costa Rica													
2002	C	71 144	17.8	C	15 004	3.8	14.0	C	793	11.1	...	...	...
2003	C	72 938	17.8	C	15 800	3.9	14.0	C	737	10.1	...	...	2.100
2004	C	72 247	17.3	C	15 949	3.8	13.5	C	668	9.2	...	...	2.000
2005	C	71 548	16.8	C	16 139	3.8	13.0	C	700	9.8	...	...	2.000
2006	C	71 291	16.4	C	16 766	3.9	12.5	C	691	9.7	...	...	...
Cuba													
2002	C	141 276	12.6	C	73 882	6.6	6.0	C	922	6.5	...	...	1.675
2003	C	136 795	12.2	C	78 434	7.0	5.2	C	859	6.3	III75.1	79.0	1.628
2004	C	127 192	11.3	C*	81 095	7.2	4.1	C*	736	5.8	...	...	1.543
2005	C	120 716	10.7	C	84 824	7.5	3.2	C	746	6.2	...	...	1.493
2006	C	111 323	9.9	C	80 840	7.2	2.7	C	589	5.3	...	...	1.393
Dominica - Dominique													
2002	+C	1 081	15.4	+C	594[7]	8.4	6.9		...	...	...	...	...
2003				+C	557[7]	...			...	...	...	...	...
Dominican Republic - République dominicaine													
2002	+U	203 228	...	+U	27 309	...	...	+U	571	...	...	...	...
2003	+U	209 069	...	+U	29 821	...	...	+U	472	...	...	...	...
2004	+U	198 304	...	+U	34 325	...	...	+U	365	...	...	...	2.798
2005	+U	183 819	...	+U	33 949	...	...	+U	377	...	69.2[10]	75.5[10]	2.766
2006		...	...		...	...	...		...	...	...	...	2.734
El Salvador													
2002	C	129 363	19.8	C	27 458	4.2	15.6	C	1 284	9.9	...	...	...
2003	C	124 476	18.8	C	29 377	4.4	14.3	C	1 322	10.6	...	...	...
2004	C	119 710	17.7	C	30 058	4.4	13.3	C	1 255	10.5	...	...	...
2005	C	112 769	16.4	C	30 933	4.5	11.9	C	1 097	9.7	VI67.7	73.7	...
2006	C	107 111	15.3	C	31 453	4.5	10.8	C	1 013	9.5	...	...	...
Greenland - Groenland													
2002	C	940	16.6	C	435	7.7	8.9	C	10	...	...	...	2.488
2003	C	895	15.8	C	412	7.3	8.5	C	8	...	V64.1	69.5	2.361
2004	C	893	15.7	C	475	8.3	7.3	C	10	...	...	...	2.380
2005	C	887	15.6	C	466	8.2	7.4	C	7	...	...	...	2.330
2006	C	842	14.8	C	440	7.7	7.1	C	13	...	V65.7	71.0	2.222
Guadeloupe													
2002	C	6 995[5]	16.0	C	2 584[5]	5.9	10.1	C	45[5]	...	74.6	81.5	2.200
2003	C	7 047[5]	16.1	C	2 636[5]	6.0	10.1	C	56[5]	...	...	...	...
2004	C	7 273[5]	16.4	C	2 676[5]	6.0	10.3	C	50[5]	...	...	...	...
2005	C	7 551[5]	16.9	C	2 904[5]	6.5	10.4		...	...	...	...	...
2006	C	7 193[5]	15.7	C	2 902[5]	6.3	9.4		...	...	...	...	...

4. Vital statistics summary and expectation of life at birth: 2002 - 2006
Aperçu des statistiques de l'état civil et espérance de vie à la naissance: 2002 - 2006 (continued - suite)

Continent, country or area and year / Continent, pays ou zone et année	Code[a]	Live births Naissances vivantes Number Nombre	Crude birth rate Taux brut de natalité	Code[a]	Deaths Décès Number Nombre	Crude death rate Taux brut de mortalité	Rate of natural increase Taux d'accrois-sement naturel	Code[a]	Infant deaths Décès d'enfants de moins d'un an Number Nombre	Rate (per 1000 births) Taux (par 1000 naiss-ances)	Male[b] Masculin[b]	Female[b] Féminin[b]	Total fertility rate L'indice synthétique de fécondité
AMERICA, NORTH - AMÉRIQUE DU NORD													
Guatemala													
2002	C	387 287	32.3	C	66 089	5.5	26.8		...	...	...	...	...
2003	C	375 092	31.0	C	66 695	5.5	25.5	C	11 022	29.4	...	...	...
2004	C	383 704	31.0	C	66 991	5.4	25.6	C	10 038	26.2	...	...	3.959
2005	C	374 066	29.5	C	71 039	5.6	23.9	C	9 947	26.6	...	...	3.738
2006	C	368 399	28.3	C	69 756	5.4	22.9	C	9 042	24.5	...	...	3.570
Haiti - Haïti[7]													
2002		...	...	U	7 657	...			...	...	...	...	...
2003		...	...	U	8 011	...			...	...	...	...	...
Honduras													
2002	+U	216 145	...	+U	34 379	...	...	+U	7 059				
2003	+U	218 173	...	+U	34 754	...	...	+U	6 902				
2004	+U	220 040	...	+U	35 075	...	...	+U	6 740				
2005	+U	221 759	...	+U	35 356	...	...	+U	6 566				
2006	+U	222 512	...	+U	35 682	...	...	+U	6 400				
Jamaica - Jamaïque													
2002	C	48 627[11]	18.6	U	17 018[12]	...	...	U	1 036[11]	...	[III]72.8	76.5	2.044
2003	C	47 110[11]	17.9	U	16 699[12]	...	...	U	1 004[11]	...	71.3	77.1	2.067
2004	C	47 127[11]	17.9	U	16 905[12]	...	...	U	1 004[11]	...	...	...	...
2005	C	47 255[11]	17.8	U	17 552[12]	...	...	U	1 007[11]	...	...	...	...
2006	C	46 277[11]	17.4	U	16 317[12]	...	...		...	...	...	...	...
Martinique													
2002	C	5 446[5]	14.0	C	2 681[5]	6.9	7.1	C	33	...	75.4	82.2	1.900
2003	C	5 430[5]	13.9	C	2 725[5]	7.0	6.9	C	33	...	...	...	...
2004	C	5 255[5]	13.3	C	2 647[5]	6.7	6.6	C	27	...	...	...	...
2005	C	5 032[5]	12.7	C	2 610[5]	6.6	6.1		...	...	...	...	...
2006	C	5 370[5]	13.4	C	2 663[5]	6.7	6.8		...	...	...	...	...
Mexico - Mexique													
2002	+U	2 209 308[13]	...	+C	457 680[13]	4.5	...	+U	36 546[13]	...	...	...	2.285
2003	+U	2 165 318[13]	...	+C	470 692[13]	4.6	...	+U	33 331[13]	...	...	...	2.333
2004	+U	2 154 927[13]	...	+C	472 273[13]	4.6	...	+U	32 758[13]	...	...	...	2.247
2005	+U	2 567 906[13]	...	+C	493 957[13]	4.8	...	+U	32 590[13]	...	71.9	77.4	2.203
2006		...	...	+C	493 296[13]	4.7	...	+U	30 890[13]	...	...	...	2.167
Netherlands Antilles - Antilles néerlandaises													
2002	C	2 442[14]	14.0	C	1 220[15]	7.0	7.0	C	17	...	[V]72.1	78.7	2.068
2003	C	2 488[14]	13.9	C	1 374[15]	7.7	6.2	C	19	...	...	...	2.059
2004	C	2 357[14]	12.9	C	1 412[15]	7.7	5.2	C	20	...	[III]70.6	79.0	1.879
2005	C	2 553[14]	13.8	C	1 304[15]	7.0	6.7		...	...	...	...	...
2006	C	2 578[14]	13.6	C	1 323[15]	7.0	6.6		...	...	...	...	...
Nicaragua													
2002	+U	121 361	...	+U	15 070	...	...	+U	2 217				
2003	+U	120 784	...	+U	15 379	...	...	+U	2 008				
2004	+U	121 402	...	+U	14 975	...	...	+U	1 827				
2005	+U	121 380	...	+U	16 770	...	...	+U	1 970	...	[VI]67.2	71.9	
Panama													
2002	C	61 671	20.2	U	12 428	...	...	U	885				
2003	C	61 753	19.8	U	13 248	...	...	U	940				
2004	C	62 743	19.8	U	13 475	...	...	U	932				
2005	C	63 645	19.7	U	14 180	...	...	U	980				
2006	C	65 764	20.0	U	14 358	...	...	U	971				
Puerto Rico - Porto Rico													
2002	C	52 871	13.7	C	28 098	7.3	6.4	C	516	9.8	73.2	80.9	1.817
2003	C	50 803	13.1	C	28 356	7.3	5.8	C	498	9.8	...	...	1.760
2004	C	51 239	13.2	C	29 066	7.5	5.7	C	416	8.1	[III]73.7	81.1	1.776
2005	C	50 687	13.0	C	29 702	7.6	5.4	C	472	9.3	[III]73.7	80.9	1.755

Continent, country or area and year / Continent, pays ou zone et année	Live births - Naissances vivantes			Deaths - Décès			Rate of natural increase - Taux d'accroissement naturel	Infant deaths - Décès d'enfants de moins d'un an			Expectation of life at birth - Espérance de vie à la naissance		Total fertility rate - L'indice synthétique de fécondité
	Code[a]	Number Nombre	Crude birth rate Taux brut de natalité	Code[a]	Number Nombre	Crude death rate Taux brut de mortalité	Taux d'accroissement naturel	Code[a]	Number Nombre	Rate (per 1000 births) Taux (par 1000 naissances)	Male[b] Masculin[b]	Female[b] Féminin[b]	
AMERICA, NORTH - AMÉRIQUE DU NORD													
Saint Lucia - Sainte-Lucie													
2002	C	2 598	16.3	C	960	6.0	10.3	C	36	...	72.0	76.7	...
2003	C	2 486	15.5	C	1 046	6.5	9.0	C	37	...	...	...	...
2004	C	2 322	14.3	C	1 114	6.9	7.4	C	45	...	...	...	...
2005	C*	2 298	13.9	C*	1 107	6.7	7.2	C*	46	...	69.9	75.7	...
Saint Vincent and the Grenadines - Saint Vincent-et-les Grenadines													
2002	+C	1 985	18.4	+C	766	7.1	11.3	+C	35	...	...	...	...
2003	+C	1 923	18.3	+C	790	7.5	10.8	+C	35	...	...	...	...
2004	+C	1 804	17.3	+C	812	7.8	9.5	+C	33	...	...	...	...
2005	+C	1 779	17.1	+C	813	7.8	9.3	+C	29	...	...	...	...
Trinidad and Tobago - Trinité-et-Tobago													
2002	C	16 990	13.3	C	9 797	7.7	5.6	C	412	24.2	...	...	...
Turks Caicos Islands - Îles Turques et Caïques													
2002	C	153	7.3	C	48	2.3	5.0	C	2	...	...	...	...
2003	C	213	8.5	C	61	2.4	6.0	C	2	...	...	...	...
2004	C	300	10.9	C	46	1.7	9.2	C	-	...	...	...	...
2005	C	318	10.4	C	53	1.7	8.7	C	1	...	...	...	...
2006	C	409	12.3	C	73	2.2	10.1						
United States - États-Unis													
2002	C	4 021 726	14.0	C	2 443 387	8.5	5.5	C	28 034	7.0	74.5	79.9	2.013
2003	C	4 089 950	14.1	C	2 448 288	8.4	5.6	C	28 025	6.9	74.8	80.1	2.043
2004	C	4 112 052	14.0	C	2 397 615	8.2	5.8	C	27 936	6.8	75.2	80.4	2.050
2005	C	4 138 349	14.0	C	2 448 017	8.3	5.7	C	28 440	6.9	...	...	2.040
2006	C*	4 265 996	14.2	C*	2 416 000	8.1	6.2	C*	28 100	6.6	...	...	...
United States Virgin Islands - Îles Vierges américaines													
2002	C	1 634	15.0	C	617[7]	5.7	9.3	C*	5	...	...	...	...
2003	C	1 522	14.0	C	631	5.8	8.2	C	12	...	...	...	...
2004	C	1 574	14.4	C	626	5.7	8.7	C	13	...	...	...	...
2005	C	1 599	14.7		...								...
AMERICA, SOUTH - AMÉRIQUE DU SUD													
Argentina - Argentine													
2002	C	694 684	18.5	C	291 190	7.8	10.8	C	11 703	16.8	...	...	...
2003	C	697 952	18.4	C	302 064	8.0	10.5	C	11 494	16.5	...	...	2.406
2004	C	736 261	19.3	C	294 051	7.7	11.6	C	10 576	14.4	...	...	2.501
2005	C	712 220	18.5	C	293 529	7.6	10.8	C	9 507	13.3	...	...	2.389
2006	+C	696 451	17.9	C	292 313	7.5	10.4	C	8 986	12.9	...	...	...
Bolivia - Bolivie													
2002	U	208 693	...		...	...	...		...	...	...	...	...
2003	U	184 179	...		...	...	...		...	...	...	...	...
2004	U	149 094	...		...	...	...		...	...	...	...	...
2005	U	113 170	...		...	...	...		...	...	...	...	...
Brazil - Brésil[16]													
2002	U	2 581 055	...	U	958 475	...	...	U	45 243	...	67.3	74.9	2.160
2003	U	2 822 462	...	U	977 717	...	...	U	48 039	...	...	...	2.330
2004	U	2 813 704	...	U	998 725	...	...	U	41 851	...	...	...	2.310
2005	U	2 874 542	...	U	979 854	...	...	U	39 259	...	68.1	75.8	2.290
2006	U	2 798 964	...	U	1 023 545	...	...	U	37 677	...	...	...	...
Chile - Chili													
2002	C	238 981	15.3	C	81 079	5.2	10.1	C	1 964	8.2	[II]74.4	80.4	2.000
2003	C	234 486	14.9	C	83 672	5.3	9.6	C	1 935	8.3	...	...	1.900

Continent, country or area and year / Continent, pays ou zone et année	Co-de[a]	Number Nombre	Crude birth rate Taux brut de natalité	Co-de[a]	Number Nombre	Crude death rate Taux brut de mortalité	Rate of natural increase Taux d'accrois-sement naturel	Co-de[a]	Number Nombre	Rate (per 1000 births) Taux (par 1000 naiss-ances)	Male[b] Masculin[b]	Female[b] Féminin[b]	Total fertility rate L'indice synthétique de fécondité
AMERICA, SOUTH - AMÉRIQUE DU SUD													
Chile - Chili													
2004	C	230 352	14.3	C	86 138	5.4	9.0	C	2 034	8.8	...	...	1.910
2005	C	230 831	14.2	C	86 102	5.3	8.9	C	1 911	8.3	VI75.5[10]	81.5[10]	1.930
Colombia - Colombie													
2002	U	700 455	...	U	192 262	...	...	U	12 640	...	...	...	...
2003	U	710 702	...	U	193 267	...	...	U	12 335	...	...	...	...
2004	U	723 099	...	U	188 933	...	...	U	11 772	...	...	...	...
2005	U	719 968	...	U	189 022	...	...	U	11 456	...	VI69.2	75.3	...
2006	U*	711 457	...	U*	189 760	...	...	U*	10 722	...	VI69.4	75.5	...
Ecuador - Équateur[17]													
2002	U	183 792	...	U	55 549	...	...	U	4 530	...	...	...	...
2003	U	178 549	...	U	53 521	...	...	U	3 985	...	...	...	...
2004	U	168 893	...	U	54 729	...	...	U	3 942	...	...	...	...
2005	U	168 324	...	U	56 825	...	...	U	3 717	...	VI71.3	77.2	...
2006	U	185 056	...	U	57 940	...	...	U	3 715	...	...	...	...
Falkland Islands (Malvinas) - Îles Falkland (Malvinas)													
2002	+C	30	...	+C	18	...	...	...	...	...	...	...	...
2003	+C	34	...	+C	20	...	...	...	...	...	...	...	...
2004	+C	44	...	+C	15	...	...	...	...	...	...	...	...
2005	+C	18	...	+C	19	...	...	...	...	...	...	...	...
2006	+C	27	...	+C	20	...	...	...	...	...	...	...	...
French Guiana - Guyane française													
2002	C	5 249[5]	29.9	C	656[5]	3.7	26.2	C	52[5]	...	72.5	79.2	3.900
2003	C	5 553[5]	30.7	C	692[5]	3.8	26.8	C	58[5]	...	71.3	79.7	...
2004	C	5 312[5]	28.4	C	719[5]	3.8	24.9	C	55[5]	...	...	...	...
2005	C	5 998[5]	30.0	C	705[5]	3.5	26.5		...	...	...	...	...
2006	C	6 276[5]	31.9	C	711[5]	3.6	28.2		...	...	...	...	...
Guyana													
2002		...	...	+C	5 003	6.7	...		...	...	...	...	...
2003		...	...	+C	4 986	6.6	...		...	...	...	...	...
2004		...	...	+C	5 141	6.8	...		...	...	...	...	...
Paraguay													
2003	U	45 669	...	U	19 593	...	...	U	674	...	...	...	...
2004	U	49 857	...	U	20 283	...	...	U	647	...	...	...	...
2005	U	51 444	...	U	17 360	...	...	U	539	...	VI68.6	73.1	...
Peru - Pérou[16]													
2002	+U	355 870[18]	...	+U	80 862[19]	...	...	+U	6 511[20]	...	...	...	2.890
2003	+U	373 600[18]	...	+U	85 198[19]	...	...	+U	7 122[20]	...	...	...	2.830
2004	+U	344 804[18]	...	+U	94 149[19]	...	...		...	...	...	...	...
Suriname													
2002	C	10 188	21.4	C	3 125	6.6	14.8	C	148	14.5	...	...	...
2003	C	9 634	20.0	C	3 154	6.5	13.4	C	109	11.3	...	...	...
2004	C	9 062	18.6	C	3 319	6.8	11.8	C	120	13.2	...	...	2.244
2005	C	8 657	17.4	C	3 392	6.8	10.6	C	130	15.7	...	...	2.120
Uruguay													
2002	C	51 953	15.7	C	31 628	9.6	6.1	C	708	13.6	...	...	2.210
2003	C	50 631	15.3	C	32 587	9.9	5.5	C*	757	15.0	71.3	79.2	...
2004	C	50 052	15.2	C	32 222	9.8	5.4	C	659	13.2	71.7	78.9	2.075
2005	C	46 944	14.2	C	32 319	9.8	4.4	C*	601	12.8	72.0	79.4	2.045
2006	C	47 410	14.3	C	31 056	9.4	4.9	C*	497	10.5	72.1	79.5	2.030
Venezuela (Bolivarian Republic of) - Venezuela (République bolivarienne du)[16]													
2002	C	492 678	19.5	C	105 388	4.2	15.4	C	7 645	15.5	70.8	76.6	...
2003	C	555 614	21.6	C	118 562	4.6	17.0		...	...	...	...	...
2004	C	637 799	24.4	C	110 946	4.2	20.2		...	...	...	...	2.690

4. Vital statistics summary and expectation of life at birth: 2002 - 2006
Aperçu des statistiques de l'état civil et espérance de vie à la naissance: 2002 - 2006 (continued - suite)

Continent, country or area and year / Continent, pays ou zone et année	Code[a]	Live births / Naissances vivantes Number Nombre	Crude birth rate Taux brut de natalité	Code[a]	Deaths / Décès Number Nombre	Crude death rate Taux brut de mortalité	Rate of natural increase Taux d'accrois-sement naturel	Code[a]	Infant deaths / Décès d'enfants de moins d'un an Number Nombre	Rate (per 1000 births) Taux (par 1000 naiss-ances)	Expectation of life at birth / Espérance de vie à la naissance Male[b] Masculin[b]	Female[b] Féminin[b]	Total fertility rate L'indice synthétique de fécondité
AMERICA, SOUTH - AMÉRIQUE DU SUD													
Venezuela (Bolivarian Republic of) - Venezuela (République bolivarienne du)[16]													
2005	C	665 997	25.1	C	110 301	4.2	20.9		...	...	...	...	2.650
2006	C	646 225	23.9	C	115 348	4.3	19.6		...	...	...	...	2.620
ASIA - ASIE													
Afghanistan													
2002		...			...	...	...		...	...	43.0	43.0	...
Armenia - Arménie													
2002	C	32 229[21]	10.0	C	25 554[21]	8.0	2.1	C	450[21]	14.0	69.8	75.9	1.208
2003	C	35 793[21]	11.1	C	26 014[21]	8.1	3.0	C	422[21]	11.8	69.9	75.8	1.349
2004	C	37 520[21]	11.7	C	25 679[21]	8.0	3.7	C	430[21]	11.5	70.3	76.4	1.383
2005	C	37 499[21]	11.7	C	26 379[21]	8.2	3.5	C	460[21]	12.3	70.3	76.5	1.365
2006	C	37 639[22]	11.7	C	27 202[21]	8.4	3.2	C	523[21]	13.9	...	...	1.348
Azerbaijan - Azerbaïdjan													
2002	+C	110 715[21]	13.5	+C	46 522[21]	5.7	7.9	+C	1 422[21]	12.8	69.4	75.0	1.840
2003	+C	113 467[21]	13.8	+C	49 001[21]	6.0	7.8	+C	1 451[21]	12.8	69.5	75.1	1.910
2004	+C	131 609[21]	15.8	+C	49 568[21]	6.0	9.9	+C	1 287[21]	9.8	69.6	75.2	2.050
2005	+C	141 901[21]	16.9	+C	51 962[21]	6.2	10.7	+C	1 321[21]	9.3	69.6	75.2	...
2006	+C	148 946[21]	17.6	+C	52 248[21]	6.2	11.4	+C	1 508[21]	10.1	69.6	75.1	...
Bahrain - Bahreïn													
2002	C	13 576	20.2	C	2 035	3.0	17.2	C	94	...	...	...	2.528
2003	C	14 560	21.1	C	2 114	3.1	18.1	C	107	7.3	...	...	2.600
2004	C	14 968	21.2	C	2 215	3.1	18.0	C	141	9.4	...	...	2.600
2005	C	15 198	21.0	C	2 222	3.1	17.9	C	134	8.8	73.1	77.3	2.600
2006	C	15 053	20.3	C	2 317	3.1	17.2	C	115	7.6	...	...	2.500*
Bangladesh													
2002	I	...	20.1[23]	I	...	5.1[23]	...	I	...	53.0[23]	64.5	65.4	2.550
2003	I	...	20.9[23]	I	...	5.9[23]	...	I	...	53.0[23]	64.3	65.4	2.570
2004	I	...	20.8[23]	I	...	5.8[23]	...	I	...	52.0[23]	64.4	65.7	2.510
2005	I	...	20.7[23]	I	...	5.8[23]	...	I	...	49.0[23]	64.6	65.8	2.470
2006	I	...	20.6[23]	I	...	5.6[23]	...	I	...	45.0[23]	64.7	65.9	2.410
Bhutan - Bhoutan													
2005	I	12 538[24]	19.7	I	4 498[24]	7.1	12.7	I	503[24]	40.1	65.6	66.8	3.590
Brunei Darussalam - Brunéi Darussalam													
2002	+C	7 464	21.7	+C	1 041	3.0	18.7	+C	62	...	...	...	...
2003	+C	7 047	20.2	+C	1 010	2.9	17.3	+C	67	...	...	...	...
2004	+C	7 163	19.9	+C	1 010	2.8	17.1	+C	63	...	...	...	...
2005	+C*	6 933	18.7	+C*	1 072	2.9	15.8	+C*	51	...	...	...	...
Cambodia - Cambodge													
2002	U	367 569	...	U	125 617	...	...		83	...	...	...	3.780
2003	U	375 799	...	U	124 981	...	...		80	...	...	...	3.780
2004	U	384 267	...	U	124 391	...	...		76	...	...	...	3.680
China - Chine[26]													
2002	I	16 470 000[27]	12.9	I	8 210 000[27]	6.4	6.5		...	...	...	...	...
2003	I	15 990 000[27]	12.4	I	8 250 000[27]	6.4	6.0		...	...	...	...	...
2004	I	15 930 000[27]	12.3	I	8 320 000[27]	6.4	5.9		...	...	...	...	...
2005	I	16 170 000[28]	12.4	I	8 490 000[28]	6.5	5.9		...	...	...	...	...
2006	I	...	12.1[27]	I	...	6.8[27]			...	...	...	...	...
China: Hong Kong SAR - Chine: Hong Kong RAS													
2002	C	48 209	7.1	C	34 267	5.1	2.1	C	110	2.3	78.5	84.5	0.941[25]
2003	C	46 965	7.0	C	36 971	5.5	1.5	C	109	2.3	78.5	84.4	0.901[25]

4. Vital statistics summary and expectation of life at birth: 2002 - 2006
Aperçu des statistiques de l'état civil et espérance de vie à la naissance: 2002 - 2006 (continued - suite)

Continent, country or area and year / Continent, pays ou zone et année	Code[a]	Live births / Naissances vivantes Number Nombre	Crude birth rate Taux brut de natalité	Code[a]	Deaths / Décès Number Nombre	Crude death rate Taux brut de mortalité	Rate of natural increase Taux d'accrois-sement naturel	Code[a]	Infant deaths / Décès d'enfants de moins d'un an Number Nombre	Rate (per 1000 births) Taux (par 1000 naiss-ances)	Expectation of life at birth / Espérance de vie à la naissance Male[b] Masculin[b]	Female[b] Féminin[b]	Total fertility rate L'indice synthétique de fécondité
ASIA - ASIE													
China: Hong Kong SAR - Chine: Hong Kong RAS													
2004	C	49 796	7.3	C	36 918	5.4	1.9	C	132	2.7	79.0	84.8	0.922[25]
2005	C	57 098	8.4	C	38 830	5.7	2.7	C	131	2.3	78.8	84.6	0.959[25]
2006	C	65 626	9.6	C*	37 457	5.5	4.1	C*	118	1.8	79.4	85.5	0.984[25]
China: Macao SAR - Chine: Macao RAS													
2002	C	3 162	7.2	C	1 415	3.2	4.0	C	11	...	...	...	0.813
2003	C	3 212	7.2	C	1 474	3.3	3.9	C	2	...	...	...	0.837
2004	C	3 308	7.3	C	1 533	3.4	3.9	C	10	...	IV77.5	82.1	0.855
2005	C	3 671	7.8	C	1 615	3.4	4.3	C	12	...	IV77.6	82.3	0.912
2006	C	4 058	8.1	C	1 566	3.1	5.0	C	11	...	...	...	0.954
Cyprus - Chypre[29]													
2002	C	7 883	11.1	C	5 168	7.3	3.8	C	37	...	...	...	1.491
2003	C	8 088	11.2	C	5 200	7.2	4.0	C	33	...	II77.0	81.4	1.498
2004	C	8 309	11.3	C	5 225	7.1	4.2	C	29	...	...	...	1.487
2005	C	8 243	10.9	C	5 425	7.2	3.7	C	38	...	II77.0	81.7	1.420
2006	C	8 731	11.3	C	5 127	6.7	4.7	C	27	...	...	...	1.437
Georgia - Géorgie													
2002	C	46 605[21]	10.7	C	46 446[21]	10.7	0.0	C	1 102[21]	23.6	68.0	74.8	1.420
2003	C	46 194[21]	10.7	C	46 055[21]	10.6	0.0	C	1 144[21]	24.8	69.1	74.7	1.370
2004	C	49 572[21]	11.5	C	48 793[21]	11.3	0.2	C	1 178[21]	23.8	67.8	74.9	1.440
2005	C	46 512[21]	10.7	C	42 984[21]	9.9	0.8	C	916[21]	19.7	69.3	76.7	1.350
2006	C	47 795[21]	10.9	C	42 255[21]	9.6	1.3	C	753[21]	15.8	69.8	78.5	1.400
India - Inde[30]													
2002	I	...	25.0[31]	I	...	8.1[31]	...	I	...	63.0[31]	...	...	3.000
2003	I	...	24.8[31]	I	...	8.0[31]	...	I	...	60.0[31]	V61.8	63.5	3.000
2004	I	...	24.1[31]	I	...	7.5[31]	...	I	...	58.0[31]	V62.1	63.7	2.900
2005	I	...	23.8[31]	I	...	7.6[31]	...	I	...	58.0[31]	V62.3	63.9	2.900
2006	I	...	23.5[31]	I	...	7.5[31]	...	I	...	57.0[31]	...	...	2.800
Iran (Islamic Republic of) - Iran (République islamique d')[32]													
2002	C	1 122 104	17.1	C	337 237	5.1	12.0		...	...	...	...	
2003	C	1 171 573	17.6	C	368 518	5.5	12.1		...	...	...	...	
2004	C	1 154 368	17.1	C	355 213	5.3	11.8		...	...	...	...	
2005	C	1 233 873	18.0	C	361 326	5.3	12.7		...	...	...	...	
2006	C	1 253 506	17.8	C	408 563	5.8	12.0		...	...			
Iraq													
2003	U*	691 269	...	U*	95 935	...	...		...	...			
2004	U*	840 257	...	U*	101 820	...	...	U*	10 972	...			
2005	U*	896 340	...	U*	115 775	...	...	U*	12 460	...			
Israel - Israël[33]													
2002	C	139 535	21.2	C	38 414[34]	5.8	15.4	C	752[35]	5.4	77.5	81.5	2.888
2003	C	144 936	21.7	C	38 499[36]	5.8	15.9	C	717[35]	4.9	77.7	81.9	2.945
2004	C	145 207	21.3	C	37 938[37]	5.6	15.8	C	670	4.6	78.1	82.4	2.904
2005	C	143 913	20.8	C	39 036[38]	5.6	15.1	C	628[35]	4.4	78.3	82.3	2.836
2006	C	148 170	21.0	C	38 703[39]	5.5	15.5	C	593	4.0	V78.0	82.0	2.879
Japan - Japon[40]													
2002	C	1 153 855	9.2	C	982 379	7.8	1.4	C	3 497	3.0	78.3	85.2	1.319
2003	C	1 123 610	8.9	C	1 014 951	8.0	0.9	C	3 364	3.0	78.4	85.3	1.290
2004	C	1 110 721	8.8	C	1 028 602	8.1	0.7	C	3 122	2.8	78.6	85.6	1.289
2005	C	1 062 530	8.4	C	1 083 796	8.6	-0.2	C	2 958	2.8	78.5	85.5	1.260
2006	C	1 092 674	8.7	C	1 084 450	8.6	0.1	C	2 864	2.6	79.0	85.8	1.317
Jordan - Jordanie[41]													
2002	C	146 077	29.0	U	17 220	...	...		...	...	70.6	72.4	3.700
2003	C	148 294	28.7	U	16 937	...	...		...	...	70.6	72.4	3.700
2004	C	150 248	28.4	U	17 011	...	...		...	...	70.6	72.4	3.700

4. Vital statistics summary and expectation of life at birth: 2002 - 2006
Aperçu des statistiques de l'état civil et espérance de vie à la naissance: 2002 - 2006 (continued - suite)

Continent, country or area and year / Continent, pays ou zone et année	Live births / Naissances vivantes			Deaths / Décès			Rate of natural increase Taux d'accrois-sement naturel	Infant deaths / Décès d'enfants de moins d'un an			Expectation of life at birth / Espérance de vie à la naissance		Total fertility rate L'indice synthétique de fécondité
	Code[a]	Number Nombre	Crude birth rate Taux brut de natalité	Code[a]	Number Nombre	Crude death rate Taux brut de mortalité		Code[a]	Number Nombre	Rate (per 1000 births) Taux (par 1000 naiss-ances)	Male[b] Masculin[b]	Female[b] Féminin[b]	
ASIA - ASIE													
Jordan - Jordanie[41]													
2005	C	152 276	28.1	U	17 883	...	...		...	...	70.6	72.4	3.700
2006	C	162 972	29.4	U	20 397	...	...		...	...	...	...	...
Kazakhstan													
2002	C	227 171[21]	15.3	C	149 381[21]	10.1	5.2	C	3 849[21]	16.9	60.7	71.5	1.880
2003	C	247 946[21]	16.6	C	155 277[21]	10.4	6.2	C	3 806[21]	15.4	60.5	71.5	2.030
2004	C	273 028[21]	18.2	C	152 250[21]	10.1	8.0	C	3 901[21]	14.3	60.6	72.0	2.210
2005	C	278 977[21]	18.4	C	157 121[21]	10.4	8.0	C	4 213[21]	15.1	60.3	71.8	2.220
2006	C	301 756[21]	19.7	C	157 210[21]	10.3	9.4	C	4 154[21]	13.8	...	...	2.360
Korea (Republic of) - Corée (République de)													
2002	C	494 625[42]	10.3	C	246 515[43]	5.1	5.2	C	2 545[44]	5.1	73.4	80.4	1.170
2003	C	493 471[42]	10.2	C	245 817[43]	5.1	5.1	C	2 470[44]	5.0	73.9	80.8	1.190
2004	C	476 052[42]	9.8	C	245 771[43]	5.1	4.7	C	2 209[44]	4.6	74.5	81.4	1.160
2005	C	438 062[42]	9.0	C	245 511[43]	5.0	4.0	C	1 822[44]	4.2	75.1	81.9	1.080
2006	C	451 514[42]	9.2	C	243 934[43]	5.0	4.2	C	1 709[44]	3.8	75.7	82.4	1.130
Kuwait - Koweït													
2002	C	43 490	19.2	C	4 342	1.9	17.3	C	418	9.6	...	...	4.146
2003	C	43 982	18.9	C	4 424	1.9	17.0	C	412	9.4	...	...	4.064
2004	C	47 274	19.8	C	4 793	2.0	17.8	C	422	8.9	...	...	4.101
2005	C	50 941	20.7	C	4 784	1.9	18.8	C	420	8.2	...	...	4.155
2006	C	52 759	...	C	5 247	...	...	C	456	8.6	...	...	...
Kyrgyzstan - Kirghizistan													
2002	C	101 012	20.2	C	35 235	7.1	13.2	C	2 128	21.1	64.4	72.1	2.465
2003	C	105 490	20.9	C	35 941	7.1	13.8	C	2 186	20.7	...	...	2.521
2004	C	109 939	21.6	C	35 061	6.9	14.7	C	2 812[45]	25.6	64.4	72.3	2.582
2005	C	109 839	21.4	C	36 992	7.2	14.2	C	3 258	29.7	64.2	71.9	2.531
2006	C	120 737	23.3	C	38 566	7.4	15.8	C	3 526	29.2	63.5	72.1	2.735
Lao People's Democratic Republic - République démocratique populaire lao[46]													
2005		...	...		...	...	...		...	...	55.0	63.0	4.500
Lebanon - Liban													
2002	C	76 405	...	C	17 294	...	...		...	...	...	...	...
2003	C	71 702	...	C	17 187	...	...		...	...	...	...	...
2004	C	73 900	19.7	C	17 774	4.7	14.9		...	...	...	...	...
2005	C	73 973	...	C	18 012	...	...		...	...	...	...	...
2006	C	72 790	...	C	18 787	...	...		...	...	...	...	...
Malaysia - Malaisie													
2002	C	484 037	19.7	C	105 982	4.3	15.4	C	3 126	6.5	70.7	75.3	2.552
2003	C	480 083	19.2	C	111 644	4.5	14.7	C	3 148	6.6	70.9	75.6	2.488
2004	C	477 768	18.7	C	112 700	4.4	14.3	C	3 105	6.5	71.7	76.1	2.438
2005	C*	466 208	17.8	C*	113 531	4.3	13.5	C*	3 105	6.7	70.6	76.4	2.340*
2006	C*	482 700	18.1	C*	117 400	4.4	13.7	C*	3 200	6.6	...	...	2.384*
Maldives													
2002	C	5 003	17.8	C	1 113	4.0	13.9	C	89	...	70.1	71.2	...
2003	C	5 157	18.1	C	1 030	3.6	14.5	C	72	...	70.4	71.3	...
2004	C	5 220	18.0	C	1 015	3.5	14.5	C	76	...	71.1	72.1	...
2005	C	5 543	18.9	C	1 027	3.5	15.4	C	67	...	71.7	72.7	...
2006	C	5 829	19.5	C	1 084	3.6	15.9	C	92	...	...	...	...
Mongolia - Mongolie													
2002	C	46 922	19.1	C	15 857	6.4	12.6	C	1 390	29.6	...	...	2.100
2003	C	45 723	18.4	C	16 006	6.4	11.9	C	1 051	23.0	...	...	2.000
2004	C	45 501	18.1	C	16 404	6.5	11.6	C	1 016	22.3	...	...	2.000
2005	C	45 326	17.8	C	16 480	6.5	11.3	C	938	20.7	...	...	1.948
2006	C	49 092	19.0	C	16 682	6.5	12.6	C	937	19.1	x62.6	69.4	2.067
Myanmar													
2002	U	753 989	...	U	214 680	...	...	U	37 693	...	...	...	...
2003	U	685 443	...	U	197 716	...	...	U	31 873	...	...	...	...

4. Vital statistics summary and expectation of life at birth: 2002 - 2006
Aperçu des statistiques de l'état civil et espérance de vie à la naissance: 2002 - 2006 (continued - suite)

Continent, country or area and year / Continent, pays ou zone et année	Code[a]	Live births - Naissances vivantes Number Nombre	Crude birth rate Taux brut de natalité	Code[a]	Deaths - Décès Number Nombre	Crude death rate Taux brut de mortalité	Rate of natural increase Taux d'accrois-sement naturel	Code[a]	Infant deaths - Décès d'enfants de moins d'un an Number Nombre	Rate (per 1000 births) Taux (par 1000 naiss-ances)	Expectation of life at birth - Espérance de vie à la naissance Male[b] Masculin[b]	Female[b] Féminin[b]	Total fertility rate L'indice synthétique de fécondité
ASIA - ASIE													
Myanmar													
2004	U	791 600	...	U	230 683	...	...	U	36 812	...	...	...	2.150[47]
2005	U	836 124	...	U	242 549	...	...	U	38 872	...	62.5[47]	66.6[47]	2.110[47]
Nepal - Népal													
2005		...			...	...	...		...	...	62.3	63.1	3.600
2006		...			...	...	...		...	...	62.9	63.7	3.500
Occupied Palestinian Territory - Territoire palestinien occupé													
2002	U	106 511	...	U	10 316	...	...	U	1 126	...	...	...	
2003	U	106 355	...	U	10 207	...	...	U	1 150	...	...	...	4.600
2004	U	111 245	...	U	10 029	...	...	U	1 103	...	...	...	
2005	U	109 439	...	U	9 645	...	...	U	1 057	...	...	...	4.600
2006	U	108 874	...	U	9 938	...	...	U	906	...	...	...	
Oman													
2002	U	40 222[48]	...	U	2 564[48]	...	...	U	332[48]	...	72.2	75.4	3.600
2003	U	40 062[48]	...	U	2 701[48]	...	...	U	335[48]	...	73.1	75.4	3.560
2004	U	40 584[48]	...	U	2 743[48]	...	...	U	336[48]	...	73.2	75.4	3.190
2005	U	42 065[48]	...	U	2 849[48]	...	...	U	315[48]	...	73.2	74.4	3.130
2006	U	44 116[48]	...	U	3 027[48]	...	...	U	381[48]	...	73.2	75.4	...
Pakistan[49]													
2003	I	3 683 290[50]	25.0	I	970 428[50]	6.6	18.4	I	280 729[50]	76.2	64.7[50]	65.6[50]	3.900[50]
2005	I	3 772 494[51]	24.6	I	1 019 467[51]	6.6	17.9	I	289 169[51]	76.7	...	...	3.800[51]
Philippines													
2002	C	1 666 773	21.0	C	396 297	5.0	16.0	C	23 778	14.3	...	...	2.500
2003	C	1 669 442	20.6	C	396 331	4.9	15.7	C	22 844	13.7	...	...	2.600
2004	C	1 710 994	20.7	C	403 191	4.9	15.8	C	22 557	13.2	...	...	...
Qatar													
2002	C	12 200	17.9	C	1 220	1.8	16.1	C	107	8.8	...	...	2.766
2003	C	12 856	17.9	C	1 311	1.8	16.1	C	137	10.7	...	...	2.864
2004	C	13 190	17.4	C	1 341	1.8	15.7	C	113	8.6	76.1	75.6	2.780
2005	C	13 401	16.8	C	1 545	1.9	14.9	C	110	8.2	[III]75.1	75.6	2.600
2006	C	14 120	15.1	C	1 750	1.9	13.2	C	114	8.1	76.7	76.7	2.710
Saudi Arabia - Arabie saoudite													
2002	...	560 746	...	...	88 728	...	...	...	11 432	...	...	...	...
2003	...	567 433	...	...	89 976	...	...	...	11 297	...	...	...	...
2004	...	574 211	...	...	91 243	...	...	...	11 165	...	...	...	3.320
2005	...	582 582	...	...	92 487	...	...	...	11 078	...	...	...	3.280
2006	...	589 223	...	...	93 752	...	...	...	10 954	...	...	...	3.220
Singapore - Singapour													
2002	C	40 760	9.8	+C	15 820	3.8	6.0	+C	123	3.0	76.6	80.7	1.370
2003	C	37 485	9.0	+C	16 036	3.8	5.1	+C	100	2.7	77.0	80.9	1.250
2004	C	37 174	8.8	+C	15 860	3.7	5.0	+C	82	...	77.4	81.3	1.240
2005	C	37 492	8.6	+C	16 215	3.7	4.9	+C	95	...	77.9	81.6	1.240
2006	C	38 317	8.5	+C	16 393	3.7	4.9	+C	117	3.1	...	...	1.260
Sri Lanka													
2002	+C*	363 549	19.1	+C*	110 637	5.8	13.3		...	...	...	...	...
2003	+C*	363 343	10.9	+C*	114 310	5.9	12.9		...	...	...	...	...
2004	+C*	360 220	18.5	+C*	112 568	5.8	12.7		...	...	...	...	...
2005	+C*	370 424	18.8	+C*	129 822	6.6	12.2		...	...	...	...	...
Syrian Arab Republic - République arabe syrienne[52]													
2002	U	574 918	...	U	62 184	...	...		...	...	...	...	...
2003	U	609 774	...	U	62 880	...	...		...	...	...	...	...
2004	U	598 221	...	U	62 496	...	...		...	...	...	...	...
2005	U	634 170	...	U	73 035	...	...		...	...	...	...	...
2006	U	656 599	...	U	72 534	...	...		...	...	...	...	...

4. Vital statistics summary and expectation of life at birth: 2002 - 2006
Aperçu des statistiques de l'état civil et espérance de vie à la naissance: 2002 - 2006 (continued - suite)

Continent, country or area and year / Continent, pays ou zone et année	Live births Naissances vivantes			Deaths Décès			Rate of natural increase Taux d'accroissement naturel	Infant deaths Décès d'enfants de moins d'un an			Expectation of life at birth Espérance de vie à la naissance		Total fertility rate L'indice synthétique de fécondité
	Code[a]	Number Nombre	Crude birth rate Taux brut de natalité	Code[a]	Number Nombre	Crude death rate Taux brut de mortalité		Code[a]	Number Nombre	Rate (per 1000 births) Taux (par 1000 naissances)	Male[b] Masculin[b]	Female[b] Féminin[b]	
ASIA - ASIE													
Tajikistan - Tadjikistan[21]													
2002	I	175 599[53]	27.3	C	31 142	4.8	22.4		...	...	...	...	...
2003	I	177 938[53]	27.1	C	33 185	5.0	22.0		...	...	...	...	...
2004	I	179 600[53]	26.8	C	29 700	4.4	22.3		...	...	...	...	...
2005	I	180 800[53]	26.4	C	31 500	4.6	21.8		...	...	...	...	...
2006	I	186 500[53]	26.7	C	32 000	4.6	22.1		...	...	...	...	...
Thailand - Thaïlande													
2002	+U	782 911	...	+U	380 364	...	...	+U	5 105	...	...	...	...
2003	+U	742 183	...	+U	384 131	...	...	+U	5 349	...	...	...	...
2004	+U	813 069	...	+U	393 592	...	...	+U	6 061	...	...	...	...
2005	+U	809 485	...	+U	395 374	...	...	+U	6 183	...	...	...	...
Turkey - Turquie													
2002	I	1 362 000[54]	19.7	I	429 000[54]	6.2	13.5	I	36 365[54]	26.7	...	...	2.240
2003	I	1 361 000[54]	19.4	I	436 000[54]	6.2	13.2	I	34 842[54]	25.6	...	...	2.220
2004	I	1 360 000[54]	19.1	I	443 000[54]	6.2	12.9	I	33 456[54]	24.6	68.8[54]	73.6[54]	2.210
2005	I	1 361 000[54]	18.9	I	450 000[54]	6.2	12.6	I	32 120[54]	23.6	...	...	2.190
2006	I	1 362 000[54]	18.7	I	456 000[54]	6.2	12.4	I	30 781[54]	22.6	69.1	74.0	2.180
United Arab Emirates - Émirats arabes unis													
2002	...	58 070	...	...	5 994	...	...	...	...	...	...	...	...
2003	...	61 165	...	...	6 002	...	...	...	477	...	...	...	...
2004	...	63 113	...	...	6 123	...	...		...	...	...	...	...
2005	...	64 623	...	...	6 361	...	...		...	...	...	...	...
2006	...	62 969	...	...	6 563	...	...		...	...	...	...	...
Yemen - Yémen													
2002	U	189 341	...	U	21 157	...	...		...	...	...	...	...
2003	U	130 112	...	U	20 346	...	...		...	...	...	...	6.200
2004	U	153 945	...	U	22 255	...	...		...	...	60.2	62.0	6.100
2005	U	152 792	...	U	19 653	...	...		...	...	...	...	...
2006		...	...	U	20 607	...	...		...	...	...	...	...
EUROPE													
Åland Islands - Îles d'Åland[55]													
2002	C	269	10.3	C	236	9.0	1.3	C	1	...	79.2	84.4	...
2003	C	262	10.0	C	268	10.2	-0.2	C	2	...	77.3	84.1	...
2004	C	281	10.6	C	262	9.9	0.7	C	1	...	76.1	84.0	...
2005	C	268	10.1	C	259	9.7	0.3	C	-	...	78.8	81.1	1.717
2006	C	295	11.0	C	257	9.6	1.4	C	-	...	...	...	1.867
Albania - Albanie													
2002	C	45 515	14.7	C	16 248	5.3	9.5	C	466	10.2	...	...	1.946
2003	C	47 012	15.1	C	17 967	5.8	9.3	C	395	8.4	...	...	1.980
2004	C	43 022	13.8	C	17 749	5.7	8.1	C	336	7.8	...	...	1.800
2005	C	39 612	12.6	C	17 427	5.5	7.1	C	303	7.6	...	...	1.600
2006	C	34 229	10.9	C	16 935	5.4	5.5	C	253	7.4	...	...	1.400
Andorra - Andorre													
2002	C	749	10.7	C	218	3.1	7.9	C	-	...	...	...	1.370
2003	C	721	9.7	C	221	3.0	6.9	C	-	...	...	...	1.190
2004	C	814	10.5	C	281	3.6	6.9	C	2	...	...	...	1.210
2005	C	828	10.4	C	276	3.5	7.0	C	5	...	...	...	1.231
2006	C	843	10.3	C	260	3.2	7.2	C	3	...	...	...	1.226
Austria - Autriche													
2002	C	78 399	9.7	C	76 131	9.4	0.3	C	318	4.1	75.8	81.7	1.393
2003	C	76 944	9.5	C	77 209	9.5	0.0	C	343	4.5	75.9	81.6	1.378
2004	C	78 968	9.7	C	74 292	9.1	0.6	C	353	4.5	76.4	82.1	1.419
2005	C	78 190	9.5	C	75 189	9.1	0.4	C	327	4.2	75.5	81.5	1.407
2006	C	77 914	9.4	C	74 295	9.0	0.4	C	281	3.6	75.5	81.5	1.405

Continent, country or area and year / Continent, pays ou zone et année	Live births Naissances vivantes			Deaths Décès			Rate of natural increase Taux d'accroissement naturel	Infant deaths Décès d'enfants de moins d'un an			Expectation of life at birth Espérance de vie à la naissance		Total fertility rate L'indice synthétique de fécondité
	Code[a]	Number Nombre	Crude birth rate Taux brut de natalité	Code[a]	Number Nombre	Crude death rate Taux brut de mortalité		Code[a]	Number Nombre	Rate (per 1000 births) Taux (par 1000 naissances)	Male[b] Masculin[b]	Female[b] Féminin[b]	
EUROPE													
Belarus - Bélarus													
2002	C	88 743[21]	8.9	C	146 655[21]	14.8	-5.8	C	695[21]	7.8	62.3	74.1	1.222
2003	C	88 512[21]	9.0	C	143 200[21]	14.5	-5.5	C	685[21]	7.7	62.7	74.7	1.206
2004	C	88 943[21]	9.1	C	140 064[21]	14.3	-5.2	C	614[21]	6.9	63.2	75.0	1.201
2005	C	90 508[21]	9.3	C	141 857[21]	14.5	-5.3	C	640[21]	7.1	...	...	1.210
2006	C	96 721[21]	9.9	C	138 426[21]	14.2	-4.3	C	587[21]	6.1	63.6	75.5	1.287
Belgium - Belgique													
2002	C	111 225[56]	10.8	C	105 642[56]	10.2	0.5	C	551	5.0	...	...	
2003	C	112 591[56]	10.9	C	107 628[56]	10.4	0.5	C	538	4.8	...	...	
2004	C	116 048[56]	11.1	C	101 929[56]	9.8	1.4	C	549	4.7	76.5	82.4	
2005	C	117 799[56]	11.2	C	102 963[56]	9.8	1.4	C	515	4.4	...	...	
2006	C	121 382[56]	11.5	C	101 587[56]	9.6	1.9		...	...	...	...	
Bosnia and Herzegovina - Bosnie-Herzégovine													
2002	C	35 587	9.3	C	30 155	7.9	1.4	C	334	9.4	71.3	76.7	1.230
2003	C	35 234	0.2	C	31 757	8.3	0.9	C	268	7.6	71.3	76.7	1.215
2004	C	35 151	9.1	C	32 616	8.5	0.7	C	253	7.2	...	...	1.217
2005	C	34 627	9.0	C	34 402	9.0	0.1	C	233	6.7	...	...	1.214
2006	C	34 033	8.9	C	33 221	8.6	0.2	C	255	7.5	...	...	...
Bulgaria - Bulgarie													
2002	C	66 499	8.5	C	112 617	14.3	-5.9	C	887	13.3	68.5	75.4	1.212
2003	C	67 359	8.6	C	111 927	14.3	-5.7	C	831	12.3	[III]68.7	75.6	1.232
2004	C	69 886	9.0	C	110 110	14.2	-5.2	C	814	11.6	[III]69.1	76.2	1.285
2005	C	71 075	9.2	C	113 374	14.6	-5.5	C	739	10.4	[III]69.0	76.3	1.310
2006	C	73 978	9.6	C	113 438	14.7	-5.1	C	720	9.7	[III]69.1	76.3	1.377
Channel Islands: Guernsey - Îles Anglo-Normandes: Guernesey													
2002	C	549	...	C	561	...	...		...	...	...	...	...
2003	C	650	...	C	564	...	...		...	...	...	...	...
2004	C	586	9.7	C	537	8.9	0.8		...	...	...	...	...
2005	C	638	...	C	525	...	...		...	...	...	...	...
2006	C	598	9.8	C	498	8.2	1.6		...	...	...	...	...
Channel Islands: Jersey - Îles Anglo-Normandes: Jersey													
2002	+C	930	10.6	+C	841	9.6	1.0		...	...	...	...	
2003	+C	1 005	11.5	+C	760	8.7	2.8		...	...	...	...	
2004	+C	971	11.1	+C	748	8.5	2.5		...	...	...	...	
2005	+C	969	11.0	+C	752	8.5	2.5		...	...	...	...	
2006	+C	950	10.7	+C	759	8.5	2.1		...	...	...	...	
Croatia - Croatie													
2002	C	40 094	9.0	C	50 569	11.4	-2.4	C	282	7.0	...	...	1.340
2003	C	39 668	8.9	C	52 575	11.8	-2.9	C	251	6.3	...	...	1.327
2004	C	40 307	9.1	C	49 756	11.2	-2.1	C	245	6.1	...	...	1.346
2005	C	42 492	9.6	C	51 790	11.7	-2.1	C	242	5.7	...	...	1.420
2006	C	41 446	9.3	C	50 378	11.3	-2.0	C	215	5.2	...	...	1.381
Czech Republic - République tchèque													
2002	C	97 878	9.6	C	108 243	10.6	-1.0	C	385	3.9	72.1	78.5	1.171
2003	C	93 685	9.2	C	111 288	10.9	-1.7	C	365	3.9	72.0	78.5	1.179
2004	C	97 664	9.6	C	107 177	10.5	-0.9	C	366	3.7	72.5	79.0	1.226
2005	C	102 211	10.0	C	107 938	10.5	-0.6	C	347	3.4	72.9	79.1	1.282
2006	C	105 831	10.3	C	104 441	10.2	0.1	C	352	3.3	73.4	79.7	1.328
Denmark - Danemark[57]													
2002	C	64 075	11.9	C	58 610	10.9	1.0	C	284	4.4	74.8	79.4	1.723
2003	C	64 599	12.0	C	57 574	10.7	1.3	C	286	4.4	[II]74.9	79.5	1.758
2004	C	64 609	12.0	C	55 806	10.3	1.6	C	283	4.4	[II]75.2	79.9	1.784
2005	C	64 282	11.9	C	54 962	10.1	1.7	C	280	4.4	[II]75.6	80.2	1.799
2006	C	64 984	12.0	C	55 477	10.2	1.7	C	250	3.8	[II]75.9	80.4	1.850

4. Vital statistics summary and expectation of life at birth: 2002 - 2006
Aperçu des statistiques de l'état civil et espérance de vie à la naissance: 2002 - 2006 (continued - suite)

Continent, country or area and year / Continent, pays ou zone et année	Code[a]	Live births / Naissances vivantes Number Nombre	Crude birth rate Taux brut de natalité	Code[a]	Deaths / Décès Number Nombre	Crude death rate Taux brut de mortalité	Rate of natural increase Taux d'accrois-sement naturel	Code[a]	Infant deaths / Décès d'enfants de moins d'un an Number Nombre	Rate (per 1000 births) Taux (par 1000 naiss-ances)	Expectation of life at birth / Espérance de vie à la naissance Male[b] Masculin[b]	Female[b] Féminin[b]	Total fertility rate L'indice synthétique de fécondité
EUROPE													
Estonia - Estonie													
2002	C	13 001	9.6	C	18 355	13.5	-3.9	C	74	...	64.8	76.3	1.372
2003	C	13 036	9.6	C	18 152	13.4	-3.8	C	91	...	66.1	77.1	1.371
2004	C	13 992	10.4	C	17 685	13.1	-2.7	C	90	...	66.4	77.8	1.465
2005	C	14 350	10.7	C	17 316	12.9	-2.2	C	78	...	67.2	78.1	1.497
2006	C	14 877	11.1	C	17 316	12.9	-1.8	C	66	...	...	...	1.545
Faeroe Islands - Îles Féroé													
2002	C	709	15.0	C	392	8.3	6.7		...	...	...	...	...
2003	C	705	14.7	C	404	8.4	6.3		...	...	...	...	...
2004	C	713	14.8	C	379	7.9	6.9		...	...	...	...	...
2005	C	712	14.8	C	419	8.7	6.1		...	...	...	...	...
2006	C	661	13.7	C	416	8.6	5.1		...	...	...	...	...
Finland - Finlande[58]													
2002	C	55 555[59]	10.7	C	49 418[59]	9.5	1.2	C	168[59]	3.0	74.9	81.5	1.718
2003	C	56 630[59]	10.9	C	48 996[59]	9.4	1.5	C	176[59]	3.1	75.1	81.8	1.760
2004	C	57 758[59]	11.0	C	47 600[59]	9.1	1.9	C	191[59]	3.3	75.3	82.3	1.800
2005	C	57 745[59]	11.0	C	47 928[59]	9.1	1.9	C	174[59]	3.0	75.5	82.3	1.803
2006	C	58 840[59]	11.2	C	48 065[59]	9.1	2.0	C	167[59]	2.8	75.8	82.8	1.837
France[60]													
2002	C	761 630[61]	12.7	C	535 144[61]	8.9	3.8	C	3 114[61]	4.1	75.8	83.0	1.868
2003	C	761 464[61]	12.6	C	552 339[61]	9.2	3.5	C	3 053[61]	4.0	75.9	82.9	1.875
2004	C	767 816[61]	12.7	C	509 429[61]	8.4	4.3	C	2 988[61]	3.9	76.7	83.8	1.897
2005	C	774 355[61]	12.7	C	527 533[61]	8.6	4.0	C	2 775[61]	3.6	76.8	83.8	1.921
2006	C	796 896[61]	13.0	C*	520 300[61]	8.5	4.5		...	...	...	...	1.983
Germany - Allemagne													
2002	C	719 250	8.7	C	841 686	10.2	-1.5	C	3 036	4.2	75.7	81.3	1.341
2003	C	706 721	8.6	C	853 946	10.3	-1.8	C	2 990	4.2	75.8	81.3	1.340
2004	C	705 622	8.6	C	818 271	9.9	-1.4	C	2 918	4.1	III75.9	81.5	1.355
2005	C	685 795	8.3	C	830 227	10.1	-1.8	C	2 696	3.9	III76.2	81.8	1.340
2006	C	672 724	8.2	C	821 627	10.0	-1.8	C	2 579	3.8	III76.6	82.1	1.331
Gibraltar													
2002	+C	371[62]	13.0	C	242[62]	8.5	4.5		...	...	...	...	...
2003	+C	372[62]	13.0	C	234[62]	8.2	4.8	C	2	...	...	...	...
2004	+C	421[62]	14.7	C	242[62]	8.4	6.2		...	...	...	...	...
2005	+C	418[62]	14.5	C	249[62]	8.6	5.9	C	1	...	...	...	...
2006	+C	373[62]	12.8	C	230[62]	7.9	5.0	C	1	...	...	...	...
Greece - Grèce													
2002	C	103 838	9.5	C	103 915	9.5	0.0	C	600	5.8	76.2	81.1	1.270
2003	C	104 420	9.5	C	105 529	9.6	-0.1	C	420	4.0	76.5	81.3	1.288
2004	C	105 655	9.6	C	104 942	9.5	0.1	C	429	4.1	76.6	81.3	1.300
2005	C	107 545	9.7	C	105 091	9.5	0.2	C	409	3.8	76.8	81.7	1.338
2006	C	112 042	10.0	C	105 476	9.5	0.6	C	415	3.7	77.1	82.0	1.410
Hungary - Hongrie													
2002	C	96 804	9.5	C	132 833	13.1	-3.5	C	693	7.2	68.3	76.6	1.305
2003	C	94 647	9.3	C	135 823	13.4	-4.1	C	690	7.3	68.3	76.5	1.276
2004	C	95 137	9.4	C	132 492	13.1	-3.7	C	628	6.6	68.6	76.9	1.285[63]
2005	C	97 496	9.7	C	135 732	13.5	-3.8	C	607	6.2	68.6	76.9	1.317[63]
2006	C	99 871	9.9	C	131 603	13.1	-3.2	C	571	5.7	69.0	77.4	1.350[63]
Iceland - Islande													
2002	C	4 049	14.1	C	1 821	6.3	7.7	C	9	...	78.6	82.5	1.932
2003	C	4 143	14.3	C	1 827	6.3	8.0	C	10	...	II79.0	82.4	1.990
2004	C	4 234	14.5	C	1 824	6.2	8.2	C	12	...	78.9	83.2	2.033
2005	C	4 280	14.5	C	1 838	6.2	8.3	C	10	...	II79.2	83.3	2.052
2006	C	4 415	14.5	C	1 903	6.3	8.3	C	6	...	II79.4	83.0	2.074
Ireland - Irlande													
2002	C	60 503	15.4	C	29 683[64]	7.6	7.9	C	305	5.0	75.1	80.3	1.978
2003	C	61 529	15.5	C	29 074[64]	7.3	8.2	C	326	5.3	...	...	1.980
2004	C	61 972	15.3	C	28 665[64]	7.1	8.2	C	287	4.6	...	...	1.950

4. Vital statistics summary and expectation of life at birth: 2002 - 2006
Aperçu des statistiques de l'état civil et espérance de vie à la naissance: 2002 - 2006 (continued - suite)

Continent, country or area and year / Continent, pays ou zone et année	Co-de[a]	Live births Naissances vivantes Number Nombre	Crude birth rate Taux brut de natalité	Co-de[a]	Deaths Décès Number Nombre	Crude death rate Taux brut de mortalité	Rate of natural increase Taux d'accrois-sement naturel	Co-de[a]	Infant deaths Décès d'enfants de moins d'un an Number Nombre	Rate (per 1000 births) Taux (par 1000 naiss-ances)	Expectation of life at birth Espérance de vie à la naissance Male[b] Masculin[b]	Female[b] Féminin[b]	Total fertility rate L'indice synthétique de fécondité
EUROPE													
Ireland - Irlande													
2005	+C*	61 042[64]	14.8	+C*	27 441[64]	6.6	8.1	+C*	244[64]	4.0	...	...	1.882
2006	+C*	64 237[64]	15.2	+C*	27 479[64]	6.5	8.7	+C*	237[64]	3.7	...	...	1.905
Isle of Man - Îles de Man													
2002	+C	903	11.7	+C	877	11.4	0.3	+C	3	...	...	...	...
2003	+C	860	11.1	+C	852	11.0	0.1	+C	6	...	...	...	...
2004	+C	862	11.1	+C	798	10.3	0.8	+C	2	...	...	...	...
2005	+C	901	11.6	+C	775	9.9	1.6			...	...	...	...
2006	+C	905	11.3	+C	768	9.6	1.7		...	...	...	...	...
Italy - Italie													
2002	C	538 198	9.4	C	557 393	9.8	-0.3	C	2 197	4.1	77.1	83.0	1.270
2003	C	544 063	9.4	C	586 468	10.2	-0.7	C	2 033	3.7	77.2	82.8	1.285
2004	C	562 599	9.7	C	545 051	9.4	0.3	C	2 609	4.6	77.9	83.7	1.334
2005	C	554 022	9.5	C	567 304	9.7	-0.2	C	2 555	4.6	...	...	1.319
2006	C	560 010	9.5	C	557 892	0.5	0.0	C	2 379	4.2	...	...	1.352
Latvia - Lettonie													
2002	C	20 044	8.6	C	32 498	13.9	-5.3	C	197	9.8	65.4	76.8	1.232
2003	C	21 006	9.0	C	32 437	13.9	-4.9	C	198	9.4	65.9	76.9	1.290
2004	C	20 334	8.8	C	32 024	13.8	-5.1	C	191	9.4	67.1	77.2	1.240
2005	C	21 497	9.3	C	32 777	14.2	-4.9	C	168	7.8	65.6	77.4	1.309
2006	C	22 264	9.7	C	33 098	14.5	-4.7	C	170	7.6	65.9	76.8	1.353
Liechtenstein													
2002	C	395	11.7	C	215	6.4	5.3	C	1	...	...	...	1.492
2003	C	347	10.2	C	217	6.4	3.8	C	1	...	...	...	1.357
2004	C	372	10.8	C	198	5.7	5.0	C	1	...	...	...	1.458
2005	C	381	11.0	C	215	6.2	4.8	C	1	...	...	...	1.510
2006	C*	361	10.3	C*	220	6.3	4.0	C*	2	...	...	...	1.400
Lithuania - Lituanie													
2002	C	30 014	8.7	C	41 072	11.8	-3.2	C	238[21]	7.9	66.2	77.6	1.236
2003	C	30 598	8.9	C	40 990	11.9	-3.0	C	206[21]	6.7	66.5	77.8	1.262
2004	C	30 419	8.9	C	41 340	12.0	-3.2	C	240[21]	7.9	66.4	77.7	1.260
2005	C	30 541	8.9	C	43 799	12.8	-3.9	C	209[21]	6.8	65.4	77.4	1.272
2006	C	31 265	9.2	C	44 813	13.2	-4.0	C	213[21]	6.8	65.3	77.1	1.306
Luxembourg													
2002	C	5 345	12.0	C	3 744	8.4	3.6	C	27	...	III74.8	81.0	1.625
2003	C	5 303	11.7	C	4 053	9.0	2.8	C	26	...	...	...	1.634
2004	C	5 452	11.9	C	3 578	7.8	4.1	C	21	...	...	...	1.656
2005	C	5 371	11.5	C	3 621	7.8	3.8	C	14	...	...	...	1.624
2006	C	5 514	11.7	C	3 766	8.0	3.8	C	14	...	...	...	1.644
Malta - Malte													
2002	C	3 918	10.1	C	3 031	7.8	2.3	C	23	...	75.8	80.5	1.460
2003	C	4 050	10.2	C	3 164	7.9	2.2	C	23	...	76.4	80.4	1.480
2004	C	3 887	9.7	C	2 999	7.5	2.2	C	23	...	76.7	80.5	1.370
2005	C	3 858	9.6	C	3 130	7.8	1.8	C	23	...	77.7	81.4	1.370
2006	C	3 885	9.6	C	3 216	7.9	1.6	C	14	...	76.8	81.2	1.410
Moldova													
2002	C	35 705[65]	9.9	C	41 852[65]	11.6	-1.7	C	528[65]	14.8	64.4	71.7	1.211
2003	C	36 471[65]	10.1	C	43 079[65]	11.9	-1.8	C	522[65]	14.3	64.5	71.6	1.219
2004	C	38 272[65]	10.6	C	41 668[65]	11.6	-0.9	C	464[65]	12.1	64.5	72.2	1.257
2005	C	37 695[65]	10.5	C	44 689[65]	12.4	-1.9	C	468[65]	12.4	...	...	1.219
2006	C	37 587[65]	10.5	C	43 137[65]	12.0	-1.5	C	442[65]	11.8	64.6	72.2	1.229
Monaco													
2002	C	771	...	C	564	...	...		...	...	...	...	...
2003	C	842	...	C	617	...	...		...	...	...	...	...
2004	C	825	...	C	525	...	...		...	...	...	...	...
2005	C	894	...	C	601	...	...		...	...	...	...	...
2006	C	880[66]	...	C	535[66]	...	...		...	...	...	...	...
Montenegro													
2002	C	8 499	13.8	C	5 513	8.9	4.8	C	92	...	...	...	...
2003	C	8 342	13.4	C	5 704	9.2	4.3	C	92	...	...	...	1.830

87

4. Vital statistics summary and expectation of life at birth: 2002 - 2006
Aperçu des statistiques de l'état civil et espérance de vie à la naissance: 2002 - 2006 (continued - suite)

Continent, country or area and year / Continent, pays ou zone et année	Live births / Naissances vivantes Code[a]	Live births / Naissances vivantes Number Nombre	Live births / Naissances vivantes Crude birth rate Taux brut de natalité	Deaths / Décès Code[a]	Deaths / Décès Number Nombre	Deaths / Décès Crude death rate Taux brut de mortalité	Rate of natural increase Taux d'accrois-sement naturel	Infant deaths / Décès d'enfants de moins d'un an Code[a]	Infant deaths / Décès d'enfants de moins d'un an Number Nombre	Infant deaths / Décès d'enfants de moins d'un an Rate (per 1000 births) Taux (par 1000 naiss-ances)	Expectation of life at birth Espérance de vie à la naissance Male[b] Masculin[b]	Expectation of life at birth Espérance de vie à la naissance Female[b] Féminin[b]	Total fertility rate L'indice synthétique de fécondité
EUROPE													
Montenegro													
2004	C	7 848	12.6	C	5 707	9.2	3.4	C	61	...	...	...	1.710
2005	C	7 352	11.8	C	5 839	9.4	2.4	C	70	...	...	...	1.600
2006	C	7 531	...	C	5 968	...	...	C	83	...	...	...	...
Netherlands - Pays-Bas													
2002	C	202 083[67]	12.5	C	142 355[67]	8.8	3.7	C	1 014[67]	5.0	76.0	80.7	1.731
2003	C	200 297[67]	12.3	C	141 936[67]	8.7	3.6	C	962[67]	4.8	76.2	80.9	1.747
2004	C	194 007[67]	11.9	C	136 553[67]	8.4	3.5	C	852[67]	4.4	76.9	81.4	1.726
2005	C	187 910[67]	11.5	C	136 402[67]	8.4	3.2	C	928[67]	4.9	77.2	81.6	1.708
2006	C	185 057[67]	11.3	C	135 372[67]	8.3	3.0	C	820[67]	4.4	77.4	81.7	1.720
Norway - Norvège[68]													
2002	C	55 434	12.2	C	44 465[69]	9.8	2.4	C	192[69]	3.5	76.5	81.5	1.754
2003	C	56 458	12.4	C	42 478[69]	9.3	3.1	C	190[69]	3.4	77.0	81.9	1.797
2004	C	56 951	12.4	C	41 200[69]	9.0	3.4	C	185[69]	3.2	77.5	82.3	1.828
2005	C	56 756	12.3	C	41 232[69]	8.9	3.4	C	175[69]	3.1	77.7	82.5	1.836
2006	C	58 545	12.6	C	41 253[69]	8.9	3.7	C	185[69]	3.2	78.1	82.7	1.904
Poland - Pologne													
2002	C	353 765	9.3	C	359 486	9.4	-0.1	C	2 662	7.5	70.4	78.8	1.249
2003	C	351 072	9.2	C	365 230	9.6	-0.4	C	2 470	7.0	70.5	78.9	1.222
2004	C	356 131	9.3	C	363 522	9.5	-0.2	C	2 423	6.8	70.7	79.2	1.227
2005	C	364 383	9.5	C	368 285	9.7	-0.1	C	2 340	6.4	70.8	79.4	1.243
2006	C	374 244	9.8	C	369 686	9.7	0.1	C	2 238	6.0	70.4	79.0	1.267
Portugal													
2002	C	114 383[70]	11.0	C	106 258[71]	10.2	0.8	C	574[71]	5.0	II73.4	80.4	1.473
2003	C	112 515[70]	10.8	C	108 795[71]	10.4	0.4	C	466[71]	4.1	II73.7	80.6	1.444
2004	C	109 298[70]	10.4	C	102 010[71]	9.7	0.7	C	418[71]	3.8	II74.5	81.0	1.403
2005	C	109 399[70]	10.4	C	107 462[71]	10.2	0.2	C	382[71]	3.5	II74.9	81.4	1.408
2006	C	105 449[70]	10.0	C*	101 990[71]	9.6	0.3	C*	349[71]	3.3	II75.2	81.8	1.362
Romania - Roumanie													
2002	C	210 529	9.7	C	269 666	12.4	-2.7	C	3 648	17.3	67.6	74.9	1.254
2003	C	212 459	9.8	C	266 575	12.3	-2.5	C	3 546	16.7	67.4	74.8	1.270
2004	C	216 261	10.0	C	258 890	11.9	-2.0	C	3 641	16.8	...	...	1.291
2005	C	221 020	10.2	C	262 101	12.1	-1.9	C	3 310	15.0	68.2	75.5	1.319
2006	C	219 483	10.2	C	258 094	12.0	-1.8	C	3 052	13.9	III68.7	75.8	1.313
Russian Federation - Fédération de Russie													
2002	C	1 396 967[21]	9.6	C	2 332 272[21]	16.1	-6.4	C	18 407[21]	13.2	58.7	71.9	1.322
2003	C	1 477 301[21]	10.2	C	2 365 826[21]	16.4	-6.1	C	18 142[21]	12.3	58.6	71.8	1.319
2004	C	1 502 477[21]	10.4	C	2 295 402[21]	16.0	-5.5	C	17 339[21]	11.5	58.9	72.3	1.340
2005	C	1 457 376[21]	10.2	C	2 303 935[21]	16.1	-5.9	C	16 073[21]	11.0	58.9	72.4	1.287
2006	C	1 479 637[21]	10.4	C	2 166 703[21]	15.2	-4.8	C	15 079[21]	10.2	60.4	73.2	1.296
San Marino - Saint-Marin													
2002	+C	295	10.4	+C	203	7.1	3.2	+C	2	...	...	...	1.206
2003	+C	300	10.3	+C	216	7.5	2.8	+C	2	...	...	...	1.250
2004	+C	306	10.4	+C	185	6.3	4.0	+C	1	...	...	...	1.255
2005	+C	284	9.2	+C	219	7.1	2.1	+C	-	...	...	...	...
2006	+C	302	9.6	+C	225	7.2	2.5	+C	-	...	...	...	...
Serbia - Serbie													
2002	+C	78 101[72]	10.4	+C	102 785[72]	13.7	-3.3	+C	790[72]	10.1	...	...	1.591
2003	+C	79 025[72]	10.6	+C	103 946[72]	13.9	-3.3	+C	711[72]	9.0	III69.6	75.0	1.575
2004	+C	78 186[72]	10.5	+C	104 320[72]	14.0	-3.5	+C	633[72]	8.1	...	...	1.453
2005	+C	72 180[72]	9.7	+C	106 771[72]	14.3	-4.6	+C	579[72]	8.0	69.9	75.4	1.453
2006	+C	70 997[72]	9.6	+C	102 884[72]	13.9	-4.3	+C	525[72]	7.4	70.6	75.9	1.432
Slovakia - Slovaquie													
2002	C	50 841	9.5	C	51 532	9.6	-0.1	C	388	7.6	69.9	77.6	1.190
2003	C	51 713	9.6	C	52 230	9.7	-0.1	C	406	7.9	69.8	77.6	1.199
2004	C	53 747	10.0	C	51 852	9.6	0.4	C	365	6.8	70.3	77.8	1.241
2005	C	54 430	10.1	C	53 475	9.9	0.2	C	392	7.2	70.1	77.9	1.253
2006	C	53 904	10.0	C	53 301	9.9	0.1	C	355	6.6	70.4	78.2	1.239

4. Vital statistics summary and expectation of life at birth: 2002 - 2006
Aperçu des statistiques de l'état civil et espérance de vie à la naissance: 2002 - 2006 (continued - suite)

Continent, country or area and year / Continent, pays ou zone et année	Live births / Naissances vivantes			Deaths / Décès			Rate of natural increase / Taux d'accrois-sement naturel	Infant deaths / Décès d'enfants de moins d'un an			Expectation of life at birth / Espérance de vie à la naissance		Total fertility rate / L'indice synthétique de fécondité
	Code[a]	Number Nombre	Crude birth rate Taux brut de natalité	Code[a]	Number Nombre	Crude death rate Taux brut de mortalité		Code[a]	Number Nombre	Rate (per 1000 births) Taux (par 1000 naiss-ances)	Male[b] Masculin[b]	Female[b] Féminin[b]	
EUROPE													
Slovenia - Slovénie													
2002	C	17 501	8.8	C	18 701	9.4	-0.6	C	67	...	73.2	80.7	1.212
2003	C	17 321	8.7	C	19 451	9.7	-1.1	C	69	...	72.5	80.3	1.202
2004	C	17 961	9.0	C	18 523	9.3	-0.3	C	66	...	II73.5	81.1	1.247
2005	C	18 157	9.1	C	18 825	9.4	-0.3	C	75	...	II74.1	81.3	1.262
2006	C	18 932	9.4	C	18 180	9.1	0.4	C	64	...	II74.8	81.9	1.314
Spain - Espagne													
2002	C	418 846	10.1	C	368 618	8.9	1.2	C	1 737	4.1	II76.3	83.0	1.263
2003	C	441 881	10.5	C	384 828	9.2	1.4	C	1 733	3.9	...	...	1.310
2004	C	454 591	10.6	C	371 934	8.7	1.9	C	1 813	4.0	II76.7	83.2	1.329
2005	C	466 371	10.7	C	387 355	8.9	1.8	C	1 765	3.8	II77.0	83.5	1.346
2006	C	481 102	10.9	C	371 267	8.4	2.5	C	1 812	3.8	...	...	1.373
Sweden - Suède													
2002	C	95 815[73]	10.7	C	95 009	10.6	0.1	C	313	3.3	77.7	82.1	1.650
2003	C	99 157[70]	11.1	C	92 961	10.4	0.7	C	308	3.1	77.9	82.4	1.720
2004	C	100 928[73]	11.2	C	90 532	10.1	1.2	C	314	3.1	78.4	82.7	1.752
2005	C	101 346[73]	11.2	C	91 710	10.2	1.1	C	246	2.4	78.4	82.8	1.769
2006	C	105 913[73]	11.7	C	91 177	10.0	1.6	C	297	2.8	78.7	82.9	1.853
Switzerland - Suisse													
2002	C	72 372	9.9	C	61 768	9.6	1.0	O	326	4.5	77.6	83.0	1.390
2003	C	71 848	9.8	C	63 070	8.6	1.2	C	311	4.3	77.9	83.0	1.385
2004	C	73 082	9.9	C	60 180	8.1	1.7	C	309	4.2	78.2	83.3	1.416
2005	C	72 903	9.8	C	61 124	8.2	1.6	C	308	4.2	II78.6	83.7	1.420
2006	C	73 371	9.8	C	60 283	8.1	1.7	C	325	4.4	II78.9	83.9	1.437
The Former Yugoslav Rep. of Macedonia - L'ex-République yougoslave de Macédoine													
2002	C	27 761	13.7	C	17 962	8.8	4.8	C	283	10.2	70.8	75.7	...
2003	C	27 011	13.3	C	18 006	8.9	4.4	C	305	11.3	71.1	75.7	1.540
2004	C	23 361	11.5	C	17 944	8.8	2.7	C	308	13.2	71.4	75.9	1.520
2005	C	22 482	11.0	C	18 406	9.0	2.0	C	287	12.8	71.6	75.9	1.457
2006	C	22 585	11.1	C	18 630	9.1	1.9	C	260	11.5	...	...	1.460
Ukraine													
2002	C	390 688[21]	8.1	C	754 911	15.7	-7.6	C	4 023[21]	10.3	...	...	1.095
2003	C	408 589[21]	8.5	C	765 408	16.0	-7.5	C	3 882[21]	9.5	II62.6	74.1	1.147
2004	C	427 259[21]	9.0	C	761 261	16.1	-7.1	C	4 024[21]	9.4	II62.6	74.1	1.192[74]
2005	C	426 086[21]	9.1	C	781 961	16.6	-7.6	C	4 259[21]	10.0	...	...	1.211[74]
2006	C	460 368[75]	9.8	C	758 092[76]	16.2	-6.4	C	4 433[75]	9.6	II62.4	74.1	1.254[74]
United Kingdom - Royaume-Uni[77]													
2002	C	668 777[78]	11.3	C	606 283	10.2	1.1	C	3 499	5.2	...	...	1.640
2003	C	695 549[78]	11.7	C*	611 188	10.3	1.4	C*	3 686	5.3	...	...	1.710
2004	C*	715 996[79]	12.0	C*	584 600	9.8	2.2	C	3 606	5.0	...	...	1.780
2005	C*	722 600[79]	12.0	C*	582 900	9.7	2.3	C*	3 670	5.1	...	...	1.840
2006	C*	748 600	12.4	C*	572 200	9.4	2.9	C*	3 740	5.0	...	...	...
OCEANIA - OCÉANIE													
American Samoa - Samoas américaines													
2002	C	1 629	26.8	C	295	4.9	21.9	C	27	...	...	...	...
2003	C	1 608	25.7	C	257	4.1	21.6	C	20	...	...	...	...
2004	C	1 713	26.7	C	289	4.5	22.2	C	26	...	...	...	...
2005	C	1 720	26.3	C	279	4.3	22.0	C	12	...	...	...	...
2006	C	1 442	21.6	C	267	4.0	17.6	C	17	...	...	...	...

Continent, country or area and year / Continent, pays ou zone et année	Live births / Naissances vivantes			Deaths / Décès			Rate of natural increase / Taux d'accrois-sement naturel	Infant deaths / Décès d'enfants de moins d'un an			Expectation of life at birth / Espérance de vie à la naissance		Total fertility rate / L'indice synthétique de fécondité
	Code[a]	Number Nombre	Crude birth rate Taux brut de natalité	Code[a]	Number Nombre	Crude death rate Taux brut de mortalité		Code[a]	Number Nombre	Rate (per 1000 births) Taux (par 1000 naiss-ances)	Male[b] Masculin[b]	Female[b] Féminin[b]	

OCEANIA - OCÉANIE

Australia - Australie
2002	+C	250 988	12.8	+C	133 707	6.8	6.0	+C	1 264	5.0	III77.4	82.6	1.759
2003	+C	251 161	12.6	+C	132 292	6.6	6.0	+C	1 199	4.8	III77.8	82.8	1.754
2004	+C	254 246	12.6	+C	132 508	6.6	6.0	+C	1 184	4.7	III78.1	83.0	1.774
2005	+C	259 791	12.7	+C	130 714	6.4	6.3	+C	1 302	5.0	III78.5	83.3	1.806
2006	+C*	266 815	12.9	+C*	134 398	6.5	6.4	+C	1 262	4.7	...	...	...

Cook Islands - Îles Cook[80]
2002	+C	292	15.9	+C	97	5.3	10.6	+C	2	...	...	...	...
2003	+C	298	16.2	+C	87	4.7	11.5	+C	5	...	...	...	...
2004	+C	295	14.5	+C	99	4.9	9.7	+C	5	...	...	...	...
2005	+C	280	13.9	+C	91	4.5	9.4	+C	6	...	...	...	...
2006	+C*	278	13.4	+C*	85	4.1	9.3	+C*	3	...	...	...	...

Fiji - Fidji
2002	+C	16 987	20.9	+C	5 133	6.3	14.6	+C	320	18.8	...	...	2.500
2003	+C	17 701	21.7	+C	5 068	6.2	15.5	+C	304	17.2	...	...	2.600
2004	+C	17 189	20.9	+C	5 628	6.9	14.1	+C	338	19.7	...	...	...

French Polynesia - Polynésie française
2002	C	4 763	19.6	C	1 127	4.6	14.9	C	32	...	...	...	...
2003	C	4 501	18.2	C	1 122	4.5	13.7	C	31	...	...	...	...
2004	C	4 431	17.7	C	1 130	4.5	13.2	C	20	...	...	...	...
2005	C	4 469	17.6	C	1 265	5.0	12.6	C	28	...	...	...	...

Guam
2002	C	3 222[81]	20.0	C	658[81]	4.1	15.9	C	20[81]	...	76.0	80.6	3.110
2003	C	3 298[81]	19.8	C	700[81]	4.2	15.6	C	37[81]	...	74.8	81.0	2.700
2004	C	3 427[81]	20.6	C	691[81]	4.2	16.5	C	42[81]	...	75.1	81.3	...
2005	C*	3 187[81]	18.9	C*	697[81]	4.1	14.8		...	...	...	...	...

Marshall Islands - Îles Marshall
2002	+U	1 355	...		...	...	...		...	...	66.5	70.2	...
2003	+U	1 565	...	+U	306	...	...		...	...	66.8	70.4	...
2004	+U	1 512	...	+U	263	...	...		...	...	67.0	70.6	...
2005	+U	1 589	...	+U	302	...	...		...	...	...	...	...
2006	+U	1 576	...	+U	318	...	...		...	...	...	...	...

Micronesia, Federated States of - Micronésie, États Fédérés de La
| 2002 | U | 2 446 | ... | U | 539 | ... | ... | | ... | ... | ... | ... | ... |
| 2003 | U | 2 483 | ... | U | 427 | ... | ... | | ... | ... | ... | ... | ... |

Nauru
| 2002 | C | 219 | 21.8 | C | 75 | 7.5 | 14.3 | | ... | ... | VI52.5 | 58.2 | ... |

New Caledonia - Nouvelle-Calédonie
2002	C	4 194	18.9	C	1 121	5.1	13.9	C	29	...	...	...	...
2003	C	4 102	18.2	C	1 121	5.0	13.2	C	24	...	71.3	77.3	...
2004	C	4 006	17.4	C	1 100	4.8	12.6	C	25	...	...	...	...
2005	C	4 035	...	C	1 139	...	...		...	...	...	...	...
2006	C	4 224	...	C	1 115	...	...		...	...	...	...	...

New Zealand - Nouvelle-Zélande
2002	+C	54 021	13.7	+C	28 065[71]	7.1	6.6	+C	300[71]	5.6	III76.3	81.1	1.896
2003	+C	56 134	14.0	+C	28 010[71]	7.0	7.0	+C	277[71]	4.9	III76.7	81.2	1.952
2004	+C	58 073	14.3	+C	28 419[71]	7.0	7.3	+C	324[71]	5.6	III77.0	81.3	2.012
2005	+C	57 745	14.1	+C	27 034[71]	6.6	7.5	+C	295[71]	5.1	III77.5	81.7	2.003
2006	+C	59 193	14.1	+C	28 245[71]	6.7	7.4	+C	300[71]	5.1	III77.9	81.9	2.053

Niue - Nioué
2002	C	25[82]	...	C	13[83]	...	...	C	-	...	...	...	...
2003	C	33[82]	19.2	C	16[83]	...	...		...	...	...	...	...
2004	C	18[82]	...	C	18[83]	...	...		...	...	...	...	...

4. Vital statistics summary and expectation of life at birth: 2002 - 2006
Aperçu des statistiques de l'état civil et espérance de vie à la naissance: 2002 - 2006 (continued - suite)

Continent, country or area and year / Continent, pays ou zone et année	Live births - Naissances vivantes			Deaths - Décès			Rate of natural increase Taux d'accrois-sement naturel	Infant deaths - Décès d'enfants de moins d'un an			Expectation of life at birth Espérance de vie à la naissance		Total fertility rate L'indice synthétique de fécondité
	Code[a]	Number Nombre	Crude birth rate Taux brut de natalité	Code[a]	Number Nombre	Crude death rate Taux brut de mortalité		Code[a]	Number Nombre	Rate (per 1000 births) Taux (par 1000 naiss-ances)	Male[b] Masculin[b]	Female[b] Féminin[b]	
OCEANIA - OCÉANIE													
Northern Mariana Islands - Îles Mariannes septentrionales													
2002	U	*1 289*	...	U	*155*	...	...	U	*10*	...	...	...	...
2003	U	*1 355*	...	U	*144*	...	...			...	...	...	...
2004	U	*1 439*	...	U	*165*	...	...			...	...	...	...
2005	U	*1 335*	...	U	*189*	...	...			...	...	...	...
Palau - Palaos													
2002	C	259	13.0	C	134	6.7	6.3	C	6	...	...	...	...
2003	C	312	15.4	C	136	6.7	8.7	C	2	...	...	...	...
2004	C	259	12.6	C	142	6.9	5.7	C	7	...	...	...	...
2005	C	279	14.0	C	134	6.7	7.3	C	6	...	...	...	...
2006	C	259	12.0	C	144	6.6	5.3	C	2	...	...	...	...
Papua New Guinea - Papouasie-Nouvelle-Guinée													
2002	I	*187 645*	...	U	*7 573*	...	...	U	*2 230*	...	...	...	...
2003	U	*192 817*	...	U	*7 054*	...	...	U	*2 082*	...	...	...	...
Samoa													
2002	C*	2 826	15.8	U*	*355*	...	...			...	...	...	...
2003	C*	2 070	11.5	U*	*551*	...	...			...	...	...	...
2004	C*	1 679	9.2	U*	*547*	...	...			...	...	...	...
Tokelau - Tokélaou													
2002	...	*20*	...	...	...	...	...			...	...	...	...
Tonga													
2002	+C	2 662	26.4	+C	591	5.9	20.5	+C	26	...	...	...	...
2003	+C	2 781	27.4	+C	617	6.1	21.3	+C	34	...	...	...	3.900
2004	+C*	2 628	...	+C*	559	...	...	+C*	35	...	...	...	...
Tuvalu													
2002	U	*156*	...	U	*87*	...	...	U	*4*	...	[VI]61.7	65.1	3.700
2003	U	*185*	...	U	*83*	...	...	U	*4*	...	...	...	...
2004	U	*190*	...	U	*89*	...	...	U	*5*	...	...	...	...
2005	U	*231*	...	U	*64*	...	...	U	*6*	...	...	...	...
2006	U	*184*	...	U	*31*	...	...			...	...	...	...
Wallis and Futuna Islands - Îles Wallis et Futuna													
2002	C	262	...	C	67	...	...			...	...	...	...
2003	C	290	19.4	C	88	5.9	13.5			...	...	...	...
2004	C	241	...	C	72	...	...			...	...	...	...
2005	C	223	...	C	65	...	...			...	...	...	...
2006	C	220	...	C	77	...	...			...	...	...	...

FOOTNOTES - NOTES

Italics: data from civil registers which are incomplete or of unknown completeness. -
Italiques: données incomplètes ou dont le degré d'exactitude n'est pas connu, provenant des registres de l'état civil.

* Provisional -
Données provisoires.

[a] 'Code' indicates the source of data, as follows:
C - Civil registration, estimated over 90% complete
U - Civil registration, estimated less than 90% complete
I - Other source, estimated reliable
+ - Data tabulated by date of registration rather than occurence.
... - Information not available

Le 'Code' indique la source des données, comme suit:
C - Registres de l'état civil considérés complets à 90 p. 100 au moins.

U - Registres de l'état civil qui ne sont pas considérés complets à 90 p. 100 au moins.
I - Autre source, considérée fiable.
+ - Données exploitées selon la date de l'enregistrement et non la date de l'événement.
... - Information non disponible.

[b] A Roman number in front of the data for males specifiies the range of the reference period of life expectancy for males and females presented on the row. For example, a reference year of 2005 and a range of V years means that the reference period for the life expectancy is 2001 - 2005. The absence of a Roman number means the reference period is one year and the reference period therefore coincides with the reference year.

Un chiffre romain devant la donnée relative aux hommes indique l'étendue de la période de référence concernant l'espérance de vie des hommes et des femmes présentée dans la ligne. Par exemple, une année de référence 2005 et une étendue de V signifie que la période de référence pour l'espérance de vie est 2001-2005. L'absence de chiffre romain signifie que la période de référence est d'un an et donc coïncide avec l'année de référence.

[1] Excluding live-born infants who died before their birth was registered. For Algerian population only. - Non compris les enfants nés vivants décédés avant l'enregistrement de leur naissance. Pour la population algérienne seulement.

[2] Data from civil registration centers of Brazzaville, Pointe-Noire, Dolisie, Nkayi, Mossendijo and Ouesso communes. - Données issues des centres d'enregistrement des faits d'état-civil des communes de Brazzaville, Pointe-Noire, Dolisie, Nkayi, Mossendijo et Ouesso.

[3] Data refer to national projections. - Les données se réfèrent aux projections nationales.

[4] Projections based on the 1998 Malawi Population and Housing Census. - Les projections sont basées sur les résultats du recensement de la population et de l'habitat de Malawi de 1998.

[5] Excluding live-born infants who died before their birth was registered. - Non compris les enfants nés vivants décédés avant l'enregistrement de leur naissance.

[6] Data are for 12 months preceding the census date. - Les données portent sur les 12 mois précédant la date du recensement.

[7] Source: World Health Organization. - Source : Organisation mondiale de la santé.

[8] Excluding non-residents and foreign service personnel and their dependants. - À l'exclusion des non-résidents et du personnel diplomatique et de leurs charges de famille.

[9] Including Canadian residents temporarily in the United States, but excluding United States residents temporarily in Canada. - Y compris les résidents canadiens se trouvant temporairement aux Etats-Unis, mais ne comprenant pas les résidents des Etats-Unis se trouvant temporairement au Canada.

[10] Data refer to national projections for 2005 - 2010. - Les données se rapportent aux prévisions nationales pour 2005-2010.

[11] Including adjustment for underenumeration. - Y compris l'ajustement pour sous-dénombrement.

[12] Adjusted for undercoverage of infant deaths and sudden and violent deaths. - Ajusté pour la sous-estimation de la mortalité infantile, du nombre de morts soudaines et de morts violentes.

[13] Data exclude visitors. - Les données non compris des visiteurs.

[14] Data refer to births to mothers resident in the Netherlands Antilles (including births outside the Netherlands Antilles to resident mothers, excluding births to non-resident mothers). - Ces données concernent les enfants nés de femmes qui résidaient aux Antilles néerlandaises (y compris ceux qui sont nés hors des Antilles néerlandaises). Elles ne concernent pas les enfants nés de non-résidentes.

[15] Data refer to deaths of residents of the Netherlands Antilles (including those that died outside the Netherlands Antilles). Data exclude deaths by non-residents. - Ces données concernent les décès de résidents des Antilles néerlandaises (y compris ceux survenus hors des Antilles néerlandaises). Elles ne concernent pas les décès des non-résidents.

[16] Excluding Indian jungle population. - Non compris les Indiens de la jungle.

[17] Excluding nomadic Indian tribes. - Non compris les tribus d'Indiens nomades.

[18] Data refer to registered live births only. - Les données concernent les naissances vivantes enregistrées seulement.

[19] Data refer to registered deaths only. - Les données se rapportent aux décès enregistrés seulement.

[20] Data refer to registered infant deaths only. - Les données se rapportent aux décès enregistrés d'enfants de moins de 1 an seulement.

[21] Excluding infants born alive of less than 28 weeks' gestation, of less than 1 000 grams in weight and 35 centimeters in length, who die within seven days of birth. - Non compris les enfants nés vivants après moins de 28 semaines de gestations, pesant moins de 1 000 grammes, mesurant moins de 35 centimètres et décédés dans les sept jours qui ont suivi leur naissance.

[22] Excluding infants born alive of less than 28 weeks' gestation, of less than 1 000 grams in weight and 35 centimeters in length, who die within seven days of birth. Since 16 October 2005 the definition of WHO on livebirths has been put into force in accordance with 10th revision of the International Classification of Diseases. - Non compris les enfants nés vivants après moins de 28 semaines de gestations, pesant moins de 1 000 grammes, mesurant moins de 35 centimètres et décédés dans les sept jours qui ont suivi leur naissance. Depuis le 16 octobre 2005, la définition de l'OMS concernant les naissances vivantes est en vigueur conformément à la dixième révision de la Classification internationale des maladies.

[23] Rates were obtained by the Sample Vital Registration System of Bangladesh. - Taux obtenus au moyen du Sample Vital Registration System du Bangladesh.

[24] For 2005, data refer to last twelve months preceding census in May 2005. - Pour 2005, les données se rapportent aux douze mois précédant le recensement de mai 2005.

[25] The fertility rates have been compiled using a population denominator which has excluded female foreign domestic helpers. - Les taux de fécondité ont été compilés pour une population (en dénominateur) ne comprenant pas les domestiques étrangères.

[26] For statistical purposes, the data for China do not include those for the Hong Kong Special Administrative Region (Hong Kong SAR), Macao Special Administrative Region (Macao SAR) and Taiwan province of China. - Pour la présentation des statistiques, les données pour la Chine ne comprennent pas la Région Administrative Spéciale de Hong Kong (Hong Kong RAS), la Région Administrative Spéciale de Macao (Macao RAS) et Taïwan province de Chine.

[27] Data have been estimated on the basis of the annual National Sample Surveys on Population Changes. - Les données ont été estimées sur la base de l'enquête annuelle "National Sample Survey on Population Changes".

[28] Data for 2005 are estimated from the National Sample Survey of 1 Per cent population. - Les données pour 2005 ont été estimées à partir de l'enquête nationale qui a porté sur un échantillon de 1 % de la population.

[29] Data refer to government controlled areas. - Les données se rapportent aux zones contrôlées par le Gouvernement.

[30] Including data for the Indian-held part of Jammu and Kashmir, the final status of which has not yet been determined. - Y compris les données pour la partie du Jammu et du Cachemire occupée par l'Inde dont le statut définitif n'a pas encore été déterminé.

[31] Rates were obtained by the Sample Registration System of India, actually a large demographic survey. - Les taux ont été obtenus par le Système de l'enregistrement par échantillon de l'Inde qui est une large enquête démographique.

[32] Data relate to the Iranian Year which begins on 21 March and ends on 20 March of the following year. - Les données concernent l'année iranienne, qui commence le 21 mars et se termine le 20 mars de l'année suivante.

[33] Including data for East Jerusalem and Israeli residents in certain other territories under occupation by Israeli military forces since June 1967. - Y compris les données pour Jérusalem-Est et les résidents israéliens dans certains autres territoires occupés depuis 1967 par les forces armées israéliennes.

[34] As of 2002, data on deaths include deaths abroad of Israeli residents who were out of the country for less than a year (there were 109 deaths of Israelis abroad in 2002). - Depuis 2002, les données sur les décès comprennent les décès à l'étranger de résidents israéliens qui ont quitté le pays depuis moins d'un an (en 2002, 109 Israéliens sont morts à l'étranger).

[35] Data include deaths abroad of Israeli residents who were out of the country for less than a year. - Y compris les décès à l'étranger de résidents israéliens qui ont quitté le pays depuis moins d'un an.

[36] Data include 182 deaths abroad of Israeli residents who were out of the country for less than a year. - Y compris les décès à l'étranger de 182 résidents israéliens qui ont quitté le pays depuis moins d'un an.

[37] Data include 183 deaths abroad of Israeli residents who were out of the country for less than a year. - Y compris les décès à l'étranger de 183 résidents israéliens qui ont quitté le pays depuis moins d'un an.

[38] Data include 30 (preliminary figure) deaths abroad of Israeli residents who were out of the country for less than a year. - Y compris les décès à l'étranger de 30 résidents israéliens (chiffres préliminaires) qui ont quitté le pays depuis moins d'un an.

[39] Data include 141 deaths abroad of Israeli residents who were out of the country for less than a year. - Y compris les décès à l'étranger de 141 résidents israéliens qui ont quitté le pays depuis moins d'un an.

[40] Data refer to Japanese nationals in Japan only. - Les données se raportent aux nationaux japonais au Japon seulement.

[41] Excluding data for Jordanian territory under occupation since June 1967 by Israeli military forces. Excluding foreigners, including registered Palestinian refugees. - Non compris les données pour le territoire jordanien occupé depuis juin 1967 par les forces armées israéliennes. Non compris les étrangers, mais y compris les réfugiés de Palestine enregistrés.

[42] Excluding alien armed forces, civilian aliens employed by armed forces, and foreign diplomatic personnel and their dependants. Including Koreans abroad. - Non compris les militaires étrangers, les civils étrangers employés par les forces armées ni le personnel diplomatique étranger et les membres de leur famille les accompagnant. Y compris les Coréens à l'étranger.

[43] Including Korean deaths abroad. Excluding alien armed forces, civilian aliens employed by armed forces, and foreign diplomatic personnel and their dependants. - Y compris les décès de Coréens survenus à l'étranger. Non compris les militaires étrangers, les civils étrangers employés par les forces armées ni le personnel diplomatique étranger et les membres de leur famille les accompagnant.

[44] Excluding alien armed forces, civilian aliens employed by armed forces, and foreign diplomatic personnel and their dependants. Including nationals outside the country. - Non compris les militaires étrangers, les civils étrangers employés par les forces armées ni le personnel diplomatique étranger et les membres de leur famille les accompagnant. Y compris les nationaux hors du pays.

[45] Since 2004, WHO criteria have been adopted in the country. - Depuis 2004, le pays a adopté les critères de l'OMS.

[46] Data estimated from population and housing census 2005. - Données dérivées du recensement de population et du logement de 2005.

[47] Data refer to urban areas only. - Données ne concernant que les zones urbaines.

[48] Data refer to the recorded events in Ministry of Health hospitals and health centres only. - Les données se rapportent aux faits d'état civil enregistrés dans les hôpitaux et les dispensaires du Ministère de la santé seulement.

[49] Excluding data for the Pakistan-held part of Jammu and Kashmir, the final status of which has not yet been determined. - Non compris les données concernant la partie du Jammu et Cachemire occupée par le Pakistan dont le statut définitif n'a pas été déterminé.

[50] Data based on Pakistan Demographic Survey (PDS 2003). - Données extraites de l'enquête démographique effectuée par le Pakistan en 2003.

[51] Data based on Pakistan Demographic Survey (PDS 2005). - Données extraites de l'enquête démographique effectuée par le Pakistan en 2005.

[52] Excluding nomad population and Palestinian refugees. Excluding live-born infants who died before their birth was registered. - Non compris la population nomade et les réfugiés de Palestine. Non compris les enfants nés vivants décédés avant l'enregistrement de leur naissance.

[53] Including an upward adjustment for under-registration. - Y compris un ajustement pour sous-enregistrement.

[54] Based on the results of the Population Demographic Survey. - D'après les résultats de la Population Demographic Survey.

[55] Also included in Finland. - Comprise aussi dans Finlande.

[56] Including armed forces stationed outside the country, but excluding alien armed forces stationed in the area. - Y compris les militaires nationaux hors du pays, mais non compris les militaires étrangers en garnison sur le territoire.

[57] Excluding Faeroe Islands and Greenland shown separately, if available. - Non compris les Iles Féroé et le Gröenland, qui font l'objet de rubriques distinctes, si disponible.

[58] Including Aland Islands. Y compris les Iles d'Aland.

[59] Including nationals temporarily outside the country. - Y compris les nationaux se trouvant temporairement hors du pays.

[60] Excluding Overseas Departments, namely, French Guiana, Guadeloupe, Martinique and Reunion, shown separately, if available. - Non compris les départements d'outre mer, c'est-à-dire la Guyane française, la Guadeloupe, la Martinique et la Réunion, qui font l'objet de rubriques distinctes, si disponible.

[61] Including armed forces stationed outside the country. - Y compris les militaires nationaux hors du pays.

[62] Excluding armed forces. - Non compris les militaires en garnison.

[63] Computations are based on five-year age-specific fertility rates by age completed - Calcul basé sur les taux de fécondité par âge sur cinq ans.

[64] Events registered within one year of occurrence. - Evénements enregistrés dans l'année qui suit l'événement.

[65] Excluding infants born alive of less than 28 weeks' gestation, of less than 1 000 grams in weight and 35 centimeters in length, who die within seven days of birth. Data do not include information for Transnistria and the municipality of Bender. - Non compris les enfants nés vivants après moins de 28 semaines de gestations, pesant moins de 1 000 grammes, mesurant moins de 35 centimètres et décédés dans les sept jours qui ont suivi leur naissance. Les données ne tiennent pas compte de l'information sur la Transnistria et la municipalité de Bender.

[66] Including residents outside the country. - Y compris les résidents hors du pays.

[67] Including residents outside the country if listed in a Netherlands population register. - Y compris les résidents hors du pays, s'ils sont inscrits sur un registre de population néerlandais.

[68] Excluding Svalbard and Jan Mayen Island shown separately, if available. - Non compris Svalbard et Jan Mayen qui font l'objet de rubriques distinctes, si disponible.

[69] Including residents temporarily outside the country. - Y compris les résidents se trouvant temporairement hors du pays.

[70] Data refer to resident mothers. - Données concernant les mères résidentes.

[71] For resident population only. - Pour la population résidante seulement.

[72] Without data for Kosovo and Metohia. - Sans les données pour le Kosovo and Metohie.

[73] Based on the results of the Total Population Register. - Selon les résultats du recensement complet de la population.

[74] Data based on fertility for range of two years shown under the year ending. - Données fournies sur la base de la fécondité pour une période de deux années consécutives ; les données qui apparaissent sont celles de l'année finale de cette période.

[75] Data refer to births with weight 500g and more (if weight is unknown - with length 25 centimeters and more, or with gestation during 22 weeks or more). - Données concernant les nouveau-nés de 500 grammes ou plus (si le poids est inconnu – de 25 centimètres de long ou plus, ou après une grossesse de 22 semaines ou plus).

[76] Before 2006, data exclude death happened within 7 days after birth, which was born with less then 26 weeks of gestation, with weight less then 1000 grams and length and less then 35 centimeters long. - Avant 2006, données excluant les décès survenus dans les sept jours après la naissance, les enfants nés après moins de 26 semaines de gestation, les enfants pesant moins d'un kilogramme et de moins de 35 centimètres.

[77] Excluding Channel Islands and Isle of Man, shown separately, if available. - Non compris les îles Anglo-Normandes et l'île de Man, qui font l'objet de rubriques distinctes, si disponible.

[78] Data revised to exclude births in Northern Ireland to non-residents of Northern Ireland. Data tabulated by date of occurrence for England and Wales, and by date of registration for Northern Ireland and Scotland. - Données révisées pour exclure les naissances en Irlande du Nord de non-résidents de l'Irlande du Nord. Données exploitées selon la date de l'événement pour l'Angleterre et le pays de Galles, et selon la date de l'enregistrement pour l'Irlande du Nord et l'Ecosse.

[79] Data tabulated by date of occurrence for England and Wales, and by date of registration for Northern Ireland and Scotland. - Données exploitées selon la date de l'événement pour l'Angleterre et le pays de Galles, et selon la date de l'enregistrement pour l'Irlande du Nord et l'Ecosse.

[80] Excluding Niue, shown separately, which is part of Cook Islands, but because of remoteness is administered separately. - Non compris Nioué, qui fait l'objet d'une rubrique distincte et qui fait partie des îles Cook, mais qui, en raison de son éloignement, est administrée séparément.

[81] Including United States military personnel, their dependants and contract employees. - Y compris les militaires des Etats-Unis, les membres de leur famille les accompagnant et les agents contractuels des Etats-Unis.

[82] Includes children born in New Zealand to women resident in Niue who chose to travel to New Zealand to give birth. - Y compris les enfants nés en Nouvelle-Zélande de femmes résidant à Nioué qui ont choisi de se rendre en Nouvelle-Zélande pour accoucher.

[83] Includes deaths occurred in New Zealand but buried in Niue and deaths occurred in Niue but buried elsewhere. - Y compris les personnes décédées en Nouvelle-Zélande qui sont enterrées à Nioué et les personnes décédées à Nioué qui sont enterrées ailleurs.

Table 5

Table 5 presents national estimates of mid-year population for all available years between 1997 and 2006.

Description of variables: Mid-year estimates of the total population are those provided by national statistical offices. They refer to the *de facto* or *de jure* population on 1 July. In cases where the national statistical office provided data referring to the beginning or the end of a year the average was calculated by the Statistics Division. The data are presented in thousands, rounded by the Statistics Division.

For certain countries or areas, there is a discrepancy between the mid-year population estimates shown in this table and those shown in subsequent tables for the same year. Usually this discrepancy arises because the estimates for a given year are revised and the remaining tabulations are not.

For some countries or areas the figures presented in this table and the figures used to calculate rates in subsequent tables are not the same, as these countries have provided a reference population for vital events that is different than the total population.

Unless otherwise indicated, all estimates relate to the population within present geographical boundaries. Major exceptions to this principle are explained in footnotes.

Reliability of data: Reliable mid-year population estimates are those that are based on a complete census (or on a sample survey) and have been adjusted on a basis of a continuous population register or on the balance of births, deaths and migration. Reliable mid-year estimates appear in roman type. Mid-year estimates that are not calculated on this basis are considered less reliable and are shown in *italics*.

Limitations: Statistics on estimates of the mid-year total population are subject to the same qualifications as have been set forth for population statistics in general in section 3 of the Technical Notes.

International comparability of mid-year population estimates is also affected by the fact that some of these estimates refer to the *de jure*, and not the *de facto*, population. These are indicated in the column titled "Code". The difference between the *de facto* and the *de jure* population is discussed in section 3.1.1 of the Technical Notes.

Earlier data: Estimates of mid-year population have been shown in previous issues of the *Demographic Yearbook*. Information on the years and specific topics covered is presented in the Historical Index.

Tableau 5

Le tableau 5 présente des estimations nationales de la population en milieu d'année pour le plus grand nombre possible d'années entre 1997 et 2006.

Description des variables : les estimations de la population totale en milieu d'année sont celles qui ont été communiquées par les services nationaux de statistique. Elles correspondent à la population de fait ou se réfèrent à la population de droit, au 1er juillet. Lorsque la date est différente, cela est signalé par une note. Sauf indication contraire, tous les chiffres sont exprimés en milliers. Les données ont été arrondies par la Division de statistique de l'ONU.

Pour certains pays ou territoires, il existe une différence entre les estimations de la population en milieu d'année et celles présentées dans les tableaux suivants pour la même année. Généralement, les différences apparaissent parce que les estimations de l'année ont été révisées mais que les autres tabulations ne l'ont pas été.

Pour certains pays ou territoires, les données présentées dans ce tableau sont différentes des données utilisées pour calculer les taux dans les tableaux suivants, parce que ces pays ont fourni une population de référence pour les événements démographiques différente de la population totale.

Sauf indication contraire, toutes les estimations se rapportent à la population présente sur le territoire actuel des pays ou zones considérés. Les principales exceptions à cette règle sont expliquées en note.

Fiabilité des données : les estimations de la population en milieu d'année sont considérées sûres quand elles sont fondées sur un recensement complet (ou sur une enquête par sondage) et ont été ajustées en fonction des données provenant d'un registre permanent de population ou en fonction des naissances, décès et mouvements migratoires qui ont eu lieu pendant la période. Les estimations considérées comme sûres et apparaissent en caractères romains. Les estimations dont le calcul n'a pas été effectué sur cette base sont considérées comme moins sûres et apparaissent en italique.

Insuffisance des données : les statistiques concernant les estimations de la population totale en milieu d'année appellent toutes les réserves qui ont été formulées à la section 3 des Notes techniques à propos des statistiques de la population en général.

Le fait que certaines des estimations concernant la population en milieu d'année se réfèrent à la population de droit et non à la population de fait influe sur la comparabilité internationale. Ces cas ont été signalés dans la colonne « Code ». La différence entre la population de fait et la population de droit est expliquée à la section 3.1.1 des Notes techniques.

Données publiées antérieurement : des estimations de la population en milieu d'année ont été publiées dans des éditions antérieures de l'*Annuaire démographique*. Pour plus de précisions concernant les années et les sujets pour lesquels des données ont été publiées, se reporter à l'index.

5. Estimates of mid-year population: 1997 - 2006
Estimations de la population au milieu de l'année: 1997 - 2006

Continent and country or area / Continent et pays ou zone	Code[a]	Population estimates (in thousands) — Estimations (en milliers)									
		1997	1998	1999	2000	2001	2002	2003	2004	2005	2006
AFRICA - AFRIQUE											
Algeria - Algérie	DJ	29 045	29 507	29 965	30 416	30 872	31 332	31 848	32 364	32 906	33 481
Benin - Bénin	DF	5 639	5 816	5 990	6 169	*6 417	...	...	...	...	...
Botswana	DF	1 533	1 572	1 611	1 653	...	1 650	1 673	1 693	1 708	1 720
Burkina Faso	DJ	10 561	10 816	11 078	11 347	11 623	11 906	12 197	12 496	12 802	...
Burundi	DF	6 194	6 300	6 483	...	...	...	...	...	...	...
Cameroon - Cameroun[1]	DF	14 298	14 439	...	15 292	15 731	16 170	16 626	17 000	...	...
Cape Verde - Cap-Vert	DF	407	417	428	435	445	453	461	468	475	483
Central African Republic - République centrafricaine	DF	3 245	...	...	...	...	...	3 151	...	...	...
Chad - Tchad[1]	DF	6 932	7 105	7 283	...	8 322	...	...	...	...	...
Congo	DF	2 663	2 738	2 815	2 893	2 974	3 058	3 143	3 231	...	...
Côte d'Ivoire	DF	15 383	15 366	15 881	16 402	16 928	17 461	18 001	18 546	19 097	19 658
Djibouti	DF	755	795	840	...	...	...	...	...	...	...
Egypt - Égypte	DF	60 080	61 341	62 639	63 975	65 298	66 628	67 965	69 304	70 653	72 009
Ethiopia - Éthiopie	DF	58 117	59 882	61 672	63 495	65 374	67 220	69 127	71 066	...	75 067
Gabon	DF	1 120	1 148	1 177	1 206	*1 237	*1 268	*1 300	...	...	...
Gambia - Gambie	DF	...	...	1 385	1 393	1 420	...	...	...	1 436	1 510
Ghana	DF	18 305	18 885	19 484	18 412	...	...	...	...	...	...
Guinea-Bissau - Guinée-Bissau[1]	DF	...	...	...	...	1 211	1 238	1 267	1 296	1 326	1 357
Kenya	DF	27 793	28 611	29 453	30 150	31 121	32 118	33 142	34 191	35 267	36 433
Lesotho	DF	2 012	2 055	2 100	2 144	...	...	...	...	...	...
Liberia - Libéria	DF	2 879	...	...	...	...	...	...	...	...	...
Libyan Arab Jamahiriya - Jamahiriya arabe libyenne[2]	DF	4 648	4 772	4 958	5 125	5 300	5 484	...	...	...	...
Madagascar	DF	13 803	14 222	14 650	15 085	15 529	15 981	16 441	17 206	17 730	...
Malawi[1]	DF	10 441	...	*10 153	*10 475	*10 816	*11 175	*11 549	*11 938	*12 341	*12 758
Mali	...	9 325	...	9 969	10 384	10 525	10 813	11 111	11 419	11 732	12 214
Mauritania - Mauritanie	DF	2 421	2 493	2 568	2 645	2 724	...	...	...	2 906	...
Mauritius - Maurice	DJ	1 148	1 160	1 175	1 187	1 200	1 210	1 223	1 233	1 243	1 253
Morocco - Maroc	DF	27 310	27 775	28 238	28 705	29 170	29 631	30 088	30 540	30 172	*30 506
Mozambique[3]	DF	16 543	16 917	17 299	17 691	*17 656	...	...	...	*19 420	...
Namibia - Namibie	DF	...	...	...	*1 817	...	...	...	...	...	...
Niger	DJ	9 574	9 871	10 177	10 493	11 090	11 456	11 834	12 225	12 628	13 045
Nigeria - Nigéria[1]	DF	...	...	...	115 224	118 801	122 444	126 153	129 175	133 767	140 004
Réunion	DF	687	698	710	722	735	748	764	769	779	...
Sao Tome and Principe - Sao Tomé-et-Principe	DF	129	131	133	135	...	140	143	146	149	*152
Senegal - Sénégal	DJ	8 742	8 964	9 193	9 427	9 667	9 913	10 165	10 564	10 848	*11 000
Seychelles	DF	77	79	80	81	81	84	83	82	83	85
Sierra Leone	DF	4 625	4 730	4 836	4 944	5 054	5 167	5 280	...	...	...
South Africa - Afrique du Sud[3]	DF	41 227	42 131	43 054	43 686	44 561	45 454	46 430	46 587	46 888	47 391
Sudan - Soudan	DF	28 507	29 266	30 326	31 081	31 627	32 468	33 334	34 512	35 397	36 297
Swaziland	DF	...	952	977	1 003	1 030	1 056	1 081	1 105	1 126	1 146
Togo	DF	4 269	4 406	4 506	4 629	4 740	4 854	4 970	5 090	5 337	5 337
Tunisia - Tunisie	DF	9 215	9 333	9 456	9 564	9 674	9 782	9 840	9 941	10 029	10 126
Uganda - Ouganda	DF	20 507	21 175	21 864	22 575	23 310	24 069	24 851	25 660	26 495	27 357
United Republic of Tanzania - République Unie de Tanzanie	DF	29 984	...	...	...	...	...	...	36 308	37 379	38 251
Zambia - Zambie	DF	9 780	10 096	10 407	...	10 089	10 409	10 744	11 090	...	11 799
Zimbabwe	DF	12 294	12 685	13 079	...	12 960	...	...	...	...	12 225[4]
AMERICA, NORTH - AMÉRIQUE DU NORD											
Anguilla	DF	10	11	11	11	12	12	12	13	14	*14
Antigua and Barbuda - Antigua-et-Barbuda	DF	69	70	71	72	77	78	80	81	83	...
Aruba	DJ	86	88	90	91	92	93	95	98	101	103
Bahamas	DF	288	293	298	...	308	312	317	321	325	330
Barbados - Barbade	DF	265	265	267	269	270	271	272	272	273	274[5]
Belize	DF	230	239	243	250	257	265	274	283	292	301
Bermuda - Bermudes	DJ	62	62	63	63	62	63	63	63	64	64
British Virgin Islands - Îles Vierges britanniques	DF	19	19	20	20	21	21	21	22	...	...
Canada	DJ	29 907[6]	30 157[6]	30 404[6]	30 689[6]	31 021[7]	31 373[7]	31 676[7]	31 995[7]	32 312[8]	32 649[8]

5. Estimates of mid-year population: 1997 - 2006
Estimations de la population au milieu de l'année: 1997 - 2006 (continued - suite)

Continent and country or area / Continent et pays ou zone	Code[a]	Population estimates (in thousands) - Estimations (en milliers)									
		1997	1998	1999	2000	2001	2002	2003	2004	2005	2006
AMERICA, NORTH - AMÉRIQUE DU NORD											
Cayman Islands - Îles Caïmanes	DJ	36	38	...	40	41	42	44	44	48	52
Costa Rica	DJ	3 271	3 341	3 413	3 810	3 907	3 998	4 089	4 179	4 266	4 354
Cuba	DJ	11 009	11 055	11 095	11 130	11 157	11 184	11 215	11 236	11 243	11 241
Dominica - Dominique	DF	72	72	72	72	71	70	...	71		
Dominican Republic - République dominicaine	DF	8 144	8 276	8 410	8 554	8 683	8 815	8 948	9 082	9 226	9 354
El Salvador	DF	5 908	6 031	6 154	6 276	6 397	6 518	6 638	6 757	6 875	6 991
Greenland - Groenland[9]	DJ	56	56	56	56	56	57	57	57	57	57
Grenada - Grenade	DF	100	100	101	101	101	...	...	...		
Guadeloupe	DJ	414	419	424	432	428	437	439	445	*446	*458
Guatemala[3]	DF	10 517	10 799	11 088	11 385	11 678	11 987	12 084	12 390	12 701	13 019
Haiti - Haïti	DJ	7 492	7 647	7 803	7 959	8 132	...	...	...		
Honduras	DF	5 908	6 057	6 211	6 369	6 530	6 695	6 861	7 028	7 197	7 367
Jamaica - Jamaïque	DJ	2 534	2 557	2 574	2 589	2 604	2 615	2 626	2 638	2 650	2 663
Martinique	DJ	376	379	382	385	387	389	391	394	398	400
Mexico - Mexique	DJ	94 478	95 790	97 115	98 439	99 716	100 909	102 000	103 002	103 947	104 874
Montserrat	DF	6[10]	4	5	5	...	...	...	...		
Netherlands Antilles - Antilles néerlandaises	DJ	193	192	186	179	174	175	179	183	185	190
Nicaragua	DJ	4 674	4 803	4 936	5 106	5 174	5 243	5 314	5 385	5 457	5 530
Panama	DF	2 719	2 764	2 809	2 856	2 897	3 060	3 116	3 172	3 228	3 284
Puorto Rico - Purto Rico[11]	DJ	3 716	3 748	3 782	3 816	3 840	3 859	3 879	3 895	3 912	3 928
Saint Kitts and Nevis - Saint-Kitts-et-Nevis	DF	41	40	42	40	*46	...	...	...		
Saint Lucia - Sainte-Lucie	DF	150	152	154	156	158	159	161	162	165	*167
Saint Vincent and the Grenadines - Saint Vincent-et-les Grenadines	DF	112	112	112	110	...	108	105	105	104	...
Trinidad and Tobago - Trinité-et-Tobago	DF	1 275	1 278	1 284	1 290	1 267	1 276	1 282	...	...	...
Turks Caicos Islands - Îles Turques et Caïques	DJ	16	17	17	18	20	21	25	27	31	33
United States - États-Unis[12]	DJ	272 647	275 854	279 040	282 193	285 108	287 985	290 850	293 623	296 410	299 398
United States Virgin Islands - Îles Vierges américaines	DJ	108	109	109	109[11]	109[11]	109[11]	109[11]	109[11]	109[11]	109[11]
AMERICA, SOUTH - AMÉRIQUE DU SUD											
Argentina - Argentine	DF	35 604	36 005	36 399	36 784	37 156	37 516	37 870	38 226	38 592	38 971
Bolivia - Bolivie	DF	7 845	8 035	8 229	8 428	8 624	8 824	9 025	9 227	9 427	9 627
Brazil - Brésil[13]	DF	163 780	166 252	168 754	171 280	173 822	176 391	178 985	181 586	184 184	186 771
Chile - Chili	DF	14 622	14 822	15 018	15 211	15 402	15 589	15 774	16 093	16 267	16 433
Colombia - Colombie[14]	DF	38 646	39 201	39 746	40 282	40 806	41 327	41 847	42 368	42 889	43 405
Ecuador - Équateur[15]	DF	11 773	11 948	12 121	12 299	12 480	12 661	12 843	13 027	13 215	13 408
French Guiana - Guyane française	DJ	148	153	158	164	170	175	181	*187	*200	*197
Guyana	DF	775	773	771	742	744	748	752[16]	755	758	760
Paraguay	DF	5 085	5 219	5 356	5 346	5 456	5 567	5 677	5 788	5 899	6 009
Peru - Pérou[3]	DF	24 712	25 180	25 621	25 982	26 315	26 636	26 888	27 076	27 179	27 377
Suriname	DJ	446	452	458	464	470	476	483	487	499	*504
Uruguay[3]	DF	3 256	3 274	3 289	3 301	3 308	3 309	3 304	3 302	3 306	3 314
Venezuela (Bolivarian Republic of) - Venezuela (République bolivarienne du)[17]	DF	22 959	23 413	23 867	24 311	24 766	25 220	25 674	26 127	26 577	27 031
ASIA - ASIE											
Afghanistan	DF	20 350	20 760	21 200	21 770	22 080	22 930	...	...	...	22 576[18]
Armenia - Arménie	DJ	3 242	3 235	3 229	3 221	3 214	3 212	3 211	3 214	3 218	3 221
Azerbaijan - Azerbaïdjan	DF	7 838	7 913	7 983	8 049	8 111	8 172	8 234	8 307	*8 392	*8 485
Bahrain - Bahreïn	DF	589	605	621	638	655	672	689	707	725	743
Bangladesh	DF	124 300	126 200	*128 100	129 300	131 000	132 900	134 800	136 700	138 600	140 600

Continent and country or area / Continent et pays ou zone	Code[a]	Population estimates (in thousands) Estimations (en milliers)									
		1997	1998	1999	2000	2001	2002	2003	2004	2005	2006
ASIA - ASIE											
Bhutan - Bhoutan	DF	550	560	570	580	591	602	613	624	...	647
Brunei Darussalam - Brunéi Darussalam	DF	302	310	317	325	333	344	350	360	370	*383
Cambodia - Cambodge[19]	DF	10 368	12 242[20]	12 462[20]	12 688[20]	12 922[20]	13 164[20]	13 415[20]	13 091[20]	*13 661[20]	...
China - Chine[21]	DF	1 230 075[22]	1 241 935[22]	1 252 735[22]	1 262 645[22]	1 271 850[23]	1 280 400[23]	1 288 400[23]	1 296 075[23]	1 303 720[24]	1 311 020[23]
China: Hong Kong SAR - Chine: Hong Kong RAS	DJ	6 489	6 544	6 607	6 665	6 714	6 744	6 731	6 784	6 813	6 857
China: Macao SAR - Chine: Macao RAS	DJ	417	422	427	431	434	438	444	455	473	499
Cyprus - Chypre[25]	DJ	670	679	686	694	701	710	721	737	758	771
Georgia - Géorgie	DF	4 532	4 487	4 453	4 418	4 387	4 357	4 329	4 318	4 361	4 398
India - Inde[26]	DF	960 497	978 981	997 556	1 016 210	1 034 931	1 051 258	1 068 065	1 084 757	1 101 318	1 117 734
Indonesia - Indonésie	DJ	201 353	204 393	207 437	...	208 643	211 439	214 251	217 077	*219 898	*222 051
Iran (Islamic Republic of) - Iran (République islamique d')[27]	DJ	60 939	61 836	62 746	63 664	64 528	65 540	66 480	67 477	68 467	*70 603
Iraq	DF	22 046	22 702	23 382	24 086	24 813	25 565	26 340	27 139	27 963	28 810
Israel - Israël[28]	DJ	5 829	5 971	6 125	6 289	6 439	6 570	6 690	6 809	6 930	7 054
Japan - Japon[29]	DF	126 057	126 400	126 631	126 843	127 149	127 445	127 718	127 761	127 773	127 756
Jordan - Jordanie[30]	DF	4 445	4 565	4 681	4 798	4 918	5 038	5 164	5 290	5 412	5 537
Kazakhstan	DF	15 334	15 073	14 928	14 884	14 858	14 859	14 909	15 013	15 147	15 308
Korea (Dem. People's Republic of) - Corée (Rép. populaire dém. de)	DF	22 355	22 554	22 754	22 963	23 149	23 313	23 464	23 612	...	...
Korea (Republic of) - Corée (République de)	DJ	45 954	46 287	46 617	47 008	47 357	47 622	47 859	48 039	48 138	48 297
Kuwait - Koweït	DF	1 980	2 027	2 107	2 138	2 183	2 262	2 325	2 391	2 457	...
Kyrgyzstan - Kirghizistan	DF	4 725	4 797	4 865	4 915	4 955	4 993	5 039	5 093	5 144	5 192
Lao People's Democratic Republic - République démocratique populaire lao	DF	...	...	5 091	5 218[31]	5 377[31]	5 526[31]	5 679[31]	5 836[31]	5 679[32]	5 747[32]
Lebanon - Liban[33]	DF	...	...	...	...	...	...	...	3 755		
Malaysia - Malaisie	DF	20 996	21 475	21 852	23 495	24 013	24 527	25 048	25 581	26 128	26 640
Maldives	DF	259	267	278	271	276	281	285	289	294	298
Mongolia - Mongolie	DF	2 273	2 281	2 332	2 390	2 425	2 459	2 490	2 519	2 548	2 579
Myanmar	DF	46 402	48 160	49 133	50 125	51 138	52 171	53 224	54 299	...	...
Nepal - Népal	DJ	21 331	21 843	22 367	*22 904	...	23 701	24 250	24 797	25 343	25 887
Occupied Palestinian Territory - Territoire palestinien occupé	DF	2 783	2 897	3 019	3 149	3 275	3 394	3 515	3 638	3 762	3 888
Oman	DF	2 256	2 288	2 325	2 401	2 478	2 538	...	2 416	2 514	2 577
Pakistan[34]	DF	128 420	131 510	134 510	138 945	141 765	144 560	147 335	150 135	153 455	*156 770
Philippines	DJ	73 527	75 155	76 783	76 348	77 926	79 504	81 081	82 664	*85 237	*86 973
Qatar	DF	530	557	586	617	649	682	718	756	796	936
Saudi Arabia - Arabie saoudite	DF	19 039	19 506	19 985	20 476	20 979	21 495	22 023	22 564	23 119	23 679
Singapore - Singapour	DF	3 796	3 927	3 959	4 028	4 138	4 176	4 186	4 238	4 342	4 484
Sri Lanka	DF	18 552	18 774	19 043	19 359	18 732	19 007	19 253	19 462	*19 668	*19 886
Syrian Arab Republic - République arabe syrienne[35]	DF	15 100	15 597	16 110	16 320	16 720	17 130	17 550	17 832	18 269	18 717
Tajikistan - Tadjikistan	DF	...	6 103	6 064	6 188	6 313	6 441	6 573	6 710	6 850	6 992
Thailand - Thaïlande	DJ	60 602	61 156	61 564	62 406[1]	62 914[1]	63 482[1]	64 019[1]	64 177[1]	64 839[1]	65 306[1]
Turkey - Turquie	DF	64 064	65 215	66 350	67 420	68 365	69 302	70 231	71 152	72 065	72 974
Turkmenistan - Turkménistan	DF	...	4 859	...	4 892	4 974	5 052	5 124	...	...	...
United Arab Emirates - Émirats arabes unis	DF	2 590	2 717	2 855	2 995	3 167	3 349	3 551	3 761	...	4 229
Uzbekistan - Ouzbékistan	DF	23 560	24 051	23 954	24 650	24 964	25 272	25 568	...	...	...
Viet Nam	DF	74 307	75 456	76 597	77 635	78 686	79 727	80 902	82 032	83 106	*84 156
Yemen - Yémen	DF	16 484	17 072	17 671	18 261	17 727	18 267	18 822	19 395	19 984	20 592
EUROPE											
Åland Islands - Îles d'Åland[36]	DF	25	26	26	26	26	26	26	26	27	27
Albania - Albanie	DF	3 075	3 055	3 054	3 061	3 074	3 093	3 111	3 127	3 142	3 151
Andorra - Andorre[9]	DF	66	66	66	66	67	70	75	78	80	82
Austria - Autriche	DJ	7 968	7 977	7 992	8 012	8 043	8 084	8 118	8 175	8 233	8 282
Belarus - Bélarus	DF	10 117	10 072	10 035	10 005	9 971	9 925	9 874	9 825	9 775	9 733
Belgium - Belgique	DJ	10 181	10 203	10 226	10 251	10 287	10 333	10 372	10 417	10 473	10 542
Bosnia and Herzegovina - Bosnie-Herzégovine	DF	3 738	3 653	3 725	3 781	3 798	3 828	3 832	3 843	3 843	3 843

5. Estimates of mid-year population: 1997 - 2006
Estimations de la population au milieu de l'année: 1997 - 2006 (continued - suite)

Continent and country or area / Continent et pays ou zone	Code[a]	Population estimates (in thousands) - Estimations (en milliers)									
		1997	1998	1999	2000	2001	2002	2003	2004	2005	2006
EUROPE											
Bulgaria - Bulgarie	DF	8 312	8 257	8 211	8 170	7 913	7 869	7 824	7 781	7 740	7 699
Channel Islands: Guernsey - Îles Anglo-Normandes: Guernesey	DF	59	59	60	60	...	...	...	60	...	61[37]
Channel Islands: Jersey - Îles Anglo-Normandes: Jersey	DF	...	...	...	...	87	88	88	88	88	89
Croatia - Croatie	DJ	4 572	4 501	4 554	4 381	...	4 443	4 442	4 439	4 442	4 440
Czech Republic - République tchèque	DJ	10 304	10 295	10 283	10 273	10 224	10 201	10 202	10 207	10 234	10 287
Denmark - Danemark[38]	DJ	5 284	5 301	5 327	5 337	5 359	5 374	5 387	5 401	5 416	5 435
Estonia - Estonie	DF	1 400	1 386	1 376	1 370	1 364	1 359	1 354	1 349	1 346	1 344
Faeroe Islands - Îles Féroé	DJ	44	45	45	46	47	47	48	48	48	48
Finland - Finlande[39]	DJ	5 140	5 153	5 165	5 176	5 188	5 201	5 213	5 228	5 246	5 266
France[40]	DJ	58 207	58 398	58 673	59 049	59 454	59 863	60 264	'60 643	'60 996	'61 353
Germany - Allemagne	DJ	82 052	82 029	82 087	82 188	82 340	82 482	82 520	82 501	82 464	82 366
Gibraltar[41]	DF	27	27	27	27	...	29	29	29	29	29
Greece - Grèce[42]	DF	10 777	10 835	10 883	10 917	10 950	10 988	11 024	11 062	11 104	11 149
Holy See - Saint-Siège[43]	DF	...	1	...	...	...	...	...	...	...	...
Hungary - Hongrie	DF	10 155	10 114	10 068	10 024	10 188	10 159	10 130	10 107	10 087	10 071
Iceland - Islande[9]	DJ	271	274	277	281	285	288	289	293	296	304
Ireland - Irlande[44]	DF	3 664	3 703	3 742	3 790	3 847	...	3 979	4 044	4 131	4 235
Isle of Man - Îles de Man	DJ	72	74	...	75	...	77	77	70	78	...
Italy Italie	DJ	56 890	56 907	56 916	56 942	56 977	57 157	57 605	58 175	58 607	58 941
Latvia - Lettonie	DJ	2 433	2 410	2 390	2 373	2 355	2 339	2 325	2 313	2 301	2 288
Liechtenstein	DF	31	32	32	33	33	34	34	34	35	35
Lithuania - Lituanie	DJ	3 575	3 549	3 524	3 500	3 481	3 469	3 454	3 436	3 414	3 394
Luxembourg	DJ	419	425	430	436	442	446	452	458	465	473
Malta - Malte[45]	DJ	377	379	380	383	385	387	399	401	404	406
Moldova[46]	DJ	3 654	3 653	3 647	3 640	3 631	3 623	3 613	3 604	3 595	3 585
Monaco	DJ	32	...	33	...	...	...	...	...	...	...
Montenegro	...	643	647	651	654	658[47]	618[47]	620	622	623	...
Netherlands - Pays-Bas	DJ	15 611	15 707	15 812	15 926	16 046	16 149	16 225	16 282	16 320	16 346
Norway - Norvège[48]	DJ	4 405	4 431	4 462	4 491	4 514	4 538	4 565	4 592	4 623	4 661
Poland - Pologne[49]	DF	38 292	38 283	38 270	38 256	38 251	38 232	38 195	38 180	38 161	38 132
Portugal	DJ	10 091	10 129	10 172	10 226	10 293	10 368	10 441	10 502	10 549	10 584
Romania - Roumanie	DJ	22 546	22 503	22 458	22 435	22 408	21 795	21 734	21 673	21 624	21 584
Russian Federation - Fédération de Russie	DJ	147 915	147 671	147 215	146 597	145 976	145 306	144 566	143 821	143 114	142 487
San Marino - Saint-Marin[9]	DF	26	28	28	27	28	28	29	29	31	31
Serbia - Serbie	DJ	9 957	7 568[50]	7 540[50]	7 516[50]	7 503[50]	7 500[50]	7 481[50]	7 463[50]	7 441[50]	7 412[50]
Slovakia - Slovaquie	DJ	5 383	5 391	5 395	5 401	5 380	5 379	5 379	5 383	5 387	5 391
Slovenia - Slovénie	DJ	1 987	1 983	1 986	1 990	1 992	1 996	1 997	1 997	2 001	2 009
Spain - Espagne	DJ	39 583	39 722	39 927	40 264	40 721	41 314	42 005	42 692	43 398	44 068
Sweden - Suède[9]	DJ	8 846	8 851	8 858	8 872	8 896	8 925	8 958	8 994	9 030	9 081
Switzerland - Suisse	DJ	7 089	7 110	7 144	7 184	7 227	7 285	7 339	7 390	7 437	7 484
The Former Yugoslav Rep. of Macedonia - L'ex-République yougoslave de Macédoine	DF	1 997	2 008	2 017	2 024	2 035	2 031	2 027	2 033	2 037	2 040
Ukraine	...	50 595	50 144	49 674[51]	49 177[51]	48 690	48 230	47 813	47 271	'47 075	'46 757
United Kingdom - Royaume-Uni[52]	DF	58 314[53]	58 475[53]	58 684[53]	58 886[53]	59 113[53]	59 323[53]	59 557	59 846	60 238	60 587
OCEANIA - OCÉANIE											
American Samoa Samoa américaines[11]	DJ	55[54]	56[54]	57[54]	58	59	61	63	64	66	67
Australia - Australie[3]	DJ	18 518	18 711	18 926	19 153	19 413	19 655	19 903	20 140	20 409	'20 701
Cook Islands - Îles Cook[55]	DF	18	17	16	18	18	18	18	20	20	'21
Fiji - Fidji	DF	788	795	802	807	810	811	816	822	825	830
French Polynesia - Polynésie française	DF	223	226	228	235	239	243	247	251	255	256
Guam[11]	DJ	147	150	153	...	158	161	167	166	'169	'171
Kiribati	DF	'83	...	...	...	...	...	...	...	...	...
Marshall Islands - Îles Marshall	DF	61	63	51	...	...	...	...	...	...	52
Micronesia, Federated States of - Micronésie, États Fédérés de La	DJ	110	112	113	119	117	120	...	...	...	...

Continent and country or area Continent et pays ou zone	Co-de[a]	Population estimates (in thousands) - Estimations (en milliers)									
		1997	1998	1999	2000	2001	2002	2003	2004	2005	2006

OCEANIA - OCÉANIE

Continent and country or area	Code	1997	1998	1999	2000	2001	2002	2003	2004	2005	2006
Nauru	DF	*11*	*11*	*11*	*12*	*12*	*10*	...	...	...	...
New Caledonia - Nouvelle-Calédonie	DF	*201*	*204*	*208*	*213*	*217*	*221*	*226*	*230*	...	...
New Zealand - Nouvelle-Zélande	DJ	3 781	3 815	3 835	3 858	3 881	3 939	4 009	4 061	4 099	4 185
Niue - Nioué	DJ	...	...	...	...	...	2	2	2	2	2
Northern Mariana Islands - Îles Mariannes septentrionales	DF	*64*	*67*	*69*	*72*	*75*	*78*	...	...	80	82
Palau - Palaos	DF	*18*	*18*	*19*	*19*	*20*	*20*	*20*	*21*	...	22
Papua New Guinea - Papouasie-Nouvelle-Guinée	DF	*4 209*	*4 600*	...	*5 100*	...	*5 462*	...	...	...	...
Samoa	DF	...	*168*	*169*	*171*	...	*178*	*180*	*182*	*183*	*185*
Solomon Islands - Îles Salomon	DF	...	...	*405*	*415*	*426*	*437*	*448*	*460*	*471*	*483*
Tonga[56]	DF	*99*	*99*	*100*	*100*	*101*	*101*	*101*	...	...	...
Tuvalu	DF	*9*	*9*	*9*	*9*	*9*	*9*	*9*	*10*	*10*	...
Vanuatu	DF	*174*	...	...	...	...	...	...	*216*[1]	...	*221*[1]

FOOTNOTES - NOTES

Italics: estimates which are less reliable. - Italiques: estimations moins sûres.

* Provisional. - Données provisoires.

[a] 'Code' indicates source of data, as follows:
DF Estimates of population de facto - Population de fait
DJ Estimates of population de jure. - Population de droit

[1] Data refer to national projections. - Les données se réfèrent aux projections nationales.
[2] Data refer to Libyan nationals only. - Les données se raportent aux nationaux libyens seulement.
[3] Mid-year estimates have been adjusted for underenumeration, at latest census. - Les estimations au milieu de l'année tiennent compte d'un ajustement destiné à compenser les lacunes du dénombrement lors du dernier recensement.
[4] Based on the results of the population census of 2002 - D'après les résultats du recensement de la population de 2002.
[5] Data refer to 31 December. - Données se rapportent au 31 Décembre.
[6] Final intercensal estimates. - Estimations inter censitaires finales.
[7] Final postcensal estimates. - Évaluations postcensal finales.
[8] Updated postcensal estimates. - Estimations post censitaires mises à jour.
[9] Population statistics are compiled from registers. - Les statistiques de la population sont compilées à partir des registres.
[10] Around 1996 - 1997 volcanic activity on Montserrat escalated, forcing people to relocate. - Vers 1996 - 1997 l'activité volcanique a connu une recrudescence à Montserrat, forçant les habitants à s'installer ailleurs.
[11] Including armed forces stationed in the area. - Y compris les militaires en garnison sur le territoire.
[12] Excluding armed forces overseas and civilian citizens absent from country for an extended period of time. - Non compris les militaires à l'étranger, et les civils hors du pays pendant une période prolongée.
[13] Data include persons in remote areas, military personnel outside the country, merchant seamen at sea, civilian seasonal workers outside the country, and other civilians outside the country, and exclude nomads, foreign military, civilian aliens temporarily in the country, transients on ships and Indian jungle population. - Y compris les personnes vivant dans des régions éloignées, le personel militaire en dehors du pays, les marins marchands, les ouvriers saisonniers en dehors du pays, et autres civils en dehors du pays, et non compris les nomades, les militaires étrangers, les étrangers civils temporairement dans le pays, les transiteurs sur des bateaux et les Indiens de la jungle.
[14] Data have been adjusted on the basis of the Population Census of 2005. - Données ajustées sur la base du recensement de la population de 2005.
[15] Excluding nomadic Indian tribes. - Non compris les tribus d'Indiens nomades.
[16] Data for 2003 have been adjusted on the basis of the Population Census of 2002. - Les données de 2003 ont été ajustées sur la base du recensement de population de 2002.

[17] Excluding Indian jungle population. - Non compris les Indiens de la jungle.
[18] Data refer to the settled population based on the 1979 Population Census and the latest household prelisting. The refugees of Afghanistan in Iran, Pakistan and estimated 1.5 million nomads are not included. The so adjusted total population of the country for 2006 is 24.1 million of which 12.3 million males and 11.8 million females. - Les données se rapportent à la population stationnaire sur la base du recensement de 1979 et du recensement préliminaire des logements le plus récent. Sont exclus les réfugiés d'Afghanistan en Iran et au Pakistan et les nomades estimés à 1,5 million. La population totale du pays ainsi ajustée pour 2006 comprend 24,1 millions de personnes (12,3 millions d'hommes et 11,8 millions de femmes).
[19] Excluding foreign diplomatic personnel and their dependants. - Non compris le personnel diplomatique étranger et les membres de leur famille les accompagnant.
[20] From 1998 based on census result. - Depuis 1998, à partir des résultats de recensement.
[21] For statistical purposes, the data for China do not include those for the Hong Kong Special Administrative Region (Hong Kong SAR), Macao Special Administrative Region (Macao SAR) and Taiwan province of China. - Pour la présentation des statistiques, les données pour la Chine ne comprennent pas la Région Administrative Spéciale de Hong Kong (Hong Kong RAS), la Région Administrative Spéciale de Macao (Macao RAS) et Taïwan province de Chine.
[22] Data for the period 1990 to 2000 have been adjusted on the basis of the Population Census of 2000. - Les données pour la période allant de 1990 à 2000 ont été ajustées à partir des résultats du recensement de la population de 2000.
[23] Data have been estimated on the basis of the annual National Sample Surveys on Population Changes. - Les données ont été estimées sur la base de l'enquête annuelle "National Sample Survey on Population Changes".
[24] Data for 2005 are estimated from the National Sample Survey of 1 Per cent population. - Les données pour 2005 ont été estimées à partir de l'enquête nationale qui a porté sur un échantillon de 1 % de la population.
[25] Data refer to government controlled areas. - Les données se rapportent aux zones contrôlées par le Gouvernement.
[26] Including data for the Indian-held part of Jammu and Kashmir, the final status of which has not yet been determined. - Y compris les données pour la partie du Jammu et du Cachemire occupée par l'Inde dont le statut définitif n'a pas encore été déterminé.
[27] Data relate to the Iranian Year which begins on 21 March and ends on 20 March of the following year. - Les données concernent l'année iranienne, qui commence le 21 mars et se termine le 20 mars de l'année suivante.
[28] Including data for East Jerusalem and Israeli residents in certain other territories under occupation by Israeli military forces since June 1967. - Y compris les données pour Jérusalem-Est et les résidents israéliens dans certains autres territoires occupés depuis 1967 par les forces armées israéliennes.
[29] Excluding diplomatic personnel outside the country and foreign military and civilian personnel and their dependants stationed in the area. - Non compris le personnel diplomatique hors du pays ni les militaires et agents civils étrangers en poste sur le territoire et les membres de leur famille les accompagnant.
[30] Excluding data for Jordanian territory under occupation since June 1967 by Israeli military forces. Excluding foreigners, including registered Palestinian refugees. - Non compris les données pour le territoire jordanien occupé depuis

juin 1967 par les forces armées israéliennes. Non compris les étrangers, mais y compris les réfugiés de Palestine enregistrés.

[31] From year 2000-2004, calculated based on Population census 1995 structure and growth rate at year 2000. - Pour les années 2000 à 2004, on a pris pour base la structure issue du recensement de population de 1995 et le taux de croissance de 2000.

[32] Data based on the results of the 2005 Population and Housing Census. - Données fondées sur les résultats du recensement de la population et de l'habitat de 2005.

[33] Based on households sample survey. - Basé sur une enquête sur un échantillon de ménages.

[34] Excluding data for the Pakistan-held part of Jammu and Kashmir, the final status of which has not yet been determined. - Non compris les données concernant la partie du Jammu et Cachemire occupée par le Pakistan dont le statut définitif n'a pas été déterminé.

[35] Including Palestinian refugees. - Y compris les réfugiés de Palestine.

[36] Also included in Finland. - Comprise aussi dans Finlande.

[37] Data refer to 1st March. - Données se rapportent au 1er Mars.

[38] Population statistics are compiled from registers. Excluding Faeroe Islands and Greenland shown separately, if available. - Les statistiques de la population sont compilées à partir des registres. Non compris les Iles Féroé et le Gröenland, qui font l'objet de rubriques distinctes, si disponible.

[39] Population statistics are compiled from registers. Including Aland Islands. - Les statistiques de la population sont compilées à partir des registres. Y compris les Îles d'Åland.

[40] Excluding Overseas Departments, namely, French Guiana, Guadeloupe, Martinique and Reunion, shown separately, if available. Excluding diplomatic personnel outside the country and including members of alien armed forces not living in military camps and foreign diplomatic personnel not living in embassies or consulates. - Non compris les départements d'outre mer, c'est-à-dire la Guyane française, la Guadeloupe, la Martinique et la Réunion, qui font l'objet de rubriques distinctes, si disponible. Non compris le personnel diplomatique hors du pays et y compris les militaires étrangers ne vivant pas dans des camps militaires et le personnel diplomatique étranger ne vivant pas dans les ambassades ou les consulats.

[41] Excluding families of military personnel, visitors and transients. - Non compris les familles des militaires, ni les visiteurs et transients.

[42] Excluding armed forces stationed outside the country, but including alien armed forces stationed in the area. - Non compris les militaires en garnison hors du pays, mais y compris les militaires étrangers en garnison sur le territoire.

[43] Data refer to the Vatican City State. Population statistics are compiled from registers. - Les données se rapportent à l'Etat de la Cité du Vatican. Les statistiques de la population sont compilées à partir des registres.

[44] Data refer to 15th of April. - Données se rapportent au 15 Avril.

[45] Including civilian nationals temporarily outside the country. - Y compris les civils nationaux temporairement hors du pays.

[46] Data do not include information for Transnistria and the municipality of Bender. - Les données ne tiennent pas compte de l'information sur la Transnistria et la municipalité de Bender.

[47] Starting from 1997 until 2001 data is de facto and from 2002 and later data is de jure. - De 1997 à 2001, les données sont de fait, à partir de 2002 elles sont de jure.

[48] Excluding Svalbard and Jan Mayen Island shown separately, if available. Including residents temporarily outside the country. - Non compris Svalbard et Jan Mayen qui font l'objet de rubriques distinctes, si disponible. Y compris les résidents se trouvant temporairement hors du pays.

[49] Excluding civilian aliens within country, but including civilian nationals temporarily outside country. - Non compris les civils étrangers dans le pays, mais y compris les civils nationaux temporairement hors du pays.

[50] Without data for Kosovo and Metohia. - Sans les données pour le Kosovo and Metohie.

[51] Starting from 1997 until 1999 data is de facto and from 2000 and later data is de jure. - De 1997 à 1999, les données sont de fait, à partir de 2000 elles sont de jure.

[52] Excluding Channel Islands and Isle of Man, shown separately, if available. - Non compris les îles Anglo-Normandes et l'île de Man, qui font l'objet de rubriques distinctes, si disponible.

[53] Population estimates for 1994 to 2002 were revised in light of the local studies. - Les estimations de la population pour les années 1994 à 2002 ont été révisées en fonction d'études locales.

[54] Population estimates for the years 1991 to 1999 have been smoothed using the 1995 mid-decade household survey and the year 2000 census. - L'estimation de la population a été lissée pour les années entre 1991 et 1999 en utilisant l'enquête des ménages de 1995 et le recensement de l'année 2000.

[55] Excluding Niue, shown separately, which is part of Cook Islands, but because of remoteness is administered separately. - Non compris Nioué, qui fait l'objet d'une rubrique distincte et qui fait partie des îles Cook, mais qui, en raison de son éloignement, est administrée séparément.

[56] Based on the results of the 1996 population census not necessarily mid year estimated. - À partir des résultats du recensement de la population de 1996, pas nécessairement des estimations en milieu d'année.

Table 6

Table 6 presents urban and total population by sex for as many years as possible between 1997 and 2006.

Description of variables: Data are from nation-wide population censuses or are estimates, some of which are based on sample surveys of population carried out among all segments of the population. The results of censuses are identified by a code following the date in the stub; sample surveys are further identified by footnotes; other data are generally estimates, the characteristics of which (*de jure* or *de facto)* are also indicated with a code.

Estimates of urban population presented in this table have been limited to countries or areas for which estimates have been based on the results of sample surveys or have been constructed by the component method from the results of a population census or sample survey. Distributions that result from the estimated total population being distributed by urban/rural residence according to percentages in each group at the time of a census or sample survey have not been included in this table.

Urban is defined according to the national census definition. The definition for each country is set forth at the end of the technical notes to this table.

Percentage computation: Percentages urban are the number of persons residing in an area defined as "urban" per 100 total population. They are calculated by the United Nations Statistics Division. In very few cases the data for total population has been revised but the data for the urban and rural population has not been. These data are footnoted accordingly. In these cases, particular caution should be used in interpreting the figures for percentage urban.

Reliability of data: Estimates that are believed to be less reliable are set in *italics* rather than in roman type. Classification in terms of reliability is based on the method of construction of the total population estimate discussed in the technical notes for table 3.

Limitations: Statistics on urban population by sex are subject to the same qualifications as have been set forth for population statistics in general, as discussed in section 3 of the Technical Notes.

The basic limitations imposed by variations in the definition of the total population and in the degree of under-enumeration are perhaps more important in relation to urban/rural than to any other distributions. The classification by urban and rural is affected by variations in defining usual residence for purposes of sub-national tabulations. Likewise, the geographical differentials in the degree of under-enumeration in censuses affect the comparability of these categories throughout the table. The distinction between *de facto* and *de jure* population is also very important with respect to urban/rural distributions. The difference between the *de facto* and the *de jure* population is discussed at length in section 3.1.1 of the Technical Notes.

A most important and specific limitation, however, lies in the national differences in the definition of urban. Because the distinction between urban and rural areas is made in so many different ways, the definitions have been included at the end of this table. The definitions are necessarily brief and, where the classification as urban involves administrative civil divisions, they are often given in the terminology of the particular country or area. As a result of variations in terminology, it may appear that differences between countries or areas are greater than they actually are. On the other hand, similar or identical terms (for example, town, village, district) as used in different countries or areas may have quite different meanings.

It will be seen from an examination of the definitions that they fall roughly into three major types: (1) classification of localities as urban based on size; (2) classification of administrative centres of minor civil divisions as urban and the remainder of the division as rural; and (3) classification of minor civil divisions on a set of criteria, which may include type of local government, number of inhabitants or proportion of population engaged in agriculture.

The designation of areas as urban or rural is so closely bound to historical, political, cultural, and administrative considerations that the process of developing uniform definitions and procedures moves very slowly. Not only do the definitions differ from one country or area to the other, but, they may also no longer reflect the original intention for distinguishing urban from rural. The criteria once established on the basis of administrative subdivisions (as most of these are) become fixed and resistant to change. For this reason, comparisons of time-series data may be severely affected because the definitions used become outdated. Special care must be taken in comparing data from censuses with those from sample surveys because the definitions of urban used may differ.

Despite their shortcomings, however, statistics on urban and rural population are useful in describing the diversity within the population of a country or area.

The definition of urban/rural areas is based on both qualitative and quantitative criteria that may include any combination of the following: size of population, population density, distance between built-up areas, predominant type of economic activity, conformity to legal or administrative status and urban characteristics such as specific services and facilities[1]. Although statistics classified by urban/rural areas are widely available, no international standard definition appears to be possible at this time since the meaning differs from one country or area to another. The urban/rural classification of population used here is reported according to the national definition.

Earlier data: Urban and total population by sex have been shown in previous issues of the Demographic Yearbook. For information on specific years covered, readers should consult the Historical Index.

DEFINITION OF "URBAN"

AFRICA

Botswana: Agglomeration of 5 000 or more inhabitants where 75 per cent of the economic activity is non-agricultural.
Burundi: Commune of Bujumbura.
Comoros: Administrative centres of prefectures and localities of 5 000 or more inhabitants.
Egypt: Governorates of Cairo, Alexandria, Port Said, Ismailia, Suez, frontier governorates and capitals of other governorates, as well as district capitals (Markaz).
Equatorial Guinea: District centres and localities with 300 dwellings and/or 1 500 inhabitants or more.
Ethiopia: Localities of 2 000 or more inhabitants.
Liberia: Localities of 2 000 or more inhabitants.
Malawi: All townships and town planning areas and all district centres.
Mauritius: Towns with proclaimed legal limits.
Niger: Capital city, capitals of the departments and districts
Senegal: Agglomerations of 10 000 or more inhabitants.
South Africa: Places with some form of local authority.
Sudan: Localities of administrative and/or commercial importance or with population of 5 000 or more inhabitants.
Swaziland: Localities proclaimed as urban.
Tunisia: Population living in communes.
United Republic of Tanzania: 16 gazetted townships.
Zambia: Localities of 5 000 or more inhabitants, the majority of whom all depend on non-agricultural activities.

AMERICA, NORTH

Canada: Places of 1 000 or more inhabitants, having a population density of 400 or more per square kilometre.
Costa Rica: Administrative centres of cantons.
Cuba: Population living in a nucleus of 2 000 or more inhabitants.
Dominican Republic: Administrative centres of municipalities and municipal districts, some of which include suburban zones of rural character.
El Salvador: Administrative centres of municipalities.
Greenland: Localities of 200 or more inhabitants.
Guatemala: Municipality of Guatemala Department and officially recognized centres of other departments and municipalities.
Haiti: Administrative centres of communes.
Honduras: Localities of 2 000 or more inhabitants, having essentially urban characteristics.
Mexico: Localities of 2 500 or more inhabitants.
Nicaragua: Administrative centres of municipalities and localities of 1 000 or more inhabitants with streets and electric light.
Panama: Localities of 1 500 or more inhabitants having essentially urban characteristics. Beginning 1970, localities of 1 500 or more inhabitants with such urban characteristics as streets, water supply systems, sewerage systems and electric light.
Puerto Rico: Agglomerations of 2 500 or more inhabitants, generally having population densities of 1 000 persons per square mile or more. Two types of urban areas: urbanized areas of 50 000 or more inhabitants and urban clusters of at least 2 500 and less than 50 000 inhabitants.
United States: Agglomerations of 2 500 or more inhabitants, generally having population densities of 1 000 persons per square mile or more. Two types of urban areas: urbanized areas of 50 000 or more inhabitants and urban clusters of at least 2 500 and less than 50 000 inhabitants.
U.S. Virgin Islands: Agglomerations of 2 500 or more inhabitants, generally having population densities of 1 000 persons per square mile or more. Two types of urban areas: urbanized areas of 50 000 or more inhabitants and urban clusters of

at least 2 500 and less than 50 000 inhabitants. (As of Census 2000, no urbanized areas are identified in the U.S. Virgin Islands.)

AMERICA, SOUTH

Argentina: Populated centres with 2 000 or more inhabitants.
Bolivia: Localities of 2 000 or more inhabitants.
Brazil: Urban and suburban zones of administrative centres of municipalities and districts.
Chile: Populated centres which have definite urban characteristics such as certain public and municipal services.
Ecuador: Capitals of provinces and cantons.
Falkland Islands (Malvinas): Town of Stanley.
Paraguay: Cities, towns and administrative centres of departments and districts.
Peru: Populated centres with 100 or more dwellings.
Suriname: The districts of Paramaribo and Wanica.
Uruguay: Cities.
Venezuela, Bolivarian Republic: Centres with a population of 1 000 or more inhabitants.

ASIA

Armenia: Cities and urban-type localities, officially designated as such, usually according to the criteria of number of inhabitants and predominance of agricultural, or number of non-agricultural workers and their families.
Azerbaijan: Cities and urban-type localities, officially designated as such, usually according to the criteria of number of inhabitants and predominance of agricultural, or number of non-agricultural workers and their families.
Bahrain: Communes or villages of 2 500 or more inhabitants.
Cambodia: Towns.
China: Cities only refer to the cities proper of those designated by the State Council. In the case of cities with district establishment, the city proper refers to the whole administrative area of the district if its population density is 1 500 people per kilometre or higher; or the seat of the district government and other areas of streets under the administration of the district if the population density is less than 1 500 people per kilometre. In the case of cities without district establishment, the city proper refers to the seat of the city government and other areas of streets under the administration of the city. For the city district with the population density below 1 500 people per kilometre and the city without district establishment, if the urban construction of the district or city government seat has extended to some part of the neighboring designated town(s) or township(s), the city proper does include the whole administrative area of the town(s) or township(s).
Cyprus: Urban areas are those defined by local town plans.
Georgia: Cities and urban-type localities, officially designated as such, usually according to the criteria of number of inhabitants and predominance of agricultural, or number of non-agricultural workers and their families.
India: Towns (places with municipal corporation, municipal area committee, town committee, notified area committee or cantonment board); also, all places having 5 000 or more inhabitants, a density of not less than 1 000 persons per square mile or 400 per square kilometre, pronounced urban characteristics and at least three fourths of the adult male population employed in pursuits other than agriculture.
Indonesia: Places with urban characteristics.
Iran (Islamic Republic of): Every district with a municipality.
Israel: All settlements of more than 2 000 inhabitants, except those where at least one third of households, participating in the civilian labour force, earn their living from agriculture.
Japan: City (shi) having 50 000 or more inhabitants with 60 per cent or more of the houses located in the main built-up areas and 60 per cent or more of the population (including their dependants) engaged in manufacturing, trade or other urban type of business. Alternatively, a shi having urban facilities and conditions as defined by the prefectural order is considered as urban.
Kazakhstan: Cities and urban-type localities, officially designated as such, usually according to the criteria of number of inhabitants and predominance of agricultural, or number of non-agricultural workers and their families.
Korea, Republic of: For estimates: Places with 50 000 or more inhabitants. For census: the figures are composed in the basis of the minor administrative divisions such as Dongs (mostly urban areas) and Eups or Myeons (rural areas).
Kyrgyzstan: Cities and urban-type localities, officially designated as such, usually according to the criteria of number of inhabitants and predominance of agricultural, or number of non-agricultural workers and their families.
Malaysia: Gazetted areas with population of 10 000 and more.
Maldives: Malé, the capital.
Mongolia: Capital and district centres.
Pakistan: Places with municipal corporation, town committee or cantonment.
Sri Lanka: Urban sector comprises of all municipal and urban council areas.
Syrian Arab Republic: Cities, Mohafaza centres and Mantika centres, and communities with 20 000 or more inhabitants.
Tajikistan: Cities and urban-type localities, officially designated as such, usually according to the criteria of number of inhabitants and predominance of agricultural, or number of non-agricultural workers and their families.

Thailand: Municipal areas.

Turkey: Population of settlement places, 20 001 and over.

Turkmenistan: Cities and urban-type localities, officially designated as such, usually according to the criteria of number of inhabitants and predominance of agricultural, or number of non-agricultural workers and their families.

Uzbekistan: Cities and urban-type localities, officially designated as such, usually according to the criteria of number of inhabitants and predominance of agricultural, or number of non-agricultural workers and their families.

Viet Nam: Urban areas include inside urban districts of cities, urban quarters and towns. All other local administrative units (communes) belong to rural areas.

EUROPE

Albania: Towns and other industrial centres of more than 400 inhabitants.

Austria: Communes of more than 5 000 inhabitants.

Belarus: Cities and urban-type localities, officially designated as such, usually according to the criteria of number of inhabitants and predominance of agricultural, or number of non-agricultural workers and their families.

Bulgaria: Towns, that is, localities legally established as urban.

Czech Republic: Localities with 2 000 or more inhabitants.

Estonia: Cities and urban-type localities, officially designated as such, usually according to the criteria of number of inhabitants and predominance of agricultural, or number of non-agricultural workers and their families.

Finland: Urban communes. 1970: Localities.

France: Communes containing an agglomeration of more than 2 000 inhabitants living in contiguous houses or with not more than 200 metres between houses, also communes of which the major portion of the population is part of a multicommunal agglomeration of this nature.

Greece: Population of municipalities and communes in which the largest population centre has 10 000 or more inhabitants. Including also the population of the 18 urban agglomerations, as these were defined at the census of 1991, namely: Greater Athens, Thessaloniki, Patra, Iraklio, Volos, Chania, Irannina, Chalkida, Agrinio, Kalamata, Katerini, Kerkyra, Salamina, Chios, Egio, Rethymno, Ermoupolis, and Sparti.

Hungary: Budapest and all legally designated towns.

Iceland: Localities of 200 or more inhabitants.

Ireland: Cities and towns including suburbs of 1 500 or more inhabitants.

Latvia: Cities and urban-type localities, officially designated as such, usually according to the criteria of number of inhabitants and predominance of agricultural, or number of non-agricultural workers and their families.

Lithuania: Urban population refers to persons who live in cities and towns, i.e., the population areas with closely built permanent dwellings and with the resident population of more than 3 000 of which 2/3 of employees work in industry, social infrastructure and business. In a number of towns the population may be less than 3 000 since these areas had already the states of "town" before the law was enforced (July 1994)

Moldova: Cities and urban-type localities, officially designated as such, usually according to the criteria of number of inhabitants and predominance of agricultural, or number of non-agricultural workers and their families.

Netherlands: Urban: Municipalities with a population of 2 000 and more inhabitants. Semi-urban: Municipalities with a population of less than 2 000 but with not more than 20 per cent of their economically active male population engaged in agriculture, and specific residential municipalities of commuters.

Norway: Localities of 200 or more inhabitants.

Poland: Towns and settlements of urban type, e.g. workers' settlements, fishermen's settlements, health resorts.

Portugal: Agglomeration of 10 000 or more inhabitants.

Romania: Cities, municipalities and other towns.

Russian Federation: Cities and urban-type localities, officially designated as such, usually according to the criteria of number of inhabitants and predominance of agricultural, or number of non-agricultural workers and their families.

Slovakia: 138 cities with 5 000 inhabitants or more.

Spain: Localities of 2 000 or more inhabitants.

Switzerland: Communes of 10 000 or more inhabitants, including suburbs.

Ukraine: Cities and urban-type localities, officially designated as such, usually according to the criteria of number of inhabitants and predominance of agricultural, or number of non-agricultural workers and their families.

United Kingdom: Settlements where the population is 10 000 or above.

OCEANIA

American Samoa: Agglomerations of 2 500 or more inhabitants, generally having population densities of 1 000 persons per square mile or more. Two types of urban areas: urbanized areas of 50 000 or more inhabitants and urban clusters of at least 2 500 and less than 50 000 inhabitants. (As of Census 2000, no urbanized areas are identified in American Samoa.)

Guam: Agglomerations of 2 500 or more inhabitants, generally having population densities of 1 000 persons per square mile or more, referred to as "urban clusters".

New Caledonia: Nouméa and communes of Païta, Nouvel Dumbéa and Mont-Dore.

New Zealand: All cities, plus boroughs, town districts, townships and country towns with a population of 1 000 or more.

Northern Mariana Islands: Agglomerations of 2 500 or more inhabitants, generally having population densities of 1 000 persons per square mile or more. Two types of urban areas: urbanized areas of 50 000 or more inhabitants and urban clusters of at least 2 500 and less than 50 000 inhabitants.

Vanuatu: Luganville centre and Vila urban.

NOTES

[1] For further information, see *Social and Demographic Statistics: Classifications of Size and Type of Locality and Urban/Rural Areas.* E/CN.3/551, United Nations, New York, 1980.

Tableau 6

Le tableau 6 présente des données sur la population urbaine et la population totale selon le sexe pour le plus grand nombre possible d'années entre 1997 et 2006.

Description des variables : les données proviennent de recensements de la population ou sont des estimations fondées, dans certains cas, sur des enquêtes par sondage portant sur toute la population. Le code qui figure dans la deuxième colonne du tableau indique comment les données ont été obtenues ; les enquêtes par sondage sont en outre signalées par une note en fin de tableau ; toutes les autres données sont en général des estimations et la colonne « Code » indique si elles portent sur la population de fait ou la population de droit.

Les estimations de la population urbaine qui figurent dans le tableau 6 ne concernent que les pays ou zones pour lesquels les estimations se fondent sur les résultats d'une enquête par sondage ou ont été établies par la méthode des composantes à partir des résultats d'un recensement de la population ou d'une enquête par sondage. Les répartitions selon le lieu de résidence (zone urbaine ou rurale) obtenues en appliquant à l'estimation de la population totale les pourcentages enregistrés pour chaque groupe lors d'un recensement ou d'une enquête par sondage n'ont pas été reproduites dans le tableau 6.

Le sens donné au terme « urbain » est conforme aux définitions utilisées dans les recensements nationaux. La définition pour chaque pays figure à la fin des présentes notes technique.

Calcul des pourcentages : les pourcentages de la population urbaine sont calculés par la Division de statistique de l'Organisation des Nations Unies et représentent le nombre de personnes qui vivent dans des régions considérées comme urbaines pour 100 personnes de la population totale. Dans de très rares cas, les données pour la population totale ont été révisées mais les données pour la population urbaine et la population rurale ne l'ont pas été. Ces données sont indiquées en note. Dans ces cas, les proportions de population urbaine ou rurale sont à interpréter avec précaution.

Fiabilité des données : les estimations considérées comme moins sûres sont indiquées en italique plutôt qu'en caractères romains. Le classement du point de vue de la fiabilité est fondé sur la méthode utilisée pour établir l'estimation de la population totale qui figure au tableau 3 (voir les explications dans les notes techniques relatives à ce même tableau).

Insuffisance des données : les statistiques de la population urbaine selon le sexe appellent toutes les réserves qui ont été formulées à la section 3 des Notes techniques à propos des statistiques de la population en général.

Les limitations fondamentales imposées par les variations de la définition de la population totale et par les lacunes du recensement se font peut-être sentir davantage dans la répartition de la population en population urbaine et population rurale que dans sa répartition suivant toute autre caractéristique. De fait, des différences dans la définition du lieu de résidence habituel utilisée pour l'exploitation des données à l'échelon sous-national influent sur la classification en population urbaine et en population rurale. De même, les différences de degré de sous-dénombrement suivant la zone, à l'occasion des recensements, ont une incidence sur la comparabilité de ces deux catégories dans l'ensemble du tableau. La distinction entre population de fait et population de droit est également très importante du point de vue de la répartition de la population en population urbaine et en population rurale. Cette distinction est expliquée en détail à la section 3.1.1 des Notes techniques.

Toutefois, la difficulté la plus importante tient aux différences de définition du terme « urbain » selon le pays. Les distinctions faites entre « zone urbaine » et « zone rurale » varient tellement que les définitions utilisées ont été reproduites à la fin des notes techniques du tableau 6. Les définitions sont forcément brèves et, lorsque le classement en « zone urbaine » repose sur des divisions administratives, on a souvent désigné celles-ci par le nom qu'elles portent dans la zone ou le pays considéré. Par suite des variations dans la terminologie, les différences entre pays ou zones peuvent sembler plus grandes qu'elles ne le sont réellement. Il se peut aussi que des termes similaires ou identiques, tels que ville, village ou district, aient des significations très différentes selon les pays ou zones.

On constatera, en examinant les définitions adoptées par les différents pays ou zones, qu'elles peuvent être ramenées à trois types principaux : 1) les localités dépassant certaines dimensions sont classées parmi les zones urbaines ; 2) les centres administratifs de petites circonscriptions administratives sont classées parmi les zones urbaines, le reste de la circonscription étant considéré comme zone rurale ; 3) les petites divisions administratives sont classées parmi les zones urbaines selon un critère déterminé, qui peut être soit le type d'administration locale, soit le nombre d'habitants, soit le pourcentage de la population exerçant une activité agricole.

La distinction entre régions urbaines et régions rurales est si étroitement liée à des considérations d'ordre historique, politique, culturel et administratif que l'on ne peut progresser que très lentement vers des définitions et des méthodes uniformes. Non seulement les définitions sont différentes d'une zone ou d'un pays à un autre, mais on n'y retrouve parfois même plus l'intention originale de distinguer les régions rurales des régions urbaines. Lorsque la classification est fondée, en particulier, sur le critère des circonscriptions administratives (comme la plupart le sont), elle a tendance à devenir rigide avec le temps et à décourager toute modification. Pour cette raison, la comparaison des données appartenant à des séries chronologiques risque d'être gravement faussée du fait que les définitions employées sont désormais périmées. Il faut être particulièrement prudent lorsque l'on compare des données issues de recensements avec des données provenant d'enquêtes par sondage, car il se peut que les définitions du terme « urbain » auxquelles ces données se réfèrent respectivement soient différentes.

Malgré leurs insuffisances, les statistiques sur la population urbaine et rurale permettent de mettre en évidence la diversité de la population d'un pays ou d'une zone.

La distinction entre « zone urbaine » et « zone rurale » repose sur une série de critères qualitatifs aussi bien que quantitatifs, notamment l'effectif de la population, la densité de peuplement, la distance entre îlots d'habitations, le type prédominant d'activité économique, le statut juridique ou administratif, et les caractéristiques d'une agglomération urbaine, c'est-à-dire l'existence de services publics et d'équipements collectifs[1]. Bien que les statistiques différenciant les zones urbaines des zones rurales soient très répandues, il ne paraît pas possible pour le moment d'adopter une classification internationale type de ces zones, vu la diversité des interprétations nationales. La classification de la population en population urbaine et population rurale retenue ici est celle qui correspond aux définitions nationales.

Données publiées antérieurement : des statistiques concernant la population urbaine et la population totale selon le sexe ont été publiées dans des éditions antérieures de l'*Annuaire démographique*. Pour plus de précisions concernant les années pour lesquelles ces données ont été publiées, se reporter à l'index historique.

DÉFINITIONS DU TERME « URBAIN »

AFRIQUE

Afrique du Sud : Zones dotées d'une administration locale.
Botswana : Agglomération de 5 000 habitants ou plus dont 75 p. 100 de l'activité économique n'est pas de type agricole.
Burundi : Commune de Bujumbura.
Comores : Chefs-lieux de préfectures et localités de 5 000 habitants ou plus.
Égypte : Chefs-lieux des gouvernorats du Caire, d'Alexandrie, de Port Saïd, d'Ismaïlia, de Suez ; chefs-lieux des gouvernorats frontaliers, autres chefs-lieux de gouvernorat et chefs-lieux de district (Markaz).
Éthiopie : Localités de 2 000 habitants ou plus.
Guinée équatoriale : Chefs-lieux de district et localités comprenant 300 habitations et/ou 1 500 habitants ou plus.
Libéria : Localités de 2 000 habitants ou plus.
Malawi : Toutes les villes et zones urbanisées et tous les chefs-lieux de district.
Maurice : Villes ayant des limites officiellement définies.
Niger: Ville capital, villes capitales de départements ou de districts.
République-Unie de Tanzanie : 16 townships érigées en communes.
Sénégal : Agglomérations de 10 000 habitants ou plus.
Soudan : Centres administratifs et/ou commerciaux ou localités ayant une population de 5 000 habitants ou plus.
Swaziland : Localités déclarées urbaines.
Tunisie : Population vivant dans les communes.
Zambie : Localités de 5 000 habitants ou plus dont l'activité économique prédominante n'est pas de type agricole.

AMÉRIQUE DU NORD

Canada : Agglomérations de 1 000 habitants ou plus ayant une densité de population d'au moins 400 habitants au kilomètre carré.

Costa Rica : Chefs-lieux de canton.

Cuba : Population vivant dans des agglomérations de 2 000 habitants ou plus.

El Salvador : Chefs-lieux de municipios.

États-Unis : Agglomérations de 2 500 habitants ou plus ayant généralement une densité de population d'au moins 1 000 habitants au mile carré. Deux types de zones urbaines : zones urbanisées de 50 000 habitants ou plus et groupements urbains comptant au moins 2 500 habitants mais moins de 50 000.

Groenland : Localités d'au moins 200 habitants.

Guatemala : Municipio du département de Guatemala et centres administratifs officiels d'autres départements et municipios.

Haïti : Chefs-lieux de communes.

Honduras : Localités d'au moins 2 000 habitants ayant des caractéristiques essentiellement urbaines.

Îles Vierges américaines : Agglomérations de 2 500 habitants ou plus ayant généralement une densité de population d'au moins 1 000 habitants au mile carré. Deux types de zones urbaines : zones urbanisées de 50 000 habitants ou plus et groupements urbains comptant au moins 2 500 habitants mais moins de 50 000. (D'après les résultats du recensement de 2000, les Îles Vierges américaines ne comptent aucune zone urbanisée.)

Mexique : Localités d'au moins 2 500 habitants.

Nicaragua : Chefs-lieux de municipios et agglomérations d'au moins 1 000 habitants dotées de rues et de l'éclairage électrique.

Panama : Localités d'au moins 1 500 habitants ayant des caractéristiques essentiellement urbaines. À partir de 1970, localités de 1 500 habitants ou plus présentant des caractéristiques urbaines, telles que rues, éclairage électrique, systèmes d'approvisionnement en eau et réseaux d'égouts.

Porto Rico : Agglomérations de 2 500 habitants ou plus ayant généralement une densité de population d'au moins 1 000 habitants au mile carré. Deux types de zones urbaines : zones urbanisées de 50 000 habitants ou plus et groupements urbains comptant au moins 2 500 habitants mais moins de 50 000.

République dominicaine : Chefs-lieux de municipios et districts municipaux, dont certains comprennent des zones suburbaines ayant des caractéristiques rurales.

AMÉRIQUE DU SUD

Argentine : Centres comptant au moins 2 000 habitants.

Bolivie : Localités de 2 000 habitants ou plus.

Brésil : Zones urbaines et suburbaines des chefs lieux de municipalités et de districts.

Chili : Centres de peuplement ayant des caractéristiques nettement urbaines (présence de certains services publics et municipaux).

Équateur : Capitales des provinces et chefs-lieux de canton.

Îles Falkland (Malvinas) : Ville de Stanley.

Paraguay : Grandes villes, villes et chefs-lieux des départements et des districts.

Pérou : Centres de peuplement comptant plus de 100 logements.

Suriname : Les districts de Paramaribo et de Wanica.

Uruguay : Villes.

Venezuela : Centres de 1 000 habitants ou plus.

ASIE

Arménie : Grandes villes et localités de type urbain, officiellement désignées comme telles, généralement sur la base du nombre d'habitants et de la prédominance des travailleurs agricoles ou non agricoles avec leur famille.

Azerbaïdjan : Grandes villes et localités de type urbain, officiellement désignées comme telles, généralement sur la base du nombre d'habitants et de la prédominance des travailleurs agricoles ou non agricoles avec leur famille.

Bahreïn : Communes ou villages comptant au moins 2 500 habitants.

Cambodge : Villes.

Chine : Villes désignées comme telles par le Conseil d'État. Dans le cas de villes ayant rang de district, la ville s'entend comme l'ensemble de la zone administrative qui relève du district si sa densité est d'au moins 1 500 habitants au kilomètre carré ou comme le siège des autorités du district et les rues qui relèvent du district si sa densité est inférieure à 1 500 habitants au kilomètre carré. Dans le cas des villes qui n'ont pas rang de district, la ville s'entend comme le siège des autorités de la commune et les rues qui relèvent des autorités de la commune. Dans le cas des villes ayant rang de district qui comptent moins de 1 500 habitants au kilomètre carré et des villes n'ayant pas rang de district, si l'urbanisation du siège du district ou du siège des autorités de la commune a empiété sur une partie de la ou des localités voisines, la ville inclut alors l'ensemble de la zone administrative desdites localités.

Chypre : Zones désignées comme urbaines dans les plans d'urbanisme locaux.

Géorgie : Grandes villes et localités de type urbain, officiellement désignées comme telles, généralement sur la base du nombre d'habitants et de la prédominance des travailleurs agricoles ou non agricoles avec leur famille.

Inde : Villes [localités dotées d'une charte municipale, d'un comité de zone municipale, d'un comité de zone déclarée urbaine ou d'un comité de zone de regroupement (cantonnement)] ; également toutes les localités qui ont une population de 5 000 habitants au moins, une densité de population d'au moins 1 000 habitants au mile carré ou 400 au kilomètre carré, des caractéristiques urbaines prononcées et où les trois quarts au moins des adultes de sexe masculin ont une occupation non agricole.

Indonésie : Localités présentant des caractéristiques urbaines.

Iran (République islamique d') : Tous les districts comptant une municipalité.

Israël : Tous les lieux comptant au moins 2 000 habitants, à l'exception de ceux où le tiers au moins des chefs de ménage faisant partie de la population civile active vivent de l'agriculture.

Japon : Villes (shi), comptant au moins 50 000 habitants, où 60 p. 100 au moins des logements sont situés dans les principales zones bâties, et dont 60 p. 100 au moins de population (y compris les personnes à charge) exercent un métier dans l'industrie, le commerce et d'autres branches d'activités essentiellement urbaines. Tout shi possédant les équipements et présentant les caractéristiques définies comme urbaines par l'administration préfectorale est également considéré comme zone urbaine.

Kazakhstan : Grandes villes et localités de type urbain, officiellement désignées comme telles, généralement sur la base du nombre d'habitants et de la prédominance des travailleurs agricoles ou non agricoles avec leur famille.

Kirghizistan : Grandes villes et localités de type urbain, officiellement désignées comme telles, généralement sur la base du nombre d'habitants et de la prédominance des travailleurs agricoles ou non agricoles avec leur famille.

Malaisie : Zones déclarées « zones urbaines » et comptant au moins 10 000 habitants.

Maldives : Malé (capitale).

Mongolie : Capitale et chefs-lieux de district.

Ouzbékistan : Grandes villes et localités de type urbain, officiellement désignées comme telles, généralement sur la base du nombre d'habitants et de la prédominance des travailleurs agricoles ou non agricoles avec leur famille.

Pakistan : Localités dotées d'une charte municipale ou d'un comité municipal et regroupements (cantonments).

République arabe syrienne : Villes, chefs-lieux de district (Mohafaza) et chefs-lieux de sous district (Mantika), et communes d'au moins 20 000 habitants.

République de Corée : Pour les estimations : localités de 50 000 habitants ou plus. Pour recensements, les données sont établies sont la base des divisions administratives mineures comme les Dongs (principalement en zone urbaines) et des Eups ou Myeons (en zones rurales).

Sri Lanka : Secteur urbain composé de toutes les zones municipales et zones dotées d'un conseil urbain.

Tadjikistan : Grandes villes et localités de type urbain, officiellement désignées comme telles, généralement sur la base du nombre d'habitants et de la prédominance des travailleurs agricoles ou non agricoles avec leur famille.

Thaïlande : Zones municipales.

Turkménistan : Grandes villes et localités de type urbain, officiellement désignées comme telles, généralement sur la base du nombre d'habitants et de la prédominance des travailleurs agricoles ou non agricoles avec leur famille.

Turquie : Population d'établissements humains s'établissant à plus de 20 000 personnes.

Viet Nam : Zones urbaines comprises à l'intérieur des districts urbains des villes ainsi que des quartiers urbains et des localités. Toutes les autres unités administratives locales (communes) sont considérées comme zones rurales.

Yémen : Définition non communiquée.

EUROPE

Albanie : Villes et autres centres industriels de plus de 400 habitants.

Autriche : Communes de plus de 5 000 habitants.

Bélarus : Grandes villes et localités de type urbain, officiellement désignées comme telles, généralement sur la base du nombre d'habitants et de la prédominance des travailleurs agricoles ou non agricoles avec leur famille.

Bulgarie : Villes, c'est-à-dire localités reconnues comme urbaines.

Espagne : Localités de 2 000 habitants et plus.

Estonie : Grandes villes et localités de type urbain, officiellement désignées comme telles, généralement sur la base du nombre d'habitants et de la prédominance des travailleurs agricoles ou non agricoles avec leur famille.

Fédération de Russie : Grandes villes et localités de type urbain, officiellement désignées comme telles, généralement sur la base du nombre d'habitants et de la prédominance des travailleurs agricoles ou non agricoles avec leur famille.

Finlande : Communes urbaines. 1970 : Localités.

France : Communes comprenant une agglomération de plus de 2 000 habitants vivant dans des habitations contiguës ou qui ne sont pas distantes les unes des autres de plus de 200 mètres et communes où la majeure partie de la population vit dans une agglomération regroupant plusieurs communes de cette nature.

Grèce : Municipalités et communes de 10 000 habitants ou plus pour l'agglomération. Y compris également 18 agglomérations urbaines, selon la définition qui en a été donnée lors du recensement de 1991, à savoir : Athènes et sa banlieue, Thessalonique, Patras, Héraklion, Volos, Chania, Ioannina, Chalkida, Agrinio, Kalamata, Katerini, Kerkyra, Salamine, Chios, Egio, Rethymno, Ermoupolis et Sparte.

Hongrie : Budapest et toutes les autres localités reconnues officiellement comme urbaines.

Irlande : Localités, y compris leur banlieues, comptant 1 500 habitants ou plus.

Islande : Localités de 200 habitants ou plus.

Lettonie : Grandes villes et localités de type urbain, officiellement désignées comme telles, généralement sur la base du nombre d'habitants et de la prédominance des travailleurs agricoles ou non agricoles avec leur famille.

Lituanie : Par population urbaine, on entend les personnes qui vivent dans des villes ou des localités, à savoir les zones habitées comportant des logements permanents proches les uns des autres et dont la population est d'au moins 3 000 habitants, les deux tiers desquels étant employés dans le secteur industriel, l'infrastructure sociale ou le commerce. Un certain nombre de villes peuvent compter moins de 3 000 habitants dans la mesure où elles avaient acquis le statut de ville avant l'entrée en vigueur de la nouvelle loi en juillet 1994.

Moldova : Grandes villes et localités de type urbain, officiellement désignées comme telles, généralement sur la base du nombre d'habitants et de la prédominance des travailleurs agricoles ou non agricoles avec leur famille.

Norvège : Localités de 200 habitants ou plus.

Pays Bas : Zones urbaines : municipalités comptant au moins 2 000 habitants. Zones semi-urbaines : municipalités comptant moins de 2 000 habitants, mais où 20 p. 100 au maximum de la population active de sexe masculin pratiquent l'agriculture, et certaines municipalités de caractère résidentiel dont les habitants travaillent ailleurs.

Pologne : Villes et zones de type urbain, par exemple groupements de travailleurs ou de pêcheurs et stations climatiques.

Portugal : Agglomérations d'au moins 10 000 habitants.

République tchèque : Localités d'au moins 2 000 habitants.

Roumanie : Grandes villes, municipalités et autres villes.

Royaume Uni: Agglomérations de population de 10 000 habitants ou plus.

Slovaquie : 138 localités comptant 5 000 habitants ou plus.

Suisse : Communes de 10 000 habitants ou plus, et leurs banlieues.

Ukraine : Grandes villes et localités de type urbain, officiellement désignées comme telles, généralement sur la base du nombre d'habitants et de la prédominance des travailleurs agricoles ou non agricoles avec leur famille.

OCÉANIE

Guam : Agglomérations de 2 500 habitants ou plus ayant généralement une densité de population d'au moins 1 000 habitants au mile carré et considérées comme étant des groupements urbains.

Îles Mariannes septentrionales : Agglomérations de 2 500 habitants ou plus ayant généralement une densité de population d'au moins 1 000 habitants au mile carré. Deux types de zones urbaines : zones urbanisées de 50 000 habitants ou plus et groupements urbains comptant au moins 2 500 habitants mais moins de 50 000.

Nouvelle-Calédonie : Nouméa et communes de Païta, Dumbéa et Mont-Dore.

Nouvelle-Zélande : Grandes villes, boroughs, chefs-lieux, municipalités et chefs-lieux de comté d'au moins 1 000 habitants.

Samoa américaines : Agglomérations de 2 500 habitants ou plus ayant généralement une densité de population d'au moins 1 000 habitants au mile carré. Deux types de zones urbaines : zones urbanisées de 50 000 habitants ou plus et groupements urbains comptant au moins 2 500 habitants mais moins de 50 000. (D'après les résultats du recensement de 2000, les Samoa américaines ne comptent aucune zone urbanisée.)

Vanuatu : Centre de Luganville et Port-Vila.

NOTES

[1] Pour plus de précisions, voir *Social and Demographic Statistics: Classifications of Size and Type of Locality and Urban/Rural Areas*, E/CN.3/551, publication des Nations Unies, New York, 1980.

6. Total and urban population by sex: 1997 - 2006
Population totale et population urbaine selon le sexe: 1997 - 2006

Continent, country or area, and date / Continent, pays ou zone et date	Code[a]	Both sexes - Les deux sexes			Male - Masculin			Female - Féminin		
			Urban - Urbaine			Urban - Urbaine			Urban - Urbaine	
		Total	Number Nombre	Percent P.100	Total	Number Nombre	Percent P.100	Total	Number Nombre	Percent P.100
AFRICA - AFRIQUE										
Algeria - Algérie										
1 VII 1997 ....ESDJ		29 045 000	...	...	14 722 612	...	...	14 322 388	...	...
25 VI 1998............CDJC		29 100 867	16 966 939	58.3	14 698 589	8 563 287	58.3	14 402 278	8 403 652	58.3
1 VII 1998 ....ESDJ		29 507 000	...	...	14 957 049	...	...	14 550 451	...	...
1 VII 1999 ....ESDJ		29 965 000	...	...	15 132 000	...	...	14 833 000	...	...
1 VII 2000 ....ESDJ		30 416 000	...	...	15 357 000	...	...	15 059 000	...	...
1 VII 2001 ....ESDJ		30 871 734	...	...	15 598 261	...	...	15 273 473	...	...
1 VII 2002 ....ESDJ		31 332 033	...	...	15 830 343	...	...	15 501 690	...	...
1 VII 2003 ....ESDJ		31 847 995	...	...	16 090 568	...	...	15 757 427	...	...
Benin - Bénin										
1 VII 1997 ....ESDF		5 638 987	2 177 515	38.6	...	...	...	...	...	...
1 VII 1998 ....ESDF		5 816 488	2 278 190	39.2	...	...	...	...	...	...
1 VII 1999 ....ESDF		5 990 396	2 383 244	39.8	...	...	...	...	...	...
1 VII 2000 ....ESDF		6 169 084	2 492 967	40.4	3 013 705	1 220 905	40.5	3 155 379	1 272 062	40.3
1 VII 2001* ....ESDF		6 416 692	...	...	3 136 516	...	...	3 280 176	...	...
11 II 2002............CDJC		6 769 914	2 630 133	38.9	3 284 119	1 280 418	39.0	3 485 795	1 349 715	38.7
Botswana										
1 VII 1997 ....ESDF		1 533 393	...	...	730 180	...	...	794 204	...	...
1 VII 1998 ....ESDF		1 571 728	...	...	757 669	...	...	814 059	...	...
1 VII 1999 ....ESDF		1 611 021	...	...	779 010	...	...	832 011	...	...
1 VII 2000 ....ESDF		1 653 061	...	...	799 735	...	...	853 326	...	...
17 VIII 2001 ....CDFC		1 680 863	910 480[1]	54.2	813 488	428 856	52.7	867 375	481 624	55.5
1 VII 2002 ....ESDF		1 649 659	375 461	22.8	795 938	...	...	853 721	...	...
1 VII 2003 ....ESDF		1 673 184	384 940	23.0	809 278	...	...	863 906	...	...
1 VII 2004 ....ESDF		1 692 731	393 528	23.2	820 577	191 287	23.3	872 155	202 241	23.2
1 VII 2005 ....ESDF		1 708 327	...	...	829 850	...	...	878 477	...	...
1 VII 2006 ....ESDF		1 719 996	...	...	837 114	...	...	882 882	...	...
Burkina Faso										
1 VII 1997 ....ESDJ		10 561 129	1 647 584	15.6	5 091 453	834 631	16.4	5 469 676	812 954	14.9
1 VII 1998 ....ESDJ		10 816 222	1 695 441	15.7	5 215 231	858 953	16.5	5 600 991	836 487	14.9
1 VII 1999 ....ESDJ		11 078 076	1 744 784	15.7	5 342 307	884 033	16.5	5 735 768	860 751	15.0
1 VII 2000 ....ESDJ		11 346 880	1 795 663	15.8	5 472 776	909 895	16.6	5 874 104	885 767	15.1
1 VII 2001 ....ESDJ		11 622 833	1 848 126	15.9	5 606 733	936 565	16.7	6 016 100	911 561	15.2
1 VII 2002 ....ESDJ		11 906 137	1 902 225	16.0	5 744 279	964 067	16.8	6 161 858	938 158	15.2
1 VII 2003 ....ESDJ		12 197 002	1 958 013	16.1	5 885 516	992 431	16.9	6 311 486	965 582	15.3
1 VII 2004 ....ESDJ		12 495 643	2 015 546	16.1	6 030 550	1 021 683	16.9	6 465 093	993 863	15.4
1 VII 2005 ....ESDJ		12 802 282	2 074 879	16.2	6 179 489	1 051 853	17.0	6 622 793	1 023 026	15.4
9 XII 2006* ....CDJC		13 730 258	2 766 383	20.1	6 635 318	1 380 320	20.8	7 094 940	1 386 063	19.5
Burundi										
1 VII 1997 ....ESDF		6 194 220	473 284	7.6	3 011 678	240 554	8.0	3 182 542	232 730	7.3
1 VII 1998 ....ESDF		6 300 489	493 297	7.8	3 064 211	...	...	3 236 278	...	...
1 VII 1999 ....ESDF		6 482 662	...	...	3 152 810	...	...	3 329 852	...	...
Cameroon - Cameroun[2]										
1 VII 1997 ....ESDF		14 297 617	6 748 475	47.2	...	...	...	...	...	...
1 VII 1998 ....ESDF		14 439 000	6 960 000	48.2	...	...	...	...	...	...
1 VII 2001 ....ESDF		15 731 000	8 023 000	51.0	...	...	...	...	...	...
1 VII 2002 ....ESDF		16 170 000	8 392 000	51.9	...	...	...	...	...	...
1 VII 2003 ....ESDF		16 626 000	8 779 000	52.8	...	...	...	...	...	...
1 VII 2004 ....ESDF		17 000 000	9 086 000	53.4	...	...	...	...	...	...
Cape Verde - Cap-Vert										
1 VII 1997 ....ESDF		406 513	...	...	193 636	...	...	212 877	...	...
1 VII 1998 ....ESDF		417 200	...	...	198 946	...	...	218 254	...	...
1 VII 1999 ....ESDF		428 230	...	...	204 433	...	...	223 797	...	...
16 VI 2000............CDFC		436 863	235 470	53.9	211 479	114 928	54.3	225 384	120 542	53.5
1 VII 2001 ....ESDF		444 683	242 484	54.5	215 288	118 351	55.0	229 395	124 133	54.1
1 VII 2002 ....ESDF		452 714	249 794	55.2	219 211	121 924	55.6	233 503	127 870	54.8
1 VII 2003 ....ESDF		460 968	257 412	55.8	223 253	125 652	56.3	237 715	131 759	55.4
1 VII 2004 ....ESDF		468 164	...	...	226 560	...	...	241 604	...	...
1 VII 2005 ....ESDF		475 465	...	...	230 063	...	...	245 402	...	...
1 VII 2006 ....ESDF		483 090	...	...	233 729	...	...	249 361	...	...

Continent, country or area, and date / Continent, pays ou zone et date	Code[a]	Both sexes - Les deux sexes			Male - Masculin			Female - Féminin		
		Total	Urban - Urbaine Number/Nombre	Urban - Urbaine Percent P.100	Total	Urban - Urbaine Number/Nombre	Urban - Urbaine Percent P.100	Total	Urban - Urbaine Number/Nombre	Urban - Urbaine Percent P.100
AFRICA - AFRIQUE										
Central African Republic - République centrafricaine										
8 XII 2003 ....CDFC		3 151 072	1 194 851	37.9	1 569 446	598 880	38.2	1 581 626	595 969	37.7
Comoros - Comores										
1 IX 2003 ....CDFC		575 660[3]	160 865	27.9	...	...	...	...	...	...
Congo										
1 VII 1997 ....ESDF		2 663 354	...	...	1 297 053	...	...	1 366 301	...	...
1 VII 1998 ....ESDF		2 737 928	...	...	1 333 371	...	...	1 404 557	...	...
1 VII 1999 ....ESDF		2 814 590	...	...	1 370 705	...	...	1 443 885	...	...
1 VII 2000 ....ESDF		2 893 398	...	...	1 409 085	...	...	1 484 313	...	...
1 VII 2001 ....ESDF		2 974 413	...	...	1 448 539	...	...	1 525 874	...	...
1 VII 2002 ....ESDF		3 057 697	...	...	1 489 098	...	...	1 568 599	...	...
1 VII 2003 ....ESDF		3 143 313	...	...	1 530 793	...	...	1 612 520	...	...
1 VII 2004 ....ESDF		3 231 326	...	...	1 573 656	...	...	1 657 670	...	...
Côte d'Ivoire										
21 XI 1998............CDFC		15 366 672	6 529 138	42.5	7 844 621	...	...	7 522 050	...	...
1 VII 1999 ....ESDF		15 881 066	...	...	8 107 236	...	...	7 773 828	...	...
1 VII 2000 ....ESDF		16 401 514	...	...	8 372 518	...	...	8 028 996	...	...
1 VII 2001 ....ESDF		16 928 324	...	...	8 640 647	...	...	8 287 679	...	...
1 VII 2002 ....ESDF		17 461 446	...	...	8 911 589	...	...	8 549 848	...	...
1 VII 2003 ....ESDF		18 000 876	...	...	9 185 374	...	...	8 815 505	...	...
1 VII 2004 ....ESDF		18 545 968	...	...	9 461 591	...	...	9 084 374	...	...
1 VII 2005 ....ESDF		19 096 988	...	...	9 740 427	...	...	9 356 561	...	...
1 VII 2006 ....ESDF		19 657 738	...	...	10 023 964	...	...	9 633 774	...	...
Egypt - Égypte										
1 VII 1997 ....ESDF		60 080 063	25 589 396	42.6	30 736 254	13 091 232	42.6	29 343 809	12 498 164	42.6
1 VII 1998 ....ESDF		61 340 882	26 123 481	42.6	31 379 023	13 363 507	42.6	29 961 859	12 759 974	42.6
1 VII 1999 ....ESDF		62 638 849	26 589 809	42.4	32 034 553	13 632 299	42.6	30 604 296	13 008 893	42.5
1 VII 2000 ....ESDF		63 974 724	27 144 976	42.4	32 714 157	...	...	31 260 567	...	...
1 VII 2001 ....ESDF		65 298 293	28 168 172	43.1	33 378 636	...	...	31 919 657	...	...
1 VII 2002 ....ESDF		66 627 610	28 553 755	42.9	34 052 407	...	...	32 575 203	...	...
1 VII 2003 ....ESDF		67 965 096	29 130 214	42.9	34 720 973	...	...	33 244 123	...	...
1 VII 2004 ....ESDF		69 303 902	29 652 904	42.8	35 379 626	...	...	33 924 276	...	...
1 VII 2005 ....ESDF		70 653 326	30 187 331	42.7	36 037 030	...	...	34 616 296	...	...
1 VII 2006 ....ESDF		72 008 900	30 699 375	42.6	36 725 501	...	...	35 283 399	...	...
11 XI 2006[4]..........CDFC		72 798 031	...	...	37 219 056	...	...	35 578 975	...	...
Equatorial Guinea - Guinée équatoriale										
1 II 2002............CDFC		1 014 999	...	...	501 387	...	...	513 612	...	...
Ethiopia - Éthiopie										
1 VII 1997 ....ESDF		58 117 000	8 315 000	14.3	29 202 000	4 094 000	14.0	28 915 000	4 221 000	14.6
1 VII 1998 ....ESDF		59 882 000	8 691 000	14.5	30 071 000	4 299 000	14.3	29 811 000	4 392 000	14.7
1 VII 1999 ....ESDF		61 672 000	9 074 000	14.7	30 956 000	4 504 000	14.5	30 716 000	4 570 000	14.9
1 VII 2000 ....ESDF		63 494 702	9 472 971	14.9	...	...	...	...	...	...
1 VII 2001 ....ESDF		65 374 320	9 883 138	15.1	32 815 082	4 938 725	15.1	32 559 238	4 944 413	15.2
1 VII 2002 ....ESDF		67 220 000	10 307 000	15.3	33 707 000	5 134 000	15.2	33 513 000	5 173 000	15.4
1 VII 2003 ....ESDF		69 127 000	10 745 000	15.5	34 653 000	5 347 000	15.4	34 474 000	5 398 000	15.7
1 VII 2004 ....ESDF		71 066 000	11 199 000	15.8	35 618 000	5 568 000	15.6	35 448 000	5 631 000	15.9
Gambia - Gambie										
15 IV 2003*...........CDFC		1 364 507	...	...	676 726	...	...	687 781	...	...
Ghana										
26 III 2000............CDFC		18 912 079	8 274 270	43.8	9 357 382	4 043 830	43.2	9 554 697	4 230 440	44.3
Kenya										
1 VII 1997 ....ESDF		27 793 345	...	...	14 425 000	...	...	14 520 000	...	...
1 VII 1998 ....ESDF		28 611 152	...	...	14 772 000	...	...	14 858 000	...	...
1 VII 1999 ....ESDF		29 453 024	5 429 790	18.4	14 342 209	...	...	15 110 815	...	...
24 VIII 1999 ....CDFC		28 686 607	3 539 888	12.3	14 205 589	1 933 437	13.6	14 481 018	1 606 451	11.1
1 VII 2000 ....ESDF		30 149 656	5 234 577	17.4	14 846 350	3 096 394	20.9	15 303 306	2 138 183	14.0
1 VII 2001 ....ESDF		31 120 677	5 421 964	17.4	15 341 600	3 209 419	20.9	15 779 077	2 212 546	14.0
1 VII 2002 ....ESDF		32 117 987	5 613 669	17.5	15 850 411	3 325 186	21.0	16 267 576	2 288 483	14.1
1 VII 2003 ....ESDF		33 141 617	5 809 612	17.5	16 372 798	3 443 644	21.0	16 768 819	2 365 968	14.1
1 VII 2004 ....ESDF		34 191 382	6 009 718	17.6	16 908 648	3 564 746	21.1	17 282 734	2 444 972	14.1
1 VII 2005 ....ESDF		35 267 222	6 213 505	17.6	17 457 906	3 688 113	21.1	17 809 316	2 525 392	14.2
1 VII 2006 ....ESDF		36 432 866	...	...	18 052 944	...	...	18 379 922	...	...

6. Total and urban population by sex: 1997 - 2006
Population totale et population urbaine selon le sexe: 1997 - 2006 (continued - suite)

Continent, country or area, and date / Continent, pays ou zone et date	Code[a]	Both sexes - Les deux sexes			Male - Masculin			Female - Féminin		
		Total	Urban - Urbaine		Total	Urban - Urbaine		Total	Urban - Urbaine	
			Number Nombre	Percent P.100		Number Nombre	Percent P.100		Number Nombre	Percent P.100

AFRICA - AFRIQUE

Lesotho

1 VII 1997 .... ESDF		2 011 644	...	...	991 216	...	...	1 020 399	...	...
1 VII 1998 .... ESDF		2 055 449	...	...	1 013 911	...	...	1 041 504	...	...
1 VII 1999 .... ESDF		2 099 646	...	...	1 036 504	...	...	1 063 142	...	...
1 VII 2000 .... ESDF		2 144 146	...	...	1 059 014	...	...	1 085 132	...	...
1 VII 2001 .... SSDJ		2 157 537	288 895	13.4	1 065 484	131 861	12.4	1 092 053	157 034	14.4
9 IV 2006* .... CDJC		1 880 661	447 970	23.8	916 281	207 848	22.7	964 380	240 122	24.9

Liberia - Libéria

1 VII 1997 .... ESDF		2 879 366	1 307 463	45.4	...	...	...	...	...	...

Libyan Arab Jamahiriya - Jamahiriya arabe libyenne[5]

1 VII 1997 .... ESDF		4 647 520	...	...	2 288 420	...	...	2 359 100	...	...
1 VII 1998 .... ESDF		4 772 430	...	...	2 350 628	...	...	2 421 802	...	...
1 VII 1999 .... FSDF		4 957 663	...	...	2 444 700	...	...	2 512 957	...	...
1 VII 2000 .... ESDF		5 124 519	...	...	2 528 980	...	...	2 595 539	...	...
1 VII 2001 .... ESDF		5 299 943	...	...	2 682 254	...	...	2 617 689	...	...
1 VII 2002 .... ESDF		5 484 426	...	...	2 773 333	...	...	2 711 093	...	...

Madagascar

1 VII 1997 .... ESDF		13 803 000	3 391 000	24.6	...	...	...	...	...	...
1 VII 1998 .... ESDF		14 222 000	3 562 000	25.0	7 091 000[6]	1 745 000	24.6	7 132 000[6]	1 817 000	25.5
1 VII 1999 .... ESDF		14 650 000	3 741 000	25.5	7 306 000[6]	1 834 000	25.1	7 343 000[6]	1 907 000	26.0
1 VII 2000 .... ESDF		15 085 000	3 927 000	26.0	7 526 000	1 926 000	25.6	7 559 000	2 001 000	26.5
1 VII 2001 .... ESDF		15 529 000	4 122 000	26.5	...	...	...	...	...	...
1 VII 2002 .... ESDF		15 981 000	4 327 000	27.1	...	...	...	...	...	...
1 VII 2003 .... ESDF		16 441 000	4 544 000	27.6	...	...	...	...	...	...
1 VII 2004 .... ESDF		17 206 280	4 232 745	24.6	...	...	...	...	...	...

Malawi

1 IX 1998 .... CDFC		9 933 868	1 435 436	14.4	4 867 563	742 839	15.3	5 066 305	692 597	13.7
1 VII 1999*[2] .... ESDF		10 152 753	...	...	4 978 411	...	...	5 174 342	...	...
1 VII 2000*[2] .... ESDF		10 475 257	...	...	5 138 486	...	...	5 336 771	...	...
1 VII 2001*[2] .... ESDF		10 816 294	...	...	5 307 972	...	...	5 508 322	...	...
1 VII 2002*[2] .... ESDF		11 174 648	...	...	5 486 254	...	...	5 688 394	...	...
1 VII 2003*[2] .... ESDF		11 548 841	...	...	5 672 569	...	...	5 876 272	...	...
1 VII 2004*[2] .... ESDF		11 937 934	...	...	5 866 452	...	...	6 071 472	...	...
1 VII 2005*[2] .... ESDF		12 341 170	1 783 289	14.4	6 067 563	...	...	6 273 607	...	...

Mali

1 IV 1998 .... CDFC		9 926 219[7]	2 691 782[7]	27.1	4 905 510[7]	1 344 623	27.4	5 020 709[7]	1 347 159	26.8
1 I 1999 .... ESDF		9 968 933	2 726 550	27.4	4 934 237	1 365 851	27.7	5 034 696	1 360 699	27.0
1 I 2000 .... ESDF		10 243 339	2 868 329	28.0	5 069 994	1 436 707	28.3	5 173 346	1 431 622	27.7
1 I 2001 .... ESDF		10 524 600	3 018 079	28.7	5 209 227	1 511 556	29.0	5 315 375	1 506 523	28.3
1 I 2002 .... ESDF		10 813 478	3 176 399	29.4	5 352 318	1 590 701	29.7	5 461 160	1 585 697	29.0
1 I 2003 .... ESDF		11 111 219	3 344 066	30.1	5 499 912	1 674 538	30.4	5 611 305	1 669 528	29.8
1 I 2004 .... ESDF		11 419 483	3 522 033	30.8	5 652 867	1 763 554	31.2	5 766 615	1 758 478	30.5
1 I 2005 .... ESDF		11 732 416	3 707 315	31.6	5 808 166	1 856 224	32.0	5 924 252	1 851 091	31.2
1 I 2006 .... ESDF		12 051 021	3 900 404	32.4	5 966 339	1 952 802	32.7	6 084 681	1 947 601	32.0

Mauritania - Mauritanie

1 XI 2000 .... CDFC		2 548 157	...	...	1 240 414	...	...	1 307 743	...	...
1 VII 2005 .... ESDF		2 905 727	...	...	1 450 418	...	...	1 455 309	...	...

Mauritius - Maurice

1 VII 1997 .... ESDJ		1 148 284	494 446	43.1	571 169	244 867	42.9	577 115	249 579	43.2
1 VII 1998 .... ESDJ		1 160 421	498 138	42.9	576 620	246 300	42.7	583 801	251 750	43.1
1 VII 1999 .... ESDJ		1 175 267	502 958	42.8	583 169	248 362	42.6	592 098	254 596	43.0
1 VII 2000 .... ESDJ		1 186 873	506 357	42.7	588 212	249 678	42.4	598 661	256 679	42.9
2 VII 2000 .... CDJC		1 178 848	503 045	42.7	583 756	247 844	42.5	595 092	255 201	42.9
1 VII 2001 .... ESDJ		1 199 881	510 822	42.6	594 490	251 721	42.3	605 391	259 101	42.8
1 VII 2002 .... ESDJ		1 210 203	513 761	42.5	599 165	252 848	42.2	611 038	260 913	42.7
1 VII 2003 .... ESDJ		1 222 811	518 368	42.4	605 084	255 077	42.2	617 727	263 291	42.6
1 VII 2004 .... ESDJ		1 233 386	521 588	42.3	610 108	256 542	42.0	623 278	265 046	42.5
1 VII 2005 .... ESDJ		1 243 253	524 318	42.2	614 786	257 785	41.9	628 467	266 533	42.4
1 VII 2006 .... ESDJ		1 252 698	527 138	42.1	619 243	259 028	41.8	633 455	268 110	42.3

Mayotte

5 VIII 1997 .... CDJC		131 368	...	...	66 600	...	...	64 768	...	...
30 VII 2002 .... CDJC		160 301	...	...	80 281	...	...	80 020	...	...

Continent, country or area, and date / Continent, pays ou zone et date	Code[a]	Both sexes - Les deux sexes			Male - Masculin			Female - Féminin		
		Total	Urban - Urbaine		Total	Urban - Urbaine		Total	Urban - Urbaine	
			Number Nombre	Percent P.100		Number Nombre	Percent P.100		Number Nombre	Percent P.100
AFRICA - AFRIQUE										
Morocco - Maroc										
1 VII 1997	ESDF	27 310 000	14 524 000	53.2	13 588 000	7 173 000	52.8	13 722 000	7 351 000	53.6
1 VII 1998	ESDF	27 775 000	14 957 000	53.9	13 819 000	7 373 000	53.4	13 956 000	7 584 000	54.3
1 VII 1999	ESDF	28 238 000	15 401 000	54.5	14 049 000	7 580 000	54.0	14 189 000	7 821 000	55.1
1 VII 2000	ESDF	28 705 000	15 849 000	55.2	14 281 000	7 787 000	54.5	14 424 000	8 062 000	55.9
1 VII 2001	ESDF	29 170 000	16 307 000	55.9	14 512 000	8 000 000	55.1	14 658 000	8 307 000	56.7
1 VII 2002	ESDF	29 631 000	16 772 000	56.6	14 742 000	8 217 000	55.7	14 889 000	8 555 000	57.5
1 VII 2003	ESDF	30 088 000	17 244 000	57.3	14 972 000	8 438 000	56.4	15 116 000	8 806 000	58.3
1 VII 2004	ESDF	30 540 000	17 723 000	58.0	...	...	...	...	...	...
1 IX 2004	CDFC	29 680 069	16 339 561	55.1	14 640 662	8 022 273	54.8	15 039 407	8 317 288	55.3
Mozambique										
1 VII 1997[8]	ESDF	16 542 740	...	...	7 831 001	...	...	8 711 739	...	...
1 VIII 1997[9]	CDFC	16 099 246	4 601 132	28.6	7 714 306	2 274 116	29.5	8 384 940	2 327 016	27.8
1 VII 1998[8]	ESDF	16 916 638	...	...	7 979 434	...	...	8 937 204	...	...
1 VII 1999[8]	ESDF	17 299 184	...	...	8 130 680	...	...	9 168 504	...	...
1 VII 2000[8]	ESDF	17 690 584	...	...	8 284 793	...	...	9 405 791	...	...
1 VII 2005*[8]	ESDF	19 420 036	...	...	9 368 425	...	...	10 051 611	...	...
Namibia - Namibie										
1 VII 2000*	ESDF	1 816 600	...	...	886 900	...	...	929 600	...	...
27 VIII 2001	CDFC	1 830 330	603 612	33.0	887 721[10]	300 358[10]	33.8	942 572[10]	303 236[10]	32.2
Niger										
1 VII 1997	ESDJ	9 574 274	1 521 647	15.9	4 769 563	764 464	16.0	4 804 711	757 183	15.8
1 VII 1998	ESDJ	9 871 076	1 576 639	16.0	4 918 547	790 858	16.1	4 952 529	785 781	15.9
1 VII 1999	ESDJ	10 177 080	1 633 578	16.1	5 072 184	818 138	16.1	5 104 896	815 440	16.0
1 VII 2000	ESDJ	10 492 569	1 692 532	16.1	5 230 620	846 331	16.2	5 261 949	846 201	16.1
20 V 2001*	CDFC	10 790 352	...	...	5 380 287	...	...	5 410 065	...	...
1 VII 2001	ESDJ	11 090 256	1 804 243	16.3	5 531 534	902 637	16.3	5 558 722	901 606	16.2
1 VII 2002	ESDJ	11 456 235	1 863 783	16.3	5 714 075	932 424	16.3	5 742 160	931 359	16.2
1 VII 2003	ESDJ	11 834 290	1 925 288	16.3	5 902 639	963 194	16.3	5 931 651	962 094	16.2
1 VII 2004	ESDJ	12 224 822	1 988 822	16.3	6 097 426	994 979	16.3	6 127 396	993 843	16.2
1 VII 2005	ESDJ	12 628 241	2 054 453	16.3	6 298 641	1 027 814	16.3	6 329 600	1 026 640	16.2
Nigeria - Nigéria										
1 VII 2000[2]	ESDF	115 224 312	...	...	57 750 754	...	...	57 473 558	...	...
1 VII 2001[2]	ESDF	118 800 696	...	...	59 538 640	...	...	59 262 056	...	...
1 VII 2002[2]	ESDF	122 443 748	...	...	61 369 212	...	...	61 074 536	...	...
1 VII 2003[2]	ESDF	126 152 844	...	...	63 241 808	...	...	62 911 036	...	...
1 VII 2004[2]	ESDF	129 175 000	...	...	64 459 000	...	...	64 716 000	...	...
1 VII 2005[2]	ESDF	133 767 000	...	...	67 111 000	...	...	48 531 000	...	...
21 III 2006*	CDFC	140 003 542	...	...	71 709 859	...	...	68 293 683	...	...
Réunion										
8 III 1999	CDJC	706 180	...	...	347 076	...	...	359 104	...	...
1 VII 1999	ESDF	709 900	...	...	349 100	...	...	360 800	...	...
1 VII 2000	ESDF	722 200	...	...	355 100	...	...	367 100	...	...
1 VII 2001	ESDF	734 700	...	...	361 200	...	...	373 500	...	...
1 VII 2002	ESDF	747 554	...	...	373 861	...	...	373 693	...	...
1 VII 2003	ESDF	764 000	...	...	375 400	...	...	388 600	...	...
1 VII 2004	ESDF	768 808	...	...	377 607	...	...	391 201	...	...
Rwanda										
16 VIII 2002	CDJC	8 128 553	1 372 604	16.9	3 879 448	727 172	18.7	4 249 105	645 432	15.2
Saint Helena ex. dep. - Sainte-Hélène sans dép.										
8 III 1998	CDFC	5 157	884	17.1	2 612	452	17.3	2 545	432	17.0
Saint Helena: Ascension - Sainte-Hélène: Ascension										
8 III 1998	CDJC	712	...	...	458	...	...	254	...	...
Sao Tome and Principe - Sao Tomé-et-Principe										
1 VII 1997	ESDF	129 178	...	...	63 958	...	...	65 220	...	...
1 VII 1998	ESDF	131 234	...	...	65 002	...	...	66 232	...	...
1 VII 1999	ESDF	133 323	...	...	66 063	...	...	67 260	...	...
1 VII 2000	ESDF	135 445	...	...	67 141	...	...	68 304	...	...
25 VIII 2001	CDJC	137 599	75 013	54.5	68 236	36 455	53.4	69 363	38 558	55.6

Continent, country or area, and date / Continent, pays ou zone et date	Code[a]	Both sexes - Les deux sexes Total	Urban - Urbaine Number Nombre	Urban - Urbaine Percent P.100	Male - Masculin Total	Urban - Urbaine Number Nombre	Urban - Urbaine Percent P.100	Female - Féminin Total	Urban - Urbaine Number Nombre	Urban - Urbaine Percent P.100
AFRICA - AFRIQUE										
Sao Tome and Principe - Sao Tomé-et-Principe										
1 VII 2002	ESDF	140 365	...	...	69 515	...	...	70 850	...	...
1 VII 2003	ESDF	143 186	...	...	70 821	...	...	72 365	...	...
1 VII 2004	ESDF	146 056	...	...	72 153	...	...	73 903	...	...
1 VII 2005	ESDF	148 968	...	...	73 506	...	...	75 462	...	...
1 VII 2006	ESDF	151 912	...	...	74 876	...	...	77 036	...	...
Senegal - Sénégal										
1 VII 1997	ESDJ	8 741 686	...	...	4 208 744	...	...	4 532 942	...	...
1 VII 1998	ESDJ	8 964 295	...	...	4 305 771	...	...	4 658 524	...	...
1 VII 1999	ESDJ	9 192 572	...	...	4 415 174	...	...	4 777 398	...	...
1 VII 2000	ESDJ	9 426 663	...	...	4 619 065	...	...	4 807 598	...	...
1 VII 2001	ESDJ	9 666 715	...	...	4 740 557	...	...	4 926 158	...	...
1 VII 2002	ESDJ	9 912 880	...	...	4 865 222	...	...	5 047 658	...	...
8 XII 2002	CDJC	9 855 338	4 007 590	40.7	4 846 126	1 984 761	41.0	5 009 212	2 022 829	40.4
1 VII 2003	ESDJ	10 165 314	...	...	5 000 053	...	...	5 165 260	...	...
1 VII 2004	ESDJ	10 564 303	...	...	5 069 869	...	...	5 494 434	...	...
1 VII 2005	ESDJ	10 848 051	...	...	5 315 545	...	...	5 532 506	...	...
Seychelles										
1 VII 1997	ESDF	77 319	...	...	38 545	...	...	38 774	...	...
29 VIII 1997	CDFC	75 876	...	...	37 589	...	...	38 287	...	...
1 VII 1998	ESDF	78 846	...	...	39 359	...	...	39 487	...	...
1 VII 1999	ESDF	80 410	...	...	40 199	...	...	40 211	...	...
1 VII 2000	ESDF	81 131	...	...	40 249	...	...	40 882	...	...
1 VII 2001	ESDF	81 202	...	...	39 973	...	...	41 229	...	...
1 VII 2002	ESDF	83 723	...	...	41 990	...	...	41 733	...	...
26 VIII 2002[11]	CDJC	81 755	...	...	40 751	...	...	41 004	...	...
1 VII 2003	ESDF	82 781	...	...	40 859	...	...	41 922	...	...
1 VII 2004	ESDF	82 475	...	...	40 652	...	...	41 823	...	...
1 VII 2005	ESDF	82 852	...	...	41 233	...	...	41 619	...	...
1 VII 2006	ESDF	84 600	...	...	42 875	...	...	41 725	...	...
Sierra Leone										
1 VII 1997	ESDF	4 625 013	1 638 198	35.4	...	...	...	...	...	...
1 VII 1998	ESDF	4 729 579	1 682 456	35.6	...	...	...	...	...	...
1 VII 1999	ESDF	4 836 011	1 727 184	35.7	...	...	...	...	...	...
1 VII 2000	ESDF	4 944 310	1 772 379	35.8	...	...	...	...	...	...
1 VII 2001	ESDF	5 054 476	1 818 044	36.0	...	...	...	...	...	...
1 VII 2002	ESDF	5 166 508	1 864 177	36.1	...	...	...	...	...	...
1 VII 2003	ESDF	5 280 406	1 910 779	36.2	...	...	...	...	...	...
4 XII 2004	CDFC	4 976 871	...	...	2 420 218	...	...	2 556 653	...	...
Somalia - Somalie[12]										
1 VII 2002	SSDF	6 799 079	2 310 817	34.0	3 499 523	1 168 410	33.4	3 299 556	1 142 407	34.6
South Africa - Afrique du Sud										
1 VII 1997[8]	ESDF	41 226 700	22 107 800	53.6	19 857 000	10 836 700	54.6	21 369 700	11 271 100	52.7
1 VII 1998[8]	ESDF	42 130 500	22 565 300	53.6	20 330 100	11 073 800	54.5	21 800 400	11 491 500	52.7
1 VII 1999[8]	ESDF	43 054 306	23 032 381	53.5	20 814 425	11 316 037	54.4	22 239 881	11 716 344	52.7
1 VII 2000[8]	ESDF	43 685 699	23 125 194	52.9	21 016 530	11 273 108	53.6	22 669 169	11 852 086	52.3
1 VII 2001[8]	ESDF	44 560 644	23 501 443	52.7	21 438 993	11 439 101	53.4	23 121 651	12 062 342	52.2
10 X 2001*	CDFC	44 819 778	...	...	21 434 041	...	...	23 385 737	...	...
1 VII 2002[8]	ESDF	45 454 211	23 888 278	52.6	21 870 730	11 612 775	53.1	23 583 481	12 275 503	52.1
1 VII 2003[8]	ESDF	46 429 823	...	...	22 150 308	...	...	24 279 515	...	...
1 VII 2004[8]	ESDF	46 586 607	...	...	22 987 410	...	...	23 599 197	...	...
1 VII 2005[8]	ESDF	46 888 200	...	...	23 070 300	...	...	23 817 900	...	...
1 VII 2006[8]	ESDF	47 390 900	...	...	23 327 600	...	...	24 063 300	...	...
Sudan - Soudan										
1 VII 1997	ESDF	28 506 732	...	...	14 444 769	...	...	14 061 963	...	...
1 VII 1998	ESDF	29 266 405	...	...	14 738 449	...	...	14 527 956	...	...
1 VII 1999	ESDF	30 326 000	...	...	15 276 000	...	...	15 050 000	...	...
1 VII 2000	ESDF	31 081 000	...	...	15 602 227	...	...	15 478 773	...	...
1 VII 2001	ESDF	31 626 526	...	...	16 014 575	...	...	15 611 951	...	...
1 VII 2002	ESDF	32 468 401	...	...	16 440 837	...	...	16 027 564	...	...
1 VII 2003	ESDF	33 333 648	...	...	16 793 306	...	...	16 540 342	...	...
1 VII 2004	ESDF	34 512 000	...	...	17 390 000	...	...	17 122 000	...	...

Continent, country or area, and date / Continent, pays ou zone et date	Code[a]	Both sexes - Les deux sexes			Male - Masculin			Female - Féminin		
		Total	Urban - Urbaine		Total	Urban - Urbaine		Total	Urban - Urbaine	
			Number Nombre	Percent P.100		Number Nombre	Percent P.100		Number Nombre	Percent P.100

AFRICA - AFRIQUE

Swaziland										
11 V 1997 ....CDFC		929 718	214 428	23.1	440 154	106 256	24.1	489 564	108 172	22.1
Tunisia - Tunisie										
1 VII 1997 ....ESDF		9 214 900	...	...	4 647 000	...	...	4 567 900	...	...
1 VII 1998 ....ESDF		9 333 300	...	...	4 709 000	...	...	4 624 300	...	...
Uganda - Ouganda										
1 VII 1997 ....ESDF		20 507 300	2 302 500	11.2	...	...	...	...	...	...
1 VII 1998 ....ESDF		21 174 700	2 418 400	11.4	...	...	...	...	...	...
1 VII 1999 ....ESDF		21 863 900	2 540 100	11.6	...	...	...	...	...	...
1 VII 2000 ....ESDF		22 575 400	2 668 000	11.8	...	...	...	...	...	...
1 VII 2001 ....ESDF		23 310 100	2 802 400	12.0	...	...	...	...	...	...
1 VII 2002 ....ESDF		24 068 800	2 943 500	12.2	...	...	...	...	...	...
12 IX 2002............CDFC		24 442 084	2 999 387	12.3	11 929 803	1 449 684	12.2	12 512 281	1 549 703	12.4
1 VII 2003 ....ESDF		24 850 700	3 091 400	12.4	...	...	...	...	...	...
1 VII 2004 ....ESDF		25 659 500	3 247 000	12.7	...	...	...	...	...	...
1 VII 2005 ....ESDF		26 494 600	3 410 500	12.9	...	...	...	...	...	...
1 VII 2006 ....ESDF		27 356 900	3 582 200	13.1	...	...	...	...	...	...
United Republic of Tanzania - République Unie de Tanzanie										
24 VIII 2002* ....CDFC		34 443 603	...	...	16 829 861	...	...	17 613 742		
Zambia - Zambie										
1 VII 1999 ....ESDF		10 406 681	...	...	5 198 440	...	...	5 208 241	...	...
25 X 2000 ....CDFC		9 337 425	3 347 069	35.8	4 594 290	1 662 739	36.2	4 743 135	1 684 330	35.5
Zimbabwe										
1 VII 1997 ....ESDF		12 293 953	...	...	6 000 009	...	...	6 293 944	...	...
18 VIII 1997 ....SSDF		11 789 274	3 826 580	32.5	5 647 090	1 906 476	33.8	6 142 184	1 920 104	31.3
1 VII 1999 ....ESDF		13 079 127	...	...	6 382 092	...	...	6 697 035	...	...
17 VIII 2002 ....CDFC		11 631 657	4 029 707	34.6	5 634 180	1 988 176	35.3	5 997 477	2 041 531	34.0

AMERICA, NORTH - AMÉRIQUE DU NORD

Anguilla										
9 V 2001 ....CDFC		11 430	...	...	5 628	...	...	5 802	...	...
1 VII 2001 ....ESDF		11 561	...	...	5 701	...	...	5 860	...	...
Antigua and Barbuda - Antigua-et-Barbuda										
1 VII 2000 ....ESDF		72 310	...	...	34 858	...	...	37 452	...	...
28 V 2001 ....CDFC		77 426	...	...	37 002	...	...	40 424	...	...
1 VII 2001 ....ESDF		76 886	...	...	36 107	...	...	40 779	...	...
1 VII 2002 ....ESDF		78 320	...	...	36 780	...	...	41 540	...	...
1 VII 2003 ....ESDF		79 781	...	...	37 467	...	...	42 314	...	...
1 VII 2004 ....ESDF		81 270	...	...	38 166	...	...	43 104	...	...
1 VII 2005 ....ESDF		82 786	...	...	38 878	...	...	43 908	...	...
Aruba										
1 VII 1997 ....ESDJ		86 302	...	...	42 175	...	...	44 127	...	...
1 VII 1998 ....ESDJ		88 452	...	...	43 027	...	...	45 425	...	...
1 VII 1999 ....ESDJ		89 659	...	...	43 362	...	...	46 297	...	...
1 VII 2000 ....ESDJ		90 600	...	...	43 594	...	...	47 005	...	...
14 X 2000 ....CDJC		90 508	...	...	43 435	...	...	47 073	...	...
1 VII 2001 ....ESDJ		91 870	...	...	44 042	...	...	47 828	...	...
1 VII 2002 ....ESDJ		93 310	...	...	44 651	...	...	48 659	...	...
1 VII 2003 ....ESDJ		95 076	...	...	45 461	...	...	49 615	...	...
1 VII 2004 ....ESDJ		97 658	...	...	46 657	...	...	51 001	...	...
1 VII 2005 ....ESDJ		100 629	...	...	48 030	...	...	52 599	...	...
1 VII 2006 ....ESDJ		102 819	...	...	49 053	...	...	53 766	...	...
Bahamas										
1 VII 1997 ....ESDF		288 467	...	...	142 312	...	...	146 155	...	...
1 VII 1998 ....ESDF		293 261	...	...	144 786	...	...	148 475	...	...
1 VII 1999 ....ESDF		298 050	...	...	147 241	...	...	150 809	...	...
1 V 2000 ....CDFC		303 611	2 578 256	849.2	147 715	124 582	84.3	155 896	133 244	85.5
1 VII 2001 ....ESDF		307 800	...	...	149 600	...	...	158 200	...	...

Continent, country or area, and date / Continent, pays ou zone et date	Code[a]	Both sexes - Les deux sexes			Male - Masculin			Female - Féminin		
		Total	Urban - Urbaine		Total	Urban - Urbaine		Total	Urban - Urbaine	
			Number Nombre	Percent P.100		Number Nombre	Percent P.100		Number Nombre	Percent P.100
AMERICA, NORTH - AMÉRIQUE DU NORD										
Bahamas										
1 VII 2002 .... ESDF		312 100	...	...	151 700	...	...	160 400	...	...
1 VII 2003 .... ESDF		316 900	...	...	154 100	...	...	162 800	...	...
1 VII 2004 .... ESDF		320 800	...	...	155 900	...	...	164 900	...	...
1 VII 2005 .... ESDF		325 200	...	...	158 000	...	...	167 200	...	...
1 VII 2006 .... ESDF		329 500	...	...	160 100	...	...	169 400	...	...
Barbados - Barbade										
1 V 2000 .... CDFC		250 010	...	...	119 926	...	...	130 084	...	...
Belize										
1 VII 1997 .... ESDF		230 000	115 975	50.4	114 500	55 350	48.3	115 500	60 625	52.5
1 VII 1998 .... ESDF		238 500	120 110	50.4	118 500	57 095	48.2	120 000	63 015	52.5
1 VII 1999 .... ESDF		243 055	118 125	48.6	122 745	58 750	47.9	120 310	59 750	49.7
12 V 2000 .... CDFC		240 204	114 541	47.7	121 278	56 565	46.6	118 926	57 976	48.7
1 VII 2000 .... ESDF		249 800	121 455	48.6	126 080	59 985	47.6	123 720	61 470	49.7
1 VII 2001 .... ESDF		257 310	125 830	48.9	129 890	62 160	47.9	127 420	63 370	49.7
1 VII 2002 .... ESDF		265 200	130 500	49.2	133 900	64 400	48.1	131 300	66 100	50.3
1 VII 2003 .... ESDF		273 700	135 600	49.5	138 300	67 000	48.4	135 400	60 000	50.7
1 VII 2004 .... ESDF		282 600	141 000	49.9	142 700	69 500	48.7	139 900	71 500	51.1
1 VII 2005 .... ESDF		291 800	146 600	50.2	147 400	72 200	49.0	144 400	74 400	51.5
1 VII 2006 .... ESDF		301 386	152 583	50.6	149 676	73 495	49.1	151 710	79 089	52.1
Bermuda - Bermudes										
1 VII 1997 .... ESDJ		61 957	...	...	30 107	...	...	31 850	...	...
1 VII 1998 .... ESDJ		62 277	...	...	31 258	...	...	31 019	...	...
1 VII 1999 .... ESDJ		62 656	...	...	30 433	...	...	32 223	...	...
20 V 2000[13] .... CDJC		62 059	...	...	29 802	...	...	32 257	...	...
1 VII 2000 .... ESDJ		63 023	...	...	30 628	...	...	32 395	...	...
1 VII 2001 .... ESDJ		62 455	...	...	29 969	...	...	32 486	...	...
1 VII 2002 .... ESDJ		62 754	...	...	30 092	...	...	32 662	...	...
1 VII 2003 .... ESDJ		63 042	...	...	30 205	...	...	32 837	...	...
1 VII 2004 .... ESDJ		63 320	...	...	30 323	...	...	32 997	...	...
1 VII 2005 .... ESDJ		63 571	...	...	30 424	...	...	33 147	...	...
1 VII 2006 .... ESDJ		63 797	...	...	30 504	...	...	33 293	...	...
British Virgin Islands - Îles Vierges britanniques										
21 V 2001 .... CDFC		20 647	...	...	10 627	...	...	10 020	...	...
Canada										
1 VII 1997[14] .... ESDJ		29 907 172	23 397 908	78.2	14 800 432	...	...	15 106 740	...	...
1 VII 1998[14] .... ESDJ		30 157 082	23 704 015	78.6	14 927 226	...	...	15 229 856	...	...
1 VII 1999[14] .... ESDJ		30 403 878	...	...	15 052 451	...	...	15 351 427	...	...
1 VII 2000[14] .... ESDJ		30 689 035	...	...	15 196 709	...	...	15 492 326	...	...
15 V 2001 .... CDJC		30 007 095[15]	23 908 105	79.7	14 706 850	11 594 915	78.8	15 300 245	12 313 190	80.5
1 VII 2001[16] .... ESDJ		31 021 251	...	...	15 364 404	...	...	15 656 847	...	...
1 VII 2002[16] .... ESDJ		31 372 587	...	...	15 538 572	...	...	15 834 015	...	...
1 VII 2003[16] .... ESDJ		31 676 077	...	...	15 688 977	...	...	15 987 100	...	...
1 VII 2004[16] .... ESDJ		31 995 199	...	...	15 846 832	...	...	16 148 367	...	...
1 VII 2005[17] .... ESDJ		32 312 077	...	...	16 003 804	...	...	16 308 273	...	...
16 V 2006 .... CDJC		31 612 895	...	...	15 475 970	...	...	16 136 925	...	...
1 VII 2006[17] .... ESDJ		32 649 482	...	...	16 170 723	...	...	16 478 759	...	...
Cayman Islands - Îles Caïmanes										
10 X 1999[18] .... CDJC		39 020	...	...	19 033	...	...	19 987	...	...
1 VII 2004 .... ESDJ		44 240	...	...	21 235	...	...	23 005	...	...
1 VII 2006 .... ESDJ		51 992	...	...	26 340	...	...	25 652	...	...
Costa Rica										
1 VII 1997 .... ESDJ		3 270 700	1 419 407	43.4	1 630 815	689 949	42.3	1 639 885	729 458	44.5
1 VII 1998 .... ESDJ		3 340 909	1 440 272	43.1	1 662 735	693 376	41.7	1 678 174	746 896	44.5
1 VII 1999 .... ESDJ		3 412 613	1 576 288	46.2	1 688 946	757 345	44.8	1 723 667	818 943	47.5
26 VI 2000 .... CDJC		3 810 179	2 249 296	59.0	1 902 614	1 096 138	57.6	1 907 565	1 153 158	60.5
1 VII 2000 .... ESDJ		3 810 187	2 249 301	59.0	1 890 808	1 100 259	58.2	1 919 379	1 149 042	59.9
1 VII 2001 .... ESDJ		3 906 742	2 305 723	59.0	1 935 168	1 119 394	57.8	1 971 574	1 186 329	60.2
1 VII 2002 .... ESDJ		3 997 883	2 359 158	59.0	1 983 715	1 147 227	57.8	2 014 168	1 211 931	60.2
1 VII 2003 .... ESDJ		4 088 773	2 412 542	59.0	2 017 467	1 167 617	57.9	2 071 306	1 244 925	60.1

Continent, country or area, and date / Continent, pays ou zone et date	Code[a]	Both sexes - Les deux sexes			Male - Masculin			Female - Féminin		
		Total	Urban - Urbaine		Total	Urban - Urbaine		Total	Urban - Urbaine	
			Number Nombre	Percent P.100		Number Nombre	Percent P.100		Number Nombre	Percent P.100
AMERICA, NORTH - AMÉRIQUE DU NORD										
Costa Rica										
1 VII 2004 ....ESDJ		4 178 755	2 465 255	59.0	2 062 468	1 191 560	57.8	2 116 287	1 273 695	60.2
1 VII 2005 ....ESDJ		4 266 185	2 516 602	59.0	2 116 648	1 231 912	58.2	2 149 537	1 284 690	59.8
1 VII 2006 ....ESDJ		4 353 843	2 567 797	59.0	2 146 610	1 243 202	57.9	2 207 233	1 324 595	60.0
Cuba										
1 VII 1997 ....ESDJ		11 008 659	8 263 940	75.1	...	...	...	...	...	...
1 VII 1998 ....ESDJ		11 055 405	8 325 827	75.3						
1 VII 1999 ....ESDJ		11 094 972	8 363 577	75.4	5 509 823	4 059 126	73.7	5 585 149	4 304 451	77.1
1 VII 2000 ....ESDJ		11 129 665	8 417 965	75.6	5 548 671	4 111 545	74.1	5 580 994	4 306 420	77.2
1 VII 2001 ....ESDJ		11 157 364	8 467 052	75.9	5 586 835	4 163 395	74.5	5 570 529	4 303 657	77.3
1 VII 2002 ....ESDJ		11 184 457	8 483 688	75.9	5 601 052	4 172 285	74.5	5 583 405	4 311 403	77.2
6 IX 2002 ....CDJC		11 177 743	8 479 329	75.9	5 597 233	4 169 722	74.5	5 580 510	4 309 607	77.2
1 VII 2003 ....ESDJ		11 215 229	8 501 628	75.8	5 616 275	4 181 234	74.4	5 598 954	4 320 394	77.2
1 VII 2004 ....ESDJ		11 235 687	8 503 738	75.7	5 626 690	4 183 047	74.3	5 608 997	4 320 691	77.0
1 VII 2005 ....ESDJ		11 242 519	8 497 885	75.6	5 629 843	4 180 296	74.3	5 612 676	4 317 589	76.9
1 VII 2006 ....ESDJ		11 241 440	8 490 101	75.5	5 629 168	4 176 538	74.2	5 612 272	4 313 563	76.9
Dominica - Dominique										
1 VII 1997 ....ESDF		72 183	...	...	36 906	...	...	35 277	...	...
1 VII 1998 ....ESDF		72 042	...	...	36 678	...	...	35 364	...	...
1 VII 1999 ....ESDF		71 814	...	...	36 561	...	...	35 253	...	...
1 VII 2000 ....ESDF		71 544	...	...	35 744	...	...	35 800	...	...
12 V 2001[19] ....CDFC		69 625	...	...	35 073	...	...	34 552	...	...
1 VII 2001 ....ESDF		70 922	...	...	35 241	...	...	35 681	...	...
1 VII 2002 ....ESDF		70 382	...	...	35 472	...	...	34 910	...	...
Dominican Republic - République dominicaine										
1 VII 1997 ....ESDF		8 144 347	4 645 617	57.0	4 087 412	2 297 938	56.2	4 056 935	2 347 680	57.9
1 VII 1998 ....ESDF		8 276 260	4 781 840	57.8	4 151 935	2 365 996	57.0	4 124 325	2 415 844	58.6
1 VII 1999 ....ESDF		8 410 015	4 921 083	58.5	4 217 318	2 435 539	57.8	4 192 697	2 485 544	59.3
1 VII 2000 ....ESDF		8 553 739	5 068 203	59.3	4 287 520	2 508 903	58.5	4 266 219	2 559 300	60.0
1 VII 2001 ....ESDF		8 683 486	5 211 082	60.0	4 350 825	2 580 145	59.3	4 332 661	2 630 937	60.7
1 VII 2002 ....ESDF		8 814 805	5 356 886	60.8	4 414 856	2 652 818	60.1	4 399 949	2 704 068	61.5
20 X 2002 ....CDJC		8 562 541	5 446 704	63.6	4 265 215	2 648 064	62.1	4 297 326	2 798 640	65.1
1 VII 2003 ....ESDF		8 947 515	5 505 541	61.5	4 479 514	2 726 880	60.9	4 468 001	2 778 661	62.2
1 VII 2004 ....ESDF		9 081 562	5 657 044	62.3	4 544 777	2 802 331	61.7	4 536 785	2 854 714	62.9
1 VII 2005 ....ESDF		9 226 449	5 817 420	63.1	4 615 274	2 882 076	62.4	4 611 175	2 935 344	63.7
1 VII 2006 ....ESDF		9 353 705	5 962 130	63.7	4 677 227	2 954 105	63.2	4 676 478	3 008 025	64.3
El Salvador										
1 VII 1997 ....ESDF		5 908 460	3 394 950	57.5	2 896 114	1 629 017	56.2	3 012 346	1 765 933	58.6
1 VII 1998 ....ESDF		6 031 326	3 485 465	57.8	2 957 835	1 673 250	56.6	3 073 491	1 812 215	59.0
1 VII 1999 ....ESDF		6 154 311	3 575 957	58.1	3 019 645	1 717 489	56.9	3 134 666	1 858 468	59.3
1 VII 2000 ....ESDF		6 276 037	3 665 747	58.4	3 080 704	1 761 327	57.2	3 195 333	1 904 420	59.6
1 VII 2001 ....ESDF		6 396 890	3 754 903	58.7	3 141 208	1 804 804	57.5	3 255 682	1 950 099	59.9
1 VII 2002 ....ESDF		6 517 798	3 843 878	59.0	3 201 720	1 848 194	57.7	3 316 078	1 995 684	60.2
1 VII 2003 ....ESDF		6 638 168	3 932 569	59.2	3 261 938	1 891 429	58.0	3 376 230	2 041 140	60.5
1 VII 2004 ....ESDF		6 757 408	4 020 878	59.5	3 321 564	1 934 445	58.2	3 435 844	2 086 433	60.7
1 VII 2005 ....ESDF		6 874 926	4 108 703	59.8	3 380 300	1 977 177	58.5	3 494 626	2 131 526	61.0
1 VII 2006 ....ESDF		6 990 658	4 195 925	60.0	3 438 107	2 019 556	58.7	3 552 551	2 176 369	61.3
Greenland - Groenland[20]										
1 VII 1997 ....ESDJ		56 024	45 420	81.1	29 872	24 043	80.5	26 152	21 378	81.7
1 VII 1998 ....ESDJ		56 076	45 489	81.1	29 904	24 092	80.6	26 172	21 397	81.8
1 VII 1999 ....ESDJ		56 087	45 523	81.2	29 941	24 189	80.8	26 146	21 334	81.6
1 VII 2000 ....CDJC		56 124	45 714	81.5	29 989	24 257	80.9	26 135	21 457	82.1
1 VII 2001 ....ESDJ		56 394	46 125	81.8	30 102	24 454	81.2	26 292	21 671	82.4
1 VII 2002 ....ESDJ		56 609	46 462	82.1	30 215	24 626	81.5	26 394	21 836	82.7
1 VII 2003 ....ESDJ		56 766	46 746	82.3	30 292	24 771	81.8	26 474	21 975	83.0
1 VII 2004 ....ESDJ		56 912	...	...	30 327	...	...	26 585	...	...
1 VII 2005 ....ESDJ		56 935	...	...	30 251	...	...	26 685	...	...
1 VII 2006 ....ESDJ		56 775	...	...	30 094	...	...	26 681	...	...
Grenada - Grenade										
1 VII 1997 ....ESDF		99 500	...	...	49 300	...	...	50 200	...	...
1 VII 1998 ....ESDF		100 100	...	...	49 600	...	...	50 500	...	...
1 VII 1999 ....ESDF		100 700	...	...	49 800	...	...	50 900	...	...

Continent, country or area, and date / Continent, pays ou zone et date	Code[a]	Both sexes - Les deux sexes Total	Urban - Urbaine Number Nombre	Urban - Urbaine Percent P.100	Male - Masculin Total	Urban - Urbaine Number Nombre	Urban - Urbaine Percent P.100	Female - Féminin Total	Urban - Urbaine Number Nombre	Urban - Urbaine Percent P.100
AMERICA, NORTH - AMÉRIQUE DU NORD										
Grenada - Grenade										
1 VII 2000	ESDF	101 400	...	...	50 100	...	...	51 300	...	...
25 V 2001	CDFC	102 632	...	...	50 481	...	...	52 151	...	...
Guadeloupe										
1 VII 1997	ESDJ	413 824	...	...	199 635	...	...	214 190	...	...
1 VII 1998	ESDJ	418 876	...	...	201 713	...	...	217 163	...	...
8 III 1999	CDJC	422 222	...	...	203 146	...	...	219 076	...	...
1 VII 1999	ESDJ	423 570	...	...	203 607	...	...	219 963	...	...
1 VII 2000	ESDJ	427 928	...	...	205 433	...	...	222 495	...	...
1 VII 2001	ESDJ	432 453	...	...	207 453	...	...	225 000	...	...
1 VII 2003	ESDJ	438 820	...	...	210 130	...	...	228 690	...	...
Guatemala[8]										
1 VII 1997	ESDF	10 517 448	...	...	5 306 910	...	...	5 210 538	...	...
1 VII 1998	ESDF	10 799 133	...	...	5 447 743	...	...	5 351 390	...	...
1 VII 1999	ESDF	11 088 362	...	...	5 592 313	...	...	5 496 049	...	...
1 VII 2000	ESDF	11 385 338	...	...	5 740 720	...	...	5 644 618	...	...
1 VII 2001	ESDF	11 678 411			5 888 426	...	...	5 789 985	...	...
Haiti - Haïti										
1 VII 1997	ESDJ	7 491 762	2 531 060	33.8	...	...	...	...	...	...
1 VII 1998	ESDJ	7 647 496	2 630 383	34.4	...	...	...	...	...	...
1 VII 1999	ESDJ	7 803 230	2 731 843	35.0	...	...	...	...	...	...
1 VII 2000	ESDJ	7 958 964	2 835 433	35.6	...	...	...	...	...	...
Honduras										
1 VII 1997	ESDF	5 908 069	2 587 337	43.8	...	...	...	...	...	...
1 VII 1998	ESDF	6 056 942	2 689 721	44.4	...	...	...	...	...	...
1 VII 1999	ESDF	6 211 412	2 796 156	45.0	...	...	...	...	...	...
1 VII 2000	ESDF	6 369 188	2 907 091	45.6	...	...	...	...	...	...
1 VII 2001	ESDF	6 530 331	3 022 150	46.3	3 228 483	1 439 896	44.6	3 301 848	1 582 254	47.9
28 VII 2001	CDFC	6 071 200	...	...	3 000 530			3 070 670		
1 VII 2002	ESDF	6 694 761	3 140 880	46.9	3 308 253	1 497 291	45.3	3 386 508	1 643 589	48.5
1 VII 2003	ESDF	6 860 842	3 260 934	47.5	3 388 874	1 555 369	45.9	3 471 968	1 705 565	49.1
1 VII 2004	ESDF	7 028 389	3 382 254	48.1	3 470 259	1 614 104	46.5	3 558 130	1 768 150	49.7
1 VII 2005	ESDF	7 197 303	3 504 730	48.7	3 552 360	1 673 434	47.1	3 644 943	1 831 296	50.2
1 VII 2006	ESDF	7 367 021	3 628 228	49.2	3 634 900	1 733 290	47.7	3 732 121	1 894 938	50.8
Jamaica - Jamaïque										
1 VII 1997	ESDJ	2 534 090	...	...	1 245 598	...	...	1 288 492	...	...
1 VII 1998	ESDJ	2 556 821	...	...	1 257 205	...	...	1 299 616	...	...
1 VII 1999	ESDJ	2 574 313	...	...	1 266 232	...	...	1 308 081	...	...
1 VII 2000	ESDJ	2 589 393	1 345 867	52.0	1 274 076	641 652	50.4	1 315 317	704 231	53.5
1 VII 2001	ESDJ	2 604 098	1 353 511	52.0	1 281 752	645 517	50.4	1 322 346	707 993	53.5
10 IX 2001	CDJC	2 607 632	1 355 347	52.0	1 283 548	646 422	50.4	1 324 084	708 925	53.5
1 VII 2002	ESDJ	2 615 248	1 359 292	52.0	1 287 663	648 494	50.4	1 327 585	710 798	53.5
1 VII 2003	ESDJ	2 625 708	1 364 719	52.0	1 293 121	651 243	50.4	1 332 587	713 476	53.5
1 VII 2004	ESDJ	2 638 074	1 371 144	52.0	1 299 406	654 407	50.4	1 338 668	716 736	53.5
1 VII 2005	ESDJ	2 650 402	1 377 546	52.0	1 305 639	657 546	50.4	1 344 763	720 000	53.5
1 VII 2006	ESDJ	2 663 106	1 384 145	52.0	1 312 025	660 763	50.4	1 351 081	723 383	53.5
Martinique										
1 VII 1997	ESDJ	375 547	...	...	178 702	...	...	196 845	...	...
1 VII 1998	ESDJ	379 042	...	...	180 005	...	...	199 038	...	...
8 III 1999	CDJC	381 325	...	...	180 910	...	...	200 415	...	...
1 VII 1999	ESDJ	382 090	...	...	181 140	...	...	200 951	...	...
1 VII 2000	ESDJ	384 615	...	...	182 044	...	...	202 571	...	...
1 VII 2001	ESDJ	387 135	...	...	182 935	...	...	204 200	...	...
1 VII 2002	ESDJ	389 455	...	...	183 727	...	...	205 729	...	...
1 VII 2003	ESDJ	390 552	...	...	184 084	...	...	206 468	...	...
Mexico - Mexique										
1 VII 1997	ESDJ	94 478 046	74 760 965	79.1	46 903 095	...	...	47 574 951	...	...
1 VII 1998	ESDJ	95 790 135	76 083 002	79.4	47 502 593	...	...	48 287 542	...	...
1 VII 1999	ESDJ	97 114 831	77 348 051	79.6	48 111 343	...	...	49 003 488	...	...
14 II 2000	CDJC	97 483 412	72 759 822	74.6	47 592 253	35 317 569	74.2	49 891 159	37 442 253	75.0
1 VII 2000	ESDJ	98 438 557	73 515 485	74.7	48 722 412	...	...	49 716 145	...	...
1 VII 2001	ESDJ	99 715 527	74 840 402	75.1	49 312 382	...	...	50 403 145	...	...
1 VII 2002	ESDJ	100 909 374	76 108 582	75.4	49 862 638	...	...	51 046 736	...	...
1 VII 2003	ESDJ	101 999 555	77 303 384	75.8	50 361 179	...	...	51 638 376	...	...

6. Total and urban population by sex: 1997 - 2006
Population totale et population urbaine selon le sexe: 1997 - 2006 (continued - suite)

Continent, country or area, and date / Continent, pays ou zone et date	Code[a]	Both sexes - Les deux sexes	Urban - Urbaine		Male - Masculin	Urban - Urbaine		Female - Féminin	Urban - Urbaine	
		Total	Number Nombre	Percent P.100	Total	Number Nombre	Percent P.100	Total	Number Nombre	Percent P.100

AMERICA, NORTH - AMÉRIQUE DU NORD

Mexico - Mexique										
1 VII 2004 ....ESDJ		103 001 867	78 436 582	76.2	50 814 580	...	...	52 187 287	...	...
1 VII 2005 ....ESDJ		103 946 866	79 528 445	76.5	51 238 427	...	...	52 708 439	...	...
17 X 2005 ....CDJC		103 263 388	78 986 852	76.5	50 249 955	38 300 417	76.2	53 013 433	40 686 435	76.7
1 VII 2006 ....ESDJ		104 874 282	80 609 788	76.9	51 654 642	...	...	53 219 640	...	...
Montserrat										
1 VII 1997[21] ....ESDF		6 094	...	...	3 019	...	...	3 075	...	...
1 VII 1998 ....ESDF		3 595	...	...	1 944	...	...	1 651	...	...
1 VII 1999 ....ESDF		4 771	...	...	2 536	...	...	2 235	...	...
1 VII 2000 ....ESDF		5 274	...	...	2 793	...	...	2 481	...	...
12 V 2001 ....CDFC		4 491	...	...	2 418	...	...	2 073	...	...
Netherlands Antilles - Antilles néerlandaises										
1 VII 1997 ....ESDJ		193 373	...	...	92 010	...	...	101 363	...	...
1 VII 1998 ....ESDJ		192 052	...	...	91 253	...	...	100 800	...	...
1 VII 1999 ....ESDJ		186 176	...	...	88 162	...	...	98 014	...	...
1 VII 2000 ....ESDJ		179 225	...	...	84 459	...	...	94 766	...	...
29 I 2001 ....CDJC		175 653	...	...	82 521	...	...	93 132	...	...
1 VII 2001 ....ESDJ		174 145	...	...	81 747	...	...	92 398	...	...
1 VII 2002 ....ESDJ		174 603	...	...	81 818	...	...	92 793	...	...
1 VII 2003 ....ESDJ		178 681	...	...	83 556	...	...	95 125	...	...
1 VII 2004 ....ESDJ		183 115	...	...	85 456	...	...	97 659	...	...
1 VII 2005 ....ESDJ		185 378	...	...	86 276	...	...	99 102	...	...
1 VII 2006 ....ESDJ		189 500	...	...	88 146	...	...	101 356	...	...
Nicaragua										
1 VII 1997 ....ESDJ		4 674 199	2 621 328	56.1	2 324 066	1 264 550	54.4	2 350 133	1 356 778	57.7
1 VII 1998 ....ESDJ		4 803 102	2 710 381	56.4	2 388 742	1 309 236	54.8	2 414 360	1 401 145	58.0
1 VII 1999 ....ESDJ		4 935 559	2 802 340	56.8	2 455 217	1 355 417	55.2	2 480 342	1 446 923	58.3
1 VII 2000 ....ESDJ		5 105 680	2 856 185	55.9	2 551 144	1 374 025	53.9	2 554 536	1 482 160	58.0
1 VII 2001 ....ESDJ		5 173 571	2 910 342	56.3	2 583 831	1 400 209	54.2	2 589 740	1 510 133	58.3
1 VII 2002 ....ESDJ		5 243 082	2 966 357	56.6	2 617 291	1 426 993	54.5	2 625 791	1 539 364	58.6
1 VII 2003 ....ESDJ		5 313 803	3 023 106	56.9	2 651 331	1 454 281	54.9	2 662 472	1 568 825	58.9
1 VII 2004 ....ESDJ		5 385 315	3 082 134	57.2	2 685 742	1 483 453	55.2	2 699 573	1 598 681	59.2
4 VI 2005 ....CDJC		5 144 553	2 877 002	55.9	2 535 461	1 369 108	54.0	2 609 092	1 507 894	57.8
1 VII 2005 ....CDJC		5 457 208	3 140 854	57.6	2 720 336	1 511 552	55.6	2 736 872	1 629 302	59.5
1 VII 2006 ....ESDJ		5 529 758	3 199 962	57.9	2 755 239	1 540 746	55.9	2 774 519	1 659 216	59.8
Panama										
1 VII 1997 ....ESDF		2 718 686	1 508 703	55.5	1 373 349	735 709	53.6	1 345 337	772 994	57.5
1 VII 1998 ....ESDF		2 763 612	1 540 742	55.8	1 395 475	751 450	53.8	1 368 137	789 292	57.7
1 VII 1999 ....ESDF		2 809 280	1 572 780	56.0	1 417 957	767 186	54.1	1 391 323	805 594	57.9
14 V 2000 ....CDFC		2 839 177	...	...	1 432 566	...	...	1 406 611	...	...
1 VII 2000 ....ESDF		2 855 703	1 604 823	56.2	1 440 801	782 928	54.3	1 414 902	821 895	58.1
1 VII 2004 ....ESDF		3 172 360	...	...	1 600 879	...	...	1 571 481	...	...
1 VII 2005 ....ESDF		3 228 186	2 050 965	63.5	1 628 720	1 011 700	62.1	1 599 466	1 039 265	65.0
1 VII 2006 ....ESDF		3 283 959	2 093 871	63.8	1 656 469	1 033 634	62.4	1 627 490	1 060 237	65.1
Puerto Rico - Porto Rico[22]										
1 VII 1997 ....ESDJ		3 715 726	...	...	1 792 139	...	...	1 923 587	...	...
1 VII 1998 ....ESDJ		3 748 150	...	...	1 806 604	...	...	1 941 546	...	...
1 VII 1999 ....ESDJ		3 782 143	...	...	1 821 772	...	...	1 960 371	...	...
1 IV 2000 ....CDJC		3 808 610	3 594 948[23]	94.4	1 833 577	1 723 589	94.0	1 975 033	1 871 359	94.8
1 VII 2000 ....ESDJ		3 815 893	3 604 039[24]	94.4	1 836 799	...	...	1 979 094	...	...
1 VII 2001 ....ESDJ		3 839 810	...	...	1 847 559	...	...	1 992 251	...	...
1 VII 2002 ....ESDJ		3 858 806	...	...	1 855 781	...	...	2 003 025	...	...
1 VII 2003 ....ESDJ		3 878 532	...	...	1 865 170	...	...	2 013 362	...	...
1 VII 2004 ....ESDJ		3 894 855	...	...	1 871 657	...	...	2 023 198	...	...
1 VII 2005 ....ESDJ		3 912 054	...	...	1 879 236	...	...	2 032 818	...	...
1 VII 2006 ....ESDJ		3 927 776	...	...	1 886 031	...	...	2 041 745	...	...
Saint Kitts and Nevis - Saint-Kitts-et-Nevis										
1 VII 1997 ....ESDF		40 740	...	...	20 550	...	...	20 190	...	...
1 VII 1998 ....ESDF		40 130	...	...	20 230	...	...	19 900	...	...
1 VII 1999 ....ESDF		42 460	...	...	21 360	...	...	21 100	...	...

Continent, country or area, and date / Continent, pays ou zone et date	Code[a]	Both sexes - Les deux sexes Total	Urban - Urbaine Number Nombre	Urban - Urbaine Percent P.100	Male - Masculin Total	Urban - Urbaine Number Nombre	Urban - Urbaine Percent P.100	Female - Féminin Total	Urban - Urbaine Number Nombre	Urban - Urbaine Percent P.100
AMERICA, NORTH - AMÉRIQUE DU NORD										
Saint Kitts and Nevis - Saint-Kitts-et-Nevis										
1 VII 2000	ESDF	40 410	...	...	20 400	...	...	20 010	...	...
14 V 2001	CDFC	45 841	...	...	22 784	...	...	23 057	...	...
1 VII 2001*	ESDF	46 111	...	...	22 919	...	...	23 192	...	...
Saint Lucia - Sainte-Lucie										
1 VII 1997	ESDF	149 621	44 256	29.6	73 114	21 620	29.6	76 552	22 636	29.6
1 VII 1998	ESDF	151 972	44 932	29.6	74 320	21 976	29.6	77 632	22 956	29.6
1 VII 1999	ESDF	153 703	...	...	75 266	...	...	78 437	...	...
1 VII 2000	ESDF	155 996	...	...	76 494	...	...	79 502	...	...
22 V 2001	CDFC	157 164	43 316	27.6	76 741	20 711	27.0	80 423	22 605	28.1
1 VII 2002	ESDF	159 133	...	...	77 868	...	...	81 265	...	...
1 VII 2003	ESDF	160 673	...	...	78 618	...	...	82 055	...	...
1 VII 2004	ESDF	162 434	...	...	79 407	...	...	83 027	...	...
1 VII 2005	ESDF	164 791	...	...	80 595	...	...	84 196	...	...
1 VII 2006*	ESDF	166 838	...	...	81 681	...	...	85 157	...	...
Saint Pierre and Miquelon - Saint Pierre-et-Miquelon										
8 III 1999	CDFC	6 316	...	...	3 147	...	...	3 169	...	...
Saint Vincent and the Grenadines - Saint Vincent-et-les Grenadines										
1 VII 1997	ESDF	111 655	48 761	43.7	55 713	...	...	55 942	...	...
1 VII 1998	ESDF	111 810	48 839	43.7	55 378	...	...	56 432	...	...
1 VII 1999	ESDF	112 030	...	...	55 925	...	...	56 105	...	...
1 VII 2000	ESDF	109 790	...	...	54 774	...	...	55 016	...	...
14 V 2001[19]	CDFC	109 022	49 590	45.5	55 456	24 809	44.7	53 566	24 781	46.3
1 VII 2002	ESDF	107 854	48 535	45.0	54 434	...	...	53 420	...	...
1 VII 2003	ESDF	105 158	42 063	40.0	53 494	...	...	51 664	...	...
1 VII 2004	ESDF	104 555	41 822	40.0	53 187	...	...	51 368	...	...
1 VII 2005	ESDF	103 751	...	...	52 778	...	...	50 973	...	...
Trinidad and Tobago - Trinité-et-Tobago										
1 VII 1997	ESDF	1 274 799	...	...	636 340	...	...	638 459	...	...
1 VII 1998	ESDF	1 277 675	...	...	638 096	...	...	639 579	...	...
1 VII 1999	ESDF	1 283 863	...	...	640 914	...	...	642 949	...	...
15 V 2000	CDFC	1 262 366	...	...	633 051	...	...	629 315	...	...
1 VII 2000	ESDF	1 290 000	...	...	643 700	...	...	642 900	...	...
1 VII 2001	ESDF	1 266 800	...	...	635 200	...	...	631 600	...	...
1 VII 2002	ESDF	1 275 700	...	...	639 700	...	...	636 000	...	...
1 VII 2003	ESDF	1 282 400	...	...	642 000	...	...	640 400	...	...
Turks Caicos Islands - Îles Turques et Caïques										
20 VIII 2001	CDFC	19 886	...	...	9 897	...	...	9 989	...	...
1 VII 2002	ESDJ	20 900	...	...	10 402	...	...	10 498	...	...
1 VII 2003	ESDJ	25 143	...	...	12 513	...	...	12 630	...	...
1 VII 2004	ESDJ	27 496	...	...	13 684	...	...	13 812	...	...
1 VII 2005	ESDJ	30 602	...	...	15 230	...	...	15 372	...	...
1 VII 2006	ESDJ	33 202	...	...	16 524	...	...	16 678	...	...
United States - États-Unis[25]										
1 VII 1997	ESDJ	272 646 925	...	...	133 473 526	...	...	139 173 399	...	...
1 VII 1998	ESDJ	275 854 104	...	...	135 129 904	...	...	140 724 200	...	...
1 VII 1999	ESDJ	279 040 168	...	...	136 802 873	...	...	142 237 295	...	...
1 IV 2000	CDJC	281 421 906	222 360 539	79.0	138 053 563	108 375 797	78.5	143 368 343	113 984 742	79.5
1 VII 2000	ESDJ	282 193 477	...	...	138 469 724	...	...	143 723 753	...	...
1 VII 2001	ESDJ	285 107 923	...	...	140 015 885	...	...	145 092 038	...	...
1 VII 2002	ESDJ	287 984 799	...	...	141 542 448	...	...	146 442 351	...	...
1 VII 2003	ESDJ	290 850 005	...	...	143 057 818	...	...	147 792 187	...	...
1 VII 2004	ESDJ	293 622 764	...	...	144 528 730	...	...	149 094 034	...	...

6. Total and urban population by sex: 1997 - 2006
Population totale et population urbaine selon le sexe: 1997 - 2006 (continued - suite)

Continent, country or area, and date / Continent, pays ou zone et date	Code[a]	Both sexes - Les deux sexes			Male - Masculin			Female - Féminin		
		Total	Urban - Urbaine		Total	Urban - Urbaine		Total	Urban - Urbaine	
			Number Nombre	Percent P.100		Number Nombre	Percent P.100		Number Nombre	Percent P.100
AMERICA, NORTH - AMÉRIQUE DU NORD										
United States - États-Unis[25]										
1 VII 2005 .... ESDJ		296 410 404	...	...	145 999 746	...	...	150 410 658	...	...
1 VII 2006 .... ESDJ		299 398 484	...	...	147 512 152	...	...	151 886 332	...	...
United States Virgin Islands - Îles Vierges américaines[22]										
1 IV 2000 .... CDJC		108 612	...	...	51 864	...	...	56 748	...	...
1 VII 2000 .... ESDJ		108 637	...	...	51 876	...	...	56 761	...	...
1 VII 2001 .... ESDJ		108 749	...	...	51 920	...	...	56 829	...	...
1 VII 2002 .... ESDJ		108 810	...	...	51 952	...	...	56 858	...	...
AMERICA, SOUTH - AMÉRIQUE DU SUD										
Argentina - Argentine										
1 VII 1997 .... ESDF		35 604 362	...	...	17 459 211	...	...	18 145 151	...	...
1 VII 1998 .... ESDF		36 005 387	...	...	17 650 012	...	...	18 355 375	...	...
1 VII 1999 .... ESDF		36 398 577	...	...	17 837 342	...	...	18 561 235	...	...
1 VII 2000 .... ESDF		36 783 859	32 902 070	89.4	18 021 900	15 957 354	88.5	18 761 959	16 944 716	90.3
1 VII 2001 .... ESDF		37 156 195	33 312 347	89.7	18 201 249	16 161 696	88.8	18 954 946	17 150 651	90.5
18 XI 2001 .... CDFC		36 260 130	32 431 950	89.4	17 659 072	15 629 299	88.5	18 601 058	16 802 651	90.3
1 VII 2002 .... ESDF		37 515 632	33 709 927	89.9	18 374 920	16 361 823	89.0	19 140 712	17 348 104	90.6
1 VII 2003 .... ESDF		37 869 730	34 101 536	90.0	18 546 570	16 559 682	89.3	19 323 160	17 541 854	90.8
1 VII 2004 .... ESDF		38 226 051	34 493 965	90.2	18 719 869	16 758 540	89.5	19 506 182	17 735 425	90.9
1 VII 2005 .... ESDF		38 592 150	34 894 057	90.4	18 898 472	16 961 698	89.8	19 693 678	17 932 359	91.1
1 VII 2006 .... ESDF		38 970 611	35 304 205	90.6	19 083 828	17 170 659	90.0	19 886 783	18 133 546	91.2
Bolivia - Bolivie										
1 VII 1997 .... ESDF		7 845 341	4 731 628	60.3	3 900 250	2 305 130	59.1	3 945 092	2 426 497	61.5
1 VII 1998 .... ESDF		8 035 143	4 888 033	60.8	3 996 143	2 380 830	59.6	4 039 000	2 507 204	62.1
1 VII 1999 .... ESDF		8 229 487	5 047 016	61.3	4 094 229	2 457 763	60.0	4 135 259	2 589 253	62.6
1 VII 2000 .... ESDF		8 427 789	5 208 601	61.8	4 194 195	2 536 032	60.5	4 233 594	2 672 569	63.1
1 VII 2001 .... ESDF		8 624 268	5 373 504	62.3	4 293 345	2 615 967	60.9	4 330 924	2 757 537	63.7
5 IX 2001 .... CDFC		8 274 325	5 165 230	62.4	4 123 850	2 517 106	61.0	4 150 475	2 648 124	63.8
1 VII 2002 .... ESDF		8 823 743	5 541 707	62.8	4 393 968	2 697 501	61.4	4 429 776	2 844 206	64.2
1 VII 2003 .... ESDF		9 024 922	5 712 138	63.3	4 495 426	2 780 137	61.8	4 529 495	2 932 001	64.7
1 VII 2004 .... ESDF		9 226 511	5 883 724	63.8	4 597 081	2 863 378	62.3	4 629 430	3 020 347	65.2
1 VII 2005 .... ESDF		9 427 219	6 055 392	64.2	4 698 293	2 946 725	62.7	4 728 926	3 108 667	65.7
1 VII 2006 .... ESDF		9 627 269	6 227 367	64.7	4 799 178	3 030 290	63.1	4 828 091	3 197 077	66.2
Brazil - Brésil[26]										
1 VII 1997 .... ESDF		163 779 827	...	...	80 755 823	...	...	83 024 004	...	...
1 VII 1998 .... ESDF		166 252 088	...	...	81 940 241	...	...	84 311 847	...	...
1 VII 1999 .... ESDF		168 753 552	...	...	83 139 277	...	...	85 614 275	...	...
1 VII 2000 .... ESDF		171 279 882	...	...	84 350 720	...	...	86 929 162	...	...
1 VIII 2000 .... CDJC		169 799 170	137 953 959	81.2	83 576 015	66 882 993	80.0	86 223 155	71 070 966	82.4
1 VII 2001 .... ESDF		173 821 934	...	...	85 569 888	...	...	88 252 046	...	...
1 VII 2002 .... ESDF		176 391 015	...	...	86 802 515	...	...	89 588 500	...	...
1 VII 2003 .... ESDF		178 985 306	...	...	88 047 716	...	...	90 937 590	...	...
1 VII 2004 .... ESDF		181 586 030	...	...	89 296 014	...	...	92 290 016	...	...
1 VII 2005 .... ESDF		184 184 264	...	...	90 542 990	...	...	93 641 274	...	...
1 VII 2006 .... ESDF		186 770 562	...	...	91 784 158	...	...	94 986 404	...	...
Chile - Chili										
1 VII 1997 .... ESDF		14 622 354	12 420 506	84.9	7 236 189	6 052 039	83.6	7 386 165	6 368 467	86.2
1 VII 1998 .... ESDF		14 821 714	12 623 059	85.2	7 336 118	6 153 975	83.9	7 485 596	6 469 084	86.4
1 VII 1999 .... ESDF		15 017 760	12 822 253	85.4	7 434 317	6 254 131	84.1	7 583 443	6 568 122	86.6
1 VII 2000 .... ESDF		15 211 308	13 018 924	85.6	7 531 173	6 352 945	84.4	7 680 135	6 665 979	86.8
1 VII 2001 .... ESDF		15 401 952	13 216 121	85.8	7 626 482	6 451 736	84.6	7 775 470	6 764 385	87.0
24 IV 2002 .... CDFC		15 116 435	13 090 113	86.6	7 447 695	6 366 311	85.5	7 668 740	6 723 802	87.7
1 VII 2002 .... ESDF		15 589 147	13 409 844	86.0	7 719 986	6 548 696	84.8	7 869 161	6 861 148	87.2
1 VII 2003 .... ESDF		15 773 504	13 600 704	86.2	7 811 991	6 644 151	85.1	7 961 513	6 956 553	87.4
1 VII 2004 .... ESDF		16 093 378	13 966 203	86.8	7 966 110	6 832 205	85.8	8 127 268	7 133 998	87.8

Continent, country or area, and date / Continent, pays ou zone et date	Code[a]	Both sexes - Les deux sexes			Male - Masculin			Female - Féminin		
		Total	Urban - Urbaine		Total	Urban - Urbaine		Total	Urban - Urbaine	
			Number Nombre	Percent P.100		Number Nombre	Percent P.100		Number Nombre	Percent P.100
AMERICA, SOUTH - AMÉRIQUE DU SUD										
Chile - Chili										
1 VII 2005 .... ESDF		16 267 278	14 123 527	86.8	8 052 564	6 910 230	85.8	8 214 714	7 213 297	87.8
1 VII 2006 .... ESDF		16 432 674	14 272 454	86.9	8 134 314	6 983 850	85.9	8 298 360	7 288 604	87.8
Colombia - Colombie										
1 VII 1997 .... ESDF		38 646 043[27]	28 048 220[28]	72.6	19 068 757[27]	...	...	19 577 286[27]	...	...
1 VII 1998 .... ESDF		39 201 321[27]	28 734 719[28]	73.3	19 343 246[27]	...	...	19 858 075[27]	...	...
1 VII 1999 .... ESDF		39 745 714[27]	29 435 181[28]	74.1	19 612 492[27]	...	...	20 133 222[27]	...	...
1 VII 2000 .... ESDF		40 282 217[27]	30 125 776[28]	74.8	19 877 987[27]	...	...	20 404 230[27]	...	...
1 VII 2001 .... ESDF		40 806 313[27]	30 772 485[28]	75.4	20 137 593[27]	...	...	20 668 720[27]	...	...
1 VII 2002 .... ESDF		41 327 459[27]	31 428 374[28]	76.0	20 395 870[27]	...	...	20 931 589[27]	...	...
1 VII 2003 .... ESDF		41 847 421[27]	32 101 585[28]	76.7	20 653 652[27]	...	...	21 193 769[27]	...	...
1 VII 2004 .... ESDF		42 367 528[27]	32 787 008[28]	77.4	20 911 536[27]	...	...	21 455 992[27]	...	...
22 V 2005 .... CDFC		41 468 384	...	...	20 336 117			21 132 267		
1 VII 2005 .... ESDF		42 888 592[27]	31 890 892	74.4	21 169 835[27]	...	...	21 718 757[27]	...	...
1 VII 2006 .... ESDF		43 405 387[27]	32 399 518	74.6	21 425 328	...	...	21 980 059		
Ecuador - Équateur[29]										
1 VII 1997 .... ESDF		11 772 871	6 953 116	59.1	5 914 629	3 433 722	58.1	5 858 242	3 519 394	60.1
1 VII 1998 .... ESDF		11 947 586	7 118 271	59.6	6 001 552	3 517 425	58.6	5 946 036	3 600 846	60.6
1 VII 1999 .... ESDF		12 120 981	7 282 105	60.1	6 087 690	3 600 349	59.1	6 033 294	3 681 756	61.0
1 VII 2000 .... ESDF		12 298 745	7 450 308	60.6	6 175 859	3 685 298	59.7	6 122 886	3 765 010	61.5
1 VII 2001 .... ESDF		12 479 924	7 633 850	61.2	6 265 558	3 778 158	60.3	6 214 366	3 855 692	62.0
25 XI 2001 .... CDFC		12 156 608	7 431 355	61.1	6 018 353	3 625 962	60.2	6 138 255	3 805 393	62.0
1 VII 2002 .... ESDF		12 660 728	7 817 018	61.7	6 354 906	3 870 667	60.9	6 305 821	3 946 351	62.6
1 VII 2003 .... ESDF		12 842 578	8 001 231	62.3	6 444 656	3 963 574	61.5	6 397 920	4 037 657	63.1
1 VII 2004 .... ESDF		13 026 891	8 187 908	62.9	6 535 564	4 057 642	62.1	6 491 327	4 130 266	63.6
1 VII 2005 .... ESDF		13 215 089	...	...	6 628 368	...	...	6 586 721	...	...
1 VII 2006 .... ESDF		13 408 270	...	...	6 723 629	...	...	6 684 641	...	...
Falkland Islands (Malvinas) - Îles Falkland (Malvinas)[30]										
8 IV 2001 .... CDFC		2 913	...	...	1 598	...	...	1 315	...	...
8 X 2006 .... CDFC		2 955	...	...	1 569	...	...	1 386	...	...
French Guiana - Guyane française										
1 VII 1997 .... ESDJ		147 590	...	...	74 698			72 892		
1 VII 1998 .... ESDJ		153 001	...	...	77 177			75 825		
8 III 1999 .... CDJC		156 790	...	...	78 963			77 827		
1 VII 1999 .... ESDJ		158 444	...	...	79 670			78 774		
1 VII 2000 .... ESDJ		163 979	...	...	82 200			81 779		
1 VII 2001 .... ESDJ		169 667	...	...	84 782			84 885		
1 VII 2002 .... ESDJ		175 426	...	...	87 387			88 039		
1 I 2004 .... ESDJ		184 451	...	...	91 522			92 929		
Guyana										
1 VII 1997 .... ESDF		775 137	...	...	381 910			393 227		
1 VII 1998 .... ESDF		773 432	...	...	381 070			392 362		
1 VII 1999 .... ESDF		770 584	...	...	379 667			390 917		
1 VII 2000 .... ESDF		742 000	...	...	365 583			376 417		
1 VII 2001 .... ESDF		743 600	...	...	366 372			377 228		
1 VII 2002 .... ESDF		747 712	...	...	371 351			376 361		
15 IX 2002 .... CDFC		751 223	...	...	376 034			375 189		
1 VII 2003[31] .... ESDF		752 498	...	...	070 075			375 823		
1 VII 2004 .... ESDF		755 061	...	...	377 958			377 103		
1 VII 2005 .... ESDF		757 637	...	...	379 245			378 393		
1 VII 2006 .... ESDF		760 218	...	...	380 536			379 682		
Paraguay										
1 VII 2000 .... ESDF		5 346 267	...	...	2 705 524	...	...	2 640 743		
1 VII 2001 .... ESDF		5 456 418	...	...	2 761 141	...	...	2 695 278	...	...
1 VII 2002 .... ESDF		5 566 852	...	...	2 816 687	...	...	2 750 164	...	...
28 VIII 2002 .... CDFC		5 163 198	2 928 437	56.7	2 603 242	1 422 339	54.6	2 559 956	1 506 098	58.8
1 VII 2003 .... ESDF		5 677 448	...	...	2 872 186	...	...	2 805 262	...	...
1 VII 2004 .... ESDF		5 788 088	...	...	2 927 657	...	...	2 860 430	...	...
1 VII 2005 .... ESDF		5 898 651	...	...	2 983 123	...	...	2 915 528	...	...
1 VII 2006 .... ESDF		6 009 143	...	...	3 038 590	...	...	2 970 553	...	...

6. Total and urban population by sex: 1997 - 2006
Population totale et population urbaine selon le sexe: 1997 - 2006 (continued - suite)

Continent, country or area, and date / Continent, pays ou zone et date	Code[a]	Both sexes - Les deux sexes Total	Urban - Urbaine Number Nombre	Urban - Urbaine Percent P.100	Male - Masculin Total	Urban - Urbaine Number Nombre	Urban - Urbaine Percent P.100	Female - Féminin Total	Urban - Urbaine Number Nombre	Urban - Urbaine Percent P.100
AMERICA, SOUTH - AMÉRIQUE DU SUD										
Peru - Pérou										
1 VII 1997[8] .... ESDF		24 711 703	17 640 917[28]	71.4	12 298 872	8 849 804[28]	72.0	12 412 831	8 791 113[28]	70.8
1 VII 1998[8] .... ESDF		25 180 030	17 978 819[28]	71.4	12 535 109	9 017 356[28]	71.9	12 644 921	8 961 463[28]	70.9
1 VII 1999[8] .... ESDF		25 621 425	18 312 557[28]	71.5	12 757 768	9 182 458[28]	72.0	12 863 657	9 130 099[28]	71.0
1 VII 2000[8] .... ESDF		25 982 485	18 647 242[28]	71.8	12 942 242	9 348 264[28]	72.2	13 040 243	9 298 978[28]	71.3
1 VII 2001[8] .... ESDF		26 314 853	18 980 589[28]	72.1	13 112 799	9 513 198[28]	72.5	13 202 054	9 467 391[28]	71.7
1 VII 2002[8] .... ESDF		26 635 640	19 310 309[28]	72.5	13 277 178	9 676 260[28]	72.9	13 358 462	9 634 049[28]	72.1
1 VII 2003[8] .... ESDF		26 887 768	19 638 160[28]	73.0	13 408 286	9 838 166[28]	73.4	13 479 482	9 799 994[28]	72.7
1 VII 2004[8] .... ESDF		27 075 697	19 966 180[28]	73.7	13 507 941	9 999 924[28]	74.0	13 567 756	9 966 256[28]	73.5
1 VII 2005[8] .... ESDF		27 179 432	...	...	13 570 520	...	...	13 608 912	...	...
18 VII 2005*[32] .... CDFC		26 152 265			13 061 026			13 091 239		
1 VII 2006[8] .... ESDF		27 377 172	20 371 596	74.4	13 666 871	10 067 586	73.7	13 710 301	10 304 010	75.2
Suriname										
1 VII 1997 .... ESDJ		445 647	...	...	223 857	...	...	221 790	...	...
1 VII 1998 .... ESDJ		451 629	...	...	226 621	...	...	225 008	...	...
1 VII 1999 .... ESDJ		457 692	...	...	229 664	...	...	228 028	...	...
1 VII 2000 .... ESDJ		463 837	...	...	232 747	...	...	231 090	...	...
1 VII 2001 .... ESDJ		470 064	...	...	236 276	...	...	233 788	...	...
1 VII 2002 .... ESDJ		476 374	...	...	239 447	...	...	236 927	...	...
31 III 2003*[33] .... CDJC		481 146	...	...	241 837	...	...	239 292	...	...
1 VII 2003 .... ESDJ		482 769	...	...	242 662	...	...	240 107	...	...
2 VIII 2004[34] .... CDJC		492 829	328 932	66.7	247 846[35]	164 297[35]	66.3	244 618[35]	164 370[35]	67.2
1 VII 2005 .... ESDJ		498 543	...	...	250 906	...	...	247 637	...	...
1 VII 2006* .... ESDJ		504 257	...	...	253 783	...	...	250 474	...	...
Uruguay										
1 VII 1997[8] .... ESDF		3 256 182	2 996 846	92.0	1 578 874	1 429 782	90.6	1 677 308	1 567 064	93.4
1 VII 1998[8] .... ESDF		3 273 777	3 019 947	92.2	1 586 775	1 441 116	90.8	1 687 002	1 578 831	93.6
1 VII 1999[8] .... ESDF		3 288 819	3 040 697	92.5	1 593 452	1 451 298	91.1	1 695 368	1 589 399	93.7
1 VII 2000[8] .... ESDF		3 300 847	3 058 437	92.7	1 598 685	1 460 013	91.3	1 702 162	1 598 424	93.9
1 VII 2001[8] .... ESDF		3 308 356	3 071 727	92.8	1 601 593	1 466 408	91.6	1 706 763	1 605 319	94.1
1 VII 2002[8] .... ESDF		3 308 527	3 077 804	93.0	1 600 814	1 469 148	91.8	1 707 713	1 608 656	94.2
1 VII 2003[8] .... ESDF		3 303 540	3 078 812	93.2	1 597 362	1 469 246	92.0	1 706 177	1 609 565	94.3
1 VI 2004[36] .... CDFC		3 241 003	2 974 714	91.8	1 565 533	1 415 362	90.4	1 675 470	1 559 352	93.1
1 VII 2004[8] .... ESDF		3 301 732	3 083 096	93.4	1 595 635	1 471 098	92.2	1 706 097	1 611 998	94.5
1 VII 2005[8] .... ESDF		3 305 723	3 089 988	93.5	1 597 040	1 474 638	92.3	1 708 683	1 615 350	94.5
1 VII 2006[8] .... ESDF		3 314 466	3 101 685	93.6	1 601 024	1 480 779	92.5	1 713 442	1 620 906	94.6
Venezuela (Bolivarian Republic of) - Venezuela (République bolivarienne du)[37]										
1 VII 1997 .... ESDF		22 958 680	20 123 896	87.7	11 559 949	10 021 295	86.7	11 398 731	10 102 601	88.6
1 VII 1998 .... ESDF		23 412 742	20 534 451	87.7	11 784 967	10 222 629	86.7	11 627 775	10 311 822	88.7
1 VII 1999 .... ESDF		23 867 393	20 945 043	87.8	12 010 280	10 423 959	86.8	11 857 113	10 521 084	88.7
1 VII 2000 .... ESDF		24 310 896	21 345 288	87.8	12 229 953	10 620 092	86.8	12 080 943	10 725 196	88.8
1 VII 2001 .... ESDF		24 765 581	21 754 766	87.8	12 454 204	10 820 038	86.9	12 311 377	10 934 728	88.8
30 X 2001 .... CDFC		23 054 210	...	...	11 402 869	...	...	11 651 341	...	...
1 VII 2002 .... ESDF		25 219 910	22 163 339	87.9	12 678 275	11 021 146	86.9	12 541 635	11 142 193	88.8
1 VII 2003 .... ESDF		25 673 550	...	...	12 901 999	...	...	12 771 551	...	...
1 VII 2004 .... ESDF		26 127 351	...	...	13 125 804	...	...	13 001 547	...	...
1 VII 2005 .... ESDF		26 577 423	...	...	13 347 732	...	...	13 229 691	...	...
1 VII 2006 .... ESDF		27 030 656	...	...	13 570 418	...	...	13 460 238	...	...
ASIA - ASIE										
Afghanistan										
1 VII 2002 .... ESDF		22 930 000	4 463 000[38]	19.5	10 453 500[38]	2 332 600[38]	22.3	9 844 300[38]	2 130 400[38]	21.6
1 VII 2006[39] .... ESDF		22 575 900	4 862 100	21.5	11 545 800	2 503 100	21.7	11 030 100	2 359 000	21.4
Armenia - Arménie										
1 VII 1997 .... ESDJ		3 242 100	2 130 651	65.7	1 554 242	1 016 310	65.4	1 687 858	1 114 341	66.0
1 VII 1998 .... ESDJ		3 235 151	2 117 251	65.4	1 553 260	1 011 028	65.1	1 681 891	1 106 223	65.8
1 VII 1999 .... ESDJ		3 229 499	2 103 700	65.1	1 552 362	1 002 727	64.6	1 677 138	1 100 974	65.6

Continent, country or area, and date / Continent, pays ou zone et date	Code[a]	Both sexes - Les deux sexes			Male - Masculin			Female - Féminin		
		Total	Urban - Urbaine		Total	Urban - Urbaine		Total	Urban - Urbaine	
			Number Nombre	Percent P.100		Number Nombre	Percent P.100		Number Nombre	Percent P.100
ASIA - ASIE										
Armenia - Arménie										
1 VII 2000 ....ESDJ		3 221 106	2 086 054	64.8	1 544 397	988 741	64.0	1 676 709	1 097 313	65.4
1 VII 2001 ....ESDJ		3 214 095	2 070 947	64.4	1 542 728	977 820	63.4	1 671 367	1 093 127	65.4
10 X 2001[40] ....CDFC		3 002 594	1 945 514	64.8	1 407 220	898 977	63.9	1 595 374	1 046 537	65.6
1 VII 2002 ....ESDJ		3 211 593	2 063 913	64.3	1 542 974	974 775	63.2	1 668 619	1 089 138	65.3
1 VII 2003 ....ESDJ		3 211 267	2 061 952	64.2	1 545 168	975 356	63.1	1 666 099	1 086 596	65.2
1 VII 2004 ....ESDJ		3 214 030	2 061 984	64.2	1 548 713	976 728	63.1	1 665 317	1 085 256	65.2
1 VII 2005 ....ESDJ		3 217 535	2 062 472	64.1	1 552 382	978 396	63.0	1 665 153	1 084 076	65.1
1 VII 2006 ....ESDJ		3 221 094	2 064 268	64.1	1 555 755	980 272	63.0	1 665 339	1 083 996	65.1
Azerbaijan - Azerbaïdjan										
1 VII 1997 ....ESDF		7 838 300	4 070 200	51.9	3 864 300	2 006 500	51.9	3 974 000	2 063 700	51.9
1 VII 1998 ....ESDF		7 913 000	4 072 600	51.5	3 882 100	1 993 500	51.4	4 030 900	2 079 100	51.6
27 I 1999 ....CDJC		7 953 438	4 053 584	51.0	3 883 155	1 970 022	50.7	4 070 283	2 083 562	51.2
1 VII 1999 ....ESDF		7 982 800	4 074 600	51.0	3 899 600	1 981 300	50.8	4 083 200	2 093 300	51.3
1 VII 2000 ....ESDF		8 048 600	4 096 900	50.9	3 936 400	1 994 300	50.7	4 112 200	2 102 600	51.1
1 VII 2001 ....ESDF		8 111 200	4 118 800	50.8	3 971 600	2 006 800	50.5	4 139 600	2 112 000	51 0
1 VII 2002 ....ESDF		8 172 000	4 142 200	50.7	4 005 900	2 020 200	50.4	4 166 100	2 122 000	50.9
1 VII 2003 ....ESDF		8 234 100	4 242 000	51.5	4 040 800	2 070 800	51.2	4 193 300	2 171 200	51.8
1 VII 2004 ....ESDF		8 306 500	4 276 300	51.5	4 081 100	2 089 500	51.2	4 225 400	2 186 800	51.8
Bahrain - Bahreïn										
1 VII 1997 ....ESDF		589 115	...	...	339 372	...	...	249 743	...	...
1 VII 1998 ....ESDF		604 842	...	...	348 100	...	...	256 742	...	...
1 VII 1999 ....ESDF		620 989	...	...	357 056	...	...	263 933	...	...
1 VII 2000 ....ESDF		637 582	...	...	366 247	...	...	271 335	...	...
7 IV 2001 ....CDJC		650 604	571 385[41]	87.8	373 649	328 817[41]	88.0	276 955	242 568[41]	87.6
1 VII 2001 ....ESDF		654 619	...	...	375 674	...	...	278 945	...	...
1 VII 2002 ....ESDF		672 123	...	...	386 220	...	...	285 903	...	...
1 VII 2003 ....ESDF		689 418	...	...	396 278	...	...	293 140	...	...
1 VII 2004 ....ESDF		707 160	...	...	406 617	...	...	300 543	...	...
1 VII 2005 ....ESDF		724 645	...	...	416 755	...	...	307 890	...	...
1 VII 2006 ....ESDF		742 562	...	...	427 164	...	...	315 397	...	...
Bangladesh										
1 VII 1997 ....ESDF		124 300 000	...	...	63 900 000	...	...	60 400 000	...	...
1 VII 1998 ....ESDF		126 200 000	...	...	64 800 000	...	...	61 400 000	...	...
1 VII 1999* ....ESDF		128 100 000	...	...	65 900 000	...	...	62 200 000	...	...
1 VII 2000 ....ESDF		129 300 000	...	...	66 300 000	...	...	63 000 000	...	...
22 I 2001[42] ....CDFC		130 522 598	31 077 952	23.8	67 731 320	16 844 256	24.9	62 791 278	14 233 696	22.7
1 VII 2002 ....ESDF		132 900 000	30 600 000	23.0	68 200 000	...	...	64 700 000	...	...
1 VII 2003 ....ESDF		134 800 000	31 300 000	23.2	69 100 000	...	...	65 700 000	...	...
1 VII 2004 ....ESDF		136 700 000	32 400 000	23.7	70 100 000	...	...	66 600 000	...	...
1 VII 2005 ....ESDF		138 600 000	33 600 000	24.2	71 000 000	...	...	67 600 000	...	...
1 VII 2006 ....ESDF		140 600 000	34 600 000	24.6	72 000 000	...	...	68 600 000	...	...
Bhutan - Bhoutan										
1 VII 2000 ....ESDF		580 297	...	...	342 324[28]	...	...	335 610[28]	...	...
1 VII 2001 ....ESDF		590 543	...	...	352 935[28]	...	...	346 014[28]	...	...
1 VII 2002 ....ESDF		601 582	...	...	361 759[28]	...	...	354 665[28]	...	...
1 VII 2003 ....ESDF		612 515	...	...	370 805[28]	...	...	363 535[28]	...	...
1 VII 2004 ....ESDF		623 647	...	...	380 090[28]	...	...	372 610[28]	...	...
30 V 2005 ....CDFC		634 982	...	...	333 595	...	...	301 387	...	...
1 VII 2006 ....ESDF		646 851	...	...	339 403	...	...	307 448	...	...
Brunei Darussalam - Brunéi Darussalam										
1 VII 1997 ....ESDF		301 700	...	...	155 600	...	...	146 100	...	...
1 VII 1998 ....ESDF		309 500	...	...	159 000	...	...	150 500	...	...
1 VII 1999 ....ESDF		316 900	...	...	162 200	...	...	154 700	...	...
1 VII 2000 ....ESDF		324 800	...	...	165 500	...	...	159 300	...	...
1 VII 2001 ....ESDF		332 800	...	...	168 900	...	...	163 900	...	...
21 VIII 2001* ....CDFC		332 844	238 699	71.7	168 974	120 046	71.0	163 870	118 653	72.4
1 VII 2002 ....ESDF		344 200	...	...	180 600	...	...	163 600	...	...
1 VII 2003 ....ESDF		349 600	...	...	182 500	...	...	167 100	...	...
1 VII 2004 ....ESDF		359 700	...	...	189 400	...	...	170 300	...	...
1 VII 2005 ....ESDF		370 100	...	...	195 300	...	...	174 800	...	...

Continent, country or area, and date / Continent, pays ou zone et date	Code[a]	Both sexes - Les deux sexes			Male - Masculin			Female - Féminin		
		Total	Urban - Urbaine		Total	Urban - Urbaine		Total	Urban - Urbaine	
			Number Nombre	Percent P.100		Number Nombre	Percent P.100		Number Nombre	Percent P.100

ASIA - ASIE

Cambodia - Cambodge[43]

3 III 1998 . . . . CDFC		11 437 656	1 795 575	15.7	5 511 408	878 186	15.9	5 926 248	917 389	15.5
1 VII 2004[44] . . . . SSDF		12 824 170	1 920 752	15.0	6 197 128	932 126	15.0	6 627 042	988 626	14.9

China - Chine[45]

1 VII 1997[46] . . . . ESDF		1 230 075 000	383 765 000[47]	31.2	626 655 000	...	...	603 420 000	...	...
1 VII 1998[46] . . . . ESDF		1 241 935 000	405 285 000[47]	32.6	635 355 000	...	...	606 580 000	...	...
1 VII 1999[46] . . . . ESDF		1 252 735 000	426 780 000[47]	34.1	643 160 000	...	...	609 575 000	...	...
1 VII 2000[46] . . . . ESDF		1 262 645 000	448 270 000[47]	35.5	650 645 000	...	...	612 000 000	...	...
1 XI 2000[48] . . . . CDJC		1 242 612 226	458 770 983	36.9	640 275 969	235 264 707	36.7	602 336 257	223 506 276	37.1
1 VII 2001[49] . . . . ESDF		1 271 850 000	469 850 000[47]	36.9	655 545 000	...	...	616 305 000	...	...
1 VII 2002[49] . . . . ESDF		1 280 400 000	491 380 000[47]	38.4	658 935 000	...	...	621 465 000	...	...
1 VII 2003[49] . . . . ESDF		1 288 400 000	512 940 000[47]	39.8	663 355 000	...	...	625 045 000	...	...
1 VII 2004[49] . . . . ESDF		1 296 075 000	533 295 000[47]	41.1	667 660 000	...	...	628 415 000	...	...
1 VII 2005[50] . . . . ESDF		1 303 720 000	552 475 000[47]	42.4	671 755 000	...	...	631 965 000	...	...
1 VII 2006[49] . . . . ESDF		1 311 020 000	569 590 000[47]	43.4	675 515 000	...	...	635 505 000	...	...

China: Hong Kong SAR - Chine: Hong Kong RAS

1 VII 1997 . . . . ESDJ		6 489 300	...	...	3 235 400	...	...	3 253 900	...	...
1 VII 1998 . . . . ESDJ		6 543 700	...	...	3 249 900	...	...	3 293 800	...	...
1 VII 1999 . . . . ESDJ		6 606 500	...	...	3 264 700	...	...	3 341 800	...	...
1 VII 2000 . . . . ESDJ		6 665 000	...	...	3 276 500	...	...	3 388 500	...	...
14 III 2001[51] . . . . CDJC		6 708 389	...	...	3 285 344	...	...	3 423 045	...	...
1 VII 2001 . . . . ESDJ		6 714 300	...	...	3 282 000	...	...	3 432 300	...	...
1 VII 2002 . . . . ESDJ		6 744 100	...	...	3 279 600	...	...	3 464 500	...	...
1 VII 2003 . . . . ESDJ		6 730 800	...	...	3 259 100	...	...	3 471 700	...	...
1 VII 2004 . . . . ESDJ		6 783 500	...	...	3 266 800	...	...	3 516 700	...	...
1 VII 2005 . . . . ESDJ		6 813 200	...	...	3 264 000	...	...	3 549 200	...	...
1 VII 2006 . . . . ESDJ		6 857 100	...	...	3 270 100	...	...	3 587 000	...	...
14 VII 2006 . . . . CDJC		6 864 346	...	...	3 272 956	...	...	3 591 390	...	...

China: Macao SAR - Chine: Macao RAS

1 VII 1997 . . . . ESDJ		417 295	...	...	201 320	...	...	215 975	...	...
1 VII 1998 . . . . ESDJ		422 304	...	...	203 535	...	...	218 769	...	...
1 VII 1999 . . . . ESDJ		427 411	...	...	205 322	...	...	222 089	...	...
1 VII 2000 . . . . ESDJ		430 569	...	...	206 686	...	...	223 883	...	...
1 VII 2001 . . . . ESDJ		433 903	...	...	208 235	...	...	225 668	...	...
23 VIII 2001 . . . . CDJC		435 235	...	...	208 865	...	...	226 370	...	...
1 VII 2002 . . . . ESDJ		438 408	...	...	210 218	...	...	228 190	...	...
1 VII 2003 . . . . ESDJ		443 600	...	...	212 866	...	...	230 734	...	...
1 VII 2004 . . . . ESDJ		454 661	...	...	218 122	...	...	236 539	...	...
1 VII 2005 . . . . ESDJ		473 457	...	...	227 600	...	...	245 857	...	...
1 VII 2006 . . . . ESDJ		498 852	...	...	243 009	...	...	255 843	...	...
19 VIII 2006[52] . . . . CDJC		502 113	...	...	245 167	...	...	256 946	...	...

Cyprus - Chypre[53]

1 VII 1997 . . . . ESDJ		670 400	...	...	330 900	...	...	339 500	...	...
1 VII 1998 . . . . ESDJ		678 900	...	...	334 600	...	...	344 300	...	...
1 VII 1999 . . . . ESDJ		686 400	...	...	337 800	...	...	348 600	...	...
1 VII 2000 . . . . ESDJ		693 600	...	...	341 000	...	...	352 600	...	...
1 VII 2001 . . . . ESDJ		701 300	...	...	344 300	...	...	357 000	...	...
1 X 2001[54] . . . . CDJC		689 565	474 450	68.8	338 497	231 128	68.3	351 068	243 322	69.3
1 VII 2002 . . . . ESDJ		709 600	...	...	347 900	...	...	361 700	...	...
1 VII 2003 . . . . ESDJ		720 600	...	...	353 700	...	...	366 900	...	...
1 VII 2004 . . . . ESDJ		737 100	...	...	363 000	...	...	374 100	...	...
1 VII 2005 . . . . ESDJ		758 000	...	...	373 600	...	...	384 400	...	...
1 VII 2006 . . . . ESDJ		770 900	...	...	380 100	...	...	390 800	...	...

Georgia - Géorgie

1 VII 1997 . . . . ESDF		4 531 700	2 389 200	52.7	...	...	...	...	...	...
1 VII 1998 . . . . ESDF		4 487 400	2 352 000	52.4	...	...	...	...	...	...
1 VII 1999 . . . . ESDF		4 452 500	2 323 200	52.2	...	...	...	...	...	...
1 VII 2000 . . . . ESDF		4 418 300	2 294 500	51.9	...	...	...	...	...	...
1 VII 2001 . . . . ESDF		4 386 500	2 282 800	52.0	2 300 700	...	...	2 085 800	...	...
17 I 2002 . . . . CDJC		4 371 535	2 284 796	52.3	2 061 753	1 048 593	50.9	2 309 782	1 236 203	53.5
1 VII 2002 . . . . ESDF		4 357 100	2 275 800	52.2	...	...	...	...	...	...
1 VII 2003 . . . . ESDF		4 328 900	2 259 600	52.2	2 045 500	...	...	2 283 400	...	...

Continent, country or area, and date / Continent, pays ou zone et date	Code[a]	Both sexes - Les deux sexes Total	Urban - Urbaine Number Nombre	Urban - Urbaine Percent P.100	Male - Masculin Total	Urban - Urbaine Number Nombre	Urban - Urbaine Percent P.100	Female - Féminin Total	Urban - Urbaine Number Nombre	Urban - Urbaine Percent P.100
ASIA - ASIE										
Georgia - Géorgie										
1 VII 2004	ESDF	4 318 400	2 255 000	52.2	...	...	...	...	...	...
1 VII 2005	ESDF	4 361 400	2 284 000	52.4	...	...	...	...	...	...
1 VII 2006	ESDF	4 398 000	2 309 700	52.5	2 081 700	...	...	2 316 300	...	...
India - Inde[55]										
1 VII 1997	ESDF	960 496 569	259 230 163	27.0	498 354 143	136 508 102	27.4	462 142 426	122 722 061	26.6
1 VII 1998	ESDF	978 980 920	266 283 953	27.2	507 668 333	140 183 037	27.6	471 312 587	126 100 916	26.8
1 VII 1999	ESDF	997 556 080	273 525 428	27.4	516 933 647	143 962 574	27.8	480 622 433	129 562 854	27.0
1 VII 2000	ESDF	1 016 209 642	280 992 154	27.7	526 131 774	147 866 984	28.1	490 077 868	133 125 170	27.2
1 III 2001[56]	CDFC	1 028 610 328	286 119 689	27.8	532 156 772	150 554 098	28.3	496 453 556	135 565 591	27.3
1 VII 2001	ESDF	1 034 930 863	288 732 422[57]	27.9	535 244 661[57]	151 922 010[57]	28.4	499 686 202[57]	136 810 412[57]	27.4
1 VII 2002	ESDF	1 051 258 250	295 388 359	28.1	543 896 774	155 423 847	28.6	507 361 477	139 964 511	27.6
1 VII 2003	ESDF	1 068 065 117	302 416 034	28.3	552 616 508	159 117 861	28.8	515 448 609	143 298 173	27.8
1 VII 2004	ESDF	1 084 756 558	309 506 730	28.5	561 281 181	162 846 812	29.0	523 475 376	146 659 918	28.0
1 VII 2005	ESDF	1 101 317 709	316 648 000	28.8	569 882 367	166 604 533	29.2	531 435 342	150 043 467	28.2
1 VII 2006	ESDF	1 117 733 826	323 827 490	29.0	578 411 677	170 384 885	29.5	539 322 149	153 442 605	28.5
Indonesia - Indonésie										
1 VII 1997	E3DJ	201 353 100	70 914 000[28]	38.2	100 200 800	...	...	101 140 300	...	...
1 VII 1998	ESDJ	204 392 500	80 275 300[28]	39.3	101 719 200	...	...	102 673 300	...	...
1 VII 1999	ESDJ	207 437 100	83 718 400[28]	40.4	103 234 400	...	...	104 202 700	...	...
30 VI 2000[58]	CDFC	206 264 595	86 601 850	42.0	103 417 180	43 368 496	41.9	102 847 415	43 233 354	42.0
1 VII 2003	ESDJ	214 251 300	...	...	107 335 600	...	...	106 915 700	...	...
31 X 2005[59]	SSDF	213 375 287	92 005 069	43.1	107 274 528	46 055 993	42.9	106 100 759	45 949 076	43.3
Iran (Islamic Republic of) - Iran (République islamique d')										
1 VII 1997[60]	ESDJ	60 938 837	37 826 305	62.1	31 011 770	19 249 804	62.1	29 927 067	18 576 501	62.1
1 VII 1998[60]	ESDJ	61 835 591	38 839 280	62.8	...	...	...	...	...	...
1 VII 1999[60]	ESDJ	62 745 540	39 856 570	63.5	...	...	...	...	...	...
1 VII 2000[60]	ESDJ	63 663 942	40 873 494	64.2	...	...	...	...	...	...
1 VII 2001[60]	ESDJ	64 528 159	42 173 587	65.4	...	...	...	...	...	...
1 VII 2002[60]	ESDJ	65 540 239	43 054 650	65.7	...	...	...	...	...	...
1 VII 2003[60]	ESDJ	66 480 365	43 892 714	66.0	...	...	...	...	...	...
1 VII 2004[60]	ESDJ	67 477 499	44 190 104	65.5	34 350 656	22 669 195	66.0	33 126 843	21 520 909	65.0
1 VII 2005[60]	ESDJ	68 467 369	45 650 230	66.7	34 801 582	23 316 275	67.0	33 665 787	22 333 955	66.3
28 X 2006*	CDJC	70 495 782	...	...	35 866 362	...	...	34 629 420	...	...
Iraq										
1 VII 1997	ESDF	22 046 000	...	...	10 987 000	...	...	11 059 000	...	...
16 X 1997[61]	CDFC	19 184 543	12 945 776	67.5	9 536 570	6 466 325	67.8	9 647 973	6 479 451	67.2
1 VII 1998	ESDF	22 702 000	...	...	11 328 000	...	...	11 374 000	...	...
1 VII 1999	ESDF	23 382 000	...	...	11 682 000	...	...	11 700 000	...	...
1 VII 2000	ESDF	24 086 000	...	...	12 047 000	...	...	12 039 000	...	...
1 VII 2001	ESDF	24 813 000	...	...	12 424 000	...	...	12 389 000	...	...
1 VII 2002	ESDF	25 565 000	...	...	12 814 000	...	...	12 751 000	...	...
1 VII 2003	ESDF	26 340 000	...	...	13 216 000	...	...	13 124 000	...	...
1 VII 2004	ESDF	27 139 000	...	...	13 629 000	...	...	13 510 000	...	...
1 VII 2005	ESDF	27 963 000	...	...	14 055 000	...	...	13 908 000	...	...
1 VII 2006	ESDF	28 810 441	19 226 476	66.7	14 493 207	9 698 293	66.9	14 317 234	9 528 183	66.6
Israel - Israël[62]										
1 VII 1997	ESDJ	5 829 000	5 294 100	90.8	2 875 400	2 599 900	90.4	2 953 500	2 694 300	91.2
1 VII 1998	ESDJ	5 970 700	5 418 400	90.7	...	...	...	...	...	...
1 VII 1999	ESDJ	6 125 300	5 554 200	90.7	3 021 743	...	...	3 103 533	...	...
1 VII 2000	ESDJ	6 289 200	5 696 100	90.6	3 102 400	2 797 800	90.2	3 186 800	2 898 300	90.9
1 VII 2001	ESDJ	6 439 000	5 900 700	91.6	3 176 600	2 900 200	91.3	3 262 500	3 000 500	92.0
1 VII 2002	ESDJ	6 569 900	6 017 300	91.6	3 241 700	2 958 200	91.3	3 328 200	3 059 100	91.9
1 VII 2003	ESDJ	6 689 700	6 122 400	91.5	3 301 800	3 010 900	91.2	3 387 900	3 111 600	91.8
1 VII 2004	ESDJ	6 809 000	6 226 900	91.5	3 362 000	3 063 600	91.1	3 447 000	3 163 300	91.8
1 VII 2005	ESDJ	6 930 128	6 359 940	91.8	3 423 132	3 131 229	91.5	3 506 996	3 228 711	92.1
1 VII 2006	ESDJ	7 053 707	6 475 600[63]	91.8	3 485 501	3 189 511[63]	91.5	3 568 206	3 286 089[63]	92.1
Japan - Japon										
1 VII 1997[64]	ESDF	126 057 000	...	...	61 782 000	...	...	64 275 000	...	...
1 VII 1998[64]	ESDF	126 400 000	...	...	61 910 000	...	...	64 490 000	...	...
1 VII 1999[64]	ESDF	126 631 000	...	...	61 996 000	...	...	64 635 000	...	...
1 VII 2000[64]	ESDF	126 843 000	...	...	62 063 000	...	...	64 780 000	...	...

Continent, country or area, and date / Continent, pays ou zone et date	Code[a]	Both sexes - Les deux sexes			Male - Masculin			Female - Féminin		
		Total	Urban - Urbaine		Total	Urban - Urbaine		Total	Urban - Urbaine	
			Number Nombre	Percent P.100		Number Nombre	Percent P.100		Number Nombre	Percent P.100

ASIA - ASIE

Japan - Japon
1 X 2000[64]........CDFC		126 925 843	99 865 289	78.7	62 110 764	49 005 691	78.9	64 815 079	50 859 598	78.5
1 VII 2001[64].......ESDF		127 149 000	...	...	62 178 000	...	...	64 971 000	...	...
1 VII 2002[64].......ESDF		127 445 000	...	...	62 278 000	...	...	65 167 000	...	...
1 VII 2003[64].......ESDF		127 718 000	...	...	62 370 000	...	...	65 348 000	...	...
1 VII 2004[64].......ESDF		127 761 000	...	...	62 355 000	...	...	65 406 000	...	...
1 VII 2005[64].......ESDF		127 773 000	...	...	62 332 000	...	...	65 441 000	...	...
1 X 2005 ....CDJC		127 767 994	110 264 324	86.3	62 348 977	53 886 000	86.4	65 419 017	56 378 324	86.2
1 VII 2006[64].......ESDF		127 756 000	...	...	62 314 000	...	...	65 442 000	...	...

Jordan - Jordanie[65]
1 VII 1997 ....ESDF		4 444 500	3 499 300	78.7	2 320 000	...	...	2 124 500	...	...
1 VII 1998 ....ESDF		4 564 500	3 594 200	78.7	2 382 650	...	...	2 181 850	...	...
1 VII 1999 ....ESDF		4 680 500	3 685 550	78.7	2 443 200	...	...	2 237 300	...	...
1 VII 2000 ....ESDF		4 797 500	3 871 450	80.7	2 487 300	...	...	2 310 200	...	...
1 VII 2001 ....ESDF		4 917 500	4 062 600	82.6	2 532 550	...	...	2 384 950	...	...
1 VII 2002 ....ESDF		5 038 000	4 162 150	82.6	2 594 600	...	...	2 443 400	...	...
1 VII 2003 ....ESDF		5 164 000	4 266 150	82.6	2 659 500	...	...	2 504 500	...	...
1 VII 2004 ....ESDF		5 290 000	4 369 800	82.6	2 725 600	...	...	2 564 400	...	...
1 X 2004 ....CDFC		5 103 639	3 997 383	78.3	2 626 287	2 055 431	78.3	2 477 352	1 941 952	78.4
1 VII 2005 ....ESDF		5 411 500	4 469 800	82.6	2 789 400	...	...	2 622 100	...	...
1 VII 2006 ....ESDF		5 536 500	4 573 100	82.6	2 853 850	...	...	2 682 650	...	...

Kazakhstan
1 VII 1997 ....ESDF		15 334 405	8 567 329	55.9	7 393 786	4 014 495	54.3	7 940 619	4 552 834	57.3
1 VII 1998 ....ESDF		15 072 983	8 434 080	56.0	7 263 077	3 945 189	54.3	7 809 906	4 488 891	57.5
26 II 1999 ....CDJC		14 953 126	8 377 303	56.0	7 201 785	3 918 556	54.4	7 751 341	4 458 747	57.5
1 VII 1999 ....ESDF		14 928 373	8 406 019	56.3	7 190 238	3 933 622	54.7	7 738 135	4 472 397	57.8
1 VII 2000 ....ESDF		14 883 626	8 405 483	56.5	7 168 613	3 933 997	54.9	7 715 013	4 471 486	58.0
1 VII 2001 ....ESDF		14 858 335	8 421 366	56.7	7 156 582	3 942 353	55.1	7 701 753	4 479 013	58.2
1 VII 2002 ....ESDF		14 858 948	8 443 242	56.8	7 156 816	3 952 649	55.2	7 702 132	4 490 593	58.3
1 VII 2003 ....ESDF		14 909 018	8 487 697	56.9	7 179 583	3 971 520	55.3	7 729 435	4 516 177	58.4
1 VII 2004 ....ESDF		15 012 985	8 566 447	57.1	7 227 960	4 005 199	55.4	7 785 025	4 561 248	58.6
1 VII 2005 ....ESDF		15 147 029	8 655 586	57.1	7 290 852	4 044 092	55.5	7 856 177	4 611 494	58.7
1 VII 2006 ....ESDF		15 308 084	8 764 884	57.3	7 367 032	4 094 572	55.6	7 941 052	4 670 312	58.8

Korea (Republic of) - Corée (République de)
1 VII 1997 ....ESDJ		45 953 580	...	...	23 148 092	...	...	22 805 488	...	...
1 VII 1998 ....ESDJ		46 286 503	...	...	23 295 727	...	...	22 990 776	...	...
1 VII 1999 ....ESDJ		46 616 677	...	...	23 457 837	...	...	23 158 840	...	...
1 VII 2000 ....ESDJ		47 008 111	...	...	23 666 769	...	...	23 341 342	...	...
1 XI 2000[66].......CDFC		46 136 101	36 755 144	79.7	23 158 582	18 484 139	79.8	22 977 519	18 271 005	79.5
1 VII 2001 ....ESDJ		47 357 362	...	...	23 843 136	...	...	23 514 226	...	...
1 VII 2002 ....ESDJ		47 622 179	...	...	23 970 035	...	...	23 652 144	...	...
1 VII 2003 ....ESDJ		47 859 311	...	...	24 089 703	...	...	23 769 608	...	...
1 VII 2004 ....ESDJ		48 039 415	...	...	24 165 488	...	...	23 873 927	...	...
1 VII 2005 ....ESDJ		48 138 077	...	...	24 190 906	...	...	23 947 171	...	...
1 XI 2005[67].......CDJC		47 278 951	38 514 753	81.5	23 623 954	19 258 840	81.5	23 654 997	19 255 913	81.4
1 VII 2006 ....ESDJ		48 297 184	...	...	24 267 609	...	...	24 029 575	...	...

Kuwait - Koweït
1 VII 1997 ....ESDF		1 979 689	...	...	1 195 171	...	...	784 518	...	...
1 VII 1998 ....ESDF		2 027 103	...	...	1 226 774	...	...	800 329	...	...
1 VII 1999 ....ESDF		2 107 195	...	...	1 278 822	...	...	828 373	...	...
1 VII 2000 ....ESDF		2 138 115	...	...	1 287 369	...	...	850 746	...	...
1 VII 2001 ....ESDF		2 182 609	...	...	1 305 391	...	...	877 218	...	...
1 VII 2002 ....ESDF		2 261 956	...	...	1 355 300	...	...	906 656	...	...
1 VII 2003 ....ESDF		2 325 440	...	...	1 392 820	...	...	932 620	...	...
1 VII 2004 ....ESDF		2 390 591	...	...	1 432 051	...	...	958 540	...	...
20 IV 2005*.........CDFC		2 213 403	...	...	1 310 067	...	...	903 336	...	...
1 VII 2005 ....ESDF		2 457 257	...	...	1 472 312	...	...	984 945	...	...

Kyrgyzstan - Kirghizistan
1 VII 1997 ....ESDF		4 724 900	1 675 900	35.5	2 328 100	800 500	34.4	2 396 800	875 400	36.5
1 VII 1998 ....ESDF		4 797 000	1 696 900	35.4	2 365 200	811 200	34.3	2 431 800	885 700	36.4
24 III 1999.........CDFC		4 850 734	1 713 836	35.3	2 392 579	819 550	34.3	2 458 155	894 286	36.4
1 VII 1999 ....ESDF		4 864 600	1 717 100	35.3	2 399 900	821 100	34.2	2 464 700	896 000	36.4
1 VII 2000 ....ESDF		4 915 300	1 738 800	35.4	2 425 800	831 300	34.3	2 489 500	907 500	36.5

Continent, country or area, and date / Continent, pays ou zone et date	Code[a]	Both sexes - Les deux sexes			Male - Masculin			Female - Féminin		
		Total	Urban - Urbaine		Total	Urban - Urbaine		Total	Urban - Urbaine	
			Number Nombre	Percent P.100		Number Nombre	Percent P.100		Number Nombre	Percent P.100
ASIA - ASIE										
Kyrgyzstan - Kirghizistan										
1 VII 2001 . . . . ESDF		4 954 800	1 760 600	35.5	2 445 900	841 900	34.4	2 508 900	918 700	36.6
1 VII 2002 . . . . ESDF		4 993 200	1 763 600	35.3	2 465 500	843 400	34.2	2 527 700	920 200	36.4
1 VII 2003 . . . . ESDF		5 038 600	1 785 700	35.4	2 488 900	854 000	34.3	2 549 700	931 700	36.5
1 VII 2004 . . . . ESDF		5 092 800	1 816 400	35.7	2 516 400	868 300	34.5	2 576 400	948 100	36.8
1 VII 2005 . . . . ESDF		5 143 500	1 830 400	35.6	2 542 300	875 100	34.4	2 601 200	955 300	36.7
1 VII 2006 . . . . ESDF		5 192 000	1 839 000	35.4	2 566 700	879 700	34.3	2 625 300	959 300	36.5
Lao People's Democratic Republic - République démocratique populaire lao										
1 VII 1997[68] . . . . SSDF		5 087 322	...	...	2 521 009	...	...	2 566 313	...	...
1 VII 1999 . . . . ESDF		5 091 100	...	...	2 516 100	...	...	2 575 000	...	...
1 VII 2000[69] . . . . ESDF		5 218 300	...	...	2 579 000	...	...	2 639 300	...	...
1 VII 2001[69] . . . . ESDF		5 377 000	...	...	2 657 000	...	...	2 720 000	...	...
1 VII 2002[69] . . . . ESDF		5 526 000	...	...	2 731 000	...	...	2 795 000	...	...
1 VII 2003[69] . . . . ESDF		5 679 000	...	...	2 807 000	...	...	2 872 000	...	...
1 VII 2004[69] . . . . ESDF		5 836 000	...	...	2 884 000	...	...	2 952 000	...	...
1 III 2005 . . . . CDJC		5 621 982			2 800 551			2 821 431		
1 VII 2005 . . . . ESDF		5 679 000[70]	...	...	2 806 400	...	...	2 872 600	...	...
1 VII 2006[70] . . . . ESDF		5 747 000	...	...	2 864 000	...	...	2 883 000	...	...
Lebanon - Liban[71]										
1 I 2004 . . . . ESDF		3 755 034	...	...	1 868 322	...	...	1 886 712	...	...
Malaysia - Malaisie										
1 VII 1997 . . . . ESDF		20 995 951	...	...	10 650 205	...	...	10 345 746	...	...
1 VII 1998 . . . . ESDF		21 475 488	...	...	10 891 958	...	...	10 583 530	...	...
1 VII 1999 . . . . ESDF		21 852 454	...	...	11 081 226	...	...	10 771 228	...	...
1 VII 2000 . . . . ESDF		23 494 891	...	...	11 965 620	...	...	11 529 271	...	...
5 VII 2000[72] . . . . CDJC		23 274 690	14 426 871	62.0	11 853 432	7 318 396	61.7	11 421 258	7 108 475	62.2
1 VII 2001 . . . . ESDF		24 012 900	...	...	12 227 400	...	...	11 785 500	...	...
1 VII 2002 . . . . ESDF		24 526 500	...	...	12 487 100	...	...	12 039 500	...	...
1 VII 2003 . . . . ESDF		25 048 300	...	...	12 751 900	...	...	12 296 400	...	...
1 VII 2004 . . . . ESDF		25 580 900	...	...	13 023 300	...	...	12 557 700	...	...
1 VII 2005 . . . . ESDF		26 127 700	...	...	13 302 800	...	...	12 824 900	...	...
1 VII 2006 . . . . ESDF		26 640 200	...	...	13 562 600	...	...	13 077 600	...	...
Maldives										
1 VII 1997 . . . . ESDF		258 678	...	...	131 545	...	...	127 133	...	...
1 VII 1998 . . . . ESDF		267 464	...	...	135 986	...	...	131 478	...	...
1 VII 1999 . . . . ESDF		277 579	...	...	141 073	...	...	136 506	...	...
31 III 2000 . . . . CDFC		270 101	74 069	27.4	137 200	38 559	28.1	132 901	35 510	26.7
1 VII 2000 . . . . ESDF		271 410	...	...	137 697	...	...	133 713	...	...
1 VII 2001 . . . . ESDF		275 975	75 680	27.4	140 100	39 398[28]	28.1	135 875	36 282[28]	26.7
1 VII 2002 . . . . ESDF		280 549	76 934	27.4	142 357	40 051[28]	28.1	138 192	36 884[28]	26.7
1 VII 2003 . . . . ESDF		285 066	78 173	27.4	144 599	40 695[28]	28.1	140 467	37 477[28]	26.7
1 VII 2004 . . . . ESDF		289 480	79 383	27.4	146 799	41 326[28]	28.2	142 681	38 058[28]	26.7
1 VII 2005 . . . . ESDF		293 746	...	...	148 929	...	...	144 817	...	...
21 III 2006 . . . . CDFC		298 968	103 693	34.7	151 459	51 992	34.3	147 509	51 701	35.0
1 VII 2006 . . . . ESDF		298 333	...	...	151 201	...	...	147 132	...	...
Mongolia - Mongolie										
1 VII 1997 . . . . ESDF		2 273 112	1 186 605	52.2	1 119 654	577 519	51.6	1 153 458	609 086	52.8
1 VII 1998 . . . . ESDF		2 280 751	1 176 278	51.6	1 121 068	568 895	50.7	1 159 683	607 383	52.4
1 VII 1999 . . . . ESDF		2 332 394	1 264 012	54.2	1 151 535	613 955	53.3	1 180 859	650 057	55.0
5 I 2000 . . . . CDFC		2 373 493	1 344 516	56.6	1 177 981	657 081	55.8	1 195 512	687 435	57.5
1 VII 2000 . . . . ESDF		2 390 491	1 360 747	56.9	1 186 258	664 991	56.1	1 204 233	695 756	57.8
1 VII 2001 . . . . ESDF		2 425 017	1 387 045	57.2	1 202 132	677 838	56.4	1 222 885	709 207	58.0
1 VII 2002 . . . . ESDF		2 458 963	1 409 034	57.3	1 218 894	688 417	56.5	1 240 069	720 617	58.1
1 VII 2003 . . . . ESDF		2 489 702	1 442 589	57.9	1 235 164	705 367	57.1	1 254 538	737 222	58.8
1 VII 2004 . . . . ESDF		2 518 573	1 481 205	58.8	1 249 487	723 856	57.9	1 269 086	757 349	59.7
1 VII 2005 . . . . ESDF		2 547 751	1 520 763	59.7	1 263 962	741 689	58.7	1 283 789	779 074	60.7
1 VII 2006 . . . . ESDF		2 578 587	1 561 417	60.6	1 268 249	756 004	59.6	1 310 338	805 413	61.5
Myanmar										
1 VII 1997 . . . . ESDF		46 402 000	...	...	23 039 000	...	...	23 363 000	...	...
1 VII 1998 . . . . ESDF		48 160 000	...	...	23 914 000	...	...	24 246 000	...	...
1 VII 1999 . . . . ESDF		49 133 000	...	...	24 404 000	...	...	24 729 000	...	...

Continent, country or area, and date / Continent, pays ou zone et date	Code[a]	Both sexes - Les deux sexes			Male - Masculin			Female - Féminin		
		Total	Urban - Urbaine		Total	Urban - Urbaine		Total	Urban - Urbaine	
			Number Nombre	Percent P.100		Number Nombre	Percent P.100		Number Nombre	Percent P.100
ASIA - ASIE										
Myanmar										
1 VII 2000	ESDF	50 125 000	...	...	24 907 000	...	...	25 218 000	...	...
1 VII 2001	ESDF	51 138 000	...	...	25 421 000	...	...	25 717 000	...	...
1 VII 2002	ESDF	52 171 000	...	...	25 941 000	...	...	26 230 000	...	...
1 VII 2003	ESDF	53 224 000	...	...	26 467 000	...	...	26 757 000	...	...
1 VII 2004	ESDF	54 299 000	...	...	27 000 000	...	...	27 299 000	...	...
Nepal - Népal										
1 VII 1999	ESDJ	22 367 048	...	...	11 167 503			11 199 545	...	...
22 VI 2001[73]	CDJC	23 151 423	...	...	11 563 921			11 587 502	...	...
1 VII 2002	ESDJ	23 701 451	...	...	11 845 495			11 855 956	...	...
1 VII 2003	ESDJ	24 249 996	...	...	12 126 262			12 123 734	...	...
1 VII 2004	ESDJ	24 797 059	...	...	12 406 222			12 390 837	...	...
1 VII 2005	ESDJ	25 342 638	...	...	12 685 375			12 657 263	...	...
1 VII 2006	ESDJ	25 886 736	...	...	12 963 722			12 923 014	...	...
Occupied Palestinian Territory - Territoire palestinien occupé										
1 VII 1997	ESDF	2 783 084	1 992 780[74]	71.6	1 404 481	...	...	1 378 603	...	...
9 XII 1997[75]	CDFC	2 601 669	...	...	1 322 264			1 279 405	...	...
1 VII 1998	ESDF	2 897 113	2 074 825[74]	71.6	1 462 821	...	...	1 434 292	...	...
1 VII 1999	ESDF	3 019 158	2 162 657[74]	71.6	1 525 297	...	...	1 493 861	...	...
1 VII 2000	ESDF	3 149 448	2 256 470[74]	71.6	1 592 028	...	...	1 557 419	...	...
1 VII 2001	ESDF	3 275 389	2 346 926[74]	71.7	1 656 513	...	...	1 618 876	...	...
1 VII 2002	ESDF	3 394 046	2 432 044[74]	71.7	1 717 239	...	...	1 676 807	...	...
1 VII 2003	ESDF	3 514 868	2 519 018[74]	71.7	1 779 088	...	...	1 735 780	...	...
1 VII 2004	ESDF	3 637 529	2 607 633[74]	71.7	1 841 894	...	...	1 795 635	...	...
1 VII 2005	ESDF	3 762 005	2 697 879[74]	71.7	1 905 642	...	...	1 856 363	...	...
1 VII 2006	ESDF	3 888 292	2 789 773[74]	71.7	1 970 327	...	...	1 917 965	...	...
Oman										
1 VII 1997	ESDF	2 255 609	...	...	1 320 084			935 525	...	...
1 VII 1998	ESDF	2 287 642	...	...	1 333 557			954 085	...	...
1 VII 1999	ESDF	2 325 438	...	...	1 365 775			959 663	...	...
1 VII 2000	ESDF	2 401 256	...	...	1 401 589			999 667	...	...
1 VII 2001	ESDF	2 477 687	...	...	1 451 041			1 026 646	...	...
1 VII 2002	ESDF	2 537 742	...		1 443 316			1 094 426	...	
7 XII 2003	CDFC	2 340 815	1 673 480	71.5	1 313 239	950 471	72.4	1 027 576	723 009	70.4
1 VII 2004	ESDF	2 415 576	...		1 360 891			1 054 685	...	
1 VII 2005	ESDF	2 513 530	...		1 458 845			1 054 685	...	
1 VII 2006	ESDF	2 577 062	1 842 376	71.5	1 498 143	1 084 297	72.4	1 078 919	759 134	70.4
Pakistan[76]										
2 III 1998	CDFC	130 579 571	42 458 339	32.5	67 840 137	22 419 286	33.0	62 739 434	20 039 053	31.9
1 VII 1998	ESDF	131 510 000	42 910 000	32.6	68 290 000	22 100 000	32.4	63 220 000	20 810 000	32.9
1 VII 2000	ESDF	138 945 000	...	...	72 300 000	...	...	66 645 000	...	...
1 VII 2001	ESDF	141 765 000	...	...	73 770 000	...	...	67 995 000	...	...
1 VII 2002	ESDF	144 560 000	...	...	75 225 000	...	...	69 335 000	...	...
1 VII 2003	ESDF	147 335 000	...	...	76 670 000	...	...	70 665 000	...	...
1 VII 2004	ESDF	150 135 000	...	...	78 125 000	...	...	72 010 000	...	...
1 VII 2005	ESDF	153 455 000	...	...	79 745 000	...	...	73 710 000	...	...
1 I 2006	ESDF	155 360 000	...		80 630 000			74 730 000	...	
Philippines										
1 VII 1997	ESDJ	73 526 941	...	...	36 051 342[28]			35 498 448[28]	...	...
1 VII 1998	ESDJ	75 154 743	...	...	36 851 141[28]			36 296 635[28]	...	...
1 VII 1999	ESDJ	76 782 548	...	...	37 650 939[28]			37 094 817[28]	...	...
1 V 2000	CDJC	76 504 077	...	...	38 524 267			37 979 810	...	...
1 VII 2000	ESDJ	76 348 114	...	...	38 452 927			37 895 187	...	...
1 VII 2001	ESDJ	77 925 894	...	...	39 242 185			38 683 709	...	...
1 VII 2002	ESDJ	79 503 675	...	...	40 031 449			39 472 226	...	...
1 VII 2003	ESDJ	81 081 457	...	...	40 820 706			40 260 751	...	...
Qatar										
1 III 1997	CDFC	522 023	...	...	342 459			179 564	...	...
1 VII 1997	ESDF	529 823	...	...	353 474			176 349	...	...
1 VII 1998	ESDF	557 335	...	...	371 829			185 506	...	...
1 VII 1999	ESDF	586 275	...	...	391 136			195 139	...	...
1 VII 2000	ESDF	616 719	...	...	411 447			205 272	...	...

Continent, country or area, and date / Continent, pays ou zone et date	Code[a]	Both sexes - Les deux sexes			Male - Masculin			Female - Féminin		
		Total	Urban - Urbaine		Total	Urban - Urbaine		Total	Urban - Urbaine	
			Number Nombre	Percent P.100		Number Nombre	Percent P.100		Number Nombre	Percent P.100
ASIA - ASIE										
Qatar										
1 VII 2001 ....ESDF		648 744	...	...	432 812	...	...	215 932	...	...
1 VII 2002 ....ESDF		682 434	...	...	455 289	...	...	227 145	...	...
1 VII 2003 ....ESDF		717 766	...	...	478 860	...	...	238 906	...	...
16 III 2004............CDFC		744 029	...	...	496 382	...	...	247 647	...	...
1 VII 2004 ....ESDF		756 486	...	...	504 693	...	...	251 793	...	...
1 VII 2005 ....ESDF		796 186	...	...	531 056	...	...	265 130	...	...
1 VII 2006 ....ESDF		936 287	...	...	666 543	...	...	269 744	...	...
Saudi Arabia - Arabie saoudite										
1 VII 1997 ....ESDF		19 038 517	...	...	10 606 265	...	...	8 432 251	...	...
1 VII 1998 ....ESDF		19 506 225	...	...	10 857 670	...	...	8 648 555	...	...
1 VII 1999 ....ESDF		19 985 423	...	...	11 115 026	...	...	8 870 397	...	...
1 VII 2000 ....ESDF		20 476 393	...	...	11 378 473	...	...	9 097 920	...	...
1 VII 2001 ....ESDF		20 979 424	...	...	11 648 157	...	...	9 331 268	...	...
1 VII 2002 ....ESDF		21 494 814	...	...	11 924 224	...	...	9 570 590	...	...
1 VII 2003 ....ESDF		22 022 864	...	...	12 206 825	...	...	9 816 039	...	...
1 VII 2004 ....ESDF		22 563 886	...	...	12 493 910	...	...	10 069 976	...	...
15 IX 2004............CDFC		22 678 262	...	...	12 557 240	...	...	10 121 022	...	...
1 VII 2005 ....ESDF		23 118 994	...	...	12 791 330	...	...	10 327 664	...	...
1 VII 2006 ....ESDF		23 678 849	...	...	13 090 840	...	...	10 588 009	...	...
Singapore - Singapour										
1 VII 1997 ....ESDJ		3 123 400	...	...	1 565 800	...	...	1 557 700	...	...
1 VII 1998 ....ESDJ		3 180 000	...	...	1 591 800	...	...	1 588 200	...	...
1 VII 1999 ....ESDJ		3 229 700	...	...	1 614 800	...	...	1 614 900	...	...
1 VII 2000[77] ....CDFC		4 017 700	...	...	2 061 800	...	...	1 955 900	...	...
1 VII 2000 ....ESDJ		3 273 400	...	...	1 634 700	...	...	1 638 700	...	...
1 VII 2001 ....ESDJ		3 325 900	...	...	1 658 600	...	...	1 667 300	...	...
1 VII 2002 ....ESDJ		3 382 900	...	...	1 684 300	...	...	1 698 600	...	...
1 VII 2004 ....ESDJ		3 486 900	...	...	1 732 800	...	...	1 754 100	...	...
1 VII 2006 ....ESDJ		3 608 400	...	...	1 787 600	...	...	1 820 800	...	...
Sri Lanka										
1 VII 1997 ....ESDF		18 552 000	...	...	9 457 000	...	...	9 095 000	...	...
1 VII 1998 ....ESDF		18 774 000	...	...	9 570 000	...	...	9 204 000	...	...
1 VII 1999 ....ESDF		19 043 000	...	...	9 707 000	...	...	9 336 000	...	...
1 VII 2001 ....ESDF		18 732 400	...	...	9 267 300	...	...	9 465 100	...	...
17 VII 2001*[78] ....CDFC		16 864 544	2 467 171	14.6	8 343 964	1 246 983	14.9	8 520 580	1 220 188	14.3
1 VII 2002 ....ESDF		19 007 410	...	...	9 402 966	...	...	9 604 444	...	...
1 VII 2003* ....ESDF		19 252 000	...	...	9 510 000	...	...	9 742 000	...	...
1 VII 2004* ....ESDF		19 462 000	...	...	9 615 000	...	...	9 847 000	...	...
1 VII 2005* ....ESDF		19 668 000	...	...	9 718 000	...	...	9 950 000	...	...
1 VII 2006* ....ESDF		19 886 000	...	...	9 826 000	...	...	10 060 000	...	...
Syrian Arab Republic - République arabe syrienne[79]										
1 VII 1997 ....ESDF		15 100 000	...	...	7 723 000	...	...	7 377 000	...	...
1 VII 1998 ....ESDF		15 597 000	...	...	7 978 000	...	...	7 619 000	...	...
1 VII 1999 ....ESDF		16 110 000	...	...	8 240 000	...	...	7 870 000	...	...
1 VII 2000 ....ESDF		16 320 000			8 343 000			7 977 000	...	...
1 VII 2001 ....ESDF		16 720 000	8 376 000	50.1	8 552 000	4 319 000	50.5	8 168 000	4 057 000	49.7
1 VII 2002 ....ESDF		17 130 000	8 599 000	50.2	8 763 000	4 439 000	50.7	8 367 000	4 160 000	49.7
1 VII 2003 ....ESDF		17 550 000	8 806 000	50.2	8 979 000	4 541 000	50.0	8 571 000	4 265 000	49.8
1 VII 2004 ....ESDF		17 832 000	9 540 000	53.5	9 151 000	4 895 000	53.5	8 681 000	4 645 000	53.5
1 VII 2005 ....ESDF		18 269 000	9 774 000	53.5	9 340 000	5 015 000	53.7	8 929 000	4 759 000	53.3
1 VII 2006 ....ESDF		18 717 000	10 013 000	53.5	9 563 000	5 139 000	53.7	9 154 000	4 874 000	53.2
Tajikistan - Tadjikistan										
1 VII 1999 ....ESDF		6 064 048	1 609 723	26.5	3 036 700	800 020	26.3	3 027 349	809 703	26.7
20 I 2000 ....CDFC		6 127 493	1 626 027	26.5	3 069 100	808 650	26.3	3 058 393	817 377	26.7
1 VII 2000 ....ESDF		6 188 366	1 642 401	26.5	3 099 855	817 233	26.4	3 088 512	825 168	26.7
1 VII 2001 ....ESDF		6 312 757	1 675 211	26.5	3 163 111	834 679	26.4	3 149 646	840 533	26.7
1 VII 2002 ....ESDF		6 441 009	1 705 240	26.5	3 228 657	850 898	26.4	3 212 352	854 343	26.6
1 VII 2003 ....ESDF		6 573 225	1 738 839	26.5	3 296 212	868 891	26.4	3 277 013	869 948	26.5
1 VII 2004 ....ESDF		6 710 200	1 774 850	26.5	...	...	...	...	...	...
1 VII 2005 ....ESDF		6 850 350	1 808 350	26.4	...	...	...	...	...	...
1 VII 2006 ....ESDF		6 992 050	1 841 250	26.3	...	...	...	...	...	...

Continent, country or area, and date / Continent, pays ou zone et date	Code[a]	Both sexes - Les deux sexes			Male - Masculin			Female - Féminin		
		Total	Urban - Urbaine		Total	Urban - Urbaine		Total	Urban - Urbaine	
			Number Nombre	Percent P.100		Number Nombre	Percent P.100		Number Nombre	Percent P.100
ASIA - ASIE										
Thailand - Thaïlande										
1 VII 1997 ....ESDJ		60 602 000	...	...	30 245 000	...	...	30 357 000	...	...
1 VII 1998 ....ESDJ		61 155 888	...	...	30 443 716	...	...	30 712 172	...	...
1 VII 1999 ....ESDJ		61 563 980	...	...	30 620 906	...	...	30 943 074	...	...
1 IV 2000..........CDJC		60 617 200	18 833 700	31.1	29 850 100	9 085 400	30.4	30 767 100	9 748 300	31.7
1 VII 2000[2] ....ESDJ		62 406 000	...	...	31 105 000	...	...	31 301 000	...	...
1 VII 2001[2] ....ESDJ		62 914 000	...	...	31 348 000	...	...	31 566 000	...	...
1 VII 2002[2] ....ESDJ		63 482 287	20 731 494	32.7	31 623 509	10 072 055	31.8	31 858 778	10 659 439	33.5
1 VII 2003[2] ....ESDJ		64 018 857	20 990 626	32.8	31 883 154	10 188 273	32.0	32 135 703	10 802 353	33.6
1 VII 2004[2] ....ESDJ		64 177 484	19 300 414	30.1	31 574 765	9 261 252	29.3	32 602 719	10 039 162	30.8
1 VII 2005[2] ....ESDJ		64 838 628	19 538 420	30.1	31 848 905	9 360 642	29.4	32 989 723	10 177 778	30.9
1 VII 2006[2] ....ESDJ		65 305 736	19 792 296	30.3	32 060 034	9 474 510	29.6	33 245 702	10 317 786	31.0
Timor-Leste										
11 VII 2004* ....CDFC		924 642	...	...	467 757	...	...	456 885	...	...
Turkey - Turquie										
1 VII 1997 ....ESDF		64 064 000	36 670 310	57.2	32 383 000	...	...	31 682 000	...	...
1 VII 1998 ....ESDF		65 215 000	37 724 702	57.8	32 956 000	...	...	32 259 000	...	...
1 VII 1999 ....ESDF		66 350 000	38 783 705	58.5	33 521 000	...	...	32 829 000	...	...
1 VII 2000 ....ESDF		67 420 000	39 818 088	59.1	34 053 000	...	...	33 367 000	...	...
22 X 2000 ....CDFC		67 803 927	44 006 274	64.9	34 346 735	22 427 603	65.3	33 457 192	21 578 671	64.5
1 VII 2001 ....ESDF		68 365 000	40 790 867	59.7	34 519 000	...	...	33 846 000	...	...
1 VII 2002 ....ESDF		69 302 000	41 770 289	60.3	34 981 000	...	...	34 320 000	...	...
1 VII 2003 ....ESDF		70 231 000	42 756 206	60.9	35 441 000	...	...	34 790 000	...	...
1 VII 2004 ....ESDF		71 152 000	43 748 475	61.5	35 897 000	...	...	35 255 000	...	...
1 VII 2005 ....ESDF		72 065 000	44 746 949	62.1	36 349 000	...	...	35 716 000	...	...
1 VII 2006 ....ESDF		72 974 000	45 753 990	62.7	36 797 000	...	...	36 177 000	...	...
United Arab Emirates - Émirats arabes unis										
1 VII 1997 ....ESDF		2 590 000	...	...	1 755 000	...	...	869 000	...	...
1 VII 1998 ....ESDF		2 717 000	...	...	1 861 000	...	...	915 000	...	...
1 VII 1999 ....ESDF		2 855 000	...	...	1 975 000	...	...	963 000	...	...
5 XII 2005 ....CDFC		4 106 427	3 384 839	82.4	2 806 141	...	...	1 300 286	...	...
1 VII 2006 ....ESDF		4 229 000	...	...	2 895 000	...	...	1 334 000	...	...
Uzbekistan - Ouzbékistan										
1 VII 1997 ....ESDF		23 560 400	8 931 400	37.9	11 710 400	4 394 700	37.5	11 850 000	4 536 700	38.3
1 VII 1998 ....ESDF		24 051 000	9 109 700	37.9	...	...	...	...	...	...
1 VII 1999 ....ESDF		23 953 922	9 037 904	37.7	11 913 994	4 450 641	37.4	12 039 928	4 587 263	38.1
1 VII 2000 ....ESDF		24 650 415	9 195 435	37.3	12 278 626	4 538 871	37.0	12 371 789	4 656 564	37.6
1 VII 2001 ....ESDF		24 964 433	9 256 101	37.1	12 442 510	4 573 055	36.8	12 521 923	4 683 046	37.4
Viet Nam										
1 VII 1997 ....ESDF		74 306 900	16 835 400	22.7	36 473 100	...	...	37 833 800	...	...
1 VII 1998 ....ESDF		75 456 300	17 464 600	23.1	37 059 700	...	...	38 366 600	...	...
1 IV 1999 ....CDFC		76 323 173	18 076 823	23.7	37 469 117	8 825 112	23.6	38 854 056	9 251 711	23.8
1 VII 1999 ....ESDF		76 596 700	18 081 600	23.6	37 662 100	...	...	38 934 600	...	...
1 VII 2000 ....ESDF		77 635 400	18 771 900	24.2	38 166 400	...	...	39 469 000	...	...
1 VII 2001 ....ESDF		78 685 800	19 469 300	24.7	38 684 200	...	...	40 001 600	...	...
1 VII 2002 ....ESDF		79 727 379	20 022 142	25.1	39 197 378	...	...	40 530 001	...	...
1 VII 2003 ....ESDF		80 902 400	20 869 500	25.8	39 755 400	...	...	41 147 000	...	...
1 VII 2004 ....ESDF		82 031 700	21 737 200	26.5	40 310 500	...	...	41 721 200	...	...
1 VII 2005 ....ESDF		83 106 300	22 336 800	26.9	40 846 200	...	...	42 260 100	...	...
1 VII 2006* ....ESDF		84 155 800	22 823 600	27.1	41 354 700	...	...	42 801 100	...	...
Yemen - Yémen										
1 VII 1997 ....ESDF		16 484 000	4 130 000	25.1	8 229 000	...	...	8 255 000	...	...
1 VII 1998 ....ESDF		17 072 000	...	...	8 532 000	...	...	8 540 000	...	...
1 VII 1999 ....ESDF		17 671 000	...	...	8 837 000	...	...	8 834 000	...	...
1 VII 2000 ....ESDF		18 261 000	4 802 000	26.3	9 143 000	2 587 000	28.3	9 118 000	2 215 000	24.3
1 VII 2001* ....ESDF		18 863 000	...	...	9 448 000	...	...	9 415 000	...	...
1 VII 2002* ....ESDF		19 495 000	...	...	9 772 000	...	...	9 723 000	...	...
16 XII 2004 ....CDFC		19 685 161	5 637 756	28.6	10 036 953	3 012 256	30.0	9 648 208	2 625 500	27.2
1 VII 2006 ....ESDF		20 591 738	...	...	10 503 044	...	...	10 088 695	...	...

Continent, country or area, and date / Continent, pays ou zone et date	Code[a]	Both sexes - Les deux sexes Total	Urban - Urbaine Number Nombre	Urban - Urbaine Percent P.100	Male - Masculin Total	Urban - Urbaine Number Nombre	Urban - Urbaine Percent P.100	Female - Féminin Total	Urban - Urbaine Number Nombre	Urban - Urbaine Percent P.100
EUROPE										
Åland Islands - Îles d'Åland[80]										
1 VII 1997	ESDF	25 325	10 404	41.1	12 419	4 891	39.4	12 906	5 513	42.7
1 VII 1998	ESDF	25 509	10 471	41.0	12 510	4 923	39.4	12 999	5 549	42.7
1 VII 1999	ESDF	25 666	10 513	41.0	12 609	4 959	39.3	13 057	5 555	42.5
1 VII 2000	ESDF	25 741	10 490	40.8	12 670	4 946	39.0	13 072	5 544	42.4
1 VII 2001	ESDF	25 892	10 549	40.7	12 750	4 967	39.0	13 142	5 582	42.5
1 VII 2002	ESDF	26 133	10 621	40.6	12 866	5 004	38.9	13 267	5 617	42.3
1 VII 2003	ESDF	26 302	10 629	40.4	12 945	5 011	38.7	13 358	5 619	42.1
1 VII 2004	ESDF	26 439	10 669	40.4	13 030	5 036	38.7	13 409	5 633	42.0
1 VII 2005	ESDF	26 648	10 746	40.3	13 174	5 087	38.6	13 475	5 660	42.0
1 VII 2006	ESDF	26 845	10 802	40.2	13 299	5 123	38.5	13 546	5 680	41.9
Albania - Albanie										
1 VII 1997	ESDF	3 074 832	1 211 925	39.4	...	...	...	...	...	...
1 VII 1998	ESDF	3 055 331	1 227 208	40.2	...	...	...	...	...	...
1 VII 1999	ESDF	3 053 831	1 234 975	40.4	...	...	...	...	...	...
1 VII 2000	ESDF	3 060 908	1 249 919	40.8	...	...	...	...	...	...
1 IV 2001	CDFC	3 069 300	1 292 800	42.1	1 530 500			1 538 800		
1 VII 2001	ESDF	3 073 733	1 312 963	42.7	1 532 598	648 278	42.3	1 541 135	664 685	43.1
1 VII 2002	ESDF	3 093 465	1 347 871	43.6	1 542 211	625 060	40.5	1 551 254	722 811	46.6
1 VII 2003	ESDF	3 111 163	1 375 367	44.2	1 550 728	636 985	41.1	1 560 435	738 382	47.3
1 VII 2004	ESDF	3 127 263	1 406 443	45.0	1 558 376	661 335	42.4	1 568 887	745 108	47.5
1 VII 2005	ESDF	3 142 065	1 468 522	46.7	1 565 316	671 848	42.9	1 576 749	796 864	50.5
1 VII 2006	ESDF	3 160 886	1 528 877	48.5	1 580 446	711 123	45.0	1 570 440	817 754	52.1
Andorra - Andorre[20]										
1 VII 1997	ESDF	65 592	...	...	34 387	...	...	31 205	...	...
1 VII 1998	ESDF	65 924	...	...	34 463	...	...	31 461	...	...
1 VII 1999	ESDF	65 908	...	...	34 351	...	...	31 557	...	...
1 VII 2000	CDFC	66 089	...	...	34 344	...	...	31 745	...	...
1 VII 2000	ESDF	66 089	...	...	34 344	...	...	31 746	...	...
1 VII 2001	ESDF	66 747	...	...	34 612	...	...	32 135	...	...
1 VII 2002	ESDF	69 740	...	...	36 194	...	...	33 546	...	...
1 VII 2003	ESDF	74 598	...	...	38 834	...	...	35 764	...	...
1 VII 2004	ESDF	77 712	...	...	40 530	...	...	37 183	...	...
1 VII 2005	ESDF	79 886	...	...	41 746	...	...	38 140	...	...
1 VII 2006	ESDF	82 180	...	...	43 016	...	...	39 164	...	...
Austria - Autriche										
1 VII 1997	ESDJ	7 968 041	...	...	3 846 162	...	...	4 121 879	...	...
1 VII 1998	ESDJ	7 976 789	...	...	3 852 166	...	...	4 124 623	...	...
1 VII 1999	ESDJ	7 992 323	...	...	3 862 180	...	...	4 130 143	...	...
1 VII 2000	ESDJ	8 011 566	...	...	3 874 717	...	...	4 136 849	...	...
15 V 2001	CDJC	8 032 926	5 368 693	66.8	3 889 189	2 564 828	65.9	4 143 737	2 803 865	67.7
1 VII 2001	ESDJ	8 043 046	...	...	3 894 129	...	...	4 148 917	...	...
1 VII 2002	ESDJ	8 083 797	...	...	3 918 990	...	...	4 164 807	...	...
1 VII 2003	ESDJ	8 117 754	...	...	3 938 582	...	...	4 179 172	...	...
1 VII 2004	ESDJ	8 174 733	...	...	3 969 190	...	...	4 205 543	...	...
1 VII 2005	ESDJ	8 233 306	...	...	4 001 861	...	...	4 231 445	...	...
1 VII 2006	ESDJ	8 281 948	...	...	4 028 658	...	...	4 253 290	...	...
Belarus - Bélarus										
1 VII 1997	ESDF	10 117 433	6 942 035	68.6	4 745 259	3 268 636	68.9	5 372 174	3 673 399	68.4
1 VII 1998	ESDF	10 071 963	6 952 014	69.0	4 728 026	3 274 360	69.3	5 343 937	3 677 654	68.8
16 II 1999	CDJC	10 045 237	6 061 516	60.3	4 717 621	3 270 106	60.5	5 327 616	3 682 320	60.1
1 VII 1999	ESDF	10 035 210	6 971 629	69.5	4 711 688	3 282 317	69.7	5 323 522	3 689 312	69.3
1 VII 2000	ESDF	10 004 958	6 999 510	70.0	4 695 465	3 291 885	70.1	5 309 493	3 707 625	69.8
1 VII 2001	ESDF	9 970 688	7 022 386	70.4	4 677 096	3 298 787	70.5	5 293 592	3 723 599	70.3
1 VII 2002	ESDF	9 924 766	7 034 721	70.9	4 652 109	3 299 920	70.9	5 272 657	3 734 801	70.8
1 VII 2003	ESDF	9 873 826	7 040 950	71.3	4 623 963	3 297 535	71.3	5 249 863	3 743 415	71.3
1 VII 2004	ESDF	9 824 568	7 050 685	71.8	4 596 633	3 296 800	71.7	5 227 935	3 753 885	71.8
1 VII 2005	ESDF	9 775 307	7 057 463	72.2	4 569 189	3 294 851	72.1	5 206 118	3 762 612	72.3
1 VII 2006	ESDF	9 732 501	7 066 903	72.6	4 545 164	3 294 559	72.5	5 187 337	3 772 344	72.7
Belgium - Belgique										
1 VII 1997	ESDJ	10 181 245	...	...	4 977 226	...	...	5 204 019	...	...
1 VII 1998	ESDJ	10 203 008	...	...	4 988 195	...	...	5 214 813	...	...
1 VII 1999	ESDJ	10 226 419	...	...	4 999 866	...	...	5 226 553	...	...
1 VII 2000	ESDJ	10 251 250	...	...	5 012 017	...	...	5 239 233	...	...

Continent, country or area, and date / Continent, pays ou zone et date	Code[a]	Both sexes - Les deux sexes Total	Urban - Urbaine Number Nombre	Urban - Urbaine Percent P.100	Male - Masculin Total	Urban - Urbaine Number Nombre	Urban - Urbaine Percent P.100	Female - Féminin Total	Urban - Urbaine Number Nombre	Urban - Urbaine Percent P.100
EUROPE										
Belgium - Belgique										
1 VII 2001	ESDJ	10 286 570	...	...	5 030 154	...	...	5 256 416	...	...
1 X 2001	CDJC	10 296 350	...	...	5 035 446	...	...	5 260 904	...	...
1 VII 2002	ESDJ	10 332 785	...	...	5 054 587	...	...	5 278 198	...	...
1 VII 2003	ESDJ	10 372 469	...	...	5 075 268	...	...	5 297 201	...	...
1 VII 2004	ESDJ	10 417 122	...	...	5 097 709	...	...	5 319 413	...	...
1 VII 2005	ESDJ	10 472 842	...	...	5 125 387	...	...	5 347 455	...	...
1 VII 2006	ESDJ	10 541 893	...	...	5 159 947	...	...	5 381 946	...	...
Bosnia and Herzegovina - Bosnie-Herzégovine										
1 VII 1997	ESDF	3 737 865	...	...	1 831 554	...	...	1 906 311	...	...
1 VII 1998	ESDF	3 653 364	...	...	1 790 148	...	...	1 863 216	...	...
1 VII 1999	ESDF	3 724 672	...	...	1 825 089	...	...	1 899 583	...	...
1 VII 2000	ESDF	3 781 497	...	...	1 852 934	...	...	1 928 563	...	...
1 VII 2001	ESDF	3 797 937	...	...	1 860 989	...	...	1 936 948	...	...
1 VII 2002	ESDF	3 828 397	...	...	1 875 915	...	...	1 952 482	...	...
1 VII 2003	ESDF	3 832 301	...	...	1 877 827	...	...	1 954 474	...	...
1 VII 2004	ESDF	3 842 527	...	...	1 882 838	...	...	1 959 689	...	...
1 VII 2005	ESDF	3 842 537	...	...	1 882 843	...	...	1 959 694	...	...
1 VII 2006	ESDF	3 842 762	...	...	1 882 953	...	...	1 959 809	...	...
Bulgaria - Bulgarie										
1 VII 1997	ESDF	8 312 068	5 623 899	67.7	4 061 233	2 734 426	67.3	4 250 835	2 889 473	68.0
1 VII 1998	ESDF	8 256 786	5 603 501	67.9	4 029 518	2 720 430	67.5	4 227 268	2 883 071	68.2
1 VII 1999	ESDF	8 210 624	5 587 165	68.0	4 002 616	2 708 093	67.7	4 208 008	2 879 072	68.4
1 VII 2000	ESDF	8 170 172	5 577 216	68.3	3 979 292	2 700 131	67.9	4 190 880	2 877 085	68.7
1 III 2001	CDFC	7 928 901	5 474 534	69.0	3 862 465	2 651 312	68.6	4 066 436	2 823 222	69.4
1 VII 2001	ESDF	7 913 301	5 477 604	69.2	3 853 710	2 652 367	68.8	4 059 591	2 825 237	69.6
1 VII 2002	ESDF	7 868 900	5 467 777	69.5	3 828 882	2 644 285	69.1	4 040 018	2 823 492	69.9
1 VII 2003	ESDF	7 823 557	5 459 344	69.8	3 803 501	2 636 908	69.3	4 020 056	2 822 436	70.2
1 VII 2004	ESDF	7 781 161	5 440 536	69.9	3 779 224	2 624 031	69.4	4 001 937	2 816 505	70.4
1 VII 2005	ESDF	7 739 900	5 424 661	70.1	3 755 469	2 613 346	69.6	3 984 431	2 811 315	70.6
1 VII 2006	ESDF	7 699 020	5 428 388	70.5	3 732 130	2 613 030	70.0	3 966 890	2 815 358	71.0
Channel Islands: Guernsey - Îles Anglo-Normandes: Guernesey										
1 VII 1998	ESDF	59 050	...	...	28 434	...	...	30 616	...	...
1 VII 1999	ESDF	60 268	...	...	29 042	...	...	31 226	...	...
29 IV 2001	CDJC	59 807	...	...	29 138	...	...	30 669	...	...
1 VII 2004	ESDF	60 382	...	...	29 841	...	...	30 541	...	...
1 III 2006[81]	ESDF	61 029	...	...	30 034	...	...	30 995	...	...
Channel Islands: Jersey - Îles Anglo-Normandes: Jersey										
11 III 2001	CDJC	87 186	...	...	42 485	...	...	44 701	...	...
Croatia - Croatie										
1 VII 1997	ESDJ	4 572 474	...	...	2 197 442	...	...	2 375 032	...	...
1 VII 1998	ESDJ	4 501 149	...	...	2 163 164	...	...	2 337 985	...	...
1 VII 1999	ESDJ	4 553 769	...	...	2 188 455	...	...	2 365 314	...	...
1 VII 2000	ESDJ	4 381 000	...	...	2 105 000	...	...	2 276 000	...	...
31 III 2001	CDJC	4 437 460	2 471 328	55.7	2 135 900	1 171 950	54.9	2 301 560	1 299 378	56.5
1 VII 2002	ESDJ	4 442 900	...	...	2 138 400	...	...	2 304 500	...	...
1 VII 2003	ESDJ	4 441 800	...	...	2 137 600	...	...	2 304 100	...	...
1 VII 2004	ESDJ	4 439 400	...	...	2 136 900	...	...	2 302 500	...	...
1 VII 2005	ESDJ	4 441 900	...	...	2 138 600	...	...	2 303 300	...	...
1 VII 2006	ESDJ	4 440 022	...	...	2 138 934	...	...	2 301 088	...	...
Czech Republic - République tchèque										
1 VII 1997	ESDJ	10 303 642	7 692 120	74.7	5 010 531	...	...	5 293 111	...	...
1 VII 1998	ESDJ	10 294 943	7 675 220	74.6	5 007 480	...	...	5 287 463	...	...
1 VII 1999	ESDJ	10 282 784	7 659 954	74.5	5 002 823	...	...	5 279 961	...	...
1 VII 2000	ESDJ	10 272 503	7 641 415	74.4	4 999 326	3 694 433	73.9	5 273 177	3 946 982	74.9
1 III 2001	CDJC	10 230 060	7 564 200	73.9	4 982 071	3 657 775	73.4	5 247 989	3 906 425	74.4
1 VII 2001	ESDJ	10 224 192	7 559 732	73.9	4 978 951	3 655 116	73.4	5 245 241	3 904 616	74.4
1 VII 2002	ESDJ	10 200 774	7 536 154	73.9	4 964 598	3 640 572	73.3	5 236 176	3 895 582	74.4

6. Total and urban population by sex: 1997 - 2006
Population totale et population urbaine selon le sexe: 1997 - 2006 (continued - suite)

Continent, country or area, and date / Continent, pays ou zone et date	Code[a]	Both sexes - Les deux sexes			Male - Masculin			Female - Féminin		
		Total	Urban - Urbaine		Total	Urban - Urbaine		Total	Urban - Urbaine	
			Number Nombre	Percent P.100		Number Nombre	Percent P.100		Number Nombre	Percent P.100
EUROPE										
Czech Republic - République tchèque										
1 VII 2003 . . . . ESDJ		10 201 651	7 533 782	73.8	4 968 189	3 640 805	73.3	5 233 462	3 892 977	74.4
1 VII 2004 . . . . ESDJ		10 206 923	7 526 698	73.7	4 971 730	3 637 603	73.2	5 235 193	3 889 095	74.3
1 VII 2005 . . . . ESDJ		10 234 092	7 552 515	73.8	4 991 439	3 655 100	73.2	5 242 653	3 897 415	74.3
1 VII 2006 . . . . ESDJ		10 287 189	7 574 397	73.6	5 026 184	3 671 881	73.1	5 261 005	3 902 516	74.2
Denmark - Danemark[82]										
1 VII 1997 . . . . ESDJ		5 284 220	...	...	2 610 070	...	...	2 674 150	...	...
1 VII 1998 . . . . ESDJ		5 301 304	...	...	2 618 854	...	...	2 682 450	...	...
1 VII 1999 . . . . ESDJ		5 327 358	...	...	2 632 641	...	...	2 694 717	...	...
1 VII 2000 . . . . ESDJ		5 337 344	...	...	2 637 878	...	...	2 699 466	...	...
1 I 2001 . . . . CDJC		5 349 212			2 644 319			2 704 893		
1 VII 2001 . . . . ESDJ		5 358 783			2 649 233			2 709 551		
1 VII 2002 . . . . ESDJ		5 374 255			2 657 341			2 716 914		
1 VII 2003 . . . . ESDJ		5 387 174			2 664 526			2 722 648		
1 VII 2004 . . . . ESDJ		5 401 177			2 671 907			2 729 270		
1 XII 2005 . . . . ESDJ		5 415 978			2 679 857			2 736 121		
1 VII 2000 . . . . E3DJ		5 434 507	...	...	2 690 179	...	...	2 744 300	...	...
Estonia - Estonie										
1 VII 1997 . . . . ESDF		1 399 535	1 011 012[28]	72.2	646 245	462 004[28]	71.5	753 290	549 008[28]	72.9
1 VII 1998 . . . . ESDF		1 386 156	1 003 119[28]	72.4	639 629	457 641[28]	71.5	746 527	545 478[28]	73.1
1 VII 1999 . . . . ESDF		1 375 654	997 188[28]	72.5	634 484	454 363[28]	71.6	741 170	542 825[28]	73.2
31 III 2000 . . . . CDJC		1 370 052	923 211	67.4	631 851	415 515	65.8	738 201	507 696	68.8
1 VII 2000 . . . . ESDF		1 369 515	947 308	69.2	631 579	426 593	67.5	737 936	520 715	70.6
1 VII 2001 . . . . ESDF		1 364 101	943 944	69.2	629 020	424 985	67.6	735 081	518 959	70.6
1 VII 2002 . . . . ESDF		1 358 644	940 465	69.2	626 276	423 224	67.6	732 368	517 241	70.6
1 VII 2003 . . . . ESDF		1 353 557	937 201	69.2	623 705	421 604	67.6	729 852	515 597	70.6
1 VII 2004 . . . . ESDF		1 349 290	934 665	69.3	621 525	420 309	67.6	727 765	514 356	70.7
1 VII 2005 . . . . ESDF		1 346 097	932 985	69.3	619 949	419 513	67.7	726 148	513 472	70.7
1 VII 2006 . . . . ESDF		1 343 547	931 855	69.4	618 772	419 103	67.7	724 775	512 752	70.7
Faeroe Islands - Îles Féroé										
1 VII 1997 . . . . ESDJ		43 993	...	...	22 688	...	...	21 305	...	...
1 VII 1998 . . . . ESDJ		44 504	...	...	22 983	...	...	21 521	...	...
1 VII 1999 . . . . ESDJ		45 063	...	...	23 305	...	...	21 758	...	...
1 VII 2000 . . . . ESDJ		45 749	...	...	23 676	...	...	22 073	...	...
1 VII 2001 . . . . ESDJ		46 553	...	...	24 116	...	...	22 437	...	...
1 VII 2002 . . . . ESDJ		47 315	...	...	24 534	...	...	22 781	...	...
1 VII 2003 . . . . ESDJ		47 923	...	...	24 873	...	...	23 051	...	...
1 VII 2004 . . . . ESDJ		48 258	...	...	25 070	...	...	23 188	...	...
1 VII 2005 . . . . ESDJ		48 260	...	...	25 074	...	...	23 187	...	...
1 VII 2006 . . . . ESDJ		48 267	...	...	25 083	...	...	23 184	...	...
Finland - Finlande[83]										
1 VII 1997 . . . . ESDJ		5 139 835	3 064 503	59.6	2 504 847	1 451 773	58.0	2 634 988	1 589 177	60.3
1 VII 1998 . . . . ESDJ		5 153 498	3 089 077	59.9	2 512 587	1 476 277	58.8	2 640 911	1 612 800	61.1
1 VII 1999 . . . . ESDJ		5 165 474	3 112 147	60.2	2 519 551	1 488 063	59.1	2 645 924	1 624 084	61.4
1 VII 2000 . . . . ESDJ		5 176 209	3 157 401	61.0	2 526 184	1 511 406	59.8	2 650 025	1 645 995	62.1
31 XII 2000 . . . . CDJC		5 181 115	3 167 668	61.1	2 529 341	1 516 812	60.0	2 651 774	1 650 856	62.3
1 VII 2001 . . . . ESDJ		5 188 008	3 179 283	61.3	2 533 469	1 523 008	60.1	2 654 539	1 656 275	62.4
1 VII 2002 . . . . ESDJ		5 200 598	3 217 447	61.9	2 541 257	1 543 243	60.7	2 659 342	1 674 204	63.0
1 VII 2003 . . . . ESDJ		5 213 014	3 234 178	62.0	2 548 905	1 552 734	60.9	2 664 109	1 681 445	63.1
1 VII 2004 . . . . ESDJ		5 228 172	3 245 435	62.1	2 557 485	1 559 747	61.0	2 670 687	1 685 689	63.1
1 VII 2005 . . . . ESDJ		5 246 096	3 285 197	62.6	2 567 214	1 580 650	61.6	2 678 882	1 704 547	63.6
1 VII 2006 . . . . ESDJ		5 266 268	3 316 388	63.0	2 578 046	1 597 209	62.0	2 688 222	1 719 179	64.0
France[84]										
1 VII 1997 . . . . ESDJ		58 207 490	...	...	28 275 964	...	...	29 931 526	...	...
1 VII 1998 . . . . ESDJ		58 397 788	...	...	28 361 163	...	...	30 036 625	...	...
8 III 1999 . . . . CDJC		58 520 688	...	...	28 419 419	...	...	30 101 269	...	...
1 VII 1999 . . . . ESDJ		58 673 079	...	...	28 492 821	...	...	30 180 258	...	...
1 VII 2000 . . . . ESDJ		59 049 351	...	...	28 677 892	...	...	30 371 465	...	...
1 VII 2001 . . . . ESDJ		59 454 461	...	...	28 877 376	...	...	30 577 085	...	...
1 VII 2002 . . . . ESDJ		59 863 266	...	...	29 079 470	...	...	30 783 796	...	...
1 VII 2003 . . . . ESDJ		60 264 196	...	...	29 279 506	...	...	30 984 690	...	...
1 VII 2004* . . . . ESDJ		60 643 307	...	...	29 466 783	...	...	31 176 524	...	...

6. Total and urban population by sex: 1997 - 2006
Population totale et population urbaine selon le sexe: 1997 - 2006 (continued - suite)

Continent, country or area, and date / Continent, pays ou zone et date	Code[a]	Both sexes - Les deux sexes			Male - Masculin			Female - Féminin		
		Total	Urban - Urbaine		Total	Urban - Urbaine		Total	Urban - Urbaine	
			Number Nombre	Percent P.100		Number Nombre	Percent P.100		Number Nombre	Percent P.100
EUROPE										
France[84]										
1 VII 2005*	ESDJ	60 995 911	...	...	29 638 708	...	...	31 357 203	...	...
1 I 2006*	CDJC	61 166 822	...	...	29 722 384	...	...	31 444 438	...	...
Germany - Allemagne										
1 VII 1997	ESDJ	82 051 698	...	...	39 989 139	...	...	42 062 559	...	...
1 VII 1998	ESDJ	82 028 947	...	...	39 992 272	...	...	42 036 675	...	...
1 VII 1999	ESDJ	82 086 582	...	...	40 047 972	...	...	42 038 610	...	...
1 VII 2000	ESDJ	82 187 614	...	...	40 115 959	...	...	42 071 655	...	...
1 VII 2001	ESDJ	82 339 777	...	...	40 214 370	...	...	42 125 407	...	...
1 VII 2002	ESDJ	82 482 309	...	...	40 310 430	...	...	42 171 879	...	...
1 VII 2003	ESDJ	82 520 176	...	...	40 349 200	...	...	42 170 976	...	...
28 III 2004[85]	SSDJ	82 491 000	...	...	40 330 000	...	...	42 161 000	...	...
1 VII 2004	ESDJ	82 501 274	...	...	40 350 091	...	...	42 151 183	...	...
1 VII 2005	ESDJ	82 464 344	...	...	40 348 986	...	...	42 115 358	...	...
1 VII 2006	ESDJ	82 365 810	...	...	40 317 807	...	...	42 048 003	...	...
Gibraltar[86]										
1 VII 1997	ESDF	27 139	...	...	13 550	...	...	13 588	...	...
1 VII 1998	ESDF	27 025	...	...	13 419	...	...	13 606	...	...
1 VII 1999	ESDF	27 114	...	...	13 460	...	...	13 654	...	...
1 VII 2000	ESDF	27 118	...	...	13 453	...	...	13 665	...	...
12 XI 2001	CDFC	27 495	...	...	13 644	...	...	13 851	...	...
1 VII 2002	ESDF	28 520	...	...	14 300	...	...	14 220	...	...
1 VII 2003	ESDF	28 562	...	...	14 342	...	...	14 220	...	...
1 VII 2004	ESDF	28 704	...	...	14 410	...	...	14 294	...	...
1 VII 2005	ESDF	28 827	...	...	14 422	...	...	14 406	...	...
1 VII 2006	ESDF	29 066	...	...	14 545	...	...	14 521	...	...
Greece - Grèce										
1 VII 1997[87]	ESDF	10 776 531		...	5 337 781	...	...	5 438 750	...	...
1 VII 1998[87]	ESDF	10 834 910		...	5 366 820	...	...	5 468 090	...	...
1 VII 1999[87]	ESDF	10 882 607		...	5 389 881	...	...	5 492 726	...	...
1 VII 2000[87]	ESDF	10 917 457		...	5 406 043	...	...	5 511 414	...	...
18 III 2001[88]	CDFC	10 964 020		...	5 431 816	...	...	5 532 204	...	...
1 VII 2001[87]	ESDF	10 949 953		...	5 421 043	...	...	5 528 910	...	...
1 VII 2002[87]	ESDF	10 987 559		...	5 439 332	...	...	5 548 227	...	...
1 VII 2003[87]	ESDF	11 023 532		...	5 456 496	...	...	5 567 036	...	...
1 VII 2004[87]	ESDF	11 061 735		...	5 475 529	...	...	5 586 206	...	...
1 VII 2005[87]	ESDF	11 103 929		...	5 497 372	...	...	5 606 557	...	...
1 VII 2006[87]	ESDF	11 148 533		...	5 520 164	...	...	5 628 369	...	...
Holy See - Saint-Siège[89]										
1 VII 1998	ESDF	786	...	...	604	...	...	182	...	...
1 VII 2000*	CDFC	798	...	...	529	...	...	269	...	...
Hungary - Hongrie										
1 VII 1997	ESDF	10 154 900	6 402 241[90]	63.0	4 852 592	3 016 070[90]	62.2	5 302 309	3 386 171[90]	63.9
1 VII 1998	ESDF	10 113 574	6 431 702[90]	63.6	4 829 734	3 028 148[90]	62.7	5 283 840	3 403 554[90]	64.4
1 VII 1999	ESDF	10 067 507	6 385 626[90]	63.4	4 804 690	3 003 675[90]	62.5	5 262 817	3 381 951[90]	64.3
1 VII 2000	ESDF	10 024 222	6 364 276[90]	63.5	4 781 701	2 991 619[90]	62.6	5 242 522	3 372 657[90]	64.3
1 II 2001	CDFC	10 198 315	6 572 880	64.5	4 850 650	3 091 857	63.7	5 347 665	3 481 023	65.1
1 VII 2001	ESDF	10 187 576	6 544 089[90]	64.2	4 843 996	3 073 458[90]	63.4	5 343 580	3 470 631[90]	64.9
1 VII 2002	ESDF	10 158 608	6 607 159[90]	65.0	4 827 718	3 101 463[90]	64.2	5 330 890	3 505 696[90]	65.8
1 VII 2003	ESDF	10 129 552	6 568 539[90]	64.8	4 811 285	3 079 592[90]	64.0	5 318 268	3 488 947[90]	65.6
1 VII 2004	ESDF	10 107 146	6 571 923[90]	65.0	4 798 614	3 078 582[90]	64.2	5 308 532	3 493 342[90]	65.8
1 VII 2005	ESDF	10 087 065	6 670 187	66.1	4 788 847	3 125 833	65.3	5 298 218	3 544 354	66.9
1 VII 2006	ESDF	10 071 370	6 749 388[91]	67.0	4 781 829	3 163 716[91]	66.2	5 289 541	3 585 673[91]	67.8
Iceland - Islande[20]										
1 VII 1997	ESDJ	270 915	249 293	92.0	135 779	124 196	91.5	135 136	125 097	92.6
1 VII 1998	ESDJ	273 794	252 356	92.2	137 092	125 634	91.6	136 702	126 722	92.7
1 VII 1999	ESDJ	277 184	255 910	92.3	138 783	127 433	91.8	138 401	128 477	92.8
1 VII 2000	CDJC	281 154	259 661	92.4	140 718	129 258	91.9	140 436	130 403	92.9
1 VII 2000	ESDJ	281 154	259 661	92.4	140 718	129 258	91.9	140 436	130 403	92.9
1 VII 2001	ESDJ	285 054	263 409	92.4	142 660	131 217	92.0	142 308	132 192	92.9
1 VII 2002	ESDJ	287 559	266 010	92.5	143 860	132 371	92.0	143 699	133 639	93.0
1 VII 2003	ESDJ	289 272	267 957	92.6	144 713	133 340	92.1	144 559	134 617	93.1
1 VII 2004	ESDJ	292 587	270 931	92.6	146 697	134 827	91.9	145 890	136 104	93.3

Continent, country or area, and date / Continent, pays ou zone et date	Code[a]	Both sexes - Les deux sexes			Male - Masculin			Female - Féminin		
		Total	Urban - Urbaine		Total	Urban - Urbaine		Total	Urban - Urbaine	
			Number Nombre	Percent P.100		Number Nombre	Percent P.100		Number Nombre	Percent P.100
EUROPE										
Iceland - Islande[20]										
1 VII 2005 . . . . ESDJ		295 864	275 017	93.0	148 449	137 003	92.3	147 415	138 014	93.6
1 VII 2006 . . . . ESDJ		304 334	281 961	92.6	154 287	141 673	91.8	150 047	140 288	93.5
Ireland - Irlande										
15 IV 1997[92] . . . . ESDF		3 664 313	...	...	1 819 394	...	...	1 844 919	...	...
15 IV 1998[92] . . . . ESDF		3 703 082	...	...	1 838 859	...	...	1 864 223	...	...
15 IV 1999[92] . . . . ESDF		3 741 647	...	...	1 858 613	...	...	1 883 034	...	...
15 IV 2000[92] . . . . ESDF		3 789 536	...	...	1 882 946	...	...	1 906 590	...	...
15 IV 2001[92] . . . . ESDF		3 847 198	...	...	1 913 128	...	...	1 934 070	...	...
28 IV 2002 . . . . CDFC		3 917 203	2 334 300	59.6	1 946 164	1 133 500	58.2	1 971 039	1 200 800	60.9
15 IV 2003[92] . . . . ESDF		3 978 862	...	...	1 977 208	...	...	2 001 654	...	...
15 IV 2004[92] . . . . ESDF		4 043 763	...	...	2 011 159	...	...	2 032 604	...	...
15 IV 2005[92] . . . . ESDF		4 130 722	...	...	2 058 952	...	...	2 071 770	...	...
15 IV 2006[92] . . . . ESDF		4 234 872	...	...	2 116 062	...	...	2 118 810	...	...
23 IV 2006 . . . . CDFC		4 239 848	...	...	2 121 171	...	...	2 118 677	...	...
Isle of Man - Îles de Man										
1 VII 1997 . . . . ESDJ		72 452	...	...	35 166	...	...	37 286	...	...
1 VII 2000 . . . . ESDJ		74 001	...	...	35 634	...	...	38 327	...	...
29 IV 2001 . . . . CDJC		76 315	...	...	37 372	...	...	38 943	...	...
1 VII 2002 . . . . ESDJ		77 156	...	...	37 827	...	...	39 330	...	...
1 VII 2003 . . . . ESDJ		77 464	...	...	38 019	...	...	39 444	...	...
1 VII 2004 . . . . ESDJ		77 581	...	...	38 111	...	...	39 470	...	...
1 VII 2005 . . . . ESDJ		78 003	...	...	38 360	...	...	39 643	...	...
23 IV 2006 . . . . CDJC		80 058	...	...	39 523	...	...	40 535	...	...
Italy - Italie										
1 VII 1997 . . . . ESDJ		56 890 372	...	...	27 569 176	...	...	29 321 196	...	...
1 VII 1998 . . . . ESDJ		56 906 744	...	...	27 567 663	...	...	29 339 081	...	...
1 VII 1999 . . . . ESDJ		56 916 317	...	...	27 563 368	...	...	29 352 949	...	...
1 VII 2000 . . . . ESDJ		56 942 108	...	...	27 569 657	...	...	29 372 451	...	...
1 VII 2001 . . . . ESDJ		56 977 217	...	...	27 581 784	...	...	29 395 433	...	...
21 X 2001 . . . . CDFC		57 110 144	...	...	27 617 335	...	...	29 492 809	...	...
1 VII 2002 . . . . ESDJ		57 157 406	...	...	27 676 733	...	...	29 480 674	...	...
1 VII 2003 . . . . ESDJ		57 604 658	...	...	27 917 416	...	...	29 687 242	...	...
1 VII 2004 . . . . ESDJ		58 175 310	...	...	28 222 706	...	...	29 952 604	...	...
1 VII 2005 . . . . ESDJ		58 607 043	...	...	28 451 846	...	...	30 155 197	...	...
1 VII 2006 . . . . ESDJ		58 941 499	...	...	28 622 665	...	...	30 318 835	...	...
Latvia - Lettonie										
1 VII 1997 . . . . ESDJ		2 432 851	1 668 743	68.6	1 121 142	757 156	67.5	1 311 709	911 587	69.5
1 VII 1998 . . . . ESDJ		2 410 019	1 649 491	68.4	1 110 461	746 363	67.2	1 299 558	903 128	69.5
1 VII 1999 . . . . ESDJ		2 390 482	1 630 335	68.2	1 101 163	735 684	66.8	1 289 319	894 651	69.4
31 III 2000 . . . . CDJC		2 377 383	1 618 144	68.1	1 094 964	729 745	66.6	1 282 419	888 399	69.3
1 VII 2000 . . . . ESDJ		2 372 985	1 614 159	68.0	1 092 871	727 722	66.6	1 280 114	886 437	69.2
1 VII 2001 . . . . ESDJ		2 355 011	1 599 272	67.9	1 084 484	720 359	66.4	1 270 527	878 913	69.2
1 VII 2002 . . . . ESDJ		2 338 624	1 586 220	67.8	1 076 587	713 616	66.3	1 262 037	872 604	69.1
1 VII 2003 . . . . ESDJ		2 325 342	1 576 965	67.8	1 070 697	709 024	66.2	1 254 645	867 941	69.2
1 VII 2004 . . . . ESDJ		2 312 819	1 570 406	67.9	1 065 627	706 082	66.3	1 247 192	864 324	69.3
1 VII 2005 . . . . ESDJ		2 300 512	1 563 372[93]	68.0	1 060 101	702 490	66.3	1 240 411	860 882	69.4
1 VII 2006 . . . . ESDJ		2 287 948	1 554 766	68.0	1 054 159	697 812	66.2	1 233 789	856 954	69.5
Liechtenstein										
1 VII 1997 . . . . ESDF		31 232	...	...	15 192	...	...	16 040	...	...
1 VII 1998 . . . . ESDF		31 668	...	...	15 418	...	...	16 250	...	...
1 VII 1999 . . . . ESDF		32 221	...	...	15 702	...	...	16 519	...	...
1 VII 2000 . . . . ESDF		32 673	...	...	15 912	...	...	16 761	...	...
5 XII 2000 . . . . CDFC		33 307	...	...	16 420	...	...	16 887	...	...
1 VII 2001 . . . . ESDF		33 104	...	...	16 195	...	...	16 909	...	...
1 VII 2002 . . . . ESDF		33 678	...	...	16 514	...	...	17 164	...	...
1 VII 2003 . . . . ESDF		34 022	...	...	16 725	...	...	17 297	...	...
1 VII 2004 . . . . ESDF		34 477	...	...	16 974	...	...	17 503	...	...
1 VII 2005 . . . . ESDF		34 734	...	...	17 100	...	...	17 634	...	...
1 VII 2006 . . . . ESDF		35 010	...	...	17 256	...	...	17 754	...	...
Lithuania - Lituanie										
1 VII 1997 . . . . ESDJ		3 575 137	2 413 579	67.5	1 678 747	1 120 359	66.7	1 896 390	1 293 220	68.2
1 VII 1998 . . . . ESDJ		3 549 331	2 387 853	67.3	1 664 607	1 105 127	66.4	1 884 724	1 282 726	68.1
1 VII 1999 . . . . ESDJ		3 524 238	2 367 146	67.2	1 650 931	1 092 628	66.2	1 873 307	1 274 518	68.0

Continent, country or area, and date / Continent, pays ou zone et date	Code[a]	Both sexes - Les deux sexes			Male - Masculin			Female - Féminin		
		Total	Urban - Urbaine		Total	Urban - Urbaine		Total	Urban - Urbaine	
			Number Nombre	Percent P.100		Number Nombre	Percent P.100		Number Nombre	Percent P.100
EUROPE										
Lithuania - Lituanie										
1 VII 2000	ESDJ	3 499 536	2 345 640	67.0	1 637 616	1 079 945	65.9	1 861 920	1 265 695	68.0
6 IV 2001	CDJC	3 483 972	2 332 098	66.9	1 629 148	1 071 986	65.8	1 854 824	1 260 112	67.9
1 VII 2001	ESDJ	3 481 292	2 330 184	66.9	1 627 704	1 070 901	65.8	1 853 588	1 259 283	67.9
1 VII 2002	ESDJ	3 469 070	2 321 713	66.9	1 620 891	1 065 912	65.8	1 848 179	1 255 801	67.9
1 VII 2003	ESDJ	3 454 205	2 307 326	66.8	1 612 996	1 058 108	65.6	1 841 209	1 249 218	67.8
1 VII 2004	ESDJ	3 435 591	2 289 399	66.6	1 603 421	1 048 397	65.4	1 832 170	1 241 002	67.7
1 VII 2005	ESDJ	3 414 304	2 275 118	66.6	1 592 402	1 040 296	65.3	1 821 902	1 234 822	67.8
1 VII 2006	ESDJ	3 394 082	2 264 535	66.7	1 581 807	1 034 128	65.4	1 812 275	1 230 407	67.9
Luxembourg										
1 VII 1998	ESDJ	424 700	...	...	209 716	...	...	216 734	...	...
1 VII 1999	ESDJ	430 475	...	...	211 978	...	...	218 497	...	...
1 VII 2000	ESDJ	436 300	...	...	214 958	...	...	221 343	...	...
15 II 2001	CDJC	439 539	...	...	216 541	...	...	222 998	...	...
1 VII 2001	ESDJ	441 525	...	...	217 562	...	...	223 963	...	...
1 VII 2002	ESDJ	446 175	...	...	219 916	...	...	226 259	...	...
1 VII 2003	ESDJ	451 631	...	...	222 859	...	...	228 772	...	...
1 VII 2004	ESDJ	458 095	...	...	226 432	...	...	231 663	...	...
1 VII 2005	ESDJ	465 158	...	...	230 128	...	...	235 030	...	...
1 VII 2006	ESDJ	472 637	...	...	233 946	...	...	238 691	...	...
Malta - Malte[94]										
1 VII 1997	ESDJ	376 513	...	...	186 664	...	...	189 849	...	...
1 VII 1998	ESDJ	378 518	...	...	187 689	...	...	190 829	...	...
1 VII 1999	ESDJ	380 201	...	...	188 589	...	...	191 612	...	...
1 VII 2000	ESDJ	382 525	...	...	189 720	...	...	192 805	...	...
31 XII 2001	ESDJ	394 641	...	...	195 363	...	...	199 278	...	...
31 XII 2002	ESDJ	397 296	...	...	196 836	...	...	200 460	...	...
1 VII 2003	ESDJ	398 582	...	...	197 468	...	...	201 114	...	...
1 VII 2004	ESDJ	401 306	...	...	198 860	...	...	202 446	...	...
1 VII 2005	ESDJ	403 509	...	...	200 104	...	...	203 405	...	...
21 XI 2005	CDJC	404 962	...	...	200 819	...	...	204 143	...	...
1 VII 2006	ESDJ	406 453	...	...	201 747	...	...	204 706	...	...
Moldova[95]										
1 VII 1997	ESDJ	3 654 208	1 525 600	41.7	1 749 374	733 792	41.9	1 904 834	791 808	41.6
1 VII 1998	ESDJ	3 652 741	1 519 851	41.6	1 748 683	732 340	41.9	1 904 058	787 511	41.4
1 VII 1999	ESDJ	3 647 001	1 515 473	41.6	1 745 826	731 531	41.9	1 901 175	783 942	41.2
1 VII 2000	ESDJ	3 639 592	1 500 283	41.2	1 742 535	724 447	41.6	1 897 057	775 836	40.9
1 VII 2001	ESDJ	3 631 462	1 485 810	40.9	1 739 081	717 661	41.3	1 892 381	768 149	40.6
1 VII 2002	ESDJ	3 623 062	1 484 676	41.0	1 735 430	716 822	41.3	1 887 632	767 854	40.7
1 VII 2003	ESDJ	3 612 874	1 481 035	41.0	1 730 861	714 970	41.3	1 882 013	766 065	40.7
1 VII 2004	ESDJ	3 603 940	1 476 980	41.0	1 726 630	712 971	41.3	1 877 310	764 009	40.7
5 X 2004*	CDFC	3 388 071	1 308 911	38.6	1 632 519	615 387	37.7	1 755 549	693 521	39.5
1 VII 2005	ESDJ	3 595 187	1 472 929	41.0	1 722 105	710 796	41.3	1 873 082	762 133	40.7
1 VII 2006	ESDJ	3 585 209	1 481 398	41.3	1 720 139	706 649	41.1	1 865 070	774 749	41.5
Monaco										
21 VI 2000	CDJC	32 020	...	...	15 544	...	...	16 476	...	...
Montenegro										
1 VII 1997	ESDF	643 405	...	...	320 009	...	...	323 396	...	...
1 VII 1998	ESDF	647 118	...	...	321 841	...	...	325 277	...	...
1 VII 1999	ESDF	650 758	...	...	323 686	...	...	327 072	...	...
1 VII 2000	ESDF	654 274	...	...	325 458	...	...	328 816	...	...
1 VII 2001	ESDF	658 223[96]	...	...	327 538	...	...	330 685	...	...
1 VII 2002	ESDJ	617 511[96]	...	...	304 814	...	...	312 697	...	...
31 III 2003	CDJC	620 145	...	...	305 225	...	...	314 920	...	...
1 VII 2003	ESDJ	620 279	385 205	62.1	305 745	187 299	61.3	314 534	197 906	62.9
1 VII 2004	ESDJ	622 118	387 501	62.3	306 428	188 266	61.4	315 690	199 235	63.1
1 VII 2005	ESDJ	623 277	389 678	62.5	306 839	189 222	61.7	316 439	200 456	63.3
Netherlands - Pays-Bas										
1 VII 1997	ESDJ	15 610 650	9 672 061	62.0	7 718 439	4 742 767	61.4	7 892 211	4 929 294	62.5
1 VII 1998	ESDJ	15 707 209	9 755 092	62.1	7 766 673	4 785 289	61.6	7 940 536	4 969 803	62.6
1 VII 1999	ESDJ	15 812 088	9 974 948	63.1	7 819 794	4 895 568	62.6	7 992 294	5 079 381	63.6
1 VII 2000	ESDJ	15 925 513	10 052 552	63.1	7 878 086	4 936 601	62.7	8 047 427	5 115 951	63.6
1 VII 2001	ESDJ	16 046 180	10 371 945	64.6	7 940 911	5 098 272	64.2	8 105 269	5 273 673	65.1
1 I 2002[97]	CDJC	16 105 285	10 447 684	64.9	7 971 967	5 137 422	64.4	8 133 318	5 310 262	65.3

Continent, country or area, and date / Continent, pays ou zone et date	Code[a]	Both sexes - Les deux sexes			Male - Masculin			Female - Féminin		
		Total	Urban - Urbaine		Total	Urban - Urbaine		Total	Urban - Urbaine	
			Number Nombre	Percent P.100		Number Nombre	Percent P.100		Number Nombre	Percent P.100
EUROPE										
Netherlands - Pays-Bas										
1 VII 2002	ESDJ	16 148 929	10 482 679	64.9	7 993 719	5 155 143	64.5	8 155 210	5 327 536	65.3
1 VII 2003	ESDJ	16 225 302	10 556 424	65.1	8 030 693	5 191 871	64.7	8 194 610	5 364 553	65.5
1 VII 2004	ESDJ	16 281 779	10 687 028	65.6	8 055 947	5 255 716	65.2	8 225 833	5 431 312	66.0
1 VII 2005	ESDJ	16 319 868	10 764 171	66.0	8 071 693	5 292 532	65.6	8 248 175	5 471 640	66.3
1 VII 2006	ESDJ	16 346 101	10 803 902	66.1	8 082 961	5 311 812	65.7	8 263 141	5 492 090	66.5
Norway - Norvège[98]										
1 VII 1997	ESDJ	4 405 157	...	...	2 178 625	...	...	2 226 532	...	...
1 VII 1998	ESDJ	4 431 464	...	...	2 192 333	...	...	2 239 132	...	...
1 VII 1999	ESDJ	4 461 913	...	...	2 208 350	...	...	2 253 564	...	...
1 VII 2000	ESDJ	4 490 967	...	...	2 224 221	...	...	2 266 746	...	...
1 VII 2001	ESDJ	4 513 751	...	...	2 236 618	...	...	2 277 134	...	...
3 XI 2001[20]	CDJC	4 520 947	3 458 699	76.5	2 240 281	1 694 153	75.6	2 280 666	1 764 546	77.4
1 VII 2002	ESDJ	4 538 159	...	...	2 249 021	...	...	2 289 139	...	...
1 VII 2003	ESDJ	4 564 855	...	...	2 262 578	...	...	2 302 277	...	...
1 VII 2004	ESDJ	4 591 910	...	...	2 276 560	...	...	2 315 351	...	...
1 VII 2005	ESDJ	4 623 291	...	...	2 293 026	...	...	2 330 266	...	...
1 VII 2006	ESDJ	4 660 677	...	...	2 313 885	...	...	2 346 792	...	...
Poland - Pologne[99]										
1 VII 1997	ESDF	38 292 000	23 693 000	61.9	18 610 000	11 317 000	60.8	19 682 000	12 376 000	62.9
1 VII 1998	ESDF	38 283 000	23 689 000	61.9	18 590 000	11 303 000	60.8	19 693 000	12 386 000	62.9
1 VII 1999	ESDF	38 270 000	23 668 000	61.8	18 566 000	11 281 000	60.8	19 704 000	12 387 000	62.9
1 VII 2000	ESDF	38 255 945	23 691 220	61.9	18 541 844	11 284 476	60.9	19 714 101	12 406 744	62.9
1 VII 2001	ESDF	38 250 790	23 656 606	61.8	18 532 945	11 261 781	60.8	19 717 845	12 394 825	62.9
20 V 2002	CDFC	38 230 080	23 610 365	61.8	18 516 403	11 234 165	60.7	19 713 677	12 376 200	62.8
1 VII 2002	ESDF	38 232 301	23 607 932	61.7	18 517 179	11 232 736	60.7	19 715 122	12 375 196	62.8
1 VII 2003	ESDF	38 195 177	23 543 325	61.6	18 492 950	11 195 269	60.5	19 702 227	12 348 056	62.7
1 VII 2004	ESDF	38 180 249	23 490 202	61.5	18 478 368	11 162 807	60.4	19 701 881	12 327 395	62.6
1 VII 2005	ESDF	38 161 313	23 450 597	61.5	18 460 730	11 135 706	60.3	19 700 583	12 314 891	62.5
1 VII 2006	ESDF	38 132 277	23 400 565	61.4	18 436 101	11 103 869	60.2	19 696 176	12 296 696	62.4
Portugal										
1 VII 1997	ESDJ	10 091 120	...	...	4 864 760	...	...	5 226 360	...	...
1 VII 1998	ESDJ	10 129 290	...	...	4 884 189	...	...	5 245 102	...	...
1 VII 1999	ESDJ	10 171 949	...	...	4 906 235	...	...	5 265 714	...	...
1 VII 2000	ESDJ	10 225 836	...	...	4 934 469	...	...	5 291 367	...	...
12 III 2001*	CDFC	10 148 259	5 573 842	54.9	4 862 699	2 638 617	54.3	5 285 560	2 935 225	55.5
1 VII 2001	ESDJ	10 292 999	...	...	4 969 817	...	...	5 323 183	...	...
1 VII 2002	ESDJ	10 368 403	...	...	5 009 592	...	...	5 358 811	...	...
1 VII 2003	ESDJ	10 441 075	...	...	5 048 278	...	...	5 392 798	...	...
1 VII 2004	ESDJ	10 501 970	...	...	5 080 324	...	...	5 421 647	...	...
1 VII 2005	ESDJ	10 549 424	...	...	5 105 041	...	...	5 444 383	...	...
1 VII 2006	ESDJ	10 584 344	...	...	5 122 840	...	...	5 461 504	...	...
Romania - Roumanie										
1 VII 1997	ESDJ	22 545 925	12 404 690	55.0	11 041 414	6 007 827	54.4	11 504 511	6 396 863	55.6
1 VII 1998	ESDJ	22 502 803	12 347 886	54.9	11 012 110	5 971 134	54.2	11 490 693	6 376 752	55.5
1 VII 1999	ESDJ	22 458 022	12 302 729	54.8	10 984 529	5 943 708	54.1	11 473 493	6 359 021	55.4
1 VII 2000	ESDJ	22 435 205	12 244 598	54.6	10 968 854	5 907 848	53.9	11 466 351	6 336 750	55.3
1 VII 2001	ESDJ	22 408 393	12 243 748	54.6	10 949 490	5 903 537	53.9	11 458 903	6 340 211	55.3
18 III 2002	CDJC	21 680 974	...	...	10 568 741	...	...	11 112 233	...	...
1 VII 2002	ESDJ	21 794 793	11 608 735	53.3	10 642 538	5 579 042	52.4	11 152 255	6 029 693	54.1
1 VII 2003	ESDJ	21 733 556	11 600 157	53.4	10 606 245	5 566 401	52.5	11 127 311	6 033 756	54.2
1 VII 2004	ESDJ	21 673 328	11 895 598	54.9	10 571 606	5 704 297	54.0	11 101 722	6 191 301	55.8
1 VII 2005	ESDJ	21 623 849	11 879 897	54.9	10 543 518	5 692 516	54.0	11 080 331	6 187 381	55.8
1 VII 2006	ESDJ	21 584 365	11 913 938	55.2	10 521 189	5 704 872	54.2	11 063 176	6 209 066	56.1
Russian Federation - Fédération de Russie										
1 VII 1997	ESDJ	147 915 361	108 149 286	73.1	69 278 223	50 363 061	72.7	78 637 138	57 786 225	73.5
1 VII 1998	ESDJ	147 670 784	108 082 033	73.2	69 134 739	50 292 483	72.7	78 536 045	57 789 550	73.6
1 VII 1999	ESDJ	147 214 776	107 736 374	73.2	68 878 518	50 071 789	72.7	78 336 258	57 664 585	73.6
1 VII 2000	ESDJ	146 596 869	107 245 610	73.2	68 518 623	49 763 462	72.6	78 078 246	57 482 148	73.6
1 VII 2001	ESDJ	145 976 482	106 898 541	73.2	68 130 474	49 504 491	72.7	77 846 008	57 394 050	73.7
1 VII 2002	ESDJ	145 306 497	106 523 307	73.3	67 706 316	49 224 967	72.7	77 600 181	57 298 340	73.8
9 X 2002[100]	CDJC	145 166 731	106 429 049	73.3	67 605 133	49 149 510	72.7	77 561 598	57 279 539	73.9
1 VII 2003	ESDJ	144 565 934	106 069 837	73.4	67 257 276	48 917 406	72.7	77 308 658	57 152 431	73.9

Continent, country or area, and date / Continent, pays ou zone et date	Code[a]	Both sexes - Les deux sexes			Male - Masculin			Female - Féminin		
		Total	Urban - Urbaine		Total	Urban - Urbaine		Total	Urban - Urbaine	
			Number Nombre	Percent P.100		Number Nombre	Percent P.100		Number Nombre	Percent P.100
EUROPE										
Russian Federation - Fédération de Russie										
1 VII 2004 . . . . ESDJ	143 821 215	105 268 883	73.2	66 813 322	48 452 954	72.5	77 007 893	56 815 929	73.8
1 VII 2005 . . . . ESDJ	143 113 876	104 412 086	73.0	66 383 146	47 962 554	72.3	76 730 730	56 449 532	73.6
1 VII 2006 . . . . ESDJ	142 487 259	103 941 621	72.9	66 006 266	47 667 046	72.2	76 480 993	56 274 575	73.6
San Marino - Saint-Marin[20]										
1 VII 1997 . . . . ESDF	25 823	23 085	89.4	12 757	11 404	89.4	13 066	11 681	89.4
1 VII 1998 . . . . ESDF	27 685	...	...	13 557	...	...	14 128	...	...
1 VII 1999 . . . . ESDF	28 106	...	...	13 733	...	...	14 373	...	...
1 VII 2000 . . . . CDFC	26 941	22 738	84.4	13 185	11 787	89.4	13 756	10 951	79.6
1 VII 2000 . . . . ESDF	26 941	22 738	84.4	13 185	11 787	89.4	13 756	10 951	79.6
1 VII 2001 . . . . ESDF	27 634	...	...	13 548	...	...	14 086	...	...
1 VII 2002 . . . . ESDF	28 486	...	...	13 946	...	...	14 540	...	...
1 VII 2003 . . . . ESDF	28 992	...	...	14 207	...	...	14 785	...	...
1 VII 2004 . . . . ESDF	29 421	...	...	14 422	...	...	14 999	...	...
1 VII 2005 . . . . ESDF	30 913	...	...	15 058	...	...	15 855	...	...
1 VII 2006 . . . . ESDF	31 359	...	...	15 309	...	...	16 050	...	...
Serbia - Serbie										
1 VII 1997 . . . . ESDJ	9 956 662	5 078 893	51.0	4 936 345	2 523 092	51.1	5 020 317	2 555 801	50.9
1 VII 1998[101] . . . . ESDJ	7 567 745	4 206 039	55.6	3 686 518	2 017 237	54.7	3 881 227	2 188 802	56.4
1 VII 1999[101] . . . . ESDJ	7 540 401	4 204 900	55.8	3 669 187	2 013 781	54.9	3 871 214	2 191 119	56.6
1 VII 2000[101] . . . . ESDJ	7 516 346	4 206 307	56.0	3 655 777	2 012 848	55.1	3 860 569	2 193 459	56.8
1 VII 2001[101] . . . . ESDJ	7 503 433	4 206 307	56.1	3 648 533	2 012 848	55.2	3 854 900	2 193 459	56.9
31 III 2002[101] . . . . CDJC	7 498 001			3 645 930	...	...	3 852 071		
1 VII 2002[101] . . . . ESDJ	7 500 031	4 241 006	56.5	3 647 190	2 027 187	55.6	3 852 841	2 213 819	57.5
1 VII 2003[101] . . . . ESDJ	7 480 591	4 239 980	56.7	3 637 789	2 026 423	55.7	3 842 802	2 213 557	57.6
1 VII 2004[101] . . . . ESDJ	7 463 157	4 249 544	56.9	3 629 194	2 030 310	55.9	3 833 963	2 219 234	57.9
1 VII 2005[101] . . . . ESDJ	7 440 769	4 257 880	57.2	3 618 040	2 033 179	56.2	3 822 729	2 224 701	58.2
1 VII 2006[101] . . . . ESDJ	7 411 569	4 263 386	57.5	3 603 698	2 034 616	56.5	3 807 871	2 228 770	58.5
Slovakia - Slovaquie										
1 VII 1997 . . . . ESDJ	5 383 233	3 066 450	57.0	...	...	...	...	...	...
1 VII 1998 . . . . ESDJ	5 390 866	3 066 457	56.9	...	...	...	...	...	...
1 VII 1999 . . . . ESDJ	5 395 324	3 061 062	56.7	...	...	...	...	...	...
1 VII 2000 . . . . ESDJ	5 400 679	3 059 010	56.6	...	...	...	...	...	...
25 V 2001 . . . . CDJC	5 379 455	3 022 106	56.2	2 612 515	1 453 638	55.6	2 766 940	1 568 468	56.7
1 VII 2001 . . . . ESDJ	5 379 780	3 017 527	56.1	...	...	...	...	...	...
1 VII 2002 . . . . ESDJ	5 378 809	3 011 737	56.0	2 611 452	1 447 959	55.4	2 767 357	1 563 778	56.5
1 VII 2003 . . . . ESDJ	5 378 950	3 001 776	55.8	2 610 872	1 442 174	55.2	2 768 078	1 559 602	56.3
1 VII 2004 . . . . ESDJ	5 382 574	2 994 284	55.6	2 612 313	1 438 019	55.0	2 770 261	1 556 265	56.2
1 VII 2005 . . . . ESDJ	5 387 285	2 989 291	55.5	2 614 912	1 435 469	54.9	2 772 373	1 553 822	56.0
1 VII 2006 . . . . ESDJ	5 391 184	2 989 769	55.5	2 616 924	1 435 472	54.9	2 774 260	1 554 297	56.0
Slovenia - Slovénie										
1 VII 1997 . . . . ESDJ	1 986 848	...	...	969 155	...	...	1 017 693	...	...
1 VII 1998 . . . . ESDJ	1 982 603	...	...	966 513	...	...	1 016 090	...	...
1 VII 1999 . . . . ESDJ	1 985 557	...	...	968 463	...	...	1 017 094	...	...
1 VII 2000 . . . . ESDJ	1 990 272	...	...	972 581	...	...	1 017 691	...	...
1 VII 2001 . . . . ESDJ	1 992 035	...	...	973 711	...	...	1 018 324	...	...
31 III 2002* . . . . CDJC	1 964 036	997 772[102]	50.8	958 576	479 356[102]	50.0	1 005 460	518 416[102]	51.6
1 VII 2002 . . . . ESDJ	1 995 718	975 163[102]	48.9	976 111[102]	462 513[102]	47.4	1 019 607[102]	512 650[102]	50.3
1 VII 2003 . . . . ESDJ	1 996 773	971 513[102]	48.7	977 436[102]	460 811[102]	47.1	1 019 337[102]	510 702[102]	50.1
1 VII 2004 . . . . ESDJ	1 997 004	968 989[102]	48.5	977 092[102]	459 504[102]	47.0	1 019 912[102]	509 485[102]	50.0
1 VII 2005 . . . . ESDJ	2 001 114	965 538[102]	48.3	980 070[102]	457 869[102]	46.7	1 021 044[102]	507 669[102]	49.7
1 VII 2006 . . . . ESDJ	2 008 516	962 740[102]	47.9	985 876[102]	456 764[102]	46.3	1 022 640[102]	505 976[102]	49.5
Spain - Espagne										
1 VII 1997 . . . . ESDJ	39 583 381	...	...	19 382 107	...	...	20 201 274	...	...
1 VII 1998 . . . . ESDJ	39 722 075	...	...	19 448 294	...	...	20 273 781	...	...
1 VII 1999 . . . . ESDJ	39 927 224	...	...	19 547 393	...	...	20 379 831	...	...
1 VII 2000 . . . . ESDJ	40 264 162	...	...	19 719 334[28]	...	...	20 544 828[28]	...	...
1 VII 2001 . . . . ESDJ	40 721 447	...	...	19 956 780[28]	...	...	20 764 667[28]	...	...
1 XI 2001 . . . . CDFC	40 847 371	...	...	20 012 882	...	...	20 834 489	...	...
1 VII 2002 . . . . ESDJ	41 314 019	...	...	20 266 005	...	...	21 048 014	...	...
1 VII 2003 . . . . ESDJ	42 004 575	...	...	20 626 192	...	...	21 378 383	...	...
1 VII 2004 . . . . ESDJ	42 691 751	...	...	20 987 670	...	...	21 704 081	...	...

6. Total and urban population by sex: 1997 - 2006
Population totale et population urbaine selon le sexe: 1997 - 2006 (continued - suite)

Continent, country or area, and date / Continent, pays ou zone et date	Code[a]	Both sexes - Les deux sexes			Male - Masculin			Female - Féminin		
		Total	Urban - Urbaine		Total	Urban - Urbaine		Total	Urban - Urbaine	
			Number Nombre	Percent P.100		Number Nombre	Percent P.100		Number Nombre	Percent P.100
EUROPE										
Spain - Espagne										
1 VII 2005	ESDJ	43 398 190	...	...	21 367 297	...	...	22 030 893	...	...
1 VII 2006	ESDJ	44 068 244	...	...	21 725 232	...	...	22 343 012	...	...
Sweden - Suède[20]										
1 VII 1997	ESDJ	8 846 062	...	...	4 370 816	...	...	4 475 247	...	...
1 VII 1998	ESDJ	8 850 974	...	...	4 373 767	...	...	4 477 208	...	...
1 VII 1999	ESDJ	8 857 874	...	...	4 377 870	...	...	4 480 006	...	...
1 VII 2000	CDJC	8 872 110	...	...	4 386 436	...	...	4 485 674	...	...
1 VII 2000	ESDJ	8 872 110	...	...	4 386 436	...	...	4 485 674	...	...
1 VII 2001	ESDJ	8 895 963	...	...	4 400 600	...	...	4 495 363	...	...
1 VII 2002	ESDJ	8 924 958	...	...	4 417 776	...	...	4 507 182	...	...
1 VII 2003	ESDJ	8 958 229	...	...	4 436 882	...	...	4 521 348	...	...
1 VII 2004	ESDJ	8 993 531	...	...	4 456 484	...	...	4 537 048	...	...
1 VII 2005	ESDJ	9 029 572	...	...	4 476 431	...	...	4 553 142	...	...
1 VII 2006	ESDJ	9 080 505	...	...	4 505 037	...	...	4 575 468	...	...
Switzerland - Suisse										
1 VII 1997	ESDJ	7 088 906	5 162 464	72.8	3 461 432	2 499 651	72.2	3 627 474	2 662 813	73.4
1 VII 1998	ESDJ	7 110 002	5 177 539	72.8	3 471 966	2 507 740	72.2	3 638 036	2 669 799	73.4
1 VII 1999	ESDJ	7 143 991	5 205 470	72.9	3 489 699	2 522 742	72.3	3 654 292	2 682 728	73.4
1 VII 2000	ESDJ	7 184 250	5 241 276	73.0	3 510 203	2 541 235	72.4	3 674 047	2 700 041	73.5
5 XII 2000	CDJC	7 204 055	4 871 989	67.6	3 519 698	2 357 890	67.0	3 684 357	2 514 099	68.2
1 VII 2001	ESDJ	7 226 647	5 279 814	73.1	3 529 342	2 559 297	72.5	3 697 305	2 720 517	73.6
1 VII 2002	ESDJ	7 284 754	5 329 197	73.2	3 559 690	2 585 292	72.6	3 725 064	2 743 905	73.7
1 VII 2003	ESDJ	7 339 002	5 372 785	73.2	3 588 285	2 608 318	72.7	3 750 717	2 764 467	73.7
1 VII 2004	ESDJ	7 389 626	5 412 574	73.2	3 615 118	2 629 384	72.7	3 774 508	2 783 190	73.7
1 VII 2005	ESDJ	7 437 116	5 450 033	73.3	3 640 600	2 649 755	72.8	3 796 516	2 800 278	73.8
1 VII 2006	ESDJ	7 483 935	5 487 270	73.3	3 665 931	2 670 092	72.8	3 818 004	2 817 178	73.8
The Former Yugoslav Rep. of Macedonia - L'ex-République yougoslave de Macédoine										
1 VII 1997	ESDF	1 996 869	1 189 442	59.6	999 595	590 300	59.1	997 274	599 142	60.1
1 VII 1998	ESDF	2 007 523	...	...	1 004 771	...	...	1 002 752	...	...
1 VII 1999	ESDF	2 017 142	...	...	1 009 369	...	...	1 007 773	...	...
1 VII 2002	ESDF	2 031 153	...	...	1 019 616	...	...	1 019 035	...	...
1 XI 2002	CDJC	2 022 547	...	...	1 015 377	...	...	1 007 170	...	...
1 VII 2003	ESDF	2 026 773	...	...	1 017 274	...	...	1 009 499	...	...
1 VII 2004	ESDF	2 032 544	...	...	1 019 903	...	...	1 012 641	...	...
1 VII 2005	ESDF	2 036 855	...	...	1 021 772	...	...	1 015 083	...	...
1 VII 2006	ESDF	2 040 228	...	...	1 023 069	...	...	1 017 159	...	...
Ukraine										
1 VII 1997	ESDF	50 594 600	34 521 800	68.2	...	...	...	...	...	...
1 VII 1998	ESDF	50 144 450	34 271 600	68.3	...	...	...	...	...	...
1 VII 1999	ESDF	49 673 950[103]	34 017 400	68.5	...	...	...	...	...	...
1 VII 2000	ESDJ	49 176 500[103]	32 768 879	66.6	22 642 532	15 171 760	67.0	26 246 748	17 597 119	67.0
1 VII 2001	ESDJ	48 690 151	32 448 930	66.6	22 423 360	14 992 532	66.9	26 028 896	17 456 398	67.1
5 XII 2001	CDFC	48 240 902	32 290 729	66.9	22 316 317	14 903 592	66.8	25 924 585	17 387 137	67.1
1 VII 2002	ESDJ	48 230 283	32 181 723	66.7	22 214 426	14 843 215	66.8	25 817 580	17 338 508	67.2
1 VII 2003	ESDJ	47 812 949	31 981 796	66.9	22 019 672	14 732 101	66.9	25 612 922	17 249 695	67.3
1 VII 2004	ESDJ	47 271 271	...	...	21 840 401	...	...	25 430 870	...	...
United Kingdom Royaume-Uni[104]										
1 VII 1997[105]	ESDF	58 314 249	...	...	28 371 035	...	...	29 943 214	...	...
1 VII 1998[105]	ESDF	58 474 943	...	...	28 458 360	...	...	30 016 583	...	...
1 VII 1999[105]	ESDF	58 684 427	...	...	28 578 474	...	...	30 105 953	...	...
1 VII 2000[105]	ESDF	58 886 065	...	...	28 690 450	...	...	30 195 615	...	...
29 IV 2001[105]	CDFC	58 789 187	47 007 427	80.0	28 579 867	22 769 606	79.7	30 209 320	24 237 821	80.2
1 VII 2001[105]	ESDF	59 113 497	...	...	28 832 420	...	...	30 281 077	...	...
1 VII 2002[105]	ESDF	59 323 498	...	...	28 964 375	...	...	30 359 123	...	...
1 VII 2003	ESDF	59 557 337	...	...	29 108 774	...	...	30 448 563	...	...
1 VII 2004	ESDF	59 845 842	...	...	29 277 960	...	...	30 567 882	...	...
1 VII 2005	ESDF	60 238 383	...	...	29 497 036	...	...	30 741 347	...	...
1 VII 2006	ESDF	60 587 349	...	...	29 693 967	...	...	30 893 382	...	...

Continent, country or area, and date / Continent, pays ou zone et date	Code[a]	Both sexes - Les deux sexes Total	Urban - Urbaine Number Nombre	Urban - Urbaine Percent P.100	Male - Masculin Total	Urban - Urbaine Number Nombre	Urban - Urbaine Percent P.100	Female - Féminin Total	Urban - Urbaine Number Nombre	Urban - Urbaine Percent P.100
OCEANIA - OCÉANIE										
American Samoa - Samoas américaines[22]										
1 IV 2000 . . . . CDJC	CDJC	57 291	...	...	29 264	...	...	28 027	...	...
Australia - Australie										
1 VII 1997[8] . . . . ESDJ	ESDJ	18 517 564	...	...	9 203 171	...	...	9 314 393	...	...
1 VII 1998[8] . . . . ESDJ	ESDJ	18 711 271	...	...	9 294 674	...	...	9 416 597	...	...
1 VII 1999[8] . . . . ESDJ	ESDJ	18 925 855	...	...	9 396 548	...	...	9 529 307	...	...
1 VII 2000[8] . . . . ESDJ	ESDJ	19 153 380	...	...	9 505 331	...	...	9 648 049	...	...
. 1 VII 2001[8] . . . . ESDJ	ESDJ	19 413 240	15 744 532	81.1	9 630 652	7 764 126	80.6	9 782 588	7 980 406	81.6
7 VIII 2001 . . . . CDJC	CDJC	18 769 249	16 344 412	87.1	9 270 466	8 003 865	86.3	9 498 783	8 340 547	87.8
1 VII 2002[8] . . . . ESDJ	ESDJ	19 654 875	...	...	9 756 969	...	...	9 897 906	...	...
1 VII 2003[8] . . . . ESDJ	ESDJ	19 902 738	...	...	9 882 364	...	...	10 020 374	...	...
1 VII 2004[8] . . . . ESDJ	ESDJ	20 139 792	17 503 103	86.9	10 005 472	8 639 350	86.3	10 134 320	8 863 753	87.5
1 VII 2005[8] . . . . ESDJ	ESDJ	20 409 146	...	...	10 144 053	...	...	10 265 093	...	...
1 VII 2006*[8] . . . . ESDJ	ESDJ	20 701 488	17 231 649	83.2	10 290 338	8 522 861	82.8	10 411 150	8 708 788	83.6
8 VIII 2006 . . . . CDFC	CDFC	20 061 646	...	...	9 896 500	...	...	10 165 146	...	...
Cook Islands - Îles Cook[106]										
1 XII 2001 . . . . CDFC	CDFC	18 027	...	...	9 303	...	...	8 724	...	...
1 XII 2006* . . . . CDFC	CDFC	19 569	...	...	9 932	...	...	9 637	...	...
French Polynesia - Polynésie française										
1 VII 1999 . . . . ESDF	ESDF	227 525	...	...	117 738	...	...	109 787	...	...
Guam[22]										
1 VII 1997 . . . . ESDJ	ESDJ	146 799	56 008	38.2	...	...	...	...	...	...
1 VII 1998 . . . . ESDJ	ESDJ	149 724	57 124	38.2	...	...	...	...	...	...
1 VII 1999 . . . . ESDJ	ESDJ	152 590	58 217	38.2	...	...	...	...	...	...
1 IV 2000 . . . . CDJC	CDJC	154 805	144 129[23]	93.1	79 181	...	...	75 624	...	...
1 VII 2001 . . . . ESDJ	ESDJ	158 330	147 411[23]	93.1	...	...	...	...	...	...
1 VII 2002 . . . . ESDJ	ESDJ	161 057	149 950[23]	93.1	...	...	...	...	...	...
1 VII 2003 . . . . ESDJ	ESDJ	166 593	152 311[23]	91.4	...	...	...	...	...	...
1 VII 2004 . . . . ESDJ	ESDJ	166 090	154 636[23]	93.1	...	...	...	...	...	...
Kiribati										
7 XI 2000* . . . . CDFC	CDFC	84 494	36 717	43.5	41 646	17 822	42.8	42 848	18 895	44.1
7 XII 2005 . . . . CDFC	CDFC	92 533	40 311	43.6	45 612	19 435	42.6	46 921	20 876	44.5
Marshall Islands - Îles Marshall										
1 VII 1997 . . . . ESDF	ESDF	60 851	...	...	30 999	...	...	29 852	...	...
1 VII 1998 . . . . ESDF	ESDF	63 301	...	...	32 235	...	...	31 066	...	...
1 VI 1999 . . . . CDFC	CDFC	50 848	...	...	26 034	...	...	24 814	...	...
1 VII 1999 . . . . ESDF	ESDF	50 840	...	...	26 026	...	...	24 814	...	...
1 VII 2006 . . . . ESDF	ESDF	52 163	...	...	26 746	...	...	25 417	...	...
Micronesia, Federated States of - Micronésie, États Fédérés de La										
1 VII 1997 . . . . ESDJ	ESDJ	110 073	...	...	...	...	...	38 928	...	...
1 IV 2000 . . . . CDJC	CDJC	107 008	...	...	54 191	...	...	52 817	...	...
Nauru										
1 VII 2002 . . . . ESDF	ESDF	10 065	...	...	5 136	...	...	4 929	...	...
New Caledonia - Nouvelle-Calédonie										
1 VII 1997 . . . . ESDF	ESDF	200 894	...	...	102 772	...	...	98 158	...	...
1 VII 1998 . . . . ESDF	ESDF	204 316	...	...	104 413	...	...	99 939	...	...
1 VII 1999 . . . . ESDF	ESDF	207 612	...	...	105 996	...	...	101 662	...	...
1 I 2003 . . . . ESDF	ESDF	225 735	...	...	111 314[28]	...	...	107 663[28]	...	...
1 VII 2004 . . . . ESDF	ESDF	230 068	133 815	58.2	112 716	...	...	109 242	...	...
31 VIII 2004* . . . . CDFC	CDFC	230 789	...	...	116 485	...	...	114 304	...	...
New Zealand - Nouvelle-Zélande										
1 VII 1997 . . . . ESDJ	ESDJ	3 781 400	3 237 800	85.6	1 863 700	...	...	1 917 700	...	...
1 VII 1998 . . . . ESDJ	ESDJ	3 815 000	3 269 700	85.7	1 877 800	...	...	1 937 200	...	...
1 VII 1999 . . . . ESDJ	ESDJ	3 835 100	3 289 300	85.8	1 884 900	...	...	1 950 200	...	...
1 VII 2000 . . . . ESDJ	ESDJ	3 857 800	3 310 100	85.8	1 893 800	...	...	1 964 000	...	...
6 III 2001 . . . . CDJC	CDJC	3 820 749	...	...	1 863 309	...	...	1 957 440	...	...

Continent, country or area, and date / Continent, pays ou zone et date	Code[a]	Both sexes - Les deux sexes			Male - Masculin			Female - Féminin		
		Total	Urban - Urbaine		Total	Urban - Urbaine		Total	Urban - Urbaine	
			Number Nombre	Percent P.100		Number Nombre	Percent P.100		Number Nombre	Percent P.100
OCEANIA - OCÉANIE										
New Zealand - Nouvelle-Zélande										
1 VII 2001	ESDJ	3 880 500	3 331 400	85.8	1 903 200	...	...	1 977 300	...	...
1 VII 2002	ESDJ	3 939 100	3 385 000	85.9	1 934 000	...	...	2 005 100	...	...
1 VII 2003	ESDJ	4 009 200	3 449 300	86.0	1 971 300	...	...	2 037 900	...	...
1 VII 2004	ESDJ	4 061 400	3 497 100	86.1	1 997 700	...	...	2 063 700	...	...
1 VII 2005	ESDJ	4 098 900	3 530 500	86.1	2 017 100	1 724 600	85.5	2 081 800	1 805 900	86.7
7 III 2006	CDFC	4 143 282	...	...	2 021 277	...	...	2 122 005	...	...
1 VII 2006	ESDJ	4 184 600	3 604 400	86.1	2 048 300[6]	1 750 300[6]	85.5	2 136 200[6]	1 854 100[6]	86.8
Niue - Nioué										
17 VIII 1997	CDFC	2 088	...	...	1 053	...	...	1 035	...	...
7 IX 2001	CDFC	1 788	...	...	897	...	...	891	...	...
1 VII 2004	ESDJ	1 761	...	...	866	...	...	895	...	...
1 VII 2005	ESDJ	1 746	...	...	849	...	...	896	...	...
1 VII 2006	ESDJ	1 679	...	...	815	...	...	864	...	...
7 IX 2006	CDFC	1 625	...	...	802	...	...	823	...	...
Norfolk Island - Île Norfolk										
7 VIII 2001	CDFC	2 037	...	...	1 017	...	...	1 020	...	...
8 VIII 2006	CDFC	2 523	...	...	1 218	...	...	1 305	...	...
Northern Mariana Islands - Îles Mariannes septentrionales										
1 VII 1997	ESDF	63 763	...	...	31 311	...	...	32 452	...	...
1 VII 1998	ESDF	66 559	...	...	32 475	...	...	34 084	...	...
1 VII 1999	ESDF	69 341	...	...	33 636	...	...	35 705	...	...
1 IV 2000	CDFC	69 221	...	...	31 984	...	...	37 237	...	...
1 VII 2000	ESDF	72 101	...	...	34 790	...	...	37 311	...	...
1 VII 2001	ESDF	74 847	...	...	35 941	...	...	38 906	...	...
1 VII 2002	ESDF	77 588	...	...	37 093	...	...	40 495	...	...
Palau - Palaos										
1 VII 1997	ESDF	18 061	...	...	9 618	...	...	8 443	...	...
1 VII 1998	ESDF	18 494	...	...	9 842	...	...	8 652	...	...
1 VII 1999	ESDF	18 882	...	...	10 039	...	...	8 843	...	...
15 IV 2000	CDFC	19 129	13 303	69.5	10 450	...	...	8 679	...	...
1 VII 2000	ESDF	19 257	...	...	10 229	...	...	9 028	...	...
1 VII 2001	ESDF	19 626	...	...	10 415	...	...	9 211	...	...
1 VII 2002	ESDF	19 976	...	...	10 590	...	...	9 386	...	...
1 IV 2005	CDJC	19 907	15 399	77.4	10 699	...	...	9 208	...	...
Papua New Guinea - Papouasie-Nouvelle-Guinée										
1 VII 1997	ESDF	4 209 335	...	...	2 218 293	...	...	1 991 042	...	...
9 VII 2000	CDFC	5 190 786	686 301	13.2	2 691 744	372 453	13.8	2 499 042	313 848	12.6
1 VII 2002	ESDF	5 461 940	...	...	2 826 212	...	...	2 635 722	...	...
Samoa										
5 XI 2001	CDFC	176 710	38 836	22.0	92 050	19 837	21.6	84 660	18 999	22.4
1 VII 2002	ESDF	178 329	39 192	22.0	92 893	20 019	21.6	85 436	19 173	22.4
1 VII 2003	ESDF	179 962	39 551	22.0	93 744	20 202	21.6	86 218	19 349	22.4
1 VII 2004	ESDF	181 611	39 913	22.0	94 603	20 387	21.6	87 008	19 526	22.4
1 VII 2005	ESDF	183 275	40 279	22.0	95 470	20 574	21.6	87 805	19 705	22.4
1 VII 2006	ESDF	184 955	40 648	22.0	96 345	20 763	21.6	88 610	19 885	22.4
5 XI 2006*	CDFC	179 186	...	...	92 961	...	...	86 225	...	...
Solomon Islands - Îles Salomon										
21 XI 1999	CDFC	409 042	...	...	211 381	...	...	197 661	...	...
1 VII 2003	ESDF	448 286	...	...	231 267	...	...	217 019	...	...
1 VII 2004	ESDF	460 110	...	...	237 626	...	...	222 484	...	...
1 VII 2005	ESDF	471 266	...	...	242 927	...	...	228 339	...	...
1 VII 2006	ESDF	483 083	...	...	248 944	...	...	234 139	...	...
Tokelau - Tokélaou										
11 X 2001	CDFC	1 537	...	...	761	...	...	776	...	...
19 X 2006	CDFC	1 151	...	...	583	...	...	568	...	...

6. Total and urban population by sex: 1997 - 2006
Population totale et population urbaine selon le sexe: 1997 - 2006 (continued - suite)

Continent, country or area, and date / Continent, pays ou zone et date	Code[a]	Both sexes - Les deux sexes			Male - Masculin			Female - Féminin		
		Total	Urban - Urbaine		Total	Urban - Urbaine		Total	Urban - Urbaine	
			Number Nombre	Percent P.100		Number Nombre	Percent P.100		Number Nombre	Percent P.100
OCEANIA - OCÉANIE										
Tonga										
1 VII 1997[107]	ESDF	98 591	...	...	50 037	...	...	48 553	...	...
1 VII 1998[107]	ESDF	99 264	...	...	50 406	...	...	48 856	...	...
1 VII 1999[107]	ESDF	99 821	...	...	50 731	...	...	49 088	...	...
1 VII 2000[107]	ESDF	100 283	...	...	51 017	...	...	49 264	...	...
1 VII 2001[107]	ESDF	100 673	...	...	51 272	...	...	49 400	...	...
1 VII 2002[107]	ESDF	101 002	...	...	51 473	...	...	49 528	...	...
1 VII 2003[107]	ESDF	101 405	...	...	51 710	...	...	49 694	...	...
30 XI 2006*	CDFC	101 134	...	...	51 197	...	...	49 937	...	...
Tuvalu										
1 XI 2002	CDFC	9 561	...	...	4 729	2 281	48.2	4 832	2 211	45.8
Vanuatu										
16 XI 1999	CDJC	186 678	40 094	21.5	95 682	20 726	21.7	90 996	19 368	21.3
1 VII 2004[2]	ESDF	215 541	...	...	110 441[108]	...	...	105 399[108]	...	...
1 VII 2006	ESDF	221 417[2]	...	...	113 034	...	...	108 383	...	...
Wallis and Futuna Islands - Îles Wallis et Futuna										
22 VII 2003	CDFC	14 944	...	...	7 494	...	...	7 450	...	...

FOOTNOTES - NOTES

Italics: estimates which are less reliable. - Italiques: estimations moins sûres.

* Provisional. - Données provisoires.

[a] 'Code' indicates the source of data, as follows:
CDFC - Census, de facto, complete tabulation
CDFS - Census, de facto, sample tabulation
CDJC - Census, de jure, complete tabulation
CDJS - Census, de jure, sample tabulation
SSDF - Sample survey, de facto
SSDJ - Sample survey, de jure
ESDF - Estimates, de facto
ESDJ - Estimates, de jure
Le 'Code' indique la source des données, comme suit:
CDFC - Recensement, population de fait, tabulation complète
CDFS - Recensement, population de fait, tabulation par sondage
CDJC - Recensement, population de droit, tabulation complète
CDJS - Recensement, population de droit, tabulation par sondage
SSDF - Enquête par sondage, population de fait
SSDJ - Enquête par sondage, population de droit
ESDF - Données estimatées, population de fait
ESDJ - Données estimatées, population de droit

[1] Series not strictly comparable due to differences of definitions of "urban". - Les séries ne sont pas strictement comparables en raison de différences existant dans la définition des "regions urbaines".

[2] Data refer to national projections. - Les données se réfèrent aux projections nationales.

[3] Excluding Mayotte. - Non compris Mayotte.

[4] Exclude border population. - À l'exception de la population frontalière.

[5] Data refer to Libyan nationals only. - Les données se raportent aux nationaux libyens seulement.

[6] Because of rounding, totals are not in all cases the sum of the parts. - Les chiffres étant arrondis, les totaux ne correspondent pas toujours rigoureusement à la somme des chiffres partiels.

[7] Including residents outside the country. - Y compris les résidents hors du pays.

[8] Mid-year estimates have been adjusted for underenumeration, at latest census. - Les estimations au millieu de l'année tiennent compte d'un ajustement destiné à compenser les lacunes du dénombrement lors du dernier recensement.

[9] Census results have been adjusted for underenumeration, estimated at 5.1 per cent. - Les résultats du recensement ont été ajustées pour compenser les lacunes du dénombrement, estimées à 5,1 p. 100.

[10] The number of males and/or females excludes persons whose sex is not stated (18 urban, 19 rural). - Il n'est pas tenu compte dans le nombre d'hommes et de femmes des personnes dont le sexe n'est pas indiqué (18 en zone urbaine et 19 en zone rurale).

[11] Data exclude adjustment for underenumeration, estimated at 2.4 per cent. - Les données n'ont pas été ajustées pour compenser les lacunes du dénombrement, estimées à 2,4 p. 100.

[12] Based on results of a Socio Economic Survey. - Basé sur les résultats d'une enquête Socio-Economique.

[13] Excluding the institutional population. - Non compris la population dans les institutions.

[14] Final intercensal estimates. - Estimations inter censitaires finales.

[15] Census data unadjusted for net census undercoverage. - Les chiffres des recensement ne sont pas ajustés pour le sous-dénombrement net du recensement.

[16] Final postcensal estimates. - Évaluations postcensal finales.

[17] Updated postcensal estimates. - Estimations post censitaires mises à jour.

[18] Excluding 390 residents of institutions. - À l'exclusion de 390 personnes en établissements de soins.

[19] Excluding persons residing in institutions. - Non compris les personnes dans les institutions.

[20] Population statistics are compiled from registers. - Les statistiques de la population sont compilées à partir des registres.

[21] Around 1996 - 1997 volcanic activity on Montserrat escalated, forcing people to relocate. - Vers 1996 - 1997 l'activité volcanique a connu une recrudescence à Montserrat, forçant les habitants à s'installer ailleurs.

[22] Including armed forces stationed in the area. - Y compris les militaires en garnison sur le territoire.

[23] Definition of urban and rural distribution changed from the year 2000. - La définition des régions urbaines et rurales a changée depuis 2000.

[24] Definition of urban and rural distribution changed from the year 2000. Unrevised data. - La définition des régions urbaines et rurales a changée depuis 2000. Les données n'ont pas été revisées.

[25] Excluding armed forces overseas and civilian citizens absent from country for an extended period of time. - Non compris les militaires à l'étranger, et les civils hors du pays pendant une période prolongée.

[26] Data include persons in remote areas, military personnel outside the country, merchant seamen at sea, civilian seasonal workers outside the country, and other civilians outside the country, and exclude nomads, foreign military, civilian aliens temporarily in the country, transients on ships and Indian jungle population. - Y

compris les personnes vivant dans des régions éloignées, le personel militaire en dehors du pays, les marins marchands, les ouvriers saisonniers en dehors du pays, et autres civils en dehors du pays, et non compris les nomades, les militaires étrangers, les étrangers civils temporairement dans le pays, les transiteurs sur des bateaux et les Indiens de la jungle.

[27] Data have been adjusted on the basis of the Population Census of 2005. - Données ajustées sur la base du recensement de la population de 2005.

[28] Unrevised data. - Les données n'ont pas été révisées.

[29] Excluding nomadic Indian tribes. - Non compris les tribus d'Indiens nomades.

[30] A dispute exists between the governments of Argentina and the United Kingdom of Great Britain and Northern Ireland concerning sovereignty over the Falkland Islands (Malvinas). - La souveraineté sur les îles Falkland (Malvinas) fait l'objet d'un différend entre le Gouvernement argentin et le Gouvernement du Royaume-Uni de Grande-Bretagne et d'Irlande du Nord.

[31] Data for 2003 have been adjusted on the basis of the Population Census of 2002. - Les données de 2003 ont été ajustées sur la base du recensement de population de 2002.

[32] The population for the year 2005 corresponds to the population actually enumerated in the census conducted between 18 July and 20 August 2005. The total (adjusted) population is 27 219 264 inhabitants. - La population pour 2005 correspond à la population effectivement dénombrée lors du recensement réalisé entre le 18 juillet et le 20 août 2005. La population totale (après ajustement) compte 27 219 264 habitants.

[33] Data for the total population include 17 diplomats. - La population totale indiquée comprend 17 diplomates.

[34] The previous census was conducted only 16 months earlier (on 31 Mar 2003) but it was repeated because all of its data were destroyed in a fire before they could be fully processed, analyzed, and reported. - Le recensement précédent a eu lieu seulement 16 mois auparavant (le 31 mars 2003), mais a dû être refait parce que toutes les données ont été détruites dans un incendie avant que l'on n'ait pu les traiter et les analyser.

[35] Figures for male and female population do not add up to the figure for total population, because they exclude 365 persons of unknown sex (265 urban and 100 rural). - Les chiffres relatifs à la population masculine et féminine ne correspondent pas au chiffre de la population totale, parce que l'on en a exclu 365 personnes de sexe inconnu (265 en zones urbaines et 100 en zones rurales).

[36] Data refer to resident population in Uruguay according to Census Phase 1, carried out between the months of June and July 2004. - Les données se rapportent à la population résidente en Uruguay d'après la phase 1 du recensement, qui a eu lieu entre juin et juillet 2004.

[37] Excluding Indian jungle population. - Non compris les Indiens de la jungle.

[38] For urban/rural distribution, data refer to the settled population based on the 1979 Population Census; an estimated 1.5 million nomads are not included. For 2002 total population was the only figure revised. - Pour la distribution urbaine/rurale, les données se rapportent à la population sédentaire sur la base du recensement de 1979; les nomades, estimées a 1.5 million, ne sont pas inclus. Pour 2002, l'effectif total de la population est le seul chiffre révisé.

[39] Data refer to the settled population based on the 1979 Population Census and the latest household prelisting. The refugees of Afghanistan in Iran, Pakistan and estimated 1.5 million nomads are not included. The so adjusted total population of the country for 2006 is 24.1 million of which 12.3 million males and 11.8 million females. - Les données se rapportent à la population stationnaire sur la base du recensement de 1979 et du recensement préliminaire des logements le plus récent. Sont exclus les réfugiés d'Afghanistan en Iran et au Pakistan et les nomades estimés à 1,5 million. La population totale du pays ainsi ajustée pour 2006 comprend 24,1 millions de personnes (12,3 millions d'hommes et 11,8 millions de femmes).

[40] The methodology used for calculating the number of the de facto and de jure population in the 2001 census data differs as follows from the methodology used in previous censuses: the duration that defines a person as being ' temporary present ' or 'temporary absent' is now 'under one year'. The previously applied definition was for '6 months'. - La méthode utilisée pour dénombrer la population de fait et la population de droit dans le contexte du recensement de 2001 diffère de celle qui a été appliquée lors des recensements antérieurs en ce que la durée considérée pour définir la ' présence temporaire 'ou' l'absence temporaire' était dorénavant fixée à 'moins d'un an' alors qu'elle était de '6 mois' auparavant.

[41] Excluding usual residents not in country at time of census (Total 4053, Male 2238, Female 1815) - À l'exclusion des résidents habituels qui n'étaient pas dans le pays au moment du recensement (au total 4 053 personnes dont 2 238 hommes et 1 815 femmes).

[42] Census results have been adjusted for underenumeration, estimated at 4.96 per cent. - Les données ont été ajustées pour compenser les lacunes du dénombrement, estimées à 4,96 %.

[43] Excluding foreign diplomatic personnel and their dependants. - Non compris le personnel diplomatique étranger et les membres de leur famille les accompagnant.

[44] Based on Cambodia Intercensal Population Survey. Data exclude institutional, homeless households and transient poulation. - Les données ne comprennent pas la population des institutions, les ménages sans abri et la population de passage.

[45] For statistical purposes, the data for China do not include those for the Hong Kong Special Administrative Region (Hong Kong SAR), Macao Special Administrative Region (Macao SAR) and Taiwan province of China. - Pour la présentation des statistiques, les données pour la Chine ne comprennent pas la Région Administrative Spéciale de Hong Kong (Hong Kong RAS), la Région Administrative Spéciale de Macao (Macao RAS) et Taïwan province de Chine.

[46] Data for the period 1990 to 2000 have been adjusted on the basis of the Population Census of 2000. - Les données pour la période allant de 1990 à 2000 ont été ajustées à partir des résultats du recensement de la population de 2000.

[47] The military personnel are classified as urban population. - Le personnel militaire est classé dans la population urbaine.

[48] For the civilian population of 31 provinces, municipalities and autonomous regions. - Pour la population civile seulement de 31 provinces, municipalités et régions autonomes.

[49] Data have been estimated on the basis of the annual National Sample Surveys on Population Changes. - Les données ont été estimées sur la base de l'enquête annuelle "National Sample Survey on Population Changes".

[50] Data for 2005 are estimated from the National Sample Survey of 1 Per cent population. - Les données pour 2005 ont été estimées à partir de l'enquête nationale qui a porté sur un échantillon de 1 % de la population.

[51] For 2001, data refer to Hong Kong resident population at the census moment, which covers usual residents and mobile residents. Usual residents refer to two categories of people: (1) Hong Kong permanent residents who had stayed in Hong Kong for at least three months during the six months before or for at least three months during the six months after the census moment, regardless of whether they were in Hong Kong or not at the census moment; and (2) Hong Kong non-permanent residents who were in Hong Kong at the census moment. Mobile Residents, they are Hong Kong permanent residents who had stayed in Hong Kong for at least one month but less than three months during the six months before or for at least one month but less than three months during the six months after the census moment, regardless of whether they were in Hong Kong or not at the census moment. - Pour 2001, les données se rapportent à la population résidente à Hong Kong au moment du recensement. Cette population est composée des résidants habituels et des résidants mobiles. La population résidente est partagée en deux catégories: (1) les résidents permanents qui ont habité à Hong Kong au moins trois mois pendant les six mois précédents ou les six mois suivants le recensement; (2) les habitants non-permanents de Hong Kong qui étaient à Hong Kong au moment du recensement. La population mobile se rapporte aux résidents permanents de Hong Kong qui ont habité à Hong Kong pendant les six mois après le recensement pour une période comprise entre un mois et trois mois, indépendamment du fait qu'ils étaient à Hong Kong au moment du recensement au pays.

[52] Data derived from the By-Census 2006 held during 19 to 31 of August 2006. - Donnes dérivées du recensement partiel de 2006 organisé entre les 19 et 31 août 2006.

[53] Data refer to government controlled areas. - Les données se rapportent aux zones contrôlées par le Gouvernement.

[54] Data include all population irrespective of citizenship, who at the time of the census resided in the country or intended to reside for a period of at least one year. It does not distinguish between those present or absent at the time of census. - Les chiffres comprennent toute la population, quelle que soit la nationalité, qui à l'époque de recensement avait résidé dans le pays, ou avait l'intention de résider, pendant une période d'au moins un an. Il n'y a pas de distinction entre les personnes présentes ou absentes au moment du recensement.

[55] Including data for the Indian-held part of Jammu and Kashmir, the final status of which has not yet been determined. - Y compris les données pour la partie du Jammu et du Cachemire occupée par l'Inde dont le statut définitif n'a pas encore été déterminé.

[56] Data exclude Mao-Maram, Paomata and Purul sub-divisions of Senapati district of Manipur. The population of Manipur including the estimated population of the three sub-divisions of Senapati district is 2,291,125 (Males 1,161,173 and females 1,129,952). - Non compris les subdivisions Mao-Maram Paomata et Purul du district de Senapati dans l'État du Manipur. Cet État compte 2 291 125 habitants (1 161 173 hommes et 1 129 952 femmes), y compris la population estimative des trois subdivisions du district de Senapati.

[57] Excluding estimated Population of Mao Maram, Paomata and Purul sub-divisions of Senapati district of Manipur. - Hormis la population estimée de Mao Maram, Paomata et les subdivisions Purul du district Senapati de Manipur.

[58] The figure includes an estimated population of 459 557 persons in urban and 1 857 659 persons in rural areas that were not directly enumerated, and a population of 566 403 persons in urban and 1 717 578 persons in rural areas that decline the participation. Also included are 421 399 non permanent residents (the homeless, the crew of ships carrying national flag, boat/floating house people, remote located tribesmen and refugees.) - Y compris la population estimée a 459 557 personnes dans les zones urbaines et de 1 857 659 personnes dans les zones rurales qui n'ont pas été énumérées directement, aussi que 566 403 personnes qui non pas répondu dans les zones urbaines et de 1 717 578 personnes dans les zones rurales. Y compris 421 399 résidants non permanents (les sans abri, l'équipage des bateaux portant le pavillon national, les habitants des embarcations ou des maisons flottantes, les habitants des tribus isolées et les réfugiés.)

[59] Intercensal Population Survey. - Étude démographique entre deux recensements.

[60] Data relate to the Iranian Year which begins on 21 March and ends on 20 March of the following year. - Les données concernent l'année iranienne, qui commence le 21 mars et se termine le 20 mars de l'année suivante.

[61] For the 1997 population census, data exclude population in three autonomous provinces in the north of the country. - Pour le recensement de 1997, la population des trois provinces autonomes dans le nord du pays est exclue.

[62] Including data for East Jerusalem and Israeli residents in certain other territories under occupation by Israeli military forces since June 1967. - Y compris les données pour Jérusalem-Est et les résidents israéliens dans certains autres territoires occupés depuis 1967 par les forces armées israéliennes.

[63] Excluding residents who had been registered in the Israeli localities (the Jewish localities) in the Gaza Area and northern Samaria, which were evacuated in August 2005, but did not notify the Ministry of Interior of their new address. These residents are included in total. - Hors résidents enregistrés dans les localités d'Israel (localités juives) de la Bande de Gaza (verfify) et du nord de la Samarie, qui ont été évacués en Août 2005, mais qui n'ont pas notifié leur nouvelle adresse au ministère de l'intérieur. Ces résidents sont inclus dans le total.

[64] Excluding diplomatic personnel outside the country and foreign military and civilian personnel and their dependants stationed in the area. - Non compris le personnel diplomatique hors du pays ni les militaires et agents civils étrangers en poste sur le territoire et les membres de leur famille les accompagnant.

[65] Excluding data for Jordanian territory under occupation since June 1967 by Israeli military forces. Excluding foreigners, including registered Palestinian refugees. - Non compris les données pour le territoire jordanien occupé depuis juin 1967 par les forces armées israéliennes. Non compris les étrangers, mais y compris les réfugiés de Palestine enregistrés.

[66] Excluding foreigners. Including diplomats and their families abroad, but excluding foreign diplomats, foreign military personnal, and their families in the country. - Non compris étrangers. Y compris le personnel diplomatique et les membres de leurs familles à l'étranger, mais sans tenir compte du personnel diplomatique et militaire étranger et des membres de leurs familles.

[67] Excluding usual residents not in country at time of census. - À l'exclusion des résidents habituels qui ne sont pas dans le pays au moment du recensement.

[68] For 1997, based on Lao expenditure and consumption survey 1997/98. - Les données se rapportent à l'Enquête sur la consommation et les dépenses des ménages du Laos du 1997/98.

[69] From year 2000-2004, calculated based on Population census 1995 structure and growth rate at year 2000. - Pour les années 2000 à 2004, on a pris pour base la structure issue du recensement de population de 1995 et le taux de croissance de 2000.

[70] Data based on the results of the 2005 Population and Housing Census. - Données fondées sur les résultats du recensement de la population et de l'habitat de 2005.

[71] Based on households sample survey. - Basé sur une enquête sur un échantillon de ménages.

[72] Excluding Malaysian citizens and permanent residents who were away or intended to be away from the country for more than six months. Excluding Malaysian military, naval and diplomatic personnel and their families outside the country, and tourists, businessman who intended to be in Malaysia for less than six months. Census results have been adjusted for underenumeration. - Non compris les citoyens malaisiens et les résidents permanents qui étaient ou qui ont prévu d'être hors du pays pour six mois ou plus. Non compris le personnel militaire Malaisien, le personnel naval ou diplomatique et leurs familles hors du pays, et les touristes et les hommes d'affaires qui avaient l'intention de rester en Malaisie moins de six mois. Les résultats du recensement ont été ajustées pour compenser les lacunes du dénombrement

[73] Data including estimated population from household listing from Village Development Committees and Wards which could not be enumerated at the time of census. - Les données incluent la population estimée par les listes des ménages des comités de développement des villages et des circonscriptions qui n'ont pas pu être énumérée au moment du recensement.

[74] Data for urban including population in refugee camps. - Les données pour la population urbaine comprennent la population dans les camps réfugiés.

[75] Total population does not include Palestinian population living in those parts of Jerusalem governorate which were annexed by Israel in 1967, amounting to 210 209 persons. Likewise, the results does not include the estimates of not enumerated population based on the findings of the post enumeration study, i.e 83 805 persons. - Les données relatives à la population totale ne comprennent pas la population palestinienne -équivalent à 210 209 personnes - habitant dans les territoires du gouvernorat de Jérusalem qui ont été annexés par Israël en 1967. Egalement, les données ne tiennent pas compte des estimations de la population calculée sur la base des résultats de l'enquête postcensitaire, équivalent à 83 805 personnes.

[76] Excluding data for the Pakistan-held part of Jammu and Kashmir, the final status of which has not yet been determined. - Non compris les données concernant la partie du Jammu et Cachemire occupée par le Pakistan dont le statut définitif n'a pas été déterminé.

[77] Excluding transients afloat and non-locally domiciled military and civilian services personnel and their dependants and visitors. - Non compris les personnes de passage à bord de navires ni les militaires et agents civils non-résidents et les membres de leur famille les accompagnants et visiteurs.

[78] The Population and Housing Census 2001 did not cover the whole area of the country due to the security problems; the Census was complete in 18 districts only; in three districts it was not possible to conduct it; and in four districts it was partially conducted. - Le recensement de la population et de l'habitat en 2001 n'a pas couvert la totalité du pays pour des problèmes de sécurité ; le recensement a été complété seulement en 18 districts ; dans 3 districts ça n'a pas été possible de conduire le recensement et dans 4 districts il a été partialement conduit.

[79] Including Palestinian refugees. - Y compris les réfugiés de Palestine.

[80] Also included in Finland. - Comprise aussi dans Finlande.

[81] Data refer to 1st March. - Données se rapportent au 1er Mars.

[82] Population statistics are compiled from registers. Excluding Faeroe Islands and Greenland shown separately, if available. - Les statistiques de la population sont compilées à partir des registres. Non compris les Iles Féroé et le Gröenland, qui font l'objet de rubriques distinctes, si disponible.

[83] Population statistics are compiled from registers. Including Aland Islands. - Les statistiques de la population sont compilées à partir des registres. Y compris les Îles d'Åland.

[84] Excluding Overseas Departments, namely, French Guiana, Guadeloupe, Martinique and Reunion, shown separately, if available. Excluding diplomatic personnel outside the country and including members of alien armed forces not living in military camps and foreign diplomatic personnel not living in embassies or consulates. - Non compris les départements d'outre mer, c'est-à-dire la Guyane française, la Guadeloupe, la Martinique et la Réunion, qui font l'objet de rubriques distinctes, si disponible. Non compris le personnel diplomatique hors du pays et y compris les militaires étrangers ne vivant pas dans des camps militaires et le personnel diplomatique étranger ne vivant pas dans les ambassades ou les consulats.

[85] Data of the microcensus - a 1% household sample survey - refer to a single reference week in spring (usually last week in April). Excluding homeless persons. Excluding foreign military personnel and foreign diplomatic and consular personnel and their family members in the country. - Les données du microrecensement (enquête sur les ménages, réalisée sur un échantillon de 1 %) concernent une seule semaine de référence au printemps (habituellement la dernière semaine d'avril). Non compris les personnes sans domicile fixe. Non compris le personnel militaire étranger, le personnel diplomatique et consulaire étranger et les membres de leur famille se trouvant dans le pays.

[86] Excluding families of military personnel, visitors and transients. - Non compris les familles des militaires, ni les visiteurs et transients.

[87] Excluding armed forces stationed outside the country, but including alien armed forces stationed in the area. - Non compris les militaires en garnison hors du pays, mais y compris les militaires étrangers en garnison sur le territoire.

[88] Census data including armed forces stationed outside the country, but excluding alien armed forces stationed in the area. - Les données de recensement comprennent les militaires se trouvant hors du pays, mais comprennent pas les militaires étrangers en poste sur le territoire.

[89] Data refer to the Vatican City State. Population statistics are compiled from registers. - Les données se rapportent à l'Etat de la Cité du Vatican. Les statistiques de la population sont compilées à partir des registres.

[90] The regional grouping (urban/rural) was made from 1990 to 2000 according to the administrative division of 1 January 2000 and from 2001 according to the administrative division of 1 January 2004. - Pour les années 1990 à 2000, le découpage régional (zone urbaine/rurale) correspond au découpage administratif en vigueur au 1er janvier 2000; à partir de 2001, il correspond à celui en vigueur au 1er janvier 2004.

⁹¹ According to the administrative division on 1 January 2006. - D'après la division en circonscriptions administratives au 1er janvier 2006.

⁹² Data refer to 15th of April. - Données se rapportent au 15 Avril.

⁹³ Urban and rural population is given according to the 2007 administrative division. - Les données sur la population urbaine et la population rurale correspondent aux divisions administratives de 2007.

⁹⁴ Including civilian nationals temporarily outside the country. - Y compris les civils nationaux temporairement hors du pays.

⁹⁵ Data do not include information for Transnistria and the municipality of Bender. - Les données ne tiennent pas compte de l'information sur la Transnistria et la municipalité de Bender.

⁹⁶ Starting from 1997 until 2001 data is de facto and from 2002 and later data is de jure. - De 1997 à 2001, les données sont de fait, à partir de 2002 elles sont de jure.

⁹⁷ Census result, based on compilation of continuous accounting and sample surveys. - Les résultat du recensement, d'après les résultats des dénombrements et enquêtes par sondage continue.

⁹⁸ Including residents temporarily outside the country. Excluding Svalbard and Jan Mayen Island shown separately, if available. - Y compris les résidents se trouvant temporairement hors du pays. Non compris Svalbard et Jan Mayen qui font l'objet de rubriques distinctes, si disponible.

⁹⁹ Excluding civilian aliens within country, but including civilian nationals temporarily outside country. - Non compris les civils étrangers dans le pays, mais y compris les civils nationaux temporairement hors du pays.

¹⁰⁰ Figures were updated taking into account the results of the 2002 All-Russian population census. - Les chiffres ont été calculés compte tenu des résultats du recensement de la population de la Fédération de Russie de 2002.

¹⁰¹ Without data for Kosovo and Metohia. - Sans les données pour le Kosovo and Metohie.

¹⁰² Excluding citizens temporarily residing abroad, the sum by urban and rural does not add up to the total. - Les nationaux se trouvant provisoirement à l'étranger ne sont pas pris en compte. La somme des chiffres disponibles pour les zones urbaines et rurales ne correspond donc pas au total.

¹⁰³ Starting from 1997 until 1999 data is de facto and from 2000 and later data is de jure. - De 1997 à 1999, les données sont de fait, à partir de 2000 elles sont de jure.

¹⁰⁴ Excluding Channel Islands and Isle of Man, shown separately, if available. - Non compris les îles Anglo-Normandes et l'île de Man, qui font l'objet de rubriques distinctes, si disponible.

¹⁰⁵ Population estimates for 1994 to 2002 were revised in light of the local studies. - Les estimations de la population pour les années 1994 à 2002 ont été révisées en fonction d'études locales.

¹⁰⁶ Excluding Niue, shown separately, which is part of Cook Islands, but because of remoteness is administered separately. - Non compris Nioué, qui fait l'objet d'une rubrique distincte et qui fait partie des îles Cook, mais qui, en raison de son éloignement, est administrée séparément.

¹⁰⁷ Based on the results of the 1996 population census not necessarily mid year estimated. - À partir des résultats du recensement de la population de 1996, pas nécessairement des estimations en milieu d'année.

¹⁰⁸ Figures for male and female do not add up to the total, reason for discrepancy not ascertained. - La some des données pour la population masculine et pour la population féminine n'est pas égale au total, les raisons de cette différence ne sont pas expliquées.

Table 7

Table 7 presents population by age, sex and urban/rural residence for the latest available year.

Description of variables: Data in this table are either population census figures or estimates, some of which are based on sample surveys. Data refer to the de facto population unless otherwise noted.

The reference date of the census or estimate appears in the stub of the table. In general, the estimates refer to mid-year (1 July).

Age is defined as age at last birthday, that is, the difference between the date of birth and the reference date of the age distribution expressed in completed solar years. The age classification used in this table is the following: under 1 year, 1-4 years, 5-year groups through 95-99 years, and 100 years or over.

Statistics are presented for one year, the most recent available. However, if more complete disaggregation is available for an earlier year, both are displayed.

The urban/rural classification of population by age and sex is that provided by each country or area; it is presumed to be based on the national census definitions of urban population that have been set forth at the end of the technical notes to table 6.

Estimates of population by age and sex presented in this table have been limited to countries or areas for which estimates have been based on the results of a sample survey or have been constructed by the component method from the results of a population census or sample survey. Estimations derived from distributing estimated total population according to percentages in each age-sex group at the time of a census or sample survey are not included in this table.

Reliability of data: Estimates which are believed to be less reliable are set in *italics* rather than in roman type. No attempt has been made to take account of age-reporting accuracy, the evaluation of which has been described in section 3.1.3 of the Technical Notes. However, the Whipple's Index presented in table 1c of the Demographic Yearbook Special Census Topic Volume 1 (Basic population characteristics) provides an assessment of age heaping for 145 countries for censuses being held between 1985 and 2003.

Limitations: Statistics on population by age and sex are subject to the same qualifications as have been set forth for population statistics in general and age distributions in particular, as discussed in sections 3 and 3.1.3, respectively, of the Technical Notes.

Comparability of population data classified by age and sex is limited by variations in the definition of total population, discussed in detail in section 3 of the Technical Notes, and by the accuracy of the original enumeration. Both factors are more important in relation to certain age groups than to others. For example, under-enumeration is known to be more prevalent among infants and young children than among older persons. Similarly, the exclusion from the total population of certain groups that tend to be of selected ages (such as the armed forces) can markedly affect the age structure and its comparability with that for other countries or areas. Consideration should be given to the implications of these basic limitations in using the data.

In addition to these general qualifications are the special problems of comparability that arise in relation to age statistics in particular. Age distributions of population are known to suffer from certain deficiencies that have their origin in irregularities in age reporting. Although some of the irregularities tend to be obscured or eliminated when data are tabulated in five-year age groups rather than by single years, precision still continues to be affected, though the degree of distortion is not always readily seen.

Another factor limiting comparability is the age classification employed by the various countries or areas. Age may be based on the year of birth rather than the age at last birthday, in other words, calculated using the day, month and year of birth. Distributions based only on the year of birth are footnoted when known.

The absence of frequencies in the unknown age group does not necessarily indicate completely accurate reporting and tabulation of the age item. The unknowns may have been eliminated by assigning ages to them before tabulation, or by proportionately distributing the unknown category across the age groups after tabulation.

As noted in connection with table 5, intercensal estimates of total population are usually revised to accord with the results of a census of population if inexplicable discontinuities appear to exist. Postcensal age-sex distributions, however, are less likely to be revised in this way. When it is known that a total population estimate for a given year has been revised and the corresponding age distribution has not been, the age distribution is shown as provisional. Distributions of this type should be used with caution when studying trends over a period of years, though their utility for studying age structure for the specified year is probably unimpaired.

The comparability of data by urban/rural residence is affected by the national definitions of urban and rural used in tabulating these data. When known, the definitions of urban used in national population censuses are presented at the end of the technical notes for table 6. As discussed in detail in the technical notes for table 6, these definitions vary considerably from one country or area to another.

Earlier data: Population by age, sex and urban/rural residence has been shown in previous issues of the *Demographic Yearbook*. For more information on specific topics, and years for which data are reported, readers should consult the Historical Index. In addition, population by single years of age, sex and urban/rural residence are shown in the *Demographic Yearbook* Special Census Topics table 1 available online at http://unstats.un.org/unsd/demographic/products/dyb/dybcens.htm.

Tableau 7

Le tableau 7 présente les données les plus récentes dont on dispose sur la population selon l'âge, le sexe et le lieu de résidence (zone urbaine ou rurale).

Description des variables : les données de ce tableau proviennent de recensements de la population ou correspondent à des estimations fondées, dans certains cas, sur des enquêtes par sondage. Sauf indication contraire, elles se rapportent à la population de fait.

La date du recensement ou de l'estimation figure dans la colonne de gauche du tableau. En général, les estimations se rapportent au milieu de l'année (1er juillet).

L'âge désigne l'âge au dernier anniversaire, c'est-à-dire la différence entre la date de naissance et la date de référence de la répartition par âge exprimée en années solaires révolues. La classification par âge utilisée dans ce tableau est la suivante : moins d'un an, 1 à 4 ans, groupes quinquennaux jusqu'à 95-99 ans et 100 ans ou plus.

Les statistiques portent sur une année, qui correspond à celle pour laquelle on dispose des statistiques les plus récentes. Toutefois, si l'on dispose de répartitions plus complètes pour des années antérieures, les statistiques sont alors présentées pour les deux années.

La classification par zones urbaines et rurales de la population selon l'âge et le sexe est celle qui est communiquée par chaque pays ou zone ; on part du principe qu'elle repose sur les définitions de la population urbaine utilisées pour les recensements de la population nationaux telles qu'elles sont reproduites à la fin des notes techniques du tableau 6.

Les estimations de la population selon l'âge et le sexe qui figurent dans ce tableau ne concernent que les pays ou zones pour lesquels les estimations sont fondées sur les résultats d'une enquête par sondage ou ont été établies par la méthode des composantes à partir des résultats d'un recensement de la population ou d'une enquête par sondage. Les répartitions par âge et par sexe obtenues en appliquant à l'estimation de la population totale les pourcentages enregistrés pour les divers groupes d'âge pour chaque sexe lors d'un recensement ou d'une enquête par sondage n'ont pas été reproduites dans ce tableau.

Fiabilité des données : les estimations considérées comme moins sûres sont indiquées en italique plutôt qu'en caractères romains. On n'a pas tenu compte des inexactitudes dans les déclarations d'âge, dont la méthode d'évaluation est exposée à la section 3.1.3 des Notes techniques. Cependant, l'index de Whipple présenté au tableau 1 c) du volume 1 de l'Annuaire démographique, qui est consacré aux recensements et porte sur les caractéristiques de la population, fournit une évaluation de l'exactitude des déclarations d'âge faites à l'occasion des recensements effectués entre 1985 et 2003 dans 145 pays.

Insuffisance des données : les statistiques de la population selon l'âge et le sexe appellent les mêmes réserves que celles qui ont été formulées aux sections 3 et 3.1.3 des Notes techniques à propos des statistiques de la population en général et des répartitions par âge en particulier.

La comparabilité des statistiques de la population selon l'âge et le sexe pâtit du manque d'uniformité dans la définition de la population totale (voir la section 3 des Notes techniques) et des lacunes des dénombrements. L'influence de ces deux facteurs varie selon les groupes d'âge. Ainsi, le dénombrement des enfants de moins d'un an et des jeunes enfants comporte souvent plus de lacunes que celui des personnes plus âgées. De même, le fait que certains groupes de personnes appartenant souvent à des groupes d'âge déterminés, par exemple les militaires, ne soient pas pris en compte dans la population totale peut influer sensiblement sur la structure par âge et sur la comparabilité des données avec celles d'autres ~~s ou zones. Il conviendra de tenir compte de ces facteurs fondamentaux lorsque l'on utilisera les ~~ du tableau.

~~és d'ordre général, la comparabilité pose des problèmes particuliers lorsqu'il s'agit des ~~ les répartitions de la population selon l'âge présentent certaines imperfections ~~clarations d'âge. Certaines de ces anomalies ont tendance à s'estomper ou à ~~se les données par groupes d'âge quinquennaux et non par années d'âge, mais ~~bsiste, même s'il n'est pas toujours facile de voir à quel point il y a distorsion.

~~rabilité dépend également de la classification par âge employée dans les divers ~~tenu peut être défini par date exacte (jour, mois et année) de naissance ou par celle

152

du dernier anniversaire. Lorsqu'elles étaient connues, les répartitions établies seulement d'après l'année de la naissance ont été signalées en note à la fin du tableau.

Si aucun nombre ne figure dans la rangée réservée aux âges inconnus, cela ne signifie pas nécessairement que les déclarations d'âge et l'exploitation des données par âge aient été tout à fait exactes. C'est souvent une indication que l'on a attribué un âge aux personnes d'âge inconnu avant l'exploitation des données ou qu'elles ont été réparties proportionnellement entre les différents groupes après cette opération.

Comme on l'a indiqué à propos du tableau 5, les estimations intercensitaires de la population totale sont d'ordinaire rectifiées d'après les résultats des recensements de population si l'on constate des discontinuités inexplicables. Les données postcensitaires concernant la répartition de la population par âge et par sexe ont toutefois moins de chance d'être rectifiées de cette manière. Lorsque l'on savait qu'une estimation de la population totale pour une année donnée avait été rectifiée sans qu'il en soit de même pour la répartition par âge correspondante, cette dernière a été indiquée comme ayant un caractère provisoire. Les répartitions de ce type doivent être utilisées avec prudence lorsque l'on étudie les tendances sur un certain nombre d'années, quoique leur utilité pour l'étude de la structure par âge de la population pour l'année visée reste probablement entière.

La comparabilité des données selon le lieu de résidence (zone urbaine ou rurale) peut être limitée par les définitions nationales des termes « urbain » et « rural » utilisées pour la mise en tableaux de ces données. Les définitions du terme « urbain » utilisées pour les recensements nationaux de population ont été présentées à la fin des notes techniques du tableau 6 lorsqu'elles étaient connues. Comme on l'a précisé dans les notes techniques relatives au tableau 6, ces définitions varient considérablement d'un pays ou d'une zone à l'autre.

Données publiées antérieurement : des statistiques concernant la population selon l'âge, le sexe et le lieu de résidence (zone urbaine ou rurale) ont été présentées dans des éditions antérieures de l'*Annuaire démographique*. Pour plus de précisions concernant les années et les sujets pour lesquels des données ont été publiées, se reporter à l'index historique.

7. Population by age, sex and urban/rural residence: latest available year, 1997 - 2006
Population selon l'âge, le sexe et la résidence, urbaine/rurale: dernière année disponible, 1997 - 2006

Continent, country or area, date, code and age (in years) / Continent, pays ou zone, date, code et âge (en années)	Total			Urban - Urbaine			Rural - Rurale		
	Both sexes Les deux sexes	Male Masculin	Female Féminin	Both sexes Les deux sexes	Male Masculin	Female Féminin	Both sexes Les deux sexes	Male Masculin	Female Féminin
AFRICA - AFRIQUE									
Algeria - Algérie									
1 VII 2003 (ESDJ)									
Total	31 847 995	16 090 568	15 757 427	...	...	...	...	...	...
0	604 019	308 412	295 607	...	...	...	...	...	...
1 - 4	2 310 513	1 180 730	1 129 783	...	...	...	...	...	...
5 - 9	3 224 819	1 647 090	1 577 729	...	...	...	...	...	...
10 - 14	3 642 440	1 856 114	1 786 326	...	...	...	...	...	...
15 - 19	3 808 498	1 939 408	1 869 089	...	...	...	...	...	...
20 - 24	3 522 547	1 791 140	1 731 407	...	...	...	...	...	...
25 - 29	2 959 388	1 493 925	1 465 463	...	...	...	...	...	...
30 - 34	2 508 416	1 259 600	1 248 816	...	...	...	...	...	...
35 - 39	2 102 178	1 056 627	1 045 551	...	...	...	...	...	...
40 - 44	1 680 817	845 183	835 634	...	...	...	...	...	...
45 - 49	1 378 726	694 140	684 586	...	...	...	...	...	...
50 - 54	1 081 550	545 636	535 914	...	...	...	...	...	...
55 - 59	776 901	382 388	394 513	...	...	...	...	...	...
60 - 64	659 350	320 650	338 700	...	...	...	...	...	...
65 - 69	591 984	286 760	305 224	...	...	...	...	...	...
70 - 74	452 969	219 670	233 299	...	...	...	...	...	...
75 - 79	282 819	137 992	144 827	...	...	...	...	...	...
80 +	260 063	125 104	134 959	...	...	...	...	...	...
Benin - Bénin									
11 II 2002 (CDJC)									
Total	6 769 914	3 284 119	3 485 795	2 630 133	1 280 418	1 349 715	4 139 781	2 003 701	2 136 080
0	235 342	118 243	117 099	82 945	41 797	41 148	152 397	76 446	75 951
1 - 4	939 907	475 297	464 610	309 993	157 189	152 804	629 914	318 108	311 806
5 - 9	1 155 377	589 653	565 724	380 207	188 422	191 785	775 170	401 231	373 939
10 - 14	838 749	438 376	400 373	332 753	162 989	169 764	505 996	275 387	230 609
15 - 19	653 251	321 984	331 267	294 811	144 462	150 349	358 440	177 522	180 918
20 - 24	563 947	243 515	320 432	262 496	123 275	139 221	301 451	120 240	181 211
25 - 29	532 056	228 090	303 966	232 948	107 420	125 528	299 108	120 670	178 438
30 - 34	414 166	192 429	221 737	180 416	88 668	91 748	233 750	103 761	129 989
35 - 39	340 632	157 551	183 081	143 773	69 970	73 803	196 859	87 581	109 278
40 - 44	264 488	125 792	138 696	109 427	54 554	54 873	155 061	71 238	83 823
45 - 49	196 056	94 805	101 251	81 020	40 280	40 740	115 036	54 525	60 511
50 - 54	167 901	81 461	86 440	63 992	31 615	32 377	103 909	49 846	54 063
55 - 59	93 493	46 214	47 279	36 952	18 405	18 547	56 541	27 809	28 732
60 - 64	116 796	53 543	63 253	38 629	17 488	21 141	78 167	36 055	42 112
65 - 69	63 847	28 630	35 217	22 857	10 048	12 809	40 990	18 582	22 408
70 - 74	71 231	32 523	38 708	22 048	9 550	12 498	49 183	22 973	26 210
75 - 79	32 158	14 609	17 549	10 617	4 473	6 144	21 541	10 136	11 405
80 - 84	41 705	18 397	23 308	11 461	4 501	6 960	30 244	13 896	16 348
85 - 89	13 113	6 037	7 076	3 860	1 497	2 363	9 253	4 540	4 713
90 - 94	12 256	5 945	6 311	3 413	1 457	1 956	8 843	4 488	4 355
95 +	23 098	10 753	12 345	5 317	2 201	3 116	17 781	8 552	9 229
Unknown - Inconnu	345	272	73	198	157	41	147	115	32
Botswana[1]									
1 VII 2004 (ESDF)									
Total	1 711 334	828 082	883 252	393 528	191 287	202 241	1 317 806	636 795	681 011
0 - 4	...	...	...	39 462	19 821	19 641	142 574	71 938	70 636
0	40 211	20 179	20 032	...	...	...	...	...	...
1 - 4	182 036	91 759	90 277	...	...	...	...	...	...
5 - 9	209 001	105 382	103 619	36 523	17 780	18 743	172 478	87 602	84 876
10 - 14	206 554	104 108	102 446	35 391	16 470	18 921	171 163	87 638	83 525
15 - 19	200 428	100 765	99 663	42 174	18 910	23 264	158 254	81 855	76 399
20 - 24	184 195	92 070	92 125	58 457	28 634	29 823	125 738	63 436	62 302
25 - 29	160 484	78 938	81 546	54 633	26 777	27 856	105 851	52 161	53 690
30 - 34	124 469	61 673	62 796	41 938	21 392	20 546	82 531	40 281	42 250
35 - 39	88 744	42 494	46 250	27 627	14 270	13 357	61 117	28 224	32 893
40 - 44	68 717	28 867	39 850	19 497	9 029	10 468	49 220	19 838	29 382
45 - 49	59 897	23 659	36 238	14 618	6 738	7 880	45 279	16 921	28 358
50 - 54	45 006	18 356	26 650	9 248	4 692	4 556	35 758	13 664	22 094
55 - 59	33 955	14 131	19 824	5 674	2 896	2 778	28 281	11 235	17 046
60 - 64	29 417	12 772	16 645	3 332	1 711	1 621	26 085	11 061	15 024
65 - 69	24 103	10 638	13 465	1 995	972	1 023	22 108	9 666	12 442

Continent, country or area, date, code and age (in years) Continent, pays ou zone, date, code et âge (en années)	Total			Urban - Urbaine			Rural - Rurale		
	Both sexes Les deux sexes	Male Masculin	Female Féminin	Both sexes Les deux sexes	Male Masculin	Female Féminin	Both sexes Les deux sexes	Male Masculin	Female Féminin
AFRICA - AFRIQUE									
Botswana[1]									
1 VII 2004 (ESDF)									
70 - 74	16 916	7 281	9 635	1 066	469	597	15 850	6 812	9 038
75 + ...	37 201	15 010	22 191	1 893	726	1 167	35 308	14 284	21 024
Burkina Faso									
1 VII 2005 (ESDJ)									
Total..................	12 802 282	6 182 079	6 620 203	...	...	...	...	...	...
0 - 4	2 510 678	1 251 348	1 259 330	...	...	...	...	...	...
5 - 9	2 161 350	1 098 299	1 063 051	...	...	...	...	...	...
10 - 14	1 681 117	865 540	815 577	...	...	...	...	...	...
15 - 19	1 332 664	651 425	681 239	...	...	...	...	...	...
20 - 24	959 180	424 059	535 121	...	...	...	...	...	...
25 - 29	830 284	357 298	472 986	...	...	...	...	...	...
30 - 34	679 849	300 735	379 114	...	...	...	...	...	...
40 - 44	577 757	255 271	322 486	...	...	...	...	...	...
45 - 49	453 009	205 521	247 488	...	...	...	...	...	...
50 - 54	387 808	179 647	208 161	...	...	...	...	...	...
55 - 59	316 611	148 463	168 148	...	...	...	...	...	...
60 - 64	270 079	130 724	139 355	...	...	...	...	...	...
65 - 69	215 896	105 703	110 193	...	...	...	...	...	...
70 - 74	169 261	84 144	85 117	...	...	...	...	...	...
75 - 79	125 232	61 177	64 055	...	...	...	...	...	...
80 - 84	75 746	37 813	37 933	...	...	...	...	...	...
85 + ...	55 761	24 912	30 849	...	...	...	...	...	...
Cape Verde - Cap-Vert									
1 VII 2003 (ESDF)									
Total..................	460 968	223 254	237 715	257 412	125 652	131 759	203 556	97 600	105 956
0 - 4	58 940	30 004	28 936	30 116	15 352	14 765	28 823	14 652	14 171
5 - 9	61 218	30 867	30 351	30 927	15 643	15 284	30 291	15 224	15 067
10 - 14	64 803	32 445	32 358	34 166	16 918	17 248	30 636	15 526	15 110
15 - 19	57 898	28 923	28 975	33 909	16 551	17 358	23 990	12 372	11 618
20 - 24	42 677	21 383	21 294	26 883	13 427	13 456	15 794	7 956	7 838
25 - 29	31 691	15 870	15 821	20 027	9 970	10 057	11 664	5 901	5 763
30 - 34	27 198	13 321	13 877	16 627	8 322	8 306	10 570	4 999	5 571
35 - 39	26 745	12 770	13 975	16 748	8 330	8 419	9 996	4 440	5 556
40 - 44	22 729	10 461	12 268	13 844	6 826	7 018	8 886	3 635	5 251
45 - 49	16 084	6 733	9 351	9 359	4 438	4 921	6 726	2 296	4 430
50 - 54	9 378	3 674	5 704	5 496	2 386	3 110	3 882	1 288	2 594
55 - 59	5 466	2 224	3 242	2 921	1 271	1 651	2 545	953	1 592
60 - 64	7 569	2 919	4 650	3 580	1 404	2 176	3 989	1 515	2 474
65 - 69	9 285	3 660	5 625	4 224	1 629	2 595	5 062	2 032	3 030
70 - 74	7 654	3 244	4 410	3 316	1 270	2 046	4 338	1 974	2 364
75 - 79	5 041	2 183	2 858	2 264	853	1 410	2 778	1 330	1 448
80 + ...	6 593	2 573	4 020	3 005	1 064	1 941	3 589	1 510	2 079
1 VII 2006 (ESDF)									
Total..................	483 090	233 729	249 361	...	...	...	...	...	...
0 - 4	58 400	29 324	29 076	...	...	...	...	...	...
5 - 9	57 530	28 927	28 603	...	...	...	...	...	...
10 - 14	62 164	31 160	31 004	...	...	...	...	...	...
15 - 19	63 275	31 560	31 715	...	...	...	...	...	...
20 - 24	50 262	24 985	25 277	...	...	...	...	...	...
25 - 29	36 543	18 195	18 348	...	...	...	...	...	...
30 - 34	28 097	13 842	14 255	...	...	...	...	...	...
35 - 39	26 822	12 828	13 994	...	...	...	...	...	...
40 - 44	25 501	12 061	13 440	...	...	...	...	...	...
45 - 49	19 975	8 914	11 061	...	...	...	...	...	...
50 - 54	13 463	5 468	7 995	...	...	...	...	...	...
55 - 59	6 988	2 840	4 148	...	...	...	...	...	...
60 - 64	5 701	2 250	3 451	...	...	...	...	...	...
65 - 69	8 752	3 397	5 355	...	...	...	...	...	...
70 - 74	8 002	3 239	4 763	...	...	...	...	...	...
75 - 79	6 108	2 580	3 528	...	...	...	...	...	...
80 + ...	5 507	2 159	3 348	...	...	...	...	...	...

7. Population by age, sex and urban/rural residence: latest available year, 1997 - 2006
Population selon l'âge, le sexe et la résidence, urbaine/rurale: dernière année disponible, 1997 - 2006 (continued - suite)

Continent, country or area, date, code and age (in years) / Continent, pays ou zone, date, code et âge (en années)	Total			Urban - Urbaine			Rural - Rurale		
	Both sexes Les deux sexes	Male Masculin	Female Féminin	Both sexes Les deux sexes	Male Masculin	Female Féminin	Both sexes Les deux sexes	Male Masculin	Female Féminin
AFRICA - AFRIQUE									
Congo									
1 VII 2004 (ESDF)									
Total.....................	3 231 326	...	...	...	...	...	...	...	...
0 - 4.....................	544 478	...	...	...	...	...	...	...	...
5 - 9.....................	484 376	...	...	...	...	...	...	...	...
10 - 14...................	414 902	...	...	...	...	...	...	...	...
15 - 19...................	357 708	...	...	...	...	...	...	...	...
20 - 24...................	291 466	...	...	...	...	...	...	...	...
25 - 29...................	231 040	...	...	...	...	...	...	...	...
30 - 34...................	171 583	...	...	...	...	...	...	...	...
35 - 39...................	142 178	...	...	...	...	...	...	...	...
40 - 44...................	130 546	...	...	...	...	...	...	...	...
45 - 49...................	116 005	...	...	...	...	...	...	...	...
50 - 54...................	95 970	...	...	...	...	...	...	...	...
55 - 59...................	80 783	...	...	...	...	...	...	...	...
60 - 64...................	66 565	...	...	...	...	...	...	...	...
65 - 69...................	48 793	...	...	...	...	...	...	...	...
70 +.....................	54 933	...	...	...	...	...	...	...	...
Egypt - Égypte									
1 VII 2000 (ESDF)									
Total.....................	63 976 000	32 695 000	31 281 000	...	...	...	...	...	...
0 - 4.....................	7 394 000	3 783 000	3 611 000	...	...	...	...	...	...
5 - 9.....................	8 225 000	4 245 000	3 980 000	...	...	...	...	...	...
10 - 14...................	8 481 000	4 392 000	4 089 000	...	...	...	...	...	...
15 - 19...................	7 445 000	3 882 000	3 563 000	...	...	...	...	...	...
20 - 24...................	5 474 000	2 848 000	2 626 000	...	...	...	...	...	...
25 - 29...................	4 714 000	2 266 000	2 448 000	...	...	...	...	...	...
30 - 34...................	4 293 000	2 149 000	2 144 000	...	...	...	...	...	...
35 - 39...................	4 164 000	2 064 000	2 100 000	...	...	...	...	...	...
40 - 44...................	3 422 000	1 740 000	1 682 000	...	...	...	...	...	...
45 - 49...................	2 909 000	1 516 000	1 393 000	...	...	...	...	...	...
50 - 54...................	2 180 000	1 071 000	1 109 000	...	...	...	...	...	...
55 - 59...................	1 593 000	835 000	758 000	...	...	...	...	...	...
60 - 64...................	1 510 000	761 000	749 000	...	...	...	...	...	...
65 - 69...................	1 003 000	546 000	457 000	...	...	...	...	...	...
70 - 74...................	667 000	339 000	328 000	...	...	...	...	...	...
75 +.....................	502 000	258 000	244 000	...	...	...	...	...	...
Ethiopia - Éthiopie[2]									
1 VII 2004 (ESDF)									
Total.....................	71 066 000	35 618 000	35 448 000	11 199 000	5 568 000	5 631 000	59 867 000	30 050 000	29 817 000
0 - 4.....................	11 917 056	6 014 178	5 902 878	1 393 080	725 408	667 672	10 524 357	5 289 011	5 235 347
5 - 9.....................	10 421 979	5 263 051	5 158 928	1 326 399	673 204	653 194	9 095 835	4 590 015	4 505 820
10 - 14...................	8 339 406	4 231 901	4 107 506	1 211 825	601 515	610 310	7 127 670	3 630 453	3 497 217
15 - 19...................	7 711 167	3 915 017	3 796 150	1 306 124	633 484	672 639	6 404 983	3 281 509	3 123 475
20 - 24...................	6 758 895	3 431 134	3 327 761	1 285 452	625 694	659 757	5 473 275	2 805 340	2 667 935
25 - 29...................	5 671 553	2 854 595	2 816 959	1 118 289	551 599	566 690	4 553 085	2 302 877	2 250 208
30 - 34...................	4 561 471	2 249 158	2 312 313	893 161	448 377	444 784	3 668 161	1 800 673	1 867 489
35 - 39...................	3 705 298	1 797 673	1 907 625	704 491	353 537	350 954	3 000 700	1 444 054	1 556 646
40 - 44...................	2 936 161	1 395 857	1 540 304	516 131	255 593	260 538	2 419 980	1 140 222	1 279 758
45 - 49...................	2 390 190	1 140 061	1 250 128	400 411	199 348	201 063	1 989 754	940 690	1 049 064
50 - 54...................	1 940 461	948 128	992 333	311 877	156 709	155 168	1 628 576	791 409	837 166
55 - 59...................	1 533 568	759 770	773 797	239 310	118 269	121 041	1 294 259	641 502	652 757
60 - 64...................	1 158 467	583 393	575 075	179 619	85 210	94 409	978 853	498 189	480 664
65 - 69...................	852 130	432 577	419 552	133 357	61 337	72 020	718 777	371 247	347 529
70 - 74...................	579 410	295 965	283 445	89 239	39 851	49 388	490 176	256 121	234 055
75 +.....................	588 788	305 542	283 246	90 236	38 864	51 372	498 558	266 687	231 871
Ghana									
26 III 2000 (CDFC)									
Total.....................	18 912 079	9 357 382	9 554 697	8 274 270	4 043 830	4 230 440	10 637 809	5 313 552	5 324 257
0........................	525 258	262 041	263 217	196 042	98 044	97 998	329 216	163 997	165 219
1 - 4.....................	2 244 163	1 117 729	1 126 434	837 690	415 237	422 453	1 406 473	702 492	703 981
5 - 9.....................	2 775 206	1 390 652	1 384 554	1 053 432	517 610	535 822	1 721 774	873 042	848 732
10 - 14...................	2 262 216	1 151 131	1 111 085	963 577	461 218	502 359	1 298 639	689 913	608 726
15 - 19...................	1 883 753	961 162	922 591	918 094	441 479	476 615	965 659	519 683	445 976
20 - 24...................	1 600 820	763 051	837 769	836 838	407 200	429 638	763 982	355 851	408 131

156

Continent, country or area, date, code and age (in years) / Continent, pays ou zone, date, code et âge (en années)	Total			Urban - Urbaine			Rural - Rurale		
	Both sexes Les deux sexes	Male Masculin	Female Féminin	Both sexes Les deux sexes	Male Masculin	Female Féminin	Both sexes Les deux sexes	Male Masculin	Female Féminin
AFRICA - AFRIQUE									
Ghana									
26 III 2000 (CDFC)									
25 - 29	1 487 299	695 494	791 805	747 897	358 913	388 984	739 402	336 581	402 821
30 - 34	1 206 809	566 439	640 370	582 893	279 843	303 050	623 916	286 596	337 320
35 - 39	1 029 765	490 864	538 901	485 638	231 910	253 728	544 127	258 954	285 173
40 - 44	886 931	443 284	443 647	403 917	201 666	202 251	483 014	241 618	241 396
45 - 49	720 357	377 315	343 042	318 875	167 117	151 758	401 482	210 198	191 284
50 - 54	568 369	279 950	288 419	240 038	120 107	119 931	328 331	159 843	168 488
55 - 59	355 842	182 843	172 999	154 952	80 607	74 345	200 890	102 236	98 654
60 - 64	366 351	177 347	189 004	142 687	70 401	72 286	223 664	106 946	116 718
65 - 69	258 709	129 090	129 619	103 807	51 472	52 335	154 902	77 618	77 284
70 - 74	225 158	106 513	118 645	83 860	38 523	45 337	141 298	67 990	73 308
75 - 79	144 830	74 268	70 562	56 031	27 696	28 335	88 799	46 572	42 227
80 - 84	140 847	66 941	73 906	52 469	24 266	28 203	88 378	42 675	45 703
85 - 89	107 558	58 254	49 304	46 202	25 229	20 973	61 356	33 025	28 331
90 - 94	57 242	28 258	28 984	22 228	10 699	11 529	35 014	17 559	17 455
95 + ...	64 596	34 756	29 840	27 103	14 593	12 510	37 493	20 163	17 330
Kenya									
1 VII 2005 (ESDF)									
Total....................	35 267 222	17 457 906	17 809 316	6 213 505	3 688 113	2 525 392	29 053 718	13 769 794	15 283 924
0 - 4....................	6 238 991	3 150 182	3 088 809	982 463	542 222	440 241	5 256 528	2 607 960	2 648 568
5 - 9....................	4 694 561	2 367 882	2 326 679	634 554	347 165	287 388	4 060 007	2 020 717	2 039 291
10 - 14	3 973 404	2 001 411	1 971 993	471 546	262 014	209 532	3 501 858	1 739 397	1 762 461
15 - 19	4 082 140	2 061 657	2 020 483	631 251	340 802	290 450	3 450 889	1 720 855	1 730 033
20 - 24	3 627 797	1 833 154	1 794 643	910 302	537 287	373 015	2 717 495	1 295 867	1 421 628
25 - 29	2 953 347	1 398 489	1 554 858	812 771	480 022	332 749	2 140 576	918 467	1 222 109
30 - 34	2 387 831	1 119 233	1 268 598	602 678	380 498	222 181	1 785 153	738 735	1 046 417
35 - 39	1 778 184	864 349	913 835	391 067	266 270	124 797	1 387 117	598 079	789 038
40 - 44	1 394 011	685 786	708 225	275 799	191 704	84 096	1 118 212	494 082	624 129
45 - 49	1 038 421	507 834	530 587	177 566	125 206	52 361	860 855	382 628	478 226
50 - 54	829 200	403 131	426 069	122 953	86 594	36 359	706 247	316 537	389 710
55 - 59	681 227	329 709	351 518	76 409	52 171	24 238	604 818	277 538	327 280
60 - 64	546 365	262 036	284 329	50 927	32 721	18 206	495 438	229 315	266 123
65 - 69	420 546	193 429	227 117	30 973	19 350	11 623	389 573	174 079	215 494
70 - 74	300 941	136 132	164 809	21 116	12 614	8 502	279 825	123 518	156 307
75 + ...	320 257	143 493	176 764	21 129	11 474	9 655	299 128	132 019	167 109
Lesotho									
1 VII 2001 (SSDJ)									
Total....................	2 157 537	1 065 484	1 092 053	288 895	131 861	157 034	1 868 642	933 623	935 019
0....................	45 867	24 441	21 426	5 590	3 177	2 413	40 277	21 264	19 013
1 - 4....................	184 467	92 420	92 047	21 097	10 832	10 265	163 370	81 588	81 782
5 - 9....................	250 417	127 720	122 697	27 655	13 408	14 247	222 762	114 312	108 450
10 - 14	280 429	141 486	138 943	29 492	14 094	15 398	250 937	127 392	123 545
15 - 19	286 404	145 591	140 813	35 686	14 075	21 611	250 719	131 517	119 202
20 - 24	225 779	116 163	109 616	35 176	14 235	20 941	190 603	101 928	88 675
25 - 29	159 700	79 705	79 995	30 051	12 477	17 574	129 648	67 227	62 421
30 - 34	114 507	56 175	58 332	23 915	11 542	12 373	90 592	44 633	45 959
35 - 39	110 264	55 375	54 889	21 547	11 162	10 385	88 717	44 213	44 504
40 - 44	93 645	43 925	49 720	15 044	7 468	7 576	78 602	36 457	42 145
45 - 49	81 488	41 152	40 336	11 468	5 651	5 817	70 019	35 501	34 518
50 - 54	77 212	33 959	43 253	9 388	3 592	5 796	67 824	30 367	37 457
55 - 59	56 352	28 197	28 155	5 927	2 782	3 145	50 425	25 415	25 010
60 - 64	48 107	21 105	27 002	4 770	1 866	2 904	43 337	19 239	24 098
65 - 69	49 001	21 165	27 836	4 284	1 949	2 335	44 717	19 216	25 501
70 - 74	29 628	11 671	17 957	1 801	843	958	27 828	10 829	16 999
75 + ...	45 242	14 815	30 427	3 208	982	2 226	42 033	13 832	28 201
Unknown - Inconnu	19 028	10 419	8 609	2 796	1 726	1 070	16 232	8 693	7 539
Malawi									
1 IX 1998 (CDFC)									
Total....................	9 933 868	4 867 563	5 066 305	1 435 436	742 839	692 597	8 498 432	4 124 724	4 373 708
0....................	368 325	182 508	185 817	49 018	24 549	24 469	319 307	157 959	161 348
1 - 4....................	1 292 065	641 117	650 948	166 030	83 011	83 019	1 126 035	558 106	567 929
5 - 9....................	1 440 370	714 830	725 540	183 924	90 095	93 829	1 256 446	624 735	631 711
10 - 14	1 232 500	616 445	616 055	180 430	84 521	95 909	1 052 070	531 924	520 146
15 - 19	1 087 936	527 865	560 071	179 240	88 044	91 196	908 696	439 821	468 875

7. Population by age, sex and urban/rural residence: latest available year, 1997 - 2006
Population selon l'âge, le sexe et la résidence, urbaine/rurale: dernière année disponible, 1997 - 2006 (continued - suite)

Continent, country or area, date, code and age (in years) / Continent, pays ou zone, date, code et âge (en années)	Total			Urban - Urbaine			Rural - Rurale		
	Both sexes Les deux sexes	Male Masculin	Female Féminin	Both sexes Les deux sexes	Male Masculin	Female Féminin	Both sexes Les deux sexes	Male Masculin	Female Féminin
AFRICA - AFRIQUE									
Malawi									
1 IX 1998 (CDFC)									
20 - 24	979 060	435 138	543 922	185 677	89 626	96 051	793 383	345 512	447 871
25 - 29	792 465	393 913	398 552	152 217	85 808	66 409	640 248	308 105	332 143
30 - 34	601 241	303 080	298 161	105 241	60 855	44 386	496 000	242 225	253 775
35 - 39	484 827	239 043	245 784	75 067	42 734	32 333	409 760	196 309	213 451
40 - 44	360 709	180 167	180 542	50 294	30 145	20 149	310 415	150 022	160 393
45 - 49	332 756	166 258	166 498	38 650	23 268	15 382	294 106	142 990	151 116
50 - 54	238 846	120 193	118 653	24 745	15 195	9 550	214 101	104 998	109 103
55 - 59	175 226	89 909	85 317	14 921	9 171	5 750	160 305	80 738	79 567
60 - 64	153 084	72 251	80 833	10 405	5 973	4 432	142 679	66 278	76 401
65 - 69	139 320	65 655	73 665	7 818	4 226	3 592	131 502	61 429	70 073
70 - 74	98 049	45 310	52 739	4 936	2 407	2 529	93 113	42 903	50 210
75 - 79	65 485	32 151	33 334	2 936	1 489	1 447	62 549	30 662	31 887
80 - 84	45 632	20 495	25 137	1 968	873	1 095	43 664	19 622	24 042
85 - 89	25 214	11 540	13 674	1 042	463	579	24 172	11 077	13 095
90 - 94	11 167	5 180	5 987	521	227	294	10 646	4 953	5 693
95 +	9 591	4 515	5 076	356	159	197	9 235	4 356	4 879
1 VII 2005 (ESDF)[3]									
Total	12 341 170	6 067 563	6 273 607	1 783 289	...	...	10 557 881	...	...
0	457 583	227 502	230 081	60 897	...	...	396 686	...	...
1 - 4	1 605 175	799 172	806 003	206 265	...	...	1 398 910	...	...
5 - 9	1 789 419	891 057	898 362	228 495	...	...	1 560 924	...	...
10 - 14	1 531 175	768 417	762 758	224 154	...	...	1 307 021	...	...
15 - 19	1 351 579	658 000	693 579	222 676	...	...	1 128 903	...	...
20 - 24	1 216 318	542 413	673 906	230 673	...	...	985 646	...	...
25 - 29	984 505	491 024	493 481	189 104	...	...	795 401	...	...
30 - 34	746 941	377 798	369 143	130 744	...	...	616 197	...	...
35 - 39	602 316	297 974	304 342	93 258	...	...	509 058	...	...
40 - 44	448 121	224 584	223 537	62 482	...	...	385 639	...	...
45 - 49	413 394	207 246	206 148	48 016	...	...	365 378	...	...
50 - 54	296 726	149 824	146 902	30 742	...	...	265 985	...	...
55 - 59	217 689	112 074	105 615	18 537	...	...	199 152	...	...
60 - 64	190 181	90 063	100 118	12 926	...	...	177 255	...	...
65 - 69	173 082	81 841	91 241	9 713	...	...	163 369	...	...
70 - 74	121 809	56 480	65 329	6 132	...	...	115 677	...	...
75 - 79	81 354	40 077	41 277	3 647	...	...	77 707	...	...
80 - 84	56 690	25 548	31 142	2 445	...	...	54 245	...	...
85 - 89	31 324	14 385	16 939	1 295	...	...	30 030	...	...
90 - 94	13 873	6 457	7 416	647	...	...	13 226	...	...
95 +	11 916	5 629	6 287	442	...	...	11 472	...	...
Mali									
1 IV 1998 (CDJC)									
Total	9 709 570	4 804 745	4 904 825	2 614 841	1 309 621	1 305 220	7 094 729	3 495 124	3 599 605
0 - 4	1 664 300	839 795	824 505	394 798	199 839	194 959	1 269 502	639 956	629 546
5 - 9	1 627 268	830 211	797 057	387 621	196 124	191 497	1 239 647	634 087	605 560
10 - 14	1 227 098	637 495	589 603	340 917	170 681	170 236	886 181	466 814	419 367
15 - 19	1 021 750	492 480	529 270	313 002	147 667	165 335	708 748	344 813	363 935
20 - 24	773 917	364 333	409 584	246 230	122 593	123 637	527 687	241 740	285 947
25 - 29	648 030	292 369	355 661	199 937	96 978	102 959	448 093	195 391	252 702
30 - 34	572 134	264 339	307 795	168 907	83 909	84 998	403 227	180 430	222 797
35 - 39	484 352	233 444	250 908	142 538	73 329	69 209	341 814	160 115	181 699
40 - 44	401 782	194 819	206 963	111 861	59 475	52 386	289 921	135 344	154 577
45 - 49	309 015	156 517	152 498	83 404	44 470	38 934	225 611	112 047	113 564
50 - 54	280 669	136 501	144 168	69 208	34 825	34 383	211 461	101 676	109 785
55 - 59	205 322	107 461	97 861	49 697	26 230	23 467	155 625	81 231	74 394
60 - 64	201 703	100 684	101 019	44 471	22 049	22 422	157 232	78 635	78 597
65 - 69	129 879	69 606	60 273	28 324	14 597	13 727	101 555	55 009	46 546
70 - 74	107 360	54 940	52 420	22 374	10 936	11 438	84 986	44 004	40 982
75 +	54 991	29 751	25 240	11 552	5 919	5 633	43 439	23 832	19 607
Mauritania - Mauritanie									
1 VII 2005 (ESDF)									
Total	2 905 727	1 450 418	1 455 309	...	...	...	...	...	...
0 - 4	473 161	242 179	230 982	...	...	...	...	...	...
5 - 9	417 913	214 175	203 738	...	...	...	...	...	...

7. Population by age, sex and urban/rural residence: latest available year, 1997 - 2006
Population selon l'âge, le sexe et la résidence, urbaine/rurale: dernière année disponible, 1997 - 2006 (continued - suite)

Continent, country or area, date, code and age (in years) / Continent, pays ou zone, date, code et âge (en années)	Total Both sexes Les deux sexes	Total Male Masculin	Total Female Féminin	Urban - Urbaine Both sexes Les deux sexes	Urban - Urbaine Male Masculin	Urban - Urbaine Female Féminin	Rural - Rurale Both sexes Les deux sexes	Rural - Rurale Male Masculin	Rural - Rurale Female Féminin
AFRICA - AFRIQUE									
Mauritania - Mauritanie									
1 VII 2005 (ESDF)									
10 - 14	360 193	185 840	174 353	...	...	...	...	...	...
15 - 19	300 592	153 780	146 812	...	...	...	...	...	...
20 - 24	267 559	130 687	136 872	...	...	...	...	...	...
25 - 29	213 382	100 660	112 722	...	...	...	...	...	...
30 - 34	186 169	87 170	98 999	...	...	...	...	...	...
35 - 39	152 901	72 861	80 040	...	...	...	...	...	...
40 - 44	133 205	63 934	69 271	...	...	...	...	...	...
45 - 49	103 483	51 959	51 524	...	...	...	...	...	...
50 - 54	94 773	46 624	48 149	...	...	...	...	...	...
55 - 59	61 455	30 423	31 032	...	...	...	...	...	...
60 - 64	40 130	20 549	19 581	...	...	...	...	...	...
65 - 69	41 849	20 925	20 924	...	...	...	...	...	...
70 - 74	24 539	12 283	12 256	...	...	...	...	...	...
75 +	34 423	16 369	18 054	...	...	...	...	...	...
Mauritius - Maurice									
2 VII 2000 (CDJC)									
Total	1 178 848	583 756	595 092	503 045	247 844	255 201	675 803	335 912	339 891
0	18 915	9 574	9 341	7 127	3 608	3 519	11 788	5 966	5 822
1 - 4	75 388	38 066	37 322	29 620	14 938	14 682	45 768	23 128	22 640
5 - 9	105 189	53 037	52 152	42 660	21 428	21 232	62 529	31 609	30 920
10 - 14	97 740	49 428	48 312	41 020	20 818	20 202	56 720	28 610	28 110
15 - 19	102 088	51 671	50 417	41 369	20 985	20 384	60 719	30 686	30 033
20 - 24	110 892	55 108	55 784	44 167	21 778	22 389	66 725	33 330	33 395
25 - 29	93 797	46 749	47 048	36 979	18 021	18 958	56 818	28 728	28 090
30 - 34	99 515	49 064	49 551	40 103	10 077	20 126	60 412	20 007	20 425
35 - 39	101 946	51 621	50 325	44 743	22 491	22 252	57 203	29 130	28 073
40 - 44	90 406	45 798	44 608	40 283	20 482	19 801	50 123	25 316	24 807
45 - 49	77 931	39 133	38 798	35 122	17 793	17 329	42 809	21 340	21 469
50 - 54	56 939	27 790	29 149	25 928	12 558	13 370	31 011	15 232	15 779
55 - 59	40 491	19 228	21 263	19 033	9 016	10 017	21 458	10 212	11 246
60 - 64	33 097	15 301	17 796	16 474	7 711	8 763	16 623	7 590	9 033
65 - 69	25 768	11 758	14 010	13 159	6 067	7 092	12 609	5 691	6 918
70 - 74	21 694	9 491	12 203	11 050	4 886	6 164	10 644	4 605	6 039
75 - 79	14 910	6 047	8 863	7 697	3 128	4 569	7 213	2 919	4 294
80 - 84	7 132	2 584	4 548	3 713	1 372	2 341	3 419	1 212	2 207
85 - 89	3 498	1 049	2 449	1 916	564	1 352	1 582	485	1 097
90 - 94	1 104	272	832	637	163	474	467	109	358
95 +	289	42	247	173	31	142	116	11	105
Unknown - Inconnu	119	45	74	72	29	43	47	16	31
1 VII 2006 (ESDJ)									
Total	1 252 698	619 243	633 455	...	...	...	...	...	...
0 - 4	94 526	48 063	46 463	...	...	...	...	...	...
5 - 9	98 351	50 040	48 311	...	...	...	...	...	...
10 - 14	106 917	53 960	52 957	...	...	...	...	...	...
15 - 19	101 339	51 333	50 006	...	...	...	...	...	...
20 - 24	97 341	49 199	48 142	...	...	...	...	...	...
25 - 29	113 237	56 466	56 771	...	...	...	...	...	...
30 - 34	94 834	46 965	47 869	...	...	...	...	...	...
35 - 39	95 178	47 521	47 657	...	...	...	...	...	...
40 - 44	103 091	51 671	51 420	...	...	...	...	...	...
45 - 49	89 635	44 985	44 650	...	...	...	...	...	...
50 - 54	76 123	37 770	38 353	...	...	...	...	...	...
55 - 59	60 356	29 177	31 179	...	...	...	...	...	...
60 - 64	38 627	17 793	20 834	...	...	...	...	...	...
65 - 69	29 101	13 068	16 033	...	...	...	...	...	...
70 - 74	22 200	9 547	12 653	...	...	...	...	...	...
75 - 79	15 666	6 223	9 443	...	...	...	...	...	...
80 - 84	10 519	3 873	6 646	...	...	...	...	...	...
85 +	5 657	1 589	4 068	...	...	...	...	...	...
Mayotte									
30 VII 2002 (CDJC)									
Total	160 301	80 281	80 020	...	...	...	...	...	...
0 - 4	26 132	13 303	12 829	...	...	...	...	...	...

Continent, country or area, date, code and age (in years) / Continent, pays ou zone, date, code et âge (en annèes)	Total			Urban - Urbaine			Rural - Rurale		
	Both sexes Les deux sexes	Male Masculin	Female Féminin	Both sexes Les deux sexes	Male Masculin	Female Féminin	Both sexes Les deux sexes	Male Masculin	Female Féminin
AFRICA - AFRIQUE									
Mayotte									
30 VII 2002 (CDJC)									
5 - 9	23 142	11 624	11 518	...	...	...	...	...	...
10 - 14	18 289	9 192	9 097	...	...	...	...	...	...
15 - 19	17 342	8 356	8 986	...	...	...	...	...	...
20 - 24	15 100	6 770	8 330	...	...	...	...	...	...
25 - 29	14 405	6 618	7 787	...	...	...	...	...	...
30 - 34	13 131	6 977	6 154	...	...	...	...	...	...
35 - 39	8 317	4 343	3 974	...	...	...	...	...	...
40 - 44	6 876	3 655	3 221	...	...	...	...	...	...
45 - 49	4 868	2 658	2 210	...	...	...	...	...	...
50 - 54	4 196	2 320	1 876	...	...	...	...	...	...
55 - 59	2 604	1 393	1 211	...	...	...	...	...	...
60 - 64	2 215	1 171	1 044	...	...	...	...	...	...
65 - 69	1 287	710	577	...	...	...	...	...	...
70 - 74	1 218	623	595	...	...	...	...	...	...
75 - 79	492	265	227	...	...	...	...	...	...
80 - 84	376	161	215	...	...	...	...	...	...
85 - 89	137	65	72	...	...	...	...	...	...
90 - 94	95	40	55	...	...	...	...	...	...
95 +	79	37	42	...	...	...	...	...	...
Morocco - Maroc									
1 IX 2004 (CDFC)									
Total	29 680 069	14 640 662	15 039 407	16 339 561	8 022 273	8 317 288	13 340 508	6 618 389	6 722 119
0 - 4	2 924 464	1 488 631	1 435 833	1 465 885	745 267	720 618	1 458 579	743 364	715 215
5 - 9	3 055 158	1 552 440	1 502 718	1 511 682	766 172	745 510	1 543 476	786 268	757 208
10 - 14	3 281 000	1 666 632	1 614 368	1 642 135	828 764	813 371	1 638 865	837 868	800 997
15 - 19	3 148 590	1 564 900	1 583 690	1 636 889	813 086	823 803	1 511 701	751 814	759 887
20 - 24	2 947 700	1 426 174	1 521 526	1 625 648	787 591	838 057	1 322 052	638 583	683 469
25 - 29	2 482 273	1 190 111	1 292 162	1 424 367	673 033	751 334	1 057 906	517 078	540 828
30 - 34	2 203 371	1 054 069	1 149 302	1 318 733	625 462	693 271	884 638	428 607	456 031
35 - 39	1 891 551	897 812	993 739	1 180 871	554 909	625 962	710 680	342 903	367 777
40 - 44	1 860 474	892 083	968 391	1 159 631	557 317	602 314	700 843	334 766	366 077
45 - 49	1 489 679	758 044	731 635	936 838	480 462	456 376	552 841	277 582	275 259
50 - 54	1 227 188	627 433	599 755	737 394	386 568	350 826	489 794	240 865	248 929
55 - 59	759 563	370 969	388 594	437 721	215 386	222 335	321 842	155 583	166 259
60 - 64	740 891	340 722	400 169	399 888	182 093	217 795	341 003	158 629	182 374
65 - 69	535 064	261 046	274 018	289 607	137 352	152 255	245 457	123 694	121 763
70 - 74	503 367	236 107	267 260	259 229	119 385	139 844	244 138	116 722	127 416
75 +	596 301	294 664	301 637	291 761	137 447	154 314	304 540	157 217	147 323
Unknown - Inconnu	33 435	18 825	14 610	21 282	11 979	9 303	12 153	6 846	5 307
Mozambique									
1 VIII 1997 (CDJC)									
Total	15 278 334	7 320 948	7 957 386	4 454 859	2 201 292	2 253 567	10 823 475	5 119 656	5 703 819
0	535 237	263 539	271 698	138 601	68 743	69 858	396 636	194 796	201 840
1 - 4	2 206 319	1 089 667	1 116 652	558 601	277 008	281 593	1 647 718	812 659	835 059
5 - 9	2 225 996	1 112 321	1 113 675	617 241	304 392	312 849	1 608 755	807 929	800 826
10 - 14	1 825 665	947 236	878 429	600 911	301 921	298 990	1 224 754	645 315	579 439
15 - 19	1 628 405	774 327	854 078	564 519	287 073	277 446	1 063 886	487 254	576 632
20 - 24	1 464 727	637 113	827 614	461 071	217 269	243 802	1 003 656	419 844	583 812
25 - 29	1 163 574	509 109	654 465	345 841	161 031	184 810	817 733	348 078	469 655
30 - 34	887 710	410 148	477 562	284 119	137 905	146 214	603 591	272 243	331 348
35 - 39	802 208	373 813	428 395	246 954	126 347	120 607	555 254	247 466	307 788
40 - 44	573 193	270 046	303 147	173 329	90 578	82 751	399 864	179 468	220 396
45 - 49	539 168	257 070	282 098	139 708	72 415	67 293	399 460	184 655	214 805
50 - 54	390 962	178 902	212 060	95 508	48 098	47 410	295 454	130 804	164 650
55 - 59	336 356	162 122	174 234	76 557	39 078	37 479	259 799	123 044	136 755
60 - 64	239 431	114 335	125 096	57 172	27 663	29 509	182 259	86 672	95 587
65 - 69	209 713	100 425	109 288	44 486	20 277	24 209	165 227	80 148	85 079
70 - 74	98 014	47 407	50 607	21 390	9 542	11 848	76 624	37 865	38 759
75 - 79	84 387	41 529	42 858	16 670	7 113	9 557	67 717	34 416	33 301
80 - 84	32 631	15 305	17 326	6 162	2 542	3 620	26 469	12 763	13 706
85 - 89	20 033	9 041	10 992	3 795	1 361	2 434	16 238	7 680	8 558
90 - 94	7 179	3 537	3 642	1 114	430	684	6 065	3 107	2 958
95 +	7 426	3 956	3 470	1 110	506	604	6 316	3 450	2 866

7. Population by age, sex and urban/rural residence: latest available year, 1997 - 2006
Population selon l'âge, le sexe et la résidence, urbaine/rurale: dernière année disponible, 1997 - 2006 (continued - suite)

Continent, country or area, date, code and age (in years) / Continent, pays ou zone, date, code et âge (en années)	Total			Urban - Urbaine			Rural - Rurale		
	Both sexes Les deux sexes	Male Masculin	Female Féminin	Both sexes Les deux sexes	Male Masculin	Female Féminin	Both sexes Les deux sexes	Male Masculin	Female Féminin
AFRICA - AFRIQUE									
Mozambique									
1 VII 2000 (ESDF)									
Total	17 690 584	8 284 793	9 405 791	...	...	...	...	...	...
0 - 4	3 139 293	1 514 640	1 624 653	...	...	...	...	...	...
5 - 9	2 664 689	1 282 460	1 382 229	...	...	...	...	...	...
10 - 14	2 208 552	1 059 016	1 149 536	...	...	...	...	...	...
15 - 19	1 966 758	940 308	1 026 450	...	...	...	...	...	...
20 - 24	1 540 328	743 941	796 387	...	...	...	...	...	...
25 - 29	1 312 794	598 600	714 194	...	...	...	...	...	...
30 - 34	1 023 631	438 932	584 699	...	...	...	...	...	...
35 - 39	858 865	372 869	485 996	...	...	...	...	...	...
40 - 44	745 586	341 179	404 407	...	...	...	...	...	...
45 - 49	621 564	286 675	334 889	...	...	...	...	...	...
50 - 54	496 069	226 219	269 850	...	...	...	...	...	...
55 - 59	388 778	173 800	214 978	...	...	...	...	...	...
60 - 64	289 060	126 794	162 266	...	...	...	...	...	...
65 - 69	201 364	86 207	115 157	...	...	...	...	...	...
70 - 74	124 004	50 747	73 257	...	...	...	...	...	...
75 - 79	66 792	26 277	40 515	...	...	...	...	...	...
80 +	42 457	16 129	26 328	...	...	...	...	...	...
Namibia - Namibie									
27 VIII 2001 (CDFC)									
Total	1 830 330	887 721	942 572	603 612	300 358[4]	303 236[4]	1 226 718	587 363[4]	639 336[4]
0 - 4	241 229	120 044	121 185	67 484	33 494	33 990	173 745	86 550	87 195
0	46 852	23 281	23 571	...	...	...	...	...	...
1 - 4	194 377	96 763	97 614	...	...	...	...	...	...
5 - 9	246 964	121 785	125 179	59 123	28 683	30 440	187 841	93 102	94 739
10 - 14	230 287	113 081	117 206	55 162	25 564	29 598	175 125	87 517	87 608
15 - 19	202 298	99 307	102 991	55 865	25 383	30 482	146 433	73 924	72 509
20 - 24	174 484	86 382	88 102	70 592	34 483	36 109	103 892	51 899	51 993
25 - 29	150 783	74 304	76 479	73 635	37 316	36 319	77 148	36 988	40 160
30 - 34	118 529	57 125	61 404	58 312	29 851	28 461	60 217	27 274	32 943
35 - 39	96 416	45 083	51 333	46 071	23 521	22 550	50 345	21 562	28 783
40 - 44	74 050	34 170	39 880	33 152	16 966	16 186	40 898	17 204	23 694
45 - 49	57 749	26 942	30 807	23 576	12 615	10 961	34 173	14 327	19 846
50 - 54	47 779	21 999	25 780	16 798	9 193	7 605	30 981	12 806	18 175
55 - 59	35 209	16 600	18 609	10 890	5 893	4 997	24 319	10 707	13 612
60 - 64	34 378	15 569	18 809	8 512	4 192	4 320	25 866	11 377	14 489
65 - 69	25 262	11 399	13 863	5 458	2 596	2 862	19 804	8 803	11 001
70 - 74	22 052	9 313	12 739	3 707	1 619	2 088	18 345	7 694	10 651
75 - 79	16 007	6 382	9 625	2 531	1 068	1 463	13 476	5 314	8 162
80 - 84	13 818	5 359	8 459	1 753	680	1 073	12 065	4 679	7 386
85 - 89	5 407	2 033	3 374	973	341	632	4 434	1 692	2 742
90 - 94	2 555	927	1 628	376	152	224	2 179	775	1 404
95 +	2 712	897	1 815	262	111	151	2 450	786	1 664
Unknown - Inconnu	32 325	19 020	13 305	9 362	6 637	2 725	22 963	12 383	10 580
Niger[5]									
1 VII 2006 (ESDJ)									
Total	12 929 300	6 470 600	6 458 700	2 295 300	1 151 700	1 143 600	10 634 000	5 318 900	5 315 100
0 - 4	2 454 500	1 257 600	1 196 900	337 600	170 900	166 700	2 116 900	1 086 700	1 030 200
5 - 9	2 190 400	1 128 900	1 061 500	360 200	183 300	176 900	1 830 200	945 600	884 600
10 - 14	1 731 900	878 700	853 200	355 700	179 800	175 900	1 376 200	698 900	677 300
15 - 19	1 250 800	616 500	634 300	273 100	136 500	136 600	977 700	480 000	497 700
20 - 24	986 400	473 700	512 700	187 300	94 000	93 300	799 100	379 700	419 400
25 - 29	849 900	398 400	451 500	150 500	77 000	79 500	693 400	321 400	372 000
30 - 34	735 700	347 900	387 800	138 100	66 600	71 500	597 600	281 300	316 300
35 - 39	654 600	323 700	330 900	122 100	61 300	60 800	532 500	262 400	270 100
40 - 44	543 400	273 700	269 700	98 900	51 500	47 400	444 500	222 200	222 300
45 - 49	405 800	206 600	199 200	72 900	37 800	35 100	332 900	168 800	164 100
50 - 54	321 700	163 000	158 700	57 400	27 500	29 900	264 300	135 500	128 800
55 - 59	267 500	131 000	136 500	47 200	21 900	25 300	220 300	109 100	111 200
60 - 64	198 100	96 500	101 600	33 500	17 900	15 600	164 600	78 600	86 000
65 - 69	118 100	59 400	58 700	19 600	10 700	8 900	98 500	48 700	49 800
70 - 74	78 700	40 500	38 200	13 200	6 300	6 900	65 500	34 200	31 300

7. Population by age, sex and urban/rural residence: latest available year, 1997 - 2006
Population selon l'âge, le sexe et la résidence, urbaine/rurale: dernière année disponible, 1997 - 2006 (continued - suite)

Continent, country or area, date, code and age (in years) / Continent, pays ou zone, date, code et âge (en annèes)	Total			Urban - Urbaine			Rural - Rurale		
	Both sexes Les deux sexes	Male Masculin	Female Féminin	Both sexes Les deux sexes	Male Masculin	Female Féminin	Both sexes Les deux sexes	Male Masculin	Female Féminin
AFRICA - AFRIQUE									
Niger[5]									
1 VII 2006 (ESDJ)									
75 - 79	54 800	28 400	26 400	9 500	3 300	6 200	45 300	25 100	20 200
80 +	87 000	46 100	40 900	12 500	5 400	7 100	74 500	40 700	33 800
Nigeria - Nigéria[6]									
1 VII 2003 (ESDF)									
Total	126 152 844	63 241 808	62 911 036	...	...	...	...	...	...
0 - 4	22 090 300	11 214 033	10 876 267	...	...	...	...	...	...
5 - 9	18 333 245	9 362 226	8 971 019	...	...	...	...	...	...
10 - 14	15 408 885	7 804 986	7 603 899	...	...	...	...	...	...
15 - 19	12 867 025	6 446 554	6 420 471	...	...	...	...	...	...
20 - 24	10 991 665	5 543 883	5 447 782	...	...	...	...	...	...
25 - 29	9 891 507	4 951 575	4 939 932	...	...	...	...	...	...
30 - 34	8 076 673	3 913 158	4 163 515	...	...	...	...	...	...
35 - 39	6 511 687	3 017 320	3 494 367	...	...	...	...	...	...
40 - 44	5 541 919	2 616 888	2 925 031	...	...	...	...	...	...
45 - 49	4 682 410	2 287 112	2 395 298	...	...	...	...	...	...
50 - 54	3 658 941	1 835 806	1 823 135	...	...	...	...	...	...
55 - 59	2 708 234	1 411 256	1 296 978	...	...	...	...	...	...
60 - 64	1 983 965	1 050 256	933 709	...	...	...	...	...	...
65 - 69	1 357 083	726 454	630 629	...	...	...	...	...	...
70 - 74	950 824	501 708	449 116	...	...	...	...	...	...
75 - 79	612 840	309 402	303 438	...	...	...	...	...	...
80 +	485 641	249 191	236 450	...	...	...	...	...	...
Réunion									
1 VII 2004 (ESDJ)									
Total	768 808	377 607	391 201	...	...	...	...	...	...
0 - 4	71 930	36 411	35 519	...	...	...	...	...	...
5 - 9	65 184	33 594	31 590	...	...	...	...	...	...
10 - 14	70 090	35 753	34 338	...	...	...	...	...	...
15 - 19	69 963	35 471	34 492	...	...	...	...	...	...
20 - 24	63 276	31 776	31 500	...	...	...	...	...	...
25 - 29	51 936	25 236	26 700	...	...	...	...	...	...
30 - 34	54 625	26 227	28 398	...	...	...	...	...	...
35 - 39	64 738	31 385	33 353	...	...	...	...	...	...
40 - 44	60 007	29 454	30 553	...	...	...	...	...	...
45 - 49	48 331	23 682	24 649	...	...	...	...	...	...
50 - 54	39 885	19 654	20 231	...	...	...	...	...	...
55 - 59	29 165	14 336	14 829	...	...	...	...	...	...
60 - 64	23 794	11 430	12 364	...	...	...	...	...	...
65 - 69	19 589	8 961	10 628	...	...	...	...	...	...
70 - 74	13 974	6 085	7 890	...	...	...	...	...	...
75 - 79	10 529	4 259	6 270	...	...	...	...	...	...
80 - 84	7 018	2 469	4 549	...	...	...	...	...	...
85 - 89	2 981	874	2 107	...	...	...	...	...	...
90 +	1 796	554	1 242	...	...	...	...	...	...
Rwanda									
16 VIII 2002 (CDJC)									
Total	8 128 553	3 879 448	4 249 105	1 372 604	727 172	645 432	6 755 949	3 152 276	3 603 673
0	325 221	161 653	163 568	46 968	23 496	23 472	278 253	138 157	140 096
1 - 4	995 010	493 437	501 573	147 083	73 621	73 462	847 927	419 816	428 111
5 - 9	1 141 039	563 351	577 688	157 009	77 648	79 361	984 030	485 703	498 327
10 - 14	1 095 225	536 876	558 349	149 787	71 947	77 840	945 438	464 929	480 509
15 - 19	1 078 839	526 563	552 276	184 874	89 576	95 298	893 965	436 987	456 978
20 - 24	810 681	382 561	428 120	177 151	98 145	79 006	633 530	284 416	349 114
25 - 29	555 509	253 180	302 329	130 102	74 049	56 053	425 407	179 131	246 276
30 - 34	448 439	208 742	239 697	100 840	59 871	40 969	347 599	148 871	198 728
35 - 39	382 636	177 816	204 820	76 430	46 117	30 313	306 206	131 699	174 507
40 - 44	363 067	168 934	194 133	63 795	38 834	24 961	299 272	130 100	169 172
45 - 49	268 262	122 615	145 647	43 450	26 007	17 443	224 812	96 608	128 204
50 - 54	193 382	86 925	106 457	30 845	17 673	13 172	162 537	69 252	93 285
55 - 59	123 868	50 480	73 388	18 782	9 561	9 221	105 086	40 919	64 167
60 - 64	111 809	45 221	66 588	15 483	7 293	8 190	96 326	37 928	58 398
65 - 69	84 928	35 178	49 750	11 333	5 166	6 167	73 595	30 012	43 583
70 - 74	71 020	30 970	40 050	8 790	4 025	4 765	62 230	26 945	35 285

Continent, country or area, date, code and age (in years) / Continent, pays ou zone, date, code et âge (en années)	Total			Urban - Urbaine			Rural - Rurale		
	Both sexes Les deux sexes	Male Masculin	Female Féminin	Both sexes Les deux sexes	Male Masculin	Female Féminin	Both sexes Les deux sexes	Male Masculin	Female Féminin
AFRICA - AFRIQUE									
Rwanda									
16 VIII 2002 (CDJC)									
75 - 79	37 989	16 255	21 734	4 451	1 923	2 528	33 538	14 332	19 206
80 - 84	26 788	12 081	14 707	3 295	1 378	1 917	23 493	10 703	12 790
85 +	14 841	6 610	8 231	2 136	842	1 294	12 705	5 768	6 937
Saint Helena ex. dep. - Sainte-Hélène sans dép.									
8 III 1998 (CDJC)									
Total	4 913	2 481	2 432	...	...	...	...	...	...
0	60	33	27	...	...	...	...	...	...
1 - 4	252	139	113	...	...	...	...	...	...
5 - 9	369	197	172	...	...	...	...	...	...
10 - 14	368	199	169	...	...	...	...	...	...
15 - 19	452	217	235	...	...	...	...	...	...
20 - 24	300	154	146	...	...	...	...	...	...
25 - 29	370	185	185	...	...	...	...	...	...
30 - 34	329	150	179	...	...	...	...	...	...
35 - 39	391	181	210	...	...	...	...	...	...
40 - 44	336	181	155	...	...	...	...	...	...
45 - 49	340	173	167	...	...	...	...	...	...
50 - 54	346	200	146	...	...	...	...	...	...
55 - 59	230	124	106	...	...	...	...	...	...
60 - 64	202	127	75	...	...	...	...	...	...
65 - 69	190	86	104	...	...	...	...	...	...
70 - 74	143	51	92	...	...	...	...	...	...
75 - 79	111	41	70	...	...	...	...	...	...
80 - 84	69	25	44	...	...	...	...	...	...
85 - 89	26	7	19	...	...	...	...	...	...
90 - 94	18	7	11	...	...	...	...	...	...
95 +	1	-	1	...	...	...	...	...	...
Unknown - Inconnu	10	4	6	...	...	...	...	...	...
Saint Helena: Ascension - Sainte-Hélène: Ascension									
8 III 1998 (CDJC)									
Total	712	458	254	...	...	...	...	...	...
0	8	4	4	...	...	...	...	...	...
1 - 4	15	9	6	...	...	...	...	...	...
5 - 9	30	11	19	...	...	...	...	...	...
10 - 14	37	21	16	...	...	...	...	...	...
15 - 19	30	21	9	...	...	...	...	...	...
20 - 24	93	55	38	...	...	...	...	...	...
25 - 29	115	81	34	...	...	...	...	...	...
30 - 34	105	67	38	...	...	...	...	...	...
35 - 39	68	42	26	...	...	...	...	...	...
40 - 44	67	43	24	...	...	...	...	...	...
45 - 49	63	42	21	...	...	...	...	...	...
50 - 54	49	37	12	...	...	...	...	...	...
55 - 59	25	21	4	...	...	...	...	...	...
60 - 64	5	2	3	...	...	...	...	...	...
65 - 69	1	1	-	...	...	...	...	...	...
70 +	1	1	-	...	...	...	...	...	...
Sao Tome and Principe - Sao Tomé-et-Principe									
25 VIII 2001 (CDFC)									
Total	136 554	67 422	69 132	73 907	35 679	38 228	62 647	31 743	30 904
0	4 588	2 299	2 289	2 433	1 221	1 212	2 155	1 078	1 077
1 - 4	16 111	8 149	7 962	8 440	4 325	4 115	7 671	3 824	3 847
5 - 9	18 794	9 587	9 207	9 780	4 972	4 808	9 014	4 615	4 399
10 - 14	18 468	9 416	9 052	9 829	4 883	4 946	8 639	4 533	4 106
15 - 19	17 311	8 663	8 648	9 762	4 701	5 061	7 549	3 962	3 587
20 - 24	13 981	6 870	7 111	7 926	3 783	4 143	6 055	3 087	2 968
25 - 29	9 703	4 795	4 908	5 333	2 564	2 769	4 370	2 231	2 139
30 - 34	7 684	3 700	3 984	4 235	1 960	2 275	3 449	1 740	1 709
35 - 39	6 567	3 050	3 517	3 639	1 632	2 007	2 928	1 418	1 510
40 - 44	5 367	2 465	2 902	3 066	1 413	1 653	2 301	1 052	1 249

Continent, country or area, date, code and age (in years) Continent, pays ou zone, date, code et âge (en années)	Total			Urban - Urbaine			Rural - Rurale		
	Both sexes Les deux sexes	Male Masculin	Female Féminin	Both sexes Les deux sexes	Male Masculin	Female Féminin	Both sexes Les deux sexes	Male Masculin	Female Féminin
AFRICA - AFRIQUE									
Sao Tome and Principe - Sao Tomé-et-Principe 25 VIII 2001 (CDFC)									
45 - 49	3 984	1 864	2 120	2 261	1 026	1 235	1 723	838	885
50 - 54	3 020	1 408	1 612	1 659	758	901	1 361	650	711
55 - 59	2 397	1 119	1 278	1 247	559	688	1 150	560	590
60 - 64	2 710	1 301	1 409	1 288	568	720	1 422	733	689
65 - 69	2 108	1 043	1 065	1 014	482	532	1 094	561	533
70 - 74	1 648	780	868	829	366	463	819	414	405
75 - 79	1 124	513	611	593	251	342	531	262	269
80 - 84	616	262	354	349	140	209	267	122	145
85 +	373	138	235	224	75	149	149	63	86
Senegal - Sénégal 8 XII 2002 (CDJC)									
Total	9 855 338	4 846 119	5 009 219	...	...	...	...	...	...
0 - 9	2 904 741	1 473 605	1 431 136	...	...	...	...	...	...
10 - 19	2 500 075	1 225 258	1 274 817	...	...	...	...	...	...
20 - 29	1 664 387	804 011	860 376	...	...	...	...	...	...
30 - 39	1 080 665	503 549	577 116	...	...	...	...	...	...
40 - 49	728 232	354 177	374 055	...	...	...	...	...	...
50 - 59	448 617	223 087	225 530	...	...	...	...	...	...
60 - 69	291 578	145 123	146 455	...	...	...	...	...	...
70 - 79	168 550	84 775	83 775	...	...	...	...	...	...
80 - 89	50 736	25 408	25 328	...	...	...	...	...	...
90 +	17 757	7 126	10 631	...	...	...	...	...	...
31 XII 2002 (ESDJ)									
Total	9 856 145	4 812 096	5 044 049	4 472 867	2 176 338	2 296 529	5 383 278	2 635 758	2 747 520
0 - 4	1 396 011	725 436	670 575	540 412	282 408	258 004	855 599	443 028	412 571
5 - 9	1 425 971	739 950	686 021	527 762	271 844	255 918	898 209	468 106	430 103
10 - 14	1 289 319	658 358	630 961	557 386	276 522	280 864	731 933	381 836	350 097
15 - 19	1 168 374	558 305	610 069	579 770	273 149	306 621	588 604	285 156	303 448
20 - 24	959 723	446 822	512 901	508 140	237 658	270 482	451 583	209 164	242 419
25 - 29	772 787	350 167	422 620	394 247	184 840	209 407	378 540	165 327	213 213
30 - 34	625 810	279 009	346 801	314 614	145 862	168 752	311 196	133 147	178 049
35 - 39	503 200	220 367	282 833	251 349	113 057	138 292	251 851	107 310	144 541
40 - 44	419 262	196 261	223 001	206 247	100 334	105 913	213 015	95 927	117 088
45 - 49	314 237	155 833	158 404	161 336	80 908	80 428	152 901	74 925	77 976
50 - 54	278 642	134 998	143 644	131 682	65 842	65 840	146 960	69 156	77 804
55 - 59	171 436	85 926	85 510	80 404	39 673	40 731	91 032	46 253	44 779
60 - 64	180 125	85 511	94 614	75 125	35 707	39 418	105 000	49 804	55 196
65 - 69	112 922	58 685	54 237	49 083	23 920	25 163	63 839	34 765	29 074
70 - 74	112 041	53 339	58 702	45 116	21 034	24 082	66 925	32 305	34 620
75 - 79	57 616	31 086	26 530	23 930	12 032	11 898	33 686	19 054	14 632
80 +	68 669	32 043	36 626	26 264	11 548	14 716	42 405	20 495	21 910
Seychelles 1 VII 2005 (ESDF)									
Total	82 852	41 233	41 619	...	...	...	...	...	...
0 - 4	6 861	3 441	3 420	...	...	...	...	...	...
5 - 9	6 399	3 270	3 129	...	...	...	...	...	...
10 - 14	7 191	3 716	3 475	...	...	...	...	...	...
15 - 19	7 280	3 747	3 533	...	...	...	...	...	...
20 - 24	7 180	3 759	3 421	...	...	...	...	...	...
25 - 29	7 091	3 615	3 476	...	...	...	...	...	...
30 - 34	7 133	3 530	3 603	...	...	...	...	...	...
35 - 39	6 787	3 243	3 544	...	...	...	...	...	...
40 - 44	6 257	3 079	3 178	...	...	...	...	...	...
45 - 49	5 807	3 047	2 760	...	...	...	...	...	...
50 - 54	3 334	1 790	1 544	...	...	...	...	...	...
55 - 59	2 902	1 485	1 417	...	...	...	...	...	...
60 - 64	2 019	987	1 032	...	...	...	...	...	...
65 - 69	2 053	858	1 195	...	...	...	...	...	...
70 - 74	1 762	709	1 053	...	...	...	...	...	...
75 - 79	1 300	503	797	...	...	...	...	...	...
80 +	1 496	454	1 042	...	...	...	...	...	...

Continent, country or area, date, code and age (in years) / Continent, pays ou zone, date, code et âge (en années)	Total			Urban - Urbaine			Rural - Rurale		
	Both sexes Les deux sexes	Male Masculin	Female Féminin	Both sexes Les deux sexes	Male Masculin	Female Féminin	Both sexes Les deux sexes	Male Masculin	Female Féminin
AFRICA - AFRIQUE									
Sierra Leone									
1 VII 2003 (ESDF)									
Total	5 280 406	2 606 045	2 674 361	...	...	...	...	...	...
0	205 242	102 685	102 557	...	...	...	...	...	...
1 - 4	657 985	331 968	326 016	...	...	...	...	...	...
5 - 9	794 093	399 695	394 398	...	...	...	...	...	...
10 - 14	516 752	273 918	242 834	...	...	...	...	...	...
15 - 19	513 263	240 312	272 951	...	...	...	...	...	...
20 - 24	408 352	182 703	225 649	...	...	...	...	...	...
25 - 29	423 009	188 100	234 910	...	...	...	...	...	...
30 - 34	329 828	149 713	180 116	...	...	...	...	...	...
35 - 39	297 142	146 203	150 940	...	...	...	...	...	...
40 - 44	220 272	108 870	111 402	...	...	...	...	...	...
45 - 49	193 199	104 586	88 612	...	...	...	...	...	...
50 - 54	155 484	80 832	74 652	...	...	...	...	...	...
55 - 59	111 025	60 805	50 221	...	...	...	...	...	...
60 - 64	116 884	59 762	57 122	...	...	...	...	...	...
65 - 69	84 034	44 224	39 811	...	...	...	...	...	...
70 - 74	67 884	36 953	30 932	...	...	...	...	...	...
75 - 79	50 153	27 772	22 381	...	...	...	...	...	...
80 - 84	38 623	19 711	18 912	...	...	...	...	...	...
85 - 89	27 246	14 469	12 777	...	...	...	...	...	...
90 +	34 069	17 392	16 677	...	...	...	...	...	...
Unknown - Inconnu	35 894	15 402	20 492	...	...	...	...	...	...
Somalia - Somalie									
1 VII 2002 (SSDF)									
Total	6 799 079	3 499 523	3 299 556	2 310 817	1 168 410	1 142 407	4 488 262	2 331 113	2 157 149
0 - 4	1 235 105	634 959	600 146	408 646	206 987	201 659	826 459	427 972	398 487
5 - 9	1 049 189	544 431	504 758	352 471	179 293	173 178	696 718	365 138	331 580
10 - 14	870 180	455 323	414 857	297 807	151 845	145 962	572 373	303 478	268 895
15 - 19	725 723	373 328	352 395	250 718	125 641	125 077	475 005	247 687	227 318
20 - 24	581 690	280 786	300 904	202 030	95 671	106 359	379 660	185 115	194 545
25 - 29	491 651	231 254	260 397	170 250	78 983	91 267	321 401	152 271	169 130
30 - 34	428 269	198 101	230 168	146 024	67 081	78 943	282 245	131 020	151 225
35 - 39	366 113	175 050	191 063	123 698	58 860	64 838	242 415	116 190	126 225
40 - 44	311 989	164 941	147 048	104 080	54 778	49 302	207 909	110 163	97 746
45 - 49	248 939	139 351	109 588	82 971	46 198	36 773	165 968	93 153	72 815
50 - 54	174 517	105 972	68 545	58 869	35 355	23 514	115 648	70 617	45 031
55 - 59	124 841	79 206	45 635	42 868	26 625	16 243	81 973	52 581	29 392
60 - 64	80 530	51 293	29 237	28 988	17 492	11 496	51 542	33 801	17 741
65 - 69	51 554	32 843	18 711	19 396	11 603	7 793	32 158	21 240	10 918
70 - 74	28 997	17 795	11 202	11 675	6 878	4 797	17 322	10 917	6 405
75 - 79	12 860	6 152	6 708	5 828	3 320	2 508	7 032	2 832	4 200
80 +	16 932	8 738	8 194	4 498	1 800	2 698	12 434	6 938	5 496
South Africa - Afrique du Sud[7]									
1 VII 2006 (ESDF)									
Total	47 390 900	23 327 600	24 063 300	...	...	...	...	...	...
0 - 4	5 164 500	2 600 900	2 563 600	...	...	...	...	...	...
5 - 9	5 012 500	2 522 600	2 489 500	...	...	...	...	...	...
10 - 14	5 089 800	2 556 800	2 533 000	...	...	...	...	...	...
15 - 19	4 938 000	2 476 900	2 461 100	...	...	...	...	...	...
20 - 24	4 653 800	2 332 800	2 321 000	...	...	...	...	...	...
25 - 29	4 271 100	2 166 900	2 104 200	...	...	...	...	...	...
30 - 34	3 841 500	1 932 500	1 909 000	...	...	...	...	...	...
35 - 39	2 842 100	1 393 500	1 448 600	...	...	...	...	...	...
40 - 44	2 428 200	1 158 300	1 269 900	...	...	...	...	...	...
45 - 49	2 215 000	1 052 600	1 162 400	...	...	...	...	...	...
50 - 54	1 820 800	855 200	965 600	...	...	...	...	...	...
55 - 59	1 455 100	670 200	784 900	...	...	...	...	...	...
60 - 64	1 269 600	586 500	683 100	...	...	...	...	...	...
65 - 69	974 800	437 000	537 800	...	...	...	...	...	...
70 - 74	672 400	290 500	381 900	...	...	...	...	...	...
75 - 79	405 600	168 200	237 200	...	...	...	...	...	...
80 +	336 400	125 900	210 500	...	...	...	...	...	...

Continent, country or area, date, code and age (in years) / Continent, pays ou zone, date, code et âge (en années)	Total			Urban - Urbaine			Rural - Rurale		
	Both sexes Les deux sexes	Male Masculin	Female Féminin	Both sexes Les deux sexes	Male Masculin	Female Féminin	Both sexes Les deux sexes	Male Masculin	Female Féminin
AFRICA - AFRIQUE									
Swaziland									
11 V 1997 (CDFC)									
Total.....................	929 718	440 154	489 564	214 428	106 256	108 172	715 290	333 898	381 392
0	24 405	12 049	12 356	5 123	2 519	2 604	19 282	9 530	9 752
1 - 4	111 992	55 480	56 512	19 744	9 701	10 043	92 248	45 779	46 469
5 - 9	139 245	68 976	70 269	22 232	10 663	11 569	117 013	58 313	58 700
10 - 14	137 487	68 200	69 287	22 036	9 908	12 128	115 451	58 292	57 159
15 - 19	112 356	54 775	57 581	24 504	10 716	13 788	87 852	44 059	43 793
20 - 24	85 094	38 807	46 287	27 184	12 804	14 380	57 910	26 003	31 907
25 - 29	68 043	30 147	37 896	24 731	12 610	12 121	43 312	17 537	25 775
30 - 34	52 156	21 988	30 168	18 103	9 257	8 846	34 053	12 731	21 322
35 - 39	45 802	19 645	26 157	15 043	7 841	7 202	30 759	11 804	18 955
40 - 44	35 505	16 165	19 340	11 090	6 128	4 962	24 415	10 037	14 378
45 - 49	30 371	14 461	15 910	8 627	5 068	3 559	21 744	9 393	12 351
50 - 54	23 316	10 799	12 517	5 756	3 413	2 343	17 560	7 386	10 174
55 - 59	17 920	8 758	9 162	3 759	2 275	1 484	14 161	6 483	7 678
60 - 64	13 866	6 325	7 541	2 349	1 298	1 051	11 517	5 027	6 490
65 - 69	10 152	4 645	5 507	1 340	710	630	8 812	3 935	4 877
70 - 74	7 301	2 924	4 377	766	343	423	6 535	2 581	3 954
75 - 79	5 269	2 175	3 094	527	256	271	4 742	1 919	2 823
80 - 84	3 085	1 161	1 924	266	110	156	2 819	1 051	1 768
85 - 89	1 765	707	1 058	145	64	81	1 620	643	977
90 - 94	731	264	467	61	25	36	670	239	431
95 + ...	959	371	588	63	34	29	896	337	559
Unknown - Inconnu	2 898	1 332	1 566	979	513	466	1 919	819	1 100
Tunisia - Tunisie									
1 VII 1998 (ESDF)									
Total.....................	9 333 300	4 709 000	4 624 300	...	...	...	...	...	...
0 - 4	978 500	500 700	477 800	...	...	...	...	...	...
5 - 9	1 015 200	519 500	495 700	...	...	...	...	...	...
10 - 14	1 058 900	541 400	517 500	...	...	...	...	...	...
15 - 19	1 006 100	514 400	491 700	...	...	...	...	...	...
20 - 24	898 500	455 600	443 000	...	...	...	...	...	...
25 - 29	795 900	395 900	399 900	...	...	...	...	...	...
30 - 34	714 800	351 200	363 600	...	...	...	...	...	...
35 - 39	621 900	310 300	311 600	...	...	...	...	...	...
40 - 44	512 500	257 400	255 100	...	...	...	...	...	...
45 - 49	384 400	190 800	193 700	...	...	...	...	...	...
50 - 54	291 800	142 200	149 600	...	...	...	...	...	...
55 - 59	266 800	131 200	135 600	...	...	...	...	...	...
60 - 64	255 000	127 100	127 900	...	...	...	...	...	...
65 - 69	208 200	105 500	102 700	...	...	...	...	...	...
70 - 74	145 800	74 200	71 600	...	...	...	...	...	...
75 - 79	94 700	48 500	46 200	...	...	...	...	...	...
80 + ...	84 100	43 000	41 000	...	...	...	...	...	...
Uganda - Ouganda									
12 IX 2002 (CDFC)									
Total.....................	24 442 084	11 929 803	12 512 281	2 999 387	1 449 684	1 549 703	21 442 697	10 480 119	10 962 578
0	1 007 407	505 006	502 401	104 439	52 481	51 958	902 968	452 525	450 443
1 - 4	3 537 016	1 767 120	1 769 896	347 233	172 444	174 789	3 189 783	1 594 676	1 595 107
5 - 9	4 001 052	1 998 157	2 002 895	399 119	193 271	205 848	3 601 933	1 804 886	1 797 047
10 - 14	3 509 151	1 757 111	1 752 040	391 236	180 572	210 664	3 117 915	1 576 539	1 541 376
15 - 19	2 708 143	1 324 222	1 383 921	407 299	180 461	226 838	2 300 844	1 143 761	1 157 083
20 - 24	2 175 580	981 994	1 193 586	392 217	180 869	211 348	1 783 363	801 125	982 238
25 - 29	1 778 541	831 129	947 412	308 026	152 765	155 261	1 470 515	678 364	792 151
30 - 34	1 420 073	708 138	711 935	215 168	116 304	98 864	1 204 905	591 834	613 071
35 - 39	1 020 968	492 372	528 596	138 208	72 826	65 382	882 760	419 546	463 214
40 - 44	828 317	400 433	427 884	96 870	50 662	46 208	731 447	349 771	381 676
45 - 49	542 862	257 694	285 168	58 821	30 676	28 145	484 041	227 018	257 023
50 - 54	486 060	223 345	262 715	44 728	22 839	21 889	441 332	200 506	240 826
55 - 59	325 875	149 792	176 083	25 198	12 690	12 508	300 677	137 102	163 575
60 - 64	363 765	173 325	190 440	24 371	11 139	13 232	339 394	162 186	177 208
65 - 69	226 029	115 081	110 948	14 175	6 657	7 518	211 854	108 424	103 430
70 - 74	217 160	102 858	114 302	12 538	5 157	7 381	204 622	97 701	106 921
75 - 79	105 318	54 213	51 105	6 582	2 824	3 758	98 736	51 389	47 347

7. Population by age, sex and urban/rural residence: latest available year, 1997 - 2006
Population selon l'âge, le sexe et la résidence, urbaine/rurale: dernière année disponible, 1997 - 2006 (continued - suite)

Continent, country or area, date, code and age (in years) / Continent, pays ou zone, date, code et âge (en années)	Total			Urban - Urbaine			Rural - Rurale		
	Both sexes Les deux sexes	Male Masculin	Female Féminin	Both sexes Les deux sexes	Male Masculin	Female Féminin	Both sexes Les deux sexes	Male Masculin	Female Féminin
AFRICA - AFRIQUE									
Uganda - Ouganda									
12 IX 2002 (CDFC)									
80 - 84	112 785	52 143	60 642	7 542	2 926	4 616	105 243	49 217	56 026
85 - 89	31 184	15 009	16 175	2 146	821	1 325	29 038	14 188	14 850
90 - 94	27 871	13 036	14 835	2 126	786	1 340	25 745	12 250	13 495
95 +	16 927	7 625	9 302	1 345	514	831	15 582	7 111	8 471
United Republic of Tanzania - République Unie de Tanzanie									
24 VIII 2002 (CDFC)									
Total	34 443 603	16 829 861	17 613 742	...	...	...	...	...	...
0 - 4	5 664 907	2 830 545	2 834 362	...	...	...	...	...	...
5 - 9	5 130 448	2 573 993	2 556 455	...	...	...	...	...	...
10 - 14	4 443 257	2 233 401	2 209 856	...	...	...	...	...	...
15 - 19	3 595 735	1 761 329	1 834 406	...	...	...	...	...	...
20 - 24	3 148 513	1 402 077	1 746 436	...	...	...	...	...	...
25 - 29	2 801 965	1 309 661	1 492 304	...	...	...	...	...	...
30 - 34	2 229 046	1 087 599	1 141 447	...	...	...	...	...	...
35 - 39	1 669 873	824 338	845 535	...	...	...	...	...	...
40 - 44	1 348 508	669 549	678 959	...	...	...	...	...	...
45 - 49	984 823	478 522	506 301	...	...	...	...	...	...
50 - 54	883 820	428 501	455 319	...	...	...	...	...	...
55 - 59	590 667	290 117	300 550	...	...	...	...	...	...
60 - 64	604 956	287 502	317 454	...	...	...	...	...	...
65 - 69	439 671	213 635	226 036	...	...	...	...	...	...
70 - 74	377 852	180 246	197 606	...	...	...	...	...	...
75 - 79	221 354	113 205	108 149	...	...	...	...	...	...
80 +	308 208	145 641	162 567	...	...	...	...	...	...
Zambia - Zambie									
25 X 2000 (CDFC)									
Total	9 337 425	4 594 290	4 743 135	3 347 069	1 662 739	1 684 330	5 990 356	2 931 551	3 058 805
0	339 228	168 841	170 387	101 775	50 699	51 076	237 453	118 142	119 311
1 - 4	1 317 492	656 948	660 544	420 759	209 814	210 945	896 733	447 134	449 599
5 - 9	1 461 082	729 181	731 901	500 572	247 117	253 455	960 510	482 064	478 446
10 - 14	1 205 646	601 279	604 367	428 831	206 305	222 526	776 815	394 974	381 841
15 - 19	1 069 996	513 320	556 676	415 197	195 518	219 679	654 799	317 802	336 997
20 - 24	908 672	416 083	492 589	376 695	174 331	202 364	531 977	241 752	290 225
25 - 29	741 148	361 901	379 247	308 436	155 070	153 366	432 712	206 831	225 881
30 - 34	557 873	282 439	275 434	225 707	119 524	106 183	332 166	162 915	169 251
35 - 39	429 987	211 356	218 631	169 148	87 763	81 385	260 839	123 593	137 246
40 - 44	325 776	161 179	164 597	125 995	66 050	59 945	199 781	95 129	104 652
45 - 49	245 320	122 486	122 834	91 507	50 128	41 379	153 813	72 358	81 455
50 - 54	203 612	97 850	105 762	65 547	37 513	28 034	138 065	60 337	77 728
55 - 59	144 838	71 905	72 933	39 418	22 860	16 558	105 420	49 045	56 375
60 - 64	131 475	62 678	68 797	29 438	15 308	14 130	102 037	47 370	54 667
65 - 69	100 493	52 499	47 994	20 294	10 642	9 652	80 199	41 857	38 342
70 - 74	68 935	37 066	31 869	12 763	6 634	6 129	56 172	30 432	25 740
75 - 79	40 649	23 301	17 348	7 217	3 793	3 424	33 432	19 508	13 924
80 - 84	24 242	13 311	10 931	4 418	2 206	2 212	19 824	11 105	8 719
85 +	20 961	10 667	10 294	3 352	1 464	1 888	17 609	9 203	8 406
Zimbabwe									
17 VIII 2002 (CDFC)									
Total	11 631 657	5 634 180	5 997 477	4 029 707	1 988 176	2 041 531	7 601 950	3 646 004	3 955 946
0	340 331	170 054	170 277	117 756	59 103	58 653	222 575	110 951	111 624
1 - 4	1 335 738	668 008	667 730	422 397	210 186	212 211	913 341	457 822	455 519
5 - 9	1 533 700	764 453	769 247	424 731	207 986	216 745	1 108 969	550 407	552 502
10 - 14	1 512 244	754 587	757 657	381 331	180 444	200 887	1 130 913	574 143	556 770
15 - 19	1 503 576	736 686	766 890	511 394	217 513	293 881	992 182	519 173	473 009
20 - 24	1 222 907	564 034	658 873	566 584	260 105	306 479	656 323	303 929	352 394
25 - 29	987 777	473 984	513 793	474 294	242 497	231 797	513 483	231 487	281 996
30 - 34	730 127	369 836	360 291	345 675	191 527	154 148	384 452	178 309	206 143
35 - 39	504 489	235 692	268 797	222 381	116 670	105 711	282 108	119 022	163 086
40 - 44	434 429	194 702	239 727	168 100	87 760	80 340	266 329	106 942	159 387
45 - 49	356 605	165 437	191 168	128 388	70 668	57 720	228 217	94 769	133 448
50 - 54	301 258	128 029	173 229	87 458	48 199	39 259	213 800	79 830	133 970

Continent, country or area, date, code and age (in years) / Continent, pays ou zone, date, code et âge (en années)	Total			Urban - Urbaine			Rural - Rurale		
	Both sexes Les deux sexes	Male Masculin	Female Féminin	Both sexes Les deux sexes	Male Masculin	Female Féminin	Both sexes Les deux sexes	Male Masculin	Female Féminin

AFRICA - AFRIQUE

Zimbabwe
17 VIII 2002 (CDFC)

55 - 59	210 915	98 417	112 498	55 467	31 214	24 253	155 448	67 203	88 245
60 - 64	193 867	94 447	99 420	42 546	23 384	19 162	151 321	71 063	80 258
65 - 69	132 152	64 301	67 851	26 735	14 234	12 501	105 417	50 067	55 350
70 - 74	122 775	60 311	62 464	20 371	10 602	9 769	102 404	49 709	52 695
75 +	328 522	143 900	184 622	23 687	10 598	13 089	140 574	61 352	79 222
75 - 79	64 470	29 997	34 473	...	...	...	...	...	...
80 - 84	59 045	26 764	32 281	...	...	...	...	...	...
85 - 89	19 084	7 727	11 357	...	...	...	...	...	...
90 - 94	9 188	3 752	5 436	...	...	...	...	...	...
95 +	12 474	3 710	8 764	...	...	...	...	...	...
Unknown - Inconnu	44 506	19 252	25 254	10 412	5 486	4 926	34 094	13 766	20 328

AMERICA, NORTH - AMÉRIQUE DU NORD

Anguilla[8]
9 V 2001 (CDFC)

Total	11 430	5 628	5 802	...	...	...	...	...	...
0	252	131	121	...	...	...	...	...	...
1 - 4	821	394	427	...	...	...	...	...	...
5 - 9	993	502	491	...	...	...	...	...	...
10 - 14	1 136	563	573	...	...	...	...	...	...
15 - 19	966	477	489	...	...	...	...	...	...
20 - 24	788	375	413	...	...	...	...	...	...
25 - 29	873	440	433	...	...	...	...	...	...
30 - 34	999	494	505	...	...	...	...	...	...
35 - 39	1 040	507	533	...	...	...	...	...	...
40 - 44	881	429	452	...	...	...	...	...	...
45 - 49	714	364	350	...	...	...	...	...	...
50 - 54	468	236	232	...	...	...	...	...	...
55 - 59	323	166	157	...	...	...	...	...	...
60 - 64	304	144	160	...	...	...	...	...	...
65 - 69	288	159	129	...	...	...	...	...	...
70 - 74	211	82	129	...	...	...	...	...	...
75 - 79	155	65	90	...	...	...	...	...	...
80 - 84	102	52	50	...	...	...	...	...	...
85 - 89	79	31	48	...	...	...	...	...	...
90 - 94	30	15	15	...	...	...	...	...	...
95 +	7	2	5	...	...	...	...	...	...

Antigua and Barbuda - Antigua-et-Barbuda
1 VII 2005 (ESDF)

Total	82 786	38 878	43 908	...	...	...	...	...	...
0	1 537	765	772	...	...	...	...	...	...
1 - 4	6 269	3 230	3 039	...	...	...	...	...	...
5 - 9	7 954	3 966	3 988	...	...	...	...	...	...
10 - 14	7 635	3 699	3 937	...	...	...	...	...	...
15 - 19	6 812	3 230	3 582	...	...	...	...	...	...
20 - 24	6 527	3 119	3 408	...	...	...	...	...	...
25 - 29	6 889	3 169	3 719	...	...	...	...	...	...
30 - 34	7 518	3 344	4 174	...	...	...	...	...	...
35 - 39	7 199	3 251	3 948	...	...	...	...	...	...
40 - 44	5 977	2 697	3 280	...	...	...	...	...	...
45 - 49	4 658	2 176	2 482	...	...	...	...	...	...
50 - 54	3 518	1 659	1 859	...	...	...	...	...	...
55 - 59	2 573	1 162	1 411	...	...	...	...	...	...
60 - 64	2 028	929	1 099	...	...	...	...	...	...
65 - 69	1 700	778	922	...	...	...	...	...	...
70 - 74	1 442	633	809	...	...	...	...	...	...
75 - 79	1 100	507	593	...	...	...	...	...	...
80 - 84	783	332	451	...	...	...	...	...	...
85 - 89	437	160	278	...	...	...	...	...	...

Continent, country or area, date, code and age (in years) Continent, pays ou zone, date, code et âge (en années)	Total			Urban - Urbaine			Rural - Rurale		
	Both sexes Les deux sexes	Male Masculin	Female Féminin	Both sexes Les deux sexes	Male Masculin	Female Féminin	Both sexes Les deux sexes	Male Masculin	Female Féminin
AMERICA, NORTH - AMÉRIQUE DU NORD									
Antigua and Barbuda - Antigua-et-Barbuda									
1 VII 2005 (ESDF)									
90 - 94	197	65	132	...	...	...	...	...	...
95 +	32	9	23	...	...	...	...	...	...
Aruba									
1 VII 2006 (ESDJ)									
Total	102 819	49 053	53 766	...	...	...	...	...	...
0 - 4	6 428	3 271	3 158	...	...	...	...	...	...
5 - 9	7 400	3 763	3 637	...	...	...	...	...	...
10 - 14	7 718	3 918	3 800	...	...	...	...	...	...
15 - 19	7 197	3 613	3 584	...	...	...	...	...	...
20 - 24	5 900	2 932	2 968	...	...	...	...	...	...
25 - 29	6 355	2 964	3 391	...	...	...	...	...	...
30 - 34	7 645	3 602	4 043	...	...	...	...	...	...
35 - 39	8 894	4 204	4 690	...	...	...	...	...	...
40 - 44	9 850	4 657	5 193	...	...	...	...	...	...
45 - 49	9 203	4 327	4 875	...	...	...	...	...	...
50 - 54	7 423	3 442	3 981	...	...	...	...	...	...
55 - 59	5 695	3 672	3 023	...	...	...	...	...	...
60 - 64	4 233	1 967	2 267	...	...	...	...	...	...
65 - 69	3 346	1 491	1 855	...	...	...	...	...	...
70 - 74	2 490	1 048	1 443	...	...	...	...	...	...
75 - 79	1 535	644	891	...	...	...	...	...	...
80 - 84	819	334	485	...	...	...	...	...	...
85 - 89	422	139	283	...	...	...	...	...	...
90 - 94	184	50	133	...	...	...	...	...	...
95 +	83	16	67	...	...	...	...	...	...
Bahamas									
1 V 2000 (CDFC)									
Total	303 611	147 715	155 896	...	...	...	...	...	...
0	5 908	2 929	2 979	...	...	...	...	...	...
1 - 4	23 212	11 737	11 475	...	...	...	...	...	...
5 - 9	31 648	16 014	15 634	...	...	...	...	...	...
10 - 14	28 561	14 149	14 412	...	...	...	...	...	...
15 - 19	26 439	13 355	13 084	...	...	...	...	...	...
20 - 24	24 772	12 140	12 632	...	...	...	...	...	...
25 - 29	26 904	13 110	13 794	...	...	...	...	...	...
30 - 34	26 117	12 601	13 516	...	...	...	...	...	...
35 - 39	25 887	12 438	13 449	...	...	...	...	...	...
40 - 44	21 014	9 971	11 043	...	...	...	...	...	...
45 - 49	15 827	7 617	8 210	...	...	...	...	...	...
50 - 54	11 978	5 749	6 229	...	...	...	...	...	...
55 - 59	10 142	4 768	5 374	...	...	...	...	...	...
60 - 64	8 011	3 750	4 261	...	...	...	...	...	...
65 - 69	5 806	2 651	3 155	...	...	...	...	...	...
70 - 74	4 072	1 689	2 383	...	...	...	...	...	...
75 - 79	2 615	1 039	1 576	...	...	...	...	...	...
80 - 84	1 919	714	1 205	...	...	...	...	...	...
85 - 89	914	293	621	...	...	...	...	...	...
90 +	451	137	314	...	...	...	...	...	...
Unknown - Inconnu	1 414	864	550	...	...	...	...	...	...
Barbados - Barbade									
1 V 2000 (CDFC)									
Total	250 010	119 926	130 084	...	...	...	...	...	...
0 - 4	17 239	8 763	8 476	...	...	...	...	...	...
5 - 9	18 749	9 479	9 270	...	...	...	...	...	...
10 - 14	18 613	9 425	9 188	...	...	...	...	...	...
15 - 19	18 636	9 434	9 202	...	...	...	...	...	...
20 - 24	17 804	8 913	8 891	...	...	...	...	...	...
25 - 29	19 738	9 758	9 980	...	...	...	...	...	...
30 - 34	19 588	9 574	10 014	...	...	...	...	...	...
35 - 39	21 257	10 155	11 102	...	...	...	...	...	...
40 - 44	20 055	9 544	10 511	...	...	...	...	...	...

7. Population by age, sex and urban/rural residence: latest available year, 1997 - 2006
Population selon l'âge, le sexe et la résidence, urbaine/rurale: dernière année disponible, 1997 - 2006 (continued - suite)

Continent, country or area, date, code and age (in years) Continent, pays ou zone, date, code et âge (en années)	Total			Urban - Urbaine			Rural - Rurale		
	Both sexes Les deux sexes	Male Masculin	Female Féminin	Both sexes Les deux sexes	Male Masculin	Female Féminin	Both sexes Les deux sexes	Male Masculin	Female Féminin
AMERICA, NORTH - AMÉRIQUE DU NORD									
Barbados - Barbade									
1 V 2000 (CDFC)									
45 - 49	16 774	8 007	8 767	...	...	...	...	...	...
50 - 54	13 638	6 563	7 075	...	...	...	...	...	...
55 - 59	9 583	4 376	5 207	...	...	...	...	...	...
60 - 64	8 925	3 969	4 956	...	...	...	...	...	...
65 - 69	8 319	3 648	4 671	...	...	...	...	...	...
70 +	21 092	8 318	12 774	...	...	...	...	...	...
Belize									
1 VII 2006 (ESDF)									
Total	301 298	149 598	151 700	151 994	73 576	78 418	149 394	76 101	73 293
0 - 4	36 761	18 145	18 616	17 720	8 446	9 274	19 808	10 070	9 738
5 - 9	40 974	20 850	20 124	19 294	9 792	9 502	21 574	11 011	10 563
10 - 14	40 474	20 611	19 862	19 185	9 790	9 395	21 185	10 775	10 410
15 - 19	33 960	17 192	16 769	16 629	8 785	7 844	17 246	8 369	8 877
20 - 24	24 423	11 939	12 484	12 728	5 973	6 755	11 631	5 939	5 692
25 - 29	20 990	9 733	11 256	11 262	5 018	6 244	9 673	4 693	4 980
30 - 34	20 405	9 522	10 883	11 277	5 183	6 094	9 075	4 318	4 757
35 - 39	18 464	8 747	9 718	9 745	4 294	5 451	8 672	4 433	4 239
40 - 44	15 793	7 735	8 058	8 174	3 931	4 243	7 579	3 787	3 792
45 - 49	12 378	6 295	6 083	6 555	3 305	3 250	5 791	2 976	2 815
50 - 54	9 686	4 983	4 703	5 176	2 385	2 791	4 485	2 586	1 899
55 - 59	6 637	3 363	3 274	3 385	1 636	1 749	3 235	1 720	1 515
60 - 64	5 692	2 913	2 778	2 838	1 376	1 462	2 839	1 531	1 308
65 - 69	4 877	2 547	2 330	2 584	1 201	1 383	2 281	1 341	940
70 - 74	3 867	2 073	1 794	2 203	999	1 204	1 654	1 069	585
75 - 79	2 708	1 374	1 333	1 511	716	795	1 191	656	535
80 - 84	1 582	782	800	794	327	467	784	453	331
85 +	1 629	794	835	934	419	515	691	374	317
Bermuda - Bermudes[9]									
1 VII 2006 (ESDJ)									
Total	63 797	30 504	33 293	...	...	...	...	...	...
0 - 4	3 848	1 981	1 867	...	...	...	...	...	...
5 - 9	3 845	1 929	1 916	...	...	...	...	...	...
10 - 14	3 848	1 935	1 913	...	...	...	...	...	...
15 - 19	3 704	1 829	1 875	...	...	...	...	...	...
20 - 24	3 516	1 725	1 791	...	...	...	...	...	...
25 - 29	4 017	1 868	2 149	...	...	...	...	...	...
30 - 34	4 692	2 247	2 445	...	...	...	...	...	...
35 - 39	5 253	2 593	2 660	...	...	...	...	...	...
40 - 44	5 882	2 931	2 951	...	...	...	...	...	...
45 - 49	5 668	2 714	2 954	...	...	...	...	...	...
50 - 54	4 742	2 264	2 478	...	...	...	...	...	...
55 - 59	4 044	1 942	2 102	...	...	...	...	...	...
60 - 64	3 212	1 481	1 731	...	...	...	...	...	...
65 - 69	2 342	1 040	1 302	...	...	...	...	...	...
70 - 74	2 065	908	1 157	...	...	...	...	...	...
75 - 79	1 484	584	900	...	...	...	...	...	...
80 - 84	995	345	650	...	...	...	...	...	...
85 +	640	188	452	...	...	...	...	...	...
British Virgin Islands - Îles Vierges britanniques									
21 V 2001 (CDFC)									
Total	20 647	10 627	10 020	...	...	...	...	...	...
0 - 4	1 787	913	874	...	...	...	...	...	...
5 - 9	1 865	946	919	...	...	...	...	...	...
10 - 14	1 768	880	888	...	...	...	...	...	...
15 - 19	1 529	778	751	...	...	...	...	...	...
20 - 24	1 465	752	713	...	...	...	...	...	...
25 - 29	1 483	756	727	...	...	...	...	...	...
30 - 34	1 826	913	913	...	...	...	...	...	...
35 - 39	2 085	1 091	994	...	...	...	...	...	...
40 - 44	1 910	991	919	...	...	...	...	...	...
45 - 49	1 501	777	724	...	...	...	...	...	...

Continent, country or area, date, code and age (in years) Continent, pays ou zone, date, code et âge (en années)	Total			Urban - Urbaine			Rural - Rurale		
	Both sexes Les deux sexes	Male Masculin	Female Féminin	Both sexes Les deux sexes	Male Masculin	Female Féminin	Both sexes Les deux sexes	Male Masculin	Female Féminin
AMERICA, NORTH - AMÉRIQUE DU NORD									
British Virgin Islands - Îles Vierges britanniques									
21 V 2001 (CDFC)									
50 - 54	1 128	614	514	...	...	...	...	...	...
55 - 59	774	421	353	...	...	...	...	...	...
60 - 64	523	267	256	...	...	...	...	...	...
65 - 69	337	177	160	...	...	...	...	...	...
70 - 74	282	145	137	...	...	...	...	...	...
75 - 79	204	113	91	...	...	...	...	...	...
80 +	180	93	87	...	...	...	...	...	...
Canada[1]									
1 VII 2003 (ESDJ)									
Total	31 629 677	15 661 734	15 967 943	25 212 723	12 355 256	12 854 903	6 416 976	3 306 472	3 113 035
0	330 644	169 512	161 132	266 115	136 475	129 645	64 529	33 037	31 492
1 - 4	1 383 658	707 774	675 884	1 102 100	563 751	538 349	281 558	144 028	137 545
5 - 9	1 949 702	998 569	951 133	1 524 480	780 199	744 285	425 232	218 384	206 833
10 - 14	2 117 613	1 084 753	1 032 860	1 619 935	828 418	791 540	497 678	256 350	241 340
15 - 19	2 120 545	1 088 772	1 031 773	1 645 028	840 027	804 942	475 517	248 740	226 832
20 - 24	2 188 501	1 119 035	1 069 466	1 836 847	928 955	907 537	351 654	190 079	161 946
25 - 20	2 118 132	1 073 969	1 044 163	1 793 207	906 422	886 635	324 930	167 559	157 518
30 - 34	2 228 713	1 124 790	1 103 923	1 841 469	928 696	912 757	387 243	190 101	101 172
35 - 39	2 481 199	1 247 414	1 233 785	1 993 776	999 796	993 876	487 428	247 599	239 908
40 - 44	2 719 324	1 364 310	1 355 014	2 154 925	1 072 864	1 081 808	564 388	291 456	273 212
45 - 49	2 515 743	1 251 593	1 264 150	1 975 279	971 446	1 003 640	540 474	280 153	260 504
50 - 54	2 176 497	1 078 752	1 097 745	1 696 925	831 506	865 385	479 588	247 236	232 350
55 - 59	1 842 459	913 922	928 537	1 410 796	689 298	721 465	431 656	224 617	207 067
60 - 64	1 396 800	684 822	711 978	1 069 033	512 657	556 262	327 784	172 155	155 722
65 - 69	1 147 902	552 166	595 736	892 139	417 080	474 989	255 758	135 080	120 737
70 - 74	1 039 113	484 186	554 927	829 340	373 391	455 502	209 773	110 784	99 420
75 - 79	839 427	358 752	480 675	689 192	283 797	404 920	150 230	74 955	75 759
80 - 84	583 656	221 629	362 027	486 967	178 027	308 751	96 688	43 596	53 281
85 - 89	296 953	97 229	199 724	252 975	79 576	173 340	43 973	17 659	26 378
90 +	153 096	39 785	113 311	132 195	32 875	99 275	20 895	6 904	14 019
1 VII 2006 (ESDJ)									
Total	32 623 490	16 155 454	16 468 036	...	...	...	...	...	...
0 - 4	1 712 848	877 078	835 770	...	...	...	...	...	...
5 - 9	1 844 308	944 083	900 225	...	...	...	...	...	...
10 - 14	2 087 453	1 069 711	1 017 742	...	...	...	...	...	...
15 - 19	2 170 044	1 111 764	1 058 280	...	...	...	...	...	...
20 - 24	2 261 041	1 156 668	1 104 373	...	...	...	...	...	...
25 - 29	2 234 356	1 128 748	1 105 608	...	...	...	...	...	...
30 - 34	2 225 613	1 122 908	1 102 705	...	...	...	...	...	...
35 - 39	2 356 247	1 185 181	1 171 066	...	...	...	...	...	...
40 - 44	2 704 272	1 359 795	1 344 477	...	...	...	...	...	...
45 - 49	2 675 933	1 336 739	1 339 194	...	...	...	...	...	...
50 - 54	2 367 940	1 172 346	1 195 594	...	...	...	...	...	...
55 - 59	2 084 957	1 029 994	1 054 963	...	...	...	...	...	...
60 - 64	1 584 237	778 463	805 774	...	...	...	...	...	...
65 - 69	1 228 181	591 130	637 051	...	...	...	...	...	...
70 - 74	1 044 888	490 294	554 594	...	...	...	...	...	...
75 - 79	879 069	387 897	491 172	...	...	...	...	...	...
80 - 84	639 451	249 744	389 707	...	...	...	...	...	...
85 - 89	344 336	115 656	228 680	...	...	...	...	...	...
90 +	178 316	47 255	131 061	...	...	...	...	...	...
Cayman Islands - Îles Caïmanes									
1 VII 2006 (ESDJ)									
Total	51 992	26 340	25 652	...	...	...	...	...	...
0 - 14	8 749	4 625	4 124	...	...	...	...	...	...
15 - 19	2 727	1 494	1 233	...	...	...	...	...	...
20 - 24	2 766	1 507	1 259	...	...	...	...	...	...
25 - 34	10 622	5 396	5 226	...	...	...	...	...	...
35 - 44	11 425	5 687	5 738	...	...	...	...	...	...
45 - 54	8 223	4 063	4 160	...	...	...	...	...	...

Continent, country or area, date, code and age (in years) Continent, pays ou zone, date, code et âge (en années)	Total			Urban - Urbaine			Rural - Rurale		
	Both sexes Les deux sexes	Male Masculin	Female Féminin	Both sexes Les deux sexes	Male Masculin	Female Féminin	Both sexes Les deux sexes	Male Masculin	Female Féminin
AMERICA, NORTH - **AMÉRIQUE DU NORD**									
Cayman Islands - Îles Caïmanes									
1 VII 2006 (ESDJ)									
55 - 64	4 169	2 208	1 961	...	...	...	...	...	...
65 +	3 311	1 360	1 951	...	...	...	...	...	...
Costa Rica									
1 VII 2006 (ESDJ)									
Total	4 353 843	2 146 610	2 207 233	2 567 797	1 243 202	1 324 595	1 786 046	903 408	882 638
0 - 4	337 287	176 191	161 096	183 917	94 748	89 169	153 370	81 443	71 927
5 - 9	401 258	202 996	198 262	208 769	106 838	101 931	192 489	96 158	96 331
10 - 14	435 001	230 190	204 811	232 916	124 240	108 676	202 085	105 950	96 135
15 - 19	463 645	235 191	228 454	269 302	135 199	134 103	194 343	99 992	94 351
20 - 24	412 322	206 401	205 921	256 748	129 591	127 157	155 574	76 810	78 764
25 - 29	335 701	160 691	175 010	209 063	99 099	109 964	126 638	61 592	65 046
30 - 39	601 888	285 009	316 879	348 733	163 588	185 145	253 155	121 421	131 734
40 - 49	578 491	283 429	295 062	355 872	167 749	188 123	222 619	115 680	106 939
50 - 59	385 775	181 887	203 888	250 934	116 271	134 663	134 841	65 616	69 225
60 - 69	205 833	94 470	111 363	126 085	52 490	73 595	79 748	41 980	37 768
70 +	192 850	88 054	104 796	123 159	51 965	71 194	69 691	36 089	33 602
Unknown - Inconnu	3 792	2 101	1 691	2 299	1 424	875	1 493	677	816
Cuba									
1 VII 2006 (ESDJ)									
Total	11 241 440	5 629 168	5 612 272	8 490 101	4 176 538	4 313 563	2 751 339	1 452 630	1 298 709
0 - 4	640 875	329 995	310 880	468 294	241 201	227 093	172 581	88 794	83 787
5 - 9	717 741	370 063	347 678	523 820	269 946	253 874	193 921	100 117	93 804
10 - 14	743 111	380 901	362 210	543 333	277 820	265 513	199 778	103 081	96 697
15 - 19	852 240	438 153	414 087	632 246	322 952	309 294	219 994	115 201	104 793
20 - 24	759 971	391 730	368 241	568 102	290 126	277 976	191 869	101 604	90 265
25 - 29	692 582	357 609	334 973	511 749	263 368	248 381	180 833	94 241	86 592
30 - 34	974 818	496 410	478 408	722 161	365 568	356 593	252 657	130 842	121 815
35 - 39	1 056 583	529 860	526 723	791 456	391 508	399 948	265 127	138 352	126 775
40 - 44	1 061 655	527 743	533 912	826 801	404 611	422 190	234 854	123 132	111 722
45 - 49	716 604	352 100	364 504	553 919	266 244	287 675	162 685	85 856	76 829
50 - 54	644 356	315 092	329 264	501 582	239 003	262 579	142 774	76 089	66 685
55 - 59	599 474	291 896	307 578	469 200	222 588	246 612	130 274	69 308	60 966
60 - 64	514 717	250 703	264 014	401 291	189 255	212 036	113 426	61 448	51 978
65 - 69	422 291	206 945	215 346	326 758	153 587	173 171	95 533	53 358	42 175
70 - 74	304 357	145 380	158 977	233 879	105 501	128 378	70 478	39 879	30 599
75 - 79	236 445	111 036	125 409	182 796	80 103	102 693	53 649	30 933	22 716
80 - 84	155 254	70 512	84 742	119 812	50 088	69 724	35 442	20 424	15 018
85 +	148 366	63 040	85 326	112 902	43 069	69 833	35 464	19 971	15 493
Dominica - Dominique									
12 V 2001 (CDFC)									
Total	68 635	34 549	34 086	...	...	...	...	...	...
0 - 4	6 087	3 059	3 028	...	...	...	...	...	...
5 - 9	7 277	3 770	3 507	...	...	...	...	...	...
10 - 14	6 847	3 395	3 452	...	...	...	...	...	...
15 - 19	6 570	3 293	3 277	...	...	...	...	...	...
20 - 24	4 409	2 326	2 083	...	...	...	...	...	...
25 - 29	4 934	2 481	2 453	...	...	...	...	...	...
30 - 34	5 456	2 753	2 703	...	...	...	...	...	...
35 - 39	5 100	2 710	2 390	...	...	...	...	...	...
40 - 44	4 310	2 306	2 004	...	...	...	...	...	...
45 - 49	3 428	1 857	1 571	...	...	...	...	...	...
50 - 54	2 717	1 400	1 317	...	...	...	...	...	...
55 - 59	2 303	1 153	1 150	...	...	...	...	...	...
60 - 64	2 175	975	1 200	...	...	...	...	...	...
65 - 69	2 241	1 041	1 200	...	...	...	...	...	...
70 - 74	1 778	831	947	...	...	...	...	...	...
75 - 79	1 285	568	717	...	...	...	...	...	...
80 - 84	895	347	548	...	...	...	...	...	...
85 +	823	284	539	...	...	...	...	...	...

7. Population by age, sex and urban/rural residence: latest available year, 1997 - 2006
Population selon l'âge, le sexe et la résidence, urbaine/rurale: dernière année disponible, 1997 - 2006 (continued - suite)

Continent, country or area, date, code and age (in years) / Continent, pays ou zone, date, code et âge (en années)	Total			Urban - Urbaine			Rural - Rurale		
	Both sexes Les deux sexes	Male Masculin	Female Féminin	Both sexes Les deux sexes	Male Masculin	Female Féminin	Both sexes Les deux sexes	Male Masculin	Female Féminin
AMERICA, NORTH - AMÉRIQUE DU NORD									
Dominican Republic - République dominicaine									
1 VII 2005 (ESDF)									
Total	9 226 449	4 615 274	4 611 175	5 816 828	2 881 652	2 935 176	3 409 621	1 733 622	1 675 999
0 - 4	1 053 698	537 020	516 678	647 199	333 736	313 462	406 499	203 284	203 216
5 - 9	1 012 877	515 417	497 460	610 854	313 263	297 591	402 023	202 154	199 869
10 - 14	1 003 497	509 330	494 167	613 179	309 875	303 304	390 318	199 455	190 863
15 - 19	939 086	472 387	466 699	594 518	294 994	299 524	344 568	177 393	167 175
20 - 24	858 031	426 160	431 871	560 000	274 859	285 141	298 031	151 301	146 730
25 - 29	752 009	370 156	381 853	495 914	242 677	253 237	256 095	127 479	128 616
30 - 34	671 024	328 762	342 262	439 246	213 800	225 445	231 778	114 962	116 817
35 - 39	598 719	294 757	303 962	391 353	190 886	200 466	207 366	103 871	103 496
40 - 44	529 396	263 036	266 360	341 232	167 303	173 930	188 164	95 733	92 430
45 - 49	447 748	223 705	224 043	287 124	140 961	146 163	160 624	82 744	77 880
50 - 54	358 315	179 332	178 983	224 993	110 493	114 500	133 322	68 839	64 483
55 - 59	274 722	137 121	137 601	170 336	83 126	87 211	104 386	53 995	50 390
60 - 64	213 703	106 527	107 176	129 578	62 264	67 314	84 125	44 263	39 862
65 - 69	184 331	91 256	93 075	111 233	52 921	58 312	73 098	38 335	34 763
70 - 74	141 054	69 467	71 587	84 217	39 297	44 920	56 837	30 170	26 667
75 - 79	94 982	46 287	48 695	57 425	26 094	31 331	37 557	20 193	17 364
80 +	93 257	44 554	48 703	58 427	25 104	33 323	34 830	19 450	15 380
El Salvador									
1 VII 2003 (ESDF)									
Total	6 638 168	3 261 938	3 376 230	3 932 569	1 891 429	2 041 140	2 705 599	1 370 509	1 335 090
0	162 479	83 082	79 397	87 126	44 566	42 560	75 353	38 516	36 837
1 - 4	644 889	329 352	315 537	342 656	174 855	167 801	302 233	154 497	147 736
5 - 9	777 836	396 371	381 465	438 845	222 691	216 154	338 991	173 680	165 311
10 - 14	720 117	365 942	354 175	404 131	203 433	200 698	315 986	162 509	153 477
15 - 19	661 005	334 785	326 220	358 075	177 949	180 126	302 930	156 836	146 094
20 - 24	660 518	333 143	327 375	374 723	183 684	191 039	285 795	149 459	136 336
25 - 29	638 627	318 847	319 780	380 057	183 630	196 427	258 570	135 217	123 353
30 - 34	509 962	246 818	263 144	324 396	152 402	171 994	185 566	94 416	91 150
35 - 39	387 053	178 680	208 373	259 673	117 642	142 031	127 380	61 038	66 342
40 - 44	309 588	140 553	169 035	210 767	94 677	116 090	98 821	45 876	52 945
45 - 49	268 869	124 218	144 651	176 322	80 071	96 251	92 547	44 147	48 400
50 - 54	225 211	105 929	119 282	143 766	66 453	77 313	81 445	39 476	41 969
55 - 59	186 454	88 100	98 354	116 650	53 968	62 682	69 804	34 132	35 672
60 - 64	146 201	68 603	77 598	90 734	41 238	49 496	55 467	27 365	28 102
65 - 69	122 667	56 429	66 238	76 373	33 785	42 588	46 294	22 644	23 650
70 - 74	97 128	43 336	53 792	61 565	26 420	35 145	35 563	16 916	18 647
75 - 79	64 745	27 429	37 316	42 647	17 583	25 064	22 098	9 846	12 252
80 +	54 819	20 321	34 498	44 063	16 382	27 681	10 756	3 939	6 817
Greenland - Groenland									
1 I 2005 (ESDJ)									
Total	56 969	30 319	26 650	47 086	24 884	22 202	9 883	5 435	4 448
0	797	405	392	639	324	315	158	81	77
1 - 4	3 540	1 793	1 747	2 866	1 449	1 417	674	344	330
5 - 9	4 763	2 419	2 344	3 833	1 969	1 864	930	450	480
10 - 14	5 220	2 638	2 582	4 187	2 128	2 059	1 033	510	523
15 - 19	4 483	2 256	2 227	3 739	1 872	1 867	744	384	360
20 - 24	3 943	2 054	1 889	3 292	1 680	1 612	651	374	277
25 - 29	3 428	1 790	1 638	2 832	1 436	1 396	596	354	242
30 - 34	3 635	2 001	1 634	3 015	1 660	1 355	620	341	279
35 - 39	5 627	3 025	2 602	4 000	2 601	2 198	928	524	404
40 - 44	5 627	3 030	2 597	4 736	2 518	2 218	891	512	379
45 - 49	4 442	2 537	1 905	3 721	2 102	1 619	721	435	286
50 - 54	3 431	1 955	1 476	2 863	1 610	1 253	568	345	223
55 - 59	2 637	1 627	1 010	2 228	1 362	866	409	265	144
60 - 64	2 253	1 291	962	1 862	1 064	798	391	227	164
65 - 69	1 317	699	618	1 056	557	499	261	142	119
70 - 74	970	467	503	806	388	418	164	79	85
75 - 79	575	238	337	483	192	291	92	46	46
80 - 84	188	70	118	152	52	100	36	18	18
85 - 89	68	16	52	54	13	41	14	3	11

Continent, country or area, date, code and age (in years) / Continent, pays ou zone, date, code et âge (en années)	Total			Urban - Urbaine			Rural - Rurale		
	Both sexes Les deux sexes	Male Masculin	Female Féminin	Both sexes Les deux sexes	Male Masculin	Female Féminin	Both sexes Les deux sexes	Male Masculin	Female Féminin
AMERICA, NORTH - AMÉRIQUE DU NORD									
Greenland - Groenland									
1 I 2005 (ESDJ)									
90 - 94	23	8	15	22	7	15	1	1	-
95 +	2	-	2	1	-	1	1	-	1
1 VII 2006 (ESDJ)[10]									
Total	56 775	30 094	26 681	...	...	...	...	...	...
0 - 4	4 356	2 212	2 145	...	...	...	...	...	...
5 - 9	4 538	2 307	2 231	...	...	...	...	...	...
10 - 14	5 033	2 544	2 489	...	...	...	...	...	...
15 - 19	4 628	2 330	2 298	...	...	...	...	...	...
20 - 24	4 018	2 054	1 964	...	...	...	...	...	...
25 - 29	3 576	1 868	1 708	...	...	...	...	...	...
30 - 34	3 419	1 863	1 556	...	...	...	...	...	...
35 - 39	4 878	2 596	2 282	...	...	...	...	...	...
40 - 44	5 706	3 065	2 641	...	...	...	...	...	...
45 - 49	4 713	2 651	2 062	...	...	...	...	...	...
50 - 54	3 552	2 014	1 538	...	...	...	...	...	...
55 - 59	2 716	1 628	1 089	...	...	...	...	...	...
60 - 64	2 322	1 345	977	...	...	...	...	...	...
65 - 69	1 424	782	642	...	...	...	...	...	...
70 - 74	975	478	498	...	...	...	...	...	...
75 - 79	618	255	363	...	...	...	...	...	...
80 - 84	221	85	136	...	...	...	...	...	...
85 - 89	65	17	48	...	...	...	...	...	...
90 +	24	5	19	...	...	...	...	...	...
Grenada - Grenade									
1 VII 2000 (ESDF)									
Total	101 308	50 200	51 108	...	...	...	...	...	...
0 - 4	10 412	5 292	5 120	...	...	...	...	...	...
5 - 9	11 547	5 798	5 749	...	...	...	...	...	...
10 - 14	13 546	6 837	6 709	...	...	...	...	...	...
15 - 19	11 911	6 077	5 834	...	...	...	...	...	...
20 - 24	9 267	4 686	4 581	...	...	...	...	...	...
25 - 29	7 290	3 883	3 407	...	...	...	...	...	...
30 - 34	5 977	2 999	2 978	...	...	...	...	...	...
35 - 39	6 537	3 294	3 243	...	...	...	...	...	...
40 - 44	5 364	2 628	2 736	...	...	...	...	...	...
45 - 49	3 780	1 955	1 825	...	...	...	...	...	...
50 - 54	2 904	1 371	1 533	...	...	...	...	...	...
55 - 59	2 472	1 160	1 312	...	...	...	...	...	...
60 - 64	2 383	1 078	1 305	...	...	...	...	...	...
65 - 69	2 356	1 010	1 346	...	...	...	...	...	...
70 +	5 562	2 132	3 430	...	...	...	...	...	...
Guadeloupe									
1 I 2004 (ESDJ)									
Total	442 953	211 832	231 121	...	...	...	...	...	...
0	6 918	3 479	3 439	...	...	...	...	...	...
1 - 4	28 700	14 770	13 930	...	...	...	...	...	...
5 - 9	33 521	17 124	16 397	...	...	...	...	...	...
10 - 14	37 037	18 794	18 243	...	...	...	...	...	...
15 - 19	34 828	17 666	17 162	...	...	...	...	...	...
20 - 24	30 258	15 313	14 945	...	...	...	...	...	...
25 - 29	24 245	11 873	12 372	...	...	...	...	...	...
30 - 34	32 983	14 998	17 985	...	...	...	...	...	...
35 - 39	36 262	16 333	19 929	...	...	...	...	...	...
40 - 44	35 808	16 938	18 870	...	...	...	...	...	...
45 - 49	29 796	13 907	15 889	...	...	...	...	...	...
50 - 54	25 806	11 849	13 957	...	...	...	...	...	...
55 - 59	21 525	10 241	11 284	...	...	...	...	...	...
60 - 64	16 754	7 757	8 997	...	...	...	...	...	...
65 - 69	14 621	6 800	7 821	...	...	...	...	...	...
70 - 74	11 500	5 074	6 426	...	...	...	...	...	...
75 - 79	9 590	4 034	5 556	...	...	...	...	...	...
80 - 84	6 741	2 748	3 993	...	...	...	...	...	...

Continent, country or area, date, code and age (in years) / Continent, pays ou zone, date, code et âge (en années)	Total			Urban - Urbaine			Rural - Rurale		
	Both sexes Les deux sexes	Male Masculin	Female Féminin	Both sexes Les deux sexes	Male Masculin	Female Féminin	Both sexes Les deux sexes	Male Masculin	Female Féminin
AMERICA, NORTH - AMÉRIQUE DU NORD									
Guadeloupe									
1 I 2004 (ESDJ)									
85 - 89	3 626	1 400	2 226	...	...	...	...	...	...
90 + ...	2 434	734	1 700	...	...	...	...	...	...
Guatemala[11]									
1 VII 2005 (ESDF)									
Total.................	12 699 780	6 197 399	6 502 381	6 345 918	3 059 570	3 286 348	6 353 862	3 137 829	3 216 033
0 - 4.................	2 036 312	1 035 549	1 000 763	866 844	447 724	419 120	1 169 468	587 825	581 643
5 - 9.................	1 823 642	921 924	901 718	790 225	405 750	384 475	1 033 417	516 174	517 243
10 - 14.................	1 624 119	815 791	808 328	755 292	378 704	376 587	868 827	437 087	431 741
15 - 19.................	1 379 574	685 359	694 215	715 501	351 554	363 947	664 073	333 805	330 268
20 - 24.................	1 180 264	571 385	608 879	636 046	306 874	329 172	544 218	264 511	279 707
25 - 29.................	952 695	446 309	506 386	523 699	243 461	280 237	428 996	202 848	226 149
30 - 34.................	753 145	340 378	412 767	416 357	184 973	231 384	336 788	155 405	181 383
35 - 39.................	600 160	270 907	329 253	326 576	144 824	181 752	273 584	126 083	147 501
40 - 44.................	492 747	225 243	267 504	270 162	120 913	149 248	222 585	104 330	118 256
45 - 49.................	409 688	191 635	218 053	221 123	100 439	120 685	188 565	91 196	97 368
50 - 54.................	367 062	175 311	191 751	201 790	92 775	109 014	165 272	82 536	82 737
55 - 59.................	310 913	149 593	161 320	171 480	79 044	92 436	139 433	70 549	68 884
60 - 64.................	233 643	113 686	119 957	128 803	58 925	69 878	104 840	54 761	50 079
65 - 69.................	192 992	94 128	98 864	111 865	51 579	60 285	81 127	42 549	38 579
70 - 74.................	156 267	74 463	81 804	93 750	42 080	51 669	62 517	32 383	30 135
75 - 79.................	107 429	50 340	57 089	66 759	29 241	37 519	40 670	21 099	19 570
80 +.................	79 128	35 398	43 730	49 648	20 709	28 939	29 480	14 689	14 791
Haiti - Haïti									
1 VII 1999 (ESDJ)									
Total.................	7 803 232	3 834 240	3 968 992	2 731 843	1 234 809	1 497 034	5 071 389	2 599 431	2 471 958
0.................	242 106	122 835	119 271	68 885	36 499	32 386	173 221	86 336	86 885
1 - 4.................	913 669	462 018	451 651	252 773	130 783	121 990	660 896	331 235	329 661
5 - 9.................	1 034 513	521 302	513 211	321 389	154 420	166 969	713 124	366 882	346 242
10 - 14.................	925 920	466 007	459 913	363 812	161 340	202 472	562 108	304 667	257 441
15 - 19.................	810 881	407 544	403 337	375 052	156 361	218 691	435 829	251 183	184 646
20 - 24.................	696 906	347 026	349 880	337 696	153 000	184 696	359 210	194 026	165 184
25 - 29.................	612 995	301 403	311 592	272 739	124 048	148 691	340 256	177 355	162 901
30 - 34.................	526 616	255 640	270 976	198 846	88 085	110 761	327 770	167 555	160 215
35 - 39.................	452 327	216 102	236 225	135 215	57 299	77 916	317 112	158 803	158 309
40 - 44.................	370 430	173 392	197 038	106 911	42 010	64 901	263 519	131 382	132 137
45 - 49.................	306 075	141 518	164 557	71 946	29 912	42 034	234 129	111 606	122 523
50 - 54.................	247 324	114 254	133 070	70 080	31 126	38 954	177 244	83 128	94 116
55 - 59.................	201 858	93 663	108 195	51 060	22 494	28 566	150 798	71 169	79 629
60 - 64.................	161 143	74 625	86 518	40 580	18 949	21 631	120 563	55 676	64 887
65 - 69.................	122 392	56 450	65 942	28 310	12 719	15 591	94 082	43 731	50 351
70 - 74.................	84 796	38 744	46 052	18 717	7 726	10 991	66 079	31 018	35 061
75 - 79.................	52 884	23 831	29 053	11 309	5 008	6 301	41 575	18 823	22 752
80 +.................	40 397	17 886	22 511	6 523	3 030	3 493	33 874	14 856	19 018
Honduras									
1 VII 2003 (ESDF)									
Total.................	6 860 842	3 388 874	3 471 968	3 260 934	1 555 369	1 705 565	3 599 908	1 833 505	1 766 403
0.................	211 122	107 546	103 576	92 446	47 136	45 310	118 676	60 410	58 266
1 - 4.................	820 813	416 615	404 198	340 186	174 013	166 173	480 627	242 602	238 025
5 - 9.................	949 750	480 017	469 733	389 928	198 612	191 316	559 822	281 405	278 417
10 - 14.................	837 102	421 803	415 299	362 885	180 041	182 844	474 217	241 762	232 455
15 - 19.................	743 031	372 741	370 290	362 858	170 460	192 398	380 173	202 281	177 892
20 - 24.................	660 060	330 232	329 828	352 858	165 359	187 499	310 395	164 874	145 521
25 - 29.................	559 428	276 591	282 837	299 286	142 499	156 787	260 142	134 092	126 050
30 - 34.................	453 592	221 413	232 179	242 678	113 600	129 078	210 914	107 813	103 101
35 - 39.................	358 774	170 994	187 780	190 971	87 412	103 559	167 803	83 582	84 221
40 - 44.................	292 742	137 740	155 002	153 583	69 630	83 953	139 159	68 110	71 049
45 - 49.................	244 002	114 465	129 537	124 151	56 039	68 112	119 851	58 426	61 425
50 - 54.................	196 270	91 939	104 331	97 646	43 561	54 085	98 624	48 378	50 246
55 - 59.................	152 017	71 521	80 496	72 441	32 030	40 411	79 576	39 491	40 085
60 - 64.................	119 860	56 175	63 685	55 043	23 792	31 251	64 817	32 383	32 434
65 - 69.................	95 844	44 359	51 485	44 728	18 795	25 933	51 116	25 564	25 552
70 - 74.................	70 413	32 212	38 201	33 351	13 867	19 484	37 062	18 345	18 717

Continent, country or area, date, code and age (in years) / Continent, pays ou zone, date, code et âge (en années)	Total			Urban - Urbaine			Rural - Rurale		
	Both sexes Les deux sexes	Male Masculin	Female Féminin	Both sexes Les deux sexes	Male Masculin	Female Féminin	Both sexes Les deux sexes	Male Masculin	Female Féminin
AMERICA, NORTH - AMÉRIQUE DU NORD									
Honduras									
1 VII 2003 (ESDF)									
75 - 79	49 736	22 968	26 768	24 076	9 963	14 113	25 660	13 005	12 655
80 + ...	43 093	19 542	23 551	21 819	8 560	13 259	21 274	10 982	10 292
Jamaica - Jamaïque									
1 VII 2005 (ESDJ)									
Total.....................	2 650 405	1 305 640	1 344 765	1 379 562	657 689	721 874	1 270 843	647 951	622 891
0 - 4.....................	240 823	122 758	118 065	121 937	62 249	59 688	118 886	60 509	58 377
5 - 9.....................	273 420	138 800	134 620	134 380	67 772	66 609	139 040	71 028	68 011
10 - 14	277 040	141 779	135 261	136 192	69 297	66 895	140 848	72 482	68 366
15 - 19	250 573	127 118	123 455	128 270	63 639	64 632	122 303	63 479	58 823
20 - 24	211 724	102 838	108 886	117 585	55 302	62 283	94 139	47 536	46 603
25 - 29	211 568	100 842	110 726	119 418	54 668	64 750	92 150	46 174	45 976
30 - 34	210 237	99 781	110 456	117 896	53 684	64 212	92 341	46 097	46 244
35 - 39	207 198	97 978	109 220	115 195	51 941	63 254	92 003	46 037	45 966
40 - 44	175 264	86 518	88 746	95 350	44 522	50 828	79 914	41 996	37 918
45 - 49	123 943	61 219	62 724	67 696	31 661	36 034	56 247	29 558	26 690
50 - 54	106 727	55 279	51 448	56 631	27 782	28 848	50 096	27 497	22 600
55 - 59	80 735	41 874	38 861	40 693	20 018	20 675	40 042	21 856	18 186
60 - 64	66 998	32 699	34 299	32 420	15 004	17 416	34 578	17 695	16 883
65 - 69	62 580	30 177	32 403	29 138	13 288	15 850	33 442	16 889	16 553
70 - 74	55 798	26 529	29 269	25 389	11 398	13 990	30 409	15 131	15 279
75 - 79	42 144	18 758	23 386	18 575	7 574	11 001	23 570	11 184	12 386
80 - 84	26 881	10 915	15 966	11 445	4 280	7 165	15 436	6 635	8 801
85 + ...	26 752	9 778	16 973	11 354	3 609	7 745	15 398	6 169	9 229
Martinique									
1 I 2004 (ESDJ)									
Total.....................	392 756	184 877	207 879	...	...	...	...	...	...
0	5 348	2 734	2 614	...	...	...	...	...	...
1 - 4	22 112	11 180	10 932	...	...	...	...	...	...
5 - 9	26 268	13 248	13 020	...	...	...	...	...	...
10 - 14	31 293	15 676	15 617	...	...	...	...	...	...
15 - 19	31 576	15 917	15 659	...	...	...	...	...	...
20 - 24	25 844	13 091	12 753	...	...	...	...	...	...
25 - 29	20 030	9 556	10 474	...	...	...	...	...	...
30 - 34	27 167	12 185	14 982	...	...	...	...	...	...
35 - 39	32 249	14 386	17 863	...	...	...	...	...	...
40 - 44	33 178	15 439	17 739	...	...	...	...	...	...
45 - 49	27 437	12 762	14 675	...	...	...	...	...	...
50 - 54	23 531	10 741	12 790	...	...	...	...	...	...
55 - 59	19 693	9 073	10 620	...	...	...	...	...	...
60 - 64	15 768	7 303	8 465	...	...	...	...	...	...
65 - 69	15 599	7 142	8 457	...	...	...	...	...	...
70 - 74	12 522	5 484	7 038	...	...	...	...	...	...
75 - 79	10 256	4 304	5 952	...	...	...	...	...	...
80 - 84	6 821	2 615	4 206	...	...	...	...	...	...
85 - 89	3 674	1 301	2 373	...	...	...	...	...	...
90 + ...	2 390	740	1 650	...	...	...	...	...	...
Mexico - Mexique									
17 X 2005 (CDJC)									
Total.....................	103 263 388	50 249 955	53 013 433	78 986 852	38 300 417	40 686 435	24 276 536	11 949 538	12 326 998
0	1 866 929	953 071	913 858	1 375 346	701 965	673 381	491 583	251 106	240 477
1 - 4	8 319 314	4 222 842	4 096 472	6 099 968	3 098 431	3 001 537	2 219 346	1 124 411	1 094 935
5 - 9	10 511 738	5 339 127	5 172 611	7 612 581	3 868 547	3 744 034	2 899 157	1 470 580	1 428 577
10 - 14	10 952 123	5 545 910	5 406 213	7 809 172	3 950 685	3 858 487	3 142 951	1 595 225	1 547 726
15 - 19	10 109 021	4 995 906	5 113 115	7 519 867	3 724 606	3 795 261	2 589 154	1 271 300	1 317 854
20 - 24	8 964 629	4 253 440	4 711 189	7 051 808	3 376 247	3 675 561	1 912 821	877 193	1 035 628
25 - 29	8 103 358	3 805 724	4 297 634	6 430 726	3 033 228	3 397 498	1 672 632	772 496	900 136
30 - 34	7 933 951	3 745 974	4 187 977	6 362 249	3 001 742	3 360 507	1 571 702	744 232	827 470
35 - 39	7 112 526	3 371 372	3 741 154	5 690 767	2 688 582	3 002 185	1 421 759	682 790	738 969
40 - 44	6 017 268	2 871 549	3 145 719	4 827 524	2 293 754	2 533 770	1 189 744	577 795	611 949
45 - 49	5 015 255	2 388 149	2 627 106	3 986 038	1 885 334	2 100 704	1 029 217	502 815	526 402
50 - 54	4 090 650	1 959 720	2 130 930	3 227 317	1 530 942	1 696 375	863 333	428 778	434 555
55 - 59	3 117 071	1 497 981	1 619 090	2 392 022	1 135 166	1 256 856	725 049	362 815	362 234

Continent, country or area, date, code and age (in years) / Continent, pays ou zone, date, code et âge (en années)	Total			Urban - Urbaine			Rural - Rurale		
	Both sexes Les deux sexes	Male Masculin	Female Féminin	Both sexes Les deux sexes	Male Masculin	Female Féminin	Both sexes Les deux sexes	Male Masculin	Female Féminin
AMERICA, NORTH - AMÉRIQUE DU NORD									
Mexico - Mexique									
17 X 2005 (CDJC)									
60 - 64	2 622 476	1 243 788	1 378 688	1 935 880	900 574	1 035 306	686 596	343 214	343 382
65 - 69	1 958 069	922 592	1 035 477	1 428 290	654 658	773 632	529 779	267 934	261 845
70 - 74	1 496 691	703 277	793 414	1 082 372	489 557	592 815	414 319	213 720	200 599
75 - 79	1 048 315	490 840	557 475	747 992	334 692	413 300	300 323	156 148	144 175
80 - 84	657 011	296 351	360 660	468 965	201 082	267 883	188 046	95 269	92 777
85 - 89	345 154	150 617	194 537	244 298	100 594	143 704	100 856	50 023	50 833
90 - 94	132 325	54 391	77 934	93 124	35 731	57 393	39 201	18 660	20 541
95 - 99	61 145	24 439	36 706	40 465	14 930	25 535	20 680	9 509	11 171
100 +	17 649	6 696	10 953	10 007	3 491	6 516	7 642	3 205	4 437
Unknown - Inconnu	2 810 720	1 406 199	1 404 521	2 550 074	1 275 879	1 274 195	260 646	130 320	130 326
1 VII 2006 (ESDJ)									
Total	104 874 282	51 654 642	53 219 640	...	...	...	...	...	...
0	1 962 477	1 003 472	959 005	...	...	...	...	...	...
1 - 4	8 151 684	4 169 320	3 982 364	...	...	...	...	...	...
5 - 9	11 098 391	5 668 296	5 430 095	...	...	...	...	...	...
10 - 14	10 938 290	5 558 839	5 379 451	...	...	...	...	...	...
15 - 19	10 444 014	5 244 082	5 199 932	...	...	...	...	...	...
20 - 24	9 571 997	4 704 306	4 867 691	...	...	...	...	...	...
25 - 29	8 857 579	4 294 196	4 563 383	...	...	...	...	...	...
30 - 34	8 394 200	4 072 404	4 321 790	...	...	...	...	...	...
35 - 39	7 594 088	3 695 304	3 898 784	...	...	...	...	...	...
40 - 44	6 601 900	3 213 152	3 388 748	...	...	...	...	...	...
45 - 49	5 464 192	2 648 121	2 816 071	...	...	...	...	...	...
50 - 54	4 279 443	2 057 903	2 221 540	...	...	...	...	...	...
55 - 59	3 327 300	1 586 061	1 741 239	...	...	...	...	...	...
60 - 64	2 599 981	1 225 454	1 374 527	...	...	...	...	...	...
65 - 69	1 990 616	925 176	1 065 440	...	...	...	...	...	...
70 - 74	1 453 770	663 211	790 559	...	...	...	...	...	...
75 - 79	993 809	441 944	551 865	...	...	...	...	...	...
80 - 84	619 875	266 833	353 042	...	...	...	...	...	...
85 - 89	323 273	134 293	188 980	...	...	...	...	...	...
90 - 94	148 502	59 470	89 032	...	...	...	...	...	...
95 - 99	49 630	19 240	30 390	...	...	...	...	...	...
100 +	9 191	3 485	5 706	...	...	...	...	...	...
Montserrat									
12 V 2001 (CDFC)									
Total	4 491	2 418	2 073	...	...	...	...	...	...
0 - 4	311	153	158	...	...	...	...	...	...
5 - 9	277	153	124	...	...	...	...	...	...
10 - 14	281	148	133	...	...	...	...	...	...
15 - 19	273	149	124	...	...	...	...	...	...
20 - 24	206	113	93	...	...	...	...	...	...
25 - 29	319	169	150	...	...	...	...	...	...
30 - 34	346	176	170	...	...	...	...	...	...
35 - 39	382	211	171	...	...	...	...	...	...
40 - 44	325	171	154	...	...	...	...	...	...
45 - 49	335	196	139	...	...	...	...	...	...
50 - 54	282	170	112	...	...	...	...	...	...
55 - 59	239	136	103	...	...	...	...	...	...
60 - 64	203	108	95	...	...	...	...	...	...
65 - 69	148	76	72	...	...	...	...	...	...
70 - 74	169	94	75	...	...	...	...	...	...
75 - 79	139	72	67	...	...	...	...	...	...
80 - 84	107	47	60	...	...	...	...	...	...
85 - 89	67	32	35	...	...	...	...	...	...
90 - 94	38	14	24	...	...	...	...	...	...
95 +	21	9	12	...	...	...	...	...	...
Unknown - Inconnu	23	21	2	...	...	...	...	...	...

Continent, country or area, date, code and age (in years) / Continent, pays ou zone, date, code et âge (en années)	Total			Urban - Urbaine			Rural - Rurale		
	Both sexes Les deux sexes	Male Masculin	Female Féminin	Both sexes Les deux sexes	Male Masculin	Female Féminin	Both sexes Les deux sexes	Male Masculin	Female Féminin
AMERICA, NORTH - AMÉRIQUE DU NORD									
Netherlands Antilles - Antilles néerlandaises									
1 VII 2006 (ESDJ)									
Total.	189 500	88 146	101 355	...	...	...	...	...	...
0 - 4	13 652	6 914	6 738	...	...	...	...	...	...
5 - 9	14 257	7 175	7 082	...	...	...	...	...	...
10 - 14	15 386	7 742	7 644	...	...	...	...	...	...
15 - 19	14 001	6 960	7 041	...	...	...	...	...	...
20 - 24	10 361	4 938	5 423	...	...	...	...	...	...
25 - 29	10 601	4 865	5 737	...	...	...	...	...	...
30 - 34	13 419	6 155	7 264	...	...	...	...	...	...
35 - 39	15 568	7 102	8 466	...	...	...	...	...	...
40 - 44	16 818	7 576	9 243	...	...	...	...	...	...
45 - 49	15 637	6 964	8 674	...	...	...	...	...	...
50 - 54	12 933	5 766	7 167	...	...	...	...	...	...
55 - 59	10 685	4 901	5 785	...	...	...	...	...	...
60 - 64	8 142	3 652	4 490	...	...	...	...	...	...
65 - 69	6 158	2 707	3 451	...	...	...	...	...	...
70 - 74	4 838	2 122	2 716	...	...	...	...	...	...
75 - 79	3 256	1 330	1 927	...	...	...	...	...	...
80 - 84	2 117	772	1 345	...	...	...	...	...	...
85 +	1 675	511	1 165	...	...	...	...	...	...
Nicaragua									
1 VII 2005 (ESDJ)									
Total.	5 457 208	2 720 336	2 736 872	3 140 854	1 511 552	1 629 302	2 316 354	1 208 784	1 107 570
0 - 4	672 455	343 130	329 325	347 013	177 124	169 889	325 442	166 006	159 436
5 - 9	693 677	353 907	339 770	372 884	189 029	183 855	320 793	164 878	155 915
10 - 14	703 201	357 159	346 042	390 798	195 006	195 792	312 403	162 153	150 250
15 - 19	623 677	313 155	310 522	353 483	171 662	181 821	270 194	141 493	128 701
20 - 24	560 765	279 115	281 650	324 357	154 423	169 934	236 408	124 692	111 716
25 - 29	458 598	223 079	235 519	276 680	129 399	147 281	181 918	93 680	88 238
30 - 34	373 458	180 491	192 967	234 445	108 580	125 865	139 013	71 911	67 102
35 - 39	306 231	149 402	156 829	191 266	89 647	101 619	114 965	59 755	55 210
40 - 44	256 202	124 889	131 313	160 165	74 579	85 586	96 037	50 310	45 727
45 - 49	215 751	104 592	111 159	131 630	60 632	70 998	84 121	43 960	40 161
50 - 54	167 246	82 212	85 034	101 171	46 410	54 761	66 075	35 802	30 273
55 - 59	119 466	61 751	57 715	71 254	34 215	37 039	48 212	27 536	20 676
60 - 64	95 217	48 028	47 189	57 028	26 492	30 536	38 189	21 536	16 653
65 - 69	74 655	36 888	37 767	45 147	20 405	24 742	29 508	16 483	13 025
70 - 74	58 515	27 772	30 743	35 515	15 150	20 365	23 000	12 622	10 378
75 - 79	39 934	18 622	21 312	24 476	10 144	14 332	15 458	8 478	6 980
80 +	38 160	16 144	22 016	23 542	8 655	14 887	14 618	7 489	7 129
Panama									
1 VII 2000 (ESDF)									
Total.	2 855 703	1 440 801	1 414 902	1 604 823	782 928	821 895	1 250 880	657 873	593 007
0	59 949	30 595	29 354	30 248	15 460	14 788	29 701	15 135	14 566
1 - 4	241 433	123 553	117 880	121 253	62 069	59 184	120 180	61 484	58 696
5 - 9	300 852	153 986	146 866	150 849	77 061	73 786	150 003	76 925	73 079
10 - 14	291 489	148 579	142 911	148 812	75 471	73 342	142 678	73 109	69 569
15 - 19	271 684	137 805	133 878	146 537	73 631	72 906	125 147	64 174	60 974
20 - 24	254 772	129 237	125 536	146 169	72 295	73 875	108 605	56 944	51 661
25 - 29	250 152	125 922	124 230	150 336	71 923	78 413	99 816	53 999	45 817
30 - 34	230 835	115 884	114 951	141 488	67 582	73 906	89 347	48 302	41 045
35 - 39	203 446	101 421	102 025	126 268	59 890	66 378	77 178	41 531	35 647
40 - 44	170 180	84 702	85 478	105 158	50 101	55 057	65 022	34 601	30 421
45 - 49	140 684	70 369	70 315	86 739	41 477	45 262	53 945	28 892	25 053
50 - 54	115 342	58 278	57 064	69 710	33 225	36 485	45 632	25 053	20 579
55 - 59	93 684	47 379	46 305	53 771	25 760	28 011	39 913	21 619	18 294
60 - 64	73 087	36 664	36 423	40 256	18 795	21 461	32 831	17 869	14 962
65 - 69	55 236	27 712	27 524	30 061	13 914	16 147	25 175	13 798	11 377
70 - 74	43 900	21 495	22 405	24 076	10 692	13 384	19 824	10 803	9 021
75 - 79	30 250	14 158	16 092	17 010	7 216	9 794	13 240	6 942	6 298
80 +	28 727	13 063	15 664	16 083	6 367	9 716	12 644	6 696	5 948

7. Population by age, sex and urban/rural residence: latest available year, 1997 - 2006
Population selon l'âge, le sexe et la résidence, urbaine/rurale: dernière année disponible, 1997 - 2006 (continued - suite)

Continent, country or area, date, code and age (in years) — Continent, pays ou zone, date, code et âge (en annèes)	Total			Urban - Urbaine			Rural - Rurale		
	Both sexes Les deux sexes	Male Masculin	Female Féminin	Both sexes Les deux sexes	Male Masculin	Female Féminin	Both sexes Les deux sexes	Male Masculin	Female Féminin
AMERICA, NORTH - AMÉRIQUE DU NORD									
Panama									
1 VII 2006 (ESDF)									
Total....................	3 283 959	1 656 469	1 627 490	...	...	...	...	...	...
0 - 4.....................	345 075	176 208	168 867	...	...	...	...	...	...
5 - 9.....................	332 782	169 919	162 863	...	...	...	...	...	...
10 - 14...................	311 909	159 197	152 712	...	...	...	...	...	...
15 - 19...................	302 064	153 919	148 145	...	...	...	...	...	...
20 - 24...................	282 585	143 601	138 984	...	...	...	...	...	...
25 - 29...................	266 603	134 923	131 680	...	...	...	...	...	...
30 - 34...................	263 104	132 469	130 635	...	...	...	...	...	...
35 - 39...................	244 441	122 883	121 558	...	...	...	...	...	...
40 - 44...................	211 442	105 789	105 653	...	...	...	...	...	...
45 - 49...................	175 069	87 052	88 017	...	...	...	...	...	...
50 - 54...................	143 081	71 107	71 974	...	...	...	...	...	...
55 - 59...................	115 497	57 850	57 647	...	...	...	...	...	...
60 - 64...................	92 979	46 371	46 608	...	...	...	...	...	...
65 - 69...................	70 241	34 763	35 478	...	...	...	...	...	...
70 - 74...................	53 174	26 002	27 172	...	...	...	...	...	...
75 - 79...................	38 088	18 127	19 961	...	...	...	...	...	...
80 +.....................	35 825	16 289	19 536	...	...	...	...	...	...
Puerto Rico - Porto Rico[12]									
1 VII 2006 (ESDJ)									
Total....................	3 927 776	1 886 031	2 041 745	...	...	...	...	...	...
0	49 929	25 555	24 374	...	...	...	...	...	...
1 - 4....................	201 675	103 029	98 646	...	...	...	...	...	...
5 - 9....................	284 942	145 609	139 333	...	...	...	...	...	...
10 - 14...................	302 626	155 005	147 621	...	...	...	...	...	...
15 - 19...................	296 387	150 471	145 916	...	...	...	...	...	...
20 - 24...................	290 226	145 710	144 516	...	...	...	...	...	...
25 - 29...................	284 404	139 587	144 817	...	...	...	...	...	...
30 - 34...................	268 935	131 056	137 879	...	...	...	...	...	...
35 - 39...................	262 196	126 006	136 190	...	...	...	...	...	...
40 - 44...................	265 094	124 769	140 325	...	...	...	...	...	...
45 - 49...................	255 773	118 535	137 238	...	...	...	...	...	...
50 - 54...................	236 075	108 485	127 590	...	...	...	...	...	...
55 - 59...................	231 156	105 705	125 451	...	...	...	...	...	...
60 - 64...................	194 474	88 701	105 773	...	...	...	...	...	...
65 - 69...................	158 321	72 032	86 289	...	...	...	...	...	...
70 - 74...................	126 025	55 972	70 053	...	...	...	...	...	...
75 - 79...................	93 386	39 894	53 492	...	...	...	...	...	...
80 +.....................	126 152	49 910	76 242	...	...	...	...	...	...
Saint Kitts and Nevis - Saint-Kitts-et-Nevis									
1 VII 2000 (ESDF)									
Total....................	40 410	20 400	20 010	...	...	...	...	...	...
0 - 4.....................	4 250	2 130	2 120	...	...	...	...	...	...
5 - 9.....................	4 100	2 140	1 960	...	...	...	...	...	...
10 - 14...................	4 040	2 120	1 920	...	...	...	...	...	...
15 - 19...................	3 870	2 000	1 870	...	...	...	...	...	...
20 - 24...................	3 620	1 880	1 740	...	...	...	...	...	...
25 - 29...................	3 240	1 640	1 600	...	...	...	...	...	...
30 - 34...................	3 100	1 550	1 550	...	...	...	...	...	...
35 - 39...................	2 910	1 430	1 480	...	...	...	...	...	...
40 - 44...................	2 520	1 270	1 250	...	...	...	...	...	...
45 - 49...................	1 880	900	980	...	...	...	...	...	...
50 - 54...................	1 390	710	680	...	...	...	...	...	...
55 - 59...................	1 100	560	540	...	...	...	...	...	...
60 - 64...................	820	400	420	...	...	...	...	...	...
65 - 69...................	840	410	430	...	...	...	...	...	...
70 - 74...................	810	380	430	...	...	...	...	...	...
75 - 79...................	700	330	370	...	...	...	...	...	...
80 - 84...................	470	240	230	...	...	...	...	...	...
85 +.....................	750	310	440	...	...	...	...	...	...

7. Population by age, sex and urban/rural residence: latest available year, 1997 - 2006
Population selon l'âge, le sexe et la résidence, urbaine/rurale: dernière année disponible, 1997 - 2006 (continued - suite)

Continent, country or area, date, code and age (in years) / Continent, pays ou zone, date, code et âge (en annèes)	Total			Urban - Urbaine			Rural - Rurale		
	Both sexes Les deux sexes	Male Masculin	Female Féminin	Both sexes Les deux sexes	Male Masculin	Female Féminin	Both sexes Les deux sexes	Male Masculin	Female Féminin
AMERICA, NORTH - AMÉRIQUE DU NORD									
Saint Lucia - Sainte-Lucie									
22 V 2001 (CDFC)									
Total...................	157 164	76 741	80 423	42 310	20 208	22 102	111 559	54 897	56 662
0	973	458	515	238	120	118	735	338	397
1 - 4	12 958	6 485	6 473	3 203	1 627	1 576	9 755	4 858	4 897
5 - 9	16 382	8 260	8 122	3 906	1 963	1 943	12 476	6 297	6 179
10 - 14	16 605	8 323	8 282	4 023	2 005	2 018	12 582	6 318	6 264
15 - 19	16 348	8 051	8 297	4 296	2 116	2 180	12 052	5 935	6 117
20 - 24	13 369	6 635	6 734	3 886	1 947	1 939	9 483	4 688	4 795
25 - 29	12 572	6 112	6 460	3 592	1 788	1 804	8 980	4 324	4 656
30 - 34	11 419	5 652	5 767	2 822	1 481	1 341	8 597	4 171	4 426
35 - 39	11 167	5 397	5 770	3 238	1 576	1 662	7 929	3 821	4 108
40 - 44	9 041	4 410	4 631	2 531	1 193	1 338	6 510	3 217	3 293
45 - 49	6 811	3 401	3 410	2 109	995	1 114	4 702	2 406	2 296
50 - 54	5 830	2 926	2 904	1 958	1 000	958	3 872	1 926	1 946
55 - 59	4 479	2 103	2 376	1 353	599	754	3 126	1 504	1 622
60 - 64	3 856	1 788	2 068	1 030	416	614	2 826	1 372	1 454
65 - 69	3 573	1 661	1 912	1 043	440	603	2 530	1 221	1 309
70 - 74	2 776	1 326	1 450	909	399	510	1 867	927	940
75 - 79	2 217	991	1 226	684	283	401	1 533	708	825
80 - 84	1 570	647	923	483	176	307	1 087	471	616
85 - 89	897	352	545	272	81	191	625	271	354
90 - 94	323	128	195	120	39	81	203	89	114
95 + ...	143	53	90	54	18	36	89	35	54
1 VII 2006 (ESDF)									
Total...................	166 838	81 681	85 157	...	...	...	...	...	...
0 - 4	14 382	7 165	7 217	...	...	...	...	...	...
5 - 9	15 001	7 488	7 513	...	...	...	...	...	...
10 - 14	17 231	8 703	8 528	...	...	...	...	...	...
15 - 19	17 645	8 752	8 893	...	...	...	...	...	...
20 - 24	16 312	8 020	8 292	...	...	...	...	...	...
25 - 29	13 812	6 751	7 061	...	...	...	...	...	...
30 - 34	12 744	6 156	6 588	...	...	...	...	...	...
35 - 39	11 792	5 688	6 104	...	...	...	...	...	...
40 - 44	11 304	5 460	5 844	...	...	...	...	...	...
45 - 49	9 088	4 437	4 651	...	...	...	...	...	...
50 - 54	6 768	3 426	3 342	...	...	...	...	...	...
55 - 59	5 206	2 529	2 677	...	...	...	...	...	...
60 - 64	4 156	1 926	2 230	...	...	...	...	...	...
65 - 69	3 563	1 658	1 905	...	...	...	...	...	...
70 - 74	3 076	1 442	1 634	...	...	...	...	...	...
75 - 79	2 000	925	1 075	...	...	...	...	...	...
80 + ...	2 758	1 155	1 603	...	...	...	...	...	...
Saint Vincent and the Grenadines - Saint Vincent-et-les Grenadines[13]									
14 V 2001 (CDFC)									
Total...................	106 253	53 626	52 627	...	...	...	...	...	...
0 - 4	9 975	5 128	4 847	...	...	...	...	...	...
5 - 9	11 457	5 739	5 718	...	...	...	...	...	...
10 - 14	11 143	5 650	5 493	...	...	...	...	...	...
15 - 19	11 293	5 676	5 617	...	...	...	...	...	...
20 - 24	9 715	4 975	4 740	...	...	...	...	...	...
25 - 29	8 515	4 350	4 165	...	...	...	...	...	...
30 - 34	7 672	4 018	3 654	...	...	...	...	...	...
35 - 39	8 069	4 194	3 875	...	...	...	...	...	...
40 - 44	6 695	3 447	3 248	...	...	...	...	...	...
45 - 49	4 729	2 415	2 314	...	...	...	...	...	...
50 - 54	3 733	1 938	1 795	...	...	...	...	...	...
55 - 59	2 783	1 393	1 390	...	...	...	...	...	...
60 - 64	2 734	1 310	1 424	...	...	...	...	...	...
65 - 69	2 551	1 226	1 325	...	...	...	...	...	...
70 - 74	1 951	891	1 060	...	...	...	...	...	...
75 - 79	1 514	634	880	...	...	...	...	...	...

Continent, country or area, date, code and age (in years) / Continent, pays ou zone, date, code et âge (en années)	Total			Urban - Urbaine			Rural - Rurale		
	Both sexes Les deux sexes	Male Masculin	Female Féminin	Both sexes Les deux sexes	Male Masculin	Female Féminin	Both sexes Les deux sexes	Male Masculin	Female Féminin
AMERICA, NORTH - AMÉRIQUE DU NORD									
Saint Vincent and the Grenadines - Saint Vincent-et-les Grenadines[13]									
14 V 2001 (CDFC)									
80 - 84	943	385	558	...	...	...	...	...	...
85 +	781	257	524	...	...	...	...	...	...
Unknown - Inconnu	-	-	-	...	...	...	...	...	...
Trinidad and Tobago - Trinité-et-Tobago									
1 VII 1999 (ESDF)									
Total	1 283 863	640 914	642 949	...	...	...	...	...	...
0 - 4	86 272	43 501	42 771	...	...	...	...	...	...
5 - 9	108 030	55 286	52 744	...	...	...	...	...	...
10 - 14	128 496	65 242	63 254	...	...	...	...	...	...
15 - 19	125 851	64 835	61 016	...	...	...	...	...	...
20 - 24	116 913	60 316	56 597	...	...	...	...	...	...
25 - 29	107 970	54 735	53 235	...	...	...	...	...	...
30 - 34	102 098	51 124	50 974	...	...	...	...	...	...
35 - 39	102 869	50 435	52 434	...	...	...	...	...	...
40 - 44	94 053	47 403	46 650	...	...	...	...	...	...
45 - 49	79 996	39 595	40 401	...	...	...	...	...	...
50 - 54	61 988	30 951	31 037	...	...	...	...	...	...
55 - 59	48 415	23 125	25 290	...	...	...	...	...	...
60 - 64	34 697	16 917	17 780	...	...	...	...	...	...
65 +	86 215	37 449	48 766	...	...	...	...	...	...
Turks Caicos Islands - Îles Turques et Caïques									
20 VIII 2001 (CDFC)									
Total	19 886	9 896	9 990	...	...	...	...	...	...
0 - 4	2 324	1 053	1 271	...	...	...	...	...	...
5 - 14	3 369	1 683	1 686	...	...	...	...	...	...
15 - 24	2 663	1 270	1 393	...	...	...	...	...	...
25 - 49	9 168	4 688	4 480	...	...	...	...	...	...
50 - 64	1 605	868	737	...	...	...	...	...	...
65 +	757	334	423	...	...	...	...	...	...
United States - États-Unis[14]									
1 IV 2000 (CDJC)									
Total	281 421 906	138 053 563	143 368 343	222 360 539	108 375 797	113 984 742	59 061 367	29 677 766	29 383 601
0	3 805 648	1 949 017	1 856 631	3 108 179	1 591 301	1 516 878	697 469	357 716	339 753
1 - 4	15 370 150	7 861 716	7 508 434	12 426 799	6 352 829	6 073 970	2 943 351	1 508 887	1 434 464
5 - 9	20 549 505	10 523 277	10 026 228	16 303 052	8 338 164	7 964 888	4 246 453	2 185 113	2 061 340
10 - 14	20 528 072	10 520 197	10 007 875	15 865 132	8 114 898	7 750 234	4 662 940	2 405 299	2 257 641
15 - 19	20 219 890	10 391 004	9 828 886	15 862 692	8 092 790	7 769 902	4 357 198	2 298 214	2 058 984
20 - 24	18 964 001	9 687 814	9 276 187	16 062 564	8 150 162	7 912 402	2 901 437	1 537 652	1 363 785
25 - 29	19 381 336	9 798 760	9 582 576	16 247 338	8 210 254	8 037 084	3 133 998	1 588 506	1 545 492
30 - 34	20 510 388	10 321 769	10 188 619	16 761 355	8 449 017	8 312 338	3 749 033	1 872 752	1 876 281
35 - 39	22 706 664	11 318 696	11 387 968	17 967 717	8 957 072	9 010 645	4 738 947	2 361 624	2 377 323
40 - 44	22 441 863	11 129 102	11 312 761	17 434 999	8 608 239	8 826 760	5 006 864	2 520 863	2 486 001
45 - 49	20 092 404	9 889 506	10 202 898	15 431 618	7 528 331	7 903 287	4 660 786	2 361 175	2 299 611
50 - 54	17 585 548	8 607 724	8 977 824	13 395 145	6 480 878	6 914 267	4 190 403	2 126 846	2 063 557
55 - 59	13 469 237	6 508 729	6 960 508	10 060 185	4 791 948	5 268 237	3 409 052	1 716 781	1 692 271
60 - 64	10 805 447	5 136 627	5 668 820	8 026 903	3 738 462	4 288 441	2 778 544	1 398 165	1 380 379
65 - 69	9 533 545	4 400 362	5 133 183	7 180 256	3 236 555	3 943 701	2 353 289	1 163 807	1 189 482
70 - 74	8 857 441	3 902 912	4 954 529	6 865 515	2 943 669	3 921 846	1 991 926	959 243	1 032 683
75 - 79	7 415 813	3 044 456	4 371 357	5 901 375	2 007 060	3 521 106	1 514 438	677 187	837 251
80 - 84	4 945 367	1 834 897	3 110 470	3 982 799	1 445 556	2 537 243	962 568	389 341	573 227
85 - 89	2 789 818	876 501	1 913 317	2 274 316	695 943	1 578 373	515 502	180 558	334 944
90 - 94	1 112 531	282 325	830 206	920 357	227 019	693 338	192 174	55 306	136 868
95 - 99	286 784	58 115	228 669	239 942	47 265	192 677	46 842	10 850	35 992
100 +	50 454	10 057	40 397	42 301	8 176	34 125	8 153	1 881	6 272
1 VII 2005 (ESDJ)									
Total	296 410 404	145 999 746	150 410 658	...	...	...	...	...	...
0	4 106 627	2 101 135	2 005 492	...	...	...	...	...	...
1 - 4	16 197 097	8 280 211	7 916 886	...	...	...	...	...	...

Continent, country or area, date, code and age (in years) / Continent, pays ou zone, date, code et âge (en années)	Total			Urban - Urbaine			Rural - Rurale		
	Both sexes Les deux sexes	Male Masculin	Female Féminin	Both sexes Les deux sexes	Male Masculin	Female Féminin	Both sexes Les deux sexes	Male Masculin	Female Féminin
AMERICA, NORTH - AMÉRIQUE DU NORD									
United States - États-Unis[14]									
1 VII 2005 (ESDJ)									
5 - 9	19 538 793	9 993 397	9 545 396	...	...	...	...	...	...
10 - 14	20 857 743	10 681 835	10 175 908	...	...	...	...	...	...
15 - 19	21 038 989	10 790 223	10 248 766	...	...	...	...	...	...
20 - 24	21 037 860	10 856 936	10 180 924	...	...	...	...	...	...
25 - 29	20 065 702	10 268 169	9 797 533	...	...	...	...	...	...
30 - 34	20 077 210	10 153 091	9 924 119	...	...	...	...	...	...
35 - 39	21 001 954	10 563 375	10 438 579	...	...	...	...	...	...
40 - 44	22 860 510	11 376 664	11 483 846	...	...	...	...	...	...
45 - 49	22 484 523	11 106 575	11 377 948	...	...	...	...	...	...
50 - 54	19 997 742	9 788 780	10 208 962	...	...	...	...	...	...
55 - 59	17 353 678	8 425 070	8 928 608	...	...	...	...	...	...
60 - 64	13 001 863	6 201 648	6 800 215	...	...	...	...	...	...
65 - 69	10 131 444	4 721 791	5 409 653	...	...	...	...	...	...
70 - 74	8 508 369	3 807 605	4 700 764	...	...	...	...	...	...
75 - 79	7 411 813	3 117 774	4 294 039	...	...	...	...	...	...
80 - 84	5 642 549	2 161 671	3 480 878	...	...	...	...	...	...
85 - 89	3 210 503	1 092 012	2 118 491	...	...	...	...	...	...
90 - 94	1 414 938	404 657	1 010 281	...	...	...	...	...	...
95 - 99	400 393	93 114	307 279	...	...	...	...	...	...
100 +	70 104	14 013	56 091	...	...	...	...	...	...
United States Virgin Islands - Îles Vierges américaines[12]									
1 IV 2000 (CDJC)									
Total	108 612	...	...	...	...	...	...	...	...
0 - 4	8 553	...	...	...	...	...	...	...	...
5 - 9	10 176	...	...	...	...	...	...	...	...
10 - 14	9 676	...	...	...	...	...	...	...	...
15 - 19	8 688	...	...	...	...	...	...	...	...
20 - 24	5 916	...	...	...	...	...	...	...	...
25 - 34	13 705	...	...	...	...	...	...	...	...
35 - 44	15 746	...	...	...	...	...	...	...	...
45 - 54	15 521	...	...	...	...	...	...	...	...
55 - 59	6 757	...	...	...	...	...	...	...	...
60 - 64	4 757	...	...	...	...	...	...	...	...
65 - 74	5 845	...	...	...	...	...	...	...	...
75 - 84	2 505	...	...	...	...	...	...	...	...
85 +	767	...	...	...	...	...	...	...	...
AMERICA, SOUTH - AMÉRIQUE DU SUD									
Argentina - Argentine									
1 VII 2005 (ESDF)									
Total	38 592 150	18 898 472	19 693 678	34 894 057	16 961 698	17 932 359	3 698 093	1 936 774	1 761 319
0 - 4	3 329 198	1 693 479	1 635 719	2 918 049	1 488 141	1 429 908	411 149	205 338	205 811
0	665 439	338 643	326 796	...	...	...	...	...	...
1 - 4	2 663 759	1 354 836	1 308 923	...	...	...	...	...	...
5 - 9	3 419 104	1 738 020	1 681 084	2 993 762	1 525 211	1 468 551	425 342	212 809	212 533
10 - 14	3 456 317	1 755 899	1 700 418	3 060 166	1 556 344	1 503 822	396 151	199 555	196 596
15 - 19	3 361 395	1 705 978	1 655 417	3 022 703	1 527 187	1 495 516	338 692	178 791	159 901
20 - 24	3 225 378	1 629 984	1 595 394	2 938 711	1 477 950	1 460 761	286 667	152 034	134 633
25 - 29	3 268 243	1 641 925	1 626 318	2 999 963	1 501 016	1 498 947	268 280	140 909	127 371
30 - 34	2 732 974	1 367 895	1 365 079	2 506 251	1 248 597	1 257 654	226 723	119 298	107 425
35 - 39	2 398 695	1 195 951	1 202 744	2 196 309	1 086 570	1 109 739	202 386	109 381	93 005
40 - 44	2 261 291	1 117 097	1 144 194	2 065 328	1 009 217	1 056 111	195 963	107 880	88 083
45 - 49	2 119 022	1 024 468	1 094 554	1 933 827	923 523	1 010 304	185 195	100 945	84 250
50 - 54	1 975 521	953 838	1 021 683	1 800 662	857 541	943 121	174 859	96 297	78 562
55 - 59	1 722 476	822 699	899 777	1 570 198	737 371	832 827	152 278	85 328	66 950
60 - 64	1 449 366	680 458	768 908	1 319 570	607 934	711 636	129 796	72 524	57 272
65 - 69	1 221 234	549 019	672 215	1 118 457	493 177	625 280	102 777	55 842	46 935
70 - 74	1 035 416	438 837	596 579	952 950	395 628	557 322	82 466	43 209	39 257

7. Population by age, sex and urban/rural residence: latest available year, 1997 - 2006
Population selon l'âge, le sexe et la résidence, urbaine/rurale: dernière année disponible, 1997 - 2006 (continued - suite)

Continent, country or area, date, code and age (in years) / Continent, pays ou zone, date, code et âge (en années)	Total			Urban - Urbaine			Rural - Rurale		
	Both sexes Les deux sexes	Male Masculin	Female Féminin	Both sexes Les deux sexes	Male Masculin	Female Féminin	Both sexes Les deux sexes	Male Masculin	Female Féminin
AMERICA, SOUTH - AMÉRIQUE DU SUD									
Argentina - Argentine									
1 VII 2005 (ESDF)									
75 - 79	813 712	318 893	494 819	752 951	287 828	465 123	60 761	31 065	29 696
80 +	802 808	264 032	538 776	744 200	238 463	505 737	58 608	25 569	33 039
1 VII 2006 (ESDF)									
Total	38 970 611	19 083 828	19 886 783	...	...	...	...	...	...
0 - 4	3 335 240	1 696 718	1 638 522	...	...	...	...	...	...
5 - 9	3 399 182	1 727 996	1 671 186	...	...	...	...	...	...
10 - 14	3 456 504	1 756 088	1 700 416	...	...	...	...	...	...
15 - 19	3 382 643	1 717 102	1 665 541	...	...	...	...	...	...
20 - 24	3 238 391	1 637 640	1 600 751	...	...	...	...	...	...
25 - 29	3 290 041	1 653 784	1 636 257	...	...	...	...	...	...
30 - 34	2 832 066	1 417 740	1 414 326	...	...	...	...	...	...
35 - 39	2 444 972	1 219 550	1 225 422	...	...	...	...	...	...
40 - 44	2 279 925	1 128 336	1 151 589	...	...	...	...	...	...
45 - 49	2 139 201	1 036 319	1 102 882	...	...	...	...	...	...
50 - 54	1 999 568	963 891	1 035 677	...	...	...	...	...	...
55 - 59	1 760 017	840 039	919 978	...	...	...	...	...	...
60 - 64	1 480 507	694 800	785 707	...	...	...	...	...	...
65 - 69	1 236 765	556 954	679 811	...	...	...	...	...	...
70 - 74	1 040 690	441 346	599 344	...	...	...	...	...	...
75 - 79	823 122	322 568	500 554	...	...	...	...	...	...
80 +	831 777	272 957	558 820	...	...	...	...	...	...
Bolivia - Bolivie									
1 VII 2003 (ESDF)									
Total	9 024 922	4 495 426	4 529 495	5 713 606	2 780 802	2 932 804	3 311 316	1 714 625	1 596 692
0 - 4	...	...	...	744 336	377 941	366 395	507 820	260 704	247 117
0	254 798	129 963	124 834	...	...	...	...	...	...
1 - 4	997 358	508 681	488 678	...	...	...	...	...	...
5 - 9	1 166 265	594 608	571 657	692 312	349 521	342 790	473 953	245 087	228 866
10 - 14	1 073 561	546 244	527 317	675 965	336 689	339 276	397 596	209 555	188 041
15 - 19	932 510	472 358	460 151	630 783	309 369	321 414	301 727	162 989	138 737
20 - 24	814 526	409 846	404 680	572 694	281 691	291 003	241 832	128 155	113 677
25 - 29	721 254	359 771	361 483	494 257	239 881	254 376	226 998	119 890	107 107
30 - 34	624 992	309 212	315 780	427 459	204 574	222 885	197 533	104 638	92 895
35 - 39	512 151	251 779	260 373	334 677	158 910	175 767	177 474	92 868	84 606
40 - 44	432 316	210 816	221 500	280 542	132 378	148 164	151 775	78 438	73 336
45 - 49	366 481	176 834	189 646	229 283	107 308	121 975	137 198	69 526	67 671
50 - 54	302 980	144 864	158 116	182 392	84 279	98 113	120 587	60 584	60 003
55 - 59	243 463	115 925	127 538	140 577	64 747	75 830	102 886	51 178	51 708
60 - 64	191 980	90 333	101 647	103 324	46 382	56 942	88 655	43 950	44 705
65 - 69	155 368	71 595	83 774	82 620	36 420	46 200	72 748	35 175	37 574
70 - 74	116 485	52 380	64 104	60 079	25 772	34 307	56 405	26 608	29 797
75 - 79	73 314	31 963	41 351	39 546	16 287	23 258	33 768	15 676	18 092
80 +	45 120	18 254	26 866	22 759	8 652	14 107	22 361	9 602	12 759
1 VII 2006 (ESDF)									
Total	9 627 269	4 799 178	4 828 091	...	...	...	...	...	...
0	265 157	135 288	129 868	...	...	...	...	...	...
1 - 4	1 022 322	521 187	501 135	...	...	...	...	...	...
5 - 9	1 198 737	611 181	587 556	...	...	...	...	...	...
10 - 14	1 135 680	578 457	557 223	...	...	...	...	...	...
15 - 19	1 006 825	510 944	495 882	...	...	...	...	...	...
20 - 24	876 469	442 185	434 285	...	...	...	...	...	...
25 - 29	767 145	384 014	383 130	...	...	...	...	...	...
30 - 34	683 878	339 150	344 728	...	...	...	...	...	...
35 - 39	567 781	279 793	287 987	...	...	...	...	...	...
40 - 44	469 536	229 661	239 875	...	...	...	...	...	...
45 - 49	398 492	193 132	205 360	...	...	...	...	...	...
50 - 54	329 979	157 842	172 137	...	...	...	...	...	...
55 - 59	270 534	128 460	142 074	...	...	...	...	...	...
60 - 64	208 815	98 236	110 578	...	...	...	...	...	...
65 - 69	166 751	76 888	89 863	...	...	...	...	...	...
70 - 74	124 009	55 640	68 368	...	...	...	...	...	...

7. Population by age, sex and urban/rural residence: latest available year, 1997 - 2006
Population selon l'âge, le sexe et la résidence, urbaine/rurale: dernière année disponible, 1997 - 2006 (continued - suite)

Continent, country or area, date, code and age (in years) / Continent, pays ou zone, date, code et âge (en années)	Total			Urban - Urbaine			Rural - Rurale		
	Both sexes Les deux sexes	Male Masculin	Female Féminin	Both sexes Les deux sexes	Male Masculin	Female Féminin	Both sexes Les deux sexes	Male Masculin	Female Féminin
AMERICA, SOUTH - AMÉRIQUE DU SUD									
Bolivia - Bolivie									
1 VII 2006 (ESDF)									
75 - 79	82 728	35 957	46 770	...	...	...	...	...	...
80 +	52 433	21 163	31 270	...	...	...	...	...	...
Brazil - Brésil[15]									
1 VIII 2000 (CDJC)									
Total	169 799 170	83 576 015	86 223 155	137 953 959	66 882 993	71 070 966	31 845 211	16 693 022	15 152 189
0	3 213 310	1 635 916	1 577 394	2 518 464	1 282 941	1 235 523	694 846	352 975	341 871
1 - 4	13 162 418	6 691 010	6 471 408	10 242 356	5 207 423	5 034 933	2 920 062	1 483 587	1 436 475
5 - 9	16 542 327	8 402 353	8 139 974	12 821 519	6 500 814	6 320 705	3 720 808	1 901 539	1 819 269
10 - 14	17 348 067	8 777 639	8 570 428	13 530 190	6 803 898	6 726 292	3 817 877	1 973 741	1 844 136
15 - 19	17 939 815	9 019 130	8 920 685	14 403 539	7 132 822	7 270 717	3 536 276	1 886 308	1 649 968
20 - 24	16 141 515	8 048 218	8 093 297	13 352 132	6 549 365	6 802 767	2 789 383	1 498 853	1 290 530
25 - 29	13 849 665	6 814 328	7 035 337	11 570 969	5 606 425	5 964 544	2 278 696	1 207 903	1 070 793
30 - 34	13 028 944	6 363 983	6 664 961	10 918 396	5 248 443	5 669 953	2 110 548	1 115 540	995 008
35 - 39	12 261 529	5 955 875	6 305 654	10 326 271	4 929 130	5 397 141	1 935 258	1 026 745	908 513
40 - 44	10 546 694	5 116 439	5 430 255	8 913 019	4 249 804	4 663 215	1 633 675	866 635	767 040
45 - 49	8 721 541	4 216 418	4 505 123	7 309 621	3 472 375	3 837 246	1 411 920	744 043	667 877
50 - 54	7 062 601	3 415 678	3 646 923	5 833 659	2 764 708	3 068 951	1 228 942	650 970	577 972
55 - 59	5 444 715	2 585 244	2 859 471	4 387 995	2 032 135	2 355 860	1 056 720	553 109	503 611
60 - 64	4 600 929	2 153 209	2 447 720	3 712 213	1 676 323	2 035 890	888 716	476 886	411 830
65 - 69	3 581 106	1 639 325	1 941 781	2 916 899	1 284 812	1 632 087	664 207	354 513	309 694
70 - 74	2 742 302	1 229 329	1 512 973	2 249 617	966 115	1 283 502	492 685	263 214	229 471
75 - 79	1 779 587	780 571	999 016	1 456 665	610 767	845 898	322 922	169 804	153 118
80 - 84	1 036 034	428 501	607 533	841 798	331 002	510 796	194 236	97 499	96 737
85 - 89	534 871	208 088	326 783	436 121	160 379	275 742	98 750	47 709	51 041
90 - 94	180 426	65 117	115 309	147 784	50 531	97 253	32 642	14 586	18 056
95 - 99	56 198	19 221	36 977	45 682	14 899	30 783	10 516	4 322	6 194
100 +	24 576	10 423	14 153	19 050	7 882	11 168	5 526	2 541	2 985
1 VII 2006 (ESDF)									
Total	186 770 562	91 784 158	94 986 404	...	...	...	...	...	...
0 - 4	18 103 960	9 191 486	8 912 474	...	...	...	...	...	...
5 - 9	17 160 388	8 703 192	8 457 196	...	...	...	...	...	...
10 - 14	16 483 958	8 347 253	8 136 705	...	...	...	...	...	...
15 - 19	17 110 663	8 634 519	8 476 144	...	...	...	...	...	...
20 - 24	17 830 018	8 953 548	8 876 470	...	...	...	...	...	...
25 - 29	16 183 394	8 074 746	8 108 648	...	...	...	...	...	...
30 - 34	14 326 804	7 117 920	7 208 884	...	...	...	...	...	...
35 - 39	13 550 118	6 648 256	6 901 862	...	...	...	...	...	...
40 - 44	12 843 021	6 162 387	6 680 634	...	...	...	...	...	...
45 - 49	10 888 536	5 169 687	5 718 849	...	...	...	...	...	...
50 - 54	8 692 193	4 090 451	4 601 742	...	...	...	...	...	...
55 - 59	6 775 234	3 177 430	3 597 804	...	...	...	...	...	...
60 - 64	5 201 071	2 396 934	2 804 137	...	...	...	...	...	...
65 - 69	4 234 849	1 936 671	2 298 178	...	...	...	...	...	...
70 - 74	3 051 419	1 352 848	1 698 571	...	...	...	...	...	...
75 - 79	2 175 186	932 908	1 242 278	...	...	...	...	...	...
80 +	2 159 750	893 922	1 265 828	...	...	...	...	...	...
Chile - Chili									
1 VII 2006 (ESDF)									
Total	16 432 674	8 134 314	8 298 360	14 272 454	6 983 850	7 288 604	2 160 220	1 150 464	1 009 756
0 - 4	1 239 635	631 321	608 314	1 087 369	553 513	533 856	152 266	77 808	74 458
5 - 9	1 310 000	666 787	643 213	1 138 883	579 259	559 624	171 117	87 528	83 589
10 - 14	1 456 584	741 051	715 533	1 257 366	638 598	618 768	199 218	102 453	96 765
15 - 19	1 468 190	746 142	722 048	1 266 261	640 594	625 667	201 929	105 548	96 381
20 - 24	1 350 171	684 494	665 677	1 179 942	591 149	588 793	170 229	93 345	76 884
25 - 29	1 201 033	605 947	595 086	1 060 914	529 574	531 340	140 119	76 373	63 746
30 - 34	1 225 810	614 983	610 827	1 079 741	536 978	542 763	146 069	78 005	68 064
35 - 39	1 238 440	618 523	619 917	1 079 685	534 021	545 664	158 755	84 502	74 253
40 - 44	1 255 704	624 448	631 256	1 089 136	533 606	555 530	166 568	90 842	75 726
45 - 49	1 122 138	555 405	566 733	975 748	473 949	501 799	146 390	81 456	64 934
50 - 54	900 770	442 330	458 440	784 269	377 278	406 991	116 501	65 052	51 449
55 - 59	727 764	352 370	375 394	630 534	298 666	331 868	97 230	53 704	43 526
60 - 64	595 937	282 296	313 641	511 412	236 470	274 942	84 525	45 826	38 699

7. Population by age, sex and urban/rural residence: latest available year, 1997 - 2006
Population selon l'âge, le sexe et la résidence, urbaine/rurale: dernière année disponible, 1997 - 2006 (continued - suite)

Continent, country or area, date, code and age (in years) / Continent, pays ou zone, date, code et âge (en années)	Total			Urban - Urbaine			Rural - Rurale		
	Both sexes Les deux sexes	Male Masculin	Female Féminin	Both sexes Les deux sexes	Male Masculin	Female Féminin	Both sexes Les deux sexes	Male Masculin	Female Féminin
AMERICA, SOUTH - AMÉRIQUE DU SUD									
Chile - Chili									
1 VII 2006 (ESDF)									
65 - 69	454 163	208 832	245 331	383 473	170 898	212 575	70 690	37 934	32 756
70 - 74	356 491	155 902	200 589	298 825	125 691	173 134	57 666	30 211	27 455
75 - 79	264 110	108 526	155 584	223 260	87 557	135 703	40 850	20 969	19 881
80 +	265 734	94 957	170 777	225 636	76 049	149 587	40 098	18 908	21 190
Colombia - Colombie									
1 VII 2006 (ESDF)									
Total	43 405 387	21 425 328	21 980 059	...	...	...	...	...	...
0 - 4	4 316 261	2 205 283	2 110 978	...	...	...	...	...	...
5 - 9	4 445 103	2 266 982	2 178 121	...	...	...	...	...	...
10 - 14	4 500 956	2 306 902	2 194 054	...	...	...	...	...	...
15 - 19	4 233 539	2 167 094	2 066 445	...	...	...	...	...	...
20 - 24	3 791 922	1 884 930	1 906 992	...	...	...	...	...	...
25 - 29	3 418 635	1 675 329	1 743 306	...	...	...	...	...	...
30 - 34	3 023 034	1 467 176	1 555 858	...	...	...	...	...	...
35 - 39	2 987 231	1 435 672	1 551 559	...	...	...	...	...	...
40 - 44	2 851 635	1 369 639	1 481 996	...	...	...	...	...	...
45 - 49	2 432 088	1 162 401	1 269 687	...	...	...	...	...	...
50 51	1 956 531	937 837	1 018 694	...	...	...	...	...	...
55 - 59	1 550 311	744 255	806 056	...	...	...	...	...	...
60 - 64	1 176 472	563 172	613 300	...	...	...	...	...	...
65 - 69	958 527	449 019	509 508	...	...	...	...	...	...
70 - 74	741 043	339 930	401 113	...	...	...	...	...	...
75 - 79	501 819	227 712	274 107	...	...	...	...	...	...
80 +	520 280	221 995	298 285	...	...	...	...	...	...
Ecuador - Équateur[16]									
1 VII 2004 (ESDF)									
Total	13 026 891	6 535 564	6 491 327	8 187 908	4 057 642	4 130 266	4 838 983	2 477 922	2 361 061
0 - 4	...	...	...	845 152	436 348	408 804	603 550	302 713	300 837
0	289 789	147 951	141 838	...	...	...	...	...	...
1 - 4	1 158 913	591 110	567 803	...	...	...	...	...	...
5 - 9	1 441 016	734 425	706 591	836 049	427 823	408 226	604 967	306 602	298 365
10 - 14	1 388 671	706 484	682 187	823 734	415 692	408 042	564 937	290 792	274 145
15 - 19	1 333 679	676 728	656 951	845 605	417 825	427 780	488 074	258 903	229 171
20 - 24	1 212 307	612 337	599 970	810 941	400 445	410 496	401 366	211 892	189 474
25 - 29	1 078 378	542 390	535 988	747 747	370 239	377 508	330 631	172 151	158 480
30 - 34	961 155	481 345	479 810	669 833	332 454	337 379	291 322	148 891	142 431
35 - 39	850 352	424 450	425 902	573 835	284 859	288 976	276 517	139 591	136 926
40 - 44	732 296	364 669	367 627	477 753	236 161	241 592	254 543	128 508	126 035
45 - 49	627 106	310 951	316 155	389 964	191 248	198 716	237 142	119 703	117 439
50 - 54	524 929	259 110	265 819	320 750	155 727	165 023	204 179	103 383	100 796
55 - 59	388 289	191 007	197 282	232 525	111 128	121 397	155 764	79 879	75 885
60 - 64	315 353	153 704	161 649	188 353	88 492	99 861	127 000	65 212	61 788
65 - 69	256 073	123 154	132 919	151 767	69 992	81 775	104 306	53 162	51 144
70 - 74	196 820	93 022	103 798	115 227	51 777	63 450	81 593	41 245	40 348
75 - 79	140 537	65 267	75 270	82 153	36 021	46 132	58 384	29 246	29 138
80 +	131 228	57 460	73 768	76 520	31 411	45 109	54 708	26 049	28 659
1 VII 2005 (ESDF)									
Total	13 215 089	6 628 368	6 586 721	...	...	...	...	...	...
0 - 4	1 445 080	737 258	707 822	...	...	...	...	...	...
5 - 9	1 446 824	737 543	709 281	...	...	...	...	...	...
10 - 14	1 393 402	709 081	684 321	...	...	...	...	...	...
15 - 19	1 341 419	680 849	660 570	...	...	...	...	...	...
20 - 24	1 226 894	619 791	607 103	...	...	...	...	...	...
25 - 29	1 094 290	550 287	544 003	...	...	...	...	...	...
30 - 34	976 014	488 676	487 338	...	...	...	...	...	...
35 - 39	867 949	433 025	434 924	...	...	...	...	...	...
40 - 44	750 456	373 564	376 892	...	...	...	...	...	...
45 - 49	642 240	318 410	323 830	...	...	...	...	...	...
50 - 54	548 106	270 440	277 666	...	...	...	...	...	...
55 - 59	405 117	199 246	205 871	...	...	...	...	...	...
60 - 64	325 144	158 469	166 675	...	...	...	...	...	...
65 - 69	264 095	127 014	137 081	...	...	...	...	...	...

7. Population by age, sex and urban/rural residence: latest available year, 1997 - 2006
Population selon l'âge, le sexe et la résidence, urbaine/rurale: dernière année disponible, 1997 - 2006 (continued - suite)

Continent, country or area, date, code and age (in years) / Continent, pays ou zone, date, code et âge (en années)	Total			Urban - Urbaine			Rural - Rurale		
	Both sexes Les deux sexes	Male Masculin	Female Féminin	Both sexes Les deux sexes	Male Masculin	Female Féminin	Both sexes Les deux sexes	Male Masculin	Female Féminin
AMERICA, SOUTH - AMÉRIQUE DU SUD									
Ecuador - Équateur[16]									
1 VII 2005 (ESDF)									
70 - 74	203 903	96 338	107 565	...	...	...	...	...	...
75 - 79	146 633	68 066	78 567	...	...	...	...	...	...
80 +	137 523	60 311	77 212	...	...	...	...	...	...
Falkland Islands (Malvinas) - Îles Falkland (Malvinas)[17]									
8 X 2006 (CDFC)									
Total	2 955	1 569	1 386	...	...	...	...	...	...
0 - 4	156	79	77	...	...	...	...	...	...
5 - 9	161	75	86	...	...	...	...	...	...
10 - 14	154	71	83	...	...	...	...	...	...
15 - 19	155	90	65	...	...	...	...	...	...
20 - 24	207	89	118	...	...	...	...	...	...
25 - 29	232	126	106	...	...	...	...	...	...
30 - 34	266	131	135	...	...	...	...	...	...
35 - 39	291	165	126	...	...	...	...	...	...
40 - 44	261	156	105	...	...	...	...	...	...
45 - 49	249	128	121	...	...	...	...	...	...
50 - 54	215	123	92	...	...	...	...	...	...
55 - 59	194	113	81	...	...	...	...	...	...
60 - 64	148	87	61	...	...	...	...	...	...
65 - 69	98	57	41	...	...	...	...	...	...
70 - 74	68	36	32	...	...	...	...	...	...
75 - 79	48	18	30	...	...	...	...	...	...
80 +	52	25	27	...	...	...	...	...	...
French Guiana - Guyane française									
1 I 2005 (ESDJ)									
Total	197 997	98 956	99 041	...	...	...	...	...	...
0 - 4	26 319	13 398	12 921	...	...	...	...	...	...
5 - 9	23 808	12 008	11 800	...	...	...	...	...	...
10 - 14	21 102	10 622	10 480	...	...	...	...	...	...
15 - 19	18 148	9 165	8 983	...	...	...	...	...	...
20 - 24	14 218	6 993	7 225	...	...	...	...	...	...
25 - 29	14 744	7 120	7 624	...	...	...	...	...	...
30 - 34	15 644	7 464	8 180	...	...	...	...	...	...
35 - 39	14 729	7 229	7 500	...	...	...	...	...	...
40 - 44	13 155	6 641	6 514	...	...	...	...	...	...
45 - 49	10 610	5 391	5 219	...	...	...	...	...	...
50 - 54	8 432	4 337	4 095	...	...	...	...	...	...
55 - 59	6 042	3 193	2 849	...	...	...	...	...	...
60 - 64	3 695	1 954	1 741	...	...	...	...	...	...
65 - 69	2 617	1 294	1 323	...	...	...	...	...	...
70 - 74	1 880	924	956	...	...	...	...	...	...
75 - 79	1 253	576	677	...	...	...	...	...	...
80 - 84	851	374	477	...	...	...	...	...	...
85 - 89	449	183	266	...	...	...	...	...	...
90 +	301	90	211	...	...	...	...	...	...
Guyana									
15 IX 2002 (CDFC)									
Total	751 223	376 034	375 189	213 705	103 127	110 578	537 518	272 907	264 611
0 - 4	88 996	45 291	43 705	22 436	11 372	11 064	66 560	33 919	32 642
5 - 9	96 671	49 119	47 552	25 254	12 909	12 345	71 416	36 210	35 206
10 - 14	81 497	41 218	40 279	22 393	11 215	11 178	59 104	30 002	29 101
15 - 19	66 922	33 496	33 426	19 559	9 737	9 822	47 363	23 759	23 604
20 - 24	64 409	31 908	32 501	19 443	9 301	10 142	44 966	22 608	22 359
25 - 29	61 086	30 232	30 854	18 068	8 439	9 629	43 017	21 792	21 225
30 - 34	57 942	29 088	28 854	16 403	7 687	8 717	41 538	21 401	20 137
35 - 39	52 735	26 441	26 295	14 716	6 779	7 937	38 020	19 662	18 358
40 - 44	46 488	23 338	23 150	13 203	6 194	7 009	33 285	17 144	16 141
45 - 49	35 810	17 952	17 859	10 609	4 910	5 699	25 202	13 042	12 160
50 - 54	28 149	14 207	13 942	8 459	4 008	4 450	19 690	10 198	9 492
55 - 59	18 129	8 980	9 149	5 539	2 628	2 911	12 590	6 352	6 238

7. Population by age, sex and urban/rural residence: latest available year, 1997 - 2006
Population selon l'âge, le sexe et la résidence, urbaine/rurale: dernière année disponible, 1997 - 2006 (continued - suite)

Continent, country or area, date, code and age (in years) Continent, pays ou zone, date, code et âge (en années)	Total			Urban - Urbaine			Rural - Rurale		
	Both sexes Les deux sexes	Male Masculin	Female Féminin	Both sexes Les deux sexes	Male Masculin	Female Féminin	Both sexes Les deux sexes	Male Masculin	Female Féminin
AMERICA, SOUTH - AMÉRIQUE DU SUD									
Guyana 15 IX 2002 (CDFC)									
60 - 64	15 005	7 191	7 813	4 540	2 081	2 459	10 465	5 110	5 354
65 - 69	11 741	5 575	6 167	3 671	1 649	2 021	8 071	3 925	4 145
70 - 74	8 543	3 965	4 578	2 784	1 212	1 571	5 759	2 753	3 006
75 + ...	11 746	5 217	6 529	3 977	1 640	2 337	7 769	3 577	4 192
Unknown - Inconnu	5 354	2 818	2 536	2 699	1 394	1 305	2 655	1 424	1 231
Paraguay 28 VIII 2002 (CDFC)									
Total.................	5 163 198	2 603 242	2 559 956	2 928 437	1 422 339	1 506 098	2 234 761	1 180 903	1 053 858
0	115 558	59 043	56 515	62 098	31 869	30 229	53 460	27 174	26 286
1 - 4	491 743	250 996	240 747	256 692	130 582	126 110	235 051	120 414	114 637
5 - 9	663 294	338 199	325 095	341 612	173 363	168 249	321 682	164 836	156 846
10 - 14	644 714	328 120	316 594	331 808	165 636	166 172	312 906	162 484	150 422
15 - 19	576 807	292 731	284 076	327 674	156 108	171 566	249 133	136 623	112 510
20 - 24	472 545	238 527	234 018	294 654	139 622	155 032	177 891	98 905	78 986
25 - 29	359 766	179 299	180 467	221 966	105 928	116 038	137 800	73 371	64 429
30 - 34	333 192	167 025	166 167	204 138	98 568	105 570	129 054	68 457	60 597
35 - 39	307 521	153 333	154 188	186 657	89 705	96 952	120 864	63 628	57 236
40 - 44	284 082	145 797	138 285	170 959	84 148	86 811	113 123	61 649	51 474
45 - 49	227 719	116 069	111 650	135 829	66 659	69 170	91 890	49 410	42 480
50 - 54	182 317	93 396	88 921	106 049	52 006	54 043	76 268	41 390	34 878
55 - 59	135 707	68 353	67 354	78 597	37 878	40 719	57 110	30 475	26 635
60 - 64	114 843	56 778	58 065	64 874	29 968	34 906	49 969	26 810	23 159
65 - 69	80 528	38 292	42 236	45 618	20 151	25 467	34 910	18 141	16 769
70 - 74	70 708	33 286	37 422	40 227	17 320	22 907	30 481	15 966	14 515
75 - 79	47 931	21 703	26 228	27 650	11 307	16 343	20 281	10 396	9 885
80 - 84	29 287	12 433	16 854	16 753	6 289	10 464	12 534	6 144	6 390
85 - 89	16 412	6 750	9 662	9 573	3 548	6 025	6 839	3 202	3 637
90 + ...	8 524	3 112	5 412	5 009	1 684	3 325	3 515	1 428	2 087
1 VII 2006 (ESDF)									
Total.................	6 009 143	3 430 620	2 578 523	...	...	...	...	...	...
0 - 4	731 068	394 950	336 118	...	...	...	...	...	...
5 - 9	710 225	379 500	330 725	...	...	...	...	...	...
10 - 14	685 692	359 102	326 590	...	...	...	...	...	...
15 - 19	650 985	343 939	307 046	...	...	...	...	...	...
20 - 24	594 810	339 917	254 893	...	...	...	...	...	...
25 - 29	483 744	305 175	178 569	...	...	...	...	...	...
30 - 34	386 439	249 694	136 745	...	...	...	...	...	...
35 - 39	346 708	218 789	127 919	...	...	...	...	...	...
40 - 44	312 090	191 154	120 936	...	...	...	...	...	...
45 - 49	272 936	164 212	108 724	...	...	...	...	...	...
50 - 54	233 113	138 741	94 372	...	...	...	...	...	...
55 - 59	179 979	104 557	75 422	...	...	...	...	...	...
60 - 64	135 903	78 654	57 249	...	...	...	...	...	...
65 - 69	105 775	59 631	46 144	...	...	...	...	...	...
70 - 74	73 616	41 696	31 920	...	...	...	...	...	...
75 - 79	56 643	32 337	24 306	...	...	...	...	...	...
80 + ...	49 417	28 572	20 845	...	...	...	...	...	...
Peru - Pérou[18] 1 VII 2006 (ESDF)									
Total.................	27 377 172	13 666 871	13 710 301	20 371 596	10 067 586	10 304 010	7 005 576	3 599 285	3 406 291
0 - 4	2 769 420	1 406 069	1 363 351	1 874 493	955 613	918 880	894 927	450 456	444 471
5 - 9	2 835 901	1 445 008	1 390 893	1 962 909	999 462	963 447	872 992	445 546	427 446
10 - 14	2 898 586	1 479 327	1 419 259	2 014 619	1 023 421	991 108	883 967	455 906	428 061
15 - 19	2 727 188	1 382 694	1 344 494	2 003 971	1 001 421	1 002 550	723 217	381 273	341 944
20 - 24	2 588 444	1 309 559	1 278 885	1 995 489	995 020	1 000 469	592 955	314 539	278 416
25 - 29	2 382 616	1 199 280	1 183 336	1 870 455	929 263	941 192	512 161	270 017	242 144
30 - 34	2 086 088	1 030 561	1 055 527	1 656 396	808 098	848 298	429 692	222 463	207 229
35 - 39	1 834 790	892 342	942 448	1 440 628	692 496	748 132	394 162	199 846	194 316
40 - 44	1 578 199	759 250	818 949	1 241 469	589 254	652 215	336 730	169 996	166 734
45 - 49	1 338 111	645 494	692 617	1 042 817	496 202	546 615	295 294	149 292	146 002
50 - 54	1 110 439	545 208	565 231	869 524	422 421	447 103	240 915	122 787	118 128
55 - 59	883 746	434 005	449 741	682 070	332 511	349 559	201 676	101 494	100 182

7. Population by age, sex and urban/rural residence: latest available year, 1997 - 2006
Population selon l'âge, le sexe et la résidence, urbaine/rurale: dernière année disponible, 1997 - 2006 (continued - suite)

Continent, country or area, date, code and age (in years) / Continent, pays ou zone, date, code et âge (en années)	Total			Urban - Urbaine			Rural - Rurale		
	Both sexes Les deux sexes	Male Masculin	Female Féminin	Both sexes Les deux sexes	Male Masculin	Female Féminin	Both sexes Les deux sexes	Male Masculin	Female Féminin
AMERICA, SOUTH - AMÉRIQUE DU SUD									
Peru - Pérou[18]									
1 VII 2006 (ESDF)									
60 - 64	695 011	341 374	353 637	513 872	250 534	263 338	181 139	90 840	90 299
65 - 69	551 826	271 239	280 587	405 025	197 329	207 696	146 801	73 910	72 891
70 - 74	427 473	209 684	217 789	311 493	150 814	160 679	115 980	58 870	57 110
75 - 79	320 042	156 955	163 087	231 102	111 097	120 005	88 940	45 858	43 082
80 +	349 292	158 822	190 470	255 264	112 630	142 634	94 028	46 192	47 836
Suriname[19]									
2 VIII 2004 (CDJC)									
Total	492 829	248 046	244 783	328 932[20]	164 444[20]	164 488[20]	163 897[20]	83 602[20]	80 295[20]
0 - 4	51 837	26 252	25 585	31 603[20]	16 152[20]	15 451[20]	20 234[20]	10 100[20]	10 134[20]
0	9 872	4 995	4 854	5 944[20]	3 028[20]	2 903[20]	3 928[20]	1 967[20]	1 951[20]
1 - 4	41 965	21 238	20 713	...	...	...	...	...	...
5 - 9	49 409	25 200	24 209	30 886[20]	15 639[20]	15 247[20]	18 523[20]	9 561[20]	8 962[20]
10 - 14	45 143	22 889	22 254	28 942[20]	14 536[20]	14 406[20]	16 201[20]	8 353[20]	7 848[20]
15 - 19	46 508	23 465	23 043	31 775[20]	16 181[20]	15 594[20]	14 733[20]	7 284[20]	7 449[20]
20 - 24	43 843	22 437	21 406	30 989[20]	16 056[20]	14 933[20]	12 854[20]	6 381[20]	6 473[20]
25 - 29	37 901	19 006	18 895	25 895[20]	12 853[20]	13 042[20]	12 006[20]	6 153[20]	5 853[20]
30 - 34	38 994	19 828	19 166	26 462[20]	13 226[20]	13 236[20]	12 532[20]	6 602[20]	5 930[20]
35 - 39	37 279	19 179	18 100	25 388[20]	12 845[20]	12 543[20]	11 891[20]	6 334[20]	5 557[20]
40 - 44	33 985	17 657	16 328	23 386[20]	11 870[20]	11 516[20]	10 599[20]	5 787[20]	4 812[20]
45 - 49	25 635	12 643	12 992	17 893[20]	8 565[20]	9 328[20]	7 742[20]	4 078[20]	3 664[20]
50 - 54	20 420	9 933	10 487	14 421[20]	6 955[20]	7 466[20]	5 999[20]	2 978[20]	3 021[20]
55 - 59	14 982	6 955	8 027	10 487[20]	4 806[20]	5 681[20]	4 495[20]	2 149[20]	2 346[20]
60 - 64	13 259	6 200	7 059	9 309[20]	4 428[20]	4 881[20]	3 950[20]	1 772[20]	2 178[20]
65 - 69	10 602	5 148	5 454	7 101[20]	3 521[20]	3 580[20]	3 501[20]	1 627[20]	1 874[20]
70 - 74	8 659	4 103	4 556	5 745[20]	2 708[20]	3 037[20]	2 914[20]	1 395[20]	1 519[20]
75 - 79	5 152	2 419	2 733	3 410[20]	1 576[20]	1 834[20]	1 742[20]	843[20]	899[20]
80 - 84	2 853	1 235	1 618	1 905[20]	779[20]	1 126[20]	948[20]	456[20]	492[20]
85 - 89	1 075	392	677	770[20]	274[20]	496[20]	305[20]	118[20]	181[20]
90 - 94	460	184	276	371[20]	157[20]	214[20]	89[20]	27[20]	62[20]
95 +	129	34	95	94[20]	24[20]	70[20]	35[20]	10[20]	25[20]
Unknown - Inconnu	4 704	2 885	1 819	2 100[20]	1 293[20]	807[20]	2 604[20]	1 592[20]	1 012[20]
1 VII 2006 (ESDJ)									
Total	504 257[21]	253 783	250 474	...	...	...	...	...	...
0 - 4	53 561[21]	27 180	26 381	...	...	...	...	...	...
5 - 9	51 034[21]	26 080	24 954	...	...	...	...	...	...
10 - 14	46 634[21]	23 693	22 941	...	...	...	...	...	...
15 - 19	48 042[21]	24 288	23 754	...	...	...	...	...	...
20 - 24	45 289[21]	23 224	22 065	...	...	...	...	...	...
25 - 29	39 174[21]	19 684	19 490	...	...	...	...	...	...
30 - 34	40 286[21]	20 527	19 759	...	...	...	...	...	...
35 - 39	38 528[21]	19 861	18 667	...	...	...	...	...	...
40 - 44	35 102[21]	18 273	16 829	...	...	...	...	...	...
45 - 49	26 473[21]	13 084	13 389	...	...	...	...	...	...
50 - 54	21 090[21]	10 281	10 809	...	...	...	...	...	...
55 - 59	15 471[21]	7 197	8 274	...	...	...	...	...	...
60 - 64	13 691[21]	6 416	7 275	...	...	...	...	...	...
65 - 69	10 950[21]	5 330	5 620	...	...	...	...	...	...
70 - 74	8 944[21]	4 247	4 697	...	...	...	...	...	...
75 - 79	5 321[21]	2 504	2 817	...	...	...	...	...	...
80 +	4 667[21]	1 914	2 753	...	...	...	...	...	...
Uruguay[18]									
1 VII 2006 (ESDF)									
Total	3 314 466	1 601 024	1 713 442	3 101 685	1 480 779	1 620 906	212 781	120 245	92 536
0 - 4	244 381	124 946	119 435	229 914	117 460	112 454	14 467	7 486	6 981
5 - 9	268 264	137 016	131 248	251 875	128 535	123 340	16 389	8 481	7 908
10 - 14	272 349	139 164	133 185	255 898	130 487	125 411	16 451	8 677	7 774
15 - 19	265 003	135 077	129 926	249 578	126 512	123 066	15 425	8 565	6 860
20 - 24	249 073	125 551	123 522	234 556	117 210	117 346	14 517	8 341	6 176
25 - 29	244 385	121 173	123 212	229 687	112 824	116 863	14 698	8 349	6 349
30 - 34	230 158	113 665	116 493	215 518	105 318	110 200	14 640	8 347	6 293

188

7. Population by age, sex and urban/rural residence: latest available year, 1997 - 2006
Population selon l'âge, le sexe et la résidence, urbaine/rurale: dernière année disponible, 1997 - 2006 (continued - suite)

Continent, country or area, date, code and age (in years) / Continent, pays ou zone, date, code et âge (en années)	Total			Urban - Urbaine			Rural - Rurale		
	Both sexes Les deux sexes	Male Masculin	Female Féminin	Both sexes Les deux sexes	Male Masculin	Female Féminin	Both sexes Les deux sexes	Male Masculin	Female Féminin
AMERICA, SOUTH - AMÉRIQUE DU SUD									
Uruguay[18]									
1 VII 2006 (ESDF)									
35 - 39	207 722	101 585	106 137	193 600	93 521	100 079	14 122	8 064	6 058
40 - 44	209 200	101 791	107 409	194 907	93 507	101 400	14 293	8 284	6 009
45 - 49	199 775	97 161	102 614	186 126	89 135	96 991	13 649	8 026	5 623
50 - 54	181 825	87 321	94 504	168 669	79 529	89 140	13 156	7 792	5 364
55 - 59	157 692	74 609	83 083	145 452	67 270	78 182	12 240	7 339	4 901
60 - 64	141 915	65 768	76 147	130 917	59 066	71 851	10 998	6 702	4 296
65 - 69	125 013	55 582	69 431	115 661	49 942	65 719	9 352	5 640	3 712
70 - 74	115 404	48 196	67 208	107 887	43 756	64 131	7 517	4 440	3 077
75 - 79	93 453	36 745	56 708	88 252	33 780	54 472	5 201	2 965	2 236
80 - 84	61 121	21 911	39 210	57 999	20 283	37 716	3 122	1 628	1 494
85 - 89	31 768	9 924	21 844	30 124	9 159	20 965	1 644	765	879
90 - 94	11 905	2 904	9 001	11 232	2 635	8 597	673	269	404
95 +	4 060	935	3 125	3 833	850	2 983	227	85	142
Venezuela (Bolivarian Republic of) - Venezuela (République bolivarienne du)[22]									
1 VII 2002 (ESDF)									
Total	25 219 910	12 678 275	12 541 635	22 163 339	11 021 146	11 142 193	3 056 571	1 657 129	1 399 442
0 - 4	...	...	...	2 365 585	1 212 601	1 152 984	431 255	216 828	214 427
0	566 727	289 817	276 910	...	...	...	...	...	...
1 - 4	2 230 113	1 139 612	1 090 501	...	...	...	...	...	...
5 - 9	2 731 128	1 394 224	1 336 904	2 338 027	1 195 058	1 142 969	393 101	199 166	193 935
10 - 14	2 712 386	1 383 578	1 328 808	2 355 253	1 197 602	1 157 651	357 133	185 976	171 157
15 - 19	2 568 391	1 306 597	1 261 794	2 258 881	1 135 863	1 123 018	309 510	170 734	138 776
20 - 24	2 336 801	1 182 579	1 154 222	2 075 006	1 035 987	1 039 019	261 795	146 592	115 203
25 - 29	2 055 341	1 034 449	1 020 892	1 827 634	907 988	919 646	227 707	126 461	101 246
30 - 34	1 871 230	938 046	933 184	1 675 269	828 977	846 292	195 961	109 069	86 892
35 - 39	1 744 170	872 099	872 071	1 567 126	772 287	794 839	177 044	99 812	77 232
40 - 44	1 506 179	751 648	754 531	1 358 018	667 128	690 890	148 161	84 520	63 641
45 - 49	1 266 420	631 252	635 168	1 141 806	559 946	581 860	124 614	71 306	53 308
50 - 54	1 044 891	520 661	524 230	935 412	457 944	477 468	109 479	62 717	46 762
55 - 59	800 903	396 302	404 601	708 958	343 000	365 958	91 945	53 302	38 643
60 - 64	590 879	287 629	303 250	516 207	244 396	271 811	74 672	43 233	31 439
65 - 69	450 395	214 998	235 397	391 277	180 798	210 479	59 118	34 200	24 918
70 - 74	344 553	160 308	184 245	299 965	135 041	164 924	44 588	25 267	19 321
75 - 79	232 921	104 448	128 473	203 220	87 769	115 451	29 701	16 679	13 022
80 +	166 482	70 028	96 454	145 695	58 761	86 934	20 787	11 267	9 520
1 VII 2006 (ESDF)									
Total	27 030 656	13 570 418	13 460 238	...	...	...	...	...	...
0 - 4	2 856 707	1 460 640	1 396 067	...	...	...	...	...	...
5 - 9	2 759 835	1 409 395	1 350 440	...	...	...	...	...	...
10 - 14	2 721 953	1 389 093	1 332 860	...	...	...	...	...	...
15 - 19	2 699 011	1 373 741	1 325 270	...	...	...	...	...	...
20 - 24	2 503 978	1 266 811	1 237 167	...	...	...	...	...	...
25 - 29	2 271 616	1 142 181	1 129 435	...	...	...	...	...	...
30 - 34	1 976 161	989 242	986 919	...	...	...	...	...	...
35 - 39	1 835 406	915 953	919 453	...	...	...	...	...	...
40 - 44	1 697 633	845 497	852 136	...	...	...	...	...	...
45 - 49	1 426 744	708 896	717 848	...	...	...	...	...	...
50 - 54	1 202 803	596 434	606 369	...	...	...	...	...	...
55 - 59	965 302	170 299	489 983	...	...	...	...	...	...
60 - 64	719 188	351 303	367 885	...	...	...	...	...	...
65 - 69	518 392	247 676	270 716	...	...	...	...	...	...
70 - 74	386 812	180 043	206 769	...	...	...	...	...	...
75 - 79	280 119	126 443	153 676	...	...	...	...	...	...
80 +	204 916	87 671	117 245	...	...	...	...	...	...

7. Population by age, sex and urban/rural residence: latest available year, 1997 - 2006
Population selon l'âge, le sexe et la résidence, urbaine/rurale: dernière année disponible, 1997 - 2006 (continued - suite)

Continent, country or area, date, code and age (in years) / Continent, pays ou zone, date, code et âge (en années)	Total			Urban - Urbaine			Rural - Rurale		
	Both sexes Les deux sexes	Male Masculin	Female Féminin	Both sexes Les deux sexes	Male Masculin	Female Féminin	Both sexes Les deux sexes	Male Masculin	Female Féminin
ASIA - ASIE									
Armenia - Arménie									
1 VII 2006 (ESDJ)									
Total	3 221 094	1 555 755	1 665 339	2 064 268	980 272	1 083 996	1 156 826	575 483	581 343
0	37 151	19 823	17 328	23 455	12 401	11 054	13 697	7 423	6 274
1 - 4	141 574	75 977	65 598	89 117	47 287	41 830	52 457	28 690	23 768
5 - 9	206 296	109 737	96 559	121 568	64 218	57 350	84 728	45 519	39 209
10 - 14	264 650	136 299	128 351	154 428	79 492	74 936	110 222	56 807	53 415
15 - 19	320 102	162 359	157 743	192 004	96 929	95 075	128 098	65 430	62 668
20 - 24	307 513	154 487	153 026	197 281	97 593	99 688	110 232	56 894	53 338
25 - 29	259 428	128 571	130 857	174 035	85 416	88 619	85 393	43 155	42 238
30 - 34	214 031	103 670	110 361	142 809	68 572	74 237	71 222	35 098	36 124
35 - 39	200 306	95 708	104 598	126 054	58 743	67 311	74 252	36 965	37 287
40 - 44	245 508	116 028	129 480	152 801	69 012	83 789	92 707	47 016	45 691
45 - 49	264 140	125 565	138 575	175 294	80 109	95 185	88 846	45 456	43 390
50 - 54	198 258	92 063	106 195	141 400	63 887	77 513	56 858	28 176	28 682
55 - 59	139 198	63 223	75 975	103 572	46 636	56 936	35 626	16 587	19 039
60 - 64	75 120	32 610	42 510	53 980	23 385	30 595	21 140	9 225	11 915
65 - 69	134 269	56 912	77 357	88 332	37 615	50 717	45 937	19 297	26 640
70 - 74	95 908	40 600	55 308	58 162	24 345	33 817	37 746	16 255	21 491
75 - 79	78 122	30 610	47 512	45 735	17 529	28 206	32 387	13 081	19 306
80 - 84	29 466	8 958	20 508	18 237	5 488	12 749	11 229	3 470	7 759
85 +	10 054	2 555	7 499	6 005	1 616	4 389	4 050	940	3 110
Azerbaijan - Azerbaïdjan									
1 VII 2004 (ESDF)									
Total	8 306 500	4 081 100	4 225 400	4 276 300	2 089 500	2 186 800	4 030 200	1 991 600	2 038 600
0	122 600	66 200	56 400	55 000	29 900	25 100	67 600	36 300	31 300
1 - 4	445 900	239 600	206 300	200 300	108 600	91 700	245 600	131 000	114 600
5 - 9	674 900	353 600	321 300	303 300	160 500	142 800	371 600	193 100	178 500
10 - 14	906 800	466 100	440 700	444 800	229 400	215 400	462 000	236 700	225 300
15 - 19	906 400	463 500	442 900	468 800	240 200	228 600	437 600	223 300	214 300
20 - 24	768 100	387 900	380 200	402 200	203 000	199 200	365 900	184 900	181 000
25 - 29	650 500	315 400	335 100	334 300	160 000	174 300	316 200	155 400	160 800
30 - 34	620 600	293 500	327 100	308 600	140 300	168 300	312 000	153 200	158 800
35 - 39	670 100	315 500	354 600	342 400	156 800	185 600	327 700	158 700	169 000
40 - 44	693 300	331 300	362 000	382 400	181 300	201 100	310 900	150 000	160 900
45 - 49	542 200	262 600	279 600	314 200	152 500	161 700	228 000	110 100	117 900
50 - 54	347 200	167 200	180 000	212 300	103 100	109 200	134 900	64 100	70 800
55 - 59	203 400	96 100	107 300	126 300	60 400	65 900	77 100	35 700	41 400
60 - 64	182 900	83 300	99 600	102 500	47 200	55 300	80 400	36 100	44 300
65 - 69	248 600	109 400	139 200	124 100	54 800	69 300	124 500	54 600	69 900
70 - 74	167 200	73 300	93 900	78 800	33 700	45 100	88 400	39 600	48 800
75 - 79	92 600	37 800	54 800	46 300	18 300	28 000	46 300	19 500	26 800
80 - 84	38 300	12 400	25 900	19 200	6 300	12 900	19 100	6 100	13 000
85 - 89	13 800	3 800	10 000	6 300	2 000	4 300	7 500	1 800	5 700
90 - 94	7 200	1 700	5 500	2 800	800	2 000	4 400	900	3 500
95 - 99	2 500	600	1 900	800	200	600	1 700	400	1 300
100 +	1 400	300	1 100	600	200	400	800	100	700
1 VII 2006 (ESDF)									
Total	8 484 550	...	...	...	...	...	...	...	...
0 - 4	620 300	...	...	...	...	...	...	...	...
5 - 9	587 900	...	...	...	...	...	...	...	...
10 - 14	840 650	...	...	...	...	...	...	...	...
15 - 19	929 200	...	...	...	...	...	...	...	...
20 - 24	828 350	...	...	...	...	...	...	...	...
25 - 29	689 600	...	...	...	...	...	...	...	...
30 - 34	610 250	...	...	...	...	...	...	...	...
35 - 39	652 800	...	...	...	...	...	...	...	...
40 - 44	686 150	...	...	...	...	...	...	...	...
45 - 49	626 950	...	...	...	...	...	...	...	...
50 - 54	403 650	...	...	...	...	...	...	...	...
55 - 59	267 700	...	...	...	...	...	...	...	...
60 - 64	139 850	...	...	...	...	...	...	...	...
65 - 69	238 650	...	...	...	...	...	...	...	...
70 +	362 550	...	...	...	...	...	...	...	...

Continent, country or area, date, code and age (in years) / Continent, pays ou zone, date, code et âge (en annèes)	Total			Urban - Urbaine			Rural - Rurale		
	Both sexes Les deux sexes	Male Masculin	Female Féminin	Both sexes Les deux sexes	Male Masculin	Female Féminin	Both sexes Les deux sexes	Male Masculin	Female Féminin
ASIA - ASIE									
Bahrain - Bahreïn[7]									
1 VII 2006 (ESDF)									
Total..................	742 562	427 164	315 397	...	...	...	...	...	...
0	11 392	5 986	5 406	...	...	...	...	...	...
1 - 4	52 362	26 703	25 659	...	...	...	...	...	...
5 - 9	71 315	36 109	35 206	...	...	...	...	...	...
10 - 14	67 496	34 778	32 718	...	...	...	...	...	...
15 - 19	58 482	30 200	28 283	...	...	...	...	...	...
20 - 24	67 446	36 988	30 459	...	...	...	...	...	...
25 - 29	79 934	49 390	30 544	...	...	...	...	...	...
30 - 34	83 328	51 648	31 680	...	...	...	...	...	...
35 - 39	75 361	46 039	29 322	...	...	...	...	...	...
40 - 44	63 660	40 874	22 787	...	...	...	...	...	...
45 - 49	43 503	28 835	14 668	...	...	...	...	...	...
50 - 54	24 544	16 234	8 310	...	...	...	...	...	...
55 - 59	14 081	8 210	5 872	...	...	...	...	...	...
60 - 64	10 899	5 668	5 231	...	...	...	...	...	...
65 - 69	7 339	3 616	3 722	...	...	...	...	...	...
70 - 74	5 592	2 862	2 731	...	...	...	...	...	...
75 + ...	5 825	3 026	2 799	...	...	...	...	...	...
Bhutan - Bhoutan									
30 V 2005 (CDFC)									
Total..................	634 982	333 595	301 387	196 111	105 559	90 552	438 871	228 036	210 835
0	12 314	6 096	6 218	4 108	2 050	2 058	8 206	4 046	4 160
1 - 4	50 239	25 393	24 846	15 095	7 659	7 436	35 144	17 734	17 410
5 - 9	70 399	35 547	34 852	19 254	9 589	9 665	51 145	25 958	25 187
10 - 14	77 007	38 728	38 279	22 332	10 904	11 428	54 675	27 824	26 851
15 - 19	75 236	37 504	37 732	27 628	13 659	13 969	47 608	23 845	23 763
20 - 24	70 574	40 254	30 320	28 922	16 884	12 038	41 652	23 370	18 282
25 - 29	57 358	31 386	25 972	21 766	12 170	9 596	35 592	19 216	16 376
30 - 34	42 806	23 208	19 598	15 161	8 527	6 634	27 645	14 681	12 964
35 - 39	38 729	21 124	17 605	13 061	7 613	5 448	25 668	13 511	12 157
40 - 44	29 900	16 022	13 878	8 475	5 068	3 407	21 425	10 954	10 471
45 - 49	27 662	14 895	12 767	6 664	3 984	2 680	20 998	10 911	10 087
50 - 54	22 047	11 779	10 268	4 509	2 769	1 740	17 538	9 010	8 528
55 - 59	16 392	8 764	7 628	2 700	1 532	1 168	13 692	7 232	6 460
60 - 64	14 574	7 564	7 010	2 134	1 084	1 050	12 440	6 480	5 960
65 - 69	11 361	5 999	5 362	1 621	845	776	9 740	5 154	4 586
70 - 74	8 742	4 493	4 249	1 233	579	654	7 509	3 914	3 595
75 - 79	5 245	2 677	2 568	741	337	404	4 504	2 340	2 164
80 - 84	2 884	1 452	1 432	452	200	252	2 432	1 252	1 180
85 - 89	1 082	528	554	193	80	113	889	448	441
90 - 94	297	121	176	40	19	21	257	102	155
95 - 99	104	48	56	18	6	12	86	42	44
100 + ...	30	13	17	4	1	3	26	12	14
1 VII 2006 (ESDF)									
Total..................	646 851	339 403	307 448	...	...	...	...	...	...
0 - 4	65 100	32 702	32 398	...	...	...	...	...	...
5 - 9	68 780	34 808	33 972	...	...	...	...	...	...
10 - 14	76 190	38 420	37 770	...	...	...	...	...	...
15 - 19	75 810	37 404	38 406	...	...	...	...	...	...
20 - 24	72 016	40 330	31 686	...	...	...	...	...	...
25 - 29	60 311	33 428	26 883	...	...	...	...	...	...
30 - 34	44 844	24 282	20 562	...	...	...	...	...	...
35 - 39	39 547	21 568	17 979	...	...	...	...	...	...
40 - 44	31 182	16 759	14 423	...	...	...	...	...	...
45 - 49	27 970	15 037	12 933	...	...	...	...	...	...
50 - 54	23 088	12 340	10 748	...	...	...	...	...	...
55 - 59	16 973	9 074	7 899	...	...	...	...	...	...
60 - 64	14 593	7 582	7 011	...	...	...	...	...	...
65 - 69	11 581	6 079	5 502	...	...	...	...	...	...
70 - 74	8 865	4 567	4 298	...	...	...	...	...	...
75 - 79	5 469	2 794	2 675	...	...	...	...	...	...
80 + ...	4 532	2 229	2 303	...	...	...	...	...	...

Continent, country or area, date, code and age (in years) / Continent, pays ou zone, date, code et âge (en années)	Total			Urban - Urbaine			Rural - Rurale		
	Both sexes Les deux sexes	Male Masculin	Female Féminin	Both sexes Les deux sexes	Male Masculin	Female Féminin	Both sexes Les deux sexes	Male Masculin	Female Féminin

ASIA - ASIE

Brunei Darussalam - Brunéi Darussalam
21 VIII 2001 (CDFC)

Total	332 844	168 974	163 870	238 699	120 046	118 653	94 145	48 928	45 217
0 - 14	100 912	52 304	48 608	72 076	37 396	34 680	28 836	14 908	13 928
15 - 19	27 963	14 014	13 949	20 019	10 085	9 934	7 944	3 929	4 015
20 - 24	32 604	15 390	17 214	23 592	10 885	12 707	9 012	4 505	4 507
25 - 29	35 773	17 884	17 889	25 856	12 573	13 283	9 917	5 311	4 606
30 - 34	34 375	16 878	17 497	24 973	11 931	13 042	9 402	4 947	4 455
35 - 39	28 764	14 581	14 183	21 112	10 461	10 651	7 652	4 120	3 532
40 - 44	24 198	12 984	11 214	17 808	9 544	8 264	6 390	3 440	2 950
45 - 49	17 149	9 150	7 999	12 402	6 637	5 765	4 747	2 513	2 234
50 - 54	10 687	5 542	5 145	7 609	4 013	3 596	3 078	1 529	1 549
55 - 59	6 140	3 249	2 891	4 153	2 197	1 956	1 987	1 052	935
60 - 64	4 962	2 432	2 530	3 217	1 544	1 673	1 745	888	857
65 - 69	3 757	1 768	1 989	2 366	1 102	1 264	1 391	666	725
70 - 74	2 441	1 263	1 178	1 530	758	772	911	505	406
75 - 79	1 582	793	789	1 027	492	535	555	301	254
80 - 84	844	423	421	548	264	284	296	159	137
85 - 89	397	188	209	252	98	154	145	90	55
90 - 94	197	86	111	111	47	64	86	39	47
95 - 99	66	33	33	33	14	19	33	19	14
100 +	33	12	21	15	5	10	18	7	11
1 VII 2004 (ESDF)									
Total	357 800	186 200	171 600	...	...	...	...	...	...
0	7 200	3 700	3 500	...	...	...	...	...	...
1 - 4	45 500	23 800	21 700	...	...	...	...	...	...
5 - 9	34 800	18 100	16 700	...	...	...	...	...	...
10 - 14	32 300	16 900	15 400	...	...	...	...	...	...
15 - 19	28 500	14 500	14 000	...	...	...	...	...	...
20 - 24	33 500	16 300	17 200	...	...	...	...	...	...
25 - 29	37 300	19 400	17 900	...	...	...	...	...	...
30 - 34	35 800	18 400	17 400	...	...	...	...	...	...
35 - 39	29 800	15 700	14 100	...	...	...	...	...	...
40 - 44	25 300	14 100	11 200	...	...	...	...	...	...
45 - 49	17 700	9 700	8 000	...	...	...	...	...	...
50 - 54	10 900	5 800	5 100	...	...	...	...	...	...
55 - 59	6 200	3 300	2 900	...	...	...	...	...	...
60 - 64	5 000	2 500	2 500	...	...	...	...	...	...
65 - 69	3 600	1 700	1 900	...	...	...	...	...	...
70 - 74	2 300	1 200	1 100	...	...	...	...	...	...
75 - 79	1 200	600	600	...	...	...	...	...	...
80 - 84	700	400	300	...	...	...	...	...	...
85 +	200	100	100	...	...	...	...	...	...

Cambodia - Cambodge
3 III 1998 (CDFC)

Total	11 437 656	5 511 408	5 926 248	1 795 575	878 186	917 389	9 642 081	4 633 222	5 008 859
0	231 609	118 075	113 534	32 869	16 851	16 018	198 740	101 224	97 516
1 - 4	1 235 183	629 217	605 966	160 680	82 377	78 303	1 074 503	546 840	527 663
5 - 9	1 772 820	903 976	868 844	239 934	122 652	117 282	1 532 886	781 324	751 562
10 - 14	1 658 196	851 139	807 057	246 998	126 217	120 781	1 411 198	724 922	686 276
15 - 19	1 344 258	664 184	680 074	233 677	113 229	120 448	1 110 581	550 955	559 626
20 - 24	745 687	354 100	391 587	128 884	63 561	65 323	616 803	290 539	326 264
25 - 29	888 540	426 968	461 572	157 736	79 241	78 495	730 804	347 727	383 077
30 - 34	782 682	370 090	412 592	137 139	69 093	68 046	645 543	300 997	344 546
35 - 39	695 868	325 331	370 537	123 310	61 255	62 055	572 558	264 076	308 482
40 - 44	497 067	199 722	297 345	92 433	40 499	51 934	404 634	159 223	245 411
45 - 49	415 931	175 052	240 879	72 681	32 868	39 813	343 250	142 184	201 066
50 - 54	312 463	132 413	180 050	50 505	22 227	28 278	261 958	110 186	151 772
55 - 59	256 930	110 189	146 741	37 186	16 284	20 902	219 744	93 905	125 839
60 - 64	204 994	86 602	118 392	28 433	11 627	16 806	176 561	74 975	101 586
65 - 69	166 928	70 660	96 268	21 891	8 614	13 277	145 037	62 046	82 991
70 - 74	112 213	46 769	65 444	14 851	5 535	9 316	97 362	41 234	56 128
75 - 79	67 528	27 838	39 690	9 135	3 337	5 798	58 393	24 501	33 892
80 - 84	30 652	12 159	18 493	4 288	1 515	2 773	26 364	10 644	15 720

7. Population by age, sex and urban/rural residence: latest available year, 1997 - 2006
Population selon l'âge, le sexe et la résidence, urbaine/rurale: dernière année disponible, 1997 - 2006 (continued - suite)

Continent, country or area, date, code and age (in years) / Continent, pays ou zone, date, code et âge (en années)	Total			Urban - Urbaine			Rural - Rurale		
	Both sexes Les deux sexes	Male Masculin	Female Féminin	Both sexes Les deux sexes	Male Masculin	Female Féminin	Both sexes Les deux sexes	Male Masculin	Female Féminin
ASIA - ASIE									
Cambodia - Cambodge									
3 III 1998 (CDFC)									
85 - 89	13 368	5 029	8 339	1 874	592	1 282	11 494	4 437	7 057
90 - 94	2 867	1 026	1 841	453	157	296	2 414	869	1 545
95 +	1 872	869	1 003	618	455	163	1 254	414	840
1 VII 2004 (SSDF)[23]									
Total	12 824 170	6 197 128	6 627 042	...	...	...	...	...	...
0	314 512	165 946	148 566	...	...	...	...	...	...
1 - 4	1 105 489	567 442	538 047	...	...	...	...	...	...
5 - 9	1 638 623	847 582	791 040	...	...	...	...	...	...
10 - 14	1 892 316	967 807	924 509	...	...	...	...	...	...
15 - 19	1 499 278	761 411	737 867	...	...	...	...	...	...
20 - 24	1 305 670	633 237	672 433	...	...	...	...	...	...
25 - 29	717 482	345 923	371 559	...	...	...	...	...	...
30 - 34	814 752	388 580	426 172	...	...	...	...	...	...
35 - 39	797 807	372 679	425 128	...	...	...	...	...	...
40 - 44	687 814	305 922	381 893	...	...	...	...	...	...
45 - 49	529 666	213 901	315 765	...	...	...	...	...	...
50 - 54	429 213	174 662	254 552	...	...	...	...	...	...
55 - 59	331 469	140 436	191 033	...	...	...	...	...	...
60 - 64	258 291	109 132	149 159	...	...	...	...	...	...
65 - 69	200 689	84 610	116 079	...	...	...	...	...	...
70 - 74	143 581	54 578	89 003	...	...	...	...	...	...
75 - 79	89 402	35 620	53 782	...	...	...	...	...	...
80 - 84	44 885	19 066	25 820	...	...	...	...	...	...
85 - 89	16 012	5 401	10 612	...	...	...	...	...	...
90 - 94	5 144	2 135	3 009	...	...	...	...	...	...
95 +	2 075	1 058	1 017	...	...	...	...	...	...
China - Chine[24]									
1 XI 2000 (CDJC)									
Total	1242612226	640 275 969	602 336 257	458 770 983	235 264 707	223 506 276	783 841 243	405 011 262	378 829 981
0	13 793 799	7 460 206	6 333 593	4 449 020	2 376 585	2 072 435	9 344 779	5 083 621	4 261 158
1 - 4	55 184 575	30 188 488	24 996 087	17 669 697	9 525 854	8 143 843	37 514 878	20 662 634	16 852 244
5 - 9	90 152 587	48 303 208	41 849 379	26 588 363	14 180 433	12 407 930	63 564 224	34 122 775	29 441 449
10 - 14	125 396 633	65 344 739	60 051 894	35 802 884	18 701 307	17 101 577	89 593 749	46 643 432	42 950 317
15 - 19	103 031 165	52 878 170	50 152 995	42 231 585	21 086 911	21 144 674	60 799 580	31 791 259	29 008 321
20 - 24	94 573 174	47 937 766	46 635 408	41 021 887	20 651 361	20 370 526	53 551 287	27 286 405	26 264 882
25 - 29	117 602 265	60 230 758	57 371 507	48 788 516	24 820 721	23 967 795	68 813 749	35 410 037	33 403 712
30 - 34	127 314 298	65 360 456	61 953 842	49 723 640	25 760 568	23 963 072	77 590 658	39 599 888	37 990 770
35 - 39	109 147 295	56 141 391	53 005 904	44 518 164	23 269 889	21 248 275	64 629 131	32 871 502	31 757 629
40 - 44	81 242 945	42 243 187	38 999 758	33 518 610	17 499 183	16 019 427	47 724 335	24 744 004	22 980 331
45 - 49	85 521 045	43 939 603	41 581 442	31 708 705	16 245 324	15 463 382	53 812 339	27 694 279	26 118 060
50 - 54	63 304 200	32 804 125	30 500 075	22 335 748	11 462 314	10 873 434	40 968 452	21 341 811	19 626 641
55 - 59	46 370 375	24 061 506	22 308 869	16 004 389	8 077 159	7 927 230	30 365 986	15 984 347	14 381 639
60 - 64	41 703 848	21 674 478	20 029 370	14 944 552	7 519 377	7 425 175	26 759 296	14 155 101	12 604 195
65 - 69	34 780 460	17 549 348	17 231 112	12 174 470	6 128 605	6 045 865	22 605 990	11 420 743	11 185 247
70 - 74	25 574 149	12 436 154	13 137 995	8 479 487	4 216 193	4 263 294	17 094 662	8 219 961	8 874 701
75 - 79	15 928 330	7 175 811	8 752 519	5 000 134	2 291 543	2 708 591	10 928 196	4 884 268	6 043 928
80 - 84	7 989 158	3 203 868	4 785 290	2 472 016	1 004 359	1 467 657	5 517 142	2 199 509	3 317 633
85 - 89	3 030 698	1 056 941	1 973 757	994 079	347 550	646 529	2 036 619	709 391	1 327 228
90 - 94	783 594	229 758	553 836	276 586	80 189	196 397	507 008	149 569	357 439
95 - 99	169 756	51 373	118 383	62 255	17 827	44 428	107 501	33 546	73 955
100 +	17 877	4 635	13 242	6 195	1 455	4 740	11 682	3 180	8 502
China: Hong Kong SAR - Chine: Hong Kong RAS									
1 VII 2006 (ESDJ)									
Total	6 857 100	3 270 100	3 587 000	...	...	...	...	...	...
0	42 600	22 900	19 700	...	...	...	...	...	...
1 - 4	170 400	87 500	82 900	...	...	...	...	...	...
5 - 9	314 100	162 300	151 800	...	...	...	...	...	...
10 - 14	412 100	211 300	200 800	...	...	...	...	...	...
15 - 19	436 200	222 300	213 900	...	...	...	...	...	...
20 - 24	472 400	225 600	246 800	...	...	...	...	...	...
25 - 29	502 300	223 800	278 500	...	...	...	...	...	...
30 - 34	548 400	238 800	309 600	...	...	...	...	...	...

Continent, country or area, date, code and age (in years) / Continent, pays ou zone, date, code et âge (en années)	Total			Urban - Urbaine			Rural - Rurale		
	Both sexes Les deux sexes	Male Masculin	Female Féminin	Both sexes Les deux sexes	Male Masculin	Female Féminin	Both sexes Les deux sexes	Male Masculin	Female Féminin
ASIA - ASIE									
China: Hong Kong SAR - Chine: Hong Kong RAS									
1 VII 2006 (ESDJ)									
35 - 39	579 400	248 000	331 400	...	...	...	...	...	...
40 - 44	669 700	304 400	365 300	...	...	...	...	...	...
45 - 49	659 400	323 700	335 700	...	...	...	...	...	...
50 - 54	531 600	264 000	267 600	...	...	...	...	...	...
55 - 59	422 500	214 700	207 800	...	...	...	...	...	...
60 - 64	243 900	127 600	116 300	...	...	...	...	...	...
65 - 69	241 800	125 200	116 600	...	...	...	...	...	...
70 - 74	228 300	112 400	115 900	...	...	...	...	...	...
75 - 79	178 600	82 300	96 300	...	...	...	...	...	...
80 - 84	112 700	44 800	67 900	...	...	...	...	...	...
85 +	90 700	28 500	62 200	...	...	...	...	...	...
China: Macao SAR - Chine: Macao RAS									
1 VII 2006 (ESDJ)									
Total	498 852	243 009	255 843	...	...	...	...	...	...
0 - 4	16 587	8 658	7 929	...	...	...	...	...	...
5 - 9	23 971	12 505	11 466	...	...	...	...	...	...
10 - 14	36 052	18 483	17 569	...	...	...	...	...	...
15 - 19	47 340	23 907	23 433	...	...	...	...	...	...
20 - 24	43 983	21 045	22 938	...	...	...	...	...	...
25 - 29	35 098	16 623	18 475	...	...	...	...	...	...
30 - 34	39 642	18 146	21 496	...	...	...	...	...	...
35 - 39	41 979	18 314	23 665	...	...	...	...	...	...
40 - 44	49 744	22 748	26 996	...	...	...	...	...	...
45 - 49	49 923	25 328	24 595	...	...	...	...	...	...
50 - 54	38 831	20 615	18 216	...	...	...	...	...	...
55 - 59	25 737	13 803	11 934	...	...	...	...	...	...
60 - 64	14 315	7 421	6 894	...	...	...	...	...	...
65 - 69	9 677	5 011	4 666	...	...	...	...	...	...
70 - 74	9 205	3 979	5 226	...	...	...	...	...	...
75 +	16 768	6 423	10 345	...	...	...	...	...	...
Cyprus - Chypre[25]									
1 X 2001 (CDJC)									
Total	689 565	338 497	351 068	474 450	231 128	243 322	215 115	107 369	107 746
0	8 024	4 068	3 956	5 443	2 765	2 678	2 581	1 303	1 278
1 - 4	34 558	17 625	16 933	23 296	11 821	11 475	11 262	5 804	5 458
5 - 9	51 718	26 502	25 216	34 111	17 402	16 709	17 607	9 100	8 507
10 - 14	53 178	27 396	25 782	35 772	18 332	17 440	17 406	9 064	8 342
15 - 19	54 603	28 132	26 471	36 725	18 872	17 853	17 878	9 260	8 618
20 - 24	51 803	26 208	25 595	36 231	18 178	18 053	15 572	8 030	7 542
25 - 29	48 272	23 096	25 176	35 248	16 654	18 594	13 024	6 442	6 582
30 - 34	48 233	22 682	25 551	34 899	16 196	18 703	13 334	6 486	6 848
35 - 39	51 561	24 813	26 748	36 645	17 304	19 341	14 916	7 509	7 407
40 - 44	52 289	25 602	26 687	37 070	17 786	19 284	15 219	7 816	7 403
45 - 49	45 580	22 705	22 875	32 005	15 647	16 358	13 575	7 058	6 517
50 - 54	42 587	21 027	21 560	30 186	14 803	15 383	12 401	6 224	6 177
55 - 59	34 554	16 930	17 624	24 216	11 883	12 333	10 338	5 047	5 291
60 - 64	30 747	14 968	15 779	20 763	10 239	10 524	9 984	4 729	5 255
65 - 69	25 445	11 905	13 540	16 669	7 943	8 726	8 776	3 962	4 814
70 - 74	20 965	9 375	11 590	13 157	5 885	7 272	7 808	3 490	4 318
75 - 79	15 974	7 073	8 901	9 899	4 338	5 561	6 075	2 735	3 340
80 - 84	9 802	4 232	5 570	6 010	2 522	3 488	3 792	1 710	2 082
85 - 89	5 861	2 423	3 438	3 523	1 368	2 155	2 338	1 055	1 283
90 - 94	1 975	825	1 150	1 269	532	737	706	293	413
95 - 99	411	148	263	252	89	163	159	59	100
100 +	40	14	26	25	8	17	15	6	9
Unknown - Inconnu	1 385	748	637	1 036	561	475	349	187	162
1 VII 2006 (ESDJ)									
Total	770 919	380 132	390 787	...	...	...	...	...	...
0	8 694	4 531	4 163	...	...	...	...	...	...
1 - 4	32 346	16 658	15 688	...	...	...	...	...	...
5 - 9	43 960	22 410	21 550	...	...	...	...	...	...

Continent, country or area, date, code and age (in years) / Continent, pays ou zone, date, code et âge (en années)	Total			Urban - Urbaine			Rural - Rurale		
	Both sexes Les deux sexes	Male Masculin	Female Féminin	Both sexes Les deux sexes	Male Masculin	Female Féminin	Both sexes Les deux sexes	Male Masculin	Female Féminin
ASIA - ASIE									
Cyprus - Chypre[25]									
1 VII 2006 (ESDJ)									
10 - 14	53 357	27 331	26 026	...	...	...	...	...	...
15 - 19	55 519	28 341	27 178	...	...	...	...	...	...
20 - 24	64 327	32 007	32 320	...	...	...	...	...	...
25 - 29	64 440	32 454	31 986	...	...	...	...	...	...
30 - 34	57 483	28 448	29 035	...	...	...	...	...	...
35 - 39	53 723	26 138	27 585	...	...	...	...	...	...
40 - 44	56 359	27 543	28 816	...	...	...	...	...	...
45 - 49	55 840	27 659	28 181	...	...	...	...	...	...
50 - 54	48 785	24 088	24 697	...	...	...	...	...	...
55 - 59	45 105	22 005	23 100	...	...	...	...	...	...
60 - 64	36 237	17 548	18 689	...	...	...	...	...	...
65 - 69	31 164	15 100	16 064	...	...	...	...	...	...
70 - 74	24 000	11 124	12 876	...	...	...	...	...	...
75 - 79	18 256	7 979	10 277	...	...	...	...	...	...
80 - 84	11 895	5 040	6 855	...	...	...	...	...	...
85 - 89	5 949	2 428	3 521	...	...	...	...	...	...
90 - 94	2 707	1 023	1 684	...	...	...	...	...	...
95 - 99	651	248	403	...	...	...	...	...	...
100 +	122	29	93	...	...	...	...	...	...
Georgia - Géorgie									
1 VII 2000 (ESDF)[1]									
Total	4 945 553	2 364 247	2 581 306	2 860 786	1 348 715	1 512 071	2 084 767	1 015 532	1 069 235
0	42 247	22 938	19 309	26 206	14 152	12 054	16 041	8 786	7 255
1 - 4	197 055	104 267	92 788	119 229	63 120	56 109	77 826	41 147	36 679
5 - 9	361 619	185 741	175 878	208 452	107 038	101 414	153 167	78 703	74 464
10 - 14	409 671	209 366	200 305	229 154	116 874	112 280	180 517	92 492	88 025
15 - 19	388 789	198 066	190 723	222 064	113 224	108 840	166 725	84 842	81 883
20 - 24	376 407	191 927	184 480	213 454	108 613	104 841	162 953	83 314	79 639
25 - 29	350 129	181 759	168 370	213 415	110 488	102 927	136 714	71 271	65 443
30 - 34	363 659	175 712	187 947	214 156	100 573	113 583	149 503	75 139	74 364
35 - 39	403 179	191 543	211 636	241 215	109 394	131 821	161 964	82 149	79 815
40 - 44	353 366	168 218	185 148	216 428	98 958	117 470	136 938	69 260	67 678
45 - 49	305 841	143 921	161 920	193 528	88 504	105 024	112 313	55 417	56 896
50 - 54	216 111	100 444	115 667	137 119	62 640	74 479	78 992	37 804	41 188
55 - 59	225 223	99 437	125 786	130 629	56 530	74 099	94 594	42 907	51 687
60 - 64	280 405	126 438	153 967	155 346	68 463	86 883	125 059	57 975	67 084
65 - 69	242 085	102 877	139 208	123 373	51 091	72 282	118 712	51 786	66 926
70 - 74	218 503	85 840	132 663	111 805	41 553	70 252	106 698	44 287	62 411
75 - 79	113 417	34 835	78 582	56 587	16 900	39 687	56 830	17 935	38 895
80 - 84	59 039	24 600	34 439	29 156	12 606	16 550	29 883	11 994	17 889
85 - 89	27 302	11 583	15 719	13 332	5 601	7 731	13 970	5 982	7 988
90 - 94	8 410	3 605	4 805	4 432	1 819	2 613	3 978	1 786	2 192
95 - 99	2 730	1 020	1 710	1 510	527	983	1 220	493	727
100 +	366	110	256	196	47	149	170	63	107
1 VII 2006 (ESDF)									
Total	4 398 000	2 081 700	2 316 300	...	...	...	...	...	...
0	46 500	24 600	21 900	...	...	...	...	...	...
1 - 4	185 000	97 350	87 650	...	...	...	...	...	...
5 - 9	249 850	131 000	118 850	...	...	...	...	...	...
10 - 14	313 150	160 400	152 750	...	...	...	...	...	...
15 - 19	369 650	187 400	182 250	...	...	...	...	...	...
20 - 24	355 800	178 950	176 850	...	...	...	...	...	...
25 - 29	326 450	161 800	164 650	...	...	...	...	...	...
30 - 34	310 700	151 500	159 200	...	...	...	...	...	...
35 - 39	299 350	143 250	156 100	...	...	...	...	...	...
40 - 44	326 750	152 550	174 200	...	...	...	...	...	...
45 - 49	325 900	151 750	174 150	...	...	...	...	...	...
50 - 54	275 750	126 900	148 850	...	...	...	...	...	...
55 - 59	230 850	104 750	126 100	...	...	...	...	...	...
60 - 64	145 100	63 200	81 900	...	...	...	...	...	...
65 - 69	235 150	97 850	137 300	...	...	...	...	...	...
70 - 74	167 800	69 250	98 550	...	...	...	...	...	...
75 - 79	135 250	51 600	83 650	...	...	...	...	...	...

7. Population by age, sex and urban/rural residence: latest available year, 1997 - 2006
Population selon l'âge, le sexe et la résidence, urbaine/rurale: dernière année disponible, 1997 - 2006 (continued - suite)

Continent, country or area, date, code and age (in years) / Continent, pays ou zone, date, code et âge (en années)	Total			Urban - Urbaine			Rural - Rurale		
	Both sexes Les deux sexes	Male Masculin	Female Féminin	Both sexes Les deux sexes	Male Masculin	Female Féminin	Both sexes Les deux sexes	Male Masculin	Female Féminin
ASIA - ASIE									
Georgia - Géorgie									
1 VII 2006 (ESDF)									
80 - 84	65 100	20 300	44 800	...	...	...	...	...	...
85 +	33 900	7 300	26 600	...	...	...	...	...	...
India - Inde[26]									
1 III 2001 (CDFC)									
Total	1028610328	532 156 772	496 453 556	286 119 689	150 554 098	135 565 591	742 490 639	381 602 674	360 887 965
0 - 4	110 447 164	57 119 612	53 327 552	25 338 754	13 262 414	12 076 340	85 108 410	43 857 198	41 251 212
5 - 9	128 316 790	66 734 833	61 581 957	29 860 545	15 640 135	14 220 410	98 456 245	51 094 698	47 361 547
10 - 14	124 846 858	65 632 877	59 213 981	32 464 536	17 030 132	15 434 404	92 382 322	48 602 745	43 779 577
15 - 19	100 215 890	53 939 991	46 275 899	30 154 067	16 191 573	13 962 494	70 061 823	37 748 418	32 313 405
20 - 24	89 764 132	46 321 150	43 442 982	28 365 228	15 193 668	13 171 560	61 398 904	31 127 482	30 271 422
25 - 29	83 422 393	41 557 546	41 864 847	25 737 253	13 180 373	12 556 880	57 685 140	28 377 173	29 307 967
30 - 34	74 274 044	37 361 916	36 912 128	22 445 165	11 673 137	10 772 028	51 828 879	25 688 779	26 140 100
35 - 39	70 574 085	36 038 727	34 535 358	21 615 541	11 157 103	10 458 438	48 958 544	24 881 624	24 076 920
40 - 44	55 738 297	29 878 715	25 859 582	17 173 126	9 458 276	7 714 850	38 565 171	20 420 439	18 144 732
45 - 49	47 408 976	24 867 886	22 541 090	14 453 974	7 844 213	6 609 761	32 955 002	17 023 673	15 931 329
50 - 54	36 587 559	19 851 608	16 735 951	10 809 961	6 038 917	4 771 044	25 777 598	13 812 691	11 964 907
55 - 59	27 653 347	13 583 022	14 070 325	7 682 278	4 010 268	3 672 010	19 971 069	9 572 754	10 398 315
60 - 64	27 516 779	13 586 347	13 930 432	6 864 810	3 439 621	3 425 189	20 651 969	10 146 726	10 505 243
65 - 69	19 806 955	9 472 103	10 334 852	4 990 199	2 401 397	2 588 802	14 816 756	7 070 706	7 746 050
70 - 74	14 708 644	7 527 688	7 180 956	3 579 168	1 780 696	1 798 472	11 129 476	5 746 992	5 382 484
75 - 79	6 551 225	3 263 209	3 288 016	1 721 085	851 088	869 997	4 830 140	2 412 121	2 418 019
80 +	8 038 718	3 918 980	4 119 738	2 022 345	935 920	1 086 425	6 016 373	2 983 060	3 033 313
Unknown - Inconnu	2 738 472	1 500 562	1 237 910	841 654	465 167	376 487	1 896 818	1 035 395	861 423
Indonesia - Indonésie[27]									
31 X 2005 (SSDF)									
Total	213 375 287	107 274 528	106 100 759	92 005 069	46 055 993	45 949 076	121 370 218	61 218 535	60 151 683
0 - 4	19 095 151	9 732 578	9 362 573	8 117 666	4 129 250	3 988 416	10 977 485	5 603 328	5 374 157
5 - 9	21 563 945	11 089 478	10 474 467	8 573 265	4 417 551	4 155 714	12 990 680	6 671 927	6 318 753
10 - 14	21 306 096	10 956 648	10 349 448	8 472 639	4 343 105	4 129 534	12 833 457	6 613 543	6 219 914
15 - 19	19 796 921	10 103 778	9 693 143	8 585 104	4 254 987	4 330 117	11 211 817	5 848 791	5 363 026
20 - 24	19 445 179	9 533 960	9 911 219	9 594 049	4 647 995	4 946 054	9 851 130	4 885 965	4 965 165
25 - 29	18 680 093	9 078 324	9 601 769	8 955 039	4 392 942	4 562 097	9 725 054	4 685 382	5 039 672
30 - 34	17 420 029	8 543 620	8 876 409	7 945 419	3 905 345	4 040 074	9 474 610	4 638 275	4 836 335
35 - 39	16 454 100	8 186 060	8 268 040	7 267 101	3 642 139	3 624 962	9 186 999	4 543 921	4 643 078
40 - 44	14 489 902	7 273 553	7 216 349	6 311 684	3 162 768	3 148 916	8 178 218	4 110 785	4 067 433
45 - 49	12 382 818	6 303 669	6 079 149	5 294 629	2 706 752	2 587 877	7 088 189	3 596 917	3 491 272
50 - 54	9 941 064	5 175 796	4 765 268	4 154 253	2 167 922	1 986 331	5 786 811	3 007 874	2 778 937
55 - 59	7 262 179	3 755 532	3 506 647	2 830 595	1 440 270	1 390 325	4 431 584	2 315 262	2 116 322
60 - 64	5 611 827	2 748 283	2 863 544	2 193 103	1 079 057	1 114 046	3 418 724	1 669 226	1 749 498
65 - 69	4 112 165	1 957 037	2 155 128	1 565 522	750 321	815 201	2 546 643	1 206 716	1 339 927
70 - 74	2 989 927	1 448 024	1 541 903	1 101 672	519 815	581 857	1 888 255	928 209	960 046
75 - 79	1 573 741	786 789	786 952	604 849	297 376	307 473	968 892	489 413	479 479
80 - 84	797 616	392 368	405 248	283 683	136 765	146 918	513 933	255 603	258 330
85 - 89	287 470	135 751	151 719	97 793	36 302	61 491	189 677	99 449	90 228
90 - 94	104 195	48 039	56 156	40 139	18 078	22 061	64 056	29 961	34 095
95 +	60 869	25 241	35 628	16 865	7 253	9 612	44 004	17 988	26 016
Iran (Islamic Republic of) - Iran (République islamique d')[28]									
1 VII 2005 (ESDJ)									
Total	68 467 369	34 801 582	33 665 787	45 650 230	23 316 275	22 333 955	22 817 140	11 485 308	11 331 832
0	1 184 820	597 647	587 173	727 317	356 467	370 850	457 503	241 180	216 323
1 - 4	4 876 120	2 509 011	2 367 108	3 003 588	1 545 528	1 458 060	1 872 532	963 483	909 049
5 - 9	7 179 426	3 688 505	3 490 921	4 408 829	2 263 160	2 145 669	2 770 597	1 425 345	1 345 251
10 - 14	7 039 567	3 685 380	3 354 187	4 412 828	2 308 219	2 104 609	2 626 739	1 377 162	1 249 578
15 - 19	8 699 798	4 498 984	4 200 814	5 704 368	2 918 032	2 786 336	2 995 431	1 580 952	1 414 478
20 - 24	7 495 211	3 740 990	3 754 221	5 128 370	2 618 524	2 509 846	2 366 842	1 122 466	1 244 375
25 - 29	5 698 538	2 831 638	2 866 900	3 900 751	1 956 914	1 943 837	1 797 788	874 724	923 064
30 - 34	4 780 634	2 393 631	2 387 003	3 295 280	1 657 622	1 637 658	1 485 354	736 009	749 345
35 - 39	4 561 614	2 238 113	2 323 501	3 308 678	1 626 511	1 682 167	1 252 936	611 602	641 334
40 - 44	3 999 313	2 044 606	1 954 707	2 878 480	1 489 784	1 388 696	1 120 833	554 822	566 011
45 - 49	3 489 945	1 778 347	1 711 599	2 546 710	1 305 974	1 240 737	943 235	472 373	470 862
50 - 54	2 834 437	1 414 749	1 419 687	1 986 046	1 023 448	962 598	848 391	391 302	457 089

196

Continent, country or area, date, code and age (in years) / Continent, pays ou zone, date, code et âge (en années)	Total			Urban - Urbaine			Rural - Rurale		
	Both sexes Les deux sexes	Male Masculin	Female Féminin	Both sexes Les deux sexes	Male Masculin	Female Féminin	Both sexes Les deux sexes	Male Masculin	Female Féminin
ASIA - ASIE									
Iran (Islamic Republic of) - Iran (République islamique d')[28]									
1 VII 2005 (ESDJ)									
55 - 59	1 986 428	987 604	998 824	1 384 972	715 765	669 208	601 455	271 839	329 617
60 - 64	1 514 901	773 864	741 037	1 030 604	545 936	484 667	484 298	227 928	256 370
65 - 69	1 099 452	565 387	534 065	692 892	353 353	339 540	406 560	212 034	194 526
70 - 74	982 703	497 599	485 104	600 899	302 576	298 323	381 804	195 023	186 781
75 - 79	584 895	311 253	273 642	365 857	186 541	179 316	219 038	124 712	94 326
80 - 84	342 227	189 024	153 203	201 765	106 905	94 860	140 462	82 119	58 343
85 - 89	73 001	35 896	37 105	46 182	25 040	21 142	26 819	10 855	15 964
90 - 94	24 408	10 967	13 440	14 851	6 065	8 786	9 557	4 902	4 655
95 +	19 932	8 388	11 544	10 964	3 912	7 052	8 968	4 476	4 493
Iraq									
1 VII 2006 (ESDF)									
Total	28 810 441	14 493 207	14 317 234	19 226 476	9 698 293	9 528 183	9 583 965	4 794 914	4 789 051
0 - 4	4 823 031	2 470 619	2 352 412	3 011 078	1 542 445	1 468 633	1 811 953	928 174	883 779
5 - 9	4 096 803	2 100 848	1 995 955	2 594 620	1 330 408	1 264 212	1 502 183	770 440	731 743
10 - 14	3 499 328	1 778 133	1 721 195	2 251 580	1 142 832	1 108 748	1 247 748	635 301	612 447
15 - 19	3 112 057	1 581 928	1 530 129	2 041 800	1 037 920	1 003 880	1 070 257	544 008	526 249
20 - 24	2 665 333	1 352 937	1 312 396	1 787 631	908 513	879 118	877 702	444 424	433 278
25 - 29	2 274 142	1 148 603	1 125 539	1 552 732	786 100	766 242	721 410	362 113	359 297
30 - 34	1 911 789	958 166	953 623	1 330 997	670 674	660 323	580 792	287 492	293 300
35 - 39	1 576 202	782 115	794 087	1 116 756	558 982	557 774	459 446	223 133	236 313
40 - 44	1 243 985	605 888	638 097	901 010	445 230	455 780	342 975	160 658	182 317
45 - 49	995 094	480 159	514 935	728 904	358 077	370 827	266 190	122 082	144 108
50 - 54	767 578	367 813	399 765	566 215	277 099	289 116	201 363	90 714	110 649
55 - 59	593 872	283 651	310 221	439 235	214 275	224 960	154 637	69 376	85 261
60 - 64	440 719	211 750	228 969	324 771	158 873	165 898	115 948	52 877	63 071
65 - 69	316 589	149 636	166 953	232 552	111 606	120 946	84 037	38 030	46 007
70 - 74	208 280	95 371	112 909	152 200	70 383	81 817	56 080	24 988	31 092
75 - 79	129 497	57 074	72 423	92 226	40 705	51 521	37 271	16 369	20 902
80 +	156 142	68 516	87 626	102 169	43 781	58 388	53 973	24 735	29 238
Israel - Israël[29]									
1 VII 2006 (ESDJ)									
Total	7 053 707	3 485 501	3 568 206	6 475 600[30]	3 189 511[30]	3 286 089[30]	573 712[30]	293 647[30]	280 065[30]
0	145 379	74 648	70 731	132 365[30]	67 953[30]	64 412[30]	12 862[30]	6 615[30]	6 247[30]
1 - 4	573 853	294 154	279 699	521 941[30]	267 584[30]	254 357[30]	51 339[30]	26 272[30]	25 068[30]
5 - 9	670 367	344 112	326 255	609 860[30]	313 038[30]	296 822[30]	59 961[30]	30 794[30]	29 167[30]
10 - 14	609 656	312 437	297 219	552 076[30]	282 474[30]	269 602[30]	57 070[30]	29 726[30]	27 345[30]
15 - 19	576 078	294 658	281 421	519 798[30]	264 694[30]	255 104[30]	55 843[30]	29 713[30]	26 130[30]
20 - 24	564 572	287 367	277 205	518 383[30]	262 760[30]	255 623[30]	45 565[30]	24 237[30]	21 329[30]
25 - 29	543 940	273 332	270 609	502 727[30]	252 042[30]	250 685[30]	40 834[30]	21 086[30]	19 749[30]
30 - 34	521 922	262 588	259 334	482 956[30]	242 870[30]	240 086[30]	38 786[30]	19 626[30]	19 160[30]
35 - 39	438 839	218 438	220 401	401 856[30]	200 072[30]	201 785[30]	36 770[30]	18 253[30]	18 517[30]
40 - 44	389 630	191 401	198 229	355 859[30]	174 402[30]	181 457[30]	33 555[30]	16 897[30]	16 658[30]
45 - 49	380 818	184 187	196 631	349 397[30]	168 148[30]	181 249[30]	31 232[30]	15 941[30]	15 291[30]
50 - 54	372 685	179 073	193 613	343 798[30]	164 149[30]	179 649[30]	28 703[30]	14 822[30]	13 881[30]
55 - 59	346 643	165 538	181 105	321 950[30]	152 780[30]	169 170[30]	24 580[30]	12 692[30]	11 889[30]
60 - 64	221 750	105 477	116 273	205 413[30]	97 125[30]	108 288[30]	16 305[30]	8 328[30]	7 977[30]
65 - 69	204 634	93 523	111 111	192 742[30]	87 372[30]	105 370[30]	11 878[30]	6 139[30]	5 739[30]
70 - 74	170 129	74 875	95 254	160 373[30]	70 243[30]	90 130[30]	9 743[30]	4 627[30]	5 116[30]
75 - 79	141 827	59 033	82 794	134 112[30]	55 742[30]	78 371[30]	7 706[30]	3 289[30]	4 418[30]
80 - 84	107 809	41 875	65 934	101 697[30]	39 266[30]	62 431[30]	6 105[30]	2 604[30]	3 501[30]
85 - 89	48 231	19 695	28 537	45 299[30]	18 437[30]	26 862[30]	2 932[30]	1 258[30]	1 674[30]
90 +	24 952	9 095	15 857	23 003[30]	8 364[30]	14 639[30]	1 946[30]	732[30]	1 214[30]
Japan - Japon									
1 X 2005 (CDJC)									
Total	127 767 994	62 348 977	65 419 017	110 264 324	53 886 000	56 378 324	17 503 670	8 462 977	9 040 693
0 - 4	5 578 087	2 854 502	2 723 585	4 852 006	2 482 703	2 369 303	726 081	371 799	354 282
5 - 9	5 928 495	3 036 503	2 891 992	5 109 001	2 616 615	2 492 386	819 494	419 888	399 606
10 - 14	6 014 652	3 080 678	2 933 974	5 127 976	2 626 071	2 501 905	886 676	454 607	432 069
15 - 19	6 568 380	3 373 430	3 194 950	5 651 131	2 902 583	2 748 548	917 249	470 847	446 402
20 - 24	7 350 598	3 754 822	3 595 776	6 502 213	3 325 698	3 176 515	848 385	429 124	419 261

Continent, country or area, date, code and age (in years) Continent, pays ou zone, date, code et âge (en années)	Total			Urban - Urbaine			Rural - Rurale		
	Both sexes Les deux sexes	Male Masculin	Female Féminin	Both sexes Les deux sexes	Male Masculin	Female Féminin	Both sexes Les deux sexes	Male Masculin	Female Féminin
ASIA - ASIE									
Japan - Japon									
1 X 2005 (CDJC)									
25 - 29	8 280 049	4 198 551	4 081 498	7 321 003	3 708 770	3 612 233	959 046	489 781	469 265
30 - 34	9 754 857	4 933 265	4 821 592	8 660 059	4 375 975	4 284 084	1 094 798	557 290	537 508
35 - 39	8 735 781	4 402 787	4 332 994	7 742 640	3 907 842	3 834 798	993 141	494 945	498 196
40 - 44	8 080 596	4 065 470	4 015 126	7 062 486	3 557 472	3 505 014	1 018 110	507 998	510 112
45 - 49	7 725 861	3 867 500	3 858 361	6 616 303	3 310 680	3 305 623	1 109 558	556 820	552 738
50 - 54	8 796 499	4 383 240	4 413 259	7 480 089	3 718 540	3 761 549	1 316 410	664 700	651 710
55 - 59	10 255 164	5 077 369	5 177 795	8 818 349	4 353 419	4 464 930	1 436 815	723 950	712 865
60 - 64	8 544 629	4 154 529	4 390 100	7 385 888	3 589 046	3 796 842	1 158 741	565 483	593 258
65 - 69	7 432 610	3 545 006	3 887 604	6 353 609	3 033 231	3 320 378	1 079 001	511 775	567 226
70 - 74	6 637 497	3 039 743	3 597 754	5 584 991	2 560 738	3 024 253	1 052 506	479 005	573 501
75 - 79	5 262 801	2 256 317	3 006 484	4 347 080	1 866 530	2 480 550	915 721	389 787	525 934
80 - 84	3 412 393	1 222 635	2 189 758	2 791 585	1 002 599	1 788 986	620 808	220 036	400 772
85 - 89	1 849 260	555 126	1 294 134	1 508 536	453 182	1 055 354	340 724	101 944	238 780
90 - 94	840 870	210 586	630 284	685 165	172 256	512 909	155 705	38 330	117 375
95 - 99	211 221	41 426	169 795	171 626	33 755	137 871	39 595	7 671	31 924
100 +	25 353	3 760	21 593	20 442	3 037	17 405	4 911	723	4 188
Unknown - Inconnu	482 341	291 732	190 609	472 146	285 258	186 888	10 195	6 474	3 721
1 VII 2006 (ESDF)[31]									
Total	127 756 000	62 314 000	65 442 000	...	...	...	...	...	...
0 - 4	5 530 000	2 833 000	2 697 000	...	...	...	...	...	...
5 - 9	5 940 000	3 045 000	2 895 000	...	...	...	...	...	...
10 - 14	6 014 000	3 082 000	2 932 000	...	...	...	...	...	...
15 - 19	6 472 000	3 321 000	3 151 000	...	...	...	...	...	...
20 - 24	7 349 000	3 764 000	3 585 000	...	...	...	...	...	...
25 - 29	8 085 000	4 108 000	3 977 000	...	...	...	...	...	...
30 - 34	9 693 000	4 909 000	4 784 000	...	...	...	...	...	...
35 - 39	9 100 000	4 591 000	4 508 000	...	...	...	...	...	...
40 - 44	8 025 000	4 039 000	3 987 000	...	...	...	...	...	...
45 - 49	7 696 000	3 855 000	3 841 000	...	...	...	...	...	...
50 - 54	8 495 000	4 235 000	4 260 000	...	...	...	...	...	...
55 - 59	10 825 000	5 362 000	5 463 000	...	...	...	...	...	...
60 - 64	8 152 000	3 964 000	4 188 000	...	...	...	...	...	...
65 - 69	7 542 000	3 603 000	3 938 000	...	...	...	...	...	...
70 - 74	6 787 000	3 118 000	3 669 000	...	...	...	...	...	...
75 - 79	5 377 000	2 316 000	3 061 000	...	...	...	...	...	...
80 - 84	3 614 000	1 326 000	2 287 000	...	...	...	...	...	...
85 +	3 060 000	842 000	2 218 000	...	...	...	...	...	...
Jordan - Jordanie[32]									
1 X 2004 (CDFC)									
Total	5 103 639	2 626 287	2 477 352	3 997 383	2 055 431	1 941 952	1 106 256	570 856	535 400
0	122 757	62 643	60 114	94 974	48 529	46 445	27 783	14 114	13 669
1 - 4	527 574	270 573	257 001	408 893	209 140	199 753	118 681	61 433	57 248
5 - 9	642 871	329 133	313 738	495 583	253 774	241 809	147 288	75 359	71 929
10 - 14	610 129	313 083	297 046	469 321	240 723	228 598	140 808	72 360	68 448
15 - 19	559 838	287 693	272 145	431 275	221 213	210 062	128 563	66 480	62 083
20 - 24	540 193	279 600	260 593	421 400	217 092	204 308	118 793	62 508	56 285
25 - 29	456 261	239 774	216 487	355 950	186 570	169 380	100 311	53 204	47 107
30 - 34	399 169	207 178	191 991	316 235	164 238	151 997	82 934	42 940	39 994
35 - 39	323 426	167 737	155 689	259 736	134 829	124 907	63 690	32 908	30 782
40 - 44	241 400	123 945	117 455	196 923	101 442	95 481	44 477	22 503	21 974
45 - 49	170 456	87 098	83 358	138 372	70 890	67 482	32 084	16 208	15 876
50 - 54	128 240	64 607	63 633	102 179	51 210	50 969	26 061	13 397	12 664
55 - 59	113 721	55 765	57 956	92 893	45 618	47 275	20 828	10 147	10 681
60 - 64	98 787	52 084	46 703	80 269	42 634	37 635	18 518	9 450	9 068
65 - 69	71 823	37 095	34 728	57 484	29 956	27 528	14 339	7 139	7 200
70 - 74	46 820	23 467	23 353	36 958	18 503	18 455	9 862	4 964	4 898
75 - 79	24 268	12 651	11 617	19 160	9 923	9 237	5 108	2 728	2 380
80 +	...	...	...	16 376	7 369	9 007	5 684	2 768	2 916
80 - 84	13 585	6 144	7 441	...	...	...	...	...	...
85 - 89	5 032	2 444	2 588	...	...	...	...	...	...
90 - 94	2 316	1 012	1 304	...	...	...	...	...	...
95 +	1 127	537	590	...	...	...	...	...	...
Unknown - Inconnu	3 846	2 024	1 822	3 402	1 778	1 624	444	246	198

Continent, country or area, date, code and age (in years) / Continent, pays ou zone, date, code et âge (en années)	Total			Urban - Urbaine			Rural - Rurale		
	Both sexes Les deux sexes	Male Masculin	Female Féminin	Both sexes Les deux sexes	Male Masculin	Female Féminin	Both sexes Les deux sexes	Male Masculin	Female Féminin
ASIA - ASIE									
Jordan - Jordanie[32]									
31 XII 2006 (ESDF)									
Total	5 600 000	2 886 600	2 713 400	...	...	...	...	...	...
0 - 4	714 190	366 600	347 590	...	...	...	...	...	...
5 - 9	705 770	361 980	343 790	...	...	...	...	...	...
10 - 14	670 270	344 660	325 610	...	...	...	...	...	...
15 - 19	614 570	316 370	298 200	...	...	...	...	...	...
20 - 24	593 140	307 420	285 720	...	...	...	...	...	...
25 - 29	501 260	263 840	237 420	...	...	...	...	...	...
30 - 34	438 600	228 040	210 560	...	...	...	...	...	...
35 - 39	355 410	184 740	170 670	...	...	...	...	...	...
40 - 44	264 870	136 250	128 620	...	...	...	...	...	...
45 - 49	187 280	95 840	91 440	...	...	...	...	...	...
50 - 54	140 740	71 010	69 730	...	...	...	...	...	...
55 - 59	124 700	61 200	63 500	...	...	...	...	...	...
60 - 64	108 430	57 150	51 280	...	...	...	...	...	...
65 - 69	79 210	40 815	38 395	...	...	...	...	...	...
70 - 74	51 400	25 775	25 625	...	...	...	...	...	...
75 - 79	26 550	13 913	12 637	...	...	...	...	...	...
80 - 84	15 090	7 022	8 068	...	...	...	...	...	...
85 - 89	5 280	2 400	2 880	...	...	...	...	...	...
90 - 94	2 450	1 285	1 165	...	...	...	...	...	...
95 +	790	290	500	...	...	...	...	...	...
Kazakhstan									
1 VII 2006 (ESDF)									
Total	15 308 084	7 367 032	7 941 052	8 764 884	4 094 572	4 670 312	6 543 200	3 272 460	3 270 740
0	286 942	147 296	139 646	167 609	86 140	81 469	119 333	61 156	58 177
1 - 4	983 466	504 183	479 283	548 319	281 456	266 863	435 147	222 727	212 420
5 - 9	1 084 286	555 783	528 503	541 813	278 297	263 516	542 473	277 486	264 987
10 - 14	1 331 435	678 614	652 821	649 023	330 707	318 316	682 412	347 907	334 505
15 - 19	1 567 466	796 204	771 262	823 791	415 430	408 361	743 675	380 774	362 901
20 - 24	1 449 497	733 988	715 509	811 181	403 406	407 775	638 316	330 582	307 734
25 - 29	1 241 818	622 490	619 328	754 631	362 283	392 348	487 187	260 207	226 980
30 - 34	1 149 899	566 568	583 331	680 919	319 600	361 319	468 980	246 968	222 012
35 - 39	1 064 972	520 562	544 410	640 625	300 102	340 523	424 347	220 460	203 887
40 - 44	1 090 067	522 460	567 607	654 430	302 670	351 760	435 637	219 790	215 847
45 - 49	1 056 298	497 475	558 823	645 497	293 985	351 512	410 801	203 490	207 311
50 - 54	825 482	374 812	450 670	509 866	223 724	286 142	315 616	151 088	164 528
55 - 59	641 298	281 770	359 528	402 769	171 026	231 743	238 529	110 744	127 785
60 - 64	334 227	138 725	195 502	198 117	78 755	119 362	136 110	59 970	76 140
65 - 69	521 889	205 334	316 555	312 459	116 097	196 362	209 430	89 237	120 193
70 - 74	280 402	104 635	175 767	172 626	60 729	111 897	107 776	43 906	63 870
75 - 79	234 524	75 961	158 563	148 171	45 190	102 981	86 353	30 771	55 582
80 - 84	113 916	29 158	84 758	72 725	18 031	54 694	41 191	11 127	30 064
85 - 89	35 210	7 884	27 326	21 977	5 014	16 963	13 233	2 870	10 363
90 - 94	11 724	2 227	9 497	6 743	1 408	5 335	4 981	819	4 162
95 - 99	2 525	632	1 893	1 260	370	890	1 265	262	1 003
100 +	741	271	470	333	152	181	408	119	289
Korea (Republic of) - Corée (République de)[33]									
1 XI 2005 (CDJC)									
Total	47 041 434	23 465 650	23 575 784	38 337 699	19 145 912	19 191 787	8 703 735	4 319 738	4 383 997
0	413 805	213 786	200 019	343 865	177 539	166 326	69 940	36 247	33 693
1 - 4	1 968 545	1 023 515	945 030	1 624 142	844 076	780 066	344 403	179 439	164 964
5 - 9	3 168 887	1 654 228	1 514 659	2 624 437	1 370 557	1 253 880	544 450	283 671	260 779
10 - 14	3 434 891	1 816 318	1 618 573	2 898 270	1 533 726	1 364 544	536 621	282 592	254 029
15 - 19	3 100 523	1 626 378	1 474 145	2 629 214	1 378 088	1 251 126	471 309	248 290	223 019
20 - 24	3 662 123	1 915 902	1 746 221	3 147 034	1 611 993	1 535 041	515 089	303 909	211 180
25 - 29	3 671 847	1 858 332	1 813 515	3 174 220	1 589 865	1 584 355	497 627	268 467	229 160
30 - 34	4 096 282	2 059 913	2 036 369	3 485 192	1 739 536	1 745 656	611 090	320 377	290 713
35 - 39	4 112 785	2 065 668	2 047 117	3 474 836	1 726 349	1 748 487	637 949	339 319	298 630
40 - 44	4 123 041	2 082 427	2 040 614	3 479 360	1 738 972	1 740 388	643 681	343 455	300 226
45 - 49	3 900 899	1 961 859	1 939 040	3 252 059	1 626 493	1 625 566	648 840	335 366	313 474
50 - 54	2 855 297	1 426 597	1 428 700	2 314 379	1 157 586	1 156 793	540 918	269 011	271 907
55 - 59	2 278 438	1 126 997	1 151 441	1 773 373	882 089	891 284	505 065	244 908	260 157

Continent, country or area, date, code and age (in years) Continent, pays ou zone, date, code et âge (en années)	Total			Urban - Urbaine			Rural - Rurale		
	Both sexes Les deux sexes	Male Masculin	Female Féminin	Both sexes Les deux sexes	Male Masculin	Female Féminin	Both sexes Les deux sexes	Male Masculin	Female Féminin
ASIA - ASIE									
Korea (Republic of) - Corée (République de)[33]									
1 XI 2005 (CDJC)									
60 - 64	1 888 853	897 384	991 469	1 370 485	665 921	704 564	518 368	231 463	286 905
65 - 69	1 680 067	755 949	924 118	1 106 537	508 208	598 329	573 530	247 741	325 789
70 - 74	1 252 734	514 241	738 493	773 269	319 475	453 794	479 465	194 766	284 699
75 - 79	766 870	270 632	496 238	466 206	161 741	304 465	300 664	108 891	191 773
80 - 84	432 259	136 705	295 554	261 192	79 567	181 625	171 067	57 138	113 929
85 +	233 288	58 819	174 469	139 629	34 131	105 498	93 659	24 688	68 971
Kuwait - Koweït									
1 VII 2005 (ESDF)									
Total	2 457 257	1 472 312	984 945	...	...	...	...	...	...
0	40 594	20 324	20 270	...	...	...	...	...	...
1 - 4	165 576	82 830	82 746	...	...	...	...	...	...
5 - 9	196 268	98 766	97 502	...	...	...	...	...	...
10 - 14	173 895	88 459	85 436	...	...	...	...	...	...
15 - 19	163 833	83 369	80 464	...	...	...	...	...	...
20 - 24	218 493	123 740	94 753	...	...	...	...	...	...
25 - 29	324 139	208 595	115 544	...	...	...	...	...	...
30 - 34	310 399	203 918	106 481	...	...	...	...	...	...
35 - 39	280 178	185 862	94 316	...	...	...	...	...	...
40 - 44	210 080	137 879	72 201	...	...	...	...	...	...
45 - 49	151 117	100 932	50 185	...	...	...	...	...	...
50 - 54	93 824	62 454	31 370	...	...	...	...	...	...
55 - 59	54 612	34 570	20 042	...	...	...	...	...	...
60 - 64	31 577	18 527	13 050	...	...	...	...	...	...
65 - 69	20 495	11 385	9 110	...	...	...	...	...	...
70 - 74	11 250	5 636	5 614	...	...	...	...	...	...
75 - 79	5 972	2 869	3 103	...	...	...	...	...	...
80 - 84	2 915	1 290	1 625	...	...	...	...	...	...
85 +	2 040	907	1 133	...	...	...	...	...	...
Kyrgyzstan - Kirghizistan[34]									
1 VII 2006 (ESDJ)									
Total	5 164 206	2 552 828	2 611 378	1 803 566	862 336	941 230	3 360 640	1 690 492	1 670 148
0	112 166	57 506	54 660	35 837	18 443	17 394	76 329	39 063	37 266
1 - 4	405 565	207 474	198 091	126 717	64 676	62 041	278 848	142 798	136 050
5 - 9	494 482	252 305	242 177	140 389	71 776	68 613	354 093	180 529	173 564
10 - 14	575 031	291 336	283 695	164 204	82 854	81 350	410 827	208 482	202 345
15 - 19	586 353	296 382	289 971	175 297	86 938	88 359	411 056	209 444	201 612
20 - 24	513 660	258 186	255 474	170 363	81 716	88 647	343 297	176 470	166 827
25 - 29	430 788	216 614	214 174	184 979	88 861	96 118	245 809	127 753	118 056
30 - 34	381 704	191 039	190 665	151 724	72 409	79 315	229 980	118 630	111 350
35 - 39	346 018	172 479	173 539	140 408	67 236	73 172	205 610	105 243	100 367
40 - 44	324 358	158 605	165 753	127 283	60 327	66 956	197 075	98 278	98 797
45 - 49	293 285	141 869	151 416	114 632	53 464	61 168	178 653	88 405	90 248
50 - 54	207 010	98 548	108 462	81 649	37 520	44 129	125 361	61 028	64 333
55 - 59	144 719	67 859	76 860	59 609	26 941	32 668	85 110	40 918	44 192
60 - 64	66 303	30 567	35 736	26 656	11 534	15 122	39 647	19 033	20 614
65 - 69	101 563	43 839	57 724	39 263	16 037	23 226	62 300	27 802	34 498
70 - 74	73 314	30 110	43 204	25 791	9 645	16 146	47 523	20 465	27 058
75 - 79	61 403	23 737	37 666	21 491	7 188	14 303	39 912	16 549	23 363
80 - 84	29 800	10 020	19 780	11 176	3 127	8 049	18 624	6 893	11 731
85 - 89	10 551	2 839	7 712	3 981	1 111	2 870	6 570	1 728	4 842
90 - 94	3 802	855	2 947	1 328	307	1 021	2 474	548	1 926
95 - 99	1 845	500	1 345	551	173	378	1 294	327	967
100 +	486	159	327	238	53	185	248	106	142
Lao People's Democratic Republic - République démocratique populaire lao[35]									
1 VII 2006 (ESDF)									
Total	5 747 000	2 864 000	2 883 000	...	...	...	...	...	...
0 - 4	736 900	370 800	366 200	...	...	...	...	...	...
5 - 9	739 300	373 400	365 900	...	...	...	...	...	...
10 - 14	771 400	394 000	377 500	...	...	...	...	...	...
15 - 19	671 900	337 600	334 200	...	...	...	...	...	...

Continent, country or area, date, code and age (in years) Continent, pays ou zone, date, code et âge (en annèes)	Total			Urban - Urbaine			Rural - Rurale		
	Both sexes Les deux sexes	Male Masculin	Female Féminin	Both sexes Les deux sexes	Male Masculin	Female Féminin	Both sexes Les deux sexes	Male Masculin	Female Féminin
ASIA - ASIE									
Lao People's Democratic Republic - République démocratique populaire lao[35]									
1 VII 2006 (ESDF)									
20 - 24	532 500	262 800	269 700	...	...	...	...	...	...
25 - 29	439 800	216 200	223 500	...	...	...	...	...	...
30 - 34	365 400	179 000	186 400	...	...	...	...	...	...
35 - 39	334 100	166 100	168 000	...	...	...	...	...	...
40 - 44	276 200	137 400	138 800	...	...	...	...	...	...
45 - 49	233 000	116 700	116 300	...	...	...	...	...	...
50 - 54	186 300	91 100	95 200	...	...	...	...	...	...
55 - 59	134 100	65 300	68 700	...	...	...	...	...	...
60 - 64	106 400	50 700	55 700	...	...	...	...	...	...
65 - 69	81 100	38 900	42 300	...	...	...	...	...	...
70 - 74	60 200	28 000	32 300	...	...	...	...	...	...
75 +	79 000	36 500	42 500	...	...	...	...	...	...
Malaysia - Malaisie									
5 VII 2000 (CDJC)[36]									
Total	23 274 690	11 853 432	11 421 258	14 426 871	7 318 396	7 108 475	8 847 819	4 535 036	4 312 783
0 - 4	2 612 744	1 347 633	1 265 111	1 574 757	812 456	762 301	1 037 987	535 177	502 810
5 - 9	2 646 527	1 364 984	1 281 543	1 534 452	792 619	741 933	1 112 075	572 465	539 610
10 - 14	2 491 777	1 276 348	1 215 429	1 383 003	709 140	673 863	1 108 774	667 208	541 566
15 - 19	2 367 021	1 195 803	1 171 218	1 408 673	707 968	700 705	958 348	487 835	470 513
20 - 24	2 087 173	1 050 916	1 036 257	1 436 911	708 607	728 304	650 262	342 309	307 953
25 - 29	1 921 052	972 668	948 384	1 315 940	653 627	662 313	605 112	319 041	286 071
30 - 34	1 800 196	915 814	884 382	1 207 148	606 473	600 675	593 048	309 341	283 707
35 - 39	1 705 044	866 212	838 832	1 141 371	577 947	563 424	563 673	288 265	275 408
40 - 44	1 487 498	764 706	722 792	976 771	504 183	472 588	510 727	260 523	250 204
45 - 49	1 168 527	604 844	563 683	743 757	389 417	354 340	424 770	215 427	209 343
50 - 54	918 868	480 261	438 607	562 704	298 115	264 589	356 164	182 146	174 018
55 - 59	616 598	320 119	296 479	356 078	186 312	169 766	260 520	133 807	126 713
60 - 64	551 027	274 216	276 811	306 351	153 941	152 410	244 676	120 275	124 401
65 - 69	346 725	164 943	181 782	189 063	89 783	99 280	157 662	75 160	82 502
70 - 74	264 119	125 883	138 236	138 716	64 354	74 362	125 403	61 529	63 874
75 +	289 794	128 082	161 712	151 176	63 554	87 622	138 618	64 528	74 090
1 VII 2006 (ESDF)									
Total	26 640 200	13 562 600	13 077 600	...	...	...	...	...	...
0 - 4	3 080 400	1 589 900	1 490 500	...	...	...	...	...	...
5 - 9	2 875 300	1 480 300	1 395 000	...	...	...	...	...	...
10 - 14	2 676 300	1 380 700	1 295 500	...	...	...	...	...	...
15 - 19	2 555 800	1 305 600	1 250 200	...	...	...	...	...	...
20 - 24	2 415 100	1 225 800	1 189 300	...	...	...	...	...	...
25 - 29	2 153 800	1 088 600	1 065 200	...	...	...	...	...	...
30 - 34	1 947 400	984 000	963 400	...	...	...	...	...	...
35 - 39	1 857 800	941 300	916 600	...	...	...	...	...	...
40 - 44	1 694 700	861 000	833 700	...	...	...	...	...	...
45 - 49	1 475 000	754 700	720 300	...	...	...	...	...	...
50 - 54	1 227 200	629 500	597 700	...	...	...	...	...	...
55 - 59	894 500	460 300	434 200	...	...	...	...	...	...
60 - 64	637 300	326 000	311 400	...	...	...	...	...	...
65 - 69	472 900	230 400	242 500	...	...	...	...	...	...
70 - 74	317 300	146 600	170 700	...	...	...	...	...	...
75 +	359 300	157 900	201 400	...	...	...	...	...	...
Maldives[37]									
21 III 2006 (CDFC)									
Total	298 968	151 459	147 509	103 693	51 992	51 701	195 275	99 467	95 808
0	5 462	2 777	2 685	1 601	832	769	3 861	1 945	1 916
1 - 4	20 709	10 585	10 124	5 743	2 912	2 831	14 966	7 673	7 293
5 - 9	29 867	15 352	14 515	7 538	3 829	3 709	22 329	11 523	10 806
10 - 14	36 999	19 111	17 888	10 082	5 171	4 911	26 917	13 940	12 977
15 - 19	39 904	20 155	19 749	15 656	7 457	8 199	24 248	12 698	11 550
20 - 24	34 809	16 933	17 876	15 535	7 401	8 134	19 274	9 532	9 742
25 - 29	24 581	11 915	12 666	10 176	5 054	5 122	14 405	6 861	7 544
30 - 34	20 635	10 022	10 613	8 137	4 089	4 048	12 498	5 933	6 565
35 - 39	18 174	8 780	9 394	6 616	3 381	3 235	11 558	5 399	6 159

Continent, country or area, date, code and age (in years) Continent, pays ou zone, date, code et âge (en années)	Total			Urban - Urbaine			Rural - Rurale		
	Both sexes Les deux sexes	Male Masculin	Female Féminin	Both sexes Les deux sexes	Male Masculin	Female Féminin	Both sexes Les deux sexes	Male Masculin	Female Féminin
ASIA - ASIE									
Maldives[37]									
21 III 2006 (CDFC)									
40 - 44	15 871	7 828	8 043	5 529	2 731	2 798	10 342	5 097	5 245
45 - 49	13 569	6 872	6 697	4 394	2 207	2 187	9 175	4 665	4 510
50 - 54	7 936	4 147	3 789	2 601	1 415	1 186	5 335	2 732	2 603
55 - 59	5 859	3 046	2 813	1 863	987	876	3 996	2 059	1 937
60 - 64	5 566	2 852	2 714	1 520	752	768	4 046	2 100	1 946
65 - 69	5 678	3 014	2 664	1 265	619	646	4 413	2 395	2 018
70 - 74	4 186	2 333	1 853	765	363	402	3 421	1 970	1 451
75 - 79	2 377	1 444	933	409	217	192	1 968	1 227	741
80 - 84	1 064	617	447	204	92	112	860	525	335
85 - 89	396	241	155	94	48	46	302	193	109
90 - 94	159	89	70	34	14	20	125	75	50
95 +	84	52	32	19	8	11	65	44	21
Unknown - Inconnu	5 083	3 294	1 789	3 912	2 413	1 499	1 171	881	290
Mongolia - Mongolie									
5 I 2000 (CDFC)									
Total	2 373 493	1 177 981	1 195 512	1 344 516	657 081	687 435	1 028 977	520 900	508 077
0	49 804	25 356	24 448	23 778	12 119	11 659	26 026	13 237	12 789
1 - 4	196 219	99 126	97 093	91 687	46 096	45 591	104 532	53 030	51 502
5 - 9	285 664	144 315	141 349	150 401	75 700	74 701	135 263	68 615	66 648
10 - 14	317 434	159 294	158 140	179 974	89 670	90 304	137 460	69 624	67 836
15 - 19	263 358	133 327	130 031	154 244	75 040	79 204	109 114	58 287	50 827
20 - 24	235 751	118 023	117 728	135 694	66 010	69 684	100 057	52 013	48 044
25 - 29	216 652	107 962	108 690	125 644	61 274	64 370	91 008	46 688	44 320
30 - 34	187 872	92 473	95 399	113 537	54 332	59 205	74 335	38 141	36 194
35 - 39	172 606	84 846	87 760	108 347	52 275	56 072	64 259	32 571	31 688
40 - 44	127 220	62 619	64 601	79 563	38 840	40 723	47 657	23 779	23 878
45 - 49	82 888	40 562	42 326	50 873	25 089	25 784	32 015	15 473	16 542
50 - 54	57 835	27 707	30 128	35 016	17 094	17 922	22 819	10 613	12 206
55 - 59	55 895	27 379	28 516	30 397	15 011	15 386	25 498	12 368	13 130
60 - 64	42 292	20 778	21 514	21 889	10 658	11 231	20 403	10 120	10 283
65 - 69	35 415	15 982	19 433	18 480	8 145	10 335	16 935	7 837	9 098
70 - 74	20 239	8 766	11 473	10 946	4 579	6 367	9 293	4 187	5 106
75 - 79	14 843	5 832	9 011	7 963	3 197	4 766	6 880	2 635	4 245
80 - 84	7 036	2 329	4 707	3 777	1 281	2 496	3 259	1 048	2 211
85 - 89	3 376	991	2 385	1 746	519	1 227	1 630	472	1 158
90 - 94	869	257	612	441	125	316	428	132	296
95 - 99	196	53	143	104	24	80	92	29	63
100 +	29	4	25	15	3	12	14	1	13
1 VII 2006 (ESDF)									
Total	2 578 587	1 268 250	1 310 337	...	...	...	...	...	...
0	43 987	22 044	21 943	...	...	...	...	...	...
1 - 4	183 446	91 938	91 508	...	...	...	...	...	...
5 - 9	259 792	130 145	129 647	...	...	...	...	...	...
10 - 14	300 924	150 919	150 005	...	...	...	...	...	...
15 - 19	304 598	152 730	151 867	...	...	...	...	...	...
20 - 24	265 579	131 370	134 209	...	...	...	...	...	...
25 - 29	231 077	113 452	117 625	...	...	...	...	...	...
30 - 34	207 956	102 289	105 667	...	...	...	...	...	...
35 - 39	188 819	92 205	96 614	...	...	...	...	...	...
40 - 44	164 026	79 620	84 406	...	...	...	...	...	...
45 - 49	126 235	61 547	64 688	...	...	...	...	...	...
50 - 54	87 125	42 300	44 825	...	...	...	...	...	...
55 - 59	64 230	30 910	33 320	...	...	...	...	...	...
60 - 64	51 716	24 125	27 591	...	...	...	...	...	...
65 - 69	40 491	18 678	21 813	...	...	...	...	...	...
70 +	58 587	23 977	34 610	...	...	...	...	...	...
Myanmar									
1 VII 2004 (ESDF)									
Total	54 299 000	27 000 000	27 299 000	...	...	...	...	...	...
0 - 4	6 407 000	3 235 000	3 172 000	...	...	...	...	...	...
5 - 9	5 933 000	2 974 000	2 959 000	...	...	...	...	...	...
10 - 14	5 382 000	2 715 000	2 667 000	...	...	...	...	...	...
15 - 19	4 824 000	2 512 000	2 312 000	...	...	...	...	...	...

7. Population by age, sex and urban/rural residence: latest available year, 1997 - 2006
Population selon l'âge, le sexe et la résidence, urbaine/rurale: dernière année disponible, 1997 - 2006 (continued - suite)

Continent, country or area, date, code and age (in years) / Continent, pays ou zone, date, code et âge (en années)	Total Both sexes Les deux sexes	Total Male Masculin	Total Female Féminin	Urban - Urbaine Both sexes Les deux sexes	Urban - Urbaine Male Masculin	Urban - Urbaine Female Féminin	Rural - Rurale Both sexes Les deux sexes	Rural - Rurale Male Masculin	Rural - Rurale Female Féminin
ASIA - ASIE									
Myanmar									
1 VII 2004 (ESDF)									
20 - 24	4 748 000	2 429 000	2 319 000	...	...	...	...	...	...
25 - 29	4 490 000	2 265 000	2 225 000	...	...	...	...	...	...
30 - 34	4 135 000	2 059 000	2 076 000	...	...	...	...	...	...
35 - 39	3 760 000	1 845 000	1 915 000	...	...	...	...	...	...
40 - 44	3 287 000	1 604 000	1 683 000	...	...	...	...	...	...
45 - 49	2 759 000	1 340 000	1 419 000	...	...	...	...	...	...
50 - 54	2 293 000	1 107 000	1 186 000	...	...	...	...	...	...
55 - 59	1 818 000	872 000	946 000	...	...	...	...	...	...
60 - 64	1 478 000	698 000	780 000	...	...	...	...	...	...
65 +	2 985 000	1 345 000	1 640 000	...	...	...	...	...	...
Nepal - Népal									
22 VI 2001 (CDJC)									
Total	22 736 934	11 359 378	11 377 556	...	...	...	...	...	...
0	494 813	252 519	242 294	...	...	...	...	...	...
1 - 4	2 260 400	1 143 196	1 117 204	...	...	...	...	...	...
5 - 9	3 211 442	1 633 087	1 578 355	...	...	...	...	...	...
10 - 14	2 981 932	1 533 806	1 448 126	...	...	...	...	...	...
15 - 19	2 389 002	1 185 826	1 203 176	...	...	...	...	...	...
20 - 24	2 016 768	946 742	1 070 026	...	...	...	...	...	...
25 - 29	1 725 478	821 014	904 464	...	...	...	...	...	...
30 - 34	1 489 503	726 040	763 463	...	...	...	...	...	...
35 - 39	1 310 653	651 351	659 302	...	...	...	...	...	...
40 - 44	1 088 044	539 993	548 051	...	...	...	...	...	...
45 - 49	923 373	469 695	453 678	...	...	...	...	...	...
50 - 54	766 054	392 659	373 395	...	...	...	...	...	...
55 - 59	602 093	318 610	283 483	...	...	...	...	...	...
60 - 64	520 908	262 255	258 653	...	...	...	...	...	...
65 - 69	387 223	196 053	191 170	...	...	...	...	...	...
70 - 74	273 789	141 678	132 111	...	...	...	...	...	...
75 - 79	165 764	82 335	83 429	...	...	...	...	...	...
80 - 84	84 255	41 192	43 063	...	...	...	...	...	...
85 - 89	27 947	13 630	14 317	...	...	...	...	...	...
90 - 94	11 421	5 082	6 339	...	...	...	...	...	...
95 +	6 072	2 615	3 457	...	...	...	...	...	...
Occupied Palestinian Territory - Territoire palestinien occupé									
1 VII 2006 (ESDF)									
Total	3 888 292	1 970 327	1 917 965	...	...	...	...	...	...
0 - 4	671 289	342 406	328 883	...	...	...	...	...	...
5 - 9	599 474	305 826	293 648	...	...	...	...	...	...
10 - 14	506 728	257 597	249 131	...	...	...	...	...	...
15 - 19	420 441	213 864	206 577	...	...	...	...	...	...
20 - 24	339 209	173 885	165 324	...	...	...	...	...	...
25 - 29	285 586	145 948	139 638	...	...	...	...	...	...
30 - 34	241 756	122 842	118 914	...	...	...	...	...	...
35 - 39	202 324	103 439	98 885	...	...	...	...	...	...
40 - 44	167 474	86 814	80 660	...	...	...	...	...	...
45 - 49	129 266	66 713	62 553	...	...	...	...	...	...
50 - 54	88 829	45 056	43 773	...	...	...	...	...	...
55 - 59	67 743	32 978	34 765	...	...	...	...	...	...
60 - 64	51 545	23 060	28 485	...	...	...	...	...	...
65 - 09	41 395	17 799	23 596	...	...	...	...	...	...
70 - 74	34 236	14 552	19 684	...	...	...	...	...	...
75 - 79	22 472	9 442	13 030	...	...	...	...	...	...
80 +	18 525	8 106	10 419	...	...	...	...	...	...
Oman									
1 VII 2006 (ESDF)									
Total	2 577 062	1 498 143	1 078 919	...	...	...	...	...	...
0 - 4	251 725	129 358	122 367	...	...	...	...	...	...
5 - 9	253 314	131 178	122 136	...	...	...	...	...	...
10 - 14	280 482	144 757	135 725	...	...	...	...	...	...
15 - 19	290 054	148 914	141 140	...	...	...	...	...	...

Continent, country or area, date, code and age (in years) / Continent, pays ou zone, date, code et âge (en années)	Total			Urban - Urbaine			Rural - Rurale		
	Both sexes Les deux sexes	Male Masculin	Female Féminin	Both sexes Les deux sexes	Male Masculin	Female Féminin	Both sexes Les deux sexes	Male Masculin	Female Féminin
ASIA - ASIE									
Oman									
1 VII 2006 (ESDF)									
20 - 24	294 079	156 885	137 194	...	...	...	...	...	...
25 - 29	302 036	181 703	120 333	...	...	...	...	...	...
30 - 34	251 860	165 400	86 460	...	...	...	...	...	...
35 - 39	194 021	133 360	60 661	...	...	...	...	...	...
40 - 44	156 250	109 644	46 606	...	...	...	...	...	...
45 - 49	107 773	75 888	31 885	...	...	...	...	...	...
50 - 54	72 858	49 657	23 201	...	...	...	...	...	...
55 - 59	44 866	28 056	16 810	...	...	...	...	...	...
60 - 64	32 666	19 304	13 362	...	...	...	...	...	...
65 - 69	18 649	10 538	8 111	...	...	...	...	...	...
70 - 74	13 694	7 231	6 463	...	...	...	...	...	...
75 - 79	5 210	2 642	2 568	...	...	...	...	...	...
80 +	7 525	3 628	3 897	...	...	...	...	...	...
Pakistan[38]									
1 VII 2003 (SSDJ)									
Total	138 979 270	71 741 403	67 237 867	49 640 104	25 819 279	23 820 825	89 339 166	45 922 123	43 417 043
0 - 4	18 874 090	9 641 577	9 232 513	5 798 058	2 932 025	2 866 033	13 076 032	6 709 552	6 366 480
5 - 9	20 770 885	10 696 306	10 074 579	6 545 959	3 370 981	3 174 978	14 224 926	7 325 326	6 899 601
10 - 14	19 004 548	9 998 775	9 005 773	6 682 490	3 508 172	3 174 318	12 322 058	6 490 603	5 831 455
15 - 19	16 304 449	8 586 808	7 717 641	6 335 209	3 356 840	2 978 369	9 969 240	5 229 967	4 739 272
20 - 24	12 807 395	6 573 668	6 233 727	5 037 368	2 680 281	2 357 087	7 770 027	3 893 387	3 876 640
25 - 29	9 704 504	4 842 061	4 862 443	3 755 282	1 893 606	1 861 676	5 949 222	2 948 455	3 000 767
30 - 34	7 706 844	3 751 378	3 955 465	2 877 291	1 462 892	1 414 399	4 829 553	2 288 486	2 541 066
35 - 39	7 338 853	3 624 659	3 714 194	2 800 153	1 396 436	1 403 717	4 538 701	2 228 223	2 310 477
40 - 44	6 082 558	3 110 905	2 971 653	2 331 614	1 216 237	1 115 376	3 750 944	1 894 667	1 856 277
45 - 49	5 625 302	2 899 571	2 725 731	2 216 767	1 155 448	1 061 319	3 408 535	1 744 123	1 664 412
50 - 54	4 245 641	2 255 598	1 990 043	1 563 957	850 028	713 930	2 681 684	1 405 570	1 276 114
55 - 59	3 095 898	1 644 139	1 451 759	1 160 460	606 560	553 900	1 935 438	1 037 579	897 859
60 - 64	2 709 743	1 472 941	1 236 802	933 107	513 221	419 886	1 776 636	959 720	816 915
65 - 69	1 903 851	1 059 937	843 915	675 240	371 961	303 279	1 228 611	687 976	540 635
70 - 74	1 336 807	759 803	577 004	450 996	247 618	203 378	885 810	512 185	373 626
75 - 79	645 190	354 323	290 867	215 784	114 212	101 572	429 406	240 111	189 294
80 - 84	474 912	272 801	202 111	157 114	87 558	69 556	317 798	185 244	132 555
85 +	347 801	196 152	151 649	103 256	55 205	48 051	244 545	140 947	103 598
Philippines									
1 VII 2003 (ESDJ)									
Total	81 081 457	40 820 706	40 260 751	...	...	...	...	...	...
0 - 4	9 633 446	4 923 339	4 710 107	...	...	...	...	...	...
5 - 9	9 416 816	4 825 448	4 591 368	...	...	...	...	...	...
10 - 14	9 046 260	4 650 500	4 395 760	...	...	...	...	...	...
15 - 19	8 359 222	4 254 885	4 104 337	...	...	...	...	...	...
20 - 24	7 591 134	3 825 549	3 765 585	...	...	...	...	...	...
25 - 29	6 799 991	3 404 184	3 395 807	...	...	...	...	...	...
30 - 34	6 016 620	3 001 529	3 015 091	...	...	...	...	...	...
35 - 39	5 245 030	2 619 599	2 625 431	...	...	...	...	...	...
40 - 44	4 485 000	2 245 860	2 239 140	...	...	...	...	...	...
45 - 49	3 748 090	1 877 697	1 870 393	...	...	...	...	...	...
50 - 54	3 046 766	1 523 354	1 523 412	...	...	...	...	...	...
55 - 59	2 412 086	1 194 640	1 217 446	...	...	...	...	...	...
60 - 64	1 836 897	895 575	941 322	...	...	...	...	...	...
65 - 69	1 362 119	650 983	711 136	...	...	...	...	...	...
70 - 74	956 336	443 008	513 328	...	...	...	...	...	...
75 - 79	621 662	274 907	346 755	...	...	...	...	...	...
80 +	503 982	209 649	294 333	...	...	...	...	...	...
Qatar									
1 VII 2006 (ESDF)									
Total	936 287	666 543	269 744	...	...	...	...	...	...
0	15 906	8 223	7 683	...	...	...	...	...	...
1 - 4	59 170	30 471	28 699	...	...	...	...	...	...
5 - 9	70 769	36 241	34 528	...	...	...	...	...	...
10 - 14	66 494	34 100	32 395	...	...	...	...	...	...
15 - 19	53 097	29 867	23 230	...	...	...	...	...	...
20 - 24	74 831	59 784	15 047	...	...	...	...	...	...

7. Population by age, sex and urban/rural residence: latest available year, 1997 - 2006
Population selon l'âge, le sexe et la résidence, urbaine/rurale: dernière année disponible, 1997 - 2006 (continued - suite)

Continent, country or area, date, code and age (in years) / Continent, pays ou zone, date, code et âge (en années)	Total			Urban - Urbaine			Rural - Rurale		
	Both sexes Les deux sexes	Male Masculin	Female Féminin	Both sexes Les deux sexes	Male Masculin	Female Féminin	Both sexes Les deux sexes	Male Masculin	Female Féminin
ASIA - ASIE									
Qatar									
1 VII 2006 (ESDF)									
25 - 29	105 635	84 089	21 546	...	...	...	...	...	...
30 - 34	119 501	92 671	26 830	...	...	...	...	...	...
35 - 39	106 698	84 017	22 682	...	...	...	...	...	...
40 - 44	95 527	74 861	20 667	...	...	...	...	...	...
45 - 49	74 374	58 669	15 705	...	...	...	...	...	...
50 - 54	46 953	37 604	9 349	...	...	...	...	...	...
55 - 59	24 985	19 856	5 129	...	...	...	...	...	...
60 - 64	11 523	8 805	2 718	...	...	...	...	...	...
65 - 69	5 135	3 596	1 539	...	...	...	...	...	...
70 - 74	3 034	2 040	994	...	...	...	...	...	...
75 - 79	1 442	936	506	...	...	...	...	...	...
80 +	1 211	714	497	...	...	...	...	...	...
Saudi Arabia - Arabie saoudite									
1 VII 2006 (ESDF)									
Total	23 678 849	13 090 839	10 588 009						
0 - 4	2 754 108	1 399 669	1 354 439						
5 - 9	2 595 789	1 310 112	1 285 677						
10 - 14	2 430 136	1 215 671	1 214 465						
15 - 19	2 206 139	1 093 786	1 112 353	...	...	...	...	...	...
20 - 24	2 095 772	1 081 896	1 013 876						
25 - 29	2 316 893	1 329 970	986 922						
30 - 34	2 336 313	1 402 957	933 355						
35 - 39	1 992 635	1 237 652	754 983						
40 - 44	1 532 030	988 595	543 437	...	...	...	...	...	...
45 - 49	1 119 319	716 867	402 452						
50 - 54	779 419	483 487	295 933						
55 - 59	513 520	300 719	212 801						
60 - 64	348 682	189 197	159 485	...	...	...	...	...	...
65 - 69	244 232	126 042	118 189						
70 - 74	170 480	86 502	83 979						
75 - 79	112 027	57 538	54 489						
80 +	131 354	70 180	61 174						
Singapore - Singapour									
1 VII 2005 (ESDJ)									
Total	3 543 900	1 758 000	1 785 900	...	...	...	...	...	...
0 - 4	201 500	103 700	97 800	...	...	...	...	...	...
5 - 9	241 800	124 700	117 100	...	...	...	...	...	...
10 - 14	263 100	135 300	127 800	...	...	...	...	...	...
15 - 19	237 500	122 000	115 500	...	...	...	...	...	...
20 - 24	221 900	111 900	110 000	...	...	...	...	...	...
25 - 29	253 100	120 500	132 600	...	...	...	...	...	...
30 - 34	302 100	145 100	157 000	...	...	...	...	...	...
35 - 39	308 000	151 100	156 900	...	...	...	...	...	...
40 - 44	329 400	165 700	163 700	...	...	...	...	...	...
45 - 49	313 200	158 100	155 100	...	...	...	...	...	...
50 - 54	259 400	130 800	128 600	...	...	...	...	...	...
55 - 59	201 900	100 700	101 300	...	...	...	...	...	...
60 - 64	120 200	58 700	61 500	...	...	...	...	...	...
65 - 69	103 600	49 500	54 100	...	...	...	...	...	...
70 - 74	78 800	36 100	42 600	...	...	...	...	...	...
75 - 79	55 300	24 100	31 200	...	...	...	...	...	...
80 - 84	29 800	12 300	17 500	...	...	...	...	...	...
85 +	23 300	7 800	15 500	...	...	...	...	...	...
Sri Lanka									
1 VII 2006 (ESDF)									
Total	19 886 000	9 826 000	10 060 000	...	...	...	...	...	...
0 - 4	1 719 000	874 000	845 000	...	...	...	...	...	...
5 - 9	1 769 000	894 000	875 000	...	...	...	...	...	...
10 - 14	1 809 000	924 000	885 000	...	...	...	...	...	...
15 - 19	1 938 000	992 000	946 000	...	...	...	...	...	...
20 - 24	1 830 000	904 000	926 000	...	...	...	...	...	...
25 - 29	1 552 000	747 000	805 000	...	...	...	...	...	...

7. Population by age, sex and urban/rural residence: latest available year, 1997 - 2006
Population selon l'âge, le sexe et la résidence, urbaine/rurale: dernière année disponible, 1997 - 2006 (continued - suite)

Continent, country or area, date, code and age (in years) / Continent, pays ou zone, date, code et âge (en années)	Total Both sexes Les deux sexes	Total Male Masculin	Total Female Féminin	Urban - Urbaine Both sexes Les deux sexes	Urban - Urbaine Male Masculin	Urban - Urbaine Female Féminin	Rural - Rurale Both sexes Les deux sexes	Rural - Rurale Male Masculin	Rural - Rurale Female Féminin
ASIA - ASIE									
Sri Lanka									
1 VII 2006 (ESDF)									
30 - 34	1 491 000	727 000	764 000	...	...	...	...	...	...
35 - 39	1 472 000	717 000	755 000	...	...	...	...	...	...
40 - 44	1 362 000	668 000	694 000	...	...	...	...	...	...
45 - 49	1 204 000	590 000	614 000	...	...	...	...	...	...
50 - 54	1 084 000	531 000	553 000	...	...	...	...	...	...
55 - 59	795 000	383 000	412 000	...	...	...	...	...	...
60 - 64	587 000	285 000	302 000	...	...	...	...	...	...
65 - 69	488 000	226 000	262 000	...	...	...	...	...	...
70 - 74	358 000	167 000	191 000	...	...	...	...	...	...
75 +	428 000	197 000	231 000	...	...	...	...	...	...
Syrian Arab Republic - République arabe syrienne[39]									
1 VII 2004 (ESDF)									
Total	17 980 000	9 199 000	8 781 000	9 022 000	4 652 000	4 370 000	8 958 000	4 547 000	4 411 000
0	412 000	202 000	210 000	202 000	102 000	100 000	210 000	100 000	110 000
1 - 4	1 778 000	915 000	863 000	831 000	433 000	398 000	947 000	482 000	465 000
5 - 9	2 409 000	1 253 000	1 156 000	1 106 000	577 000	529 000	1 303 000	676 000	627 000
10 - 14	2 520 000	1 304 000	1 216 000	1 199 000	619 000	580 000	1 321 000	685 000	636 000
15 - 19	2 325 000	1 226 000	1 099 000	1 150 000	604 000	546 000	1 175 000	622 000	553 000
20 - 24	1 678 000	879 000	799 000	865 000	461 000	404 000	813 000	418 000	395 000
25 - 29	1 264 000	589 000	675 000	645 000	312 000	333 000	619 000	277 000	342 000
30 - 34	1 049 000	491 000	558 000	556 000	265 000	291 000	493 000	226 000	267 000
35 - 39	1 047 000	506 000	541 000	573 000	274 000	299 000	474 000	232 000	242 000
40 - 44	843 000	424 000	419 000	472 000	247 000	225 000	371 000	177 000	194 000
45 - 49	650 000	328 000	322 000	364 000	186 000	178 000	286 000	142 000	144 000
50 - 54	579 000	290 000	289 000	310 000	158 000	152 000	269 000	132 000	137 000
55 - 59	392 000	199 000	193 000	221 000	112 000	109 000	171 000	87 000	84 000
60 - 64	383 000	203 000	180 000	204 000	112 000	92 000	179 000	91 000	88 000
65 +	651 000	390 000	261 000	324 000	190 000	134 000	327 000	200 000	127 000
Tajikistan - Tadjikistan									
20 I 2000 (CDFC)									
Total	6 127 493	3 069 100	3 058 393	1 626 027	808 650	817 377	4 501 466	2 260 450	2 241 016
0 - 4	882 056	448 631	433 425	208 724	106 293	102 431	673 332	342 338	330 994
5 - 9	881 672	448 632	433 040	212 443	108 483	103 960	669 229	340 149	329 080
10 - 14	853 037	431 095	421 942	207 945	104 701	103 244	645 092	326 394	318 698
15 - 19	669 877	338 197	331 680	173 413	91 078	82 335	496 464	247 119	249 345
20 - 24	533 897	266 028	267 869	144 104	73 209	70 895	389 793	192 819	196 974
25 - 29	468 281	231 206	237 075	131 529	62 116	69 413	336 752	169 090	167 662
30 - 34	414 647	204 261	210 386	123 866	59 797	64 069	290 781	144 464	146 317
35 - 39	385 740	190 676	195 064	116 943	57 232	59 711	268 797	133 444	135 353
40 - 44	287 391	142 315	145 076	87 145	42 544	44 601	200 246	99 771	100 475
45 - 49	195 629	96 581	99 048	61 137	29 526	31 611	134 492	67 055	67 437
50 - 54	119 095	59 790	59 305	38 191	18 451	19 740	80 904	41 339	39 565
55 - 59	98 741	52 455	46 286	29 067	14 613	14 454	69 674	37 842	31 832
60 - 64	113 545	56 552	56 993	33 028	15 794	17 234	80 517	40 758	39 759
65 - 69	93 942	45 159	48 783	24 311	11 323	12 988	69 631	33 836	35 795
70 - 74	67 749	33 684	34 065	18 090	7 948	10 142	49 659	25 736	23 923
75 - 79	36 227	14 508	21 719	9 846	3 481	6 365	26 381	11 027	15 354
80 - 84	14 111	5 220	8 891	3 707	1 226	2 481	10 404	3 994	6 410
85 - 89	7 237	2 664	4 573	1 815	609	1 206	5 422	2 055	3 367
90 - 94	2 613	901	1 712	486	147	339	2 127	754	1 373
95 - 99	1 486	439	1 047	183	65	118	1 303	374	929
100 +	517	106	411	53	14	39	464	92	372
Unknown - Inconnu	3	-	3	1	-	1	2	-	2
Thailand - Thaïlande[3]									
1 VII 2006 (ESDJ)									
Total	65 305 736	32 060 034	33 245 702	19 792 296	9 474 510	10 317 786	45 513 440	22 585 524	22 927 916
0 - 4	4 881 454	2 482 906	2 398 548	1 390 659	701 889	688 770	3 490 795	1 781 017	1 709 778
5 - 9	4 752 901	2 435 397	2 317 504	1 279 124	648 471	630 653	3 473 777	1 786 926	1 686 851
10 - 14	5 176 438	2 646 343	2 530 095	1 384 377	697 797	686 580	3 792 061	1 948 546	1 843 515
15 - 19	5 243 553	2 677 657	2 565 896	1 454 162	725 468	728 694	3 789 391	1 952 189	1 837 202
20 - 24	5 313 321	2 695 912	2 617 409	1 653 594	810 506	843 088	3 659 727	1 885 406	1 774 321
25 - 29	5 347 860	2 696 420	2 651 440	1 870 970	905 665	965 305	3 476 890	1 790 755	1 686 135

Continent, country or area, date, code and age (in years) Continent, pays ou zone, date, code et âge (en années)	Total			Urban - Urbaine			Rural - Rurale		
	Both sexes Les deux sexes	Male Masculin	Female Féminin	Both sexes Les deux sexes	Male Masculin	Female Féminin	Both sexes Les deux sexes	Male Masculin	Female Féminin
ASIA - ASIE									
Thailand - Thaïlande[3]									
1 VII 2006 (ESDJ)									
30 - 34	5 454 165	2 674 150	2 780 015	1 888 962	901 024	987 938	3 565 203	1 773 126	1 792 077
35 - 39	5 516 007	2 649 938	2 866 069	1 796 380	842 791	953 589	3 719 627	1 807 147	1 912 480
40 - 44	5 270 842	2 531 017	2 739 825	1 646 384	769 079	877 305	3 624 458	1 761 938	1 862 520
45 - 49	4 765 479	2 289 840	2 475 639	1 463 711	685 086	778 625	3 301 768	1 604 754	1 697 014
50 - 54	3 832 933	1 835 881	1 997 052	1 157 952	540 758	617 194	2 674 981	1 295 123	1 379 858
55 - 59	2 887 252	1 377 204	1 510 048	853 544	398 349	455 195	2 033 708	978 855	1 054 853
60 - 64	2 228 531	1 045 357	1 183 174	635 610	291 598	344 012	1 592 921	753 759	839 162
65 - 69	1 820 032	830 911	989 121	520 454	231 627	288 827	1 299 578	599 284	700 294
70 - 74	1 344 139	591 594	752 545	377 794	160 735	217 059	966 345	430 859	535 486
75 - 79	825 481	349 019	476 462	230 734	93 717	137 017	594 747	255 302	339 445
80 +	645 348	250 488	394 860	187 885	69 950	117 935	457 463	180 538	276 925
Turkey - Turquie									
22 X 2000 (CDFC)									
Total	67 803 927	34 346 735	33 457 192	44 006 274	22 427 603	21 578 671	23 797 653	11 919 132	11 878 521
0	1 244 675	640 760	603 915	782 345	402 411	379 934	462 330	238 349	223 981
1 - 4	5 340 147	2 755 930	2 584 217	3 305 208	1 705 098	1 600 110	2 034 939	1 050 832	984 107
5 - 9	6 756 617	3 485 746	3 270 871	4 239 171	2 186 546	2 052 625	2 517 446	1 299 200	1 218 246
10 - 14	6 878 656	3 570 657	3 307 990	4 390 792	2 300 010	2 090 782	2 487 864	1 270 647	1 217 217
15 - 19	7 209 475	3 691 218	3 518 257	4 740 001	2 485 382	2 254 619	2 469 474	1 205 836	1 263 638
20 - 24	6 690 146	3 426 714	3 263 432	4 616 663	2 412 166	2 204 497	2 073 483	1 014 548	1 058 935
25 - 29	5 895 255	2 976 430	2 918 825	4 043 777	2 043 057	2 000 720	1 851 478	933 373	918 105
30 - 34	5 009 655	2 552 370	2 457 285	3 438 737	1 744 883	1 693 854	1 570 918	807 487	763 431
35 - 39	4 854 387	2 453 579	2 400 808	3 324 212	1 671 781	1 652 431	1 530 175	781 798	748 377
40 - 44	4 068 756	2 083 531	1 985 225	2 781 023	1 424 039	1 356 984	1 287 733	659 492	1 356 984
45 - 49	3 368 769	1 710 757	1 658 012	2 251 799	1 153 832	1 097 967	1 116 970	556 925	560 045
50 - 54	2 717 349	1 356 391	1 360 958	1 724 916	874 700	850 216	992 433	481 691	510 742
55 - 59	2 058 422	1 016 254	1 042 168	1 225 906	612 521	613 385	832 516	403 733	428 783
60 - 64	1 829 288	864 299	964 989	1 030 176	484 922	545 254	799 112	379 377	419 735
65 - 69	1 645 517	794 881	850 636	883 840	417 194	466 646	761 677	377 687	383 990
70 - 74	1 172 643	517 870	654 773	635 253	270 034	365 219	537 390	247 836	289 554
75 - 79	577 597	254 443	323 154	321 179	135 075	186 104	256 418	119 368	137 050
80 - 84	246 692	98 797	147 895	137 630	52 964	84 666	109 062	45 833	63 229
85 - 89	138 361	55 298	83 063	77 087	28 707	48 380	61 274	26 591	34 683
90 - 94	52 426	18 616	33 810	28 975	9 770	19 205	23 451	8 846	14 605
95 - 99	19 504	7 402	12 102	10 919	4 100	6 819	8 585	3 302	5 283
100 +	6 209	2 256	3 953	3 183	1 118	2 065	3 026	1 138	1 888
Unknown - Inconnu	23 381	12 536	10 845	13 482	7 293	6 189	9 899	5 243	4 656
1 VII 2004 (ESDF)[7]									
Total	71 152 000	35 895 000	35 255 000	...	...	...	...	...	...
0	1 307 000	668 000	639 000	...	...	...	...	...	...
1 - 4	5 454 000	2 782 000	2 671 000	...	...	...	...	...	...
5 - 9	7 100 000	3 614 000	3 485 000	...	...	...	...	...	...
10 - 14	6 649 000	3 385 000	3 262 000	...	...	...	...	...	...
15 - 19	6 273 000	3 210 000	3 065 000	...	...	...	...	...	...
20 - 24	6 693 000	3 423 000	3 268 000	...	...	...	...	...	...
25 - 29	6 730 000	3 436 000	3 294 000	...	...	...	...	...	...
30 - 34	6 051 000	3 073 000	2 978 000	...	...	...	...	...	...
35 - 39	5 054 000	2 541 000	2 512 000	...	...	...	...	...	...
40 - 44	4 446 000	2 246 000	2 200 000	...	...	...	...	...	...
45 - 49	3 873 000	1 975 000	1 900 000	...	...	...	...	...	...
50 - 54	3 145 000	1 589 000	1 555 000	...	...	...	...	...	...
55 - 59	2 346 000	1 164 000	1 183 000	...	...	...	...	...	...
60 - 64	1 950 000	944 000	1 006 000	...	...	...	...	...	...
65 - 69	1 645 000	774 000	873 000	...	...	...	...	...	...
70 - 74	1 190 000	542 000	647 000	...	...	...	...	...	...
75 +	1 246 000	529 000	717 000	...	...	...	...	...	...
Turkmenistan - Turkménistan[7]									
1 VII 2003 (ESDF)									
Total	5 123 940	2 571 866	2 552 073	...	...	...	...	...	...
0 - 4	571 355	277 748	293 607	...	...	...	...	...	...
5 - 9	613 767	300 841	312 925	...	...	...	...	...	...
10 - 14	645 136	316 247	328 889	...	...	...	...	...	...

Continent, country or area, date, code and age (in years) / Continent, pays ou zone, date, code et âge (en années)	Total			Urban - Urbaine			Rural - Rurale		
	Both sexes Les deux sexes	Male Masculin	Female Féminin	Both sexes Les deux sexes	Male Masculin	Female Féminin	Both sexes Les deux sexes	Male Masculin	Female Féminin
ASIA - ASIE									
Turkmenistan - Turkménistan[7]									
1 VII 2003 (ESDF)									
15 - 19	579 113	284 926	294 186	...	...	...	...	...	...
20 - 24	479 053	235 762	243 291	...	...	...	...	...	...
25 - 29	423 109	210 578	212 531	...	...	...	...	...	...
30 - 34	380 948	194 438	186 510	...	...	...	...	...	...
35 - 39	341 403	173 922	167 481	...	...	...	...	...	...
40 - 44	316 309	161 800	154 509	...	...	...	...	...	...
45 - 49	233 504	120 701	112 803	...	...	...	...	...	...
50 - 54	161 151	84 220	76 931	...	...	...	...	...	...
55 - 59	85 927	44 454	41 472	...	...	...	...	...	...
60 - 64	92 992	49 068	43 924	...	...	...	...	...	...
65 - 69	76 006	41 263	34 743	...	...	...	...	...	...
70 - 74	61 177	34 393	26 784	...	...	...	...	...	...
75 +	62 987	41 503	21 484	...	...	...	...	...	...
United Arab Emirates - Émirats arabes unis									
1 VII 2006 (ESDF)									
Total	4 229 000	2 895 000	1 334 000	...	...	...	...	...	...
0 - 4	289 526	149 518	140 008	...	...	...	...	...	...
5 - 9	276 385	143 677	132 708	...	...	...	...	...	...
10 - 14	255 292	134 136	121 156	...	...	...	...	...	...
15 - 19	237 882	124 423	113 459	...	...	...	...	...	...
20 - 24	446 336	280 635	165 701	...	...	...	...	...	...
25 - 29	683 152	500 172	182 980	...	...	...	...	...	...
30 - 34	661 389	506 717	154 672	...	...	...	...	...	...
35 - 39	516 826	399 855	116 971	...	...	...	...	...	...
40 - 44	351 946	271 277	80 669	...	...	...	...	...	...
45 - 49	232 547	179 895	52 652	...	...	...	...	...	...
50 - 54	142 950	110 609	32 341	...	...	...	...	...	...
55 - 59	68 988	52 803	16 185	...	...	...	...	...	...
60 - 64	28 047	19 332	8 715	...	...	...	...	...	...
65 - 69	14 778	9 385	5 393	...	...	...	...	...	...
70 - 74	9 597	5 506	4 091	...	...	...	...	...	...
75 - 79	4 368	2 495	1 873	...	...	...	...	...	...
80 +	8 991	4 565	4 426	...	...	...	...	...	...
Unknown - Inconnu	-	-	-	...	...	...	...	...	...
Uzbekistan - Ouzbékistan									
1 VII 2001 (ESDF)									
Total	24 964 433	12 442 510	12 521 923	9 256 101	4 573 055	4 683 046	15 708 332	7 869 455	7 838 877
0	513 043	263 408	249 635	158 893	81 393	77 500	354 150	182 015	172 135
1 - 4	2 219 863	1 138 212	1 081 651	693 448	355 999	337 449	1 526 415	782 213	744 202
5 - 9	3 237 989	1 653 776	1 584 213	1 015 989	519 360	496 629	2 222 000	1 134 416	1 087 584
10 - 14	3 203 022	1 627 673	1 575 349	1 049 577	533 870	515 707	2 153 445	1 093 803	1 059 642
15 - 19	2 821 926	1 422 296	1 399 630	984 385	497 725	486 660	1 837 541	924 571	912 970
20 - 24	2 296 834	1 157 998	1 138 836	841 326	425 348	415 978	1 455 508	732 650	722 858
25 - 29	2 030 200	1 023 174	1 007 026	788 176	397 184	390 992	1 242 024	625 990	616 034
30 - 34	1 749 557	861 368	888 189	726 099	372 846	353 253	1 023 458	488 522	534 936
35 - 39	1 672 397	816 665	855 732	660 932	323 492	337 440	1 011 465	493 173	518 292
40 - 44	1 479 057	728 780	750 277	612 755	297 460	315 295	866 302	431 320	434 982
45 - 49	1 034 628	506 734	527 894	464 375	223 425	240 950	570 253	283 309	286 944
50 - 54	696 648	337 634	359 014	340 008	161 069	178 939	356 640	176 565	180 075
55 - 59	394 997	197 700	197 297	185 073	88 314	96 759	209 924	109 386	100 538
60 - 64	553 697	265 428	288 269	254 409	115 715	138 694	299 288	149 713	149 575
65 - 69	399 550	185 653	213 897	171 869	75 277	96 592	227 681	110 376	117 305
70 - 74	325 230	143 466	181 764	146 702	57 100	89 602	178 528	86 366	92 162
75 - 79	185 449	67 568	117 881	87 515	27 439	60 076	97 934	40 129	57 805
80 - 84	78 794	23 459	55 335	39 138	10 729	28 409	39 656	12 730	26 926
85 - 89	41 343	10 761	30 582	20 793	4 904	15 889	20 550	5 857	14 693
90 - 94	19 195	6 220	12 975	9 150	2 774	6 376	10 045	3 446	6 599
95 - 99	10 114	4 171	5 943	4 954	1 461	3 493	5 160	2 710	2 450
100 +	900	366	534	535	171	364	365	195	170

7. Population by age, sex and urban/rural residence: latest available year, 1997 - 2006
Population selon l'âge, le sexe et la résidence, urbaine/rurale: dernière année disponible, 1997 - 2006 (continued - suite)

Continent, country or area, date, code and age (in years) Continent, pays ou zone, date, code et âge (en années)	Total			Urban - Urbaine			Rural - Rurale		
	Both sexes Les deux sexes	Male Masculin	Female Féminin	Both sexes Les deux sexes	Male Masculin	Female Féminin	Both sexes Les deux sexes	Male Masculin	Female Féminin
ASIA - ASIE									
Uzbekistan - Ouzbékistan									
1 VII 2003 (ESDF)[7]									
Total....................	25 567 663	12 809 713	12 757 950	...	...	...	...	...	...
0 - 4.....................	2 584 779	1 257 871	1 326 908	...	...	...	...	...	...
5 - 9.....................	3 057 832	1 492 224	1 565 608	...	...	...	...	...	...
10 - 14...................	3 247 432	1 593 319	1 654 113	...	...	...	...	...	...
15 - 19...................	3 036 011	1 502 977	1 533 033	...	...	...	...	...	...
20 - 24...................	2 440 283	1 210 643	1 229 640	...	...	...	...	...	...
25 - 29...................	2 077 200	1 032 960	1 044 240	...	...	...	...	...	...
30 - 34...................	1 852 315	929 765	922 550	...	...	...	...	...	...
35 - 39...................	1 654 410	848 383	806 026	...	...	...	...	...	...
40 - 44...................	1 586 930	807 669	779 261	...	...	...	...	...	...
45 - 49...................	1 170 247	595 727	574 520	...	...	...	...	...	...
50 - 54...................	821 154	423 337	397 817	...	...	...	...	...	...
55 - 59...................	426 436	218 173	208 263	...	...	...	...	...	...
60 - 64...................	499 732	256 051	243 680	...	...	...	...	...	...
65 - 69...................	416 696	220 394	196 302	...	...	...	...	...	...
70 - 74...................	324 533	182 720	141 812	...	...	...	...	...	...
75 +.....................	371 669	237 497	134 172	...	...	...	...	...	...
Viet Nam									
1 IV 1999 (CDFC)									
Total....................	76 323 173	37 469 117	38 854 056	18 076 823	8 825 112	9 251 711	58 246 350	28 644 005	29 602 345
0.........................	1 263 599	647 832	615 767	232 977	120 215	112 762	1 030 622	527 617	503 005
1 - 4.....................	5 908 643	3 034 911	2 873 732	1 184 870	611 659	573 211	4 723 773	2 423 252	2 300 521
5 - 9.....................	9 033 162	4 634 400	4 398 762	1 746 284	899 731	846 553	7 286 878	3 734 669	3 552 209
10 - 14...................	9 066 562	4 654 315	4 412 247	1 775 015	913 513	861 502	7 291 547	3 740 802	3 550 745
15 - 19...................	8 222 280	4 141 058	4 081 222	1 902 373	944 176	958 197	6 319 907	3 196 882	3 123 025
20 - 24...................	6 925 387	3 430 084	3 495 303	1 787 592	869 997	917 595	5 137 795	2 560 087	2 577 708
25 - 29...................	6 568 174	3 281 300	3 286 874	1 730 659	845 461	885 198	4 837 515	2 435 839	2 401 676
30 - 34...................	6 033 706	3 003 421	3 030 285	1 582 568	776 373	806 195	4 451 138	2 227 048	2 224 090
35 - 39...................	5 586 620	2 726 540	2 860 080	1 547 320	759 866	787 454	4 039 300	1 966 674	2 072 626
40 - 44...................	4 550 060	2 180 363	2 369 697	1 317 660	641 149	676 511	3 232 400	1 539 214	1 693 186
45 - 49...................	3 137 258	1 465 289	1 671 969	872 584	405 712	466 872	2 264 674	1 059 577	1 205 097
50 - 54...................	2 104 316	964 240	1 140 076	571 834	259 517	312 317	1 532 482	704 723	827 759
55 - 59...................	1 787 007	782 143	1 004 864	463 473	209 785	253 688	1 323 534	572 358	751 176
60 - 64...................	1 747 308	759 708	987 600	409 484	179 982	229 502	1 337 824	579 726	758 098
65 - 69...................	1 646 775	725 600	921 175	367 000	164 733	202 267	1 279 775	560 867	718 908
70 - 74...................	1 211 104	500 522	710 582	262 578	111 897	150 681	948 526	388 625	559 901
75 - 79...................	821 749	307 069	514 680	170 797	63 805	106 992	650 952	243 264	407 688
80 - 84...................	418 244	144 203	274 041	89 323	30 036	59 287	328 921	114 167	214 754
85 +.....................	291 219	86 119	205 100	62 432	17 505	44 927	228 787	68 614	160 173
Yemen - Yémen									
1 VII 2006 (ESDF)									
Total....................	20 591 738	10 503 044	10 088 695	...	...	...	...	...	...
0 - 4.....................	3 073 462	1 571 014	1 502 448	...	...	...	...	...	...
5 - 9.....................	3 195 246	1 639 947	1 555 299	...	...	...	...	...	...
10 - 14...................	3 000 920	1 583 760	1 417 160	...	...	...	...	...	...
15 - 19...................	2 590 188	1 323 652	1 266 536	...	...	...	...	...	...
20 - 24...................	1 978 780	1 010 858	967 923	...	...	...	...	...	...
25 - 29...................	1 538 806	763 518	775 287	...	...	...	...	...	...
30 - 34...................	1 011 506	510 135	501 371	...	...	...	...	...	...
35 - 39...................	949 562	450 513	499 049	...	...	...	...	...	...
40 - 44...................	761 317	371 245	390 072	...	...	...	...	...	...
45 - 49...................	611 627	296 781	314 846	...	...	...	...	...	...
50 - 54...................	521 800	266 566	255 234	...	...	...	...	...	...
55 - 59...................	300 708	157 077	143 631	...	...	...	...	...	...
60 - 64...................	339 573	178 319	161 254	...	...	...	...	...	...
65 - 69...................	191 515	101 044	90 471	...	...	...	...	...	...
70 - 74...................	228 689	119 441	109 248	...	...	...	...	...	...
75 - 79...................	98 404	53 306	45 098	...	...	...	...	...	...
80 - 84...................	104 406	53 979	50 427	...	...	...	...	...	...
85 +.....................	82 411	44 212	38 199	...	...	...	...	...	...
Unknown - Inconnu.......	12 818	7 675	5 144	...	...	...	...	...	...

Continent, country or area, date, code and age (in years) / Continent, pays ou zone, date, code et âge (en années)	Total			Urban - Urbaine			Rural - Rurale		
	Both sexes Les deux sexes	Male Masculin	Female Féminin	Both sexes Les deux sexes	Male Masculin	Female Féminin	Both sexes Les deux sexes	Male Masculin	Female Féminin
EUROPE									
Åland Islands - Îles d'Åland[40]									
1 VII 2006 (ESDF)									
Total................	26 923	13 352	13 571	...	...	...	...	...	...
0 - 4....................	1 423	740	683	...	...	...	...	...	...
5 - 9....................	1 523	799	724	...	...	...	...	...	...
10 - 14..................	1 698	857	841	...	...	...	...	...	...
15 - 19..................	1 699	891	808	...	...	...	...	...	...
20 - 24..................	1 274	665	609	...	...	...	...	...	...
25 - 29..................	1 474	760	714	...	...	...	...	...	...
30 - 34..................	1 677	876	801	...	...	...	...	...	...
35 - 39..................	1 885	930	955	...	...	...	...	...	...
40 - 44..................	1 979	1 002	977	...	...	...	...	...	...
45 - 49..................	1 863	905	958	...	...	...	...	...	...
50 - 54..................	2 041	982	1 059	...	...	...	...	...	...
55 - 59..................	2 026	1 012	1 014	...	...	...	...	...	...
60 - 64..................	1 798	916	882	...	...	...	...	...	...
65 - 69..................	1 288	675	613	...	...	...	...	...	...
70 - 74..................	1 038	497	541	...	...	...	...	...	...
75 - 79..................	848	378	470	...	...	...	...	...	...
80 - 84..................	735	279	456	...	...	...	...	...	...
85 - 89..................	414	122	292	...	...	...	...	...	...
90 - 94..................	179	58	121	...	...	...	...	...	...
95 - 99..................	57	8	49	...	...	...	...	...	...
100 +....................	4	-	4	...	...	...	...	...	...
Albania - Albanie									
1 VII 2006 (ESDF)									
Total................	3 150 886	1 580 446	1 570 440	...	...	...	...	...	...
0 - 4....................	240 177	125 415	114 832	...	...	...	...	...	...
5 - 9....................	261 258	136 186	125 145	...	...	...	...	...	...
10 - 14..................	294 291	151 933	142 420	...	...	...	...	...	...
15 - 19..................	315 781	162 121	153 712	...	...	...	...	...	...
20 - 24..................	288 647	142 768	145 851	...	...	...	...	...	...
25 - 29..................	226 520	109 128	117 328	...	...	...	...	...	...
30 - 34..................	206 510	99 123	107 325	...	...	...	...	...	...
35 - 39..................	208 936	101 433	107 455	...	...	...	...	...	...
40 - 44..................	211 315	104 942	106 358	...	...	...	...	...	...
45 - 49..................	207 787	105 576	102 230	...	...	...	...	...	...
50 - 54..................	165 892	85 120	80 799	...	...	...	...	...	...
55 - 59..................	136 769	70 113	66 677	...	...	...	...	...	...
60 - 64..................	112 190	57 186	55 017	...	...	...	...	...	...
65 - 69..................	102 853	51 456	51 395	...	...	...	...	...	...
70 - 74..................	76 384	38 046	38 335	...	...	...	...	...	...
75 - 79..................	52 126	24 018	28 078	...	...	...	...	...	...
80 - 84..................	26 698	10 295	16 359	...	...	...	...	...	...
85 - 89..................	12 945	4 519	8 398	...	...	...	...	...	...
90 - 94..................	3 312	947	2 355	...	...	...	...	...	...
95 +....................	495	122	371	...	...	...	...	...	...
Andorra - Andorre[41]									
31 XII 2006 (ESDF)									
Total................	81 222	42 517	38 705	...	...	...	...	...	...
0 - 4....................	3 801	2 011	1 790	...	...	...	...	...	...
5 - 9....................	4 354	2 263	2 091	...	...	...	...	...	...
10 - 14..................	3 912	2 091	1 821	...	...	...	...	...	...
15 - 19..................	3 732	1 934	1 798	...	...	...	...	...	...
20 - 24..................	4 983	2 554	2 429	...	...	...	...	...	...
25 - 29..................	7 051	3 632	3 419	...	...	...	...	...	...
30 - 34..................	8 134	4 172	3 962	...	...	...	...	...	...
35 - 39..................	7 871	4 090	3 781	...	...	...	...	...	...
40 - 44..................	7 706	4 102	3 604	...	...	...	...	...	...
45 - 49..................	6 617	3 573	3 044	...	...	...	...	...	...
50 - 54..................	5 417	2 970	2 447	...	...	...	...	...	...
55 - 59..................	4 507	2 464	2 043	...	...	...	...	...	...
60 - 64..................	3 577	1 930	1 647	...	...	...	...	...	...
65 - 69..................	2 451	1 256	1 195	...	...	...	...	...	...
70 - 74..................	2 227	1 172	1 055	...	...	...	...	...	...

7. Population by age, sex and urban/rural residence: latest available year, 1997 - 2006
Population selon l'âge, le sexe et la résidence, urbaine/rurale: dernière année disponible, 1997 - 2006 (continued - suite)

Continent, country or area, date, code and age (in years) / Continent, pays ou zone, date, code et âge (en années)	Total			Urban - Urbaine			Rural - Rurale		
	Both sexes Les deux sexes	Male Masculin	Female Féminin	Both sexes Les deux sexes	Male Masculin	Female Féminin	Both sexes Les deux sexes	Male Masculin	Female Féminin
EUROPE									
Andorra - Andorre[41]									
31 XII 2006 (ESDF)									
75 - 79	1 995	980	1 015	...	...	...	...	...	...
80 - 84	1 424	677	747	...	...	...	...	...	...
85 - 89	781	341	440	...	...	...	...	...	...
90 - 94	380	161	219	...	...	...	...	...	...
95 +	302	144	158	...	...	...	...	...	...
Austria - Autriche									
15 V 2001 (CDJC)									
Total	8 032 926	3 889 189	4 143 737	5 368 693	2 564 828	2 803 865	2 664 233	1 324 361	1 339 872
0	77 060	39 641	37 419	50 942	26 172	24 770	26 118	13 469	12 649
1 - 4	332 964	170 439	162 525	215 492	110 553	104 939	117 472	59 886	57 586
5 - 9	469 735	240 593	229 142	296 471	151 887	144 584	173 264	88 706	84 558
10 - 14	473 723	242 791	230 932	294 674	151 245	143 429	179 049	91 546	87 503
15 - 19	483 957	247 452	236 505	300 985	153 733	147 252	182 972	93 719	89 253
20 - 24	472 777	240 171	232 606	309 267	154 636	154 631	163 510	85 535	77 975
25 - 29	539 031	268 179	270 852	364 619	178 639	185 980	174 412	89 540	84 872
30 - 34	668 281	337 121	331 160	456 030	227 926	228 104	212 251	109 195	103 056
35 - 39	704 872	358 748	346 124	473 632	239 432	234 200	231 240	119 316	111 924
40 - 44	625 783	316 280	309 503	416 601	207 478	209 123	209 182	108 802	100 380
45 - 49	525 207	261 903	263 304	352 245	172 161	180 084	172 962	89 742	83 220
50 - 54	514 535	255 906	258 629	356 937	174 415	182 522	157 508	81 491	76 107
55 - 59	452 265	220 827	231 438	326 907	157 892	169 015	125 358	62 935	62 423
60 - 64	451 057	217 191	233 866	305 628	145 952	159 676	145 429	71 239	74 190
65 - 69	332 596	152 844	179 752	215 372	97 381	117 991	117 224	55 463	61 761
70 - 74	327 321	140 193	187 128	217 723	90 939	126 784	109 598	49 254	60 344
75 - 79	290 140	97 886	192 254	202 551	66 803	135 748	87 589	31 083	56 506
80 - 84	151 242	45 800	105 442	108 554	32 170	76 384	42 688	13 630	29 058
85 - 89	96 166	25 556	70 610	70 458	18 358	52 100	25 708	7 198	18 510
90 - 94	37 255	8 413	28 842	28 193	6 138	22 055	9 062	2 275	6 787
95 +	6 959	1 255	5 704	5 412	918	4 494	1 547	337	1 210
1 VII 2006 (ESDJ)									
Total	8 281 948	4 028 658	4 253 290	...	...	...	...	...	...
0	77 902	39 805	38 097	...	...	...	...	...	...
1 - 4	321 313	164 885	156 428	...	...	...	...	...	...
5 - 9	423 263	217 041	206 222	...	...	...	...	...	...
10 - 14	481 429	246 855	234 574	...	...	...	...	...	...
15 - 19	493 448	252 867	240 581	...	...	...	...	...	...
20 - 24	526 464	266 025	260 439	...	...	...	...	...	...
25 - 29	522 783	264 022	258 761	...	...	...	...	...	...
30 - 34	567 920	283 048	284 872	...	...	...	...	...	...
35 - 39	682 501	344 096	338 405	...	...	...	...	...	...
40 - 44	713 746	362 060	351 686	...	...	...	...	...	...
45 - 49	629 537	316 830	312 707	...	...	...	...	...	...
50 - 54	523 910	259 059	264 851	...	...	...	...	...	...
55 - 59	500 739	246 012	254 727	...	...	...	...	...	...
60 - 64	434 704	208 653	226 051	...	...	...	...	...	...
65 - 69	432 585	203 752	228 833	...	...	...	...	...	...
70 - 74	302 651	134 071	168 580	...	...	...	...	...	...
75 - 79	279 634	113 597	166 037	...	...	...	...	...	...
80 - 84	221 548	68 672	152 876	...	...	...	...	...	...
85 - 89	96 575	26 243	70 332	...	...	...	...	...	...
90 - 94	39 257	9 092	30 165	...	...	...	...	...	...
95 +	10 039	1 073	8 066	...	...	...	...	...	...
Belarus - Bélarus									
1 VII 2006 (ESDF)									
Total	9 732 501	4 545 164	5 187 337	7 066 903	3 294 559	3 772 344	2 665 598	1 250 605	1 414 993
0	93 072	47 810	45 262	68 531	35 291	33 240	24 541	12 519	12 022
1 - 4	354 102	181 989	172 113	262 168	134 783	127 385	91 934	47 206	44 728
5 - 9	455 824	234 229	221 595	327 232	168 278	158 954	128 592	65 951	62 641
10 - 14	557 950	286 329	271 621	390 475	200 555	189 920	167 475	85 774	81 701
15 - 19	771 017	394 823	376 194	589 713	297 735	291 978	181 304	97 088	84 216
20 - 24	828 110	421 443	406 667	656 546	329 195	327 351	171 564	92 248	79 316
25 - 29	732 518	372 488	360 030	593 726	300 758	292 968	138 792	71 730	67 062
30 - 34	686 566	341 560	345 006	530 471	260 307	270 164	156 095	81 253	74 842

Continent, country or area, date, code and age (in years) / Continent, pays ou zone, date, code et âge (en années)	Total			Urban - Urbaine			Rural - Rurale		
	Both sexes Les deux sexes	Male Masculin	Female Féminin	Both sexes Les deux sexes	Male Masculin	Female Féminin	Both sexes Les deux sexes	Male Masculin	Female Féminin
EUROPE									
Belarus - Bélarus									
1 VII 2006 (ESDF)									
35 - 39	672 593	330 378	342 215	501 951	240 310	261 641	170 642	90 068	80 574
40 - 44	753 128	366 332	386 796	564 649	265 003	299 646	188 479	101 329	87 150
45 - 49	819 285	391 929	427 356	619 048	284 383	334 665	200 237	107 546	92 691
50 - 54	680 984	315 637	365 347	521 341	232 755	288 586	159 643	82 882	76 761
55 - 59	568 275	255 297	312 978	431 045	188 629	242 416	137 230	66 668	70 562
60 - 64	338 121	141 056	197 065	229 717	96 489	133 228	108 404	44 567	63 837
65 - 69	477 455	180 972	296 483	299 390	114 562	184 828	178 065	66 410	111 655
70 - 74	374 587	129 024	245 563	194 888	67 097	127 791	179 699	61 927	117 772
75 - 79	321 810	99 268	222 542	159 559	49 681	109 878	162 251	49 587	112 664
80 - 84	172 265	39 970	132 295	86 314	20 607	65 707	85 951	19 363	66 588
85 +	74 839	14 630	60 209	40 139	8 141	31 998	34 700	6 489	28 211
Belgium - Belgique									
1 I 2006 (ESDJ)									
Total	10 511 382	5 143 821	5 367 561	...	...	...	...	...	...
0	118 366	60 747	57 619	...	...	...	...	...	...
1 - 4	580 368	296 868	283 500	...	...	...	...	...	...
5 - 9	592 003	302 269	289 734	...	...	...	...	...	...
10 - 14	623 731	319 008	304 723	...	...	...	...	...	...
15 - 19	632 604	323 106	309 498	...	...	...	...	...	...
20 - 24	637 168	320 284	316 884	...	...	...	...	...	...
25 - 29	667 765	335 194	332 571	...	...	...	...	...	...
30 - 34	703 395	354 866	348 529	...	...	...	...	...	...
35 - 39	766 820	388 525	378 295	...	...	...	...	...	...
40 - 44	818 710	413 953	404 757	...	...	...	...	...	...
45 - 49	782 371	393 789	388 582	...	...	...	...	...	...
50 - 54	714 021	357 987	356 034	...	...	...	...	...	...
55 - 59	675 073	336 999	338 074	...	...	...	...	...	...
60 - 64	508 336	248 736	259 600	...	...	...	...	...	...
65 - 69	487 826	230 477	257 349	...	...	...	...	...	...
70 - 74	462 644	207 712	254 932	...	...	...	...	...	...
75 - 79	392 695	161 235	231 460	...	...	...	...	...	...
80 - 84	286 129	103 843	182 286	...	...	...	...	...	...
85 - 89	115 585	35 057	80 528	...	...	...	...	...	...
90 - 94	51 424	11 898	39 526	...	...	...	...	...	...
95 - 99	11 416	1 865	9 551	...	...	...	...	...	...
100 +	1 298	150	1 148	...	...	...	...	...	...
Bulgaria - Bulgarie									
1 VII 2006 (ESDF)									
Total	7 699 020	3 732 130	3 966 890	5 428 388	2 613 030	2 815 358	2 270 632	1 119 100	1 151 532
0	69 445	35 700	33 745	51 532	26 441	25 091	17 913	9 259	8 654
1 - 4	271 067	139 573	131 494	197 021	101 441	95 580	74 046	38 132	35 914
5 - 9	321 281	165 083	156 198	225 652	115 858	109 794	95 629	49 225	46 404
10 - 14	377 689	193 647	184 042	262 998	134 690	128 308	114 691	58 957	55 734
15 - 19	501 419	256 895	244 524	366 517	186 592	179 925	134 902	70 303	64 599
20 - 24	534 709	274 272	260 437	418 228	212 254	205 974	116 481	62 018	54 463
25 - 29	570 706	292 383	278 323	441 104	222 903	218 201	129 602	69 480	60 122
30 - 34	570 806	290 586	280 220	436 765	219 899	216 866	134 041	70 687	63 354
35 - 39	541 864	274 419	267 445	406 833	202 163	204 670	135 031	72 256	62 775
40 - 44	515 899	258 434	257 465	384 652	188 082	196 570	131 247	70 352	60 895
45 - 49	537 868	266 208	271 660	401 966	193 837	208 129	135 902	72 371	63 531
50 - 54	546 041	264 898	281 143	403 819	191 639	212 180	142 222	73 259	68 963
55 - 59	558 432	264 255	294 177	396 484	184 822	211 662	161 948	79 433	82 515
60 - 64	455 180	208 316	246 864	291 936	134 094	157 842	163 244	74 222	89 022
65 - 69	391 500	172 317	219 183	227 347	98 918	128 429	164 153	73 399	90 754
70 - 74	384 402	162 664	221 738	211 777	86 192	125 585	172 625	76 472	96 153
75 - 79	290 270	116 873	173 397	161 782	62 950	98 832	128 488	53 923	74 565
80 - 84	183 004	68 342	114 662	100 090	36 002	64 088	82 914	32 340	50 574
85 - 89	58 073	20 750	37 323	31 642	10 950	20 692	26 431	9 800	16 631
90 - 94	16 386	5 551	10 835	8 710	2 805	5 905	7 676	2 746	4 930
95 - 99	2 709	889	1 820	1 406	462	944	1 303	427	876
100 +	270	75	195	127	36	91	143	39	104

Continent, country or area, date, code and age (in years) / Continent, pays ou zone, date, code et âge (en années)	Total			Urban - Urbaine			Rural - Rurale		
	Both sexes Les deux sexes	Male Masculin	Female Féminin	Both sexes Les deux sexes	Male Masculin	Female Féminin	Both sexes Les deux sexes	Male Masculin	Female Féminin
EUROPE									
Channel Islands: Guernsey - Îles Anglo-Normandes: Guernesey									
1 III 2006 (ESDF)									
Total.....................	61 029	30 034	30 995	...	...	...	...	...	...
0 - 9	6 095	3 159	2 936	...	...	...	...	...	...
10 - 19	7 281	3 703	3 578	...	...	...	...	...	...
20 - 29	7 876	3 993	3 883	...	...	...	...	...	...
30 - 39	9 020	4 440	4 580	...	...	...	...	...	...
40 - 49	9 566	4 751	4 815	...	...	...	...	...	...
50 - 59	8 525	4 305	4 220	...	...	...	...	...	...
60 - 69	5 721	2 859	2 862	...	...	...	...	...	...
70 - 79	4 231	1 884	2 347	...	...	...	...	...	...
80 - 89	2 248	827	1 421	...	...	...	...	...	...
90 + ...	466	113	353	...	...	...	...	...	...
Croatia - Croatie									
31 III 2001 (CDJC)									
Total.....................	4 437 460	2 135 900	2 301 560	2 471 328	1 171 950	1 299 378	1 966 132	963 950	1 002 182
0	42 942	22 097	20 845	23 438	12 112	11 326	19 504	9 985	9 519
1 - 4	194 580	99 621	94 959	104 707	53 579	51 128	89 873	46 042	43 831
5 - 9	248 528	127 274	121 254	134 027	68 669	65 358	114 501	58 605	55 896
10 - 14	268 584	137 175	131 409	144 935	74 118	70 817	123 649	63 057	60 592
15 - 19	298 606	152 676	145 930	165 511	84 240	81 271	133 095	68 436	64 659
20 - 24	305 631	155 739	149 892	176 487	88 565	87 922	129 144	67 174	61 970
25 - 29	294 497	148 666	145 831	171 776	84 620	87 156	122 721	64 046	58 675
30 - 34	295 431	147 920	147 511	169 076	82 749	86 327	126 355	65 171	61 184
35 - 39	317 273	158 506	158 767	177 369	85 563	91 806	139 904	72 943	66 961
40 - 44	333 403	166 499	166 904	189 206	89 569	99 637	144 197	76 930	67 267
45 - 49	333 576	168 290	165 286	195 040	93 697	101 343	138 536	74 593	63 943
50 - 54	299 773	148 224	151 549	178 220	84 433	93 787	121 553	63 791	57 762
55 - 59	229 775	108 673	121 102	134 170	61 988	72 182	95 605	46 685	48 920
60 - 64	262 016	120 667	141 349	142 207	65 853	76 354	119 809	54 814	64 995
65 - 69	252 947	110 459	142 488	131 008	58 413	72 595	121 939	52 046	69 893
70 - 74	203 885	81 884	122 001	102 578	41 358	61 220	101 307	40 526	60 781
75 - 79	137 201	44 149	93 052	69 924	22 818	47 106	67 277	21 331	45 946
80 - 84	56 954	17 040	39 914	29 302	8 963	20 339	27 652	8 077	19 575
85 - 89	30 833	8 682	22 151	16 108	4 575	11 533	14 725	4 107	10 618
90 - 94	10 265	2 571	7 694	5 386	1 310	4 076	4 879	1 261	3 618
95 - 99	1 371	302	1 069	753	153	600	618	149	469
100 + ...	84	21	63	54	16	38	30	5	25
Unknown - Inconnu	19 305	8 765	10 540	10 046	4 589	5 457	9 259	4 176	5 083
1 VII 2006 (ESDJ)									
Total.....................	4 440 022	2 138 934	2 301 088	...	...	...	...	...	...
0	41 680	21 431	20 249	...	...	...	...	...	...
1 - 4	163 396	83 997	79 399	...	...	...	...	...	...
5 - 9	240 027	122 938	117 089	...	...	...	...	...	...
10 - 14	252 615	129 277	123 338	...	...	...	...	...	...
15 - 19	272 184	138 846	133 338	...	...	...	...	...	...
20 - 24	304 090	155 130	148 960	...	...	...	...	...	...
25 - 29	312 664	158 726	153 938	...	...	...	...	...	...
30 - 34	300 275	151 437	148 838	...	...	...	...	...	...
35 - 39	297 860	149 187	148 673	...	...	...	...	...	...
40 - 44	320 024	159 576	160 448	...	...	...	...	...	...
45 - 49	332 950	165 274	167 676	...	...	...	...	...	...
50 - 54	332 897	165 628	167 269	...	...	...	...	...	...
55 - 59	294 479	143 130	151 349	...	...	...	...	...	...
60 - 64	218 894	100 863	118 031	...	...	...	...	...	...
65 - 69	241 576	106 536	135 040	...	...	...	...	...	...
70 - 74	219 581	89 996	129 585	...	...	...	...	...	...
75 - 79	160 756	59 450	101 306	...	...	...	...	...	...
80 - 84	92 280	26 826	65 454	...	...	...	...	...	...
85 + ...	41 794	10 686	31 108	...	...	...	...	...	...

Continent, country or area, date, code and age (in years) / Continent, pays ou zone, date, code et âge (en années)	Total			Urban - Urbaine			Rural - Rurale		
	Both sexes Les deux sexes	Male Masculin	Female Féminin	Both sexes Les deux sexes	Male Masculin	Female Féminin	Both sexes Les deux sexes	Male Masculin	Female Féminin
EUROPE									
Czech Republic - République tchèque									
31 XII 2006 (ESDJ)									
Total	10 287 189	5 026 184	5 261 005	7 574 397	3 671 881	3 902 516	2 712 792	1 354 303	1 358 489
0	105 775	54 541	51 234	78 041	40 246	37 795	27 734	14 295	13 439
1 - 4	387 834	199 244	188 590	282 545	145 506	137 039	105 289	53 738	51 551
5 - 9	450 045	231 306	218 739	321 685	165 021	156 664	128 360	66 285	62 075
10 - 14	535 860	274 974	260 886	381 607	195 576	186 031	154 253	79 398	74 855
15 - 19	651 247	333 223	318 024	474 858	242 365	232 493	176 389	90 858	85 531
20 - 24	694 953	356 689	338 264	511 605	262 216	249 389	183 348	94 473	88 875
25 - 29	829 472	424 645	404 827	616 687	314 819	301 868	212 785	109 826	102 959
30 - 34	902 760	461 730	441 030	666 225	338 388	327 837	236 535	123 342	113 193
35 - 39	708 610	362 618	345 992	522 494	264 202	258 292	186 116	98 416	87 700
40 - 44	701 559	357 652	343 907	521 642	262 693	258 949	179 917	94 959	84 958
45 - 49	652 845	329 481	323 364	479 795	238 909	240 886	173 050	90 572	82 478
50 - 54	763 858	378 166	385 692	564 249	275 129	289 120	199 609	103 037	96 572
55 - 59	778 943	378 098	400 845	574 748	274 241	300 507	204 195	103 857	100 338
60 - 64	640 991	300 913	340 078	481 995	222 939	259 056	158 996	77 974	81 022
65 - 69	450 751	202 212	248 539	335 450	149 583	185 867	115 301	52 629	62 672
70 - 74	370 844	154 885	215 959	273 121	113 533	159 588	97 723	41 352	56 371
75 - 79	325 288	123 091	202 197	239 617	90 661	148 956	85 671	32 430	53 241
80 - 84	222 369	71 992	150 377	164 754	53 470	111 284	57 615	18 522	39 093
85 - 89	82 377	23 546	58 831	61 037	17 319	43 718	21 340	6 227	15 113
90 - 94	24 912	5 958	18 954	18 121	4 224	13 897	6 791	1 734	5 057
95 - 99	5 456	1 133	4 323	3 840	787	3 053	1 616	346	1 270
100 +	440	87	353	281	54	227	159	33	126
Denmark - Danemark[42]									
1 VII 2006 (ESDJ)									
Total	5 434 567	2 690 179	2 744 388	...	...	...	...	...	...
0	64 453	33 009	31 444	...	...	...	...	...	...
1 - 4	259 654	132 698	126 956	...	...	...	...	...	...
5 - 9	338 509	173 340	165 169	...	...	...	...	...	...
10 - 14	351 372	180 371	171 001	...	...	...	...	...	...
15 - 19	318 373	163 583	154 790	...	...	...	...	...	...
20 - 24	292 180	148 470	143 710	...	...	...	...	...	...
25 - 29	326 799	164 047	162 752	...	...	...	...	...	...
30 - 34	382 553	191 861	190 692	...	...	...	...	...	...
35 - 39	395 731	200 952	194 779	...	...	...	...	...	...
40 - 44	417 777	212 206	205 571	...	...	...	...	...	...
45 - 49	372 942	188 678	184 264	...	...	...	...	...	...
50 - 54	359 784	180 980	178 804	...	...	...	...	...	...
55 - 59	371 884	185 992	185 892	...	...	...	...	...	...
60 - 64	353 483	176 235	177 248	...	...	...	...	...	...
65 - 69	251 091	121 592	129 499	...	...	...	...	...	...
70 - 74	196 582	91 237	105 345	...	...	...	...	...	...
75 - 79	157 487	68 411	89 076	...	...	...	...	...	...
80 - 84	119 164	45 495	73 669	...	...	...	...	...	...
85 - 89	69 473	22 402	47 071	...	...	...	...	...	...
90 - 94	28 033	7 260	20 773	...	...	...	...	...	...
95 - 99	6 554	1 267	5 287	...	...	...	...	...	...
100 +	689	93	596	...	...	...	...	...	...
Estonia - Estonie									
1 VII 2006 (ESDF)									
Total	1 343 547	618 772	724 775	931 855	419 103	512 752	411 692	199 669	212 023
0 - 4	67 677	34 788	32 889	47 308	24 309	22 999	20 369	10 479	9 890
5 - 9	61 321	31 683	29 638	40 815	21 089	19 726	20 506	10 594	9 912
10 - 14	72 089	36 901	35 188	45 292	23 181	22 111	26 797	13 720	13 077
15 - 19	104 295	53 515	50 780	67 653	34 682	32 971	36 642	18 833	17 809
20 - 24	104 466	53 020	51 446	70 638	35 561	35 077	33 828	17 459	16 369
25 - 29	95 354	48 392	46 962	71 799	35 038	36 761	23 555	13 354	10 201
30 - 34	92 831	46 347	46 484	68 684	33 474	35 210	24 147	12 873	11 274
35 - 39	90 174	44 044	46 130	63 388	30 450	32 938	26 786	13 594	13 192
40 - 44	91 249	43 823	47 426	63 059	29 381	33 678	28 190	14 442	13 748
45 - 49	96 514	45 172	51 342	67 468	30 283	37 185	29 046	14 889	14 157
50 - 54	91 653	41 672	49 981	65 243	28 378	36 865	26 410	13 294	13 116

7. Population by age, sex and urban/rural residence: latest available year, 1997 - 2006
Population selon l'âge, le sexe et la résidence, urbaine/rurale: dernière année disponible, 1997 - 2006 (continued - suite)

Continent, country or area, date, code and age (in years) / Continent, pays ou zone, date, code et âge (en années)	Total			Urban - Urbaine			Rural - Rurale		
	Both sexes Les deux sexes	Male Masculin	Female Féminin	Both sexes Les deux sexes	Male Masculin	Female Féminin	Both sexes Les deux sexes	Male Masculin	Female Féminin
EUROPE									
Estonia - Estonie									
1 VII 2006 (ESDF)									
55 - 59	84 215	36 982	47 233	59 653	25 076	34 577	24 562	11 906	12 656
60 - 64	64 363	27 015	37 348	43 347	17 294	26 053	21 016	9 721	11 295
65 - 69	74 041	28 720	45 321	52 045	19 459	32 586	21 996	9 261	12 735
70 - 74	58 556	20 840	37 716	40 061	13 783	26 278	18 495	7 057	11 438
75 - 79	49 206	15 495	33 711	34 730	10 787	23 943	14 476	4 708	9 768
80 - 84	29 173	6 941	22 232	19 988	4 672	15 316	9 185	2 269	6 916
85 - 89	10 514	2 227	8 287	6 973	1 491	5 482	3 541	736	2 805
90 - 94	4 397	867	3 530	2 801	517	2 284	1 596	350	1 246
95 - 99	1 078	188	890	643	102	541	435	86	349
100 +	147	22	125	76	13	63	71	9	62
Unknown - Inconnu	234	118	116	191	83	108	43	35	8
Finland - Finlande[43]									
1 VII 2006 (ESDJ)									
Total	5 266 268	2 578 046	2 688 222	3 316 388	1 597 209	1 719 179	1 949 880	980 837	969 043
0	58 264	29 679	28 585	38 170	19 446	18 725	20 094	10 234	9 861
1 - 4	228 274	116 690	111 583	143 412	73 412	70 000	84 861	43 278	41 583
5 - 9	291 318	148 775	142 543	175 692	89 567	86 126	115 626	59 209	56 417
10 - 14	326 187	166 242	159 946	194 199	98 778	95 421	131 989	67 464	64 525
15 - 19	323 145	165 131	158 014	197 328	98 489	98 839	125 817	66 642	59 175
20 - 24	332 970	170 285	162 685	244 644	120 671	123 974	88 326	49 016	38 712
25 - 29	331 071	169 301	161 770	246 031	124 773	121 258	85 040	44 528	40 512
30 - 34	312 289	160 300	151 989	217 098	111 662	105 437	95 191	48 639	46 553
35 - 39	342 096	174 100	167 997	224 140	113 496	110 645	117 956	60 604	57 352
40 - 44	376 893	191 361	185 532	238 797	119 728	119 070	138 096	71 633	66 463
45 - 49	377 207	190 173	187 035	231 829	114 545	117 284	145 379	75 628	69 751
50 - 54	392 628	196 544	196 084	238 396	115 250	123 147	154 232	81 294	72 938
55 - 59	413 483	206 127	207 356	251 895	121 006	130 889	161 588	85 121	76 467
60 - 64	305 505	149 366	156 139	186 885	88 437	98 448	118 620	60 929	57 692
65 - 69	250 766	117 412	133 354	146 696	66 114	80 582	104 070	51 298	52 772
70 - 74	205 846	91 169	114 678	117 771	49 889	67 882	88 075	41 280	46 796
75 - 79	181 604	71 905	109 699	102 071	38 388	63 684	79 533	33 517	46 016
80 - 84	125 560	41 144	84 416	69 940	21 733	48 207	55 620	19 411	36 209
85 - 89	62 579	16 463	46 117	35 156	8 749	26 408	27 423	7 714	19 709
90 - 94	23 393	4 986	18 407	13 292	2 610	10 682	10 101	2 376	7 726
95 - 99	4 817	845	3 972	2 741	441	2 300	2 076	404	1 672
100 +	379	53	326	208	31	177	171	23	149
France[44]									
1 VII 2005 (ESDJ)									
Total	60 995 911	29 638 708	31 357 203	...	...	...	...	...	...
0	767 392	392 747	374 645	...	...	...	...	...	...
1 - 4	3 067 832	1 567 960	1 499 872	...	...	...	...	...	...
5 - 9	3 701 394	1 895 546	1 805 848	...	...	...	...	...	...
10 - 14	3 697 811	1 893 654	1 804 157	...	...	...	...	...	...
15 - 19	3 928 586	2 003 179	1 925 407	...	...	...	...	...	...
20 - 24	3 941 630	1 989 427	1 952 203	...	...	...	...	...	...
25 - 29	3 802 373	1 911 518	1 890 855	...	...	...	...	...	...
30 - 34	4 260 328	2 136 090	2 124 238	...	...	...	...	...	...
35 - 39	4 323 356	2 150 492	2 172 864	...	...	...	...	...	...
40 - 44	4 379 410	2 160 422	2 218 988	...	...	...	...	...	...
45 - 49	4 235 177	2 077 435	2 157 742	...	...	...	...	...	...
50 - 54	4 152 086	2 040 293	2 111 793	...	...	...	...	...	...
55 - 59	4 006 477	1 978 810	2 027 667	...	...	...	...	...	...
60 - 64	2 707 046	1 324 777	1 382 269	...	...	...	...	...	...
65 - 69	2 559 485	1 203 094	1 356 391	...	...	...	...	...	...
70 - 74	2 496 686	1 104 473	1 392 213	...	...	...	...	...	...
75 - 79	2 151 856	877 933	1 273 923	...	...	...	...	...	...
80 - 84	1 670 856	609 345	1 061 511	...	...	...	...	...	...
85 - 89	642 668	202 899	439 769	...	...	...	...	...	...
90 - 94	387 427	96 721	290 706	...	...	...	...	...	...
95 - 99	99 299	18 751	80 548	...	...	...	...	...	...
100 +	16 736	3 142	13 594	...	...	...	...	...	...

Continent, country or area, date, code and age (in years). / Continent, pays ou zone, date, code et âge (en années)	Total			Urban - Urbaine			Rural - Rurale		
	Both sexes Les deux sexes	Male Masculin	Female Féminin	Both sexes Les deux sexes	Male Masculin	Female Féminin	Both sexes Les deux sexes	Male Masculin	Female Féminin
EUROPE									
Germany - Allemagne									
1 VII 2006 (ESDJ)									
Total	82 365 810	40 317 807	42 048 003	...	...	...	...	...	...
0	679 405	348 734	330 671	...	...	...	...	...	...
1 - 4	2 857 411	1 465 658	1 391 753	...	...	...	...	...	...
5 - 9	3 934 265	2 017 904	1 916 361	...	...	...	...	...	...
10 - 14	4 073 184	2 089 653	1 983 531	...	...	...	...	...	...
15 - 19	4 798 748	2 460 792	2 337 956	...	...	...	...	...	...
20 - 24	4 850 620	2 461 404	2 389 216	...	...	...	...	...	...
25 - 29	4 885 549	2 474 656	2 410 893	...	...	...	...	...	...
30 - 34	4 897 014	2 488 757	2 408 257	...	...	...	...	...	...
35 - 39	6 543 832	3 350 602	3 193 230	...	...	...	...	...	...
40 - 44	7 199 985	3 691 585	3 508 400	...	...	...	...	...	...
45 - 49	6 439 546	3 273 689	3 165 857	...	...	...	...	...	...
50 - 54	5 659 534	2 832 935	2 826 599	...	...	...	...	...	...
55 - 59	4 979 750	2 478 599	2 501 151	...	...	...	...	...	...
60 - 64	4 486 255	2 204 673	2 281 582	...	...	...	...	...	...
65 - 69	5 415 613	2 590 255	2 825 358	...	...	...	...	...	...
70 - 74	3 864 937	1 759 243	2 105 694	...	...	...	...	...	...
75 - 79	3 058 381	1 254 517	1 803 864	...	...	...	...	...	...
80 - 84	2 160 974	676 508	1 484 466	...	...	...	...	...	...
85 - 89	994 492	261 071	733 421	...	...	...	...	...	...
90 - 94	427 925	93 813	334 112	...	...	...	...	...	...
95 +	158 390	42 759	115 631	...	...	...	...	...	...
Gibraltar[45]									
12 XI 2001 (CDFC)									
Total	27 495	13 644	13 851	...	...	...	...	...	...
0	143	74	69	...	...	...	...	...	...
1 - 4	1 315	693	622	...	...	...	...	...	...
5 - 9	1 773	932	841	...	...	...	...	...	...
10 - 14	1 831	956	875	...	...	...	...	...	...
15 - 19	1 801	917	884	...	...	...	...	...	...
20 - 24	1 764	912	852	...	...	...	...	...	...
25 - 29	1 770	867	903	...	...	...	...	...	...
30 - 34	1 916	959	957	...	...	...	...	...	...
35 - 39	2 044	1 008	1 036	...	...	...	...	...	...
40 - 44	1 995	987	1 008	...	...	...	...	...	...
45 - 49	1 904	988	916	...	...	...	...	...	...
50 - 54	1 944	1 056	888	...	...	...	...	...	...
55 - 59	1 610	844	766	...	...	...	...	...	...
60 - 64	1 379	691	688	...	...	...	...	...	...
65 - 69	1 247	611	636	...	...	...	...	...	...
70 - 74	1 037	477	560	...	...	...	...	...	...
75 - 79	895	329	566	...	...	...	...	...	...
80 - 84	605	186	419	...	...	...	...	...	...
85 - 89	306	100	206	...	...	...	...	...	...
90 - 94	134	25	109	...	...	...	...	...	...
95 +	34	9	25	...	...	...	...	...	...
Unknown - Inconnu	48	23	25	...	...	...	...	...	...
Greece - Grèce[46]									
1 VII 2006 (ESDF)									
Total	11 148 533	5 520 164	5 628 369	...	...	...	...	...	...
0	109 674	56 589	53 085	...	...	...	...	...	...
1 - 4	419 968	216 689	203 279	...	...	...	...	...	...
5 - 9	513 506	263 670	249 836	...	...	...	...	...	...
10 - 14	551 896	283 934	267 962	...	...	...	...	...	...
15 - 19	593 174	307 820	285 354	...	...	...	...	...	...
20 - 24	716 847	373 717	343 130	...	...	...	...	...	...
25 - 29	840 244	438 080	402 164	...	...	...	...	...	...
30 - 34	865 521	445 709	419 812	...	...	...	...	...	...
35 - 39	885 787	451 107	434 680	...	...	...	...	...	...
40 - 44	807 125	405 028	402 097	...	...	...	...	...	...
45 - 49	791 928	392 913	399 015	...	...	...	...	...	...
50 - 54	725 043	359 343	365 700	...	...	...	...	...	...
55 - 59	683 598	333 356	350 242	...	...	...	...	...	...

7. Population by age, sex and urban/rural residence: latest available year, 1997 - 2006
Population selon l'âge, le sexe et la résidence, urbaine/rurale: dernière année disponible, 1997 - 2006 (continued - suite)

Continent, country or area, date, code and age (in years) / Continent, pays ou zone, date, code et âge (en annèes)	Total			Urban - Urbaine			Rural - Rurale		
	Both sexes Les deux sexes	Male Masculin	Female Féminin	Both sexes Les deux sexes	Male Masculin	Female Féminin	Both sexes Les deux sexes	Male Masculin	Female Féminin
EUROPE									
Greece - Grèce[46]									
1 VII 2006 (ESDF)									
60 - 64	576 893	275 149	301 744	...	...	...	...	...	...
65 - 69	600 085	272 857	327 228	...	...	...	...	...	...
70 - 74	580 249	260 623	319 626	...	...	...	...	...	...
75 - 79	468 739	205 336	263 403	...	...	...	...	...	...
80 - 84	263 765	111 252	152 513	...	...	...	...	...	...
85 - 89	113 105	48 588	64 517	...	...	...	...	...	...
90 - 94	30 451	13 323	17 128	...	...	...	...	...	...
95 - 99	8 194	4 347	3 847	...	...	...	...	...	...
100 +	2 741	734	2 007	...	...	...	...	...	...
Hungary - Hongrie									
1 VII 2006 (ESDF)									
Total	10 071 370	4 781 829	5 289 541	6 749 388[47]	3 163 716[47]	3 585 673[47]	3 321 982[47]	1 618 113[47]	1 703 869[47]
0	97 681	50 165	47 516	65 286[47]	33 504[47]	31 782[47]	32 396[47]	16 661[47]	15 735[47]
1 - 4	382 587	196 761	185 826	250 298[47]	128 508[47]	121 790[47]	132 290[47]	68 253[47]	64 037[47]
5 - 9	487 273	249 778	237 495	305 058[47]	156 296[47]	148 762[47]	182 215[47]	93 482[47]	88 733[47]
10 - 14	574 007	293 901	280 107	360 102[47]	183 893[47]	176 209[47]	213 906[47]	110 008[47]	103 898[47]
15 - 19	625 430	319 504	305 926	414 392[47]	209 157[47]	205 235[47]	211 038[47]	110 347[47]	100 691[47]
20 - 24	668 886	340 204	328 682	454 416[47]	228 211[47]	226 206[47]	214 470[47]	111 994[47]	102 476[47]
25 - 29	802 922	410 257	392 666	566 248[47]	284 971[47]	281 277[47]	236 674[47]	125 286[47]	111 389[47]
30 - 34	805 888	409 785	396 103	560 564[47]	281 712[47]	278 852[47]	245 324[47]	128 073[17]	117 252[47]
35 - 39	709 311	358 884	350 428	477 392[47]	239 216[47]	238 177[47]	231 919[47]	119 668[47]	112 251[47]
40 - 44	605 557	301 278	304 280	394 950[47]	192 574[47]	202 377[47]	210 607[47]	108 704[47]	101 903[47]
45 - 49	675 944	328 028	347 917	439 089[47]	206 732[47]	232 357[47]	236 856[47]	121 296[47]	115 560[47]
50 - 54	797 181	378 711	418 470	540 619[47]	248 914[47]	291 705[47]	256 562[47]	129 797[47]	126 765[47]
55 - 59	674 841	311 758	363 084	461 746[47]	208 241[47]	253 505[47]	213 096[47]	103 517[47]	109 579[47]
60 - 64	565 947	249 328	316 620	391 139[47]	170 922[47]	220 217[47]	174 809[47]	78 406[47]	96 403[47]
65 - 69	484 116	197 008	287 108	323 217[47]	131 490[47]	191 727[47]	160 899[47]	65 519[47]	95 381[47]
70 - 74	416 975	159 453	257 522	274 221[47]	105 498[47]	168 723[47]	142 755[47]	53 955[47]	88 800[47]
75 - 79	339 866	119 631	220 235	226 328[47]	80 468[47]	145 860[47]	113 539[47]	39 164[47]	74 375[47]
80 - 84	227 240	70 859	156 381	152 815[47]	47 520[47]	105 296[47]	74 425[47]	23 340[47]	51 085[47]
85 - 89	88 794	25 437	63 357	61 954[47]	17 906[47]	44 048[47]	26 840[47]	7 531[47]	19 309[47]
90 +	40 926	11 103	29 823	29 559[47]	7 988[47]	21 572[47]	11 367[47]	3 115[47]	8 252[47]
Iceland - Islande									
1 VII 2006 (ESDJ)									
Total	304 334	154 287	150 047	281 961	141 673	140 288	22 373	12 614	9 759
0	4 469	2 280	2 189	4 234	2 161	2 073	235	119	116
1 - 4	16 866	8 534	8 332	15 948	8 050	7 898	918	484	434
5 - 9	21 346	10 878	10 468	19 988	10 190	9 798	1 358	688	670
10 - 14	22 686	11 616	11 070	21 020	10 775	10 245	1 666	841	825
15 - 19	22 727	11 709	11 018	20 890	10 719	10 171	1 837	990	847
20 - 24	21 701	11 062	10 639	20 141	10 182	9 959	1 560	880	680
25 - 29	22 553	11 578	10 975	21 244	10 822	10 422	1 309	756	553
30 - 34	22 232	11 557	10 675	20 824	10 701	10 123	1 408	856	552
35 - 39	21 023	10 945	10 078	19 453	9 999	9 454	1 570	946	624
40 - 44	22 480	11 474	11 006	20 600	10 355	10 245	1 880	1 119	761
45 - 49	22 021	11 521	10 500	20 245	10 489	9 756	1 776	1 032	744
50 - 54	19 446	10 073	9 373	17 870	9 123	8 747	1 576	950	626
55 - 59	16 668	8 626	8 042	15 333	7 856	7 477	1 335	770	565
60 - 64	12 857	6 471	6 386	11 821	5 883	5 938	1 036	588	448
65 - 69	9 347	4 586	4 761	8 553	4 140	4 413	794	446	348
70 - 74	8 737	4 129	4 608	8 013	3 739	4 274	724	390	334
75 - 79	7 835	3 575	4 260	7 169	3 178	3 991	666	397	269
80 - 84	5 221	2 195	3 026	4 836	1 998	2 838	385	197	188
85 - 89	2 836	1 087	1 749	2 600	966	1 634	236	121	115
90 - 94	1 011	333	678	924	295	629	87	38	49
95 - 99	238	52	186	224	47	177	14	5	9
100 +	34	6	28	31	5	26	3	1	2
Ireland - Irlande									
28 IV 2002 (CDFC)									
Total	3 917 203	1 946 164	1 971 039	2 334 282	1 133 507	1 200 775	1 582 921	812 657	770 264
0	54 499	27 805	26 694	34 126	17 447	16 679	20 373	10 358	10 015
1 - 4	223 131	114 235	108 896	132 464	67 852	64 612	90 667	46 383	44 284

7. Population by age, sex and urban/rural residence: latest available year, 1997 - 2006
Population selon l'âge, le sexe et la résidence, urbaine/rurale: dernière année disponible, 1997 - 2006 (continued - sulto)

Continent, country or area, date, code and age (in years) Continent, pays ou zone, date, code et âge (en années)	Total			Urban - Urbaine			Rural - Rurale		
	Both sexes Les deux sexes	Male Masculin	Female Féminin	Both sexes Les deux sexes	Male Masculin	Female Féminin	Both sexes Les deux sexes	Male Masculin	Female Féminin

EUROPE

Ireland - Irlande
28 IV 2002 (CDFC)

5 - 9	264 090	135 890	128 200	148 750	76 507	72 243	115 340	59 383	55 957
10 - 14	285 708	146 114	139 594	156 518	79 813	76 705	129 190	66 301	62 889
15 - 19	313 188	160 413	152 775	180 794	90 629	90 165	132 394	69 784	62 610
20 - 24	328 334	165 292	163 042	229 323	110 629	118 694	99 011	54 663	44 348
25 - 29	312 693	156 100	156 593	218 159	106 459	111 700	94 534	49 641	44 893
30 - 34	304 676	152 377	152 299	198 557	98 235	100 322	106 119	54 142	51 977
35 - 39	290 906	144 530	146 376	175 440	85 989	89 451	115 466	58 541	56 925
40 - 44	271 984	135 301	136 683	156 586	76 632	79 954	115 398	58 669	56 729
45 - 49	249 604	124 981	124 623	139 387	67 871	71 516	110 217	57 110	53 107
50 - 54	230 843	116 585	114 258	128 125	62 642	65 483	102 718	53 943	48 775
55 - 59	197 294	99 827	97 467	109 812	53 573	56 239	87 482	46 254	41 228
60 - 64	154 252	77 559	76 693	87 940	42 559	45 381	66 312	35 000	31 312
65 - 69	133 474	65 290	68 184	75 006	34 910	40 096	58 468	30 380	28 088
70 - 74	112 129	51 719	60 410	61 997	26 751	35 246	50 132	24 968	25 164
75 - 79	89 815	37 377	52 438	48 176	18 610	29 566	41 639	18 767	22 872
80 - 84	58 857	22 283	36 574	31 005	10 617	20 388	27 852	11 666	16 186
85 - 89	29 629	9 444	20 185	15 533	4 387	11 146	14 096	5 057	9 039
90 - 94	9 871	2 617	7 254	5 329	1 201	4 128	4 542	1 416	3 126
95 - 99	1 972	379	1 593	1 115	168	947	857	211	646
100 +	254	46	208	140	26	114	114	20	94

23 IV 2006 (CDFC)

Total	4 239 848	2 121 171	2 118 677	...	...	...	...	...	...
0	61 076	31 273	29 803	...	...	...	...	...	...
0 - 14	864 449	443 044	421 405	...	...	...	...	...	...
15 - 24	632 732	321 007	311 725	...	...	...	...	...	...
25 - 44	1 345 873	681 988	663 885	...	...	...	...	...	...
45 - 64	928 868	468 037	460 831	...	...	...	...	...	...
65 +	467 926	207 095	260 831	...	...	...	...	...	...

Isle of Man - Îles de Man
23 IV 2006 (CDJC)

Total	80 058	39 523	40 535	...	...	...	...	...	...
0 - 4	4 110	2 147	1 963	...	...	...	...	...	...
5 - 9	4 509	2 391	2 118	...	...	...	...	...	...
10 - 14	4 918	2 510	2 408	...	...	...	...	...	...
15 - 19	4 924	2 537	2 387	...	...	...	...	...	...
20 - 24	4 384	2 223	2 161	...	...	...	...	...	...
25 - 29	4 485	2 206	2 279	...	...	...	...	...	...
30 - 34	5 179	2 492	2 687	...	...	...	...	...	...
35 - 39	6 031	3 019	3 012	...	...	...	...	...	...
40 - 44	6 385	3 227	3 158	...	...	...	...	...	...
45 - 49	5 829	2 884	2 945	...	...	...	...	...	...
50 - 54	5 243	2 695	2 548	...	...	...	...	...	...
55 - 59	5 777	2 938	2 839	...	...	...	...	...	...
60 - 64	4 597	2 282	2 315	...	...	...	...	...	...
65 - 69	3 833	1 909	1 924	...	...	...	...	...	...
70 - 74	3 084	1 469	1 615	...	...	...	...	...	...
75 - 79	2 722	1 150	1 572	...	...	...	...	...	...
80 - 84	2 099	816	1 283	...	...	...	...	...	...
85 - 89	1 203	414	789	...	...	...	...	...	...
90 - 94	559	172	387	...	...	...	...	...	...
95 +	187	42	145	...	...	...	...	...	...

Italy - Italie
1 VII 2004 (ESDJ)

Total	58 175 310	28 222 706	29 952 604	...	...	...	...	...	...
0	547 567	280 828	266 740	...	...	...	...	...	...
1 - 4	2 163 171	1 109 737	1 053 434	...	...	...	...	...	...
5 - 9	2 671 964	1 375 453	1 296 511	...	...	...	...	...	...
10 - 14	2 840 330	1 458 787	1 381 543	...	...	...	...	...	...
15 - 19	2 888 282	1 483 714	1 404 568	...	...	...	...	...	...
20 - 24	3 226 972	1 647 804	1 579 169	...	...	...	...	...	...
25 - 29	3 990 359	2 022 724	1 967 635	...	...	...	...	...	...
30 - 34	4 613 815	2 331 991	2 281 824	...	...	...	...	...	...
35 - 39	4 816 156	2 428 326	2 387 831	...	...	...	...	...	...

Continent, country or area, date, code and age (in years) / Continent, pays ou zone, date, code et âge (en années)	Total			Urban - Urbaine			Rural - Rurale		
	Both sexes Les deux sexes	Male Masculin	Female Féminin	Both sexes Les deux sexes	Male Masculin	Female Féminin	Both sexes Les deux sexes	Male Masculin	Female Féminin
EUROPE									
Italy - Italie									
1 VII 2004 (ESDJ)									
40 - 44	4 483 752	2 242 154	2 241 599	...	...	...	...	...	...
45 - 49	3 955 775	1 963 059	1 992 716	...	...	...	...	...	...
50 - 54	3 710 420	1 826 050	1 884 370	...	...	...	...	...	...
55 - 59	3 688 019	1 802 812	1 885 208	...	...	...	...	...	...
60 - 64	3 324 821	1 592 418	1 732 403	...	...	...	...	...	...
65 - 69	3 210 418	1 498 987	1 711 431	...	...	...	...	...	...
70 - 74	2 856 672	1 265 721	1 590 952	...	...	...	...	...	...
75 - 79	2 354 807	957 683	1 397 124	...	...	...	...	...	...
80 - 84	1 679 797	601 537	1 078 261	...	...	...	...	...	...
85 - 89	674 998	210 658	464 341	...	...	...	...	...	...
90 - 94	389 499	104 189	285 311	...	...	...	...	...	...
95 - 99	79 292	16 616	62 676	...	...	...	...	...	...
100 +	8 429	1 465	6 964	...	...	...	...	...	...
Latvia - Lettonie									
1 VII 2006 (ESDI)									
Total	2 287 948	1 054 159	1 233 789	1 554 766	697 812	856 954	733 182	356 347	376 835
0 - 4	103 732	53 105	50 627	70 171	35 894	34 277	33 561	17 211	16 350
0	21 933	11 166	10 767	...	...	...	...	...	...
1 - 4	81 799	41 939	39 860	...	...	...	...	...	...
5 - 9	94 707	48 449	46 258	60 508	30 920	29 588	34 199	17 529	16 670
10 - 14	125 066	63 915	61 151	76 796	39 117	37 679	48 270	24 798	23 472
15 - 19	178 654	91 137	87 517	112 819	57 159	55 660	65 835	33 978	31 857
20 - 24	180 856	92 063	88 793	121 923	60 918	61 005	58 933	31 145	27 788
25 - 29	159 527	80 958	78 569	112 088	55 337	56 751	47 439	25 621	21 818
30 - 34	160 530	80 936	79 594	112 577	55 124	57 453	47 953	25 812	22 141
35 - 39	157 853	77 947	79 906	108 107	51 742	56 365	49 746	26 205	23 541
40 - 44	163 803	79 696	84 107	111 138	52 045	59 093	52 665	27 651	25 014
45 - 49	171 880	81 788	90 092	118 563	53 968	64 595	53 317	27 820	25 497
50 - 54	149 577	68 571	81 006	105 828	46 362	59 466	43 749	22 209	21 540
55 - 59	135 990	59 934	76 056	97 168	40 907	56 261	38 822	19 027	19 795
60 - 64	117 978	48 937	69 041	79 746	31 803	47 943	38 232	17 134	21 098
65 - 69	130 549	50 566	79 983	90 693	34 174	56 519	39 856	16 392	23 464
70 - 74	99 130	34 561	64 569	67 029	22 973	44 056	32 101	11 588	20 513
75 - 79	82 883	25 567	57 316	57 935	17 988	39 947	24 948	7 579	17 369
80 - 84	49 143	10 591	38 552	34 172	7 536	26 636	14 971	3 055	11 916
85 - 89	17 275	3 775	13 500	11 691	2 675	9 016	5 584	1 100	4 484
90 - 94	7 010	1 332	5 678	4 610	942	3 668	2 400	390	2 010
95 - 99	1 611	293	1 318	1 069	199	870	542	94	448
100 +	194	38	156	135	29	106	59	9	50
Liechtenstein									
1 VII 2006 (ESDF)									
Total	35 010	17 256	17 754	...	...	...	...	...	...
0 - 4	1 859	955	904	...	...	...	...	...	...
5 - 9	2 028	1 009	1 019	...	...	...	...	...	...
10 - 14	2 131	1 053	1 078	...	...	...	...	...	...
15 - 19	2 136	1 107	1 029	...	...	...	...	...	...
20 - 24	2 161	1 087	1 074	...	...	...	...	...	...
25 - 29	2 213	1 139	1 074	...	...	...	...	...	...
30 - 34	2 538	1 235	1 303	...	...	...	...	...	...
35 - 39	3 078	1 545	1 533	...	...	...	...	...	...
40 - 44	2 983	1 488	1 495	...	...	...	...	...	...
45 - 49	2 903	1 402	1 501	...	...	...	...	...	...
50 - 54	2 567	1 281	1 286	...	...	...	...	...	...
55 - 59	2 350	1 237	1 113	...	...	...	...	...	...
60 - 64	1 961	982	979	...	...	...	...	...	...
65 - 69	1 372	672	700	...	...	...	...	...	...
70 - 74	945	410	535	...	...	...	...	...	...
75 - 79	756	317	439	...	...	...	...	...	...
80 - 84	589	194	395	...	...	...	...	...	...
85 - 89	306	106	200	...	...	...	...	...	...
90 - 94	112	34	78	...	...	...	...	...	...
95 - 99	19	3	16	...	...	...	...	...	...
100 +	3	-	3	...	...	...	...	...	...

7. Population by age, sex and urban/rural residence: latest available year, 1997 - 2006
Population selon l'âge, le sexe et la résidence, urbaine/rurale: dernière année disponible, 1997 - 2006 (continued - suite)

Continent, country or area, date, code and age (in years) / Continent, pays ou zone, date, code et âge (en années)	Total			Urban - Urbaine			Rural - Rurale		
	Both sexes Les deux sexes	Male Masculin	Female Féminin	Both sexes Les deux sexes	Male Masculin	Female Féminin	Both sexes Les deux sexes	Male Masculin	Female Féminin
EUROPE									
Lithuania - Lituanie									
1 VII 2006 (ESDJ)									
Total.....................	3 394 082	1 581 807	1 812 275	2 264 535	1 034 128	1 230 407	1 129 547	547 679	581 868
0.....................	30 714	15 644	15 070	20 151	10 263	9 888	10 563	5 381	5 182
1 - 4.....................	120 696	61 912	58 784	76 206	39 095	37 111	44 490	22 817	21 673
5 - 9.....................	175 053	90 119	84 934	111 733	57 452	54 281	63 320	32 667	30 653
10 - 14.....................	222 795	113 914	108 881	141 042	72 000	69 042	81 753	41 914	39 839
15 - 19.....................	268 398	136 998	131 400	170 832	86 703	84 129	97 566	50 295	47 271
20 - 24.....................	263 264	133 973	129 291	176 463	87 856	88 607	86 801	46 117	40 684
25 - 29.....................	226 131	114 921	111 210	164 795	80 315	84 480	61 336	34 606	26 730
30 - 34.....................	232 138	115 356	116 782	168 819	81 748	87 071	63 319	33 608	29 711
35 - 39.....................	248 671	121 992	126 679	172 767	82 855	89 912	75 904	39 137	36 767
40 - 44.....................	261 801	127 707	134 094	180 837	85 053	95 784	80 964	42 654	38 310
45 - 49.....................	258 343	122 108	136 235	178 822	80 811	98 011	79 521	41 297	38 224
50 - 54.....................	208 866	96 408	112 458	145 489	63 999	81 490	63 377	32 409	30 968
55 - 59.....................	184 281	81 111	103 170	126 131	52 992	73 139	58 150	28 119	30 031
60 - 64.....................	168 390	70 354	98 036	110 277	44 553	65 724	58 113	25 801	32 312
65 - 69.....................	164 183	64 237	99 946	104 691	39 897	64 794	59 492	24 340	35 152
70 - 74.....................	143 483	51 849	91 634	86 452	30 984	55 468	57 031	20 865	36 166
75 - 79.....................	114 305	37 185	77 120	68 585	22 532	46 053	45 720	14 653	31 067
80 - 84.....................	67 768	17 475	50 293	39 507	10 075	29 432	28 261	7 400	20 861
85 - 89.....................	23 671	5 812	17 859	13 686	3 280	10 406	9 985	2 532	7 453
90 - 94.....................	8 613	1 961	6 652	5 405	1 175	4 230	3 208	786	2 422
95 - 99.....................	2 166	666	1 500	1 583	430	1 153	583	236	347
100 +.....................	352	105	247	262	60	202	90	45	45
Luxembourg									
1 VII 2006 (ESDJ)									
Total.....................	472 637	233 946	238 691	...	...	...	...	...	...
0.....................	5 430	2 799	2 631	...	...	...	...	...	...
1 - 4.....................	22 395	11 651	10 744	...	...	...	...	...	...
5 - 9.....................	29 512	15 106	14 406	...	...	...	...	...	...
10 - 14.....................	29 553	15 103	14 450	...	...	...	...	...	...
15 - 19.....................	27 636	14 133	13 503	...	...	...	...	...	...
20 - 24.....................	28 089	14 375	13 714	...	...	...	...	...	...
25 - 29.....................	31 507	15 821	15 686	...	...	...	...	...	...
30 - 34.....................	35 396	17 662	17 734	...	...	...	...	...	...
35 - 39.....................	39 965	20 062	19 903	...	...	...	...	...	...
40 - 44.....................	40 297	20 578	19 719	...	...	...	...	...	...
45 - 49.....................	36 209	18 412	17 797	...	...	...	...	...	...
50 - 54.....................	31 418	15 954	15 464	...	...	...	...	...	...
55 - 59.....................	27 265	14 003	13 262	...	...	...	...	...	...
60 - 64.....................	21 548	10 788	10 760	...	...	...	...	...	...
65 - 69.....................	19 115	9 049	10 066	...	...	...	...	...	...
70 - 74.....................	16 773	7 572	9 201	...	...	...	...	...	...
75 - 79.....................	15 001	6 332	8 669	...	...	...	...	...	...
80 - 84.....................	9 254	3 012	6 242	...	...	...	...	...	...
85 - 89.....................	4 277	1 169	3 108	...	...	...	...	...	...
90 - 94.....................	1 724	352	1 372	...	...	...	...	...	...
95 +.....................	273	13	260	...	...	...	...	...	...
Malta - Malte									
1 VII 2006 (ESDJ)									
Total.....................	406 453	201 747	204 706	...	...	...	...	...	...
0.....................	4 017	2 071	1 946	...	...	...	...	...	...
1 - 4.....................	15 804	8 067	7 737	...	...	...	...	...	...
5 - 9.....................	22 641	11 591	11 050	...	...	...	...	...	...
10 - 14.....................	26 528	13 654	12 874	...	...	...	...	...	...
15 - 19.....................	28 693	14 698	13 995	...	...	...	...	...	...
20 - 24.....................	29 393	15 097	14 296	...	...	...	...	...	...
25 - 29.....................	29 926	15 500	14 426	...	...	...	...	...	...
30 - 34.....................	28 225	14 491	13 734	...	...	...	...	...	...
35 - 39.....................	24 826	12 665	12 161	...	...	...	...	...	...
40 - 44.....................	27 233	13 888	13 345	...	...	...	...	...	...
45 - 49.....................	30 436	15 264	15 172	...	...	...	...	...	...
50 - 54.....................	28 994	14 546	14 448	...	...	...	...	...	...
55 - 59.....................	30 814	15 330	15 484	...	...	...	...	...	...

Continent, country or area, date, code and age (in years) / Continent, pays ou zone, date, code et âge (en années)	Total			Urban - Urbaine			Rural - Rurale		
	Both sexes Les deux sexes	Male Masculin	Female Féminin	Both sexes Les deux sexes	Male Masculin	Female Féminin	Both sexes Les deux sexes	Male Masculin	Female Féminin
EUROPE									
Malta - Malte									
1 VII 2006 (ESDJ)									
60 - 64	23 075	11 204	11 871	...	...	...	...	...	...
65 - 69	17 625	8 224	9 401	...	...	...	...	...	...
70 - 74	15 087	6 529	8 558	...	...	...	...	...	...
75 - 79	11 012	4 435	6 577	...	...	...	...	...	...
80 - 84	7 418	2 890	4 528	...	...	...	...	...	...
85 - 89	3 426	1 239	2 187	...	...	...	...	...	...
90 +	1 280	364	916	...	...	...	...	...	...
Moldova[48]									
1 I 2006 (ESDJ)									
Total	3 589 936	1 719 368	1 870 568	1 469 828	709 160	760 668	2 120 108	1 010 208	1 109 900
0 - 4	181 669	93 772	87 897	64 705	33 723	30 982	116 964	60 049	56 915
5 - 9	203 408	104 412	98 996	68 461	35 352	33 109	134 947	69 060	65 887
10 - 14	272 799	139 487	133 312	95 529	49 105	46 424	177 270	90 382	86 888
15 - 19	349 138	177 563	171 575	133 930	68 249	65 681	215 208	109 314	105 894
20 - 24	349 754	176 624	173 130	134 121	68 517	65 604	215 633	108 107	107 526
25 - 29	304 114	153 879	150 235	122 352	62 724	59 628	181 762	91 155	90 607
30 - 34	266 897	132 266	134 631	118 987	57 893	61 094	147 910	74 373	73 537
35 - 39	216 458	106 361	110 097	110 481	56 788	53 693	105 977	49 573	56 404
40 - 44	252 139	119 199	132 940	115 905	54 279	61 626	136 234	64 920	71 314
45 - 49	285 000	133 877	151 123	131 082	60 215	70 867	153 918	73 662	80 256
50 - 54	246 984	114 415	132 569	114 241	52 309	61 932	132 743	62 106	70 637
55 - 59	186 343	84 245	102 098	87 101	40 426	46 675	99 242	43 819	55 423
60 - 64	122 126	51 661	70 465	48 269	22 004	26 265	73 857	29 657	44 200
65 - 69	127 296	51 321	75 975	49 813	21 036	28 777	77 483	30 285	47 198
70 - 74	98 769	38 084	60 685	31 880	12 842	19 038	66 889	25 242	41 647
75 - 79	73 121	25 793	47 328	24 039	8 375	15 664	49 082	17 418	31 664
80 - 84	38 336	11 856	26 480	12 618	3 679	8 939	25 718	8 177	17 541
85 +	15 585	4 553	11 032	6 314	1 644	4 670	9 271	2 909	6 362
Monaco									
21 VI 2000 (CDJC)									
Total	32 020	15 544	16 476	...	...	...	...	...	...
0	145	69	76	...	...	...	...	...	...
1 - 4	1 223	644	579	...	...	...	...	...	...
5 - 9	1 462	747	715	...	...	...	...	...	...
10 - 14	1 407	746	661	...	...	...	...	...	...
15 - 19	1 337	706	631	...	...	...	...	...	...
20 - 24	1 297	661	636	...	...	...	...	...	...
25 - 29	1 638	830	808	...	...	...	...	...	...
30 - 34	2 346	1 184	1 162	...	...	...	...	...	...
35 - 39	2 386	1 205	1 181	...	...	...	...	...	...
40 - 44	2 328	1 151	1 177	...	...	...	...	...	...
45 - 49	2 178	1 107	1 071	...	...	...	...	...	...
50 - 54	2 584	1 264	1 320	...	...	...	...	...	...
55 - 59	2 405	1 163	1 242	...	...	...	...	...	...
60 - 64	2 083	1 018	1 065	...	...	...	...	...	...
65 - 69	1 794	854	940	...	...	...	...	...	...
70 - 74	1 704	803	901	...	...	...	...	...	...
75 - 79	1 598	704	894	...	...	...	...	...	...
80 - 84	937	347	590	...	...	...	...	...	...
85 - 89	669	216	453	...	...	...	...	...	...
90 - 94	374	96	278	...	...	...	...	...	...
95 - 99	96	20	76	...	...	...	...	...	...
100 +	11	2	9	...	...	...	...	...	...
Unknown - Inconnu	18	7	11	...	...	...	...	...	...
Montenegro									
1 VII 2005 (ESDJ)									
Total	623 277	306 839	316 439	389 678	189 222	200 456	233 600	117 617	115 983
0	7 608	3 955	3 653	5 955	3 099	2 857	1 653	857	796
1 - 4	32 446	16 825	15 621	21 794	11 385	10 410	10 652	5 441	5 212
5 - 9	41 691	21 538	20 153	25 956	13 384	12 572	15 736	8 155	7 581
10 - 14	44 850	23 240	21 610	28 168	14 562	13 607	16 682	8 679	8 003
15 - 19	48 434	24 827	23 607	30 696	15 743	14 953	17 738	9 085	8 654
20 - 24	50 240	25 620	24 621	32 191	16 025	16 166	18 050	9 595	8 455

Continent, country or area, date, code and age (in years) / Continent, pays ou zone, date, code et âge (en années)	Total			Urban - Urbaine			Rural - Rurale		
	Both sexes Les deux sexes	Male Masculin	Female Féminin	Both sexes Les deux sexes	Male Masculin	Female Féminin	Both sexes Les deux sexes	Male Masculin	Female Féminin
EUROPE									
Montenegro									
1 VII 2005 (ESDJ)									
25 - 29	46 344	23 172	23 172	29 900	14 472	15 429	16 444	8 701	7 744
30 - 34	42 712	21 016	21 697	27 289	12 974	14 315	15 423	8 042	7 382
35 - 39	41 245	20 470	20 775	26 243	12 442	13 801	15 002	8 028	6 974
40 - 44	43 851	21 791	22 060	28 410	13 510	14 900	15 442	8 281	7 161
45 - 49	44 446	22 386	22 061	29 026	14 106	14 920	15 421	8 280	7 141
50 - 54	42 291	21 072	21 219	27 752	13 546	14 207	14 539	7 526	7 013
55 - 59	32 875	15 504	17 372	20 870	9 810	11 060	12 006	5 694	6 312
60 - 64	25 855	11 740	14 115	14 653	6 648	8 005	11 202	5 092	6 110
65 - 69	29 533	13 403	16 130	16 268	7 374	8 894	13 265	6 029	7 236
70 - 74	22 462	9 894	12 568	11 857	5 240	6 617	10 605	4 654	5 951
75 - 79	15 359	6 429	8 930	7 556	3 135	4 421	7 803	3 295	4 509
80 - 84	7 506	2 791	4 715	3 551	1 302	2 250	3 955	1 490	2 466
85 - 89	2 172	744	1 428	962	307	655	1 210	437	773
90 - 94	1 004	306	698	433	115	318	571	191	380
95 - 99	284	95	189	116	34	82	168	61	107
100 +	75	25	50	36	14	22	40	11	29
Netherlands - Pays-Bas									
1 I 2006 (ESDJ)									
Total	16 334 210	8 077 407	8 256 803	10 793 720	5 306 687	5 487 033	5 540 490	2 770 720	2 769 770
0	187 172	95 904	91 268	127 776	65 461	62 315	59 396	30 443	28 953
1 - 4	800 980	409 666	391 314	526 495	269 414	257 081	274 485	140 252	134 233
5 - 9	998 577	510 917	487 660	634 333	324 340	309 993	364 244	186 577	177 667
10 - 14	997 855	510 266	487 589	628 720	321 301	307 419	369 135	188 965	180 170
15 - 19	991 042	506 372	484 670	644 134	326 105	318 029	346 908	180 267	166 641
20 - 24	964 744	487 458	477 286	698 261	344 604	353 657	266 483	142 854	123 629
25 - 29	991 875	497 244	494 631	731 835	363 080	368 755	260 040	134 164	125 876
30 - 34	1 124 946	563 294	561 652	796 734	400 106	396 628	328 212	163 188	165 024
35 - 39	1 308 275	662 351	645 924	879 157	447 218	431 939	429 118	215 133	213 985
40 - 44	1 314 697	666 242	648 455	863 523	437 865	425 658	451 174	228 377	222 797
45 - 49	1 218 156	614 181	603 975	790 781	397 227	393 554	427 375	216 954	210 421
50 - 54	1 119 525	564 124	555 401	719 533	359 980	359 553	399 992	204 144	195 848
55 - 59	1 147 612	579 927	567 685	730 101	367 098	363 003	417 511	212 829	204 682
60 - 64	838 295	420 695	417 600	517 842	257 606	260 236	320 453	163 089	157 364
65 - 69	695 946	338 845	357 101	436 437	209 763	226 674	259 509	129 082	130 427
70 - 74	579 264	266 238	313 026	367 085	165 856	201 229	212 179	100 382	111 797
75 - 79	468 233	195 660	272 573	305 602	125 628	179 974	162 631	70 032	92 599
80 - 84	336 415	120 325	216 090	225 338	79 421	145 917	111 077	40 904	70 173
85 - 89	171 369	50 508	120 861	115 991	33 436	82 555	55 378	17 072	38 306
90 - 94	64 398	14 692	49 706	43 909	9 568	34 341	20 489	5 124	15 365
95 - 99	13 464	2 305	11 159	9 216	1 492	7 724	4 248	813	3 435
100 +	1 370	193	1 177	917	118	799	453	75	378
Norway - Norvège[49]									
3 XI 2001 (CDJC)									
Total	4 520 947	2 240 281	2 280 666	3 458 699	1 694 153	1 764 546	1 018 422	522 925	495 497
0	57 205	29 340	27 865	44 798	23 002	21 796	11 828	6 048	5 780
1 - 4	240 268	123 153	117 115	186 738	95 742	90 996	51 255	26 232	25 023
5 - 9	307 650	158 230	149 420	235 620	121 061	114 559	69 433	35 833	33 600
10 - 14	300 609	153 989	146 620	227 068	116 054	111 014	71 100	36 697	34 403
15 - 19	267 596	137 494	130 102	199 238	102 194	97 044	66 278	34 188	32 090
20 - 24	273 126	138 679	134 447	211 551	106 040	105 511	59 030	31 337	27 693
25 - 29	316 989	160 678	156 311	255 685	128 167	127 518	57 993	30 759	27 234
30 - 34	351 386	178 688	172 698	280 044	141 397	138 647	67 654	35 193	32 461
35 - 39	338 689	173 595	165 094	265 141	134 740	130 401	70 226	36 890	33 336
40 - 44	319 293	162 807	156 486	246 090	124 014	122 076	70 273	37 050	33 223
45 - 49	309 642	157 276	152 366	236 578	118 274	118 304	70 375	37 421	32 954
50 - 54	301 283	154 010	147 273	227 967	114 779	113 188	70 543	37 669	32 874
55 - 59	269 320	136 414	132 906	203 022	101 540	101 482	63 778	33 413	30 365
60 - 64	190 808	93 953	96 855	140 947	67 923	73 024	47 966	25 008	22 958
65 - 69	163 197	77 766	85 431	119 675	55 351	64 324	41 888	21 553	20 335
70 - 74	161 097	73 389	87 708	118 670	52 350	66 320	40 811	20 243	20 568
75 - 79	151 839	63 682	88 157	111 134	44 980	66 154	38 918	17 898	21 020
80 - 84	113 628	41 784	71 844	83 558	29 286	54 272	28 500	11 877	16 623
85 - 89	60 467	18 752	41 715	44 821	12 816	32 005	14 644	5 617	9 027

Continent, country or area, date, code and age (in years) / Continent, pays ou zone, date, code et âge (en années)	Total			Urban - Urbaine			Rural - Rurale		
	Both sexes Les deux sexes	Male Masculin	Female Féminin	Both sexes Les deux sexes	Male Masculin	Female Féminin	Both sexes Les deux sexes	Male Masculin	Female Féminin
EUROPE									
Norway - Norvège[49]									
3 XI 2001 (CDJC)									
90 - 94	22 093	5 668	16 425	16 645	3 797	12 848	4 988	1 744	3 244
95 - 99	4 307	849	3 458	3 333	580	2 753	872	239	633
100 +	455	85	370	376	66	310	69	16	53
1 VII 2006 (ESDJ)[50]									
Total	4 660 677	2 313 885	2 346 792	...	...	...	...	...	...
0	57 852	29 621	28 231	...	...	...	...	...	...
1 - 4	230 732	117 703	113 030	...	...	...	...	...	...
5 - 9	304 151	155 891	148 261	...	...	...	...	...	...
10 - 14	313 636	161 268	152 369	...	...	...	...	...	...
15 - 19	303 723	155 675	148 048	...	...	...	...	...	...
20 - 24	276 753	140 826	135 927	...	...	...	...	...	...
25 - 29	288 325	145 090	143 235	...	...	...	...	...	...
30 - 34	331 944	167 791	164 153	...	...	...	...	...	...
35 - 39	357 730	181 961	175 769	...	...	...	...	...	...
40 - 44	339 035	173 456	165 579	...	...	...	...	...	...
45 - 49	319 489	162 587	156 902	...	...	...	...	...	...
50 - 54	305 087	154 671	150 416	...	...	...	...	...	...
55 - 59	297 699	151 384	146 315	...	...	...	...	...	...
60 - 64	250 491	125 677	124 814	...	...	...	...	...	...
65 - 69	179 067	86 617	92 451	...	...	...	...	...	...
70 - 74	149 306	68 903	80 404	...	...	...	...	...	...
75 - 79	138 641	60 180	78 461	...	...	...	...	...	...
80 - 84	115 921	44 510	71 412	...	...	...	...	...	...
85 - 89	69 771	22 362	47 409	...	...	...	...	...	...
90 - 94	25 425	6 531	18 894	...	...	...	...	...	...
95 - 99	5 330	1 083	4 247	...	...	...	...	...	...
100 +	574	103	471	...	...	...	...	...	...
Unknown - Inconnu	-	-	-	...	...	...	...	...	...
Poland - Pologne									
1 I 2006 (ESDF)									
Total	38 132 277	18 436 101	19 696 176	23 400 565	11 103 869	12 296 696	14 731 712	7 332 232	7 399 480
0	366 586	188 332	178 254	212 686	109 495	103 191	153 900	78 837	75 063
1 - 4	1 417 459	728 761	688 698	805 462	414 412	391 050	611 997	314 349	297 648
5 - 9	1 949 623	999 688	949 935	1 059 322	543 432	515 890	890 301	456 256	434 045
10 - 14	2 370 975	1 211 853	1 159 122	1 278 520	653 716	624 804	1 092 455	558 137	534 318
15 - 19	2 828 744	1 446 766	1 381 978	1 624 454	827 352	797 102	1 204 290	619 414	584 876
20 - 24	3 300 278	1 678 849	1 621 429	2 036 061	1 025 118	1 010 943	1 264 217	653 731	610 486
25 - 29	3 112 418	1 578 005	1 534 413	1 996 027	996 574	999 453	1 116 391	581 431	534 960
30 - 34	2 801 457	1 418 504	1 382 953	1 768 484	885 950	882 534	1 032 973	532 554	500 419
35 - 39	2 398 734	1 212 384	1 186 350	1 447 956	720 750	727 206	950 778	491 634	459 144
40 - 44	2 463 389	1 236 842	1 226 547	1 481 132	719 635	761 497	982 257	517 207	465 050
45 - 49	2 951 770	1 458 808	1 492 962	1 868 828	884 260	984 568	1 082 942	574 548	508 394
50 - 54	3 001 054	1 454 473	1 546 581	1 996 557	928 371	1 068 186	1 004 497	526 102	478 395
55 - 59	2 543 674	1 202 915	1 340 759	1 711 370	786 027	925 343	832 304	416 888	415 416
60 - 64	1 535 516	695 881	839 635	1 014 222	451 855	562 367	521 294	244 026	277 268
65 - 69	1 522 023	651 612	870 411	966 068	404 961	561 107	555 955	246 651	309 304
70 - 74	1 389 967	557 571	832 396	856 592	339 663	516 929	533 375	217 908	315 467
75 - 79	1 121 673	406 288	715 385	662 079	238 668	423 411	459 594	167 620	291 974
80 - 84	692 511	211 984	480 527	402 343	120 633	281 710	290 168	91 351	198 817
85 +	364 426	96 585	267 841	212 402	52 997	159 405	152 024	43 588	108 436
Portugal									
12 III 2001 (CDFC)									
Total	10 356 117	5 000 141	5 355 976	5 680 711	2 713 204	2 967 507	4 675 406	2 286 937	2 388 469
0	110 914	56 866	54 048	63 392	32 505	30 887	47 522	24 361	23 161
1 - 4	428 577	219 103	209 474	238 914	122 152	116 762	189 663	96 951	92 712
5 - 9	537 521	275 199	262 322	291 377	149 224	142 153	246 144	125 975	120 169
10 - 14	579 590	296 385	283 205	306 265	156 159	150 106	273 325	140 226	133 099
15 - 19	688 686	351 422	337 264	364 989	185 544	179 445	323 697	165 878	157 819
20 - 24	790 901	400 087	390 814	446 459	222 820	223 639	344 442	177 267	167 175
25 - 29	814 661	409 243	405 418	477 253	237 314	239 939	337 408	171 929	165 479
30 - 34	761 457	379 363	382 094	436 577	215 220	221 357	324 880	164 143	160 737
35 - 39	770 781	378 783	391 998	431 579	208 353	223 226	339 202	170 430	168 772
40 - 44	728 518	357 528	370 990	410 550	197 035	213 515	317 968	160 493	157 475

Continent, country or area, date, code and age (in years) / Continent, pays ou zone, date, code et âge (en années)	Total			Urban - Urbaine			Rural - Rurale		
	Both sexes Les deux sexes	Male Masculin	Female Féminin	Both sexes Les deux sexes	Male Masculin	Female Féminin	Both sexes Les deux sexes	Male Masculin	Female Féminin
EUROPE									
Portugal									
12 III 2001 (CDFC)									
45 - 49	686 134	333 382	352 752	392 185	186 726	205 459	293 949	146 656	147 293
50 - 54	642 516	309 484	333 032	373 939	178 079	195 860	268 577	131 405	137 172
55 - 59	571 452	268 899	302 553	320 755	151 997	168 758	250 697	116 902	133 795
60 - 64	550 916	256 179	294 737	289 014	133 942	155 072	261 902	122 237	139 665
65 - 69	538 165	244 230	293 935	271 583	120 482	151 101	266 582	123 748	142 834
70 - 74	453 962	196 615	257 347	225 235	93 945	131 290	228 727	102 670	126 057
75 - 79	348 066	143 439	204 627	169 460	66 449	103 011	178 606	76 990	101 616
80 - 84	201 706	76 014	125 692	96 249	33 700	62 549	105 457	42 314	63 143
85 - 89	108 419	36 167	72 252	53 184	16 295	36 889	55 235	19 872	35 363
90 - 94	36 063	10 241	25 822	18 088	4 583	13 505	17 975	5 658	12 317
95 - 99	6 523	1 417	5 106	3 350	639	2 711	3 173	778	2 395
100 +	589	95	494	314	41	273	275	54	221
1 VII 2006 (ESDJ)									
Total	10 584 344	5 122 840	5 461 504	...	...	...	...	...	...
0	107 048	55 121	51 927	...	...	...	...	...	...
1 - 4	443 115	228 865	214 250	...	...	...	...	...	...
5 - 9	543 396	278 024	265 372	...	...	...	...	...	...
10 - 14	547 377	279 809	267 568	...	...	...	...	...	...
15 - 19	588 248	300 395	287 853	...	...	...	...	...	...
20 - 24	691 033	351 785	339 249	...	...	...	...	...	...
25 - 29	801 786	404 971	396 816	...	...	...	...	...	...
30 - 34	841 399	422 457	418 942	...	...	...	...	...	...
35 - 39	785 807	391 696	394 112	...	...	...	...	...	...
40 - 44	786 089	386 819	399 270	...	...	...	...	...	...
45 - 49	740 559	363 121	377 438	...	...	...	...	...	...
50 - 54	683 934	330 853	353 082	...	...	...	...	...	...
55 - 59	640 635	306 411	334 224	...	...	...	...	...	...
60 - 64	564 563	262 154	302 409	...	...	...	...	...	...
65 - 69	521 790	238 102	283 688	...	...	...	...	...	...
70 - 74	490 476	214 588	275 888	...	...	...	...	...	...
75 - 79	383 245	156 824	226 421	...	...	...	...	...	...
80 - 84	256 537	96 560	159 977	...	...	...	...	...	...
85 - 89	118 985	40 326	78 659	...	...	...	...	...	...
90 - 94	39 553	11 541	28 012	...	...	...	...	...	...
95 - 99	8 092	2 284	5 808	...	...	...	...	...	...
100 +	683	140	543	...	...	...	...	...	...
Romania - Roumanie									
1 VII 2006 (ESDJ)									
Total	21 584 365	10 521 189	11 063 176	11 913 938	5 704 872	6 209 066	9 670 427	4 816 317	4 854 110
0	218 633	112 496	106 137	119 019	61 332	57 687	99 614	51 164	48 450
1 - 4	839 171	431 615	407 556	420 713	216 360	204 353	418 458	215 255	203 203
5 - 9	1 098 663	563 176	535 487	509 929	261 480	248 449	588 734	301 696	287 038
10 - 14	1 177 605	602 816	574 789	574 019	293 811	280 208	603 586	309 005	294 581
15 - 19	1 653 027	842 934	810 093	935 210	472 141	463 069	717 817	370 793	347 024
20 - 24	1 599 535	818 547	780 988	966 974	485 451	481 523	632 561	333 096	299 465
25 - 29	1 778 735	911 059	867 676	1 066 742	531 832	534 910	711 993	379 227	332 766
30 - 34	1 689 369	863 241	826 128	955 171	472 446	482 725	734 198	390 795	343 403
35 - 39	1 869 153	944 770	924 383	1 105 237	527 133	578 104	763 916	417 637	346 279
40 - 44	1 192 648	596 863	595 785	730 337	340 614	389 723	462 311	256 249	206 062
45 - 49	1 463 532	720 761	742 771	937 510	436 904	500 606	526 022	283 857	242 165
50 - 54	1 528 720	739 441	789 279	976 666	467 551	509 115	552 054	271 890	280 164
55 - 59	1 310 266	621 161	689 105	748 939	358 939	390 000	561 327	262 222	299 105
60 - 64	977 303	447 270	530 033	486 557	223 362	263 195	490 746	223 908	266 838
65 - 69	1 041 631	453 301	588 330	477 817	207 697	270 120	563 814	245 604	318 210
70 - 74	913 325	383 397	529 928	388 486	160 277	228 209	524 839	223 120	301 719
75 - 79	675 967	269 993	405 974	281 856	109 686	172 170	394 111	160 307	233 804
80 - 84	391 080	143 476	247 604	160 006	55 321	104 685	231 074	88 155	142 919
85 - 89	116 666	38 378	78 288	50 574	15 573	35 001	66 092	22 805	43 287
90 - 94	39 672	13 091	26 581	18 193	5 679	12 514	21 479	7 412	14 067
95 - 99	8 235	2 960	5 275	3 472	1 136	2 336	4 763	1 824	2 939
100 +	1 429	443	986	511	147	364	918	296	622

7. Population by age, sex and urban/rural residence: latest available year, 1997 - 2006
Population selon l'âge, le sexe et la résidence, urbaine/rurale: dernière année disponible, 1997 - 2006 (continued - suite)

Continent, country or area, date, code and age (in years) Continent, pays ou zone, date, code et âge (en années)	Total			Urban - Urbaine			Rural - Rurale		
	Both sexes Les deux sexes	Male Masculin	Female Féminin	Both sexes Les deux sexes	Male Masculin	Female Féminin	Both sexes Les deux sexes	Male Masculin	Female Féminin
EUROPE									
Russian Federation - Fédération de Russie									
1 VII 2006 (ESDJ)									
Total....................	142 487 259	66 006 266	76 480 993	103 941 621	47 667 046	56 274 575	38 545 638	18 339 220	20 206 418
0........................	1 455 816	747 695	708 121	1 031 290	530 262	501 028	424 526	217 433	207 093
1 - 4....................	5 673 996	2 911 158	2 762 838	3 998 080	2 053 769	1 944 311	1 675 916	857 389	818 527
5 - 9....................	6 396 691	3 273 101	3 123 590	4 336 940	2 221 406	2 115 534	2 059 751	1 051 695	1 008 056
10 - 14..................	7 536 087	3 850 887	3 685 200	5 046 393	2 579 501	2 466 892	2 489 694	1 271 386	1 218 308
15 - 19..................	11 456 442	5 835 460	5 620 982	7 978 324	4 039 334	3 938 990	3 478 118	1 796 126	1 681 992
20 - 24..................	12 537 730	6 339 470	6 198 260	9 650 513	4 832 511	4 818 002	2 887 217	1 506 959	1 380 258
25 - 29..................	11 107 187	5 547 352	5 559 835	8 519 208	4 214 253	4 304 955	2 587 979	1 333 099	1 254 880
30 - 34..................	10 368 546	5 144 043	5 224 503	7 907 608	3 898 330	4 009 278	2 460 938	1 245 713	1 215 225
35 - 39..................	9 438 139	4 645 260	4 792 879	7 009 564	3 419 160	3 590 404	2 428 575	1 226 100	1 202 475
40 - 44..................	10 658 534	5 137 055	5 521 479	7 773 852	3 677 150	4 096 702	2 884 682	1 459 905	1 424 777
45 - 49..................	12 060 316	5 685 938	6 374 378	8 824 324	4 051 268	4 773 056	3 235 992	1 634 670	1 601 322
50 - 54..................	10 725 063	4 868 051	5 857 012	8 003 786	3 536 309	4 467 477	2 721 277	1 331 742	1 389 535
55 - 59..................	8 787 638	3 843 019	4 944 619	6 707 482	2 870 673	3 836 809	2 080 156	972 346	1 107 810
60 - 64..................	4 371 640	1 773 964	2 597 676	3 294 318	1 325 784	1 968 534	1 077 322	448 180	629 142
65 - 69..................	7 533 440	2 805 793	4 727 647	5 369 625	1 973 543	3 396 082	2 163 815	832 250	1 331 565
70 - 74..................	4 767 069	1 631 378	3 135 691	3 254 243	1 086 292	2 167 951	1 512 826	545 086	967 740
75 - 79..................	4 403 655	1 308 577	3 095 078	2 984 090	877 917	2 106 173	1 419 565	430 660	988 905
80 - 84..................	2 188 092	472 034	1 716 058	1 536 776	339 777	1 196 999	651 316	132 257	519 059
85 - 89..................	692 848	132 180	560 668	489 072	98 647	390 425	203 776	33 533	170 243
90 - 94..................	264 401	43 744	220 657	183 502	33 512	149 990	80 899	10 232	70 667
95 - 99..................	49 016	7 823	41 193	33 598	5 933	27 665	15 418	1 890	13 528
100 +....................	14 913	2 284	12 629	9 033	1 715	7 318	5 880	569	5 311
San Marino - Saint-Marin									
1 VII 2004 (ESDF)									
Total....................	29 457	14 442	15 015	...	...	...	...	...	...
0........................	308	160	149	...	...	...	...	...	...
1 - 4....................	1 274	678	596	...	...	...	...	...	...
5 - 9....................	1 508	800	708	...	...	...	...	...	...
10 - 14..................	1 383	707	676	...	...	...	...	...	...
15 - 19..................	1 292	672	620	...	...	...	...	...	...
20 - 24..................	1 519	779	740	...	...	...	...	...	...
25 - 29..................	2 038	983	1 055	...	...	...	...	...	...
30 - 34..................	2 559	1 256	1 304	...	...	...	...	...	...
35 - 39..................	2 863	1 385	1 478	...	...	...	...	...	...
40 - 44..................	2 617	1 297	1 320	...	...	...	...	...	...
45 - 49..................	2 067	1 054	1 013	...	...	...	...	...	...
50 - 54..................	1 876	932	944	...	...	...	...	...	...
55 - 59..................	1 819	892	927	...	...	...	...	...	...
60 - 64..................	1 526	751	775	...	...	...	...	...	...
65 - 69..................	1 383	688	696	...	...	...	...	...	...
70 - 74..................	1 207	553	655	...	...	...	...	...	...
75 - 79..................	946	413	533	...	...	...	...	...	...
80 - 84..................	765	290	475	...	...	...	...	...	...
85 - 89..................	321	102	219	...	...	...	...	...	...
90 - 94..................	163	47	116	...	...	...	...	...	...
95 - 99..................	29	9	20	...	...	...	...	...	...
100 +....................	2	-	2	...	...	...	...	...	...
Serbia - Serbie[51]									
1 VII 2006 (ESDJ)									
Total....................	7 411 569	3 603 698	3 807 871	4 263 386	2 034 616	2 228 770	3 148 183	1 569 082	1 579 101
0........................	71 088	36 576	34 512	46 442	23 890	22 552	24 646	12 686	11 960
1 - 4....................	308 670	158 784	149 886	188 041	96 802	91 239	120 629	61 982	58 647
5 - 9....................	364 248	186 377	177 871	198 829	102 150	96 679	165 419	84 227	81 192
10 - 14..................	413 607	212 228	201 379	230 244	118 289	111 955	183 363	93 939	89 424
15 - 19..................	456 348	233 817	222 531	260 944	133 009	127 935	195 404	100 808	94 596
20 - 24..................	506 071	257 773	248 298	306 447	153 310	153 137	199 624	104 463	95 161
25 - 29..................	515 849	262 060	253 789	322 867	159 715	163 152	192 982	102 345	90 637
30 - 34..................	501 489	251 583	249 906	306 434	149 395	157 039	195 055	102 188	92 867
35 - 39..................	475 882	236 563	239 319	281 975	136 104	145 871	193 907	100 459	93 448
40 - 44..................	490 837	242 360	248 477	289 672	137 826	151 846	201 165	104 534	96 631
45 - 49..................	532 008	261 980	270 028	315 107	148 084	167 023	216 901	113 896	103 005

Continent, country or area, date, code and age (in years) / Continent, pays ou zone, date, code et âge (en années)	Total			Urban - Urbaine			Rural - Rurale		
	Both sexes Les deux sexes	Male Masculin	Female Féminin	Both sexes Les deux sexes	Male Masculin	Female Féminin	Both sexes Les deux sexes	Male Masculin	Female Féminin
EUROPE									
Serbia - Serbie[51]									
1 VII 2006 (ESDJ)									
50 - 54	606 617	299 629	306 988	360 865	170 468	190 397	245 752	129 161	116 591
55 - 59	532 389	256 760	275 629	321 083	149 524	171 559	211 306	107 236	104 070
60 - 64	358 505	166 849	191 656	201 631	92 072	109 559	156 874	74 777	82 097
65 - 69	406 210	183 484	222 726	216 369	96 211	120 158	189 841	87 273	102 568
70 - 74	385 685	167 601	218 084	190 466	82 638	107 828	195 219	84 963	110 256
75 - 79	280 353	114 335	166 018	128 544	50 396	78 148	151 809	63 939	87 870
80 - 84	146 232	53 418	92 814	68 513	24 607	43 906	77 719	28 811	48 908
85 - 89	44 171	15 945	28 226	20 294	7 069	13 225	23 877	8 876	15 001
90 - 94	10 485	3 771	6 714	5 575	1 910	3 665	4 910	1 861	3 049
95 - 99	3 452	1 318	2 134	2 052	785	1 267	1 400	533	867
100 +	1 373	487	886	992	362	630	381	125	256
Slovakia - Slovaquie									
1 VII 2006 (ESDJ)									
Total	5 391 184	2 616 924	2 774 260	2 989 769	1 435 472	1 554 297	2 401 415	1 181 452	1 219 963
0	53 930	27 686	26 244	28 477	14 676	13 801	25 453	13 010	12 443
1 - 4	207 885	106 728	101 157	107 227	55 039	52 188	100 658	51 689	48 969
5 - 9	279 383	143 195	136 188	137 396	70 229	67 167	141 987	72 966	69 021
10 - 14	341 456	174 535	166 921	175 390	89 411	85 979	166 066	85 124	80 942
15 - 19	403 595	206 052	197 543	223 606	114 122	109 484	179 989	91 930	88 059
20 - 24	445 081	227 202	217 879	254 060	129 691	124 369	191 021	97 511	93 510
25 - 29	469 608	239 413	230 195	271 869	137 926	133 943	197 739	101 487	96 252
30 - 34	437 916	222 332	215 584	247 418	124 150	123 268	190 498	98 182	92 316
35 - 39	363 060	183 365	179 695	201 961	98 747	103 214	161 099	84 618	76 481
40 - 44	381 362	191 029	190 333	219 072	105 003	114 069	162 290	86 026	76 264
45 - 49	394 992	196 802	198 190	233 251	111 334	121 917	161 741	85 468	76 273
50 - 54	402 542	196 342	206 200	241 472	114 250	127 222	161 070	82 092	78 978
55 - 59	332 597	157 452	175 145	194 432	90 384	104 048	138 165	67 068	71 097
60 - 64	240 043	106 623	133 420	132 983	58 450	74 533	107 060	48 173	58 887
65 - 69	197 961	82 661	115 300	102 733	42 927	59 806	95 228	39 734	55 494
70 - 74	169 066	65 715	103 351	85 576	33 870	51 706	83 490	31 845	51 645
75 - 79	135 936	48 110	87 826	66 945	24 254	42 691	68 991	23 856	45 135
80 - 84	89 448	28 255	61 193	43 487	14 125	29 362	45 961	14 130	31 831
85 - 89	30 925	9 317	21 608	15 195	4 739	10 456	15 730	4 578	11 152
90 - 94	10 860	3 044	7 816	5 386	1 543	3 843	5 474	1 501	3 973
95 - 99	2 929	843	2 086	1 513	465	1 048	1 416	378	1 038
100 +	609	223	386	320	137	183	289	86	203
Slovenia - Slovénie									
1 VII 2006 (ESDJ)									
Total	2 008 516	985 876	1 022 640	962 740[52]	456 764[52]	505 976[52]	992 507[52]	491 002[52]	501 505[52]
0	18 440	9 433	9 007	8 817[52]	4 492[52]	4 325[52]	9 420[52]	4 837[52]	4 583[52]
1 - 4	71 506	36 806	34 703	33 276[52]	17 157[52]	16 119[52]	37 181[52]	19 103[52]	18 078[52]
5 - 9	91 766	47 277	44 489	41 415[52]	21 371[52]	20 044[52]	49 214[52]	25 336[52]	23 878[52]
10 - 14	99 749	51 301	48 448	44 434[52]	22 803[52]	21 631[52]	54 209[52]	27 902[52]	26 307[52]
15 - 19	121 567	62 453	59 114	56 061[52]	28 588[52]	27 473[52]	63 661[52]	32 700[52]	30 961[52]
20 - 24	137 699	71 089	66 610	64 034[52]	32 622[52]	31 412[52]	68 985[52]	35 307[52]	33 678[52]
25 - 29	153 741	79 744	73 997	72 618[52]	37 080[52]	35 538[52]	74 994[52]	38 548[52]	36 446[52]
30 - 34	149 365	77 259	72 106	69 299[52]	34 625[52]	34 674[52]	73 437[52]	37 943[52]	35 494[52]
35 - 39	146 754	74 773	71 981	67 459[52]	32 719[52]	34 740[52]	72 862[52]	37 248[52]	35 614[52]
40 - 44	156 625	79 521	77 104	74 529[52]	35 598[52]	38 931[52]	75 715[52]	38 958[52]	36 757[52]
45 - 49	154 731	78 790	75 941	74 601[52]	35 468[52]	39 133[52]	74 252[52]	38 580[52]	35 672[52]
50 - 54	156 669	80 671	75 998	78 483[52]	38 108[52]	40 375[52]	73 378[52]	38 650[52]	34 728[52]
55 - 59	134 000	67 632	66 368	67 764[52]	32 506[52]	35 258[52]	63 249[52]	32 794[52]	30 455[52]
60 - 64	99 566	47 630	51 936	50 837[52]	22 972[52]	27 865[52]	47 228[52]	23 548[52]	23 680[52]
65 - 69	96 734	44 398	52 336	48 549[52]	21 699[52]	26 850[52]	47 073[52]	22 023[52]	25 050[52]
70 - 74	85 363	35 310	50 053	42 835[52]	17 653[52]	25 182[52]	41 919[52]	17 355[52]	24 564[52]
75 - 79	68 382	24 632	43 750	34 072[52]	12 154[52]	21 918[52]	33 912[52]	12 303[52]	21 609[52]
80 - 84	43 031	11 835	31 196	21 908[52]	6 282[52]	15 626[52]	20 869[52]	5 447[52]	15 422[52]
85 - 89	15 289	3 743	11 546	7 843[52]	2 017[52]	5 826[52]	7 360[52]	1 696[52]	5 664[52]
90 - 94	6 033	1 284	4 749	3 109[52]	692[52]	2 417[52]	2 891[52]	587[52]	2 304[52]
95 - 99	1 383	279	1 104	728[52]	148[52]	580[52]	647[52]	131[52]	516[52]
100 +	123	16	107	69[52]	10[52]	59[52]	51[52]	6[52]	45[52]

Continent, country or area, date, code and age (in years) / Continent, pays ou zone, date, code et âge (en années)	Total			Urban - Urbaine			Rural - Rurale		
	Both sexes Les deux sexes	Male Masculin	Female Féminin	Both sexes Les deux sexes	Male Masculin	Female Féminin	Both sexes Les deux sexes	Male Masculin	Female Féminin
EUROPE									
Spain - Espagne									
1 VII 2006 (ESDJ)									
Total....................	44 068 244	21 725 232	22 343 012	...	...	...	...	...	...
0 - 4.....................	2 259 396	1 162 856	1 096 540	...	...	...	...	...	...
5 - 9.....................	2 060 398	1 057 678	1 002 720	...	...	...	...	...	...
10 - 14...................	2 073 652	1 065 078	1 008 574	...	...	...	...	...	...
15 - 19...................	2 288 987	1 176 093	1 112 894	...	...	...	...	...	...
20 - 24...................	2 850 807	1 459 361	1 391 446	...	...	...	...	...	...
25 - 29...................	3 682 358	1 899 661	1 782 697	...	...	...	...	...	...
30 - 34...................	3 874 841	2 004 187	1 870 654	...	...	...	...	...	...
35 - 39...................	3 674 100	1 881 315	1 792 785	...	...	...	...	...	...
40 - 44...................	3 468 777	1 750 917	1 717 860	...	...	...	...	...	...
45 - 49...................	3 121 210	1 558 405	1 562 805	...	...	...	...	...	...
50 - 54...................	2 678 732	1 325 153	1 353 579	...	...	...	...	...	...
55 - 59...................	2 476 591	1 210 072	1 266 519	...	...	...	...	...	...
60 - 64...................	2 202 020	1 061 310	1 140 710	...	...	...	...	...	...
65 - 69...................	1 852 847	869 044	983 803	...	...	...	...	...	...
70 - 74...................	1 929 742	869 815	1 059 927	...	...	...	...	...	...
75 - 79...................	1 607 806	680 368	927 438	...	...	...	...	...	...
80 - 84...................	1 113 292	428 671	684 621	...	...	...	...	...	...
85 - 89...................	570 553	188 741	381 812	...	...	...	...	...	...
90 - 94...................	222 386	61 739	160 647	...	...	...	...	...	...
95 - 99...................	54 277	13 440	40 837	...	...	...	...	...	...
100 +....................	5 472	1 328	4 144	...	...	...	...	...	...
Sweden - Suède[41]									
1 VII 2006 (ESDJ)									
Total....................	9 080 505	4 505 037	4 575 468	...	...	...	...	...	...
0........................	103 917	53 410	50 507	...	...	...	...	...	...
1 - 4.....................	400 548	205 295	195 253	...	...	...	...	...	...
5 - 9.....................	468 354	240 476	227 878	...	...	...	...	...	...
10 - 14...................	582 364	298 382	283 982	...	...	...	...	...	...
15 - 19...................	609 051	312 630	296 421	...	...	...	...	...	...
20 - 24...................	534 422	273 492	260 930	...	...	...	...	...	...
25 - 29...................	545 898	278 176	267 722	...	...	...	...	...	...
30 - 34...................	606 160	308 419	297 741	...	...	...	...	...	...
35 - 39...................	634 732	323 200	311 532	...	...	...	...	...	...
40 - 44...................	646 213	330 170	316 043	...	...	...	...	...	...
45 - 49...................	584 649	296 591	288 058	...	...	...	...	...	...
50 - 54...................	580 056	292 807	287 249	...	...	...	...	...	...
55 - 59...................	621 670	311 914	309 756	...	...	...	...	...	...
60 - 64...................	589 066	296 215	292 851	...	...	...	...	...	...
65 - 69...................	426 408	208 994	217 414	...	...	...	...	...	...
70 - 74...................	347 405	162 301	185 104	...	...	...	...	...	...
75 - 79...................	310 886	135 478	175 408	...	...	...	...	...	...
80 - 84...................	256 515	102 610	153 905	...	...	...	...	...	...
85 - 89...................	157 361	54 681	102 680	...	...	...	...	...	...
90 - 94...................	60 051	16 740	43 311	...	...	...	...	...	...
95 - 99...................	13 406	2 845	10 561	...	...	...	...	...	...
100 +....................	1 374	212	1 162	...	...	...	...	...	...
Switzerland - Suisse									
1 VII 2006 (ESDJ)									
Total....................	7 483 935	3 665 931	3 818 004	...	...	...	...	...	...
0........................	36 496	18 777	17 719	...	...	...	...	...	...
1 - 4.....................	292 022	150 096	141 926	...	...	...	...	...	...
5 - 9.....................	387 386	199 410	187 976	...	...	...	...	...	...
10 - 14...................	426 998	219 200	207 798	...	...	...	...	...	...
15 - 19...................	445 524	228 745	216 779	...	...	...	...	...	...
20 - 24...................	442 574	223 586	218 988	...	...	...	...	...	...
25 - 29...................	466 983	232 323	234 660	...	...	...	...	...	...
30 - 34...................	508 375	252 609	255 766	...	...	...	...	...	...
35 - 39...................	592 951	295 397	297 554	...	...	...	...	...	...
40 - 44...................	641 009	323 407	317 602	...	...	...	...	...	...
45 - 49...................	576 448	290 576	285 872	...	...	...	...	...	...
50 - 54...................	508 354	255 621	252 733	...	...	...	...	...	...
55 - 59...................	478 255	238 724	239 531	...	...	...	...	...	...

Continent, country or area, date, code and age (in years) / Continent, pays ou zone, date, code et âge (en années)	Total			Urban - Urbaine			Rural - Rurale		
	Both sexes Les deux sexes	Male Masculin	Female Féminin	Both sexes Les deux sexes	Male Masculin	Female Féminin	Both sexes Les deux sexes	Male Masculin	Female Féminin
EUROPE									
Switzerland - Suisse									
1 VII 2006 (ESDJ)									
60 - 64	438 844	217 263	221 581	...	...	...	...	...	...
65 - 69	338 476	160 621	177 855	...	...	...	...	...	...
70 - 74	294 087	133 110	160 977	...	...	...	...	...	...
75 - 79	246 440	102 787	143 653	...	...	...	...	...	...
80 - 84	188 680	70 452	118 228	...	...	...	...	...	...
85 - 89	110 137	36 633	73 504	...	...	...	...	...	...
90 - 94	48 315	13 360	34 955	...	...	...	...	...	...
95 +	15 581	3 234	12 347	...	...	...	...	...	...
The Former Yugoslav Rep. of Macedonia - L'ex-République yougoslave de Macédoine									
1 VII 2006 (ESDF)									
Total	2 040 228	1 023 069	1 017 159	...	...	...	...	...	...
0	22 298	11 392	10 906	...	...	...	...	...	...
1 - 4	92 399	47 700	44 699	...	...	...	...	...	...
5 - 9	127 145	65 645	61 500	...	...	...	...	...	...
10 - 14	149 523	76 912	72 611	...	...	...	...	...	...
15 - 19	162 091	83 449	78 642	...	...	...	...	...	...
20 - 24	165 305	84 763	80 542	...	...	...	...	...	...
25 - 29	158 513	81 597	76 916	...	...	...	...	...	...
30 - 34	151 643	77 119	74 524	...	...	...	...	...	...
35 - 39	147 700	74 922	72 778	...	...	...	...	...	...
40 - 44	147 772	75 184	72 588	...	...	...	...	...	...
45 - 49	145 509	74 089	71 420	...	...	...	...	...	...
50 - 54	137 034	69 174	67 860	...	...	...	...	...	...
55 - 59	116 170	56 428	59 742	...	...	...	...	...	...
60 - 64	88 714	42 468	46 246	...	...	...	...	...	...
65 - 69	80 628	37 815	42 813	...	...	...	...	...	...
70 - 74	70 251	31 969	38 282	...	...	...	...	...	...
75 - 79	44 511	19 157	25 354	...	...	...	...	...	...
80 - 84	22 849	9 322	13 527	...	...	...	...	...	...
85 - 89	6 946	2 849	4 097	...	...	...	...	...	...
90 - 94	1 883	742	1 141	...	...	...	...	...	...
95 +	493	167	326	...	...	...	...	...	...
Unknown - Inconnu	851	206	645	...	...	...	...	...	...
Ukraine									
5 XII 2001 (CDFC)									
Total	48 240 902	22 316 317	25 924 585	32 290 729	14 903 592	17 387 137	15 950 173	7 412 725	8 537 448
0	358 166	183 728	174 438	219 819	112 829	106 990	138 347	70 899	67 448
1 - 4	1 616 029	828 496	787 533	971 165	498 793	472 372	644 864	329 703	315 161
5 - 9	2 559 107	1 311 943	1 247 164	1 566 939	804 013	762 926	992 168	507 930	484 238
10 - 14	3 416 561	1 750 539	1 666 022	2 233 242	1 145 140	1 088 102	1 183 319	605 399	577 920
15 - 19	3 891 568	1 989 538	1 902 030	2 843 968	1 451 113	1 392 855	1 047 600	538 425	509 175
20 - 24	3 489 588	1 766 985	1 722 603	2 502 035	1 257 873	1 244 162	987 553	509 112	478 441
25 - 29	3 402 010	1 700 516	1 701 494	2 372 359	1 174 123	1 198 236	1 029 651	526 393	503 258
30 - 34	3 204 103	1 586 043	1 618 060	2 195 441	1 060 601	1 134 840	1 008 662	525 442	483 220
35 - 39	3 417 079	1 660 397	1 756 682	2 372 481	1 117 635	1 254 846	1 044 598	542 762	501 836
40 - 44	3 828 331	1 833 438	1 994 893	2 704 764	1 254 682	1 450 082	1 123 567	578 756	544 811
45 - 49	3 470 419	1 623 194	1 847 225	2 491 185	1 132 099	1 359 086	979 234	491 095	488 139
50 - 54	3 182 588	1 454 550	1 728 038	2 279 654	1 022 278	1 257 376	902 934	432 272	470 662
55 - 59	2 062 711	892 852	1 169 859	1 362 264	590 267	771 997	700 447	302 585	397 862
60 - 64	3 364 050	1 398 332	1 965 718	2 160 327	898 221	1 262 106	1 203 723	500 111	703 612
65 - 69	2 158 171	868 633	1 289 538	1 283 340	522 241	761 099	874 831	346 392	528 439
70 - 74	2 239 064	806 587	1 432 477	1 292 298	475 502	816 796	946 766	331 085	615 681
75 - 79	1 500 920	416 155	1 084 765	845 122	240 075	605 047	655 798	176 080	479 718
80 - 84	618 819	147 952	470 867	340 633	86 630	254 003	278 186	61 322	216 864
85 - 89	324 697	65 475	259 222	177 221	38 841	138 380	147 476	26 634	120 842
90 - 94	100 593	18 643	81 950	49 709	9 981	39 728	50 884	8 662	42 222
95 - 99	15 119	2 419	12 700	7 261	1 255	6 006	7 858	1 164	6 694
100 +	1 549	199	1 350	661	106	555	888	93	795
Unknown - Inconnu	19 660	9 703	9 957	18 841	9 294	9 547	819	409	410

7. Population by age, sex and urban/rural residence: latest available year, 1997 - 2006
Population selon l'âge, le sexe et la résidence, urbaine/rurale: dernière année disponible, 1997 - 2006 (continued - suite)

Continent, country or area, date, code and age (in years) / Continent, pays ou zone, date, code et âge (en années)	Total			Urban - Urbaine			Rural - Rurale		
	Both sexes Les deux sexes	Male Masculin	Female Féminin	Both sexes Les deux sexes	Male Masculin	Female Féminin	Both sexes Les deux sexes	Male Masculin	Female Féminin

EUROPE

Ukraine
1 VII 2004 (ESDJ)

Total	47 271 271	21 840 401	25 430 870	...	...	...	...	...	...
0	414 634	213 119	201 515	...	...	...	...	...	...
1 - 4	1 533 811	789 224	744 587	...	...	...	...	...	...
5 - 9	2 225 162	1 139 772	1 085 390	...	...	...	...	...	...
10 - 14	2 944 446	1 509 276	1 435 170	...	...	...	...	...	...
15 - 19	3 757 321	1 920 789	1 836 532	...	...	...	...	...	...
20 - 24	3 709 786	1 889 845	1 819 941	...	...	...	...	...	...
25 - 29	3 410 477	1 710 972	1 699 506	...	...	...	...	...	...
30 - 34	3 291 742	1 631 230	1 660 512	...	...	...	...	...	...
35 - 39	3 142 690	1 532 714	1 609 977	...	...	...	...	...	...
40 - 44	3 680 850	1 759 871	1 920 979	...	...	...	...	...	...
45 - 49	3 575 003	1 670 590	1 904 414	...	...	...	...	...	...
50 - 54	3 304 191	1 501 526	1 802 665	...	...	...	...	...	...
55 - 59	2 410 760	1 051 150	1 359 610	...	...	...	...	...	...
60 - 64	2 432 159	995 315	1 436 844	...	...	...	...	...	...
65 - 69	2 811 124	1 107 662	1 703 462	...	...	...	...	...	...
70 - 74	1 801 864	653 321	1 148 544	...	...	...	...	...	...
75 - 79	1 661 403	504 979	1 156 424	...	...	...	...	...	...
80 - 84	770 993	181 430	589 563	...	...	...	...	...	...
85 - 89	264 206	54 641	209 565	...	...	...	...	...	...
90 - 94	112 772	20 434	92 338	...	...	...	...	...	...
95 - 99	14 144	2 305	11 840	...	...	...	...	...	...
100 +	1 738	240	1 498	...	...	...	...	...	...

United Kingdom - Royaume-Uni[53]
29 IV 2001 (CDFC)

Total	58 789 194	28 579 869	30 209 325	47 007 427	22 769 606	24 237 821	11 781 767	5 810 263	5 971 504
0	660 025	337 154	322 871	545 015	278 159	266 856	115 010	58 995	56 015
1 - 4	2 826 228	1 448 534	1 377 694	2 305 860	1 181 014	1 124 846	520 368	267 520	252 848
5 - 9	3 738 042	1 914 727	1 823 315	3 009 441	1 541 475	1 467 966	728 601	373 252	355 349
10 - 14	3 880 557	1 987 606	1 892 951	3 103 939	1 588 218	1 515 721	776 618	399 388	377 230
15 - 19	3 663 782	1 870 508	1 793 274	2 968 710	1 505 467	1 463 243	695 072	365 041	330 031
20 - 24	3 545 984	1 765 257	1 780 727	3 041 392	1 493 532	1 547 860	504 592	271 725	232 867
25 - 29	3 867 015	1 895 469	1 971 546	3 299 342	1 610 026	1 689 316	567 673	285 443	282 230
30 - 34	4 493 532	2 199 767	2 293 765	3 723 844	1 824 665	1 899 179	769 688	375 102	394 586
35 - 39	4 625 777	2 277 678	2 348 099	3 727 542	1 835 623	1 891 919	898 235	442 055	456 180
40 - 44	4 151 613	2 056 545	2 095 068	3 290 231	1 629 251	1 660 980	861 382	427 294	434 088
45 - 49	3 735 986	1 851 391	1 884 595	2 911 582	1 441 854	1 469 728	824 404	409 537	414 867
50 - 54	4 040 576	2 003 158	2 037 418	3 082 777	1 526 738	1 556 039	957 799	476 420	481 379
55 - 59	3 339 004	1 651 396	1 687 608	2 514 831	1 238 414	1 276 417	824 173	412 982	411 191
60 - 64	2 880 074	1 409 684	1 470 390	2 203 267	1 070 975	1 132 292	676 807	338 709	338 098
65 - 69	2 596 939	1 241 382	1 355 557	2 005 735	948 325	1 057 410	591 204	293 057	298 147
70 - 74	2 339 319	1 059 156	1 280 163	1 821 307	812 938	1 008 369	518 012	246 218	271 794
75 - 79	1 967 088	817 738	1 149 350	1 542 567	632 032	910 535	424 521	185 706	238 815
80 - 84	1 313 592	482 707	830 885	1 030 404	373 231	657 173	283 188	109 476	173 712
85 - 89	752 035	226 520	525 515	589 543	174 135	415 408	162 492	52 385	110 107
90 - 94	293 961	68 682	225 279	229 205	52 178	177 027	64 756	16 504	48 252
95 - 99	68 655	12 920	55 735	53 532	9 866	43 666	15 123	3 054	12 069
100 +	9 410	1 890	7 520	7 361	1 490	5 871	2 049	400	1 649

1 VII 2006 (ESDF)

Total	60 587 349	29 693 967	30 893 382	...	...	...	...	...	...
0 - 4	3 496 220	1 790 204	1 706 016	...	...	...	...	...	...
5 - 9	3 489 826	1 784 718	1 705 108	...	...	...	...	...	...
10 - 14	3 751 360	1 924 421	1 826 939	...	...	...	...	...	...
15 - 19	3 996 150	2 060 105	1 936 045	...	...	...	...	...	...
20 - 24	4 023 910	2 048 086	1 975 824	...	...	...	...	...	...
25 - 29	3 856 127	1 930 356	1 925 771	...	...	...	...	...	...
30 - 34	4 040 223	2 010 058	2 030 165	...	...	...	...	...	...
35 - 39	4 598 749	2 281 272	2 317 477	...	...	...	...	...	...
40 - 44	4 663 075	2 305 197	2 357 878	...	...	...	...	...	...
45 - 49	4 150 621	2 055 769	2 094 852	...	...	...	...	...	...
50 - 54	3 683 049	1 820 077	1 862 972	...	...	...	...	...	...
55 - 59	3 909 968	1 927 796	1 982 172	...	...	...	...	...	...

Continent, country or area, date, code and age (in years) / Continent, pays ou zone, date, code et âge (en années)	Total			Urban - Urbaine			Rural - Rurale		
	Both sexes Les deux sexes	Male Masculin	Female Féminin	Both sexes Les deux sexes	Male Masculin	Female Féminin	Both sexes Les deux sexes	Male Masculin	Female Féminin
EUROPE									
United Kingdom - Royaume-Uni[53]									
1 VII 2006 (ESDF)									
60 - 64	3 240 134	1 584 429	1 655 705	...	...	...	...	...	...
65 - 69	2 690 897	1 292 923	1 397 974	...	...	...	...	...	...
70 - 74	2 338 222	1 086 437	1 251 785	...	...	...	...	...	...
75 - 79	1 959 315	849 315	1 110 000	...	...	...	...	...	...
80 - 84	1 456 345	563 887	892 458	...	...	...	...	...	...
85 - 89	820 237	273 380	546 857	...	...	...	...	...	...
90 + ...	422 921	105 537	317 384	...	...	...	...	...	...
OCEANIA - OCÉANIE									
American Samoa - Samoas américaines[12]									
1 IV 2000 (CDJC)									
Total.................	57 291	29 264	28 027	...	...	...	...	...	...
0 - 4.................	7 820	4 008	3 812	...	...	...	...	...	...
5 - 9.................	7 788	4 058	3 730	...	...	...	...	...	...
10 - 14.................	6 604	3 389	3 215	...	...	...	...	...	...
15 - 19.................	5 223	2 747	2 476	...	...	...	...	...	...
20 - 24.................	4 476	2 328	2 148	...	...	...	...	...	...
25 - 29.................	4 356	2 218	2 138	...	...	...	...	...	...
30 - 34.................	4 351	2 167	2 184	...	...	...	...	...	...
35 - 39.................	4 059	1 980	2 079	...	...	...	...	...	...
40 - 44.................	3 302	1 654	1 648	...	...	...	...	...	...
45 - 49.................	2 660	1 331	1 329	...	...	...	...	...	...
50 - 54.................	2 073	1 071	1 002	...	...	...	...	...	...
55 - 59.................	1 474	817	657	...	...	...	...	...	...
60 - 64.................	1 204	636	568	...	...	...	...	...	...
65 - 69.................	790	407	383	...	...	...	...	...	...
70 - 74.................	555	231	324	...	...	...	...	...	...
75 +.................	556	222	334	...	...	...	...	...	...
Australia - Australie									
1 VII 2006 (ESDJ)									
Total.................	20 701 488	10 290 338	10 411 150	17 231 649	8 522 861	8 708 788	3 469 839	1 767 477	1 702 362
0 - 4.................	1 308 651	672 183	636 468	1 085 661	557 306	528 355	222 990	114 877	108 113
5 - 9.................	1 340 779	687 357	653 422	1 089 290	557 659	531 631	251 489	129 698	121 791
10 - 14.................	1 400 713	719 258	681 455	1 132 412	580 720	551 692	268 301	138 538	129 763
15 - 19.................	1 414 666	726 266	688 400	1 188 711	606 789	581 922	225 955	119 477	106 478
20 - 24.................	1 469 432	747 927	721 505	1 308 888	663 056	645 832	160 544	84 871	75 673
25 - 29.................	1 406 466	708 376	698 090	1 242 936	625 379	617 557	163 530	82 997	80 533
30 - 34.................	1 493 153	743 386	749 767	1 292 900	643 576	649 324	200 253	99 810	100 443
35 - 39.................	1 527 431	759 543	767 888	1 294 818	643 128	651 690	232 613	116 415	116 198
40 - 44.................	1 534 709	762 579	772 130	1 278 134	633 218	644 916	256 575	129 361	127 214
45 - 49.................	1 495 288	741 136	754 152	1 230 792	605 775	625 017	264 496	135 361	129 135
50 - 54.................	1 363 680	679 033	684 647	1 114 075	549 246	564 829	249 605	129 787	119 818
55 - 59.................	1 271 559	636 723	634 836	1 029 336	510 564	518 772	242 223	126 159	116 064
60 - 64.................	987 847	496 072	491 775	784 895	390 914	393 981	202 952	105 158	97 794
65 - 69.................	779 169	385 226	393 943	614 069	299 188	314 881	165 100	86 038	79 062
70 - 74.................	629 138	302 778	326 360	500 701	236 890	263 811	128 437	65 888	62 549
75 - 79.................	551 488	252 158	299 330	444 809	199 835	244 974	106 679	52 323	54 356
80 - 84.................	405 328	166 000	239 328	333 439	134 515	198 924	71 889	31 485	40 404
85 +.................	...	...	...	265 783	85 103	180 680	56 208	19 234	36 974
85 - 89.................	214 338	75 405	138 933						
90 - 94.................	85 816	24 167	61 649	...	...	...	...	...	...
95 - 99.................	19 396	4 305	15 091						
100 +.................	2 441	460	1 981						
8 VIII 2006 (CDJC)									
Total.................	19 855 288	9 799 252	10 056 036	...	...	...	...	...	...
0 - 4.................	1 260 403	647 403	613 000						
5 - 9.................	1 308 863	671 402	637 461						
10 - 14.................	1 367 940	702 538	665 402	...	...	...	...	...	...
15 - 19.................	1 356 910	695 795	661 115	...	...	...	...	...	...

Continent, country or area, date, code and age (in years) / Continent, pays ou zone, date, code et âge (en années)	Total			Urban - Urbaine			Rural - Rurale		
	Both sexes Les deux sexes	Male Masculin	Female Féminin	Both sexes Les deux sexes	Male Masculin	Female Féminin	Both sexes Les deux sexes	Male Masculin	Female Féminin
OCEANIA - OCÉANIE									
Australia - Australie									
8 VIII 2006 (CDJC)									
20 - 24	1 347 362	681 649	665 713	...	...	...	...	...	...
25 - 29	1 276 929	635 794	641 135	...	...	...	...	...	...
30 - 34	1 399 459	685 255	714 204	...	...	...	...	...	...
35 - 39	1 466 184	715 177	751 007	...	...	...	...	...	...
40 - 44	1 471 658	722 075	749 583	...	...	...	...	...	...
45 - 49	1 446 725	711 198	735 527	...	...	...	...	...	...
50 - 54	1 315 787	648 874	666 913	...	...	...	...	...	...
55 - 59	1 234 602	615 562	619 040	...	...	...	...	...	...
60 - 64	958 077	480 563	477 514	...	...	...	...	...	...
65 - 69	757 386	373 606	383 780	...	...	...	...	...	...
70 - 74	616 051	294 845	321 206	...	...	...	...	...	...
75 - 79	543 611	247 506	296 105	...	...	...	...	...	...
80 - 84	404 484	164 961	239 523	...	...	...	...	...	...
85 - 89	214 319	75 538	138 781	...	...	...	...	...	...
90 - 94	85 732	24 255	61 477	...	...	...	...	...	...
95 - 99	19 649	4 454	15 195	...	...	...	...	...	...
100 +	3 157	802	2 355	...	...	...	...	...	...
Cook Islands - Îles Cook[54]									
1 XII 2006 (CDFC)									
Total	19 569	9 932	9 637	...	...	...	...	...	...
0 - 14	5 098	2 649	2 449	...	...	...	...	...	...
15 - 44	8 865	4 405	4 460	...	...	...	...	...	...
45 - 59	3 287	1 689	1 598	...	...	...	...	...	...
60 +	2 319	1 189	1 130	...	...	...	...	...	...
French Polynesia - Polynésie française									
1 I 1999 (ESDF)									
Total	227 525	117 738	109 787	...	...	...	...	...	...
0	4 268	2 177	2 091	...	...	...	...	...	...
1 - 4	18 470	9 604	8 866	...	...	...	...	...	...
5 - 9	25 518	13 178	12 340	...	...	...	...	...	...
10 - 14	25 533	13 055	12 478	...	...	...	...	...	...
15 - 19	22 126	11 290	10 836	...	...	...	...	...	...
20 - 24	19 077	9 884	9 193	...	...	...	...	...	...
25 - 29	19 574	10 141	9 433	...	...	...	...	...	...
30 - 34	19 667	10 179	9 488	...	...	...	...	...	...
35 - 39	17 032	8 941	8 091	...	...	...	...	...	...
40 - 44	14 421	7 640	6 781	...	...	...	...	...	...
45 - 49	11 037	5 830	5 207	...	...	...	...	...	...
50 - 54	9 001	4 790	4 211	...	...	...	...	...	...
55 - 59	7 202	3 845	3 357	...	...	...	...	...	...
60 - 64	5 518	2 899	2 619	...	...	...	...	...	...
65 - 69	3 998	2 042	1 956	...	...	...	...	...	...
70 - 74	2 600	1 244	1 356	...	...	...	...	...	...
75 - 79	1 365	585	780	...	...	...	...	...	...
80 +	1 118	414	704	...	...	...	...	...	...
Guam[12]									
1 IV 2000 (CDJC)									
Total	154 805	79 181	75 624	...	...	...	...	...	...
0	3 535	1 862	1 673	...	...	...	...	...	...
1 - 4	13 250	6 945	6 305	...	...	...	...	...	...
5 - 9	16 090	8 270	7 820	...	...	...	...	...	...
10 - 14	14 281	7 232	7 049	...	...	...	...	...	...
15 - 19	12 379	6 273	6 106	...	...	...	...	...	...
20 - 24	11 989	6 140	5 849	...	...	...	...	...	...
25 - 29	12 944	6 584	6 360	...	...	...	...	...	...
30 - 34	12 906	6 727	6 179	...	...	...	...	...	...
35 - 39	12 751	6 692	6 059	...	...	...	...	...	...
40 - 44	10 390	5 344	5 046	...	...	...	...	...	...
45 - 49	9 042	4 608	4 434	...	...	...	...	...	...
50 - 54	7 506	3 813	3 693	...	...	...	...	...	...
55 - 59	4 993	2 548	2 445	...	...	...	...	...	...
60 - 64	4 534	2 190	2 344	...	...	...	...	...	...

Continent, country or area, date, code and age (in years) Continent, pays ou zone, date, code et âge (en années)	Total			Urban - Urbaine			Rural - Rurale		
	Both sexes Les deux sexes	Male Masculin	Female Féminin	Both sexes Les deux sexes	Male Masculin	Female Féminin	Both sexes Les deux sexes	Male Masculin	Female Féminin
OCEANIA - OCÉANIE									
Guam[12]									
1 IV 2000 (CDJC)									
65 - 69	3 399	1 628	1 771	...	...	...	...	...	...
70 - 74	2 461	1 287	1 174	...	...	...	...	...	...
75 - 79	1 384	681	703	...	...	...	...	...	...
80 - 84	616	234	382	...	...	...	...	...	...
85 - 89	248	83	165	...	...	...	...	...	...
90 - 94	79	30	49	...	...	...	...	...	...
95 - 99	22	9	13	...	...	...	...	...	...
100 +	6	1	5	...	...	...	...	...	...
Kiribati									
7 XII 2005 (CDFC)									
Total	92 533	45 612	46 921	40 311	19 435	20 876	52 222	26 177	26 045
0 - 4	10 917	5 613	5 304	4 587	2 379	2 208	6 330	3 234	3 096
5 - 9	12 466	6 315	6 151	4 908	2 438	2 470	7 558	3 877	3 681
10 - 14	10 810	5 597	5 213	4 297	2 185	2 112	6 513	3 412	3 101
15 - 19	10 793	5 511	5 282	4 634	2 288	2 346	6 159	3 223	2 936
20 - 24	8 574	4 247	4 327	4 568	2 132	2 436	4 006	2 115	1 891
25 - 29	6 782	3 274	3 508	3 385	1 631	1 754	3 397	1 643	1 754
30 - 34	5 561	2 631	2 930	2 567	1 196	1 371	2 994	1 435	1 559
35 - 39	6 459	3 095	3 364	2 774	1 304	1 470	3 685	1 791	1 894
40 - 44	5 253	2 575	2 678	2 286	1 093	1 193	2 967	1 482	1 485
45 - 49	4 298	2 046	2 252	1 915	905	1 010	2 383	1 141	1 242
50 - 54	3 150	1 479	1 671	1 396	639	757	1 754	840	914
55 - 59	2 450	1 143	1 307	1 038	458	580	1 412	685	727
60 - 64	1 740	802	938	708	309	399	1 032	493	539
65 - 69	1 288	547	741	516	219	297	772	328	444
70 - 74	1 111	428	683	403	150	253	708	278	430
75 +	881	309	572	329	109	220	552	200	352
Marshall Islands - Îles Marshall									
1 VII 2006 (ESDF)									
Total	52 163	26 746	25 417	...	...	...	...	...	...
0 - 4	7 508	3 853	3 655	...	...	...	...	...	...
5 - 9	7 352	3 803	3 549	...	...	...	...	...	...
10 - 14	6 501	3 322	3 179	...	...	...	...	...	...
15 - 19	6 837	3 533	3 304	...	...	...	...	...	...
20 - 24	5 945	3 067	2 878	...	...	...	...	...	...
25 - 29	3 684	1 857	1 827	...	...	...	...	...	...
30 - 34	2 590	1 302	1 288	...	...	...	...	...	...
35 - 39	2 355	1 205	1 150	...	...	...	...	...	...
40 - 44	2 253	1 154	1 099	...	...	...	...	...	...
45 - 49	2 041	1 004	1 037	...	...	...	...	...	...
50 - 54	1 796	948	848	...	...	...	...	...	...
55 - 59	1 343	728	615	...	...	...	...	...	...
60 - 64	762	403	359	...	...	...	...	...	...
65 - 69	473	232	241	...	...	...	...	...	...
70 - 74	334	160	174	...	...	...	...	...	...
75 +	388	173	215	...	...	...	...	...	...
Micronesia, Federated States of - Micronésie, États Fédérés de La									
1 IV 2000 (CDJC)									
Total	107 008	54 191	52 817	...	...	...	...	...	...
0	2 906	1 528	1 378	...	...	...	...	...	...
1 - 4	11 877	6 051	5 826	...	...	...	...	...	...
5 - 9	14 169	7 310	6 859	...	...	...	...	...	...
10 - 14	14 220	7 481	6 739	...	...	...	...	...	...
15 - 19	13 237	6 754	6 483	...	...	...	...	...	...
20 - 24	9 525	4 886	4 639	...	...	...	...	...	...
25 - 29	7 603	3 695	3 908	...	...	...	...	...	...
30 - 34	6 489	3 124	3 365	...	...	...	...	...	...
35 - 39	6 015	2 994	3 021	...	...	...	...	...	...
40 - 44	5 559	2 801	2 758	...	...	...	...	...	...
45 - 49	4 647	2 393	2 254	...	...	...	...	...	...

Continent, country or area, date, code and age (in years) / Continent, pays ou zone, date, code et âge (en années)	Total			Urban - Urbaine			Rural - Rurale		
	Both sexes Les deux sexes	Male Masculin	Female Féminin	Both sexes Les deux sexes	Male Masculin	Female Féminin	Both sexes Les deux sexes	Male Masculin	Female Féminin
OCEANIA - OCÉANIE									
Micronesia, Federated States of - Micronésie, États Fédérés de La									
1 IV 2000 (CDJC)									
50 - 54	3 209	1 654	1 555	...	...	...	...	...	...
55 - 59	1 898	899	999	...	...	...	...	...	...
60 - 64	1 733	830	903	...	...	...	...	...	...
65 - 69	1 487	699	788	...	...	...	...	...	...
70 - 74	993	457	536	...	...	...	...	...	...
75 - 79	727	310	417	...	...	...	...	...	...
80 - 84	328	138	190	...	...	...	...	...	...
85 +	386	187	199	...	...	...	...	...	...
New Caledonia - Nouvelle-Calédonie									
1 I 2004 (ESDF)									
Total	221 958	112 716	109 242	...	...	...	...	...	...
0	4 067	2 105	1 962	...	...	...	...	...	...
1 - 4	17 225	8 761	8 464	...	...	...	...	...	...
5 - 9	21 083	10 821	10 262	...	...	...	...	...	...
10 - 14	21 016	10 924	10 002	...	...	...	...	...	...
15 - 19	19 551	10 040	9 511	...	...	...	...	...	...
20 - 24	18 594	9 255	9 339	...	...	...	...	...	...
25 - 29	18 367	8 862	9 505	...	...	...	...	...	...
30 - 34	17 999	9 236	8 763	...	...	...	...	...	...
35 - 39	16 479	8 464	8 015	...	...	...	...	...	...
40 - 44	14 964	7 604	7 360	...	...	...	...	...	...
45 - 49	12 255	6 221	6 034	...	...	...	...	...	...
50 - 54	10 517	5 523	4 994	...	...	...	...	...	...
55 - 59	9 394	5 105	4 289	...	...	...	...	...	...
60 - 64	7 220	3 717	3 503	...	...	...	...	...	...
65 - 69	5 226	2 605	2 621	...	...	...	...	...	...
70 - 74	3 788	1 768	2 020	...	...	...	...	...	...
75 - 79	2 441	1 053	1 388	...	...	...	...	...	...
80 +	1 772	652	1 120	...	...	...	...	...	...
New Zealand - Nouvelle-Zélande									
7 III 2006 (CDFC)									
Total	4 143 282	...	...	...	...	...	...	...	...
0 - 4	277 257	...	...	...	...	...	...	...	...
5 - 9	287 952	...	...	...	...	...	...	...	...
10 - 14	307 719	...	...	...	...	...	...	...	...
15 - 19	306 981	...	...	...	...	...	...	...	...
20 - 24	284 925	...	...	...	...	...	...	...	...
25 - 29	255 330	...	...	...	...	...	...	...	...
30 - 34	285 519	...	...	...	...	...	...	...	...
35 - 39	308 091	...	...	...	...	...	...	...	...
40 - 44	319 224	...	...	...	...	...	...	...	...
45 - 49	299 160	...	...	...	...	...	...	...	...
50 - 54	259 857	...	...	...	...	...	...	...	...
55 - 59	244 011	...	...	...	...	...	...	...	...
60 - 64	191 691	...	...	...	...	...	...	...	...
65 - 09	158 751	...	...	...	...	...	...	...	...
70 - 74	122 523	...	...	...	...	...	...	...	...
75 - 79	103 971	...	...	...	...	...	...	...	...
80 - 84	73 242	...	...	...	...	...	...	...	...
85 - 89	38 412	...	...	...	...	...	...	...	...
90 - 94	14 841	...	...	...	...	...	...	...	...
95 - 99	3 258	...	...	...	...	...	...	...	...
100 +	558	...	...	...	...	...	...	...	...
1 VII 2006 (ESDJ)									
Total	4 184 580[7]	2 048 340	2 136 260	3 604 440[7]	1 750 350	1 824 130	580 150[7]	297 980	282 140
0 - 4	286 000[7]	146 210	139 790	246 390[7]	126 030	120 370	39 610[7]	20 180	19 430
0	59 060[7]	30 150	28 910	...	...	...	...	...	...
1 - 4	226 940[7]	116 060	110 880	...	...	...	...	...	...
5 - 9	291 880[7]	149 230	142 650	247 050[7]	126 170	120 890	44 820[7]	23 060	21 760

7. Population by age, sex and urban/rural residence: latest available year, 1997 - 2006

Population selon l'âge, le sexe et la résidence, urbaine/rurale: dernière année disponible, 1997 - 2006 (continued - suite)

Continent, country or area, date, code and age (in years) / Continent, pays ou zone, date, code et âge (en années)	Total			Urban - Urbaine			Rural - Rurale		
	Both sexes Les deux sexes	Male Masculin	Female Féminin	Both sexes Les deux sexes	Male Masculin	Female Féminin	Both sexes Les deux sexes	Male Masculin	Female Féminin
OCEANIA - OCÉANIE									
New Zealand - Nouvelle-Zélande									
1 VII 2006 (ESDJ)									
10 - 14	310 430[7]	159 520	150 920	260 530[7]	133 610	126 920	49 910[7]	25 910	24 000
15 - 19	313 560[7]	159 400	154 160	273 210[7]	137 880	135 340	40 350[7]	21 530	18 820
20 - 24	291 180[7]	145 850	145 330	267 620[7]	132 880	134 740	23 570[7]	12 980	10 590
25 - 29	260 370[7]	126 770	133 600	235 270[7]	114 240	121 030	25 100[7]	12 530	12 570
30 - 34	286 010[7]	136 320	149 700	251 280[7]	119 430	131 850	34 730[7]	16 880	17 850
35 - 39	312 560[7]	149 140	163 430	269 030[7]	128 200	140 830	43 530[7]	20 940	22 600
40 - 44	322 490[7]	155 940	166 540	272 260[7]	131 200	141 060	50 230[7]	24 740	25 490
45 - 49	305 160[7]	149 120	156 040	254 900[7]	123 470	131 430	50 260[7]	25 640	24 610
50 - 54	263 650[7]	129 930	133 720	218 660[7]	106 580	112 070	44 990[7]	23 340	21 650
55 - 59	243 010[7]	120 080	122 930	201 070[7]	98 350	102 720	41 940[7]	21 730	20 210
60 - 64	186 660[7]	91 900	94 760	155 090[7]	75 170	79 920	31 570[7]	16 730	14 840
65 - 69	155 530[7]	75 620	79 910	131 320[7]	62 470	68 860	24 210[7]	13 150	11 050
70 - 74	120 170[7]	57 380	62 790	104 670[7]	48 800	55 870	15 500[7]	8 580	6 910
75 - 79	103 600[7]	47 570	56 030	93 090[7]	41 810	21 290	10 510[7]	5 760	4 750
80 - 84	74 180[7]	30 180	44 000	68 390[7]	27 290	41 100	5 790[7]	2 890	2 890
85 +	...	...	...	54 610[7]	16 770	37 840	3 530[7]	1 410	2 120
85 - 89	39 080[7]	13 160	25 920	...	...	...	...	...	...
90 +	19 060[7]	5 020	14 040	...	...	...	...	...	...
Niue - Nioué									
1 VII 2006 (ESDJ)									
Total	1 679	815	864	...	...	...	...	...	...
0 - 4	137	58	79	...	...	...	...	...	...
5 - 9	136	65	71	...	...	...	...	...	...
10 - 14	145	77	68	...	...	...	...	...	...
15 - 19	175	96	79	...	...	...	...	...	...
20 - 24	137	56	81	...	...	...	...	...	...
25 - 29	103	53	50	...	...	...	...	...	...
30 - 34	97	49	48	...	...	...	...	...	...
35 - 39	96	50	46	...	...	...	...	...	...
40 - 44	101	50	51	...	...	...	...	...	...
45 - 49	104	60	44	...	...	...	...	...	...
50 - 54	121	60	61	...	...	...	...	...	...
55 - 59	67	27	40	...	...	...	...	...	...
60 - 64	61	30	31	...	...	...	...	...	...
65 - 69	82	32	50	...	...	...	...	...	...
70 - 74	62	30	32	...	...	...	...	...	...
75 +	55	22	33	...	...	...	...	...	...
Norfolk Island - Île Norfolk									
8 VIII 2006 (CDFC)									
Total	2 523	1 218	1 305	...	...	...	...	...	...
0 - 4	116	60	56	...	...	...	...	...	...
5 - 9	127	67	60	...	...	...	...	...	...
10 - 14	116	58	58	...	...	...	...	...	...
15 - 19	78	34	44	...	...	...	...	...	...
20 - 24	64	22	42	...	...	...	...	...	...
25 - 29	96	48	48	...	...	...	...	...	...
30 - 34	140	70	70	...	...	...	...	...	...
35 - 39	156	78	78	...	...	...	...	...	...
40 - 44	170	86	84	...	...	...	...	...	...
45 - 49	194	95	99	...	...	...	...	...	...
50 - 54	212	95	117	...	...	...	...	...	...
55 - 59	255	126	129	...	...	...	...	...	...
60 - 64	222	109	113	...	...	...	...	...	...
65 - 69	184	81	103	...	...	...	...	...	...
70 +	377	182	195	...	...	...	...	...	...
Unknown - Inconnu	16	7	9	...	...	...	...	...	...

Continent, country or area, date, code and age (in years) / Continent, pays ou zone, date, code et âge (en années)	Total			Urban - Urbaine			Rural - Rurale		
	Both sexes Les deux sexes	Male Masculin	Female Féminin	Both sexes Les deux sexes	Male Masculin	Female Féminin	Both sexes Les deux sexes	Male Masculin	Female Féminin
OCEANIA - OCÉANIE									
Northern Mariana Islands - Îles Mariannes septentrionales[55]									
1 VII 2003 (ESDF)[56]									
Total	63 419	27 488	35 931	56 941	24 932	32 009	6 478	2 556	3 922
0 - 4	4 555	2 498	2 057	4 230	2 285	1 945	325	213	112
5 - 9	5 534	2 836	2 698	5 212	2 656	2 556	322	180	142
10 - 14	4 586	2 362	2 224	4 322	2 216	2 106	264	145	119
15 - 19	3 825	1 848	1 977	3 538	1 684	1 854	287	165	122
20 - 24	7 253	1 671	5 582	6 101	1 492	4 609	1 152	179	973
25 - 29	8 449	2 405	6 044	7 055	2 026	5 029	1 394	379	1 015
30 - 34	8 085	2 900	5 185	7 168	2 597	4 571	917	303	614
35 - 39	6 330	3 033	3 297	5 928	2 834	3 094	402	199	203
40 - 44	5 117	2 615	2 502	4 547	2 320	2 227	569	294	275
45 - 49	4 105	2 270	1 835	3 815	2 102	1 713	290	168	122
50 - 54	2 263	1 240	1 023	1 995	1 107	888	268	133	135
55 - 59	1 505	729	776	1 339	623	716	166	106	60
60 - 64	886	616	270	804	564	240	82	52	30
65 - 69	370	246	124	333	209	124	38	38	-
70 - 74	329	95	234	327	93	234	2	2	-
75 +	227	124	103	227	124	103	-	-	-
1 VII 2005 (ESDF)									
Total	65 927	30 712	35 215	...	...	...	...	...	...
0 - 4	5 335	2 775	2 560	...	...	...	...	...	...
5 - 9	5 244	2 961	2 283	...	...	...	...	...	...
10 - 14	5 621	3 034	2 587	...	...	...	...	...	...
15 - 19	4 971	2 235	2 736	...	...	...	...	...	...
20 - 24	6 260	1 634	4 626	...	...	...	...	...	...
25 - 29	6 238	1 837	4 401	...	...	...	...	...	...
30 - 34	6 576	2 860	3 716	...	...	...	...	...	...
35 - 39	6 562	3 177	3 385	...	...	...	...	...	...
40 - 44	6 000	3 140	2 860	...	...	...	...	...	...
45 - 49	5 148	2 763	2 385	...	...	...	...	...	...
50 - 54	3 207	1 837	1 370	...	...	...	...	...	...
55 - 59	2 124	1 131	993	...	...	...	...	...	...
60 - 64	1 174	583	591	...	...	...	...	...	...
65 - 69	662	413	249	...	...	...	...	...	...
70 - 74	308	142	166	...	...	...	...	...	...
75 +	498	190	308	...	...	...	...	...	...
Palau - Palaos									
1 IV 2005 (CDJC)									
Total	19 907	10 699	9 208	...	...	...	...	...	...
0 - 4	1 363	685	678	...	...	...	...	...	...
5 - 9	1 521	805	716	...	...	...	...	...	...
10 - 14	1 914	964	950	...	...	...	...	...	...
15 - 19	1 462	715	747	...	...	...	...	...	...
20 - 24	1 266	712	554	...	...	...	...	...	...
25 - 29	1 583	942	641	...	...	...	...	...	...
30 - 34	1 856	1 072	784	...	...	...	...	...	...
35 - 39	1 965	1 132	833	...	...	...	...	...	...
40 - 44	1 887	1 096	791	...	...	...	...	...	...
45 - 49	1 534	842	692	...	...	...	...	...	...
50 - 54	1 102	624	558	...	...	...	...	...	...
55 - 59	732	393	339	...	...	...	...	...	...
60 - 64	506	254	252	...	...	...	...	...	...
65 - 69	373	170	203	...	...	...	...	...	...
70 - 74	257	119	138	...	...	...	...	...	...
75 - 79	214	71	143	...	...	...	...	...	...
80 - 84	151	56	95	...	...	...	...	...	...
85 +	141	47	94	...	...	...	...	...	...
Papua New Guinea - Papouasie-Nouvelle-Guinée									
9 VII 2000 (CDFC)									
Total	5 190 786	2 691 744	2 499 042	686 301	372 453	313 848	4 504 485	2 319 291	2 185 194
0	125 718	65 539	60 179	16 930	8 991	7 939	108 788	56 548	52 240

Continent, country or area, date, code and age (in years) Continent, pays ou zone, date, code et âge (en années)	Total			Urban - Urbaine			Rural - Rurale		
	Both sexes Les deux sexes	Male Masculin	Female Féminin	Both sexes Les deux sexes	Male Masculin	Female Féminin	Both sexes Les deux sexes	Male Masculin	Female Féminin
OCEANIA - OCÉANIE									
Papua New Guinea - Papouasie-Nouvelle-Guinée									
9 VII 2000 (CDFC)									
1 - 4	600 962	312 237	288 725	71 219	37 178	34 041	529 743	275 059	254 684
5 - 9	727 370	381 339	346 031	86 078	45 216	40 862	641 292	336 123	305 169
10 - 14	620 874	330 965	289 909	75 022	39 374	35 648	545 852	291 591	254 261
15 - 19	554 481	293 277	261 204	78 912	41 679	37 233	475 569	251 598	223 971
20 - 24	474 801	239 863	234 938	79 915	43 166	36 749	394 886	196 697	198 189
25 - 29	448 414	219 680	228 734	70 866	37 802	33 064	377 548	181 878	195 670
30 - 34	384 260	191 662	192 598	57 156	30 983	26 173	327 104	160 679	166 425
35 - 39	330 337	166 656	163 681	48 585	26 512	22 073	281 752	140 144	141 608
40 - 44	252 368	128 910	123 458	36 195	20 956	15 239	216 173	107 954	108 219
45 - 49	198 757	104 867	93 890	25 337	15 595	9 742	173 420	89 272	84 148
50 - 54	151 013	79 899	71 114	16 428	10 414	6 014	134 585	69 485	65 100
55 - 59	108 708	59 308	49 400	9 692	6 131	3 561	99 016	53 177	45 839
60 - 64	89 503	48 530	40 973	6 723	4 247	2 476	82 780	44 283	38 497
65 - 69	57 221	31 351	25 870	3 641	2 141	1 500	53 580	29 210	24 370
70 - 74	35 134	19 657	15 477	1 930	1 105	825	33 204	18 552	14 652
75 - 79	16 864	9 782	7 082	880	498	382	15 984	9 284	6 700
80 - 84	8 669	5 041	3 628	489	295	194	8 180	4 746	3 434
85 - 89	3 315	1 984	1 331	176	99	77	3 139	1 885	1 254
90 +	2 017	1 197	820	127	71	56	1 890	1 126	764
Samoa									
5 XI 2001 (CDFC)									
Total	176 710	92 050	84 660	...	...	...	...	...	...
0 - 4	26 028	13 631	12 397	...	...	...	...	...	...
5 - 9	24 917	13 024	11 893	...	...	...	...	...	...
10 - 14	20 985	10 948	10 037	...	...	...	...	...	...
15 - 19	17 608	9 488	8 120	...	...	...	...	...	...
20 - 24	14 281	7 549	6 732	...	...	...	...	...	...
25 - 29	13 197	6 910	6 287	...	...	...	...	...	...
30 - 34	12 258	6 545	5 713	...	...	...	...	...	...
35 - 39	10 385	5 378	5 007	...	...	...	...	...	...
40 - 44	8 855	4 628	4 227	...	...	...	...	...	...
45 - 49	6 833	3 538	3 295	...	...	...	...	...	...
50 - 54	5 081	2 538	2 543	...	...	...	...	...	...
55 - 59	4 417	2 217	2 200	...	...	...	...	...	...
60 - 64	3 659	1 835	1 824	...	...	...	...	...	...
65 - 69	2 975	1 452	1 523	...	...	...	...	...	...
70 - 74	2 272	1 036	1 236	...	...	...	...	...	...
75 - 79	1 639	731	908	...	...	...	...	...	...
80 - 84	680	312	368	...	...	...	...	...	...
85 - 89	240	80	160	...	...	...	...	...	...
90 - 94	64	18	46	...	...	...	...	...	...
95 - 99	27	5	22	...	...	...	...	...	...
100 +	6	1	5	...	...	...	...	...	...
Unknown - Inconnu	303	186	117	...	...	...	...	...	...
Tokelau - Tokélaou									
19 X 2006 (CDFC)									
Total	1 151	583	568	...	...	...	...	...	...
0 - 4	123	63	60	...	...	...	...	...	...
5 - 9	143	66	77	...	...	...	...	...	...
10 - 14	155	86	69	...	...	...	...	...	...
15 - 19	115	69	46	...	...	...	...	...	...
20 - 24	66	31	35	...	...	...	...	...	...
25 - 29	52	30	22	...	...	...	...	...	...
30 - 34	65	29	36	...	...	...	...	...	...
35 - 39	72	36	36	...	...	...	...	...	...
40 - 44	69	34	35	...	...	...	...	...	...
45 - 49	67	31	36	...	...	...	...	...	...
50 - 54	48	26	22	...	...	...	...	...	...
55 - 59	46	21	25	...	...	...	...	...	...
60 - 64	36	22	14	...	...	...	...	...	...
65 - 69	33	12	21	...	...	...	...	...	...

7. Population by age, sex and urban/rural residence: latest available year, 1997 - 2006
Population selon l'âge, le sexe et la résidence, urbaine/rurale: dernière année disponible, 1997 - 2006 (continued - suite)

Continent, country or area, date, code and age (in years) Continent, pays ou zone, date, code et âge (en années)	Total			Urban - Urbaine			Rural - Rurale		
	Both sexes Les deux sexes	Male Masculin	Female Féminin	Both sexes Les deux sexes	Male Masculin	Female Féminin	Both sexes Les deux sexes	Male Masculin	Female Féminin
OCEANIA - OCÉANIE									
Tokelau - Tokélaou									
19 X 2006 (CDFC)									
70 - 74	23	10	13	...	...	...	...	...	...
75 +	38	17	21	...	...	...	...	...	...
Tonga									
31 XII 2002 (ESDF)									
Total	101 002	51 473	49 528	...	...	...	...	...	...
0 - 4	12 179	6 295	5 884	...	...	...	...	...	...
5 - 9	12 686	6 577	6 109	...	...	...	...	...	...
10 - 14	11 795	6 303	5 492	...	...	...	...	...	...
15 - 19	11 980	6 241	5 739	...	...	...	...	...	...
20 - 24	9 942	5 111	4 831	...	...	...	...	...	...
25 - 29	7 057	3 564	3 493	...	...	...	...	...	...
30 - 34	6 284	3 207	3 077	...	...	...	...	...	...
35 - 39	5 382	2 723	2 659	...	...	...	...	...	...
40 - 44	4 541	2 186	2 355	...	...	...	...	...	...
45 - 49	4 029	1 908	2 121	...	...	...	...	...	...
50 - 54	3 397	1 572	1 825	...	...	...	...	...	...
55 - 59	3 105	1 467	1 638	...	...	...	...	...	...
60 - 64	2 775	1 393	1 382	...	...	...	...	...	...
65 - 69	2 277	1 167	1 110	...	...	...	...	...	...
70 - 74	1 668	840	828	...	...	...	...	...	...
75 +	1 904	919	985	...	...	...	...	...	...
Tuvalu									
1 XI 2002 (CDFC)									
Total	9 561	4 729	4 832	...	...	...	...	...	...
0	182	92	90	...	...	...	...	...	...
1 - 4	996	528	468	...	...	...	...	...	...
5 - 9	1 201	612	589	...	...	...	...	...	...
10 - 14	1 079	591	488	...	...	...	...	...	...
15 - 19	826	474	352	...	...	...	...	...	...
20 - 24	682	326	356	...	...	...	...	...	...
25 - 29	523	245	278	...	...	...	...	...	...
30 - 34	545	278	267	...	...	...	...	...	...
35 - 39	684	331	353	...	...	...	...	...	...
40 - 44	697	310	387	...	...	...	...	...	...
45 - 49	580	261	319	...	...	...	...	...	...
50 - 54	467	199	268	...	...	...	...	...	...
55 - 59	276	129	147	...	...	...	...	...	...
60 - 64	280	131	149	...	...	...	...	...	...
65 - 69	207	84	123	...	...	...	...	...	...
70 - 74	167	75	92	...	...	...	...	...	...
75 - 79	101	40	61	...	...	...	...	...	...
80 - 84	56	20	36	...	...	...	...	...	...
85 - 89	10	1	9	...	...	...	...	...	...
90 +	2	2	-	...	...	...	...	...	...
Vanuatu[57]									
1 VII 2004 (ESDF)									
Total	215 541	110 141	105 399	...	...	...	...	...	...
0 - 4	33 815	17 435	16 380	...	...	...	...	...	...
5 - 9	27 846	14 474	13 372	...	...	...	...	...	...
10 - 14	27 125	14 025	13 100	...	...	...	...	...	...
15 - 19	23 437	12 132	11 305	...	...	...	...	...	...
20 - 24	18 951	9 684	9 267	...	...	...	...	...	...
25 - 29	16 235	8 027	8 207	...	...	...	...	...	...
30 - 34	14 670	7 175	7 494	...	...	...	...	...	...
35 - 39	12 560	6 214	6 346	...	...	...	...	...	...
40 - 44	10 429	5 221	5 208	...	...	...	...	...	...
45 - 49	8 303	4 221	4 082	...	...	...	...	...	...
50 - 54	6 476	3 333	3 143	...	...	...	...	...	...
55 - 59	5 083	2 632	2 452	...	...	...	...	...	...
60 - 64	3 824	1 996	1 828	...	...	...	...	...	...
65 - 69	2 714	1 417	1 296	...	...	...	...	...	...
70 - 74	1 810	957	854	...	...	...	...	...	...
75 +	2 265	1 198	1 066	...	...	...	...	...	...

FOOTNOTES - NOTES

Italics: estimates which are less reliable. - Italiques: estimations moins sûres.

'Code' indicates the source of data, as follows:
CDFC - Census,de facato, complete tabulation
CDFS - Census, de facto, sample tabulation
CDJC - Census, de jure, complete tabulation
CDJS - Census, de jure, sample tabulation
SSDF - Sample survey, de facto
SSDJ - Sample survey, de jure
ESDF - Estimates, de facto
ESDJ - Estimates, de jure

Le 'Code' indique la source des données, comme suit:
CDFC - Recensement, population de fait, tabulation complète
CDFS - Recensement, population de fait, tabulation par sondage
CDJC - Recensement, population de droit, tabulation complète
CDJS - Recensement, population de droit, tabulation par sondage
SSDF - Enquête par sondage, population de fait
SSDJ - Enquête par sondage, population de droit
ESDF - Estimations, population de fait
ESDJ - Estimations, population de droit

[1] Unrevised data. - Les données n'ont pas été révisées.

[2] Data as reported by national statistical authorities. Figures for urban and rural do not add up to the total. - Données comme déclarées par les autorités statistiques nationales. Les données pour la population urbaine et la population rurale ne s'ajoutent pas au total.

[3] Data refer to national projections. - Les données se réfèrent aux projections nationales.

[4] The number of males and/or females excludes persons whose sex is not stated (18 urban, 19 rural). - Il n'est pas tenu compte dans le nombre d'hommes et de femmes des personnes dont le sexe n'est pas indiqué (18 en zone urbaine et 19 en zone rurale).

[5] Data refer to national projections. Unrevised data. - Les données se réfèrent aux projections nationales. Les données n'ont pas été révisées.

[6] Data refer to national projections. Data as reported by national statistical authorities. - Les données se réfèrent aux projections nationales. Les données comme elles ont été déclarées par l'institut national de la statistique.

[7] Because of rounding, totals are not in all cases the sum of the parts. - Les chiffres étant arrondis, les totaux ne correspondent pas toujours rigoureusement à la somme des chiffres partiels.

[8] Total population excludes persons who were not contacted at the time of the census. - La population non comprend pas les personnes qui n'ont pas été contactées à l'heure du recensement.

[9] Includes race not stated and Bermudian status not stated. - Comprend les personnes de race non déclarée et dont le statut de ressortissant bermudien n'est pas déclaré.

[10] Data as reported by national statistical authorities. Summation of frequencies gives a different total; reason for discrepancy not ascertained. Population statistics are compiled from registers. - Les données comme elles ont été déclarées par l'institut national de la statistique. La somme des fréquences un total différent; on ne sait pas comment s'explique la divergence. Les statistiques de la population sont compilées à partir des registres.

[11] Reason for discrepancy between these figures and corresponding figures shown elsewhere not ascertained. - On ne sait pas comment s'explique la divergence entre ces chiffres et les chiffres correspondants indiqués ailleurs.

[12] Including armed forces stationed in the area. - Y compris les militaires en garnison sur le territoire.

[13] Excluding adjustment for underenumeration. Excluding persons residing in institutions. - Les données n'ont pas été ajustées pour compenser les lacunes du dénombrement. Non compris les personnes dans les institutions.

[14] Excluding armed forces overseas and civilian citizens absent from country for an extended period of time. - Non compris les militaires à l'étranger, et les civils hors du pays pendant une période prolongée.

[15] Data include persons in remote areas, military personnel outside the country, merchant seamen at sea, civilian seasonal workers outside the country, and other civilians outside the country, and exclude nomads, foreign military, civilian aliens temporarily in the country, transients on ships and Indian jungle population. - Y compris les personnes vivant dans des régions éloignées, le personel militaire en dehors du pays, les marins marchands, les ouvriers saisonniers en dehors du pays, et autres civils en dehors du pays, et non compris les nomades, les militaires étrangers, les étrangers civils temporairement dans le pays, les transiteurs sur des bateaux et les Indiens de la jungle.

[16] Excluding nomadic Indian tribes. - Non compris les tribus d'Indiens nomades.

[17] A dispute exists between the governments of Argentina and the United Kingdom of Great Britain and Northern Ireland concerning sovereignty over the Falkland Islands (Malvinas). - La souveraineté sur les îles Falkland (Malvinas) fait l'objet d'un différend entre le Gouvernement argentin et le Gouvernement du Royaume-Uni de Grande-Bretagne et d'Irlande du Nord.

[18] Mid-year estimates have been adjusted for underenumeration, at latest census. - Les estimations au millieu de l'année tiennent compte d'un ajustement destiné à compenser les lacunes du dénombrement lors du dernier recensement.

[19] Totals may not add up because cases with age unknown and/or sex unknown have been prorated. - Les totaux peuvent ne pas tomber juste du fait que l'on a calculé au prorata les cas pour lesquels l'âge ou le sexe n'était pas connu.

[20] The districts of Paramaribo and Wanica are considered urban areas, whereas the rest of the districts are considered more or less rural districts (areas). - Les districts de Paramaribo et de Wanica sont considérés comme des zones urbaines, les autres districts étant considérés comme des zones rurales à divers degrés.

[21] The unknown age and sex is proportionately distributed over all age groups and both sexes. - La population d'âge ou de sexe inconnu est répartie proportionnellement dans tous les groupes d'âge et dans chaque sexe.

[22] Excluding Indian jungle population. - Non compris les Indiens de la jungle.

[23] Based on Cambodia Intercensal Population Survey. Data exclude institutional, homeless households and transient poulation. - Les données ne comprennent pas la population des institutions, les ménages sans abri et la population de passage.

[24] For statistical purposes, the data for China do not include those for the Hong Kong Special Administrative Region (Hong Kong SAR), Macao Special Administrative Region (Macao SAR) and Taiwan province of China. - Pour la présentation des statistiques, les données pour la Chine ne comprennent pas la Région Administrative Spéciale de Hong Kong (Hong Kong RAS), la Région Administrative Spéciale de Macao (Macao RAS) et Taïwan province de Chine.

[25] Data refer to government controlled areas. - Les données se rapportent aux zones contrôlées par le Gouvernement.

[26] Including data for the Indian-held part of Jammu and Kashmir, the final status of which has not yet been determined. Data exclude Mao-Maram, Paomata and Purul sub-divisions of Senapati district of Manipur. The population of Manipur including the estimated population of the three sub-divisions of Senapati district is 2,291,125 (Males 1,161,173 and females 1,129,952). - Y compris les données pour la partie du Jammu et du Cachemire occupée par l'Inde dont le statut définitif n'a pas encore été déterminé. Non compris les subdivisions Mao-Maram Paomata et Purul du district de Senapati dans l'État du Manipur. Cet État compte 2 291 125 habitants (1 161 173 hommes et 1 129 952 femmes), y compris la population estimative des trois subdivisions du district de Senapati.

[27] Intercensal Population Survey. - Étude démographique entre deux recensements.

[28] Data relate to the population for the Iranian Year 1384 (21 March 2005-20 March 2006). - Les données concernent la population pour l'année iranienne 1384 (21 mars 2005-20 mars 2006).

[29] Including data for East Jerusalem and Israeli residents in certain other territories under occupation by Israeli military forces since June 1967. Because of rounding, totals are not in all cases the sum of the parts. - Y compris les données pour Jérusalem-Est et les résidents israéliens dans certains autres territoires occupés depuis 1967 par les forces armées israéliennes. Les chiffres étant arrondis, les totaux ne correspondent pas toujours rigoureusement à la somme des chiffres partiels.

[30] Excluding residents who had been registered in the Israeli localities (the Jewish localities) in the Gaza Area and northern Samaria, which were evacuated in August 2005, but did not notify the Ministry of Interior of their new address. These residents are included in total. - Hors résidents enregistrés dans les localités d'Israel (localités juives) et du nord de la Bande de Gaza (verfify) et du nord de la Samarie, qui ont été évacués en Août 2005, mais qui n'ont pas notifié leur nouvelle adresse au ministère de l'intérieur. Ces résidents sont inclus dans le total.

[31] Because of rounding, totals are not in all cases the sum of the parts. Excluding diplomatic personnel outside the country and foreign military and civilian personnel and their dependants stationed in the area. - Les chiffres étant arrondis, les totaux ne correspondent pas toujours rigoureusement à la somme des chiffres partiels. Non compris le personnel diplomatique hors du pays ni les militaires et agents civils étrangers en poste sur le territoire et les membres de leur famille les accompagnant.

[32] Excluding data for Jordanian territory under occupation since June 1967 by Israeli military forces. Excluding foreigners, including registered Palestinian refugees. - Non compris les données pour le territoire jordanien occupé depuis juin 1967 par les forces armées israéliennes. Non compris les étrangers, mais y compris les réfugiés de Palestine enregistrés.

[33] Excluding foreigners. - Non compris étrangers.

Data refer to constant population as reported by national statistical authorities, meaning that it does not include migrant population. - Les données se rapportent à la population constante déclarée par les autorités statistiques nationales; la population migrante n'est donc pas comprise.

35 Data based on the results of the 2005 Population and Housing Census. Because of rounding, totals are not in all cases the sum of the parts. - Données fondées sur les résultats du recensement de la population et de l'habitat de 2005. Les chiffres étant arrondis, les totaux ne correspondent pas toujours rigoureusement à la somme des chiffres partiels.

36 Excluding Malaysian citizens and permanent residents who were away or intended to be away from the country for more than six months. Excluding Malaysian military, naval and diplomatic personnel and their families outside the country, and tourists, businessman who intended to be in Malaysia for less than six months. Census results have been adjusted for underenumeration. - Non compris les citoyens malaisiens et les résidents permanents qui étaient ou qui ont prévu d'être hors du pays pour six mois ou plus. Non compris le personnel militaire Malaisien, le personnel naval ou diplomatique et leurs familles hors du pays, et les touristes et les hommes d'affaires qui avaient l'intention de rester en Malaisie moins de six mois. Les résultats du recensement ont été ajustées pour compenser les lacunes du dénombrement

37 Total Population is taken as de facto and de jure together. - Population totale considérée comme de fait et de droit.

38 Data based on Pakistan Demographic Survey 2003. These estimates do not reflect completely accurately the actual population and vital events of the country. Excluding data for the Pakistan-held part of Jammu and Kashmir, the final status of which has not yet been determined. - D'après les résultats de Pakistan démographique par sondage 2003. Ces estimations ne dénotent pas d'une manière complètement ponctuelle la population actuelle et les statistiques de l'état civil du pays. Non compris les données concernant la partie du Jammu et Cachemiro occupée par le Pakistan dont le statut définitif n'a pas été déterminé.

39 Including Palestinian refugees. - Y compris les réfugiés de Palestine.

40 Also included in Finland. - Comprise aussi dans Finlande.

41 Population statistics are compiled from registers. - Les statistiques de la population sont compilées à partir des registres.

42 Population statistics are compiled from registers. Excluding Faeroe Islands and Greenland shown separately, if available. - Les statistiques de la population sont compilées à partir des registres. Non compris les Îles Féroé et le Gröenland, qui font l'objet de rubriques distinctes, si disponible.

43 Including Aland Islands. - Y compris les Îles d'Åland.

44 Excluding Overseas Departments, namely, French Guiana, Guadeloupe, Martinique and Reunion, shown separately, if available. Excluding diplomatic personnel outside the country and including members of alien armed forces not living in military camps and foreign diplomatic personnel not living in embassies or consulates. - Non compris les départements d'outre mer, c'est-à-dire la Guyane française, la Guadeloupe, la Martinique et la Réunion, qui font l'objet de rubriques distinctes, si disponible. Non compris le personnel diplomatique hors du pays et y compris les militaires étrangers ne vivant pas dans des camps militaires et le personnel diplomatique étranger ne vivant pas dans les ambassades ou les consulats.

45 Excluding families of military personnel, visitors and transients. - Non compris les familles des militaires, ni les visiteurs et transients.

46 Excluding armed forces stationed outside the country, but including alien armed forces stationed in the area. - Non compris les militaires en garnison hors du pays, mais y compris les militaires étrangers en garnison sur le territoire.

47 According to the administrative division on 1 January 2006. - D'après la division en circonscriptions administratives au 1er janvier 2006.

48 Data do not include information for Transnistria and the municipality of Bender. - Les données ne tiennent pas compte de l'information sur la Transnistria et la municipalité de Bender.

49 Excluding Svalbard and Jan Mayen Island shown separately, if available. - Non compris Svalbard et Jan Mayen qui font l'objet de rubriques distinctes, si disponible.

50 Including residents temporarily outside the country. - Y compris les résidents se trouvant temporairement hors du pays.

51 Without data for Kosovo and Metohia. - Sans les données pour le Kosovo and Metohie.

52 Excluding citizens temporarily residing abroad, the sum by urban and rural does not add up to the total. - Les nationaux se trouvant provisoirement à l'étranger ne sont pas pris en compte. La somme des chiffres disponibles pour les zones urbaines et rurales ne correspond donc pas au total.

53 Excluding Channel Islands and Isle of Man, shown separately, if available. - Non compris les îles Anglo-Normandes et l'île de Man, qui font l'objet de rubriques distinctes, si disponible.

54 Excluding Niue, shown separately, which is part of Cook Islands, but because of remoteness is administered separately. - Non compris Nioué, qui fait l'objet d'une rubrique distincte et qui fait partie des îles Cook, mais qui, en raison de son éloignement, est administrée séparément.

55 Data refer to Saipan only. - Saipan seulement.

56 Based on results of a sample survey. - D'après les résultats d'une enquête par sondage.

57 Figures for male and female do not add up to the total, reason for discrepancy not ascertained. Data refer to national projections. - La some des données pour la population masculine et pour la population féminine n'est pas égale au total, les raisons de cette différence ne sont pas expliquées. Les données se réfèrent aux projections nationales.

Table 8

Table 8 presents population of capital cities and cities of 100 000 or more inhabitants for the latest available year from 1987 - 2006.

Description of variables: Since the way in which cities are delimited differs from one country or area to another, the table not only presents data for the so-called city proper, but also for the urban agglomeration, if available.

City proper is defined as a locality with legally fixed boundaries and an administratively recognized urban status, usually characterized by some form of local government.

Urban agglomeration has been defined as comprising the city or town proper and also the suburban fringe or densely settled territory lying outside of, but adjacent to, the city boundaries.

For some countries or areas, however, the data relate to entire administrative divisions known, for example, as shi or municipalities (municipios) which are composed of a populated centre and adjoining territory, some of which may contain other, often separate urban localities or may be distinctively rural in character. For this group of countries or areas the type of civil division is given in a footnote.

The surface area of the city or urban agglomeration is presented, when available.

City names are presented in the original language of the country or area in which the cities are located. In cases where the original names are not in the Roman alphabet, they have been Romanized. Cities are listed in English alphabetical order.

Capital cities are shown in the table regardless of their population size. The names of the capital cities are printed in capital letters. The designation of any specific city as a capital city is as reported by the country or area.

The table also covers cities whose urban agglomeration's population exceeds 100 000; that is, while the urban agglomeration should have a population of 100 000 or more to be included in the table, the city proper may be of a smaller population size.

The reference date of each population figure appears in the stub of the table. Estimates based on results of sample surveys and city censuses as well as those derived from other sources are noted in the "code" column.

Reliability of data: Specific information is generally not available on the reliability of the estimates of the population of cities or urban agglomerations presented in this table.

In the absence of such quality assessment, data from population censuses, sample surveys and city censuses are considered to be reliable and, therefore, set in roman type. Other estimates are considered to be reliable if they are based on a complete census (or a sample survey), and have been adjusted by a continuous population register or adjusted on the basis of the calculated balance of births, deaths, and migration.

Limitations: Statistics on the population of capital cities and cities of 100 000 or more inhabitants are subject to the same qualifications as have been set forth for population statistics in general as discussed in section 3 of the Technical Notes.

International comparability of data on city population is limited to a great extent by variations in national concepts and definitions. Although an effort is made to reduce the sources of non-comparability somewhat by presenting the data for both city proper and urban agglomeration, many serious problems of comparability remain.

Data presented in the "city proper" column for some countries represent an urban administrative area legally distinguished from surrounding rural territory, while for other countries these data represent a commune or an equally small administrative unit. In still other countries, the administrative units may be relatively extensive and thereby include considerable territories beyond the urban centre itself.

City data are also especially affected by whether the data refer to *de facto* or *de jure* population, as well as variations among countries in how each of these concepts is applied. With reference to the total population, the difference between the *de facto* and *de jure* population is discussed at length in section 3.1.1 of the Technical Notes.

Data on city populations based on intercensal estimates present additional problems: comparability is impaired by the different methods used in making the estimates and by the loss of precision in applying to selected segments of the population, methods best suited for the whole population. For example, it is far more difficult to apply the component method of estimating population growth to cities than it is to the entire country.

Births and deaths occurring in the cities do not all originate in the population present in or resident of that area. Therefore, the use of natural increase to estimate the probable size of the city population is a potential source of error. Internal migration is another component of population change that cannot be measured with accuracy in many areas. Because of these factors, estimates in this table may be less valuable in general and in particular limited for purposes of international comparison.

City data, even when set in roman type, are often not as reliable as estimates for the total population of the country or area. Furthermore, because the sources of these data include censuses (national or city), surveys and estimates, the years to which they refer vary widely. In addition, because city boundaries may alter over time, comparisons covering different years should be carried out with caution.

Earlier data: Population of capital cities and cities with a population of 100 000 or more have been shown in previous issues of the *Demographic Yearbook*. For more information on specific topics and years for which data are reported, readers should consult the Historical Index.

Tableau 8

Le tableau 8 présente les données les plus récentes (1987 - 2006) dont on dispose sur la population des capitales et des villes de 100 000 habitants ou plus.

Description des variables : étant donné que les villes ne sont pas délimitées de la même manière dans tous les pays ou zones, on s'est efforcé de donner, dans ce tableau, des chiffres correspondant non seulement aux villes proprement dites, mais aussi, le cas échéant, aux agglomérations urbaines.

On entend par villes proprement dites les localités qui ont des limites juridiquement définies et sont administrativement considérées comme villes, ce qui se caractérise généralement par l'existence d'une autorité locale.

L'agglomération urbaine comprend, par définition, la ville proprement dite ainsi que la proche banlieue, c'est-à-dire la zone fortement peuplée qui est extérieure, mais contiguë aux limites de la ville.

En outre, dans certains pays ou zones, les données se rapportent à des divisions administratives entières, connues par exemple sous le nom de shi ou de municipios, qui comportent une agglomération et le territoire avoisinant, lequel peut englober d'autres agglomérations urbaines tout à fait distinctes ou être à caractère essentiellement rural. Pour ce groupe de pays ou zones, le type de division administrative est indiqué en note.

On trouvera à la fin du tableau la superficie de la ville ou agglomération urbaine chaque fois que possible.

Les noms des villes sont indiqués dans la langue du pays ou zone où ces villes sont situées. Les noms de villes qui ne sont pas à l'origine libellés en caractères latins ont été romanisés. Les villes sont énumérées dans l'ordre alphabétique anglais.

Les capitales figurent dans le tableau quel que soit le chiffre de leur population et leur nom a été imprimé en lettres majuscules. Ne sont indiquées comme capitales que les villes ainsi désignées par le pays ou zone intéressé.

En ce qui concerne les autres villes, le tableau indique celles dont la population est égale ou supérieure à 100 000 habitants. Ce chiffre limite s'applique à l'agglomération urbaine et non à la ville proprement dite, dont la population peut être moindre.

L'année à laquelle se réfère le chiffre correspondant à chaque population figure dans la colonne de gauche du tableau. La colonne « Code » permet de savoir si les estimations sont fondées sur les résultats d'enquêtes par sondage ou de recensements municipaux ou sont tirées d'autres sources.

Fiabilité des données : on ne possède généralement pas de renseignements précis sur la fiabilité des estimations de la population des villes ou agglomérations urbaines présentées dans ce tableau.

Les données provenant de recensements de la population, d'enquêtes par sondage ou de recensements municipaux sont jugées sûres et figurent par conséquent en caractères romains. D'autres estimations sont considérées comme sûres si elles sont fondées sur un recensement complet (ou une enquête par sondage) et ont été ajustées en fonction des données provenant d'un registre permanent de population ou en fonction de la balance, établie par le calcul des naissances, des décès et des migrations.

Insuffisance des données : les statistiques portant sur la population des capitales et des villes de 100 000 habitants ou plus appellent toutes les réserves qui ont été formulées à la section 3 des Notes techniques à propos des statistiques de la population en général.

La comparabilité internationale des données portant sur la population des villes est compromise dans une large mesure par la diversité des définitions nationales. Bien que l'on se soit efforcé de réduire les facteurs de non-comparabilité en présentant à la fois dans le tableau les données relatives aux villes proprement dites et celles concernant les agglomérations urbaines, de graves problèmes de comparabilité n'en subsistent pas moins.

Pour certains pays, les données figurant dans la colonne intitulée « Ville proprement dite » correspondent à une zone administrative urbaine juridiquement distincte du territoire rural environnant,

242

tandis que pour d'autres pays ces données correspondent à une commune ou petite unité administrative analogue. Pour d'autres encore, les unités administratives en cause peuvent être relativement étendues et englober par conséquent un vaste territoire au-delà du centre urbain lui-même.

L'emploi de données se rapportant tantôt à la population de fait, tantôt à la population de droit, ainsi que les différences de traitement de ces deux notions d'un pays à l'autre influent particulièrement sur les statistiques urbaines. En ce qui concerne la population totale, la différence entre population de fait et population de droit est expliquée en détail à la section 3.1.1 des Notes techniques.

Les statistiques relatives à la population urbaine qui sont fondées sur des estimations intercensitaires posent encore plus de problèmes que les données issues de recensement. Leur comparabilité est compromise par la diversité des méthodes employées pour établir les estimations et par l'imprécision qui résulte de l'application de certaines méthodes à telles ou telles composantes de la population alors qu'elles sont conçues pour être appliquées à l'ensemble de la population. La méthode des composantes, par exemple, est beaucoup plus difficile à appliquer en vue de l'estimation de l'accroissement de la population lorsqu'il s'agit de villes que lorsqu'il s'agit d'un pays tout entier.

Les naissances et décès qui surviennent dans les villes ne correspondent pas tous à la population présente ou résidente. En conséquence, des erreurs peuvent se produire si l'on établit pour les villes des estimations fondées sur l'accroissement naturel de la population. Les migrations intérieures constituent un second élément d'estimation que, dans bien des régions, on ne peut pas toujours mesurer avec exactitude. Pour ces raisons, les estimations présentées dans ce tableau risquent dans l'ensemble d'être peu fiables et leur valeur est particulièrement limitée du point de vue des comparaisons internationales.

Même lorsqu'elles figurent en caractères romains, il arrive souvent que les statistiques urbaines ne soient pas aussi fiables que les estimations concernant la population totale de la zone ou du pays considéré. De surcroît, comme ces statistiques proviennent aussi bien de recensements (nationaux ou municipaux) que d'enquêtes ou d'estimations, les années auxquelles elles se rapportent sont extrêmement variables. Enfin, comme les limites urbaines varient parfois d'une époque à une autre, il y a lieu d'être prudent lorsque l'on compare des données se rapportant à des années différentes.

Données publiées antérieurement : des statistiques concernant la population des capitales et des villes de 100 000 habitants ou plus ont été présentées dans des éditions antérieures de l'*Annuaire démographique*. Pour plus de précisions concernant les années et les sujets pour lesquels des données ont été publiées, se reporter à l'index.

8. Population of capital cities and cities of 100 000 or more inhabitants: latest available year, 1987 - 2006
Population des capitales et des villes de 100 000 habitants ou plus: dernière année disponible, 1987 - 2006

Continent, country or area, date and city / Continent, pays ou zone, date et ville	Code[1]	City proper — Ville proprement dite Population				Urban agglomeration — Agglomération urbaine Population			
		Both sexes Les deux sexes	Male Masculin	Female Féminin	Surface area Superficie (km²)	Both sexes Les deux sexes	Male Masculin	Female Féminin	Surface area Superficie (km²)
AFRICA — AFRIQUE									
Algeria — Algérie									
25 VI 1998									
ALGER (EL DJAZAIR)	CDJC	1 569 897	...	...	...	...	...	...	...
Annaba	CDJC	352 523	...	...	...	...	...	...	...
Batna	CDJC	246 800	...	...	...	...	...	...	...
Béchar	CDJC	134 523	...	...	...	...	...	...	...
Bejaïa	CDJC	144 405	...	...	...	...	...	...	...
Biskra	CDJC	177 060	...	...	...	...	...	...	...
Blida (El Boulaïda)	CDJC	229 788	...	...	...	...	...	...	...
Bordj Bou Arreridj	CDJC	129 004	...	...	...	...	...	...	...
Bordj el Kiffan	CDJC	103 690	...	...	...	...	...	...	...
Chlef (Ech Cheliff)	CDJC	174 314	...	...	...	...	...	...	...
Constantine (Qacentina)	CDJC	465 021	...	...	...	...	...	...	...
El Djelfa	CDJC	158 679	...	...	...	...	...	...	...
El Eulma	CDJC	104 758	...	...	...	...	...	...	...
El Oued (El Wad)	CDJC	105 151	...	...	...	...	...	...	...
Ghardaïa	CDJC	127 959	...	...	...	...	...	...	...
Guelma	CDJC	108 682	...	...	...	...	...	...	...
Jijel	CDJC	106 306	...	...	...	...	...	...	...
Medea (Lemdiyya)	CDJC	128 427	...	...	...	...	...	...	...
Mostaganem	CDJC	125 911	...	...	...	...	...	...	...
M'Sila	CDJC	102 514	...	...	...	...	...	...	...
Oran (Wahran)	CDJC	705 335	...	...	...	...	...	...	...
Ouargla (Wargla)	CDJC	139 381	...	...	...	...	...	...	...
Relizane	CDJC	104 644	...	...	...	...	...	...	...
Saïda	CDJC	113 533	...	...	...	...	...	...	...
Sétif (Stif)	CDJC	214 842	...	...	...	...	...	...	...
Sidi-bel-Abbès	CDJC	183 931	...	...	...	...	...	...	...
Skikda	CDJC	153 531	...	...	...	...	...	...	...
Souk Ahras	CDJC	114 512	...	...	...	...	...	...	...
Tebessa	CDJC	154 335	...	...	...	...	...	...	...
Tiaert	CDJC	148 850	...	...	...	...	...	...	...
Tlemcen (Tilimsen)	CDJC	156 258	...	...	...	...	...	...	...
Tougourt	CDJC	114 183	...	...	...	...	...	...	...
Angola									
1 VII 1993									
Huambo	ESDF	...	...	...	...	400 000	...	...	...
LUANDA	ESDF	...	...	...	...	1 822 407	855 676	936 731	...
Benin — Bénin									
1 VII 2000									
Cotonou	ESDF	650 660	318 752	331 908	79	...	...	...	...
Parakou	ESDF	144 627	73 603	71 024	441	...	...	...	...
PORTO-NOVO	ESDF	232 756	113 737	119 019	50	...	...	...	...
Botswana									
17 VIII 2001									
Francistown	CDFC	83 023	40 147	42 876	79	113 315	...	...	...
GABORONE	CDFC	186 007	91 851	94 156	169	282 150	...	...	...
Burkina Faso									
9 XII 2006									
Bobo Dioulasso	CDJC	435 543	215 968	219 575	...	...	...	...	...
OUAGADOUGOU	CDJC	1 181 702	596 396	585 306	...	...	...	...	...
Burundi									
16 VIII 1990									
BUJUMBURA	CDFC	235 440	129 195	106 245	...	...	...	...	...
Cameroon — Cameroun									
1 VII 1998									
Bafoussam	ESDF	205 620	...	...	...	...	...	...	...
Bamenda	ESDF	252 083	...	...	...	...	...	...	...
Bertoua	ESDF	129 067	...	...	...	...	...	...	...
Douala	ESDF	1 382 900	...	...	...	...	...	...	...
Edéa	ESDF	101 200	...	...	...	...	...	...	...
Garoua	ESDF	293 081	...	...	...	...	...	...	...
Kousséri	ESDF	233 280	...	...	...	...	...	...	...

8. Population of capital cities and cities of 100 000 or more inhabitants: latest available year, 1987 - 2006
Population des capitales et des villes de 100 000 habitants ou plus: dernière année disponible, 1987 - 2006
(continued — suite)

Continent, country or area, date and city / Continent, pays ou zone, date et ville	Code[1]	City proper — Ville proprement dite Population				Urban agglomeration — Agglomération urbaine Population			
		Both sexes Les deux sexes	Male Masculin	Female Féminin	Surface area Superficie (km²)	Both sexes Les deux sexes	Male Masculin	Female Féminin	Surface area Superficie (km²)
AFRICA — AFRIQUE									
Cameroon — Cameroun									
1 VII 1998									
Kumba	ESDF	110 860	...	...	...	...	...	...	...
Loum	ESDF	115 781	...	...	...	...	...	...	...
Maroua	ESDF	225 469	...	...	...	...	...	...	...
Ngaoundéré	ESDF	156 804	...	...	...	...	...	...	...
Nkongsamba	ESDF	104 908	...	...	...	...	...	...	...
YAOUNDE	ESDF	1 293 000	...	...	...	...	...	...	...
Cape Verde — Cap-Vert									
23 VI 1990									
PRAIA	CDFC	61 644	...	...	...	...	...	...	...
Central African Republic — République centrafricaine									
8 XII 1988									
BANGUI	CDFC	451 690	...	...	...	...	...	...	...
Chad — Tchad									
8 IV 1993									
N'DJAMENA	CDFC	530 965	...	...	...	...	...	...	...
Comoros — Comores									
15 IX 1991									
MORONI	CDFC	30 365	...	...	...	...	...	...	...
Côte d'Ivoire									
1 III 1988									
Abidjan	CDFC	1 929 079	...	...	...	...	...	...	...
Bouake	CDFC	329 850	...	...	...	362 192	...	...	...
Daloa	CDFC	121 842	...	...	...	127 923	...	...	...
Korhogo	CDFC	109 445	...	...	...	112 888	...	...	...
YAMOUSSOUKRO	CDFC	106 786	...	...	...	126 191	...	...	...
Djibouti									
1 VII 1995									
DJIBOUTI	ESDF	383 000	...	...	...	...	...	...	...
Egypt — Égypte									
19 XI 1996									
Alexandria	CDFC	3 339 076	1 707 477	1 631 599	...	...	...	...	...
Al Orizah	CDFC	100 482	53 081	47 401	...	...	...	...	...
Assyût	CDFC	343 662	182 151	161 511	...	...	...	...	...
Aswan	CDFC	219 541	111 640	107 901	...	...	...	...	...
Banha	CDFC	135 892	69 154	66 738	...	...	...	...	...
Beni-Suef	CDFC	171 734	87 105	84 629	...	...	...	...	...
CAIRO	CDFC	6 800 992	3 486 260	3 314 732	...	...	...	...	...
Damanhûr	CDFC	209 423	107 965	101 458	...	...	...	...	...
El-Mahalla El-Kubra	CDFC	394 924	199 100	195 824	...	...	...	...	...
Faiyûm	CDFC	260 830	134 462	126 368	...	...	...	...	...
Giza	CDFC	2 221 817	1 139 665	1 082 152	...	...	...	...	...
Imbaba	CDFC	523 265	266 793	256 472	...	...	...	...	...
Ismailia	CDFC	255 134	129 004	126 130	...	...	...	...	...
Kafr-El-Dwar	CDFC	101 056	51 491	49 565	...	...	...	...	...
Kena	CDFC	155 382	79 038	76 344	...	...	...	...	...
Luxer	CDFC	153 758	79 753	74 005	...	...	...	...	...
Mansûra	CDFC	369 409	187 622	181 787	...	...	...	...	...
Menia	CDFC	201 440	103 428	98 012	...	...	...	...	...
Port Said	CDFC	472 335	242 502	229 833	...	...	...	...	...
Shebin-El-Kom	CDFC	156 794	79 868	76 926	...	...	...	...	...
Shubra-El-Khema	CDFC	870 776	449 271	421 505	...	...	...	...	...
Sohag	CDFC	170 417	85 918	84 499	...	...	...	...	...
Suez	CDFC	417 527	214 133	203 394	...	...	...	...	...
Tanta	CDFC	372 893	188 594	184 299	...	...	...	...	...
Zagazig	CDFC	267 469	136 094	131 375	...	...	...	...	...
11 XI 2006									
CAIRO	CDFC	6 758 581	3 433 198	3 325 383	...	...	...	...	...
Eritrea — Érythrée									
1 VII 1990									
ASMARA	ESDF	358 100	...	...	...	...	...	...	...

8. Population of capital cities and cities of 100 000 or more inhabitants: latest available year, 1987 - 2006
Population des capitales et des villes de 100 000 habitants ou plus: dernière année disponible, 1987 - 2006
(continued — suite)

Continent, country or area, date and city Continent, pays ou zone, date et ville	Code[1]	City proper — Ville proprement dite Population				Urban agglomeration — Agglomération urbaine Population			
		Both sexes Les deux sexes	Male Masculin	Female Féminin	Surface area Superficie (km²)	Both sexes Les deux sexes	Male Masculin	Female Féminin	Surface area Superficie (km²)
AFRICA — AFRIQUE									
Ethiopia — Éthiopie									
1 VII 2002									
ADDIS ABABA	ESDF	2 646 000	1 273 000	1 373 000	...	...	...	...	...
Awassa	ESDF	103 725	52 308	51 417	...	...	...	...	...
Bahir Dar	ESDF	140 084	72 736	67 348	28	...	...	...	...
Debre Zeit	ESDF	108 632	53 648	54 984	...	...	...	...	...
Dessie	ESDF	141 616	72 578	69 038	15	...	...	...	...
Dire Dawa	ESDF	237 012	118 880	118 132	18	...	...	...	...
Gondar	ESDF	163 097	82 229	80 868	40	...	...	...	...
Harar	ESDF	105 000	53 000	52 000	...	...	...	...	...
Jimma	ESDF	131 708	67 138	64 570	...	...	...	...	...
Mekele	ESDF	141 433	71 990	69 443	24	...	...	...	...
Nazareth	ESDF	189 362	94 822	94 540	...	...	...	...	...
Gabon									
31 VII 1993									
LIBREVILLE	CDFC	362 386	184 192	178 194	...	418 616	212 383	206 233	...
Gambia — Gambie									
15 IV 1993									
BANJUL	CDFC	42 326	22 268	20 058	12	...	...	...	...
Ghana									
26 III 2000									
ACCRA	CDFC	1 658 937	817 404	841 533	...	...	...	...	...
Kumasi	CDFC	1 170 270	587 012	583 258	...	...	...	...	...
Sekondi	CDFC	114 157	56 697	57 460	...	...	...	...	...
Takoradi	CDFC	175 436	86 794	88 642	...	...	...	...	...
Tamale	CDFC	202 317	100 854	101 463	...	...	...	...	...
Tema	CDFC	141 479	68 467	73 012	...	...	...	...	...
Guinea — Guinée									
1 XII 1996									
CONAKRY	CDFC	1 091 500	...	...	...	...	...	...	...
Kankan	CDFC	...	...	...	...	261 341	...	...	...
Kindia	CDFC	...	...	...	...	287 607	...	...	...
Labé	CDFC	...	...	...	...	249 515	...	...	...
Nzérékoré	CDFC	...	...	...	...	282 772	...	...	...
Guinea-Bissau — Guinée-Bissau									
1 XII 1991									
BISSAU	CDFC	197 600	...	...	...	...	...	...	...
Kenya									
1 VII 2006									
Kisumu	ESDF	600 789	...	...	475	...	...	...	...
Mombasa	ESDF	862 092	...	...	230	...	...	...	...
NAIROBI	ESDF	2 948 109	...	...	696	...	...	...	...
Nakuru	ESDF	1 571 162	...	...	290	...	...	...	...
Libyan Arab Jamahiriya — Jamahiriya arabe libyenne									
1 VII 1990									
Al Khums	ESDJ	200 000	...	...	...	...	...	...	...
BENGHAZI[2]	ESDJ	800 000	...	...	...	...	...	...	...
Misurata	ESDJ	360 000	...	...	...	...	...	...	...
Sebha	ESDJ	150 000	...	...	...	...	...	...	...
TRIPOLI[2]	ESDJ	1 500 000	...	...	...	...	...	...	...
Zuwarah	ESDJ	280 000	...	...	...	...	...	...	...
Madagascar									
1 VII 2005									
ANTANANARIVO[3]	ESDF	1 015 140	495 393	519 747	...	...	...	...	...
Antsirabe	ESDF	...	...	...	...	180 180	87 691	92 489	...
Fianarantsoa	ESDF	...	...	...	...	165 220	80 410	84 810	...
Mahajanga	ESDF	...	...	...	...	152 785	74 359	78 426	...
Toamasina	ESDF	...	...	...	...	203 469	99 026	104 443	...
Toliara	ESDF	...	...	...	...	113 993	55 479	58 514	...
Malawi									
1 VII 2005									
Blantyre City	ESDF	711 233	366 847	344 386	...	...	...	...	...

8. Population of capital cities and cities of 100 000 or more inhabitants: latest available year, 1987 - 2006
Population des capitales et des villes de 100 000 habitants ou plus: dernière année disponible, 1987 - 2006
(continued — suite)

Continent, country or area, date and city Continent, pays ou zone, date et ville	Code[1]	City proper — Ville proprement dite Population				Urban agglomeration — Agglomération urbaine Population			
		Both sexes Les deux sexes	Male Masculin	Female Féminin	Surface area Superficie (km²)	Both sexes Les deux sexes	Male Masculin	Female Féminin	Surface area Superficie (km²)
AFRICA — AFRIQUE									
Malawi									
1 VII 2005									
LILONGWE	ESDF	669 114	346 358	322 756	...	...	...	...	...
Mali									
1 IV 1998									
BAMAKO	CDJC	1 016 296	514 967	501 329	252	...	...	...	...
Gao	CDJC	394 594	193 517	201 077	...	...	...	...	...
Kayes	CDJC	1 374 316	671 678	702 638	...	...	...	...	...
Koulikoro	CDJC	1 570 507	778 332	792 175	...	...	...	...	...
Mopti	CDJC	1 478 505	730 771	747 734	...	...	...	...	...
Ségou	CDJC	1 675 357	831 386	843 971	...	...	...	...	...
Sikasso	CDJC	1 782 157	880 108	902 049	...	...	...	...	...
Tombouctou	CDJC	476 793	232 978	243 815	...	...	...	...	...
Mauritania — Mauritanie									
1 XI 2000									
NOUAKCHOTT	CDFC	558 195	...	...	...	...	...	...	...
Mauritius — Maurice									
1 VII 2006									
Beau Bassin-Rose Hill	ESDJ	108 921	53 071	55 850	20	...	...	...	...
PORT LOUIS	ESDJ	148 872	70 870	75 002	46	...	...	...	...
Vacoas - Phoenix	ESDJ	106 011	52 188	53 823	54	...	...	...	...
Morocco — Maroc[4]									
1 VII 2003									
Agadir	ESDF	494 000	...	...	...	...	...	...	...
Béni-Mellal	ESDF	998 000	...	...	...	...	...	...	...
Casablanca (Dar-el-Beida)[5]	ESDF	3 389 000	...	...	...	...	...	...	...
El-Jadida	ESDF	1 102 000	...	...	...	...	...	...	...
Fès	ESDF	1 185 000	...	...	...	...	...	...	...
Kénitra	ESDF	598 000	...	...	...	...	...	...	...
Khouribga	ESDF	336 000	...	...	...	...	...	...	...
Marrakech[5]	ESDF	1 068 000	...	...	...	...	...	...	...
Meknès[5]	ESDF	680 000	...	...	...	...	...	...	...
Mohammedia	ESDF	223 000	...	...	...	...	...	...	...
Oujda	ESDF	486 000	...	...	...	...	...	...	...
RABAT	ESDF	673 000	...	...	...	...	...	...	...
Safi	ESDF	906 000	...	...	...	...	...	...	...
Salé	ESDF	880 000	...	...	...	...	...	...	...
Tanger	ESDF	782 000	...	...	...	...	...	...	...
Tétouan	ESDF	652 000	...	...	...	...	...	...	...
Mozambique									
1 VIII 1997									
Beira	CDFC	397 368	...	...	...	...	...	...	...
Chimoio	CDFC	171 056	...	...	...	...	...	...	...
MAPUTO	CDFC	966 837	...	...	...	1 391 499	...	...	...
Matola	CDFC	424 662	...	...	...	...	...	...	...
Mocuba	CDFC	124 650	...	...	...	...	...	...	...
Nacala	CDFC	158 248	...	...	...	...	...	...	...
Nampula	CDFC	303 346	...	...	...	...	...	...	...
Quelimane	CDFC	150 116	...	...	...	...	...	...	...
Tete	CDFC	101 984	...	...	...	...	...	...	...
Namibia — Namibie									
27 VIII 2001									
WINDHOEK	CDFC	...	...	...	...	233 529	117 306	116 222	...
Niger[6]									
20 V 2001									
NIAMEY	CDJC	707 951	358 500	349 451	...	...	...	...	...
Nigeria — Nigéria									
26 XI 1991									
Aba	CDFC	500 183	...	...	...	...	...	...	...
Abeokuta	CDFC	352 735	...	...	...	...	...	...	...
ABUJA	CDFC	107 069	...	...	...	378 671	...	...	...
Ado-Ekiti	CDFC	156 122	...	...	...	...	...	...	...
Akure	CDFC	239 124	...	...	...	...	...	...	...

8. Population of capital cities and cities of 100 000 or more inhabitants: latest available year, 1987 - 2006
Population des capitales et des villes de 100 000 habitants ou plus: dernière année disponible, 1987 - 2006
(continued — suite)

Continent, country or area, date and city / Continent, pays ou zone, date et ville	Code[1]	City proper — Ville proprement dite Population				Urban agglomeration — Agglomération urbaine Population			
		Both sexes Les deux sexes	Male Masculin	Female Féminin	Surface area Superficie (km²)	Both sexes Les deux sexes	Male Masculin	Female Féminin	Surface area Superficie (km²)
AFRICA — AFRIQUE									
Nigeria — Nigéria									
26 XI 1991									
Awka	CDFC	104 682	...	...	...	...	...	...	...
Bauchi	CDFC	206 537	...	...	...	...	...	...	...
Benin City	CDFC	762 719	...	...	...	...	...	...	...
Bida	CDFC	111 245	...	...	...	...	...	...	...
Calabar	CDFC	310 839	...	...	...	...	...	...	...
Damaturu	CDFC	141 897	...	...	...	...	...	...	...
Ede	CDFC	142 363	...	...	...	...	...	...	...
Effon-Alaiye	CDFC	158 977	...	...	...	...	...	...	...
Enugu	CDFC	407 756	...	...	...	...	...	...	...
Gboko	CDFC	101 281	...	...	...	...	...	...	...
Gombe	CDFC	163 604	...	...	...	...	...	...	...
Gusau	CDFC	132 393	...	...	...	...	...	...	...
Ibadan	CDFC	1 835 300	...	...	...	...	...	...	...
Ife	CDFC	186 856	...	...	...	...	...	...	...
Ijebu-Ode	CDFC	124 313	...	...	...	...	...	...	...
Ikare	CDFC	103 843	...	...	...	...	...	...	...
Ikire	CDFC	111 435	...	...	...	...	...	...	...
Ikorodu	CDFC	184 674	...	...	...	...	...	...	...
Ikot Ekpene	CDFC	119 402	...	...	...	...	...	...	...
Ilawe-Ekiti	CDFC	104 049	...	...	...	...	...	...	...
Ilesha	CDFC	139 445	...	...	...	...	...	...	...
Ilorin	CDFC	532 089	...	...	...	...	...	...	...
Ise	CDFC	108 136	...	...	...	...	...	...	...
Iseyin	CDFC	170 936	...	...	...	...	...	...	...
Iwo	CDFC	125 645	...	...	...	...	...	...	...
Jimeta	CDFC	141 724	...	...	...	...	...	...	...
Jos	CDFC	510 300	...	...	...	...	...	...	...
Kaduna	CDFC	993 642	...	...	...	...	...	...	...
Kano	CDFC	2 166 554	...	...	...	...	...	...	...
Katsina	CDFC	259 315	...	...	...	...	...	...	...
Lagos	CDFC	5 195 247	...	...	...	...	...	...	...
Maiduguri	CDFC	618 278	...	...	...	...	...	...	...
Makurdi	CDFC	151 515	...	...	...	...	...	...	...
Minna	CDFC	189 191	...	...	...	...	...	...	...
Mubi	CDFC	128 900	...	...	...	...	...	...	...
Nnewi	CDFC	121 065	...	...	...	...	...	...	...
Ogbomosho	CDFC	433 030	...	...	...	...	...	...	...
Okene	CDFC	312 775	...	...	...	...	...	...	...
Okpogho	CDFC	105 127	...	...	...	...	...	...	...
Ondo	CDFC	146 051	...	...	...	...	...	...	...
Onitsha	CDFC	350 280	...	...	...	...	...	...	...
Oshogbo	CDFC	250 951	...	...	...	...	...	...	...
Owerri	CDFC	119 711	...	...	...	...	...	...	...
Owo	CDFC	157 181	...	...	...	...	...	...	...
Oyo	CDFC	369 894	...	...	...	...	...	...	...
Port Harcourt	CDFC	703 421	...	...	...	...	...	...	...
Sagamu	CDFC	127 513	...	...	...	...	...	...	...
Sango Otta	CDFC	103 332	...	...	...	...	...	...	...
Sapele	CDFC	109 576	...	...	...	...	...	...	...
Sokoto	CDFC	329 639	...	...	...	...	...	...	...
Suleja	CDFC	105 075	...	...	...	...	...	...	...
Ugep	CDFC	134 773	...	...	...	...	...	...	...
Umuahia	CDFC	147 167	...	...	...	...	...	...	...
Warri	CDFC	363 382	...	...	...	...	...	...	...
Zaria	CDFC	612 257	...	...	...	...	...	...	...
Réunion									
1 VII 2002									
SAINT-DENIS[7]	ESDF	134 042	63 922	70 120	143	...	...	...	...
Rwanda									
15 VIII 1991									
KIGALI	CDJC	233 640	125 550	108 090	...	...	...	...	...

8. Population of capital cities and cities of 100 000 or more inhabitants: latest available year, 1987 - 2006
Population des capitales et des villes de 100 000 habitants ou plus: dernière année disponible, 1987 - 2006
(continued — suite)

Continent, country or area, date and city Continent, pays ou zone, date et ville	Code[1]	City proper — Ville proprement dite Population				Urban agglomeration — Agglomération urbaine Population			
		Both sexes Les deux sexes	Male Masculin	Female Féminin	Surface area Superficie (km²)	Both sexes Les deux sexes	Male Masculin	Female Féminin	Surface area Superficie (km²)
AFRICA — AFRIQUE									
Saint Helena ex. dep. — Sainte-Hélène sans dép. 8 III 1998									
JAMESTOWN	CDFC	884	452	432	4	...	...	...	...
Sao Tome and Principe — Sao Tomé-et-Principe 25 VIII 2001									
SAO TOME	CDJC	...	...	...	...	49 957	24 003	25 954	...
Senegal — Sénégal 1 VII 1999									
DAKAR	ESDF	879 703	...	...	500	1 976 533	...	...	...
Kaolack	ESDF	227 915	...	...	...	...	...	...	...
Mbour	ESDF	135 619	...	...	...	...	...	...	...
Pikine-Guediawaye[8]	ESDF	1 096 830	...	...	...	...	...	...	...
Saint Louis	ESDF	147 961	...	...	...	...	...	...	...
Thiès	ESDF	256 113	...	...	...	...	...	...	...
Ziguinchor	ESDF	199 871	...	...	...	...	...	...	...
Seychelles 29 VIII 1997									
VICTORIA	CDFC	...	...	...	...	24 701	...	...	...
Somalia — Somalie 1 VII 2001									
MOGADISHU	ESDF	*1 212 000*	...	...	...	...	...	...	...
South Africa — Afrique du Sud 10 X 1996									
Alexandra	CDFC	171 284	...	...	...	...	...	...	...
Benoni	CDFC	366 343	...	...	...	...	...	...	...
Bloemfontein	CDFC	350 504	...	...	...	...	...	...	...
Boksburg	CDFC	263 179	...	...	...	...	...	...	...
Botshabelo	CDFC	177 971	...	...	...	...	...	...	...
CAPE TOWN[9]	CDFC	987 007	...	...	...	...	...	...	...
Durban	CDFC	669 242	...	...	...	...	...	...	...
Germiston	CDFC	164 252	...	...	...	...	...	...	...
Johannesburg	CDFC	752 349	...	...	...	...	...	...	...
Kathlehong	CDFC	344 803	...	...	...	...	...	...	...
Kempton Park	CDFC	344 426	...	...	...	...	...	...	...
Khayelitsa	CDFC	314 239	...	...	...	...	...	...	...
Kimberley	CDFC	206 070	...	...	...	...	...	...	...
Mangaung	CDFC	176 525	...	...	...	...	...	...	...
Pietermaritzburg	CDFC	405 385	...	...	...	...	...	...	...
Port Elizabeth	CDFC	775 255	...	...	...	...	...	...	...
PRETORIA[9]	CDFC	692 348	340 363	351 985	...	...	...	...	...
Roodepoort	CDFC	279 340	...	...	...	...	...	...	...
Soweto	CDFC	904 165	...	...	...	...	...	...	...
Springs	CDFC	163 304	...	...	...	...	...	...	...
Tembisa	CDFC	237 676	...	...	...	...	...	...	...
Umlazi	CDFC	339 715	...	...	...	...	...	...	...
Vereeniging	CDFC	379 638	...	...	...	...	...	...	...
Sudan — Soudan 15 IV 1993									
Al-Fasher	CDFC	141 884	...	...	...	...	...	...	...
Al-Gadarif	CDFC	191 164	...	...	...	...	...	...	...
Al-Gezira	CDFC	211 362	...	...	...	...	...	...	...
Al-Obeid	CDFC	229 425	...	...	...	...	...	...	...
Juba	CDFC	114 980	...	...	...	...	...	...	...
Kassala	CDFC	234 022	...	...	...	...	...	...	...
KHARTOUM	CDFC	947 483	...	...	...	2 910 773	...	...	...
Khartoum North	CDFC	700 887	...	...	...	...	...	...	...
Kosti	CDFC	173 599	...	...	...	...	...	...	...
Nyala	CDFC	227 183	...	...	...	...	...	...	...
Omdurman	CDFC	1 271 403	...	...	...	...	...	...	...
Port Sudan	CDFC	308 195	...	...	...	...	...	...	...

8. Population of capital cities and cities of 100 000 or more inhabitants: latest available year, 1987 - 2006
Population des capitales et des villes de 100 000 habitants ou plus: dernière année disponible, 1987 - 2006
(continued — suite)

Continent, country or area, date and city / Continent, pays ou zone, date et ville	Code[1]	City proper — Ville proprement dite Population				Urban agglomeration — Agglomération urbaine Population			
		Both sexes Les deux sexes	Male Masculin	Female Féminin	Surface area Superficie (km²)	Both sexes Les deux sexes	Male Masculin	Female Féminin	Surface area Superficie (km²)
AFRICA — AFRIQUE									
Togo									
1 VII 1990									
LOME	ESDF	450 000	...	...	...	...	...	...	...
Tunisia — Tunisie									
1 VII 1998									
Bizerte	ESDF	105 520	...	...	...	...	...	...	...
Gabes	ESDF	104 950	...	...	...	...	...	...	...
Kairouan	ESDF	110 280	...	...	...	...	...	...	...
Sfax	ESDF	248 800	...	...	...	...	...	...	...
TUNIS	ESDF	702 330	...	...	...	...	...	...	...
Uganda — Ouganda									
12 IX 2002									
Gulu	CDFC	113 144	...	...	...	...	...	...	...
KAMPALA	CDFC	1 208 544	588 433	620 111	...	...	...	...	...
United Republic of Tanzania — République Unie de Tanzanie									
28 VIII 1988									
Arusha	CDFC	134 708	69 875	64 833	...	...	...	...	...
Dar es Salaam	CDFC	1 360 850	715 925	644 925	...	...	...	...	...
DODOMA	CDFC	203 833	101 437	102 396	...	...	...	...	...
Mbeya	CDFC	152 844	74 259	78 585	...	...	...	...	...
Morogoro	CDFC	117 760	59 144	58 616	...	...	...	...	...
Mwanza	CDFC	223 013	113 779	109 234	...	...	...	...	...
Shinyanga	CDFC	100 724	50 117	50 607	...	...	...	...	...
Tanga	CDFC	187 455	96 259	91 196	...	...	...	...	...
Zanzibar	CDFC	157 634	77 787	79 847	...	...	...	...	...
Western Sahara — Sahara occidental									
1 VII 1999									
EL AAIUN	ESDF	169 000	...	...	...	...	...	...	...
Zambia — Zambie									
1 VII 2000									
Chingola	ESDF	164 964	82 643	82 321	1 678	...	...	...	...
Kabwe	ESDF	170 387	84 041	86 346	1 572	...	...	...	...
Kitwe	ESDF	362 423	180 865	181 558	777	...	...	...	...
Luanshya	ESDF	144 009	72 449	71 560	811	...	...	...	...
LUSAKA	ESDF	1 057 212	528 891	528 321	360	...	...	...	...
Mufulira	ESDF	137 272	68 253	69 019	1 637	...	...	...	...
Ndola	ESDF	371 221	185 043	186 178	1 103	...	...	...	...
Zimbabwe									
17 VIII 2002									
Bulawayo	CDFC	676 650	323 550	353 100	479	...	...	...	...
Gweru	CDFC	140 806	67 689	73 117	...	...	...	...	...
HARARE	CDFC	1 435 784	720 021	715 763	872	...	...	...	...
Mutare	CDFC	170 466	85 006	85 460	...	...	...	...	...
AMERICA, NORTH — AMERIQUE DU NORD									
Anguilla									
1 VII 2001									
THE VALLEY	ESDF	4 904	...	...	...	...	...	...	...
Antigua and Barbuda — Antigua-et-Barbuda									
28 V 1991									
ST. JOHN	CDFC	22 342	...	...	...	...	...	...	...
Aruba									
6 X 1991									
ORANJESTAD	CDJC	20 045	9 441	10 604	...	...	...	...	...
Bahamas									
1 V 2000									
NASSAU	CDFC	...	...	...	...	210 832	101 558	109 274	80

8. Population of capital cities and cities of 100 000 or more inhabitants: latest available year, 1987 - 2006
Population des capitales et des villes de 100 000 habitants ou plus: dernière année disponible, 1987 - 2006
(continued — suite)

Continent, country or area, date and city / Continent, pays ou zone, date et ville	Code[1]	City proper — Ville proprement dite Population				Urban agglomeration — Agglomération urbaine Population			
		Both sexes Les deux sexes	Male Masculin	Female Féminin	Surface area Superficie (km²)	Both sexes Les deux sexes	Male Masculin	Female Féminin	Surface area Superficie (km²)
AMERICA, NORTH — AMERIQUE DU NORD									
Belize									
1 VII 2000									
BELMOPAN	ESDF	8 305	4 050	4 255	...	...	...	...	...
Bermuda — Bermudes[10]									
20 V 2000									
HAMILTON	CDJC	969	508	461	0	...	...	...	...
British Virgin Islands — Iles Vierges britanniques									
1 VII 1992									
ROAD TOWN	ESDF	3 500	...	...	...	...	...	...	...
Canada									
1 VII 2006									
Abbotsford	ESDJ	...	...	...	...	161 911	81 342	80 569	626
Calgary	ESDJ	...	...	...	...	1 107 242	557 909	549 333	5 083
Chicoutimi-Jonquière	ESDJ	...	...	...	...	152 132	75 446	76 686	1 754
Edmonton	ESDJ	...	...	...	...	1 050 046	525 622	524 424	9 419
Halifax	ESDJ	...	...	...	...	382 203	186 216	195 987	5 496
Hamilton	ESDJ	...	...	...	...	716 230	352 099	364 131	1 372
Kingston	ESDJ	...	...	...	...	154 971	76 508	78 463	1 907
Kitchener	ESDJ	...	...	...	...	463 644	230 887	202 757	827
London	ESDJ	...	...	...	...	465 720	227 837	237 883	2 333
Montréal	ESDJ	...	...	...	...	3 666 280	1 794 951	1 871 329	4 047
Oshawa	ESDJ	...	...	...	...	344 374	170 531	173 843	903
OTTAWA	ESDJ	...	...	...	...	1 158 314	569 246	589 068	5 318
Québec	ESDJ	...	...	...	...	723 263	352 710	370 553	3 154
Regina	ESDJ	...	...	...	...	198 316	97 307	101 009	3 408
St. Catharines	ESDJ	...	...	...	...	396 754	194 153	202 601	1 406
St. John's	ESDJ	...	...	...	...	181 394	87 602	93 792	805
Saint John	ESDJ	...	...	...	...	125 944	60 978	64 966	3 360
Saskatoon	ESDJ	...	...	...	...	235 464	115 420	120 044	5 192
Sherbrooke	ESDJ	...	...	...	...	164 685	80 426	84 259	1 108
Sudbury	ESDJ	...	...	...	...	161 983	79 586	82 397	3 536
Thunder Bay	ESDJ	...	...	...	...	125 359	61 930	63 429	2 548
Toronto	ESDJ	...	...	...	...	5 406 324	2 658 925	2 747 399	5 903
Trois-Rivières	ESDJ	...	...	...	...	142 614	68 975	73 639	880
Vancouver	ESDJ	...	...	...	...	2 236 068	1 106 382	1 129 686	2 879
Victoria	ESDJ	...	...	...	...	334 332	161 185	173 147	695
Windsor	ESDJ	...	...	...	...	332 066	164 954	167 112	1 023
Winnipeg	ESDJ	...	...	...	...	706 749	347 883	358 866	4 151
Cayman Islands — Iles Caïmanes									
10 X 1999									
GEORGE TOWN	CDFC	20 626	10 191	10 435	...	...	...	...	...
Costa Rica									
1 VII 2006									
Alajuela	ESDJ	249 121	126 977	122 144	388	...	...	...	...
Cartago	ESDJ	146 522	73 885	72 637	288	...	...	...	...
Heredia	ESDJ	116 041	57 248	58 793	283	...	...	...	...
Puntarenas	ESDJ	115 609	59 807	55 802	1 842	...	...	...	...
SAN JOSE	ESDJ	344 747	170 082	174 665	45	...	...	...	...
Cuba									
1 VII 2006									
Bayamo	ESDF	146 260	...	...	...	...	...	...	...
Camagüey	ESDF	306 702	...	...	...	...	...	...	...
Ciego de Avila	ESDF	109 379	...	...	...	...	...	...	...
Cienfuegos	ESDF	142 420	...	...	...	...	...	...	...
Guantánamo	ESDF	208 579	...	...	...	...	...	...	...
Holguín	ESDF	274 805	...	...	...	...	...	...	...
LA HABANA	ESDF	2 174 790	...	...	727	...	...	...	...
Las Tunas	ESDF	149 532	...	...	...	...	...	...	...
Matanzas	ESDF	129 864	...	...	...	...	...	...	...
Pinar del Río	ESDF	137 701	...	...	...	...	...	...	...

251

8. Population of capital cities and cities of 100 000 or more inhabitants: latest available year, 1987 - 2006
Population des capitales et des villes de 100 000 habitants ou plus: dernière année disponible, 1987 - 2006
(continued — suite)

Continent, country or area, date and city / Continent, pays ou zone, date et ville	Code[1]	City proper — Ville proprement dite Population				Urban agglomeration — Agglomération urbaine Population			
		Both sexes Les deux sexes	Male Masculin	Female Féminin	Surface area Superficie (km²)	Both sexes Les deux sexes	Male Masculin	Female Féminin	Surface area Superficie (km²)
AMERICA, NORTH — AMERIQUE DU NORD									
Cuba									
1 VII 2006									
Santa Clara	ESDF	208 739	...	...	...	...	...	...	...
Santiago de Cuba	ESDF	425 990	...	...	...	...	...	...	...
Dominica — Dominique									
12 V 1991									
ROSEAU	CDFC	16 243	...	...	...	...	...	...	...
Dominican Republic — République dominicaine									
1 VII 2001									
San Pedro de Macoris	ESDF	*266 629*	...	...	...	...	...	...	...
Santiago de los Caballeros	ESDF	*836 614*	...	...	...	...	...	...	...
SANTO DOMINGO	ESDF	*2 677 056*	...	...	...	...	...	...	...
El Salvador[11]									
1 VII 2003									
Ahuachapan	ESDF	115 521	57 593	57 928	245	...	...	...	...
Apopa	ESDF	192 728	91 699	100 830	52	...	...	...	...
Ciudad Delgado	ESDF	164 069	78 063	85 837	33	...	...	...	...
Cuscatancingo	ESDF	104 640	49 787	54 745	5	...	...	...	...
Ilopango	ESDF	144 985	68 983	75 852	35	...	...	...	...
Mejicanos	ESDF	200 917	95 596	105 114	22	...	...	...	...
Nueva San Salvador	ESDF	175 286	86 161	89 097	112	...	...	...	...
SAN SALVADOR	ESDF	497 844	236 873	261 836	886	...	...	...	...
San Martin	ESDF	123 663	58 838	64 697	56	...	...	...	...
San Miguel	ESDF	259 197	128 026	131 171	594	...	...	...	...
Santa Ana	ESDF	261 568	129 155	132 413	400	...	...	...	...
Sonsonate	ESDF	103 490	51 402	52 088	233	...	...	...	...
Soyapango	ESDF	290 412	138 177	152 739	30	...	...	...	...
Greenland — Groenland									
1 VII 2000									
NUUK (GODTHAB)	ESDJ	13 552	7 265	6 287		...	...	...	...
Guadeloupe									
8 III 1999									
BASSE-TERRE	CDJC	12 377	5 687	6 690	...	44 747	21 252	23 495	...
Pointe-à-Pitre	CDJC	...	...	...	...	171 773	...	...	...
Guatemala									
1 VII 2001									
GUATEMALA	ESDF	*1 022 001*	*491 891*	*530 110*	*228*	...	...	...	...
Escuintla	ESDF	*114 626*	*57 893*	*56 733*	*332*	...	...	...	...
Mixco	ESDF	*452 134*	*221 928*	*230 206*	*99*	...	...	...	...
Quetzaltenango	ESDF	*152 223*	*76 272*	*75 951*	*120*	...	...	...	...
Villa Nueva	ESDF	*390 329*	*192 238*	*198 091*	*114*	...	...	...	...
Haiti — Haïti									
1 VII 1999									
Cap-Haitien	ESDJ	*113 555*	*50 064*	*63 491*	10	...	...	...	...
Carrefour	ESDJ	*336 222*	*146 838*	*189 384*	23	...	...	...	...
Delmas	ESDJ	*284 079*	*124 774*	*159 305*	26	...	...	...	...
PORT-AU-PRINCE	ESDJ	*990 558*	*436 170*	*554 388*	21	...	...	...	...
Honduras									
1 VII 2003									
La Ceiba	ESDF	137 815	67 691	70 124		...	...	...	...
San Pedro Sula	ESDF	518 736	251 514	267 222		...	...	...	...
TEGUCIGALPA	ESDF	858 437	411 687	446 749		...	...	...	...
Jamaica — Jamaïque									
10 IX 2001									
KINGSTON	CDJC	579 137	272 587	306 550	22	...	...	...	...
Portmore	CDJC	156 467	72 292	84 175	...	...	...	...	...
Spanish Town	CDJC	131 510	63 791	67 719	...	...	...	...	...
Martinique									
8 III 1999									
FORT-DE-FRANCE	CDJC	94 152	42 812	51 340	...	134 796	61 705	73 091	...

8. Population of capital cities and cities of 100 000 or more inhabitants: latest available year, 1987 - 2006
Population des capitales et des villes de 100 000 habitants ou plus: dernière année disponible, 1987 - 2006
(continued — suite)

Continent, country or area, date and city — Continent, pays ou zone, date et ville	Code[1]	City proper — Ville proprement dite Population				Urban agglomeration — Agglomération urbaine Population			
		Both sexes Les deux sexes	Male Masculin	Female Féminin	Surface area Superficie (km²)	Both sexes Les deux sexes	Male Masculin	Female Féminin	Surface area Superficie (km²)
AMERICA, NORTH — AMERIQUE DU NORD									
Mexico — Mexique[12,13]									
1 VII 2006									
Acapulco (de Juárez)	ESDJ	...	...	...	...	638 084	...	...	...
Aguascalientes	ESDJ	...	...	...	...	718 643	...	...	...
Campeche	ESDJ	216 473	...	...	...	...	...	...	...
Cancun	ESDJ	...	...	...	...	545 138	...	...	...
Celaya	ESDJ	320 881	...	...	...	...	...	...	...
Chihuahua	ESDJ	...	...	...	...	766 513	...	...	...
Ciudad Del Carmen	ESDJ	160 500	...	...	...	...	...	...	...
Ciudad Victoria	ESDJ	282 527	...	...	...	...	...	...	...
Coatzacoalcos	ESDJ	...	...	...	...	423 095	...	...	...
Colimas	ESDJ	...	...	...	...	227 198	...	...	...
Cuernavaca	ESDJ	...	...	...	...	725 033	...	...	...
Culiacán Rosales	ESDJ	620 768	...	...	...	...	...	...	...
Durango (Victoria de Durango)	ESDJ	479 450	...	...	...	...	...	...	...
Guadalajara	ESDJ	...	...	...	...	3 833 866	...	...	...
Hermosillo	ESDJ	661 057	...	...	...	...	...	...	...
Irapuato	FSDJ	346 706	...	...	...	...	...	...	...
Juárez	ESDJ	...	...	...	...	1 333 234	...	...	...
La Paz	ESDJ	...	...	...	...	192 157	...	...	...
León (de los Aldama)	ESDJ	...	...	...	...	1 284 692	...	...	...
Manzanillo	ESDJ	114 630	...	...	...	...	...	...	...
Matamoros	ESDJ	...	...	...	...	430 923	...	...	...
Mérida	ESDJ	...	...	...	...	889 435	...	...	...
Mexicali	ESDJ	...	...	...	...	668 736	...	...	...
MEXICO, CIUDAD DE	ESDJ	...	...	...	...	18 204 964	...	...	...
Monclova	ESDJ	...	...	...	...	267 575	...	...	...
Monterrey	ESDJ	...	...	...	...	3 473 088	...	...	...
Morelia	ESDJ	...	...	...	...	654 303	...	...	...
Nuevo Laredo	ESDJ	...	...	...	...	355 666	...	...	...
Oaxaca de Juárez	ESDJ	...	...	...	...	500 338	...	...	...
Orizaba	ESDJ	...	...	...	...	481 444	...	...	...
Pachuca (de Soto)	ESDJ	...	...	...	...	321 799	...	...	...
Puebla de Zaragoza	ESDJ	...	...	...	...	1 887 827	...	...	...
Querétaro	ESDJ	...	...	...	...	695 149	...	...	...
Reynosa	ESDJ	...	...	...	...	532 192	...	...	...
Salamanca	ESDJ	145 860	...	...	...	...	...	...	...
Saltillo	ESDJ	...	...	...	...	701 570	...	...	...
San Luis Potosí	ESDJ	...	...	...	...	934 645	...	...	...
Tampico	ESDJ	...	...	...	...	644 494	...	...	...
Tepic	ESDJ	...	...	...	...	303 613	...	...	...
Tijuana	ESDJ	...	...	...	...	1 311 774	...	...	...
Tlaxcala	ESDJ	...	...	...	...	503 693	...	...	...
Toluca (de Lerdo)	ESDJ	...	...	...	...	1 069 710	...	...	...
Torreón	ESDJ	...	...	...	...	883 021	...	...	...
Tuxtla Gutiérrez	ESDJ	...	...	...	...	501 681	...	...	...
Veracruz	ESDJ	...	...	...	...	637 345	...	...	...
Villahermosa	ESDJ	...	...	...	...	378 618	...	...	...
Zacatecas	ESDJ	...	...	...	...	235 325	...	...	...
Netherlands Antilles — Antilles néerlandaises									
27 I 1992									
WILLEMSTAD	CDJC	2 345	...	...	...				
Nicaragua									
03 VI 2005									
Leon	CDJC	...	...	...	...	139 433	64 973	74 460	...
MANAGUA	CDJC	...	...	...	...	908 892	430 389	478 503	...
Panama									
1 VII 2000									
PANAMA[14]	ESDF	484 261	230 747	253 514	107	...	...	...	...
San Miguelito	ESDF	331 692	161 901	169 791	50	...	...	...	...

8. Population of capital cities and cities of 100 000 or more inhabitants: latest available year, 1987 - 2006
Population des capitales et des villes de 100 000 habitants ou plus: dernière année disponible, 1987 - 2006
(continued — suite)

Continent, country or area date and city / Continent, pays ou zone, date et ville	Code[1]	City proper — Ville proprement dite Population				Urban agglomeration — Agglomération urbaine Population			
		Both sexes Les deux sexes	Male Masculin	Female Féminin	Surface area Superficie (km²)	Both sexes Les deux sexes	Male Masculin	Female Féminin	Surface area Superficie (km²)
AMERICA, NORTH — AMERIQUE DU NORD									
Puerto Rico — Porto Rico[15]									
1 VII 2006									
Arecibo	ESDJ	102 216	...	...	327	...	...	...	...
Bayamón	ESDJ	221 546	...	...	115	...	...	...	...
Caguas	ESDJ	142 769	...	...	152	...	...	...	...
Carolina	ESDJ	187 578	...	...	118	...	...	...	...
Guaynabo	ESDJ	102 525	...	...	70	...	...	...	...
Ponce	ESDJ	181 267	...	...	301	...	...	...	...
SAN JUAN	ESDJ	426 618	...	...	124	...	...	...	...
Saint Lucia — Sainte-Lucie									
22 V 2001									
CASTRIES	CDFC	11 092	5 238	5 854	...	...	...	...	...
Saint Pierre and Miquelon — Saint Pierre-et-Miquelon									
8 III 1999									
SAINT-PIERRE	CDFC	5 618	...	...	...	...	...	...	...
Saint Vincent and the Grenadines — Saint Vincent-et-les Grenadines									
12 V 1991									
KINGSTOWN	CDFC	15 466	...	...	...	...	...	...	...
Trinidad and Tobago — Trinité-et-Tobago									
1 VII 1996									
PORT-OF-SPAIN	ESDF	43 396	20 739	22 657	12	...	...	...	...
Turks and Caicos Islands — Iles Turques et Caïques									
1 VII 2006									
GRAND TURK	ESDF	*5 718*	*2 846*	*2 872*	*17*	...	...	...	...
United States — Etats-Unis[16,17]									
1 VII 2005									
Abilene (TX)	ESDJ	114 757	...	...	273	...	...	...	...
Akron (OH)	ESDJ	210 795	...	...	161	...	...	...	...
Albuquerque (NM)	ESDJ	494 236	...	...	479	...	...	...	...
Alexandria (VA)[18]	ESDJ	135 337	...	...	39	...	...	...	...
Allentown (PA)	ESDJ	106 992	...	...	45	...	...	...	...
Amarillo (TX)	ESDJ	183 021	...	...	243	...	...	...	...
Anaheim (CA)[19]	ESDJ	331 804	...	...	127	...	...	...	...
Anchorage (AK)	ESDJ	275 043	...	...	4 396	...	...	...	...
Ann Arbor (MI)	ESDJ	113 271	...	...	70	...	...	...	...
Antioch (CA)	ESDJ	100 631	...	...	70	...	...	...	...
Arlington (TX)[20]	ESDJ	362 805	...	...	246	...	...	...	...
Arlington (VA)[18]	ESDJ	195 965	...	...	67	...	...	...	...
Arvada (CO)[21]	ESDJ	103 966	...	...	90	...	...	...	...
Athens (GA)	ESDJ	103 238	...	...	301	...	...	...	...
Atlanta (GA)	ESDJ	470 688	...	...	341	...	...	...	...
Augusta-Richmond (GA)	ESDJ	190 782	...	...	783	...	...	...	...
Aurora (CO)[21]	ESDJ	297 235	...	...	379	...	...	...	...
Aurora (IL)[22]	ESDJ	168 181	...	...	107	...	...	...	...
Austin (TX)	ESDJ	690 252	...	...	688	...	...	...	...
Bakersfield (CA)	ESDJ	295 536	...	...	304	...	...	...	...
Baltimore (MD)	ESDJ	635 815	...	...	210	...	...	...	...
Baton Rouge (LA)	ESDJ	222 064	...	...	199	...	...	...	...
Beaumont (TX)	ESDJ	111 799	...	...	214	...	...	...	...
Bellevue (WA)[23]	ESDJ	117 137	...	...	82	...	...	...	...
Berkeley (CA)[24]	ESDJ	100 744	...	...	27	...	...	...	...
Birmingham (AL)	ESDJ	231 483	...	...	388	...	...	...	...
Boise City (ID)	ESDJ	193 161	...	...	176	...	...	...	...
Boston (MA)	ESDJ	559 034	...	...	125	...	...	...	...
Bridgeport (CT)	ESDJ	139 008	...	...	41	...	...	...	...
Brownsville (TX)	ESDJ	167 493	...	...	340	...	...	...	...
Buffalo (NY)	ESDJ	279 745	...	...	105	...	...	...	...

8. Population of capital cities and cities of 100 000 or more inhabitants: latest available year, 1987 - 2006
Population des capitales et des villes de 100 000 habitants ou plus: dernière année disponible, 1987 - 2006
(continued — suite)

Continent, country or area, date and city / Continent, pays ou zone, date et ville	Code[1]	City proper — Ville proprement dite Population				Urban agglomeration — Agglomération urbaine Population			
		Both sexes Les deux sexes	Male Masculin	Female Féminin	Surface area Superficie (km²)	Both sexes Les deux sexes	Male Masculin	Female Féminin	Surface area Superficie (km²)
AMERICA, NORTH — AMERIQUE DU NORD									
United States — Etats-Unis[16,17]									
1 VII 2005									
Burbank (CA)[19]	ESDJ	104 108	...	...	45	...	...	...	...
Cambridge (MA)[25]	ESDJ	100 135	...	...	17	...	...	...	...
Cape Coral (FL)	ESDJ	140 010	...	...	273	...	...	...	...
Carrollton (TX)[20]	ESDJ	118 870	...	...	93	...	...	...	...
Cary (NC)	ESDJ	106 439	...	...	122	...	...	...	...
Cedar Rapids (IA)	ESDJ	123 119	...	...	174	...	...	...	...
Chandler (AZ)[26]	ESDJ	234 939	...	...	165	...	...	...	...
Charleston (SC)	ESDJ	106 712	...	...	262	...	...	...	...
Charlotte (NC)	ESDJ	610 949	...	...	697	...	...	...	...
Chattanooga (TN)	ESDJ	154 762	...	...	349	...	...	...	...
Chesapeake (VA)[27]	ESDJ	218 968	...	...	883	...	...	...	...
Chicago (IL)	ESDJ	2 842 518	...	...	588	...	...	...	...
Chula Vista (CA)[28]	ESDJ	210 497	...	...	130	...	...	...	...
Cincinnati (OH)	ESDJ	308 728	...	...	202	...	...	...	...
Clarksville (TN)	ESDJ	112 878	...	...	246	...	...	...	...
Clearwater (FL)[20]	ESDJ	108 687	...	...	66	...	...	...	...
Cleveland (OH)	ESDJ	452 208	...	...	201	...	...	...	...
Colorado Springs (CO)	ESDJ	369 815	...	...	493	...	...	...	...
Columbia (SC)	ESDJ	117 088	...	...	324	...	...	...	...
Columbus (GA)	ESDJ	185 271	...	...	560	...	...	...	...
Columbus (OH)	ESDJ	730 657	...	...	563	...	...	...	...
Concord (CA)	ESDJ	123 252	...	...	79	...	...	...	...
Coral Springs (FL)[30]	ESDJ	128 804	...	...	62	...	...	...	...
Corona (CA)[31]	ESDJ	149 387	...	...	98	...	...	...	...
Corpus Christi (TX)	ESDJ	283 474	...	...	412	...	...	...	...
Costa Mesa (CA)[19]	ESDJ	109 830	...	...	41	...	...	...	...
Dallas (TX)	ESDJ	1 213 825	...	...	881	...	...	...	...
Daly City (CA)[24]	ESDJ	100 339	...	...	20	...	...	...	...
Dayton (OH)	ESDJ	158 873	...	...	144	...	...	...	...
Denton (TX)	ESDJ	104 153	...	...	176	...	...	...	...
Denver (CO)	ESDJ	557 917	...	...	397	...	...	...	...
Des Moines (IA)	ESDJ	194 163	...	...	204	...	...	...	...
Detroit (MI)	ESDJ	886 671	...	...	359	...	...	...	...
Downey (CA)[19]	ESDJ	109 718	...	...	32	...	...	...	...
Durham (NC)	ESDJ	204 845	...	...	266	...	...	...	...
El Monte (CA)[19]	ESDJ	122 513	...	...	25	...	...	...	...
El Paso (TX)	ESDJ	598 590	...	...	645	...	...	...	...
Elizabeth (NJ)[32]	ESDJ	125 809	...	...	32	...	...	...	...
Elk Grove (CA)	ESDJ	112 338	...	...	108	...	...	...	...
Erie (PA)	ESDJ	102 612	...	...	49	...	...	...	...
Escondido (CA)[28]	ESDJ	134 085	...	...	95	...	...	...	...
Eugene (OR)	ESDJ	144 515	...	...	107	...	...	...	...
Evansville (IN)	ESDJ	115 918	...	...	106	...	...	...	...
Fairfield (CA)	ESDJ	104 476	...	...	98	...	...	...	...
Fayetteville (NC)	ESDJ	129 928	...	...	164	...	...	...	...
Flint (MI)	ESDJ	118 551	...	...	87	...	...	...	...
Fontana (CA)[31]	ESDJ	163 860	...	...	95	...	...	...	...
Fort Collins (CO)	ESDJ	128 026	...	...	133	...	...	...	...
Fort Lauderdale (FL)[30]	ESDJ	167 380	...	...	83	...	...	...	...
Fort Wayne (IN)	ESDJ	223 341	...	...	245	...	...	...	...
Fort Worth (TX)[20]	ESDJ	624 067	...	...	864	...	...	...	...
Fremont (CA)[24]	ESDJ	200 468	...	...	199	...	...	...	...
Fresno (CA)	ESDJ	461 116	...	...	277	...	...	...	...
Fullerton (CA)[19]	ESDJ	132 787	...	...	58	...	...	...	...
Gainesville (FL)	ESDJ	108 184	...	...	137	...	...	...	...
Garden Grove (CA)[19]	ESDJ	166 075	...	...	47	...	...	...	...
Garland (TX)[20]	ESDJ	216 346	...	...	148	...	...	...	...
Gilbert (AZ)[26]	ESDJ	173 989	...	...	146	...	...	...	...
Glendale (AZ)[26]	ESDJ	239 435	...	...	149	...	...	...	...

8. Population of capital cities and cities of 100 000 or more inhabitants: latest available year, 1987 - 2006
Population des capitales et des villes de 100 000 habitants ou plus: dernière année disponible, 1987 - 2006
(continued — suite)

Continent, country or area, date and city / Continent, pays ou zone, date et ville	Code[1]	City proper — Ville proprement dite Population				Urban agglomeration — Agglomération urbaine Population			
		Both sexes Les deux sexes	Male Masculin	Female Féminin	Surface area Superficie (km²)	Both sexes Les deux sexes	Male Masculin	Female Féminin	Surface area Superficie (km²)
AMERICA, NORTH — AMERIQUE DU NORD									
United States — Etats-Unis[16,17]									
1 VII 2005									
Glendale (CA)[19]	ESDJ	200 065	...	...	79	...	...	...	...
Grand Prairie (TX)[20]	ESDJ	144 337	...	...	186	...	...	...	...
Grand Rapids (MI)	ESDJ	193 780	...	...	115	...	...	...	...
Green Bay (WI)	ESDJ	101 203	...	...	118	...	...	...	...
Greensboro (NC)	ESDJ	231 962	...	...	285	...	...	...	...
Hampton (VA)[27]	ESDJ	145 579	...	...	134	...	...	...	...
Hartford (CT)	ESDJ	124 397	...	...	45	...	...	...	...
Hayward (CA)[24]	ESDJ	140 293	...	...	115	...	...	...	...
Henderson (NV)[33]	ESDJ	232 146	...	...	251	...	...	...	...
Hialeah (FL)[30]	ESDJ	220 485	...	...	55	...	...	...	...
Hollywood (FL)[30]	ESDJ	145 629	...	...	71	...	...	...	...
Honolulu (HI)	ESDJ	377 379	...	...	222	...	...	...	...
Houston (TX)	ESDJ	2 016 582	...	...	1 524	...	...	...	...
Huntington Beach (CA)[19]	ESDJ	194 457	...	...	68	...	...	...	...
Huntsville (AL)	ESDJ	166 313	...	...	479	...	...	...	...
Independence (MO)[34]	ESDJ	110 208	...	...	201	...	...	...	...
Indianapolis (IN)	ESDJ	784 118	...	...	936	...	...	...	...
Inglewood (CA)[19]	ESDJ	114 467	...	...	24	...	...	...	...
Irvine (CA)[19]	ESDJ	186 852	...	...	126	...	...	...	...
Irving (TX)[20]	ESDJ	193 649	...	...	173	...	...	...	...
Jackson (MS)	ESDJ	177 977	...	...	272	...	...	...	...
Jacksonville (FL)	ESDJ	782 623	...	...	1 934	...	...	...	...
Jersey City (NJ)[32]	ESDJ	239 614	...	...	39	...	...	...	...
Joliet (IL)[22]	ESDJ	136 208	...	...	118	...	...	...	...
Kansas City (KS)[34]	ESDJ	144 210	...	...	323	...	...	...	...
Kansas City (MO)	ESDJ	444 965	...	...	813	...	...	...	...
Killeen (TX)[35]	ESDJ	100 233	...	...	94	...	...	...	...
Knoxville (TN)	ESDJ	180 130	...	...	253	...	...	...	...
Lafayette (LA)	ESDJ	112 030	...	...	125	...	...	...	...
Lakewood	ESDJ	140 671	...	...	108	...	...	...	...
Lancaster (CA)	ESDJ	134 032	...	...	243	...	...	...	...
Lansing (MI)	ESDJ	115 518	...	...	93	...	...	...	...
Laredo (TX)	ESDJ	208 754	...	...	216	...	...	...	...
Las Vegas (NV)	ESDJ	545 147	...	...	344	...	...	...	...
Lexington-Fayette (KY)	ESDJ	268 080	...	...	737	...	...	...	...
Lincoln (NE)	ESDJ	239 213	...	...	210	...	...	...	...
Little Rock (AR)	ESDJ	184 564	...	...	303	...	...	...	...
Long Beach (CA)[19]	ESDJ	474 014	...	...	132	...	...	...	...
Los Angeles (CA)	ESDJ	3 844 829	...	...	1 217	...	...	...	...
Louisville (KY)	ESDJ	556 429	...	...	842	...	...	...	...
Lowell (MA)[25]	ESDJ	103 111	...	...	36	...	...	...	...
Lubbock (TX)	ESDJ	209 737	...	...	298	...	...	...	...
Madison (WI)	ESDJ	221 551	...	...	195	...	...	...	...
Manchester (NH)	ESDJ	109 691	...	...	86	...	...	...	...
McAllen (TX)	ESDJ	123 622	...	...	122	...	...	...	...
Memphis (TN)	ESDJ	672 277	...	...	787	...	...	...	...
Mesa (AZ)[26]	ESDJ	442 780	...	...	336	...	...	...	...
Mesquite (TX)[20]	ESDJ	129 902	...	...	113	...	...	...	...
Miami (FL)	ESDJ	386 417	...	...	93	...	...	...	...
Milwaukee (WI)	ESDJ	578 887	...	...	249	...	...	...	...
Minneapolis (MN)	ESDJ	372 811	...	...	142	...	...	...	...
Miramar (FL)	ESDJ	106 623	...	...	77	...	...	...	...
Mobile (AL)	ESDJ	191 544	...	...	305	...	...	...	...
Modesto (CA)	ESDJ	207 011	...	...	93	...	...	...	...
Montgomery (AL)	ESDJ	200 127	...	...	406	...	...	...	...
Moreno Valley (CA)[31]	ESDJ	178 367	...	...	132	...	...	...	...
Naperville (IL)[22]	ESDJ	141 579	...	...	100	...	...	...	...
Nashville-Davidson (TN)	ESDJ	549 110	...	...	1 224	...	...	...	...
New Haven (CT)	ESDJ	124 791	...	...	49	...	...	...	...

8. Population of capital cities and cities of 100 000 or more inhabitants: latest available year, 1987 - 2006
Population des capitales et des villes de 100 000 habitants ou plus: dernière année disponible, 1987 - 2006
(continued — suite)

Continent, country or area, date and city Continent, pays ou zone, date et ville	Code[1]	City proper — Ville proprement dite Population				Urban agglomeration — Agglomération urbaine Population			
		Both sexes Les deux sexes	Male Masculin	Female Féminin	Surface area Superficie (km²)	Both sexes Les deux sexes	Male Masculin	Female Féminin	Surface area Superficie (km²)
AMERICA, NORTH — AMERIQUE DU NORD									
United States — Etats-Unis[16,17]									
1 VII 2005									
New Orleans (LA)	ESDJ	454 863	...	...	438	...	...	...	...
New York (NY)	ESDJ	8 143 197	...	...	783	...	...	...	...
Newark (NJ)[32]	ESDJ	280 666	...	...	62	...	...	...	...
Newport News (VA)[27]	ESDJ	179 899	...	...	177	...	...	...	...
Norfolk (VA)[27]	ESDJ	231 954	...	...	139	...	...	...	...
Norman (OK)	ESDJ	101 719	...	...	460	...	...	...	...
North Las Vegas (NV)[33]	ESDJ	176 635	...	...	206	...	...	...	...
Norwalk (CA)[19]	ESDJ	105 834	...	...	25	...	...	...	...
Oakland (CA)[24]	ESDJ	395 274	...	...	145	...	...	...	...
Oceanside (CA)[28]	ESDJ	166 108	...	...	105	...	...	...	...
Oklahoma City (OK)	ESDJ	531 324	...	...	1 572	...	...	...	...
Olathe (KS)	ESDJ	111 334	...	...	144	...	...	...	...
Omaha (NE)	ESDJ	414 521	...	...	304	...	...	...	...
Ontario (CA)[19]	ESDJ	172 679	...	...	129	...	...	...	...
Orange (CA)[19]	ESDJ	134 950	...	...	62	...	...	...	...
Orlando (FL)	ESDJ	213 223	...	...	260	...	...	...	...
Overland Park (KS)[34]	ESDJ	164 811	...	...	161	...	...	...	...
Oxnard (CA)	ESDJ	183 628	...	...	70	...	...	...	...
Palmdale (CA)[36]	ESDJ	134 570	...	...	274	...	...	...	...
Pasadena (CA)[19]	ESDJ	143 731	...	...	60	...	...	...	...
Pasadena (TX)[37]	ESDJ	143 852	...	...	117	...	...	...	...
Paterson (NJ)[32]	ESDJ	149 843	...	...	22	...	...	...	...
Pembroke Pines (FL)[30]	ESDJ	150 380	...	...	85	...	...	...	...
Peoria (AZ)[26]	ESDJ	138 200	...	...	456	...	...	...	...
Peoria (IL)	ESDJ	112 685	...	...	119	...	...	...	...
Philadelphia (PA)	ESDJ	1 463 281	...	...	347	...	...	...	...
Phoenix (AZ)	ESDJ	1 461 575	...	...	1 328	...	...	...	...
Pittsburgh (PA)	ESDJ	316 718	...	...	144	...	...	...	...
Plano (TX)[20]	ESDJ	250 096	...	...	186	...	...	...	...
Pomona (CA)[19]	ESDJ	153 787	...	...	59	...	...	...	...
Pompano Beach (FL)	ESDJ	104 179	...	...	62	...	...	...	...
Port St. Lucie (FL)	ESDJ	131 692	...	...	288	...	...	...	...
Portland (OR)	ESDJ	533 427	...	...	348	...	...	...	...
Portsmouth (VA)[27]	ESDJ	100 169	...	...	86	...	...	...	...
Providence (RI)	ESDJ	176 862	...	...	48	...	...	...	...
Provo (UT)	ESDJ	113 459	...	...	103	...	...	...	...
Pueblo (CO)	ESDJ	103 495	...	...	120	...	...	...	...
Raleigh (NC)	ESDJ	341 530	...	...	339	...	...	...	...
Rancho Cucamonga (CA)[19]	ESDJ	169 353	...	...	100	...	...	...	...
Reno (NV)	ESDJ	203 550	...	...	187	...	...	...	...
Richmond (CA)	ESDJ	102 186	...	...	78	...	...	...	...
Richmond (VA)	ESDJ	193 777	...	...	156	...	...	...	...
Riverside (CA)	ESDJ	290 086	...	...	205	...	...	...	...
Rochester (NY)	ESDJ	211 091	...	...	93	...	...	...	...
Rockford (IL)	ESDJ	152 916	...	...	151	...	...	...	...
Roseville (CA)	ESDJ	105 940	...	...	81	...	...	...	...
Sacramento (CA)	ESDJ	456 441	...	...	252	...	...	...	...
St. Louis (MO)	ESDJ	344 362	...	...	160	...	...	...	...
St. Paul (MN)[38]	ESDJ	275 150	...	...	135	...	...	...	...
St. Petersburg (FL)[29]	ESDJ	249 079	...	...	159	...	...	...	...
Salem (OR)	ESDJ	148 751	...	...	120	...	...	...	...
Salinas (CA)	ESDJ	140 401	...	...	50	...	...	...	...
Salt Lake City (UT)	ESDJ	178 097	...	...	283	...	...	...	...
San Antonio (TX)	ESDJ	1 256 509	...	...	1 088	...	...	...	...
San Bernardino (CA)[31]	ESDJ	198 550	...	...	153	...	...	...	...
San Buenaventura (CA)[39]	ESDJ	104 017	...	...	56	...	...	...	...
San Diego (CA)	ESDJ	1 255 540	...	...	844	...	...	...	...
San Francisco (CA)	ESDJ	739 426	...	...	121	...	...	...	...
San Jose (CA)	ESDJ	912 332	...	...	456	...	...	...	...

8. Population of capital cities and cities of 100 000 or more inhabitants: latest available year, 1987 - 2006
Population des capitales et des villes de 100 000 habitants ou plus: dernière année disponible, 1987 - 2006
(continued — suite)

Continent, country or area, date and city / Continent, pays ou zone, date et ville	Code[1]	City proper — Ville proprement dite Population				Urban agglomeration — Agglomération urbaine Population			
		Both sexes Les deux sexes	Male Masculin	Female Féminin	Surface area Superficie (km²)	Both sexes Les deux sexes	Male Masculin	Female Féminin	Surface area Superficie (km²)
AMERICA, NORTH — AMERIQUE DU NORD									
United States — Etats-Unis[16,17]									
1 VII 2005									
Santa Ana (CA)[19]	ESDJ	340 368	...	...	70	...	...	...	...
Santa Clara (CA)[40]	ESDJ	105 402	...	...	48	...	...	...	...
Santa Clarita (CA)	ESDJ	168 253	...	...	133	...	...	...	...
Santa Rosa (CA)	ESDJ	153 158	...	...	105	...	...	...	...
Savannah (GA)	ESDJ	128 453	...	...	223	...	...	...	...
Scottsdale (AZ)[26]	ESDJ	226 013	...	...	479	...	...	...	...
Seattle (WA)	ESDJ	573 911	...	...	217	...	...	...	...
Shreveport (LA)	ESDJ	198 874	...	...	273	...	...	...	...
Simi Valley (CA)	ESDJ	118 687	...	...	109	...	...	...	...
Sioux Falls (SD)	ESDJ	139 517	...	...	163	...	...	...	...
South Bend (IN)	ESDJ	105 262	...	...	104	...	...	...	...
Spokane (WA)	ESDJ	196 818	...	...	150	...	...	...	...
Springfield (IL)	ESDJ	115 668	...	...	145	...	...	...	...
Springfield (MA)	ESDJ	151 732	...	...	83	...	...	...	...
Springfield (MO)	ESDJ	150 298	...	...	203	...	...	...	...
Stamford (CT)[41]	ESDJ	120 045	...	...	98	...	...	...	...
Sterling Heights (MI)[42]	ESDJ	128 034	...	...	95	...	...	...	...
Stockton (CA)	ESDJ	286 926	...	...	147	...	...	...	...
Sunnyvale (CA)[40]	ESDJ	128 902	...	...	57	...	...	...	...
Syracuse (NY)	ESDJ	141 683	...	...	65	...	...	...	...
Tacoma (WA)[23]	ESDJ	195 898	...	...	130	...	...	...	...
Tallahassee (FL)	ESDJ	158 500	...	...	256	...	...	...	...
Tampa (FL)	ESDJ	325 989	...	...	303	...	...	...	...
Tempe (AZ)[26]	ESDJ	161 143	...	...	104	...	...	...	...
Thornton (CO)	ESDJ	105 182	...	...	78	...	...	...	...
Thousand Oaks (CA)	ESDJ	124 359	...	...	142	...	...	...	...
Toledo (OH)	ESDJ	301 285	...	...	209	...	...	...	...
Topeka (KS)	ESDJ	121 946	...	...	148	...	...	...	...
Torrance (CA)[19]	ESDJ	142 384	...	...	53	...	...	...	...
Tucson (AZ)	ESDJ	515 526	...	...	583	...	...	...	...
Tulsa (OK)	ESDJ	382 457	...	...	509	...	...	...	...
Vallejo (CA)	ESDJ	117 483	...	...	78	...	...	...	...
Vancouver (WA)[43]	ESDJ	157 493	...	...	112	...	...	...	...
Virginia Beach (VA)	ESDJ	438 415	...	...	643	...	...	...	...
Visalia (CA)	ESDJ	108 669	...	...	84	...	...	...	...
Waco (TX)	ESDJ	120 465	...	...	225	...	...	...	...
Warren (MI)[42]	ESDJ	135 311	...	...	89	...	...	...	...
WASHINGTON (DC)	ESDJ	550 521	...	...	158	...	...	...	...
Waterbury (CT)	ESDJ	107 902	...	...	74	...	...	...	...
West Covina (CA)[19]	ESDJ	108 185	...	...	42	...	...	...	...
West Valley City (UT)[44]	ESDJ	113 300	...	...	92	...	...	...	...
Westminster (CO)[21]	ESDJ	105 084	...	...	84	...	...	...	...
Wichita (KS)	ESDJ	354 865	...	...	391	...	...	...	...
Winston-Salem (NC)	ESDJ	193 755	...	...	284	...	...	...	...
Worcester (MA)	ESDJ	175 898	...	...	97	...	...	...	...
Yonkers (NY)[32]	ESDJ	196 425	...	...	47	...	...	...	...
United States Virgin Islands — Iles Vierges américaines[15]									
1 IV 2000									
CHARLOTTE AMALIE	CDFC	11 004	...	...	...	18 914	...	...	...
AMERICA, SOUTH — AMERIQUE DU SUD									
Argentina — Argentine									
15 V 1991									
Avellaneda	CDFC	344 024	...	...	...	...	...	...	...
Bahía Blanca	CDFC	260 096	...	...	...	...	...	...	...
BUENOS AIRES	CDFC	2 965 403	...	...	...	11 298 030	...	...	...

8. Population of capital cities and cities of 100 000 or more inhabitants: latest available year, 1987 - 2006
Population des capitales et des villes de 100 000 habitants ou plus: dernière année disponible, 1987 - 2006
(continued — suite)

Continent, country or area, date and city / Continent, pays ou zone, date et ville	Code[1]	City proper — Ville proprement dite Population				Urban agglomeration — Agglomération urbaine Population			
		Both sexes Les deux sexes	Male Masculin	Female Féminin	Surface area Superficie (km²)	Both sexes Les deux sexes	Male Masculin	Female Féminin	Surface area Superficie (km²)
AMERICA, SOUTH — AMERIQUE DU SUD									
Argentina — Argentine									
15 V 1991									
Catamarca	CDFC	109 882	...	...	...	132 626	...	...	...
Comodoro Rivadavia	CDFC	124 104	...	...	...	...	...	...	...
Concordia	CDFC	116 485	...	...	...	...	...	...	...
Córdoba	CDFC	1 157 507	...	...	...	1 208 554	...	...	...
Corrientes	CDFC	258 103	...	...	...	...	...	...	...
Formosa	CDFC	147 636	...	...	...	...	...	...	...
General San Martín	CDFC	406 809	...	...	...	...	...	...	...
La Matanza	CDFC	1 120 088	...	...	...	...	...	...	...
Lanus	CDFC	468 561	...	...	...	...	...	...	...
La Plata	CDFC	521 936	...	...	...	642 979	...	...	...
Lomas de Zamora	CDFC	574 330	...	...	...	...	...	...	...
Mar del Plata	CDFC	512 880	...	...	...	...	...	...	...
Mendoza	CDFC	121 620	...	...	...	773 113	...	...	...
Morón	CDFC	643 553	...	...	...	...	...	...	...
Neuquén	CDFC	167 296	...	...	...	183 579	...	...	...
Paraná	CDFC	207 041	...	...	...	211 936	...	...	...
Posadas	CDFC	201 273	...	...	...	210 755	...	...	...
Quilmes	CDFC	511 234	...	...	...	...	...	...	...
Resistencia	CDFC	229 212	...	...	...	292 287	...	...	...
Río Cuarto	CDFC	134 355	...	...	...	138 853	...	...	...
Rosario	CDFC	907 718	...	...	...	1 118 905	...	...	...
Salta	CDFC	367 550	...	...	...	370 904	...	...	...
San Fernando	CDFC	141 063	...	...	...	...	...	...	...
San Isidro	CDFC	299 023	...	...	...	...	...	...	...
San Juan	CDFC	119 423	...	...	...	352 691	...	...	...
San Miguel de Tucumán	CDFC	470 809	...	...	...	622 324	...	...	...
San Nicolás	CDFC	119 302	...	...	...	...	...	...	...
San Salvador de Jujuy	CDFC	178 748	...	...	...	180 102	...	...	...
Santa Fé	CDFC	353 063	...	...	...	406 388	...	...	...
Santiago del Estero	CDFC	189 947	...	...	...	263 471	...	...	...
Vicente López	CDFC	289 505	...	...	...	...	...	...	...
Bolivia — Bolivie									
1 VII 2006									
Cochabamba	ESDF	*586 813*	*280 091*	*306 722*	...	...	...	...	...
El Alto	ESDF	*827 239*	*405 040*	*422 198*	...	...	...	...	...
LA PAZ[45]	ESDF	*835 167*	*397 542*	*437 625*	...	...	...	...	...
Oruro	ESDF	*216 620*	*104 279*	*112 342*	...	...	...	...	...
Potosí	ESDF	*149 246*	*71 761*	*77 485*	...	...	...	...	...
Santa Cruz	ESDF	*1 397 692*	*679 977*	*717 715*	...	...	...	...	...
SUCRE[45]	ESDF	*247 259*	*119 116*	*128 143*	...	...	...	...	...
Tarija	ESDF	*170 906*	*82 438*	*88 468*	...	...	...	...	...
Brazil — Brésil[11]									
1 VII 2005									
Abaeteluba	ESDF	*133 316*	...	...	*1 090*	...	...	...	...
Açailândia	ESDF	*106 357*	...	...	...	...	...	...	...
Aguas Lindas de Goiás	ESDF	*168 919*	...	...	...	...	...	...	...
Alagoinhas	ESDF	*139 818*	...	...	*761*	...	...	...	...
Almirante Tamandaré	ESDF	*113 589*	...	...	...	...	...	...	...
Alvorada	ESDF	*214 953*	...	...	...	...	...	...	...
Americana	ESDF	*203 845*	...	...	...	...	...	...	...
Ananindeua	ESDF	*498 095*	...	...	*485*	...	...	...	...
Anápolis	ESDF	*318 808*	...	...	...	...	...	...	...
Angra dos Reis	ESDF	*144 137*	...	...	...	...	...	...	...
Aparecida de Goiania	ESDF	*453 104*	...	...	...	...	...	...	...
Apucarana	ESDF	*117 260*	...	...	*556*	...	...	...	...
Aracaju	ESDF	*505 286*	...	...	*151*	...	...	...	...
Araçatuba	ESDF	*181 598*	...	...	*2 668*	...	...	...	...
Araguaina	ESDF	*130 105*	...	...	...	...	...	...	...
Araguario	ESDF	*109 876*	...	...	...	...	...	...	...

8. Population of capital cities and cities of 100 000 or more inhabitants: latest available year, 1987 - 2006
Population des capitales et des villes de 100 000 habitants ou plus: dernière année disponible, 1987 - 2006
(continued — suite)

Continent, country or area, date and city Continent, pays ou zone, date et ville	Code[1]	City proper — Ville proprement dite Population				Urban agglomeration — Agglomération urbaine Population			
		Both sexes Les deux sexes	Male Masculin	Female Féminin	Surface area Superficie (km²)	Both sexes Les deux sexes	Male Masculin	Female Féminin	Surface area Superficie (km²)
AMERICA, SOUTH — AMERIQUE DU SUD									
Brazil — Brésil[11]									
1 VII 2005									
Arapiraca	ESDF	202 390	...	...	...	...	...	...	...
Arapongas	ESDF	100 855	...	...	...	...	...	...	...
Araraquara	ESDF	199 657	...	...	...	...	...	...	...
Araras	ESDF	116 566	...	...	...	...	...	...	...
Araruama	ESDF	110 378	...	...	...	...	...	...	...
Araucária	ESDF	118 313	...	...	...	...	...	...	...
Atibaia	ESDF	129 751	...	...	...	...	...	...	...
Bagé	ESDF	122 461	...	...	7 185	...	...	...	...
Barbacena	ESDF	124 601	...	...	...	...	...	...	...
Barueri	ESDF	265 549	...	...	...	...	...	...	...
Barra Mansa	ESDF	176 151	...	...	830	...	...	...	...
Barreiras	ESDF	138 037	...	...	...	...	...	...	...
Barretos	ESDF	110 195	...	...	...	...	...	...	...
Bauru	ESDF	356 680	...	...	702	...	...	...	...
Belém	ESDF	1 428 368	...	...	736	...	...	...	...
Belford Roxo	ESDF	489 002	...	...	...	...	...	...	...
Belo Horizonte	ESDF	2 399 920	...	...	335	...	...	...	...
Bento Gonçalves	ESDF	104 423	...	...	...	...	...	...	...
Betim	ESDF	407 003	...	...	376	...	...	...	...
Birigui	ESDF	108 472	...	...	...	...	...	...	...
Blumenou	ESDF	298 603	...	...	509	...	...	...	...
Boa Vista	ESDF	249 655	...	...	...	...	...	...	...
Botucatu	ESDF	121 274	...	...	...	...	...	...	...
Bragança	ESDF	103 751	...	...	...	...	...	...	...
Bragança Paulista	ESDF	143 621	...	...	770	...	...	...	...
BRASILIA	ESDF	2 383 784	...	...	5 794	...	...	...	...
Cabo de Santo Agostinho	ESDF	172 150	...	...	...	...	...	...	...
Cabo Frio	ESDF	165 591	...	...	...	...	...	...	...
Cachoeirinha	ESDF	121 880	...	...	...	...	...	...	...
Cachoeiro de Itapemirim	ESDF	198 150	...	...	892	...	...	...	...
Camacari	ESDF	197 144	...	...	718	...	...	...	...
Camaragibe	ESDF	150 354	...	...	...	...	...	...	...
Cametá	ESDF	106 816	...	...	...	...	...	...	...
Campina Grande	ESDF	379 871	...	...	970	...	...	...	...
Campinas	ESDF	1 059 420	...	...	781	...	...	...	...
Campo Grande	ESDF	765 247	...	...	8 091	...	...	...	...
Campo Largo	ESDF	107 756	...	...	...	...	...	...	...
Campos dos Goytacazes	ESDF	429 667	...	...	4 536	...	...	...	...
Canoas	ESDF	333 322	...	...	...	...	...	...	...
Carapicuíba	ESDF	389 634	...	...	...	...	...	...	...
Cariacica	ESDF	361 058	...	...	279	...	...	...	...
Caruaru	ESDF	283 152	...	...	936	...	...	...	...
Cascavel	ESDF	284 083	...	...	2 074	...	...	...	...
Castanhal	ESDF	158 462	...	...	1 003	...	...	...	...
Catanduva	ESDF	116 984	...	...	...	...	...	...	...
Caucaia	ESDF	313 584	...	...	1 293	...	...	...	...
Caxias	ESDF	144 387	...	...	6 724	...	...	...	...
Caxias do Sul	ESDF	412 053	...	...	1 601	...	...	...	...
Chapecó	ESDF	173 262	...	...	...	...	...	...	...
Codo	ESDF	115 098	...	...	4 923	...	...	...	...
Colatina	ESDF	111 789	...	...	2 094	...	...	...	...
Colombo	ESDF	231 787	...	...	...	...	...	...	...
Conselheiro Lafaiete	ESDF	113 019	...	...	...	...	...	...	...
Contagem	ESDF	603 376	...	...	167	...	...	...	...
Coronel Fabriciano	ESDF	104 851	...	...	...	...	...	...	...
Corumbá	ESDF	101 089	...	...	...	...	...	...	...
Cotia	ESDF	179 685	...	...	...	...	...	...	...
Crato	ESDF	115 087	...	...	...	...	...	...	...
Criciúma	ESDF	188 233	...	...	...	...	...	...	...

8. Population of capital cities and cities of 100 000 or more inhabitants: latest available year, 1987 - 2006
Population des capitales et des villes de 100 000 habitants ou plus: dernière année disponible, 1987 - 2006
(continued — suite)

Continent, country or area, date and city / Continent, pays ou zone, date et ville	Code[1]	City proper — Ville proprement dite Population				Urban agglomeration — Agglomération urbaine Population			
		Both sexes Les deux sexes	Male Masculin	Female Féminin	Surface area Superficie (km²)	Both sexes Les deux sexes	Male Masculin	Female Féminin	Surface area Superficie (km²)
AMERICA, SOUTH — AMERIQUE DU SUD									
Brazil — Brésil[11]									
1 VII 2005									
Cubatao	ESDF	121 002	...	...	...	...	...	...	...
Cuiabá	ESDF	542 861	...	...	3 922	...	...	...	...
Curitiba	ESDF	1 788 559	...	...	427	...	...	...	...
Diadema	ESDF	395 333	...	...	...	...	...	...	...
Divinópolis	ESDF	207 983	...	...	716	...	...	...	...
Dourados	ESDF	186 357	...	...	4 082	...	...	...	...
Duque de Caxias	ESDF	855 010	...	...	463	...	...	...	...
Embu	ESDF	245 855	...	...	...	...	...	...	...
Erechim	ESDF	100 251	...	...	...	...	...	...	...
Feira de Santana	ESDF	535 820	...	...	1 344	...	...	...	...
Ferraz de Vasconcelos	ESDF	176 532	...	...	...	...	...	...	...
Florianópolis	ESDF	406 564	...	...	440	...	...	...	...
Fortaleza	ESDF	2 416 920	...	...	336	...	...	...	...
Foz do Iguaçu	ESDF	309 113	...	...	596	...	...	...	...
Franca	ESDF	328 121	...	...	...	...	...	...	...
Francisco Morato	ESDF	170 585	...	...	...	...	...	...	...
Franco da Rocha	ESDF	124 816	...	...	...	...	...	...	...
Garanhuns	ESDF	128 398	...	...	456	...	...	...	...
Goiânia	ESDF	1 220 412	...	...	788	...	...	...	...
Governador Valadares	ESDF	259 405	...	...	2 447	...	...	...	...
Gravatai	ESDF	270 763	...	...	...	...	...	...	...
Guaratinguetá	ESDF	113 012	...	...	...	...	...	...	...
Guaíba	ESDF	105 808	...	...	...	...	...	...	...
Guarapari	ESDF	108 120	...	...	...	...	...	...	...
Guarapuava	ESDF	169 007	...	...	5 365	...	...	...	...
Guarujá	ESDF	305 171	...	...	...	...	...	...	...
Guarulhos	ESDF	1 283 253	...	...	...	...	...	...	...
Hortolandia	ESDF	201 795	...	...	...	...	...	...	...
Ibirité	ESDF	173 617	...	...	...	...	...	...	...
Ilhéus	ESDF	220 932	...	...	1 712	...	...	...	...
Imperatriz	ESDF	232 560	...	...	6 014	...	...	...	...
Indaiatuba	ESDF	181 124	...	...	...	...	...	...	...
Ipatinga	ESDF	236 463	...	...	231	...	...	...	...
Itabiraí	ESDF	107 721	...	...	...	...	...	...	...
Itaboraí	ESDF	220 981	...	...	569	...	...	...	...
Itabuna	ESDF	205 070	...	...	...	...	...	...	...
Itajaí	ESDF	168 088	...	...	...	...	...	...	...
Itapetininga	ESDF	143 097	...	...	2 035	...	...	...	...
Itapecerica da Serra	ESDF	162 239	...	...	...	...	...	...	...
Itapevi	ESDF	202 683	...	...	...	...	...	...	...
Itapipoca	ESDF	107 012	...	...	...	...	...	...	...
Itaquaquecetuba	ESDF	352 755	...	...	...	...	...	...	...
Itu	ESDF	156 100	...	...	640	...	...	...	...
Jaboatao dos Guarapes	ESDF	651 355	...	...	...	...	...	...	...
Jacareí	ESDF	211 559	...	...	...	...	...	...	...
Jandira	ESDF	113 323	...	...	...	...	...	...	...
Jaraguá do Sul	ESDF	131 786	...	...	...	...	...	...	...
Jaú	ESDF	125 399	...	...	...	...	...	...	...
Jequié	ESDF	148 992	...	...	3 113	...	...	...	...
Ji-Paraná	ESDF	113 453	...	...	...	...	...	...	...
Joao Pessoa	ESDF	672 081	...	...	...	...	...	...	...
Joinville	ESDF	106 051	...	...	1 080	...	...	...	...
Juazeiro	ESDF	208 299	...	...	5 615	...	...	...	...
Juàzeiro do Norte	ESDF	240 638	...	...	...	...	...	...	...
Juiz de Fora	ESDF	509 125	...	...	1 424	...	...	...	...
Jundiaí	ESDF	348 621	...	...	432	...	...	...	...
Lages	ESDF	168 384	...	...	5 287	...	...	...	...
Lauro de Freitas	ESDF	146 150	...	...	...	...	...	...	...
Limeira	ESDF	279 554	...	...	...	...	...	...	...

8. Population of capital cities and cities of 100 000 or more inhabitants: latest available year, 1987 - 2006
Population des capitales et des villes de 100 000 habitants ou plus: dernière année disponible, 1987 - 2006
(continued — suite)

Continent, country or area, city and city / Continent, pays ou zone, date et ville	Code[1]	City proper — Ville proprement dite Population				Urban agglomeration — Agglomération urbaine Population			
		Both sexes Les deux sexes	Male Masculin	Female Féminin	Surface area Superficie (km²)	Both sexes Les deux sexes	Male Masculin	Female Féminin	Surface area Superficie (km²)

AMERICA, SOUTH — AMERIQUE DU SUD

Brazil — Brésil[11]
1 VII 2005

Linhares	ESDF	123 000	...	...	4 388	...	...	...	...
Londrina	ESDF	495 696	...	...	2 129	...	...	...	...
Luziânia	ESDF	187 262	...	...	4 653	...	...	...	...
Macae	ESDF	160 725	...	...		...	...	...	...
Macapá	ESDF	368 367	...	...	...	...	...	...	...
Maceió	ESDF	922 458	...	...	517	...	...	...	...
Magé	ESDF	237 000	...	...	744	...	...	...	...
Manaus	ESDF	1 688 524	...	...	11 349	...	...	...	...
Maraba	ESDF	200 801	...	...	14 320	...	...	...	...
Maracanau	ESDF	196 422	...	...	...	...	...	...	...
Maranguape	ESDF	100 279	...	...		...	...	...	...
Marília	ESDF	224 093	...	...	1 194	...	...	...	...
Maringá	ESDF	324 397	...	...	490	...	...	...	...
Mauá	ESDF	413 943	...	...		...	...	...	...
Mesquita	ESDF	185 552	...	...		...	...	...	...
Moji das Cruzes	ESDF	372 419	...	...	749	...	...	...	...
Moji-Guaçu	ESDF	141 559	...	...	960	...	...	...	...
Montes Claros	ESDF	348 991	...	...	4 135	...	...	...	...
Mossoró	ESDF	229 787	...	...	2 108	...	...	...	...
Natal	ESDF	789 896	...	...	...	...	...	...	...
Nilópolis	ESDF	150 475	...	...		...	...	...	...
Niterói	ESDF	476 669	...	...	131	...	...	...	...
Nossa Senhora do Socorro	ESDF	179 060	...	...	...	...	...	...	...
Nova Friburgo	ESDF	178 102	...	...	930	...	...	...	...
Nova Iguaçu	ESDF	844 583	...	...	795	...	...	...	...
Nôvo Hamburgo	ESDF	258 754	...	...	...	...	...	...	...
Olinda	ESDF	387 494	...	...		...	...	...	...
Ourinhos	ESDF	106 350	...	...		...	...	...	...
Osasco	ESDF	714 950	...	...		...	...	...	...
Palhoça	ESDF	128 102	...	...		...	...	...	...
Palmas	ESDF	220 889	...	...		...	...	...	...
Paranaguá	ESDF	147 934	...	...	1 015	...	...	...	...
Parintins	ESDF	112 636	...	...		...	...	...	...
Parnaíba	ESDF	143 675	...	...	1 053	...	...	...	...
Parnamirim	ESDF	170 055	...	...		...	...	...	...
Passo Fundo	ESDF	188 302	...	...	1 596	...	...	...	...
Paulo Afonso	ESDF	103 776	...	...	...	...	...	...	...
Passos	ESDF	106 516	...	...		...	...	...	...
Patos de Minas	ESDF	139 354	...	...	3 336	...	...	...	...
Paulista	ESDF	299 744	...	...		...	...	...	...
Pelotas	ESDF	346 452	...	...	1 924	...	...	...	...
Petrolina	ESDF	260 004	...	...	6 116	...	...	...	...
Petrópolis	ESDF	310 216	...	...	771	...	...	...	...
Pindamonhangaba	ESDF	143 737	...	...	719	...	...	...	...
Pinhais	ESDF	123 288	...	...	...	...	...	...	...
Piracicaba	ESDF	366 442	...	...	1 426	...	...	...	...
Poços de Caldas	ESDF	154 477	...	...	533	...	...	...	...
Poà	ESDF	110 213	...	...		...	...	...	...
Ponta Grossa	ESDF	304 973	...	...	2 212	...	...	...	...
Porto Alegre	ESDF	1 440 939	...	...		...	...	...	...
Porto Seguro	ESDF	140 692	...	...	...	...	...	...	...
Porto Velho	ESDF	380 974	...	...		...	...	...	...
Pouso Alegre	ESDF	125 209	...	...		...	...	...	...
Praia Grande	ESDF	245 386	...	...		...	...	...	...
Presidente Prudente	ESDF	206 704	...	...	554	...	...	...	...
Queimados	ESDF	139 118	...	...		...	...	...	...
Recife	ESDF	1 515 052	...	...		...	...	...	...
Resende	ESDF	119 729	...	...	...	...	...	...	...
Ribeirao das Neves	ESDF	322 969	...	...	...	...	...	...	...

8. Population of capital cities and cities of 100 000 or more inhabitants: latest available year, 1987 - 2006
Population des capitales et des villes de 100 000 habitants ou plus: dernière année disponible, 1987 - 2006
(continued — suite)

Continent, country or area, date and city Continent, pays ou zone, date et ville	Code[1]	City proper — Ville proprement dite Population				Urban agglomeration — Agglomération urbaine Population			
		Both sexes Les deux sexes	Male Masculin	Female Féminin	Surface area Superficie (km²)	Both sexes Les deux sexes	Male Masculin	Female Féminin	Surface area Superficie (km²)
AMERICA, SOUTH — AMERIQUE DU SUD									
Brazil — Brésil[11]									
1 VII 2005									
Ribeirao Prêto	ESDF	559 650	...	...	...	...	...	...	...
Ribeirao Pires	ESDF	118 864	...	...	...	...	...	...	...
Rio Branco	ESDF	314 127	...	...	...	...	...	...	...
Rio Claro	ESDF	190 373	...	...	503	...	...	...	...
Rio de Janeiro	ESDF	6 136 652	...	...	1 256	...	...	...	...
Rio Grande	ESDF	196 982	...	...	2 825	...	...	...	...
Rio Verde	ESDF	136 229	...	...	9 136	...	...	...	...
Rondonópolis	ESDF	169 814	...	...	4 594	...	...	...	...
Sabára	ESDF	134 282	...	...	...	...	...	...	...
Salvador	ESDF	2 714 018	...	...	313	...	...	...	...
Santa Bárbara D'Oeste	ESDF	188 417	...	...	...	...	...	...	...
Santa Cruz do Sul	ESDF	119 803	...	...	...	...	...	...	...
Santa Luzia (Minas Gerais)	ESDF	219 699	...	...	...	...	...	...	...
Santa Maria	ESDF	270 073	...	...	3 279	...	...	...	...
Salto	ESDF	108 552	...	...	...	...	...	...	...
Santa Rita	ESDF	131 684	...	...	...	...	...	...	...
Santarém	ESDF	276 074	...	...	...	...	...	...	...
Santo André	ESDF	673 234	...	...	...	...	...	...	...
Santos	ESDF	418 375	...	...	725	...	...	...	...
Sao Bernardo do Campo	ESDF	803 906	...	...	319	...	...	...	...
Sao Caetano do Sul	ESDF	133 241	...	...	...	...	...	...	...
Sao Carlo	ESDF	218 702	...	...	1 120	...	...	...	...
Sao Gonçalo	ESDF	973 372	...	...	...	...	...	...	...
Sao Joao de Meriti	ESDF	466 996	...	...	...	...	...	...	...
Sao José	ESDF	201 103	...	...	...	...	...	...	...
Sao José de Ribamar	ESDF	134 593	...	...	...	...	...	...	...
Sao José do Rio Prêto	ESDF	415 508	...	...	586	...	...	...	...
Sao José dos Campos	ESDF	610 965	...	...	1 186	...	...	...	...
Sao José dos Pinhais	ESDF	261 125	...	...	923	...	...	...	...
Sao Leopoldo	ESDF	212 498	...	...	...	...	...	...	...
Sao Luís	ESDF	998 385	...	...	822	...	...	...	...
Sao Paulo	ESDF	11 016 703	...	...	1 493	...	...	...	...
Sao Vicente	ESDF	329 370	...	...	...	...	...	...	...
Sapucaia do Sul	ESDF	135 956	...	...	...	...	...	...	...
Serra	ESDF	394 370	...	...	549	...	...	...	...
Sertaozinho	ESDF	106 407	...	...	...	...	...	...	...
Sete Lagoas	ESDF	215 069	...	...	...	...	...	...	...
Simoes Filho	ESDF	109 930	...	...	...	...	...	...	...
Sobral	ESDF	175 814	...	...	1 646	...	...	...	...
Sorocaba	ESDF	578 068	...	...	...	...	...	...	...
Sumaré	ESDF	237 900	...	...	208	...	...	...	...
Susano	ESDF	280 318	...	...	...	...	...	...	...
Taboao da Serra	ESDF	225 405	...	...	...	...	...	...	...
Taubaté	ESDF	271 660	...	...	...	...	...	...	...
Tatuí	ESDF	107 115	...	...	...	...	...	...	...
Teixeira de Freitas	ESDF	123 557	...	...	...	...	...	...	...
Teófilo Otoni	ESDF	127 530	...	...	...	...	...	...	...
Teresina	ESDF	801 971	...	...	1 356	...	...	...	...
Teresópolis	ESDF	150 921	...	...	768	...	...	...	...
Timon	ESDF	146 139	...	...	1 702	...	...	...	...
Toledo	ESDF	107 033	...	...	...	...	...	...	...
Uberaba	ESDF	295 094	...	...	4 524	...	...	...	...
Uberlândia	ESDF	600 368	...	...	4 040	...	...	...	...
Uruguaiana	ESDF	136 364	...	...	6 763	...	...	...	...
Valparaiso de Goiás	ESDF	123 921	...	...	...	...	...	...	...
Varginha	ESDF	124 502	...	...	...	...	...	...	...
Várzea Grande	ESDF	254 736	...	...	900	...	...	...	...
Várzea Paulista	ESDF	110 449	...	...	...	...	...	...	...
Viamao	ESDF	261 971	...	...	...	...	...	...	...

8. Population of capital cities and cities of 100 000 or more inhabitants: latest available year, 1987 - 2006
Population des capitales et des villes de 100 000 habitants ou plus: dernière année disponible, 1987 - 2006
(continued — suite)

Continent, country or area and city — Continent, pays ou zone, date et ville	Code[1]	City proper — Ville proprement dite Population				Urban agglomeration — Agglomération urbaine Population			
		Both sexes Les deux sexes	Male Masculin	Female Féminin	Surface area Superficie (km²)	Both sexes Les deux sexes	Male Masculin	Female Féminin	Surface area Superficie (km²)
AMERICA, SOUTH — AMERIQUE DU SUD									
Brazil — Brésil[11]									
1 VII 2005									
Vila Velha	ESDF	405 374	...	...	...	...	...	...	...
Vitória	ESDF	317 085	...	...	...	...	...	...	...
Vitória da Conquista	ESDF	290 042	...	...	3 743	...	...	...	...
Vitória de Santo Antao	ESDF	125 563	...	...	344	...	...	...	...
Volta Redonda	ESDF	258 145	...	...	...	...	...	...	...
Chile — Chili									
30 VI 2006									
Antofagasta	ESDF	341 942	177 640	164 302	...	...	...	...	...
Arica	ESDF	173 222	83 391	89 831	...	...	...	...	...
Calama	ESDF	144 913	74 026	70 887	...	...	...	...	...
Chillán	ESDF	153 012	72 383	80 629	...	...	...	...	...
Concepción	ESDF	219 994	106 285	113 709	...	...	...	...	...
Copiapó	ESDF	145 292	72 875	72 417	...	...	...	...	...
Coquimbo	ESDF	167 952	81 474	86 478	...	...	...	...	...
Iquique	ESDF	178 356	86 755	91 601	...	...	...	...	...
La Serena	ESDF	175 064	84 791	90 273	...	...	...	...	...
Los Angeles	ESDF	129 450	62 636	66 814	...	...	...	...	...
Osorno	ESDF	142 169	69 293	72 876	...	...	...	...	...
Puente Alto	ESDF	626 310	307 076	319 234	...	...	...	...	...
Puerto Montt	ESDF	175 970	87 947	88 023	...	...	...	...	...
Punta Arenas	ESDF	120 017	60 244	59 773	...	...	...	...	...
Quilpué	ESDF	145 001	70 287	74 714	...	...	...	...	...
Rancagua	ESDF	226 798	112 126	114 672	...	...	...	...	...
San Bernardo	ESDF	276 016	135 906	140 110	...	...	...	...	...
SANTIAGO[46]	ESDF	5 890 745	2 860 572	3 030 173	...	...	...	...	...
Talca	ESDF	203 911	97 969	105 942	...	...	...	...	...
Talcahuano	ESDF	156 835	75 833	81 002	...	...	...	...	...
Temuco	ESDF	247 275	118 051	129 224	...	...	...	...	...
Valdivia	ESDF	134 829	65 511	69 318	...	...	...	...	...
Valparaíso	ESDF	275 063	136 143	138 920	...	...	...	...	...
Viña del Mar	ESDF	292 062	139 901	152 161	...	...	...	...	...
Colombia — Colombie[47]									
1 VII 2006									
Apartadó	ESDF	...	...	...	...	135 654	...	...	607
Armenia	ESDF	...	...	...	...	282 534	...	...	115
Barrancabermeja	ESDF	...	...	...	...	190 545	...	...	1 274
Barranquilla	ESDF	...	...	...	...	1 154 642	...	...	166
Bello	ESDF	...	...	...	...	380 324	...	...	151
Bucaramanga	ESDF	...	...	...	...	518 351	...	...	154
Buenaventura	ESDF	...	...	...	...	335 644	...	...	6 785
Buga	ESDF	...	...	...	...	116 657	...	...	873
Cali	ESDF	...	...	...	...	2 144 953	...	...	552
Cartagena	ESDF	...	...	...	...	902 311	...	...	570
Cartago	ESDF	...	...	...	...	125 335	...	...	260
Chia	ESDF	...	...	...	...	100 813	...	...	76
Ciénaga	ESDF	...	...	...	...	102 193	...	...	1 366
Cúcuta	ESDF	...	...	...	...	593 952	...	...	1 098
Dos Quebradas	ESDF	...	...	...	...	181 275	...	...	80
Duitama	ESDF	...	...	...	...	108 126	...	...	229
Envigado	ESDF	...	...	...	...	178 641	...	...	51
Facatativa	ESDF	...	...	...	...	109 997	...	...	160
Florencia (Caquetá)	ESDF	...	...	...	...	146 284	...	...	2 292
Floridablanca	ESDF	...	...	...	...	256 281	...	...	101
Fusagasuga	ESDF	...	...	...	...	111 420	...	...	206
Girón	ESDF	...	...	...	...	139 935	...	...	681
Ibagué	ESDF	...	...	...	...	504 089	...	...	1 439
Ipiales	ESDF	...	...	...	...	111 762	...	...	1 707
Itagüi	ESDF	...	...	...	...	239 053	...	...	17
Lorica	ESDF	...	...	...	...	111 023	...	...	890

8. Population of capital cities and cities of 100 000 or more inhabitants: latest available year, 1987 - 2006
Population des capitales et des villes de 100 000 habitants ou plus: dernière année disponible, 1987 - 2006
(continued — suite)

Continent, country or area, date and city Continent, pays ou zone, date et ville	Code[1]	City proper — Ville proprement dite Population				Urban agglomeration — Agglomération urbaine Population			
		Both sexes Les deux sexes	Male Masculin	Female Féminin	Surface area Superficie (km²)	Both sexes Les deux sexes	Male Masculin	Female Féminin	Surface area Superficie (km²)
AMERICA, SOUTH — AMERIQUE DU SUD									
Colombia — Colombie[47]									
1 VII 2006									
Magangué	ESDF	...	...	...	...	121 628	...	...	1 102
Maicao	ESDF	...	...	...	...	127 489	...	...	2 229
Malambo	ESDF	...	...	...	...	103 340	...	...	108
Manizales	ESDF	...	...	...	...	381 752	...	...	477
Medellín	ESDF	...	...	...	...	2 238 626	...	...	387
Montería	ESDF	...	...	...	...	384 937	...	...	3 043
Neiva	ESDF	...	...	...	...	319 253	...	...	1 468
Palmira	ESDF	...	...	...	...	286 355	...	...	1 044
Pasto	ESDF	...	...	...	...	388 347	...	...	1 181
Pereira	ESDF	...	...	...	...	446 269	...	...	702
Piedecuesta	ESDF	...	...	...	...	120 364	...	...	481
Pitalito	ESDF	...	...	...	...	104 834	...	...	653
Popayán	ESDF	...	...	...	...	259 690	...	...	464
Quibdo	ESDF	...	...	...	...	113 240	...	...	3 075
Riohacha	ESDF	...	...	...	...	176 180	...	...	3 276
Rionogro	ESDF	...	...	...	...	102 483	...	...	198
SANTA FE DE BOGOTA	ESDF	...	...	...	...	6 945 216	...	...	1 605
Santa Marta	ESDF	...	...	...	...	421 703	...	...	2 369
Sincelejo	ESDF	...	...	...	...	241 456	...	...	292
Soacha	ESDF	...	...	...	...	412 922	...	...	187
Sogamoso	ESDF	...	...	...	...	116 946	...	...	214
Soledad	ESDF	...	...	...	...	476 335	...	...	67
Tuluá	ESDF	...	...	...	...	189 758	...	...	818
Tumaco	ESDF	...	...	...	...	163 874	...	...	3 778
Tunja	ESDF	...	...	...	...	157 650	...	...	118
Turbo	ESDF	...	...	...	...	125 398	...	...	3 090
Uribia	ESDF	...	...	...	...	123 175	...	...	7 904
Valledupar	ESDF	...	...	...	...	364 264	...	...	4 225
Villavicencio	ESDF	...	...	...	...	390 293	...	...	1 328
Yopal	ESDF	...	...	...	...	110 076	...	...	2 532
Zipaquira	ESDF	...	...	...	...	103 721	...	...	194
Ecuador — Equateur									
1 VII 2003									
Ambato	ESDF	169 103	...	...	27	...	...	...	...
Cuenca	ESDF	303 994	...	...	47	...	...	...	...
Durán	ESDF	183 731	...	...	...	...	...	...	...
Esmeraldas	ESDF	103 063	...	...	8	...	...	...	...
Guayaquil	ESDF	2 090 039	...	...	193	...	...	...	...
Ibarra	ESDF	118 116	...	...	39	...	...	...	...
Loja	ESDF	129 429	...	...	21	...	...	...	...
Machala	ESDF	217 266	...	...	23	...	...	...	...
Manta	ESDF	193 232	...	...	38	...	...	...	...
Milagro	ESDF	119 420	...	...	17	...	...	...	...
Portoviejo	ESDF	194 916	...	...	38	...	...	...	...
Quevedo	ESDF	128 068	...	...	20	...	...	...	...
QUITO	ESDF	1 482 447	...	...	170	...	...	...	...
Riobamba	ESDF	140 558	...	...	24	...	...	...	...
Santo Domingo de los Colorados	ESDF	211 689	...	...	43	...	...	...	...
Falkland Islands (Malvinas) — Iles Falkland (Malvinas)									
8 X 2006									
STANLEY	CDFC	2 115	...	...	...	...	...	...	...
French Guiana — Guyane Française									
8 III 1999									
CAYENNE[7]	CDJC	50 395	24 496	25 899	24	65 933	32 394	33 539	70
Guyana									
1 VII 2001									
GEORGETOWN	ESDF	...	...	...	...	280 000	...	...	...

8. Population of capital cities and cities of 100 000 or more inhabitants: latest available year, 1987 - 2006
Population des capitales et des villes de 100 000 habitants ou plus: dernière année disponible, 1987 - 2006
(continued — suite)

Continent, country or area, date and city Continent, pays ou zone, date et ville	Code[1]	City proper — Ville proprement dite Population				Urban agglomeration — Agglomération urbaine Population			
		Both sexes Les deux sexes	Male Masculin	Female Féminin	Surface area Superficie (km²)	Both sexes Les deux sexes	Male Masculin	Female Féminin	Surface area Superficie (km²)
AMERICA, SOUTH — AMERIQUE DU SUD									
Paraguay									
28 VIII 2002									
ASUNCION[48]	CDFC	513 399	...	...	117	1 620 483	...	...	...
Capiatá	CDFC	154 469	...	...	...	...	...	...	...
Ciudad del Este	CDFC	223 350	...	...	57	333 535	...	...	...
Fernando de la Mora	CDFC	114 332	...	...	...	...	...	...	...
Lambaré	CDFC	119 984	...	...	...	...	...	...	...
Luque	CDFC	170 433	...	...	...	...	...	...	...
San Lorenzo	CDFC	202 745	...	...	91	...	...	...	...
Peru — Pérou[49]									
18 VII 2005									
Arequipa	CDFC	783 000	...	...	...	...	...	...	...
Ayacucho	CDFC	161 586	...	...	...	...	...	...	...
Cajamarca	CDFC	129 079	...	...	...	...	...	...	...
Callao	CDFC	567 042	...	...	...	...	...	...	...
Chiclayo	CDFC	500 561	...	...	...	...	...	...	...
Chimbote	CDFC	328 386	...	...	...	...	...	...	...
Chincha Alta	CDFC	140 477	...	...	...	...	...	...	...
Cuzco	CDFC	326 405	...	...	...	...	...	...	...
Huancayo	CDFC	306 954	...	...	...	...	...	...	...
Huánuco	CDFC	142 738	...	...	...	...	...	...	...
Ica	CDFC	205 807	...	...	...	...	...	...	...
Iquitos	CDFC	356 549	...	...	...	...	...	...	...
Juliaca	CDFC	208 553	...	...	...	...	...	...	...
LIMA	CDFC	5 681 941	...	...	...	...	...	...	...
Piura	CDFC	361 832	...	...	...	...	...	...	...
Pucallpa	CDFC	248 878	...	...	...	...	...	...	...
Puno	CDFC	118 008	...	...	...	...	...	...	...
Sullana	CDFC	175 078	...	...	...	...	...	...	...
Tacna	CDFC	230 146	...	...	...	...	...	...	...
Tarapoto	CDFC	108 042	...	...	...	...	...	...	...
Trujillo	CDFC	644 547	...	...	...	...	...	...	...
Suriname									
2 VIII 2004									
PARAMARIBO	CDFC	...	...	...	...	242 946	120 292	122 405	182
Uruguay									
30 VI 2006									
MONTEVIDEO	ESDF	1 345 010	627 495	717 515	530	...	...	...	...
Venezuela (Bolivarian Republic of) - Venezuela (République bolivarienne du)									
1 VII 1998									
Acarigua-Araure	ESDF	227 684	...	...	1 065	...	...	...	...
Barcelona	ESDF	301 595	...	...	463	...	...	...	...
Barcelona-Puerto La Cruz	ESDF	484 149	...	...	707	...	...	...	...
Barinas	ESDF	221 558	...	...	848	...	...	...	...
Barquisimeto	ESDF	810 809	...	...	2 645	...	...	...	...
Cabimas	ESDF	213 290	...	...	175	...	...	...	...
CARACAS	ESDF	1 975 294	...	...	433	...	...	...	...
Carúpano	ESDF	116 107	...	...	203	...	...	...	...
Catia la Mar	ESDF	117 013	...	...	76	...	...	...	...
Ciudad Bolívar	ESDF	278 525	...	...	5 851	...	...	...	...
Ciudad Guayana	ESDF	641 998	...	...	1 612	...	...	...	...
Coro	ESDF	167 048	...	...	438	...	...	...	...
Cumaná	ESDF	265 621	...	...	405	...	...	...	...
Guarenas	ESDF	169 202	...	...	180	...	...	...	...
Los Teques	ESDF	176 292	...	...	98	...	...	...	...
Maracaibo	ESDF	1 706 547	...	...	604	...	...	...	...
Maracay	ESDF	458 761	...	...	169	...	...	...	...
Maturín	ESDF	262 167	...	...	...	...	...	...	...
Mérida	ESDF	272 437	...	...	482	...	...	...	...

8. Population of capital cities and cities of 100 000 or more inhabitants: latest available year, 1987 - 2006
Population des capitales et des villes de 100 000 habitants ou plus: dernière année disponible, 1987 - 2006
(continued — suite)

Continent, country or area, date and city / Continent, pays ou zone, date et ville	Code[1]	City proper — Ville proprement dite Population				Urban agglomeration — Agglomération urbaine Population			
		Both sexes Les deux sexes	Male Masculin	Female Féminin	Surface area Superficie (km²)	Both sexes Les deux sexes	Male Masculin	Female Féminin	Surface area Superficie (km²)
AMERICA, SOUTH — AMERIQUE DU SUD									
Venezuela (Bolivarian Republic of) - Venezuela (République bolivarienne du)									
1 VII 1998									
Puerto Cabello	ESDF	176 347	...	...	309				...
Punto Fijo	ESDF	118 126	...	...	31				...
San Cristóbal	ESDF	272 374	...	...	248				...
San Fernando de Apure	ESDF	121 949	...	...	...				...
Turmero	ESDF	203 434	...	...	208				...
Valencia	ESDF	1 263 888	...	...	1 212				...
Valera	ESDF	121 090	...	...	55				...
ASIA — ASIE									
Afghanistan									
1 VII 1988									
Herat	ESDF	*177 300*	...	...	...				...
KABUL	ESDF	*1 424 400*	...	...	...				...
Kandahar (Quandahar)	ESDF	*225 500*	...	...	...				...
Mazar-i-Sharif	ESDF	*130 600*	...	...	...				...
Armenia — Arménie									
1 VII 2006									
Leninakan(Gyumzi)	ESDJ	148 000	70 542	77 458	50				...
Vanadzor (Kirovakan)	ESDJ	105 300	50 011	55 289	25				...
YEREVAN	ESDJ	1 104 398	515 699	588 699	227				...
Azerbaijan — Azerbaïdjan									
1 VII 2004									
BAKU	ESDF	1 847 500	901 700	945 800	2 130				...
Ganja	ESDF	303 800	146 100	157 700	110				...
Sumgayit	ESDF	291 600	143 400	148 200	80				...
Bahrain — Bahreïn									
1 VII 2006									
MANAMA	ESDF	176 909	113 503	63 406	30				...
Bangladesh									
22 I 2001									
Barisal	CDFC	...	...	...	...	192 810	103 785	89 025	20
Bogra	CDFC	...	...	...	...	154 807	82 368	72 439	11
Brahmanbaria	CDFC	...	...	...	...	129 278	66 890	62 388	18
Chittagong	CDFC	...	...	...	...	2 023 489	1 127 516	895 973	168
Comilla	CDFC	...	...	...	...	166 519	88 927	77 592	11
DHAKA	CDFC	...	...	...	...	5 333 571	3 025 395	2 308 176	154
Dinajpur	CDFC	...	...	...	...	157 914	82 068	75 846	19
Gazipur	CDFC	...	...	...	...	122 801	65 522	57 279	49
Jamalpur	CDFC	...	...	...	...	120 955	62 059	58 896	53
Jessore	CDFC	...	...	...	...	176 655	94 203	82 452	15
Kadamrasul	CDFC	...	...	...	...	128 561	66 799	61 762	6
Khulna	CDFC	...	...	...	...	770 498	412 661	357 837	60
Mymensingh	CDFC	...	...	...	...	227 204	119 172	108 032	22
Naogaon	CDFC	...	...	...	...	124 046	65 406	58 640	37
Narayanganj	CDFC	...	...	...	...	241 393	131 168	110 225	13
Narsingdi	CDFC	...	...	...	...	124 204	67 575	56 629	9
Nawabganj	CDFC	...	...	...	...	152 223	75 375	76 848	34
Pabna	CDFC	...	...	...	...	116 305	60 666	55 639	27
Rajshahi	CDFC	...	...	...	...	388 811	208 525	180 286	97
Rangpur	CDFC	...	...	...	...	241 310	124 296	117 014	51
Saidpur	CDFC	...	...	...	...	112 609	58 289	54 320	34
Sirajganj	CDFC	...	...	...	...	128 144	66 673	61 471	28
Tangail	CDFC	...	...	...	...	128 785	66 856	61 929	29
Tongi	CDFC	...	...	...	...	283 099	156 335	126 764	30

8. Population of capital cities and cities of 100 000 or more inhabitants: latest available year, 1987 - 2006
Population des capitales et des villes de 100 000 habitants ou plus: dernière année disponible, 1987 - 2006
(continued — suite)

Continent, country or area, date and city / Continent, pays ou zone, date et ville	Code[1]	City proper — Ville proprement dite Population				Urban agglomeration — Agglomération urbaine Population			
		Both sexes Les deux sexes	Male Masculin	Female Féminin	Surface area Superficie (km²)	Both sexes Les deux sexes	Male Masculin	Female Féminin	Surface area Superficie (km²)
ASIA — ASIE									
Bhutan — Bhoutan									
30 V 2005									
THIMPHU	CDFC	79 185	42 465	36 720	...	...	...	...	...
Brunei Darussalam — Brunéi Darussalam									
21 VIII 2001									
BANDAR SERI BEGAWAN	CDFC	27 285	13 639	13 646	...	...	...	...	...
Cambodia — Cambodge									
1 VII 2002									
Bat Dambang	ESDF	*171 382*	*82 785*	*88 597*	*114*	...	...	...	...
PHNOM PENH	ESDF	*703 963*	*339 763*	*364 200*	*21*	*1 234 444*	...	...	...
Seam Reab	ESDF	*140 966*	*69 052*	*71 914*	*292*	...	...	...	...
China — Chine									
1 VII 1999									
Chiayi	ESDF	264 286	133 270	131 016		...	...	...	...
Hsinchu	ESDF	359 087	183 682	175 405		...	...	...	...
Kaohsiung[50]	ESDF	1 468 586	744 243	724 343		...	...	...	...
Keelung	ESDF	383 272	196 952	186 320		...	...	...	...
Taichung	ESDF	930 175	461 069	469 106		...	...	...	...
Tainan	ESDF	725 445	366 061	359 384		...	...	...	...
Taipei[50]	ESDF	2 640 322	1 310 368	1 329 954		...	...	...	...
1 XI 2000									
Acheng	CDJC	638 894	327 774	311 120		...	...	...	...
Akesu	CDJC	561 822	295 811	266 011		...	...	...	...
Aletai	CDJC	178 510	91 207	87 303		...	...	...	...
Anda	CDJC	473 091	243 349	229 742		...	...	...	...
An'guo	CDJC	378 830	189 944	188 886		...	...	...	...
Ankang	CDJC	843 426	443 270	400 156		...	...	...	...
Anlu	CDJC	611 990	314 089	297 901		...	...	...	...
Anning	CDJC	295 173	161 481	133 692		...	...	...	...
Anqing	CDJC	582 751	293 884	288 867		...	...	...	...
Anqiu	CDJC	1 096 782	554 403	542 379		...	...	...	...
Anshan	CDJC	1 556 285	787 838	768 447		...	...	...	...
Anshun	CDJC	767 307	395 894	371 413		...	...	...	...
Anyang	CDJC	768 992	390 120	378 872		...	...	...	...
Atushi	CDJC	200 345	101 867	98 478		...	...	...	...
Baicheng	CDJC	484 979	244 453	240 526		...	...	...	...
Baise	CDJC	340 483	177 310	163 173		...	...	...	...
Baishan	CDJC	335 400	172 109	163 291		...	...	...	...
Baiyin	CDJC	460 982	243 672	217 310		...	...	...	...
Baoding	CDJC	902 496	455 625	446 871		...	...	...	...
Baoji	CDJC	600 377	308 493	291 884		...	...	...	...
Baoshan	CDJC	846 865	430 076	416 789		...	...	...	...
Baotou	CDJC	1 671 181	862 495	808 686		...	...	...	...
Bazhong	CDJC	1 185 862	616 323	569 539		...	...	...	...
Bazhou	CDJC	557 901	285 321	272 580		...	...	...	...
Beian	CDJC	442 474	226 743	215 731		...	...	...	...
Beihai	CDJC	558 635	290 544	268 091		...	...	...	...
BEIJING (PEKING)	CDJC	11 509 595	6 020 903	5 488 692		...	...	...	...
Beiliu	CDJC	1 049 035	557 967	491 068		...	...	...	...
Beining	CDJC	527 217	270 153	257 064		...	...	...	...
Beipiao	CDJC	573 836	291 584	282 252		...	...	...	...
Bengbu	CDJC	809 399	413 444	395 955		...	...	...	...
Benxi	CDJC	980 069	495 102	484 967		...	...	...	...
Bijie	CDJC	1 128 230	589 537	538 693		...	...	...	...
Binzhou	CDJC	600 883	299 952	300 931		...	...	...	...
Bole	CDJC	224 869	116 506	108 363		...	...	...	...
Botou	CDJC	550 888	280 209	270 679		...	...	...	...
Bozhou	CDJC	1 351 939	697 126	654 813		...	...	...	...
Cangzhou	CDJC	443 561	223 648	219 913		...	...	...	...
Cenxi	CDJC	731 623	384 212	347 411		...	...	...	...
Changchun	CDJC	3 225 557	1 647 216	1 578 341		...	...	...	...

8. Population of capital cities and cities of 100 000 or more inhabitants: latest available year, 1987 - 2006
Population des capitales et des villes de 100 000 habitants ou plus: dernière année disponible, 1987 - 2006
(continued — suite)

Continent, country or area, date and city / Continent, pays ou zone, date et ville	Code[1]	City proper — Ville proprement dite Population				Urban agglomeration — Agglomération urbaine Population			
		Both sexes Les deux sexes	Male Masculin	Female Féminin	Surface area Superficie (km²)	Both sexes Les deux sexes	Male Masculin	Female Féminin	Surface area Superficie (km²)
ASIA — ASIE									
China — Chine									
1 XI 2000									
Changde	CDJC	1 346 739	686 467	660 272	...	...	...	...	...
Changge	CDJC	646 306	332 022	314 284	...	...	...	...	...
Changji	CDJC	387 169	202 275	184 894	...	...	...	...	...
Changle	CDJC	689 815	358 963	330 852	...	...	...	...	...
Changning	CDJC	795 223	428 332	366 891	...	...	...	...	...
Changsha	CDJC	2 122 873	1 099 304	1 023 569	...	...	...	...	...
Changshu	CDJC	1 239 637	598 034	641 603	...	...	...	...	...
Changyi	CDJC	683 182	340 763	342 419	...	...	...	...	...
Changzhi	CDJC	648 981	332 246	316 735	...	...	...	...	...
Changzhou	CDJC	1 081 845	552 850	528 995	...	...	...	...	...
Chaohu	CDJC	778 864	396 961	381 903	...	...	...	...	...
Chaoyang (Guangdong)	CDJC	2 470 812	1 256 428	1 214 384	...	...	...	...	...
Chaoyang (Liaoning)	CDJC	475 038	238 128	236 910	...	...	...	...	...
Chaozhou	CDJC	363 582	181 260	182 322	...	...	...	...	...
Chengde	CDJC	437 251	221 221	216 030	...	...	...	...	...
Chengdu	CDJC	4 333 541	2 258 996	2 074 545	...	...	...	...	...
Chenghai	CDJC	860 003	428 157	431 846	...	...	...	...	...
Chenzhou	CDJC	655 014	340 799	314 215	...	...	...	...	...
Chibi	CDJC	510 926	267 233	243 693	...	...	...	...	...
Chifeng	CDJC	1 153 723	589 450	564 273	...	...	...	...	...
Chishui	CDJC	251 780	130 227	121 553	...	...	...	...	...
Chizhou	CDJC	555 489	280 395	275 094	...	...	...	...	...
Chongqing	CDJC	9 691 901	5 013 398	4 678 503	...	...	...	...	...
Chongzhou	CDJC	650 698	330 345	320 353	...	...	...	...	...
Chuxiong	CDJC	503 682	261 315	242 367	...	...	...	...	...
Chuzhou	CDJC	493 735	251 117	242 618	...	...	...	...	...
Cixi	CDJC	1 214 537	615 279	599 258	...	...	...	...	...
Conghua	CDJC	517 552	264 150	253 402	...	...	...	...	...
Daan	CDJC	430 512	219 682	210 830	...	...	...	...	...
Dafeng	CDJC	756 766	383 391	373 375	...	...	...	...	...
Dali	CDJC	521 169	262 564	258 605	...	...	...	...	...
Dalian	CDJC	3 245 191	1 641 485	1 603 706	...	...	...	...	...
Dandong	CDJC	780 414	389 277	391 137	...	...	...	...	...
Dangyang	CDJC	495 946	253 125	242 821	...	...	...	...	...
Danjiangkou	CDJC	501 126	262 922	238 204	...	...	...	...	...
Danyang	CDJC	877 232	442 296	434 936	...	...	...	...	...
Danzhou	CDJC	835 465	442 636	392 829	...	...	...	...	...
Daqing	CDJC	1 380 051	704 765	675 286	...	...	...	...	...
Dashiqiao	CDJC	714 670	370 713	343 957	...	...	...	...	...
Datong	CDJC	1 526 744	785 754	740 990	...	...	...	...	...
Daye	CDJC	873 859	460 417	413 442	...	...	...	...	...
Dazhou	CDJC	384 525	192 819	191 706	...	...	...	...	...
Dehui	CDJC	878 349	448 146	430 203	...	...	...	...	...
Dengfeng	CDJC	609 085	321 081	288 004	...	...	...	...	...
Dengta	CDJC	502 149	259 895	242 254	...	...	...	...	...
Dengzhou	CDJC	1 290 656	677 791	612 865	...	...	...	...	...
Dexing	CDJC	297 784	155 178	142 606	...	...	...	...	...
Deyang	CDJC	628 876	324 823	304 053	...	...	...	...	...
Dezhou	CDJC	552 445	277 994	274 451	...	...	...	...	...
Dingzhou	CDJC	1 107 903	559 214	548 689	...	...	...	...	...
Dongfang	CDJC	358 318	188 840	169 478	...	...	...	...	...
Donggang	CDJC	640 340	324 344	315 996	...	...	...	...	...
Dongguan	CDJC	6 445 777	3 035 742	3 410 035	...	...	...	...	...
Dongsheng	CDJC	252 566	129 512	123 054	...	...	...	...	...
Dongtai	CDJC	1 164 653	583 122	581 531	...	...	...	...	...
Dongxing	CDJC	108 131	58 939	49 192	...	...	...	...	...
Dongyang	CDJC	753 094	375 565	377 529	...	...	...	...	...
Dongying	CDJC	788 844	407 241	381 603	...	...	...	...	...
Dujiangyan	CDJC	621 980	314 845	307 135	...	...	...	...	...
Dunhua	CDJC	480 834	247 966	232 868	...	...	...	...	...

8. Population of capital cities and cities of 100 000 or more inhabitants: latest available year, 1987 - 2006
Population des capitales et des villes de 100 000 habitants ou plus: dernière année disponible, 1987 - 2006
(continued — suite)

Continent, country or area, date and city / Continent, pays ou zone, date et ville	Code[1]	City proper — Ville proprement dite Population				Urban agglomeration — Agglomération urbaine Population			
		Both sexes Les deux sexes	Male Masculin	Female Féminin	Surface area Superficie (km²)	Both sexes Les deux sexes	Male Masculin	Female Féminin	Surface area Superficie (km²)
ASIA — ASIE									
China — Chine									
1 XI 2000									
Dunhuang	CDJC	187 578	96 679	90 899		...	...	...	...
Duyun	CDJC	463 426	241 421	222 005		...	...	...	...
Enping	CDJC	464 898	240 765	224 133		...	...	...	...
Enshi	CDJC	755 725	397 284	358 441		...	...	...	...
Emeishan	CDJC	423 070	217 201	205 869		...	...	...	...
Ezhou	CDJC	1 023 285	533 940	489 345		...	...	...	...
Fangchenggang	CDJC	422 514	233 979	188 535		...	...	...	...
Feicheng	CDJC	948 602	476 032	472 570		...	...	...	...
Fengcheng (Jiangxi)	CDJC	1 216 412	644 029	572 383		...	...	...	...
Fengcheng (Liaoning)	CDJC	560 384	288 402	271 982		...	...	...	...
Fenghua	CDJC	471 558	239 252	232 306		...	...	...	...
Fengnan	CDJC	550 872	285 442	265 430		...	...	...	...
Fengzhen	CDJC	264 204	137 562	126 642		...	...	...	...
Fenyang	CDJC	387 046	199 129	187 917		...	...	...	...
Foshan	CDJC	768 656	398 973	369 683		...	...	...	...
Fuan	CDJC	554 057	296 379	257 678		...	...	...	...
Fuding	CDJC	521 070	276 419	244 651		...	...	...	...
Fujin	CDJC	420 579	215 650	204 929		...	...	...	...
Fukang	CDJC	152 965	80 372	72 593		...	...	...	...
Fuqing	CDJC	1 174 540	597 890	576 650		...	...	...	...
Fuquan	CDJC	292 720	155 972	136 748		...	...	...	...
Fushun	CDJC	1 434 447	722 549	711 898		...	...	...	...
Fuxin	CDJC	627 855	311 912	315 943		...	...	...	...
Fuyang (Anhui)	CDJC	628 633	324 172	304 461		...	...	...	...
Fuyang (Zhejiang)	CDJC	1 719 057	878 560	840 497		...	...	...	...
Fuzhou (Fujian)	CDJC	2 124 435	1 086 638	1 037 797		...	...	...	...
Fuzhou (Jiangxi)	CDJC	1 007 391	533 936	473 455		...	...	...	...
Gaizhou	CDJC	883 811	455 641	428 170		...	...	...	...
Ganzhou	CDJC	494 600	254 272	240 328		...	...	...	...
Gaoan	CDJC	788 329	416 678	371 651		...	...	...	...
Gaobeidian	CDJC	538 582	268 027	270 555		...	...	...	...
Gaocheng	CDJC	758 269	380 317	377 952		...	...	...	...
Gaomi	CDJC	842 403	420 956	421 447		...	...	...	...
Gaoming	CDJC	301 041	159 746	141 295		...	...	...	...
Gaoping	CDJC	471 671	236 439	235 232		...	...	...	...
Gaoyao	CDJC	625 125	314 474	310 651		...	...	...	...
Gaoyou	CDJC	797 752	392 863	404 889		...	...	...	...
Gaozhou	CDJC	1 219 132	639 497	579 635		...	...	...	...
Geermu	CDJC	135 897	73 572	62 325		...	...	...	...
Gejiu	CDJC	453 311	243 377	209 934		...	...	...	...
Genhe	CDJC	157 337	80 485	76 852		...	...	...	...
Gongyi	CDJC	777 202	395 784	381 418		...	...	...	...
Gongzhuling	CDJC	1 041 735	532 134	509 601		...	...	...	...
Guang'an	CDJC	1 093 103	561 454	531 649		...	...	...	...
Guanghan	CDJC	577 298	289 596	287 702		...	...	...	...
Guangshui	CDJC	885 936	458 607	427 329		...	...	...	...
Guangyuan	CDJC	905 057	467 422	437 635		...	...	...	...
Guangzhou	CDJC	8 524 826	4 445 052	4 079 774		...	...	...	...
Guigang	CDJC	1 413 128	731 298	681 830		...	...	...	...
Guilin	CDJC	804 571	414 004	390 567		...	...	...	...
Guiping	CDJC	1 359 035	716 617	642 418		...	...	...	...
Guixi	CDJC	535 517	282 662	252 855		...	...	...	...
Guiyang	CDJC	2 985 105	1 568 544	1 416 561		...	...	...	...
Gujiao	CDJC	205 702	110 105	95 597		...	...	...	...
Haerbin	CDJC	3 481 504	1 759 609	1 721 895		...	...	...	...
Haicheng	CDJC	1 181 130	606 805	574 325		...	...	...	...
Haikou	CDJC	830 192	431 774	398 418		...	...	...	...
Hailaer	CDJC	262 184	132 849	129 335		...	...	...	...
Hailin	CDJC	435 677	222 525	213 152		...	...	...	...
Hailun	CDJC	720 008	368 751	351 257		...	...	...	...

8. Population of capital cities and cities of 100 000 or more inhabitants: latest available year, 1987 - 2006
Population des capitales et des villes de 100 000 habitants ou plus: dernière année disponible, 1987 - 2006
(continued — suite)

Continent, country or area, date and city / Continent, pays ou zone, date et ville	Code[1]	City proper — Ville proprement dite Population				Urban agglomeration — Agglomération urbaine Population			
		Both sexes Les deux sexes	Male Masculin	Female Féminin	Surface area Superficie (km²)	Both sexes Les deux sexes	Male Masculin	Female Féminin	Surface area Superficie (km²)
ASIA — ASIE									
China — Chine									
1 XI 2000									
Haimen	CDJC	942 952	431 066	511 886	...	...	...	...	...
Haining	CDJC	666 080	331 349	334 731	...	...	...	...	...
Haiyang	CDJC	654 594	329 202	325 392	...	...	...	...	...
Hami	CDJC	388 714	201 005	187 709	...	...	...	...	...
Hancheng	CDJC	387 041	201 881	185 160	...	...	...	...	...
Hanchuan	CDJC	1 057 396	552 093	505 303	...	...	...	...	...
Handan	CDJC	1 329 734	693 882	635 852	...	...	...	...	...
Hangzhou	CDJC	2 451 319	1 301 103	1 150 216	...	...	...	...	...
Hanzhong	CDJC	503 871	258 142	245 729	...	...	...	...	...
Hebi	CDJC	495 336	260 212	235 124	...	...	...	...	...
Hechi	CDJC	318 348	167 526	150 822	...	...	...	...	...
Hechuan	CDJC	1 420 520	732 503	688 017	...	...	...	...	...
Hefei	CDJC	1 659 075	879 749	779 326	...	...	...	...	...
Hegang	CDJC	694 640	354 262	340 378	...	...	...	...	...
Heihe	CDJC	192 764	97 488	95 276	...	...	...	...	...
Hejian	CDJC	757 581	383 621	373 960	...	...	...	...	...
Hejin	CDJC	368 572	195 677	172 895	...	...	...	...	...
Helong	CDJC	215 266	110 051	105 215	...	...	...	...	...
Hengshui	CDJC	422 761	212 417	210 344	...	...	...	...	...
Hengyang	CDJC	879 051	450 222	428 829	...	...	...	...	...
Heshan (Guangdong)	CDJC	405 779	202 461	203 318	...	...	...	...	...
Heshan (Guangxi)	CDJC	131 249	69 205	62 044	...	...	...	...	...
Hetian	CDJC	186 127	94 034	92 093	...	...	...	...	...
Heyuan	CDJC	227 773	115 330	112 443	...	...	...	...	...
Heze	CDJC	1 280 031	656 790	623 241	...	...	...	...	...
Hezhou	CDJC	850 023	446 208	403 815	...	...	...	...	...
Honghu	CDJC	877 775	459 997	417 778	...	...	...	...	...
Hongjiang	CDJC	485 061	250 434	234 627	...	...	...	...	...
Houma	CDJC	225 123	113 997	111 126	...	...	...	...	...
Huadian	CDJC	444 415	228 624	215 791	...	...	...	...	...
Huaian	CDJC	1 200 679	619 541	581 138	...	...	...	...	...
Huaibei	CDJC	741 195	382 444	358 751	...	...	...	...	...
Huaihua	CDJC	346 522	178 221	168 301	...	...	...	...	...
Huainan	CDJC	1 357 228	701 205	656 023	...	...	...	...	...
Huaiyin	CDJC	555 052	282 186	272 866	...	...	...	...	...
Huanggang	CDJC	373 568	194 607	178 961	...	...	...	...	...
Huanghua	CDJC	483 273	251 128	232 145	...	...	...	...	...
Huangshan	CDJC	406 200	208 004	198 196	...	...	...	...	...
Huangshi (Hubei)	CDJC	653 722	334 712	319 010	...	...	...	...	...
Huayin	CDJC	242 488	125 006	117 482	...	...	...	...	...
Huaying	CDJC	352 257	183 962	168 295	...	...	...	...	...
Huazhou	CDJC	1 007 796	529 550	478 246	...	...	...	...	...
Huhehaote	CDJC	1 406 955	724 328	682 627	...	...	...	...	...
Huixian	CDJC	776 326	394 763	381 563	...	...	...	...	...
Huiyang	CDJC	862 822	429 006	433 816	...	...	...	...	...
Huizhou	CDJC	591 686	292 216	299 470	...	...	...	...	...
Hulin	CDJC	311 509	160 842	150 667	...	...	...	...	...
Huludao	CDJC	900 936	456 211	444 725	...	...	...	...	...
Hunchun	CDJC	211 091	108 873	102 218	...	...	...	...	...
Huozhou	CDJC	274 955	142 316	132 639	...	...	...	...	...
Huzhou	CDJC	1 145 414	573 421	571 993	...	...	...	...	...
Jiamusi	CDJC	859 944	433 369	426 575	...	...	...	...	...
Jian (Jiangxi)	CDJC	473 113	244 476	228 637	...	...	...	...	...
Jian (Jilin)	CDJC	239 849	124 475	115 374	...	...	...	...	...
Jiande	CDJC	473 062	242 606	230 456	...	...	...	...	...
Jiangdu	CDJC	1 053 023	512 151	540 872	...	...	...	...	...
Jiangjin	CDJC	1 322 890	686 106	636 784	...	...	...	...	...
Jiangmen	CDJC	536 317	271 693	264 624	...	...	...	...	...
Jiangshan	CDJC	473 222	241 301	231 921	...	...	...	...	...
Jiangyan	CDJC	861 321	419 333	441 988	...	...	...	...	...

8. Population of capital cities and cities of 100 000 or more inhabitants: latest available year, 1987 - 2006
Population des capitales et des villes de 100 000 habitants ou plus: dernière année disponible, 1987 - 2006
(continued — suite)

Continent, country or area, date and city / Continent, pays ou zone, date et ville	Code[1]	City proper — Ville proprement dite Population				Urban agglomeration — Agglomération urbaine Population			
		Both sexes Les deux sexes	Male Masculin	Female Féminin	Surface area Superficie (km²)	Both sexes Les deux sexes	Male Masculin	Female Féminin	Surface area Superficie (km²)
ASIA — ASIE									
China — Chine									
1 XI 2000									
Jiangyin	CDJC	1 315 472	665 719	649 753	...	...	...	...	...
Jiangyou	CDJC	849 761	436 112	413 649	...	...	...	...	...
Jian'ou	CDJC	478 651	249 624	229 027	...	...	...	...	...
Jianyang (Sichuan)	CDJC	1 412 523	728 353	684 170	...	...	...	...	...
Jianyang (Fujian)	CDJC	317 848	167 066	150 782	...	...	...	...	...
Jiaohe	CDJC	474 109	243 510	230 599	...	...	...	...	...
Jiaonan	CDJC	827 771	419 331	408 440	...	...	...	...	...
Jiaozhou	CDJC	783 478	388 207	395 271	...	...	...	...	...
Jiaozuo	CDJC	747 299	384 395	362 904	...	...	...	...	...
Jiaxing	CDJC	881 923	445 646	436 277	...	...	...	...	...
Jiayuguan	CDJC	159 541	85 959	73 582	...	...	...	...	...
Jieshou	CDJC	640 878	327 384	313 494	...	...	...	...	...
Jiexiu	CDJC	372 993	190 675	182 318	...	...	...	...	...
Jieyang	CDJC	633 570	324 831	308 739	...	...	...	...	...
Jilin	CDJC	1 953 134	984 762	968 372	...	...	...	...	...
Jimo	CDJC	1 111 202	553 261	557 941	...	...	...	...	...
Ji'nan	CDJC	2 999 934	1 539 067	1 460 867	...	...	...	...	...
Jinchang	CDJC	204 902	106 725	98 177	...	...	...	...	...
Jincheng	CDJC	304 221	157 663	146 558	...	...	...	...	...
Jingdezhen	CDJC	444 720	228 747	215 973	...	...	...	...	...
Jinggangshan	CDJC	145 769	74 722	71 047	...	...	...	...	...
Jinghong	CDJC	443 672	229 846	213 826	...	...	...	...	...
Jingjiang	CDJC	639 665	316 885	322 780	...	...	...	...	...
Jingmen	CDJC	583 373	300 284	283 089	...	...	...	...	...
Jingzhou	CDJC	1 177 150	598 951	578 199	...	...	...	...	...
Jinhua	CDJC	424 859	216 773	208 086	...	...	...	...	...
Jining (Shandong)	CDJC	1 050 522	530 322	520 200	...	...	...	...	...
Jining (Inner Mongolia)	CDJC	272 448	136 913	135 535	...	...	...	...	...
Jinjiang	CDJC	1 479 259	772 066	707 193	...	...	...	...	...
Jinshi	CDJC	243 242	126 619	116 623	...	...	...	...	...
Jintan	CDJC	533 350	256 798	276 552	...	...	...	...	...
Jinzhong	CDJC	534 357	274 957	259 400	...	...	...	...	...
Jinzhou (Liaoning)	CDJC	861 991	430 777	431 214	...	...	...	...	...
Jinzhou (Hebei)	CDJC	520 942	265 012	255 930	...	...	...	...	...
Jishou	CDJC	294 297	151 422	142 875	...	...	...	...	...
Jiujiang	CDJC	551 329	280 126	271 203	...	...	...	...	...
Jiuquan	CDJC	346 258	177 943	168 315	...	...	...	...	...
Jiutai	CDJC	799 729	411 067	388 662	...	...	...	...	...
Jixi	CDJC	910 782	467 547	443 235	...	...	...	...	...
Jiyuan	CDJC	626 478	323 554	302 924	...	...	...	...	...
Jizhou	CDJC	373 825	187 005	186 820	...	...	...	...	...
Jurong	CDJC	594 316	302 713	291 603	...	...	...	...	...
Kaifeng	CDJC	796 171	398 133	398 038	...	...	...	...	...
Kaili	CDJC	433 236	230 692	202 544	...	...	...	...	...
Kaiping	CDJC	668 692	326 560	342 132	...	...	...	...	...
Kaiyuan (Liaoning)	CDJC	529 736	271 422	258 314	...	...	...	...	...
Kaiyuan (Yunnan)	CDJC	292 039	152 771	139 268	...	...	...	...	...
Kashi (Xinjiang)	CDJC	340 640	172 136	168 504	...	...	...	...	...
Kelamayi	CDJC	270 232	143 500	126 732	...	...	...	...	...
Kuerle	CDJC	381 943	199 344	182 599	...	...	...	...	...
Kuitun	CDJC	285 299	148 740	136 559	...	...	...	...	...
Kunming	CDJC	3 035 406	1 615 096	1 420 310	...	...	...	...	...
Kunshan	CDJC	750 074	377 433	372 641	...	...	...	...	...
Laiwu	CDJC	1 233 525	626 549	606 976	...	...	...	...	...
Laixi	CDJC	728 796	366 400	362 396	...	...	...	...	...
Laiyang	CDJC	897 681	453 293	444 388	...	...	...	...	...
Laizhou	CDJC	889 361	450 192	439 169	...	...	...	...	...
Langfang	CDJC	715 388	363 094	352 294	...	...	...	...	...
Langzhong	CDJC	787 809	400 390	387 419	...	...	...	...	...
Lanxi	CDJC	607 196	314 090	293 106	...	...	...	...	...

8. Population of capital cities and cities of 100 000 or more inhabitants: latest available year, 1987 - 2006
Population des capitales et des villes de 100 000 habitants ou plus: dernière année disponible, 1987 - 2006
(continued — suite)

Continent, country or area, date and city / Continent, pays ou zone, date et ville	Code[1]	City proper — Ville proprement dite Population				Urban agglomeration — Agglomération urbaine Population			
		Both sexes Les deux sexes	Male Masculin	Female Féminin	Surface area Superficie (km²)	Both sexes Les deux sexes	Male Masculin	Female Féminin	Surface area Superficie (km²)
ASIA — ASIE									
China — Chine									
1 XI 2000									
Lanzhou	CDJC	2 087 759	1 092 661	995 098	...	...	...	...	...
Laohekou	CDJC	509 468	257 204	252 264	...	...	...	...	...
Lasa	CDJC	223 001	117 004	105 997	...	...	...	...	...
Lechang	CDJC	423 444	223 788	199 656	...	...	...	...	...
Leiyang	CDJC	1 180 235	631 431	548 804	...	...	...	...	...
Leizhou	CDJC	1 268 298	674 213	594 085	...	...	...	...	...
Leling	CDJC	615 833	313 642	302 191	...	...	...	...	...
Lengshuijiang	CDJC	339 701	175 071	164 630	...	...	...	...	...
Leping	CDJC	729 639	381 937	347 702	...	...	...	...	...
Leqing	CDJC	1 162 765	605 494	557 271	...	...	...	...	...
Leshan	CDJC	1 120 158	567 028	553 130	...	...	...	...	...
Lianjiang	CDJC	1 205 764	642 214	563 550	...	...	...	...	...
Lianyuan	CDJC	996 893	521 941	474 952	...	...	...	...	...
Lianyungang	CDJC	687 242	354 350	332 892	...	...	...	...	...
Lianzhou	CDJC	409 360	212 292	197 068	...	...	...	...	...
Liaocheng	CDJC	950 319	474 976	475 343	...	...	...	...	...
Liaoyang	CDJC	728 492	365 833	362 659	...	...	...	...	...
Liaoyuan	CDJC	462 233	234 701	227 532	...	...	...	...	...
Lichuan	CDJC	786 984	417 988	368 996	...	...	...	...	...
Liling	CDJC	934 396	484 127	450 269	...	...	...	...	...
Lin'an	CDJC	514 238	261 852	252 386	...	...	...	...	...
Linfen	CDJC	724 403	367 377	357 026	...	...	...	...	...
Lingbao	CDJC	722 890	377 872	345 018	...	...	...	...	...
Linghai	CDJC	647 310	332 906	314 404	...	...	...	...	...
Lingwu	CDJC	249 890	128 364	121 526	...	...	...	...	...
Lingyuan	CDJC	620 121	324 554	295 567	...	...	...	...	...
Linhai	CDJC	948 618	479 625	468 993	...	...	...	...	...
Linhe	CDJC	510 965	260 835	250 130	...	...	...	...	...
Linjiang	CDJC	184 901	94 904	89 997	...	...	...	...	...
Linqing	CDJC	694 247	348 411	345 836	...	...	...	...	...
Linxia	CDJC	202 498	104 017	98 481	...	...	...	...	...
Linxiang	CDJC	448 452	235 723	212 729	...	...	...	...	...
Linyi	CDJC	1 938 510	988 940	949 570	...	...	...	...	...
Linzhou	CDJC	982 254	501 659	480 595	...	...	...	...	...
Lishi	CDJC	235 678	121 253	114 425	...	...	...	...	...
Lishui	CDJC	348 241	178 908	169 333	...	...	...	...	...
Liuan	CDJC	1 559 037	807 902	751 135	...	...	...	...	...
Liupanshui	CDJC	995 055	523 692	471 363	...	...	...	...	...
Liuyang	CDJC	1 307 572	680 610	626 962	...	...	...	...	...
Liuzhou	CDJC	1 220 392	634 909	585 483	...	...	...	...	...
Liyang	CDJC	740 871	375 694	365 177	...	...	...	...	...
Longhai	CDJC	816 318	415 936	400 382	...	...	...	...	...
Longjing	CDJC	261 551	132 150	129 401	...	...	...	...	...
Longkou	CDJC	671 335	337 507	333 828	...	...	...	...	...
Longquan	CDJC	250 398	131 534	118 864	...	...	...	...	...
Longyan	CDJC	543 731	298 481	245 250	...	...	...	...	...
Loudi	CDJC	398 577	205 172	193 405	...	...	...	...	...
Lucheng	CDJC	213 944	111 293	102 651	...	...	...	...	...
Lufeng	CDJC	1 164 767	600 959	563 808	...	...	...	...	...
Luoding	CDJC	866 190	449 131	417 059	...	...	...	...	...
Luohe	CDJC	304 105	150 273	153 832	...	...	...	...	...
Luoyang	CDJC	1 491 680	759 425	732 255	...	...	...	...	...
Luquan	CDJC	397 449	202 340	195 109	...	...	...	...	...
Luxi (Yunnan)	CDJC	337 406	172 038	165 368	...	...	...	...	...
Luzhou	CDJC	1 252 884	636 652	616 232	...	...	...	...	...
Maanshan	CDJC	567 576	292 994	274 582	...	...	...	...	...
Macheng	CDJC	1 129 047	595 391	533 656	...	...	...	...	...
Manzhouli	CDJC	181 112	92 853	88 259	...	...	...	...	...
Maoming	CDJC	644 301	335 713	308 588	...	...	...	...	...
Meihekou	CDJC	617 674	317 226	300 448	...	...	...	...	...

8. Population of capital cities and cities of 100 000 or more inhabitants: latest available year, 1987 - 2006
Population des capitales et des villes de 100 000 habitants ou plus: dernière année disponible, 1987 - 2006
(continued — suite)

Continent, country or area, date and city / Continent, pays ou zone, date et ville	Code[1]	City proper — Ville proprement dite Population				Urban agglomeration — Agglomération urbaine Population			
		Both sexes Les deux sexes	Male Masculin	Female Féminin	Surface area Superficie (km²)	Both sexes Les deux sexes	Male Masculin	Female Féminin	Surface area Superficie (km²)
ASIA — ASIE									
China — Chine									
1 XI 2000									
Meishan	CDJC	799 309	402 889	396 420	...	...	...	...	...
Meixian	CDJC	313 821	160 925	152 896	...	...	...	...	...
Meizhou	CDJC	354 302	178 658	175 644	...	...	...	...	...
Mianyang	CDJC	1 162 962	604 414	558 548	...	...	...	...	...
Mianzhu	CDJC	515 830	263 098	252 732	...	...	...	...	...
Miluo	CDJC	658 867	342 113	316 754	...	...	...	...	...
Mingguang	CDJC	569 585	290 126	279 459	...	...	...	...	...
Miquan	CDJC	180 952	95 368	85 584	...	...	...	...	...
Mishan	CDJC	438 277	224 565	213 712	...	...	...	...	...
Mudanjiang	CDJC	1 014 206	512 000	502 206	...	...	...	...	...
Muling	CDJC	310 096	158 623	151 473	...	...	...	...	...
Nan'an	CDJC	1 385 276	700 218	685 058	...	...	...	...	...
Nanchang	CDJC	1 844 253	952 504	891 749	...	...	...	...	...
Nanchong	CDJC	1 771 920	922 452	849 468	...	...	...	...	...
Nanchuan	CDJC	631 853	326 307	305 546	...	...	...	...	...
Nan'gong	CDJC	467 356	234 978	232 378	...	...	...	...	...
Nanhai	CDJC	2 133 741	1 111 731	1 022 010	...	...	...	...	...
Nanjing	CDJC	3 624 234	1 935 931	1 688 303	...	...	...	...	...
Nankang	CDJC	694 987	338 836	356 151	...	...	...	...	...
Nanning	CDJC	1 766 701	924 916	841 785	...	...	...	...	...
Nanping	CDJC	488 818	257 352	231 466	...	...	...	...	...
Nantong	CDJC	771 386	386 206	385 180	...	...	...	...	...
Nanxiong	CDJC	372 844	185 330	187 514	...	...	...	...	...
Nanyang	CDJC	1 584 715	814 822	769 893	...	...	...	...	...
Nehe	CDJC	672 295	343 873	328 422	...	...	...	...	...
Neijiang	CDJC	1 391 931	709 053	682 878	...	...	...	...	...
Ning'an	CDJC	437 328	223 201	214 127	...	...	...	...	...
Ningbo	CDJC	1 567 499	804 850	762 649	...	...	...	...	...
Ningde	CDJC	400 293	213 131	187 162	...	...	...	...	...
Ningguo	CDJC	381 842	199 915	181 927	...	...	...	...	...
Panjin	CDJC	602 541	309 377	293 164	...	...	...	...	...
Panshi	CDJC	530 470	273 219	257 251	...	...	...	...	...
Panzhihua	CDJC	690 739	363 585	327 154	...	...	...	...	...
Penglai	CDJC	500 408	252 726	247 682	...	...	...	...	...
Pengzhou	CDJC	770 749	389 697	381 052	...	...	...	...	...
Pingdingshan	CDJC	900 903	470 362	430 541	...	...	...	...	...
Pingdu	CDJC	1 321 975	670 685	651 290	...	...	...	...	...
Pinghu	CDJC	507 899	249 848	258 051	...	...	...	...	...
Pingliang	CDJC	454 996	236 426	218 570	...	...	...	...	...
Pingxiang (Jiangxi)	CDJC	783 445	402 198	381 247	...	...	...	...	...
Pingxiang (Guangxi)	CDJC	107 046	57 445	49 601	...	...	...	...	...
Pizhou	CDJC	1 539 922	791 332	748 590	...	...	...	...	...
Pulandian	CDJC	757 844	385 636	372 208	...	...	...	...	...
Puning	CDJC	1 856 402	954 242	902 160	...	...	...	...	...
Putian	CDJC	443 926	216 578	227 348	...	...	...	...	...
Puyang	CDJC	448 290	229 387	218 903	...	...	...	...	...
Qian'an	CDJC	632 704	323 330	309 374	...	...	...	...	...
Qianjiang	CDJC	992 438	506 290	486 148	...	...	...	...	...
Qidong	CDJC	1 057 073	495 819	561 254	...	...	...	...	...
Qingdao	CDJC	2 720 972	1 359 527	1 361 445	...	...	...	...	...
Qingtongxia	CDJC	248 640	129 121	119 519	...	...	...	...	...
Qingyuan	CDJC	506 680	258 819	247 861	...	...	...	...	...
Qingzhen	CDJC	471 305	248 079	223 226	...	...	...	...	...
Qingzhou	CDJC	894 468	450 090	444 378	...	...	...	...	...
Qinhuangdao	CDJC	817 487	411 355	406 132	...	...	...	...	...
Qinyang	CDJC	446 404	224 725	221 679	...	...	...	...	...
Qinzhou	CDJC	1 035 504	578 428	457 076	...	...	...	...	...
Qionghai	CDJC	449 845	236 560	213 285	...	...	...	...	...
Qionglai	CDJC	631 577	321 382	310 195	...	...	...	...	...
Qiongshan	CDJC	678 149	355 557	322 592	...	...	...	...	...

8. Population of capital cities and cities of 100 000 or more inhabitants: latest available year, 1987 - 2006
Population des capitales et des villes de 100 000 habitants ou plus: dernière année disponible, 1987 - 2006
(continued — suite)

Continent, country or area, date and city / Continent, pays ou zone, date et ville	Code[1]	City proper — Ville proprement dite Population				Urban agglomeration — Agglomération urbaine Population			
		Both sexes Les deux sexes	Male Masculin	Female Féminin	Surface area Superficie (km²)	Both sexes Les deux sexes	Male Masculin	Female Féminin	Surface area Superficie (km²)
ASIA — ASIE									
China — Chine									
1 XI 2000									
Qiqihaer	CDJC	1 540 089	776 191	763 898	...	...	...	...	...
Qitaihe	CDJC	486 704	254 500	232 204	...	...	...	...	...
Qixia	CDJC	651 357	331 148	320 209	...	...	...	...	...
Quanzhou	CDJC	1 192 286	616 826	575 460	...	...	...	...	...
Qufu	CDJC	625 313	317 685	307 628	...	...	...	...	...
Qujing	CDJC	648 956	333 756	315 200	...	...	...	...	...
Quzhou	CDJC	286 271	148 054	138 217	...	...	...	...	...
Renhuai	CDJC	520 759	270 091	250 668	...	...	...	...	...
Renqiu	CDJC	768 900	390 649	378 251	...	...	...	...	...
Rizhao	CDJC	1 148 190	576 050	572 140	...	...	...	...	...
Rongcheng	CDJC	732 147	368 156	363 991	...	...	...	...	...
Rugao	CDJC	1 362 533	659 720	702 813	...	...	...	...	...
Ruian	CDJC	1 207 788	627 593	580 195	...	...	...	...	...
Ruichang	CDJC	398 844	209 755	189 089	...	...	...	...	...
Ruijin	CDJC	535 499	280 328	255 171	...	...	...	...	...
Ruili	CDJC	155 210	80 532	74 678	...	...	...	...	...
Rushan	CDJC	580 326	291 047	289 279	...	...	...	...	...
Ruzhou	CDJC	923 245	474 090	449 155	...	...	...	...	...
Sanhe	CDJC	456 882	229 788	227 094	...	...	...	...	...
Sanmenxia	CDJC	288 746	149 846	138 900	...	...	...	...	...
Sanming	CDJC	337 105	178 031	159 074	...	...	...	...	...
Sanshui	CDJC	440 119	230 835	209 284	...	...	...	...	...
Sanya	CDJC	482 296	254 293	228 003	...	...	...	...	...
Shahe	CDJC	474 260	243 171	231 089	...	...	...	...	...
Shanghai	CDJC	14 348 535	7 414 274	6 934 261	...	...	...	...	...
Shangqiu	CDJC	1 428 983	729 319	699 664	...	...	...	...	...
Shangrao	CDJC	327 703	164 698	163 005	...	...	...	...	...
Shangyu	CDJC	722 523	354 917	367 606	...	...	...	...	...
Shangzhi	CDJC	582 764	298 966	283 798	...	...	...	...	...
Shangzhou	CDJC	530 883	279 160	251 723	...	...	...	...	...
Shantou	CDJC	1 270 112	636 189	633 923	...	...	...	...	...
Shanwei	CDJC	409 677	211 746	197 931	...	...	...	...	...
Shaoguan	CDJC	535 979	282 515	253 464	...	...	...	...	...
Shaowu	CDJC	288 401	151 117	137 284	...	...	...	...	...
Shaoxing	CDJC	633 118	310 860	322 258	...	...	...	...	...
Shaoyang	CDJC	607 868	309 563	298 305	...	...	...	...	...
Shengzhou	CDJC	671 221	345 614	325 607	...	...	...	...	...
Shenyang	CDJC	5 303 053	2 700 380	2 602 673	...	...	...	...	...
Shenzhen	CDJC	7 008 831	3 454 392	3 554 439	...	...	...	...	...
Shenzhou	CDJC	568 558	289 086	279 472	...	...	...	...	...
Shifang	CDJC	432 579	218 447	214 132	...	...	...	...	...
Shihezi	CDJC	590 115	305 253	284 862	...	...	...	...	...
Shijiazhuang	CDJC	1 969 975	1 005 476	964 499	...	...	...	...	...
Shishi	CDJC	498 786	264 700	234 086	...	...	...	...	...
Shishou	CDJC	602 649	310 486	292 163	...	...	...	...	...
Shiyan	CDJC	589 824	309 552	280 272	...	...	...	...	...
Shizuishan	CDJC	314 296	163 261	151 035	...	...	...	...	...
Shouguang	CDJC	1 081 991	548 020	533 971	...	...	...	...	...
Shuangcheng	CDJC	749 182	382 673	366 509	...	...	...	...	...
Shuangliao	CDJC	404 499	206 071	198 428	...	...	...	...	...
Shuangyashan	CDJC	487 294	248 542	238 752	...	...	...	...	...
Shulan	CDJC	660 065	340 293	319 772	...	...	...	...	...
Shunde	CDJC	1 694 152	893 580	800 572	...	...	...	...	...
Shuozhou	CDJC	563 896	290 621	273 275	...	...	...	...	...
Sihui	CDJC	409 804	209 936	199 868	...	...	...	...	...
Simao	CDJC	230 834	120 071	110 763	...	...	...	...	...
Siping	CDJC	492 841	247 416	245 425	...	...	...	...	...
Songyuan	CDJC	538 469	273 101	265 368	...	...	...	...	...
Songzi	CDJC	859 941	437 980	421 961	...	...	...	...	...
Suihua	CDJC	800 207	405 382	394 825	...	...	...	...	...

8. Population of capital cities and cities of 100 000 or more inhabitants: latest available year, 1987 - 2006
Population des capitales et des villes de 100 000 habitants ou plus: dernière année disponible, 1987 - 2006
(continued — suite)

Continent, country or area, date and city / Continent, pays ou zone, date et ville	Code[1]	City proper — Ville proprement dite Population				Urban agglomeration — Agglomération urbaine Population			
		Both sexes Les deux sexes	Male Masculin	Female Féminin	Surface area Superficie (km²)	Both sexes Les deux sexes	Male Masculin	Female Féminin	Surface area Superficie (km²)
ASIA — ASIE									
China — Chine									
1 XI 2000									
Suining	CDJC	1 355 388	696 590	658 798	...	...	...	...	...
Suizhou	CDJC	1 598 752	818 936	779 816	...	...	...	...	...
Suqian	CDJC	244 651	124 719	119 932	...	...	...	...	...
Suzhou (Anhui)	CDJC	1 601 181	819 067	782 114	...	...	...	...	...
Suzhou (Jiangsu)	CDJC	1 344 709	686 919	657 790	...	...	...	...	...
Tacheng	CDJC	149 210	76 056	73 154	...	...	...	...	...
Taian	CDJC	1 538 211	775 346	762 865	...	...	...	...	...
Taicang	CDJC	515 063	250 788	264 275	...	...	...	...	...
Taishan	CDJC	948 716	478 773	469 943	...	...	...	...	...
Taixing	CDJC	1 235 454	618 158	617 296	...	...	...	...	...
Taiyuan	CDJC	2 558 382	1 321 216	1 237 166	...	...	...	...	...
Taizhou (Zhejiang)	CDJC	1 491 963	766 497	725 466	...	...	...	...	...
Taizhou (Jiangsu)	CDJC	607 660	303 078	304 582	...	...	...	...	...
Tangshan	CDJC	1 711 311	863 091	848 220	...	...	...	...	...
Taonan	CDJC	441 096	224 878	216 218	...	...	...	...	...
Tengzhou	CDJC	1 548 817	811 999	736 818	...	...	...	...	...
Tianchang	CDJC	590 745	297 550	293 195	...	...	...	...	...
Tianjin	CDJC	7 499 181	3 825 069	3 674 112	...	...	...	...	...
Tianmen	CDJC	1 613 739	849 283	764 456	...	...	...	...	...
Tianshui	CDJC	1 146 986	594 508	552 478	...	...	...	...	...
Tiefa	CDJC	239 636	121 471	118 165	...	...	...	...	...
Tieli	CDJC	354 601	181 024	173 577	...	...	...	...	...
Tieling	CDJC	433 799	217 795	216 004	...	...	...	...	...
Tongcheng	CDJC	660 772	321 098	339 674	...	...	...	...	...
Tongchuan	CDJC	404 257	211 294	192 963	...	...	...	...	...
Tonghua	CDJC	460 148	231 960	228 188	...	...	...	...	...
Tongjiang	CDJC	164 595	85 426	79 169	...	...	...	...	...
Tongliao	CDJC	793 913	400 930	392 983	...	...	...	...	...
Tongling	CDJC	362 477	188 130	174 347	...	...	...	...	...
Tongren	CDJC	308 583	163 632	144 951	...	...	...	...	...
Tongshi	CDJC	100 836	53 146	47 690	...	...	...	...	...
Tongxiang	CDJC	713 399	360 567	352 832	...	...	...	...	...
Tongzhou	CDJC	1 371 498	652 777	718 721	...	...	...	...	...
Tulufan	CDJC	251 652	129 183	122 469	...	...	...	...	...
Tumen	CDJC	132 368	67 067	65 301	...	...	...	...	...
Urumqi	CDJC	1 753 298	911 328	841 970	...	...	...	...	...
Wafangdian	CDJC	956 063	489 377	466 686	...	...	...	...	...
Wanning	CDJC	513 604	272 751	240 853	...	...	...	...	...
Wanyuan	CDJC	536 685	278 918	257 767	...	...	...	...	...
Weifang	CDJC	1 380 300	696 720	683 580	...	...	...	...	...
Weihai	CDJC	609 219	307 867	301 352	...	...	...	...	...
Weihui	CDJC	464 371	233 151	231 220	...	...	...	...	...
Weinan	CDJC	888 866	451 028	437 838	...	...	...	...	...
Wenchang	CDJC	509 271	260 432	248 839	...	...	...	...	...
Wendeng	CDJC	675 061	335 330	339 731	...	...	...	...	...
Wenling	CDJC	1 162 783	604 031	558 752	...	...	...	...	...
Wenzhou	CDJC	1 915 548	1 028 001	887 547	...	...	...	...	...
Wuan	CDJC	720 196	373 108	347 088	...	...	...	...	...
Wuchang	CDJC	888 782	454 587	434 195	...	...	...	...	...
Wuchuan	CDJC	822 482	429 336	393 146	...	...	...	...	...
Wudalianchi	CDJC	338 689	176 002	162 687	...	...	...	...	...
Wugang (Hunan)	CDJC	694 847	363 904	330 943	...	...	...	...	...
Wugang (Henan)	CDJC	313 089	164 347	148 742	...	...	...	...	...
Wuhai	CDJC	427 553	223 947	203 606	...	...	...	...	...
Wuhan	CDJC	8 312 700	4 306 729	4 005 971	...	...	...	...	...
Wuhu	CDJC	697 197	359 560	337 637	...	...	...	...	...
Wujiang	CDJC	857 104	426 423	430 681	...	...	...	...	...
Wujin	CDJC	1 420 204	719 200	701 004	...	...	...	...	...
Wulanhaote	CDJC	269 162	135 406	133 756	...	...	...	...	...
Wusu	CDJC	190 359	100 288	90 071	...	...	...	...	...

8. **Population of capital cities and cities of 100 000 or more inhabitants: latest available year, 1987 - 2006**
Population des capitales et des villes de 100 000 habitants ou plus: dernière année disponible, 1987 - 2006
(continued — suite)

Continent, country or area, date and city / Continent, pays ou zone, date et ville	Code[1]	City proper — Ville proprement dite Population				Urban agglomeration — Agglomération urbaine Population			
		Both sexes Les deux sexes	Male Masculin	Female Féminin	Surface area Superficie (km²)	Both sexes Les deux sexes	Male Masculin	Female Féminin	Surface area Superficie (km²)
ASIA — ASIE									
China — Chine									
1 XI 2000									
Wuwei	CDJC	946 506	488 872	457 634	...	...	...	...	...
Wuxi	CDJC	1 425 766	732 231	693 535	...	...	...	...	...
Wuxian	CDJC	1 128 429	557 717	570 712	...	...	...	...	...
Wuxue	CDJC	719 426	381 959	337 467	...	...	...	...	...
Wuyishan	CDJC	212 156	112 006	100 150	...	...	...	...	...
Wuzhong	CDJC	355 442	181 909	173 533	...	...	...	...	...
Wuzhou	CDJC	381 043	193 424	187 619	...	...	...	...	...
Xiamen	CDJC	2 053 070	1 061 697	991 373	...	...	...	...	...
Xi'an	CDJC	4 481 508	2 320 642	2 160 866	...	...	...	...	...
Xiangcheng	CDJC	1 052 468	546 760	505 708	...	...	...	...	...
Xiangfan	CDJC	871 388	443 899	427 489	...	...	...	...	...
Xiangtan	CDJC	707 783	363 619	344 164	...	...	...	...	...
Xiangxiang	CDJC	807 718	413 489	394 229	...	...	...	...	...
Xianning	CDJC	567 598	295 836	271 762	...	...	...	...	...
Xiantao	CDJC	1 474 078	774 487	699 591	...	...	...	...	...
Xianyang	CDJC	953 860	493 153	460 707	...	...	...	...	...
Xiaogan	CDJO	883 123	454 917	428 206	...	...	...	...	...
Xiaoshan	CDJC	1 233 348	613 229	620 119	...	...	...	...	...
Xiaoyi	CDJC	414 154	215 941	198 213	...	...	...	...	...
Xichang	CDJC	615 212	318 658	296 554	...	...	...	...	...
Xifeng	CDJC	317 669	163 228	154 441	...	...	...	...	...
Xilin'haote	CDJC	173 796	89 527	84 269	...	...	...	...	...
Xingcheng	CDJC	524 527	269 567	254 960	...	...	...	...	...
Xinghua	CDJC	1 441 659	745 856	695 803	...	...	...	...	...
Xingning	CDJC	871 507	436 749	434 758	...	...	...	...	...
Xingping	CDJC	551 523	284 879	266 644	...	...	...	...	...
Xingtai	CDJC	536 282	272 661	263 621	...	...	...	...	...
Xingyang	CDJC	619 840	316 049	303 791	...	...	...	...	...
Xingyi	CDJC	719 605	375 079	344 526	...	...	...	...	...
Xinhui	CDJC	932 425	467 557	464 868	...	...	...	...	...
Xi'ning	CDJC	854 466	440 359	414 107	...	...	...	...	...
Xinji	CDJC	623 219	314 536	308 683	...	...	...	...	...
Xinle	CDJC	439 644	220 811	218 833	...	...	...	...	...
Xinmi	CDJC	779 014	406 291	372 723	...	...	...	...	...
Xinmin	CDJC	653 719	333 683	320 036	...	...	...	...	...
Xintai	CDJC	1 344 395	687 569	656 826	...	...	...	...	...
Xinxiang	CDJC	775 941	394 224	381 717	...	...	...	...	...
Xinyang	CDJC	1 255 750	644 031	611 719	...	...	...	...	...
Xinyi (Guangdong)	CDJC	907 978	464 088	443 890	...	...	...	...	...
Xinyi (Jiangsu)	CDJC	962 656	491 509	471 147	...	...	...	...	...
Xinyu	CDJC	778 391	408 940	369 451	...	...	...	...	...
Xinzheng	CDJC	609 173	315 462	293 711	...	...	...	...	...
Xinzhou	CDJC	496 608	251 708	244 900	...	...	...	...	...
Xishan	CDJC	1 181 073	599 540	581 533	...	...	...	...	...
Xuancheng	CDJC	822 707	428 470	394 237	...	...	...	...	...
Xuanwei	CDJC	1 292 825	691 846	600 979	...	...	...	...	...
Xuchang	CDJC	373 387	188 476	184 911	...	...	...	...	...
Xuzhou	CDJC	1 679 626	866 686	812 940	...	...	...	...	...
Yaan	CDJC	334 475	171 237	163 238	...	...	...	...	...
Yakeshi	CDJC	405 806	207 451	198 355	...	...	...	...	...
Yan'an	CDJC	403 868	209 240	194 628	...	...	...	...	...
Yancheng	CDJC	683 663	347 576	336 087	...	...	...	...	...
Yangchun	CDJC	840 581	440 930	399 651	...	...	...	...	...
Yangjiang	CDJC	538 069	276 769	261 300	...	...	...	...	...
Yangquan	CDJC	655 317	346 209	309 108	...	...	...	...	...
Yangzhong	CDJC	301 672	150 538	151 134	...	...	...	...	...
Yangzhou	CDJC	711 993	362 425	349 568	...	...	...	...	...
Yanji	CDJC	432 339	223 342	208 997	...	...	...	...	...
Yanshi	CDJC	816 026	414 890	401 136	...	...	...	...	...
Yantai	CDJC	1 724 404	871 452	852 952	...	...	...	...	...

8. Population of capital cities and cities of 100 000 or more inhabitants: latest available year, 1987 - 2006
Population des capitales et des villes de 100 000 habitants ou plus: dernière année disponible, 1987 - 2006
(continued — suite)

Continent, country or area, date and city / Continent, pays ou zone, date et ville	Code[1]	City proper — Ville proprement dite Population				Urban agglomeration — Agglomération urbaine Population			
		Both sexes Les deux sexes	Male Masculin	Female Féminin	Surface area Superficie (km²)	Both sexes Les deux sexes	Male Masculin	Female Féminin	Surface area Superficie (km²)
ASIA — ASIE									
China — Chine									
1 XI 2000									
Yibin	CDJC	809 099	419 397	389 702	...	...	...	...	...
Yichang	CDJC	712 738	371 510	341 228	...	...	...	...	...
Yicheng	CDJC	522 835	266 340	256 495	...	...	...	...	...
Yichun (Jiangxi)	CDJC	920 357	480 945	439 412	...	...	...	...	...
Yichun (Heilongjiang)	CDJC	814 016	413 071	400 945	...	...	...	...	...
Yidu	CDJC	385 779	196 716	189 063	...	...	...	...	...
Yima	CDJC	136 543	73 411	63 132	...	...	...	...	...
Yinchuan	CDJC	807 487	415 203	392 284	...	...	...	...	...
Yingcheng	CDJC	650 485	340 907	309 578	...	...	...	...	...
Yingde	CDJC	810 446	421 964	388 482	...	...	...	...	...
Yingkou	CDJC	698 059	353 751	344 308	...	...	...	...	...
Yingtan	CDJC	178 406	92 050	86 356	...	...	...	...	...
Yi'ning	CDJC	357 519	179 862	177 657	...	...	...	...	...
Yiwu	CDJC	912 670	461 103	451 567	...	...	...	...	...
Yixing	CDJC	1 164 275	592 095	572 180	...	...	...	...	...
Yiyang	CDJC	1 228 881	629 842	599 039	...	...	...	...	...
Yizheng	CDJC	610 356	311 144	299 212	...	...	...	...	...
Yizhou	CDJC	549 434	288 084	261 350	...	...	...	...	...
Yong'an	CDJC	334 852	180 109	154 743	...	...	...	...	...
Yongcheng	CDJC	1 264 607	654 047	610 560	...	...	...	...	...
Yongchuan	CDJC	984 730	507 848	476 882	...	...	...	...	...
Yongkang	CDJC	557 067	290 946	266 121	...	...	...	...	...
Yongji	CDJC	421 244	214 446	206 798	...	...	...	...	...
Yongzhou	CDJC	976 539	508 021	468 518	...	...	...	...	...
Yuanjiang	CDJC	700 236	363 730	336 506	...	...	...	...	...
Yuanping	CDJC	471 853	244 751	227 102	...	...	...	...	...
Yucheng	CDJC	494 301	248 103	246 198	...	...	...	...	...
Yueyang	CDJC	912 993	471 170	441 823	...	...	...	...	...
Yuhang	CDJC	817 715	419 877	397 838	...	...	...	...	...
Yulin (Shaanxi)	CDJC	451 337	232 951	218 386	...	...	...	...	...
Yulin (Guangxi)	CDJC	918 229	491 729	426 500	...	...	...	...	...
Yumen	CDJC	188 931	99 832	89 099	...	...	...	...	...
Yuncheng	CDJC	604 381	304 489	299 892	...	...	...	...	...
Yunfu	CDJC	261 636	136 789	124 847	...	...	...	...	...
Yunzhou	CDJC	598 387	303 581	294 806	...	...	...	...	...
Yushu	CDJC	1 155 670	592 213	563 457	...	...	...	...	...
Yuxi	CDJC	409 044	206 139	202 905	...	...	...	...	...
Yuyao	CDJC	852 719	429 835	422 884	...	...	...	...	...
Yuzhou	CDJC	1 122 669	587 728	534 941	...	...	...	...	...
Zaoyang	CDJC	1 054 374	538 588	515 786	...	...	...	...	...
Zaozhuang	CDJC	1 996 798	1 025 190	971 608	...	...	...	...	...
Zengcheng	CDJC	899 644	466 540	433 104	...	...	...	...	...
Zhalantun	CDJC	409 051	211 922	197 129	...	...	...	...	...
Zhangjiagang	CDJC	957 223	466 771	490 452	...	...	...	...	...
Zhangjiajie	CDJC	453 723	234 454	219 269	...	...	...	...	...
Zhangjiakou	CDJC	903 348	455 048	448 300	...	...	...	...	...
Zhangping	CDJC	264 757	140 779	123 978	...	...	...	...	...
Zhangqiu	CDJC	977 324	485 925	491 399	...	...	...	...	...
Zhangshu	CDJC	527 823	273 691	254 132	...	...	...	...	...
Zhangye	CDJC	486 688	248 469	238 219	...	...	...	...	...
Zhangzhou	CDJC	567 884	291 597	276 287	...	...	...	...	...
Zhanjiang	CDJC	1 350 665	707 187	643 478	...	...	...	...	...
Zhaodong	CDJC	832 657	424 694	407 963	...	...	...	...	...
Zhaoqing	CDJC	507 834	254 086	253 748	...	...	...	...	...
Zhaotong	CDJC	727 959	377 931	350 028	...	...	...	...	...
Zhaoyuan	CDJC	593 705	297 504	296 201	...	...	...	...	...
Zhengzhou	CDJC	2 589 387	1 347 037	1 242 350	...	...	...	...	...
Zhenjiang	CDJC	695 663	364 429	331 234	...	...	...	...	...
Zhijiang	CDJC	508 835	257 013	251 822	...	...	...	...	...
Zhongshan	CDJC	2 363 322	1 175 587	1 187 735	...	...	...	...	...

8. Population of capital cities and cities of 100 000 or more inhabitants: latest available year, 1987 - 2006
Population des capitales et des villes de 100 000 habitants ou plus: dernière année disponible, 1987 - 2006
(continued — suite)

Continent, country or area, date and city Continent, pays ou zone, date et ville	Code[1]	City proper — Ville proprement dite Population				Urban agglomeration — Agglomération urbaine Population			
		Both sexes Les deux sexes	Male Masculin	Female Féminin	Surface area Superficie (km²)	Both sexes Les deux sexes	Male Masculin	Female Féminin	Surface area Superficie (km²)
ASIA — ASIE									
China — Chine									
1 XI 2000									
Zhongxiang	CDJC	1 021 998	516 758	505 240	...	...	...	...	...
Zhoukou	CDJC	323 738	162 443	161 295	...	...	...	...	...
Zhoushan	CDJC	715 685	362 426	353 259	...	...	...	...	...
Zhuanghe	CDJC	835 062	422 677	412 385	...	...	...	...	...
Zhucheng	CDJC	1 053 695	531 390	522 305	...	...	...	...	...
Zhuhai	CDJC	833 908	414 067	419 841	...	...	...	...	...
Zhuji	CDJC	1 070 675	535 820	534 855	...	...	...	...	...
Zhumadian	CDJC	338 036	170 485	167 551	...	...	...	...	...
Zhuozhou	CDJC	546 754	275 834	270 920	...	...	...	...	...
Zhuzhou	CDJC	879 996	454 057	425 939	...	...	...	...	...
Zibo	CDJC	2 817 479	1 429 838	1 387 641	...	...	...	...	...
Zigong	CDJC	1 051 384	532 479	518 905	...	...	...	...	...
Zixing	CDJC	351 581	181 632	169 949	...	...	...	...	...
Ziyang	CDJC	1 016 034	527 326	488 708	...	...	...	...	...
Zoucheng	CDJC	1 101 003	571 761	529 242	...	...	...	...	...
Zunhua	CDJC	683 662	348 121	335 541	...	...	...	...	...
Zunyi	CDJC	691 694	358 839	332 855	...	...	...	...	...
China : Hong Kong SAR — Chine - Hong Kong RAS									
1 VII 2006									
HONG KONG	ESDJ	6 857 100	3 270 100	3 587 000	1 104	...	...	...	...
China : Macao SAR — Chine - Macao RAS									
1 VII 2006									
MACAO	ESDJ	498 852	243 009	255 843	29	...	...	...	...
Cyprus — Chypre									
1 I 2006									
LEFKOSIA[51]	ESDJ	...	...	...	...	224 500	...	...	...
Lemesos[52]	ESDJ	...	...	...	...	176 900	...	...	...
Georgia — Géorgie									
1 VII 2003									
Batumi	ESDF	120 200	...	...	...	...	...	...	...
Kutaisi	ESDF	183 800	...	...	...	...	...	...	...
Rustavi	ESDF	115 000	...	...	...	...	...	...	...
TBILISI	ESDF	1 059 600	...	...	...	...	...	...	...
India — Inde[53]									
1 III 2001									
Abohar	CDFC	124 303	66 434	57 869	23	...	...	...	...
Achalpur	CDFC	107 304	55 678	51 626	...	...	...	...	...
Adilabad	CDFC	108 233	55 023	53 210	...	128 196	64 883	63 313	...
Adityapur	CDFC	119 221	63 855	55 366	...	...	...	...	...
Adoni	CDFC	155 969	78 908	77 061	30	161 125	81 577	79 548	...
Agartala	CDFC	189 327	94 398	94 929	16	...	...	...	...
Agra	CDFC	1 259 979	674 902	585 077	121	1 321 410	708 622	612 788	141
Ahmedabad	CDFC	3 515 361	1 863 886	1 651 475	...	4 519 278	2 397 728	2 121 550	...
Ahmednagar	CDFC	307 455	159 409	148 046	18	347 396	184 604	162 792	30
Aizawl	CDFC	229 714	116 983	112 731	110	...	...	...	...
Ajmer	CDFC	485 197	253 854	231 343	242	490 138	256 379	233 759	...
Akola	CDFC	399 978	206 433	193 545	23	...	...	...	...
Alandur	CDFC	146 154	74 784	71 370	...	...	...	...	...
Alappuzha	CDFC	177 079	85 708	91 371	70	202 727	137 232	145 495	84
Aligarh	CDFC	667 732	357 152	310 580	34	...	...	...	...
Alipurduar	CDFC	...	...	...	...	114 069	58 527	55 542	20
Allahabad	CDFC	990 298	549 754	440 544	...	1 049 579	581 876	467 703	...
Alwal	CDFC	106 424	56 562	49 862	...	...	...	...	...
Alwar	CDFC	260 245	139 141	121 104	...	265 850	143 238	122 612	58
Ambala	CDFC	139 222	73 956	65 266	17	168 003	92 610	75 393	38
Ambala Sadar	CDFC	106 378	55 461	50 917	...	...	...	...	...
Ambarnath	CDFC	203 795	107 378	96 417	...	...	...	...	...
Ambattur	CDFC	302 492	156 237	146 255	...	...	...	...	...

8. Population of capital cities and cities of 100 000 or more inhabitants: latest available year, 1987 - 2000
Population des capitales et des villes de 100 000 habitants ou plus: dernière année disponible, 1987 - 2006
(continued — suite)

Continent, country or area, date and city Continent, pays ou zone, date et ville	Code[1]	City proper — Ville proprement dite Population				Urban agglomeration — Agglomération urbaine Population			
		Both sexes Les deux sexes	Male Masculin	Female Féminin	Surface area Superficie (km²)	Both sexes Les deux sexes	Male Masculin	Female Féminin	Surface area Superficie (km²)
ASIA — ASIE									
India — Inde[53]									
1 III 2001									
Amravati	CDFC	549 370	283 789	265 581	122	...	...	...	...
Amritsar	CDFC	975 695	524 127	451 568	...	1 011 327	543 638	467 689	...
Amroha	CDFC	164 890	86 836	78 054	6	...	...	...	...
Anand	CDFC	130 462	68 032	62 430	...	218 064	115 183	102 881	...
Anantapur	CDFC	220 951	112 273	108 678	...	243 359	123 976	119 383	...
Anklesvar	CDFC	...	...	...	...	112 648	60 265	52 383	...
Arcot	CDFC	...	...	...	...	126 975	62 938	64 037	19
Arrah	CDFC	203 395	109 876	93 519	31	...	...	...	...
Asansol	CDFC	486 304	256 551	229 753	25	1 090 171	576 813	513 358	223
Ashoknagar Kalyangarh	CDFC	111 475	56 340	55 135	...	...	...	...	...
Aurangabad	CDFC	872 667	458 869	413 798	139	891 841	468 815	423 026	148
Avadi	CDFC	230 913	119 187	111 726	...	...	...	...	...
Azamgarh	CDFC	104 943	51 284	53 659	...	...	...	...	...
Bahadurgarh	CDFC	119 839	65 835	54 004	...	131 924	72 851	59 073	...
Baharampur	CDFC	160 168	81 795	78 373	17	170 343	87 038	83 305	19
Bahraich	CDFC	168 376	89 532	78 844	13	...	...	...	...
Baidyabati	CDFC	108 231	56 429	51 802	...	...	...	...	...
Baleshwar	CDFC	106 032	55 637	50 395	...	156 274	82 034	74 240	42
Ballia	CDFC	102 226	55 123	47 103	...	...	...	...	...
Bally	CDFC	261 575	149 810	111 765	12	...	...	...	...
Balurghat	CDFC	135 516	68 822	66 694	...	143 095	72 687	70 408	8
Banda	CDFC	134 822	72 663	62 159	...	139 387	75 172	64 215	...
Bangalore	CDFC	4 292 223	2 240 956	2 051 267	...	5 686 844	2 983 926	2 702 918	446
Bangaon	CDFC	102 115	52 489	49 626	...	...	...	...	...
Bankura	CDFC	128 811	66 333	62 478	19	...	...	...	...
Bansberia	CDFC	104 453	55 403	49 050	...	...	...	...	...
Baranagar	CDFC	250 615	132 701	117 914	7	...	...	...	...
Barasat	CDFC	231 515	118 367	113 148	...	...	...	...	...
Barddhaman	CDFC	285 871	148 824	137 047	23	...	...	...	...
Bareilly	CDFC	699 839	368 022	331 817	107	729 800	386 418	343 382	124
Baripada	CDFC	...	...	...	...	100 593	53 610	46 983	...
Barrackpur	CDFC	144 331	76 268	68 063	14	...	...	...	...
Barshi	CDFC	104 786	53 894	50 892	...	...	...	...	...
Basirhat	CDFC	113 120	57 876	55 244	22	...	...	...	...
Basti	CDFC	106 985	56 813	50 172	...	...	...	...	...
Batala	CDFC	126 646	67 026	59 620	...	147 753	78 342	69 411	...
Bathinda	CDFC	217 389	117 359	100 030	97	...	...	...	...
Beawar	CDFC	123 701	64 394	59 307	...	125 923	65 569	60 354	18
Begusarai	CDFC	...	...	...	...	107 203	57 349	49 854	...
Belgaum	CDFC	399 600	204 846	194 754	142	506 235	261 862	244 373	155
Bellary	CDFC	317 000	163 082	153 918	66	...	...	...	...
Bettiah	CDFC	116 692	61 803	54 889	...	...	...	...	...
Bhadravati	CDFC	160 392	81 260	79 132	...	...	...	...	...
Bhadreswar	CDFC	105 944	57 991	47 953	...	...	...	...	...
Bhagalpur	CDFC	340 349	182 704	157 645	30	349 709	187 627	162 082	31
Bhalswa Jahangir Pur	CDFC	151 427	83 289	68 138	...	...	...	...	...
Bharatpur	CDFC	204 456	109 809	94 647	41	205 104	110 148	94 956	51
Bharuch	CDFC	148 391	76 568	71 823	...	176 531	91 273	85 258	...
Bhatpara	CDFC	441 956	243 065	198 891	16	...	...	...	...
Bhavani	CDFC	...	...	...	...	104 285	52 804	51 481	...
Bhavnagar	CDFC	510 958	267 019	243 939	...	517 578	270 458	247 120	...
Bheemavaram	CDFC	137 327	69 487	67 840	26	141 975	71 938	70 037	...
Bhilai Nagar	CDFC	553 837	289 853	263 984	89	...	...	...	...
Bhilwara	CDFC	280 185	148 642	131 543	118	...	...	...	...
Bhind	CDFC	153 768	83 009	70 759	17	...	...	...	...
Bhiwandi	CDFC	598 703	367 858	230 845	26	621 390	382 493	238 897	28
Bhiwani	CDFC	169 424	91 726	77 698	28	...	...	...	...
Bhopal	CDFC	1 433 875	755 685	678 190	285	1 454 830	766 602	688 228	...
Bhubaneswar	CDFC	647 302	360 476	286 826	125	657 477	365 848	291 629	...
Bhusawal	CDFC	172 366	89 187	83 179	13	187 524	97 192	90 332	25

8. Population of capital cities and cities of 100 000 or more inhabitants: latest available year, 1987 - 2006
Population des capitales et des villes de 100 000 habitants ou plus: dernière année disponible, 1987 - 2006
(continued — suite)

Continent, country or area, date and city / Continent, pays ou zone, date et ville	Code[1]	City proper — Ville proprement dite Population				Urban agglomeration — Agglomération urbaine Population			
		Both sexes Les deux sexes	Male Masculin	Female Féminin	Surface area Superficie (km²)	Both sexes Les deux sexes	Male Masculin	Female Féminin	Surface area Superficie (km²)
ASIA — ASIE									
India — Inde[53]									
1 III 2001									
Bid	CDFC	138 091	71 790	66 301	8	...	...	...	...
Bidar	CDFC	172 298	89 715	82 583	...	173 678	90 449	83 229	47
Bidhan Nagar	CDFC	167 848	85 215	82 633	...	...	...	...	...
Bihar	CDFC	231 972	121 813	110 159	24	...	...	...	...
Bijapur	CDFC	245 946	126 554	119 392	...	253 307	130 237	123 070	75
Bikaner	CDFC	529 007	282 450	246 557	166	...	...	...	...
Bilaspur	CDFC	265 178	137 273	127 905	36	330 291	170 898	159 393	46
Birnagar	CDFC	...	...	...		115 104	59 179	55 925	...
Bokaro Steel City	CDFC	394 173	213 044	181 129	163	497 855	268 668	229 187	183
Bommanahalli	CDFC	201 220	108 040	93 180	...	...	...	...	...
Botad	CDFC	100 059	52 668	47 391	...	...	...	...	...
Brahmapur	CDFC	289 724	150 089	139 635	80	...	...	...	...
Budaun	CDFC	148 138	78 294	69 844	4	...	...	...	...
Bulandshahr	CDFC	176 256	93 066	83 190	12	...	...	...	...
Burhanpur	CDFC	194 360	100 031	94 329	13	...	...	...	...
Byatarayanapura	CDFC	180 931	94 683	86 248		...	...	...	...
Chakdaha	CDFC	...	...	...	...	101 278	51 321	49 957	
Champdani	CDFC	103 232	57 874	45 358	...	...	...	...	...
Chandan Nagar	CDFC	162 166	84 222	77 944	10	...	...	...	...
Chandausi	CDFC	103 757	55 167	48 590	...	...	...	...	...
Chandigarh	CDFC	808 796	451 387	357 409	70	...	...	...	...
Chandrapur	CDFC	297 612	148 499	149 113	56	...	...	...	...
Chapra	CDFC	178 835	96 077	82 758	17	...	...	...	...
Chennai (Madras)	CDFC	4 216 268	2 161 605	2 054 663	174	6 424 624	3 294 328	3 130 296	612
Cherthala	CDFC	...	...	...	...	141 512	68 740	72 772	93
Chhatarpur	CDFC	...	...	...		109 021	58 393	50 628	...
Chhindwara	CDFC	122 309	63 583	58 726	...	153 635	79 889	73 746	...
Chikmagalur	CDFC	101 022	51 611	49 411	...	...	...	...	...
Chirala	CDFC	...	...	...	...	166 877	83 262	83 615	48
Chirkunda	CDFC	...	...	...	...	106 200	56 528	49 672	...
Chitradurga	CDFC	122 594	62 811	59 783	...	125 060	64 075	60 985	16
Chittoor	CDFC	152 966	77 044	75 922	33	...	...	...	...
Churu	CDFC	...	...	...		101 853	53 099	48 754	...
Coimbatore	CDFC	923 085	476 056	447 029	106	1 446 034	743 161	702 873	317
Coonoor	CDFC	...	...	...	...	101 234	51 089	50 145	...
Cuddalore	CDFC	158 569	80 113	78 456	28	...	...	...	...
Cuddapah	CDFC	125 725	63 165	62 560	42	260 899	132 297	128 602	78
Cuttack	CDFC	535 139	286 192	248 947	122	587 637	314 435	273 202	153
Dallo Pura	CDFC	132 628	71 349	61 279	...	...	...	...	...
Damoh	CDFC	112 160	58 898	53 262	...	127 939	67 244	60 695	36
Darbhanga	CDFC	266 834	142 042	124 792	19	...	...	...	...
Darjiling	CDFC	107 530	53 325	54 205	...	109 163	54 131	55 032	...
Dasarahalli	CDFC	263 636	143 225	120 411		...	...	...	...
Davangere	CDFC	363 780	187 603	176 177	...	...	...	...	...
Dehradun	CDFC	447 808	236 852	210 956	37	527 859	279 653	248 206	86
Dehri	CDFC	119 007	63 552	55 455	...	...	...	...	...
Delhi[54]	CDFC	9 817 439	5 378 658	4 438 781	431	12 791 458	7 021 896	5 769 562	624
Delhi Cantonment	CDFC	124 452	75 700	48 752	...	...	...	...	...
Deoghar	CDFC	...	...	...	...	112 501	61 405	51 096	...
Deoli	CDFC	119 432	66 575	52 857	...	...	...	...	...
Deoria	CDFC	104 222	54 737	49 485	...	...	...	...	...
Dewas	CDFC	230 658	120 610	110 048	100	...	...	...	...
Dhanbad	CDFC	198 963	108 400	90 563	23	1 064 357	578 602	485 755	201
Dharmavaram	CDFC	103 400	52 799	50 601	...	...	...	...	...
Dhule	CDFC	341 473	177 631	163 842	46	...	...	...	...
Dibrugarh	CDFC	122 523	65 736	56 787	15	137 879	74 239	63 640	16
Dimapur	CDFC	107 382	61 595	45 787	...	...	...	...	...
Dinapur Nizamat	CDFC	130 339	69 024	61 315	...	...	...	...	...
Dindigul	CDFC	196 619	98 969	97 650	14	...	...	...	...
Dohad	CDFC	...	...	...	...	112 087	57 765	54 322	...

8. Population of capital cities and cities of 100 000 or more inhabitants: latest available year, 1987 - 2006
Population des capitales et des villes de 100 000 habitants ou plus: dernière année disponible, 1987 - 2006
(continued — suite)

Continent, country or area, date and city Continent, pays ou zone, date et ville	Code[1]	City proper — Ville proprement dite Population				Urban agglomeration — Agglomération urbaine Population			
		Both sexes Les deux sexes	Male Masculin	Female Féminin	Surface area Superficie (km²)	Both sexes Les deux sexes	Male Masculin	Female Féminin	Surface area Superficie (km²)
ASIA — ASIE									
India — Inde[53]									
1 III 2001									
Dumdum	CDFC	101 319	52 868	48 451	...	...	...	...	...
Durg	CDFC	231 182	118 896	112 286	51	...	...	...	...
Durgapur	CDFC	492 996	263 426	229 570	154	...	...	...	...
Durg-Bhilai Nagar	CDFC	...	...	...	...	923 559	480 432	443 127	183
Eluru	CDFC	189 772	92 405	97 367	15	215 343	104 987	110 356	...
English Bazar	CDFC	161 448	82 932	78 516	...	224 392	115 454	108 938	19
Erode	CDFC	151 184	76 726	74 458	8	391 169	199 306	191 863	132
Etah	CDFC	107 098	56 960	50 138	...	...	...	...	...
Etawah	CDFC	211 460	112 833	98 627	9	...	...	...	...
Faizabad	CDFC	144 924	76 078	68 846	33	208 164	114 252	93 912	63
Faridabad	CDFC	1 054 981	580 548	474 433	178	...	...	...	...
Farrukhabad-cum-Fategarh	CDFC	227 876	120 783	107 093	17	242 558	129 608	112 950	21
Fatehpur	CDFC	151 757	79 836	71 921	57	...	...	...	...
Firozabad	CDFC	278 801	147 980	130 821	9	432 213	230 477	201 736	12
Gadag-Betgeri	CDFC	154 849	78 672	76 177	35	...	...	...	...
Gajuwaka	CDFC	258 944	133 461	125 483	...	...	...	...	...
Gandhinagar	CDFC	195 891	103 814	92 077	57	...	...	...	...
Ganganagar	CDFC	210 788	115 412	95 376	21	222 833	121 877	100 956	...
Gangawati	CDFC	...	...	...	...	101 397	51 253	50 144	...
Gaya	CDFC	383 197	203 252	179 945	29	394 185	209 926	184 259	32
Ghatlodiya	CDFC	106 259	56 040	50 219	...	...	...	...	...
Ghaziabad	CDFC	968 521	521 408	447 113	64	...	...	...	...
Ghazipur	CDFC	...	...	...	...	103 283	54 321	48 962	...
Giridih	CDFC	...	...	...	...	105 212	55 154	50 058	...
Godhra	CDFC	121 852	63 143	58 709	...	131 144	67 933	63 211	...
Gonda	CDFC	122 164	67 400	54 764	...	...	...	...	...
Gondiya	CDFC	120 878	61 435	59 443	18	...	...	...	...
Gorakhpur	CDFC	624 570	330 450	294 120	137	...	...	...	...
Gudivada	CDFC	112 245	55 439	56 806	13	...	...	...	...
Gudiyatham	CDFC	...	...	...	...	100 021	49 822	50 199	...
Gulbarga	CDFC	427 929	222 623	205 306	...	435 631	226 848	208 783	43
Guna	CDFC	137 132	72 462	64 670	46	...	...	...	...
Guntakul	CDFC	117 403	59 364	58 039	52	...	...	...	...
Guntur	CDFC	514 707	257 939	256 768	30	...	...	...	...
Gurgaon	CDFC	173 542	92 985	80 557	15	229 243	123 370	105 873	24
Guruvayur	CDFC	...	...	...	...	138 676	64 550	74 126	50
Guwahati	CDFC	808 021	441 347	366 674	217	814 575	445 649	368 926	...
Gwalior	CDFC	826 919	442 484	384 435	290	865 800	465 388	400 412	303
Habra	CDFC	127 695	65 263	62 432	18	239 170	121 603	117 567	37
Hajipur	CDFC	119 276	63 762	55 514	...	...	...	...	...
Haldia	CDFC	170 695	89 886	80 809	69	...	...	...	...
Haldwani-cum-Kathgodam	CDFC	129 140	68 826	60 314	11	159 020	84 611	74 409	...
Halisahar	CDFC	124 479	67 124	57 355	...	...	...	...	...
Hanumangarh	CDFC	129 654	69 583	60 071	...	...	...	...	...
Haora (Howrah)	CDFC	1 008 704	547 969	460 735	52	...	...	...	...
Hapur	CDFC	211 987	112 962	99 025	14	...	...	...	...
Hardoi	CDFC	112 474	59 877	52 597	...	...	...	...	...
Hardwar	CDFC	175 010	94 650	80 360	15	220 433	119 159	101 274	42
Hassan	CDFC	117 386	60 225	57 161	...	133 317	68 337	64 980	27
Hathras	CDFC	123 243	65 908	57 335	8	126 352	67 568	58 784	...
Hazaribag	CDFC	127 243	67 905	59 338	...	135 446	72 296	63 150	...
Hindupur	CDFC	125 056	64 159	60 897	38	...	...	...	...
Hisar	CDFC	256 810	140 240	116 570	45	263 070	143 816	119 254	49
Hoshiarpur	CDFC	148 243	78 946	69 297	28	...	...	...	...
Hospet	CDFC	163 284	83 430	79 854	28	...	...	...	...
Hubli-Dharwad	CDFC	786 018	403 270	382 748	191	...	...	...	...
Hugli-Chinsurah	CDFC	170 201	86 728	83 473	17	...	...	...	...
Hyderabad	CDFC	3 449 878	1 773 899	1 675 979	...	5 533 640	2 854 938	2 678 702	...
Ichalakaranji	CDFC	257 572	135 988	121 584	30	285 795	150 934	134 861	38
Imphal	CDFC	217 275	107 593	109 682	33	245 967	121 588	124 379	37

8. Population of capital cities and cities of 100 000 or more inhabitants: latest available year, 1987 - 2006
Population des capitales et des villes de 100 000 habitants ou plus: dernière année disponible, 1987 - 2006
(continued — suite)

Continent, country or area, date and city / Continent, pays ou zone, date et ville	Code[1]	City proper — Ville proprement dite Population				Urban agglomeration — Agglomération urbaine Population			
		Both sexes Les deux sexes	Male Masculin	Female Féminin	Surface area Superficie (km²)	Both sexes Les deux sexes	Male Masculin	Female Féminin	Surface area Superficie (km²)
ASIA — ASIE									
India — Inde[53]									
1 III 2001									
Indore	CDFC	1 597 441	839 843	757 598	...	1 639 044	861 758	777 286	165
Itarsi	CDFC	...	...	...	...	109 288	57 118	52 170	...
Jabalpur	CDFC	951 469	496 829	454 640	154	1 117 200	588 556	528 644	224
Jagadhri	CDFC	101 300	55 910	45 390	...	...	...	...	...
Jagdalpur	CDFC	...	...	...	...	103 216	53 048	50 168	...
Jaipur	CDFC	2 324 319	1 239 711	1 084 608	200	...	...	...	...
Jalandhar	CDFC	701 223	376 925	324 298	80	709 255	381 116	328 139	...
Jalgaon	CDFC	368 579	193 464	175 115	62	...	...	...	...
Jalna	CDFC	235 529	121 728	113 801	82	...	...	...	...
Jalpaiguri	CDFC	100 212	50 570	49 642	...	...	...	...	...
Jammu	CDFC	378 431	206 061	172 370	...	607 642	330 769	276 873	...
Jamnagar	CDFC	447 734	235 093	212 641	...	558 462	292 954	265 508	...
Jamshedpur	CDFC	570 349	300 081	270 268	60	1 101 804	580 336	521 468	160
Jamuria	CDFC	129 456	68 741	60 715	...	...	...	...	...
Jaunpur	CDFC	159 996	84 179	76 817	25	...	...	...	...
Jetpur Navagadh	CDFC	104 311	54 772	49 539	...	...	...	...	...
Jhansi	CDFC	383 248	203 003	180 245	48	463 281	246 495	216 706	83
Jhunjhunun	CDFC	100 476	52 814	47 662	...	...	...	...	...
Jind	CDFC	136 089	73 557	62 532	...	...	...	...	...
Jodhpur	CDFC	846 408	450 816	395 592	79	856 034	455 860	400 174	...
Jorhat	CDFC	...	...	...	60	135 091	71 837	63 254	69
Junagadh	CDFC	168 686	86 935	81 751	...	252 138	130 318	121 820	...
Kaithal	CDFC	117 226	63 090	54 136	...	...	...	...	...
Kakinada	CDFC	289 920	143 905	146 015	39	368 672	183 619	185 053	58
Kalol	CDFC	100 021	53 098	46 923	...	112 025	59 532	52 493	...
Kalyan	CDFC	1 193 266	633 395	559 871	225	...	...	...	...
Kamarhati	CDFC	314 334	168 633	145 701	11	...	...	...	...
Kamptee	CDFC	...	...	...	...	137 056	71 633	65 423	36
Kancheepuram	CDFC	152 984	77 058	75 926	12	188 349	94 942	93 407	40
Kanchrapara	CDFC	126 118	65 197	60 921	13	...	...	...	...
Kanhangad	CDFC	...	...	...	...	129 364	61 954	67 410	84
Kannur	CDFC	...	...	...	...	498 175	237 101	261 074	145
Kanpur	CDFC	2 532 138	1 354 581	1 177 557	267	2 690 486	1 440 140	1 250 346	299
Kapra	CDFC	159 176	82 914	76 262	...	...	...	...	...
Karaikkudi	CDFC	...	...	...	...	125 185	62 230	62 955	79
Karawal Nagar	CDFC	148 549	80 364	68 185	...	...	...	...	...
Karimnagar	CDFC	203 819	104 514	99 305	24	215 782	110 479	105 303	...
Karnal	CDFC	210 476	112 263	98 213	22	222 017	118 428	103 589	24
Karur	CDFC	...	...	...	...	153 123	77 130	75 993	19
Katihar	CDFC	175 169	93 567	81 602	25	190 862	102 126	88 736	...
Khammam	CDFC	158 022	80 072	77 950	...	196 763	100 255	96 508	26
Khandwa	CDFC	171 976	88 859	83 117	36	...	...	...	...
Khanna	CDFC	103 059	55 290	47 769	...	...	...	...	...
Kharagpur	CDFC	207 984	107 506	100 478	91	296 323	152 700	143 623	125
Khardaha	CDFC	116 252	61 254	54 998	...	...	...	...	...
Khargone	CDFC	...	...	...	...	103 980	54 236	49 744	...
Kirari Suleman Nagar	CDFC	153 874	84 908	68 966	...	...	...	...	...
Kishangarh	CDFC	116 156	61 025	55 131	...	...	...	...	...
Koch Bihar	CDFC	...	...	...	...	102 922	52 186	50 736	...
Kochi	CDFC	596 473	295 351	301 122	109	1 355 406	670 462	684 944	373
Kolar	CDFC	113 299	57 773	55 526	...	...	...	...	...
Kolhapur	CDFC	485 183	251 958	233 225	67	497 554	258 400	239 154	67
Kolkata (Calcutta)[55]	CDFC	4 580 544	2 506 029	2 074 515	185	13 216 546	7 072 114	6 144 432	897
Kollam	CDFC	361 441	177 586	183 855	41	379 975	186 842	193 133	68
Korba	CDFC	315 695	165 028	150 667	35	...	...	...	...
Kota	CDFC	695 899	369 897	326 002	221	704 731	374 570	330 161	...
Kothagudem	CDFC	...	...	...	...	105 265	52 377	52 888	35
Kottayam	CDFC	...	...	...	...	172 867	84 915	87 952	64
Kozhikode	CDFC	436 527	211 785	224 742	96	880 168	428 984	451 184	233
Krishnanagar	CDFC	139 070	70 512	68 558	16	148 645	75 381	73 264	...

8. Population of capital cities and cities of 100 000 or more inhabitants: latest available year, 1987 - 2006
Population des capitales et des villes de 100 000 habitants ou plus: dernière année disponible, 1987 - 2006
(continued — suite)

Continent, country or area, date and city / Continent, pays ou zone, date et ville	Code[1]	City proper — Ville proprement dite Population				Urban agglomeration — Agglomération urbaine Population			
		Both sexes Les deux sexes	Male Masculin	Female Féminin	Surface area Superficie (km²)	Both sexes Les deux sexes	Male Masculin	Female Féminin	Surface area Superficie (km²)
ASIA — ASIE									
India — Inde[53]									
1 III 2001									
Krishnarajapura	CDFC	187 453	98 107	89 346	...	...	...	...	...
Kukatpalle	CDFC	290 591	152 159	138 432	...	...	...	...	...
Kulti	CDFC	290 057	152 947	137 110	...	...	...	...	...
Kumbakonam	CDFC	140 021	69 607	70 414	13	160 827	80 012	80 815	15
Kurnool	CDFC	267 739	135 859	131 880	15	320 619	163 071	157 548	46
L.B. Nagar	CDFC	261 987	135 636	126 351	...	...	...	...	...
Lakhimpur	CDFC	120 566	64 804	55 762	...	...	...	...	...
Lalitpur	CDFC	111 810	58 901	52 909	...	...	...	...	...
Latur	CDFC	299 828	156 477	143 351	21	...	...	...	...
Loni	CDFC	120 659	64 976	55 683	...	...	...	...	...
Lucknow	CDFC	2 207 340	1 165 932	1 041 408	310	2 266 933	1 199 273	1 067 660	338
Ludhiana	CDFC	1 395 053	789 868	605 185	135	...	...	...	...
Machilipatnam	CDFC	183 370	91 400	91 970	27	...	...	...	...
Madanapalle	CDFC	...	...	...	...	107 262	54 507	52 755	...
Madhyamgram	CDFC	155 503	79 716	75 787	...	...	...	...	...
Madurai	CDFC	922 913	466 909	456 004	47	1 194 665	604 728	589 937	115
Mahadevapura	CDFC	135 597	72 803	62 794	...	...	...	...	...
Mahbubnagar	CDFC	130 849	67 019	63 830	14	139 483	71 508	67 975	...
Mahesana	CDFC	...	...	...	...	141 367	74 928	66 439	...
Maheshtala	CDFC	389 214	204 734	184 480	...	...	...	...	...
Mainpuri	CDFC	...	...	...	...	102 007	54 043	47 964	...
Malappuram	CDFC	...	...	...	...	170 364	83 669	86 695	111
Malegaon	CDFC	409 190	208 744	200 446	13	...	...	...	...
Malerkotla	CDFC	106 802	56 872	49 930	...	...	...	...	...
Malkajgiri	CDFC	175 000	90 000	85 000	...	...	...	...	...
Mancherial	CDFC	...	...	...	...	118 047	60 371	57 676	...
Mandsaur	CDFC	116 483	60 269	56 214	...	117 532	60 860	56 672	...
Mandya	CDFC	131 211	66 630	64 581	17	...	...	...	...
Mangalore	CDFC	398 745	200 234	198 511	75	538 560	269 176	269 384	155
Mango	CDFC	166 091	87 322	78 769	...	...	...	...	...
Mathura	CDFC	298 827	159 249	139 578	9	319 235	171 516	147 719	22
Maunath Bhanjan	CDFC	210 071	108 696	101 375	9	...	...	...	...
Medinipur	CDFC	153 349	78 365	74 984	15	...	...	...	...
Meerut	CDFC	1 074 229	571 074	503 155	142	1 167 399	624 904	542 495	178
Mira-Bhayandar	CDFC	520 301	286 458	233 843	...	...	...	...	...
Mirzapur-cum-Vindhyachal	CDFC	205 264	109 872	95 392	39	...	...	...	...
Modinagar	CDFC	112 918	60 260	52 658	10	139 642	74 570	65 072	17
Moga	CDFC	124 624	66 843	57 781	...	134 242	71 996	62 246	...
Moradabad	CDFC	641 240	340 217	301 023	34	...	...	...	...
Morena	CDFC	150 890	82 281	68 609	96	...	...	...	...
Mormugoa	CDFC	...	...	...	...	104 689	55 927	48 762	...
Motihari	CDFC	101 506	54 629	46 877	...	109 250	59 517	49 733	...
Mughalsarai	CDFC	...	...	...	...	116 246	61 572	54 674	...
Mumbai (Bombay)	CDFC	11 914 398	6 577 902	5 336 496	466	16 368 084	8 979 172	7 388 912	1 041
Munger	CDFC	187 311	100 374	86 937	18	...	...	...	...
Murwara (Katni)	CDFC	186 738	97 666	89 072	107	...	...	...	...
Muzaffarnagar	CDFC	316 452	166 998	149 454	...	331 403	174 877	156 526	12
Muzaffarpur	CDFC	305 465	163 907	141 558	26	...	...	...	...
Mysore	CDFC	742 261	377 132	365 129	103	785 800	399 904	385 896	129
Nabadwip	CDFC	115 036	58 268	56 768	...	125 346	63 544	61 802	...
Nadiad	CDFC	192 799	100 452	92 347	...	196 679	102 469	94 210	...
Nagaon	CDFC	107 471	56 888	50 583	...	123 054	64 976	58 078	...
Nagercoil	CDFC	208 149	103 075	105 074	24	...	...	...	...
Nagpur	CDFC	2 051 320	1 058 692	992 628	217	2 122 965	1 097 723	1 025 242	229
Naihati	CDFC	215 432	113 706	101 726	4	...	...	...	...
Nala Sopara	CDFC	184 664	99 629	85 035	...	...	...	...	...
Nalgonda	CDFC	110 651	56 495	54 156	...	111 745	57 042	54 703	...
Nanded	CDFC	430 598	224 766	205 832	21	...	...	...	...
Nandyal	CDFC	151 771	76 914	74 857	15	156 216	79 145	77 071	...
Nangloi Jat	CDFC	150 371	82 358	68 013	...	...	...	...	...

8. Population of capital cities and cities of 100 000 or more inhabitants: latest available year, 1987 - 2006
Population des capitales et des villes de 100 000 habitants ou plus: dernière année disponible, 1987 - 2006
(continued — suite)

Continent, country or area, date and city Continent, pays ou zone, date et ville	Code[1]	City proper — Ville proprement dite Population				Urban agglomeration — Agglomération urbaine Population			
		Both sexes Les deux sexes	Male Masculin	Female Féminin	Surface area Superficie (km²)	Both sexes Les deux sexes	Male Masculin	Female Féminin	Surface area Superficie (km²)

ASIA — ASIE

India — Inde[53]
1 III 2001

Nashik	CDFC	1 076 967	579 638	497 329	259	1 152 048	619 962	532 086	322
Navghar-Manikpur	CDFC	116 700	61 806	54 894	...	...	...	...	...
Navi Mumbai (New Bombay)	CDFC	703 947	395 891	308 056	...	...	...	...	...
Navsari	CDFC	134 009	69 766	64 243	...	229 323	122 335	106 988	...
Neemuch	CDFC	107 496	56 509	50 987	...	112 691	59 250	53 441	...
Nellore	CDFC	378 947	191 283	187 664	48	404 922	204 269	200 653	...
NEW DELHI[56,57]	CDFC	294 783	161 596	133 187	...	...	...	...	...
Neyveli	CDFC	128 133	65 632	62 501	97	138 387	70 920	67 467	116
Nizamabad	CDFC	286 956	145 457	141 499	37	...	...	...	...
Noida	CDFC	293 908	162 306	131 602	90	...	...	...	...
North Barrackpur	CDFC	123 523	63 827	59 696	...	...	...	...	...
North Dumdum	CDFC	220 032	112 868	107 164	...	...	...	...	...
Ongole	CDFC	149 589	76 134	73 455	8	152 945	77 862	75 083	20
Orai	CDFC	139 444	74 974	64 470	...	...	...	...	...
Ozhukarai	CDFC	217 623	110 038	107 585	...	...	...	...	...
Palakkad	CDFC	130 736	64 293	66 443	30	197 281	96 790	100 491	59
Palanpur	CDFC	110 383	58 019	52 364	...	122 279	64 343	57 936	...
Pali	CDFC	187 571	99 258	88 313	84	...	...	...	...
Pallavaram	CDFC	143 984	73 152	70 832	...	...	...	...	...
Palwal	CDFC	100 528	53 577	46 951	...	...	...	...	...
Panchkula Urban Estate	CDFC	140 992	75 925	65 067	...	...	...	...	...
Panihati	CDFC	348 379	180 068	168 311	19	...	...	...	...
Panipat	CDFC	261 665	143 565	118 100	21	353 983	194 697	159 286	...
Panvel	CDFC	104 031	54 967	49 064	...	...	...	...	...
Parbhani	CDFC	259 170	133 892	125 278	58	...	...	...	...
Patan	CDFC	112 038	59 031	53 007	...	113 568	59 889	53 679	...
Pathankot	CDFC	159 559	87 505	72 054	...	168 275	91 998	76 277	...
Patiala	CDFC	302 870	162 465	140 405	...	323 309	173 412	149 897	...
Patna	CDFC	1 376 950	749 868	627 082	107	1 707 429	925 857	781 572	129
Phagwara	CDFC	...	...	...	...	102 111	55 224	46 887	...
Phusro	CDFC	...	...	...	...	174 367	93 656	80 711	84
Pilibhit	CDFC	124 082	65 824	58 258	10	...	...	...	...
Pimpri Chinchwad	CDFC	1 006 417	543 436	462 981	...	...	...	...	...
Pollachi	CDFC	...	...	...	...	127 993	64 417	63 576	43
Pondicherry	CDFC	220 749	109 386	111 363	20	505 715	253 336	252 379	67
Porbandar	CDFC	133 083	68 261	64 822	...	197 414	101 882	95 532	...
Port Blair	CDFC	100 186	55 507	44 679	...	...	...	...	...
Proddatur	CDFC	164 932	82 826	82 106	7	...	...	...	...
Pudukkottai	CDFC	108 947	54 537	54 410	...	...	...	...	...
Pune	CDFC	2 540 069	1 325 694	1 214 375	146	3 755 525	1 980 941	1 774 584	423
Puri	CDFC	157 610	82 229	75 381	17	...	...	...	...
Purnia	CDFC	171 235	92 573	78 662	45	196 757	106 051	90 706	60
Puruliya	CDFC	113 766	59 171	54 595	...	...	...	...	...
Quthbullapur	CDFC	225 816	118 463	107 353	...	...	...	...	...
Rae Bareli	CDFC	169 285	88 961	80 324	50	...	...	...	...
Raichur	CDFC	205 634	105 714	99 920	...	...	...	...	...
Raiganj	CDFC	165 222	87 489	77 733	11	175 064	92 742	82 322	15
Raigarh	CDFC	110 987	57 465	53 522	...	115 740	59 916	55 824	...
Raipur	CDFC	605 131	314 369	290 762	...	699 264	364 034	335 230	64
Rajahmundry	CDFC	313 347	158 027	155 320	52	408 341	205 655	202 686	64
Rajapalayam	CDFC	121 982	61 080	60 902	11	...	...	...	...
Rajarhat Gopalpur	CDFC	271 781	140 179	131 602	...	...	...	...	...
Rajkot	CDFC	966 642	506 915	459 727	...	1 002 160	525 797	476 363	...
Rajnandgaon	CDFC	143 727	72 964	70 763	93	...	...	...	...
Rajpur Sonarpur	CDFC	336 390	173 591	162 799	...	...	...	...	...
Ramagundam	CDFC	235 540	120 307	115 233	28	236 623	120 871	115 752	...
Rampur	CDFC	281 549	146 621	134 928	20	...	...	...	...
Ranaghat	CDFC	...	...	...	...	145 172	73 804	71 368	25
Ranchi	CDFC	846 454	450 514	395 940	177	862 850	459 251	403 599	182
Raniganj	CDFC	122 891	65 360	57 531	...	...	...	...	...

8. Population of capital cities and cities of 100 000 or more inhabitants: latest available year, 1987 - 2006
Population des capitales et des villes de 100 000 habitants ou plus: dernière année disponible, 1987 - 2006
(continued — suite)

Continent, country or area, date and city / Continent, pays ou zone, date et ville	Code[1]	City proper — Ville proprement dite Population				Urban agglomeration — Agglomération urbaine Population			
		Both sexes Les deux sexes	Male Masculin	Female Féminin	Surface area Superficie (km²)	Both sexes Les deux sexes	Male Masculin	Female Féminin	Surface area Superficie (km²)
ASIA — ASIE									
India — Inde[53]									
1 III 2001									
Ratlam	CDFC	221 267	113 982	107 285	39	233 480	120 473	113 007	41
Raurkela	CDFC	224 601	121 028	103 573	133	484 292	258 466	225 826	157
Rewa	CDFC	183 232	98 476	84 756	55	...	...	...	...
Rewari	CDFC	100 946	54 111	46 835	...	...	...	...	...
Rishra	CDFC	113 259	62 602	50 657	...	...	...	...	...
Robertson Pet	CDFC	141 294	70 568	70 726	...	156 961	78 574	78 387	...
Rohtak	CDFC	286 773	154 153	132 620	28	294 537	158 299	136 238	...
Roorkee	CDFC	...	...	...	...	114 811	63 861	50 950	...
S.A.S. Nagar (Mohali)	CDFC	123 284	65 570	57 714	...	...	...	...	...
Sagar	CDFC	232 321	122 491	109 830	36	309 164	163 018	146 146	52
Saharanpur	CDFC	452 925	239 456	213 469	25	...	...	...	...
Saharasa	CDFC	124 015	67 010	57 005	...	...	...	...	...
Salem	CDFC	693 236	352 770	340 466	20	748 513	381 042	367 471	93
Sambalpur	CDFC	154 164	79 914	74 250	50	226 966	117 954	109 012	90
Sambhal	CDFC	182 930	97 264	85 666	16	...	...	...	...
Sangli-Miraj-Kupwad	CDFC	436 639	224 195	212 444	...	447 632	229 852	217 780	...
Santipur	CDFC	138 195	70 084	68 111	25	...	...	...	...
Sasaram	CDFC	131 042	69 665	61 377	...	...	...	...	...
Satara	CDFC	108 043	55 935	52 108	...	...	...	...	...
Satna	CDFC	225 468	120 203	105 265	...	229 323	122 335	106 988	...
Sawai Madhopur	CDFC	...	...	...	...	101 994	53 942	48 052	...
Secunderabad	CDFC	204 182	103 274	100 908	...	...	...	...	...
Serampore	CDFC	197 955	105 613	92 342	6	...	...	...	...
Serilingampalle	CDFC	150 525	75 462	75 063	...	...	...	...	...
Shahjahanpur	CDFC	297 932	162 796	135 136	13	323 166	176 910	146 256	23
Shillong	CDFC	132 876	66 129	66 747	10	267 881	134 416	133 465	25
Shimla	CDFC	142 161	80 772	61 389	32	144 578	82 424	62 154	35
Shimoga	CDFC	274 105	140 107	133 998	...	...	...	...	...
Shivapuri	CDFC	146 859	78 395	68 464	81	...	...	...	...
Sikar	CDFC	184 904	96 327	88 577	23	185 506	96 646	88 860	...
Silchar	CDFC	142 393	72 727	69 666	16	184 285	94 321	89 964	...
Siliguri	CDFC	470 275	249 942	220 333	16	...	...	...	...
Singrauli	CDFC	185 580	100 342	85 238	...	...	...	...	...
Sirsa	CDFC	160 129	85 802	74 327	19	...	...	...	...
Sitapur	CDFC	151 827	79 682	72 145	26	...	...	...	...
Sivakasi	CDFC	...	...	...	...	121 312	60 923	60 389	13
Siwan	CDFC	108 172	57 223	50 949	...	...	...	...	...
Solapur	CDFC	873 037	444 885	428 152	...	...	...	...	...
Sonipat	CDFC	216 213	117 654	98 559	28	225 151	122 488	102 663	...
South Dum Dum	CDFC	392 150	200 182	191 968	11	...	...	...	...
Srikakulam	CDFC	109 666	54 788	54 878	...	117 066	58 613	58 453	...
Srinagar	CDFC	894 940	481 750	413 190	...	971 357	523 017	448 340	...
Sultan Pur Majra	CDFC	163 716	88 313	75 403	...	...	...	...	...
Sultanpur	CDFC	100 085	53 163	46 922	...	...	...	...	...
Surat	CDFC	2 433 787	1 372 307	1 061 480	...	2 811 466	1 597 093	1 214 373	...
Surendranagar Dudhrej	CDFC	156 417	81 430	74 987	...	...	...	...	...
Tadepalligudem	CDFC	102 303	50 476	51 827	...	...	...	...	...
Tambaram	CDFC	137 609	70 181	67 428	...	...	...	...	...
Tenali	CDFC	149 839	74 868	74 971	15	...	...	...	...
Thane	CDFC	1 261 517	674 660	586 857	144	...	...	...	...
Thanesar	CDFC	120 072	65 786	54 286	...	122 704	67 239	55 465	...
Thanjavur	CDFC	215 725	106 950	108 775	15	...	...	...	...
Thiruvananthapuram	CDFC	744 739	365 899	378 840	142	889 191	437 009	452 182	178
Thoothukkudi (Tuticorin)	CDFC	216 058	107 781	108 277	13	242 860	121 205	121 655	140
Thrissur	CDFC	317 474	154 188	163 286	...	330 067	160 386	169 681	88
Tinsukia	CDFC	...	...	...	...	108 102	59 515	48 587	...
Tiruchchirappalli	CDFC	746 062	373 541	372 521	23	847 131	424 541	422 590	166
Tirunelveli	CDFC	411 298	203 173	208 125	15	431 603	213 399	218 204	87
Tirupati	CDFC	227 657	117 786	109 871	16	302 678	154 845	147 833	20
Tiruppur	CDFC	346 551	180 629	165 922	44	542 787	282 872	259 915	91

8. Population of capital cities and cities of 100 000 or more inhabitants: latest available year, 1987 - 2006
Population des capitales et des villes de 100 000 habitants ou plus: dernière année disponible, 1987 - 2006
(continued — suite)

Continent, country or area, date and city / Continent, pays ou zone, date et ville	Code[1]	City proper — Ville proprement dite Population				Urban agglomeration — Agglomération urbaine Population			
		Both sexes Les deux sexes	Male Masculin	Female Féminin	Surface area Superficie (km²)	Both sexes Les deux sexes	Male Masculin	Female Féminin	Surface area Superficie (km²)
ASIA — ASIE									
India — Inde[53]									
1 III 2001									
Tiruvannamalai	CDFC	130 301	66 026	64 275	14	...	...	...	...
Tiruvottiyur	CDFC	211 768	108 938	102 830	...	...	...	...	...
Titagarh	CDFC	124 198	70 608	53 590	3	...	...	...	...
Tonk	CDFC	135 663	70 135	65 528	...	...	...	...	...
Tumkur	CDFC	248 592	129 215	119 377	...	...	...	...	...
Udaipur	CDFC	389 317	205 319	183 998	64	...	...	...	...
Udupi	CDFC	113 039	55 933	57 106	...	127 060	62 644	64 416	73
Ujjain	CDFC	429 933	223 745	206 188	...	430 669	224 223	206 446	92
Ulhasnagar	CDFC	472 943	251 610	221 333	22	...	...	...	...
Uluberia	CDFC	202 095	105 735	96 360	...	...	...	...	...
Unnao	CDFC	144 917	76 474	68 443	16	...	...	...	...
Uppal Kalan	CDFC	118 259	61 299	56 960	...	...	...	...	...
Uttarpara Kotrung	CDFC	150 204	78 661	71 543	...	...	...	...	...
Vadakara	CDFC	...	...	...	...	123 965	59 743	64 222	39
Vadodara	CDFC	1 306 035	684 130	621 905	...	1 492 398	783 237	709 161	...
Valsad	CDFC	...	...	...	...	145 050	75 322	70 328	...
Vaniyambadi	CDFC	...	...	...	...	103 841	51 668	52 173	...
Varanasi	CDFC	1 100 748	584 514	516 234	83	1 211 749	644 922	566 827	105
Vasai	CDFC	...	...	...	...	174 382	91 121	83 261	...
Vejalpur	CDFC	113 304	58 828	54 476	...	...	...	...	...
Vellore	CDFC	177 413	88 048	89 365	12	388 211	193 779	194 432	62
Veraval	CDFC	141 207	72 074	69 133	...	157 869	80 813	77 056	...
Vidisha	CDFC	125 457	66 579	58 878	...	...	...	...	...
Vijayawada	CDFC	825 436	436 366	389 070	...	1 011 152	531 084	480 068	105
Virar	CDFC	118 945	63 762	55 183	...	...	...	...	...
Visakhapatnam	CDFC	969 608	489 038	480 570	78	1 329 472	674 080	655 392	318
Vizianagarm	CDFC	174 324	86 111	88 213	21	195 462	96 771	98 691	30
Wadhwan	CDFC	...	...	...	...	219 828	114 217	105 611	...
Warangal	CDFC	528 570	267 820	260 750	57	577 190	292 709	284 481	67
Wardha	CDFC	111 070	57 447	53 623	8	...	...	...	...
Yamunanagar	CDFC	189 587	101 888	87 699	16	306 640	166 324	140 316	42
Yavatmal	CDFC	122 906	62 838	60 068	10	141 970	72 883	69 087	13
Indonesia — Indonésie									
1 VII 2003									
Ambon	ESDF	*224 160*	...	...	359	...	...	...	...
Balikpapan	ESDF	*429 568*	...	...	503	...	...	...	...
Banda Aceh	ESDF	*269 943*	...	...	61	...	...	...	...
Bandar Lampung	ESDF	*789 755*	...	...	193	...	...	...	...
Bandjarmasin	ESDF	*567 345*	...	...	72	...	...	...	...
Bandung	ESDF	*2 231 139*	...	...	1 670	...	...	...	...
Batam	ESDF	*547 550*	...	...	969	...	...	...	...
Bengkulu	ESDF	*254 693*	...	...	145	...	...	...	...
Binjai	ESDF	*226 468*	...	...	9	...	...	...	...
Bitung	ESDF	*163 074*	...	...	304	...	...	...	...
Blitar	ESDF	*123 327*	...	...	33	...	...	...	...
Bogor	ESDF	*816 911*	...	...	119	...	...	...	...
Cirebon	ESDF	*273 311*	...	...	37	...	...	...	...
Denpasar	ESDF	*502 873*	...	...	124	...	...	...	...
Gorontalo	ESDF	*145 828*	...	...	65	...	...	...	...
JAKARTA	ESDF	*8 640 184*	...	...	740	...	...	...	...
Jambi	ESDF	*444 551*	...	...	205	...	...	...	...
Jayapura	ESDF	*192 961*	...	...	740	...	...	...	...
Kediri	ESDF	*252 126*	...	...	63	...	...	...	...
Madiun	ESDF	*170 408*	...	...	34	...	...	...	...
Magelang	ESDF	*121 079*	...	...	18	...	...	...	...
Makasar (Ujung Pandang)	ESDF	*1 151 245*	...	...	199	...	...	...	...
Malang	ESDF	*770 483*	...	...	145	...	...	...	...
Manado	ESDF	*412 425*	...	...	157	...	...	...	...
Mataram	ESDF	*341 770*	...	...	61	...	...	...	...
Medan	ESDF	*1 983 659*	...	...	265	...	...	...	...

8. Population of capital cities and cities of 100 000 or more inhabitants: latest available year, 1987 - 2006
Population des capitales et des villes de 100 000 habitants ou plus: dernière année disponible, 1987 - 2006
(continued — suite)

Continent, country or area, date and city Continent, pays ou zone, date et ville	Code[1]	City proper — Ville proprement dite Population				Urban agglomeration — Agglomération urbaine Population			
		Both sexes Les deux sexes	Male Masculin	Female Féminin	Surface area Superficie (km²)	Both sexes Les deux sexes	Male Masculin	Female Féminin	Surface area Superficie (km²)
ASIA — ASIE									
Indonesia — Indonésie									
1 VII 2003									
Mojokerto	ESDF	112 137	...	...	16	...	...	...	...
Padang	ESDF	770 451	...	...	694	...	...	...	...
Pekalongan	ESDF	272 208	...	...	45	...	...	...	...
Pakanbaru	ESDF	672 480	...	...	632	...	...	...	...
Palangkaraya	ESDF	166 017	...	...	2 400	...	...	...	...
Palembang	ESDF	1 290 599	...	...	369	...	...	...	...
Pangkal Pinang	ESDF	158 163	...	...	89	...	...	...	...
Pare Pare	ESDF	113 290	...	...	99	...	...	...	...
Pasuruan	ESDF	176 987	...	...	35	...	...	...	...
Pematang Siantar	ESDF	224 446	...	...	80	...	...	...	...
Pontianak	ESDF	483 224	...	...	108	...	...	...	...
Probolinggo	ESDF	200 465	...	...	57	...	...	...	...
Salatiga	ESDF	160 592	...	...	57	...	...	...	...
Samarinda	ESDF	563 570	...	...	781	...	...	...	...
Semarang	ESDF	1 396 059	...	...	374	...	...	...	...
Sukabumi	ESDF	269 987	...	...	48	...	...	...	...
Surabaya	ESDF	2 689 728	...	...	351	...	...	...	...
Surakarta	ESDF	492 325	...	...	44	...	...	...	...
Tangerang	ESDF	1 471 396	...	...	187	...	...	...	...
Tanjung Balai	ESDF	145 572	...	...	68	...	...	...	...
Tebing Tinggi	ESDF	132 982	...	...	32	...	...	...	...
Tegal	ESDF	242 423	...	...	35	...	...	...	...
Yogyakarta	ESDF	392 239	...	...	33	...	...	...	...
Iran (Islamic Republic of) — Iran (République islamique d')									
1 VII 2003									
Abadan	ESDJ	277 998	...	...	...	...	...	...	...
Ahwaz	ESDJ	949 054	...	...	...	...	...	...	...
Amol	ESDJ	195 588	...	...	...	...	...	...	...
Andimeshk	ESDJ	133 932	...	...	...	...	...	...	...
Arak	ESDJ	476 568	...	...	...	...	...	...	...
Ardabil	ESDJ	390 651	...	...	...	...	...	...	...
Babol	ESDJ	196 569	...	...	...	...	...	...	...
Bandar-e-Abbas	ESDJ	315 075	...	...	...	...	...	...	...
Birjand	ESDJ	186 893	...	...	...	...	...	...	...
Bojnurd	ESDJ	182 465	...	...	...	...	...	...	...
Borujerd	ESDJ	244 205	...	...	...	...	...	...	...
Bukand	ESDJ	173 005	...	...	...	...	...	...	...
Bushehr	ESDJ	150 411	...	...	...	...	...	...	...
Dezful	ESDJ	241 544	...	...	...	...	...	...	...
Esfahan	ESDJ	1 523 006	...	...	...	...	...	...	...
Gonbad-e-Kavus	ESDJ	125 215	...	...	...	...	...	...	...
Gorgan	ESDJ	241 085	...	...	...	...	...	...	...
Hamadan	ESDJ	494 378	...	...	...	...	...	...	...
Ilam	ESDJ	141 915	...	...	...	...	...	...	...
Islam Shahr (Qasemabad)	ESDJ	273 520	...	...	...	...	...	...	...
Karaj	ESDJ	1 212 220	...	...	...	...	...	...	...
Kashan	ESDJ	244 877	...	...	...	...	...	...	...
Kerman	ESDJ	529 748	...	...	...	...	...	...	...
Kermanshah	ESDJ	816 428	...	...	...	...	...	...	...
Khomeini shahr	ESDJ	181 110	...	...	...	...	...	...	...
Khoramabad	ESDJ	313 177	...	...	...	...	...	...	...
Khoramshahr	ESDJ	142 506	...	...	...	...	...	...	...
Khoy	ESDJ	166 974	...	...	...	...	...	...	...
Mahabad	ESDJ	137 173	...	...	...	...	...	...	...
Malayer	ESDJ	169 060	...	...	...	...	...	...	...
Marvadsht	ESDJ	125 072	...	...	...	...	...	...	...
Maraqeh	ESDJ	155 350	...	...	...	...	...	...	...
Mashhad	ESDJ	2 070 604	...	...	...	...	...	...	...
Masjed Soleyman	ESDJ	132 496	...	...	...	...	...	...	...

8. Population of capital cities and cities of 100 000 or more inhabitants: latest available year, 1987 - 2006
Population des capitales et des villes de 100 000 habitants ou plus: dernière année disponible, 1987 - 2006
(continued — suite)

Continent, country or area, date and city / Continent, pays ou zone, date et ville	Code[1]	City proper — Ville proprement dite Population				Urban agglomeration — Agglomération urbaine Population			
		Both sexes Les deux sexes	Male Masculin	Female Féminin	Surface area Superficie (km²)	Both sexes Les deux sexes	Male Masculin	Female Féminin	Surface area Superficie (km²)
ASIA — ASIE									
Iran (Islamic Republic of) — Iran (République islamique d')									
1 VII 2003									
Najafabad	ESDJ	*204 637*	...	...	...	...	...	...	...
Neyshabur	ESDJ	*205 842*	...	...	...	...	...	...	...
Orumiyeh	ESDJ	*601 478*	...	...	...	...	...	...	...
Qaem shahr	ESDJ	*168 359*	...	...	...	...	...	...	...
Qazvin	ESDJ	*306 984*	...	...	...	...	...	...	...
Qarchak	ESDJ	*165 462*	...	...	...	...	...	...	...
Qods	ESDJ	*236 463*	...	...	...	...	...	...	...
Qom	ESDJ	*986 922*	...	...	...	...	...	...	...
Rasht	ESDJ	*519 481*	...	...	...	...	...	...	...
Sabzewar	ESDJ	*215 278*	...	...	...	...	...	...	...
Sanandaj	ESDJ	*327 969*	...	...	...	...	...	...	...
Saqez	ESDJ	*148 445*	...	...	...	...	...	...	...
Sari	ESDJ	*253 052*	...	...	...	...	...	...	...
Shahr Kord	ESDJ	*121 337*	...	...	...	...	...	...	...
Shahrud	ESDJ	*128 642*	...	...	...	...	...	...	...
Shiraz	ESDJ	*1 197 847*	...	...	...	...	...	...	...
Sirjan	ESDJ	*197 303*	...	...	...	...	...	...	...
Tabriz	ESDJ	*1 365 476*	...	...	...	...	...	...	...
TEHRAN	ESDJ	*7 188 936*	...	...	...	...	...	...	...
Varamin	ESDJ	*187 178*	...	...	...	...	...	...	...
Yazd	ESDJ	*432 233*	...	...	...	...	...	...	...
Zabol	ESDJ	*118 424*	...	...	...	...	...	...	...
Zahedan	ESDJ	*534 771*	...	...	...	...	...	...	...
Zanjan	ESDJ	*346 253*	...	...	...	...	...	...	...
Iraq									
17 X 1987									
Adhamiyah	CDFC	464 151	...	...	...	...	...	...	...
Amara	CDFC	208 797	...	...	...	...	...	...	...
BAGHDAD[58]	CDFC	3 841 268	...	...	...	...	...	...	...
Basra	CDFC	406 296	...	...	...	...	...	...	...
Diwaniya	CDFC	196 519	...	...	...	...	...	...	...
Erbil	CDFC	485 968	...	...	...	...	...	...	...
Hilla	CDFC	268 834	...	...	...	...	...	...	...
Kadhimain	CDFC	521 444	...	...	...	...	...	...	...
Karradah Sharqiyah	CDFC	235 554	...	...	...	...	...	...	...
Kerbala	CDFC	296 705	...	...	...	...	...	...	...
Kirkuk	CDFC	418 624	...	...	...	...	...	...	...
Kut	CDFC	183 183	...	...	...	...	...	...	...
Majnoon	CDFC	244 545	...	...	...	...	...	...	...
Mosul	CDFC	664 221	...	...	...	...	...	...	...
Najaf	CDFC	309 010	...	...	...	...	...	...	...
Nasariya	CDFC	265 937	...	...	...	...	...	...	...
Ramadi	CDFC	192 556	...	...	...	...	...	...	...
Sulamaniya	CDFC	364 096	...	...	...	...	...	...	...
Israel — Israël									
1 VII 2006									
Ashdod	ESDJ	202 383	99 402	102 982	47	...	...	...	...
Ashqelon	ESDJ	107 156	52 224	54 931	48	...	...	...	...
Bat Yam	ESDJ	129 566	61 189	68 377	8	...	...	...	...
Be'er Sheva	ESDJ	185 256	90 024	95 232	50	...	...	...	...
Bene Beraq	ESDJ	146 499	73 540	72 959	7	...	...	...	...
Haifa	ESDJ	266 662	128 031	138 632	64	...	...	...	...
Holon	ESDJ	166 635	80 210	86 426	19	...	...	...	...
JERUSALEM[59,60]	ESDJ	726 638	361 859	364 778	125	...	...	...	...
Netanya	ESDJ	172 600	83 325	89 276	29	...	...	...	...
Petah Tiqwa	ESDJ	181 789	88 078	93 711	36	...	...	...	...
Ramat Gan	ESDJ	129 016	60 590	68 426	13	...	...	...	...
Rehovot	ESDJ	103 793	50 684	53 109	23	...	...	...	...
Rishon Leziyyon	ESDJ	220 758	107 654	113 104	59	...	...	...	...

8. Population of capital cities and cities of 100 000 or more inhabitants: latest available year, 1987 - 2006
Population des capitales et des villes de 100 000 habitants ou plus: dernière année disponible, 1987 - 2006
(continued — suite)

Continent, country or area, date and city / Continent, pays ou zone, date et ville	Code[1]	City proper — Ville proprement dite Population				Urban agglomeration — Agglomération urbaine Population			
		Both sexes Les deux sexes	Male Masculin	Female Féminin	Surface area Superficie (km²)	Both sexes Les deux sexes	Male Masculin	Female Féminin	Surface area Superficie (km²)
ASIA — ASIE									
Israel — Israël									
1 VII 2006									
Tel Aviv-Yafo	ESDJ	381 650	183 892	197 759	52	...	...	...	...
Japan — Japon[61,62,63]									
01 X 2005									
Abiko	CDFC	131 205	64 853	66 352	43	...	...	...	...
Ageo	CDFC	220 232	110 102	110 130	46	...	...	...	...
Aizuwakamatsu	CDFC	122 248	58 067	64 181	343	...	...	...	...
Akashi	CDFC	291 027	141 749	149 278	49	...	...	...	...
Akishima	CDFC	110 143	55 446	54 697	17	...	...	...	...
Akita	CDFC	333 109	158 107	175 002	906	...	...	...	...
Amagasaki	CDFC	462 647	226 084	236 563	50	...	...	...	...
Anjo	CDFC	170 250	87 022	83 228	86	...	...	...	...
Aomori	CDFC	311 508	145 965	165 543	825	...	...	...	...
Asahikawa	CDFC	355 004	165 387	189 617	748	...	...	...	...
Asaka	CDFC	124 393	65 460	58 933	18	...	...	...	...
Ashikaga	CDFC	159 756	78 120	81 636	178	...	...	...	...
Atsugi	CDFC	222 403	116 150	106 253	94	...	...	...	...
Beppu	CDFC	126 959	57 392	69 567	125	...	...	...	...
Chiba	CDFC	924 319	462 961	461 358	272	...	...	...	...
Chigasaki	CDFC	228 420	113 272	115 148	36	...	...	...	...
Chikusei	CDFC	112 581	55 795	56 786	205	...	...	...	...
Chofu	CDFC	216 119	109 098	107 021	22	...	...	...	...
Daito	CDFC	126 504	62 840	63 664	18	...	...	...	...
Ebetsu	CDFC	125 601	60 807	64 794	188	...	...	...	...
Ebina	CDFC	123 764	63 089	60 675	26	...	...	...	...
Fuchu	CDFC	245 623	127 575	118 048	29	...	...	...	...
Fuji	CDFC	236 474	117 069	119 405	214	...	...	...	...
Fujieda	CDFC	129 248	62 921	66 327	141	...	...	...	...
Fujimi	CDFC	104 748	52 491	52 257	20	...	...	...	...
Fujimino	CDFC	101 960	51 349	50 611	15	...	...	...	...
Fujinomiya	CDFC	121 779	60 113	61 666	315	...	...	...	...
Fujisawa	CDFC	396 014	198 365	197 649	70	...	...	...	...
Fukaya	CDFC	103 529	51 692	51 837	69	...	...	...	...
Fukui	CDFC	252 220	122 750	129 470	341	...	...	...	...
Fukuoka	CDFC	1 401 279	673 097	728 182	341	...	...	...	...
Fukushima	CDFC	290 869	140 013	150 856	746	...	...	...	...
Fukuyama	CDFC	418 509	201 999	216 510	461	...	...	...	...
Funabashi	CDFC	569 835	288 667	281 168	86	...	...	...	...
Gifu	CDFC	399 931	189 633	210 298	195	...	...	...	...
Habikino	CDFC	118 695	56 447	62 248	26	...	...	...	...
Hachinohe	CDFC	244 700	117 446	127 254	305	...	...	...	...
Hachioji	CDFC	560 012	286 154	273 858	186	...	...	...	...
Hadano	CDFC	168 317	86 664	81 653	104	...	...	...	...
Hakodate	CDFC	294 264	134 868	159 396	678	...	...	...	...
Hakusan	CDFC	109 450	53 129	56 321	755	...	...	...	...
Hamamatsu	CDFC	804 032	399 704	404 328	1 511	...	...	...	...
Handa	CDFC	115 845	57 626	58 219	47	...	...	...	...
Higashihiroshima	CDFC	184 430	93 960	90 470	635	...	...	...	...
Higashikurume	CDFC	115 330	57 123	58 207	13	...	...	...	...
Higashimurayama	CDFC	144 929	71 635	73 294	17	...	...	...	...
Higashiosaka	CDFC	513 821	251 708	262 113	62	...	...	...	...
Hikone	CDFC	109 779	54 136	55 643	98	...	...	...	...
Himeji	CDFC	482 304	232 553	249 751	276	...	...	...	...
Hino	CDFC	176 538	90 636	85 902	28	...	...	...	...
Hirakata	CDFC	404 044	195 236	208 808	65	...	...	...	...
Hiratsuka	CDFC	258 958	132 156	126 802	68	...	...	...	...
Hirosaki	CDFC	173 221	79 299	93 922	274	...	...	...	...
Hiroshima	CDFC	1 154 391	559 345	595 046	905	...	...	...	...
Hitachi	CDFC	199 218	99 212	100 006	226	...	...	...	...
Hitachinaka	CDFC	153 639	77 331	76 308	99	...	...	...	...
Hofu	CDFC	116 818	56 332	60 486	189	...	...	...	...

8. Population of capital cities and cities of 100 000 or more inhabitants: latest available year, 1987 - 2006
Population des capitales et des villes de 100 000 habitants ou plus: dernière année disponible, 1987 - 2006
(continued — suite)

Continent, country or area, date and city / Continent, pays ou zone, date et ville	Code[1]	City proper — Ville proprement dite Population				Urban agglomeration — Agglomération urbaine Population			
		Both sexes Les deux sexes	Male Masculin	Female Féminin	Surface area Superficie (km²)	Both sexes Les deux sexes	Male Masculin	Female Féminin	Surface area Superficie (km²)
ASIA — ASIE									
Japan — Japon[61,62,63]									
01 X 2005									
Ibaraki	CDFC	267 961	131 135	136 826	77	...	...	...	...
Ichihara	CDFC	280 255	143 404	136 851	368	...	...	...	...
Ichikawa	CDFC	466 608	239 659	226 949	57	...	...	...	...
Ichinomiya	CDFC	100 623	48 675	51 948	558	...	...	...	...
Ichinomiya	CDFC	371 687	181 614	190 073	114	...	...	...	...
Iida	CDFC	108 624	51 706	56 918	659	...	...	...	...
Ikeda	CDFC	101 616	49 682	51 934	22	...	...	...	...
Ikoma	CDFC	113 686	53 937	59 749	53	...	...	...	...
Ikoma	CDFC	125 818	60 793	65 025	1 133	...	...	...	...
Imabari	CDFC	173 983	80 745	93 238	420	...	...	...	...
Inazawa	CDFC	136 965	67 754	69 211	79	...	...	...	...
Iruma	CDFC	148 576	73 574	75 002	45	...	...	...	...
Isahaya	CDFC	144 034	68 154	75 880	312	...	...	...	...
Isehara	CDFC	100 579	51 630	48 949	56	...	...	...	...
Isesaki	CDFC	202 447	101 019	101 428	139	...	...	...	...
Ishinomaki	CDFC	167 324	80 553	86 771	550	...	...	...	...
Itami	CDFC	192 250	94 232	98 018	25	...	...	...	...
Iwaki	CDFC	354 492	172 169	182 323	1 231	...	...	...	...
Iwakuni	CDFC	103 507	49 240	54 267	222	...	...	...	...
Iwata	CDFC	170 899	86 262	84 637	164	...	...	...	...
Izumi (Osaka)	CDFC	177 856	86 339	91 517	85	...	...	...	...
Izumo	CDFC	146 307	69 901	76 406	543	...	...	...	...
Joetsu	CDFC	208 082	100 884	107 198	973	...	...	...	...
Kadoma	CDFC	131 706	65 229	66 477	12	...	...	...	...
Kagoshima	CDFC	604 367	281 389	322 978	547	...	...	...	...
Kakamigahara	CDFC	144 174	70 696	73 478	88	...	...	...	...
Kakegawa	CDFC	117 857	58 862	58 995	266	...	...	...	...
Kakogawa	CDFC	267 100	130 694	136 406	139	...	...	...	...
Kamagaya	CDFC	102 812	50 969	51 843	21	...	...	...	...
Kamakura	CDFC	171 158	81 443	89 715	40	...	...	...	...
Kanazawa	CDFC	454 607	220 679	233 928	468	...	...	...	...
Karatsu	CDFC	128 564	59 962	68 602	425	...	...	...	...
Kariya	CDFC	142 134	74 800	67 334	50	...	...	...	...
Kashihara	CDFC	124 728	59 792	64 936	40	...	...	...	...
Kashiwa	CDFC	380 963	190 138	190 825	115	...	...	...	...
Kasuga	CDFC	108 402	52 815	55 587	14	...	...	...	...
Kasugai	CDFC	295 802	147 732	148 070	93	...	...	...	...
Kasukabe	CDFC	238 506	118 931	119 575	66	...	...	...	...
Kawachinagano	CDFC	117 239	55 618	61 621	110	...	...	...	...
Kawagoe	CDFC	333 795	168 943	164 852	109	...	...	...	...
Kawaguchi	CDFC	480 079	246 310	233 769	56	...	...	...	...
Kawanishi	CDFC	157 668	74 928	82 740	53	...	...	...	...
Kawasaki	CDFC	1 327 011	687 080	639 931	143	...	...	...	...
Kiryu	CDFC	128 037	61 796	66 241	275	...	...	...	...
Kisarazu	CDFC	122 234	60 947	61 287	139	...	...	...	...
Kishiwada	CDFC	201 000	96 866	104 134	72	...	...	...	...
Kitakyushu[64]	CDFC	993 525	466 779	526 746	488	...	...	...	...
Kitami	CDFC	110 715	53 484	57 231	421	...	...	...	...
Kobe	CDFC	1 525 393	724 427	800 966	552	...	...	...	...
Kochi	CDFC	333 484	155 025	178 459	264	...	...	...	...
Kodaira	CDFC	183 796	91 756	92 040	20	...	...	...	...
Kofu	CDFC	194 244	95 535	98 709	172	...	...	...	...
Koga	CDFC	145 265	72 399	72 866	124	...	...	...	...
Koganei	CDFC	114 112	57 696	56 416	11	...	...	...	...
Kokubunji	CDFC	117 604	58 889	58 715	11	...	...	...	...
Komaki	CDFC	147 182	74 526	72 656	63	...	...	...	...
Komatsu	CDFC	109 084	52 782	56 302	371	...	...	...	...
Konosu	CDFC	119 594	59 595	59 999	67	...	...	...	...
Koriyama	CDFC	338 834	167 071	171 763	757	...	...	...	...
Koshigaya	CDFC	315 792	158 721	157 071	60	...	...	...	...

8. Population of capital cities and cities of 100 000 or more inhabitants: latest available year, 1987 - 2006
Population des capitales et des villes de 100 000 habitants ou plus: dernière année disponible, 1987 - 2006
(continued — suite)

Continent, country or area, date and city Continent, pays ou zone, date et ville	Code[1]	City proper — Ville proprement dite Population				Urban agglomeration — Agglomération urbaine Population			
		Both sexes Les deux sexes	Male Masculin	Female Féminin	Surface area Superficie (km²)	Both sexes Les deux sexes	Male Masculin	Female Féminin	Surface area Superficie (km²)
ASIA — ASIE									
Japan — Japon[61,62,63]									
01 X 2005									
Kumagaya	CDFC	191 107	95 743	95 364	137				
Kumamoto	CDFC	669 603	316 048	353 555	267	...	...	...	...
Kurashiki	CDFC	469 377	227 334	242 043	354	...	...	...	...
Kure	CDFC	251 003	120 435	130 568	353	...	...	...	...
Kurume	CDFC	306 434	145 210	161 224	230	...	...	...	...
Kusatsu	CDFC	121 159	63 071	58 088	48	...	...	...	...
Kushiro	CDFC	181 516	86 007	95 509	222	...	...	...	...
Kuwana	CDFC	138 963	68 145	70 818	137	...	...	...	...
Kyoto	CDFC	1 474 811	703 210	771 601	828	...	...	...	...
Machida	CDFC	405 534	200 197	205 337	72	...	...	...	...
Maebashi	CDFC	318 584	155 480	163 104	241	...	...	...	...
Marugame	CDFC	110 085	53 090	56 995	112	...	...	...	...
Matsubara	CDFC	127 276	61 776	65 500	17	...	...	...	...
Matsudo	CDFC	472 579	237 562	235 017	61	...	...	...	...
Matsue	CDFC	196 603	94 638	101 965	530	...	...	...	...
Matsumoto	CDFC	227 627	112 083	115 544	919	...	...	...	...
Matsusaka	CDFC	168 973	81 320	87 653	624	...	...	...	...
Matsuyama	CDFC	514 937	242 463	272 474	429	...	...	...	...
Mihara	CDFC	104 196	49 729	54 467	471	...	...	...	...
Minoh	CDFC	127 135	61 286	65 849	48	...	...	...	...
Misato	CDFC	128 278	65 307	62 971	30	...	...	...	...
Mishima	CDFC	112 241	55 054	57 187	62	...	...	...	...
Mitaka	CDFC	177 016	88 579	88 437	16	...	...	...	...
Mito	CDFC	262 603	127 435	135 168	217	...	...	...	...
Miyakonojo	CDFC	133 062	62 426	70 636	306	...	...	...	...
Miyazaki	CDFC	310 123	145 263	164 860	287	...	...	...	...
Moriguchi	CDFC	147 465	71 972	75 493	13	...	...	...	...
Morioka	CDFC	287 192	137 262	149 930	489	...	...	...	...
Musashino	CDFC	137 525	66 628	70 897	11	...	...	...	...
Nagano	CDFC	378 512	183 065	195 447	731	...	...	...	...
Nagaoka	CDFC	236 344	115 726	120 618	526	...	...	...	...
Nagareyama	CDFC	152 641	75 643	76 998	35	...	...	...	...
Nagasaki	CDFC	442 699	203 292	239 407	339	...	...	...	...
Nagoya	CDFC	2 215 062	1 099 582	1 115 480	326	...	...	...	...
Naha	CDFC	312 393	150 463	161 930	39	...	...	...	...
Nara	CDFC	370 102	174 469	195 633	277	...	...	...	...
Narashino	CDFC	158 785	80 308	78 477	21	...	...	...	...
Narita	CDFC	100 717	50 592	50 125	131	...	...	...	...
Nasushiobara	CDFC	115 032	57 184	57 848	593	...	...	...	...
Neyagawa	CDFC	241 816	118 593	123 223	25	...	...	...	...
Niigata	CDFC	785 134	378 725	406 409	650	...	...	...	...
Niihama	CDFC	123 952	59 190	64 762	234	...	...	...	...
Niiza	CDFC	153 305	77 310	75 995	23	...	...	...	...
Nishio	CDFC	104 321	52 584	51 737	76	...	...	...	...
Nishinomiya	CDFC	465 337	221 205	244 132	99	...	...	...	...
Nishitokyo	CDFC	189 735	94 046	95 689	16	...	...	...	...
Nobeoka	CDFC	121 635	56 816	64 819	284	...	...	...	...
Noda	CDFC	151 240	75 797	75 443	104	...	...	...	...
Numazu	CDFC	208 005	102 259	105 746	187	...	...	...	...
Obihiro	CDFC	170 580	81 906	88 674	619	...	...	...	...
Odawara	CDFC	198 741	97 501	101 240	114	...	...	...	...
Ogaki	CDFC	151 030	73 398	77 632	80	...	...	...	...
Oita	CDFC	462 317	221 539	240 778	501	...	...	...	...
Okayama	CDFC	674 746	324 623	350 123	659	...	...	...	...
Okazaki	CDFC	354 704	179 294	175 410	227	...	...	...	...
Okinawa	CDFC	126 400	60 896	65 504	49	...	...	...	...
Ome	CDFC	142 354	71 731	70 623	103	...	...	...	...
Omuta	CDFC	131 090	59 452	71 638	82	...	...	...	...
Onomichi	CDFC	114 486	54 018	60 468	212	...	...	...	...
Osaka	CDFC	2 628 811	1 280 325	1 348 486	222	...	...	...	...

8. Population of capital cities and cities of 100 000 or more inhabitants: latest available year, 1987 - 2006
Population des capitales et des villes de 100 000 habitants ou plus: dernière année disponible, 1987 - 2006
(continued — suite)

Continent, country or area, date and city / Continent, pays ou zone, date et ville	Code[1]	City proper — Ville proprement dite Population				Urban agglomeration — Agglomération urbaine Population			
		Both sexes Les deux sexes	Male Masculin	Female Féminin	Surface area Superficie (km²)	Both sexes Les deux sexes	Male Masculin	Female Féminin	Surface area Superficie (km²)
ASIA — ASIE									
Japan — Japon[61,62,63]									
01 X 2005									
Ota	CDFC	213 299	107 556	105 743	176	...	...	...	...
Otaru	CDFC	142 161	64 436	77 725	243	...	...	...	...
Otsu	CDFC	301 672	146 353	155 319	302	...	...	...	...
Oyama	CDFC	160 150	80 723	79 427	172	...	...	...	...
Saga	CDFC	206 967	98 013	108 954	355	...	...	...	...
Sagamihara	CDFC	628 698	318 986	309 712	90	...	...	...	...
Saijo	CDFC	113 371	54 144	59 227	509	...	...	...	...
Saitama	CDFC	1 176 314	590 972	585 342	217	...	...	...	...
Sakai	CDFC	830 966	400 294	430 672	150	...	...	...	...
Saku	CDFC	100 462	49 041	51 421	424	...	...	...	...
Sakura	CDFC	171 246	84 050	87 196	104	...	...	...	...
Sanda	CDFC	113 572	54 881	58 691	210	...	...	...	...
Sanjo	CDFC	104 749	50 660	54 089	432	...	...	...	...
Sano	CDFC	123 926	60 917	63 009	356	...	...	...	...
Sapporo	CDFC	1 880 863	889 054	991 809	1 121	...	...	...	...
Sasebo	CDFC	248 041	116 726	131 315	308	...	...	...	...
Satsumasendai	CDFC	102 370	48 195	54 175	684	...	...	...	...
Sayama	CDFC	158 074	80 072	78 002	49	...	...	...	...
Sendai	CDFC	1 025 098	500 597	524 501	784	...	...	...	...
Seto	CDFC	131 925	65 471	66 454	112	...	...	...	...
Shibata	CDFC	104 634	50 431	54 203	533	...	...	...	...
Shimonoseki	CDFC	290 693	134 741	155 952	716	...	...	...	...
Shizuoka	CDFC	700 886	340 999	359 887	1 374	...	...	...	...
Shunan	CDFC	152 387	73 058	79 329	656	...	...	...	...
Soka	CDFC	236 316	120 673	115 643	27	...	...	...	...
Suita	CDFC	353 885	173 154	180 731	36	...	...	...	...
Suzuka	CDFC	193 114	96 577	96 537	195	...	...	...	...
Tachikawa	CDFC	172 566	85 889	86 677	24	...	...	...	...
Tajimi	CDFC	103 821	50 283	53 538	78	...	...	...	...
Takamatsu	CDFC	337 902	163 509	174 393	274	...	...	...	...
Takaoka	CDFC	167 685	80 216	87 469	151	...	...	...	...
Takarazuka	CDFC	219 862	103 495	116 367	102	...	...	...	...
Takasaki	CDFC	245 100	120 607	124 493	111	...	...	...	...
Takatsuki	CDFC	351 826	170 102	181 724	105	...	...	...	...
Tama	CDFC	145 877	73 140	72 737	21	...	...	...	...
Toda	CDFC	116 696	61 254	55 442	18	...	...	...	...
Tokai	CDFC	104 339	54 737	49 602	43	...	...	...	...
Tokorozawa	CDFC	336 100	169 176	166 924	72	...	...	...	...
Tokushima	CDFC	267 833	127 241	140 592	191	...	...	...	...
TOKYO[65]	CDFC	8 489 653	4 210 749	4 278 904	621	12 576 601	6 264 895	6 311 706	2 187
Tomakomai	CDFC	172 758	83 935	88 823	561	...	...	...	...
Tondabayashi	CDFC	123 837	58 946	64 891	40	...	...	...	...
Toride	CDFC	111 327	54 899	56 428	70	...	...	...	...
Tottori	CDFC	201 740	98 333	103 407	766	...	...	...	...
Toyama	CDFC	421 239	204 407	216 832	1 242	...	...	...	...
Toyota	CDFC	412 141	218 286	193 855	918	...	...	...	...
Toyohashi	CDFC	372 479	186 116	186 363	261	...	...	...	...
Toyokawa	CDFC	120 967	60 337	60 630	65	...	...	...	...
Toyonaka	CDFC	386 623	186 440	200 183	36	...	...	...	...
Tsu	CDFC	165 182	80 544	84 638	102	...	...	...	...
Tsuchiura	CDFC	135 058	67 254	67 804	82	...	...	...	...
Tsukuba	CDFC	200 528	103 110	97 418	284	...	...	...	...
Tsuruoka	CDFC	142 384	67 676	74 708	1 311	...	...	...	...
Tsuyama	CDFC	110 569	52 418	58 151	506	...	...	...	...
Ube	CDFC	178 955	85 444	93 511	288	...	...	...	...
Ueda	CDFC	123 680	60 383	63 297	177	...	...	...	...
Uji	CDFC	189 591	92 286	97 305	68	...	...	...	...
Urasoe	CDFC	106 049	52 128	53 921	19	...	...	...	...
Urayasu	CDFC	155 290	79 275	76 015	17	...	...	...	...
Uruma	CDFC	113 535	56 598	56 937	86	...	...	...	...

8. Population of capital cities and cities of 100 000 or more inhabitants: latest available year, 1987 - 2006
Population des capitales et des villes de 100 000 habitants ou plus: dernière année disponible, 1987 - 2006
(continued — suite)

Continent, country or area, date and city / Continent, pays ou zone, date et ville	Code[1]	City proper — Ville proprement dite Population				Urban agglomeration — Agglomération urbaine Population			
		Both sexes Les deux sexes	Male Masculin	Female Féminin	Surface area Superficie (km²)	Both sexes Les deux sexes	Male Masculin	Female Féminin	Surface area Superficie (km²)
ASIA — ASIE									
Japan — Japon[61,62,63]									
01 X 2005									
Utsunomiya	CDFC	457 673	229 006	228 667	312	...	...	...	...
Wakayama	CDFC	375 591	176 825	198 766	209	...	...	...	...
Yachiyo	CDFC	180 729	89 601	91 128	51	...	...	...	...
Yaizu	CDFC	120 109	58 484	61 625	46	...	...	...	...
Yamagata	CDFC	256 012	122 903	133 109	381	...	...	...	...
Yamaguchi	CDFC	191 677	91 263	100 414	730	...	...	...	...
Yamato	CDFC	221 220	111 802	109 418	27	...	...	...	...
Yao	CDFC	273 487	132 627	140 860	42	...	...	...	...
Yatsushiro	CDFC	136 886	63 823	73 063	680	...	...	...	...
Yokkaichi	CDFC	303 845	149 692	154 153	205	...	...	...	...
Yokohama	CDFC	3 579 628	1 803 579	1 776 049	437	...	...	...	...
Yokosuka	CDFC	426 178	214 029	212 149	101	...	...	...	...
Yokote	CDFC	103 652	48 811	54 841	694	...	...	...	...
Yonago	CDFC	149 584	71 053	78 531	132	...	...	...	...
Zama	CDFC	128 174	65 860	62 314	18	...	...	...	...
Jordan — Jordanie									
31 XII 2006									
AMMAN	ESDF	*1 152 540*	*592 767*	*559 773*		...	...	...	...
Irbid	ESDF	*269 140*	*138 145*	*130 995*		...	...	...	...
Russiefa	ESDF	*248 512*	*129 233*	*119 279*		...	...	...	...
Zarqa	ESDF	*431 278*	*222 817*	*208 461*		...	...	...	...
Kazakhstan									
1 I 2006									
Aktau	ESDF	165 931	80 409	85 522		...	...	...	...
Aktobe	ESDF	258 014	119 330	138 684		...	...	...	...
Almaty	ESDF	1 247 896	566 189	681 707		...	...	...	...
ASTANA	ESDF	550 438	267 869	282 569		...	...	...	...
Atirau	ESDF	175 737	82 809	92 928		...	...	...	...
Ekibastuz	ESDF	132 455	62 146	70 309		...	...	...	...
Karaganda	ESDF	446 139	202 935	243 204		...	...	...	...
Koktshetau	ESDF	129 885	59 159	70 726		...	...	...	...
Kustanai	ESDF	207 802	93 896	113 906		...	...	...	...
Kyzylorda	ESDF	183 716	88 121	95 595		...	...	...	...
Pavlodar	ESDF	304 809	138 790	166 019		...	...	...	...
Petropavlovsk (Severo-Kazakhstanskaya oblast)	ESDF	190 092	85 068	105 024		...	...	...	...
Rudni	ESDF	120 006	55 495	64 511		...	...	...	...
Semipalatinsk	ESDF	281 814	126 909	154 905		...	...	...	...
Shimkent	ESDF	526 140	250 046	276 094		...	...	...	...
Taldykorgan	ESDF	106 900	47 744	59 156		...	...	...	...
Taraz	ESDF	336 057	154 100	181 957		...	...	...	...
Temirtau	ESDF	170 667	78 600	92 067		...	...	...	...
Uralsk	ESDF	230 070	104 509	125 561		...	...	...	...
Ust-Kamenogorsk	ESDF	288 509	129 671	158 838		...	...	...	...
Korea (Dem. People's Republic of) — Corée (Rép. populaire dém. de)									
31 XII 1993									
Chongjin	CDFC	582 480	...	...	...	...	...	...	...
Haeju	CDFC	229 172	...	...		...	...	...	...
Hamhung	CDFC	709 730	...	...		...	...	...	...
Hyesan	CDFC	178 020	...	...		...	...	...	...
Kaesong	CDFC	334 433	...	...		...	...	...	...
Kanggye	CDFC	223 410	...	...		...	...	...	...
Nampho	CDFC	731 448	...	...		...	...	...	...
Phyongsong	CDFC	272 934	...	...		...	...	...	...
PYONGYANG	CDFC	2 741 260	...	...		...	...	...	...
Sariwon	CDFC	254 146	...	...		...	...	...	...
Sinuiji	CDFC	326 011	...	...		...	...	...	...
Wonsan	CDFC	300 148	...	...		...	...	...	...

8. Population of capital cities and cities of 100 000 or more inhabitants: latest available year, 1987 - 2006
Population des capitales et des villes de 100 000 habitants ou plus: dernière année disponible, 1987 - 2006
(continued — suite)

Continent, country or area, date and city Continent, pays ou zone, date et ville	Code[1]	City proper — Ville proprement dite Population				Urban agglomeration — Agglomération urbaine Population			
		Both sexes Les deux sexes	Male Masculin	Female Féminin	Surface area Superficie (km²)	Both sexes Les deux sexes	Male Masculin	Female Féminin	Surface area Superficie (km²)

ASIA — ASIE

Korea (Republic of) — Corée
(République de)
 1 XI 2000

Andong	CDFC	182 098	89 823	92 275	1 518	...	...	...	...
Asan	CDFC	180 763	90 812	89 951	...	...	...	...	...
Boryeong	CDFC	109 535	55 390	54 145	...	...	...	...	...
Bucheon (Puchon)	CDFC	761 389	384 935	376 454	53	...	...	...	...
Busan (Pusan)	CDFC	3 662 884	1 827 062	1 835 822	748	...	...	...	...
Changwon	CDFC	517 410	265 941	251 469	293	...	...	...	...
Cheonan	CDFC	417 835	212 874	204 961	637	...	...	...	...
Cheongju	CDFC	586 700	292 144	294 556	153	...	...	...	...
Chuncheon	CDFC	252 547	125 605	126 942	1 117	...	...	...	...
Chungju	CDFC	217 927	110 540	107 387	984	...	...	...	...
Daegu (Taegu)	CDFC	2 480 578	1 247 562	1 233 016	885	...	...	...	...
Daejeon (Taejon)	CDFC	1 368 207	690 600	677 607	539	...	...	...	...
Gangneung (Kangnung)	CDFC	228 232	113 826	114 406	1 039	...	...	...	...
Geoje	CDFC	168 022	87 169	80 853	...	...	...	...	...
Gimcheon	CDFC	147 855	73 629	74 226	...	...	...	...	...
Gimhae (Kimhae)	CDFC	331 979	167 255	164 724	463	...	...	...	...
Gimje	CDFC	102 589	50 067	52 522	...	...	...	...	...
Gongju	CDFC	130 376	64 537	65 839	...	...	...	...	...
Goyang	CDFC	763 971	381 072	382 899	...	...	...	...	...
Gumi (Kumi)	CDFC	341 550	173 253	168 297	127	...	...	...	...
Gunpo (Kunpo)	CDFC	263 760	133 013	130 747	36	...	...	...	...
Gunsan (Kunsan)	CDFC	272 715	138 537	134 178	388	...	...	...	...
Gwangju (Kwangchu)	CDFC	1 352 797	674 228	678 569	501	...	...	...	...
Gwangmyeong (Kwangmyong)	CDFC	334 089	167 115	166 974	38	...	...	...	...
Gwangyang	CDFC	132 639	67 629	65 010	...	...	...	...	...
Gyeongju (Kyongju)	CDFC	275 842	136 891	138 951	1 324	...	...	...	...
Gyeongsan	CDFC	228 206	114 162	114 044	...	...	...	...	...
Icheon	CDFC	179 719	88 460	91 259	...	...	...	...	...
Iksan (Iri)	CDFC	323 687	161 231	162 456	507	...	...	...	...
Incheon	CDFC	2 475 139	1 250 383	1 224 756	955	...	...	...	...
Jecheon (Chechon)	CDFC	143 710	72 855	70 855	882	...	...	...	...
Jeju (Cheju)	CDFC	279 996	138 932	141 064	255	...	...	...	...
Jeongeup	CDFC	129 152	62 902	66 250	...	...	...	...	...
Jeonju (Chonchu)	CDFC	616 468	306 661	309 807	206	...	...	...	...
Jinhae (Chinhae)	CDFC	127 578	64 317	63 261	...	...	...	...	...
Jinju (Chinju)	CDFC	339 791	168 576	171 215	712	...	...	...	...
Masan	CDFC	434 371	218 050	216 321	329	...	...	...	...
Miryang	CDFC	115 962	56 855	59 107	...	...	...	...	...
Mokpo	CDFC	250 480	125 922	124 558	46	...	...	...	...
Nonsan	CDFC	137 452	68 799	68 653	...	...	...	...	...
Pohang	CDFC	515 714	264 319	251 395	1 126	...	...	...	...
Sacheon	CDFC	111 078	55 285	55 793	...	...	...	...	...
Sangju	CDFC	116 493	57 152	59 341	...	...	...	...	...
Seongnam	CDFC	914 590	461 011	453 579	141	...	...	...	...
Seosan	CDFC	143 154	73 100	70 054	...	...	...	...	...
SEOUL	CDFC	9 895 217	4 966 993	4 928 224	605	...	...	...	...
Suncheon	CDFC	265 930	133 064	132 866	907	...	...	...	...
Suwon (Puwan)	CDFC	946 704	476 639	470 065	121	...	...	...	...
Tongyeong	CDFC	123 842	62 017	61 825	...	...	...	...	...
Uijeongbu (Eujeongbu)	CDFC	355 380	177 657	177 723	81	...	...	...	...
Ulsan	CDFC	1 014 428	522 062	492 366	1 055	...	...	...	...
Wonju	CDFC	268 352	134 901	133 451	865	...	...	...	...
Yangsan	CDFC	191 975	96 551	95 424	...	...	...	...	...
Yeongcheon	CDFC	111 392	55 176	56 216	...	...	...	...	...
Yeongju	CDFC	126 507	63 556	62 951	...	...	...	...	...
Yeosu	CDFC	303 233	152 836	150 397	45	...	...	...	...
1 VII 2006									
Busan (Pusan)	ESDF	*3 554 003*	*1 767 568*	*1 786 435*	*765*	...	...	...	...
Daegu (Taegu)	ESDF	*2 484 022*	*1 247 963*	*1 236 059*	*884*	...	...	...	...

8. Population of capital cities and cities of 100 000 or more inhabitants: latest available year, 1987 - 2006
Population des capitales et des villes de 100 000 habitants ou plus: dernière année disponible, 1987 - 2006
(continued — suite)

Continent, country or area, date and city Continent, pays ou zone, date et ville	Code[1]	City proper — Ville proprement dite Population				Urban agglomeration — Agglomération urbaine Population			
		Both sexes Les deux sexes	Male Masculin	Female Féminin	Surface area Superficie (km²)	Both sexes Les deux sexes	Male Masculin	Female Féminin	Surface area Superficie (km²)
ASIA — ASIE									
Korea (Republic of) — Corée (République de)									
1 VII 2006									
Daejeon (Taejon)	ESDF	1 476 736	743 507	733 229	540	...	...	...	...
Gwangju (Kwangchu)	ESDF	1 443 226	720 228	722 998	501	...	...	...	...
Incheon	ESDF	2 596 317	1 313 256	1 283 061	1 002	...	...	...	...
SEOUL	ESDF	10 020 123	4 994 996	5 025 127	605	...	...	...	...
Ulsan	ESDF	1 074 516	556 396	518 120	1 057	...	...	...	...
Kuwait — Koweït									
1 VII 2004									
Hawalli	ESDF	125 877	90 219	35 658	...	...	...	...	...
KUWAIT CITY	ESDF	44 424	36 947	7 477	...	...	...	...	...
Salmiya	ESDF	197 161	121 724	75 437	...	...	...	...	...
Kyrgyzstan — Kirghizistan									
1 VII 2006									
BISHKEK	ESDJ	790 600	377 200	413 400	...	802 600	383 200	419 400	127
Osh	ESDJ	223 700	106 900	116 800	...	249 900	119 900	130 000	182
Lao People's Democratic Republic — République démocratique populaire lao									
1 III 1995									
VIENTIANE	CDFC	...	...	...	...	528 100	...	...	...
Lebanon — Liban									
31 XII 2006									
BEIRUT	ESDF	361 366	166 282	195 084	...	...	...	...	...
Malaysia — Malaisie									
14 VIII 1991									
Alor Setar	CDFC	124 412	...	...	...	164 444	...	...	...
George Town	CDFC	219 603	...	...	...	...	...	...	...
Ipoh	CDFC	382 853	...	...	...	468 841	...	...	...
Johore Bharu	CDFC	328 436	...	...	...	441 703	...	...	...
Klang	CDFC	243 355	...	...	...	368 379	...	...	...
Kota Bahru	CDFC	219 582	...	...	...	234 581	...	...	...
Kota Kinabalu	CDFC	76 120	...	...	...	160 184	...	...	...
KUALA LUMPUR	CDFC	1 145 342	...	...	...	...	...	...	...
Kuala Terengganu	CDFC	228 119	...	...	...	...	...	...	...
Kuantan	CDFC	199 484	...	...	...	202 445	...	...	...
Kuching	CDFC	148 059	...	...	...	277 905	...	...	...
Petaling Jaya	CDFC	254 350	...	...	...	350 995	...	...	...
Sandakan	CDFC	125 841	...	...	...	156 675	...	...	...
Seleyang Baru	CDFC	124 228	...	...	...	134 197	...	...	...
Seremban	CDFC	182 869	...	...	...	193 237	...	...	...
Shah Alam	CDFC	102 019	...	...	...	117 027	...	...	...
Sibu	CDFC	126 381	...	...	...	133 479	...	...	...
Sungai Petani	CDFC	114 763	...	...	...	116 977	...	...	...
Taiping	CDFC	183 261	...	...	...	200 324	...	...	...
Maldives									
21 III 2006									
MALE	CDFC	103 693	51 993	51 701	2	...	...	...	...
Mongolia — Mongolie									
1 VII 2006									
ULAANBAATAR	ESDF	979 780	473 130	506 650	212	...	...	...	...
Nepal — Népal									
22 VI 2001									
Biratnagar	CDJC	166 674	87 664	79 010	58	...	...	...	...
Birgunj	CDJC	112 484	60 956	51 528	21	...	...	...	...
KATHMANDU	CDJC	671 846	360 103	311 743	49	...	...	...	...
Lalitpur	CDJC	162 991	84 502	78 489	15	...	...	...	...
Pokhara	CDJC	156 312	79 563	76 749	55	...	...	...	...

8. Population of capital cities and cities of 100 000 or more inhabitants: latest available year, 1987 - 2006
Population des capitales et des villes de 100 000 habitants ou plus: dernière année disponible, 1987 - 2006
(continued — suite)

Continent, country or area, date and city / Continent, pays ou zone, date et ville	Code[1]	City proper — Ville proprement dite Population				Urban agglomeration — Agglomération urbaine Population			
		Both sexes Les deux sexes	Male Masculin	Female Féminin	Surface area Superficie (km²)	Both sexes Les deux sexes	Male Masculin	Female Féminin	Surface area Superficie (km²)
ASIA — ASIE									
Occupied Palestinian Territory — Territoire palestinien occupé									
1 VII 2006									
Gaza	ESDF	409 680	...	...	...	...	...	...	...
Hebron	ESDF	166 003	...	...	...	...	...	...	...
Khan Yunis	ESDF	130 607	...	...	...	...	...	...	...
Nablus	ESDF	134 116	...	...	...	...	...	...	...
Oman									
7 VII 2003									
AsSeeb	CDFC	223 449	128 068	95 381	...	...	...	...	...
AsSuwayq	CDFC	101 122	54 997	46 125	...	...	...	...	...
Bawshar	CDFC	150 420	91 687	58 733	...	...	...	...	...
MUSCAT	CDFC	24 893	13 695	11 198	...	...	...	...	...
Mutrah	CDFC	153 526	96 878	56 648	...	...	...	...	...
Salalah	CDFC	156 530	92 489	64 041	...	...	...	...	...
Sohar	CDFC	104 312	57 695	46 617	...	...	...	...	...
Pakistan[66]									
2 III 1998									
Abbotabad	CDFC	106 101	61 698	44 403	...	...	...	...	...
Bahawalnagar	CDFC	111 313	57 779	53 534	...	...	...	...	...
Bahawalpur	CDFC	408 395	222 228	186 167	...	...	...	...	...
Burewala	CDFC	152 097	78 726	73 371	...	...	...	...	...
Chiniot	CDFC	172 522	90 474	82 048	...	...	...	...	...
Chishtian	CDFC	102 287	52 427	49 860	...	...	...	...	...
Dadu	CDFC	102 550	53 508	49 042	...	...	...	...	...
Daska	CDFC	102 883	52 359	50 524	...	...	...	...	...
Dera Ghazi Khan	CDFC	190 542	98 738	91 804	...	...	...	...	...
Faisalabad (Lyallpur)	CDFC	2 008 861	1 053 085	955 776	...	...	...	...	...
Gojra	CDFC	117 872	60 598	57 294	...	...	...	...	...
Gujranwala	CDFC	1 132 509	588 512	543 997	...	...	...	...	...
Gujrat	CDFC	251 792	128 524	123 268	...	...	...	...	...
Hafizabad	CDFC	133 678	69 231	64 447	...	...	...	...	...
Hyderabad	CDFC	1 166 894	612 283	554 611	...	...	...	...	...
ISLAMABAD	CDFC	529 180	290 717	238 463	...	...	...	...	...
Jacobabad	CDFC	138 780	71 854	66 926	...	...	...	...	...
Jaranwala	CDFC	106 785	55 819	51 166	...	...	...	...	...
Jhang	CDFC	293 366	153 123	140 243	...	...	...	...	...
Jhelum	CDFC	147 392	79 169	68 223	...	...	...	...	...
Kamoke	CDFC	152 288	78 848	73 440	...	...	...	...	...
Karachi	CDFC	9 339 023	5 029 900	4 309 123	...	...	...	...	...
Kasur	CDFC	245 321	129 553	115 768	...	...	...	...	...
Khairpur	CDFC	105 637	55 358	50 279	...	...	...	...	...
Khanewal	CDFC	133 986	69 145	64 841	...	...	...	...	...
Khanpur	CDFC	120 382	62 371	58 011	...	...	...	...	...
Kohat	CDFC	126 627	71 505	55 122	...	...	...	...	...
Lahore	CDFC	5 143 495	2 707 220	2 436 275	...	...	...	...	...
Larkana	CDFC	270 283	140 622	129 661	...	...	...	...	...
Mangora	CDFC	173 868	91 742	82 126	...	...	...	...	...
Mardan	CDFC	245 926	129 247	116 679	...	...	...	...	...
Mirpur Khas	CDFC	189 671	97 940	91 731	...	...	...	...	...
Multan	CDFC	1 197 384	637 911	559 473	...	...	...	...	...
Muridke	CDFC	111 951	58 210	53 741	...	...	...	...	...
Muzaffargharh	CDFC	123 404	66 556	56 848	...	...	...	...	...
Nawabshah	CDFC	189 244	98 116	91 128	...	...	...	...	...
Okara	CDFC	201 815	104 245	97 570	...	...	...	...	...
Pakpattan	CDFC	109 033	56 676	52 357	...	...	...	...	...
Peshawar	CDFC	982 816	521 901	460 915	...	...	...	...	...
Quetta	CDFC	565 137	307 759	257 378	...	...	...	...	...
Rahimyar Khan	CDFC	233 537	121 446	112 091	...	...	...	...	...
Rawalpindi	CDFC	1 409 768	750 530	659 238	...	...	...	...	...
Sadiqabad	CDFC	144 391	75 217	69 174	...	...	...	...	...
Sahiwal	CDFC	208 778	108 992	99 786	...	...	...	...	...

8. Population of capital cities and cities of 100 000 or more inhabitants: latest available year, 1987 - 2006
Population des capitales et des villes de 100 000 habitants ou plus: dernière année disponible, 1987 - 2006
(continued — suite)

Continent, country or area, date and city Continent, pays ou zone, date et ville	Code[1]	City proper — Ville proprement dite Population				Urban agglomeration — Agglomération urbaine Population			
		Both sexes Les deux sexes	Male Masculin	Female Féminin	Surface area Superficie (km²)	Both sexes Les deux sexes	Male Masculin	Female Féminin	Surface area Superficie (km²)
ASIA — ASIE									
Pakistan[66]									
2 III 1998									
Sargodha	CDFC	458 440	239 837	218 603	...	...	...	...	...
Shakkarpur	CDFC	134 883	69 713	65 170	...	...	...	...	...
Sheikhu Pura	CDFC	280 263	146 739	133 524	...	...	...	...	...
Sialkote	CDFC	421 502	227 398	194 104	...	...	...	...	...
Sukkur	CDFC	335 551	175 679	159 872	...	...	...	...	...
Tandoadam	CDFC	104 907	54 670	50 237	...	...	...	...	...
Wah Cantonment	CDFC	198 891	104 230	94 661	...	...	...	...	...
Philippines									
1 V 2000									
Angeles	CDJC	267 788	132 972	134 816	60	...	...	...	...
Bacolod	CDJC	429 076	209 729	219 347	156	...	...	...	...
Bago	CDJC	141 721	72 777	68 944	402	...	...	...	...
Baguio	CDJC	252 386	124 208	128 178	58	...	...	...	...
Basilan	CDJC	332 828	166 413	166 415	...	...	...	...	...
Batangas	CDJC	247 588	123 740	123 848	283	...	...	...	...
Butuan	CDJC	267 279	135 735	131 544	816	...	...	...	...
Cabanatuan	CDJC	222 859	111 461	111 398	283	...	...	...	...
Cadiz	CDJC	141 954	72 701	69 253	467	...	...	...	...
Cagayan de Oro	CDJC	461 877	228 524	233 353	413	...	...	...	...
Calbayog	CDJC	147 187	75 157	72 030	...	...	...	...	...
Caloocan	CDJC	1 177 604	587 890	589 714	56	...	...	...	...
Cebu	CDJC	718 821	351 640	367 181	281	...	...	...	...
Cotabato	CDJC	163 849	79 853	83 996	144	...	...	...	...
Dagupan	CDJC	130 328	64 468	65 860	37	...	...	...	...
Davao	CDJC	1 147 116	573 242	573 874	1 211	...	...	...	...
Digos	CDJC	125 171	63 107	62 064	...	...	...	...	...
Dumaguete	CDJC	102 265	49 378	52 887	34	...	...	...	...
General Santos	CDJC	411 822	207 496	264 326	402	...	...	...	...
Gingoog	CDJC	102 379	52 302	50 077	...	...	...	...	...
Iligan	CDJC	285 061	141 641	143 420	673	...	...	...	...
Iloilo	CDJC	366 391	177 620	188 771	56	...	...	...	...
Kabankalan	CDJC	149 769	76 479	73 290	697	...	...	...	...
Kalookan (Caloocan)	CDJC	1 177 604	587 890	589 714	56	...	...	...	...
Kidapawan	CDJC	101 205	51 278	49 927	...	...	...	...	...
Koronadal	CDJC	133 786	67 493	66 293	...	...	...	...	...
Lapu-Lapu	CDJC	217 019	106 099	110 920	...	...	...	...	...
Las Piñas	CDJC	472 780	229 776	243 004	33	...	...	...	...
Legasp	CDJC	157 010	78 141	78 869	154	...	...	...	...
Lipa	CDJC	218 447	109 938	108 509	209	...	...	...	...
Lucena City	CDJC	196 075	97 380	98 695	80	...	...	...	...
Makati	CDJC	471 379	226 422	244 957	18	...	...	...	...
Malabalay	CDJC	123 672	63 381	60 291	969	...	...	...	...
Malabon	CDJC	338 855	168 587	170 268	...	...	...	...	...
Malolos	CDJC	175 291	86 600	88 691	67	...	...	...	...
Mandaue	CDJC	259 728	128 501	131 227	12	...	...	...	...
Mandaluyong	CDJC	278 474	135 287	143 187	9	...	...	...	...
MANILA	CDJC	1 581 082	770 491	810 591	614	...	...	...	...
Marawi	CDJC	131 090	63 110	67 980	23	...	...	...	...
Marikina	CDJC	391 170	191 585	199 585	22	...	...	...	...
Muntinlupa	CDJC	379 310	187 381	191 929	40	...	...	...	...
Naga	CDJC	137 810	68 040	69 770	84	...	...	...	...
Navotas	CDJC	230 403	115 697	114 706	...	...	...	...	...
Olongapo	CDJC	194 260	95 585	98 675	185	...	...	...	...
Ormoc	CDJC	154 297	78 612	75 685	...	...	...	...	...
Ozamis	CDJC	110 420	54 986	55 434	...	...	...	...	...
Pagadian	CDJC	142 585	71 009	71 576	332	...	...	...	...
Paranaque	CDJC	449 811	217 828	231 983	47	...	...	...	...
Pasay	CDJC	354 908	175 041	179 867	14	...	...	...	...
Pasig	CDJC	505 058	246 047	259 011	48	...	...	...	...
Puerto Princesa	CDJC	161 912	83 045	78 867	2 381	...	...	...	...

8. Population of capital cities and cities of 100 000 or more inhabitants: latest available year, 1987 - 2006
Population des capitales et des villes de 100 000 habitants ou plus: dernière année disponible, 1987 - 2006
(continued — suite)

Continent, country or area, date and city / Continent, pays ou zone, date et ville	Code[1]	City proper — Ville proprement dite Population				Urban agglomeration — Agglomération urbaine Population			
		Both sexes Les deux sexes	Male Masculin	Female Féminin	Surface area Superficie (km²)	Both sexes Les deux sexes	Male Masculin	Female Féminin	Surface area Superficie (km²)
ASIA — ASIE									
Philippines									
1 V 2000									
Quezon City	CDJC	2 173 831	1 064 780	1 109 051	172	...	...	...	...
Roxas	CDJC	126 352	62 542	63 810	95	...	...	...	...
Sagay City	CDJC	129 765	65 935	63 830	330	...	...	...	...
San Carlos (Negros Occidental)	CDJC	118 259	60 073	58 186	452	...	...	...	...
San Carlos (Pangasinan)	CDJC	154 264	77 652	76 612	...	...	...	...	...
San Fernando City	CDJC	221 857	111 798	110 059	68	...	...	...	...
San Juan	CDJC	117 680	54 604	63 076	6	...	...	...	...
San Pablo	CDJC	207 927	102 685	105 242	...	...	...	...	...
Silay	CDJC	107 722	54 419	53 303	215	...	...	...	...
Surigao	CDJC	118 534	59 253	59 281	225	...	...	...	...
Tacloban	CDJC	178 639	88 490	90 149	...	...	...	...	...
Taguig	CDJC	467 375	233 712	233 663	...	...	...	...	...
Tagum	CDJC	179 531	90 004	89 527	...	...	...	...	...
Tarlac	CDJC	262 481	132 532	129 949	...	...	...	...	...
Toledo	CDJC	141 174	71 719	69 455	...	...	...	...	...
Tuguegarao	CDJC	120 645	60 270	60 375	145	...	...	...	...
Valenzuela	CDJC	485 433	244 373	241 060	47	...	...	...	...
Zamboanga	CDJC	601 794	302 089	299 705	464	...	...	...	...
Qatar									
1 VII 2006									
Al-Rayyan	ESDF	...	...	...	...	349 046	232 866	116 180	...
DOHA	ESDF	...	...	...	...	421 164	280 980	140 184	...
Saudi Arabia — Arabie saoudite									
15 IX 2004									
Abha	CDFC	201 912	113 102	88 810	...	...	...	...	...
Ad-Dammam	CDFC	744 321	450 494	293 827	...	...	...	...	...
Al-Hawiyah	CDFC	132 078	69 481	62 597	...	...	...	...	...
Al-Hufuf	CDFC	287 841	155 924	131 917	...	...	...	...	...
Al-Jubayl	CDFC	222 544	135 659	86 885	...	...	...	...	...
Al-Kharj	CDFC	200 958	109 112	91 846	...	...	...	...	...
Al-Khubar	CDFC	165 799	101 818	63 981	...	...	...	...	...
Al-Madinah	CDFC	918 889	493 929	424 960	...	...	...	...	...
Al-Mubarraz	CDFC	285 067	150 449	134 618	...	...	...	...	...
Al-Qurrayyat	CDFC	100 436	52 869	47 567	...	...	...	...	...
Ar'ar	CDFC	145 237	77 744	67 493	...	...	...	...	...
Ath-Thuqbah	CDFC	191 826	117 165	74 661	...	...	...	...	...
At-Ta'if	CDFC	521 273	274 531	246 742	...	...	...	...	...
Buraydah	CDFC	378 422	211 317	167 105	...	...	...	...	...
Hafar al-Batin	CDFC	231 978	122 781	109 197	...	...	...	...	...
Ha'il	CDFC	267 005	142 015	124 990	...	...	...	...	...
Jiddah	CDFC	2 801 481	1 619 932	1 181 549	...	...	...	...	...
Jizan	CDFC	100 694	57 988	42 706	...	...	...	...	...
Khamis Mushayt	CDFC	372 695	208 397	164 298	...	...	...	...	...
Makkah	CDFC	1 294 168	704 672	589 496	...	...	...	...	...
Najran (Aba as-Suud)	CDFC	246 880	133 405	113 475	...	...	...	...	...
RIYADH	CDFC	4 087 152	2 354 246	1 732 906	...	...	...	...	...
Sekaka	CDFC	122 686	66 672	56 014	...	...	...	...	...
Tabuk	CDFC	441 351	241 913	199 438	...	...	...	...	...
Unayzah	CDFC	128 930	71 841	57 089	...	...	...	...	...
Yanbu al-Bahr	CDFC	188 430	105 966	82 464	...	...	...	...	...
Singapore — Singapour									
1 VII 2006									
SINGAPORE	ESDF	4 483 900	...	...	...	...	...	...	...
Sri Lanka									
1 VII 1990									
COLOMBO	ESDF	615 000	...	...	...	...	...	...	...
Dehiwala-Mount Lavinia	ESDF	196 000	...	...	...	...	...	...	...
Jaffna	ESDF	129 000	...	...	...	...	...	...	...
Kandy	ESDF	104 000	...	...	...	...	...	...	...
Moratuwa	ESDF	170 000	...	...	...	...	...	...	...

8. Population of capital cities and cities of 100 000 or more inhabitants: latest available year, 1987 - 2006
Population des capitales et des villes de 100 000 habitants ou plus: dernière année disponible, 1987 - 2006
(continued — suite)

Continent, country or area, date and city Continent, pays ou zone, date et ville	Code[1]	City proper — Ville proprement dite Population				Urban agglomeration — Agglomération urbaine Population			
		Both sexes Les deux sexes	Male Masculin	Female Féminin	Surface area Superficie (km²)	Both sexes Les deux sexes	Male Masculin	Female Féminin	Surface area Superficie (km²)
ASIA — ASIE									
Syrian Arab Republic — République arabe syrienne									
1 VII 2000									
Aleppo	ESDF	*3 818 000*	*1 968 000*	*1 850 000*	...	...	...	...	...
Al-Hasakeh	ESDF	*1 295 000*	*657 000*	*638 000*	...	...	...	...	...
Al-Kamishli	ESDF	*467 120*	*229 542*	*237 578*	...	...	...	...	...
Al-Rakka	ESDF	*708 000*	*360 000*	*348 000*	...	...	...	...	...
DAMASCUS	ESDF	*1 675 000*	*865 000*	*810 000*	...	...	...	...	...
Deir El-Zor	ESDF	*803 000*	*404 000*	*399 000*	...	...	...	...	...
Hama	ESDF	*1 525 000*	*780 000*	*745 000*	...	...	...	...	...
Homs	ESDF	*1 365 000*	*698 000*	*667 000*	...	...	...	...	...
Lattakia	ESDF	*890 000*	*455 000*	*435 000*	...	...	...	...	...
Tajikistan — Tadjikistan									
1 VII 1993									
DUSHANBE	ESDJ	528 600							
Thailand — Thaïlande									
1 VII 2006									
BANGKOK	ESDJ	...	...	...	...	*6 858 000*	*3 232 000*	*3 626 000*	*1 569*
Buri Ram	ESDJ	...	...	...	...	*206 648*	*94 170*	*112 478*	*10 323*
Chachoengsao	ESDJ	...	...	...	...	*125 229*	*60 799*	*64 430*	*5 351*
Chaiyaphum	ESDJ	...	...	...	...	*151 536*	*77 336*	*74 200*	*12 778*
Chanthaburi	ESDJ	...	...	...	...	*147 599*	*74 480*	*73 119*	*6 338*
Chiang Mai	ESDJ	...	...	...	...	*379 391*	*176 196*	*203 195*	*20 107*
Chiang Rai	ESDJ	...	...	...	...	*241 328*	*115 157*	*126 171*	*11 678*
Chon Buri	ESDJ	...	...	...	...	*565 687*	*259 223*	*306 464*	*4 363*
Kalasin	ESDJ	...	...	...	...	*213 104*	*102 132*	*110 972*	*6 947*
KamphaengPhet	ESDJ	...	...	...	...	*110 518*	*51 500*	*59 018*	*8 608*
Kanchanaburi	ESDJ	...	...	...	...	*159 670*	*80 981*	*78 689*	*19 483*
Khon Kaen	ESDJ	...	...	...	...	*326 474*	*159 656*	*166 818*	*10 886*
Lampang	ESDJ	...	...	...	...	*216 935*	*101 266*	*115 669*	*12 534*
Loei	ESDJ	...	...	...	...	*102 534*	*50 169*	*52 365*	*11 425*
Lop Buri	ESDJ	...	...	...	...	*138 696*	*71 494*	*67 202*	*6 200*
Nakhon Pathom	ESDJ	...	...	...	...	*235 125*	*116 376*	*118 749*	*2 168*
Nakhon Ratchasima	ESDJ	...	...	...	...	*530 993*	*243 628*	*287 365*	*20 494*
Nakhon Sawan	ESDJ	...	...	...	...	*199 045*	*92 134*	*106 911*	*9 598*
Nakhon Si Thammarat	ESDJ	...	...	...	...	*269 433*	*121 851*	*147 582*	*9 942*
Narathiwat	ESDJ	...	...	...	...	*181 685*	*85 914*	*95 771*	*4 475*
Nong Bua Lam Phu	ESDJ	...	...	...	...	*151 831*	*78 919*	*72 912*	*3 859*
Nong Khai	ESDJ	...	...	...	...	*184 911*	*93 767*	*91 144*	*7 332*
Nonthaburi	ESDJ	...	...	...	...	*714 853*	*339 954*	*374 899*	*1 004*
Pathum Thani	ESDJ	...	...	...	...	*312 411*	*149 091*	*163 320*	*1 526*
Pattani	ESDJ	...	...	...	...	*104 295*	*57 279*	*47 016*	*1 940*
Phayao	ESDJ	...	...	...	...	*112 671*	*55 143*	*57 528*	*6 335*
Phetchabun	ESDJ	...	...	...	...	*147 432*	*73 678*	*73 754*	*12 668*
Phetchaburi	ESDJ	...	...	...	...	*149 623*	*69 510*	*80 113*	*6 225*
Phitsanulok	ESDJ	...	...	...	...	*135 417*	*67 904*	*67 513*	*10 816*
Phra Nakhon Si Ayutthaya	ESDJ	...	...	...	...	*249 049*	*116 955*	*132 094*	*2 557*
Phuket	ESDJ	...	...	...	...	*126 373*	*59 270*	*67 103*	*543*
Prachuap Khiri Khan	ESDJ	...	...	...	...	*146 822*	*71 053*	*75 769*	*6 368*
Ratchaburi	ESDJ	...	...	...	...	*259 981*	*121 693*	*138 288*	*5 196*
Rayong	ESDJ	...	...	...	...	*201 197*	*95 066*	*106 131*	*3 552*
Roi Et	ESDJ	...	...	...	...	*161 400*	*77 319*	*84 081*	*8 299*
Sakon Nakhon	ESDJ	...	...	...	...	*136 225*	*68 431*	*67 794*	*9 606*
Samut Prakan	ESDJ	...	...	...	...	*737 472*	*342 766*	*394 706*	*622*
Samut Sakhon	ESDJ	...	...	...	...	*197 688*	*102 014*	*95 674*	*872*
Saraburi	ESDJ	...	...	...	...	*246 295*	*119 886*	*126 409*	*3 576*
Si Sa Ket	ESDJ	...	...	...	...	*132 804*	*66 495*	*66 309*	*8 840*
Songkhla	ESDJ	...	...	...	...	*501 406*	*247 213*	*254 193*	*7 394*
Sukhothai	ESDJ	...	...	...	...	*107 815*	*47 215*	*60 600*	*6 596*
Suphan Buri	ESDJ	...	...	...	...	*132 526*	*61 834*	*70 692*	*5 358*
Surat Thani	ESDJ	...	...	...	...	*335 445*	*164 324*	*171 121*	*12 892*
Surin	ESDJ	...	...	...	...	*105 018*	*50 405*	*54 613*	*8 124*

8. Population of capital cities and cities of 100 000 or more inhabitants: latest available year, 1987 - 2006
Population des capitales et des villes de 100 000 habitants ou plus: dernière année disponible, 1987 - 2006
(continued — suite)

Continent, country or area, date and city — Continent, pays ou zone, date et ville	Code[1]	City proper — Ville proprement dite Population				Urban agglomeration — Agglomération urbaine Population			
		Both sexes Les deux sexes	Male Masculin	Female Féminin	Surface area Superficie (km²)	Both sexes Les deux sexes	Male Masculin	Female Féminin	Surface area Superficie (km²)
ASIA — ASIE									
Thailand — Thaïlande									
1 VII 2006									
Tak	ESDJ	...	...	...	...	104 021	49 411	54 610	16 407
Trang	ESDJ	...	...	...	...	123 768	61 090	62 678	4 918
Ubon Ratchathani	ESDJ	...	...	...	...	254 091	119 731	134 360	15 745
Udon Thani	ESDJ	...	...	...	...	366 222	196 826	169 396	11 730
Yala	ESDJ	...	...	...	...	115 890	58 747	57 143	4 521
Timor-Leste									
1 VII 2001									
DILI	ESDF	56 000	...	...	...	...	...	...	...
Turkey — Turquie									
1 VII 2003									
Adana[67]	ESDF	...	...	...	...	1 187 098	...	...	...
Adiyaman	ESDF	203 880	...	...	...	...	...	...	...
Afyon	ESDF	137 411	...	...	...	...	...	...	...
Aksaray	ESDF	141 521	...	...	...	...	...	...	...
ANKARA[68]	ESDF	...	...	...	...	3 729 453	...	...	...
Antalya	ESDF	670 229	...	...	...	...	...	...	...
Aydin	ESDF	152 918	...	...	...	...	...	...	...
Balikesir	ESDF	227 428	...	...	...	...	...	...	...
Bandirma	ESDF	102 733	...	...	...	...	...	...	...
Batman	ESDF	277 349	...	...	...	...	...	...	...
Bursa[69]	ESDF	...	...	...	...	1 305 059	...	...	...
Ceyhan	ESDF	114 956	...	...	...	...	...	...	...
Corlu	ESDF	164 431	...	...	...	...	...	...	...
Corum	ESDF	173 960	...	...	...	...	...	...	...
Denizli	ESDF	295 319	...	...	...	...	...	...	...
Derince[70]	ESDF	101 744	...	...	...	...	...	...	...
Diyarbakir	ESDF	595 951	...	...	...	...	...	...	...
Edirne	ESDF	122 932	...	...	...	...	...	...	...
Elazig	ESDF	281 560	...	...	...	...	...	...	...
Erzincan	ESDF	110 196	...	...	...	...	...	...	...
Erzurum	ESDF	396 092	...	...	...	...	...	...	...
Eskisehir	ESDF	498 836	...	...	...	...	...	...	...
Gaziantep[71]	ESDF	...	...	...	...	926 458	...	...	...
Gebze	ESDF	282 938	...	...	...	...	...	...	...
Hatay	ESDF	149 607	...	...	...	...	...	...	...
İçel	ESDF	568 388	...	...	...	...	...	...	...
Inegol	ESDF	115 096	...	...	...	...	...	...	...
Iskenderun	ESDF	158 695	...	...	...	...	...	...	...
Isparta	ESDF	157 913	...	...	...	...	...	...	...
Istanbul[72]	ESDF	...	...	...	...	9 555 719	...	...	...
Izmir[73]	ESDF	...	...	...	...	2 299 584	...	...	...
Kahramanmaras	ESDF	354 891	...	...	...	...	...	...	...
Karaman	ESDF	113 687	...	...	...	...	...	...	...
Kayseri[74]	ESDF	...	...	...	...	566 162	...	...	...
Kirikkale	ESDF	208 086	...	...	...	...	...	...	...
Kiziltepe	ESDF	130 904	...	...	...	...	...	...	...
Kocaeli	ESDF	194 055	...	...	...	...	...	...	...
Konya[75]	ESDF	...	...	...	...	810 957	...	...	...
Kütahya	ESDF	175 905	...	...	...	...	...	...	...
Malatya	ESDF	412 724	...	...	...	...	...	...	...
Manisa	ESDF	230 223	...	...	...	...	...	...	...
Nazilli	ESDF	112 269	...	...	...	...	...	...	...
Ordu	ESDF	113 756	...	...	...	...	...	...	...
Osmaniye	ESDF	189 238	...	...	...	...	...	...	...
Sakarya	ESDF	283 516	...	...	...	...	...	...	...
Samsun	ESDF	377 927	...	...	...	...	...	...	...
Sanliurfa	ESDF	411 159	...	...	...	...	...	...	...
Siirt	ESDF	106 966	...	...	...	...	...	...	...
Sivas	ESDF	256 914	...	...	...	...	...	...	...
Siverek	ESDF	149 236	...	...	...	...	...	...	...

8. Population of capital cities and cities of 100 000 or more inhabitants: latest available year, 1987 - 2006
Population des capitales et des villes de 100 000 habitants ou plus: dernière année disponible, 1987 - 2006
(continued — suite)

Continent, country or area, date and city — Continent, pays ou zone, date et ville	Code[1]	City proper — Ville proprement dite Population				Urban agglomeration — Agglomération urbaine Population			
		Both sexes Les deux sexes	Male Masculin	Female Féminin	Surface area Superficie (km²)	Both sexes Les deux sexes	Male Masculin	Female Féminin	Surface area Superficie (km²)
ASIA — ASIE									
Turkey — Turquie									
1 VII 2003									
Tarsus	ESDF	222 693	...	...	...	...	...	...	...
Tekirdag	ESDF	113 285	...	...	...	...	...	...	...
Tokat	ESDF	121 694	...	...	...	...	...	...	...
Trabzon	ESDF	228 013	...	...	...	...	...	...	...
Turhal	ESDF	103 225	...	...	...	...	...	...	...
Usak	ESDF	145 758	...	...	...	...	...	...	...
Van	ESDF	324 352	...	...	...	...	...	...	...
Viransehir	ESDF	144 731	...	...	...	...	...	...	...
Turkmenistan — Turkménistan									
1 VII 1990									
ASHKHABAD	ESDF	407 000	...	...	...	...	...	...	...
Chardzhou	ESDF	164 000	...	...	...	...	...	...	...
Tashauz	ESDF	114 000	...	...	...	...	...	...	...
United Arab Emirates — Emirats Arabes Unis									
1 VII 2002									
ABU DHABI	ESDF	527 000	359 000	168 000		...	...	...	...
Ajman	ESDF	205 000	122 000	83 000		...	...	...	...
Al-Ayn	ESDF	328 000	215 000	113 000		...	...	...	...
Al-Sharjah	ESDF	488 000	317 000	171 000		...	...	...	...
Dubai	ESDF	1 089 000	759 000	330 000		...	...	...	...
Uzbekistan — Ouzbékistan									
1 VII 2001									
Almalyk	ESDF	113 114	56 317	56 797		...	...	...	...
Andizhan	ESDF	338 366	165 159	173 207		...	...	...	...
Angren	ESDF	128 757	64 060	64 697		...	...	...	...
Banjzak	ESDF	131 512	68 441	63 071		...	...	...	...
Bukhara	ESDF	237 361	118 613	118 748		...	...	...	...
Chirchik	ESDF	141 742	70 203	71 539		...	...	...	...
Fergana	ESDF	183 037	87 142	95 895		...	...	...	...
Karshi	ESDF	204 690	104 159	100 531		...	...	...	...
Kokand	ESDF	197 450	95 872	101 578		...	...	...	...
Margilan	ESDF	149 646	73 899	75 747		...	...	...	...
Namangan	ESDF	391 297	197 962	193 335		...	...	...	...
Navoi	ESDF	138 082	70 577	67 505		...	...	...	...
Nukus	ESDF	212 012	103 918	108 094		...	...	...	...
Samarkand	ESDF	361 339	178 608	182 731		...	...	...	...
TASHKENT	ESDF	2 137 218	1 043 213	1 094 005		...	...	...	...
Termez	ESDF	116 467	60 031	56 436		...	...	...	...
Urgentch	ESDF	138 609	67 667	70 942		...	...	...	...
Viet Nam									
1 VII 1992									
Buonmathuot	ESDF	282 095	...	...	...	...	...	...	...
Campha	ESDF	209 086	...	...	...	...	...	...	...
Cantho	ESDF	215 587	...	...	...	...	...	...	...
Dalat	ESDF	106 409	...	...	...	...	...	...	...
Da Nang	ESDF	382 674	...	...	...	...	...	...	...
Haiphong	ESDF	783 133	...	...	22	...	...	...	...
HANOI	ESDF	1 073 760	...	...	46	...	...	...	...
Ho Chi Minh[76]	ESDF	3 015 743	...	...	140	...	...	...	...
Hon Gai	ESDF	127 484	...	...	...	...	...	...	...
Hué	ESDF	219 149	...	...	...	...	...	...	...
Longxuyen	ESDF	132 681	...	...	...	...	...	...	...
Mytho	ESDF	108 404	...	...	...	...	...	...	...
Namdinh	ESDF	171 699	...	...	...	...	...	...	...
Nhatrang	ESDF	221 331	...	...	...	...	...	...	...
Qui Nhon	ESDF	163 385	...	...	...	...	...	...	...
Rach Gia	ESDF	141 132	...	...	...	...	...	...	...
Thai Nguyen	ESDF	127 643	...	...	...	...	...	...	...
Vinh	ESDF	112 455	...	...	...	...	...	...	...

8. Population of capital cities and cities of 100 000 or more inhabitants: latest available year, 1987 - 2006
Population des capitales et des villes de 100 000 habitants ou plus: dernière année disponible, 1987 - 2006
(continued — suite)

Continent, country or area, date and city / Continent, pays ou zone, date et ville	Code[1]	City proper — Ville proprement dite Population				Urban agglomeration — Agglomération urbaine Population			
		Both sexes Les deux sexes	Male Masculin	Female Féminin	Surface area Superficie (km²)	Both sexes Les deux sexes	Male Masculin	Female Féminin	Surface area Superficie (km²)
ASIA — ASIE									
Viet Nam									
1 VII 1992									
Vungtau	ESDF	*145 145*	...	...	...	...	...	...	...
Yemen — Yémen									
16 XII 1994									
Adan	CDFC	398 294	...	...	...	...	...	...	...
Al-Hudaydah (Hodeidah)	CDFC	298 452	...	...	...	...	...	...	...
Al-Mukalla	CDFC	122 359	...	...	...	...	...	...	...
Ibb	CDFC	103 312	...	...	...	...	...	...	...
SANA'A	CDFC	954 448	...	...	...	...	...	...	...
Ta'izz	CDFC	317 571	...	...	...	...	...	...	...
EUROPE									
Albania — Albanie[77]									
1 VII 2003									
TIRANA	ESDF	392 863	194 006	198 857	31	...	...	...	...
Andorra — Andorre									
31 XII 2006									
ANDORRA LA VELLA	ESDF	...	...	...	...	*24 211*	*12 267*	*11 944*	...
Austria — Autriche[78,79]									
1 I 2006									
Graz	ESDJ	244 604	117 116	127 488	128	...	...	...	...
Innsbruck	ESDJ	116 851	55 329	61 522	105	...	...	...	...
Klagenfurt	ESDJ	92 160	42 673	49 487	120	...	...	...	...
Linz	ESDJ	188 362	89 285	99 077	96	...	...	...	...
Salzburg	ESDJ	148 473	69 615	78 858	66	...	...	...	...
WIEN	ESDJ	1 651 437	788 461	862 976	415	...	...	...	...
Belarus — Bélarus									
1 VII 2006									
Baranovichi	ESDF	167 911	77 765	90 146	50	...	...	...	...
Bobruisk	ESDF	218 756	102 058	116 698	90	...	...	...	...
Borisov	ESDF	149 788	70 652	79 136	46	...	...	...	...
Brest	ESDF	302 348	139 140	163 208	75	...	...	...	...
Gomel	ESDF	...	...	...	...	492 032	224 323	267 709	118
Grodno	ESDF	320 166	147 515	172 651	93	...	...	...	...
Lida	ESDF	96 278	45 254	51 024	38	...	...	...	...
MINSK	ESDF	1 789 098	826 797	962 301	306	...	...	...	...
Mogilev	ESDF	368 481	169 991	198 490	108	...	...	...	...
Mozir	ESDF	111 693	53 330	58 363	38	...	...	...	...
Novopolotsk	ESDF	...	...	...	...	106 764	50 784	55 980	54
Orsha	ESDF	...	...	...	...	139 994	66 633	73 361	51
Pinsk	ESDF	129 779	60 705	69 074	44	...	...	...	...
Soligorsk	ESDF	100 805	47 716	53 089	11	...	...	...	...
Vitebsk	ESDF	...	...	...	...	352 247	157 421	194 826	96
Belgium — Belgique[80]									
1 I 2006									
Antwerpen (Anvers)	ESDJ	461 496	226 280	235 216	2 256	...	...	...	...
Brugge	ESDJ	117 224	56 769	60 455	846	...	...	...	...
BRUXELLES (BRUSSEL)	ESDJ	144 784	72 270	72 514	4 440	1 018 804	489 684	529 120	6 312
Charleroi	ESDJ	201 300	97 421	103 879	1 972	...	...	...	...
Gent (Gand)	ESDJ	233 120	114 061	119 059	1 492	...	...	...	...
Liège (Luik)	ESDJ	187 086	91 363	95 723	2 696	...	...	...	...
Namur	ESDJ	107 178	51 489	55 689	610	...	...	...	...
Bosnia and Herzegovina — Bosnie-Herzégovine									
31 III 1991									
Banja Luka	ESDJ	195 994	...	...	1 239	...	...	...	...
Doboj	ESDJ	102 624	...	...	697	...	...	...	...
Mostar	ESDJ	127 034	...	...	1 227	...	...	...	...
Prijedor	ESDJ	112 635	...	...	834	...	...	...	...
SARAJEVO	ESDJ	529 021	...	...	2 095	...	...	...	...

8. Population of capital cities and cities of 100 000 or more inhabitants: latest available year, 1987 - 2006
Population des capitales et des villes de 100 000 habitants ou plus: dernière année disponible, 1987 - 2006
(continued — suite)

Continent, country or area, date and city Continent, pays ou zone, date et ville	Code[1]	City proper — Ville proprement dite Population				Urban agglomeration — Agglomération urbaine Population			
		Both sexes Les deux sexes	Male Masculin	Female Féminin	Surface area Superficie (km²)	Both sexes Les deux sexes	Male Masculin	Female Féminin	Surface area Superficie (km²)
EUROPE									
Bosnia and Herzegovina — Bosnie-Herzégovine 31 III 1991									
Tuzla	ESDJ	131 866	...	...	303	...	...	...	...
Zenica	ESDJ	145 837	...	...	505	...	...	...	...
Bulgaria — Bulgarie[47,81] 1 VII 2006									
Bourgas	ESDF	189 066	90 975	98 091	...	...	...	...	...
Pleven	ESDF	113 541	54 738	58 803	...	...	...	...	...
Plovdiv	ESDF	342 768	163 134	179 633	...	...	...	...	...
Rousse	ESDF	157 533	75 697	81 836	...	...	...	...	...
SOFIA	ESDF	1 151 220	545 041	606 178	...	...	...	...	...
Stara Zagora	ESDF	141 538	68 590	72 948	...	...	...	...	...
Varna	ESDF	311 630	151 080	160 550	...	...	...	...	...
Channel Islands: Guernsey — Iles Anglo-Normandes: Guernesey 29 IV 2001									
ST. PETER PORT	CDJC	16 488	...	...		...	...	...	...
Channel Islands — Iles Anglo-Normandes: Jersey 11 III 2001									
ST. HELIER	CDJC	28 310	13 669	14 641	9	...	...	...	...
Croatia — Croatie 1 VII 2001									
Osijek	ESDJ	90 411	41 592	48 819	...	114 616	53 497	61 119	...
Rijeka	ESDJ	143 800	68 382	75 418	...	144 043	68 511	75 532	...
Split	ESDJ	175 140	83 720	91 420	...	188 694	90 484	98 210	...
ZAGREB	ESDJ	691 724	321 507	370 217	1 405	779 145	363 992	415 153	...
Czech Republic — République tchéque 1 VII 2005									
Brno	ESDJ	366 904	174 257	192 647	230	...	...	...	...
Hradec Králové	ESDJ	94 436	45 015	49 421	106	...	...	...	...
Liberec	ESDJ	97 596	46 424	51 172	106	...	...	...	...
Olomouc	ESDJ	100 491	47 379	53 112	103	...	...	...	...
Ostrava	ESDJ	310 681	149 780	160 901	214	...	...	...	...
Plzen	ESDJ	162 659	78 173	84 486	138	...	...	...	...
PRAHA	ESDJ	1 176 116	563 147	612 969	496	...	...	...	...
Östí nad Labem	ESDJ	94 021	45 360	48 661	94	...	...	...	...
Denmark — Danemark 1 VII 2006									
Ålborg	ESDJ	163 505	81 285	82 220	560	...	...	...	...
Århus	ESDJ	294 273	144 143	150 130	469	...	...	...	...
KOBENHAVN	ESDJ	500 543	246 810	253 733	88	...	...	...	...
Odense	ESDJ	186 614	91 264	95 350	304	...	...	...	...
Estonia — Estonie 1 VII 2006									
TALLINN	ESDF	396 523	178 906	217 617	158	...	...	...	...
Tartu	ESDF	101 853	45 464	56 389	39	...	...	...	...
Faeroe Islands — Iles Féroé 1 VII 1992									
THORSHAVN	ESDJ	14 671	...	...	63	16 218	...	...	79
Finland — Finlande 1 VII 2006									
Espoo	ESDJ	233 362	114 330	119 031	312	...	...	...	...
HELSINKI	ESDJ	562 713	262 485	300 228	186	...	...	...	...
Jyvaskyla	ESDJ	84 586	40 247	44 340	106	...	...	...	...
Lahti	ESDJ	98 590	46 473	52 116	135	...	...	...	...
Oulu	ESDJ	129 570	63 167	66 403	369	...	...	...	...
Tampere	ESDJ	205 352	98 458	106 895	523	...	...	...	...
Turku	ESDJ	175 111	81 938	93 174	246	...	...	...	...
Vantaa	ESDJ	188 496	92 172	96 324	241	...	...	...	...

8. Population of capital cities and cities of 100 000 or more inhabitants: latest available year, 1987 - 2006
Population des capitales et des villes de 100 000 habitants ou plus: dernière année disponible, 1987 - 2006
(continued — suite)

Continent, country or area, date and city — Continent, pays ou zone, date et ville	Code[1]	City proper — Ville proprement dite Population				Urban agglomeration — Agglomération urbaine Population			
		Both sexes Les deux sexes	Male Masculin	Female Féminin	Surface area Superficie (km²)	Both sexes Les deux sexes	Male Masculin	Female Féminin	Surface area Superficie (km²)

EUROPE

France[82,83]
  8 III 1999

Aix-en-Provence	CDJC	134 280	62 220	72 060	186	...	...	...	...
Amiens	CDJC	135 406	63 513	71 893	49	...	...	...	...
Angers	CDJC	151 406	69 235	82 171	43	...	...	...	...
Besançon	CDJC	117 693	54 692	63 001	65	...	...	...	...
Bordeaux	CDJC	215 277	99 637	115 640	49	...	...	...	...
Boulogne-Billancourt	CDJC	106 384	49 840	56 544	6	...	...	...	...
Brest	CDJC	149 495	71 431	78 064	50	...	...	...	...
Caen	CDJC	114 079	52 605	61 474	26	...	...	...	...
Clermont-Ferrand	CDJC	136 968	63 702	73 266	43	...	...	...	...
Dijon	CDJC	150 144	69 331	80 813	40	...	...	...	...
Grenoble	CDJC	153 531	73 311	80 220	18	...	...	...	...
Le Havre	CDJC	190 806	90 882	99 924	47	...	...	...	...
Le Mans	CDJC	145 994	68 982	77 012	53	...	...	...	...
Lille[84]	CDJC	184 445	86 196	98 249	30	...	...	...	...
Limoges	CDJC	134 055	62 106	71 949	77	...	...	...	...
Lyon[85]	CDJC	444 852	206 422	238 430	48	...	...	...	...
Marseille	CDJC	796 525	376 082	420 443	241	...	...	...	...
Metz	CDJC	123 720	59 670	64 050	42	...	...	...	...
Montpellier	CDJC	225 748	103 437	122 311	57	...	...	...	...
Mulhouse	CDJC	110 129	53 963	56 166	22	...	...	...	...
Nantes	CDJC	270 474	126 599	143 875	65	...	...	...	...
Nancy	CDJC	103 533	47 345	56 188	15	...	...	...	...
Nice	CDJC	343 166	157 148	186 018	72	...	...	...	...
Nîmes	CDJC	133 391	62 451	70 940	162	...	...	...	...
Orléans	CDJC	113 077	53 728	59 349	27	...	...	...	...
PARIS	CDJC	2 125 017	995 844	1 129 173	105	...	...	...	...
Perpignan	CDJC	105 027	47 870	57 157	68	...	...	...	...
Reims	CDJC	187 183	88 707	98 476	47	...	...	...	...
Rennes	CDJC	206 221	95 224	110 997	50	...	...	...	...
Rouen	CDJC	106 356	49 432	56 924	21	...	...	...	...
Saint-Étienne	CDJC	180 393	84 135	96 258	80	...	...	...	...
Strasbourg[84]	CDJC	263 682	124 926	138 756	78	...	...	...	...
Toulon	CDJC	160 549	74 964	85 585	43	...	...	...	...
Toulouse	CDJC	390 174	185 107	205 067	118	...	...	...	...
Tours	CDJC	132 637	60 117	72 520	34	...	...	...	...
Villeurbanne	CDJC	124 451	59 519	64 932	15	...	...	...	...

Germany — Allemagne
  1 VII 1999

Aachen	ESDJ	243 825	121 671	122 154	161	...	...	...	...
Augsburg	ESDJ	254 867	121 846	133 021	147	...	...	...	...
Bergisch Gladbach	ESDJ	106 150	50 723	55 427	83	...	...	...	...
BERLIN	ESDJ	3 386 667	1 644 575	1 742 092	891	...	...	...	...
Bielefeld	ESDJ	321 125	152 701	168 424	258	...	...	...	...
Bochum	ESDJ	392 830	190 433	202 397	145	...	...	...	...
Bonn	ESDJ	301 048	143 416	157 632	141	...	...	...	...
Bottrop	ESDJ	121 097	58 490	62 607	101	...	...	...	...
Braunschweig	ESDJ	246 322	119 350	126 972	192	...	...	...	...
Bremen	ESDJ	540 330	259 439	280 891	327	...	...	...	...
Bremerhaven	ESDJ	122 735	59 991	62 744	78	...	...	...	...
Chemnitz	ESDJ	263 222	125 123	138 099	176	...	...	...	...
Cottbus	ESDJ	110 894	53 712	57 182	150	...	...	...	...
Darmstadt	ESDJ	137 776	67 680	70 096	122	...	...	...	...
Dortmund	ESDJ	590 213	286 880	303 333	280	...	...	...	...
Dresden	ESDJ	476 668	229 565	247 103	237	...	...	...	...
Duisburg	ESDJ	519 793	252 735	267 058	233	...	...	...	...
Düsseldorf	ESDJ	568 855	268 630	300 225	217	...	...	...	...
Erfurt	ESDJ	201 267	96 937	104 330	269	...	...	...	...
Erlangen	ESDJ	100 750	48 939	51 811	77	...	...	...	...
Essen	ESDJ	599 515	286 350	313 165	210	...	...	...	...
Frankfurt am Main	ESDJ	643 821	314 431	329 390	248	...	...	...	...

8. Population of capital cities and cities of 100 000 or more inhabitants: latest available year, 1987 - 2006
Population des capitales et des villes de 100 000 habitants ou plus: dernière année disponible, 1987 - 2006
(continued — suite)

Continent, country or area, date and city / Continent, pays ou zone, date et ville	Code[1]	City proper — Ville proprement dite Population				Urban agglomeration — Agglomération urbaine Population			
		Both sexes Les deux sexes	Male Masculin	Female Féminin	Surface area Superficie (km²)	Both sexes Les deux sexes	Male Masculin	Female Féminin	Surface area Superficie (km²)
EUROPE									
Germany — Allemagne									
1 VII 1999									
Freiburg im Breisgau	ESDJ	202 455	96 025	106 430	153	...	...	...	...
Fürth	ESDJ	109 771	52 773	56 998	63	...	...	...	...
Gelsenkirchen	ESDJ	281 979	135 781	146 198	105	...	...	...	...
Gera	ESDJ	114 718	55 211	59 507	152	...	...	...	...
Göttingen	ESDJ	124 775	60 334	64 441	117	...	...	...	...
Hagen	ESDJ	205 201	98 338	106 863	160	...	...	...	...
Halle	ESDJ	254 360	121 314	133 046	135	...	...	...	...
Hamburg	ESDJ	1 704 735	824 686	880 049	755	...	...	...	...
Hamm	ESDJ	181 804	89 307	92 497	226	...	...	...	...
Hannover	ESDJ	514 718	245 017	269 701	204	...	...	...	...
Heidelberg	ESDJ	139 672	65 694	73 978	109	...	...	...	...
Heilbronn	ESDJ	119 526	58 400	61 126	100	...	...	...	...
Herne	ESDJ	175 661	85 577	90 084	51	...	...	...	...
Hildesheim	ESDJ	104 013	48 910	55 103	93	...	...	...	...
Ingolstadt	ESDJ	114 826	56 417	58 409	133	...	...	...	...
Kaiserslautern	ESDJ	100 025	49 247	50 778	140	...	...	...	...
Karlsruhe	ESDJ	277 204	134 775	142 429	173	...	...	...	...
Kassel	ESDJ	196 211	93 058	103 153	107	...	...	...	...
Kiel	ESDJ	233 795	113 274	120 521	117	...	...	...	...
Koblenz	ESDJ	108 003	51 340	56 663	105	...	...	...	...
Köln	ESDJ	962 507	466 543	495 964	405	...	...	...	...
Krefeld	ESDJ	241 769	117 087	124 682	138	...	...	...	...
Leipzig	ESDJ	489 532	235 789	253 743	176	...	...	...	...
Leverkusen	ESDJ	160 841	78 116	82 725	79	...	...	...	...
Lübeck	ESDJ	213 326	101 024	112 302	214	...	...	...	...
Ludwigshafen am Rhein	ESDJ	163 771	81 257	82 514	78	...	...	...	...
Magdeburg	ESDJ	235 073	112 839	122 234	193	...	...	...	...
Mainz	ESDJ	183 134	89 093	94 041	98	...	...	...	...
Mannheim	ESDJ	307 730	151 145	156 585	145	...	...	...	...
Moers	ESDJ	106 837	51 824	55 013	68	...	...	...	...
Mönchengladbach	ESDJ	263 697	126 721	136 976	170	...	...	...	...
Mülheim an der Ruhr	ESDJ	173 895	82 677	91 218	91	...	...	...	...
München	ESDJ	1 194 560	571 363	623 197	311	...	...	...	...
Münster (Westf.)	ESDJ	264 670	123 825	140 845	303	...	...	...	...
Neuss	ESDJ	149 702	72 522	77 180	99	...	...	...	...
Nürnberg	ESDJ	486 628	233 415	253 213	186	...	...	...	...
Oberhausen	ESDJ	222 349	107 562	114 787	77	...	...	...	...
Offenbach am Main	ESDJ	116 627	57 539	59 088	45	...	...	...	...
Oldenburg	ESDJ	154 125	73 572	80 553	103	...	...	...	...
Osnabrück	ESDJ	164 539	77 981	86 558	120	...	...	...	...
Paderborn	ESDJ	137 647	67 010	70 637	179	...	...	...	...
Pforzheim	ESDJ	117 227	55 738	61 489	98	...	...	...	...
Potsdam	ESDJ	128 983	62 651	66 332	109	...	...	...	...
Recklinghausen	ESDJ	125 022	60 456	64 566	66	...	...	...	...
Regensburg	ESDJ	125 236	59 600	65 636	81	...	...	...	...
Remscheid	ESDJ	120 125	57 923	62 202	75	...	...	...	...
Reutlingen	ESDJ	110 343	53 564	56 779	87	...	...	...	...
Rostock	ESDJ	203 279	99 627	103 652	181	...	...	...	...
Saarbrücken	ESDJ	183 836	87 875	95 961	167	...	...	...	...
Salzgitter	ESDJ	112 934	54 808	58 126	224	...	...	...	...
Schwerin	ESDJ	102 878	49 428	53 450	130	...	...	...	...
Siegen	ESDJ	109 225	53 585	55 640	115	...	...	...	...
Solingen	ESDJ	165 583	79 712	85 871	89	...	...	...	...
Stuttgart	ESDJ	582 443	284 977	297 466	207	...	...	...	...
Ulm	ESDJ	116 103	56 511	59 592	119	...	...	...	...
Wiesbaden	ESDJ	268 716	129 032	139 684	204	...	...	...	...
Witten	ESDJ	103 384	49 545	53 839	72	...	...	...	...
Wolfsburg	ESDJ	121 954	59 761	62 193	204	...	...	...	...
Wuppertal	ESDJ	368 993	176 350	192 643	168	...	...	...	...
Würzburg	ESDJ	127 350	58 801	68 549	88	...	...	...	...

8. Population of capital cities and cities of 100 000 or more inhabitants: latest available year, 1987 - 2006
Population des capitales et des villes de 100 000 habitants ou plus: dernière année disponible, 1987 - 2006
(continued — suite)

Continent, country or area, date and city — Continent, pays ou zone, date et ville	Code[1]	City proper — Ville proprement dite Population				Urban agglomeration — Agglomération urbaine Population			
		Both sexes Les deux sexes	Male Masculin	Female Féminin	Surface area Superficie (km²)	Both sexes Les deux sexes	Male Masculin	Female Féminin	Surface area Superficie (km²)
EUROPE									
Germany — Allemagne									
1 VII 1999									
Zwickau	ESDJ	104 146	49 513	54 633	73	...	...	...	...
Gibraltar									
14 X 1991									
GIBRALTAR	CDFC	28 074	...	...	...	...	...	...	...
Greece — Grèce[86]									
18 III 2001									
ATHINAI	CDJC	789 166	374 900	414 266	39	...	...	...	...
Calithèa	CDJC	115 150	54 137	61 013	5	...	...	...	...
Iraclion	CDJC	135 761	66 956	68 805	52	...	...	...	...
Larissa	CDJC	131 095	64 000	67 095	88	...	...	...	...
Patrai	CDJC	168 530	82 981	85 549	57	...	...	...	...
Pésterion	CDJC	146 743	72 391	74 352	10	...	...	...	...
Pireas	CDJC	181 933	87 362	94 571	...	...	...	...	...
Thessaloniki	CDJC	385 406	180 122	205 284	...	...	...	...	...
Holy See — Saint-Slège[87]									
1 VII 1988									
VATICAN CITY	ESDF	766	...	...	...	...	...	...	...
Hungary — Hongrie									
1 VII 2006									
BUDAPEST	ESDF	1 697 117	773 982	923 134	525	...	...	...	...
Debrecen	ESDF	204 104	94 592	109 512	462	...	...	...	...
Györ	ESDF	128 272	60 388	67 884	175	...	...	...	...
Kecskemét	ESDF	109 341	50 682	58 659	321	...	...	...	...
Miskolc	ESDF	173 526	80 238	93 288	237	...	...	...	...
Nyiregyhaza	ESDF	116 126	53 796	62 330	275	...	...	...	...
Pécs	ESDF	156 382	71 854	84 528	163	...	...	...	...
Szeged	ESDF	164 071	75 307	88 764	281	...	...	...	...
Székesfehérvar	ESDF	101 450	47 628	53 821	171	...	...	...	...
Iceland — Islande[88,89]									
1 VII 2006									
REYKJAVIK	ESDJ	116 091	57 454	58 637	100	189 867	94 265	95 602	...
Ireland — Irlande									
28 IV 2002									
Cork	CDFC	123 062	59 263	63 799	40	186 239	90 348	95 891	...
DUBLIN	CDFC	495 781	237 813	257 968	118	1 004 614	485 209	519 405	...
Isle of Man — Ile de Man									
23 IV 2006									
DOUGLAS	CDJC	26 218	13 000	13 218	...	...	...	...	
Italy — Italie									
1 VII 2006									
Ancona	ESDJ	101 671	48 365	53 306	124	...	...	...	...
Bari	ESDJ	325 984	157 100	168 884	116	...	...	...	...
Bergamo	ESDJ	115 921	54 198	61 724	40	...	...	...	...
Bologna	ESDJ	373 384	174 629	198 756	141	...	...	...	...
Brescia	ESDJ	190 552	90 274	100 277	91	...	...	...	...
Cagliari	ESDJ	159 852	74 526	85 326	86	...	...	...	...
Catania	ESDJ	302 854	142 822	160 032	181	...	...	...	...
Ferrara	ESDJ	132 842	62 092	70 751	404	...	...	...	...
Firenze	ESDJ	366 434	171 390	195 044	102	...	...	...	...
Foggia	ESDJ	153 590	74 117	79 472	508	...	...	...	...
Forli	ESDJ	113 041	54 510	58 531	228	...	...	...	...
Genova	ESDJ	618 001	290 002	327 668	244	...	...		
Giugliano in Campania	ESDJ	109 418	53 896	55 522	94	...	...	...	...
Latina	ESDJ	113 503	54 627	58 876	278	...	...	...	...
Livorno	ESDJ	160 518	76 705	83 813	104	...	...	...	...
Messina	ESDJ	245 741	117 243	128 498	211	...	...	...	...
Milano	ESDJ	1 306 086	617 637	688 449	182	...	...	...	...
Modena	ESDJ	180 274	86 701	93 574	183	...	...	...	...
Monza	ESDJ	121 703	58 470	63 233	33	...	...	...	...
Napoli	ESDJ	979 690	466 666	513 024	117	...	...	...	...

8. Population of capital cities and cities of 100 000 or more inhabitants: latest available year, 1987 - 2006
Population des capitales et des villes de 100 000 habitants ou plus: dernière année disponible, 1987 - 2006
(continued — suite)

Continent, country or area, date and city / Continent, pays ou zone, date et ville	Code[1]	City proper — Ville proprement dite Population				Urban agglomeration — Agglomération urbaine Population			
		Both sexes Les deux sexes	Male Masculin	Female Féminin	Surface area Superficie (km²)	Both sexes Les deux sexes	Male Masculin	Female Féminin	Surface area Superficie (km²)
EUROPE									
Italy — Italie									
1 VII 2006									
Novara	ESDJ	102 706	49 252	53 454	103	...	...	...	...
Padova	ESDJ	210 643	99 177	111 466	93	...	...	...	...
Palermo	ESDJ	668 686	318 460	350 226	159	...	...	...	...
Parma	ESDJ	176 429	83 750	92 680	261	...	...	...	...
Perugia	ESDJ	161 667	77 089	84 578	450	...	...	...	...
Pescara	ESDJ	122 430	57 692	64 738	33	...	...	...	...
Prato	ESDJ	184 742	90 440	94 302	98	...	...	...	...
Ravenna	ESDJ	150 070	73 076	76 994	653	...	...	...	...
Reggio di Calabria	ESDJ	184 274	88 616	95 658	236	...	...	...	...
Reggio nell'Emilia	ESDJ	158 598	77 382	81 216	232	...	...	...	...
Rimini	ESDJ	136 602	65 928	70 674	134	...	...	...	...
ROMA	ESDJ	2 626 640	1 234 647	1 391 993	1 308	...	...	...	...
Salerno	ESDJ	133 805	62 520	71 284	59	...	...	...	...
Sassari	ESDJ	128 252	61 770	66 482	546	...	...	...	...
Siracusa	ESDJ	123 148	59 990	63 158	204	...	...	...	...
Taranto	ESDJ	196 976	93 795	103 180	210	...	...	...	...
Terni	ESDJ	109 692	51 966	57 726	212	...	...	...	...
Torino	ESDJ	900 588	429 749	470 840	130	...	...	...	...
Trento	ESDJ	111 381	53 370	58 011	158	...	...	...	...
Trieste	ESDJ	205 710	96 058	109 652	84	...	...	...	...
Venezia	ESDJ	269 357	127 676	141 681	416	...	...	...	...
Verona	ESDJ	260 049	123 730	136 320	207	...	...	...	...
Vicenza	ESDJ	114 250	54 444	59 806	81	...	...	...	...
Latvia — Lettonie[90]									
1 VII 2006									
Daugavpils	ESDF	108 787	48 426	60 361	73	...	...	...	...
RIGA	ESDF	725 032	322 365	402 667	307	...	...	...	...
Liechtenstein[91]									
30 VI 2006									
VADUZ	ESDF	5 050	2 441	2 609	17	...	...	...	...
Lithuania — Lituanie									
1 VII 2006									
Kaunas	ESDJ	359 374	161 319	198 055	157	...	...	...	...
Klaipeda	ESDJ	186 626	85 901	100 725	98	...	...	...	...
Panevezhis	ESDJ	114 948	52 336	62 612	50	...	...	...	...
Shauliai	ESDJ	128 717	58 581	70 136	81	...	...	...	...
VILNIUS	ESDJ	542 303	246 279	296 024	394	...	...	...	...
Luxembourg									
1 VII 2006									
LUXEMBOURG-VILLE	ESDJ	83 165	...	...	51	...	...	...	...
Malta — Malte[92]									
1 VII 2006									
VALLETTA	ESDJ	6 306	3 071	3 235	1	...	...	...	...
Moldova — Moldova									
1 VII 2004									
Balti	ESDJ	144 200	...	...	...	148 900	...	...	...
KISHINEV	ESDJ	661 200	...	...	121	780 100	...	...	...
Monaco									
1 VII 2000									
MONACO	ESDJ	*32 020*	*15 544*	*16 476*	...	...	...	...	...
Netherlands — Pays-Bas[93]									
1 I 2006									
Almere	ESDJ	178 466	88 519	89 947	130	...	...	...	...
Amersfoort	ESDJ	136 999	66 944	70 055	63	165 888	81 165	84 723	122
AMSTERDAM	ESDJ	743 079	366 128	376 951	165	1 021 254	501 581	519 673	366
Apeldoorn	ESDJ	156 051	76 639	79 412	340	...	...	...	...
Arnhem	ESDJ	142 195	70 245	71 950	98	143 697	70 981	72 716	126
Breda	ESDJ	169 709	82 352	87 357	127	...	...	...	...
Dordrecht	ESDJ	118 821	58 189	60 632	80	245 482	120 395	125 087	158
Ede	ESDJ	107 048	52 358	54 690	318	...	...	...	...

8. Population of capital cities and cities of 100 000 or more inhabitants: latest available year, 1987 - 2006
Population des capitales et des villes de 100 000 habitants ou plus: dernière année disponible, 1987 - 2006
(continued — suite)

Continent, country or area, date and city Continent, pays ou zone, date et ville	Code[1]	City proper — Ville proprement dite Population				Urban agglomeration — Agglomération urbaine Population			
		Both sexes Les deux sexes	Male Masculin	Female Féminin	Surface area Superficie (km²)	Both sexes Les deux sexes	Male Masculin	Female Féminin	Surface area Superficie (km²)
EUROPE									
Netherlands — Pays-Bas[93]									
1 I 2006									
Eindhoven	ESDJ	209 172	105 649	103 523	88	322 410	161 874	160 536	199
Emmen	ESDJ	108 589	53 647	54 942	337	...	...	...	...
Enschede	ESDJ	154 377	78 542	75 835	141	...	...	...	...
Geleen-Sittard	ESDJ	...	...	...	...	140 230	69 081	71 149	122
Groningen	ESDJ	180 729	89 411	91 318	80	199 836	98 450	101 386	125
Haarlem	ESDJ	147 015	71 245	75 770	29	189 639	91 216	98 423	76
Haarlemmermeer	ESDJ	135 136	67 379	67 757	180	...	...	...	...
Heerlen-Kerkrade	ESDJ	...	...	...	...	209 634	103 123	106 511	109
Leiden	ESDJ	118 069	57 542	60 527	22	249 769	121 951	127 818	87
Maastricht	ESDJ	120 175	57 886	62 289	57	...	...	...	...
Nijmegen	ESDJ	159 522	76 275	83 247	54	...	...	...	...
Rotterdam	ESDJ	588 697	288 275	300 422	206	991 578	485 630	505 948	330
s-Hertogenbosch	ESDJ	134 717	66 243	68 474	85	159 952	78 635	81 317	118
The Hague	ESDJ	475 627	233 638	241 989	83	621 512	302 812	318 700	...
Tilburg	ESDJ	200 380	99 067	101 313	116	222 526	110 077	112 449	158
Utrecht	ESDJ	280 949	135 514	145 435	96	416 093	202 036	214 057	168
Zaanstad	ESDJ	140 270	69 166	71 104	74	...	...	...	...
Zoetermeer	ESDJ	116 979	57 296	59 683	35	...	...	...	...
Zwolle	ESDJ	113 078	54 875	58 203	112	...	...	...	...
Norway — Norvège									
1 VII 2006									
Bergen	ESDJ	243 389	120 315	123 074	445	...	...	...	...
OSLO	ESDJ	543 514	265 874	277 640	426	...	...	...	...
Stavanger	ESDJ	116 236	57 652	58 584	68	...	...	...	...
Trondheim	ESDJ	160 172	79 247	80 924	322	...	...	...	...
Poland — Pologne[94]									
1 VII 2006									
Bialystok	ESDF	295 210	138 562	156 648	102	...	...	...	...
Bielsko-Biala	ESDF	176 678	83 400	93 278	125	...	...	...	...
Bydgoszcz	ESDF	364 953	171 206	193 747	175	...	...	...	...
Bytom	ESDF	187 205	90 634	96 571	69	...	...	...	...
Chorzów	ESDF	114 434	54 555	59 879	33	...	...	...	...
Czestochowa	ESDF	246 129	116 029	130 100	160	...	...	...	...
Dabrowa Górnicza	ESDF	129 753	62 628	67 125	189	...	...	...	...
Elblag	ESDF	127 055	60 806	66 249	80	...	...	...	...
Gdansk	ESDF	457 630	216 934	240 696	266	...	...	...	...
Gdynia	ESDF	252 443	120 508	131 935	135	...	...	...	...
Gliwice	ESDF	199 099	96 053	103 046	134	...	...	...	...
Gorzów Wielkopolski	ESDF	125 204	59 623	65 581	86	...	...	...	...
Kalisz	ESDF	108 575	50 708	57 867	69	...	...	...	...
Katowice	ESDF	315 996	149 601	166 395	165	...	...	...	...
Kielce	ESDF	207 718	98 575	109 143	110	...	...	...	...
Koszalin	ESDF	107 783	51 324	56 459	83	...	...	...	...
Kraków	ESDF	756 757	354 087	402 670	327	...	...	...	...
Legnica	ESDF	105 485	49 983	55 502	56	...	...	...	...
Lódz	ESDF	764 168	348 042	416 126	293	...	...	...	...
Lublin	ESDF	354 272	163 436	190 836	147	...	...	...	...
Olsztyn	ESDF	174 693	81 083	93 610	88	...	...	...	...
Opole	ESDF	128 034	59 961	68 073	97	...	...	...	...
Plock	ESDF	127 307	61 016	66 291	88	...	...	...	...
Poznan	ESDF	566 546	263 949	302 597	262	...	...	...	...
Radom	ESDF	228 372	108 190	118 102	112	...	...	...	...
Ruda Slaska	ESDF	145 929	71 144	74 785	78	...	...	...	...
Rybnik	ESDF	141 382	69 363	72 019	148	...	...	...	...
Rzeszów	ESDF	163 155	77 002	86 153	68	...	...	...	...
Sosnowiec	ESDF	225 202	107 111	118 091	91	...	...	...	...
Szczecin	ESDF	410 809	195 234	215 575	301	...	...	...	...
Tarnów	ESDF	117 109	55 667	61 442	72	...	...	...	...
Torun	ESDF	207 381	96 210	111 171	116	...	...	...	...
Tychy	ESDF	130 842	63 499	67 343	82	...	...	...	...

8. Population of capital cities and cities of 100 000 or more inhabitants: latest available year, 1987 - 2006
Population des capitales et des villes de 100 000 habitants ou plus: dernière année disponible, 1987 - 2006
(continued — suite)

Continent, country or area, date and city / Continent, pays ou zone, date et ville	Code[1]	City proper — Ville proprement dite Population				Urban agglomeration — Agglomération urbaine Population			
		Both sexes Les deux sexes	Male Masculin	Female Féminin	Surface area Superficie (km²)	Both sexes Les deux sexes	Male Masculin	Female Féminin	Surface area Superficie (km²)

EUROPE

Poland — Pologne[94]
1 VII 2006

Walbrzych	ESDF	125 773	59 367	66 406	85	...	...	...	...
WARSZAWA	ESDF	1 700 536	783 387	917 149	517	...	...	...	...
Wloclawek	ESDF	119 608	56 339	63 269	84	...	...	...	...
Wroclaw	ESDF	635 280	297 258	338 022	293	...	...	...	...
Zabrze	ESDF	190 610	92 259	98 351	80	...	...	...	...
Zielona Góra	ESDF	118 201	55 414	62 787	58	...	...	...	...

Portugal
1 VII 2006

Amadora	ESDF	175 000	83 711	91 290	24	...	...	...	...
LISBOA	ESDF	514 773	234 391	280 382	85	...	...	...	...
Porto	ESDF	230 628	104 502	126 125	41	...	...	...	...

Romania — Roumanie
1 VII 2006

Arad	ESDJ	167 980	78 483	89 497	267	...	...	...	...
Bacau	ESDJ	179 507	86 276	93 231	43	...	...	...	...
Baia Mare	ESDJ	140 581	67 456	73 125	233	...	...	...	...
Botosani	ESDJ	116 286	55 735	60 551	41	...	...	...	...
Braila	ESDJ	216 814	103 710	113 104	33	...	...	...	...
Brasov	ESDJ	281 375	134 551	146 824	267	...	...	...	...
BUCURESTI	ESDJ	1 931 236	899 426	1 031 810	238	...	...	...	...
Buzau	ESDJ	135 861	65 082	70 779	81	...	...	...	...
Cluj-Napoca	ESDJ	305 620	143 774	161 846	180	...	...	...	...
Constanta	ESDJ	305 550	144 522	161 028	127	...	...	...	...
Craiova	ESDJ	300 587	144 000	156 587	81	...	...	...	...
Drobeta Turnu-Severin	ESDJ	109 134	52 813	56 321	55	...	...	...	...
Focsani	ESDJ	100 782	48 158	52 624	...	...	...	...	...
Galati	ESDJ	296 697	143 990	152 707	246	...	...	...	...
Iasi	ESDJ	316 716	149 299	167 417	94	...	...	...	...
Oradea	ESDJ	205 956	97 282	108 674	111	...	...	...	...
Piatra Neamt	ESDJ	108 940	51 968	56 972	77	...	...	...	...
Pitesti	ESDJ	170 217	81 494	88 723	41	...	...	...	...
Ploiesti	ESDJ	231 620	109 283	122 337	58	...	...	...	...
Rimnicu Vilcea	ESDJ	111 658	53 660	57 998	90	...	...	...	...
Satu-Mare	ESDJ	114 678	54 236	60 442	150	...	...	...	...
Sibiu	ESDJ	154 452	72 356	82 096	122	...	...	...	...
Suceava	ESDJ	106 508	51 329	55 179	52	...	...	...	...
Timisoara	ESDJ	303 796	142 366	161 430	49	...	...	...	...
Tirgu-Mures	ESDJ	146 448	69 587	76 861	130	...	...	...	...

Russian Federation — Fédération de Russie[95,96]
1 VII 2006

Abakan	ESDJ	163 546	75 049	88 497	...	...	...	...	...
Achinsk	ESDJ	112 172	50 536	61 636	...	113 456	...	...	...
Almetievsk	ESDJ	141 781	65 992	75 789	...	...	...	...	...
Angarsk	ESDJ	244 919	112 154	132 765	...	...	...	...	...
Arkhangelsk	ESDJ	349 175	155 629	193 546	...	355 198	...	...	...
Armavir	ESDJ	190 351	85 089	105 262	...	208 822	...	...	...
Artem (Primorskiy Krai)	ESDJ	...	...	...	...	111 659	...	...	...
Arzamas	ESDJ	106 563	48 233	58 330	...	...	...	...	...
Asbest	ESDJ	...	...	...	...	104 445	...	...	...
Astrakhan	ESDJ	499 570	228 206	271 364	...	...	...	...	...
Balakovo	ESDJ	199 135	90 213	108 922	...	200 396	...	...	...
Balashikha	ESDJ	183 839	86 035	97 804	...	...	...	...	...
Barnaul	ESDJ	602 160	268 010	334 150	...	651 530	...	...	...
Bataisk	ESDJ	103 560	48 843	54 717	...	...	...	...	...
Belgorod	ESDJ	346 194	156 959	189 235	...	...	...	...	...
Belovo	ESDJ	...	...	...	...	145 712	...	...	...
Berezniki	ESDJ	167 649	74 730	92 919	...	...	...	...	...
Biisk	ESDJ	224 190	99 954	124 236	...	225 678	...	...	...

8. Population of capital cities and cities of 100 000 or more inhabitants: latest available year, 1987 - 2006
Population des capitales et des villes de 100 000 habitants ou plus: dernière année disponible, 1987 - 2006
(continued — suite)

Continent, country or area, date and city — Continent, pays ou zone, date et ville	Code[1]	City proper — Ville proprement dite Population				Urban agglomeration — Agglomération urbaine Population			
		Both sexes Les deux sexes	Male Masculin	Female Féminin	Surface area Superficie (km²)	Both sexes Les deux sexes	Male Masculin	Female Féminin	Surface area Superficie (km²)

EUROPE

Russian Federation — Fédération de Russie[95,96]

1 VII 2006

Blagoveshchensk (Amurskaya oblast)	ESDJ	210 616	96 554	114 062	...	215 892	...	...	...
Bratsk	ESDJ	254 018	115 033	138 985	...	...	...	...	...
Bryansk	ESDJ	418 097	185 995	232 102	...	436 508	...	...	...
Chaykovsky	ESDJ	...	...	...	...	108 714	...	...	...
Cheboksary	ESDJ	441 836	197 971	243 865	...	453 494	...	...	...
Chelyabinsk	ESDJ	1 092 231	490 191	602 040	...	...	...	...	...
Cherepovets	ESDJ	308 115	140 674	167 441	...	...	...	...	...
Cherkessk	ESDJ	116 610	52 157	64 453	...	...	...	...	...
Chita	ESDJ	306 018	142 671	163 347	...	306 404	...	...	...
Derbent	ESDJ	106 981	51 277	55 704	...	...	...	...	...
Dimitrovgrad	ESDJ	127 510	59 233	68 277	...	...	...	...	...
Dzerzhinsk (Novgorodskaya oblast)	ESDJ	251 197	111 824	139 373	...	259 982	...	...	...
Ekaterinoburg	ESDJ	1 311 764	590 558	721 206	...	1 342 977	...	...	...
Elektrostal	ESDJ	146 064	65 500	80 564	...	...	...	...	...
Elets	ESDJ	113 084	51 144	61 940	...	...	...	...	...
Elista	ESDJ	102 895	46 515	56 380	...	106 916	...	...	...
Engels	ESDJ	197 827	90 572	107 255	...	233 920	...	...	...
Glazov	ESDJ	99 997	45 149	54 848	...	...	...	...	...
Groznyi	ESDJ	220 120	100 728	119 392	...	...	...	...	...
Hasaviurt	ESDJ	125 526	60 143	65 383	...	...	...	...	...
Irkutsk	ESDJ	576 973	259 353	317 620	...	...	...	...	...
Ivanovo	ESDJ	411 012	179 987	231 025	...	...	...	...	...
Izhevsk	ESDJ	617 558	277 676	339 882	...	...	...	...	...
Kaliningrad (Kaliningradskaya oblast)	ESDJ	423 007	197 712	225 295	...	...	...	...	...
Kaliningrad (Moskovskaya oblast)	ESDJ	173 196	77 652	95 544	...	...	...	...	...
Kaluga	ESDJ	328 300	145 736	182 564	...	342 234	...	...	...
Kamensk-Uralsky	ESDJ	182 051	81 184	100 867	...	183 591	...	...	...
Kamyshin	ESDJ	120 903	57 537	63 366	...	...	...	...	...
Kansk	ESDJ	100 963	46 352	54 611	...	...	...	...	...
Kazan	ESDJ	1 114 325	494 775	619 550	...	...	...	...	...
Kemerovo	ESDJ	519 984	232 818	287 166	...	...	...	...	...
Khabarovsk	ESDJ	577 737	267 638	310 099	...	...	...	...	...
Khimki	ESDJ	180 535	81 744	98 791	...	...	...	...	...
Kirov	ESDJ	467 361	205 954	261 407	...	489 236	...	...	...
Kiselevsk	ESDJ	103 511	47 078	56 433	...	108 087	...	...	...
Kislovodsk	ESDJ	128 618	58 187	70 431	...	134 250	...	...	...
Kolomna	ESDJ	147 970	68 151	79 819	...	...	...	...	...
Komsomolsk-na-Amure	ESDJ	272 429	126 690	145 739	...	...	...	...	...
Kopeysk	ESDJ	...	...	...	...	139 780	...	...	...
Kostroma	ESDJ	273 933	122 391	151 542	...	...	...	...	...
Kovrov	ESDJ	151 272	69 905	81 367	...	...	...	...	...
Krasnodar	ESDJ	709 686	322 422	387 264	...	779 320	...	...	...
Krasnoyarsk	ESDJ	924 046	416 451	507 595	...	924 768	...	...	...
Kurgan	ESDJ	328 206	146 529	181 677	...	...	...	...	...
Kursk	ESDJ	405 705	180 909	224 796	...	...	...	...	...
Kyzyl	ESDJ	108 720	49 968	58 752	...	...	...	...	...
Leninsk-Kuznetsky	ESDJ	107 141	49 444	57 697	...	100 516	...	...	...
Lipetsk	ESDJ	502 735	228 891	273 844	...	...	...	...	...
Lyubertsy	ESDJ	158 800	70 307	88 493	...	...	...	...	...
Magadan	ESDJ	100 108	46 771	53 337	...	107 438	...	...	...
Magnitogorsk	ESDJ	411 861	188 113	223 748	...	...	...	...	...
Maikop	ESDJ	156 730	70 354	86 376	...	175 480	...	...	...
Makhachkala	ESDJ	466 626	223 209	243 417	...	552 170	...	...	...
Mezhdurechensk	ESDJ	103 592	48 321	55 271	...	...	...	...	...
Miass	ESDJ	154 088	69 542	84 546	...	167 714	...	...	...

8. Population of capital cities and cities of 100 000 or more inhabitants: latest available year, 1987 - 2006
Population des capitales et des villes de 100 000 habitants ou plus: dernière année disponible, 1987 - 2006
(continued — suite)

Continent, country or area, date and city / Continent, pays ou zone, date et ville	Code[1]	City proper — Ville proprement dite Population				Urban agglomeration — Agglomération urbaine Population			
		Both sexes Les deux sexes	Male Masculin	Female Féminin	Surface area Superficie (km²)	Both sexes Les deux sexes	Male Masculin	Female Féminin	Surface area Superficie (km²)
EUROPE									
Russian Federation — Fédération de Russie[95,96]									
1 VII 2006									
MOSKVA	ESDJ	10 433 869	4 961 764	5 472 105	...	...	...	...	...
Murmansk	ESDJ	319 244	147 241	172 003	...	...	...	...	...
Murom	ESDJ	121 445	53 851	67 594	...	...	...	...	...
Mytishchi	ESDJ	162 240	72 515	89 725	...	...	...	...	...
Naberezhnye Tchelny	ESDJ	506 778	234 126	272 652	...	...	...	...	...
Nakhodka	ESDJ	170 850	82 811	88 039	...	171 860	...	...	...
Naltchik	ESDJ	270 898	121 737	149 161	...	296 620	...	...	...
Nazran	ESDJ	131 244	62 483	68 761	...	...	...	...	...
Nefteyugansk	ESDJ	113 819	55 937	57 882	...	...	...	...	...
Neftekamsk	ESDJ	118 049	54 646	63 403	...	129 122	...	...	...
Nevinnomyssk	ESDJ	129 591	60 722	68 869	...	...	...	...	...
Nizhnekamsk	ESDJ	226 778	105 983	120 795	...	...	...	...	...
Nizhenvartovsk	ESDJ	241 402	118 266	123 136	...	...	...	...	...
Nizhny Tagil	ESDJ	378 626	173 408	205 218	...	...	...	...	...
Nizhny Novgorod	ESDJ	1 280 949	565 062	715 887	...	1 289 112	...	...	...
Noginsk	ESDJ	116 111	52 217	63 894	...	...	...	...	...
Norilsk	ESDJ	211 256	105 193	106 063	...	212 426	...	...	...
Novocheboksarsk	ESDJ	125 745	58 885	66 860	...	126 031	...	...	...
Novocherkassk	ESDJ	178 743	84 995	93 748	...	...	...	...	...
Novokuybishevsk	ESDJ	111 661	50 076	61 585	...	113 740	...	...	...
Novokuznetsk	ESDJ	561 647	253 260	308 387	...	...	...	...	...
Novomoskovsk (Tulskaya oblast)	ESDJ	126 743	56 692	70 051	...	...	...	...	...
Novorossiysk	ESDJ	229 931	109 903	120 028	...	281 468	...	...	...
Novoshakhtinsk	ESDJ	114 989	52 258	62 731	...	...	...	...	...
Novosibirsk	ESDJ	1 394 469	633 243	761 226	...	...	...	...	...
Novotroitsk	ESDJ	103 551	49 296	54 255	...	110 994	...	...	...
Obninsk	ESDJ	105 363	48 402	56 961	...	...	...	...	...
Odintsovo	ESDJ	130 939	61 877	69 062	...	...	...	...	...
Oktyabrsky	ESDJ	107 723	49 600	58 123	...	...	...	...	...
Omsk	ESDJ	1 136 799	516 884	619 915	...	...	...	...	...
Orekhovo-Zuevo	ESDJ	122 035	53 228	68 807	...	...	...	...	...
Orel	ESDJ	324 458	144 213	180 245	...	...	...	...	...
Orenburg	ESDJ	531 731	242 805	288 926	...	546 904	...	...	...
Orsk	ESDJ	246 540	109 045	137 495	...	251 006	...	...	...
Penza	ESDJ	509 597	229 229	280 368	...	...	...	...	...
Perm	ESDJ	991 741	444 607	547 134	...	991 748	...	...	...
Pervouralsk	ESDJ	133 240	59 920	73 320	...	158 424	...	...	...
Petropavlovsk-Kamchatsky	ESDJ	195 168	97 233	97 935	...	...	...	...	...
Petrozavodsk	ESDJ	265 663	116 956	148 707	...	...	...	...	...
Podolsk	ESDJ	179 459	79 961	99 498	...	...	...	...	...
Prokopyevsk	ESDJ	215 689	97 659	118 030	...	216 904	...	...	...
Pskov	ESDJ	195 952	87 491	108 461	...	...	...	...	...
Pyatigorsk	ESDJ	139 420	62 529	76 891	...	205 404	...	...	...
Rostov-na-Donu	ESDJ	1 053 254	479 299	573 955	...	...	...	...	...
Rubtsovsk	ESDJ	157 942	74 762	83 180	...	...	...	...	...
Ryazan	ESDJ	512 744	231 910	280 834	...	...	...	...	...
Rybinsk	ESDJ	213 968	95 544	118 424	...	...	...	...	...
Salavat	ESDJ	156 616	74 938	81 678	...	...	...	...	...
Samara (Samarskaya oblast)	ESDJ	1 141 173	511 991	629 182	...	1 141 234	...	...	...
Saransk	ESDJ	296 243	131 526	164 717	...	323 330	...	...	...
Sarapyul	ESDJ	99 855	44 837	55 018	...	...	...	...	...
Saratov	ESDJ	845 758	377 392	468 366	...	...	...	...	...
Sergiev Posad	ESDJ	111 937	50 518	61 419	...	...	...	...	...
Serov	ESDJ	98 257	43 734	54 523	...	100 154	...	...	...
Serpukhov	ESDJ	124 615	56 355	68 260	...	...	...	...	...
Severodvinsk	ESDJ	194 233	89 357	104 876	...	196 126	...	...	...
Seversk	ESDJ	107 340	50 088	57 252	...	113 968	...	...	...
Shakhty	ESDJ	246 806	111 765	135 041	...	...	...	...	...
Shchelkovo	ESDJ	112 930	52 657	60 273	...	...	...	...	...

8. Population of capital cities and cities of 100 000 or more inhabitants: latest available year, 1987 - 2006
Population des capitales et des villes de 100 000 habitants ou plus: dernière année disponible, 1987 - 2006
(continued — suite)

Continent, country or area, date and city / Continent, pays ou zone, date et ville	Code[1]	City proper — Ville proprement dite Population				Urban agglomeration — Agglomération urbaine Population			
		Both sexes Les deux sexes	Male Masculin	Female Féminin	Surface area Superficie (km²)	Both sexes Les deux sexes	Male Masculin	Female Féminin	Surface area Superficie (km²)
EUROPE									
Russian Federation — Fédération de Russie[95,96]									
1 VII 2006									
Smolensk	ESDJ	317 821	140 655	177 166	...	...	...	...	...
Sochi	ESDJ	330 264	149 953	180 311	...	400 166	...	...	...
Solikamsk	ESDJ	98 761	45 528	53 233	...	...	...	...	...
St. Petersburg	ESDJ	4 575 902	2 050 178	2 525 724	...	...	...	...	...
Starsy Oskol	ESDJ	218 657	100 227	118 430	...	...	...	...	...
Stavropol	ESDJ	359 072	164 173	194 899	...	359 269	...	...	...
Sterlitamak	ESDJ	265 854	120 975	144 879	...	...	...	...	...
Surgut	ESDJ	290 221	141 542	148 679	...	...	...	...	...
Syktivkar	ESDJ	229 247	104 018	125 229	...	244 645	...	...	...
Syzran	ESDJ	180 617	81 849	98 768	...	181 473	...	...	...
Taganrog	ESDJ	266 511	119 188	147 323	...	...	...	...	...
Tambov	ESDJ	283 144	126 075	157 069	...	...	...	...	...
Tobolsk	ESDJ	100 312	45 713	54 599	...	104 544	...	...	...
Tolyatti	ESDJ	705 093	329 600	375 484	...	717 760	...	...	...
Tomsk	ESDJ	491 442	226 908	264 534	...	511 064	...	...	...
Tula	ESDJ	506 495	222 956	283 539	...	...	...	...	...
Tver	ESDJ	405 573	177 958	227 615	...	...	...	...	...
Tyumen	ESDJ	546 167	251 411	294 756	...	574 592	...	...	...
Ufa	ESDJ	1 026 097	466 976	559 121	...	1 033 276	...	...	...
Uhta	ESDJ	103 389	49 011	54 378	...	127 110	...	...	...
Ulan-Ude	ESDJ	345 398	158 399	186 999	...	375 168	...	...	...
Ulyanovsk	ESDJ	614 447	279 693	334 754	...	635 526	...	...	...
Ussuriisk	ESDJ	154 326	74 285	80 041	...	168 049	...	...	...
Ust-Ulimsk	ESDJ	98 937	47 038	51 899	...	...	...	...	...
Velikie Luky	ESDJ	101 738	44 987	56 751	...	...	...	...	...
Velikiy Novgorod	ESDJ	217 199	94 331	122 868	...	...	...	...	...
Vladikavkaz (Osetinskaya ASSR)	ESDJ	313 914	146 380	167 534	...	331 126	...	...	...
Vladimir	ESDJ	340 267	152 907	187 360	...	...	...	...	...
Vladivostok	ESDJ	582 246	271 910	310 336	...	608 778	...	...	...
Volgodonsk	ESDJ	170 490	77 681	92 809	...	...	...	...	...
Volgograd	ESDJ	988 997	449 429	539 568	...	1 023 299	...	...	...
Vologda	ESDJ	286 623	127 259	159 364	...	294 311	...	...	...
Volzhsky	ESDJ	307 893	140 811	167 082	...	318 784	...	...	...
Vorkuta	ESDJ	...	...	...	...	121 950	...	...	...
Voronezh	ESDJ	843 531	376 439	467 092	...	923 678	...	...	...
Yakutsk	ESDJ	242 414	111 014	131 400	...	263 451	...	...	...
Yaroslave	ESDJ	603 872	267 597	336 275	...	...	...	...	...
Yoshkar-ola	ESDJ	250 605	112 547	138 058	...	275 454	...	...	...
Yuzhno-Sakhalinsk	ESDJ	173 275	80 619	92 656	...	180 799	...	...	...
Zelenodolsk	ESDJ	99 118	44 346	54 772	...	...	...	...	...
Zheleznodorozhny	ESDJ	117 705	52 993	64 712	...	...	...	...	...
Zheleznogorsk	ESDJ	...	...	...	...	102 900	...	...	...
Zhukovsky	ESDJ	101 646	46 301	55 345	...	...	...	...	...
Zlatoust	ESDJ	189 842	86 296	103 546	...	192 258	...	...	...
San Marino — Saint-Marin									
1 VII 2004									
SAN MARINO	ESDF	4 464	2 168	2 296	...	...	...	...	...
Serbia — Serbie[97]									
30 VI 2006									
BELGRADE	ESDJ	1 306 168	609 860	696 308	389	1 602 861	758 008	844 853	3 215
Cacak	ESDJ	73 667	35 333	38 334	38	116 534	56 557	59 977	642
Kragujevac	ESDJ	146 764	70 969	75 795	83	174 920	84 971	89 949	847
Kraljevo	ESDJ	64 044	30 889	33 155	22	120 304	58 944	61 360	1 529
NIS	ESDJ	181 317	87 273	94 044	43	254 164	124 182	129 982	597
NoviSad	ESDJ	248 241	116 045	132 196	103	314 192	148 710	165 482	699
Kruševac	ESDJ	56 955	27 094	29 861	11	129 370	62 880	66 490	854
Leskovac	ESDJ	68 721	33 546	35 175	24	153 084	76 195	76 889	1 025
Pancevo	ESDJ	92 283	44 384	47 899	162	126 388	61 473	64 915	756
Šabac	ESDJ	54 621	25 784	28 837	31	120 626	58 858	61 768	795

8. Population of capital cities and cities of 100 000 or more inhabitants: latest available year, 1987 - 2006
Population des capitales et des villes de 100 000 habitants ou plus: dernière année disponible, 1987 - 2006
(continued — suite)

Continent, country or area, date and city / Continent, pays ou zone, date et ville	Code[1]	City proper — Ville proprement dite Population				Urban agglomeration — Agglomération urbaine Population			
		Both sexes Les deux sexes	Male Masculin	Female Féminin	Surface area Superficie (km²)	Both sexes Les deux sexes	Male Masculin	Female Féminin	Surface area Superficie (km²)
EUROPE									
Serbia — Serbie[97]									
30 VI 2006									
Smederevo	ESDJ	63 577	30 919	32 658	40	109 379	53 894	55 485	481
Subotica	ESDJ	107 134	50 843	56 291	164	146 238	70 172	76 066	1 007
Zrenjanin	ESDJ	78 252	37 374	40 878	50	128 527	62 321	66 206	1 327
Slovakia — Slovaquie									
1 VII 2006									
BRATISLAVA	ESDJ	425 609	199 100	226 509	383	...	...	...	...
Kosice	ESDJ	234 904	112 083	122 821	243	...	...	...	...
Slovenia — Slovénie									
30 VI 2006									
LJUBLJANA	ESDJ	246 472	114 442	132 030	164	248 139	115 261	132 878	171
Maribor	ESDJ	89 951	42 238	47 713	38	104 767	49 522	55 245	99
Spain — Espagne[98]									
1 I 2006									
Albacete	ESDJ	161 508	79 498	82 010	12 431	...	...	...	...
Alcalá de Henares	ESDJ	201 380	101 351	100 029	...	...	...	...	...
Alcobendas	ESDJ	104 118	50 765	53 353	...	...	...	...	...
Alcorcón	ESDJ	164 633	81 380	83 253	...	...	...	...	...
Algeciras	ESDJ	112 937	57 853	55 084	...	...	...	...	...
Alicante	ESDJ	322 431	156 772	165 659	2 008	...	...	...	...
Almería	ESDJ	185 309	91 235	94 074	2 962	...	...	...	...
Badajoz	ESDJ	143 748	69 853	73 895	15 302	...	...	...	...
Badalona	ESDJ	221 520	112 117	109 403	...	...	...	...	...
Barcelona	ESDJ	1 605 602	761 870	843 732	991	...	...	...	...
Bilbao	ESDJ	354 145	167 652	186 493	413	...	...	...	...
Burgos	ESDJ	173 676	83 580	90 096	1 084	...	...	...	...
Cádiz	ESDJ	130 561	62 374	68 187	112	...	...	...	...
Cartagena	ESDJ	208 609	106 497	102 112	...	...	...	...	...
Castellón de la Plana	ESDJ	172 110	85 208	86 902	1 075	...	...	...	...
Córdoba	ESDJ	322 867	155 543	167 324	12 533	...	...	...	...
Coruña(A)	ESDJ	243 320	113 431	129 889	...	...	...	...	...
Donostia - San Sebastián	ESDJ	183 308	86 116	97 192	615	...	...	...	...
DosHermanas	ESDJ	114 672	56 871	57 801	...	...	...	...	...
Elche	ESDJ	219 032	109 595	109 437	...	...	...	...	...
Fuenlabrada	ESDJ	193 715	98 089	95 626	...	...	...	...	...
Getafe	ESDJ	156 320	77 584	78 736	...	...	...	...	...
Gijón	ESDJ	274 472	130 229	144 243	...	...	...	...	...
Granada	ESDJ	237 929	110 698	127 231	882	...	...	...	...
Hospitalet de Llobregat	ESDJ	248 150	121 707	126 443	...	...	...	...	...
Huelva	ESDJ	145 763	70 688	75 075	1 513	...	...	...	...
Jaén	ESDJ	116 769	56 459	60 310	4 243	...	...	...	...
Jérez de la Frontera	ESDJ	199 544	97 424	102 120	...	...	...	...	...
La Coruña	ESDJ	243 320	113 431	129 889	376	...	...	...	...
Las Palmas de Gran Canaria	ESDJ	377 056	184 295	192 761	1 005	...	...	...	...
Leganés	ESDJ	182 471	90 850	91 621	...	...	...	...	...
León	ESDJ	136 985	63 255	73 730	392	...	...	...	...
Lleida	ESDJ	125 677	62 347	63 330	2 120	...	...	...	...
Logroño	ESDJ	147 036	71 617	75 419	796	...	...	...	...
MADRID	ESDJ	3 128 600	1 469 284	1 659 316	6 058	...	...	...	...
Málaga	ESDJ	560 631	270 672	289 959	3 930	...	...	...	...
Marbella	ESDJ	125 519	61 899	63 620	...	...	...	...	...
Mataró	ESDJ	118 748	59 683	59 065	...	...	...	...	...
Móstoles	ESDJ	206 301	102 998	103 303	...	...	...	...	...
Murcia	ESDJ	416 996	207 800	209 196	8 865	...	...	...	...
Ourense	ESDJ	108 137	50 362	57 775	845	...	...	...	...
Oviedo	ESDJ	214 883	100 072	114 811	1 866	...	...	...	...
Palma de Mallorca	ESDJ	375 048	183 443	191 605	2 008	...	...	...	...
PalmasdeGranCanaria	ESDJ	377 056	184 295	192 761	...	...	...	...	...
Pamplona	ESDJ	195 769	93 775	101 994	238	...	...	...	...
Reus	ESDJ	101 767	50 697	51 070	...	...	...	...	...
Sabadell	ESDJ	200 545	98 312	102 233	...	...	...	...	...

8. Population of capital cities and cities of 100 000 or more inhabitants: latest available year, 1987 - 2006
Population des capitales et des villes de 100 000 habitants ou plus: dernière année disponible, 1987 - 2006
(continued — suite)

Continent, country or area, date and city / Continent, pays ou zone, date et ville	Code[1]	City proper — Ville proprement dite Population				Urban agglomeration — Agglomération urbaine Population			
		Both sexes Les deux sexes	Male Masculin	Female Féminin	Surface area Superficie (km²)	Both sexes Les deux sexes	Male Masculin	Female Féminin	Surface area Superficie (km²)

EUROPE

Spain — Espagne[98]
1 I 2006

Salamanca	ESDJ	159 754	74 349	85 405	386	...	...	...	...
San Cristóbal de La Laguna	ESDJ	142 161	69 995	72 166	...	...	...	...	...
Santa Coloma de Gramanet	ESDJ	119 056	60 583	58 473	...	...	...	...	...
Santa Cruz de Tenerife	ESDJ	223 148	107 638	115 510	1 506	...	...	...	...
Santander	ESDJ	182 926	85 243	97 683	348	...	...	...	...
Sevilla	ESDJ	704 414	335 792	368 622	1 413	...	...	...	...
Tarragona	ESDJ	131 158	64 783	66 375	624	...	...	...	...
Terrassa	ESDJ	199 817	99 579	100 238	...	...	...	...	...
TorrejóndeArdoz	ESDJ	112 114	55 605	56 509	...	...	...	...	...
Valencia	ESDJ	805 304	388 401	416 903	1 346	...	...	...	...
Valladolid	ESDJ	319 943	152 976	166 967	1 975	...	...	...	...
Vigo	ESDJ	293 255	139 869	153 386		...	...	...	...
Vitoria-Gasteiz	ESDJ	227 568	112 028	115 540	2 768	...	...	...	...
Zaragoza	ESDJ	649 181	314 460	334 721	10 631	...	...	...	...

Sweden — Suède
1 VII 2006

Göteborg	ESDJ	487 350	240 504	246 846	449	883 764	438 391	445 373	...
Helsingborg	ESDJ	122 726	59 742	62 984	346	...	...	...	...
Jönköping	ESDJ	121 580	59 684	61 896	1 485	...	...	...	...
Linköping	ESDJ	138 108	69 451	68 657	1 431	...	...	...	...
Malmö	ESDJ	273 758	133 203	140 555	154	609 356	299 912	309 444	...
Norrköping	ESDJ	125 053	61 765	63 288	1 491	...	...	...	...
Orebro	ESDJ	128 356	62 372	65 984	1 371	...	...	...	...
STOCKHOLM	ESDJ	776 962	377 296	399 666	187	1 904 025	936 029	967 996	...
Umeå	ESDJ	110 997	55 257	55 740	2 316	...	...	...	...
Uppsala	ESDJ	184 248	89 934	94 314	2 465	...	...	...	...
Västerås	ESDJ	132 427	65 560	66 867	956	...	...	...	...

Switzerland — Suisse
1 I 2006

Baden-Brugg	ESDJ	18 318	8 875	9 443	13	108 977	54 075	54 902	124
Bâle	ESDJ	163 930	77 795	86 135	24	486 146	234 771	251 375	481
BERNE	ESDJ	122 178	57 289	64 889	52	343 789	164 598	179 191	493
Genève	ESDJ	178 722	84 267	94 455	16	493 445	236 890	256 555	457
Lausanne	ESDJ	117 388	55 375	62 013	41	310 028	149 234	160 794	312
Lugano	ESDJ	49 223	22 827	26 396	26	127 351	60 301	67 050	226
Luzern	ESDJ	57 533	26 781	30 752	16	199 202	96 999	102 203	198
Olten-Zofingen	ESDJ	16 633	8 037	8 596	11	104 644	51 514	53 130	179
St. Gallen	ESDJ	70 316	33 699	36 617	39	145 270	70 502	74 768	175
Winterthur	ESDJ	93 546	45 330	48 216	68	128 654	62 851	65 803	151
Zürich	ESDJ	347 517	168 441	179 076	88	1 101 710	541 246	560 464	937

The Former Yougoslav Rep. of Macedonia — L'ex-République yougoslave de Macédoine
1 VII 2006

SKOPLJE	ESDF	522 187	256 424	265 763	...	...	...	...	...

Ukraine
01 I 2005

Alchevsk	ESDJ	116 472	53 523	62 949	30	...	...	...	...
Berdyansk	ESDJ	119 505	53 458	66 047	41	122 694	54 971	67 723	205
Bila Tserkva (Belaya Tserkov)	ESDJ	200 865	93 471	107 394	42	...	...	...	...
Cherkasy	ESDJ	290 796	133 856	156 940	60	291 570	134 262	157 308	76
Chernihiv	ESDJ	294 677	136 812	157 865	49	...	...	...	...
Chernivtsy	ESDJ	238 492	109 710	128 782	71	...	...	...	...
Dnieprodzerzhynsk	ESDJ	248 980	112 364	136 616	84	255 882	115 491	140 391	138
Dnipropetrovsk	ESDJ	1 044 094	476 165	567 929	250	1 046 365	477 278	569 087	405
Donetsk (Donestskaya oblast)	ESDJ	991 310	441 714	549 596	305	1 008 002	449 307	558 695	557
Enakievo (Yenakievo)	ESDJ	96 928	43 317	53 611	41	151 930	68 891	83 039	425
Evpotoriya	ESDJ	103 662	46 266	57 396	21	118 670	53 069	65 601	54
Horlivka	ESDJ	276 873	124 786	152 087	162	298 514	134 597	163 917	399
Ivano-Frankivsk	ESDJ	216 626	102 690	113 936	34	232 040	109 938	122 102	90

8. Population of capital cities and cities of 100 000 or more inhabitants: latest available year, 1987 - 2006
Population des capitales et des villes de 100 000 habitants ou plus: dernière année disponible, 1987 - 2006
(continued — suite)

Continent, country or area, date and city / Continent, pays ou zone, date et ville	Code[1]	City proper — Ville proprement dite Population				Urban agglomeration — Agglomération urbaine Population			
		Both sexes Les deux sexes	Male Masculin	Female Féminin	Surface area Superficie (km²)	Both sexes Les deux sexes	Male Masculin	Female Féminin	Surface area Superficie (km²)
EUROPE									
Ukraine									
01 I 2005									
Kerch	ESDJ	153 858	69 573	84 285	43	...	...	...	...
Kharkiv	ESDJ	1 445 173	660 732	784 441	239	...	...	...	...
Kherson	ESDJ	315 676	142 769	172 907	58	353 128	160 153	192 975	304
Khmelnytskiy (Hmilnyk)	ESDJ	253 068	117 864	135 204	50	...	...	...	...
KYIV (KIEV)	ESDJ	2 625 094	1 217 865	1 407 229	834	...	...	...	...
Kirovohrad	ESDJ	245 226	111 387	133 839	59	253 256	115 031	138 225	74
Kramatorsk	ESDJ	174 440	77 909	96 531	53	208 839	93 877	114 962	349
Krasny Lutch	ESDJ	89 642	41 547	48 095	39	136 916	63 728	73 188	181
Kremenchuh	ESDJ	230 222	105 746	124 476	44	...	...	...	...
Kryviy Rig	ESDJ	695 168	316 203	378 965	243	698 599	317 925	380 674	470
Lysychansk	ESDJ	111 160	50 443	60 717	45	128 454	58 383	70 071	87
Luhansk	ESDJ	449 314	200 381	248 933	120	488 290	218 590	269 700	269
Lutsk	ESDJ	199 832	90 707	109 125	43	...	...	...	...
Lviv	ESDJ	727 061	342 015	385 046	94	752 285	353 969	398 316	168
Makyivka	ESDJ	374 301	170 162	204 139	161	415 715	189 508	226 207	460
Mariupol	ESDJ	479 045	219 290	259 755	134	501 158	229 739	271 419	200
Melitopol	ESDJ	159 135	72 385	86 750	47	...	...	...	...
Mykolayiv (Nikolaevskaya oblast)	ESDJ	504 516	229 322	275 194	112	...	...	...	...
Nikopol	ESDJ	133 828	60 310	73 518	46	...	...	...	...
Odessa	ESDJ	989 468	458 474	530 994	130	...	...	...	...
Pavlohrad	ESDJ	114 691	53 344	61 347	48	...	...	...	...
Poltava	ESDJ	302 939	139 355	163 584	77	...	...	...	...
Rivne	ESDJ	244 448	112 289	132 159	40	...	...	...	...
Sevastopol	ESDJ	338 508	154 201	184 307	55	376 645	171 922	204 723	866
Simpheropol	ESDJ	336 250	148 412	187 838	49	357 999	158 359	199 640	90
Siverodonetsk	ESDJ	116 679	52 509	64 170	22	126 626	57 224	69 402	65
Slovyansk	ESDJ	119 937	52 632	67 305	59	139 740	61 742	77 998	74
Stakhanov	ESDJ	84 538	37 342	47 196	43	101 506	45 029	56 477	83
Sumy	ESDJ	281 396	128 337	153 059	62	284 227	129 661	154 566	127
Ternopil	ESDJ	219 238	102 603	116 635	34	...	...	...	...
Uzhhorod	ESDJ	115 468	53 672	61 796	23	...	...	...	...
Vinnytsya	ESDJ	358 403	165 241	193 162	56	...	...	...	...
Zaporizhya	ESDJ	795 422	360 836	434 586	169	798 034	362 008	436 026	328
Zhytomyr	ESDJ	276 618	128 194	148 424	55	...	...	...	...
United Kingdom — Royaume-Uni[99]									
29 IV 2001									
Aberdeen	ESDF	...	...	...	...	212 125	103 818	108 307	...
Aberdeenshire	ESDF	...	...	...	...	226 871	112 470	114 401	...
Aldershot	ESDF	...	...	...	...	243 344	121 127	122 217	...
Angus	ESDF	...	...	...	...	108 400	52 458	55 942	...
Basildon/North Benfleet	ESDF	...	...	...	...	101 492	48 649	52 843	...
Bedford/Kempston	ESDF	...	...	...	...	101 928	50 341	51 587	...
Belfast[100]	ESDF	...	...	...	...	276 459	129 321	147 138	...
Birkenhead	ESDF	...	...	...	...	319 675	152 133	167 542	...
Blackburn/Darwen	ESDF	...	...	...	...	136 655	66 834	69 821	...
Blackpool	ESDF	...	...	...	...	261 088	124 698	136 390	...
Bournemouth	ESDF	...	...	...	...	383 713	182 875	200 838	...
Brighton/Worthing/Littlehampton	ESDF	...	...	...	...	461 181	220 275	240 906	...
Bristol	ESDF	...	...	...	...	551 066	269 689	281 377	...
Burnley/Nelson	ESDF	...	...	...	...	149 796	72 657	77 139	...
Cambridge	ESDF	...	...	...	...	131 465	65 343	66 122	...
Cardiff[101]	ESDF	...	...	...	...	327 706	156 272	171 434	...
Cheltenham/Charlton Kings	ESDF	...	...	...	...	110 320	53 526	56 794	...
Chesterfield/Staveley	ESDF	...	...	...	...	100 879	49 204	51 675	...
Colchester	ESDF	...	...	...	...	104 390	51 652	52 738	...
Coventry/Bedworth	ESDF	...	...	...	...	336 452	166 666	169 786	...
Crawley	ESDF	...	...	...	...	180 177	88 404	91 773	...
Dearne Valley	ESDF	...	...	...	...	207 726	100 992	106 734	...
Derby	ESDF	...	...	...	...	236 738	115 644	121 094	...
Doncaster	ESDF	...	...	...	...	127 851	62 127	65 724	...

8. Population of capital cities and cities of 100 000 or more inhabitants: latest available year, 1987 - 2006
Population des capitales et des villes de 100 000 habitants ou plus: dernière année disponible, 1987 - 2006
(continued — suite)

Continent, country or area, date and city / Continent, pays ou zone, date et ville	Code[1]	City proper — Ville proprement dite Population				Urban agglomeration — Agglomération urbaine Population			
		Both sexes Les deux sexes	Male Masculin	Female Féminin	Surface area Superficie (km²)	Both sexes Les deux sexes	Male Masculin	Female Féminin	Surface area Superficie (km²)

EUROPE

United Kingdom — Royaume-Uni[99]
  29 IV 2001

Dumfries & Galloway	ESDF	...	...	...	...	147 765	71 303	76 462	...
Dundee	ESDF	...	...	...	...	145 663	69 140	76 523	...
East Ayrshire	ESDF	...	...	...	...	130 235	57 842	62 393	...
East Dunbartonshire	ESDF	...	...	...	...	108 243	52 014	56 229	...
Eastbourne	ESDF	...	...	...	...	106 562	49 369	57 193	...
Edinburgh[102]	ESDF	...	...	...	...	448 624	214 711	233 913	...
Exeter	ESDF	...	...	...	...	106 772	52 045	54 727	...
Falkirk	ESDF	...	...	...	...	145 191	70 016	75 175	...
Fife	ESDF	...	...	...	...	349 429	167 628	181 801	...
Glasgow	ESDF	...	...	...	...	577 869	272 309	305 560	...
Gloucester	ESDF	...	...	...	...	136 203	66 669	69 534	...
Grimsby/Cleethorpes	ESDF	...	...	...	...	138 842	67 360	71 482	...
Hastings/Bexhill	ESDF	...	...	...	...	126 386	59 247	67 139	...
High Wycombe	ESDF	...	...	...	...	118 229	57 857	60 372	...
Highland	ESDF	...	...	...	...	208 914	102 297	106 617	...
Ipswich	ESDF	...	...	...	...	141 658	69 468	72 190	...
Kingston-upon-Hull	ESDF	...	...	...	...	301 416	146 926	154 490	...
Leicester	ESDF	...	...	...	...	441 213	214 060	227 153	...
Lincoln	ESDF	...	...	...	...	104 221	50 794	53 427	...
Liverpool	ESDF	...	...	...	...	816 216	389 119	427 097	...
LONDON[103]	ESDF	...	...	...	...	8 278 251	4 007 297	4 270 954	...
Luton/Dunstable	ESDF	...	...	...	...	236 318	117 707	118 611	...
Manchester	ESDF	...	...	...	...	2 244 931	1 090 898	1 154 033	...
Mansfield	ESDF	...	...	...	...	158 114	76 884	81 230	...
Milton Keynes	ESDF	...	...	...	...	184 506	91 441	93 065	...
Newport	ESDF	...	...	...	...	139 298	66 884	72 414	...
North Ayrshire	ESDF	...	...	...	...	135 817	64 238	71 579	...
North Lanarkshire	ESDF	...	...	...	...	321 067	153 966	167 101	...
Northampton	ESDF	...	...	...	...	197 199	96 670	100 529	...
Norwich	ESDF	...	...	...	...	194 839	94 523	100 316	...
Nottingham	ESDF	...	...	...	...	666 358	327 851	338 507	...
Nuneaton	ESDF	...	...	...	...	132 236	64 837	67 399	...
Oxford	ESDF	...	...	...	...	143 016	70 462	72 554	...
Perth & Kinross	ESDF	...	...	...	...	134 949	65 172	69 777	...
Peterborough	ESDF	...	...	...	...	136 292	66 139	70 153	...
Plymouth	ESDF	...	...	...	...	243 795	119 076	124 719	...
Portsmouth	ESDF	...	...	...	...	442 252	216 341	225 911	...
Preston	ESDF	...	...	...	...	264 601	129 665	134 936	...
Reading/Wokingham	ESDF	...	...	...	...	369 804	185 475	184 329	...
Renfrewshire	ESDF	...	...	...	...	172 867	82 525	90 342	...
Scottish Borders	ESDF	...	...	...	...	106 764	51 361	55 403	...
Sheffield	ESDF	...	...	...	...	640 720	312 619	328 101	...
Slough	ESDF	...	...	...	...	141 848	70 286	71 562	...
South Ayrshire	ESDF	...	...	...	...	112 097	53 406	58 691	...
South Lanarkshire	ESDF	...	...	...	...	302 216	144 206	158 010	...
Southampton	ESDF	...	...	...	...	304 400	151 534	152 866	...
Southend	ESDF	...	...	...	...	269 415	129 650	139 765	...
Southport/Formby	ESDF	...	...	...	...	115 882	54 337	61 545	...
St Albans/Hatfield	ESDF	...	...	...	...	114 710	56 585	58 125	...
Sunderland	ESDF	...	...	...	...	182 974	88 892	94 082	...
Swansea	ESDF	...	...	...	...	270 506	130 648	139 858	...
Swindon	ESDF	...	...	...	...	155 432	77 551	77 881	...
Teesside	ESDF	...	...	...	...	365 323	176 475	188 848	...
Telford	ESDF	...	...	...	...	138 241	67 770	70 471	...
Thanet	ESDF	...	...	...	...	119 144	56 266	62 878	...
The Medway Towns	ESDF	...	...	...	...	231 659	114 069	117 590	...
The Potteries	ESDF	...	...	...	...	362 403	176 467	185 936	...
Torbay	ESDF	...	...	...	...	110 366	52 551	57 815	...
Tyneside	ESDF	...	...	...	...	879 996	425 119	454 877	...
Warrington	ESDF	...	...	...	...	158 195	77 334	80 861	...

8. Population of capital cities and cities of 100 000 or more inhabitants: latest available year, 1987 - 2006
Population des capitales et des villes de 100 000 habitants ou plus: dernière année disponible, 1987 - 2006
(continued — suite)

Continent, country or area, date and city Continent, pays ou zone, date et ville	Code[1]	City proper — Ville proprement dite Population				Urban agglomeration — Agglomération urbaine Population			
		Both sexes Les deux sexes	Male Masculin	Female Féminin	Surface area Superficie (km²)	Both sexes Les deux sexes	Male Masculin	Female Féminin	Surface area Superficie (km²)
EUROPE									
United Kingdom — Royaume-Uni[99]									
29 IV 2001									
West Lothian	ESDF	...	...	...	...	158 714	76 701	82 013	...
West Midlands	ESDF	...	...	...	...	2 284 093	1 109 397	1 174 696	...
West Yorkshire	ESDF	...	...	...	...	1 499 465	724 818	774 647	...
Wigan	ESDF	...	...	...	...	166 840	81 254	85 586	...
York	ESDF	...	...	...	...	137 505	66 142	71 363	...
OCEANIA — OCEANIE									
American Samoa — Samoa américaines[15]									
1 IV 2000									
PAGO PAGO	CDJC	4 278	2 086	2 192	...	...	...	...	...
Australia — Australie[104]									
30 VI 2005									
Adelaide[105]	ESDJ	1 129 145	554 962	574 183	1 830	...	...	...	...
Albury-Wodonga[106]	ESDJ	100 175	49 498	50 677	4 410	...	...	...	...
Brisbane[105]	ESDJ	1 790 921	888 980	901 941	5 900	...	...	...	...
Cairns[106]	ESDJ	123 775	62 490	61 285	490	...	...	...	...
CANBERRA[105]	ESDJ	325 405	161 193	164 212	810	...	...	...	...
Darwin[105]	ESDJ	111 179	59 093	52 086	3 120	...	...	...	...
Geelong[106]	ESDJ	165 827	80 851	84 976	390	...	...	...	...
Gold Coast-Tweed[106]	ESDJ	540 115	267 325	272 790	1 320	...	...	...	...
Wollongong[106]	ESDJ	274 838	137 510	137 328	1 090	...	...	...	...
Greater Hobart[105]	ESDJ	203 527	99 485	104 042	1 360	...	...	...	...
Launceston[106]	ESDJ	103 221	50 357	52 864	800	...	...	...	...
Melbourne[105]	ESDJ	3 635 508	1 792 547	1 842 961	7 690	...	...	...	...
Newcastle[106]	ESDJ	508 597	251 625	256 972	4 050	...	...	...	...
Perth[105]	ESDJ	1 478 039	733 953	744 086	5 390	...	...	...	...
Sunshine Coast[106]	ESDJ	215 059	105 235	109 824	460	...	...	...	...
Sydney[105]	ESDJ	4 255 954	2 115 723	2 140 231	12 140	...	...	...	...
Toowoomba[106]	ESDJ	119 486	57 923	61 563	550	...	...	...	...
Townsville[106]	ESDJ	149 207	75 645	73 562	460	...	...	...	...
Cook Islands — Iles Cook									
1 XII 2001									
RAROTONGA	CDFC	12 188	...	...	...	...	...	...	...
Fiji — Fidji									
31 VIII 1996									
SUVA	CDFC	77 366	38 518	38 848	...	167 975	83 910	84 065	...
French Polynesia — Polynésie française									
7 XI 2002									
PAPEETE	CDFC	26 181	...	...	...	124 864	...	...	...
Guam[15]									
1 IV 2000									
AGANA	CDJC	1 100	672	428	3	...	...	...	...
Kiribati									
7 XI 2000									
TARAWA	CDFC	...	...	...	...	36 717	...	...	...
Marshall Islands — Iles Marshall									
1 VI 1999									
MAJURO	CDFC	23 676	12 075	11 601	...	...	...	...	...
Micronesia, Federated States of — Micronésie, États fédérés de									
1 IV 2000									
PALIKIR	CDJC	6 227	...	...	...	...	...	...	...
Nauru									
17 IV 1992									
YAREN	CDFC	672	...	...	...	...	...	...	...

8. Population of capital cities and cities of 100 000 or more inhabitants: latest available year, 1987 - 2006
Population des capitales et des villes de 100 000 habitants ou plus: dernière année disponible, 1987 - 2006
(continued — suite)

Continent, country or area, date and city / Continent, pays ou zone, date et ville	Code[1]	City proper — Ville proprement dite Population				Urban agglomeration — Agglomération urbaine Population			
		Both sexes Les deux sexes	Male Masculin	Female Féminin	Surface area Superficie (km²)	Both sexes Les deux sexes	Male Masculin	Female Féminin	Surface area Superficie (km²)
OCEANIA — OCEANIE									
New Caledonia — Nouvelle-Calédonie									
16 IV 1996									
NOUMEA	CDFC	76 293	38 443	37 850	46	118 823	60 327	58 496	1 643
New Zealand — Nouvelle-Zélande[107,108,109]									
1 VII 2006									
Auckland	ESDJ	428 300	209 600	218 700	664	1 272 800	621 800	650 900	1 084
Christchurch	ESDJ	361 800	175 500	186 300	1 540	374 500	181 700	192 800	608
Dunedin[110]	ESDJ	122 300	58 800	63 500	3 342	114 400	54 800	59 600	255
Hamilton	ESDJ	134 400	64 700	69 700	98	191 700	92 800	99 000	1 099
Lower hutt	ESDJ	101 300	49 600	51 700	377	...	...	...	...
Manukau	ESDJ	347 100	169 400	177 700	683	...	...	...	...
Napier-Hastings	ESDJ	...	...	...	...	121 900	58 800	63 200	389
Northshore	ESDJ	216 900	106 200	110 700	129	...	...	...	...
Tauranga	ESDJ	106 700	51 100	55 600	168	112 100	53 800	58 300	178
Waitakere	ESDJ	195 300	95 400	100 000	367	...	...	...	...
WELLINGTON	ESDJ	187 700	91 200	96 500	290	375 600	183 400	192 200	447
Niue — Nioué									
13 IX 2001									
ALOFI	CDFC	615	...	...	...	...	...	...	...
Norfolk Island — Ile Norfolk									
1 VII 1997									
KINGSTON	ESDF	*800*	...	...	...	...	...	...	...
Northern Mariana Islands — Iles Mariannes du Nord									
1 IV 2000									
GARAPAN	CDFC	3 588	...	...	...	...	...	...	...
Palau — Palaos									
15 IV 2000									
KOROR	CDFC	10 600	...	...	...	...	...	...	...
Papua New Guinea — Papouasie-Nouvelle-Guinée									
9 VII 2000									
PORT MORESBY	CDFC	254 158	138 974	115 184	...	...	...	...	...
Pitcairn									
1 VII 1993									
ADAMSTOWN	ESDF	53	...	...	5	...	...	...	...
Samoa									
1 XI 2001									
APIA	CDFC	38 836	...	...	...	...	...	...	...
Solomon Islands — Iles Salomon									
21 XI 1999									
HONIARA	CDFC	49 107	...	...	...	...	...	...	...
Tonga									
1 VII 2000									
NUKU'ALOFA	ESDF	21 538	10 625	10 913	...	30 336	15 115	15 221	...
Tuvalu									
1 XI 2002									
FUNAFUTI	CDFC	4 492	2 281	2 211	...	...	...	...	...
Vanuatu									
16 XI 1999									
PORT VILA	CDFC	29 356	...	...	...	...	...	...	...
Wallis and Futuna Islands — Iles Wallis et Futuna									
3 X 1996									
META-UTU	CDFC	1 137	...	...	...	...	...	...	...

GENERAL NOTES - NOTES GENERALES

The capital city of each country is shown in capital letters. Figures in italics are estimates of questionable reliability. For definition of city proper and urban agglomeration, method of evaluation and limitations of data see

Technical Notes for this table. — Le nom de la capitale de chaque pays est imprimé en majuscules. Les chiffres en italique sont des estimations dont la fiabilité n'est pas assurée. Pour la définition de la ville proprement dite et de l'agglomération urbaine, et pour les méthodes d'évaluation et les insuffisances de données, voir les notes techniques pour ce tableau.

FOOTNOTES - NOTES

[1] 'Code' indicates the source of data, as follows:
CDFC - Census, de facto, complete tabulation
CDFS - Census, de facto, sample tabulation
CDJC - Census, de jure, complete tabulation
CDJS - Census, de jure, sample tabulation
SSDF - Sample survey, de facto
SSDJ - Sample survey, de jure
ESDF - Estimates, de facto
ESDJ - Estimates, de jure
Le 'Code' indique la source des données, comme suit:
CDFC - Recensement, population de fait, tabulation complète
CDFS - Recensement, population de fait, tabulation par sondage
CDJC - Recensement, population de droit, tabulation complète
CDJS - Recensement, population de droit, tabulation par sondage
SSDF - Enquête par sondage, population de fait
SSDJ - Enquête par sondage, population de droit
ESDF - Données estimées, population de fait
ESDJ - Données estimées, population de droit

[2] Dual capitals. — Le pays a deux capitales.

[3] For the urban commune of Antananarivo. — Pour la commune urbaine d'Antananarivo.

[4] Data for city proper refer to population in municipalities. - Les données concernant la ville proprement dite se rapportent a la population des municipalités.

[5] Data include those for two or more cities. - Les données présentées concernent deux villes ou plus.

[6] Data for cities proper refer to communes. — Les données pour les villes se réfèrent aux communes.

[7] For communes which may contain rural areas as well as urban centre. — Commune(s) pouvant comprendre un centre urbain et une zone rurale.

[8] Included in urban agglomeration of Dakar. — Comprise dans l'agglomération urbaine de Dakar.

[9] Pretoria is the administrative capital, Cape Town the legislative capital. — Pretoria est la capital administrative, Le Cap la capitale législative.

[10] Excluding persons residing in institutions. — Non compris les personnes dans les institutions.

[11] For municipalities which may contain an urban centre as well as a rural area. — Pour les municipalités qui peuvent comprendre un centre urbain et aussi une zone rurale.

[12] The definition of locality is based on the 2000 Population census. - La localité est définie suivant le recensement général de la population de 2000.

[13] Urban agglomeration (Metropolitan area) refers to 2 or more municipalities where there is only one urban concentration. - L'agglomération urbaine (zone métropolitaine) se rapporte à 2 municipalités ou plus où il y a seulement une concentration urbaine.

[14] Including municipalities of Bella Vista, Betania, Calidonia, Curundu, El Chorillo, Juan Diaz, Parque Lefevre, Pedregal, Pueblo Nuevo, Rio Abajo, San Felipe, San Francisco and Santa Ana. — Y compris les municipalités de Bella Vista, Betania, Calidonia, Curundu, El Chorillo, Juan Diaz, Parque Lefevre, Pedregal, Pueblo Nuevo, Rio Abajo, San Felipe, San Francisco et Santa Ana.

[15] Including armed forces stationed in the area. — Y compris les militaires en garnison sur le territoire.

[16] Excluding armed forces overseas and civilian citizens absent from country for extended period of time. — Non compris les militaires à l'étranger et les civils hors du pays pendant une période prolongée.

[17] City refers to a type of incorporated place in 49 states and the District of Columbia, that has an elected government and provides a range of government functions and services. Also included are Honolulu, Hawaii Census Designated Place (CDP), for which the Census Bureau reports data under agreement with the State of Hawaii (instead of the combined city and county of Honolulu), and Arlington, VA CDP (which is coextensive with Arlington County - an entirely urban county that provides the same levels of services and functions as a municipality. - Par ville, on entend un lieu doté de la personnalité morale dans 49 États et dans le district de Columbia, qui a un gouvernement élu et fournit tout un ensemble de fonctions et de services publics. Sont également inclus Honolulu, lieu chargé du recensement pour Hawaii, pour lequel le Census Bureau établit les données en accord avec l'État de Hawaii (au lieu de la ville et du comté d'Honolulu), et Arlington, lieu chargé du recensement pour la Virginie, qui est de même étendue que le comté d'Arlington, lequel est un comté entièrement urbain qui offre les mêmes niveaux de services et de fonctions qu'une municipalité.

[18] Included in urban agglomeration of Washington, DC--VA--MD. — Comprise dans l'agglomération urbaine de Washington, DC--VA--MD

[19] Included in urban agglomeration of Los Angeles--Long Beach--Santa Ana, CA. — Comprise dans l'agglomération urbaine de Los Angeles--Long Beach--Santa Ana, CA.

[20] Included in urban agglomeration of Dallas--Fort Worth--Arlington, TX. — Comprise dans l'agglomération urbaine de Dallas--Fort Worth--Arlington, TX.

[21] Included in urban agglomeration of Denver--Aurora, CO. — Comprise dans l'agglomération urbaine de Denver--Aurora, CO.

[22] Included in urban agglomeration of Chicago, IL--IN. — Comprise dans l'agglomération urbaine de Chicago, IL--IN.

[23] Included in urban agglomeration of Seattle, WA. — Comprise dans l'agglomération urbaine de Seattle, WA.

[24] Included in urban agglomeration of San Francisco--Oakland, CA. — Comprise dans l'agglomération urbaine de San Francisco--Oakland, CA.

[25] Included in urban agglomeration of Boston, MA--NH--RI. — Comprise dans l'agglomération urbaine de Boston, MA--NH--RI.

[26] Included in urban agglomeration of Phoenix--Mesa, AZ. — Comprise dans l'agglomération urbaine de Phoenix--Mesa, AZ.

[27] Included in urban agglomeration of Virginia Beach, VA. — Comprise dans l'agglomération urbaine de Virginia Beach, VA.

[28] Included in urban agglomeration of San Diego, CA. — Comprise dans l'agglomération urbaine de San Diego, CA.

[29] Included in urban agglomeration of Tampa--St. Petersburg, FL. — Comprise dans l'agglomération urbaine de Tampa--St. Petersburg, FL.

[30] Included in urban agglomeration of Miami, FL. — Comprise dans l'agglomération urbaine de Miami, FL.

[31] Included in urban agglomeration of Riverside--San Bernardino, CA. — Comprise dans l'agglomération urbaine de Riverside--San Bernardino, CA.

[32] Included in urban agglomeration of New York--Newark, NY--NJ--CT. — Comprise dans l'agglomération urbaine de New York--Newark, NY--NJ--CT.

[33] Included in urban agglomeration of Las Vegas, NV. — Comprise dans l'agglomération urbaine de Las Vegas, NV.

[34] Included in urban agglomeration of Kansas City, MO--KS. — Comprise dans l'agglomération urbaine de Kansas City, MO--KS.

[35] Data for urban agglomeration refer to Killeen-Temple 'metropolitan statistical area'. — Les données pour l'agglomération urbaine se rapportent à la 'zone métropolitaine statistique' de Killeen-Temple.

[36] Included in urban agglomeration of Lancaster--Palmdale, CA. — Comprise dans l'agglomération urbaine de Lancaster--Palmdale, CA.

[37] Included in urban agglomeration of Houston, TX. — Comprise dans l'agglomération urbaine de Houston, TX.

[38] Included in urban agglomeration of Minneapolis--St. Paul, MN. — Comprise dans l'agglomération urbaine de Minneapolis--St. Paul, MN.

[39] Included in urban agglomeration of Oxnard, CA. — Comprise dans l'agglomération urbaine de Oxnard, CA.

[40] Included in urban agglomeration of San Jose, CA. — Comprise dans l'agglomération urbaine de San Jose, CA.

[41] Included in urban agglomeration of Bridgeport--Stamford, CT--NY. — Comprise dans l'agglomération urbaine de Bridgeport--Stamford, CT--NY.

[42] Included in urban agglomeration of Detroit, MI. — Comprise dans l'agglomération urbaine de Detroit, MI.

[43] Included in urban agglomeration of Portland, OR--WA. — Comprise dans l'agglomération urbaine de Portland, OR--WA.

[44] Included in urban agglomeration of Salt Lake City, UT. — Comprise dans l'agglomération urbaine de Salt Lake City, UT.

[45] La Paz is the actual capital and the seat of the Government but Sucre is the legal capital and the seat of the judiciary. — La Paz est la capitale effective et le siège du gouvernement, mais Sucre est la capitale constitutionnelle et la siège du pouvoir judiciaire.

[46] 'Metropolitan area' Grand Santiago. — 'Zone métropolitaine' Grand Santiago.

[47] Urban agglomeration refers to the urban part of the municipality with a proper city center. - L'agglomération urbaine se rapporte à la partie urbaine de la municipalité avec un centre de la ville.

[48] Data for urban agglomeration refer to 'metropolitan area', comprising Asuncion proper and localities of Trinidad, Zeballos Cué, Campo Grande and Lamboré. — Les données pour l'agglomération urbaine se rapportent à la 'zone métropolitaine' comprenant la ville d'Asuncion proprement dite et les localités de Trinidad, Zeballos Cué, Campo Grande et Lamboré.

[49] City population refers to urban population of districts within the city. - La population des villes se rapporte à la population urbaine des districts compris dans la ville.

[50] For municipalities which may contain rural area as well as urban centre. — Pour les municipalités qui peuvent comprendre un centre urbaine et une zone rurale.

[51] Lefkosia urban agglomeration is composed of Lefkosia municipality, Agios Dometios, Egkomi, Strovolos, Aglangia, Lakatameia, Anthoupoli, Latsia and Geri. — L'agglomération urbaine de Lefkosia comprend la municipalité de Lefkosia et Agios Dometios, Egkomi, Strovolos, Aglangia, Lakatameia, Anthoupoli, Latsia et Geri.

[52] Lemesos urban agglomeration is composed of Lemesos municipality, Mesa Geitonia, Agios Athanasios, Germasogeia, Pano Polemidia, Ypsonas, Kato Polemidia, and parts of Mouttagiaka, Agios Tychon, Parekklisia, Monagrouli, Moni, Pyrgos and Tserkezoi. — L'agglomération urbaine de Lemesos comprend la municipalité de Lemesos et Mesa Geitonia, Agios Athanasios, Germasogeia, Pano Polemidia, Ypsonas, Kato Polemidia, et certaines parties des Mouttagiaka, Agios Tychon, Parekklisia, Monagrouli, Moni, Pyrgos et Tserkezoi.

[53] Including data for the India-held part of Jammu and Kashmir, the final status of which has not yet been determined. Excluding cities for Assam

state. — Y compris les données concernant la partie de Jammu-et-Cachemire occupée par l'Inde, dont le statut définitif n'a pas encore été déterminé. Non compris les villes de l'état d'Assam.

[54] Data for urban agglomeration includes New Delhi. — Les données pour l'agglomération urbaine y compris New Delhi.

[55] Data for urban agglomeration include Bally, Baranagar, Barrackpur, Bhatpara, Calcutta Municipal Corporation, Chandan Nagar, Garden Reach, Houghly-Chinsura, Howrah, Jadarpur, Kamarhati, Naihati, Panihati, Serampore, South Dum Dum, South Suburban, and Titagarh. — Les données pour l'agglomération urbaine y compris Bally, Baranagar, Barrackpur, Bhatpara, Calcutta Municipal Corporation, Chandan Nagar, Garden Reach, Houghly Chinsura, Howrah, Jadarpur, Kamarhati, Naihati, Panihati, Serampopre, South Dum Dum, South Suburban et Titagarh.

[56] Included in urban agglomeration of Delhi. — Comprise dans l'agglomération urbaine de Delhi.

[57] Data refer to the New Delhi Municipal Council. — Les données se rapportent au New Delhi Municipal Council.

[58] Including Karkh, Rassaiah, Adhamiya and Kadhimain Qadha Centres and Maamoon, Mansour and Karradah-Sharqiyah Nahlyas. — Y compris les cazas de Karkh, Adhamiya et Kadhimain ainsi que les nahiyas de Maamoon, Mansour et Karradah-Sharqiyah.

[59] Designation and data provided by Israel. The position of the United Nations on the question of Jerusalem is contained in General Assembly resolution 181 (II) and subsequent resolutions of the General Assembly and the Security Council concerning this question. — Appellation et données fournies par Israel. La position des Nations Unies concernant la question de Jérusalem est décrite dans la résolution 181 (II) de l'Assemblée générale et résolutions ultérieures de l'Assemblée générale et du Conseil de sécurité sur cette question.

[60] Including East Jerusalem. — Y compris Jérusalem-Est.

[61] Excluding diplomatic personnel outside country and foreign military and civilian personnel and their dependants stationed in the area. — Non compris le personnel diplomatique hors du territoire, les militaires et agents civils étrangers en poste sur le territoire et les membres de leur famille les accompagnant.

[62] Except for Tokyo, all data refer to shi, a minor division which may include some scattered or rural population as well as an urban centre. — Sauf pour Tokyo, toutes les données se rapportent à des shi, petites divisions administratives qui peuvent comprendre des peuplements dispersés ou ruraux en plus d'un centre urbain.

[63] Data excluding Hokkaido region. — Non compris la région de Hokkaido.

[64] Including Kokura, Moji, Tobata, Wakamatsu and Yahata (Yawata). — Y compris Kokura, Moji, Tobata, Wakamatsu et Yahata (Yawata).

[65] Data for city proper refer to 23 wards (ku) of the old city. The urban agglomeration figures refer to Tokyo-to (Tokyo Prefecture), comprising the 23 wards plus 14 urban counties (shi), 18 towns (machi) and 8 villages (mura). The 'Tokyo Metropolitan Area' comprises the 23 wards of Tokyo-to plus 21 cities, 20 towns and 2 villages. The 'Keihin Metropolitan Area' (Tokyo-Yokohama Metropolitan Area) plus 9 cities (one of which is Yokohama City) and two towns, with a total population of 20 485 542 on 1 October 1965. — Les données concernant la ville proprement dite se rapportent aux 23 circonscriptions de la vieille ville. Les chiffres pour l'agglomération urbaine se rapportent à Tokyo-to (préfecture de Tokyo), comprenant les 23 circonscriptions plus 14 cantons urbains (Shi), 18 villes (machi) et 8 villages (mura). La 'zone métropolitaine de Tokyo' comprend les 23 circonscriptions de Tokyo-to plus 21 municipalités, 20 villes et 2 villages. La 'zone métropolitaine de Keihin' (zone métropolitaine de Tokyo-Yokohama) comprend la zone métropolitaine de Tokyo, plus 9 municipalités, dont l'une est Yokohama et 2 villes, elle comptait 20 485 542 habitants au 1er octobre 1965.

[66] Excluding data for the Pakistan-held part of Jammu and Kashmir, the final status of which has not yet been determined, and for Junagardh, Manavadar, Gilgit and Baltistan. — Non compris les données pour la partie de Jammu-Cachemire occupée par le Pakistan dont le status definitif n'a pas encore été déterminé, et le Junagardh, le Manavadar, le Gilgit et le Baltistan.

[67] Covers Seyhan and Yuregir districts in Adana. - Y compris la population des districts de Seyhan et de Yuregir.

[68] Covers Altindag, Cankaya, Etimesgut, Golbasi, Kecioren, Mamak, Sincan, and Yenimahalle districts in Ankara. - Y compris la population des districts de Altindag, de Cankaya, de Etimesgut, de Golbasi, de Kecioren, de Mamak, de Sincan, et de Yenimahalle.

[69] Covers Nilufer, Osmangazi and Yildirim districts in Bursa. - Y compris la population des districts de Nilufer, de Osmangazi et de Yildirim.

[70] District centre. — Le centre du district.

[71] Covers Sahinbey and Sehitkamil districts in Gaziantep. - Y compris la population des districts de Sahinbey et de Sehitkamil.

[72] Covers Adalar, Avcilar, Bagcilar, Bahcelievler, Bakirkoy, Bayrampasa, Besiktas, Beykoz, Beyoglu, Eminonu, Esenler, Eyup, Fatih, Gaziosmanpasa, Gungoren, Kadikoy, Kagithane, Kartal, Kucukcekmece, Maltepe, Pendik, Sariyer, Sisli, Sultanbeyli, Tuzla, Umraniye, Uskudar, Zentinburnu districts in Istanbul. - Y compris la population des districts de Adalar, de Avcilar, de Bagcilar, de Bahcelievler, de Bakirkoy, de Bayrampasa, de Besiktas, de Beykoz, de Beyoglu, de Eminonu, de Esenler,

de Eyup, de Fatih, de Gaziosmanpasa, de Gungoren, de Kadikoy, de Kagithane, de Kartal, de Kucukcekmece, de Maltepe, de Pendik, de Sariyer, de Sisli, de Sultanbeyli, de Tuzla, de Umraniye, de Uskudar, et de Zentinburnu.

[73] Covers Bolcova, Bornova, Buca, Cigli, Gaziemir, Guzelbahce, Karsiyaka, Konak and Narlidere districts in Izmir. - Y compris la population des districts de Bolcova, de Bornova, de Buca, de Cigli, de Gaziemir, de Guzelbahce, de Karsiyaka, de Konak et de Narlidere.

[74] Covers Kocasinan and Melikgazi districts in Kayseri. - Y compris la population des districts de Kocasinan et de Melikgazi.

[75] Covers Karatay, Meram and Selcuklu districts Konya. - Y compris la population des districts de Karatay, de Meram et de Selcuklu.

[76] Including Cholon. — Y compris Cholon.

[77] City is defined as a residential center that has a zoning and urbanisation plan approved by law. - Une ville est définie comme centre résidentiel soumis à un règlement de zonage et à un plan d'urbanisation approuvés par voie législative.

[78] City proper refers to commune or municipality. - La ville proprement dite se rapporte à la commune ou à la municipalité

[79] Urban agglomeration refers to core area of an urban region. The core area consists of a densely inhabited area and of urban localities in short distance as well as of next situated urban localities, in case of mutual commuting to work (at least 35 index points). - Par agglomération urbaine, on entend la zone centrale d'une région urbaine, qui est constituée d'une zone de peuplement dense et des localités urbaines avoisinantes, ainsi que des localités urbaines situées un peu plus loin, les habitants des unes allant travailler dans les autres (35 points d'indice au minimum).

[80] Data for cities proper refer to communes which may contain an urban centre and a rural area. — Les données concernant les villes proprement dites se rapportent à des communes qui peuvent comprendre un centre urbain et une zone rurale.

[81] City is a settlement with a status of city according to the administrative-territorial division of the country at the end of the respective year. - La ville est une agglomération avec un statut de ville selon la division administratif-territoriale du pays à la fin de l'année respective.

[82] Data for cities proper refer to communes which are centres for urban agglomeration. — Les données concernant les villes proprement dites se rapportent à des communes qui sont des centres d'agglomérations urbaines.

[83] De jure population, but excluding diplomatic personnel outside the country and including foreign diplomatic personnel not living in embassies or consulates. — Population de droit, mais non compris le personnel diplomatique hors du pays et y compris le personnel diplomatique étranger qui ne vit pas dans les ambassades ou les consulats.

[84] Data refer to French territory of this international agglomeration. — Les données se rapportent aux habitants de cette agglomération internationale qui vivent en territoire francais.

[85] Including Villeurbanne. — Y compris Villeurbanne.

[86] Including armed forces stationed outside the country but excluding alien armed forces stationed in the area. — Y compris les militaires en garnison hors du pays, mais non compris les militaires étrangers en garnison sur le territoire.

[87] Data refer to the Vatican City State. — Les données se rapportent à l'Etat de la cité du Vatican.

[88] The boundaries of a city are related to the boundaries of a commune. - Les limites d'une ville correspondent aux limites d'une commune.

[89] The urban agglomeration of the capital area is much bigger and includes the following communes: Bessastaðahreppur, Garðabær, Hafnarfjörður, Kjósarhreppur, Kópavogur, Mosfellsbær ,Reykjavík, Seltjarnarnes. - L'agglomération urbaine de la capitale est beaucoup plus étendue et comprend les communes suivantes : Bessastaðahreppur, Garðabær, Hafnarfjörður, Kjósarhreppur, Kópavogur, Mosfellsbær ,Reykjavík, Seltjarnarnes.

[90] City is populated area with no less than 2 000 resident population, which is approved by the Cabinet of Ministers'. - Une ville est une zone de peuplement comptant au moins 2 000 habitants, selon une réglementation approuvée par le Cabinet ministériel.

[91] Population is not classified as 'urban' or 'rural'. About 95% of the population in Liechtenstein are living in a community with a population of 2000 and more. - La population n'est pas classée en 'urbaine' et 'rurale'. Environ 95 % de la population du Liechtenstein vit en agglomération comptant plus de 2 000 habitants.

[92] Including civilian nationals temporarily outside the country. — Y compris les civils nationaux temporairement hors du pays.

[93] Data for cities proper refer to administrative units (municipalities). — Les données concernant les villes proprement dites se rapportent à des unités administratives (municipalités).

[94] City is defined as administratively separated area entitled to civil (municipal) rights. Urban agglomeration is not defined. - Une ville est définie comme une zone administrativement distincte dotée de droits municipaux. Il n'y a pas de définition de l'agglomération urbaine.

[95] City is defined as industrial and cultural centers according to the legislation. - Une ville est définie comme centre culturel et industriel, conformément à la législation.

[96] Urban agglomeration includes the city and its populated localities subordinated to its authority. - Une agglomération urbaine comprend la ville et les localités peuplées qui relèvent de la même autorité.

[97] Data for Urban agglomeration refer to communes which are administrative division.- Les données pour l'agglomération urbaine se rapportent aux communes qui sont des divisions administrative.

[98] 2001 data refer to municipals with 100 000 + population. Les données de 2001 font référence aux municipalités de plus de 100 000 habitants.

[99] Data to urban areas with 100,000+ residents. — Les données se rapportent aux zones urbaines avec plus de 100 000 résidents.

[100] Capital of Northern Ireland. — Capitale de l'Irlande du Nord.

[101] Capital of Wales for certain purposes. — Considérée à certains égards comme la capitale du pays de Galles.

[102] Capital of Scotland. — Capitale de l'Ecosse.

[103] 'Greater London' conurbation as reconstituted in 1965 and comprising 32 new Greater London Boroughs. — Ensemble urbain du 'Grand Londres', tel qu'il a été reconstitué en 1965, comprenant 32 nouveaux Greater London Boroughs.

[104] For all regions it is not possible to distinguish between 'city proper' and 'urban agglomeration' areas, therefore data has been include under 'city proper'. - Il n'est pas possible de distinguer pour toutes les régions entre 'ville proprement dite' et 'agglomération urbaine', et les données sont donc présentées sous 'ville proprement dite'.

[105] Statistical division, which is a relatively stable area that includes a large buffer around each city to reduce the need to change boundaries as the city grows. - Division statistique, définie comme zone relativement stable comprenant une zone-tampon assez étendue autour de chaque ville, ce qui permet de ne pas avoir à en modifier aussi souvent les limites à mesure que la ville s'étend.

[106] Statistical district, which includes a much smaller buffer and basically just represent the urban area of that city. - District statistique, comprenant une zone-tampon beaucoup plus restreinte, et représentant pour l'essentiel la seule zone urbaine de la ville considérée.

[107] Excludes inland water and oceanic areas. - Exclut les eaux intérieures et les zones océaniques.

[108] A city is a territorial authority which is a distinct entity, is predominantly urban in character, has a minimum population of 50,000 and is a major centre of activity within its parent region. - Une ville est une collectivité territoriale qui constitue une entité distincte, est à prédominance urbaine, compte au moins 50 000 habitants et est un grand centre d'activité dans la région où elle est située.

[109] Urban agglomerations refer to main urban areas that are centres with populations of 30,000 or more. - Les agglomérations urbaines désignent les principales zones urbaines qui sont des centres de population comptant au moins 30 000 habitants.

[110] The Territorial Authority of Dunedin City (3341.53 sq km) includes a large hinterland of rural area. The Dunedin 'Urban Area' (255.13 sq km) is the area of Dunedin City that is urban. - La collectivité territoriale de Dunedin (3 341,53 kilomètres carrés) comprend de vastes étendues rurales. La 'zone urbaine' de Dunedin (255,13 kilomètres carrés) correspond à la zone urbanisée de la ville de Dunedin.

Table 9

Table 9 presents live births and live-birth rates by urban/rural residence for as many years as possible between 2002 and 2006.

Description of variables: Live birth is defined as the complete expulsion or extraction from its mother of a product of conception, irrespective of the duration of pregnancy, which after such separation, breathes or shows any other evidence of life such as beating of the heart, pulsation of the umbilical cord, or definite movements of voluntary muscles, whether or not the umbilical cord has been cut or the placenta is attached; each product of such a birth is considered live-born[1].

Statistics on the number of live births are obtained from civil registers unless otherwise noted. For those countries or areas where civil registration statistics on live births are considered reliable (estimated completeness of 90 per cent or more) the birth rates shown have been calculated on the basis of registered live births. However, for countries or areas where civil registration of live births is non-existent or considered unreliable (estimated completeness of less than 90 per cent or of unknown completeness), estimates provided by national statistical authorities are presented and are identified by the code "|" in the first column.

Rate computation: Crude live-birth rates are the annual number of live births per 1 000 mid-year population.

Rates by urban/rural residence are the annual number of live births, in the appropriate urban or rural category, per 1 000 corresponding mid-year population. Rates are calculated only for data considered complete, that is, coded with a "C" and for estimates, coded "|". These rates are calculated by the Statistics Division of the United Nations based on the appropriate reference population (for example: total population, nationals only etc.) if known and available. If the reference population is not known or unavailable the total population is used to calculate the rates. Therefore, if the population that is used to calculate the rates is different from the correct reference population, the rates presented might under- or overstate the true situation in a country or area.

Rates presented in this table are limited to those countries or areas having a minimum number of 30 live births in a given year.

In addition, some rates were obtained from sample surveys, using different methods[2]; to distinguish them from civil registration data, estimated rates are identified by a footnote.

Reliability of data: Each country or area has been asked to indicate the estimated completeness of the live births recorded in its civil register. These national assessments are indicated by the quality codes (C) and (U) that appear in the first column of this table.

"C" indicates that the data are estimated to be virtually complete, that is, representing at least 90 per cent of the live births occurring each year, while "U" indicates that data are estimated to be incomplete, that is, representing less than 90 per cent of the live births occurring each year. A third code (...) indicates that no information was provided regarding completeness.

Data from civil registers that are reported as incomplete or of unknown completeness (coded "U" or "...") are considered unreliable. They appear in italics in this table and rates are not calculated for these data.

These quality codes apply only to data from civil registers. If data from other sources are presented, the symbol (|) is shown instead of the quality code. For more information about the quality of vital statistics data in general, and the information available on the basis of the completeness estimates in particular, see section 4.2 of the Technical Notes.

Limitations: Statistics on live births are subject to the same qualifications as have been set forth for vital statistics in general and birth statistics in particular as discussed in section 4 of the Technical Notes.

The reliability of data, an indication of which is described above, is an important factor in considering the limitations. In addition, some live births are tabulated by date of registration and not by date of occurrence; these have been indicated by a plus sign "+". Whenever the lag between the date of occurrence and date of registration is prolonged and, therefore, a large proportion of the live-birth registrations are delayed, birth statistics for any given year may be seriously affected.

323

Another factor that limits international comparability is the practice of some countries or areas not to include in live-birth statistics infants who were born alive but died before the registration of the birth or within the first 24 hours of life, thus underestimating the total number of life births. Statistics of this type are footnoted.

In addition, it should be noted that rates are affected also by the quality and limitations of the population estimates that are used in their computation. The problems of under-enumeration or over-enumeration and, to some extent, the differences in definition of total population have been discussed in section 3 of the Technical Notes dealing with population data in general, and specific information pertaining to individual countries or areas is given in the footnotes to table 3.

The rates estimated from the results of sample surveys are subject to possibilities of considerable error as a result of omissions in reporting of births, or as a result of erroneous reporting of births that occurred outside the reference period. However, rates estimated from sample surveys have the advantage of the availability of a built-in and strictly corresponding population base.

It should be emphasized that crude birth rates - like crude death, marriage and divorce rates - may be seriously affected by the age-sex structure of the populations to which they relate. Nevertheless, they do provide a simple measure of the level of and changes in natality.

The urban/rural classification of birth may refer to the residence of mother or the place of delivery, as the national practices vary and is provided by each country or area. In addition, the comparability of data by urban/rural residence is affected by the national definition of urban and rural used in tabulating these data. It is assumed, in the absence of specific information to the contrary, that the definitions of urban and rural used in connection with the national population census were also used in the compilation of the vital statistics for each country or area. However, it cannot be ruled out that, for a given country or area, different definitions of urban and rural are used for the vital statistics data and the population census data respectively. When known, the definitions of urban used in national population census are presented at the end of the technical notes to table 6. As discussed in detail in the technical notes to table 6, these definitions vary considerably from one area or country to another. Urban/rural differentials in vital rates may also be affected by whether the vital events have been tabulated in terms of place of occurrence or place of usual residence. This problem is discussed in more detail in section 4.1.4.1 of the Technical notes.

Earlier data: Live births have been shown in each issue of the *Demographic Yearbook*. Data included in this table update the series covering a period of years as follows:

Issue	Years Covered
Special Edition on Natality, CD, 1999	
- Numbers	1980 - 1999
- Rates	1985 - 1999
Historical Supplement, CD, 1997	1948 – 1997
1992	1983 – 1992
1986	1967 – 1986
1981	1962 – 1981
Historical Supplement, 1979	1948 - 1977

For further information on years covered prior to 1948, readers should consult the Historical Index.

NOTES

[1] *Principles and Recommendations for a Vital Statistics System Revision 2,* Sales No. E. 01.XVII.10, United Nations, New York, 2001.
[2] *Manual X: Indirect Techniques for Demographic Estimation,* United Nations publication, Sales No. E.83.XIII.2, United Nations, New York, 1983.

Tableau 9

Le tableau 9 présente des données sur les naissances vivantes et les taux bruts de natalité selon le lieu de résidence (zone urbaine ou rurale) pour le plus grand nombre d'années possible entre 2002 et 2006.

Description des variables : La naissance vivante est l'expulsion ou l'extraction complète du corps de la mère, indépendamment de la durée de gestation, d'un produit de la conception qui, après cette séparation, respire ou manifeste tout autre signe de vie, tel que battement de cœur, pulsation du cordon ombilical ou contraction effective d'un muscle soumis à l'action de la volonté, que le cordon ombilical ait été coupé ou non et que le placenta soit ou non demeuré attaché ; tout produit d'une telle naissance est considéré comme « enfant né vivant »[1].

Sauf indication contraire, les statistiques relatives au nombre de naissances vivantes sont établies sur la base des registres de l'état civil. Pour les pays ou zones où les statistiques obtenues auprès des services de l'état civil sont jugées sûres (complétude estimée à 90 p. 100 ou plus), les taux de natalité indiqués ont été calculés par la Division de statistique de l'ONU d'après les naissances vivantes enregistrées. En revanche, pour les pays ou zones où les services de l'état civil n'enregistrent pas les naissances vivantes et ceux où l'enregistrement des naissances vivantes est de qualité douteuse (complétude estimée à moins de 90 p. 100 ou degré de complétude inconnu), on a présenté, autant que possible, des taux estimatifs nationaux signalés par le code '|'.

Calcul des taux : Les taux bruts de natalité représentent le nombre annuel de naissances vivantes pour 1 000 habitants au milieu de l'année.

Les taux selon le lieu de résidence (zone urbaine ou rurale) représentent le nombre annuel de naissances vivantes, classées selon la catégorie urbaine ou rurale appropriée pour 1 000 habitants au milieu de l'année. Les taux ont été calculés seulement pour les données considérées complètes, c'est-à-dire celles associées au code 'C'. Ces taux sont calculés par la division de statistique des Nations Unies sur la base de la population de référence adéquate (par exemple : population totale, nationaux seulement, etc.) si connue et disponible. Si la population de référence n'est pas connue ou n'est pas disponible, la population totale est utilisée pour calculer les taux. Par conséquent, si la population utilisée pour calculer les taux est différente de la population de référence adéquate, les taux présentés sont susceptibles de sous ou sur estimer la situation réelle d'un pays ou d'un territoire.

Les taux présentés dans ce tableau se rapportent seulement aux pays ou zones où l'on a enregistré un nombre minimal de 30 naissances vivantes au cours d'une année donnée.

Dans certains cas, les données ont été calculées à partir d'enquêtes par sondage, en utilisant différentes techniques indirectes d'estimation démographique[2]. Pour les distinguer des données qui proviennent des registres de l'état civil, les taux estimatifs ont été signalés par une note.

Fiabilité des données : Il a été demandé à chaque pays ou zone d'indiquer le degré estimatif de complétude des données sur les naissances vivantes figurant dans ses registres d'état civil. Ces évaluations nationales sont signalées par les codes de qualité 'C' et 'U' qui apparaissent dans la deuxième colonne du tableau.

La lettre 'C' indique que les données sont jugées à peu près complètes, c'est-à-dire qu'elles représentent au moins 90 p. 100 des naissances vivantes survenues chaque année ; la lettre 'U' signifie que les données sont jugées incomplètes, c'est-à-dire qu'elles représentent moins de 90 p. 100 des naissances vivantes survenues chaque année. Un troisième code, '...', indique qu'aucun renseignement n'a été communiqué quant à la complétude des données.

Les données provenant des registres de l'état civil qui sont déclarées incomplètes ou dont le degré de complétude n'est pas connu (code 'U' ou '...') sont jugées douteuses. Elles apparaissent en italique dans le tableau. Les taux pour ces données ne sont pas calculés.

Les codes de qualité ne s'appliquent qu'aux données provenant des registres de l'état civil. Si l'on présente des données autres que celles de l'état civil, le signe '|' est utilisé à la place du code de qualité. Pour plus de précisions sur la qualité des données reposant sur les statistiques de l'état civil en général et les estimations de complétude en particulier, voir la section 4.2 des Notes techniques.

Insuffisance des données : Les statistiques concernant les naissances vivantes appellent toutes les réserves qui ont été formulées à propos des statistiques de l'état civil en général et des statistiques des naissances en particulier (voir la section 4 des Notes techniques).

La fiabilité des données, au sujet de laquelle des indications ont été fournies plus haut, est un facteur important. Il faut également tenir compte du fait que, dans certains cas, les données relatives aux naissances vivantes sont exploitées selon la date de l'enregistrement et non selon la date de l'événement ; ces cas ont été signalés par le signe '+'. Chaque fois que le décalage entre l'événement et son enregistrement est grand et qu'une forte proportion des naissances vivantes fait l'objet d'un enregistrement tardif, les statistiques des naissances vivantes pour une année donnée peuvent être considérablement faussées.

Un autre facteur qui nuit à la comparabilité internationale est la pratique de certains pays ou zones qui consiste à ne pas inclure dans les statistiques des naissances vivantes les enfants nés vivants mais décédés avant l'enregistrement de leur naissance ou dans les 24 heures qui ont suivi la naissance, pratique qui conduit à sous-estimer le nombre total de naissances vivantes. Lorsque ce facteur a joué, cela a été signalé en note à la fin du tableau.

La qualité et les limitations des estimations concernant la population ont également une incidence sur le calcul des taux. Les problèmes liés au sur-dénombrement ou au sous-dénombrement et, dans une certaine mesure, aux différences dans la définition de la population totale ont été abordés à la section 3 des Notes techniques relative aux données sur la population en général et des précisions sur certains pays ou zones sont données dans les notes se rapportant au tableau 3.

Les taux estimatifs fondés sur les résultats d'enquêtes par sondage comportent des possibilités d'erreurs considérables dues soit à des omissions dans les déclarations, soit au fait que l'on a déclaré à tort des naissances survenues en réalité hors de la période considérée. Toutefois, les taux estimatifs fondés sur les résultats d'enquêtes par sondage présentent un gros avantage : le chiffre de population utilisé comme base est, par définition, rigoureusement correspondant.

Il faut souligner que les taux bruts de natalité, de même que les taux bruts de mortalité, de nuptialité et de divortialité, peuvent varier très sensiblement selon la structure par âge et par sexe de la population à laquelle ils se rapportent. Ils offrent néanmoins un moyen simple de mesurer le niveau et l'évolution de la natalité.

La classification des naissances selon le lieu de résidence (zone urbaine ou rurale) peut se rapporter au lieu de résidence de la mère ou au lieu d'occurrence et correspond à celle indiquée par chaque pays ou zone. En outre, la comparabilité des données selon le lieu de résidence (zone urbaine ou rurale) peut être limitée par les définitions nationales des termes « urbain » et « rural » utilisées pour la mise en tableaux de ces données. En l'absence d'indications contraires, on a supposé que les mêmes définitions avaient servi pour le recensement national de la population et pour l'établissement des statistiques de l'état civil pour chaque pays ou zone. Toutefois, il n'est pas exclu que, pour une zone ou un pays donné, des définitions différentes aient été retenues. Les définitions du terme « urbain » utilisées pour les recensements nationaux de population ont été présentées à la fin des notes techniques du tableau 6 lorsqu'elles étaient connues. Comme on l'a précisé dans les notes techniques relatives au tableau 6, ces définitions varient considérablement d'un pays ou d'une zone à l'autre. La différence entre ces taux pour les zones urbaines et rurales pourra aussi être faussée selon que les faits d'état civil auront été classés d'après le lieu de l'événement ou le lieu de résidence habituel. Ce problème est examiné plus en détail à la section 4.1.4.1 des Notes techniques.

Données publiées antérieurement : Les différentes éditions de l'*Annuaire démographique* contiennent des données sur les naissances vivantes. Les données qui figurent dans le tableau 9 actualisent les données qui portaient sur les périodes suivantes :

Éditions	Années considérées
Édition spéciale sur les statistiques de la natalité (CD-ROM), 1999	
- Nombre	1980 – 1999

- Taux	1985 – 1999
Supplément historique (CD-ROM), 1997	1948 – 1997
1992	1983 – 1992
1986	1967 – 1986
1981	1962 – 1981
Supplément rétrospectif, 1979	1948 – 1977

Pour plus de détails concernant les années antérieures à 1948, se reporter à l'index historique.

NOTES

[1] *Principes et recommandations pour un système de statistique de l'état civil, deuxième révision,* numéro de vente : F.01.XVII.10, publication des Nations Unies, New York, 2003.
[2] *Manuel X, techniques indirectes d'estimation démographique,* numéro de vente : F.83.XIII.2, publication des Nations Unies, New York, 1984.

9. Live births and crude birth rates, by urban/rural residence: 2002 - 2006
Naissances vivantes et taux bruts de natalité selon la résidence, urbaine/rurale: 2002 - 2006

Continent, country or area, and urban/rural residence / Continent, pays ou zone et résidence, urbaine/rurale	Co- de[a]	Number - Nombre					Rate - Taux				
		2002	2003	2004	2005	2006	2002	2003	2004	2005	2006
AFRICA - AFRIQUE											
Algeria - Algérie[1]											
Total	C	616 963	649 000	669 000	703 000	739 000	19.7	20.4	20.7	21.4	22.1
Cape Verde - Cap-Vert											
Total	C	13 123	13 334	...	...	...	29.0	28.9	...	...	...
Congo[2]											
Total	+U	40 708	44 132	44 473	...	...	...	...	...	...	...
Egypt - Égypte											
Total	C	1 766 589	1 777 418	1 779 500	1 800 972	1 853 746	26.5	26.2	25.7	25.5	25.7
Urban - Urbaine	C	769 122	769 791	712 431	723 044	740 228	26.9	26.4	24.0	24.0	24.1
Rural - Rurale	C	997 467	1 007 627	1 067 069	1 077 928	1 113 518	26.2	25.9	26.9	26.6	27.0
Kenya											
Total	U	494 941	495 433	...	...	...	...	...	...	...	...
Libyan Arab Jamahiriya - Jamahiriya arabe libyenne											
Total	C	111 053	...	...	...	...	20.2	...	...	...	...
Malawi											
Total[3]	I	567 241	578 978	...	...	...	50.8	50.1	...	...	...
Total	U	...	...	...	...	614 410	...	...	...	...	...
Mauritius - Maurice											
Total	+C	19 983	19 343	19 230	18 820	17 604	16.5	15.8	15.6	15.1	14.1
Urban - Urbaine	+C	7 930	7 580	7 268	7 115	6 691	15.4	14.6	13.9	13.6	12.7
Rural - Rurale	+C	12 053	11 763	11 962	11 705	10 913	17.3	16.7	16.8	16.3	15.0
Mayotte											
Total	C	7 128	7 197	7 452	...	...	44.5	...	...	...	...
Urban - Urbaine	C	4 480	...	...	...	...	...	...	...	...	...
Rural - Rurale	C	2 648	...	...	...	...	...	...	...	...	...
Réunion[4]											
Total	C	14 789	14 427	14 545	*14 799	*14 495	19.8	18.9	18.9	*19.0	*18.5
Saint Helena ex. dep. - Sainte-Hélène sans dép.											
Total	C	39	37	34	34	...	...	...	...	...	...
Seychelles											
Total	+C	1 481	1 498	1 435	1 536	1 467	17.7	18.1	17.4	18.5	17.3
South Africa - Afrique du Sud											
Total	U	899 286	875 748	897 514	848 043	...	...	...	...	...	...
Zambia - Zambie[3]											
Total	I	...	...	...	...	509 766	...	...	...	...	43.2
AMERICA, NORTH - AMÉRIQUE DU NORD											
Anguilla											
Total	+C	169	139	164	167	*183	14.2	11.4	13.1	12.2	*12.8
Aruba											
Total	C	1 228	1 244	1 193	1 234	1 227	13.2	13.1	12.2	12.3	11.9
Bahamas											
Total	U	...	5 054	...	...	...	...	...	...	...	...
Barbados - Barbade											
Total	+C	*3 812	...	...	...	...	*14.1	...	...	...	...
Belize											
Total	U	7 553	7 440	8 083	8 396	...	...	...	...	...	...
Bermuda - Bermudes[5]											
Total	C	830	834	831	835	798	13.2	13.2	13.1	13.1	12.5
British Virgin Islands - Îles Vierges britanniques											
Total	C	253	269	318	...	...	12.1	12.6	14.7	...	...
Canada[6]											
Total	C	328 802	335 202	337 422	342 176	*350 181	10.5	10.6	10.5	10.6	*10.7
Cayman Islands - Îles Caïmanes											
Total	C	583	623	611	699	710	13.7	14.3	13.8	14.5	13.7
Costa Rica											
Total	C	71 144	72 938	72 247	71 548	71 291	17.8	17.8	17.3	16.8	16.4
Urban - Urbaine	C	...	...	31 203	30 602	...	...	...	12.7	12.2	...
Rural - Rurale	C	...	...	41 044	40 946	...	...	...	24.0	23.4	...

9. Live births and crude birth rates, by urban/rural residence: 2002 - 2006
Naissances vivantes et taux bruts de natalité selon la résidence, urbaine/rurale: 2002 - 2006 (continued - suite)

Continent, country or area, and urban/rural residence / Continent, pays ou zone et résidence, urbaine/rurale	Co-de[a]	Number - Nombre					Rate - Taux				
		2002	2003	2004	2005	2006	2002	2003	2004	2005	2006
AMERICA, NORTH - AMÉRIQUE DU NORD											
Cuba											
Total	C	141 276	136 795	127 192	120 716	111 323	12.6	12.2	11.3	10.7	9.9
Urban - Urbaine	C	103 994	100 429	92 129	88 922	83 389	12.3	11.8	10.8	10.5	9.8
Rural - Rurale	C	37 282	36 366	35 063	31 794	27 934	13.8	13.4	12.8	11.6	10.2
Dominica - Dominique											
Total	+C	1 081	...	...	...	...	15.4	...	...	...	...
Dominican Republic - République dominicaine											
Total	+U	*203 228*	*209 069*	*198 304*	*183 819*	...	...	...	...	...	...
Urban - Urbaine[7]	+U	*147 553*	*148 907*	*133 802*	*128 936*	...	...	...	...	...	...
Rural - Rurale[7]	+U	*50 752*	*51 371*	*56 306*	*46 634*	...	...	...	...	...	...
El Salvador											
Total	C	129 363	124 476	119 710	112 769	107 111	19.8	18.8	17.7	16.4	15.3
Urban - Urbaine	C	77 779	73 311	71 430	69 236	70 810	20.2	18.6	17.8	16.9	16.9
Rural - Rurale	C	51 584	51 165	48 280	43 533	36 301	19.3	18.9	17.6	15.7	13.0
Greenland - Groenland											
Total	C	940	895	893	887	842	16.6	15.8	15.7	15.6	14.8
Urban - Urbaine	C	745	717	...	...	...	16.0	15.3	...	...	...
Rural - Rurale	C	195	178	...	...	...	19.2	17.8	...	...	...
Guadeloupe[4]											
Total	C	6 995	7 047	7 273	7 551	7 193	16.0	16.1	16.4	16.9	15.7
Guatemala											
Total	C	387 287	375 092	383 704	374 066	368 399	32.3	31.0	31.0	29.5	28.3
Urban - Urbaine	C	...	...	...	160 158	158 159	...	...	...	...	...
Rural - Rurale	C	...	...	...	213 908	210 240	...	...	...	...	...
Honduras											
Total	+U	*216 145*	*218 173*	*220 040*	*221 759*	*222 512*	...	...	...	...	...
Urban - Urbaine	+U	*93 370*	*95 182*	*96 862*	*98 408*	*99 818*	...	...	...	...	...
Rural - Rurale	+U	*122 775*	*122 991*	*123 178*	*123 351*	*122 694*	...	...	...	...	...
Jamaica - Jamaïque[8]											
Total	C	48 627	47 110	47 127	47 255	46 277	18.6	17.9	17.9	17.8	17.4
Martinique[4]											
Total	C	5 446	5 430	5 255	5 032	5 370	14.0	13.9	13.3	12.7	13.4
Mexico - Mexique[9]											
Total	+U	*2 209 308*	*2 165 318*	*2 154 927*	*2 567 906*	...	...	...	...	...	...
Urban - Urbaine[7]	+U	*1 613 460*	*1 564 908*	*1 575 037*	*1 776 726*	...	...	...	...	...	...
Rural - Rurale[7]	+U	*556 615*	*550 595*	*531 186*	*643 618*	...	...	...	...	...	...
Netherlands Antilles - Antilles néerlandaises[10]											
Total	C	2 442	2 488	2 357	2 553	2 578	14.0	13.9	12.9	13.8	13.6
Nicaragua											
Total	+U	*121 361*	*120 784*	*121 402*	*121 380*	...	...	...	...	...	...
Urban - Urbaine	+U	*65 465*	*63 105*	*62 412*	*62 960*	...	...	...	...	...	...
Rural - Rurale	+U	*55 896*	*57 679*	*58 990*	*58 420*	...	...	...	...	...	...
Panama											
Total	C	61 671	61 753	62 743	63 645	65 764	20.2	19.8	19.8	19.7	20.0
Urban - Urbaine	C	38 167	38 568	38 797	38 902	40 113	...	...	...	19.0	19.2
Rural - Rurale	C	23 504	23 185	23 946	24 743	25 651	...	...	...	21.0	21.6
Puerto Rico - Porto Rico											
Total	C	52 871	50 803	51 239	50 687	...	13.7	13.1	13.2	13.0	...
Urban - Urbaine[7]	C	...	26 642	26 866	27 809	...	...	...	...	...	...
Rural - Rurale[7]	C	...	24 151	24 355	22 867	...	...	...	...	...	...
Saint Lucia - Sainte-Lucie											
Total	C	2 598	2 486	2 322	*2 298	...	16.3	15.5	14.3	*13.9	...
Saint Vincent and the Grenadines - Saint Vincent-et-les Grenadines											
Total	+C	1 985	1 923	1 804	1 779	...	18.4	18.3	17.3	17.1	...
Trinidad and Tobago - Trinité-et-Tobago											
Total	C	16 990	...	...	...	...	13.3	...	...	...	...
Turks Caicos Islands - Îles Turques et Caïques											
Total	C	153	213	300	318	409	7.3	8.5	10.9	10.4	12.3
United States - États-Unis											
Total	C	4 021 726	4 089 950	4 112 052	4 138 349	*4 265 996	14.0	14.1	14.0	14.0	*14.2

9. Live births and crude birth rates, by urban/rural residence: 2002 - 2006
Naissances vivantes et taux bruts de natalité selon la résidence, urbaine/rurale: 2002 - 2006 (continued - suite)

Continent, country or area, and urban/rural residence / Continent, pays ou zone et résidence, urbaine/rurale	I. B. de[a]	Number - Nombre					Rate - Taux				
		2002	2003	2004	2005	2006	2002	2003	2004	2005	2006
AMERICA, NORTH - **AMÉRIQUE DU NORD**											
United States Virgin Islands - Îles Vierges américaines											
Total....................	C	1 634	1 522	1 574	1 599	...	15.0	14.0	14.4	14.7	...
AMERICA, SOUTH - **AMÉRIQUE DU SUD**											
Argentina - Argentine											
Total....................	C	694 684	697 952	736 261	712 220	...	18.5	18.4	19.3	18.5	...
Total....................	+C	...	...	...	...	696 451	...	...	...	...	17.9
Bolivia - Bolivie											
Total....................	U	208 693	184 179	149 094	113 170	...	...	...	...	...	...
Brazil - Brésil[11]											
Total....................	U	2 581 055	2 822 462	2 813 704	2 874 542	2 798 964	...	...	...	...	...
Chile - Chili											
Total....................	C	238 981	234 486	230 352	230 831	...	15.3	14.9	14.3	14.2	...
Urban - Urbaine	C	213 171	209 572	204 612	205 297	...	15.9	15.4	14.7	14.5	...
Rural - Rurale	C	25 810	24 914	25 740	25 534	...	11.8	11.5	12.1	11.9	...
Colombia - Colombie											
Total....................	U	700 455	710 702	723 099	719 968	*711 457	...	...	...	...	...
Urban - Urbaine[7]	U	539 729	546 406	554 045	554 388	*553 077	...	...	...	...	...
Rural - Rurale[7]	U	148 599	149 345	154 369	152 392	*147 090	...	...	...	...	...
Ecuador - Équateur[12]											
Total....................	U	183 792	178 549	168 893	168 324	185 056	...	...	...	...	...
Urban - Urbaine	U	143 377	137 189	132 618	131 539		...	...	...	...	...
Rural - Rurale	U	40 415	41 360	36 275	36 785	...	...	...	...	...	...
Falkland Islands (Malvinas) - Îles Falkland (Malvinas)											
Total....................	+C	30	34	44	18	27	...	...	...	...	...
French Guiana - Guyane française[4]											
Total....................	C	5 249	5 553	5 312	5 998	6 276	29.9	30.7	28.4	30.0	31.9
Paraguay											
Total....................	U	...	45 669	49 857	51 444	...	...	...	...	...	...
Peru - Pérou[13]											
Total....................	+U	355 870	373 600	344 804	...	...	...	...	...	...	...
Suriname											
Total....................	C	10 188	9 634	9 062	8 657	...	21.4	20.0	18.6	17.4	...
Urban - Urbaine[14]........	C	6 298[7]	6 053	5 632	5 427	...	...	...	...	...	...
Rural - Rurale[14]..........	C	3 670[7]	3 581	3 430	3 230	...	...	...	...	...	...
Uruguay											
Total....................	C	51 953	50 631	50 052	46 944	47 410	15.7	15.3	15.2	14.2	14.3
Venezuela (Bolivarian Republic of) - Venezuela (République bolivarienne du)[11]											
Total....................	C	492 678	555 614	637 799	665 997	646 225	19.5	21.6	24.4	25.1	23.9
ASIA - ASIE											
Armenia - Arménie[15]											
Total....................	C	32 229	35 793	37 520	37 499	37 639[16]	10.0	11.1	11.7	11.7	11.7
Urban - Urbaine	C	20 804	22 629	23 628	23 762	23 793[16]	10.1	11.0	11.5	11.5	11.5
Rural - Rurale	C	11 425	13 164	13 892	13 737	13 846[16]	10.0	11.5	12.1	11.9	12.0
Azerbaijan - Azerbaïdjan[15]											
Total....................	+C	110 715	113 467	131 609	141 901	148 946	13.5	13.8	15.8	16.9	17.6
Urban - Urbaine	+C	49 733	51 057	59 026	...	...	12.0	12.0	13.8	...	...
Rural - Rurale	+C	60 982	62 410	72 583	...	...	15.1	15.6	18.0	...	...
Bahrain - Bahreïn											
Total....................	C	13 576	14 560	14 968	15 198	15 053	20.2	21.1	21.2	21.0	20.3

9. Live births and crude birth rates, by urban/rural residence: 2002 - 2006
Naissances vivantes et taux bruts de natalité selon la résidence, urbaine/rurale: 2002 - 2006 (continued - suite)

Continent, country or area, and urban/rural residence / Continent, pays ou zone et résidence, urbaine/rurale	Code[a]	Number - Nombre					Rate - Taux				
		2002	2003	2004	2005	2006	2002	2003	2004	2005	2006

ASIA - ASIE

Bangladesh[17]											
Total	I	...	...	...	...	...	20.1	20.9	20.8	20.7	20.6
Urban - Urbaine	I	...	...	...	...	...	16.6	17.9	17.8	17.8	17.5
Rural - Rurale	I	...	...	...	...	...	21.0	21.7	21.6	21.7	21.7
Bhutan - Bhoutan[18]											
Total	I	...	...	...	12 538	...	...	...	...	19.7	...
Urban - Urbaine	I	...	...	...	3 845	...	...	...	...	...	...
Rural - Rurale	I	...	...	...	8 693	...	...	...	...	...	...
Brunei Darussalam - Brunéi Darussalam											
Total	+C	7 464	7 047	7 163	*6 933	...	21.7	20.2	19.9	*18.7	...
Cambodia - Cambodge											
Total	U	367 569	375 799	384 267	...	...	...	...	...	...	...
China - Chine[19]											
Total	I	16 470 000[20]	15 990 000[20]	15 930 000[20]	16 170 000[21]	...	12.9	12.4	12.3	12.4	12.1[20]
China: Hong Kong SAR - Chine: Hong Kong RAS											
Total	C	48 209	46 965	49 796	57 098	65 626	7.1	7.0	7.3	8.4	9.6
China: Macao SAR - Chine: Macao RAS											
Total	C	3 162	3 212	3 308	3 671	4 058	7.2	7.2	7.3	7.8	8.1
Cyprus - Chypre[22]											
Total	C	7 883	8 088	8 309	8 243	8 731	11.1	11.2	11.3	10.9	11.3
Urban - Urbaine[7]	C	4 806	4 854	5 366	5 672	5 184	...	...	...	...	...
Rural - Rurale[7]	C	2 637	2 692	2 863	2 512	2 875	...	...	...	...	...
Georgia - Géorgie[15]											
Total	C	46 605	46 194	49 572	46 512	47 795	10.7	10.7	11.5	10.7	10.9
Urban - Urbaine	C	...	34 589	...	...	...	...	15.3	...	...	...
Rural - Rurale	C	...	11 605	...	...	...	...	5.6	...	...	...
India - Inde[23]											
Total	I	...	...	...	...	...	25.0	24.8	24.1	23.8	23.5
Urban - Urbaine	I	...	...	...	...	...	20.0	19.8	19.0	19.1	18.8
Rural - Rurale	I	...	...	...	...	...	26.6	26.4	25.9	25.6	25.2
Iran (Islamic Republic of) - Iran (République islamique d')[24]											
Total	C	1 122 104	1 171 573	1 154 368	1 233 873	1 253 506	17.1	17.6	17.1	18.0	17.8
Urban - Urbaine	C	734 332	768 845	759 162	815 445	844 813	17.1	17.5	17.2	17.9	...
Rural - Rurale	C	387 772	402 728	395 206	418 428	408 693	17.2	17.8	17.0	18.3	...
Iraq											
Total	U	...	*691 269	*840 257	*896 340	...	...	...	...	...	...
Israel - Israël[25]											
Total	C	139 535	144 936	145 207	143 913	148 170	21.2	21.7	21.3	20.8	21.0
Urban - Urbaine[7]	C	126 795	131 658	131 794	130 294	133 924	21.1	21.5	21.2	20.5	20.7
Rural - Rurale[7]	C	12 738	13 272	13 404	13 517	14 084	23.1	23.4	23.0	23.7	24.5
Japan - Japon[26]											
Total	C	1 153 855	1 123 610	1 110 721	1 062 530	1 092 674	9.2	8.9	8.8	8.4	8.7
Urban - Urbaine[7]	C	939 091	917 627	916 299	917 831	984 329	...	...	...	...	...
Rural - Rurale[7]	C	214 569	205 813	194 246	144 529	108 169	...	...	...	...	...
Jordan - Jordanie[27]											
Total	C	146 077	148 294	150 248	152 276	162 972	29.0	28.7	28.4	28.1	29.4
Kazakhstan[15]											
Total	C	227 171	247 946	273 028	278 977	301 756	15.3	16.6	18.2	18.4	19.7
Urban - Urbaine	C	122 151	138 680	155 997	163 952	175 582	14.5	16.3	18.2	18.9	20.0
Rural - Rurale	C	105 020	109 266	117 031	115 025	126 174	16.4	17.0	18.2	17.7	19.3
Korea (Republic of) - Corée (République de)[28]											
Total[29]	C	494 625	493 471	476 052	438 062	451 514	10.3	10.2	9.8	9.0	9.2
Urban - Urbaine	C	402 385	400 980	388 402	357 588	371 084	10.5	10.4	10.0	9.2	9.4
Rural - Rurale	C	89 660	86 525	84 303	77 406	77 020	9.0	8.8	8.7	8.0	8.2
Kuwait - Koweït											
Total	C	43 490	43 982	47 274	50 941	52 759	19.2	18.9	19.8	20.7	...
Kyrgyzstan - Kirghizistan											
Total	C	101 012	105 490	109 939	109 839	120 737	20.2	20.9	21.6	21.4	23.3
Urban - Urbaine	C	30 195	31 866	37 381	35 600	39 414	17.1	17.8	20.6	19.4	21.4
Rural - Rurale	C	70 817	73 624	72 558	74 239	81 323	21.9	22.6	22.1	22.4	24.3

9. Live births and crude birth rates, by urban/rural residence: 2002 - 2006
Naissances vivantes et taux bruts de natalité selon la résidence, urbaine/rurale: 2002 - 2006 (continued - suite)

Continent, country or area, and urban/rural residence / Continent, pays ou zone et résidence, urbaine/rurale	Code[a]	Number - Nombre					Rate - Taux				
		2002	2003	2004	2005	2006	2002	2003	2004	2005	2006
ASIA - ASIE											
Lebanon - Liban											
Total	C	76 405	71 702	73 900	73 973	72 790	...	...	19.7	...	...
Malaysia - Malaisie											
Total	C	484 037	480 083	477 768	*466 208	*482 700	19.7	19.2	18.7	*17.8	*18.1
Maldives											
Total	C	5 003	5 157	5 220	5 543	5 829	17.8	18.1	18.0	18.9	19.5
Urban - Urbaine	C	1 878	1 966	2 145	2 457	2 707	24.4	25.1	27.0	...	...
Rural - Rurale	C	3 125	3 191	3 075	3 086	3 122	15.3	15.4	14.6	...	...
Mongolia - Mongolie											
Total	C	46 922	45 723	45 501	45 326	49 092	19.1	18.4	18.1	17.8	19.0
Urban - Urbaine	C	24 067	24 315	25 812	26 462	29 717	17.1	16.9	17.4	17.4	19.0
Rural - Rurale	C	22 855	21 408	19 689	18 864	19 375	21.8	20.4	19.0	18.4	19.0
Myanmar											
Total	U	753 989	685 443	791 600	836 124		...	...	...	...	...
Urban - Urbaine	U	240 539	228 981	228 680	233 307		...	...	...	...	...
Rural - Rurale	U	513 450	456 462	562 920	602 817		...	...	...	...	...
Occupied Palestinian Territory - Territoire palestinien occupé											
Total	U	106 511	106 355	111 245	109 439	108 874	...	...	...	...	...
Oman[30]											
Total	U	40 222	40 062	40 584	42 065	44 116	...	...	...	...	...
Pakistan[31]											
Total	I	...	3 683 290[32]	...	3 772 494[33]	...	...	25.0	...	24.6	...
Urban - Urbaine	I	...	1 194 081[32]	...	1 226 151[33]	...	...	...	...	...	...
Rural - Rurale	I	...	2 489 209[32]	...	2 546 343[33]	...	...	...	...	...	...
Philippines											
Total	C	1 666 773	1 669 442	1 710 994	...	...	21.0	20.6	20.7	...	...
Qatar											
Total	C	12 200	12 856	13 190	13 401	14 120	17.9	17.9	17.4	16.8	15.1
Saudi Arabia - Arabie saoudite											
Total	...	560 746	567 433	574 211	582 582	589 223	...	...	...	...	...
Singapore - Singapour											
Total	C	40 760	37 485	37 174	37 492	38 317	9.8	9.0	8.8	8.6	8.5
Sri Lanka											
Total	+C	*363 549	*363 343	*360 220	*370 424	...	*19.1	*18.9	*18.5	*18.8	...
Syrian Arab Republic - République arabe syrienne[34]											
Total	U	574 918	609 774	598 221	634 170	656 599	...	...	...	...	...
Tajikistan - Tadjikistan[35]											
Total	I	175 599	177 938	179 600	180 800	186 500	27.3	27.1	26.8	26.4	26.7
Urban - Urbaine	I	42 823	45 182	...	...	...	25.1	26.0	...	...	...
Rural - Rurale	I	132 776	132 756	...	...	...	28.0	27.5	...	...	...
Thailand - Thaïlande											
Total	+U	782 911	742 183	813 069	809 485		...	...	...	...	...
Turkey - Turquie[36]											
Total	I	1 362 000	1 361 000	1 360 000	1 361 000	1 362 000	19.7	19.4	19.1	18.9	18.7
United Arab Emirates - Émirats arabes unis											
Total	...	58 070	61 165	63 113	64 623	62 969	...	...	...	...	...
Yemen - Yémen											
Total	U	189 341	130 112	153 945	152 792		...	...	...	...	...
EUROPE											
Åland Islands - Îles d'Åland[37]											
Total	C	269	262	281	268	295	10.3	10.0	10.6	10.1	11.0
Urban - Urbaine	C	113	102	122	94	113	10.6	9.6	11.4	8.7	10.5
Rural - Rurale	C	156	160	159	174	182	10.1	10.2	10.1	10.9	11.3
Albania - Albanie											
Total	C	45 515	47 012	43 022	39 612	34 229	14.7	15.1	13.8	12.6	10.9
Urban - Urbaine	C	19 450	19 447	18 859	...	...	14.4	14.1	13.4	...	...
Rural - Rurale	C	26 065	27 565	24 163	...	...	14.9	15.9	14.0	...	...

9. Live births and crude birth rates, by urban/rural residence: 2002 - 2006
Naissances vivantes et taux bruts de natalité selon la résidence, urbaine/rurale: 2002 - 2006 (continued - suite)

Continent, country or area, and urban/rural residence / Continent, pays ou zone et résidence, urbaine/rurale	Code[a]	Number - Nombre					Rate - Taux				
		2002	2003	2004	2005	2006	2002	2003	2004	2005	2006
EUROPE											
Andorra - Andorre											
Total	C	749	721	814	828	843	10.7	9.7	10.5	10.4	10.3
Austria - Autriche											
Total	C	78 399	76 944	78 968	78 190	77 914	9.7	9.5	9.7	9.5	9.4
Belarus - Bélarus[15]											
Total	C	88 743	88 512	88 943	90 508	96 721	8.9	9.0	9.1	9.3	9.9
Urban - Urbaine	C	65 091	64 814	65 038	66 259	71 186	9.3	9.2	9.2	9.4	10.1
Rural - Rurale	C	23 652	23 698	23 905	24 249	25 535	8.2	8.4	8.6	8.9	9.6
Belgium - Belgique[38]											
Total	C	111 225	112 591	116 048	117 799	121 382	10.8	10.9	11.1	11.2	11.5
Bosnia and Herzegovina - Bosnie-Herzégovine											
Total	C	35 587	35 234	35 151	34 627	34 033	9.3	9.2	9.1	9.0	8.9
Bulgaria - Bulgarie											
Total	C	66 499	67 359	69 886	71 075	73 978	8.5	8.6	9.0	9.2	9.6
Urban - Urbaine	C	47 779	48 597	50 390	52 280	55 043	8.7	8.9	9.3	9.6	10.1
Rural - Rurale	C	18 720	18 762	19 496	18 795	18 935	7.8	7.9	8.3	8.1	8.3
Channel Islands: Guernsey - Îles Anglo-Normandes: Guernesey											
Total	C	549	650	586	638	598	...	...	9.7	...	9.8
Channel Islands: Jersey - Îles Anglo-Normandes: Jersey											
Total	+C	930	1 005	971	969	950	10.6	11.5	11.1	11.0	10.7
Croatia - Croatie											
Total	C	40 094	39 668	40 307	42 492	41 446	9.0	8.9	9.1	9.6	9.3
Urban - Urbaine	C	22 539	21 837	22 420	23 421	23 085	...	...	...	...	...
Rural - Rurale	C	17 555	17 831	17 887	19 071	18 361	...	...	...	...	...
Czech Republic - République tchèque											
Total	C	97 878	93 685	97 664	102 211	105 831	9.6	9.2	9.6	10.0	10.3
Urban - Urbaine	C	73 482	69 120	72 231	75 719	78 561	9.8	9.2	9.6	10.0	10.4
Rural - Rurale	C	24 396	24 565	25 433	26 492	27 270	9.2	9.2	9.5	9.9	10.1
Denmark - Danemark[39]											
Total	C	64 075	64 599	64 609	64 282	64 984	11.9	12.0	12.0	11.9	12.0
Estonia - Estonie											
Total	C	13 001	13 036	13 992	14 350	14 877	9.6	9.6	10.4	10.7	11.1
Urban - Urbaine	C	8 840	9 049	9 892	10 233	10 554	9.4	9.7	10.6	11.0	11.3
Rural - Rurale	C	4 161	3 987	4 100	4 117	4 323	10.0	9.6	9.9	10.0	10.5
Faeroe Islands - Îles Féroé											
Total	C	709	705	713	712	661	15.0	14.7	14.8	14.8	13.7
Finland - Finlande[40]											
Total	C	55 555	56 630	57 758	57 745	58 840	10.7	10.9	11.0	11.0	11.2
Urban - Urbaine	C	36 263	37 303	37 816	38 181	39 003	11.3	11.5	11.7	11.6	11.8
Rural - Rurale	C	19 292	19 327	19 942	19 564	19 837	9.7	9.8	10.1	10.0	10.2
France[41]											
Total	C	761 630	761 464	767 816	774 355	796 896	12.7	12.6	12.7	12.7	13.0
Urban - Urbaine[42]	C	577 724	574 477	578 024	581 681	596 949	...	...	...	...	...
Rural - Rurale[42]	C	182 454	185 572	188 475	191 223	198 494	...	...	...	...	...
Germany - Allemagne											
Total	C	719 250	706 721	705 622	685 795	672 724	8.7	8.6	8.6	8.3	8.2
Gibraltar[43]											
Total	+C	371	372	421	418	373	13.0	13.0	14.7	14.5	12.8
Greece - Grèce											
Total	C	103 030	104 420	106 666	107 545	112 042	9.5	9.5	9.6	9.7	10.0
Urban - Urbaine	C	...	...	...	73 816	76 996	...	...	...	...	...
Rural - Rurale	C	...	...	...	33 729	35 046	...	...	...	...	...
Hungary - Hongrie											
Total	C	96 804	94 647	95 137	97 496	99 871	9.5	9.3	9.4	9.7	9.9
Urban - Urbaine[44]	C	60 753	59 280	60 331	63 785	66 223	9.2	9.0	9.2	9.6	9.8
Rural - Rurale[44]	C	35 248	34 465	33 983	32 860	32 789	9.9	9.7	9.6	9.6	9.9
Iceland - Islande											
Total	C	4 049	4 143	4 234	4 280	4 415	14.1	14.3	14.5	14.5	14.5
Urban - Urbaine	C	3 823	3 906	...	4 054	4 204	14.4	14.6	...	14.7	14.9
Rural - Rurale	C	226	237	...	226	211	10.5	11.1	...	10.8	9.4

9. Live births and crude birth rates, by urban/rural residence: 2002 - 2006
Naissances vivantes et taux bruts de natalité selon la résidence, urbaine/rurale: 2002 - 2006 (continued - suite)

Continent, country or area, and urban/rural residence / Continent, pays ou zone et résidence, urbaine/rurale	Code[a]	Number - Nombre					Rate - Taux				
		2002	2003	2004	2005	2006	2002	2003	2004	2005	2006
EUROPE											
Ireland - Irlande											
Total	C	60 503	61 529	61 972	...	...	15.4	15.5	15.3	...	...
Total[45]	+C	...	...	...	*61 042	*64 237	...	...	...	*14.8	*15.2
Isle of Man - Îles de Man											
Total	+C	903	860	862	901	905	11.7	11.1	11.1	11.6	11.3
Italy - Italie											
Total	C	538 198	544 063	562 599	554 022	560 010	9.4	9.4	9.7	9.5	9.5
Latvia - Lettonie											
Total	C	20 044	21 006	20 334	21 497	22 264	8.6	9.0	8.8	9.3	9.7
Urban - Urbaine	C	12 938	13 891	13 820	14 591	15 342	8.2	8.8	8.8	9.3	9.9
Rural - Rurale	C	7 106	7 115	6 514	6 906	6 922	9.4	9.5	8.8	9.4	9.4
Liechtenstein											
Total	C	395	347	372	381	*361	11.7	10.2	10.8	11.0	*10.3
Lithuania - Lituanie											
Total	C	30 014	30 598	30 419	30 541	31 265	8.7	8.9	8.9	8.9	9.2
Urban - Urbaine	C	18 697	19 140	19 464	19 914	20 691	8.1	8.3	8.5	8.8	9.1
Rural - Rurale	C	11 317	11 458	10 955	10 627	10 574	9.9	10.0	9.6	9.3	9.4
Luxembourg											
Total	C	5 345	5 303	5 452	5 371	5 514	12.0	11.7	11.9	11.5	11.7
Malta - Malte											
Total	C	3 918	4 050	3 887	3 858	3 885	10.1	10.2	9.7	9.6	9.6
Moldova[46]											
Total	C	35 705	36 471	38 272	37 695	37 587	9.9	10.1	10.6	10.5	10.5
Urban - Urbaine	C	12 747	12 788	14 060	13 583	13 579	8.6	8.6	9.5	9.2	9.2
Rural - Rurale	C	22 958	23 683	24 212	24 112	24 008	10.7	11.1	11.4	11.4	11.4
Monaco											
Total	C	771	842	825	894	880[47]	...	...	...	...	...
Montenegro											
Total	C	8 499	8 342	7 848	7 352	7 531	13.8	13.4	12.6	11.8	...
Urban - Urbaine	C	...	6 328	6 144	5 786	...	...	16.4	15.9	14.8	...
Rural - Rurale	C	...	2 014	1 704	1 566	...	...	8.6	7.3	6.7	...
Netherlands - Pays-Bas[48]											
Total	C	202 083	200 297	194 007	187 910	185 057	12.5	12.3	11.9	11.5	11.3
Urban - Urbaine	C	132 825	132 805	130 945	128 609	126 775	12.7	12.6	12.3	11.9	11.7
Rural - Rurale	C	69 258	67 492	63 062	59 301	58 282	12.2	11.9	11.3	10.7	10.5
Norway - Norvège[49]											
Total	C	55 434	56 458	56 951	56 756	58 545	12.2	12.4	12.4	12.3	12.6
Poland - Pologne											
Total	C	353 765	351 072	356 131	364 383	374 244	9.3	9.2	9.3	9.5	9.8
Urban - Urbaine	C	197 434	199 583	204 898	211 200	218 000	8.4	8.5	8.7	9.0	9.3
Rural - Rurale	C	156 331	151 489	151 233	153 183	156 244	10.7	10.3	10.3	10.4	10.6
Portugal[50]											
Total	C	114 383	112 515	109 298	109 399	105 449	11.0	10.8	10.4	10.4	10.0
Romania - Roumanie											
Total	C	210 529	212 459	216 261	221 020	219 483	9.7	9.8	10.0	10.2	10.2
Urban - Urbaine	C	98 190	100 915	111 348	117 780	119 477	8.5	8.7	9.4	9.9	10.0
Rural - Rurale	C	112 339	111 544	104 913	103 240	100 006	11.0	11.0	10.7	10.6	10.3
Russian Federation - Fédération de Russie[15]											
Total	C	1 396 967	1 477 301	1 502 477	1 457 376	1 479 637	9.6	10.2	10.4	10.2	10.4
Urban - Urbaine	C	998 056	1 050 565	1 074 247	1 036 870	1 044 540	9.4	9.9	10.2	9.9	10.0
Rural - Rurale	C	398 911	426 736	428 230	420 506	435 097	10.3	11.1	11.1	10.9	11.3
San Marino - Saint-Marin											
Total	+C	295	300	306	284	302	10.4	10.3	10.4	9.2	9.6
Serbia - Serbie[51]											
Total	+C	78 101	79 025	78 186	72 180	70 997	10.4	10.6	10.5	9.7	9.6
Urban - Urbaine	+C	47 786	47 968	47 998	46 754	46 401	11.3	11.3	11.3	11.0	10.9
Rural - Rurale	+C	30 315	31 057	30 188	25 426	24 596	9.3	9.6	9.4	8.0	7.8
Slovakia - Slovaquie											
Total	C	50 841	51 713	53 747	54 430	53 904	9.5	9.6	10.0	10.1	10.0
Urban - Urbaine	C	26 321	26 798	28 399	28 816	28 411	8.7	8.9	9.5	9.6	9.5
Rural - Rurale	C	24 520	24 915	25 348	25 614	25 493	10.4	10.5	10.6	10.7	10.6
Slovenia - Slovénie											
Total	C	17 501	17 321	17 961	18 157	18 932	8.8	8.7	9.0	9.1	9.4
Urban - Urbaine	C	8 400	8 425	8 745	8 869	9 190	8.6	8.7	9.0	9.2	9.5
Rural - Rurale	C	9 101	8 896	9 216	9 288	9 742	9.3	9.1	9.4	9.4	9.8

Continent, country or area, and urban/rural residence / Continent, pays ou zone et résidence, urbaine/rurale	Code[a]	Number - Nombre					Rate - Taux				
		2002	2003	2004	2005	2006	2002	2003	2004	2005	2006

EUROPE

Spain - Espagne											
Total	C	418 846	441 881	454 591	466 371	481 102	10.1	10.5	10.6	10.7	10.9
Sweden - Suède[52]											
Total	C	95 815	99 157	100 928	101 346	105 913	10.7	11.1	11.2	11.2	11.7
Switzerland - Suisse											
Total	C	72 372	71 848	73 082	72 903	73 371	9.9	9.8	9.9	9.8	9.8
Urban - Urbaine	C	52 917	52 789	53 844	54 021	54 465	9.9	9.8	9.9	9.9	9.9
Rural - Rurale	C	19 455	19 059	19 238	18 882	18 906	9.9	9.7	9.7	9.5	9.5
The Former Yugoslav Rep. of Macedonia - L'ex-République yougoslave de Macédoine											
Total	C	27 761	27 011	23 361	22 482	22 585	13.7	13.3	11.5	11.0	11.1
Urban - Urbaine	C	14 909	...	...	12 519	12 653	...	...	...	...	...
Rural - Rurale	C	12 852	...	...	9 963	9 932	...	...	...	...	...
Ukraine											
Total	C	390 688[15]	408 589[15]	427 259[15]	426 086[15]	460 368[53]	8.1	8.5	9.0	9.1	9.8
Urban - Urbaine	C	248 877[15]	266 415[15]	284 361[15]	284 257[15]	306 635[53]	7.7	8.3	...	...	...
Rural - Rurale	C	141 811[15]	142 174[15]	142 898[15]	141 829[15]	153 733[53]	8.9	9.1	...	...	...
United Kingdom - Royaume-Uni[54]											
Total	C	668 777[55]	695 549[55]	*715 996[56]	*722 600[56]	*748 600	11.3	11.7	*12.0	*12.0	*12.4

OCEANIA - OCÉANIE

American Samoa - Samoas américaines											
Total	C	1 629	1 608	1 713	1 720	1 442	26.8	25.7	26.7	26.3	21.6
Australia - Australie											
Total	+C	250 988	251 161	254 246	259 791	*266 815	12.8	12.6	12.6	12.7	*12.9
Urban - Urbaine	+C	165 041	166 906	169 901	176 079	...	...	...	9.7	...	...
Rural - Rurale	+C	85 947	84 255	84 345	83 712	...	...	...	32.6	...	...
Cook Islands - Îles Cook[57]											
Total	+C	292	298	295	280	*278	15.9	16.2	14.5	13.9	*13.4
Fiji - Fidji											
Total	+C	16 987	17 701	17 189	...	...	20.9	21.7	20.9	...	...
Urban - Urbaine	+C	7 592	8 332	8 508	...	...	...	...	...	...	...
Rural - Rurale	+C	9 395	9 369	8 681	...	...	...	...	...	...	...
French Polynesia - Polynésie française											
Total	C	4 763	4 501	4 431	4 469	...	19.6	18.2	17.7	17.6	...
Guam[58]											
Total	C	3 222	3 298	3 427	*3 187	...	20.0	19.8	20.6	*18.9	...
Marshall Islands - Îles Marshall											
Total	+U	1 355	1 565	1 512	1 589	1 576	...	...	...	...	...
Micronesia, Federated States of - Micronésie, États Fédérés de La											
Total	U	2 446	2 483	...	...	...	...	...	...	...	...
Nauru											
Total	C	219	...	...	...	...	21.8	...	...	...	...
New Caledonia - Nouvelle-Calédonie											
Total	C	4 194	4 102	4 006	4 035	4 224	18.9	18.2	17.4	...	...
New Zealand - Nouvelle-Zélande											
Total	+C	54 021	56 134	58 073	57 745	59 193	13.7	14.0	14.3	14.1	14.1
Urban - Urbaine[7]	+C	47 068	49 166	50 933	50 300	51 540	13.9	14.3	14.6	14.2	14.3
Rural - Rurale[7]	+C	6 896	6 878	7 060	7 391	7 518	12.5	12.3	12.5	13.0	13.0
Niue - Nioué[59]											
Total	C	25	33	18	...	...	...	19.2	...	...	...

Continent, country or area, and urban/rural residence / Continent, pays ou zone et résidence, urbaine/rurale	Code [a]	Number - Nombre					Rate - Taux				
		2002	2003	2004	2005	2006	2002	2003	2004	2005	2006
OCEANIA - OCÉANIE											
Northern Mariana Islands - Îles Mariannes septentrionales											
Total	U	1 289	1 355	1 439	1 335		...	...	...	...	...
Palau - Palaos											
Total	C	259	312	259	279	259	13.0	15.4	12.6	14.0	12.0
Papua New Guinea - Papouasie-Nouvelle-Guinée											
Total	U	187 645	192 817	...	...	...	...	...	...	...	...
Samoa											
Total	C	*2 826	*2 070	*1 679	...	...	*15.8	*11.5	*9.2	...	...
Tokelau - Tokélaou											
Total	...	20	...	...	...	...	...	...	...	...	...
Tonga											
Total	+C	2 662	2 781	*2 628	...	...	26.4	27.4	...	...	...
Tuvalu											
Total	U	156	185	190	231	184	...	...	...	...	...
Wallis and Futuna Islands - Îles Wallis et Futuna											
Total	C	262	290	241	223	220	...	19.4	...	...	...

FOOTNOTES - NOTES

Italics: data from civil registers which are incomplete or of unknown completeness. -
Italiques: données incomplètes ou dont le degré d'exactitude n'est pas connu, provenant des registres de l'état civil.

* Provisional. -
Données provisoires.

[a] 'Code' indicates the source of data, as follows:
C - Civil registration, estimated over 90% complete
U - Civil registration, estimated less than 90% complete
| - Other source, estimated reliable
+ - Data tabulated by date of registration rather than occurence.
... - Information not available

Le 'Code' indique la source des données, comme suit:
C - Registres de l'état civil considérés complets à 90 p. 100 au moins.
U - Registres de l'état civil qui ne sont pas considérés complets à 90 p. 100 au moins.
| - Autre source, considérée pas douteuses.
+ - Données exploitées selon la date de l'enregistrement et non la date de l'événement.
... - Information pas disponible.

[1] Excluding live-born infants who died before their birth was registered. For Algerian population only. - Non compris les enfants nés vivants décédés avant l'enregistrement de leur naissance. Pour la population algérienne seulement.
[2] Data from civil registration centers of Brazzaville, Pointe-Noire, Dolisie, Nkayi, Mossendijo and Ouesso communes. - Données issues des centres d'enregistrement des faits d'état-civil des communes de Brazzaville, Pointe-Noire, Dolisie, Nkayi, Mossendijo et Ouesso.
[3] Data refer to national projections. - Les données se réfèrent aux projections nationales.
[4] Excluding live-born infants who died before their birth was registered. - Non compris les enfants nés vivants décédés avant l'enregistrement de leur naissance.
[5] Excluding non-residents and foreign service personnel and their dependants. - À l'exclusion des non-résidents et du personnel diplomatique et de leurs charges de famille.
[6] Including Canadian residents temporarily in the United States, but excluding United States residents temporarily in Canada. - Y compris les résidents canadiens se trouvant temporairement aux Etats-Unis, mais ne comprenant pas les résidents des Etats-Unis se trouvant temporairement au Canada.

[7] The total number includes 'Unknown residence', but the categories urban and rural do not. - Le nombre total inclue 'Résidence inconnue ', mais les catégories Urbain et Rural ne l'incluent pas.
[8] Including adjustment for underenumeration. - Y compris l'ajustement pour sous-dénombrement.
[9] Data exclude visitors. - Les données non compris des visiteurs.
[10] Data refer to births to mothers resident in the Netherlands Antilles (including births outside the Netherlands Antilles to resident mothers, excluding births to non-resident mothers). - Ces données concernent les enfants nés de femmes qui résidaient aux Antilles néerlandaises (y compris ceux qui sont nés hors des Antilles néerlandaises). Elles ne concernent pas les enfants nés de non-résidentes.
[11] Excluding Indian jungle population. - Non compris les Indiens de la jungle.
[12] Excluding nomadic Indian tribes. - Non compris les tribus d'Indiens nomades.
[13] Excluding Indian jungle population. Data refer to registered live births only. - Non compris les Indiens de la jungle. Les données concernent les naissances vivantes enregistrées seulement.
[14] The districts of Paramaribo and Wanica are considered urban areas, whereas the rest of the districts are considered more or less rural districts (areas). - Les districts de Paramaribo et de Wanica sont considérés comme des zones urbaines, les autres districts étant considérés comme des zones rurales à divers degrés.
[15] Excluding infants born alive of less than 28 weeks' gestation, of less than 1 000 grams in weight and 35 centimeters in length, who die within seven days of birth. - Non compris les enfants nés vivants après moins de 28 semaines de gestations, pesant moins de 1 000 grammes, mesurant moins de 35 centimètres et décédés dans les sept jours qui ont suivi leur naissance.
[16] Since 16 October 2005 the definition of WHO on livebirths has been put into force in accordance with 10th revision of the International Classification of Diseases. - Depuis le 16 octobre 2005, la définition de l'OMS concernant les naissances vivantes est en vigueur conformément à la dixième révision de la Classification internationale des maladies.
[17] Rates were obtained by the Sample Vital Registration System of Bangladesh. - Taux obtenus au moyen du Sample Vital Registration System du Bangladesh.
[18] For 2005, data refer to last twelve months preceding census in May 2005. - Pour 2005, les données se rapportent aux douze mois précédant le recensement de mai 2005.
[19] For statistical purposes, the data for China do not include those for the Hong Kong Special Administrative Region (Hong Kong SAR), Macao Special Administrative Region (Macao SAR) and Taiwan province of China. - Pour la présentation des statistiques, les données pour la Chine ne comprennent pas la Région Administrative Spéciale de Hong Kong (Hong Kong RAS), la Région Administrative Spéciale de Macao (Macao RAS) et Taïwan province de Chine.

²⁰ Data have been estimated on the basis of the annual National Sample Surveys on Population Changes. - Les données ont été estimées sur la base de l'enquête annuelle "National Sample Survey on Population Changes".

²¹ Data for 2005 are estimated from the National Sample Survey of 1 Per cent population. - Les données pour 2005 ont été estimées à partir de l'enquête nationale qui a porté sur un échantillon de 1 % de la population.

²² Data refer to government controlled areas. - Les données se rapportent aux zones contrôlées par le Gouvernement.

²³ Including data for the Indian-held part of Jammu and Kashmir, the final status of which has not yet been determined. Rates were obtained by the Sample Registration System of India, actually a large demographic survey. - Y compris les données pour la partie du Jammu et du Cachemire occupée par l'Inde dont le statut définitif n'a pas encore été déterminé. Les taux ont été obtenus par le Système de l'enregistrement par échantillon de l'Inde qui est une large enquête démographique.

²⁴ Data relate to the Iranian Year which begins on 21 March and ends on 20 March of the following year. - Les données concernent l'année iranienne, qui commence le 21 mars et se termine le 20 mars de l'année suivante.

²⁵ Including data for East Jerusalem and Israeli residents in certain other territories under occupation by Israeli military forces since June 1967. - Y compris les données pour Jérusalem-Est et les résidents israéliens dans certains autres territoires occupés depuis 1967 par les forces armées israéliennes.

²⁶ Data refer to Japanese nationals in Japan only. - Les données se raportent aux nationaux japonais au Japon seulement.

²⁷ Excluding data for Jordanian territory under occupation since June 1967 by Israeli military forces. Excluding foreigners, including registered Palestinian refugees. - Non compris les données pour le territoire jordanien occupé depuis juin 1967 par les forces armées israéliennes. Non compris les étrangers, mais y compris les réfugiés de Palestine enregistrés.

²⁸ Excluding alien armed forces, civilian aliens employed by armed forces, and foreign diplomatic personnel and their dependants. - Non compris les militaires étrangers, les civils étrangers employés par les forces armées ni le personnel diplomatique étranger et les membres de leur famille les accompagnant.

²⁹ Including Koreans abroad. - Y compris les Coréens à l'étranger.

³⁰ Data refer to the recorded events in Ministry of Health hospitals and health centres only. - Les données se rapportent aux faits d'état civil enregistrés dans les hôpitaux et les dispensaires du Ministère de la santé seulement.

³¹ Excluding data for the Pakistan-held part of Jammu and Kashmir, the final status of which has not yet been determined. - Non compris les données concernant la partie du Jammu et Cachemire occupée par le Pakistan dont le statut définitif n'a pas été déterminé.

³² Data based on Pakistan Demographic Survey (PDS 2003) . - Données extraites de l'enquête démographique effectuée par le Pakistan en 2003.

³³ Data based on Pakistan Demographic Survey (PDS 2005). - Données extraites de l'enquête démographique effectuée par le Pakistan en 2005.

³⁴ Excluding nomad population and Palestinian refugees. Excluding live-born infants who died before their birth was registered. - Non compris la population nomade et les réfugiés de Palestine. Non compris les enfants nés vivants décédés avant l'enregistrement de leur naissance.

³⁵ Excluding infants born alive of less than 28 weeks' gestation, of less than 1 000 grams in weight and 35 centimeters in length, who die within seven days of birth. Including an upward adjustment for under-registration. - Non compris les enfants nés vivants après moins de 28 semaines de gestations, pesant moins de 1 000 grammes, mesurant moins de 35 centimètres et décédés dans les sept jours qui ont suivi leur naissance. Y compris un ajustement pour sous-enregistrement.

³⁶ Based on the results of the Population Demographic Survey. - D'après les résultats de la Population Demographic Survey.

³⁷ Also included in Finland. - Comprise aussi dans Finlande.

³⁸ Including armed forces stationed outside the country, but excluding alien armed forces stationed in the area. - Y compris les militaires nationaux hors du pays, mais non compris les militaires étrangers en garnison sur le territoire.

³⁹ Excluding Faeroe Islands and Greenland shown separately, if available. - Non compris les Iles Féroé et le Gröenland, qui font l'objet de rubriques distinctes, si disponible.

⁴⁰ Including nationals temporarily outside the country. Including Aland Islands. - Y compris les nationaux se trouvant temporairement hors du pays. Y compris les Îles d'Åland.

⁴¹ Including armed forces stationed outside the country. Excluding Overseas Departments, namely, French Guiana, Guadeloupe, Martinique and Reunion, shown separately, if available. - Y compris les militaires nationaux hors du pays. Non compris les départements d'outre mer, c'est-à-dire la Guyane française, la Guadeloupe, la Martinique et la Réunion, qui font l'objet de rubriques distinctes, si disponible.

⁴² Urban/rural figures, excluding nationals outside the country. - Les chiffres urbaine/rurale, non compris les nationaux hors du pays.

⁴³ Excluding armed forces. - Non compris les militaires en garnison.

⁴⁴ Total includes the data of foreigners, persons of unknown residence and homeless, but the categories urban and rural do not. - Total incluant les étrangers, les personnes de résidence inconnue et les sans-abri, ce qui n'est pas le cas pour les catégories urbaines et rurales.

⁴⁵ Events registered within one year of occurrence. - Evénements enregistrés dans l'année qui suit l'événement.

⁴⁶ Excluding infants born alive of less than 28 weeks' gestation, of less than 1 000 grams in weight and 35 centimeters in length, who die within seven days of birth. Data do not include information for Transnistria and the municipality of Bender. - Non compris les enfants nés vivants après moins de 28 semaines de gestations, pesant moins de 1 000 grammes, mesurant moins de 35 centimètres et décédés dans les sept jours qui ont suivi leur naissance. Les données ne tiennent pas compte de l'information sur la Transnistria et la municipalité de Bender.

⁴⁷ Including residents outside the country. - Y compris les résidents hors du pays.

⁴⁸ Including residents outside the country if listed in a Netherlands population register. - Y compris les résidents hors du pays, s'ils sont inscrits sur un registre de population néerlandais.

⁴⁹ Excluding Svalbard and Jan Mayen Island shown separately, if available. - Non compris Svalbard et Jan Mayen qui font l'objet de rubriques distinctes, si disponible.

⁵⁰ Data refer to resident mothers. - Données concernant les mères résidentes.

⁵¹ Without data for Kosovo and Metohia. - Sans les données pour le Kosovo and Metohie.

⁵² Based on the results of the Total Population Register. - Selon les résultats du recensement complet de la population.

⁵³ Data refer to births with weight 500g and more (if weight is unknown - with length 25 centimeters and more, or with gestation during 22 weeks or more). - Données concernant les nouveau-nés de 500 grammes ou plus (si le poids est inconnu – de 25 centimètres de long ou plus, ou après une grossesse de 22 semaines ou plus).

⁵⁴ Excluding Channel Islands and Isle of Man, shown separately, if available. - Non compris les îles Anglo-Normandes et l'île de Man, qui font l'objet de rubriques distinctes, si disponible.

⁵⁵ Data revised to exclude births in Northern Ireland to non-residents of Northern Ireland. Data tabulated by date of occurrence for England and Wales, and by date of registration for Northern Ireland and Scotland. - Données révisées pour exclure les naissances en Irlande du Nord de non-résidents de l'Irlande du Nord. Données exploitées selon la date de l'événement pour l'Angleterre et le pays de Galles, et selon la date de l'enregistrement pour l'Irlande du Nord et l'Ecosse.

⁵⁶ Data tabulated by date of occurrence for England and Wales, and by date of registration for Northern Ireland and Scotland. - Données exploitées selon la date de l'événement pour l'Angleterre et le pays de Galles, et selon la date de l'enregistrement pour l'Irlande du Nord et l'Ecosse.

⁵⁷ Excluding Niue, shown separately, which is part of Cook Islands, but because of remoteness is administered separately. - Non compris Nioué, qui fait l'objet d'une rubrique distincte et qui fait partie des îles Cook, mais qui, en raison de son éloignement, est administrée séparément.

⁵⁸ Including United States military personnel, their dependants and contract employees. - Y compris les militaires des Etats-Unis, les membres de leur famille les accompagnant et les agents contractuels des Etats-Unis.

⁵⁹ Includes children born in New Zealand to women resident in Niue who chose to travel to New Zealand to give birth. - Y compris les enfants nés en Nouvelle-Zélande de femmes résidant à Nioué qui ont choisi de se rendre en Nouvelle-Zélande pour accoucher.

Table 10

Table 10 presents live births by age of mother, sex of the child and urban/rural residence for the latest available year.

Description of variables: Age is defined as age at last birthday, that is, the difference between the date of birth and the date of the occurrence of the event, expressed in completed solar years. The age classification used in this table is the following: under 15 years, 5-year age groups through 45-49 years, and 50 years and over.

Reliability of data: Data from civil registers of live births which are reported as incomplete (less than 90 per cent completeness) or of unknown completeness are considered unreliable and are set in *italics* rather than in roman type. Table 9 and the technical notes for that table provide more detailed information on the completeness of live-birth registration. For more information about the quality of vital statistics data in general, see section 4.2 of the Technical Notes.

Limitations: Statistics on live births by age of mother are subject to the same qualifications as have been set forth for vital statistics in general and birth statistics in particular as discussed in section 4 of the Technical Notes.

The reliability of the data described above, is an important factor in considering the limitations. In addition, some live births are tabulated by date of registration and not by date of occurrence; these are indicated in the table by a plus sign "+". Whenever the lag between the date of occurrence and date of registration is prolonged and, therefore, a large proportion of the live-birth registrations are delayed, birth statistics for any given year may be seriously affected. For example, the age of the mother will almost always refer to the date of registration rather than to the date of birth of the child. Hence, in those countries or areas where registration of births is delayed, possibly for years, statistics on births by age of mother should be used with caution.

Another factor which limits international comparability is the practice of some countries or areas of not including in live-birth statistics infants who were born alive but died before the registration of the birth or within the first 24 hours of life, thus underestimating the total number of live births. Statistics of this type are footnoted.

Because these statistics are classified according to age, they are subject to the limitations with respect to accuracy of age reporting similar to those already discussed in connection with section 3.1.3 of the Technical Notes. The factors influencing the accuracy of reporting may be somewhat dissimilar in vital statistics (because of the differences in the method of taking a census and registering a birth) but, in general, the same errors can be observed. The absence of frequencies in the unknown age group does not necessarily indicate completely accurate reporting and tabulation of the age item. It is often an indication that the unknowns have been eliminated by assigning ages to them before tabulation, or by proportionate distribution after tabulation.

On the other hand, large frequencies in the unknown age category may indicate that a large proportion of the births are born outside of wedlock, the records for which tend to be incomplete in so far as characteristics of the parents are concerned.

Another limitation of age reporting may result from calculating age of mother at birth of child (or at time of registration) from year of birth rather than from day, month and year of birth. Information on this factor is given in footnotes when known.

In few countries, data by age refer to deliveries rather than to live births causing under-enumeration in the event of a multiple birth. This practice leads to lack of strict comparability, both among countries or areas relying on this practice and between data shown in this table and table 9.

The comparability of data by urban/rural residence is affected by the national definitions of urban and rural used in tabulating these data. It is assumed, in the absence of specific information to the contrary, that the definitions of urban and rural used in connection with the national population census were also used in the compilation of the vital statistics for each country or area. However, the possibility cannot be excluded that, for a given country or area, the same definitions of urban and rural are not used for both the vital statistics data and the population census data. When known, the definitions of urban used in national population censuses are presented at the end of table 6. As discussed in detail in the technical notes for table 6, these definitions vary considerably from one country or area to another.

Earlier data: Live births by age of mother have been shown for the latest available year in each issue of the Yearbook. Data included in this table update the series covering period of years as follows:

Issue	Years Covered
Special Edition on Natality, CD, 1999	1990 – 1998
Historical Supplement CD, 1997	1948 – 1997
1992	1983 – 1992
1986	1977 – 1988
1981	1972 – 1980
Historical Supplement, 1979	1948 - 1977

For further information on years covered prior to 1948, readers should consult the Historical Index.

Tableau 10

Le tableau 10 présente les données les plus récentes dont on dispose sur les naissances vivantes selon l'âge de la mère, le sexe de l'enfant et le lieu de résidence (zone urbaine ou rurale).

Description des variables : L'âge désigne l'âge au dernier anniversaire, c'est-à-dire la différence entre la date de naissance et la date de l'événement exprimée en années solaires révolues. La classification par âge utilisée dans ce tableau comprend les catégories suivantes : moins de 15 ans, groupes quinquennaux jusqu'à 45-49 ans, 50 ans et plus, et âge inconnu.

Fiabilité des données : Les données sur les naissances vivantes provenant des registres de l'état civil qui sont déclarées incomplètes (degré de complétude inférieur à 90 p. 100) ou dont le degré de complétude n'est pas connu sont jugées douteuses et apparaissent en italique et non en caractères romains. Le tableau 9 et les notes techniques qui s'y rapportent présentent des renseignements plus détaillés sur le degré de complétude de l'enregistrement des naissances vivantes. Pour plus de précisions sur la qualité des statistiques de l'état civil en général, voir la section 4.2 des Notes techniques.

Insuffisance des données : Les statistiques relatives aux naissances vivantes selon l'âge de la mère appellent toutes les réserves qui ont été formulées à propos des statistiques de l'état civil en général et des statistiques de naissances en particulier (voir la section 4 des Notes techniques).

La fiabilité des données, au sujet de laquelle des indications ont été données plus haut, est un facteur important. Il faut également tenir compte du fait que, dans certains cas, les données relatives aux naissances vivantes sont exploitées selon la date de l'enregistrement et non la date de l'événement ; ces cas ont été signalés dans le tableau par le signe '+'. Chaque fois que le décalage entre l'événement et son enregistrement est grand et qu'une forte proportion des naissances vivantes fait l'objet d'un enregistrement tardif, les statistiques des naissances vivantes pour une année donnée peuvent être considérablement faussées. Par exemple, l'âge de la mère représente presque toujours son âge à la date de l'enregistrement et non à la date de la naissance de l'enfant. Ainsi, dans les pays ou zones où l'enregistrement des naissances est tardif, le retard atteignant parfois plusieurs années, il faut utiliser avec prudence les statistiques concernant les naissances selon l'âge de la mère.

Un autre facteur qui nuit à la comparabilité internationale est la pratique de certains pays ou zones qui consiste à ne pas inclure dans les statistiques des naissances vivantes les enfants nés vivants mais décédés avant l'enregistrement de leur naissance ou dans les 24 heures qui ont suivi la naissance, pratique qui conduit à sous-estimer le nombre total de naissances vivantes. Quand pareil facteur a joué, cela a été signalé en note à la fin du tableau.

Étant donné que les statistiques du tableau 10 sont classées selon l'âge, elles appellent les mêmes réserves concernant l'exactitude des déclarations d'âge que celles formulées à la section 3.1.3 des Notes techniques. Dans le cas des statistiques de l'état civil, les facteurs qui interviennent à cet égard sont parfois différents, étant donné que le recensement de la population et l'enregistrement des naissances se font par des méthodes différentes, mais, d'une manière générale, les erreurs observées seront les mêmes. Si aucun nombre ne figure dans la rangée réservée aux âges inconnus, cela ne signifie pas nécessairement que les déclarations d'âge et l'exploitation des données par âge ont été tout à fait exactes. C'est souvent une indication que l'on a attribué un âge aux personnes d'âge inconnu avant l'exploitation des données ou qu'elles ont été réparties proportionnellement entre les différents groupes après cette opération.

À l'inverse, lorsque le nombre des personnes d'âge inconnu est important, cela peut signifier que la proportion de naissances parmi les mères célibataires est élevée, étant donné qu'en pareil cas l'acte de naissance ne contient pas tous les renseignements concernant les parents.

Les déclarations par âge peuvent comporter des distorsions, du fait que l'âge de la mère au moment de la naissance d'un enfant (ou de la déclaration de naissance) est donné par année de naissance et non par date exacte (jour, mois et année).

Dans quelques pays, la classification par âges se réfère aux accouchements, et non aux naissances vivantes, ce qui conduit à un sous-dénombrement en cas de naissances gémellaires. Cette pratique nuit à la comparabilité des données, à la fois entre pays ou zones qui recourent à cette méthode et entre les données présentées dans le tableau 10 et celles du tableau 9.

La comparabilité des données selon le lieu de résidence (zone urbaine ou rurale) peut être limitée par les définitions nationales des termes « urbain » et « rural » utilisées pour la mise en tableaux de ces données. En l'absence d'indications contraires, on a supposé que les mêmes définitions avaient servi pour le recensement national de la population et pour l'établissement des statistiques de l'état civil pour chaque pays ou zone. Toutefois, il n'est pas exclu que, pour une zone ou un pays donné, des définitions différentes aient été retenues. Les définitions du terme « urbain » utilisées pour les recensements nationaux de population ont été présentées à la fin des notes techniques du tableau 6 lorsqu'elles étaient connues. Comme on l'a précisé dans les notes techniques relatives au tableau 6, ces définitions varient considérablement d'un pays ou d'une zone à l'autre.

Données publiées antérieurement : Les différentes éditions de l'*Annuaire démographique* regroupent les dernières statistiques dont on disposait à l'époque sur les naissances vivantes selon l'âge de la mère. Les données qui figurent dans le tableau 10 actualisent les données qui portaient sur les périodes suivantes :

Éditions	Années considérées
Édition spéciale sur les statistiques de la natalité (CD-ROM), 1999	1990 – 1998
Supplément historique (CD-ROM), 1997	1948 – 1997
1992	1983 – 1992
1986	1977 – 1988
1981	1972 – 1980
Supplément rétrospectif, 1979	1948 – 1977

Pour plus de détails concernant les années antérieures à 1948, se reporter à l'index historique.

Continent, country or area, code, date and age (in years) / Continent, pays ou zone, code, date et âge (en années)	Total — Both sexes Les deux sexes	Total — Male Masculin	Total — Female Féminin	Urban - Urbaine — Both sexes Les deux sexes	Urban - Urbaine — Male Masculin	Urban - Urbaine — Female Féminin	Rural - Rurale — Both sexes Les deux sexes	Rural - Rurale — Male Masculin	Rural - Rurale — Female Féminin
AFRICA - AFRIQUE									
Egypt - Égypte									
2006 (C)									
Total..................	1 853 746	951 085	902 661	740 228	378 370	361 858	1 113 518	572 715	540 803
0 - 14.................	-	-	-	-	-	-	-	-	-
15 - 19................	77 837	36 171	41 666	33 634	14 589	19 045	44 203	21 582	22 621
20 - 24................	433 135	223 554	209 581	153 339	79 053	74 286	279 796	144 501	135 295
25 - 29................	483 538	248 979	234 559	183 482	94 152	89 330	300 056	154 827	145 229
30 - 34................	250 837	127 874	122 963	100 079	50 918	49 161	150 758	76 956	73 802
35 - 39................	121 711	62 184	59 527	48 811	24 527	24 284	72 900	37 657	35 243
40 - 44................	34 751	17 797	16 954	15 321	7 787	7 534	19 430	10 010	9 420
45 +..................	6 972	3 472	3 500	2 734	1 337	1 397	4 238	2 135	2 103
Unknown - Inconnu......	444 965	231 054	213 911	202 828	106 007	96 821	242 137	125 047	117 090
Kenya									
2000 (U)									
Total..................	*470 712*	...	...	...	...	...	...	...	...
0 - 14.................	*1 033*	...	...	...	...	...	...	...	...
15 - 19................	*72 510*	...	...	...	...	...	...	...	...
20 - 24................	*151 037*	...	...	...	...	...	...	...	...
25 - 29................	*117 804*	...	...	...	...	...	...	...	...
30 - 34................	*76 286*	...	...	...	...	...	...	...	...
35 - 39................	*33 301*	...	...	...	...	...	...	...	...
40 - 44................	*9 096*	...	...	...	...	...	...	...	...
45 - 49................	*1 571*	...	...	...	...	...	...	...	...
50 +..................	*218*	...	...	...	...	...	...	...	...
Unknown - Inconnu......	*7 856*	...	...	...	...	...	...	...	...
Libyan Arab Jamahiriya - Jamahiriya arabe libyenne									
2002 (C)									
Total..................	111 053	57 722	53 331	...	...	...	...	...	...
0 - 19.................	1 196	592	604	...	...	...	...	...	...
20 - 24................	15 018	7 845	7 173	...	...	...	...	...	...
25 - 29................	32 713	16 877	15 836	...	...	...	...	...	...
30 - 34................	33 325	17 384	15 941	...	...	...	...	...	...
35 - 39................	18 702	9 777	8 925	...	...	...	...	...	...
40 - 44................	6 422	3 296	3 126	...	...	...	...	...	...
45 +..................	676	364	312	...	...	...	...	...	...
Unknown - Inconnu......	3 001	1 587	1 414	...	...	...	...	...	...
Mauritius - Maurice									
2006 (C)									
Total..................	17 320	8 882	8 438	...	...	...	...	...	...
0 - 14.................	27	11	16	...	...	...	...	...	...
15 - 19................	1 602	828	774	...	...	...	...	...	...
20 - 24................	4 495	2 336	2 159	...	...	...	...	...	...
25 - 29................	5 773	2 982	2 791	...	...	...	...	...	...
30 - 34................	2 978	1 483	1 495	...	...	...	...	...	...
35 - 39................	1 371	693	678	...	...	...	...	...	...
40 - 44................	379	187	192	...	...	...	...	...	...
45 - 49................	27	17	10	...	...	...	...	...	...
50 +..................	1	1	-	...	...	...	...	...	...
Unknown - Inconnu......	667	344	323	...	...	...	...	...	...
Morocco - Maroc									
2001 (C)									
Total..................	541 298	277 242	264 056	282 380[1]	144 818[1]	137 562[1]	258 297[1]	132 082[1]	126 215[1]
0 - 14.................	1 016	525	491	457[1]	234[1]	223[1]	559[1]	291[1]	268[1]
15 - 19................	45 049	23 151	21 898	19 695[1]	10 164[1]	9 531[1]	25 327[1]	12 973[1]	12 354[1]
20 - 24................	131 163	67 353	63 810	62 623[1]	32 254[1]	30 369[1]	68 480[1]	35 068[1]	33 412[1]
25 - 29................	136 599	69 989	66 610	73 246[1]	37 596[1]	35 650[1]	63 288[1]	32 360[1]	30 928[1]
30 - 34................	117 851	60 300	57 551	66 841[1]	34 234[1]	32 607[1]	50 954[1]	26 040[1]	24 914[1]
35 - 39................	75 484	38 586	36 898	43 396[1]	22 230[1]	21 166[1]	32 054[1]	16 336[1]	15 718[1]
40 - 44................	27 453	13 958	13 495	13 819[1]	6 959[1]	6 860[1]	13 624[1]	6 991[1]	6 633[1]
45 - 49................	3 974	1 998	1 976	1 445[1]	713[1]	732[1]	2 528[1]	1 284[1]	1 244[1]
50 +..................	1 105	556	549	313[1]	157[1]	156[1]	791[1]	399[1]	392[1]
Unknown - Inconnu......	1 604	826	778	545[1]	277[1]	268[1]	692[1]	340[1]	352[1]

10. Live births by age of mother, sex of the child and urban/rural residence: latest available year, 1997 - 2006
Naissances vivantes selon l'âge de la mère, le sexe de l'enfant et la résidence, urbaine/rurale: dernière année disponible, 1997 - 2006 (continued - suite)

Continent, country or area, date, code and age (in years) / Continent, pays ou zone, code, date et âge (en années)	Total			Urban - Urbaine			Rural - Rurale		
	Both sexes Les deux sexes	Male Masculin	Female Féminin	Both sexes Les deux sexes	Male Masculin	Female Féminin	Both sexes Les deux sexes	Male Masculin	Female Féminin
AFRICA - AFRIQUE									
Namibia - Namibie[2]									
2001 (I)									
Total	45 157	22 643	22 514	15 352	7 678	7 674	29 805	14 965	14 840
12 - 14	74	37	37	16	4	12	58	33	25
15 - 19	5 278	2 638	2 640	1 377	665	712	3 901	1 973	1 928
20 - 24	11 964	5 997	5 967	3 827	1 930	1 897	8 137	4 067	4 070
25 - 29	11 056	5 563	5 493	4 389	2 231	2 158	6 667	3 332	3 335
30 - 34	8 429	4 259	4 170	3 217	1 621	1 596	5 212	2 638	2 574
35 - 39	5 292	2 636	2 656	1 793	882	911	3 499	1 754	1 745
40 - 44	2 383	1 187	1 196	613	297	316	1 770	890	880
45 +	681	326	355	120	48	72	561	278	283
Réunion[3]									
2003 (C)									
Total	14 427	7 412	7 015	...	...	...	...	...	...
0 - 19	1 241	596	645	...	...	...	...	...	...
20 - 24	3 054	1 596	1 458	...	...	...	...	...	...
25 - 29	3 925	2 046	1 879	...	...	...	...	...	...
30 - 34	3 478	1 788	1 690	...	...	...	...	...	...
35 - 39	2 110	1 064	1 046	...	...	...	...	...	...
40 - 44	596	309	287	...	...	...	...	...	...
45 +	23	13	10	...	...	...	...	...	...
Saint Helena ex. dep. - Sainte-Hélène sans dép.									
2000 (C)									
Total	56	32	24	...	...	...	...	...	...
15 - 19	7	3	4	...	...	...	...	...	...
20 - 24	16	10	6	...	...	...	...	...	...
25 - 29	12	5	7	...	...	...	...	...	...
30 - 34	13	9	4	...	...	...	...	...	...
35 - 39	7	4	3	...	...	...	...	...	...
40 - 44	1	1	-	...	...	...	...	...	...
Seychelles									
2006 (+C)									
Total	1 467	757	710	...	...	...	...	...	...
0 - 14	4	-	4	...	...	...	...	...	...
15 - 19	196	107	89	...	...	...	...	...	...
20 - 24	364	193	171	...	...	...	...	...	...
25 - 29	422	199	223	...	...	...	...	...	...
30 - 34	301	166	135	...	...	...	...	...	...
35 - 39	149	77	72	...	...	...	...	...	...
40 - 44	30	15	15	...	...	...	...	...	...
45 +	1	-	1	...	...	...	...	...	...
South Africa - Afrique du Sud									
1999 (U)									
Total	1 363 800	...	...	...	...	...	...	...	...
15 - 19	195 560	...	...	...	...	...	...	...	...
20 - 24	362 872	...	...	...	...	...	...	...	...
25 - 29	339 586	...	...	...	...	...	...	...	...
30 - 34	246 119	...	...	...	...	...	...	...	...
35 - 39	140 344	...	...	...	...	...	...	...	...
40 - 44	52 428	...	...	...	...	...	...	...	...
45 - 49	13 437	...	...	...	...	...	...	...	...
50 +	4 439	...	...	...	...	...	...	...	...
Unknown - Inconnu	9 015	...	...	...	...	...	...	...	...
Swaziland[4]									
1997 (I)									
Total	31 087	...	...	6 915	...	...	24 172	...	...
15 - 19	4 192	...	...	897	...	...	3 295	...	...
20 - 24	8 927	...	...	2 107	...	...	6 820	...	...
25 - 29	7 537	...	...	1 895	...	...	5 642	...	...
30 - 34	4 893	...	...	1 021	...	...	3 872	...	...
35 - 39	3 413	...	...	664	...	...	2 749	...	...
40 - 44	1 247	...	...	194	...	...	1 053	...	...
45 - 49	564	...	...	78	...	...	486	...	...

10. Live births by age of mother, sex of the child and urban/rural residence: latest available year, 1997 - 2006
Naissances vivantes selon l'âge de la mère, le sexe de l'enfant et la résidence, urbaine/rurale: dernière année disponible, 1997 - 2006 (continued - suite)

Continent, country or area, date, code and age (in years) Continent, pays ou zone, code, date et âge (en années)	Total			Urban - Urbaine			Rural - Rurale		
	Both sexes Les deux sexes	Male Masculin	Female Féminin	Both sexes Les deux sexes	Male Masculin	Female Féminin	Both sexes Les deux sexes	Male Masculin	Female Féminin
AFRICA - AFRIQUE									
Swaziland[4]									
1997 (I)									
50 +.....................	230	...	...	32	...	...	198	...	...
Unknown - Inconnu.......	84	...	...	27	...	...	57	...	...
Tunisia - Tunisie									
1998 (C)									
Total.....................	166 718	...	...	...	...	...	...	...	...
15 - 19	3 650	...	...	...	...	...	...	...	...
20 - 24	28 802	...	...	...	...	...	...	...	...
25 - 29	44 260	...	...	...	...	...	...	...	...
30 - 34	39 518	...	...	...	...	...	...	...	...
35 - 39	19 869	...	...	...	...	...	...	...	...
40 - 44	5 327	...	...	...	...	...	...	...	...
45 + ...	650	...	...	...	...	...	...	...	...
Unknown - Inconnu.......	2 446	...	...	...	...	...	...	...	...
AMERICA, NORTH - AMÉRIQUE DU NORD									
Anguilla									
2005 (+C)									
Total.....................	167	...	...	...	...	...	...	...	...
0 - 14....................	3	...	...	...	...	...	...	...	...
15 - 19	21	...	...	...	...	...	...	...	...
20 - 24	47	...	...	...	...	...	...	...	...
25 - 29	46	...	...	...	...	...	...	...	...
30 - 34	29	...	...	...	...	...	...	...	...
35 - 39	16	...	...	...	...	...	...	...	...
40 + ...	4	...	...	...	...	...	...	...	...
Unknown - Inconnu.......	1	...	...	...	...	...	...	...	...
Aruba									
2006 (C)									
Total.....................	1 227	615	612	...	...	...	...	...	...
0 - 14....................	3	2	1	...	...	...	...	...	...
15 - 19	152	83	69	...	...	...	...	...	...
20 - 24	309	157	152	...	...	...	...	...	...
25 - 29	316	164	152	...	...	...	...	...	...
30 - 34	234	109	125	...	...	...	...	...	...
35 - 39	165	71	94	...	...	...	...	...	...
40 - 44	47	28	19	...	...	...	...	...	...
45 - 49	1	1	-	...	...	...	...	...	...
50 + ...	-	-	-	...	...	...	...	...	...
Bahamas									
2001 (U)									
Total.....................	4 495	2 305	2 190	...	...	...	...	...	...
0 - 14....................	5	3	2	...	...	...	...	...	...
15 - 19	568	282	286	...	...	...	...	...	...
20 - 24	1 120	567	553	...	...	...	...	...	...
25 - 29	1 154	602	552	...	...	...	...	...	...
30 - 34	904	460	444	...	...	...	...	...	...
35 - 39	601	319	282	...	...	...	...	...	...
40 - 44	125	63	62	...	...	...	...	...	...
45 - 49	10	5	5	...	...	...	...	...	...
Unknown - Inconnu.......	8	4	4	...	...	...	...	...	...
Belize									
1997 (U)									
Total.....................	5 738	2 921	2 817	2 354	1 152	1 202	3 384	1 769	1 615
0 - 14....................	17	8	9	4	2	2	13	6	7
15 - 19	993	504	489	392	202	190	601	302	299
20 - 24	1 762	907	855	759	368	391	1 003	539	464
25 - 29	1 350	660	690	566	271	295	784	389	395
30 - 34	804	419	385	327	161	166	477	258	219
35 - 39	422	228	194	159	85	74	263	143	120
40 - 44	105	55	50	37	21	16	68	34	34

10. Live births by age of mother, sex of the child and urban/rural residence: latest available year, 1997 - 2006
Naissances vivantes selon l'âge de la mère, le sexe de l'enfant et la résidence, urbaine/rurale: dernière année disponible, 1997 - 2006 (continued - suite)

Continent, country or area, date, code and age (in years) / Continent, pays ou zone, code, date et âge (en années)	Total			Urban - Urbaine			Rural - Rurale		
	Both sexes Les deux sexes	Male Masculin	Female Féminin	Both sexes Les deux sexes	Male Masculin	Female Féminin	Both sexes Les deux sexes	Male Masculin	Female Féminin
AMERICA, NORTH - AMÉRIQUE DU NORD									
Belize									
1997 (U)									
45 +.....................	15	6	9	5	2	3	10	4	6
Unknown - Inconnu.......	270	134	136	105	40	65	165	94	71
2002 (U)									
Total[5].....................	7 356	...	...	...	...	...	...	...	...
0 - 14.....................	22	...	...	...	...	...	...	...	...
15 - 19.....................	1 237	...	...	...	...	...	...	...	...
20 - 24.....................	2 233	...	...	...	...	...	...	...	...
25 - 29.....................	1 712	...	...	...	...	...	...	...	...
30 - 34.....................	1 106	...	...	...	...	...	...	...	...
35 - 39.....................	566	...	...	...	...	...	...	...	...
40 - 44.....................	165	...	...	...	...	...	...	...	...
45 +.....................	17	...	...	...	...	...	...	...	...
Unknown - Inconnu.......	298	...	...	...	...	...	...	...	...
Bermuda - Bermudes									
2003 (C)									
Total.....................	834	...	...	...	...	...	...	...	...
15 - 19.....................	79	...	...	...	...	...	...	...	...
20 - 24.....................	116	...	...	...	...	...	...	...	...
25 - 29.....................	203	...	...	...	...	...	...	...	...
30 - 34.....................	250	...	...	...	...	...	...	...	...
35 - 39.....................	148	...	...	...	...	...	...	...	...
40 +.....................	38	...	...	...	...	...	...	...	...
Canada[6]									
2005 (C)									
Total.....................	342 176	175 376	166 800	...	...	...	...	...	...
0 - 14.....................	118	60	58	...	...	...	...	...	...
15 - 19.....................	13 895	7 184	6 711	...	...	...	...	...	...
20 - 24.....................	55 318	28 372	26 946	...	...	...	...	...	...
25 - 29.....................	105 566	54 041	51 525	...	...	...	...	...	...
30 - 34.....................	107 524	54 966	52 558	...	...	...	...	...	...
35 - 39.....................	49 526	25 413	24 113	...	...	...	...	...	...
40 - 44.....................	9 728	5 076	4 652	...	...	...	...	...	...
45 - 49.....................	396	209	187	...	...	...	...	...	...
50 +.....................	22	11	11	...	...	...	...	...	...
Unknown - Inconnu.......	83	44	39	...	...	...	...	...	...
Costa Rica									
2006 (C)									
Total.....................	71 291	...	...	...	...	...	...	...	...
0 - 14.....................	469	...	...	...	...	...	...	...	...
15 - 19.....................	13 527	...	...	...	...	...	...	...	...
20 - 24.....................	22 089	...	...	...	...	...	...	...	...
25 - 29.....................	17 372	...	...	...	...	...	...	...	...
30 - 34.....................	10 630	...	...	...	...	...	...	...	...
35 - 39.....................	5 363	...	...	...	...	...	...	...	...
40 - 44.....................	1 361	...	...	...	...	...	...	...	...
45 +.....................	76	...	...	...	...	...	...	...	...
Unknown - Inconnu.......	404	...	...	...	...	...	...	...	...
Cuba									
2006 (C)									
Total.....................	111 323	57 502	53 821	83 389	42 978	40 411	27 934	14 524	13 410
0 - 14.....................	372	200	172	219	122	97	153	78	75
15 - 19.....................	16 956	8 874	8 082	11 296	5 885	5 411	5 660	2 909	2 671
20 - 24.....................	32 169	16 616	15 553	23 938	12 325	11 613	8 231	4 291	3 940
25 - 29.....................	25 370	13 010	12 360	19 485	10 018	9 467	5 885	2 992	2 893
30 - 34.....................	23 209	12 022	11 187	18 048	9 350	8 698	5 161	2 672	2 489
35 - 39.....................	11 089	5 693	5 396	8 703	4 417	4 286	2 386	1 276	1 110
40 - 44.....................	2 057	1 027	1 030	1 620	814	806	437	213	224
45 - 49.....................	50	33	17	38	25	13	12	8	4
50 +.....................	34	18	16	28	14	14	6	4	2
Unknown - Inconnu.......	17	9	8	14	8	6	3	1	2

10. Live births by age of mother, sex of the child and urban/rural residence: latest available year, 1997 - 2006
Naissances vivantes selon l'âge de la mère, le sexe de l'enfant et la résidence, urbaine/rurale: dernière année disponible,
1997 - 2006 (continued - suite)

Continent, country or area, date, code and age (in years) / Continent, pays ou zone, code, date et âge (en années)	Total			Urban - Urbaine			Rural - Rurale		
	Both sexes Les deux sexes	Male Masculin	Female Féminin	Both sexes Les deux sexes	Male Masculin	Female Féminin	Both sexes Les deux sexes	Male Masculin	Female Féminin
AMERICA, NORTH - AMÉRIQUE DU NORD									
Dominican Republic - République dominicaine									
2005 (+U)									
Total	183 819[7]	92 856[7]	90 963[7]	128 936	65 523	63 413	46 634	23 290	23 344
0 - 14	3 302[7]	1 615[7]	1 687[7]	1 982	1 005	977	1 219	565	654
15 - 19	35 426[7]	17 933[7]	17 493[7]	23 484	11 941	11 543	10 808	5 431	5 377
20 - 24	55 678[7]	28 172[7]	27 506[7]	39 636	20 170	19 466	14 437	7 186	7 251
25 - 29	43 749[7]	22 140[7]	21 609[7]	32 645	16 535	16 110	9 988	5 060	4 928
30 - 34	24 840[7]	12 659[7]	12 181[7]	18 860	9 635	9 225	5 325	2 691	2 634
35 - 39	10 989[7]	5 583[7]	5 406[7]	8 181	4 189	3 992	2 545	1 270	1 275
40 - 44	3 081[7]	1 519[7]	1 562[7]	2 027	1 014	1 013	959	461	498
45 - 49	713[7]	334[7]	376[7]	395	189	206	296	134	162
50 +	379[7]	184[7]	195[7]	230	113	117	137	65	72
Unknown - Inconnu	5 665[7]	2 717[7]	2 948[7]	1 496	732	764	920	427	493
El Salvador									
2006 (C)									
Total	107 111	56 111	51 000	70 810	37 151	33 659	36 301	18 960	17 341
0 - 14	1 163	617	546	642	359	283	521	258	263
15 - 19	21 836	11 404	10 432	13 692	7 144	6 548	8 144	4 260	3 884
20 - 24	30 351	16 044	14 307	20 206	10 710	9 496	10 145	5 334	4 811
25 - 29	26 478	13 791	12 687	18 231	9 494	8 737	8 247	4 297	3 950
30 - 34	16 395	8 495	7 900	11 259	5 894	5 365	5 136	2 601	2 535
35 - 39	7 929	4 226	3 703	5 127	2 701	2 426	2 802	1 525	1 277
40 - 44	2 418	1 248	1 170	1 358	693	665	1 060	555	505
45 - 49	238	132	106	131	71	60	107	61	46
50 +	20	12	8	12	7	5	8	5	3
Unknown - Inconnu	283	142	141	152	78	74	131	64	67
Greenland - Groenland									
2003 (C)									
Total	895	480	415	717	386	331	178	94	84
0 - 14	1	1	-	-	-	-	1	1	-
15 - 19	100	52	48	83	40	43	17	12	5
20 - 24	262	144	118	208	123	85	54	21	33
25 - 29	203	104	99	158	77	81	45	27	18
30 - 34	179	93	86	142	75	67	37	18	19
35 - 39	128	72	56	107	57	50	21	15	6
40 - 44	20	13	7	18	13	5	2	-	2
45 - 49	2	1	1	1	1	-	1	-	1
2006 (C)									
Total	842	...	...	...	...	...	...	...	...
0 - 14	-	...	...	...	...	...	...	...	...
15 - 19	128	...	...	...	...	...	...	...	...
20 - 24	246	...	...	...	...	...	...	...	...
25 - 29	228	...	...	...	...	...	...	...	...
30 - 34	127	...	...	...	...	...	...	...	...
35 - 39	89	...	...	...	...	...	...	...	...
40 - 44	23	...	...	...	...	...	...	...	...
45 - 49	1	...	...	...	...	...	...	...	...
50 +	-	...	...	...	...	...	...	...	...
Grenada - Grenade									
2000 (+C)									
Total	1 883	...	...	...	...	...	...	...	...
0 - 14	9	...	...	...	...	...	...	...	...
15 - 19	310	...	...	...	...	...	...	...	...
20 - 24	490	...	...	...	...	...	...	...	...
25 - 29	452	...	...	...	...	...	...	...	...
30 - 34	339	...	...	...	...	...	...	...	...
35 - 39	208	...	...	...	...	...	...	...	...
40 - 44	73	...	...	...	...	...	...	...	...
45 +	2	...	...	...	...	...	...	...	...
Guadeloupe									
2003 (C)									
Total	7 047	3 543	3 504	...	...	...	...	...	...
0 - 14	7	2	5	...	...	...	...	...	...

10. Live births by age of mother, sex of the child and urban/rural residence: latest available year, 1997 - 2006
Naissances vivantes selon l'âge de la mère, le sexe de l'enfant et la résidence, urbaine/rurale: dernière année disponible, 1997 - 2006 (continued - suite)

Continent, country or area, date, code and age (in years) Continent, pays ou zone, code, date et âge (en annèes)	Total			Urban - Urbaine			Rural - Rurale		
	Both sexes Les deux sexes	Male Masculin	Female Féminin	Both sexes Les deux sexes	Male Masculin	Female Féminin	Both sexes Les deux sexes	Male Masculin	Female Féminin
AMERICA, NORTH - **AMÉRIQUE DU NORD**									
Guadeloupe 2003 (C)									
15 - 19	431	215	216	...	...	...	...	...	...
20 - 24	1 148	588	560	...	...	...	...	...	...
25 - 29	1 815	912	903	...	...	...	...	...	...
30 - 34	2 001	1 005	996	...	...	...	...	...	...
35 - 39	1 280	637	643	...	...	...	...	...	...
40 - 44	352	177	175	...	...	...	...	...	...
45 + ...	13	7	6	...	...	...	...	...	...
Guatemala 2006 (C)									
Total.......................	368 399	187 190	181 209	...	...	...	...	...	...
0 - 14....................	2 209	1 101	1 108	...	...	...	...	...	...
15 - 19	65 284	33 335	31 949	...	...	...	...	...	...
20 - 24	107 634	54 736	52 898	...	...	...	...	...	...
25 - 29	86 944	44 413	42 531	...	...	...	...	...	...
30 - 34	56 080	28 468	27 612	...	...	...	...	...	...
35 - 39	32 668	16 478	16 190	...	...	...	...	...	...
40 - 44	12 790	6 341	6 449	...	...	...	...	...	...
45 - 49	2 280	1 141	1 139	...	...	...	...	...	...
50 + ...	1 009	487	522	...	...	...	...	...	...
Unknown - Inconnu	1 501	690	811	...	...	...	...	...	...
Jamaica - Jamaïque[8] 2006 (C)									
Total.......................	42 387	21 671	20 716	...	...	...	...	...	...
0 - 14....................	211	111	100	...	...	...	...	...	...
15 - 19	7 809	4 029	3 780	...	...	...	...	...	...
20 - 24	11 699	5 972	5 727	...	...	...	...	...	...
25 - 29	9 283	4 722	4 561	...	...	...	...	...	...
30 - 34	7 339	3 781	3 558	...	...	...	...	...	...
35 - 39	4 455	2 280	2 175	...	...	...	...	...	...
40 - 44	1 496	232	764	...	...	...	...	...	...
45 + ...	79	35	44	...	...	...	...	...	...
Unknown - Inconnu	16	9	7	...	...	...	...	...	...
Martinique[9] 2003 (C)									
Total.......................	5 430	2 774	2 656	...	...	...	...	...	...
0 - 14....................	6	3	3	...	...	...	...	...	...
15 - 19	397	217	180	...	...	...	...	...	...
20 - 24	812	397	415	...	...	...	...	...	...
25 - 29	1 330	698	632	...	...	...	...	...	...
30 - 34	1 554	759	795	...	...	...	...	...	...
35 - 39	1 038	541	497	...	...	...	...	...	...
40 - 44	283	155	128	...	...	...	...	...	...
45 + ...	10	4	6	...	...	...	...	...	...
Mexico - Mexique 2005 (+U)									
Total.......................	2 567 906	1 284 304	1 283 009	1 776 726[1]	897 076[1]	879 449[1]	643 618[1]	323 483[1]	319 958[1]
0 - 14....................	9 880	4 956	4 919	5 639[1]	2 863[1]	2 775[1]	3 516[1]	1 728[1]	1 785[1]
15 - 19	412 368	209 771	202 518	283 530[1]	144 396[1]	139 106[1]	116 089[1]	58 980[1]	57 072[1]
20 - 24	728 815	369 979	358 729	518 046[1]	263 334[1]	254 662[1]	192 744[1]	97 615[1]	95 082[1]
25 - 29	618 381	313 455	304 839	453 543[1]	230 481[1]	223 017[1]	151 824[1]	76 472[1]	75 315[1]
30 - 34	417 702	211 594	206 045	311 310[1]	150 100[1]	153 181[1]	98 322[1]	49 405[1]	48 889[1]
35 - 39	187 204	93 965	93 205	132 917[1]	66 791[1]	66 114[1]	50 304[1]	25 218[1]	25 068[1]
40 - 44	49 220	24 697	24 514	30 919[1]	15 555[1]	15 355[1]	17 026[1]	8 511[1]	8 515[1]
45 - 49	6 225	3 071	3 152	3 296[1]	1 625[1]	1 671[1]	2 690[1]	1 332[1]	1 356[1]
50 + ...	1 873	928	945	815[1]	391[1]	424[1]	833[1]	435[1]	398[1]
Unknown - Inconnu	136 238	51 888	84 143	36 711[1]	13 540[1]	23 144[1]	10 270[1]	3 787[1]	6 478[1]
Montserrat 1999 (+C)									
Total.......................	45	19	26	...	...	...	...	...	...
0 - 14....................	-	-	-	...	...	...	...	...	...
15 - 19	7	5	2	...	...	...	...	...	...
20 - 24	10	4	6	...	...	...	...	...	...

10. Live births by age of mother, sex of the child and urban/rural residence: latest available year, 1997 - 2006
Naissances vivantes selon l'âge de la mère, le sexe de l'enfant et la résidence, urbaine/rurale: dernière année disponible, 1997 - 2006 (continued - suite)

Continent, country or area, date, code and age (in years) / Continent, pays ou zone, code, date et âge (en années)	Total Both sexes Les deux sexes	Total Male Masculin	Total Female Féminin	Urban - Urbaine Both sexes Les deux sexes	Urban - Urbaine Male Masculin	Urban - Urbaine Female Féminin	Rural - Rurale Both sexes Les deux sexes	Rural - Rurale Male Masculin	Rural - Rurale Female Féminin
AMERICA, NORTH - AMÉRIQUE DU NORD									
Montserrat									
1999 (+C)									
25 - 29	11	4	7	...	...	...	...	...	...
30 - 34	12	4	8	...	...	...	...	...	...
35 - 39	5	2	3	...	...	...	...	...	...
40 - 44	-	-	-	...	...	...	...	...	...
45 - 49	-	-	-	...	...	...	...	...	...
50 +	-	-	-	...	...	...	...	...	...
Unknown - Inconnu	-	-	-	...	...	...	...	...	...
Netherlands Antilles - Antilles néerlandaises[10]									
2004 (C)									
Total	2 357	1 230	1 127	...	...	...	...	...	...
0 - 14	6	1	5	...	...	...	...	...	...
15 - 19	259	129	130	...	...	...	...	...	...
20 - 24	447	239	208	...	...	...	...	...	...
25 - 29	558	296	262	...	...	...	...	...	...
30 - 34	601	308	293	...	...	...	...	...	...
35 - 39	362	190	172	...	...	...	...	...	...
40 - 44	86	44	42	...	...	...	...	...	...
45 - 49	7	3	4	...	...	...	...	...	...
50 +	-	-	-	...	...	...	...	...	...
Unknown - Inconnu	31	20	11	...	...	...	...	...	...
Nicaragua									
2005 (+U)									
Total	121 380	63 001	58 379	62 960	32 687	30 273	58 420	30 314	28 106
0 - 14	1 441	753	688	689	360	329	752	393	359
15 - 19	31 846	16 476	15 370	15 932	8 267	7 665	15 914	8 209	7 705
20 - 24	39 579	20 696	18 883	21 308	11 191	10 117	18 271	9 505	8 766
25 - 29	25 244	13 065	12 179	13 667	7 031	6 636	11 577	6 034	5 543
30 - 34	14 126	7 348	6 778	7 283	3 754	3 529	6 843	3 594	3 249
35 - 39	7 034	3 634	3 400	3 263	1 687	1 576	3 771	1 947	1 824
40 - 44	1 832	901	931	740	361	379	1 092	540	552
45 - 49	245	114	131	71	34	37	174	80	94
50 +	33	14	19	7	2	5	26	12	14
Panama									
1999 (C)									
Total	64 248	33 077	31 171	32 724	16 894	15 830	31 524	16 183	15 341
0 - 14	537	290	247	205	114	91	332	176	156
15 - 19	12 126	6 288	5 838	5 594	2 893	2 701	6 532	3 395	3 137
20 - 24	18 281	9 435	8 846	9 344	4 846	4 498	8 937	4 589	4 348
25 - 29	15 488	7 964	7 524	8 369	4 321	4 048	7 119	3 643	3 476
30 - 34	10 451	5 314	5 137	5 822	2 989	2 833	4 629	2 325	2 304
35 - 39	4 925	2 581	2 344	2 553	1 309	1 244	2 372	1 272	1 100
40 - 44	1 076	528	548	448	226	222	628	302	326
45 - 49	95	46	49	14	9	5	81	37	44
50 +	23	9	14	1	-	1	22	9	13
Unknown - Inconnu	1 246	622	624	374	187	187	872	435	437
2006 (C)									
Total	65 764	...	...	...	...	...	...	...	...
0 - 14	513	...	...	...	...	...	...	...	...
15 - 19	11 987	...	...	...	...	...	...	...	...
20 - 24	19 271	...	...	...	...	...	...	...	...
25 - 29	15 498	...	...	...	...	...	...	...	...
30 - 34	11 196	...	...	...	...	...	...	...	...
35 - 39	5 546	...	...	...	...	...	...	...	...
40 - 44	1 329	...	...	...	...	...	...	...	...
45 - 49	98	...	...	...	...	...	...	...	...
50 +	17	...	...	...	...	...	...	...	...
Unknown - Inconnu	309	...	...	...	...	...	...	...	...
Puerto Rico - Porto Rico									
2000 (C)									
Total	59 460	30 593	28 867	30 464[1]	15 589[1]	14 875[1]	28 967[1]	14 991[1]	13 976[1]
0 - 14	272	155	117	115[1]	62[1]	53[1]	156[1]	93[1]	63[1]

10. Live births by age of mother, sex of the child and urban/rural residence: latest available year, 1997 - 2006
Naissances vivantes selon l'âge de la mère, le sexe de l'enfant et la résidence, urbaine/rurale: dernière année disponible, 1997 - 2006 (continued - suite)

Continent, country or area, date, code and age (in years) Continent, pays ou zone, code, date et âge (en annèes)	Total			Urban - Urbaine			Rural - Rurale		
	Both sexes Les deux sexes	Male Masculin	Female Féminin	Both sexes Les deux sexes	Male Masculin	Female Féminin	Both sexes Les deux sexes	Male Masculin	Female Féminin
AMERICA, NORTH - AMÉRIQUE DU NORD									
Puerto Rico - Porto Rico									
2000 (C)									
15 - 19	11 118	5 735	5 383	4 972[1]	2 552[1]	2 420[1]	6 140[1]	3 181[1]	2 959[1]
20 - 24	19 423	10 005	9 418	9 360[1]	4 804[1]	4 556[1]	10 057[1]	5 197[1]	4 860[1]
25 - 29	15 152	7 806	7 346	8 167[1]	4 169[1]	3 998[1]	6 983[1]	3 637[1]	3 346[1]
30 - 34	8 902	4 515	4 387	5 123[1]	2 586[1]	2 537[1]	3 779[1]	1 929[1]	1 850[1]
35 - 39	3 762	1 974	1 788	2 243[1]	1 176[1]	1 067[1]	1 518[1]	797[1]	721[1]
40 - 44	748	362	386	437[1]	218[1]	219[1]	311[1]	144[1]	167[1]
45 - 49	29	14	15	18[1]	7[1]	11[1]	10[1]	7[1]	3[1]
Unknown - Inconnu	54	27	27	29[1]	15[1]	14[1]	13[1]	6[1]	7[1]
2005 (C)									
Total.	50 687	25 999	24 688	...	...	...	...	...	...
0 - 14	206	99	107	...	...	...	...	...	...
15 - 19	8 934	4 660	4 274	...	...	...	...	...	...
20 - 24	16 049	8 218	7 831	...	...	...	...	...	...
25 - 29	13 447	6 843	6 604	...	...	...	...	...	...
30 - 34	7 965	4 083	3 882	...	...	...	...	...	...
35 - 30	3 300	1 691	1 609	...	...	...	...	...	...
40 - 44	738	377	361	...	...	...	...	...	...
45 - 49	35	21	14	...	...	...	...	...	...
50 + ...	2	2	-	...	...	...	...	...	...
Unknown - Inconnu	11	5	6	...	...	...	...	...	...
Saint Kitts and Nevis - Saint-Kitts-et-Nevis									
2001 (+C)									
Total.	803	...	...	...	...	...	...	...	...
10 - 14	3	...	...	...	...	...	...	...	...
15 - 19	164	...	...	...	...	...	...	...	...
20 - 24	241	...	...	...	...	...	...	...	...
25 - 29	166	...	...	...	...	...	...	...	...
30 - 34	148	...	...	...	...	...	...	...	...
35 - 39	67	...	...	...	...	...	...	...	...
40 + ...	14	...	...	...	...	...	...	...	...
Saint Lucia - Sainte-Lucie									
2005* (C)									
Total.	2 298	...	...	...	...	...	...	...	...
0 - 14	7	...	...	...	...	...	...	...	...
15 - 19	390	...	...	...	...	...	...	...	...
20 - 24	639	...	...	...	...	...	...	...	...
25 - 29	549	...	...	...	...	...	...	...	...
30 - 34	396	...	...	...	...	...	...	...	...
35 - 39	245	...	...	...	...	...	...	...	...
40 - 44	62	...	...	...	...	...	...	...	...
45 + ...	10	...	...	...	...	...	...	...	...
Saint Vincent and the Grenadines - Saint Vincent-et-les Grenadines									
2003 (+C)									
Total.	1 923	975	948	...	...	...	...	...	...
0 - 14	10	4	6	...	...	...	...	...	...
15 - 19	388	193	195	...	...	...	...	...	...
20 - 24	547	286	261	...	...	...	...	...	...
25 - 29	430	208	222	...	...	...	...	...	...
30 - 34	304	163	141	...	...	...	...	...	...
35 - 39	182	82	100	...	...	...	...	...	...
40 - 44	55	34	21	...	...	...	...	...	...
45 - 49	4	2	2	...	...	...	...	...	...
50 + ...	-	-	-	...	...	...	...	...	...
Unknown - Inconnu	3	3	-	...	...	...	...	...	...
Trinidad and Tobago - Trinité-et-Tobago									
2002 (C)									
Total.	16 990	8 613	8 377	...	...	...	...	...	...
0 - 14	28	16	12	...	...	...	...	...	...

10. Live births by age of mother, sex of the child and urban/rural residence: latest available year, 1997 - 2006
Naissances vivantes selon l'âge de la mère, le sexe de l'enfant et la résidence, urbaine/rurale: dernière année disponible, 1997 - 2006 (continued - suite)

Continent, country or area, date, code and age (in years) — Continent, pays ou zone, code, date et âge (en années)	Total			Urban - Urbaine			Rural - Rurale		
	Both sexes Les deux sexes	Male Masculin	Female Féminin	Both sexes Les deux sexes	Male Masculin	Female Féminin	Both sexes Les deux sexes	Male Masculin	Female Féminin
AMERICA, NORTH - AMÉRIQUE DU NORD									
Trinidad and Tobago - Trinité-et-Tobago 2002 (C)									
15 - 19	2 377	1 257	1 120	...	...	...	...	...	...
20 - 24	5 275	2 706	2 569	...	...	...	...	...	...
25 - 29	4 328	2 195	2 133	...	...	...	...	...	...
30 - 34	2 919	1 426	1 493	...	...	...	...	...	...
35 - 39	1 652	812	840	...	...	...	...	...	...
40 - 44	364	175	189	...	...	...	...	...	...
45 +	11	8	3	...	...	...	...	...	...
Unknown - Inconnu	36	18	18	...	...	...	...	...	...
Turks Caicos Islands - Îles Turques et Caïques 2005 (C)									
Total	318	158	160	...	...	...	...	...	...
0 - 14	1	-	1	...	...	...	...	...	...
15 - 19	28	13	15	...	...	...	...	...	...
20 - 24	65	29	36	...	...	...	...	...	...
25 - 29	83	40	43	...	...	...	...	...	...
30 - 34	76	47	29	...	...	...	...	...	...
35 - 39	52	23	29	...	...	...	...	...	...
40 - 44	11	5	6	...	...	...	...	...	...
45 +	2	1	1	...	...	...	...	...	...
United States - États-Unis 2004 (C)									
Total	4 112 052	...	...	...	...	...	...	...	...
0 - 14	6 781	...	...	...	...	...	...	...	...
15 - 19	415 262	...	...	...	...	...	...	...	...
20 - 24	1 034 454	...	...	...	...	...	...	...	...
25 - 29	1 104 485	...	...	...	...	...	...	...	...
30 - 34	965 663	...	...	...	...	...	...	...	...
35 - 39	475 606	...	...	...	...	...	...	...	...
40 - 44	103 679	...	...	...	...	...	...	...	...
45 - 49	5 748	...	...	...	...	...	...	...	...
50 +	374	...	...	...	...	...	...	...	...
United States Virgin Islands - Îles Vierges américaines 1997 (C)									
Total[11]	2 124	...	...	...	...	...	...	...	...
0 - 14	5	...	...	...	...	...	...	...	...
15 - 19	349	...	...	...	...	...	...	...	...
20 - 24	555	...	...	...	...	...	...	...	...
25 - 29	568	...	...	...	...	...	...	...	...
30 - 34	413	...	...	...	...	...	...	...	...
35 - 39	190	...	...	...	...	...	...	...	...
40 - 44	44	...	...	...	...	...	...	...	...
45 +	-	...	...	...	...	...	...	...	...
AMERICA, SOUTH - AMÉRIQUE DU SUD									
Argentina - Argentine 2006 (+C)									
Total	696 451	...	...	...	...	...	...	...	...
0 - 14	2 766	...	...	...	...	...	...	...	...
15 - 19	103 885	...	...	...	...	...	...	...	...
20 - 24	174 342	...	...	...	...	...	...	...	...
25 - 29	176 931	...	...	...	...	...	...	...	...
30 - 34	139 003	...	...	...	...	...	...	...	...
35 - 39	73 177	...	...	...	...	...	...	...	...
40 - 44	19 866	...	...	...	...	...	...	...	...
45 - 49	1 405	...	...	...	...	...	...	...	...

Continent, country or area, date, code and age (in years) / Continent, pays ou zone, code, date et âge (en années)	Total			Urban - Urbaine			Rural - Rurale		
	Both sexes Les deux sexes	Male Masculin	Female Féminin	Both sexes Les deux sexes	Male Masculin	Female Féminin	Both sexes Les deux sexes	Male Masculin	Female Féminin
AMERICA, SOUTH - AMÉRIQUE DU SUD									
Argentina - Argentine									
2006 (+C)									
50 +	83	...	...	...	...	...	...	...	...
Unknown - Inconnu	4 993	...	...	...	...	...	...	...	...
Brazil - Brésil[5]									
2006 (U)									
Total	2 803 759	1 439 402	1 364 357	...	...	...	...	...	...
0 - 14	22 159	11 368	10 791	...	...	...	...	...	...
15 - 19	551 051	282 783	268 268	...	...	...	...	...	...
20 - 24	833 275	429 393	403 882	...	...	...	...	...	...
25 - 29	680 961	349 217	331 744	...	...	...	...	...	...
30 - 34	428 072	219 322	208 750	...	...	...	...	...	...
35 - 39	210 439	107 505	102 934	...	...	...	...	...	...
40 - 44	56 579	28 907	27 672	...	...	...	...	...	...
45 - 49	4 226	2 136	2 090	...	...	...	...	...	...
50 +	324	168	156	...	...	...	...	...	...
Unknown - Inconnu	16 673	8 603	8 070	...	...	...	...	...	...
Chile - Chili									
2005 (C)									
Total	230 831	118 534	112 297	...	...	...	...	...	...
0 - 14	935	445	490	...	...	...	...	...	...
15 - 19	35 143	18 193	16 950	...	...	...	...	...	...
20 - 24	54 032	27 664	26 368	...	...	...	...	...	...
25 - 29	53 401	27 425	25 976	...	...	...	...	...	...
30 - 34	49 906	25 662	24 244	...	...	...	...	...	...
35 - 39	28 810	14 725	14 085	...	...	...	...	...	...
40 - 44	8 234	4 238	3 996	...	...	...	...	...	...
45 - 49	364	178	186	...	...	...	...	...	...
50 +	6	4	2	...	...	...	...	...	...
Unknown - Inconnu	-	-	-	...	...	...	...	...	...
Colombia - Colombie									
2006* (U)									
Total	711 457	365 169	346 288	553 077[1]	283 976[1]	269 101[1]	147 090[1]	75 518[1]	71 572[1]
0 - 14	6 479	3 389	3 090	4 308[1]	2 252[1]	2 056[1]	2 017[1]	1 066[1]	951[1]
15 - 19	156 234	80 184	76 050	114 987[1]	58 927[1]	56 060[1]	38 474[1]	19 835[1]	18 639[1]
20 - 24	210 548	108 287	102 261	163 809[1]	84 295[1]	79 514[1]	43 591[1]	22 419[1]	21 172[1]
25 - 29	161 333	82 690	78 643	129 636[1]	66 494[1]	63 142[1]	29 435[1]	15 086[1]	14 349[1]
30 - 34	100 219	51 286	48 933	81 067[1]	41 543[1]	39 524[1]	17 856[1]	9 080[1]	8 776[1]
35 - 39	56 231	28 866	27 365	44 719[1]	22 952[1]	21 767[1]	10 771[1]	5 550[1]	5 221[1]
40 - 44	16 001	8 246	7 755	12 098[1]	6 257[1]	5 841[1]	3 685[1]	1 871[1]	1 814[1]
45 - 49	1 333	650	683	845[1]	420[1]	425[1]	456[1]	211[1]	245[1]
50 +	172	77	95	108[1]	43[1]	65[1]	57[1]	31[1]	26[1]
Unknown - Inconnu	2 907	1 494	1 413	1 500[1]	793[1]	707[1]	748[1]	369[1]	379[1]
Ecuador - Équateur[12]									
2004 (U)									
Total	168 893	85 999	82 894	132 618	67 598	65 020	36 275	18 401	17 874
0 - 14	1 908	981	927	1 555	796	759	353	185	168
15 - 19	29 145	14 987	14 158	22 490	11 555	10 935	6 655	3 432	3 223
20 - 24	50 760	25 781	24 979	39 743	20 159	19 584	11 017	5 622	5 395
25 - 29	38 133	19 409	18 724	30 697	15 660	15 037	7 436	3 749	3 687
30 - 34	25 313	12 915	12 398	20 023	10 264	9 759	5 290	2 651	2 639
35 - 39	13 869	6 991	6 878	10 633	5 374	5 259	3 236	1 617	1 619
40 - 44	4 953	2 531	2 422	3 449	1 792	1 657	1 504	739	765
45 - 49	662	311	351	446	203	243	216	108	108
50 +	-	-	-	-	-	-	-	-	-
Unknown - Inconnu	4 150	2 093	2 057	3 582	1 795	1 787	568	298	270
2005 (U)									
Total	168 324	...	...	...	...	...	...	...	...
0 - 14	614	...	...	...	...	...	...	...	...
15 - 19	29 030	...	...	...	...	...	...	...	...
20 - 24	50 551	...	...	...	...	...	...	...	...
25 - 29	39 315	...	...	...	...	...	...	...	...
30 - 34	25 284	...	...	...	...	...	...	...	...
35 - 39	13 978	...	...	...	...	...	...	...	...

10. Live births by age of mother, sex of the child and urban/rural residence: latest available year, 1997 - 2006
Naissances vivantes selon l'âge de la mère, le sexe de l'enfant et la résidence, urbaine/rurale: dernière année disponible, 1997 - 2006 (continued - suite)

Continent, country or area, date, code and age (in years) Continent, pays ou zone, code, date et âge (en annèes)	Total			Urban - Urbaine			Rural - Rurale		
	Both sexes Les deux sexes	Male Masculin	Female Féminin	Both sexes Les deux sexes	Male Masculin	Female Féminin	Both sexes Les deux sexes	Male Masculin	Female Féminin
AMERICA, SOUTH - AMÉRIQUE DU SUD									
Ecuador - Équateur[12]									
2005 (U)									
40 - 44	4 761	...	...	...	...	...	...	...	...
45 - 49	682	...	...	...	...	...	...	...	...
50 +	-	...	...	...	...	...	...	...	...
Unknown - Inconnu	4 109	...	...	...	...	...	...	...	...
French Guiana - Guyane française[3]									
2003 (C)									
Total	5 553	2 842	2 711	...	...	...	...	...	...
0 - 14	62	32	30	...	...	...	...	...	...
15 - 19	830	431	399	...	...	...	...	...	...
20 - 24	1 292	695	597	...	...	...	...	...	...
25 - 29	1 405	705	700	...	...	...	...	...	...
30 - 34	1 157	596	561	...	...	...	...	...	...
35 - 39	624	299	325	...	...	...	...	...	...
40 - 44	173	78	95	...	...	...	...	...	...
45 - 49	10	6	4	...	...	...	...	...	...
50 +	-	-	-	...	...	...	...	...	...
Peru - Pérou[13]									
2004 (+U)									
Total	344 804	176 441	168 363	...	...	...	...	...	...
12 - 14	996	530	466	...	...	...	...	...	...
15 - 19	45 455	23 226	22 229	...	...	...	...	...	...
20 - 24	91 076	46 690	44 386	...	...	...	...	...	...
25 - 29	86 864	44 593	42 271	...	...	...	...	...	...
30 - 34	67 304	34 344	32 960	...	...	...	...	...	...
35 - 39	39 462	20 244	19 218	...	...	...	...	...	...
40 - 44	12 063	6 025	6 038	...	...	...	...	...	...
45 - 49	1 140	563	577	...	...	...	...	...	...
50 +	137	64	73	...	...	...	...	...	...
Unknown - Inconnu	307	162	145	...	...	...	...	...	...
Suriname									
2005 (C)									
Total	8 657	...	...	...	...	...	...	...	...
0 - 14	67	...	...	...	...	...	...	...	...
15 - 19	1 368	...	...	...	...	...	...	...	...
20 - 24	2 476	...	...	...	...	...	...	...	...
25 - 29	2 142	...	...	...	...	...	...	...	...
30 - 34	1 576	...	...	...	...	...	...	...	...
35 - 39	814	...	...	...	...	...	...	...	...
40 - 44	188	...	...	...	...	...	...	...	...
45 +	26	...	...	...	...	...	...	...	...
Unknown - Inconnu	-	...	...	...	...	...	...	...	...
Uruguay									
2004 (C)									
Total	50 052	...	...	...	...	...	...	...	...
0 - 14	184	...	...	...	...	...	...	...	...
15 - 19	7 427	...	...	...	...	...	...	...	...
20 - 24	11 976	...	...	...	...	...	...	...	...
25 - 29	12 672	...	...	...	...	...	...	...	...
30 - 34	10 023	...	...	...	...	...	...	...	...
35 - 39	5 285	...	...	...	...	...	...	...	...
40 - 44	1 603	...	...	...	...	...	...	...	...
45 - 49	96	...	...	...	...	...	...	...	...
50 +	6	...	...	...	...	...	...	...	...
Unknown - Inconnu	780	...	...	...	...	...	...	...	...
Venezuela (Bolivarian Republic of) - Venezuela (République bolivarienne du)[14]									
2002 (C)									
Total	492 678	254 969	237 709	...	...	...	...	...	...
0 - 14	5 148	2 660	2 488	...	...	...	...	...	...

10. Live births by age of mother, sex of the child and urban/rural residence: latest available year, 1997 - 2006
Naissances vivantes selon l'âge de la mère, le sexe de l'enfant et la résidence, urbaine/rurale: dernière année disponible, 1997 - 2006 (continued - suite)

Continent, country or area, date, code and age (in years) Continent, pays ou zone, code, date et âge (en années)	Total			Urban - Urbaine			Rural - Rurale		
	Both sexes Les deux sexes	Male Masculin	Female Féminin	Both sexes Les deux sexes	Male Masculin	Female Féminin	Both sexes Les deux sexes	Male Masculin	Female Féminin
AMERICA, SOUTH - **AMÉRIQUE DU SUD**									
Venezuela (Bolivarian **Republic of) - Venezuela** **(République bolivarienne** **du)[14]**									
2002 (C)									
15 - 19	100 062	51 874	48 188	...	...	...	...	...	...
20 - 24	146 417	75 965	70 452	...	...	...	...	...	...
25 - 29	110 318	56 888	53 430	...	...	...	...	...	...
30 - 34	73 522	38 081	35 441	...	...	...	...	...	...
35 - 39	36 756	18 951	17 805	...	...	...	...	...	...
40 - 44	10 443	5 408	5 035	...	...	...	...	...	...
45 - 49	1 376	685	691	...	...	...	...	...	...
50 +	412	186	226	...	...	...	...	...	...
Unknown - Inconnu	8 224	4 271	3 953	...	...	...	...	...	...
ASIA - ASIE									
Armenia - Arménie[15]									
2006 (C)									
Total	37 639	...	...	23 793	...	...	13 846	...	...
15 - 19	4 000	...	...	1 954	...	...	2 046	...	...
20 - 24	18 169	...	...	10 821	...	...	7 348	...	...
25 - 29	10 436	...	...	7 310	...	...	3 126	...	...
30 - 34	3 615	...	...	2 695	...	...	920	...	...
35 - 39	1 168	...	...	835	...	...	333	...	...
40 - 44	239	...	...	170	...	...	69	...	...
45 - 49	12	...	...	8	...	...	4	...	...
50 +	-	...	...	-	...	...	-	...	...
Azerbaijan - Azerbaïdjan[16]									
2004 (+C)									
Total	131 609	71 009	60 600	59 026	32 047	26 979	72 583	38 962	33 621
15 - 19	13 739	7 115	6 624	4 695	2 432	2 263	9 044	4 683	4 361
20 - 24	54 902	28 884	26 018	23 512	12 400	11 112	31 390	16 484	14 906
25 - 29	35 916	19 610	16 306	17 555	9 515	8 040	18 361	10 095	8 266
30 - 34	16 846	9 599	7 247	8 361	4 826	3 535	8 485	4 773	3 712
35 - 39	7 790	4 504	3 286	3 696	2 200	1 496	4 094	2 304	1 790
40 - 44	2 189	1 189	1 000	1 088	617	471	1 101	572	529
45 - 49	204	96	108	104	51	53	100	45	55
50 +	23	12	11	15	6	9	8	6	2
Bahrain - Bahreïn									
2006 (C)									
Total	15 053	...	...	...	...	...	...	...	...
0 - 14	3	...	...	...	...	...	...	...	...
15 - 19	424	...	...	...	...	...	...	...	...
20 - 24	3 370	...	...	...	...	...	...	...	...
25 - 29	4 794	...	...	...	...	...	...	...	...
30 - 34	3 665	...	...	...	...	...	...	...	...
35 - 39	2 059	...	...	...	...	...	...	...	...
40 - 44	683	...	...	...	...	...	...	...	...
45 - 49	49	...	...	...	...	...	...	...	...
50 +	4	...	...	...	...	...	...	...	...
Unknown - Inconnu	2	...	...	...	...	...	...	...	...
Bhutan - Bhoutan[17]									
2005 (I)									
Total	12 538	6 306	6 232	3 845	1 943	1 902	8 693	4 363	4 330
15 - 19	1 376	711	665	309	158	151	1 067	553	514
20 - 24	4 211	2 156	2 055	1 388	702	686	2 823	1 454	1 369
25 - 29	3 677	1 814	1 863	1 332	670	662	2 345	1 144	1 201
30 - 34	1 753	880	873	518	265	253	1 235	615	620
35 - 39	960	463	497	215	110	105	745	353	392
40 - 44	434	207	227	64	30	34	370	177	193
45 - 49	127	75	52	19	8	11	108	67	41

10. Live births by age of mother, sex of the child and urban/rural residence: latest available year, 1997 - 2006
Naissances vivantes selon l'âge de la mère, le sexe de l'enfant et la résidence, urbaine/rurale: dernière année disponible, 1997 - 2006 (continued - suite)

Continent, country or area, date, code and age (in years) / Continent, pays ou zone, code, date et âge (en annèes)	Total			Urban - Urbaine			Rural - Rurale		
	Both sexes Les deux sexes	Male Masculin	Female Féminin	Both sexes Les deux sexes	Male Masculin	Female Féminin	Both sexes Les deux sexes	Male Masculin	Female Féminin
ASIA - ASIE									
Brunei Darussalam - Brunéi Darussalam									
2002 (+C)									
Total	7 464	3 818	3 646	...	...	...	...	...	...
0 - 14	7	4	3	...	...	...	...	...	...
15 - 19	387	187	200	...	...	...	...	...	...
20 - 24	1 585	819	766	...	...	...	...	...	...
25 - 29	2 125	1 072	1 053	...	...	...	...	...	...
30 - 34	1 967	994	973	...	...	...	...	...	...
35 - 39	1 052	560	492	...	...	...	...	...	...
40 - 44	317	169	148	...	...	...	...	...	...
45 - 49	21	12	9	...	...	...	...	...	...
50 +	-	-	-	...	...	...	...	...	...
Unknown - Inconnu	3	1	2	...	...	...	...	...	...
Cambodia - Cambodge									
2004 (U)									
Total	320 594[5]	...	...	40 790[18]	...	...	279 843[18]	...	...
15 - 19	23 238	...	...	2 097	...	...	21 140	...	...
20 - 24	106 787	...	...	11 172	...	...	95 615	...	...
25 - 29	66 573	...	...	9 448	...	...	57 125	...	...
30 - 34	57 861	...	...	8 609	...	...	49 252	...	...
35 - 39	43 391	...	...	6 945	...	...	36 446	...	...
40 - 44	19 386	...	...	2 066	...	...	17 320	...	...
45 - 49	3 358	...	...	453	...	...	2 945	...	...
China: Hong Kong SAR - Chine: Hong Kong RAS									
2006 (C)									
Total	65 626	34 595	31 031	...	...	...	...	...	...
0 - 14	9	2	7	...	...	...	...	...	...
15 - 19	885	455	430	...	...	...	...	...	...
20 - 24	9 071	4 713	4 358	...	...	...	...	...	...
25 - 29	18 814	9 902	8 912	...	...	...	...	...	...
30 - 34	23 035	12 219	10 816	...	...	...	...	...	...
35 - 39	11 750	6 206	5 544	...	...	...	...	...	...
40 - 44	1 958	1 043	915	...	...	...	...	...	...
45 - 49	100	52	48	...	...	...	...	...	...
50 +	2	1	1	...	...	...	...	...	...
Unknown - Inconnu	2	2	-	...	...	...	...	...	...
China: Macao SAR - Chine: Macao RAS									
2006 (C)									
Total	4 058	2 113	1 945	...	...	...	...	...	...
0 - 14	-	-	-	...	...	...	...	...	...
15 - 19	82	40	42	...	...	...	...	...	...
20 - 24	691	348	343	...	...	...	...	...	...
25 - 29	1 128	577	551	...	...	...	...	...	...
30 - 34	1 340	716	624	...	...	...	...	...	...
35 - 39	674	356	318	...	...	...	...	...	...
40 - 44	133	71	62	...	...	...	...	...	...
45 - 49	7	3	4	...	...	...	...	...	...
50 +	3	2	1	...	...	...	...	...	...
Unknown - Inconnu	-	-	-	...	...	...	...	...	...
Cyprus - Chypre[19]									
2006 (C)									
Total	8 731	4 559	4 172	5 184[1]	2 659[1]	2 525[1]	2 875[1]	1 536[1]	1 339[1]
0 - 14	-	-	-	-[1]	-[1]	-[1]	-[1]	-[1]	-[1]
15 - 19	176	88	88	81[1]	33[1]	48[1]	59[1]	33[1]	26[1]
20 - 24	1 417	755	662	677[1]	361[1]	316[1]	602[1]	323[1]	279[1]
25 - 29	3 208	1 661	1 547	1 888[1]	938[1]	950[1]	1 101[1]	607[1]	494[1]
30 - 34	2 618	1 385	1 233	1 699[1]	904[1]	795[1]	753[1]	384[1]	369[1]
35 - 39	1 027	526	501	662[1]	336[1]	326[1]	280[1]	148[1]	132[1]
40 - 44	218	113	105	139[1]	72[1]	67[1]	67[1]	32[1]	35[1]
45 - 49	25	8	17	18[1]	5[1]	13[1]	5[1]	2[1]	3[1]

Continent, country or area, date, code and age (in years) / Continent, pays ou zone, code, date et âge (en années)	Total			Urban - Urbaine			Rural - Rurale		
	Both sexes Les deux sexes	Male Masculin	Female Féminin	Both sexes Les deux sexes	Male Masculin	Female Féminin	Both sexes Les deux sexes	Male Masculin	Female Féminin
ASIA - ASIE									
Cyprus - Chypre[19]									
2006 (C)									
50 + ...	6	2	4	4[1]	2[1]	2[1]	-[1]	-[1]	-[1]
Unknown - Inconnu	36	21	15	16[1]	8[1]	8[1]	8[1]	7[1]	1[1]
Georgia - Géorgie[16]									
2001 (C)									
Total.....................	40 416	21 906	18 510	25 078	13 427	11 651	15 338	8 479	6 859
0 - 14...................	86	45	41	53	31	22	33	14	19
15 - 19...................	4 814	2 557	2 257	2 769	1 440	1 329	2 045	1 117	928
20 - 24...................	15 733	8 392	7 341	9 193	4 883	4 310	6 540	3 509	3 031
25 - 29...................	9 640	5 334	4 306	6 397	3 501	2 896	3 243	1 833	1 410
30 - 34...................	5 992	3 291	2 701	3 896	2 098	1 798	2 096	1 193	903
35 - 39...................	3 058	1 686	1 372	2 046	1 097	949	1 012	589	423
40 - 44...................	809	449	360	535	287	248	274	162	112
45 - 49...................	146	80	66	89	42	47	57	38	19
50 + ...	38	17	21	26	11	15	12	6	6
Unknown - Inconnu	100	55	45	74	37	37	26	18	8
2006 (C)									
Total.....................	47 795	25 236	22 559	...	...	...	...	...	...
0 - 14...................	25	13	12	...	...	...	...	...	...
15 - 19...................	6 608	3 478	3 130	...	...	...	...	...	...
20 - 24...................	17 666	9 301	8 365	...	...	...	...	...	...
25 - 29...................	12 409	6 487	5 922	...	...	...	...	...	...
30 - 34...................	6 831	3 673	3 158	...	...	...	...	...	...
35 - 39...................	2 929	1 597	1 332	...	...	...	...	...	...
40 - 44...................	791	423	368	...	...	...	...	...	...
45 - 49...................	87	49	38	...	...	...	...	...	...
50 + ...	34	15	19	...	...	...	...	...	...
Unknown - Inconnu	415	200	215	...	...	...	...	...	...
Iraq[20]									
2000 (U)									
Total.....................	471 886	...	...	...	...	...	...	...	...
15 - 19...................	21 367	...	...	...	...	...	...	...	...
20 - 24...................	115 973	...	...	...	...	...	...	...	...
25 - 29...................	149 287	...	...	...	...	...	...	...	...
30 - 34...................	110 981	...	...	...	...	...	...	...	...
35 - 39...................	52 196	...	...	...	...	...	...	...	...
40 - 44...................	16 717	...	...	...	...	...	...	...	...
45 + ...	5 365	...	...	...	...	...	...	...	...
Israel - Israël[21]									
2006 (C)									
Total.....................	148 170	76 078	72 092	133 924[1]	68 816[1]	65 108[1]	14 084[1]	7 182[1]	6 902[1]
0 - 14...................	5	1	4	5[1]	1[1]	4[1]	-[1]	-[1]	-[1]
15 - 19...................	3 961	2 012	1 949	3 704[1]	1 893[1]	1 811[1]	256[1]	119[1]	137[1]
20 - 24...................	29 414	15 167	14 247	27 187[1]	14 028[1]	13 159[1]	2 163[1]	1 110[1]	1 053[1]
25 - 29...................	46 177	23 714	22 463	42 062[1]	21 602[1]	20 460[1]	4 069[1]	2 085[1]	1 984[1]
30 - 34...................	42 389	21 756	20 633	37 803[1]	19 413[1]	18 390[1]	4 556[1]	2 331[1]	2 225[1]
35 - 39...................	20 752	10 625	10 127	18 265[1]	9 374[1]	8 891[1]	2 477[1]	1 244[1]	1 233[1]
40 - 44...................	4 712	2 428	2 284	4 198[1]	2 159[1]	2 039[1]	509[1]	266[1]	243[1]
45 - 49...................	410	203	207	381[1]	189[1]	192[1]	29[1]	14[1]	15[1]
50 + ...	73	37	36	69[1]	36[1]	33[1]	4[1]	1[1]	3[1]
Unknown - Inconnu	277	135	142	250[1]	121[1]	129[1]	21[1]	12[1]	9[1]
Japan - Japon[22]									
2006 (C)									
Total.....................	1 092 674	560 439	532 235	984 329[1]	504 907[1]	479 422[1]	108 169[1]	55 449[1]	52 720[1]
0 - 14...................	41	27	14	40[1]	26[1]	14[1]	1[1]	1[1]	-[1]
15 - 19...................	15 933	8 190	7 743	14 103[1]	7 254[1]	6 849[1]	1 829[1]	936[1]	893[1]
20 - 24...................	130 230	67 201	63 029	114 311[1]	59 029[1]	55 282[1]	15 917[1]	8 171[1]	7 746[1]
25 - 29...................	335 771	172 401	163 370	300 478[1]	154 267[1]	146 211[1]	35 257[1]	18 120[1]	17 137[1]
30 - 34...................	417 776	214 014	203 762	379 196[1]	194 317[1]	184 879[1]	38 486[1]	19 646[1]	18 840[1]
35 - 39...................	170 775	87 498	83 277	156 044[1]	79 945[1]	76 099[1]	14 696[1]	7 538[1]	7 158[1]
40 - 44...................	21 608	10 832	10 776	19 668[1]	9 819[1]	9 849[1]	1 932[1]	1 011[1]	921[1]
45 - 49...................	522	267	255	474[1]	242[1]	232[1]	48[1]	25[1]	23[1]

10. Live births by age of mother, sex of the child and urban/rural residence: latest available year, 1997 - 2006
Naissances vivantes selon l'âge de la mère, le sexe de l'enfant et la résidence, urbaine/rurale: dernière année disponible, 1997 - 2006 (continued - suite)

Continent, country or area, date, code and age (in years) / Continent, pays ou zone, code, date et âge (en années)	Total			Urban - Urbaine			Rural - Rurale		
	Both sexes Les deux sexes	Male Masculin	Female Féminin	Both sexes Les deux sexes	Male Masculin	Female Féminin	Both sexes Les deux sexes	Male Masculin	Female Féminin
ASIA - ASIE									
Japan - Japon[22]									
2006 (C)									
50 +	9	5	4	7[1]	5[1]	2[1]	2[1]	-[1]	2[1]
Unknown - Inconnu	9	4	5	8[1]	3[1]	5[1]	1[1]	1[1]	-[1]
Kazakhstan[16]									
2006 (C)									
Total	301 756	155 104	146 652	175 582	90 402	85 180	126 174	64 702	61 472
0 - 14	31	18	13	19	10	9	12	8	4
15 - 19	21 429	10 898	10 531	12 405	6 344	6 061	9 024	4 554	4 470
20 - 24	102 851	53 057	49 794	58 776	30 280	28 496	44 075	22 777	21 298
25 - 29	86 895	44 610	42 285	51 204	26 294	24 910	35 691	18 316	17 375
30 - 34	55 398	28 347	27 051	32 735	16 849	15 886	22 663	11 498	11 165
35 - 39	28 041	14 487	13 554	16 339	8 525	7 814	11 702	5 962	5 740
40 - 44	6 526	3 371	3 155	3 746	1 918	1 828	2 780	1 453	1 327
45 - 49	303	166	137	156	79	77	147	87	60
50 +	20	11	9	11	7	4	9	4	5
Unknown - Inconnu	262	139	123	191	96	95	71	43	28
Korea (Republic of) - Corée (République de)[23]									
2006 (C)									
Total	451 514[24]	233 845[24]	217 669[24]	371 084	192 149	178 935	77 020	40 000	37 020
0 - 14	33[24]	17[24]	16[24]	31	17	14	2	-	2
15 - 19	3 236[24]	1 808[24]	1 428[24]	2 377	1 350	1 027	854	456	398
20 - 24	30 801[24]	15 904[24]	14 897[24]	22 309	11 582	10 727	8 401	4 280	4 121
25 - 29	173 711[24]	89 737[24]	83 974[24]	141 115	72 764	68 351	31 699	16 517	15 182
30 - 34	189 454[24]	98 060[24]	91 394[24]	160 681	83 229	77 452	27 097	14 012	13 085
35 - 39	47 628[24]	24 930[24]	22 698[24]	39 422	20 558	18 864	7 564	4 038	3 526
40 - 44	5 398[24]	2 770[24]	2 628[24]	4 199	2 175	2 024	1 120	560	560
45 - 49	357[24]	152[24]	205[24]	252	117	135	98	33	65
50 +	35[24]	22[24]	13[24]	27	17	10	8	5	3
Unknown - Inconnu	861[24]	445[24]	416[24]	671	340	331	177	99	78
Kuwait - Koweït									
2006 (C)									
Total	52 759	26 923	25 836	...	...	...	...	...	...
15 - 19	1 287	680	607	...	...	...	...	...	...
20 - 24	11 328	5 745	5 583	...	...	...	...	...	...
25 - 29	16 526	8 449	8 077	...	...	...	...	...	...
30 - 34	12 998	6 676	6 322	...	...	...	...	...	...
35 - 39	6 863	3 489	3 374	...	...	...	...	...	...
40 - 44	1 935	982	953	...	...	...	...	...	...
45 +	226	119	107	...	...	...	...	...	...
Unknown - Inconnu	1 596	783	813	...	...	...	...	...	...
Kyrgyzstan - Kirghizistan									
2006 (C)									
Total	120 737	61 987	58 750	39 414	20 320	19 094	81 323	41 667	39 656
0 - 14	2	2	-	-	-	-	2	2	-
15 - 19	8 232	4 306	3 926	2 401	1 248	1 153	5 831	3 058	2 773
20 - 24	44 451	22 805	21 646	13 771	7 129	6 642	30 680	15 676	15 004
25 - 29	34 008	17 417	16 591	11 354	5 842	5 512	22 654	11 575	11 079
30 - 34	19 962	10 240	9 722	6 848	3 541	3 307	13 114	6 699	6 415
35 - 39	10 412	5 321	5 091	3 690	1 879	1 811	6 722	3 442	3 280
40 - 44	2 919	1 482	1 437	1 028	528	500	1 891	954	937
45 - 49	494	278	216	147	61	86	347	217	130
50 +	28	12	16	6	2	4	22	10	12
Unknown - Inconnu	229	124	105	169	90	79	60	34	26
Malaysia - Malaisie									
2004 (C)									
Total	477 768	246 726	231 042	...	...	...	...	...	...
0 - 14	564	286	278	...	...	...	...	...	...
15 - 19	15 793	8 139	7 654	...	...	...	...	...	...
20 - 24	84 516	43 836	40 680	...	...	...	...	...	...
25 - 29	153 014	79 130	73 884	...	...	...	...	...	...
30 - 34	127 824	65 873	61 951	...	...	...	...	...	...
35 - 39	70 925	36 518	34 407	...	...	...	...	...	...

10. Live births by age of mother, sex of the child and urban/rural residence: latest available year, 1997 - 2006
Naissances vivantes selon l'âge de la mère, le sexe de l'enfant et la résidence, urbaine/rurale: dernière année disponible, 1997 - 2006 (continued - suite)

Continent, country or area, date, code and age (in years) Continent, pays ou zone, code, date et âge (en années)	Total			Urban - Urbaine			Rural - Rurale		
	Both sexes Les deux sexes	Male Masculin	Female Féminin	Both sexes Les deux sexes	Male Masculin	Female Féminin	Both sexes Les deux sexes	Male Masculin	Female Féminin
ASIA - ASIE									
Malaysia - Malaisie									
2004 (C)									
40 - 44	21 168	10 891	10 277	...	...	...	...	...	...
45 - 49	1 948	1 013	935	...	...	...	...	...	...
50 +	134	73	61	...	...	...	...	...	...
Unknown - Inconnu	1 882	967	915	...	...	...	...	...	...
Maldives									
2006 (C)									
Total	5 829	3 008[25]	2 820[25]	2 707	1 381[25]	1 325[25]	3 122	1 627	1 495
0 - 14	1	-	1	-	-	-	1	-	1
15 - 19	288	147	141	100	50	50	188	97	91
20 - 24	2 091	1 076	1 015	999	509	490	1 092	567	525
25 - 29	1 733	909[25]	823[25]	889	477[25]	411[25]	844	432	412
30 - 34	1 048	540	508	480	239	241	568	301	267
35 - 39	526	264	262	206	95	111	320	169	151
40 - 44	132	68	64	32	11	21	100	57	43
45 - 49	9	4	5	1	-	1	8	4	4
50 +	1	-	1	-	-	-	1	-	1
Mongolia Mongolie									
1998 (C)									
Total	49 256	24 999	24 257	22 393	11 320	11 073	26 863	13 679	13 184
0 - 14	50	19	31	16	8	8	34	11	23
15 - 19	3 658	1 811	1 847	1 451	734	717	2 207	1 077	1 130
20 - 24	17 857	9 078	8 779	7 720	3 906	3 814	10 137	5 172	4 965
25 - 29	14 919	7 613	7 306	6 876	3 479	3 397	8 043	4 134	3 909
30 - 34	7 893	3 987	3 906	3 950	1 988	1 962	3 943	1 999	1 944
35 - 39	3 678	1 854	1 824	1 873	948	925	1 805	906	899
40 - 44	982	518	464	424	215	209	558	303	255
45 - 49	188	104	84	71	36	35	117	68	49
50 +	31	15	16	12	6	6	19	9	10
2006 (C)									
Total	49 092	25 055	24 037	29 717	...	...	19 375	...	...
0 - 14	28	15	13	17	...	...	11	...	...
15 - 19	2 992	1 567	1 425	1 939	...	...	1 053	...	...
20 - 24	16 859	8 518	8 341	9 952	...	...	6 907	...	...
25 - 29	15 194	7 659	7 535	8 991	...	...	6 203	...	...
30 - 34	8 840	4 585	4 255	5 474	...	...	3 366	...	...
35 - 39	3 989	2 096	1 893	2 541	...	...	1 448	...	...
40 - 44	1 048	543	505	717	...	...	331	...	...
45 - 49	118	57	61	71	...	...	47	...	...
50 +	24	15	9	15	...	...	9	...	...
Oman[20]									
1999 (U)									
Total	44 067	...	...	...	...	...	...	...	...
15 - 19	4 096	...	...	...	...	...	...	...	...
20 - 24	13 224	...	...	...	...	...	...	...	...
25 - 29	11 504	...	...	...	...	...	...	...	...
30 - 34	7 759	...	...	...	...	...	...	...	...
35 - 39	5 563	...	...	...	...	...	...	...	...
40 - 44	1 739	...	...	...	...	...	...	...	...
45 +	182	...	...	...	...	...	...	...	...
Pakistan[26]									
2005 (I)									
Total	3 772 494	1 993 492	1 779 002	1 226 151	653 480	572 671	2 546 343	1 340 012	1 206 331
15 - 19	161 490	90 049	71 441	32 480	16 115	16 365	129 010	73 934	55 076
20 - 24	1 050 830	556 310	494 520	338 217	172 425	165 792	712 613	383 885	328 728
25 - 29	1 166 365	611 186	555 179	399 554	214 071	185 483	766 811	397 115	369 696
30 - 34	754 513	395 425	359 088	262 585	142 356	120 229	491 928	253 069	238 859
35 - 39	425 352	222 186	203 166	142 496	80 113	62 383	282 856	142 073	140 783
40 - 44	161 914	86 273	75 641	38 358	21 167	17 191	123 556	65 106	58 450
45 +	52 030	32 063	19 967	12 461	7 233	5 228	39 569	24 830	14 739
Philippines									
2003 (C)									
Total	1 669 442	868 749	800 693	...	...	...	...	...	...
0 - 14	829	422	407	...	...	...	...	...	...

10. Live births by age of mother, sex of the child and urban/rural residence: latest available year, 1997 - 2006
Naissances vivantes selon l'âge de la mère, le sexe de l'enfant et la résidence, urbaine/rurale: dernière année disponible, 1997 - 2006 (continued - suite)

Continent, country or area, date, code and age (in years) / Continent, pays ou zone, code, date et âge (en années)	Total			Urban - Urbaine			Rural - Rurale		
	Both sexes Les deux sexes	Male Masculin	Female Féminin	Both sexes Les deux sexes	Male Masculin	Female Féminin	Both sexes Les deux sexes	Male Masculin	Female Féminin
ASIA - ASIE									
Philippines									
2003 (C)									
15 - 19	123 036	64 147	58 889	...	...	...	...	...	...
20 - 24	472 211	246 027	226 184	...	...	...	...	...	...
25 - 29	458 341	239 200	219 141	...	...	...	...	...	...
30 - 34	340 211	177 132	163 079	...	...	...	...	...	...
35 - 39	193 825	100 206	93 619	...	...	...	...	...	...
40 - 44	68 400	35 260	33 140	...	...	...	...	...	...
45 - 49	8 124	4 145	3 979	...	...	...	...	...	...
50 + ...	728	346	382	...	...	...	...	...	...
Unknown - Inconnu	3 737	1 864	1 873	...	...	...	...	...	...
Qatar									
2006 (C)									
Total....................	14 120	7 196	6 924	...	...	...	...	...	...
0 - 14....................	-	-	-	...	...	...	...	...	...
15 - 19	366	194	172	...	...	...	...	...	...
20 - 24	2 741	1 413	1 328	...	...	...	...	...	...
25 - 29	4 353	2 232	2 121	...	...	...	...	...	...
30 - 34	3 765	1 881	1 884	...	...	...	...	...	...
35 - 39	2 145	1 080	1 065	...	...	...	...	...	...
40 - 44	667	356	311	...	...	...	...	...	...
45 - 49	70	36	34	...	...	...	...	...	...
50 + ...	9	3	6	...	...	...	...	...	...
Unknown - Inconnu	4	1	3	...	...	...	...	...	...
Saudi Arabia - Arabie saoudite									
2005 (...)									
Total....................	582 582	298 396	284 186	...	...	...	...	...	...
15 - 19	25 652	13 139	12 513	...	...	...	...	...	...
20 - 24	153 901	78 827	75 074	...	...	...	...	...	...
25 - 29	194 252	99 495	94 757	...	...	...	...	...	...
30 - 34	135 325	69 313	66 012	...	...	...	...	...	...
35 - 39	57 941	29 677	28 264	...	...	...	...	...	...
40 - 44	14 373	7 362	7 011	...	...	...	...	...	...
45 - 49	1 137	583	555	...	...	...	...	...	...
Singapore - Singapour									
2006 (C)									
Total....................	38 317	19 750	18 567	...	...	...	...	...	...
0 - 14....................	11	5	6	...	...	...	...	...	...
15 - 19	827	444	383	...	...	...	...	...	...
20 - 24	3 501	1 787	1 714	...	...	...	...	...	...
25 - 29	11 099	5 681	5 418	...	...	...	...	...	...
30 - 34	15 284	7 882	7 402	...	...	...	...	...	...
35 - 39	6 471	3 388	3 083	...	...	...	...	...	...
40 - 44	1 095	548	547	...	...	...	...	...	...
45 - 49	29	15	14	...	...	...	...	...	...
50 + ...	-	-	-	...	...	...	...	...	...
Unknown - Inconnu	-	-	-	...	...	...	...	...	...
Sri Lanka									
2001 (+C)									
Total....................	358 581	183 409	175 172	...	...	...	...	...	...
0 - 14....................	118	68	50	...	...	...	...	...	...
15 - 19	27 515	14 105	13 410	...	...	...	...	...	...
20 - 24	92 239	47 239	45 000	...	...	...	...	...	...
25 - 29	105 303	54 028	51 275	...	...	...	...	...	...
30 - 34	83 231	42 415	40 816	...	...	...	...	...	...
35 - 39	39 712	20 259	19 453	...	...	...	...	...	...
40 - 44	9 597	4 875	4 722	...	...	...	...	...	...
45 - 49	816	399	417	...	...	...	...	...	...
50 + ...	50	21	29	...	...	...	...	...	...
Tajikistan - Tadjikistan[16]									
1999 (U)									
Total....................	114 015	60 552	53 463	23 602	12 650	10 952	90 413	47 902	42 511
15 - 19	10 026	5 239	4 787	2 207	1 156	1 051	7 819	4 083	3 736
20 - 24	38 400	20 275	18 125	8 093	4 355	3 738	30 307	15 920	14 387

358

10. Live births by age of mother, sex of the child and urban/rural residence: latest available year, 1997 - 2006
Naissances vivantes selon l'âge de la mère, le sexe de l'enfant et la résidence, urbaine/rurale: dernière année disponible, 1997 - 2006 (continued - suite)

Continent, country or area, date, code and age (in years) Continent, pays ou zone, code, date et âge (en années)	Total			Urban - Urbaine			Rural - Rurale		
	Both sexes Les deux sexes	Male Masculin	Female Féminin	Both sexes Les deux sexes	Male Masculin	Female Féminin	Both sexes Les deux sexes	Male Masculin	Female Féminin
ASIA - ASIE									
Tajikistan - Tadjikistan[16]									
1999 (U)									
25 - 29	30 752	16 431	14 321	6 394	3 414	2 980	24 358	13 017	11 341
30 - 34	20 245	10 744	9 501	4 144	2 223	1 921	16 101	8 521	7 580
35 - 39	10 957	5 873	5 084	2 116	1 153	963	8 841	4 720	4 121
40 - 44	2 819	1 532	1 287	441	226	215	2 378	1 306	1 072
45 - 49	234	128	106	31	17	14	203	111	92
50 +	37	25	12	5	4	1	32	21	11
Unknown - Inconnu	545	305	240	171	102	69	374	203	171
Thailand - Thaïlande									
1999 (+U)									
Total	772 604	398 608	373 996	116 268	59 796	56 472	656 336	338 812	317 524
0 - 14	1 525	817	708	161	77	84	1 364	740	624
15 - 19	91 785	47 478	44 307	9 485	4 984	4 501	82 300	42 494	39 806
20 - 24	215 558	111 265	104 293	25 069	12 898	12 171	190 489	98 367	92 122
25 - 29	217 409	112 172	105 237	30 889	15 857	15 032	186 520	96 315	90 205
30 - 34	146 305	75 426	70 879	25 943	13 219	12 724	120 362	62 207	58 155
35 - 39	63 192	32 560	30 632	11 438	5 914	5 524	51 754	26 646	25 108
40 - 44	15 125	7 746	7 379	2 031	1 049	982	13 094	6 697	6 397
45 - 49	1 748	893	855	129	67	62	1 619	826	793
50 +	227	124	103	7	3	4	220	121	99
Unknown - Inconnu	19 730	10 127	9 603	11 116	5 728	5 388	8 614	4 399	4 215
2005 (+U)									
Total	809 485	416 474	393 011	...	...	...	...	...	...
0 - 14	2 549	1 301	1 248	...	...	...	...	...	...
15 - 19	113 048	58 207	54 841	...	...	...	...	...	...
20 - 24	207 269	106 613	100 656	...	...	...	...	...	...
25 - 29	220 696	113 676	107 020	...	...	...	...	...	...
30 - 34	164 735	84 673	80 062	...	...	...	...	...	...
35 - 39	78 749	40 531	38 218	...	...	...	...	...	...
40 - 44	18 809	9 667	9 142	...	...	...	...	...	...
45 - 49	1 364	667	697	...	...	...	...	...	...
50 +	78	43	35	...	...	...	...	...	...
Unknown - Inconnu	2 188	1 096	1 092	...	...	...	...	...	...
Turkey - Turquie[27]									
1997 (I)									
Total	1 377 000		...	...	...	...	...	...	...
0 - 14	-	...	...	...	...	...	...	...	...
15 - 19	165 000	...	...	...	...	...	...	...	...
20 - 24	531 000	...	...	...	...	...	...	...	...
25 - 29	387 000	...	...	...	...	...	...	...	...
30 - 34	182 000	...	...	...	...	...	...	...	...
35 - 39	79 000	...	...	...	...	...	...	...	...
40 - 44	28 000	...	...	...	...	...	...	...	...
45 +	5 000	...	...	...	...	...	...	...	...
United Arab Emirates - Émirats arabes unis									
2003 (...)									
Total	61 165	31 241	29 924	...	...	...	...	...	...
15 - 19	2 647	1 415	1 232	...	...	...	...	...	...
20 - 24	12 551	6 386	6 165	...	...	...	...	...	...
25 - 29	18 710	9 605	9 105	...	...	...	...	...	...
30 - 34	14 699	7 484	7 215	...	...	...	...	...	...
35 - 39	7 670	3 876	3 794	...	...	...	...	...	...
40 - 44	2 796	1 409	1 387	...	...	...	...	...	...
45 - 49	620	316	304	...	...	...	...	...	...
50 +	101	51	50	...	...	...	...	...	...
Unknown - Inconnu	1 371	699	672	...	...	...	...	...	...
Uzbekistan - Ouzbékistan[16]									
2000 (C)									
Total	527 580	...	...	163 834	...	...	363 746	...	...
15 - 19	28 179	...	...	10 217	...	...	17 962	...	...
20 - 24	228 743	...	...	69 369	...	...	159 374	...	...
25 - 29	160 082	...	...	48 315	...	...	111 767	...	...
30 - 34	78 316	...	...	25 084	...	...	53 232	...	...

10. Live births by age of mother, sex of the child and urban/rural residence: latest available year, 1997 - 2006
Naissances vivantes selon l'âge de la mère, le sexe de l'enfant et la résidence, urbaine/rurale: dernière année disponible, 1997 - 2006 (continued - suite)

Continent, country or area, date, code and age (in years) / Continent, pays ou zone, code, date et âge (en années)	Total			Urban - Urbaine			Rural - Rurale		
	Both sexes Les deux sexes	Male Masculin	Female Féminin	Both sexes Les deux sexes	Male Masculin	Female Féminin	Both sexes Les deux sexes	Male Masculin	Female Féminin
ASIA - ASIE									
Uzbekistan - Ouzbékistan[16]									
2000 (C)									
35 - 39	26 866	...	...	9 095	...	...	17 771	...	...
40 - 44	4 979	...	...	1 639	...	...	3 340	...	...
45 - 49	348	...	...	96	...	...	252	...	...
50 +	67	...	...	19	...	...	48	...	...
EUROPE									
Åland Islands - Îles d'Åland[28]									
2006 (C)									
Total	295	...	...	...	...	...	...	...	...
0 - 19	5	...	...	...	...	...	...	...	...
20 - 24	26	...	...	...	...	...	...	...	...
25 - 29	88	...	...	...	...	...	...	...	...
30 - 34	102	...	...	...	...	...	...	...	...
35 - 39	59	...	...	...	...	...	...	...	...
40 +	15	...	...	...	...	...	...	...	...
Albania - Albanie									
2004 (C)									
Total	43 022	22 859	20 163	18 859	10 001	8 858	24 163	12 858	11 305
15 - 19	2 249	1 213	1 036	1 001	539	462	1 248	674	574
20 - 24	13 516	7 006	6 510	5 508	2 849	2 659	8 008	4 157	3 851
25 - 29	14 476	7 669	6 807	6 269	3 311	2 958	8 207	4 358	3 849
30 - 34	8 491	4 597	3 894	3 991	2 161	1 830	4 500	2 436	2 064
35 - 39	3 239	1 800	1 439	1 532	855	677	1 707	945	762
40 - 44	736	419	317	346	185	161	390	234	156
45 - 49	64	38	26	36	22	14	28	16	12
50 +	12	7	5	5	2	3	7	5	2
Unknown - Inconnu	239	110	129	171	77	94	68	33	35
2006 (C)									
Total	34 229	...	...	...	...	...	...	...	...
0 - 19	1 985	...	...	...	...	...	...	...	...
20 - 24	11 213	...	...	...	...	...	...	...	...
25 - 29	11 233	...	...	...	...	...	...	...	...
30 - 34	6 440	...	...	...	...	...	...	...	...
35 - 39	2 469	...	...	...	...	...	...	...	...
40 - 44	502	...	...	...	...	...	...	...	...
45 - 49	46	...	...	...	...	...	...	...	...
50 +	15	...	...	...	...	...	...	...	...
Unknown - Inconnu	326	...	...	...	...	...	...	...	...
Andorra - Andorre									
2006 (C)									
Total	843	445	398	...	...	...	...	...	...
0 - 14	-	-	-	...	...	...	...	...	...
15 - 19	19	10	9	...	...	...	...	...	...
20 - 24	93	46	47	...	...	...	...	...	...
25 - 29	219	120	99	...	...	...	...	...	...
30 - 34	322	167	155	...	...	...	...	...	...
35 - 39	142	78	64	...	...	...	...	...	...
40 - 44	46	24	22	...	...	...	...	...	...
45 - 49	1	-	1	...	...	...	...	...	...
50 +	1	-	1	...	...	...	...	...	...
Austria - Autriche									
2006 (C)									
Total	77 914	39 745	38 169	...	...	...	...	...	...
0 - 14	18	13	5	...	...	...	...	...	...
15 - 19	2 874	1 469	1 405	...	...	...	...	...	...
20 - 24	13 956	7 125	6 831	...	...	...	...	...	...
25 - 29	23 635	12 066	11 569	...	...	...	...	...	...
30 - 34	23 357	11 921	11 436	...	...	...	...	...	...
35 - 39	11 610	5 886	5 724	...	...	...	...	...	...
40 - 44	2 364	1 222	1 142	...	...	...	...	...	...

Continent, country or area, date, code and age (in years) / Continent, pays ou zone, code, date et âge (en années)	Total			Urban - Urbaine			Rural - Rurale		
	Both sexes Les deux sexes	Male Masculin	Female Féminin	Both sexes Les deux sexes	Male Masculin	Female Féminin	Both sexes Les deux sexes	Male Masculin	Female Féminin
EUROPE									
Austria - Autriche									
2006 (C)									
45 - 49	96	41	55	...	...	...	...	...	...
50 +	4	2	2	...	...	...	...	...	...
Belarus - Bélarus[16]									
2006 (C)									
Total	96 721	49 849	46 872	71 186	36 851	34 335	25 535	12 998	12 537
0 - 14	10	5	5	7	4	3	3	1	2
15 - 19	8 238	4 234	4 004	5 007	2 604	2 403	3 231	1 630	1 601
20 - 24	36 120	18 613	17 507	25 928	13 424	12 504	10 192	5 189	5 003
25 - 29	29 846	15 372	14 474	23 031	11 896	11 135	6 815	3 476	3 339
30 - 34	15 950	8 229	7 721	12 385	6 397	5 988	3 565	1 832	1 733
35 - 39	5 488	2 846	2 642	4 077	2 145	1 932	1 411	701	710
40 - 44	935	488	447	651	334	317	284	154	130
45 - 49	47	23	24	32	16	16	15	7	8
50 +	-	-	-	-	-	-	-	-	-
Unknown - Inconnu	87	39	48	68	31	37	19	8	11
Bosnia and Herzegovina - Bosnie-Herzégovine									
2006 (C)									
Total	34 033	...	...	...	...	...	...	...	...
0 - 14	7	...	...	...	...	...	...	...	...
15 - 19	2 065	...	...	...	...	...	...	...	...
20 - 24	9 964	...	...	...	...	...	...	...	...
25 - 29	11 370	...	...	...	...	...	...	...	...
30 - 34	6 969	...	...	...	...	...	...	...	...
35 - 39	2 555	...	...	...	...	...	...	...	...
40 - 44	507	...	...	...	...	...	...	...	...
45 - 49	29	...	...	...	...	...	...	...	...
50 +	1	...	...	...	...	...	...	...	...
Unknown - Inconnu	566	...	...	...	...	...	...	...	...
Bulgaria - Bulgarie									
2006 (C)									
Total	73 978	38 108	35 870	55 043	28 322	26 721	18 935	9 786	9 149
0 - 14	383	198	185	250	134	116	133	64	69
15 - 19	9 861	4 967	4 894	5 827	2 962	2 865	4 034	2 005	2 029
20 - 24	20 716	10 699	10 017	13 826	7 121	6 705	6 890	3 578	3 312
25 - 29	23 428	12 177	11 251	18 711	9 672	9 039	4 717	2 505	2 212
30 - 34	14 627	7 555	7 072	12 256	6 314	5 942	2 371	1 241	1 130
35 - 39	4 355	2 207	2 148	3 668	1 864	1 804	687	343	344
40 - 44	571	285	286	474	239	235	97	46	51
45 - 49	25	17	8	19	13	6	6	4	2
50 +	-	-	-	-	-	-	-	-	-
Unknown - Inconnu	12	3	9	12	3	9	-	-	-
Channel Islands: Guernsey - Îles Anglo-Normandes: Guernesey									
2000 (C)									
Total	644	336	308	...	...	...	...	...	...
15 - 19	42	15	27	...	...	...	...	...	...
20 - 24	84	49	35	...	...	...	...	...	...
25 - 29	192	101	91	...	...	...	...	...	...
30 - 34	200	102	98	...	...	...	...	...	...
35 - 39	106	60	46	...	...	...	...	...	...
40 - 44	20	9	11	...	...	...	...	...	...
Croatia - Croatie									
2006 (C)									
Total	41 446	21 469	19 977	23 085	11 934	11 151	18 361	9 535	8 826
0 - 14	5	4	1	3	3	-	2	1	1
15 - 19	1 823	944	879	656	340	316	1 167	604	563
20 - 24	9 074	4 768	4 306	3 915	2 112	1 803	5 159	2 656	2 503
25 - 29	14 748	7 685	7 063	8 260	4 228	4 032	6 488	3 457	3 031
30 - 34	10 806	5 526	5 280	6 969	3 582	3 387	3 837	1 944	1 893
35 - 39	4 146	2 091	2 055	2 761	1 393	1 368	1 385	698	687
40 - 44	776	412	364	474	248	226	302	164	138

10. Live births by age of mother, sex of the child and urban/rural residence: latest available year, 1997 - 2006
Naissances vivantes selon l'âge de la mère, le sexe de l'enfant et la résidence, urbaine/rurale: dernière année disponible,
1997 - 2006 (continued - suite)

Continent, country or area, date, code and age (in years) / Continent, pays ou zone, code, date et âge (en années)	Total			Urban - Urbaine			Rural - Rurale		
	Both sexes Les deux sexes	Male Masculin	Female Féminin	Both sexes Les deux sexes	Male Masculin	Female Féminin	Both sexes Les deux sexes	Male Masculin	Female Féminin
EUROPE									
Croatia - Croatie									
2006 (C)									
45 - 49	46	24	22	30	16	14	16	8	8
50 +	-	-	-	-	-	-	-	-	-
Unknown - Inconnu	22	15	7	17	12	5	5	3	2
Czech Republic - République tchèque									
2006 (C)									
Total	105 831	54 612	51 219	78 561	40 557	38 004	27 270	14 055	13 215
0 - 14	19	13	6	16	10	6	3	3	-
15 - 19	3 471	1 792	1 679	2 589	1 330	1 259	882	462	420
20 - 24	15 884	8 150	7 734	11 197	5 710	5 487	4 687	2 440	2 247
25 - 29	41 935	21 695	20 240	30 328	15 707	14 621	11 607	5 988	5 619
30 - 34	34 198	17 649	16 549	26 341	13 627	12 714	7 857	4 022	3 835
35 - 39	8 861	4 567	4 294	6 942	3 591	3 351	1 919	976	943
40 - 44	1 406	718	688	1 106	557	549	300	161	139
45 - 49	55	26	29	40	23	17	15	3	12
50 +	2	2	-	2	2	-	-	-	-
Unknown - Inconnu	-	-	-	-	-	-	-	-	-
Denmark - Danemark[29]									
2006 (C)									
Total	64 984	33 404	31 580	...	...	...	...	...	...
0 - 14	4	1	3	...	...	...	...	...	...
15 - 19	921	505	416	...	...	...	...	...	...
20 - 24	6 290	3 254	3 036	...	...	...	...	...	...
25 - 29	20 892	10 750	10 142	...	...	...	...	...	...
30 - 34	24 986	12 832	12 154	...	...	...	...	...	...
35 - 39	10 044	5 104	4 940	...	...	...	...	...	...
40 - 44	1 796	931	865	...	...	...	...	...	...
45 - 49	50	27	23	...	...	...	...	...	...
50 +	1	-	1	...	...	...	...	...	...
Unknown - Inconnu	-	-	-	...	...	...	...	...	...
Estonia - Estonie									
2006 (C)									
Total	14 877	7 756	7 121	10 554	5 513	5 041	4 323	2 243	2 080
0 - 14	3	1	2	-	-	-	3	1	2
15 - 19	1 107	568	539	645	321	324	462	247	215
20 - 24	3 556	1 838	1 718	2 397	1 251	1 146	1 159	587	572
25 - 29	4 799	2 529	2 270	3 575	1 875	1 700	1 224	654	570
30 - 34	3 463	1 792	1 671	2 588	1 344	1 244	875	448	427
35 - 39	1 625	858	767	1 126	599	527	499	259	240
40 - 44	309	161	148	212	117	95	97	44	53
45 - 49	12	6	6	8	3	5	4	3	1
50 +	3	3	-	3	3	-	-	-	-
Unknown - Inconnu	-	-	-	-	-	-	-	-	-
Faeroe Islands - Îles Féroé									
2005 (C)									
Total	713	...	...	...	...	...	...	...	...
0 - 14	-	...	...	...	...	...	...	...	...
15 - 19	24	...	...	...	...	...	...	...	...
20 - 24	119	...	...	...	...	...	...	...	...
25 - 29	229	...	...	...	...	...	...	...	...
30 - 34	196	...	...	...	...	...	...	...	...
35 - 39	124	...	...	...	...	...	...	...	...
40 - 44	19	...	...	...	...	...	...	...	...
45 - 49	2	...	...	...	...	...	...	...	...
50 +	-	...	...	...	...	...	...	...	...
Finland - Finlande[30]									
2006 (C)									
Total	58 840	30 005	28 835	39 003	19 919	19 084	19 837	10 086	9 751
0 - 14	3	1	2	2	-	2	1	1	-
15 - 19	1 492	782	710	970	504	466	522	278	244
20 - 24	9 506	4 715	4 791	6 301	3 102	3 199	3 205	1 613	1 592
25 - 29	18 887	9 642	9 245	12 533	6 415	6 118	6 354	3 227	3 127
30 - 34	17 924	9 190	8 734	12 081	6 210	5 871	5 843	2 980	2 863

10. Live births by age of mother, sex of the child and urban/rural residence: latest available year, 1997 - 2006
Naissances vivantes selon l'âge de la mère, le sexe de l'enfant et la résidence, urbaine/rurale: dernière année disponible, 1997 - 2006 (continued - suite)

Continent, country or area, date, code and age (in years) / Continent, pays ou zone, code, date et âge (en annèes)	Total			Urban - Urbaine			Rural - Rurale		
	Both sexes Les deux sexes	Male Masculin	Female Féminin	Both sexes Les deux sexes	Male Masculin	Female Féminin	Both sexes Les deux sexes	Male Masculin	Female Féminin
EUROPE									
Finland - Finlande[30]									
2006 (C)									
35 - 39	8 902	4 624	4 278	5 768	3 015	2 753	3 134	1 609	1 525
40 - 44	2 037	1 008	1 029	1 291	648	643	746	360	386
45 - 49	85	43	42	54	25	29	31	18	13
50 +	4	-	4	3	-	3	1	-	1
Unknown - Inconnu	-	-	-	-	-	-	-	-	-
France[31]									
2006 (C)									
Total	796 896	407 846	389 050	596 949[32]	305 440[32]	291 509[32]	198 494[32]	101 690[32]	96 804[32]
0 - 14	49	23	26	42[32]	19[32]	23[32]	7[32]	4[32]	3[32]
15 - 19	14 577	7 520	7 057	12 448[32]	6 410[32]	6 038[32]	2 111[32]	1 099[32]	1 012[32]
20 - 24	108 803	55 685	53 118	87 220[32]	44 525[32]	42 695[32]	21 446[32]	11 103[32]	10 343[32]
25 - 29	253 052	129 790	123 262	185 733[32]	95 260[32]	90 473[32]	66 972[32]	34 358[32]	32 614[32]
30 - 34	258 924	132 568	126 356	188 938[32]	96 850[32]	92 088[32]	69 461[32]	35 456[32]	34 005[32]
35 - 39	130 047	66 151	63 896	97 564[32]	49 579[32]	47 985[32]	32 143[32]	16 403[32]	15 740[32]
40 - 44	29 867	15 299	14 568	23 685[32]	12 123[32]	11 562[32]	6 101[32]	3 132[32]	2 969[32]
45 - 49	1 500	772	728	1 253[32]	640[32]	613[32]	242[32]	131[32]	111[32]
50 +	77	38	39	66[32]	34[32]	32[32]	11[32]	4[32]	7[32]
Unknown - Inconnu	-	-	-	-[32]	-[32]	-[32]	-[32]	-[32]	-[32]
Germany - Allemagne									
2006 (C)									
Total	672 724	345 816	326 908	...	...	...	...	...	...
0 - 14	141	66	75	...	...	...	...	...	...
15 - 19	23 626	12 164	11 462	...	...	...	...	...	...
20 - 24	108 190	55 645	52 545	...	...	...	...	...	...
25 - 29	198 538	101 857	96 681	...	...	...	...	...	...
30 - 34	198 712	101 966	96 746	...	...	...	...	...	...
35 - 39	119 465	61 663	57 802	...	...	...	...	...	...
40 - 44	23 195	12 008	11 187	...	...	...	...	...	...
45 - 49	826	428	398	...	...	...	...	...	...
50 +	31	19	12	...	...	...	...	...	...
Gibraltar									
2002 (C)									
Total	375	...	...	...	...	...	...	...	...
15 - 19	25	...	...	...	...	...	...	...	...
20 - 24	59	...	...	...	...	...	...	...	...
25 - 29	120	...	...	...	...	...	...	...	...
30 - 34	115	...	...	...	...	...	...	...	...
35 - 39	46	...	...	...	...	...	...	...	...
40 - 44	10	...	...	...	...	...	...	...	...
Greece - Grèce									
2006 (C)									
Total	112 042	57 739	54 303	76 996	39 734	37 262	35 046	18 005	17 041
0 - 14	80	37	43	52	25	27	28	12	16
15 - 19	3 231	1 680	1 551	1 813	945	868	1 418	735	683
20 - 24	15 274	7 829	7 445	8 761	4 516	4 245	6 513	3 313	3 200
25 - 29	33 884	17 350	16 534	22 017	11 260	10 757	11 867	6 090	5 777
30 - 34	38 161	19 795	18 366	27 957	14 498	13 459	10 204	5 297	4 907
35 - 39	17 844	9 210	8 634	13 626	7 068	6 558	4 218	2 142	2 076
40 - 44	3 196	1 648	1 548	2 477	1 274	1 203	719	374	345
45 - 49	335	170	165	260	131	129	75	39	36
50 +	37	20	17	33	17	16	4	3	1
Unknown - Inconnu	-	-	-	-	-	-	-	-	-
Hungary - Hongrie									
2006 (C)									
Total	99 871	51 116	48 755	66 223[33]	33 950	32 273	32 789[33]	16 710	16 079
0 - 14	89	45	44	41[33]	21	20	48[33]	24	24
15 - 19	6 039	3 047	2 992	3 015[33]	1 521	1 494	2 974[33]	1 506	1 468
20 - 24	15 858	8 106	7 752	8 603[33]	4 372	4 231	7 046[33]	3 621	3 425
25 - 29	35 142	18 077	17 065	23 593[33]	12 125	11 468	11 249[33]	5 789	5 460
30 - 34	31 000	15 894	15 106	22 532[33]	11 648	10 884	8 253[33]	4 131	4 122
35 - 39	10 193	5 175	5 018	7 379[33]	3 740	3 639	2 742[33]	1 399	1 343
40 - 44	1 486	740	746	1 015[33]	499	516	458[33]	232	226

10. Live births by age of mother, sex of the child and urban/rural residence: latest available year, 1997 - 2006
Naissances vivantes selon l'âge de la mère, le sexe de l'enfant et la résidence, urbaine/rurale: dernière année disponible, 1997 - 2006 (continued - suite)

Continent, country or area, date, code and age (in years) / Continent, pays ou zone, code, date et âge (en années)	Total			Urban - Urbaine			Rural - Rurale		
	Both sexes Les deux sexes	Male Masculin	Female Féminin	Both sexes Les deux sexes	Male Masculin	Female Féminin	Both sexes Les deux sexes	Male Masculin	Female Féminin
EUROPE									
Hungary - Hongrie									
2006 (C)									
45 - 49	64	32	32	45[33]	24	21	19[33]	8	11
50 +	-	-	-	-[33]	-	-	-[33]	-	-
Unknown - Inconnu	-	-	-	-[33]	-	-	-[33]	-	-
Iceland - Islande									
2006 (C)									
Total	4 415	2 258	2 157	4 204	2 154	2 050	211	104	107
0 - 14	-	-	-	-	-	-	-	-	-
15 - 19	150	85	65	140	75	65	10	10	-
20 - 24	842	395	447	802	378	424	40	17	23
25 - 29	1 404	731	673	1 338	697	641	66	34	32
30 - 34	1 274	658	616	1 224	637	587	50	21	29
35 - 39	619	317	302	584	300	284	35	17	18
40 - 44	123	69	54	113	64	49	10	5	5
45 - 49	3	3	-	3	3	-	-	-	-
50 +	-	-	-	-	-	-	-	-	-
Unknown - Inconnu	-	-	-	-	-	-	-	-	-
Ireland - Irlande									
1999 (+C)[34]									
Total	53 354	27 508	25 846	30 827	15 973	14 854	22 527	11 535	10 992
0 - 14	11	3	8	8	1	7	3	2	1
15 - 19	3 290	1 732	1 558	2 152	1 146	1 006	1 138	586	552
20 - 24	7 503	3 937	3 566	4 780	2 542	2 238	2 723	1 395	1 328
25 - 29	13 576	6 942	6 634	7 850	4 046	3 804	5 726	2 896	2 830
30 - 34	17 614	9 049	8 565	9 888	5 096	4 792	7 726	3 953	3 773
35 - 39	9 377	4 850	4 527	5 146	2 651	2 495	4 231	2 199	2 032
40 - 44	1 638	828	810	846	413	433	792	415	377
45 - 49	72	34	38	35	18	17	37	16	21
50 +	1	1	-	1	1	-	-	-	-
Unknown - Inconnu	272	132	140	121	59	62	151	73	78
2006* (+C)[35]									
Total	64 237	33 085	31 152	...	...	...	...	...	...
0 - 14	10	7	3	...	...	...	...	...	...
15 - 19	2 352	1 239	1 113	...	...	...	...	...	...
20 - 24	8 345	4 345	4 000	...	...	...	...	...	...
25 - 29	14 891	7 616	7 275	...	...	...	...	...	...
30 - 34	22 002	11 426	10 576	...	...	...	...	...	...
35 - 39	13 856	7 029	6 827	...	...	...	...	...	...
40 - 44	2 648	1 348	1 300	...	...	...	...	...	...
45 - 49	94	52	42	...	...	...	...	...	...
50 +	4	1	3	...	...	...	...	...	...
Unknown - Inconnu	35	22	13	...	...	...	...	...	...
Italy - Italie[36]									
2005 (C)									
Total	544 030[5]	280 606	263 424	...	...	...	...	...	...
0 - 14	3	2	1	...	...	...	...	...	...
15 - 19	9 416	4 863	4 553	...	...	...	...	...	...
20 - 24	50 715	26 262	24 453	...	...	...	...	...	...
25 - 29	135 713	69 895	65 818	...	...	...	...	...	...
30 - 34	198 611	102 392	96 219	...	...	...	...	...	...
35 - 39	117 659	60 755	56 904	...	...	...	...	...	...
40 - 44	23 874	12 310	11 564	...	...	...	...	...	...
45 - 49	880	467	413	...	...	...	...	...	...
50 +	113	59	54	...	...	...	...	...	...
Unknown - Inconnu	7 046	3 601	3 445	...	...	...	...	...	...
Latvia - Lettonie									
2006 (C)									
Total	22 264	11 312	10 952	15 342	7 777	7 565	6 922	3 535	3 387
0 - 14	3	2	1	2	2	-	1	-	1
15 - 19	1 545	782	763	883	458	425	662	324	338
20 - 24	5 979	3 054	2 925	3 834	1 919	1 915	2 145	1 135	1 010
25 - 29	6 804	3 415	3 389	4 972	2 505	2 467	1 832	910	922
30 - 34	4 973	2 538	2 435	3 600	1 824	1 776	1 373	714	659
35 - 39	2 366	1 225	1 141	1 660	878	782	706	347	359

Continent, country or area, date, code and age (in years) Continent, pays ou zone, code, date et âge (en années)	Total			Urban - Urbaine			Rural - Rurale		
	Both sexes Les deux sexes	Male Masculin	Female Féminin	Both sexes Les deux sexes	Male Masculin	Female Féminin	Both sexes Les deux sexes	Male Masculin	Female Féminin
EUROPE									
Latvia - Lettonie									
2006 (C)									
40 - 44	559	279	280	363	178	185	196	101	95
45 - 49	30	14	16	24	10	14	6	4	2
50 + ...	1	-	1	-	-	-	1	-	1
Unknown - Inconnu	4	3	1	4	3	1	-	-	-
Liechtenstein									
2006* (C)									
Total....................	361	184	177	...	...	...	...	...	...
0 - 19...................	4	3	1	...	...	...	...	...	...
20 - 24..................	43	19	24	...	...	...	...	...	...
25 - 29..................	60	31	29	...	...	...	...	...	...
30 - 34..................	156	83	73	...	...	...	...	...	...
35 - 39..................	77	38	39	...	...	...	...	...	...
40 - 44..................	20	10	10	...	...	...	...	...	...
45 - 49..................	1	-	1	...	...	...	...	...	...
50 + ...	-			...	...	...	...	...	...
Lithuania - Lituanie									
2006 (C)									
Total....................	31 265	15 880	15 385	20 691	10 518	10 173	10 574	5 362	5 212
0 - 14...................	10	6	4	7	5	2	3	1	2
15 - 19..................	2 545	1 298	1 247	1 240	610	630	1 305	688	617
20 - 24..................	8 304	4 152	4 152	4 887	2 478	2 409	3 417	1 674	1 743
25 - 29..................	10 384	5 291	5 093	7 384	3 724	3 660	3 000	1 567	1 433
30 - 34..................	6 638	3 411	3 227	4 849	2 503	2 346	1 789	908	881
35 - 39..................	2 765	1 423	1 342	1 927	1 004	923	838	419	419
40 - 44..................	592	286	306	381	184	197	211	102	109
45 - 49..................	24	11	13	13	8	5	11	3	8
50 + ...	-	-	-	-	-	-	-	-	-
Unknown - Inconnu	3	2	1	3	2	1	-	-	-
Luxembourg									
2006 (C)									
Total....................	5 514	2 826	2 688	...	...	...	...	...	...
0 - 14...................	1	-	1	...	...	...	...	...	...
15 - 19..................	140	62	78	...	...	...	...	...	...
20 - 24..................	747	383	364	...	...	...	...	...	...
25 - 29..................	1 550	818	732	...	...	...	...	...	...
30 - 34..................	1 877	965	912	...	...	...	...	...	...
35 - 39..................	1 016	492	524	...	...	...	...	...	...
40 - 44..................	173	99	74	...	...	...	...	...	...
45 - 49..................	4	3	1	...	...	...	...	...	...
50 + ...	-	-	-	...	...	...	...	...	...
Unknown - Inconnu	6	4	2	...	...	...	...	...	...
Malta - Malte									
2006 (C)									
Total....................	3 885	2 039	1 846	...	...	...	...	...	...
0 - 19...................	234	125	109	...	...	...	...	...	...
20 - 24..................	653	360	293	...	...	...	...	...	...
25 - 29..................	1 389	731	658	...	...	...	...	...	...
30 - 34..................	1 161	601	560	...	...	...	...	...	...
35 - 39..................	377	186	191	...	...	...	...	...	...
40 - 44..................	69	35	34	...	...	...	...	...	...
45 - 49..................	2	1	1	...	...	...	...	...	...
50 + ...	-	-	-	...	...	...	...	...	...
Unknown - Inconnu	-	-	-	...	...	...	...	...	...
Moldova[37]									
2006 (C)									
Total....................	37 587	19 310	18 277	13 579	6 910	6 669	24 008	12 400	11 608
0 - 14...................	8	5	3	4	3	1	4	2	2
15 - 19..................	4 873	2 513	2 360	1 165	596	569	3 709	1 917	1 792
20 - 24..................	14 762	7 584	7 178	4 696	2 373	2 323	10 066	5 211	4 855
25 - 29..................	10 537	5 415	5 122	4 376	2 256	2 120	6 160	3 159	3 001
30 - 34..................	5 237	2 695	2 542	2 356	1 187	1 169	2 881	1 508	1 373
35 - 39..................	1 815	918	897	849	426	423	966	492	474
40 - 44..................	350	178	172	132	69	63	218	109	109

Continent, country or area, date and age (in years) / Continent, pays ou zone, code, date et âge (en années)	Total			Urban - Urbaine			Rural - Rurale		
	Both sexes Les deux sexes	Male Masculin	Female Féminin	Both sexes Les deux sexes	Male Masculin	Female Féminin	Both sexes Les deux sexes	Male Masculin	Female Féminin
EUROPE									
Moldova[37]									
2006 (C)									
45 - 49	4	1	3	1	-	1	3	1	2
50 +	-	-	-	-	-	-	-	-	-
Unknown - Inconnu	1	1	-	-	-	-	1	1	-
Montenegro									
2005 (C)									
Total	7 352	3 883	3 469	5 786	3 051	2 735	1 566	832	734
0 - 14	3	2	1	1	1	-	2	1	1
15 - 19	373	191	182	262	130	132	111	61	50
20 - 24	1 954	1 025	929	1 478	762	716	476	263	213
25 - 29	2 426	1 264	1 162	1 929	1 021	908	497	243	254
30 - 34	1 637	901	736	1 327	717	610	310	184	126
35 - 39	696	364	332	560	301	259	136	63	73
40 - 44	167	83	84	141	70	71	26	13	13
45 - 49	13	10	3	13	10	3	-	-	-
50 +	2	1	1	2	1	1	-	-	-
Unknown - Inconnu	81	42	39	73	38	35	8	4	4
Netherlands - Pays-Bas[38]									
2006 (C)									
Total	185 057	94 979	90 078	126 775	65 033	61 742	58 282	29 946	28 336
0 - 14	-	-	-	-	-	-	-	-	-
15 - 19	1 859	932	927	1 466	747	719	393	185	208
20 - 24	16 344	8 374	7 970	12 377	6 311	6 066	3 967	2 063	1 904
25 - 29	49 342	25 311	24 031	33 211	17 086	16 125	16 131	8 225	7 906
30 - 34	70 987	36 554	34 433	47 507	24 475	23 032	23 480	12 079	11 401
35 - 39	39 951	20 445	19 506	27 426	13 951	13 475	12 525	6 494	6 031
40 - 44	6 328	3 250	3 078	4 616	2 381	2 235	1 712	869	843
45 - 49	241	110	131	168	80	88	73	30	43
50 +	5	3	2	4	2	2	1	1	-
Norway - Norvège[39]									
2006 (C)									
Total	58 545	29 989	28 556	...	...	...	...	...	...
0 - 14	3	1	2	...	...	...	...	...	...
15 - 19	1 292	675	617	...	...	...	...	...	...
20 - 24	8 196	4 206	3 990	...	...	...	...	...	...
25 - 29	18 220	9 274	8 946	...	...	...	...	...	...
30 - 34	20 164	10 298	9 866	...	...	...	...	...	...
35 - 39	9 130	4 709	4 421	...	...	...	...	...	...
40 - 44	1 478	789	689	...	...	...	...	...	...
45 - 49	60	35	25	...	...	...	...	...	...
50 +	2	2	-	...	...	...	...	...	...
Unknown - Inconnu	-	-	-	...	...	...	...	...	...
Poland - Pologne									
2006 (C)									
Total	374 244	192 518	181 726	218 000	112 322	105 678	156 244	80 196	76 048
0 - 14	44	26	18	27	18	9	17	8	9
15 - 19	19 186	9 853	9 333	9 916	5 104	4 812	9 270	4 749	4 521
20 - 24	93 569	48 100	45 469	47 278	24 356	22 922	46 291	23 744	22 547
25 - 29	139 853	72 056	67 797	84 704	43 756	40 948	55 149	28 300	26 849
30 - 34	86 825	44 609	42 216	55 598	28 549	27 049	31 227	16 060	15 167
35 - 39	28 487	14 667	13 820	17 046	8 789	8 257	11 441	5 878	5 563
40 - 44	5 975	3 059	2 916	3 267	1 675	1 592	2 708	1 384	1 324
45 - 49	304	148	156	163	75	88	141	73	68
50 +	1	-	1	1	-	1	-	-	-
Portugal[36]									
2006 (C)									
Total	105 449	54 057	51 392	...	...	...	...	...	...
0 - 14	73	37	36	...	...	...	...	...	...
15 - 19	4 831	2 519	2 312	...	...	...	...	...	...
20 - 24	15 458	7 843	7 615	...	...	...	...	...	...
25 - 29	31 640	16 139	15 501	...	...	...	...	...	...
30 - 34	35 088	18 125	16 963	...	...	...	...	...	...
35 - 39	15 132	7 714	7 418	...	...	...	...	...	...
40 - 44	3 063	1 591	1 472	...	...	...	...	...	...

10. Live births by age of mother, sex of the child and urban/rural residence: latest available year, 1997 - 2006
Naissances vivantes selon l'âge de la mère, le sexe de l'enfant et la résidence, urbaine/rurale: dernière année disponible, 1997 - 2006 (continued - suite)

Continent, country or area, date, code and age (in years) Continent, pays ou zone, code, date et âge (en années)	Total			Urban - Urbaine			Rural - Rurale		
	Both sexes Les deux sexes	Male Masculin	Female Féminin	Both sexes Les deux sexes	Male Masculin	Female Féminin	Both sexes Les deux sexes	Male Masculin	Female Féminin
EUROPE									
Portugal[36]									
2006 (C)									
45 - 49	154	85	69	...	...	...	...	...	...
50 +	6	2	4	...	...	...	...	...	...
Unknown - Inconnu	4	2	2	...	...	...	...	...	...
Romania - Roumanie									
2006 (C)									
Total	219 483	112 779	106 704	119 477	61 499	57 978	100 006	51 280	48 726
0 - 14	551	304	247	196	111	85	355	193	162
15 - 19	28 329	14 532	13 797	10 328	5 297	5 031	18 001	9 235	8 766
20 - 24	54 533	28 082	26 451	24 808	12 795	12 013	29 725	15 287	14 438
25 - 29	71 721	36 816	34 905	43 563	22 451	21 112	28 158	14 365	13 793
30 - 34	44 580	22 827	21 753	28 570	14 630	13 940	16 010	8 197	7 813
35 - 39	17 537	9 059	8 478	10 857	5 619	5 238	6 680	3 440	3 240
40 - 44	2 104	1 094	1 010	1 091	570	521	1 013	524	489
45 - 49	127	65	62	63	26	37	64	39	25
50 +	1	-	1	1	-	1	-	-	-
Unknown - Inconnu	-	-	-	-	-	-	-	-	-
Russian Federation - Fédération de Russie[16]									
2006 (C)									
Total	1 479 637	...	...	1 044 540	...	...	435 097	...	...
0 - 14	332	...	...	187	...	...	145	...	...
15 - 19	160 092	...	...	95 899	...	...	64 193	...	...
20 - 24	531 018	...	...	358 582	...	...	172 436	...	...
25 - 29	434 309	...	...	323 074	...	...	111 235	...	...
30 - 34	244 383	...	...	186 161	...	...	58 222	...	...
35 - 39	89 420	...	...	66 283	...	...	23 137	...	...
40 - 44	17 253	...	...	12 018	...	...	5 235	...	...
45 - 49	929	...	...	625	...	...	304	...	...
50 +	44	...	...	40	...	...	4	...	...
Unknown - Inconnu	1 857	...	...	1 671	...	...	186	...	...
San Marino - Saint-Marin									
2004 (+C)									
Total	306	...	...	...	...	...	...	...	...
15 - 19	1								
20 - 24	15								
25 - 29	69								
30 - 34	134								
35 - 39	75								
40 - 44	11								
45 - 49	1								
Serbia - Serbie[40]									
2006 (+C)									
Total	70 997	36 599	34 398	46 401	23 903	22 498	24 596	12 696	11 900
0 - 14	55	29	26	37	19	18	18	10	8
15 - 19	5 045	2 592	2 453	2 413	1 221	1 192	2 632	1 371	1 261
20 - 24	19 478	10 054	9 424	11 040	5 722	5 318	8 438	4 332	4 106
25 - 29	23 525	12 019	11 506	15 897	8 126	7 771	7 628	3 893	3 735
30 - 34	15 845	8 229	7 616	11 754	6 110	5 644	4 091	2 119	1 972
35 - 39	5 631	2 936	2 695	4 219	2 171	2 048	1 412	765	647
40 - 44	985	513	472	713	367	346	272	146	126
45 - 49	65	32	33	44	20	24	21	12	9
50 +	16	12	4	10	0	4	3	3	-
Unknown - Inconnu	352	183	169	271	138	133	81	45	36
Slovakia - Slovaquie									
2006 (C)									
Total	53 904	27 682	26 222	28 411	14 614	13 797	25 493	13 068	12 425
0 - 14	35	20	15	15	9	6	20	11	9
15 - 19	3 986	2 094	1 892	1 608	844	764	2 378	1 250	1 128
20 - 24	12 332	6 377	5 955	5 418	2 812	2 606	6 914	3 565	3 349
25 - 29	19 473	9 965	9 508	10 663	5 473	5 190	8 810	4 492	4 318
30 - 34	13 394	6 844	6 550	8 092	4 144	3 948	5 302	2 700	2 602
35 - 39	3 954	2 012	1 942	2 219	1 135	1 084	1 735	877	858
40 - 44	694	351	343	381	191	190	313	160	153

10. Live births by age of mother, sex of the child and urban/rural residence: latest available year, 1997 - 2006
Naissances vivantes selon l'âge de la mère, le sexe de l'enfant et la résidence, urbaine/rurale: dernière année disponible, 1997 - 2006 (continued - suite)

Continent, country or area, date, code and num (in years) Continent, pays ou zone, code, date et âge (en années)	Total			Urban - Urbaine			Rural - Rurale		
	Both sexes Les deux sexes	Male Masculin	Female Féminin	Both sexes Les deux sexes	Male Masculin	Female Féminin	Both sexes Les deux sexes	Male Masculin	Female Féminin
EUROPE									
Slovakia - Slovaquie									
2006 (C)									
45 - 49	33	17	16	13	5	8	20	12	8
50 +	3	2	1	2	1	1	1	1	-
Slovenia - Slovénie									
2006 (C)									
Total	18 932	9 762	9 170	9 190	4 701	4 489	9 742	5 061	4 681
0 - 14	1	-	1	1	-	1	-	-	-
15 - 19	279	137	142	134	68	66	145	69	76
20 - 24	2 617	1 372	1 245	1 139	608	531	1 478	764	714
25 - 29	7 346	3 755	3 591	3 296	1 655	1 641	4 050	2 100	1 950
30 - 34	6 213	3 169	3 044	3 262	1 638	1 624	2 951	1 531	1 420
35 - 39	2 107	1 114	993	1 170	621	549	937	493	444
40 - 44	353	205	148	178	103	75	175	102	73
45 - 49	14	10	4	10	8	2	4	2	2
50 +	2	-	2	-	-	-	2	-	2
Unknown - Inconnu	-	-	-	-	-	-	-	-	-
Spain - Espagne									
2005 (C)									
Total	466 371	240 201	226 170	...	...	...	...	...	...
0 - 14	153	74	79	...	...	...	...	...	...
15 - 19	12 878	6 660	6 218	...	...	...	...	...	...
20 - 24	44 355	22 845	21 510	...	...	...	...	...	...
25 - 29	115 145	59 671	55 474	...	...	...	...	...	...
30 - 34	183 215	94 006	89 209	...	...	...	...	...	...
35 - 39	94 105	48 482	45 623	...	...	...	...	...	...
40 - 44	15 729	8 071	7 658	...	...	...	...	...	...
45 - 49	733	363	370	...	...	...	...	...	...
50 +	58	29	29	...	...	...	...	...	...
Sweden - Suède									
2006 (C)									
Total	105 913	54 483	51 430	...	...	...	...	...	...
0 - 14	6	6	-	...	...	...	...	...	...
15 - 19	1 758	969	789	...	...	...	...	...	...
20 - 24	12 426	6 314	6 112	...	...	...	...	...	...
25 - 29	30 400	15 644	14 756	...	...	...	...	...	...
30 - 34	39 057	19 942	19 115	...	...	...	...	...	...
35 - 39	18 493	9 674	8 819	...	...	...	...	...	...
40 - 44	3 628	1 866	1 762	...	...	...	...	...	...
45 - 49	140	66	74	...	...	...	...	...	...
50 +	5	2	3	...	...	...	...	...	...
Switzerland - Suisse									
2006 (C)									
Total	73 371	37 766	35 605	54 423	27 989	26 434	18 948	9 777	9 171
0 - 14	6	5	1	4	3	1	2	2	-
15 - 19	982	522	460	756	404	352	226	118	108
20 - 24	8 275	4 283	3 992	6 211	3 198	3 013	2 064	1 085	979
25 - 29	20 004	10 288	9 716	14 253	7 388	6 865	5 751	2 900	2 851
30 - 34	26 298	13 552	12 746	19 449	9 985	9 464	6 849	3 567	3 282
35 - 39	14 877	7 635	7 242	11 463	5 864	5 599	3 414	1 771	1 643
40 - 44	2 832	1 428	1 404	2 214	1 107	1 107	618	321	297
45 - 49	93	50	43	69	37	32	24	13	11
50 +	4	3	1	4	3	1	-	-	-
The Former Yugoslav Rep. of Macedonia - L'ex-République yougoslave de Macédoine									
2006 (C)									
Total	22 585	11 629	10 956	12 653	6 444	6 209	9 932	5 185	4 747
0 - 14	29	17	12	23	12	11	6	5	1
15 - 19	1 589	837	752	781	402	379	808	435	373
20 - 24	6 438	3 306	3 132	3 210	1 639	1 571	3 228	1 667	1 561
25 - 29	8 132	4 164	3 968	4 714	2 370	2 344	3 418	1 794	1 624
30 - 34	4 614	2 374	2 240	2 809	1 455	1 354	1 805	919	886
35 - 39	1 552	807	745	964	487	477	588	320	268

10. Live births by age of mother, sex of the child and urban/rural residence: latest available year, 1997 - 2006
Naissances vivantes selon l'âge de la mère, le sexe de l'enfant et la résidence, urbaine/rurale: dernière année disponible, 1997 - 2006 (continued - suite)

Continent, country or area, date, code and age (in years) / Continent, pays ou zone, code, date et âge (en années)	Total			Urban - Urbaine			Rural - Rurale		
	Both sexes Les deux sexes	Male Masculin	Female Féminin	Both sexes Les deux sexes	Male Masculin	Female Féminin	Both sexes Les deux sexes	Male Masculin	Female Féminin
EUROPE									
The Former Yugoslav Rep. of Macedonia - L'ex-République yougoslave de Macédoine									
2006 (C)									
40 - 44	215	112	103	140	69	71	75	43	32
45 - 49	10	7	3	7	5	2	3	2	1
50 + ...	1	-	1	-	-	-	1	-	1
Unknown - Inconnu	5	5	-	5	5	-	-	-	-
Ukraine[41]									
2006 (C)									
Total..................	460 368	...	...	306 635	...	...	153 733	...	...
0 - 14.................	149	...	...	79	...	...	70	...	...
15 - 19	49 672	...	...	27 640	...	...	22 032	...	...
20 - 24	172 622	...	...	111 034	...	...	61 588	...	...
25 - 29	135 711	...	...	95 205	...	...	40 506	...	...
30 - 34	71 739	...	...	51 229	...	...	20 510	...	...
35 - 39	24 774	...	...	17 455	...	...	7 319	...	...
40 - 44	4 433	...	...	2 985	...	...	1 448	...	...
45 - 49	210	...	...	144	...	...	66	...	...
50 + ...	7	...	...	5	...	...	2	...	...
Unknown - Inconnu	1 051	...	...	859	...	...	192	...	...
United Kingdom - Royaume-Uni[42]									
2004 (C)									
Total..................	715 996	...	...	...	...	...	...	...	...
10 - 14	226	...	...	...	...	...	...	...	...
15 - 19	50 525	...	...	...	...	...	...	...	...
20 - 24	134 615	...	...	...	...	...	...	...	...
25 - 29	179 050	...	...	...	...	...	...	...	...
30 - 34	213 619	...	...	...	...	...	...	...	...
35 - 39	114 852	...	...	...	...	...	...	...	...
40 - 44	22 107	...	...	...	...	...	...	...	...
45 - 49	923	...	...	...	...	...	...	...	...
Unknown - Inconnu	26	...	...	...	...	...	...	...	...
OCEANIA - OCÉANIE									
American Samoa - Samoas américaines									
2006 (C)									
Total..................	1 442	...	...	...	...	...	...	...	...
0 - 14.................	1	...	...	...	...	...	...	...	...
15 - 19	110	...	...	...	...	...	...	...	...
20 - 24	342	...	...	...	...	...	...	...	...
25 - 29	410	...	...	...	...	...	...	...	...
30 - 34	303	...	...	...	...	...	...	...	...
35 - 39	218	...	...	...	...	...	...	...	...
40 - 44	55	...	...	...	...	...	...	...	...
45 - 49	3	...	...	...	...	...	...	...	...
Australia - Australie[43]									
2005 (+C)									
Total..................	259 791	133 428	126 363	170 079	90 505	85 574	83 712	42 923	40 789
0 - 14.................	85	45	40	47	23	24	38	22	16
15 - 19	10 659	5 479	5 180	6 258	3 182	3 076	4 401	2 297	2 104
20 - 24	36 482	18 821	17 661	22 608	11 568	11 040	13 874	7 253	6 621
25 - 29	69 420	35 750	33 670	45 320	23 381	21 939	24 100	12 369	11 731
30 - 34	89 158	45 594	43 564	62 622	32 143	30 479	26 536	13 451	13 085
35 - 39	44 873	23 028	21 845	32 563	16 741	15 822	12 310	6 287	6 023
40 - 44	8 376	4 297	4 079	6 124	3 169	2 955	2 252	1 128	1 124
45 - 49	335	187	148	243	134	109	92	53	39
50 + ...	23	11	12	19	9	10	4	3	3
Unknown - Inconnu	380	216	164	275	155	120	105	61	44

10. Live births by age of mother, sex of the child and urban/rural residence: latest available year, 1997 - 2006
Naissances vivantes selon l'âge de la mère, le sexe de l'enfant et la résidence, urbaine/rurale: dernière année disponible, 1997 - 2006 (continued - suite)

Continent, country or area, date, code and age (in years) / Continent, pays ou zone, code, date et âge (en années)	Total			Urban - Urbaine			Rural - Rurale		
	Both sexes Les deux sexes	Male Masculin	Female Féminin	Both sexes Les deux sexes	Male Masculin	Female Féminin	Both sexes Les deux sexes	Male Masculin	Female Féminin
OCEANIA - OCÉANIE									
Fiji - Fidji									
2004 (+C)									
Total.....................	17 189	8 944	8 245	...	...	...	...	...	...
0 - 14..................	7	1	6	...	...	...	...	...	...
15 - 19................	1 194	622	572	...	...	...	...	...	...
20 - 24................	5 684	2 961	2 723	...	...	...	...	...	...
25 - 29................	5 126	2 665	2 461	...	...	...	...	...	...
30 - 34................	3 033	1 526	1 507	...	...	...	...	...	...
35 - 39................	1 592	868	724	...	...	...	...	...	...
40 - 44................	464	254	210	...	...	...	...	...	...
45 - 49................	43	23	20	...	...	...	...	...	...
50 +....................	-	-	-	...	...	...	...	...	...
Unknown - Inconnu......	46	24	22	...	...	...	...	...	...
Guam[44]									
2004 (C)									
Total.....................	3 427	1 783	1 644	3 007	1 565	1 442	420	218	202
10 - 14................	2	1	1	2	1	1	-	-	-
15 - 19................	352	168	184	320	154	166	32	14	18
20 - 24................	887	486	401	764	413	351	123	73	50
25 - 29................	939	483	456	811	422	389	128	61	67
30 - 34................	738	393	345	661	352	309	77	41	36
35 - 39................	395	196	199	344	168	176	51	28	23
40 - 44................	102	50	52	95	50	45	7	-	7
45 - 49................	10	5	5	8	4	4	2	1	1
50 +....................	-	-	-	-	-	-	-	-	-
Unknown - Inconnu......	2	1	1	2	1	1	-	-	-
Marshall Islands - Îles Marshall[45]									
2005 (+U)									
Total.....................	1 589	...	...	...	...	...	...	...	...
0 - 14..................	3	...	...	...	...	...	...	...	...
15 - 19................	296	...	...	...	...	...	...	...	...
20 - 24................	563	...	...	...	...	...	...	...	...
25 - 29................	388	...	...	...	...	...	...	...	...
30 - 34................	215	...	...	...	...	...	...	...	...
35 - 39................	93	...	...	...	...	...	...	...	...
40 - 44................	26	...	...	...	...	...	...	...	...
45 - 49................	4	...	...	...	...	...	...	...	...
Unknown - Inconnu......	1	...	...	...	...	...	...	...	...
Micronesia, Federated States of - Micronésie, États Fédérés de La									
2003 (U)									
Total[46].................	2 485	...	...	...	...	...	...	...	...
10 - 14................	10	...	...	...	...	...	...	...	...
15 - 19................	329	...	...	...	...	...	...	...	...
20 - 24................	675	...	...	...	...	...	...	...	...
25 - 29................	649	...	...	...	...	...	...	...	...
30 - 34................	401	...	...	...	...	...	...	...	...
35 - 39................	275	...	...	...	...	...	...	...	...
40 - 44................	108	...	...	...	...	...	...	...	...
45 +...................	11	...	...	...	...	...	...	...	...
Unknown - Inconnu......	27	...	...	...	...	...	...	...	...
New Caledonia - Nouvelle-Calédonie									
2003 (C)									
Total.....................	4 102	...	...	...	...	...	...	...	...
0 - 14..................	-	...	...	...	...	...	...	...	...
15 - 19................	190	...	...	...	...	...	...	...	...
20 - 24................	1 017	...	...	...	...	...	...	...	...
25 - 29................	1 215	...	...	...	...	...	...	...	...
30 - 34................	1 030	...	...	...	...	...	...	...	...
35 - 39................	518	...	...	...	...	...	...	...	...
40 - 44................	130	...	...	...	...	...	...	...	...
45 - 49................	2	...	...	...	...	...	...	...	...

10. Live births by age of mother, sex of the child and urban/rural residence: latest available year, 1997 - 2006
Naissances vivantes selon l'âge de la mère, le sexe de l'enfant et la résidence, urbaine/rurale: dernière année disponible, 1997 - 2006 (continued - suite)

Continent, country or area, date, code and age (in years) / Continent, pays ou zone, code, date et âge (en années)	Total			Urban - Urbaine			Rural - Rurale		
	Both sexes Les deux sexes	Male Masculin	Female Féminin	Both sexes Les deux sexes	Male Masculin	Female Féminin	Both sexes Les deux sexes	Male Masculin	Female Féminin
OCEANIA - OCÉANIE									
New Zealand - Nouvelle-Zélande[47]									
2006 (+C)									
Total	59 193	30 240	28 953	51 540	26 276	25 264	7 518	3 892	3 626
0 - 14	35	12	23	32	12	20	2	-	2
15 - 19	4 338	2 218	2 120	3 849	1 957	1 892	482	254	228
20 - 24	10 308	5 236	5 072	9 165	4 655	4 510	1 099	559	540
25 - 29	14 082	7 251	6 831	12 252	6 279	5 973	1 799	956	843
30 - 34	17 867	9 105	8 762	15 440	7 874	7 566	2 407	1 223	1 184
35 - 39	10 401	5 333	5 068	8 952	4 569	4 383	1 421	747	674
40 - 44	2 054	1 037	1 017	1 761	890	871	289	145	144
45 - 49	107	48	59	88	40	48	19	8	11
50 +	1	-	1	1	-	1	-	-	-
Northern Mariana Islands - Îles Mariannes septentrionales									
2002 (U)									
Total	1 289	...	...	...	...	...	...	...	...
0 - 19	110	...	...	...	...	...	...	...	...
20 - 24	298	...	...	...	...	...	...	...	...
25 - 29	347	...	...	...	...	...	...	...	...
30 - 34	317	...	...	...	...	...	...	...	...
35 - 39	182	...	...	...	...	...	...	...	...
40 +	35	...	...	...	...	...	...	...	...
Unknown - Inconnu	-	...	...	...	...	...	...	...	...
Palau - Palaos									
2003 (C)									
Total	312	163	149	...	...	...	...	...	...
15 - 19	21	13	8	...	...	...	...	...	...
20 - 24	71	34	37	...	...	...	...	...	...
25 - 29	81	40	41	...	...	...	...	...	...
30 - 34	63	35	28	...	...	...	...	...	...
35 - 39	56	29	27	...	...	...	...	...	...
40 - 44	16	11	5	...	...	...	...	...	...
45 - 49	4	1	3	...	...	...	...	...	...
Tonga									
2000 (+C)									
Total	2 471	...	...	...	...	...	...	...	...
0 - 14	2	...	...	...	...	...	...	...	...
15 - 19	101	...	...	...	...	...	...	...	...
20 - 24	528	...	...	...	...	...	...	...	...
25 - 29	695	...	...	...	...	...	...	...	...
30 - 34	688	...	...	...	...	...	...	...	...
35 - 39	314	...	...	...	...	...	...	...	...
40 - 44	122	...	...	...	...	...	...	...	...
45 - 49	14	...	...	...	...	...	...	...	...
Unknown - Inconnu	7	...	...	...	...	...	...	...	...
Tuvalu									
2003 (U)									
Total	239	...	...	...	...	...	...	...	...
15 - 19	17	...	...	...	...	...	...	...	...
20 - 24	76	...	...	...	...	...	...	...	...
25 - 29	53	...	...	...	...	...	...	...	...
30 - 34	35	...	...	...	...	...	...	...	...
35 - 39	37	...	...	...	...	...	...	...	...
40 - 44	20	...	...	...	...	...	...	...	...
45 - 49	-	...	...	...	...	...	...	...	...
Wallis and Futuna Islands - Îles Wallis et Futuna									
2006 (C)									
Total	220	...	...	...	...	...	...	...	...
15 - 19	7	...	...	...	...	...	...	...	...
20 - 24	45	...	...	...	...	...	...	...	...
25 - 29	74	...	...	...	...	...	...	...	...
30 - 34	58	...	...	...	...	...	...	...	...

10. Live births by age of mother, sex of the child and urban/rural residence: latest available year, 1997 - 2006
Naissances vivantes selon l'âge de la mère, le sexe de l'enfant et la résidence, urbaine/rurale: dernière année disponible, 1997 - 2006 (continued - suite)

Continent, country or area, date, code and age (in years) / Continent, pays ou zone, code, date et âge (en années)	Total			Urban - Urbaine			Rural - Rurale		
	Both sexes Les deux sexes	Male Masculin	Female Féminin	Both sexes Les deux sexes	Male Masculin	Female Féminin	Both sexes Les deux sexes	Male Masculin	Female Féminin
OCEANIA - OCÉANIE									
Wallis and Futuna Islands - Îles Wallis et Futuna									
2006 (C)									
35 - 39	20	...	...	...	...	...	...	...	...
40 - 44	10	...	...	...	...	...	...	...	...

FOOTNOTES - NOTES

Italics: estimates which are less reliable. - Italiques: estimations moins sûres.

* Provisional. - Données provisoires.

'Code' indicates the source of data, as follows:
C - Civil registration, estimated over 90% complete
U - Civil registration, estimated less than 90% complete
| - Other source, estimated reliable
+ - Data tabulated by date of registration rather than occurrence.
... - Information not available

Le 'Code' indique la source des données, comme suit:
C - Registres de l'état civil considérés complets à 90 p. 100 au moins.
U - Registres de l'état civil qui ne sont pas considérés complets à 90 p. 100 au moins.
| - Autre source, considérée fiable.
+ - Données exploitées selon la date de l'enregistrement et non la date de l'événement.
... - Information non disponible.

[1] The total number includes 'Unknown residence', but the categories urban and rural do not. - Le nombre total inclue 'Résidence inconnue ', mais les catégories Urbain et Rural ne l'incluent pas.

[2] For 2001, data refer to last twelve months preceding census in August 2001. - Pour 2001, les données se rapportent aux douze mois précédant le recensement d'août 2001.

[3] Excluding live-born infants who died before their birth was registered. - Non compris les enfants nés vivants décédés avant l'enregistrement de leur naissance.

[4] Data for 1997 refer to last twelve months preceding population and housing census of 1997. - Les données pour 1997 se réfèrent au douze mois précédant le recensement de population et de l'habitat de 1997.

[5] Data as reported by national statistical authorities; they may differ from data presented in other tables. - Les données comme elles ont été déclarées par l'institut national de la statistique; elles peuvent être différentes de celles présentées dans d'autres tableaux.

[6] Including Canadian residents temporarily in the United States, but excluding United States residents temporarily in Canada. - Y compris les résidents canadiens se trouvant temporairement aux Etats-Unis, mais ne comprenant pas les résidents des Etats-Unis se trouvant temporairement au Canada.

[7] Including persons of unknown residence. - Y compris les personnes d'état résidence inconnu.

[8] Excluding adjustment for underenumeration. - Les données n'ont pas été ajustées pour compenser les lacunes du dénombrement.

[9] Age classification is based on year of birth of mother rather than the exact age of mother at birth of child. Excluding live-born infants who died before their birth was registered. - Le classement selon l'âge est basé sur l'année de naissance de la mère et non sur l'age exacte de la mère au moment de naissance de l'enfant. Non compris les enfants nés vivants décédés avant l'enregistrement de leur naissance.

[10] Data refer to births to mothers resident in the Netherlands Antilles (including births outside the Netherlands Antilles to resident mothers, excluding births to non-resident mothers). - Ces données concernent les enfants nés de femmes qui résidaient aux Antilles néerlandaises (y compris ceux qui sont nés hors des Antilles néerlandaises). Elles ne concernent pas les enfants nés de non-résidentes.

[11] Reason for discrepancy between these figures and corresponding figures shown elsewhere not ascertained. - On ne sait pas comment s'explique la divergence entre ces chiffres et les chiffres correspondants indiqués ailleurs.

[12] Excluding nomadic Indian tribes. - Non compris les tribus d'Indiens nomades.

[13] Excluding Indian jungle population. Data refer to registered live births only. - Non compris les Indiens de la jungle. Les données concernent les naissances vivantes enregistrées seulement.

[14] Excluding Indian jungle population. - Non compris les Indiens de la jungle.

[15] Excluding infants born alive of less than 28 weeks' gestation, of less than 1 000 grams in weight and 35 centimeters in length, who die within seven days of birth. Since 16 October 2005 the definition of WHO on livebirths has been put into force in accordance with 10th revision of the International Classification of Diseases. - Non compris les enfants nés vivants après moins de 28 semaines de gestations, pesant moins de 1 000 grammes, mesurant moins de 35 centimètres et décédés dans les sept jours qui ont suivi leur naissance. Depuis le 16 octobre 2005, la définition de l'OMS concernant les naissances vivantes est en vigueur conformément à la dixième révision de la Classification internationale des maladies.

[16] Excluding infants born alive of less than 28 weeks' gestation, of less than 1 000 grams in weight and 35 centimeters in length, who die within seven days of birth. - Non compris les enfants nés vivants après moins de 28 semaines de gestations, pesant moins de 1 000 grammes, mesurant moins de 35 centimètres et décédés dans les sept jours qui ont suivi leur naissance.

[17] For 2005, data refer to last twelve months preceding census in May 2005. - Pour 2005, les données se rapportent aux douze mois précédant le recensement de mai 2005.

[18] Figures for urban and rural areas do not add up to the total; reason for discrepancy not ascertained. - La somme des données pour la résidence urbaine et rurale n'est pas égale au total; on ne sait pas comment s'explique la divergence.

[19] Data refer to government controlled areas. - Les données se rapportent aux zones contrôlées par le Gouvernement.

[20] Published by the United Nations Economic and Social Commission for Western Asia. - Publié par la Commission économique et sociale des Nations Unies pour l'Asie occidentale.

[21] Including data for East Jerusalem and Israeli residents in certain other territories under occupation by Israeli military forces since June 1967. - Y compris les données pour Jérusalem-Est et les résidents israéliens dans certains autres territoires occupés depuis 1967 par les forces armées israéliennes.

[22] Data refer to Japanese nationals in Japan only. - Les données se raportent aux nationaux japonais au Japon seulement.

[23] Excluding alien armed forces, civilian aliens employed by armed forces, and foreign diplomatic personnel and their dependants. - Non compris les militaires étrangers, les civils étrangers employés par les forces armées ni le personnel diplomatique étranger et les membres de leur famille les accompagnant.

[24] Including Koreans abroad. - Y compris les Coréens à l'étranger.

[25] Figures for male and female categories do not add up to the total, since they do not include the category "Unknown". - La somme des chiffres indiqués pour les sexes masculin et féminin n'est pas égale au total parce qu'elle n'inclut pas la catégorie " inconnue ".

[26] Excluding data for the Pakistan-held part of Jammu and Kashmir, the final status of which has not yet been determined. Data based on Pakistan Demographic Survey (PDS 2005). - Non compris les données concernant la partie du Jammu et Cachemire occupée par le Pakistan dont le statut définitif n'a pas été déterminé. Données extraites de l'enquête démographique effectuée par le Pakistan en 2005.

[27] Based on the results of the Population Growth Survey. Data as reported by national statistical authorities; they may differ from data presented in other tables. - D'après les résultats de la 'Population Growth Survey.' Les données comme elles ont été déclarées par l'institut national de la statistique; elles peuvent être différentes de celles présentées dans d'autres tableaux.

[28] Also included in Finland. - Comprise aussi dans Finlande.

[29] Excluding Faeroe Islands and Greenland shown separately, if available. - Non compris les Iles Féroé et le Gröenland, qui font l'objet de rubriques distinctes, si disponible.

[30] Including nationals temporarily outside the country. Including Aland Islands. - Y compris les nationaux se trouvant temporairement hors du pays. Y compris les Îles d'Åland.

[31] Including armed forces stationed outside the country. Excluding Overseas Departments, namely, French Guiana, Guadeloupe, Martinique and Reunion, shown separately, if available. - Y compris les militaires nationaux hors du pays. Non compris les départements d'outre mer, c'est-à-dire la Guyane française, la Guadeloupe, la Martinique et la Réunion, qui font l'objet de rubriques distinctes, si disponible.

[32] Urban/rural figures, excluding nationals outside the country. - Les chiffres urbaine/rurale, non compris les nationaux hors du pays.

[33] Total includes the data of foreigners, persons of unknown residence and homeless, but the categories urban and rural do not. - Total incluant les étrangers, les personnes de résidence inconnue et les sans-abri, ce qui n'est pas le cas pour les catégories urbaines et rurales.

[34] Births registered within one year of occurrence. - Naissances enregistrées dans l'année qui suit l'événement.

[35] Events registered within one year of occurrence. - Evénements enregistrés dans l'année qui suit l'événement.

[36] Data refer to resident mothers. - Données concernant les mères résidentes.

[37] Data do not include information for Transnistria and the municipality of Bender. Excluding infants born alive of less than 28 weeks' gestation, of less than 1 000 grams in weight and 35 centimetres in length, who die within seven days of birth. - Les données ne tiennent pas compte de l'information sur la Transnistria et la municipalité de Bender. Non compris les enfants nés vivants après moins de 28 semaines de gestations, pesant moins de 1 000 grammes, mesurant moins de 35 centimètres et décédés dans les sept jours qui ont suivi leur naissance.

[38] Including residents outside the country if listed in a Netherlands population register. - Y compris les résidents hors du pays, s'ils sont inscrits sur un registre de population néerlandais.

[39] Age classification is based on year of birth of mother rather than the exact age of mother at birth of child. Excluding Svalbard and Jan Mayen Island shown separately, if available. - Le classement selon l'âge est basé sur l'année de naissance de la mère et non sur l'age exacte de la mère au moment de naissance de l'enfant. Non compris Svalbard et Jan Mayen qui font l'objet de rubriques distinctes, si disponible.

[40] Without data for Kosovo and Metohia. - Sans les données pour le Kosovo et Metohie.

[41] Data refer to births with weight 500g and more (if weight is unknown - with length 25 centimeters and more, or with gestation during 22 weeks or more). - Données concernant les nouveau-nés de 500 grammes ou plus (si le poids est inconnu – de 25 centimètres de long ou plus, ou après une grossesse de 22 semaines ou plus).

[42] Excluding Channel Islands and Isle of Man, shown separately, if available. Data tabulated by date of occurrence for England and Wales, and by date of registration for Northern Ireland and Scotland. - Non compris les îles Anglo-Normandes et l'île de Man, qui font l'objet de rubriques distinctes, si disponible. Données exploitées selon la date de l'événement pour l'Angleterre et le pays de Galles, et selon la date de l'enregistrement pour l'Irlande du Nord et l'Ecosse.

[43] Data is referred to in Australia as 'nuptial' births. Data includes; births born in wedlock where age of father is unknown and ; births born out of wedlock and where the father has not acknowledged the birth and age of father is therefore unknown. - L'Australie utilise le terme « nuptial » pour qualifier ces naissances. Les données se rapportent aux enfants légitimes pour lesquels l'âge du père n'est pas connu et aux naissances hors mariage non reconnues par le père et pour lesquelles l'âge du père n'est par conséquent pas connu.

[44] Including United States military personnel, their dependants and contract employees. - Y compris les militaires des Etats-Unis, les membres de leur famille les accompagnant et les agents contractuels des Etats-Unis.

[45] Excluding United States military personnel, their dependants and contract employees. - Non compris les militaires des Etats-Unis, les membres de leur famille les accompagnant et les agents contractuels des Etats-Unis.

[46] The total births by year may not match due to late births report coming from the Outer Islands of Yap. - Le total des naissances annuelles peut ne pas correspondre, les îles extérieures de Yap ayant communiqué leurs données tardivement.

[47] For resident population only. - Pour la population résidante seulement.

Table 11

Table 11 presents live-birth rates by age of mother and urban/rural residence for the latest available year.

Description of variables: Age is defined as age at last birthday preceding the live birth, that is, the difference between the date of birth and the date of the occurrence of the event, expressed in completed solar years. The age classification used in this table is the following: under 20 years, 5-year age groups through 40-44 years, and 45 years or over.

Rate computation: Live-birth rates specific to age of mother are the annual number of births to women in each age group (as shown in table 10) per 1 000 female population in the same age group.

Birth rates by age of mother and urban/rural residence are the annual number of live births that occurred to a specific age-urban/rural group (as shown in table 10) per 1 000 females in the corresponding age-urban/rural group. These rates are calculated by the Statistics Division of the United Nations.

Since relatively few births occur to women below 15 or above 50 years of age, birth rates for women under 20 years of age and for those 45 years of age or over are computed on the female population aged 15-19 and 45-49, respectively. Similarly, the rate for women of "All ages" is based on all live births irrespective of age of mother, and is computed on the female population aged 15-49 years. This rate for "All ages" is known as the general fertility rate.

Births to mothers of unknown age are distributed proportionately across the age groups, by the Statistics Division of the United Nations, in accordance with the distribution of births by age of mother prior to the calculation of the rates.

The population used in computing the rates is the estimated or enumerated distribution of females by age. First priority is given to an estimate for the mid-point of the same year (as shown in table 7), second priority to census returns of the year to which the births referred, and third priority to an estimate for some other point of time in the year.

Rates presented in this table are limited to those for countries or areas having at least a total of 100 live births in a given year.

Reliability of data: Rates are not computed if the data on live births from civil registers are reported as incomplete (less than 90 per cent completeness) or of unknown completeness. Table 9 and the technical notes for that table provide more detailed information on the completeness of live-birth registration. For more information about the quality of vital statistics data in general, and the information available on the basis of the completeness of estimates in particular, see section 4.2 of the Technical Notes.

Limitations: Rates shown in this table are subject to the same limitations that affect the corresponding frequencies and are set forth in the technical notes for table 10. These include differences in the completeness of registration, the treatment of infants who were born alive but died before the registration of the birth or within the first 24 hours of life, the method used to determine age of mother and the quality of the reported information relating to age of mother. In addition, some rates are based on births tabulated by date of registration and not by date of occurrence; these have been indicated by a plus sign "+".

The effect of including delayed registration on the distribution of births by age of mother may be noted in the age-specific fertility rates for women at older ages. In some cases, high age-specific rates for women aged 45 years and over may reflect age of mother at registration of birth and not fertility at these older ages.

The comparability of data by urban/rural residence is affected by the national definitions of urban and rural used in tabulating these data. It is assumed, in the absence of specific information to the contrary, that the definitions of urban and rural used in connection with the national population census were also used in the compilation of the vital statistics for each country or area. However, it is possible that, for a given country or area, the definitions of urban and rural used for both the vital statistics data and the population census data are not the same. When known, the definitions of urban used in national population censuses are presented at the end of the technical notes for table 6. As discussed in detail in the technical notes for table 6, these definitions vary considerably from one country or area to another.

In addition to problems of comparability, vital rates classified by urban/rural residence are also subject to certain special types of bias. If, when calculating vital rates, different definitions of urban are used in connection with the vital events and the population data and if this results in a net difference between the numerator and denominator of the rate in the population at risk, then the vital rates would be biased. Urban/rural differentials in vital rates may also be affected by whether the vital events have been tabulated in terms of place of occurrence or place of usual residence. This problem is discussed in more detail in section 4.1.4.1 of the Technical Notes.

Earlier data: Live-birth rates specific for age of mother have been shown for the latest available year in each issue of the Yearbook. Data included in this table update the series covering a period of years as follows:

Issue	Years Covered
Special Topic on Natality, CD, 1999	1990 – 1998
Historical Supplement CD, 1997	1948 – 1997
1992	1983 – 1992
1986	1977 – 1985
1981	1972 – 1980
Historical Supplement, 1979	1948 - 1977

Tableau 11

Tableau 11

Le tableau 11 présente les taux des naissances vivantes selon l'âge de la mère et selon le lieu de résidence (zone urbaine ou rurale) correspondant aux données les plus récentes dont on dispose.

Description des variables : l'âge désigne l'âge au dernier anniversaire précédant la naissance, c'est-à-dire la différence entre la date de naissance et la date de l'événement, exprimée en années solaires révolues. La classification par âge utilisée dans le tableau 11 comprend les catégories suivantes : moins de 20 ans, groupes quinquennaux jusqu'à 40-44 ans, et 45 et plus.

Calcul des taux : les taux des naissances vivantes selon l'âge de la mère représentent le nombre annuel de naissances dans chaque groupe d'âge (voir tableau 10) pour 1 000 femmes des mêmes groupes d'âge.

Les taux de natalité selon l'âge de la mère et le lieu de résidence (zone urbaine ou rurale) représentent le nombre annuel de naissances vivantes intervenues dans un groupe d'âge donné parmi la population urbaine ou rurale (comme il est indiqué au tableau 10) pour 1 000 femmes du groupe d'âge correspondant parmi la population urbaine ou rurale. Ces taux ont été calculés par la Division de statistique de l'ONU.

Étant donné que le nombre de naissances parmi les femmes de moins de 15 ans ou de plus de 50 ans est relativement peu élevé, les taux de natalité parmi les femmes âgées de moins de 20 ans et celles de 45 ans et plus ont été calculés sur la base des populations féminines âgées de 15 à 19 ans et de 45 à 49 ans, respectivement. De même, le taux pour les femmes de « tous âges » est fondé sur la totalité des naissances vivantes, indépendamment de l'âge de la mère et ce chiffre est rapporté à l'effectif de la population féminine âgée de 15 à 49 ans. Ce taux « tous âges » est le taux global de fécondité.

Les naissances pour lesquelles l'âge de la mère était inconnu ont été réparties par la Division de statistique de l'ONU, avant le calcul des taux, suivant les proportions observées pour celles où l'âge de la mère était connu.

Les chiffres de population utilisés pour le calcul des taux proviennent de dénombrements ou de répartitions estimatives de la population féminine selon l'âge. On a utilisé de préférence les estimations de la population au milieu de l'année considérée selon les chiffres du tableau 7 ; à défaut, on s'est contenté des données censitaires se rapportant à l'année des naissances et, si ces données manquaient également, d'estimations établies à un autre moment de l'année.

Les taux présentés dans ce tableau ne concernent que les pays ou zones où l'on a enregistré un total d'au moins 100 naissances vivantes dans une année donnée.

Fiabilité des données : on a choisi de ne pas faire figurer dans le tableau 11 des taux calculés à partir de données sur les naissances vivantes issues de registres de l'état civil qui sont déclarées incomplètes (degré de complétude inférieur à 90 p. 100) ou dont le degré de complétude n'est pas connu. Le tableau 9 et les notes techniques qui s'y rapportent présentent des renseignements plus détaillés sur le degré de complétude de l'enregistrement des naissances vivantes. Pour plus de précisions sur la qualité des données reposant sur les statistiques de l'état civil en général et les estimations de complétude en particulier, voir la section 4.2 des Notes techniques.

Insuffisance des données : les taux du tableau 11 appellent les mêmes réserves que celles concernant les fréquences correspondantes (voir à ce sujet les notes techniques relatives au tableau 10). Leurs imperfections tiennent notamment au degré de complétude de l'enregistrement, au classement des enfants nés vivants décédés avant l'enregistrement de leur naissance ou dans les 24 heures qui ont suivi la naissance, à la méthode utilisée pour déterminer l'âge de la mère et à l'exactitude des renseignements concernant l'âge de la mère. En outre, dans certains cas, les données relatives aux naissances sont exploitées selon la date de l'enregistrement et non selon la date de l'événement ; ces cas ont été signalés par le signe '+'.

On peut se rendre compte, d'après les taux relatifs aux groupes d'âge les plus avancés, des conséquences que peut avoir l'inclusion, dans les statistiques des naissances selon l'âge de la mère, des naissances enregistrées tardivement. Dans certains cas, il se peut que des taux élevés pour le groupe d'âge 45 ans et plus ne traduisent pas le niveau de fécondité de ce groupe d'âge, mais l'âge de la mère au moment où la naissance a été enregistrée.

La comparabilité des données selon le lieu de résidence (zone urbaine ou rurale) peut être limitée par les définitions nationales des termes « urbain » et « rural » utilisées pour le classement de ces données. En l'absence d'indications contraires, on a supposé que les mêmes définitions avaient servi pour le recensement national de la population et pour l'établissement des statistiques de l'état civil pour chaque pays ou zone. Toutefois, il n'est pas exclu que, pour une zone ou un pays donné, des définitions différentes aient été retenues. Les définitions du terme « urbain » utilisées pour les recensements nationaux de population ont été présentées à la fin du tableau 6 lorsqu'elles étaient connues. Comme on l'a précisé dans les notes techniques relatives au tableau 6, ces définitions varient considérablement d'un pays ou d'une zone à l'autre.

Outre les problèmes de comparabilité, les taux démographiques classés selon le lieu de résidence (zone urbaine ou rurale) sont également sujets à des distorsions particulières. Si l'on utilise des définitions différentes du terme « urbain » pour classer les faits d'état civil et les données relatives à la population lors du calcul des taux et qu'il en résulte une différence nette entre le numérateur et le dénominateur pour le taux de la population exposée au risque, les taux démographiques s'en trouveront faussés. La différence entre ces taux pour les zones urbaines et rurales pourra aussi être faussée selon que les faits d'état civil auront été classés d'après le lieu de l'événement ou d'après le lieu de résidence habituel. Ce problème est examiné plus en détail à la section 4.1.4.1 des Notes techniques.

Données publiées antérieurement : les différentes éditions de l'*Annuaire démographique* regroupent les statistiques les plus récentes dont on disposait à l'époque sur les taux de naissances vivantes selon l'âge de la mère. Les données qui figurent dans le tableau 11 actualisent les données qui portaient sur les périodes suivantes :

Éditions	Années considérées
Édition spéciale sur les statistiques de la natalité (CD-ROM), 1999	1990 – 1990
Supplément historique (CD-ROM), 1997	1948 – 1997
1992	1983 – 1992
1986	1977 – 1985
1981	1972 – 1980
Supplément rétrospectif, 1979	1948 - 1977

11. Live-birth rates by age of mother and urban/rural residence: latest available year, 1997 - 2006
Naissances vivantes, taux selon l'âge de la mère et la résidence, urbaine/rurale: dernière année disponible, 1997 - 2006

Continent, country or area, year, and age of mother (in years) / Continent, pays ou zone, année et âge de la mère (en années)	Rate - Taux		
	Total Total	Urban Urbaine	Rural Rurale
AFRICA - AFRIQUE			
Egypt - Égypte			
1999			
Total	108.4	...	...
0 - 19	18.7	...	...
20 - 24	194.8	...	...
25 - 29	228.7	...	...
30 - 34	164.5	...	...
35 - 39	88.6	...	...
40 - 44	25.9	...	...
45 +	6.7	...	...
Mauritius - Maurice			
2006			
Total	50.0	...	...
15 - 19	33.3	...	...
20 - 24	97.1	...	...
25 - 29	105.8	...	...
30 - 34	64.7	...	...
35 - 39	29.9	...	...
40 - 44	7.7	...	...
45 - 49	♦0.6	...	...
Morocco - Maroc			
2001			
Total	66.7	57.5[1]	80.5[1]
15 - 19	28.3	23.3[1]	33.9[1]
20 - 24	88.3	74.5[1]	106.0[1]
25 - 29	102.3	90.2[1]	120.9[1]
30 - 34	104.4	89.9[1]	132.0[1]
35 - 39	73.6	63.4[1]	93.7[1]
40 - 44	32.1	24.9[1]	45.4[1]
45 - 49	5.9	3.4[1]	10.0[1]
Namibia - Namibie[2]			
2001			
Total	100.1	84.8	110.4
15 - 19	51.2	45.2	53.8
20 - 24	135.8	106.0	156.5
25 - 29	144.6	120.8	166.0
30 - 34	137.3	113.0	158.2
35 - 39	103.1	79.5	121.6
40 - 44	59.8	37.9	74.7
45 +	22.1	10.9	28.3
Réunion[3]			
1999			
Total	72.0	...	...
0 - 19	35.1	...	...
20 - 24	115.9	...	...
25 - 29	143.0	...	...
30 - 34	107.1	...	...
35 - 39	61.3	...	...
40 - 44	15.1	...	...
45 +	♦1.3	...	...
Swaziland[4]			
1997			
Total	133.2	106.6	143.5
15 - 19	73.0	65.3	75.4
20 - 24	193.4	147.1	214.3
25 - 29	199.4	157.0	219.4
30 - 34	162.6	115.9	182.0
35 - 39	130.8	92.6	145.4
40 - 44	64.7	39.3	73.4
45 - 49	35.5	22.0	39.4
Tunisia - Tunisie			
1998			
Total	67.8	...	...
15 - 19	7.5	...	...
20 - 24	66.0	...	...
25 - 29	112.3	...	...

Continent, country or area, year, and age of mother (in years) / Continent, pays ou zone, année et âge de la mère (en années)	Rate - Taux		
	Total Total	Urban Urbaine	Rural Rurale
AFRICA - AFRIQUE			
Tunisia - Tunisie			
1998			
30 - 34	110.3	...	...
35 - 39	64.7	...	...
40 - 44	21.2	...	...
45 +	3.4	...	...
AMERICA, NORTH - AMÉRIQUE DU NORD			
Anguilla			
2001 (+)			
Total	57.6	...	...
15 - 19	♦59.6	...	...
20 - 24	136.3	...	...
25 - 29	102.2	...	...
30 - 34	♦49.8	...	...
35 - 39	♦37.7	...	...
40 +	♦8.8	...	...
Aruba			
2006			
Total	42.7	...	...
15 - 19	42.4	...	...
20 - 24	104.1	...	...
25 - 29	93.2	...	...
30 - 34	57.9	...	...
35 - 39	35.2	...	...
40 - 44	9.1	...	...
45 - 49	♦0.2	...	...
Bermuda - Bermudes			
2003			
Total	48.9	...	...
15 - 19	42.4	...	...
20 - 24	68.8	...	...
25 - 29	91.9	...	...
30 - 34	93.5	...	...
35 - 39	52.2	...	...
40 +	6.6	...	...
Canada[5]			
2005			
Total	41.8	...	...
15 - 19	13.3	...	...
20 - 24	50.5	...	...
25 - 29	97.4	...	...
30 - 34	97.6	...	...
35 - 39	42.1	...	...
40 - 44	7.1	...	...
45 - 49	0.3	...	...
Costa Rica			
2006			
Total	58.4	...	...
15 - 19	59.5	...	...
20 - 24	107.9	...	...
25 - 29	99.8	...	...
Cuba			
2006			
Total	36.9	36.2	38.9
15 - 19	41.0	36.5	54.0
20 - 24	87.4	86.1	91.2
25 - 29	75.7	78.5	68.0
30 - 34	48.5	50.6	42.4
35 - 39	21.1	21.8	18.8
40 - 44	3.9	3.8	3.9
45 - 49	0.1	0.1	♦0.2

11. Live-birth rates by age of mother and urban/rural residence: latest available year, 1997 - 2006
Naissances vivantes, taux selon l'âge de la mère et la résidence, urbaine/rurale: dernière année disponible, 1997 - 2006
(continued - suite)

Continent, country or area, year, and age of mother (in years) / Continent, pays ou zone, année et âge de la mère (en années)	Rate - Taux			Continent, country or area, year, and age of mother (in years) / Continent, pays ou zone, année et âge de la mère (en années)	Rate - Taux		
	Total / Total	Urban / Urbaine	Rural / Rurale		Total / Total	Urban / Urbaine	Rural / Rurale
AMERICA, NORTH - AMÉRIQUE DU NORD				**AMERICA, NORTH - AMÉRIQUE DU NORD**			
El Salvador				Martinique[7]			
2003				2003			
Total	70.8	67.0	77.0	35 - 39	57.2		
15 - 19	75.0	73.9	76.4	40 - 44	16.7	...	...
20 - 24	117.5	122.0	111.3	45 +	♦0.7	...	...
25 - 29	95.1	96.3	93.2	Netherlands Antilles - Antilles néerlandaises[8]			
30 - 34	67.4	62.6	76.5	2004			
35 - 39	43.5	35.1	61.3	Total	47.0		
40 - 44	16.6	10.7	29.6	15 - 19	40.3		
45 - 49	2.1	1.2	3.8	20 - 24	95.6	...	...
Greenland - Groenland				25 - 29	103.7	...	...
2006				30 - 34	80.6	...	...
Total	58.0	...	...	35 - 39	42.4	...	...
15 - 19	55.7	...	...	40 - 44	9.5	...	...
20 - 24	125.3	...	...	45 - 49	♦0.9	...	...
25 - 29	133.5	...	...	Panama			
30 - 34	81.6	...	...	2006			
35 - 39	39.0	...	...	Total	76.1		
40 - 44	♦8.7	...	...	15 - 19	81.3		
45 - 49	♦0.5	...	...	20 - 24	139.3	...	...
Grenada - Grenade				25 - 29	118.3	...	...
2000 (¹)				30 - 34	86.1	...	...
Total	76.5	...	...	35 - 39	45.8	...	...
15 - 19	53.1	...	...	40 - 44	12.6	...	...
20 - 24	107.0	...	...	45 - 49	1.1	...	...
25 - 29	132.7	...	...	Puerto Rico - Porto Rico			
30 - 34	113.8	...	...	2005			
35 - 39	64.1	...	...	Total	51.3		
40 - 44	26.7	...	...	15 - 19	61.0		
45 +	♦1.1	...	...	20 - 24	109.7	...	...
Guadeloupe				25 - 29	92.7	...	...
2003				30 - 34	58.3	...	...
Total	60.4	...	...	35 - 39	24.1	...	...
15 - 19	25.5	...	...	40 - 44	5.3	...	...
20 - 24	81.3	...	...	45 - 49	0.3	...	...
25 - 29	132.3	...	...	Saint Kitts and Nevis - Saint-Kitts-et-Nevis			
30 - 34	108.6	...	...	2000 (+)			
35 - 39	64.6	...	...	Total	80.0		
40 - 44	19.3	...	...	15 - 19	85.6		
45 +	♦0.8	...	...	20 - 24	140.2	...	...
Guatemala				25 - 29	123.1	...	...
1999				30 - 34	80.0	...	...
Total	141.2	...	...	35 - 39	57.4	...	...
15 - 19	107.5	...	...	40 - 44	♦20.0	...	...
20 - 24	210.8	...	...	45 +	♦1.0	...	...
25 - 29	192.9	...	...	Saint Lucia - Sainte-Lucie			
30 - 34	162.3	...	...	2005*			
35 - 39	128.0	...	...	Total	49.4		
40 - 44	60.0	...	...	15 - 19	44.1		
45 - 49	10.8	...	...	20 - 24	78.8	...	...
Jamaica - Jamaïque[6]				25 - 29	79.8	...	...
2004				30 - 34	60.7	...	...
Total	61.5	...	...	35 - 39	40.4	...	...
15 - 19	62.6	...	...	40 - 44	10.9	...	...
20 - 24	103.3	...	...	45 +	♦2.3	...	...
25 - 29	06.2	...	...	Saint Vincent and the Grenadines - Saint Vincent-et-les Grenadines[9]			
30 - 34	70.4	...	...	2001 (+)			
35 - 39	45.2	...	...	Total	76.4	...	...
40 - 44	16.3	...	...	15 - 19	71.8	...	...
45 - 49	1.1	...	...	20 - 24	121.3	...	...
Martinique[7]				25 - 29	120.7	...	...
2003				30 - 34	97.2	...	...
Total	52.3	...	...				
15 - 19	25.9	...	...				
20 - 24	67.7	...	...				
25 - 29	116.7	...	...				
30 - 34	99.2	...	...				

11. Live-birth rates by age of mother and urban/rural residence: latest available year, 1997 - 2006
Naissances vivantes, taux selon l'âge de la mère et la résidence, urbaine/rurale: dernière année disponible, 1997 - 2006
(continued - suite)

Continent, country or area, year, and age of mother (in years) / Continent, pays ou zone, année et âge de la mère (en années)	Rate - Taux		
	Total Total	Urban Urbaine	Rural Rurale

AMERICA, NORTH - AMÉRIQUE DU NORD

Saint Vincent and the Grenadines - Saint Vincent-et-les Grenadines[9]
2001 (+)

35 - 39	53.9	...	...
40 - 44	14.2	...	...
45 - 49	♦0.9	...	...

Trinidad and Tobago - Trinité-et-Tobago
1997

Total	52.2	...	...
15 - 19	42.7	...	...
20 - 24	97.0	...	...
25 - 29	88.0	...	...
30 - 34	70.0	...	...
35 - 39	35.3	...	...
40 - 44	9.4	...	...
45 +	♦0.6	...	...

Turks Caicos Islands - Îles Turques et Caïques
2001

Total	46.1	...	...

United States - États-Unis
2004

Total	56.1	...	...
15 - 19	41.2	...	...
20 - 24	101.8	...	...
25 - 29	115.2	...	...
30 - 34	95.4	...	...
35 - 39	45.3	...	...
40 - 44	9.0	...	...
45 - 49	0.5	...	...

AMERICA, SOUTH - AMÉRIQUE DU SUD

Argentina - Argentine
2006 (+)

Total	71.1	...	...
15 - 19	62.8	...	...
20 - 24	109.7	...	...
25 - 29	108.9	...	...
30 - 34	99.0	...	...
35 - 39	60.1	...	...
40 - 44	17.4	...	...
45 - 49	1.3	...	...

Chile - Chili
2005

Total	52.8	...	...
15 - 19	48.8	...	...
20 - 24	82.9	...	...
25 - 29	92.0	...	...
30 - 34	80.7	...	...
35 - 39	46.4	...	...
40 - 44	13.0	...	...
45 - 49	0.7	...	...

French Guiana - Guyane française[3]
2003

Total	118.5	...	...
15 - 19	104.0	...	...
20 - 24	201.8	...	...
25 - 29	236.5	...	...
30 - 34	144.0	...	...
35 - 39	84.7	...	...

AMERICA, SOUTH - AMÉRIQUE DU SUD

French Guiana - Guyane française[3]
2003

40 - 44	27.3	...	...
45 - 49	♦2.1	...	...

Suriname
2004

Total	69.7	...	...
15 - 19	63.7	...	...
20 - 24	118.6	...	...
25 - 29	120.7	...	...
30 - 34	85.2	...	...
35 - 39	46.5	...	...
40 - 44	13.9	...	...
45 +	♦1.0	...	...

Uruguay
2004

Total	62.1	...	...
15 - 19	58.2	...	...
20 - 24	98.1	...	...
25 - 29	102.7	...	...
30 - 34	90.0	...	...
35 - 39	50.6	...	...
40 - 44	14.9	...	...
45 - 49	1.0	...	...

Venezuela (Bolivarian Republic of) - Venezuela (République bolivarienne du)[10]
2002

Total	74.3	...	...
15 - 19	80.6	...	...
20 - 24	129.0	...	...
25 - 29	109.9	...	...
30 - 34	80.1	...	...
35 - 39	42.9	...	...
40 - 44	14.1	...	...
45 - 49	2.2	...	...

ASIA - ASIE

Armenia - Arménie[11]
2006

Total	40.7	39.4	43.2
15 - 19	25.4	20.6	32.6
20 - 24	118.7	108.5	137.8
25 - 29	79.8	82.5	74.0
30 - 34	32.8	36.3	25.5
35 - 39	11.2	12.4	8.9
40 - 44	1.8	2.0	1.5
45 - 49	♦0.1	♦0.1	♦0.1

Azerbaijan - Azerbaïdjan[12]
2004 (+)

Total	53.0	44.8	62.4
15 - 19	31.0	20.5	42.2
20 - 24	144.4	118.0	173.4
25 - 29	107.2	100.7	114.2
30 - 34	51.5	49.7	53.4
35 - 39	22.0	19.9	24.2
40 - 44	6.0	5.4	6.8
45 - 49	0.7	0.6	0.8

Bahrain - Bahreïn
2006

Total	80.2	...	...
15 - 19	15.0	...	...
20 - 24	110.7	...	...

11. Live-birth rates by age of mother and urban/rural residence: latest available year, 1997 - 2006
Naissances vivantes, taux selon l'âge de la mère et la résidence, urbaine/rurale: dernière année disponible, 1997 - 2006
(continued - suite)

Continent, country or area, year, and age of mother (in years) / Continent, pays ou zone, année et âge de la mère (en années)	Rate - Taux		
	Total Total	Urban Urbaine	Rural Rurale

ASIA - ASIE

	Total	Urban	Rural
Bahrain - Bahreïn			
2006			
25 - 29	157.0	...	...
30 - 34	115.7	...	...
35 - 39	70.2	...	...
40 - 44	30.0	...	...
45 - 49	3.3	...	...
Bhutan - Bhoutan[13]			
2005			
Total	79.4	71.5	83.5
15 - 19	36.5	22.1	44.9
20 - 24	138.9	115.3	154.4
25 - 29	141.6	138.8	143.2
30 - 34	89.4	78.1	95.3
35 - 39	54.5	39.5	61.3
40 - 44	31.3	18.8	35.3
45 - 49	9.9	♦7.1	10.7
Brunei Darussalam - Brunéi Darussalam			
2001 (+)			
Total	73.7	...	...
15 - 19	20.6	...	...
20 - 24	90.9	...	...
25 - 29	125.0	...	...
30 - 34	108.1	...	...
35 - 39	68.0	...	...
40 - 44	24.5	...	...
45 - 49	♦1.8	...	...
China: Hong Kong SAR - Chine: Hong Kong RAS			
2006			
Total	31.5	...	...
15 - 19	4.1	...	...
20 - 24	36.8	...	...
25 - 29	67.6	...	...
30 - 34	74.4	...	...
35 - 39	35.5	...	...
40 - 44	5.4	...	...
45 - 49	0.3	...	...
China: Macao SAR - Chine: Macao RAS			
2006			
Total	25.1	...	...
15 - 19	3.5	...	...
20 - 24	30.1	...	...
25 - 29	61.1	...	...
30 - 34	62.3	...	...
35 - 39	28.5	...	...
40 - 44	4.9	...	...
45 - 49	♦0.3	...	...
Cyprus - Chypre[14]			
2006			
Total	42.6	...	...
15 - 19	6.5	...	...
20 - 24	44.0	...	...
25 - 29	100.7	...	...
30 - 34	90.5	...	...
35 - 39	37.4	...	...
40 - 44	7.6	...	...
45 - 49	♦0.9	...	...
Georgia - Géorgie[12]			
2006			
Total	40.3	...	...
15 - 19	36.6	...	...
20 - 24	100.8	...	...
25 - 29	76.0	...	...

ASIA - ASIE

	Total	Urban	Rural
Georgia - Géorgie[12]			
2006			
30 - 34	43.3	...	...
35 - 39	18.9	...	...
40 - 44	4.6	...	...
45 - 49	0.5	...	...
Israel - Israël[15]			
2006			
Total	87.0	85.5[1]	102.9[1]
15 - 19	14.1	14.5[1]	9.8[1]
20 - 24	106.3	106.6[1]	101.6[1]
25 - 29	171.0	168.1[1]	206.3[1]
30 - 34	163.8	157.8[1]	238.1[1]
35 - 39	94.3	90.7[1]	134.0[1]
40 - 44	23.8	23.2[1]	30.6[1]
45 - 49	2.1	2.1[1]	♦1.9[1]
Japan - Japon[16]			
2006			
Total	39.3	...	...
15 - 19	5.1	...	...
20 - 24	36.3	...	...
25 - 29	81.4	...	...
30 - 34	87.3	...	...
35 - 39	37.9	...	...
40 - 44	5.4	...	...
45 - 49	0.1	...	...
Kazakhstan[12]			
2006			
Total	69.2	67.2	72.2
15 - 19	27.8	30.4	24.9
20 - 24	143.9	144.3	143.3
25 - 29	140.4	130.6	157.3
30 - 34	95.1	90.7	102.1
35 - 39	51.6	48.0	57.4
40 - 44	11.5	10.7	12.9
45 - 49	0.5	0.4	0.7
Korea (Republic of) - Corée (République de)[17]			
2005			
Total	33.4[18]	31.8	41.5
15 - 19	2.1[18]	1.8	3.7
20 - 24	18.9[18]	15.7	41.9
25 - 29	97.0[18]	89.8	143.0
30 - 34	88.0[18]	86.3	92.9
35 - 39	20.1[18]	19.3	22.7
40 - 44	2.6[18]	2.3	3.6
45 - 49	0.2[18]	0.2	0.3
Kuwait - Koweït			
2005			
Total	83.0	...	...
15 - 19	16.1	...	...
20 - 24	118.8	...	...
25 - 29	142.5	...	...
30 - 34	120.0	...	...
36 - 39	74.1	...	...
40 - 44	27.0	...	...
45 - 49	4.1	...	...
Kyrgyzstan - Kirghizistan			
2006			
Total	83.8	71.2	91.7
15 - 19	28.4	27.3	28.9
20 - 24	174.3	156.0	184.0
25 - 29	159.1	118.6	192.0
30 - 34	104.9	86.7	117.9
35 - 39	60.1	50.6	67.0

11. Live-birth rates by age of mother and urban/rural residence: latest available year, 1997 - 2006
Naissances vivantes, taux selon l'âge de la mère et la résidence, urbaine/rurale: dernière année disponible, 1997 - 2006
(continued - suite)

Continent, country or area, year, and age of mother (in years) / Continent, pays ou zone, année et âge de la mère (en années)	Rate - Taux		
	Total Total	Urban Urbaine	Rural Rurale

ASIA - ASIE

Kyrgyzstan - Kirghizistan			
2006			
40 - 44	17.6	15.4	19.2
45 - 49	3.3	2.4	3.8
Malaysia - Malaisie			
2004			
Total	71.4	...	...
15 - 19	12.9	...	...
20 - 24	74.3	...	...
25 - 29	151.2	...	...
30 - 34	136.5	...	...
35 - 39	79.7	...	...
40 - 44	26.8	...	...
45 - 49	2.9	...	...
Maldives			
2006			
Total	68.5	80.3	60.8
15 - 19	14.6	12.2	16.3
20 - 24	117.0	122.8	112.1
25 - 29	136.8	173.6	111.9
30 - 34	98.7	118.6	86.5
35 - 39	56.0	63.7	52.0
40 - 44	16.4	11.4	19.1
45 - 49	♦1.3	♦0.5	♦1.8
Mongolia - Mongolie			
2006			
Total	65.0	...	...
15 - 19	19.7	...	...
20 - 24	125.6	...	...
25 - 29	129.2	...	...
30 - 34	83.7	...	...
35 - 39	41.3	...	...
40 - 44	12.4	...	...
45 - 49	1.8	...	...
Pakistan[19]			
2003			
Total	114.5	97.9	124.5
15 - 19	23.7	14.2	29.7
20 - 24	163.1	137.1	178.9
25 - 29	229.6	219.3	236.1
30 - 34	190.0	169.2	201.6
35 - 39	112.7	93.4	124.5
40 - 44	49.0	34.2	57.8
45 +	18.8	11.2	23.7
Philippines			
2003			
Total	79.4	...	...
15 - 19	30.0	...	...
20 - 24	125.7	...	...
25 - 29	135.3	...	...
30 - 34	113.1	...	...
35 - 39	74.0	...	...
40 - 44	30.6	...	...
45 - 49	4.4	...	...
Qatar			
2006			
Total	96.9	...	...
15 - 19	15.8	...	...
20 - 24	182.2	...	...
25 - 29	202.1	...	...
30 - 34	140.4	...	...
35 - 39	94.6	...	...
40 - 44	32.3	...	...
45 - 49	4.5	...	...

Continent, country or area, year, and age of mother (in years) / Continent, pays ou zone, année et âge de la mère (en années)	Rate - Taux		
	Total Total	Urban Urbaine	Rural Rurale

ASIA - ASIE

Saudi Arabia - Arabie saoudite[20]			
2004			
Total	93.4	...	...
15 - 19	14.7	...	...
20 - 24	66.1	...	...
25 - 29	228.3	...	...
30 - 34	117.5	...	...
35 - 39	97.9	...	...
40 - 44	58.7	...	...
45 - 49	22.8	...	...
Singapore - Singapour			
2005			
Total	37.8	...	...
15 - 19	7.3	...	...
20 - 24	33.8	...	...
25 - 29	83.8	...	...
30 - 34	93.0	...	...
35 - 39	38.9	...	...
40 - 44	6.5	...	...
45 - 49	0.3	...	...
Turkey - Turquie[21]			
1997			
Total	81.1	...	...
15 - 19	50.0	...	...
20 - 24	173.6	...	...
25 - 29	144.9	...	...
30 - 34	73.3	...	...
35 - 39	36.1	...	...
40 - 44	15.5	...	...
45 +	3.4	...	...
Uzbekistan - Ouzbékistan[12]			
2000			
Total	82.7	65.7	93.6
15 - 19	21.1	21.8	20.7
20 - 24	205.4	167.9	227.5
25 - 29	161.4	123.6	185.9
30 - 34	89.7	73.0	100.6
35 - 39	31.5	26.6	34.7
40 - 44	7.0	5.4	8.2
45 - 49	0.7	0.4	0.9

EUROPE

Åland Islands - Îles d'Åland[22]			
2006			
Total	50.7	...	...
0 - 19	♦6.2	...	...
20 - 24	♦42.7	...	...
25 - 29	123.2	...	...
30 - 34	127.3	...	...
35 - 39	61.8	...	...
40 +	♦7.8	...	...
Albania - Albanie			
2006			
Total	40.7	...	...
0 - 19	13.0	...	...
20 - 24	77.6	...	...
25 - 29	96.7	...	...
30 - 34	60.6	...	...
35 - 39	23.2	...	...
40 - 44	4.8	...	...
45 - 49	0.5	...	...

11. Live-birth rates by age of mother and urban/rural residence: latest available year, 1997 - 2006
Naissances vivantes, taux selon l'âge de la mère et la résidence, urbaine/rurale: dernière année disponible, 1997 - 2006
(continued - suite)

Continent, country or area, year, and age of mother (in years) / Continent, pays ou zone, année et âge de la mère (en années)	Rate - Taux			Continent, country or area, year, and age of mother (in years) / Continent, pays ou zone, année et âge de la mère (en années)	Rate - Taux		
	Total Total	Urban Urbaine	Rural Rurale		Total Total	Urban Urbaine	Rural Rurale
EUROPE				EUROPE			
Andorra - Andorre				Denmark - Danemark[23]			
2006				2006			
Total	38.3	...	...	30 - 34	131.0	...	...
15 - 19	♦10.6	...	...	35 - 39	51.6	...	...
20 - 24	38.3	...	...	40 - 44	8.7	...	...
25 - 29	64.1	...	...	45 - 49	0.3	...	...
30 - 34	81.3	...	...	Estonia - Estonie			
35 - 39	37.6	...	...	2006			
40 - 44	12.8	...	...	Total	43.6	43.1	44.8
45 - 49	♦0.3	...	...	15 - 19	21.4	19.2	25.7
Austria - Autriche				20 - 24	69.4	67.7	73.2
2006				25 - 29	102.7	97.3	122.5
Total	38.1	...	...	30 - 34	74.2	73.7	75.8
15 - 19	11.9	...	...	35 - 39	35.5	34.6	37.9
20 - 24	53.6	...	...	40 - 44	6.4	6.2	7.0
25 - 29	91.3	...	...	45 - 49	♦0.2	♦0.2	♦0.3
30 - 34	82.0	...	...	Finland - Finlande[24]			
35 - 39	34.3	...	...	2006			
40 - 44	6.7	...	...	Total	50.1	49.0	52.4
45 - 49	0.3	...	...	15 - 19	9.4	9.8	8.8
Belarus - Bélarus[12]				20 - 24	58.4	50.8	82.8
2006				25 - 29	116.8	103.4	156.8
Total	36.6	34.3	45.1	30 - 34	117.9	114.6	125.5
15 - 19	21.9	17.2	38.4	35 - 39	53.0	52.1	54.6
20 - 24	88.9	79.3	128.6	40 - 44	11.0	10.8	11.2
25 - 29	83.0	78.7	101.7	45 - 49	0.5	0.5	0.4
30 - 34	46.3	45.9	47.7	France[25]			
35 - 39	16.1	15.6	17.5	2005			
40 - 44	2.4	2.2	3.3	Total	53.6	...	...
45 - 49	0.1	0.1	♦0.2	15 - 19	7.8	...	...
Bulgaria - Bulgarie				20 - 24	55.0	...	...
2006				25 - 29	128.1	...	...
Total	39.8	38.5	44.1	30 - 34	121.4	...	...
15 - 19	40.3	32.4	62.4	35 - 39	56.0	...	...
20 - 24	79.6	67.1	126.5	40 - 44	12.9	...	...
25 - 29	84.2	85.8	78.5	45 - 49	0.7	...	...
30 - 34	52.2	56.5	37.4	Germany - Allemagne			
35 - 39	16.3	17.9	10.9	2006			
40 - 44	2.2	2.4	1.6	Total	34.7	...	...
45 - 49	♦0.1	♦0.1	♦0.1	15 - 19	10.1	...	...
Croatia - Croatie				20 - 24	45.3	...	...
2006				25 - 29	82.4	...	...
Total	39.0	...	...	30 - 34	82.5	...	...
15 - 19	13.7	...	...	35 - 39	37.4	...	...
20 - 24	60.9	...	...	40 - 44	6.6	...	...
25 - 29	95.9	...	...	45 - 49	0.3	...	...
30 - 34	72.6	...	...	Gibraltar			
35 - 39	27.9	...	...	2001			
40 - 44	4.8	...	...	Total	60.9	...	...
45 - 49	0.3	...	...	15 - 19	♦24.9	...	...
Czech Republic - République tchèque				20 - 24	77.5	...	...
2006				25 - 29	168.3	...	...
Total	42.1	42.0	42.2	30 - 34	110.8	...	...
15 - 19	10.9	11.1	10.3	35 - 39	43.4	...	...
20 - 24	47.0	44.9	52.7	40 - 44	♦7.9	...	...
25 - 29	103.6	100.5	112.7	Greece - Grèce			
30 - 34	77.5	80.3	69.4	2006			
35 - 39	25.6	26.9	21.9	Total	41.7	...	...
40 - 44	4.1	4.3	3.5	15 - 19	11.3	...	...
45 - 49	0.2	0.2	♦0.2	20 - 24	44.5	...	...
Denmark - Danemark[23]				25 - 29	84.3	...	...
2006				30 - 34	90.9	...	...
Total	52.6	...	...	35 - 39	41.1	...	...
15 - 19	5.9	...	...	40 - 44	7.9	...	...
20 - 24	43.8	...	...	45 - 49	0.8	...	...
25 - 29	128.4	...	...				

11. Live-birth rates by age of mother and urban/rural residence: latest available year, 1997 - 2006
Naissances vivantes, taux selon l'âge de la mère et la résidence, urbaine/rurale: dernière année disponible, 1997 - 2006
(continued - suite)

Continent, country or area, year, and age of mother (in years) / Continent, pays ou zone, année et âge de la mère (en années)	Rate - Taux		
	Total / Total	Urban / Urbaine	Rural / Rurale
EUROPE			
Hungary - Hongrie 2006			
Total	41.2	39.8[26]	43.1[26]
15 - 19	19.7	14.7[26]	29.5[26]
20 - 24	48.2	38.0[26]	68.8[26]
25 - 29	89.5	83.9[26]	101.0[26]
30 - 34	78.3	80.8[26]	70.4[26]
35 - 39	29.1	31.0[26]	24.4[26]
40 - 44	4.9	5.0[26]	4.5[26]
45 - 49	0.2	0.2[26]	◆0.2[26]
Iceland - Islande 2006			
Total	59.0	59.9	44.3
15 - 19	13.6	13.8	◆11.8
20 - 24	79.1	80.5	58.8
25 - 29	127.9	128.4	119.3
30 - 34	119.3	120.9	90.6
35 - 39	61.4	61.8	56.1
40 - 44	11.2	11.0	◆13.1
45 - 49	◆0.3	◆0.3	-
Ireland - Irlande[27] 2006* (+)			
Total	57.9	...	...
15 - 19	16.4	...	...
20 - 24	48.8	...	...
25 - 29	79.4	...	...
30 - 34	131.9	...	...
35 - 39	89.3	...	...
40 - 44	17.8	...	...
45 - 49	0.7	...	...
Italy - Italie[28] 2004			
Total	40.0	...	...
15 - 19	7.0	...	...
20 - 24	33.6	...	...
25 - 29	73.9	...	...
30 - 34	89.8	...	...
35 - 39	49.2	...	...
40 - 44	9.9	...	...
45 - 49	0.4	...	...
Latvia - Lettonie 2006			
Total	37.8	37.3	39.0
15 - 19	17.7	15.9	20.8
20 - 24	67.3	62.9	77.2
25 - 29	86.6	87.6	84.0
30 - 34	62.5	62.7	62.0
35 - 39	29.6	29.5	30.0
40 - 44	6.6	6.1	7.8
45 - 49	0.3	◆0.4	◆0.2
Liechtenstein 2006*			
Total	40.1	...	...
0 - 19	◆3.9	...	...
20 - 24	40.0	...	...
25 - 29	55.9	...	...
30 - 34	119.7	...	...
35 - 39	50.2	...	...
40 - 44	◆13.4	...	...
45 - 49	◆0.7	...	...
Lithuania - Lituanie 2006			
Total	35.3	32.9	41.0
15 - 19	19.4	14.7	27.6
20 - 24	64.2	55.2	84.0
25 - 29	93.4	87.4	112.2
EUROPE			
Lithuania - Lituanie 2006			
30 - 34	56.8	55.7	60.2
35 - 39	21.8	21.4	22.8
40 - 44	4.4	4.0	5.5
45 - 49	◆0.2	◆0.1	◆0.3
Luxembourg 2006			
Total	46.7	...	...
15 - 19	10.4	...	...
20 - 24	54.5	...	...
25 - 29	98.9	...	...
30 - 34	106.0	...	...
35 - 39	51.1	...	...
40 - 44	8.8	...	...
45 - 49	◆0.2	...	...
Malta - Malte 2006			
Total	40.0	...	...
0 - 19	16.7	...	...
20 - 24	45.7	...	...
25 - 29	96.3	...	...
30 - 34	84.5	...	...
35 - 39	31.0	...	...
40 - 44	5.2	...	...
45 - 49	◆0.1	...	...
Moldova[29] 2006			
Total	37.1	30.1	42.7
15 - 19	28.7	16.8	36.8
20 - 24	86.7	61.1	107.8
25 - 29	71.7	68.8	73.8
30 - 34	40.0	40.0	40.0
35 - 39	16.0	16.1	16.0
40 - 44	2.7	2.2	3.1
45 - 49	-	-	-
Montenegro 2005			
Total	46.5	55.4	29.3
15 - 19	16.0	17.7	12.9
20 - 24	80.2	92.6	56.6
25 - 29	105.9	126.6	64.5
30 - 34	76.3	93.9	42.2
35 - 39	33.9	41.1	19.6
40 - 44	7.7	9.6	◆3.6
45 - 49	◆0.6	◆0.9	-
Netherlands - Pays-Bas[30] 2006			
Total	47.2	47.2	47.4
15 - 19	3.8	4.6	2.4
20 - 24	34.2	35.0	32.1
25 - 29	99.8	90.1	128.1
30 - 34	126.4	119.8	142.3
35 - 39	61.9	63.5	58.5
40 - 44	9.8	10.8	7.7
45 - 49	0.4	0.4	0.3
Norway - Norvège[31] 2006			
Total	53.7	...	...
15 - 19	8.7	...	...
20 - 24	60.3	...	...
25 - 29	127.2	...	...
30 - 34	122.8	...	...
35 - 39	51.9	...	...
40 - 44	8.9	...	...
45 - 49	0.4	...	...

11. Live-birth rates by age of mother and urban/rural residence: latest available year, 1997 - 2006
Naissances vivantes, taux selon l'âge de la mère et la résidence, urbaine/rurale: dernière année disponible, 1997 - 2006
(continued - suite)

Continent, country or area, year, and age of mother (in years) / Continent, pays ou zone, année et âge de la mère (en années)	Rate - Taux			Continent, country or area, year, and age of mother (in years) / Continent, pays ou zone, année et âge de la mère (en années)	Rate - Taux		
	Total / Total	Urban / Urbaine	Rural / Rurale		Total / Total	Urban / Urbaine	Rural / Rurale
EUROPE				**EUROPE**			
Poland - Pologne				**Slovakia - Slovaquie**			
2006				2006			
Total	38.1	35.4	42.7	25 - 29	84.6	79.6	91.5
15 - 19	13.9	12.4	15.8	30 - 34	62.1	65.6	57.4
20 - 24	57.7	46.8	75.8	35 - 39	22.0	21.5	22.7
25 - 29	91.1	84.8	103.1	40 - 44	3.6	3.3	4.1
30 - 34	62.8	63.0	62.4	45 - 49	0.2	♦0.1	♦0.3
35 - 39	24.0	23.4	24.9	**Slovenia - Slovénie**			
40 - 44	4.9	4.3	5.8	2006			
45 - 49	0.2	0.2	0.3	Total	38.1	38.0	39.8
Portugal[28]				15 - 19	4.7	4.9	4.7
2006				20 - 24	39.3	36.3	43.9
Total	40.3	...	...	25 - 29	99.3	92.7	111.1
15 - 19	16.8	...	...	30 - 34	86.2	94.1	83.1
20 - 24	45.6	...	...	35 - 39	29.3	33.7	26.3
25 - 29	79.7	...	...	40 - 44	4.6	4.6	4.8
30 - 34	83.8	...	...	45 - 49	♦0.2	♦0.3	♦0.1
35 - 39	38.4	...	...	**Spain - Espagne**			
40 - 44	7.7	...	...	2005			
45 - 49	0.4	...	...	Total	41.9	...	...
Romania - Roumanie				15 - 19	11.5	...	...
2006				20 - 24	31.0	...	...
Total	39.6	34.8	47.2	25 - 29	64.3	...	...
15 - 19	35.0	22.3	51.9	30 - 34	100.4	...	...
20 - 24	69.8	51.5	99.3	35 - 39	53.4	...	...
25 - 29	82.7	81.4	84.6	40 - 44	9.4	...	...
30 - 34	54.0	59.2	46.6	45 - 49	0.5	...	...
35 - 39	19.0	18.8	19.3	**Sweden - Suède**			
40 - 44	3.5	2.8	4.9	2006			
45 - 49	0.2	0.1	0.3	Total	52.0	...	...
Russian Federation - Fédération de Russie[12]				15 - 19	5.9	...	...
2006				20 - 24	47.6	...	...
Total	37.7	35.4	44.6	25 - 29	113.6	...	...
15 - 19	28.5	24.4	38.2	30 - 34	131.2	...	...
20 - 24	85.8	74.5	125.0	35 - 39	59.4	...	...
25 - 29	78.2	75.2	88.7	40 - 44	11.5	...	...
30 - 34	46.8	46.5	47.9	45 - 49	0.5	...	...
35 - 39	18.7	18.5	19.2	**Switzerland - Suisse**			
40 - 44	3.1	2.9	3.7	2006			
45 - 49	0.1	0.1	0.2	Total	40.2	...	...
San Marino - Saint-Marin				15 - 19	4.5	...	...
2004 (+)				20 - 24	37.8	...	...
Total	40.7	...	...	25 - 29	85.2	...	...
15 - 19	♦1.6	...	...	30 - 34	102.8	...	...
20 - 24	♦20.3	...	...	35 - 39	50.0	...	...
25 - 29	65.4	...	...	40 - 44	8.9	...	...
30 - 34	102.8	...	...	45 - 49	0.3	...	...
35 - 39	50.7	...	...	**The Former Yugoslav Rep. of Macedonia - L'ex-République yougoslave de Macédoine**			
40 - 44	♦8.3	...	...	2006			
45 - 49	♦1.0	...	...	Total	42.8	...	...
Serbia - Serbie[32]				15 - 19	20.2	...	...
2006 (+)				20 - 24	80.0	...	...
Total	41.0	43.5	36.9	25 - 29	105.7	...	...
15 - 19	22.8	19.0	27.9	30 - 34	61.9	...	...
20 - 24	78.8	72.5	89.0	35 - 39	21.3	...	...
25 - 29	93.2	98.0	84.4	40 - 44	3.0	...	...
30 - 34	63.7	75.3	44.2	45 - 49	♦0.1	...	...
35 - 39	23.6	29.1	15.2	**Ukraine[33]**			
40 - 44	4.0	4.7	2.8	2004			
45 - 49	0.2	0.3	♦0.2	Total	34.3	...	...
Slovakia - Slovaquie				15 - 19	29.4	...	...
2006				20 - 24	93.4	...	...
Total	37.7	34.2	42.5	25 - 29	70.6	...	...
15 - 19	20.2	14.7	27.0	30 - 34	35.5	...	...
20 - 24	56.6	43.6	73.9	35 - 39	12.3	...	...

11. Live-birth rates by age of mother and urban/rural residence: latest available year, 1997 - 2006
Naissances vivantes, taux selon l'âge de la mère et la résidence, urbaine/rurale: dernière année disponible, 1997 - 2006
(continued - suite)

Continent, country or area, year and age of mother (in years) / Continent, pays ou zone, année et âge de la mère (en années)	Total Total	Urban Urbaine	Rural Rurale
EUROPE			
Ukraine[33]			
2004			
40 - 44	2.2	...	...
45 - 49	0.1	...	...
United Kingdom - Royaume-Uni[34]			
2004			
Total	49.8	...	...
15 - 19	26.7	...	...
20 - 24	71.5	...	...
25 - 29	97.6	...	...
30 - 34	97.5	...	...
35 - 39	48.5	...	...
40 - 44	9.8	...	...
45 - 49	0.5	...	...
OCEANIA - OCÉANIE			
American Samoa - Samoas américaines			
2000			
Total	123.6	...	...
15 - 19	56.1	...	...
20 - 24	199.3	...	...
25 - 29	238.5	...	...
30 - 34	180.4	...	...
35 - 39	102.0	...	...
40 - 44	26.7	...	...
45 - 49	-	...	...
Australia - Australie			
2004 (+)			
Total	50.7	...	...
0 - 19	16.3	...	...
20 - 24	53.4	...	...
25 - 29	102.5	...	...
30 - 34	114.4	...	...
35 - 39	57.4	...	...
40 - 44	10.6	...	...
45 +	0.5	...	...

Continent, country or area, year and age of mother (in years) / Continent, pays ou zone, année et âge de la mère (en années)	Total Total	Urban Urbaine	Rural Rurale
OCEANIA - OCÉANIE			
New Caledonia - Nouvelle-Calédonie			
2003			
Total	71.2	...	...
15 - 19	20.3	...	...
20 - 24	109.2	...	...
25 - 29	129.5	...	...
30 - 34	118.9	...	...
35 - 39	64.8	...	...
40 - 44	18.3	...	...
45 - 49	♦0.3	...	...
New Zealand - Nouvelle-Zélande[35]			
2006 (+)			
Total	55.4	55.0	56.7
15 - 19	28.1	28.4	25.6
20 - 24	70.9	68.0	103.8
25 - 29	105.4	101.2	143.1
30 - 34	119.4	117.1	134.8
35 - 39	63.6	63.6	62.9
40 - 44	12.3	12.5	11.3
45 - 49	0.7	0.7	♦0.8
Palau - Palaos			
2000			
Total	55.7	...	...
15 - 19	♦24.8	...	...
20 - 24	93.3	...	...
25 - 29	94.5	...	...
30 - 34	74.7	...	...
35 - 39	47.0	...	...
40 - 44	♦29.6	...	...
45 - 49	♦1.9	...	...
Tonga			
1999 (+)			
Total	110.2	...	...
15 - 19	28.3	...	...
20 - 24	129.1	...	...
25 - 29	221.6	...	...
30 - 34	202.8	...	...
35 - 39	129.0	...	...
40 - 44	49.6	...	...
45 - 49	♦3.2	...	...

FOOTNOTES - NOTES

♦ Rates based on 30 or fewer births. - Taux basés sur 30 naissances ou moins.

* Provisional. - Données provisoires.

+ Data tabulated by date of registration rather than occurence. - Données exploitées selon la date de l'enregistrement et non la date de l'événement.

[1] The total number includes 'Unknown residence', but the categories urban and rural do not. - Le nombre total inclue 'Résidence inconnue ', mais les catégories Urbain et Rural ne l'incluent pas.

[2] For 2001, data refer to last twelve months preceding census in August 2001. - Pour 2001, les données se rapportent aux douze mois précédant le recensement d'août 2001.

[3] Excluding live-born infants who died before their birth was registered. - Non compris les enfants nés vivants décédés avant l'enregistrement de leur naissance.

[4] Data for 1997 refer to last twelve months preceding population and housing census of 1997. - Les données pour 1997 se réfèrent au douze mois précédant le recensement de population et de l'habitat de 1997.

[5] Including Canadian residents temporarily in the United States, but excluding United States residents temporarily in Canada. - Y compris les résidents canadiens se trouvant temporairement aux Etats-Unis, mais ne comprenant pas les résidents des Etats-Unis se trouvant temporairement au Canada.

[6] Including births to non-resident mothers. - Y compris les naissances chez des mères non résidentes.

[7] Excluding live-born infants who died before their birth was registered. Age classification is based on year of birth of mother rather than the exact age of mother at birth of child. - Non compris les enfants nés vivants décédés avant l'enregistrement de leur naissance. Le classement selon l'âge est basé sur l'année de naissance de la mère et non sur l'age exacte de la mère au moment de naissance de l'enfant.

[8] Data refer to births to mothers resident in the Netherlands Antilles (including births outside the Netherlands Antilles to resident mothers, excluding births to non-resident mothers). - Ces données concernent les enfants nés de femmes qui résidaient aux Antilles néerlandaises (y compris ceux qui sont nés hors des Antilles néerlandaises). Elles ne concernent pas les enfants nés de non-résidentes.

[9] Data as reported by national statistical authorities; they may differ from data presented in other tables. - Les données comme elles ont été déclarées par

l'institut national de la statistique; elles peuvent être différentes de celles présentées dans d'autres tableaux.

[10] Excluding Indian jungle population. - Non compris les Indiens de la jungle.

[11] Excluding infants born alive of less than 28 weeks' gestation, of less than 1 000 grams in weight and 35 centimeters in length, who die within seven days of birth. Since 16 October 2005 the definition of WHO on livebirths has been put into force in accordance with 10th revision of the International Classification of Diseases. - Non compris les enfants nés vivants après moins de 28 semaines de gestations, pesant moins de 1 000 grammes, mesurant moins de 35 centimètres et décédés dans les sept jours qui ont suivi leur naissance. Depuis le 16 octobre 2005, la définition de l'OMS concernant les naissances vivantes est en vigueur conformément à la dixième révision de la Classification internationale des maladies.

[12] Excluding infants born alive of less than 28 weeks' gestation, of less than 1 000 grams in weight and 35 centimeters in length, who die within seven days of birth. - Non compris les enfants nés vivants après moins de 28 semaines de gestations, pesant moins de 1 000 grammes, mesurant moins de 35 centimètres et décédés dans les sept jours qui ont suivi leur naissance.

[13] For 2005, data refer to last twelve months preceding census in May 2005. - Pour 2005, les données se rapportent aux douze mois précédant le recensement de mai 2005.

[14] Data refer to government controlled areas. - Les données se rapportent aux zones contrôlées par le Gouvernement.

[15] Including data for East Jerusalem and Israeli residents in certain other territories under occupation by Israeli military forces since June 1967. - Y compris les données pour Jérusalem-Est et les résidents israéliens dans certains autres territoires occupés depuis 1967 par les forces armées israéliennes.

[16] Data refer to Japanese nationals in Japan only. - Les données se raportent aux nationaux japonais au Japon seulement.

[17] Excluding alien armed forces, civilian aliens employed by armed forces, and foreign diplomatic personnel and their dependants. - Non compris les militaires étrangers, les civils étrangers employés par les forces armées ni le personnel diplomatique étranger et les membres de leur famille les accompagnant.

[18] Including Koreans abroad. - Y compris les Coréens à l'étranger.

[19] Excluding data for the Pakistan-held part of Jammu and Kashmir, the final status of which has not yet been determined. Data based on Pakistan Demographic Survey (PDS 2003) . - Non compris les données concernant la partie du Jammu et Cachemire occupée par le Pakistan dont le statut définitif n'a pas été déterminé. Données extraites de l'enquête démographique effectuée par le Pakistan en 2003.

[20] For 2004, data refer to last twelve months preceding the census in September 2004. - Pour 2004, les données se rapportent aux douze mois précédant le recensement septembre 2004.

[21] Based on the results of the Population Growth Survey. Data as reported by national statistical authorities; they may differ from data presented in other tables. - D'après les résultats de la 'Population Growth Survey.' Les données comme elles ont été déclarées par l'institut national de la statistique; elles peuvent être différentes de celles présentées dans d'autres tableaux.

[22] Also included in Finland. - Comprise aussi dans Finlande.

[23] Excluding Faeroe Islands and Greenland shown separately, if available. - Non compris les Iles Féroé et le Gröenland, qui font l'objet de rubriques distinctes, si disponible.

[24] Including nationals temporarily outside the country. Including Aland Islands. - Y compris les nationaux se trouvant temporairement hors du pays. Y compris les Îles d'Åland.

[25] Excluding Overseas Departments, namely, French Guiana, Guadeloupe, Martinique and Reunion, shown separately, if available. Including armed forces stationed outside the country. Age classification is based on year of birth of mother rather than the exact age of mother at birth of child. - Non compris les départements d'outre mer, c'est-à-dire la Guyane française, la Guadeloupe, la Martinique et la Réunion, qui font l'objet de rubriques distinctes, si disponible. Y compris les militaires nationaux hors du pays. Le classement selon l'âge est basé sur l'année de naissance de la mère et non sur l'age exacte de la mère au moment de naissance de l'enfant.

[26] Total includes the data of foreigners, persons of unknown residence and homeless, but the categories urban and rural do not. - Total incluant les étrangers, les personnes de résidence inconnue et les sans-abri, ce qui n'est pas le cas pour les catégories urbaines et rurales.

[27] Events registered within one year of occurrence. - Evénements enregistrés dans l'année qui suit l'événement.

[28] Data refer to resident mothers. - Données concernant les mères résidentes.

[29] Excluding infants born alive of less than 28 weeks' gestation, of less than 1 000 grams in weight and 35 centimeters in length, who die within seven days of birth. Data do not include information for Transnistria and the municipality of Bender. - Non compris les enfants nés vivants après moins de 28 semaines de gestations, pesant moins de 1 000 grammes, mesurant moins de 35 centimètres et décédés dans les sept jours qui ont suivi leur naissance. Les données ne tiennent pas compte de l'information sur la Transnistria et la municipalité de Bender.

[30] Including residents outside the country if listed in a Netherlands population register. - Y compris les résidents hors du pays, s'ils sont inscrits sur un registre de population néerlandais.

[31] Age classification is based on year of birth of mother rather than the exact age of mother at birth of child. Excluding Svalbard and Jan Mayen Island shown separately, if available. - Le classement selon l'âge est basé sur l'année de naissance de la mère et non sur l'age exacte de la mère au moment de naissance de l'enfant. Non compris Svalbard et Jan Mayen qui font l'objet de rubriques distinctes, si disponible.

[32] Without data for Kosovo and Metohia. - Sans les données pour le Kosovo and Metohie.

[33] Age classification based on year of birth rather than on completed years of age. Excluding infants born alive of less than 28 weeks' gestation, of less than 1 000 grams in weight and 35 centimeters in length, who die within seven days of birth. - La classification par âge est fondée sur l'année de naissance et non sur l'âge en années révolues. Non compris les enfants nés vivants après moins de 28 semaines de gestations, pesant moins de 1 000 grammes, mesurant moins de 35 centimètres et décédés dans les sept jours qui ont suivi leur naissance.

[34] Data tabulated by date of occurrence for England and Wales, and by date of registration for Northern Ireland and Scotland. Excluding Channel Islands and Isle of Man, shown separately, if available. - Données exploitées selon la date de l'événement pour l'Angleterre et le pays de Galles, et selon la date de l'enregistrement pour l'Irlande du Nord et l'Ecosse. Non compris les îles Anglo-Normandes et l'île de Man, qui font l'objet de rubriques distinctes, si disponible.

[35] For resident population only. - Pour la population résidante seulement.

Table 12

Table 12 presents late foetal deaths and late foetal-death ratios by urban/rural residence for as many years as possible between 2002 and 2006.

Description of variables: Late foetal deaths are foetal deaths[i] of 28 or more completed weeks of gestation. Foetal deaths of unknown gestational age are included with those 28 or more weeks.

Statistics on the number of late foetal deaths are obtained from civil registers unless otherwise noted.

The urban/rural classification of late foetal deaths is as provided by each country or area; it is presumed to be based on the national census definitions of urban population that have been set forth at the end of the technical notes for table 6.

Ratio computation: Late foetal-death ratios are the annual number of late foetal deaths per 1 000 live births (as shown in table 9) in the same year. The live-birth base was adopted because it is assumed to be more comparable from one country or area to another than the sum of live births and foetal deaths.

Ratios by urban/rural residence are the annual number of late foetal deaths, in the appropriate urban or rural category, per 1 000 corresponding live births (as shown in table 9). These ratios are calculated by the Statistics Division of the United Nations.

Ratios presented in this table are limited to those for countries or areas and urban/rural areas having at least a total of 30 late foetal deaths in a given year.

Reliability of data: Each country or area is asked to indicate the estimated completeness of the late foetal deaths recorded in its civil register. These national assessments are indicated by the quality codes, C and U that appear in the first column of this table.

C indicates that the data are estimated to be virtually complete, that is, representing at least 90 per cent of the late foetal deaths occurring each year, while U indicates that data are estimated to be incomplete, that is, representing less than 90 per cent of the late foetal deaths occurring each year. The code ... indicates that no information was provided regarding completeness.

Data from civil registers which are reported as incomplete or of unknown completeness (coded U or ...) are considered unreliable. They appear in italics in this table. Ratios are not computed for data so coded.

For more information about the quality of vital statistics data in general, see section 4.2 of the Technical Notes.

Limitations: Statistics on late foetal deaths are subject to the same qualifications as have been set forth for vital statistics in general and foetal-death statistics in particular as discussed in section 4 of the Technical Notes.

The reliability of the data is a very important factor. Of all vital statistics, the registration of foetal deaths is probably the most incomplete.

Variation in the definition of foetal deaths, and in particular late foetal deaths, also limits international comparability. The criterion of 28 or more completed weeks of gestation to distinguish late foetal deaths is not universally used; some countries or areas use different durations of gestation or other criteria such as size of the foetus. In addition, the difficulty of accurately determining gestational age further reduces comparability. However, to promote comparability, late foetal deaths shown in this table are restricted to those of at least 28 or more completed weeks of gestation. Wherever this is not possible a footnote is provided.

Another factor introducing variation in the definition of late foetal deaths is the practice by some countries or areas of including in late foetal-death statistics infants who were born alive but died before the registration of the birth or within the first 24 hours of life, thus overestimating the total number of late foetal deaths. This has also the effect of inflating the late foetal-death ratios unduly by decreasing the birth denominator and increasing the foetal-death numerator. Statistics of this type are footnoted.

388

In addition, late foetal-death ratios are subject to the limitations of the data on live births with which they have been calculated. These have been set forth in the technical notes for table 9.

Regarding the computation of the ratios, it must be pointed out that when late foetal deaths and live births are both under registered, the resulting ratios may be of reasonable magnitude. For the countries or areas where live-birth registration is poorest, the late foetal-death ratios may be the largest, effectively masking the completeness of the base data. For this reason, possible variations in birth-registration completeness as well as the reported completeness of late foetal deaths must always be borne in mind in evaluating late foetal-death ratios.

In addition to the indirect effect of live-birth under-registration, late foetal-death ratios may be seriously affected by date-of-registration tabulation of live births. When the annual number of live births registered and reported fluctuates over a wide range due to changes in legislation or to special needs for proof of birth on the part of large segments of the population, then the late foetal-death ratios will also fluctuate, but inversely. Because of these effects, data for countries or areas known to tabulate live births by date of registration should be used with caution.

Finally, it may be noted that the counting of live-born infants as late foetal deaths, because they died before the registration of the birth or within the first 24 hours of life, has the effect of inflating the late foetal-death ratios unduly by decreasing the birth denominator and increasing the foetal-death numerator. This factor should not be overlooked in using data from this table.

The comparability of data by urban/rural residence is affected by the national definitions of urban and rural used in tabulating these data. It is assumed, in the absence of specific information to the contrary, that the definitions of urban and rural used in connection with the national population census were also used in the compilation of the vital statistics for each country or area. However, it cannot be excluded that, for a given country or area, different definitions of urban and rural are used for the vital statistics data and the population census data respectively. When known, the definitions of urban used in national population censuses are presented at the end of the technical notes for table 6. As discussed in detail in the technical notes for table 6, these definitions vary considerably from one country or area to another.

Urban/rural differentials in late foetal death ratios may also be affected by whether the late foetal deaths and live births have been tabulated in terms of place of occurrence or place of usual residence. This problem is discussed in more detail in section 4.1.4.1 of the Technical Notes.

Earlier data: Late foetal deaths and late foetal-death ratios have been shown in each issue of the Demographic Yearbook beginning with the 1951 issue. A special topic CD on natality published in 2001 presents the data for all available years from 1990 to 1998. For more information on specific topics, and years for which data are reported, readers should consult the Historical Index.

NOTES

[i] For definition, see section 4.1.1.3 of the Technical Notes.

Tableau 12

Le tableau 12 présente des données sur les morts fœtales tardives et les rapports de mortinatalité selon le lieu de résidence (zone urbaine ou rurale) pour le plus grand nombre d'années possible entre 2002 et 2006.

Description des variables : Par mort fœtale tardive, on entend le décès d'un fœtus[1] survenu après 28 semaines complètes de gestation au moins. Les morts fœtales pour lesquelles la durée de la période de gestation n'est pas connue sont comprises dans cette catégorie.

Sauf indication contraire, les statistiques du nombre de morts fœtales tardives sont établies sur la base des registres de l'état civil.

La classification des morts fœtales tardives selon le lieu de résidence (zone urbaine ou rurale) est celle qui a été communiquée par chaque pays ou zone ; on part du principe qu'elle repose sur les définitions de la population urbaine utilisées pour les recensements nationaux, telles qu'elles sont reproduites à la fin des notes techniques du tableau 6.

Calcul des rapports : les rapports de mortinatalité représentent le nombre annuel de morts fœtales tardives pour 1 000 naissances vivantes (telles qu'elles sont présentées au tableau 9) survenues pendant la même année. On a pris pour base de calcul les naissances vivantes parce que l'on pense qu'elle sont plus facilement comparables d'un pays ou d'une zone à l'autre que la somme des naissances vivantes et des morts fœtales.

Les rapports selon le lieu de résidence (zone urbaine ou rurale) représentent le nombre annuel de morts fœtales tardives, classées selon la catégorie urbaine ou rurale appropriée pour 1 000 naissances vivantes (telles qu'elles sont présentées au tableau 9) survenues parmi la population correspondante. Ces rapports ont été calculés par la Division de statistique de l'ONU.

Les rapports présentés dans le tableau 12 ne concernent que les pays ou zones où l'on a enregistré un total d'au moins 1 000 morts fœtales tardives pendant une année donnée.

Fiabilité des données : il a été demandé à chaque pays ou zone d'indiquer le degré estimatif de complétude des données sur les morts fœtales tardives figurant dans ses registres d'état civil. Ces évaluations nationales sont signalées par les codes de qualité 'C', 'U' et '...' qui apparaissent dans la deuxième colonne du tableau.

La lettre 'C' indique que les données sont jugées à peu près complètes, c'est-à-dire qu'elles représentent au moins 90 p. 100 des morts fœtales tardives survenues chaque année ; la lettre 'U' signifie que les données sont jugées incomplètes, c'est-à-dire qu'elles représentent moins de 90 p.100 des morts fœtales tardives survenues chaque année. Le code '...' indique qu'aucun renseignement n'a été communiqué quant à la complétude des données.

Les données provenant des registres de l'état civil qui sont déclarées incomplètes ou dont le degré de complétude n'est pas connu (code 'U' ou '...') sont jugées douteuses. Elles apparaissent en italique dans le tableau ; les rapports, dans ces cas, n'ont pas été calculés.

Pour plus de précisions sur la qualité des données reposant sur les statistiques de l'état civil en général, voir la section 4.2 des Notes techniques.

Insuffisance des données : les statistiques des morts fœtales tardives appellent toutes les réserves qui ont été formulées à propos des statistiques de l'état civil en général et des statistiques concernant les morts fœtales en particulier (voir la section 4 des Notes techniques).

La fiabilité des données est un facteur très important. Les statistiques concernant les morts fœtales sont probablement les moins complètes de toutes les statistiques de l'état civil.

L'hétérogénéité des définitions de la mort fœtale et, en particulier, de la mort fœtale tardive nuit aussi à la comparabilité internationale des données. Le critère des 28 semaines complètes de gestation au moins n'est pas universellement utilisé ; certains pays ou zones retiennent des critères différents pour la durée de la période de gestation ou d'autres critères tels que la taille du fœtus. De surcroît, la comparabilité est rendue malaisée par le fait qu'il est difficile d'établir avec précision l'âge gestationnel. Pour faciliter les comparaisons, les morts fœtales tardives considérées ici sont exclusivement celles qui sont survenues au terme de 28 semaines de gestation au moins. Les exceptions sont signalées en note.

Un autre facteur d'hétérogénéité dans la définition de la mort fœtale tardive est la pratique de certains pays ou zones qui consiste à inclure dans les statistiques des morts fœtales tardives les enfants nés vivants mais décédés avant l'enregistrement de leur naissance ou dans les 24 heures qui ont suivi la naissance, pratique qui conduit à surestimer le nombre total des morts fœtales tardives. Cela donne aussi des rapports de mortinatalité exagérés parce que le dénominateur (nombre de naissances) se trouve alors diminué et le numérateur (morts fœtales) augmenté. Quand pareil facteur a joué, cela a été signalé en note.

Les rapports de mortinatalité appellent en outre toutes les réserves qui ont été formulées à propos des statistiques des naissances vivantes qui ont servi à leur calcul (voir à ce sujet les notes techniques relatives au tableau 9).

En ce qui concerne le calcul des rapports, il convient de noter que, si l'enregistrement des morts fœtales tardives et celui des naissances vivantes sont loin d'être exhaustifs, les rapports de mortinatalité peuvent être raisonnables. C'est parfois pour les pays ou zones où l'enregistrement des naissances vivantes laisse le plus à désirer que les rapports de mortinatalité sont les plus élevés, ce qui masque le caractère incomplet des données de base. Aussi, pour porter un jugement sur la qualité des rapports de mortinatalité, il ne faut jamais oublier que la complétude de l'enregistrement des naissances comme celle de l'enregistrement des morts fœtales tardives peuvent varier sensiblement.

Hormis les effets indirects des lacunes de l'enregistrement des naissances vivantes, il arrive que les rapports de mortinatalité soient considérablement faussés lorsque l'exploitation des données relatives aux naissances se fait d'après la date de l'enregistrement. Si le nombre des naissances vivantes enregistrées vient à varier notablement d'une année à l'autre par suite de modifications de la législation ou parce que de très nombreuses personnes ont besoin de se procurer une attestation de naissance, les rapports de mortinatalité varient également, mais en sens inverse. Il convient donc d'utiliser avec prudence le données des pays ou zones où les statistiques sont établies d'après la date de l'enregistrement.

Enfin, on notera que l'inclusion parmi les morts fœtales tardives des décès d'enfants nés vivants qui sont décédés avant l'enregistrement de leur naissance ou dans les 24 heures qui ont suivi la naissance conduit à des rapports de mortinatalité exagérés parce que le dénominateur (nombre de naissances) se trouve alors diminué et le numérateur (morts fœtales) augmenté. Il importe de ne pas négliger ce facteur lorsque l'on utilise les données du tableau 12.

La comparabilité des données selon le lieu de résidence (zone urbaine ou rurale) peut être limitée par les définitions nationales des termes « urbain » et « rural » utilisées pour la mise en tableaux de ces données. En l'absence d'indications contraires, on a supposé que les mêmes définitions avaient servi pour le recensement national de la population et pour l'établissement des statistiques de l'état civil pour chaque pays ou zone. Toutefois, il n'est pas exclu que, pour une zone ou un pays donné, des définitions différentes aient été retenues. Les définitions du terme « urbain » utilisées pour les recensements nationaux de population ont été présentées à la fin des notes techniques du tableau 6 lorsqu'elles étaient connues. Comme on l'a précisé dans les notes techniques relatives au tableau 6, ces définitions varient considérablement d'un pays ou d'une zone à l'autre.

La différence entre les rapports de mortinatalité pour les zones urbaines et rurales pourra aussi être faussée selon que les morts fœtales tardives et les naissances vivantes auront été classées d'après le lieu de l'événement ou le lieu de résidence habituel. Ce problème est examiné plus en détail à la section 4.1.4.1 des Notes techniques.

Données publiées antérieurement : les éditions de l'*Annuaire démographique* parues à partir de 1951 contiennent des statistiques concernant les morts fœtales tardives et les rapports de mortinatalité. Un CD-ROM sur la natalité paru en 2001 présente les données pour toutes les années disponibles de 1990 à 1998. Pour plus de précisions concernant les années et les sujets pour lesquels des données ont été publiées, se reporter à l'index.

---

[1] Pour la définition, voir la section 4.1.1.3 des Notes techniques.

12. Late foetal deaths and late foetal death ratios, by urban/rural residence: 2002 - 2006
Morts foetales tardives et rapports de mortinatalité, selon la résidence, urbaine/rurale: 2002 - 2006

Continent, country or area, and urban/rural residence / Continent, pays ou zone et résidence, urbaine/rurale	Code	Number - Nombre					Ratio - Rapport				
		2002	2003	2004	2005	2006	2002	2003	2004	2005	2006
AFRICA - AFRIQUE											
Algeria - Algérie											
Total	+C	17 135	...	...	...	...	27.8	...	...	...	...
Egypt - Égypte											
Total	+U	4 745	4 605	4 201	4 218	4 557	...	...	...	...	...
Urban - Urbaine	+U	3 842	3 567	3 436	3 549	3 869	...	...	...	...	...
Rural - Rurale	+U	903	1 038	765	669	688	...	...	...	...	...
Mauritius - Maurice											
Total	+C	203	220	191	185	147	10.2	11.4	9.9	9.8	8.4
Urban - Urbaine	+C	86	79	70	65	49	10.8	10.4	9.6	9.1	7.3
Rural - Rurale	+C	117	141	121	120	98	9.7	12.0	10.1	10.3	9.0
Réunion											
Total	C	...	...	159	170	...	...	...	10.9	11.5	...
Seychelles											
Total	+C	...	...	6	13	7	...	...	...	...	...
AMERICA, NORTH - AMÉRIQUE DU NORD											
Bermuda - Bermudes											
Total	C	...	...	...	...	...	...	...	...	...	...
Canada[1]											
Total	C	1 028	1 027	972	1 012	...	3.1	3.1	2.9	3.0	...
Costa Rica											
Total	C	465	471	524	503	550	6.5	6.5	7.3	7.0	7.7
Cuba[2]											
Total	C	1 983	1 868	1 675	1 642	1 680	14.0	13.7	13.2	13.6	15.1
El Salvador											
Total	C	617	535	572	460	378	4.8	4.3	4.8	4.1	3.5
Urban - Urbaine	C	550	461	510	410	348	7.1	6.3	7.1	5.9	4.9
Rural - Rurale	C	67	74	62	50	30	1.3	1.4	1.3	1.1	0.8
Guadeloupe											
Total	C	118	151	140	157	...	16.9	21.4	19.2	20.8	...
Guatemala											
Total	C	2 903	2 865	3 016	3 136	2 980	7.5	7.6	7.9	8.4	8.1
Martinique											
Total	C	89	118	98	88	...	16.3	21.7	18.6	17.5	...
Mexico - Mexique[3]											
Total	+U	14 965	14 508	14 090	13 633	12 812	...	...	...	...	...
Urban - Urbaine	+U	10 951	10 734	10 390	10 101	9 584	...	...	...	...	...
Rural - Rurale	+U	3 696	3 556	3 422	3 385	3 098	...	...	...	...	...
Puerto Rico - Porto Rico											
Total	C	234	206	198	189	...	4.4	4.1	3.9	3.7	...
Urban - Urbaine[4]	C	138	113	124	109	...	...	4.2	4.6	3.9	...
Rural - Rurale[4]	C	90	87	64	74	...	...	3.6	2.6	3.2	...
Saint Lucia - Sainte-Lucie											
Total	C	51	36	39	*31	...	19.6	14.5	16.8	*13.5	...
Saint Vincent and the Grenadines - Saint Vincent-et-les Grenadines											
Total	+C	16	...	...	...	...	...	...	...	...	...
Turks Caicos Islands - Îles Turques et Caïques[5]											
Total	C	2	5[6]	1	...	...	...	...	...	...	...
United States - États-Unis											
Total	C	12 871	12 485	12 761	...	...	3.2	3.1	3.1	...	...
AMERICA, SOUTH - AMÉRIQUE DU SUD											
Argentina - Argentine											
Total	C	4 850	4 663	3 812	5 048	4 983	7.0	6.7	5.2	7.1	7.2
Brazil - Brésil[7]											
Total	U	...	30 201	28 852	26 257	25 564	...	...	...	...	...

12. Late foetal deaths and late foetal death ratios, by urban/rural residence: 2002 - 2006
Morts foetales tardives et rapports de mortinatalité, selon la résidence, urbaine/rurale: 2002 - 2006 (continued - suite)

Continent, country or area, and urban/rural residence / Continent, pays ou zone et résidence, urbaine/rurale	Co-de	Number - Nombre					Ratio - Rapport				
		2002	2003	2004	2005	2006	2002	2003	2004	2005	2006
AMERICA, SOUTH - AMÉRIQUE DU SUD											
Chile - Chili[8]											
Total	C	1 197	1 404	1 510	1 841	...	5.0	6.0	6.6	8.0	...
Urban - Urbaine	C	1 044	1 220	1 365	1 740	...	4.9	5.8	6.7	8.5	...
Rural - Rurale	C	153	184	145	101	...	5.9	7.4	5.6	4.0	...
Colombia - Colombie[9]											
Total	...	6 121	8 542	8 897	11 428	12 504	...	...	...	...	...
Urban - Urbaine[4]	...	3 951	6 119	6 400	8 405	9 469	...	...	...	...	...
Rural - Rurale[4]	...	1 705	1 886	1 798	2 312	2 370	...	...	...	...	...
Ecuador - Équateur[10]											
Total	...	2 685	2 298	2 098	...	...	...	...	...	...	...
Urban - Urbaine	...	2 372	1 992	1 879	...	...	...	...	...	...	...
Rural - Rurale	...	313	306	219	...	...	...	...	...	...	...
French Guiana - Guyane française											
Total	C	72	69	60	63	...	13.7	12.4	11.3	10.5	...
Suriname											
Total	...	194	248	243	155	138	...	...	...	...	...
Uruguay											
Total	C	...	...	*458	...	...	...	...	*9.2	...	...
Venezuela (Bolivarian Republic of) - Venezuela (République bolivarienne du)[7]											
Total	...	3 852	...	...	...	...	...	...	...	...	...
ASIA - ASIE											
Armenia - Arménie											
Total	C	236	289	290	358	662[11]	7.3	8.1	7.7	9.5	17.6
Urban - Urbaine	C	196	227	224	284	456[11]	9.4	10.0	9.5	12.0	19.2
Rural - Rurale	C	40	62	66	74	206[11]	3.5	4.7	4.8	5.4	14.9
Azerbaijan - Azerbaïdjan											
Total	+C	443	431	479	...	...	4.0	3.8	3.6		
Bahrain - Bahreïn											
Total	...	19	15	34	38	39	...	...	...	...	...
China: Hong Kong SAR - Chine: Hong Kong RAS											
Total	...	308	189	164	218	...	...	...	...	...	...
China: Macao SAR - Chine: Macao RAS											
Total	C	8	8	4	5	9					
Georgia - Géorgie											
Total	C	726	811	870	739	712	15.6	17.6	17.6	15.9	14.9
Urban - Urbaine	C	...	791	...	...	...	...	22.9	...	...	...
Rural - Rurale	C	...	20	...	...	...	...	...	...	...	...
Israel - Israël[12]											
Total	C	549[13]	560	420[14]	494	566	3.9	3.9	2.9	3.4	3.8
Urban - Urbaine[4]	C	498[13]	503	378[14]	437	500	3.9	3.8	2.9	3.4	3.7
Rural - Rurale[4]	C	46[13]	53	34[14]	54	62	3.6	4.0	2.5	4.0	4.4
Japan - Japon[15]											
Total	C	2 850	2 692	2 487	2 401	2 367	2.5	2.4	2.2	2.3	2.2
Urban - Urbaine[4]	C	2 288	2 161	2 057	2 083	2 137	2.4	2.4	2.2	2.3	2.2
Rural - Rurale[4]	C	561	529	430	318	227	2.6	2.6	2.2	2.2	2.1
Kazakhstan											
Total	C	1 740	1 708	1 729	1 882	1 987	7.7	7.1	6.3	6.7	6.6
Urban - Urbaine	C	1 050	1 169	1 196	1 324	1 416	8.6	8.4	7.7	8.1	8.1
Rural - Rurale	C	698	599	533	558	571	6.6	5.5	4.6	4.9	4.5
Kuwait - Koweït											
Total	C	325	307	355	375	347	7.5	7.0	7.5	7.4	6.6
Kyrgyzstan - Kirghizistan											
Total	C	759	879	1 437[16]	1 586	1 621	7.5	8.3	13.1	14.4	13.4
Urban - Urbaine	C	395	470	962[16]	1 022	1 066	13.1	14.7	25.7	28.7	27.0
Rural - Rurale	C	364	409	475[16]	564	555	5.1	5.6	6.5	7.6	6.8

12. Late foetal deaths and late foetal death ratios, by urban/rural residence: 2002 - 2006
Morts foetales tardives et rapports de mortinatalité, selon la résidence, urbaine/rurale: 2002 - 2006 (continued - suite)

Continent, country or area, and urban/rural residence / Continent, pays ou zone et résidence, urbaine/rurale	Code	Number - Nombre					Ratio - Rapport				
		2002	2003	2004	2005	2006	2002	2003	2004	2005	2006
ASIA - ASIE											
Malaysia - Malaisie											
Total	C	1 989	2 030	2 003	*2 075	*2 100	4.1	4.2	4.2	*4.5	*4.4
Maldives[8]											
Total	...	61	71	47	41	59	...	...	...	...	...
Urban - Urbaine	...	27	28	20	12	27	...	...	...	...	...
Rural - Rurale	...	34	43	27	29	32	...	...	...	...	...
Myanmar											
Urban - Urbaine	U	1 911	1 819	1 794	1 778	...	...	...	...	...	...
Oman[17]											
Total	U	376	381	344	387	367	...	...	...	...	...
Philippines											
Total	...	4 645	4 386	...	...	...	...	...	...	...	...
Qatar											
Total	C	62	81	64	97	79	5.1	6.3	4.9	7.2	5.6
Singapore - Singapour											
Total	+C	114	95	115	102	99	2.8	2.5	3.1	2.7	2.6
Tajikistan - Tadjikistan											
Total	C	1 096	1 043	...	...	...	6.2	5.9	...	...	...
Urban - Urbaine	C	940	899	...	...	...	22.0	19.9	...	...	...
Rural - Rurale	C	156	144	...	...	...	1.2	1.1	...	...	...
EUROPE											
Åland Islands - Îles d'Åland[18]											
Total	C	1	1	-	1		...	...	...	...	...
Andorra - Andorre											
Total	C	-	3	5	-	1	...	...	...	...	...
Austria - Autriche											
Total	C	338	307	313	289	313	4.3	4.0	4.0	3.7	4.0
Belarus - Bélarus											
Total	C	...	...	...	326	352	...	...	...	3.6	3.6
Urban - Urbaine	C	...	...	...	237	250	...	...	...	3.6	3.5
Rural - Rurale	C	...	...	...	89	102	...	...	...	3.7	4.0
Belgium - Belgique											
Total	C	...	493	437	442	...	...	4.4	3.8	3.8	...
Bosnia and Herzegovina - Bosnie-Herzégovine											
Total	C	138	150	168	147	160	3.9	4.3	4.8	4.2	4.7
Bulgaria - Bulgarie											
Total	C	539	549	547	565	517	8.1	8.2	7.8	7.9	7.0
Urban - Urbaine	C	323	348	339	363	349	6.8	7.2	6.7	6.9	6.3
Rural - Rurale	C	216	201	208	202	168	11.5	10.7	10.7	10.7	8.9
Croatia - Croatie[19]											
Total	C	189	180	179	186	182	4.7	4.5	4.4	4.4	4.4
Urban - Urbaine	C	108	94	107	105	99	4.8	4.3	4.8	4.5	4.3
Rural - Rurale	C	81	86	72	81	83	4.6	4.8	4.0	4.2	4.5
Czech Republic - République tchèque											
Total	C	261	272	265	287	299	2.7	2.9	2.7	2.8	2.8
Urban - Urbaine	C	207	209	162	195	213	2.8	3.0	2.2	2.6	2.7
Rural - Rurale	C	54	63	103	92	86	2.2	2.6	4.0	3.5	3.2
Denmark - Danemark[20]											
Total	C	224	239	316	246	...	3.5	3.7	4.9	3.8	...
Estonia - Estonie											
Total	C	74	63	63	88	56	5.7	4.8	4.5	6.1	3.8
Urban - Urbaine	C	47	45	49	60	38	5.3	5.0	5.0	5.9	3.6
Rural - Rurale	C	27	18	14	28	18	...	...	...	...	...
Finland - Finlande[21]											
Total	C	134	133	117	113	139	2.4	2.3	2.0	2.0	2.4
Urban - Urbaine	C	82	84	73	77	88	2.3	2.3	1.9	2.0	2.3
Rural - Rurale	C	52	49	44	36	51	2.7	2.5	2.2	1.8	2.6
France[22]											
Total	C	6 259[24]	6 862	7 054	6 964	7 531	8.2	9.0	9.2	9.0	9.5
Urban - Urbaine[23]	C	4 840[24]	5 309	5 469	5 370	5 824	8.4	9.2	9.5	9.2	9.8
Rural - Rurale[23]	C	1 373[24]	1 477	1 510	1 518	1 643	7.5	8.0	8.0	7.9	8.3

394

12. Late foetal deaths and late foetal death ratios, by urban/rural residence: 2002 - 2006
Morts foetales tardives et rapports de mortinatalité, selon la résidence, urbaine/rurale: 2002 - 2006 (continued - suite)

Continent, country or area, and urban/rural residence / Continent, pays ou zone et résidence, urbaine/rurale	Code	Number - Nombre					Ratio - Rapport				
		2002	2003	2004	2005	2006	2002	2003	2004	2005	2006
EUROPE											
Germany - Allemagne											
Total	C	2 700	2 699	2 728	2 487	2 420	3.8	3.8	3.9	3.6	3.6
Greece - Grèce											
Total	C	441	416	408	346	316	4.2	4.0	3.9	3.2	2.8
Urban - Urbaine	C	...	...	...	244	226	...	...	...	3.3	2.9
Rural - Rurale	C	...	...	...	102	90	...	...	...	3.0	2.6
Hungary - Hongrie[25]											
Total	C	523	530	476	506	489	5.4	5.6	5.0	5.2	4.9
Urban - Urbaine[26]	C	306	291	267	305	271	5.0	4.9	4.4	4.8	4.1
Rural - Rurale[26]	C	208	237	208	201	211	5.9	6.9	6.1	6.1	6.4
Iceland - Islande											
Total	C	7	4	15	8	13	...	...	...	...	...
Urban - Urbaine	C	7	4	...	7	12	...	...	...	...	...
Rural - Rurale	C	-	-	...	1	1	...	...	...	...	...
Ireland - Irlande											
Total	C	274	258	236	...	...	4.5	4.2	3.8	...	...
Italy - Italie[8]											
Total	C	1 721	1 702	1 658	...	...	3.2	3.1	2.9	...	...
Latvia - Lettonie											
Total	C	176	130	136	132	154	8.8	6.2	6.7	6.1	6.9
Urban - Urbaine	C	108	76	90	79	103	8.3	5.5	6.5	5.4	6.7
Rural - Rurale	C	68	54	46	53	51	9.6	7.6	7.1	7.7	7.4
Lithuania - Lituanie[19]											
Total	C	193	168	150	152	137	6.4	5.5	4.9	5.0	4.4
Urban - Urbaine	C	125	106	81	86	79	6.7	5.5	4.2	4.3	3.8
Rural - Rurale	C	68	62	69	66	58	6.0	5.4	6.3	6.2	5.5
Luxembourg											
Total	C	20	17	16	21	14	...	...	...	...	...
Malta - Malte											
Total	C	...	18	15	8	10	...	...	...	...	...
Montenegro											
Total	C	...	42	38	27	...	...	5.0	4.8	...	...
Urban - Urbaine	C	...	25	28	24	...	...	...	...	...	...
Rural - Rurale	C	...	17	10	3	...	...	...	...	...	...
Netherlands - Pays-Bas[27]											
Total	C	945	928	795	760	642	4.7	4.6	4.1	4.0	3.5
Urban - Urbaine	C	617	631	527	517	456	4.6	4.8	4.0	4.0	3.6
Rural - Rurale	C	328	297	268	243	186	4.7	4.4	4.2	4.1	3.2
Norway - Norvège[28]											
Total	C	197	213	210	182	201	3.6	3.8	3.7	3.2	3.4
Poland - Pologne											
Total	C	1 372	1 322	1 342	1 283	1 338	3.9	3.8	3.8	3.5	3.6
Urban - Urbaine	C	703	687	715	687	710	3.6	3.4	3.5	3.3	3.3
Rural - Rurale	C	669	635	627	596	628	4.3	4.2	4.1	3.9	4.0
Portugal[29]											
Total	C	388	349	294	306	324	3.4	3.1	2.7	2.8	3.1
Romania - Roumanie											
Total	C	1 319	1 290	1 314	1 262	1 143	6.3	6.1	6.1	5.7	5.2
Urban - Urbaine	C	602	569	633	589	538	6.1	5.6	5.7	5.0	4.5
Rural - Rurale	C	717	721	681	673	605	6.4	6.5	6.5	6.5	6.0
Russian Federation - Fédération de Russie											
Total	C	8 998	9 043	8 745	8 328	7 934	6.4	6.1	5.8	5.7	5.4
Urban - Urbaine	C	6 687	6 624	6 416	6 035	5 678	6.7	6.3	6.0	5.8	5.4
Rural - Rurale	C	2 311	2 419	2 329	2 293	2 256	5.8	5.7	5.4	5.5	5.2
San Marino - Saint-Marin											
Total	+C	-	2	-	-	...	...	...	...	...	...
Serbia - Serbie[30]											
Total	+C	432	411	419	361	365	5.5	5.2	5.4	5.0	5.1
Slovakia - Slovaquie											
Total	C	194	217	211	195	218	3.8	4.2	3.9	3.6	4.0
Urban - Urbaine	C	95	114	92	93	98	3.6	4.3	3.2	3.2	3.4
Rural - Rurale	C	99	103	119	102	120	4.0	4.1	4.7	4.0	4.7
Slovenia - Slovénie											
Total	C	69	58	62	76	57	3.9	3.3	3.5	4.2	3.0
Urban - Urbaine	C	43	45	32	...	...	5.1	5.3	3.7	...	...
Rural - Rurale	C	50	49	30	...	...	5.5	5.5	3.3	...	...

12. Late foetal deaths and late foetal death ratios, by urban/rural residence: 2002 - 2006
Morts foetales tardives et rapports de mortinatalité, selon la résidence, urbaine/rurale: 2002 - 2006 (continued - suite)

Continent, country or area, and urban/rural residence — Continent, pays ou zone et résidence, urbaine/rurale	Co-dé	Number - Nombre					Ratio - Rapport				
		2002	2003	2004	2005	2006	2002	2003	2004	2005	2006
EUROPE											
Spain - Espagne											
Total....................	C	1 470	1 494	1 438	1 169	1 528	3.5	3.4	3.2	2.5	3.2
Sweden - Suède											
Total....................	C	339	347	318	301	319	3.5	3.5	3.2	3.0	3.0
Switzerland - Suisse											
Total....................	C	255	306	276	307	342	3.5	4.3	3.8	4.2	4.7
Urban - Urbaine	C	186	232	206	210	249	3.5	4.4	3.8	3.9	4.6
Rural - Rurale	C	69	74	70	97	93	3.5	3.9	3.6	5.1	4.9
The Former Yugoslav Rep. of Macedonia - L'ex-République yougoslave de Macédoine											
Total....................	C	291	232	258	215	201	10.5	8.6	11.0	9.6	8.9
Urban - Urbaine	C	187	...	...	102	112	12.5	...	...	8.1	8.9
Rural - Rurale	C	104	...	...	113	89	8.1	...	...	11.3	9.0
Ukraine											
Total....................	C	1 837	1 969	1 986	2 242	2 314	4.7	4.8	4.6	5.3	5.0
Urban - Urbaine	C	1 270	1 361	1 398	1 489	1 532	5.1	5.1	4.9	5.2	5.0
Rural - Rurale	C	567	608	588	753	782	4.0	4.3	4.1	5.3	5.1
United Kingdom - Royaume-Uni[31]											
Total....................	C	3 772	3 989	3 962	...	...	5.6	5.7	5.5	...	...
OCEANIA - OCÉANIE											
Australia - Australie[9]											
Total....................	+C	728	759	732	757	...	2.9	3.0	2.9	2.9	...
Urban - Urbaine	+C	472	504	439	513	...	2.9	3.0	2.6	2.9	...
Rural - Rurale	+C	256	255	293	244	...	3.0	3.0	3.5	2.9	...
French Polynesia - Polynésie française											
Total....................	C	17	35	...	...	...	...	7.8	...	...	...
New Caledonia - Nouvelle-Calédonie											
Total....................	+C	30	25	...	...	...	7.2	...	...	...	...
New Zealand - Nouvelle-Zélande[32]											
Total....................	+C	167	169	228	174	162	3.1	3.0	3.9	3.0	2.7
Urban - Urbaine	+C	150	150	210	156	139	3.2	3.1	4.1	3.1	2.7
Rural - Rurale	+C	17	19	18	18	23	...	...	...	...	...
Palau - Palaos											
Total....................	C	2	2	18	5	6	...	...	...	...	...
Papua New Guinea - Papouasie-Nouvelle-Guinée											
Total....................	U	*1 080*	*991*	...	...	...	...	...	...	...	...

FOOTNOTES - NOTES

Italics: data from civil registers which are incomplete or of unknown completeness. - Italiques: données incomplètes ou dont le degré d'exactitude n'est pas connu, provenant des registres de l'état civil.

* Provisional. - Données provisoires.

[1] Including Canadian residents temporarily in the United States, but excluding United States residents temporarily in Canada. - Y compris les résidents canadiens se trouvant temporairement aux Etats-Unis, mais ne comprenant pas les résidents des Etats-Unis se trouvant temporairement au Canada.

[2] Late foetal death is indicated by the fact that the foetus is at least 500 grams or more in weight. - Les décès foetaux tardifs sont caractérisés par le fait que le foetus pèse au moins 500 grammes

[3] Excluding late foetal deaths to mothers residing aboad which occurred in the country. The total number includes 'Unknown residence', but the categories urban and rural do not. - À l'exclusion des fausses couches tardives de mères

résidant à l'étranger qui sont survenues dans le pays. Le nombre total inclue 'Résidence inconnue ', mais les catégories Urbain et Rural ne l'incluent pas.

[4] The total number includes 'Unknown residence', but the categories urban and rural do not. - Le nombre total inclue 'Résidence inconnue ', mais les catégories Urbain et Rural ne l'incluent pas.

[5] Includes some underreporting of foetal deaths especially among those under 28 weeks gestational age. - Des décès intra-utérins n'ont sans doute pas été déclarés, surtout parmi ceux qui sont survenus à moins de 28 semaines de gestation.

[6] For 2003, two of the 5 still births are to non Turks and Caicos nationals. - Pour 2003, deux des cinq mortinaissances concernent des personnes qui n'étaient pas ressortissantes des Îles Turques et Caïques.

[7] Excluding Indian jungle population. - Non compris les Indiens de la jungle.

[8] Data refer to total foetal deaths. - Y compris toutes les morts foetales.

[9] Data include unknown gestational weeks. - Les données comprennnent les cas où le nombre de semaines de gestation n'est pas connu.

[10] Excluding nomadic Indian tribes. - Non compris les tribus d'Indiens nomades.

[11] Since 16 October 2005 the definition of WHO on stillbirths has been put into force in accordance with 10th revision of the International Classification of Diseases. - Depuis le 16 octobre 2005, la définition de l'OMS de la mort fœtale est en vigueur conformément à la dixième révision de la Classification internationale des maladies.

[12] Including data for East Jerusalem and Israeli residents in certain other territories under occupation by Israeli military forces since June 1967. - Y compris les données pour Jérusalem-Est et les résidents israéliens dans certains autres territoires occupés depuis 1967 par les forces armées israéliennes.

[13] Data include 9 foetal deaths of unknown gestational age and weight over 1000 grams. - Y compris neuf décès intra-utérins pour lesquels l'âge gestationnel est inconnu et le poids est supérieur à 1 000 grammes.

[14] Data include 8 foetal deaths of unknown gestational age and weight over 1000 grams. - Y compris huit décès intra-utérins pour lesquels l'âge gestationnel est inconnu et le poids est supérieur à 1 000 grammes.

[15] Data refer to Japanese nationals in Japan only. Data exclude the unknown duration of pregnancy. - Les données se raportent aux nationaux japonais au Japon seulement. Exception faite des grossesses dont la durée n'est pas connue.

[16] Since 2004, WHO criteria have been adopted in the country. - Depuis 2004, le pays a adopté les critères de l'OMS.

[17] Data refer to the recorded events in Ministry of Health hospitals and health centres only. - Les données se rapportent aux faits d'état civil enregistrés dans les hôpitaux et les dispensaires du Ministère de la santé seulement.

[18] Also included in Finland. - Comprise aussi dans Finlande.

[19] Late foetal death is defined as an infant born without any signs of life, weighing at least 500 grams, after during of pregnancy of at least 22 weeks. - On dit qu'il y a mort intra-utérine tardive lorsqu'un enfant pesant au minimum 500 grammes naît sans donner aucun signe de vie au terme d'une grossesse qui a duré au moins 22 semaines.

[20] Excluding Faeroe Islands and Greenland shown separately, if available. - Non compris les Iles Féroé et le Gröenland, qui font l'objet de rubriques distinctes, si disponible.

[21] Including nationals temporarily outside the country. Including Aland Islands. - Y compris les nationaux se trouvant temporairement hors du pays. Y compris les Îles d'Åland.

[22] Foetal deaths after at least 180 days (6 calendar months or 26 weeks) of gestation. Excluding Overseas Departments, namely, French Guiana, Guadeloupe, Martinique and Reunion, shown separately, if available. - Morts foetales survenues après 180 jours (6 mois civils ou 26 semaines) au moins de gestation. Non compris les départements d'outre mer, c'est-à-dire la Guyane française, la Guadeloupe, la Martinique et la Réunion, qui font l'objet de rubriques distinctes, si disponible.

[23] Urban/rural figures, excluding nationals outside the country. - Les chiffres urbaine/rurale, non compris les nationaux hors du pays.

[24] The strong increase in still births number is due to a legislative change: according to a circular of November 2001, a still birth bulletin is now drawn up after 22 weeks of amenorrhea or for a 500 g weight. These new criteria take the place of the 180 days of gestation, existing in the registry declaration. - La forte évolution du nombre d'enfants sans vie est liée à un changement législatif: selon une circulaire de novembre 2001, un acte d'enfant sans vie correspond désormais au terme de vingt-deux semaines d'aménorrhée ou à un poids de 500 grammes. Ces critères se substituent au délai de 180 jours de gestation prévu dans l'état civil.

[25] Late foetal death is indicated by the fact that the foetus is at least 24 (it has been 28 weeks until 1996) completed weeks of gestational and does not show any sign of life after the separation from its mother; the foetus has to be 30 cm or more in length or 500 grams or more in weight if its gestational age cannot be determined. - Pour qu'il y ait mort foetale tardive, il faut que le décès d'un foetus survienne après 24 semaines complètes de gestation au moins (28 semaines jusqu'en 1996), que le foetus n'ait pas donné signe de vie après avoir été séparé de la mère, qu'il mesure 30 centimètres au moins ou pèse 500 grammes si la durée de la période de gestation n'est pas connue.

[26] Total includes the data of foreigners, persons of unknown residence and homeless, but the categories urban and rural do not. - Total incluant les étrangers, les personnes de résidence inconnue et les sans-abri, ce qui n'est pas le cas pour les catégories urbaines et rurales.

[27] Including residents outside the country if listed in a Netherlands population register. - Y compris les résidents hors du pays, s'ils sont inscrits sur un registre de population néerlandais.

[28] Excluding Svalbard and Jan Mayen Island shown separately, if available. - Non compris Svalbard et Jan Mayen qui font l'objet de rubriques distinctes, si disponible.

[29] Data refer to resident mothers. - Données concernant les mères résidentes.

[30] Without data for Kosovo and Metohia. - Sans les données pour le Kosovo and Metohie.

[31] Excluding Channel Islands and Isle of Man, shown separately, if available. - Non compris les îles Anglo-Normandes et l'île de Man, qui font l'objet de rubriques distinctes, si disponible.

[32] For resident population only. - Pour la population résidante seulement.

Table 13

Table 13 presents legally induced abortions for as many years as possible between 1997 and 2006.

Description of variables: There are two major categories of abortion: spontaneous and induced. Induced abortions are those initiated by deliberate action undertaken with the intention of terminating pregnancy; all other abortions are considered spontaneous.

The induction of abortion is subject to governmental regulation in most, if not all, countries or areas. This regulation varies from complete prohibition in some countries or areas to abortion on request, with services provided by governmental health authorities, in others. More generally, governments have attempted to define the conditions under which a pregnancy may lawfully be terminated and have established procedures for authorizing abortion in individual cases.

In an effort to provide more complete interpretation of these statistics, countries or areas providing data on legally induced abortions have been requested to communicate grounds for legally induced abortions in their country or area. This information is presented in table 13-1 below.

Reliability of data: Unlike data on live births and foetal deaths, which are generally collected through systems of vital registration, data on abortion are collected from a variety of sources. Because of this, the quality specification, showing the completeness of civil registers, which is presented for other tables, does not appear here.

Limitations: With regard to the collection of information on abortions, a variety of sources are used, but hospital records are the most common source of information. This implies that most cases that have no contact with hospitals are missed. Data from other sources are probably also incomplete. The data in the present table are limited to legally induced abortions, which, by their nature, might be assumed to be more complete than data on all induced abortions.

Earlier data: Legally induced abortions have been shown previously in all issues of the *Demographic Yearbook* since the 1971 issue.

13-1 Grounds for legally induced abortions

Country	Grounds for abortion					
	(a) Continuation of pregnancy would involve risk to the life of the pregnant woman greater than if the pregnancy were terminated.	(b) Continuation of pregnancy would involve risk of injury to the physical health of the pregnant woman greater than if the pregnancy were terminated.	(c) Continuation of pregnancy would involve risk of injury to the mental health of the pregnant woman greater than if the pregnancy were terminated.	(d) Continuation of pregnancy would involve risk of injury to the mental or physical health of any existing children of the family greater than if the pregnancy were terminated.	(e) There is a substantial risk that if the child were born it would suffer from such physical or mental abnormalities as to be seriously handicapped.	(f) Other
Canada	x	x	x			
Mexico		x				
China Hong Kong SAR	x	x	x	x	x	
Israel	x	x	x		x	x
Japan	x	x				x
Singapore	x	x	x	x	x	x
Czech Rep.	x	x	x		x	
Denmark	x	x	x	x	x	
Estonia	x	x	x	x	x	
Finland	x	x	x		x	x

Country	Grounds for abortion					
	(a) Continuation of pregnancy would involve risk to the life of the pregnant woman greater than if the pregnancy were terminated.	(b) Continuation of pregnancy would involve risk of injury to the physical health of the pregnant woman greater than if the pregnancy were terminated.	(c) Continuation of pregnancy would involve risk of injury to the mental health of the pregnant woman greater than if the pregnancy were terminated.	(d) Continuation of pregnancy would involve risk of injury to the mental or physical health of any existing children of the family greater than if the pregnancy were terminated.	(e) There is a substantial risk that if the child were born it would suffer from such physical or mental abnormalities as to be seriously handicapped.	(f) Other
Germany	x	x	x			x
Greece	x	x	x	x	x	
Hungary	x	x	x	x	x	
Iceland	x	x	x	x	x	x
Italy	x	x	x		x	x
Latvia	x	x	x		x	
Lithuania						x
Netherlands	x	x	x		x	
Norway	x	x	x	x	x	x
Poland	x	x			x	x
Republic of Moldova	x	x	x	x	x	
United Kingdom	x	x	x	x	x	
New Zealand	x	x	x		x	x

Tableau 13

Ce tableau présente des données relatives aux avortements provoqués légalement, pour le plus grand nombre d'années possible entre 1997 et 2006.

Description des variables : l'avortement peut être spontané ou provoqué. L'avortement provoqué est celui qui résulte de manœuvres délibérées, entreprises afin d'interrompre la grossesse ; tous les autres avortements sont considérés comme spontanés.

L'interruption délibérée de la grossesse fait l'objet d'une réglementation officielle dans la plupart des pays ou zones, sinon dans tous. Cette réglementation va de l'interdiction totale à l'autorisation de l'avortement sur demande, pratiqué par des services de santé publique. Le plus souvent, les gouvernements se sont efforcés de définir les circonstances dans lesquelles la grossesse peut être interrompue licitement et de fixer une procédure d'autorisation.

Dans un effort de fournir une interprétation plus complète de ces statistiques, les pays ou les zones fournissant des données sur des avortements légalement induits ont été demandés pour communiquer des raisons pour des avortements légalement induits dans leur pays ou zone. Cette information est présentée dans le tableau 13-1 ci-dessous.

Fiabilité des données : à la différence des données sur les naissances vivantes et les morts fœtales, qui proviennent généralement des registres d'état civil, les données sur l'avortement sont tirées de sources diverses. Aussi ne trouve-t-on pas ici une évaluation de la qualité des données semblable à celle qui indique, pour les autres tableaux, le degré d'exhaustivité des données de l'état civil.

Insuffisance des données : en ce qui concerne les renseignements sur l'avortement, un grand nombre de sources sont utilisées, les relevés hospitaliers restant cependant la source la plus commune. Il s'ensuit que la plupart des cas qui ne passent pas par les hôpitaux sont ignorés. Il faut aussi tenir compte du fait que les données provenant d'autres sources sont probablement incomplètes. Les données du tableau 13 se limitent aux avortements provoqués pour raisons légales dont on peut supposer, en raison de leur nature même, que les statistiques sont plus complètes que les données concernant l'ensemble des avortements provoqués.

Données publiées antérieurement : des statistiques concernant les avortements provoqués pour raisons légales sont publiées dans *l'Annuaire démographique* depuis 1971.

13-1 Motifs d'autorisation pour avortements provoqués légalement

Pays ou zone	Motifs d'autorisation					
	(a) La non-interruption de la grossesse comporterait, pour la vie de la femme enceinte, un risque plus grave que celui de l'avortement.	(b) La non-interruption de la grossesse comporterait, pour la santé physique de la femme enceinte, un risque plus grave que celui de l'avortement.	(c) La non-interruption de la grossesse comporterait, pour la santé mentale de la femme, un risque plus grave que celui de l'avortement.	(d) La non-interruption de la grossesse comporterait, pour la santé mentale ou physique d'un enfant déjà né dans la famille, un risque plus grave que celui de l'avortement.	(e) L'enfant né à terme courrait un risque important de souffrir d'anomalies physiques ou mentales entraînant pour lui un grave handicap.	(f) Autres motifs.
Canada	x	x	x			
Mexique		x				
Chine: Hong Kong RAS	x	x	x	x	x	
Israël	x	x	x		x	x
Japon	x	x				x
Singapour	x	x	x	x	x	x
République tchèque	x	x	x		x	

400

Pays ou zone	Motifs d'autorisation					
	(a) La non-interruption de la grossesse comporterait, pour la vie de la femme enceinte, un risque plus grave que celui de l'avortement.	(b) La non-interruption de la grossesse comporterait, pour la santé physique de la femme enceinte, un risque plus grave que celui de l'avortement.	(c) La non-interruption de la grossesse comporterait, pour la santé mentale de la femme, un risque plus grave que celui de l'avortement.	(d) La non-interruption de la grossesse comporterait, pour la santé mentale ou physique d'un enfant déjà né dans la famille, un risque plus grave que celui de l'avortement.	(e) L'enfant né à terme courrait un risque important de souffrir d'anomalies physiques ou mentales entraînant pour lui un grave handicap.	(f) Autres motifs.
Danemark	x	x	x	x	x	
Estonie	x	x	x	x	x	
Finlande	x	x	x		x	x
Allemagne	x	x	x			x
Grèce	x	x	x	x	x	
Hongrie	x	x	x	x	x	
Islande	x	x	x	x	x	x
Italie	x	x	x		x	x
Lettonie	x	x	x		x	
Lituanie						x
Pays-Bas	x	x	x		x	
Norvège	x	x	x	x	x	x
Pologne	x	x			x	x
République de Moldova	x	x	x	x	x	
Royaume-Uni	x	x	x	x	x	
Nouvelle Zélande	x	x	x		x	x

13. Legally induced abortions: 1997 - 2006
Avortements provoqués légalement: 1997 - 2006

Continent and country or area Continent et pays ou zone	1997	1998	1999	2000	2001	2002	2003	2004	2005	2006
AFRICA - AFRIQUE										
Réunion	4 729	4 652	4 522	4 404	4 339	4 385	...	...	...	...
Seychelles	362	411	536	495	461	460	440	435	413	443
South Africa - Afrique du Sud[1]	...	28 978	...	...	...	...	...	...	...	...
AMERICA, NORTH - AMÉRIQUE DU NORD										
Anguilla	...	...	...	...	...	27	24	26	21	...
Canada	111 709	110 331	105 666	105 427	106 418	105 154[2]	103 768[2]	100 039[2]	96 815[2]	...
Costa Rica	8 705	8 850	9 160	9 711	8 220	8 332	8 967	8 074	7 974	...
Cuba	80 097	75 109	80 037	76 293	69 563	70 823[3]	65 628[3]	67 277[3]	62 530[3]	...
Dominican Republic - République dominicaine	22 911	31 068	...	...	20 187	28 091	24 899	26 438	29 167	...
Greenland - Groenland	843	915	842	944	809	821	869	...	899	...
Mexico - Mexique[4]	561	595	614	541	571	591	676	752	735	799
Panama[5]	...	...	...	11	...	...	...	...	...	...
Puerto Rico - Porto Rico	...	...	...	...	1 229	...	7 781	9 215	6 713	...
Turks Caicos Islands - Îles Turques et Caïques[6]	...	...	...	...	...	39	32	43	32	...
ASIA - ASIE										
Armenia - Arménie	25 266	18 286	14 403	11 769	10 419	9 372	10 290	10 487	10 925	11 132
Azerbaijan - Azerbaïdjan	25 182	24 914	20 878	17 501	18 332	16 606	16 903	19 798	...	...
Bahrain - Bahreïn	1 592	1 680	1 658	1 655	1 747	1 749	...	...	...	...
China: Hong Kong SAR - Chine: Hong Kong RAS	23 939	22 086	20 891	21 375	20 235	18 651	17 420	15 880	14 190	...
Israel - Israël[7]	19 210	18 500	18 372	18 689	19 131	19 126	19 671	19 712	19 090	19 452
Japan - Japon[8]	337 799	333 220	337 288	341 146	341 588	329 326	319 831	301 673	289 127	276 352
Kazakhstan	156 222	148 799	137 808	...	...	...	...	...	...	...
Kyrgyzstan - Kirghizistan[9]	31 598	28 090	25 790	22 044	23 390	18 995	19 225	19 984	20 035	14 914
Mongolia - Mongolie	12 870	9 135	9 200	11 837	12 056	9 977	10 472	8 919	9 064	12 594
Qatar	97	71	124	177	127	121	131	172	169	...
Singapore - Singapour	13 827	13 838	13 753	13 734	13 140	12 749	12 272	12 070	11 482	12 032
Tajikistan - Tadjikistan	...	...	21 234	22 066	19 087	21 104	18 822	20 500	19 400	17 500
EUROPE										
Åland Islands - Îles d'Åland[10]	57	64	76	59	59	61	70	59	68	53
Albania - Albanie	22 103	18 944	19 930	21 004	17 125	17 500	12 087	10 517	9 403	9 552
Belarus - Bélarus	152 660	145 339	135 824	121 895	101 402	89 895	80 174	71 700	64 655	58 516
Belgium - Belgique	...	11 999	12 734	13 762	14 775	14 791	15 595	...	...	...
Bulgaria - Bulgarie	87 896	79 842	72 382	61 378	51 165	50 824	48 035	47 223	41 795	37 272
Channel Islands: Guernsey - Îles Anglo-Normandes: Guernesey	57	104	92	89						
Croatia - Croatie	10 036	8 907	8 064	7 534	6 574	6 191	5 923	5 232	4 563	4 733
Czech Republic - République tchèque	45 022	42 959	39 382	34 623	32 528	31 142	29 298	27 574	26 453	25 352
Denmark - Danemark[11]	17 152	16 592	16 271	15 681	15 315	14 991	15 622	14 674	15 103	15 053
Estonia - Estonie[12]	16 615	15 798	14 503	12 743	11 653	10 834	10 619	10 074	9 610	9 378
Faeroe Islands - Îles Féroé	38	59	47	49	42	49	37	44	29	41
Finland - Finlande[13]	10 250	10 751	10 837	10 932	10 738	10 974	10 767	11 162	10 969	10 645
France[14]	188 477	195 368	196 295	...	201 434	204 931	202 594	209 907	...	...
Germany - Allemagne	130 890	131 795	130 471	134 609	134 964	130 387	128 030	129 650	124 023	119 710
Greece - Grèce	12 853	11 838	11 824	18 015	22 223	16 173	15 782	...	...	...
Hungary - Hongrie	74 564	68 971	65 981	59 249	56 404	56 075	53 789	52 539	48 689	46 324
Iceland - Islande	921	...	935	987	984	926	951	889	867	...
Italy - Italie	140 166	138 354	138 708	...	132 073	131 039	124 118	...	...	...
Latvia - Lettonie	21 768	19 964	18 031	17 240	15 647	14 685	14 508	13 723	12 785	11 825
Lithuania - Lituanie[15]	22 680	21 022	18 846	16 259	13 677	12 495	11 513	10 644	9 972	9 536
Moldova	...	31 293	27 908	20 395	16 028	15 739	17 551	17 965	16 642	15 742
Montenegro	...	...	...	...	...	...	...	...	1 952	
Netherlands - Pays-Bas	...	24 141	...	...	...	...	...	...	...	...
Norway - Norvège[16]	...	14 028	14 251	14 635	13 887	13 557	13 888	14 071	13 989	14 132

Continent and country or area Continent et pays ou zone	Number - Nombre									
	1997	1998	1999	2000	2001	2002	2003	2004	2005	2006
EUROPE										
Poland - Pologne[17]	3 171[18]	312	151	138	123	159	174	199	225	339
Romania - Roumanie	347 126	271 496	259 888	257 865	254 855	247 608	224 807	191 038	163 359	150 246
Russian Federation - Fédération de Russie	...	...	...	...	2 014 710	1 944 481	1 864 647	1 797 567	1 732 289	1 582 398
Serbia - Serbie[19]	...	...	...	...	...	30 794[20]	...	29 856[20]	26 645[20]	25 665
Slovakia - Slovaquie	...	21 109	19 949	...	18 026	17 382	16 222	15 307	14 427	14 243
Slovenia - Slovénie	9 712	9 116	8 707	8 429	7 799	7 327	6 873	6 403	5 851	5 632
Spain - Espagne	46 902	53 847	58 399	63 756	69 857	77 125	79 788	84 985	91 664	...
Sweden - Suède	31 443	31 008	30 712	30 980	31 772	33 365	34 473	34 454	34 978	36 045
The Former Yugoslav Rep. of Macedonia - L'ex-République yougoslave de Macédoine	12 028	...	...	...	...	...	...	...	...	...
Ukraine	596 740	525 329	495 760	434 223	369 750	345 967	315 835	289 065	263 590	229 618
United Kingdom - Royaume-Uni[21]	191 855	199 887	195 394	197 366	197 913	...	...	...	...	...
OCEANIA - OCÉANIE										
New Caledonia - Nouvelle-Calédonie	1 528	1 466	...	...	...	...	...	...	...	...
New Zealand - Nouvelle-Zélande	15 208	15 029	15 501	16 103	16 410	17 380	18 511	18 211	17 531	17 934

FOOTNOTES - NOTES

* Provisional. - Données provisoires

1 Data refer to both 1997 and 1998. - Les données se rapportent à 1997 et à 1998.

2 Data excludes abortions performed on non-Canadian residents. - À l'exclusion des avortements pratiqués sur des résidents non canadiens.

3 Late foetal death is indicated by the fact that the foetus is at least 500 grams or more in weight. - Les décès foetaux tardifs sont caractérisés par le fait que le foetus pèse au moins 500 grammes

4 Excluding abortions to mothers living abroad which occurred in the country. - À l'exclusion des avortements, survenus dans le pays, de mères résidant à l'étranger.

5 Data refer to abortions granted for medical reasons by the Comision Multidisciplinaria Nacional de Aborto Terapéutico. - Les données se réfèrent aux avortements autorisés pour des raisons médicales par la Comision Multidisciplinaria Nacional de Aborto Terapéutico.

6 For abortions performed in hospitals at Grand Turk and Providenciales. - Pour des avortements exécutés dans les hôpitaux dans Grand Turk et Providenciales.

7 Legally induced abortions are applications to commissions for termination of pregnancy and not authorizations. Including data for East Jerusalem and Israeli residents in certain other territories under occupation by Israeli military forces since June 1967. - Les données relatives aux avortements provoqués légalement se rapportent aux demandes d'autorisation et non aux autorisations elles-mêmes. Y compris les données pour Jérusalem-Est et les résidents israéliens dans certains autres territoires occupés depuis 1967 par les forces armées israéliennes.

8 Data refer to Japanese nationals in Japan only. - Les données se raportent aux nationaux japonais au Japon seulement.

9 Data on abortions are based on administrative reporting of Ministry of Health. - Les données sur les avortements reposent sur les rapports administratifs du Ministère de la santé.

10 Also included in Finland. - Comprise aussi dans Finlande.

11 Excluding Faeroe Islands and Greenland shown separately, if available. - Non compris les Iles Féroé et le Gröenland, qui font l'objet de rubriques distinctes, si disponible.

12 Data refer to the legally induced abortions if the woman's place of residence is in Estonia - Données concernant les avortements légaux de femmes dont le lieu de résidence est l'Estonie.

13 Including Aland Islands. - Y compris les Îles d'Åland.

14 Excluding Overseas Departments, namely, French Guiana, Guadeloupe, Martinique and Reunion, shown separately, if available. Total only contains women between 15 and 49 years old. - Non compris les départements d'outre mer, c'est-à-dire la Guyane française, la Guadeloupe, la Martinique et la Réunion,

qui font l'objet de rubriques distinctes, si disponible. Le total se rapporte uniquement aux femmes dont l'âge est compris entre 15 et 49 ans.

15 Data refer to requested abortions only and exclude abortions due to therapeutic reasons. - Les données se rapportent seulement aux interruptions volontaires de grossesse et excluent les avortements effectués pour des rasions thérapeutiques.

16 Excluding Svalbard and Jan Mayen Island shown separately, if available. - Non compris Svalbard et Jan Mayen qui font l'objet de rubriques distinctes, si disponible.

17 Based on hospital and polyclinic records. - D'après les registres des hôpitaux et des polycliniques.

18 From 1993, a restrictive legal adjustment binds in Poland. In 1997 regulations were moderated briefly and only that year women were able to have an abortion if they had difficult life conditions - Depuis 1993, un ajustement légal restrictif lie en Pologne. En 1997 le règlement a été modéré brièvement et seulement cette année les femmes pouvaient avoir un avortement si elles avaient des conditions difficiles de vie

19 Without data for Kosovo and Metohia. - Sans les données pour le Kosovo and Metohie.

20 Data refer to institutions included in the Health Institutions Network Plan in the Republic of Serbia. - Les données se rapportent aux institutions membres du "Health Institutions Network Plan" de la République de Serbie.

21 Excluding Channel Islands and Isle of Man, shown separately, if available. For resident population only. - Non compris les îles Anglo-Normandes et l'Île de Man, qui font l'objet de rubriques distinctes, si disponible. Pour la population résidante seulement.

Table 14

Table 14 presents legally induced abortions by age and number of previous live births of women for the latest available year.

Description of variables: Age is defined as age at last birthday, that is, the difference between the date of birth and the date of the occurrence of the event, expressed in complete solar years. The age classification used in this table is the following: under 15 years, 5-year age groups through 45-49 years and 50 years and over.

Except where otherwise indicated, eight categories are used in classifying the number of previous live births: 0 through 5, 6 or more live births, and, if required, number of live births unknown.

In an effort to provide more complete interpretation of these statistics, countries or areas providing data on legally induced abortions have been requested to communicate grounds for legally induced abortions in their country or area. This information is presented in table 13-1 above.

Reliability of data: Unlike data on live births and foetal deaths, which are generally collected through systems of vital registration, data on abortion are collected from a variety of sources. Because of this, the quality specification, showing the completeness of civil registers, which is presented for other tables, does not appear here.

Limitations: With regard to the collection of information on abortions, a variety of sources are used, but hospital records are the most common source of information. This implies that most cases that have no contact with hospitals are missed. Data from other sources are probably also incomplete. The data in the present table are limited to legally induced abortions, which, by their nature, might be assumed to be more complete than data on all induced abortions.

In addition, deficiencies in the reporting of age and number of previous live births of the woman, differences in the method used for obtaining the age of the woman, and the proportion of abortions for which age or previous live births of the woman are unknown must all be taken into account in using these data.

Earlier data: Legally induced abortions by age and previous live births of women have been shown previously in most issues of the *Demographic Yearbook* since the 1971 issue. For more information on specific topics and years for which data are reported, readers should consult the Index.

Tableau 14

Le tableau 14 présente les données les plus récentes dont on dispose sur les avortements provoqués pour des raisons légales, selon l'âge de la mère et le nombre de naissances vivantes précédentes.

Description des variables : Les notes techniques du tableau 13 contiennent une classification des avortements provoqués légalement. L'âge considéré est l'âge au dernier anniversaire, c'est-à-dire la différence entre la date de naissance et la date de l'avortement, exprimée en années solaires révolues. La classification par âge utilisée dans le tableau 14 est la suivante : moins de 15 ans, groupes quinquennaux jusqu'à 45-49 ans, 50 ans et plus, et âge inconnu.

Sauf indication contraire, les naissances vivantes antérieures sont classées dans les huit catégories suivantes: 0 à 5 naissances vivantes, 6 naissances vivantes ou plus et, le cas échéant, nombre de naissances vivantes inconnu.

Afin de fournir une interprétation plus complète de ces statistiques, il a été demandé aux pays ou zones fournissant des données de communiquer les motifs d'avortement autorisés par la loi. Cette information est présentée dans le tableau 13-1.

Fiabilité des données : à la différence des données sur les naissances vivantes et les morts fœtales, qui proviennent généralement des registres d'état civil, les données sur l'avortement sont tirées de sources diverses. Aussi ne trouve-t-on pas ici une évaluation de la qualité des données semblable à celle qui indique, pour les autres tableaux, le degré d'exhaustivité des données de l'état civil.

Insuffisance des données : en ce qui concerne les renseignements sur l'avortement, un grand nombre de sources sont utilisées, les relevés hospitaliers restant cependant la source la plus commune. Il s'ensuit que la plupart des cas qui ne passent pas par les hôpitaux sont ignorés. Il faut aussi tenir compte du fait que les données provenant d'autres sources sont probablement incomplètes. Les données du tableau 14 se limitent aux avortements provoqués pour raisons légales dont on peut supposer, en raison de leur nature même, que les statistiques sont plus complètes que les données concernant l'ensemble des avortements provoqués.

En outre, on doit tenir compte, lorsque l'on utilise ces données, des erreurs de déclaration de l'âge de la mère et du nombre des naissances vivantes précédentes, de l'hétérogénéité des méthodes de calcul de l'âge de la mère et de la proportion d'avortements pour lesquels l'âge de la mère ou le nombre des naissances vivantes ne sont pas connus.

Données publiées antérieurement : Depuis 1971, la plupart des éditions de l'*Annuaire démographique* contiennent des statistiques concernant les avortements provoqués pour raisons légales, selon l'âge de la mère et le nombre de naissances vivantes antérieures. Pour plus de précisions concernant les années et les sujets pour lesquels des données ont été publiées, se reporter à l'index.

14. Legally induced abortions by age and number of previous live births of women: latest available year, 1997 - 2006
Avortments provoqués légalement selon l'âge de la femme et selon le nombre des naissances vivantes précédentes: dernière année disponible, 1997 - 2006

Continent, country or area, year and age Continent, pays ou zone, année et âge	Total	\multicolumn{8}{c}{Number of previous live births Nombre des naissances vivantes précédentes}	Unknown - Inconnu
		0	1	2	3	4	5	6+	
AMERICA, NORTH - AMÉRIQUE DU NORD									
Canada[1]									
2005									
Total	96 815	...	...	...	...	...	...	...	...
0 - 14	284	...	...	...	...	...	...	...	...
15 - 19	16 065	...	...	...	...	...	...	...	...
20 - 24	30 359	...	...	...	...	...	...	...	...
25 - 29	21 419	...	...	...	...	...	...	...	...
30 - 34	14 450	...	...	...	...	...	...	...	...
35 - 39	9 973	...	...	...	...	...	...	...	...
40 - 44	4 263	...	...	...	...	...	...	...	...
45 +	-	...	...	...	...	...	...	...	...
Unknown - Inconnu	2	...	...	...	...	...	...	...	...
Mexico - Mexique[2]									
2006									
Total	799	142	204	178	71	27	9	8	160
0 - 14	3	1	-	-	-	-	-	-	2
15 - 19	92	30	20	6	-	-	-	1	35
20 - 24	187	47	47	35	9	-	-	-	49
25 - 29	180	27	49	48	18	8	-	-	30
30 - 34	148	15	37	43	20	8	2	2	21
35 - 39	109	10	27	30	18	5	4	3	12
40 - 44	26	4	6	7	3	3	-	2	-
45 - 49	-	-	-	-	-	-	-	-	-
50 +	-	-	-	-	-	-	-	-	-
Unknown - Inconnu	54	8	18	9	3	3	3	-	11
Panama[3]									
2000									
Total	11	7	3	-	-	-	-	1	-
15 - 19	2	2	-	-	-	-	-	-	-
20 - 24	4	3	1	-	-	-	-	-	-
25 - 29	2	1	1	-	-	-	-	-	-
30 - 34	2	-	1	-	-	-	-	1	-
35 +	1	1	-	-	-	-	-	-	-
Puerto Rico - Porto Rico									
2005									
Total	6 713	...	...	...	...	...	...	...	...
0 - 14	7	...	...	...	...	...	...	...	...
15 - 19	787	...	...	...	...	...	...	...	...
20 - 24	2 158	...	...	...	...	...	...	...	...
25 - 29	1 485	...	...	...	...	...	...	...	...
30 - 34	881	...	...	...	...	...	...	...	...
35 - 39	257	...	...	...	...	...	...	...	...
40 - 44	94	...	...	...	...	...	...	...	...
45 - 49	3	...	...	...	...	...	...	...	...
50 +	-	...	...	...	...	...	...	...	...
Unknown - Inconnu	1 041	...	...	...	...	...	...	...	...
Turks Caicos Islands - Îles Turques et Caïques[4]									
2005									
Total	32	...	...	...	...	...	...	...	...
15 - 19	4	...	...	...	...	...	...	...	...
20 - 24	7	...	...	...	...	...	...	...	...
25 - 29	9	...	...	...	...	...	...	...	...
30 - 34	6	...	...	...	...	...	...	...	...
35 - 39	4	...	...	...	...	...	...	...	...
40 - 44	1	...	...	...	...	...	...	...	...
45 +	1	...	...	...	...	...	...	...	...
ASIA - ASIE									
Armenia - Arménie									
2006									
Total	11 132	...	...	...	...	...	...	...	...
15 - 19	531	...	...	...	...	...	...	...	...
20 - 34	8 200	...	...	...	...	...	...	...	...
35 +	2 401	...	...	...	...	...	...	...	...

14. Legally induced abortions by age and number of previous live births of women: latest available year, 1997 - 2006
Avortments provoqués légalement selon l'âge de la femme et selon le nombre des naissances vivantes précédentes:
dernière année disponible, 1997 - 2006 (continued - suite)

Continent, country or area, year and age Continent, pays ou zone, année et âge	Total	Number of previous live births Nombre des naissances vivantes précédentes							Unknown - Inconnu
		0	1	2	3	4	5	6+	
ASIA - ASIE									
Azerbaijan - Azerbaïdjan									
2004									
Total	19 798	...	...	...	...	...	...	...	...
0 - 14	-	...	...	...	...	...	...	...	...
15 - 19	725	...	...	...	...	...	...	...	...
20 - 24	4 552	...	...	...	...	...	...	...	...
25 - 29	6 681	...	...	...	...	...	...	...	...
30 - 34	4 830	...	...	...	...	...	...	...	...
35 +	3 010	...	...	...	...	...	...	...	...
China: Hong Kong SAR - Chine: Hong Kong RAS									
2005									
Total	14 190	7 995	2 764	2 774	547	^110	...	...	-
0 - 14	28	28	-	-	-	^_	...	...	-
15 - 19	1 260	1 215	41	4	-	^_	...	...	-
20 - 24	3 258	2 924	259	58	15	^2	...	...	-
25 - 29	2 883	2 007	554	281	35	^6	...	...	-
30 - 34	2 740	1 136	786	701	103	^14	...	...	-
35 - 39	2 518	516	735	1 012	208	^47	...	...	-
40 - 44	1 353	159	354	644	162	^34	...	...	-
45 +	150	10	35	74	24	^7	...	...	-
Unknown - Inconnu	-	-	-	-	-	^_	...	...	-
Israel - Israël[5]									
2006									
Total	19 485	8 230	2 832	3 861	2 410	945	413	318	476
0 - 14	75	71	1	-	-	-	-	-	3
15 - 19	2 716	2 476	84	15	3	1	-	-	137
20 - 24	3 977	3 040	484	245	48	10	-	-	150
25 - 29	3 957	1 666	885	835	340	93	36	18	84
30 - 34	3 983	678	850	1 325	640	262	117	60	51
35 - 39	3 112	221	381	1 006	881	337	150	120	16
40 - 44	1 451	45	126	390	452	221	102	109	6
45 - 49	138	8	10	37	42	20	8	11	2
50 +	8	1	4	-	1	1	-	-	1
Unknown - Inconnu	68	24	7	8	3	-	-	-	26
Japan - Japon[6]									
2006									
Total	276 352	...	...	...	...	...	...	...	...
0 - 14	340	...	...	...	...	...	...	...	...
15 - 19	27 027	...	...	...	...	...	...	...	...
20 - 24	68 563	...	...	...	...	...	...	...	...
25 - 29	57 698	...	...	...	...	...	...	...	...
30 - 34	57 516	...	...	...	...	...	...	...	...
35 - 39	45 856	...	...	...	...	...	...	...	...
40 - 44	17 725	...	...	...	...	...	...	...	...
45 - 49	1 572	...	...	...	...	...	...	...	...
50 +	26	...	...	...	...	...	...	...	...
Unknown - Inconnu	29	...	...	...	...	...	...	...	...
Kazakhstan									
1999									
Total	137 808	...	...	...	...	...	...	...	...
0 - 14	177	...	...	...	...	...	...	...	...
15 - 18	8 971	...	...	...	...	...	...	...	...
19 - 35	105 204	...	...	...	...	...	...	...	...
36 +	23 456	...	...	...	...	...	...	...	...
Unknown - Inconnu	-	...	...	...	...	...	...	...	...
Kyrgyzstan - Kirghizistan[7]									
2005									
Total	20 035	...	...	...	...	...	...	...	...
0 - 14	5	...	...	...	...	...	...	...	...
15 - 19	1 827	...	...	...	...	...	...	...	...
20 - 24	4 463	...	...	...	...	...	...	...	...
25 - 29	4 779	...	...	...	...	...	...	...	...
30 - 34	4 455	...	...	...	...	...	...	...	...
35 - 39	3 025	...	...	...	...	...	...	...	...
40 - 44	1 349	...	...	...	...	...	...	...	...
45 +	132	...	...	...	...	...	...	...	...

14. Legally induced abortions by age and number of previous live births of women: latest available year, 1997 - 2006
Avortments provoqués légalement selon l'âge de la femme et selon le nombre des naissances vivantes précédentes: dernière année disponible, 1997 - 2006 (continued - suite)

Continent, country or area, year and age / Continent, pays ou zone, année et âge	Total	Number of previous live births / Nombre des naissances vivantes précédentes								Unknown - Inconnu
		0	1	2	3	4	5	6+	

ASIA - ASIE

Singapore - Singapour
2006
Total	12 032	7 931	2 825	885	267	^124	...	...	...
0 - 14	20	19	1	-	-	^-	...	...	...
15 - 19	1 371	1 159	185	21	6	^-	...	...	...
20 - 24	3 044	2 108	703	173	49	^11	...	...	...
25 - 29	2 706	1 765	601	249	53	^38	...	...	...
30 - 34	2 366	1 459	617	183	70	^37	...	...	...
35 - 39	1 700	969	499	162	49	^21	...	...	...
40 - 44	762	420	203	87	35	^17	...	...	...
45 +	63	32	16	10	5	^-	...	...	...

Tajikistan - Tadjikistan
2003
Total	18 822	...	...	...	...	...	...	...	...
0 - 14	2	...	...	...	...	...	...	...	...
15 - 19	1 493	...	...	...	...	...	...	...	...
20 - 34	11 830	...	...	...	...	...	...	...	...
35 +	5 497	...	...	...	...	...	...	...	...

EUROPE

Åland Islands - Îles d'Åland[8]
2006
Total	53	...	...	...	...	...	...	...	...
0 - 14	-	...	...	...	...	...	...	...	...
15 - 19	11	...	...	...	...	...	...	...	...
20 - 24	14	...	...	...	...	...	...	...	...
25 - 29	11	...	...	...	...	...	...	...	...
30 - 34	7	...	...	...	...	...	...	...	...
35 - 39	6	...	...	...	...	...	...	...	...
40 - 44	3	...	...	...	...	...	...	...	...
45 - 49	1	...	...	...	...	...	...	...	...
50 +	-	...	...	...	...	...	...	...	...
Unknown - Inconnu	-	...	...	...	...	...	...	...	...

Belarus - Bélarus
2006
Total	58 516	...	...	...	...	...	...	...	...
0 - 14	28	...	...	...	...	...	...	...	...
15 - 19	5 731	...	...	...	...	...	...	...	...
20 - 24	14 905	...	...	...	...	...	...	...	...
25 - 29	14 743	...	...	...	...	...	...	...	...
30 - 34	11 510	...	...	...	...	...	...	...	...
35 - 39	7 867	...	...	...	...	...	...	...	...
40 - 44	3 286	...	...	...	...	...	...	...	...
45 +	446	...	...	...	...	...	...	...	...

Belgium - Belgique
2003
Total	15 595	...	...	...	...	...	...	...	...
0 - 14	65	...	...	...	...	...	...	...	...
15 - 19	2 097	...	...	...	...	...	...	...	...
20 - 24	4 032	...	...	...	...	...	...	...	...
25 - 29	3 411	...	...	...	...	...	...	...	...
30 - 34	3 001	...	...	...	...	...	...	...	...
35 - 39	2 107	...	...	...	...	...	...	...	...
40 - 44	810	...	...	...	...	...	...	...	...
45 - 49	67	...	...	...	...	...	...	...	...
50 +	1	...	...	...	...	...	...	...	...
Unknown - Inconnu	4	...	...	...	...	...	...	...	...

Bulgaria - Bulgarie
2006
Total	37 272	...	...	...	...	...	...	...	...
0 - 14	166	...	...	...	...	...	...	...	...
15 - 19	3 490	...	...	...	...	...	...	...	...
20 - 24	8 775	...	...	...	...	...	...	...	...
25 - 29	10 431	...	...	...	...	...	...	...	...
30 - 34	8 015	...	...	...	...	...	...	...	...
35 - 39	4 976	...	...	...	...	...	...	...	...

14. Legally induced abortions by age and number of previous live births of women: latest available year, 1997 - 2006
Avortments provoqués légalement selon l'âge de la femme et selon le nombre des naissances vivantes précédentes: dernière année disponible, 1997 - 2006 (continued - suite)

Continent, country or area, year and age / Continent, pays ou zone, année et âge	Total	Number of previous live births / Nombre des naissances vivantes précédentes							Unknown - Inconnu
		0	1	2	3	4	5	6+	
EUROPE									
Bulgaria - Bulgarie									
2006									
40 - 44	1 326	...	...	...	...	...	...	...	...
45 - 49	92	...	...	...	...	...	...	...	...
50 +	1	...	...	...	...	...	...	...	...
Unknown - Inconnu	-	...	...	...	...	...	...	...	...
Channel Islands: Guernsey - Îles Anglo-Normandes: Guernesey									
2000									
Total	89	46	21	11	9	1	1	-	-
0 - 14	1	1	-	-	-	-	-	-	-
15 - 19	12	11	1	-	-	-	-	-	-
20 - 24	30	17	13	-	-	-	-	-	-
25 - 29	18	11	3	3	1	-	-	-	-
30 - 34	15	4	3	4	2	1	1	-	-
35 - 39	10	1	1	4	4	-	-	-	-
40 - 44	3	1	-	-	2	-	-	-	-
45 +	-								
Croatia - Croatie									
2006									
Total	4 733	1 397	907	1 540	568	173	45	49	54
0 - 14	3	2	-	-	-	-	-	-	1
15 - 19	411	362	25	12	1	-	-	-	11
20 - 24	858	525	186	111	21	4	3	-	8
25 - 29	912	229	237	310	90	23	4	6	13
30 - 34	1 002	107	221	436	159	49	8	14	8
35 - 39	922	67	147	427	176	60	17	20	8
40 - 44	440	34	60	200	93	30	11	8	4
45 - 49	39	3	7	15	13	-	1	-	-
50 +	2	1	-	-	-	1	-	-	-
Unknown - Inconnu	144	67	24	29	15	6	1	1	1
Czech Republic - République tchèque									
2006									
Total	25 352	6 939	6 436	8 745	2 395	566	161	110	-
0 - 14	46	44	2	-	-	-	-	-	-
15 - 19	2 269	1 990	246	32	1	-	-	-	-
20 - 24	4 637	2 600	1 370	526	120	17	3	1	-
25 - 29	5 667	1 521	1 908	1 704	388	106	26	14	-
30 - 34	6 312	580	1 756	2 968	739	174	57	38	-
35 - 39	4 302	154	830	2 367	701	160	52	38	-
40 - 44	1 939	46	301	1 043	412	98	21	18	-
45 - 49	177	4	21	104	34	11	2	1	-
50 +	3	-	2	1	-	-	-	-	-
Unknown - Inconnu	-								
Denmark - Danemark[9]									
2006									
Total	15 053	...	...	...	...	...	...	...	...
15 - 19	2 518	...	...	...	...	...	...	...	...
20 - 24	3 138	...	...	...	...	...	...	...	...
25 - 29	2 861	...	...	...	...	...	...	...	...
30 - 34	2 973	...	...	...	...	...	...	...	...
35 - 39	2 373	...	...	...	...	...	...	...	...
40 - 44	1 107	...	...	...	...	...	...	...	...
45 - 49	83	...	...	...	...	...	...	...	...
50 +		...	...	...	...	...	...	...	...
Estonia - Estonie									
2006									
Total	9 378	2 628	3 310	2 407	754	174	69	34	2
0 - 14	20	20	-	-	-	-	-	-	-
15 - 19	1 298	1 092	193	13	-	-	-	-	-
20 - 24	2 304	1 046	995	234	23	5	-	-	1
25 - 29	2 038	337	962	554	144	29	11	1	-
30 - 34	1 699	87	591	697	232	56	20	15	1
35 - 39	1 438	30	424	623	258	64	28	11	-
40 - 44	531	12	134	263	90	19	9	4	-
45 - 49	50	4	11	23	7	1	1	3	-
50 +	-								
Unknown - Inconnu	-								

14. Legally induced abortions by age and number of previous live births of women: latest available year, 1997 - 2006
Avortments provoqués légalement selon l'âge de la femme et selon le nombre des naissances vivantes précédentes:
dernière année disponible, 1997 - 2006 (continued - suite)

Continent, country or area, year and age Continent, pays ou zone, année et âge	Total	Number of previous live births Nombre des naissances vivantes précédentes							
		0	1	2	3	4	5	6+	Unknown - Inconnu
EUROPE									
Faeroe Islands - Îles Féroé									
2005									
Total....................................	29	...	...	...	...	...	...	...	...
0 - 14...................................	-	...	...	...	...	...	...	...	...
15 - 19..................................	6	...	...	...	...	...	...	...	...
20 - 24..................................	2	...	...	...	...	...	...	...	...
25 - 29..................................	5	...	...	...	...	...	...	...	...
30 - 34..................................	8	...	...	...	...	...	...	...	...
35 - 39..................................	5	...	...	...	...	...	...	...	...
40 - 44..................................	3	...	...	...	...	...	...	...	...
45 - 49..................................	-	...	...	...	...	...	...	...	...
50 + ...	-	...	...	...	...	...	...	...	...
Finland - Finlande[10]									
2006									
Total....................................	10 645	5 593	1 982	1 843	872	264	63	27	1
0 - 14...................................	65	65	-	-	-	-	-	-	-
15 - 19..................................	2 163	2 012	136	15	-	-	-	-	-
20 - 24..................................	2 947	2 005	655	252	31	4	-	-	-
25 - 29..................................	1 985	886	471	431	151	37	7	1	1
30 - 34..................................	1 511	353	327	478	250	80	16	7	-
35 - 39..................................	1 322	190	254	448	303	91	26	10	-
40 - 44..................................	610	77	135	205	122	50	13	8	-
45 - 49..................................	40	5	4	13	15	2	-	1	-
50 + ...	2	-	-	1	-	-	1	-	-
Unknown - Inconnu	-	-	-	-	-	-	-	-	-
France[11]									
2004									
Total....................................	209 907	...	...	...	...	...	...	...	...
0 - 14...................................	-	...	...	...	...	...	...	...	...
15 - 19..................................	28 925	...	...	...	...	...	...	...	...
20 - 24..................................	52 929	...	...	...	...	...	...	...	...
25 - 29..................................	44 001	...	...	...	...	...	...	...	...
30 - 34..................................	40 512	...	...	...	...	...	...	...	...
35 - 39..................................	29 706	...	...	...	...	...	...	...	...
40 - 44..................................	12 521	...	...	...	...	...	...	...	...
45 - 49..................................	1 313	...	...	...	...	...	...	...	...
50 + ...	-	...	...	...	...	...	...	...	...
Germany - Allemagne									
2006									
Total....................................	119 710	48 760	31 055	27 726	8 776	2 344	673	376	-
0 - 14...................................	542	541	1	-	-	-	-	-	-
15 - 19..................................	15 209	13 804	1 282	115	7	1	-	-	-
20 - 24..................................	27 876	17 330	7 383	2 589	456	95	18	5	-
25 - 29..................................	26 530	9 262	8 668	6 331	1 706	419	102	42	-
30 - 34..................................	21 580	4 260	6 358	7 489	2 483	705	194	91	-
35 - 39..................................	19 106	2 619	5 255	7 557	2 620	699	226	130	-
40 - 44..................................	8 211	888	1 979	3 341	1 389	393	122	99	-
45 - 49..................................	640	52	125	299	112	32	11	9	-
50 + ...	16	4	4	5	3	-	-	-	-
Unknown - Inconnu	-	-	-	-	-	-	-	-	-
Greece - Grèce									
2003									
Total....................................	15 782	...	...	...	...	...	...	...	...
0 - 14...................................	8	...	...	...	...	...	...	...	...
15 - 19..................................	569	...	...	...	...	...	...	...	...
20 - 29..................................	5 934	...	...	...	...	...	...	...	...
30 - 39..................................	7 557	...	...	...	...	...	...	...	...
40 - 49..................................	1 345	...	...	...	...	...	...	...	...
50 + ...	48	...	...	...	...	...	...	...	...
Unknown - Inconnu	321	...	...	...	...	...	...	...	...
Hungary - Hongrie									
2006									
Total....................................	46 324	12 495	11 012	11 966	6 666	2 471	944	770	...
0 - 14...................................	175	171	4	-	-	-	-	-	...
15 - 19..................................	5 325	4 080	974	228	41	2	-	-	...
20 - 24..................................	9 138	4 029	2 603	1 520	747	183	40	16	...
25 - 29..................................	10 984	2 662	2 874	2 692	1 658	701	253	144	...
30 - 34..................................	10 605	1 182	2 578	3 447	2 008	796	338	256	...
35 - 39..................................	7 369	298	1 515	2 870	1 605	562	248	271	...

14. Legally induced abortions by age and number of previous live births of women: latest available year, 1997 - 2006
Avortments provoqués légalement selon l'âge de la femme et selon le nombre des naissances vivantes précédentes: dernière année disponible, 1997 - 2006 (continued - suite)

Continent, country or area, year and age Continent, pays ou zone, année et âge	Total	Number of previous live births Nombre des naissances vivantes précédentes							Unknown - Inconnu
		0	1	2	3	4	5	6+	
EUROPE									
Hungary - Hongrie									
2006									
40 - 44	2 532	63	436	1 113	560	220	63	77	
45 - 49	194	9	28	95	47	7	2	6	
50 + ...	2	1	-	1	-	-	-	-	
Iceland - Islande									
2005									
Total.................	867	348	239	164	87	29	-	-	
0 - 14.................	2	...	...	...	...	...	...	...	...
15 - 19	163	...	...	...	...	...	...	...	...
20 - 24	253	...	...	...	...	...	...	...	...
25 - 29	193	...	...	...	...	...	...	...	...
30 - 34	127	...	...	...	...	...	...	...	...
35 - 39	82	...	...	...	...	...	...	...	...
40 - 44	45	...	...	...	...	...	...	...	...
45 + ...	2	...	...	...	...	...	...	...	...
Italy - Italie									
2003									
Total.................	124 118	52 804	28 193	30 616	9 001	2 007	464	216	817
0 - 14.................	255	242	3	1	-	-	-	-	9
15 - 19	9 725	8 722	744	114	13	2	1	-	129
20 - 24	24 074	17 042	4 694	1 757	251	47	4	3	276
25 - 29	28 656	13 633	7 686	5 655	1 212	217	44	11	198
30 - 34	27 794	7 948	7 527	9 078	2 470	502	107	52	110
35 - 39	22 877	3 840	5 299	9 387	3 273	734	180	95	69
40 - 44	9 580	1 147	2 016	4 191	1 604	449	113	46	14
45 - 49	760	76	133	333	149	47	12	9	1
50 + ...	36	9	9	12	4	1	1	-	-
Unknown - Inconnu	361	145	82	88	25	8	2	-	11
Latvia - Lettonie[12]									
2006									
Total.................	11 825	...	...	...	...	...	...	...	...
0 - 14.................	10	...	...	...	...	...	...	...	...
15 - 19	1 318	...	...	...	...	...	...	...	...
20 - 24	2 795	...	...	...	...	...	...	...	...
25 - 29	2 639	...	...	...	...	...	...	...	...
30 - 34	2 378	...	...	...	...	...	...	...	...
35 - 39	1 845	...	...	...	...	...	...	...	...
40 - 44	777	...	...	...	...	...	...	...	...
45 - 49	62	...	...	...	...	...	...	...	...
50 + ...	1	...	...	...	...	...	...	...	...
Unknown - Inconnu	-	...	...	...	...	...	...	...	...
Lithuania - Lituanie[13]									
2006									
Total.................	9 536	...	...	...	...	...	...	...	...
0 - 14.................	6	...	...	...	...	...	...	...	...
15 - 19	890	...	...	...	...	...	...	...	...
20 - 24	2 233	...	...	...	...	...	...	...	...
25 - 29	2 047	...	...	...	...	...	...	...	...
30 - 34	1 945	...	...	...	...	...	...	...	...
35 - 39	1 573	...	...	...	...	...	...	...	...
40 - 44	748	...	...	...	...	...	...	...	...
45 - 49	94	...	...	...	...	...	...	...	...
50 + ...	-	...	...	...	...	...	...	...	...
Unknown - Inconnu	-	...	...	...	...	...	...	...	...
Moldova									
2006									
Total.................	15 742	...	...	...	...	...	...	...	...
0 - 14.................	18	...	...	...	...	...	...	...	...
15 - 19	1 410	...	...	...	...	...	...	...	...
20 - 34	11 884	...	...	...	...	...	...	...	...
35 + ...	2 430	...	...	...	...	...	...	...	...
Montenegro									
2005									
Total.................	1 952	307	283	677	473	139	45	26	2
0 - 14.................	3	-	2	1	-	-	-	-	-
15 - 16	5	5	-	-	-	-	-	-	-
17 - 19	46	31	7	4	2	1	-	-	1
20 - 29	685	179	155	219	98	21	10	3	-

14. Legally induced abortions by age and number of previous live births of women: latest available year, 1997 - 2006
Avortments provoqués légalement selon l'âge de la femme et selon le nombre des naissances vivantes précédentes:
dernière année disponible, 1997 - 2006 (continued - suite)

Continent, country or area, year and age Continent, pays ou zone, année et âge	Number of previous live births Nombre des naissances vivantes précédentes								
	Total	0	1	2	3	4	5	6+	Unknown - Inconnu
EUROPE									
Montenegro									
2005									
30 - 39	982	80	108	365	286	91	33	18	1
40 - 49	223	11	11	86	82	26	2	5	-
50 +	4	1	-	1	2	-	-	-	-
Unknown - Inconnu	4	-	-	1	3	-	-	-	-
Norway - Norvège[14]									
2006									
Total	14 132	...	...	...	...	...	...	...	...
0 - 14	37	...	...	...	...	...	...	...	...
15 - 19	2 307	...	...	...	...	...	...	...	...
20 - 24	3 740	...	...	...	...	...	...	...	...
25 - 29	2 904	...	...	...	...	...	...	...	...
30 - 34	2 495	...	...	...	...	...	...	...	...
35 - 39	1 877	...	...	...	...	...	...	...	...
40 - 44	694	...	...	...	...	...	...	...	...
45 - 49	55	...	...	...	...	...	...	...	...
50 +	-	...	...	...	...	...	...	...	...
Unknown - Inconnu	23	...	...	...	...	...	...	...	...
Poland - Pologne[15]									
2006									
Total	339	...	...	...	...	...	...	...	...
15 - 19	24	...	...	...	...	...	...	...	...
20 - 24	81	...	...	...	...	...	...	...	...
25 - 29	112	...	...	...	...	...	...	...	...
30 - 34	72	...	...	...	...	...	...	...	...
35 +	50	...	...	...	...	...	...	...	...
Romania - Roumanie									
2006									
Total	150 246	...	...	...	...	...	...	...	...
0 - 14	616	...	...	...	...	...	...	...	...
15 - 19	16 656	...	...	...	...	...	...	...	...
20 - 24	30 732	...	...	...	...	...	...	...	...
25 - 29	37 085	...	...	...	...	...	...	...	...
30 - 34	32 951	...	...	...	...	...	...	...	...
35 - 39	25 260	...	...	...	...	...	...	...	...
40 - 44	6 319	...	...	...	...	...	...	...	...
45 - 49	595	...	...	...	...	...	...	...	...
50 +	32	...	...	...	...	...	...	...	...
Russian Federation - Fédération de Russie									
2006									
Total	1 582 398	...	...	...	...	...	...	...	...
0 - 14	1 062	...	...	...	...	...	...	...	...
15 - 19	161 156	...	...	...	...	...	...	...	...
20 - 34	1 123 654	...	...	...	...	...	...	...	...
35 +	296 526	...	...	...	...	...	...	...	...
Serbia - Serbie[16]									
2005									
Total	26 645	6 069	5 196	11 480	2 865	712	191	132	...
0 - 14	4	4	-	-	-	-	-	-	...
15 - 19	916	686	167	51	7	3	-	2	...
20 - 24	3 739	1 706	1 011	834	143	36	5	4	...
25 - 29	6 036	1 529	1 459	2 324	533	142	30	19	...
30 - 34	7 106	1 062	1 350	3 522	836	224	69	43	...
35 - 39	5 789	721	834	3 076	859	195	57	47	...
40 - 44	2 730	314	338	1 503	432	100	28	15	...
45 - 49	314	46	32	165	55	12	2	2	...
50 +	11	1	5	5	-	-	-	-	...
Slovakia - Slovaquie									
2006									
Total	14 243	4 000	3 712	4 340	1 387	468	165	171	...
0 - 14	12	12	-	-	-	-	-	-	...
15 - 19	1 181	994	148	31	8	-	-	-	...
20 - 24	2 812	1 499	840	366	79	23	3	2	...
25 - 29	3 434	974	1 150	928	247	84	31	20	...
30 - 34	3 495	348	982	1 484	433	139	63	46	...
35 - 39	2 292	127	447	1 062	409	141	42	64	...
40 - 44	964	41	137	446	201	76	25	38	...

14. Legally induced abortions by age and number of previous live births of women: latest available year, 1997 - 2006
Avortments provoqués légalement selon l'âge de la femme et selon le nombre des naissances vivantes précédentes: dernière année disponible, 1997 - 2006 (continued - suite)

Continent, country or area, year and age / Continent, pays ou zone, année et âge	Total	Number of previous live births / Nombre des naissances vivantes précédentes							
		0	1	2	3	4	5	6+	Unknown - Inconnu
EUROPE									
Slovakia - Slovaquie									
2006									
45 - 49	52	5	8	22	10	5	1	1	...
50 + ...	1	-	-	1	-	-	-	-	...
Slovenia - Slovénie									
2006									
Total...............................	5 632	1 901	1 228	1 900	477	91	20	14	1
0 - 14...............................	5	5	-	-	-	-	-	-	-
15 - 19	430	412	14	2	2	-	-	-	-
20 - 24	1 029	750	202	62	12	2	1	-	-
25 - 29	1 243	464	395	317	60	6	-	1	-
30 - 34	1 203	163	327	553	127	23	5	5	-
35 - 39	1 127	76	194	627	185	31	10	4	-
40 - 44	535	26	88	308	79	25	4	4	1
45 - 49	60	5	8	31	12	4	-	-	-
50 + ...	-	-	-	-	-	-	-	-	-
Unknown - Inconnu	-	-	-	-	-	-	-	-	-
Spain - Espagne									
2004									
Total...............................	84 985	42 757	19 962	15 023	4 772	1 400	^741	...	330
0 - 14...............................	369	365	1	-	-	-	^_	...	3
15 - 19	11 677	10 415	1 057	145	16	4	^_	...	40
20 - 24	22 461	15 193	5 127	1 680	353	33	^13	...	62
25 - 29	20 309	9 931	5 541	3 457	981	239	^77	...	83
30 - 34	15 212	4 630	4 381	4 186	1 329	424	^195	...	67
35 - 39	10 572	1 777	2 846	3 757	1 373	476	^288	...	55
40 - 44	4 072	414	949	1 665	661	211	^153	...	19
45 - 49	313	32	60	133	59	13	^15	...	1
50 + ...	-	-	-	-	-	-	^_	...	-
Sweden - Suède[17]									
2006									
Total...............................	36 045	19 390	5 498	6 918	2 708	788	236	114	393
0 - 14...............................	236	230	1	-	-	-	-	-	5
15 - 19	7 296	6 945	225	19	6	-	-	-	101
20 - 24	8 638	6 735	1 294	430	63	9	-	-	107
25 - 29	6 740	3 402	1 530	1 314	339	57	15	4	79
30 - 34	5 851	1 343	1 246	2 131	789	216	55	22	49
35 - 39	4 904	529	839	2 081	977	304	92	53	29
40 - 44	2 188	191	338	864	490	192	64	27	22
45 - 49	170	8	21	72	40	10	10	8	1
50 + ...	2	-	-	1	1	-	-	-	-
Unknown - Inconnu	20	7	4	6	3	-	-	-	-
Ukraine									
2006									
Total...............................	229 618	...	...	...	...	...	...	...	...
0 - 14...............................	106	...	...	...	...	...	...	...	...
15 - 19	23 195	...	...	...	...	...	...	...	...
20 - 34	168 290	...	...	...	...	...	...	...	...
35 + ...	38 027	...	...	...	...	...	...	...	...
United Kingdom - Royaume-Uni[18]									
2000									
Total...............................	197 366	105 328	37 645	33 532	13 982	4 683	1 414	753	29
0 - 14...............................	1 170	1 165	4	1	-	-	-	-	-
15 - 19	40 225	35 254	4 393	528	40	4	-	-	6
20 - 24	53 590	35 263	11 732	5 183	1 150	222	25	9	6
25 - 29	42 680	20 273	9 640	8 295	3 212	953	231	71	5
30 - 34	31 928	8 925	7 004	9 504	4 339	1 491	455	205	5
35 - 39	20 684	3 562	3 711	7 438	3 771	1 433	485	279	5
40 - 44	6 526	794	1 081	2 375	1 359	542	203	171	1
45 - 49	490	62	66	189	108	36	14	15	-
50 + ...	25	4	4	9	2	2	1	3	-
Unknown - Inconnu	48	26	10	10	1	-	-	-	1
2001									
Total...............................	197 913	...	...	...	...	...	...	...	...
0 - 14...............................	1 157	...	...	...	...	...	...	...	...
15 - 19	40 387	...	...	...	...	...	...	...	...
20 - 24	54 878	...	...	...	...	...	...	...	...
25 - 29	41 126	...	...	...	...	...	...	...	...
30 - 34	31 921	...	...	...	...	...	...	...	...

14. Legally induced abortions by age and number of previous live births of women: latest available year, 1997 - 2006
Avortments provoqués légalement selon l'âge de la femme et selon le nombre des naissances vivantes précédentes:
dernière année disponible, 1997 - 2006 (continued - suite)

Continent, country or area, year and age Continent, pays ou zone, année et âge	Total Total	0	1	2	3	4	5	6+	Unknown - Inconnu
EUROPE									
United Kingdom - Royaume-Uni[18]									
2001									
35 - 39	21 096	...	...	...	...	...	...	...	...
40 - 44	6 833	...	...	...	...	...	...	...	...
45 - 49	513	...	...	...	...	...	...	...	...
50 +	-	...	...	...	...	...	...	...	...
Unknown - Inconnu	2	...	...	...	...	...	...	...	...
OCEANIA - OCÉANIE									
New Zealand - Nouvelle-Zélande									
2006									
Total	17 934	9 078	3 401	3 013	1 397	640	244	161	...
0 - 14	105	105	-	-	-	-	-	-	...
15 - 19	3 978	3 436	473	66	2	1	-	-	...
20 - 24	5 314	3 293	1 218	599	162	36	6	-	...
25 - 29	3 530	1 304	767	801	398	182	52	26	...
30 - 34	2 497	578	486	729	368	204	81	51	...
35 - 39	1 777	279	331	571	310	157	73	56	...
40 - 44	691	81	115	236	150	55	29	25	...
45 - 49	42	2	11	11	7	5	3	3	...
50 +	-	-	-	-	-	-	-	-	...

FOOTNOTES - NOTES

* Provisional. - Données provisoires.

^ Indicates an open-ended group, for example 4+. - indique un groupe d'âge ouvert, par exemple 4 ou plus.

[1] Data excludes abortions performed on non-Canadian residents. - À l'exclusion des avortements pratiqués sur des résidents non canadiens.

[2] Data refer to 'Therapeutic Abortions'. According to the Mexican law, only the induced abortions, prescribed by medical reasons and induced because of pregnancy coming from sexual agression, are considered as legal. Excluding abortions to mothers living abroad which occurred in the country. - Les données se rapportent aux « interruptions volontaires de grossesse pour des motifs thérapeutiques ». D'après la loi mexicaine, seuls sont considérés légaux les avortements déclenchés pour des raisons médicales ou parce que la grossesse est le résultat d'une agression sexuelle. À l'exclusion des avortements, survenus dans le pays, de mères résidant à l'étranger.

[3] Data refer to abortions granted for medical reasons by the Comision Multidisciplinaria Nacional de Aborto Terapéutico. - Les données se référent aux avortements autorisés pour des raisons médicales par la Comision Multidisciplinaria Nacional de Aborto Terapéutico.

[4] For abortions performed in hospitals at Grand Turk and Providenciales. - Pour des avortements exécutés dans les hôpitaux dans Grand Turk et Providenciales.

[5] Including data for East Jerusalem and Israeli residents in certain other territories under occupation by Israeli military forces since June 1967. Legally induced abortions are applications to commissions for termination of pregnancy and not authorizations. - Y compris les données pour Jérusalem-Est et les résidents israéliens dans certains autres territoires occupés depuis 1967 par les forces armées israéliennes. Les données relatives aux avortements provoqués légalement se rapportent aux demandes d'autorisation et non aux autorisations elles-mêmes.

[6] Data refer to Japanese nationals in Japan only. - Les données se raportent aux nationaux japonais au Japon seulement.

[7] Data on abortions are based on administrative reporting of Ministry of Health. - Les données sur les avortements reposent sur les rapports administratifs du Ministère de la santé.

[8] Also included in Finland. - Comprise aussi dans Finlande.

[9] Excluding Faeroe Islands and Greenland shown separately, if available. - Non compris les Îles Féroé et le Grôenland, qui font l'objet de rubriques distinctes, si disponible.

[10] Including Aland Islands. - Y compris les Îles d'Åland.

[11] Excluding Overseas Departments, namely, French Guiana, Guadeloupe, Martinique and Reunion, shown separately, if available. - Non compris les départements d'outre mer, c'est-à-dire la Guyane française, la Guadeloupe, la Martinique et la Réunion, qui font l'objet de rubriques distinctes, si disponible.

[12] Source: based on the results of the Health Statistics and Medical Technology State Agency under the Ministry of Health. - Source : Chiffres basés sur les résultats de l'Agence nationale de statistiques sanitaires et de technologie médicale du Ministère de la santé.

[13] Data refer to requested abortions only and exclude abortions due to therapeutic reasons. - Les données se rapportent seulement aux interruptions volontaires de grossesse et excluent les avortements effectués pour des rasions thérapeutiques.

[14] Excluding Svalbard and Jan Mayen Island shown separately, if available. - Non compris Svalbard et Jan Mayen qui font l'objet de rubriques distinctes, si disponible.

[15] Based on hospital and polyclinic records. - D'après les registres des hôpitaux et des polycliniques.

[16] Without data for Kosovo and Metohia. - Sans les données pour le Kosovo and Metohie.

[17] Abortion by previous deliveries of mother rather than previous live births of mother. - Avortements selon les accouchements précédents de la mère plutôt que selon les naissances vivantes de la mère.

[18] For resident population only. Excluding Channel Islands and Isle of Man, shown separately, if available. - Pour la population résidante seulement. Non compris les îles Anglo-Normandes et l'île de Man, qui font l'objet de rubriques distinctes, si disponible.

Table 15

Table 15 presents infant deaths and infant mortality rates by urban/rural residence for as many years as possible between 2002 and 2006.

Description of variables: Infant deaths are deaths of live-born infants under one year of age.

Statistics on the number of infant deaths are obtained from civil registers unless otherwise noted. Infant mortality rates are, in most instances, calculated from data on registered infant deaths and registered live births for a country or area where civil registration is considered reliable (that is, with an estimated completeness of 90 per cent or more).

The urban/rural classification of infant deaths is that provided by each reporting country or area; it is presumed to be based on the national census definitions of urban population that have been set forth at the end of the technical notes of table 6.

Rate computation: Infant mortality rates are the annual number of deaths of infants under one year of age per 1 000 live births (as shown in table 9) in the same year.

Rates by urban/rural residence are the annual number of infant deaths, in the appropriate urban or rural category, per 1 000 corresponding live births (as shown in table 9). These rates have been calculated by the Statistics Division of the United Nations.

Rates presented in this table have been limited to those for countries or areas having at least a total of 100 infant deaths in a given year and for which the quality code is represented by a C or a symbol |.

Reliability of data: Each country or area has been asked to indicate the estimated completeness of the infant deaths recorded in its civil register. These national assessments are indicated by the quality codes C, U and | that appear in the first column of this table.

C indicates that the data are estimated to be virtually complete, that is, representing at least 90 per cent of the infant deaths occurring each year, while U indicates that data are estimated to be incomplete that is, representing less than 90 per cent of the infant deaths occurring each year. The code I indicates that the source of data is not civil registration, but is still considered reliable. The code ... indicates that no information was provided regarding completeness.

Data from civil registers that are reported as incomplete or of unknown completeness (coded U or ...) are considered unreliable. They appear in italics in this table; rates are not computed for data so coded.

Limitations: Statistics on infant deaths are subject to the same qualifications as have been set forth for vital statistics in general and death statistics in particular as discussed in section 4 of the Technical Notes.

The reliability of the data, an indication of which is described above, is an important factor in considering the limitations. In addition, some infant deaths are tabulated by date of registration and not by date of occurrence; these have been indicated by a plus sign (+). Whenever the lag between the date of occurrence and date of registration is prolonged and, therefore, a large proportion of the infant-death registrations are delayed, infant-death statistics for any given year may be seriously affected.

Another factor that limits international comparability is the practice of some countries or areas not to include in infant-death statistics infants who were born alive but died before the registration of the birth or within the first 24 hours of life, thus underestimating the total number of infant deaths. Statistics of this type are footnoted.

The method of reckoning age at death for infants may also introduce non-comparability. If year alone, rather than completed minutes, hours, days and months elapsed since birth, is used to calculate age at time of death, many of the infants who died during the eleventh month of life and some of those who died at younger ages will be classified as having completed one year of age and thus be excluded. The effect would be to underestimate the number of infant deaths. Information on this factor is given in footnotes when known. Reckoning of infant age is further discussed in the technical notes for table 16.

In addition, infant mortality rates are subject to the limitations of the data on live births with which they have been calculated. These have been set forth in the technical notes for table 9.

Because the two components of the infant mortality rate, infant deaths in the numerator and live births in the denominator, are both obtained from systems of civil registration, the limitations which affect live-birth statistics are very similar to those which have been mentioned above in connection with the infant-death statistics. It is important to consider the reliability of the data (the completeness of registration) and the method of tabulation (by date of occurrence or by date of registration) of live-birth statistics as well as infant-death statistics, both of which are used to calculate infant mortality rates. The quality code and use of italics to indicate unreliable data presented in this table refer only to infant deaths. Similarly, the indication of the basis of tabulation (the use of the symbol (+) to indicate data tabulated by date of registration) presented in this table also refers only to infant deaths. Table 9 provides the corresponding information for live births.

If the registration of infant deaths is more complete than the registration of live births, then infant mortality rates would be biased upwards. If, however, the registration of live births is more complete than registration of infant deaths, infant mortality rates would be biased downwards. If both infant deaths and live births are tabulated by registration, it should be noted that deaths tend to be more promptly reported than births.

Infant mortality rates may be seriously affected by the practice of some countries or areas of not considering infants that were born alive but died before the registration of the birth or within the first 24 hours of life as live-birth and subsequently infant death. Although this practice results in both the number of infant deaths in the numerator and the number of live births in the denominator being underestimated, its impact is greater on the numerator of the infant mortality rate. As a result this practice causes infant mortality rates to be biased downwards.

Infant mortality rates will also be underestimated if the method of reckoning age at death results in an underestimation of the number of infant deaths. This point has been discussed above.

Because of all these factors care should be taken in comparing and rank ordering infant mortality rates.

With respect to the method of calculating infant mortality rates used in this table, it should be noted that no adjustment was made to take account of the fact that a proportion of the infant deaths that occur during a given year are deaths of infants that were born during the preceding year and hence are not taken from the universe of births used to compute the rates. However, unless the number of live births or infant deaths is changing rapidly, the error involved is insignificant.

The comparability of data by urban/rural residence is affected by the national definitions of urban and rural used in tabulating these data. It is assumed, in the absence of specific information to the contrary, that the definitions of urban and rural used in connection with the national population census were also used in the compilation of the vital statistics for each country or area. However, it cannot be denied that, for some countries or areas, different definitions of urban and rural may be used for the vital statistics data and the population census data respectively. When known, the definitions of urban used in national population censuses are presented at the end of the technical notes for table 6. As discussed in detail in the technical notes for table 6, these definitions vary considerably from one country or area to another.

Urban/rural differentials in infant mortality rates may also be affected by whether the infant deaths and live births have been tabulated in terms of place of occurrence or place of usual residence. This problem is discussed in more detail in section 4.1.4.1 of the Technical Notes.

Earlier data: Infant deaths and infant mortality rates have been shown in previous issues of the *Demographic Yearbook*. For more information on specific topics and years for which data are reported, readers should consult the Historical Index.

Tableau 15

Le tableau 15 présente des données sur les décès d'enfants de moins d'un an et les taux de mortalité infantile selon le lieu de résidence (zone urbaine ou rurale) pour le plus grand nombre d'années possible entre 2002 et 2006.

Description des variables : les chiffres se rapportent aux décès d'enfants de moins d'un an.

Sauf indication contraire, les statistiques concernant le nombre de décès d'enfants de moins d'un an sont établies à partir des registres de l'état civil. Dans la plupart des cas, les taux de mortalité infantile sont calculés à partir des données relatives aux décès enregistrés d'enfants de moins d'un an et aux naissances vivantes enregistrées dans un pays ou une zone lorsque les registres de l'état civil sont jugés fiables (exhaustivité estimée à 90 p. 100 ou plus).

La classification des décès d'enfants de moins d'un an selon le lieu de résidence (zone urbaine ou rurale) est celle qui a été communiquée par chaque pays ou zone ; on part du principe qu'elle repose sur les définitions de la population urbaine utilisées pour les recensements nationaux, telles qu'elles sont reproduites à la fin des notes techniques du tableau 6.

Calcul des taux : Les taux de mortalité infantile représentent le nombre annuel de décès d'enfants de moins d'un an pour 1 000 naissances vivantes (fréquences du tableau 9) survenues pendant la même année.

Les taux selon le lieu de résidence (zone urbaine ou rurale) représentent le nombre annuel de décès d'enfants de moins d'un an, classés selon la catégorie urbaine ou rurale appropriée pour 1 000 naissances vivantes survenues parmi la population correspondante (fréquences du tableau 9). Ces taux ont été calculés par la Division de statistique de l'ONU.

Les taux présentés dans ce tableau se rapportent seulement aux pays ou zones où l'on a enregistré au moins un total de 100 décès d'enfants de moins d'un an au cours d'une année donnée et pour lesquels le code de qualité est soit 'C', soit 'I'.

Fiabilité des données : il a été demandé à chaque pays ou zone d'indiquer le degré estimatif de complétude des données sur les décès d'enfants de moins d'un an figurant dans ses registres d'état civil. Ces évaluations nationales sont signalées par les codes de qualité 'C', 'U' et 'I' qui apparaissent dans la deuxième colonne du tableau.

La lettre 'C' indique que les données sont jugées à peu près complètes, c'est-à-dire qu'elles représentent au moins 90 p. 100 des décès d'enfants de moins d'un an survenus chaque année ; la lettre 'U' signifie que les données sont jugées incomplètes, c'est-à-dire qu'elles représentent moins de 90 p.100 des décès d'enfants de moins d'un an survenus chaque année. Le symbole 'I' indique que la source des données n'est pas un registre de l'état civil, mais est quand même considérée fiable. Le code '...' dénote qu'aucun renseignement n'a été communiqué quant à la complétude des données.

Les données provenant des registres de l'état civil qui sont déclarées incomplètes ou dont le degré de complétude n'est pas connu (code 'U' ou '...') sont jugées douteuses. Elles apparaissent en italique dans le tableau ; les taux, dans ces cas là, n'ont pas été calculés.

Insuffisance des données : les statistiques des décès d'enfants de moins d'un an appellent toutes les réserves qui ont été formulées à propos des statistiques de l'état civil en général et des statistiques concernant les décès en particulier (voir la section 4 des notes techniques).

La fiabilité des données, au sujet de laquelle des indications ont été fournies plus haut, est un facteur important. Il faut également tenir compte du fait que, dans certains cas, les données relatives aux décès d'enfants de moins d'un an sont exploitées selon la date de l'enregistrement et non la date de l'événement ; ces cas ont été signalés par le signe '+'. Chaque fois que le décalage entre l'événement et son enregistrement est grand et qu'une forte proportion des décès d'enfants de moins d'un an fait l'objet d'un enregistrement tardif, les statistiques des décès d'enfants de moins d'un an pour une année donnée peuvent être considérablement faussées.

Un autre facteur qui nuit à la comparabilité internationale est la pratique de certains pays ou zones qui consiste à ne pas inclure dans les statistiques des décès d'enfants de moins d'un an les enfants nés vivants mais décédés avant l'enregistrement de leur naissance ou dans les 24 heures qui ont suivi la naissance, pratique qui conduit à sous-estimer le nombre total de décès d'enfants de moins d'un an. Quand pareil facteur a joué, cela a été signalé en note.

Les méthodes appliquées pour calculer l'âge au moment du décès peuvent également nuire à la comparabilité des données. Si l'on utilise à cet effet l'année seulement, et non pas les minutes, heures, jours et mois qui se sont écoulés depuis la naissance, de nombreux enfants décédés au cours du onzième mois qui a suivi leur naissance et certains enfants décédés encore plus jeunes seront classés comme décédés à un an révolu et donc exclus des données. Cette pratique conduit à sous-estimer le nombre de décès d'enfants de moins d'un an. Les renseignements dont on dispose sur ce facteur apparaissent en note à la fin du tableau. La question du calcul de l'âge au moment du décès est examinée plus en détail dans les notes techniques se rapportant au tableau 16.

Les taux de mortalité infantile appellent en outre toutes les réserves qui ont été formulées à propos des statistiques des naissances vivantes qui ont servi à leur calcul (voir à ce sujet les notes techniques relatives au tableau 9).

Les deux composantes du taux de mortalité infantile - décès d'enfants de moins d'un an au numérateur et naissances vivantes au dénominateur - étant obtenues à partir des registres de l'état civil, les statistiques des naissances vivantes appellent des réserves presque identiques à celles qui ont été formulées plus haut à propos des statistiques des décès d'enfants de moins d'un an. Il importe de prendre en considération la fiabilité des données (complétude de l'enregistrement) et le mode d'exploitation (selon la date de l'événement ou selon la date de l'enregistrement) dans le cas des statistiques des naissances vivantes tout comme dans le cas de celles des décès d'enfants de moins d'un an, puisque les unes et les autres servent au calcul des taux de mortalité infantile. Dans le tableau 15, le code de qualité et l'emploi de caractères italiques pour signaler les données moins sûres ne concernent que les décès d'enfants de moins d'un an. L'indication du mode d'exploitation des données (emploi du signe '+' pour signaler les données exploitées selon la date de l'enregistrement) ne porte là aussi que sur les décès d'enfants de moins d'un an. Le tableau 9 contient les renseignements correspondants pour les naissances vivantes.

Si l'enregistrement des décès d'enfants de moins d'un an est plus complet que l'enregistrement des naissances vivantes, les taux de mortalité infantile seront entachés d'une erreur par excès. En revanche, si l'enregistrement des naissances vivantes est plus complet que l'enregistrement des décès d'enfants de moins d'un an, les taux de mortalité infantile seront entachés d'une erreur par défaut. Si les décès d'enfants de moins d'un an et les naissances vivantes sont exploitées selon la date de l'enregistrement, il convient de ne pas perdre de vue que les décès sont, en règle générale, déclarés plus rapidement que les naissances.

Les taux de mortalité infantile peuvent être gravement faussés par la pratique de certains pays ou zones qui consiste à ne pas classer dans les naissances vivantes et ensuite dans les décès d'enfants de moins d'un an les enfants nés vivants mais décédés soit avant l'enregistrement de leur naissance, soit dans les 24 heures qui ont suivi la naissance. Cette pratique conduit à sous-estimer aussi bien le nombre des décès d'enfants de moins d'un an, qui constitue le numérateur, que le nombre des naissances vivantes, qui constitue le dénominateur, mais c'est pour le numérateur du taux de mortalité infantile que la distorsion est la plus marquée. Ce système a pour effet d'introduire une erreur par défaut dans les taux de mortalité infantile.

Les taux de mortalité infantile seront également sous-estimés si la méthode utilisée pour calculer l'âge au moment du décès conduit à sous-estimer le nombre de décès d'enfants de moins d'un an. Cette question a été examinée plus haut.

Tous ces facteurs sont importants et il faut donc en tenir compte lorsque l'on compare et classe les taux de mortalité infantile.

En ce qui concerne la méthode de calcul des taux de mortalité infantile utilisée dans le tableau, il convient de noter qu'il n'a pas été tenu compte du fait qu'une partie des décès survenus pendant une année donnée sont des décès d'enfants nés l'année précédente et ne correspondent donc pas à l'ensemble des naissances utilisé pour le calcul des taux. Toutefois, l'erreur n'est pas grave, à moins que le nombre des naissances vivantes ou des décès d'enfants de moins d'un an ne varie rapidement.

La comparabilité des données selon le lieu de résidence (zone urbaine ou rurale) peut être limitée par les définitions nationales des termes « urbain » et « rural » utilisées pour la mise en tableaux de ces données. En l'absence d'indications contraires, on a supposé que les mêmes définitions avaient servi pour le recensement national de la population et pour l'établissement des statistiques de l'état civil pour chaque pays ou zone. Toutefois, il n'est pas exclu que, pour une zone ou un pays donné, des définitions différentes aient été retenues. Les définitions du terme « urbain » utilisées pour les recensements nationaux de population ont été présentées à la fin des notes techniques du tableau 6 lorsqu'elles étaient connues. Comme on l'a précisé dans les notes techniques relatives au tableau 6, ces définitions varient considérablement d'un pays ou d'une zone à l'autre.

La différence entre les taux de mortalité infantile pour les zones urbaines et rurales pourra aussi être faussée selon que les décès d'enfants de moins d'un an et les naissances vivantes auront été classés d'après le lieu de l'événement ou le lieu de résidence habituel. Ce problème est examiné plus en détail à la section 4.1.4.1 des Notes techniques.

Données publiées antérieurement : Des statistiques concernant les décès d'enfants de moins d'un an et les taux de mortalité infantile ont déjà été présentées dans des éditions antérieures de l'*Annuaire démographique*. Pour plus de précisions concernant les années et les sujets pour lesquels des données ont été publiées, se reporter à l'index historique.

15. Infant deaths and infant mortality rates, by urban/rural residence: 2002 - 2006
Décès d'enfants de moins d'un an et taux de mortalité infantile, selon la résidence, urbaine/rurale: 2002 - 2006

Continent, country or area, and urban/rural residence / Continent, pays ou zone et résidence, urbaine/rurale	Code	Number - Nombre					Rate - Taux				
		2002	2003	2004	2005	2006	2002	2003	2004	2005	2006
AFRICA - AFRIQUE											
Algeria - Algérie[1]											
Total	U	19 850	...	...	...	...	...	...	...	...	...
Egypt - Égypte											
Total	C	37 904	38 859	40 177	36 146	35 952	21.5	21.9	22.6	20.1	19.4
Urban - Urbaine	C	15 825	17 021	16 954	16 676	17 792	20.6	22.1	23.8	23.1	24.0
Rural - Rurale	C	22 079	21 838	23 223	19 470	18 160	22.1	21.7	21.8	18.1	16.3
Ghana											
Total	...	34 293	...	...	...	...	...	...	...	...	...
Kenya											
Total	U	35 940	35 515	35 321	35 252	35 786	...	...	...	...	...
Mauritius - Maurice											
Total	+C	297	250	277	248	249	14.9	12.9	14.4	13.2	14.1
Urban - Urbaine	+C	102	93	90	92	79	12.9				
Rural - Rurale	+C	195	157	187	156	170	16.2	13.3	15.6	13.3	15.6
Réunion											
Total	C	91	*107	...	...	...	...	*7.4	...	...	...
Saint Helena ex. dep. - Sainte-Hélène sans dép.											
Total	C	...	1	...	1	...	...	...	...	...	...
Seychelles											
Total	+C	26	24	17	16	14	...	...	...	...	...
AMERICA, NORTH - AMÉRIQUE DU NORD											
Anguilla											
Total	+C	2	2	-	3	*1	...	...	...	...	...
Aruba											
Total	+U	3	3	3	6	8	...	...	...	...	...
Bahamas											
Total	C	...	87	...	...	...	...	...	...	...	...
Barbados - Barbade											
Total	+C	*54	...	...	...	...	...	...	...	...	...
Belize											
Total	U	145	...	112	137	...	...	...	...	...	...
Bermuda - Bermudes											
Total	C	-	2	-	2	6	...	...	...	...	...
Canada[2]											
Total	C	1 762	1 765	1 775	1 863	...	5.4	5.3	5.3	5.4	...
Cayman Islands - Îles Caïmanes											
Total	C	...	...	...	4	7	...	...	...	...	...
Costa Rica											
Total	C	793	737	668	700	691	11.1	10.1	9.2	9.8	9.7
Cuba											
Total	C	922	859	*736	746	589	6.5	6.3	*5.8	6.2	5.3
Urban - Urbaine	C	719	671	...	584	475	6.9	6.7	...	6.6	5.7
Rural - Rurale	C	203	188	...	162	114	5.4	5.2	...	5.1	4.1
Dominican Republic - République dominicaine											
Total	+U	571	472	365	377	...	...	...	...	...	...
Urban - Urbaine[3]	+U	439	347	197	285	...	...	...	...	...	...
Rural - Rurale[3]	+U	93	77	72	64	...	...	...	...	...	...
El Salvador											
Total	C	1 284	1 322	1 255	1 097	1 013	9.9	10.6	10.5	9.7	9.5
Urban - Urbaine	C	821	847	781	718	822	10.6	11.6	10.9	10.4	11.6
Rural - Rurale	C	463	475	474	379	191	9.0	9.3	9.8	8.7	5.3
Greenland - Groenland											
Total	C	10	8	10	7	13	...	...	...	...	...
Urban - Urbaine	C	7	8	...	...	...	...	...	...	...	...
Rural - Rurale	C	3	-	...	...	...	...	...	...	...	...
Guadeloupe[4]											
Total	C	45	56	50	...	...	...	...	...	...	...

15. Infant deaths and infant mortality rates, by urban/rural residence: 2002 - 2006
Décès d'enfants de moins d'un an et taux de mortalité infantile, selon la résidence, urbaine/rurale: 2002 - 2006 (continued - suite)

Continent, country or area, and urban/rural residence / Continent, pays ou zone et résidence, urbaine/rurale	Co-de[a]	Number - Nombre					Rate - Taux				
		2002	2003	2004	2005	2006	2002	2003	2004	2005	2006
AMERICA, NORTH - AMÉRIQUE DU NORD											
Guatemala											
Total	C	...	11 022	10 038	9 947	9 042	...	29.4	26.2	26.6	24.5
Urban - Urbaine	C	...	...	...	5 062	4 993	...	...	...	31.6	31.6
Rural - Rurale	C	...	...	...	4 885	4 049	...	...	...	22.8	19.3
Honduras											
Total	+U	7 059	6 902	6 740	6 566	6 400	...	...	...	...	...
Urban - Urbaine	+U	2 180	2 162	2 135	2 104	2 077	...	...	...	...	...
Rural - Rurale	+U	4 879	4 740	4 605	4 462	4 323	...	...	...	...	...
Jamaica - Jamaïque[5]											
Total	U	1 036	1 004	1 004	1 007	...	...	...	...	...	...
Martinique											
Total	C	33	33	27	...	...	...	...	...	...	...
Mexico - Mexique[6]											
Total	+U	36 546	33 331	32 758	32 590	30 890	...	...	...	...	...
Urban - Urbaine[3]	+U	27 207	25 073	24 433	24 372	23 057	...	...	...	...	...
Rural - Rurale[3]	+U	8 498	7 714	7 671	7 639	7 263	...	...	...	...	...
Netherlands Antilles - Antilles néerlandaises											
Total	C	17	19	20	...	...	...	...	...	...	...
Nicaragua											
Total	+U	2 217	2 008	1 827	1 970	...	...	...	...	...	...
Urban - Urbaine	+U	1 168	1 091	1 073	934	...	...	...	...	...	...
Rural - Rurale	+U	1 049	917	754	1 036	...	...	...	...	...	...
Panama											
Total	U	885	940	932	980	971	...	...	...	...	...
Urban - Urbaine	U	488	500	546	533	490	...	...	...	...	...
Rural - Rurale	U	397	440	386	447	481	...	...	...	...	...
Puerto Rico - Porto Rico											
Total	C	516	498	416	472	...	9.8	9.8	8.1	9.3	...
Urban - Urbaine	C	...	297[3]	246[3]	285	...	...	11.1	9.2	10.2	...
Rural - Rurale	C	...	199[3]	169[3]	187	...	...	8.2	6.9	8.2	...
Saint Lucia - Sainte-Lucie											
Total	C	36	37	45	*46	...	...	...	...	...	...
Saint Vincent and the Grenadines - Saint Vincent-et-les Grenadines											
Total	+C	35	35	33	29	...	...	...	...	...	...
Trinidad and Tobago - Trinité-et-Tobago											
Total	C	412	...	...	...	...	24.2	...	...	...	...
Turks Caicos Islands - Îles Turques et Caïques											
Total	C	2	2	-	1	...	...	...	...	...	...
United States - États-Unis											
Total	C	28 034	28 025	27 936	28 440	*28 100	7.0	6.9	6.8	6.9	*6.6
United States Virgin Islands - Îles Vierges américaines											
Total	C	*5	12	13	...	...	...	...	...	...	...
AMERICA, SOUTH - AMÉRIQUE DU SUD											
Argentina - Argentine											
Total	C	11 703	11 494	10 576	9 507	8 986	16.8	16.5	14.4	13.3	12.9
Brazil - Brésil[7]											
Total	U	45 243	48 039	41 851	39 259	37 677	...	...	...	...	...
Chile - Chili											
Total	C	1 964	1 935	2 034	1 911	...	8.2	8.3	8.8	8.3	...
Urban - Urbaine	C	1 715	1 691	1 773	1 637	...	8.0	8.1	8.7	8.0	...
Rural - Rurale	C	249	244	261	274	...	9.6	9.8	10.1	10.7	...
Colombia - Colombie											
Total	U	12 640	12 335	11 772	11 456	*10 722	...	...	...	...	...
Urban - Urbaine[3]	U	8 970	8 894	8 445	8 160	*7 565	...	...	...	...	...
Rural - Rurale[3]	U	2 922	2 755	2 664	2 643	*2 645	...	...	...	...	...

15. Infant deaths and infant mortality rates, by urban/rural residence: 2002 - 2006
Décès d'enfants de moins d'un an et taux de mortalité infantile, selon la résidence, urbaine/rurale: 2002 - 2006 (continued - suite)

Continent, country or area, and urban/rural residence / Continent, pays ou zone et résidence, urbaine/rurale	Co-de[n]	Number - Nombre					Rate - Taux				
		2002	2003	2004	2005	2006	2002	2003	2004	2005	2006
AMERICA, SOUTH - AMÉRIQUE DU SUD											
Ecuador - Équateur[8]											
Total....................	U	4 530	3 985	3 942	3 717	3 715	...	...	...	...	...
Urban - Urbaine	U	3 420	3 085	3 121	...	...	...	...	...	...	...
Rural - Rurale	U	1 110	900	821	...	...	...	...	...	...	...
French Guiana - Guyane française[4]											
Total....................	C	52	58	55	...		...				
Paraguay											
Total....................	U	...	674	647	539	...	...	...	...	...	...
Peru - Pérou[9]											
Total....................	+U	6 511	7 122	...			...	...	...	...	...
Suriname											
Total....................	C	148	109	120	136	...	14.5	11.3	13.2	15.7	...
Urban - Urbaine[10]........	C	112	69	67	87	...	17.8	...	...	...	...
Rural - Rurale[10]..........	C	34	36	49	48	...	...	...	...	...	...
Uruguay											
Total....................	C	708	*757	659	*601	*497	13.6	*15.0	13.2	*12.8	*10.5
Venezuela (Bolivarian Republic of) - Venezuela (République bolivarienne du)[7]											
Total....................	C	7 645	...				15.5	...	...	...	...
ASIA - ASIE											
Armenia - Arménie[11]											
Total....................	C	450	422	430	460	523	14.0	11.8	11.5	12.3	13.9
Urban - Urbaine	C	300	311	311	351	389	14.4	13.7	13.2	14.8	16.3
Rural - Rurale	C	150	111	119	109	134	13.1	8.4	8.6	7.9	9.7
Azerbaijan - Azerbaïdjan[11]											
Total....................	+C	1 422	1 451	1 287	1 321	1 508	12.8	12.8	9.8	9.3	10.1
Urban - Urbaine	+C	554	633	605	...	...	11.1	12.4	10.2	...	...
Rural - Rurale	+C	868	818	682	...	...	14.2	13.1	9.4	...	...
Bahrain - Bahreïn											
Total....................	C	94	107	141	134	115	...	7.3	9.4	8.8	7.6
Bangladesh[12]											
Total....................	I	...	...	...	...	...	53.0	53.0	52.0	49.0	45.0
Urban - Urbaine	I	...	...	...	...	...	37.0	40.0	41.0	44.0	38.0
Rural - Rurale	I	...	...	...	...	...	57.0	57.0	55.0	51.0	47.0
Bhutan - Bhoutan[13]											
Total....................	I	...	...	...	503	...	...	...	...	40.1	...
Urban - Urbaine	I	...	...	...	126		...	...	...	32.8	...
Rural - Rurale	I	...	...	...	377		...	...	...	43.4	...
Brunei Darussalam - Brunéi Darussalam											
Total....................	+C	62	67	63	*51	...	...	...	...	...	...
Cambodia - Cambodge											
Total....................	...	83	80	76	...		...	...	...	...	...
China: Hong Kong SAR - Chine: Hong Kong RAS											
Total....................	C	110	109	132	131	*118	2.3	2.3	2.7	2.3	*1.8
China: Macao SAR - Chine: Macao RAS											
Total....................	C	11	2	10	12	11	...	...	...	...	...
Cyprus - Chypre[14]											
Total....................	C	37	33	29	38	27	...	...	...	...	...
Georgia - Géorgie[11]											
Total....................	C	1 102	1 144	1 178	916	753	23.6	24.8	23.8	19.7	15.8
Urban - Urbaine	C	...	1 057	...	...	...	...	30.6	...	...	...
Rural - Rurale	C	...	87	...	...	...	...	...	...	...	...
India - Inde[15]											
Total....................	I	...	...	...	...	...	63.0	60.0	58.0	58.0	57.0
Urban - Urbaine	I	...	...	...	...	...	40.0	38.0	40.0	40.0	39.0
Rural - Rurale	I	...	...	...	...	...	69.0	66.0	64.0	64.0	62.0

15. Infant deaths and infant mortality rates, by urban/rural residence: 2002 - 2006
Décès d'enfants de moins d'un an et taux de mortalité infantile, selon la résidence, urbaine/rurale: 2002 - 2006 (continued - suite)

Continent, country or area, and urban/rural residence / Continent, pays ou zone et résidence, urbaine/rurale	Code[a]	Number - Nombre					Rate - Taux				
		2002	2003	2004	2005	2006	2002	2003	2004	2005	2006
ASIA - ASIE											
Iraq											
Total	U	...	...	*10 972	*12 460	...	...	...	...	...	...
Israel - Israël[16]											
Total	C	752[17]	717[17]	670	628[17]	593	5.4	4.9	4.6	4.4	4.0
Urban - Urbaine	C	678	641	597	551	529	5.3	4.9	4.5	4.2	4.0
Rural - Rurale	C	73	74	73	76	64	...	...	...	...	...
Japan - Japon[18]											
Total	C	3 497	3 364	3 122	2 958	2 864	3.0	3.0	2.8	2.8	2.6
Urban - Urbaine[3]	C	2 815	2 728	2 591	2 544	2 581	3.0	3.0	2.8	2.8	2.6
Rural - Rurale[3]	C	672	631	529	407	280	3.1	3.1	2.7	2.8	2.6
Kazakhstan[11]											
Total	C	3 849	3 806	3 901	4 213	4 154	16.9	15.4	14.3	15.1	13.8
Urban - Urbaine	C	2 211	2 340	2 418	2 711	2 730	18.1	16.9	15.5	16.5	15.5
Rural - Rurale	C	1 638	1 466	1 483	1 502	1 424	15.6	13.4	12.7	13.1	11.3
Korea (Republic of) - Corée (République de)[19]											
Total	C	2 545	2 470	2 209	1 822	1 709	5.1	5.0	4.6	4.2	3.8
Urban - Urbaine	C	2 156	1 984	1 759	1 438	1 359	5.4	4.9	4.5	4.0	3.7
Rural - Rurale	C	385	483	447	382	348	4.3	5.6	5.3	4.9	4.5
Kuwait - Koweït											
Total	C	418	412	422	420	456	9.6	9.4	8.9	8.2	8.6
Kyrgyzstan - Kirghizistan											
Total	C	2 128	2 186	2 812[20]	3 258	3 526	21.1	20.7	25.6	29.7	29.2
Urban - Urbaine	C	852	880	1 427[20]	1 617	1 802	28.2	27.6	38.2	45.4	45.7
Rural - Rurale	C	1 276	1 306	1 385[20]	1 641	1 724	10.0	17.7	19.1	22.1	21.2
Malaysia - Malaisie											
Total	C	3 126	3 148	3 105	*3 105	*3 200	6.5	6.6	6.5	*6.7	*6.6
Maldives											
Total	C	89	72	76	67	92	...	...	...	...	...
Urban - Urbaine	C	28	16	21	29	36	...	...	...	...	...
Rural - Rurale	C	61	56	55	38	56	...	...	...	...	...
Mongolia - Mongolie											
Total	C	1 390	1 051	1 016	938	937	29.6	23.0	22.3	20.7	19.1
Urban - Urbaine	C	626	520	531	520	583	26.0	21.4	20.6	19.7	19.6
Rural - Rurale	C	764	531	485	418	354	33.4	24.8	24.6	22.2	18.3
Myanmar											
Total	U	37 693	31 873	36 812	38 872	...	...	...	...	...	...
Urban - Urbaine	U	11 638	10 378	10 340	10 531	...	...	...	...	...	...
Rural - Rurale	U	26 055	21 495	26 472	28 341	...	...	...	...	...	...
Occupied Palestinian Territory - Territoire palestinien occupé											
Total	U	1 126	1 150	1 103	1 057	906	...	...	...	...	...
Oman[21]											
Total	U	332	335	336	315	381	...	...	...	...	...
Pakistan[22]											
Total	I	...	280 729[23]	...	289 169[24]	...	...	76.2	...	76.7	...
Urban - Urbaine	I	...	80 199[23]	...	82 299[24]	...	...	67.2	...	67.1	...
Rural - Rurale	I	...	200 530[23]	...	206 870[24]	...	...	80.6	...	81.2	...
Philippines											
Total	C	23 778	22 844	22 557	...	...	14.3	13.7	13.2	...	...
Qatar											
Total	C	107	137	113	110	114	8.8	10.7	8.6	8.2	8.1
Saudi Arabia - Arabie saoudite											
Total	...	11 432	11 297	11 165	11 078	10 954	...	...	...	...	...
Singapore - Singapour											
Total	+C	123	100	82	95	117	3.0	2.7	...	...	3.1
Thailand - Thaïlande											
Total	+U	5 105	5 349	6 061	6 183	...	...	...	...	...	...
Turkey - Turquie[25]											
Total	I	36 365	34 842	33 456	32 120	30 781	26.7	25.6	24.6	23.6	22.6
United Arab Emirates - Émirats arabes unis											
Total	...	...	477	...	...	...	...	...	...	...	...

15. Infant deaths and infant mortality rates, by urban/rural residence: 2002 - 2006
Décès d'enfants de moins d'un an et taux de mortalité infantile, selon la résidence, urbaine/rurale: 2002 - 2006 (continued - suite)

Continent, country or area, and urban/rural residence / Continent, pays ou zone et résidence, urbaine/rurale	Code[a]	Number - Nombre					Rate - Taux				
		2002	2003	2004	2005	2006	2002	2003	2004	2005	2006
EUROPE											
Åland Islands - Îles d'Åland[26]											
Total.................	C	1	2	1	-	-	...	...	...	...	...
Urban - Urbaine	C	-	-	1	-	-	...	...	...	...	...
Rural - Rurale	C	1	2	-	-	-	...	...	...	...	...
Albania - Albanie											
Total.................	C	466	395	336	303	253	10.2	8.4	7.8	7.6	7.4
Andorra - Andorre											
Total.................	C	-	-	2	5	3	...	...	...	...	...
Austria - Autriche											
Total.................	C	318	343	353	327	281	4.1	4.5	4.5	4.2	3.6
Belarus - Bélarus[11]											
Total.................	C	695	685	614	640	587	7.8	7.7	6.9	7.1	6.1
Urban - Urbaine	C	454	440	386	398	407	7.0	6.8	5.9	6.0	5.7
Rural - Rurale	C	241	245	228	242	180	10.2	10.3	9.5	10.0	7.0
Belgium - Belgique											
Total.................	C	551	538	549	515	...	5.0	4.8	4.7	4.4	...
Bosnia and Herzegovina - Bosnie-Herzégovine											
Total.................	C	334	268	253	233	255	9.4	7.6	7.2	6.7	7.5
Bulgaria - Bulgarie											
Total.................	C	887	831	814	739	720	13.3	12.3	11.6	10.4	9.7
Urban - Urbaine	C	571	522	516	464	472	12.0	10.7	10.2	8.9	8.6
Rural - Rurale	C	316	309	298	275	248	16.9	16.5	15.3	14.6	13.1
Croatia - Croatie											
Total.................	C	282	251	245	242	215	7.0	6.3	6.1	5.7	5.2
Urban - Urbaine	C	144	135	132	151	113	6.4	6.2	5.9	6.4	4.9
Rural - Rurale	C	138	116	113	91	102	7.9	6.5	6.3	...	5.6
Czech Republic - République tchèque											
Total.................	C	385	365	366	347	352	3.9	3.9	3.7	3.4	3.3
Urban - Urbaine	C	288	266	268	261	268	3.9	3.8	3.7	3.4	3.4
Rural - Rurale	C	97	99	98	86	84	...	...	...	...	...
Denmark - Danemark[27]											
Total.................	C	284	286	283	280	250	4.4	4.4	4.4	4.4	3.8
Estonia - Estonie											
Total.................	C	74	91	90	78	66	...	...	...	...	...
Urban - Urbaine	C	53	59	58	53	47	...	...	...	...	...
Rural - Rurale	C	21	32	32	25	19	...	...	...	...	...
Finland - Finlande[28]											
Total.................	C	168	176	191	174	167	3.0	3.1	3.3	3.0	2.8
Urban - Urbaine	C	109	107	121	103	109	3.0	2.9	3.2	2.7	2.8
Rural - Rurale	C	59	69	70	71	58	...	...	...	...	...
France[29]											
Total.................	C	3 114	3 053	2 988	2 775	...	4.1	4.0	3.9	3.6	...
Urban - Urbaine[30]........	C	2 437	2 403	2 321	2 139	...	4.2	4.2	4.0	3.7	...
Rural - Rurale[30]..........	C	657	625	633	610	...	3.6	3.4	3.4	3.2	...
Germany - Allemagne											
Total.................	C	3 036	2 990	2 918	2 696	2 579	4.2	4.2	4.1	3.9	3.8
Gibraltar											
Total.................	C	...	2	...	1	1	...	...	...	...	...
Greece - Grèce											
Total.................	C	600	420	429	409	415	5.8	4.0	4.1	3.8	3.7
Urban - Urbaine	C	...	...	319	302	299	...	...	...	4.1	3.9
Rural - Rurale	C	...	...	110	107	116	...	...	...	3.2	3.3
Hungary - Hongrie											
Total.................	C	693	690	628	607	571	7.2	7.3	6.6	6.2	5.7
Urban - Urbaine[31]........	C	421	375	384	369	349	6.9	6.3	6.4	5.8	5.3
Rural - Rurale[31]..........	C	269	308	236	228	215	7.6	8.9	6.9	6.9	6.6
Iceland - Islande											
Total.................	C	9	10	12	10	6	...	...	...	...	...
Urban - Urbaine	C	9	10	...	10	6	...	...	...	...	...
Rural - Rurale	C	-	-	...	-	-	...	...	...	...	...
Ireland - Irlande											
Total.................	C	305	326	287	...	...	5.0	5.3	4.6	...	...
Total[32].................	+C	...	...	...	*244	*237	...	...	...	*4.0	*3.7

15. Infant deaths and infant mortality rates, by urban/rural residence: 2002 - 2006
Décès d'enfants de moins d'un an et taux de mortalité infantile, selon la résidence, urbaine/rurale: 2002 - 2006 (continued - suite)

Continent, country or area, and urban/rural residence / Continent, pays ou zone et résidence, urbaine/rurale	Code[a]	Number - Nombre					Rate - Taux				
		2002	2003	2004	2005	2006	2002	2003	2004	2005	2006
EUROPE											
Isle of Man - Îles de Man											
Total	+C	3	6	2	...	...	...	...	...	...	...
Italy - Italie											
Total	C	2 197	2 033	2 609	2 555	2 379	4.1	3.7	4.6	4.6	4.2
Latvia - Lettonie											
Total	C	197	198	191	168	170	9.8	9.4	9.4	7.8	7.6
Urban - Urbaine	C	105	129	117	102	99	8.1	9.3	8.5	7.0	...
Rural - Rurale	C	92	69	74	66	71	...	...	...	...	...
Liechtenstein											
Total	C	1	1	1	1	*2	...	...	...	...	...
Lithuania - Lituanie[11]											
Total	C	238	206	240	209	213	7.9	6.7	7.9	6.8	6.8
Urban - Urbaine	C	128	108	133	135	167	6.8	5.6	6.8	6.8	8.1
Rural - Rurale	C	110	98	107	74	46	9.7	...	9.8	...	...
Luxembourg											
Total	C	27	26	21	14	14	...	...	...	...	...
Malta - Malte											
Total	C	23	23	23	23	14	...	...	...	...	...
Moldova[33]											
Total	C	528	522	464	468	442	14.8	14.3	12.1	12.4	11.8
Urban - Urbaine	C	192	178	167	177	177	15.1	13.9	11.9	13.0	13.0
Rural - Rurale	C	336	344	297	291	265	14.6	14.5	12.3	12.1	11.0
Montenegro											
Total	C	92	92	61	70	83	...	...	...	...	...
Urban - Urbaine	C	...	86	52	65	...	...	...	...	...	...
Rural - Rurale	C	...	6	9	5	...	...	...	...	...	...
Netherlands - Pays-Bas[34]											
Total	C	1 014	962	852	928	820	5.0	4.8	4.4	4.9	4.4
Urban - Urbaine	C	670	627	554	650	538	5.0	4.7	4.2	5.1	4.2
Rural - Rurale	C	344	335	298	278	282	5.0	5.0	4.7	4.7	4.8
Norway - Norvège[35]											
Total	C	192	190	185	175	185	3.5	3.4	3.2	3.1	3.2
Poland - Pologne											
Total	C	2 662	2 470	2 423	2 340	2 238	7.5	7.0	6.8	6.4	6.0
Urban - Urbaine	C	1 551	1 446	1 462	1 339	1 343	7.9	7.2	7.1	6.3	6.2
Rural - Rurale	C	1 111	1 024	961	1 001	895	7.1	6.8	6.4	6.5	5.7
Portugal[36]											
Total	C	574	466	418	382	*349	5.0	4.1	3.8	3.5	*3.3
Romania - Roumanie											
Total	C	3 648	3 546	3 641	3 310	3 052	17.3	16.7	16.8	15.0	13.9
Urban - Urbaine	C	1 426	1 381	1 555	1 458	1 341	14.5	13.7	14.0	12.4	11.2
Rural - Rurale	C	2 222	2 165	2 086	1 852	1 711	19.8	19.4	19.9	17.9	17.1
Russian Federation - Fédération de Russie[11]											
Total	C	18 407	18 142	17 339	16 073	15 079	13.2	12.3	11.5	11.0	10.2
Urban - Urbaine	C	12 511	12 235	11 596	10 716	9 839	12.5	11.6	10.8	10.3	9.4
Rural - Rurale	C	5 896	5 907	5 743	5 357	5 240	14.8	13.8	13.4	12.7	12.0
San Marino - Saint-Marin											
Total	+C	2	2	1	-	-	...	...	...	...	...
Serbia - Serbie[37]											
Total	+C	790	711	633	579	525	10.1	9.0	8.1	8.0	7.4
Urban - Urbaine	+C	529	451	435	378	352	11.1	9.4	9.1	8.1	7.6
Rural - Rurale	+C	261	260	198	201	173	8.6	8.4	6.6	7.9	7.0
Slovakia - Slovaquie											
Total	C	388	406	365	392	355	7.6	7.9	6.8	7.2	6.6
Urban - Urbaine	C	191	176	171	188	153	7.3	6.6	6.0	6.5	5.4
Rural - Rurale	C	197	230	194	204	202	8.0	9.2	7.7	8.0	7.9
Slovenia - Slovénie											
Total	C	67	69	66	75	64	...	...	...	...	...
Urban - Urbaine	C	37	37	34	26	37	...	...	...	...	...
Rural - Rurale	C	30	32	32	49	27	...	...	...	...	...
Spain - Espagne											
Total	C	1 737	1 733	1 813	1 765	1 812	4.1	3.9	4.0	3.8	3.8
Sweden - Suède											
Total	C	313	308	314	246	297	3.3	3.1	3.1	2.4	2.8

15. Infant deaths and infant mortality rates, by urban/rural residence: 2002 - 2006
Décès d'enfants de moins d'un an et taux de mortalité infantile, selon la résidence, urbaine/rurale: 2002 - 2006 (continued - suite)

Continent, country or area, and urban/rural residence / Continent, pays ou zone et résidence, urbaine/rurale	Code[a]	Number - Nombre					Rate - Taux				
		2002	2003	2004	2005	2006	2002	2003	2004	2005	2006
EUROPE											
Switzerland - Suisse											
Total	C	326	311	309	308	325	4.5	4.3	4.2	4.2	4.4
Urban - Urbaine	C	242	225	220	223	255	4.6	4.3	4.1	4.1	4.7
Rural - Rurale	C	84	86	89	85	70	...	...	...	...	...
The Former Yugoslav Rep. of Macedonia - L'ex-République yougoslave de Macédoine											
Total	C	283	305	308	287	260	10.2	11.3	13.2	12.8	11.5
Urban - Urbaine	C	157	...	...	151	144	10.5	...	...	12.1	11.4
Rural - Rurale	C	126	...	...	136	116	9.8	...	...	13.7	11.7
Ukraine											
Total	C	4 023[11]	3 882[11]	4 024[11]	4 259[11]	4 433[38]	10.3	9.5	9.4	10.0	9.6
Urban - Urbaine	C	2 543[11]	2 531[11]	2 584[11]	2 675[11]	2 828[38]	10.2	9.5	9.1	9.4	9.2
Rural - Rurale	C	1 480[11]	1 351[11]	1 440[11]	1 584[11]	1 605[38]	10.4	9.5	10.1	11.2	10.4
United Kingdom - Royaume-Uni[39]											
Total	C	3 499	*3 686	3 606	*3 670	*3 740	5.2	*5.3	5.0	*5.1	*5.0
OCEANIA - OCÉANIE											
American Samoa - Samoas américaines											
Total	C	27	20	26	12	17	...	...	...	...	...
Australia - Australie											
Total	+C	1 264	1 199	1 184	1 302	1 262	5.0	4.8	4.7	5.0	4.7
Urban - Urbaine	+C	779	740	766	858	...	4.7	4.4	4.5	4.9	...
Rural - Rurale	+C	485	459	418	444	...	5.6	5.4	5.0	5.3	...
Cook Islands - Îles Cook[40]											
Total	+C	2	5	5	6	*3	...	...	...	...	...
Fiji - Fidji											
Total	+C	320	304	338	...	...	18.8	17.2	19.7	...	...
French Polynesia - Polynésie française											
Total	C	32	31	20	28	...	...	...	...	...	...
Guam[41]											
Total	C	20	37	42	...	...	...	...	...	...	...
New Caledonia - Nouvelle-Calédonie											
Total	C	29	24	25	...	...	...	...	...	...	...
New Zealand - Nouvelle-Zélande[36]											
Total	+C	300	277	324	295	300	5.6	4.9	5.6	5.1	5.1
Urban - Urbaine[3]	+C	255	231	274	246	251	5.4	4.7	5.4	4.9	4.9
Rural - Rurale[3]	+C	24	27	33	26	33	...	...	...	...	...
Niue - Nioué											
Total	C	-	...	...	...	...	...	...	...	...	...
Northern Mariana Islands - Îles Mariannes septentrionales											
Total	U	*10*	...	...	...	...	...	...	...	...	...
Palau - Palaos											
Total	C	6	2	7	6	2	...	...	...	...	...
Papua New Guinea - Papouasie-Nouvelle-Guinée											
Total	U	*2 230*	*2 082*	...	...	...	...	...	...	...	...
Tonga											
Total	+C	26	34	*35	...	...	...	...	...	...	...
Tuvalu											
Total	U	*4*	*4*	5	6	...	...	...	...	...	...

FOOTNOTES - NOTES

Italics: data from civil registers which are incomplete or of unknown completeness. - Italiques: données incomplètes ou dont le degré d'exactitude n'est pas connu, provenant des registres de l'état civil.

* Provisional. - Données provisoires.

^a 'Code' indicates the source of data, as follows:

C - Civil registration, estimated over 90% complete
U - Civil registration, estimated less than 90% complete
| - Other source, estimated reliable
+ - Data tabulated by date of registration rather than occurence.
... - Information not available

Le 'Code' indique la source des données, comme suit:
C - Registres de l'état civil considérés complets à 90 p. 100 au moins.
U - Registres de l'état civil qui ne sont pas considérés complets à 90 p. 100 au moins.
| - Autre source, considérée pas douteuses.
+ - Données exploitées selon la date de l'enregistrement et non la date de l'événement.
... - Information pas disponible.

[1] Excluding live-born infants who died before their birth was registered. For Algerian population only. - Non compris les enfants nés vivants décédés avant l'enregistrement de leur naissance. Pour la population algérienne seulement.

[2] Including Canadian residents temporarily in the United States, but excluding United States residents temporarily in Canada. - Y compris les résidents canadiens se trouvant temporairement aux Etats-Unis, mais ne comprenant pas les résidents des Etats-Unis se trouvant temporairement au Canada.

[3] The total number includes 'Unknown residence', but the categories urban and rural do not. - Le nombre total inclue 'Résidence inconnue ', mais les catégories Urbain et Rural ne l'incluent pas.

[4] Excluding live-born infants who died before their birth was registered. - Non compris les enfants nés vivants décédés avant l'enregistrement de leur naissance.

[5] Including adjustment for underenumeration. - Y compris l'ajustement pour sous-dénombrement.

[6] Data exclude visitors. - Les données non compris des visiteurs.

[7] Excluding Indian jungle population. - Non compris les Indiens de la jungle.

[8] Excluding nomadic Indian tribes. - Non compris les tribus d'Indiens nomades.

[9] Excluding Indian jungle population. Data refer to registered Infant deaths only. - Non compris les Indiens de la jungle. Les données se rapportent aux décès enregistrés d'enfants de moins de 1 an seulement.

[10] The total number includes 'Unknown residence', but the categories urban and rural do not. The districts of Paramaribo and Wanica are considered urban areas, whereas the rest of the districts are considered more or less rural districts (areas). - Le nombre total inclue 'Résidence inconnue , mais les catégories Urbain et Rural ne l'incluent pas. Les districts de Paramaribo et de Wanica sont considérés comme des zones urbaines, les autres districts étant considérés comme des zones rurales à divers degrés.

[11] Excluding infants born alive of less than 28 weeks' gestation, of less than 1 000 grams in weight and 35 centimeters in length, who die within seven days of birth. - Non compris les enfants nés vivants après moins de 28 semaines de gestations, pesant moins de 1 000 grammes, mesurant moins de 35 centimètres et décédés dans les sept jours qui ont suivi leur naissance.

[12] Rates were obtained by the Sample Vital Registration System of Bangladesh. - Taux obtenus au moyen du Sample Vital Registration System du Bangladesh.

[13] For 2005, data refer to last twelve months preceding census in May 2005. - Pour 2005, les données se rapportent aux douze mois précédant le recensement de mai 2005.

[14] Data refer to government controlled areas. - Les données se rapportent aux zones contrôlées par le Gouvernement.

[15] Rates were obtained by the Sample Registration System of India, actually a large demographic survey. Including data for the Indian-held part of Jammu and Kashmir, the final status of which has not yet been determined. - Les taux ont été obtenus par le Système de l'enregistrement par échantillon de l'Inde qui est une large enquête démographique. Y compris les données pour la partie du Jammu et du Cachemire occupée par l'Inde dont le statut définitif n'a pas encore été déterminé.

[16] Including data for East Jerusalem and Israeli residents in certain other territories under occupation by Israeli military forces since June 1967. - Y compris les données pour Jérusalem-Est et les résidents israéliens dans certains autres territoires occupés depuis 1967 par les forces armées israéliennes.

[17] Data include deaths abroad of Israeli residents who were out of the country for less than a year. - Y compris les décès à l'étranger de résidents israéliens qui ont quitté le pays depuis moins d'un an.

[18] Data refer to Japanese nationals in Japan only. - Les données se raportent aux nationaux japonais au Japon seulement.

[19] Excluding alien armed forces, civilian aliens employed by armed forces, and foreign diplomatic personnel and their dependants. Including nationals outside the country. - Non compris les militaires étrangers, les civils étrangers employés par les forces armées ni le personnel diplomatique étranger et les membres de leur famille les accompagnant. Y compris les nationaux hors du pays.

[20] Since 2004, WHO criteria have been adopted in the country. - Depuis 2004, le pays a adopté les critères de l'OMS.

[21] Data refer to the recorded events in Ministry of Health hospitals and health centres only. - Les données se rapportent aux faits d'état civil enregistrés dans les hôpitaux et les dispensaires du Ministère de la santé seulement.

[22] Excluding data for the Pakistan-held part of Jammu and Kashmir, the final status of which has not yet been determined. - Non compris les données concernant la partie du Jammu et Cachemire occupée par le Pakistan dont le statut définitif n'a pas été déterminé.

[23] Data based on Pakistan Demographic Survey (PDS 2003) . - Données extraites de l'enquête démographique effectuée par le Pakistan en 2003.

[24] Data based on Pakistan Demographic Survey (PDS 2005). - Données extraites de l'enquête démographique effectuée par le Pakistan en 2005.

[25] Based on the results of the Population Demographic Survey. - D'après les résultats de la Population Demographic Survey.

[26] Also included in Finland. - Comprise aussi dans Finlande.

[27] Excluding Faeroe Islands and Greenland shown separately, if available. - Non compris les Iles Féroé et le Gröenland, qui font l'objet de rubriques distinctes, si disponible.

[28] Including nationals temporarily outside the country. Including Aland Islands. - Y compris les nationaux se trouvant temporairement hors du pays. Y compris les Îles d'Åland.

[29] Including armed forces stationed outside the country. Excluding Overseas Departments, namely, French Guiana, Guadeloupe, Martinique and Reunion, shown separately, if available. - Y compris les militaires nationaux hors du pays. Non compris les départements d'outre mer, c'est-à-dire la Guyane française, la Guadeloupe, la Martinique et la Réunion, qui font l'objet de rubriques distinctes, si disponible.

[30] Urban/rural figures, excluding nationals outside the country. - Les chiffres urbaine/rurale, non compris les nationaux hors du pays.

[31] Total includes the data of foreigners, persons of unknown residence and homeless, but the categories urban and rural do not. - Total incluant les étrangers, les personnes de résidence inconnue et les sans-abri, ce qui n'est pas le cas pour les catégories urbaines et rurales.

[32] Events registered within one year of occurrence. - Evénements enregistrés dans l'année qui suit l'événement.

[33] Excluding infants born alive of less than 28 weeks' gestation, of less than 1 000 grams in weight and 35 centimetre in length, who die within seven days of birth. Data do not include information for Transnistria and the municipality of Bender. - Non compris les enfants nés vivants après moins de 28 semaines de gestation, pesant moins de 1 000 grammes, mesurant moins de 35 centimètres et décédés dans les sept jours qui ont suivi leur naissance. Les données ne tiennent pas compte de l'information sur la Transnistria et la municipalité de Bender.

[34] Including residents outside the country if listed in a Netherlands population register. - Y compris les résidents hors du pays, s'ils sont inscrits sur un registre de population néerlandais.

[35] Including residents temporarily outside the country. Excluding Svalbard and Jan Mayen Island shown separately, if available. - Y compris les résidents se trouvant temporairement hors du pays. Non compris Svalbard et Jan Mayen qui font l'objet de rubriques distinctes, si disponible.

[36] For resident population only. - Pour la population résidante seulement.

[37] Without data for Kosovo and Metohia. - Sans les données pour le Kosovo et Metohie.

[38] Data refer to births with weight 500g and more (if weight is unknown - with length 25 centimeters and more, or with gestation during 22 weeks or more). - Données concernant les nouveau-nés de 500 grammes ou plus (si le poids est inconnu – de 25 centimètres de long ou plus, ou après une grossesse de 22 semaines ou plus).

[39] Excluding Channel Islands and Isle of Man, shown separately, if available. - Non compris les îles Anglo-Normandes et l'île de Man, qui font l'objet de rubriques distinctes, si disponible.

[40] Including Niue, shown separately, which is part of Cook Islands, but because of remoteness is administered separately. - Non compris Nioué, qui fait l'objet d'une rubrique distincte et qui fait partie des îles Cook, mais qui, en raison de son éloignement, est administrée séparément.

[41] Including United States military personnel, their dependants and contract employees. - Y compris les militaires des Etats-Unis, les membres de leur famille les accompagnant et les agents contractuels des Etats-Unis.

Table 16

Table 16 presents infant deaths and infant mortality rates by age and sex for latest available year.

Description of variables. Age is defined as hours, days and months of life completed, based on the difference between the hour, day, month and year of birth and the hour, day, month and year of death. The age classification used in this table has been expanded from previous years and is now as follows: Main categories are "under 1 day", "1-6 days", "7-27 days" and "28days – 11 months". Additional subcategories are shown within "7-27 days" and "28 days to 11 months" wherever available.

Rate computation: Infant mortality rates are the annual number of deaths of infants under one year of age per 1 000 live births (as shown in table 9) in the same year.

Infant mortality rates by age and sex are the annual number of infant deaths that occurred in a specific age-sex group per 1 000 live births in the corresponding sex group (as shown in table 9). These rates have been calculated by the Statistics Division of the United Nations. The denominator for all these rates, regardless of age of infant at death, is the number of live births by sex.

Infant deaths of unknown age are included only in the rate for under one year of age. Deaths under the category of sex "unknown" are included in the rate for the total and, hence, these rates, shown in the first column of the table, should agree with the infant mortality rates shown in table 15. Discrepancies are explained in footnotes.

Rates presented in this table have been limited to those for countries or areas having at least a total of 1 000 deaths in a given year. Moreover, rates specific for individual sub-categories based on 30 or fewer infant deaths are identified by the symbol (♦).

Reliability of data: Data from civil registers of infant deaths which are reported as incomplete (less than 90 percent completeness) or of unknown completeness are considered unreliable and are set in italics rather than in roman type. Rates on these data are not computed. Tables 9 and 15 and the technical notes for these tables provide more detailed information on the completeness of infant death registration. For more information about the quality of vital statistics data in general, and the information available on the basis of the completeness of estimates in particular, see section 4.2 of the Technical Notes.

Limitations: Statistics on infant deaths by age and sex are subject to the same qualifications as have been set forth for vital statistics in general and death statistics in particular as discussed in section 4 of the Technical Notes.

The reliability of the data, an indication of which is described above, is an important factor in considering the limitations. In addition, some infant deaths are tabulated by date of registration and not by date of occurrence; these have been indicated by a plus sign (+). Whenever the lag between the date of occurrence and date of registration is prolonged and, therefore, a large proportion of the infant-death registrations are delayed, infant-death statistics for any given year may be seriously affected.

Another factor that limits international comparability is the practice of some countries or areas of not including in infant-death statistics infants who were born alive but died before the registration of the birth or within the first 24 hours of life, thus underestimating the total number of infant deaths. Statistics of this type are footnoted. In this table in particular, this practice may contribute to the lack of comparability among deaths under one year, under 28 days, under one week and under one day.

Variation in the method of reckoning age at the time of death may also introduce non-comparability. Although it is to some degree a limiting factor throughout the age span, it is an especially important consideration with respect to deaths at ages under one day and under one week (early neonatal deaths) and under 28 days (neonatal deaths). As noted above, the recommended method of reckoning infant age at death is to calculate duration of life in minutes, hours and days, as appropriate. This gives age in completed units of time. In some countries or areas, however, infant age is calculated to the nearest day only, that is, age at death for an infant is the difference between the day, month and year of birth and the day, month and year of death. The result of this procedure is to classify as deaths at age one day, many deaths of infants that occurred before the infants had completed 24 hours of life. The under-one-day class is thus understated while the frequency in the 1-6-day age group is inflated.

A special limitation on comparability of neonatal (under 28 days) deaths is the variation in the classification of infant age used. It is evident from the footnotes that some countries or areas continue to report infant age in calendar, rather than lunar month (4-week or 28-day) periods. This failure to tabulate infant deaths under 4 weeks of age in terms of completed days introduces another source of variation between countries or areas. Deaths classified as occurring under one month usually connote deaths within any one calendar month; these frequencies are not strictly comparable with those referring to deaths within 4 weeks or 27 completed days.

In addition, infant mortality rates by age and sex are subject to the limitations of the data on live births with which they have been calculated. These have been set forth in the technical notes for table 9. These limitations have also been discussed in the technical notes for table 15.

In addition, it should be noted that infant mortality rates by age are affected by the problems related to the practice of excluding infants who were born alive but died before the registration of the birth or within the first 24 hours of life from both infant-death and live-birth statistics and the problems related to the reckoning of infant age at death. These factors, which have been described above, may affect certain age groups more than others. In so far as the numbers of infant deaths for the various age groups are underestimated or overestimated, the corresponding rates for the various age groups will also be underestimated or overestimated. The youngest age groups are more likely to be underestimated than other age groups; the youngest age group (under one day) is likely to be the most seriously affected.

Earlier data: Infant deaths and infant mortality rates by age and sex have been shown in previous issues of the *Demographic Yearbook*. For information on specific years covered, readers should consult the Historical Index.

Tableau 16

Le tableau 16 présente les données les plus récentes dont on dispose sur les décès d'enfants de moins d'un an et les taux de mortalité infantile selon l'âge et le sexe.

Description des variables : l'âge est exprimé en heures, jours et mois révolus et est calculé en retranchant la date de la naissance (heure, jour, mois et année) de celle du décès (heure, jour, mois et année). Les tranches d'âge utilisées dans ce tableau ont été étendues par rapport aux années précédentes et se présentent désormais comme suit : les catégories principales sont « moins d'un jour », « 1-6 jours », « 7-27 jours » et « 28 jours à 11 mois ». Des sous-catégories additionnelles pour « 7-27 jours » et « 28 jours à 11 mois » sont présentées lorsque disponibles.

Calcul des taux : les taux de mortalité infantile selon l'âge et le sexe représentent le nombre annuel de décès d'enfants de moins d'un an selon l'âge et le sexe pour 1 000 naissances vivantes d'enfants du même sexe (fréquences du tableau 9) survenues au cours de l'année considérée.

Les taux de mortalité infantile selon l'âge et le sexe représentent le nombre annuel de décès d'enfants de moins d'un an intervenu dans un groupe d'âge donné parmi la population de sexe masculin ou féminin (fréquences du tableau 9) pour 1 000 naissances vivantes survenues parmi la population du même sexe. Ces taux ont été calculés par la Division de statistique de l'ONU. Le dénominateur de tous ces taux, quel que soit l'âge de l'enfant au moment du décès, est le nombre de naissances vivantes selon le sexe.

Il n'est tenu compte des décès d'enfants d'âge « inconnu » que pour le calcul du taux relatif à l'ensemble des décès de moins d'un an. Étant donné que les décès d'enfants de sexe inconnu sont compris dans le numérateur des taux concernant le total qui figurent dans la deuxième colonne du tableau 16, les chiffres obtenus devraient concorder avec les taux de mortalité infantile du tableau 15. Les divergences sont expliquées en note.

Les taux présentés dans le tableau 16 ne concernent que les pays ou zones où l'on a enregistré un total d'au moins 1 000 décès au cours d'une année donnée. Les taux relatifs à des sous-catégories qui sont fondées sur un nombre égal ou inférieur à 30 décès d'enfants âgés de moins d'un an sont signalés par le signe '♦'.

Fiabilité des données : les données relatives aux décès d'enfants de moins d'un an provenant de registres de l'état civil qui sont déclarées incomplètes (degré de complétude inférieur à 90 p.100) ou dont le degré de complétude n'est pas connu sont jugées douteuses et apparaissent en italique et non en caractères romains. Les taux à partir de ces données n'ont pas été calculés. Les tableaux 9 et 15 et les notes techniques se rapportant à ces tableaux comportent des renseignements plus détaillés sur le degré de complétude de l'enregistrement des décès d'enfants de moins d'un an. Pour plus de précisions sur la qualité des données reposant sur les statistiques de l'état civil en général et les estimations de complétude en particulier, voir la section 4.2 des Notes techniques.

Insuffisance des données : les statistiques des décès d'enfants de moins d'un an selon l'âge et le sexe appellent toutes les réserves qui ont été formulées à propos des statistiques de l'état civil en général et des statistiques concernant les décès en particulier (voir la section 4 des Notes techniques).

La fiabilité des données, au sujet de laquelle des indications ont été fournies plus haut, est un facteur important. Il faut également tenir compte du fait que, dans certains cas, les données relatives aux décès d'enfants de moins d'un an sont exploitées selon la date de l'enregistrement et non la date de l'événement ; ces cas ont été signalés par le signe '+'. Chaque fois que le décalage entre l'événement et son enregistrement est grand et qu'une forte proportion des décès d'enfants de moins d'un an fait l'objet d'un enregistrement tardif, les statistiques des décès d'enfants de moins d'un an pour une année donnée peuvent être considérablement faussées.

Un autre facteur qui nuit à la comparabilité internationale est la pratique de certains pays ou zones qui consiste à ne pas inclure dans les statistiques des décès d'enfants de moins d'un an les enfants nés vivants mais décédés soit avant l'enregistrement de leur naissance, soit dans les 24 heures qui ont suivi la naissance, pratique qui conduit à sous-estimer le nombre total de décès d'enfants de moins d'un an. Quand pareil facteur a joué, cela a été signalé en note. Dans le tableau 16 en particulier, ce système peut limiter la comparabilité des données concernant les décès d'enfants de moins d'un an, de moins de 28 jours, de moins d'une semaine et de moins d'un jour.

Le manque d'uniformité des méthodes suivies pour calculer l'âge au moment du décès nuit également à la comparabilité des données. Ce facteur influe dans une certaine mesure sur les données relatives à la mortalité à tous les âges, mais il a des répercussions particulièrement marquées sur les statistiques des décès de moins d'un jour et de moins d'une semaine (mortalité néo-natale précoce) et de moins de 28 jours (mortalité néo-natale). Comme on l'a dit, l'âge d'un enfant de moins d'un an à son décès est calculé, selon la méthode recommandée, en évaluant la durée de vie en minutes, heures et jours, selon le cas. L'âge est ainsi exprimé en unités de temps révolues. Toutefois, dans certains pays ou zones, l'âge de ces enfants est ramené au jour le plus proche en retranchant la date de la naissance (jour, mois et année) de celle du décès (jour, mois et année). Il s'ensuit que de nombreux décès survenus dans les vingt-quatre heures qui suivent la naissance sont classés comme décès d'un jour. Dans ces conditions, les données concernant les décès de moins d'un jour sont entachées d'une erreur par défaut et celles qui se rapportent aux décès de 1 à 6 jours d'une erreur par excès.

La comparabilité des données relatives à la mortalité néo-natale (moins de 28 jours) est influencée par un facteur spécial : l'hétérogénéité de la classification par âge utilisée pour les enfants de moins d'un an. Les notes figurant à la fin des tableaux montrent que, dans un certain nombre de pays ou zones, on continue d'utiliser le mois civil au lieu du mois lunaire (4 semaines ou 28 jours).

Lorsque les données relatives aux décès de moins de 4 semaines ne sont pas exploitées sur la base de l'âge en jours révolus, il existe une nouvelle cause de non-comparabilité internationale. Les décès de moins d'un mois sont généralement ceux qui se produisent au cours d'un mois civil ; les taux calculés sur la base de ces données ne sont pas strictement comparables à ceux qui sont établis à partir des données concernant les décès survenus dans les 4 semaines ou 27 jours révolus qui suivent la naissance.

Les taux de mortalité infantile selon l'âge et le sexe appellent en outre toutes les réserves qui ont été formulées à propos des statistiques des naissances vivantes qui ont servi à leur calcul (voir à ce sujet les notes techniques relatives au tableau 9). Ces insuffisances ont également été examinées dans les notes techniques relatives au tableau 15.

Il convient de signaler aussi que les taux de mortalité infantile selon l'âge peuvent être gravement faussés par la pratique qui consiste à ne pas classer dans les naissances vivantes et ensuite dans les décès d'enfants de moins d'un an les enfants nés vivants mais décédés soit avant l'enregistrement de leur naissance, soit dans les 24 heures qui ont suivi la naissance, et par les problèmes que pose le calcul de l'âge de l'enfant au moment du décès. Ces facteurs, qui ont été décrits plus haut, peuvent fausser les statistiques concernant certains groupes d'âge plus que d'autres. Si le nombre des décès d'enfants de moins d'un an pour chaque groupe d'âge est sous-estimé ou surestimé, les taux correspondants pour chacun de ces groupes d'âge seront eux aussi sous-estimés ou surestimés. Les risques de sous-estimation sont plus grands pour les groupes les plus jeunes ; c'est pour le groupe d'âge le plus jeune de tous (moins d'un jour) que les données risquent de comporter les plus grosses erreurs.

Données publiées antérieurement : Des statistiques des décès d'enfants de moins d'un an et des taux de mortalité infantile selon l'âge et le sexe ont déjà été présentées dans des éditions antérieures de l'*Annuaire démographique*. Pour plus de précisions concernant les années pour lesquelles ces données ont été publiées, se reporter à l'index.

16. Infant deaths and infant mortality rates by age and sex: latest available year, 1997 - 2006
Décès d'enfants de moins d'un an et taux de mortalité infantile selon l'âge et le sexe: dernière année disponible, 1997 - 2006

Continent, country or area, year and age (in days) Continent, pays ou zone, année et âge (en jours)	Number - Nombre			Rate - Taux		
	Both sexes Les deux sexes	Male Masculin	Female Féminin	Both sexes Les deux sexes	Male Masculin	Female Féminin
AFRICA - AFRIQUE						
Egypt - Égypte						
2006 (C)						
Total	35 952	19 624	16 328	19.4	20.6	18.1
Less than 1 day - Moins de 1 jour[1]	-	-	-	-	-	-
1 - 6 days - 1 - 6 jours	8 649	5 192	3 457	4.7	5.5	3.8
7 - 27 days - 7 - 27 jours	8 716	4 994	3 722	4.7	5.3	4.1
7 - 13 days - 7 - 13 jours	4 117	2 405	1 712	2.2	2.5	1.9
14 - 20 days - 14 - 20 jours	2 823	1 613	1 210	1.5	1.7	1.3
21 - 27 days - 21 - 27 jours	1 776	976	800	1.0	1.0	0.9
28 days - 11 months - 28 jours - 11 mois	18 587	9 438	9 149	10.0	9.9	10.1
28 days - 1 month - 28 jours - 1 mois	4 123	2 179	1 944	2.2	2.3	2.2
2 months - 2 mois	2 876	1 470	1 406	1.6	1.5	1.6
3 months - 3 mois	2 294	1 140	1 154	1.2	1.2	1.3
4 months - 4 mois	2 076	996	1 080	1.1	1.0	1.2
5 months - 5 mois	1 501	763	738	0.8	0.8	0.8
6 months - 6 mois	1 830	931	899	1.0	1.0	1.0
7 months - 7 mois	1 044	546	498	0.6	0.6	0.6
8 months - 8 mois	874	436	438	0.5	0.5	0.5
9 months - 9 mois	859	425	434	0.5	0.4	0.5
10 months - 10 mois	622	313	309	0.3	0.3	0.3
11 months - 11 mois	488	239	249	0.3	0.3	0.3
Mauritius - Maurice						
2006 (+C)						
Total	249	138	111	...	...	...
Less than 1 day - Moins de 1 jour	35	19	16	...	...	...
1 - 6 days - 1 - 6 jours	90	45	45	...	...	...
7 - 27 days - 7 - 27 jours	61	39	22	...	...	...
7 - 13 days - 7 - 13 jours	35	20	15	...	...	...
14 - 20 days - 14 - 20 jours	11	8	3	...	...	...
21 - 27 days - 21 - 27 jours	15	11	4	...	...	...
28 days - 11 months - 28 jours - 11 mois	63	35	28	...	...	...
28 days - 1 month - 28 jours - 1 mois	20	12	8	...	...	...
2 months - 2 mois	8	3	5	...	...	...
3 months - 3 mois	10	6	4	...	...	...
4 months - 4 mois	3	2	1	...	...	...
5 months - 5 mois	5	3	2	...	...	...
6 months - 6 mois	4	3	1	...	...	...
7 months - 7 mois	3	2	1	...	...	...
8 months - 8 mois	4	1	3	...	...	...
9 months - 9 mois	2	1	1	...	...	...
10 months - 10 mois	1		1	...	...	...
11 months - 11 mois	3	2	1	...	...	...
Unknown - Inconnu	-	-	-	...	...	...
Morocco - Maroc						
2001 (U)						
Total	7 379	4 022	3 357	...	...	...
Less than 28 days - Moins de 28 jours	1 638	912	726	...	...	...
28 days - 11 months - 28 jours - 11 mois	5 729	3 103	2 626	...	...	...
28 days - 1 month - 28 jours - 1 mois	1 331	733	598	...	...	...
2 months - 2 mois	941	556	385	...	...	...
3 months - 3 mois	753	421	332	...	...	...
4 months - 4 mois	610	320	290	...	...	...
5 months - 5 mois	512	274	238	...	...	...
6 months - 6 mois	405	212	193	...	...	...
7 months - 7 mois	339	174	165	...	...	...
8 months - 8 mois	321	156	165	...	...	...
9 months - 9 mois	234	118	116	...	...	...
10 months - 10 mois	186	94	92	...	...	...
11 months - 11 mois	97	45	52	...	...	...
Unknown - Inconnu	12	7	5	...	...	...
Réunion						
2003* (C)						
Total	107	59	48	...	...	...
Less than 1 day - Moins de 1 jour	43	26	17	...	...	...
1 - 6 days - 1 - 6 jours	19	12	7	...	...	...
7 - 27 days - 7 - 27 jours	16	7	9	...	...	...
7 - 13 days - 7 - 13 jours	2	1	1	...	...	...
14 - 20 days - 14 - 20 jours	6	1	5	...	...	...

16. Infant deaths and infant mortality rates by age and sex: latest available year, 1997 - 2006
Décès d'enfants de moins d'un an et taux de mortalité infantile selon l'âge et le sexe: dernière année disponible, 1997 - 2006 (continued - suite)

Continent, country or area, year and age (in days) Continent, pays ou zone, année et âge (en jours)	Number - Nombre			Rate - Taux		
	Both sexes Les deux sexes	Male Masculin	Female Féminin	Both sexes Les deux sexes	Male Masculin	Female Féminin
AFRICA - AFRIQUE						
Réunion						
2003* (C)						
21 - 27 days - 21 - 27 jours	8	5	3	...	...	...
28 days - 11 months - 28 jours - 11 mois	29	14	15	...	...	...
28 days - 1 month - 28 jours - 1 mois	-	-	-	...	...	...
2 months - 2 mois	6	2	4	...	...	...
3 months - 3 mois	6	5	1	...	...	...
4 months - 4 mois	3	2	1	...	...	...
5 months - 5 mois	3	1	2	...	...	...
6 months - 6 mois	3	2	1	...	...	...
7 months - 7 mois	1	-	1	...	...	...
8 months - 8 mois	-	-	-	...	...	...
9 months - 9 mois	4	2	2	...	...	...
10 months - 10 mois	-	-	-	...	...	...
11 months - 11 mois	3	-	3	...	...	...
Unknown - Inconnu	-	-	-	...	...	...
Saint Helena ex. dep. - Sainte-Hélène sans dép.						
2005 (C)						
Total	1	1		...	...	...
Less than 1 day - Moins de 1 jour	-	-		...	...	...
1 - 6 days - 1 - 6 jours	1	1	-	...	...	...
7 - 27 days - 7 - 27 jours	-	-		...	...	...
28 days - 11 months - 28 jours - 11 mois	-	-		...	...	...
Unknown - Inconnu	-	-		...	...	...
Seychelles						
2006 (+C)						
Total	14	5	9	...	...	...
Less than 1 day - Moins de 1 jour	5	1	4	...	...	...
1 - 6 days - 1 - 6 jours	2	1	1	...	...	...
7 - 27 days - 7 - 27 jours	2	-	2	...	...	...
7 - 13 days - 7 - 13 jours	1	-	1	...	...	...
14 - 20 days - 14 - 20 jours	-	-	-	...	...	...
21 - 27 days - 21 - 27 jours	1	-	1	...	...	...
28 days - 11 months - 28 jours - 11 mois	5	3	2	...	...	...
28 days - 1 month - 28 jours - 1 mois	1	1	-	...	...	...
2 months - 2 mois	-	-	-	...	...	...
3 months - 3 mois	-	-	-	...	...	...
4 months - 4 mois	1	-	1	...	...	...
5 months - 5 mois	2	2	-	...	...	...
6 months - 6 mois	1	-	1	...	...	...
7 months - 7 mois	-	-	-	...	...	...
8 months - 8 mois	-	-	-	...	...	...
9 months - 9 mois	-	-	-	...	...	...
10 months - 10 mois	-	-	-	...	...	...
11 months - 11 mois	-	-	-	...	...	...
Unknown - Inconnu	-	-	-	...	...	...
Tunisia - Tunisie						
1998 (U)						
Total	3 098	1 775	1 323	...	...	...
Less than 1 day - Moins de 1 jour	464	281	183	...	...	...
1 - 6 days - 1 - 6 jours	847	485	362	...	...	...
7 - 27 days - 7 - 27 jours	559	332	227	...	...	...
7 - 13 days - 7 - 13 jours	282	160	122	...	...	...
14 - 20 days - 14 - 20 jours	173	114	59	...	...	...
21 - 27 days - 21 - 27 jours	104	58	46	...	...	...
28 days - 11 months - 28 jours - 11 mois	1 227	677	550	...	...	...
28 days - 1 month - 28 jours - 1 mois	292	165	127	...	...	...
2 months - 2 mois	220	124	96	...	...	...
3 months - 3 mois	168	92	76	...	...	...
4 months - 4 mois	132	72	60	...	...	...
5 months - 5 mois	89	54	35	...	...	...
6 months - 6 mois	75	40	35	...	...	...
7 months - 7 mois	51	33	18	...	...	...
8 months - 8 mois	64	35	29	...	...	...
9 months - 9 mois	58	28	30	...	...	...
10 months - 10 mois	40	16	24	...	...	...
11 months - 11 mois	38	18	20	...	...	...
Unknown - Inconnu	1	-	1	...	...	...

16. Infant deaths and infant mortality rates by age and sex: latest available year, 1997 - 2006
Décès d'enfants de moins d'un an et taux de mortalité infantile selon l'âge et le sexe: dernière année disponible, 1997 - 2006 (continued - suite)

Continent, country or area, year and age (in days) / Continent, pays ou zone, année et âge (en jours)	Number - Nombre			Rate - Taux		
	Both sexes Les deux sexes	Male Masculin	Female Féminin	Both sexes Les deux sexes	Male Masculin	Female Féminin
AMERICA, NORTH - AMÉRIQUE DU NORD						
Bahamas						
2001 (C)						
Total..........	37	23	14	...	...	...
Less than 7 days - Moins de 7 jours................	8	7	1	...	...	...
7 - 27 days - 7 - 27 jours................	15	8	7	...	...	...
28 days - 11 months - 28 jours - 11 mois..........	14	8	6	...	...	...
28 days - 2 months - 28 jours - 2 mois..........	7	5	2	...	...	...
3 months - 3 mois..........	4	2	2	...	...	...
4 - 8 month - 4 - 8 mois..........	3	1	2	...	...	...
9 - 11 months - 9 - 11 mois..........	-	-	-	...	...	...
Canada[2]						
2005 (C)						
Total..........	1 863	1 030	833	5.4	5.9	5.0
Less than 1 day - Moins de 1 jour..................	916	500	416	2.7	2.9	2.5
1 - 6 days - 1 - 6 jours..........	242	135	107	0.7	0.8	0.6
7 - 27 days - 7 - 27 jours..........	252	132	120	0.7	0.8	0.7
7 - 13 days - 7 - 13 jours..........	129	73	56	0.4	0.4	0.3
14 - 20 days - 14 - 20 jours..........	74	36	38	0.2	0.2	0.2
21 - 27 days - 21 - 27 jours..........	49	23	26	0.1	♦0.1	♦0.2
28 days - 11 months - 28 jours - 11 mois..........	453	263	190	1.3	1.5	1.1
28 days - 1 month - 28 jours - 1 mois..........	129	76	53	0.4	0.4	0.3
2 months - 2 mois..........	75	41	34	0.2	0.2	0.2
3 months - 3 mois..........	47	31	16	0.1	0.2	♦0.1
4 months - 4 mois..........	52	31	21	0.2	0.2	♦0.1
5 months - 5 mois..........	30	17	13	0.1	♦0.1	♦0.1
6 months - 6 mois..........	29	14	15	♦0.1	♦0.1	♦0.1
7 months - 7 mois..........	19	12	7	♦0.1	♦0.1	-
8 months - 8 mois..........	20	13	7	♦0.1	♦0.1	-
9 months - 9 mois..........	21	10	11	♦0.1	♦0.1	♦0.1
10 months - 10 mois..........	14	7	7	-	-	-
11 months - 11 mois..........	17	11	6	-	♦0.1	-
Unknown - Inconnu..........	-	-	-	-	-	-
Cayman Islands - Îles Caïmanes						
2006 (C)						
Total..........	7	3	4	...	...	...
Less than 1 day - Moins de 1 jour..........	5	1	4	...	...	...
1 - 6 days - 1 - 6 jours..........	2	2	-	...	...	...
7 - 27 days - 7 - 27 jours..........	-	-	-	...	...	...
28 days - 11 months - 28 jours - 11 mois..........	-	-	-	...	...	...
Costa Rica						
2005 (C)						
Total..........	700	383	317	...	...	...
Less than 1 day - Moins de 1 jour..........	207	118	89	...	...	...
1 - 6 days - 1 - 6 jours..........	190	103	87	...	...	...
7 - 27 days - 7 - 27 jours..........	111	63	48	...	...	...
7 - 13 days - 7 - 13 jours..........	68	41	27	...	...	...
14 - 20 days - 14 - 20 jours..........	27	16	11	...	...	...
21 - 27 days - 21 - 27 jours..........	16	6	10	...	...	...
28 days - 11 months - 28 jours - 11 mois..........	192	99	93	...	...	...
28 days - 1 month - 28 jours - 1 mois..........	47	24	23	...	...	...
2 months - 2 mois..........	36	21	15	...	...	...
3 months - 3 mois..........	20	6	14	...	...	...
4 months - 4 mois..........	17	11	6	...	...	...
5 months - 5 mois..........	11	7	4	...	...	...
6 months - 6 mois..........	11	6	5	...	...	...
7 months - 7 mois..........	11	6	5	...	...	...
8 months - 8 mois..........	11	3	8	...	...	...
9 months - 9 mois..........	10	5	5	...	...	...
10 months - 10 mois..........	8	5	3	...	...	...
11 months - 11 mois..........	10	5	5	...	...	...
Cuba						
2005 (C)						
Total..........	746	412	334	...	...	...
Less than 1 day - Moins de 1 jour..........	75	35	40	...	...	...
1 - 6 days - 1 - 6 jours..........	183	107	76	...	...	...
7 - 27 days - 7 - 27 jours..........	151	78	73	...	...	...
7 - 13 days - 7 - 13 jours..........	85	47	38	...	...	...
14 - 20 days - 14 - 20 jours..........	41	20	21	...	...	...

16. Infant deaths and infant mortality rates by age and sex: latest available year, 1997 - 2006
Décès d'enfants de moins d'un an et taux de mortalité infantile selon l'âge et le sexe: dernière année disponible, 1997 - 2006 (continued - suite)

Continent, country or area, year and age (in days) / Continent, pays ou zone, année et âge (en jours)	Number - Nombre			Rate - Taux		
	Both sexes Les deux sexes	Male Masculin	Female Féminin	Both sexes Les deux sexes	Male Masculin	Female Féminin
AMERICA, NORTH - AMÉRIQUE DU NORD						
Cuba						
2005 (C)						
21 - 27 days - 21 - 27 jours	25	11	14	...	...	...
28 days - 11 months - 28 jours - 11 mois	337	192	145	...	...	...
28 days - 1 month - 28 jours - 1 mois	90	48	42	...	...	...
2 months - 2 mois	63	43	20	...	...	...
3 months - 3 mois	48	25	23	...	...	...
4 months - 4 mois	31	19	12	...	...	...
5 months - 5 mois	27	18	9	...	...	...
6 months - 6 mois	14	8	6	...	...	...
7 months - 7 mois	14	6	8	...	...	...
8 months - 8 mois	12	7	5	...	...	...
9 months - 9 mois	16	7	9	...	...	...
10 months - 10 mois	11	6	5	...	...	...
11 months - 11 mois	11	5	6	...	...	...
El Salvador						
2006 (C)						
Total	1 013	571	442	9.5	10.2	8.7
Less than 1 day - Moins de 1 jour	130	68	62	1.2	1.2	1.2
1 - 6 days - 1 - 6 jours	151	87	64	1.4	1.6	1.3
7 - 27 days - 7 - 27 jours	154	93	61	1.4	1.7	1.2
7 - 13 days - 7 - 13 jours	69	43	26	0.6	0.8	♦0.5
14 - 20 days - 14 - 20 jours	47	29	18	0.4	♦0.5	♦0.4
21 - 27 days - 21 - 27 jours	38	21	17	0.4	♦0.4	♦0.3
28 days - 11 months - 28 jours - 11 mois	578	323	255	5.4	5.8	5.0
28 days - 1 month - 28 jours - 1 mois	134	73	61	1.3	1.3	1.2
2 months - 2 mois	86	52	34	0.8	0.9	0.7
3 months - 3 mois	55	30	25	0.5	0.5	♦0.5
4 months - 4 mois	59	34	25	0.6	0.6	♦0.5
5 months - 5 mois	42	23	19	0.4	♦0.4	♦0.4
6 months - 6 mois	44	28	16	0.4	♦0.5	♦0.3
7 months - 7 mois	38	18	20	0.4	♦0.3	♦0.4
8 months - 8 mois	39	22	17	0.4	♦0.4	♦0.3
9 months - 9 mois	43	30	13	0.4	0.5	♦0.3
10 months - 10 mois	17	6	11	♦0.2	♦0.1	♦0.2
11 months - 11 mois	21	7	14	♦0.2	♦0.1	♦0.3
Greenland - Groenland						
2006 (C)						
Total	13	7	6	...	...	...
Less than 1 day - Moins de 1 jour	8	5	3	...	...	...
1 - 6 days - 1 - 6 jours	-	-	-	...	...	...
7 - 27 days - 7 - 27 jours	-	-	-	...	...	...
28 days - 11 months - 28 jours - 11 mois	5	2	3	...	...	...
28 days - 1 month - 28 jours - 1 mois	5	2	3	...	...	...
2 - 11 months - 2 - 11 mois	-	-	-	...	...	...
Guadeloupe[3]						
2003 (C)						
Total	56	34	22	...	...	...
Less than 1 day - Moins de 1 jour	13	5	8	...	...	...
1 - 6 days - 1 - 6 jours	8	4	4	...	...	...
7 - 27 days - 7 - 27 jours	19	12	7	...	...	...
7 - 13 days - 7 - 13 jours	5	3	2	...	...	...
14 - 20 days - 14 - 20 jours	10	5	5	...	...	...
21 - 27 days - 21 - 27 jours	4	4	-	...	...	...
28 days - 11 months - 28 jours - 11 mois	16	13	3	...	...	...
28 days - 1 month - 28 jours - 1 mois	7	6	1	...	...	...
2 months - 2 mois	4	2	2	...	...	...
3 months - 3 mois	3	3	-	...	...	...
4 months - 4 mois	1	1	-	...	...	...
5 months - 5 mois	-	-	-	...	...	...
6 months - 6 mois	1	1	-	...	...	...
7 months - 7 mois	-	-	-	...	...	...
8 months - 8 mois	-	-	-	...	...	...
9 months - 9 mois	-	-	-	...	...	...
10 months - 10 mois	-	-	-	...	...	...
11 months - 11 mois	-	-	-	...	...	...
Unknown - Inconnu	-	-	-	...	...	...

16. Infant deaths and infant mortality rates by age and sex: latest available year, 1997 - 2006
Décès d'enfants de moins d'un an et taux de mortalité infantile selon l'âge et le sexe: dernière année disponible, 1997 - 2006 (continued - suite)

Continent, country or area, year and age (in days) Continent, pays ou zone, année el âge (en jours)	Number - Nombre			Rate - Taux		
	Both sexes Les deux sexes	Male Masculin	Female Féminin	Both sexes Les deux sexes	Male Masculin	Female Féminin

AMERICA, NORTH - AMÉRIQUE DU NORD

Guatemala
2006 (C)

Total	9 042	5 012	4 030	24.5	26.8	22.2
Less than 1 day - Moins de 1 jour	842	478	364	2.3	2.6	2.0
1 - 6 days - 1 - 6 jours	2 040	1 162	878	5.5	6.2	4.8
7 - 27 days - 7 - 27 jours	1 209	681	528	3.3	3.6	2.9
7 - 13 days - 7 - 13 jours	550	318	232	1.5	1.7	1.3
14 - 20 days - 14 - 20 jours	359	185	174	1.0	1.0	1.0
21 - 27 days - 21 - 27 jours	300	178	122	0.8	1.0	0.7
28 days - 11 months - 28 jours - 11 mois	4 951	2 691	2 260	13.4	14.4	12.5
28 days - 1 month - 28 jours - 1 mois	1 017	564	453	2.8	3.0	2.5
2 months - 2 mois	773	402	371	2.1	2.1	2.0
3 months - 3 mois	527	274	253	1.4	1.5	1.4
4 months - 4 mois	438	248	190	1.2	1.3	1.0
5 months - 5 mois	323	162	161	0.9	0.9	0.9
6 months - 6 mois	367	211	156	1.0	1.1	0.9
7 months - 7 mois	332	171	161	0.9	0.9	0.9
8 months - 8 mois	297	166	131	0.8	0.9	0.7
9 months - 9 mois	296	170	126	0.8	0.9	0.7
10 months - 10 mois	282	152	130	0.8	0.8	0.7
11 months - 11 mois	299	171	128	0.8	0.9	0.7

Martinique
2003 (C)

Total	33	14	19	...	...	...
Less than 1 day - Moins de 1 jour	9	4	5	...	...	...
1 - 6 days - 1 - 6 jours	11	5	6	...	...	...
7 - 27 days - 7 - 27 jours	4	1	3	...	...	...
7 - 13 days - 7 - 13 jours	4	1	3	...	...	...
14 - 20 days - 14 - 20 jours	-	-	-	...	...	...
21 - 27 days - 21 - 27 jours	-	-	-	...	...	...
28 days - 11 months - 28 jours - 11 mois	9	4	5	...	...	...
28 days - 1 month - 28 jours - 1 mois	3	1	2	...	...	...
2 months - 2 mois	1	1	-	...	...	...
3 months - 3 mois	1	-	1	...	...	...
4 months - 4 mois	-	-	-	...	...	...
5 months - 5 mois	-	-	-	...	...	...
6 months - 6 mois	1	-	1	...	...	...
7 months - 7 mois	2	1	1	...	...	...
8 months - 8 mois	-	-	-	...	...	...
9 months - 9 mois	-	-	-	...	...	...
10 months - 10 mois	1	1	-	...	...	...
11 months - 11 mois	-	-	-	...	...	...
Unknown - Inconnu	-	-	-	...	...	...

Mexico - Mexique[4]
2006 (+U)

Total	30 890	17 369	13 442	...	...	...
Less than 1 day - Moins de 1 jour	6 608	3 647	2 909	...	...	...
1 - 6 days - 1 - 6 jours	7 468	4 388	3 068	...	...	...
7 - 27 days - 7 - 27 jours	5 253	2 937	2 310	...	...	...
7 - 13 days - 7 - 13 jours	2 706	1 537	1 169	...	...	...
14 - 20 days - 14 - 20 jours	1 518	827	688	...	...	...
21 - 27 days - 21 - 27 jours	1 029	573	453	...	...	...
28 days - 11 months - 28 jours - 11 mois	11 560	6 396	5 155	...	...	...
28 days - 1 month - 28 jours - 1 mois	3 141	1 783	1 351	...	...	...
2 months - 2 mois	2 133	1 193	940	...	...	...
3 months - 3 mois	1 494	847	647	...	...	...
4 months - 4 mois	1 073	595	477	...	...	...
5 months - 5 mois	804	433	370	...	...	...
6 months - 6 mois	727	383	344	...	...	...
7 months - 7 mois	537	282	255	...	...	...
8 months - 8 mois	509	264	245	...	...	...
9 months - 9 mois	414	219	195	...	...	...
10 months - 10 mois	353	180	173	...	...	...
11 months - 11 mois	375	217	158	...	...	...
Unknown - Inconnu	1	1	-	...	...	...

16. Infant deaths and infant mortality rates by age and sex: latest available year, 1997 - 2006
Décès d'enfants de moins d'un an et taux de mortalité infantile selon l'âge et le sexe: dernière année disponible, 1997 - 2006 (continued - suite)

Continent, country or area, year and age (in days) / Continent, pays ou zone, année et âge (en jours)	Number - Nombre			Rate - Taux		
	Both sexes Les deux sexes	Male Masculin	Female Féminin	Both sexes Les deux sexes	Male Masculin	Female Féminin
AMERICA, NORTH - AMÉRIQUE DU NORD						
Netherlands Antilles - Antilles néerlandaises						
2004 (C)						
Total...............	20	13	7	...	...	...
Less than 1 day - Moins de 1 jour	4	3	1	...	...	...
1 - 6 days - 1 - 6 jours............	5	2	3	...	...	...
7 - 27 days - 7 - 27 jours	3	2	1	...	...	...
7 - 13 days - 7 - 13 jours	-	-	-	...	...	...
14 - 20 days - 14 - 20 jours............	2	1	1	...	...	...
21 - 27 days - 21 - 27 jours............	1	1	-	...	...	...
28 days - 11 months - 28 jours - 11 mois............	8	6	2	...	...	...
28 days - 1 month - 28 jours - 1 mois............	4	3	1	...	...	...
2 months - 2 mois............	3	3	-	...	...	...
3 months - 3 mois............	-	-	-	...	...	...
4 months - 4 mois............	1	-	1	...	...	...
5 - 11 months - 5 - 11 mois	-	-	-	...	...	...
Nicaragua						
2005 (+U)						
Total...............	1 970	1 125	845	...	...	...
Less than 1 day - Moins de 1 jour	291	159	132	...	...	...
1 - 6 days - 1 - 6 jours............	765	449	316	...	...	...
7 - 27 days - 7 - 27 jours	310	179	131	...	...	...
7 - 13 days - 7 - 13 jours	196	112	84	...	...	...
14 - 20 days - 14 - 20 jours............	69	39	30	...	...	...
21 - 27 days - 21 - 27 jours............	45	28	17	...	...	...
28 days - 11 months - 28 jours - 11 mois............	604	338	266	...	...	...
28 days - 1 month - 28 jours - 1 mois............	125	71	54	...	...	...
2 months - 2 mois............	80	44	36	...	...	...
3 months - 3 mois............	66	37	29	...	...	...
4 months - 4 mois............	58	35	23	...	...	...
5 months - 5 mois............	40	23	17	...	...	...
6 months - 6 mois............	59	35	24	...	...	...
7 months - 7 mois............	41	19	22	...	...	...
8 months - 8 mois............	43	22	21	...	...	...
9 months - 9 mois............	36	24	12	...	...	...
10 months - 10 mois	29	12	17	...	...	...
11 months - 11 mois............	27	16	11	...	...	...
Unknown - Inconnu	-	-	-	...	...	...
Panama						
2006 (U)						
Total...............	971	562	409	...	...	...
Less than 1 day - Moins de 1 jour	145	82	63	...	...	...
1 - 6 days - 1 - 6 jours............	184	115	69	...	...	...
7 - 27 days - 7 - 27 jours	167	91	76	...	...	...
7 - 13 days - 7 - 13 jours	76	44	32	...	...	...
14 - 20 days - 14 - 20 jours............	54	31	23	...	...	...
21 - 27 days - 21 - 27 jours............	37	16	21	...	...	...
28 days - 11 months - 28 jours - 11 mois............	475	274	201	...	...	...
28 days - 1 month - 28 jours - 1 mois............	102	62	40	...	...	...
2 months - 2 mois............	84	52	32	...	...	...
3 months - 3 mois............	55	33	22	...	...	...
4 months - 4 mois............	50	33	17	...	...	...
5 months - 5 mois............	37	19	18	...	...	...
6 months - 6 mois............	37	19	18	...	...	...
7 months - 7 mois............	28	19	9	...	...	...
8 months - 8 mois............	21	10	11	...	...	...
9 months - 9 mois............	20	10	10	...	...	...
10 months - 10 mois	18	5	13	...	...	...
11 months - 11 mois............	23	12	11	...	...	...
Puerto Rico - Porto Rico						
2005 (C)						
Total...............	472	252	220	...	...	...
Less than 1 day - Moins de 1 jour	100	46	54	...	...	...
1 - 6 days - 1 - 6 jours	144	87	57	...	...	...
7 - 27 days - 7 - 27 jours	93	43	50	...	...	...
7 - 13 days - 7 - 13 jours	48	23	25	...	...	...
14 - 20 days - 14 - 20 jours............	25	14	11	...	...	...
21 - 27 days - 21 - 27 jours............	20	6	14	...	...	...

16. Infant deaths and infant mortality rates by age and sex: latest available year, 1997 - 2006
Décès d'enfants de moins d'un an et taux de mortalité infantile selon l'âge et le sexe: dernière année disponible, 1997 - 2006 (continued - suite)

Continent, country or area, year and age (in days) / Continent, pays ou zone, année et âge (en jours)	Number - Nombre			Rate - Taux		
	Both sexes Les deux sexes	Male Masculin	Female Féminin	Both sexes Les deux sexes	Male Masculin	Female Féminin
AMERICA, NORTH - AMÉRIQUE DU NORD						
Puerto Rico - Porto Rico						
2005 (C)						
28 days - 11 months - 28 jours - 11 mois	134	75	59	...	...	...
28 days - 1 month - 28 jours - 1 mois	44	23	21	...	...	...
2 months - 2 mois	23	13	10	...	...	...
3 months - 3 mois	18	8	10	...	...	...
4 months - 4 mois	16	8	8	...	...	...
5 months - 5 mois	18	14	4	...	...	...
6 months - 6 mois	3	1	2	...	...	...
7 months - 7 mois	2	2	-	...	...	...
8 months - 8 mois	5	2	3	...	...	...
9 months - 9 mois	4	3	1	...	...	...
10 months - 10 mois	-	-	-	...	...	...
11 months - 11 mois	1	1	-	...	...	...
Unknown - Inconnu	1	1	-	...	...	...
Saint Lucia - Sainte-Lucie						
2002 (C)						
Total	36	17	19	...	...	...
Less than 1 day - Moins de 1 jour	11	5	6	...	...	...
1 - 6 days - 1 - 6 jours	16	6	10	...	...	...
7 - 27 days - 7 - 27 jours	2	1	1	...	...	...
7 - 20 days - 7 - 20 jours	-	-	-	...	...	...
21 - 27 days - 21 - 27 jours	2	1	1	...	...	...
28 days - 11 months - 28 jours - 11 mois	7	5	2	...	...	...
28 days - 1 month - 28 jours - 1 mois	-	-	-	...	...	...
2 months - 2 mois	1	1	-	...	...	...
3 months - 3 mois	1	1	-	...	...	...
4 months - 4 mois	1	1	-	...	...	...
5 months - 5 mois	1	1	-	...	...	...
6 months - 6 mois	-	-	-	...	...	...
7 months - 7 mois	-	-	-	...	...	...
8 months - 8 mois	2	1	1	...	...	...
9 months - 9 mois	-	-	-	...	...	...
10 months - 10 mois	1	-	1	...	...	...
11 months - 11 mois	-	-	-	...	...	...
Unknown - Inconnu	-	-	-	...	...	...
Saint Vincent and the Grenadines - Saint Vincent-et-les Grenadines						
2005 (+C)						
Total	29	17	12	...	...	...
Less than 1 day - Moins de 1 jour	6	3	3	...	...	...
1 - 6 days - 1 - 6 jours	11	6	5	...	...	...
7 - 27 days - 7 - 27 jours	3	2	1	...	...	...
28 days - 11 months - 28 jours - 11 mois	9	6	3	...	...	...
28 days - 1 month - 28 jours - 1 mois	-	-	-	...	...	...
2 - 11 months - 2 - 11 mois	9	6	3	...	...	...
Trinidad and Tobago - Trinité-et-Tobago						
2002 (C)						
Total	412	247	165	...	...	...
Less than 1 day - Moins de 1 jour	91	51	40	...	...	...
1 - 6 days - 1 - 6 jours	148	92	56	...	...	...
7 - 27 days - 7 - 27 jours	105	71	34	...	...	...
7 - 13 days - 7 - 13 jours	66	44	22	...	...	...
14 - 20 days - 14 - 20 jours	21	16	5	...	...	...
21 - 27 days - 21 - 27 jours	18	11	7	...	...	...
28 days - 11 months - 28 jours - 11 mois	68	33	35	...	...	...
28 days - 1 month - 28 jours - 1 mois	25	12	13	...	...	...
2 - 3 months - 2 - 3 mois	4	2	2	...	...	...
4 - 6 months - 4 - 6 mois	18	9	9	...	...	...
7 - 9 months - 7 - 9 mois	11	4	7	...	...	...
10 - 11 months - 10 - 11 mois	10	6	4	...	...	...
Unknown - Inconnu	-	-	-	...	...	...
United States - États-Unis						
2003 (C)						
Total	28 025	15 902	12 123	6.9	7.6	6.1
Less than 1 day - Moins de 1 jour	11 469	6 387	5 082	2.8	3.1	2.5
1 - 6 days - 1 - 6 jours	3 664	2 123	1 541	0.9	1.0	0.8
7 - 27 days - 7 - 27 jours	3 760	2 126	1 634	0.9	1.0	0.8
7 - 13 days - 7 - 13 jours	1 650	923	727	0.4	0.4	0.4

16. Infant deaths and infant mortality rates by age and sex: latest available year, 1997 - 2006
Décès d'enfants de moins d'un an et taux de mortalité infantile selon l'âge et le sexe: dernière année disponible, 1997 - 2006 (continued - suite)

Continent, country or area, year and age (in days) / Continent, pays ou zone, année et âge (en jours)	Number - Nombre			Rate - Taux		
	Both sexes Les deux sexes	Male Masculin	Female Féminin	Both sexes Les deux sexes	Male Masculin	Female Féminin
AMERICA, NORTH - AMÉRIQUE DU NORD						
United States - États-Unis						
2003 (C)						
14 - 20 days - 14 - 20 jours	1 203	688	515	0.3	0.3	0.3
21 - 27 days - 21 - 27 jours	907	515	392	0.2	0.2	0.2
28 days - 11 months - 28 jours - 11 mois	9 132	5 266	3 866	2.2	2.5	1.9
28 days - 1 month - 28 jours - 1 mois	2 544	1 437	1 107	0.6	0.7	0.6
2 months - 2 mois	1 747	1 030	717	0.4	0.5	0.4
3 months - 3 mois	1 301	776	525	0.3	0.4	0.3
4 months - 4 mois	901	534	367	0.2	0.3	0.2
5 months - 5 mois	682	389	293	0.2	0.2	0.1
6 months - 6 mois	502	300	202	0.1	0.1	0.1
7 months - 7 mois	366	201	165	0.1	0.1	0.1
8 months - 8 mois	347	192	155	0.1	0.1	0.1
9 months - 9 mois	299	164	135	0.1	0.1	0.1
10 months - 10 mois	232	129	103	0.1	0.1	0.1
11 months - 11 mois	211	114	97	0.1	0.1	-
AMERICA, SOUTH - AMÉRIQUE DU SUD						
Argentina - Argentine						
2006 (C)						
Total	8 986	5 063[5]	3 911[5]	12.9	14.1	11.7
Less than 7 days - Moins de 7 jours	4 312	2 465[5]	1 838[5]	6.2	6,8	5.5
7 - 27 days - 7 - 27 jours	1 591	898[6]	691[5]	2.3	2.5	2.1
28 days - 11 months - 28 jours - 11 mois	3 083	1 700[5]	1 382[5]	4.4	4.7	4.1
Brazil - Brésil[6]						
2006 (U)						
Total	37 698	20 264[5]	16 289[5]	...	...	...
Less than 1 day - Moins de 1 jour	8 904	4 379[5]	3 891[5]	...	...	...
1 - 6 days - 1 - 6 jours	10 264	6 018[5]	4 211[5]	...	...	...
7 - 27 days - 7 - 27 jours	6 001	3 312[5]	2 651[5]	...	...	...
7 - 13 days - 7 - 13 jours	3 172	1 762[5]	1 401[5]	...	...	...
14 - 20 days - 14 - 20 jours	1 707	918[5]	771[5]	...	...	...
21 - 27 days - 21 - 27 jours	1 122	632[5]	479[5]	...	...	...
28 days - 11 months - 28 jours - 11 mois	12 529	6 555	5 536	...	...	...
28 days - 1 month - 28 jours - 1 mois	3 178	1 762[5]	1 379[5]	...	...	...
2 months - 2 mois	1 939	1 056[5]	856[5]	...	...	...
3 months - 3 mois	1 518	821[5]	682[5]	...	...	...
4 months - 4 mois	1 175	662[5]	503[5]	...	...	...
5 months - 5 mois	949	555[5]	385[5]	...	...	...
6 months - 6 mois	881	476[5]	395[5]	...	...	...
7 months - 7 mois	716	57[5]	354[5]	...	...	...
8 months - 8 mois	668	359[5]	305[5]	...	...	...
9 months - 9 mois	550	307[5]	240[5]	...	...	...
10 months - 10 mois	476	250[5]	215[5]	...	...	...
11 months - 11 mois	479	250[5]	222[5]	...	...	...
Chile - Chili						
2005 (C)						
Total	1 911	1 071	840	8.3	9.0	7.5
Less than 1 day - Moins de 1 jour	648	353	295	2.8	3.0	2.6
1 - 6 days - 1 - 6 jours	361	219	142	1.6	1.8	1.3
7 - 27 days - 7 - 27 jours	245	126	119	1.1	1.1	1.1
7 - 13 days - 7 - 13 jours	127	65	62	0.6	0.5	0.6
14 - 20 days - 14 - 20 jours	63	28	35	0.3	♦0.2	0.3
21 - 27 days - 21 - 27 jours	55	33	22	0.2	0.3	♦0.2
28 days - 11 months - 28 jours - 11 mois	657	373	284	2.8	3.1	2.5
28 days - 1 month - 28 jours - 1 mois	165	90	75	0.7	0.8	0.7
2 months - 2 mois	114	71	43	0.5	0.6	0.4
3 months - 3 mois	84	48	36	0.4	0.4	0.3
4 months - 4 mois	72	47	25	0.3	0.4	♦0.2
5 months - 5 mois	48	24	24	0.2	♦0.2	♦0.2
6 months - 6 mois	41	23	18	0.2	♦0.2	♦0.2
7 months - 7 mois	42	22	20	0.2	♦0.2	♦0.2
8 months - 8 mois	25	12	13	♦0.1	♦0.1	♦0.1
9 months - 9 mois	21	12	9	♦0.1	♦0.1	♦0.1

16. Infant deaths and infant mortality rates by age and sex: latest available year, 1997 - 2006

Décès d'enfants de moins d'un an et taux de mortalité infantile selon l'âge et le sexe: dernière année disponible, 1997 - 2006 (continued - suite)

Continent, country or area, year and age (in days) Continent, pays ou zone, année et âge (en jours)	Number - Nombre			Rate - Taux		
	Both sexes Les deux sexes	Male Masculin	Female Féminin	Both sexes Les deux sexes	Male Masculin	Female Féminin
AMERICA, SOUTH - AMÉRIQUE DU SUD						
Chile - Chili						
2005 (C)						
10 months - 10 mois	20	10	10	◆0.1	◆0.1	◆0.1
11 months - 11 mois	25	14	11	◆0.1	◆0.1	◆0.1
Unknown - Inconnu	-	-	-	-	-	-
Colombia - Colombie						
2006* (U)						
Total	10 722	6 074[5]	4 646[5]	...	...	...
Less than 1 day - Moins de 1 jour	2 186	1 236[5]	948[5]	...	...	...
1 - 6 days - 1 - 6 jours	2 194	1 281	913	...	...	...
7 - 27 days - 7 - 27 jours	1 823	1 026	797	...	...	...
7 - 13 days - 7 - 13 jours	951	529	422	...	...	...
14 - 20 days - 14 - 20 jours	534	309	225	...	...	...
21 - 27 days - 21 - 27 jours	338	188	150	...	...	...
28 days - 11 months - 28 jours - 11 mois	4 231	2 364	1 867	...	...	...
28 days - 1 month - 28 jours - 1 mois	985	577	408	...	...	...
2 months - 2 mois	665	364	301	...	...	...
3 months - 3 mois	500	291	209	...	...	...
4 months - 4 mois	390	223	167	...	...	...
5 months - 5 mois	337	176	161	...	...	...
6 months - 6 mois	284	155	129	...	...	...
7 months - 7 mois	255	142	113	...	...	...
8 months - 8 mois	272	159	113	...	...	...
9 months - 9 mois	197	100	97	...	...	...
10 months - 10 mois	176	85	91	...	...	...
11 months - 11 mois	170	92	78	...	...	...
Unknown - Inconnu	288	167	121	...	...	...
Ecuador - Équateur[7]						
2004 (U)						
Total	3 942	2 241	1 701	...	...	...
Less than 1 day - Moins de 1 jour	760	420	340	...	...	...
1 - 6 days - 1 - 6 jours	829	498	331	...	...	...
7 - 27 days - 7 - 27 jours	568	331	237	...	...	...
7 - 13 days - 7 - 13 jours	287	179	108	...	...	...
14 - 20 days - 14 - 20 jours	162	83	79	...	...	...
21 - 27 days - 21 - 27 jours	119	69	50	...	...	...
28 days - 11 months - 28 jours - 11 mois	1 785	992	793	...	...	...
28 days - 1 month - 28 jours - 1 mois	255	148	107	...	...	...
2 months - 2 mois	306	175	131	...	...	...
3 months - 3 mois	231	124	107	...	...	...
4 months - 4 mois	171	86	85	...	...	...
5 months - 5 mois	155	79	76	...	...	...
6 months - 6 mois	130	68	62	...	...	...
7 months - 7 mois	120	72	48	...	...	...
8 months - 8 mois	119	71	48	...	...	...
9 months - 9 mois	98	53	45	...	...	...
10 months - 10 mois	100	56	44	...	...	...
11 months - 11 mois	100	60	40	...	...	...
French Guiana - Guyane française[3]						
2003 (C)						
Total	58	32	26	...	...	...
Less than 1 day - Moins de 1 jour	10	3	7	...	...	...
1 - 6 days - 1 - 6 jours	15	10	5	...	...	...
7 - 27 days - 7 - 27 jours	16	12	4	...	...	...
7 - 13 days - 7 - 13 jours	7	5	2	...	...	...
14 - 20 days - 14 - 20 jours	4	3	1	...	...	...
21 - 27 days - 21 - 27 jours	5	4	1	...	...	...
28 days - 11 months - 28 jours - 11 mois	17	7	10	...	...	...
28 days - 1 month - 28 jours - 1 mois	5	3	2	...	...	...
2 months - 2 mois	2	-	2	...	...	...
3 months - 3 mois	-	-	-	...	...	...
4 months - 4 mois	1		1	...	...	...
5 months - 5 mois	2	1	1	...	...	...
6 months - 6 mois	3	1	2	...	...	...
7 months - 7 mois	2	1	1	...	...	...
8 months - 8 mois	2	1	1	...	...	...
9 months - 9 mois	-	-	-	...	...	...

16. Infant deaths and infant mortality rates by age and sex: latest available year, 1997 - 2006
Décès d'enfants de moins d'un an et taux de mortalité infantile selon l'âge et le sexe: dernière année disponible, 1997 - 2006 (continued - suite)

Continent, country or area, year and age (in days) / Continent, pays ou zone, année et âge (en jours)	Number - Nombre			Rate - Taux		
	Both sexes Les deux sexes	Male Masculin	Female Féminin	Both sexes Les deux sexes	Male Masculin	Female Féminin
AMERICA, SOUTH - AMÉRIQUE DU SUD						
French Guiana - Guyane française[3]						
2003 (C)						
10 months - 10 mois	-	-	-	...	...	...
11 months - 11 mois	-	-	-	...	...	...
Peru - Pérou[8]						
2003 (+U)						
Total	7 122	3 886[5]	3 233[5]	...	...	...
Less than 1 day - Moins de 1 jour	1 256	701[5]	553[5]	...	...	...
1 - 6 days - 1 - 6 jours	1 503	836	667	...	...	...
7 - 27 days - 7 - 27 jours	1 160	647	513	...	...	...
7 - 13 days - 7 - 13 jours	501	295	206	...	...	...
14 - 20 days - 14 - 20 jours	373	200	173	...	...	...
21 - 27 days - 21 - 27 jours	286	152	134	...	...	...
28 days - 11 months - 28 jours - 11 mois	3 203	1 702[5]	1 500[5]	...	...	...
28 days - 1 month - 28 jours - 1 mois	990	548	442	...	...	...
2 months - 2 mois	578	305	273	...	...	...
3 months - 3 mois	345	185	160	...	...	...
4 months - 4 mois	265	128	137	...	...	...
5 months - 5 mois	195	100	95	...	...	...
6 months - 6 mois	172	84[5]	87[5]	...	...	...
7 months - 7 mois	142	78	64	...	...	...
8 months - 8 mois	149	85	64	...	...	...
9 months - 9 mois	132	71	61	...	...	...
10 months - 10 mois	104	55	49	...	...	...
11 months - 11 mois	131	63	68	...	...	...
Uruguay						
2000 (C)						
Total	742	434[5]	304[5]	...	...	...
Less than 1 day - Moins de 1 jour	152	87[5]	61[5]	...	...	...
1 - 6 days - 1 - 6 jours	124	74	50	...	...	...
7 - 27 days - 7 - 27 jours	142	90	52	...	...	...
7 - 13 days - 7 - 13 jours	71	46	25	...	...	...
14 - 20 days - 14 - 20 jours	42	27	15	...	...	...
21 - 27 days - 21 - 27 jours	29	17	12	...	...	...
28 days - 11 months - 28 jours - 11 mois	324	183	141	...	...	...
28 days - 1 month - 28 jours - 1 mois	96	62	34	...	...	...
2 months - 2 mois	46	23	23	...	...	...
3 months - 3 mois	44	25	19	...	...	...
4 months - 4 mois	33	19	14	...	...	...
5 months - 5 mois	26	15	11	...	...	...
6 months - 6 mois	18	10	8	...	...	...
7 months - 7 mois	12	7	5	...	...	...
8 months - 8 mois	14	7	7	...	...	...
9 months - 9 mois	17	7	10	...	...	...
10 months - 10 mois	9	6	3	...	...	...
11 months - 11 mois	9	2	7	...	...	...
Venezuela (Bolivarian Republic of) - Venezuela (République bolivarienne du)[9]						
2001 (C)						
Total	8 158	4 710	3 448	15.4	17.1	13.5
Less than 28 days - Moins de 28 jours	5 657	3 288	2 369	10.7	12.0	9.3
28 days - 11 months - 28 jours - 11 mois	2 501	1 422	1 079	4.7	5.2	4.2
28 days - 1 month - 28 jours - 1 mois	461	250	211	0.9	0.9	0.8
2 months - 2 mois	367	222	145	0.7	0.8	0.6
3 months - 3 mois	291	165	126	0.5	0.6	0.5
4 months - 4 mois	265	154	111	0.5	0.6	0.4
5 months - 5 mois	229	126	103	0.4	0.5	0.4
6 months - 6 mois	197	112	85	0.4	0.4	0.3
7 months - 7 mois	194	106	88	0.4	0.4	0.3
8 months - 8 mois	176	97	79	0.3	0.4	0.3
9 months - 9 mois	178	101	77	0.3	0.4	0.3
10 - 11 months - 10 - 11 mois	143	89	54	0.3	0.3	0.2

16. Infant deaths and infant mortality rates by age and sex: latest available year, 1997 - 2006
Décès d'enfants de moins d'un an et taux de mortalité infantile selon l'âge et le sexe: dernière année disponible, 1997 - 2006 (continued - suite)

Continent, country or area, year and age (in days) / Continent, pays ou zone, année et âge (en jours)	Number - Nombre			Rate - Taux		
	Both sexes Les deux sexes	Male Masculin	Female Féminin	Both sexes Les deux sexes	Male Masculin	Female Féminin
ASIA - ASIE						
Armenia - Arménie[10]						
2006 (C)						
Total	523	315	208	...	...	...
Less than 1 day - Moins de 1 jour	104	60	44	...	...	...
1 - 6 days - 1 - 6 jours	230	141	89	...	...	...
7 - 27 days - 7 - 27 jours	67	45	22	...	...	...
7 - 13 days - 7 - 13 jours	46	32	14	...	...	...
14 - 20 days - 14 - 20 jours	11	6	5	...	...	...
21 - 27 days - 21 - 27 jours	10	7	3	...	...	...
28 days - 11 months - 28 jours - 11 mois	122	69	53	...	...	...
28 days - 1 month - 28 jours - 1 mois	24	8	16	...	...	...
2 months - 2 mois	12	11	1	...	...	...
3 months - 3 mois	18	9	9	...	...	...
4 months - 4 mois	18	7	11	...	...	...
5 months - 5 mois	14	10	4	...	...	...
6 months - 6 mois	5	4	1	...	...	...
7 months - 7 mois	14	9	5	...	...	...
8 months - 8 mois	5	3	2	...	...	...
9 months - 9 mois	3	3	-	...	...	...
10 months - 10 mois	4	2	2	...	...	...
11 months - 11 mois	5	3	2	...	...	...
Azerbaijan - Azerbaïdjan[10]						
2004 (+C)						
Total	1 287	757	530	9.8	10.7	8.7
Less than 1 day - Moins de 1 jour	111	69	42	0.8	1.0	0.7
1 - 6 days - 1 - 6 jours	192	139	53	1.5	2.0	0.9
7 - 27 days - 7 - 27 jours	56	31	25	0.4	0.4	♦0.4
7 - 13 days - 7 - 13 jours	27	14	13	♦0.2	♦0.2	♦0.2
14 - 20 days - 14 - 20 jours	20	12	8	♦0.2	♦0.2	♦0.1
21 - 27 days - 21 - 27 jours	9	5	4	♦0.1	♦0.1	♦0.1
28 days - 11 months - 28 jours - 11 mois	928	518	410	7.1	7.3	6.8
28 days - 1 month - 28 jours - 1 mois	3	2	1	-	-	-
2 months - 2 mois	69	46	23	0.5	0.6	♦0.4
3 months - 3 mois	115	68	47	0.9	1.0	0.8
4 months - 4 mois	131	72	59	1.0	1.0	1.0
5 months - 5 mois	95	52	43	0.7	0.7	0.7
6 months - 6 mois	92	53	39	0.7	0.7	0.6
7 months - 7 mois	91	49	42	0.7	0.7	0.7
8 months - 8 mois	106	53	53	0.8	0.7	0.9
9 months - 9 mois	75	41	34	0.6	0.6	0.6
10 months - 10 mois	70	36	34	0.5	0.5	0.6
11 months - 11 mois	81	46	35	0.6	0.6	0.6
Bahrain - Bahreïn						
2006 (C)						
Total	115	60	55	...	...	...
Less than 7 days - Moins de 7 jours	34	14	20	...	...	...
7 - 27 days - 7 - 27 jours	22	14	8	...	...	...
28 days - 11 months - 28 jours - 11 mois	59	32	27	...	...	...
China: Hong Kong SAR - Chine: Hong Kong RAS						
2005 (C)						
Total	131	78	53	...	...	...
Less than 1 day - Moins de 1 jour	21	13	8	...	...	...
1 - 6 days - 1 - 6 jours	39	24	15	...	...	...
7 - 27 days - 7 - 27 jours	27	10	17	...	...	...
7 - 13 days - 7 - 13 jours	14	5	9	...	...	...
14 - 20 days - 14 - 20 jours	12	5	7	...	...	...
21 - 27 days - 21 - 27 jours	1	-	1	...	...	...
28 days - 11 months - 28 jours - 11 mois	44	31	13	...	...	...
28 days - 1 month - 28 jours - 1 mois	8	4	4	...	...	...
2 months - 2 mois	8	6	2	...	...	...
3 months - 3 mois	8	6	2	...	...	...
4 months - 4 mois	3	3	-	...	...	...
5 months - 5 mois	3	2	1	...	...	...
6 months - 6 mois	7	4	3	...	...	...
7 months - 7 mois	2	2	-	...	...	...
8 months - 8 mois	-	-	-	...	...	...
9 months - 9 mois	-	-	-	...	...	...
10 months - 10 mois	4	3	1	...	...	...

16. Infant deaths and infant mortality rates by age and sex: latest available year, 1997 - 2006
Décès d'enfants de moins d'un an et taux de mortalité infantile selon l'âge et le sexe: dernière année disponible, 1997 - 2006 (continued - suite)

Continent, country or area, year and age (in days)	Number - Nombre			Rate - Taux		
Continent, pays ou zone, année et âge (en jours)	Both sexes Les deux sexes	Male Masculin	Female Féminin	Both sexes Les deux sexes	Male Masculin	Female Féminin

	Both sexes Les deux sexes	Male Masculin	Female Féminin	Both sexes Les deux sexes	Male Masculin	Female Féminin
ASIA - ASIE						
China: Hong Kong SAR - Chine: Hong Kong RAS						
2005 (C)						
11 months - 11 mois................................	1	1	-	...	...	...
Unknown - Inconnu	-	-	-	...	...	...
China: Macao SAR - Chine: Macao RAS						
2006 (C)						
Total........................	11	6	5	...	...	...
Less than 1 day - Moins de 1 jour	4	2	2	...	...	...
1 - 6 days - 1 - 6 jours................................	-	-	-	...	...	...
7 - 27 days - 7 - 27 jours	3	2	1	...	...	...
7 - 13 days - 7 - 13 jours	2	1	1	...	...	...
14 - 20 days - 14 - 20 jours	1	1	-	...	...	...
21 - 27 days - 21 - 27 jours	-	-	-	...	...	...
28 days - 11 months - 28 jours - 11 mois........	4	2	2	...	...	...
28 days - 1 month - 28 jours - 1 mois	-	-	-	...	...	...
2 months - 2 mois	1	-	1	...	...	...
3 months - 3 mois	-	-	-	...	...	...
4 months - 4 mois	1	-	1	...	...	...
5 months - 5 mois	-	-	-	...	...	...
6 months - 6 mois	-	-	-	...	...	...
7 months - 7 mois	-	-	-	...	...	...
8 months - 8 mois	1	1	-	...	...	...
9 months - 9 mois	1	1	-	...	...	...
10 months - 10 mois	-	-	-	...	...	...
11 months - 11 mois	-	-	-	...	...	...
Cyprus - Chypre[11]						
2006 (C)						
Total........................	27	16	11	...	...	...
Less than 1 day - Moins de 1 jour	9	5	4	...	...	...
1 - 6 days - 1 - 6 jours................................	6	4	2	...	...	...
7 - 27 days - 7 - 27 jours	4	3	1	...	...	...
28 days - 11 months - 28 jours - 11 mois........	7	4	3	...	...	...
28 days - 1 month - 28 jours - 1 mois	1	-	1	...	...	...
2 months - 2 mois	3	3	-	...	...	...
3 months - 3 mois	1	1	-	...	...	...
4 months - 4 mois	-	-	-	...	...	...
5 months - 5 mois	-	-	-	...	...	...
6 months - 6 mois	-	-	-	...	...	...
7 months - 7 mois	-	-	-	...	...	...
8 months - 8 mois	1	-	1	...	...	...
9 months - 9 mois	1	-	1	...	...	...
10 months - 10 mois	-	-	-	...	...	...
11 months - 11 mois	-	-	-	...	...	...
Unknown - Inconnu	1	-	1	...	...	...
Georgia - Géorgie[10]						
2006 (C)						
Total........................	753	395	358	...	...	...
Less than 1 day - Moins de 1 jour	467	222	245	...	...	...
1 - 6 days - 1 - 6 jours................................	197	126	71	...	...	...
7 - 27 days - 7 - 27 jours	38	23	15	...	...	...
7 - 13 days - 7 - 13 jours	19	13	6	...	...	...
14 - 20 days - 14 - 20 jours	13	5	8	...	...	...
21 - 27 days - 21 - 27 jours	6	5	1	...	...	...
28 days - 11 months - 28 jours - 11 mois........	51	26	25	...	...	...
28 days - 1 month - 28 jours - 1 mois	14	9	5	...	...	...
2 months - 2 mois	10	5	5	...	...	...
3 months - 3 mois	6	2	4	...	...	...
4 months - 4 mois	5	1	4	...	...	...
5 months - 5 mois	6	3	3	...	...	...
6 months - 6 mois	1	-	1	...	...	...
7 months - 7 mois	2	2	-	...	...	...
8 months - 8 mois	5	2	3	...	...	...
9 months - 9 mois	-	-	-	...	...	...
10 months - 10 mois	-	-	-	...	...	...
11 months - 11 mois	2	2	-	...	...	...

16. Infant deaths and infant mortality rates by age and sex: latest available year, 1997 - 2006
Décès d'enfants de moins d'un an et taux de mortalité infantile selon l'âge et le sexe: dernière année disponible, 1997 - 2006 (continued - suite)

Continent, country or area, year and age (in days) Continent, pays ou zone, année et âge (en jours)	Number - Nombre			Rate - Taux		
	Both sexes Les deux sexes	Male Masculin	Female Féminin	Both sexes Les deux sexes	Male Masculin	Female Féminin
ASIA - ASIE						
Israel - Israël[12]						
2006 (C)						
Total	593	335[5]	255[5]	...	...	...
Less than 1 day - Moins de 1 jour	130	71[5]	56[5]	...	...	...
1 - 6 days - 1 - 6 jours	108	57	51	...	...	...
7 - 27 days - 7 - 27 jours	111	67	44	...	...	...
7 - 13 days - 7 - 13 jours	50	26	24	...	...	...
14 - 20 days - 14 - 20 jours	39	28	11	...	...	...
21 - 27 days - 21 - 27 jours	22	13	9	...	...	...
28 days - 11 months - 28 jours - 11 mois	244	140	104	...	...	...
28 days - 1 month - 28 jours - 1 mois	68	36	32	...	...	...
2 months - 2 mois	36	20	16	...	...	...
3 months - 3 mois	28	17	11	...	...	...
4 months - 4 mois	26	16	10	...	...	...
5 months - 5 mois	16	9	7	...	...	...
6 months - 6 mois	7	4	3	...	...	...
7 months - 7 mois	18	13	5	...	...	...
8 months - 8 mois	16	10	6	...	...	...
9 months - 9 mois	11	7	4	...	...	...
10 months - 10 mois	11	7	4	...	...	...
11 months - 11 mois	7	1	6	...	...	...
Japan - Japon[13]						
2006 (C)						
Total	2 864	1 556	1 308	2.6	2.8	2.5
Less than 1 day - Moins de 1 jour	644	336	308	0.6	0.6	0.6
1 - 6 days - 1 - 6 jours	409	231	178	0.4	0.4	0.3
7 - 27 days - 7 - 27 jours	391	215	176	0.4	0.4	0.3
7 - 13 days - 7 - 13 jours	164	94	70	0.2	0.2	0.1
14 - 20 days - 14 - 20 jours	128	68	60	0.1	0.1	0.1
21 - 27 days - 21 - 27 jours	99	53	46	0.1	0.1	0.1
28 days - 11 months - 28 jours - 11 mois	1 420	774	646	1.3	1.4	1.2
28 days - 1 month - 28 jours - 1 mois	301	167	134	0.3	0.3	0.3
2 months - 2 mois	207	105	102	0.2	0.2	0.2
3 months - 3 mois	166	85	81	0.2	0.2	0.2
4 months - 4 mois	144	72	72	0.1	0.1	0.1
5 months - 5 mois	132	79	53	0.1	0.1	0.1
6 months - 6 mois	112	71	41	0.1	0.1	0.1
7 months - 7 mois	86	46	40	0.1	0.1	0.1
8 months - 8 mois	93	49	44	0.1	0.1	0.1
9 months - 9 mois	61	36	25	0.1	0.1	-
10 months - 10 mois	57	29	28	0.1	◆0.1	◆0.1
11 months - 11 mois	61	35	26	0.1	0.1	-
Kazakhstan[10]						
2006 (C)						
Total	4 154	2 397	1 757	13.8	15.5	12.0
Less than 1 day - Moins de 1 jour	415	246	169	1.4	1.6	1.2
1 - 6 days - 1 - 6 jours	1 630	970	660	5.4	6.3	4.5
7 - 27 days - 7 - 27 jours	615	349	266	2.0	2.3	1.8
7 - 13 days - 7 - 13 jours	364	220	144	1.2	1.4	1.0
14 - 20 days - 14 - 20 jours	138	68	70	0.5	0.4	0.5
21 - 27 days - 21 - 27 jours	113	61	52	0.4	0.4	0.4
28 days - 11 months - 28 jours - 11 mois	1 492	831	661	4.9	5.4	4.5
28 days - 1 month - 28 jours - 1 mois	370	217	153	1.2	1.4	1.0
2 months - 2 mois	226	120	106	0.7	0.8	0.7
3 months - 3 mois	170	93	77	0.6	0.6	0.5
4 months - 4 mois	154	90	64	0.5	0.6	0.4
5 months - 5 mois	111	61	50	0.4	0.4	0.3
6 months - 6 mois	112	61	51	0.4	0.4	0.3
7 months - 7 mois	116	65	51	0.4	0.4	0.3
8 months - 8 mois	70	42	28	0.2	0.3	◆0.2
9 months - 9 mois	71	38	33	0.2	0.2	0.2
10 months - 10 mois	55	29	26	0.2	◆0.2	◆0.2
11 months - 11 mois	37	15	22	0.1	◆0.1	◆0.2
Unknown - Inconnu	2	1	1	-	-	-
Korea (Republic of) - Corée (République de)[14]						
2006 (C)						
Total	1 709	959	750	3.8	4.1	3.4
Less than 7 days - Moins de 7 jours	622	371	251	1.4	1.6	1.2

16. Infant deaths and infant mortality rates by age and sex: latest available year, 1997 - 2006
Décès d'enfants de moins d'un an et taux de mortalité infantile selon l'âge et le sexe: dernière année disponible, 1997 - 2006 (continued - suite)

Continent, country or area, year and age (in days) / Continent, pays ou zone, année et âge (en jours)	Number - Nombre			Rate - Taux		
	Both sexes Les deux sexes	Male Masculin	Female Féminin	Both sexes Les deux sexes	Male Masculin	Female Féminin
ASIA - ASIE						
Korea (Republic of) - Corée (République de)[14]						
2006 (C)						
7 - 27 days - 7 - 27 jours	357	185	172	0.8	0.8	0.8
28 days - 11 months - 28 jours - 11 mois	730	403	327	1.6	1.7	1.5
28 days - 1 month - 28 jours - 1 mois	200	104	96	0.4	0.4	0.4
2 - 11 months - 2 - 11 mois	530	299	231	1.2	1.3	1.1
Kuwait - Koweït						
2006 (C)						
Total	456	245	211	...	...	...
Less than 1 day - Moins de 1 jour	119	66	53	...	...	...
1 - 6 days - 1 - 6 jours	85	49	36	...	...	...
7 - 27 days - 7 - 27 jours	83	37	46	...	...	...
7 - 13 days - 7 - 13 jours	45	20	25	...	...	...
14 - 20 days - 14 - 20 jours	22	12	10	...	...	...
21 - 27 days - 21 - 27 jours	16	5	11	...	...	...
28 days - 11 months - 28 jours - 11 mois	169	93	76	...	...	...
28 days - 1 month - 28 jours - 1 mois	58	36	22	...	...	...
2 months - 2 mois	29	14	15	...	...	...
3 months - 3 mois	22	14	8	...	...	...
4 months - 4 mois	13	9	4	...	...	...
5 months - 5 mois	11	2	9	...	...	...
6 months - 6 mois	15	9	6	...	...	...
7 months - 7 mois	2	1	1	...	...	...
8 months - 8 mois	4	1	3	...	...	...
9 months - 9 mois	10	4	6	...	...	...
10 months - 10 mois	2	1	1	...	...	...
11 months - 11 mois	3	2	1	...	...	...
Kyrgyzstan - Kirghizistan[15]						
2006 (C)						
Total	3 526	1 970	1 556	29.2	31.8	26.5
Less than 1 day - Moins de 1 jour	947	523	424	7.8	8.4	7.2
1 - 6 days - 1 - 6 jours	1 218	679	539	10.1	11.0	9.2
7 - 27 days - 7 - 27 jours	295	167	128	2.4	2.7	2.2
7 - 13 days - 7 - 13 jours	176	103	73	1.5	1.7	1.2
14 - 20 days - 14 - 20 jours	71	40	31	0.6	0.6	0.5
21 - 27 days - 21 - 27 jours	48	24	24	0.4	♦0.4	♦0.4
28 days - 11 months - 28 jours - 11 mois	1 066	601	465	8.8	9.7	7.9
28 days - 1 month - 28 jours - 1 mois	235	143	92	1.9	2.3	1.6
2 months - 2 mois	135	79	56	1.1	1.3	1.0
3 months - 3 mois	111	63	48	0.9	1.0	0.8
4 months - 4 mois	121	66	55	1.0	1.1	0.9
5 months - 5 mois	95	50	45	0.8	0.8	0.8
6 months - 6 mois	80	52	28	0.7	0.8	♦0.5
7 months - 7 mois	76	36	40	0.6	0.6	0.7
8 months - 8 mois	72	39	33	0.6	0.6	0.6
9 months - 9 mois	54	26	28	0.4	♦0.4	♦0.5
10 months - 10 mois	44	21	23	0.4	♦0.3	♦0.4
11 months - 11 mois	43	26	17	0.4	♦0.4	♦0.3
Malaysia - Malaisie						
2004 (C)						
Total	3 105	1 784	1 321	6.5	7.2	5.7
Less than 1 day - Moins de 1 jour	443	262	181	0.9	1.1	0.8
1 - 6 days - 1 - 6 jours	834	500	334	1.7	2.0	1.4
7 - 27 days - 7 - 27 jours	492	268	224	1.0	1.1	1.0
28 days - 11 months - 28 jours - 11 mois	1 336	754	582	2.8	3.1	2.5
28 days - 2 months - 28 jours - 2 mois	568	335	233	1.2	1.4	1.0
3 - 5 months - 3 - 5 mois	393	216	177	0.8	0.9	0.8
6 - 8 months - 6 - 8 mois	220	122	98	0.5	0.5	0.4
9 - 11 months - 9 - 11 mois	155	81	74	0.3	0.3	0.3
Maldives						
2006 (C)						
Total	92	54	38	...	...	...
Less than 7 days - Moins de 7 jours	51	33	18	...	...	...
7 - 27 days - 7 - 27 jours	16	7	9	...	...	...
28 days - 11 months - 28 jours - 11 mois	25	14	11	...	...	...

Continent, country or area, year and age (in days) Continent, pays ou zone, année et âge (en jours)	Number - Nombre			Rate - Taux		
	Both sexes Les deux sexes	Male Masculin	Female Féminin	Both sexes Les deux sexes	Male Masculin	Female Féminin
ASIA - ASIE						
Occupied Palestinian Territory - Territoire palestinien occupé						
2006 (U)						
Total.........	906	500	406	...	...	...
Less than 1 day - Moins de 1 jour	52	24	28	...	...	...
1 - 6 days - 1 - 6 jours.........................	202	129	73	...	...	...
7 - 27 days - 7 - 27 jours..........................	165	94	71	...	...	...
7 - 13 days - 7 - 13 jours	86	51	35	...	...	...
14 - 20 days - 14 - 20 jours.....................	43	22	21	...	...	...
21 - 27 days - 21 - 27 jours.....................	36	21	15	...	...	...
28 days - 11 months - 28 jours - 11 mois	487	253	234	...	...	...
28 days - 1 month - 28 jours - 1 mois	113	65	48	...	...	...
2 months - 2 mois..........................	62	25	37	...	...	...
3 months - 3 mois..........................	61	35	26	...	...	...
4 months - 4 mois..........................	58	31	27	...	...	...
5 months - 5 mois..........................	37	20	17	...	...	...
6 months - 6 mois..........................	38	20	18	...	...	...
7 months - 7 mois..........................	27	10	17	...	...	...
8 months - 8 mois..........................	26	15	11	...	...	...
9 months - 9 mois..........................	21	9	12	...	...	...
10 months - 10 mois..........................	24	13	11	...	...	...
11 months - 11 mois..........................	20	10	10	...	...	...
Pakistan[16]						
2005 (I)						
Total.........	289 169	168 960	120 209	76.7	84.8	67.6
Less than 1 day - Moins de 1 jour	30 052	18 699	11 353	8.0	9.4	6.4
1 - 6 days - 1 - 6 jours.........................	113 531	68 118	45 413	30.1	34.2	25.5
7 - 27 days - 7 - 27 jours..........................	38 734	23 374	15 359	10.3	11.7	8.6
7 - 13 days - 7 - 13 jours	22 706	11 353	11 353	6.0	5.7	6.4
14 - 20 days - 14 - 20 jours.....................	13 357	11 353	2 003	3.5	5.7	1.1
21 - 27 days - 21 - 27 jours.....................	2 671	668	2 003	0.7	0.3	1.1
28 days - 11 months - 28 jours - 11 mois.	106 852	58 768	48 084	28.3	29.5	27.0
28 days - 1 month - 28 jours - 1 mois	26 713	12 689	14 025	7.1	6.4	7.9
2 months - 2 mois..........................	14 692	6 678	8 014	3.9	3.3	4.5
3 months - 3 mois..........................	19 367	10 685	8 682	5.1	5.4	4.9
4 months - 4 mois..........................	8 014	5 343	2 671	2.1	2.7	1.5
5 months - 5 mois..........................	6 678	3 339	3 339	1.8	1.7	1.9
6 months - 6 mois..........................	8 682	5 343	3 339	2.3	2.7	1.9
7 months - 7 mois..........................	4 007	2 003	2 003	1.1	1.0	1.1
8 months - 8 mois..........................	5 343	2 003	3 339	1.4	1.0	1.9
9 months - 9 mois..........................	6 010	4 675	1 336	1.6	2.3	0.8
10 months - 10 mois..........................	4 007	3 339	668	1.1	1.7	0.4
11 months - 11 mois..........................	3 339	2 671	668	0.9	1.3	0.4
Philippines						
2003 (C)						
Total.........	22 844	13 329	9 515	13.7	15.3	11.9
Less than 1 day - Moins de 1 jour	4 466	2 560	1 906	2.7	2.9	2.4
1 - 6 days - 1 - 6 jours.........................	5 936	3 619	2 317	3.6	4.2	2.9
7 - 27 days - 7 - 27 jours..........................	2 742	1 637	1 105	1.6	1.9	1.4
7 - 13 days - 7 - 13 jours	1 502	901	601	0.9	1.0	0.8
14 - 20 days - 14 - 20 jours.....................	697	405	292	0.4	0.5	0.4
21 - 27 days - 21 - 27 jours.....................	543	331	212	0.3	0.4	0.3
28 days - 11 months - 28 jours - 11 mois.....................	9 700	5 513	4 187	5.8	6.3	5.2
28 days - 1 month - 28 jours - 1 mois	2 026	1 202	824	1.2	1.4	1.0
2 months - 2 mois..........................	1 274	722	552	0.8	0.8	0.7
3 months - 3 mois..........................	951	532	419	0.6	0.6	0.5
4 months - 4 mois..........................	779	404	375	0.5	0.5	0.5
5 months - 5 mois..........................	711	399	312	0.4	0.5	0.4
6 months - 6 mois..........................	736	415	321	0.4	0.5	0.4
7 months - 7 mois..........................	760	421	339	0.5	0.5	0.4
8 months - 8 mois..........................	766	429	337	0.5	0.5	0.4
9 months - 9 mois..........................	643	368	275	0.4	0.5	0.3
10 months - 10 mois..........................	519	310	209	0.3	0.4	0.3
11 months - 11 mois..........................	535	311	224	0.3	0.4	0.3
Qatar						
2006 (C)						
Total.........	114	65	49	...	...	...
Less than 1 day - Moins de 1 jour[1]	-	-	-	...	...	...
1 - 6 days - 1 - 6 jours.........................	51	34	17	...	...	...

Continent, country or area, year and age (in days) / Continent, pays ou zone, année et âge (en jours)	Number - Nombre			Rate - Taux		
	Both sexes Les deux sexes	Male Masculin	Female Féminin	Both sexes Les deux sexes	Male Masculin	Female Féminin
ASIA - ASIE						
Qatar						
2006 (C)						
7 - 27 days - 7 - 27 jours	27	12	15	...	...	...
7 - 13 days - 7 - 13 jours	14	8	6	...	...	...
14 - 20 days - 14 - 20 jours	7	1	6	...	...	...
21 - 27 days - 21 - 27 jours	6	3	3	...	...	...
28 days - 11 months - 28 jours - 11 mois	36	19	17	...	...	...
28 days - 1 month - 28 jours - 1 mois	6	1	5	...	...	...
2 months - 2 mois	4	2	2	...	...	...
3 months - 3 mois	6	4	2	...	...	...
4 months - 4 mois	4	2	2	...	...	...
5 months - 5 mois	1	-	1	...	...	...
6 months - 6 mois	4	3	1	...	...	...
7 months - 7 mois	2	1	1	...	...	...
8 months - 8 mois	3	1	2	...	...	...
9 months - 9 mois	3	2	1	...	...	...
10 months - 10 mois	3	3	-	...	...	...
11 months - 11 mois	-	-	-	...	...	...
Unknown - Inconnu	-	-	-	...	...	...
Singapore - Singapour						
2006 (+C)						
Total	117	61	56	...	...	...
Less than 1 day - Moins de 1 jour	16	8	8	...	...	...
1 - 6 days - 1 - 6 jours	30	18	12	...	...	...
7 - 27 days - 7 - 27 jours	24	13	11	...	...	...
7 - 13 days - 7 - 13 jours	13	7	6	...	...	...
14 - 20 days - 14 - 20 jours	7	3	4	...	...	...
21 - 27 days - 21 - 27 jours	4	3	1	...	...	...
28 days - 11 months - 28 jours - 11 mois	47	22	25	...	...	...
28 days - 1 month - 28 jours - 1 mois	9	5	4	...	...	...
2 months - 2 mois	11	7	4	...	...	...
3 months - 3 mois	5	2	3	...	...	...
4 months - 4 mois	7	1	6	...	...	...
5 months - 5 mois	4	3	1	...	...	...
6 months - 6 mois	3	1	2	...	...	...
7 months - 7 mois	3	1	2	...	...	...
8 months - 8 mois	1	1	-	...	...	...
9 months - 9 mois	1	-	1	...	...	...
10 months - 10 mois	1	1	-	...	...	...
11 months - 11 mois	2	-	2	...	...	...
Unknown - Inconnu	-	-	-	...	...	...
Thailand - Thaïlande						
2005 (+U)						
Total	6 183	3 450	2 733	...	...	...
Less than 1 day - Moins de 1 jour	711	378	333	...	...	...
1 - 6 days - 1 - 6 jours	1 813	1 041	772	...	...	...
7 - 27 days - 7 - 27 jours	1 121	644	477	...	...	...
7 - 13 days - 7 - 13 jours	585	342	243	...	...	...
14 - 20 days - 14 - 20 jours	338	192	146	...	...	...
21 - 27 days - 21 - 27 jours	198	110	88	...	...	...
28 days - 11 months - 28 jours - 11 mois	2 538	1 387	1 151	...	...	...
28 days - 1 month - 28 jours - 1 mois	672	365	307	...	...	...
2 months - 2 mois	452	252	200	...	...	...
3 months - 3 mois	284	153	131	...	...	...
4 months - 4 mois	237	133	104	...	...	...
5 months - 5 mois	195	108	87	...	...	...
6 months - 6 mois	166	91	75	...	...	...
7 months - 7 mois	156	95	61	...	...	...
8 months - 8 mois	110	61	49	...	...	...
9 months - 9 mois	100	48	52	...	...	...
10 months - 10 mois	89	46	43	...	...	...
11 months - 11 mois	77	35	42	...	...	...
Turkey - Turquie[17]						
1999 (U)						
Total	15 870	8 931	6 939	...	...	...
1 - 6 days - 1 - 6 jours	8 483	4 876	3 607	...	...	...
7 - 27 days - 7 - 27 jours	1 978	1 093	885	...	...	...
7 - 13 days - 7 - 13 jours	1 119	636	483	...	...	...

16. Infant deaths and infant mortality rates by age and sex: latest available year, 1997 - 2006
Décès d'enfants de moins d'un an et taux de mortalité infantile selon l'âge et le sexe: dernière année disponible, 1997 - 2006 (continued - sulte)

Continent, country or area, year and age (in days) Continent, pays ou zone, année et âge (en jours)	Number - Nombre			Rate - Taux		
	Both sexes Les deux sexes	Male Masculin	Female Féminin	Both sexes Les deux sexes	Male Masculin	Female Féminin
ASIA - ASIE						
Turkey - Turquie[17]						
1999 (U)						
14 - 20 days - 14 - 20 jours	582	308	274	...	...	...
21 - 27 days - 21 - 27 jours	277	149	128	...	...	...
28 days - 11 months - 28 jours - 11 mois	5 409	2 962	2 447	...	...	...
28 days - 1 month - 28 jours - 1 mois	993	545	448	...	...	...
2 months - 2 mois	799	438	361	...	...	...
3 months - 3 mois	759	416	343	...	...	...
4 months - 4 mois	540	287	253	...	...	...
5 months - 5 mois	607	345	262	...	...	...
6 months - 6 mois	592	347	245	...	...	...
7 months - 7 mois	325	165	160	...	...	...
8 months - 8 mois	277	152	125	...	...	...
9 months - 9 mois	193	91	102	...	...	...
10 months - 10 mois	194	108	86	...	...	...
11 months - 11 mois	130	68	62	...	...	...
Uzbekistan - Ouzbékistan[10]						
2000 (C)						
Total	10 091	5 805	4 286	19.1	21.4	16.7
Less than 1 day - Moins de 1 jour	607	355	252	1.2	1.3	1.0
1 - 6 days - 1 - 6 jours	2 179	1 352	827	4.1	5.0	3.2
7 - 27 days - 7 - 27 jours	1 279	731	548	2.4	2.7	2.1
7 - 13 days - 7 - 13 jours	719	421	298	1.4	1.6	1.2
14 - 20 days - 14 - 20 jours	343	192	151	0.7	0.7	0.6
21 - 27 days - 21 - 27 jours	217	118	99	0.4	0.4	0.4
28 days - 11 months - 28 jours - 11 mois	6 026	3 367	2 659	11.4	12.4	10.4
28 days - 1 month - 28 jours - 1 mois	976	582	394	1.8	2.1	1.5
2 months - 2 mois	680	363	317	1.3	1.3	1.2
3 months - 3 mois	693	411	282	1.3	1.5	1.1
4 months - 4 mois	691	377	314	1.3	1.4	1.2
5 months - 5 mois	612	324	288	1.2	1.2	1.1
6 months - 6 mois	538	293	245	1.0	1.1	1.0
7 months - 7 mois	486	269	217	0.9	1.0	0.8
8 months - 8 mois	445	259	186	0.8	1.0	0.7
9 months - 9 mois	388	204	184	0.7	0.8	0.7
10 months - 10 mois	274	150	124	0.5	0.6	0.5
11 months - 11 mois	243	135	108	0.5	0.5	0.4
EUROPE						
Albania - Albanie						
2006 (C)						
Total	253	...	...	...	...	...
Less than 1 day - Moins de 1 jour	10	...	...	...	...	...
1 - 6 days - 1 - 6 jours	40	...	...	...	...	...
7 - 27 days - 7 - 27 jours	21	...	...	...	...	...
28 days - 11 months - 28 jours - 11 mois	182	...	...	...	...	...
28 days - 1 month - 28 jours - 1 mois	35	...	...	...	...	...
2 - 11 months - 2 - 11 mois	147	...	...	...	...	...
Andorra - Andorre						
2006 (C)						
Total	3	3	-	...	...	...
Less than 1 day - Moins de 1 jour	-	-	-	...	...	...
1 - 6 days - 1 - 6 jours	-	-	-	...	...	...
7 - 27 days - 7 - 27 jours	1	1	-	...	...	...
28 days - 11 months - 28 jours - 11 mois	2	2	-	...	...	...
28 days - 1 month - 28 jours - 1 mois	-	-	-	...	...	...
2 months - 2 mois	-	-	-	...	...	...
3 months - 3 mois	-	-	-	...	...	...
4 months - 4 mois	-	-	-	...	...	...
5 months - 5 mois	-	-	-	...	...	...
6 months - 6 mois	-	-	-	...	...	...
7 months - 7 mois	-	-	-	...	...	...
8 months - 8 mois	-	-	-	...	...	...
9 months - 9 mois	-	-	-	...	...	...
10 months - 10 mois	-	-	-	...	...	...

16. Infant deaths and infant mortality rates by age and sex: latest available year, 1997 - 2006
Décès d'enfants de moins d'un an et taux de mortalité infantile selon l'âge et le sexe: dernière année disponible, 1997 - 2006 (continued - suite)

Continent, country or area, year and age (in days) Continent, pays ou zone, année et âge (en jours)	Number - Nombre			Rate - Taux		
	Both sexes Les deux sexes	Male Masculin	Female Féminin	Both sexes Les deux sexes	Male Masculin	Female Féminin
EUROPE						
Andorra - Andorre						
2006 (C)						
11 months - 11 mois...............	2	2	-	...	...	...
Unknown - Inconnu	-	-	-	...	...	...
Austria - Autriche						
2006 (C)						
Total........................	281	163	118	...	...	...
Less than 1 day - Moins de 1 jour	110	62	48	...	...	...
1 - 6 days - 1 - 6 jours................	42	30	12	...	...	...
7 - 27 days - 7 - 27 jours...............	44	25	19	...	...	...
7 - 13 days - 7 - 13 jours............	22	17	5	...	...	...
14 - 20 days - 14 - 20 jours............	12	6	6	...	...	...
21 - 27 days - 21 - 27 jours............	10	2	8	...	...	...
28 days - 11 months - 28 jours - 11 mois............	85	46	39	...	...	...
28 days - 1 month - 28 jours - 1 mois	26	13	13	...	...	...
2 months - 2 mois	18	12	6	...	...	...
3 months - 3 mois	10	6	4	...	...	...
4 months - 4 mois	7	6	1	...	...	...
5 months - 5 mois	5	3	2	...	...	...
6 months - 6 mois	2	-	2	...	...	...
7 months - 7 mois	5	2	3	...	...	...
8 months - 8 mois	3	1	2	...	...	...
9 months - 9 mois	5	1	4	...	...	...
10 months - 10 mois	1	1	-	...	...	...
11 months - 11 mois...............	3	1	2	...	...	...
Unknown - Inconnu	-	-	-	...	...	...
Belarus - Belarus[10]						
2006 (C)						
Total........................	587	333	254	...	...	...
Less than 1 day - Moins de 1 jour	106	66	40	...	...	...
1 - 6 days - 1 - 6 jours................	133	71	62	...	...	...
7 - 27 days - 7 - 27 jours...............	63	43	20	...	...	...
7 - 13 days - 7 - 13 jours............	29	18	11	...	...	...
14 - 20 days - 14 - 20 jours............	21	16	5	...	...	...
21 - 27 days - 21 - 27 jours............	13	9	4	...	...	...
28 days - 11 months - 28 jours - 11 mois............	285	153	132	...	...	...
28 days - 1 month - 28 jours - 1 mois	80	47	33	...	...	...
2 months - 2 mois	62	33	29	...	...	...
3 months - 3 mois	37	20	17	...	...	...
4 months - 4 mois	22	10	12	...	...	...
5 months - 5 mois	24	12	12	...	...	...
6 months - 6 mois	15	12	3	...	...	...
7 months - 7 mois	12	4	8	...	...	...
8 months - 8 mois	12	5	7	...	...	...
9 months - 9 mois	9	4	5	...	...	...
10 months - 10 mois	6	5	1	...	...	...
11 months - 11 mois...............	6	1	5	...	...	...
Unknown - Inconnu	-	-	-	...	...	...
Belgium - Belgique						
2000 (C)						
Total........................	554	305	249	...	...	...
Less than 1 day - Moins de 1 jour	91	46	45	...	...	...
1 - 6 days - 1 - 6 jours................	153	85	68	...	...	...
7 - 27 days - 7 - 27 jours...............	90	56	34	...	...	...
28 days - 11 months - 28 jours - 11 mois............	220	118	102	...	...	...
Bosnia and Herzegovina - Bosnie-Herzégovine						
2006 (C)						
Total........................	255	158	97	...	...	...
Less than 1 day - Moins de 1 jour	60	38	22	...	...	...
1 - 6 days - 1 - 6 jours................	104	66	38	...	...	...
7 - 27 days - 7 - 27 jours...............	40	21	19	...	...	...
28 days - 11 months - 28 jours - 11 mois............	51	33	18	...	...	...
28 days - 1 month - 28 jours - 1 mois	-	-	-	...	...	...
2 - 11 months - 2 - 11 mois	51	33	18	...	...	...
Bulgaria - Bulgarie						
2006 (C)						
Total........................	720	371	349	...	...	...
Less than 1 day - Moins de 1 jour	119	51	68	...	...	...

Continent, country or area, year and age (in days) / Continent, pays ou zone, année et âge (en jours)	Number - Nombre			Rate - Taux		
	Both sexes Les deux sexes	Male Masculin	Female Féminin	Both sexes Les deux sexes	Male Masculin	Female Féminin
EUROPE						
Bulgaria - Bulgarie						
2006 (C)						
1 - 6 days - 1 - 6 jours	160	88	72	...	...	...
7 - 27 days - 7 - 27 jours	119	63	56	...	...	...
7 - 13 days - 7 - 13 jours	64	35	29	...	...	...
14 - 20 days - 14 - 20 jours	27	11	16	...	...	...
21 - 27 days - 21 - 27 jours	28	17	11	...	...	...
28 days - 11 months - 28 jours - 11 mois	322	169	153	...	...	...
28 days - 1 month - 28 jours - 1 mois	103	58	45	...	...	...
2 months - 2 mois	51	22	29	...	...	...
3 months - 3 mois	33	21	12	...	...	...
4 months - 4 mois	32	12	20	...	...	...
5 months - 5 mois	26	13	13	...	...	...
6 months - 6 mois	24	15	9	...	...	...
7 months - 7 mois	8	1	7	...	...	...
8 months - 8 mois	19	12	7	...	...	...
9 months - 9 mois	8	4	4	...	...	...
10 months - 10 mois	9	6	3	...	...	...
11 months - 11 mois	9	5	4	...	...	...
Croatia - Croatie						
2006 (C)						
Total	215	105	110	...	...	...
Less than 1 day - Moins de 1 jour	71	40	31	...	...	...
1 - 6 days - 1 - 6 jours	60	28	32	...	...	...
7 - 27 days - 7 - 27 jours	30	12	18	...	...	...
7 - 13 days - 7 - 13 jours	12	3	9	...	...	...
14 - 20 days - 14 - 20 jours	12	5	7	...	...	...
21 - 27 days - 21 - 27 jours	6	4	2	...	...	...
28 days - 11 months - 28 jours - 11 mois	54	25	29	...	...	...
28 days - 1 month - 28 jours - 1 mois	15	5	10	...	...	...
2 months - 2 mois	11	4	7	...	...	...
3 months - 3 mois	7	6	1	...	...	...
4 months - 4 mois	6	3	3	...	...	...
5 months - 5 mois	3	1	2	...	...	...
6 months - 6 mois	5	4	1	...	...	...
7 months - 7 mois	3	1	2	...	...	...
8 months - 8 mois	2	-	2	...	...	...
9 months - 9 mois	2	1	1	...	...	...
10 months - 10 mois	-	-	-	...	...	...
11 months - 11 mois	-	-	-	...	...	...
Unknown - Inconnu	-	-	-	...	...	...
Czech Republic - République tchèque						
2006 (C)						
Total	352	214	138	...	...	...
Less than 1 day - Moins de 1 jour	50	32	18	...	...	...
1 - 6 days - 1 - 6 jours	100	63	37	...	...	...
7 - 27 days - 7 - 27 jours	96	50	46	...	...	...
7 - 13 days - 7 - 13 jours	59	33	26	...	...	...
14 - 20 days - 14 - 20 jours	22	12	10	...	...	...
21 - 27 days - 21 - 27 jours	15	5	10	...	...	...
28 days - 11 months - 28 jours - 11 mois	106	69	37	...	...	...
28 days - 1 month - 28 jours - 1 mois	21	16	5	...	...	...
2 months - 2 mois	17	9	8	...	...	...
3 months - 3 mois	20	9	11	...	...	...
4 months - 4 mois	10	7	3	...	...	...
5 months - 5 mois	6	5	1	...	...	...
6 months - 6 mois	6	4	2	...	...	...
7 months - 7 mois	5	4	1	...	...	...
8 months - 8 mois	7	5	2	...	...	...
9 months - 9 mois	5	3	2	...	...	...
10 months - 10 mois	6	5	1	...	...	...
11 months - 11 mois	3	2	1	...	...	...
Unknown - Inconnu	-	-	-	...	...	...
Denmark - Danemark[18]						
2006 (C)						
Total	250	141	109	...	...	...
Less than 1 day - Moins de 1 jour	112	65	47	...	...	...
1 - 6 days - 1 - 6 jours	59	26	33	...	...	...

16. Infant deaths and infant mortality rates by age and sex: latest available year, 1997 - 2006
Décès d'enfants de moins d'un an et taux de mortalité infantile selon l'âge et le sexe: dernière année disponible, 1997 - 2006 (continued - suite)

Continent, country or area, year and age (in days) Continent, pays ou zone, année et âge (en jours)	Number - Nombre			Rate - Taux		
	Both sexes Les deux sexes	Male Masculin	Female Féminin	Both sexes Les deux sexes	Male Masculin	Female Féminin
EUROPE						
Denmark - Danemark[18]						
2006 (C)						
7 - 27 days - 7 - 27 jours	34	23	11	...	...	...
28 days - 11 months - 28 jours - 11 mois.........................	45	27	18	...	...	...
Estonia - Estonie						
2006 (C)						
Total................	66	44	22	...	...	...
Less than 1 day - Moins de 1 jour	12	6	6	...	...	...
1 - 6 days - 1 - 6 jours.................	13	8	5	...	...	...
7 - 27 days - 7 - 27 jours	15	12	3	...	...	...
7 - 13 days - 7 - 13 jours	9	7	2	...	...	...
14 - 20 days - 14 - 20 jours	3	2	1	...	...	...
21 - 27 days - 21 - 27 jours	3	3	-	...	...	...
28 days - 11 months - 28 jours - 11 mois...	26	18	8	...	...	...
28 days - 1 month - 28 jours - 1 mois	5	4	1	...	...	...
2 months - 2 mois.........	4	1	3	...	...	...
3 months - 3 mois.................	2	2	-	...	...	...
4 months - 4 mois.................	3	2	1	...	...	...
5 months - 5 mois.................	1	1	-	...	...	...
6 months - 6 mois.................	1	1	-	...	...	...
7 months - 7 mois.................	3	1	2	...	...	...
8 months - 8 mois.................	1	1	-	...	...	...
9 months - 9 mois.................	5	5	-	...	...	...
10 months - 10 mois.................	1	-	1	...	...	...
11 months - 11 mois.................	-	-	-	...	...	...
Unknown - Inconnu	-	-	-	...	...	...
Finland - Finlande[19]						
2006 (C)						
Total................	107	00	71	...	...	...
Less than 1 day - Moins de 1 jour	47	25	22	...	...	...
1 - 6 days - 1 - 6 jours.................	42	26	16	...	...	...
7 - 27 days - 7 - 27 jours	27	13	14	...	...	...
7 - 13 days - 7 - 13 jours	14	6	8	...	...	...
14 - 20 days - 14 - 20 jours	11	7	4	...	...	...
21 - 27 days - 21 - 27 jours	2	-	2	...	...	...
28 days - 11 months - 28 jours - 11 mois...	49	32	17	...	...	...
28 days - 1 month - 28 jours - 1 mois	8	4	4	...	...	...
2 months - 2 mois.........	14	9	5	...	...	...
3 months - 3 mois.................	5	4	1	...	...	...
4 months - 4 mois.................	6	5	1	...	...	...
5 months - 5 mois.................	6	5	1	...	...	...
6 months - 6 mois.................	4	3	1	...	...	...
7 months - 7 mois.................	2	1	1	...	...	...
8 months - 8 mois.................	2	1	1	...	...	...
9 months - 9 mois.................	-	-	-	...	...	...
10 months - 10 mois.................	1	-	1	...	...	...
11 months - 11 mois.................	1	-	1	...	...	...
Unknown - Inconnu	-	-	-	...	...	...
France[20]						
2005 (C)						
Total................	2 775	1 583	1 192	3.6	4.0	3.2
Less than 1 day - Moins de 1 jour	614	340	274	0.8	0.9	0.7
1 - 6 days - 1 - 6 jours.................	585	317	268	0.8	0.8	0.7
7 - 27 days - 7 - 27 jours	599.	349	250	0.8	0.9	0.7
7 - 13 days - 7 - 13 jours	284	168	116	0.4	0.4	0.3
14 - 20 days - 14 - 20 jours	182	106	76	0.2	0.3	0.2
21 - 27 days - 21 - 27 jours	133	75	58	0.2	0.2	0.2
28 days - 11 months - 28 jours - 11 mois...	977	577	400	1.3	1.5	1.1
28 days - 1 month - 28 jours - 1 mois	310	174	136	0.4	0.4	0.4
2 months - 2 mois.........	147	86	61	0.2	0.2	0.2
3 months - 3 mois.................	122	80	42	0.2	0.2	0.1
4 months - 4 mois.................	85	47	38	0.1	0.1	0.1
5 months - 5 mois.................	64	41	23	0.1	0.1	♦0.1
6 months - 6 mois.................	67	35	32	0.1	0.1	0.1
7 months - 7 mois.................	48	29	19	0.1	♦0.1	♦0.1
8 months - 8 mois.................	45	27	18	0.1	♦0.1	-
9 months - 9 mois.................	33	22	11	-	♦0.1	-
10 months - 10 mois.................	31	20	11	-	♦0.1	-

Continent, country or area, year and age (in days) / Continent, pays ou zone, année et âge (en jours)	Number - Nombre			Rate - Taux		
	Both sexes Les deux sexes	Male Masculin	Female Féminin	Both sexes Les deux sexes	Male Masculin	Female Féminin
EUROPE						
France[20]						
2005 (C)						
11 months - 11 mois	25	16	9	-	-	-
Unknown - Inconnu	-	-	-	-	-	-
Germany - Allemagne						
2006 (C)						
Total	2 579	1 429	1 150	3.8	4.1	3.5
Less than 1 day - Moins de 1 jour	760	407	353	1.1	1.2	1.1
1 - 6 days - 1 - 6 jours	564	308	256	0.8	0.9	0.8
7 - 27 days - 7 - 27 jours	414	244	170	0.6	0.7	0.5
7 - 13 days - 7 - 13 jours	184	113	71	0.3	0.3	0.2
14 - 20 days - 14 - 20 jours	137	79	58	0.2	0.2	0.2
21 - 27 days - 21 - 27 jours	93	52	41	0.1	0.2	0.1
28 days - 11 months - 28 jours - 11 mois	841	470	371	1.3	1.4	1.1
28 days - 1 month - 28 jours - 1 mois	203	126	77	0.3	0.4	0.2
2 months - 2 mois	136	73	63	0.2	0.2	0.2
3 months - 3 mois	94	54	40	0.1	0.2	0.1
4 months - 4 mois	82	49	33	0.1	0.1	0.1
5 months - 5 mois	81	42	39	0.1	0.1	0.1
6 months - 6 mois	58	30	28	0.1	0.1	♦0.1
7 months - 7 mois	55	32	23	0.1	0.1	♦0.1
8 months - 8 mois	41	16	25	0.1	-	♦0.1
9 months - 9 mois	38	22	16	0.1	♦0.1	-
10 months - 10 mois	23	12	11	-	-	-
11 months - 11 mois	30	14	16	-	-	-
Gibraltar						
2006 (C)						
Total	1	1	-	...	...	...
Less than 7 days - Moins de 7 jours	-	-	-	...	...	...
7 - 27 days - 7 - 27 jours	-	-	-	...	...	...
28 days - 11 months - 28 jours - 11 mois	1	1	-	...	...	...
28 days - 2 months - 28 jours - 2 mois	-	-	-	...	...	...
3 months - 3 mois	1	1	-	...	...	...
4 - 11 months - 4 - 11 mois	-	-	-	...	...	...
Greece - Grèce						
2006 (C)						
Total	415	215	200	...	...	...
Less than 1 day - Moins de 1 jour	73	38	35	...	...	...
1 - 6 days - 1 - 6 jours	107	59	48	...	...	...
7 - 27 days - 7 - 27 jours	101	54	47	...	...	...
7 - 13 days - 7 - 13 jours	50	26	24	...	...	...
14 - 20 days - 14 - 20 jours	35	19	16	...	...	...
21 - 27 days - 21 - 27 jours	16	9	7	...	...	...
28 days - 11 months - 28 jours - 11 mois	134	64	70	...	...	...
28 days - 1 month - 28 jours - 1 mois	57	20	37	...	...	...
2 months - 2 mois	25	14	11	...	...	...
3 months - 3 mois	8	4	4	...	...	...
4 months - 4 mois	11	7	4	...	...	...
5 months - 5 mois	11	8	3	...	...	...
6 months - 6 mois	10	7	3	...	...	...
7 months - 7 mois	3	1	2	...	...	...
8 months - 8 mois	5	-	5	...	...	...
9 months - 9 mois	1	1	-	...	...	...
10 months - 10 mois	2	2	-	...	...	...
11 months - 11 mois	1	-	1	...	...	...
Unknown - Inconnu	-	-	-	...	...	...
Hungary - Hongrie						
2006 (C)						
Total	571	323	248	...	...	...
Less than 1 day - Moins de 1 jour	114	60	54	...	...	...
1 - 6 days - 1 - 6 jours	164	92	72	...	...	...
7 - 27 days - 7 - 27 jours	94	54	40	...	...	...
7 - 13 days - 7 - 13 jours	45	26	19	...	...	...
14 - 20 days - 14 - 20 jours	23	15	8	...	...	...
21 - 27 days - 21 - 27 jours	26	13	13	...	...	...
28 days - 11 months - 28 jours - 11 mois	199	117	82	...	...	...
28 days - 1 month - 28 jours - 1 mois	65	38	27	...	...	...
2 months - 2 mois	35	23	12	...	...	...

Continent, country or area, year and age (in days)	Number - Nombre			Rate - Taux		
Continent, pays ou zone, année et âge (en jours)	Both sexes Les deux sexes	Male Masculin	Female Féminin	Both sexes Les deux sexes	Male Masculin	Female Féminin
EUROPE						
Hungary - Hongrie						
2006 (C)						
3 months - 3 mois	29	16	13	...	...	...
4 months - 4 mois	15	10	5	...	...	...
5 months - 5 mois	19	11	8	...	...	...
6 months - 6 mois	10	6	4	...	...	...
7 months - 7 mois	7	4	3	...	...	...
8 months - 8 mois	4	2	2	...	...	...
9 months - 9 mois	2	2	-	...	...	...
10 months - 10 mois	8	4	4	...	...	...
11 months - 11 mois	5	1	4	...	...	...
Iceland - Islande						
2006 (C)						
Total	6	3	3	...	...	...
Less than 1 day - Moins de 1 jour	1	-	1	...	...	...
1 - 6 days - 1 - 6 jours	2	1	1	...	...	...
7 - 27 days - 7 - 27 jours	1	1	-	...	...	...
7 - 13 days - 7 - 13 jours	-	-	-	...	...	...
14 - 20 days - 14 - 20 jours	1	1	-	...	...	...
21 - 27 days - 21 - 27 jours	-	-	-	...	...	...
28 days - 11 months - 28 jours - 11 mois	2	1	1	...	...	...
28 days - 1 month - 28 jours - 1 mois	-	-	-	...	...	...
2 months - 2 mois	-	-	-	...	...	...
3 months - 3 mois	-	-	-	...	...	...
4 months - 4 mois	-	-	-	...	...	...
5 months - 5 mois	1	-	1	...	...	...
6 months - 6 mois	-	-	-	...	...	...
7 months - 7 mois	1	1	-	...	...	...
8 months - 8 mois	-	-	-	...	...	...
9 months - 9 mois	-	-	-	...	...	...
10 months - 10 mois	-	-	-	...	...	...
11 months - 11 mois	-	-	-	...	...	...
Ireland - Irlande[21]						
2006* (+C)						
Total	238	136	102	...	...	...
Less than 1 day - Moins de 1 jour	86	48	38	...	...	...
1 - 6 days - 1 - 6 jours	43	23	20	...	...	...
7 - 27 days - 7 - 27 jours	39	20	19	...	...	...
7 - 13 days - 7 - 13 jours	20	11	9	...	...	...
14 - 20 days - 14 - 20 jours	12	5	7	...	...	...
21 - 27 days - 21 - 27 jours	7	4	3	...	...	...
28 days - 11 months - 28 jours - 11 mois	69	45	24	...	...	...
28 days - 1 month - 28 jours - 1 mois	24	17	7	...	...	...
2 months - 2 mois	11	8	3	...	...	...
3 months - 3 mois	5	3	2	...	...	...
4 months - 4 mois	7	3	4	...	...	...
5 months - 5 mois	4	3	1	...	...	...
6 months - 6 mois	8	5	3	...	...	...
7 months - 7 mois	2	1	1	...	...	...
8 months - 8 mois	3	2	1	...	...	...
9 months - 9 mois	2	2	-	...	...	...
10 months - 10 mois	3	1	2	...	...	...
11 months - 11 mois	-	-	-	...	...	...
Unknown - Inconnu	-	-	-	...	...	...
Isle of Man - Îles de Man						
2004 (+C)						
Total	2	1	1	...	...	...
Less than 7 days - Moins de 7 jours	-	-	-	...	...	...
7 - 27 days - 7 - 27 jours	1	-	1	...	...	...
7 - 13 days - 7 - 13 jours	1	-	1	...	...	...
14 - 27 days - 14 - 27 jours	-	-	-	...	...	...
28 days - 11 months - 28 jours - 11 mois	1	1	-	...	...	...
28 days - 4 months - 28 jours - 4 mois	-	-	-	...	...	...
5 months - 5 mois	1	1	-	...	...	...
6 - 11 months - 6 - 11 mois	-	-	-	...	...	...

16. Infant deaths and infant mortality rates by age and sex: latest available year, 1997 - 2006
Décès d'enfants de moins d'un an et taux de mortalité infantile selon l'âge et le sexe: dernière année disponible, 1997 - 2006 (continued - suite)

Continent, country or area, year and age (in days) / Continent, pays ou zone, année et âge (en jours)	Number - Nombre			Rate - Taux		
	Both sexes Les deux sexes	Male Masculin	Female Féminin	Both sexes Les deux sexes	Male Masculin	Female Féminin
EUROPE						
Italy - Italie[22]						
2004 (C)						
Total...........	2 168	1 189	979	3.9	4.1	3.6
Less than 1 day - Moins de 1 jour.............	568	310	258	1.0	1.1	0.9
1 - 6 days - 1 - 6 jours.............	567	320	247	1.0	1.1	0.9
7 - 27 days - 7 - 27 jours.............	429	222	207	0.8	0.8	0.8
7 - 13 days - 7 - 13 jours.............	223	108	115	0.4	0.4	0.4
14 - 20 days - 14 - 20 jours.............	122	67	55	0.2	0.2	0.2
21 - 27 days - 21 - 27 jours.............	84	47	37	0.1	0.2	0.1
28 days - 11 months - 28 jours - 11 mois.............	604	337	267	1.1	1.2	1.0
28 days - 1 month - 28 jours - 1 mois.............	210	120	90	0.4	0.4	0.3
2 months - 2 mois.............	84	40	44	0.1	0.1	0.2
3 months - 3 mois.............	59	35	24	0.1	0.1	♦0.1
4 months - 4 mois.............	60	29	31	0.1	♦0.1	0.1
5 months - 5 mois.............	40	25	15	0.1	♦0.1	♦0.1
6 months - 6 mois.............	35	19	16	0.1	♦0.1	♦0.1
7 months - 7 mois.............	31	18	13	0.1	♦0.1	-
8 months - 8 mois.............	29	19	10	♦0.1	♦0.1	-
9 months - 9 mois.............	23	13	10	-	-	-
10 months - 10 mois.............	18	11	7	-	-	-
11 months - 11 mois.............	15	8	7	-	-	-
Latvia - Lettonie						
2006 (C)						
Total...........	170	93	77	...	...	...
Less than 1 day - Moins de 1 jour.............	23	14	9	...	...	...
1 - 6 days - 1 - 6 jours.............	57	30	27	...	...	...
7 - 27 days - 7 - 27 jours.............	24	16	8	...	...	...
7 - 13 days - 7 - 13 jours.............	15	9	6	...	...	...
14 - 20 days - 14 - 20 jours.............	8	6	2	...	...	...
21 - 27 days - 21 - 27 jours.............	1	1	-	...	...	...
28 days - 11 months - 28 jours - 11 mois.............	66	33	33	...	...	...
28 days - 1 month - 28 jours - 1 mois.............	3	-	3	...	...	...
2 months - 2 mois.............	10	5	5	...	...	...
3 months - 3 mois.............	19	11	8	...	...	...
4 months - 4 mois.............	11	4	7	...	...	...
5 months - 5 mois.............	4	4	-	...	...	...
6 months - 6 mois.............	3	1	2	...	...	...
7 months - 7 mois.............	5	2	3	...	...	...
8 months - 8 mois.............	3	2	1	...	...	...
9 months - 9 mois.............	1	1	-	...	...	...
10 months - 10 mois.............	2	-	2	...	...	...
11 months - 11 mois.............	5	3	2	...	...	...
Unknown - Inconnu.............	-	-	-	...	...	...
Lithuania - Lituanie[10]						
2006 (C)						
Total...........	213	116	97	...	...	...
Less than 1 day - Moins de 1 jour.............	36	16	20	...	...	...
1 - 6 days - 1 - 6 jours.............	55	34	21	...	...	...
7 - 27 days - 7 - 27 jours.............	31	20	11	...	...	...
7 - 13 days - 7 - 13 jours.............	14	8	6	...	...	...
14 - 20 days - 14 - 20 jours.............	8	5	3	...	...	...
21 - 27 days - 21 - 27 jours.............	9	7	2	...	...	...
28 days - 11 months - 28 jours - 11 mois.............	91	46	45	...	...	...
28 days - 1 month - 28 jours - 1 mois.............	29	13	16	...	...	...
2 months - 2 mois.............	11	6	5	...	...	...
3 months - 3 mois.............	11	6	5	...	...	...
4 months - 4 mois.............	11	6	5	...	...	...
5 months - 5 mois.............	4	3	1	...	...	...
6 months - 6 mois.............	3	2	1	...	...	...
7 months - 7 mois.............	5	3	2	...	...	...
8 months - 8 mois.............	8	4	4	...	...	...
9 months - 9 mois.............	4	2	2	...	...	...
10 months - 10 mois.............	3	-	3	...	...	...
11 months - 11 mois.............	2	1	1	...	...	...
Unknown - Inconnu.............	-	-	-	...	...	...

16. Infant deaths and infant mortality rates by age and sex: latest available year, 1997 - 2006
Décès d'enfants de moins d'un an et taux de mortalité infantile selon l'âge et le sexe: dernière année disponible, 1997 - 2006 (continued - suite)

Continent, country or area, year and age (in days) / Continent, pays ou zone, année et âge (en jours)	Number - Nombre			Rate - Taux		
	Both sexes Les deux sexes	Male Masculin	Female Féminin	Both sexes Les deux sexes	Male Masculin	Female Féminin
EUROPE						
Luxembourg						
2006 (C)						
Total	14	9	5	...	...	...
Less than 1 day - Moins de 1 jour	3	3	-	...	...	...
1 - 6 days - 1 - 6 jours	1	1	-	...	...	...
7 - 27 days - 7 - 27 jours	4	3	1	...	...	...
7 - 13 days - 7 - 13 jours	4	3	1	...	...	...
14 - 20 days - 14 - 20 jours	-	-	-	...	...	...
21 - 27 days - 21 - 27 jours	-	-	-	...	...	...
28 days - 11 months - 28 jours - 11 mois	6	2	4	...	...	...
28 days - 1 month - 28 jours - 1 mois	3	1	2	...	...	...
2 months - 2 mois	2	1	1	...	...	...
3 months - 3 mois	-	-	-	...	...	...
4 months - 4 mois	1	-	1	...	...	...
5 months - 5 mois	-	-	-	...	...	...
6 months - 6 mois	-	-	-	...	...	...
7 months - 7 mois	-	-	-	...	...	...
8 months - 8 mois	-	-	-	...	...	...
9 months - 9 mois	-	-	-	...	...	...
10 months - 10 mois	-	-	-	...	...	...
11 months - 11 mois	-	-	-	...	...	...
Unknown - Inconnu	-	-	-	...	...	...
Malta - Malte						
2006 (C)						
Total	14	10	4	...	...	...
Less than 7 days - Moins de 7 jours	-	-	-	...	...	...
7 - 27 days - 7 - 27 jours	9	6	3	...	...	...
7 - 20 days - 7 - 20 jours	-	-	-	...	...	...
21 - 27 days - 21 - 27 jours	9	6	3	...	...	...
28 days - 11 months - 28 jours - 11 mois	-	-	-	...	...	...
Unknown - Inconnu	5	4	1	...	...	...
Moldova[23]						
2006 (C)						
Total	442	243	199	...	...	...
Less than 1 day - Moins de 1 jour	60	39	21	...	...	...
1 - 6 days - 1 - 6 jours	140	82	58	...	...	...
7 - 27 days - 7 - 27 jours	62	36	26	...	...	...
7 - 13 days - 7 - 13 jours	36	24	12	...	...	...
14 - 20 days - 14 - 20 jours	18	9	9	...	...	...
21 - 27 days - 21 - 27 jours	8	3	5	...	...	...
28 days - 11 months - 28 jours - 11 mois	180	86	94	...	...	...
28 days - 1 month - 28 jours - 1 mois	50	21	29	...	...	...
2 months - 2 mois	36	13	23	...	...	...
3 months - 3 mois	24	16	8	...	...	...
4 months - 4 mois	17	9	8	...	...	...
5 months - 5 mois	19	12	7	...	...	...
6 months - 6 mois	9	4	5	...	...	...
7 months - 7 mois	10	4	6	...	...	...
8 months - 8 mois	5	3	2	...	...	...
9 months - 9 mois	2	-	2	...	...	...
10 months - 10 mois	6	4	2	...	...	...
11 months - 11 mois	2	-	2	...	...	...
Unknown - Inconnu	-	-	-	...	...	...
Montenegro						
2005 (C)						
Total	70	39	31	...	...	...
Less than 1 day - Moins de 1 jour	18	9	9	...	...	...
1 - 6 days - 1 - 6 jours	22	13	9	...	...	...
7 - 27 days - 7 - 27 jours	14	11	3	...	...	...
7 - 13 days - 7 - 13 jours	9	7	2	...	...	...
14 - 20 days - 14 - 20 jours	2	1	1	...	...	...
21 - 27 days - 21 - 27 jours	3	3	-	...	...	...
28 days - 11 months - 28 jours - 11 mois	16	6	10	...	...	...
28 days - 1 month - 28 jours - 1 mois	9	3	6	...	...	...
2 months - 2 mois	-	-	-	...	...	...
3 months - 3 mois	-	-	-	...	...	...
4 months - 4 mois	2	1	1	...	...	...
5 months - 5 mois	2	-	2	...	...	...

16. Infant deaths and infant mortality rates by age and sex: latest available year, 1997 - 2006
Décès d'enfants de moins d'un an et taux de mortalité infantile selon l'âge et le sexe: dernière année disponible, 1997 - 2006 (continued - suite)

Continent, country or area, year and age (in days) / Continent, pays ou zone, année et âge (en jours)	Number - Nombre			Rate - Taux		
	Both sexes Les deux sexes	Male Masculin	Female Féminin	Both sexes Les deux sexes	Male Masculin	Female Féminin
EUROPE						
Montenegro						
2005 (C)						
6 months - 6 mois	-	-	-	...	...	...
7 months - 7 mois	1	-	1	...	...	...
8 months - 8 mois	1	1	-	...	...	...
9 months - 9 mois	-	-	-	...	...	...
10 months - 10 mois	-	-	-	...	...	...
11 months - 11 mois	1	1	-	...	...	...
Unknown - Inconnu	-	-	-	...	...	...
Netherlands - Pays-Bas[24]						
2006 (C)						
Total	820	468	352	...	...	...
Less than 1 day - Moins de 1 jour	250	141	109	...	...	...
1 - 6 days - 1 - 6 jours	219	131	88	...	...	...
7 - 27 days - 7 - 27 jours	150	87	63	...	...	...
7 - 13 days - 7 - 13 jours	79	44	35	...	...	...
14 - 20 days - 14 - 20 jours	42	26	16	...	...	...
21 - 27 days - 21 - 27 jours	29	17	12	...	...	...
28 days - 11 months - 28 jours - 11 mois	200	108	92	...	...	...
28 days - 1 month - 28 jours - 1 mois	58	28	30	...	...	...
2 months - 2 mois	26	13	13	...	...	...
3 months - 3 mois	16	8	8	...	...	...
4 months - 4 mois	20	10	10	...	...	...
5 months - 5 mois	23	12	11	...	...	...
6 months - 6 mois	10	8	2	...	...	...
7 months - 7 mois	14	8	6	...	...	...
8 months - 8 mois	12	7	5	...	...	...
9 months - 9 mois	6	4	2	...	...	...
10 months - 10 mois	9	7	2	...	...	...
11 months - 11 mois	6	3	3	...	...	...
Norway - Norvège[25]						
2006 (C)						
Total	185	111	74	...	...	...
Less than 1 day - Moins de 1 jour	47	35	12	...	...	...
1 - 6 days - 1 - 6 jours	56	31	25	...	...	...
7 - 27 days - 7 - 27 jours	41	24	17	...	...	...
7 - 13 days - 7 - 13 jours	20	10	10	...	...	...
14 - 20 days - 14 - 20 jours	13	8	5	...	...	...
21 - 27 days - 21 - 27 jours	8	6	2	...	...	...
28 days - 11 months - 28 jours - 11 mois	41	21	20	...	...	...
28 days - 1 month - 28 jours - 1 mois	12	7	5	...	...	...
2 months - 2 mois	5	3	2	...	...	...
3 months - 3 mois	8	5	3	...	...	...
4 months - 4 mois	2	1	1	...	...	...
5 months - 5 mois	2	1	1	...	...	...
6 months - 6 mois	3	1	2	...	...	...
7 months - 7 mois	3	2	1	...	...	...
8 months - 8 mois	3	-	3	...	...	...
9 months - 9 mois	2	1	1	...	...	...
10 months - 10 mois	1	-	1	...	...	...
11 months - 11 mois	-	-	-	...	...	...
Unknown - Inconnu	-	-	-	...	...	...
Poland - Pologne						
2006 (C)						
Total	2 238	1 278	960	6.0	6.6	5.3
Less than 1 day - Moins de 1 jour	592	322	270	1.6	1.7	1.5
1 - 6 days - 1 - 6 jours	632	375	257	1.7	1.9	1.4
7 - 27 days - 7 - 27 jours	399	244	155	1.1	1.3	0.9
7 - 13 days - 7 - 13 jours	200	130	70	0.5	0.7	0.4
14 - 20 days - 14 - 20 jours	115	66	49	0.3	0.3	0.3
21 - 27 days - 21 - 27 jours	84	48	36	0.2	0.2	0.2
28 days - 11 months - 28 jours - 11 mois	615	337	278	1.6	1.8	1.5
28 days - 1 month - 28 jours - 1 mois	243	137	106	0.6	0.7	0.6
2 months - 2 mois	93	51	42	0.2	0.3	0.2
3 months - 3 mois	65	34	31	0.2	0.2	0.2
4 months - 4 mois	44	24	20	0.1	♦0.1	♦0.1
5 months - 5 mois	34	18	16	0.1	♦0.1	♦0.1
6 months - 6 mois	31	16	15	0.1	♦0.1	♦0.1

16. Infant deaths and infant mortality rates by age and sex: latest available year, 1997 - 2006
Décès d'enfants de moins d'un an et taux de mortalité infantile selon l'âge et le sexe: dernière année disponible, 1997 - 2006 (continued - suite)

Continent, country or area, year and age (in days) / Continent, pays ou zone, année et âge (en jours)	Number - Nombre			Rate - Taux		
	Both sexes Les deux sexes	Male Masculin	Female Féminin	Both sexes Les deux sexes	Male Masculin	Female Féminin
EUROPE						
Poland - Pologne						
2006 (C)						
7 months - 7 mois........................	30	14	16	0.1	♦0.1	♦0.1
8 months - 8 mois........................	26	16	10	♦0.1	♦0.1	♦0.1
9 months - 9 mois........................	16	6	10	-	-	♦0.1
10 months - 10 mois......................	21	15	6	♦0.1	♦0.1	-
11 months - 11 mois......................	12	6	6	-	-	-
Portugal[26]						
2006* (C)						
Total....................................	349	209	140	...	...	...
Less than 1 day - Moins de 1 jour	76	37	39	...	...	...
1 - 6 days - 1 - 6 jours..................	88	53	35	...	...	...
7 - 27 days - 7 - 27 jours................	60	42	18	...	...	...
7 - 13 days - 7 - 13 jours.............	30	25	5	...	...	...
14 - 20 days - 14 - 20 jours...........	19	10	9	...	...	...
21 - 27 days - 21 - 27 jours...........	11	7	4	...	...	...
28 days - 11 months - 28 jours - 11 mois.....................	125	77	48	...	...	...
28 days - 1 month - 28 jours - 1 mois	33	21	12	...	...	...
2 months - 2 mois.....................	23	14	9	...	...	...
3 months - 3 mois.....................	16	8	8	...	...	...
4 months - 4 mois.....................	15	11	4	...	...	...
5 months - 5 mois.....................	8	3	5	...	...	...
6 months - 6 mois.....................	11	8	3	...	...	...
7 months - 7 mois.....................	3	3	-	...	...	...
8 months - 8 mois.....................	8	5	3	...	...	...
9 months - 9 mois.....................	2	2	-	...	...	...
10 months - 10 mois...................	3	1	2	...	...	...
11 months - 11 mois...................	3	1	2	...	...	...
Unknown - Inconnu	-	-	-	...	...	...
Romania - Roumanie						
2006 (C)						
Total....................................	3 052	1 704	1 348	13.9	15.1	12.6
Less than 1 day - Moins de 1 jour	242	145	97	1.1	1.3	0.9
1 - 6 days - 1 - 6 jours..................	948	562	386	4.3	5.0	3.6
7 - 27 days - 7 - 27 jours................	509	274	235	2.3	2.4	2.2
7 - 13 days - 7 - 13 jours.............	254	141	113	1.2	1.3	1.1
14 - 20 days - 14 - 20 jours...........	153	77	76	0.7	0.7	0.7
21 - 27 days - 21 - 27 jours...........	102	56	46	0.5	0.5	0.4
28 days - 11 months - 28 jours - 11 mois....	1 353	723	630	6.2	6.4	5.9
28 days - 1 month - 28 jours - 1 mois	391	203	188	1.8	1.8	1.8
2 months - 2 mois.....................	273	160	113	1.2	1.4	1.1
3 months - 3 mois.....................	166	88	78	0.8	0.8	0.7
4 months - 4 mois.....................	137	73	64	0.6	0.6	0.6
5 months - 5 mois.....................	102	52	50	0.5	0.5	0.5
6 months - 6 mois.....................	75	37	38	0.3	0.3	0.4
7 months - 7 mois.....................	61	25	36	0.3	♦0.2	0.3
8 months - 8 mois.....................	34	23	11	0.2	♦0.2	♦0.1
9 months - 9 mois.....................	43	24	19	0.2	♦0.2	♦0.2
10 months - 10 mois...................	35	16	19	0.2	♦0.1	♦0.2
11 months - 11 mois...................	36	22	14	0.2	♦0.2	♦0.1
Unknown - Inconnu	-	-	-	-	-	-
Russian Federation - Fédération de Russie[10]						
2006 (C)						
Total....................................	15 079	8 660	6 419	10.2	11.4	8.9
Less than 1 day - Moins de 1 jour	1 959	1 124	835	1.3	1.5	1.2
1 - 6 days - 1 - 6 jours..................	4 336	2 585	1 751	2.9	3.4	2.4
7 - 27 days - 7 - 27 jours................	2 669	1 572	1 097	1.8	2.1	1.5
7 - 13 days - 7 - 13 jours.............	1 405	847	558	0.9	1.1	0.8
14 - 20 days - 14 - 20 jours...........	738	446	292	0.5	0.6	0.4
21 - 27 days - 21 - 27 jours...........	526	279	247	0.4	0.4	0.3
28 days - 11 months - 28 jours - 11 mois....	6 098	3 371	2 727	4.1	4.4	3.8
28 days - 1 month - 28 jours - 1 mois	1 746	998	748	1.2	1.3	1.0
2 months - 2 mois.....................	1 069	612	457	0.7	0.8	0.6
3 months - 3 mois.....................	750	422	328	0.5	0.6	0.5
4 months - 4 mois.....................	611	334	277	0.4	0.4	0.4
5 months - 5 mois.....................	452	235	217	0.3	0.3	0.3
6 months - 6 mois.....................	362	194	168	0.2	0.3	0.2
7 months - 7 mois.....................	307	150	157	0.2	0.2	0.2

Continent, country or area, year and age (in days) / Continent, pays ou zone, année et âge (en jours)	Number - Nombre			Rate - Taux		
	Both sexes Les deux sexes	Male Masculin	Female Féminin	Both sexes Les deux sexes	Male Masculin	Female Féminin
EUROPE						
Russian Federation - Fédération de Russie[10]						
2006 (C)						
8 months - 8 mois	265	136	129	0.2	0.2	0.2
9 months - 9 mois	191	101	90	0.1	0.1	0.1
10 months - 10 mois	178	102	76	0.1	0.1	0.1
11 months - 11 mois	167	87	80	0.1	0.1	0.1
Unknown - Inconnu	17	8	9	-	-	-
San Marino - Saint-Marin						
2003 (+C)						
Total	2	1	1	...	...	...
Less than 1 day - Moins de 1 jour	1	-	1	...	...	...
7 - 27 days - 7 - 27 jours	1	1	-	...	...	...
28 days - 11 months - 28 jours - 11 mois.	-	-	-	...	...	...
Serbia - Serbie[27]						
2006 (+C)						
Total	525	311	214	...	...	...
Less than 1 day - Moins de 1 jour	154	94	60	...	...	...
1 - 6 days - 1 - 6 jours	127	77	50	...	...	...
7 - 27 days - 7 - 27 jours	88	56	32	...	...	...
7 - 13 days - 7 - 13 jours	47	32	15	...	...	...
14 - 20 days - 14 - 20 jours	24	12	12	...	...	...
21 - 27 days - 21 - 27 jours	17	12	5	...	...	...
28 days - 11 months - 28 jours - 11 mois.	156	84	72	...	...	...
28 days - 1 month - 28 jours - 1 mois	56	26	30	...	...	...
2 months - 2 mois	20	10	10	...	...	...
3 months - 3 mois	22	14	8	...	...	...
4 months - 4 mois	20	10	10	...	...	...
5 months - 5 mois	13	7	6	...	...	...
6 months - 6 mois	6	4	2	...	...	...
7 months - 7 mois	4	4	-	...	...	...
8 months - 8 mois	4	2	2	...	...	...
9 months - 9 mois	4	2	2	...	...	...
10 months - 10 mois	4	3	1	...	...	...
11 months - 11 mois.	3	2	1	...	...	...
Slovakia - Slovaquie						
2006 (C)						
Total	355	204	151	...	...	...
Less than 1 day - Moins de 1 jour	56	30	26	...	...	...
1 - 6 days - 1 - 6 jours	75	46	29	...	...	...
7 - 27 days - 7 - 27 jours	59	35	24	...	...	...
7 - 13 days - 7 - 13 jours	35	20	15	...	...	...
14 - 20 days - 14 - 20 jours	9	5	4	...	...	...
21 - 27 days - 21 - 27 jours	15	10	5	...	...	...
28 days - 11 months - 28 jours - 11 mois.	165	93	72	...	...	...
28 days - 1 month - 28 jours - 1 mois	46	28	18	...	...	...
2 months - 2 mois	33	15	18	...	...	...
3 months - 3 mois	27	16	11	...	...	...
4 months - 4 mois	12	8	4	...	...	...
5 months - 5 mois	11	4	7	...	...	...
6 months - 6 mois	5	5	-	...	...	...
7 months - 7 mois	9	3	6	...	...	...
8 months - 8 mois	8	4	4	...	...	...
9 months - 9 mois	4	3	1	...	...	...
10 months - 10 mois	6	4	2	...	...	...
11 months - 11 mois.	4	3	1	...	...	...
Slovenia - Slovénie						
2006 (C)						
Total	64	32	32	...	...	...
Less than 1 day - Moins de 1 jour	23	11	12	...	...	...
1 - 6 days - 1 - 6 jours	12	8	4	...	...	...
7 - 27 days - 7 - 27 jours	12	5	7	...	...	...
7 - 13 days - 7 - 13 jours	3	2	1	...	...	...
14 - 20 days - 14 - 20 jours	7	2	5	...	...	...
21 - 27 days - 21 - 27 jours	2	1	1	...	...	...
28 days - 11 months - 28 jours - 11 mois.	17	8	9	...	...	...
28 days - 1 month - 28 jours - 1 mois	4	2	2	...	...	...
2 months - 2 mois	4	2	2	...	...	...
3 months - 3 mois	4	2	2	...	...	...

16. Infant deaths and infant mortality rates by age and sex: latest available year, 1997 - 2006
Décès d'enfants de moins d'un an et taux de mortalité infantile selon l'âge et le sexe: dernière année disponible, 1997 - 2006 (continued - suite)

Continent, country or area, year and age (in days) / Continent, pays ou zone, année et âge (en jours)	Number - Nombre			Rate - Taux		
	Both sexes Les deux sexes	Male Masculin	Female Féminin	Both sexes Les deux sexes	Male Masculin	Female Féminin
EUROPE						
Slovenia - Slovénie						
2006 (C)						
4 months - 4 mois	1	1	-	...	...	...
5 months - 5 mois	3	1	2	...	...	...
6 months - 6 mois	-	-	-	...	...	...
7 months - 7 mois	-	-	-	...	...	...
8 months - 8 mois	-	-	-	...	...	...
9 months - 9 mois	1	-	1	...	...	...
10 months - 10 mois	-	-	-	...	...	...
11 months - 11 mois	-	-	-	...	...	...
Unknown - Inconnu	-	-	-	...	...	...
Spain - Espagne						
2005 (C)						
Total	1 765	1 017	748	3.8	4.2	3.3
Less than 1 day - Moins de 1 jour	379	218	161	0.8	0.9	0.7
1 - 6 days - 1 - 6 jours	382	219	163	0.8	0.9	0.7
7 - 27 days - 7 - 27 jours	366	224	142	0.8	0.9	0.6
7 - 13 days - 7 - 13 jours	195	123	72	0.4	0.5	0.3
14 - 20 days - 14 - 20 jours	106	65	41	0.2	0.3	0.2
21 - 27 days - 21 - 27 jours	65	36	29	0.1	0.1	♦0.1
28 days - 11 months - 28 jours - 11 mois	638	356	282	1.4	1.5	1.2
28 days - 1 month - 28 jours - 1 mois	186	101	85	0.4	0.4	0.4
2 months - 2 mois	106	72	34	0.2	0.3	0.2
3 months - 3 mois	88	50	38	0.2	0.2	0.2
4 months - 4 mois	56	22	34	0.1	♦0.1	0.2
5 months - 5 mois	41	30	11	0.1	0.1	-
6 months - 6 mois	32	14	18	0.1	♦0.1	♦0.1
7 months - 7 mois	30	16	14	0.1	♦0.1	♦0.1
8 months - 8 mois	23	9	14	-	-	♦0.1
9 months - 9 mois	28	19	9	♦0.1	♦0.1	-
10 months - 10 mois	21	12	9	-	-	-
11 months - 11 mois	27	11	16	♦0.1	-	♦0.1
Unknown - Inconnu	-	-	-	-	-	-
Sweden - Suède						
2006 (C)						
Total	296	165	131	...	...	...
Less than 1 day - Moins de 1 jour	77	40	37	...	...	...
1 - 6 days - 1 - 6 jours	75	37	38	...	...	...
7 - 27 days - 7 - 27 jours	42	26	16	...	...	...
7 - 13 days - 7 - 13 jours	23	14	9	...	...	...
14 - 20 days - 14 - 20 jours	11	7	4	...	...	...
21 - 27 days - 21 - 27 jours	8	5	3	...	...	...
28 days - 11 months - 28 jours - 11 mois	102	62	40	...	...	...
28 days - 1 month - 28 jours - 1 mois	30	18	12	...	...	...
2 months - 2 mois	12	8	4	...	...	...
3 months - 3 mois	12	10	2	...	...	...
4 months - 4 mois	10	6	4	...	...	...
5 months - 5 mois	14	6	8	...	...	...
6 months - 6 mois	10	8	2	...	...	...
7 months - 7 mois	5	3	2	...	...	...
8 months - 8 mois	3	2	1	...	...	...
9 months - 9 mois	2	-	2	...	...	...
10 months - 10 mois	2	1	1	...	...	...
11 months - 11 mois	2	-	2	...	...	...
Switzerland - Suisse						
2006 (C)						
Total	325	182	143	...	...	...
Less than 1 day - Moins de 1 jour	155	80	75	...	...	...
1 - 6 days - 1 - 6 jours	63	41	22	...	...	...
7 - 27 days - 7 - 27 jours	32	18	14	...	...	...
7 - 13 days - 7 - 13 jours	17	11	6	...	...	...
14 - 20 days - 14 - 20 jours	7	1	6	...	...	...
21 - 27 days - 21 - 27 jours	8	6	2	...	...	...
28 days - 11 months - 28 jours - 11 mois	75	43	32	...	...	...
28 days - 1 month - 28 jours - 1 mois	16	7	9	...	...	...
2 months - 2 mois	6	4	2	...	...	...
3 months - 3 mois	10	4	6	...	...	...
4 months - 4 mois	8	7	1	...	...	...

16. Infant deaths and infant mortality rates by age and sex: latest available year, 1997 - 2006
Décès d'enfants de moins d'un an et taux de mortalité infantile selon l'âge et le sexe: dernière année disponible, 1997 - 2006 (continued - suite)

Continent, country or area, year and age (in days) / Continent, pays ou zone, année et âge (en jours)	Number - Nombre			Rate - Taux		
	Both sexes Les deux sexes	Male Masculin	Female Féminin	Both sexes Les deux sexes	Male Masculin	Female Féminin
EUROPE						
Switzerland - Suisse						
2006 (C)						
5 months - 5 mois	7	6	1	...	...	...
6 months - 6 mois	1	1	-	...	...	...
7 months - 7 mois	7	4	3	...	...	...
8 months - 8 mois	3	3	-	...	...	...
9 months - 9 mois	7	3	4	...	...	...
10 months - 10 mois	5	2	3	...	...	...
11 months - 11 mois	5	2	3	...	...	...
The Former Yugoslav Rep. of Macedonia - L'ex-République yougoslave de Macédoine						
2006 (C)						
Total	260	149	111	...	...	...
Less than 1 day - Moins de 1 jour	53	25	28	...	...	...
1 - 6 days - 1 - 6 jours	92	56	36	...	...	...
7 - 27 days - 7 - 27 jours	46	28	18	...	...	...
7 - 13 days - 7 - 13 jours	31	20	11	...	...	...
14 - 20 days - 14 - 20 jours	7	4	3	...	...	...
21 - 27 days - 21 - 27 jours	8	4	4	...	...	...
28 days - 11 months - 28 jours - 11 mois	69	40	29	...	...	...
28 days - 1 month - 28 jours - 1 mois	23	9	14	...	...	...
2 months - 2 mois	8	5	3	...	...	...
3 months - 3 mois	16	11	5	...	...	...
4 months - 4 mois	2	2	-	...	...	...
5 months - 5 mois	7	6	1	...	...	...
6 months - 6 mois	4	4	-	...	...	...
7 months - 7 mois	1	1	-	...	...	...
8 months - 8 mois	3	-	3	...	...	...
9 months - 9 mois	2	1	1	...	...	...
10 months - 10 mois	1	1	-	...	...	...
11 months - 11 mois	2	-	2	...	...	...
Ukraine[28]						
2006 (C)						
Total	4 433	2 628	1 805	9.6	11.1	8.1
Less than 1 day - Moins de 1 jour	513	296	217	1.1	1.3	1.0
1 - 6 days - 1 - 6 jours	1 220	783	437	2.7	3.3	2.0
7 - 27 days - 7 - 27 jours	833	466	367	1.8	2.0	1.6
7 - 13 days - 7 - 13 jours	426	243	183	0.9	1.0	0.8
14 - 20 days - 14 - 20 jours	227	123	104	0.5	0.5	0.5
21 - 27 days - 21 - 27 jours	180	100	80	0.4	0.4	0.4
28 days - 11 months - 28 jours - 11 mois	1 867	1 083	784	4.1	4.6	3.5
28 days - 1 month - 28 jours - 1 mois	531	326	205	1.2	1.4	0.9
2 months - 2 mois	320	184	136	0.7	0.8	0.6
3 months - 3 mois	232	124	108	0.5	0.5	0.5
4 months - 4 mois	180	102	78	0.4	0.4	0.3
5 months - 5 mois	144	87	57	0.3	0.3	0.3
6 months - 6 mois	117	73	44	0.3	0.3	0.2
7 months - 7 mois	104	59	45	0.2	0.2	0.2
8 months - 8 mois	78	46	32	0.2	0.2	0.1
9 months - 9 mois	69	36	33	0.1	0.2	0.1
10 months - 10 mois	44	18	26	0.1	♦0.1	♦0.1
11 months - 11 mois	48	28	20	0.1	♦0.1	♦0.1
Unknown - Inconnu	-	-	-	-	-	-
United Kingdom - Royaume-Uni[29]						
2003* (C)						
Total	3 686	2 029	1 657	5.3	5.7	4.9
Less than 1 day - Moins de 1 jour	1 073	593	480	1.5	1.7	1.4
1 - 6 days - 1 - 6 jours	873	483	390	1.3	1.4	1.2
7 - 27 days - 7 - 27 jours	583	300	283	0.8	0.8	0.8
28 days - 11 months - 28 jours - 11 mois	1 157	653	504	1.7	1.8	1.5
OCEANIA - OCÉANIE						
Australia - Australie						
2005 (+C)						
Total	1 302	714	588	5.0	5.4	4.7
Less than 1 day - Moins de 1 jour	565	311	255	2.2	2.3	2.0

Continent, country or area, year and age (in days) Continent, pays ou zone, année et âge (en jours)	Number - Nombre			Rate - Taux		
	Both sexes Les deux sexes	Male Masculin	Female Féminin	Both sexes Les deux sexes	Male Masculin	Female Féminin
OCEANIA - OCÉANIE						
Australia - Australie						
2005 (+C)						
1 - 6 days - 1 - 6 jours	198	111	87	0.8	0.8	0.7
7 - 27 days - 7 - 27 jours	170	93	77	0.7	0.7	0.6
7 - 13 days - 7 - 13 jours	81	45	36	0.3	0.3	0.3
14 - 20 days - 14 - 20 jours	45	23	22	0.2	♦0.2	♦0.2
21 - 27 days - 21 - 27 jours	44	25	19	0.2	♦0.2	♦0.2
28 days - 11 months - 28 jours - 11 mois	368	199	169	1.4	1.5	1.3
28 days - 1 month - 28 jours - 1 mois	90	50	40	0.3	0.4	0.3
2 months - 2 mois	66	33	33	0.3	0.2	0.3
3 months - 3 mois	43	22	21	0.2	♦0.2	♦0.2
4 months - 4 mois	48	26	22	0.2	♦0.2	♦0.2
5 months - 5 mois	26	14	12	♦0.1	♦0.1	♦0.1
6 months - 6 mois	24	12	12	♦0.1	♦0.1	♦0.1
7 months - 7 mois	24	14	10	♦0.1	♦0.1	♦0.1
8 months - 8 mois	15	11	4	♦0.1	♦0.1	-
9 months - 9 mois	12	8	4	-	♦0.1	-
10 months - 10 mois	8	3	5	-	-	-
11 months - 11 mois	12	6	6	-	-	-
Unknown - Inconnu	-	-	-	-	-	-
New Caledonia - Nouvelle-Calédonie						
2003 (C)						
Total	24	14	10	...	...	...
Less than 1 day - Moins de 1 jour	5	2	3	...	...	...
1 - 6 days - 1 - 6 jours	4	3	1	...	...	...
7 - 27 days - 7 - 27 jours	3	2	1	...	...	...
7 - 13 days - 7 - 13 jours	2	1	1	...	...	...
14 - 20 days - 14 - 20 jours	1	1	-	...	...	...
21 - 27 days - 21 - 27 jours	-	-	-	...	...	...
28 days - 11 months - 28 jours - 11 mois	12	7	5	...	...	...
New Zealand - Nouvelle-Zélande[26]						
2006 (+C)						
Total	300	173	127	...	...	...
Less than 1 day - Moins de 1 jour	88	47	41	...	...	...
1 - 6 days - 1 - 6 jours	42	21	21	...	...	...
7 - 27 days - 7 - 27 jours	28	19	9	...	...	...
7 - 13 days - 7 - 13 jours	7	4	3	...	...	...
14 - 20 days - 14 - 20 jours	13	10	3	...	...	...
21 - 27 days - 21 - 27 jours	8	5	3	...	...	...
28 days - 11 months - 28 jours - 11 mois	142	86	56	...	...	...
28 days - 1 month - 28 jours - 1 mois	36	23	13	...	...	...
2 months - 2 mois	26	14	12	...	...	...
3 months - 3 mois	18	11	7	...	...	...
4 months - 4 mois	21	15	6	...	...	...
5 months - 5 mois	13	8	5	...	...	...
6 months - 6 mois	5	2	3	...	...	...
7 months - 7 mois	5	2	3	...	...	...
8 months - 8 mois	7	6	1	...	...	...
9 months - 9 mois	8	4	4	...	...	...
10 months - 10 mois	2	-	2	...	...	...
11 months - 11 mois	1	1	-	...	...	...
Tonga						
1997 (+C)						
Total	20	...	...	...	...	...
Less than 1 day - Moins de 1 jour	4	...	...	...	...	...
1 - 6 days - 1 - 6 jours	2	...	...	...	...	...
7 - 27 days - 7 - 27 jours	2	...	...	...	...	...
7 - 13 days - 7 - 13 jours	-	...	...	...	...	...
14 - 20 days - 14 - 20 jours	1	...	...	...	...	...
21 - 27 days - 21 - 27 jours	1	...	...	...	...	...
28 days - 11 months - 28 jours - 11 mois	12	...	...	...	...	...
28 days - 1 month - 28 jours - 1 mois	-	...	...	...	...	...
2 months - 2 mois	-	...	...	...	...	...
3 months - 3 mois	-	...	...	...	...	...
4 months - 4 mois	1	...	...	...	...	...
5 months - 5 mois	3	...	...	...	...	...
6 months - 6 mois	1	...	...	...	...	...
7 months - 7 mois	3	...	...	...	...	...

16. Infant deaths and infant mortality rates by age and sex: latest available year, 1997 - 2006
Décès d'enfants de moins d'un an et taux de mortalité infantile selon l'âge et le sexe: dernière année disponible, 1997 - 2006 (continued - suite)

Continent, country or area, year and age (in days) / Continent, pays ou zone, année et âge (en jours)	Number - Nombre			Rate - Taux		
	Both sexes Les deux sexes	Male Masculin	Female Féminin	Both sexes Les deux sexes	Male Masculin	Female Féminin
OCEANIA - OCÉANIE						
Tonga						
1997 (+C)						
8 months - 8 mois	-	...	...	...	...	...
9 months - 9 mois	1	...	...	...	...	...
10 months - 10 mois	1	...	...	...	...	...
11 months - 11 mois	2	...	...	...	...	...

FOOTNOTES - NOTES

Italics: data from civil registers which are incomplete or of unknown completeness. - Italiques: données incomplètes ou dont le degré d'exactitude n'est pas connu, provenant des registres de l'état civil.

◆ Rates based on 30 or fewer infant deaths. — Taux basés sur 30 décès d'enfants ou moins.

* Provisional. - Données provisoires.

'Code' indicates the source of data, as follows:
C - Civil registration, estimated over 90% complete
U - Civil registration, estimated less than 90% complete
| - Other source, estimated reliable
+ - Data tabulated by date of registration rather than occurence.
... - Information not available

Le 'Code' indique la source des données, comme suit:
C - Registres de l'état civil considérés complets à 90 p. 100 au moins.
U - Registres de l'état civil qui ne sont pas considérés complets à 90 p. 100 au moins.
| - Autre source, considérée pas douteuses.
+ - Données exploitées selon la date de l'enregistrement et non la date de l'événement.
... - Information pas disponible.

[1] Data as reported by national statistical authorities. - Les données comme elles ont été déclarées par l'institut national de la statistique.
[2] Including Canadian residents temporarily in the United States, but excluding United States residents temporarily in Canada. - Y compris les résidents canadiens se trouvant temporairement aux Etats-Unis, mais ne comprenant pas les résidents des Etats-Unis se trouvant temporairement au Canada.
[3] Excluding live-born infants who died before their birth was registered. - Non compris les enfants nés vivants décédés avant l'enregistrement de leur naissance.
[4] Data exclude visitors. - Les données non compris des visiteurs.
[5] Data for male and female categories exclude infant deaths of unknown sex. - Il n'est pas tenu compte dans les données classées par sexe des décès d'enfant de moins d'un an de sexe inconnu.
[6] Data as reported by national statistical authorities; they may differ from data presented in other tables. Excluding Indian jungle population. - Les données comme elles ont été déclarées par l'institut national de la statistique; elles peuvent être différentes de celles présentées dans d'autres tableaux. Non compris les Indiens de la jungle.
[7] Excluding nomadic Indian tribes. - Non compris les tribus d'Indiens nomades.
[8] Excluding Indian jungle population. Data refer to registered infant deaths only. - Non compris les Indiens de la jungle. Les données se rapportent aux décès enregistrés d'enfants de moins de 1 an seulement.
[9] Excluding Indian jungle population. - Non compris les Indiens de la jungle.
[10] Excluding infants born alive of less than 28 weeks' gestation, of less than 1 000 grams in weight and 35 centimeters in length, who die within seven days of birth. - Non compris les enfants nés vivants après moins de 28 semaines de gestations, pesant moins de 1 000 grammes, mesurant moins de 35 centimètres et décédés dans les sept jours qui ont suivi leur naissance.
[11] Data refer to government controlled areas. - Les données se rapportent aux zones contrôlées par le Gouvernement.
[12] Data include deaths abroad of Israeli residents who were out of the country for less than a year. Including data for East Jerusalem and Israeli residents in certain other territories under occupation by Israeli military forces since June 1967. - Y compris les décès à l'étranger de résidents israéliens qui ont quitté le pays depuis moins d'un an. Y compris les données pour Jérusalem-Est et les résidents israéliens dans certains autres territoires occupés depuis 1967 par les forces armées israéliennes.
[13] Data refer to Japanese nationals in Japan only. - Les données se raportent aux nationaux japonais au Japon seulement.
[14] Excluding alien armed forces, civilian aliens employed by armed forces, and foreign diplomatic personnel and their dependants. Including nationals outside the country. - Non compris les militaires étrangers, les civils étrangers employés par les forces armées ni le personnel diplomatique étranger et les membres de leur famille les accompagnant. Y compris les nationaux hors du pays.
[15] Since 2004, WHO criteria have been adopted in the country. - Depuis 2004, le pays a adopté les critères de l'OMS.
[16] Data based on Pakistan Demographic Survey (PDS 2005). Excluding data for the Pakistan-held part of Jammu and Kashmir, the final status of which has not yet been determined. - Données extraites de l'enquête démographique effectuée par le Pakistan en 2005. Non compris les données concernant la partie du Jammu et Cachemire occupée par le Pakistan dont le statut définitif n'a pas été déterminé.
[17] Based on the results of the Population Demographic Survey. Deaths in province and district centers. - D'après les résultats de la Population Demographic Survey. Les décès aux centres des provinces et des zones seulement.
[18] Excluding Faeroe Islands and Greenland shown separately, if available. - Non compris les Iles Féroé et le Gröenland, qui font l'objet de rubriques distinctes, si disponible.
[19] Including nationals temporarily outside the country. Including Aland Islands. - Y compris les nationaux se trouvant temporairement hors du pays. Y compris les Îles d'Åland.
[20] Including armed forces stationed outside the country. Excluding Overseas Departments, namely, French Guiana, Guadeloupe, Martinique and Reunion, shown separately, if available. - Y compris les militaires nationaux hors du pays. Non compris les départements d'outre mer, c'est-à-dire la Guyane française, la Guadeloupe, la Martinique et la Réunion, qui font l'objet de rubriques distinctes, si disponible.
[21] Events registered within one year of occurrence. - Evénements enregistrés dans l'année qui suit l'événement.
[22] Data as reported by national statistical authorities; they may differ from data presented in other tables. - Les données comme elles ont été déclarées par l'institut national de la statistique; elles peuvent être différentes de celles présentées dans d'autres tableaux.
[23] Data do not include information for Transnistria and the municipality of Bender. Excluding infants born alive of less than 28 weeks' gestation, of less than 1 000 grams in weight and 35 centimeters in length, who die within seven days of birth. - Les données ne tiennent pas compte de l'information sur la Transnistria et la municipalité de Bender. Non compris les enfants nés vivants après moins de 28 semaines de gestations, pesant moins de 1 000 grammes, mesurant moins de 35 centimètres et décédés dans les sept jours qui ont suivi leur naissance.
[24] Including residents outside the country if listed in a Netherlands population register. - Y compris les résidents hors du pays, s'ils sont inscrits sur un registre de population néerlandais.
[25] Including residents temporarily outside the country. Excluding Svalbard and Jan Mayen Island shown separately, if available. - Y compris les résidents se trouvant temporairement hors du pays. Non compris Svalbard et Jan Mayen qui font l'objet de rubriques distinctes, si disponible.
[26] For resident population only. - Pour la population résidante seulement.
[27] Without data for Kosovo and Metohia. - Sans les données pour le Kosovo et Metohie.

Table 17

Table 17 presents maternal deaths and maternal mortality rates for as many years available between 1997 and 2006.

Description of variables: Maternal deaths are defined for the purposes of the Demographic Yearbook as those caused by deliveries and complications of pregnancy, childbirth and the puerperium, within 42 days of termination of pregnancy. They are usually defined as deaths coded "38-41" for ICD-9 Basic Tabulation List or as deaths coded "A34", "O00-O95", "O98-O99" for ICD-10, respectively. However, data for ICD-10 shown in this table include deaths due to "O96" and "O97" which refer to deaths from any obstetric cause occurring more than 42 days but less than one year after delivery and death from sequelae of direct obstetric causes occurring one year or more after delivery. For details on causes and corresponding ICD codes, see technical notes for Table 21.

For further information on the definition of maternal mortality from the tenth revisions of the *International Statistical Classification of Diseases and Related Health Problems*[1], see also section 4.3 of the Technical Notes.

Statistics on maternal death presented in this table are provided by the World Health Organisation. They are limited to countries or areas that meet the criterion that cause-of-death statistics are either classified by or convertible to the ninth or tenth revisions mentioned above. Data that are classified by the tenth revision are set in bold in the table.

Rate computation: Maternal mortality rates are the annual number of maternal deaths per 100 000 live births (table 9) in the same year. These rates have been calculated by the Statistics Division of the United Nations. Rates based on 30 or fewer maternal deaths are identified by the symbol (♦).

Reliability of data: Countries and areas that have incomplete (less than 90 per cent completeness) or of unknown completeness of cause of deaths data coverage are considered to provide unreliable data, which are set in *italics* rather than in roman type. Rates on these data are not computed. Information on completeness is normally provided by the World Health Organisation, when this is not the case, information on completeness is set to coincide with that of Table 18. Similarly, the reliability of data for the completeness of cause of death is provided by the World Health Organisation[1] and it may differ from the reliability of data for the total number of reported deaths. Therefore, there are cases when the quality code in table 18 does not correspond with the typeface used in this table.

Territorial composition as set in Section 2.2 of "Technical Notes on the Statistical Tables", including or excluding certain population of a country refers only to the denominator.

Limitations: Statistics on maternal deaths are subject to the same qualifications that have been set forth for vital statistics in general and death statistics in particular as discussed in section 4 of the Technical Notes. The reliability of the data, an indication of which is described above, is an important factor in considering the limitations. In addition, maternal-death statistics are subject to all the qualifications relating to cause-of-death statistics. These have been set forth in section 4 of the Technical Notes.

Maternal mortality rates are subject to the limitations of the data on live births with which they have been calculated. These have been set forth in the technical notes for table 9. Specific information pertaining to individual countries or areas is given in the footnotes to table 9.

The calculation of the maternal mortality rates based on the total number of live births approximates the risk of dying from complications of pregnancy, childbirth or puerperium. Ideally this rate should be based on the number of women exposed to the risk of pregnancy, in other words, the number of women conceiving. Since it is impossible to know how many women have conceived, the total number of live births is used in calculating this rate.

Earlier data: Maternal deaths and maternal mortality rates have been shown in previous issues of the *Demographic Yearbook*. For information on specific years covered, the reader should consult the Index.

NOTES

[1] *International Statistical Classification of Diseases and Related Health Problems*, Tenth Revision, Volume 2, World Health Organization, Geneva, 1992.

It should however be noted that in issues prior to 1975, maternal mortality rates were calculated using the female population rather than live births. Therefore, maternal mortality rates published since 1975 are not comparable to the earlier maternal death rates.

---

[i] For more information on specific method used for countries, see "Mathers CD, Bernard C, Iburg KM, Inoue M, Ma Fat D, Shibuya K et al. *Global burden of disease in 2002: data sources, methods and results.* Geneva, World Health Organization, 2003 (GPE Discussion Paper No. 54).

Tableau 17

Ce tableau présente des statistiques et des taux de mortalité liée à la maternité pour les années disponibles entre 1997 et 2006.

Description des variables : aux fins de *l'Annuaire démographique*, les décès liés à la maternité sont ceux entraînés par l'accouchement ou les complications de la grossesse, de l'accouchement et des suites de couches dans un délai de 42 jours après la terminaison de la grossesse. Ils sont généralement associés aux codes 38 à 41 dans le cas de la liste de base pour la mise en tableaux de la CIM-9 et aux codes A34, O00 à O95 et O98 et O99 dans le cas de la CIM-10. Les statistiques associées à des codes correspondant à la CIM-10 englobent des décès de type O96 et O97, qui désignent les décès liés à des causes obstétriques se produisant après 42 jours mais moins d'un an après l'accouchement et les décès entraînés par les séquelles de complications obstétriques directes qui se produisent un an ou plus après l'accouchement. Pour plus de précisions sur les causes des décès et les codes correspondants de la CIM, voir les notes techniques correspondant au tableau 21.

Pour plus de précisions concernant les définitions de la mortalité liée à la maternité dans la dixième révision de la *Classification statistique internationale des maladies et des problèmes de santé connexes*[1], se reporter également à la section 4.3 des Notes techniques.

Les statistiques de mortalité liée à la maternité présentées dans le tableau 17 émanent de l'Organisation mondiale de la santé. Elles ne se rapportent qu'aux pays ou zones qui répondent aux critères selon lesquels les statistiques relatives à la cause des décès sont conformes à la liste de la neuvième ou de la dixième révision de la CIM ou peuvent être aisément comparées aux catégories de cette liste. Les données conformes à la dixième révision sont indiquées en gras dans le tableau.

Calcul des taux : les taux de mortalité liée à la maternité représentent le nombre annuel de décès dus à la maternité pour 100 000 naissances vivantes (fréquences du tableau 9) de la même année. Ces taux ont été calculés par la Division de statistique de l'ONU. Les taux fondés sur 30 décès liés à la maternité ou moins sont signalés par le signe '♦'.

Fiabilité des données : les statistiques relatives aux pays et aux zones pour lesquels la couverture des données concernant les causes de décès est incomplète (mois de 90 pour cent) ou dont le degré de complétude n'est pas connue sont jugés douteuses et apparaissent en *italique* et non en caractères romains. Les taux correspondant ne sont pas calculés. L'information sur la complétude est normalement fournie par l'Organisation Mondiale de la Santé. Si ce n'est pas le cas, l'information sur la complétude est reprise de tableau 18. De même, la fiabilité des données relatives aux causes de décès est fournie par l'Organisation Mondiale de la Santé et peut différer de la fiabilité des données relatives au nombre de décès enregistrés. En conséquence, il peut apparaitre de différences entre les codes de fiabilité du tableau 18 et du présent tableau.

La composition territoriale est définie dans la Section 2.2 des "Notes Techniques sur les tableaux statistiques". L'inclusion ou l'exclusion de certaines populations d'un pays ne concerne que le dénominateur.

Insuffisance des données : les statistiques de la mortalité liée à la maternité appellent toutes les réserves qui ont été formulées à propos des statistiques de l'état civil en général et des statistiques relatives à la mortalité en particulier (voir la section 4 des Notes techniques). La fiabilité des données, au sujet de laquelle des indications ont été fournies plus haut, est un facteur important. En outre, les statistiques de la mortalité liée à la maternité appellent les mêmes réserves que celles exposées à la section 4 des Notes techniques en ce qui concerne les statistiques des causes de décès.

Les taux de mortalité liée à la maternité appellent également toutes les réserves formulées à propos des statistiques des naissances vivantes qui ont servi à leur calcul (voir à ce sujet les notes techniques relatives au tableau 9). Des précisions sur certains pays ou zones sont données dans les notes se rapportant au tableau 9.

En prenant le nombre total des naissances vivantes comme base pour le calcul des taux de mortalité liée à la maternité, on obtient une mesure approximative de la probabilité de décès dus aux complications de la grossesse, de l'accouchement et des suites de couches. Idéalement, ces taux devraient être calculés sur la base du nombre de femmes exposées aux risques liés à la grossesse, c'est-à-dire sur la base du nombre de femmes qui conçoivent. Étant donné qu'il est impossible de connaître le nombre de femmes ayant conçu, c'est le nombre total de naissances vivantes que l'on utilise pour calculer ces taux.

Données publiées antérieurement : des statistiques concernant les décès liés à la maternité (nombre de décès et taux) ont déjà été présentées dans des éditions antérieures de *l'Annuaire démographique*. Pour plus de précisions concernant les années pour lesquelles ces données ont été publiées, se reporter à l'index.

Il faut souligner que, avant 1975, les taux de mortalité liée à la maternité étaient calculés sur la base de la population féminine et non sur celle du nombre de naissances vivantes. Ils ne sont donc pas comparables à ceux qui figurent dans les éditions de l'*Annuaire démographique* parues après 1975.

NOTE

[1] *Classification statistique internationale des maladies et des problèmes de santé connexes*, dixième révision, volume 2. Genève, Organisation mondiale de la santé, 1992.

Continent and country or area / Continent et pays ou zone	Code[a]	1997	1998	1999	2000	2001	2002	2003	2004	2005	2006
AFRICA - AFRIQUE											
Egypt - Égypte											
Number - Nombre	U	...	...	...	492	...	...	...	...	...	...
Mauritius - Maurice											
Number - Nombre	+C	10	4	7	3	4	1	4	3	4	...
Rate - Taux	+C	♦50.0	♦20.6	♦34.5	♦14.8	♦20.3	♦5.0	♦20.7	♦15.6	♦21.3	...
Réunion											
Number - Nombre	...	...	...	...	...	-	3	3	4	4	...
Seychelles											
Number - Nombre	+C	...	...	...	...	-	1	1	-	1	
Rate - Taux	+C	...	...	...	...	-	♦67.5	♦66.8	-	♦65.1	
South Africa - Afrique du Sud											
Number - Nombre	U	623	631	693	737	854	794	898	1 158	1 249	...
AMERICA, NORTH - AMÉRIQUE DU NORD											
Anguilla											
Number - Nombre	+...	...	...	...	-	-	...	-	-	-	-
Antigua and Barbuda - Antigua-et-Barbuda											
Number - Nombre	+U	...	...	...	...	...	...	...	...	...	...
Aruba											
Number - Nombre	C	...	...	-	...	...	...	...	...	...	...
Bahamas											
Number - Nombre	U	-	1	1	2	...	...	...	...	...	...
Barbados - Barbade											
Number - Nombre	C	...	...	...	1	-	...	...	...	...	...
Rate - Taux	C	...	...	...	♦26.6	...	...	...	...	...	...
Belize											
Number - Nombre	C	3	9	3	5	3	...	...	...	...	...
Rate - Taux	C	♦40.8	♦131.5	♦42.2	♦68.4	♦41.6	...	...	...	...	...
Bermuda - Bermudes											
Number - Nombre	...	-	-	-	-	-	...	...	...	...	...
British Virgin Islands - Îles Vierges britanniques											
Number - Nombre	...	...	-	-	-	-	...	...	...	...	...
Canada											
Number - Nombre	C	19	13	8	11	26	15	23	20	...	...
Rate - Taux	C	♦5.5	♦3.8	♦2.4	♦3.4	♦7.8	♦4.6	♦6.9	♦5.9	...	...
Cayman Islands - Îles Caïmanes											
Number - Nombre	...	...	-	-	1	...	...	...	-	...	...
Costa Rica											
Number - Nombre	+U	29	14	15	28	24	27	24	22	24	...
Cuba											
Number - Nombre	C	59	59	66	58	57	65	62	56	66	...
Rate - Taux	C	38.6	39.1	43.8	40.4	41.1	46.0	45.3	44.0	54.7	...
Dominica - Dominique											
Number - Nombre	+C	-	1	-	-	1	1	-	-	...	...
Rate - Taux	+C	-	♦81.3	-	-	♦82.4	♦92.5	...	...	...	...
Dominican Republic - République dominicaine											
Number - Nombre	U	74	64	69	51	64	...	58	85	...	...
El Salvador											
Number - Nombre	+U	42	42	23	31	28	32	27	22	23	...
Grenada - Grenade											
Number - Nombre	U	...	...	...	...	-	1	...	...	...	...
Guadeloupe											
Number - Nombre	...	...	...	...	3	2	6	4	3	1	...
Guatemala											
Number - Nombre	U	342	324	316	346	278	280	293	296	...	...
Haiti - Haïti											
Number - Nombre	...	101	...	156	...	180	135	124	...	...	...
Martinique											
Number - Nombre	...	...	...	...	2	1	2	2	1	-	...
Mexico - Mexique											
Number - Nombre	+C	1 266	1 430	1 411	1 325	1 268	1 324	1 332	1 266	1 269	...
Rate - Taux	+C	57.5	63.8	62.9	57.6	56.9	59.9	61.5	58.7	49.4	...

Continent and country or area Continent et pays ou zone	Co-de[a]	1997	1998	1999	2000	2001	2002	2003	2004	2005	2006
AMERICA, NORTH - **AMÉRIQUE DU NORD**											
Montserrat											
Number - Nombre	+C	-	-	-	1	-	-	-	...	...	...
Nicaragua											
Number - Nombre	+U	127	113	138	97	124	114	88	108	93	...
Panama											
Number - Nombre	+U	28	30	31	30	37	38	34	23	...	...
Puerto Rico - Porto Rico											
Number - Nombre	+...	13	8	10	14	6	5	8	...	5	...
Saint Kitts and Nevis - Saint-Kitts-et-Nevis											
Number - Nombre	+C	-	-	-	-	2	-	2	...	...	...
Rate - Taux	+C	-	-	-	-	♦249.1	...	...	...	...	...
Saint Lucia - Sainte-Lucie											
Number - Nombre	C	-	-	1	3	1	1	...	...	...	...
Rate - Taux	C	-	-	♦33.4	♦103.3	♦35.9	♦38.5	...	...	...	...
Saint Pierre and Miquelon - Saint Pierre-et-Miquelon											
Number - Nombre	C	...	...	...	...	...	...	...	...	-	...
Saint Vincent and the Grenadines - Saint Vincent-et-les Grenadines											
Number - Nombre	+C	1	-	1	1	-	-	-	...	...	...
Rate - Taux	+C	♦43.3	-	♦46.1	♦46.5	-	-	-	...	...	...
Trinidad and Tobago - Trinité-et-Tobago											
Number - Nombre	C	13	8	7	10	7	5	...	...	...	...
Rate - Taux	C	♦70.5	...	♦38.2	♦55.1	♦38.7	♦29.4	...	...	...	...
Turks Caicos Islands - Îles Turques et Caïques											
Number - Nombre	...	-	-	-	-	1	-	1	1	-	...
United States - États-Unis											
Number - Nombre	C	327	281	406	404	416	379	545	697	760	...
Rate - Taux	C	8.4	7.1	10.3	10.0	10.3	9.4	13.3	17.0	18.4	...
United States Virgin Islands - Îles Vierges américaines											
Number - Nombre		1	-	-	1	2	-	-	...	...	...
AMERICA, SOUTH - **AMÉRIQUE DU SUD**											
Argentina - Argentine											
Number - Nombre	+C	265	260	287	245	309	356	321	313	290	...
Rate - Taux	+C	38.3	38.1	41.8	34.9	45.2	51.2	46.0	42.5	40.7	...
Brazil - Brésil											
Number - Nombre	U	1 791	1 937	1 823	1 648	1 587	1 648	1 597	1 672	...	...
Chile - Chili											
Number - Nombre	C	61	55	60	49	45	42	33	42	48	...
Rate - Taux	C	23.5	21.4	23.9	19.7	18.3	17.6	14.1	18.2	20.8	...
Colombia - Colombie											
Number - Nombre	U	420	721	676	776	689	577	...	546	504	...
Ecuador - Équateur											
Number - Nombre	U	162	153	209	232	187	149	139	129	143	...
French Guiana Guyane française											
Number - Nombre	...	...	...	...	...	2	2	1	1	1	...
Guyana											
Number - Nombre	U	...	24	17	...	17	20	21	19	24	...
Paraguay											
Number - Nombre	+U	89	96	103	140	132	163	150	154	...	...
Peru - Pérou											
Number - Nombre	+U	246	279	261	263	...	...	...	...	...	...
Suriname											
Number - Nombre	U	5	7	4	9	...	...	...	...	...	...
Uruguay											
Number - Nombre	C	17	11	6	9	19	...	...	9	...	...
Rate - Taux	C	♦29.3	♦20.1	♦11.1	♦17.1	♦36.6	...	...	♦18.0	...	...

17. Maternal deaths and maternal death rates: 1997 - 2006
Mortalité liée à la maternité nombre de décès et taux: 1997 - 2006 (continued - suite)

Continent and country or area / Continent et pays ou zone	Code de[a]	1997	1998	1999	2000	2001	2002	2003	2004	2005	2006
AMERICA, SOUTH - AMÉRIQUE DU SUD											
Venezuela (Bolivarian Republic of) - Venezuela (République bolivarienne du)											
Number - Nombre	C	308	256	313	327	356	335	321	318	351	...
Rate - Taux	C	59.6	51.0	59.3	60.1	67.2	68.0	57.8	49.9	52.7	...
ASIA - ASIE											
Armenia - Arménie											
Number - Nombre	C	17	10	12	18	7	3	8	...	...	...
Rate - Taux	C	♦38.7	♦25.4	♦32.9	♦52.5	♦21.8	♦9.3	♦22.4	...	...	...
Azerbaijan - Azerbaïdjan											
Number - Nombre	U	41	51	51	44	27	22	21	34	...	...
Bahrain - Bahreïn											
Number - Nombre	C	2	2	3	2	3	...	...	...	...	...
Rate - Taux	C	♦14.9	♦14.9	♦21.0	♦14.3	♦22.3	...	...	...	...	...
Brunei Darussalam - Brunéi Darussalam											
Number - Nombre	+C	2	3	-	2	...	...	...	...	...	...
Rate - Taux	+C	♦26.8	♦40.5	-	♦26.7	...	...	...	...	...	...
China: Hong Kong SAR - Chine: Hong Kong RAS											
Number - Nombre	...	1	1	1	3	1	1	2	2	2	1
Cyprus - Chypre											
Number - Nombre	C	...	...	-	-	...	...	...	-	...	1
Rate - Taux	C	...	...	-	-	...	...	...	-	...	♦11.5
Georgia - Géorgie											
Number - Nombre	U	13	15	9	4	4	...	...	...	...	...
Israel - Israël											
Number - Nombre	C	12	11	9	5	9	6	3	6	...	...
Rate - Taux	C	♦9.6	♦8.5	♦6.8	♦3.7	♦6.6	♦4.3	♦2.1	♦4.1	...	...
Japan - Japon											
Number - Nombre	C	81	89	79	84	79	90	74	56	66	63
Rate - Taux	C	6.8	7.4	6.7	7.1	6.7	7.8	6.6	5.0	6.2	5.8
Kazakhstan											
Number - Nombre	U	137	122	98	94	87	80	67	63	81	100
Korea (Republic of) - Corée (République de)											
Number - Nombre	U	66	63	77	62	70	71	58	59	53	54
Kuwait - Koweït											
Number - Nombre	U	7	3	3	2	1	3	...	...	...	...
Kyrgyzstan - Kirghizistan											
Number - Nombre	U	64	35	44	44	43	54	52	56	66	67
Maldives											
Number - Nombre	+C	...	...	...	4	3	7	-	2	1	...
Rate - Taux	+C	...	...	...	♦74.1	♦61.2	♦139.9	-	♦38.3	♦18.0	...
Philippines											
Number - Nombre	U	1 513	1 579	...	...	...	...	...	...	...	...
Singapore - Singapour											
Number - Nombre	+U	1	5	2	8	4	4	2	1	4	3
Tajikistan - Tadjikistan											
Number - Nombre	U	38	57	45	36	40	57	36	37	28	...
Thailand - Thaïlande											
Number - Nombre	+U	87	63	93	102	...	114	...	...	...	...
Turkmenistan - Turkménistan											
Number - Nombre	U	21	16	...	...	...	...	...	...	...	...
Uzbekistan - Ouzbékistan											
Number - Nombre	U	62	48	80	182	...	143	151	156	145	...
EUROPE											
Albania - Albanie											
Number - Nombre	U	5	8	2	8	2	5	1	1	...	...
Austria - Autriche											
Number - Nombre	C	2	4	1	2	5	2	2	3	3	2
Rate - Taux	C	♦2.4	♦4.9	♦1.3	♦2.6	♦6.6	♦2.6	♦2.6	♦3.8	♦3.8	♦2.6

17. Maternal deaths and maternal death rates: 1997 - 2006
Mortalité liée à la maternité nombre de décès et taux: 1997 - 2006 (continued - suite)

Continent and country or area / Continent et pays ou zone	Code[a]	1997	1998	1999	2000	2001	2002	2003	2004	2005	2006
EUROPE											
Belarus - Bélarus											
Number - Nombre	C	23	26	19	20	13	17	18	...	...	...
Rate - Taux	C	♦25.7	♦28.1	♦20.4	♦21.3	♦14.2	♦19.2	♦20.3	...	...	...
Belgium - Belgique											
Number - Nombre	C	10	...	...	...	...	...	...	...	...	...
Rate - Taux	C	♦8.6	...	...	...	...	...	...	...	...	...
Bulgaria - Bulgarie											
Number - Nombre	C	12	10	16	13	13	11	4	7	...	...
Rate - Taux	C	♦18.7	♦15.3	♦22.1	♦17.6	♦19.1	♦16.5	♦5.9	♦10.0	...	...
Croatia - Croatie											
Number - Nombre	C	6	3	5	3	1	4	3	3	3	4
Rate - Taux	C	♦10.8	♦6.4	♦11.1	♦6.9	♦2.4	♦10.0	♦7.6	♦7.4	♦7.1	♦9.7
Czech Republic - République tchèque											
Number - Nombre	C	2	5	6	5	3	3	4	5	3	...
Rate - Taux	C	♦2.2	♦5.5	♦6.7	♦5.5	♦3.3	♦3.1	♦4.3	♦5.1	♦2.9	...
Denmark - Danemark											
Number - Nombre	C	5	2	4	-	2	...	...	...	...	...
Rate - Taux	C	♦7.4	♦3.0	♦6.0	-	♦3.1	...	...	...	...	...
Estonia - Estonie											
Number - Nombre	C	2	2	2	5	1	1	4	4	2	...
Rate - Taux	C	♦15.9	♦16.4	♦16.1	♦38.3	♦7.9	♦7.7	♦30.7	♦28.6	♦13.9	...
Finland - Finlande											
Number - Nombre	C	3	3	2	3	3	3	2	7	3	4
Rate - Taux	C	♦5.1	♦5.3	♦3.5	♦5.3	♦5.3	♦5.4	♦3.5	♦12.1	♦5.2	♦6.8
France											
Number - Nombre	C	70	75	55	50	56	67	56	53	41	...
Rate - Taux	C	9.6	10.2	7.4	6.5	7.3	8.8	7.4	6.9	5.3	...
Germany - Allemagne											
Number - Nombre	C	49	44	37	43	27	21	30	37	28	41
Rate - Taux	C	6.0	5.6	4.8	5.6	♦3.7	♦2.9	♦4.2	5.2	♦4.1	6.1
Greece - Grèce											
Number - Nombre	C	-	7	6	-	4	1	2	3	-	3
Rate - Taux	C	-	♦6.9	♦6.0	-	♦3.9	♦1.0	♦1.9	♦2.8	-	♦2.7
Hungary - Hongrie											
Number - Nombre	C	21	6	4	10	5	8	7	4	5	...
Rate - Taux	C	♦20.9	♦6.2	♦4.2	♦10.2	♦5.2	♦8.3	♦7.4	♦4.2	♦5.1	...
Iceland - Islande											
Number - Nombre	C	-	-	-	-	1	-	-	-	-	-
Rate - Taux	C	-	-	-	-	♦24.4	-	-	-	-	-
Ireland - Irlande											
Number - Nombre	C	3	2	1	1	3	5	-	-	2	-
Rate - Taux	C	♦5.7	♦3.7	♦1.9	♦1.8	♦5.2	♦8.3	-	-	♦3.3	-
Italy - Italie											
Number - Nombre	C	23	18	14	16	11	17	28	...	...	...
Rate - Taux	C	♦4.3	♦3.4	♦2.6	♦2.9	♦2.1	♦3.2	♦5.1	...	...	...
Latvia - Lettonie											
Number - Nombre	+C	8	9	8	5	5	1	3	2	1	2
Rate - Taux	+C	♦42.5	♦48.9	♦41.2	♦24.7	♦25.4	♦5.0	♦14.3	♦9.8	♦4.7	♦9.0
Lithuania - Lituanie											
Number - Nombre	+C	6	5	5	3	4	6	1	5	4	-
Rate - Taux	+C	♦15.9	♦13.5	♦13.7	♦8.8	♦12.7	♦20.0	♦3.3	♦16.4	♦13.1	-
Luxembourg											
Number - Nombre	+C	-	1	-	1	-	-	-	1	1	...
Rate - Taux	+C	-	♦18.6	-	♦17.5	-	-	-	♦18.3	♦18.6	...
Malta - Malte											
Number - Nombre	+C	-	1	1	-	2	-	-	-	-	...
Rate - Taux	+C	-	♦21.4	♦22.7	-	♦50.5	-	-	-	-	...
Moldova											
Number - Nombre	+U	23	15	11	10	16	11	8	9	8	6
Netherlands - Pays-Bas											
Number - Nombre	+C	15	23	19	18	14	20	8	10	16	15
Rate - Taux	+C	♦7.8	♦11.5	♦9.5	♦8.7	♦6.9	♦9.9	♦4.0	♦5.2	♦8.5	♦8.1
Norway - Norvège											
Number - Nombre	+C	1	4	5	2	3	2	7	-	2	...
Rate - Taux	+C	♦1.7	♦6.9	♦8.4	♦3.4	♦5.3	♦3.6	♦12.4	-	♦3.5	...
Poland - Pologne											
Number - Nombre	C	...	...	20	30	13	19	14	17	11	11
Rate - Taux	C	...	...	♦5.2	♦7.9	♦3.5	♦5.4	♦4.0	♦4.8	♦3.0	♦2.9

17. Maternal deaths and maternal death rates: 1997 - 2006
Mortalité liée à la maternité nombre de décès et taux: 1997 - 2006 (continued - suite)

Continent and country or area Continent et pays ou zone	Co- de[a]	1997	1998	1999	2000	2001	2002	2003	2004	2005	2006
EUROPE											
Portugal											
Number - Nombre	+C	6	9	6	3	6	8	8	...	...	...
Rate - Taux	+C	♦5.3	♦7.9	♦5.2	♦2.5	♦5.3	♦7.0	♦7.1	...	...	...
Romania - Roumanie											
Number - Nombre	+C	98	96	**98**	75	75	47	65	52	37	34
Rate - Taux	+C	41.4	40.5	**41.8**	32.0	34.0	22.3	30.6	24.0	16.7	15.5
Russian Federation - Fédération de Russie[1]											
Number - Nombre	+C	633	565	**537**	503	479	469	463	352	370	352
Rate - Taux	+C	50.2	44.0	**44.2**	39.7	36.5	33.6	31.3	23.4	25.4	23.8
San Marino - Saint-Marin											
Number - Nombre	+U	-	-	-	-	-	-	-	...	-	...
Serbia - Serbie											
Number - Nombre	+C	...	...	...	...	...	...	...	2	10	9
Rate - Taux	+C	...	...	...	...	...	...	...	♦2.6	♦13.9	♦12.7
Slovakia - Slovaquie											
Number - Nombre	C	1	5	5	1	7	4	2	3	2	...
Rate - Taux	C	♦1.7	♦8.7	♦8.9	♦1.8	♦13.7	♦7.9	♦3.9	♦5.6	♦3.7	...
Slovenia - Slovénie											
Number - Nombre	C	2	-	2	2	3	-	-	2	1	3
Rate - Taux	C	♦11.0	-	♦11.4	♦11.0	♦17.2	-	-	♦11.1	♦5.5	♦15.8
Spain - Espagne											
Number - Nombre	C	8	10	**14**	**14**	**17**	**14**	**20**	**21**	**18**	...
Rate - Taux	C	♦2.2	♦2.7	♦3.7	♦3.5	♦4.2	♦3.3	♦4.5	♦4.6	♦3.9	...
Sweden - Suède											
Number - Nombre	C	3	7	1	4	3	4	2	2	6	...
Rate - Taux	C	♦3.3	♦7.9	♦1.1	♦4.4	♦3.3	♦4.2	♦2.0	♦2.0	♦5.9	...
Switzerland - Suisse											
Number - Nombre	C	3	3	6	5	1	3	4	4	4	...
Rate - Taux	C	♦3.7	♦3.8	♦7.7	♦6.4	♦1.4	♦4.1	♦5.6	♦5.5	♦5.5	...
The Former Yugoslav Rep. of Macedonia - L'ex-République yougoslave de Macédoine											
Number - Nombre	C	1	1	2	4	4	3	1	...	...	...
Rate - Taux	C	♦3.4	♦3.4	♦7.3	♦13.6	♦14.8	♦10.8	♦3.7	...	...	...
Ukraine											
Number - Nombre	C	111	114	98	95	90	85	71	56	75	...
Rate - Taux	C	25.1	27.2	25.2	24.7	23.9	21.8	17.4	13.1	17.6	...
United Kingdom - Royaume-Uni											
Number - Nombre	+C	39	49	37	46	50	40	53	55	51	50
Rate - Taux	+C	5.4	6.8	5.3	6.8	7.5	6.0	7.6	7.7	7.1	6.7
OCEANIA - OCÉANIE											
Australia - Australie											
Number - Nombre	C	12	5	**13**	**13**	**12**	**13**	**8**	...	...	...
Rate - Taux	C	♦4.8	♦2.0	♦5.2	♦5.2	♦4.9	♦5.2	♦3.2	...	...	...
Kiribati											
Number - Nombre	U	*3*	-	*1*	-	*1*	...	...	...	...	...
New Zealand - Nouvelle-Zélande											
Number - Nombre	+C	3	3	4	5	3	8	4	4	...	...
Rate - Taux	+C	♦5.2	♦5.4	♦7.0	♦8.8	♦5.4	♦14.8	♦7.1	♦6.9	...	...

FOOTNOTES - NOTES

Data in bold refer to maternal deaths based on ICD-10 Classification, otherwise data refer to maternal deaths based on ICD-9 Classification. - Les données en typographie gras se rapportent aux décès maternelles basées sur la classification CIM-10, autrement les données se rapportent aux décès maternelles basées sur la classification CIM-9.

Italics: data from civil registers which are incomplete or of unknown completeness. - Italiques: données incomplètes ou dont le degré d'exactitude n'est pas connu, provenant des registres de l'état civil.

* Provisional. - Données provisoires.

♦ Rates based on 30 or fewer deaths. - Taux basés sur 30 décès ou moins.

[a] 'Code' indicates the source of data, as follows:
C - Civil registration, estimated over 90% complete
U - Civil registration, estimated less than 90% complete
| - Other source, estimated reliable
+ - Data tabulated by date of registration rather than occurence.
... - Information not available

Le 'Code' indique la source des données, comme suit:
C - Registres de l'état civil considérés complèts à 90 p. 100 au moins.

U - Registres de l'état civil qui ne sont pas considérés complèts à 90 p. 100 au moins.

| - Autre source, considérée pas douteuses.

+ - Données exploitées selon la date de l'enregistrement et non la date de l'événement.

... - Information pas disponible.

[1] For 2003 and before, data on cause of death do not include the Chechnya region. Therefore, rates must be used with caution as they are based on the total population, which is assumed to include all regions. - Pour 2003 et avant, les données sur les causes de décès ne comprennent par la région de Chechnya. Par conséquent, les taux doivent être utilisés avec précaution car ils sont basés sur la population totale, qui est supposée inclure toutes les régions.

473

Table 18

Table 18 presents deaths and crude death rates by urban/rural residence for as many years as possible between 2002 and 2006.

Description of variables: Death is defined as the permanent disappearance of all evidence of life at any time after live birth has taken place (post-natal cessation of vital functions without capability of resuscitation).

Statistics on the number of deaths are obtained from civil registers unless otherwise noted. For those countries or areas where civil registration statistics on deaths are considered reliable (estimated completeness of 90 per cent or more), the death rates shown have been calculated on the basis of registered deaths.

The urban/rural classification of deaths is that provided by each country or area; it is presumed to be based on the national census definitions of urban population that have been set forth at the end of the technical notes for table 6.

For certain countries, there is a discrepancy between the total number of deaths shown in this table and those shown in subsequent tables for the same year. Usually this discrepancy arises because the total number of deaths occurring in a given year is revised although the remaining tabulations are not.

Rate computation: Crude death rates are the annual number of deaths per 1 000 mid-year population.

Rates by urban/rural residence are the annual number of deaths, in the appropriate urban or rural category, per 1 000 corresponding mid-year population. These rates are calculated by the Statistics Division of the United Nations based on the appropriate reference population (for example: total population, nationals only etc.) if known and available. If the reference population is not known or unavailable the total population is used to calculate the rates. Therefore, if the population that is used to calculate the rates is different from the correct reference population, the rates presented might under- or overstate the true situation in a country or area.

Rates presented in this table are limited to those countries or areas with a minimum number of 30 deaths in a given year.

Reliability of data: Each country or area has been asked to indicate the estimated completeness of the deaths recorded in its civil register. These national assessments are indicated by the quality codes (C), (U) and (|) that appear in the first column of this table. C indicates that the data are estimated to be virtually complete, that is, representing at least 90 per cent of the deaths occurring each year, while U indicates that data are estimated to be incomplete that is, representing less than 90 per cent of the deaths occurring each year. The code (I) indicates that the source of data is different than civil registration, but still considered reliable and explained by footnote. The code (...) indicates that no information was provided regarding completeness or no assessment has been done in the country.

Data from civil registers that are reported as incomplete or of unknown completeness (code U or ...) are considered unreliable. They appear in italics in this table; rates based on these data are not computed.

Limitations: Statistics on deaths are subject to the same qualifications as have been set forth for vital statistics in general and death statistics in particular as discussed in section 4 of the Introduction.

The reliability of the data, an indication of which is described above, is an important factor in considering the limitations. In addition, some deaths are tabulated by date of registration and not by date of occurrence; these have been indicated with a plus sign (+). Whenever the lag between the date of occurrence and date of registration is prolonged and, therefore, a large proportion of the death registrations are delayed, death statistics for any given year may be seriously affected. However, delays in the registration of deaths are less common and shorter than in the registration of live births.

International comparability in mortality statistics may also be affected by the exclusion of deaths of infants who were born alive but died before the registration of the birth or within the first 24 hours of life. Statistics of this type are footnoted.

In addition, it should be noted that rates are affected also by the quality and limitations of the population estimates that are used in their computation. The problems of under-enumeration or over-enumeration and, to some extent, the differences in definition of total population have been discussed in section 3 of the Introduction dealing with population data in general, and specific information pertaining to individual countries or areas is given in the footnotes to table 3.

Estimated rates based directly on the results of sample surveys are subject to considerable error as a result of omissions in reporting deaths or as a result of erroneous reporting of those that occurred outside the period of reference. However, such rates do have the advantage of having a "built-in" and corresponding base.

It should be emphasized that crude death rates -- like other crude rates, such as of birth, marriage and divorce -- may be seriously affected by the age-sex structure of the populations to which they relate. Nevertheless, they do provide a simple measure of the level and changes in mortality.

The comparability of data by urban/rural residence is affected by the national definitions of urban and rural used in tabulating these data. It is assumed, in the absence of specific information to the contrary, that the definitions of urban and rural used in connection with the national population census were also used in the compilation of the vital statistics for each country or area. However, it cannot be excluded that, for a given country or area, different definitions of urban and rural are used for the vital statistics data and the population census data respectively. When known, the definitions of urban used in national population censuses are presented at the end of the technical notes for table 6. As discussed in detail in the technical notes for table 6, these definitions vary considerably from one country or area to another.

In addition to problems of comparability, vital rates classified by urban/rural residence are also subject to certain types of bias. If, when calculating vital rates, different definitions of urban are used in connection with the vital events and the population data and if this results in a net difference between the numerator and denominator of the rate in the population at risk, then the vital rates would be biased. Urban/rural differentials in vital rates may also be affected by whether the vital events have been tabulated in terms of place of occurrence or place of usual residence. This problem is discussed in more detail in section 4.1.4.1 of the Introduction.

Earlier data: Deaths and crude death rates have been shown in each issue of the Demographic Yearbook. Data included in this table update the series covering a period of years as follows:

Issue	Years Covered
Historical Supplement CD, 1997	1948 – 1997
1992	1983 – 1992
1985	1976 – 1985
1980	1971 – 1980
Historical Supplement, 1979	1948 – 1977

Tableau 18

Le tableau 18 présente le nombre des décès et les taux bruts de mortalité selon le lieu de résidence (zone urbaine ou rurale) pour le plus grand nombre d'années possible entre 2002 et 2006.

Description des variables : Le décès est défini comme la disparition permanente de tout signe de vie à un moment quelconque postérieur à la naissance vivante (cessation des fonctions vitales après la naissance sans possibilité de réanimation).

Sauf indication contraire, les statistiques relatives au nombre de décès sont établies sur la base des registres d'état civil. Pour les pays ou zones où les données concernant l'enregistrement des décès par les services de l'état civil sont jugées sûres (complétude estimée à 90 p. 100 ou plus), les taux de mortalité ont été calculés d'après les décès enregistrés.

La répartition des décès entre zones urbaines et zones rurales est celle qui a été communiquée par chaque pays ou zone ; on part du principe qu'elle repose sur les définitions de la population urbaine utilisées pour les recensements nationaux, qui sont reproduites à la fin des notes techniques du tableau 6.

Pour quelques pays il y a une discordance entre le nombre total des décès présenté dans ce tableau et ceux présentés après pour la même année. Habituellement ces différences apparaissent lorsque le nombre total des décès pour une certaine année a été révisé alors que les autres tabulations ne l'ont pas été.

Calcul des taux : Les taux bruts de mortalité représentent le nombre annuel de décès pour 1 000 habitants en milieu d'année.

Les taux selon le lieu de résidence (zone urbaine ou rurale) représentent le nombre annuel de décès, classés selon la catégorie urbaine ou rurale appropriée, pour 1 000 habitants en milieu d'année. Ces taux sont calculés par la division de statistique des Nations Unies sur la base de la population de référence adéquate (par exemple : population totale, nationaux seulement, etc.) si connue et disponible. Si la population de référence n'est pas connue ou n'est pas disponible, la population totale est utilisée pour calculer les taux. Par conséquent, si la population utilisée pour calculer les taux est différente de la population de référence adéquate, les taux présentés sont susceptibles de sous ou sur estimer la situation réelle d'un pays ou d'un territoire.

Les taux présentés dans ce tableau se rapportent seulement aux pays ou zones où l'on a enregistré un nombre minimal de 30 décès au cours d'une année donnée.

Fiabilité des données : Il a été demandé à chaque pays ou zone d'indiquer le degré estimatif de complétude des données sur les décès d'enfants de moins d'un an figurant dans ses registres d'état civil. Ces évaluations nationales sont signalées par les codes de qualité 'C', 'U' et 'I' qui apparaissent dans la deuxième colonne du tableau.

La lettre 'C' indique que les données sont jugées à peu près complètes, c'est-à-dire qu'elles représentent au moins 90 p. 100 des décès d'enfants de moins d'un an survenus chaque année ; la lettre 'U' signifie que les données sont jugées incomplètes, c'est-à-dire qu'elles représentent moins de 90 p.100 des décès d'enfants de moins d'un an survenus chaque année. Le symbole 'I' indique que la source des données est fiable mais n'est pas un registre de l'état civil ; le symbole, dans ce cas, est accompagné par une note explicative. Le code '...' dénote qu'aucun renseignement n'a été communiqué quant à la complétude des données.

Les données provenant des registres de l'état civil qui sont déclarées incomplètes ou dont le degré de complétude n'est pas connu (code 'U' ou '...') sont jugées douteuses. Elles apparaissent en italique dans le présent tableau et les taux correspondants n'ont pas été calculés.

Insuffisance des données : Les statistiques relatives à la mortalité appellent les mêmes réserves que celles qui ont été formulées à propos des statistiques de l'état civil en général et des statistiques relatives aux décès en particulier (voir la section 4 des Introduction).

La fiabilité des données, au sujet de laquelle des indications ont été fournies plus haut, est un facteur important. Il faut également tenir compte du fait que, dans certains cas, les décès sont classés par date d'enregistrement et non par date d'occurrence ; ces cas ont été signalés par le signe '+'. Chaque fois que le décalage entre le décès et son enregistrement est grand et qu'une forte proportion des décès fait l'objet d'un enregistrement tardif, les statistiques relatives aux décès survenus pendant l'année peuvent être considérablement faussées.

En règle générale, toutefois, les décès sont enregistrés beaucoup plus rapidement que les naissances vivantes, et les retards prolongés sont rares.

Un autre facteur qui nuit à la comparabilité internationale est la pratique qui consiste à ne pas inclure dans les statistiques de la mortalité les enfants nés vivants mais décédés avant l'enregistrement de leur naissance ou dans les 24 heures qui ont suivi la naissance. Quand pareil facteur a joué, cela a été signalé en note à la fin du tableau.

Il convient de noter par ailleurs que l'exactitude des taux dépend également de la qualité et des limitations des estimations de la population qui sont utilisées pour leur calcul. Le problème des erreurs par excès ou par défaut commises lors du dénombrement et, dans une certaine mesure, le problème de l'hétérogénéité des définitions de la population totale ont été examinés à la section 3 de l'Introduction, relative à la population en général ; des indications concernant certains pays ou zones sont données en note à la fin du tableau 3.

Les taux estimatifs fondés directement sur les résultats d'enquêtes par sondage comportent des possibilités d'erreurs considérables dues soit à des omissions dans les déclarations des décès, soit au fait que l'on a déclaré à tort des décès survenus en réalité hors de la période considérée. Toutefois, ces taux présentent un avantage : le chiffre de population utilisé comme base est connu par définition et rigoureusement correspondant.

Il faut souligner que les taux bruts de mortalité, de même que les taux bruts de natalité, de nuptialité et de divortialité, peuvent varier très sensiblement selon la composition par âge et par sexe de la population à laquelle ils se rapportent. Ils offrent néanmoins un moyen simple de mesurer le niveau et l'évolution de la mortalité.

La comparabilité des données selon le lieu de résidence (zone urbaine ou rurale) peut être limitée par les définitions nationales des termes « urbain » et « rural » utilisées pour le classement de ces données. En l'absence d'indications contraires, on a supposé que les mêmes définitions avaient servi pour le recensement national de la population et pour l'établissement des statistiques de l'état civil pour chaque pays ou zone. Toutefois, il n'est pas exclu que, pour une zone ou un pays donné, des définitions différentes aient été retenues. Les définitions du terme « urbain » utilisées pour les recensements nationaux de population ont été présentées à la fin du tableau 6 lorsqu'elles étaient connues. Comme on l'a précisé dans les notes techniques relatives au tableau 6, ces définitions varient considérablement d'un pays ou d'une zone à l'autre.

Outre les problèmes de comparabilité, les taux démographiques classés selon le lieu de résidence « urbaine » ou « rurale » sont également sujets à des distorsions particulières. Si l'on utilise des définitions différentes du terme « urbain » pour classer les faits d'état civil et les données relatives à la population lors du calcul des taux et qu'il en résulte une différence nette entre le numérateur et le dénominateur pour le taux de la population exposée au risque, les taux démographiques s'en trouveront faussés. La différence entre ces taux pour les zones urbaines et rurales pourra aussi être faussée selon que les faits d'état civil auront été classés d'après le lieu où ils se sont produits ou d'après le lieu de résidence habituel. Ce problème est examiné plus en détail à la section 4.1.4.1 de l' Introduction.

Données publiées antérieurement : les différentes éditions de l'*Annuaire démographique* contiennent des statistiques des décès et des taux bruts de mortalité. Les données qui figurent dans le tableau 18 actualisent les données qui portaient sur les périodes suivantes :

Éditions	Années considérées
Supplément historique (CD-ROM), 1997	1948 – 1997
1992	1983 – 1992
1985	1976 – 1985
1980	1971 – 1980
Supplément rétrospectif, 1979	1948 – 1977

18. Deaths and crude death rates, by urban/rural residence: 2002 - 2006
Décès et taux bruts de mortalité, selon la résidence, urbaine/rurale: 2002 - 2000

Continent, country or area, and urban/rural residence / Continent, pays ou zone et résidence, urbaine/rurale	Code[a]	Number - Nombre					Rate - Taux				
		2002	2003	2004	2005	2006	2002	2003	2004	2005	2006
AFRICA - AFRIQUE											
Algeria - Algérie[1]											
Total	U	126 557	145 000	141 000	147 000	144 000	...	...	...	...	...
Egypt - Égypte											
Total	C	424 034	440 149	440 790	450 646	451 863	6.4	6.5	6.4	6.4	6.3
Urban - Urbaine	C	204 377	211 719	195 491	198 588	214 008	7.2	7.3	6.6	6.6	7.0
Rural - Rurale	C	219 657	228 430	245 299	252 058	237 855	5.8	5.9	6.2	6.2	5.8
Ghana											
Total	...		34 682								
Kenya											
Total	U	171 800	174 950	178 051	168 919	174 856	...	...	...	...	...
Libyan Arab Jamahiriya - Jamahiriya arabe libyenne											
Total	U	19 362					...	...	...	...	...
Malawi											
Total[2]	I	217 205	213 705	...	...	...	19.4	18.5	...	...	...
Total	U	...	...	...	...	207 641	...	...	...	...	...
Mauritius - Maurice											
Total	+C	8 310	8 520	8 475	8 646	9 162	6.9	7.0	6.9	7.0	7.3
Urban - Urbaine	+C	3 702	3 942	3 914	3 988	4 142	7.2	7.6	7.5	7.6	7.9
Rural - Rurale	+C	4 608	4 578	4 561	4 658	5 020	6.6	6.5	6.4	6.5	6.9
Mayotte											
Total	C	...	...	513			...	...	...	...	...
Réunion[3]											
Total	C	4 004	*4 022	3 884	4 357	*4 323	5.4	*5.3	5.1	5.6	*5.5
Saint Helena ex. dep. - Sainte-Hélène sans dép.											
Total	C	52	44	33	39		...	...	...	...	...
Seychelles											
Total	+C	647	668	611	673	664	7.7	8.1	7.4	8.1	7.8
South Africa - Afrique du Sud											
Total	U	499 925	553 718	572 350	591 213		...	...	...	...	...
Zambia - Zambie[2]											
Total	I	...	...	...	...	152 549	...	...	...	...	12.9
Zimbabwe[4]											
Total	I	200 294	...	...	...	...	17.2	...	...	...	...
Urban - Urbaine	I	50 364	...	...	...	...	12.5	...	...	...	...
Rural - Rurale	I	149 930	...	...	...	...	19.7	...	...	...	...
AMERICA, NORTH - AMÉRIQUE DU NORD											
Anguilla											
Total	+C	52	65	53	62	*59	4.4	5.3	4.2	4.5	*4.1
Antigua and Barbuda - Antigua-et-Barbuda[5]											
Total	+C	444	...	...	...	...	5.7	...	...	...	...
Aruba											
Total	C	492	501	502	482	537	5.3	5.3	5.1	4.8	5.2
Bahamas											
Total	C	...	1 649	...	...	...	...	5.2	...	...	...
Barbados - Barbade											
Total	+C	*2 285	...	...	...	...	*8.4	...	...	...	...
Belize											
Total	U	1 284	1 277	1 298	1 369		...	...	...	...	...
Bermuda - Bermudes[6]											
Total	C	404	434	406	437	461	6.4	6.9	6.4	6.9	7.2
British Virgin Islands - Îles Vierges britanniques											
Total	C	97	104	120	...	...	4.6	4.9	5.5	...	...
Canada[7]											
Total	C	223 603	226 169	226 584	230 132	*233 415	7.1	7.1	7.1	7.1	*7.1
Cayman Islands - Îles Caïmanes											
Total	C	120	153	165	170	182	2.8	3.5	3.7	3.5	3.5

18. Deaths and crude death rates, by urban/rural residence: 2002 - 2006
Décès et taux bruts de mortalité, selon la résidence, urbaine/rurale: 2002 - 2006 (continued - suite)

Continent, country or area, and urban/rural residence / Continent, pays ou zone et résidence, urbaine/rurale	Code[a]	Number - Nombre					Rate - Taux				
		2002	2003	2004	2005	2006	2002	2003	2004	2005	2006
AMERICA, NORTH - AMÉRIQUE DU NORD											
Costa Rica											
Total	C	15 004	15 800	15 949	16 139	16 766	3.8	3.9	3.8	3.8	3.9
Cuba											
Total	C	73 882	78 434	*81 095	84 824	80 840	6.6	7.0	*7.2	7.5	7.2
Urban - Urbaine	C	60 167[8]	64 200[8]	*68 587	69 969	67 111	7.1	7.6	*8.1	8.2	7.9
Rural - Rurale	C	13 697[8]	14 224[8]	*12 508	14 855	13 729	5.1	5.2	*4.6	5.4	5.0
Dominica - Dominique[5]											
Total	+C	594	557	...	...	...	8.4	...	...	...	...
Dominican Republic - République dominicaine											
Total	+U	27 309	29 821	34 325	33 949	...	...	...	...	...	...
Urban - Urbaine[8]	+U	19 990	21 899	25 435	25 969	...	...	...	...	...	...
Rural - Rurale[8]	+U	5 990	5 987	6 708	6 824	...	...	...	...	...	...
El Salvador											
Total	C	27 458	29 377	30 058	30 933	31 453	4.2	4.4	4.4	4.5	4.5
Urban - Urbaine	C	19 595	20 856	20 576	21 612	24 682	5.1	5.3	5.1	5.3	5.9
Rural - Rurale	C	7 863	8 521	9 482	9 321	6 771	2.9	3.1	3.5	3.4	2.4
Greenland - Groenland											
Total	C	435	412	475	466	440	7.7	7.3	8.3	8.2	7.7
Urban - Urbaine	C	344	340	...	...	...	7.4	7.3	...	...	...
Rural - Rurale	C	91	72	...	...	...	9.0	7.2	...	...	...
Guadeloupe[3]											
Total	C	2 584	2 636	2 676	2 904	2 902	5.9	6.0	6.0	6.5	6.3
Guatemala											
Total	C	66 089	66 695	66 991	71 039	69 756	5.5	5.5	5.4	5.6	5.4
Urban - Urbaine	C	...	...	...	38 444	38 897	...	...	...	...	...
Rural - Rurale	C	...	...	...	32 595	30 859	...	...	...	...	...
Haiti - Haïti[5]											
Total	U	7 657	8 011	...	...	...	...	...	...	...	...
Honduras											
Total	+U	34 379	34 754	35 075	35 356	35 682	...	...	...	...	...
Urban - Urbaine	+U	13 030	13 459	13 867	14 251	14 654	...	...	...	...	...
Rural - Rurale	+U	21 349	21 295	21 208	21 105	21 028	...	...	...	...	...
Jamaica - Jamaïque[9]											
Total	U	17 018	16 699	16 905	17 552	16 317	...	...	...	...	...
Martinique[3]											
Total	C	2 681	2 725	2 647	2 610	2 663	6.9	7.0	6.7	6.6	6.7
Mexico - Mexique[10]											
Total	+C	457 680	470 692	472 273	493 957	493 296	4.5	4.6	4.6	4.8	4.7
Urban - Urbaine[8]	+C	342 331	354 633	353 951	370 267	370 811	4.5	4.6	4.5	4.7	4.6
Rural - Rurale[8]	+C	107 345	109 167	110 999	116 657	116 393	4.3	4.4	4.5	4.8	4.8
Netherlands Antilles - Antilles néerlandaises[11]											
Total	C	1 220	1 374	1 412	1 304	1 323	7.0	7.7	7.7	7.0	7.0
Nicaragua											
Total	+U	15 070	15 379	14 975	16 770	...	...	...	...	...	...
Urban - Urbaine	+U	9 805	10 180	10 489	10 931	...	...	...	...	...	...
Rural - Rurale	+U	5 265	5 199	4 486	5 839	...	...	...	...	...	...
Panama											
Total	U	12 428	13 248	13 475	14 180	14 358	...	...	...	...	...
Urban - Urbaine	U	8 214	8 638	9 815	...	...	...	...	...	...	...
Rural - Rurale	U	4 214	4 610	3 660	...	...	...	...	...	...	...
Puerto Rico - Porto Rico											
Total	C	28 098	28 356	29 066	29 702	...	7.3	7.3	7.5	7.6	...
Urban - Urbaine[8]	C	15 026	15 038	15 627	16 000	...	...	...	...	...	...
Rural - Rurale[8]	C	13 009	13 283	13 423	13 617	...	...	...	...	...	...
Saint Lucia - Sainte-Lucie											
Total	C	960	1 046	1 114	*1 107	...	6.0	6.5	6.9	*6.7	...
Saint Vincent and the Grenadines - Saint Vincent-et-les Grenadines											
Total	+C	766	790	812	813	...	7.1	7.5	7.8	7.8	...
Trinidad and Tobago - Trinité-et-Tobago											
Total	C	9 797	...	...	...	...	7.7	...	...	...	...

18. Deaths and crude death rates, by urban/rural residence: 2002 - 2006
Décès et taux bruts de mortalité, selon la résidence, urbaine/rurale: 2002 - 2006 (continued - suite)

Continent, country or area, and urban/rural residence / Continent, pays ou zone et résidence, urbaine/rurale	Code[a]	Number - Nombre					Rate - Taux				
		2002	2003	2004	2005	2006	2002	2003	2004	2005	2006
AMERICA, NORTH - AMÉRIQUE DU NORD											
Turks Caicos Islands - Îles Turques et Caïques											
Total	C	48	61	46	53	73	2.3	2.4	1.7	1.7	2.2
United States - États-Unis											
Total	C	2 443 387	2 448 288	2 397 615	2 448 017	*2 416 000	8.5	8.4	8.2	8.3	*8.1
United States Virgin Islands - Îles Vierges américaines											
Total	C	617[5]	631	626	...	...	5.7	5.8	5.7	...	...
AMERICA, SOUTH - AMÉRIQUE DU SUD											
Argentina - Argentine											
Total	C	291 190	302 064	294 051	293 529	292 313	7.8	8.0	7.7	7.6	7.5
Brazil - Brésil[12]											
Total	U	958 475	977 717	998 725	979 854	1 023 545	...	...	...	...	...
Chile - Chili											
Total	C	81 079	83 672	86 138	86 102	...	5.2	5.3	5.4	5.3	...
Urban - Urbaine	C	69 209	72 647	74 920	73 900	...	5.2	5.3	5.4	5.2	...
Rural - Rurale	C	11 870	11 025	11 218	12 202	...	5.4	5.1	5.3	5.7	...
Colombia - Colombie											
Total	U	192 262	193 267	188 933	189 022	*189 760	...	...	...	...	...
Urban - Urbaine[8]	U	143 237	145 545	144 135	146 173	*146 349	...	...	...	...	...
Rural - Rurale[8]	U	38 094	38 028	36 720	36 123	*36 903	...	...	...	...	...
Ecuador - Équateur[13]											
Total	U	55 549	53 521	54 729	56 825	57 940	...	...	...	...	...
Urban - Urbaine	U	42 236	40 585	41 783	...	...	...	...	...	...	...
Rural - Rurale	U	13 313	12 936	12 946	...	...	...	...	...	...	...
Falkland Islands (Malvinas) - Îles Falkland (Malvinas)											
Total	+C	18	20	15	19	20	...	...	...	...	...
French Guiana - Guyane française[3]											
Total	C	656	692	719	705	711	3.7	3.8	3.8	3.5	3.6
Guyana											
Total	+C	5 003	4 986	5 141	...	...	6.7	6.6	6.8	...	...
Paraguay											
Total	U	...	19 593	20 283	17 360	...	...	...	...	...	...
Peru - Pérou[14]											
Total	+U	80 862	85 198	94 149	...	...	...	...	...	...	...
Suriname											
Total	C	3 125	3 154	3 319	3 392	...	6.6	6.5	6.8	6.8	...
Urban - Urbaine[15]	C	2 188	2 166	2 298	2 308	...	...	...	...	...	...
Rural - Rurale[15]	C	937	988	1 021	1 084	...	...	...	...	...	...
Uruguay											
Total	C	31 628	32 587	32 222	32 319	31 056	9.6	9.9	9.8	9.8	9.4
Venezuela (Bolivarian Republic of) - Venezuela (République bolivarienne du)[12]											
Total	C	105 388	118 562	110 946	110 301	115 348	4.2	4.6	4.2	4.2	4.3
ASIA - ASIE											
Armenia - Arménie[16]											
Total	C	25 554	26 014	25 679	26 379	27 202	8.0	8.1	8.0	8.2	8.4
Urban - Urbaine	C	16 737	16 870	16 531	17 128	17 689	8.1	8.2	8.0	8.3	8.6
Rural - Rurale	C	8 817	9 144	9 148	9 251	9 513	7.7	8.0	7.9	8.0	8.2
Azerbaijan - Azerbaïdjan[16]											
Total	+C	46 522	49 001	49 568	51 962	52 248	5.7	6.0	6.0	6.2	6.2
Urban - Urbaine	+C	23 605	24 999	25 867	...	...	5.7	5.9	6.0	...	...
Rural - Rurale	+C	22 917	24 002	23 701	...	...	5.7	6.0	5.9	...	...

18. Deaths and crude death rates, by urban/rural residence: 2002 - 2006
Décès et taux bruts de mortalité, selon la résidence, urbaine/rurale: 2002 - 2006 (continued - suite)

Continent, country or area, and urban/rural residence / Continent, pays ou zone et résidence, urbaine/rurale	Code[a]	Number - Nombre					Rate - Taux				
		2002	2003	2004	2005	2006	2002	2003	2004	2005	2006
ASIA - ASIE											
Bahrain - Bahreïn											
Total	C	2 035	2 114	2 215	2 222	2 317	3.0	3.1	3.1	3.1	3.1
Bangladesh[17]											
Total	I	...	...	...	...	...	5.1	5.9	5.8	5.8	5.6
Urban - Urbaine	I	...	...	...	...	...	3.8	4.7	4.4	4.9	4.4
Rural - Rurale	I	...	...	...	...	...	5.4	6.2	6.1	6.1	6.0
Bhutan - Bhoutan[18]											
Total	I	...	...	...	4 498	...	...	...	...	7.1	...
Urban - Urbaine	I	...	...	...	1 048	...	...	...	...	...	...
Rural - Rurale	I	...	...	...	3 450	...	...	...	...	...	...
Brunei Darussalam - Brunéi Darussalam											
Total	+C	1 041	1 010	1 010	*1 072	...	3.0	2.9	2.8	*2.9	...
Cambodia - Cambodge											
Total	U	125 617	124 981	124 391	...	...	...	...	...	...	...
China - Chine[19]											
Total	I	8 210 000[20]	8 250 000[20]	8 320 000[20]	8 490 000[21]	...	6.4	6.4	6.4	6.5	6.8[20]
China: Hong Kong SAR - Chine: Hong Kong RAS											
Total	C	34 267	36 971	36 918	38 830	*37 457	5.1	5.5	5.4	5.7	*5.5
China: Macao SAR - Chine: Macao RAS											
Total	C	1 415	1 474	1 533	1 615	1 566	3.2	3.3	3.4	3.4	3.1
Cyprus - Chypre[22]											
Total	C	5 168	5 200	5 225	5 425	5 127	7.3	7.2	7.1	7.2	6.7
Georgia - Géorgie[16]											
Total	C	46 446	46 055	48 793	42 984	42 255	10.7	10.6	11.3	9.9	9.6
Urban - Urbaine	C	...	28 887	...	...	...	...	12.8	...	...	...
Rural - Rurale	C	...	17 168	...	...	...	...	8.3	...	...	...
India - Inde[23]											
Total	I	...	...	...	...	...	8.1	8.0	7.5	7.6	7.5
Urban - Urbaine	I	...	...	...	...	...	6.1	6.0	5.8	6.0	6.0
Rural - Rurale	I	...	...	...	...	...	8.7	8.7	8.2	8.1	8.1
Iran (Islamic Republic of) - Iran (République islamique d')[24]											
Total	C	337 237	368 518	355 213	361 326	408 563	5.1	5.5	5.3	5.3	5.8
Urban - Urbaine	C	234 091	265 239	240 872	238 235	...	5.4	6.0	5.5	5.2	...
Rural - Rurale	C	103 146	103 279	114 341	123 091	...	4.6	4.6	4.9	5.4	...
Iraq											
Total	U	...	*95 935	*101 820	*115 775	...	...	...	...	...	...
Israel - Israël[25]											
Total	C	38 414[26]	38 499[27]	37 938[28]	39 036[29]	38 703[30]	5.8	5.8	5.6	5.6	5.5
Urban - Urbaine	C	35 967	36 086	35 526	36 595	36 302	6.0	5.9	5.7	5.8	5.6
Rural - Rurale	C	2 442	2 407	2 411	2 432	2 395	4.4	4.2	4.1	4.3	4.2
Japan - Japon[31]											
Total	C	982 379	1 014 951	1 028 602	1 083 796	1 084 450	7.8	8.0	8.1	8.6	8.6
Urban - Urbaine[8]	C	724 274	750 810	773 413	877 007	936 383	...	...	...	...	...
Rural - Rurale[8]	C	256 004	261 979	253 197	204 723	146 174	...	...	...	...	...
Jordan - Jordanie[32]											
Total	U	17 220	16 937	17 011	17 883	20 397	...	...	...	...	...
Kazakhstan[16]											
Total	C	149 381	155 277	152 250	157 121	157 210	10.1	10.4	10.1	10.4	10.3
Urban - Urbaine	C	95 470	99 595	98 025	100 651	100 526	11.3	11.7	11.4	11.6	11.5
Rural - Rurale	C	53 911	55 682	54 225	56 470	56 684	8.4	8.7	8.4	8.7	8.7
Korea (Republic of) - Corée (République de)[33]											
Total[34]	C	246 515	245 817	245 771	245 511	243 934	5.1	5.1	5.1	5.0	5.0
Urban - Urbaine	C	156 559	156 802	158 419	159 797	159 877	4.1	4.1	4.1	4.1	4.1
Rural - Rurale	C	88 760	87 661	85 774	84 089	82 391	9.0	8.9	8.8	8.7	8.7
Kuwait - Koweït											
Total	C	4 342	4 424	4 793	4 784	5 247	1.9	1.9	2.0	1.9	...
Kyrgyzstan - Kirghizistan											
Total	C	35 235	35 941	35 061	36 992	38 566	7.1	7.1	6.9	7.2	7.4
Urban - Urbaine	C	13 583	13 943	14 108	14 526	14 930	7.7	7.8	7.8	7.9	8.1
Rural - Rurale	C	21 652	21 998	20 953	22 466	23 636	6.7	6.8	6.4	6.8	7.0

Continent, country or area, and urban/rural residence / Continent, pays ou zone et résidence, urbaine/rurale	Co-de[a]	Number - Nombre					Rate - Taux				
		2002	2003	2004	2005	2006	2002	2003	2004	2005	2006
ASIA - ASIE											
Lebanon - Liban											
Total.	C	17 294	17 187	17 774	18 012	18 787	...	...	4.7	...	...
Malaysia - Malaisie											
Total.	C	105 982	111 644	112 700	*113 531	*117 400	4.3	4.5	4.4	*4.3	*4.4
Maldives											
Total.	C	1 113	1 030	1 015	1 027	1 084	4.0	3.6	3.5	3.5	3.6
Urban - Urbaine	C	347	297	294	327	354	4.5	3.8	3.7	...	...
Rural - Rurale	C	766	733	721	700	730	3.8	3.5	3.4	...	...
Mongolia - Mongolie											
Total.	C	15 857	16 006	16 404	16 480	16 682	6.4	6.4	6.5	6.5	6.5
Urban - Urbaine	C	8 981	9 480	10 183	10 148	10 811	6.4	6.6	6.9	6.7	6.9
Rural - Rurale	C	6 876	6 526	6 221	6 332	5 871	6.5	6.2	6.0	6.2	5.8
Myanmar											
Total.	U	*214 680*	*197 716*	*230 683*	*242 549*		...	...	...	...	...
Urban - Urbaine	U	*69 870*	*64 428*	*66 325*	*67 344*		...	...	...	...	...
Rural - Rurale	U	*144 810*	*133 288*	*164 358*	*175 205*		...	...	...	...	...
Occupied Palestinian Territory - Territoire palestinien occupé											
Total.	U	*10 316*	*10 207*	*10 029*	*9 645*	*9 938*					
Oman[35]											
Total.	U	*2 564*	*2 701*	*2 743*	*2 849*	*3 027*	...	...	...	...	...
Pakistan[36]											
Total.	I	...	970 428[37]	...	1 019 467[38]	...	...	6.6	...	6.6	...
Urban - Urbaine	I	...	309 451[37]	...	321 394[38]	...	...	...	...	...	...
Rural - Rurale	I	...	660 977[37]	...	698 073[38]	...	...	...	...	...	...
Philippines											
Total.	C	396 297	396 331	403 191	...	...	5.0	4.9	4.9	...	...
Qatar											
Total.	C	1 220	1 311	1 341	1 545	1 750	1.8	1.8	1.8	1.9	1.9
Saudi Arabia - Arabie saoudite											
Total.	...	*88 728*	*89 976*	*91 243*	*92 487*	*93 752*	...	...	...	...	...
Singapore - Singapour											
Total.	+C	15 820	16 036	15 860	16 215	16 393	3.8	3.8	3.7	3.7	3.7
Sri Lanka											
Total.	+C	*110 637	*114 310	*112 568	*129 822	...	*5.8	*5.9	*5.8	*6.6	...
Syrian Arab Republic - République arabe syrienne[39]											
Total.	U	*62 184*	*62 880*	*62 496*	*73 035*	*72 534*	...	...	...	...	...
Tajikistan - Tadjikistan[16]											
Total.	C	31 142	33 185	29 700	31 500	32 000	4.8	5.0	4.4	4.6	4.6
Urban - Urbaine	C	9 274	9 722	...	...	...	5.4	5.6	...	...	...
Rural - Rurale	C	21 868	23 463	...	...	...	4.6	4.9	...	...	...
Thailand - Thaïlande											
Total.	+U	*380 364*	*384 131*	*393 592*	*395 374*		...	...	...	...	...
Turkey - Turquie[40]											
Total.	I	429 000	436 000	443 000	450 000	456 000	6.2	6.2	6.2	6.2	6.2
United Arab Emirates - Émirats arabes unis											
Total.	...	*5 994*	*6 002*	*6 123*	*6 361*	*6 563*	...	...	...	...	...
Yemen - Yémen											
Total.	U	*21 157*	*20 346*	*22 255*	*19 653*	*20 607*	...	...	...	...	...
EUROPE											
Åland Islands - Îles d'Åland[41]											
Total.	C	236	268	262	259	257	9.0	10.2	9.9	9.7	9.6
Urban - Urbaine	C	104	102	109	110	91	9.8	9.6	10.2	10.2	8.4
Rural - Rurale	C	132	166	153	149	166	8.5	10.6	9.7	9.4	10.3
Albania - Albanie											
Total.	C	16 248	17 967	17 749	17 427	16 935	5.3	5.8	5.7	5.5	5.4
Urban - Urbaine	C	8 560	8 923	9 248	7 040	...	6.4	6.5	6.6	4.8	...
Rural - Rurale	C	7 688	9 044	8 501	10 387	...	4.4	5.2	4.9	6.2	...

18. Deaths and crude death rates, by urban/rural residence: 2002 - 2006
Décès et taux bruts de mortalité, selon la résidence, urbaine/rurale: 2002 - 2006 (continued - suite)

Continent, country or area, and urban/rural residence / Continent, pays ou zone et résidence, urbaine/rurale	Code[a]	Number - Nombre					Rate - Taux				
		2002	2003	2004	2005	2006	2002	2003	2004	2005	2006
EUROPE											
Andorra - Andorre											
Total	C	218	221	281	276	260	3.1	3.0	3.6	3.5	3.2
Austria - Autriche											
Total	C	76 131	77 209	74 292	75 189	74 295	9.4	9.5	9.1	9.1	9.0
Belarus - Bélarus[16]											
Total	C	146 655	143 200	140 064	141 857	138 426	14.8	14.5	14.3	14.5	14.2
Urban - Urbaine	C	77 020	75 420	74 486	76 452	75 437	10.9	10.7	10.6	10.8	10.7
Rural - Rurale	C	69 635	67 780	65 578	65 405	62 989	24.1	23.9	23.6	24.1	23.6
Belgium - Belgique[42]											
Total	C	105 642	107 628	101 929	102 963	101 587	10.2	10.4	9.8	9.8	9.6
Bosnia and Herzegovina - Bosnie-Herzégovine											
Total	C	30 155	31 757	32 616	34 402	33 221	7.9	8.3	8.5	9.0	8.6
Bulgaria - Bulgarie											
Total	C	112 617	111 927	110 110	113 374	113 438	14.3	14.3	14.2	14.6	14.7
Urban - Urbaine	C	63 765	64 495	64 638	65 309	66 352	11.7	11.8	11.9	12.0	12.2
Rural - Rurale	C	48 852	47 432	45 472	48 065	47 086	20.3	20.1	19.4	20.8	20.7
Channel Islands: Guernsey - Îles Anglo-Normandes: Guernsey											
Total	C	561	564	537	525	498	...	...	8.9	...	8.2
Channel Islands: Jersey - Îles Anglo-Normandes: Jersey											
Total	+C	841	760	748	752	759	9.6	8.7	8.5	8.5	8.5
Croatia - Croatie											
Total	C	50 569	52 575	49 756	51 790	50 378	11.4	11.8	11.2	11.7	11.3
Urban - Urbaine	C	24 984	25 976	24 418	25 899	25 144	...	...	...	...	...
Rural - Rurale	C	25 585	26 599	25 338	25 891	25 234	...	...	...	...	...
Czech Republic - République tchèque											
Total	C	108 243	111 288	107 177	107 938	104 441	10.6	10.9	10.5	10.5	10.2
Urban - Urbaine	C	78 023	80 561	77 674	78 141	75 900	10.4	10.7	10.3	10.3	10.0
Rural - Rurale	C	30 220	30 727	29 503	29 797	28 541	11.3	11.5	11.0	11.1	10.5
Denmark - Danemark[43]											
Total	C	58 610	57 574	55 806	54 962	55 477	10.9	10.7	10.3	10.1	10.2
Estonia - Estonie											
Total	C	18 355	18 152	17 685	17 316	17 316	13.5	13.4	13.1	12.9	12.9
Urban - Urbaine	C	11 953[8]	11 596[8]	11 432[8]	11 053[8]	10 431	12.7	12.4	12.2	11.8	11.2
Rural - Rurale	C	6 276[8]	6 547[8]	6 250[8]	6 262[8]	6 885	15.0	15.7	15.1	15.2	16.7
Faeroe Islands - Îles Féroé											
Total	C	392	404	379	419	416	8.3	8.4	7.9	8.7	8.6
Finland - Finlande[44]											
Total	C	49 418	48 996	47 600	47 928	48 065	9.5	9.4	9.1	9.1	9.1
Urban - Urbaine	C	27 591	27 156	26 715	27 009	27 199	8.6	8.4	8.2	8.2	8.2
Rural - Rurale	C	21 827	21 840	20 885	20 919	20 866	11.0	11.0	10.5	10.7	10.7
France[45]											
Total	C	535 144	552 339	509 429	527 533	*520 300	8.9	9.2	8.4	8.6	*8.5
Urban - Urbaine[46]	C	379 292	393 958	360 779	373 576	...	...	...	...	...	...
Rural - Rurale[46]	C	153 896	156 493	146 823	152 218	...	...	...	...	...	...
Germany - Allemagne											
Total	C	841 686	853 946	818 271	830 227	821 627	10.2	10.3	9.9	10.1	10.0
Gibraltar[47]											
Total	C	242	234	242	249	230	8.5	8.2	8.4	8.6	7.9
Greece - Grèce											
Total	C	103 915	105 529	104 942	105 091	105 476	9.5	9.6	9.5	9.5	9.5
Urban - Urbaine	C	57 288	58 197	58 300	58 022	57 700	...	...	...	...	...
Rural - Rurale	C	46 627	47 332	46 642	47 069	47 776	...	...	...	...	...
Hungary - Hongrie											
Total	C	132 833	135 823	132 492	135 732	131 603	13.1	13.4	13.1	13.5	13.1
Urban - Urbaine[48]	C	83 112	84 106	82 363	85 546	84 656	12.6	12.8	12.5	12.8	12.5
Rural - Rurale[48]	C	49 128	51 086	49 473	49 479	46 233	13.8	14.3	14.0	14.5	13.9
Iceland - Islande											
Total	C	1 821	1 827	1 824	1 838	1 903	6.3	6.3	6.2	6.2	6.3
Urban - Urbaine	C	1 658	1 676	1 672	1 693	1 750	6.2	6.3	6.2	6.2	6.2
Rural - Rurale	C	163	151	152	145	153	7.6	7.1	7.0	7.0	6.8

18. Deaths and crude death rates, by urban/rural residence: 2002 - 2006
Décès et taux bruts de mortalité, selon la résidence, urbaine/rurale: 2002 - 2006 (continued - suite)

Continent, country or area and urban/rural residence / Continent, pays ou zone et résidence, urbaine/rurale	Code[a]	Number - Nombre					Rate - Taux				
		2002	2003	2004	2005	2006	2002	2003	2004	2005	2006

EUROPE

Ireland - Irlande[49]											
Total.	C	29 683	29 074	28 665	...	...	7.6	7.3	7.1	...	...
Total.	+C	...	...	...	*27 441	*27 479	...	...	...	*6.6	*6.5
Isle of Man - Îles de Man											
Total.	+C	877	852	798	775	768	11.4	11.0	10.3	9.9	9.6
Italy - Italie											
Total.	C	557 393	586 468	545 051	567 304	557 892	9.8	10.2	9.4	9.7	9.5
Latvia - Lettonie											
Total.	C	32 498	32 437	32 024	32 777	33 098	13.9	13.9	13.8	14.2	14.5
Urban - Urbaine	C	21 059	21 038	20 814	21 186	21 535	13.3	13.3	13.3	13.6	13.9
Rural - Rurale	C	11 439	11 399	11 210	11 591	11 563	15.2	15.2	15.1	15.7	15.8
Liechtenstein											
Total.	C	215	217	198	215	*220	6.4	6.4	5.7	6.2	*6.3
Lithuania - Lituanie											
Total.	C	41 072	40 990	41 340	43 799	44 813	11.8	11.9	12.0	12.8	13.2
Urban - Urbaine	C	23 175	23 082	23 550	25 067	26 194	10.0	10.0	10.3	11.0	11.6
Rural - Rurale	C	17 897	17 908	17 790	18 732	18 619	15.6	15.6	15.5	16.4	16.5
Luxembourg											
Total.	C	3 744	4 053	3 578	3 621	3 766	8.4	9.0	7.8	7.8	8.0
Malta - Malte											
Total.	C	3 031	3 164	2 999	3 130	3 216	7.8	7.9	7.5	7.8	7.9
Moldova[50]											
Total.	C	41 852	43 079	41 668	44 689	43 137	11.6	11.9	11.6	12.4	12.0
Urban - Urbaine	C	13 229	13 650	13 319	14 199	13 764	8.9	9.2	9.0	9.6	9.3
Rural - Rurale	C	28 623	29 429	28 349	30 490	29 373	13.4	13.8	13.3	14.4	14.0
Monaco											
Total.	C	564	617	525	601	535[51]	...	...	...	...	...
Montenegro											
Total.	C	5 513	5 704	5 707	5 839	5 968	8.9	9.2	9.2	9.4	...
Urban - Urbaine	C	...	3 798	3 585	3 571	...	...	9.9	9.3	9.2	...
Rural - Rurale	C	...	1 906	2 122	2 268	...	...	8.1	9.0	9.7	...
Netherlands - Pays-Bas[52]											
Total.	C	142 355	141 936	136 553	136 402	135 372	8.8	8.7	8.4	8.4	8.3
Urban - Urbaine	C	94 926	94 744	91 388	91 282	90 611	9.1	9.0	8.6	8.5	8.4
Rural - Rurale	C	47 429	47 192	45 165	45 120	44 761	8.4	8.3	8.1	8.1	8.1
Norway - Norvège[53]											
Total.	C	44 465	42 478	41 200	41 232	41 253	9.8	9.3	9.0	8.9	8.9
Poland - Pologne											
Total.	C	359 486	365 230	363 522	368 285	369 686	9.4	9.6	9.5	9.7	9.7
Urban - Urbaine	C	213 629	216 349	216 515	219 403	222 219	9.0	9.2	9.2	9.4	9.5
Rural - Rurale	C	145 857	148 881	147 007	148 882	147 467	10.0	10.2	10.0	10.1	10.0
Portugal[54]											
Total.	C	106 258	108 795	102 010	107 462	101 990	10.2	10.4	9.7	10.2	9.6
Romania - Roumanie											
Total.	C	269 666	266 575	258 890	262 101	258 094	12.4	12.3	11.9	12.1	12.0
Urban - Urbaine	C	113 225	112 283	114 316	116 809	116 384	9.8	9.7	9.6	9.8	9.8
Rural - Rurale	C	156 441	154 292	144 574	145 292	141 710	15.4	15.2	14.8	14.9	14.7
Russian Federation - Fédération de Russie[16]											
Total.	C	2 332 272	2 365 826	2 295 402	2 303 935	2 166 703	16.1	16.4	16.0	16.1	15.2
Urban - Urbaine	C	1 638 822	1 657 569	1 606 894	1 595 762	1 501 245	15.4	15.6	15.3	15.3	14.4
Rural - Rurale	C	693 450	708 257	688 508	708 173	665 458	17.9	18.4	17.9	18.3	17.3
San Marino - Saint-Marin											
Total.	+C	203	216	185	219	225	7.1	7.5	6.3	7.1	7.2
Serbia - Serbie[55]											
Total.	+C	102 785	103 946	104 320	106 771	102 884	13.7	13.9	14.0	14.3	13.9
Urban - Urbaine	+C	51 727	51 817	52 701	54 937	53 073	12.2	12.2	12.4	12.9	12.4
Rural - Rurale	+C	51 058	52 129	51 619	51 834	49 811	15.7	16.1	16.1	16.3	15.8
Slovakia - Slovaquie											
Total.	C	51 532	52 230	51 852	53 475	53 301	9.6	9.7	9.6	9.9	9.9
Urban - Urbaine	C	24 737	25 272	25 041	26 111	26 157	8.2	8.4	8.4	8.7	8.7
Rural - Rurale	C	26 795	26 958	26 811	27 364	27 144	11.3	11.3	11.2	11.4	11.3
Slovenia - Slovénie											
Total.	C	18 701	19 451	18 523	18 825	18 180	9.4	9.7	9.3	9.4	9.1
Urban - Urbaine	C	8 684	8 983	8 725	8 791	8 571	8.9	9.2	9.0	9.1	8.9
Rural - Rurale	C	10 017	10 468	9 798	10 034	9 609	10.3	10.7	10.0	10.2	9.7

Continent, country or area, and urban/rural residence / Continent, pays ou zone et résidence, urbaine/rurale	Co-de[a]	Number - Nombre					Rate - Taux				
		2002	2003	2004	2005	2006	2002	2003	2004	2005	2006
EUROPE											
Spain - Espagne											
Total	C	368 618	384 828	371 934	387 355	371 267	8.9	9.2	8.7	8.9	8.4
Sweden - Suède											
Total	C	95 009	92 961	90 532	91 710	91 177	10.6	10.4	10.1	10.2	10.0
Switzerland - Suisse											
Total	C	61 768	63 070	60 180	61 124	60 283	8.5	8.6	8.1	8.2	8.1
Urban - Urbaine	C	45 180	46 125	43 993	44 575	44 255	8.5	8.6	8.1	8.2	8.1
Rural - Rurale	C	16 588	16 945	16 187	16 549	16 028	8.5	8.6	8.2	8.3	8.0
The Former Yugoslav Rep. of Macedonia - L'ex-République yougoslave de Macédoine											
Total	C	17 962	18 006	17 944	18 406	18 630	8.8	8.9	8.8	9.0	9.1
Urban - Urbaine	C	10 452	10 597	...	10 645	10 931	...	...	...	...	...
Rural - Rurale	C	7 510	7 409	...	7 761	7 699	...	...	...	...	...
Ukraine											
Total	C	754 911	765 408	761 261	781 961	758 092[56]	15.7	16.0	16.1	16.6	16.2
Urban - Urbaine	C	454 406	459 965	460 492	471 561	461 774[56]	14.1	14.4	...	...	...
Rural - Rurale	C	300 505	305 443	300 769	310 400	296 318[56]	19.0	19.5	...	...	...
United Kingdom - Royaume-Uni[57]											
Total	C	606 283	*611 188	*584 600	*582 900	*572 200	10.2	*10.3	*9.8	*9.7	*9.4
OCEANIA - OCÉANIE											
American Samoa - Samoas américaines											
Total	C	295	257	289	279	267	4.9	4.1	4.5	4.3	4.0
Australia - Australie											
Total	+C	133 707	132 292	132 508	130 714	*134 398	6.8	6.6	6.6	6.4	*6.5
Urban - Urbaine	+C	85 378	84 753	84 569	84 311	...	...	...	4.8	...	...
Rural - Rurale	+C	48 329	47 539	47 939	46 403	...	...	...	18.5	...	...
Cook Islands - Îles Cook[58]											
Total	+C	97	87	99	91	*85	5.3	4.7	4.9	4.5	*4.1
Fiji - Fidji											
Total	+C	5 133	5 068	5 628	...	...	6.3	6.2	6.9	...	...
Urban - Urbaine	+C	3 091	3 211	...	...	...	...	...	...	...	...
Rural - Rurale	+C	2 042	1 857	...	...	...	...	...	...	...	...
French Polynesia - Polynésie française											
Total	C	1 127	1 122	1 130	1 265	...	4.6	4.5	4.5	5.0	...
Guam[59]											
Total	C	658	700	691	*697	...	4.1	4.2	4.2	*4.1	...
Marshall Islands - Îles Marshall											
Total	+U	...	306	263	302	318	...	...	...	...	...
Micronesia, Federated States of - Micronésie, États Fédérés de La											
Total	U	539	427	...	...	...	...	...	...	...	...
Nauru											
Total	C	75	...	...	...	...	7.5	...	...	...	...
New Caledonia - Nouvelle-Calédonie											
Total	C	1 121	1 121	1 100	1 139	1 115	5.1	5.0	4.8	...	...
New Zealand - Nouvelle-Zélande[54]											
Total	+C	28 065	28 010	28 419	27 034	28 245	7.1	7.0	7.0	6.6	6.7
Urban - Urbaine[8]	+C	25 390	25 279	25 684	24 275	25 398	7.5	7.3	7.3	6.9	7.0
Rural - Rurale[8]	+C	2 611	2 654	2 653	2 628	2 711	4.7	4.7	4.7	4.6	4.7
Niue - Nioué[60]											
Total	C	13	16	18	...	...	...	...	...	...	...
Northern Mariana Islands - Îles Mariannes septentrionales											
Total	U	155	144	165	189	...	...	...	...	...	...

18. Deaths and crude death rates, by urban/rural residence: 2002 - 2006
Décès et taux bruts de mortalité, selon la résidence, urbaine/rurale. 2002 - 2006 (continued - suite)

Continent, country or area, and urban/rural residence / Continent, pays ou zone et résidence, urbaine/rurale	Code[a]	Number - Nombre					Rate - Taux				
		2002	2003	2004	2005	2006	2002	2003	2004	2005	2006
OCEANIA - OCÉANIE											
Palau - Palaos											
Total....................	C	134	136	142	134	144	6.7	6.7	6.9	6.7	6.6
Papua New Guinea - Papouasie-Nouvelle-Guinée											
Total....................	U	7 573	7 054	...	...	...	...	...	...	...	...
Samoa											
Total....................	U	*355	*551	*547	...	...	...	...	...	...	...
Tonga											
Total....................	+C	591	617	*559	...		5.9	6.1	...	...	...
Tuvalu											
Total....................	U	87	83	89	64	31	...	...	...	...	...
Wallis and Futuna Islands - Îles Wallis et Futuna											
Total....................	C	67	88	72	65	77	...	5.9			

FOOTNOTES - NOTES

Italics: data from civil registers which are incomplete or of unknown completeness. -
Italiques: données incomplètes ou dont le degré d'exactitude n'est pas connu, provenant des registres de l'état civil.

* Provisional. -
Données provisoires.

[a] 'Code' indicates the source of data, as follows:
C - Civil registration, estimated over 90% complete
U - Civil registration, estimated less than 90% complete
| - Other source, estimated reliable
+ - Data tabulated by date of registration rather than occurence.
... - Information not available

Le 'Code' indique la source des données, comme suit:
C - Registres de l'état civil considérés complets à 90 p. 100 au moins.
U - Registres de l'état civil qui ne sont pas considérés complets à 90 p. 100 au moins.
| - Autre source, considérée pas douteuses.
+ - Données exploitées selon la date de l'enregistrement et non la date de l'événement.
... - Information pas disponible.

[1] Excluding live-born infants who died before their birth was registered. For Algerian population only. - Non compris les enfants nés vivants décédés avant l'enregistrement de leur naissance. Pour la population algérienne seulement.
[2] Data refer to national projections. - Les données se réfèrent aux projections nationales.
[3] Excluding live-born infants who died before their birth was registered. - Non compris les enfants nés vivants décédés avant l'enregistrement de leur naissance.
[4] Data are for 12 months preceding the census date. - Les données portent sur les 12 mois précédant la date du recensement.
[5] Source: World Health Organization. - Source : Organisation mondiale de la santé.
[6] Excluding non-residents and foreign service personnel and their dependants. - À l'exclusion des non-résidents et du personnel diplomatique et de leurs charges de famille.
[7] Including Canadian residents temporarily in the United States, but excluding United States residents temporarily in Canada. - Y compris les résidents canadiens se trouvant temporairement aux Etats-Unis, mais ne comprenant pas les résidents des Etats-Unis se trouvant temporairement au Canada.
[8] The total number includes 'Unknown residence', but the categories urban and rural do not. - Le nombre total inclue 'Résidence inconnue ', mais les catégories Urbain et Rural ne l'incluent pas.
[9] Adjusted for undercoverage of infant deaths and sudden and violent deaths. - Ajusté pour la sous-estimation de la mortalité infantile, du nombre de morts soudaines et de morts violentes.

[10] Data exclude visitors. - Les données non compris des visiteurs.
[11] Data refer to deaths of residents of the Netherlands Antilles (including those that died outside the Netherlands Antilles). Data exclude deaths by non-residents. - Ces données concernent les décès de résidents des Antilles néerlandaises (y compris ceux survenus hors des Antilles néerlandaises). Elles ne concernent pas les décès des non-résidents.
[12] Excluding Indian jungle population. - Non compris les Indiens de la jungle.
[13] Excluding nomadic Indian tribes. - Non compris les tribus d'Indiens nomades.
[14] Excluding Indian jungle population. Data refer to registered deaths only. - Non compris les Indiens de la jungle. Les données se rapportent aux décès enregistrés seulement.
[15] The districts of Paramaribo and Wanica are considered urban areas, whereas the rest of the districts are considered more or less rural districts (areas). - Les districts de Paramaribo et de Wanica sont considérés comme des zones urbaines, les autres districts étant considérés comme des zones rurales à divers degrés.
[16] Excluding infants born alive of less than 28 weeks' gestation, of less than 1 000 grams in weight and 35 centimeters in length, who die within seven days of birth. - Non compris les enfants nés vivants après moins de 28 semaines de gestation, pesant moins de 1 000 grammes, mesurant moins de 35 centimètres et décédés dans les sept jours qui ont suivi leur naissance.
[17] Rates were obtained by the Sample Vital Registration System of Bangladesh. - Taux obtenus au moyen du Sample Vital Registration System du Bangladesh.
[18] For 2005, data refer to last twelve months preceding census in May 2005. - Pour 2005, les données se rapportent aux douze mois précédant le recensement de mai 2005.
[19] For statistical purposes, the data for China do not include those for the Hong Kong Special Administrative Region (Hong Kong SAR), Macao Special Administrative Region (Macao SAR) and Taiwan province of China. - Pour la présentation des statistiques, les données pour la Chine ne comprennent pas la Région Administrative Spéciale de Hong Kong (Hong Kong RAS), la Région Administrative Spéciale de Macao (Macao RAS) et Taïwan province de Chine.
[20] Data have been estimated on the basis of the annual National Sample Surveys on Population Changes. - Les données ont été estimées sur la base de l'enquête annuelle "National Sample Survey on Population Changes".
[21] Data for 2005 are estimated from the National Sample Survey of 1 Per cent population. - Les données pour 2005 ont été estimées à partir de l'enquête nationale qui a porté sur un échantillon de 1 % de la population.
[22] Data refer to government controlled areas. - Les données se rapportent aux zones contrôlées par le Gouvernement.
[23] Rates were obtained by the Sample Registration System of India, actually a large demographic survey. Including data for the Indian-held part of Jammu and Kashmir, the final status of which has not yet been determined. - Les taux ont été obtenus par le Système de l'enregistrement par échantillon de l'Inde qui est une large enquête démographique. Y compris les données pour la partie du Jammu et du Cachemire occupée par l'Inde dont le statut définitif n'a pas encore été déterminé.
[24] Data relate to the Iranian Year which begins on 21 March and ends on 20 March of the following year. - Les données concernent l'année iranienne, qui commence le 21 mars et se termine le 20 mars de l'année suivante.

²⁵ Including data for East Jerusalem and Israeli residents in certain other territories under occupation by Israeli military forces since June 1967. - Y compris les données pour Jérusalem-Est et les résidents israéliens dans certains autres territoires occupés depuis 1967 par les forces armées israéliennes.

²⁶ As of 2002, data on deaths include deaths abroad of Israeli residents who were out of the country for less than a year (there were 109 deaths of Israelis abroad in 2002). - Depuis 2002, les données sur les décès comprennent les décès à l'étranger de résidents israéliens qui ont quitté le pays depuis moins d'un an (en 2002, 109 Israéliens sont morts à l'étranger).

²⁷ Data include 182 deaths abroad of Israeli residents who were out of the country for less than a year. - Y compris les décès à l'étranger de 182 résidents israéliens qui ont quitté le pays depuis moins d'un an.

²⁸ Data include 183 deaths abroad of Israeli residents who were out of the country for less than a year. - Y compris les décès à l'étranger de 183 résidents israéliens qui ont quitté le pays depuis moins d'un an.

²⁹ Data include 30 (preliminary figure) deaths abroad of Israeli residents who were out of the country for less than a year. - Y compris les décès à l'étranger de 30 résidents israéliens (chiffres préliminaires) qui ont quitté le pays depuis moins d'un an.

³⁰ Data include 141 deaths abroad of Israeli residents who were out of the country for less than a year. - Y compris les décès à l'étranger de 141 résidents israéliens qui ont quitté le pays depuis moins d'un an.

³¹ Data refer to Japanese nationals in Japan only. - Les données se raportent aux nationaux japonais au Japon seulement.

³² Excluding data for Jordanian territory under occupation since June 1967 by Israeli military forces. Excluding foreigners, including registered Palestinian refugees. - Non compris les données pour le territoire jordanien occupé depuis juin 1967 par les forces armées israéliennes. Non compris les étrangers, mais y compris les réfugiés de Palestine enregistrés.

³³ Excluding alien armed forces, civilian aliens employed by armed forces, and foreign diplomatic personnel and their dependants. - Non compris les militaires étrangers, les civils étrangers employés par les forces armées ni le personnel diplomatique étranger et les membres de leur famille les accompagnant.

³⁴ Including Korean deaths abroad. - Y compris les décès de Coréens survenus à l'étranger.

³⁵ Data refer to the recorded events in Ministry of Health hospitals and health centres only. - Les données se rapportent aux faits d'état civil enregistrés dans les hôpitaux et les dispensaires du Ministère de la santé seulement.

³⁶ Excluding data for the Pakistan-held part of Jammu and Kashmir, the final status of which has not yet been determined. - Non compris les données concernant la partie du Jammu et Cachemire occupée par le Pakistan dont le statut définitif n'a pas été déterminé.

³⁷ Data based on Pakistan Demographic Survey (PDS 2003) . - Données extraites de l'enquête démographique effectuée par le Pakistan en 2003.

³⁸ Data based on Pakistan Demographic Survey (PDS 2005). - Données extraites de l'enquête démographique effectuée par le Pakistan en 2005.

³⁹ Excluding nomad population and Palestinian refugees. Excluding live-born infants who died before their birth was registered. - Non compris la population nomade et les réfugiés de Palestine. Non compris les enfants nés vivants décédés avant l'enregistrement de leur naissance.

⁴⁰ Based on the results of the Population Demographic Survey. - D'après les résultats de la Population Demographic Survey.

⁴¹ Also included in Finland. - Comprise aussi dans Finlande.

⁴² Including armed forces stationed outside the country, but excluding alien armed forces stationed in the area. - Y compris les militaires nationaux hors du pays, mais non compris les militaires étrangers en garnison sur le territoire.

⁴³ Excluding Faeroe Islands and Greenland shown separately, if available. - Non compris les Iles Féroé et le Gröenland, qui font l'objet de rubriques distinctes, si disponible.

⁴⁴ Including nationals temporarily outside the country. Including Aland Islands. - Y compris les nationaux se trouvant temporairement hors du pays. Y compris les Îles d'Åland.

⁴⁵ Including armed forces stationed outside the country. Excluding Overseas Departments, namely, French Guiana, Guadeloupe, Martinique and Reunion, shown separately, if available. - Y compris les militaires nationaux hors du pays. Non compris les départements d'outre mer, c'est-à-dire la Guyane française, la Guadeloupe, la Martinique et la Réunion, qui font l'objet de rubriques distinctes, si disponible.

⁴⁶ Urban/rural figures, excluding nationals outside the country. - Les chiffres urbaine/rurale, non compris les nationaux hors du pays.

⁴⁷ Excluding armed forces. - Non compris les militaires en garnison.

⁴⁸ Total includes the data of foreigners, persons of unknown residence and homeless, but the categories urban and rural do not. - Total incluant les étrangers, les personnes de résidence inconnue et les sans-abri, ce qui n'est pas le cas pour les catégories urbaines et rurales.

⁴⁹ Events registered within one year of occurrence. - Evénements enregistrés dans l'année qui suit l'événement.

⁵⁰ Data do not include information for Transnistria and the municipality of Bender. Excluding infants born alive of less than 28 weeks' gestation, of less than 1 000 grams in weight and 35 centimeters in length, who die within seven days of birth. - Les données ne tiennent pas compte de l'information sur la Transnistria et la municipalité de Bender. Non compris les enfants nés vivants après moins de 28 semaines de gestations, pesant moins de 1 000 grammes, mesurant moins de 35 centimètres et décédés dans les sept jours qui ont suivi leur naissance.

⁵¹ Including residents outside the country. - Y compris les résidents hors du pays.

⁵² Including residents outside the country if listed in a Netherlands population register. - Y compris les résidents hors du pays, s'ils sont inscrits sur un registre de population néerlandais.

⁵³ Including residents temporarily outside the country. Excluding Svalbard and Jan Mayen Island shown separately, if available. - Y compris les résidents se trouvant temporairement hors du pays. Non compris Svalbard et Jan Mayen qui font l'objet de rubriques distinctes, si disponible.

⁵⁴ For resident population only. - Pour la population résidante seulement.

⁵⁵ Without data for Kosovo and Metohia. - Sans les données pour le Kosovo and Metohie.

⁵⁶ Before 2006, data exclude death happened within 7 days after birth, which was born with less then 26 weeks of gestation, with weight less then 1000 grams and length and less then 35 centimeters long. - Avant 2006, données excluant les décès survenus dans les sept jours après la naissance, les enfants nés après moins de 26 semaines de gestation, les enfants pesant moins d'un kilogramme et de moins de 35 centimètres.

⁵⁷ Excluding Channel Islands and Isle of Man, shown separately, if available. - Non compris les îles Anglo-Normandes et l'île de Man, qui font l'objet de rubriques distinctes, si disponible.

⁵⁸ Excluding Niue, shown separately, which is part of Cook Islands, but because of remoteness is administered separately. - Non compris Nioué, qui fait l'objet d'une rubrique distincte et qui fait partie des îles Cook, mais qui, en raison de son éloignement, est administrée séparément.

⁵⁹ Including United States military personnel, their dependants and contract employees. - Y compris les militaires des Etats-Unis, les membres de leur famille les accompagnant et les agents contractuels des Etats-Unis.

⁶⁰ Includes deaths occurred in New Zealand but buried in Niue and deaths occurred in Niue but buried elsewhere. - Y compris les personnes décédées en Nouvelle-Zélande qui sont enterrées à Nioué et les personnes décédées à Nioué qui sont enterrées ailleurs.

Table 19

Table 19 presents deaths by age, sex and urban/rural residence for latest available year.

Description of variables: Age is defined as age at last birthday, that is, the difference between the date of birth and the date of the occurrence of the event, expressed in completed solar years. The age classification used in this table is the following: under 1 year, 1-4 years, 5-year age groups through 95-99 years, and 100 years or over.

The urban/rural classification of deaths is that provided by each country or area; it is presumed to be based on the national census definitions of urban population that have been set forth at the end of the technical notes for table 6.

Reliability of data: Data from civil registers of deaths that are reported as incomplete (less than 90 per cent completeness) or of unknown completeness are considered unreliable and are set in italics rather than in roman type. Table 18 and the technical notes for that table provide more detailed information on the completeness of death registration. For more information about the quality of vital statistics data in general and the information available on the basis of the completeness estimates in particular, see section 4.2 of the Introduction.

Limitations: Statistics on deaths by age and sex are subject to the same qualifications as are set forth for vital statistics in general and death statistics in particular as discussed in section 4 of the Introduction.

The reliability of the data is an important factor in considering the limitations. In addition, some deaths are tabulated by date of registration and not by date of occurrence; these have been indicated by a plus sign (+). Whenever the lag between the date of occurrence and date of registration is prolonged and, therefore, a large proportion of the death registrations are delayed, death statistics for any given year may be seriously affected. However, delays in the registration of deaths are less common and shorter than in the registration of live births.

International comparability in mortality statistics may also be affected by the exclusion of deaths of infants who were born alive but died before the registration of the birth or within the first 24 hours of life. Statistics of this type are footnoted.

Because these statistics are classified according to age, they are subject to the limitations with respect to accuracy of age reporting similar to those already discussed in connection with section 3.1.3 of the Introduction. The factors influencing the accuracy of reporting may be somewhat dissimilar in vital statistics (because of the differences in the method of taking a census and registering a death) but, in general, the same errors can be observed.

The absence of frequencies in the unknown age group does not necessarily indicate completely accurate reporting and tabulation of the age item. It is often an indication that the unknowns have been eliminated by assigning ages to them before tabulation, or by proportionate distribution after tabulation.

International comparability of statistics on deaths by age is also affected by the use of different methods to determine age at death. If age is obtained from an item that simply requests age at death in completed years or is derived from information on year of birth and death rather than from information on complete date (day, month and year) of birth and death, the number of deaths classified in the under-one-year age group will tend to be reduced and the number of deaths in the next age group will tend to be somewhat increased. A similar bias may affect other age groups but its impact is usually negligible. Information on this factor is given in the footnotes when known.

The comparability of data by urban/rural residence is affected by the national definitions of urban and rural used in tabulating these data. It is assumed, in the absence of specific information to the contrary, that the definitions of urban and rural used in connection with the national population census were also used in the compilation of the vital statistics for each country or area. However, it cannot be excluded that, for a given country or area, different definitions of urban and rural are used for the vital statistics data and the population census data respectively. When known, the definitions of urban used in national population censuses are presented at the end of the technical notes for table 6. As discussed in detail in the technical notes for table 6, these definitions vary considerably from one country or area to another.

Earlier data: Deaths by age and sex have been shown for the latest available year in each issue of the Yearbook since the 1955 issue. Data included in this table update the series covering a period of years as follows:

Issue	Years Covered
Historical Supplement CD, 1997	1948 – 1997
1996	1987 – 1995
1992	1983 – 1992
1985	1976 – 1984
1980	1971 – 1979
Historical Supplement, 1979	1948 - 1977

Data have been presented by urban/rural residence in each regular issue of the Yearbook since the 1967 issue.

Tableau 19

Le tableau 19 présente les données les plus récentes dont on dispose sur les décès selon l'âge, le sexe et le lieu de résidence (zone urbaine ou rurale).

Description des variables : L'âge considéré est l'âge au dernier anniversaire, c'est-à-dire la différence entre la date de naissance et la date du décès, exprimée en années solaires révolues. La classification par âge est la suivante : moins d'un an, 1 à 4 ans, groupes quinquennaux jusqu'à 95-99 ans et 100 ans et plus.

La classification des décès selon le lieu de résidence (zone urbaine ou rurale) est celle qui a été communiquée par chaque pays ou zone ; on part du principe qu'elle repose sur les définitions de la population urbaine utilisées pour les recensements nationaux, qui sont reproduites à la fin des notes techniques du tableau 6.

Fiabilité des données : Les données sur les décès issues des registres d'état civil qui sont déclarées incomplètes (degré d'exhaustivité inférieur à 90 p.100) ou dont le degré d'exhaustivité n'est pas connu sont jugées douteuses et apparaissent en italique et non en caractères romains. Le tableau 18 et les notes techniques s'y rapportant présentent des renseignements plus détaillés sur le degré d'exhaustivité de l'enregistrement des décès. Pour plus de précisions sur la qualité des statistiques de l'état civil en général et le degré de complétude en particulier, voir la section 4.2 des Introduction.

Insuffisance des données : Les statistiques des décès selon l'âge et le sexe appellent les mêmes réserves que les statistiques de l'état civil en général et les statistiques relatives à la mortalité en particulier (voir la section 4 des Introduction).

La fiabilité des données est un facteur important. Il faut également tenir compte du fait que, dans certains cas, les données relatives aux décès sont classées par date d'enregistrement et non par date d'occurrence ; ces cas ont été signalés par le signe '+'. Chaque fois que le décalage entre le décès et son enregistrement est grand et qu'une forte proportion des décès fait l'objet d'un enregistrement tardif, les statistiques des décès de l'année peuvent être considérablement faussées.

En règle générale, toutefois, les décès sont enregistrés beaucoup plus rapidement que les naissances vivantes, et les retards prolongés sont rares.

Un autre facteur qui nuit à la comparabilité internationale est la pratique de certains pays ou zones qui consiste à ne pas inclure dans les statistiques des décès les enfants nés vivants mais décédés avant l'enregistrement de leur naissance ou dans les 24 heures qui ont suivi la naissance, pratique qui conduit à sous-évaluer le nombre de décès à moins d'un an. Quand pareil facteur a joué, cela a été signalé en note à la fin du tableau.

Étant donné que les statistiques relatives à la mortalité sont classées selon l'âge, elles appellent les mêmes réserves concernant l'exactitude des déclarations d'âge que celles qui ont été formulées à la section 3.1.3 des Introduction. Dans le cas des données d'état civil, les facteurs qui interviennent à cet égard sont parfois un peu différents, du fait que le recensement et l'enregistrement des décès se font par des méthodes différentes, mais, d'une manière générale, les erreurs observées sont les mêmes.

Si aucun nombre ne figure dans la rangée réservée aux âges inconnus, cela ne signifie pas nécessairement que les déclarations d'âge et le classement par âge sont tout à fait exacts. C'est souvent une indication que l'on a attribué un âge aux personnes d'âge inconnu avant l'exploitation des données ou qu'elles ont été réparties proportionnellement entre les différents groupes après cette opération.

Le manque d'uniformité des méthodes suivies pour obtenir l'âge au moment du décès nuit également à la comparabilité internationale des données. Si l'âge est connu, soit d'après la réponse à une simple question sur l'âge du décès en années révolues, soit d'après l'année de la naissance et l'année du décès, et non d'après des renseignements concernant la date exacte (jour, mois et année) de la naissance et du décès, le nombre de décès classés dans la catégorie « moins d'un an » sera entaché d'une erreur par défaut et le chiffre figurant dans la catégorie suivante d'une erreur par excès.

Les données pour les autres groupes d'âge pourront être entachées d'une distorsion analogue, mais les répercussions seront généralement négligeables. Les imperfections, lorsqu'elles étaient connues, ont été signalées en note à la fin du tableau.

La comparabilité des données selon le lieu de résidence (zone urbaine ou rurale) peut être limitée par les définitions nationales des termes « urbain » et « rural » utilisées pour le classement de ces données. En l'absence d'indications contraires, on a supposé que les mêmes définitions avaient servi pour le recensement national de la population et pour l'établissement des statistiques de l'état civil pour chaque pays ou zone. Toutefois, il n'est pas exclu que, pour une zone ou un pays donné, des définitions différentes aient été retenues. Les définitions du terme « urbain » utilisées pour les recensements nationaux de population ont été présentées à la fin du tableau 6 lorsqu'elles étaient connues. Comme on l'a précisé dans les notes techniques relatives au tableau 6, ces définitions varient considérablement d'un pays ou d'une zone à l'autre.

Données publiées antérieurement : Les éditions de l'*Annuaire démographique* parues depuis 1955 présentent les statistiques les plus récentes dont on disposait à l'époque sur les décès selon l'âge et le sexe. Les données qui figurent dans le tableau 19 actualisent les données qui portaient sur les périodes suivantes :

Éditions	Années considérées
Supplément historique (CD-ROM), 1997	1948 – 1997
1996	1987 – 1995
1992	1983 – 1992
1985	1976 – 1984
1980	1971 – 1979
Supplément rétrospectif, 1979	1948 - 1977

Des données selon le lieu de résidence (zone urbaine ou rurale) ont été présentées dans toutes les éditions de l'*Annuaire* depuis celle de 1967, exception faite des éditions spéciales.

19. Deaths by age, sex and urban/rural residence: latest available year, 1997 - 2006
Décès selon l'âge, le sexe et la résidence, urbaine/rurale: dernière année disponible, 1997 - 2006

Continent, country or area, date, code and age (in years) / Continent, pays ou zone, date, code et âge (en années)	Total			Urban - Urbaine			Rural - Rurale		
	Both sexes Les deux sexes	Male Masculin	Female Féminin	Both sexes Les deux sexes	Male Masculin	Female Féminin	Both sexes Les deux sexes	Male Masculin	Female Féminin
AFRICA - AFRIQUE									
Algeria - Algérie[1]									
1998 (+U)									
Total.....................	131 708	73 352	58 356	...	...	...	...	...	...
0	21 169	12 009	9 160	...	...	...	...	...	...
1 - 4	4 475	2 378	2 097	...	...	...	...	...	...
5 - 9	2 759	1 592	1 167	...	...	...	...	...	...
10 - 14	2 272	1 373	899	...	...	...	...	...	...
15 - 19	3 017	1 947	1 070	...	...	...	...	...	...
20 - 24	3 425	2 335	1 090	...	...	...	...	...	...
25 - 29	3 508	2 355	1 153	...	...	...	...	...	...
30 - 34	3 216	1 958	1 258	...	...	...	...	...	...
35 - 39	3 195	1 770	1 425	...	...	...	...	...	...
40 - 44	3 468	1 959	1 509	...	...	...	...	...	...
45 - 49	3 771	2 135	1 636	...	...	...	...	...	...
50 - 54	3 777	2 184	1 593	...	...	...	...	...	...
55 - 59	5 113	2 908	2 205	...	...	...	...	...	...
60 - 64	7 616	4 227	3 389	...	...	...	...	...	...
65 - 69	8 962	4 937	4 025	...	...	...	...	...	...
70 - 74	10 320	5 732	4 588	...	...	...	...	...	...
75 - 79	11 346	6 241	5 105	...	...	...	...	...	...
80 + ...	30 299	15 312	14 987	...	...	...	...	...	...
Botswana[2]									
2001 (I)									
Total.....................	20 823	10 800	10 023	10 041	5 204	4 837	10 782	5 596	5 186
0	1 576	815	761	718	364	354	858	451	407
1 - 4	1 187	637	550	551	294	257	636	343	293
5 - 9	484	251	233	210	118	92	274	133	141
10 - 14	249	114	135	112	51	61	137	63	74
15 - 19	386	179	207	192	88	104	194	91	103
20 - 24	1 090	388	702	520	197	323	570	191	379
25 - 29	2 091	848	1 243	1 056	443	613	1 035	405	630
30 - 34	2 376	1 235	1 141	1 208	631	577	1 168	604	564
35 - 39	2 039	1 132	907	997	550	447	1 042	582	460
40 - 44	1 595	910	685	842	483	359	753	427	326
45 - 49	1 334	814	520	702	422	280	632	392	240
50 - 54	858	529	329	418	253	165	440	276	164
55 - 59	669	416	253	333	208	125	336	208	128
60 - 64	638	386	252	316	197	119	322	189	133
65 - 69	673	374	299	308	154	154	365	220	145
70 - 74	601	322	279	261	131	130	340	191	149
75 - 79	569	315	254	256	144	112	313	171	142
80 + ...	1 634	740	894	762	329	433	872	411	461
Unknown - Inconnu	774	395	379	279	147	132	495	248	247
Egypt - Égypte									
2006 (C)									
Total.....................	451 863	249 758	202 105	214 008	124 523	89 485	237 855	125 235	112 620
0	35 952	19 624	16 328	17 792	10 423	7 369	18 160	9 201	8 959
1 - 4	11 026	6 006	5 020	4 300	2 486	1 814	6 726	3 520	3 206
5 - 9	5 239	3 025	2 214	2 415	1 428	987	2 824	1 597	1 227
10 - 14	3 976	2 416	1 560	1 987	1 255	732	1 989	1 161	828
15 - 19	6 091	4 018	2 073	3 375	2 297	1 078	2 716	1 721	995
20 - 24	6 838	4 350	2 488	3 889	2 639	1 250	2 949	1 711	1 238
25 - 29	7 153	4 436	2 717	4 092	2 679	1 413	3 061	1 757	1 304
30 - 34	6 602	3 940	2 662	3 629	2 300	1 329	2 973	1 640	1 333
35 - 39	8 503	5 223	3 280	4 445	2 823	1 622	4 058	2 400	1 658
40 - 44	12 701	8 050	4 651	6 515	4 191	2 324	6 186	3 859	2 327
45 - 49	19 203	12 861	6 342	9 858	6 537	3 321	9 345	6 324	3 021
50 - 54	31 324	20 083	11 241	16 414	10 564	5 850	14 910	9 519	5 391
55 - 59	36 853	23 078	13 775	19 531	12 457	7 074	17 322	10 621	6 701
60 - 64	38 080	22 209	15 871	19 530	11 774	7 756	18 550	10 435	8 115
65 - 69	43 806	24 860	18 946	20 650	12 180	8 470	23 156	12 680	10 476
70 - 74	49 511	25 981	23 530	22 528	12 221	10 307	26 983	13 760	13 223
75 - 79	46 654	23 502	23 152	20 128	10 654	9 474	26 526	12 848	13 678
80 - 84	36 985	16 919	20 066	14 804	7 262	7 542	22 181	9 657	12 524

19. Deaths by age, sex and urban/rural residence: latest available year, 1997 - 2006
Décès selon l'âge, le sexe et la résidence, urbaine/rurale: dernière année disponible, 1997 - 2006 (continued - suite)

Continent, country or area, date, code and age (in years) Continent, pays ou zone, date, code et âge (en années)	Total			Urban - Urbaine			Rural - Rurale		
	Both sexes Les deux sexes	Male Masculin	Female Féminin	Both sexes Les deux sexes	Male Masculin	Female Féminin	Both sexes Les deux sexes	Male Masculin	Female Féminin
AFRICA - AFRIQUE									
Egypt - Égypte									
2006 (C)									
85 + ...	34 137	13 017	21 120	13 039	5 410	7 629	21 098	7 607	13 491
Unknown - Inconnu	11 229	6 160	5 069	5 087	2 943	2 144	6 142	3 217	2 925
Kenya									
2002 (U)									
Total.....................	206 089	107 108	98 981	...	...	...	...	...	...
0	32 459	16 735	15 724	...	...	...	...	...	...
1 - 4	22 623	12 166	10 457	...	...	...	...	...	...
5 - 14	11 035	5 889	5 146	...	...	...	...	...	...
15 - 24	15 157	6 083	9 074	...	...	...	...	...	...
25 - 34	29 921	13 485	16 436	...	...	...	...	...	...
35 - 44	27 720	14 714	13 006	...	...	...	...	...	...
45 - 54	19 896	11 770	8 126	...	...	...	...	...	...
55 - 74	26 196	15 183	11 013	...	...	...	...	...	...
75 + ...	21 082	11 083	9 999	...	...	...	...	...	...
Libyan Arab Jamahiriya -									
Jamahiriya arabe libyenne									
2002 (U)									
Total.....................	19 362	11 278	8 084	...	...	...	...	...	...
0	2 194	1 190	1 004	...	...	...	...	...	...
1 - 4	891	546	345	...	...	...	...	...	...
5 - 9	267	142	125	...	...	...	...	...	...
10 - 19	670	432	238	...	...	...	...	...	...
20 - 29	1 100	824	276	...	...	...	...	...	...
30 - 39	1 287	820	467	...	...	...	...	...	...
40 - 49	1 118	621	497	...	...	...	...	...	...
50 - 59	1 492	860	632	...	...	...	...	...	...
60 - 69	2 936	1 754	1 182	...	...	...	...	...	...
70 - 79	3 812	2 254	1 558	...	...	...	...	...	...
80 + ...	3 595	1 835	1 760	...	...	...	...	...	...
Malawi[3]									
1998 (I)									
Total.....................	208 040	113 856	94 184	22 186	12 404	9 782	185 854	101 452	84 402
0	44 928	24 977	19 951	5 241	2 968	2 273	39 687	22 009	17 678
1 - 4	59 930	32 821	27 109	6 180	3 435	2 745	53 750	29 386	24 364
5 - 9	16 717	9 200	7 517	1 628	926	702	15 089	8 274	6 815
10 - 14	9 638	4 849	4 789	801	440	361	8 837	4 409	4 428
15 - 19	7 130	3 427	3 703	672	336	336	6 458	3 091	3 367
20 - 24	11 710	6 947	4 763	1 240	629	611	10 470	6 318	4 152
25 - 29	9 290	4 853	4 437	1 168	548	620	8 122	4 305	3 817
30 - 34	8 797	4 481	4 316	1 168	621	547	7 629	3 860	3 769
35 - 39	7 036	3 678	3 358	969	553	416	6 067	3 125	2 942
40 - 44	6 338	3 713	2 625	822	527	295	5 516	3 186	2 330
45 - 49	5 639	3 705	1 934	587	388	199	5 052	3 317	1 735
50 - 54	3 677	2 160	1 517	461	310	151	3 216	1 850	1 366
55 - 59	3 872	1 739	2 133	335	200	135	3 537	1 539	1 998
60 - 64	2 921	1 620	1 301	259	152	107	2 662	1 468	1 194
65 - 69	2 695	1 257	1 438	156	90	66	2 539	1 167	1 372
70 - 74	2 228	1 358	870	131	76	55	2 097	1 282	815
75 - 79	1 599	942	657	104	64	40	1 495	878	617
80 81	1 516	842	674	92	52	40	1 424	790	634
85 + ...	2 379	1 287	1 092	172	80	83	2 207	1 198	1 009
Mauritius - Maurice									
2006 (+C)									
Total.....................	9 162	5 036	4 126	...	...	...	...	...	...
0	249	138	111	...	...	...	...	...	...
1 - 4	49	28	21	...	...	...	...	...	...
5 - 9	24	13	11	...	...	...	...	...	...
10 - 14	29	14	15	...	...	...	...	...	...
15 - 19	60	37	23	...	...	...	...	...	...
20 - 24	87	55	32	...	...	...	...	...	...
25 - 29	121	92	29	...	...	...	...	...	...
30 - 34	136	102	34	...	...	...	...	...	...
35 - 39	239	165	74	...	...	...	...	...	...

Continent, country or area, date, code and age (in years) / Continent, pays ou zone, date, code et âge (en années)	Total			Urban - Urbaine			Rural - Rurale		
	Both sexes Les deux sexes	Male Masculin	Female Féminin	Both sexes Les deux sexes	Male Masculin	Female Féminin	Both sexes Les deux sexes	Male Masculin	Female Féminin
AFRICA - AFRIQUE									
Mauritius - Maurice									
2006 (+C)									
40 - 44	360	257	103	...	...	...	...	...	...
45 - 49	452	319	133	...	...	...	...	...	...
50 - 54	601	384	217	...	...	...	...	...	...
55 - 59	715	451	264	...	...	...	...	...	...
60 - 64	779	470	309	...	...	...	...	...	...
65 - 69	874	505	369	...	...	...	...	...	...
70 - 74	988	561	427	...	...	...	...	...	...
75 - 79	1 089	581	508	...	...	...	...	...	...
80 - 84	1 072	447	625	...	...	...	...	...	...
85 +	1 238	417	821	...	...	...	...	...	...
Morocco - Maroc									
2001 (U)									
Total	95 612	62 023	33 589	55 745[4]	34 330[4]	21 415[4]	39 787[4]	27 639[4]	12 148[4]
0	7 379	4 022	3 357	2 804[4]	1 566[4]	1 238[4]	4 569[4]	2 453[4]	2 116[4]
1 - 4	3 066	1 590	1 476	965[4]	521[4]	444[4]	2 100[4]	1 068[4]	1 032[4]
5 - 9	1 300	787	513	518[4]	323[4]	195[4]	782[4]	464[4]	318[4]
10 - 14	1 346	805	541	617[4]	381[4]	236[4]	727[4]	423[4]	304[4]
15 - 19	1 954	1 174	780	1 064[4]	664[4]	400[4]	889[4]	509[4]	380[4]
20 - 24	2 721	1 734	987	1 522[4]	991[4]	531[4]	1 195[4]	740[4]	455[4]
25 - 29	2 685	1 679	1 006	1 491[4]	959[4]	532[4]	1 189[4]	716[4]	473[4]
30 - 34	2 784	1 685	1 099	1 689[4]	1 051[4]	638[4]	1 093[4]	632[4]	461[4]
35 - 39	2 884	1 716	1 168	1 821[4]	1 094[4]	727[4]	1 058[4]	619[4]	439[4]
40 - 44	3 683	2 272	1 411	2 400[4]	1 479[4]	921[4]	1 279[4]	791[4]	488[4]
45 - 49	3 798	2 476	1 322	2 538[4]	1 635[4]	903[4]	1 255[4]	837[4]	418[4]
50 - 54	4 385	2 925	1 460	2 899[4]	1 899[4]	1 000[4]	1 484[4]	1 024[4]	460[4]
55 - 59	4 949	3 229	1 720	3 244[4]	1 998[4]	1 246[4]	1 698[4]	1 228[4]	470[4]
60 - 64	8 122	5 290	2 832	5 114[4]	3 093[4]	2 021[4]	3 003[4]	2 194[4]	809[4]
65 - 69	9 255	6 243	3 012	5 926[4]	3 671[4]	2 255[4]	3 322[4]	2 568[4]	754[4]
70 - 74	11 272	7 590	3 682	6 932[4]	4 182[4]	2 750[4]	4 337[4]	3 406[4]	931[4]
75 - 79	9 110	6 417	2 693	5 560[4]	3 552[4]	2 008[4]	3 543[4]	2 859[4]	684[4]
80 +	14 063	9 896	4 167	8 111[4]	5 022[4]	3 089[4]	5 942[4]	4 868[4]	1 074[4]
Unknown - Inconnu	856	493	363	530[4]	249[4]	281[4]	322[4]	240[4]	82[4]
Mozambique[5]									
1997 (I)									
Total	385 754	206 737	179 017	70 750	39 060	31 690	315 004	167 677	147 327
0	99 947	54 065	45 882	16 506	9 132	7 374	83 441	44 933	38 508
1 - 4	123 644	66 656	56 988	16 230	8 766	7 464	107 414	57 890	49 524
5 - 9	31 778	17 034	14 744	4 267	2 367	1 900	27 511	14 667	12 844
10 - 14	14 914	8 144	6 770	2 407	1 337	1 070	12 507	6 807	5 700
15 - 19	12 169	5 896	6 273	2 624	1 379	1 245	9 545	4 517	5 028
20 - 24	10 633	4 883	5 750	2 691	1 328	1 363	7 942	3 555	4 387
25 - 29	9 556	4 643	4 913	2 606	1 378	1 228	6 950	3 265	3 685
30 - 34	8 691	4 610	4 081	2 490	1 454	1 036	6 201	3 156	3 045
35 - 39	8 180	4 411	3 769	2 340	1 350	990	5 840	3 061	2 779
40 - 44	7 276	4 092	3 184	2 158	1 289	869	5 118	2 803	2 315
45 - 49	7 208	4 194	3 014	2 130	1 307	823	5 078	2 887	2 191
50 - 54	7 386	4 227	3 159	2 191	1 299	892	5 195	2 928	2 267
55 - 59	5 300	3 090	2 210	1 484	890	594	3 816	2 200	1 616
60 - 64	7 853	4 380	3 473	2 309	1 293	1 016	5 544	3 087	2 457
65 - 69	5 348	2 962	2 386	1 608	911	697	3 740	2 051	1 689
70 - 74	5 008	2 897	2 111	1 536	855	681	3 472	2 042	1 430
75 - 79	3 440	1 918	1 522	1 054	589	465	2 386	1 329	1 057
80 +	6 610	3 512	3 098	1 751	894	857	4 859	2 618	2 241
Unknown - Inconnu	10 813	5 123	5 690	2 368	1 242	1 126	8 445	3 881	4 564
Namibia - Namibie[6]									
2001 (I)									
Total	25 061	12 338[7]	12 137[7]	6 529	3 354[7]	3 175[7]	18 532	9 063[7]	8 962[7]
0 - 4	4 631	2 180[7]	2 343[7]	1 084	487[7]	582[7]	3 547	1 693[7]	1 761[7]
5 - 9	938	461[7]	447[7]	174	90[7]	83[7]	764	371[7]	364[7]
10 - 14	508	246[7]	256[7]	110	48[7]	60[7]	398	198[7]	196[7]
15 - 19	658	317[7]	330[7]	173	81[7]	88[7]	485	236[7]	242[7]
20 - 24	1 240	492[7]	740[7]	334	149[7]	184[7]	906	343[7]	556[7]

Continent, country or area, date, code and age (in years) / Continent, pays ou zone, date, code et âge (en années)	Total			Urban - Urbaine			Rural - Rurale		
	Both sexes Les deux sexes	Male Masculin	Female Féminin	Both sexes Les deux sexes	Male Masculin	Female Féminin	Both sexes Les deux sexes	Male Masculin	Female Féminin
AFRICA - AFRIQUE									
Namibia - Namibie[6]									
2001 (|)									
25 - 29	1 791	799[7]	989[7]	502	228[7]	274[7]	1 289	571[7]	715[7]
30 - 34	2 032	1 029[7]	988[7]	545	278[7]	264[7]	1 487	751[7]	724[7]
35 - 39	1 845	1 003[7]	837[7]	532	290[7]	241[7]	1 313	713[7]	596[7]
40 - 44	1 370	753[7]	615[7]	406	220[7]	186[7]	964	533[7]	429[7]
45 - 49	1 099	609[7]	485[7]	323	181[7]	142[7]	776	428[7]	343[7]
50 - 54	866	547[7]	317[7]	289	182[7]	107[7]	577	365[7]	210[7]
55 - 59	699	419[7]	279[7]	208	121[7]	87[7]	491	298[7]	192[7]
60 - 64	761	431[7]	315[7]	244	137[7]	105[7]	517	294[7]	210[7]
65 - 69	576	310[7]	260[7]	160	89[7]	69[7]	416	221[7]	191[7]
70 - 74	729	405[7]	322[7]	203	100[7]	101[7]	526	305[7]	221[7]
75 - 79	571	266[7]	291[7]	147	71[7]	73[7]	424	195[7]	218[7]
80 - 84	539	228[7]	299[7]	139	54[7]	84[7]	400	174[7]	215[7]
85 - 89	361	162[7]	189[7]	92	40[7]	50[7]	269	122[7]	139[7]
90 - 94	246	102[7]	138[7]	50	22[7]	28[7]	196	80[7]	110[7]
95 +	373	131[7]	242[7]	52	23[7]	29[7]	321	108[7]	213[7]
Unknown - Inconnu	3 228	1 448[7]	1 455[7]	762	384[7]	338[7]	2 466	1 064[7]	1 117[7]
Réunion[8]									
2003* (C)									
Total	4 022	2 311	1 711	...	...	...	...	...	...
0	107	59	48	...	...	...	...	...	...
1 - 4	19	11	8	...	...	...	...	...	...
5 - 9	9	4	5	...	...	...	...	...	...
10 - 14	14	8	6	...	...	...	...	...	...
15 - 19	38	30	8	...	...	...	...	...	...
20 - 24	44	34	10	...	...	...	...	...	...
25 - 29	36	26	10	...	...	...	...	...	...
30 - 34	81	52	29	...	...	...	...	...	...
35 - 39	126	93	33	...	...	...	...	...	...
40 - 44	159	118	41	...	...	...	...	...	...
45 - 49	196	144	52	...	...	...	...	...	...
50 - 54	222	162	60	...	...	...	...	...	...
55 - 59	234	165	69	...	...	...	...	...	...
60 - 64	267	178	89	...	...	...	...	...	...
65 - 69	396	258	138	...	...	...	...	...	...
70 - 74	425	264	161	...	...	...	...	...	...
75 - 79	478	268	210	...	...	...	...	...	...
80 - 84	482	220	262	...	...	...	...	...	...
85 +	689	217	472	...	...	...	...	...	...
Saint Helena ex. dep. - Sainte-Hélène sans dép.									
2005 (C)									
Total	39	21	18	...	...	...	...	...	...
0	1	1	-	...	...	...	...	...	...
1 - 4	-	-	-	...	...	...	...	...	...
5 - 9	-	-	-	...	...	...	...	...	...
10 - 14	-	-	-	...	...	...	...	...	...
15 - 19	-	-	-	...	...	...	...	...	...
20 - 24	-	-	-	...	...	...	...	...	...
25 - 29	-	-	-	...	...	...	...	...	...
30 - 34	-	-	-	...	...	...	...	...	...
35 - 39	-	-	-	...	...	...	...	...	...
40 - 44	-	-	-	...	...	...	...	...	...
45 - 49	2	2	-	...	...	...	...	...	...
50 - 54	1	1	-	...	...	...	...	...	...
55 - 59	2	2	-	...	...	...	...	...	...
60 - 64	1	-	1	...	...	...	...	...	...
65 - 69	3	2	1	...	...	...	...	...	...
70 - 74	4	2	2	...	...	...	...	...	...
75 - 79	8	7	1	...	...	...	...	...	...
80 - 84	8	-	8	...	...	...	...	...	...
85 - 89	3	1	2	...	...	...	...	...	...
90 - 94	3	2	1	...	...	...	...	...	...

19. Deaths by age, sex and urban/rural residence: latest available year, 1997 - 2006
Décès selon l'âge, le sexe et la résidence, urbaine/rurale: dernière année disponible, 1997 - 2006 (continued - suite)

Continent, country or area, date, code and age (in years) / Continent, pays ou zone, date, code et âge (en années)	Total			Urban - Urbaine			Rural - Rurale		
	Both sexes Les deux sexes	Male Masculin	Female Féminin	Both sexes Les deux sexes	Male Masculin	Female Féminin	Both sexes Les deux sexes	Male Masculin	Female Féminin
AFRICA - AFRIQUE									
Saint Helena ex. dep. - Sainte-Hélène sans dép.									
2005 (C)									
95 - 99	2	1	1	...	...	...	...	...	...
100 +	1	-	1	...	...	...	...	...	...
Unknown - Inconnu	-	-	-	...	...	...	...	...	...
Seychelles									
2006 (+C)									
Total	664	356	308	...	...	...	...	...	...
0	14	5	9	...	...	...	...	...	...
1 - 4	2	2	-	...	...	...	...	...	...
5 - 9	4	2	2	...	...	...	...	...	...
10 - 14	8	2	6	...	...	...	...	...	...
15 - 19	5	4	1	...	...	...	...	...	...
20 - 24	6	3	3	...	...	...	...	...	...
25 - 29	9	6	3	...	...	...	...	...	...
30 - 34	10	3	7	...	...	...	...	...	...
35 - 39	15	13	2	...	...	...	...	...	...
40 - 44	25	15	10	...	...	...	...	...	...
45 - 49	30	22	8	...	...	...	...	...	...
50 - 54	26	18	8	...	...	...	...	...	...
55 - 59	34	27	7	...	...	...	...	...	...
60 - 64	44	25	19	...	...	...	...	...	...
65 - 69	60	40	20	...	...	...	...	...	...
70 - 74	75	37	38	...	...	...	...	...	...
75 - 79	91	51	40	...	...	...	...	...	...
80 - 84	88	42	46	...	...	...	...	...	...
85 +	118	39	79	...	...	...	...	...	...
South Africa - Afrique du Sud									
2005 (U)									
Total	591 213	297 517[7]	292 017[7]	...	...	...	...	...	...
0 - 4	61 461	31 941[7]	28 977[7]	...	...	...	...	...	...
5 - 9	6 098	3 315[7]	2 762[7]	...	...	...	...	...	...
10 - 14	3 968	2 119[7]	1 833[7]	...	...	...	...	...	...
15 - 19	9 224	4 691[7]	4 482[7]	...	...	...	...	...	...
20 - 24	25 029	10 330[7]	14 614[7]	...	...	...	...	...	...
25 - 29	45 982	19 055[7]	26 823[7]	...	...	...	...	...	...
30 - 34	59 360	28 472[7]	30 786[7]	...	...	...	...	...	...
35 - 39	55 011	29 048[7]	25 870[7]	...	...	...	...	...	...
40 - 44	48 367	27 107[7]	21 180[7]	...	...	...	...	...	...
45 - 49	41 323	24 114[7]	17 135[7]	...	...	...	...	...	...
50 - 54	36 094	21 261[7]	14 777[7]	...	...	...	...	...	...
55 - 59	32 640	19 445[7]	13 148[7]	...	...	...	...	...	...
60 - 64	29 749	16 615[7]	13 100[7]	...	...	...	...	...	...
65 - 69	31 247	16 184[7]	15 028[7]	...	...	...	...	...	...
70 - 74	27 757	12 801[7]	14 923[7]	...	...	...	...	...	...
75 - 79	27 884	12 081[7]	15 768[7]	...	...	...	...	...	...
80 - 84	20 098	8 355[7]	11 722[7]	...	...	...	...	...	...
85 - 89	15 648	5 401[7]	10 230[7]	...	...	...	...	...	...
90 +	11 051	3 244[7]	7 793[7]	...	...	...	...	...	...
Unknown - Inconnu	3 222	1 938[7]	1 066[7]	...	...	...	...	...	...
Swaziland[5]									
1997 (I)									
Total	8 480	4 714	3 766	1 370	753	617	7 110	3 961	3 149
0 - 4	2 043	1 068	975	301	165	136	1 742	903	839
5 - 9	191	104	87	29	15	14	162	89	73
10 - 14	143	74	69	23	12	11	120	62	58
15 - 19	258	123	135	42	20	22	216	103	113
20 - 24	455	199	256	86	39	47	369	160	209
25 - 29	603	317	286	112	62	50	491	255	236
30 - 34	577	321	256	97	54	43	480	267	213
35 - 39	529	315	214	95	49	46	434	266	168
40 - 44	489	309	180	86	54	32	403	255	148
45 - 49	434	287	147	81	49	32	353	238	115

19. Deaths by age, sex and urban/rural residence: latest available year, 1997 - 2006
Décès selon l'âge, le sexe et la résidence, urbaine/rurale: dernière année disponible, 1997 - 2006 (continued - suite)

Continent, country or area, date, code and age (in years) / Continent, pays ou zone, date, code et âge (en annèes)	Total			Urban - Urbaine			Rural - Rurale		
	Both sexes Les deux sexes	Male Masculin	Female Féminin	Both sexes Les deux sexes	Male Masculin	Female Féminin	Both sexes Les deux sexes	Male Masculin	Female Féminin

AFRICA - AFRIQUE

Swaziland[5]
1997 (I)

50 - 54	439	274	165	78	48	30	361	226	135
55 - 59	358	235	123	64	40	24	294	195	99
60 - 64	365	237	128	50	25	25	315	212	103
65 - 69	305	195	110	43	31	12	262	164	98
70 - 74	315	189	126	41	22	19	274	167	107
75 + ...	745	341	404	97	41	56	648	300	348
Unknown - Inconnu	231	126	105	45	27	18	186	99	87

Tunisia - Tunisie
1998 (U)

Total....................	42 571	25 319	17 252	...	...	...	...	...	...
0	3 098	1 775	1 323	...	...	...	...	...	...
1 - 4	2 096	1 196	900	...	...	...	...	...	...
5 - 9	412	252	160	...	...	...	...	...	...
10 - 14	382	236	146	...	...	...	...	...	...
15 - 19	578	408	170	...	...	...	...	...	...
20 - 24	653	459	194	...	...	...	...	...	...
25 - 29	612	425	187	...	...	...	...	...	...
30 - 34	801	528	273	...	...	...	...	...	...
35 - 39	812	519	293	...	...	...	...	...	...
40 - 44	998	631	367	...	...	...	...	...	...
45 - 49	1 161	737	424	...	...	...	...	...	...
50 - 54	1 267	805	462	...	...	...	...	...	...
55 - 59	1 833	1 152	681	...	...	...	...	...	...
60 - 64	2 920	1 843	1 077	...	...	...	...	...	...
65 - 69	4 337	2 673	1 664	...	...	...	...	...	...
70 - 74	4 918	2 943	1 975	...	...	...	...	...	...
75 - 79	5 201	2 930	2 271	...	...	...	...	...	...
80 + ...	10 199	5 681	4 518	...	...	...	...	...	...
Unknown - Inconnu	293	126	167	...	...	...	...	...	...

Zimbabwe[9]
2002 (I)

Total....................	200 294	103 741	96 553	50 364	26 779	23 585	149 930	76 962	72 968
0	23 672	12 887	10 785	6 770	3 697	3 073	16 902	9 190	7 712
1 - 4	16 231	8 688	7 543	3 523	1 943	1 580	12 708	6 745	5 963
5 - 9	5 166	2 793	2 373	1 160	641	519	4 006	2 152	1 854
10 - 14	3 599	1 946	1 653	896	488	408	2 703	1 458	1 245
15 - 19	4 165	1 802	2 363	940	417	523	3 225	1 385	1 840
20 - 24	9 623	3 440	6 183	2 366	882	1 484	7 257	2 558	4 699
25 - 29	17 414	6 930	10 484	4 464	1 788	2 676	12 950	5 142	7 808
30 - 34	21 358	10 286	11 072	5 763	2 897	2 866	15 595	7 389	8 206
35 - 39	19 611	10 176	9 435	5 549	3 046	2 503	14 062	7 130	6 932
40 - 44	15 322	8 608	6 714	4 223	2 448	1 775	11 099	6 160	4 939
45 - 49	11 993	6 907	5 086	3 327	2 003	1 324	8 666	4 904	3 762
50 - 54	8 845	5 029	3 816	2 354	1 360	994	6 491	3 669	2 822
55 - 59	6 229	3 857	2 372	1 555	959	596	4 674	2 898	1 776
60 - 64	5 910	3 649	2 261	1 410	865	545	4 500	2 784	1 716
65 - 69	4 504	2 682	1 822	1 051	626	425	3 453	2 056	1 397
70 - 74	4 638	2 810	1 828	954	587	367	3 684	2 223	1 461
75 + ...	11 781	6 066	5 715	2 048	1 091	957	9 733	4 975	4 758
Unknown - Inconnu	10 233	5 185	5 048	2 011	1 041	970	8 222	4 144	4 078

AMERICA, NORTH - AMÉRIQUE DU NORD

Anguilla
2004 (+C)

Total....................	53	25	28	...	...	...	...	...	...
0	-	-	-	...	...	...	...	...	...
1 - 4	-	-	-	...	...	...	...	...	...
5 - 9	-	-	-	...	...	...	...	...	...
10 - 14	-	-	-	...	...	...	...	...	...
15 - 19	-	-	-	...	...	...	...	...	...

Continent, country or area, date, code and age (in years) / Continent, pays ou zone, date, code et âge (en années)	Total			Urban - Urbaine			Rural - Rurale		
	Both sexes Les deux sexes	Male Masculin	Female Féminin	Both sexes Les deux sexes	Male Masculin	Female Féminin	Both sexes Les deux sexes	Male Masculin	Female Féminin
AMERICA, NORTH - AMÉRIQUE DU NORD									
Anguilla									
2004 (+C)									
20 - 24	1	1	-	...	...	...	...	...	...
25 - 29	-	-	-	...	...	...	...	...	...
30 - 34	1	-	1	...	...	...	...	...	...
35 - 39	3	2	1	...	...	...	...	...	...
40 - 44	2	1	1	...	...	...	...	...	...
45 - 49	2	2	-	...	...	...	...	...	...
50 - 54	3	1	2	...	...	...	...	...	...
55 - 59	-	-	-	...	...	...	...	...	...
60 - 64	2	2	-	...	...	...	...	...	...
65 - 69	5	2	3	...	...	...	...	...	...
70 - 74	6	1	5	...	...	...	...	...	...
75 - 79	5	2	3	...	...	...	...	...	...
80 - 84	4	2	2	...	...	...	...	...	...
85 +	19	9	10	...	...	...	...	...	...
Antigua and Barbuda - Antigua-et-Barbuda[10]									
2002 (+C)									
Total	444	234	210	...	...	...	...	...	...
0	21	14	7	...	...	...	...	...	...
1 - 4	3	2	1	...	...	...	...	...	...
5 - 9	1	-	1	...	...	...	...	...	...
10 - 14	2	1	1	...	...	...	...	...	...
15 - 19	2	2	-	...	...	...	...	...	...
20 - 24	9	6	3	...	...	...	...	...	...
25 - 29	3	3	-	...	...	...	...	...	...
30 - 34	11	8	3	...	...	...	...	...	...
35 - 39	10	8	2	...	...	...	...	...	...
40 - 44	13	5	8	...	...	...	...	...	...
45 - 49	13	6	7	...	...	...	...	...	...
50 - 54	16	7	9	...	...	...	...	...	...
55 - 59	18	9	9	...	...	...	...	...	...
60 - 64	24	15	9	...	...	...	...	...	...
65 - 69	28	17	11	...	...	...	...	...	...
70 - 74	52	27	25	...	...	...	...	...	...
75 - 79	48	30	18	...	...	...	...	...	...
80 - 84	64	32	32	...	...	...	...	...	...
85 - 89	54	25	29	...	...	...	...	...	...
90 - 94	30	10	20	...	...	...	...	...	...
95 +	22	7	15	...	...	...	...	...	...
Aruba									
2006 (C)									
Total	537	301	236	...	...	...	...	...	...
0	8	3	5	...	...	...	...	...	...
1 - 4	3	2	1	...	...	...	...	...	...
5 - 9	-	-	-	...	...	...	...	...	...
10 - 14	1	1	-	...	...	...	...	...	...
15 - 19	6	3	3	...	...	...	...	...	...
20 - 24	5	4	1	...	...	...	...	...	...
25 - 29	7	4	3	...	...	...	...	...	...
30 - 34	7	7	-	...	...	...	...	...	...
35 - 39	10	8	2	...	...	...	...	...	...
40 - 44	15	11	4	...	...	...	...	...	...
45 - 49	16	12	4	...	...	...	...	...	...
50 - 54	20	11	9	...	...	...	...	...	...
55 - 59	23	15	8	...	...	...	...	...	...
60 - 64	47	32	15	...	...	...	...	...	...
65 - 69	68	41	27	...	...	...	...	...	...
70 - 74	75	42	33	...	...	...	...	...	...
75 - 79	68	42	26	...	...	...	...	...	...
80 - 84	58	30	28	...	...	...	...	...	...
85 - 89	56	22	34	...	...	...	...	...	...

Continent, country or area, date, code and age (in years) / Continent, pays ou zone, date, code et âge (en années)	Total			Urban - Urbaine			Rural - Rurale		
	Both sexes Les deux sexes	Male Masculin	Female Féminin	Both sexes Les deux sexes	Male Masculin	Female Féminin	Both sexes Les deux sexes	Male Masculin	Female Féminin
AMERICA, NORTH - AMÉRIQUE DU NORD									
Aruba									
2006 (C)									
90 - 94	30	10	20	...	...	...	...	...	...
95 + ...	14	1	13	...	...	...	...	...	...
Bahamas									
2001 (C)									
Total...................	1 609	879	730	...	...	...	...	...	...
0	37	23	14	...	...	...	...	...	...
1 - 4	14	6	8	...	...	...	...	...	...
5 - 9	7	5	2	...	...	...	...	...	...
10 - 14	7	3	4	...	...	...	...	...	...
15 - 19	22	17	5	...	...	...	...	...	...
20 - 24	25	17	8	...	...	...	...	...	...
25 - 29	62	40	22	...	...	...	...	...	...
30 - 34	86	55	31	...	...	...	...	...	...
35 - 39	97	58	39	...	...	...	...	...	...
40 - 44	118	78	40	...	...	...	...	...	...
45 - 49	106	64	42	...	...	...	...	...	...
50 - 54	91	53	38	...	...	...	...	...	...
55 - 59	108	63	45	...	...	...	...	...	...
60 - 64	111	71	40	...	...	...	...	...	...
65 - 69	145	80	65	...	...	...	...	...	...
70 - 74	126	64	62	...	...	...	...	...	...
75 - 79	120	60	60	...	...	...	...	...	...
80 - 84	141	72	69	...	...	...	...	...	...
85 - 89	108	37	71	...	...	...	...	...	...
90 - 94	52	7	45	...	...	...	...	...	...
95 - 99	19	6	13	...	...	...	...	...	...
100 + ...	7	-	7	...	...	...	...	...	...
Barbados - Barbade[10]									
2001 (+C)									
Total...................	1 712	784	928	...	...	...	...	...	...
0	32	15	17	...	...	...	...	...	...
1 - 4	5	2	3	...	...	...	...	...	...
5 - 9	2	1	1	...	...	...	...	...	...
10 - 14	1	1	-	...	...	...	...	...	...
15 - 19	9	7	2	...	...	...	...	...	...
20 - 24	16	12	4	...	...	...	...	...	...
25 - 29	26	18	8	...	...	...	...	...	...
30 - 34	32	16	16	...	...	...	...	...	...
35 - 39	31	16	15	...	...	...	...	...	...
40 - 44	51	29	22	...	...	...	...	...	...
45 - 49	45	31	14	...	...	...	...	...	...
50 - 54	53	33	20	...	...	...	...	...	...
55 - 59	66	34	32	...	...	...	...	...	...
60 - 64	84	39	45	...	...	...	...	...	...
65 - 69	107	55	52	...	...	...	...	...	...
70 - 74	175	82	93	...	...	...	...	...	...
75 - 79	192	89	103	...	...	...	...	...	...
80 - 84	285	137	148	...	...	...	...	...	...
85 - 89	260	106	154	...	...	...	...	...	...
90 - 94	145	46	99	...	...	...	...	...	...
95 + ...	92	14	78	...	...	...	...	...	...
Unknown - Inconnu	3	1	2	...	...	...	...	...	...
Belize									
2001 (U)									
Total...................	1 261	...	...	...	...	...	...	...	...
0	120	...	...	...	...	...	...	...	...
1 - 4	32	...	...	...	...	...	...	...	...
5 - 9	15	...	...	...	...	...	...	...	...
10 - 14	12	...	...	...	...	...	...	...	...
15 - 19	35	...	...	...	...	...	...	...	...
20 - 24	41	...	...	...	...	...	...	...	...
25 - 29	54	...	...	...	...	...	...	...	...

19. Deaths by age, sex and urban/rural residence: latest available year, 1997 - 2006
Décès selon l'âge, le sexe et la résidence, urbaine/rurale: dernière année disponible, 1997 - 2006 (continued - suite)

Continent, country or area, date, code and age (in years) / Continent, pays ou zone, date, code et âge (en années)	Total			Urban Urbaine			Rural - Rurale		
	Both sexes Les deux sexes	Male Masculin	Female Féminin	Both sexes Les deux sexes	Male Masculin	Female Féminin	Both sexes Les deux sexes	Male Masculin	Female Féminin
AMERICA, NORTH - AMÉRIQUE DU NORD									
Belize									
2001 (U)									
30 - 34	51	...	...	...	...	...	...	...	...
35 - 39	56	...	...	...	...	...	...	...	...
40 - 44	53	...	...	...	...	...	...	...	...
45 - 49	62	...	...	...	...	...	...	...	...
50 - 54	53	...	...	...	...	...	...	...	...
55 - 59	57	...	...	...	...	...	...	...	...
60 - 64	68	...	...	...	...	...	...	...	...
65 - 69	98	...	...	...	...	...	...	...	...
70 - 74	122	...	...	...	...	...	...	...	...
75 - 79	87	...	...	...	...	...	...	...	...
80 +	239	...	...	...	...	...	...	...	...
Unknown - Inconnu	6	...	...	...	...	...	...	...	...
Bermuda - Bermudes									
2003 (C)									
Total	434	...	...	...	...	...	...	...	...
0 - 14	2	...	...	...	...	...	...	...	...
15 - 24	2	...	...	...	...	...	...	...	...
25 - 44	31	...	...	...	...	...	...	...	...
45 - 64	81	...	...	...	...	...	...	...	...
65 - 84	197	...	...	...	...	...	...	...	...
85 +	121	...	...	...	...	...	...	...	...
British Virgin Islands - Îles Vierges britanniques[10]									
1998 (C)									
Total	85	50	35	...	...	...	...	...	...
0	3	2	1	...	...	...	...	...	...
1 - 4	-	-	-	...	...	...	...	...	...
5 - 9	1	1	-	...	...	...	...	...	...
10 - 14	-	-	-	...	...	...	...	...	...
15 - 19	2	2	-	...	...	...	...	...	...
20 - 24	2	2	-	...	...	...	...	...	...
25 - 29	2	2	-	...	...	...	...	...	...
30 - 34	1	1	-	...	...	...	...	...	...
35 - 39	5	1	4	...	...	...	...	...	...
40 - 44	2	1	1	...	...	...	...	...	...
45 - 49	5	3	2	...	...	...	...	...	...
50 - 54	6	6	-	...	...	...	...	...	...
55 - 59	3	1	2	...	...	...	...	...	...
60 - 64	1	1	-	...	...	...	...	...	...
65 - 69	3	2	1	...	...	...	...	...	...
70 - 74	11	7	4	...	...	...	...	...	...
75 - 79	15	8	7	...	...	...	...	...	...
80 - 84	9	5	4	...	...	...	...	...	...
85 - 89	8	3	5	...	...	...	...	...	...
90 - 94	3	1	2	...	...	...	...	...	...
95 +	3	1	2	...	...	...	...	...	...
Canada[11]									
2005 (C)									
Total	230 132	116 006	114 126	...	...	...	...	...	...
0	1 863	1 030	833	...	...	...	...	...	...
1 - 4	282	170	112	...	...	...	...	...	...
5 - 9	198	120	78	...	...	...	...	...	...
10 - 14	311	186	125	...	...	...	...	...	...
15 - 19	986	672	314	...	...	...	...	...	...
20 - 24	1 342	973	369	...	...	...	...	...	...
25 - 29	1 265	920	345	...	...	...	...	...	...
30 - 34	1 541	1 043	498	...	...	...	...	...	...
35 - 39	2 177	1 412	765	...	...	...	...	...	...
40 - 44	3 874	2 418	1 456	...	...	...	...	...	...
45 - 49	5 828	3 521	2 307	...	...	...	...	...	...
50 - 54	7 937	4 812	3 125	...	...	...	...	...	...
55 - 59	10 878	6 665	4 213	...	...	...	...	...	...

Continent, country or area, date, code and age (in years) / Continent, pays ou zone, date, code et âge (en années)	Total			Urban - Urbaine			Rural - Rurale		
	Both sexes Les deux sexes	Male Masculin	Female Féminin	Both sexes Les deux sexes	Male Masculin	Female Féminin	Both sexes Les deux sexes	Male Masculin	Female Féminin
AMERICA, NORTH - AMÉRIQUE DU NORD									
Canada[11]									
2005 (C)									
60 - 64	13 269	8 045	5 224	...	...	...	...	...	...
65 - 69	16 400	9 945	6 455	...	...	...	...	...	...
70 - 74	23 429	13 760	9 669	...	...	...	...	...	...
75 - 79	31 682	17 391	14 291	...	...	...	...	...	...
80 - 84	38 443	18 707	19 736	...	...	...	...	...	...
85 - 89	34 288	14 090	20 198	...	...	...	...	...	...
90 +	34 136	10 124	24 012	...	...	...	...	...	...
Unknown - Inconnu	3	2	1	...	...	...	...	...	...
Cayman Islands - Îles Caïmanes									
2005 (C)									
Total	170	94	76	...	...	...	...	...	...
0	4	2	2	...	...	...	...	...	...
1 - 4	1	1	-	...	...	...	...	...	...
5 - 9	-	-	-	...	...	...	...	...	...
10 - 14	-	-	-	...	...	...	...	...	...
15 - 19	1	1	-	...	...	...	...	...	...
20 - 24	4	4	-	...	...	...	...	...	...
25 - 29	3	3	-	...	...	...	...	...	...
30 - 34	8	4	4	...	...	...	...	...	...
35 - 39	2	2	-	...	...	...	...	...	...
40 - 44	7	3	4	...	...	...	...	...	...
45 - 49	5	2	3	...	...	...	...	...	...
50 - 54	7	3	4	...	...	...	...	...	...
55 - 59	9	5	4	...	...	...	...	...	...
60 - 64	14	10	4	...	...	...	...	...	...
65 - 69	12	10	2	...	...	...	...	...	...
70 - 74	24	16	8	...	...	...	...	...	...
75 - 79	18	9	9	...	...	...	...	...	...
80 - 84	12	6	6	...	...	...	...	...	...
85 +	39	13	26	...	...	...	...	...	...
Unknown - Inconnu	-	-	-	...	...	...	...	...	...
Costa Rica									
2006 (C)									
Total	16 766	9 697	7 069	...	...	...	...	...	...
0	692	398	294	...	...	...	...	...	...
1 - 4	99	54	45	...	...	...	...	...	...
5 - 9	91	52	39	...	...	...	...	...	...
10 - 14	107	70	37	...	...	...	...	...	...
15 - 19	241	172	69	...	...	...	...	...	...
20 - 24	347	256	91	...	...	...	...	...	...
25 - 29	380	289	91	...	...	...	...	...	...
30 - 34	342	242	100	...	...	...	...	...	...
30 - 39	760	534	226	...	...	...	...	...	...
35 - 39	418	292	126	...	...	...	...	...	...
40 - 44	556	378	178	...	...	...	...	...	...
40 - 49	1 273	832	441	...	...	...	...	...	...
45 - 49	717	454	263	...	...	...	...	...	...
50 - 54	855	523	332	...	...	...	...	...	...
50 - 59	1 755	1 067	688	...	...	...	...	...	...
55 - 59	900	544	356	...	...	...	...	...	...
60 - 64	1 052	622	430	...	...	...	...	...	...
60 - 69	2 398	1 426	972	...	...	...	...	...	...
65 - 69	1 346	804	542	...	...	...	...	...	...
70 - 74	1 505	897	608	...	...	...	...	...	...
75 - 79	1 959	1 123	836	...	...	...	...	...	...
80 - 84	1 842	1 000	842	...	...	...	...	...	...
85 +	3 292	1 506	1 786	...	...	...	...	...	...
Unknown - Inconnu	25	21	4	...	...	...	...	...	...

19. Deaths by age, sex and urban/rural residence: latest available year, 1997 - 2006
Décès selon l'âge, le sexe et la résidence, urbaine/rurale: dernière année disponible, 1997 - 2006 (continued - suite)

Continent, country or area, date, code and age (in years) — Continent, pays ou zone, date, code et âge (en années)	Total			Urban - Urbaine			Rural - Rurale		
	Both sexes Les deux sexes	Male Masculin	Female Féminin	Both sexes Les deux sexes	Male Masculin	Female Féminin	Both sexes Les deux sexes	Male Masculin	Female Féminin
AMERICA, NORTH - AMÉRIQUE DU NORD									
Cuba									
2005 (C)									
Total	84 824	45 878	38 946	69 969	37 055	32 914	14 855	8 823	6 032
0	746	412	334	584	325	259	162	87	75
1 - 4	219	126	93	168	94	74	51	32	19
5 - 9	146	102	44	113	79	34	33	23	10
10 - 14	200	122	78	149	93	56	51	29	22
15 - 19	415	264	151	322	205	117	93	59	34
20 - 24	497	332	165	397	268	129	100	64	36
25 - 29	625	416	209	501	337	164	124	79	45
30 - 34	964	642	322	738	490	248	226	152	74
35 - 39	1 469	912	557	1 155	728	427	314	184	130
40 - 44	2 009	1 227	782	1 645	1 015	630	364	212	152
45 - 49	2 314	1 395	919	1 886	1 142	744	428	253	175
50 - 54	3 359	2 004	1 355	2 792	1 673	1 119	567	331	236
55 - 59	4 707	2 789	1 918	3 908	2 326	1 582	799	463	336
60 - 64	6 087	3 609	2 478	5 125	3 035	2 090	962	574	388
65 - 69	7 298	4 223	3 075	6 112	3 538	2 574	1 186	685	501
70 - 74	9 002	5 107	3 895	7 466	4 173	3 293	1 536	934	602
75 - 79	11 165	6 099	5 066	9 290	4 935	4 355	1 875	1 164	711
80 - 84	11 860	6 103	5 757	9 884	4 901	4 983	1 976	1 202	774
85 - 89	10 835	5 207	5 628	8 938	4 119	4 819	1 897	1 088	809
90 - 94	7 300	3 213	4 087	5 921	2 418	3 503	1 379	795	584
95 - 99	2 918	1 279	1 639	2 352	958	1 394	566	321	245
100 +	682	289	393	520	200	320	162	89	73
Unknown - Inconnu	7	6	1	3	3	-	4	3	1
Dominica - Dominique[10]									
2003 (+C)									
Total	557	297	260	...	...	...	...	...	...
0	20	11	9	...	...	...	...	...	...
1 - 4	3	1	2	...	...	...	...	...	...
5 - 9	-	-	-	...	...	...	...	...	...
10 - 14	2	2	-	...	...	...	...	...	...
15 - 19	3	3	-	...	...	...	...	...	...
20 - 24	8	6	2	...	...	...	...	...	...
25 - 29	9	9	-	...	...	...	...	...	...
30 - 34	7	4	3	...	...	...	...	...	...
35 - 39	11	8	3	...	...	...	...	...	...
40 - 44	19	16	3	...	...	...	...	...	...
45 - 49	18	8	10	...	...	...	...	...	...
50 - 54	20	8	12	...	...	...	...	...	...
55 - 59	18	9	9	...	...	...	...	...	...
60 - 64	25	16	9	...	...	...	...	...	...
65 - 69	41	24	17	...	...	...	...	...	...
70 - 74	64	38	26	...	...	...	...	...	...
75 - 79	59	37	22	...	...	...	...	...	...
80 - 84	81	37	44	...	...	...	...	...	...
85 - 89	67	35	32	...	...	...	...	...	...
90 - 94	43	12	31	...	...	...	...	...	...
95 +	24	3	21	...	...	...	...	...	...
Unknown - Inconnu	15	10	5	...	...	...	...	...	...
Dominican Republic - République dominicaine									
2005 (+U)									
Total	33 949	19 086	14 458	25 969[4]	14 512[4]	11 457[4]	6 824[4]	3 921[4]	2 903[4]
0	377	218	159	311[4]	189[4]	122[4]	44[4]	22[4]	22[4]
1 - 4	182	113	69	127[4]	81[4]	46[4]	41[4]	22[4]	19[4]
5 - 9	167	106	61	125[4]	77[4]	48[4]	37[4]	24[4]	13[4]
10 - 14	259	143	116	206[4]	112[4]	94[4]	50[4]	29[4]	21[4]
15 - 19	573	393	180	462[4]	319[4]	143[4]	92[4]	62[4]	30[4]
20 - 24	848	627	221	700[4]	516[4]	184[4]	118[4]	86[4]	32[4]
25 - 29	996	684	312	828[4]	570[4]	258[4]	150[4]	102[4]	48[4]
30 - 34	1 151	763	388	918[4]	611[4]	307[4]	196[4]	125[4]	71[4]
35 - 39	1 256	805	451	976[4]	632[4]	344[4]	243[4]	149[4]	94[4]

Continent, country or area, date, code and age (in years) / Continent, pays ou zone, date, code et âge (en années)	Total			Urban - Urbaine			Rural - Rurale		
	Both sexes Les deux sexes	Male Masculin	Female Féminin	Both sexes Les deux sexes	Male Masculin	Female Féminin	Both sexes Les deux sexes	Male Masculin	Female Féminin
AMERICA, NORTH - AMÉRIQUE DU NORD									
Dominican Republic - République dominicaine 2005 (+U)									
40 - 44	1 274	830	444	1 029[4]	667[4]	362[4]	213[4]	140[4]	73[4]
45 - 49	1 299	813	486	1 021[4]	646[4]	375[4]	240[4]	142[4]	98[4]
50 - 54	1 615	942	673	1 272[4]	743[4]	529[4]	299[4]	174[4]	125[4]
55 - 59	1 698	1 049	649	1 327[4]	823[4]	504[4]	320[4]	199[4]	121[4]
60 - 64	1 902	1 144	758	1 464[4]	898[4]	566[4]	369[4]	204[4]	165[4]
65 - 69	2 475	1 416	1 059	1 895[4]	1 064[4]	831[4]	504[4]	305[4]	199[4]
70 +	13 294	7 207	6 087	9 732[4]	5 182[4]	4 550[4]	3 144[4]	1 791[4]	1 353[4]
Unknown - Inconnu	4 538	1 833	2 750	3 576[4]	1 382[4]	2 194[4]	764[4]	345[4]	419[4]
El Salvador 2006 (C)									
Total	31 453	18 452	13 001	24 682	14 342	10 340	6 771	4 110	2 661
0	1 013	571	442	822	472	350	191	99	92
1 - 4	366	198	168	282	159	123	84	39	45
5 - 9	220	119	101	166	89	77	54	30	24
10 - 14	280	174	106	226	141	85	54	33	21
15 - 19	968	752	216	786	602	184	182	150	32
20 - 24	1 296	1 070	226	1 068	872	196	228	198	30
25 - 29	1 614	1 354	260	1 300	1 098	202	314	256	58
30 - 34	1 272	976	296	1 017	782	235	255	194	61
35 - 39	1 253	937	316	1 003	756	247	250	181	69
40 - 44	1 275	879	396	1 010	686	324	265	193	72
45 - 49	1 311	862	449	1 058	687	371	253	175	78
50 - 54	1 423	897	526	1 116	703	413	307	194	113
55 - 59	1 668	1 043	625	1 317	824	493	351	219	132
60 - 64	1 798	1 028	770	1 427	798	629	371	230	141
65 - 69	2 346	1 265	1 081	1 824	961	863	522	304	218
70 - 74	2 438	1 249	1 189	1 850	917	933	588	332	256
75 - 79	3 022	1 485	1 537	2 313	1 096	1 217	709	389	320
80 - 84	2 905	1 432	1 473	2 225	1 082	1 143	680	350	330
85 +	4 985	2 161	2 824	3 872	1 617	2 255	1 113	544	569
Greenland - Groenland 2003 (C)									
Total	412	235	177	340	197	143	72	38	34
0	8	6	2	8	6	2	-	-	-
1 - 4	4	2	2	3	2	1	1	-	1
5 - 9	1	-	1	1	-	1	-	-	-
10 - 14	2	2	-	2	2	-	-	-	-
15 - 19	12	7	5	11	7	4	1	-	1
20 - 24	17	13	4	15	11	4	2	2	-
25 - 29	5	3	2	5	3	2	-	-	-
30 - 34	10	5	5	5	2	3	5	3	2
35 - 39	16	12	4	13	10	3	3	2	1
40 - 44	15	11	4	13	10	3	2	1	1
45 - 49	21	13	8	17	9	8	4	4	-
50 - 54	23	13	10	18	10	8	5	3	2
55 - 59	36	25	11	31	21	10	5	4	1
60 - 64	32	18	14	26	16	10	6	2	4
65 - 69	61	40	21	48	34	14	13	6	7
70 - 74	64	29	35	50	23	27	14	6	8
75 - 79	38	19	19	34	17	17	4	2	2
80 - 84	32	13	19	27	11	16	5	2	3
85 +	15	4	11	13	3	10	2	1	1
Grenada - Grenade 2000 (+C)									
Total	716	365	351	...	...	...	...	...	...
0	27	10	17	...	...	...	...	...	...
1 - 4	1	1	-	...	...	...	...	...	...
5 - 9	1	1	-	...	...	...	...	...	...
10 - 14	4	4	-	...	...	...	...	...	...
15 - 19	8	2	6	...	...	...	...	...	...
20 - 24	11	9	2	...	...	...	...	...	...

Continent, country or area, date, code and age (in years) / Continent, pays ou zone, date, code et âge (en années)	Total			Urban - Urbaine			Rural - Rurale		
	Both sexes Les deux sexes	Male Masculin	Female Féminin	Both sexes Les deux sexes	Male Masculin	Female Féminin	Both sexes Les deux sexes	Male Masculin	Female Féminin
AMERICA, NORTH - AMÉRIQUE DU NORD									
Grenada - Grenade									
2000 (+C)									
25 - 29	17	13	4	...	...	...	...	...	...
30 - 34	21	11	10	...	...	...	...	...	...
35 - 39	17	7	10	...	...	...	...	...	...
40 - 44	14	9	5	...	...	...	...	...	...
45 - 49	21	13	8	...	...	...	...	...	...
50 - 54	27	15	12	...	...	...	...	...	...
55 - 59	24	17	7	...	...	...	...	...	...
60 - 64	50	30	20	...	...	...	...	...	...
65 - 69	61	35	26	...	...	...	...	...	...
70 - 74	81	52	29	...	...	...	...	...	...
75 - 79	96	50	46	...	...	...	...	...	...
80 - 84	69	27	42	...	...	...	...	...	...
85 - 89	84	34	50	...	...	...	...	...	...
90 - 94	52	16	36	...	...	...	...	...	...
95 - 99	24	8	16	...	...	...	...	...	...
100 +	6	1	5	...	...	...	...	...	...
Guadeloupe[8]									
2003 (C)									
Total	2 636	1 405	1 231	...	...	...	...	...	...
0	56	34	22	...	...	...	...	...	...
1 - 4	9	5	4	...	...	...	...	...	...
5 - 9	5	4	1	...	...	...	...	...	...
10 - 14	5	3	2	...	...	...	...	...	...
15 - 19	21	18	3	...	...	...	...	...	...
20 - 24	23	19	4	...	...	...	...	...	...
25 - 29	23	17	6	...	...	...	...	...	...
30 - 34	39	31	8	...	...	...	...	...	...
35 - 39	60	40	20	...	...	...	...	...	...
40 - 44	76	47	29	...	...	...	...	...	...
45 - 49	102	71	31	...	...	...	...	...	...
50 - 54	112	87	25	...	...	...	...	...	...
55 - 59	128	85	43	...	...	...	...	...	...
60 - 64	177	96	81	...	...	...	...	...	...
65 - 69	213	126	87	...	...	...	...	...	...
70 - 74	257	141	116	...	...	...	...	...	...
75 - 79	316	180	136	...	...	...	...	...	...
80 - 84	356	185	171	...	...	...	...	...	...
85 - 89	329	124	205	...	...	...	...	...	...
90 - 94	205	65	140	...	...	...	...	...	...
95 - 99	96	19	77	...	...	...	...	...	...
100 +	28	8	20	...	...	...	...	...	...
Guatemala									
2006 (C)									
Total	69 756	40 650	29 106	38 897	23 196	15 701	30 859	17 454	13 405
0	9 042	5 012	4 030	4 993	2 787	2 206	4 049	2 225	1 824
1 - 4	3 567	1 900	1 667	1 198	658	540	2 369	1 242	1 127
5 - 9	1 016	556	460	416	243	173	600	313	287
10 - 14	922	519	403	468	271	197	454	248	206
15 - 19	2 271	1 597	674	1 430	1 082	348	841	515	326
20 - 24	3 053	2 342	711	1 963	1 576	387	1 090	766	324
25 - 29	3 227	2 448	779	2 055	1 599	456	1 172	849	323
30 - 34	2 777	2 054	723	1 674	1 288	386	1 103	766	337
35 - 39	2 721	1 905	816	1 635	1 182	453	1 086	723	363
40 - 44	2 765	1 835	930	1 611	1 093	518	1 154	742	412
45 - 49	2 829	1 803	1 026	1 687	1 112	575	1 142	691	451
50 - 54	3 048	1 846	1 202	1 806	1 096	710	1 242	750	492
55 - 59	3 342	1 857	1 485	1 957	1 130	827	1 385	727	658
60 - 64	3 420	1 870	1 550	1 968	1 097	871	1 452	773	679
65 - 69	3 955	2 124	1 831	2 177	1 158	1 019	1 778	966	812
70 +	21 532	10 787	10 745	11 729	5 723	6 006	9 803	5 064	4 739
Unknown - Inconnu	269	195	74	130	101	29	139	94	45

19. Deaths by age, sex and urban/rural residence: latest available year, 1997 - 2006
Décès selon l'âge, le sexe et la résidence, urbaine/rurale: dernière année disponible, 1997 - 2006 (continued - suite)

Continent, country or area, date, code and age (in years) Continent, pays ou zone, date, code et âge (en années)	Total			Urban - Urbaine			Rural - Rurale		
	Both sexes Les deux sexes	Male Masculin	Female Féminin	Both sexes Les deux sexes	Male Masculin	Female Féminin	Both sexes Les deux sexes	Male Masculin	Female Féminin

AMERICA, NORTH -
AMÉRIQUE DU NORD

Haiti - Haïti[10]
2003 (U)

Total	8 011	4 135	3 876	...	...	...	...	...	...
0	724	388	336	...	...	...	...	...	...
1 - 4	501	270	231	...	...	...	...	...	...
5 - 9	161	85	76	...	...	...	...	...	...
10 - 14	135	66	69	...	...	...	...	...	...
15 - 19	216	114	102	...	...	...	...	...	...
20 - 24	324	158	166	...	...	...	...	...	...
25 - 29	371	179	192	...	...	...	...	...	...
30 - 34	442	229	213	...	...	...	...	...	...
35 - 39	392	215	177	...	...	...	...	...	...
40 - 44	434	234	200	...	...	...	...	...	...
45 - 49	363	190	173	...	...	...	...	...	...
50 - 54	346	177	169	...	...	...	...	...	...
55 - 59	316	176	140	...	...	...	...	...	...
60 - 64	397	205	192	...	...	...	...	...	...
65 - 69	378	196	182	...	...	...	...	...	...
70 - 74	460	245	215	...	...	...	...	...	...
75 - 79	416	223	193	...	...	...	...	...	...
80 - 84	417	208	209	...	...	...	...	...	...
85 - 89	266	110	156	...	...	...	...	...	...
90 - 94	162	57	105	...	...	...	...	...	...
95 +	132	48	84	...	...	...	...	...	...
Unknown - Inconnu	658	362	296	...	...	...	...	...	...

Jamaica - Jamaïque[12]
2005 (U)

Total	17 552	9 473	8 079	...	...	...	...	...	...
0	1 007	517	490	...	...	...	...	...	...
1 - 4	197	98	99	...	...	...	...	...	...
5 - 9	75	45	30	...	...	...	...	...	...
10 - 14	73	32	41	...	...	...	...	...	...
15 - 19	248	195	53	...	...	...	...	...	...
20 - 24	505	404	101	...	...	...	...	...	...
25 - 29	550	398	152	...	...	...	...	...	...
30 - 34	555	386	169	...	...	...	...	...	...
35 - 39	568	350	218	...	...	...	...	...	...
40 - 44	597	370	227	...	...	...	...	...	...
45 - 49	597	329	268	...	...	...	...	...	...
50 - 54	636	382	254	...	...	...	...	...	...
55 - 59	670	397	273	...	...	...	...	...	...
60 - 64	981	566	415	...	...	...	...	...	...
65 - 69	1 159	658	501	...	...	...	...	...	...
70 - 74	1 701	974	727	...	...	...	...	...	...
75 +	7 433	3 372	4 061	...	...	...	...	...	...

Martinique[8]
2003 (C)

Total	2 725	1 421	1 304	...	...	...	...	...	...
0	33	14	19	...	...	...	...	...	...
1 - 4	8	3	5	...	...	...	...	...	...
5 - 9	6	3	3	...	...	...	...	...	...
10 - 14	5	4	1	...	...	...	...	...	...
15 - 19	20	16	4	...	...	...	...	...	...
20 - 24	20	14	6	...	...	...	...	...	...
25 - 29	21	16	5	...	...	...	...	...	...
30 - 34	40	29	11	...	...	...	...	...	...
35 - 39	42	27	15	...	...	...	...	...	...
40 - 44	53	30	17	...	...	...	...	...	...
45 - 49	81	50	31	...	...	...	...	...	...
50 - 54	91	55	36	...	...	...	...	...	...
55 - 59	97	58	39	...	...	...	...	...	...
60 - 64	137	84	53	...	...	...	...	...	...
65 - 69	189	118	71	...	...	...	...	...	...
70 - 74	267	156	111	...	...	...	...	...	...

19. Deaths by age, sex and urban/rural residence: latest available year, 1997 - 2006
Décès selon l'âge, le sexe et la résidence, urbaine/rurale: dernière année disponible, 1997 - 2006 (continued - suite)

Continent, country or area, date, code and age (in years) / Continent, pays ou zone, date, code et âge (en années)	Total Both sexes Les deux sexes	Total Male Masculin	Total Female Féminin	Urban - Urbaine Both sexes Les deux sexes	Urban - Urbaine Male Masculin	Urban - Urbaine Female Féminin	Rural - Rurale Both sexes Les deux sexes	Rural - Rurale Male Masculin	Rural - Rurale Female Féminin
AMERICA, NORTH - AMÉRIQUE DU NORD									
Martinique[8]									
2003 (C)									
75 - 79	360	213	147	...	...	...	...	...	...
80 - 84	439	221	218	...	...	...	...	...	...
85 - 89	386	178	208	...	...	...	...	...	...
90 - 94	273	85	188	...	...	...	...	...	...
95 - 99	129	35	94	...	...	...	...	...	...
100 + ...	28	6	22	...	...	...	...	...	...
Mexico - Mexique									
2006 (+C)									
Total	493 296	273 276[7]	219 880[7]	370 811[4]	202 089[13]	168 630[13]	116 393[4]	66 756[13]	49 619[13]
0	30 890	17 369[7]	13 442[7]	23 057[4]	12 996[13]	9 994[13]	7 263[4]	4 049[13]	3 205[13]
1 - 4	6 075	3 328[7]	2 747[7]	3 986[4]	2 159[13]	1 827[13]	2 018[4]	1 123[13]	895[13]
5 - 9	2 976	1 718[7]	1 258[7]	2 012[4]	1 148[13]	864[13]	931[4]	553[13]	378[13]
10 - 14	3 678	2 201[7]	1 477[7]	2 466[4]	1 434[13]	1 032[13]	1 166[4]	744[13]	422[13]
15 - 19	7 616	5 246[7]	2 369[7]	5 381[4]	3 680[13]	1 700[13]	2 111[4]	1 479[13]	632[13]
20 - 24	9 677	7 025[7]	2 649[7]	7 095[4]	5 154[13]	1 939[13]	2 415[4]	1 737[13]	678[13]
25 - 29	10 747	7 918[7]	2 827[7]	7 982[4]	5 921[13]	2 060[13]	2 514[4]	1 805[13]	708[13]
30 - 34	12 706	9 243[7]	3 459[7]	9 474[4]	6 894[13]	2 580[13]	2 934[4]	2 091[13]	843[13]
35 - 39	14 196	9 935[7]	4 260[7]	10 574[4]	7 377[13]	3 197[13]	3 235[4]	2 226[13]	1 009[13]
40 - 44	16 773	11 262[7]	5 508[7]	12 675[4]	8 434[13]	4 240[13]	3 748[4]	2 523[13]	1 225[13]
45 - 49	20 976	13 193[7]	7 782[7]	16 025[4]	9 952[13]	6 073[13]	4 580[4]	2 937[13]	1 643[13]
50 - 54	25 377	15 261[7]	10 115[7]	19 711[4]	11 782[13]	7 929[13]	5 322[4]	3 212[13]	2 109[13]
55 - 59	30 227	17 521[7]	12 706[7]	23 710[4]	13 585[13]	10 125[13]	6 207[4]	3 698[13]	2 509[13]
60 - 64	35 117	19 427[7]	15 684[7]	27 252[4]	14 939[13]	12 310[13]	7 583[4]	4 282[13]	3 300[13]
65 - 69	41 191	22 517[7]	18 670[7]	31 530[4]	17 049[13]	14 478[13]	9 352[4]	5 266[13]	4 085[13]
70 - 74	46 504	25 000[7]	21 504[7]	35 684[4]	18 951[13]	16 733[13]	10 523[4]	5 858[13]	4 665[13]
75 - 79	50 074	25 832[7]	24 239[7]	37 787[4]	19 050[13]	18 736[13]	11 980[4]	6 598[13]	5 380[13]
80 - 84	49 011	24 494[7]	24 512[7]	36 958[4]	17 954[13]	19 001[13]	11 779[4]	6 375[13]	5 402[13]
85 - 89	37 950	17 457[7]	20 492[7]	28 232[4]	12 490[13]	15 741[13]	9 506[4]	4 855[13]	4 651[13]
90 - 94	23 604	9 833[7]	13 767[7]	17 331[4]	6 746[13]	10 582[13]	6 161[4]	3 040[13]	3 120[13]
95 - 99	12 091	4 699[7]	7 389[7]	8 623[4]	3 104[13]	5 518[13]	3 390[4]	1 563[13]	1 827[13]
100 + ...	3 975	1 423[7]	2 552[7]	2 605[4]	875[13]	1 730[13]	1 344[4]	537[13]	807[13]
Unknown - Inconnu	1 865	1 374[7]	472[7]	661[4]	415[13]	241[13]	331[4]	205[13]	126[13]
Montserrat									
1999 (+C)									
Total	59	39	20	...	...	...	...	...	...
0	-	-	-	...	...	...	...	...	...
1 - 4	-	-	-	...	...	...	...	...	...
5 - 9	-	-	-	...	...	...	...	...	...
10 - 14	-	-	-	...	...	...	...	...	...
15 - 19	1	-	1	...	...	...	...	...	...
20 - 24	-	-	-	...	...	...	...	...	...
25 - 29	-	-	-	...	...	...	...	...	...
30 - 34	-	-	-	...	...	...	...	...	...
35 - 39	-	-	-	...	...	...	...	...	...
40 - 44	-	-	-	...	...	...	...	...	...
45 - 49	1	1	-	...	...	...	...	...	...
50 - 54	1	1	-	...	...	...	...	...	...
55 - 59	2	2	-	...	...	...	...	...	...
60 - 64	3	2	1	...	...	...	...	...	...
65 - 69	3	2	1	...	...	...	...	...	...
70 - 74	7	6	1	...	...	...	...	...	...
75 - 79	5	4	1	...	...	...	...	...	...
80 - 84	15	8	7	...	...	...	...	...	...
85 - 89	11	5	6	...	...	...	...	...	...
90 + ...	9	7	2	...	...	...	...	...	...
Unknown - Inconnu	1	1	-	...	...	...	...	...	...
Netherlands Antilles - Antilles néerlandaises[14]									
2004 (C)									
Total	1 412	753	659	...	...	...	...	...	...
0	20	13	7	...	...	...	...	...	...

Continent, country or area, date, code and age (in years) / Continent, pays ou zone, date, code et âge (en années)	Total			Urban - Urbaine			Rural - Rurale		
	Both sexes Les deux sexes	Male Masculin	Female Féminin	Both sexes Les deux sexes	Male Masculin	Female Féminin	Both sexes Les deux sexes	Male Masculin	Female Féminin
AMERICA, NORTH - AMÉRIQUE DU NORD									
Netherlands Antilles - Antilles néerlandaises[14]									
2004 (C)									
1 - 4	2	1	1	...	...	...	...	...	...
5 - 9	2	2	-	...	...	...	...	...	...
10 - 14	3	3	-	...	...	...	...	...	...
15 - 19	13	10	3	...	...	...	...	...	...
20 - 24	11	8	3	...	...	...	...	...	...
25 - 29	18	11	7	...	...	...	...	...	...
30 - 34	26	19	7	...	...	...	...	...	...
35 - 39	32	23	9	...	...	...	...	...	...
40 - 44	41	26	15	...	...	...	...	...	...
45 - 49	57	32	25	...	...	...	...	...	...
50 - 54	75	45	30	...	...	...	...	...	...
55 - 59	83	54	29	...	...	...	...	...	...
60 - 64	109	63	46	...	...	...	...	...	...
65 - 69	135	77	58	...	...	...	...	...	...
70 - 74	165	86	79	...	...	...	...	...	...
75 - 79	164	94	70	...	...	...	...	...	...
80 - 84	161	79	82	...	...	...	...	...	...
85 - 89	144	56	88	...	...	...	...	...	...
90 - 94	91	34	57	...	...	...	...	...	...
95 - 99	49	15	34	...	...	...	...	...	...
100 +	11	2	9	...	...	...	...	...	...
Nicaragua									
2005 (+U)									
Total	16 770	9 717	7 053	10 931	6 214	4 717	5 839	3 503	2 336
0	1 970	1 124	846	934	520	414	1 036	604	432
1 - 4	369	189	180	153	77	76	216	112	104
5 - 9	167	102	65	71	43	28	96	59	37
10 - 14	214	123	91	97	58	39	117	65	52
15 - 19	470	323	147	293	218	75	177	105	72
20 - 24	631	467	164	383	287	96	248	180	68
25 - 29	543	390	153	343	255	88	200	135	65
30 - 34	563	425	138	349	267	82	214	158	56
35 - 39	583	402	181	391	282	109	192	120	72
40 - 44	642	424	218	439	296	143	203	128	75
45 - 49	808	518	290	551	360	191	257	158	99
50 - 54	823	508	315	572	363	209	251	145	106
55 - 59	868	475	393	613	327	286	255	148	107
60 - 64	969	561	408	652	379	273	317	182	135
65 - 69	1 179	658	521	834	457	377	345	201	144
70 - 74	1 277	722	555	912	490	422	365	232	133
75 - 79	1 386	711	675	997	497	500	389	214	175
80 +	3 308	1 595	1 713	2 347	1 038	1 309	961	557	404
Panama									
1999 (U)									
Total	11 938	6 978	4 960	7 108	4 042	3 066	4 830	2 936	1 894
0	1 005	571	434	490	284	206	515	287	228
1 - 4	302	157	145	81	42	39	221	115	106
5 - 9	122	76	46	49	25	24	73	51	22
10 - 14	95	58	37	30	17	13	65	41	24
15 - 19	222	154	68	117	84	33	105	70	35
20 - 24	302	224	78	159	119	40	143	105	38
25 - 29	332	246	86	190	139	51	142	107	35
30 - 34	369	261	108	225	103	62	144	08	16
35 - 39	329	222	107	197	128	69	132	94	38
40 - 44	396	260	136	239	158	81	157	102	55
45 - 49	411	272	139	265	178	87	146	94	52
50 - 54	496	329	167	301	210	91	195	119	76
55 - 59	514	322	192	319	198	121	195	124	71
60 - 64	663	405	258	413	251	162	250	154	96
65 - 69	817	489	328	468	268	200	349	221	128
70 - 74	1 012	594	418	620	360	260	392	234	158

Continent, country or area, date, code and age (in years) / Continent, pays ou zone, date, code et âge (en années)	Total			Urban - Urbaine			Rural - Rurale		
	Both sexes Les deux sexes	Male Masculin	Female Féminin	Both sexes Les deux sexes	Male Masculin	Female Féminin	Both sexes Les deux sexes	Male Masculin	Female Féminin
AMERICA, NORTH - AMÉRIQUE DU NORD									
Panama									
1999 (U)									
75 - 79	1 255	693	562	796	415	381	459	278	181
80 - 84	1 324	704	620	860	449	411	464	255	209
85 - 89	1 066	548	518	690	328	362	376	220	156
90 - 94	553	241	312	376	142	234	177	99	78
95 - 99	210	75	135	141	45	96	69	30	39
100 +	49	24	25	38	17	21	11	7	4
Unknown - Inconnu	94	53	41	44	22	22	50	31	19
2006 (U)									
Total	14 358	8 346	6 012	...	...	...	...	...	...
0	971	562	409	...	...	...	...	...	...
1 - 4	340	189	151	...	...	...	...	...	...
5 - 9	113	59	54	...	...	...	...	...	...
10 - 14	90	51	39	...	...	...	...	...	...
15 - 19	247	178	69	...	...	...	...	...	...
20 - 24	348	243	105	...	...	...	...	...	...
25 - 29	337	238	99	...	...	...	...	...	...
30 - 34	393	283	110	...	...	...	...	...	...
35 - 39	403	262	141	...	...	...	...	...	...
40 - 44	445	303	142	...	...	...	...	...	...
45 - 49	497	326	171	...	...	...	...	...	...
50 - 54	567	363	204	...	...	...	...	...	...
55 - 59	708	431	277	...	...	...	...	...	...
60 - 64	921	565	356	...	...	...	...	...	...
65 - 69	985	601	384	...	...	...	...	...	...
70 - 74	1 253	738	515	...	...	...	...	...	...
75 - 79	1 396	804	592	...	...	...	...	...	...
80 - 84	1 526	841	685	...	...	...	...	...	...
85 +	2 760	1 267	1 493	...	...	...	...	...	...
Unknown - Inconnu	58	42	16	...	...	...	...	...	...
Puerto Rico - Porto Rico									
2003 (C)									
Total	28 356	15 758	12 598	15 038[4]	8 095[4]	6 943[4]	13 283[4]	7 633[4]	5 650[4]
0	498	288	210	294[4]	168[4]	126[4]	198[4]	114[4]	84[4]
1 - 4	47	26	21	27[4]	15[4]	12[4]	19[4]	10[4]	9[4]
5 - 9	32	16	16	13[4]	6[4]	7[4]	19[4]	10[4]	9[4]
10 - 14	47	31	16	16[4]	11[4]	5[4]	31[4]	20[4]	11[4]
15 - 19	201	161	40	106[4]	89[4]	17[4]	95[4]	72[4]	23[4]
20 - 24	419	359	60	238[4]	204[4]	34[4]	179[4]	153[4]	26[4]
25 - 29	414	345	69	228[4]	188[4]	40[4]	185[4]	156[4]	29[4]
30 - 34	404	304	100	217[4]	163[4]	54[4]	187[4]	141[4]	46[4]
35 - 39	526	382	144	275[4]	191[4]	84[4]	249[4]	189[4]	60[4]
40 - 44	661	453	208	341[4]	232[4]	109[4]	320[4]	221[4]	99[4]
45 - 49	898	580	318	471[4]	302[4]	169[4]	426[4]	277[4]	149[4]
50 - 54	1 221	781	440	613[4]	378[4]	235[4]	608[4]	403[4]	205[4]
55 - 59	1 627	1 035	592	807[4]	518[4]	289[4]	819[4]	517[4]	302[4]
60 - 64	2 006	1 206	800	1 027[4]	614[4]	413[4]	979[4]	592[4]	387[4]
65 - 69	2 311	1 410	901	1 165[4]	703[4]	462[4]	1 145[4]	706[4]	439[4]
70 - 74	2 869	1 589	1 280	1 507[4]	833[4]	674[4]	1 360[4]	754[4]	606[4]
75 - 79	3 450	1 894	1 556	1 846[4]	975[4]	871[4]	1 602[4]	917[4]	685[4]
80 - 84	3 882	1 956	1 926	2 120[4]	1 016[4]	1 104[4]	1 761[4]	939[4]	822[4]
85 +	6 822	2 924	3 898	3 720[4]	1 482[4]	2 238[4]	3 099[4]	1 440[4]	1 659[4]
Unknown - Inconnu	21	18	3	7[4]	7[4]	-[4]	2[4]	2[4]	-[4]
2005 (C)									
Total	29 702	16 479	13 223	...	...	...	...	...	...
0	471	251	220	...	...	...	...	...	...
1 - 4	42	22	20	...	...	...	...	...	...
5 - 9	30	12	18	...	...	...	...	...	...
10 - 14	38	27	11	...	...	...	...	...	...
15 - 19	192	157	35	...	...	...	...	...	...
20 - 24	436	362	74	...	...	...	...	...	...
25 - 29	403	330	73	...	...	...	...	...	...

19. Deaths by age, sex and urban/rural residence: latest available year, 1997 - 2006
Décès selon l'âge, le sexe et la résidence, urbaine/rurale: dernière année disponible, 1997 - 2006 (continued - suite)

Continent, country or area, date, code and age (in years) / Continent, pays ou zone, date, code et âge (en annèes)	Total			Urban - Urbaine			Rural - Rurale		
	Both sexes Les deux sexes	Male Masculin	Female Féminin	Both sexes Les deux sexes	Male Masculin	Female Féminin	Both sexes Les deux sexes	Male Masculin	Female Féminin
AMERICA, NORTH - AMÉRIQUE DU NORD									
Puerto Rico - Porto Rico									
2005 (C)									
30 - 34	436	333	103	...	...	...	...	...	...
35 - 39	519	366	153	...	...	...	...	...	...
40 - 44	663	469	194	...	...	...	...	...	...
45 - 49	884	599	285	...	...	...	...	...	...
50 - 54	1 196	801	395	...	...	...	...	...	...
55 - 59	1 673	1 091	582	...	...	...	...	...	...
60 - 64	2 116	1 312	804	...	...	...	...	...	...
65 - 69	2 479	1 495	984	...	...	...	...	...	...
70 - 74	3 070	1 746	1 324	...	...	...	...	...	...
75 - 79	3 490	1 878	1 612	...	...	...	...	...	...
80 - 84	4 107	1 979	2 128	...	...	...	...	...	...
85 - 89	3 599	1 645	1 954	...	...	...	...	...	...
90 - 94	2 537	1 091	1 446	...	...	...	...	...	...
95 - 99	1 000	399	601	...	...	...	...	...	...
100 +	274	79	195	...	...	...	...	...	...
Unknown - Inconnu	47	35	12	...	...	...	...	...	...
Saint Kitts and Nevis - Saint-Kitts-et-Nevis									
2001 (+C)									
Total	352	181	171	...	...	...	...	...	...
0	10	3	7	...	...	...	...	...	...
1 - 4	6	1	5	...	...	...	...	...	...
5 - 9	3	3	-	...	...	...	...	...	...
10 - 14	2	1	1	...	...	...	...	...	...
15 - 19	2	1	1	...	...	...	...	...	...
20 - 24	2	1	1	...	...	...	...	...	...
25 - 29	6	4	2	...	...	...	...	...	...
30 - 34	5	3	2	...	...	...	...	...	...
35 - 39	8	6	2	...	...	...	...	...	...
40 - 44	9	6	3	...	...	...	...	...	...
45 - 49	22	16	6	...	...	...	...	...	...
50 - 54	9	4	5	...	...	...	...	...	...
55 - 59	12	8	4	...	...	...	...	...	...
60 - 64	13	9	4	...	...	...	...	...	...
65 - 69	19	9	10	...	...	...	...	...	...
70 - 74	29	17	12	...	...	...	...	...	...
75 - 79	63	31	32	...	...	...	...	...	...
80 - 84	56	25	31	...	...	...	...	...	...
85 +	76	33	43	...	...	...	...	...	...
Saint Lucia - Sainte-Lucie									
2005* (C)									
Total	1 107	625	482	...	...	...	...	...	...
0	46	28	18	...	...	...	...	...	...
1 - 4	7	2	5	...	...	...	...	...	...
5 - 9	2	1	1	...	...	...	...	...	...
10 - 14	7	4	3	...	...	...	...	...	...
15 - 19	14	12	2	...	...	...	...	...	...
20 - 24	19	15	4	...	...	...	...	...	...
25 - 29	24	18	6	...	...	...	...	...	...
30 - 34	33	21	12	...	...	...	...	...	...
35 - 39	25	19	6	...	...	...	...	...	...
40 - 44	40	30	10	...	...	...	...	...	...
45 - 49	38	28	10	...	...	...	...	...	...
50 - 54	49	25	24	...	...	...	...	...	...
55 - 59	42	23	19	...	...	...	...	...	...
60 - 64	82	52	30	...	...	...	...	...	...
65 - 69	103	63	40	...	...	...	...	...	...
70 - 74	88	52	36	...	...	...	...	...	...
75 - 79	114	72	42	...	...	...	...	...	...
80 - 84	154	70	84	...	...	...	...	...	...
85 +	207	84	123	...	...	...	...	...	...
Unknown - Inconnu	13	6	7	...	...	...	...	...	...

19. Deaths by age, sex and urban/rural residence: latest available year, 1997 - 2006
Décès selon l'âge, le sexe et la résidence, urbaine/rurale: dernière année disponible, 1997 - 2006 (continued - suite)

Continent, country or area, date, code and age (in years) / Continent, pays ou zone, date, code et âge (en années)	Total			Urban - Urbaine			Rural - Rurale		
	Both sexes Les deux sexes	Male Masculin	Female Féminin	Both sexes Les deux sexes	Male Masculin	Female Féminin	Both sexes Les deux sexes	Male Masculin	Female Féminin
AMERICA, NORTH - AMÉRIQUE DU NORD									
Saint Vincent and the Grenadines - Saint Vincent-et-les Grenadines									
2003 (+C)									
Total...................	790	434	356	...	...	...	...	...	...
0.....................	35	19	16	...	...	...	...	...	...
1 - 4.................	7	4	3	...	...	...	...	...	...
5 - 9.................	5	2	3	...	...	...	...	...	...
10 - 14..............	3	2	1	...	...	...	...	...	...
15 - 19..............	6	6	-	...	...	...	...	...	...
20 - 24..............	8	7	1	...	...	...	...	...	...
25 - 29..............	13	12	1	...	...	...	...	...	...
30 - 34..............	20	12	8	...	...	...	...	...	...
35 - 39..............	31	18	13	...	...	...	...	...	...
40 - 44..............	23	14	9	...	...	...	...	...	...
45 - 49..............	27	19	8	...	...	...	...	...	...
50 - 54..............	33	21	12	...	...	...	...	...	...
55 - 59..............	45	28	17	...	...	...	...	...	...
60 - 64..............	50	37	13	...	...	...	...	...	...
65 - 69..............	69	40	29	...	...	...	...	...	...
70 - 74..............	85	42	43	...	...	...	...	...	...
75 - 79..............	89	38	51	...	...	...	...	...	...
80 - 84..............	99	49	50	...	...	...	...	...	...
85 +.................	137	59	78	...	...	...	...	...	...
Unknown - Inconnu.......	5	5	-	...	...	...	...	...	...
Trinidad and Tobago - Trinité-et-Tobago									
2002 (C)									
Total...................	9 797	5 564	4 233	...	...	...	...	...	...
0.....................	412	247	165	...	...	...	...	...	...
1 - 4.................	53	22	31	...	...	...	...	...	...
5 - 9.................	23	10	13	...	...	...	...	...	...
10 - 14..............	36	22	14	...	...	...	...	...	...
15 - 19..............	118	77	41	...	...	...	...	...	...
20 - 24..............	196	138	58	...	...	...	...	...	...
25 - 29..............	211	127	84	...	...	...	...	...	...
30 - 34..............	244	165	79	...	...	...	...	...	...
35 - 39..............	342	220	122	...	...	...	...	...	...
40 - 44..............	354	229	125	...	...	...	...	...	...
45 - 49..............	467	301	166	...	...	...	...	...	...
50 - 54..............	558	354	204	...	...	...	...	...	...
55 - 59..............	678	420	258	...	...	...	...	...	...
60 - 64..............	792	472	320	...	...	...	...	...	...
65 - 69..............	866	499	367	...	...	...	...	...	...
70 - 74..............	1 028	583	445	...	...	...	...	...	...
75 - 79..............	1 037	575	462	...	...	...	...	...	...
80 - 84..............	977	521	456	...	...	...	...	...	...
85 +.................	1 394	572	822	...	...	...	...	...	...
Unknown - Inconnu.......	11	10	1	...	...	...	...	...	...
Turks Caicos Islands - Îles Turques et Caïques									
2005 (C)									
Total...................	53	32	21	...	...	...	...	...	...
0.....................	1	1	-	...	...	...	...	...	...
1 - 4.................	-	-	-	...	...	...	...	...	...
5 - 9.................	-	-	-	...	...	...	...	...	...
10 - 14..............	1	1	-	...	...	...	...	...	...
15 - 19..............	1	1	-	...	...	...	...	...	...
20 - 24..............	-	-	-	...	...	...	...	...	...
25 - 29..............	2	2	-	...	...	...	...	...	...
30 - 34..............	8	5	3	...	...	...	...	...	...
35 - 39..............	3	2	1	...	...	...	...	...	...
40 - 44..............	3	1	2	...	...	...	...	...	...
45 - 49..............	1	1	-	...	...	...	...	...	...

Continent, country or area, date, code and age (in years) / Continent, pays ou zone, date, code et âge (en annèes)	Total			Urban - Urbaine			Rural - Rurale		
	Both sexes Les deux sexes	Male Masculin	Female Féminin	Both sexes Les deux sexes	Male Masculin	Female Féminin	Both sexes Les deux sexes	Male Masculin	Female Féminin
AMERICA, NORTH - AMÉRIQUE DU NORD									
Turks Caicos Islands - Îles Turques et Caïques									
2005 (C)									
50 - 54	2	-	2	...	...	...	...	...	...
55 - 59	2	2	-	...	...	...	...	...	...
60 - 64	2	2	-	...	...	...	...	...	...
65 - 69	-	-	-	...	...	...	...	...	...
70 - 74	3	3	-	...	...	...	...	...	...
75 - 79	6	1	5	...	...	...	...	...	...
80 - 84	5	3	2	...	...	...	...	...	...
85 +	11	5	6	...	...	...	...	...	...
Unknown - Inconnu	2	2	-	...	...	...	...	...	...
United States - États-Unis									
2004 (C)									
Total	2 397 615	1 181 668	1 215 947	...	...	...	...	...	...
0	27 936	15 718	12 218	...	...	...	...	...	...
1 - 4	4 785	2 649	2 136	...	...	...	...	...	...
5 - 9	2 888	1 645	1 243	...	...	...	...	...	...
10 - 14	3 946	2 354	1 592	...	...	...	...	...	...
15 - 19	13 706	9 678	4 028	...	...	...	...	...	...
20 - 24	19 715	14 909	4 806	...	...	...	...	...	...
25 - 29	18 771	13 554	5 217	...	...	...	...	...	...
30 - 34	22 097	14 805	7 292	...	...	...	...	...	...
35 - 39	31 944	20 485	11 459	...	...	...	...	...	...
40 - 44	53 418	33 192	20 226	...	...	...	...	...	...
45 - 49	77 927	48 514	29 413	...	...	...	...	...	...
50 - 54	99 770	62 649	37 121	...	...	...	...	...	...
55 - 59	121 163	73 400	47 763	...	...	...	...	...	...
60 - 64	143 534	84 632	58 902	...	...	...	...	...	...
65 - 69	171 984	98 455	73 529	...	...	...	...	...	...
70 - 74	227 682	124 436	103 246	...	...	...	...	...	...
75 - 79	310 746	160 308	150 438	...	...	...	...	...	...
80 - 84	373 484	173 361	200 123	...	...	...	...	...	...
85 +	671 773	226 650	445 123	...	...	...	...	...	...
Unknown - Inconnu	346	274	72	...	...	...	...	...	...
United States Virgin Islands - Îles Vierges américaines[10]									
2002 (C)									
Total	617	371	246	...	...	...	...	...	...
0	8	1	7	...	...	...	...	...	...
1 - 4	1	-	1	...	...	...	...	...	...
5 - 9	-	-	-	...	...	...	...	...	...
10 - 14	1	-	1	...	...	...	...	...	...
15 - 19	11	10	1	...	...	...	...	...	...
20 - 24	13	11	2	...	...	...	...	...	...
25 - 29	13	9	4	...	...	...	...	...	...
30 - 34	13	10	3	...	...	...	...	...	...
35 - 39	26	19	7	...	...	...	...	...	...
40 - 44	15	10	5	...	...	...	...	...	...
45 - 49	25	16	9	...	...	...	...	...	...
50 - 54	28	17	11	...	...	...	...	...	...
55 - 59	50	34	16	...	...	...	...	...	...
60 - 64	57	39	18	...	...	...	...	...	...
65 - 69	57	41	16	...	...	...	...	...	...
70 - 74	57	32	25	...	...	...	...	...	...
75 - 79	66	37	29	...	...	...	...	...	...
80 - 84	66	32	34	...	...	...	...	...	...
85 - 89	62	32	30	...	...	...	...	...	...
90 - 94	36	17	19	...	...	...	...	...	...
95 +	11	3	8	...	...	...	...	...	...
Unknown - Inconnu	1	1	-	...	...	...	...	...	...

Continent, country or area, date, code and age (in years) / Continent, pays ou zone, date, code et âge (en années)	Total Both sexes Les deux sexes	Total Male Masculin	Total Female Féminin	Urban - Urbaine Both sexes Les deux sexes	Urban - Urbaine Male Masculin	Urban - Urbaine Female Féminin	Rural - Rurale Both sexes Les deux sexes	Rural - Rurale Male Masculin	Rural - Rurale Female Féminin
AMERICA, SOUTH - AMÉRIQUE DU SUD									
Argentina - Argentine									
2006 (C)									
Total	292 313	154 479[7]	137 647[7]	...	...	...	...	...	...
0	8 986	5 063[7]	3 911[7]	...	...	...	...	...	...
1 - 4	1 592	877[7]	715[7]	...	...	...	...	...	...
5 - 9	892	490[7]	402[7]	...	...	...	...	...	...
10 - 14	1 082	655[7]	427[7]	...	...	...	...	...	...
15 - 19	2 398	1 669[7]	717[7]	...	...	...	...	...	...
20 - 24	2 987	2 211[7]	774[7]	...	...	...	...	...	...
25 - 29	3 141	2 219[7]	920[7]	...	...	...	...	...	...
30 - 34	3 191	2 109[7]	1 079[7]	...	...	...	...	...	...
35 - 39	3 919	2 501[7]	1 417[7]	...	...	...	...	...	...
40 - 44	5 125	3 208[7]	1 915[7]	...	...	...	...	...	...
45 - 49	7 873	4 970[7]	2 900[7]	...	...	...	...	...	...
50 - 54	11 623	7 424[7]	4 197[7]	...	...	...	...	...	...
55 - 59	16 091	10 464[7]	5 620[7]	...	...	...	...	...	...
60 - 64	20 714	13 268[7]	7 443[7]	...	...	...	...	...	...
65 - 69	24 796	15 668[7]	9 122[7]	...	...	...	...	...	...
70 - 74	31 690	19 086[7]	12 589[7]	...	...	...	...	...	...
75 - 79	40 298	21 879[7]	18 405[7]	...	...	...	...	...	...
80 - 84	42 532	19 712[7]	22 801[7]	...	...	...	...	...	...
85 +	62 858	20 664[7]	42 162[7]	...	...	...	...	...	...
Unknown - Inconnu	525	342[7]	131[7]	...	...	...	...	...	...
Brazil - Brésil[15]									
2006 (U)									
Total	1 023 545	593 172	430 373	...	...	...	...	...	...
0	37 677	21 300	16 377	...	...	...	...	...	...
1 - 4	7 652	4 199	3 453	...	...	...	...	...	...
5 - 9	4 700	2 758	1 942	...	...	...	...	...	...
10 - 14	5 613	3 422	2 191	...	...	...	...	...	...
15 - 19	18 236	14 363	3 873	...	...	...	...	...	...
20 - 24	26 211	21 301	4 910	...	...	...	...	...	...
25 - 29	26 299	20 478	5 821	...	...	...	...	...	...
30 - 34	26 575	19 734	6 841	...	...	...	...	...	...
35 - 39	31 497	22 130	9 367	...	...	...	...	...	...
40 - 44	40 179	27 199	12 980	...	...	...	...	...	...
45 - 49	50 160	32 742	17 418	...	...	...	...	...	...
50 - 54	59 349	38 122	21 227	...	...	...	...	...	...
55 - 59	67 794	42 510	25 284	...	...	...	...	...	...
60 - 64	74 755	45 382	29 373	...	...	...	...	...	...
65 - 69	90 073	53 156	36 917	...	...	...	...	...	...
70 - 74	100 901	56 785	44 116	...	...	...	...	...	...
75 - 79	111 374	58 666	52 708	...	...	...	...	...	...
80 - 84	100 139	49 141	50 998	...	...	...	...	...	...
85 - 89	75 240	32 471	42 769	...	...	...	...	...	...
90 - 94	44 801	17 163	27 638	...	...	...	...	...	...
95 - 99	16 413	5 735	10 678	...	...	...	...	...	...
100 +	3 755	1 097	2 658	...	...	...	...	...	...
Unknown - Inconnu	4 152	3 318	834	...	...	...	...	...	...
Chile - Chili									
2005 (C)									
Total	86 102	46 369	39 733	73 900	38 957	34 943	12 202	7 412	4 790
0	1 911	1 071	840	1 637	912	725	274	159	115
1 - 4	339	190	149	271	150	121	68	40	28
5 - 9	225	133	92	191	112	79	34	21	13
10 - 14	278	162	116	218	124	94	60	38	22
15 - 19	747	546	201	609	461	148	138	85	53
20 - 24	941	758	183	779	614	165	162	144	18
25 - 29	983	761	222	828	637	191	155	124	31
30 - 34	1 302	975	327	1 076	800	276	226	175	51
35 - 39	1 622	1 151	471	1 339	940	399	283	211	72
40 - 44	2 244	1 512	732	1 880	1 255	625	364	257	107
45 - 49	2 846	1 848	998	2 465	1 573	892	381	275	106

19. Deaths by age, sex and urban/rural residence: latest available year, 1997 - 2006
Décès selon l'âge, le sexe et la résidence, urbaine/rurale: dernière année disponible, 1997 - 2006 (continued - suite)

Continent, country or area, date, code and age (in years) / Continent, pays ou zone, date, code et âge (en années)	Total			Urban - Urbaine			Rural - Rurale		
	Both sexes Les deux sexes	Male Masculin	Female Féminin	Both sexes Les deux sexes	Male Masculin	Female Féminin	Both sexes Les deux sexes	Male Masculin	Female Féminin
AMERICA, SOUTH - AMÉRIQUE DU SUD									
Chile - Chili									
2005 (C)									
50 - 54	3 486	2 170	1 316	3 006	1 843	1 163	480	327	153
55 - 59	4 661	2 956	1 705	4 047	2 551	1 496	614	405	209
60 - 64	6 127	3 764	2 363	5 280	3 180	2 100	847	584	263
65 - 69	7 493	4 528	2 965	6 400	3 809	2 591	1 093	719	374
70 - 74	9 681	5 624	4 057	8 340	4 784	3 556	1 341	840	501
75 - 79	12 047	6 469	5 578	10 349	5 440	4 909	1 698	1 029	669
80 - 84	11 281	5 370	5 911	9 685	4 476	5 209	1 596	894	702
85 - 89	9 497	3 753	5 744	8 173	3 106	5 067	1 324	647	677
90 - 94	6 055	2 011	4 044	5 294	1 678	3 616	761	333	428
95 - 99	1 974	538	1 436	1 723	449	1 274	251	89	162
100 + ...	362	79	283	310	63	247	52	16	36
Colombia - Colombie									
2006* (U)									
Total..................	189 760	109 585[7]	80 151[7]	146 349[4]	81 936[13]	64 406[13]	36 903[4]	22 821[13]	14 077[13]
0	10 722	6 074[7]	4 646[7]	7 565[4]	4 293[13]	3 270[13]	2 645[4]	1 490[13]	1 155[13]
1 - 4	2 350	1 263[7]	1 087[7]	1 460[4]	784[13]	676[13]	821[4]	445[13]	376[13]
5 - 9	1 300	761[7]	538[7]	827[4]	493[13]	334[13]	434[4]	244[13]	189[13]
10 - 14	1 380	833[7]	547[7]	927[4]	557[13]	370[13]	418[4]	251[13]	167[13]
15 - 19	4 358	3 258[7]	1 098[7]	3 048[4]	2 307[13]	739[13]	1 056[4]	759[13]	297[13]
20 - 24	6 467	5 317[7]	1 148[7]	4 561[4]	3 756[13]	804[13]	1 411[4]	1 148[13]	263[13]
25 - 29	6 793	5 526[7]	1 266[7]	4 743[4]	3 806[13]	937[13]	1 425[4]	1 162[13]	263[13]
30 - 34	5 756	4 597[7]	1 158[7]	4 054[4]	3 176[13]	878[13]	1 216[4]	977[13]	239[13]
35 - 39	5 897	4 233[7]	1 661[7]	4 262[4]	2 971[13]	1 289[13]	1 225[4]	906[13]	318[13]
40 - 44	6 218	4 174[7]	2 044[7]	4 759[4]	3 104[13]	1 655[13]	1 156[4]	821[13]	335[13]
45 - 49	7 227	4 562[7]	2 665[7]	5 511[4]	3 348[13]	2 163[13]	1 426[4]	975[13]	451[13]
50 - 54	8 310	4 998[7]	3 312[7]	6 554[4]	3 836[13]	2 718[13]	1 466[4]	943[13]	523[13]
55 - 59	9 588	5 698[7]	3 889[7]	7 576[4]	4 421[13]	3 155[13]	1 726[4]	1 067[13]	659[13]
60 - 64	11 173	6 387[7]	4 786[7]	8 813[4]	4 963[13]	3 850[13]	2 082[4]	1 244[13]	838[13]
65 - 69	14 852	8 414[7]	6 437[7]	11 750[4]	6 476[13]	5 274[13]	2 800[4]	1 735[13]	1 064[13]
70 - 74	18 047	9 674[7]	8 372[7]	14 278[4]	7 496[13]	6 782[13]	3 419[4]	1 967[13]	1 451[13]
75 - 79	21 468	11 431[7]	10 037[7]	17 146[4]	8 906[13]	8 240[13]	4 000[4]	2 332[13]	1 668[13]
80 - 84	19 181	9 485[7]	9 696[7]	15 526[4]	7 462[13]	8 064[13]	3 387[4]	1 874[13]	1 513[13]
85 + ...	27 647	12 074[7]	15 573[7]	22 691[4]	9 578[13]	13 113[13]	4 607[4]	2 332[13]	2 275[13]
Unknown - Inconnu	1 026	826[7]	191[7]	298[4]	203[13]	95[13]	183[4]	149[13]	33[13]
Ecuador - Équateur[16]									
2004 (U)									
Total..................	54 729	31 292	23 437	41 783	23 947	17 836	12 946	7 345	5 601
0	3 942	2 241	1 701	3 121	1 789	1 332	821	452	369
1 - 4	1 595	885	710	1 067	605	462	528	280	248
5 - 14	1 327	788	539	948	564	384	379	224	155
15 - 49	12 277	8 441	3 836	9 549	6 643	2 906	2 728	1 798	930
50 - 64	8 296	4 875	3 421	6 473	3 768	2 705	1 823	1 107	716
65 + ...	27 239	14 025	13 214	20 587	10 549	10 038	6 652	3 476	3 176
Unknown - Inconnu	53	37	16	38	29	9	15	8	7
2006 (U)									
Total..................	57 940	32 775	25 165	...	...	...	...	...	...
0	3 715	2 048	1 667	...	...	...	...	...	...
1 - 4	1 357	742	615	...	...	...	...	...	...
5 - 14	1 322	737	585	...	...	...	...	...	...
15 - 49	12 752	8 799	3 953	...	...	...	...	...	...
50 - 64	8 819	5 222	3 597	...	...	...	...	...	...
65 + ...	29 877	15 163	14 714	...	...	...	...	...	...
Unknown - Inconnu	98	64	34	...	...	...	...	...	...
French Guiana - Guyane française[8]									
2003 (C)									
Total..................	692	435	257	...	...	...	...	...	...
0	58	32	26	...	...	...	...	...	...
1 - 4	17	10	7	...	...	...	...	...	...
5 - 9	3	1	2	...	...	...	...	...	...
10 - 14	6	5	1	...	...	...	...	...	...

Continent, country or area, date, code and age (in years) / Continent, pays ou zone, date, code et âge (en années)	Total			Urban - Urbaine			Rural - Rurale		
	Both sexes Les deux sexes	Male Masculin	Female Féminin	Both sexes Les deux sexes	Male Masculin	Female Féminin	Both sexes Les deux sexes	Male Masculin	Female Féminin
AMERICA, SOUTH - AMÉRIQUE DU SUD									
French Guiana - Guyane française[8]									
2003 (C)									
15 - 19	15	10	5	...	...	...	...	...	...
20 - 24	17	11	6	...	...	...	...	...	...
25 - 29	31	25	6	...	...	...	...	...	...
30 - 34	26	18	8	...	...	...	...	...	...
35 - 39	38	28	10	...	...	...	...	...	...
40 - 44	34	24	10	...	...	...	...	...	...
45 - 49	38	26	12	...	...	...	...	...	...
50 - 54	44	33	11	...	...	...	...	...	...
55 - 59	36	25	11	...	...	...	...	...	...
60 - 64	45	29	16	...	...	...	...	...	...
65 - 69	43	28	15	...	...	...	...	...	...
70 - 74	47	36	11	...	...	...	...	...	...
75 - 79	50	37	13	...	...	...	...	...	...
80 - 84	49	19	30	...	...	...	...	...	...
85 - 89	53	24	29	...	...	...	...	...	...
90 - 94	23	8	15	...	...	...	...	...	...
95 - 99	15	4	11	...	...	...	...	...	...
100 +	4	2	2	...	...	...	...	...	...
Guyana[10]									
2003 (+C)									
Total	4 986	2 898	2 088	...	...	...	...	...	...
0	290	157	133	...	...	...	...	...	...
1 - 4	72	40	32	...	...	...	...	...	...
5 - 9	33	21	12	...	...	...	...	...	...
10 - 14	43	24	19	...	...	...	...	...	...
15 - 19	64	39	25	...	...	...	...	...	...
20 - 24	148	97	51	...	...	...	...	...	...
25 - 29	175	120	55	...	...	...	...	...	...
30 - 34	263	169	94	...	...	...	...	...	...
35 - 39	274	188	86	...	...	...	...	...	...
40 - 44	277	195	82	...	...	...	...	...	...
45 - 49	305	197	108	...	...	...	...	...	...
50 - 54	338	207	131	...	...	...	...	...	...
55 - 59	339	212	127	...	...	...	...	...	...
60 - 64	377	228	149	...	...	...	...	...	...
65 - 69	401	226	175	...	...	...	...	...	...
70 - 74	418	214	204	...	...	...	...	...	...
75 - 79	441	224	217	...	...	...	...	...	...
80 - 84	291	145	146	...	...	...	...	...	...
85 - 89	220	97	123	...	...	...	...	...	...
90 - 94	104	39	65	...	...	...	...	...	...
95 - 99	36	12	24	...	...	...	...	...	...
100 +	77	47	30	...	...	...	...	...	...
Paraguay									
2001 (I)[17]									
Total	38 514	20 073[7]	15 948[7]	23 907	12 238[7]	10 148[7]	14 607	7 835[7]	5 800[7]
0	3 898	2 219[7]	1 662[7]	2 076	1 156[7]	911[7]	1 822	1 063[7]	751[7]
1 - 4	1 666	939[7]	720[7]	745	419[7]	322[7]	921	520[7]	398[7]
5 - 9	554	308[7]	242[7]	289	163[7]	123[7]	265	145[7]	119[7]
10 - 14	446	255[7]	189[7]	213	104[7]	108[7]	233	151[7]	81[7]
15 - 19	1 019	640[7]	379[7]	582	380[7]	202[7]	437	260[7]	177[7]
20 - 24	1 208	863[7]	340[7]	675	488[7]	183[7]	533	375[7]	157[7]
25 - 29	1 061	754[7]	302[7]	641	461[7]	177[7]	420	293[7]	125[7]
30 - 34	927	626[7]	297[7]	581	401[7]	177[7]	346	225[7]	120[7]
35 - 39	1 115	664[7]	449[7]	681	405[7]	275[7]	434	259[7]	174[7]
40 - 44	1 222	730[7]	489[7]	781	465[7]	314[7]	441	265[7]	175[7]
45 - 49	1 550	929[7]	619[7]	1 035	632[7]	402[7]	515	297[7]	217[7]
50 - 54	1 765	999[7]	763[7]	1 176	658[7]	516[7]	589	341[7]	247[7]
55 - 59	1 703	997[7]	702[7]	1 134	668[7]	463[7]	569	329[7]	239[7]
60 - 64	2 378	1 333[7]	1 039[7]	1 560	882[7]	674[7]	818	451[7]	365[7]

Continent, country or area, date, code and age (in years) / Continent, pays ou zone, date, code et âge (en années)	Total			Urban - Urbaine			Rural - Rurale		
	Both sexes Les deux sexes	Male Masculin	Female Féminin	Both sexes Les deux sexes	Male Masculin	Female Féminin	Both sexes Les deux sexes	Male Masculin	Female Féminin
AMERICA, SOUTH - AMÉRIQUE DU SUD									
Paraguay									
2001 (I)[17]									
65 - 69	2 373	1 278[7]	1 093[7]	1 622	848[7]	774[7]	751	430[7]	319[7]
70 - 74	2 996	1 744[7]	1 246[7]	2 026	1 162[7]	860[7]	970	582[7]	386[7]
75 - 79	2 793	1 483[7]	1 300[7]	1 740	877[7]	860[7]	1 053	606[7]	440[7]
80 - 84	2 846	1 377[7]	1 465[7]	1 889	876[7]	1 010[7]	957	501[7]	455[7]
85 - 89	2 220	1 006[7]	1 209[7]	1 485	652[7]	831[7]	735	354[7]	378[7]
90 +	1 912	670[7]	1 227[7]	1 236	394[7]	835[7]	676	276[7]	392[7]
Unknown - Inconnu	2 862	259[7]	216[7]	1 740	147[7]	131[7]	1 122	112[7]	85[7]
2005 (U)									
Total	17 360	9 658[7]	7 614[7]	...	...	...	...	...	...
0	539	294[7]	240[7]	...	...	...	...	...	...
1 - 4	272	160[7]	111[7]	...	...	...	...	...	...
5 - 9	150	89[7]	60[7]	...	...	...	...	...	...
10 - 14	161	107[7]	54[7]	...	...	...	...	...	...
15 - 19	338	228[7]	109[7]	...	...	...	...	...	...
20 - 24	477	355[7]	122[7]	...	...	...	...	...	...
25 - 29	392	260[7]	123[7]	...	...	...	...	...	...
30 - 34	401	274[7]	127[7]	...	...	...	...	...	...
35 - 39	431	277[7]	151[7]	...	...	...	...	...	...
40 - 44	585	359[7]	220[7]	...	...	...	...	...	...
45 - 49	687	420[7]	261[7]	...	...	...	...	...	...
50 - 54	922	563[7]	356[7]	...	...	...	...	...	...
55 - 59	974	574[7]	399[7]	...	...	...	...	...	...
60 - 64	1 203	705[7]	491[7]	...	...	...	...	...	...
65 - 69	1 334	746[7]	587[7]	...	...	...	...	...	...
70 - 74	1 603	887[7]	705[7]	...	...	...	...	...	...
75 - 79	1 925	1 044[7]	871[7]	...	...	...	...	...	...
80 - 84	1 792	891[7]	892[7]	...	...	...	...	...	...
85 +	2 930	1 269[7]	1 647[7]	...	...	...	...	...	...
Unknown - Inconnu	244	148[7]	88[7]	...	...	...	...	...	...
Peru - Pérou[18]									
2003 (+U)									
Total	85 198	45 261[7]	39 909[7]	...	...	...	...	...	...
0	7 122	3 886[7]	3 233[7]	...	...	...	...	...	...
1 - 4	1 914	990[7]	923[7]	...	...	...	...	...	...
5 - 9	887	523	364	...	...	...	...	...	...
10 - 14	854	486	368	...	...	...	...	...	...
15 - 19	1 440	849	591	...	...	...	...	...	...
20 - 24	2 009	1 251	758	...	...	...	...	...	...
25 - 29	2 030	1 276	754	...	...	...	...	...	...
30 - 34	2 221	1 424	797	...	...	...	...	...	...
35 - 39	2 468	1 486[7]	981[7]	...	...	...	...	...	...
40 - 44	2 696	1 601[7]	1 094[7]	...	...	...	...	...	...
45 - 49	2 984	1 669	1 315	...	...	...	...	...	...
50 - 54	3 630	2 013	1 617	...	...	...	...	...	...
55 - 59	3 993	2 230[7]	1 762[7]	...	...	...	...	...	...
60 - 64	5 041	2 734	2 307	...	...	...	...	...	...
65 - 69	6 123	3 325	2 798	...	...	...	...	...	...
70 - 74	7 853	4 308	3 545	...	...	...	...	...	...
75 - 79	8 488	4 602[7]	3 885[7]	...	...	...	...	...	...
80 - 84	8 679	4 397[7]	4 281[7]	...	...	...	...	...	...
85 - 89	7 160	3 277	3 883	...	...	...	...	...	...
90 - 94	4 589	1 869	2 720	...	...	...	...	...	...
95 - 99	2 258	752	1 506	...	...	...	...	...	...
100 +	460	145	315	...	...	...	...	...	...
Unknown - Inconnu	299	168[7]	112[7]	...	...	...	...	...	...
Suriname									
2005 (C)									
Total	3 392	1 950	1 442	2 308[19]	1 328[19]	980[19]	1 051[19]	605[19]	446[19]
0	136	76	60	87[19]	49[19]	38[19]	48[19]	26[19]	22[19]
1 - 4	47	28	19	29[19]	18[19]	11[19]	18[19]	10[19]	8[19]

19. Deaths by age, sex and urban/rural residence: latest available year, 1997 - 2006
Décès selon l'âge, le sexe et la résidence, urbaine/rurale: dernière année disponible, 1997 - 2006 (continued - suite)

Continent, country or area, date, code and age (in years) / Continent, pays ou zone, date, code et âge (en années)	Total			Urban - Urbaine			Rural - Rurale		
	Both sexes Les deux sexes	Male Masculin	Female Féminin	Both sexes Les deux sexes	Male Masculin	Female Féminin	Both sexes Les deux sexes	Male Masculin	Female Féminin
AMERICA, SOUTH - AMÉRIQUE DU SUD									
Suriname									
2005 (C)									
5 - 9	23	13	10	16[19]	9[19]	7[19]	7[19]	4[19]	3[19]
10 - 14	21	10	11	15[19]	7[19]	8[19]	6[19]	3[19]	3[19]
15 - 19	42	24	18	32[19]	18[19]	14[19]	10[19]	6[19]	4[19]
20 - 24	82	49	33	55[19]	33[19]	22[19]	25[19]	14[19]	11[19]
25 - 29	85	54	31	59[19]	35[19]	24[19]	35[19]	29[19]	6[19]
30 - 34	135	100	35	95[19]	69[19]	26[19]	37[19]	28[19]	9[19]
35 - 39	119	78	41	82[19]	54[19]	28[19]	34[19]	22[19]	12[19]
40 - 44	154	103	51	106[19]	70[19]	36[19]	42[19]	30[19]	12[19]
45 - 49	154	113	41	112[19]	82[19]	30[19]	37[19]	27[19]	10[19]
50 - 54	181	116	65	118[19]	77[19]	41[19]	57[19]	35[19]	22[19]
55 - 59	204	131	73	149[19]	98[19]	51[19]	52[19]	31[19]	21[19]
60 - 64	292	166	126	204[19]	118[19]	86[19]	82[19]	44[19]	38[19]
65 - 69	310	175	135	206[19]	118[19]	88[19]	102[19]	55[19]	47[19]
70 - 74	424	229	195	282[19]	161[19]	121[19]	140[19]	68[19]	72[19]
75 - 79	365	196	169	230[19]	121[19]	109[19]	133[19]	75[19]	58[19]
80 - 84	285	146	139	188[19]	94[19]	94[19]	97[19]	52[19]	45[19]
85 - 89	197	88	109	134[19]	56[19]	78[19]	63[19]	32[19]	31[19]
90 - 94	98	39	59	82[19]	30[19]	52[19]	15[19]	9[19]	6[19]
95 - 99	31	12	19	23[19]	8[19]	15[19]	8[19]	4[19]	4[19]
100 +	7	4	3	4[19]	3[19]	1[19]	3[19]	1[19]	2[19]
Uruguay									
2002 (C)									
Total	31 628	16 796[7]	14 819[7]	...	...	...	...	...	...
0	708	401[7]	304[7]	...	...	...	...	...	...
1 - 4	104	69	35	...	...	...	...	...	...
5 - 9	63	31	32	...	...	...	...	...	...
10 - 14	67	42	25	...	...	...	...	...	...
15 - 19	182	139	43	...	...	...	...	...	...
20 - 24	249	199	50	...	...	...	...	...	...
25 - 29	260	196	64	...	...	...	...	...	...
30 - 34	301	200	101	...	...	...	...	...	...
35 - 39	339	218[7]	120[7]	...	...	...	...	...	...
40 - 44	494	273	221	...	...	...	...	...	...
45 - 49	754	467	287	...	...	...	...	...	...
50 - 54	1 108	724	384	...	...	...	...	...	...
55 - 59	1 501	990	511	...	...	...	...	...	...
60 - 64	2 095	1 422	673	...	...	...	...	...	...
65 - 69	2 842	1 818	1 024	...	...	...	...	...	...
70 - 74	3 938	2 395[7]	1 542[7]	...	...	...	...	...	...
75 +	16 534	7 149[7]	9 381[7]	...	...	...	...	...	...
Unknown - Inconnu	89	63[7]	22[7]	...	...	...	...	...	...
Venezuela (Bolivarian Republic of) - Venezuela (République bolivarienne du)[15]									
2002 (C)									
Total	105 388	64 917	40 471	...	...	...	...	...	...
0	7 645	4 406	3 239	...	...	...	...	...	...
1 - 4	1 937	1 077	860	...	...	...	...	...	...
5 - 9	829	493	336	...	...	...	...	...	...
10 - 14	1 061	668	393	...	...	...	...	...	...
15 - 19	3 540	2 929	611	...	...	...	...	...	...
20 - 24	5 301	4 579	722	...	...	...	...	...	...
25 - 29	4 293	3 578	715	...	...	...	...	...	...
30 - 34	3 957	3 002	955	...	...	...	...	...	...
35 - 39	3 621	2 586	1 035	...	...	...	...	...	...
40 - 44	4 168	2 795	1 373	...	...	...	...	...	...
45 - 49	4 878	3 164	1 714	...	...	...	...	...	...
50 - 54	5 518	3 549	1 969	...	...	...	...	...	...
55 - 59	5 802	3 719	2 083	...	...	...	...	...	...
60 - 64	6 494	4 032	2 462	...	...	...	...	...	...

Continent, country or area, date, code and age (in years) / Continent, pays ou zone, date, code et âge (en années)	Total			Urban - Urbaine			Rural - Rurale		
	Both sexes Les deux sexes	Male Masculin	Female Féminin	Both sexes Les deux sexes	Male Masculin	Female Féminin	Both sexes Les deux sexes	Male Masculin	Female Féminin
AMERICA, SOUTH - AMÉRIQUE DU SUD									
Venezuela (Bolivarian Republic of) - Venezuela (République bolivarienne du)[15]									
2002 (C)									
65 - 69	7 964	4 746	3 218	...	...	...	...	...	...
70 - 74	9 145	5 339	3 806	...	...	...	...	...	...
75 - 79	9 369	5 076	4 293	...	...	...	...	...	...
80 - 84	8 247	4 164	4 083	...	...	...	...	...	...
85 - 89	6 270	2 793	3 477	...	...	...	...	...	...
90 - 94	3 518	1 463	2 055	...	...	...	...	...	...
95 - 99	1 201	420	781	...	...	...	...	...	...
100 +	364	133	231	...	...	...	...	...	...
Unknown - Inconnu	266	206	60	...	...	...	...	...	...
ASIA - ASIE									
Armenia - Arménie[20]									
2006 (C)									
Total	27 202	14 125	13 077	17 689	9 297	8 392	9 513	4 828	4 685
0	523	315	208	389	228	161	134	87	47
1 - 4	72	32	40	44	20	24	28	12	16
5 - 9	42	24	18	24	13	11	18	11	7
10 - 14	43	24	19	23	11	12	20	13	7
15 - 19	125	95	30	72	54	18	53	41	12
20 - 24	182	128	54	129	91	38	53	37	16
25 - 29	195	142	53	134	101	33	61	41	20
30 - 34	235	169	66	171	127	44	64	42	22
35 - 39	319	227	92	218	161	57	101	66	35
40 - 44	670	457	213	458	313	145	212	144	68
45 - 49	1 055	732	323	725	493	232	330	239	91
50 - 54	1 316	906	410	977	667	310	339	239	100
55 - 59	1 440	956	484	1 076	712	364	364	244	120
60 - 64	1 259	768	491	896	549	347	363	219	144
65 - 69	3 627	2 134	1 493	2 518	1 485	1 033	1 109	649	460
70 - 74	4 264	2 272	1 992	2 667	1 414	1 253	1 597	858	739
75 - 79	5 713	2 772	2 941	3 450	1 650	1 800	2 263	1 122	1 141
80 - 84	3 597	1 332	2 265	2 239	809	1 430	1 358	523	835
85 +	2 525	640	1 885	1 479	399	1 080	1 046	241	805
Azerbaijan - Azerbaïdjan[20]									
2004 (+C)									
Total	49 568	26 039	23 529	25 867	13 797	12 070	23 701	12 242	11 459
0	1 287	757	530	605	385	220	682	372	310
1 - 4	726	405	321	139	69	70	587	336	251
5 - 9	336	191	145	130	68	62	206	123	83
10 - 14	315	200	115	126	75	51	189	125	64
15 - 19	438	279	159	228	139	89	210	140	70
20 - 24	586	393	193	304	213	91	282	180	102
25 - 29	647	429	218	332	231	101	315	198	117
30 - 34	931	659	272	518	361	157	413	298	115
35 - 39	1 264	858	406	696	488	208	568	370	198
40 - 44	1 873	1 255	618	1 077	749	328	796	506	290
45 - 49	2 270	1 557	713	1 384	953	431	886	604	282
50 - 54	2 431	1 557	874	1 549	1 011	538	882	546	336
55 - 59	2 323	1 491	832	1 493	979	514	830	512	318
60 - 64	3 493	2 108	1 385	2 057	1 246	811	1 436	862	574
65 - 69	7 684	4 301	3 383	3 924	2 249	1 675	3 760	2 052	1 708
70 - 74	8 158	4 225	3 933	4 008	2 025	1 983	4 150	2 200	1 950
75 - 79	6 696	3 114	3 582	3 455	1 500	1 955	3 241	1 614	1 627
80 - 84	3 703	1 208	2 495	1 928	573	1 355	1 775	635	1 140
85 - 89	1 983	532	1 451	1 000	263	737	983	269	714
90 - 94	1 379	334	1 045	587	147	440	792	187	605

Continent, country or area, date, code and age (in years) / Continent, pays ou zone, date, code et âge (en années)	Total			Urban - Urbaine			Rural - Rurale		
	Both sexes Les deux sexes	Male Masculin	Female Féminin	Both sexes Les deux sexes	Male Masculin	Female Féminin	Both sexes Les deux sexes	Male Masculin	Female Féminin
ASIA - ASIE									
Azerbaijan - Azerbaïdjan[20]									
2004 (+C)									
95 - 99	501	113	388	182	42	140	319	71	248
100 + ...	544	73	471	145	31	114	399	42	357
Bahrain - Bahreïn									
2006 (C)									
Total	2 317	1 379	938	...	...	...	...	...	...
0	115	60	55	...	...	...	...	...	...
1 - 4	37	17	20	...	...	...	...	...	...
5 - 9	24	14	10	...	...	...	...	...	...
10 - 14	11	8	3	...	...	...	...	...	...
15 - 19	33	24	9	...	...	...	...	...	...
20 - 24	51	38	13	...	...	...	...	...	...
25 - 29	81	61	20	...	...	...	...	...	...
30 - 34	99	71	28	...	...	...	...	...	...
35 - 39	84	56	28	...	...	...	...	...	...
40 - 44	101	67	34	...	...	...	...	...	...
45 - 49	147	105	42	...	...	...	...	...	...
50 - 54	152	102	50	...	...	...	...	...	...
55 - 59	136	94	42	...	...	...	...	...	...
60 - 64	132	72	60	...	...	...	...	...	...
65 - 69	208	113	95	...	...	...	...	...	...
70 - 74	257	132	125	...	...	...	...	...	...
75 + ...	649	345	304	...	...	...	...	...	...
Bhutan - Bhoutan[21]									
2005 (I)									
Total	4 498	2 390	2 108	1 048	568	480	3 450	1 822	1 628
0	503	270	233	126	60	66	377	210	167
1 - 4	269	143	126	77	45	32	192	98	94
5 - 9	139	85	54	49	36	13	90	49	41
10 - 14	88	46	42	14	4	10	74	42	32
15 - 19	126	65	61	19	13	6	107	52	55
20 - 24	123	65	58	28	15	13	95	50	45
25 - 29	133	74	59	36	22	14	97	52	45
30 - 34	145	79	66	32	19	13	113	60	53
35 - 39	182	107	75	60	40	20	122	67	55
40 - 44	174	95	79	42	21	21	132	74	58
45 - 49	250	129	121	71	36	35	179	93	86
50 - 54	204	113	91	41	26	15	163	87	76
55 - 59	239	126	113	66	30	36	173	96	77
60 - 64	291	145	146	57	28	29	234	117	117
65 - 69	331	163	168	76	35	41	255	128	127
70 - 74	368	188	180	59	29	30	309	159	150
75 + ...	933	497	436	195	109	86	738	388	350
Brunei Darussalam - Brunéi Darussalam									
2004 (+C)									
Total	1 010	559	451	...	...	...	...	...	...
0 - 4	70	37	33	...	...	...	...	...	...
5 - 9	12	10	2	...	...	...	...	...	...
10 - 14	10	6	4	...	...	...	...	...	...
15 - 19	12	8	4	...	...	...	...	...	...
20 - 24	19	14	5	...	...	...	...	...	...
25 - 29	21	15	6	...	...	...	...	...	...
30 - 34	36	19	17	...	...	...	...	...	...
35 - 39	37	20	17	...	...	...	...	...	...
40 - 44	47	26	21	...	...	...	...	...	...
45 - 49	55	33	22	...	...	...	...	...	...
50 - 54	52	31	21	...	...	...	...	...	...
55 - 59	62	25	37	...	...	...	...	...	...
60 - 64	54	31	23	...	...	...	...	...	...
65 - 69	98	55	43	...	...	...	...	...	...
70 + ...	425	229	196	...	...	...	...	...	...

19. Deaths by age, sex and urban/rural residence: latest available year, 1997 - 2006
Décès selon l'âge, le sexe et la résidence, urbaine/rurale: dernière année disponible, 1997 - 2006 (continued - suite)

Continent, country or area, date, code and age (in years) / Continent, pays ou zone, date, code et âge (en années)	Total			Urban - Urbaine			Rural - Rurale		
	Both sexes Les deux sexes	Male Masculin	Female Féminin	Both sexes Les deux sexes	Male Masculin	Female Féminin	Both sexes Les deux sexes	Male Masculin	Female Féminin
ASIA - ASIE									
China - Chine[22]									
1999 (...)									
Total....................	7 420 000	4 140 000	3 280 000	...	...	...	...	...	...
0 - 4.....................	474 000	237 000	237 000	...	...	...	...	...	...
5 - 9.....................	40 000	22 000	18 000	...	...	...	...	...	...
10 - 14...................	33 000	20 000	13 000	...	...	...	...	...	...
15 - 19...................	72 000	38 000	34 000	...	...	...	...	...	...
20 - 24...................	104 000	59 000	45 000	...	...	...	...	...	...
25 - 29...................	165 000	87 000	78 000	...	...	...	...	...	...
30 - 34...................	180 000	112 000	68 000	...	...	...	...	...	...
35 - 39...................	147 000	93 000	54 000	...	...	...	...	...	...
40 - 44...................	229 000	150 000	79 000	...	...	...	...	...	...
45 - 49...................	306 000	199 000	107 000	...	...	...	...	...	...
50 - 54...................	286 000	177 000	109 000	...	...	...	...	...	...
55 - 59...................	414 000	242 000	172 000	...	...	...	...	...	...
60 - 64...................	673 000	432 000	241 000	...	...	...	...	...	...
65 - 69...................	906 000	540 000	366 000	...	...	...	...	...	...
70 - 74...................	1 028 000	594 000	434 000	...	...	...	...	...	...
75 - 79...................	947 000	528 000	419 000	...	...	...	...	...	...
80 - 84...................	799 000	381 000	418 000	...	...	...	...	...	...
85 - 89...................	423 000	174 000	249 000	...	...	...	...	...	...
90 +.....................	193 000	54 000	139 000	...	...	...	...	...	...
China: Hong Kong SAR - Chine: Hong Kong RAS									
2006* (C)									
Total....................	37 457	20 983	16 474	...	...	...	...	...	...
0........................	118	65	53	...	...	...	...	...	...
1 - 4.....................	36	22	14	...	...	...	...	...	...
5 - 9.....................	32	20	12	...	...	...	...	...	...
10 - 14...................	46	25	21	...	...	...	...	...	...
15 - 19...................	68	42	26	...	...	...	...	...	...
20 - 24...................	124	88	36	...	...	...	...	...	...
25 - 29...................	215	149	66	...	...	...	...	...	...
30 - 34...................	277	160	117	...	...	...	...	...	...
35 - 39...................	412	238	174	...	...	...	.т	...	...
40 - 44...................	714	431	283	...	...	...	...	...	...
45 - 49...................	1 043	653	390	...	...	...	...	...	...
50 - 54...................	1 503	965	538	...	...	...	...	...	...
55 - 59...................	1 770	1 210	560	...	...	...	...	...	...
60 - 64...................	1 771	1 261	510	...	...	...	...	...	...
65 - 69...................	2 742	1 932	810	...	...	...	...	...	...
70 - 74...................	4 530	3 009	1 521	...	...	...	...	...	...
75 - 79...................	5 916	3 627	2 289	...	...	...	...	...	...
80 - 84...................	6 345	3 407	2 938	...	...	...	...	...	...
85 +.....................	9 795	3 679	6 116	...	...	...	...	...	...
China: Macao SAR - Chine: Macao RAS									
2006 (C)									
Total....................	1 566	887	679	...	...	...	...	...	...
0........................	11	6	5	...	...	...	...	...	...
1 - 4.....................	2	1	1	...	...	...	...	...	...
5 - 9.....................	1	1	-	...	...	...	...	...	...
10 - 14...................	-	-	-	...	...	...	...	...	...
15 - 19...................	6	3	3	...	...	...	...	...	...
20 - 24...................	16	7	9	...	...	...	...	...	...
25 - 29...................	12	8	4	...	...	...	...	...	...
30 - 34...................	24	13	11	...	...	...	...	...	...
35 - 39...................	21	13	8	...	...	...	...	...	...
40 - 44...................	62	38	24	...	...	...	...	...	...
45 - 49...................	79	51	28	...	...	...	...	...	...
50 - 54...................	99	74	25	...	...	...	...	...	...
55 - 59...................	104	70	34	...	...	...	...	...	...
60 - 64...................	90	70	20	...	...	...	...	...	...
65 - 69...................	103	76	27	...	...	...	...	...	...
70 - 74...................	158	102	56	...	...	...	...	...	...

19. Deaths by age, sex and urban/rural residence: latest available year, 1997 - 2006
Décès selon l'âge, le sexe et la résidence, urbaine/rurale: dernière année disponible, 1997 - 2006 (continued - suite)

Continent, country or area, date, code and age (in years) / Continent, pays ou zone, date, code et âge (en années)	Total			Urban - Urbaine			Rural Rurale		
	Both sexes Les deux sexes	Male Masculin	Female Féminin	Both sexes Les deux sexes	Male Masculin	Female Féminin	Both sexes Les deux sexes	Male Masculin	Female Féminin
ASIA - ASIE									
China: Macao SAR - Chine: Macao RAS									
2006 (C)									
75 - 79	207	119	88	...	...	...	...	...	...
80 - 84	240	115	125	...	...	...	...	...	...
85 +	331	120	211	...	...	...	...	...	...
Cyprus - Chypre[23]									
2006 (C)									
Total	5 127	2 623	2 504	...	...	...	...	...	...
0	27	16	11	...	...	...	...	...	...
1 - 4	8	6	2	...	...	...	...	...	...
5 - 9	4	3	1	...	...	...	...	...	...
10 - 14	5	3	2	...	...	...	...	...	...
15 - 19	26	16	10	...	...	...	...	...	...
20 - 24	35	29	6	...	...	...	...	...	...
25 - 29	34	28	6	...	...	...	...	...	...
30 - 34	32	20	12	...	...	...	...	...	...
35 - 39	32	20	12	...	...	...	...	...	...
40 - 44	50	27	23	...	...	...	...	...	...
45 - 49	83	50	33	...	...	...	...	...	...
50 - 54	120	70	50	...	...	...	...	...	...
55 - 59	182	116	66	...	...	...	...	...	...
60 - 64	243	163	80	...	...	...	...	...	...
65 - 69	374	233	141	...	...	...	...	...	...
70 - 74	495	286	209	...	...	...	...	...	...
75 - 79	749	377	372	...	...	...	...	...	...
80 - 84	898	382	516	...	...	...	...	...	...
85 - 89	848	356	492	...	...	...	...	...	...
90 - 94	561	250	311	...	...	...	...	...	...
95 - 99	139	60	79	...	...	...	...	...	...
100 +	182	112	70	...	...	...	...	...	...
Georgia - Géorgie[20]									
2001 (C)									
Total	39 339	19 569	19 770	21 600	11 077	10 523	17 739	8 492	9 247
0	478	301	177	439	280	159	39	21	18
1 - 4	58	26	32	29	10	19	29	16	13
5 - 9	40	29	11	27	21	6	13	8	5
10 - 14	74	53	21	50	36	14	24	17	7
15 - 19	183	114	69	99	66	33	84	48	36
20 - 24	208	137	71	134	88	46	74	49	25
25 - 29	370	271	99	231	169	62	139	102	37
30 - 34	463	350	113	270	204	66	193	146	47
35 - 39	668	506	162	427	327	100	241	179	62
40 - 44	953	711	242	629	484	145	324	227	97
45 - 49	1 156	857	299	778	584	194	378	273	105
50 - 54	1 294	924	370	890	635	255	404	289	115
55 - 59	1 311	877	434	823	568	255	488	309	179
60 - 64	3 440	1 980	1 460	2 067	1 242	825	1 373	738	635
65 - 69	5 046	2 936	2 110	2 693	1 560	1 133	2 353	1 376	977
70 - 74	7 055	3 787	3 268	3 703	1 965	1 738	3 352	1 822	1 530
75 - 79	6 361	2 713	3 648	3 381	1 361	2 020	2 980	1 352	1 628
80 - 84	4 249	1 361	2 888	2 177	676	1 501	2 072	685	1 387
85 - 89	3 498	997	2 501	1 775	512	1 263	1 723	485	1 238
90 - 94	1 558	413	1 145	636	175	461	922	238	684
95 - 99	487	97	390	165	37	128	322	60	262
100 +	301	75	226	93	25	68	208	50	158
Unknown - Inconnu	88	54	34	84	52	32	4	2	2
2006 (C)									
Total	42 255	22 458	19 797	...	...	...	...	...	...
0	753	395	358	...	...	...	...	...	...
1 - 4	57	31	26	...	...	...	...	...	...
5 - 9	57	36	21	...	...	...	...	...	...
10 - 14	67	38	29	...	...	...	...	...	...
15 - 19	129	93	36	...	...	...	...	...	...
20 - 24	279	207	72	...	...	...	...	...	...

Continent, country or area, date, code and age (in years) / Continent, pays ou zone, date, code et âge (en années)	Total			Urban - Urbaine			Rural - Rurale		
	Both sexes Les deux sexes	Male Masculin	Female Féminin	Both sexes Les deux sexes	Male Masculin	Female Féminin	Both sexes Les deux sexes	Male Masculin	Female Féminin
ASIA - ASIE									
Georgia - Géorgie[20]									
2006 (C)									
25 - 29	378	293	85	...	...	...	...	...	...
30 - 34	523	405	118	...	...	...	...	...	...
35 - 39	668	513	155	...	...	...	...	...	...
40 - 44	1 061	803	258	...	...	...	...	...	...
45 - 49	1 448	1 102	346	...	...	...	...	...	...
50 - 54	1 864	1 365	499	...	...	...	...	...	...
55 - 59	1 996	1 419	577	...	...	...	...	...	...
60 - 64	1 886	1 179	707	...	...	...	...	...	...
65 - 69	5 581	3 329	2 252	...	...	...	...	...	...
70 - 74	6 091	3 414	2 677	...	...	...	...	...	...
75 - 79	7 805	3 858	3 947	...	...	...	...	...	...
80 - 84	6 426	2 468	3 958	...	...	...	...	...	...
85 +	5 186	1 510	3 676	...	...	...	...	...	...
Israel - Israël[24]									
2006 (C)									
Total	38 703[25]	19 192[7]	19 508[7]	36 302[4]	17 970[13]	18 331[13]	2 395[4]	1 220[13]	1 173[13]
0	593	335[7]	255[7]	529[4]	302[13]	226[13]	64[4]	33[13]	29[13]
1 - 4	184	110[7]	74[7]	161[4]	95[13]	66[13]	23[4]	15[13]	8[13]
5 - 9	97	62[7]	35[7]	88[4]	57[13]	31[13]	9[4]	5[13]	4[13]
10 - 14	77	43[7]	34[7]	62[4]	34[13]	28[13]	15[4]	9[13]	6[13]
15 - 19	199	144[7]	55[7]	177[4]	126[13]	51[13]	22[4]	18[13]	4[13]
20 - 24	331	262[7]	69[7]	286[4]	222[13]	64[13]	44[4]	39[13]	5[13]
25 - 29	273	195[7]	78[7]	245[4]	170[13]	75[13]	28[4]	25[13]	3[13]
30 - 34	304	206[7]	98[7]	283[4]	195[13]	88[13]	20[4]	11[13]	9[13]
35 - 39	341	231[7]	110[7]	306[4]	208[13]	98[13]	35[4]	23[13]	12[13]
40 - 44	536	328[7]	208[7]	509[4]	308[13]	201[13]	27[4]	20[13]	7[13]
45 - 49	759	481[7]	278[7]	718[4]	458[13]	260[13]	41[4]	23[13]	18[13]
50 - 54	1 163	748[7]	415[7]	1 094[4]	699[13]	395[13]	68[4]	49[13]	19[13]
55 - 59	1 666	1 022[7]	644[7]	1 568[4]	964[13]	604[13]	98[4]	58[13]	40[13]
60 - 64	1 681	1 023[7]	658[7]	1 578[4]	954[13]	624[13]	102[4]	68[13]	34[13]
65 - 69	2 668	1 571[7]	1 097[7]	2 541[4]	1 489[13]	1 052[13]	126[4]	82[13]	44[13]
70 - 74	3 804	2 050[7]	1 754[7]	3 613[4]	1 945[13]	1 668[13]	191[4]	105[13]	86[13]
75 - 79	5 429	2 745[7]	2 684[7]	5 156[4]	2 616[13]	2 540[13]	273[4]	129[13]	144[13]
80 - 84	7 055	3 069[7]	3 986[7]	6 663[4]	2 884[13]	3 779[13]	392[4]	185[13]	207[13]
85 +	11 542	4 567[7]	6 975[7]	10 725[4]	4 244[13]	6 481[13]	816[4]	323[13]	493[13]
Japan - Japon[26]									
2006 (C)									
Total	1 084 450	581 370	503 080	...	...	...	...	...	...
0	2 864	1 556	1 308	...	...	...	...	...	...
1 - 4	1 076	600	476	...	...	...	...	...	...
5 - 9	612	347	265	...	...	...	...	...	...
10 - 14	573	357	216	...	...	...	...	...	...
15 - 19	1 778	1 206	572	...	...	...	...	...	...
20 - 24	3 168	2 170	998	...	...	...	...	...	...
25 - 29	3 948	2 630	1 318	...	...	...	...	...	...
30 - 34	5 624	3 748	1 876	...	...	...	...	...	...
35 - 39	7 387	4 845	2 542	...	...	...	...	...	...
40 - 44	10 065	6 613	3 452	...	...	...	...	...	...
45 - 49	15 297	10 238	5 059	...	...	...	...	...	...
50 - 54	26 373	17 651	8 722	...	...	...	...	...	...
55 - 59	51 068	35 161	15 907	...	...	...	...	...	...
60 - 64	58 267	40 979	17 200	...	...	...	...	...	...
65 - 69	79 279	54 158	25 121	...	...	...	...	...	...
70 - 74	117 346	77 682	39 664	...	...	...	...	...	...
75 - 79	159 251	99 667	59 584	...	...	...	...	...	...
80 - 84	178 396	93 674	84 722	...	...	...	...	...	...
85 - 89	166 753	69 592	97 161	...	...	...	...	...	...
90 - 94	130 488	43 024	87 464	...	...	...	...	...	...
95 - 99	53 976	13 320	40 656	...	...	...	...	...	...
100 +	10 340	1 734	8 606	...	...	...	...	...	...
Unknown - Inconnu	521	418	103	...	...	...	...	...	...

19. Deaths by age, sex and urban/rural residence: latest available year, 1997 - 2006
Décès selon l'âge, le sexe et la résidence, urbaine/rurale: dernière année disponible, 1997 - 2006 (continued - suite)

Continent, country or area, date, code and age (in years) / Continent, pays ou zone, date, code et âge (en années)	Total			Urban - Urbaine			Rural - Rurale		
	Both sexes Les deux sexes	Male Masculin	Female Féminin	Both sexes Les deux sexes	Male Masculin	Female Féminin	Both sexes Les deux sexes	Male Masculin	Female Féminin
ASIA - ASIE									
Kazakhstan[20]									
2006 (C)									
Total	157 210	89 370	67 840	100 526	57 284	43 242	56 684	32 086	24 598
0	4 154	2 397	1 757	2 730	1 572	1 158	1 424	825	599
1 - 4	1 140	649	491	506	288	218	634	361	273
5 - 9	508	312	196	254	153	101	254	159	95
10 - 14	648	410	238	309	187	122	339	223	116
15 - 19	1 675	1 148	527	891	625	266	784	523	261
20 - 24	3 204	2 354	850	2 018	1 485	533	1 186	869	317
25 - 29	4 444	3 463	981	2 971	2 338	633	1 473	1 125	348
30 - 34	5 419	4 200	1 219	3 662	2 842	820	1 757	1 358	399
35 - 39	5 888	4 378	1 510	3 937	2 932	1 005	1 951	1 446	505
40 - 44	8 064	6 022	2 042	5 411	4 061	1 350	2 653	1 961	692
45 - 49	10 565	7 624	2 941	7 187	5 217	1 970	3 378	2 407	971
50 - 54	11 520	8 195	3 325	7 652	5 511	2 141	3 868	2 684	1 184
55 - 59	12 364	8 284	4 080	8 152	5 481	2 671	4 212	2 803	1 409
60 - 64	8 806	5 433	3 373	5 339	3 301	2 038	3 467	2 132	1 335
65 - 69	19 750	11 514	8 236	12 020	6 910	5 110	7 730	4 604	3 126
70 - 74	14 983	7 881	7 102	9 211	4 730	4 481	5 772	3 151	2 621
75 - 79	18 951	8 095	10 856	12 165	5 053	7 112	6 786	3 042	3 744
80 - 84	13 114	3 967	9 147	8 441	2 539	5 902	4 673	1 428	3 245
85 - 89	6 343	1 490	4 853	4 013	900	3 113	2 330	590	1 740
90 - 94	3 513	709	2 804	2 224	453	1 771	1 289	256	1 033
95 - 99	1 030	188	842	563	103	460	467	85	382
100 +	356	37	319	137	16	121	219	21	198
Unknown - Inconnu	771	620	151	733	587	146	38	33	5
Korea (Republic of) - Corée (République de)[27]									
2006 (C)									
Total	243 934[28]	134 724[28]	109 210[28]	159 877	88 247	71 630	82 391	45 479	36 912
0	1 709[28]	959[28]	750[28]	1 359	757	602	348	201	147
1 - 4	547[28]	294[28]	253[28]	426	227	199	121	67	54
5 - 9	499[28]	290[28]	209[28]	338	201	137	158	86	72
10 - 14	516[28]	330[28]	186[28]	398	255	143	114	72	42
15 - 19	957[28]	643[28]	314[28]	734	498	236	216	144	72
20 - 24	1 493[28]	945[28]	548[28]	1 138	713	425	340	228	112
25 - 29	2 097[28]	1 380[28]	717[28]	1 632	1 050	582	458	327	131
30 - 34	2 826[28]	1 839[28]	987[28]	2 103	1 329	774	707	502	205
35 - 39	4 624[28]	3 142[28]	1 482[28]	3 517	2 343	1 174	1 084	783	301
40 - 44	7 259[28]	5 272[28]	1 987[28]	5 388	3 838	1 550	1 832	1 413	419
45 - 49	11 513[28]	8 606[28]	2 907[28]	8 593	6 336	2 257	2 850	2 233	617
50 - 54	12 714[28]	9 456[28]	3 258[28]	9 407	6 939	2 468	3 231	2 462	769
55 - 59	13 936[28]	10 290[28]	3 646[28]	10 069	7 481	2 588	3 756	2 734	1 022
60 - 64	17 627[28]	12 561[28]	5 066[28]	12 211	8 726	3 485	5 286	3 746	1 540
65 - 69	25 938[28]	17 508[28]	8 430[28]	16 787	11 260	5 527	8 992	6 137	2 855
70 - 74	31 036[28]	18 538[28]	12 498[28]	19 255	11 222	8 033	11 604	7 207	4 397
75 - 79	33 742[28]	16 558[28]	17 184[28]	20 872	9 857	11 015	12 630	6 558	6 072
80 - 84	34 368[28]	14 108[28]	20 260[28]	21 052	8 217	12 835	13 041	5 729	7 312
85 - 89	24 481[28]	8 297[28]	16 184[28]	15 053	4 859	10 194	9 255	3 336	5 919
90 - 94	12 083[28]	2 901[28]	9 182[28]	7 296	1 665	5 631	4 696	1 200	3 496
95 +	3 952[28]	802[28]	3 150[28]	2 247	474	1 773	1 664	312	1 352
Unknown - Inconnu	17[28]	5[28]	12[28]	2	-	2	8	2	6
Kuwait - Koweït									
2006 (C)									
Total	5 247	3 428	1 819	...	...	...	...	...	...
0	456	245	211	...	...	...	...	...	...
1 - 4	77	42	35	...	...	...	...	...	...
5 - 9	59	38	21	...	...	...	...	...	...
10 - 14	31	19	12	...	...	...	...	...	...
15 - 19	106	85	21	...	...	...	...	...	...
20 - 24	161	128	33	...	...	...	...	...	...
25 - 29	215	174	41	...	...	...	...	...	...
30 - 34	214	174	40	...	...	...	...	...	...
35 - 39	282	231	51	...	...	...	...	...	...

19. Deaths by age, sex and urban/rural residence: latest available year, 1997 - 2006
Décès selon l'âge, le sexe et la résidence, urbaine/rurale: dernière année disponible, 1997 - 2006 (continued - suite)

Continent, country or area, date, code and age (in years) / Continent, pays ou zone, date, code et âge (en années)	Total			Urban - Urbaine			Rural - Rurale		
	Both sexes Les deux sexes	Male Masculin	Female Féminin	Both sexes Les deux sexes	Male Masculin	Female Féminin	Both sexes Les deux sexes	Male Masculin	Female Féminin
ASIA - ASIE									
Kuwait - Koweït									
2006 (C)									
40 - 44	287	231	56	...	...	...	...	...	...
45 - 49	367	286	81	...	...	...	...	...	...
50 - 54	349	267	82	...	...	...	...	...	...
55 - 59	325	237	88	...	...	...	...	...	...
60 - 64	374	218	156	...	...	...	...	...	...
65 - 69	410	239	171	...	...	...	...	...	...
70 - 74	420	228	192	...	...	...	...	...	...
75 - 79	386	211	175	...	...	...	...	...	...
80 - 84	277	130	147	...	...	...	...	...	...
85 +	307	171	136	...	...	...	...	...	...
Unknown - Inconnu	144	74	70	...	...	...	...	...	...
Kyrgyzstan - Kirghizistan									
2006 (C)									
Total	38 566	21 502	17 064	14 930	8 341	6 589	23 636	13 161	10 475
0	3 526	1 970	1 556	1 802	997	805	1 724	973	751
1 - 4	661	361	300	123	68	55	538	293	245
5 - 9	178	104	74	37	24	13	141	80	61
10 - 14	208	133	75	56	33	23	152	100	52
15 - 19	338	217	121	101	69	32	237	148	89
20 - 24	614	401	213	210	145	65	404	256	148
25 - 29	829	601	228	293	222	71	536	379	157
30 - 34	1 119	832	287	415	310	105	704	522	182
35 - 39	1 332	955	377	510	354	156	822	601	221
40 - 44	1 766	1 278	488	727	534	193	1 039	744	295
45 - 49	2 287	1 624	663	931	675	256	1 356	949	407
50 - 54	2 375	1 613	762	970	669	301	1 405	944	461
55 - 59	2 355	1 540	815	1 034	674	360	1 321	866	455
60 - 64	1 724	1 065	659	698	433	265	1 026	632	394
65 - 69	3 809	2 147	1 662	1 469	821	648	2 340	1 326	1 014
70 - 74	4 100	2 268	1 832	1 441	801	640	2 659	1 467	1 192
75 - 79	4 959	2 372	2 587	1 766	797	969	3 193	1 575	1 618
80 - 84	3 292	1 203	2 089	1 265	408	857	2 027	795	1 232
85 - 89	1 646	472	1 174	597	164	433	1 049	308	741
90 - 94	803	203	600	309	67	242	494	136	358
95 - 99	341	62	279	83	19	64	258	43	215
100 +	238	26	212	27	2	25	211	24	187
Unknown - Inconnu	66	55	11	66	55	11	-	-	-
Malaysia - Malaisie									
2004 (C)									
Total	112 700	65 126	47 574	...	...	...	...	...	...
0	3 105	1 784	1 321	...	...	...	...	...	...
1 - 4	939	529	410	...	...	...	...	...	...
5 - 9	776	459	317	...	...	...	...	...	...
10 - 14	900	558	342	...	...	...	...	...	...
15 - 19	1 969	1 493	476	...	...	...	...	...	...
20 - 24	2 283	1 746	537	...	...	...	...	...	...
25 - 29	2 249	1 681	568	...	...	...	...	...	...
30 - 34	2 669	1 989	680	...	...	...	...	...	...
35 - 39	3 194	2 277	917	...	...	...	...	...	...
40 - 44	4 275	2 934	1 341	...	...	...	...	...	...
45 - 49	5 627	3 780	1 847	...	...	...	...	...	...
50 - 54	6 806	4 347	2 459	...	...	...	...	...	...
55 - 59	8 238	5 276	2 962	...	...	...	...	...	...
60 - 64	9 660	6 027	3 633	...	...	...	...	...	...
65 - 69	12 816	7 448	5 368	...	...	...	...	...	...
70 - 74	12 622	6 848	5 774	...	...	...	...	...	...
75 - 79	12 469	6 397	6 072	...	...	...	...	...	...
80 - 84	10 635	4 763	5 872	...	...	...	...	...	...
85 +	11 465	4 790	6 675	...	...	...	...	...	...
Unknown - Inconnu	3	-	3	...	...	...	...	...	...

19. Deaths by age, sex and urban/rural residence: latest available year, 1997 - 2006
Décès selon l'âge, le sexe et la résidence, urbaine/rurale: dernière année disponible, 1997 - 2006 (continued - suite)

Continent, country or area, date, code and age (in years) / Continent, pays ou zone, date, code et âge (en années)	Total Both sexes Les deux sexes	Total Male Masculin	Total Female Féminin	Urban - Urbaine Both sexes Les deux sexes	Urban - Urbaine Male Masculin	Urban - Urbaine Female Féminin	Rural - Rurale Both sexes Les deux sexes	Rural - Rurale Male Masculin	Rural - Rurale Female Féminin
ASIA - ASIE									
Maldives									
2006 (C)									
Total	1 084	649	435	354	211	143	730	438	292
0	92	54	38	36	20	16	56	34	22
1 - 4	15	9	6	2	2	-	13	7	6
5 - 9	14	9	5	5	2	3	9	7	2
10 - 14	16	8	8	8	3	5	8	5	3
15 - 19	16	8	8	9	4	5	7	4	3
20 - 24	21	17	4	12	10	2	9	7	2
25 - 29	14	10	4	7	4	3	7	6	1
30 - 34	12	8	4	5	4	1	7	4	3
35 - 39	10	7	3	3	2	1	7	5	2
40 - 44	16	12	4	5	3	2	11	9	2
45 - 49	40	22	18	21	14	7	19	8	11
50 - 54	37	23	14	20	15	5	17	8	9
55 - 59	48	26	22	21	11	10	27	15	12
60 - 64	88	52	36	34	19	15	54	33	21
65 - 69	115	67	48	30	18	12	85	49	36
70 +	530	317	213	136	80	56	394	237	157
Mongolia - Mongolie									
1998 (C)									
Total	15 860	8 535	7 325	8 779	4 714	4 044	7 081	3 790	3 251
0	1 741	960	781	936	506	409	805	423	342
1 - 4	767	405	362	367	194	173	400	211	189
5 - 9	143	83	60	62	36	26	81	47	34
10 - 14	150	89	61	82	49	33	68	40	28
15 - 19	236	142	94	143	86	57	93	56	37
20 - 24	398	215	183	257	139	118	141	76	65
25 - 29	454	297	157	270	177	93	184	120	64
30 - 34	543	332	211	338	207	131	205	125	80
35 - 39	712	433	279	436	265	171	276	168	108
40 - 44	644	386	258	401	240	161	243	146	97
45 - 49	730	414	316	442	251	191	288	163	125
50 - 54	850	454	396	513	274	239	337	180	157
55 - 59	1 113	637	476	620	355	265	493	282	211
60 - 64	1 299	720	579	645	339	306	654	381	273
65 - 69	1 605	849	756	889	470	419	716	379	337
70 +	4 475	2 119	2 356	2 378	1 126	1 252	2 097	993	1 104
2006 (C)									
Total	16 682	9 954	6 728	10 811	...	...	5 871	...	...
0	937	502	435	583	...	...	354	...	...
1 - 4	255	143	112	109	...	...	146	...	...
5 - 9	86	51	35	55	...	...	31	...	...
10 - 14	110	70	40	56	...	...	54	...	...
15 - 19	222	139	83	137	...	...	85	...	...
20 - 24	351	240	111	222	...	...	129	...	...
25 - 29	504	370	134	330	...	...	174	...	...
30 - 34	618	471	147	458	...	...	160	...	...
35 - 39	838	613	225	583	...	...	255	...	...
40 - 44	1 183	826	357	839	...	...	344	...	...
45 - 49	1 322	903	419	939	...	...	383	...	...
50 - 54	1 318	910	408	911	...	...	407	...	...
55 - 59	1 177	763	414	805	...	...	372	...	...
60 - 64	1 284	780	504	843	...	...	441	...	...
65 - 69	1 552	926	626	951	...	...	601	...	...
70 - 74	1 564	821	743	965	...	...	599	...	...
75 - 79	1 321	660	661	798	...	...	523	...	...
80 - 84	992	403	589	601	...	...	391	...	...
85 - 89	642	236	406	382	...	...	260	...	...
90 - 94	296	88	208	180	...	...	116	...	...
95 - 99	98	35	63	57	...	...	41	...	...
100 +	12	4	8	7	...	...	5	...	...

19. Deaths by age, sex and urban/rural residence: latest available year, 1997 - 2006
Décès selon l'âge, le sexe et la résidence, urbaine/rurale: dernière année disponible, 1997 - 2006 (continued - suite)

Continent, country or area, date, code and age (in years) / Continent, pays ou zone, date, code et âge (en annèes)	Total			Urban - Urbaine			Rural - Rurale		
	Both sexes Les deux sexes	Male Masculin	Female Féminin	Both sexes Les deux sexes	Male Masculin	Female Féminin	Both sexes Les deux sexes	Male Masculin	Female Féminin
ASIA - ASIE									
Myanmar									
2005 (U)									
Total....................	242 549	...	...	67 344	...	...	175 205	...	...
0	38 872	...	...	10 531	...	...	28 341	...	...
1 - 4	20 358	...	...	5 804	...	...	14 554	...	...
5 - 9	10 488	...	...	2 442	...	...	8 046	...	...
10 - 14	7 865	...	...	1 169	...	...	6 696	...	...
15 - 19	6 726	...	...	1 598	...	...	5 128	...	...
20 - 24	6 689	...	...	1 650	...	...	5 039	...	...
25 - 29	7 016	...	...	1 729	...	...	5 287	...	...
30 - 34	6 774	...	...	1 882	...	...	4 892	...	...
35 - 39	7 402	...	...	2 133	...	...	5 269	...	...
40 - 44	7 484	...	...	2 286	...	...	5 198	...	...
45 - 49	7 984	...	...	2 755	...	...	5 229	...	...
50 - 54	9 365	...	...	3 622	...	...	5 743	...	...
55 - 59	10 458	...	...	4 195	...	...	6 263	...	...
60 - 64	11 391	...	...	4 553	...	...	6 838	...	...
65 - 69	23 252	...	...	5 300	...	...	17 952	...	...
70 - 74	21 817	...	...	5 190	...	...	16 627	...	...
75 - 79	16 011	...	...	3 785	...	...	12 226	...	...
80 - 84	12 520	...	...	2 855	...	...	9 665	...	...
85 + ...	9 786	...	...	3 708	...	...	6 078	...	...
Unknown - Inconnu	291	...	...	157	...	...	134	...	...
Nepal - Népal[29]									
2001 (|)									
Total....................	106 789	59 544	47 245	...	...	...	...	...	...
0	13 037	6 956	6 081	...	...	...	...	...	...
1 - 4	9 790	5 590	4 200	...	...	...	...	...	...
5 - 9	3 320	1 726	1 594	...	...	...	...	...	...
10 - 14	2 304	1 332	972	...	...	...	...	...	...
15 - 19	2 523	1 293	1 230	...	...	...	...	...	...
20 - 24	2 747	1 449	1 298	...	...	...	...	...	...
25 - 29	2 688	1 429	1 259	...	...	...	...	...	...
30 - 34	2 474	1 303	1 172	...	...	...	...	...	...
35 - 39	2 839	1 594	1 244	...	...	...	...	...	...
40 - 44	2 970	1 828	1 142	...	...	...	...	...	...
45 - 49	3 553	2 027	1 526	...	...	...	...	...	...
50 - 54	4 662	2 771	1 891	...	...	...	...	...	...
55 - 59	6 115	3 612	2 503	...	...	...	...	...	...
60 - 64	8 337	4 710	3 626	...	...	...	...	...	...
65 - 69	8 667	4 764	3 903	...	...	...	...	...	...
70 - 74	9 606	5 512	4 093	...	...	...	...	...	...
75 - 79	8 113	4 657	3 456	...	...	...	...	...	...
80 + ...	13 042	6 990	6 052	...	...	...	...	...	...
Occupied Palestinian Territory - Territoire palestinien occupé									
2006 (U)									
Total....................	9 938	5 749	4 189	...	...	...	...	...	...
0	906	500	406	...	...	...	...	...	...
1 - 4	343	186	157	...	...	...	...	...	...
5 - 9	146	88	58	...	...	...	...	...	...
10 - 14	168	101	67	...	...	...	...	...	...
15 - 19	323	269	54	...	...	...	...	...	...
20 - 24	370	326	44	...	...	...	...	...	...
25 - 29	259	215	44	...	...	...	...	...	...
30 - 34	201	145	56	...	...	...	...	...	...
35 - 39	188	122	66	...	...	...	...	...	...
40 - 44	239	163	76	...	...	...	...	...	...
45 - 49	294	200	94	...	...	...	...	...	...
50 - 54	362	221	141	...	...	...	...	...	...
55 - 59	583	350	233	...	...	...	...	...	...
60 - 64	660	351	309	...	...	...	...	...	...
65 - 69	874	408	466	...	...	...	...	...	...
70 - 74	1 001	524	477	...	...	...	...	...	...

Continent, country or area, date, code and age (in years) / Continent, pays ou zone, date, code et âge (en années)	Total			Urban - Urbaine			Rural - Rurale		
	Both sexes Les deux sexes	Male Masculin	Female Féminin	Both sexes Les deux sexes	Male Masculin	Female Féminin	Both sexes Les deux sexes	Male Masculin	Female Féminin
ASIA - ASIE									
Occupied Palestinian Territory - Territoire palestinien occupé									
2006 (U)									
75 - 79	1 197	597	600	...	...	...	...	...	...
80 - 84	865	465	400	...	...	...	...	...	...
85 - 89	529	274	255	...	...	...	...	...	...
90 - 94	206	127	79	...	...	...	...	...	...
95 - 99	159	91	68	...	...	...	...	...	...
100 +	65	26	39	...	...	...	...	...	...
Oman[30]									
2006 (U)									
Total	3 027	...	...	...	...	...	...	...	...
0	381	...	...	...	...	...	...	...	...
1 - 4	57	...	...	...	...	...	...	...	...
5 - 14	65	...	...	...	...	...	...	...	...
15 - 44	407	...	...	...	...	...	...	...	...
45 +	2 117	...	...	...	...	...	...	...	...
Pakistan[31]									
2005 (I)									
Total	1 019 467	579 377	440 090	321 394	182 358	139 036	698 073	397 019	301 054
0 - 4	368 059	211 759	156 300	103 537	60 612	42 925	264 522	151 147	113 375
5 - 9	23 661	12 863	10 798	3 115	420	2 695	20 547	12 443	8 103
10 - 14	15 408	8 412	6 996	4 014	1 556	2 458	11 394	6 856	4 538
15 - 19	16 574	7 309	9 266	2 963	687	2 276	13 612	6 622	6 990
20 - 24	23 454	10 197	13 257	8 416	5 008	3 407	15 038	5 188	9 850
25 - 29	19 050	9 934	9 116	4 741	3 192	1 549	14 309	6 742	7 568
30 - 34	16 415	8 425	7 990	4 961	2 235	2 725	11 454	6 190	5 264
35 - 39	20 240	10 672	9 568	6 092	2 948	3 145	14 148	7 724	6 424
40 - 44	24 539	14 051	10 488	8 858	5 001	3 857	15 682	9 050	6 631
45 - 49	28 193	17 196	10 997	13 154	8 650	4 504	15 039	8 546	6 493
50 - 54	45 835	23 314	22 521	17 065	8 785	8 280	28 770	14 529	14 241
55 - 59	45 765	27 898	17 867	17 794	9 419	8 375	27 970	18 479	9 492
60 - 64	65 863	40 859	25 003	24 394	15 594	8 800	41 469	25 265	16 203
65 - 69	53 933	26 352	27 581	18 842	7 971	10 871	35 091	18 382	16 710
70 - 74	66 763	37 156	29 607	21 605	13 187	8 418	45 159	23 970	21 187
75 - 79	48 494	24 009	24 486	18 834	11 345	7 489	29 660	12 663	16 997
80 - 84	44 377	24 463	22 915	13 818	6 549	7 269	30 559	14 913	15 646
85 +	92 843	67 508	25 334	29 193	19 199	9 994	63 650	48 310	15 340
Philippines									
2004 (C)									
Total	403 191	237 750	165 441	...	...	...	...	...	...
0	22 557	13 219	9 338	...	...	...	...	...	...
1 - 4	8 648	4 818	3 830	...	...	...	...	...	...
5 - 9	5 153	2 908	2 245	...	...	...	...	...	...
10 - 14	4 668	2 747	1 921	...	...	...	...	...	...
15 - 19	6 948	4 473	2 475	...	...	...	...	...	...
20 - 24	10 080	7 050	3 030	...	...	...	...	...	...
25 - 29	11 238	7 769	3 469	...	...	...	...	...	...
30 - 34	13 028	8 935	4 093	...	...	...	...	...	...
35 - 39	15 540	10 495	5 045	...	...	...	...	...	...
40 - 44	18 265	12 235	6 030	...	...	...	...	...	...
45 - 49	22 103	14 938	7 165	...	...	...	...	...	...
50 - 54	26 495	17 806	8 689	...	...	...	...	...	...
55 - 59	28 572	19 163	9 409	...	...	...	...	...	...
60 - 64	32 586	21 079	11 507	...	...	...	...	...	...
65 - 69	35 886	21 922	13 964	...	...	...	...	...	...
70 - 74	36 565	21 035	15 530	...	...	...	...	...	...
75 - 79	34 601	18 103	16 498	...	...	...	...	...	...
80 - 84	31 333	14 199	17 134	...	...	...	...	...	...
85 +	38 205	14 493	23 712	...	...	...	...	...	...
Unknown - Inconnu	720	363	357	...	...	...	...	...	...

19. Deaths by age, sex and urban/rural residence: latest available year, 1997 - 2006
Décès selon l'âge, le sexe et la résidence, urbaine/rurale: dernière année disponible, 1997 - 2006 (continued - suite)

Continent, country or area, date, code and age (in years) / Continent, pays ou zone, date, code et âge (en années)	Total			Urban - Urbaine			Rural - Rurale		
	Both sexes Les deux sexes	Male Masculin	Female Féminin	Both sexes Les deux sexes	Male Masculin	Female Féminin	Both sexes Les deux sexes	Male Masculin	Female Féminin
ASIA - ASIE									
Qatar									
2006 (C)									
Total	1 750	1 274	476	...	...	...	...	...	...
0	114	65	49	...	...	...	...	...	...
1 - 4	37	18	19	...	...	...	...	...	...
5 - 9	15	6	9	...	...	...	...	...	...
10 - 14	18	12	6	...	...	...	...	...	...
15 - 19	63	52	11	...	...	...	...	...	...
20 - 24	97	90	7	...	...	...	...	...	...
25 - 29	112	97	15	...	...	...	...	...	...
30 - 34	103	95	8	...	...	...	...	...	...
35 - 39	111	101	10	...	...	...	...	...	...
40 - 44	119	101	18	...	...	...	...	...	...
45 - 49	123	104	19	...	...	...	...	...	...
50 - 54	137	119	18	...	...	...	...	...	...
55 - 59	108	86	22	...	...	...	...	...	...
60 - 64	112	67	45	...	...	...	...	...	...
65 - 69	112	66	46	...	...	...	...	...	...
70 - 74	138	72	66	...	...	...	...	...	...
75 - 79	95	45	50	...	...	...	...	...	...
80 - 84	64	40	24	...	...	...	...	...	...
85 - 89	43	26	17	...	...	...	...	...	...
90 - 94	19	8	11	...	...	...	...	...	...
95 - 99	10	4	6	...	...	...	...	...	...
100 +	-	-	-	...	...	...	...	...	...
Saudi Arabia - Arabie saoudite									
2005 (...)									
Total	92 486	54 253	38 233	...	...	...	...	...	...
0 - 4	12 889	6 692	6 197	...	...	...	...	...	...
5 - 9	977	524	453	...	...	...	...	...	...
10 - 14	977	566	411	...	...	...	...	...	...
15 - 19	1 350	791	559	...	...	...	...	...	...
20 - 24	1 695	998	697	...	...	...	...	...	...
25 - 29	2 248	1 371	877	...	...	...	...	...	...
30 - 34	2 750	1 681	1 069	...	...	...	...	...	...
35 - 39	3 309	2 131	1 178	...	...	...	...	...	...
40 - 44	3 997	2 698	1 299	...	...	...	...	...	...
45 - 49	4 754	3 266	1 488	...	...	...	...	...	...
50 - 54	5 285	3 629	1 656	...	...	...	...	...	...
55 - 59	5 538	3 658	1 880	...	...	...	...	...	...
60 - 64	6 116	3 756	2 360	...	...	...	...	...	...
65 - 69	6 924	3 985	2 939	...	...	...	...	...	...
70 - 74	8 082	4 448	3 634	...	...	...	...	...	...
75 - 79	8 176	4 484	3 692	...	...	...	...	...	...
80 +	17 419	9 575	7 844	...	...	...	...	...	...
Singapore - Singapour									
2006 (+C)									
Total	16 393	8 967[7]	7 424[7]	...	...	...	...	...	...
0	117	61	56	...	...	...	...	...	...
1 - 4	26	16	10	...	...	...	...	...	...
5 - 9	26	14	12	...	...	...	...	...	...
10 - 14	50	31	19	...	...	...	...	...	...
15 - 19	61	43	18	...	...	...	...	...	...
20 - 24	141	96	45	...	...	...	...	...	...
25 - 29	155	100	55	...	...	...	...	...	...
30 - 34	211	132	79	...	...	...	...	...	...
35 - 39	251	163	88	...	...	...	...	...	...
40 - 44	458	296	162	...	...	...	...	...	...
45 - 49	644	409	235	...	...	...	...	...	...
50 - 54	917	576	341	...	...	...	...	...	...
55 - 59	1 214	758	456	...	...	...	...	...	...
60 - 64	1 136	718	418	...	...	...	...	...	...
65 - 69	1 604	991	613	...	...	...	...	...	...
70 - 74	1 914	1 146	768	...	...	...	...	...	...

19. Deaths by age, sex and urban/rural residence: latest available year, 1997 - 2006
Décès selon l'âge, le sexe et la résidence, urbaine/rurale: dernière année disponible, 1997 - 2006 (continued - suite)

Continent, country or area, date, code and age (in years) / Continent, pays ou zone, date, code et âge (en années)	Total			Urban - Urbaine			Rural - Rurale		
	Both sexes Les deux sexes	Male Masculin	Female Féminin	Both sexes Les deux sexes	Male Masculin	Female Féminin	Both sexes Les deux sexes	Male Masculin	Female Féminin
ASIA - ASIE									
Singapore - Singapour									
2006 (+C)									
75 - 79	2 378	1 268	1 110	...	...	...	...	...	...
80 - 84	2 023	997	1 026	...	...	...	...	...	...
85 - 89	1 623	686	937	...	...	...	...	...	...
90 - 94	949	332	617	...	...	...	...	...	...
95 - 99	414	104	310	...	...	...	...	...	...
100 + ...	66	18	48	...	...	...	...	...	...
Unknown - Inconnu	15	12	1	...	...	...	...	...	...
Sri Lanka									
2001 (+C)									
Total.....................	112 858	70 646	42 212	...	...	...	...	...	...
0	4 519	2 576	1 943	...	...	...	...	...	...
1 - 4....................	919	493	426	...	...	...	...	...	...
5 - 14..................	1 436	825	611	...	...	...	...	...	...
15 - 24	4 706	3 395	1 311	...	...	...	...	...	...
25 - 34	5 593	4 345	1 248	...	...	...	...	...	...
35 - 44	7 977	6 261	1 716	...	...	...	...	...	...
45 - 54	12 524	9 239	3 285	...	...	...	...	...	...
55 - 64	15 854	10 890	4 964	...	...	...	...	...	...
65 - 74	23 552	14 220	9 332	...	...	...	...	...	...
75 + ...	35 778	18 402	17 376	...	...	...	...	...	...
Thailand - Thaïlande									
1999 (+U)									
Total.....................	362 593	213 427	149 166	36 796	21 674	15 122	325 797	191 753	134 044
0	5 003	2 765	2 238	711	359	352	4 292	2 406	1 886
1 - 4....................	5 948	3 193	2 755	451	246	205	5 497	2 947	2 550
5 - 9....................	3 040	1 804	1 236	184	106	78	2 856	1 698	1 158
10 - 14	2 162	1 300	862	181	112	69	1 981	1 188	793
15 - 19	6 504	4 861	1 643	553	408	145	5 951	4 453	1 498
20 - 24	11 727	8 192	3 535	1 280	972	308	10 447	7 220	3 227
25 - 29	22 108	16 139	5 969	1 860	1 447	413	20 248	14 692	5 556
30 - 34	23 928	18 116	5 812	2 242	1 715	527	21 686	16 401	5 285
35 - 39	20 640	15 414	5 226	2 120	1 607	513	18 520	13 807	4 713
40 - 44	18 982	13 089	5 893	2 120	1 480	640	16 862	11 609	5 253
45 - 49	18 489	12 071	6 418	2 107	1 380	727	16 382	10 691	5 691
50 - 54	18 660	11 727	6 933	2 017	1 267	750	16 643	10 460	6 183
55 - 59	21 563	13 072	8 491	2 322	1 419	903	19 241	11 653	7 588
60 - 64	27 435	16 057	11 378	3 029	1 810	1 219	24 406	14 247	10 159
65 - 69	31 442	17 504	13 938	3 299	1 895	1 404	28 143	15 609	12 534
70 - 74	32 171	17 261	14 910	3 202	1 660	1 542	28 969	15 601	13 368
75 - 79	30 537	15 485	15 052	2 971	1 449	1 522	27 566	14 036	13 530
80 - 84	26 406	11 901	14 505	2 803	1 203	1 600	23 603	10 698	12 905
85 + ...	32 613	12 063	20 550	3 292	1 118	2 174	29 321	10 945	18 376
Unknown - Inconnu	3 235	1 413	1 822	52	21	31	3 183	1 392	1 791
2005 (+U)									
Total.....................	395 374	225 622	169 752	...	...	...	...	...	...
0	6 183	3 450	2 733	...	...	...	...	...	...
1 - 4....................	2 536	1 453	1 083	...	...	...	...	...	...
5 - 9....................	2 419	1 472	947	...	...	...	...	...	...
10 - 14	2 492	1 529	963	...	...	...	...	...	...
15 - 19	6 287	4 957	1 330	...	...	...	...	...	...
20 - 24	8 297	6 475	1 822	...	...	...	...	...	...
25 - 29	11 749	8 344	3 405	...	...	...	...	...	...
30 - 34	15 442	10 951	4 491	...	...	...	...	...	...
35 - 39	18 012	12 832	5 180	...	...	...	...	...	...
40 - 44	20 102	14 078	6 024	...	...	...	...	...	...
45 - 49	22 061	14 915	7 146	...	...	...	...	...	...
50 - 54	24 397	15 701	8 696	...	...	...	...	...	...
55 - 59	25 976	15 856	10 120	...	...	...	...	...	...
60 - 64	28 431	16 649	11 782	...	...	...	...	...	...
65 - 69	36 414	20 539	15 875	...	...	...	...	...	...
70 - 74	41 607	22 090	19 517	...	...	...	...	...	...
75 - 79	42 417	21 262	21 155	...	...	...	...	...	...
80 - 84	35 484	16 111	19 373	...	...	...	...	...	...

Continent, country or area, date, code and age (in years) / Continent, pays ou zone, date, code et âge (en années)	Total			Urban - Urbaine			Rural - Rurale		
	Both sexes Les deux sexes	Male Masculin	Female Féminin	Both sexes Les deux sexes	Male Masculin	Female Féminin	Both sexes Les deux sexes	Male Masculin	Female Féminin
ASIA - ASIE									
Thailand - Thaïlande									
2005 (+U)									
85 +	43 689	16 454	27 235	...	...	...	...	...	...
Unknown - Inconnu	1 379	504	875	...	...	...	...	...	...
United Arab Emirates - Émirats arabes unis									
2003 (...)									
Total	6 002	4 305	1 697	...	...	...	...	...	...
0	477	272	205	...	...	...	...	...	...
1 - 4	132	74	58	...	...	...	...	...	...
5 - 9	94	59	35	...	...	...	...	...	...
10 - 14	79	57	22	...	...	...	...	...	...
15 - 19	174	134	40	...	...	...	...	...	...
20 - 24	253	221	32	...	...	...	...	...	...
25 - 29	302	249	53	...	...	...	...	...	...
30 - 34	297	256	41	...	...	...	...	...	...
35 - 39	308	269	39	...	...	...	...	...	...
40 - 44	405	347	58	...	...	...	...	...	...
45 - 49	515	437	78	...	...	...	...	...	...
50 - 54	502	411	91	...	...	...	...	...	...
55 - 59	357	284	73	...	...	...	...	...	...
60 - 64	565	348	217	...	...	...	...	...	...
65 - 69	418	225	193	...	...	...	...	...	...
70 - 74	386	204	182	...	...	...	...	...	...
75 - 79	244	147	97	...	...	...	...	...	...
80 +	378	209	169	...	...	...	...	...	...
Unknown - Inconnu	116	102	14	...	...	...	...	...	...
Uzbekistan - Ouzbékistan[20]									
2000 (C)									
Total	135 598	70 794	64 804	61 130	32 195	28 935	74 468	38 599	35 869
0	10 091	5 805	4 286	3 703	2 136	1 567	6 388	3 669	2 719
1 - 4	5 417	2 925	2 492	1 177	645	532	4 240	2 280	1 960
5 - 9	1 474	886	588	423	251	172	1 051	635	416
10 - 14	1 436	852	584	442	260	182	994	592	402
15 - 19	2 001	1 289	712	709	475	234	1 292	814	478
20 - 24	2 849	1 758	1 091	1 155	789	366	1 694	969	725
25 - 29	3 427	2 177	1 250	1 501	1 023	478	1 926	1 154	772
30 - 34	3 660	2 403	1 257	1 657	1 185	472	2 003	1 218	785
35 - 39	4 181	2 759	1 422	1 993	1 407	586	2 188	1 352	836
40 - 44	5 086	3 277	1 809	2 584	1 789	795	2 502	1 488	1 014
45 - 49	5 290	3 445	1 845	2 797	1 924	873	2 493	1 521	972
50 - 54	5 765	3 647	2 118	3 140	2 052	1 088	2 625	1 595	1 030
55 - 59	6 104	3 794	2 310	3 056	1 990	1 066	3 048	1 804	1 244
60 - 64	12 287	7 257	5 030	5 897	3 603	2 294	6 390	3 654	2 736
65 - 69	14 077	7 757	6 320	6 312	3 601	2 711	7 765	4 156	3 609
70 - 74	17 094	8 713	8 381	8 142	4 010	4 132	8 952	4 703	4 249
75 - 79	12 547	4 824	7 723	6 043	2 111	3 932	6 504	2 713	3 791
80 - 84	8 807	2 836	5 971	4 430	1 285	3 145	4 377	1 551	2 826
85 - 89	7 198	2 312	4 886	3 747	1 011	2 736	3 451	1 301	2 150
90 - 94	3 782	1 295	2 487	1 515	421	1 094	2 267	874	1 393
95 - 99	1 963	579	1 384	511	167	344	1 452	412	1 040
100 +	1 062	204	858	196	60	136	866	144	722
EUROPE									
Aland Islands - Îles d'Åland[32]									
2006 (C)									
Total	257	122	135	...	...	...	...	...	...
0 - 4	-	-	-	...	...	...	...	...	...
5 - 14	-	-	-	...	...	...	...	...	...
15 - 29	-	-	-	...	...	...	...	...	...
30 - 44	3	3	-	...	...	...	...	...	...
45 - 59	16	8	8	...	...	...	...	...	...
60 - 64	14	11	3	...	...	...	...	...	...

19. Deaths by age, sex and urban/rural residence: latest available year, 1997 - 2006
Décès selon l'âge, le sexe et la résidence, urbaine/rurale: dernière année disponible, 1997 - 2006 (continued - suite)

Continent, country or area, date, code and age (in years) / Continent, pays ou zone, date, code et âge (en années)	Total			Urban - Urbaine			Rural - Rurale		
	Both sexes Les deux sexes	Male Masculin	Female Féminin	Both sexes Les deux sexes	Male Masculin	Female Féminin	Both sexes Les deux sexes	Male Masculin	Female Féminin
EUROPE									
Åland Islands - Îles d'Åland[32]									
2006 (C)									
65 - 69	17	12	5	...	...	...	...	...	...
70 - 74	24	16	8	...	...	...	...	...	...
75 - 79	33	21	12	...	...	...	...	...	...
80 - 84	39	10	29	...	...	...	...	...	...
85 - 89	57	29	28	...	...	...	...	...	...
90 +	54	12	42	...	...	...	...	...	...
Albania - Albanie									
2004 (C)									
Total	17 749	9 950	7 799	9 248	5 267	3 981	8 501	4 683	3 818
0	336	181	155	124	67	57	212	114	98
1 - 4	237	132	105	76	43	33	161	89	72
5 - 9	164	108	56	51	35	16	113	73	40
10 - 14	140	86	54	49	32	17	91	54	37
15 - 19	157	106	51	65	50	15	92	56	36
20 - 24	219	147	72	96	66	30	123	81	42
25 - 29	181	140	41	94	71	23	87	69	18
30 - 34	225	159	66	112	83	29	113	76	37
35 - 39	244	160	84	128	86	42	116	74	42
40 - 44	365	249	116	223	153	70	142	96	46
45 - 49	469	313	156	277	183	94	192	130	62
50 - 54	586	397	189	366	245	121	220	152	68
55 - 59	676	451	225	386	261	125	290	190	100
60 - 64	1 248	820	428	706	458	248	542	362	180
65 - 69	1 720	1 158	562	973	658	315	747	500	247
70 - 74	2 428	1 478	950	1 328	811	517	1 100	667	433
75 - 79	2 608	1 462	1 146	1 429	801	628	1 179	661	518
80 - 84	2 768	1 256	1 512	1 419	641	778	1 349	615	734
85 - 89	1 652	719	933	750	325	425	902	394	508
90 - 94	936	298	638	430	140	290	506	158	348
95 - 99	300	103	197	127	43	84	173	60	113
100 +	90	27	63	39	15	24	51	12	39
2006 (C)									
Total	16 935	...	...	...	...	...	...	...	...
0	253	...	...	...	...	...	...	...	...
1 - 4	161	...	...	...	...	...	...	...	...
5 - 9	120	...	...	...	...	...	...	...	...
10 - 14	99	...	...	...	...	...	...	...	...
15 - 19	137	...	...	...	...	...	...	...	...
20 - 24	156	...	...	...	...	...	...	...	...
25 - 29	162	...	...	...	...	...	...	...	...
30 - 34	171	...	...	...	...	...	...	...	...
35 - 39	225	...	...	...	...	...	...	...	...
40 - 44	299	...	...	...	...	...	...	...	...
45 - 49	452	...	...	...	...	...	...	...	...
50 - 54	590	...	...	...	...	...	...	...	...
55 - 59	671	...	...	...	...	...	...	...	...
60 - 64	1 026	...	...	...	...	...	...	...	...
65 - 69	1 490	...	...	...	...	...	...	...	...
70 - 74	2 349	...	...	...	...	...	...	...	...
75 - 79	2 702	...	...	...	...	...	...	...	...
80 - 84	2 582	...	...	...	...	...	...	...	...
85 +	3 290	...	...	...	...	...	...	...	...
Andorra - Andorre									
2006 (C)									
Total	260	144	116	...	...	...	...	...	...
0	3	3	-	...	...	...	...	...	...
15 - 19	1	1	-	...	...	...	...	...	...
20 - 24	4	3	1	...	...	...	...	...	...
25 - 29	1	1	-	...	...	...	...	...	...
30 - 34	6	3	3	...	...	...	...	...	...
35 - 39	8	3	5	...	...	...	...	...	...
40 - 44	2	1	1	...	...	...	...	...	...
45 - 49	12	7	5	...	...	...	...	...	...

Continent, country or area, date, code and age (in years) Continent, pays ou zone, date, code et âge (en années)	Total			Urban - Urbaine			Rural - Rurale		
	Both sexes Les deux sexes	Male Masculin	Female Féminin	Both sexes Les deux sexes	Male Masculin	Female Féminin	Both sexes Les deux sexes	Male Masculin	Female Féminin

EUROPE

Andorra - Andorre
2006 (C)

50 - 54	13	10	3	...	...	...	...	...	...
55 - 59	17	12	5	...	...	...	...	...	...
60 - 64	13	8	5	...	...	...	...	...	...
65 - 69	14	10	4	...	...	...	...	...	...
70 - 74	22	14	8	...	...	...	...	...	...
75 - 79	21	13	8	...	...	...	...	...	...
80 - 84	42	23	19	...	...	...	...	...	...
85 - 89	43	15	28	...	...	...	...	...	...
90 - 94	26	12	14	...	...	...	...	...	...
95 - 99	10	5	5	...	...	...	...	...	...
100 +	2	-	2	...	...	...	...	...	...

Austria - Autriche
1999 (C)

Total	78 200	35 880	42 320	46 752	20 596	26 156	31 448	15 284	16 164
0	341	176	165	191	100	91	150	76	74
1 - 4	98	67	31	51	37	14	47	30	17
5 - 9	51	28	23	25	11	14	26	17	9
10 - 14	72	36	36	38	17	21	34	19	15
15 - 19	276	197	79	116	78	38	160	119	41
20 - 24	330	257	73	177	136	41	153	121	32
25 - 29	348	251	97	183	132	51	165	119	46
30 - 34	512	352	160	313	201	112	199	151	48
35 - 39	806	550	256	472	324	148	334	226	108
40 - 44	1 075	714	361	621	406	215	454	308	146
45 - 49	1 433	922	511	848	523	325	585	399	186
50 - 54	2 251	1 468	783	1 425	916	509	826	552	274
55 - 59	3 554	2 373	1 181	2 238	1 464	774	1 316	909	407
60 - 64	3 939	2 654	1 285	2 194	1 461	733	1 745	1 193	552
65 - 69	6 004	3 939	2 065	3 267	2 091	1 176	2 737	1 848	889
70 - 74	8 963	5 084	3 879	5 131	2 793	2 338	3 832	2 291	1 541
75 - 79	12 409	5 726	6 683	7 297	3 256	4 041	5 112	2 470	2 642
80 - 84	10 218	3 965	6 253	6 134	2 373	3 761	4 084	1 592	2 492
85 +	25 520	7 121	18 399	16 031	4 277	11 754	9 489	2 844	6 645

2006 (C)

Total	74 295	34 757	39 538	...	...	...	...	...	...
0	281	163	118	...	...	...	...	...	...
1 - 4	70	42	28	...	...	...	...	...	...
5 - 9	41	24	17	...	...	...	...	...	...
10 - 14	55	32	23	...	...	...	...	...	...
15 - 19	243	181	62	...	...	...	...	...	...
20 - 24	297	222	75	...	...	...	...	...	...
25 - 29	258	183	75	...	...	...	...	...	...
30 - 34	341	231	110	...	...	...	...	...	...
35 - 39	577	402	175	...	...	...	...	...	...
40 - 44	936	604	332	...	...	...	...	...	...
45 - 49	1 365	922	443	...	...	...	...	...	...
50 - 54	1 928	1 295	633	...	...	...	...	...	...
55 - 59	3 094	2 063	1 031	...	...	...	...	...	...
60 - 64	3 968	2 641	1 327	...	...	...	...	...	...
65 - 69	5 634	3 594	2 040	...	...	...	...	...	...
70 - 74	6 517	3 930	2 587	...	...	...	...	...	...
75 - 79	10 373	5 582	4 791	...	...	...	...	...	...
80 - 84	14 760	5 902	8 858	...	...	...	...	...	...
85 - 89	11 505	3 731	7 774	...	...	...	...	...	...
90 - 94	0 055	2 202	6 363	...	...	...	...	...	...
95 - 99	3 027	653	2 374	...	...	...	...	...	...
100 +	370	68	302	...	...	...	...	...	...

Belarus - Bélarus[20]
2006 (C)

Total	138 426	73 227	65 199	75 437	41 747	33 690	62 989	31 480	31 509
0	587	333	254	407	226	181	180	107	73
1 - 4	192	104	88	98	53	45	94	51	43
5 - 9	108	72	36	63	40	23	45	32	13

19. Deaths by age, sex and urban/rural residence: latest available year, 1997 - 2006
Décès selon l'âge, le sexe et la résidence, urbaine/rurale: dernière année disponible, 1997 - 2006 (continued - suite)

Continent, country or area, date, code and age (in years) Continent, pays ou zone, date, code et âge (en années)	Total			Urban - Urbaine			Rural - Rurale		
	Both sexes Les deux sexes	Male Masculin	Female Féminin	Both sexes Les deux sexes	Male Masculin	Female Féminin	Both sexes Les deux sexes	Male Masculin	Female Féminin
EUROPE									
Belarus - Bélarus[20]									
2006 (C)									
10 - 14	114	65	49	77	44	33	37	21	16
15 - 19	518	381	137	307	216	91	211	165	46
20 - 24	1 060	839	221	643	498	145	417	341	76
25 - 29	1 588	1 265	323	1 025	804	221	563	461	102
30 - 34	2 164	1 740	424	1 362	1 082	280	802	658	144
35 - 39	2 712	2 100	612	1 602	1 205	397	1 110	895	215
40 - 44	4 343	3 386	957	2 665	2 019	646	1 678	1 367	311
45 - 49	6 681	5 176	1 505	4 181	3 158	1 023	2 500	2 018	482
50 - 54	7 934	5 940	1 994	5 174	3 810	1 364	2 760	2 130	630
55 - 59	10 052	7 032	3 020	6 804	4 726	2 078	3 248	2 306	942
60 - 64	8 638	5 957	2 681	5 268	3 658	1 610	3 370	2 299	1 071
65 - 69	15 972	9 924	6 048	9 260	5 875	3 385	6 712	4 049	2 663
70 - 74	18 005	9 521	8 484	8 943	4 666	4 277	9 062	4 855	4 207
75 - 79	22 949	10 160	12 789	11 231	4 988	6 243	11 718	5 172	6 546
80 - 84	19 084	5 698	13 386	9 093	2 869	6 224	9 991	2 829	7 162
85 - 89	8 635	2 107	6 528	4 148	1 067	3 081	4 487	1 040	3 447
90 - 94	5 038	977	4 061	2 229	497	1 732	2 809	480	2 329
95 - 99	1 570	284	1 286	615	121	494	955	163	792
100 +	327	42	285	103	14	89	224	28	196
Unknown - Inconnu	155	124	31	139	111	28	16	13	3
Belgium - Belgique[33]									
2006 (C)									
Total	101 587	50 412	51 175	...	...	...	...	...	...
0	489	269	220	...	...	...	...	...	...
1 - 4	109	62	47	...	...	...	...	...	...
5 - 9	64	36	28	...	...	...	...	...	...
10 - 14	73	41	32	...	...	...	...	...	...
15 - 19	223	147	76	...	...	...	...	...	...
20 - 24	356	285	71	...	...	...	...	...	...
25 - 29	424	306	118	...	...	...	...	...	...
30 - 34	543	380	163	...	...	...	...	...	...
35 - 39	797	532	265	...	...	...	...	...	...
40 - 44	1 279	824	455	...	...	...	...	...	...
45 - 49	2 080	1 332	748	...	...	...	...	...	...
50 - 54	3 016	1 889	1 127	...	...	...	...	...	...
55 - 59	4 254	2 759	1 495	...	...	...	...	...	...
60 - 64	5 073	3 343	1 730	...	...	...	...	...	...
65 - 69	6 702	4 287	2 415	...	...	...	...	...	...
70 - 74	10 264	6 298	3 966	...	...	...	...	...	...
75 - 79	15 552	8 647	6 905	...	...	...	...	...	...
80 - 84	20 094	9 517	10 577	...	...	...	...	...	...
85 - 89	15 052	5 646	9 406	...	...	...	...	...	...
90 - 94	10 646	3 030	7 616	...	...	...	...	...	...
95 - 99	3 872	713	3 159	...	...	...	...	...	...
100 +	625	69	556	...	...	...	...	...	...
Bosnia and Herzegovina - Bosnie-Herzégovine									
2006 (C)									
Total	33 221	17 308	15 913	...	...	...	...	...	...
0	255	158	97	...	...	...	...	...	...
1 - 4	37	22	15	...	...	...	...	...	...
5 - 9	33	20	13	...	...	...	...	...	...
10 - 14	51	25	26	...	...	...	...	...	...
15 - 19	93	64	29	...	...	...	...	...	...
20 - 24	149	106	43	...	...	...	...	...	...
25 - 29	171	120	51	...	...	...	...	...	...
30 - 34	200	135	65	...	...	...	...	...	...
35 - 39	266	179	87	...	...	...	...	...	...
40 - 44	553	375	178	...	...	...	...	...	...
45 - 49	944	610	334	...	...	...	...	...	...
50 - 54	1 599	1 093	506	...	...	...	...	...	...
55 - 59	1 946	1 292	654	...	...	...	...	...	...
60 - 64	2 229	1 391	838	...	...	...	...	...	...

19. Deaths by age, sex and urban/rural residence: latest available year, 1997 - 2006
Décès selon l'âge, le sexe et la résidence, urbaine/rurale: dernière année disponible, 1997 - 2006 (continued - suite)

Continent, country or area, date, code and age (in years) / Continent, pays ou zone, date, code et âge (en années)	Total			Urban - Urbaine			Rural - Rurale		
	Both sexes Les deux sexes	Male Masculin	Female Féminin	Both sexes Les deux sexes	Male Masculin	Female Féminin	Both sexes Les deux sexes	Male Masculin	Female Féminin
EUROPE									
Bosnia and Herzegovina - Bosnie-Herzégovine									
2006 (C)									
65 - 69	4 553	2 694	1 859	...	...	...	...	...	...
70 - 74	6 212	3 321	2 891	...	...	...	...	...	...
75 - 79	6 437	3 081	3 356	...	...	...	...	...	...
80 - 84	4 504	1 626	2 878	...	...	...	...	...	...
85 - 89	1 884	595	1 289	...	...	...	...	...	...
90 - 94	806	284	522	...	...	...	...	...	...
95 - 99	213	75	138	...	...	...	...	...	...
100 +	30	11	19	...	...	...	...	...	...
Unknown - Inconnu	56	31	25	...	...	...	...	...	...
Bulgaria - Bulgarie									
2006 (C)									
Total	113 438	60 503	52 935	66 352	35 518	30 834	47 086	24 985	22 101
0	720	371	349	472	247	225	248	124	124
1 - 4	137	81	56	86	52	34	51	29	22
5 - 9	111	59	52	72	32	40	39	27	12
10 - 14	104	63	41	64	33	31	40	30	10
15 - 19	259	180	79	168	125	43	91	55	36
20 - 24	413	311	102	307	235	72	106	76	30
25 - 29	488	374	114	381	291	90	107	83	24
30 - 34	646	450	196	461	318	143	185	132	53
35 - 39	969	657	312	661	430	231	308	227	81
40 - 44	1 583	1 073	510	1 089	721	368	494	352	142
45 - 49	2 746	1 942	804	1 855	1 284	571	891	658	233
50 - 54	4 557	3 224	1 333	3 131	2 159	972	1 426	1 065	361
55 - 59	6 972	4 969	2 003	4 632	3 224	1 408	2 340	1 745	595
60 - 64	8 156	5 558	2 598	5 074	3 448	1 626	3 082	2 110	972
65 - 69	10 395	6 478	3 917	6 202	3 857	2 345	4 193	2 621	1 572
70 - 74	16 251	9 100	7 151	8 978	4 992	3 986	7 273	4 108	3 165
75 - 79	20 579	10 064	10 515	11 604	5 664	5 940	8 975	4 400	4 575
80 - 84	21 995	9 397	12 598	12 146	5 101	7 045	9 849	4 296	5 553
85 - 89	10 552	4 128	6 424	5 826	2 223	3 603	4 726	1 905	2 821
90 - 94	4 686	1 669	3 017	2 536	875	1 661	2 150	794	1 356
95 - 99	1 004	324	680	546	188	358	458	136	322
100 +	115	31	84	61	19	42	54	12	42
Channel Islands: Guernsey - Îles Anglo-Normandes: Guernesey									
2000 (C)									
Total	565	264	301	...	...	...	...	...	...
0	4	3	1	...	...	...	...	...	...
1 - 4	1	-	1	...	...	...	...	...	...
15 - 19	4	3	1	...	...	...	...	...	...
20 - 24	1	-	1	...	...	...	...	...	...
25 - 29	1	1	-	...	...	...	...	...	...
30 - 34	2	1	1	...	...	...	...	...	...
35 - 39	2	2	-	...	...	...	...	...	...
40 - 44	4	4	-	...	...	...	...	...	...
45 - 49	7	5	2	...	...	...	...	...	...
50 - 54	13	9	4	...	...	...	...	...	...
55 - 59	13	7	6	...	...	...	...	...	...
60 - 64	30	15	15	...	...	...	...	...	...
65 - 69	45	29	16	...	...	...	...	...	...
70 - 74	57	27	30	...	...	...	...	...	...
75 - 79	71	38	33	...	...	...	...	...	...
80 - 84	103	55	48	...	...	...	...	...	...
85 - 89	108	45	63	...	...	...	...	...	...
90 - 94	68	14	54	...	...	...	...	...	...
95 - 99	24	3	21	...	...	...	...	...	...
100 +	5	2	3	...	...	...	...	...	...
Unknown - Inconnu	2	1	1	...	...	...	...	...	...

Continent, country or area, date, code and age (in years) Continent, pays ou zone, date, code et âge (en années)	Total			Urban - Urbaine			Rural - Rurale		
	Both sexes Les deux sexes	Male Masculin	Female Féminin	Both sexes Les deux sexes	Male Masculin	Female Féminin	Both sexes Les deux sexes	Male Masculin	Female Féminin
EUROPE									
Croatia - Croatie									
2006 (C)									
Total....................	50 378	25 329	25 049	25 144	12 565	12 579	25 234	12 764	12 470
0.........................	215	105	110	113	52	61	102	53	49
1 - 4.....................	39	22	17	19	10	9	20	12	8
5 - 9.....................	33	19	14	19	9	10	14	10	4
10 - 14...................	33	21	12	19	12	7	14	9	5
15 - 19...................	112	81	31	53	39	14	59	42	17
20 - 24...................	214	161	53	109	80	29	105	81	24
25 - 29...................	213	169	44	113	88	25	100	81	19
30 - 34...................	211	157	54	111	82	29	100	75	25
35 - 39...................	352	253	99	170	121	49	182	132	50
40 - 44...................	620	447	173	279	194	85	341	253	88
45 - 49...................	1 215	876	339	585	388	197	630	488	142
50 - 54...................	1 964	1 426	538	996	685	311	968	741	227
55 - 59...................	2 568	1 844	724	1 389	950	439	1 179	894	285
60 - 64...................	2 912	1 970	942	1 526	996	530	1 386	974	412
65 - 69...................	4 901	3 119	1 782	2 424	1 481	943	2 477	1 638	839
70 - 74...................	7 610	4 346	3 264	3 745	2 171	1 574	3 865	2 175	1 690
75 - 79...................	9 455	4 585	4 870	4 620	2 267	2 353	4 835	2 318	2 517
80 - 84...................	9 240	3 311	5 929	4 533	1 653	2 880	4 707	1 658	3 049
85 - 89...................	5 016	1 492	3 524	2 545	797	1 748	2 471	695	1 776
90 - 94...................	2 643	726	1 917	1 349	378	971	1 294	348	946
95 - 99...................	717	171	546	363	91	272	354	80	274
100 +....................	77	15	62	50	11	39	27	4	23
Unknown - Inconnu.......	18	13	5	14	10	4	4	3	1
Czech Republic - République tchèque									
2006 (C)									
Total....................	104 441	52 706	51 735	75 900	37 877	38 023	28 541	14 829	13 712
0.........................	352	214	138	268	163	105	84	51	33
1 - 4.....................	76	42	34	56	35	21	20	7	13
5 - 9.....................	64	44	20	43	29	14	21	15	6
10 - 14...................	67	49	18	53	37	16	14	12	2
15 - 19...................	248	189	59	171	130	41	77	59	18
20 - 24...................	421	325	96	304	236	68	117	89	28
25 - 29...................	453	348	105	317	245	72	136	103	33
30 - 34...................	613	437	176	458	325	133	155	112	43
35 - 39...................	784	542	242	562	378	184	222	164	58
40 - 44...................	1 308	877	431	937	627	310	371	250	121
45 - 49...................	2 221	1 549	672	1 603	1 091	512	618	458	160
50 - 54...................	4 267	3 000	1 267	3 170	2 195	975	1 097	805	292
55 - 59...................	6 792	4 622	2 170	4 913	3 298	1 615	1 879	1 324	555
60 - 64...................	8 521	5 683	2 838	6 303	4 126	2 177	2 218	1 557	661
65 - 69...................	8 762	5 531	3 231	6 332	3 923	2 409	2 430	1 608	822
70 - 74...................	11 712	6 658	5 054	8 440	4 774	3 666	3 272	1 884	1 388
75 - 79...................	17 057	8 325	8 732	12 286	5 987	6 299	4 771	2 338	2 433
80 - 84...................	20 158	7 999	12 159	14 729	5 763	8 966	5 429	2 236	3 193
85 - 89...................	11 546	3 937	7 609	8 348	2 820	5 528	3 198	1 117	2 081
90 - 94...................	6 997	1 917	5 080	5 126	1 399	3 727	1 871	518	1 353
95 - 99...................	1 834	385	1 449	1 339	271	1 068	495	114	381
100 +....................	188	33	155	142	25	117	46	8	38
Unknown - Inconnu.......	-	-	-	-	-	-	-	-	-
Denmark - Danemark[34]									
2006 (C)									
Total....................	55 477	27 197	28 280	...	...	...	...	...	...
0.........................	250	141	109	...	...	...	...	...	...
1 - 4.....................	39	24	15	...	...	...	...	...	...
5 - 9.....................	34	20	14	...	...	...	...	...	...
10 - 14...................	41	26	15	...	...	...	...	...	...
15 - 19...................	111	75	36	...	...	...	...	...	...
20 - 24...................	145	118	27	...	...	...	...	...	...
25 - 29...................	149	105	44	...	...	...	...	...	...
30 - 34...................	234	168	66	...	...	...	...	...	...
35 - 39...................	392	263	129	...	...	...	...	...	...

19. Deaths by age, sex and urban/rural residence: latest available year, 1997 - 2006
Décès selon l'âge, le sexe et la résidence, urbaine/rurale: dernière année disponible, 1997 - 2006 (continued - suite)

Continent, country or area, date, code and age (in years) / Continent, pays ou zone, date, code et âge (en années)	Total			Urban - Urbaine			Rural - Rurale		
	Both sexes Les deux sexes	Male Masculin	Female Féminin	Both sexes Les deux sexes	Male Masculin	Female Féminin	Both sexes Les deux sexes	Male Masculin	Female Féminin
EUROPE									
Denmark - Danemark[34]									
2006 (C)									
40 - 44	706	444	262	...	...	...	...	...	...
45 - 49	1 025	667	358	...	...	...	...	...	...
50 - 54	1 772	1 115	657	...	...	...	...	...	...
55 - 59	2 668	1 631	1 037	...	...	...	...	...	...
60 - 64	3 912	2 408	1 504	...	...	...	...	...	...
65 - 69	4 300	2 499	1 801	...	...	...	...	...	...
70 - 74	5 718	3 230	2 488	...	...	...	...	...	...
75 - 79	7 588	4 028	3 560	...	...	...	...	...	...
80 - 84	9 104	4 357	4 747	...	...	...	...	...	...
85 - 89	8 856	3 464	5 392	...	...	...	...	...	...
90 - 94	5 916	1 855	4 061	...	...	...	...	...	...
95 + ...	2 517	559	1 958	...	...	...	...	...	...
Estonia - Estonie									
2006 (C)									
Total.................	17 316	8 853	8 463	10 431	5 281	5 150	6 885	3 572	3 313
0.................	66	44	22	44	27	17	22	17	5
1 - 4.................	19	11	8	12	7	5	7	4	3
5 - 9.................	13	7	6	5	4	1	8	3	5
10 - 14.................	14	9	5	4	3	1	10	6	4
15 - 19.................	75	58	17	39	28	11	36	30	6
20 - 24.................	132	105	27	93	71	22	39	34	5
25 - 29.................	150	122	28	119	99	20	31	23	8
30 - 34.................	171	137	34	110	88	22	61	49	12
35 - 39.................	200	155	45	128	96	32	72	59	13
40 - 44.................	353	272	81	228	173	55	125	99	26
45 - 49.................	569	429	140	331	242	89	238	187	51
50 - 54.................	915	660	255	584	402	182	331	258	73
55 - 59.................	1 148	795	353	711	467	244	437	328	109
60 - 64.................	1 254	839	415	685	445	240	569	394	175
65 - 69.................	1 823	1 173	650	1 095	688	407	728	485	243
70 - 74.................	2 046	1 189	857	1 226	691	535	820	498	322
75 - 79.................	2 712	1 269	1 443	1 685	803	882	1 027	466	561
80 - 84.................	2 591	822	1 769	1 566	493	1 073	1 025	329	696
85 - 89.................	1 554	407	1 147	883	235	648	671	172	499
90 - 94.................	1 074	247	827	630	148	482	444	99	345
95 - 99.................	365	73	292	199	43	156	166	30	136
100 +.................	45	6	39	28	5	23	17	1	16
Unknown - Inconnu	27	24	3	26	23	3	1	1	-
Finland - Finlande[35]									
2006 (C)									
Total.................	48 065	24 315	23 750	27 199	13 523	13 676	20 866	10 792	10 074
0.................	167	96	71	109	64	45	58	32	26
1 - 4.................	29	14	15	9	5	4	20	9	11
5 - 9.................	33	15	18	19	9	10	14	6	8
10 - 14.................	44	30	14	23	13	10	21	17	4
15 - 19.................	163	124	39	87	66	21	76	58	18
20 - 24.................	237	194	43	176	146	30	61	48	13
25 - 29.................	210	164	46	150	114	36	60	50	10
30 - 34.................	258	193	65	166	131	35	92	62	30
35 - 39.................	394	284	110	244	169	75	150	115	35
40 - 44.................	666	461	205	418	282	136	248	179	69
45 - 49.................	1 122	791	331	703	487	216	419	304	115
50 - 54.................	1 841	1 251	590	1 136	763	373	705	488	217
55 - 59.................	2 044	2 005	839	1 695	1 155	540	1 149	850	299
60 - 64.................	2 883	1 996	887	1 752	1 177	575	1 131	819	312
65 - 69.................	3 450	2 302	1 148	1 947	1 251	696	1 503	1 051	452
70 - 74.................	4 523	2 870	1 653	2 487	1 529	958	2 036	1 341	695
75 - 79.................	6 774	3 796	2 978	3 731	2 050	1 681	3 043	1 746	1 297
80 - 84.................	8 430	3 701	4 729	4 582	1 967	2 615	3 848	1 734	2 114
85 - 89.................	7 330	2 428	4 902	4 069	1 310	2 759	3 261	1 118	2 143
90 - 94.................	4 914	1 252	3 662	2 714	659	2 055	2 200	593	1 607
95 - 99.................	1 555	315	1 240	866	159	707	689	156	533

19. Deaths by age, sex and urban/rural residence: latest available year, 1997 - 2006
Décès selon l'âge, le sexe et la résidence, urbaine/rurale: dernière année disponible, 1997 - 2006 (continued - suite)

Continent, country or area, date, code and age (in years) Continent, pays ou zone, date, code et âge (en années)	Total			Urban - Urbaine			Rural - Rurale		
	Both sexes Les deux sexes	Male Masculin	Female Féminin	Both sexes Les deux sexes	Male Masculin	Female Féminin	Both sexes Les deux sexes	Male Masculin	Female Féminin
EUROPE									
Finland - Finlande[35]									
2006 (C)									
100 +.....................	198	33	165	116	17	99	82	16	66
Unknown - Inconnu.......	-	-	-	-	-	-	-	-	-
France[36]									
2005 (C)									
Total.....................	527 533	270 634	256 899	373 576[37]	187 684[37]	185 892[37]	152 218[37]	81 733[37]	70 485[37]
0	2 775	1 583	1 192	2 139[37]	1 219[37]	920[37]	610[37]	347[37]	263[37]
1 - 4.....................	601	332	269	439[37]	244[37]	195[37]	148[37]	76[37]	72[37]
5 - 9.....................	368	215	153	255[37]	143[37]	112[37]	104[37]	64[37]	40[37]
10 - 14.....................	408	245	163	283[37]	169[37]	114[37]	107[37]	64[37]	43[37]
15 - 19.....................	1 507	1 087	420	973[37]	679[37]	294[37]	515[37]	399[37]	116[37]
20 - 24.....................	2 312	1 751	561	1 632[37]	1 210[37]	422[37]	637[37]	505[37]	132[37]
25 - 29.....................	2 251	1 663	588	1 654[37]	1 210[37]	444[37]	546[37]	413[37]	133[37]
30 - 34.....................	3 321	2 354	967	2 480[37]	1 745[37]	735[37]	772[37]	553[37]	219[37]
35 - 39.....................	4 889	3 259	1 630	3 624[37]	2 398[37]	1 226[37]	1 193[37]	811[37]	382[37]
40 - 44.....................	7 938	5 270	2 668	5 880[37]	3 889[37]	1 991[37]	1 969[37]	1 319[37]	650[37]
45 - 49.....................	13 144	8 877	4 267	9 710[37]	6 523[37]	3 187[37]	3 325[37]	2 270[37]	1 055[37]
50 - 54.....................	18 997	13 092	5 905	14 034[37]	9 553[37]	4 481[37]	4 839[37]	3 453[37]	1 386[37]
55 - 59.....................	25 402	17 800	7 602	18 256[37]	12 689[37]	5 567[37]	6 995[37]	5 002[37]	1 993[37]
60 - 64.....................	23 431	16 139	7 292	16 790[37]	11 470[37]	5 320[37]	6 474[37]	4 550[37]	1 924[37]
65 - 69.....................	32 278	21 745	10 533	22 752[37]	15 093[37]	7 659[37]	9 352[37]	6 520[37]	2 832[37]
70 - 74.....................	49 531	31 666	17 865	34 510[37]	21 678[37]	12 832[37]	14 855[37]	9 868[37]	4 987[37]
75 - 79.....................	70 064	40 332	29 732	48 426[37]	27 121[37]	21 305[37]	21 459[37]	13 085[37]	8 374[37]
80 - 84.....................	96 969	48 064	48 905	67 065[37]	32 326[37]	34 739[37]	29 789[37]	15 667[37]	14 122[37]
85 - 89.....................	64 217	26 104	38 113	46 186[37]	18 277[37]	27 909[37]	17 956[37]	7 786[37]	10 170[37]
90 - 94.....................	72 170	21 985	50 185	51 199[37]	15 132[37]	36 067[37]	20 924[37]	6 834[37]	14 090[37]
95 - 99.....................	29 671	6 365	23 306	21 412[37]	4 427[37]	16 985[37]	8 237[37]	1 930[37]	6 307[37]
100 +.....................	5 289	706	4 583	3 877[37]	489[37]	3 388[37]	1 412[37]	217[37]	1 195[37]
Germany - Allemagne									
2006 (C)									
Total.....................	821 627	385 940	435 687	...	...	...	...	...	...
0	2 579	1 429	1 150	...	...	...	...	...	...
1 - 4.....................	528	302	226	...	...	...	...	...	...
5 - 9.....................	355	217	138	...	...	...	...	...	...
10 - 14.....................	429	239	190	...	...	...	...	...	...
15 - 19.....................	1 498	1 044	454	...	...	...	...	...	...
20 - 24.....................	2 020	1 478	542	...	...	...	...	...	...
25 - 29.....................	2 103	1 510	593	...	...	...	...	...	...
30 - 34.....................	2 659	1 815	844	...	...	...	...	...	...
35 - 39.....................	5 477	3 640	1 837	...	...	...	...	...	...
40 - 44.....................	10 524	6 993	3 531	...	...	...	...	...	...
45 - 49.....................	16 535	10 840	5 695	...	...	...	...	...	...
50 - 54.....................	23 591	15 644	7 947	...	...	...	...	...	...
55 - 59.....................	31 075	20 595	10 480	...	...	...	...	...	...
60 - 64.....................	42 135	27 833	14 302	...	...	...	...	...	...
65 - 69.....................	74 864	49 189	25 675	...	...	...	...	...	...
70 - 74.....................	88 847	54 632	34 215	...	...	...	...	...	...
75 - 79.....................	120 838	65 222	55 616	...	...	...	...	...	...
80 - 84.....................	148 007	58 443	89 564	...	...	...	...	...	...
85 - 89.....................	116 443	36 169	80 274	...	...	...	...	...	...
90 - 94.....................	92 582	21 952	70 630	...	...	...	...	...	...
95 - 99.....................	33 988	6 162	27 826	...	...	...	...	...	...
100 +.....................	4 550	592	3 958	...	...	...	...	...	...
Greece - Grèce									
2006 (C)									
Total.....................	105 476	55 290	50 186	57 700	29 761	27 939	47 776	25 529	22 247
0	415	215	200	299	146	153	116	69	47
1 - 4.....................	64	27	37	42	21	21	22	6	16
5 - 9.....................	59	38	21	37	24	13	22	14	8
10 - 14.....................	64	43	21	44	32	12	20	11	9
15 - 19.....................	251	189	62	156	111	45	95	78	17
20 - 24.....................	490	414	76	323	267	56	167	147	20
25 - 29.....................	584	473	111	422	342	80	162	131	31

Continent, country or area, date, code and age (in years) Continent, pays ou zone, date, code et âge (en années)	Total			Urban - Urbaine			Rural - Rurale		
	Both sexes Les deux sexes	Male Masculin	Female Féminin	Both sexes Les deux sexes	Male Masculin	Female Féminin	Both sexes Les deux sexes	Male Masculin	Female Féminin
EUROPE									
Greece - Grèce									
2006 (C)									
30 - 34	602	463	139	410	313	97	192	150	42
35 - 39	856	635	221	554	406	148	302	229	73
40 - 44	1 115	791	324	717	490	227	398	301	97
45 - 49	1 749	1 187	562	1 119	715	404	630	472	158
50 - 54	2 635	1 816	819	1 703	1 118	585	932	698	234
55 - 59	3 664	2 541	1 123	2 309	1 589	720	1 355	952	403
60 - 64	4 522	3 105	1 417	2 678	1 787	891	1 844	1 318	526
65 - 69	7 328	4 801	2 527	4 157	2 661	1 496	3 171	2 140	1 031
70 - 74	12 029	7 475	4 554	6 650	4 041	2 609	5 379	3 434	1 945
75 - 79	18 084	9 765	8 319	9 807	5 084	4 723	8 277	4 681	3 596
80 - 84	19 468	9 051	10 417	10 449	4 709	5 740	9 019	4 342	4 677
85 - 89	15 842	6 436	9 406	8 283	3 214	5 069	7 559	3 222	4 337
90 - 94	11 219	4 311	6 908	5 534	2 040	3 494	5 685	2 271	3 414
95 - 99	3 755	1 317	2 438	1 728	570	1 158	2 027	747	1 280
100 +	681	197	484	279	81	198	402	116	286
Hungary - Hongrie									
2006 (C)									
Total	131 603	67 851	63 752	84 656[38]	42 516[38]	42 140[38]	46 233[38]	24 788[38]	21 445[38]
0	571	323	248	349[38]	200[38]	149[38]	215[38]	119[38]	96[38]
1 - 4	125	67	58	71[38]	35[38]	36[38]	51[38]	31[38]	20[38]
5 - 9	49	33	16	29[38]	20[38]	9[38]	19[38]	12[38]	7[38]
10 - 14	118	76	42	64[38]	40[38]	24[38]	53[38]	35[38]	18[38]
15 - 19	259	188	71	166[38]	122[38]	44[38]	87[38]	63[38]	24[38]
20 - 24	335	255	80	203[38]	155[38]	48[38]	112[38]	86[38]	26[38]
25 - 29	552	415	137	343[38]	252[38]	91[38]	180[38]	139[38]	41[38]
30 - 34	805	578	227	478[38]	329[38]	149[38]	292[38]	216[38]	76[38]
35 - 39	1 228	881	347	722[38]	496[38]	226[38]	473[38]	357[38]	116[38]
40 - 44	2 177	1 554	623	1 224[38]	850[38]	374[38]	900[38]	659[38]	241[38]
45 - 49	4 575	3 239	1 336	2 689[38]	1 874[38]	815[38]	1 829[38]	1 320[38]	509[38]
50 - 54	8 188	5 782	2 406	5 118[38]	3 485[38]	1 633[38]	2 958[38]	2 199[38]	759[38]
55 - 59	9 338	6 488	2 850	5 847[38]	3 956[38]	1 891[38]	3 400[38]	2 459[38]	941[38]
60 - 64	10 553	6 994	3 559	6 852[38]	4 417[38]	2 435[38]	3 637[38]	2 527[38]	1 110[38]
65 - 69	12 530	7 668	4 862	7 837[38]	4 702[38]	3 135[38]	4 639[38]	2 922[38]	1 717[38]
70 - 74	15 517	8 506	7 011	9 816[38]	5 322[38]	4 494[38]	5 652[38]	3 149[38]	2 503[38]
75 - 79	19 909	9 352	10 557	12 773[38]	5 947[38]	6 826[38]	7 105[38]	3 386[38]	3 719[38]
80 - 84	22 125	8 617	13 508	14 396[38]	5 588[38]	8 808[38]	7 697[38]	3 014[38]	4 683[38]
85 - 89	13 074	4 243	8 831	8 892[38]	2 912[38]	5 980[38]	4 164[38]	1 324[38]	2 840[38]
90 - 94	7 321	2 065	5 256	5 166[38]	1 432[38]	3 734[38]	2 144[38]	631[38]	1 513[38]
95 - 99	1 997	477	1 520	1 431[38]	345[38]	1 086[38]	564[38]	131[38]	433[38]
100 +	252	45	207	189[38]	36[38]	153[38]	62[38]	9[38]	53[38]
Unknown - Inconnu	5	5	-	1[38]	1[38]	-[38]	-[38]	-[38]	-[38]
Iceland - Islande									
2006 (C)									
Total	1 903	959	944	1 750	870	880	153	89	64
0	6	3	3	6	3	3	-	-	-
1 - 4	4	2	2	4	2	2	-	-	-
5 - 9	1	-	1	1	-	1	-	-	-
10 - 14	4	3	1	4	3	1	-	-	-
15 - 19	12	6	6	11	5	6	1	1	-
20 - 24	14	11	3	13	10	3	1	1	-
25 - 29	15	13	2	13	12	1	2	1	1
30 - 34	11	8	3	8	5	3	3	3	-
35 - 39	13	9	4	12	8	4	1	1	-
40 - 44	20	12	8	19	12	7	1	-	1
45 - 49	37	24	13	37	24	13	-	-	-
50 - 54	55	32	23	52	30	22	3	2	1
55 - 59	85	46	39	77	43	34	8	3	5
60 - 64	98	63	35	96	61	35	2	2	-
65 - 69	131	72	59	115	64	51	16	8	8
70 - 74	174	102	72	162	92	70	12	10	2
75 - 79	265	132	133	251	121	130	14	11	3
80 - 84	301	155	146	279	139	140	22	16	6

19. Deaths by age, sex and urban/rural residence: latest available year, 1997 - 2006
Décès selon l'âge, le sexe et la résidence, urbaine/rurale: dernière année disponible, 1997 - 2006 (continued - suite)

Continent, country or area, date, code and age (in years) / Continent, pays ou zone, date, code et âge (en années)	Total			Urban - Urbaine			Rural - Rurale		
	Both sexes Les deux sexes	Male Masculin	Female Féminin	Both sexes Les deux sexes	Male Masculin	Female Féminin	Both sexes Les deux sexes	Male Masculin	Female Féminin
EUROPE									
Iceland - Islande									
2006 (C)									
85 - 89	346	155	191	315	138	177	31	17	14
90 - 94	222	87	135	198	76	122	24	11	13
95 - 99	70	21	49	61	19	42	9	2	7
100 +	19	3	16	16	3	13	3	-	3
Ireland - Irlande[39]									
1999 (+C)									
Total	31 683	16 480	15 203	17 288	8 599	8 689	14 395	7 881	6 514
0	293	160	133	195	108	87	98	52	46
1 - 4	68	39	29	37	25	12	31	14	17
5 - 9	41	28	13	20	14	6	21	14	7
10 - 14	56	37	19	31	19	12	25	18	7
15 - 19	171	123	48	90	64	26	81	59	22
20 - 24	233	179	54	130	103	27	103	76	27
25 - 29	196	149	47	109	83	26	87	66	21
30 - 34	222	153	69	141	94	47	81	59	22
35 - 39	279	174	105	178	111	67	101	63	38
40 - 44	406	243	163	232	143	89	174	100	74
45 - 49	637	392	245	409	249	160	228	143	85
50 - 54	888	553	335	514	301	213	374	252	122
55 - 59	1 226	777	449	747	460	287	479	317	162
60 - 64	1 675	1 065	610	1 003	626	377	672	439	233
65 - 69	2 606	1 630	976	1 485	897	588	1 121	733	388
70 - 74	3 961	2 375	1 586	2 224	1 300	924	1 737	1 075	662
75 - 79	5 492	3 005	2 487	2 877	1 499	1 378	2 615	1 506	1 109
80 - 84	5 601	2 666	2 935	2 823	1 221	1 602	2 778	1 445	1 333
85 +	7 632	2 732	4 900	4 043	1 282	2 761	3 589	1 450	2 139
2006* (+C)									
Total	27 479	14 111	13 368	...	...	...	...	...	...
0	238	136	102	...	...	...	...	...	...
1 - 4	33	21	12	...	...	...	...	...	...
5 - 9	29	22	7	...	...	...	...	...	...
10 - 14	36	19	17	...	...	...	...	...	...
15 - 19	145	96	49	...	...	...	...	...	...
20 - 24	206	161	45	...	...	...	...	...	...
25 - 29	208	149	59	...	...	...	...	...	...
30 - 34	210	152	58	...	...	...	...	...	...
35 - 39	230	152	78	...	...	...	...	...	...
40 - 44	365	217	148	...	...	...	...	...	...
45 - 49	581	324	257	...	...	...	...	...	...
50 - 54	834	521	313	...	...	...	...	...	...
55 - 59	1 192	707	485	...	...	...	...	...	...
60 - 64	1 552	952	600	...	...	...	...	...	...
65 - 69	2 032	1 265	767	...	...	...	...	...	...
70 - 74	2 865	1 816	1 049	...	...	...	...	...	...
75 - 79	4 052	2 240	1 812	...	...	...	...	...	...
80 - 84	4 931	2 360	2 571	...	...	...	...	...	...
85 - 89	4 356	1 766	2 590	...	...	...	...	...	...
90 - 94	2 541	841	1 700	...	...	...	...	...	...
95 - 99	713	171	542	...	...	...	...	...	...
100 +	130	23	107	...	...	...	...	...	...
Unknown - Inconnu	-	-	-	...	...	...	...	...	...
Isle of Man - Îles de Man									
2004 (+C)									
Total	798	390	408	...	...	...	...	...	...
0	2	1	1	...	...	...	...	...	...
1 - 4	-	-	-	...	...	...	...	...	...
5 - 9	-	-	-	...	...	...	...	...	...
10 - 14	1	1	-	...	...	...	...	...	...
15 - 19	3	3	-	...	...	...	...	...	...
20 - 24	5	4	1	...	...	...	...	...	...
25 - 29	3	3	-	...	...	...	...	...	...
30 - 34	3	1	2	...	...	...	...	...	...
35 - 39	6	5	1	...	...	...	...	...	...

Continent, country or area, date, code and age (in years) / Continent, pays ou zone, date, code et âge (en années)	Total			Urban - Urbaine			Rural - Rurale		
	Both sexes Les deux sexes	Male Masculin	Female Féminin	Both sexes Les deux sexes	Male Masculin	Female Féminin	Both sexes Les deux sexes	Male Masculin	Female Féminin
EUROPE									
Isle of Man - Îles de Man									
2004 (+C)									
40 - 44	7	4	3	...	...	...	...	...	...
45 - 49	11	5	6	...	...	...	...	...	...
50 - 54	17	8	9	...	...	...	...	...	...
55 - 59	31	18	13	...	...	...	...	...	...
60 - 64	33	19	14	...	...	...	...	...	...
65 - 69	60	45	15	...	...	...	...	...	...
70 - 74	82	46	36	...	...	...	...	...	...
75 - 79	118	59	59	...	...	...	...	...	...
80 - 84	169	77	92	...	...	...	...	...	...
85 - 89	111	43	68	...	...	...	...	...	...
90 - 94	96	36	60	...	...	...	...	...	...
95 +	40	12	28	...	...	...	...	...	...
Italy - Italie									
2004 (C)									
Total	545 051	272 864	272 187	...	...	...	...	...	...
0	2 168	1 189	979	...	...	...	...	...	...
1 - 4	377	199	178	...	...	...	...	...	...
5 - 9	254	145	109	...	...	...	...	...	...
10 - 14	342	212	130	...	...	...	...	...	...
15 - 19	1 063	777	286	...	...	...	...	...	...
20 - 24	1 690	1 346	344	...	...	...	...	...	...
25 - 29	2 184	1 679	505	...	...	...	...	...	...
30 - 34	2 781	1 988	793	...	...	...	...	...	...
35 - 39	3 865	2 646	1 219	...	...	...	...	...	...
40 - 44	5 610	3 667	1 943	...	...	...	...	...	...
45 - 49	7 592	4 801	2 791	...	...	...	...	...	...
50 - 54	11 453	7 264	4 189	...	...	...	...	...	...
55 - 59	17 874	11 625	6 249	...	...	...	...	...	...
60 - 64	26 142	17 196	8 946	...	...	...	...	...	...
65 - 69	39 852	25 820	14 032	...	...	...	...	...	...
70 - 74	59 477	36 897	22 580	...	...	...	...	...	...
75 - 79	84 065	47 357	36 708	...	...	...	...	...	...
80 - 84	105 547	49 898	55 649	...	...	...	...	...	...
85 - 89	75 148	29 323	45 825	...	...	...	...	...	...
90 - 94	71 759	22 905	48 854	...	...	...	...	...	...
95 - 99	22 572	5 351	17 221	...	...	...	...	...	...
100 +	3 201	553	2 648	...	...	...	...	...	...
Unknown - Inconnu	35	26	9	...	...	...	...	...	...
Latvia - Lettonie									
2006 (C)									
Total	33 098	16 621	16 477	21 535	10 736	10 799	11 563	5 885	5 678
0	170	93	77	99	55	44	71	38	33
1 - 4	32	19	13	18	11	7	14	8	6
5 - 9	33	21	12	21	13	8	12	8	4
10 - 14	27	16	11	16	10	6	11	6	5
15 - 19	102	73	29	54	40	14	48	33	15
20 - 24	183	151	32	122	99	23	61	52	9
25 - 29	225	173	52	159	123	36	66	50	16
30 - 34	350	284	66	235	189	46	115	95	20
35 - 39	564	422	142	385	281	104	179	141	38
40 - 44	792	616	176	523	397	126	269	219	50
45 - 49	1 314	965	349	892	638	254	422	327	95
50 - 54	1 728	1 218	510	1 175	798	377	553	420	133
55 - 59	2 211	1 520	691	1 505	1 004	501	706	516	190
60 - 64	2 571	1 721	850	1 589	1 035	554	982	686	296
65 - 69	3 581	2 236	1 345	2 288	1 383	905	1 293	853	440
70 - 74	4 035	2 223	1 812	2 531	1 361	1 170	1 504	862	642
75 - 79	5 050	2 324	2 726	3 360	1 563	1 797	1 690	761	929
80 - 84	4 809	1 356	3 453	3 172	945	2 227	1 637	411	1 226
85 - 89	2 818	692	2 126	1 796	449	1 347	1 022	243	779
90 - 94	1 753	363	1 390	1 118	253	865	635	110	525
95 - 99	637	116	521	406	73	333	231	43	188

19. Deaths by age, sex and urban/rural residence: latest available year, 1997 - 2006
Décès selon l'âge, le sexe et la résidence, urbaine/rurale: dernière année disponible, 1997 - 2006 (continued - suite)

Continent, country or area, date, code and age (in years) / Continent, pays ou zone, date, code et âge (en années)	Total			Urban - Urbaine			Rural - Rurale		
	Both sexes Les deux sexes	Male Masculin	Female Féminin	Both sexes Les deux sexes	Male Masculin	Female Féminin	Both sexes Les deux sexes	Male Masculin	Female Féminin
EUROPE									
Latvia - Lettonie									
2006 (C)									
100 +	107	14	93	66	12	54	41	2	39
Unknown - Inconnu	6	5	1	5	4	1	1	1	-
Liechtenstein									
2006* (C)									
Total	220	105	115	...	...	...	...	...	...
0 - 9	2	1	1	...	...	...	...	...	...
10 - 14	-	-	-	...	...	...	...	...	...
15 - 19	-	-	-	...	...	...	...	...	...
20 - 29	5	4	1	...	...	...	...	...	...
30 - 39	3	2	1	...	...	...	...	...	...
40 - 49	7	5	2	...	...	...	...	...	...
50 - 59	14	10	4	...	...	...	...	...	...
60 - 69	35	20	15	...	...	...	...	...	...
70 - 79	41	26	15	...	...	...	...	...	...
80 - 89	70	24	46	...	...	...	...	...	...
90 - 99	43	13	30	...	...	...	...	...	...
100 +	-	-	-	...	...	...	...	...	...
Lithuania - Lituanie									
2006 (C)									
Total	44 813	23 809	21 004	26 194	13 904	12 290	18 619	9 905	8 714
0	213	116	97	167	93	74	46	23	23
1 - 4	52	26	26	30	16	14	22	10	12
5 - 9	54	38	16	32	24	8	22	14	8
10 - 14	55	35	20	31	19	12	24	16	8
15 - 19	205	155	50	100	75	25	105	80	25
20 - 24	314	264	50	164	135	29	150	129	21
25 - 29	423	338	85	262	210	52	161	128	33
30 - 34	589	459	130	341	265	76	248	194	54
35 - 39	894	677	217	549	414	135	345	263	82
40 - 44	1 417	1 100	317	826	625	201	591	475	116
45 - 49	1 979	1 463	516	1 239	911	328	740	552	188
50 - 54	2 432	1 815	617	1 542	1 128	414	890	687	203
55 - 59	2 925	2 106	819	1 846	1 294	552	1 079	812	267
60 - 64	3 591	2 478	1 113	2 188	1 501	687	1 403	977	426
65 - 69	4 351	2 793	1 558	2 599	1 684	915	1 752	1 109	643
70 - 74	5 307	3 003	2 304	3 020	1 656	1 364	2 287	1 347	940
75 - 79	6 499	2 965	3 534	3 731	1 733	1 998	2 768	1 232	1 536
80 - 84	6 470	2 131	4 339	3 684	1 158	2 526	2 786	973	1 813
85 - 89	3 696	1 039	2 657	2 024	562	1 462	1 672	477	1 195
90 - 94	2 240	504	1 736	1 218	255	963	1 022	249	773
95 - 99	940	245	695	521	121	400	419	124	295
100 +	167	59	108	80	25	55	87	34	53
Unknown - Inconnu	-	-	-	-	-	-	-	-	-
Luxembourg									
2006 (C)									
Total	3 766	1 812	1 954	...	...	...	...	...	...
0	14	9	5	...	...	...	...	...	...
1 - 4	4	1	3	...	...	...	...	...	...
5 - 9	3	2	1	...	...	...	...	...	...
10 - 14	2	2	-	...	...	...	...	...	...
15 - 19	5	2	3	...	...	...	...	...	...
20 - 24	17	13	4	...	...	...	...	...	...
25 - 29	17	7	10	...	...	...	...	...	...
30 - 34	20	13	7	...	...	...	...	...	...
35 - 39	50	33	17	...	...	...	...	...	...
40 - 44	68	47	21	...	...	...	...	...	...
45 - 49	95	59	36	...	...	...	...	...	...
50 - 54	147	91	56	...	...	...	...	...	...
55 - 59	174	122	52	...	...	...	...	...	...
60 - 64	228	147	81	...	...	...	...	...	...
65 - 69	276	181	95	...	...	...	...	...	...
70 - 74	385	233	152	...	...	...	...	...	...
75 - 79	601	322	279	...	...	...	...	...	...

19. Deaths by age, sex and urban/rural residence: latest available year, 1997 - 2006
Décès selon l'âge, le sexe et la résidence, urbaine/rurale: dernière année disponible, 1997 - 2006 (continued - suite)

Continent, country or area, date, code and age (in years) / Continent, pays ou zone, date, code et âge (en annèes)	Total			Urban - Urbaine			Rural - Rurale		
	Both sexes Les deux sexes	Male Masculin	Female Féminin	Both sexes Les deux sexes	Male Masculin	Female Féminin	Both sexes Les deux sexes	Male Masculin	Female Féminin
EUROPE									
Luxembourg									
2006 (C)									
80 - 84	595	237	358	...	...	...	...	...	...
85 - 89	518	161	357	...	...	...	...	...	...
90 - 94	420	108	312	...	...	...	...	...	...
95 - 99	115	21	94	...	...	...	...	...	...
100 +	12	1	11	...	...	...	...	...	...
Unknown - Inconnu	-	-	-	...	...	...	...	...	...
Malta - Malte									
2006 (C)									
Total	3 216	1 667	1 549	...	...	...	...	...	...
0	14	10	4	...	...	...	...	...	...
1 - 4	4	1	3	...	...	...	...	...	...
5 - 9	-	-	-	...	...	...	...	...	...
10 - 14	6	3	3	...	...	...	...	...	...
15 - 19	9	7	2	...	...	...	...	...	...
20 - 24	13	12	1	...	...	...	...	...	...
25 - 29	6	6	-	...	...	...	...	...	...
30 - 34	17	11	6	...	...	...	...	...	...
35 - 39	16	13	3	...	...	...	...	...	...
40 - 44	39	25	14	...	...	...	...	...	...
45 - 49	60	31	29	...	...	...	...	...	...
50 - 54	87	64	23	...	...	...	...	...	...
55 - 59	149	88	61	...	...	...	...	...	...
60 - 64	188	114	74	...	...	...	...	...	...
65 - 69	259	157	102	...	...	...	...	...	...
70 - 74	392	236	156	...	...	...	...	...	...
75 - 79	494	265	229	...	...	...	...	...	...
80 - 84	605	292	313	...	...	...	...	...	...
85 - 89	496	213	283	...	...	...	...	...	...
90 +	362	119	243	...	...	...	...	...	...
Moldova[40]									
2006 (C)									
Total	43 137	22 499	20 638	13 764	7 396	6 368	29 373	15 103	14 270
0	442	243	199	177	99	78	265	144	121
1 - 4	85	50	35	26	15	11	59	35	24
5 - 9	71	46	25	23	13	10	48	33	15
10 - 14	101	59	42	20	12	8	81	47	34
15 - 19	211	146	65	78	56	22	133	90	43
20 - 24	269	196	73	90	67	23	179	129	50
25 - 29	399	309	90	164	140	24	235	169	66
30 - 34	560	415	145	234	177	57	326	238	88
35 - 39	781	595	186	294	215	79	487	380	107
40 - 44	1 393	989	404	487	345	142	906	644	262
45 - 49	2 461	1 758	703	906	640	266	1 555	1 118	437
50 - 54	3 170	2 154	1 016	1 201	806	395	1 969	1 348	621
55 - 59	3 509	2 159	1 350	1 350	863	487	2 159	1 296	863
60 - 64	3 241	1 786	1 455	1 049	610	439	2 192	1 176	1 016
65 - 69	4 960	2 727	2 233	1 579	913	666	3 381	1 814	1 567
70 - 74	5 875	2 831	3 044	1 740	839	901	4 135	1 992	2 143
75 - 79	6 672	2 923	3 749	1 879	791	1 088	4 793	2 132	2 661
80 - 84	5 039	1 834	3 205	1 422	491	931	3 617	1 343	2 274
85 - 89	2 653	887	1 766	719	219	500	1 934	668	1 266
90 - 94	963	308	655	262	70	192	701	238	463
95 - 99	235	74	161	54	12	42	181	62	119
100 +	47	10	37	10	3	7	37	7	30
Montenegro									
2005 (C)									
Total	5 839	3 082	2 757	3 571	1 891	1 680	2 268	1 191	1 077
0	70	39	31	65	36	29	5	3	2
1 - 4	12	10	2	10	9	1	2	1	1
5 - 9	7	3	4	7	3	4	-	-	-
10 - 14	8	7	1	4	4	-	4	3	1
15 - 19	16	11	5	10	7	3	6	4	2
20 - 24	38	27	11	24	18	6	14	9	5

Continent, country or area, date, code and age (in years) / Continent, pays ou zone, date, code et âge (en années)	Total			Urban - Urbaine			Rural - Rurale		
	Both sexes Les deux sexes	Male Masculin	Female Féminin	Both sexes Les deux sexes	Male Masculin	Female Féminin	Both sexes Les deux sexes	Male Masculin	Female Féminin
EUROPE									
Montenegro									
2005 (C)									
25 - 29	45	28	17	29	15	14	16	13	3
30 - 34	37	28	9	29	21	8	8	7	1
35 - 39	61	40	21	48	30	18	13	10	3
40 - 44	88	58	30	60	35	25	28	23	5
45 - 49	187	117	70	129	73	56	58	44	14
50 - 54	279	187	92	206	135	71	73	52	21
55 - 59	353	249	104	247	168	79	106	81	25
60 - 64	431	266	165	289	177	112	142	89	53
65 - 69	716	416	300	453	259	194	263	157	106
70 - 74	873	492	381	531	310	221	342	182	160
75 - 79	1 082	510	572	622	283	339	460	227	233
80 - 84	809	342	467	432	185	247	377	157	220
85 - 89	385	141	244	206	74	132	179	67	112
90 - 94	241	76	165	123	34	89	118	42	76
95 - 99	77	25	52	35	11	24	42	14	28
100 +	24	10	14	12	4	8	12	6	6
Unknown - Inconnu	-	-	-	-	-	-	-	-	-
Netherlands - Pays-Bas[41]									
2006 (C)									
Total	135 372	65 294	70 078	90 611	42 777	47 834	44 761	22 517	22 244
0	738	423	315	482	267	215	256	156	100
1 - 4	239	133	106	164	98	66	75	35	40
5 - 9	109	63	46	57	32	25	52	31	21
10 - 14	104	53	51	60	31	29	44	22	22
15 - 19	217	143	74	133	82	51	84	61	23
20 - 24	335	246	89	227	165	62	108	81	27
25 - 29	356	235	121	247	162	85	109	73	36
30 - 34	550	338	212	387	244	143	163	94	69
35 - 39	930	553	377	634	380	254	296	173	123
40 - 44	1 472	840	632	1 025	604	421	447	236	211
45 - 49	2 463	1 356	1 107	1 665	911	754	798	445	353
50 - 54	3 851	2 166	1 685	2 619	1 476	1 143	1 232	690	542
55 - 59	5 873	3 440	2 433	3 972	2 348	1 624	1 901	1 092	809
60 - 64	7 741	4 789	2 952	5 081	3 116	1 965	2 660	1 673	987
65 - 69	9 364	5 848	3 516	6 085	3 724	2 361	3 279	2 124	1 155
70 - 74	13 266	8 138	5 128	8 653	5 158	3 495	4 613	2 980	1 633
75 - 79	19 000	10 608	8 392	12 546	6 828	5 718	6 454	3 780	2 674
80 - 84	24 060	11 585	12 475	16 299	7 724	8 575	7 761	3 861	3 900
85 - 89	23 115	8 833	14 282	15 666	5 852	9 814	7 449	2 981	4 468
90 - 94	15 223	4 253	10 970	10 258	2 763	7 495	4 965	1 490	3 475
95 - 99	5 439	1 102	4 337	3 721	724	2 997	1 718	378	1 340
100 +	927	149	778	630	88	542	297	61	236
Norway - Norvège[42]									
2006 (C)									
Total	41 253	19 628	21 625	...	...	...	...	...	...
0	185	111	74	...	...	...	...	...	...
1 - 4	42	25	17	...	...	...	...	...	...
5 - 9	36	16	20	...	...	...	...	...	...
10 - 14	20	17	3	...	...	...	...	...	...
15 - 19	112	77	35	...	...	...	...	...	...
20 - 24	160	121	39	...	...	...	...	...	...
25 - 29	180	140	40	...	...	...	...	...	...
30 - 34	230	160	70	...	...	...	...	...	...
35 - 39	302	199	103	...	...	...	...	...	...
40 - 44	376	228	148	...	...	...	...	...	...
45 - 49	659	385	274	...	...	...	...	...	...
50 - 54	970	600	370	...	...	...	...	...	...
55 - 59	1 501	914	587	...	...	...	...	...	...
60 - 64	2 099	1 293	806	...	...	...	...	...	...
65 - 69	2 241	1 414	827	...	...	...	...	...	...
70 - 74	3 155	1 868	1 287	...	...	...	...	...	...
75 - 79	5 153	2 834	2 319	...	...	...	...	...	...
80 - 84	7 899	3 823	4 076	...	...	...	...	...	...

19. Deaths by age, sex and urban/rural residence: latest available year, 1997 - 2006
Décès selon l'âge, le sexe et la résidence, urbaine/rurale: dernière année disponible, 1997 - 2006 (continued - suite)

Continent, country or area, date, code and age (in years) Continent, pays ou zone, date, code et âge (en années)	Total			Urban - Urbaine			Rural - Rurale		
	Both sexes Les deux sexes	Male Masculin	Female Féminin	Both sexes Les deux sexes	Male Masculin	Female Féminin	Both sexes Les deux sexes	Male Masculin	Female Féminin
EUROPE									
Norway - Norvège[42]									
2006 (C)									
85 - 89	8 413	3 328	5 085	...	...	...	...	...	...
90 - 94	5 445	1 630	3 815	...	...	...	...	...	...
95 - 99	1 817	395	1 422	...	...	...	...	...	...
100 +	258	50	208	...	...	...	...	...	...
Unknown - Inconnu	-	-	-	...	...	...	...	...	...
Poland - Pologne									
2006 (C)									
Total	369 686	198 299	171 387	222 219	117 812	104 407	147 467	80 487	66 980
0	2 238	1 278	960	1 343	784	559	895	494	401
1 - 4	388	214	174	208	114	94	180	100	80
5 - 9	305	183	122	141	86	55	164	97	67
10 - 14	441	274	167	216	127	89	225	147	78
15 - 19	1 304	962	342	640	464	176	664	498	166
20 - 24	2 243	1 819	424	1 226	963	263	1 017	856	161
25 - 29	2 307	1 858	449	1 327	1 043	284	980	815	165
30 - 34	2 873	2 243	630	1 720	1 304	416	1 153	939	214
35 - 39	4 232	3 250	982	2 548	1 890	658	1 684	1 360	324
40 - 44	7 241	5 398	1 843	4 336	3 133	1 203	2 905	2 265	640
45 - 49	14 710	10 812	3 898	9 372	6 643	2 729	5 338	4 169	1 169
50 - 54	22 932	16 544	6 388	14 998	10 437	4 561	7 934	6 107	1 827
55 - 59	28 145	19 782	8 363	18 884	12 838	6 046	9 261	6 944	2 317
60 - 64	23 673	16 083	7 590	15 824	10 460	5 364	7 849	5 623	2 226
65 - 69	33 225	21 595	11 630	21 028	13 321	7 707	12 197	8 274	3 923
70 - 74	44 868	26 289	18 579	27 391	15 617	11 774	17 477	10 672	6 805
75 - 79	57 232	28 491	28 741	33 258	16 269	16 989	23 974	12 222	11 752
80 - 84	58 469	22 753	35 716	33 151	12 653	20 498	25 318	10 100	15 218
85 - 89	34 240	11 255	22 985	18 381	5 825	12 556	15 859	5 430	10 429
90 - 94	21 098	5 525	15 573	11 915	2 931	8 984	9 183	2 594	6 589
95 - 99	6 719	1 542	5 177	3 813	818	2 995	2 906	724	2 182
100 +	803	149	654	499	92	407	304	57	247
Unknown - Inconnu	-	-	-	-	-	-	-	-	-
Portugal[43]									
2006 (C)									
Total	101 990	53 473	48 517	...	...	...	...	...	...
0	349	209	140	...	...	...	...	...	...
1 - 4	115	66	49	...	...	...	...	...	...
5 - 9	84	45	39	...	...	...	...	...	...
10 - 14	93	63	30	...	...	...	...	...	...
15 - 19	247	178	69	...	...	...	...	...	...
20 - 24	388	300	88	...	...	...	...	...	...
25 - 29	501	371	130	...	...	...	...	...	...
30 - 34	774	579	195	...	...	...	...	...	...
35 - 39	1 175	841	334	...	...	...	...	...	...
40 - 44	1 690	1 227	463	...	...	...	...	...	...
45 - 49	2 287	1 668	619	...	...	...	...	...	...
50 - 54	2 895	2 050	845	...	...	...	...	...	...
55 - 59	3 847	2 682	1 165	...	...	...	...	...	...
60 - 64	4 932	3 237	1 695	...	...	...	...	...	...
65 - 69	7 189	4 718	2 471	...	...	...	...	...	...
70 - 74	11 332	6 865	4 467	...	...	...	...	...	...
75 - 79	15 830	8 793	7 037	...	...	...	...	...	...
80 - 84	19 340	9 269	10 071	...	...	...	...	...	...
85 - 89	15 677	6 309	9 368	...	...	...	...	...	...
90 - 94	9 740	3 131	6 609	...	...	...	...	...	...
95 - 99	3 048	772	2 276	...	...	...	...	...	...
100 +	431	76	355	...	...	...	...	...	...
Unknown - Inconnu	26	24	2	...	...	...	...	...	...
Romania - Roumanie									
2006 (C)									
Total	258 094	136 264	121 830	116 384	61 994	54 390	141 710	74 270	67 440
0	3 052	1 704	1 348	1 341	743	598	1 711	961	750
1 - 4	548	302	246	210	119	91	338	183	155
5 - 9	334	198	136	128	84	44	206	114	92

543

Continent, country or area, date, code and age (in years) / Continent, pays ou zone, date, code et âge (en années)	Total			Urban - Urbaine			Rural - Rurale		
	Both sexes Les deux sexes	Male Masculin	Female Féminin	Both sexes Les deux sexes	Male Masculin	Female Féminin	Both sexes Les deux sexes	Male Masculin	Female Féminin
EUROPE									
Romania - Roumanie									
2006 (C)									
10 - 14	365	231	134	147	83	64	218	148	70
15 - 19	941	628	313	458	298	160	483	330	153
20 - 24	1 020	744	276	543	382	161	477	362	115
25 - 29	1 421	1 036	385	742	532	210	679	504	175
30 - 34	1 839	1 311	528	883	607	276	956	704	252
35 - 39	3 348	2 357	991	1 680	1 132	548	1 668	1 225	443
40 - 44	3 841	2 729	1 112	1 964	1 321	643	1 877	1 408	469
45 - 49	8 146	5 831	2 315	4 593	3 133	1 460	3 553	2 698	855
50 - 54	13 063	9 179	3 884	7 696	5 308	2 388	5 367	3 871	1 496
55 - 59	15 686	10 776	4 910	8 721	5 980	2 741	6 965	4 796	2 169
60 - 64	16 893	11 113	5 780	8 519	5 588	2 931	8 374	5 525	2 849
65 - 69	26 951	16 518	10 433	12 482	7 688	4 794	14 469	8 830	5 639
70 - 74	36 656	19 875	16 781	15 815	8 532	7 283	20 841	11 343	9 498
75 - 79	44 769	21 657	23 112	18 484	8 886	9 598	26 285	12 771	13 514
80 - 84	43 883	18 042	25 841	17 145	6 740	10 405	26 738	11 302	15 436
85 - 89	20 653	7 173	13 480	8 386	2 760	5 626	12 267	4 413	7 854
90 - 94	11 643	3 879	7 764	5 115	1 689	3 426	6 528	2 190	4 338
95 - 99	2 788	902	1 886	1 214	360	854	1 574	542	1 032
100 +	254	79	175	118	29	89	136	50	86
Unknown - Inconnu	-	-	-	-	-	-	-	-	-
Russian Federation - Fédération de Russie[20]									
2006 (C)									
Total	2 166 703	1 148 561	1 018 142	1 501 245	796 734	704 511	665 458	351 827	313 631
0	15 079	8 660	6 419	9 839	5 627	4 212	5 240	3 033	2 207
1 - 4	3 968	2 287	1 681	2 321	1 360	961	1 647	927	720
5 - 9	2 273	1 387	886	1 326	786	540	947	601	346
10 - 14	2 807	1 807	1 000	1 706	1 075	631	1 101	732	369
15 - 19	12 684	9 126	3 558	7 886	5 610	2 276	4 798	3 516	1 282
20 - 24	27 399	21 586	5 813	18 848	14 808	4 040	8 551	6 778	1 773
25 - 29	42 400	33 888	8 512	31 052	24 774	6 278	11 348	9 114	2 234
30 - 34	50 481	39 814	10 667	36 822	28 930	7 892	13 659	10 884	2 775
35 - 39	54 732	41 977	12 755	38 532	29 308	9 224	16 200	12 669	3 531
40 - 44	82 896	63 160	19 736	57 352	43 344	14 008	25 544	19 816	5 728
45 - 49	125 595	94 084	31 511	86 777	64 414	22 363	38 818	29 670	9 148
50 - 54	155 656	113 586	42 070	110 326	79 953	30 373	45 330	33 633	11 697
55 - 59	171 040	118 008	53 032	123 622	84 780	38 842	47 418	33 228	14 190
60 - 64	112 271	73 230	39 041	80 091	52 183	27 908	32 180	21 047	11 133
65 - 69	258 319	153 132	105 187	177 696	104 825	72 871	80 623	48 307	32 316
70 - 74	239 408	121 930	117 478	159 199	79 826	79 373	80 209	42 104	38 105
75 - 79	334 688	137 324	197 364	225 351	91 364	133 987	109 337	45 960	63 377
80 - 84	242 832	62 957	179 875	170 048	44 748	125 300	72 784	18 209	54 575
85 - 89	122 775	24 610	98 165	85 826	17 996	67 830	36 949	6 614	30 335
90 - 94	74 998	11 977	63 021	51 045	8 922	42 123	23 953	3 055	20 898
95 - 99	17 972	2 447	15 525	11 700	1 768	9 932	6 272	679	5 593
100 +	2 260	255	2 005	1 212	170	1 042	1 048	85	963
Unknown - Inconnu	14 170	11 329	2 841	12 668	10 163	2 505	1 502	1 166	336
San Marino - Saint-Marin									
2004 (+C)									
Total	185	94	91	...	...	...	...	...	...
0	1	1	-	...	...	...	...	...	...
1 - 14	-	-	-	...	...	...	...	...	...
15 - 19	2	2	-	...	...	...	...	...	...
20 - 24	2	2	-	...	...	...	...	...	...
25 - 29	-	-	-	...	...	...	...	...	...
30 - 34	1	-	1	...	...	...	...	...	...
35 - 39	-	-	-	...	...	...	...	...	...
40 - 44	3	-	3	...	...	...	...	...	...
45 - 49	2	-	2	...	...	...	...	...	...
50 - 54	7	5	2	...	...	...	...	...	...
55 - 59	9	6	3	...	...	...	...	...	...
60 - 64	8	6	2	...	...	...	...	...	...
65 - 69	12	7	5	...	...	...	...	...	...

19. Deaths by age, sex and urban/rural residence: latest available year, 1997 - 2006
Décès selon l'âge, le sexe et la résidence, urbaine/rurale: dernière année disponible, 1997 - 2006 (continued - suite)

Continent, country or area, date, code and age (in years) / Continent, pays ou zone, date, code et âge (en années)	Total Both sexes Les deux sexes	Total Male Masculin	Total Female Féminin	Urban - Urbaine Both sexes Les deux sexes	Urban - Urbaine Male Masculin	Urban - Urbaine Female Féminin	Rural - Rurale Both sexes Les deux sexes	Rural - Rurale Male Masculin	Rural - Rurale Female Féminin
EUROPE									
San Marino - Saint-Marin									
2004 (+C)									
70 - 74	14	9	5	...	...	...	...	...	...
75 - 79	22	13	9	...	...	...	...	...	...
80 - 84	35	16	19	...	...	...	...	...	...
85 - 89	34	16	18	...	...	...	...	...	...
90 - 94	27	7	20	...	...	...	...	...	...
95 - 99	5	4	1	...	...	...	...	...	...
100 + ...	1	-	1	...	...	...	...	...	...
Serbia - Serbie[44]									
2006 (+C)									
Total..................	102 884	52 325	50 559	53 073	27 178	25 895	49 811	25 147	24 664
0	525	311	214	352	195	157	173	116	57
1 - 4	93	46	47	59	27	32	34	19	15
5 - 9	71	47	24	35	23	12	36	24	12
10 - 14	63	39	24	45	28	17	18	11	7
15 - 19	177	125	52	102	71	31	75	54	21
20 - 24	341	256	85	224	169	55	117	87	30
25 - 29	409	296	113	285	197	88	124	99	25
30 - 34	486	339	147	309	227	82	177	112	65
35 - 39	655	429	226	378	240	138	277	189	88
40 - 44	1 209	702	427	700	437	263	509	345	164
45 - 49	2 311	1 519	792	1 384	891	493	927	628	299
50 - 54	4 595	3 085	1 510	2 777	1 795	982	1 818	1 290	528
55 - 59	6 215	4 142	2 073	3 766	2 431	1 335	2 449	1 711	738
60 - 64	6 350	4 059	2 291	3 678	2 279	1 399	2 672	1 780	892
65 - 69	11 149	6 498	4 651	6 155	3 560	2 595	4 994	2 938	2 056
70 - 74	17 404	9 338	8 066	8 760	4 775	3 985	8 644	4 563	4 081
75 - 79	21 263	9 910	11 353	10 189	4 735	5 454	11 074	5 175	5 899
80 - 84	18 152	6 939	11 213	8 493	3 205	5 288	9 659	3 734	5 925
85 + ...	11 343	4 118	7 225	5 332	1 855	3 477	6 011	2 263	3 748
Unknown - Inconnu	73	47	26	50	38	12	23	9	14
Slovakia - Slovaquie									
2006 (C)									
Total..................	53 301	28 091	25 210	26 157	13 708	12 449	27 144	14 383	12 761
0	355	204	151	153	83	70	202	121	81
1 - 4	72	44	28	31	17	14	41	27	14
5 - 9	59	37	22	20	12	8	39	25	14
10 - 14	58	39	19	35	27	8	23	12	11
15 - 19	147	107	40	72	48	24	75	59	16
20 - 24	262	213	49	141	115	26	121	98	23
25 - 29	307	245	62	159	132	27	148	113	35
30 - 34	410	319	91	216	168	48	194	151	43
35 - 39	568	425	143	276	195	81	292	230	62
40 - 44	972	714	258	498	351	147	474	363	111
45 - 49	1 822	1 352	470	924	657	267	898	695	203
50 - 54	2 963	2 123	840	1 625	1 126	499	1 338	997	341
55 - 59	3 562	2 502	1 060	1 882	1 258	624	1 680	1 244	436
60 - 64	3 803	2 563	1 240	1 932	1 254	678	1 871	1 309	562
65 - 69	4 819	3 037	1 782	2 393	1 469	924	2 426	1 568	858
70 - 74	6 547	3 623	2 924	3 161	1 736	1 425	3 386	1 887	1 499
75 - 79	8 532	4 095	4 437	4 031	1 948	2 083	4 501	2 147	2 354
80 - 84	9 321	3 629	5 692	4 405	1 728	2 677	4 916	1 901	3 015
85 - 89	5 017	1 713	3 304	2 436	841	1 595	2 581	872	1 709
90 - 94	2 814	875	1 939	1 340	439	901	1 474	436	1 038
95 - 99	811	213	598	388	94	294	423	119	304
100 + ...	80	19	61	39	10	29	41	9	32
Slovenia - Slovénie									
2006 (C)									
Total..................	18 180	9 270	8 910	8 571	4 316	4 255	9 609	4 954	4 655
0	64	32	32	37	21	16	27	11	16
1 - 4	10	7	3	5	4	1	5	3	2
5 - 9	10	5	5	2	1	1	8	4	4
10 - 14	12	8	4	4	3	1	8	5	3
15 - 19	53	38	15	23	17	6	30	21	9

19. Deaths by age, sex and urban/rural residence: latest available year, 1997 - 2006
Décès selon l'âge, le sexe et la résidence, urbaine/rurale: dernière année disponible, 1997 - 2006 (continued - suite)

Continent, country or area, date, code and age (in years) Continent, pays ou zone, date, code et âge (en années)	Total			Urban - Urbaine			Rural - Rurale		
	Both sexes Les deux sexes	Male Masculin	Female Féminin	Both sexes Les deux sexes	Male Masculin	Female Féminin	Both sexes Les deux sexes	Male Masculin	Female Féminin
EUROPE									
Slovenia - Slovénie									
2006 (C)									
20 - 24	104	84	20	42	31	11	62	53	9
25 - 29	105	87	18	50	40	10	55	47	8
30 - 34	102	83	19	47	36	11	55	47	8
35 - 39	144	111	33	55	42	13	89	69	20
40 - 44	302	229	73	136	109	27	166	120	46
45 - 49	478	358	120	216	157	59	262	201	61
50 - 54	871	620	251	431	290	141	440	330	110
55 - 59	1 052	770	282	497	356	141	555	414	141
60 - 64	1 135	777	358	558	370	188	577	407	170
65 - 69	1 557	1 040	517	730	480	250	827	560	267
70 - 74	2 276	1 359	917	1 077	635	442	1 199	724	475
75 - 79	2 938	1 493	1 445	1 372	682	690	1 566	811	755
80 - 84	3 209	1 152	2 057	1 494	542	952	1 715	610	1 105
85 - 89	1 895	572	1 323	899	273	626	996	299	697
90 - 94	1 373	343	1 030	664	179	485	709	164	545
95 - 99	443	92	351	205	43	162	238	49	189
100 +	47	10	37	27	5	22	20	5	15
Unknown - Inconnu	-	-	-	-	-	-	-	-	-
Spain - Espagne									
2005 (C)									
Total	387 355	201 769	185 586	...	...	...	...	...	...
0	1 765	1 017	748	...	...	...	...	...	...
1 - 4	380	223	157	...	...	...	...	...	...
5 - 9	229	125	104	...	...	...	...	...	...
10 - 14	281	176	105	...	...	...	...	...	...
15 - 19	914	680	234	...	...	...	...	...	...
20 - 24	1 430	1 090	340	...	...	...	...	...	...
25 - 29	1 846	1 410	436	...	...	...	...	...	...
30 - 34	2 568	1 864	704	...	...	...	...	...	...
35 - 39	3 763	2 657	1 106	...	...	...	...	...	...
40 - 44	5 310	3 713	1 597	...	...	...	...	...	...
45 - 49	7 307	5 021	2 286	...	...	...	...	...	...
50 - 54	9 505	6 806	2 699	...	...	...	...	...	...
55 - 59	13 238	9 525	3 713	...	...	...	...	...	...
60 - 64	16 905	12 002	4 903	...	...	...	...	...	...
65 - 69	23 721	16 357	7 364	...	...	...	...	...	...
70 - 74	40 546	26 159	14 387	...	...	...	...	...	...
75 - 79	57 516	33 474	24 042	...	...	...	...	...	...
80 - 84	73 005	36 157	36 848	...	...	...	...	...	...
85 - 89	64 022	24 717	39 305	...	...	...	...	...	...
90 - 94	44 812	14 000	30 812	...	...	...	...	...	...
95 - 99	15 697	4 071	11 626	...	...	...	...	...	...
100 +	2 595	525	2 070	...	...	...	...	...	...
Unknown - Inconnu	-	-	-	...	...	...	...	...	...
Sweden - Suède									
2006 (C)									
Total	91 177	44 177	47 000	...	...	...	...	...	...
0	297	165	132	...	...	...	...	...	...
1 - 4	70	34	36	...	...	...	...	...	...
5 - 9	43	30	13	...	...	...	...	...	...
10 - 14	53	35	18	...	...	...	...	...	...
15 - 19	190	125	65	...	...	...	...	...	...
20 - 24	268	185	83	...	...	...	...	...	...
25 - 29	236	173	63	...	...	...	...	...	...
30 - 34	303	182	121	...	...	...	...	...	...
35 - 39	446	286	160	...	...	...	...	...	...
40 - 44	693	436	257	...	...	...	...	...	...
45 - 49	1 013	608	405	...	...	...	...	...	...
50 - 54	1 799	1 108	691	...	...	...	...	...	...
55 - 59	3 022	1 834	1 188	...	...	...	...	...	...
60 - 64	4 625	2 802	1 823	...	...	...	...	...	...
65 - 69	5 347	3 322	2 025	...	...	...	...	...	...
70 - 74	7 374	4 367	3 007	...	...	...	...	...	...

19. Deaths by age, sex and urban/rural residence: latest available year, 1997 - 2006
Décès selon l'âge, le sexe et la résidence, urbaine/rurale: dernière année disponible, 1997 - 2006 (continued - suite)

Continent, country or area, date, code and age (in years) / Continent, pays ou zone, date, code et âge (en années)	Total			Urban - Urbaine			Rural - Rurale		
	Both sexes Les deux sexes	Male Masculin	Female Féminin	Both sexes Les deux sexes	Male Masculin	Female Féminin	Both sexes Les deux sexes	Male Masculin	Female Féminin
EUROPE									
Sweden - Suède									
2006 (C)									
75 - 79	11 319	6 297	5 022	...	...	...	...	...	...
80 - 84	17 145	8 659	8 486	...	...	...	...	...	...
85 - 89	18 935	8 131	10 804	...	...	...	...	...	...
90 - 94	12 757	4 215	8 542	...	...	...	...	...	...
95 - 99	4 556	1 075	3 481	...	...	...	...	...	...
100 +	686	108	578	...	...	...	...	...	...
Switzerland - Suisse									
2006 (C)									
Total	60 283	29 220	31 063	44 209	21 006	23 203	16 074	8 214	7 860
0	325	182	143	255	139	116	70	43	27
1 - 4	52	29	23	32	16	16	20	13	7
5 - 9	45	27	18	26	13	13	19	14	5
10 - 14	47	28	19	26	14	12	21	14	7
15 - 19	153	102	51	101	70	31	52	32	20
20 - 24	198	144	54	142	102	40	56	42	14
25 - 29	240	171	69	178	125	53	62	46	16
30 - 34	291	190	101	226	140	86	65	50	15
35 - 39	435	287	148	331	218	113	104	69	35
40 - 44	698	440	258	519	328	191	179	112	67
45 - 49	1 049	641	408	767	479	288	282	162	120
50 - 54	1 439	882	557	1 045	628	417	394	254	140
55 - 59	2 285	1 461	824	1 709	1 064	645	576	397	179
60 - 64	3 087	1 968	1 119	2 285	1 419	866	802	549	253
65 - 69	3 589	2 231	1 358	2 678	1 642	1 036	911	589	322
70 - 74	5 212	3 141	2 071	3 823	2 248	1 575	1 389	893	496
75 - 79	7 686	4 282	3 404	5 578	3 075	2 503	2 108	1 207	901
80 - 84	10 482	5 124	5 358	7 647	3 673	3 974	2 835	1 451	1 384
85 - 89	11 074	4 473	6 601	7 958	3 140	4 818	3 116	1 333	1 783
90 - 94	8 351	2 617	5 734	6 170	1 882	4 288	2 181	735	1 446
95 - 99	3 091	717	2 374	2 366	537	1 829	725	180	545
100 +	454	83	371	347	54	293	107	29	78
The Former Yugoslav Rep. of Macedonia - L'ex-République yougoslave de Macédoine									
2006 (C)									
Total	18 630	10 000	8 630	10 931	5 905	5 026	7 699	4 095	3 604
0	260	149	111	144	81	63	116	68	48
1 - 4	31	18	13	16	10	6	15	8	7
5 - 9	17	8	9	8	3	5	9	5	4
10 - 14	24	15	9	14	7	7	10	8	2
15 - 19	53	35	18	34	22	12	19	13	6
20 - 24	83	60	23	54	39	15	29	21	8
25 - 29	77	56	21	52	38	14	25	18	7
30 - 34	105	62	43	65	42	23	40	20	20
35 - 39	160	97	63	90	54	36	70	43	27
40 - 44	280	175	105	168	109	59	112	66	46
45 - 49	538	365	173	356	237	119	182	128	54
50 - 54	914	644	270	595	407	188	319	237	82
55 - 59	1 143	750	393	758	505	253	385	245	140
60 - 64	1 395	853	542	900	561	339	495	292	203
65 - 69	1 983	1 149	834	1 206	713	493	777	436	341
70 - 74	3 004	1 638	1 366	1 742	965	777	1 262	673	589
75 - 79	3 431	1 673	1 758	1 933	923	1 010	1 498	750	748
80 - 84	3 018	1 347	1 671	1 689	740	949	1 329	607	722
85 +	2 114	906	1 208	1 107	449	658	1 007	457	550
Ukraine									
2006 (C)									
Total	758 092	386 989	371 103	461 774	240 961	220 813	296 318	146 028	150 290
0	4 433	2 628	1 805	2 828	1 720	1 108	1 605	908	697
1 - 4	1 102	613	489	585	328	257	517	285	232
5 - 9	689	431	258	387	248	139	302	183	119
10 - 14	807	510	297	452	284	168	355	226	129

Continent, country or area, date, code and age (in years) / Continent, pays ou zone, date, code et âge (en années)	Total			Urban - Urbaine			Rural - Rurale		
	Both sexes Les deux sexes	Male Masculin	Female Féminin	Both sexes Les deux sexes	Male Masculin	Female Féminin	Both sexes Les deux sexes	Male Masculin	Female Féminin
EUROPE									
Ukraine									
2006 (C)									
15 - 19	2 668	1 894	774	1 588	1 113	475	1 080	781	299
20 - 24	5 475	4 265	1 210	3 513	2 685	828	1 962	1 580	382
25 - 29	8 837	6 795	2 042	6 082	4 590	1 492	2 755	2 205	550
30 - 34	12 925	9 865	3 060	8 953	6 695	2 258	3 972	3 170	802
35 - 39	16 055	12 142	3 913	10 763	7 945	2 818	5 292	4 197	1 095
40 - 44	23 784	18 172	5 612	15 987	11 999	3 988	7 797	6 173	1 624
45 - 49	34 845	26 231	8 614	23 307	17 167	6 140	11 538	9 064	2 474
50 - 54	42 873	31 259	11 614	28 755	20 683	8 072	14 118	10 576	3 542
55 - 59	51 479	35 227	16 252	34 714	23 665	11 049	16 765	11 562	5 203
60 - 64	47 223	30 486	16 737	29 355	18 955	10 400	17 868	11 531	6 337
65 - 69	99 486	58 627	40 859	61 810	36 238	25 572	37 676	22 389	15 287
70 - 74	85 411	44 490	40 921	50 286	26 151	24 135	35 125	18 339	16 786
75 - 79	126 679	53 453	73 226	74 310	31 672	42 638	52 369	21 781	30 588
80 - 84	105 360	31 112	74 248	59 626	17 751	41 875	45 734	13 361	32 373
85 - 89	50 854	11 867	38 987	28 476	7 016	21 460	22 378	4 851	17 527
90 - 94	29 069	5 466	23 603	15 944	3 245	12 699	13 125	2 221	10 904
95 - 99	7 064	1 212	5 852	3 538	646	2 892	3 526	566	2 960
100 +	833	127	706	394	62	332	439	65	374
Unknown - Inconnu	141	117	24	121	103	18	20	14	6
United Kingdom - Royaume-Uni[45]									
2005* (C)									
Total	582 663	276 803	305 860	...	...	...	...	...	...
0	3 671	2 104	1 567	...	...	...	...	...	...
1 - 4	588	328	260	...	...	...	...	...	...
5 - 9	336	186	150	...	...	...	...	...	...
10 - 14	485	284	201	...	...	...	...	...	...
15 - 19	1 345	909	436	...	...	...	...	...	...
20 - 24	1 876	1 337	539	...	...	...	...	...	...
25 - 29	2 039	1 408	631	...	...	...	...	...	...
30 - 34	2 995	2 006	989	...	...	...	...	...	...
35 - 39	4 654	3 006	1 648	...	...	...	...	...	...
40 - 44	6 930	4 225	2 705	...	...	...	...	...	...
45 - 49	9 738	5 868	3 870	...	...	...	...	...	...
50 - 54	13 892	8 297	5 595	...	...	...	...	...	...
55 - 59	22 734	13 589	9 145	...	...	...	...	...	...
60 - 64	29 549	18 036	11 513	...	...	...	...	...	...
65 - 69	41 515	24 598	16 917	...	...	...	...	...	...
70 - 74	59 200	34 220	24 980	...	...	...	...	...	...
75 - 79	84 915	44 962	39 953	...	...	...	...	...	...
80 - 84	109 294	50 805	58 489	...	...	...	...	...	...
85 - 89	91 279	35 277	56 002	...	...	...	...	...	...
90 - 94	67 100	19 790	47 310	...	...	...	...	...	...
95 - 99	24 337	5 035	19 302	...	...	...	...	...	...
100 +	4 181	532	3 649	...	...	...	...	...	...
Unknown - Inconnu	10	1	9	...	...	...	...	...	...
OCEANIA - OCÉANIE									
American Samoa - Samoas américaines									
2006 (C)									
Total	267	156	111	...	...	...	...	...	...
0	17	9	8	...	...	...	...	...	...
1 - 4	7	3	4	...	...	...	...	...	...
5 - 9	1	1	-	...	...	...	...	...	...
10 - 14	5	2	3	...	...	...	...	...	...
15 - 19	3	-	3	...	...	...	...	...	...
20 - 24	5	4	1	...	...	...	...	...	...
25 - 29	4	3	1	...	...	...	...	...	...
30 - 34	5	5	-	...	...	...	...	...	...
35 - 39	10	6	4	...	...	...	...	...	...

19. Deaths by age, sex and urban/rural residence: latest available year, 1997 - 2006
Décès selon l'âge, le sexe et la résidence, urbaine/rurale: dernière année disponible, 1997 - 2006 (continued - suite)

Continent, country or area, date, code and age (in years) / Continent, pays ou zone, date, code et âge (en années)	Total			Urban - Urbaine			Rural - Rurale		
	Both sexes Les deux sexes	Male Masculin	Female Féminin	Both sexes Les deux sexes	Male Masculin	Female Féminin	Both sexes Les deux sexes	Male Masculin	Female Féminin
OCEANIA - OCÉANIE									
American Samoa - Samoas américaines									
2006 (C)									
40 - 44	9	4	5	...	...	...	...	...	...
45 - 49	19	10	9	...	...	...	...	...	...
50 - 54	18	11	7	...	...	...	...	...	...
55 - 59	21	13	8	...	...	...	...	...	...
60 - 64	23	15	8	...	...	...	...	...	...
65 - 69	27	18	9	...	...	...	...	...	...
70 - 74	31	22	9	...	...	...	...	...	...
75 - 79	28	19	9	...	...	...	...	...	...
80 - 84	13	6	7	...	...	...	...	...	...
85 +	21	5	16	...	...	...	...	...	...
Australia - Australie									
2005 (+C)									
Total	130 714	67 241	63 473	84 311	42 585	41 726	46 403	24 656	21 747
0	1 302	714	588	858	459	399	444	255	189
1 - 4	243	139	104	132	71	61	111	68	43
5 - 9	145	86	59	86	57	29	59	29	30
10 - 14	141	81	60	83	47	36	58	34	24
15 - 19	497	347	150	291	209	82	206	138	68
20 - 24	812	612	200	491	369	122	321	243	78
25 - 29	864	644	220	527	403	124	337	241	96
30 - 34	1 141	814	327	723	522	201	418	292	126
35 - 39	1 364	895	469	800	527	273	564	368	196
40 - 44	2 059	1 313	746	1 245	792	453	814	521	293
45 - 49	2 813	1 759	1 054	1 724	1 054	670	1 089	705	384
50 - 54	3 796	2 352	1 444	2 369	1 413	956	1 427	939	488
55 - 59	5 356	3 385	1 971	3 414	2 159	1 255	1 942	1 226	716
60 - 64	6 669	4 167	2 502	4 017	2 496	1 521	2 652	1 671	981
65 - 69	8 843	5 606	3 237	5 501	3 449	2 052	3 342	2 157	1 185
70 - 74	11 885	7 244	4 641	7 448	4 462	2 986	4 437	2 782	1 655
75 - 79	18 197	10 597	7 600	11 532	6 575	4 957	6 665	4 022	2 643
80 - 84	23 264	11 752	11 512	15 348	7 699	7 649	7 916	4 053	3 863
85 - 89	20 855	8 597	12 258	13 794	5 719	8 075	7 061	2 878	4 183
90 - 94	14 651	4 774	9 877	9 920	3 177	6 743	4 731	1 597	3 134
95 - 99	4 916	1 210	3 706	3 385	824	2 561	1 531	386	1 145
100 +	876	141	735	622	102	521	253	39	214
Unknown - Inconnu	25	12	13	-	-	-	25	12	13
Fiji - Fidji									
2004 (+C)									
Total	5 628	3 150	2 478	...	...	...	...	...	...
0	316	180	136	...	...	...	...	...	...
1 - 4	83	53	30	...	...	...	...	...	...
5 - 9	47	27	20	...	...	...	...	...	...
10 - 14	51	24	27	...	...	...	...	...	...
15 - 19	100	61	39	...	...	...	...	...	...
20 - 24	103	58	45	...	...	...	...	...	...
25 - 29	116	71	45	...	...	...	...	...	...
30 - 34	124	64	60	...	...	...	...	...	...
35 - 39	140	89	51	...	...	...	...	...	...
40 - 44	247	138	109	...	...	...	...	...	...
45 - 49	371	232	139	...	...	...	...	...	...
50 - 54	463	267	196	...	...	...	...	...	...
55 - 59	527	321	206	...	...	...	...	...	...
60 - 64	641	366	275	...	...	...	...	...	...
65 - 69	569	323	246	...	...	...	...	...	...
70 - 74	597	311	286	...	...	...	...	...	...
75 - 79	414	219	195	...	...	...	...	...	...
80 - 84	361	191	170	...	...	...	...	...	...
85 - 89	223	97	126	...	...	...	...	...	...
90 - 94	81	40	41	...	...	...	...	...	...
95 +	54	18	36	...	...	...	...	...	...
Unknown - Inconnu	-	-	-	...	...	...	...	...	...

19. Deaths by age, sex and urban/rural residence: latest available year, 1997 - 2006

Décès selon l'âge, le sexe et la résidence, urbaine/rurale: dernière année disponible, 1997 - 2006 (continued - suite)

Continent, country or area, date, code and age (in years) / Continent, pays ou zone, date, code et âge (en années)	Total			Urban - Urbaine			Rural - Rurale		
	Both sexes Les deux sexes	Male Masculin	Female Féminin	Both sexes Les deux sexes	Male Masculin	Female Féminin	Both sexes Les deux sexes	Male Masculin	Female Féminin
OCEANIA - OCÉANIE									
Guam[46]									
2004 (C)									
Total....................	691	426	265	...	...	...	...	...	...
0.........................	42	25	17	...	...	...	...	...	...
1 - 4.....................	4	1	3	...	...	...	...	...	...
5 - 9.....................	3	3	-	...	...	...	...	...	...
10 - 14...................	5	3	2	...	...	...	...	...	...
15 - 19...................	13	9	4	...	...	...	...	...	...
20 - 24...................	16	12	4	...	...	...	...	...	...
25 - 29...................	12	7	5	...	...	...	...	...	...
30 - 34...................	20	16	4	...	...	...	...	...	...
35 - 39...................	19	17	2	...	...	...	...	...	...
40 - 44...................	39	30	9	...	...	...	...	...	...
45 - 49...................	37	24	13	...	...	...	...	...	...
50 - 54...................	52	40	12	...	...	...	...	...	...
55 - 59...................	60	36	24	...	...	...	...	...	...
60 - 64...................	56	29	27	...	...	...	...	...	...
65 - 69...................	59	32	27	...	...	...	...	...	...
70 - 74...................	65	40	25	...	...	...	...	...	...
75 - 79...................	77	47	30	...	...	...	...	...	...
80 - 84...................	53	31	22	...	...	...	...	...	...
85 +.....................	59	24	35	...	...	...	...	...	...
Marshall Islands - Îles Marshall									
2005 (+U)									
Total....................	302	166	136	...	...	...	...	...	...
0.........................	46	33	13	...	...	...	...	...	...
1 - 4.....................	19	8	11	...	...	...	...	...	...
5 - 9.....................	3	1	2	...	...	...	...	...	...
10 - 14...................	2	-	2	...	...	...	...	...	...
15 - 19...................	6	5	1	...	...	...	...	...	...
20 - 24...................	9	7	2	...	...	...	...	...	...
25 - 29...................	4	4	-	...	...	...	...	...	...
30 - 34...................	7	5	2	...	...	...	...	...	...
35 - 39...................	4	1	3	...	...	...	...	...	...
40 - 44...................	13	8	5	...	...	...	...	...	...
45 - 49...................	12	7	5	...	...	...	...	...	...
50 - 54...................	23	11	12	...	...	...	...	...	...
55 - 59...................	29	16	13	...	...	...	...	...	...
60 - 64...................	21	11	10	...	...	...	...	...	...
65 +.....................	104	49	55	...	...	...	...	...	...
Micronesia, Federated States of - Micronésie, États Fédérés de La									
2003 (U)									
Total....................	427	...	...	...	...	...	...	...	...
0.........................	21	...	...	...	...	...	...	...	...
1 - 4.....................	20	...	...	...	...	...	...	...	...
5 - 9.....................	8	...	...	...	...	...	...	...	...
10 - 14...................	4	...	...	...	...	...	...	...	...
15 - 19...................	14	...	...	...	...	...	...	...	...
20 - 24...................	8	...	...	...	...	...	...	...	...
25 - 29...................	13	...	...	...	...	...	...	...	...
30 - 34...................	6	...	...	...	...	...	...	...	...
35 - 39...................	10	...	...	...	...	...	...	...	...
40 - 44...................	19	...	...	...	...	...	...	...	...
45 - 49...................	21	...	...	...	...	...	...	...	...
50 - 54...................	47	...	...	...	...	...	...	...	...
55 - 59...................	33	...	...	...	...	...	...	...	...
60 - 64...................	32	...	...	...	...	...	...	...	...
65 - 69...................	50	...	...	...	...	...	...	...	...
70 +.....................	121	...	...	...	...	...	...	...	...

19. Deaths by age, sex and urban/rural residence: latest available year, 1997 - 2006
Décès selon l'âge, le sexe et la résidence, urbaine/rurale: dernière année disponible, 1997 - 2006 (continued - suite)

Continent, country or area, date, code and age (in years) / Continent, pays ou zone, date, code et âge (en années)	Total			Urban - Urbaine			Rural - Rurale		
	Both sexes Les deux sexes	Male Masculin	Female Féminin	Both sexes Les deux sexes	Male Masculin	Female Féminin	Both sexes Les deux sexes	Male Masculin	Female Féminin

OCEANIA - OCÉANIE

New Caledonia - Nouvelle-Calédonie
2003 (C)

Total	1 121	666	455	...	...	...	...	...	...
0	24	14	10	...	...	...	...	...	...
1 - 4	10	9	1	...	...	...	...	...	...
5 - 9	8	4	4	...	...	...	...	...	...
10 - 14	5	2	3	...	...	...	...	...	...
15 - 19	12	7	5	...	...	...	...	...	...
20 - 24	30	22	8	...	...	...	...	...	...
25 - 29	22	13	9	...	...	...	...	...	...
30 - 34	28	22	6	...	...	...	...	...	...
35 - 39	27	16	11	...	...	...	...	...	...
40 - 44	36	26	10	...	...	...	...	...	...
45 - 49	47	29	18	...	...	...	...	...	...
50 - 54	56	32	24	...	...	...	...	...	...
55 - 59	101	65	36	...	...	...	...	...	...
60 - 64	89	60	29	...	...	...	...	...	...
65 - 69	136	82	54	...	...	...	...	...	...
70 - 74	142	92	50	...	...	...	...	...	...
75 - 79	134	74	60	...	...	...	...	...	...
80 - 84	91	42	49	...	...	...	...	...	...
85 - 89	72	32	40	...	...	...	...	...	...
90 - 94	35	21	14	...	...	...	...	...	...
95 +	16	2	14	...	...	...	...	...	...

New Zealand - Nouvelle-Zélande[43]
2006 (+C)

Total	28 245	13 924	14 321	25 398[4]	12 223[4]	13 175[4]	2 711[4]	1 623[4]	1 088[4]
0	300	173	127	251[4]	143[4]	108[4]	33[4]	19[4]	14[4]
1 - 4	59	33	26	50[4]	31[4]	19[4]	9[4]	2[4]	7[4]
5 - 9	35	24	11	26[4]	16[4]	10[4]	9[4]	8[4]	1[4]
10 - 14	44	26	18	33[4]	19[4]	14[4]	11[4]	7[4]	4[4]
15 - 19	199	139	60	165[4]	113[4]	52[4]	32[4]	25[4]	7[4]
20 - 24	177	130	47	144[4]	104[4]	40[4]	32[4]	26[4]	6[4]
25 - 29	169	120	49	144[4]	101[4]	43[4]	21[4]	17[4]	4[4]
30 - 34	208	139	69	176[4]	116[4]	60[4]	28[4]	19[4]	9[4]
35 - 39	296	176	120	253[4]	145[4]	108[4]	39[4]	27[4]	12[4]
40 - 44	438	247	191	364[4]	199[4]	165[4]	70[4]	46[4]	24[4]
45 - 49	657	373	284	537[4]	296[4]	241[4]	112[4]	72[4]	40[4]
50 - 54	852	483	369	725[4]	405[4]	320[4]	122[4]	75[4]	47[4]
55 - 59	1 243	727	516	1 050[4]	611[4]	439[4]	189[4]	114[4]	75[4]
60 - 64	1 534	926	608	1 308[4]	780[4]	528[4]	217[4]	142[4]	75[4]
65 - 69	2 022	1 199	823	1 734[4]	1 019[4]	715[4]	277[4]	173[4]	104[4]
70 - 74	2 685	1 547	1 138	2 352[4]	1 333[4]	1 019[4]	323[4]	207[4]	116[4]
75 - 79	3 831	2 123	1 708	3 471[4]	1 891[4]	1 580[4]	345[4]	223[4]	122[4]
80 - 84	4 634	2 299	2 335	4 279[4]	2 077[4]	2 202[4]	344[4]	215[4]	129[4]
85 - 89	4 484	1 819	2 665	4 206[4]	1 691[4]	2 515[4]	265[4]	124[4]	141[4]
90 - 94	3 098	956	2 142	2 915[4]	885[4]	2 030[4]	175[4]	67[4]	108[4]
95 - 99	1 078	228	850	1 023[4]	213[4]	810[4]	48[4]	13[4]	35[4]
100 +	202	37	165	192[4]	35[4]	157[4]	10[4]	2[4]	8[4]

Northern Mariana Islands - Îles Mariannes septentrionales
2005 (U)

Total	188	107	81	...	...	...	...	...	...
0	5	1	4	...	...	...	...	...	...
1 - 4	4	3	1	...	...	...	...	...	...
5 - 9	-	-	-	...	...	...	...	...	...
10 - 14	3	2	1	...	...	...	...	...	...
15 - 19	1	-	1	...	...	...	...	...	...
20 - 24	3	2	1	...	...	...	...	...	...
25 - 29	10	3	7	...	...	...	...	...	...
30 - 34	11	9	2	...	...	...	...	...	...

19. Deaths by age, sex and urban/rural residence: latest available year, 1997 - 2006
Décès selon l'âge, le sexe et la résidence, urbaine/rurale: dernière année disponible, 1997 - 2006 (continued - suite)

Continent, country or area, date, code and age (in years) / Continent, pays ou zone, date, code et âge (en années)	Total			Urban - Urbaine			Rural - Rurale		
	Both sexes Les deux sexes	Male Masculin	Female Féminin	Both sexes Les deux sexes	Male Masculin	Female Féminin	Both sexes Les deux sexes	Male Masculin	Female Féminin
OCEANIA - OCÉANIE									
Northern Mariana Islands - Îles Mariannes septentrionales									
2005 (U)									
35 - 39	7	4	3	...	...	...	...	...	...
40 - 44	11	6	5	...	...	...	...	...	...
45 - 49	7	6	1	...	...	...	...	...	...
50 - 54	17	13	4	...	...	...	...	...	...
55 - 59	19	11	8	...	...	...	...	...	...
60 - 64	20	9	11	...	...	...	...	...	...
65 - 69	20	14	6	...	...	...	...	...	...
70 - 74	20	11	9	...	...	...	...	...	...
75 - 79	13	6	7	...	...	...	...	...	...
80 - 84	8	5	3	...	...	...	...	...	...
85 - 89	5	1	4	...	...	...	...	...	...
90 - 94	2	-	2	...	...	...	...	...	...
95 - 99	2	1	1	...	...	...	...	...	...
100 +	-	-	-	...	...	...	...	...	...
Palau - Palaos									
2003 (C)									
Total	136	79	57	...	...	...	...	...	...
0	3	1	2	...	...	...	...	...	...
1 - 14	5	4	1	...	...	...	...	...	...
15 - 24	7	4	3	...	...	...	...	...	...
25 - 44	17	12	5	...	...	...	...	...	...
45 - 64	33	29	4	...	...	...	...	...	...
65 +	71	29	42	...	...	...	...	...	...
Unknown - Inconnu	-	-	-	...	...	...	...	...	...
Tonga									
2000 (+C)									
Total	653	334	319	...	...	...	...	...	...
0	28	12	16	...	...	...	...	...	...
1 - 9	23	10	13	...	...	...	...	...	...
10 - 19	14	10	4	...	...	...	...	...	...
20 - 29	21	10	11	...	...	...	...	...	...
30 - 39	16	5	11	...	...	...	...	...	...
40 - 49	33	20	13	...	...	...	...	...	...
50 - 59	78	37	41	...	...	...	...	...	...
60 - 69	116	67	49	...	...	...	...	...	...
70 +	299	151	148	...	...	...	...	...	...
Unknown - Inconnu	25	12	13	...	...	...	...	...	...
Tuvalu									
2005 (U)									
Total	59	33	26	...	...	...	...	...	...
0	6	5	1	...	...	...	...	...	...
1 - 4	2	1	1	...	...	...	...	...	...
5 - 9	-	-	-	...	...	...	...	...	...
10 - 14	-	-	-	...	...	...	...	...	...
15 - 19	-	-	-	...	...	...	...	...	...
20 - 24	1	1	-	...	...	...	...	...	...
25 - 29	-	-	-	...	...	...	...	...	...
30 - 34	1	1	-	...	...	...	...	...	...
35 - 39	2	2	-	...	...	...	...	...	...
40 - 44	2	2	-	...	...	...	...	...	...
45 - 49	3	3	-	...	...	...	...	...	...
50 - 54	6	3	3	...	...	...	...	...	...
55 - 59	4	3	1	...	...	...	...	...	...
60 - 64	7	2	5	...	...	...	...	...	...
65 - 69	6	2	4	...	...	...	...	...	...
70 - 74	1	-	1	...	...	...	...	...	...
75 - 79	8	4	4	...	...	...	...	...	...
80 - 84	8	3	5	...	...	...	...	...	...
85 - 89	2	1	1	...	...	...	...	...	...

Continent, country or area, date, code and age (in years) / Continent, pays ou zone, date, code et âge (en années)	Total			Urban - Urbaine			Rural - Rurale		
	Both sexes Les deux sexes	Male Masculin	Female Féminin	Both sexes Les deux sexes	Male Masculin	Female Féminin	Both sexes Les deux sexes	Male Masculin	Female Féminin
OCEANIA - OCÉANIE									
Wallis and Futuna Islands - Îles Wallis et Futuna									
2006 (C)									
Total.....................	77	31	46	...	...	...	...	...	...
0..........................	-	-	-	...	...	...	...	...	...
1 - 4......................	-	-	-	...	...	...	...	...	...
5 - 9......................	1	-	1	...	...	...	...	...	...
10 - 14....................	-	-	-	...	...	...	...	...	...
15 - 19....................	2	2	-	...	...	...	...	...	...
20 - 24....................	2	2	-	...	...	...	...	...	...
25 - 29....................	1	1	-	...	...	...	...	...	...
30 - 34....................	1	-	1	...	...	...	...	...	...
35 - 39....................	-	-	-	...	...	...	...	...	...
40 - 44....................	4	2	2	...	...	...	...	...	...
45 - 49....................	-	-	-	...	...	...	...	...	...
50 - 54....................	-	-	-	...	...	...	...	...	...
55 - 59....................	2	1	1	...	...	...	...	...	...
60 - 64....................	13	5	8	...	...	...	...	...	...
65 - 69....................	11	2	9	...	...	...	...	...	...
70 - 74....................	8	3	5	...	...	...	...	...	...
75 - 79....................	11	4	7	...	...	...	...	...	...
80 - 84....................	7	3	4	...	...	...	...	...	...
85 - 89....................	10	4	6	...	...	...	...	...	...
90 - 94....................	4	2	2	...	...	...	...	...	...
95 +......................	-	-	-	...	...	...	...	...	...

FOOTNOTES - NOTES

Italics: estimates which are less reliable. - Italiques: estimations moins sûres.

*
Provisional. -
Données provisoires.

'Code' indicates the source of data, as follows:
C - Civil registration, estimated over 90% complete
U - Civil registration, estimated less than 90% complete
| - Other source, estimated reliable
+ - Data tabulated by date of registration rather than occurence.
... - Information not available

Le 'Code' indique la source des données, comme suit:
C - Registres de l'état civil considérés complets à 90 p. 100 au moins.
U - Registres de l'état civil qui ne sont pas considérés complets à 90 p. 100 au moins.
| - Autre source, considérée pas douteuses.
+ - Données exploitées selon la date de l'enregistrement et non la date de l'événement.
... - Information pas disponible.

[1] Excluding live-born infants who died before their birth was registered. For Algerian population only. - Non compris les enfants nés vivants décédés avant l'enregistrement de leur naissance. Pour la population algérienne seulement.
[2] For 2001, data refer to last twelve months preceding census in August 2001. - Pour 2001, les données se rapportent aux douze mois précédant le recensement d'août 2001.
[3] Based on the results of the population census. - D'après les résultats du recensement de la population.
[4] The total number includes 'Unknown residence', but the categories urban and rural do not. - Le nombre total inclue 'Résidence inconnue ', mais les catégories Urbain et Rural ne l'incluent pas.
[5] Data for 1997 refer to last twelve months preceding population and housing census of 1997. - Les données pour 1997 se réfèrent au douze mois précédant le recensement de population et de l'habitat de 1997.
[6] Deaths for 2001 refer to the period January-August 2001. - Le chiffre des décès de 2001 correspond à la période allant de janvier à août 2001.

[7] Figures for male and female categories do not add up to the total, since they do not include the category "Unknown". - La somme des chiffres indiqués pour les sexes masculin et féminin n'est pas égale au total parce qu'elle n'inclut pas la catégorie " inconnue ".
[8] Excluding live-born infants who died before their birth was registered. - Non compris les enfants nés vivants décédés avant l'enregistrement de leur naissance.
[9] Data are for 12 months preceding the census date. - Les données portent sur les 12 mois précédant la date du recensement.
[10] Source: World Health Organization. - Source : Organisation mondiale de la santé.
[11] Including Canadian residents temporarily in the United States, but excluding United States residents temporarily in Canada. - Y compris les résidents canadiens se trouvant temporairement aux Etats-Unis, mais ne comprenant pas les résidents des Etats-Unis se trouvant temporairement au Canada.
[12] Adjusted for undercoverage of infant deaths and sudden and violent deaths. - Ajusté pour la sous-estimation de la mortalité infantile, du nombre de morts soudaines et de morts violentes.
[13] Figures for male and female categories do not add up to the total, since they do not include the category "Unknown". The total number includes 'Unknown residence', but the categories urban and rural do not. - La somme des chiffres indiqués pour les sexes masculin et féminin n'est pas égale au total parce qu'elle n'inclut pas la catégorie " inconnue ". Le nombre total inclue 'Résidence inconnue ', mais les catégories Urbain et Rural ne l'incluent pas.
[14] Data refer to deaths of residents of the Netherlands Antilles (including those that died outside the Netherlands Antilles). Data exclude deaths by non-residents. - Ces données concernent les décès de résidents des Antilles néerlandaises (y compris ceux survenus hors des Antilles néerlandaises). Elles ne concernent pas les décès des non-résidents.
[15] Excluding Indian jungle population. - Non compris les Indiens de la jungle
[16] Excluding nomadic Indian tribes. - Non compris les tribus d'Indiens nomades.
[17] For 2001, data were collected from population census held on August 2002, referring to events in calendar year 2001. - Pour 2001, les données sont tirées du recensement de la population réalisé en août 2002, concernant des événements de l'année civile 2001.

[18] Data refer to registered deaths only. Excluding Indian jungle population. - Les données se rapportent aux décès enregistrés seulement. Non compris les Indiens de la jungle.

[19] The total number includes 'Unknown residence', but the categories urban and rural do not. The districts of Paramaribo and Wanica are considered urban areas, whereas the rest of the districts are considered more or less rural districts (areas). - Le nombre total inclue 'Résidence inconnue ', mais les catégories Urbain et Rural ne l'incluent pas. Les districts de Paramaribo et de Wanica sont considérés comme des zones urbaines, les autres districts étant considérés comme des zones rurales à divers degrés.

[20] Excluding infants born alive of less than 28 weeks' gestation, of less than 1 000 grams in weight and 35 centimeters in length, who die within seven days of birth. - Non compris les enfants nés vivants après moins de 28 semaines de gestations, pesant moins de 1 000 grammes, mesurant moins de 35 centimètres et décédés dans les sept jours qui ont suivi leur naissance.

[21] For 2005, data refer to last twelve months preceding census in May 2005. - Pour 2005, les données se rapportent aux douze mois précédant le recensement de mai 2005.

[22] For statistical purposes, the data for China do not include those for the Hong Kong Special Administrative Region (Hong Kong SAR), Macao Special Administrative Region (Macao SAR) and Taiwan province of China. - Pour la présentation des statistiques, les données pour la Chine ne comprennent pas la Région Administrative Spéciale de Hong Kong (Hong Kong RAS), la Région Administrative Spéciale de Macao (Macao RAS) et Taïwan province de Chine.

[23] Data refer to government controlled areas. - Les données se rapportent aux zones contrôlées par le Gouvernement.

[24] Including data for East Jerusalem and Israeli residents in certain other territories under occupation by Israeli military forces since June 1967. - Y compris les données pour Jérusalem-Est et les résidents israéliens dans certains autres territoires occupés depuis 1967 par les forces armées israéliennes.

[25] Data include 141 deaths abroad of Israeli residents who were out of the country for less than a year. - Y compris les décès à l'étranger de 141 résidents israéliens qui ont quitté le pays depuis moins d'un an.

[26] Data refer to Japanese nationals in Japan only. - Les données se raportent aux nationaux japonais au Japon seulement.

[27] Excluding alien armed forces, civilian aliens employed by armed forces, and foreign diplomatic personnel and their dependants. - Non compris les militaires étrangers, les civils étrangers employés par les forces armées ni le personnel diplomatique étranger et les membres de leur famille les accompagnant.

[28] Including Korean deaths abroad. - Y compris les décès de Coréens survenus à l'étranger.

[29] For 2001, data refer to last twelve months preceding census on June 2001. - Pour 2001, les données se rapportent aux douze mois précédant le recensement juin 2001.

[30] Data refer to the recorded events in Ministry of Health hospitals and health centres only. - Les données se rapportent aux faits d'état civil enregistrés dans les hôpitaux et les dispensaires du Ministère de la santé seulement.

[31] Data based on Pakistan Demographic Survey (PDS 2005). Excluding data for the Pakistan-held part of Jammu and Kashmir, the final status of which has not yet been determined. - Données extraites de l'enquête démographique effectuée par le Pakistan en 2005. Non compris les données concernant la partie du Jammu et Cachemire occupée par le Pakistan dont le statut définitif n'a pas été déterminé.

[32] Also included in Finland. - Comprise aussi dans Finlande.

[33] Including armed forces stationed outside the country, but excluding alien armed forces stationed in the area. - Y compris les militaires nationaux hors du pays, mais non compris les militaires étrangers en garnison sur le territoire.

[34] Excluding Faeroe Islands and Greenland shown separately, if available. - Non compris les Iles Féroé et le Gröenland, qui font l'objet de rubriques distinctes, si disponible.

[35] Including nationals temporarily outside the country. Including Aland Islands. - Y compris les nationaux se trouvant temporairement hors du pays. Y compris les Îles d'Åland.

[36] Including armed forces stationed outside the country. Excluding Overseas Departments, namely, French Guiana, Guadeloupe, Martinique and Reunion, shown separately, if available. - Y compris les militaires nationaux hors du pays. Non compris les départements d'outre mer, c'est-à-dire la Guyane française, la Guadeloupe, la Martinique et la Réunion, qui font l'objet de rubriques distinctes, si disponible.

[37] Urban/rural figures, excluding nationals outside the country. - Les chiffres urbaine/rurale, non compris les nationaux hors du pays.

[38] Total includes the data of foreigners, persons of unknown residence and homeless, but the categories urban and rural do not. - Total incluant les étrangers, les personnes de résidence inconnue et les sans-abri, ce qui n'est pas le cas pour les catégories urbaines et rurales.

[39] Events registered within one year of occurrence. - Evénements enregistrés dans l'année qui suit l'événement.

[40] Data do not include information for Transnistria and the municipality of Bender. Excluding infants born alive of less than 28 weeks' gestation, of less than 1 000 grams in weight and 35 centimeters in length, who die within seven days of birth. - Les données ne tiennent pas compte de l'information sur la Transnistria et la municipalité de Bender. Non compris les enfants nés vivants après moins de 28 semaines de gestations, pesant moins de 1 000 grammes, mesurant moins de 35 centimètres et décédés dans les sept jours qui ont suivi leur naissance.

[41] Including residents outside the country if listed in a Netherlands population register. - Y compris les résidents hors du pays, s'ils sont inscrits sur un registre de population néerlandais.

[42] Including residents temporarily outside the country. Excluding Svalbard and Jan Mayen Island shown separately, if available. - Y compris les résidents se trouvant temporairement hors du pays. Non compris Svalbard et Jan Mayen qui font l'objet de rubriques distinctes, si disponible.

[43] For resident population only. - Pour la population résidante seulement.

[44] Without data for Kosovo and Metohia. - Sans les données pour le Kosovo et Metohie.

[45] Excluding Channel Islands and Isle of Man, shown separately, if available. - Non compris les îles Anglo-Normandes et l'île de Man, qui font l'objet de rubriques distinctes, si disponible.

[46] Including United States military personnel, their dependants and contract employees. - Y compris les militaires des Etats-Unis, les membres de leur famille les accompagnant et les agents contractuels des Etats-Unis.

Table 20

Table 20 presents death rates by age, sex and urban/rural residence for the latest available year.

Description of variables: Age is defined as age at last birthday, that is, the difference between the date of birth and the date of the occurrence of the event, expressed in completed solar years. The age classification used in this table is the following: under 1 year, 1-4 years, 5-year age groups through 95-99, and 100 years or over.

The urban/rural classification of deaths is that provided by each country or area; it is presumed to be based on the national census definition of urban population that have been set forth at the end of the technical notes for table 6.

Rate computation: Death rates specific for age and sex are the annual number of deaths in each age-sex group (as shown in table 19) per 1 000 population in the same age-sex group.

Death rates by age, sex and urban/rural residence are the annual number of deaths that occurred in a specific age-sex-urban/rural group (as shown in table 19) per 1 000 population in the corresponding age-sex-urban/rural group (as shown in table 7). These rates are calculated by the Statistics Division of the United Nations.

Deaths at unknown age and the population of unknown age are excluded from age-specific rate calculations but are part of the death rate for all ages combined.

Death rates for infants under one year of age in this table differ from the infant mortality rates shown elsewhere, because the latter are computed per 1 000 live births rather than per 1 000 population.

The population used in computing the rates is estimated or enumerated distributions by age and sex. First priority was given to an estimate for the mid-point of the same year (as shown in table 7), second priority to census returns of the year to which the deaths referred and third priority to an estimate for some other point of time in the year.

Rates presented in this table have been limited to those for countries or areas having at least a total of 1 000 deaths in a given year. Moreover, rates specific for individual sub-categories that are based on 30 or fewer deaths are identified by the symbol (♦).

Reliability of data: Rates are not computed if data from civil registers of deaths are reported as incomplete (less than 90 per cent completeness) or of unknown completeness, and therefore deemed unreliable. Table 18 and the technical notes for that table provide more detailed information on the completeness of death registration. For more information about the quality of vital statistics, see section 4.2 of the Introduction.

Limitations: Rates shown in this table are subject to the same limitations that affect the corresponding frequencies and are set forth in the technical notes for table 19. These include differences in the completeness of registration, the treatment of infants who were born alive but died before the registration of their birth or within the first 24 hours of life, the method used to determine age at death and the quality of the reported information relating to age at death. In addition, some rates are based on deaths tabulated by date of registration and not by date of occurrence; these have been indicated with a plus sign (+).

The problem of obtaining precise correspondence between deaths (numerator) and population (denominator) as regards the inclusion or exclusion of armed forces, refugees, displaced persons and other special groups is particularly difficult where age-specific death rates are concerned. This is the case for Japan and Malta. For Japan, deaths refer to Japanese nationals only while the population include foreigners except foreign military and civilian personnel and their dependants stationed in the area. Similarly for Malta, deaths are for Maltese nationals only while the population include foreigners who hold work and resident permit and reside in the country. One should also note that male rates in the age range 20 to 40 years may be especially affected by this non-correspondence, and care should be exercised in using these rates for comparative purposes.

Even when deaths and population do correspond conceptually, comparability of the rates may be affected by abnormal conditions such as absence from the country or area of large numbers of young men in the military forces or working abroad as temporary workers. Death rates may appear high in the younger ages, simply because a large section of the able-bodied members of the age group, whose death rates under normal conditions might be less than the average for persons of their age, is not included.

Also, in a number of cases the rates shown here for all ages combined differ from crude death rates shown elsewhere, because in this table they are computed on the population for which an appropriate age-sex distribution was available, while the crude death rates shown elsewhere may utilize a different total population. The population by age and sex might refer to a census date within the year rather than to the mid-point, or it might be more or less inclusive as regards ethnic groups, armed forces and so forth. In a few instances, the difference is attributable to the fact that the rates in this table were computed on the mean population whereas the corresponding rates in other tables were computed on an estimate for 1 July.

The comparability of data by urban/rural residence is affected by the national definitions of urban and rural used in tabulating these data. It is assumed, in the absence of specific information to the contrary, that the definitions of urban and rural used in connection with the national population census were also used in the compilation of the vital statistics for each country or area. However, it cannot be excluded that, for a given country or area, different definitions of urban and rural are used for the vital statistics data and the population census data respectively. When known, the definitions of urban used in national population censuses are presented at the end of the technical notes for table 6. As discussed in detail in the technical notes for table 6, these definitions vary considerably from one country or area to another.

In addition to problems of comparability, vital rates classified by urban/rural residence are also subject to certain special types of bias. If, when calculating vital rates, different definitions of urban are used in connection with the vital events and the population data and if this results in a net difference between the numerator and denominator of the rate in the population at risk, then the vital rates would be biased. Urban/rural differentials in vital rates may also be affected by whether the vital events have been tabulated in terms of place of occurrence or place of usual residence. This problem is discussed in more detail in section 4.1.4.1 of the Introduction.

Earlier data: Death rates specific for age and sex have been shown for the latest available year in many of the issues of the Yearbook since the 1955 issue. Data included in this table update the series shown in the Yearbook and in the Special Supplements covering a period of years as follows:

Issue	Years Covered
Historical Supplement CD, 1997	1948 – 1997
1996	1987 - 1995
1992	1983 – 1992
1985	1976 – 1984
1980	1971 – 1979
Historical Supplement, 1979	1948 - 1977

Tableau 20

Le tableau 20 présente les taux de mortalité selon l'âge et le sexe et selon le lieu de résidence (zone urbaine ou rurale) correspondant à la dernière année disponible.

Description des variables : L'âge considéré est l'âge au dernier anniversaire, c'est-à-dire la différence entre la date de naissance et la date du décès, exprimée en années solaires révolues. La classification par âge est la suivante : moins d'un an, 1 à 4 ans, groupes quinquennaux jusqu'à 95-99 ans et 100 ans et plus.

La classification des décès selon le lieu de résidence (zone urbaine ou rurale) est celle qui a été communiquée par chaque pays ou zone ; on part du principe qu'elle repose sur les définitions de la population urbaine utilisées pour les recensements nationaux, qui sont reproduites à la fin des notes techniques du tableau 6.

Calcul des taux : les taux de mortalité selon l'âge et le sexe représentent le nombre annuel de décès survenus pour chaque sexe et chaque groupe d'âge (fréquences du tableau 19) pour 1 000 personnes du même groupe.

Les taux de mortalité selon l'âge, le sexe et le lieu de résidence (zone urbaine ou rurale) représentent le nombre annuel de décès survenus dans un groupe d'âge et de sexe donné parmi la population urbaine ou rurale (fréquences du tableau 19) pour 1 000 personnes du même groupe parmi la population urbaine ou rurale. Ces taux ont été calculés par la Division de statistique de l'ONU.

On n'a pas tenu compte des décès à un âge inconnu ni de la population d'âge inconnu, sauf dans les taux de mortalité pour tous les âges combinés.

Il convient de noter que, dans ce tableau, les taux de mortalité des groupes de moins d'un an sont différents des taux de mortalité infantile qui figurent dans d'autres tableaux, ces derniers ayant été établis pour 1 000 naissances vivantes et non pour 1 000 habitants.

Les chiffres de population utilisés pour le calcul des taux proviennent de dénombrements ou de répartitions estimatives de la population selon l'âge et le sexe. On a utilisé de préférence les estimations de la population au milieu de l'année considérée selon les chiffres du tableau 7 ; à défaut, on s'est contenté des données censitaires se rapportant à l'année des décès et, si ces données manquaient également, d'estimations établies à un autre moment de l'année.

Les taux présentés dans le tableau 20 ne se rapportent qu'aux pays ou zones où l'on a enregistré un total d'au moins 1 000 décès pendant l'année. Les taux relatifs à des sous-catégories, qui sont fondés sur 30 décès ou moins, sont signalés par le signe '♦'.

Fiabilité des données : on a choisi de ne pas faire figurer dans le tableau 20 des taux calculés à partir de données sur les décès issues de registres d'état civil qui sont déclarées incomplètes (degré d'exhaustivité inférieur à 90 p. 100) ou dont le degré d'exhaustivité n'est pas connu. Le tableau 18 et les notes techniques s'y rapportant présentent des renseignements plus détaillés sur le degré d'exhaustivité de l'enregistrement des décès. Pour plus de précisions sur la qualité des statistiques de l'état civil, voir la section 4.2 de l'introduction.

Insuffisance des données : les taux présentés dans le tableau 20 appellent les mêmes réserves que celles formulées à propos des fréquences correspondantes (voir à ce sujet les notes techniques se rapportant au tableau 19). Leurs imperfections tiennent notamment aux différences d'exhaustivité de l'enregistrement, au classement des enfants nés vivants mais décédés avant l'enregistrement de leur naissance ou dans les 24 heures qui ont suivi la naissance, à la méthode utilisée pour obtenir l'âge au moment du décès, et à la qualité des déclarations concernant l'âge au moment du décès. En outre, dans certains cas, les données relatives aux décès sont classées par date d'enregistrement et non par date de l'événement ; ces cas ont été signalés par le signe '+'.

S'agissant des taux de mortalité par âge, il est particulièrement difficile d'établir une correspondance exacte entre les décès (numérateur) et la population (dénominateur) du fait de l'inclusion ou de l'exclusion des militaires, des réfugiés, des personnes déplacées et d'autres groupes spéciaux. C'est le cas pour le Japon et Malte. Pour le Japon, les décès se rapportent aux seuls citoyens japonais alors que la population inclut les étrangers à l'exception des militaires étrangers et des personnels civils ainsi que leurs familles stationnés dans le pays. De même, pour Malte, les décès se rapportent aux nationaux alors que la population inclut les étrangers titulaires d'un permis de séjour et de travail qui résident dans le pays. Les taux de mortalité pour le sexe masculin dans les groupes d'âge de 20 à 40 ans peuvent être tout particulièrement influencés par ce manque de correspondance, et il importe d'être prudent quand on les utilise dans des comparaisons. Il convient d'ajouter que, même lorsque population et décès correspondent, la comparabilité des taux peut être compromise par des conditions anormales telles que l'absence du pays ou de la zone d'un grand nombre de jeunes gens qui sont sous les drapeaux ou qui travaillent à l'étranger comme travailleurs temporaires. Il arrive ainsi que les taux de mortalité paraissent élevés parmi les groupes les plus jeunes simplement parce que l'on en a exclu un grand nombre d'individus en bonne santé pour lesquels le taux de mortalité pourrait être, dans des conditions normales, inférieur à la moyenne observée pour les personnes du même âge.

De même, les taux indiqués pour tous les âges combinés diffèrent dans plusieurs cas des taux bruts de mortalité qui figurent dans d'autres tableaux, parce qu'ils se rapportent à une population pour laquelle on disposait d'une répartition par âge et par sexe appropriée, tandis que les taux bruts de mortalité indiqués ailleurs peuvent avoir été calculés sur la base d'un chiffre de population totale différent. Ainsi, il est possible que les chiffres de population par âge et par sexe proviennent d'un recensement effectué dans le courant de l'année et non au milieu de l'année, et qu'ils se différencient des autres chiffres de population en excluant ou en incluant certains groupes ethniques, les militaires, etc. Quelquefois, la différence tient à ce que les taux du tableau 20 ont été calculés sur la base de la population moyenne, alors que les taux correspondants des autres tableaux reposent sur une estimation au 1er juillet. Les écarts de cet ordre sont insignifiants, mais il n'en a pas été tenu compte dans le tableau.

La comparabilité des données selon le lieu de résidence (zone urbaine ou rurale) peut être limitée par les définitions nationales des termes « urbain » et « rural » utilisées pour le classement de ces données. En l'absence d'indications contraires, on a supposé que les mêmes définitions avaient servi pour le recensement national de la population et pour l'établissement des statistiques de l'état civil pour chaque pays ou zone. Toutefois, il n'est pas exclu que, pour une zone ou un pays donné, des définitions différentes aient été retenues. Les définitions du terme « urbain » utilisées pour les recensements nationaux de population ont été présentées à la fin du tableau 6 lorsqu'elles étaient connues. Comme on l'a précisé dans les notes techniques relatives au tableau 6, ces définitions varient considérablement d'un pays ou d'une zone à l'autre.

Outre les problèmes de comparabilité, les taux démographiques classés selon le lieu de résidence (zone urbaine ou rurale) sont également sujets à des distorsions particulières. Si l'on utilise des définitions différentes du terme « urbain » pour classer les faits d'état civil et les données relatives à la population lors du calcul des taux et qu'il en résulte une différence nette entre le numérateur et le dénominateur pour le taux de la population exposée au risque, les taux démographiques s'en trouveront faussés. La différence entre ces taux pour les zones urbaines et rurales pourra aussi être faussée selon que les faits d'état civil auront été classés d'après le lieu où ils se sont produits ou d'après le lieu de résidence habituel.

Ce problème est examiné plus en détail à la section 4.1.4.1 de l'introduction.

Données publiées antérieurement : un certain nombre d'éditions de l'*Annuaire* parues depuis 1955 présentent les statistiques les plus récentes dont on disposait à l'époque sur les taux de mortalité selon l'âge et le sexe. Les données du tableau 20 actualisent celles qui figuraient dans les éditions de l'*Annuaire démographique* et dans les *Suppléments spéciaux* qui portaient sur les périodes suivantes :

Éditions	Années considérées
Supplément historique (CD-ROM), 1997	1948 – 1997
1996	1987 - 1995
1992	1983 – 1992
1985	1976 – 1984
1980	1971 – 1979
Supplément rétrospectif, 1979	1948 - 1977

20. Death rates specific for age, sex and urban/rural residence: latest available year, 1997 - 2006
Taux de mortalité selon l'âge, le sexe et la résidence, urbaine/rurale: dernière année disponible, 1997 - 2006

Continent, country or area, date, code and age (in years) / Continent, pays ou zone, date, code et âge (en années)	Total			Urban - Urbaine			Rural - Rurale		
	Both sexes Les deux sexes	Male Masculin	Female Féminin	Both sexes Les deux sexes	Male Masculin	Female Féminin	Both sexes Les deux sexes	Male Masculin	Female Féminin

AFRICA - AFRIQUE

Botswana[1]
2001 (|)

Total	12.4	13.3	11.6	11.0	12.1	10.0	14.0	14.5	13.4
0 - 4	14.1	14.7	13.5	13.3	13.7	12.9	14.9	15.7	14.1
0	36.8	37.5	36.1	...	...	...	...	...	...
1 - 4	7.8	8.3	7.2	...	...	...	...	...	...
5 - 9	2.3	2.4	2.2	2.1	2.5	1.8	2.5	2.4	2.7
10 - 14	1.2	1.1	1.3	1.1	1.1	1.2	1.2	1.1	1.4
15 - 19	1.9	1.8	2.0	1.7	1.8	1.7	2.1	1.8	2.4
20 - 24	6.4	4.8	7.8	4.7	3.9	5.4	9.5	6.5	12.4
25 - 29	14.2	11.8	16.4	10.8	9.4	12.0	20.8	16.4	25.2
30 - 34	20.9	22.5	19.4	16.4	17.7	15.1	29.2	31.2	27.3
35 - 39	21.4	25.4	17.9	16.9	19.6	14.5	28.6	35.0	23.3
40 - 44	20.9	25.8	16.7	18.6	22.5	15.0	24.2	31.0	18.9
45 - 49	21.0	27.5	15.3	19.9	25.0	15.3	22.4	30.9	15.4
50 - 54	19.0	24.5	14.0	18.3	22.4	14.3	19.8	26.9	13.7
55 - 59	20.1	26.5	14.3	20.9	27.5	14.9	19.4	25.6	13.8
60 - 64	22.3	28.9	16.5	25.3	35.3	17.2	20.0	24.3	16.0
65 - 69	26.4	33.7	20.8	29.0	35.6	24.5	24.6	32.4	18.0
70 - 74	28.4	36.2	22.8	32.2	43.2	25.6	26.1	32.6	20.8
75 +	60.1	73.2	51.6	70.4	92.8	58.2	53.4	62.5	46.9

Egypt - Égypte
1999 (C)

Total	6.4	6.8	6.0	...	...	...	...	...	...
0	34.3	35.4	33.2	...	...	...	...	...	...
1 - 4	2.4	2.4	2.4	...	...	...	...	...	...
5 - 9	0.7	0.8	0.6	...	...	...	...	...	...
10 - 14	0.6	0.7	0.6	...	...	...	...	...	...
15 - 19	0.8	1.0	0.7	...	...	...	...	...	...
20 - 24	1.2	1.4	0.9	...	...	...	...	...	...
25 - 29	1.2	1.6	0.9	...	...	...	...	...	...
30 - 34	1.4	1.8	1.1	...	...	...	...	...	...
35 - 39	2.1	2.6	1.6	...	...	...	...	...	...
40 - 44	3.3	4.2	2.3	...	...	...	...	...	...
45 - 49	5.8	7.3	4.3	...	...	...	...	...	...
50 - 54	10.3	12.9	7.8	...	...	...	...	...	...
55 - 59	15.5	17.9	12.7	...	...	...	...	...	...
60 - 64	22.9	26.1	19.6	...	...	...	...	...	...
65 - 69	43.1	44.4	41.5	...	...	...	...	...	...
70 - 74	71.3	72.7	69.7	...	...	...	...	...	...
75 +	199.5	175.9	224.8	...	...	...	...	...	...

Malawi[2]
1998 (|)

Total	20.9	23.4	18.6	15.5	16.7	14.1	21.9	24.6	19.3
0	122.0	136.9	107.4	106.9	120.9	92.9	124.3	139.3	109.6
1 - 4	46.4	51.2	41.6	37.2	41.4	33.1	47.7	52.7	42.9
5 - 9	11.6	12.9	10.4	8.9	10.3	7.5	12.0	13.2	10.8
10 - 14	7.8	7.9	7.8	4.4	5.2	3.8	8.4	8.3	8.5
15 - 19	6.6	6.5	6.6	3.7	3.8	3.7	7.1	7.0	7.2
20 - 24	12.0	16.0	8.8	6.7	7.0	6.4	13.2	18.3	9.3
25 - 29	11.7	12.3	11.1	7.7	6.4	9.3	12.7	14.0	11.5
30 - 34	14.6	14.8	14.5	11.1	10.2	12.3	15.4	15.9	14.9
35 - 39	14.5	15.4	13.7	12.9	12.9	12.9	14.8	15.9	13.8
40 - 44	17.6	20.6	14.5	16.3	17.5	14.6	17.8	21.2	14.5
45 - 49	16.9	22.3	11.6	15.2	16.7	12.9	17.2	23.2	11.5
50 - 54	16.4	18.0	12.8	18.6	20.4	15.8	15.0	17.6	12.5
55 - 59	22.1	19.3	25.0	22.5	21.8	23.5	22.1	10.1	25.1
60 - 64	19.1	22.4	16.1	24.9	25.4	24.1	18.7	22.1	15.6
65 - 69	19.3	19.1	19.5	20.0	21.3	18.4	19.3	19.0	19.6
70 - 74	22.7	30.0	16.5	26.5	31.6	21.7	22.5	29.9	16.2
75 - 79	24.4	29.3	19.7	35.4	43.0	27.6	23.9	28.6	19.3
80 - 84	33.2	41.1	26.8	46.7	59.6	36.5	32.6	40.3	26.4
85 +	51.7	60.6	44.1	89.6	104.8	77.6	50.1	58.8	42.6

20. Death rates specific for age, sex and urban/rural residence: latest available year, 1997 - 2006
Taux de mortalité selon l'âge, le sexe et la résidence, urbaine/rurale: dernière année disponible, 1997 - 2006 (continued - suite)

Continent, country or area, date, code and age (in years) / Continent, pays ou zone, date, code et âge (en années)	Total			Urban - Urbaine			Rural - Rurale		
	Both sexes Les deux sexes	Male Masculin	Female Féminin	Both sexes Les deux sexes	Male Masculin	Female Féminin	Both sexes Les deux sexes	Male Masculin	Female Féminin

AFRICA - AFRIQUE

Mauritius - Maurice
2006 (+C)

Total	7.3	8.1	6.5	...	...	...	...	...	...
0 - 4	3.2	3.5	2.8	...	...	...	...	...	...
5 - 9	◆0.2	◆0.3	◆0.2	...	...	...	...	...	...
10 - 14	◆0.3	◆0.3	◆0.3	...	...	...	...	...	...
15 - 19	0.6	0.7	◆0.5	...	...	...	...	...	...
20 - 24	0.9	1.1	0.7	...	...	...	...	...	...
25 - 29	1.1	1.6	◆0.5	...	...	...	...	...	...
30 - 34	1.4	2.2	0.7	...	...	...	...	...	...
35 - 39	2.5	3.5	1.6	...	...	...	...	...	...
40 - 44	3.5	5.0	2.0	...	...	...	...	...	...
45 - 49	5.0	7.1	3.0	...	...	...	...	...	...
50 - 54	7.9	10.2	5.7	...	...	...	...	...	...
55 - 59	11.8	15.5	8.5	...	...	...	...	...	...
60 - 64	20.2	26.4	14.8	...	...	...	...	...	...
65 - 69	30.0	38.6	23.0	...	...	...	...	...	...
70 - 74	44.5	58.8	33.7	...	...	...	...	...	...
75 - 79	69.5	93.4	53.8	...	...	...	...	...	...
80 - 84	101.9	115.4	94.0	...	...	...	...	...	...
85 +	218.8	262.4	201.8	...	...	...	...	...	...

Mozambique[3]
1997 (I)

Total	25.2	28.2	22.5	15.9	17.7	14.1	29.1	32.8	25.8
0	186.7	205.1	168.9	119.1	132.8	105.6	210.4	230.7	190.8
1 - 4	56.0	61.2	51.0	29.1	31.6	26.5	65.2	71.2	59.3
5 - 9	14.3	15.3	13.2	6.9	7.8	6.1	17.1	18.2	16.0
10 - 14	8.2	8.6	7.7	4.0	4.4	3.6	10.2	10.5	9.8
15 - 19	7.5	7.6	7.3	4.6	4.8	4.5	9.0	9.3	8.7
20 - 24	7.3	7.7	6.9	5.8	6.1	5.6	7.9	8.5	7.5
25 - 29	8.2	9.1	7.5	7.5	8.6	6.6	8.5	9.4	7.8
30 - 34	9.8	11.2	8.5	8.8	10.5	7.1	10.3	11.6	9.2
35 - 39	10.2	11.8	8.8	9.5	10.7	8.2	10.5	12.4	9.0
40 - 44	12.7	15.2	10.5	12.5	14.2	10.5	12.8	15.6	10.5
45 - 49	13.4	16.3	10.7	15.2	18.0	12.2	12.7	15.6	10.2
50 - 54	18.9	23.6	14.9	22.9	27.0	18.8	17.6	22.4	13.8
55 - 59	15.8	19.1	12.7	19.4	22.8	15.8	14.7	17.9	11.8
60 - 64	32.8	38.3	27.8	40.4	46.7	34.4	30.4	35.6	25.7
65 - 69	25.5	29.5	21.8	36.1	44.9	28.8	22.6	25.6	19.9
70 - 74	51.1	61.1	41.7	71.8	89.6	57.5	45.3	53.9	36.9
75 - 79	40.8	46.2	35.5	63.2	82.8	48.7	35.2	38.6	31.7
80 +	98.3	110.3	87.4	143.7	184.7	116.7	88.2	97.0	79.8

Namibia - Namibie[4]
2001 (I)

Total	13.7	13.9[5]	12.9[5]	10.8	11.2[5]	10.5[5]	15.1	15.4[5]	14.0[5]
0 - 4	19.2	18.2[5]	19.3[5]	16.1	14.5[5]	17.1[5]	20.4	19.6[5]	20.2[5]
5 - 9	3.8	3.8[5]	3.6[5]	2.9	3.1[5]	2.7[5]	4.1	4.0[5]	3.8[5]
10 - 14	2.2	2.2[5]	2.2[5]	2.0	1.9[5]	2.0[5]	2.3	2.3[5]	2.2[5]
15 - 19	3.3	3.2[5]	3.2[5]	3.1	3.2[5]	2.9[5]	3.3	3.2[5]	3.3[5]
20 - 24	7.1	5.7[5]	8.4[5]	4.7	4.3[5]	5.1[5]	8.7	6.6[5]	10.7[5]
25 - 29	11.9	10.8[5]	12.9[5]	6.8	6.1[5]	7.5[5]	16.7	15.4[5]	17.8[5]
30 - 34	17.1	18.0[5]	16.1[5]	9.3	9.3[5]	9.3[5]	24.7	27.5[5]	22.0[5]
35 - 39	19.1	22.2[5]	16.3[5]	11.5	12.3[5]	10.7[5]	26.1	33.1[5]	20.7[5]
40 - 44	18.5	22.0[5]	15.4[5]	12.2	13.0[5]	11.5[5]	23.6	31.0[5]	18.1[5]
45 - 49	19.0	22.6[5]	15.7[5]	13.7	14.3[5]	13.0[5]	22.7	29.9[5]	17.3[5]
50 - 54	18.1	24.9[5]	12.3[5]	17.2	19.8[5]	14.1[5]	18.6	28.5[5]	11.6[5]
55 - 59	19.9	25.2[5]	15.0[5]	19.1	20.5[5]	17.4[5]	20.2	27.8[5]	14.1[5]
60 - 64	22.1	27.7[5]	16.7[5]	28.7	32.7[5]	24.3[5]	20.0	25.8[5]	14.5[5]
65 - 69	22.8	27.2[5]	18.8[5]	29.3	34.3[5]	24.1[5]	21.0	25.1[5]	17.4[5]
70 - 74	33.1	43.5[5]	25.3[5]	54.8	61.8[5]	48.4[5]	28.7	39.6[5]	20.7[5]
75 - 79	35.7	41.7[5]	30.2[5]	58.1	66.5[5]	49.9[5]	31.5	36.7[5]	26.7[5]
80 - 84	39.0	42.5[5]	35.3[5]	79.3	79.4[5]	78.3[5]	33.2	37.2[5]	29.1[5]
85 - 89	66.8	79.7[5]	56.0[5]	94.6	117.3[5]	79.1[5]	60.7	72.1[5]	50.7[5]

560

20. Death rates specific for age, sex and urban/rural residence: latest available year, 1997 - 2006
Taux de mortalité selon l'âge, le sexe et la résidence, urbaine/rurale: dernière année disponible, 1997 - 2006 (continued - suite)

Continent, country or area, date, code and age (in years) / Continent, pays ou zone, date, code et âge (en annèes)	Total			Urban - Urbaine			Rural - Rurale		
	Both sexes Les deux sexes	Male Masculin	Female Féminin	Both sexes Les deux sexes	Male Masculin	Female Féminin	Both sexes Les deux sexes	Male Masculin	Female Féminin
AFRICA - AFRIQUE									
Namibia - Namibie[4]									
2001 (I)									
90 - 94	96.3	110.0[5]	84.8[5]	133.0	♦144.7[5]	♦125.0[5]	89.9	103.2[5]	78.3[5]
95 +	137.5	146.0[5]	133.3[5]	198.5	♦207.2[5]	♦192.1[5]	131.0	137.4[5]	128.0[5]
Réunion[6]									
1999 (C)									
Total	5.4	6.5	4.4	...	...	...	...	...	...
0	35.7	40.1	31.4	...	...	...	...	...	...
1 - 4	♦0.5	♦0.6	♦0.4	...	...	...	...	...	...
5 - 9	♦0.2	♦0.2	♦0.1	...	...	...	...	...	...
10 - 14	♦0.3	♦0.3	♦0.3	...	...	...	...	...	...
15 - 19	0.5	♦0.9	♦0.2	...	...	...	...	...	...
20 - 24	0.9	1.6	♦0.3	...	...	...	...	...	...
25 - 29	1.0	1.3	♦0.6	...	...	...	...	...	...
30 - 34	1.6	2.3	♦0.9	...	...	...	...	...	...
35 - 39	1.5	2.4	♦0.7	...	...	...	...	...	...
40 - 44	3.2	4.8	1.5	...	...	...	...	...	...
45 - 49	4.7	6.7	2.7	...	...	...	...	...	...
50 - 54	7.3	11.1	3.4	...	...	...	...	...	...
55 - 59	9.9	14.6	5.3	...	...	...	...	...	...
60 - 64	14.8	20.5	9.6	...	...	...	...	...	...
65 - 69	21.0	29.1	14.1	...	...	...	...	...	...
70 - 74	31.5	45.8	20.4	...	...	...	...	...	...
75 - 79	46.6	64.2	34.9	...	...	...	...	...	...
80 - 84	77.9	106.5	63.3	...	...	...	...	...	...
85 - 89	108.9	134.4	98.2	...	...	...	...	...	...
90 - 94	160.1	183.5	151.5	...	...	...	...	...	...
95 - 99	180.8	♦123.7	203.3	...	...	...	...	...	...
100 +	♦321.4	♦400.0	♦304.3	...	...	...	...	...	...
Swaziland[3]									
1997 (I)									
Total	9.1	10.7	7.7	6.4	7.1	5.7	9.9	11.9	8.3
0 - 4	15.0	15.8	14.2	12.1	13.5	10.8	15.6	16.3	14.9
5 - 9	1.4	1.5	1.2	♦1.3	♦1.4	♦1.2	1.4	1.5	1.2
10 - 14	1.0	1.1	1.0	♦1.0	♦1.2	♦0.9	1.0	1.1	1.0
15 - 19	2.3	2.2	2.3	1.7	♦1.9	♦1.6	2.5	2.3	2.6
20 - 24	5.3	5.1	5.5	3.2	3.0	3.3	6.4	6.2	6.6
25 - 29	8.9	10.5	7.5	4.5	4.9	4.1	11.3	14.5	9.2
30 - 34	11.1	14.6	8.5	5.4	5.8	4.9	14.1	21.0	10.0
35 - 39	11.5	16.0	8.2	6.3	6.2	6.4	14.1	22.5	8.9
40 - 44	13.8	19.1	9.3	7.8	8.8	6.4	16.5	25.4	10.3
45 - 49	14.3	19.8	9.2	9.4	9.7	9.0	16.2	25.3	9.3
50 - 54	18.8	25.4	13.2	13.6	14.1	♦12.8	20.6	30.6	13.3
55 - 59	20.0	26.8	13.4	17.0	17.6	♦16.2	20.8	30.1	12.9
60 - 64	26.3	37.5	17.0	21.3	♦19.3	♦23.8	27.4	42.2	15.9
65 - 69	30.0	42.0	20.0	32.1	43.7	♦19.0	29.7	41.7	20.1
70 - 74	43.1	64.6	28.8	53.5	♦64.1	♦44.9	41.9	64.7	27.1
75 +	63.1	72.9	56.7	91.3	83.8	97.7	60.3	71.6	53.1
Zimbabwe[7]									
2002 (I)									
Total	17.2	18.4	16.1	12.5	13.5	11.6	19.7	21.1	18.4
0	69.6	75.8	63.3	57.5	62.6	52.4	75.9	82.8	69.1
1 - 4	12.2	13.0	11.3	8.3	9.2	7.4	13.9	14.7	13.1
5 - 9	3.4	3.7	3.1	2.7	3.1	2.4	3.6	3.9	3.4
10 - 14	2.4	2.6	2.2	2.3	2.7	2.0	2.4	2.5	2.2
15 - 19	2.8	2.4	3.1	1.8	1.9	1.8	3.3	2.7	3.9
20 - 24	7.9	6.1	9.4	4.2	3.4	4.8	11.1	8.4	13.3
25 - 29	17.6	14.6	20.4	9.4	7.4	11.5	25.2	22.2	27.7
30 - 34	29.3	27.8	30.7	16.7	15.1	18.6	40.6	41.4	39.8
35 - 39	38.9	43.2	35.1	25.0	26.1	23.7	49.8	59.9	42.5
40 - 44	35.3	44.2	28.0	25.1	27.9	22.1	41.7	57.6	31.0
45 - 49	33.6	41.8	26.6	25.9	28.3	22.9	38.0	51.7	28.2
50 - 54	29.4	39.3	22.0	26.9	28.2	25.3	30.4	46.0	21.1
55 - 59	29.5	39.2	21.1	28.0	30.7	24.6	30.1	43.1	20.1
60 - 64	30.5	38.6	22.7	33.1	37.0	28.4	29.7	39.2	21.4

20. Death rates specific for age, sex and urban/rural residence: latest available year, 1997 - 2006
Taux de mortalité selon l'âge, le sexe et la résidence, urbaine/rurale: dernière année disponible, 1997 - 2006 (continued - suite)

Continent, country or area, date, code and age (in years) / Continent, pays ou zone, date, code et âge (en années)	Total			Urban - Urbaine			Rural - Rurale		
	Both sexes Les deux sexes	Male Masculin	Female Féminin	Both sexes Les deux sexes	Male Masculin	Female Féminin	Both sexes Les deux sexes	Male Masculin	Female Féminin
AFRICA - AFRIQUE									
Zimbabwe[7]									
2002 (I)									
65 - 69	34.1	41.7	26.9	39.3	44.0	34.0	32.8	41.1	25.2
70 - 74	37.8	46.6	29.3	46.8	55.4	37.6	36.0	44.7	27.7
75 +	35.9	42.2	31.0	86.5	102.9	73.1	69.2	81.1	60.1
AMERICA, NORTH - AMÉRIQUE DU NORD									
Bahamas									
2000 (C)									
Total	5.4	6.1	4.7	...	...	...	...	...	...
0	8.8	♦8.9	♦8.7	...	...	...	...	...	...
1 - 4	♦0.8	♦0.9	♦0.8	...	...	...	...	...	...
5 - 9	♦0.4	♦0.6	♦0.3	...	...	...	...	...	...
10 - 14	♦0.4	♦0.4	♦0.4	...	...	...	...	...	...
15 - 19	♦0.6	♦0.9	♦0.3	...	...	...	...	...	...
20 - 24	1.6	♦2.1	♦1.1	...	...	...	...	...	...
25 - 29	2.9	3.3	2.5	...	...	...	...	...	...
30 - 34	2.9	3.7	♦2.2	...	...	...	...	...	...
35 - 39	4.1	5.5	2.8	...	...	...	...	...	...
40 - 44	5.1	7.2	3.3	...	...	...	...	...	...
45 - 49	6.3	8.1	4.5	...	...	...	...	...	...
50 - 54	8.4	11.3	5.8	...	...	...	...	...	...
55 - 59	10.5	14.3	7.1	...	...	...	...	...	...
60 - 64	14.2	18.1	10.8	...	...	...	...	...	...
65 - 69	22.2	27.2	18.1	...	...	...	...	...	...
70 - 74	29.2	33.7	26.0	...	...	...	...	...	...
75 - 79	43.6	50.0	39.3	...	...	...	...	...	...
80 - 84	71.4	72.8	70.5	...	...	...	...	...	...
85 - 89	102.8	146.8	82.1	...	...	...	...	...	...
90 +	184.0	248.2	156.1	...	...	...	...	...	...
Canada[8]									
2005 (C)									
Total	7.1	7.3	7.0	...	...	...	...	...	...
0	5.5	6.0	5.1	...	...	...	...	...	...
1 - 4	0.2	0.2	0.2	...	...	...	...	...	...
5 - 9	0.1	0.1	0.1	...	...	...	...	...	...
10 - 14	0.1	0.2	0.1	...	...	...	...	...	...
15 - 19	0.5	0.6	0.3	...	...	...	...	...	...
20 - 24	0.6	0.8	0.3	...	...	...	...	...	...
25 - 29	0.6	0.8	0.3	...	...	...	...	...	...
30 - 34	0.7	0.9	0.5	...	...	...	...	...	...
35 - 39	0.9	1.2	0.7	...	...	...	...	...	...
40 - 44	1.4	1.8	1.1	...	...	...	...	...	...
45 - 49	2.2	2.7	1.8	...	...	...	...	...	...
50 - 54	3.4	4.2	2.7	...	...	...	...	...	...
55 - 59	5.4	6.7	4.1	...	...	...	...	...	...
60 - 64	8.8	10.8	6.8	...	...	...	...	...	...
65 - 69	13.7	17.3	10.4	...	...	...	...	...	...
70 - 74	22.5	28.2	17.5	...	...	...	...	...	...
75 - 79	36.7	46.0	29.4	...	...	...	...	...	...
80 - 84	61.5	77.4	51.5	...	...	...	...	...	...
85 - 89	106.3	131.6	93.8	...	...	...	...	...	...
90 +	201.4	227.1	192.2	...	...	...	...	...	...
Costa Rica									
2006 (C)									
Total	3.9	4.5	3.2	...	...	...	...	...	...
0 - 4	2.3	2.6	2.1	...	...	...	...	...	...
5 - 9	0.2	0.3	0.2	...	...	...	...	...	...
10 - 14	0.2	0.3	0.2	...	...	...	...	...	...
15 - 19	0.5	0.7	0.3	...	...	...	...	...	...
20 - 24	0.8	1.2	0.4	...	...	...	...	...	...
25 - 29	1.1	1.8	0.5	...	...	...	...	...	...

20. Death rates specific for age, sex and urban/rural residence: latest available year, 1997 - 2006
Taux de mortalité selon l'âge, le sexe et la résidence, urbaine/rurale: dernière année disponible, 1997 - 2006 (continued - suite)

Continent, country or area, date, code and age (in years) / Continent, pays ou zone, date, code et âge (en années)	Total			Urban - Urbaine			Rural - Rurale		
	Both sexes Les deux sexes	Male Masculin	Female Féminin	Both sexes Les deux sexes	Male Masculin	Female Féminin	Both sexes Les deux sexes	Male Masculin	Female Féminin
AMERICA, NORTH - AMÉRIQUE DU NORD									
Costa Rica									
2006 (C)									
30 - 39	1.3	1.9	0.7	...	...	...	...	...	...
40 - 49	2.2	2.9	1.5	...	...	...	...	...	...
50 - 59	4.5	5.9	3.4	...	...	...	...	...	...
60 - 69	11.7	15.1	8.7	...	...	...	...	...	...
70 +	44.6	51.4	38.9	...	...	...	...	...	...
Cuba									
2005 (C)									
Total	7.5	8.1	6.9	8.2	8.9	7.6	5.4	6.1	4.7
0	6.1	6.5	5.6	6.5	7.0	6.0	4.9	5.1	4.6
1 - 4	0.4	0.4	0.4	0.4	0.5	0.4	0.3	0.4	♦0.3
5 - 9	0.2	0.3	0.1	0.2	0.3	0.1	0.2	♦0.2	♦0.1
10 - 14	0.3	0.3	0.2	0.3	0.3	0.2	0.2	♦0.3	♦0.2
15 - 19	0.5	0.6	0.4	0.5	0.6	0.4	0.4	0.5	0.3
20 - 24	0.7	0.9	0.5	0.7	1.0	0.5	0.5	0.7	0.4
25 - 29	0.8	1.1	0.6	0.9	1.2	0.6	0.6	0.8	0.5
30 - 34	0.9	1.2	0.6	1.0	1.3	0.7	0.9	1.1	0.6
35 - 39	1.4	1.7	1.0	1.4	1.8	1.0	1.2	1.3	1.0
40 - 44	2.0	2.4	1.5	2.1	2.6	1.6	1.6	1.8	1.4
45 - 49	3.4	4.2	2.6	3.6	4.5	2.7	2.7	3.1	2.4
50 - 54	5.2	6.3	4.1	5.5	6.9	4.2	4.0	4.4	3.6
55 - 59	8.0	9.8	6.3	8.5	10.7	6.5	6.3	6.9	5.6
60 - 64	12.0	14.5	9.6	12.9	16.2	10.0	8.6	9.4	7.6
65 - 69	10.3	12.3	8.4	11.2	14.0	8.7	7.4	7.6	7.2
70 - 74	23.1	28.3	18.7	24.7	32.0	19.1	17.8	18.7	16.4
75 +	305.6	354.6	269.1	325.5	398.2	279.3	237.5	251.0	220.1
El Salvador									
2003 (C)									
Total	4.4	5.2	3.7	5.3	6.3	4.4	3.1	3.7	2.5
0	8.1	9.0	7.2	9.7	10.7	8.7	6.3	7.1	5.5
1 - 4	0.7	0.8	0.7	0.8	0.9	0.7	0.6	0.7	0.6
5 - 9	0.3	0.3	0.2	0.3	0.3	0.3	0.2	0.3	♦0.2
10 - 14	0.4	0.4	0.3	0.4	0.5	0.4	0.3	0.3	♦0.2
15 - 19	1.1	1.7	0.6	1.5	2.3	0.7	0.7	1.0	0.4
20 - 24	1.8	2.9	0.7	2.3	3.8	0.9	1.1	1.7	0.5
25 - 29	2.0	3.2	0.8	2.4	4.0	0.9	1.3	2.0	0.6
30 - 34	2.1	3.4	0.9	2.3	3.9	0.9	1.6	2.5	0.7
35 - 39	3.0	4.7	1.5	3.2	5.2	1.6	2.5	3.9	1.2
40 - 44	3.6	5.4	2.0	3.8	6.0	2.0	3.1	4.4	2.1
45 - 49	4.5	6.6	2.8	4.8	7.2	2.8	4.0	5.3	2.7
50 - 54	5.9	7.7	4.3	6.7	8.8	4.9	4.6	5.9	3.3
55 - 59	8.1	10.8	5.7	9.1	12.2	6.5	6.5	8.6	4.4
60 - 64	12.8	14.9	10.9	14.9	17.9	12.3	9.4	10.5	8.3
65 - 69	17.6	20.8	14.8	19.8	23.4	16.8	14.0	16.8	11.2
70 - 74	25.5	30.0	21.9	28.3	33.9	24.0	20.7	23.8	17.9
75 - 79	42.2	50.5	36.2	46.4	56.4	39.5	34.2	39.9	29.5
80 +	132.9	162.9	115.2	119.5	137.8	108.6	187.8	267.3	141.9
Guadeloupe[6]									
2003 (C)									
Total	6.0	6.7	5.4	...	...	...	...	...	...
0	8.1	9.7	♦6.5	...	...	...	...	...	...
1 - 4	♦0.3	♦0.3	♦0.3	...	...	...	...	...	...
5 - 9	♦0.1	♦0.2	♦0.1	...	...	...	...	...	...
10 - 14	♦0.1	♦0.2	♦0.1	...	...	...	...	...	...
15 - 19	♦0.6	♦1.0	♦0.2	...	...	...	...	...	...
20 - 24	♦0.8	♦1.3	♦0.3	...	...	...	...	...	...
25 - 29	♦0.9	♦1.3	♦0.4	...	...	...	...	...	...
30 - 34	1.1	2.0	♦0.4	...	...	...	...	...	...
35 - 39	1.6	2.4	♦1.0	...	...	...	...	...	...
40 - 44	2.2	2.8	♦1.6	...	...	...	...	...	...
45 - 49	3.5	5.3	2.0	...	...	...	...	...	...
50 - 54	4.5	7.5	♦1.9	...	...	...	...	...	...
55 - 59	6.3	8.7	4.1	...	...	...	...	...	...

20. Death rates specific for age, sex and urban/rural residence: latest available year, 1997 - 2006
Taux de mortalité selon l'âge, le sexe et la résidence, urbaine/rurale: dernière année disponible, 1997 - 2006 (continued - suite)

Continent, country or area, date, code and age (in years) / Continent, pays ou zone, date, code et âge (en années)	Total			Urban - Urbaine			Rural - Rurale		
	Both sexes Les deux sexes	Male Masculin	Female Féminin	Both sexes Les deux sexes	Male Masculin	Female Féminin	Both sexes Les deux sexes	Male Masculin	Female Féminin
AMERICA, NORTH - AMÉRIQUE DU NORD									
Guadeloupe[6]									
2003 (C)									
60 - 64	10.9	12.7	9.3	...	...	...	...	...	...
65 - 69	14.9	19.1	11.2	...	...	...	...	...	...
70 - 74	22.7	28.5	18.2	...	...	...	...	...	...
75 - 79	34.1	45.4	25.6	...	...	...	...	...	...
80 - 84	53.8	68.2	43.8	...	...	...	...	...	...
85 - 89	96.8	98.9	95.6	...	...	...	...	...	...
90 +	148.6	142.2	151.2	...	...	...	...	...	...
Guatemala									
1999 (C)									
Total	5.8	6.6	5.0	...	...	...	...	...	...
0 - 4	10.1	10.8	9.3	...	...	...	...	...	...
5 - 9	0.7	0.7	0.7	...	...	...	...	...	...
10 - 14	0.7	0.8	0.5	...	...	...	...	...	...
15 - 19	1.4	1.7	1.0	...	...	...	...	...	...
20 - 24	2.1	2.9	1.3	...	...	...	...	...	...
25 - 29	2.6	3.7	1.5	...	...	...	...	...	...
30 - 34	3.4	4.8	2.1	...	...	...	...	...	...
35 - 39	4.4	6.2	2.7	...	...	...	...	...	...
40 - 44	5.4	7.1	3.7	...	...	...	...	...	...
45 - 49	6.9	9.0	4.8	...	...	...	...	...	...
50 - 54	8.8	10.9	6.7	...	...	...	...	...	...
55 - 59	10.8	12.3	9.3	...	...	...	...	...	...
60 - 64	15.2	17.5	12.9	...	...	...	...	...	...
65 +	52.5	56.5	48.8	...	...	...	...	...	...
Martinique[6]									
2003 (C)									
Total	7.0	7.7	6.3	...	...	...	...	...	...
0	6.2	♦5.2	♦7.3	...	...	...	...	...	...
1 - 4	♦0.4	♦0.3	♦0.5	...	...	...	...	...	...
5 - 9	♦0.2	♦0.2	♦0.2	...	...	...	...	...	...
10 - 14	♦0.2	♦0.2	♦0.1	...	...	...	...	...	...
15 - 19	♦0.6	♦1.0	♦0.3	...	...	...	...	...	...
20 - 24	♦0.8	♦1.1	♦0.5	...	...	...	...	...	...
25 - 29	♦1.0	♦1.6	♦0.4	...	...	...	...	...	...
30 - 34	1.4	♦2.2	♦0.7	...	...	...	...	...	...
35 - 39	1.3	♦1.8	♦0.8	...	...	...	...	...	...
40 - 44	1.7	2.4	♦1.0	...	...	...	...	...	...
45 - 49	3.0	4.1	2.2	...	...	...	...	...	...
50 - 54	4.0	5.3	2.9	...	...	...	...	...	...
55 - 59	5.2	6.7	3.9	...	...	...	...	...	...
60 - 64	8.7	11.6	6.2	...	...	...	...	...	...
65 - 69	12.2	16.7	8.4	...	...	...	...	...	...
70 - 74	22.1	29.3	16.4	...	...	...	...	...	...
75 - 79	36.8	52.1	25.8	...	...	...	...	...	...
80 - 84	65.0	84.5	52.7	...	...	...	...	...	...
85 - 89	107.2	137.0	90.4	...	...	...	...	...	...
90 +	187.0	186.1	187.3	...	...	...	...	...	...
Mexico - Mexique									
2005 (+C)									
Total	4.8	5.4[5]	4.2[5]	4.7[9]	5.2[10]	4.2[10]	4.8[9]	5.6[10]	4.1[10]
0	17.5	19.1[5]	15.7[5]	17.7[9]	19.4[10]	15.9[10]	15.5[9]	16.9[10]	14.1[10]
1 - 4	0.8	0.8[5]	0.7[5]	0.7[9]	0.7[10]	0.6[10]	1.0[9]	1.0[10]	1.0[10]
5 - 9	0.3	0.3[5]	0.3[5]	0.3[9]	0.3[10]	0.3[10]	0.3[9]	0.4[10]	0.3[10]
10 - 14	0.3	0.4[5]	0.3[5]	0.3[9]	0.4[10]	0.3[10]	0.4[9]	0.4[10]	0.3[10]
15 - 19	0.7	1.0[5]	0.5[5]	0.7[9]	1.0[10]	0.4[10]	0.8[9]	1.1[10]	0.5[10]
20 - 24	1.1	1.7[5]	0.6[5]	1.0[9]	1.5[10]	0.5[10]	1.3[9]	2.1[10]	0.6[10]
25 - 29	1.3	2.1[5]	0.7[5]	1.2[9]	1.9[10]	0.6[10]	1.6[9]	2.5[10]	0.8[10]
30 - 34	1.6	2.4[5]	0.8[5]	1.5[9]	2.2[10]	0.8[10]	1.8[9]	2.7[10]	1.0[10]
35 - 39	2.0	3.0[5]	1.1[5]	1.8[9]	2.7[10]	1.0[10]	2.2[9]	3.2[10]	1.3[10]
40 - 44	2.8	4.0[5]	1.8[5]	2.7[9]	3.7[10]	1.7[10]	3.2[9]	4.3[10]	2.1[10]
45 - 49	4.2	5.5[5]	3.0[5]	4.0[9]	5.2[10]	2.9[10]	4.4[9]	5.8[10]	3.1[10]

Continent, country or area, date, code and age (in years) / Continent, pays ou zone, date, code et âge (en annèes)	Total			Urban - Urbaine			Rural - Rurale		
	Both sexes Les deux sexes	Male Masculin	Female Féminin	Both sexes Les deux sexes	Male Masculin	Female Féminin	Both sexes Les deux sexes	Male Masculin	Female Féminin
AMERICA, NORTH - AMÉRIQUE DU NORD									
Mexico - Mexique									
2005 (+C)									
50 - 54	6.1	7.7[5]	4.6[5]	5.9[9]	7.5[10]	4.5[10]	6.1[9]	7.6[10]	4.6[10]
55 - 59	9.5	11.4[5]	7.8[5]	9.7[9]	11.6[10]	8.0[10]	8.4[9]	9.9[10]	6.9[10]
60 - 64	13.5	15.8[5]	11.4[5]	13.9[9]	16.5[10]	11.7[10]	11.4[9]	12.8[10]	10.0[10]
65 - 69	20.9	24.1[5]	18.1[5]	21.9[9]	25.5[10]	18.8[10]	17.3[9]	19.3[10]	15.2[10]
70 - 74	31.4	35.5[5]	27.8[5]	33.0[9]	38.2[10]	28.7[10]	26.1[9]	28.0[10]	24.1[10]
75 - 79	47.1	51.7[5]	43.1[5]	50.0[9]	55.9[10]	45.3[10]	38.4[9]	40.9[10]	35.7[10]
80 - 84	75.5	83.6[5]	68.8[5]	79.5[9]	89.8[10]	71.7[10]	63.3[9]	68.0[10]	58.4[10]
85 - 89	105.0	110.5[5]	100.7[5]	111.2[9]	118.4[10]	106.1[10]	87.2[9]	91.3[10]	83.2[10]
90 - 94	194.9	196.5[5]	193.7[5]	203.1[9]	208.3[10]	199.9[10]	170.7[9]	168.9[10]	172.3[10]
95 - 99	191.0	181.8[5]	197.1[5]	203.9[9]	194.0[10]	209.6[10]	160.7[9]	156.6[10]	164.3[10]
100 +	227.0	206.8[5]	239.4[5]	262.2[9]	238.0[10]	275.2[10]	175.5[9]	169.1[10]	180.1[10]
2006 (+C)									
Total	4.7	5.3[5]	4.1[5]	...	...	...	...	...	...
0	15.7	17.3[5]	14.0[5]	...	...	...	...	...	...
1 - 4	0.7	0.8[5]	0.7[5]	...	...	...	...	...	...
5 - 9	0.3	0.3[5]	0.2[5]	...	...	...	...	...	...
10 - 14	0.3	0.4[5]	0.3[5]	...	...	...	...	...	...
15 - 19	0.7	1.0[5]	0.5[5]	...	...	...	...	...	...
20 - 24	1.0	1.5[5]	0.5[5]	...	...	...	...	...	...
25 - 29	1.2	1.8[5]	0.6[5]	...	...	...	...	...	...
30 - 34	1.5	2.3[5]	0.8[5]	...	...	...	...	...	...
35 - 39	1.9	2.7[5]	1.1[5]	...	...	...	...	...	...
40 - 44	2.5	3.5[5]	1.6[5]	...	...	...	...	...	...
45 - 49	3.8	5.0[5]	2.8[5]	...	...	...	...	...	...
50 - 54	5.9	7.4[5]	4.6[5]	...	...	...	...	...	...
55 - 59	9.1	11.0[5]	7.3[5]	...	...	...	...	...	...
60 - 64	13.5	15.9[5]	11.4[5]	...	...	...	...	...	...
65 - 69	20.7	24.3[5]	17.5[5]	...	...	...	...	...	...
70 - 74	32.0	37.7[5]	27.2[5]	...	...	...	...	...	...
75 - 79	50.4	58.5[5]	43.9[5]	...	...	...	...	...	...
80 - 84	79.1	91.8[5]	69.4[5]	...	...	...	...	...	...
85 - 89	117.4	130.0[5]	108.4[5]	...	...	...	...	...	...
90 - 94	158.9	165.3[5]	154.6[5]	...	...	...	...	...	...
95 - 99	243.6	244.2[5]	243.1[5]	...	...	...	...	...	...
100 +	432.5	408.3[5]	447.2[5]	...	...	...	...	...	...
Netherlands Antilles - Antilles néerlandaises[11]									
2004 (C)									
Total	7.7	8.8	6.7	...	...	...	...	...	...
0	♦8.2	♦10.4	♦5.8	...	...	...	...	...	...
1 - 4	♦0.2	♦0.2	♦0.2	...	...	...	...	...	...
5 - 9	♦0.1	♦0.3	-	...	...	...	...	...	...
10 - 14	♦0.2	♦0.4		...	...	...	...	...	...
15 - 19	♦1.0	♦1.5	♦0.5	...	...	...	...	...	...
20 - 24	♦1.2	♦1.9	♦0.6	...	...	...	...	...	...
25 - 29	♦1.8	♦2.3	♦1.3	...	...	...	...	...	...
30 - 34	♦1.9	♦3.0	♦0.9	...	...	...	...	...	...
35 - 39	2.0	♦3.2	♦1.0	...	...	...	...	...	...
40 - 44	2.5	♦3.5	♦1.6	...	...	...	...	...	...
45 - 49	3.9	4.9	♦3.1	...	...	...	...	...	...
50 - 54	6.0	8.0	♦4.4	...	...	...	...	...	...
55 - 59	8.3	11.7	♦5.4	...	...	...	...	...	...
60 - 64	14.9	19.1	11.5	...	...	...	...	...	...
65 - 69	22.2	27.9	17.4	...	...	...	...	...	...
70 - 74	35.9	42.9	30.5	...	...	...	...	...	...
75 - 79	52.9	73.3	38.5	...	...	...	...	...	...
80 - 84	79.2	105.2	64.0	...	...	...	...	...	...
85 - 89	128.6	148.9	118.3	...	...	...	...	...	...
90 - 94	197.8	274.2	169.6	...	...	...	...	...	...

20. Death rates specific for age, sex and urban/rural residence: latest available year, 1997 - 2006
Taux de mortalité selon l'âge, le sexe et la résidence, urbaine/rurale: dernière année disponible, 1997 - 2006 (continued - suite)

Continent, country or area, date, code and age (in years) / Continent, pays ou zone, date, code et âge (en années)	Total			Urban - Urbaine			Rural - Rurale		
	Both sexes Les deux sexes	Male Masculin	Female Féminin	Both sexes Les deux sexes	Male Masculin	Female Féminin	Both sexes Les deux sexes	Male Masculin	Female Féminin
AMERICA, NORTH - AMÉRIQUE DU NORD									
Netherlands Antilles - Antilles néerlandaises[11] 2004 (C)									
95 - 99	392.0	♦384.6	395.3	...	...	...	...	...	...
100 +	♦392.9	♦200.0	♦500.0	...	...	...	...	...	...
Puerto Rico - Porto Rico 2005 (C)									
Total	7.6	8.8	6.5	...	...	...	...	...	...
0	9.3	9.7	8.9	...	...	...	...	...	...
1 - 4	0.2	♦0.2	0.2	...	...	...	...	...	...
5 - 9	♦0.1	♦0.1	♦0.1	...	...	...	...	...	...
10 - 14	0.1	♦0.2	♦0.1	...	...	...	...	...	...
15 - 19	0.6	1.0	0.2	...	...	...	...	...	...
20 - 24	1.5	2.5	0.5	...	...	...	...	...	...
25 - 29	1.4	2.4	0.5	...	...	...	...	...	...
30 - 34	1.6	2.6	0.8	...	...	...	...	...	...
35 - 39	2.0	2.9	1.1	...	...	...	...	...	...
40 - 44	2.5	3.8	1.4	...	...	...	...	...	...
45 - 49	3.5	5.1	2.1	...	...	...	...	...	...
50 - 54	5.1	7.5	3.1	...	...	...	...	...	...
55 - 59	7.3	10.4	4.7	...	...	...	...	...	...
60 - 64	11.3	15.4	7.9	...	...	...	...	...	...
65 - 69	16.1	21.3	11.7	...	...	...	...	...	...
70 - 74	25.0	32.1	19.4	...	...	...	...	...	...
75 - 79	38.5	48.4	31.0	...	...	...	...	...	...
80 +	94.1	106.6	85.8	...	...	...	...	...	...
Saint Lucia - Sainte-Lucie 2005* (C)									
Total	6.7	7.8	5.7	...	...	...	...	...	...
0 - 4	3.7	♦4.3	♦3.2	...	...	...	...	...	...
5 - 9	♦0.1	♦0.1	♦0.1	...	...	...	...	...	...
10 - 14	♦0.4	♦0.5	♦0.3	...	...	...	...	...	...
15 - 19	♦0.8	♦1.4	♦0.2	...	...	...	...	...	...
20 - 24	♦1.2	♦1.9	♦0.5	...	...	...	...	...	...
25 - 29	♦1.8	♦2.7	♦0.9	...	...	...	...	...	...
30 - 34	2.6	♦3.5	♦1.8	...	...	...	...	...	...
35 - 39	♦2.1	♦3.3	♦1.0	...	...	...	...	...	...
40 - 44	3.6	♦5.6	♦1.8	...	...	...	...	...	...
45 - 49	4.4	♦6.5	♦2.3	...	...	...	...	...	...
50 - 54	7.6	♦7.7	♦7.5	...	...	...	...	...	...
55 - 59	8.3	♦9.5	♦7.3	...	...	...	...	...	...
60 - 64	20.1	27.6	♦13.7	...	...	...	...	...	...
65 - 69	28.6	37.2	20.9	...	...	...	...	...	...
70 - 74	28.9	36.5	22.2	...	...	...	...	...	...
75 - 79	58.3	78.8	40.4	...	...	...	...	...	...
80 +	125.4	129.1	122.8	...	...	...	...	...	...
Trinidad and Tobago - Trinité-et-Tobago 1997 (C)									
Total	7.2	7.9	6.5	...	...	...	...	...	...
0	19.8	21.4	18.2	...	...	...	...	...	...
1 - 4	0.8	0.8	♦0.7	...	...	...	...	...	...
5 - 9	0.3	♦0.4	♦0.2	...	...	...	...	...	...
10 - 14	0.4	♦0.4	♦0.3	...	...	...	...	...	...
15 - 19	0.7	0.8	0.6	...	...	...	...	...	...
20 - 24	1.4	1.8	0.9	...	...	...	...	...	...
25 - 29	1.6	1.9	1.2	...	...	...	...	...	...
30 - 34	2.5	3.2	1.9	...	...	...	...	...	...
35 - 39	3.0	3.7	2.3	...	...	...	...	...	...
40 - 44	3.9	4.8	2.9	...	...	...	...	...	...
45 - 49	5.4	6.6	4.3	...	...	...	...	...	...
50 - 54	8.3	10.3	6.3	...	...	...	...	...	...
55 - 59	13.6	16.6	10.9	...	...	...	...	...	...
60 - 64	22.1	24.2	20.2	...	...	...	...	...	...

20. Death rates specific for age, sex and urban/rural residence: latest available year, 1997 - 2006
Taux de mortalité selon l'âge, le sexe et la résidence, urbaine/rurale: dernière année disponible, 1997 - 2006 (continued - suite)

Continent, country or area, date, code and age (in years) / Continent, pays ou zone, date, code et âge (en années)	Total			Urban - Urbaine			Rural - Rurale		
	Both sexes Les deux sexes	Male Masculin	Female Féminin	Both sexes Les deux sexes	Male Masculin	Female Féminin	Both sexes Les deux sexes	Male Masculin	Female Féminin
AMERICA, NORTH - AMÉRIQUE DU NORD									
Trinidad and Tobago - Trinité-et-Tobago									
1997 (C)									
65 - 69	31.7	36.0	27.8	...	...	...	...	...	...
70 - 74	44.7	60.6	32.8	...	...	...	...	...	...
75 - 79	62.6	82.7	47.8	...	...	...	...	...	...
80 +	146.2	154.8	139.3	...	...	...	...	...	...
United States - États-Unis									
2004 (C)									
Total	8.2	8.2	8.2	...	...	...	...	...	...
0	6.9	7.6	6.2	...	...	...	...	...	...
1 - 4	0.3	0.3	0.3	...	...	...	...	...	...
5 - 9	0.1	0.2	0.1	...	...	...	...	...	...
10 - 14	0.2	0.2	0.2	...	...	...	...	...	...
15 - 19	0.7	0.9	0.4	...	...	...	...	...	...
20 - 24	0.9	1.4	0.5	...	...	...	...	...	...
25 - 29	1.0	1.4	0.5	...	...	...	...	...	...
30 - 34	1.1	1.4	0.7	...	...	...	...	...	...
35 - 39	1.5	1.9	1.1	...	...	...	...	...	...
40 - 44	2.3	2.9	1.7	...	...	...	...	...	...
45 - 49	3.5	4.4	2.6	...	...	...	...	...	...
50 - 54	5.1	6.6	3.7	...	...	...	...	...	...
55 - 59	7.3	9.2	5.6	...	...	...	...	...	...
60 - 64	11.4	14.1	8.9	...	...	...	...	...	...
65 - 69	17.3	21.3	13.8	...	...	...	...	...	...
70 - 74	26.8	32.8	21.9	...	...	...	...	...	...
75 - 79	42.0	51.9	34.9	...	...	...	...	...	...
80 - 84	67.9	82.7	58.8	...	...	...	...	...	...
85 +	137.8	149.1	132.6	...	...	...	...	...	...
AMERICA, SOUTH - AMÉRIQUE DU SUD									
Argentina - Argentine									
2006 (C)									
Total	7.5	8.1[5]	6.9[5]	...	...	...	...	...	...
0 - 4	3.2	3.5[5]	2.8[5]	...	...	...	...	...	...
5 - 9	0.3	0.3[5]	0.2[5]	...	...	...	...	...	...
10 - 14	0.3	0.4[5]	0.3[5]	...	...	...	...	...	...
15 - 19	0.7	1.0[5]	0.4[5]	...	...	...	...	...	...
20 - 24	0.9	1.4[5]	0.5[5]	...	...	...	...	...	...
25 - 29	1.0	1.3[5]	0.6[5]	...	...	...	...	...	...
30 - 34	1.1	1.5[5]	0.8[5]	...	...	...	...	...	...
35 - 39	1.6	2.1[5]	1.2[5]	...	...	...	...	...	...
40 - 44	2.2	2.8[5]	1.7[5]	...	...	...	...	...	...
45 - 49	3.7	4.8[5]	2.6[5]	...	...	...	...	...	...
50 - 54	5.8	7.7[5]	4.1[5]	...	...	...	...	...	...
55 - 59	9.1	12.5[5]	6.1[5]	...	...	...	...	...	...
60 - 64	14.0	19.1[5]	9.5[5]	...	...	...	...	...	...
65 - 69	20.0	28.1[5]	13.4[5]	...	...	...	...	...	...
70 - 74	30.5	43.2[5]	21.0[5]	...	...	...	...	...	...
75 - 79	49.0	67.8[5]	36.8[5]	...	...	...	...	...	...
80 +	126.7	147.9[5]	110.3[5]	...	...	...	...	...	...
Chile - Chili									
2005 (C)									
Total	5.3	5.8	4.8	5.2	5.6	4.8	5.7	6.5	4.8
0 - 4	1.8	2.0	1.6	1.8	1.9	1.6	2.3	2.6	1.9
5 - 9	0.2	0.2	0.1	0.2	0.2	0.1	0.2	♦0.2	♦0.2
10 - 14	0.2	0.2	0.2	0.2	0.2	0.1	0.3	0.4	♦0.2
15 - 19	0.5	0.7	0.3	0.5	0.7	0.2	0.7	0.8	0.6
20 - 24	0.7	1.1	0.3	0.7	1.1	0.3	1.0	1.6	♦0.2
25 - 29	0.8	1.3	0.4	0.8	1.2	0.4	1.1	1.7	0.5

20. Death rates specific for age, sex and urban/rural residence: latest available year, 1997 - 2006
Taux de mortalité selon l'âge, le sexe et la résidence, urbaine/rurale: dernière année disponible, 1997 - 2006 (continued - suite)

Continent, country or area, date, code and age (in years) / Continent, pays ou zone, date, code et âge (en années)	Total			Urban - Urbaine			Rural - Rurale		
	Both sexes Les deux sexes	Male Masculin	Female Féminin	Both sexes Les deux sexes	Male Masculin	Female Féminin	Both sexes Les deux sexes	Male Masculin	Female Féminin
AMERICA, SOUTH - AMÉRIQUE DU SUD									
Chile - Chili									
2005 (C)									
30 - 34	1.1	1.6	0.5	1.0	1.5	0.5	1.5	2.2	0.7
35 - 39	1.3	1.9	0.8	1.2	1.8	0.7	1.8	2.5	1.0
40 - 44	1.8	2.4	1.2	1.7	2.3	1.1	2.2	2.8	1.4
45 - 49	2.6	3.4	1.8	2.6	3.4	1.8	2.7	3.5	1.7
50 - 54	4.1	5.2	3.0	4.0	5.1	3.0	4.3	5.3	3.1
55 - 59	6.6	8.7	4.7	6.7	8.9	4.7	6.5	7.8	4.9
60 - 64	10.6	13.8	7.8	10.7	14.0	7.9	10.2	13.0	6.9
65 - 69	17.3	22.8	12.7	17.6	23.6	12.8	15.9	19.4	11.7
70 - 74	27.8	37.1	20.6	28.6	39.2	21.0	23.7	28.4	18.5
75 - 79	47.0	61.6	36.9	47.7	64.1	37.1	43.3	51.0	35.2
80 +	115.4	130.8	107.0	117.4	135.9	108.1	104.3	110.3	98.9
Suriname									
2004 (C)									
Total	6.7	7.6	5.8	...	...	...	...	...	...
0	12.2	15.6	8.7	...	...	...	...	...	...
1 - 4	1.3	1.6	♦1.1	...	...	...	...	...	...
5 - 9	♦0.4	♦0.3	♦0.4	...	...	...	...	...	...
10 - 14	♦0.6	♦0.7	♦0.4	...	...	...	...	...	...
15 - 19	0.9	♦1.2	♦0.6	...	...	...	...	...	...
20 - 24	1.6	1.9	♦1.3	...	...	...	...	...	...
25 - 29	2.6	3.6	♦1.5	...	...	...	...	...	...
30 - 34	2.8	3.6	2.0	...	...	...	...	...	...
35 - 39	3.8	5.1	2.5	...	...	...	...	...	...
40 - 44	4.8	6.1	3.5	...	...	...	...	...	...
45 - 49	7.7	9.3	6.2	...	...	...	...	...	...
50 - 54	7.8	9.8	5.9	...	...	...	...	...	...
55 - 59	14.9	17.8	12.3	...	...	...	...	...	...
60 - 64	19.5	23.1	16.4	...	...	...	...	...	...
65 - 69	31.4	38.1	25.1	...	...	...	...	...	...
70 - 74	42.6	51.2	34.9	...	...	...	...	...	...
75 - 79	66.6	82.3	52.7	...	...	...	...	...	...
80 - 84	102.7	120.6	89.0	...	...	...	...	...	...
85 - 89	149.8	165.8	141.8	...	...	...	...	...	...
90 - 94	215.2	190.2	231.9	...	...	...	...	...	...
95 +	294.6	♦264.7	♦305.3	...	...	...	...	...	...
Uruguay									
2002 (C)									
Total	9.6	10.5[5]	8.7[5]	...	...	...	...	...	...
0	14.0	15.4[5]	12.3[5]	...	...	...	...	...	...
1 - 4	0.5	0.6	0.3	...	...	...	...	...	...
5 - 9	0.2	0.2	0.2	...	...	...	...	...	...
10 - 14	0.2	0.3	♦0.2	...	...	...	...	...	...
15 - 19	0.7	1.0	0.3	...	...	...	...	...	...
20 - 24	1.0	1.5	0.4	...	...	...	...	...	...
25 - 29	1.1	1.6	0.5	...	...	...	...	...	...
30 - 34	1.4	1.8	0.9	...	...	...	...	...	...
35 - 39	1.6	2.1[5]	1.1[5]	...	...	...	...	...	...
40 - 44	2.4	2.7	2.1	...	...	...	...	...	...
45 - 49	4.0	5.1	2.9	...	...	...	...	...	...
50 - 54	6.5	8.8	4.3	...	...	...	...	...	...
55 - 59	9.9	13.8	6.4	...	...	...	...	...	...
60 - 64	15.0	22.0	9.0	...	...	...	...	...	...
65 - 69	22.0	31.8	14.3	...	...	...	...	...	...
70 - 74	33.3	47.7[5]	22.7[5]	...	...	...	...	...	...
75 +	88.5	105.3[5]	78.9[5]	...	...	...	...	...	...
Venezuela (Bolivarian Republic of) - Venezuela (République bolivarienne du)[12]									
2002 (C)									
Total	4.2	5.1	3.2	...	...	...	...	...	...
0	13.5	15.2	11.7	...	...	...	...	...	...

20. Death rates specific for age, sex and urban/rural residence: latest available year, 1997 - 2006
Taux de mortalité selon l'âge, le sexe et la résidence, urbaine/rurale: dernière année disponible, 1997 - 2006 (continued - suite)

Continent, country or area, date, code and age (in years) / Continent, pays ou zone, date, code et âge (en années)	Total			Urban - Urbaine			Rural - Rurale		
	Both sexes Les deux sexes	Male Masculin	Female Féminin	Both sexes Les deux sexes	Male Masculin	Female Féminin	Both sexes Les deux sexes	Male Masculin	Female Féminin
AMERICA, SOUTH - AMÉRIQUE DU SUD									
Venezuela (Bolivarian Republic of) - Venezuela (République bolivarienne du)[12] 2002 (C)									
1 - 4	0.9	0.9	0.8	...	...	...	...	...	...
5 - 9	0.3	0.4	0.3	...	...	...	...	...	...
10 - 14	0.4	0.5	0.3	...	...	...	...	...	...
15 - 19	1.4	2.2	0.5	...	...	...	...	...	...
20 - 24	2.3	3.9	0.6	...	...	...	...	...	...
25 - 29	2.1	3.5	0.7	...	...	...	...	...	...
30 - 34	2.1	3.2	1.0	...	...	...	...	...	...
35 - 39	2.1	3.0	1.2	...	...	...	...	...	...
40 - 44	2.8	3.7	1.8	...	...	...	...	...	...
45 - 49	3.9	5.0	2.7	...	...	...	...	...	...
50 - 54	5.3	6.8	3.8	...	...	...	...	...	...
55 - 59	7.2	9.4	5.1	...	...	...	...	...	...
60 - 64	11.0	14.0	8.1	...	...	...	...	...	...
65 - 69	17.7	22.1	13.7	...	...	...	...	...	...
70 - 74	26.5	33.3	20.7	...	...	...	...	...	...
75 - 79	40.2	48.6	33.4	...	...	...	...	...	...
80 +	117.7	128.1	110.2	...	...	...	...	...	...
ASIA - ASIE									
Armenia - Arménie[13] 2006 (C)									
Total	8.4	9.1	7.9	8.6	9.5	7.7	8.2	8.4	8.1
0	14.1	15.9	12.0	16.6	18.4	14.6	9.8	11.7	7.5
1 - 4	0.5	0.4	0.6	0.5	♦0.4	♦0.6	♦0.5	♦0.4	♦0.7
5 - 9	0.2	♦0.2	♦0.2	♦0.2	♦0.2	♦0.2	♦0.2	♦0.2	♦0.2
10 - 14	0.2	♦0.2	♦0.1	♦0.1	♦0.1	♦0.2	♦0.2	♦0.2	♦0.1
15 - 19	0.4	0.6	♦0.2	0.4	0.6	♦0.2	0.4	0.6	♦0.2
20 - 24	0.6	0.8	0.4	0.7	0.9	0.4	0.5	0.7	♦0.3
25 - 29	0.8	1.1	0.4	0.8	1.2	0.4	0.7	1.0	♦0.5
30 - 34	1.1	1.6	0.6	1.2	1.9	0.6	0.9	1.2	♦0.6
35 - 39	1.6	2.4	0.9	1.7	2.7	0.8	1.4	1.8	0.9
40 - 44	2.7	3.9	1.6	3.0	4.5	1.7	2.3	3.1	1.5
45 - 49	4.0	5.8	2.3	4.1	6.2	2.4	3.7	5.3	2.1
50 - 54	6.6	9.8	3.9	6.9	10.4	4.0	6.0	8.5	3.5
55 - 59	10.3	15.1	6.4	10.4	15.3	6.4	10.2	14.7	6.3
60 - 64	16.8	23.6	11.6	16.6	23.5	11.3	17.2	23.7	12.1
65 - 69	27.0	37.5	19.3	28.5	39.5	20.4	24.1	33.6	17.3
70 - 74	44.5	56.0	36.0	45.9	58.1	37.1	42.3	52.8	34.4
75 - 79	73.1	90.6	61.9	75.4	94.1	63.8	69.9	85.8	59.1
80 - 84	122.1	148.7	110.4	122.8	147.4	112.2	120.9	150.7	107.6
85 +	251.1	250.5	251.4	246.3	247.0	246.1	258.3	256.5	258.8
Azerbaijan - Azerbaïdjan[13] 2004 (+C)									
Total	6.0	6.4	5.6	6.0	6.6	5.5	5.9	6.1	5.6
0	10.5	11.4	9.4	11.0	12.9	8.8	10.1	10.2	9.9
1 - 4	1.6	1.7	1.6	0.7	0.6	0.8	2.4	2.6	2.2
5 - 9	0.5	0.5	0.5	0.4	0.4	0.4	0.6	0.6	0.5
10 - 14	0.3	0.4	0.3	0.3	0.3	0.2	0.4	0.5	0.3
15 - 19	0.5	0.6	0.4	0.5	0.6	0.4	0.5	0.6	0.3
20 - 24	0.8	1.0	0.5	0.8	1.0	0.5	0.8	1.0	0.6
25 - 29	1.0	1.4	0.7	1.0	1.4	0.6	1.0	1.3	0.7
30 - 34	1.5	2.2	0.8	1.7	2.6	0.9	1.3	1.9	0.7
35 - 39	1.9	2.7	1.1	2.0	3.1	1.1	1.7	2.3	1.2
40 - 44	2.7	3.8	1.7	2.8	4.1	1.6	2.6	3.4	1.8
45 - 49	4.2	5.9	2.6	4.4	6.2	2.7	3.9	5.5	2.4
50 - 54	7.0	9.3	4.9	7.3	9.8	4.9	6.5	8.5	4.7
55 - 59	11.4	15.5	7.8	11.8	16.2	7.8	10.8	14.3	7.7

20. Death rates specific for age, sex and urban/rural residence: latest available year, 1997 - 2006
Taux de mortalité selon l'âge, le sexe et la résidence, urbaine/rurale: dernière année disponible, 1997 - 2006 (continued - suite)

Continent, country or area, date, code and age (in years) / Continent, pays ou zone, date, code et âge (en années)	Total			Urban - Urbaine			Rural - Rurale		
	Both sexes Les deux sexes	Male Masculin	Female Féminin	Both sexes Les deux sexes	Male Masculin	Female Féminin	Both sexes Les deux sexes	Male Masculin	Female Féminin
ASIA - ASIE									
Azerbaijan - Azerbaïdjan[13]									
2004 (+C)									
60 - 64	19.1	25.3	13.9	20.1	26.4	14.7	17.9	23.9	13.0
65 - 69	30.9	39.3	24.3	31.6	41.0	24.2	30.2	37.6	24.4
70 - 74	48.8	57.6	41.9	50.9	60.1	44.0	46.9	55.6	40.0
75 - 79	72.3	82.4	65.4	74.6	82.0	69.8	70.0	82.8	60.7
80 - 84	96.7	97.4	96.3	100.4	91.0	105.0	92.9	104.1	87.7
85 - 89	143.7	140.0	145.1	158.7	131.5	171.4	131.1	149.4	125.3
90 - 94	191.5	196.5	190.0	209.6	183.8	220.0	180.0	207.8	172.9
95 - 99	200.4	188.3	204.2	227.5	210.0	233.3	187.6	177.5	190.8
100 +	388.6	243.3	428.2	241.7	155.0	285.0	498.8	420.0	510.0
Bahrain - Bahreïn									
2006 (C)									
Total	3.1	3.2	3.0	...	...	...	...	...	...
0	10.1	10.0	10.2	...	...	...	...	...	...
1 - 4	0.7	♦0.6	♦0.8	...	...	...	...	...	...
5 - 9	♦0.3	♦0.4	♦0.3	...	...	...	...	...	...
10 - 14	♦0.2	♦0.2	♦0.1	...	...	...	...	...	...
15 - 19	0.6	♦0.8	♦0.3	...	...	...	...	...	...
20 - 24	0.8	1.0	♦0.4	...	...	...	...	...	...
25 - 29	1.0	1.2	♦0.7	...	...	...	...	...	...
30 - 34	1.2	1.4	♦0.9	...	...	...	...	...	...
35 - 39	1.1	1.2	♦1.0	...	...	...	...	...	...
40 - 44	1.6	1.6	1.5	...	...	...	...	...	...
45 - 49	3.4	3.6	2.9	...	...	...	...	...	...
50 - 54	6.2	6.3	6.0	...	...	...	...	...	...
55 - 59	9.7	11.4	7.2	...	...	...	...	...	...
60 - 64	12.1	12.7	11.5	...	...	...	...	...	...
65 - 69	28.3	31.3	25.5	...	...	...	...	...	...
70 - 74	46.0	46.1	45.8	...	...	...	...	...	...
75 +	111.4	114.0	108.6	...	...	...	...	...	...
Bhutan - Bhoutan[14]									
2005 (|)									
Total	7.1	7.2	7.0	5.3	5.4	5.3	7.9	8.0	7.7
0	40.8	44.3	37.5	30.7	29.3	32.1	45.9	51.9	40.1
1 - 4	5.4	5.6	5.1	5.1	5.9	4.3	5.5	5.5	5.4
5 - 9	2.0	2.4	1.5	2.5	3.8	♦1.3	1.8	1.9	1.6
10 - 14	1.1	1.2	1.1	♦0.6	♦0.4	♦0.9	1.4	1.5	1.2
15 - 19	1.7	1.7	1.6	♦0.7	♦1.0	♦0.4	2.2	2.2	2.3
20 - 24	1.7	1.6	1.9	♦1.0	♦0.9	♦1.1	2.3	2.1	2.5
25 - 29	2.3	2.4	2.3	1.7	♦1.8	♦1.5	2.7	2.7	2.7
30 - 34	3.4	3.4	3.4	2.1	♦2.2	♦2.0	4.1	4.1	4.1
35 - 39	4.7	5.1	4.3	4.6	5.3	♦3.7	4.8	5.0	4.5
40 - 44	5.8	5.9	5.7	5.0	♦4.1	♦6.2	6.2	6.8	5.5
45 - 49	9.0	8.7	9.5	10.7	9.0	13.1	8.5	8.5	8.5
50 - 54	9.3	9.6	8.9	9.1	♦9.4	♦8.6	9.3	9.7	8.9
55 - 59	14.6	14.4	14.8	24.4	♦19.6	30.8	12.6	13.3	11.9
60 - 64	20.0	19.2	20.8	26.7	♦25.8	♦27.6	18.8	18.1	19.6
65 - 69	29.1	27.2	31.3	46.9	41.4	52.8	26.2	24.8	27.7
70 - 74	42.1	41.8	42.4	47.9	♦50.1	♦45.9	41.2	40.6	41.7
75 +	96.8	102.7	90.8	134.7	169.5	106.8	90.1	92.5	87.5
Brunei Darussalam - Brunéi Darussalam									
2004 (+C)									
Total	2.8	3.0	2.6	...	...	...	...	...	...
0 - 4	1.3	1.3	1.3	...	...	...	...	...	...
5 - 9	♦0.3	♦0.6	♦0.1	...	...	...	...	...	...
10 - 14	♦0.3	♦0.4	♦0.3	...	...	...	...	...	...
15 - 19	♦0.4	♦0.6	♦0.3	...	...	...	...	...	...
20 - 24	♦0.6	♦0.9	♦0.3	...	...	...	...	...	...
25 - 29	♦0.6	♦0.8	♦0.3	...	...	...	...	...	...
30 - 34	1.0	♦1.0	♦1.0	...	...	...	...	...	...
35 - 39	1.2	♦1.3	♦1.2	...	...	...	...	...	...
40 - 44	1.9	♦1.8	♦1.9	...	...	...	...	...	...
45 - 49	3.1	3.4	♦2.8	...	...	...	...	...	...

20. Death rates specific for age, sex and urban/rural residence: latest available year, 1997 - 2006
Taux de mortalité selon l'âge, le sexe et la résidence, urbaine/rurale: dernière année disponible, 1997 - 2006 (continued - suite)

Continent, country or area, date, code and age (in years) / Continent, pays ou zone, date, code et âge (en années)	Total			Urban - Urbaine			Rural - Rurale		
	Both sexes Les deux sexes	Male Masculin	Female Féminin	Both sexes Les deux sexes	Male Masculin	Female Féminin	Both sexes Les deux sexes	Male Masculin	Female Féminin
ASIA - ASIE									
Brunei Darussalam - Brunéi Darussalam									
2004 (+C)									
50 - 54	4.8	5.3	♦4.1	...	...	...	...	...	...
55 - 59	10.0	♦7.6	12.8	...	...	...	...	...	...
60 - 64	10.8	12.4	♦9.2	...	...	...	...	...	...
65 - 69	27.2	32.4	22.6	...	...	...	...	...	...
70 +	96.6	99.6	93.3	...	...	...	...	...	...
China: Hong Kong SAR - Chine: Hong Kong RAS									
2006* (C)									
Total	5.5	6.4	4.6	...	...	...	...	...	...
0	2.8	2.8	2.7	...	...	...	...	...	...
1 - 4	0.2	♦0.3	♦0.2	...	...	...	...	...	...
5 - 9	0.1	♦0.1	♦0.1	...	...	...	...	...	...
10 - 14	0.1	♦0.1	♦0.1	...	...	...	...	...	...
15 - 19	0.2	0.2	♦0.1	...	...	...	...	...	...
20 - 24	0.3	0.4	0.1	...	...	...	...	...	...
25 - 29	0.4	0.7	0.2	...	...	...	...	...	...
30 - 34	0.5	0.7	0.4	...	...	...	...	...	...
35 - 39	0.7	1.0	0.5	...	...	...	...	...	...
40 - 44	1.1	1.4	0.8	...	...	...	...	...	...
45 - 49	1.6	2.0	1.2	...	...	...	...	...	...
50 - 54	2.8	3.7	2.0	...	...	...	...	...	...
55 - 59	4.2	5.6	2.7	...	...	...	...	...	...
60 - 64	7.3	9.9	4.4	...	...	...	...	...	...
65 - 69	11.3	15.4	6.9	...	...	...	...	...	...
70 - 74	19.8	26.8	13.1	...	...	...	...	...	...
75 - 79	33.1	44.1	23.8	...	...	...	...	...	...
80 - 84	56.3	76.0	43.3	...	...	...	...	...	...
85 +	108.0	129.1	98.3	...	...	...	...	...	...
China: Macao SAR - Chine: Macao RAS									
2006 (C)									
Total	3.1	3.7	2.7	...	...	...	...	...	...
0 - 4	♦0.8	♦0.8	♦0.8	...	...	...	...	...	...
5 - 9	-	♦0.1	-	...	...	...	...	...	...
10 - 14	-	-	-	...	...	...	...	...	...
15 - 19	♦0.1	♦0.1	♦0.1	...	...	...	...	...	...
20 - 24	♦0.4	♦0.3	♦0.4	...	...	...	...	...	...
25 - 29	♦0.3	♦0.5	♦0.2	...	...	...	...	...	...
30 - 34	♦0.6	♦0.7	♦0.5	...	...	...	...	...	...
35 - 39	♦0.5	♦0.7	♦0.3	...	...	...	...	...	...
40 - 44	1.2	1.7	♦0.9	...	...	...	...	...	...
45 - 49	1.6	2.0	♦1.1	...	...	...	...	...	...
50 - 54	2.5	3.6	♦1.4	...	...	...	...	...	...
55 - 59	4.0	5.1	2.8	...	...	...	...	...	...
60 - 64	6.3	9.4	♦2.9	...	...	...	...	...	...
65 - 69	10.6	15.2	♦5.8	...	...	...	...	...	...
70 - 74	17.2	25.6	10.7	...	...	...	...	...	...
75 +	46.4	55.1	41.0	...	...	...	...	...	...
Cyprus - Chypre[15]									
2006 (C)									
Total	6.7	6.9	6.4	...	...	...	...	...	...
0	♦3.1	♦3.5	♦2.6	...	...	...	...	...	...
1 - 4	♦0.2	♦0.4	♦0.1	...	...	...	...	...	...
5 - 9	♦0.1	♦0.1	-	...	...	...	...	...	...
10 - 14	♦0.1	♦0.1	♦0.1	...	...	...	...	...	...
15 - 19	♦0.5	♦0.6	♦0.4	...	...	...	...	...	...
20 - 24	0.5	♦0.9	♦0.2	...	...	...	...	...	...
25 - 29	0.5	♦0.9	♦0.2	...	...	...	...	...	...
30 - 34	0.6	♦0.7	♦0.4	...	...	...	...	...	...
35 - 39	0.6	♦0.8	♦0.4	...	...	...	...	...	...
40 - 44	0.9	♦1.0	♦0.8	...	...	...	...	...	...
45 - 49	1.5	1.8	1.2	...	...	...	...	...	...

20. Death rates specific for age, sex and urban/rural residence: latest available year, 1997 - 2006
Taux de mortalité selon l'âge, le sexe et la résidence, urbaine/rurale: dernière année disponible, 1997 - 2006 (continued - suite)

Continent, country or area, date, code and age (in years) / Continent, pays ou zone, date, code et âge (en années)	Total			Urban - Urbaine			Rural - Rurale		
	Both sexes Les deux sexes	Male Masculin	Female Féminin	Both sexes Les deux sexes	Male Masculin	Female Féminin	Both sexes Les deux sexes	Male Masculin	Female Féminin
ASIA - ASIE									
Cyprus - Chypre[15]									
2006 (C)									
50 - 54	2.5	2.9	2.0	...	...	...	...	...	...
55 - 59	4.0	5.3	2.9	...	...	...	...	...	...
60 - 64	6.7	9.3	4.3	...	...	...	...	...	...
65 - 69	12.0	15.4	8.8	...	...	...	...	...	...
70 - 74	20.6	25.7	16.2	...	...	...	...	...	...
75 - 79	41.0	47.2	36.2	...	...	...	...	...	...
80 - 84	75.5	75.8	75.3	...	...	...	...	...	...
85 - 89	142.5	146.6	139.7	...	...	...	...	...	...
90 - 94	207.2	244.4	184.7	...	...	...	...	...	...
95 - 99	213.5	241.9	196.0	...	...	...	...	...	...
100 +	1491.8	3862.1	752.7	...	...	...	...	...	...
Georgia - Géorgie[13]									
2000 (C)									
Total	8.4	8.6	8.1	7.8	8.4	7.3	9.1	8.8	9.3
0	14.2	15.9	12.2	21.0	23.7	17.8	3.1	♦3.2	♦3.0
1 - 4	0.4	0.4	♦0.3	0.4	♦0.4	♦0.3	♦0.3	♦0.4	♦0.3
5 - 9	0.1	♦0.2	♦0.1	♦0.1	♦0.2	♦0.1	♦0.1	♦0.1	♦0.1
10 - 14	0.1	0.2	♦0.1	0.1	♦0.2	♦0.1	♦0.1	♦0.1	♦0.1
15 - 19	0.4	0.4	0.3	0.3	0.4	♦0.2	0.4	0.5	0.4
20 - 24	0.6	0.9	0.3	0.7	1.1	0.3	0.5	0.7	♦0.4
25 - 29	1.0	1.4	0.4	1.0	1.6	0.4	0.9	1.2	0.6
30 - 34	1.2	1.9	0.6	1.3	2.1	0.6	1.1	1.7	0.6
35 - 39	1.8	2.8	0.9	1.9	3.1	0.9	1.6	2.3	0.9
40 - 44	2.6	4.2	1.2	2.7	4.6	1.2	2.5	3.7	1.2
45 - 49	3.8	6.0	1.8	4.1	6.7	2.0	3.1	4.8	1.4
50 - 54	5.6	8.5	3.1	6.0	9.3	3.2	4.9	7.2	2.9
55 - 59	6.8	10.2	4.1	7.5	11.8	4.3	5.7	8.1	3.7
60 - 64	13.4	17.9	9.7	14.2	20.2	9.5	12.3	15.2	9.9
65 - 69	21.6	30.3	15.2	22.2	32.1	15.2	21.0	28.5	15.1
70 - 74	35.2	46.6	27.8	36.5	50.2	28.4	33.8	43.3	27.1
75 - 79	54.1	68.8	47.5	55.5	67.5	50.4	52.6	70.1	44.6
80 - 84	77.9	57.6	92.5	79.6	54.3	99.0	76.3	61.1	86.5
85 +	164.4	109.3	204.4	146.4	96.7	181.0	182.6	121.3	228.9
2006 (C)									
Total	9.6	10.8	8.5	...	...	...	...	...	...
0	16.2	16.1	16.3	...	...	...	...	...	...
1 - 4	0.3	0.3	♦0.3	...	...	...	...	...	...
5 - 9	0.2	0.3	♦0.2	...	...	...	...	...	...
10 - 14	0.2	0.2	♦0.2	...	...	...	...	...	...
15 - 19	0.3	0.5	0.2	...	...	...	...	...	...
20 - 24	0.8	1.2	0.4	...	...	...	...	...	...
25 - 29	1.2	1.8	0.5	...	...	...	...	...	...
30 - 34	1.7	2.7	0.7	...	...	...	...	...	...
35 - 39	2.2	3.6	1.0	...	...	...	...	...	...
40 - 44	3.2	5.3	1.5	...	...	...	...	...	...
45 - 49	4.4	7.3	2.0	...	...	...	...	...	...
50 - 54	6.8	10.8	3.4	...	...	...	...	...	...
55 - 59	8.6	13.5	4.6	...	...	...	...	...	...
60 - 64	13.0	18.7	8.6	...	...	...	...	...	...
65 - 69	23.7	34.0	16.4	...	...	...	...	...	...
70 - 74	36.3	49.3	27.2	...	...	...	...	...	...
75 - 79	57.7	74.8	47.2	...	...	...	...	...	...
80 - 84	98.7	121.6	88.3	...	...	...	...	...	...
85 +	153.0	206.8	138.2	...	...	...	...	...	...
Israel - Israël[16]									
2006 (C)									
Total	5.5[17]	5.5[5]	5.5[5]	5.6[9]	5.6[10]	5.6[10]	4.2[9]	4.2[10]	4.2[10]
0	4.1	4.5[5]	3.6[5]	4.0[9]	4.4[10]	3.5[10]	5.0[9]	5.0[10]	♦4.6[10]
1 - 4	0.3	0.4[5]	0.3[5]	0.3[9]	0.4[10]	0.3[10]	♦0.4[9]	♦0.6[10]	♦0.3[10]
5 - 9	0.1	0.2[5]	0.1[5]	0.1[9]	0.2[10]	0.1[10]	♦0.2[9]	♦0.2[10]	♦0.1[10]
10 - 14	0.1	0.1[5]	0.1[5]	0.1[9]	0.1[10]	♦0.1[10]	♦0.3[9]	♦0.3[10]	♦0.2[10]
15 - 19	0.3	0.5[5]	0.2[5]	0.3[9]	0.5[10]	0.2[10]	♦0.4[9]	♦0.6[10]	♦0.2[10]
20 - 24	0.6	0.9[5]	0.2[5]	0.6[9]	0.8[10]	0.3[10]	1.0[9]	1.6[10]	♦0.2[10]

20. Death rates specific for age, sex and urban/rural residence: latest available year, 1997 - 2006
Taux de mortalité selon l'âge, le sexe et la résidence, urbaine/rurale: dernière année disponible, 1997 - 2006 (continued - suite)

Continent, country or area, date, code and age (in years) / Continent, pays ou zone, date, code et âge (en années)	Total			Urban - Urbaine			Rural - Rurale		
	Both sexes Les deux sexes	Male Masculin	Female Féminin	Both sexes Les deux sexes	Male Masculin	Female Féminin	Both sexes Les deux sexes	Male Masculin	Female Féminin
ASIA - ASIE									
Israel - Israël[16]									
2006 (C)									
25 - 29	0.5	0.7[5]	0.3[5]	0.5[9]	0.7[10]	0.3[10]	♦0.7[9]	♦1.2[10]	♦0.2[10]
30 - 34	0.6	0.8[5]	0.4[5]	0.6[9]	0.8[10]	0.4[10]	♦0.5[9]	♦0.6[10]	♦0.5[10]
35 - 39	0.8	1.1[5]	0.5[5]	0.8[9]	1.0[10]	0.5[10]	1.0[9]	♦1.3[10]	♦0.6[10]
40 - 44	1.4	1.7[5]	1.0[5]	1.4[9]	1.8[10]	1.1[10]	♦0.8[9]	♦1.2[10]	♦0.4[10]
45 - 49	2.0	2.6[5]	1.4[5]	2.1[9]	2.7[10]	1.4[10]	1.3[9]	♦1.4[10]	♦1.2[10]
50 - 54	3.1	4.2[5]	2.1[5]	3.2[9]	4.3[10]	2.2[10]	2.4[9]	3.3[10]	♦1.4[10]
55 - 59	4.8	6.2[5]	3.6[5]	4.9[9]	6.3[10]	3.6[10]	4.0[9]	4.6[10]	3.4[10]
60 - 64	7.6	9.7[5]	5.7[5]	7.7[9]	9.8[10]	5.8[10]	6.3[9]	8.2[10]	4.3[10]
65 - 69	13.0	16.8[5]	9.9[5]	13.2[9]	17.0[10]	10.0[10]	10.6[9]	13.4[10]	7.7[10]
70 - 74	22.4	27.4[5]	18.4[5]	22.5[9]	27.7[10]	18.5[10]	19.6[9]	22.7[10]	16.8[10]
75 - 79	38.3	46.5[5]	32.4[5]	38.4[9]	46.9[10]	32.4[10]	35.4[9]	39.2[10]	32.6[10]
80 - 84	65.4	73.3[5]	60.5[5]	65.5[9]	73.4[10]	60.5[10]	64.2[9]	71.1[10]	59.1[10]
85 +	157.7	158.6[5]	157.1[5]	157.0[9]	158.4[10]	156.2[10]	167.3[9]	162.3[10]	170.7[10]
Japan - Japon[18]									
2006 (C)									
Total	8.5	9.3	7.7	...	...	...	...	...	...
0 - 4	0.7	0.8	0.7	...	...	...	...	...	...
5 - 9	0.1	0.1	0.1	...	...	...	...	...	...
10 - 14	0.1	0.1	0.1	...	...	...	...	...	...
15 - 19	0.3	0.4	0.2	...	...	...	...	...	...
20 - 24	0.4	0.6	0.3	...	...	...	...	...	...
25 - 29	0.5	0.6	0.3	...	...	...	...	...	...
30 - 34	0.6	0.8	0.4	...	...	...	...	...	...
35 - 39	0.8	1.1	0.6	...	...	...	...	...	...
40 - 44	1.3	1.6	0.9	...	...	...	...	...	...
45 - 49	2.0	2.7	1.3	...	...	...	...	...	...
50 - 54	3.1	4.2	2.0	...	...	...	...	...	...
55 - 59	4.7	6.6	2.9	...	...	...	...	...	...
60 - 64	7.1	10.3	4.1	...	...	...	...	...	...
65 - 69	10.5	15.0	6.4	...	...	...	...	...	...
70 - 74	17.3	24.9	10.8	...	...	...	...	...	...
75 - 79	29.6	43.0	19.5	...	...	...	...	...	...
80 - 84	49.4	70.6	37.0	...	...	...	...	...	...
85 +	118.2	151.6	105.4	...	...	...	...	...	...
Kazakhstan[13]									
2006 (C)									
Total	10.3	12.1	8.5	11.5	14.0	9.3	8.7	9.8	7.5
0	14.5	16.3	12.6	16.3	18.2	14.2	11.9	13.5	10.3
1 - 4	1.2	1.3	1.0	0.9	1.0	0.8	1.5	1.6	1.3
5 - 9	0.5	0.6	0.4	0.5	0.5	0.4	0.5	0.6	0.4
10 - 14	0.5	0.6	0.4	0.5	0.6	0.4	0.5	0.6	0.3
15 - 19	1.1	1.4	0.7	1.1	1.5	0.7	1.1	1.4	0.7
20 - 24	2.2	3.2	1.2	2.5	3.7	1.3	1.9	2.6	1.0
25 - 29	3.6	5.6	1.6	3.9	6.5	1.6	3.0	4.3	1.5
30 - 34	4.7	7.4	2.1	5.4	8.9	2.3	3.7	5.5	1.8
35 - 39	5.5	8.4	2.8	6.1	9.8	3.0	4.6	6.6	2.5
40 - 44	7.4	11.5	3.6	8.3	13.4	3.8	6.1	8.9	3.2
45 - 49	10.0	15.3	5.3	11.1	17.7	5.6	8.2	11.8	4.7
50 - 54	14.0	21.9	7.4	15.0	24.6	7.5	12.3	17.8	7.2
55 - 59	19.3	29.4	11.3	20.2	32.0	11.5	17.7	25.3	11.0
60 - 64	26.3	39.2	17.3	26.9	41.9	17.1	25.5	35.6	17.5
65 - 69	37.8	56.1	26.0	38.5	59.5	26.0	36.9	51.6	26.0
70 - 74	53.4	75.3	40.4	53.4	77.9	40.0	53.6	71.8	41.0
75 - 79	80.8	106.6	68.5	82.1	111.8	69.1	78.6	98.9	67.4
80 - 84	115.1	136.1	107.9	116.1	140.8	107.9	113.4	128.3	107.9
85 - 89	180.1	189.0	177.6	182.6	179.5	183.5	176.1	205.6	167.9
90 - 94	299.6	318.4	295.3	329.8	321.7	332.0	258.8	312.6	248.2
95 - 99	407.9	297.5	444.8	446.8	278.4	516.9	369.2	324.4	380.9
100 +	480.4	136.5	678.7	411.4	♦105.3	668.5	536.8	♦176.5	685.1

Continent, country or area, date, code and age (in years) / Continent, pays ou zone, date, code et âge (en années)	Total			Urban - Urbaine			Rural - Rurale		
	Both sexes Les deux sexes	Male Masculin	Female Féminin	Both sexes Les deux sexes	Male Masculin	Female Féminin	Both sexes Les deux sexes	Male Masculin	Female Féminin
ASIA - ASIE									
Korea (Republic of) - Corée (République de)[19]									
2005 (C)									
Total	5.2[20]	5.8[20]	4.7[20]	4.2	4.6	3.7	9.7	10.7	8.6
0	4.4[20]	4.6[20]	4.2[20]	4.2	4.3	4.1	5.5	6.0	4.9
1 - 4	0.3[20]	0.4[20]	0.3[20]	0.3	0.3	0.2	0.5	0.5	0.4
5 - 9	0.2[20]	0.2[20]	0.2[20]	0.2	0.2	0.1	0.3	0.3	0.3
10 - 14	0.1[20]	0.2[20]	0.1[20]	0.1	0.2	0.1	0.2	0.2	0.2
15 - 19	0.3[20]	0.4[20]	0.2[20]	0.3	0.3	0.2	0.5	0.7	0.3
20 - 24	0.5[20]	0.6[20]	0.4[20]	0.4	0.5	0.4	0.9	1.0	0.6
25 - 29	0.6[20]	0.8[20]	0.5[20]	0.5	0.7	0.4	1.1	1.4	0.7
30 - 34	0.8[20]	1.1[20]	0.6[20]	0.8	1.0	0.5	1.3	1.8	0.9
35 - 39	1.2[20]	1.6[20]	0.8[20]	1.1	1.4	0.7	1.9	2.6	1.2
40 - 44	2.0[20]	2.8[20]	1.1[20]	1.7	2.4	1.0	3.3	4.8	1.7
45 - 49	3.0[20]	4.4[20]	1.6[20]	2.7	4.0	1.4	4.4	6.5	2.2
50 - 54	4.3[20]	6.4[20]	2.2[20]	3.9	5.7	2.0	5.8	9.0	2.7
55 - 59	6.0[20]	9.0[20]	3.2[20]	5.6	8.3	3.0	7.3	11.2	3.5
60 - 64	10.4[20]	15.4[20]	5.8[20]	9.7	14.1	5.5	12.0	19.0	6.4
65 - 69	15.7[20]	23.4[20]	9.4[20]	15.0	21.8	9.3	16.8	26.3	9.6
70 - 74	24.2[20]	34.3[20]	17.2[20]	24.1	33.3	17.6	24.0	35.3	16.3
75 - 79	43.7[20]	59.4[20]	35.1[20]	44.0	58.0	36.6	42.4	60.1	32.3
80 - 84	78.3[20]	101.4[20]	67.5[20]	79.1	101.3	69.4	75.2	98.6	63.4
85 +	166.7[20]	196.3[20]	156.7[20]	167.6	197.2	158.0	161.9	188.4	152.4
Kuwait - Koweït									
2005 (C)									
Total	1.9	2.1	1.7	...	...	...	...	...	...
0	10.3	11.0	9.7	...	...	...	...	...	...
1 - 4	0.5	0.6	0.5	...	...	...	...	...	...
5 - 9	0.3	♦0.3	♦0.2	...	...	...	...	...	...
10 - 14	0.3	0.4	♦0.2	...	...	...	...	...	...
15 - 19	0.6	1.0	♦0.2	...	...	...	...	...	...
20 - 24	0.6	0.9	♦0.2	...	...	...	...	...	...
25 - 29	0.7	0.9	0.3	...	...	...	...	...	...
30 - 34	0.6	0.7	0.4	...	...	...	...	...	...
35 - 39	0.8	1.0	0.5	...	...	...	...	...	...
40 - 44	1.3	1.6	0.7	...	...	...	...	...	...
45 - 49	2.0	2.5	1.1	...	...	...	...	...	...
50 - 54	3.3	3.8	2.5	...	...	...	...	...	...
55 - 59	6.1	6.5	5.4	...	...	...	...	...	...
60 - 64	10.0	10.8	9.0	...	...	...	...	...	...
65 - 69	20.7	23.6	17.1	...	...	...	...	...	...
70 - 74	33.9	33.9	33.8	...	...	...	...	...	...
75 - 79	53.6	61.7	46.1	...	...	...	...	...	...
80 - 84	69.3	86.0	56.0	...	...	...	...	...	...
85 +	137.7	149.9	128.0	...	...	...	...	...	...
Kyrgyzstan - Kirghizistan									
2006 (C)									
Total	7.5	8.4	6.5	8.3	9.7	7.0	7.0	7.8	6.3
0	31.4	34.3	28.5	50.3	54.1	46.3	22.6	24.9	20.2
1 - 4	1.6	1.7	1.5	1.0	1.1	0.9	1.9	2.1	1.8
5 - 9	0.4	0.4	0.3	0.3	♦0.3	♦0.2	0.4	0.4	0.4
10 - 14	0.4	0.5	0.3	0.3	0.4	♦0.3	0.4	0.5	0.3
15 - 19	0.6	0.7	0.4	0.6	0.8	0.4	0.6	0.7	0.4
20 - 24	1.2	1.6	0.8	1.2	1.8	0.7	1.2	1.5	0.9
25 - 29	1.9	2.8	1.1	1.6	2.5	0.7	2.2	3.0	1.3
30 - 34	2.9	4.4	1.5	2.7	4.3	1.3	3.1	4.4	1.6
35 - 39	3.8	5.5	2.2	3.6	5.3	2.1	4.0	5.7	2.2
40 - 44	5.4	8.1	2.9	5.7	8.9	2.9	5.3	7.6	3.0
45 - 49	7.8	11.4	4.4	8.1	12.6	4.2	7.6	10.7	4.5
50 - 54	11.5	16.4	7.0	11.9	17.8	6.8	11.2	15.5	7.2
55 - 59	16.3	22.7	10.6	17.3	25.0	11.0	15.5	21.2	10.3
60 - 64	26.0	34.8	18.4	26.2	37.5	17.5	25.9	33.2	19.1
65 - 69	37.5	49.0	28.8	37.4	51.2	27.9	37.6	47.7	29.4
70 - 74	55.9	75.3	42.4	55.9	83.0	39.6	56.0	71.7	44.1

20. Death rates specific for age, sex and urban/rural residence: latest available year, 1997 - 2006
Taux de mortalité selon l'âge, le sexe et la résidence, urbaine/rurale: dernière année disponible, 1997 - 2006 (continued - suite)

Continent, country or area, date, code and age (in years) / Continent, pays ou zone, date, code et âge (en années)	Total			Urban - Urbaine			Rural - Rurale		
	Both sexes Les deux sexes	Male Masculin	Female Féminin	Both sexes Les deux sexes	Male Masculin	Female Féminin	Both sexes Les deux sexes	Male Masculin	Female Féminin
ASIA - ASIE									
Kyrgyzstan - Kirghizistan									
2006 (C)									
75 - 79	80.8	99.9	68.7	82.2	110.9	67.7	80.0	95.2	69.3
80 - 84	110.5	120.1	105.6	113.2	130.5	106.5	108.8	115.3	105.0
85 - 89	156.0	166.3	152.2	150.0	147.6	150.9	159.7	178.2	153.0
90 - 94	211.2	237.4	203.6	232.7	218.2	237.0	199.7	248.2	185.9
95 - 99	184.8	124.0	207.4	150.6	♦109.8	169.3	199.4	131.5	222.3
100 +	489.7	♦163.5	648.3	♦113.4	♦37.7	♦135.1	850.8	♦226.4	1316.9
Malaysia - Malaisie									
2004 (C)									
Total	4.4	5.0	3.8	...	...	...	...	...	...
0 - 4	1.3	1.5	1.2	...	...	...	...	...	...
5 - 9	0.3	0.3	0.2	...	...	...	...	...	...
10 - 14	0.3	0.4	0.3	...	...	...	...	...	...
15 - 19	0.8	1.2	0.4	...	...	...	...	...	...
20 - 24	1.0	1.5	0.5	...	...	...	...	...	...
25 - 29	1.1	1.6	0.6	...	...	...	...	...	...
30 - 34	1.4	2.1	0.7	...	...	...	...	...	...
35 - 39	1.8	2.5	1.0	...	...	...	...	...	...
40 - 44	2.6	3.6	1.7	...	...	...	...	...	...
45 - 49	4.0	5.3	2.7	...	...	...	...	...	...
50 - 54	6.1	7.5	4.5	...	...	...	...	...	...
55 - 59	10.4	12.8	7.7	...	...	...	...	...	...
60 - 64	16.4	20.2	12.6	...	...	...	...	...	...
65 - 69	29.0	34.9	23.4	...	...	...	...	...	...
70 - 74	43.2	50.6	36.8	...	...	...	...	...	...
75 +	101.8	106.3	98.1	...	...	...	...	...	...
Maldives									
2006 (C)									
Total	3.6	4.3	2.9	3.4	4.1	2.8	3.7	4.4	3.0
0	16.8	19.4	14.2	22.5	♦24.0	♦20.8	14.5	17.5	♦11.5
1 - 4	♦0.7	♦0.9	♦0.6	♦0.3	♦0.7	-	♦0.9	♦0.9	♦0.8
5 - 9	♦0.5	♦0.6	♦0.3	♦0.7	♦0.5	♦0.8	♦0.4	♦0.6	♦0.2
10 - 14	♦0.4	♦0.4	♦0.4	♦0.8	♦0.6	♦1.0	♦0.3	♦0.4	♦0.2
15 - 19	♦0.4	♦0.4	♦0.4	♦0.6	♦0.5	♦0.6	♦0.3	♦0.3	♦0.3
20 - 24	♦0.6	♦1.0	♦0.2	♦0.8	♦1.4	♦0.2	♦0.5	♦0.7	♦0.2
25 - 29	♦0.6	♦0.8	♦0.3	♦0.7	♦0.8	♦0.6	♦0.5	♦0.9	♦0.1
30 - 34	♦0.6	♦0.8	♦0.4	♦0.6	♦1.0	♦0.2	♦0.6	♦0.7	♦0.5
35 - 39	♦0.6	♦0.8	♦0.3	♦0.5	♦0.6	♦0.3	♦0.6	♦0.9	♦0.3
40 - 44	♦1.0	♦1.5	♦0.5	♦0.9	♦1.1	♦0.7	♦1.1	♦1.8	♦0.4
45 - 49	2.9	♦3.2	♦2.7	♦4.8	♦6.3	♦3.2	♦2.1	♦1.7	♦2.4
50 - 54	4.7	♦5.5	♦3.7	♦7.7	♦10.6	♦4.2	♦3.2	♦2.9	♦3.5
55 - 59	8.2	♦8.5	♦7.8	♦11.3	♦11.1	♦11.4	♦6.8	♦7.3	♦6.2
60 - 64	15.8	18.2	13.3	22.4	♦25.3	♦19.5	13.3	15.7	♦10.8
65 - 69	20.3	22.2	18.0	♦23.7	♦29.1	♦18.6	19.3	20.5	17.8
70 +	64.1	66.4	61.0	89.2	107.8	71.5	58.4	58.8	58.0
Mongolia - Mongolie									
2006 (C)									
Total	6.5	7.8	5.1	...	...	...	...	...	...
0	21.3	22.8	19.8	...	...	...	...	...	...
1 - 4	1.4	1.6	1.2	...	...	...	...	...	...
5 - 9	0.3	0.4	0.3	...	...	...	...	...	...
10 - 14	0.4	0.5	0.3	...	...	...	...	...	...
15 - 19	0.7	0.9	0.5	...	...	...	...	...	...
20 - 24	1.3	1.8	0.8	...	...	...	...	...	...
25 - 29	2.2	3.3	1.1	...	...	...	...	...	...
30 - 34	3.0	4.6	1.4	...	...	...	...	...	...
35 - 39	4.4	6.6	2.3	...	...	...	...	...	...
40 - 44	7.2	10.4	4.2	...	...	...	...	...	...
45 - 49	10.5	14.7	6.5	...	...	...	...	...	...
50 - 54	15.1	21.5	9.1	...	...	...	...	...	...
55 - 59	18.3	24.7	12.4	...	...	...	...	...	...
60 - 64	24.8	32.3	18.3	...	...	...	...	...	...
65 - 69	38.3	49.6	28.7	...	...	...	...	...	...
70 +	84.1	93.7	77.4	...	...	...	...	...	...

20. Death rates specific for age, sex and urban/rural residence: latest available year, 1997 - 2006
Taux de mortalité selon l'âge, le sexe et la résidence, urbaine/rurale: dernière année disponible, 1997 - 2006 (continued - suite)

Continent, country or area, date, code and age (in years) Continent, pays ou zone, date, code et âge (en années)	Total			Urban - Urbaine			Rural - Rurale		
	Both sexes Les deux sexes	Male Masculin	Female Féminin	Both sexes Les deux sexes	Male Masculin	Female Féminin	Both sexes Les deux sexes	Male Masculin	Female Féminin
ASIA - ASIE									
Nepal - Népal[21]									
2001 (I)									
Total	4.7	5.2	4.2	...	...	...	...	...	...
0	26.3	27.5	25.1	...	...	...	...	...	...
1 - 4	4.3	4.9	3.8	...	...	...	...	...	...
5 - 9	1.0	1.1	1.0	...	...	...	...	...	...
10 - 14	0.8	0.9	0.7	...	...	...	...	...	...
15 - 19	1.1	1.1	1.0	...	...	...	...	...	...
20 - 24	1.4	1.5	1.2	...	...	...	...	...	...
25 - 29	1.6	1.7	1.4	...	...	...	...	...	...
30 - 34	1.7	1.8	1.5	...	...	...	...	...	...
35 - 39	2.2	2.4	1.9	...	...	...	...	...	...
40 - 44	2.7	3.4	2.1	...	...	...	...	...	...
45 - 49	3.8	4.3	3.4	...	...	...	...	...	...
50 - 54	6.1	7.1	5.1	...	...	...	...	...	...
55 - 59	10.2	11.3	8.8	...	...	...	...	...	...
60 - 64	16.0	18.0	14.0	...	...	...	...	...	...
65 - 69	22.4	24.3	20.4	...	...	...	...	...	...
70 - 74	35.1	38.9	31.0	...	...	...	...	...	...
75 - 79	48.9	56.6	41.4	...	...	...	...	...	...
80 +	100.6	111.8	90.1	...	...	...	...	...	...
Pakistan[22]									
2003 (I)									
Total	7.0	7.5	6.4	6.2	6.8	5.6	7.4	7.9	6.9
0 - 4	19.9	21.5	18.2	16.5	17.5	15.4	21.5	23.3	19.5
5 - 9	0.8	1.1	0.6	0.5	0.7	0.3	1.0	1.3	0.7
10 - 14	0.4	0.7	0.1	0.2	0.4	-	0.5	0.8	0.1
15 - 19	0.9	0.6	1.3	0.6	0.4	0.9	1.1	0.7	1.5
20 - 24	1.7	1.4	1.9	1.5	1.2	2.0	1.8	1.6	1.9
25 - 29	1.8	1.9	1.6	0.9	1.4	0.3	2.3	2.3	2.4
30 - 34	2.0	2.3	1.7	1.3	2.2	0.4	2.4	2.4	2.4
35 - 39	2.6	2.7	2.6	1.8	2.4	1.2	3.1	2.8	3.4
40 - 44	3.5	3.8	3.1	4.0	4.3	3.6	3.1	3.5	2.8
45 - 49	4.8	5.6	4.1	5.3	5.0	5.5	4.6	5.9	3.2
50 - 54	11.4	10.0	12.9	13.9	13.3	14.7	9.9	8.1	12.0
55 - 59	15.8	16.7	14.7	20.4	24.8	15.5	13.0	11.9	14.3
60 - 64	23.7	26.3	20.7	22.7	28.6	15.5	24.3	25.0	23.3
65 - 69	27.2	21.0	35.0	25.7	19.5	33.3	28.0	21.9	35.9
70 - 74	47.1	43.2	52.3	57.1	53.4	61.6	42.1	38.2	47.3
75 - 79	65.2	71.5	57.5	71.1	82.0	59.0	62.2	66.5	56.6
80 - 84	98.5	85.2	116.3	98.3	97.8	98.9	98.5	79.3	125.5
85 +	195.5	247.0	128.8	230.4	312.5	136.1	180.7	221.3	125.4
Philippines									
2003 (C)									
Total	4.9	5.7	4.0	...	...	...	...	...	...
0 - 4	3.4	3.8	3.0	...	...	...	...	...	...
5 - 9	0.6	0.6	0.5	...	...	...	...	...	...
10 - 14	0.5	0.6	0.4	...	...	...	...	...	...
15 - 19	0.8	1.0	0.6	...	...	...	...	...	...
20 - 24	1.3	1.8	0.8	...	...	...	...	...	...
25 - 29	1.6	2.2	1.0	...	...	...	...	...	...
30 - 34	2.1	2.9	1.3	...	...	...	...	...	...
35 - 39	2.9	3.9	1.8	...	...	...	...	...	...
40 - 44	4.0	5.4	2.6	...	...	...	...	...	...
45 - 49	5.7	7.7	3.7	...	...	...	...	...	...
50 - 54	8.5	11.4	5.5	...	...	...	...	...	...
55 - 59	11.1	15.0	7.2	...	...	...	...	...	...
60 - 64	17.1	22.8	11.7	...	...	...	...	...	...
65 - 69	25.7	32.8	19.1	...	...	...	...	...	...
70 - 74	37.1	45.8	29.5	...	...	...	...	...	...
75 - 79	54.5	64.6	46.6	...	...	...	...	...	...
80 +	138.5	140.4	137.2	...	...	...	...	...	...

20. Death rates specific for age, sex and urban/rural residence: latest available year, 1997 - 2006
Taux de mortalité selon l'âge, le sexe et la résidence, urbaine/rurale: dernière année disponible, 1997 - 2006 (continued - suite)

Continent, country or area, date, code and age (in years) Continent, pays ou zone, date, code et âge (en années)	Total			Urban - Urbaine			Rural - Rurale		
	Both sexes Les deux sexes	Male Masculin	Female Féminin	Both sexes Les deux sexes	Male Masculin	Female Féminin	Both sexes Les deux sexes	Male Masculin	Female Féminin
ASIA - ASIE									
Qatar									
2006 (C)									
Total...................	1.9	1.9	1.8	...	...	...	...	...	...
0........................	7.2	7.9	6.4	...	...	...	...	...	...
1 - 4....................	0.6	♦0.6	♦0.7	...	...	...	...	...	...
5 - 9....................	♦0.2	♦0.2	♦0.3	...	...	...	...	...	...
10 - 14..................	♦0.3	♦0.4	♦0.2	...	...	...	...	...	...
15 - 19..................	1.2	1.7	♦0.5	...	...	...	...	...	...
20 - 24..................	1.3	1.5	♦0.5	...	...	...	...	...	...
25 - 29..................	1.1	1.2	♦0.7	...	...	...	...	...	...
30 - 34..................	0.9	1.0	♦0.3	...	...	...	...	...	...
35 - 39..................	1.0	1.2	♦0.4	...	...	...	...	...	...
40 - 44..................	1.2	1.3	♦0.9	...	...	...	...	...	...
45 - 49..................	1.7	1.8	♦1.2	...	...	...	...	...	...
50 - 54..................	2.9	3.2	♦1.9	...	...	...	...	...	...
55 - 59..................	4.3	4.3	♦4.3	...	...	...	...	...	...
60 - 64..................	9.7	7.6	16.6	...	...	...	...	...	...
65 - 69..................	21.8	18.4	29.9	...	...	...	...	...	...
70 - 74..................	45.5	35.3	66.4	...	...	...	...	...	...
75 - 79..................	65.9	48.1	98.8	...	...	...	...	...	...
80 +....................	112.3	109.3	116.6	...	...	...	...	...	...
Saudi Arabia - Arabie saoudite[23]									
2004 (I)									
Total...................	3.3	3.7	2.9	...	...	...	...	...	...
0........................	18.4	17.7	19.0	...	...	...	...	...	...
1 - 4....................	0.5	0.4	0.6	...	...	...	...	...	...
5 - 9....................	0.9	1.0	0.8	...	...	...	...	...	...
10 - 14..................	0.7	0.8	0.5	...	...	...	...	...	...
15 - 19..................	1.3	2.1	0.5	...	...	...	...	...	...
20 - 24..................	1.5	2.4	0.5	...	...	...	...	...	...
25 - 29..................	0.8	1.0	0.4	...	...	...	...	...	...
30 - 34..................	0.6	0.6	0.5	...	...	...	...	...	...
35 - 39..................	0.8	0.7	0.8	...	...	...	...	...	...
40 - 44..................	1.4	1.4	1.5	...	...	...	...	...	...
45 - 49..................	2.3	2.6	1.8	...	...	...	...	...	...
50 - 54..................	4.5	4.4	4.7	...	...	...	...	...	...
55 - 59..................	6.2	6.5	5.9	...	...	...	...	...	...
60 - 64..................	18.5	21.4	15.3	...	...	...	...	...	...
65 - 69..................	21.8	28.7	14.2	...	...	...	...	...	...
70 - 74..................	57.4	75.8	39.8	...	...	...	...	...	...
75 - 79..................	51.5	57.3	43.7	...	...	...	...	...	...
80 +....................	114.6	115.7	113.3	...	...	...	...	...	...
Singapore - Singapour									
2005 (+C)									
Total...................	4.6	5.1	4.1	...	...	...	...	...	...
0 - 4....................	0.7	0.8	0.6	...	...	...	...	...	...
5 - 9....................	0.1	♦0.1	♦0.2	...	...	...	...	...	...
10 - 14..................	0.1	♦0.1	♦0.1	...	...	...	...	...	...
15 - 19..................	0.3	0.4	♦0.2	...	...	...	...	...	...
20 - 24..................	0.6	0.8	0.4	...	...	...	...	...	...
25 - 29..................	0.5	0.8	0.3	...	...	...	...	...	...
30 - 34..................	0.7	0.9	0.5	...	...	...	...	...	...
35 - 39..................	0.9	1.3	0.6	...	...	...	...	...	...
40 - 44..................	1.3	1.6	0.9	...	...	...	...	...	...
45 - 49..................	2.1	2.6	1.5	...	...	...	...	...	...
50 - 54..................	3.6	4.6	2.6	...	...	...	...	...	...
55 - 59..................	5.9	7.8	3.9	...	...	...	...	...	...
60 - 64..................	9.6	12.1	7.2	...	...	...	...	...	...
65 - 69..................	16.5	22.3	11.2	...	...	...	...	...	...
70 - 74..................	25.1	32.1	19.2	...	...	...	...	...	...
75 - 79..................	39.3	48.1	32.5	...	...	...	...	...	...
80 - 84..................	68.3	81.4	59.0	...	...	...	...	...	...
85 +....................	125.3	138.2	118.8	...	...	...	...	...	...

20. Death rates specific for age, sex and urban/rural residence: latest available year, 1997 - 2006
Taux de mortalité selon l'âge, le sexe et la résidence, urbaine/rurale: dernière année disponible, 1997 - 2006 (continued - suite)

Continent, country or area, date, code and age (in years) / Continent, pays ou zone, date, code et âge (en années)	Total			Urban - Urbaine			Rural - Rurale		
	Both sexes Les deux sexes	Male Masculin	Female Féminin	Both sexes Les deux sexes	Male Masculin	Female Féminin	Both sexes Les deux sexes	Male Masculin	Female Féminin
ASIA - ASIE									
Uzbekistan - Ouzbékistan[13]									
2000 (C)									
Total	5.5	5.8	5.2	6.6	7.1	6.2	4.8	5.0	4.6
0	19.1	21.4	16.6	22.6	25.4	19.6	17.5	19.6	15.3
1 - 4	2.3	2.4	2.2	1.6	1.7	1.5	2.6	2.8	2.5
5 - 9	0.4	0.5	0.4	0.4	0.5	0.3	0.5	0.6	0.4
10 - 14	0.5	0.5	0.4	0.4	0.5	0.4	0.5	0.6	0.4
15 - 19	0.7	0.9	0.5	0.7	1.0	0.5	0.7	0.9	0.5
20 - 24	1.3	1.6	1.0	1.4	1.9	0.9	1.2	1.4	1.0
25 - 29	1.7	2.2	1.3	1.9	2.5	1.2	1.6	1.9	1.3
30 - 34	2.1	2.9	1.4	2.4	3.3	1.4	2.0	2.5	1.5
35 - 39	2.5	3.4	1.7	3.0	4.3	1.7	2.2	2.7	1.6
40 - 44	3.6	4.8	2.6	4.4	6.3	2.6	3.1	3.7	2.5
45 - 49	5.4	7.2	3.7	6.2	8.9	3.7	4.7	5.8	3.6
50 - 54	9.4	12.2	6.7	10.2	14.1	6.7	8.5	10.4	6.6
55 - 59	14.2	17.6	10.8	15.3	20.9	10.2	13.2	15.0	11.3
60 - 64	22.3	27.5	17.5	23.3	31.4	16.5	21.5	24.5	18.4
65 - 69	35.9	43.2	29.7	37.2	49.2	28.2	34.8	39.0	30.9
70 - 74	52.7	61.0	46.2	54.6	69.8	45.0	51.2	55.1	47.4
75 - 79	72.9	80.3	68.9	73.8	84.7	69.0	72.1	77.2	68.8
80 - 84	114.2	129.9	108.1	115.6	127.9	111.3	112.9	131.6	104.7
85 - 89	164.0	194.7	152.6	166.2	183.1	160.8	161.7	204.8	143.4
90 - 94	195.5	192.3	197.2	171.3	152.4	179.9	215.8	219.9	213.3
95 +	316.6	202.4	394.2	156.3	168.0	151.3	460.7	220.9	700.6
EUROPE									
Albania - Albanie									
2006 (C)									
Total	5.4	...	...	...	...	...	...	...	...
0 - 4	1.7	...	...	...	...	...	...	...	...
5 - 9	0.5	...	...	...	...	...	...	...	...
10 - 14	0.3	...	...	...	...	...	...	...	...
15 - 19	0.4	...	...	...	...	...	...	...	...
20 - 24	0.5	...	...	...	...	...	...	...	...
25 - 29	0.7	...	...	...	...	...	...	...	...
30 - 34	0.8	...	...	...	...	...	...	...	...
35 - 39	1.1	...	...	...	...	...	...	...	...
40 - 44	1.4	...	...	...	...	...	...	...	...
45 - 49	2.2	...	...	...	...	...	...	...	...
50 - 54	3.6	...	...	...	...	...	...	...	...
55 - 59	4.9	...	...	...	...	...	...	...	...
60 - 64	9.1	...	...	...	...	...	...	...	...
65 - 69	14.5	...	...	...	...	...	...	...	...
70 - 74	30.8	...	...	...	...	...	...	...	...
75 - 79	51.8	...	...	...	...	...	...	...	...
80 - 84	96.7	...	...	...	...	...	...	...	...
85 +	196.4	...	...	...	...	...	...	...	...
Austria - Autriche									
2006 (C)									
Total	9.0	8.6	9.3	...	...	...	...	...	...
0	3.6	4.1	3.1	...	...	...	...	...	...
1 - 4	0.2	0.3	♦0.2	...	...	...	...	...	...
5 - 9	0.1	♦0.1	♦0.1	...	...	...	...	...	...
10 - 14	0.1	0.1	♦0.1	...	...	...	...	...	...
15 - 19	0.5	0.7	0.3	...	...	...	...	...	...
20 - 24	0.6	0.8	0.3	...	...	...	...	...	...
25 - 29	0.5	0.7	0.3	...	...	...	...	...	...
30 - 34	0.6	0.8	0.4	...	...	...	...	...	...
35 - 39	0.8	1.2	0.5	...	...	...	...	...	...
40 - 44	1.3	1.7	0.9	...	...	...	...	...	...
45 - 49	2.2	2.9	1.4	...	...	...	...	...	...
50 - 54	3.7	5.0	2.4	...	...	...	...	...	...
55 - 59	6.2	8.4	4.0	...	...	...	...	...	...

20. Death rates specific for age, sex and urban/rural residence: latest available year, 1997 - 2006
Taux de mortalité selon l'âge, le sexe et la résidence, urbaine/rurale: dernière année disponible, 1997 - 2006 (continued - suite)

Continent, country or area, date, code and age (in years) / Continent, pays ou zone, date, code et âge (en années)	Total			Urban - Urbaine			Rural - Rurale		
	Both sexes Les deux sexes	Male Masculin	Female Féminin	Both sexes Les deux sexes	Male Masculin	Female Féminin	Both sexes Les deux sexes	Male Masculin	Female Féminin
EUROPE									
Austria - Autriche									
2006 (C)									
60 - 64	9.1	12.7	5.9	...	...	...	...	...	...
65 - 69	13.0	17.6	8.9	...	...	...	...	...	...
70 - 74	21.5	29.3	15.3	...	...	...	...	...	...
75 - 79	37.1	49.1	28.9	...	...	...	...	...	...
80 - 84	66.6	85.9	57.9	...	...	...	...	...	...
85 - 89	119.1	142.2	110.5	...	...	...	...	...	...
90 - 94	220.5	252.1	210.9	...	...	...	...	...	...
95 +	338.4	365.4	331.8	...	...	...	...	...	...
Belarus - Bélarus[13]									
2006 (C)									
Total	14.2	16.1	12.6	10.7	12.7	8.9	23.6	25.2	22.3
0	6.3	7.0	5.6	5.9	6.4	5.4	7.3	8.5	6.1
1 - 4	0.5	0.6	0.5	0.4	0.4	0.4	1.0	1.1	1.0
5 - 9	0.2	0.3	0.2	0.2	0.2	◆0.1	0.3	0.5	◆0.2
10 - 14	0.2	0.2	0.2	0.2	0.2	0.2	0.2	◆0.2	◆0.2
15 - 19	0.7	1.0	0.4	0.5	0.7	0.3	1.2	1.7	0.5
20 - 24	1.3	2.0	0.5	1.0	1.5	0.4	2.4	3.7	1.0
25 - 29	2.2	3.4	0.9	1.7	2.7	0.8	4.1	6.4	1.5
30 - 34	3.2	5.1	1.2	2.6	4.2	1.0	5.1	8.1	1.9
35 - 39	4.0	6.4	1.8	3.2	5.0	1.5	6.5	9.9	2.7
40 - 44	5.8	9.2	2.5	4.7	7.6	2.2	8.9	13.5	3.6
45 - 49	8.2	13.2	3.5	6.8	11.1	3.1	12.5	18.8	5.2
50 - 54	11.7	18.8	5.5	9.9	16.4	4.7	17.3	25.7	8.2
55 - 59	17.7	27.5	9.6	15.8	25.1	8.6	23.7	34.6	13.3
60 - 64	25.5	42.2	13.6	22.9	37.9	12.1	31.1	51.6	16.8
65 - 69	33.5	54.8	20.4	30.9	51.3	18.3	37.7	61.0	23.9
70 - 74	48.1	73.8	34.5	45.9	69.5	33.5	50.4	78.4	35.7
75 - 79	71.3	102.3	57.5	70.4	100.4	56.8	72.2	104.3	58.1
80 - 84	110.8	142.6	101.2	105.3	139.2	94.7	116.2	146.1	107.6
85 +	208.0	233.1	202.0	176.8	208.7	168.6	244.2	263.7	239.8
Belgium - Belgique[24]									
2006 (C)									
Total	9.7	9.8	9.5	...	...	...	...	...	...
0	4.1	4.4	3.8	...	...	...	...	...	...
1 - 4	0.2	0.2	0.2	...	...	...	...	...	...
5 - 9	0.1	0.1	◆0.1	...	...	...	...	...	...
10 - 14	0.1	0.1	0.1	...	...	...	...	...	...
15 - 19	0.4	0.5	0.2	...	...	...	...	...	...
20 - 24	0.6	0.9	0.2	...	...	...	...	...	...
25 - 29	0.6	0.9	0.4	...	...	...	...	...	...
30 - 34	0.8	1.1	0.5	...	...	...	...	...	...
35 - 39	1.0	1.4	0.7	...	...	...	...	...	...
40 - 44	1.6	2.0	1.1	...	...	...	...	...	...
45 - 49	2.7	3.4	1.9	...	...	...	...	...	...
50 - 54	4.2	5.3	3.2	...	...	...	...	...	...
55 - 59	6.3	8.2	4.4	...	...	...	...	...	...
60 - 64	10.0	13.4	6.7	...	...	...	...	...	...
65 - 69	13.7	18.6	9.4	...	...	...	...	...	...
70 - 74	22.2	30.3	15.6	...	...	...	...	...	...
75 - 79	39.6	53.6	29.8	...	...	...	...	...	...
80 - 84	70.2	91.6	58.0	...	...	...	...	...	...
85 - 89	130.2	161.1	116.8	...	...	...	...	...	...
90 - 94	207.0	254.7	192.7	...	...	...	...	...	...
95 - 99	339.2	382.3	330.8	...	...	...	...	...	...
100 +	481.5	460.0	484.3	...	...	...	...	...	...
Bulgaria - Bulgarie									
2006 (C)									
Total	14.7	16.2	13.3	12.2	13.6	11.0	20.7	22.3	19.2
0	10.4	10.4	10.3	9.2	9.3	9.0	13.8	13.4	14.3
1 - 4	0.5	0.6	0.4	0.4	0.5	0.4	0.7	◆0.8	◆0.6
5 - 9	0.3	0.4	0.3	0.3	0.3	0.4	0.4	◆0.5	◆0.3
10 - 14	0.3	0.3	0.2	0.2	0.2	0.2	0.3	◆0.5	◆0.2
15 - 19	0.5	0.7	0.3	0.5	0.7	0.2	0.7	0.8	0.6

20. Death rates specific for age, sex and urban/rural residence: latest available year, 1997 - 2006
Taux de mortalité selon l'âge, le sexe et la résidence, urbaine/rurale: dernière année disponible, 1997 - 2006 (continued - suite)

Continent, country or area, date, code and age (in years) / Continent, pays ou zone, date, code et âge (en années)	Total			Urban - Urbaine			Rural - Rurale		
	Both sexes Les deux sexes	Male Masculin	Female Féminin	Both sexes Les deux sexes	Male Masculin	Female Féminin	Both sexes Les deux sexes	Male Masculin	Female Féminin
EUROPE									
Bulgaria - Bulgarie									
2006 (C)									
20 - 24	0.8	1.1	0.4	0.7	1.1	0.3	0.9	1.2	♦0.6
25 - 29	0.9	1.3	0.4	0.9	1.3	0.4	0.8	1.2	♦0.4
30 - 34	1.1	1.5	0.7	1.1	1.4	0.7	1.4	1.9	0.8
35 - 39	1.8	2.4	1.2	1.6	2.1	1.1	2.3	3.1	1.3
40 - 44	3.1	4.2	2.0	2.8	3.8	1.9	3.8	5.0	2.3
45 - 49	5.1	7.3	3.0	4.6	6.6	2.7	6.6	9.1	3.7
50 - 54	8.3	12.2	4.7	7.8	11.3	4.6	10.0	14.5	5.2
55 - 59	12.5	18.8	6.8	11.7	17.4	6.7	14.4	22.0	7.2
60 - 64	17.9	26.7	10.5	17.4	25.7	10.3	18.9	28.4	10.9
65 - 69	26.6	37.6	17.9	27.3	39.0	18.3	25.5	35.7	17.3
70 - 74	42.3	55.9	32.2	42.4	57.9	31.7	42.1	53.7	32.9
75 - 79	70.9	86.1	60.6	71.7	90.0	60.1	69.9	81.6	61.4
80 - 84	120.2	137.5	109.9	121.4	141.7	109.9	118.8	132.8	109.8
85 - 89	181.7	198.9	172.1	184.1	203.0	174.1	178.8	194.4	169.6
90 - 94	286.0	300.7	278.4	291.2	311.9	281.3	280.1	289.1	275.1
95 - 99	370.6	364.5	373.6	388.3	406.9	379.2	351.5	318.5	367.6
100 +	425.9	413.3	430.8	480.3	♦527.8	461.5	377.6	♦307.7	403.8
Croatia - Croatie									
2001 (C)									
Total	11.2	11.7	10.6	10.1	10.8	9.4	12.6	12.9	12.3
0	7.3	7.6	7.1	7.6	7.8	7.4	7.0	7.2	6.7
1 - 4	0.3	0.4	♦0.2	♦0.3	♦0.3	♦0.2	0.4	♦0.5	♦0.2
5 - 9	0.2	♦0.2	♦0.1	♦0.1	♦0.2	♦0.1	♦0.2	♦0.2	♦0.2
10 - 14	0.2	♦0.2	♦0.1	♦0.1	♦0.2	♦0.1	♦0.2	♦0.3	♦0.1
15 - 19	0.5	0.8	0.3	0.5	0.7	♦0.3	0.5	0.9	♦0.2
20 - 24	0.8	1.2	0.3	0.8	1.3	♦0.3	0.7	1.1	♦0.3
25 - 29	0.7	1.1	0.3	0.7	1.0	♦0.3	0.7	1.2	♦0.2
30 - 34	0.9	1.2	0.5	0.9	1.2	0.6	0.9	1.2	♦0.5
35 - 39	1.4	2.1	0.8	1.3	1.9	0.8	1.5	2.2	0.7
40 - 44	2.4	3.5	1.3	2.1	3.0	1.2	2.9	4.2	1.5
45 - 49	4.0	5.9	2.1	3.6	5.5	1.9	4.7	6.6	2.4
50 - 54	6.5	9.4	3.7	5.9	8.5	3.7	7.4	10.6	3.9
55 - 59	9.8	14.4	5.6	9.5	13.9	5.6	10.2	15.0	5.6
60 - 64	15.2	22.4	9.1	14.5	21.0	8.8	16.1	24.1	9.4
65 - 69	24.2	34.9	16.0	23.3	33.0	15.5	25.2	37.0	16.4
70 - 74	39.4	54.0	29.5	38.9	53.7	28.9	39.8	54.3	30.2
75 - 79	62.9	80.2	54.7	60.9	75.0	54.0	65.1	85.7	55.5
80 - 84	106.1	126.4	97.4	100.2	122.5	90.3	112.4	130.7	104.8
85 - 89	168.2	191.2	159.2	155.3	182.5	144.5	182.5	201.1	175.3
90 - 94	275.0	318.6	260.5	254.2	322.9	232.1	298.2	314.8	292.4
95 - 99	394.6	404.0	392.0	355.9	405.2	343.3	441.7	402.7	454.2
100 +	607.1	♦761.9	555.6	♦425.9	♦312.5	♦473.7	♦833.3	♦1800.0	♦640.0
2006 (C)									
Total	11.3	11.8	10.9	...	...	...	...	...	...
0	5.2	4.9	5.4	...	...	...	...	...	...
1 - 4	0.2	♦0.3	♦0.2	...	...	...	...	...	...
5 - 9	0.1	♦0.2	♦0.1	...	...	...	...	...	...
10 - 14	0.1	♦0.2	♦0.1	...	...	...	...	...	...
15 - 19	0.4	0.6	0.2	...	...	...	...	...	...
20 - 24	0.7	1.0	0.4	...	...	...	...	...	...
25 - 29	0.7	1.1	0.3	...	...	...	...	...	...
30 - 34	0.7	1.0	0.4	...	...	...	...	...	...
35 - 39	1.2	1.7	0.7	...	...	...	...	...	...
40 - 44	1.9	2.8	1.1	...	...	...	...	...	...
45 - 49	3.6	5.3	2.0	...	...	...	...	...	...
50 - 54	5.9	8.6	3.2	...	...	...	...	...	...
55 - 59	8.7	12.9	4.8	...	...	...	...	...	...
60 - 64	13.3	19.5	8.0	...	...	...	...	...	...
65 - 69	20.3	29.3	13.2	...	...	...	...	...	...
70 - 74	34.7	48.3	25.2	...	...	...	...	...	...
75 - 79	58.8	77.1	48.1	...	...	...	...	...	...
80 - 84	100.1	123.4	90.6	...	...	...	...	...	...
85 +	202.3	225.0	194.5	...	...	...	...	...	...

20. Death rates specific for age, sex and urban/rural residence: latest available year, 1997 - 2006
Taux de mortalité selon l'âge, le sexe et la résidence, urbaine/rurale: dernière année disponible, 1997 - 2006 (continued - suite)

Continent, country or area, date, code and age (in years) / Continent, pays ou zone, date, code et âge (en années)	Total			Urban - Urbaine			Rural - Rurale		
	Both sexes Les deux sexes	Male Masculin	Female Féminin	Both sexes Les deux sexes	Male Masculin	Female Féminin	Both sexes Les deux sexes	Male Masculin	Female Féminin
EUROPE									
Czech Republic - République tchèque									
2006 (C)									
Total	10.2	10.5	9.8	10.0	10.3	9.7	10.5	10.9	10.1
0	3.3	3.9	2.7	3.4	4.1	2.8	3.0	3.6	2.5
1 - 4	0.2	0.2	0.2	0.2	0.2	◆0.2	◆0.2	◆0.1	◆0.3
5 - 9	0.1	0.2	◆0.1	0.1	◆0.2	◆0.1	◆0.2	◆0.2	◆0.1
10 - 14	0.1	0.2	◆0.1	0.1	0.2	◆0.1	◆0.1	◆0.2	-
15 - 19	0.4	0.6	0.2	0.4	0.5	0.2	0.4	0.6	◆0.2
20 - 24	0.6	0.9	0.3	0.6	0.9	0.3	0.6	0.9	◆0.3
25 - 29	0.5	0.8	0.3	0.5	0.8	0.2	0.6	0.9	0.3
30 - 34	0.7	0.9	0.4	0.7	1.0	0.4	0.7	0.9	0.4
35 - 39	1.1	1.5	0.7	1.1	1.4	0.7	1.2	1.7	0.7
40 - 44	1.9	2.5	1.3	1.8	2.4	1.2	2.1	2.6	1.4
45 - 49	3.4	4.7	2.1	3.3	4.6	2.1	3.6	5.1	1.9
50 - 54	5.6	7.9	3.3	5.6	8.0	3.4	5.5	7.8	3.0
55 - 59	8.7	12.2	5.4	8.5	12.0	5.4	9.2	12.7	5.5
60 - 64	13.3	18.9	8.3	13.1	18.5	8.4	14.0	20.0	8.2
65 - 69	19.4	27.4	13.0	18.9	26.2	13.0	21.1	30.6	13.1
70 - 74	31.6	43.0	23.4	30.9	42.0	23.0	33.5	45.6	24.6
75 - 79	52.4	67.6	43.2	51.3	66.0	42.3	55.7	72.1	45.7
80 - 84	90.7	111.1	80.9	89.4	107.8	80.6	94.2	120.7	81.7
85 - 89	140.2	167.2	129.3	136.8	162.8	126.4	149.9	179.4	137.7
90 - 94	280.9	321.8	268.0	282.9	331.2	268.2	275.5	298.7	267.5
95 - 99	336.1	339.8	335.2	348.7	344.3	349.8	306.3	329.5	300.0
100 +	427.3	379.3	439.1	505.3	◆463.0	515.4	289.3	◆242.4	301.6
Denmark - Danemark[25]									
2006 (C)									
Total	10.2	10.1	10.3	...	...	...	...	...	...
0	3.9	4.3	3.5	...	...	...	...	...	...
1 - 4	0.2	◆0.2	◆0.1	...	...	...	...	...	...
5 - 9	0.1	◆0.1	◆0.1	...	...	...	...	...	...
10 - 14	0.1	◆0.1	◆0.1	...	...	...	...	...	...
15 - 19	0.3	0.5	0.2	...	...	...	...	...	...
20 - 24	0.5	0.8	◆0.2	...	...	...	...	...	...
25 - 29	0.5	0.6	0.3	...	...	...	...	...	...
30 - 34	0.6	0.9	0.3	...	...	...	...	...	...
35 - 39	1.0	1.3	0.7	...	...	...	...	...	...
40 - 44	1.7	2.1	1.3	...	...	...	...	...	...
45 - 49	2.7	3.5	1.9	...	...	...	...	...	...
50 - 54	4.9	6.2	3.7	...	...	...	...	...	...
55 - 59	7.2	8.8	5.6	...	...	...	...	...	...
60 - 64	11.1	13.7	8.5	...	...	...	...	...	...
65 - 69	17.1	20.6	13.9	...	...	...	...	...	...
70 - 74	29.1	35.4	23.6	...	...	...	...	...	...
75 - 79	48.2	58.9	40.0	...	...	...	...	...	...
80 - 84	76.4	95.8	64.4	...	...	...	...	...	...
85 - 89	127.5	154.6	114.6	...	...	...	...	...	...
90 - 94	211.0	255.5	195.5	...	...	...	...	...	...
95 +	347.5	411.0	332.8	...	...	...	...	...	...
Estonia - Estonie									
2006 (C)									
Total	12.9	14.3	11.7	11.2	12.6	10.0	16.7	17.9	15.6
0	4.6	5.9	◆3.2	4.3	◆5.1	◆3.5	◆5.4	◆8.0	◆2.5
1 - 4	◆0.4	◆0.4	◆0.3	◆0.3	◆0.4	◆0.3	◆0.4	◆0.5	◆0.4
5 - 9	◆0.2	◆0.2	◆0.2	◆0.1	◆0.2	◆0.1	◆0.4	◆0.3	◆0.5
10 - 14	◆0.2	◆0.2	◆0.1	◆0.1	◆0.1	-	◆0.4	◆0.4	◆0.3
15 - 19	0.7	1.1	◆0.3	0.6	0.8	◆0.3	1.0	◆1.6	◆0.3
20 - 24	1.3	2.0	◆0.5	1.3	2.0	◆0.6	1.2	2.0	◆0.3
25 - 29	1.6	2.5	◆0.6	1.7	2.8	◆0.5	1.3	◆1.8	◆0.8
30 - 34	1.8	2.9	0.7	1.6	2.6	◆0.6	2.5	3.8	◆1.0
35 - 39	2.2	3.6	1.0	2.0	3.2	1.0	2.7	4.3	◆1.0
40 - 44	3.8	6.1	1.7	3.6	5.8	1.6	4.4	6.7	◆1.9
45 - 49	5.9	9.5	2.7	4.9	8.0	2.4	8.2	12.6	3.6
50 - 54	10.0	15.8	5.1	8.9	14.2	4.9	12.6	19.5	5.6

20. Death rates specific for age, sex and urban/rural residence: latest available year, 1997 - 2006
Taux de mortalité selon l'âge, le sexe et la résidence, urbaine/rurale: dernière année disponible, 1997 - 2006 (continued - suite)

Continent, country or area, date, code and age (in years) / Continent, pays ou zone, date, code et âge (en années)	Total			Urban - Urbaine			Rural - Rurale		
	Both sexes Les deux sexes	Male Masculin	Female Féminin	Both sexes Les deux sexes	Male Masculin	Female Féminin	Both sexes Les deux sexes	Male Masculin	Female Féminin
EUROPE									
Estonia - Estonie									
2006 (C)									
55 - 59	13.8	21.8	7.6	12.1	18.9	7.1	17.9	27.9	8.7
60 - 64	19.1	30.4	10.9	15.5	25.4	9.0	26.4	39.4	15.1
65 - 69	24.8	41.1	14.4	21.2	35.5	12.6	33.3	52.9	19.2
70 - 74	34.9	57.0	22.7	30.6	50.1	20.4	44.3	70.5	28.1
75 - 79	55.5	83.1	43.0	48.8	75.2	37.0	71.6	101.4	57.6
80 - 84	91.1	122.9	81.4	81.1	110.6	72.3	112.3	147.4	101.0
85 - 89	156.5	191.1	147.0	134.6	166.0	126.0	199.1	240.9	187.8
90 - 94	236.9	269.1	228.8	217.9	268.1	·206.1	270.4	270.5	270.4
95 - 99	349.6	403.3	338.4	316.9	421.6	296.6	399.0	◆379.7	403.6
100 +	328.5	◆285.7	336.2	◆363.6	◆333.3	◆371.0	◆283.3	◆166.7	◆296.3
Finland - Finlande[26]									
2006 (C)									
Total	9.1	9.4	8.8	8.2	8.5	8.0	10.7	11.0	10.4
0	2.9	3.2	2.5	2.9	3.3	2.4	2.9	3.1	◆2.6
1 - 4	◆0.1	◆0.1	◆0.1	◆0.1	◆0.1	◆0.1	◆0.2	◆0.2	◆0.3
5 - 9	0.1	◆0.1	◆0.1	◆0.1	◆0.1	◆0.1	◆0.1	·◆0.1	◆0.1
10 - 14	0.1	◆0.2	◆0.1	◆0.1	◆0.1	◆0.1	◆0.2	◆0.3	◆0.1
15 - 19	0.5	0.8	0.2	0.4	0.7	◆0.2	0.6	0.9	◆0.3
20 - 24	0.7	1.1	0.3	0.7	1.2	◆0.2	0.7	1.0	◆0.3
25 - 29	0.6	1.0	0.3	0.6	0.9	0.3	0.7	1.1	◆0.2
30 - 34	0.8	1.2	0.4	0.8	1.2	0.3	1.0	1.3	◆0.6
35 - 39	1.2	1.6	0.7	1.1	1.5	0.7	1.3	1.9	0.6
40 - 44	1.8	2.4	1.1	1.8	2.4	1.1	1.8	2.5	1.0
45 - 49	3.0	4.2	1.8	3.0	4.3	1.8	2.9	4.0	1.6
50 - 54	4.7	6.4	3.0	4.8	6.6	3.0	4.6	6.0	3.0
55 - 59	6.9	9.7	4.0	6.7	9.5	4.1	7.1	10.0	3.9
60 - 64	9.4	13.4	5.7	9.4	13.3	5.8	9.5	13.4	5.4
65 - 69	13.8	19.6	8.6	13.3	18.9	8.6	14.4	20.5	8.6
70 - 74	22.0	31.5	14.4	21.1	30.6	14.1	23.1	32.5	14.9
75 - 79	37.3	52.8	27.1	36.6	53.4	26.4	38.3	52.1	28.2
80 - 84	67.1	90.0	56.0	65.5	90.5	54.2	69.2	89.3	58.4
85 - 89	117.1	147.5	106.3	115.7	149.7	104.5	118.9	144.9	108.7
90 - 94	210.1	251.1	198.9	204.2	252.5	192.4	217.8	249.6	208.0
95 - 99	322.8	372.8	312.2	316.0	360.5	307.5	331.9	386.1	318.8
100 +	523.1	622.6	506.9	559.0	◆557.4	559.3	479.5	◆711.1	444.4
France[27]									
2005 (C)									
Total	8.6	9.1	8.2	...	...	...	...	...	...
0	3.6	4.0	3.2	...	...	...	...	...	...
1 - 4	0.2	0.2	0.2	...	...	...	...	...	...
5 - 9	0.1	0.1	0.1	...	...	...	...	...	...
10 - 14	0.1	0.1	0.1	...	...	...	...	...	...
15 - 19	0.4	0.5	0.2	...	...	...	...	...	...
20 - 24	0.6	0.9	0.3	...	...	...	...	...	...
25 - 29	0.6	0.9	0.3	...	...	...	...	...	...
30 - 34	0.8	1.1	0.5	...	...	...	...	...	...
35 - 39	1.1	1.5	0.8	...	...	...	...	...	...
40 - 44	1.8	2.4	1.2	...	...	...	...	...	...
45 - 49	3.1	4.3	2.0	...	...	...	...	...	...
50 - 54	4.6	6.4	2.8	...	...	...	...	...	...
55 - 59	6.3	9.0	3.7	...	...	...	...	...	...
60 - 64	8.7	12.2	5.3	...	...	...	...	...	...
65 - 69	12.6	18.1	7.8	...	...	...	...	...	...
70 - 74	19.8	28.7	12.8	...	...	...	...	...	...
75 - 79	32.6	45.9	23.3	...	...	...	...	...	...
80 - 84	58.0	78.9	46.1	...	...	...	...	...	...
85 - 89	99.9	128.7	86.7	...	...	...	...	...	...
90 - 94	186.3	227.3	172.6	...	...	...	...	...	...
95 - 99	298.8	339.4	289.3	...	...	...	...	...	...
100 +	316.0	224.7	337.1	...	...	...	...	...	...

Continent, country or area, date, code and age (in years) / Continent, pays ou zone, date, code et âge (en années)	Total			Urban - Urbaine			Rural - Rurale		
	Both sexes Les deux sexes	Male Masculin	Female Féminin	Both sexes Les deux sexes	Male Masculin	Female Féminin	Both sexes Les deux sexes	Male Masculin	Female Féminin
EUROPE									
Germany - Allemagne									
2006 (C)									
Total.....................	10.0	9.6	10.4	...	...	...	...	...	...
0	3.8	4.1	3.5	...	...	...	...	...	...
1 - 4	0.2	0.2	0.2	...	...	...	...	...	...
5 - 9	0.1	0.1	0.1	...	...	...	...	...	...
10 - 14	0.1	0.1	0.1	...	...	...	...	...	...
15 - 19	0.3	0.4	0.2	...	...	...	...	...	...
20 - 24	0.4	0.6	0.2	...	...	...	...	...	...
25 - 29	0.4	0.6	0.2	...	...	...	...	...	...
30 - 34	0.5	0.7	0.4	...	...	...	...	...	...
35 - 39	0.8	1.1	0.6	...	...	...	...	...	...
40 - 44	1.5	1.9	1.0	...	...	...	...	...	...
45 - 49	2.6	3.3	1.8	...	...	...	...	...	...
50 - 54	4.2	5.5	2.8	...	...	...	...	...	...
55 - 59	6.2	8.3	4.2	...	...	...	...	...	...
60 - 64	9.4	12.6	6.3	...	...	...	...	...	...
65 - 69	13.8	19.0	9.1	...	...	...	...	...	...
70 - 74	23.0	31.1	16.2	...	...	...	...	...	...
75 - 79	39.5	52.0	30.8	...	...	...	...	...	...
80 - 84	68.5	86.4	60.3	...	...	...	...	...	...
85 - 89	117.1	138.5	109.5	...	...	...	...	...	...
90 - 94	216.4	234.0	211.4	...	...	...	...	...	...
95 +	243.3	158.0	274.9	...	...	...	...	...	...
Greece - Grèce									
2006 (C)									
Total.....................	9.5	10.0	8.9	...	...	...	...	...	...
0	3.8	3.8	3.8	...	...	...	...	...	...
1 - 4	0.2	◆0.1	0.2	...	...	...	...	...	...
5 - 9	0.1	0.1	◆0.1	...	...	...	...	...	...
10 - 14	0.1	0.2	◆0.1	...	...	...	...	...	...
15 - 19	0.4	0.6	0.2	...	...	...	...	...	...
20 - 24	0.7	1.1	0.2	...	...	...	...	...	...
25 - 29	0.7	1.1	0.3	...	...	...	...	...	...
30 - 34	0.7	1.0	0.3	...	...	...	...	...	...
35 - 39	1.0	1.4	0.5	...	...	...	...	...	...
40 - 44	1.4	2.0	0.8	...	...	...	...	...	...
45 - 49	2.2	3.0	1.4	...	...	...	...	...	...
50 - 54	3.6	5.1	2.2	...	...	...	...	...	...
55 - 59	5.4	7.6	3.2	...	...	...	...	...	...
60 - 64	7.8	11.3	4.7	...	...	...	...	...	...
65 - 69	12.2	17.6	7.7	...	...	...	...	...	...
70 - 74	20.7	28.7	14.2	...	...	...	...	...	...
75 - 79	38.6	47.6	31.6	...	...	...	...	...	...
80 - 84	73.8	81.4	68.3	...	...	...	...	...	...
85 - 89	140.1	132.5	145.8	...	...	...	...	...	...
90 - 94	368.4	323.6	403.3	...	...	...	...	...	...
95 - 99	458.3	303.0	633.7	...	...	...	...	...	...
100 +	248.4	268.4	241.2	...	...	...	...	...	...
Hungary - Hongrie									
2006 (C)									
Total.....................	13.1	14.2	12.1	12.5[28]	13.4[28]	11.8[28]	13.9[28]	15.3[28]	12.6[28]
0	5.8	6.4	5.2	5.3[28]	6.0[28]	4.7[28]	6.6[28]	7.1[28]	6.1[28]
1 - 4	0.3	0.3	0.3	0.3[28]	0.3[28]	0.3[28]	0.4[28]	0.5[28]	◆0.3[28]
5 - 9	0.1	0.1	◆0.1	◆0.1[28]	◆0.1[28]	◆0.1[28]	◆0.1[28]	◆0.1[28]	◆0.1[28]
10 - 14	0.2	0.3	0.1	0.2[28]	0.2[28]	◆0.1[28]	0.2[28]	0.3[28]	◆0.2[28]
15 - 19	0.4	0.6	0.2	0.4[28]	0.6[28]	0.2[28]	0.4[28]	0.6[28]	◆0.2[28]
20 - 24	0.5	0.7	0.2	0.4[28]	0.7[28]	0.2[28]	0.5[28]	0.8[28]	◆0.3[28]
25 - 29	0.7	1.0	0.3	0.6[28]	0.9[28]	0.3[28]	0.8[28]	1.1[28]	0.4[28]
30 - 34	1.0	1.4	0.6	0.9[28]	1.2[28]	0.5[28]	1.2[28]	1.7[28]	0.6[28]
35 - 39	1.7	2.5	1.0	1.5[28]	2.1[28]	0.9[28]	2.0[28]	3.0[28]	1.0[28]
40 - 44	3.6	5.2	2.0	3.1[28]	4.4[28]	1.8[28]	4.3[28]	6.1[28]	2.4[28]
45 - 49	6.8	9.9	3.8	6.1[28]	9.1[28]	3.5[28]	7.7[28]	10.9[28]	4.4[28]
50 - 54	10.3	15.3	5.7	9.5[28]	14.0[28]	5.6[28]	11.5[28]	16.9[28]	6.0[28]

20. Death rates specific for age, sex and urban/rural residence: latest available year, 1997 - 2006
Taux de mortalité selon l'âge, le sexe et la résidence, urbaine/rurale: dernière année disponible, 1997 - 2006 (continued - suite)

Continent, country or area, date, code and age (in years) / Continent, pays ou zone, date, code et âge (en années)	Total			Urban - Urbaine			Rural - Rurale		
	Both sexes Les deux sexes	Male Masculin	Female Féminin	Both sexes Les deux sexes	Male Masculin	Female Féminin	Both sexes Les deux sexes	Male Masculin	Female Féminin
EUROPE									
Hungary - Hongrie									
2006 (C)									
55 - 59	13.8	20.8	7.8	12.7[28]	19.0[28]	7.5[28]	16.0[28]	23.8[28]	8.6[28]
60 - 64	18.6	28.1	11.2	17.5[28]	25.8[28]	11.1[28]	20.8[28]	32.2[28]	11.5[28]
65 - 69	25.9	38.9	16.9	24.2[28]	35.8[28]	16.4[28]	28.8[28]	44.6[28]	18.0[28]
70 - 74	37.2	53.3	27.2	35.8[28]	50.4[28]	26.6[28]	39.6[28]	58.4[28]	28.2[28]
75 - 79	58.6	78.2	47.9	56.4[28]	73.9[28]	46.8[28]	62.6[28]	86.5[28]	50.0[28]
80 - 84	97.4	121.6	86.4	94.2[28]	117.6[28]	83.7[28]	103.4[28]	129.1[28]	91.7[28]
85 - 89	147.2	166.8	139.4	143.5[28]	162.6[28]	135.8[28]	155.1[28]	175.8[28]	147.1[28]
90 +	233.8	233.0	234.1	229.6[28]	227.0[28]	230.5[28]	243.7[28]	247.5[28]	242.3[28]
Iceland - Islande									
2006 (C)									
Total	6.3	6.2	6.3	6.2	6.1	6.3	6.8	7.1	6.6
0	♦1.3	♦1.3	♦1.4	♦1.4	♦1.4	♦1.4	-	-	-
1 - 4	♦0.2	♦0.2	♦0.2	♦0.3	♦0.2	♦0.3	-	-	-
5 - 9	-	-	♦0.1	♦0.1	-	♦0.1	-	-	-
10 - 14	♦0.2	♦0.3	♦0.1	♦0.2	♦0.3	♦0.1	-	-	-
15 - 19	♦0.5	♦0.5	♦0.5	♦0.5	♦0.5	♦0.6	♦0.5	♦1.0	-
20 - 24	♦0.6	♦1.0	♦0.3	♦0.6	♦1.0	♦0.3	♦0.6	♦1.1	-
25 - 29	♦0.7	♦1.1	♦0.2	♦0.6	♦1.1	♦0.1	♦1.5	♦1.3	♦1.8
30 - 34	♦0.5	♦0.7	♦0.3	♦0.4	♦0.5	♦0.3	♦2.1	♦3.5	-
35 - 39	♦0.6	♦0.8	♦0.4	♦0.6	♦0.8	♦0.4	♦0.6	♦1.1	-
40 - 44	♦0.9	♦1.0	♦0.7	♦0.9	♦1.2	♦0.7	♦0.5	-	♦1.3
45 - 49	1.7	♦2.1	♦1.2	1.8	♦2.3	♦1.3	-	-	-
50 - 54	2.8	3.2	♦2.5	2.9	♦3.3	♦2.5	♦1.9	♦2.1	♦1.6
55 - 59	5.1	5.3	4.8	5.0	5.5	4.5	♦6.0	♦3.9	♦8.8
60 - 64	7.6	9.7	5.5	8.1	10.4	5.9	♦1.9	♦3.4	-
65 - 69	14.0	15.7	12.4	13.4	15.5	11.6	♦20.2	♦17.9	♦23.0
70 - 74	19.9	24.7	15.6	20.2	24.6	16.4	♦16.6	♦25.6	♦6.0
75 - 79	33.8	36.9	31.2	35.0	38.1	32.6	♦21.0	♦27.7	♦11.2
80 - 84	57.7	70.6	48.2	57.7	69.6	49.3	♦57.1	♦81.2	♦31.9
85 - 89	122.0	142.6	109.2	121.2	142.9	108.3	131.4	♦140.5	♦121.7
90 - 94	219.6	261.3	199.1	214.3	257.6	194.0	♦275.9	♦289.5	♦265.3
95 - 99	294.1	♦403.8	263.4	272.3	♦404.3	237.3	♦642.9	♦400.0	♦777.8
100 +	♦558.8	♦500.0	♦571.4	♦516.1	♦600.0	♦500.0	♦1000.0	-	♦1500.0
Ireland - Irlande[29]									
2006* (+C)									
Total	6.5	6.7	6.3	...	...	...	...	...	...
0	3.9	4.3	3.4	...	...	...	...	...	...
1 - 4	0.1	♦0.1	♦0.1	...	...	...	...	...	...
5 - 9	♦0.1	♦0.1	♦0.1	...	...	...	...	...	...
10 - 14	0.1	♦0.1	♦0.1	...	...	...	...	...	...
15 - 19	0.5	0.6	0.3	...	...	...	...	...	...
20 - 24	0.6	0.9	0.3	...	...	...	...	...	...
25 - 29	0.5	0.8	0.3	...	...	...	...	...	...
30 - 34	0.6	0.9	0.3	...	...	...	...	...	...
35 - 39	0.7	0.9	0.5	...	...	...	...	...	...
40 - 44	1.2	1.5	1.0	...	...	...	...	...	...
45 - 49	2.1	2.4	1.9	...	...	...	...	...	...
50 - 54	3.4	4.2	2.6	...	...	...	...	...	...
55 - 59	5.3	6.2	4.3	...	...	...	...	...	...
60 - 64	8.5	10.4	6.6	...	...	...	...	...	...
65 - 69	14.1	17.8	10.5	...	...	...	...	...	...
70 - 74	24.1	32.2	16.8	...	...	...	...	...	...
75 - 79	43.7	55.6	34.5	...	...	...	...	...	...
80 - 84	76.8	97.2	64.4	...	...	...	...	...	...
85 - 89	127.3	153.1	114.1	...	...	...	...	...	...
90 - 94	196.1	225.8	184.1	...	...	...	...	...	...
95 - 99	194.8	204.3	191.9	...	...	...	...	...	...
Italy - Italie									
2004 (C)									
Total	9.4	9.7	9.1	...	...	...	...	...	...
0	4.0	4.2	3.7	...	...	...	...	...	...
1 - 4	0.2	0.2	0.2	...	...	...	...	...	...
5 - 9	0.1	0.1	0.1	...	...	...	...	...	...

20. Death rates specific for age, sex and urban/rural residence: latest available year, 1997 - 2006
Taux de mortalité selon l'âge, le sexe et la résidence, urbaine/rurale: dernière année disponible, 1997 - 2006 (continued - suite)

Continent, country or area, date, code and age (in years) / Continent, pays ou zone, date, code et âge (en années)	Total			Urban - Urbaine			Rural - Rurale		
	Both sexes Les deux sexes	Male Masculin	Female Féminin	Both sexes Les deux sexes	Male Masculin	Female Féminin	Both sexes Les deux sexes	Male Masculin	Female Féminin
EUROPE									
Italy - Italie									
2004 (C)									
10 - 14	0.1	0.1	0.1	...	...	...	...	...	...
15 - 19	0.4	0.5	0.2	...	...	...	...	...	...
20 - 24	0.5	0.8	0.2	...	...	...	...	...	...
25 - 29	0.5	0.8	0.3	...	...	...	...	...	...
30 - 34	0.6	0.9	0.3	...	...	...	...	...	...
35 - 39	0.8	1.1	0.5	...	...	...	...	...	...
40 - 44	1.3	1.6	0.9	...	...	...	...	...	...
45 - 49	1.9	2.4	1.4	...	...	...	...	...	...
50 - 54	3.1	4.0	2.2	...	...	...	...	...	...
55 - 59	4.8	6.4	3.3	...	...	...	...	...	...
60 - 64	7.9	10.8	5.2	...	...	...	...	...	...
65 - 69	12.4	17.2	8.2	...	...	...	...	...	...
70 - 74	20.8	29.2	14.2	...	...	...	...	...	...
75 - 79	35.7	49.4	26.3	...	...	...	...	...	...
80 - 84	62.8	83.0	51.6	...	...	...	...	...	...
85 - 89	111.3	139.2	98.7	...	...	...	...	...	...
90 - 94	184.2	219.8	171.2	...	...	...	...	...	...
95 - 99	284.7	322.0	274.8	...	...	...	...	...	...
100 +	379.8	377.5	380.2	...	...	...	...	...	...
Latvia - Lettonie									
2006 (C)									
Total	14.5	15.8	13.4	13.9	15.4	12.6	15.8	16.5	15.1
0 - 4	1.9	2.1	1.8	1.7	1.8	1.5	2.5	2.7	2.4
0	7.8	8.3	7.2	...	...	...	...	...	...
1 - 4	0.4	♦0.5	♦0.3	...	...	...	...	...	...
5 - 9	0.3	♦0.4	♦0.3	♦0.3	♦0.4	♦0.3	♦0.4	♦0.5	♦0.2
10 - 14	♦0.2	♦0.3	♦0.2	♦0.2	♦0.3	♦0.2	♦0.2	♦0.2	♦0.2
15 - 19	0.6	0.8	♦0.3	0.5	0.7	♦0.3	0.7	1.0	♦0.5
20 - 24	1.0	1.6	0.4	1.0	1.6	♦0.4	1.0	1.7	♦0.3
25 - 29	1.4	2.1	0.7	1.4	2.2	0.6	1.4	2.0	♦0.7
30 - 34	2.2	3.5	0.8	2.1	3.4	0.8	2.4	3.7	♦0.9
35 - 39	3.6	5.4	1.8	3.6	5.4	1.8	3.6	5.4	1.6
40 - 44	4.8	7.7	2.1	4.7	7.6	2.1	5.1	7.9	2.0
45 - 49	7.6	11.8	3.9	7.5	11.8	3.9	7.9	11.8	3.7
50 - 54	11.6	17.8	6.3	11.1	17.2	6.3	12.6	18.9	6.2
55 - 59	16.3	25.4	9.1	15.5	24.5	8.9	18.2	27.1	9.6
60 - 64	21.8	35.2	12.3	19.9	32.5	11.6	25.7	40.0	14.0
65 - 69	27.4	44.2	16.8	25.2	40.5	16.0	32.4	52.0	18.8
70 - 74	40.7	64.3	28.1	37.8	59.2	26.6	46.9	74.4	31.3
75 - 79	60.9	90.9	47.6	58.0	86.9	45.0	67.7	100.4	53.5
80 - 84	97.9	128.0	89.6	92.8	125.4	83.6	109.3	134.5	102.9
85 - 89	163.1	183.3	157.5	153.6	167.9	149.4	183.0	220.9	173.7
90 - 94	250.1	272.5	244.8	242.5	268.6	235.8	264.6	282.1	261.2
95 - 99	395.4	395.9	395.3	379.8	366.8	382.8	426.2	457.4	419.6
100 +	551.5	♦368.4	596.2	488.9	♦413.8	509.4	694.9	♦222.2	780.0
Lithuania - Lituanie									
2006 (C)									
Total	13.2	15.1	11.6	11.6	13.4	10.0	16.5	18.1	15.0
0	6.9	7.4	6.4	8.3	9.1	7.5	4.4	♦4.3	♦4.4
1 - 4	0.4	♦0.4	♦0.4	♦0.4	♦0.4	♦0.4	♦0.5	♦0.4	♦0.6
5 - 9	0.3	0.4	♦0.2	0.3	♦0.4	♦0.1	♦0.3	♦0.4	♦0.3
10 - 14	0.2	0.3	♦0.2	0.2	♦0.3	♦0.2	♦0.3	♦0.4	♦0.2
15 - 19	0.8	1.1	0.4	0.6	0.9	♦0.3	1.1	1.6	♦0.5
20 - 24	1.2	2.0	0.4	0.9	1.5	♦0.3	1.7	2.7	♦0.5
25 - 29	1.9	2.9	0.8	1.6	2.6	0.6	2.6	3.7	1.2
30 - 34	2.5	4.0	1.1	2.0	3.2	0.9	3.9	5.8	1.8
35 - 39	3.6	5.5	1.7	3.2	5.0	1.5	4.5	6.7	2.2
40 - 44	5.4	8.6	2.4	4.6	7.3	2.1	7.3	11.1	3.0
45 - 49	7.7	12.0	3.8	6.9	11.3	3.3	9.3	13.4	4.9
50 - 54	11.6	18.8	5.5	10.6	17.6	5.1	14.0	21.2	6.6
55 - 59	15.9	26.0	7.9	14.6	24.4	7.5	18.6	28.9	8.9
60 - 64	21.3	35.2	11.4	19.8	33.7	10.5	24.1	37.9	13.2
65 - 69	26.5	43.5	15.6	24.8	42.2	14.1	29.4	45.6	18.3

20. Death rates specific for age, sex and urban/rural residence: latest available year, 1997 - 2006
Taux de mortalité selon l'âge, le sexe et la résidence, urbaine/rurale: dernière année disponible, 1997 - 2006 (continued - suite)

Continent, country or area, date, code and age (in years) / Continent, pays ou zone, date, code et âge (en années)	Total			Urban - Urbaine			Rural - Rurale		
	Both sexes Les deux sexes	Male Masculin	Female Féminin	Both sexes Les deux sexes	Male Masculin	Female Féminin	Both sexes Les deux sexes	Male Masculin	Female Féminin
EUROPE									
Lithuania - Lituanie									
2006 (C)									
70 - 74	37.0	57.9	25.1	34.9	53.4	24.6	40.1	64.6	26.0
75 - 79	56.9	79.7	45.8	54.4	76.9	43.4	60.5	84.1	49.4
80 - 84	95.5	121.9	86.3	93.2	114.9	85.8	98.6	131.5	86.9
85 - 89	156.1	178.8	148.8	147.9	171.3	140.5	167.5	188.4	160.3
90 - 94	260.1	257.0	261.0	225.3	217.0	227.7	318.6	316.8	319.2
95 - 99	434.0	367.9	463.3	329.1	281.4	346.9	718.7	525.4	850.1
100 +	474.4	561.9	437.2	305.3	♦416.7	272.3	966.7	755.6	1177.8
Luxembourg									
2006 (C)									
Total	8.0	7.7	8.2	...	...	...	...	...	...
0	♦2.6	♦3.2	♦1.9	...	...	...	...	...	...
1 - 4	♦0.2	♦0.1	♦0.3	...	...	...	...	...	...
5 - 9	♦0.1	♦0.1	♦0.1	...	...	...	...	...	...
10 - 14	♦0.1	♦0.1	-	...	...	...	...	...	...
15 - 19	♦0.2	♦0.1	♦0.2	...	...	...	...	...	...
20 - 24	♦0.6	♦0.9	♦0.3	...	...	...	...	...	...
25 - 29	♦0.5	♦0.4	♦0.6	...	...	...	...	...	...
30 - 34	♦0.6	♦0.7	♦0.4	...	...	...	...	...	...
35 - 39	1.3	1.6	♦0.9	...	...	...	...	...	...
40 - 44	1.7	2.3	♦1.1	...	...	...	...	...	...
45 - 49	2.6	3.2	2.0	...	...	...	...	...	...
50 - 54	4.7	5.7	3.6	...	...	...	...	...	...
55 - 59	6.4	8.7	3.9	...	...	...	...	...	...
60 - 64	10.6	13.6	7.5	...	...	...	...	...	...
65 - 69	14.4	20.0	9.4	...	...	...	...	...	...
70 - 74	23.0	30.8	16.5	...	...	...	...	...	...
75 - 79	40.1	50.9	32.2	...	...	...	...	...	...
80 - 84	64.3	78.7	57.4	...	...	...	...	...	...
85 - 89	121.1	137.7	114.9	...	...	...	...	...	...
90 - 94	243.6	306.8	227.4	...	...	...	...	...	...
95 +	465.2	♦1692.3	403.8	...	...	...	...	...	...
Malta - Malte									
2006 (C)									
Total	7.9	8.3	7.6	...	...	...	...	...	...
0	♦3.5	♦4.8	♦2.1	...	...	...	...	...	...
1 - 4	♦0.3	♦0.1	♦0.4	...	...	...	...	...	...
5 - 9	-	-	-	...	...	...	...	...	...
10 - 14	♦0.2	♦0.2	♦0.2	...	...	...	...	...	...
15 - 19	♦0.3	♦0.5	♦0.1	...	...	...	...	...	...
20 - 24	♦0.4	♦0.8	♦0.1	...	...	...	...	...	...
25 - 29	♦0.2	♦0.4	-	...	...	...	...	...	...
30 - 34	♦0.6	♦0.8	♦0.4	...	...	...	...	...	...
35 - 39	♦0.6	♦1.0	♦0.2	...	...	...	...	...	...
40 - 44	1.4	♦1.8	♦1.0	...	...	...	...	...	...
45 - 49	2.0	2.0	♦1.9	...	...	...	...	...	...
50 - 54	3.0	4.4	♦1.6	...	...	...	...	...	...
55 - 59	4.8	5.7	3.9	...	...	...	...	...	...
60 - 64	8.1	10.2	6.2	...	...	...	...	...	...
65 - 69	14.7	19.1	10.8	...	...	...	...	...	...
70 - 74	26.0	36.1	18.2	...	...	...	...	...	...
75 - 79	44.9	59.8	34.8	...	...	...	...	...	...
80 - 84	81.6	101.0	69.1	...	...	...	...	...	...
85 - 89	144.8	171.9	129.4	...	...	...	...	...	...
90 +	282.8	326.9	265.3	...	...	...	...	...	...
Moldova[30]									
2006 (C)									
Total	12.0	13.1	11.1	9.3	10.5	8.2	14.0	14.9	13.1
0	11.7	12.6	10.8	12.7	13.7	11.6	11.1	11.9	10.4
1 - 4	0.6	0.7	0.5	♦0.5	♦0.5	♦0.4	0.6	0.7	♦0.5
5 - 9	0.4	0.4	♦0.3	♦0.3	♦0.4	♦0.3	0.4	0.5	♦0.2
10 - 14	0.4	0.4	0.3	♦0.2	♦0.2	♦0.2	0.5	0.5	0.4
15 - 19	0.6	0.8	0.4	0.6	0.8	♦0.3	0.6	0.9	0.4
20 - 24	0.8	1.1	0.4	0.6	0.9	♦0.3	0.9	1.3	0.5

20. Death rates specific for age, sex and urban/rural residence: latest available year, 1997 - 2006
Taux de mortalité selon l'âge, le sexe et la résidence, urbaine/rurale: dernière année disponible, 1997 - 2006 (continued - suite)

Continent, country or area, date, code and age (in years) / Continent, pays ou zone, date, code et âge (en années)	Total			Urban - Urbaine			Rural - Rurale		
	Both sexes Les deux sexes	Male Masculin	Female Féminin	Both sexes Les deux sexes	Male Masculin	Female Féminin	Both sexes Les deux sexes	Male Masculin	Female Féminin
EUROPE									
Moldova[30]									
2006 (C)									
25 - 29	1.3	2.1	0.6	1.3	2.2	♦0.4	1.4	1.9	0.8
30 - 34	2.2	3.2	1.1	2.0	3.1	1.0	2.2	3.3	1.2
35 - 39	3.5	5.4	1.6	2.8	4.1	1.5	4.1	6.6	1.8
40 - 44	5.6	8.3	3.1	4.3	6.6	2.4	6.5	9.5	3.7
45 - 49	8.6	13.0	4.7	7.1	10.9	3.8	9.8	14.5	5.4
50 - 54	12.8	18.7	7.6	10.7	15.9	6.4	14.5	20.8	8.7
55 - 59	18.3	24.9	12.9	15.6	21.8	10.4	20.6	27.4	15.0
60 - 64	26.6	33.9	21.0	21.6	27.5	16.6	29.9	38.5	23.8
65 - 69	39.0	53.0	29.5	32.4	44.8	23.5	43.1	58.4	33.1
70 - 74	58.7	73.0	49.6	53.8	66.4	45.7	61.0	76.2	51.5
75 - 79	88.4	107.8	77.5	77.1	93.3	68.5	93.8	114.3	81.9
80 - 84	124.8	146.6	115.0	108.6	128.8	100.4	132.5	154.4	122.3
85 +	218.1	240.4	208.7	170.4	183.2	165.6	243.0	266.2	232.5
Montenegro									
2005 (C)									
Total	9.4	10.0	8.7	9.2	10.0	8.4	9.7	10.1	9.3
0	9.2	9.9	8.5	10.9	11.6	♦10.2	♦3.0	♦3.5	♦2.5
1 - 4	♦0.4	♦0.6	♦0.1	♦0.5	♦0.8	♦0.1	♦0.2	♦0.2	♦0.2
5 - 9	♦0.2	♦0.1	♦0.2	♦0.3	♦0.2	♦0.3	-	-	-
10 - 14	♦0.2	♦0.3	-	♦0.1	♦0.3	-	♦0.2	♦0.3	♦0.1
15 - 19	♦0.3	♦0.4	♦0.2	♦0.3	♦0.4	♦0.2	♦0.3	♦0.4	♦0.2
20 - 24	0.8	♦1.1	♦0.4	♦0.7	♦1.1	♦0.4	♦0.8	♦0.9	♦0.6
25 - 29	1.0	♦1.2	♦0.7	♦1.0	♦1.0	♦0.9	♦1.0	♦1.5	♦0.4
30 - 34	0.9	♦1.3	♦0.4	♦1.1	♦1.6	♦0.6	♦0.5	♦0.9	♦0.1
35 - 39	1.5	2.0	♦1.0	1.8	♦2.4	♦1.3	♦0.9	♦1.2	♦0.4
40 - 44	2.0	2.7	♦1.4	2.1	2.6	♦1.7	♦1.8	♦2.8	♦0.7
45 - 49	4.2	5.2	3.2	4.4	5.2	3.8	3.8	5.3	♦2.0
50 - 54	6.6	8.9	4.3	7.4	10.0	5.0	5.0	6.9	♦3.0
55 - 59	10.7	16.1	6.0	11.8	17.1	7.1	8.8	14.2	♦4.0
60 - 64	16.7	22.7	11.7	19.7	26.6	14.0	12.7	17.5	8.7
65 - 69	24.2	31.0	18.6	27.8	35.1	21.8	19.8	26.0	14.6
70 - 74	38.9	49.7	30.3	44.8	59.2	33.4	32.3	39.1	26.9
75 - 79	70.4	79.3	64.1	82.3	90.3	76.7	59.0	68.9	51.7
80 - 84	107.8	122.5	99.0	121.7	142.1	109.8	95.3	105.4	89.2
85 - 89	177.3	189.6	170.9	214.1	241.0	201.5	148.0	153.5	144.9
90 - 94	240.2	248.4	236.6	284.1	295.7	279.9	206.8	219.9	200.3
95 - 99	271.6	♦264.6	275.1	301.7	♦323.5	♦292.7	250.7	♦231.4	♦261.7
100 +	♦320.0	♦400.0	♦280.0	♦338.0	♦285.7	♦372.1	♦303.8	♦545.5	♦210.5
Netherlands - Pays-Bas[31]									
2006 (C)									
Total	8.3	8.1	8.5	8.4	8.1	8.7	8.1	8.1	8.0
0	3.9	4.4	3.5	3.8	4.1	3.5	4.3	5.1	3.5
1 - 4	0.3	0.3	0.3	0.3	0.4	0.3	0.3	0.2	0.3
5 - 9	0.1	0.1	0.1	0.1	0.1	♦0.1	0.1	0.2	♦0.1
10 - 14	0.1	0.1	0.1	0.1	0.1	♦0.1	0.1	♦0.1	♦0.1
15 - 19	0.2	0.3	0.2	0.2	0.3	0.2	0.2	0.3	♦0.1
20 - 24	0.3	0.5	0.2	0.3	0.5	0.2	0.4	0.6	♦0.2
25 - 29	0.4	0.5	0.2	0.3	0.4	0.2	0.4	0.5	0.3
30 - 34	0.5	0.6	0.4	0.5	0.6	0.4	0.5	0.6	0.4
35 - 39	0.7	0.8	0.6	0.7	0.8	0.6	0.7	0.8	0.6
40 - 44	1.1	1.3	1.0	1.2	1.4	1.0	1.0	1.0	0.9
45 - 49	2.0	2.2	1.8	2.1	2.3	1.9	1.9	2.1	1.7
50 - 54	3.4	3.8	3.0	3.6	4.1	3.2	3.1	3.4	2.8
55 - 59	5.1	5.9	4.3	5.4	6.4	4.5	4.6	5.1	4.0
00 - 04	9.2	11.4	7.1	9.8	12.1	7.6	8.3	10.3	6.3
65 - 69	13.5	17.3	9.8	13.9	17.8	10.4	12.6	16.5	8.9
70 - 74	22.9	30.6	16.4	23.6	31.1	17.4	21.7	29.7	14.6
75 - 79	40.6	54.2	30.8	41.1	54.4	31.8	39.7	54.0	28.9
80 - 84	71.5	96.3	57.7	72.3	97.3	58.8	69.9	94.4	55.6
85 - 89	134.9	174.9	118.2	135.1	175.0	118.9	134.5	174.6	116.6
90 - 94	236.4	289.5	220.7	233.6	288.8	218.3	242.3	290.8	226.2
95 - 99	404.0	478.1	388.7	403.8	485.3	388.0	404.4	464.9	390.1
100 +	676.6	772.0	661.0	687.0	745.8	678.3	655.6	813.3	624.3

587

20. Death rates specific for age, sex and urban/rural residence: latest available year, 1997 - 2006
Taux de mortalité selon l'âge, le sexe et la résidence, urbaine/rurale: dernière année disponible, 1997 - 2006 (continued - suite)

Continent, country or area, date, code and age (in years) / Continent, pays ou zone, date, code et âge (en années)	Total			Urban - Urbaine			Rural - Rurale		
	Both sexes Les deux sexes	Male Masculin	Female Féminin	Both sexes Les deux sexes	Male Masculin	Female Féminin	Both sexes Les deux sexes	Male Masculin	Female Féminin
EUROPE									
Norway - Norvège[32]									
2006 (C)									
Total	8.9	8.5	9.2	...	...	...	...	...	...
0	3.2	3.7	2.6	...	...	...	...	...	...
1 - 4	0.2	♦0.2	♦0.2	...	...	...	...	...	...
5 - 9	0.1	♦0.1	♦0.1	...	...	...	...	...	...
10 - 14	♦0.1	♦0.1	-	...	...	...	...	...	...
15 - 19	0.4	0.5	0.2	...	...	...	...	...	...
20 - 24	0.6	0.9	0.3	...	...	...	...	...	...
25 - 29	0.6	1.0	0.3	...	...	...	...	...	...
30 - 34	0.7	1.0	0.4	...	...	...	...	...	...
35 - 39	0.8	1.1	0.6	...	...	...	...	...	...
40 - 44	1.1	1.3	0.9	...	...	...	...	...	...
45 - 49	2.1	2.4	1.7	...	...	...	...	...	...
50 - 54	3.2	3.9	2.5	...	...	...	...	...	...
55 - 59	5.0	6.0	4.0	...	...	...	...	...	...
60 - 64	8.4	10.3	6.5	...	...	...	...	...	...
65 - 69	12.5	16.3	8.9	...	...	...	...	...	...
70 - 74	21.1	27.1	16.0	...	...	...	...	...	...
75 - 79	37.2	47.1	29.6	...	...	...	...	...	...
80 - 84	68.1	85.9	57.1	...	...	...	...	...	...
85 - 89	120.6	148.8	107.3	...	...	...	...	...	...
90 - 94	214.2	249.6	201.9	...	...	...	...	...	...
95 - 99	340.9	364.7	334.9	...	...	...	...	...	...
100 +	449.9	487.8	441.6	...	...	...	...	...	...
Poland - Pologne									
2006 (C)									
Total	9.7	10.8	8.7	9.5	10.6	8.5	10.0	11.0	9.1
0	6.1	6.8	5.4	6.3	7.2	5.4	5.8	6.3	5.3
1 - 4	0.3	0.3	0.3	0.3	0.3	0.2	0.3	0.3	0.3
5 - 9	0.2	0.2	0.1	0.1	0.2	0.1	0.2	0.2	0.2
10 - 14	0.2	0.2	0.1	0.2	0.2	0.1	0.2	0.3	0.1
15 - 19	0.5	0.7	0.2	0.4	0.6	0.2	0.6	0.8	0.3
20 - 24	0.7	1.1	0.3	0.6	0.9	0.3	0.8	1.3	0.3
25 - 29	0.7	1.2	0.3	0.7	1.0	0.3	0.9	1.4	0.3
30 - 34	1.0	1.6	0.5	1.0	1.5	0.5	1.1	1.8	0.4
35 - 39	1.8	2.7	0.8	1.8	2.6	0.9	1.8	2.8	0.7
40 - 44	2.9	4.4	1.5	2.9	4.4	1.6	3.0	4.4	1.4
45 - 49	5.0	7.4	2.6	5.0	7.5	2.8	4.9	7.3	2.3
50 - 54	7.6	11.4	4.1	7.5	11.2	4.3	7.9	11.6	3.8
55 - 59	11.1	16.4	6.2	11.0	16.3	6.5	11.1	16.7	5.6
60 - 64	15.4	23.1	9.0	15.6	23.1	9.5	15.1	23.0	8.0
65 - 69	21.8	33.1	13.4	21.8	32.9	13.7	21.9	33.5	12.7
70 - 74	32.3	47.1	22.3	32.0	46.0	22.8	32.8	49.0	21.6
75 - 79	51.0	70.1	40.2	50.2	68.2	40.1	52.2	72.9	40.3
80 - 84	84.4	107.3	74.3	82.4	104.9	72.8	87.3	110.6	76.5
85 +	172.5	191.2	165.7	162.9	182.4	156.5	185.8	202.0	179.3
Portugal[33]									
2006 (C)									
Total	9.6	10.4	8.9	...	...	...	...	...	...
0	3.3	3.8	2.7	...	...	...	...	...	...
1 - 4	0.3	0.3	0.2	...	...	...	...	...	...
5 - 9	0.2	0.2	0.1	...	...	...	...	...	...
10 - 14	0.2	0.2	♦0.1	...	...	...	...	...	...
15 - 19	0.4	0.6	0.2	...	...	...	...	...	...
20 - 24	0.6	0.9	0.3	...	...	...	...	...	...
25 - 29	0.6	0.9	0.3	...	...	...	...	...	...
30 - 34	0.9	1.4	0.5	...	...	...	...	...	...
35 - 39	1.5	2.1	0.8	...	...	...	...	...	...
40 - 44	2.1	3.2	1.2	...	...	...	...	...	...
45 - 49	3.1	4.6	1.6	...	...	...	...	...	...
50 - 54	4.2	6.2	2.4	...	...	...	...	...	...
55 - 59	6.0	8.8	3.5	...	...	...	...	...	...
60 - 64	8.7	12.3	5.6	...	...	...	...	...	...
65 - 69	13.8	19.8	8.7	...	...	...	...	...	...

20. Death rates specific for age, sex and urban/rural residence: latest available year, 1997 - 2006
Taux de mortalité selon l'âge, le sexe et la résidence, urbaine/rurale: dernière année disponible, 1997 - 2006 (continued - suite)

Continent, country or area, date, code and age (in years) Continent, pays ou zone, date, code et âge (en années)	Total			Urban - Urbaine			Rural - Rurale		
	Both sexes Les deux sexes	Male Masculin	Female Féminin	Both sexes Les deux sexes	Male Masculin	Female Féminin	Both sexes Les deux sexes	Male Masculin	Female Féminin
EUROPE									
Portugal[33]									
2006 (C)									
70 - 74	23.1	32.0	16.2	...	...	...	...	...	...
75 - 79	41.3	56.1	31.1	...	...	...	...	...	...
80 - 84	75.4	96.0	63.0	...	...	...	...	...	...
85 - 89	131.8	156.5	119.1	...	...	...	...	...	...
90 - 94	246.3	271.3	235.9	...	...	...	...	...	...
95 - 99	376.7	338.0	391.9	...	...	...	...	...	...
100 +..................	631.0	542.9	653.8	...	...	...	...	...	...
Romania - Roumanie									
2006 (C)									
Total.....................	12.0	13.0	11.0	9.8	10.9	8.8	14.7	15.4	13.9
0	14.0	15.1	12.7	11.3	12.1	10.4	17.2	18.8	15.5
1 - 4	0.7	0.7	0.6	0.5	0.6	0.4	0.8	0.9	0.8
5 - 9	0.3	0.4	0.3	0.3	0.3	0.2	0.3	0.4	0.3
10 - 14	0.3	0.4	0.2	0.3	0.3	0.2	0.4	0.5	0.2
15 - 19	0.6	0.7	0.4	0.5	0.6	0.3	0.7	0.9	0.4
20 - 24	0.6	0.9	0.4	0.6	0.8	0.3	0.8	1.1	0.4
25 - 29	0.8	1.1	0.4	0.7	1.0	0.4	1.0	1.3	0.5
30 - 34	1.1	1.5	0.6	0.9	1.3	0.6	1.3	1.8	0.7
35 - 39	1.8	2.5	1.1	1.5	2.1	0.9	2.2	2.9	1.3
40 - 44	3.2	4.6	1.9	2.7	3.9	1.6	4.1	5.5	2.3
45 - 49	5.6	8.1	3.1	4.9	7.2	2.9	6.8	9.5	3.5
50 - 54	8.5	12.4	4.9	7.9	11.4	4.7	9.7	14.2	5.3
55 - 59	12.0	17.3	7.1	11.6	16.7	7.0	12.4	18.3	7.3
60 - 64	17.3	24.8	10.9	17.5	25.0	11.1	17.1	24.7	10.7
65 - 69	25.9	36.4	17.7	26.1	37.0	17.7	25.7	36.0	17.7
70 - 74	40.1	51.8	31.7	40.7	53.2	31.9	39.7	50.8	31.5
75 - 79	66.2	80.2	56.9	65.6	81.0	55.7	66.7	79.7	57.8
80 - 84	112.2	125.7	104.4	107.2	121.8	99.4	115.7	128.2	108.0
85 - 89	177.0	186.9	172.2	165.8	177.2	160.7	185.6	193.5	181.4
90 - 94	293.5	296.3	292.1	281.2	297.4	273.8	303.9	295.5	308.4
95 - 99	338.6	304.7	357.5	349.7	316.9	365.6	330.5	297.1	351.1
100 +....................	177.7	178.3	177.5	230.9	♦197.3	244.5	148.1	168.9	138.3
Russian Federation - Fédération de Russie[13]									
2006 (C)									
Total.....................	15.2	17.4	13.3	14.4	16.7	12.5	17.3	19.2	15.5
0	10.4	11.6	9.1	9.5	10.6	8.4	12.3	13.9	10.7
1 - 4	0.7	0.8	0.6	0.6	0.7	0.5	1.0	1.1	0.9
5 - 9	0.4	0.4	0.3	0.3	0.4	0.3	0.5	0.6	0.3
10 - 14	0.4	0.5	0.3	0.3	0.4	0.3	0.4	0.6	0.3
15 - 19	1.1	1.6	0.6	1.0	1.4	0.6	1.4	2.0	0.8
20 - 24	2.2	3.4	0.9	2.0	3.1	0.8	3.0	4.5	1.3
25 - 29	3.8	6.1	1.5	3.6	5.9	1.5	4.4	6.8	1.8
30 - 34	4.9	7.7	2.0	4.7	7.4	2.0	5.6	8.7	2.3
35 - 39	5.8	9.0	2.7	5.5	8.6	2.6	6.7	10.3	2.9
40 - 44	7.8	12.3	3.6	7.4	11.8	3.4	8.9	13.6	4.0
45 - 49	10.4	16.5	4.9	9.8	15.9	4.7	12.0	18.2	5.7
50 - 54	14.5	23.3	7.2	13.8	22.6	6.8	16.7	25.3	8.4
55 - 59	19.5	30.7	10.7	18.4	29.5	10.1	22.8	34.2	12.8
60 - 64	25.7	41.3	15.0	24.3	39.4	14.2	29.9	47.0	17.7
65 - 69	34.3	54.0	22.2	33.1	53.1	21.5	37.3	58.0	24.3
70 - 74	50.2	74.7	37.5	48.9	73.5	36.6	53.0	77.2	39.4
75 - 79	76.0	104.9	63.8	75.5	104.1	63.6	77.0	106.7	64.1
80 - 84	111.0	133.4	104.8	110.7	131.7	104.7	111.7	137.7	105.1
85 - 89	177.2	186.2	175.1	175.5	182.4	173.7	181.3	197.2	178.2
90 - 94	283.7	273.8	285.6	278.2	266.2	280.8	296.1	298.6	295.7
95 - 99	366.7	312.8	376.9	348.2	298.0	359.0	406.8	359.3	413.4
100 +....................	151.5	111.6	158.8	134.2	99.1	142.4	178.2	149.4	181.3
Serbia - Serbie[34]									
2006 (+C)									
Total.....................	13.9	14.5	13.3	12.4	13.4	11.6	15.8	16.0	15.6
0	7.4	8.5	6.2	7.6	8.2	7.0	7.0	9.1	4.8
1 - 4	0.3	0.3	0.3	0.3	♦0.3	0.4	0.3	♦0.3	♦0.3

20. Death rates specific for age, sex and urban/rural residence: latest available year, 1997 - 2006
Taux de mortalité selon l'âge, le sexe et la résidence, urbaine/rurale: dernière année disponible, 1997 - 2006 (continued - suite)

Continent, country or area, date, code and age (in years) Continent, pays ou zone, date, code et âge (en années)	Total			Urban - Urbaine			Rural - Rurale		
	Both sexes Les deux sexes	Male Masculin	Female Féminin	Both sexes Les deux sexes	Male Masculin	Female Féminin	Both sexes Les deux sexes	Male Masculin	Female Féminin
EUROPE									
Serbia - Serbie[34]									
2006 (+C)									
5 - 9	0.2	0.3	♦0.1	0.2	♦0.2	♦0.1	0.2	♦0.3	♦0.1
10 - 14	0.2	0.2	♦0.1	0.2	♦0.2	♦0.2	♦0.1	♦0.1	♦0.1
15 - 19	0.4	0.5	0.2	0.4	0.5	0.2	0.4	0.5	♦0.2
20 - 24	0.7	1.0	0.3	0.7	1.1	0.4	0.6	0.8	♦0.3
25 - 29	0.8	1.1	0.4	0.9	1.2	0.5	0.6	1.0	♦0.3
30 - 34	1.0	1.3	0.6	1.0	1.5	0.5	0.9	1.1	0.7
35 - 39	1.4	1.8	0.9	1.3	1.8	0.9	1.4	1.9	0.9
40 - 44	2.5	3.2	1.7	2.4	3.2	1.7	2.5	3.3	1.7
45 - 49	4.3	5.8	2.9	4.4	6.0	3.0	4.3	5.5	2.9
50 - 54	7.6	10.3	4.9	7.7	10.5	5.2	7.4	10.0	4.5
55 - 59	11.7	16.1	7.5	11.7	16.3	7.8	11.6	16.0	7.1
60 - 64	17.7	24.3	12.0	18.2	24.8	12.8	17.0	23.8	10.9
65 - 69	27.4	35.4	20.9	28.4	37.0	21.6	26.3	33.7	20.0
70 - 74	45.1	55.7	37.0	46.0	57.8	37.0	44.3	53.7	37.0
75 - 79	75.8	86.7	68.4	79.3	94.0	69.8	72.9	80.9	67.1
80 - 84	124.1	129.9	120.8	124.0	130.2	120.4	124.3	129.6	121.1
85 +	190.7	191.3	190.3	184.4	183.2	185.1	196.6	198.6	195.5
Slovakia - Slovaquie									
2006 (C)									
Total	9.9	10.7	9.1	8.7	9.5	8.0	11.3	12.2	10.5
0	6.6	7.4	5.8	5.4	5.7	5.1	7.9	9.3	6.5
1 - 4	0.3	0.4	♦0.3	0.3	♦0.3	♦0.3	0.4	♦0.5	♦0.3
5 - 9	0.2	0.3	♦0.2	♦0.1	♦0.2	♦0.1	0.3	♦0.3	♦0.2
10 - 14	0.2	0.2	♦0.1	0.2	♦0.3	♦0.1	♦0.1	♦0.1	♦0.1
15 - 19	0.4	0.5	0.2	0.3	0.4	♦0.2	0.4	0.6	♦0.2
20 - 24	0.6	0.9	0.2	0.6	0.9	♦0.2	0.6	1.0	♦0.2
25 - 29	0.7	1.0	0.3	0.6	1.0	♦0.2	0.7	1.1	0.4
30 - 34	0.9	1.4	0.4	0.9	1.4	0.4	1.0	1.5	0.5
35 - 39	1.6	2.3	0.8	1.4	2.0	0.8	1.8	2.7	0.8
40 - 44	2.5	3.7	1.4	2.3	3.3	1.3	2.9	4.2	1.5
45 - 49	4.6	6.9	2.4	4.0	5.9	2.2	5.6	8.1	2.7
50 - 54	7.4	10.8	4.1	6.7	9.9	3.9	8.3	12.1	4.3
55 - 59	10.7	15.9	6.1	9.7	13.9	6.0	12.2	18.5	6.1
60 - 64	15.8	24.0	9.3	14.5	21.5	9.1	17.5	27.2	9.5
65 - 69	24.3	36.7	15.5	23.3	34.2	15.4	25.5	39.5	15.5
70 - 74	38.7	55.1	28.3	36.9	51.3	27.6	40.6	59.3	29.0
75 - 79	62.8	85.1	50.5	60.2	80.3	48.8	65.2	90.0	52.2
80 - 84	104.2	128.4	93.0	101.3	122.3	91.2	107.0	134.5	94.7
85 - 89	162.2	183.9	152.9	160.3	177.5	152.5	164.1	190.5	153.2
90 - 94	259.1	287.5	248.1	248.8	284.5	234.5	269.3	290.5	261.3
95 - 99	276.9	252.7	286.7	256.4	202.2	280.5	298.7	314.8	292.9
100 +	131.4	♦85.2	158.0	121.9	♦73.0	♦158.5	141.9	♦104.7	157.6
Slovenia - Slovénie									
2006 (C)									
Total	9.1	9.4	8.7	8.9	9.4	8.4	9.7	10.1	9.3
0	3.5	3.4	3.6	4.2	♦4.7	♦3.7	♦2.9	♦2.3	♦3.5
1 - 4	♦0.1	♦0.2	♦0.1	♦0.2	♦0.2	♦0.1	♦0.1	♦0.2	♦0.1
5 - 9	♦0.1	♦0.1	♦0.1	-	-	-	♦0.2	♦0.2	♦0.2
10 - 14	♦0.1	♦0.2	♦0.1	♦0.1	♦0.1	-	♦0.1	♦0.2	♦0.1
15 - 19	0.4	0.6	♦0.3	♦0.4	♦0.6	♦0.2	♦0.5	♦0.6	♦0.3
20 - 24	0.8	1.2	♦0.3	0.7	1.0	♦0.4	0.9	1.5	♦0.3
25 - 29	0.7	1.1	♦0.2	0.7	1.1	♦0.3	0.7	1.2	♦0.2
30 - 34	0.7	1.1	♦0.3	0.7	1.0	♦0.3	0.7	1.2	♦0.2
35 - 39	1.0	1.5	0.5	0.8	1.3	♦0.4	1.2	1.9	♦0.6
40 - 44	1.9	2.9	0.9	1.8	3.1	♦0.7	2.2	3.1	1.3
45 - 49	3.1	4.5	1.6	2.9	4.4	1.5	3.5	5.2	1.7
50 - 54	5.6	7.7	3.3	5.5	7.6	3.5	6.0	8.5	3.2
55 - 59	7.9	11.4	4.2	7.3	11.0	4.0	8.8	12.6	4.6
60 - 64	11.4	16.3	6.9	11.0	16.1	6.7	12.2	17.3	7.2
65 - 69	16.1	23.4	9.9	15.0	22.1	9.3	17.6	25.4	10.7
70 - 74	26.7	38.5	18.3	25.1	36.0	17.6	28.6	41.7	19.3
75 - 79	43.0	60.6	33.0	40.3	56.1	31.5	46.2	65.9	34.9
80 - 84	74.6	97.3	65.9	68.2	86.3	60.9	82.2	112.0	71.7

20. Death rates specific for age, sex and urban/rural residence: latest available year, 1997 - 2006
Taux de mortalité selon l'âge, le sexe et la résidence, urbaine/rurale: dernière année disponible, 1997 - 2006 (continued - suite)

Continent, country or area, date, code and age (in years) / Continent, pays ou zone, date, code et âge (en années)	Total			Urban - Urbaine			Rural - Rurale		
	Both sexes Les deux sexes	Male Masculin	Female Féminin	Both sexes Les deux sexes	Male Masculin	Female Féminin	Both sexes Les deux sexes	Male Masculin	Female Féminin
EUROPE									
Slovenia - Slovénie									
2006 (C)									
85 - 89	123.9	152.8	114.6	114.6	135.3	107.4	135.3	176.3	123.1
90 - 94	227.6	267.1	216.9	213.6	258.7	200.7	245.2	279.4	236.5
95 - 99	320.3	329.7	317.9	281.6	290.5	279.3	367.9	374.0	366.3
100 + ...	382.1	♦625.0	345.8	♦391.3	♦500.0	♦372.9	♦392.2	♦833.3	♦333.3
Spain - Espagne									
2005 (C)									
Total....................	8.9	9.4	8.4	...	...	...	...	...	...
0	3.9	4.3	3.4	...	...	...	...	...	...
1 - 4	0.2	0.2	0.2	...	...	...	...	...	...
5 - 9	0.1	0.1	0.1	...	...	...	...	...	...
10 - 14	0.1	0.2	0.1	...	...	...	...	...	...
15 - 19	0.4	0.6	0.2	...	...	...	...	...	...
20 - 24	0.5	0.7	0.2	...	...	...	...	...	...
25 - 29	0.5	0.7	0.2	...	...	...	...	...	...
30 - 34	0.7	1.0	0.4	...	...	...	...	...	...
35 - 39	1.0	1.4	0.6	...	...	...	...	...	...
40 - 44	1.6	2.2	1.0	...	...	...	...	...	...
45 - 49	2.4	3.3	1.5	...	...	...	...	...	...
50 - 54	3.6	5.3	2.0	...	...	...	...	...	...
55 - 59	5.4	8.0	3.0	...	...	...	...	...	...
60 - 64	8.0	11.8	4.5	...	...	...	...	...	...
65 - 69	12.6	18.6	7.4	...	...	...	...	...	...
70 - 74	20.9	30.0	13.5	...	...	...	...	...	...
75 - 79	36.7	50.6	26.5	...	...	...	...	...	...
80 - 84	68.1	88.2	55.7	...	...	...	...	...	...
85 - 89	119.0	141.1	108.4	...	...	...	...	...	...
90 - 94	205.9	231.3	196.2	...	...	...	...	...	...
95 - 99	302.7	315.8	298.3	...	...	...	...	...	...
100 + ...	489.6	407.0	516.2	...	...	...	...	...	...
Sweden - Suède									
2006 (C)									
Total....................	10.0	9.8	10.3	...	...	...	...	...	...
0	2.9	3.1	2.6	...	...	...	...	...	...
1 - 4	0.2	0.2	0.2	...	...	...	...	...	...
5 - 9	0.1	♦0.1	♦0.1	...	...	...	...	...	...
10 - 14	0.1	0.1	♦0.1	...	...	...	...	...	...
15 - 19	0.3	0.4	0.2	...	...	...	...	...	...
20 - 24	0.5	0.7	0.3	...	...	...	...	...	...
25 - 29	0.4	0.6	0.2	...	...	...	...	...	...
30 - 34	0.5	0.6	0.4	...	...	...	...	...	...
35 - 39	0.7	0.9	0.5	...	...	...	...	...	...
40 - 44	1.1	1.3	0.8	...	...	...	...	...	...
45 - 49	1.7	2.0	1.4	...	...	...	...	...	...
50 - 54	3.1	3.8	2.4	...	...	...	...	...	...
55 - 59	4.9	5.9	3.8	...	...	...	...	...	...
60 - 64	7.9	9.5	6.2	...	...	...	...	...	...
65 - 69	12.5	15.9	9.3	...	...	...	...	...	...
70 - 74	21.2	26.9	16.2	...	...	...	...	...	...
75 - 79	36.4	46.5	28.6	...	...	...	...	...	...
80 - 84	66.8	84.4	55.1	...	...	...	...	...	...
85 - 89	120.3	148.7	105.2	...	...	...	...	...	...
90 - 94	212.4	251.8	197.2	...	...	...	...	...	...
95 - 99	339.8	377.9	329.6	...	...	...	...	...	...
100 + ...	499.3	509.4	497.4	...	...	...	...	...	...
Switzerland - Suisse									
2006 (C)									
Total....................	8.1	8.0	8.1	...	...	...	...	...	...
0	8.9	9.7	8.1	...	...	...	...	...	...
1 - 4	0.2	♦0.2	♦0.2	...	...	...	...	...	...
5 - 9	0.1	♦0.1	♦0.1	...	...	...	...	...	...
10 - 14	0.1	♦0.1	♦0.1	...	...	...	...	...	...
15 - 19	0.3	0.4	0.2	...	...	...	...	...	...
20 - 24	0.4	0.6	0.2	...	...	...	...	...	...

20. Death rates specific for age, sex and urban/rural residence: latest available year, 1997 - 2006
Taux de mortalité selon l'âge, le sexe et la résidence, urbaine/rurale: dernière année disponible, 1997 - 2006 (continued - suite)

Continent, country or area, date, code and age (in years) / Continent, pays ou zone, date, code et âge (en années)	Total			Urban - Urbaine			Rural - Rurale		
	Both sexes Les deux sexes	Male Masculin	Female Féminin	Both sexes Les deux sexes	Male Masculin	Female Féminin	Both sexes Les deux sexes	Male Masculin	Female Féminin
EUROPE									
Switzerland - Suisse									
2006 (C)									
25 - 29	0.5	0.7	0.3	...	...	...	...	...	...
30 - 34	0.6	0.8	0.4	...	...	...	...	...	...
35 - 39	0.7	1.0	0.5	...	...	...	...	...	...
40 - 44	1.1	1.4	0.8	...	...	...	...	...	...
45 - 49	1.8	2.2	1.4	...	...	...	...	...	...
50 - 54	2.8	3.5	2.2	...	...	...	...	...	...
55 - 59	4.8	6.1	3.4	...	...	...	...	...	...
60 - 64	7.0	9.1	5.1	...	...	...	...	...	...
65 - 69	10.6	13.9	7.6	...	...	...	...	...	...
70 - 74	17.7	23.6	12.9	...	...	...	...	...	...
75 - 79	31.2	41.7	23.7	...	...	...	...	...	...
80 - 84	55.6	72.7	45.3	...	...	...	...	...	...
85 - 89	100.5	122.1	89.8	...	...	...	...	...	...
90 - 94	172.8	195.9	164.0	...	...	...	...	...	...
95 +	227.5	247.4	222.3	...	...	...	...	...	...
The Former Yugoslav Rep. of Macedonia - L'ex-République yougoslave de Macédoine									
2006 (C)									
Total	9.1	9.8	8.5	...	...	...	...	...	...
0	11.7	13.1	10.2	...	...	...	...	...	...
1 - 4	0.3	♦0.4	♦0.3	...	...	...	...	...	...
5 - 9	♦0.1	♦0.1	♦0.1	...	...	...	...	...	...
10 - 14	♦0.2	♦0.2	♦0.1	...	...	...	...	...	...
15 - 19	0.3	0.4	♦0.2	...	...	...	...	...	...
20 - 24	0.5	0.7	♦0.3	...	...	...	...	...	...
25 - 29	0.5	0.7	♦0.3	...	...	...	...	...	...
30 - 34	0.7	0.8	0.6	...	...	...	...	...	...
35 - 39	1.1	1.3	0.9	...	...	...	...	...	...
40 - 44	1.9	2.3	1.4	...	...	...	...	...	...
45 - 49	3.7	4.9	2.4	...	...	...	...	...	...
50 - 54	6.7	9.3	4.0	...	...	...	...	...	...
55 - 59	9.8	13.3	6.6	...	...	...	...	...	...
60 - 64	15.7	20.1	11.7	...	...	...	...	...	...
65 - 69	24.6	30.4	19.5	...	...	...	...	...	...
70 - 74	42.8	51.2	35.7	...	...	...	...	...	...
75 - 79	77.1	87.3	69.3	...	...	...	...	...	...
80 - 84	132.1	144.5	123.5	...	...	...	...	...	...
85 +	226.8	241.1	217.1	...	...	...	...	...	...
Ukraine[35]									
2001 (C)									
Total	15.5	16.9	14.2	13.9	15.9	12.3	18.5	19.0	18.1
0	12.0	13.5	10.3	12.2	13.7	10.7	11.5	13.3	9.6
1 - 4	0.9	1.0	0.8	0.7	0.8	0.6	1.2	1.3	1.0
5 - 9	0.4	0.5	0.3	0.4	0.5	0.3	0.4	0.5	0.3
10 - 14	0.4	0.5	0.3	0.4	0.5	0.2	0.4	0.5	0.3
15 - 19	0.9	1.2	0.5	0.8	1.1	0.5	1.2	1.7	0.7
20 - 24	1.8	2.8	0.8	1.7	2.6	0.8	2.1	3.2	0.8
25 - 29	2.6	4.0	1.1	2.5	4.0	1.1	2.6	4.1	1.0
30 - 34	3.4	5.3	1.5	3.4	5.3	1.6	3.4	5.3	1.3
35 - 39	4.7	7.6	2.0	4.6	7.6	2.0	4.9	7.6	2.0
40 - 44	6.4	10.3	2.8	6.2	10.3	2.7	6.8	10.5	2.9
45 - 49	9.2	14.9	4.3	8.9	14.7	4.1	10.0	15.4	4.6
50 - 54	12.5	19.8	6.4	12.3	19.6	6.3	13.2	20.2	6.8
55 - 59	17.9	28.1	10.1	17.5	27.6	9.8	18.7	29.2	10.7
60 - 64	24.6	38.5	14.7	24.3	38.0	14.6	25.1	39.4	14.9
65 - 69	33.3	48.9	22.8	33.6	48.9	23.1	32.8	48.9	22.2
70 - 74	51.2	72.3	39.3	52.7	73.2	40.7	49.2	70.9	37.5
75 - 79	72.6	95.5	63.8	73.0	93.9	64.7	72.1	97.8	62.7
80 - 84	116.0	139.5	108.7	117.5	138.4	110.3	114.3	141.0	106.7
85 - 89	206.8	236.7	199.3	202.8	229.2	195.4	211.6	247.7	203.6
90 - 94	310.2	344.3	302.4	315.9	343.1	309.0	304.6	345.8	296.1

20. Death rates specific for age, sex and urban/rural residence: latest available year, 1997 - 2006
Taux de mortalité selon l'âge, le sexe et la résidence, urbaine/rurale: dernière année disponible, 1997 - 2006 (continued - suite)

Continent, country or area, date, code and age (in years) / Continent, pays ou zone, date, code et âge (en années)	Total			Urban - Urbaine			Rural - Rurale		
	Both sexes Les deux sexes	Male Masculin	Female Féminin	Both sexes Les deux sexes	Male Masculin	Female Féminin	Both sexes Les deux sexes	Male Masculin	Female Féminin
EUROPE									
Ukraine[35]									
2001 (C)									
95 - 99	421.3	438.2	418.1	411.0	420.7	408.9	430.9	457.0	426.4
100 +	584.9	758.8	559.3	574.9	735.8	544.1	592.3	784.9	569.8
2004 (C)									
Total	16.1	17.9	14.5	...	...	...	...	...	...
0	9.7	11.0	8.3	...	...	...	...	...	...
1 - 4	0.7	0.8	0.7	...	...	...	...	...	...
5 - 9	0.4	0.4	0.3	...	...	...	...	...	...
10 - 14	0.3	0.4	0.2	...	...	...	...	...	...
15 - 19	0.7	1.0	0.4	...	...	...	...	...	...
20 - 24	1.5	2.3	0.7	...	...	...	...	...	...
25 - 29	2.6	4.0	1.2	...	...	...	...	...	...
30 - 34	3.7	5.8	1.7	...	...	...	...	...	...
35 - 39	5.3	8.2	2.4	...	...	...	...	...	...
40 - 44	7.2	11.7	3.2	...	...	...	...	...	...
45 - 49	10.0	16.2	4.7	...	...	...	...	...	...
50 - 54	13.9	22.1	7.0	...	...	...	...	...	...
55 - 59	18.1	28.5	10.1	...	...	...	...	...	...
60 - 64	25.6	40.6	15.2	...	...	...	...	...	...
65 - 69	34.5	52.3	23.0	...	...	...	...	...	...
70 - 74	50.5	71.8	38.4	...	...	...	...	...	...
75 - 79	75.5	101.1	64.4	...	...	...	...	...	...
80 - 84	116.5	141.7	108.8	...	...	...	...	...	...
85 - 89	190.7	214.7	184.5	...	...	...	...	...	...
90 - 94	289.6	305.3	286.2	...	...	...	...	...	...
95 - 99	468.3	505.5	461.0	...	...	...	...	...	...
100 +	452.9	538.6	439.3	...	...	...	...	...	...
United Kingdom - Royaume-Uni[36]									
2005* (C)									
Total	9.7	9.4	10.0	...	...	...	...	...	...
0	5.1	5.7	4.5	...	...	...	...	...	...
1 - 4	0.2	0.2	0.2	...	...	...	...	...	...
5 - 9	0.1	0.1	0.1	...	...	...	...	...	...
10 - 14	0.1	0.1	0.1	...	...	...	...	...	...
15 - 19	0.3	0.4	0.2	...	...	...	...	...	...
20 - 24	0.5	0.7	0.3	...	...	...	...	...	...
25 - 29	0.5	0.8	0.3	...	...	...	...	...	...
30 - 34	0.7	1.0	0.5	...	...	...	...	...	...
35 - 39	1.0	1.3	0.7	...	...	...	...	...	...
40 - 44	1.5	1.9	1.2	...	...	...	...	...	...
45 - 49	2.4	2.9	1.9	...	...	...	...	...	...
50 - 54	3.8	4.6	3.0	...	...	...	...	...	...
55 - 59	5.8	7.0	4.6	...	...	...	...	...	...
60 - 64	9.5	11.9	7.2	...	...	...	...	...	...
65 - 69	15.3	18.8	12.0	...	...	...	...	...	...
70 - 74	25.3	31.6	19.9	...	...	...	...	...	...
75 - 79	43.6	53.6	36.1	...	...	...	...	...	...
80 - 84	74.0	90.1	64.0	...	...	...	...	...	...
85 - 89	120.7	142.1	110.2	...	...	...	...	...	...
90 +	228.0	245.1	222.4	...	...	...	...	...	...
OCEANIA - OCÉANIE									
Australia - Australie									
2004 (+C)									
Total	6.6	6.8	6.3	...	...	...	...	...	...
0	4.7	5.2	4.2	...	...	...	...	...	...
1 - 4	0.3	0.3	0.2	...	...	...	...	...	...
5 - 9	0.1	0.1	0.1	...	...	...	...	...	...
10 - 14	0.1	0.1	0.1	...	...	...	...	...	...
15 - 19	0.4	0.5	0.3	...	...	...	...	...	...
20 - 24	0.6	0.8	0.3	...	...	...	...	...	...

Continent, country or area, date, code and age (in years) / Continent, pays ou zone, date, code et âge (en années)	Total			Urban - Urbaine			Rural - Rurale		
	Both sexes Les deux sexes	Male Masculin	Female Féminin	Both sexes Les deux sexes	Male Masculin	Female Féminin	Both sexes Les deux sexes	Male Masculin	Female Féminin
OCEANIA - OCÉANIE									
Australia - Australie									
2004 (+C)									
25 - 29	0.7	0.9	0.4	...	...	...	...	...	...
30 - 34	0.8	1.2	0.4	...	...	...	...	...	...
35 - 39	0.9	1.2	0.6	...	...	...	...	...	...
40 - 44	1.3	1.7	0.9	...	...	...	...	...	...
45 - 49	2.0	2.4	1.6	...	...	...	...	...	...
50 - 54	2.9	3.6	2.1	...	...	...	...	...	...
55 - 59	4.4	5.4	3.4	...	...	...	...	...	...
60 - 64	7.4	9.3	5.4	...	...	...	...	...	...
65 - 69	12.0	15.2	9.0	...	...	...	...	...	...
70 - 74	20.4	26.7	14.7	...	...	...	...	...	...
75 - 79	35.2	44.8	27.2	...	...	...	...	...	...
80 - 84	61.3	76.4	51.1	...	...	...	...	...	...
85 +	137.6	156.4	128.9	...	...	...	...	...	...
New Caledonia - Nouvelle-Calédonie									
2003 (C)									
Total	5.1	6.0	4.2	...	...	...	...	...	...
0	♦5.8	♦6.5	♦5.0	...	...	...	...	...	...
1 - 4	♦0.6	♦1.0	♦0.1	...	...	...	...	...	...
5 - 9	♦0.4	♦0.4	♦0.4	...	...	...	...	...	...
10 - 14	♦0.2	♦0.2	♦0.3	...	...	...	...	...	...
15 - 19	♦0.6	♦0.7	♦0.5	...	...	...	...	...	...
20 - 24	♦1.6	♦2.4	♦0.9	...	...	...	...	...	...
25 - 29	♦1.2	♦1.4	♦1.0	...	...	...	...	...	...
30 - 34	♦1.6	♦2.4	♦0.7	...	...	...	...	...	...
35 - 39	♦1.6	♦1.9	♦1.4	...	...	...	...	...	...
40 - 44	2.5	♦3.6	♦1.4	...	...	...	...	...	...
45 - 49	4.0	♦4.8	♦3.1	...	...	...	...	...	...
50 - 54	5.3	5.7	♦4.9	...	...	...	...	...	...
55 - 59	11.3	13.4	8.8	...	...	...	...	...	...
60 - 64	12.6	16.7	♦8.4	...	...	...	...	...	...
65 - 69	27.7	33.5	22.0	...	...	...	...	...	...
70 - 74	38.4	52.4	25.7	...	...	...	...	...	...
75 - 79	59.8	74.6	48.0	...	...	...	...	...	...
80 +	121.0	149.2	104.7	...	...	...	...	...	...
New Zealand - Nouvelle-Zélande[33]									
2006 (+C)									
Total	6.7	6.8	6.7	7.0[9]	7.0[9]	7.2[9]	4.7[9]	5.4[9]	3.9[9]
0 - 4	1.3	1.4	1.1	1.2[9]	1.4[9]	1.1[9]	1.1[9]	♦1.0[9]	♦1.1[9]
0	5.1	5.7	4.4	...	...	...	...	...	...
1 - 4	0.3	0.3	♦0.2	...	...	...	...	...	...
5 - 9	0.1	♦0.2	♦0.1	♦0.1[9]	♦0.1[9]	♦0.1[9]	♦0.2[9]	♦0.3[9]	-[9]
10 - 14	0.1	♦0.2	♦0.1	0.1[9]	♦0.1[9]	♦0.1[9]	♦0.2[9]	♦0.3[9]	♦0.2[9]
15 - 19	0.6	0.9	0.4	0.6[9]	0.8[9]	0.4[9]	0.8[9]	♦1.2[9]	♦0.4[9]
20 - 24	0.6	0.9	0.3	0.5[9]	0.8[9]	0.3[9]	1.4[9]	♦2.0[9]	♦0.6[9]
25 - 29	0.6	0.9	0.4	0.6[9]	0.9[9]	0.4[9]	♦0.8[9]	♦1.4[9]	♦0.3[9]
30 - 34	0.7	1.0	0.5	0.7[9]	1.0[9]	0.5[9]	♦0.8[9]	♦1.1[9]	♦0.5[9]
35 - 39	0.9	1.2	0.7	0.9[9]	1.1[9]	0.8[9]	0.9[9]	♦1.3[9]	♦0.5[9]
40 - 44	1.4	1.6	1.1	1.3[9]	1.5[9]	1.2[9]	1.4[9]	1.9[9]	♦0.9[9]
45 - 49	2.2	2.5	1.8	2.1[9]	2.4[9]	1.8[9]	2.2[9]	2.8[9]	1.6[9]
50 - 54	3.2	3.7	2.8	3.3[9]	3.8[9]	2.9[9]	2.7[9]	3.2[9]	2.2[9]
55 - 59	5.1	6.1	4.2	5.2[9]	6.2[9]	4.3[9]	4.5[9]	5.2[9]	3.7[9]
60 - 64	8.2	10.1	6.4	8.4[9]	10.4[9]	6.6[9]	6.9[9]	8.5[9]	5.1[9]
65 - 69	13.0	15.9	10.3	13.2[9]	16.3[9]	10.4[9]	11.4[9]	13.2[9]	9.4[9]
70 - 74	22.3	27.0	18.1	22.5[9]	27.3[9]	18.2[9]	20.8[9]	24.1[9]	16.8[9]
75 - 79	37.0	44.6	30.5	37.3[9]	45.2[9]	74.2[9]	32.8[9]	38.7[9]	25.7[9]
80 - 84	62.5	76.2	53.1	62.6[9]	76.1[9]	53.6[9]	59.4[9]	74.4[9]	44.6[9]
85 +[9]	...	...	...	152.6	168.4	145.7	141.1	146.1	137.7
85 - 89	114.7	138.2	102.8	...	...	...	...	...	...
90 +	229.7	243.2	224.9	...	...	...	...	...	...

FOOTNOTES - NOTES

♦ Rates based on 30 or fewer deaths. - Taux basés sur 30 décès ou moins.

* Provisional. - Données provisoires.

'Code' indicates the source of data, as follows:
C - Civil registration, estimated over 90% complete
U - Civil registration, estimated less than 90% complete
| - Other source, estimated reliable
+ - Data tabulated by date of registration rather than occurence.
... - Information not available

Le 'Code' indique la source des données, comme suit:
C - Registres de l'état civil considérés complets à 90 p. 100 au moins.
U - Registres de l'état civil qui ne sont pas considérés complets à 90 p. 100 au moins.
| - Autre source, considérée pas douteuses.
+ - Données exploitées selon la date de l'enregistrement et non la date de l'événement.
... - Information pas disponible.

[1] For 2001, data refer to last twelve months preceding census in August 2001. - Pour 2001, les données se rapportent aux douze mois précédant le recensement d'août 2001.

[2] Based on the results of the population census. - D'après les résultats du recensement de la population.

[3] Data for 1997 refer to last twelve months preceding population and housing census of 1997. - Les données pour 1997 se réfèrent au douze mois précédant le recensement de population et de l'habitat de 1997.

[4] Deaths for 2001 refer to the period January-August 2001. - Le chiffre des décès de 2001 correspond à la période allant de janvier à août 2001.

[5] Figures for male and female categories do not add up to the total, since they do not include the category "Unknown". - La somme des chiffres indiqués pour les sexes masculin et féminin n'est pas égale au total parce qu'elle n'inclut pas la catégorie " inconnue ".

[6] Excluding live-born infants who died before their birth was registered. - Non compris les enfants nés vivants décédés avant l'enregistrement de leur naissance.

[7] Data are for 12 months preceding the census date. - Les données portent sur les 12 mois précédant la date du recensement.

[8] Including Canadian residents temporarily in the United States, but excluding United States residents temporarily in Canada. - Y compris les résidents canadiens se trouvant temporairement aux Etats-Unis, mais ne comprenant pas les résidents des Etats-Unis se trouvant temporairement au Canada.

[9] The total number includes 'Unknown residence', but the categories urban and rural do not. - Le nombre total inclue 'Résidence inconnue ', mais les catégories Urbain et Rural ne l'incluent pas.

[10] The total number includes 'Unknown residence', but the categories urban and rural do no. Figures for male and female categories do not add up to the total, since they do not include the category "Unknown". - Le nombre total inclue 'Résidence inconnue ', mais les catégories Urbain et Rural ne l'incluent pas. La somme des chiffres indiqués pour les sexes masculin et féminin n'est pas égale au total parce qu'elle n'inclut pas la catégorie " inconnue ".

[11] Data refer to deaths of residents of the Netherlands Antilles (including those that died outside the Netherlands Antilles). Data exclude deaths by non-residents. - Ces données concernent les décès de résidents des Antilles néerlandaises (y compris ceux survenus hors des Antilles néerlandaises). Elles ne concernent pas les décès des non-résidents.

[12] Excluding Indian jungle population. - Non compris les Indiens de la jungle.

[13] Excluding infants born alive of less than 28 weeks' gestation, of less than 1 000 grams in weight and 35 centimeters in length, who die within seven days of birth. - Non compris les enfants nés vivants après moins de 28 semaines de gestations, pesant moins de 1 000 grammes, mesurant moins de 35 centimètres et décédés dans les sept jours qui ont suivi leur naissance.

[14] For 2005, data refer to last twelve months preceding census in May 2005. - Pour 2005, les données se rapportent aux douze mois précédant le recensement de mai 2005.

[15] Data refer to government controlled areas. - Les données se rapportent aux zones contrôlées par le Gouvernement.

[16] Including data for East Jerusalem and Israeli residents in certain other territories under occupation by Israeli military forces since June 1967. - Y compris les données pour Jérusalem-Est et les résidents israéliens dans certains autres territoires occupés depuis 1967 par les forces armées israéliennes.

[17] Data include 141 deaths abroad of Israeli residents who were out of the country for less than a year. - Y compris les décès à l'étranger de 141 résidents israéliens qui ont quitté le pays depuis moins d'un an.

[18] Data refer to Japanese nationals in Japan only. - Les données se raportent aux nationaux japonais au Japon seulement.

[19] Excluding alien armed forces, civilian aliens employed by armed forces, and foreign diplomatic personnel and their dependants. - Non compris les militaires étrangers, les civils étrangers employés par les forces armées ni le personnel diplomatique étranger et les membres de leur famille les accompagnant.

[20] Including Korean deaths abroad. - Y compris les décès de Coréens survenus à l'étranger.

[21] For 2001, data refer to last twelve months preceding census on June 2001. - Pour 2001, les données se rapportent aux douze mois précédant le recensement juin 2001.

[22] Excluding data for the Pakistan-held part of Jammu and Kashmir, the final status of which has not yet been determined. Data based on Pakistan Demographic Survey (PDS 2003) . - Non compris les données concernant la partie du Jammu et Cachemire occupée par le Pakistan dont le statut définitif n'a pas été déterminé. Données extraites de l'enquête démographique effectuée par le Pakistan en 2003.

[23] For 2004, data refer to last twelve months preceding the census in September 2004. - Pour 2004, les données se rapportent aux douze mois précédant le recensement septembre 2004.

[24] Including armed forces stationed outside the country, but excluding alien armed forces stationed in the area. - Y compris les militaires nationaux hors du pays, mais non compris les militaires étrangers en garnison sur le territoire.

[25] Excluding Faeroe Islands and Greenland shown separately, if available. - Non compris les Iles Féroé et le Gröenland, qui font l'objet de rubriques distinctes, si disponible.

[26] Including nationals temporarily outside the country. Including Aland Islands. - Y compris les nationaux se trouvant temporairement hors du pays. Y compris les Îles d'Åland.

[27] Excluding Overseas Departments, namely, French Guiana, Guadeloupe, Martinique and Reunion, shown separately, if available. Including armed forces stationed outside the country. - Non compris les départements d'outre mer, c'est-à-dire la Guyane française, la Guadeloupe, la Martinique et la Réunion, qui font l'objet de rubriques distinctes, si disponible. Y compris les militaires nationaux hors du pays.

[28] Total includes the data of foreigners, persons of unknown residence and homeless, but the categories urban and rural do not. - Total incluant les étrangers, les personnes de résidence inconnue et les sans-abri, ce qui n'est pas le cas pour les catégories urbaines et rurales.

[29] Events registered within one year of occurrence. - Evénements enregistrés dans l'année qui suit l'événement.

[30] Excluding infants born alive of less than 28 weeks' gestation, of less than 1 000 grams in weight and 35 centimeters in length, who die within seven days of birth. Data do not include information for Transnistria and the municipality of Bender. - Non compris les enfants nés vivants après moins de 28 semaines de gestations, pesant moins de 1 000 grammes, mesurant moins de 35 centimètres et décédés dans les sept jours qui ont suivi leur naissance. Les données ne tiennent pas compte de l'information sur la Transnistria et la municipalité de Bender.

[31] Including residents outside the country if listed in a Netherlands population register. - Y compris les résidents hors du pays, s'ils sont inscrits sur un registre de population néerlandais.

[32] Including residents temporarily outside the country. Excluding Svalbard and Jan Mayen Island shown separately, if available. - Y compris les résidents se trouvant temporairement hors du pays. Non compris Svalbard et Jan Mayen qui font l'objet de rubriques distinctes, si disponible.

[33] For resident population only. - Pour la population résidante seulement.

[34] Without data for Kosovo and Metohia. - Sans les données pour le Kosovo et Metohie.

[35] Age classification based on year of birth rather than on completed years of age. Excluding infants born alive of less than 28 weeks' gestation, of less than 1 000 grams in weight and 35 centimeters in length, who die within seven days of birth. - La classification par âge est fondée sur l'année de naissance et non sur l'âge en années révolues. Non compris les enfants nés vivants après moins de 28 semaines de gestations, pesant moins de 1 000 grammes, mesurant moins de 35 centimètres et décédés dans les sept jours qui ont suivi leur naissance.

[36] Excluding Channel Islands and Isle of Man, shown separately, if available. - Non compris les îles Anglo-Normandes et l'île de Man, qui font l'objet de rubriques distinctes, si disponible.

Table 21

Table 21 presents deaths and death rates by cause and sex for the two latest available years between 2002 and 2006. A simpler version of this table was last published in the *Demographic Yearbook* 2004.

Description of variables: Causes of death are all those diseases, morbid conditions or injuries which either resulted in or contributed to death and the circumstances of the accident or violence which produced any such injuries.[1]

The underlying cause of death, rather than direct or intermediate antecedent cause, is the one recommended as the main cause for tabulation of mortality statistics. It is defined as (a) the disease or injury which initiated the train of events leading directly to death, or (b) the circumstances of the accident or violence which produced the fatal injury.[1]

Statistics on deaths by cause presented in this table are provided by the World Health Organisation. They are limited to countries or areas that meet the criterion that cause-of-death statistics are classified to the ninth or tenth revisions of the ICD. Data that are classified by the tenth revision are set in bold in the table.

Rate computation: Rates are the annual number of deaths in each cause group by sex reported for the year per 100 000 corresponding mid-year population. For certain causes, the population that more nearly approximates the population at risk is used as denominator, as specified below:
-   rates for malignant neoplasm of female breast and malignant neoplasm of cervix uteri are computed per 100 000 female population 15 years and over;
-   rates for hyperplasia of prostate are computed per 100 000 male population 50 years and over; and
-   rates for direct and indirect obstetric causes, and rates for conditions originating in the perinatal period are computed per 100 000 total live births in the same year.

As noted above, rates presented in this table have been limited to those countries or areas having a total of at least 1 000 deaths from all causes in a given year. In certain cases death rates by cause have not been calculated because the population data needed for the denominator are not available (no data on population at risk are available). Moreover, rates based on 30 or fewer deaths shown in this table are identified by the symbol (♦).

Reliability of data: Countries and areas that have incomplete (less than 90 per cent completeness) or of unknown completeness of cause of deaths data coverage are considered unreliable and are set in *italics* rather than in roman type. Rates on these data are not computed. Information on completeness is normally provided by the World Health Organisation, when this is not the case, information on completeness is set to coincide with that of Table 18. Similarly, the reliability of data for the completeness of cause of death is provided by the World Health Organisation[2] and it may differ from the reliability of data for the total number of reported deaths. Therefore, there are cases when the quality code in table 18 does not correspond with the typeface used in this table.

Territorial composition as set in Section 2.2 of "Technical Notes on the Statistical Tables", including or excluding certain population of a country refers only to the denominator.

Limitations: Statistics on deaths by cause are subject to the same qualifications as have been set forth for vital statistics in general and death statistics in particular as discussed in section 4 of the Technical Notes.

In considering cause-of-death statistics it is important to take account of the differences among countries or areas in the quality, availability, and efficiency of medical services, certification procedures, and coding practices. When a death is registered and reported for statistical purposes, the cause of death if available will be stated in the death registration form. This statement of cause may have several sources:

NOTES

[1] *International Statistical Classification of Diseases and Related Health Problems*, Tenth Revision, Volume 2, World Health Organization, Geneva, 1992
[2] For more information on specific method used for countries, see "Mathers CD, Bernard C, Iburg KM, Inoue M, Ma Fat D, Shibuya K et al. *Global burden of disease in 2002: data sources, methods and results.* Geneva, World Health Organization, 2003 (GPE Discussion Paper No. 54).

(1) If the death has been followed by an autopsy, presumably the "true" cause will have been discovered; (2) If an autopsy is not performed but the decedent was treated prior to death by a medical attendant, the reported cause of death will reflect the opinion of that physician based on observation of the patient while he or she was alive; and (3) If, on the other hand, the decedent has died without medical attendance, the body may be examined (without autopsy) by a physician who, aided by the questioning of persons who saw the patient before death, may come to a decision as to the probable cause of death. These three possible sources of information on cause of death constitute in general five degrees of decreasing accuracy in reporting.

Serious difficulties of comparability may stem also from differences in the form of death certificate being used, an increasing tendency to enter more than one cause of death on the certificate and diversity in the principles by which the primary or underlying cause is selected for statistical use when more than one is entered.

Differences in terminology used to identify the same disease also result in lack of comparability in statistics. These differences may arise in the same language in various parts of one country or area, but they are particularly troublesome between different languages.

Coding problems, and problems in interpretation of rules, arise constantly in using the various revisions of the International Statistical Classification of Diseases and Related Health Problems. Lack of uniformity between countries or areas in these interpretations and in adapting rules to national needs results in a lack of comparability that can be observed in the statistics. It is particularly evident in causes that are coded differently according to the age of the decedent, such as pneumonia, diarrhoeal diseases and others. Changing interpretations and new rules can also introduce disparities into the time series for one country or area. Hence, large increases or decreases in deaths reported from specified diseases should be examined carefully for possible explanations in terms of coding practice, before they are accepted as changes in mortality.

Further limitations of statistics by cause of death result from the periodic revision of the International Classification of Diseases. Data might not be comparable among countries or areas if different revisions of the Classification were used. Similarly, comparison over time for one country or area is not appropriate if different revisions were applied in the country. For a detailed indication of the revision that countries have used when cause of deaths data are available, see table 21-2 in the technical notes.

In addition to the qualifications explained in footnotes, particular care must be taken in using distributions with relatively large numbers of deaths attributed to ill-defined causes. Large frequencies in this category may indicate that cause of death among whole segments of the population has been undiagnosed, and the distribution of known causes in such cases is likely to be quite unrepresentative of the situation as a whole.

The possibility of error being introduced by the exclusion of deaths of infants who were born alive but died before the registration of the birth or within the first 24 hours of life should not be overlooked. These infant deaths are incorrectly classified as late foetal deaths. In several countries or areas, tabulation procedures have been devised to separate these pseudo-late-foetal deaths from true late foetal deaths and to incorporate them into the total deaths, but even in these cases there is no way of knowing the cause of death. Such distributions are footnoted.

For a further detailed discussion of the development of statistics of causes of death and the problems involved, see chapter II of the Demographic Yearbook 1951.

In addition, it should be noted that rates are affected also by the quality and limitations of the population at risk that are used in their computation. The problems of under-enumeration or over-enumeration and, to some extent, the differences in definition of population and live births have been discussed in section 3 of the Technical Notes dealing with population data in general and section 4 with vital statistics, respectively, Specific Information pertaining to individual countries or areas is given in the footnotes to table 3 on total population and to table 9 on live births.

Earlier data: Deaths and death rates by cause have been shown in the 2004 and earlier issues of the Demographic Yearbook. For information on specific years covered, readers should consult the Index.

Table 21-2. Tabulation list for ICD-9 and ICD-10 data for presentation in the Demographic Yearbook

Disease	ICD-10	ICD-9 Basic Tabulation List
All causes	**A00-Y89**	**01-56**
Certain infectious and parasitic diseases	**A00-B99**	**01-07, 184**
Intestinal infectious diseases	A00-A09	01
Tuberculosis	A15-A19	02
Tetanus[1]	A33, A35	037
Diphtheria	A36	033
Whooping cough	A37	034
Meningococcal infection	A39	036
Septicaemia	A40-A41	038
Acute poliomyelitis	A80	040
Measles	B05	042
Viral hepatitis	B15-B19	046
Human immunodeficiency virus [HIV] disease	B20-B24	184
Malaria	B50-B54	052
Neoplasms	**C00-D48**	**08-17**
Malignant neoplasms	**C00-C97**	**08-14**
Malignant neoplasm of lip, oral cavity and pharynx	C00-C14	08
Malignant neoplasm of oesophagus	C15	090
Malignant neoplasm of stomach	C16	091
Malignant neoplasm of colon, rectosigmoid junction, rectum, anus and anal canal	C18-C21	093-094
Malignant neoplasm of liver and intrahepatic bile ducts	C22	095
Malignant neoplasm of pancreas	C25	096
Malignant neoplasm of trachea, bronchus and lung	C33-C34	101
Malignant neoplasm of **female** breast	C50	113
Malignant neoplasm of cervix uteri	C53	120
Malignant neoplasm of prostate	C61	124
Malignant neoplasm of lymphoid, haematopoietic and related tissue	C81-C96	14
Disorders of the blood and blood-forming organs and certain disorders involving the immune mechanism	**D50-D89**	**20**
Anaemias	D50-D64	200
Endocrine, nutritional and metabolic diseases	**E00-E88**	**18-19, minus 184**
Diabetes mellitus	E10-E14	181
Malnutrition	E40-E46	190-192
Mental and behavioural disorders	**F01-F99**	**21**
Diseases of the nervous system	**G00-G98**	**22**
Diseases of the circulatory system	**I00-I99**	**25-30**
Acute rheumatic fever and chronic rheumatic heart diseases	I01-I09	25
Hypertensive diseases	I10-I13	26
Ischaemic heart diseases	I20-I25	27
Cerebrovascular diseases	I60-I69	29
Diseases of arteries, arterioles and capillaries	I70-I79	300-302
Diseases of the respiratory system	**J00-J98**	**31-32**
Influenza	J10-J11	322

Table 21-2. Tabulation list for ICD-9 and ICD-10 data for presentation in the Demographic Yearbook

Disease	ICD-10	ICD-9 Basic Tabulation List
Pneumonia	J12-J18	321
Chronic lower respiratory diseases	J40-J47	323-325
Diseases of the digestive system	**K00-K92**	**33-34**
Gastric and duodenal ulcer	K25-K27	341
Diseases of the liver	K70-K76	347
Diseases of the musculoskeletal system and connective tissue	**M00-M99**	**43**
Diseases of the genitourinary system	**N00-N98**	**35-37**
Disorders of kidney and ureter	N00-N28	350-351
Hyperplasia of prostate	N40	360
Pregnancy, childbirth and the puerperium	**O00-O99**	**38-41**
Pregnancy with abortive outcome	O00-O07	38
Other direct obstetric causes[1]	O10-092, O95, A34	39
Indirect obstetric causes	O98-O99	40
Certain conditions originating in the perinatal period	**P00-P96**	**45**
Congenital malformations, deformations and chromosomal abnormalities	**Q00-Q99**	**44**
Symptoms, signs and abnormal clinical and laboratory findings, not elsewhere classified	**R00-R99**	**46**
All other diseases	**H00-H95, L00-L98**	**23-24, 42**
External causes	**V01-Y89**	**E47-E56**
Accidents	**V01-X59**	**E47-E53**
Transport accidents	V01-V99	E47
Falls	W00-W19	E50
Accidental drowning and submersion	W65-W74	E521
Exposure to smoke, fire and flames	X00-X09	E51
Accidental poisoning by and exposure to noxious substances	X40-X49	E48
Intentional self-harm	**X60-X84**	**E54**
Assault	**X85-Y09**	**E55**
All other external causes	Y10-Y89	E56

---

[1] In ICD-10 obstetrical tetanus is classified to A34 but in this table it is included with the "Other direct obstetric causes".

Table 21-2. Tabulation list for ICD-9 and ICD-10 data for presentation in the Demographic Yearbook

Disease	ICD-10	ICD-9 Basic Tabulation List
All causes	**A00-Y89**	**01-56**
Certain infectious and parasitic diseases	**A00-B99**	**01-07, 184**
Intestinal infectious diseases	A00-A09	01
Tuberculosis	A15-A19	02
Tetanus[1]	A33, A35	037
Diphtheria	A36	033
Whooping cough	A37	034
Meningococcal infection	A39	036
Septicaemia	A40-A41	038
Acute poliomyelitis	A80	040
Measles	B05	042
Viral hepatitis	B15-B19	046
Human immunodeficiency virus [HIV] disease	B20-B24	184
Malaria	B50-B54	052
Neoplasms	**C00-D48**	**08-17**
Malignant neoplasms	**C00-C97**	**08-14**
Malignant neoplasm of lip, oral cavity and pharynx	C00-C14	08
Malignant neoplasm of oesophagus	C15	090
Malignant neoplasm of stomach	C16	091
Malignant neoplasm of colon, rectosigmoid junction, rectum, anus and anal canal	C18-C21	093-094
Malignant neoplasm of liver and intrahepatic bile ducts	C22	095
Malignant neoplasm of pancreas	C25	096
Malignant neoplasm of trachea, bronchus and lung	C33-C34	101
Malignant neoplasm of **female** breast	C50	113
Malignant neoplasm of cervix uteri	C53	120
Malignant neoplasm of prostate	C61	124
Malignant neoplasm of lymphoid, haematopoietic and related tissue	C81-C96	14
Disorders of the blood and blood-forming organs and certain disorders involving the immune mechanism	**D50-D89**	**20**
Anaemias	D50-D64	200
Endocrine, nutritional and metabolic diseases	**E00-E88**	**18-19, minus 184**
Diabetes mellitus	E10-E14	181
Malnutrition	E40-E46	190-192
Mental and behavioural disorders	**F01-F99**	**21**
Diseases of the nervous system	**G00-G98**	**22**
Diseases of the circulatory system	**I00-I99**	**25-30**
Acute rheumatic fever and chronic rheumatic heart diseases	I01-I09	25
Hypertensive diseases	I10-I13	26
Ischaemic heart diseases	I20-I25	27
Cerebrovascular diseases	I60-I69	29
Diseases of arteries, arterioles and capillaries	I70-I79	300-302
Diseases of the respiratory system	**J00-J98**	**31-32**
Influenza	J10-J11	322

Table 21-2. Tabulation list for ICD-9 and ICD-10 data for presentation in the Demographic Yearbook

Disease	ICD-10	ICD-9 Basic Tabulation List
Pneumonia	J12-J18	321
Chronic lower respiratory diseases	J40-J47	323-325
Diseases of the digestive system	**K00-K92**	**33-34**
Gastric and duodenal ulcer	K25-K27	341
Diseases of the liver	K70-K76	347
Diseases of the musculoskeletal system and connective tissue	**M00-M99**	**43**
Diseases of the genitourinary system	**N00-N98**	**35-37**
Disorders of kidney and ureter	N00-N28	350-351
Hyperplasia of prostate	N40	360
Pregnancy, childbirth and the puerperium	**O00-O99**	**38-41**
Pregnancy with abortive outcome	O00-O07	38
Other direct obstetric causes[1]	O10-092, O95, A34	39
Indirect obstetric causes	O98-O99	40
Certain conditions originating in the perinatal period	**P00-P96**	**45**
Congenital malformations, deformations and chromosomal abnormalities	**Q00-Q99**	**44**
Symptoms, signs and abnormal clinical and laboratory findings, not elsewhere classified	**R00-R99**	**46**
All other diseases	**H00-H95, L00-L98**	**23-24, 42**
External causes	**V01-Y89**	**E47-E56**
Accidents	**V01-X59**	**E47-E53**
Transport accidents	V01-V99	E47
Falls	W00-W19	E50
Accidental drowning and submersion	W65-W74	E521
Exposure to smoke, fire and flames	X00-X09	E51
Accidental poisoning by and exposure to noxious substances	X40-X49	E48
Intentional self-harm	**X60-X84**	**E54**
Assault	**X85-Y09**	**E55**
All other external causes	Y10-Y89	E56

---

[1] In ICD-10 obstetrical tetanus is classified to A34 but in this table it is included with the "Other direct obstetric causes".

Tableau 21

Le tableau 21 présente la statistique des décès par cause et sexe pour les deux dernières années entre 2002 et 2006. Une version plus simple a été publiée dans l'Annuaire Démographique 2004.

Description des variables : les causes des décès sont toutes les maladies, états morbides ou traumatismes qui ont abouti ou contribué au décès et les circonstances de l'accident ou de la violence qui ont entraîné ces traumatismes[1].

La cause initiale de décès, plutôt que la cause directe du décès, est recommandée pour les statistiques de la mortalité. La cause initiale de décès est définie comme : a) la maladie ou le traumatisme qui a déclenché l'évolution morbide conduisant directement au décès ; b) les circonstances de l'accident ou de la violence qui ont entraîné le traumatisme mortel[1].

Les statistiques sur les décès classés en fonction de la cause qui les a provoqués émanent de l'Organisation mondiale de la santé. Elles ne portent que sur les pays ou les zones dans lesquels les statistiques relatives à la cause des décès sont conformes à la liste de la neuvième ou de la dixième révision de la CIM. Les données conformes à la liste de la dixième révision sont indiquées en caractères gras dans le tableau.

Calcul des taux : les taux représentent le nombre annuel de décès signalés dans chaque groupe, pour l'année, dans une population de 100 000 habitants en milieu d'année.

Les taux relatifs à certaines catégories de causes correspondent aux populations les plus semblables à la population exposée comme spécifié di-dessous :
- les taux correspondant aux catégories « tumeur maligne du sein chez la femme » et « tumeur maligne du col de l'utérus » sont calculés sur une population de 100 000 femmes de 15 ans ou plus.
- les taux correspondant à la catégorie « tumeur maligne de la prostate » sont calculés sur une population de 100 000 personnes de sexe masculin âgées de 50 ans ou plus, et
- les taux pour les catégorie « décès maternels directs », « décès maternels indirects » et « affections dont l'origine se situe dans la période périnatale » sont calculés sur 100 000 naissances vivantes dans la même année.

Comme indiqué plus haut, les taux figurant dans ce tableau ne concernent que les pays ou zones où l'on a relevé au moins 1 000 décès, toutes causes confondues, dans l'année. Dans certains cas, on n'a pas calculé les taux de mortalité selon la cause car l'on ne disposait pas des informations sur la population qui étaient nécessaires pour déterminer le dénominateur (pas d'informations sur la population exposée au risque). De plus, les taux calculés sur la base de 30 décès ou moins, qui sont indiqués dans le tableau, sont signalés par le signe '♦'.

Fiabilité des données : les statistiques relatives aux pays et aux zones pour lesquels la couverture des données concernant les causes de décès est incomplète (mois de 90 pour cent) ou dont le degré de complétude n'est pas connue sont jugés douteuses et apparaissent en *italique* et non en caractères romains. Les taux correspondant ne sont pas calculés. L'information sur la complétude est normalement fournie par l'Organisation Mondiale de la Santé. Si ce n'est pas le cas, l'information sur la complétude est reprise de tableau 18. De même, la fiabilité des données relatives aux causes de décès est fournie par l'Organisation Mondiale de la Santé et peut différer de la fiabilité des données relatives au nombre de décès enregistrés. En conséquence, il peut apparaitre de différences entre les codes de fiabilité du tableau 18 et du présent tableau.

La composition territoriale est définie dans la Section 2.2 des "Notes Techniques sur les tableaux statistiques". L'inclusion ou l'exclusion de certaines populations d'un pays ne concerne que le dénominateur.

Insuffisance des données : les statistiques des décès selon la cause appellent les mêmes réserves que celles qui ont été formulées à propos des statistiques de l'état civil en général et des statistiques relatives aux décès en particulier (voir la section 4 des Notes techniques).

NOTES

[1] *Classification statistique internationale des maladies et des problèmes de santé connexes*, dixième révision, volume 2. Genève, Organisation mondiale de la santé, 1992.

Lorsque l'on étudie les statistiques des causes des décès, il importe de prendre en considération les disparités existant entre pays ou zones du point de vue de la qualité, de la disponibilité et de l'efficacité des services médicaux, ainsi que des méthodes d'établissement des certificats de décès et des procédés de codage. Lorsqu'un décès est enregistré et déclaré aux fins de statistiques, le bulletin établi doit mentionner la cause du décès si elle est connue. Or la déclaration de la cause peut émaner de plusieurs sources : 1) si le décès a été suivi d'une autopsie, il est probable qu'on en aura décelé la cause « véritable » ; 2) s'il n'y a pas eu d'autopsie mais que le défunt a reçu, avant sa mort, les soins d'un médecin, la déclaration de la cause du décès reflétera l'opinion de ce médecin fondée sur l'observation du malade alors qu'il vivait encore ; 3) si, au contraire, le défunt est mort sans avoir reçu de soins médicaux, il se peut qu'un médecin examine le corps (sans qu'il soit fait d'autopsie), auquel cas il pourra, en questionnant les personnes qui ont vu le défunt avant sa mort, se former une opinion sur la cause probable du décès. À ces trois sources de renseignements possibles correspondent généralement trois degrés décroissants d'exactitude des données.

La comparabilité est aussi parfois très difficile à assurer par suite des différences existant dans la forme des certificats de décès utilisés, de la tendance croissante à indiquer plus d'une cause de décès sur le certificat et de la diversité des principes régissant le choix de la cause principale ou initiale à retenir dans les statistiques quand le certificat indique plus d'une cause.

Les différences entre les termes utilisés pour désigner une même maladie compromettent aussi la comparabilité des statistiques. On en rencontre parfois d'une région à l'autre dans un même pays ou une même zone où toute la population parle la même langue, mais elles sont particulièrement gênantes lorsque plusieurs langues interviennent.

En outre, des problèmes de codage et d'interprétation des règles se posent constamment lorsque l'on utilise les diverses révisions de la *Classification statistique internationale des maladies et des problèmes de santé connexes*. Les pays ou zones n'interprètent pas ces règles de manière uniforme et ne les adaptent pas de la même façon à leurs besoins ; la comparabilité s'en ressent comme le montrent les statistiques. Cela est particulièrement vrai pour les causes comme la pneumonie et les maladies diarrhéiques et autres, qui sont codées différemment selon l'âge du défunt. Les changements d'interprétation et l'adoption de nouvelles règles peuvent aussi introduire des divergences dans les séries chronologiques d'un même pays ou d'une même zone. En conséquence, il convient d'examiner attentivement les cas où le nombre de décès attribués à des maladies déterminées s'accroît ou diminue fortement, pour s'assurer, avant de conclure à une évolution de la mortalité, que le changement n'est pas dû à la méthode de codage.

D'autres irrégularités statistiques résultent des révisions périodiques de la *Classification statistique internationale des maladies*. Il est possible que les données ne soient pas comparables d'un pays ou d'une zone à un autre si différentes révisions de la classification ont été utilisées. De même, il n'est pas possible de comparer les données dans le temps pour un même pays ou zone lorsque différentes révisions y ont été utilisées. Pour une description détaillée des révisions utilisées par les pays qui ont communiqué des données concernant les causes des décès, voir le tableau 21-2 dans les notes techniques.

Outre les réserves expliquées dans les notes, il faut interpréter avec circonspection les répartitions comportant un nombre relativement élevé de décès attribués à des causes mal définies. Si les chiffres donnés pour cette catégorie sont importants, c'est peut-être parce que les décès survenus parmi des pans entiers de la population n'ont fait l'objet d'aucun diagnostic ; en pareil cas, il est probable que la répartition des causes connues est loin de donner une vue exacte de la situation d'ensemble.

Il ne faut pas négliger non plus le risque d'erreur que peut présenter l'exclusion des enfants nés vivants mais décédés avant l'enregistrement de leur naissance ou dans les 24 heures qui ont suivi la naissance. Ces décès sont classés à tort dans les morts fœtales tardives. Dans plusieurs pays ou zones, les méthodes d'exploitation permettent de différencier ces pseudo-morts fœtales tardives des morts fœtales tardives véritables et de les ajouter au nombre total des décès, mais, là encore, il est impossible de connaître la cause du décès. Ces répartitions sont signalées en note.

Pour un exposé plus détaillé de l'évolution des statistiques des décès selon la cause et des problèmes qui se posent, voir le chapitre II de l'*Annuaire démographique 1951*.

De plus, il convient de noter que les taux sont également fonction de la qualité de l'évaluation de la population à risque et des caractéristiques de celle-ci dont il est tenu compte dans leur calcul. Les problèmes du sous-enregistrement et du surenregistrement et, à un certain degré, les différences entre les définitions de la population et des naissances vivantes ont été examinés, respectivement, à la section 3 des Notes techniques, qui traite des données démographiques en général, et à la section 4, qui traite des statistiques de l'état civil. Des informations sur certains pays ou certaines zones sont données dans les notes du tableau 3, relatif à la population totale, et dans celles du tableau 9, relatif aux naissances vivantes.

Données antérieures : les annuaires démographiques de 2004 et des années précédentes indiquent le nombre des décès et les taux de mortalité par cause. Pour obtenir ces informations pour une année donnée, les lecteurs doivent se reporter à l'index.

Tableau 21-2. Liste de tabulation pour les données CIM-9 et CIM-10 pour la présentation dans l'annuaire démographique

Maladie	CIM-10	CIM-9 (Liste de base pour la mise en tableaux)
Toutes causes	**A00-Y89**	**01-56**
Certaines maladies infectieuses et parasitaires	**A00-B99**	**01-07, 184**
Maladies infectieuses intestinales	A00-A09	01
Tuberculose	A15-A19	02
Tétanos[1]	A33, A35	037
Diphtérie	A36	033
Coqueluche	A37	034
Infection à méningocoques	A39	036
Septicémie	A40-A41	038
Poliomyélite aiguë	A80	040
Rougeole	B05	042
Hépatite virale	B15-B19	046
Maladies dues au virus de l'immunodéficience humaine (VIH)	B20-B24	184
Malaria	B50-B54	052
Tumeurs	**C00-D48**	**08-17**
Tumeurs malignes	**C00-C97**	**08-14**
Tumeur maligne de la lèvre, de la cavité buccale et du pharynx	C00-C14	08
Tumeur maligne de l'oesophage	C15	090
Tumeur maligne de l'estomac	C16	091
sigmoïdienne, du rectum, de l'anus et du canal anal	C18-C21	093-094
Tumeur maligne du foie et des voies bilaires intrahépatiques	C22	095
Tumeur maligne du pancréas	C25	096
Tumeur maligne de la trachée, des bronches et du poumon	C33-C34	101
Tumeur maligne du sein chez la femme	C50	113
Tumeur maligne du col de l'utérus	C53	120
Tumeur maligne de la prostate	C61	124
Tumeurs malignes primitives ou présumées primitives des tissus lymphoïde, hématopoïétique et apparentés	C81-C96	14
Maladies du sang et des organes hématopoïétiques et certains troubles du système immunitaire	**D50-D89**	**20**
Anémies	D50-D64	200
Maladies endocriniennes, nutritionnelles et métaboliques	**E00-E88**	**18-19, minus 184**
Diabète sucré	E10-E14	181
Malnutrition	E40-E46	190-192
Troubles mentaux et du comportement	**F01-F99**	**21**
Maladies du système nerveux	**G00-G98**	**22**
Maladies de l'appareil circulatoire	**I00-I99**	**25-30**
Rhumatisme articularie aigu et cardiopathies rhumatismales chroniques	I01-I09	25
Maladies hypertensives	I10-I13	26
Cardiopathies ischémiques	I20-I25	27
Maladies cérébrovasculaires	I60-I69	29
Maladies des artères, artérioles et capillaires	I70-I79	300-302

Tableau 21-2. Liste de tabulation pour les données CIM-9 et CIM-10 pour la présentation dans l'annuaire démographique

Maladie	CIM-10	CIM-9 (Liste de base pour la mise en tableaux)
Maladies de l'appareil respiratoire	**J00-J98**	**31-32**
Grippe	J10-J11	322
Pneumopathies	J12-J18	321
Maladies chroniques des voies respiratoires inférieures	J40-J47	323-325
Maladies de l'appareil digestif	**K00-K92**	**33-34**
Ulcère de l'estomac et du duodénum	K25-K27	341
Maladies du foie	K70-K76	347
Maladies du système ostéo-articularie, des muscles et du tissu conjonctif	**M00-M99**	**43**
Maladies de l'appareil génito-urinaire	**N00-N98**	**35-37**
Affections du rein et de l'uretère	N00-N28	350-351
Hyperplasie de la prostate	N40	360
Grossesse, accouchement et puerpéralité	**O00-O99**	**38-41**
Grossesse se terminant par un avortement	O00-O07	38
Autres décès maternels directs[1]	O10-092, O95, A34	39
Décès maternels indirects	O98-O99	40
Certaines affections dont l'origine se situe dans la période périnatale	**P00-P96**	**45**
Malformations congénitales et anomalies chromosomiques	**Q00-Q99**	**44**
Symptômes, signes et résultats anormaux d'examens cliniques et de laboratoire, non classés ailleurs	**R00-R99**	**46**
Toutes autres maladies	**H00-H95, L00-L98**	**23-24, 42**
Causes externes	**V01-Y89**	**E47-E56**
Accidents	**V01-X59**	**E47-E53**
Accidents de transport	V01-V99	E47
Chutes	W00-W19	E50
Noyade et submersion accidentelles	W65-W74	E521
Exposition à la fumée, au feu et aux flammes	X00-X09	E51
Intoxication accidentelle par des substances nocives et exposition à ces substances	X40-X49	E48
Lésions auto-infligées	**X60-X84**	**E54**
Agresssions	**X85-Y09**	**E55**
Toutes autres causes externes	Y10-Y89	E56

[1] Dans la Classification internationale des maladies (CIM-10), le tétanos obstétrique est classé à la rubrique A34 mais, dans ce tableau, il est inclus dans les « Autres causes obstétriques directes ».

Tableau 21-2. Liste de tabulation pour les données CIM-9 et CIM-10 pour la présentation dans l'annuaire démographique

Maladie	CIM-10	CIM-9 (Liste de base pour la mise en tableaux)
Toutes causes	**A00-Y89**	**01-56**
Certaines maladies infectieuses et parasitaires	**A00-B99**	**01-07, 184**
Maladies infectieuses intestinales	A00-A09	01
Tuberculose	A15-A19	02
Tétanos[1]	A33, A35	037
Diphtérie	A36	033
Coqueluche	A37	034
Infection à méningocoques	A39	036
Septicémie	A40-A41	038
Poliomyélite aiguë	A80	040
Rougeole	B05	042
Hépatite virale	B15-B19	046
Maladies dues au virus de l'immunodéficience humaine (VIH)	B20-B24	184
Malaria	B50-B54	052
Tumeurs	**C00-D48**	**08-17**
Tumeurs malignes	**C00-C97**	**08-14**
Tumeur maligne de la lèvre, de la cavité buccale et du pharynx	C00-C14	08
Tumeur maligne de l'oesophage	C15	090
Tumeur maligne de l'estomac	C16	091
sigmoïdienne, du rectum, de l'anus et du canal anal	C18-C21	093-094
Tumeur maligne du foie et des voies bilaires intrahépatiques	C22	095
Tumeur maligne du pancréas	C25	096
Tumeur maligne de la trachée, des bronches et du poumon	C33-C34	101
Tumeur maligne du sein chez la femme	C50	113
Tumeur maligne du col de l'utérus	C53	120
Tumeur maligne de la prostate	C61	124
Tumeurs malignes primitives ou présumées primitives des tissus lymphoïde, hématopoïétique et apparentés	C81-C96	14
Maladies du sang et des organes hématopoïétiques et certains troubles du système immunitaire	**D50-D89**	**20**
Anémies	D50-D64	200
Maladies endocriniennes, nutritionnelles et métaboliques	**E00-E88**	**18-19, minus 184**
Diabète sucré	E10-E14	181
Malnutrition	E40-E46	190-192
Troubles mentaux et du comportement	**F01-F99**	**21**
Maladies du système nerveux	**G00-G98**	**22**
Maladies de l'appareil circulatoire	**I00-I99**	**25-30**
Rhumatisme articularie aigu et cardiopathies rhumatismales chroniques	I01-I09	25
Maladies hypertensives	I10-I13	26
Cardiopathies ischémiques	I20-I25	27
Maladies cérébrovasculaires	I60-I69	29
Maladies des artères, artérioles et capillaires	I70-I79	300-302
Maladies de l'appareil respiratoire	**J00-J98**	**31-32**

Tableau 21-2. Liste de tabulation pour les données CIM-9 et CIM-10 pour la présentation dans l'annuaire démographique

Maladie	CIM-10	CIM-9 (Liste de base pour la mise en tableaux)
Grippe	J10-J11	322
Pneumopathies	J12-J18	321
Maladies chroniques des voies respiratoires inférieures	J40-J47	323-325
Maladies de l'appareil digestif	**K00-K92**	**33-34**
Ulcère de l'estomac et du duodénum	K25-K27	341
Maladies du foie	K70-K76	347
Maladies du système ostéo-articularie, des muscles et du tissu conjonctif	**M00-M99**	**43**
Maladies de l'appareil génito-urinaire	**N00-N98**	**35-37**
Affections du rein et de l'uretère	N00-N28	350-351
Hyperplasie de la prostate	N40	360
Grossesse, accouchement et puerpéralité	**O00-O99**	**38-41**
Grossesse se terminant par un avortement	O00-O07	38
Autres décès maternels directs[1]	O10-092, O95, A34	39
Décès maternels indirects	O98-O99	40
Certaines affections dont l'origine se situe dans la période périnatale	**P00-P96**	**45**
Malformations congénitales et anomalies chromosomiques	**Q00-Q99**	**44**
Symptômes, signes et résultats anormaux d'examens cliniques et de laboratoire, non classés ailleurs	**R00-R99**	**46**
Toutes autres maladies	**H00-H95, L00-L98**	**23-24, 42**
Causes externes	**V01-Y89**	**E47-E56**
Accidents	**V01-X59**	**E47-E53**
Accidents de transport	V01-V99	E47
Chutes	W00-W19	E50
Noyade et submersion accidentelles	W65-W74	E521
Exposition à la fumée, au feu et aux flammes	X00-X09	E51
Intoxication accidentelle par des substances nocives et exposition à ces substances	X40-X49	E48
Lésions auto-infligées	**X60-X84**	**E54**
Agresssions	**X85-Y09**	**E55**
Toutes autres causes externes	**Y10-Y89**	**E56**

---

[1] Dans la Classification internationale des maladies (CIM-10), le tétanos obstétrique est classé à la rubrique A34 mais, dans ce tableau, il est inclus dans les « Autres causes obstétriques directes ».

21. Death and death rates by cause and sex: 2002 - 2006
Décès et taux de mortalité par cause et sexe : 2002 - 2006

Mauritius - Maurice

Cause of death — Cause de décès	2004 (+C)				2005 (+C)			
	Male — Masculin		Female — Féminin		Male — Masculin		Female — Féminin	
	Number Nombre	Rate Taux	Number Nombre	Rate Taux	Number Nombre	Rate Taux	Number Nombre	Rate Taux
TOTAL..	4 607	755.1	3 652	585.9	4 733	769.9	3 689	587.0
Certain infectious and parasitic diseases — Certaines maladies infectieuses et parasitaires								
Total.......	71	11.6	52	8.3	83	13.5	62	9.9
Intestinal infectious diseases — Maladies infectieuses intestinales............	11	♦1.8	6	♦1.0	5	♦0.8	5	♦0.8
Tuberculosis — Tuberculose............................	13	♦2.1	2	♦0.3	11	♦1.8	2	♦0.3
Tetanus — Tétanos.......................................	-	-	-	-	-	-	1	♦0.2
Diphtheria — Diphtérie...................................	-	-	-	-	-	-	-	-
Whooping cough — Coqueluche........................	-	-	-	-	-	-	-	-
Meningococcal infection — Infection à méningocoques.............	1	♦0.2	-	-	-	-	-	-
Septicaemia — Septicémie...............................	43	7.0	41	6.6	45	7.3	45	7.2
Acute poliomyelitis — Poliomyélite aiguë.............	-	-	-	-	-	-	-	-
Measles — Rougeole.....................................	-	-	-	-	-	-	-	-
Viral hepatitis — Hépatite virale........................	-	-	1	♦0.2	3	♦0.5	1	♦0.2
Human immunodeficiency virus [HIV] disease — Maladies dues au virus de l'immunodéficience humaine (VIH)...........................	-	-	-	-	16	♦2.6	3	♦0.5
Malaria — Paludisme.....................................	-	-	1	♦0.2	-	-	1	♦0.2
Neoplasms — Tumeurs..............................	467	76.5	460	75.2	437	71.1	452	71.9
Malignant neoplasms — Tumeurs malignes								
Total........	454	74.4	461	74.0	416	67.7	436	69.4
Malignant neoplasm of lip, oral cavity and pharynx — Tumeur maligne de la lèvre, de la cavité buccale et du pharynx..............	30	♦4.9	13	♦2.1	36	5.9	11	♦1.8
Malignant neoplasm of oesophagus — Tumeur maligne de l'oesophage......	13	♦2.1	9	♦1.4	8	♦1.3	8	♦1.3
Malignant neoplasm of stomach — Tumeur maligne de l'estomac........	34	5.6	41	6.6	44	7.2	28	♦4.5
Malignant neoplasm of colon, rectosigmoid junction, rectum, anus and anal canal — Tumeur maligne du côlon, de la jonction recto-sigmoïdienne, du rectum, de l'anus et du canal anal................	51	8.4	31	5.0	37	6.0	41	6.5
Malignant neoplasm of liver and intrahepatic bile ducts — Tumeur maligne du foie et des voies bilaires intrahépatiques.............	1	♦0.2	1	♦0.2	25	♦4.1	24	♦3.8
Malignant neoplasm of pancreas — Tumeur maligne du pancréas.........	17	♦2.8	22	♦3.5	20	♦3.3	22	♦3.5
Malignant neoplasm of trachea, bronchus and lung — Tumeur maligne de la trachée, des bronches et du poumon.....................	88	14.4	34	5.5	72	11.7	37	5.9
Malignant neoplasm of female breast — Tumeur maligne du sein chez la femme........................	..	..	99	15.9	..	..	88	18.4
Malignant neoplasm of cervix uteri — Tumeur maligne du col de l'utérus......	..	..	26	..	..	..	27	♦5.6
Malignant neoplasm of prostate — Tumeur maligne de la prostate.............	48	...	..	..	42	36.6	..	..
Malignant neoplasm of lymphoid, haematopoietic and related tissue — Tumeurs malignes primitives ou présumées primitives des tissus lymphoïde, hématopoïétique et apparentés...............	31	5.1	15	♦2.4	28	♦4.6	29	♦4.6
Disorders of the blood and blood-forming organs and certain disorders involving the immune mechanism — Maladies du sang et des organes hématopoïétiques et certains troubles du système immunitaire								
Total......	12	♦2.0	11	♦1.8	8	♦1.3	10	♦1.6
Anaemias — Anémies.....................................	10	♦1.6	9	♦1.4	7	♦1.1	7	♦1.1
Endocrine, nutritional and metabolic diseases — Maladies endocriniennes, nutritionnelles et métaboliques								
Total.....	296	48.5	260	41.7	926	150.6	876	139.4
Diabetes mellitus — Diabète sucré............................	272	44.6	239	38.3	916	149.0	862	137.2
Malnutrition — Malnutrition.................................	6	♦1.0	3	♦0.5	1	♦0.2	4	♦0.6
Mental and behavioural disorders — Troubles mentaux et du comportement	58	9.5	12	♦1.9	50	8.1	4	♦0.6
Diseases of the nervous system — Maladies du système nerveux..........	63	10.3	44	7.1	77	12.5	36	5.7
Diseases of the circulatory system — Maladies de l'appareil circulatoire								
Total.........	2 173	356.2	2 014	323.1	1 700	276.5	1 444	229.8
Acute rheumatic fever and chronic rheumatic heart diseases — Rhumatisme articularie aigu et cardiopathies rhumatismales chroniques.............	2	♦0.3	1	♦0.2	2	♦0.3	3	♦0.5
Hypertensive diseases — Maladies hypertensives........	133	21.8	151	24.2	136	22.1	163	25.9
Ischaemic heart disease — Cardiopathie ischémique............	975	159.8	872	139.9	702	114.2	522	83.1
Cerebrovascular disease — Maladie cérébrovasculaire......................	654	107.2	590	94.7	498	81.0	415	66.0

Mauritius - Maurice

Cause of death — Cause de décès	2004 (+C)				2005 (+C)			
	Male — Masculin		Female — Féminin		Male — Masculin		Female — Féminin	
	Number Nombre	Rate Taux	Number Nombre	Rate Taux	Number Nombre	Rate Taux	Number Nombre	Rate Taux
Diseases of arteries, arterioles and capillaries — Maladies des artères, artérioles et capillaires	21	♦3.4	9	♦1.4	4	♦0.7	6	♦1.0
Diseases of the respiratory system — Maladies de l'appareil respiratoire								
Total........	394	64.6	253	40.6	457	74.3	288	45.8
Influenza — Grippe	-	-	-	-	-	-	-	-
Pneumonia — Pneumopathies	111	18.2	77	12.4	112	18.2	79	12.6
Chronic lower respiratory diseases — Maladies chroniques des voies respiratoires inférieures	128	21.0	96	15.4	153	24.9	99	15.8
Diseases of the digestive system — Maladies de l'appareil digestif								
Total........	340	55.7	109	17.5	295	48.0	93	14.8
Gastric and duodenal ulcer — Ulcère de l'estomac et du duodénum	6	♦1.0	9	♦1.4	11	♦1.8	6	♦1.0
Diseases of the liver — Maladies du foie	174	28.5	30	♦4.8	207	33.7	42	6.7
Diseases of the musculoskeletal system and connective tissue — Maladies du système ostéo-articularie, des muscles et du tissu conjonctif	1	♦0.2	12	♦1.9	5	♦0.8	13	♦2.1
Diseases of the genitourinary system — Maladies de l'appareil génito-urinaire								
Total........	109	17.9	70	11.2	107	17.4	91	14.5
Disorders of kidney and ureter — Affections du rein et de l'uretère	101	16.6	70	11.2	103	16.8	88	14.0
Hyperplasia of prostate — Hyperplasie de la prostate........................	1	...	..	..	-	-	..	..
Pregnancy, childbirth and the puerperium — Grossesse, accouchement et puerpéralité								
Total........	..	..	3	♦15.6	...	..	4	♦21.3
Pregnancy with abortive outcome — Grossesse se terminant par un avortement	..	...	1	♦5.2	..	...	-	-
Other direct obstetric causes — Autres décès maternels directs	..	...	2	♦10.4	..	..	4	♦21.3
Indirect obstetric causes — Décès maternels indirects........................	..	..	-	-	...	..	-	-
Certain conditions originating in the perinatal period — Certaines affections dont l'origine se situe dans la période périnatale	87	888.8	58	614.3	81	847.8	47	507.2
Congenital malformations, deformations and chromosomal abnormalities — Malformations congénitales et anomalies chromosomiques	29	♦296.3	34	360.1	37	387.3	43	464.1
Symptoms, signs and abnormal clinical and laboratory findings, not elsewhere classified — Symptômes, signes et résultats anormaux d'examens cliniques et de laboratoire, non classés ailleurs	104	17.0	124	19.9	88	14.3	97	15.4
All other diseases — Toutes autres maladies........................	1	♦0.2	4	♦0.6	4	♦0.7	6	♦1.0
External causes — Causes externes								
Total........	402	65.9	123	19.7	378	61.5	123	19.6
Accidents								
Total........	293	48.0	89	14.3	226	36.8	63	10.0
Transport accidents — Accidents de transport	141	23.1	33	5.3	106	17.2	26	♦4.1
Falls — Chutes	35	5.7	4	♦0.6	17	♦2.8	2	♦0.3
Accidental drowning and submersion — Noyade et submersion accidentelles...........	34	5.6	5	♦0.8	30	♦4.9	5	♦0.8
Exposure to smoke, fire and flames — Exposition à la fumée, au feu et aux flammes...........	22	♦3.6	20	♦3.2	12	♦2.0	12	♦1.9
Accidental poisoning by and exposure to noxious substances — Intoxication accidentelle par des substances nocives et exposition à ces substances	1	♦0.2	-	-	1	♦0.2	1	♦0.2
Intentional self-harm — Lésions auto-infligées........................	75	12.3	22	♦3.5	79	12.8	23	♦3.7
Assault — Agresssions	28	♦4.6	7	♦1.1	29	♦4.7	16	♦2.5
All other external causes — Toutes autres causes externes.................	6	♦1.0	5	♦0.8	44	7.2	21	♦3.3

21. Death and death rates by cause and sex: 2002 - 2006
Décès et taux de mortalité par cause et sexe : 2002 - 2006 (continued - suite)

Cause of death — Cause de décès	Réunion				Seychelles			
	2004 (...)		2005 (...)		2004 (+C)		2005 (+C)	
	Male — Masculin	Female — Féminin	Male — Masculin	Female — Féminin	Male — Masculin	Female — Féminin	Male — Masculin	Female — Féminin
	Number Nombre	Number Nombre	Number Nombre	Number Nombre	Number Nombre	Number Nombre	Number Nombre	Number Nombre
TOTAL.................	*2 159*	*1 721*	*2 486*	*1 879*	*329*	*282*	*386*	*287*
Certain infectious and parasitic diseases — Certaines maladies infectieuses et parasitaires								
Total........	*39*	*34*	*58*	*44*	*25*	*24*	*29*	*21*
Intestinal infectious diseases — Maladies infectieuses intestinales.............	*4*	*5*	*7*	*6*	*1*	-	*1*	-
Tuberculosis — Tuberculose..............	*2*	*3*	*1*	-	-	-	*2*	-
Tetanus — Tétanos.........	-	-	-	-	-	-	-	-
Diphtheria — Diphtérie.................	-	-	-	-	-	-	-	-
Whooping cough — Coqueluche	-	-	-	-	-	-	-	-
Meningococcal infection — Infection à méningocoques	-	-	-	-	-	-	-	-
Septicaemia — Septicémie...............	*12*	*19*	*21*	*22*	*15*	*23*	*20*	*21*
Acute poliomyelitis — Poliomyélite aiguë	-	-	-	-	-	-	-	-
Measles — Rougeole...............	-	-	-	-	-	-	-	-
Viral hepatitis — Hépatite virale	*6*	-	*4*	*5*	*1*	-	*1*	-
Human immunodeficiency virus [HIV] disease — Maladies dues au virus de l'Immunodéficience humaine (VIH)...............	*3*	-	*5*	*2*	*2*	*1*	-	-
Malaria — Paludisme..........	-	-	*1*	*1*	-	-	-	-
Neoplasms — Tumeurs	*553*	*335*	*607*	*376*	*64*	*44*	*66*	*41*
Malignant neoplasms — Tumeurs malignes								
Total.........	*531*	*320*	*574*	*352*	*63*	*44*	*66*	*41*
Malignant neoplasm of lip, oral cavity and pharynx — Tumeur maligne de la lèvre, de la cavité buccale et du pharynx	*46*	*6*	*47*	*5*	*8*	*1*	*7*	*2*
Malignant neoplasm of oesophagus — Tumeur maligne de l'oesophage	*40*	*5*	*48*	*3*	*3*	-	*1*	-
Malignant neoplasm of stomach — Tumeur maligne de l'estomac.............	*43*	*22*	*47*	*31*	*4*	*2*	*3*	*1*
Malignant neoplasm of colon, rectosigmoid junction, rectum, anus and anal canal — Tumeur maligne du côlon, de la jonction recto-sigmoïdienne, du rectum, de l'anus et du canal anal	*30*	*40*	*40*	*42*	*7*	*5*	*8*	*4*
Malignant neoplasm of liver and intrahepatic bile ducts — Tumeur maligne du foie et des voies bilaires intrahépatiques	*14*	*11*	*25*	*15*	-	-	*3*	*2*
Malignant neoplasm of pancreas — Tumeur maligne du pancréas.............	*23*	*11*	*15*	*16*	*4*	*4*	*2*	-
Malignant neoplasm of trachea, bronchus and lung — Tumeur maligne de la trachée, des bronches et du poumon	*96*	*24*	*121*	*19*	*13*	*4*	*8*	*3*
Malignant neoplasm of female breast — Tumeur maligne du sein chez la femme.........	..	*44*	..	*55*	..	*9*	..	*8*
Malignant neoplasm of cervix uteri — Tumeur maligne du col de l'utérus	..	*18*	..	*8*	..	*3*	..	*6*
Malignant neoplasm of prostate — Tumeur maligne de la prostate	*62*	..	*63*	..	*14*	..	*14*	..
Malignant neoplasm of lymphoid, haematopoietic and related tissue — Tumeurs malignes primitives ou présumées primitives des tissus lymphoïde, hématopoïétique et apparentés	*43*	*27*	*36*	*35*	-	-	-	-
Disorders of the blood and blood-forming organs and certain disorders involving the immune mechanism — Maladies du sang et des organes hématopoïétiques et certains troubles du système immunitaire								
Total.........	*12*	*5*	*16*	*8*	*4*	*3*	*4*	-
Anaemias — Anémies	*4*	*3*	*10*	*5*	*4*	*3*	*4*	-
Endocrine, nutritional and metabolic diseases — Maladies endocriniennes, nutritionnelles et métaboliques								
Total.........	*125*	*170*	*140*	*160*	*7*	*9*	*6*	*10*
Diabetes mellitus — Diabète sucré.............	*96*	*141*	*105*	*132*	*4*	*8*	*5*	*9*
Malnutrition — Malnutrition.........	*4*	*7*	*7*	*5*	*2*	-	-	-
Mental and behavioural disorders — Troubles mentaux et du comportement	*86*	*32*	*127*	*45*	*3*	*1*	*2*	*1*
Diseases of the nervous system — Maladies du système nerveux.........	*76*	*76*	*85*	*72*	*3*	*4*	*6*	*12*
Diseases of the circulatory system — Maladies de l'appareil circulatoire								
Total.........	*584*	*635*	*688*	*626*	*97*	*124*	*132*	*119*
Acute rheumatic fever and chronic rheumatic heart diseases — Rhumatisme articularie aigu et cardiopathies rhumatismales chroniques	*3*	*11*	*7*	*17*	-	-	-	-
Hypertensive diseases — Maladies hypertensives.........................	*26*	*79*	*41*	*66*	*38*	*63*	*36*	*69*
Ischaemic heart disease — Cardiopathie ischémique	*172*	*171*	*184*	*134*	*22*	*15*	*39*	*18*

Cause of death — Cause de décès	Réunion				Seychelles			
	2004 (...)		2005 (...)		2004 (+C)		2005 (+C)	
	Male — Masculin	Female — Féminin	Male — Masculin	Female — Féminin	Male — Masculin	Female — Féminin	Male — Masculin	Female — Féminin
	Number Nombre	Number Nombre	Number Nombre	Number Nombre	Number Nombre	Number Nombre	Number Nombre	Number Nombre
Cerebrovascular disease — Maladie cérébrovasculaire.....................	185	187	213	196	14	8	19	8
Diseases of arteries, arterioles and capillaries — Maladies des artères, artérioles et capillaires	44	24	47	27	...	...	...	...
Diseases of the respiratory system — Maladies de l'appareil respiratoire								
Total...	142	105	173	132	39	22	55	36
Influenza — Grippe	3	4	2	5	-	-	-	-
Pneumonia — Pneumopathies	36	29	34	46	26	14	35	23
Chronic lower respiratory diseases — Maladies chroniques des voies respiratoires inférieures	58	35	73	48	6	5	14	11
Diseases of the digestive system — Maladies de l'appareil digestif								
Total...	131	57	151	102	24	12	18	15
Gastric and duodenal ulcer — Ulcère de l'estomac et du duodénum	3	1	10	9	3	-	4	1
Diseases of the liver — Maladies du foie	83	33	80	44	11	2	5	2
Diseases of the musculoskeletal system and connective tissue — Maladies du système ostéo-articulaire, des muscles et du tissu conjonctif	12	11	6	14	1	2	-	-
Diseases of the genitourinary system — Maladies de l'appareil génito-urinaire								
Total...	43	41	37	38	16	10	13	12
Disorders of kidney and ureter — Affections du rein et de l'uretère	34	34	30	32	...	...	...	...
Hyperplasia of prostate — Hyperplasie de la prostate.................	2	..	-	..	...		...	..
Pregnancy, childbirth and the puerperium — Grossesse, accouchement et puerpéralité								
Total...	..	4	..	4	..	-	..	1
Pregnancy with abortive outcome — Grossesse se terminant par un avortement	..	1	..	..	...	-	...	..
Other direct obstetric causes — Autres décès maternels directs	..	3	..	4	...	-	...	1
Indirect obstetric causes — Décès maternels indirects...................	...	-	..	-	...	-	...	-
Certain conditions originating in the perinatal period — Certaines affections dont l'origine se situe dans la période périnatale	32	31	42	32	2	5	4	5
Congenital malformations, deformations and chromosomal abnormalities — Malformations congénitales et anomalies chromosomiques	12	10	16	14	-	3	5	2
Symptoms, signs and abnormal clinical and laboratory findings, not elsewhere classified — Symptômes, signes et résultats anormaux d'examens cliniques et de laboratoire, non classés ailleurs	90	85	85	102	11	14	15	8
All other diseases — Toutes autres maladies...............................	7	7	2	9	-	-	-	1
External causes — Causes externes								
Total...	215	83	253	101	33	5	31	3
Accidents								
Total..	137	55	166	67	...	...	...	...
Transport accidents — Accidents de transport	62	11	65	17	5	1	9	-
Falls — Chutes	22	10	28	14	2	-	3	-
Accidental drowning and submersion — Noyade et submersion accidentelles	7	-	18	2	9	2	8	1
Exposure to smoke, fire and flames — Exposition à la fumée, au feu et aux flammes	8	4	4	5	2	-	-	-
Accidental poisoning by and exposure to noxious substances — Intoxication accidentelle par des substances nocives et exposition à ces substances	5	4	3	1	...	...	...	...
Intentional self-harm — Lésions auto-infligées...........................	64	16	65	24	6	-	4	1
Assault — Agresssions	11	9	12	5	5	1	2	1
All other external causes — Toutes autres causes externes...................	3	3	10	5	...		...	...

21. Death and death rates by cause and sex: 2002 - 2006
Décès et taux de mortalité par cause et sexe : 2002 - 2006 (continued - suite)

Cause of death — Cause de décès	South Africa - Afrique du Sud				Anguilla			
	2004 (U)		2005 (U)		2005 (+...)		2006 (+...)	
	Male — Masculin	Female — Féminin	Male — Masculin	Female — Féminin	Male — Masculin	Female — Féminin	Male — Masculin	Female — Féminin
	Number Nombre	Number Nombre	Number Nombre	Number Nombre	Number Nombre	Number Nombre	Number Nombre	Number Nombre
TOTAL............	287 112	278 841	297 517	292 017	34	22	33	22
Certain infectious and parasitic diseases — Certaines maladies infectieuses et parasitaires								
Total........	65 730	66 505	69 592	71 061	-	-	-	-
Intestinal infectious diseases — Maladies infectieuses intestinales............	11 301	15 236	12 003	16 480	-	-	-	-
Tuberculosis — Tuberculose............	37 654	31 886	39 954	33 798	-	-	-	-
Tetanus — Tétanos............	17	10	19	8	-	-	-	-
Diphtheria — Diphtérie............	2	-	1	1	-	-	-	-
Whooping cough — Coqueluche............	6	7	4	11	-	-	-	-
Meningococcal infection — Infection à méningocoques............	58	50	68	53	-	-	-	-
Septicaemia — Septicémie............	1 724	1 916	1 984	2 193	-	-	-	-
Acute poliomyelitis — Poliomyélite aiguë............	4	3	5	4	-	-	-	-
Measles — Rougeole............	10	18	16	13	-	-	-	-
Viral hepatitis — Hépatite virale............	160	108	186	129	-	-	-	-
Human immunodeficiency virus [HIV] disease — Maladies dues au virus de l'immunodéficience humaine (VIH)............	6 307	6 976	6 853	7 640	-	-	-	-
Malaria — Paludisme............	402	350	366	277	-	-	-	-
Neoplasms — Tumeurs............	17 473	16 320	17 209	16 850	15	5	7	4
Malignant neoplasms — Tumeurs malignes								
Total........	16 951	15 766	16 694	16 291	15	5	7	4
Malignant neoplasm of lip, oral cavity and pharynx — Tumeur maligne de la lèvre, de la cavité buccale et du pharynx	793	307	796	318	1	-	2	-
Malignant neoplasm of oesophagus — Tumeur maligne de l'oesophage......	2 045	1 197	2 029	1 260	-	-	1	-
Malignant neoplasm of stomach — Tumeur maligne de l'estomac............	792	490	741	529	3	-	-	-
Malignant neoplasm of colon, rectosigmoid junction, rectum, anus and anal canal — Tumeur maligne du côlon, de la jonction recto-sigmoïdienne, du rectum, de l'anus et du canal anal	977	881	971	840	2	1	-	-
Malignant neoplasm of liver and intrahepatic bile ducts — Tumeur maligne du foie et des voies bilaires intrahépatiques............	1 128	607	1 044	624	1	-	1	-
Malignant neoplasm of pancreas — Tumeur maligne du pancréas............	556	525	583	531	-	-	1	-
Malignant neoplasm of trachea, bronchus and lung — Tumeur maligne de la trachée, des bronches et du poumon............	3 212	1 411	3 165	1 446	-	-	-	-
Malignant neoplasm of female breast — Tumeur maligne du sein chez la femme............	..	2 474	..	2 524	..	1	..	2
Malignant neoplasm of cervix uteri — Tumeur maligne du col de l'utérus......	..	2 535	..	2 673	..	-	..	-
Malignant neoplasm of prostate — Tumeur maligne de la prostate............	1 939	..	2 005	..	4	..	-	..
Malignant neoplasm of lymphoid, haematopoietic and related tissue — Tumeurs malignes primitives ou présumées primitives des tissus lymphoïde, hématopoïétique et apparentés............	1 202	964	1 138	1 111	1	-	-	-
Disorders of the blood and blood-forming organs and certain disorders involving the immune mechanism — Maladies du sang et des organes hématopoïétiques et certains troubles du système immunitaire								
Total........	8 293	11 136	8 384	11 359	-	-	-	-
Anaemias — Anémies............	1 064	1 993	1 154	2 027	-	-	-	-
Endocrine, nutritional and metabolic diseases — Maladies endocriniennes, nutritionnelles et métaboliques								
Total........	10 349	14 242	11 010	15 548	3	7	2	5
Diabetes mellitus — Diabète sucré............	6 641	10 251	7 044	11 372	3	5	1	5
Malnutrition — Malnutrition............	1 288	1 216	1 296	1 162	-	1	1	-
Mental and behavioural disorders — Troubles mentaux et du comportement	829	835	846	902	1	-	-	-
Diseases of the nervous system — Maladies du système nerveux............	7 686	6 998	8 011	7 738	1	-	2	2
Diseases of the circulatory system — Maladies de l'appareil circulatoire								
Total........	36 033	42 943	35 427	43 091	6	7	7	6
Acute rheumatic fever and chronic rheumatic heart diseases — Rhumatisme articularie aigu et cardiopathies rhumatismales chroniques............	186	368	186	357	-	-	-	-
Hypertensive diseases — Maladies hypertensives............	4 557	7 447	4 288	7 563	-	1	-	1
Ischaemic heart disease — Cardiopathie ischémique............	7 338	5 358	7 401	5 503	3	1	2	-

	South Africa - Afrique du Sud				Anguilla			
	2004 (U)		2005 (U)		2005 (+...)		2006 (+...)	
Cause of death — Cause de décès	Male — Masculin	Female — Féminin	Male — Masculin	Female — Féminin	Male — Masculin	Female — Féminin	Male — Masculin	Female — Féminin
	Number Nombre	Number Nombre	Number Nombre	Number Nombre	Number Nombre	Number Nombre	Number Nombre	Number Nombre
Cerebrovascular disease — Maladie cérébrovasculaire.....	10 671	14 324	10 273	14 135	1	4	1	1
Diseases of arteries, arterioles and capillaries — Maladies des artères, artérioles et capillaires	890	687	863	623	1	-	1	-
Diseases of the respiratory system — Maladies de l'appareil respiratoire								
Total.....	37 939	38 266	39 170	39 138	1	-	3	-
Influenza — Grippe.....	217	303	281	336	-	-	-	-
Pneumonia — Pneumopathies.....	20 793	23 982	21 117	23 765	-	-	-	-
Chronic lower respiratory diseases — Maladies chroniques des voies respiratoires inférieures	9 102	6 212	9 244	6 477	-	-	2	-
Diseases of the digestive system — Maladies de l'appareil digestif								
Total.....	8 379	7 946	8 168	7 948	3	-	2	-
Gastric and duodenal ulcer — Ulcère de l'estomac et du duodénum	874	857	805	770	-	-	-	-
Diseases of the liver — Maladies du foie	3 098	1 913	3 047	2 019	1	-	-	-
Diseases of the musculoskeletal system and connective tissue — Maladies du système ostéo-articularie, des muscles et du tissu conjonctif	808	1 344	910	1 408	-	-	1	-
Diseases of the genitourinary system — Maladies de l'appareil génito-urinaire								
Total.....	4 028	3 647	4 162	3 834	-	2	-	-
Disorders of kidney and ureter — Affections du rein et de l'uretère	3 600	3 084	3 726	3 271	-	1	-	-
Hyperplasia of prostate — Hyperplasie de la prostate.....	130	..	115	..	-	-	-	-
Pregnancy, childbirth and the puerperium — Grossesse, accouchement et puerpéralité								
Total.....	..	1 158	..	1 249	..	-	..	-
Pregnancy with abortive outcome — Grossesse se terminant par un avortement	..	189	..	167	..	-	..	-
Other direct obstetric causes — Autres décès maternels directs	..	782	..	828	..	-	..	-
Indirect obstetric causes — Décès maternels indirects.....	..	187	..	253	..	-	..	-
Certain conditions originating in the perinatal period — Certaines affections dont l'origine se situe dans la période périnatale	17 438	15 315	19 880	18 093	-	-	-	-
Congenital malformations, deformations and chromosomal abnormalities — Malformations congénitales et anomalies chromosomiques	960	916	1 028	945	-	-	-	2
Symptoms, signs and abnormal clinical and laboratory findings, not elsewhere classified — Symptômes, signes et résultats anormaux d'examens cliniques et de laboratoire, non classés ailleurs	31 309	37 216	33 038	39 094	-	1	1	2
All other diseases — Toutes autres maladies.....	671	899	629	850	1	-	-	1
External causes — Causes externes								
Total.....	39 187	13 155	40 053	12 909	3	-	8	-
Accidents								
Total.....	7 148	3 550	8 317	3 762	3	-	4	-
Transport accidents — Accidents de transport	3 770	1 400	3 986	1 445	1	-	3	-
Falls — Chutes	77	41	81	22	1	-	-	-
Accidental drowning and submersion — Noyade et submersion accidentelles.....	55	19	108	39	-	-	-	-
Exposure to smoke, fire and flames — Exposition à la fumée, au feu et aux flammes	71	46	170	104	-	-	-	-
Accidental poisoning by and exposure to noxious substances — Intoxication accidentelle par des substances nocives et exposition à ces substances	632	488	639	490	-	-	-	-
Intentional self-harm — Lésions auto-infligées.....	298	89	360	101	-	-	-	-
Assault — Agresssions	3 577	639	4 266	672	-	-	4	-
All other external causes — Toutes autres causes externes.....	28 164	8 877	27 110	8 374	-	-	-	-

Cause of death — Cause de décès	Antigua and Barbuda - Antigua-et-Barbuda 2003 (+U) Male — Masculin Number Nombre	2003 (+U) Female — Féminin Number Nombre	2004 (+U) Male — Masculin Number Nombre	2004 (+U) Female — Féminin Number Nombre	Bermuda - Bermudes 2002 (...) Male — Masculin Number Nombre	2002 (...) Female — Féminin Number Nombre	British Virgin Islands - Îles Vierges britanniques 2002 (...) Male — Masculin Number Nombre	2002 (...) Female — Féminin Number Nombre
TOTAL	242	209	267	244	208	210	50	45
Certain infectious and parasitic diseases — Certaines maladies infectieuses et parasitaires								
Total	5	7	6	10	9	4	-	1
Intestinal infectious diseases — Maladies infectieuses intestinales	-	-	-	-	-	-	-	-
Tuberculosis — Tuberculose	-	-	-	-	-	-	-	-
Tetanus — Tétanos	-	-	-	-	-	-	-	-
Diphtheria — Diphtérie	-	-	-	-	-	-	-	-
Whooping cough — Coqueluche	-	-	-	-	-	-	-	-
Meningococcal infection — Infection à méningocoques	-	-	-	-	-	-	-	-
Septicaemia — Septicémie	2	5	1	6	-	-	-	-
Acute poliomyelitis — Poliomyélite aiguë	-	-	-	-	-	-	-	-
Measles — Rougeole	-	-	-	-	-	-	-	-
Viral hepatitis — Hépatite virale	-	-	1	-	-	-	-	-
Human immunodeficiency virus [HIV] disease — Maladies dues au virus de l'immunodéficience humaine (VIH)	3	2	3	2	9	4	-	1
Malaria — Paludisme	-	-	-	-	-	-	-	-
Neoplasms — Tumeurs	51	30	57	46	57	65	8	8
Malignant neoplasms — Tumeurs malignes								
Total	50	29	56	40	55	63	8	8
Malignant neoplasm of lip, oral cavity and pharynx — Tumeur maligne de la lèvre, de la cavité buccale et du pharynx	2	-	1	-	1	1	-	-
Malignant neoplasm of oesophagus — Tumeur maligne de l'oesophage	2	-	-	1	4	1	-	1
Malignant neoplasm of stomach — Tumeur maligne de l'estomac	5	2	1	1	2	4	-	1
Malignant neoplasm of colon, rectosigmoid junction, rectum, anus and anal canal — Tumeur maligne du côlon, de la jonction recto-sigmoïdienne, du rectum, de l'anus et du canal anal	5	3	2	6	6	5	1	2
Malignant neoplasm of liver and intrahepatic bile ducts — Tumeur maligne du foie et des voies bilaires intrahépatiques	2	4	-	1	3	-	-	-
Malignant neoplasm of pancreas — Tumeur maligne du pancréas	1	-	3	-	2	4	1	-
Malignant neoplasm of trachea, bronchus and lung — Tumeur maligne de la trachée, des bronches et du poumon	4	1	1	1	13	6	1	1
Malignant neoplasm of female breast — Tumeur maligne du sein chez la femme	..	6	-	11	..	16	-	1
Malignant neoplasm of cervix uteri — Tumeur maligne du col de l'utérus	..	4	-	3	..	-	-	-
Malignant neoplasm of prostate — Tumeur maligne de la prostate	18	..	28	..	12	..	3	..
Malignant neoplasm of lymphoid, haematopoietic and related tissue — Tumeurs malignes primitives ou présumées primitives des tissus lymphoïde, hématopoïétique et apparentés	4	2	8	-	3	6	-	2
Disorders of the blood and blood-forming organs and certain disorders involving the immune mechanism — Maladies du sang et des organes hématopoïétiques et certains troubles du système immunitaire								
Total	5	4	6	4	3	-	-	-
Anaemias — Anémies	4	3	4	3	-	-	-	-
Endocrine, nutritional and metabolic diseases — Maladies endocriniennes, nutritionnelles et métaboliques								
Total	28	40	33	42	13	22	1	3
Diabetes mellitus — Diabète sucré	23	32	29	37	12	21	-	2
Malnutrition — Malnutrition	2	4	2	2	-	-	-	-
Mental and behavioural disorders — Troubles mentaux et du comportement	1	-	2	1	-	-	-	-
Diseases of the nervous system — Maladies du système nerveux	3	3	8	-	8	13	-	1
Diseases of the circulatory system — Maladies de l'appareil circulatoire								
Total	93	91	83	92	66	67	17	22
Acute rheumatic fever and chronic rheumatic heart diseases — Rhumatisme articulaire aigu et cardiopathies rhumatismales chroniques	-	1	-	-	-	-	-	-
Hypertensive diseases — Maladies hypertensives	16	19	15	19	2	7	11	8
Ischaemic heart disease — Cardiopathie ischémique	27	23	27	21	27	21	5	3

Cause of death — Cause de décès	Antigua and Barbuda - Antigua-et-Barbuda 2003 (+U) Male — Masculin Number Nombre	Antigua and Barbuda 2003 (+U) Female — Féminin Number Nombre	Antigua and Barbuda 2004 (+U) Male — Masculin Number Nombre	Antigua and Barbuda 2004 (+U) Female — Féminin Number Nombre	Bermuda - Bermudes 2002 (...) Male — Masculin Number Nombre	Bermuda - Bermudes 2002 (...) Female — Féminin Number Nombre	British Virgin Islands - Îles Vierges britanniques 2002 (...) Male — Masculin Number Nombre	British Virgin Islands 2002 (...) Female — Féminin Number Nombre
Cerebrovascular disease — Maladie cérébrovasculaire	19	17	20	31	19	22	-	1
Diseases of arteries, arterioles and capillaries — Maladies des artères, artérioles et capillaires	1	3	-	1	8	5	-	3
Diseases of the respiratory system — Maladies de l'appareil respiratoire								
Total	17	12	9	5	16	10	1	3
Influenza — Grippe	-	1	-	-	-	-	-	-
Pneumonia — Pneumopathies	12	8	2	2	3	5	-	-
Chronic lower respiratory diseases — Maladies chroniques des voies respiratoires inférieures	1	1	3	1	11	2	-	2
Diseases of the digestive system — Maladies de l'appareil digestif								
Total	7	5	11	7	11	9	2	1
Gastric and duodenal ulcer — Ulcère de l'estomac et du duodénum	1	-	-	-	3	1	1	-
Diseases of the liver — Maladies du foie	3	2	5	5	2	2	1	-
Diseases of the musculoskeletal system and connective tissue — Maladies du système ostéo-articulaire, des muscles et du tissu conjonctif	-	1	-	-	2	3	-	1
Diseases of the genitourinary system — Maladies de l'appareil génito-urinaire								
Total	5	3	6	3	7	5	1	-
Disorders of kidney and ureter — Affections du rein et de l'uretère	3	3	5	3	7	5	-	-
Hyperplasia of prostate — Hyperplasie de la prostate	-	..	-	..	-	..	1	..
Pregnancy, childbirth and the puerperium — Grossesse, accouchement et puerpéralité								
Total	..	-	..	-	..	-	..	-
Pregnancy with abortive outcome — Grossesse se terminant par un avortement	..	-	..	-	..	-	..	-
Other direct obstetric causes — Autres décès maternels directs	..	-	..	-	..	-	..	-
Indirect obstetric causes — Décès maternels indirects	..	-	..	-	..	-	..	-
Certain conditions originating in the perinatal period — Certaines affections dont l'origine se situe dans la période périnatale	1	-	21	9	-	-	7	-
Congenital malformations, deformations and chromosomal abnormalities — Malformations congénitales et anomalies chromosomiques	5	2	-	4	-	-	1	-
Symptoms, signs and abnormal clinical and laboratory findings, not elsewhere classified — Symptômes, signes et résultats anormaux d'examens cliniques et de laboratoire, non classés ailleurs	4	3	3	16	3	6	2	2
All other diseases — Toutes autres maladies	-	2	1	-	1	2	1	-
External causes — Causes externes								
Total	17	6	21	4	12	4	9	3
Accidents								
Total	14	6	13	2	10	3	7	2
Transport accidents — Accidents de transport	7	2	3	-	4	1	1	-
Falls — Chutes	-	-	-	-	3	1	-	-
Accidental drowning and submersion — Noyade et submersion accidentelles	1	1	3	-	2	-	6	1
Exposure to smoke, fire and flames — Exposition à la fumée, au feu et aux flammes	1	-	1	1	-	-	-	-
Accidental poisoning by and exposure to noxious substances — Intoxication accidentelle par des substances nocives et exposition à ces substances	1	-	-	-	1	1	-	-
Intentional self-harm — Lésions auto-infligées	1	-	2	-	2	1	-	-
Assault — Agresssions	2	-	4	2	-	-	1	-
All other external causes — Toutes autres causes externes	-	-	2	-	-	-	1	1

Cause of death — Cause de décès	British Virgin Islands - Îles Vierges britanniques		Canada			
	2003 (...)		2003 (C)			
	Male — Masculin	Female — Féminin	Male — Masculin		Female — Féminin	
	Number Nombre	Number Nombre	Number Nombre	Rate Taux	Number Nombre	Rate Taux
TOTAL.........	65	39	114 905	732.4	111 264	696.0
Certain infectious and parasitic diseases — Certaines maladies infectieuses et parasitaires						
Total...	1	1	1 928	12.3	1 649	10.3
Intestinal infectious diseases — Maladies infectieuses intestinales...	-	-	239	1.5	345	2.2
Tuberculosis — Tuberculose...	-	-	51	0.3	42	0.3
Tetanus — Tétanos...	-	-	-	-	-	-
Diphtheria — Diphtérie...	-	-	-	-	-	-
Whooping cough — Coqueluche...	-	-	-	-	1	◆0.0
Meningococcal infection — Infection à méningocoques...	-	-	6	◆0.0	15	◆0.1
Septicaemia — Septicémie...	1	1	738	4.7	814	5.1
Acute poliomyelitis — Poliomyélite aiguë...	-	-	-	-	-	-
Measles — Rougeole...	-	-	-	-	-	-
Viral hepatitis — Hépatite virale...	-	-	259	1.7	135	0.8
Human immunodeficiency virus [HIV] disease — Maladies dues au virus de l'immunodéficience humaine (VIH)...	-	-	373	2.4	67	0.4
Malaria — Paludisme...	-	-	-	-	-	-
Neoplasms — Tumeurs	18	8	35 440	225.9	31 983	200.1
Malignant neoplasms — Tumeurs malignes						
Total...	18	6	34 701	221.2	31 289	195.7
Malignant neoplasm of lip, oral cavity and pharynx — Tumeur maligne de la lèvre, de la cavité buccale et du pharynx...	-	-	691	4.4	327	2.0
Malignant neoplasm of oesophagus — Tumeur maligne de l'oesophage...	-	-	1 052	6.7	361	2.3
Malignant neoplasm of stomach — Tumeur maligne de l'estomac...	-	1	1 188	7.6	756	4.7
Malignant neoplasm of colon, rectosigmoid junction, rectum, anus and anal canal — Tumeur maligne du côlon, de la jonction recto sigmoïdienne, du rectum, de l'anus et du canal anal...	4	-	3 711	23.7	3 227	20.2
Malignant neoplasm of liver and intrahepatic bile ducts — Tumeur maligne du foie et des voies bilaires intrahépatiques...	-	-	945	6.0	556	3.5
Malignant neoplasm of pancreas — Tumeur maligne du pancréas...	-	-	1 687	10.8	1 754	11.0
Malignant neoplasm of trachea, bronchus and lung — Tumeur maligne de la trachée, des bronches et du poumon...	-	-	10 203	65.0	7 171	44.9
Malignant neoplasm of female breast — Tumeur maligne du sein chez la femme...	..	2	..	..	5 060	38.5
Malignant neoplasm of cervix uteri — Tumeur maligne du col de l'utérus...	..	1	..	..	377	2.9
Malignant neoplasm of prostate — Tumeur maligne de la prostate...	9	..	3 658	82.6	...	...
Malignant neoplasm of lymphoid, haematopoietic and related tissue — Tumeurs malignes primitives ou présumées primitives des tissus lymphoïde, hématopoïétique et apparentés...	1	1	3 417	21.8	2 826	17.7
Disorders of the blood and blood-forming organs and certain disorders involving the immune mechanism — Maladies du sang et des organes hématopoïétiques et certains troubles du système immunitaire						
Total...	1	1	394	2.5	540	3.4
Anaemias — Anémies...	1	1	210	1.3	322	2.0
Endocrine, nutritional and metabolic diseases — Maladies endocriniennes, nutritionnelles et métaboliques						
Total...	1	2	4 983	31.8	5 216	32.6
Diabetes mellitus — Diabète sucré...	1	2	3 991	25.4	3 979	24.9
Malnutrition — Malnutrition...	-	-	70	0.4	124	0.8
Mental and behavioural disorders — Troubles mentaux et du comportement...	2	2	2 441	15.6	4 181	26.2
Diseases of the nervous system — Maladies du système nerveux...	3	1	4 142	26.4	6 122	38.3
Diseases of the circulatory system — Maladies de l'appareil circulatoire						
Total...	23	15	37 188	237.0	37 067	231.9
Acute rheumatic fever and chronic rheumatic heart diseases — Rhumatisme articularie aigu et cardiopathies rhumatismales chroniques...	-	-	173	1.1	329	2.1
Hypertensive diseases — Maladies hypertensives...	10	11	726	4.6	1 249	7.8
Ischaemic heart disease — Cardiopathie ischémique...	7	1	22 452	143.1	18 156	113.6
Cerebrovascular disease — Maladie cérébrovasculaire...	2	1	6 332	40.4	8 951	56.0
Diseases of arteries, arterioles and capillaries — Maladies des artères, artérioles et capillaires...	-	-	2 274	14.5	2 037	12.7
Diseases of the respiratory system — Maladies de l'appareil respiratoire						

Cause of death — Cause de décès	British Virgin Islands - Îles Vierges britanniques 2003 (...)		Canada 2003 (C)			
	Male — Masculin	Female — Féminin	Male — Masculin		Female — Féminin	
	Number Nombre	Number Nombre	Number Nombre	Rate Taux	Number Nombre	Rate Taux
Total	-	2	9 481	60.4	8 991	56.2
Influenza — Grippe	-	-	84	0.5	134	0.8
Pneumonia — Pneumopathies	-	2	2 092	13.3	2 647	16.6
Chronic lower respiratory diseases — Maladies chroniques des voies respiratoires inférieures	-	-	5 468	34.9	4 694	29.4
Diseases of the digestive system — Maladies de l'appareil digestif						
Total	2	2	4 288	27.3	4 411	27.6
Gastric and duodenal ulcer — Ulcère de l'estomac et du duodénum	-	-	187	1.2	216	1.4
Diseases of the liver — Maladies du foie	1	-	1 813	11.6	1 063	6.6
Diseases of the musculoskeletal system and connective tissue — Maladies du système ostéo-articularie, des muscles et du tissu conjonctif	-		444	2.8	1 124	7.0
Diseases of the genitourinary system — Maladies de l'appareil génito-urinaire						
Total	-	-	2 211	14.1	2 471	15.5
Disorders of kidney and ureter — Affections du rein et de l'uretère	-	-	1 817	11.6	1 913	12.0
Hyperplasia of prostate — Hyperplasie de la prostate	-	..	58	1.3	..	..
Pregnancy, childbirth and the puerperium — Grossesse, accouchement et puerpéralité						
Total	..	-	..	..	23	♦6.9
Pregnancy with abortive outcome — Grossesse se terminant par un avortement	..	-	..	..	2	♦0.6
Other direct obstetric causes — Autres décès maternels directs	..	-	..	..	16	♦4.8
Indirect obstetric causes — Décès maternels indirects	..	-	..	..	4	♦1.2
Certain conditions originating in the perinatal period — Certaines affections dont l'origine se situe dans la période périnatale	1	1	552	321.5	439	268.5
Congenital malformations, deformations and chromosomal abnormalities — Malformations congénitales et anomalies chromosomiques	-	1	461	268.5	451	275.8
Symptoms, signs and abnormal clinical and laboratory findings, not elsewhere classified — Symptômes, signes et résultats anormaux d'examens cliniques et de laboratoire, non classés ailleurs	-	3	1 605	10.2	1 474	9.2
All other diseases — Toutes autres maladies	-	-	129	0.8	209	1.3
External causes — Causes externes						
Total	13	2	9 204	58.7	4 897	30.6
Accidents						
Total	9	1	5 369	34.2	3 546	22.2
Transport accidents — Accidents de transport	-	-	2 193	14.0	892	5.6
Falls — Chutes	1	-	1 024	6.5	954	6.0
Accidental drowning and submersion — Noyade et submersion accidentelles	6	1	214	1.4	52	0.3
Exposure to smoke, fire and flames — Exposition à la fumée, au feu et aux flammes	-	-	120	0.8	76	0.5
Accidental poisoning by and exposure to noxious substances — Intoxication accidentelle par des substances nocives et exposition à ces substances	-	-	615	3.9	271	1.7
Intentional self-harm — Lésions auto-infligées	1	-	2 902	18.5	862	5.4
Assault — Agresssions	1	1	323	2.1	121	0.8
All other external causes — Toutes autres causes externes	2	-	610	3.9	368	2.3

Cause of death — Cause de décès	Canada 2004 (C)				Cayman Islands - Îles Caïmanes 2004 (...)		Costa Rica 2004 (+U)	
	Male — Masculin		Female — Féminin		Male — Masculin	Female — Féminin	Male — Masculin	Female — Féminin
	Number Nombre	Rate Taux	Number Nombre	Rate Taux	Number Nombre	Number Nombre	Number Nombre	Number Nombre
TOTAL	114 513	722.6	112 071	694.0	86	76	9 048	6 901
Certain infectious and parasitic diseases — Certaines maladies infectieuses et parasitaires								
Total	2 032	12.8	1 961	12.1	-	1	238	145
Intestinal infectious diseases — Maladies infectieuses intestinales	428	2.7	600	3.7	-	-	50	56
Tuberculosis — Tuberculose	42	0.3	28	+0.2	-	-	46	16
Tetanus — Tétanos	-	-	-	-	-	-	-	-
Diphtheria — Diphtérie	-	-	-	-	-	-	-	-
Whooping cough — Coqueluche	-	-	-	-	-	-	-	1
Meningococcal infection — Infection à méningocoques	6	+0.0	8	+0.0	-	-	2	-
Septicaemia — Septicémie	737	4.7	871	5.4	-	1	14	15
Acute poliomyelitis — Poliomyélite aiguë	-	-	-	-	-	-	-	-
Measles — Rougeole	-	-	-	-	-	-	-	-
Viral hepatitis — Hépatite virale	267	1.7	142	0.9	-	-	2	10
Human immunodeficiency virus [HIV] disease — Maladies dues au virus de l'immunodéficience humaine (VIH)	345	2.2	75	0.5	-	-	93	26
Malaria — Paludisme	-	-	-	-	-	-	1	-
Neoplasms — Tumeurs	35 864	226.3	32 458	201.0	23	16	2 024	1 599
Malignant neoplasms — Tumeurs malignes								
Total	35 156	221.8	31 791	196.9	23	16	1 940	1 518
Malignant neoplasm of lip, oral cavity and pharynx — Tumeur maligne de la lèvre, de la cavité buccale et du pharynx	699	4.4	368	2.3	2	-	44	12
Malignant neoplasm of oesophagus — Tumeur maligne de l'oesophage	1 112	7.0	376	2.3	1	-	31	12
Malignant neoplasm of stomach — Tumeur maligne de l'estomac	1 163	7.3	756	4.7	-	-	399	230
Malignant neoplasm of colon, rectosigmoid junction, rectum, anus and anal canal — Tumeur maligne du côlon, de la jonction recto-sigmoïdienne, du rectum, de l'anus et du canal anal	3 882	24.5	3 437	21.3	-	3	155	147
Malignant neoplasm of liver and intrahepatic bile ducts — Tumeur maligne du foie et des voies bilaires intrahépatiques	974	6.1	536	3.3	2	1	123	69
Malignant neoplasm of pancreas — Tumeur maligne du pancréas	1 751	11.0	1 826	11.3	1	1	84	86
Malignant neoplasm of trachea, bronchus and lung — Tumeur maligne de la trachée, des bronches et du poumon	10 136	64.0	7 517	46.5	7	2	158	88
Malignant neoplasm of female breast — Tumeur maligne du sein chez la femme	..	..	4 964	37.2	..	4	..	217
Malignant neoplasm of cervix uteri — Tumeur maligne du col de l'utérus	..	..	388	2.9	..	-	..	125
Malignant neoplasm of prostate — Tumeur maligne de la prostate	3 685	80.6	..	..	3	..	301	..
Malignant neoplasm of lymphoid, haematopoietic and related tissue — Tumeurs malignes primitives ou présumées primitives des tissus lymphoïde, hématopoïétique et apparentés	3 449	21.8	2 838	17.6	-	-	223	154
Disorders of the blood and blood-forming organs and certain disorders involving the immune mechanism — Maladies du sang et des organes hématopoïétiques et certains troubles du système immunitaire								
Total	319	2.0	481	3.0	1	-	27	36
Anaemias — Anémies	145	0.9	272	1.7	1	-	17	22
Endocrine, nutritional and metabolic diseases — Maladies endocriniennes, nutritionnelles et métaboliques								
Total	5 093	32.1	5 079	31.5	3	7	383	509
Diabetes mellitus — Diabète sucré	4 020	25.4	3 803	23.6	3	7	353	478
Malnutrition — Malnutrition	83	0.5	130	0.8	-	-	8	10
Mental and behavioural disorders — Troubles mentaux et du comportement	2 576	16.3	4 264	26.4	1	-	79	50
Diseases of the nervous system — Maladies du système nerveux	4 041	25.5	6 217	38.5	-	-	219	201
Diseases of the circulatory system — Maladies de l'appareil circulatoire								
Total	36 048	227.5	36 695	227.2	21	26	2 467	2 177
Acute rheumatic fever and chronic rheumatic heart diseases — Rhumatisme articularie aigu et cardiopathies rhumatismales chroniques	145	0.9	284	1.8	1	-	18	31
Hypertensive diseases — Maladies hypertensives	792	5.0	1 329	8.2	2	6	285	299
Ischaemic heart disease — Cardiopathie ischémique	21 571	136.1	17 740	109.9	9	5	1 314	931

21. Death and death rates by cause and sex: 2002 - 2006
Décès et taux de mortalité par cause et sexe : 2002 - 2006 (continued - suite)

Cause of death — Cause de décès	Canada 2004 (C)				Cayman Islands - Îles Caïmanes 2004 (...)		Costa Rica 2004 (+U)	
	Male — Masculin		Female — Féminin		Male — Masculin	Female — Féminin	Male — Masculin	Female — Féminin
	Number Nombre	Rate Taux	Number Nombre	Rate Taux	Number Nombre	Number Nombre	Number Nombre	Number Nombre
Cerebrovascular disease — Maladie cérébrovasculaire	5 959	37.6	8 667	53.7	2	8	441	528
Diseases of arteries, arterioles and capillaries — Maladies des artères, artérioles et capillaires	2 322	14.7	2 034	12.6	-	2	93	60
Diseases of the respiratory system — Maladies de l'appareil respiratoire								
Total	9 985	63.0	9 622	59.6	11	12	835	700
Influenza — Grippe	115	0.7	181	1.1	-	-	1	1
Pneumonia — Pneumopathies	2 442	15.4	2 991	18.5	8	7	200	212
Chronic lower respiratory diseases — Maladies chroniques des voies respiratoires inférieures	5 324	33.6	4 717	29.2	2	3	450	343
Diseases of the digestive system — Maladies de l'appareil digestif								
Total	4 279	27.0	4 381	27.1	3	3	611	513
Gastric and duodenal ulcer — Ulcère de l'estomac et du duodénum	216	1.4	206	1.3	-	-	37	28
Diseases of the liver — Maladies du foie	1 799	11.4	1 032	6.4	-	1	325	190
Diseases of the musculoskeletal system and connective tissue — Maladies du système ostéo-articularie, des muscles et du tissu conjonctif	409	2.6	1 024	6.3	1	1	16	53
Diseases of the genitourinary system — Maladies de l'appareil génito-urinaire								
Total	2 365	14.9	2 514	15.6	1	3	238	144
Disorders of kidney and ureter — Affections du rein et de l'uretère	1 927	12.2	1 878	11.6	-	1	195	120
Hyperplasia of prostate — Hyperplasie de la prostate	70	1.5	..	..	-	..	8	..
Pregnancy, childbirth and the puerperium — Grossesse, accouchement et puerpéralité								
Total	..	..	20	♦5.9	..	-	..	22
Pregnancy with abortive outcome — Grossesse se terminant par un avortement	..	..	1	♦0.3	..	-	..	2
Other direct obstetric causes — Autres décès maternels directs	..	..	14	♦4.1	..	-	..	16
Indirect obstetric causes — Décès maternels indirects	..	..	5	♦1.5	..	-	..	4
Certain conditions originating in the perinatal period — Certaines affections dont l'origine se situe dans la période périnatale	543	313.3	481	293.1	1	-	187	143
Congenital malformations, deformations and chromosomal abnormalities — Malformations congénitales et anomalies chromosomiques	424	244.6	441	268.7	2	1	144	101
Symptoms, signs and abnormal clinical and laboratory findings, not elsewhere classified — Symptômes, signes et résultats anormaux d'examens cliniques et de laboratoire, non classés ailleurs	1 392	8.8	1 293	8.0	2	2	100	66
All other diseases — Toutes autres maladies	123	0.8	219	1.4	1	-	35	42
External causes — Causes externes								
Total	9 020	56.9	4 921	30.5	15	4	1 445	400
Accidents								
Total	5 336	33.7	3 524	21.8	9	3	852	286
Transport accidents — Accidents de transport	2 196	13.9	844	5.2	3	1	488	99
Falls — Chutes	1 080	6.8	1 149	7.1	1	-	71	8
Accidental drowning and submersion — Noyade et submersion accidentelles	201	1.3	50	0.3	-	-	101	16
Exposure to smoke, fire and flames — Exposition à la fumée, au feu et aux flammes	139	0.9	96	0.6	-	-	16	6
Accidental poisoning by and exposure to noxious substances — Intoxication accidentelle par des substances nocives et exposition à ces substances	681	4.3	273	1.7	1	1	1	1
Intentional self-harm — Lésions auto-infligées	2 734	17.3	879	5.4	-	-	261	33
Assault — Agresssions	366	2.3	148	0.9	4	1	215	36
All other external causes — Toutes autres causes externes	584	3.7	370	2.3	2	-	117	45

Cause of death — Cause de décès	Costa Rica		Cuba			
	2005 (+U)		2004 (C)			
	Male — Masculin	Female — Féminin	Male — Masculin		Female — Féminin	
	Number Nombre	Number Nombre	Number Nombre	Rate Taux	Number Nombre	Rate Taux
TOTAL............	8 788	6 731	43 924	780.6	37 186	663.0
Certain infectious and parasitic diseases — Certaines maladies infectieuses et parasitaires						
Total....	259	126	435	7.7	313	5.6
Intestinal infectious diseases — Maladies infectieuses intestinales....	46	45	116	2.1	119	2.1
Tuberculosis — Tuberculose....	45	12	27	+0.5	10	+0.2
Tetanus — Tétanos....	-	-	-	-	-	-
Diphtheria — Diphtérie....	-	-	-	-	-	-
Whooping cough — Coqueluche....	-	1	-	-	-	-
Meningococcal infection — Infection à méningocoques....	2	2	4	+0.1	4	+0.1
Septicaemia — Septicémie....	22	15	44	0.8	42	0.7
Acute poliomyelitis — Poliomyélite aiguë....	-	-	-	-	-	-
Measles — Rougeole....	-	-	-	-	-	-
Viral hepatitis — Hépatite virale....	7	4	59	1.0	61	1.1
Human immunodeficiency virus [HIV] disease — Maladies dues au virus de l'immunodéficience humaine (VIH)....	106	17	92	1.6	17	+0.3
Malaria — Paludisme....	-	-	-	-	-	-
Neoplasms — Tumeurs....	1 869	1 646	11 059	196.5	8 049	143.6
Malignant neoplasms — Tumeurs malignes						
Total....	1 784	1 569	10 902	193.8	7 855	140.0
Malignant neoplasm of lip, oral cavity and pharynx — Tumeur maligne de la lèvre, de la cavité buccale et du pharynx....	34	17	442	7.9	145	2.6
Malignant neoplasm of oesophagus — Tumeur maligne de l'oesophage....	35	11	393	7.0	103	1.8
Malignant neoplasm of stomach — Tumeur maligne de l'estomac....	359	200	456	8.1	304	5.4
Malignant neoplasm of colon, rectosigmoid junction, rectum, anus and anal canal — Tumeur maligne du côlon, de la jonction recto-sigmoïdienne, du rectum, de l'anus et du canal anal....	146	166	837	14.9	1 029	18.3
Malignant neoplasm of liver and intrahepatic bile ducts — Tumeur maligne du foie et des voies bilaires intrahépatiques....	83	83	333	5.9	304	5.4
Malignant neoplasm of pancreas — Tumeur maligne du pancréas....	74	86	368	6.5	286	5.1
Malignant neoplasm of trachea, bronchus and lung — Tumeur maligne de la trachée, des bronches et du poumon....	165	90	2 969	52.8	1 414	25.2
Malignant neoplasm of female breast — Tumeur maligne du sein chez la femme....	..	210	..	..	1 197	26.4
Malignant neoplasm of cervix uteri — Tumeur maligne du col de l'utérus....	..	118	..	..	431	9.5
Malignant neoplasm of prostate — Tumeur maligne de la prostate....	280	..	2 168	153.2	..	..
Malignant neoplasm of lymphoid, haematopoietic and related tissue — Tumeurs malignes primitives ou présumées primitives des tissus lymphoïde, hématopoïétique et apparentés....	195	175	804	14.3	592	10.6
Disorders of the blood and blood-forming organs and certain disorders involving the immune mechanism — Maladies du sang et des organes hématopoïétiques et certains troubles du système immunitaire						
Total....	37	33	84	1.5	99	1.8
Anaemias — Anémies....	22	18	58	1.0	71	1.3
Endocrine, nutritional and metabolic diseases — Maladies endocriniennes, nutritionnelles et métaboliques						
Total....	341	425	737	13.1	1 370	24.4
Diabetes mellitus — Diabète sucré....	310	384	631	11.2	1 248	22.2
Malnutrition — Malnutrition....	10	7	37	0.7	20	+0.4
Mental and behavioural disorders — Troubles mentaux et du comportement....	72	46	1 261	22.4	1 296	23.1
Diseases of the nervous system — Maladies du système nerveux....	242	192	681	12.1	478	8.5
Diseases of the circulatory system — Maladies de l'appareil circulatoire						
Total....	2 486	2 060	16 843	299.3	15 962	284.6
Acute rheumatic fever and chronic rheumatic heart diseases — Rhumatisme articularie aigu et cardiopathies rhumatismales chroniques....	26	30	96	1.7	137	2.4
Hypertensive diseases — Maladies hypertensives....	329	301	839	14.9	779	13.9
Ischaemic heart disease — Cardiopathie ischémique....	1 284	904	8 169	145.2	7 200	128.4
Cerebrovascular disease — Maladie cérébrovasculaire....	462	471	3 920	69.7	4 330	77.2
Diseases of arteries, arterioles and capillaries — Maladies des artères, artérioles et capillaires.....	82	50	1 672	29.7	1 611	28.7
Diseases of the respiratory system — Maladies de l'appareil respiratoire						

21. Death and death rates by cause and sex: 2002 - 2006
Décès et taux de mortalité par cause et sexe : 2002 - 2006 (continued - suite)

Cause of death — Cause de décès	Costa Rica		Cuba			
	2005 (+U)		2004 (C)			
	Male — Masculin	Female — Féminin	Male — Masculin		Female — Féminin	
	Number Nombre	Number Nombre	Number Nombre	Rate Taux	Number Nombre	Rate Taux
Total	758	680	5 123	91.0	4 416	78.7
Influenza — Grippe	2	2	-	-	-	-
Pneumonia — Pneumopathies	199	196	3 201	56.9	2 921	52.1
Chronic lower respiratory diseases — Maladies chroniques des voies respiratoires inférieures	407	344	1 748	31.1	1 365	24.3
Diseases of the digestive system — Maladies de l'appareil digestif						
Total	560	492	1 753	31.2	1 311	23.4
Gastric and duodenal ulcer — Ulcère de l'estomac et du duodénum	35	26	246	4.4	143	2.5
Diseases of the liver — Maladies du foie	295	211	800	14.2	342	6.1
Diseases of the musculoskeletal system and connective tissue — Maladies du système ostéo-articularie, des muscles et du tissu conjonctif	30	63	163	2.9	327	5.8
Diseases of the genitourinary system — Maladies de l'appareil génito-urinaire						
Total	237	174	399	7.1	319	5.7
Disorders of kidney and ureter — Affections du rein et de l'uretère	204	133	278	4.9	245	4.4
Hyperplasia of prostate — Hyperplasie de la prostate	7	..	78	5.5	..	..
Pregnancy, childbirth and the puerperium — Grossesse, accouchement et puerpéralité						
Total	..	24	..	..	56	44.0
Pregnancy with abortive outcome — Grossesse se terminant par un avortement	..	2	..	..	11	♦8.6
Other direct obstetric causes — Autres décès maternels directs	..	13	..	..	18	♦14.2
Indirect obstetric causes — Décès maternels indirects	..	9	..	..	20	♦15.7
Certain conditions originating in the perinatal period — Certaines affections dont l'origine se situe dans la période périnatale	179	147	212	322.8	142	230.8
Congenital malformations, deformations and chromosomal abnormalities — Malformations congénitales et anomalies chromosomiques	161	115	279	424.8	235	382.0
Symptoms, signs and abnormal clinical and laboratory findings, not elsewhere classified — Symptômes, signes et résultats anormaux d'examens cliniques et de laboratoire, non classés ailleurs	73	44	385	6.8	287	5.1
All other diseases — Toutes autres maladies	14	43	59	1.0	97	1.7
External causes — Causes externes						
Total	1 470	421	4 451	79.1	2 429	43.3
Accidents						
Total	882	276	2 473	44.0	1 407	25.1
Transport accidents — Accidents de transport	504	93	1 022	18.2	264	4.7
Falls — Chutes	74	8	784	13.9	982	17.5
Accidental drowning and submersion — Noyade et submersion accidentelles	122	24	244	4.3	21	♦0.4
Exposure to smoke, fire and flames — Exposition à la fumée, au feu et aux flammes	16	6	25	♦0.4	40	0.7
Accidental poisoning by and exposure to noxious substances — Intoxication accidentelle par des substances nocives et exposition à ces substances	5	1	26	♦0.5	10	♦0.2
Intentional self-harm — Lésions auto-infligées	233	41	1 144	20.3	370	6.6
Assault — Agresssions	246	55	513	9.1	146	2.6
All other external causes — Toutes autres causes externes	109	49	321	5.7	506	9.0

Cause of death — Cause de décès	Cuba				Dominica - Dominique			
	2005 (C)				2003 (+C)		2004 (+C)	
	Male — Masculin		Female — Féminin		Male — Masculin	Female — Féminin	Male — Masculin	Female — Féminin
	Number Nombre	Rate Taux	Number Nombre	Rate Taux	Number Nombre	Number Nombre	Number Nombre	Number Nombre
TOTAL............................	45 878	814.9	38 946	693.9	297	260	285	272
Certain infectious and parasitic diseases — Certaines maladies infectieuses et parasitaires								
Total..................	543	9.6	346	6.2	16	8	12	7
Intestinal infectious diseases — Maladies infectieuses intestinales............	171	3.0	161	2.9	-	-	-	-
Tuberculosis — Tuberculose................	27	◊0.5	8	◊0.1	1	1	1	-
Tetanus — Tétanos..................	-	-	-	-	-	-	-	-
Diphtheria — Diphtérie.............	-	-	-	-	-	-	-	-
Whooping cough — Coqueluche............	-	-	-	-	-	-	-	-
Meningococcal infection — Infection à méningocoques	4	◊0.1	7	◊0.1	-	-	-	-
Septicaemia — Septicémie............	46	0.8	41	0.7	4	4	3	5
Acute poliomyelitis — Poliomyélite aiguë	-	-	-	-	-	-	-	-
Measles — Rougeole..............	-	-	-	-	-	-	-	-
Viral hepatitis — Hépatite virale	61	1.1	41	0.7	-	-	-	-
Human immunodeficiency virus [HIV] disease — Maladies dues au virus de l'immunodéficience humaine (VIH)	103	1.8	17	◊0.3	10	2	7	2
Malaria — Paludisme...............	1	◊0.0	-	-	-	-	-	-
Neoplasms — Tumeurs	11 282	200.4	8 291	147.7	68	55	79	46
Malignant neoplasms — Tumeurs malignes								
Total..................	11 082	196.8	8 098	144.3	67	54	79	46
Malignant neoplasm of lip, oral cavity and pharynx — Tumeur maligne de la lèvre, de la cavité buccale et du pharynx	429	7.6	146	2.6	2	1	2	-
Malignant neoplasm of oesophagus — Tumeur maligne de l'oesophage	390	6.9	87	1.6	2	1	2	-
Malignant neoplasm of stomach — Tumeur maligne de l'estomac............	509	9.0	269	4.8	7	9	9	8
Malignant neoplasm of colon, rectosigmoid junction, rectum, anus and anal canal — Tumeur maligne du côlon, de la jonction recto-sigmoïdienne, du rectum, de l'anus et du canal anal............	835	14.8	1 099	19.6	4	5	6	2
Malignant neoplasm of liver and intrahepatic bile ducts — Tumeur maligne du foie et des voies bilaires intrahépatiques	315	5.6	348	6.2	-	1	3	1
Malignant neoplasm of pancreas — Tumeur maligne du pancréas	354	6.3	354	6.3	1	3	3	4
Malignant neoplasm of trachea, bronchus and lung — Tumeur maligne de la trachée, des bronches et du poumon............	2 991	53.1	1 493	26.6	6	5	4	1
Malignant neoplasm of female breast — Tumeur maligne du sein chez la femme.	..	..	1 208	26.5	..	13	..	4
Malignant neoplasm of cervix uteri — Tumeur maligne du col de l'utérus	..	..	459	10.1	..	3	..	6
Malignant neoplasm of prostate — Tumeur maligne de la prostate	2 260	157.1	..	..	33	..	41	..
Malignant neoplasm of lymphoid, haematopoietic and related tissue — Tumeurs malignes primitives ou présumées primitives des tissus lymphoïde, hématopoïétique et apparentés	789	14.0	538	9.6	5	2	2	7
Disorders of the blood and blood-forming organs and certain disorders involving the immune mechanism — Maladies du sang et des organes hématopoïétiques et certains troubles du système immunitaire								
Total..................	119	2.1	107	1.9	3	1	2	2
Anaemias — Anémies	86	1.5	78	1.4	3	1	2	2
Endocrine, nutritional and metabolic diseases — Maladies endocriniennes, nutritionnelles et métaboliques								
Total..................	790	14.0	1 464	26.1	21	22	17	36
Diabetes mellitus — Diabète sucré	690	12.3	1 332	23.7	13	18	14	32
Malnutrition — Malnutrition...............	21	◊0.4	21	◊0.4	-	-	1	-
Mental and behavioural disorders — Troubles mentaux et du comportement	1 386	24.6	1 485	26.5	3	2	5	1
Diseases of the nervous system — Maladies du système nerveux............	711	12.6	526	9.4	7	5	2	1
Diseases of the circulatory system — Maladies de l'appareil circulatoire								
Total..................	17 943	318.7	16 853	300.3	82	101	83	113
Acute rheumatic fever and chronic rheumatic heart diseases — Rhumatisme articularie aigu et cardiopathies rhumatismales chroniques	72	1.3	127	2.3	-	2	-	1
Hypertensive diseases — Maladies hypertensives...............	914	16.2	851	15.2	30	56	32	49
Ischaemic heart disease — Cardiopathie ischémique............	8 740	155.2	7 647	136.2	14	8	19	11

	Cuba				Dominica - Dominique			
Cause of death — Cause de décès	2005 (C)				2003 (+C)		2004 (+C)	
	Male — Masculin		Female — Féminin		Male — Masculin	Female — Féminin	Male — Masculin	Female — Féminin
	Number Nombre	Rate Taux	Number Nombre	Rate Taux	Number Nombre	Number Nombre	Number Nombre	Number Nombre
Cerebrovascular disease — Maladie cérébrovasculaire	4 259	75.7	4 512	80.4	12	14	11	21
Diseases of arteries, arterioles and capillaries — Maladies des artères, artérioles et capillaires	1 697	30.1	1 623	28.9	-	-	-	3
Diseases of the respiratory system — Maladies de l'appareil respiratoire								
Total	5 269	93.6	4 519	80.5	15	21	25	24
Influenza — Grippe	-	-	-	-	-	1	2	-
Pneumonia — Pneumopathies	3 372	59.9	3 028	53.9	4	10	10	11
Chronic lower respiratory diseases — Maladies chroniques des voies respiratoires inférieures	1 711	30.4	1 371	24.4	2	2	7	7
Diseases of the digestive system — Maladies de l'appareil digestif								
Total	1 832	32.5	1 251	22.3	14	9	10	7
Gastric and duodenal ulcer — Ulcère de l'estomac et du duodénum	204	3.6	125	2.2	-	1	-	-
Diseases of the liver — Maladies du foie	869	15.4	387	6.9	6	3	4	3
Diseases of the musculoskeletal system and connective tissue — Maladies du système ostéo-articularie, des muscles et du tissu conjonctif	212	3.8	425	7.6	-	1	-	-
Diseases of the genitourinary system — Maladies de l'appareil génito-urinaire								
Total	431	7.7	307	5.5	6	4	10	3
Disorders of kidney and ureter — Affections du rein et de l'uretère	279	5.0	250	4.5	2	3	7	3
Hyperplasia of prostate — Hyperplasie de la prostate	94	6.5	..	..	4		1	..
Pregnancy, childbirth and the puerperium — Grossesse, accouchement et puerpéralité								
Total	..	..	66	54.7	..	-	..	-
Pregnancy with abortive outcome — Grossesse se terminant par un avortement	..	..	6	♦5.0	..	-	..	-
Other direct obstetric causes — Autres décès maternels directs	..	..	39	32.3	..	-	..	-
Indirect obstetric causes — Décès maternels indirects	..	..	17	♦14.1	..	-	..	-
Certain conditions originating in the perinatal period — Certaines affections dont l'origine se situe dans la période périnatale	176	282.9	143	244.5	9	5	4	5
Congenital malformations, deformations and chromosomal abnormalities — Malformations congénitales et anomalies chromosomiques	255	409.8	223	381.2	1	1	1	1
Symptoms, signs and abnormal clinical and laboratory findings, not elsewhere classified — Symptômes, signes et résultats anormaux d'examens cliniques et de laboratoire, non classés ailleurs	371	6.6	266	4.7	28	18	14	16
All other diseases — Toutes autres maladies	69	1.2	116	2.1	1	4	3	5
External causes — Causes externes								
Total	4 489	79.7	2 558	45.6	23	3	18	5
Accidents								
Total	2 506	44.5	1 393	24.8	15	-	10	2
Transport accidents — Accidents de transport	1 051	18.7	266	4.7	5	-	7	1
Falls — Chutes	788	14.0	966	17.2	3	-	-	-
Accidental drowning and submersion — Noyade et submersion accidentelles	238	4.2	25	♦0.4	2	-	1	1
Exposure to smoke, fire and flames — Exposition à la fumée, au feu et aux flammes	32	0.6	28	♦0.5	1	-	1	-
Accidental poisoning by and exposure to noxious substances — Intoxication accidentelle par des substances nocives et exposition à ces substances	24	♦0.4	12	♦0.2	-	-	-	-
Intentional self-harm — Lésions auto-infligées	1 046	18.6	350	6.2	1	1	1	1
Assault — Agresssions	514	9.1	168	3.0	5	2	3	1
All other external causes — Toutes autres causes externes	423	7.5	647	11.5	2	-	4	1

21. Death and death rates by cause and sex: 2002 - 2006
Décès et taux de mortalité par cause et sexe : 2002 - 2006 (continued - suite)

Cause of death — Cause de décès	Dominican Republic - République dominicaine				El Salvador			
	2003 (U)		2004 (U)		2004 (+U)		2005 (+U)	
	Male — Masculin	Female — Féminin	Male — Masculin	Female — Féminin	Male — Masculin	Female — Féminin	Male — Masculin	Female — Féminin
	Number Nombre	Number Nombre	Number Nombre	Number Nombre	Number Nombre	Number Nombre	Number Nombre	Number Nombre
TOTAL................................	16 695	11 572	18 018	12 581	17 583	12 475	18 135	12 798
Certain infectious and parasitic diseases — Certaines maladies infectieuses et parasitaires								
Total...........................	1 414	889	1 384	913	1 013	640	847	624
Intestinal infectious diseases — Maladies infectieuses intestinales............	152	125	156	126	138	122	154	115
Tuberculosis — Tuberculose.............................	275	150	290	131	62	21	57	18
Tetanus — Tétanos.........................	22	3	26	12	3	3	2	-
Diphtheria — Diphtérie........................	1	2	9	-	-	-	-	-
Whooping cough — Coqueluche...............	-	-	-	-	-	2	-	-
Meningococcal infection — Infection à méningocoques	3	2	3	6	-	-	-	-
Septicaemia — Septicémie...................	113	113	142	136	397	321	302	311
Acute poliomyelitis — Poliomyélite aiguë	-	-	-	-	-	-	-	-
Measles — Rougeole	-	-	-	-	-	-	-	-
Viral hepatitis — Hépatite virale	54	34	50	26	5	2	1	2
Human immunodeficiency virus [HIV] disease — Maladies dues au virus de l'immunodéficience humaine (VIH)	696	385	627	417	389	161	299	156
Malaria — Paludisme	2	4	2	3	-	-	-	-
Neoplasms — Tumeurs	2 055	1 579	2 165	1 731	1 364	1 914	1 435	1 971
Malignant neoplasms — Tumeurs malignes								
Total...........................	1 986	1 523	2 071	1 664	1 361	1 913	1 433	1 966
Malignant neoplasm of lip, oral cavity and pharynx — Tumeur maligne de la lèvre, de la cavité buccale et du pharynx ...	90	52	89	50	35	19	51	17
Malignant neoplasm of oesophagus — Tumeur maligne de l'oesophage	34	16	32	16	32	18	42	14
Malignant neoplasm of stomach — Tumeur maligne de l'estomac.............	141	90	137	106	276	223	285	244
Malignant neoplasm of colon, rectosigmoid junction, rectum, anus and anal canal — Tumeur maligne du côlon, de la jonction recto-sigmoïdienne, du rectum, de l'anus et du canal anal ...	111	117	143	128	54	77	41	70
Malignant neoplasm of liver and intrahepatic bile ducts — Tumeur maligne du foie et des voies bilaires intrahépatiques	180	126	155	178	81	114	89	117
Malignant neoplasm of pancreas — Tumeur maligne du pancréas	48	52	48	62	44	66	53	50
Malignant neoplasm of trachea, bronchus and lung — Tumeur maligne de la trachée, des bronches et du poumon ...	248	151	257	153	98	110	111	112
Malignant neoplasm of female breast — Tumeur maligne du sein chez la femme...........................	..	214	..	243	..	128	..	109
Malignant neoplasm of cervix uteri — Tumeur maligne du col de l'utérus	..	123	..	150	..	220	..	248
Malignant neoplasm of prostate — Tumeur maligne de la prostate	681	..	762	..	175	..	167	..
Malignant neoplasm of lymphoid, haematopoietic and related tissue — Tumeurs malignes primitives ou présumées primitives des tissus lymphoïde, hématopoïétique et apparentés ...	132	93	137	109	106	85	127	128
Disorders of the blood and blood-forming organs and certain disorders involving the immune mechanism — Maladies du sang et des organes hématopoïétiques et certains troubles du système immunitaire								
Total...........................	108	88	117	100	69	81	72	70
Anaemias — Anémies	102	83	104	84	58	63	61	54
Endocrine, nutritional and metabolic diseases — Maladies endocriniennes, nutritionnelles et métaboliques								
Total...........................	665	688	799	857	606	741	626	892
Diabetes mellitus — Diabète sucré.............	535	574	654	716	403	574	425	726
Malnutrition — Malnutrition......................	81	77	112	106	126	97	122	95
Mental and behavioural disorders — Troubles mentaux et du comportement	54	23	68	18	806	34	789	48
Diseases of the nervous system — Maladies du système nerveux............	206	160	278	207	338	367	331	321
Diseases of the circulatory system — Maladies de l'appareil circulatoire								
Total...........................	4 594	3 895	5 125	4 194	2 577	2 936	2 632	2 894
Acute rheumatic fever and chronic rheumatic heart diseases — Rhumatisme articularie aigu et cardiopathies rhumatismales chroniques	16	22	12	23	2	5	3	2
Hypertensive diseases — Maladies hypertensives.....................	560	559	632	630	157	222	152	192
Ischaemic heart disease — Cardiopathie ischémique	1 928	1 420	1 992	1 503	917	939	1 094	1 012

21. Death and death rates by cause and sex: 2002 - 2006
Décès et taux de mortalité par cause et sexe : 2002 - 2006 (continued - suite)

Cause of death — Cause de décès	Dominican Republic - République dominicaine				El Salvador			
	2003 (U)		2004 (U)		2004 (+U)		2005 (+U)	
	Male — Masculin	Female — Féminin	Male — Masculin	Female — Féminin	Male — Masculin	Female — Féminin	Male — Masculin	Female — Féminin
	Number Nombre	Number Nombre	Number Nombre	Number Nombre	Number Nombre	Number Nombre	Number Nombre	Number Nombre
Cerebrovascular disease — Maladie cérébrovasculaire.....................	1 362	1 186	1 646	1 290	441	508	448	542
Diseases of arteries, arterioles and capillaries — Maladies des artères, artérioles et capillaires	149	172	95	64	15	8	14	14
Diseases of the respiratory system — Maladies de l'appareil respiratoire								
Total..	1 024	834	1 146	957	1 386	1 260	1 467	1 265
Influenza — Grippe	4	5	3	2	1	-	-	1
Pneumonia — Pneumopathies................................	416	325	446	360	798	687	900	707
Chronic lower respiratory diseases — Maladies chroniques des voies respiratoires inférieures	308	242	388	281	238	285	221	314
Diseases of the digestive system — Maladies de l'appareil digestif								
Total...	851	515	971	568	888	583	940	582
Gastric and duodenal ulcer — Ulcère de l'estomac et du duodénum	99	49	113	42	80	90	75	92
Diseases of the liver — Maladies du foie	579	350	645	374	561	270	579	245
Diseases of the musculoskeletal system and connective tissue — Maladies du système ostéo-articularie, des muscles et du tissu conjonctif	22	49	23	46	46	73	34	81
Diseases of the genitourinary system — Maladies de l'appareil génito-urinaire								
Total...	223	103	252	102	1 338	573	1 338	648
Disorders of kidney and ureter — Affections du rein et de l'uretère	156	95	190	93	1 285	538	1 267	610
Hyperplasia of prostate — Hyperplasie de la prostate.........................	51	..	50	..	34	..	27	..
Pregnancy, childbirth and the puerperium — Grossesse, accouchement et puerpéralité								
Total..	..	58	..	85	..	22	..	23
Pregnancy with abortive outcome — Grossesse se terminant par un avortement	..	8	..	9	..	-	..	4
Other direct obstetric causes — Autres décès maternels directs	..	39	..	62	..	22	..	19
Indirect obstetric causes — Décès maternels indirects........................	..	11	..	14	..	-	..	-
Certain conditions originating in the perinatal period — Certaines affections dont l'origine se situe dans la période périnatale	890	867	911	836	259	213	228	167
Congenital malformations, deformations and chromosomal abnormalities — Malformations congénitales et anomalies chromosomiques	201	224	217	167	187	157	163	143
Symptoms, signs and abnormal clinical and laboratory findings, not elsewhere classified — Symptômes, signes et résultats anormaux d'examens cliniques et de laboratoire, non classés ailleurs	999	955	1 167	1 042	2 044	1 962	2 076	2 091
All other diseases — Toutes autres maladies...............................	6	16	9	13	36	42	34	42
External causes — Causes externes								
Total..	3 383	629	3 386	745	4 626	877	5 123	936
Accidents								
Total..	1 416	276	1 250	315	1 899	521	1 842	481
Transport accidents — Accidents de transport	1 161	199	1 000	228	1 402	353	1 195	270
Falls — Chutes	13	7	16	14	149	78	213	86
Accidental drowning and submersion — Noyade et submersion accidentelles	10	1	17	11	209	51	263	47
Exposure to smoke, fire and flames — Exposition à la fumée, au feu et aux flammes	4	9	4	6	15	12	18	15
Accidental poisoning by and exposure to noxious substances — Intoxication accidentelle par des substances nocives et exposition à ces substances	2	1	2	-	18	2	19	6
Intentional self-harm — Lésions auto-infligées.................................	139	21	123	26	349	117	338	119
Assault — Agresssions	279	44	446	51	2 375	239	2 942	336
All other external causes — Toutes autres causes externes..................	1 549	288	1 567	353	3	-	1	-

21. Death and death rates by cause and sex: 2002 - 2006
Décès et taux de mortalité par cause et sexe : 2002 - 2006 (continued - suite)

Cause of death — Cause de décès	Grenada - Grenade		Guadeloupe				Guatemala	
	2002 (U)		2004 (...)		2005 (...)		2003 (U)	
	Male — Masculin	Female — Féminin	Male — Masculin	Female — Féminin	Male — Masculin	Female — Féminin	Male — Masculin	Female — Féminin
	Number Nombre	Number Nombre	Number Nombre	Number Nombre	Number Nombre	Number Nombre	Number Nombre	Number Nombre
TOTAL..	*434*	*451*	*1 463*	*1 209*	*1 597*	*1 330*	*38 383*	*28 229*
Certain infectious and parasitic diseases — Certaines maladies infectieuses et parasitaires								
Total..	*16*	*14*	*57*	*37*	*61*	*44*	*3 415*	*2 653*
Intestinal infectious diseases — Maladies infectieuses intestinales............	*2*	-	*1*	*4*	*2*	*2*	*2 235*	*1 895*
Tuberculosis — Tuberculose..............................	*1*	-	*1*	-	*2*	-	*228*	*143*
Tetanus — Tétanos..................................	*1*	-	-	-	*1*	-	*12*	*4*
Diphtheria — Diphtérie................................	-	-	-	-	-	-	-	-
Whooping cough — Coqueluche........................	-	-	-	-	-	-	*11*	*14*
Meningococcal infection — Infection à méningocoques............	-	-	-	-	-	-	-	-
Septicaemia — Septicémie............................	*8*	*11*	*20*	*12*	*20*	*16*	*339*	*283*
Acute poliomyelitis — Poliomyélite aiguë............	-	-	-	-	-	-	-	-
Measles — Rougeole................................	-	-	-	-	-	-	*2*	*5*
Viral hepatitis — Hépatite virale......................	-	-	*2*	*2*	*4*	*4*	-	-
Human immunodeficiency virus [HIV] disease — Maladies dues au virus de l'immunodéficience humaine (VIH).........	*2*	*1*	*18*	*8*	*19*	*10*	*411*	*162*
Malaria — Paludisme................................	-	-	-	-	-	-	*23*	*28*
Neoplasms — Tumeurs..................................	*74*	*58*	*368*	*237*	*419*	*279*	*2 686*	*3 309*
Malignant neoplasms — Tumeurs malignes								
Total..	*72*	*56*	*363*	*226*	*402*	*271*	*2 680*	*3 298*
Malignant neoplasm of lip, oral cavity and pharynx — Tumeur maligne de la lèvre, de la cavité buccale et du pharynx......	*1*	-	*23*	*4*	*22*	*3*	*74*	*57*
Malignant neoplasm of oesophagus — Tumeur maligne de l'oesophage	*3*	*2*	*18*	*3*	*10*	*2*	*43*	*32*
Malignant neoplasm of stomach — Tumeur maligne de l'estomac............	*2*	*3*	*31*	*16*	*40*	*20*	*612*	*664*
Malignant neoplasm of colon, rectosigmoid junction, rectum, anus and anal canal — Tumeur maligne du côlon, de la jonction recto-sigmoïdienne, du rectum, de l'anus et du canal anal......	*5*	*3*	*25*	*26*	*37*	*33*	*75*	*115*
Malignant neoplasm of liver and intrahepatic bile ducts — Tumeur maligne du foie et des voies bilaires intrahépatiques............	*2*	*1*	*10*	*6*	*18*	*9*	-	-
Malignant neoplasm of pancreas — Tumeur maligne du pancréas............	*1*	-	*21*	*13*	*21*	*16*	*57*	*77*
Malignant neoplasm of trachea, bronchus and lung — Tumeur maligne de la trachée, des bronches et du poumon............	*6*	*1*	*33*	*13*	*45*	*14*	*220*	*161*
Malignant neoplasm of female breast — Tumeur maligne du sein chez la femme..........................	..	*10*	..	*36*	..	*37*	..	*139*
Malignant neoplasm of cervix uteri — Tumeur maligne du col de l'utérus......	..	*3*	..	*6*	..	*8*	..	*213*
Malignant neoplasm of prostate — Tumeur maligne de la prostate............	*31*	..	*94*	..	*98*	..	*322*	..
Malignant neoplasm of lymphoid, haematopoietic and related tissue — Tumeurs malignes primitives ou présumées primitives des tissus lymphoïde, hématopoïétique et apparentés............	*5*	*8*	*32*	*19*	*24*	*30*	*215*	*172*
Disorders of the blood and blood-forming organs and certain disorders involving the immune mechanism — Maladies du sang et des organes hématopoïétiques et certains troubles du système immunitaire								
Total..	*5*	*5*	*8*	*8*	*10*	*7*	*170*	*202*
Anaemias — Anémies................................	*5*	*5*	*6*	*4*	*7*	*4*	*140*	*164*
Endocrine, nutritional and metabolic diseases — Maladies endocriniennes, nutritionnelles et métaboliques								
Total..	*31*	*56*	*74*	*102*	*75*	*123*	*2 403*	*2 727*
Diabetes mellitus — Diabète sucré......................	*24*	*53*	*57*	*78*	*53*	*94*	*965*	*1 270*
Malnutrition — Malnutrition............................	*2*	-	*2*	*3*	*5*	*9*	*1 127*	*1 180*
Mental and behavioural disorders — Troubles mentaux et du comportement	*2*	*2*	*45*	*21*	*47*	*14*	*1 402*	*157*
Diseases of the nervous system — Maladies du système nerveux............	*10*	*11*	*48*	*48*	*69*	*60*	*560*	*447*
Diseases of the circulatory system — Maladies de l'appareil circulatoire								
Total..	*141*	*171*	*407*	*426*	*425*	*438*	*4 723*	*4 699*
Acute rheumatic fever and chronic rheumatic heart diseases — Rhumatisme articularie aigu et cardiopathies rhumatismales chroniques............	-	-	*1*	*4*	*1*	*1*	-	*2*
Hypertensive diseases — Maladies hypertensives..................	*14*	*23*	*42*	*68*	*50*	*70*	*488*	*638*
Ischaemic heart disease — Cardiopathie ischémique..................	*21*	*24*	*64*	*52*	*56*	*44*	*1 087*	*866*

Cause of death — Cause de décès	Grenada - Grenade 2002 (U) Male — Masculin Number Nombre	Grenada - Grenade 2002 (U) Female — Féminin Number Nombre	Guadeloupe 2004 (...) Male — Masculin Number Nombre	Guadeloupe 2004 (...) Female — Féminin Number Nombre	Guadeloupe 2005 (...) Male — Masculin Number Nombre	Guadeloupe 2005 (...) Female — Féminin Number Nombre	Guatemala 2003 (U) Male — Masculin Number Nombre	Guatemala 2003 (U) Female — Féminin Number Nombre
Cerebrovascular disease — Maladie cérébrovasculaire	51	73	147	167	166	147	1 063	1 062
Diseases of arteries, arterioles and capillaries — Maladies des artères, artérioles et capillaires	8	4	19	14	22	20	108	141
Diseases of the respiratory system — Maladies de l'appareil respiratoire								
Total	48	52	64	45	63	60	6 000	5 193
Influenza — Grippe	-	-	1	1	3	5	5	8
Pneumonia — Pneumopathies	21	37	33	16	22	28	5 069	4 413
Chronic lower respiratory diseases — Maladies chroniques des voies respiratoires inférieures	9	6	11	12	21	8	490	425
Diseases of the digestive system — Maladies de l'appareil digestif								
Total	24	20	71	57	69	62	2 989	1 647
Gastric and duodenal ulcer — Ulcère de l'estomac et du duodénum	1	2	-	4	2	1	387	348
Diseases of the liver — Maladies du foie	17	12	37	16	38	13	1 588	553
Diseases of the musculoskeletal system and connective tissue — Maladies du système ostéo-articulaire, des muscles et du tissu conjonctif	-	3	7	7	6	6	79	108
Diseases of the genitourinary system — Maladies de l'appareil génito-urinaire								
Total	17	12	25	32	25	22	725	593
Disorders of kidney and ureter — Affections du rein et de l'uretère	16	11	15	28	17	19	634	515
Hyperplasia of prostate — Hyperplasie de la prostate	1	..	4	..	2	..	47	..
Pregnancy, childbirth and the puerperium — Grossesse, accouchement et puerpéralité								
Total	..	1	..	3	..	1	..	293
Pregnancy with abortive outcome — Grossesse se terminant par un avortement	..	1	..	1	-	..	..	28
Other direct obstetric causes — Autres décès maternels directs	..	-	..	2	..	1	..	265
Indirect obstetric causes — Décès maternels indirects	..	-	..	-	..	-	..	-
Certain conditions originating in the perinatal period — Certaines affections dont l'origine se situe dans la période périnatale	16	19	14	16	12	17	2 385	1 707
Congenital malformations, deformations and chromosomal abnormalities — Malformations congénitales et anomalies chromosomiques	-	2	8	9	10	11	286	272
Symptoms, signs and abnormal clinical and laboratory findings, not elsewhere classified — Symptômes, signes et résultats anormaux d'examens cliniques et de laboratoire, non classés ailleurs	8	11	90	101	121	121	2 635	2 527
All other diseases — Toutes autres maladies	9	4	2	8	6	5	114	124
External causes — Causes externes								
Total	33	10	175	52	179	60	7 811	1 571
Accidents								
Total	29	7	126	37	125	38	1 816	579
Transport accidents — Accidents de transport	5	2	65	9	51	12	305	67
Falls — Chutes	-	-	11	6	10	2	114	50
Accidental drowning and submersion — Noyade et submersion accidentelles	13	2	10	2	15	4	70	27
Exposure to smoke, fire and flames — Exposition à la fumée, au feu et aux flammes	4	2	2	4	5	3	42	20
Accidental poisoning by and exposure to noxious substances — Intoxication accidentelle par des substances nocives et exposition à ces substances	-	1	4	3	4	2	25	23
Intentional self-harm — Lésions auto-infligées	-	-	33	6	30	16	202	53
Assault — Agresssions	-	2	7	4	14	1	3 065	276
All other external causes — Toutes autres causes externes	4	1	9	5	10	5	2 728	663

21. Death and death rates by cause and sex: 2002 - 2006
Décès et taux de mortalité par cause et sexe : 2002 - 2006 (continued - suite)

Cause of death — Cause de décès	Guatemala 2004 (U) Male — Masculin Number Nombre	Guatemala 2004 (U) Female — Féminin Number Nombre	Haiti - Haïti 2002 (...) Male — Masculin Number Nombre	Haiti - Haïti 2002 (...) Female — Féminin Number Nombre	Haiti - Haïti 2003 (...) Male — Masculin Number Nombre	Haiti - Haïti 2003 (...) Female — Féminin Number Nombre	Martinique 2004 (...) Male — Masculin Number Nombre	Martinique 2004 (...) Female — Féminin Number Nombre
TOTAL	38 671	28 205	3 775	3 882	4 135	3 876	1 438	1 209
Certain infectious and parasitic diseases — Certaines maladies infectieuses et parasitaires								
Total	3 229	2 354	814	790	862	719	65	42
Intestinal infectious diseases — Maladies infectieuses intestinales	1 972	1 622	233	255	268	219	4	4
Tuberculosis — Tuberculose	218	117	119	104	148	118	1	-
Tetanus — Tétanos	12	2	30	18	27	11	-	-
Diphtheria — Diphtérie	-	1	2	5	-	-	-	-
Whooping cough — Coqueluche	' 11	10	-	-	-	-	-	-
Meningococcal infection — Infection à méningocoques	-	-	1	-	-	1	-	-
Septicaemia — Septicémie	328	293	61	52	65	55	20	15
Acute poliomyelitis — Poliomyélite aiguë	-	-	-	-	-	-	-	-
Measles — Rougeole	4	-	-	-	-	-	-	-
Viral hepatitis — Hépatite virale	3	2	20	7	11	6	3	2
Human immunodeficiency virus [HIV] disease — Maladies dues au virus de l'immunodéficience humaine (VIH)	513	167	279	292	271	219	20	6
Malaria — Paludisme	15	13	45	32	46	63	-	-
Neoplasms — Tumeurs	2 900	3 445	162	193	154	171	387	276
Malignant neoplasms — Tumeurs malignes								
Total	2 884	3 436	147	179	135	157	371	260
Malignant neoplasm of lip, oral cavity and pharynx — Tumeur maligne de la lèvre, de la cavité buccale et du pharynx	107	51	3	1	5	1	13	2
Malignant neoplasm of oesophagus — Tumeur maligne de l'oesophage	62	40	6	6	1	1	15	3
Malignant neoplasm of stomach — Tumeur maligne de l'estomac	600	684	18	14	19	5	30	21
Malignant neoplasm of colon, rectosigmoid junction, rectum, anus and anal canal — Tumeur maligne du côlon, de la jonction recto-sigmoïdienne, du rectum, de l'anus et du canal anal	98	104	7	19	3	11	30	24
Malignant neoplasm of liver and intrahepatic bile ducts — Tumeur maligne du foie et des voies bilaires intrahépatiques	-	-	17	13	9	10	18	7
Malignant neoplasm of pancreas — Tumeur maligne du pancréas	57	91	6	5	4	4	22	19
Malignant neoplasm of trachea, bronchus and lung — Tumeur maligne de la trachée, des bronches et du poumon	219	175	6	13	10	11	29	14
Malignant neoplasm of female breast — Tumeur maligne du sein chez la femme	..	170	..	29	..	26	..	45
Malignant neoplasm of cervix uteri — Tumeur maligne du col de l'utérus	..	215	..	5	..	10	..	6
Malignant neoplasm of prostate — Tumeur maligne de la prostate	366	..	44	..	49	..	94	..
Malignant neoplasm of lymphoid, haematopoietic and related tissue — Tumeurs malignes primitives ou présumées primitives des tissus lymphoïde, hématopoïétique et apparentés	237	183	14	11	8	10	44	36
Disorders of the blood and blood-forming organs and certain disorders involving the immune mechanism — Maladies du sang et des organes hématopoïétiques et certains troubles du système immunitaire								
Total	153	150	54	64	48	47	8	4
Anaemias — Anémies	117	111	51	64	45	44	5	4
Endocrine, nutritional and metabolic diseases — Maladies endocriniennes, nutritionnelles et métaboliques								
Total	2 315	2 712	229	267	206	239	68	92
Diabetes mellitus — Diabète sucré	1 024	1 303	64	98	56	104	45	66
Malnutrition — Malnutrition	981	1 101	145	153	132	117	1	9
Mental and behavioural disorders — Troubles mentaux et du comportement	1 438	118	20	8	11	4	40	20
Diseases of the nervous system — Maladies du système nerveux	574	450	50	64	89	61	64	86
Diseases of the circulatory system — Maladies de l'appareil circulatoire								
Total	4 030	3 976	430	768	570	841	392	396
Acute rheumatic fever and chronic rheumatic heart diseases — Rhumatisme articularie aigu et cardiopathies rhumatismales chroniques	2	5	2	4	-	2	2	4
Hypertensive diseases — Maladies hypertensives	722	760	95	149	102	147	38	49
Ischaemic heart disease — Cardiopathie ischémique	1 080	887	40	66	44	56	43	46

	Guatemala		Haiti - Haïti				Martinique	
Cause of death — Cause de décès	2004 (U)		2002 (...)		2003 (...)		2004 (...)	
	Male — Masculin	Female — Féminin	Male — Masculin	Female — Féminin	Male — Masculin	Female — Féminin	Male — Masculin	Female — Féminin
	Number Nombre	Number Nombre	Number Nombre	Number Nombre	Number Nombre	Number Nombre	Number Nombre	Number Nombre
Cerebrovascular disease — Maladie cérébrovasculaire	1 097	1 106	179	304	250	300	162	137
Diseases of arteries, arterioles and capillaries — Maladies des artères, artérioles et capillaires	94	100	4	5	4	6	38	24
Diseases of the respiratory system — Maladies de l'appareil respiratoire								
Total	6 075	5 231	197	156	211	205	60	58
Influenza — Grippe	9	3	6	7	7	6	-	1
Pneumonia — Pneumopathies	5 146	4 446	145	120	162	154	28	28
Chronic lower respiratory diseases — Maladies chroniques des voies respiratoires inférieures	441	414	20	11	16	21	13	11
Diseases of the digestive system — Maladies de l'appareil digestif								
Total	2 866	1 644	119	89	136	91	55	44
Gastric and duodenal ulcer — Ulcère de l'estomac et du duodénum	417	378	21	14	19	10	-	3
Diseases of the liver — Maladies du foie	1 509	564	31	25	37	23	24	4
Diseases of the musculoskeletal system and connective tissue — Maladies du système ostéo-articulaire, des muscles et du tissu conjonctif	71	114	8	8	8	5	6	4
Diseases of the genitourinary system — Maladies de l'appareil génito-urinaire								
Total	780	665	37	27	40	30	33	13
Disorders of kidney and ureter — Affections du rein et de l'uretère	690	596	19	17	23	19	22	10
Hyperplasia of prostate — Hyperplasie de la prostate	41	..	1	..	1	..	3	..
Pregnancy, childbirth and the puerperium — Grossesse, accouchement et puerpéralité								
Total	..	296	..	135	..	124	..	1
Pregnancy with abortive outcome — Grossesse se terminant par un avortement	..	22	..	8	..	16	..	-
Other direct obstetric causes — Autres décès maternels directs	..	274	..	119	..	101	..	1
Indirect obstetric causes — Décès maternels indirects	..	-	..	8	..	6	..	-
Certain conditions originating in the perinatal period — Certaines affections dont l'origine se situe dans la période périnatale	2 192	1 622	170	210	118	129	11	5
Congenital malformations, deformations and chromosomal abnormalities — Malformations congénitales et anomalies chromosomiques	297	260	30	25	28	29	7	2
Symptoms, signs and abnormal clinical and laboratory findings, not elsewhere classified — Symptômes, signes et résultats anormaux d'examens cliniques et de laboratoire, non classés ailleurs	3 601	3 320	1 083	926	1 273	1 043	120	100
All other diseases — Toutes autres maladies	111	115	15	3	8	7	9	12
External causes — Causes externes								
Total	8 039	1 733	357	149	373	131	113	54
Accidents								
Total	1 924	638	144	80	142	77	74	40
Transport accidents — Accidents de transport	321	78	78	25	59	30	36	7
Falls — Chutes	139	65	5	10	14	8	7	7
Accidental drowning and submersion — Noyade et submersion accidentelles	74	20	8	-	13	7	9	2
Exposure to smoke, fire and flames — Exposition à la fumée, au feu et aux flammes	67	23	12	16	16	13	1	1
Accidental poisoning by and exposure to noxious substances — Intoxication accidentelle par des substances nocives et exposition à ces substances	63	21	3	5	4	3	2	1
Intentional self-harm — Lésions auto-infligées	185	67	4	-	-	2	25	9
Assault — Agresssions	3 046	357	128	25	145	28	7	2
All other external causes — Toutes autres causes externes	2 884	671	81	44	86	24	7	3

Cause of death — Cause de décès	Martinique		Mexico - Mexique			
	2005 (...)		2004 (+C)			
	Male — Masculin	Female — Féminin	Male — Masculin		Female — Féminin	
	Number Nombre	Number Nombre	Number Nombre	Rate Taux	Number Nombre	Rate Taux
TOTAL..........	*1 349*	*1 268*	260 738	513.1	210 737	403.8
Certain infectious and parasitic diseases — Certaines maladies infectieuses et parasitaires						
Total..........	52	42	10 697	21.1	7 006	13.4
Intestinal infectious diseases — Maladies infectieuses intestinales..........	2	4	2 138	4.2	2 037	3.9
Tuberculosis — Tuberculose..........	1	-	1 576	3.1	803	1.5
Tetanus — Tétanos..........	-	-	28	◆0.1	15	◆0.0
Diphtheria — Diphtérie..........	-	-	-	-	-	-
Whooping cough — Coqueluche..........	-	-	4	◆0.0	5	◆0.0
Meningococcal infection — Infection à méningocoques..........	-	-	1	◆0.0	4	◆0.0
Septicaemia — Septicémie..........	24	19	1 782	3.5	1 845	3.5
Acute poliomyelitis — Poliomyélite aiguë..........	-	-	-	-	-	-
Measles — Rougeole..........	-	-	-	-	-	-
Viral hepatitis — Hépatite virale..........	5	2	453	0.9	725	1.4
Human immunodeficiency virus [HIV] disease — Maladies dues au virus de l'immunodéficience humaine (VIH)..........	9	5	3 903	7.7	816	1.6
Malaria — Paludisme..........	-	-	-	-	-	-
Neoplasms — Tumeurs..........	*352*	*301*	31 207	61.4	32 896	63.0
Malignant neoplasms — Tumeurs malignes						
Total..........	337	281	29 682	58.4	31 352	60.1
Malignant neoplasm of lip, oral cavity and pharynx — Tumeur maligne de la lèvre, de la cavité buccale et du pharynx..........	13	-	567	1.1	345	0.7
Malignant neoplasm of oesophagus — Tumeur maligne de l'oesophage..........	5	1	583	1.1	235	0.5
Malignant neoplasm of stomach — Tumeur maligne de l'estomac..........	32	27	2 788	5.5	2 447	4.7
Malignant neoplasm of colon, rectosigmoid junction, rectum, anus and anal canal — Tumeur maligne du côlon, de la jonction recto-sigmoïdienne, du rectum, de l'anus et du canal anal..........	28	32	1 544	3.0	1 600	3.1
Malignant neoplasm of liver and intrahepatic bile ducts — Tumeur maligne du foie et des voies bilaires intrahépatiques..........	12	16	2 266	4.5	2 542	4.9
Malignant neoplasm of pancreas — Tumeur maligne du pancréas..........	9	17	1 487	2.9	1 648	3.2
Malignant neoplasm of trachea, bronchus and lung — Tumeur maligne de la trachée, des bronches et du poumon..........	31	14	4 600	9.1	2 234	4.3
Malignant neoplasm of female breast — Tumeur maligne du sein chez la femme..........	..	58	..	..	4 160	...
Malignant neoplasm of cervix uteri — Tumeur maligne du col de l'utérus..........	..	9	..	..	4 239	...
Malignant neoplasm of prostate — Tumeur maligne de la prostate..........	119	..	4 505	...	..	..
Malignant neoplasm of lymphoid, haematopoietic and related tissue — Tumeurs malignes primitives ou présumées primitives des tissus lymphoïde, hématopoïétique et apparentés..........	28	31	3 592	7.1	2 877	5.5
Disorders of the blood and blood-forming organs and certain disorders involving the immune mechanism — Maladies du sang et des organes hématopoïétiques et certains troubles du système immunitaire						
Total..........	10	11	1 973	3.9	2 241	4.3
Anaemias — Anémies..........	5	8	1 628	3.2	1 934	3.7
Endocrine, nutritional and metabolic diseases — Maladies endocriniennes, nutritionnelles et métaboliques						
Total..........	48	107	34 755	68.4	40 507	77.6
Diabetes mellitus — Diabète sucré..........	35	71	28 318	55.7	33 780	64.7
Malnutrition — Malnutrition..........	2	8	4 066	8.0	4 239	8.1
Mental and behavioural disorders — Troubles mentaux et du comportement..........	41	22	3 815	7.5	554	1.1
Diseases of the nervous system — Maladies du système nerveux..........	69	71	4 516	8.9	3 662	7.0
Diseases of the circulatory system — Maladies de l'appareil circulatoire						
Total..........	311	380	53 882	106.0	53 412	102.3
Acute rheumatic fever and chronic rheumatic heart diseases — Rhumatisme articularie aigu et cardiopathies rhumatismales chroniques..........	3	2	383	0.8	779	1.5
Hypertensive diseases — Maladies hypertensives..........	33	53	5 125	10.1	7 050	13.5
Ischaemic heart disease — Cardiopathie ischémique..........	52	39	27 953	55.0	22 440	43.0
Cerebrovascular disease — Maladie cérébrovasculaire..........	109	127	12 750	25.1	14 181	27.2
Diseases of arteries, arterioles and capillaries — Maladies des artères, artérioles et capillaires.....	22	26	968	1.9	1 065	2.0
Diseases of the respiratory system — Maladies de l'appareil respiratoire						

Cause of death — Cause de décès	Martinique		Mexico - Mexique			
	2005 (...)		2004 (+C)			
	Male — Masculin	Female — Féminin	Male — Masculin		Female — Féminin	
	Number Nombre	Number Nombre	Number Nombre	Rate Taux	Number Nombre	Rate Taux
Total............	80	53	22 321	43.9	18 520	35.5
Influenza — Grippe............	3	3	1	+0.0	4	+0.0
Pneumonia — Pneumopathies............	31	18	6 629	13.0	5 685	10.9
Chronic lower respiratory diseases — Maladies chroniques des voies respiratoires inférieures	13	13	11 603	22.8	9 155	17.5
Diseases of the digestive system — Maladies de l'appareil digestif						
Total............	65	57	30 087	59.2	15 549	29.8
Gastric and duodenal ulcer — Ulcère de l'estomac et du duodénum	3	1	1 420	2.8	1 322	2.5
Diseases of the liver — Maladies du foie............	32	11	21 935	43.2	7 391	14.2
Diseases of the musculoskeletal system and connective tissue — Maladies du système ostéo-articularie, des muscles et du tissu conjonctif	11	4	872	1.7	2 035	3.9
Diseases of the genitourinary system — Maladies de l'appareil génito-urinaire						
Total............	37	25	7 226	14.2	5 897	11.3
Disorders of kidney and ureter — Affections du rein et de l'uretère	25	22	6 008	11.8	5 164	9.9
Hyperplasia of prostate — Hyperplasie de la prostate............	-	..	536	...	..	..
Pregnancy, childbirth and the puerperium — Grossesse, accouchement et puerpéralité						
Total............	..	-	..	..	1 266	58.7
Pregnancy with abortive outcome — Grossesse se terminant par un avortement	..	-	..	..	87	4.0
Other direct obstetric causes — Autres décès maternels directs	..	-	..	..	947	43.9
Indirect obstetric causes — Décès maternels indirects............	..	-	..	..	198	9.2
Certain conditions originating in the perinatal period — Certaines affections dont l'origine se situe dans la période périnatale	16	14	9 556	871.0	6 910	653.4
Congenital malformations, deformations and chromosomal abnormalities — Malformations congénitales et anomalies chromosomiques	5	5	4 720	430.2	4 286	405.3
Symptoms, signs and abnormal clinical and laboratory findings, not elsewhere classified — Symptômes, signes et résultats anormaux d'examens cliniques et de laboratoire, non classés ailleurs	98	123	4 727	9.3	4 708	9.0
All other diseases — Toutes autres maladies............	5	12	362	0.7	618	1.2
External causes — Causes externes						
Total............	149	41	40 022	78.8	10 670	20.4
Accidents						
Total............	106	28	25 745	50.7	7 956	15.2
Transport accidents — Accidents de transport	36	8	12 118	23.8	3 351	6.4
Falls — Chutes	18	3	1 766	3.5	484	0.9
Accidental drowning and submersion — Noyade et submersion accidentelles	19	-	1 879	3.7	374	0.7
Exposure to smoke, fire and flames — Exposition à la fumée, au feu et aux flammes	1	-	363	0.7	147	0.3
Accidental poisoning by and exposure to noxious substances — Intoxication accidentelle par des substances nocives et exposition à ces substances	1	1	605	1.2	264	0.5
Intentional self-harm — Lésions auto-infligées............	22	4	3 414	6.7	678	1.3
Assault — Agresssions	12	2	8 044	15.8	1 193	2.3
All other external causes — Toutes autres causes externes............	9	7	2 819	5.5	843	1.6

21. Death and death rates by cause and sex: 2002 - 2006
Décès et taux de mortalité par cause et sexe : 2002 - 2006 (continued - suite)

	Mexico - Mexique				Montserrat			
	2005 (+C)				2002 (+C)		2003 (+C)	
Cause of death — Cause de décès	Male — Masculin		Female — Féminin		Male — Masculin	Female — Féminin	Male — Masculin	Female — Féminin
	Number Nombre	Rate Taux	Number Nombre	Rate Taux	Number Nombre	Number Nombre	Number Nombre	Number Nombre
TOTAL........	272 236	531.3	221 575	420.4	21	23	30	25
Certain infectious and parasitic diseases — Certaines maladies infectieuses et parasitaires								
Total........	10 926	21.3	7 288	13.8	1	-	-	-
Intestinal infectious diseases — Maladies infectieuses intestinales...........	2 130	4.2	2 132	4.0	-	-	-	-
Tuberculosis — Tuberculose.........	1 671	3.3	817	1.6	1	-	-	-
Tetanus — Tétanos........	27	⬦0.1	11	⬦0.0	-	-	-	-
Diphtheria — Diphtérie.........	-	-	-	-	-	-	-	-
Whooping cough — Coqueluche.........	11	⬦0.0	17	⬦0.0	-	-	-	-
Meningococcal infection — Infection à méningocoques....................	2	⬦0.0	5	⬦0.0	-	-	-	-
Septicaemia — Septicémie.........	1 817	3.5	1 924	3.7	-	-	-	-
Acute poliomyelitis — Poliomyélite aiguë.........	-	-	-	-	-	-	-	-
Measles — Rougeole.........	-	-	-	-	-	-	-	-
Viral hepatitis — Hépatite virale.........	506	1.0	820	1.6	-	-	-	-
Human immunodeficiency virus [HIV] disease — Maladies dues au virus de l'immunodéficience humaine (VIH)........	3 853	7.5	796	1.5	-	-	-	-
Malaria — Paludisme.........	-	-	-	-	-	-	-	-
Neoplasms — Tumeurs........	32 550	63.5	33 757	64.0	5	3	6	7
Malignant neoplasms — Tumeurs malignes								
Total........	30 811	60.1	32 165	61.0	4	3	5	7
Malignant neoplasm of lip, oral cavity and pharynx — Tumeur maligne de la lèvre, de la cavité buccale et du pharynx.........	615	1.2	344	0.7	-	-	-	-
Malignant neoplasm of oesophagus — Tumeur maligne de l'oesophage......	619	1.2	238	0.5	-	-	1	-
Malignant neoplasm of stomach — Tumeur maligne de l'estomac.............	2 805	5.5	2 523	4.8	-	-	1	-
Malignant neoplasm of colon, rectosigmoid junction, rectum, anus and anal canal — Tumeur maligne du côlon, de la jonction recto-sigmoïdienne, du rectum, de l'anus et du canal anal.........	1 695	3.3	1 661	3.2	-	-	1	1
Malignant neoplasm of liver and intrahepatic bile ducts — Tumeur maligne du foie et des voies bilaires intrahépatiques.........	2 298	4.5	2 540	4.8	-	-	-	-
Malignant neoplasm of pancreas — Tumeur maligne du pancréas............	1 506	2.9	1 684	3.2	2	-	1	-
Malignant neoplasm of trachea, bronchus and lung — Tumeur maligne de la trachée, des bronches et du poumon.........	4 795	9.4	2 223	4.2	-	-	-	-
Malignant neoplasm of female breast — Tumeur maligne du sein chez la femme........	..	..	4 220	11.7	..	1	..	2
Malignant neoplasm of cervix uteri — Tumeur maligne du col de l'utérus......	..	..	4 270	11.9	..	-	..	-
Malignant neoplasm of prostate — Tumeur maligne de la prostate............	4 788	65.1	..	..	2	..	1	..
Malignant neoplasm of lymphoid, haematopoietic and related tissue — Tumeurs malignes primitives ou présumées primitives des tissus lymphoïde, hématopoïétique et apparentés.........	3 706	7.2	3 158	6.0	-	-	-	-
Disorders of the blood and blood-forming organs and certain disorders involving the immune mechanism — Maladies du sang et des organes hématopoïétiques et certains troubles du système immunitaire								
Total........	2 098	4.1	2 357	4.5	-	-	-	1
Anaemias — Anémies.........	1 688	3.3	1 964	3.7	-	-	-	1
Endocrine, nutritional and metabolic diseases — Maladies endocriniennes, nutritionnelles et métaboliques								
Total........	37 576	73.3	43 446	82.4	2	2	5	7
Diabetes mellitus — Diabète sucré.........	30 842	60.2	36 248	68.8	2	2	5	7
Malnutrition — Malnutrition.........	4 138	8.1	4 302	8.2	-	-	-	-
Mental and behavioural disorders — Troubles mentaux et du comportement	3 827	7.5	671	1.3	-	1	3	-
Diseases of the nervous system — Maladies du système nerveux.........	4 980	9.7	4 138	7.9	-	1	1	-
Diseases of the circulatory system — Maladies de l'appareil circulatoire								
Total........	56 323	109.9	55 385	105.1	5	12	10	8
Acute rheumatic fever and chronic rheumatic heart diseases — Rhumatisme articularie aigu et cardiopathies rhumatismales chroniques..................	383	0.7	755	1.4	-	-	-	-
Hypertensive diseases — Maladies hypertensives........................	5 328	10.4	7 548	14.3	-	1	2	1
Ischaemic heart disease — Cardiopathie ischémique........................	29 677	57.9	23 508	44.6	3	4	2	-

21. Death and death rates by cause and sex: 2002 - 2006
Décès et taux de mortalité par cause et sexe : 2002 - 2006 (continued - suite)

	Mexico - Mexique				Montserrat			
	2005 (+C)				2002 (+C)		2003 (+C)	
Cause of death — Cause de décès	Male — Masculin		Female — Féminin		Male — Masculin	Female — Féminin	Male — Masculin	Female — Féminin
	Number Nombre	Rate Taux	Number Nombre	Rate Taux	Number Nombre	Number Nombre	Number Nombre	Number Nombre
Cerebrovascular disease — Maladie cérébrovasculaire	12 875	25.1	14 493	27.5	-	1	5	3
Diseases of arteries, arterioles and capillaries — Maladies des artères, artérioles et capillaires	1 036	2.0	1 040	2.0	-	1	-	1
Diseases of the respiratory system — Maladies de l'appareil respiratoire								
Total	23 209	45.3	20 098	38.1	3	1	3	1
Influenza — Grippe	11	♦0.0	9	♦0.0	-	-	-	-
Pneumonia — Pneumopathies	6 946	13.6	6 152	11.7	-	-	1	-
Chronic lower respiratory diseases — Maladies chroniques des voies respiratoires inférieures	12 083	23.6	10 162	19.3	2	-	1	1
Diseases of the digestive system — Maladies de l'appareil digestif								
Total	31 034	60.6	16 601	31.5	2	2	-	-
Gastric and duodenal ulcer — Ulcère de l'estomac et du duodénum	1 487	2.9	1 334	2.5	1	1	-	-
Diseases of the liver — Maladies du foie	22 343	43.6	7 882	15.0	-	-	-	-
Diseases of the musculoskeletal system and connective tissue — Maladies du système ostéo-articularie, des muscles et du tissu conjonctif	1 030	2.0	2 263	4.3	-	-	-	-
Diseases of the genitourinary system — Maladies de l'appareil génito-urinaire								
Total	7 905	15.4	6 348	12.0	-	1	2	-
Disorders of kidney and ureter — Affections du rein et de l'uretère	6 381	12.5	5 462	10.4	-	1	-	-
Hyperplasia of prostate — Hyperplasie de la prostate	662	9.0	..	..	-	..	1	-
Pregnancy, childbirth and the puerperium — Grossesse, accouchement et puerpéralité								
Total	..	..	1 269	49.4	..	-	..	-
Pregnancy with abortive outcome — Grossesse se terminant par un avortement	..	..	93	3.6	..	-	..	-
Other direct obstetric causes — Autres décès maternels directs	..	..	918	35.7	..	-	..	-
Indirect obstetric causes — Décès maternels indirects	..	..	222	8.6	..	-	..	-
Certain conditions originating in the perinatal period — Certaines affections dont l'origine se situe dans la période périnatale	9 441	735.1	7 018	547.0	-	-	-	-
Congenital malformations, deformations and chromosomal abnormalities — Malformations congénitales et anomalies chromosomiques	4 889	380.7	4 327	337.3	-	-	-	-
Symptoms, signs and abnormal clinical and laboratory findings, not elsewhere classified — Symptômes, signes et résultats anormaux d'examens cliniques et de laboratoire, non classés ailleurs	4 713	9.2	4 758	9.0	-	-	-	-
All other diseases — Toutes autres maladies	361	0.7	724	1.4	2	-	-	-
External causes — Causes externes								
Total	41 374	80.7	11 127	21.1	1	-	-	1
Accidents								
Total	26 416	51.6	8 202	15.6	-	-	-	1
Transport accidents — Accidents de transport	12 912	25.2	3 500	6.6	-	-	-	-
Falls — Chutes	1 832	3.6	501	1.0	-	-	-	-
Accidental drowning and submersion — Noyade et submersion accidentelles	1 843	3.6	352	0.7	-	-	-	-
Exposure to smoke, fire and flames — Exposition à la fumée, au feu et aux flammes	492	1.0	209	0.4	-	-	-	1
Accidental poisoning by and exposure to noxious substances — Intoxication accidentelle par des substances nocives et exposition à ces substances	623	1.2	259	0.5	-	-	-	-
Intentional self-harm — Lésions auto-infligées	3 571	7.0	735	1.4	-	-	-	-
Assault — Agresssions	8 552	16.7	1 286	2.4	-	-	-	-
All other external causes — Toutes autres causes externes	2 835	5.5	904	1.7	1	-	-	-

21. Death and death rates by cause and sex: 2002 - 2006
Décès et taux de mortalité par cause et sexe : 2002 - 2006 (continued - suite)

Cause of death — Cause de décès	Nicaragua 2004 (+U) Male — Masculin Number Nombre	Nicaragua 2004 (+U) Female — Féminin Number Nombre	Nicaragua 2005 (+U) Male — Masculin Number Nombre	Nicaragua 2005 (+U) Female — Féminin Number Nombre	Panama 2003 (+U) Male — Masculin Number Nombre	Panama 2003 (+U) Female — Féminin Number Nombre	Panama 2004 (+U) Male — Masculin Number Nombre	Panama 2004 (+U) Female — Féminin Number Nombre
TOTAL	9 058	6 752	9 708	7 046	7 763	5 485	7 793	5 681
Certain infectious and parasitic diseases — Certaines maladies infectieuses et parasitaires								
Total	423	278	484	370	568	291	568	317
Intestinal infectious diseases — Maladies infectieuses intestinales	124	102	125	125	67	53	70	55
Tuberculosis — Tuberculose	116	63	126	68	117	58	86	64
Tetanus — Tétanos	3	1	4	-	-	-	-	-
Diphtheria — Diphtérie	-	-	-	-	-	-	-	-
Whooping cough — Coqueluche	-	-	-	-	-	1	1	1
Meningococcal infection — Infection à méningocoques	6	4	4	3	-	2	1	-
Septicaemia — Septicémie	60	52	87	99	48	46	58	52
Acute poliomyelitis — Poliomyélite aiguë	-	-	-	-	-	-	-	-
Measles — Rougeole	-	-	-	-	-	-	-	-
Viral hepatitis — Hépatite virale	14	9	17	11	4	2	8	6
Human immunodeficiency virus [HIV] disease — Maladies dues au virus de l'immunodéficience humaine (VIH)	69	14	65	25	311	109	323	114
Malaria — Paludisme	2	2	5	3	2	2	1	1
Neoplasms — Tumeurs	867	1 109	974	1 037	1 210	982	1 146	1 085
Malignant neoplasms — Tumeurs malignes								
Total	862	1 089	960	1 021	1 171	950	1 120	1 059
Malignant neoplasm of lip, oral cavity and pharynx — Tumeur maligne de la lèvre, de la cavité buccale et du pharynx	21	7	24	6	35	9	27	12
Malignant neoplasm of oesophagus — Tumeur maligne de l'oesophage	12	5	14	4	26	7	33	8
Malignant neoplasm of stomach — Tumeur maligne de l'estomac	131	110	144	108	152	83	112	101
Malignant neoplasm of colon, rectosigmoid junction, rectum, anus and anal canal — Tumeur maligne du côlon, de la jonction recto-sigmoïdienne, du rectum, de l'anus et du canal anal	50	56	61	51	89	81	97	98
Malignant neoplasm of liver and intrahepatic bile ducts — Tumeur maligne du foie et des voies bilaires intrahépatiques	81	101	98	90	40	37	57	45
Malignant neoplasm of pancreas — Tumeur maligne du pancréas	37	43	44	37	37	49	48	49
Malignant neoplasm of trachea, bronchus and lung — Tumeur maligne de la trachée, des bronches et du poumon	76	63	79	63	165	80	154	79
Malignant neoplasm of female breast — Tumeur maligne du sein chez la femme	..	110	..	94	..	119	..	132
Malignant neoplasm of cervix uteri — Tumeur maligne du col de l'utérus	..	238	..	218	..	146	..	133
Malignant neoplasm of prostate — Tumeur maligne de la prostate	160	..	160	..	266	..	234	..
Malignant neoplasm of lymphoid, haematopoietic and related tissue — Tumeurs malignes primitives ou présumées primitives des tissus lymphoïde, hématopoïétique et apparentés	117	106	128	82	129	99	119	101
Disorders of the blood and blood-forming organs and certain disorders involving the immune mechanism — Maladies du sang et des organes hématopoïétiques et certains troubles du système immunitaire								
Total	34	59	62	54	47	43	51	55
Anaemias — Anémies	28	50	52	49	42	40	41	43
Endocrine, nutritional and metabolic diseases — Maladies endocriniennes, nutritionnelles et métaboliques								
Total	493	700	591	700	426	541	403	537
Diabetes mellitus — Diabète sucré	389	571	474	587	341	439	312	449
Malnutrition — Malnutrition	87	106	97	04	05	78	48	66
Mental and behavioural disorders — Troubles mentaux et du comportement	213	23	222	11	32	3	18	6
Diseases of the nervous system — Maladies du système nerveux	170	119	159	132	184	125	174	149
Diseases of the circulatory system — Maladies de l'appareil circulatoire								
Total	2 127	1 962	2 134	2 069	1 936	1 527	2 029	1 604
Acute rheumatic fever and chronic rheumatic heart diseases — Rhumatisme articularie aigu et cardiopathies rhumatismales chroniques	17	26	7	21	10	16	12	10
Hypertensive diseases — Maladies hypertensives	260	238	229	216	99	88	100	78
Ischaemic heart disease — Cardiopathie ischémique	1 069	863	1 010	969	768	550	795	564

Cause of death — Cause de décès	Nicaragua				Panama			
	2004 (+U)		2005 (+U)		2003 (+U)		2004 (+U)	
	Male — Masculin	Female — Féminin	Male — Masculin	Female — Féminin	Male — Masculin	Female — Féminin	Male — Masculin	Female — Féminin
	Number Nombre	Number Nombre	Number Nombre	Number Nombre	Number Nombre	Number Nombre	Number Nombre	Number Nombre
Cerebrovascular disease — Maladie cérébrovasculaire........................	532	564	614	589	719	620	723	655
Diseases of arteries, arterioles and capillaries — Maladies des artères, artérioles et capillaires	6	9	12	13	70	48	64	48
Diseases of the respiratory system — Maladies de l'appareil respiratoire								
Total..	541	506	684	624	546	439	641	502
Influenza — Grippe	-	-	1	-	3	4	-	-
Pneumonia — Pneumopathies	237	231	351	302	180	157	202	186
Chronic lower respiratory diseases — Maladies chroniques des voies respiratoires inférieures	264	232	281	271	273	202	295	206
Diseases of the digestive system — Maladies de l'appareil digestif								
Total..	802	399	773	377	301	257	330	208
Gastric and duodenal ulcer — Ulcère de l'estomac et du duodénum	39	30	46	34	26	21	25	17
Diseases of the liver — Maladies du foie	546	177	514	183	145	92	157	78
Diseases of the musculoskeletal system and connective tissue — Maladies du système ostéo-articulaire, des muscles et du tissu conjonctif	23	62	17	76	13	34	14	40
Diseases of the genitourinary system — Maladies de l'appareil génito-urinaire								
Total..	548	189	607	192	205	145	248	171
Disorders of kidney and ureter — Affections du rein et de l'uretère	514	181	585	182	172	127	212	158
Hyperplasia of prostate — Hyperplasie de la prostate..................	26	..	19	..	17	..	19	..
Pregnancy, childbirth and the puerperium — Grossesse, accouchement et puerpéralité								
Total..	..	108	..	93	..	34	..	23
Pregnancy with abortive outcome — Grossesse se terminant par un avortement	..	5	..	1	..	8	..	4
Other direct obstetric causes — Autres décès maternels directs	..	91	..	79	..	17	..	15
Indirect obstetric causes — Décès maternels indirects........................	..	12	..	13	..	9	..	4
Certain conditions originating in the perinatal period — Certaines affections dont l'origine se situe dans la période périnatale	598	382	644	456	192	140	202	142
Congenital malformations, deformations and chromosomal abnormalities — Malformations congénitales et anomalies chromosomiques	252	202	220	189	196	160	181	134
Symptoms, signs and abnormal clinical and laboratory findings, not elsewhere classified — Symptômes, signes et résultats anormaux d'examens cliniques et de laboratoire, non classés ailleurs	285	295	301	283	654	473	623	445
All other diseases — Toutes autres maladies.............................	2	2	4	2	25	27	20	26
External causes — Causes externes								
Total..	1 680	357	1 832	381	1 228	264	1 145	237
Accidents								
Total..	875	185	958	223	713	202	656	169
Transport accidents — Accidents de transport	378	75	432	96	368	91	346	66
Falls — Chutes	52	10	64	20	72	19	52	24
Accidental drowning and submersion — Noyade et submersion accidentelles	154	19	171	25	113	22	108	18
Exposure to smoke, fire and flames — Exposition à la fumée, au feu et aux flammes	11	6	7	4	9	6	8	2
Accidental poisoning by and exposure to noxious substances — Intoxication accidentelle par des substances nocives et exposition à ces substances	17	6	12	5	23	13	17	9
Intentional self-harm — Lésions auto-infligées..................	293	100	301	90	174	21	152	35
Assault — Agressions	476	60	514	57	318	38	297	25
All other external causes — Toutes autres causes externes..................	36	12	59	11	23	3	40	8

21. Death and death rates by cause and sex: 2002 - 2006
Décès et taux de mortalité par cause et sexe : 2002 - 2006 (continued - suite)

Cause of death — Cause de décès	Puerto Rico - Porto Rico 2003 (+...) Male — Masculin Number Nombre	Puerto Rico - Porto Rico 2003 (+...) Female — Féminin Number Nombre	Puerto Rico - Porto Rico 2005 (+...) Male — Masculin Number Nombre	Puerto Rico - Porto Rico 2005 (+...) Female — Féminin Number Nombre	Saint Kitts and Nevis - Saint-Kitts-et-Nevis 2004 (+C) Male — Masculin Number Nombre	Saint Kitts and Nevis - Saint-Kitts-et-Nevis 2004 (+C) Female — Féminin Number Nombre	Saint Kitts and Nevis - Saint-Kitts-et-Nevis 2005 (+C) Male — Masculin Number Nombre	Saint Kitts and Nevis - Saint-Kitts-et-Nevis 2005 (+C) Female — Féminin Number Nombre
TOTAL.........	15 656	12 546	16 379	13 152	216	180	179	177
Certain infectious and parasitic diseases — Certaines maladies infectieuses et parasitaires								
Total.........	918	574	976	649	24	15	6	8
Intestinal infectious diseases — Maladies infectieuses intestinales...........	-	2	19	9	1	1	2	-
Tuberculosis — Tuberculose.........	11	5	11	6	-	-	-	-
Tetanus — Tétanos....	-	-	1	2	-	-	-	-
Diphtheria — Diphtérie.........	-	-	-	-	-	-	-	-
Whooping cough — Coqueluche.........	-	-	-	-	-	-	-	-
Meningococcal infection — Infection à méningocoques.........	1	-	1	1	-	-	-	-
Septicaemia — Septicémie.........	415	414	432	428	19	13	1	6
Acute poliomyelitis — Poliomyélite aiguë.........	-	-	-	-	-	-	-	-
Measles — Rougeole.........	-	-	-	-	-	-	-	-
Viral hepatitis — Hépatite virale.........	38	14	41	16	-	-	-	-
Human immunodeficiency virus [HIV] disease — Maladies dues au virus de l'immunodéficience humaine (VIH).........	379	106	387	132	4	-	2	1
Malaria — Paludisme.........	-	-	-	-	-	-	-	-
Neoplasms — Tumeurs.........	2 702	2 195	2 788	2 198	35	22	29	15
Malignant neoplasms — Tumeurs malignes								
Total.........	2 630	2 124	2 703	2 134	35	22	29	15
Malignant neoplasm of lip, oral cavity and pharynx — Tumeur maligne de la lèvre, de la cavité buccale et du pharynx.........	110	30	112	26	2	-	-	-
Malignant neoplasm of oesophagus — Tumeur maligne de l'oesophage......	121	43	109	30	1	-	-	-
Malignant neoplasm of stomach — Tumeur maligne de l'estomac...........	145	96	145	102	3	2	-	1
Malignant neoplasm of colon, rectosigmoid junction, rectum, anus and anal canal — Tumeur maligne du côlon, de la jonction recto-sigmoïdienne, du rectum, de l'anus et du canal anal.........	326	284	316	296	4	3	2	2
Malignant neoplasm of liver and intrahepatic bile ducts — Tumeur maligne du foie et des voies bilaires intrahépatiques.........	166	108	136	90	3	-	1	2
Malignant neoplasm of pancreas — Tumeur maligne du pancréas...........	107	80	115	106	-	3	3	2
Malignant neoplasm of trachea, bronchus and lung — Tumeur maligne de la trachée, des bronches et du poumon.........	378	204	336	209	2	2	1	-
Malignant neoplasm of female breast — Tumeur maligne du sein chez la femme.........	..	386	..	364	..	3	..	1
Malignant neoplasm of cervix uteri — Tumeur maligne du col de l'utérus......	..	56	..	50	..	1	..	2
Malignant neoplasm of prostate — Tumeur maligne de la prostate...........	479	..	510	..	13	..	9	..
Malignant neoplasm of lymphoid, haematopoietic and related tissue — Tumeurs malignes primitives ou présumées primitives des tissus lymphoïde, hématopoïétique et apparentés.........	250	228	271	210	1	3	5	-
Disorders of the blood and blood-forming organs and certain disorders involving the immune mechanism — Maladies du sang et des organes hématopoïétiques et certains troubles du système immunitaire								
Total.........	159	132	172	151	1	2	1	2
Anaemias — Anémies.........	91	87	96	104	1	2	1	1
Endocrine, nutritional and metabolic diseases — Maladies endocriniennes, nutritionnelles et métaboliques								
Total.........	1 436	1 630	1 689	1 710	7	7	14	24
Diabetes mellitus — Diabète sucré.........	1 203	1 316	1 373	1 417	3	3	12	18
Malnutrition — Malnutrition.........	18	28	36	31	-	1	-	-
Mental and behavioural disorders — Troubles mentaux et du comportement	166	78	203	73	1	-	5	2
Diseases of the nervous system — Maladies du système nerveux...........	668	794	756	1 101	4	3	8	5
Diseases of the circulatory system — Maladies de l'appareil circulatoire								
Total.........	4 244	4 002	4 490	3 848	69	93	50	83
Acute rheumatic fever and chronic rheumatic heart diseases — Rhumatisme articulaire aigu et cardiopathies rhumatismales chroniques.........	10	12	1	9	-	-	-	-
Hypertensive diseases — Maladies hypertensives.........	404	428	437	432	3	5	6	9
Ischaemic heart disease — Cardiopathie ischémique.........	2 258	1 939	2 444	1 826	16	17	25	19

	Puerto Rico - Porto Rico				Saint Kitts and Nevis - Saint-Kitts-et-Nevis			
	2003 (+...)		2005 (+...)		2004 (+C)		2005 (+C)	
Cause of death — Cause de décès	Male — Masculin	Female — Féminin	Male — Masculin	Female — Féminin	Male — Masculin	Female — Féminin	Male — Masculin	Female — Féminin
	Number Nombre	Number Nombre	Number Nombre	Number Nombre	Number Nombre	Number Nombre	Number Nombre	Number Nombre
Cerebrovascular disease — Maladie cérébrovasculaire......................	759	792	759	766	27	33	9	28
Diseases of arteries, arterioles and capillaries — Maladies des artères, artérioles et capillaires	110	91	129	97	-	1	-	3
Diseases of the respiratory system — Maladies de l'appareil respiratoire								
Total...........................	1 454	1 375	1 523	1 453	20	17	8	11
Influenza — Grippe	-	-	1	-	-	-	-	-
Pneumonia — Pneumopathies	542	511	588	492	6	8	2	2
Chronic lower respiratory diseases — Maladies chroniques des voies respiratoires inférieures	606	555	609	606	2	2	2	2
Diseases of the digestive system — Maladies de l'appareil digestif								
Total...........................	983	494	917	551	12	5	9	5
Gastric and duodenal ulcer — Ulcère de l'estomac et du duodénum	16	7	20	7	1	-	-	-
Diseases of the liver — Maladies du foie	605	214	568	257	6	2	7	-
Diseases of the musculoskeletal system and connective tissue — Maladies du système ostéo-articularie, des muscles et du tissu conjonctif	50	85	48	105	-	-	1	1
Diseases of the genitourinary system — Maladies de l'appareil génito-urinaire								
Total...........................	658	521	629	539	11	8	10	2
Disorders of kidney and ureter — Affections du rein et de l'uretère	571	415	552	425	10	8	8	2
Hyperplasia of prostate — Hyperplasie de la prostate........................	4	..	4	..	-	..	-	..
Pregnancy, childbirth and the puerperium — Grossesse, accouchement et puerpéralité								
Total...........................	..	8	..	5	..	-	..	-
Pregnancy with abortive outcome — Grossesse se terminant par un avortement	..	2	..	-	..	-	..	-
Other direct obstetric causes — Autres décès maternels directs	..	6	..	5	..	-	..	-
Indirect obstetric causes — Décès maternels indirects.......................	..	-	..	-	..	-	..	-
Certain conditions originating in the perinatal period — Certaines affections dont l'origine se situe dans la période périnatale	168	124	131	119	7	3	6	2
Congenital malformations, deformations and chromosomal abnormalities — Malformations congénitales et anomalies chromosomiques	82	59	74	67	-	2	1	1
Symptoms, signs and abnormal clinical and laboratory findings, not elsewhere classified — Symptômes, signes et résultats anormaux d'examens cliniques et de laboratoire, non classés ailleurs	109	98	81	88	-	1	-	4
All other diseases — Toutes autres maladies.............................	74	90	72	113	-	-	3	7
External causes — Causes externes								
Total...........................	1 785	287	1 830	382	25	2	28	5
Accidents								
Total...........................	835	202	843	258	14	2	11	3
Transport accidents — Accidents de transport	398	112	389	90	5	-	7	3
Falls — Chutes	102	36	127	58	3	2	3	-
Accidental drowning and submersion — Noyade et submersion accidentelles	42	4	30	7	3	-	-	-
Exposure to smoke, fire and flames — Exposition à la fumée, au feu et aux flammes	13	3	12	5	1	-	-	-
Accidental poisoning by and exposure to noxious substances — Intoxication accidentelle par des substances nocives et exposition à ces substances	198	15	139	21	-	-	-	-
Intentional self-harm — Lésions auto-infligées..............................	240	22	248	40	1	-	1	-
Assault — Agresssions	690	50	705	56	9	-	-	-
All other external causes — Toutes autres causes externes...................	20	13	34	28	1	-	16	2

Cause of death — Cause de décès	Saint Lucia - Sainte-Lucie 2002 (C) Male — Masculin Number Nombre	Saint Lucia - Sainte-Lucie 2002 (C) Female — Féminin Number Nombre	Saint Pierre and Miquelon - Saint Pierre-et-Miquelon 2005 (C) Male — Masculin Number Nombre	Saint Pierre and Miquelon - Saint Pierre-et-Miquelon 2005 (C) Female — Féminin Number Nombre	Saint Vincent and the Grenadines - Saint Vincent-et-les Grenadines 2002 (+C) Male — Masculin Number Nombre	Saint Vincent and the Grenadines - Saint Vincent-et-les Grenadines 2002 (+C) Female — Féminin Number Nombre	Saint Vincent and the Grenadines 2003 (+C) Male — Masculin Number Nombre	Saint Vincent and the Grenadines 2003 (+C) Female — Féminin Number Nombre
TOTAL	487	452	28	25	379	386	425	349
Certain infectious and parasitic diseases — Certaines maladies infectieuses et parasitaires								
Total	22	16	-	1	34	27	42	14
Intestinal infectious diseases — Maladies infectieuses intestinales	-	-	-	-	-	2	4	1
Tuberculosis — Tuberculose	-	-	-	-	1	-	6	-
Tetanus — Tétanos	-	-	-	-	-	-	-	-
Diphtheria — Diphtérie	-	-	-	-	-	-	-	-
Whooping cough — Coqueluche	-	-	-	-	-	-	-	-
Meningococcal infection — Infection à méningocoques	-	-	-	-	-	-	-	-
Septicaemia — Septicémie	11	13	-	-	8	11	5	2
Acute poliomyelitis — Poliomyélite aiguë	-	-	-	-	-	-	-	-
Measles — Rougeole	-	-	-	-	-	-	-	-
Viral hepatitis — Hépatite virale	-	-	-	-	-	-	-	-
Human immunodeficiency virus [HIV] disease — Maladies dues au virus de l'immunodéficience humaine (VIH)	7	2	-	-	23	13	24	10
Malaria — Paludisme	-	-	-	-	-	-	-	-
Neoplasms — Tumeurs	105	65	6	4	58	63	69	50
Malignant neoplasms — Tumeurs malignes								
Total	105	65	6	3	56	63	69	49
Malignant neoplasm of lip, oral cavity and pharynx — Tumeur maligne de la lèvre, de la cavité buccale et du pharynx	8	2	-	-	1	2	1	2
Malignant neoplasm of oesophagus — Tumeur maligne de l'oesophage	5	2	1	-	1	-	-	-
Malignant neoplasm of stomach — Tumeur maligne de l'estomac	12	7	-	-	2	7	4	3
Malignant neoplasm of colon, rectosigmoid junction, rectum, anus and anal canal — Tumeur maligne du côlon, de la jonction recto-sigmoïdienne, du rectum, de l'anus et du canal anal	6	2	2	-	5	3	5	5
Malignant neoplasm of liver and intrahepatic bile ducts — Tumeur maligne du foie et des voies bilaires intrahépatiques	4	1	1	-	1	-	3	1
Malignant neoplasm of pancreas — Tumeur maligne du pancréas	5	5	-	-	2	6	2	2
Malignant neoplasm of trachea, bronchus and lung — Tumeur maligne de la trachée, des bronches et du poumon	4	3	1	1	3	5	7	5
Malignant neoplasm of female breast — Tumeur maligne du sein chez la femme	..	11	..	1	..	6	..	6
Malignant neoplasm of cervix uteri — Tumeur maligne du col de l'utérus	..	11	..	-	..	6	..	6
Malignant neoplasm of prostate — Tumeur maligne de la prostate	41	..	1	..	23	..	34	..
Malignant neoplasm of lymphoid, haematopoietic and related tissue — Tumeurs malignes primitives ou présumées primitives des tissus lymphoïde, hématopoïétique et apparentés	8	6	-	-	8	7	4	-
Disorders of the blood and blood-forming organs and certain disorders involving the immune mechanism — Maladies du sang et des organes hématopoïétiques et certains troubles du système immunitaire								
Total	4	1	-	-	4	8	3	3
Anaemias — Anémies	3	1	-	-	4	8	1	3
Endocrine, nutritional and metabolic diseases — Maladies endocriniennes, nutritionnelles et métaboliques								
Total	43	74	2	-	33	68	61	76
Diabetes mellitus — Diabète sucré	37	67	2	-	26	63	49	71
Malnutrition — Malnutrition	3	-	-	-	4	3	6	1
Mental and behavioural disorders — Troubles mentaux et du comportement	-	-	-	2	1	-	8	1
Diseases of the nervous system — Maladies du système nerveux	6	5	2	3	9	1	6	3
Diseases of the circulatory system — Maladies de l'appareil circulatoire								
Total	118	136	9	12	112	141	120	140
Acute rheumatic fever and chronic rheumatic heart diseases — Rhumatisme articularie aigu et cardiopathies rhumatismales chroniques	1	1	-	-	1	2	-	-
Hypertensive diseases — Maladies hypertensives	11	18	-	-	22	34	47	55
Ischaemic heart disease — Cardiopathie ischémique	18	26	3	5	43	40	29	35

Cause of death — Cause de décès	Saint Lucia - Sainte-Lucie 2002 (C) Male — Masculin Number Nombre	Female — Féminin Number Nombre	Saint Pierre and Miquelon - Saint Pierre-et-Miquelon 2005 (C) Male — Masculin Number Nombre	Female — Féminin Number Nombre	Saint Vincent and the Grenadines - Saint Vincent-et-les Grenadines 2002 (+C) Male — Masculin Number Nombre	Female — Féminin Number Nombre	2003 (+C) Male — Masculin Number Nombre	Female — Féminin Number Nombre
Cerebrovascular disease — Maladie cérébrovasculaire..........	41	54	3	4	26	48	24	27
Diseases of arteries, arterioles and capillaries — Maladies des artères, artérioles et capillaires	9	11	2	1	5	6	2	6
Diseases of the respiratory system — Maladies de l'appareil respiratoire								
Total.................	35	26	1	-	36	28	26	19
Influenza — Grippe	-	-	-	-	-	-	-	-
Pneumonia — Pneumopathies.................	13	16	-	-	23	24	11	13
Chronic lower respiratory diseases — Maladies chroniques des voies respiratoires inférieures	17	7	1	-	7	-	9	3
Diseases of the digestive system — Maladies de l'appareil digestif								
Total.................	16	14	3	1	15	7	18	11
Gastric and duodenal ulcer — Ulcère de l'estomac et du duodénum	1	-	-	-	3	2	3	2
Diseases of the liver — Maladies du foie	10	11	2	-	5	2	8	3
Diseases of the musculoskeletal system and connective tissue — Maladies du système ostéo-articularie, des muscles et du tissu conjonctif	-	-	-	-	-	2	1	1
Diseases of the genitourinary system — Maladies de l'appareil génito-urinaire								
Total.................	8	9	-	-	5	5	7	2
Disorders of kidney and ureter — Affections du rein et de l'uretère	8	9	-	-	4	5	4	2
Hyperplasia of prostate — Hyperplasie de la prostate.................	-	..	-	..	-	..	-	..
Pregnancy, childbirth and the puerperium — Grossesse, accouchement et puerpéralité								
Total.................	..	1	..	-	..	-	..	-
Pregnancy with abortive outcome — Grossesse se terminant par un avortement	..	-	..	-	..	-	..	-
Other direct obstetric causes — Autres décès maternels directs	..	1	..	-	..	-	..	-
Indirect obstetric causes — Décès maternels indirects.................	..	-	..	-	..	-	..	-
Certain conditions originating in the perinatal period — Certaines affections dont l'origine se situe dans la période périnatale	14	21	-	-	20	11	17	16
Congenital malformations, deformations and chromosomal abnormalities — Malformations congénitales et anomalies chromosomiques	1	3	1	-	-	2	6	-
Symptoms, signs and abnormal clinical and laboratory findings, not elsewhere classified — Symptômes, signes et résultats anormaux d'examens cliniques et de laboratoire, non classés ailleurs	37	55	1	1	6	4	2	4
All other diseases — Toutes autres maladies.................	-	-	-	-	3	4	3	4
External causes — Causes externes								
Total.................	78	26	3	1	43	15	36	5
Accidents								
Total.................	37	16	2	-	26	10	20	5
Transport accidents — Accidents de transport	22	11	1	-	5	3	8	3
Falls — Chutes	-	1	-	-	3	2	3	1
Accidental drowning and submersion — Noyade et submersion accidentelles.................	3	1	1	-	10	-	6	1
Exposure to smoke, fire and flames — Exposition à la fumée, au feu et aux flammes	3	-	-	-	1	2	1	-
Accidental poisoning by and exposure to noxious substances — Intoxication accidentelle par des substances nocives et exposition à ces substances	-	-	-	-	-	-	-	-
Intentional self-harm — Lésions auto-infligées.................	8	4	1	1	6	1	4	-
Assault — Agresssions	32	6	-	-	11	4	10	-
All other external causes — Toutes autres causes externes.................	1	-	-	-	-	-	2	-

	Trinidad and Tobago - Trinité-et-Tobago				Turks Caicos Islands - Îles Turques et Caïques			
	2002 (C)				2004 (...)		2005 (...)	
Cause of death — Cause de décès	Male — Masculin		Female — Féminin		Male — Masculin	Female — Féminin	Male — Masculin	Female — Féminin
	Number Nombre	Rate Taux	Number Nombre	Rate Taux	Number Nombre	Number Nombre	Number Nombre	Number Nombre
TOTAL................	5 442	850.7	4 182	657.5	31	31	32	21
Certain infectious and parasitic diseases — Certaines maladies infectieuses et parasitaires								
Total....	415	64.9	259	40.7	7	2	1	1
Intestinal infectious diseases — Maladies infectieuses intestinales...........	9	♦1.4	14	♦2.2	-	-	-	-
Tuberculosis — Tuberculose....	22	♦3.4	1	♦0.2	-	-	-	-
Tetanus — Tétanos....	-		-		-	-	-	-
Diphtheria — Diphtérie....	-		-		-	-	-	-
Whooping cough — Coqueluche....	-		-		-	-	-	-
Meningococcal infection — Infection à méningocoques....	-		-		-	-	-	-
Septicaemia — Septicémie....	40	6.3	31	4.9	-	-	-	1
Acute poliomyelitis — Poliomyélite aiguë....	-		-		-	-	-	-
Measles — Rougeole....	-		-		-	-	-	-
Viral hepatitis — Hépatite virale....	5	♦0.8	3	♦0.5	-	-	-	-
Human immunodeficiency virus [HIV] disease — Maladies dues au virus de l'immunodéficience humaine (VIH)....	304	47.5	188	29.6	7	2	1	-
Malaria — Paludisme....	1	♦0.2	-		-	-	-	-
Neoplasms — Tumeurs....	725	113.3	600	94.3	1	5	3	4
Malignant neoplasms — Tumeurs malignes								
Total....	700	109.4	574	90.3	1	5	3	4
Malignant neoplasm of lip, oral cavity and pharynx — Tumeur maligne de la lèvre, de la cavité buccale et du pharynx....	14	♦2.2	7	♦1.1	-	-	-	-
Malignant neoplasm of oesophagus — Tumeur maligne de l'oesophage......	12	♦1.9	5	♦0.8	-	-	-	-
Malignant neoplasm of stomach — Tumeur maligne de l'estomac....	42	6.6	26	♦4.1	-	-	-	-
Malignant neoplasm of colon, rectosigmoid junction, rectum, anus and anal canal — Tumeur maligne du côlon, de la jonction recto-sigmoïdienne, du rectum, de l'anus et du canal anal....	56	8.8	56	8.8	-	-	-	2
Malignant neoplasm of liver and intrahepatic bile ducts — Tumeur maligne du foie et des voies bilaires intrahépatiques....	15	♦2.3	21	♦3.3	-	-	-	-
Malignant neoplasm of pancreas — Tumeur maligne du pancréas...........	26	♦4.1	25	♦3.9	-	-	-	-
Malignant neoplasm of trachea, bronchus and lung — Tumeur maligne de la trachée, des bronches et du poumon....	79	12.3	26	♦4.1	1	-	-	-
Malignant neoplasm of female breast — Tumeur maligne du sein chez la femme....	..	..	143	...		2	-	-
Malignant neoplasm of cervix uteri — Tumeur maligne du col de l'utérus......	..	..	60	...		2	-	1
Malignant neoplasm of prostate — Tumeur maligne de la prostate.............	277	....	..	...	-		2	..
Malignant neoplasm of lymphoid, haematopoietic and related tissue — Tumeurs malignes primitives ou présumées primitives des tissus lymphoïde, hématopoïétique et apparentés....	67	10.5	43	6.8	-	-	-	-
Disorders of the blood and blood-forming organs and certain disorders involving the immune mechanism — Maladies du sang et des organes hématopoïétiques et certains troubles du système immunitaire								
Total....	53	8.3	28	♦4.4	-	-	-	-
Anaemias — Anémies....	46	7.2	25	♦3.9	-	-	-	-
Endocrine, nutritional and metabolic diseases — Maladies endocriniennes, nutritionnelles et métaboliques								
Total....	694	108.5	697	109.6	4	2	-	1
Diabetes mellitus — Diabète sucré....	632	98.8	636	100.0	3	2	-	1
Malnutrition — Malnutrition....	15	♦2.3	0	♦1.4	-	-	-	-
Mental and behavioural disorders — Troubles mentaux et du comportement	21	♦3.3	15	♦2.4	-	-	-	-
Diseases of the nervous system — Maladies du système nerveux..........	109	17.0	82	12.9	-	-	-	1
Diseases of the circulatory system — Maladies de l'appareil circulatoire								
Total....	1 887	295.0	1 668	262.3	5	13	7	7
Acute rheumatic fever and chronic rheumatic heart diseases — Rhumatisme articulaire aigu et cardiopathies rhumatismales chroniques....	9	♦1.4	10	♦1.6	-	-	-	-
Hypertensive diseases — Maladies hypertensives....	177	27.7	199	31.3	-	4	3	2
Ischaemic heart disease — Cardiopathie ischémique....	977	152.7	724	113.8	2	2	-	-

	Trinidad and Tobago - Trinité-et-Tobago				Turks Caicos Islands - Îles Turques et Caïques			
	2002 (C)				2004 (...)		2005 (...)	
Cause of death — Cause de décès	Male — Masculin		Female — Féminin		Male — Masculin	Female — Féminin	Male — Masculin	Female — Féminin
	Number Nombre	Rate Taux	Number Nombre	Rate Taux	Number Nombre	Number Nombre	Number Nombre	Number Nombre
Cerebrovascular disease — Maladie cérébrovasculaire	501	78.3	502	78.9	-	-	-	-
Diseases of arteries, arterioles and capillaries — Maladies des artères, artérioles et capillaires	39	6.1	45	7.1	-	-	-	-
Diseases of the respiratory system — Maladies de l'appareil respiratoire								
Total	282	44.1	184	28.9	5	3	4	2
Influenza — Grippe	-	-	-	-	-	-	-	-
Pneumonia — Pneumopathies	123	19.2	90	14.2	1	1	3	2
Chronic lower respiratory diseases — Maladies chroniques des voies respiratoires inférieures	112	17.5	58	9.1	1	1	-	-
Diseases of the digestive system — Maladies de l'appareil digestif								
Total	245	38.3	149	23.4	-	-	1	-
Gastric and duodenal ulcer — Ulcère de l'estomac et du duodénum	38	5.9	18	♦2.8	-	-	-	-
Diseases of the liver — Maladies du foie	109	17.0	50	7.9	-	-	-	-
Diseases of the musculoskeletal system and connective tissue — Maladies du système ostéo-articularie, des muscles et du tissu conjonctif	16	♦2.5	44	6.9	-	-	-	-
Diseases of the genitourinary system — Maladies de l'appareil génito-urinaire								
Total	132	20.6	69	10.8	-	-	-	1
Disorders of kidney and ureter — Affections du rein et de l'uretère	103	16.1	59	9.3	-	-	-	1
Hyperplasia of prostate — Hyperplasie de la prostate	16	...	..	..	-	-	-	-
Pregnancy, childbirth and the puerperium — Grossesse, accouchement et puerpéralité								
Total	..	..	5	♦29.4	..	1	..	-
Pregnancy with abortive outcome — Grossesse se terminant par un avortement	..	..	-	-	..	1	..	-
Other direct obstetric causes — Autres décès maternels directs	..	..	5	♦29.4	..	-	..	-
Indirect obstetric causes — Décès maternels indirects	..	..	-	-	..	-	..	-
Certain conditions originating in the perinatal period — Certaines affections dont l'origine se situe dans la période périnatale	138	1 602.2	101	1 205.7	1	-	1	-
Congenital malformations, deformations and chromosomal abnormalities — Malformations congénitales et anomalies chromosomiques	63	731.5	52	620.7	-	-	-	-
Symptoms, signs and abnormal clinical and laboratory findings, not elsewhere classified — Symptômes, signes et résultats anormaux d'examens cliniques et de laboratoire, non classés ailleurs	73	11.4	73	11.5	3	4	-	2
All other diseases — Toutes autres maladies	13	♦2.0	18	♦2.8	-	-	-	-
External causes — Causes externes								
Total	576	90.0	138	21.7	5	1	15	2
Accidents								
Total	260	40.6	79	12.4	1	-	14	2
Transport accidents — Accidents de transport	145	22.7	34	5.3	1	-	6	1
Falls — Chutes	20	♦3.1	5	♦0.8	-	-	-	-
Accidental drowning and submersion — Noyade et submersion accidentelles	37	5.8	7	♦1.1	-	-	-	-
Exposure to smoke, fire and flames — Exposition à la fumée, au feu et aux flammes	11	♦1.7	10	♦1.6	-	-	-	-
Accidental poisoning by and exposure to noxious substances — Intoxication accidentelle par des substances nocives et exposition à ces substances	7	♦1.1	2	♦0.3	-	-	-	-
Intentional self-harm — Lésions auto-infligées	130	20.3	27	♦4.2	1	-	-	-
Assault — Agresssions	158	24.7	21	♦3.3	-	-	-	-
All other external causes — Toutes autres causes externes	28	♦4.4	11	♦1.7	3	1	1	-

21. Death and death rates by cause and sex: 2002 - 2006
Décès et taux de mortalité par cause et sexe : 2002 - 2006 (continued - suite)

United States - États-Unis

Cause of death — Cause de décès	2004 (C)				2005 (C)			
	Male — Masculin		Female — Féminin		Male — Masculin		Female — Féminin	
	Number Nombre	Rate Taux	Number Nombre	Rate Taux	Number Nombre	Rate Taux	Number Nombre	Rate Taux
TOTAL..........	1 181 668	817.6	1 215 947	815.6	1 207 675	827.2	1 240 342	824.6
Certain infectious and parasitic diseases — Certaines maladies infectieuses et parasitaires								
Total........	34 303	23.7	30 315	20.3	35 084	24.0	31 423	20.9
Intestinal infectious diseases — Maladies infectieuses intestinales............	1 647	1.1	2 744	1.8	2 230	1.5	3 484	2.3
Tuberculosis — Tuberculose.........	406	0.3	251	0.2	392	0.3	256	0.2
Tetanus — Tétanos............	1	♦0.0	3	♦0.0	-	-	1	♦0.0
Diphtheria — Diphtérie.............	-	-	-	-	-	-	-	-
Whooping cough — Coqueluche.........	10	♦0.0	6	♦0.0	19	♦0.0	12	♦0.0
Meningococcal infection — Infection à méningocoques.....................	79	0.1	59	0.0	68	0.0	55	0.0
Septicaemia — Septicémie..........	15 011	10.4	18 362	12.3	15 322	10.5	18 814	12.5
Acute poliomyelitis — Poliomyélite aiguë...	-	-	-	-	-	-	-	-
Measles — Rougeole.............	-	-	-	-	1	♦0.0	-	-
Viral hepatitis — Hépatite virale............	3 513	2.4	1 869	1.3	3 612	2.5	1 917	1.3
Human immunodeficiency virus [HIV] disease — Maladies dues au virus de l'immunodéficience humaine (VIH)..........	9 506	6.6	3 557	2.4	9 189	6.3	3 354	2.2
Malaria — Paludisme.............	8	♦0.0	-	-	4	♦0.0	2	♦0.0
Neoplasms — Tumeurs....................	293 594	203.1	273 874	183.7	297 242	203.6	275 780	183.4
Malignant neoplasms — Tumeurs malignes								
Total........	286 830	198.5	267 058	179.1	290 422	198.9	268 890	178.8
Malignant neoplasm of lip, oral cavity and pharynx — Tumeur maligne de la lèvre, de la cavité buccale et du pharynx	5 312	3.7	2 514	1.7	5 273	3.6	2 500	1.7
Malignant neoplasm of oesophagus — Tumeur maligne de l'oesophage......	10 081	7.0	2 942	2.0	10 611	7.3	2 888	1.9
Malignant neoplasm of stomach — Tumeur maligne de l'estomac............	6 958	4.8	4 901	3.3	6 752	4.6	4 762	3.2
Malignant neoplasm of colon, rectosigmoid junction, rectum, anus and anal canal — Tumeur maligne du côlon, de la jonction recto-sigmoïdienne, du rectum, de l'anus et du canal anal	26 930	18.6	26 842	18.0	26 843	18.4	26 409	17.6
Malignant neoplasm of liver and intrahepatic bile ducts — Tumeur maligne du foie et des voies bilaires intrahépatiques......	9 832	6.8	5 489	3.7	10 548	7.2	5 528	3.7
Malignant neoplasm of pancreas — Tumeur maligne du pancréas............	15 776	10.9	15 996	10.7	16 147	11.1	16 613	11.0
Malignant neoplasm of trachea, bronchus and lung — Tumeur maligne de la trachée, des bronches et du poumon.........	89 630	62.0	68 461	45.9	90 187	61.8	69 105	45.9
Malignant neoplasm of female breast — Tumeur maligne du sein chez la femme............	..	..	40 954	34.3	..	..	41 116	34.0
Malignant neoplasm of cervix uteri — Tumeur maligne du col de l'utérus......	..	..	3 850	3.2	..	..	3 924	3.2
Malignant neoplasm of prostate — Tumeur maligne de la prostate............	29 004	75.0	..	..	28 905	72.6	..	..
Malignant neoplasm of lymphoid, haematopoietic and related tissue — Tumeurs malignes primitives ou présumées primitives des tissus lymphoïde, hématopoïétique et apparentés	29 522	20.4	25 123	16.9	30 031	20.6	24 997	16.6
Disorders of the blood and blood-forming organs and certain disorders involving the immune mechanism — Maladies du sang et des organes hématopoïétiques et certains troubles du système immunitaire								
Total........	4 066	2.8	5 357	3.6	4 104	2.8	5 486	3.6
Anaemias — Anémies............	1 833	1.3	2 742	1.8	1 787	1.2	2 837	1.9
Endocrine, nutritional and metabolic diseases — Maladies endocriniennes, nutritionnelles et métaboliques								
Total........	46 482	32.2	52 531	35.2	48 651	33.3	54 473	36.2
Diabetes mellitus — Diabète sucré............	35 267	24.4	37 871	25.4	36 538	25.0	38 581	25.7
Malnutrition — Malnutrition............	1 026	0.7	1 821	1.2	1 059	0.7	1 944	1.3
Mental and behavioural disorders — Troubles mentaux et du comportement	23 382	16.2	38 142	25.6	26 519	18.2	44 947	29.9
Diseases of the nervous system — Maladies du système nerveux..........	43 313	30.0	68 438	45.9	46 736	32.0	73 974	49.2
Diseases of the circulatory system — Maladies de l'appareil circulatoire								
Total........	408 541	282.7	457 321	306.7	407 935	279.4	452 907	301.1
Acute rheumatic fever and chronic rheumatic heart diseases — Rhumatisme articularie aigu et cardiopathies rhumatismales chroniques	1 009	0.7	2 245	1.5	1 044	0.7	2 321	1.5
Hypertensive diseases — Maladies hypertensives.........	23 099	16.0	31 607	21.2	24 045	16.5	33 310	22.1
Ischaemic heart disease — Cardiopathie ischémique..........	233 538	161.6	217 788	146.1	232 115	159.0	213 572	142.0
Cerebrovascular disease — Maladie cérébrovasculaire..........	58 800	40.7	91 274	61.2	56 586	38.8	86 993	57.8

21. Death and death rates by cause and sex: 2002 - 2006
Décès et taux de mortalité par cause et sexe : 2002 - 2006 (continued - suite)

United States - États-Unis

Cause of death — Cause de décès	2004 (C)				2005 (C)			
	Male — Masculin		Female — Féminin		Male — Masculin		Female — Féminin	
	Number Nombre	Rate Taux	Number Nombre	Rate Taux	Number Nombre	Rate Taux	Number Nombre	Rate Taux
Diseases of arteries, arterioles and capillaries — Maladies des artères, artérioles et capillaires	16 816	11.6	18 738	12.6	16 895	11.6	18 563	12.3
Diseases of the respiratory system — Maladies de l'appareil respiratoire								
Total	108 659	75.2	118 426	79.4	113 549	77.8	126 125	83.9
Influenza — Grippe	421	0.3	679	0.5	657	0.5	1 155	0.8
Pneumonia — Pneumopathies	26 440	18.3	32 124	21.5	27 395	18.8	33 794	22.5
Chronic lower respiratory diseases — Maladies chroniques des voies respiratoires inférieures	58 627	40.6	63 336	42.5	62 422	42.8	68 485	45.5
Diseases of the digestive system — Maladies de l'appareil digestif								
Total	43 327	30.0	42 978	28.8	44 382	30.4	42 984	28.6
Gastric and duodenal ulcer — Ulcère de l'estomac et du duodénum	1 669	1.2	1 966	1.3	1 707	1.2	1 744	1.2
Diseases of the liver — Maladies du foie	22 659	15.7	13 363	9.0	23 284	15.9	13 499	9.0
Diseases of the musculoskeletal system and connective tissue — Maladies du système ostéo-articularie, des muscles et du tissu conjonctif	4 239	2.9	10 045	6.7	4 361	3.0	10 057	6.7
Diseases of the genitourinary system — Maladies de l'appareil génito-urinaire								
Total	26 788	18.5	33 532	22.5	27 949	19.1	34 821	23.2
Disorders of kidney and ureter — Affections du rein et de l'uretère	21 389	14.8	23 355	15.7	22 247	15.2	23 885	15.9
Hyperplasia of prostate — Hyperplasie de la prostate	507	1.3	..	..	525	1.3	..	..
Pregnancy, childbirth and the puerperium — Grossesse, accouchement et puerpéralité								
Total	..	..	697	17.0	..	..	760	18.4
Pregnancy with abortive outcome — Grossesse se terminant par un avortement	..	..	32	0.8	..	..	33	0.8
Other direct obstetric causes — Autres décès maternels directs	..	..	375	9.1	..	..	431	10.4
Indirect obstetric causes — Décès maternels indirects	..	..	133	3.2	..	..	159	3.8
Certain conditions originating in the perinatal period — Certaines affections dont l'origine se situe dans la période périnatale	8 141	386.8	6 152	306.5	8 229	388.3	6 392	316.5
Congenital malformations, deformations and chromosomal abnormalities — Malformations congénitales et anomalies chromosomiques	5 423	257.7	5 075	252.8	5 447	257.1	4 963	245.8
Symptoms, signs and abnormal clinical and laboratory findings, not elsewhere classified — Symptômes, signes et résultats anormaux d'examens cliniques et de laboratoire, non classés ailleurs	13 711	9.5	16 412	11.0	14 644	10.0	17 350	11.5
All other diseases — Toutes autres maladies	1 586	1.1	2 698	1.8	1 676	1.1	2 661	1.8
External causes — Causes externes								
Total	116 113	80.3	53 954	36.2	121 167	83.0	55 239	36.7
Accidents								
Total	70 948	49.1	39 438	26.5	75 197	51.5	40 921	27.2
Transport accidents — Accidents de transport	32 815	22.7	14 570	9.8	33 546	23.0	14 171	9.4
Falls — Chutes	9 856	6.8	8 951	6.0	10 154	7.0	9 502	6.3
Accidental drowning and submersion — Noyade et submersion accidentelles	2 594	1.8	714	0.5	2 818	1.9	764	0.5
Exposure to smoke, fire and flames — Exposition à la fumée, au feu et aux flammes	1 902	1.3	1 327	0.9	1 886	1.3	1 311	0.9
Accidental poisoning by and exposure to noxious substances — Intoxication accidentelle par des substances nocives et exposition à ces substances	13 934	9.6	7 016	4.7	15 884	10.9	7 734	5.1
Intentional self-harm — Lésions auto-infligées	25 504	17.6	6 859	4.6	25 848	17.7	6 711	4.5
Assault — Agresssions	13 418	9.3	3 747	2.5	14 173	9.7	3 714	2.5
All other external causes — Toutes autres causes externes	6 243	4.3	3 910	2.6	5 949	4.1	3 893	2.6

Cause of death — Cause de décès	United States Virgin Islands - Îles Vierges américaines				Argentina - Argentine			
	2003 (...)		2005 (...)		2004 (+C)			
	Male — Masculin	Female — Féminin	Male — Masculin	Female — Féminin	Male — Masculin		Female — Féminin	
	Number Nombre	Number Nombre	Number Nombre	Number Nombre	Number Nombre	Rate Taux	Number Nombre	Rate Taux
TOTAL	363	268	373	290	155 699	831.7	137 951	707.2
Certain infectious and parasitic diseases — Certaines maladies infectieuses et parasitaires								
Total	14	8	11	14	6 972	37.2	6 357	32.6
Intestinal infectious diseases — Maladies infectieuses intestinales	1	-	-	-	173	0.9	192	1.0
Tuberculosis — Tuberculose	-	-	-	-	440	2.4	233	1.2
Tetanus — Tétanos	-	-	-	-	6	◊0.0	7	◊0.0
Diphtheria — Diphtérie	-	-	-	-	-		-	
Whooping cough — Coqueluche	-	-	-	-	9	◊0.0	11	◊0.1
Meningococcal infection — Infection à méningocoques	-	-	-	-	14	◊0.1	15	◊0.1
Septicaemia — Septicémie	5	4	5	8	4 698	25.1	5 065	26.0
Acute poliomyelitis — Poliomyélite aiguë	-	-	-	-	-		-	
Measles — Rougeole	-	-	-	-	-		-	
Viral hepatitis — Hépatite virale	2	-	1	1	105	0.6	104	0.5
Human immunodeficiency virus [HIV] disease — Maladies dues au virus de l'immunodéficience humaine (VIH)	5	3	4	3	1 055	5.6	396	2.0
Malaria — Paludisme	-	-	-	-	-		-	
Neoplasms — Tumeurs	69	46	74	53	31 012	166.7	26 714	137.0
Malignant neoplasms — Tumeurs malignes								
Total	68	43	72	52	29 496	157.6	25 417	130.3
Malignant neoplasm of lip, oral cavity and pharynx — Tumeur maligne de la lèvre, de la cavité buccale et du pharynx	2	1	4	2	630	3.4	210	1.1
Malignant neoplasm of oesophagus — Tumeur maligne de l'oesophage	-	-	-	1	1 264	6.8	574	2.9
Malignant neoplasm of stomach — Tumeur maligne de l'estomac	7	1	4	4	1 952	10.4	1 043	5.3
Malignant neoplasm of colon, rectosigmoid junction, rectum, anus and anal canal — Tumeur maligne du côlon, de la jonction recto-sigmoïdienne, du rectum, de l'anus et du canal anal	11	12	4	5	3 165	16.9	2 811	14.4
Malignant neoplasm of liver and intrahepatic bile ducts — Tumeur maligne du foie et des voies bilaires intrahépatiques	1	1	-	1	959	5.1	745	3.8
Malignant neoplasm of pancreas — Tumeur maligne du pancréas	4	2	2	3	1 571	8.4	1 761	9.0
Malignant neoplasm of trachea, bronchus and lung — Tumeur maligne de la trachée, des bronches et du poumon	12	3	6	2	6 404	34.2	2 064	10.6
Malignant neoplasm of female breast — Tumeur maligne du sein chez la femme	..	6	..	12	..	..	5 244	36.2
Malignant neoplasm of cervix uteri — Tumeur maligne du col de l'utérus	..	5	..	4	..	..	1 007	7.0
Malignant neoplasm of prostate — Tumeur maligne de la prostate	16	..	35	..	3 680	92.9	..	..
Malignant neoplasm of lymphoid, haematopoietic and related tissue — Tumeurs malignes primitives ou présumées primitives des tissus lymphoïde, hématopoïétique et apparentés	3	2	5	5	1 955	10.4	1 792	9.2
Disorders of the blood and blood-forming organs and certain disorders involving the immune mechanism — Maladies du sang et des organes hématopoïétiques et certains troubles du système immunitaire								
Total	1	2	4	4	492	2.6	624	3.2
Anaemias — Anémies	-	1	1	2	350	1.9	469	2.4
Endocrine, nutritional and metabolic diseases — Maladies endocriniennes, nutritionnelles et métaboliques								
Total	25	23	20	26	6 141	32.8	6 454	33.1
Diabetes mellitus — Diabète sucré	18	16	18	24	4 685	25.0	4 552	23.3
Malnutrition — Malnutrition	3	2	-	-	725	3.9	714	3.7
Mental and behavioural disorders — Troubles mentaux et du comportement	10	6	6	3	1 141	6.1	1 310	6.7
Diseases of the nervous system — Maladies du système nerveux	7	8	15	10	2 058	11.0	2 224	11.4
Diseases of the circulatory system — Maladies de l'appareil circulatoire								
Total	129	109	130	131	46 238	247.0	44 645	228.9
Acute rheumatic fever and chronic rheumatic heart diseases — Rhumatisme articulaire aigu et cardiopathies rhumatismales chroniques	1	-	-	-	62	0.3	100	0.5
Hypertensive diseases — Maladies hypertensives	8	14	13	12	2 751	14.7	3 154	16.2
Ischaemic heart disease — Cardiopathie ischémique	75	51	72	78	11 241	60.0	7 379	37.8

Cause of death — Cause de décès	United States Virgin Islands - Îles Vierges américaines				Argentina Argentina			
	2003 (...)		2005 (...)		2004 (+C)			
	Male — Masculin	Female — Féminin	Male — Masculin	Female — Féminin	Male — Masculin		Female — Féminin	
	Number Nombre	Number Nombre	Number Nombre	Number Nombre	Number Nombre	Rate Taux	Number Nombre	Rate Taux
Cerebrovascular disease — Maladie cérébrovasculaire............	22	22	14	23	10 778	57.6	11 098	56.9
Diseases of arteries, arterioles and capillaries — Maladies des artères, artérioles et capillaires	1	4	4	2	1 951	10.4	1 699	8.7
Diseases of the respiratory system — Maladies de l'appareil respiratoire								
Total...	12	14	18	12	20 901	111.7	20 305	104.1
Influenza — Grippe	-	-	-	-	11	+0.1	10	+0.1
Pneumonia — Pneumopathies..........................	5	6	8	5	7 017	37.5	7 602	39.0
Chronic lower respiratory diseases — Maladies chroniques des voies respiratoires inférieures	4	4	8	5	3 356	17.9	1 716	8.8
Diseases of the digestive system — Maladies de l'appareil digestif								
Total...	21	13	17	6	6 485	34.6	4 741	24.3
Gastric and duodenal ulcer — Ulcère de l'estomac et du duodénum	-	2	-	-	210	1.1	146	0.7
Diseases of the liver — Maladies du foie	14	6	13	3	2 787	14.9	1 247	6.4
Diseases of the musculoskeletal system and connective tissue — Maladies du système ostéo-articularie, des muscles et du tissu conjonctif	-	3	2	2	236	1.3	482	2.5
Diseases of the genitourinary system — Maladies de l'appareil génito-urinaire								
Total...	5	6	11	6	4 310	23.0	4 068	20.9
Disorders of kidney and ureter — Affections du rein et de l'uretère	3	3	10	1	3 686	19.7	3 258	16.7
Hyperplasia of prostate — Hyperplasie de la prostate...............	-	..	-	..	47	1.2	..	..
Pregnancy, childbirth and the puerperium — Grossesse, accouchement et puerpéralité								
Total...	..	-	..	-	..	..	313	42.5
Pregnancy with abortive outcome — Grossesse se terminant par un avortement	..	-	..	-	..	..	94	12.8
Other direct obstetric causes — Autres décès maternels directs	..	-	..	-	..	..	166	22.5
Indirect obstetric causes — Décès maternels indirects......................	..	-	..	-	..	..	33	4.5
Certain conditions originating in the perinatal period — Certaines affections dont l'origine se situe dans la période périnatale	6	3	3	1	3 164	839.8	2 370	659.7
Congenital malformations, deformations and chromosomal abnormalities — Malformations congénitales et anomalies chromosomiques	1	2	2	3	1 510	400.8	1 335	371.6
Symptoms, signs and abnormal clinical and laboratory findings, not elsewhere classified — Symptômes, signes et résultats anormaux d'examens cliniques et de laboratoire, non classés ailleurs	5	14	5	6	11 319	60.5	10 384	53.2
All other diseases — Toutes autres maladies....................	3	3	2	1	448	2.4	878	4.5
External causes — Causes externes								
Total...	55	8	53	12	13 272	70.9	4 747	24.3
Accidents								
Total...	17	4	16	8	7 318	39.1	2 944	15.1
Transport accidents — Accidents de transport	6	2	3	2	2 868	15.3	875	4.5
Falls — Chutes	-	1	3	1	204	1.1	90	0.5
Accidental drowning and submersion — Noyade et submersion accidentelles	4	-	5	1	455	2.4	110	0.6
Exposure to smoke, fire and flames — Exposition à la fumée, au feu et aux flammes	-	-	-	-	273	1.5	145	0.7
Accidental poisoning by and exposure to noxious substances — Intoxication accidentelle par des substances nocives et exposition à ces substances	-	-	2	2	136	0.7	81	0.4
Intentional self-harm — Lésions auto-infligées....................	8	1	2	-	2 476	13.2	655	3.4
Assault — Agresssions	28	3	32	3	1 915	10.2	321	1.6
All other external causes — Toutes autres causes externes.................	2	-	3	1	1 563	8.3	827	4.2

Cause of death — Cause de décès	Argentina - Argentine 2005 (+C) Male — Masculin Number Nombre	Rate Taux	Female — Féminin Number Nombre	Rate Taux	Brazil - Brésil 2003 (U) Male — Masculin Number Nombre	Female — Féminin Number Nombre	2004 (U) Male — Masculin Number Nombre	Female — Féminin Number Nombre
TOTAL............	155 390	822.2	137 519	698.3	582 799	418 698	593 747	429 625
Certain infectious and parasitic diseases — Certaines maladies infectieuses et parasitaires								
Total.........	7 168	37.9	6 835	34.7	27 706	18 764	27 436	18 613
Intestinal infectious diseases — Maladies infectieuses intestinales............	176	0.9	170	0.9	3 111	2 864	2 824	2 582
Tuberculosis — Tuberculose............	448	2.4	233	1.2	3 672	1 314	3 670	1 310
Tetanus — Tétanos............	7	+0.0	5	+0.0	116	34	117	35
Diphtheria — Diphtérie............	-	-	-	-	3	2	1	1
Whooping cough — Coqueluche............	3	+0.0	5	+0.0	6	13	9	10
Meningococcal infection — Infection à méningocoques............	23	+0.1	9	+0.0	239	198	253	219
Septicaemia — Septicémie............	4 981	26.4	5 546	28.2	6 245	5 976	6 214	6 150
Acute poliomyelitis — Poliomyélite aiguë............	-	-	-	-	-	-	-	-
Measles — Rougeole............	-	-	-	-	1	-	1	-
Viral hepatitis — Hépatite virale............	102	0.5	116	0.6	1 128	749	1 310	811
Human immunodeficiency virus [HIV] disease — Maladies dues au virus de l'immunodéficience humaine (VIH)............	923	4.9	380	1.9	7 672	3 610	7 458	3 562
Malaria — Paludisme............	-	-	-	-	61	42	63	37
Neoplasms — Tumeurs............	31 705	167.0	27 235	138.3	72 622	62 061	76 065	64 724
Malignant neoplasms — Tumeurs malignes								
Total.........	30 192	159.8	26 019	132.1	71 800	61 180	75 231	63 892
Malignant neoplasm of lip, oral cavity and pharynx — Tumeur maligne de la lèvre, de la cavité buccale et du pharynx	597	3.2	201	1.0	4 377	928	4 418	1 045
Malignant neoplasm of oesophagus — Tumeur maligne de l'oesophage	1 340	7.1	565	2.9	4 580	1 418	4 916	1 420
Malignant neoplasm of stomach — Tumeur maligne de l'estomac............	2 005	10.6	1 038	5.3	7 711	4 027	7 951	4 131
Malignant neoplasm of colon, rectosigmoid junction, rectum, anus and anal canal — Tumeur maligne du côlon, de la jonction recto-sigmoïdienne, du rectum, de l'anus et du canal anal	3 300	17.5	2 976	15.1	4 228	4 861	4 416	5 135
Malignant neoplasm of liver and intrahepatic bile ducts — Tumeur maligne du foie et des voies bilaires intrahépatiques	959	5.1	742	3.8	3 037	2 570	3 296	2 673
Malignant neoplasm of pancreas — Tumeur maligne du pancréas............	1 684	8.9	1 824	9.3	2 461	2 432	2 713	2 814
Malignant neoplasm of trachea, bronchus and lung — Tumeur maligne de la trachée, des bronches et du poumon............	6 391	33.8	2 102	10.7	11 057	5 398	11 730	5 757
Malignant neoplasm of female breast — Tumeur maligne du sein chez la femme.........	..	..	5 361	36.5	..	9 342	..	9 789
Malignant neoplasm of cervix uteri — Tumeur maligne du col de l'utérus......	..	..	930	6.3	..	4 202	..	4 393
Malignant neoplasm of prostate — Tumeur maligne de la prostate............	3 784	93.9	..	..	8 977	..	9 590	..
Malignant neoplasm of lymphoid, haematopoietic and related tissue — Tumeurs malignes primitives ou présumées primitives des tissus lymphoïde, hématopoïétique et apparentés	2 143	11.3	1 835	9.3	5 581	4 631	5 671	4 835
Disorders of the blood and blood-forming organs and certain disorders involving the immune mechanism — Maladies du sang et des organes hématopoïétiques et certains troubles du système immunitaire								
Total.........	461	2.4	534	2.7	2 684	2 664	2 576	2 401
Anaemias — Anémies............	284	1.5	366	1.9	1 874	1 850	1 785	1 739
Endocrine, nutritional and metabolic diseases — Maladies endocriniennes, nutritionnelles et métaboliques								
Total.........	5 808	30.7	6 221	31.6	22 943	28 237	23 854	29 262
Diabetes mellitus — Diabète sucré............	4 512	23.9	4 451	22.6	15 954	21 530	16 906	22 336
Malnutrition — Malnutrition............	568	3.0	631	3.2	3 924	3 333	3 861	3 281
Mental and behavioural disorders — Troubles mentaux et du comportement	1 108	5.9	1 053	5.3	5 745	1 610	6 355	1 800
Diseases of the nervous system — Maladies du système nerveux............	1 970	10.4	2 075	10.5	7 349	6 395	7 956	7 198
Diseases of the circulatory system — Maladies de l'appareil circulatoire								
Total.........	45 178	239.1	44 312	225.0	144 643	129 377	150 381	135 116
Acute rheumatic fever and chronic rheumatic heart diseases — Rhumatisme articularie aigu et cardiopathies rhumatismales chroniques	57	0.3	96	0.5	784	1 256	796	1 253
Hypertensive diseases — Maladies hypertensives............	2 327	12.3	2 843	14.4	13 037	14 802	14 524	16 325
Ischaemic heart disease — Cardiopathie ischémique............	11 703	61.9	7 774	39.5	48 237	34 944	50 102	36 679

Cause of death — Cause de décès	Argentina - Argentine				Brazil - Brésil			
	2005 (+C)				2003 (U)		2004 (U)	
	Male — Masculin		Female — Féminin		Male — Masculin	Female — Féminin	Male — Masculin	Female — Féminin
	Number Nombre	Rate Taux	Number Nombre	Rate Taux	Number Nombre	Number Nombre	Number Nombre	Number Nombre
Cerebrovascular disease — Maladie cérébrovasculaire	9 977	52.8	10 622	53.9	45 552	43 464	46 199	44 716
Diseases of arteries, arterioles and capillaries — Maladies des artères, artérioles et capillaires	1 776	9.4	1 421	7.2	5 723	4 437	5 882	4 588
Diseases of the respiratory system — Maladies de l'appareil respiratoire								
Total	20 983	111.0	20 340	103.3	53 594	43 978	55 780	46 363
Influenza — Grippe	7	♦0.0	7	♦0.0	45	66	46	65
Pneumonia — Pneumopathies	7 205	38.1	7 857	39.9	17 893	16 504	19 277	18 213
Chronic lower respiratory diseases — Maladies chroniques des voies respiratoires inférieures	3 687	19.5	1 875	9.5	21 908	14 503	22 692	15 730
Diseases of the digestive system — Maladies de l'appareil digestif								
Total	6 938	36.7	4 811	24.4	30 506	16 375	31 500	17 154
Gastric and duodenal ulcer — Ulcère de l'estomac et du duodénum	189	1.0	149	0.8	1 881	1 102	1 835	1 200
Diseases of the liver — Maladies du foie	3 079	16.3	1 165	5.9	17 099	4 758	17 617	4 874
Diseases of the musculoskeletal system and connective tissue — Maladies du système ostéo-articularie, des muscles et du tissu conjonctif	197	1.0	455	2.3	1 067	1 933	1 056	1 946
Diseases of the genitourinary system — Maladies de l'appareil génito-urinaire								
Total	4 252	22.5	4 055	20.6	8 336	7 519	9 078	8 015
Disorders of kidney and ureter — Affections du rein et de l'uretère	3 555	18.8	3 208	16.3	6 111	5 091	6 610	5 294
Hyperplasia of prostate — Hyperplasie de la prostate	44	1.1	..	..	430	..	454	
Pregnancy, childbirth and the puerperium — Grossesse, accouchement et puerpéralité								
Total	..	..	290	40.7	..	1 597	..	1 672
Pregnancy with abortive outcome — Grossesse se terminant par un avortement	..	..	79	11.1	..	152	..	156
Other direct obstetric causes — Autres décès maternels directs	..	..	146	20.5	..	1 087	..	1 119
Indirect obstetric causes — Décès maternels indirects	..	..	51	7.2	..	301	..	318
Certain conditions originating in the perinatal period — Certaines affections dont l'origine se situe dans la période périnatale	2 864	783.2	2 053	593.1	18 241	13 549	17 541	13 174
Congenital malformations, deformations and chromosomal abnormalities — Malformations congénitales et anomalies chromosomiques	1 384	378.5	1 259	363.7	5 248	4 762	5 306	4 801
Symptoms, signs and abnormal clinical and laboratory findings, not elsewhere classified — Symptômes, signes et résultats anormaux d'examens cliniques et de laboratoire, non classés ailleurs	11 452	60.6	10 313	52.4	74 373	58 911	70 955	55 869
All other diseases — Toutes autres maladies	399	2.1	765	3.9	928	1 189	876	1 149
External causes — Causes externes								
Total	13 523	71.6	4 913	24.9	106 814	19 777	107 032	20 368
Accidents								
Total	7 490	39.6	3 002	15.2	43 491	11 108	45 939	11 509
Transport accidents — Accidents de transport	2 949	15.6	929	4.7	27 280	6 335	29 052	6 609
Falls — Chutes	249	1.3	70	0.4	4 239	1 777	4 610	2 005
Accidental drowning and submersion — Noyade et submersion accidentelles	460	2.4	102	0.5	5 052	915	5 524	905
Exposure to smoke, fire and flames — Exposition à la fumée, au feu et aux flammes	286	1.5	168	0.9	638	364	626	324
Accidental poisoning by and exposure to noxious substances — Intoxication accidentelle par des substances nocives et exposition à ces substances	235	1.2	130	0.7	179	78	171	78
Intentional self-harm — Lésions auto-infligées	2 403	12.7	666	3.4	6 256	1 604	6 311	1 704
Assault — Agresssions	1 711	9.1	317	1.6	47 082	3 937	44 519	3 830
All other external causes — Toutes autres causes externes	1 919	10.2	928	4.7	9 985	3 128	10 263	3 325

Chile - Chili

Cause of death — Cause de décès	2004 (C)				2005 (C)			
	Male — Masculin		Female — Féminin		Male — Masculin		Female — Féminin	
	Number Nombre	Rate Taux	Number Nombre	Rate Taux	Number Nombre	Rate Taux	Number Nombre	Rate Taux
TOTAL.............	46 549	584.3	39 589	487.1	46 369	575.8	39 733	483.7
Certain infectious and parasitic diseases — Certaines maladies infectieuses et parasitaires								
Total....	1 143	14.3	681	8.4	1 068	13.3	699	8.5
Intestinal infectious diseases — Maladies infectieuses intestinales............	92	1.2	127	1.6	67	0.8	134	1.6
Tuberculosis — Tuberculose................	200	2.5	67	0.8	165	2.0	68	0.8
Tetanus — Tétanos............	1	◆0.0	-	-	3	◆0.0	-	-
Diphtheria — Diphtérie............	-	-	-	-	-	-	-	-
Whooping cough — Coqueluche............	6	◆0.1	5	◆0.1	7	◆0.1	1	◆0.0
Meningococcal infection — Infection à méningocoques................	10	◆0.1	13	◆0.2	7	◆0.1	5	◆0.1
Septicaemia — Septicémie................	90	1.1	99	1.2	109	1.4	145	1.8
Acute poliomyelitis — Poliomyélite aiguë............	-	-	-	-	-	-	-	-
Measles — Rougeole............	-	-	-	-	-	-	-	-
Viral hepatitis — Hépatite virale................	32	0.4	57	0.7	31	0.4	32	0.4
Human immunodeficiency virus [HIV] disease — Maladies dues au virus de l'immunodéficience humaine (VIH)................	356	4.5	43	0.5	331	4.1	59	0.7
Malaria — Paludisme................	-	-	-	-	1	◆0.0	-	-
Neoplasms — Tumeurs................	10 683	134.1	10 090	124.1	11 034	137.0	10 360	126.1
Malignant neoplasms — Tumeurs malignes								
Total....	10 229	128.4	9 671	119.0	10 552	131.0	9 928	120.9
Malignant neoplasm of lip, oral cavity and pharynx — Tumeur maligne de la lèvre, de la cavité buccale et du pharynx................	130	1.6	60	0.7	144	1.8	52	0.6
Malignant neoplasm of oesophagus — Tumeur maligne de l'oesophage......	424	5.3	291	3.6	453	5.6	313	3.8
Malignant neoplasm of stomach — Tumeur maligne de l'estomac.............	2 027	25.4	1 025	12.6	2 044	25.4	1 048	12.8
Malignant neoplasm of colon, rectosigmoid junction, rectum, anus and anal canal — Tumeur maligne du côlon, de la jonction recto-sigmoïdienne, du rectum, de l'anus et du canal anal................	638	8.0	789	9.7	701	8.7	796	9.7
Malignant neoplasm of liver and intrahepatic bile ducts — Tumeur maligne du foie et des voies bilaires intrahépatiques................	398	5.0	365	4.5	452	5.6	357	4.3
Malignant neoplasm of pancreas — Tumeur maligne du pancréas............	389	4.9	508	6.3	393	4.9	488	5.9
Malignant neoplasm of trachea, bronchus and lung — Tumeur maligne de la trachée, des bronches et du poumon................	1 460	18.3	762	9.4	1 478	18.4	819	10.0
Malignant neoplasm of female breast — Tumeur maligne du sein chez la femme................	..	..	1 096	17.9	..	..	1 169	18.8
Malignant neoplasm of cervix uteri — Tumeur maligne du col de l'utérus......	..	..	676	11.1	..	..	677	10.9
Malignant neoplasm of prostate — Tumeur maligne de la prostate............	1 462	95.8	..	..	1 514	96.0	..	..
Malignant neoplasm of lymphoid, haematopoietic and related tissue — Tumeurs malignes primitives ou présumées primitives des tissus lymphoïde, hématopoïétique et apparentés................	804	10.1	747	9.2	801	9.9	734	8.9
Disorders of the blood and blood-forming organs and certain disorders involving the immune mechanism — Maladies du sang et des organes hématopoïétiques et certains troubles du système immunitaire								
Total....	138	1.7	161	2.0	153	1.9	176	2.1
Anaemias — Anémies................	101	1.3	116	1.4	109	1.4	145	1.8
Endocrine, nutritional and metabolic diseases — Maladies endocriniennes, nutritionnelles et métaboliques								
Total....	1 941	24.4	2 302	28.3	1 994	24.8	2 257	27.5
Diabetes mellitus — Diabète sucré................	1 607	20.2	1 808	22.2	1 597	19.8	1 785	21.7
Malnutrition — Malnutrition................	197	2.5	257	3.2	248	3.1	290	3.5
Mental and behavioural disorders — Troubles mentaux et du comportement	1 228	15.4	1 372	16.9	1 188	14.8	1 382	16.8
Diseases of the nervous system — Maladies du système nerveux..........	1 065	13.4	1 106	13.6	1 114	13.8	1 228	14.9
Diseases of the circulatory system — Maladies de l'appareil circulatoire								
Total....	12 358	155.1	11 910	146.5	12 376	153.7	11 914	145.0
Acute rheumatic fever and chronic rheumatic heart diseases — Rhumatisme articulaire aigu et cardiopathies rhumatismales chroniques................	105	1.3	174	2.1	112	1.4	169	2.1
Hypertensive diseases — Maladies hypertensives................	1 318	16.5	1 814	22.3	1 343	16.7	1 818	22.1
Ischaemic heart disease — Cardiopathie ischémique................	4 668	58.6	3 299	40.6	4 709	58.5	3 239	39.4
Cerebrovascular disease — Maladie cérébrovasculaire................	3 735	46.9	4 048	49.8	3 686	45.8	4 012	48.8

Chile - Chili

Cause of death — Cause de décès	2004 (C)				2005 (C)			
	Male — Masculin		Female — Féminin		Male — Masculin		Female — Féminin	
	Number Nombre	Rate Taux	Number Nombre	Rate Taux	Number Nombre	Rate Taux	Number Nombre	Rate Taux
Diseases of arteries, arterioles and capillaries — Maladies des artères, artérioles et capillaires	461	5.8	391	4.8	480	6.0	379	4.6
Diseases of the respiratory system — Maladies de l'appareil respiratoire								
Total	4 190	52.6	4 154	51.1	4 051	50.3	3 954	48.1
Influenza — Grippe	21	◆0.3	38	0.5	16	◆0.2	13	◆0.2
Pneumonia — Pneumopathies	1 617	20.3	1 797	22.1	1 468	18.2	1 627	19.8
Chronic lower respiratory diseases — Maladies chroniques des voies respiratoires inférieures	1 642	20.6	1 474	18.1	1 605	19.9	1 462	17.8
Diseases of the digestive system — Maladies de l'appareil digestif								
Total	4 123	51.8	2 439	30.0	3 781	47.0	2 349	28.6
Gastric and duodenal ulcer — Ulcère de l'estomac et du duodénum	126	1.6	84	1.0	122	1.5	99	1.2
Diseases of the liver — Maladies du foie	2 960	37.2	1 217	15.0	2 676	33.2	1 057	12.9
Diseases of the musculoskeletal system and connective tissue — Maladies du système ostéo-articularie, des muscles et du tissu conjonctif	143	1.8	404	5.0	115	1.4	365	4.4
Diseases of the genitourinary system — Maladies de l'appareil génito-urinaire								
Total	1 165	14.6	1 271	15.6	1 241	15.4	1 325	16.1
Disorders of kidney and ureter — Affections du rein et de l'uretère	784	9.8	766	9.4	823	10.2	786	9.6
Hyperplasia of prostate — Hyperplasie de la prostate	82	5.4	..		91	5.8	..	
Pregnancy, childbirth and the puerperium — Grossesse, accouchement et puerpéralité								
Total	..	..	42	18.2	..	..	48	20.8
Pregnancy with abortive outcome — Grossesse se terminant par un avortement	..	..	4	◆1.7	..	..	7	◆3.0
Other direct obstetric causes — Autres décès maternels directs	..	..	22	◆9.6	..	..	21	◆9.1
Indirect obstetric causes — Décès maternels indirects	..	..	16	◆6.9	..	..	17	◆7.4
Certain conditions originating in the perinatal period — Certaines affections dont l'origine se situe dans la période périnatale	483	411.3	361	319.7	449	378.8	359	319.7
Congenital malformations, deformations and chromosomal abnormalities — Malformations congénitales et anomalies chromosomiques	517	440.2	446	395.0	496	418.4	433	385.6
Symptoms, signs and abnormal clinical and laboratory findings, not elsewhere classified — Symptômes, signes et résultats anormaux d'examens cliniques et de laboratoire, non classés ailleurs	1 221	15.3	1 221	15.0	1 184	14.7	1 195	14.5
All other diseases — Toutes autres maladies	112	1.4	160	2.0	110	1.4	186	2.3
External causes — Causes externes								
Total	6 039	75.8	1 469	18.1	6 015	74.7	1 503	18.3
Accidents								
Total	3 706	46.5	1 038	12.8	3 676	45.7	1 053	12.8
Transport accidents — Accidents de transport	1 886	23.7	423	5.2	1 870	23.2	431	5.2
Falls — Chutes	402	5.0	318	3.9	409	5.1	316	3.8
Accidental drowning and submersion — Noyade et submersion accidentelles	453	5.7	60	0.7	428	5.3	60	0.7
Exposure to smoke, fire and flames — Exposition à la fumée, au feu et aux flammes	182	2.3	93	1.1	206	2.6	90	1.1
Accidental poisoning by and exposure to noxious substances — Intoxication accidentelle par des substances nocives et exposition à ces substances	41	0.5	47	0.6	77	1.0	32	0.4
Intentional self-harm — Lésions auto-infligées	1 472	18.5	263	3.2	1 401	17.4	279	3.4
Assault — Agresssions	769	9.7	84	1.0	838	10.4	108	1.3
All other external causes — Toutes autres causes externes	92	1.2	84	1.0	100	1.2	63	0.8

Cause of death — Cause de décès	Colombia - Colombie 2004 (U) Male — Masculin Number Nombre	2004 (U) Female — Féminin Number Nombre	2005 (U) Male — Masculin Number Nombre	2005 (U) Female — Féminin Number Nombre	Ecuador - Équateur 2004 (U) Male — Masculin Number Nombre	2004 (U) Female — Féminin Number Nombre	2005 (U) Male — Masculin Number Nombre	2005 (U) Female — Féminin Number Nombre
TOTAL	110 589	78 165	109 392	79 420	31 269	23 428	32 607	24 189
Certain infectious and parasitic diseases — Certaines maladies infectieuses et parasitaires								
Total	4 694	2 658	4 529	2 521	1 659	1 000	1 808	933
Intestinal infectious diseases — Maladies infectieuses intestinales	695	634	576	558	275	240	258	192
Tuberculosis — Tuberculose	805	373	687	330	504	259	558	249
Tetanus — Tétanos	24	13	29	12	14	4	9	6
Diphtheria — Diphtérie	-	-	-	-	-	-	-	-
Whooping cough — Coqueluche	1	7	8	14	-	-	1	-
Meningococcal infection — Infection à méningocoques	10	10	10	17	3	-	1	-
Septicaemia — Septicémie	643	680	758	710	356	341	336	286
Acute poliomyelitis — Poliomyélite aiguë	-	-	-	-	-	-	-	-
Measles — Rougeole	-	-	-	-	-	-	-	-
Viral hepatitis — Hépatite virale	83	69	99	66	19	11	24	12
Human immunodeficiency virus [HIV] disease — Maladies dues au virus de l'immunodéficience humaine (VIH)	1 905	521	1 836	468	404	91	515	103
Malaria — Paludisme	69	50	49	35	21	16	15	7
Neoplasms — Tumeurs	15 099	15 847	16 624	16 923	3 713	3 824	3 051	4 139
Malignant neoplasms — Tumeurs malignes								
Total	14 698	15 414	15 195	15 498	3 639	3 740	3 788	4 057
Malignant neoplasm of lip, oral cavity and pharynx — Tumeur maligne de la lèvre, de la cavité buccale et du pharynx	287	188	272	203	52	30	51	38
Malignant neoplasm of oesophagus — Tumeur maligne de l'oesophage	458	216	452	222	66	18	75	30
Malignant neoplasm of stomach — Tumeur maligne de l'estomac	2 556	1 795	2 729	1 811	822	662	849	664
Malignant neoplasm of colon, rectosigmoid junction, rectum, anus and anal canal — Tumeur maligne du côlon, de la jonction recto-sigmoïdienne, du rectum, de l'anus et du canal anal	917	1 164	920	1 100	175	226	184	220
Malignant neoplasm of liver and intrahepatic bile ducts — Tumeur maligne du foie et des voies bilaires intrahépatiques	754	925	731	857	279	294	273	364
Malignant neoplasm of pancreas — Tumeur maligne du pancréas	437	565	487	561	122	134	126	152
Malignant neoplasm of trachea, bronchus and lung — Tumeur maligne de la trachée, des bronches et du poumon	2 192	1 404	2 253	1 438	331	237	365	242
Malignant neoplasm of female breast — Tumeur maligne du sein chez la femme	..	1 853	..	1 849	..	304	..	326
Malignant neoplasm of cervix uteri — Tumeur maligne du col de l'utérus	..	1 621	..	1 693	..	235	..	292
Malignant neoplasm of prostate — Tumeur maligne de la prostate	2 239	..	2 277	..	636	..	632	..
Malignant neoplasm of lymphoid, haematopoietic and related tissue — Tumeurs malignes primitives ou présumées primitives des tissus lymphoïde, hématopoïétique et apparentés	1 448	1 259	1 531	1 307	424	360	474	333
Disorders of the blood and blood-forming organs and certain disorders involving the immune mechanism — Maladies du sang et des organes hématopoïétiques et certains troubles du système immunitaire								
Total	382	362	430	434	239	260	297	305
Anaemias — Anémies	246	265	260	259	198	226	254	262
Endocrine, nutritional and metabolic diseases — Maladies endocriniennes, nutritionnelles et métaboliques								
Total	4 288	5 476	4 260	5 362	1 650	1 985	1 603	2 018
Diabetes mellitus — Diabète sucré	3 158	4 279	3 135	4 127	1 178	1 493	1 211	1 583
Malnutrition — Malnutrition	938	928	921	927	315	331	282	321
Mental and behavioural disorders — Troubles mentaux et du comportement	24	31	22	40	237	31	230	40
Diseases of the nervous system — Maladies du système nerveux	1 389	1 110	1 440	1 171	562	419	519	425
Diseases of the circulatory system — Maladies de l'appareil circulatoire								
Total	27 839	26 398	28 802	27 012	6 402	5 709	6 648	6 099
Acute rheumatic fever and chronic rheumatic heart diseases — Rhumatisme articularie aigu et cardiopathies rhumatismales chroniques	112	172	77	162	22	30	17	34
Hypertensive diseases — Maladies hypertensives	2 668	2 914	2 391	2 775	1 289	1 184	1 444	1 392
Ischaemic heart disease — Cardiopathie ischémique	13 798	10 913	14 783	11 515	1 375	921	1 547	960

	Colombia — Colombie				Friannr - Aniialaur			
Cause of death — Cause de décès	2004 (U)		2005 (U)		2004 (U)		2005 (U)	
	Male — Masculin	Female — Féminin	Male — Masculin	Female — Féminin	Male — Masculin	Female — Féminin	Male — Masculin	Female — Féminin
	Number Nombre	Number Nombre	Number Nombre	Number Nombre	Number Nombre	Number Nombre	Number Nombre	Number Nombre
Cerebrovascular disease — Maladie cérébrovasculaire	6 228	7 444	6 364	7 459	1 539	1 408	1 499	1 558
Diseases of arteries, arterioles and capillaries — Maladies des artères, artérioles et capillaires	1 052	741	1 026	684	141	124	184	169
Diseases of the respiratory system — Maladies de l'appareil respiratoire								
Total	9 500	8 292	10 319	8 996	2 855	2 397	2 659	2 150
Influenza — Grippe	12	5	2	12	17	11	19	12
Pneumonia — Pneumopathies	2 789	2 693	3 231	3 154	1 607	1 390	1 485	1 242
Chronic lower respiratory diseases — Maladies chroniques des voies respiratoires inférieures	5 359	4 335	5 549	4 414	529	380	567	406
Diseases of the digestive system — Maladies de l'appareil digestif								
Total	4 526	4 010	4 621	4 041	1 882	1 162	2 051	1 187
Gastric and duodenal ulcer — Ulcère de l'estomac et du duodénum	453	334	456	281	156	91	176	85
Diseases of the liver — Maladies du foie	1 428	818	1 497	875	1 124	531	1 194	586
Diseases of the musculoskeletal system and connective tissue — Maladies du système ostéo-articularie, des muscles et du tissu conjonctif	361	880	454	929	52	102	65	119
Diseases of the genitourinary system — Maladies de l'appareil génito-urinaire								
Total	2 152	1 801	2 330	1 999	1 050	825	983	843
Disorders of kidney and ureter — Affections du rein et de l'uretère	1 558	1 220	1 547	1 212	1 012	817	928	835
Hyperplasia of prostate — Hyperplasie de la prostate	130	..	134	..	31	..	48	..
Pregnancy, childbirth and the puerperium — Grossesse, accouchement et puerpéralité								
Total	..	546	..	504	..	129	..	143
Pregnancy with abortive outcome — Grossesse se terminant par un avortement	..	55	..	54	..	11	..	17
Other direct obstetric causes — Autres décès maternels directs	..	363	..	328	..	116	..	119
Indirect obstetric causes — Décès maternels indirects	..	123	..	112	..	2	..	7
Certain conditions originating in the perinatal period — Certaines affections dont l'origine se situe dans la période périnatale	3 312	2 455	3 332	2 466	1 112	800	1 083	727
Congenital malformations, deformations and chromosomal abnormalities — Malformations congénitales et anomalies chromosomiques	1 571	1 277	1 465	1 176	265	238	294	260
Symptoms, signs and abnormal clinical and laboratory findings, not elsewhere classified — Symptômes, signes et résultats anormaux d'examens cliniques et de laboratoire, non classés ailleurs	1 847	1 416	1 810	1 353	3 335	3 020	3 621	3 164
All other diseases — Toutes autres maladies	354	419	397	532	3	11	4	11
External causes — Causes externes								
Total	33 251	5 187	29 557	4 961	6 253	1 516	6 891	1 626
Accidents								
Total	8 694	2 330	8 374	2 342	3 496	1 026	3 856	1 107
Transport accidents — Accidents de transport	5 110	1 372	4 843	1 286	1 448	420	1 868	510
Falls — Chutes	873	236	919	219	302	66	398	103
Accidental drowning and submersion — Noyade et submersion accidentelles	921	194	820	199	389	76	310	66
Exposure to smoke, fire and flames — Exposition à la fumée, au feu et aux flammes	81	45	77	44	66	35	70	53
Accidental poisoning by and exposure to noxious substances — Intoxication accidentelle par des substances nocives et exposition à ces substances	126	31	95	32	125	31	139	24
Intentional self-harm — Lésions auto-infligées	1 762	502	1 652	467	556	237	683	260
Assault — Agresssions	20 498	1 835	17 207	1 635	2 103	211	2 219	188
All other external causes — Toutes autres causes externes	2 297	520	2 324	517	98	42	133	71

Cause of death — Cause de décès	French Guiana - Guyane française				Guyana			
	2004 (...)		2005 (...)		2004 (U)		2005 (U)	
	Male — Masculin	Female — Féminin	Male — Masculin	Female — Féminin	Male — Masculin	Female — Féminin	Male — Masculin	Female — Féminin
	Number Nombre	Number Nombre	Number Nombre	Number Nombre	Number Nombre	Number Nombre	Number Nombre	Number Nombre
TOTAL..	442	277	452	288	2 929	2 212	2 949	2 283
Certain infectious and parasitic diseases — Certaines maladies infectieuses et parasitaires								
Total.........................	31	24	39	26	410	234	388	282
Intestinal infectious diseases — Maladies infectieuses intestinales............	1	-	2	2	31	19	37	40
Tuberculosis — Tuberculose.................................	1	2	-	1	85	33	71	25
Tetanus — Tétanos....................................	-	-	1	-	1	-	-	-
Diphtheria — Diphtérie.....................................	-	-	-	-	-	-	-	-
Whooping cough — Coqueluche........................	-	-	-	-	-	-	-	-
Meningococcal infection — Infection à méningocoques................	-	-	-	-	-	-	-	-
Septicaemia — Septicémie.............................	3	4	2	1	36	30	25	38
Acute poliomyelitis — Poliomyélite aiguë............	-	-	-	-	-	-	-	-
Measles — Rougeole..................................	-	-	-	-	-	-	-	-
Viral hepatitis — Hépatite virale......................	1	1	1	2	1	3	14	2
Human immunodeficiency virus [HIV] disease — Maladies dues au virus de l'immunodéficience humaine (VIH)........................	19	14	26	14	219	137	200	159
Malaria — Paludisme.....................................	1	-	2	-	30	8	23	12
Neoplasms — Tumeurs.........................	71	51	78	44	207	219	223	229
Malignant neoplasms — Tumeurs malignes								
Total..........................	68	50	77	41	194	208	209	216
Malignant neoplasm of lip, oral cavity and pharynx — Tumeur maligne de la lèvre, de la cavité buccale et du pharynx	2	1	2	-	10	-	4	5
Malignant neoplasm of oesophagus — Tumeur maligne de l'oesophage......	5	-	2	1	3	1	2	1
Malignant neoplasm of stomach — Tumeur maligne de l'estomac............	4	3	14	1	12	8	21	8
Malignant neoplasm of colon, rectosigmoid junction, rectum, anus and anal canal — Tumeur maligne du côlon, de la jonction recto-sigmoïdienne, du rectum, de l'anus et du canal anal.......	3	4	4	3	15	6	15	13
Malignant neoplasm of liver and intrahepatic bile ducts — Tumeur maligne du foie et des voies bilaires intrahépatiques..................	6	1	4	1	10	13	12	9
Malignant neoplasm of pancreas — Tumeur maligne du pancréas............	4	3	-	2	10	7	9	11
Malignant neoplasm of trachea, bronchus and lung — Tumeur maligne de la trachée, des bronches et du poumon.....	12	6	8	1	10	4	23	4
Malignant neoplasm of female breast — Tumeur maligne du sein chez la femme....................	..	7	..	12	..	38	..	51
Malignant neoplasm of cervix uteri — Tumeur maligne du col de l'utérus......	..	5	..	3	..	44	..	43
Malignant neoplasm of prostate — Tumeur maligne de la prostate............	10	..	13	..	59	..	78	..
Malignant neoplasm of lymphoid, haematopoietic and related tissue — Tumeurs malignes primitives ou présumées primitives des tissus lymphoïde, hématopoïétique et apparentés............	4	1	8	7	14	14	10	9
Disorders of the blood and blood-forming organs and certain disorders involving the immune mechanism — Maladies du sang et des organes hématopoïétiques et certains troubles du système immunitaire								
Total...........................	-	3	3	1	31	41	35	34
Anaemias — Anémies.................................	-	3	2	1	30	38	31	31
Endocrine, nutritional and metabolic diseases — Maladies endocriniennes, nutritionnelles et métaboliques								
Total...........................	19	22	11	11	194	264	206	292
Diabetes mellitus — Diabète sucré............................	11	11	6	9	159	226	168	243
Malnutrition — Malnutrition.................................	2	1	2	-	19	22	18	21
Mental and behavioural disorders — Troubles mentaux et du comportement	12	5	14	3	8	1	9	3
Diseases of the nervous system — Maladies du système nerveux..........	17	5	11	8	42	23	70	41
Diseases of the circulatory system — Maladies de l'appareil circulatoire								
Total...........................	74	60	77	75	923	857	913	841
Acute rheumatic fever and chronic rheumatic heart diseases — Rhumatisme articularie aigu et cardiopathies rhumatismales chroniques	1	1	1	1	7	4	3	6
Hypertensive diseases — Maladies hypertensives...................	8	4	10	14	105	142	107	113
Ischaemic heart disease — Cardiopathie ischémique....................	12	8	13	6	335	295	367	274

Cause of death — Cause de décès	French Guiana - Guyane française 2004 (...) Male — Masculin Number Nombre	2004 (...) Female — Féminin Number Nombre	2005 (...) Male — Masculin Number Nombre	2005 (...) Female — Féminin Number Nombre	Guyana 2004 (U) Male — Masculin Number Nombre	2004 (U) Female — Féminin Number Nombre	2005 (U) Male — Masculin Number Nombre	2005 (U) Female — Féminin Number Nombre
Cerebrovascular disease — Maladie cérébrovasculaire	32	29	26	27	297	261	288	297
Diseases of arteries, arterioles and capillaries — Maladies des artères, artérioles et capillaires	5	3	3	4	19	16	17	13
Diseases of the respiratory system — Maladies de l'appareil respiratoire								
Total	16	14	10	11	162	123	140	115
Influenza — Grippe	-	-	-	-	-	1	-	1
Pneumonia — Pneumopathies	6	7	2	7	85	81	76	69
Chronic lower respiratory diseases — Maladies chroniques des voies respiratoires inférieures	3	3	2	3	46	19	36	20
Diseases of the digestive system — Maladies de l'appareil digestif								
Total	8	15	12	11	207	96	199	86
Gastric and duodenal ulcer — Ulcère de l'estomac et du duodénum	-	-	1	-	21	10	21	12
Diseases of the liver — Maladies du foie	2	4	6	2	143	50	136	43
Diseases of the musculoskeletal system and connective tissue — Maladies du système ostéo-articularie, des muscles et du tissu conjonctif	-	1	2	2	3	6	4	6
Diseases of the genitourinary system — Maladies de l'appareil génito-urinaire								
Total	1	4	4	3	30	22	56	34
Disorders of kidney and ureter — Affections du rein et de l'uretère	1	3	3	2	23	18	38	30
Hyperplasia of prostate — Hyperplasie de la prostate	-	..	-	..	5	..	9	..
Pregnancy, childbirth and the puerperium — Grossesse, accouchement et puerpéralité								
Total	..	1	..	1	..	19	..	24
Pregnancy with abortive outcome — Grossesse se terminant par un avortement	..	-	..	-	..	4	..	4
Other direct obstetric causes — Autres décès maternels directs	..	1	..	1	..	7	..	17
Indirect obstetric causes — Décès maternels indirects	..	-	..	-	..	8	..	3
Certain conditions originating in the perinatal period — Certaines affections dont l'origine se situe dans la période périnatale	13	12	20	11	133	101	105	98
Congenital malformations, deformations and chromosomal abnormalities — Malformations congénitales et anomalies chromosomiques	8	4	1	8	30	32	28	18
Symptoms, signs and abnormal clinical and laboratory findings, not elsewhere classified — Symptômes, signes et résultats anormaux d'examens cliniques et de laboratoire, non classés ailleurs	57	30	50	37	24	28	28	27
All other diseases — Toutes autres maladies	2	2	-	1	-	1	-	1
External causes — Causes externes								
Total	113	24	120	35	525	145	545	152
Accidents								
Total	57	19	80	23	200	54	269	67
Transport accidents — Accidents de transport	32	4	34	7	112	27	124	34
Falls — Chutes	2	2	1	2	19	4	17	5
Accidental drowning and submersion — Noyade et submersion accidentelles	10	4	9	-	9	2	81	9
Exposure to smoke, fire and flames — Exposition à la fumée, au feu et aux flammes	1	1	3	1	-	2	5	3
Accidental poisoning by and exposure to noxious substances — Intoxication accidentelle par des substances nocives et exposition à ces substances	2	1	4	3	2	-	1	1
Intentional self-harm — Lésions auto-infligées	24	3	14	11	138	48	127	42
Assault — Agresssions	13	2	10	1	88	16	108	30
All other external causes — Toutes autres causes externes	19	-	16	-	99	27	41	13

21. Death and death rates by cause and sex: 2002 - 2006
Décès et taux de mortalité par cause et sexe : 2002 - 2006 (continued - suite)

Cause of death — Cause de décès	Paraguay				Uruguay			
	2003 (+U)		2004 (+U)		2004 (C)			
	Male — Masculin	Female — Féminin	Male — Masculin	Female — Féminin	Male — Masculin		Female — Féminin	
	Number Nombre	Number Nombre	Number Nombre	Number Nombre	Number Nombre	Rate Taux	Number Nombre	Rate Taux
TOTAL..........	11 060	8 714	12 067	9 623	16 854	1 056.3	15 320	898.0
Certain infectious and parasitic diseases — Certaines maladies infectieuses et parasitaires								
Total.........	514	392	586	428	362	22.7	310	18.2
Intestinal infectious diseases — Maladies infectieuses intestinales...........	109	105	129	137	25	+1.6	55	3.2
Tuberculosis — Tuberculose...............	104	36	131	52	42	2.6	22	+1.3
Tetanus — Tétanos...............	14	6	3	2	1	+0.1	-	-
Diphtheria — Diphtérie.............	-	1	-	-	-	-	-	-
Whooping cough — Coqueluche...............	-	2	-	-	-	-	-	-
Meningococcal infection — Infection à méningocoques...........	-	1	1	3	2	+0.1	-	-
Septicaemia — Septicémie.........	161	173	154	142	141	8.8	167	9.8
Acute poliomyelitis — Poliomyélite aiguë.............	-	-	-	-	-	-	-	-
Measles — Rougeole...........	-	-	-	-	-	-	-	-
Viral hepatitis — Hépatite virale...........	2	2	4	3	4	+0.3	5	+0.3
Human immunodeficiency virus [HIV] disease — Maladies dues au virus de l'immunodéficience humaine (VIH)...........	78	31	111	49	110	6.9	36	2.1
Malaria — Paludisme............	1	-	-	-	-	-	-	-
Neoplasms — Tumeurs	1 308	1 347	1 503	1 383	4 276	268.0	3 306	193.8
Malignant neoplasms — Tumeurs malignes								
Total.........	1 348	1 328	1 450	1 323	4 160	260.7	3 194	187.2
Malignant neoplasm of lip, oral cavity and pharynx — Tumeur maligne de la lèvre, de la cavité buccale et du pharynx...........	46	15	54	13	125	7.8	28	+1.6
Malignant neoplasm of oesophagus — Tumeur maligne de l'oesophage......	53	16	56	16	197	12.3	87	5.1
Malignant neoplasm of stomach — Tumeur maligne de l'estomac...........	134	98	138	84	246	15.4	163	9.6
Malignant neoplasm of colon, rectosigmoid junction, rectum, anus and anal canal — Tumeur maligne du côlon, de la jonction recto-sigmoïdienne, du rectum, de l'anus et du canal anal...........	68	91	111	93	410	25.7	442	25.9
Malignant neoplasm of liver and intrahepatic bile ducts — Tumeur maligne du foie et des voies bilaires intrahépatiques...........	41	40	53	29	56	3.5	25	+1.5
Malignant neoplasm of pancreas — Tumeur maligne du pancréas...........	41	45	44	58	182	11.4	226	13.2
Malignant neoplasm of trachea, bronchus and lung — Tumeur maligne de la trachée, des bronches et du poumon...........	279	69	250	67	925	58.0	199	11.7
Malignant neoplasm of female breast — Tumeur maligne du sein chez la femme...........	..	212	..	208	..	..	611	46.4
Malignant neoplasm of cervix uteri — Tumeur maligne du col de l'utérus......	..	151	..	185	..	..	78	5.9
Malignant neoplasm of prostate — Tumeur maligne de la prostate...........	223	..	266	..	646	162.6	..	..
Malignant neoplasm of lymphoid, haematopoietic and related tissue — Tumeurs malignes primitives ou présumées primitives des tissus lymphoïde, hématopoïétique et apparentés...........	109	91	128	108	295	18.5	254	14.9
Disorders of the blood and blood-forming organs and certain disorders involving the immune mechanism — Maladies du sang et des organes hématopoïétiques et certains troubles du système immunitaire								
Total.........	27	24	37	28	79	5.0	86	5.0
Anaemias — Anémies...........	17	17	21	17	54	3.4	58	3.4
Endocrine, nutritional and metabolic diseases — Maladies endocriniennes, nutritionnelles et métaboliques								
Total.........	609	799	678	951	500	31.3	541	31.7
Diabetes mellitus — Diabète sucré...........	513	710	549	813	361	22.6	370	21.7
Malnutrition — Malnutrition...........	54	44	73	79	43	2.7	34	2.0
Mental and behavioural disorders — Troubles mentaux et du comportement	48	8	68	12	157	9.8	342	20.0
Diseases of the nervous system — Maladies du système nerveux........	128	86	178	124	535	33.5	796	46.7
Diseases of the circulatory system — Maladies de l'appareil circulatoire								
Total.........	2 200	2 033	2 785	2 448	5 044	316.1	5 575	326.8
Acute rheumatic fever and chronic rheumatic heart diseases — Rhumatisme articulaire aigu et cardiopathies rhumatismales chroniques...........	8	14	12	8	16	+1.0	12	+0.7
Hypertensive diseases — Maladies hypertensives...........	165	172	277	259	218	13.7	281	16.5
Ischaemic heart disease — Cardiopathie ischémique...........	724	477	928	608	1 582	99.1	1 207	70.7

Cause of death — Cause de décès	Paraguay				Uruguay			
	2003 (+U)		2004 (+U)		2004 (C)			
	Male — Masculin	Female — Féminin	Male — Masculin	Female — Féminin	Male — Masculin		Female — Féminin	
	Number Nombre	Number Nombre	Number Nombre	Number Nombre	Number Nombre	Rate Taux	Number Nombre	Rate Taux
Cerebrovascular disease — Maladie cérébrovasculaire.......................	764	860	909	1 006	1 534	96.1	2 146	125.8
Diseases of arteries, arterioles and capillaries — Maladies des artères, artérioles et capillaires	53	48	92	50	339	21.2	261	15.3
Diseases of the respiratory system — Maladies de l'appareil respiratoire								
Total...	733	570	817	712	1 774	111.2	1 335	78.2
Influenza — Grippe	-	1	1	1	1	♦0.1	1	♦0.1
Pneumonia — Pneumopathies......................................	435	342	463	430	509	31.9	591	34.6
Chronic lower respiratory diseases — Maladies chroniques des voies respiratoires inférieures	110	59	153	84	872	54.6	327	19.2
Diseases of the digestive system — Maladies de l'appareil digestif								
Total...	402	240	466	301	643	40.3	529	31.0
Gastric and duodenal ulcer — Ulcère de l'estomac et du duodénum	34	18	32	34	37	2.3	19	♦1.1
Diseases of the liver — Maladies du foie	146	41	181	51	231	14.5	70	4.1
Diseases of the musculoskeletal system and connective tissue — Maladies du système ostéo-articularie, des muscles et du tissu conjonctif	26	27	22	50	43	2.7	84	4.9
Diseases of the genitourinary system — Maladies de l'appareil génito-urinaire								
Total...	204	131	198	164	322	20.2	297	17.4
Disorders of kidney and ureter — Affections du rein et de l'uretère	177	105	167	135	238	14.9	202	11.8
Hyperplasia of prostate — Hyperplasie de la prostate.....................	1	..	5	..	17	♦4.3	..	..
Pregnancy, childbirth and the puerperium — Grossesse, accouchement et puerpéralité								
Total...	..	150	..	154	..	..	9	♦18.0
Pregnancy with abortive outcome — Grossesse se terminant par un avortement	..	36	..	35	..	..	1	♦2.0
Other direct obstetric causes — Autres décès maternels directs	..	106	..	108	..	..	8	♦16.0
Indirect obstetric causes — Décès maternels indirects......................	..	8	..	11	..	..	-	-
Certain conditions originating in the perinatal period — Certaines affections dont l'origine se situe dans la période périnatale	489	367	524	369	164	638.4	117	480.2
Congenital malformations, deformations and chromosomal abnormalities — Malformations congénitales et anomalies chromosomiques	135	129	169	133	121	471.0	110	451.5
Symptoms, signs and abnormal clinical and laboratory findings, not elsewhere classified — Symptômes, signes et résultats anormaux d'examens cliniques et de laboratoire, non classés ailleurs	2 241	1 990	2 032	1 775	1 395	87.4	1 185	69.5
All other diseases — Toutes autres maladies.............................	15	20	21	18	81	5.1	157	9.2
External causes — Causes externes								
Total...	1 921	401	1 983	573	1 358	85.1	541	31.7
Accidents								
Total...	900	236	971	407	760	47.6	339	19.9
Transport accidents — Accidents de transport	403	91	449	114	275	17.2	83	4.9
Falls — Chutes	31	9	25	8	28	♦1.8	9	♦0.5
Accidental drowning and submersion — Noyade et submersion accidentelles	85	21	78	21	59	3.7	12	♦0.7
Exposure to smoke, fire and flames — Exposition à la fumée, au feu et aux flammes	14	5	138	180	28	♦1.8	24	♦1.4
Accidental poisoning by and exposure to noxious substances — Intoxication accidentelle par des substances nocives et exposition à ces substances	15	6	8	7	15	♦0.9	6	♦0.4
Intentional self-harm — Lésions auto-infligées.............................	129	45	160	77	417	26.1	109	6.4
Assault — Agresssions	661	61	716	47	106	6.6	45	2.6
All other external causes — Toutes autres causes externes.................	231	59	136	42	75	4.7	48	2.8

21. Death and death rates by cause and sex: 2002 - 2006
Décès et taux de mortalité par cause et sexe : 2002 - 2006 (continued - suite)

Venezuela (Bolivarian Republic of) - Venezuela (République bolivarienne du)

Cause of death — Cause de décès	2004 (C) Male — Masculin Number Nombre	Rate Taux	2004 (C) Female — Féminin Number Nombre	Rate Taux	2005 (C) Male — Masculin Number Nombre	Rate Taux	2005 (C) Female — Féminin Number Nombre	Rate Taux
TOTAL..........	70 828	539.6	46 390	356.8	71 125	532.9	46 663	352.7
Certain infectious and parasitic diseases — Certaines maladies infectieuses et parasitaires								
Total.........	3 752	28.6	2 339	18.0	3 606	27.0	2 160	16.3
Intestinal infectious diseases — Maladies infectieuses intestinales............	1 000	7.6	865	6.7	912	6.8	763	5.8
Tuberculosis — Tuberculose................	470	3.6	221	1.7	412	3.1	213	1.6
Tetanus — Tétanos..................	9	♦0.1	4	♦0.0	13	♦0.1	7	♦0.1
Diphtheria — Diphtérie..............	-	-	-	-	-	-	-	-
Whooping cough — Coqueluche..........	25	♦0.2	35	0.3	23	♦0.2	13	♦0.1
Meningococcal infection — Infection à méningocoques................	11	♦0.1	2	♦0.0	1	♦0.0	6	♦0.0
Septicaemia — Septicémie..........	337	2.6	316	2.4	294	2.2	282	2.1
Acute poliomyelitis — Poliomyélite aiguë....	-	-	-	-	-	-	-	-
Measles — Rougeole................	-	-	-	-	-	-	-	-
Viral hepatitis — Hépatite virale............	107	0.8	84	0.6	73	0.5	39	0.3
Human immunodeficiency virus [HIV] disease — Maladies dues au virus de l'immunodéficience humaine (VIH)............	1 097	8.4	299	2.3	1 145	8.6	333	2.5
Malaria — Paludisme............	21	♦0.2	14	♦0.1	11	♦0.1	6	♦0.0
Neoplasms — Tumeurs..........	9 520	72.5	9 231	71.0	9 816	73.5	9 742	73.6
Malignant neoplasms — Tumeurs malignes								
Total.........	8 835	67.3	8 672	66.7	9 084	68.1	9 070	68.6
Malignant neoplasm of lip, oral cavity and pharynx — Tumeur maligne de la lèvre, de la cavité buccale et du pharynx	210	1.6	108	0.8	213	1.6	99	0.7
Malignant neoplasm of oesophagus — Tumeur maligne de l'oesophage......	189	1.4	65	0.5	184	1.4	75	0.6
Malignant neoplasm of stomach — Tumeur maligne de l'estomac............	1 048	8.0	681	5.2	1 076	8.1	668	5.0
Malignant neoplasm of colon, rectosigmoid junction, rectum, anus and anal canal — Tumeur maligne du côlon, de la jonction recto-sigmoïdienne, du rectum, de l'anus et du canal anal....	564	4.3	628	4.8	578	4.3	592	4.5
Malignant neoplasm of liver and intrahepatic bile ducts — Tumeur maligne du foie et des voies bilaires intrahépatiques............	351	2.7	374	2.9	356	2.7	349	2.6
Malignant neoplasm of pancreas — Tumeur maligne du pancréas............	261	2.0	302	2.3	335	2.5	351	2.7
Malignant neoplasm of trachea, bronchus and lung — Tumeur maligne de la trachée, des bronches et du poumon............	1 629	12.4	976	7.5	1 646	12.3	1 021	7.7
Malignant neoplasm of female breast — Tumeur maligne du sein chez la femme.........	..	..	1 375	15.4	..	..	1 425	15.5
Malignant neoplasm of cervix uteri — Tumeur maligne du col de l'utérus......	..	..	1 116	12.5	..	..	1 210	13.2
Malignant neoplasm of prostate — Tumeur maligne de la prostate............	1 713	89.8	..	..	1 766	89.0	..	..
Malignant neoplasm of lymphoid, haematopoietic and related tissue — Tumeurs malignes primitives ou présumées primitives des tissus lymphoïde, hématopoïétique et apparentés............	928	7.1	772	5.9	920	6.9	775	5.9
Disorders of the blood and blood-forming organs and certain disorders involving the immune mechanism — Maladies du sang et des organes hématopoïétiques et certains troubles du système immunitaire								
Total.........	145	1.1	184	1.4	141	1.1	172	1.3
Anaemias — Anémies............	101	0.8	116	0.9	107	0.8	122	0.9
Endocrine, nutritional and metabolic diseases — Maladies endocriniennes, nutritionnelles et métaboliques								
Total.........	4 165	31.7	4 359	33.5	4 129	30.9	4 250	32.1
Diabetes mellitus — Diabète sucré............	3 445	26.2	3 678	28.3	3 570	26.7	3 742	28.3
Malnutrition — Malnutrition............	500	3.8	458	3.5	350	2.6	293	2.2
Mental and behavioural disorders — Troubles mentaux et du comportement	148	1.1	24	♦0.2	117	0.9	18	♦0.1
Diseases of the nervous system — Maladies du système nerveux..........	1 075	8.2	856	6.6	975	7.3	804	6.1
Diseases of the circulatory system — Maladies de l'appareil circulatoire								
Total.........	19 140	145.8	15 784	121.4	19 599	146.8	15 851	119.8
Acute rheumatic fever and chronic rheumatic heart diseases — Rhumatisme articularie aigu et cardiopathies rhumatismales chroniques............	46	0.4	92	0.7	64	0.5	80	0.6
Hypertensive diseases — Maladies hypertensives............	2 261	17.2	2 383	18.3	2 321	17.4	2 227	16.8
Ischaemic heart disease — Cardiopathie ischémique............	10 404	79.3	7 100	54.6	10 684	80.0	7 106	53.7
Cerebrovascular disease — Maladie cérébrovasculaire............	4 127	31.4	4 159	32.0	4 302	32.2	4 392	33.2

Venezuela (Bolivarian Republic of)   Venezuela (République bolivarienne du)

Cause of death — Cause de décès	2004 (C)				2005 (C)			
	Male — Masculin		Female — Féminin		Male — Masculin		Female — Féminin	
	Number Nombre	Rate Taux	Number Nombre	Rate Taux	Number Nombre	Rate Taux	Number Nombre	Rate Taux
Diseases of arteries, arterioles and capillaries — Maladies des artères, artérioles et capillaires	377	2.9	299	2.3	377	2.8	291	2.2
Diseases of the respiratory system — Maladies de l'appareil respiratoire								
Total..................	3 959	30.2	3 372	25.9	3 982	29.8	3 550	26.8
Influenza — Grippe	4	♦0.0	11	♦0.1	10	♦0.1	12	♦0.1
Pneumonia — Pneumopathies..............	1 533	11.7	1 309	10.1	1 400	10.5	1 233	9.3
Chronic lower respiratory diseases — Maladies chroniques des voies respiratoires inférieures	1 731	13.2	1 435	11.0	1 838	13.8	1 559	11.8
Diseases of the digestive system — Maladies de l'appareil digestif								
Total...................	2 921	22.3	1 685	13.0	3 158	23.7	1 695	12.8
Gastric and duodenal ulcer — Ulcère de l'estomac et du duodénum	290	2.2	178	1.4	278	2.1	176	1.3
Diseases of the liver — Maladies du foie	1 677	12.8	532	4.1	1 883	14.1	565	4.3
Diseases of the musculoskeletal system and connective tissue — Maladies du système ostéo-articularie, des muscles et du tissu conjonctif	118	0.9	464	3.6	101	0.8	393	3.0
Diseases of the genitourinary system — Maladies de l'appareil génito-urinaire								
Total..................	1 025	7.8	749	5.8	1 044	7.8	737	5.6
Disorders of kidney and ureter — Affections du rein et de l'uretère	840	6.4	633	4.9	852	6.4	618	4.7
Hyperplasia of prostate — Hyperplasie de la prostate......................	90	4.7	..	..	108	5.4	..	..
Pregnancy, childbirth and the puerperium — Grossesse, accouchement et puerpéralité								
Total..................	..	..	318	49.9	..	..	351	52.7
Pregnancy with abortive outcome — Grossesse se terminant par un avortement	..	..	55	8.6	..	..	45	6.8
Other direct obstetric causes — Autres décès maternels directs	..	..	191	29.9	..	..	229	34.4
Indirect obstetric causes — Décès maternels indirects......................	..	..	72	11.3	..	..	73	11.0
Certain conditions originating in the perinatal period — Certaines affections dont l'origine se situe dans la période périnatale	3 037	926.7	2 237	721.4	3 157	919.3	2 260	700.6
Congenital malformations, deformations and chromosomal abnormalities — Malformations congénitales et anomalies chromosomiques	1 197	365.2	935	301.5	1 160	337.8	1 023	317.1
Symptoms, signs and abnormal clinical and laboratory findings, not elsewhere classified — Symptômes, signes et résultats anormaux d'examens cliniques et de laboratoire, non classés ailleurs	412	3.1	466	3.6	338	2.5	417	3.2
All other diseases — Toutes autres maladies..................	26	♦0.2	56	0.4	24	♦0.2	38	0.3
External causes — Causes externes								
Total..................	20 190	153.8	3 331	25.6	19 778	148.2	3 202	24.2
Accidents								
Total..................	6 448	49.1	1 938	14.9	6 536	49.0	1 935	14.6
Transport accidents — Accidents de transport	4 294	32.7	1 143	8.8	4 327	32.4	1 109	8.4
Falls — Chutes	446	3.4	252	1.9	444	3.3	258	2.0
Accidental drowning and submersion — Noyade et submersion accidentelles	498	3.8	100	0.8	492	3.7	98	0.7
Exposure to smoke, fire and flames — Exposition à la fumée, au feu et aux flammes	72	0.5	32	0.2	70	0.5	38	0.3
Accidental poisoning by and exposure to noxious substances — Intoxication accidentelle par des substances nocives et exposition à ces substances	65	0.5	37	0.3	57	0.4	25	♦0.2
Intentional self-harm — Lésions auto-infligées..............................	833	6.3	201	1.5	823	6.2	188	1.4
Assault — Agresssions	6 895	52.5	453	3.5	7 180	53.8	423	3.2
All other external causes — Toutes autres causes externes...................	6 014	45.8	739	5.7	5 239	39.3	656	5.0

21. Death and death rates by cause and sex: 2002 - 2006
Décès et taux de mortalité par cause et sexe : 2002 - 2006 (continued - suite)

Armenia - Arménie

Cause of death — Cause de décès	2002 (C)				2003 (C)			
	Male — Masculin		Female — Féminin		Male — Masculin		Female — Féminin	
	Number Nombre	Rate Taux	Number Nombre	Rate Taux	Number Nombre	Rate Taux	Number Nombre	Rate Taux
TOTAL..........	13 093	848.6	12 461	746.8	13 378	865.8	12 636	758.4
Certain infectious and parasitic diseases — Certaines maladies infectieuses et parasitaires								
Total..........	199	12.9	52	3.1	187	12.1	48	2.9
Intestinal infectious diseases — Maladies infectieuses intestinales............	15	♦1.0	8	♦0.5	8	♦0.5	13	♦0.8
Tuberculosis — Tuberculose..........	150	9.7	17	♦1.0	137	8.9	18	♦1.1
Tetanus — Tétanos	1	♦0.1	1	♦0.1	-	-	-	-
Diphtheria — Diphtérie..........	...	...	...	...	...	...	...	...
Whooping cough — Coqueluche	-	...	...	...	...	...	...	...
Meningococcal infection — Infection à méningocoques..........	-	-	-	-	2	♦0.1	-	-
Septicaemia — Septicémie..........	18	♦1.2	11	♦0.7	17	♦1.1	6	♦0.4
Acute poliomyelitis — Poliomyélite aiguë	...	...	...	...	...	...	...	...
Measles — Rougeole..........	...	...	-	-	-	-	-	-
Viral hepatitis — Hépatite virale	...	...	...	...	...	...	...	...
Human immunodeficiency virus [HIV] disease — Maladies dues au virus de l'immunodéficience humaine (VIH)	1	♦0.1	-	-	...	...	...	...
Malaria — Paludisme	-	-	-	-	-	-	-	-
Neoplasms — Tumeurs	2 367	153.4	1 875	112.4	2 401	155.4	1 968	118.1
Malignant neoplasms — Tumeurs malignes								
Total..........	2 365	153.3	1 868	111.9	2 396	155.1	1 960	117.6
Malignant neoplasm of lip, oral cavity and pharynx — Tumeur maligne de la lèvre, de la cavité buccale et du pharynx	47	3.0	10	♦0.6	69	4.5	19	♦1.1
Malignant neoplasm of oesophagus — Tumeur maligne de l'oesophage	33	2.1	11	♦0.7	32	2.1	13	♦0.8
Malignant neoplasm of stomach — Tumeur maligne de l'estomac..........	267	17.3	138	8.3	285	18.4	166	10.0
Malignant neoplasm of colon, rectosigmoid junction, rectum, anus and anal canal — Tumeur maligne du côlon, de la jonction recto-sigmoïdienne, du rectum, de l'anus et du canal anal..........	159	10.3	178	10.7	156	10.1	195	11.7
Malignant neoplasm of liver and intrahepatic bile ducts — Tumeur maligne du foie et des voies bilaires intrahépatiques	...	...	...	...	...	...	...	...
Malignant neoplasm of pancreas — Tumeur maligne du pancréas	...	...	...	...	...	...	...	...
Malignant neoplasm of trachea, bronchus and lung — Tumeur maligne de la trachée, des bronches et du poumon..........	743	48.2	137	8.2	760	49.2	132	7.9
Malignant neoplasm of female breast — Tumeur maligne du sein chez la femme..........	..	..	457	...	..	..	446	34.0
Malignant neoplasm of cervix uteri — Tumeur maligne du col de l'utérus	..	..	96	...	..	..	101	7.7
Malignant neoplasm of prostate — Tumeur maligne de la prostate	107	...	..	..	122	40.1	..	..
Malignant neoplasm of lymphoid, haematopoietic and related tissue — Tumeurs malignes primitives ou présumées primitives des tissus lymphoïde, hématopoïétique et apparentés	136	8.8	114	6.8	152	9.8	105	6.3
Disorders of the blood and blood-forming organs and certain disorders involving the immune mechanism — Maladies du sang et des organes hématopoïétiques et certains troubles du système immunitaire								
Total..........	5	♦0.3	6	♦0.4	14	♦0.9	19	♦1.1
Anaemias — Anémies	3	♦0.2	4	♦0.2	10	♦0.6	13	♦0.8
Endocrine, nutritional and metabolic diseases — Maladies endocriniennes, nutritionnelles et métaboliques								
Total..........	536	34.7	1 051	63.0	613	39.7	1 164	69.9
Diabetes mellitus — Diabète sucré..........	510	33.1	1 010	60.5	581	37.6	1 127	67.6
Malnutrition — Malnutrition..........	...	...	...	...	...	...	...	...
Mental and behavioural disorders — Troubles mentaux et du comportement	34	2.2	35	2.1	9	♦0.6	12	♦0.7
Diseases of the nervous system — Maladies du système nerveux..........	129	8.4	64	3.8	121	7.8	70	4.2
Diseases of the circulatory system — Maladies de l'appareil circulatoire								
Total..........	6 654	431.2	7 373	441.9	6 836	442.4	7 417	445.2
Acute rheumatic fever and chronic rheumatic heart diseases — Rhumatisme articularie aigu et cardiopathies rhumatismales chroniques	52	3.4	95	5.7	48	3.1	93	5.6
Hypertensive diseases — Maladies hypertensives	13	♦0.8	31	1.9	121	7.8	232	13.9
Ischaemic heart disease — Cardiopathie ischémique..........	4 292	278.2	4 193	251.3	4 420	286.1	4 151	249.1
Cerebrovascular disease — Maladie cérébrovasculaire..........	1 810	117.3	2 563	153.6	1 724	111.6	2 460	147.7

Armenia - Arménie

Cause of death — Cause de décès	2002 (C)				2003 (C)			
	Male — Masculin		Female — Féminin		Male — Masculin		Female — Féminin	
	Number Nombre	Rate Taux	Number Nombre	Rate Taux	Number Nombre	Rate Taux	Number Nombre	Rate Taux
Diseases of arteries, arterioles and capillaries — Maladies des artères, artérioles et capillaires	147	9.5	93	5.6	168	10.9	110	6.6
Diseases of the respiratory system — Maladies de l'appareil respiratoire								
Total	953	61.8	509	30.5	1 021	66.1	540	32.4
Influenza — Grippe	-	-	1	♦0.1	1	♦0.1	5	♦0.3
Pneumonia — Pneumopathies	121	7.8	77	4.6	117	7.6	79	4.7
Chronic lower respiratory diseases — Maladies chroniques des voies respiratoires inférieures	...	...	...	...	...	...	...	...
Diseases of the digestive system — Maladies de l'appareil digestif								
Total	623	40.4	386	23.1	623	40.3	378	22.7
Gastric and duodenal ulcer — Ulcère de l'estomac et du duodénum	97	6.3	44	2.6	92	6.0	48	2.9
Diseases of the liver — Maladies du foie	...	...	...	...	...	...	...	...
Diseases of the musculoskeletal system and connective tissue — Maladies du système ostéo-articularie, des muscles et du tissu conjonctif	32	2.1	47	2.8	23	♦1.5	45	2.7
Diseases of the genitourinary system — Maladies de l'appareil génito-urinaire								
Total	251	16.3	141	8.5	265	17.2	166	10.0
Disorders of kidney and ureter — Affections du rein et de l'uretère	159	10.3	128	7.7	194	12.6	141	8.5
Hyperplasia of prostate — Hyperplasie de la prostate	70	...	..		36	11.8	..	
Pregnancy, childbirth and the puerperium — Grossesse, accouchement et puerpéralité								
Total	..	..	3	♦9.3	..	..	8	♦22.4
Pregnancy with abortive outcome — Grossesse se terminant par un avortement	..	..	1	♦3.1	..	..	1	♦2.8
Other direct obstetric causes — Autres décès maternels directs	..	...	...	...	...	...	...	...
Indirect obstetric causes — Décès maternels indirects	..	..	..	..	...	...	...	...
Certain conditions originating in the perinatal period — Certaines affections dont l'origine se situe dans la période périnatale	122	706.0	88	588.7	128	664.0	65	393.6
Congenital malformations, deformations and chromosomal abnormalities — Malformations congénitales et anomalies chromosomiques	95	549.8	63	421.4	80	415.0	76	460.2
Symptoms, signs and abnormal clinical and laboratory findings, not elsewhere classified — Symptômes, signes et résultats anormaux d'examens cliniques et de laboratoire, non classés ailleurs	262	17.0	517	31.0	260	16.8	413	24.8
All other diseases — Toutes autres maladies	7	♦0.5	4	♦0.2	1	♦0.1	4	♦0.2
External causes — Causes externes								
Total	824	53.4	247	14.8	796	51.5	243	14.6
Accidents								
Total	426	27.6	156	9.3	449	29.1	134	8.0
Transport accidents — Accidents de transport	140	9.1	49	2.9	159	10.3	40	2.4
Falls — Chutes	13	♦0.8	9	♦0.5	14	♦0.9	10	♦0.6
Accidental drowning and submersion — Noyade et submersion accidentelles	32	2.1	7	♦0.4	27	♦1.7	2	♦0.1
Exposure to smoke, fire and flames — Exposition à la fumée, au feu et aux flammes	7	♦0.5	3	♦0.2	9	♦0.6	8	♦0.5
Accidental poisoning by and exposure to noxious substances — Intoxication accidentelle par des substances nocives et exposition à ces substances	46	3.0	24	♦1.4	28	♦1.8	17	♦1.0
Intentional self-harm — Lésions auto-infligées	62	4.0	12	♦0.7	50	3.2	9	♦0.5
Assault — Agresssions	55	3.6	15	♦0.9	51	3.3	9	♦0.5
All other external causes — Toutes autres causes externes	281	18.2	64	3.8	246	15.9	91	5.5

Cause of death — Cause de décès	Azerbaijan - Azerbaïdjan				China: Hong Kong SAR - Chine: Hong Kong RAS			
	2003 (U)		2004 (U)		2005 (...)		2006 (...)	
	Male — Masculin	Female — Féminin	Male — Masculin	Female — Féminin	Male — Masculin	Female — Féminin	Male — Masculin	Female — Féminin
	Number Nombre	Number Nombre	Number Nombre	Number Nombre	Number Nombre	Number Nombre	Number Nombre	Number Nombre
TOTAL	25 760	23 619	26 039	23 529	21 568	17 110	21 001	16 403
Certain infectious and parasitic diseases — Certaines maladies infectieuses et parasitaires								
Total	930	372	841	283	582	484	589	471
Intestinal infectious diseases — Maladies infectieuses intestinales	71	70	82	68	5	8	7	3
Tuberculosis — Tuberculose	747	223	670	143	186	55	193	70
Tetanus — Tétanos	-	-	1	1	1	-	1	-
Diphtheria — Diphtérie	2	-	-	-	-	-	-	-
Whooping cough — Coqueluche	1	1	-	-	-	-	-	-
Meningococcal infection — Infection à méningocoques	27	17	1	-	-	1	-	1
Septicaemia — Septicémie	-	-	7	18	321	380	322	354
Acute poliomyelitis — Poliomyélite aiguë	-	-	-	-	-	-	-	-
Measles — Rougeole	3	2	6	5	-	-	-	-
Viral hepatitis — Hépatite virale	31	27	56	35	10	6	3	3
Human immunodeficiency virus [HIV] disease — Maladies dues au virus de l'immunodéficience humaine (VIH)	-	-	-	-	12	1	7	1
Malaria — Paludisme	-	1	-	1	-	2	-	-
Neoplasms — Tumeurs	3 553	2 744	3 348	2 759	7 029	4 941	7 519	4 806
Malignant neoplasms — Tumeurs malignes								
Total	3 547	2 738	3 303	2 721	7 497	4 813	7 386	4 707
Malignant neoplasm of lip, oral cavity and pharynx — Tumeur maligne de la lèvre, de la cavité buccale et du pharynx	20	15	65	38	430	144	399	127
Malignant neoplasm of oesophagus — Tumeur maligne de l'oesophage	227	130	210	160	289	75	283	76
Malignant neoplasm of stomach — Tumeur maligne de l'estomac	673	430	673	420	396	239	391	244
Malignant neoplasm of colon, rectosigmoid junction, rectum, anus and anal canal — Tumeur maligne du côlon, de la jonction recto-sigmoïdienne, du rectum, de l'anus et du canal anal	183	173	225	198	906	708	923	705
Malignant neoplasm of liver and intrahepatic bile ducts — Tumeur maligne du foie et des voies bilaires intrahépatiques	234	214	241	204	1 119	387	1 075	387
Malignant neoplasm of pancreas — Tumeur maligne du pancréas	121	118	154	150	204	190	214	183
Malignant neoplasm of trachea, bronchus and lung — Tumeur maligne de la trachée, des bronches et du poumon	725	184	697	186	2 503	1 183	2 396	1 135
Malignant neoplasm of female breast — Tumeur maligne du sein chez la femme	..	437	..	433	..	460	..	463
Malignant neoplasm of cervix uteri — Tumeur maligne du col de l'utérus	..	63	..	106	..	126	..	133
Malignant neoplasm of prostate — Tumeur maligne de la prostate	314	..	164	..	231	..	285	..
Malignant neoplasm of lymphoid, haematopoietic and related tissue — Tumeurs malignes primitives ou présumées primitives des tissus lymphoïde, hématopoïétique et apparentés	...	...	...	...	393	306	397	302
Disorders of the blood and blood-forming organs and certain disorders involving the immune mechanism — Maladies du sang et des organes hématopoïétiques et certains troubles du système immunitaire								
Total	109	109	78	53	36	56	42	53
Anaemias — Anémies	65	69	64	49	14	30	16	24
Endocrine, nutritional and metabolic diseases — Maladies endocriniennes, nutritionnelles et métaboliques								
Total	519	793	550	785	292	413	279	325
Diabetes mellitus — Diabète sucré	492	756	533	759	247	355	232	279
Malnutrition — Malnutrition	5	3	6	4	3	5	-	2
Mental and behavioural disorders — Troubles mentaux et du comportement	70	43	19	16	107	185	120	178
Diseases of the nervous system — Maladies du système nerveux	522	423	325	232	159	142	154	132
Diseases of the circulatory system — Maladies de l'appareil circulatoire								
Total	13 788	14 388	14 073	14 422	5 062	5 076	4 862	4 818
Acute rheumatic fever and chronic rheumatic heart diseases — Rhumatisme articularie aigu et cardiopathies rhumatismales chroniques	55	61	51	68	49	89	28	68
Hypertensive diseases — Maladies hypertensives	801	1 080	2 452	3 465	353	472	371	435
Ischaemic heart disease — Cardiopathie ischémique	8 991	8 284	7 171	5 423	2 176	1 827	2 049	1 700

21. Death and death rates by cause and sex: 2002 - 2006
Décès et taux de mortalité par cause et sexe : 2002 - 2006 (continued - suite)

	Azerbaijan - Azerbaïdjan				China: Hong Kong SAR - Chine: Hong Kong RAS			
	2003 (U)		2004 (U)		2005 (...)		2006 (...)	
Cause of death — Cause de décès	Male — Masculin	Female — Féminin	Male — Masculin	Female — Féminin	Male — Masculin	Female — Féminin	Male — Masculin	Female — Féminin
	Number Nombre	Number Nombre	Number Nombre	Number Nombre	Number Nombre	Number Nombre	Number Nombre	Number Nombre
Cerebrovascular disease — Maladie cérébrovasculaire	2 722	3 709	2 992	4 022	1 663	1 771	1 603	1 699
Diseases of arteries, arterioles and capillaries — Maladies des artères, artérioles et capillaires	...	...	...	...	248	171	256	163
Diseases of the respiratory system — Maladies de l'appareil respiratoire								
Total	1 736	1 456	1 662	1 548	4 159	2 917	3 932	2 678
Influenza — Grippe	2	-	24	35	14	12	6	2
Pneumonia — Pneumopathies	755	672	833	830	2 276	2 015	2 264	1 937
Chronic lower respiratory diseases — Maladies chroniques des voies respiratoires inférieures	488	419	555	446	1 598	663	1 382	542
Diseases of the digestive system — Maladies de l'appareil digestif								
Total	1 496	1 338	1 607	1 433	778	645	813	662
Gastric and duodenal ulcer — Ulcère de l'estomac et du duodénum	200	84	156	72	75	55	72	40
Diseases of the liver — Maladies du foie	1 054	1 007	1 218	1 162	317	181	328	186
Diseases of the musculoskeletal system and connective tissue — Maladies du système ostéo-articulaire, des muscles et du tissu conjonctif	52	76	15	21	47	82	50	71
Diseases of the genitourinary system — Maladies de l'appareil génito-urinaire								
Total	485	412	640	409	790	1 011	827	1 037
Disorders of kidney and ureter — Affections du rein et de l'uretère	...	...	...	...	620	684	648	682
Hyperplasia of prostate — Hyperplasie de la prostate	...	..	...	..	17	..	20	..
Pregnancy, childbirth and the puerperium — Grossesse, accouchement et puerpéralité								
Total	..	21	..	34	..	2	..	1
Pregnancy with abortive outcome — Grossesse se terminant par un avortement	..	1	..	6	..	1	..	-
Other direct obstetric causes — Autres décès maternels directs	..	19	..	25	..	1	..	1
Indirect obstetric causes — Décès maternels indirects	..	-	..	1	..	-	..	-
Certain conditions originating in the perinatal period — Certaines affections dont l'origine se situe dans la période périnatale	218	182	328	219	29	23	24	15
Congenital malformations, deformations and chromosomal abnormalities — Malformations congénitales et anomalies chromosomiques	97	83	165	110	47	42	55	42
Symptoms, signs and abnormal clinical and laboratory findings, not elsewhere classified — Symptômes, signes et résultats anormaux d'examens cliniques et de laboratoire, non classés ailleurs	595	651	857	756	329	198	372	277
All other diseases — Toutes autres maladies	4	5	12	4	120	145	99	140
External causes — Causes externes								
Total	1 586	523	1 519	445	1 402	748	1 264	697
Accidents								
Total	...	...	...	...	562	233	557	233
Transport accidents — Accidents de transport	407	141	265	65	153	50	115	61
Falls — Chutes	24	5	36	24	77	51	119	53
Accidental drowning and submersion — Noyade et submersion accidentelles	146	47	119	38	22	13	43	13
Exposure to smoke, fire and flames — Exposition à la fumée, au feu et aux flammes	215	106	143	68	1	1	11	3
Accidental poisoning by and exposure to noxious substances — Intoxication accidentelle par des substances nocives et exposition à ces substances	93	32	37	15	151	29	129	20
Intentional self-harm — Lésions auto-infligées	93	36	78	30	718	431	630	412
Assault — Agresssions	173	40	130	27	13	23	20	15
All other external causes — Toutes autres causes externes	...	...	...	...	109	61	57	37

Cyprus - Chypre

Cause of death — Cause de décès	2004 (C)				2006 (C)			
	Male — Masculin		Female — Féminin		Male — Masculin		Female — Féminin	
	Number Nombre	Rate Taux	Number Nombre	Rate Taux	Number Nombre	Rate Taux	Number Nombre	Rate Taux
TOTAL...........	2 825	778.2	2 400	641.5	2 623	690.1	2 504	640.7
Certain infectious and parasitic diseases — Certaines maladies infectieuses et parasitaires								
Total...	21	♦5.8	24	♦6.4	17	♦4.5	18	♦4.6
Intestinal infectious diseases — Maladies infectieuses intestinales............	-	-	1	♦0.3	2	♦0.5	-	-
Tuberculosis — Tuberculose...........	3	♦0.8	-	-	-	-	1	♦0.3
Tetanus — Tétanos.....................	-	-	-	-	-	-	-	-
Diphtheria — Diphtérie................	-	-	-	-	-	-	-	-
Whooping cough — Coqueluche...........	-	-	-	-	-	-	1	♦0.3
Meningococcal infection — Infection à méningocoques..............	1	♦0.3	-	-	1	♦0.3	-	-
Septicaemia — Septicémie............	12	♦3.3	17	♦4.5	9	♦2.4	11	♦2.8
Acute poliomyelitis — Poliomyélite aiguë	-	-	-	-	-	-	-	-
Measles — Rougeole..................	-	-	-	-	-	-	-	-
Viral hepatitis — Hépatite virale.....	-	-	3	♦0.8	2	♦0.5	-	-
Human immunodeficiency virus [HIV] disease — Maladies dues au virus de l'immunodéficience humaine (VIH).......................................	1	♦0.3	-	-	1	♦0.3	1	♦0.3
Malaria — Paludisme................	-	-	-	-	-	-	-	-
Neoplasms — Tumeurs....................	603	166.1	403	107.7	569	149.7	448	114.6
Malignant neoplasms — Tumeurs malignes								
Total....................	589	162.3	388	103.7	558	146.8	431	110.3
Malignant neoplasm of lip, oral cavity and pharynx — Tumeur maligne de la lèvre, de la cavité buccale et du pharynx	6	♦1.7	2	♦0.5	6	♦1.6	1	♦0.3
Malignant neoplasm of oesophagus — Tumeur maligne de l'oesophage	6	♦1.7	-	-	12	♦3.2	1	♦0.3
Malignant neoplasm of stomach — Tumeur maligne de l'estomac............	24	♦6.6	12	♦3.2	32	8.4	14	♦3.6
Malignant neoplasm of colon, rectosigmoid junction, rectum, anus and anal canal — Tumeur maligne du côlon, de la jonction recto-sigmoïdienne, du rectum, de l'anus et du canal anal.....	55	15.2	41	11.0	43	11.3	45	11.5
Malignant neoplasm of liver and intrahepatic bile ducts — Tumeur maligne du foie et des voies bilaires intrahépatiques	22	♦6.1	6	♦1.6	23	♦6.1	16	♦4.1
Malignant neoplasm of pancreas — Tumeur maligne du pancréas............	28	♦7.7	21	♦5.6	21	♦5.5	19	♦4.9
Malignant neoplasm of trachea, bronchus and lung — Tumeur maligne de la trachée, des bronches et du poumon.....	143	39.4	23	♦6.1	121	31.8	34	8.7
Malignant neoplasm of female breast — Tumeur maligne du sein chez la femme....................	..	..	88	28.9	..	..	95	29.4
Malignant neoplasm of cervix uteri — Tumeur maligne du col de l'utérus......	..	..	8	♦2.6	..	..	7	♦2.2
Malignant neoplasm of prostate — Tumeur maligne de la prostate............	82	83.5	..	..	82	76.9	..	..
Malignant neoplasm of lymphoid, haematopoietic and related tissue — Tumeurs malignes primitives ou présumées primitives des tissus lymphoïde, hématopoïétique et apparentés....................	66	18.2	36	9.6	56	14.7	44	11.3
Disorders of the blood and blood-forming organs and certain disorders involving the immune mechanism — Maladies du sang et des organes hématopoïétiques et certains troubles du système immunitaire								
Total....................	9	♦2.5	14	♦3.7	12	♦3.2	20	♦5.1
Anaemias — Anémies............	9	♦2.5	12	♦3.2	7	♦1.8	16	♦4.1
Endocrine, nutritional and metabolic diseases — Maladies endocriniennes, nutritionnelles et métaboliques								
Total....................	184	50.7	208	55.6	188	49.5	201	51.4
Diabetes mellitus — Diabète sucré............	173	47.7	184	49.2	164	43.1	170	43.5
Malnutrition — Malnutrition................	-	-	-	-	-	-	1	♦0.3
Mental and behavioural disorders — Troubles mentaux et du comportement	14	♦3.9	15	♦4.0	23	♦6.1	41	10.5
Diseases of the nervous system — Maladies du système nerveux...........	55	15.2	50	13.4	59	15.5	66	16.9
Diseases of the circulatory system — Maladies de l'appareil circulatoire								
Total....................	1 067	293.9	951	254.2	1 020	268.4	1 020	261.0
Acute rheumatic fever and chronic rheumatic heart diseases — Rhumatisme articularie aigu et cardiopathies rhumatismales chroniques	7	♦1.9	7	♦1.9	6	♦1.6	9	♦2.3
Hypertensive diseases — Maladies hypertensives....................	57	15.7	102	27.3	56	14.7	99	25.3
Ischaemic heart disease — Cardiopathie ischémique.....................	410	112.9	227	60.7	430	113.1	257	65.8
Cerebrovascular disease — Maladie cérébrovasculaire....................	204	56.2	202	54.0	225	59.2	267	68.3

Cyprus - Chypre

Cause of death — Cause de décès	2004 (C)				2006 (C)			
	Male — Masculin		Female — Féminin		Male — Masculin		Female — Féminin	
	Number Nombre	Rate Taux	Number Nombre	Rate Taux	Number Nombre	Rate Taux	Number Nombre	Rate Taux
Diseases of arteries, arterioles and capillaries — Maladies des artères, artérioles et capillaires	40	11.0	32	8.6	43	11.3	36	9.2
Diseases of the respiratory system — Maladies de l'appareil respiratoire								
Total	196	54.0	155	41.4	179	47.1	163	41.7
Influenza — Grippe	-	-	-	-	-	-	-	-
Pneumonia — Pneumopathies	51	14.0	52	13.9	39	10.3	56	14.3
Chronic lower respiratory diseases — Maladies chroniques des voies respiratoires inférieures	72	19.8	42	11.2	60	15.8	38	9.7
Diseases of the digestive system — Maladies de l'appareil digestif								
Total	95	26.2	83	22.2	83	21.8	101	25.8
Gastric and duodenal ulcer — Ulcère de l'estomac et du duodénum	7	♦1.9	6	♦1.6	6	♦1.6	6	♦1.5
Diseases of the liver — Maladies du foie	33	9.1	19	♦5.1	29	♦7.6	24	♦6.1
Diseases of the musculoskeletal system and connective tissue — Maladies du système ostéo-articulaire, des muscles et du tissu conjonctif	7	♦1.9	18	♦4.8	11	♦2.9	16	♦4.1
Diseases of the genitourinary system — Maladies de l'appareil génito-urinaire								
Total	66	18.2	61	16.3	82	21.6	76	19.4
Disorders of kidney and ureter — Affections du rein et de l'uretère	56	15.4	45	12.0	67	17.6	52	13.3
Hyperplasia of prostate — Hyperplasie de la prostate	3	♦3.1	..	..	-	-		
Pregnancy, childbirth and the puerperium — Grossesse, accouchement et puerpéralité								
Total	..	..	-	-	..	..	1	♦11.5
Pregnancy with abortive outcome — Grossesse se terminant par un avortement	..	..	-	-	..	..	-	-
Other direct obstetric causes — Autres décès maternels directs	..	..	-	-	..	..	1	♦11.5
Indirect obstetric causes — Décès maternels indirects	..	..	-	-	..	..	-	-
Certain conditions originating in the perinatal period — Certaines affections dont l'origine se situe dans la période périnatale	9	♦211.4	3	♦74.0	5	♦109.7	2	♦47.9
Congenital malformations, deformations and chromosomal abnormalities — Malformations congénitales et anomalies chromosomiques	4	♦94.0	7	♦172.8	8	♦175.5	6	♦143.8
Symptoms, signs and abnormal clinical and laboratory findings, not elsewhere classified — Symptômes, signes et résultats anormaux d'examens cliniques et de laboratoire, non classés ailleurs	264	72.7	292	78.1	178	46.8	210	53.7
All other diseases — Toutes autres maladies	6	♦1.7	16	♦4.3	4	♦1.1	13	♦3.3
External causes — Causes externes								
Total	225	62.0	100	26.7	185	48.7	102	26.1
Accidents								
Total	202	55.6	90	24.1	159	41.8	87	22.3
Transport accidents — Accidents de transport	107	29.5	21	♦5.6	77	20.3	15	♦3.8
Falls — Chutes	16	♦4.4	4	♦1.1	16	♦4.2	9	♦2.3
Accidental drowning and submersion — Noyade et submersion accidentelles	12	♦3.3	9	♦2.4	13	♦3.4	3	♦0.8
Exposure to smoke, fire and flames — Exposition à la fumée, au feu et aux flammes	3	♦0.8	2	♦0.5	3	♦0.8	1	♦0.3
Accidental poisoning by and exposure to noxious substances — Intoxication accidentelle par des substances nocives et exposition à ces substances	1	♦0.3	2	♦0.5	6	♦1.6	-	-
Intentional self-harm — Lésions auto-infligées	4	♦1.1	1	♦0.3	12	♦3.2	7	♦1.8
Assault — Agresssions	7	♦1.9	4	♦1.1	11	♦2.9	3	♦0.8
All other external causes — Toutes autres causes externes	12	♦3.3	5	♦1.3	3	♦0.8	5	♦1.3

21. Death and death rates by cause and sex: 2002 - 2006
Décès et taux de mortalité par cause et sexe : 2002 - 2006 (continued - suite)

Israel - Israël

Cause of death — Cause de décès	2003 (C)				2004 (C)			
	Male — Masculin		Female — Féminin		Male — Masculin		Female — Féminin	
	Number Nombre	Rate Taux	Number Nombre	Rate Taux	Number Nombre	Rate Taux	Number Nombre	Rate Taux
TOTAL.............	19 332	585.5	19 027	561.6	18 999	565.1	18 758	544.2
Certain infectious and parasitic diseases — Certaines maladies infectieuses et parasitaires								
Total...	512	15.5	551	16.3	491	14.6	571	16.6
Intestinal infectious diseases — Maladies infectieuses intestinales............	45	1.4	56	1.7	37	1.1	55	1.6
Tuberculosis — Tuberculose...........	15	♦0.5	9	♦0.3	11	♦0.3	4	♦0.1
Tetanus — Tétanos ...	-	-	-	-	-	-	-	-
Diphtheria — Diphtérie..........	-	-	-	-	-	-	-	-
Whooping cough — Coqueluche	-	-	-	-	2	♦0.1	-	-
Meningococcal infection — Infection à méningocoques	2	♦0.1	-	-	1	♦0.0	1	♦0.0
Septicaemia — Septicémie............	312	9.4	372	11.0	300	8.9	370	10.7
Acute poliomyelitis — Poliomyélite aiguë	1	♦0.0	1	♦0.0	-	-	-	-
Measles — Rougeole............	-	-	-	-	-	-	-	-
Viral hepatitis — Hépatite virale	75	2.3	67	2.0	78	2.3	83	2.4
Human immunodeficiency virus [HIV] disease — Maladies dues au virus de l'immunodéficience humaine (VIH) ...	18	♦0.5	8	♦0.2	12	♦0.4	8	♦0.2
Malaria — Paludisme..........	1	♦0.0	-	-	2	♦0.1	1	♦0.0
Neoplasms — Tumeurs	4 888	148.0	4 912	145.0	4 799	142.7	4 728	137.2
Malignant neoplasms — Tumeurs malignes								
Total...	4 766	144.3	4 761	140.5	4 685	139.4	4 595	133.3
Malignant neoplasm of lip, oral cavity and pharynx — Tumeur maligne de la lèvre, de la cavité buccale et du pharynx	62	1.9	38	1.1	53	1.6	20	♦0.6
Malignant neoplasm of oesophagus — Tumeur maligne de l'oesophage	77	2.3	35	1.0	69	2.1	38	1.1
Malignant neoplasm of stomach — Tumeur maligne de l'estomac............	299	9.1	185	5.5	237	7.0	191	5.5
Malignant neoplasm of colon, rectosigmoid junction, rectum, anus and anal canal — Tumeur maligne du côlon, de la jonction recto-sigmoïdienne, du rectum, de l'anus et du canal anal...	649	19.7	640	18.9	603	17.9	602	17.5
Malignant neoplasm of liver and intrahepatic bile ducts — Tumeur maligne du foie et des voies biliaires intrahépatiques	143	4.3	117	3.5	144	4.3	106	3.1
Malignant neoplasm of pancreas — Tumeur maligne du pancréas	319	9.7	332	9.8	342	10.2	303	8.8
Malignant neoplasm of trachea, bronchus and lung — Tumeur maligne de la trachée, des bronches et du poumon	952	28.8	435	12.8	1 024	30.5	444	12.9
Malignant neoplasm of female breast — Tumeur maligne du sein chez la femme.........	..	..	931	37.8	..	..	945	37.7
Malignant neoplasm of cervix uteri — Tumeur maligne du col de l'utérus	..	..	64	2.6	..	..	57	2.3
Malignant neoplasm of prostate — Tumeur maligne de la prostate	434	63.1	..	..	431	60.9	..	..
Malignant neoplasm of lymphoid, haematopoietic and related tissue — Tumeurs malignes primitives ou présumées primitives des tissus lymphoïde, hématopoïétique et apparentés	548	16.6	487	14.4	562	16.7	491	14.2
Disorders of the blood and blood-forming organs and certain disorders involving the immune mechanism — Maladies du sang et des organes hématopoïétiques et certains troubles du système immunitaire								
Total...	137	4.1	229	6.8	105	3.1	131	3.8
Anaemias — Anémies	84	2.5	167	4.9	59	1.8	84	2.4
Endocrine, nutritional and metabolic diseases — Maladies endocriniennes, nutritionnelles et métaboliques								
Total...	1 517	45.9	1 896	56.0	1 342	39.9	1 748	50.7
Diabetes mellitus — Diabète sucré...........	1 267	38.4	1 521	44.9	1 138	33.8	1 388	40.3
Malnutrition — Malnutrition............	8	♦0.2	22	♦0.6	5	♦0.1	9	♦0.3
Mental and behavioural disorders — Troubles mentaux et du comportement	272	8.2	382	11.3	292	8.7	315	9.1
Diseases of the nervous system — Maladies du système nerveux...	572	17.3	564	16.6	500	14.9	531	15.4
Diseases of the circulatory system — Maladies de l'appareil circulatoire								
Total...	5 536	167.7	5 760	170.0	5 364	159.5	5 666	164.4
Acute rheumatic fever and chronic rheumatic heart diseases — Rhumatisme articularie aigu et cardiopathies rhumatismales chroniques	23	♦0.7	68	2.0	30	♦0.9	53	1.5
Hypertensive diseases — Maladies hypertensives............	233	7.1	416	12.3	282	8.4	447	13.0
Ischaemic heart disease — Cardiopathie ischémique............	2 895	87.7	2 467	72.8	2 550	75.8	2 187	63.4
Cerebrovascular disease — Maladie cérébrovasculaire......................	1 133	34.3	1 352	39.9	1 181	35.1	1 459	42.3

21. Death and death rates by cause and sex: 2002 - 2006
Décès et taux de mortalité par cause et sexe : 2002 - 2006 (continued - suite)

Israel - Israël

Cause of death — Cause de décès	2003 (C)				2004 (C)			
	Male — Masculin		Female — Féminin		Male — Masculin		Female — Féminin	
	Number Nombre	Rate Taux	Number Nombre	Rate Taux	Number Nombre	Rate Taux	Number Nombre	Rate Taux
Diseases of arteries, arterioles and capillaries — Maladies des artères, artérioles et capillaires	160	4.8	131	3.9	191	5.7	137	4.0
Diseases of the respiratory system — Maladies de l'appareil respiratoire								
Total............	1 290	39.1	1 283	37.9	1 330	39.6	1 307	37.9
Influenza — Grippe	1	♦0.0	2	♦0.1	-	-	-	-
Pneumonia — Pneumopathies............	326	9.9	325	9.6	319	9.5	350	10.2
Chronic lower respiratory diseases — Maladies chroniques des voies respiratoires inférieures	598	18.1	512	15.1	593	17.6	492	14.3
Diseases of the digestive system — Maladies de l'appareil digestif								
Total............	602	18.2	622	18.4	622	18.5	670	19.4
Gastric and duodenal ulcer — Ulcère de l'estomac et du duodénum	33	1.0	32	0.9	23	♦0.7	36	1.0
Diseases of the liver — Maladies du foie	229	6.9	161	4.8	196	5.8	143	4.1
Diseases of the musculoskeletal system and connective tissue — Maladies du système ostéo-articulaire, des muscles et du tissu conjonctif	74	2.2	133	3.9	93	2.8	126	3.7
Diseases of the genitourinary system — Maladies de l'appareil génito-urinaire								
Total............	915	27.7	843	24.9	1 084	32.2	1 081	31.4
Disorders of kidney and ureter — Affections du rein et de l'uretère	755	22.9	598	17.7	950	28.3	860	24.9
Hyperplasia of prostate — Hyperplasie de la prostate............	14	♦2.0	..	..	9	♦1.3	..	..
Pregnancy, childbirth and the puerperium — Grossesse, accouchement et puerpéralité								
Total............	..	..	3	♦2.1	..	..	6	♦4.1
Pregnancy with abortive outcome — Grossesse se terminant par un avortement	..	..	-	-	..	..	-	-
Other direct obstetric causes — Autres décès maternels directs	..	..	3	♦2.1	..	..	6	♦4.1
Indirect obstetric causes — Décès maternels indirects............	..	..	-	-	..	..	-	-
Certain conditions originating in the perinatal period — Certaines affections dont l'origine se situe dans la période périnatale	192	258.5	159	225.0	161	215.5	147	208.5
Congenital malformations, deformations and chromosomal abnormalities — Malformations congénitales et anomalies chromosomiques	143	192.5	106	150.0	147	196.8	106	150.3
Symptoms, signs and abnormal clinical and laboratory findings, not elsewhere classified — Symptômes, signes et résultats anormaux d'examens cliniques et de laboratoire, non classés ailleurs	1 001	30.3	696	20.5	1 066	31.7	697	20.2
All other diseases — Toutes autres maladies............	156	4.7	238	7.0	154	4.6	248	7.2
External causes — Causes externes								
Total............	1 525	46.2	650	19.2	1 449	43.1	680	19.7
Accidents								
Total............	844	25.6	430	12.7	843	25.1	480	13.9
Transport accidents — Accidents de transport	364	11.0	136	4.0	388	11.5	159	4.6
Falls — Chutes	70	2.1	30	♦0.9	44	1.3	43	1.2
Accidental drowning and submersion — Noyade et submersion accidentelles............	26	♦0.8	9	♦0.3	37	1.1	7	♦0.2
Exposure to smoke, fire and flames — Exposition à la fumée, au feu et aux flammes	8	♦0.2	12	♦0.4	17	♦0.5	5	♦0.1
Accidental poisoning by and exposure to noxious substances — Intoxication accidentelle par des substances nocives et exposition à ces substances	82	2.5	7	♦0.2	73	2.2	16	♦0.5
Intentional self-harm — Lésions auto-infligées............	345	10.4	72	2.1	320	9.5	91	2.6
Assault — Agresssions	235	7.1	91	2.7	170	5.1	62	1.8
All other external causes — Toutes autres causes externes............	101	3.1	57	1.7	116	3.5	47	1.4

Japan - Japon

Cause of death — Cause de décès	2005 (C)				2006 (C)			
	Male — Masculin		Female — Féminin		Male — Masculin		Female — Féminin	
	Number Nombre	Rate Taux	Number Nombre	Rate Taux	Number Nombre	Rate Taux	Number Nombre	Rate Taux
TOTAL	584 970	949.5	498 826	772.0	581 370	944.3	503 080	778.8
Certain infectious and parasitic diseases — Certaines maladies infectieuses et parasitaires								
Total	12 211	19.8	11 327	17.5	12 223	19.9	11 788	18.2
Intestinal infectious diseases — Maladies infectieuses intestinales	733	1.2	1 019	1.6	916	1.5	1 274	2.0
Tuberculosis — Tuberculose	1 579	2.6	717	1.1	1 517	2.5	752	1.2
Tetanus — Tétanos	5	♦0.0	2	♦0.0	5	♦0.0	-	-
Diphtheria — Diphtérie	-		-		-		-	
Whooping cough — Coqueluche	-		-		-		1	♦0.0
Meningococcal infection — Infection à méningocoques	1	♦0.0	1	♦0.0	3	♦0.0	1	♦0.0
Septicaemia — Septicémie	4 045	6.6	4 459	6.9	4 257	6.9	4 605	7.1
Acute poliomyelitis — Poliomyélite aiguë	-		-		-		-	
Measles — Rougeole	1	♦0.0	2	♦0.0	-		-	
Viral hepatitis — Hépatite virale	3 093	5.0	2 949	4.6	2 856	4.6	2 959	4.6
Human immunodeficiency virus [HIV] disease — Maladies dues au virus de l'immunodéficience humaine (VIH)	62	0.1	7	♦0.0	55	0.1	5	♦0.0
Malaria — Paludisme	1	♦0.0	-	-	-		1	♦0.0
Neoplasms — Tumeurs	201 728	327.4	134 142	207.6	203 181	330.0	136 243	210.9
Malignant neoplasms — Tumeurs malignes								
Total	196 603	319.1	129 338	200.2	198 052	321.7	131 262	203.2
Malignant neoplasm of lip, oral cavity and pharynx — Tumeur maligne de la lèvre, de la cavité buccale et du pharynx	4 151	6.7	1 528	2.4	4 310	7.0	1 708	2.6
Malignant neoplasm of oesophagus — Tumeur maligne de l'oesophage	9 465	15.4	1 717	2.7	9 650	15.7	1 695	2.6
Malignant neoplasm of stomach — Tumeur maligne de l'estomac	32 643	53.0	17 668	27.3	32 745	53.2	17 670	27.4
Malignant neoplasm of colon, rectosigmoid junction, rectum, anus and anal canal — Tumeur maligne du côlon, de la jonction recto-sigmoïdienne, du rectum, de l'anus et du canal anal	22 283	36.2	18 814	29.1	22 547	36.6	18 834	29.2
Malignant neoplasm of liver and intrahepatic bile ducts — Tumeur maligne du foie et des voies bilaires intrahépatiques	23 203	37.7	11 065	17.1	22 576	36.7	11 086	17.2
Malignant neoplasm of pancreas — Tumeur maligne du pancréas	12 284	19.9	10 643	16.5	12 539	20.4	10 827	16.8
Malignant neoplasm of trachea, bronchus and lung — Tumeur maligne de la trachée, des bronches et du poumon	45 189	73.3	16 874	26.1	45 941	74.6	17 314	26.8
Malignant neoplasm of female breast — Tumeur maligne du sein chez la femme	..	..	10 721	18.9	..	..	11 177	19.6
Malignant neoplasm of cervix uteri — Tumeur maligne du col de l'utérus	..	..	2 465	4.3	..	..	2 481	4.4
Malignant neoplasm of prostate — Tumeur maligne de la prostate	9 265	38.2	..	..	9 527	38.5	..	..
Malignant neoplasm of lymphoid, haematopoietic and related tissue — Tumeurs malignes primitives ou présumées primitives des tissus lymphoïde, hématopoïétique et apparentés	11 144	18.1	8 608	13.3	11 275	18.3	8 703	13.5
Disorders of the blood and blood-forming organs and certain disorders involving the immune mechanism — Maladies du sang et des organes hématopoïétiques et certains troubles du système immunitaire								
Total	1 872	3.0	2 301	3.6	1 899	3.1	2 281	3.5
Anaemias — Anémies	650	1.1	1 018	1.6	630	1.0	959	1.5
Endocrine, nutritional and metabolic diseases — Maladies endocriniennes, nutritionnelles et métaboliques								
Total	9 974	16.2	9 752	15.1	10 056	16.3	9 549	14.8
Diabetes mellitus — Diabète sucré	7 131	11.6	6 490	10.0	7 268	11.8	6 382	9.9
Malnutrition — Malnutrition	857	1.4	813	1.3	810	1.3	710	1.1
Mental and behavioural disorders — Troubles mentaux et du comportement	1 692	2.7	2 910	4.5	1 833	3.0	3 335	5.2
Diseases of the nervous system — Maladies du système nerveux	6 650	10.8	6 354	9.8	7 220	11.7	7 031	10.9
Diseases of the circulatory system — Maladies de l'appareil circulatoire								
Total	159 268	258.5	170 207	263.4	155 787	253.1	168 999	261.6
Acute rheumatic fever and chronic rheumatic heart diseases — Rhumatisme articulaire aigu et cardiopathies rhumatismales chroniques	837	1.4	1 703	2.6	800	1.3	1 668	2.6
Hypertensive diseases — Maladies hypertensives	2 145	3.5	3 690	5.7	2 095	3.4	3 715	5.8
Ischaemic heart disease — Cardiopathie ischémique	41 970	68.1	34 533	53.4	41 296	67.1	34 133	52.8
Cerebrovascular disease — Maladie cérébrovasculaire	63 657	103.3	69 190	107.1	61 348	99.7	66 920	103.6

Japan - Japon

Cause of death — Cause de décès	2005 (C)				2006 (C)			
	Male — Masculin		Female — Féminin		Male — Masculin		Female — Féminin	
	Number Nombre	Rate Taux	Number Nombre	Rate Taux	Number Nombre	Rate Taux	Number Nombre	Rate Taux
Diseases of arteries, arterioles and capillaries — Maladies des artères, artérioles et capillaires	7 902	12.8	6 489	10.0	8 065	13.1	6 516	10.1
Diseases of the respiratory system — Maladies de l'appareil respiratoire								
Total	92 157	149.6	73 842	114.3	90 080	146.3	72 827	112.7
Influenza — Grippe	863	1.4	955	1.5	428	0.7	437	0.7
Pneumonia — Pneumopathies	57 310	93.0	49 931	77.3	56 572	91.9	50 670	78.4
Chronic lower respiratory diseases — Maladies chroniques des voies respiratoires inférieures	13 253	21.5	6 003	9.3	12 795	20.8	5 969	9.2
Diseases of the digestive system — Maladies de l'appareil digestif								
Total	22 978	37.3	18 824	29.1	23 133	37.6	19 296	29.9
Gastric and duodenal ulcer — Ulcère de l'estomac et du duodénum	1 897	3.1	1 593	2.5	1 924	3.1	1 479	2.3
Diseases of the liver — Maladies du foie	11 007	17.9	5 423	8.4	10 909	17.7	5 358	8.3
Diseases of the musculoskeletal system and connective tissue — Maladies du système ostéo-articularie, des muscles et du tissu conjonctif	1 566	2.5	3 037	4.7	1 701	2.8	3 147	4.9
Diseases of the genitourinary system — Maladies de l'appareil génito-urinaire								
Total	11 793	19.1	15 159	23.5	12 105	19.7	15 754	24.4
Disorders of kidney and ureter — Affections du rein et de l'uretère	10 770	17.5	13 288	20.6	11 063	18.0	13 792	21.4
Hyperplasia of prostate — Hyperplasie de la prostate	91	0.4	..	..	79	0.3	..	..
Pregnancy, childbirth and the puerperium — Grossesse, accouchement et puerpéralité								
Total	..	..	66	6.2	..	..	63	5.8
Pregnancy with abortive outcome — Grossesse se terminant par un avortement	..	..	3	♦0.3	..	..	5	♦0.5
Other direct obstetric causes — Autres décès maternels directs	..	..	42	4.0	..	..	36	3.3
Indirect obstetric causes — Décès maternels indirects	..	..	17	♦1.6	..	..	13	♦1.2
Certain conditions originating in the perinatal period — Certaines affections dont l'origine se situe dans la période périnatale	462	84.8	380	73.4	418	74.6	410	77.0
Congenital malformations, deformations and chromosomal abnormalities — Malformations congénitales et anomalies chromosomiques	1 163	213.4	1 161	224.3	1 155	206.1	1 151	216.3
Symptoms, signs and abnormal clinical and laboratory findings, not elsewhere classified — Symptômes, signes et résultats anormaux d'examens cliniques et de laboratoire, non classés ailleurs	11 302	18.3	23 152	35.8	12 555	20.4	25 104	38.9
All other diseases — Toutes autres maladies	379	0.6	607	0.9	393	0.6	621	1.0
External causes — Causes externes								
Total	49 775	80.8	25 605	39.6	47 631	77.4	25 481	39.4
Accidents								
Total	24 591	39.9	15 272	23.6	23 329	37.9	14 941	23.1
Transport accidents — Accidents de transport	7 015	11.4	3 013	4.7	6 258	10.2	2 790	4.3
Falls — Chutes	3 989	6.5	2 713	4.2	3 931	6.4	2 670	4.1
Accidental drowning and submersion — Noyade et submersion accidentelles	3 404	5.5	2 818	4.4	3 226	5.2	2 812	4.4
Exposure to smoke, fire and flames — Exposition à la fumée, au feu et aux flammes	972	1.6	621	1.0	959	1.6	550	0.9
Accidental poisoning by and exposure to noxious substances — Intoxication accidentelle par des substances nocives et exposition à ces substances	609	1.0	282	0.4	596	1.0	277	0.4
Intentional self-harm — Lésions auto-infligées	22 236	36.1	8 317	12.9	21 419	34.8	8 502	13.2
Assault — Agresssions	317	0.5	283	0.4	314	0.5	266	0.4
All other external causes — Toutes autres causes externes	2 631	4.3	1 733	2.7	2 569	4.2	1 772	2.7

Cause of death — Cause de décès	Kazakhstan				Korea (Republic of) - Corée (République de)			
	2005 (U)		2006 (U)		2005 (U)		2006 (U)	
	Male — Masculin	Female — Féminin	Male — Masculin	Female — Féminin	Male — Masculin	Female — Féminin	Male — Masculin	Female — Féminin
	Number Nombre	Number Nombre	Number Nombre	Number Nombre	Number Nombre	Number Nombre	Number Nombre	Number Nombre
TOTAL.............	89 013	68 106	89 370	67 840	135 405	110 106	134 724	109 210
Certain infectious and parasitic diseases — Certaines maladies infectieuses et parasitaires								
Total..........	3 209	1 079	2 891	1 005	3 438	2 130	3 353	2 096
Intestinal infectious diseases — Maladies infectieuses intestinales............	48	46	47	49	43	55	34	63
Tuberculosis — Tuberculose.................	2 775	796	2 436	671	1 991	902	1 880	853
Tetanus — Tétanos....................	-	1	-	-	5	4	4	6
Diphtheria — Diphtérie.................	-	-	-	-	-	-	-	-
Whooping cough — Coqueluche	-	1	-	-	-	-	-	-
Meningococcal infection — Infection à méningocoques	56	31	37	28	2	-	4	-
Septicaemia — Septicémie.................	182	111	190	135	535	635	545	620
Acute poliomyelitis — Poliomyélite aiguë	-	1	-	-	-	-	-	-
Measles — Rougeole......................	1	2	-	2	-	-	-	-
Viral hepatitis — Hépatite virale	38	30	38	30	517	335	535	376
Human immunodeficiency virus [HIV] disease — Maladies dues au virus de l'immunodéficience humaine (VIH)...............	57	16	69	30	66	4	72	5
Malaria — Paludisme.............	-	-	-	-	3	1	4	-
Neoplasms — Tumeurs.................	10 123	8 447	9 667	8 489	41 731	24 497	42 496	24 278
Malignant neoplasms — Tumeurs malignes								
Total.................	10 053	8 377	9 608	8 411	41 375	24 104	42 080	23 829
Malignant neoplasm of lip, oral cavity and pharynx — Tumeur maligne de la lèvre, de la cavité buccale et du pharynx	362	126	341	143	653	194	695	199
Malignant neoplasm of oesophagus — Tumeur maligne de l'oesophage	706	548	718	585	1 319	115	1 357	129
Malignant neoplasm of stomach — Tumeur maligne de l'estomac...........	1 556	922	1 483	944	7 183	3 807	7 094	3 685
Malignant neoplasm of colon, rectosigmoid junction, rectum, anus and anal canal — Tumeur maligne du côlon, de la jonction recto-sigmoïdienne, du rectum, de l'anus et du canal anal	710	830	726	841	3 293	2 778	3 453	2 824
Malignant neoplasm of liver and intrahepatic bile ducts — Tumeur maligne du foie et des voies bilaires intrahépatiques	594	428	580	402	8 253	2 709	8 305	2 667
Malignant neoplasm of pancreas — Tumeur maligne du pancréas	451	393	441	426	1 872	1 517	1 898	1 565
Malignant neoplasm of trachea, bronchus and lung — Tumeur maligne de la trachée, des bronches et du poumon	2 826	640	2 666	619	10 154	3 651	10 490	3 607
Malignant neoplasm of female breast — Tumeur maligne du sein chez la femme..........	..	1 362	..	1 384	..	1 581	..	1 609
Malignant neoplasm of cervix uteri — Tumeur maligne du col de l'utérus	..	570	..	589	..	1 067	..	1 005
Malignant neoplasm of prostate — Tumeur maligne de la prostate	372	..	323	..	909	..	1 010	..
Malignant neoplasm of lymphoid, haematopoietic and related tissue — Tumeurs malignes primitives ou présumées primitives des tissus lymphoïde, hématopoïétique et apparentés	...	...	...	...	1 858	1 405	1 921	1 317
Disorders of the blood and blood-forming organs and certain disorders involving the immune mechanism — Maladies du sang et des organes hématopoïétiques et certains troubles du système immunitaire								
Total..........	59	80	67	68	212	235	201	263
Anaemias — Anémies	38	46	39	36	124	156	116	172
Endocrine, nutritional and metabolic diseases — Maladies endocriniennes, nutritionnelles et métaboliques								
Total...........	463	834	496	838	6 292	6 138	6 139	6 126
Diabetes mellitus — Diabète sucré............	381	725	417	748	5 968	5 834	5 823	5 777
Malnutrition — Malnutrition............	30	10	28	15	11	27	27	17
Mental and behavioural disorders — Troubles mentaux et du comportement	425	142	358	149	1 942	2 567	1 952	2 426
Diseases of the nervous system — Maladies du système nerveux...........	827	594	892	563	1 997	2 136	2 121	2 282
Diseases of the circulatory system — Maladies de l'appareil circulatoire								
Total...........	40 064	41 038	40 833	40 772	27 360	29 216	27 174	29 214
Acute rheumatic fever and chronic rheumatic heart diseases — Rhumatisme articularie aigu et cardiopathies rhumatismales chroniques	267	305	261	316	111	178	106	164
Hypertensive diseases — Maladies hypertensives....................	2 291	2 684	2 326	2 676	1 605	2 934	1 603	3 020
Ischaemic heart disease — Cardiopathie ischémique....................	19 116	17 338	19 025	17 185	7 037	6 373	7 466	6 810

Cause of death — Cause de décès	Kazakhstan 2005 (U) Male — Masculin Number Nombre	2005 (U) Female — Féminin Number Nombre	2006 (U) Male — Masculin Number Nombre	2006 (U) Female — Féminin Number Nombre	Korea (Republic of) - Corée (République de) 2005 (U) Male — Masculin Number Nombre	2005 (U) Female — Féminin Number Nombre	2006 (U) Male — Masculin Number Nombre	2006 (U) Female — Féminin Number Nombre
Cerebrovascular disease — Maladie cérébrovasculaire	9 562	11 677	9 071	11 100	14 949	16 348	14 510	15 526
Diseases of arteries, arterioles and capillaries — Maladies des artères, artérioles et capillaires	...	...	...	...	637	436	627	485
Diseases of the respiratory system — Maladies de l'appareil respiratoire								
Total	5 790	3 099	5 490	2 755	8 453	5 850	8 500	5 810
Influenza — Grippe	18	29	26	20	2	4	-	-
Pneumonia — Pneumopathies	2 099	981	2 003	870	2 195	1 991	2 376	2 227
Chronic lower respiratory diseases — Maladies chroniques des voies respiratoires inférieures	3 121	1 761	2 931	1 529	4 604	2 952	4 470	2 600
Diseases of the digestive system — Maladies de l'appareil digestif								
Total	4 610	2 868	4 719	2 912	8 151	3 113	7 731	3 002
Gastric and duodenal ulcer — Ulcère de l'estomac et du duodénum	341	144	353	151	205	170	251	185
Diseases of the liver — Maladies du foie	3 431	2 108	3 522	2 173	6 708	1 717	6 156	1 468
Diseases of the musculoskeletal system and connective tissue — Maladies du système ostéo-articularie, des muscles et du tissu conjonctif	52	106	50	119	414	1 114	469	1 189
Diseases of the genitourinary system — Maladies de l'appareil génito-urinaire								
Total	838	784	819	680	1 542	1 545	1 662	1 581
Disorders of kidney and ureter — Affections du rein et de l'uretère	...	..	...	..	1 432	1 388	1 520	1 415
Hyperplasia of prostate — Hyperplasie de la prostate	...	..	...	..	46	..	58	..
Pregnancy, childbirth and the puerperium — Grossesse, accouchement et puerpéralité								
Total	..	81	..	100	...	53	...	54
Pregnancy with abortive outcome — Grossesse se terminant par un avortement	..	5	..	5	..	1	..	2
Other direct obstetric causes — Autres décès maternels directs	..	66	..	77	..	48	..	47
Indirect obstetric causes — Décès maternels indirects	..	9	..	6	..	3	..	5
Certain conditions originating in the perinatal period — Certaines affections dont l'origine se situe dans la période périnatale	1 217	878	1 231	831	476	426	482	377
Congenital malformations, deformations and chromosomal abnormalities — Malformations congénitales et anomalies chromosomiques	692	589	739	602	304	301	309	262
Symptoms, signs and abnormal clinical and laboratory findings, not elsewhere classified — Symptômes, signes et résultats anormaux d'examens cliniques et de laboratoire, non classés ailleurs	2 905	2 681	3 135	2 850	11 888	20 623	11 931	20 339
All other diseases — Toutes autres maladies	63	79	45	40	155	255	159	341
External causes — Causes externes								
Total	17 676	4 727	17 938	5 067	21 050	9 907	20 045	9 570
Accidents								
Total	...	...	...	...	10 458	4 404	10 299	4 572
Transport accidents — Accidents de transport	2 766	1 017	3 574	1 322	5 859	2 098	5 716	2 106
Falls — Chutes	459	110	466	109	1 915	1 240	2 056	1 363
Accidental drowning and submersion — Noyade et submersion accidentelles	1 146	240	914	217	686	175	592	165
Exposure to smoke, fire and flames — Exposition à la fumée, au feu et aux flammes	301	132	285	100	288	156	255	145
Accidental poisoning by and exposure to noxious substances — Intoxication accidentelle par des substances nocives et exposition à ces substances	2 463	659	2 778	820	182	94	195	101
Intentional self-harm — Lésions auto-infligées	3 283	636	3 410	676	8 053	3 994	7 249	3 439
Assault — Agresssions	1 659	518	1 570	462	422	444	400	390
All other external causes — Toutes autres causes externes	...	...	...	...	2 117	1 065	2 097	1 169

21. Death and death rates by cause and sex: 2002 - 2006
Décès et taux de mortalité par cause et sexe : 2002 - 2006 (continued - suite)

Cause of death — Cause de décès	Kuwait - Koweït 2002 (U) Male — Masculin Number Nombre	Kuwait - Koweït 2002 (U) Female — Féminin Number Nombre	Kyrgyzstan - Kirghizistan 2005 (U) Male — Masculin Number Nombre	Kyrgyzstan - Kirghizistan 2005 (U) Female — Féminin Number Nombre	Kyrgyzstan - Kirghizistan 2006 (U) Male — Masculin Number Nombre	Kyrgyzstan - Kirghizistan 2006 (U) Female — Féminin Number Nombre	Maldives 2004 (+C) Male — Masculin Number Nombre	Maldives 2004 (+C) Female — Féminin Number Nombre
TOTAL	2 755	1 587	20 399	16 593	21 504	17 064	571	420
Certain infectious and parasitic diseases — Certaines maladies infectieuses et parasitaires								
Total	77	41	827	321	873	390	47	34
Intestinal infectious diseases — Maladies infectieuses intestinales	1	2	90	83	106	103	34	24
Tuberculosis — Tuberculose	14	9	641	156	644	196	1	-
Tetanus — Tétanos	-	-	-	-	-	-	-	-
Diphtheria — Diphtérie	-	-	-	-	-	-	-	-
Whooping cough — Coqueluche	-	-	1	3	-	-	-	-
Meningococcal infection — Infection à méningocoques	-	-	9	9	17	11	-	-
Septicaemia — Septicémie	30	18	22	20	34	32	9	7
Acute poliomyelitis — Poliomyélite aiguë	-	-	-	-	-	-	-	-
Measles — Rougeole	-	-	-	-	-	-	-	-
Viral hepatitis — Hépatite virale	16	9	17	30	27	19	-	1
Human immunodeficiency virus [HIV] disease — Maladies dues au virus de l'immunodéficience humaine (VIH)	2	-	16	3	13	4	-	-
Malaria — Paludisme	1	-	-	-	-	-	-	-
Neoplasms — Tumeurs	290	262	1 672	1 427	1 623	1 484	19	21
Malignant neoplasms — Tumeurs malignes								
Total	277	252	1 635	1 405	1 593	1 457	16	18
Malignant neoplasm of lip, oral cavity and pharynx — Tumeur maligne de la lèvre, de la cavité buccale et du pharynx	6	4	65	28	81	34	2	-
Malignant neoplasm of oesophagus — Tumeur maligne de l'oesophage	7	4	81	47	89	61	-	-
Malignant neoplasm of stomach — Tumeur maligne de l'estomac	9	11	387	189	355	184	-	2
Malignant neoplasm of colon, rectosigmoid junction, rectum, anus and anal canal — Tumeur maligne du côlon, de la jonction recto-sigmoïdienne, du rectum, de l'anus et du canal anal	15	25	105	108	100	103	-	-
Malignant neoplasm of liver and intrahepatic bile ducts — Tumeur maligne du foie et des voies bilaires intrahépatiques	42	16	136	99	145	77	3	1
Malignant neoplasm of pancreas — Tumeur maligne du pancréas	14	3	67	68	58	50	-	2
Malignant neoplasm of trachea, bronchus and lung — Tumeur maligne de la trachée, des bronches et du poumon	50	11	310	87	313	99	3	1
Malignant neoplasm of female breast — Tumeur maligne du sein chez la femme	..	59	..	198	..	223	..	4
Malignant neoplasm of cervix uteri — Tumeur maligne du col de l'utérus	..	6	..	151	..	168	..	3
Malignant neoplasm of prostate — Tumeur maligne de la prostate	11	..	42	..	44	..	1	..
Malignant neoplasm of lymphoid, haematopoietic and related tissue — Tumeurs malignes primitives ou présumées primitives des tissus lymphoïde, hématopoïétique et apparentés	56	34	92	59	89	78	1	2
Disorders of the blood and blood-forming organs and certain disorders involving the immune mechanism — Maladies du sang et des organes hématopoïétiques et certains troubles du système immunitaire								
Total	10	12	30	38	24	31	3	4
Anaemias — Anémies	5	6	18	28	14	18	3	4
Endocrine, nutritional and metabolic diseases — Maladies endocriniennes, nutritionnelles et métaboliques								
Total	146	114	172	215	186	205	7	8
Diabetes mellitus — Diabète sucré	139	107	154	196	167	187	4	4
Malnutrition — Malnutrition	-	-	11	4	14	2	-	-
Mental and behavioural disorders — Troubles mentaux et du comportement	4	5	55	51	63	50	3	-
Diseases of the nervous system — Maladies du système nerveux	42	36	371	215	332	211	4	4
Diseases of the circulatory system — Maladies de l'appareil circulatoire								
Total	1 146	565	8 451	9 061	8 954	9 347	111	71
Acute rheumatic fever and chronic rheumatic heart diseases — Rhumatisme articularie aigu et cardiopathies rhumatismales chroniques	6	5	124	115	124	135	1	-
Hypertensive diseases — Maladies hypertensives	269	221	155	219	152	172	4	6
Ischaemic heart disease — Cardiopathie ischémique	543	151	4 605	4 873	4 973	5 262	34	15

Cause of death — Cause de décès	Kuwait - Koweït		Kyrgyzstan - Kirghizistan				Maldives	
	2002 (U)		2005 (U)		2006 (U)		2004 (+C)	
	Male — Masculin	Female — Féminin	Male — Masculin	Female — Féminin	Male — Masculin	Female — Féminin	Male — Masculin	Female — Féminin
	Number Nombre	Number Nombre	Number Nombre	Number Nombre	Number Nombre	Number Nombre	Number Nombre	Number Nombre
Cerebrovascular disease — Maladie cérébrovasculaire......................	114	57	3 066	3 594	3 130	3 434	27	18
Diseases of arteries, arterioles and capillaries — Maladies des artères, artérioles et capillaires	37	38	94	61	83	74	-	-
Diseases of the respiratory system — Maladies de l'appareil respiratoire								
Total..	127	94	2 216	1 619	2 347	1 649	41	32
Influenza — Grippe	-	-	50	35	47	44	-	-
Pneumonia — Pneumopathies	82	45	575	421	592	456	2	-
Chronic lower respiratory diseases — Maladies chroniques des voies respiratoires inférieures	36	41	1 425	1 067	1 530	1 017	10	10
Diseases of the digestive system — Maladies de l'appareil digestif								
Total..	67	44	1 468	823	1 643	943	6	3
Gastric and duodenal ulcer — Ulcère de l'estomac et du duodénum	7	2	90	28	74	24	1	-
Diseases of the liver — Maladies du foie	35	21	1 228	683	1 416	807	3	2
Diseases of the musculoskeletal system and connective tissue — Maladies du système ostéo-articulaire, des muscles et du tissu conjonctif	2	-	36	60	47	111	-	-
Diseases of the genitourinary system — Maladies de l'appareil génito-urinaire								
Total..	43	29	418	293	546	321	12	12
Disorders of kidney and ureter — Affections du rein et de l'uretère	43	27	403	290	523	318	12	12
Hyperplasia of prostate — Hyperplasie de la prostate.............................	-	..	13	..	16	..	-	..
Pregnancy, childbirth and the puerperium — Grossesse, accouchement et puerpéralité								
Total..	..	3	..	66	..	67	..	2
Pregnancy with abortive outcome — Grossesse se terminant par un avortement	..	-	..	1	..	6	..	-
Other direct obstetric causes — Autres décès maternels directs	..	3	..	52	..	46	..	2
Indirect obstetric causes — Décès maternels indirects.........................	..	-	..	13	..	15	..	-
Certain conditions originating in the perinatal period — Certaines affections dont l'origine se situe dans la période périnatale	90	83	1 127	859	1 208	942	13	9
Congenital malformations, deformations and chromosomal abnormalities — Malformations congénitales et anomalies chromosomiques	127	104	236	211	263	230	4	1
Symptoms, signs and abnormal clinical and laboratory findings, not elsewhere classified — Symptômes, signes et résultats anormaux d'examens cliniques et de laboratoire, non classés ailleurs	56	72	482	479	394	228	61	45
All other diseases — Toutes autres maladies...................................	2	5	5	6	16	9	-	1
External causes — Causes externes								
Total..	526	118	2 833	849	2 985	846	240	173
Accidents								
Total..	440	91	1 779	565	1 973	594	52	51
Transport accidents — Accidents de transport	316	55	564	178	626	174	2	-
Falls — Chutes	39	3	94	23	72	15	-	1
Accidental drowning and submersion — Noyade et submersion accidentelles..	18	2	189	69	201	69	49	50
Exposure to smoke, fire and flames — Exposition à la fumée, au feu et aux flammes	19	4	45	17	47	13	1	-
Accidental poisoning by and exposure to noxious substances — Intoxication accidentelle par des substances nocives et exposition à ces substances	8	10	382	112	505	143	-	-
Intentional self-harm — Lésions auto-infligées.................................	35	13	386	84	368	97	-	1
Assault — Agresssions	16	10	291	87	264	73	-	-
All other external causes — Toutes autres causes externes..................	35	4	377	113	380	82	188	121

Cause of death — Cause de décès	Maldives 2005 (+C) Male — Masculin Number Nombre	Maldives 2005 (+C) Female — Féminin Number Nombre	Singapore - Singapour 2005 (+U) Male — Masculin Number Nombre	Singapore - Singapour 2005 (+U) Female — Féminin Number Nombre	Singapore - Singapour 2006 (+U) Male — Masculin Number Nombre	Singapore - Singapour 2006 (+U) Female — Féminin Number Nombre	Tajikistan - Tadjikistan 2004 (U) Male — Masculin Number Nombre	Tajikistan - Tadjikistan 2004 (U) Female — Féminin Number Nombre
TOTAL	598	397	8 381	6 904	8 383	7 031	14 507	12 263
Certain infectious and parasitic diseases — Certaines maladies infectieuses et parasitaires								
Total	5	5	199	156	111	125	736	519
Intestinal infectious diseases — Maladies infectieuses intestinales	-	-	3	13	6	11	214	176
Tuberculosis — Tuberculose	3	1	49	15	42	19	372	245
Tetanus — Tétanos	-	-	-	-	-	-	1	-
Diphtheria — Diphtérie	-	-	-	-	-	-	...	...
Whooping cough — Coqueluche	-	-	-	-	-	-	-	-
Meningococcal infection — Infection à méningocoques	-	-	-	-	-	-	5	6
Septicaemia — Septicémie	2	3	99	110	46	79	76	51
Acute poliomyelitis — Poliomyélite aiguë	-	-	-	-	-	-	...	...
Measles — Rougeole	-	-	-	-	-	-	-	-
Viral hepatitis — Hépatite virale	-	-	16	2	7	5	...	...
Human immunodeficiency virus [HIV] disease — Maladies dues au virus de l'immunodéficience humaine (VIH)	-	-	-	-	-	-	-	-
Malaria — Paludisme	-	-	1	-	-	-	-	1
Neoplasms — Tumeurs	24	14	2 251	1 855	2 461	2 000	1 151	964
Malignant neoplasms — Tumeurs malignes								
Total	24	12	2 237	1 830	2 444	1 976	1 147	960
Malignant neoplasm of lip, oral cavity and pharynx — Tumeur maligne de la lèvre, de la cavité buccale et du pharynx	3	1	151	44	162	50	19	17
Malignant neoplasm of oesophagus — Tumeur maligne de l'oesophage	-	-	51	15	54	18	178	107
Malignant neoplasm of stomach — Tumeur maligne de l'estomac	1	-	183	139	174	120	260	181
Malignant neoplasm of colon, rectosigmoid junction, rectum, anus and anal canal — Tumeur maligne du côlon, de la jonction recto-sigmoïdienne, du rectum, de l'anus et du canal anal	1	-	320	299	346	310	59	46
Malignant neoplasm of liver and intrahepatic bile ducts — Tumeur maligne du foie et des voies bilaires intrahépatiques	7	-	222	58	239	66	...	...
Malignant neoplasm of pancreas — Tumeur maligne du pancréas	1	-	103	93	107	94	...	...
Malignant neoplasm of trachea, bronchus and lung — Tumeur maligne de la trachée, des bronches et du poumon	2	3	680	309	697	346	126	61
Malignant neoplasm of female breast — Tumeur maligne du sein chez la femme	..	1	..	302	..	354	..	97
Malignant neoplasm of cervix uteri — Tumeur maligne du col de l'utérus	..	2	..	79	..	76	..	40
Malignant neoplasm of prostate — Tumeur maligne de la prostate	3	..	69	...	90	...	30	..
Malignant neoplasm of lymphoid, haematopoietic and related tissue — Tumeurs malignes primitives ou présumées primitives des tissus lymphoïde, hématopoïétique et apparentés	1	2	125	82	147	127	100	65
Disorders of the blood and blood-forming organs and certain disorders involving the immune mechanism — Maladies du sang et des organes hématopoïétiques et certains troubles du système immunitaire								
Total	-	2	11	21	16	17	65	84
Anaemias — Anémies	-	2	1	6	4	3	53	74
Endocrine, nutritional and metabolic diseases — Maladies endocriniennes, nutritionnelles et métaboliques								
Total	4	5	285	286	281	320	299	292
Diabetes mellitus — Diabète sucré	3	3	222	273	221	305	252	248
Malnutrition — Malnutrition	-	-	-	-	-	-	...	...
Mental and behavioural disorders — Troubles mentaux et du comportement	1	-	2	-	1	1	39	33
Diseases of the nervous system — Maladies du système nerveux	2	1	35	26	31	25	292	219
Diseases of the circulatory system — Maladies de l'appareil circulatoire								
Total	37	21	2 728	2 374	2 830	2 313	6 695	6 448
Acute rheumatic fever and chronic rheumatic heart diseases — Rhumatisme articularie aigu et cardiopathies rhumatismales chroniques	-	-	11	11	12	14	95	126
Hypertensive diseases — Maladies hypertensives	12	6	192	135	239	183	1 543	1 701
Ischaemic heart disease — Cardiopathie ischémique	10	3	1 621	1 175	1 728	1 147	2 940	2 361

	Maldives		Singapore - Singapour				Tajikistan - Tadjikistan	
Cause of death — Cause de décès	2005 (+C)		2005 (+U)		2006 (+U)		2004 (U)	
	Male — Masculin	Female — Féminin	Male — Masculin	Female — Féminin	Male — Masculin	Female — Féminin	Male — Masculin	Female — Féminin
	Number Nombre	Number Nombre	Number Nombre	Number Nombre	Number Nombre	Number Nombre	Number Nombre	Number Nombre
Cerebrovascular disease — Maladie cérébrovasculaire	10	4	668	874	611	784	1 075	1 193
Diseases of arteries, arterioles and capillaries — Maladies des artères, artérioles et capillaires	-	-	56	37	74	33	582	732
Diseases of the respiratory system — Maladies de l'appareil respiratoire								
Total	24	22	1 702	1 292	1 551	1 252	1 511	1 329
Influenza — Grippe	1	-	1	-	1	1	13	9
Pneumonia — Pneumopathies	3	1	1 227	1 108	1 105	1 055	478	447
Chronic lower respiratory diseases — Maladies chroniques des voies respiratoires inférieures	4	12	441	146	411	148	...	...
Diseases of the digestive system — Maladies de l'appareil digestif								
Total	9	6	202	157	190	170	709	590
Gastric and duodenal ulcer — Ulcère de l'estomac et du duodénum	-	-	30	17	29	21	107	51
Diseases of the liver — Maladies du foie	3	3	62	23	67	27	...	...
Diseases of the musculoskeletal system and connective tissue — Maladies du système ostéo-articularie, des muscles et du tissu conjonctif	1	-	18	25	17	40	13	9
Diseases of the genitourinary system — Maladies de l'appareil génito-urinaire								
Total	9	7	253	371	252	366	373	349
Disorders of kidney and ureter — Affections du rein et de l'uretère	8	7	134	146	143	138	332	343
Hyperplasia of prostate — Hyperplasie de la prostate	1	..	1	..	-	..	26	..
Pregnancy, childbirth and the puerperium — Grossesse, accouchement et puerpéralité								
Total	..	1	..	4	..	3	..	37
Pregnancy with abortive outcome — Grossesse se terminant par un avortement	..	-	..	2	..	-	..	-
Other direct obstetric causes — Autres décès maternels directs	..	-	..	2	..	3	..	...
Indirect obstetric causes — Décès maternels indirects	..	1	..	-	..	-	..	...
Certain conditions originating in the perinatal period — Certaines affections dont l'origine se situe dans la période périnatale	4	7	17	10	21	17	306	185
Congenital malformations, deformations and chromosomal abnormalities — Malformations congénitales et anomalies chromosomiques	2	6	32	30	29	31	403	254
Symptoms, signs and abnormal clinical and laboratory findings, not elsewhere classified — Symptômes, signes et résultats anormaux d'examens cliniques et de laboratoire, non classés ailleurs	64	48	7	11	17	8	603	471
All other diseases — Toutes autres maladies	1	-	32	47	31	55	1	2
External causes — Causes externes								
Total	411	252	607	239	544	288	1 311	478
Accidents								
Total	7	4	304	94	253	116	979	359
Transport accidents — Accidents de transport	1	-	125	25	126	30	225	61
Falls — Chutes	-	-	101	44	75	50	39	5
Accidental drowning and submersion — Noyade et submersion accidentelles	4	1	12	4	7	3	156	82
Exposure to smoke, fire and flames — Exposition à la fumée, au feu et aux flammes	2	3	4	-	2	5	63	48
Accidental poisoning by and exposure to noxious substances — Intoxication accidentelle par des substances nocives et exposition à ces substances	-	-	19	5	20	8	102	25
Intentional self-harm — Lésions auto-infligées	1	-	240	119	231	141	116	56
Assault — Agresssions	-	1	11	10	9	3	115	36
All other external causes — Toutes autres causes externes	403	247	52	16	51	28	101	27

Cause of death — Cause de décès	Tajikistan - Tadjikistan		Thailand - Thaïlande		Uzbekistan - Ouzbékistan			
	2005 (U)		2002 (+U)		2004 (U)		2005 (U)	
	Male — Masculin	Female — Féminin	Male — Masculin	Female — Féminin	Male — Masculin	Female — Féminin	Male — Masculin	Female — Féminin
	Number Nombre	Number Nombre	Number Nombre	Number Nombre	Number Nombre	Number Nombre	Number Nombre	Number Nombre
TOTAL...............................	15 831	13 082	219 480	160 884	69 528	61 759	74 569	66 016
Certain infectious and parasitic diseases — Certaines maladies infectieuses et parasitaires								
Total..................	790	549	26 759	18 072	2 483	1 381	2 552	1 383
Intestinal infectious diseases — Maladies infectieuses intestinales............	290	200	753	606	68	59	69	48
Tuberculosis — Tuberculose.............................	380	242	4 761	1 990	1 893	961	1 878	906
Tetanus — Tétanos..................................	-	-	48	22	-	1	-	-
Diphtheria — Diphtérie.............................	...	...	2	6	-	-	-	-
Whooping cough — Coqueluche...............	-	-	1	-	-	-	-	-
Meningococcal infection — Infection à méningocoques......................	11	4	3	1	8	5	15	9
Septicaemia — Septicémie........................	50	51	8 045	7 761	209	142	264	181
Acute poliomyelitis — Poliomyélite aiguë...........	...	...	13	9	2	1	-	-
Measles — Rougeole..........................	...	...	3	1	-	-	1	-
Viral hepatitis — Hépatite virale.............	...	...	186	76	232	173	219	202
Human immunodeficiency virus [HIV] disease — Maladies dues au virus de l'immunodéficience humaine (VIH)......................	...	...	9 862	5 736	13	4	43	3
Malaria — Paludisme...........................	-	-	251	110	-	-	-	-
Neoplasms — Tumeurs..............................	1 203	998	26 659	19 175	4 819	4 747	4 996	4 908
Malignant neoplasms — Tumeurs malignes								
Total..................	1 202	997	26 657	19 168	4 765	4 708	4 962	4 859
Malignant neoplasm of lip, oral cavity and pharynx — Tumeur maligne de la lèvre, de la cavité buccale et du pharynx	38	23	726	398	241	138	208	135
Malignant neoplasm of oesophagus — Tumeur maligne de l'oesophage	182	116	586	143	393	358	364	319
Malignant neoplasm of stomach — Tumeur maligne de l'estomac............	282	167	540	435	900	551	918	621
Malignant neoplasm of colon, rectosigmoid junction, rectum, anus and anal canal — Tumeur maligne du côlon, de la jonction recto-sigmoïdienne, du rectum, de l'anus et du canal anal..........	65	39	701	601	233	244	235	235
Malignant neoplasm of liver and intrahepatic bile ducts — Tumeur maligne du foie et des voies bilaires intrahépatiques	...	...	7 973	3 249	376	286	384	295
Malignant neoplasm of pancreas — Tumeur maligne du pancréas............	...	...	333	246	102	102	103	99
Malignant neoplasm of trachea, bronchus and lung — Tumeur maligne de la trachée, des bronches et du poumon......	113	61	4 712	2 165	691	224	754	281
Malignant neoplasm of female breast — Tumeur maligne du sein chez la femme...........................	..	109	..	1 497	..	769	..	795
Malignant neoplasm of cervix uteri — Tumeur maligne du col de l'utérus......	..	51	..	1 258	..	444	..	412
Malignant neoplasm of prostate — Tumeur maligne de la prostate............	20	..	299	..	85	..	83	..
Malignant neoplasm of lymphoid, haematopoietic and related tissue — Tumeurs malignes primitives ou présumées primitives des tissus lymphoïde, hématopoïétique et apparentés......................	119	74	926	820	506	381	547	352
Disorders of the blood and blood-forming organs and certain disorders involving the immune mechanism — Maladies du sang et des organes hématopoïétiques et certains troubles du système immunitaire								
Total..................	79	65	1 963	1 398	145	184	138	186
Anaemias — Anémies	71	60	144	180	93	150	106	165
Endocrine, nutritional and metabolic diseases — Maladies endocriniennes, nutritionnelles et métaboliques								
Total..................	350	321	3 239	5 065	1 466	1 787	1 558	1 854
Diabetes mellitus — Diabète sucré............	316	292	2 773	4 610	1 441	1 741	1 527	1 811
Malnutrition — Malnutrition.........................	...	...	57	59	-	3	2	-
Mental and behavioural disorders — Troubles mentaux et du comportement	56	33	643	88	169	108	207	132
Diseases of the nervous system — Maladies du système nerveux..........	343	246	4 397	2 770	1 231	974	1 399	1 100
Diseases of the circulatory system — Maladies de l'appareil circulatoire								
Total..................	7 681	7 068	18 512	14 355	35 593	36 187	39 238	39 877
Acute rheumatic fever and chronic rheumatic heart diseases — Rhumatisme articularie aigu et cardiopathies rhumatismales chroniques	77	126	32	26	370	497	375	542
Hypertensive diseases — Maladies hypertensives.....................	1 754	1 788	1 725	1 488	5 225	5 129	5 830	6 020
Ischaemic heart disease — Cardiopathie ischémique........................	3 267	2 439	5 299	3 712	18 816	18 321	20 373	19 144

Cause of death — Cause de décès	Tajikistan - Tadjikistan 2005 (U) Male — Masculin Number Nombre	Tajikistan - Tadjikistan 2005 (U) Female — Féminin Number Nombre	Thailand - Thaïlande 2002 (+U) Male — Masculin Number Nombre	Thailand - Thaïlande 2002 (+U) Female — Féminin Number Nombre	Uzbekistan - Ouzbékistan 2004 (U) Male — Masculin Number Nombre	Uzbekistan - Ouzbékistan 2004 (U) Female — Féminin Number Nombre	Uzbekistan - Ouzbékistan 2005 (U) Male — Masculin Number Nombre	Uzbekistan - Ouzbékistan 2005 (U) Female — Féminin Number Nombre
Cerebrovascular disease — Maladie cérébrovasculaire	1 287	1 358	7 660	5 738	7 057	8 143	8 404	9 793
Diseases of arteries, arterioles and capillaries — Maladies des artères, artérioles et capillaires	815	1 063	418	278	1 559	2 265	1 551	2 404
Diseases of the respiratory system — Maladies de l'appareil respiratoire								
Total	1 390	1 357	16 237	9 014	6 060	4 980	6 317	5 140
Influenza — Grippe	5	11	40	33	15	18	4	8
Pneumonia — Pneumopathies	425	427	6 956	4 699	2 815	2 174	2 950	2 248
Chronic lower respiratory diseases — Maladies chroniques des voies respiratoires inférieures	...	...	4 261	1 570	1 437	1 317	1 698	1 500
Diseases of the digestive system — Maladies de l'appareil digestif								
Total	835	585	7 759	3 508	4 710	3 729	4 973	3 813
Gastric and duodenal ulcer — Ulcère de l'estomac et du duodénum	96	53	148	68	408	157	445	164
Diseases of the liver — Maladies du foie	...	...	5 187	2 091	3 809	3 195	4 039	3 300
Diseases of the musculoskeletal system and connective tissue — Maladies du système ostéo-articulaire, des muscles et du tissu conjonctif	8	10	273	350	124	209	126	179
Diseases of the genitourinary system — Maladies de l'appareil génito-urinaire								
Total	438	342	5 422	5 557	1 251	1 131	1 484	1 287
Disorders of kidney and ureter — Affections du rein et de l'uretère	379	325	5 277	5 310	1 156	1 114	1 380	1 272
Hyperplasia of prostate — Hyperplasie de la prostate	37	..	32	..	33	..	45	..
Pregnancy, childbirth and the puerperium — Grossesse, accouchement et puerpéralité								
Total	..	28	..	114	..	156	..	145
Pregnancy with abortive outcome — Grossesse se terminant par un avortement	..	1	..	21	..	2	..	1
Other direct obstetric causes — Autres décès maternels directs	..	...	..	92	..	122	..	126
Indirect obstetric causes — Décès maternels indirects	..	...	..	1	..	14	..	3
Certain conditions originating in the perinatal period — Certaines affections dont l'origine se situe dans la période périnatale	373	262	737	536	1 964	1 213	1 740	1 107
Congenital malformations, deformations and chromosomal abnormalities — Malformations congénitales et anomalies chromosomiques	383	286	597	559	390	328	361	343
Symptoms, signs and abnormal clinical and laboratory findings, not elsewhere classified — Symptômes, signes et résultats anormaux d'examens cliniques et de laboratoire, non classés ailleurs	620	483	72 147	70 913	1 673	2 173	1 753	2 110
All other diseases — Toutes autres maladies	2	1	350	393	32	32	21	16
External causes — Causes externes								
Total	1 280	448	33 786	9 017	7 418	2 440	7 706	2 436
Accidents								
Total	992	354	19 024	5 059	4 728	1 554	4 784	1 555
Transport accidents — Accidents de transport	244	65	10 837	2 601	1 943	486	1 897	496
Falls — Chutes	27	10	643	206	369	95	351	93
Accidental drowning and submersion — Noyade et submersion accidentelles	174	78	3 136	1 082	676	359	703	339
Exposure to smoke, fire and flames — Exposition à la fumée, au feu et aux flammes	58	46	143	77	173	167	149	140
Accidental poisoning by and exposure to noxious substances — Intoxication accidentelle par des substances nocives et exposition à ces substances	97	26	69	43	268	91	327	99
Intentional self-harm — Lésions auto-infligées	139	48	3 715	1 190	943	308	921	300
Assault — Agresssions	92	31	2 822	510	456	173	575	160
All other external causes — Toutes autres causes externes	57	15	8 225	2 258	1 291	405	1 426	421

Cause of death — Cause de décès	Albania - Albanie				Austria - Autriche			
	2003 (U)		2004 (U)		2005 (C)			
	Male — Masculin	Female — Féminin	Male — Masculin	Female — Féminin	Male — Masculin		Female — Féminin	
	Number Nombre	Number Nombre	Number Nombre	Number Nombre	Number Nombre	Rate Taux	Number Nombre	Rate Taux
TOTAL..........	10 012	7 953	9 949	7 799	34 986	874.2	40 203	950.1
Certain infectious and parasitic diseases — Certaines maladies infectieuses et parasitaires								
Total..........	62	43	65	38	343	8.6	292	6.9
Intestinal infectious diseases — Maladies infectieuses intestinales..........	4	3	9	4	9	+0.2	19	+0.4
Tuberculosis — Tuberculose..........	8	4	7	5	29	+0.7	23	+0.5
Tetanus — Tétanos..........	-	-	-	-	-	-	1	+0.0
Diphtheria — Diphtérie..........	-	-	1	-	-	-	-	-
Whooping cough — Coqueluche..........	-	-	-	-	-	-	-	-
Meningococcal infection — Infection à méningocoques..........	-	-	-	-	2	+0.0	4	+0.1
Septicaemia — Septicémie..........	12	10	6	5	12	+0.3	23	+0.5
Acute poliomyelitis — Poliomyélite aiguë..........	-	-	-	-	-	-	-	-
Measles — Rougeole..........	1	-	-	-	-	-	-	-
Viral hepatitis — Hépatite virale..........	1	2	4	-	174	4.3	162	3.8
Human immunodeficiency virus [HIV] disease — Maladies dues au virus de l'immunodéficience humaine (VIH)..........	-	1	1	1	61	1.5	10	+0.2
Malaria — Paludisme..........	-	-	-	-	-	-	1	+0.0
Neoplasms — Tumeurs..........	1 808	1 118	1 835	1 072	10 218	255.3	9 456	223.5
Malignant neoplasms — Tumeurs malignes								
Total..........	1 748	998	1 707	1 011	9 991	249.7	9 133	215.8
Malignant neoplasm of lip, oral cavity and pharynx — Tumeur maligne de la lèvre, de la cavité buccale et du pharynx	38	31	46	25	337	8.4	109	2.6
Malignant neoplasm of oesophagus — Tumeur maligne de l'oesophage......	19	13	35	13	249	6.2	58	1.4
Malignant neoplasm of stomach — Tumeur maligne de l'estomac..........	261	110	233	138	565	14.1	501	11.8
Malignant neoplasm of colon, rectosigmoid junction, rectum, anus and anal canal — Tumeur maligne du côlon, de la jonction recto-sigmoïdienne, du rectum, de l'anus et du canal anal..........	48	63	60	41	1 244	31.1	1 150	27.2
Malignant neoplasm of liver and intrahepatic bile ducts — Tumeur maligne du foie et des voies bilaires intrahépatiques..........	...	...	...	...	519	13.0	270	6.4
Malignant neoplasm of pancreas — Tumeur maligne du pancréas..........	63	42	91	47	630	15.7	688	16.3
Malignant neoplasm of trachea, bronchus and lung — Tumeur maligne de la trachée, des bronches et du poumon..........	507	144	464	141	2 317	57.9	1 031	24.4
Malignant neoplasm of female breast — Tumeur maligne du sein chez la femme..........	..	138	..	138	..	..	1 583	44.1
Malignant neoplasm of cervix uteri — Tumeur maligne du col de l'utérus......	..	13	..	18	..	..	180	5.0
Malignant neoplasm of prostate — Tumeur maligne de la prostate..........	156	..	134	..	1 097	88.1	..	..
Malignant neoplasm of lymphoid, haematopoietic and related tissue — Tumeurs malignes primitives ou présumées primitives des tissus lymphoïde, hématopoïétique et apparentés..........	69	67	106	59	764	19.1	753	17.8
Disorders of the blood and blood-forming organs and certain disorders involving the immune mechanism — Maladies du sang et des organes hématopoïétiques et certains troubles du système immunitaire								
Total..........	26	24	43	18	52	1.3	85	2.0
Anaemias — Anémies..........	16	14	22	11	27	+0.7	36	0.9
Endocrine, nutritional and metabolic diseases — Maladies endocriniennes, nutritionnelles et métaboliques								
Total..........	96	88	103	108	1 975	49.4	2 559	60.5
Diabetes mellitus — Diabète sucré..........	74	75	78	82	1 562	39.0	2 148	50.8
Malnutrition — Malnutrition..........	7	2	2	1	2	+0.0	-	-
Mental and behavioural disorders — Troubles mentaux et du comportement	46	36	52	55	504	12.6	186	4.4
Diseases of the nervous system — Maladies du système nerveux..........	248	212	269	204	817	20.4	1 094	25.9
Diseases of the circulatory system — Maladies de l'appareil circulatoire								
Total..........	4 738	4 256	4 679	4 212	13 048	326.0	19 588	462.9
Acute rheumatic fever and chronic rheumatic heart diseases — Rhumatisme articularie aigu et cardiopathies rhumatismales chroniques..........	11	10	25	10	54	1.3	148	3.5
Hypertensive diseases — Maladies hypertensives..........	251	288	271	266	719	18.0	1 593	37.6
Ischaemic heart disease — Cardiopathie ischémique..........	1 603	1 072	1 593	1 065	6 723	168.0	8 221	194.3

	Albania - Albanie				Austria - Autriche			
	2003 (U)		2004 (U)		2005 (C)			
Cause of death — Cause de décès	Male — Masculin	Female — Féminin	Male — Masculin	Female — Féminin	Male — Masculin		Female — Féminin	
	Number Nombre	Number Nombre	Number Nombre	Number Nombre	Number Nombre	Rate Taux	Number Nombre	Rate Taux
Cerebrovascular disease — Maladie cérébrovasculaire	1 536	1 678	1 521	1 661	2 108	52.7	3 456	81.7
Diseases of arteries, arterioles and capillaries — Maladies des artères, artérioles et capillaires	140	142	119	144	881	22.0	1 301	30.7
Diseases of the respiratory system — Maladies de l'appareil respiratoire								
Total	563	438	544	389	2 371	59.2	2 299	54.3
Influenza — Grippe	28	13	16	18	10	◆0.2	17	◆0.4
Pneumonia — Pneumopathies	246	236	210	181	617	15.4	888	21.0
Chronic lower respiratory diseases — Maladies chroniques des voies respiratoires inférieures	222	153	243	138	1 575	39.4	1 217	28.8
Diseases of the digestive system — Maladies de l'appareil digestif								
Total	187	128	195	120	1 855	46.4	1 499	35.4
Gastric and duodenal ulcer — Ulcère de l'estomac et du duodénum	9	5	12	4	88	2.2	135	3.2
Diseases of the liver — Maladies du foie	1	-	2	-	1 252	31.3	463	10.9
Diseases of the musculoskeletal system and connective tissue — Maladies du système ostéo-articularie, des muscles et du tissu conjonctif	19	22	13	24	84	2.1	222	5.2
Diseases of the genitourinary system — Maladies de l'appareil génito-urinaire								
Total	162	97	153	98	407	10.2	632	14.9
Disorders of kidney and ureter — Affections du rein et de l'uretère	128	85	119	89	368	9.2	570	13.5
Hyperplasia of prostate — Hyperplasie de la prostate	24	..	26	..	16	◆1.3	..	..
Pregnancy, childbirth and the puerperium — Grossesse, accouchement et puerpéralité								
Total	..	1	..	1	..	..	3	◆3.8
Pregnancy with abortive outcome — Grossesse se terminant par un avortement	..	-	..	-	..	..	1	◆1.3
Other direct obstetric causes — Autres décès maternels directs	..	1	..	1	..	..	2	◆2.6
Indirect obstetric causes — Décès maternels indirects	..	-	..	-	..	..	-	..
Certain conditions originating in the perinatal period — Certaines affections dont l'origine se situe dans la période périnatale	47	46	32	33	98	245.7	102	266.2
Congenital malformations, deformations and chromosomal abnormalities — Malformations congénitales et anomalies chromosomiques	29	33	32	25	118	295.9	111	289.7
Symptoms, signs and abnormal clinical and laboratory findings, not elsewhere classified — Symptômes, signes et résultats anormaux d'examens cliniques et de laboratoire, non classés ailleurs	967	1 120	1 013	1 079	191	4.8	489	11.6
All other diseases — Toutes autres maladies	13	10	16	13	15	◆0.4	37	0.9
External causes — Causes externes								
Total	941	281	905	310	2 890	72.2	1 549	36.6
Accidents								
Total	713	193	685	215	1 664	41.6	1 046	24.7
Transport accidents — Accidents de transport	298	63	278	75	584	14.6	184	4.3
Falls — Chutes	39	19	32	13	581	14.5	585	13.8
Accidental drowning and submersion — Noyade et submersion accidentelles	59	18	55	26	63	1.6	25	◆0.6
Exposure to smoke, fire and flames — Exposition à la fumée, au feu et aux flammes	16	6	5	5	20	◆0.5	24	◆0.6
Accidental poisoning by and exposure to noxious substances — Intoxication accidentelle par des substances nocives et exposition à ces substances	62	23	78	27	12	◆0.3	9	◆0.2
Intentional self-harm — Lésions auto-infligées	73	51	89	57	1 043	26.1	349	8.2
Assault — Agresssions	145	21	112	19	37	0.9	30	◆0.7
All other external causes — Toutes autres causes externes	10	16	19	19	146	3.6	124	2.9

Cause of death — Cause de décès	Austria - Autriche				Belarus - Bélarus			
	2006 (C)				2002 (C)			
	Male — Masculin		Female — Féminin		Male — Masculin		Female — Féminin	
	Number Nombre	Rate Taux	Number Nombre	Rate Taux	Number Nombre	Rate Taux	Number Nombre	Rate Taux
TOTAL.................................	34 757	862.7	39 538	929.6	77 583	1 667.7	69 075	1 310.1
Certain infectious and parasitic diseases — Certaines maladies infectieuses et parasitaires								
Total........	262	6.5	283	6.7	1 010	21.7	241	4.6
Intestinal infectious diseases — Maladies infectieuses intestinales............	13	♦0.3	36	0.8	12	♦0.3	4	♦0.1
Tuberculosis — Tuberculose.............................	27	♦0.7	20	♦0.5	815	17.5	123	2.3
Tetanus — Tétanos..................................	-	-	1	♦0.0	-	-	2	♦0.0
Diphtheria — Diphtérie.............................	-	-	-	-	-	-	-	-
Whooping cough — Coqueluche................................	-	-	-	-	-	-	-	-
Meningococcal infection — Infection à méningocoques.....................	2	♦0.0	4	♦0.1	21	♦0.5	10	♦0.2
Septicaemia — Septicémie.............................	10	♦0.2	28	♦0.7	48	1.0	32	0.6
Acute poliomyelitis — Poliomyélite aiguë..................	-	-	-	-	-	-	-	-
Measles — Rougeole................................	-	-	-	-	-	-	-	-
Viral hepatitis — Hépatite virale.............................	125	3.1	127	3.0	24	♦0.5	12	♦0.2
Human immunodeficiency virus [HIV] disease — Maladies dues au virus de l'immunodéficience humaine (VIH).............................	31	0.8	12	♦0.3	22	♦0.5	5	♦0.1
Malaria — Paludisme.............................	-	-	-	-	-	-	-	-
Neoplasms — Tumeurs..............................	10 347	256.8	9 272	218.0	11 478	246.7	7 868	149.2
Malignant neoplasms — Tumeurs malignes								
Total.........	10 094	250.6	8 962	210.7	11 395	244.9	7 776	147.5
Malignant neoplasm of lip, oral cavity and pharynx — Tumeur maligne de la lèvre, de la cavité buccale et du pharynx	333	8.3	91	2.1	518	11.1	78	1.5
Malignant neoplasm of oesophagus — Tumeur maligne de l'oesophage	264	6.6	64	1.5	322	6.9	42	0.8
Malignant neoplasm of stomach — Tumeur maligne de l'estomac............	525	13.0	491	11.5	1 774	38.1	1 174	22.3
Malignant neoplasm of colon, rectosigmoid junction, rectum, anus and anal canal — Tumeur maligne du côlon, de la jonction recto-sigmoïdienne, du rectum, de l'anus et du canal anal.	1 230	30.5	1 119	26.3	1 102	23.7	1 126	21.4
Malignant neoplasm of liver and intrahepatic bile ducts — Tumeur maligne du foie et des voies bilaires intrahépatiques	533	13.2	289	6.8	213	4.6	149	2.8
Malignant neoplasm of pancreas — Tumeur maligne du pancréas............	626	15.5	674	15.8	430	9.2	362	6.9
Malignant neoplasm of trachea, bronchus and lung — Tumeur maligne de la trachée, des bronches et du poumon.............................	2 354	58.4	1 059	24.9	3 277	70.4	386	7.3
Malignant neoplasm of female breast — Tumeur maligne du sein chez la femme.............................	..	..	1 563	43.2	..	..	1 199	27.0
Malignant neoplasm of cervix uteri — Tumeur maligne du col de l'utérus......	..	..	169	4.7	..	..	406	9.1
Malignant neoplasm of prostate — Tumeur maligne de la prostate............	1 083	85.2	..	..	705	61.8	..	..
Malignant neoplasm of lymphoid, haematopoietic and related tissue — Tumeurs malignes primitives ou présumées primitives des tissus lymphoïde, hématopoïétique et apparentés.............................	811	20.1	779	18.3	...	...	...	...
Disorders of the blood and blood-forming organs and certain disorders involving the immune mechanism — Maladies du sang et des organes hématopoïétiques et certains troubles du système immunitaire								
Total.........	58	1.4	64	1.5	31	0.7	37	0.7
Anaemias — Anémies.............................	15	♦0.4	38	0.9	21	♦0.5	22	♦0.4
Endocrine, nutritional and metabolic diseases — Maladies endocriniennes, nutritionnelles et métaboliques								
Total.........	1 909	47.4	2 563	60.3	307	6.6	478	9.1
Diabetes mellitus — Diabète sucré...............	1 521	37.8	2 120	49.8	264	5.7	443	8.4
Malnutrition — Malnutrition.............................	-	-	1	♦0.0	8	♦0.2	3	♦0.1
Mental and behavioural disorders — Troubles mentaux et du comportement	468	11.6	180	4.2	571	12.3	239	4.5
Diseases of the nervous system — Maladies du système nerveux...........	908	22.5	1 158	27.2	579	12.4	379	7.2
Diseases of the circulatory system — Maladies de l'appareil circulatoire								
Total.........	13 170	326.9	19 319	454.2	38 105	819.1	41 066	778.8
Acute rheumatic fever and chronic rheumatic heart diseases — Rhumatisme articularie aigu et cardiopathies rhumatismales chroniques..................	59	1.5	129	3.0	2	♦0.0	4	♦0.1
Hypertensive diseases — Maladies hypertensives......................	815	20.2	1 728	40.6	499	10.7	542	10.3
Ischaemic heart disease — Cardiopathie ischémique......................	6 908	171.5	8 052	189.3	25 752	553.6	26 255	497.9
Cerebrovascular disease — Maladie cérébrovasculaire.....................	2 103	52.2	3 508	82.5	8 522	183.2	11 584	219.7

Cause of death — Cause de décès	Austria - Autriche				Belarus - Bélarus			
	2006 (C)				2002 (C)			
	Male — Masculin		Female — Féminin		Male — Masculin		Female — Féminin	
	Number Nombre	Rate Taux	Number Nombre	Rate Taux	Number Nombre	Rate Taux	Number Nombre	Rate Taux
Diseases of arteries, arterioles and capillaries — Maladies des artères, artérioles et capillaires	835	20.7	1 276	30.0	...	...	...	...
Diseases of the respiratory system — Maladies de l'appareil respiratoire								
Total	2 219	55.1	2 182	51.3	4 559	98.0	1 793	34.0
Influenza — Grippe	3	♦0.1	4	♦0.1	4	♦0.1	1	♦0.0
Pneumonia — Pneumopathies	541	13.4	820	19.3	827	17.8	188	3.6
Chronic lower respiratory diseases — Maladies chroniques des voies respiratoires inférieures	1 530	38.0	1 222	28.7	3 426	73.6	1 499	28.4
Diseases of the digestive system — Maladies de l'appareil digestif								
Total	1 649	40.9	1 449	34.1	2 386	51.3	1 547	29.3
Gastric and duodenal ulcer — Ulcère de l'estomac et du duodénum	77	1.9	103	2.4	232	5.0	83	1.6
Diseases of the liver — Maladies du foie	1 120	27.8	443	10.4	1 387	29.8	939	17.8
Diseases of the musculoskeletal system and connective tissue — Maladies du système ostéo-articularie, des muscles et du tissu conjonctif	81	2.0	201	4.7	67	1.4	154	2.9
Diseases of the genitourinary system — Maladies de l'appareil génito-urinaire								
Total	455	11.3	609	14.3	657	14.1	531	10.1
Disorders of kidney and ureter — Affections du rein et de l'uretère	408	10.1	536	12.6	...	...	...	...
Hyperplasia of prostate — Hyperplasie de la prostate	9	♦0.7	..	..	...	...	..	..
Pregnancy, childbirth and the puerperium — Grossesse, accouchement et puerpéralité								
Total	..	..	2	♦2.6	..	..	17	♦19.2
Pregnancy with abortive outcome — Grossesse se terminant par un avortement	..	..	-	-	..	..	2	♦2.3
Other direct obstetric causes — Autres décès maternels directs	..	..	2	♦2.6	..	..	12	♦13.5
Indirect obstetric causes — Décès maternels indirects	..	..	-	-	..	..	3	♦3.4
Certain conditions originating in the perinatal period — Certaines affections dont l'origine se situe dans la période périnatale	116	291.9	70	183.4	134	293.5	90	208.9
Congenital malformations, deformations and chromosomal abnormalities — Malformations congénitales et anomalies chromosomiques	106	266.7	103	269.9	242	530.1	225	522.2
Symptoms, signs and abnormal clinical and laboratory findings, not elsewhere classified — Symptômes, signes et résultats anormaux d'examens cliniques et de laboratoire, non classés ailleurs	226	5.6	604	14.2	3 997	85.9	10 713	203.2
All other diseases — Toutes autres maladies	14	♦0.3	37	0.9	31	0.7	30	♦0.6
External causes — Causes externes								
Total	2 769	68.7	1 442	33.9	13 429	288.7	3 667	69.5
Accidents								
Total	1 543	38.3	977	23.0	...	...	...	...
Transport accidents — Accidents de transport	534	13.3	192	4.5	1 669	35.9	535	10.1
Falls — Chutes	507	12.6	447	10.5	938	20.2	265	5.0
Accidental drowning and submersion — Noyade et submersion accidentelles	45	1.1	24	♦0.6	1 069	23.0	203	3.9
Exposure to smoke, fire and flames — Exposition à la fumée, au feu et aux flammes	14	♦0.3	16	♦0.4	519	11.2	160	3.0
Accidental poisoning by and exposure to noxious substances — Intoxication accidentelle par des substances nocives et exposition à ces substances	20	♦0.5	18	♦0.4	2 887	62.1	821	15.6
Intentional self-harm — Lésions auto-infligées	997	24.7	296	7.0	2 789	60.0	511	9.7
Assault — Agresssions	34	0.8	32	0.8	765	16.4	373	7.1
All other external causes — Toutes autres causes externes	195	4.8	137	3.2	...	...	...	...

Cause of death — Cause de décès	Belarus - Bélarus				Bulgaria - Bulgarie			
	2003 (C)				2003 (C)			
	Male — Masculin		Female — Féminin		Male — Masculin		Female — Féminin	
	Number Nombre	Rate Taux	Number Nombre	Rate Taux	Number Nombre	Rate Taux	Number Nombre	Rate Taux
TOTAL..	**76 023**	**1 644.1**	**67 180**	**1 279.7**	**59 992**	**1 577.3**	**51 935**	**1 291.9**
Certain infectious and parasitic diseases — Certaines maladies infectieuses et parasitaires								
Total.........	**1 087**	**23.5**	**217**	**4.1**	**422**	**11.1**	**217**	**5.4**
Intestinal infectious diseases — Maladies infectieuses intestinales............	9	♦0.2	8	♦0.2	9	♦0.2	10	♦0.2
Tuberculosis — Tuberculose...	913	19.7	114	2.2	217	5.7	58	1.4
Tetanus — Tétanos.............................	1	♦0.0	-	-	1	♦0.0	-	-
Diphtheria — Diphtérie...........................	-	-	-	-	-	-	-	-
Whooping cough — Coqueluche..........................	-	-	-	-	-	-	-	-
Meningococcal infection — Infection à méningocoques	17	♦0.4	8	♦0.2	16	♦0.4	10	♦0.2
Septicaemia — Septicémie..........................	40	0.9	23	♦0.4	121	3.2	91	2.3
Acute poliomyelitis — Poliomyélite aiguë..........	-	-	-	-	-	-	-	-
Measles — Rougeole............................	-	-	-	-	-	-	-	-
Viral hepatitis — Hépatite virale	14	♦0.3	4	♦0.1	20	♦0.5	14	♦0.3
Human immunodeficiency virus [HIV] disease — Maladies dues au virus de l'immunodéficience humaine (VIH)	41	0.9	15	♦0.3				
Malaria — Paludisme	-	-	-	-	-	-	-	-
Neoplasms — Tumeurs	**11 205**	**242.3**	**7 519**	**143.2**	**9 297**	**244.4**	**6 493**	**161.5**
Malignant neoplasms — Tumeurs malignes								
Total.........	**11 120**	**240.5**	**7 416**	**141.3**	**9 260**	**243.5**	**6 465**	**160.8**
Malignant neoplasm of lip, oral cavity and pharynx — Tumeur maligne de la lèvre, de la cavité buccale et du pharynx	594	12.8	74	1.4	255	6.7	62	1.5
Malignant neoplasm of oesophagus — Tumeur maligne de l'oesophage	301	6.5	28	♦0.5	125	3.3	37	0.9
Malignant neoplasm of stomach — Tumeur maligne de l'estomac........	1 652	35.7	1 079	20.6	938	24.7	573	14.3
Malignant neoplasm of colon, rectosigmoid junction, rectum, anus and anal canal — Tumeur maligne du côlon, de la jonction recto-sigmoïdienne, du rectum, de l'anus et du canal anal	1 072	23.2	1 126	21.4	1 252	32.9	930	23.1
Malignant neoplasm of liver and intrahepatic bile ducts — Tumeur maligne du foie et des voies bilaires intrahépatiques	207	4.5	125	2.4	...	...	...	...
Malignant neoplasm of pancreas — Tumeur maligne du pancréas	402	8.7	318	6.1	503	13.2	362	9.0
Malignant neoplasm of trachea, bronchus and lung — Tumeur maligne de la trachée, des bronches et du poumon.............	3 207	69.4	365	7.0	2 585	68.0	501	12.5
Malignant neoplasm of female breast — Tumeur maligne du sein chez la femme.............	..	..	1 260	28.3	..	..	1 138	32.8
Malignant neoplasm of cervix uteri — Tumeur maligne du col de l'utérus	..	..	380	8.5	..	..	356	10.3
Malignant neoplasm of prostate — Tumeur maligne de la prostate	712	62.2	..	..	727	56.6	..	..
Malignant neoplasm of lymphoid, haematopoietic and related tissue — Tumeurs malignes primitives ou présumées primitives des tissus lymphoïde, hématopoïétique et apparentés	...	...	...	...	405	10.6	261	6.5
Disorders of the blood and blood-forming organs and certain disorders involving the immune mechanism — Maladies du sang et des organes hématopoïétiques et certains troubles du système immunitaire								
Total.........	38	0.8	25	♦0.5	66	1.7	54	1.3
Anaemias — Anémies	17	♦0.4	17	♦0.3	44	1.2	42	1.0
Endocrine, nutritional and metabolic diseases — Maladies endocriniennes, nutritionnelles et métaboliques								
Total.............	212	4.6	395	7.5	855	22.5	1 135	28.2
Diabetes mellitus — Diabète sucré.............	176	3.8	365	7.0	835	22.0	1 118	27.8
Malnutrition — Malnutrition.........................	9	♦0.2	2	♦0.0	2	♦0.1	1	♦0.0
Mental and behavioural disorders — Troubles mentaux et du comportement	**517**	**11.2**	**173**	**3.3**	**112**	**2.9**	**77**	**1.9**
Diseases of the nervous system — Maladies du système nerveux..........	**484**	**10.5**	**311**	**5.9**	**396**	**10.4**	**314**	**7.8**
Diseases of the circulatory system — Maladies de l'appareil circulatoire								
Total.........	38 253	827.3	40 516	771.8	38 393	1 009.4	37 285	927.5
Acute rheumatic fever and chronic rheumatic heart diseases — Rhumatisme articularie aigu et cardiopathies rhumatismales chroniques	2	♦0.0	1	♦0.0	91	2.4	106	2.6
Hypertensive diseases — Maladies hypertensives........................	657	14.2	839	16.0	2 312	60.8	2 613	65.0
Ischaemic heart disease — Cardiopathie ischémique.............	26 039	563.1	26 124	497.6	10 657	280.2	8 716	216.8
Cerebrovascular disease — Maladie cérébrovasculaire........................	8 443	182.6	11 230	213.9	10 201	268.2	10 976	273.0

Cause of death — Cause de décès	Belarus - Belarus				Bulgaria Bulgarie			
	2003 (C)				2003 (C)			
	Male — Masculin		Female — Féminin		Male — Masculin		Female — Féminin	
	Number Nombre	Rate Taux	Number Nombre	Rate Taux	Number Nombre	Rate Taux	Number Nombre	Rate Taux
Diseases of arteries, arterioles and capillaries — Maladies des artères, artérioles et capillaries	...	...	...	...	2 612	68.7	3 381	84.1
Diseases of the respiratory system — Maladies de l'appareil respiratoire								
Total	3 649	78.9	1 302	24.8	2 152	56.6	1 316	32.7
Influenza — Grippe	2	♦0.0	2	♦0.0	2	♦0.1	3	♦0.1
Pneumonia — Pneumopathies	710	15.4	156	3.0	915	24.1	666	16.6
Chronic lower respiratory diseases — Maladies chroniques des voies respiratoires inférieures	2 732	59.1	1 083	20.6	922	24.2	433	10.8
Diseases of the digestive system — Maladies de l'appareil digestif								
Total	2 281	49.3	1 426	27.2	1 890	49.7	869	21.6
Gastric and duodenal ulcer — Ulcère de l'estomac et du duodénum	198	4.3	72	1.4	103	2.7	61	1.5
Diseases of the liver — Maladies du foie	1 433	31.0	913	17.4	1 029	27.1	306	7.6
Diseases of the musculoskeletal system and connective tissue — Maladies du système ostéo-articularie, des muscles et du tissu conjonctif	57	1.2	115	2.2	15	♦0.4	24	♦0.6
Diseases of the genitourinary system — Maladies de l'appareil génito-urinaire								
Total	593	12.8	491	9.4	508	13.4	418	10.4
Disorders of kidney and ureter — Affections du rein et de l'uretère	...	...	...	...	445	11.7	390	9.7
Hyperplasia of prostate — Hyperplasie de la prostate	...	...	..	..	11	♦0.9	..	..
Pregnancy, childbirth and the puerperium — Grossesse, accouchement et puerpéralité								
Total	..	..	18	♦20.3	..	..	4	♦5.9
Pregnancy with abortive outcome — Grossesse se terminant par un avortement	..	..	5	♦5.6	..	..	-	-
Other direct obstetric causes — Autres décès maternels directs	..	..	7	♦7.9	..	..	4	♦5.9
Indirect obstetric causes — Décès maternels indirects	..	..	3	♦3.4	..	..	-	-
Certain conditions originating in the perinatal period — Certaines affections dont l'origine se situe dans la période périnatale	145	317.8	89	207.5	159	458.6	101	309.0
Congenital malformations, deformations and chromosomal abnormalities — Malformations congénitales et anomalies chromosomiques	248	543.5	163	380.1	122	351.9	89	272.3
Symptoms, signs and abnormal clinical and laboratory findings, not elsewhere classified — Symptômes, signes et résultats anormaux d'examens cliniques et de laboratoire, non classés ailleurs	4 237	91.6	10 867	207.0	2 567	67.5	2 513	62.5
All other diseases — Toutes autres maladies	34	0.7	23	♦0.4	11	♦0.3	14	♦0.3
External causes — Causes externes								
Total	12 983	280.8	3 530	67.2	3 027	79.6	1 012	25.2
Accidents								
Total	...	...	...	...	1 914	50.3	619	15.4
Transport accidents — Accidents de transport	1 706	36.9	535	10.2	742	19.5	230	5.7
Falls — Chutes	911	19.7	270	5.1	211	5.5	69	1.7
Accidental drowning and submersion — Noyade et submersion accidentelles	846	18.3	201	3.8	142	3.7	41	1.0
Exposure to smoke, fire and flames — Exposition à la fumée, au feu et aux flammes	555	12.0	163	3.1	68	1.8	48	1.2
Accidental poisoning by and exposure to noxious substances — Intoxication accidentelle par des substances nocives et exposition à ces substances	2 923	63.2	814	15.5	124	3.3	52	1.3
Intentional self-harm — Lésions auto-infligées	2 927	63.3	540	10.3	800	21.0	292	7.3
Assault — Agresssions	665	14.4	318	6.1	173	4.5	46	1.1
All other external causes — Toutes autres causes externes	...	...	...	...	140	3.7	55	1.4

Cause of death — Cause de décès	Bulgaria - Bulgarie				Croatia - Croatie			
	2004 (C)				2005 (C)			
	Male — Masculin		Female — Féminin		Male — Masculin		Female — Féminin	
	Number Nombre	Rate Taux	Number Nombre	Rate Taux	Number Nombre	Rate Taux	Number Nombre	Rate Taux
TOTAL	59 256	1 567.9	50 854	1 270.7	**26 066**	**1 218.8**	**25 724**	**1 116.8**
Certain infectious and parasitic diseases — Certaines maladies infectieuses et parasitaires								
Total	416	11.0	203	5.1	169	7.9	147	6.4
Intestinal infectious diseases — Maladies infectieuses intestinales	7	♦0.2	10	♦0.2	6	♦0.3	14	♦0.6
Tuberculosis — Tuberculose	203	5.4	65	1.6	60	2.8	49	2.1
Tetanus — Tétanos	-	-	1	♦0.0	-	-	3	♦0.1
Diphtheria — Diphtérie	-	-	-	-	-	-	-	-
Whooping cough — Coqueluche	-	-	-	-	-	-	-	-
Meningococcal infection — Infection à méningocoques	21	♦0.6	9	♦0.2	5	♦0.2	2	♦0.1
Septicaemia — Septicémie	113	3.0	76	1.9	53	2.5	56	2.4
Acute poliomyelitis — Poliomyélite aiguë	-	-	-	-	-	-	-	-
Measles — Rougeole	-	-	-	-	-	-	-	-
Viral hepatitis — Hépatite virale	27	♦0.7	14	♦0.3	28	♦1.3	14	♦0.6
Human immunodeficiency virus [HIV] disease — Maladies dues au virus de l'immunodéficience humaine (VIH)	-	-	-	-	3	♦0.1	-	-
Malaria — Paludisme	1	♦0.0	-	-	1	♦0.0	-	-
Neoplasms — Tumeurs	9 614	254.4	6 652	166.2	7 494	350.4	5 289	229.6
Malignant neoplasms — Tumeurs malignes								
Total	9 566	253.1	6 613	165.2	7 430	347.4	5 210	226.2
Malignant neoplasm of lip, oral cavity and pharynx — Tumeur maligne de la lèvre, de la cavité buccale et du pharynx	262	6.9	58	1.4	321	15.0	63	2.7
Malignant neoplasm of oesophagus — Tumeur maligne de l'oesophage	126	3.3	51	1.3	175	8.2	33	1.4
Malignant neoplasm of stomach — Tumeur maligne de l'estomac	918	24.3	582	14.5	556	26.0	350	15.2
Malignant neoplasm of colon, rectosigmoid junction, rectum, anus and anal canal — Tumeur maligne du côlon, de la jonction recto-sigmoïdienne, du rectum, de l'anus et du canal anal	1 225	32.4	921	23.0	998	46.7	749	32.5
Malignant neoplasm of liver and intrahepatic bile ducts — Tumeur maligne du foie et des voies bilaires intrahépatiques	...	...	...	...	244	11.4	136	5.9
Malignant neoplasm of pancreas — Tumeur maligne du pancréas	540	14.3	408	10.2	330	15.4	281	12.2
Malignant neoplasm of trachea, bronchus and lung — Tumeur maligne de la trachée, des bronches et du poumon	2 611	69.1	548	13.7	2 086	97.5	554	24.1
Malignant neoplasm of female breast — Tumeur maligne du sein chez la femme	..	..	1 144	32.9	..	..	922	47.1
Malignant neoplasm of cervix uteri — Tumeur maligne du col de l'utérus	..	..	364	10.5	..	..	105	5.4
Malignant neoplasm of prostate — Tumeur maligne de la prostate	755	58.7	..	..	636	91.9	..	..
Malignant neoplasm of lymphoid, haematopoietic and related tissue — Tumeurs malignes primitives ou présumées primitives des tissus lymphoïde, hématopoïétique et apparentés	460	12.2	316	7.9	403	18.8	333	14.5
Disorders of the blood and blood-forming organs and certain disorders involving the immune mechanism — Maladies du sang et des organes hématopoïétiques et certains troubles du système immunitaire								
Total	58	1.5	65	1.6	20	♦0.9	29	♦1.3
Anaemias — Anémies	43	1.1	52	1.3	4	♦0.2	17	♦0.7
Endocrine, nutritional and metabolic diseases — Maladies endocriniennes, nutritionnelles et métaboliques								
Total	857	22.7	1 114	27.8	453	21.2	656	28.5
Diabetes mellitus — Diabète sucré	838	22.2	1 090	27.2	439	20.5	638	27.7
Malnutrition — Malnutrition	2	♦0.1	-	-	-	-	-	-
Mental and behavioural disorders — Troubles mentaux et du comportement	127	3.4	53	1.3	338	15.8	341	14.8
Diseases of the nervous system — Maladies du système nerveux	432	11.4	291	7.3	312	14.6	310	13.5
Diseases of the circulatory system — Maladies de l'appareil circulatoire								
Total	37 601	994.9	36 463	911.1	11 343	530.4	14 686	637.6
Acute rheumatic fever and chronic rheumatic heart diseases — Rhumatisme articularie aigu et cardiopathies rhumatismales chroniques	71	1.9	107	2.7	4	♦0.2	20	♦0.9
Hypertensive diseases — Maladies hypertensives	2 213	58.6	2 485	62.1	314	14.7	589	25.6
Ischaemic heart disease — Cardiopathie ischémique	10 111	267.5	8 267	206.6	4 819	225.3	5 129	222.7
Cerebrovascular disease — Maladie cérébrovasculaire	9 903	262.0	10 661	266.4	3 373	157.7	4 781	207.6

Cause of death — Cause de décès	Bulgaria — Bulgarie 2004 (C)				Croatia — Croatie 2005 (C)			
	Male — Masculin		Female — Féminin		Male — Masculin		Female — Féminin	
	Number Nombre	Rate Taux	Number Nombre	Rate Taux	Number Nombre	Rate Taux	Number Nombre	Rate Taux
Diseases of arteries, arterioles and capillaries — Maladies des artères, artérioles et capillaires	2 511	66.4	3 220	80.5	486	22.7	860	37.3
Diseases of the respiratory system — Maladies de l'appareil respiratoire								
Total	2 022	53.5	1 170	29.2	1 817	85.0	1 363	59.2
Influenza — Grippe	3	♦0.1	2	♦0.0	13	♦0.6	25	♦1.1
Pneumonia — Pneumopathies	850	22.5	576	14.4	866	40.5	763	33.1
Chronic lower respiratory diseases — Maladies chroniques des voies respiratoires inférieures	899	23.8	443	11.1	844	39.5	498	21.6
Diseases of the digestive system — Maladies de l'appareil digestif								
Total	1 994	52.8	911	22.8	1 445	67.6	915	39.7
Gastric and duodenal ulcer — Ulcère de l'estomac et du duodénum	148	3.9	79	2.0	141	6.6	84	3.6
Diseases of the liver — Maladies du foie	1 116	29.5	347	8.7	931	43.5	349	15.2
Diseases of the musculoskeletal system and connective tissue — Maladies du système ostéo-articulaire, des muscles et du tissu conjonctif	16	♦0.4	22	♦0.5	23	♦1.1	58	2.5
Diseases of the genitourinary system — Maladies de l'appareil génito-urinaire								
Total	522	13.8	405	10.1	322	15.1	436	18.9
Disorders of kidney and ureter — Affections du rein et de l'uretère	468	12.4	367	9.2	232	10.8	315	13.7
Hyperplasia of prostate — Hyperplasie de la prostate	8	♦0.6	..	..	25	♦3.6	..	..
Pregnancy, childbirth and the puerperium — Grossesse, accouchement et puerpéralité								
Total	..	..	7	♦10.0	..	..	3	♦7.1
Pregnancy with abortive outcome — Grossesse se terminant par un avortement	..	..	1	♦1.4	..	..	-	-
Other direct obstetric causes — Autres décès maternels directs	..	..	6	♦8.6	..	..	1	♦2.4
Indirect obstetric causes — Décès maternels indirects	..	..	-	-	..	..	2	♦4.7
Certain conditions originating in the perinatal period — Certaines affections dont l'origine se situe dans la période périnatale	147	408.0	106	313.1	50	229.9	62	298.9
Congenital malformations, deformations and chromosomal abnormalities — Malformations congénitales et anomalies chromosomiques	120	333.1	91	268.8	72	331.0	69	332.7
Symptoms, signs and abnormal clinical and laboratory findings, not elsewhere classified — Symptômes, signes et résultats anormaux d'examens cliniques et de laboratoire, non classés ailleurs	2 349	62.2	2 375	59.3	249	11.6	408	17.7
All other diseases — Toutes autres maladies	11	♦0.3	16	♦0.4	9	♦0.4	24	♦1.0
External causes — Causes externes								
Total	2 970	78.6	910	22.7	1 950	91.2	928	40.3
Accidents								
Total	1 912	50.6	545	13.6	1 226	57.3	670	29.1
Transport accidents — Accidents de transport	748	19.8	236	5.9	499	23.3	139	6.0
Falls — Chutes	253	6.7	61	1.5	351	16.4	396	17.2
Accidental drowning and submersion — Noyade et submersion accidentelles	119	3.1	28	♦0.7	66	3.1	13	♦0.6
Exposure to smoke, fire and flames — Exposition à la fumée, au feu et aux flammes	67	1.8	37	0.9	28	♦1.3	13	♦0.6
Accidental poisoning by and exposure to noxious substances — Intoxication accidentelle par des substances nocives et exposition à ces substances	144	3.8	40	1.0	65	3.0	22	♦1.0
Intentional self-harm — Lésions auto-infligées	746	19.7	267	6.7	652	30.5	223	9.7
Assault — Agresssions	170	4.5	52	1.3	34	1.6	25	♦1.1
All other external causes — Toutes autres causes externes	142	3.8	46	1.1	38	1.8	10	♦0.4

Cause of death — Cause de décès	Croatia - Croatie 2006 (C)				Czech Republic - République tchèque 2004 (C)			
	Male — Masculin		Female — Féminin		Male — Masculin		Female — Féminin	
	Number Nombre	Rate Taux	Number Nombre	Rate Taux	Number Nombre	Rate Taux	Number Nombre	Rate Taux
TOTAL..........	25 329	1 184.2	25 049	1 088.6	54 190	1 090.0	52 987	1 012.1
Certain infectious and parasitic diseases — Certaines maladies infectieuses et parasitaires								
Total....	199	9.3	180	7.8	181	3.6	147	2.8
Intestinal infectious diseases — Maladies infectieuses intestinales...........	5	✦0.2	15	✦0.7	8	✦0.2	3	✦0.1
Tuberculosis — Tuberculose................	92	4.3	49	2.1	41	0.8	27	✦0.5
Tetanus — Tétanos..........	1	✦0.0	1	✦0.0	-	-	-	-
Diphtheria — Diphtérie...........	-	-	-	-	-	-	-	-
Whooping cough — Coqueluche..........	-	-	-	-	-	-	-	-
Meningococcal infection — Infection à méningocoques..........	1	✦0.0	-	-	2	✦0.0	10	✦0.2
Septicaemia — Septicémie..........	67	3.1	86	3.7	107	2.2	82	1.6
Acute poliomyelitis — Poliomyélite aiguë...........	-	-	-	-	-	-	-	-
Measles — Rougeole.........	-	-	-	-	-	-	-	-
Viral hepatitis — Hépatite virale...........	22	✦1.0	19	✦0.8	12	✦0.2	6	✦0.1
Human immunodeficiency virus [HIV] disease — Maladies dues au virus de l'immunodéficience humaine (VIH)...........	6	✦0.3	2	✦0.1	-	-	-	-
Malaria — Paludisme..........	-	-	-	-	-	-	-	-
Neoplasms — Tumeurs..........	7 426	347.2	5 274	229.2	16 280	327.5	13 024	248.8
Malignant neoplasms — Tumeurs malignes								
Total....	7 364	344.3	5 187	225.4	16 218	326.2	12 950	247.4
Malignant neoplasm of lip, oral cavity and pharynx — Tumeur maligne de la lèvre, de la cavité buccale et du pharynx...........	321	15.0	41	1.8	551	11.1	105	2.0
Malignant neoplasm of oesophagus — Tumeur maligne de l'oesophage......	190	8.9	40	1.7	359	7.2	83	1.6
Malignant neoplasm of stomach — Tumeur maligne de l'estomac......	539	25.2	317	13.8	811	16.3	598	11.4
Malignant neoplasm of colon, rectosigmoid junction, rectum, anus and anal canal — Tumeur maligne du côlon, de la jonction recto-sigmoïdienne, du rectum, de l'anus et du canal anal...........	1 028	48.1	772	33.5	2 610	52.5	1 946	37.2
Malignant neoplasm of liver and intrahepatic bile ducts — Tumeur maligne du foie et des voies bilaires intrahépatiques...........	261	12.2	156	6.8	586	11.8	373	7.1
Malignant neoplasm of pancreas — Tumeur maligne du pancréas...........	290	13.6	292	12.7	857	17.2	854	16.3
Malignant neoplasm of trachea, bronchus and lung — Tumeur maligne de la trachée, des bronches et du poumon...........	2 145	100.3	572	24.9	4 346	87.4	1 343	25.7
Malignant neoplasm of female breast — Tumeur maligne du sein chez la femme...........	..	..	830	42.3	..	..	1 998	44.4
Malignant neoplasm of cervix uteri — Tumeur maligne du col de l'utérus......	..	..	94	4.8	..	..	394	8.8
Malignant neoplasm of prostate — Tumeur maligne de la prostate...........	604	85.9	..	..	1 520	96.0	..	..
Malignant neoplasm of lymphoid, haematopoietic and related tissue —, Tumeurs malignes primitives ou présumées primitives des tissus lymphoïde, hématopoïétique et apparentés...........	406	19.0	391	17.0	1 008	20.3	945	18.1
Disorders of the blood and blood-forming organs and certain disorders involving the immune mechanism — Maladies du sang et des organes hématopoïétiques et certains troubles du système immunitaire								
Total...........	12	✦0.6	26	✦1.1	25	✦0.5	37	0.7
Anaemias — Anémies...........	4	✦0.2	16	✦0.7	9	✦0.2	12	✦0.2
Endocrine, nutritional and metabolic diseases — Maladies endocriniennes, nutritionnelles et métaboliques								
Total....	470	22.0	661	28.7	592	11.9	824	15.7
Diabetes mellitus — Diabète sucré...........	459	21.5	653	28.4	568	11.4	790	15.1
Malnutrition — Malnutrition...........	-	-	-	-	4	✦0.1	6	✦0.1
Mental and behavioural disorders — Troubles mentaux et du comportement	311	14.5	340	14.8	140	2.8	41	0.8
Diseases of the nervous system — Maladies du système nerveux..........	294	13.7	389	16.9	932	18.7	1 043	19.9
Diseases of the circulatory system — Maladies de l'appareil circulatoire								
Total....	11 229	525.0	14 382	625.0	24 919	501.2	30 123	575.4
Acute rheumatic fever and chronic rheumatic heart diseases — Rhumatisme articularie aigu et cardiopathies rhumatismales chroniques...........	11	✦0.5	16	✦0.7	78	1.6	126	2.4
Hypertensive diseases — Maladies hypertensives...........	323	15.1	531	23.1	710	14.3	893	17.1
Ischaemic heart disease — Cardiopathie ischémique...........	4 730	221.1	5 092	221.3	10 659	214.4	10 397	198.6
Cerebrovascular disease — Maladie cérébrovasculaire...........	3 369	157.5	4 706	204.5	5 797	116.6	8 669	165.6

21. Death and death rates by cause and sex: 2002 - 2006
Décès et taux de mortalité par cause et sexe : 2002 - 2006 (continued - suite)

Croatia - Croatie   Czech Republic - République tchèque

Cause of death — Cause de décès	2006 (C)				2004 (C)			
	Male — Masculin		Female — Féminin		Male — Masculin		Female — Féminin	
	Number Nombre	Rate Taux	Number Nombre	Rate Taux	Number Nombre	Rate Taux	Number Nombre	Rate Taux
Diseases of arteries, arterioles and capillaries — Maladies des artères, artérioles et capillaires	462	21.6	737	32.0	5 079	102.2	7 096	135.5
Diseases of the respiratory system — Maladies de l'appareil respiratoire								
Total	1 459	68.2	1 035	45.0	2 686	54.0	2 069	39.5
Influenza — Grippe	3	♦0.1	1	♦0.0	5	♦0.1	14	♦0.3
Pneumonia — Pneumopathies	636	29.7	547	23.8	1 231	24.8	1 144	21.9
Chronic lower respiratory diseases — Maladies chroniques des voies respiratoires inférieures	728	34.0	427	18.6	1 087	21.9	650	12.4
Diseases of the digestive system — Maladies de l'appareil digestif								
Total	1 432	66.9	889	38.6	2 583	52.0	1 954	37.3
Gastric and duodenal ulcer — Ulcère de l'estomac et du duodénum	108	5.0	118	5.1	273	5.5	298	5.7
Diseases of the liver — Maladies du foie	929	43.4	299	13.0	1 471	29.6	629	12.0
Diseases of the musculoskeletal system and connective tissue — Maladies du système ostéo-articularie, des muscles et du tissu conjonctif	22	♦1.0	59	2.6	11	♦0.2	14	♦0.3
Diseases of the genitourinary system — Maladies de l'appareil génito-urinaire								
Total	361	16.9	389	16.9	685	13.8	801	15.3
Disorders of kidney and ureter — Affections du rein et de l'uretère	273	12.8	300	13.0	601	12.1	748	14.3
Hyperplasia of prostate — Hyperplasie de la prostate	25	♦3.6	..	..	27	♦1.7	..	..
Pregnancy, childbirth and the puerperium — Grossesse, accouchement et puerpéralité								
Total	..	..	4	♦9.7	..	..	5	♦5.1
Pregnancy with abortive outcome — Grossesse se terminant par un avortement	..	..	-	-	..	..	-	-
Other direct obstetric causes — Autres décès maternels directs	..	..	2	♦4.8	..	..	4	♦4.1
Indirect obstetric causes — Décès maternels indirects	..	..	2	♦4.8	..	..	-	-
Certain conditions originating in the perinatal period — Certaines affections dont l'origine se situe dans la période périnatale	59	274.8	57	285.3	116	230.8	91	192.0
Congenital malformations, deformations and chromosomal abnormalities — Malformations congénitales et anomalies chromosomiques	64	298.1	61	305.4	49	97.5	33	69.6
Symptoms, signs and abnormal clinical and laboratory findings, not elsewhere classified — Symptômes, signes et résultats anormaux d'examens cliniques et de laboratoire, non classés ailleurs	181	8.5	339	14.7	408	8.2	362	6.9
All other diseases — Toutes autres maladies	6	♦0.3	15	♦0.7	5	♦0.1	6	♦0.1
External causes — Causes externes								
Total	1 804	84.3	949	41.2	4 578	92.1	2 413	46.1
Accidents								
Total	1 157	54.1	683	29.7	2 809	56.5	1 937	37.0
Transport accidents — Accidents de transport	512	23.9	147	6.4	981	19.7	335	6.4
Falls — Chutes	326	15.2	403	17.5	819	16.5	1 213	23.2
Accidental drowning and submersion — Noyade et submersion accidentelles	53	2.5	25	♦1.1	119	2.4	47	0.9
Exposure to smoke, fire and flames — Exposition à la fumée, au feu et aux flammes	21	♦1.0	20	♦0.9	42	0.8	27	♦0.5
Accidental poisoning by and exposure to noxious substances — Intoxication accidentelle par des substances nocives et exposition à ces substances	90	4.2	21	♦0.9	227	4.6	66	1.3
Intentional self-harm — Lésions auto-infligées	575	26.9	223	9.7	1 286	25.9	297	5.7
Assault — Agresssions	52	2.4	29	♦1.3	84	1.7	40	0.8
All other external causes — Toutes autres causes externes	20	♦0.9	14	♦0.6	399	8.0	139	2.7

Cause of death — Cause de décès	Czech Republic - République tchèque				Estonia - Estonie			
	2005 (C)				2004 (C)			
	Male — Masculin		Female — Féminin		Male — Masculin		Female — Féminin	
	Number Nombre	Rate Taux	Number Nombre	Rate Taux	Number Nombre	Rate Taux	Number Nombre	Rate Taux
TOTAL............	54 072	1 083.3	53 866	1 027.5	9 067	1 458.8	8 618	1 184.2
Certain infectious and parasitic diseases — Certaines maladies infectieuses et parasitaires								
Total.......	194	3.9	217	4.1	112	18.0	40	5.5
Intestinal infectious diseases — Maladies infectieuses intestinales...........	3	◊0.1	11	◊0.2	-	-	-	-
Tuberculosis — Tuberculose............	49	1.0	19	◊0.4	83	13.4	15	◊2.1
Tetanus — Tétanos.........	-	-	-	-	-	-	-	-
Diphtheria — Diphtérie............	-	-	-	-	-	-	-	-
Whooping cough — Coqueluche............	-	-	-	-	-	-	-	-
Meningococcal infection — Infection à méningocoques.....................	-	-	2	◊0.0	-	-	1	◊0.1
Septicaemia — Septicémie............	106	2.1	143	2.7	4	◊0.6	7	◊1.0
Acute poliomyelitis — Poliomyélite aiguë............	-	-	-	-	-	-	-	-
Measles — Rougeole............	-	-	-	-	-	-	-	-
Viral hepatitis — Hépatite virale............	14	◊0.3	10	◊0.2	3	◊0.5	1	◊0.1
Human immunodeficiency virus [HIV] disease — Maladies dues au virus de l'immunodéficience humaine (VIH)	4	◊0.1	1	◊0.0	14	◊2.3	7	◊1.0
Malaria — Paludisme............	-	-	-	-	-	-	-	-
Neoplasms — Tumeurs............	15 680	314.1	12 575	239.9	1 907	306.8	1 604	220.4
Malignant neoplasms — Tumeurs malignes								
Total.......	15 567	311.9	12 466	237.8	1 889	303.9	1 574	216.3
Malignant neoplasm of lip, oral cavity and pharynx — Tumeur maligne de la lèvre, de la cavité buccale et du pharynx.....................	518	10.4	121	2.3	61	9.8	22	◊3.0
Malignant neoplasm of oesophagus — Tumeur maligne de l'oesophage......	375	7.5	70	1.3	49	7.9	13	◊1.8
Malignant neoplasm of stomach — Tumeur maligne de l'estomac..........	755	15.1	541	10.3	184	29.6	164	22.5
Malignant neoplasm of colon, rectosigmoid junction, rectum, anus and anal canal — Tumeur maligne du côlon, de la jonction recto-sigmoïdienne, du rectum, de l'anus et du canal anal..........	2 463	49.3	1 783	34.0	168	27.0	235	32.3
Malignant neoplasm of liver and intrahepatic bile ducts — Tumeur maligne du foie et des voies bilaires intrahépatiques..........	528	10.6	342	6.5	49	7.9	34	4.7
Malignant neoplasm of pancreas — Tumeur maligne du pancréas...........	935	18.7	873	16.7	96	15.4	88	12.1
Malignant neoplasm of trachea, bronchus and lung — Tumeur maligne de la trachée, des bronches et du poumon....................	4 170	83.5	1 373	26.2	511	82.2	145	19.9
Malignant neoplasm of female breast — Tumeur maligne du sein chez la femme.	..	..	1 916	42.4	..	..	234	37.5
Malignant neoplasm of cervix uteri — Tumeur maligne du col de l'utérus......	..	..	343	7.6	..	..	58	9.3
Malignant neoplasm of prostate — Tumeur maligne de la prostate...........	1 381	85.7	..	..	207	116.2	..	..
Malignant neoplasm of lymphoid, haematopoietic and related tissue — Tumeurs malignes primitives ou présumées primitives des tissus lymphoïde, hématopoïétique et apparentés.....................	944	18.9	871	16.6	146	23.5	124	17.0
Disorders of the blood and blood-forming organs and certain disorders involving the immune mechanism — Maladies du sang et des organes hématopoïétiques et certains troubles du système immunitaire								
Total.......	38	0.8	68	1.3	3	◊0.5	13	◊1.8
Anaemias — Anémies.....................	17	◊0.3	33	0.6	1	◊0.2	5	◊0.7
Endocrine, nutritional and metabolic diseases — Maladies endocriniennes, nutritionnelles et métaboliques								
Total.......	638	12.8	848	16.2	128	20.6	190	26.1
Diabetes mellitus — Diabète sucré..........	615	12.3	809	15.4	118	19.0	168	23.1
Malnutrition — Malnutrition..........	2	◊0.0	7	◊0.1	2	◊0.3	3	◊0.4
Mental and behavioural disorders — Troubles mentaux et du comportement	217	4.3	67	1.3	108	17.4	31	4.3
Diseases of the nervous system — Maladies du système nerveux..........	969	19.4	1 102	21.0	119	19.1	111	15.3
Diseases of the circulatory system — Maladies de l'appareil circulatoire								
Total.......	24 573	492.3	30 582	583.3	4 127	664.0	5 275	724.8
Acute rheumatic fever and chronic rheumatic heart diseases — Rhumatisme articularie aigu et cardiopathies rhumatismales chroniques..................	58	1.2	120	2.3	20	◊3.2	47	6.5
Hypertensive diseases — Maladies hypertensives..........	604	12.1	827	15.8	266	42.8	389	53.5
Ischaemic heart disease — Cardiopathie ischémique..........	11 330	227.0	12 037	229.6	2 396	385.5	2 772	380.9
Cerebrovascular disease — Maladie cérébrovasculaire............	5 808	116.4	8 780	167.5	894	143.8	1 509	207.3

Cause of death — Cause de décès	Czech Republic - République tchèque				Estonia - Estonie			
	2005 (C)				2004 (C)			
	Male — Masculin		Female — Féminin		Male — Masculin		Female — Féminin	
	Number Nombre	Rate Taux	Number Nombre	Rate Taux	Number Nombre	Rate Taux	Number Nombre	Rate Taux
Diseases of arteries, arterioles and capillaries — Maladies des artères, artérioles et capillaires	3 827	76.7	5 377	102.6	163	26.2	232	31.9
Diseases of the respiratory system — Maladies de l'appareil respiratoire								
Total	3 237	64.9	2 803	53.5	404	65.0	170	23.4
Influenza — Grippe	26	♦0.5	29	♦0.6	-	-	-	-
Pneumonia — Pneumopathies	1 423	28.5	1 546	29.5	172	27.7	77	10.6
Chronic lower respiratory diseases — Maladies chroniques des voies respiratoires inférieures	1 396	28.0	895	17.1	187	30.1	80	11.0
Diseases of the digestive system — Maladies de l'appareil digestif								
Total	2 771	55.5	2 052	39.1	371	59.7	277	38.1
Gastric and duodenal ulcer — Ulcère de l'estomac et du duodénum	282	5.6	284	5.4	46	7.4	26	♦3.6
Diseases of the liver — Maladies du foie	1 581	31.7	680	13.0	196	31.5	114	15.7
Diseases of the musculoskeletal system and connective tissue — Maladies du système ostéo-articularie, des muscles et du tissu conjonctif	12	♦0.2	28	♦0.5	19	♦3.1	37	5.1
Diseases of the genitourinary system — Maladies de l'appareil génito-urinaire								
Total	694	13.9	919	17.5	71	11.4	76	10.4
Disorders of kidney and ureter — Affections du rein et de l'uretère	617	12.4	821	15.7	55	8.8	73	10.0
Hyperplasia of prostate — Hyperplasie de la prostate	14	♦0.9	..	..	13	♦7.3	..	..
Pregnancy, childbirth and the puerperium — Grossesse, accouchement et puerpéralité								
Total	..	..	3	♦2.9	..	..	4	♦28.6
Pregnancy with abortive outcome — Grossesse se terminant par un avortement	..	..	1	♦1.0	..	..	-	-
Other direct obstetric causes — Autres décès maternels directs	..	..	2	♦2.0	..	..	3	♦21.4
Indirect obstetric causes — Décès maternels indirects	..	..	-	-	..	..	1	♦7.1
Certain conditions originating in the perinatal period — Certaines affections dont l'origine se situe dans la période périnatale	123	234.5	65	130.6	24	♦334.4	25	♦366.8
Congenital malformations, deformations and chromosomal abnormalities — Malformations congénitales et anomalies chromosomiques	59	112.5	57	114.6	20	♦278.7	23	♦337.4
Symptoms, signs and abnormal clinical and laboratory findings, not elsewhere classified — Symptômes, signes et résultats anormaux d'examens cliniques et de laboratoire, non classés ailleurs	529	10.6	411	7.8	241	38.8	369	50.7
All other diseases — Toutes autres maladies	5	♦0.1	26	♦0.5	8	♦1.3	12	♦1.6
External causes — Causes externes								
Total	4 333	86.8	2 043	39.0	1 405	226.1	361	49.6
Accidents								
Total	2 691	53.9	1 579	30.1	956	153.8	259	35.6
Transport accidents — Accidents de transport	949	19.0	312	6.0	154	24.8	49	6.7
Falls — Chutes	644	12.9	830	15.8	75	12.1	41	5.6
Accidental drowning and submersion — Noyade et submersion accidentelles	151	3.0	51	1.0	67	10.8	18	♦2.5
Exposure to smoke, fire and flames — Exposition à la fumée, au feu et aux flammes	38	0.8	24	♦0.5	106	17.1	31	4.3
Accidental poisoning by and exposure to noxious substances — Intoxication accidentelle par des substances nocives et exposition à ces substances	221	4.4	93	1.8	267	43.0	56	7.7
Intentional self-harm — Lésions auto-infligées	1 272	25.5	292	5.6	264	42.5	59	8.1
Assault — Agresssions	55	1.1	41	0.8	90	14.5	19	♦2.6
All other external causes — Toutes autres causes externes	315	6.3	131	2.5	95	15.3	24	♦3.3

	Estonia - Estonie				Finland - Finlande			
	2005 (C)				2005 (C)			
Cause of death — Cause de décès	Male — Masculin		Female — Féminin		Male — Masculin		Female — Féminin	
	Number Nombre	Rate Taux	Number Nombre	Rate Taux	Number Nombre	Rate Taux	Number Nombre	Rate Taux
TOTAL..........	8 834	1 425.0	8 482	1 168.1	23 965	933.5	23 786	887.9
Certain infectious and parasitic diseases — Certaines maladies infectieuses et parasitaires								
Total.....	76	12.3	32	4.4	173	6.7	194	7.2
Intestinal infectious diseases — Maladies infectieuses intestinales...........	1	◊0.2	-	-	16	◊0.6	24	◊0.9
Tuberculosis — Tuberculose................	40	6.5	9	◊1.2	24	◊0.9	14	◊0.5
Tetanus — Tétanos......................	-	-	-	-	-	-	-	-
Diphtheria — Diphtérie..................	-	-	-	-	1	◊0.0	-	-
Whooping cough — Coqueluche............	-	-	-	-	-	-	-	-
Meningococcal infection — Infection à méningocoques..................	-	-	-	-	6	◊0.2	1	◊0.0
Septicaemia — Septicémie................	5	◊0.8	5	◊0.7	54	2.1	81	3.0
Acute poliomyelitis — Poliomyélite aiguë.....	-	-	-	-	-	-	-	-
Measles — Rougeole....................	-	-	-	-	-	-	-	-
Viral hepatitis — Hépatite virale	1	◊0.2	1	◊0.1	8	◊0.3	4	◊0.1
Human immunodeficiency virus [HIV] disease — Maladies dues au virus de l'immunodéficience humaine (VIH)........	25	◊4.0	8	◊1.1	9	◊0.4	-	-
Malaria — Paludisme....................	-	-	-	-	-	-	-	-
Neoplasms — Tumeurs................	1 957	315.7	1 568	215.9	5 616	218.8	5 240	195.6
Malignant neoplasms — Tumeurs malignes								
Total.....	1 937	312.4	1 542	212.4	5 518	214.9	5 075	189.4
Malignant neoplasm of lip, oral cavity and pharynx — Tumeur maligne de la lèvre, de la cavité buccale et du pharynx............	94	15.2	20	◊2.8	86	3.3	54	2.0
Malignant neoplasm of oesophagus — Tumeur maligne de l'oesophage......	52	8.4	7	◊1.0	134	5.2	82	3.1
Malignant neoplasm of stomach — Tumeur maligne de l'estomac...............	163	26.3	150	20.7	301	11.7	240	9.0
Malignant neoplasm of colon, rectosigmoid junction, rectum, anus and anal canal — Tumeur maligne du côlon, de la jonction recto-sigmoïdienne, du rectum, de l'anus et du canal anal............	203	32.7	210	28.9	505	19.7	544	20.3
Malignant neoplasm of liver and intrahepatic bile ducts — Tumeur maligne du foie et des voies bilaires intrahépatiques.......	50	8.1	36	5.0	216	8.4	170	6.3
Malignant neoplasm of pancreas — Tumeur maligne du pancréas.......	90	14.5	79	10.9	396	15.4	433	16.2
Malignant neoplasm of trachea, bronchus and lung — Tumeur maligne de la trachée, des bronches et du poumon..................	500	80.7	140	19.3	1 413	55.0	536	20.0
Malignant neoplasm of female breast — Tumeur maligne du sein chez la femme..................	..	..	242	...	..	..	827	37.0
Malignant neoplasm of cervix uteri — Tumeur maligne du col de l'utérus......	..	..	65	...	..	..	58	2.6
Malignant neoplasm of prostate — Tumeur maligne de la prostate...........	225	...	..	..	771	87.8	..	..
Malignant neoplasm of lymphoid, haematopoietic and related tissue — Tumeurs malignes primitives ou présumées primitives des tissus lymphoïde, hématopoïétique et apparentés............	114	18.4	117	16.1	522	20.3	524	19.6
Disorders of the blood and blood-forming organs and certain disorders involving the immune mechanism — Maladies du sang et des organes hématopoïétiques et certains troubles du système immunitaire								
Total.....	3	◊0.5	10	◊1.4	18	◊0.7	29	◊1.1
Anaemias — Anémies................	-	-	5	◊0.7	3	◊0.1	14	◊0.5
Endocrine, nutritional and metabolic diseases — Maladies endocriniennes, nutritionnelles et métaboliques								
Total.....	95	15.3	161	22.2	336	13.1	295	11.0
Diabetes mellitus — Diabète sucré...........	84	13.5	142	19.6	291	11.3	228	8.5
Malnutrition — Malnutrition................	-	-	1	◊0.1	1	◊0.0	3	◊0.1
Mental and behavioural disorders — Troubles mentaux et du comportement	132	21.3	55	7.6	858	33.4	1 869	69.8
Diseases of the nervous system — Maladies du système nerveux...........	137	22.1	114	15.7	1 189	46.3	1 606	60.0
Diseases of the circulatory system — Maladies de l'appareil circulatoire								
Total.....	4 078	657.8	5 153	709.6	9 347	364.1	10 417	388.9
Acute rheumatic fever and chronic rheumatic heart diseases — Rhumatisme articularie aigu et cardiopathies rhumatismales chroniques..............	12	◊1.9	23	◊3.2	25	◊1.0	59	2.2
Hypertensive diseases — Maladies hypertensives.........................	281	45.3	427	58.8	184	7.2	305	11.4
Ischaemic heart disease — Cardiopathie ischémique......................	2 268	365.8	2 644	364.1	5 916	230.4	5 812	217.0
Cerebrovascular disease — Maladie cérébrovasculaire......................	888	143.2	1 446	199.1	1 792	69.8	2 669	99.6

Cause of death — Cause de décès	Latvia Lettonie 2005 (C)				Finland Finlande 2005 (C)			
	Male — Masculin		Female — Féminin		Male — Masculin		Female — Féminin	
	Number Nombre	Rate Taux	Number Nombre	Rate Taux	Number Nombre	Rate Taux	Number Nombre	Rate Taux
Diseases of arteries, arterioles and capillaries — Maladies des artères, artérioles et capillaires	182	29.4	275	37.9	471	18.3	385	14.4
Diseases of the respiratory system — Maladies de l'appareil respiratoire								
Total............	331	53.4	142	19.6	1 445	56.3	1 022	38.2
Influenza — Grippe	-	-	-	-	13	♦0.5	15	♦0.6
Pneumonia — Pneumopathies	129	20.8	52	7.2	441	17.2	514	19.2
Chronic lower respiratory diseases — Maladies chroniques des voies respiratoires inférieures	147	23.7	68	9.4	820	31.9	365	13.6
Diseases of the digestive system — Maladies de l'appareil digestif								
Total............	391	63.1	299	41.2	1 428	55.6	1 038	38.7
Gastric and duodenal ulcer — Ulcère de l'estomac et du duodénum	49	7.9	29	♦4.0	146	5.7	105	3.9
Diseases of the liver — Maladies du foie	213	34.4	121	16.7	786	30.6	343	12.8
Diseases of the musculoskeletal system and connective tissue — Maladies du système ostéo-articularie, des muscles et du tissu conjonctif	16	♦2.6	50	6.9	76	3.0	217	8.1
Diseases of the genitourinary system — Maladies de l'appareil génito-urinaire								
Total............	75	12.1	70	9.6	166	6.5	284	10.6
Disorders of kidney and ureter — Affections du rein et de l'uretère	66	10.6	65	9.0	109	4.2	240	9.0
Hyperplasia of prostate — Hyperplasie de la prostate.....................	6	...		...	36	4.1		
Pregnancy, childbirth and the puerperium — Grossesse, accouchement et puerpéralité								
Total............	..	..	2	♦13.9	..	..	3	♦5.2
Pregnancy with abortive outcome — Grossesse se terminant par un avortement	..	..	-	-	..	..	-	-
Other direct obstetric causes — Autres décès maternels directs	..	..	1	♦7.0	..	..	3	♦5.2
Indirect obstetric causes — Décès maternels indirects.....................	..	..	1	♦7.0	..	..	-	-
Certain conditions originating in the perinatal period — Certaines affections dont l'origine se situe dans la période périnatale	17	♦227.1	12	♦174.8	41	139.5	36	127.0
Congenital malformations, deformations and chromosomal abnormalities — Malformations congénitales et anomalies chromosomiques	16	♦213.7	23	♦335.1	93	316.3	99	349.3
Symptoms, signs and abnormal clinical and laboratory findings, not elsewhere classified — Symptômes, signes et résultats anormaux d'examens cliniques et de laboratoire, non classés ailleurs	227	36.6	397	54.7	168	6.5	117	4.4
All other diseases — Toutes autres maladies................................	7	♦1.1	11	♦1.5	14	♦0.5	22	♦0.8
External causes — Causes externes								
Total............	1 276	205.8	383	52.7	2 997	116.7	1 298	48.5
Accidents								
Total............	844	136.1	263	36.2	2 078	80.9	959	35.8
Transport accidents — Accidents de transport	150	24.2	53	7.3	379	14.8	101	3.8
Falls — Chutes	83	13.4	44	6.1	698	27.2	541	20.2
Accidental drowning and submersion — Noyade et submersion accidentelles.....................	50	8.1	9	♦1.2	126	4.9	18	♦0.7
Exposure to smoke, fire and flames — Exposition à la fumée, au feu et aux flammes..........................	100	16.1	36	5.0	50	1.9	19	♦0.7
Accidental poisoning by and exposure to noxious substances — Intoxication accidentelle par des substances nocives et exposition à ces substances	203	32.7	59	8.1	603	23.5	196	7.3
Intentional self-harm — Lésions auto-infligées....................	220	35.5	53	7.3	722	28.1	269	10.0
Assault — Agresssions	92	14.8	31	4.3	71	2.8	30	♦1.1
All other external causes — Toutes autres causes externes...................	120	19.4	36	5.0	126	4.9	40	1.5

Cause of death — Cause de décès	Finland - Finlande 2006 (C)				France 2004 (C)			
	Male — Masculin		Female — Féminin		Male — Masculin		Female — Féminin	
	Number Nombre	Rate Taux	Number Nombre	Rate Taux	Number Nombre	Rate Taux	Number Nombre	Rate Taux
TOTAL............	24 335	943.9	23 771	884.3	263 076	892.8	246 343	790.2
Certain infectious and parasitic diseases — Certaines maladies infectieuses et parasitaires								
Total....	154	6.0	181	6.7	4 876	16.5	4 681	15.0
Intestinal infectious diseases — Maladies infectieuses intestinales............	18	◆0.7	26	◆1.0	335	1.1	520	1.7
Tuberculosis — Tuberculose............	13	◆0.5	8	◆0.3	237	0.8	191	0.6
Tetanus — Tétanos............	-	-	-	-	3	◆0.0	7	◆0.0
Diphtheria — Diphtérie............	-	-	-	-	-	-	-	-
Whooping cough — Coqueluche............	-	-	-	-	2	◆0.0	1	◆0.0
Meningococcal infection — Infection à méningocoques............	3	◆0.1	2	◆0.1	18	◆0.1	18	◆0.1
Septicaemia — Septicémie............	60	2.3	62	2.3	1 862	6.3	1 888	6.1
Acute poliomyelitis — Poliomyélite aiguë............	-	-	-	-	-	-	-	-
Measles — Rougeole............	-	-	-	-	1	◆0.0	-	-
Viral hepatitis — Hépatite virale............	1	◆0.0	2	◆0.1	388	1.3	337	1.1
Human immunodeficiency virus [HIV] disease — Maladies dues au virus de l'immunodéficience humaine (VIH)............	6	◆0.2	3	◆0.1	706	2.4	222	0.7
Malaria — Paludisme............	-	-	-	-	12	◆0.0	4	◆0.0
Neoplasms — Tumeurs............	5 853	227.0	5 193	193.2	90 688	307.8	62 021	198.9
Malignant neoplasms — Tumeurs malignes								
Total............	5 738	222.6	5 039	187.4	87 520	297.0	58 950	189.1
Malignant neoplasm of lip, oral cavity and pharynx — Tumeur maligne de la lèvre, de la cavité buccale et du pharynx............	87	3.4	58	2.2	3 538	12.0	727	2.3
Malignant neoplasm of oesophagus — Tumeur maligne de l'oesophage......	110	4.3	81	3.0	3 180	10.8	686	2.2
Malignant neoplasm of stomach — Tumeur maligne de l'estomac............	308	11.9	218	8.1	3 108	10.5	1 832	5.9
Malignant neoplasm of colon, rectosigmoid junction, rectum, anus and anal canal — Tumeur maligne du côlon, de la jonction recto-sigmoïdienne, du rectum, de l'anus et du canal anal............	545	21.1	516	19.2	8 817	29.9	7 641	24.5
Malignant neoplasm of liver and intrahepatic bile ducts — Tumeur maligne du foie et des voies bilaires intrahépatiques............	244	9.5	177	6.6	5 297	18.0	1 814	5.8
Malignant neoplasm of pancreas — Tumeur maligne du pancréas............	432	16.8	453	16.9	4 021	13.6	3 727	12.0
Malignant neoplasm of trachea, bronchus and lung — Tumeur maligne de la trachée, des bronches et du poumon............	1 464	56.8	541	20.1	21 398	72.6	5 462	17.5
Malignant neoplasm of female breast — Tumeur maligne du sein chez la femme............	..	..	856	38.1	..	..	11 199	43.7
Malignant neoplasm of cervix uteri — Tumeur maligne du col de l'utérus......	..	..	57	2.5	..	..	733	2.9
Malignant neoplasm of prostate — Tumeur maligne de la prostate............	814	90.8	..	..	9 138	98.6	..	..
Malignant neoplasm of lymphoid, haematopoietic and related tissue — Tumeurs malignes primitives ou présumées primitives des tissus lymphoïde, hématopoïétique et apparentés............	532	20.6	514	19.1	6 501	22.1	5 818	18.7
Disorders of the blood and blood-forming organs and certain disorders involving the immune mechanism — Maladies du sang et des organes hématopoïétiques et certains troubles du système immunitaire								
Total............	24	◆0.9	33	1.2	975	3.3	1 140	3.7
Anaemias — Anémies............	5	◆0.2	19	◆0.7	468	1.6	683	2.2
Endocrine, nutritional and metabolic diseases — Maladies endocriniennes, nutritionnelles et métaboliques								
Total............	295	11.4	297	11.0	8 141	27.6	10 715	34.4
Diabetes mellitus — Diabète sucré............	241	9.3	232	8.6	5 135	17.4	5 756	18.5
Malnutrition — Malnutrition............	2	◆0.1	-	-	808	2.7	1 555	5.0
Mental and behavioural disorders — Troubles mentaux et du comportement	831	32.2	1 854	69.0	6 736	22.9	9 293	29.8
Diseases of the nervous system — Maladies du système nerveux............	1 279	49.6	1 921	71.5	9 752	33.1	13 621	43.7
Diseases of the circulatory system — Maladies de l'appareil circulatoire								
Total............	9 576	371.4	10 404	387.0	69 336	235.3	77 986	250.1
Acute rheumatic fever and chronic rheumatic heart diseases — Rhumatisme articularie aigu et cardiopathies rhumatismales chroniques............	14	◆0.5	36	1.3	573	1.9	1 023	3.3
Hypertensive diseases — Maladies hypertensives............	188	7.3	351	13.1	2 752	9.3	4 960	15.9
Ischaemic heart disease — Cardiopathie ischémique............	6 065	235.3	5 668	210.8	23 122	78.5	17 535	56.2
Cerebrovascular disease — Maladie cérébrovasculaire............	1 785	69.2	2 753	102.4	13 985	47.5	19 502	62.6

21. Death and death rates by cause and sex: 2002 - 2006
Décès et taux de mortalité par cause et sexe : 2002 - 2006 (continued - suite)

Cause of death — Cause de décès	Finland — Finlande 2006 (C)				France 2004 (C)			
	Male — Masculin		Female — Féminin		Male — Masculin		Female — Féminin	
	Number Nombre	Rate Taux	Number Nombre	Rate Taux	Number Nombre	Rate Taux	Number Nombre	Rate Taux
Diseases of arteries, arterioles and capillaries — Maladies des artères, artérioles et capillaires	443	17.2	364	13.5	5 626	19.1	4 006	12.8
Diseases of the respiratory system — Maladies de l'appareil respiratoire								
Total	1 340	52.0	786	29.2	15 944	54.1	14 340	46.0
Influenza — Grippe	3	♦0.1	11	♦0.4	50	0.2	102	0.3
Pneumonia — Pneumopathies	314	12.2	304	11.3	4 402	14.9	5 097	16.3
Chronic lower respiratory diseases — Maladies chroniques des voies respiratoires inférieures	858	33.3	362	13.5	5 361	18.2	3 225	10.3
Diseases of the digestive system — Maladies de l'appareil digestif								
Total	1 385	53.7	1 024	38.1	12 270	41.6	10 633	34.1
Gastric and duodenal ulcer — Ulcère de l'estomac et du duodénum	103	4.0	111	4.1	405	1.4	420	1.3
Diseases of the liver — Maladies du foie	794	30.8	311	11.6	6 040	20.5	2 690	8.6
Diseases of the musculoskeletal system and connective tissue — Maladies du système ostéo-articularie, des muscles et du tissu conjonctif	84	3.3	203	7.6	1 226	4.2	2 255	7.2
Diseases of the genitourinary system — Maladies de l'appareil génito-urinaire								
Total	165	6.4	305	11.3	3 868	13.1	3 961	12.7
Disorders of kidney and ureter — Affections du rein et de l'uretère	123	4.8	240	8.9	3 032	10.3	3 119	10.0
Hyperplasia of prostate — Hyperplasie de la prostate	26	♦2.9	..	..	160	1.7	..	..
Pregnancy, childbirth and the puerperium — Grossesse, accouchement et puerpéralité								
Total	..	..	4	♦6.8	..	..	53	6.9
Pregnancy with abortive outcome — Grossesse se terminant par un avortement	..	..	-	-	..	..	4	♦0.5
Other direct obstetric causes — Autres décès maternels directs	..	..	3	♦5.1	..	..	44	5.7
Indirect obstetric causes — Décès maternels indirects	..	..	1	♦1.7	..	..	4	♦0.5
Certain conditions originating in the perinatal period — Certaines affections dont l'origine se situe dans la période périnatale	43	143.3	30	♦104.0	813	206.6	609	162.7
Congenital malformations, deformations and chromosomal abnormalities — Malformations congénitales et anomalies chromosomiques	86	286.6	97	336.4	801	203.6	717	191.5
Symptoms, signs and abnormal clinical and laboratory findings, not elsewhere classified — Symptômes, signes et résultats anormaux d'examens cliniques et de laboratoire, non classés ailleurs	186	7.2	101	3.8	14 613	49.6	18 028	57.8
All other diseases — Toutes autres maladies	21	♦0.8	14	♦0.5	554	1.9	1 342	4.3
External causes — Causes externes								
Total	3 013	116.9	1 324	49.3	22 483	76.3	14 948	47.9
Accidents								
Total	2 022	78.4	994	37.0	13 182	44.7	10 912	35.0
Transport accidents — Accidents de transport	341	13.2	102	3.8	4 035	13.7	1 354	4.3
Falls — Chutes	642	24.9	536	19.9	2 582	8.8	2 772	8.9
Accidental drowning and submersion — Noyade et submersion accidentelles	105	4.1	30	♦1.1	705	2.4	276	0.9
Exposure to smoke, fire and flames — Exposition à la fumée, au feu et aux flammes	83	3.2	26	♦1.0	273	0.9	194	0.6
Accidental poisoning by and exposure to noxious substances — Intoxication accidentelle par des substances nocives et exposition à ces substances	644	25.0	217	8.1	454	1.5	457	1.5
Intentional self-harm — Lésions auto-infligées	802	31.1	259	9.6	7 853	26.7	2 945	9.4
Assault — Agresssions	75	2.9	30	♦1.1	271	0.9	194	0.6
All other external causes — Toutes autres causes externes	114	4.4	41	1.5	1 177	4.0	897	2.9

Cause of death — Cause de décès	France 2005 (C)				Germany - Allemagne 2005 (C)			
	Male — Masculin		Female — Féminin		Male — Masculin		Female — Féminin	
	Number Nombre	Rate Taux	Number Nombre	Rate Taux	Number Nombre	Rate Taux	Number Nombre	Rate Taux
TOTAL...............	270 630	913.1	256 886	819.2	388 554	963.0	441 673	1 048.7
Certain infectious and parasitic diseases — Certaines maladies infectieuses et parasitaires								
Total......	4 999	16.9	4 904	15.6	5 754	14.3	6 307	15.0
Intestinal infectious diseases — Maladies infectieuses intestinales............	343	1.2	532	1.7	386	1.0	755	1.8
Tuberculosis — Tuberculose........	228	0.8	188	0.6	189	0.5	136	0.3
Tetanus — Tétanos..........	1	♦0.0	6	♦0.0	-	-	3	♦0.0
Diphtheria — Diphtérie.......	-	-	-	-	-	-	1	♦0.0
Whooping cough — Coqueluche..........	5	♦0.0	5	♦0.0	-	-	-	-
Meningococcal infection — Infection à méningocoques.................	12	♦0.0	19	♦0.1	38	0.1	16	♦0.0
Septicaemia — Septicémie.......	1 948	6.6	2 009	6.4	3 195	7.9	3 441	8.2
Acute poliomyelitis — Poliomyélite aiguë..........	-	-	-	-	-	-	-	-
Measles — Rougeole............	-	-	-	-	1	♦0.0	-	-
Viral hepatitis — Hépatite virale.............	418	1.4	343	1.1	544	1.3	520	1.2
Human immunodeficiency virus [HIV] disease — Maladies dues au virus de l'immunodéficience humaine (VIH).................	628	2.1	199	0.6	398	1.0	93	0.2
Malaria — Paludisme..........	12	♦0.0	2	♦0.0	4	♦0.0	2	♦0.0
Neoplasms — Tumeurs.............	92 106	310.8	63 303	201.9	114 542	283.9	102 386	243.1
Malignant neoplasms — Tumeurs malignes								
Total........	88 778	299.5	60 105	191.7	112 066	277.7	99 330	235.9
Malignant neoplasm of lip, oral cavity and pharynx — Tumeur maligne de la lèvre, de la cavité buccale et du pharynx..........	3 358	11.3	746	2.4	3 703	9.2	1 116	2.6
Malignant neoplasm of oesophagus — Tumeur maligne de l'oesophage......	3 258	11.0	668	2.1	3 661	9.1	1 129	2.7
Malignant neoplasm of stomach — Tumeur maligne de l'estomac......	3 045	10.3	1 789	5.7	6 211	15.4	5 089	12.1
Malignant neoplasm of colon, rectosigmoid junction, rectum, anus and anal canal — Tumeur maligne du côlon, de la jonction recto-sigmoïdienne, du rectum, de l'anus et du canal anal..........	8 748	29.5	7 851	25.0	13 696	33.9	13 843	32.9
Malignant neoplasm of liver and intrahepatic bile ducts — Tumeur maligne du foie et des voies bilaires intrahépatiques.........	5 457	18.4	1 882	6.0	3 917	9.7	2 225	5.3
Malignant neoplasm of pancreas — Tumeur maligne du pancréas......	4 192	14.1	3 857	12.3	6 544	16.2	7 031	16.7
Malignant neoplasm of trachea, bronchus and lung — Tumeur maligne de la trachée, des bronches et du poumon........	21 901	73.9	5 949	19.0	28 980	71.8	11 701	27.8
Malignant neoplasm of female breast — Tumeur maligne du sein chez la femme........	..	..	11 308	43.7	..	..	17 455	...
Malignant neoplasm of cervix uteri — Tumeur maligne du col de l'utérus......	..	..	734	2.8	..	..	1 626	...
Malignant neoplasm of prostate — Tumeur maligne de la prostate............	9 099	96.2	..	..	11 203	..	..	..
Malignant neoplasm of lymphoid, haematopoietic and related tissue — Tumeurs malignes primitives ou présumées primitives des tissus lymphoïde, hématopoïétique et apparentés.........	6 691	22.6	5 920	18.9	8 526	21.1	8 143	19.3
Disorders of the blood and blood-forming organs and certain disorders involving the immune mechanism — Maladies du sang et des organes hématopoïétiques et certains troubles du système immunitaire								
Total..........	942	3.2	1 205	3.8	823	2.0	1 300	3.1
Anaemias — Anémies.................	475	1.6	714	2.3	311	0.8	689	1.6
Endocrine, nutritional and metabolic diseases — Maladies endocriniennes, nutritionnelles et métaboliques								
Total........	8 319	28.1	10 966	35.0	11 010	27.3	17 261	41.0
Diabetes mellitus — Diabète sucré............	5 391	18.2	5 905	18.8	9 419	23.3	14 923	35.4
Malnutrition — Malnutrition..........	835	2.8	1 664	5.3	55	0.1	147	0.3
Mental and behavioural disorders — Troubles mentaux et du comportement	7 194	24.3	9 863	31.5	6 179	15.3	5 177	12.3
Diseases of the nervous system — Maladies du système nerveux..........	10 963	37.0	15 388	49.1	8 591	21.3	9 964	23.7
Diseases of the circulatory system — Maladies de l'appareil circulatoire								
Total........	70 037	236.3	79 799	254.5	152 274	377.4	215 087	510.7
Acute rheumatic fever and chronic rheumatic heart diseases — Rhumatisme articulaire aigu et cardiopathies rhumatismales chroniques........	559	1.9	1 039	3.3	678	1.7	1 656	3.9
Hypertensive diseases — Maladies hypertensives........	2 840	9.6	5 359	17.1	8 249	20.4	19 284	45.8
Ischaemic heart disease — Cardiopathie ischémique............	22 985	77.6	17 612	56.2	72 003	178.5	76 638	182.0
Cerebrovascular disease — Maladie cérébrovasculaire..................	14 328	48.3	19 578	62.4	24 786	61.4	42 331	100.5

Cause of death — Cause de décès	France 2005 (C)				Germany Allemagne 2005 (C)			
	Male — Masculin		Female — Féminin		Male — Masculin		Female — Féminin	
	Number Nombre	Rate Taux	Number Nombre	Rate Taux	Number Nombre	Rate Taux	Number Nombre	Rate Taux
Diseases of arteries, arterioles and capillaries — Maladies des artères, artérioles et capillaires	5 550	18.7	4 063	13.0	9 085	22.5	13 092	31.1
Diseases of the respiratory system — Maladies de l'appareil respiratoire								
Total..................	18 040	60.9	17 016	54.3	29 332	72.7	28 410	67.5
Influenza — Grippe	360	1.2	630	2.0	103	0.3	198	0.5
Pneumonia — Pneumopathies..........	5 136	17.3	6 035	19.2	9 476	23.5	12 223	29.0
Chronic lower respiratory diseases — Maladies chroniques des voies respiratoires inférieures	5 917	20.0	3 604	11.5	14 769	36.6	10 974	26.1
Diseases of the digestive system — Maladies de l'appareil digestif								
Total..................	12 457	42.0	10 720	34.2	21 369	53.0	21 418	50.9
Gastric and duodenal ulcer — Ulcère de l'estomac et du duodénum	448	1.5	411	1.3	1 370	3.4	1 923	4.6
Diseases of the liver — Maladies du foie	5 926	20.0	2 685	8.6	11 206	27.8	5 600	13.3
Diseases of the musculoskeletal system and connective tissue — Maladies du système ostéo-articularie, des muscles et du tissu conjonctif	1 231	4.2	2 343	7.5	686	1.7	1 338	3.2
Diseases of the genitourinary system — Maladies de l'appareil génito-urinaire								
Total..................	4 082	13.8	4 298	13.7	5 953	14.8	8 335	19.8
Disorders of kidney and ureter — Affections du rein et de l'uretère	3 154	10.6	3 335	10.6	4 719	11.7	6 401	15.2
Hyperplasia of prostate — Hyperplasie de la prostate..........	173	1.8	..	..	101	....		
Pregnancy, childbirth and the puerperium — Grossesse, accouchement et puerpéralité								
Total..................	..	..	41	5.3	..	..	28	+4.1
Pregnancy with abortive outcome — Grossesse se terminant par un avortement	..	..	3	+0.4	..	..	1	+0.1
Other direct obstetric causes — Autres décès maternels directs	..	..	34	4.4	..	..	19	+2.8
Indirect obstetric causes — Décès maternels indirects..........	..	..	4	+0.5	...	..	6	+0.9
Certain conditions originating in the perinatal period — Certaines affections dont l'origine se situe dans la période périnatale	774	195.3	587	155.3	766	217.8	575	172.1
Congenital malformations, deformations and chromosomal abnormalities — Malformations congénitales et anomalies chromosomiques	795	200.6	685	181.2	812	230.8	716	214.3
Symptoms, signs and abnormal clinical and laboratory findings, not elsewhere classified — Symptômes, signes et résultats anormaux d'examens cliniques et de laboratoire, non classés ailleurs	15 480	52.2	19 400	61.9	9 920	24.6	10 273	24.4
All other diseases — Toutes autres maladies..........	529	1.8	1 242	4.0	190	0.5	427	1.0
External causes — Causes externes								
Total..................	22 682	76.5	15 126	48.2	20 353	50.4	12 671	30.1
Accidents								
Total..................	13 454	45.4	11 210	35.7	10 712	26.5	8 409	20.0
Transport accidents — Accidents de transport	4 016	13.5	1 361	4.3	4 111	10.2	1 524	3.6
Falls — Chutes	2 579	8.7	2 754	8.8	3 788	9.4	4 760	11.3
Accidental drowning and submersion — Noyade et submersion accidentelles..........	662	2.2	271	0.9	280	0.7	120	0.3
Exposure to smoke, fire and flames — Exposition à la fumée, au feu et aux flammes	333	1.1	195	0.6	279	0.7	205	0.5
Accidental poisoning by and exposure to noxious substances — Intoxication accidentelle par des substances nocives et exposition à ces substances	559	1.9	457	1.5	526	1.3	187	0.4
Intentional self-harm — Lésions auto-infligées..........	7 826	26.4	2 881	9.2	7 523	18.6	2 737	6.5
Assault — Agresssions	277	0.9	158	0.5	247	0.6	206	0.5
All other external causes — Toutes autres causes externes..........	1 125	3.8	877	2.8	1 871	4.6	1 319	3.1

Cause of death — Cause de décès	Germany - Allemagne 2006 (C)				Greece - Grèce 2005 (C)			
	Male — Masculin		Female — Féminin		Male — Masculin		Female — Féminin	
	Number Nombre	Rate Taux	Number Nombre	Rate Taux	Number Nombre	Rate Taux	Number Nombre	Rate Taux
TOTAL	385 940	957.2	435 687	1 036.2	55 435	1 008.4	49 656	885.7
Certain infectious and parasitic diseases — Certaines maladies infectieuses et parasitaires								
Total	5 661	14.0	6 693	15.9	363	6.6	415	7.4
Intestinal infectious diseases — Maladies infectieuses intestinales	477	1.2	908	2.2	-	-	-	-
Tuberculosis — Tuberculose	216	0.5	120	0.3	52	0.9	38	0.7
Tetanus — Tétanos	1	◆0.0	4	◆0.0	2	◆0.0	2	◆0.0
Diphtheria — Diphtérie	2	◆0.0	-	-	-	-	-	-
Whooping cough — Coqueluche	-	-	-	-	-	-	-	-
Meningococcal infection — Infection à méningocoques	30	◆0.1	26	◆0.1	1	◆0.0	-	-
Septicaemia — Septicémie	3 026	7.5	3 707	8.8	201	3.7	299	5.3
Acute poliomyelitis — Poliomyélite aiguë	-	-	-	-	-	-	-	-
Measles — Rougeole	1	◆0.0	-	-	-	-	-	-
Viral hepatitis — Hépatite virale	542	1.3	516	1.2	58	1.1	40	0.7
Human immunodeficiency virus [HIV] disease — Maladies dues au virus de l'immunodéficience humaine (VIH)	420	1.0	84	0.2	26	◆0.5	2	◆0.0
Malaria — Paludisme	2	◆0.0	3	◆0.0	-	-	-	-
Neoplasms — Tumeurs	115 176	285.7	101 919	242.4	15 998	291.0	9 898	176.5
Malignant neoplasms — Tumeurs malignes								
Total	112 761	279.7	98 762	234.9	15 990	290.9	9 894	176.5
Malignant neoplasm of lip, oral cavity and pharynx — Tumeur maligne de la lèvre, de la cavité buccale et du pharynx	3 623	9.0	1 111	2.6	210	3.8	86	1.5
Malignant neoplasm of oesophagus — Tumeur maligne de l'oesophage	3 642	9.0	1 074	2.6	157	2.9	33	0.6
Malignant neoplasm of stomach — Tumeur maligne de l'estomac	5 986	14.8	4 937	11.7	782	14.2	500	8.9
Malignant neoplasm of colon, rectosigmoid junction, rectum, anus and anal canal — Tumeur maligne du côlon, de la jonction recto-sigmoïdienne, du rectum, de l'anus et du canal anal	13 756	34.1	13 469	32.0	1 135	20.6	994	17.7
Malignant neoplasm of liver and intrahepatic bile ducts — Tumeur maligne du foie et des voies bilaires intrahépatiques	4 329	10.7	2 351	5.6	175	3.2	52	0.9
Malignant neoplasm of pancreas — Tumeur maligne du pancréas	6 729	16.7	7 213	17.2	742	13.5	558	10.0
Malignant neoplasm of trachea, bronchus and lung — Tumeur maligne de la trachée, des bronches et du poumon	28 898	71.7	11 873	28.2	5 063	92.1	925	16.5
Malignant neoplasm of female breast — Tumeur maligne du sein chez la femme	..	..	17 286	47.5	..	..	1 794	37.1
Malignant neoplasm of cervix uteri — Tumeur maligne du col de l'utérus	..	..	1 492	4.1	..	..	90	1.9
Malignant neoplasm of prostate — Tumeur maligne de la prostate	11 577	81.6	..	..	1 543	83.2	..	..
Malignant neoplasm of lymphoid, haematopoietic and related tissue — Tumeurs malignes primitives ou présumées primitives des tissus lymphoïde, hématopoïétique et apparentés	8 496	21.1	8 084	19.2	1 147	20.9	830	14.8
Disorders of the blood and blood-forming organs and certain disorders involving the immune mechanism — Maladies du sang et des organes hématopoïétiques et certains troubles du système immunitaire								
Total	828	2.1	1 216	2.9	119	2.2	114	2.0
Anaemias — Anémies	333	0.8	657	1.6	39	0.7	38	0.7
Endocrine, nutritional and metabolic diseases — Maladies endocriniennes, nutritionnelles et métaboliques								
Total	10 568	26.2	16 056	38.2	687	12.5	688	12.3
Diabetes mellitus — Diabète sucré	8 816	21.9	13 492	32.1	519	9.4	544	9.7
Malnutrition — Malnutrition	55	0.1	145	0.3	-	-	-	-
Mental and behavioural disorders — Troubles mentaux et du comportement	6 680	16.0	7 397	17.6	55	1.0	84	1.5
Diseases of the nervous system — Maladies du système nerveux	9 003	22.3	10 391	24.7	557	10.1	603	10.8
Diseases of the circulatory system — Maladies de l'appareil circulatoire								
Total	149 578	371.0	209 375	497.9	23 823	433.4	25 915	462.2
Acute rheumatic fever and chronic rheumatic heart diseases — Rhumatisme articulaire aigu et cardiopathies rhumatismales chroniques	726	1.8	1 656	3.9	1	◆0.0	-	-
Hypertensive diseases — Maladies hypertensives	8 388	20.8	20 111	47.8	552	10.0	688	12.3
Ischaemic heart disease — Cardiopathie ischémique	70 378	174.6	73 811	175.5	7 997	145.5	4 732	84.4
Cerebrovascular disease — Maladie cérébrovasculaire	24 403	60.5	40 730	96.9	7 256	132.0	9 967	177.8

21. Death and death rates by cause and sex: 2002 - 2006
Décès et taux de mortalité par cause et sexe : 2002 - 2006 (continued - suite)

	Germany - Allemagne				Greece - Grèce			
	2006 (C)				2005 (C)			
Cause of death — Cause de décès	Male — Masculin		Female — Féminin		Male — Masculin		Female — Féminin	
	Number Nombre	Rate Taux	Number Nombre	Rate Taux	Number Nombre	Rate Taux	Number Nombre	Rate Taux
Diseases of arteries, arterioles and capillaries — Maladies des artères, artérioles et capillaires	8 818	21.9	11 581	27.5	631	11.5	251	4.5
Diseases of the respiratory system — Maladies de l'appareil respiratoire								
Total......	28 326	70.3	26 562	63.2	4 350	79.1	3 859	68.8
Influenza — Grippe	24	♦0.1	42	0.1	1	♦0.0	-	-
Pneumonia — Pneumopathies......	9 141	22.7	11 227	26.7	408	7.4	288	5.1
Chronic lower respiratory diseases — Maladies chroniques des voies respiratoires inférieures	14 392	35.7	10 563	25.1	760	13.8	412	7.3
Diseases of the digestive system — Maladies de l'appareil digestif								
Total......	21 153	52.5	21 820	51.9	1 414	25.7	1 038	18.5
Gastric and duodenal ulcer — Ulcère de l'estomac et du duodénum	1 413	3.5	1 894	4.5	184	3.3	140	2.5
Diseases of the liver — Maladies du foie	10 777	26.7	5 524	13.1	543	9.9	202	3.6
Diseases of the musculoskeletal system and connective tissue — Maladies du système ostéo-articularie, des muscles et du tissu conjonctif	818	2.0	1 464	3.5	146	2.7	208	3.7
Diseases of the genitourinary system — Maladies de l'appareil génito-urinaire								
Total......	6 217	15.4	8 870	21.1	676	12.3	751	13.4
Disorders of kidney and ureter — Affections du rein et de l'uretère	4 977	12.3	6 731	16.0	635	11.6	717	12.8
Hyperplasia of prostate — Hyperplasie de la prostate......	93	0.7	..	..	-	-	-	-
Pregnancy, childbirth and the puerperium — Grossesse, accouchement et puerpéralité								
Total......	..	..	41	6.1	..	..	-	-
Pregnancy with abortive outcome — Grossesse se terminant par un avortement	..	..	3	♦0.4	..	..	-	-
Other direct obstetric causes — Autres décès maternels directs	..	..	32	4.8	..	..	-	-
Indirect obstetric causes — Décès maternels indirects......	..	..	2	♦0.3	..	..	-	-
Certain conditions originating in the perinatal period — Certaines affections dont l'origine se situe dans la période périnatale	777	224.7	613	187.5	111	199.9	86	165.4
Congenital malformations, deformations and chromosomal abnormalities — Malformations congénitales et anomalies chromosomiques	732	211.7	741	226.7	94	169.3	103	198.1
Symptoms, signs and abnormal clinical and laboratory findings, not elsewhere classified — Symptômes, signes et résultats anormaux d'examens cliniques et de laboratoire, non classés ailleurs	10 164	25.2	9 814	23.3	3 785	68.9	4 866	86.8
All other diseases — Toutes autres maladies......	218	0.5	476	1.1	9	♦0.2	32	0.6
External causes — Causes externes								
Total......	20 041	49.7	12 239	29.1	3 248	59.1	996	17.8
Accidents								
Total......	10 596	26.3	8 068	19.2	2 848	51.8	877	15.6
Transport accidents — Accidents de transport	3 946	9.8	1 413	3.4	1 514	27.5	457	8.2
Falls — Chutes	3 803	9.4	4 578	10.9	352	6.4	171	3.1
Accidental drowning and submersion — Noyade et submersion accidentelles......	298	0.7	120	0.3	251	4.6	82	1.5
Exposure to smoke, fire and flames — Exposition à la fumée, au feu et aux flammes......	242	0.6	164	0.4	52	0.9	48	0.9
Accidental poisoning by and exposure to noxious substances — Intoxication accidentelle par des substances nocives et exposition à ces substances	570	1.4	188	0.4	416	7.6	58	1.0
Intentional self-harm — Lésions auto-infligées......	7 225	17.9	2 540	6.0	321	5.8	79	1.4
Assault — Agresssions	255	0.6	229	0.5	79	1.4	40	0.7
All other external causes — Toutes autres causes externes......	1 965	4.9	1 402	3.3	-	-	-	-

21. Death and death rates by cause and sex: 2002 - 2006
Décès et taux de mortalité par cause et sexe : 2002 - 2006 (continued - suite)

Cause of death — Cause de décès	Greece - Grèce 2006 (C)				Hungary - Hongrie 2004 (C)			
	Male — Masculin		Female — Féminin		Male — Masculin		Female — Féminin	
	Number Nombre	Rate Taux	Number Nombre	Rate Taux	Number Nombre	Rate Taux	Number Nombre	Rate Taux
TOTAL.........	54 951	995.5	50 017	888.7	68 381	1 425.0	64 111	1 207.7
Certain infectious and parasitic diseases — Certaines maladies infectieuses et parasitaires								
Total........	387	7.0	409	7.3	317	6.6	173	3.3
Intestinal infectious diseases — Maladies infectieuses intestinales...........	-	-	1	♦0.0	5	♦0.1	5	♦0.1
Tuberculosis — Tuberculose.............	58	1.1	23	♦0.4	194	4.0	68	1.3
Tetanus — Tétanos.................	-	-	2	♦0.0	-	-	1	♦0.0
Diphtheria — Diphtérie.............	-	-	-	-	-	-	-	-
Whooping cough — Coqueluche.............	-	-	-	-	-	-	-	-
Meningococcal infection — Infection à méningocoques..................	2	♦0.0	-	-	2	♦0.0	3	♦0.1
Septicaemia — Septicémie.................	233	4.2	327	5.8	31	0.6	46	0.9
Acute poliomyelitis — Poliomyélite aiguë.............	-	-	-	-	-	-	-	-
Measles — Rougeole.............	-	-	-	-	-	-	-	-
Viral hepatitis — Hépatite virale..............	55	1.0	38	0.7	1	♦0.0	1	♦0.0
Human immunodeficiency virus [HIV] disease — Maladies dues au virus de l'immunodéficience humaine (VIH).............	19	♦0.3	3	♦0.1	9	♦0.2	3	♦0.1
Malaria — Paludisme.............	-	-	-	-	-	-	1	♦0.0
Neoplasms — Tumeurs.........	15 723	284.8	9 948	176.7	19 100	398.0	14 956	281.7
Malignant neoplasms — Tumeurs malignes								
Total........	15 717	284.7	9 943	176.7	18 842	392.7	14 660	276.2
Malignant neoplasm of lip, oral cavity and pharynx — Tumeur maligne de la lèvre, de la cavité buccale et du pharynx	195	3.5	94	1.7	1 416	29.5	274	5.2
Malignant neoplasm of oesophagus — Tumeur maligne de l'oesophage	149	2.7	32	0.6	545	11.4	123	2.3
Malignant neoplasm of stomach — Tumeur maligne de l'estomac.............	825	14.9	496	8.8	1 081	22.5	857	16.1
Malignant neoplasm of colon, rectosigmoid junction, rectum, anus and anal canal — Tumeur maligne du côlon, de la jonction recto-sigmoïdienne, du rectum, de l'anus et du canal anal	1 136	20.6	964	17.1	2 718	56.6	2 261	42.6
Malignant neoplasm of liver and intrahepatic bile ducts — Tumeur maligne du foie et des voies bilaires intrahépatiques	134	2.4	46	0.8	614	12.8	356	6.7
Malignant neoplasm of pancreas — Tumeur maligne du pancréas	718	13.0	613	10.9	855	17.8	828	15.6
Malignant neoplasm of trachea, bronchus and lung — Tumeur maligne de la trachée, des bronches et du poumon	5 100	92.4	938	16.7	5 852	122.0	2 408	45.4
Malignant neoplasm of female breast — Tumeur maligne du sein chez la femme.........	..	..	1 870	38.5	..	..	2 285	50.4
Malignant neoplasm of cervix uteri — Tumeur maligne du col de l'utérus	..	..	95	2.0	..	..	493	10.9
Malignant neoplasm of prostate — Tumeur maligne de la prostate	1 537	81.5	..	..	1 275	86.3	..	..
Malignant neoplasm of lymphoid, haematopoietic and related tissue — Tumeurs malignes primitives ou présumées primitives des tissus lymphoïde, hématopoïétique et apparentés	1 090	19.7	879	15.6	1 053	21.9	957	18.0
Disorders of the blood and blood-forming organs and certain disorders involving the immune mechanism — Maladies du sang et des organes hématopoïétiques et certains troubles du système immunitaire								
Total........	79	1.4	83	1.5	51	1.1	82	1.5
Anaemias — Anémies.............	31	0.6	26	♦0.5	25	♦0.5	46	0.9
Endocrine, nutritional and metabolic diseases — Maladies endocriniennes, nutritionnelles et métaboliques								
Total........	714	12.9	792	14.1	1 034	21.5	1 465	27.6
Diabetes mellitus — Diabète sucré.............	618	11.2	699	12.4	975	20.3	1 387	26.1
Malnutrition — Malnutrition.............	-	-	-	-	3	♦0.1	2	♦0.0
Mental and behavioural disorders — Troubles mentaux et du comportement	47	0.9	51	0.9	540	11.4	299	5.6
Diseases of the nervous system — Maladies du système nerveux...........	568	10.3	659	11.7	875	18.2	878	16.5
Diseases of the circulatory system — Maladies de l'appareil circulatoire								
Total........	23 930	433.5	26 348	468.1	30 846	642.8	36 319	684.2
Acute rheumatic fever and chronic rheumatic heart diseases — Rhumatisme articularie aigu et cardiopathies rhumatismales chroniques	-	-	2	♦0.0	162	3.4	262	4.9
Hypertensive diseases — Maladies hypertensives.................	588	10.7	727	12.9	1 644	34.3	2 763	52.0
Ischaemic heart disease — Cardiopathie ischémique................	7 876	142.7	4 813	85.5	15 362	320.1	16 662	313.9
Cerebrovascular disease — Maladie cérébrovasculaire................	7 235	131.1	9 830	174.7	7 771	161.9	9 696	182.6

Cause of death — Cause de décès	Greece - Grèce				Hungary - Hongrie			
	2006 (C)				2004 (C)			
	Male — Masculin		Female — Féminin		Male — Masculin		Female — Féminin	
	Number Nombre	Rate Taux	Number Nombre	Rate Taux	Number Nombre	Rate Taux	Number Nombre	Rate Taux
Diseases of arteries, arterioles and capillaries — Maladies des artères, artérioles et capillaires	665	12.0	235	4.2	2 952	61.5	3 992	75.2
Diseases of the respiratory system — Maladies de l'appareil respiratoire								
Total........	4 582	83.0	4 273	75.9	2 975	62.0	2 240	42.2
Influenza — Grippe	-	-	-	-	4	♦0.1	7	♦0.1
Pneumonia — Pneumopathies........	398	7.2	404	7.2	453	9.4	423	8.0
Chronic lower respiratory diseases — Maladies chroniques des voies respiratoires inférieures	1 181	21.4	698	12.4	2 247	46.8	1 595	30.0
Diseases of the digestive system — Maladies de l'appareil digestif								
Total........	1 419	25.7	1 123	20.0	5 736	119.5	3 408	64.2
Gastric and duodenal ulcer — Ulcère de l'estomac et du duodénum	172	3.1	143	2.5	411	8.6	398	7.5
Diseases of the liver — Maladies du foie	594	10.8	227	4.0	4 302	89.7	1 769	33.3
Diseases of the musculoskeletal system and connective tissue — Maladies du système ostéo-articularie, des muscles et du tissu conjonctif	173	3.1	219	3.9	89	1.9	203	3.8
Diseases of the genitourinary system — Maladies de l'appareil génito-urinaire								
Total........	830	15.0	920	16.3	445	9.3	518	9.8
Disorders of kidney and ureter — Affections du rein et de l'uretère	788	14.3	862	15.3	355	7.4	480	9.0
Hyperplasia of prostate — Hyperplasie de la prostate........	-	..	..	..	63	4.3	..	..
Pregnancy, childbirth and the puerperium — Grossesse, accouchement et puerpéralité								
Total........	..	..	3	♦2.7	..	..	4	♦4.2
Pregnancy with abortive outcome — Grossesse se terminant par un avortement	..	..	1	♦0.9	..	..	-	-
Other direct obstetric causes — Autres décès maternels directs	..	..	1	♦0.9	..	..	4	♦4.2
Indirect obstetric causes — Décès maternels indirects........	..	..	1	♦0.9	..	..	-	-
Certain conditions originating in the perinatal period — Certaines affections dont l'origine se situe dans la période périnatale	104	180.1	90	165.7	230	471.5	166	358.1
Congenital malformations, deformations and chromosomal abnormalities — Malformations congénitales et anomalies chromosomiques	102	176.7	106	195.2	146	299.3	140	302.0
Symptoms, signs and abnormal clinical and laboratory findings, not elsewhere classified — Symptômes, signes et résultats anormaux d'examens cliniques et de laboratoire, non classés ailleurs	3 225	58.4	4 160	73.9	67	1.4	56	1.1
All other diseases — Toutes autres maladies........	5	♦0.1	15	♦0.3	14	♦0.3	14	♦0.3
External causes — Causes externes								
Total........	3 063	55.5	818	14.5	5 907	123.1	3 190	60.1
Accidents								
Total........	2 661	48.2	731	13.0	3 567	74.3	2 390	45.0
Transport accidents — Accidents de transport	1 461	26.5	341	6.1	1 249	26.0	386	7.3
Falls — Chutes	333	6.0	156	2.8	1 380	28.8	1 643	31.0
Accidental drowning and submersion — Noyade et submersion accidentelles........	192	3.5	69	1.2	147	3.1	33	0.6
Exposure to smoke, fire and flames — Exposition à la fumée, au feu et aux flammes	42	0.8	30	♦0.5	115	2.4	63	1.2
Accidental poisoning by and exposure to noxious substances — Intoxication accidentelle par des substances nocives et exposition à ces substances	378	6.8	70	1.2	114	2.4	38	0.7
Intentional self-harm — Lésions auto-infligées........	326	5.9	68	1.2	2 087	43.5	655	12.3
Assault — Agresssions	76	1.4	19	♦0.3	130	2.7	89	1.7
All other external causes — Toutes autres causes externes........	-	-	-	-	123	2.6	56	1.1

Cause of death — Cause de décès	Hungary - Hongrie 2005 (C)				Iceland - Islande 2005 (C)			
	Male — Masculin		Female — Féminin		Male — Masculin		Female — Féminin	
	Number Nombre	Rate Taux	Number Nombre	Rate Taux	Number Nombre	Rate Taux	Number Nombre	Rate Taux
TOTAL.................	69 781	1 457.2	65 951	1 244.8	944	635.9	893	605.8
Certain infectious and parasitic diseases — Certaines maladies infectieuses et parasitaires								
Total........................	307	6.4	193	3.6	2	♦1.3	10	♦6.8
Intestinal infectious diseases — Maladies infectieuses intestinales............	11	♦0.2	10	♦0.2	-	-	1	♦0.7
Tuberculosis — Tuberculose................................	138	2.9	53	1.0	-	-	-	-
Tetanus — Tétanos...............................	-	-	1	♦0.0	-	-	-	-
Diphtheria — Diphtérie.............................	-	-	-	-	-	-	-	-
Whooping cough — Coqueluche.....................	-	-	-	-	-	-	-	-
Meningococcal infection — Infection à méningocoques.....................	5	♦0.1	2	♦0.0	-	-	-	-
Septicaemia — Septicémie................	54	1.1	51	1.0	-	-	4	♦2.7
Acute poliomyelitis — Poliomyélite aiguë.............	-	-	-	-	-	-	-	-
Measles — Rougeole............................	-	-	-	-	-	-	-	-
Viral hepatitis — Hépatite virale....................	1	♦0.0	1	♦0.0	-	-	-	-
Human immunodeficiency virus [HIV] disease — Maladies dues au virus de l'immunodéficience humaine (VIH)................	6	♦0.1	-	-	-	-	-	-
Malaria — Paludisme............................	-	-	-	-	-	-	-	-
Neoplasms — Tumeurs................	17 918	374.2	14 139	266.9	294	198.0	231	156.7
Malignant neoplasms — Tumeurs malignes								
Total.......................	17 134	357.8	13 481	254.4	287	193.3	224	152.0
Malignant neoplasm of lip, oral cavity and pharynx — Tumeur maligne de la lèvre, de la cavité buccale et du pharynx	1 298	27.1	269	5.1	1	♦0.7	1	♦0.7
Malignant neoplasm of oesophagus — Tumeur maligne de l'oesophage......	495	10.3	91	1.7	11	♦7.4	4	♦2.7
Malignant neoplasm of stomach — Tumeur maligne de l'estomac............	984	20.5	738	13.9	17	♦11.5	14	♦9.5
Malignant neoplasm of colon, rectosigmoid junction, rectum, anus and anal canal — Tumeur maligne du côlon, de la jonction recto-sigmoïdienne, du rectum, do l'anus et du canal anal	2 462	51.4	2 095	39.5	25	♦16.8	26	♦17.6
Malignant neoplasm of liver and intrahepatic bile ducts — Tumeur maligne du foie et des voies bilaires intrahépatiques....................	527	11.0	315	5.9	9	♦6.1	2	♦1.4
Malignant neoplasm of pancreas — Tumeur maligne du pancréas............	808	16.9	803	15.2	18	♦12.1	13	♦8.8
Malignant neoplasm of trachea, bronchus and lung — Tumeur maligne de la trachée, des bronches et du poumon............	5 336	111.4	2 235	42.2	73	49.2	56	38.0
Malignant neoplasm of female breast — Tumeur maligne du sein chez la femme........................	..	..	2 085	46.0	..	..	31	26.9
Malignant neoplasm of cervix uteri — Tumeur maligne du col de l'utérus......	..	..	416	9.2	..	..	2	♦1.7
Malignant neoplasm of prostate — Tumeur maligne de la prostate............	1 077	71.7	..	..	55	139.8	..	..
Malignant neoplasm of lymphoid, haematopoietic and related tissue — Tumeurs malignes primitives ou présumées primitives des tissus lymphoïde, hématopoïétique et apparentés	838	17.5	857	16.2	17	♦11.5	13	♦8.8
Disorders of the blood and blood-forming organs and certain disorders involving the immune mechanism — Maladies du sang et des organes hématopoïétiques et certains troubles du système immunitaire								
Total........................	104	2.2	107	2.0	3	♦2.0	2	♦1.4
Anaemias — Anémies......................	49	1.0	49	0.9	1	♦0.7	-	-
Endocrine, nutritional and metabolic diseases — Maladies endocriniennes, nutritionnelles et métaboliques								
Total........................	1 630	34.0	2 335	44.1	16	♦10.8	15	♦10.2
Diabetes mellitus — Diabète sucré......................	1 493	31.2	2 105	39.7	10	♦6.7	11	♦7.5
Malnutrition — Malnutrition..................	5	♦0.1	11	♦0.2	-	-	1	♦0.7
Mental and behavioural disorders — Troubles mentaux et du comportement	683	14.3	407	7.7	28	♦18.9	39	26.5
Diseases of the nervous system — Maladies du système nerveux...........	910	19.0	782	14.8	57	38.4	79	53.6
Diseases of the circulatory system — Maladies de l'appareil circulatoire								
Total........................	32 636	681.5	38 302	722.9	336	226.3	320	217.1
Acute rheumatic fever and chronic rheumatic heart diseases — Rhumatisme articularie aigu et cardiopathies rhumatismales chroniques	48	1.0	94	1.8	1	♦0.7	3	♦2.0
Hypertensive diseases — Maladies hypertensives...................	2 462	51.4	3 967	74.9	9	♦6.1	9	♦6.1
Ischaemic heart disease — Cardiopathie ischémique......................	17 559	366.7	19 334	364.9	193	130.0	143	97.0
Cerebrovascular disease — Maladie cérébrovasculaire......................	6 837	142.8	8 720	164.6	65	43.8	85	57.7

Cause of death — Cause de décès	Hungary - Hongrie				Iceland - Islande			
	2005 (C)				2005 (C)			
	Male — Masculin		Female — Féminin		Male — Masculin		Female — Féminin	
	Number Nombre	Rate Taux	Number Nombre	Rate Taux	Number Nombre	Rate Taux	Number Nombre	Rate Taux
Diseases of arteries, arterioles and capillaries — Maladies des artères, artérioles et capillaires	2 581	53.9	3 396	64.1	20	*13.5	15	*10.2
Diseases of the respiratory system — Maladies de l'appareil respiratoire								
Total	3 724	77.8	2 778	52.4	85	57.3	96	65.1
Influenza — Grippe	9	*0.2	15	*0.3	11	*7.4	18	*12.2
Pneumonia — Pneumopathies	455	9.5	412	7.8	26	*17.5	34	23.1
Chronic lower respiratory diseases — Maladies chroniques des voies respiratoires inférieures	2 945	61.5	2 121	40.0	41	27.6	41	27.8
Diseases of the digestive system — Maladies de l'appareil digestif								
Total	5 345	111.6	3 160	59.6	29	*19.5	29	*19.7
Gastric and duodenal ulcer — Ulcère de l'estomac et du duodénum	412	8.6	346	6.5	4	*2.7	3	*2.0
Diseases of the liver — Maladies du foie	3 912	81.7	1 613	30.4	7	*4.7	4	*2.7
Diseases of the musculoskeletal system and connective tissue — Maladies du système ostéo-articularie, des muscles et du tissu conjonctif	119	2.5	265	5.0	2	*1.3	6	*4.1
Diseases of the genitourinary system — Maladies de l'appareil génito-urinaire								
Total	456	9.5	505	9.5	12	*8.1	17	*11.5
Disorders of kidney and ureter — Affections du rein et de l'uretère	318	6.6	449	8.5	7	*4.7	9	*6.1
Hyperplasia of prostate — Hyperplasie de la prostate	91	6.1	..		-	-	..	
Pregnancy, childbirth and the puerperium — Grossesse, accouchement et puerpéralité								
Total	..	..	5	*5.1	..	..	-	-
Pregnancy with abortive outcome — Grossesse se terminant par un avortement	..	..	1	*1.0	..	..	-	-
Other direct obstetric causes — Autres décès maternels directs	..	..	4	*4.1	..	..	-	-
Indirect obstetric causes — Décès maternels indirects	..	..	-	-	..	..	-	-
Certain conditions originating in the perinatal period — Certaines affections dont l'origine se situe dans la période périnatale	202	401.4	134	284.1	2	*91.6	4	*190.7
Congenital malformations, deformations and chromosomal abnormalities — Malformations congénitales et anomalies chromosomiques	185	367.6	154	326.5	5	*229.0	1	*47.7
Symptoms, signs and abnormal clinical and laboratory findings, not elsewhere classified — Symptômes, signes et résultats anormaux d'examens cliniques et de laboratoire, non classés ailleurs	80	1.7	64	1.2	7	*4.7	5	*3.4
All other diseases — Toutes autres maladies	40	0.8	73	1.4	-	-	1	*0.7
External causes — Causes externes								
Total	5 442	113.6	2 548	48.1	66	44.5	38	25.8
Accidents								
Total	3 225	67.3	1 829	34.5	38	25.6	26	*17.6
Transport accidents — Accidents de transport	1 183	24.7	380	7.2	14	*9.4	6	*4.1
Falls — Chutes	1 035	21.6	1 067	20.1	7	*4.7	8	*5.4
Accidental drowning and submersion — Noyade et submersion accidentelles	157	3.3	35	0.7	-	-	-	-
Exposure to smoke, fire and flames — Exposition à la fumée, au feu et aux flammes	109	2.3	66	1.2	1	*0.7	-	-
Accidental poisoning by and exposure to noxious substances — Intoxication accidentelle par des substances nocives et exposition à ces substances	106	2.2	48	0.9	4	*2.7	8	*5.4
Intentional self-harm — Lésions auto-infligées	2 028	42.3	593	11.2	24	*16.2	9	*6.1
Assault — Agresssions	107	2.2	87	1.6	3	*2.0	-	-
All other external causes — Toutes autres causes externes	82	1.7	39	0.7	1	*0.7	3	*2.0

	Iceland - Islande				Ireland - Irlande			
Cause of death — Cause de décès	2006 (C)				2005 (C)			
	Male — Masculin		Female — Féminin		Male — Masculin		Female — Féminin	
	Number Nombre	Rate Taux	Number Nombre	Rate Taux	Number Nombre	Rate Taux	Number Nombre	Rate Taux
TOTAL...........	**959**	**621.6**	**944**	**629.1**	13 904	675.3	13 537	653.4
Certain infectious and parasitic diseases — Certaines maladies infectieuses et parasitaires								
Total............	10	♦6.5	9	♦6.0	93	4.5	67	3.2
Intestinal infectious diseases — Maladies infectieuses intestinales............	-	-	-	-	13	♦0.6	7	♦0.3
Tuberculosis — Tuberculose...........	-	-	1	♦0.7	7	♦0.3	8	♦0.4
Tetanus — Tétanos...........	-	-	-	-	-	-	-	-
Diphtheria — Diphtérie...........	-	-	-	-	-	-	-	-
Whooping cough — Coqueluche...........	-	-	-	-	-	-	-	-
Meningococcal infection — Infection à méningocoques...........	-	-	-	-	5	♦0.2	1	♦0.0
Septicaemia — Septicémie...........	4	♦2.6	5	♦3.3	26	♦1.3	16	♦0.8
Acute poliomyelitis — Poliomyélite aiguë...........	-	-	-	-	-	-	-	-
Measles — Rougeole...........	-	-	-	-	-	-	1	♦0.0
Viral hepatitis — Hépatite virale...........	-	-	-	-	9	♦0.4	2	♦0.1
Human immunodeficiency virus [HIV] disease — Maladies dues au virus de l'immunodéficience humaine (VIH)...........	3	♦1.9	-	-	-	-	-	-
Malaria — Paludisme...........	-	-	-	-	1	♦0.0	-	-
Neoplasms — Tumeurs...........	**277**	**179.5**	**227**	**151.3**	3 993	193.9	3 721	179.6
Malignant neoplasms — Tumeurs malignes								
Total............	271	175.6	222	148.0	3 950	191.8	3 664	176.9
Malignant neoplasm of lip, oral cavity and pharynx — Tumeur maligne de la lèvre, de la cavité buccale et du pharynx.......	5	♦3.2	3	♦2.0	93	4.5	42	2.0
Malignant neoplasm of oesophagus — Tumeur maligne de l'oesophage	9	♦5.8	2	♦1.3	187	9.1	119	5.7
Malignant neoplasm of stomach — Tumeur maligne de l'estomac...........	10	♦6.5	10	♦6.7	199	9.7	138	6.7
Malignant neoplasm of colon, rectosigmoid junction, rectum, anus and anal canal — Tumeur maligne du côlon, de la jonction recto-sigmoïdienne, du rectum, de l'anus et du canal anal...........	30	♦19.4	23	♦15.3	530	25.7	394	19.0
Malignant neoplasm of liver and intrahepatic bile ducts — Tumeur maligne du foie et des voies bilaires intrahépatiques	8	♦5.2	3	♦2.0	29	♦1.4	17	♦0.8
Malignant neoplasm of pancreas — Tumeur maligne du pancréas...........	17	♦11.0	16	♦10.7	181	8.8	164	7.9
Malignant neoplasm of trachea, bronchus and lung — Tumeur maligne de la trachée, des bronches et du poumon...........	59	38.2	62	41.3	926	45.0	637	30.7
Malignant neoplasm of female breast — Tumeur maligne du sein chez la femme............	..	..	35	29.7	..	..	678	40.9
Malignant neoplasm of cervix uteri — Tumeur maligne du col de l'utérus......	..	..	2	♦1.7	..	..	77	4.6
Malignant neoplasm of prostate — Tumeur maligne de la prostate...........	38	92.4	..	..	537	102.6	..	..
Malignant neoplasm of lymphoid, haematopoietic and related tissue — Tumeurs malignes primitives ou présumées primitives des tissus lymphoïde, hématopoïétique et apparentés	19	♦12.3	13	♦8.7	356	17.3	287	13.9
Disorders of the blood and blood-forming organs and certain disorders involving the immune mechanism — Maladies du sang et des organes hématopoïétiques et certains troubles du système immunitaire								
Total............	1	♦0.6	4	♦2.7	38	1.8	53	2.6
Anaemias — Anémies	-	-	3	♦2.0	23	♦1.1	39	1.9
Endocrine, nutritional and metabolic diseases — Maladies endocriniennes, nutritionnelles et métaboliques								
Total............	15	♦9.7	18	♦12.0	333	16.2	329	15.9
Diabetes mellitus — Diabète sucré...........	12	♦7.8	15	♦10.0	238	11.6	220	10.6
Malnutrition — Malnutrition...........	2	♦1.3	1	♦0.7	4	♦0.2	2	♦0.1
Mental and behavioural disorders — Troubles mentaux et du comportement	30	♦19.4	45	30.0	240	11.7	276	13.3
Diseases of the nervous system — Maladies du système nerveux...........	47	30.5	76	50.7	338	16.4	385	18.6
Diseases of the circulatory system — Maladies de l'appareil circulatoire								
Total............	361	234.0	355	236.6	5 092	247.3	4 892	236.1
Acute rheumatic fever and chronic rheumatic heart diseases — Rhumatisme articularie aigu et cardiopathies rhumatismales chroniques	1	♦0.6	1	♦0.7	17	♦0.8	29	♦1.4
Hypertensive diseases — Maladies hypertensives...........	7	♦4.5	22	♦14.7	135	6.6	189	9.1
Ischaemic heart disease — Cardiopathie ischémique...........	201	130.3	162	108.0	2 839	137.9	2 225	107.4
Cerebrovascular disease — Maladie cérébrovasculaire...........	77	49.9	82	54.6	885	43.0	1 144	55.2

	Iceland - Islande				Ireland - Irlande			
	2006 (C)				2005 (C)			
Cause of death — Cause de décès	Male — Masculin		Female — Féminin		Male — Masculin		Female — Féminin	
	Number Nombre	Rate Taux	Number Nombre	Rate Taux	Number Nombre	Rate Taux	Number Nombre	Rate Taux
Diseases of arteries, arterioles and capillaries — Maladies des artères, artérioles et capillaires	13	♦8.4	14	♦9.3	309	15.0	287	13.9
Diseases of the respiratory system — Maladies de l'appareil respiratoire								
Total	69	44.7	81	54.0	1 820	88.4	2 135	103.1
Influenza — Grippe	1	♦0.6	1	♦0.7	1	♦0.0	2	♦0.1
Pneumonia — Pneumopathies	27	♦17.5	27	♦18.0	785	38.1	1 128	54.4
Chronic lower respiratory diseases — Maladies chroniques des voies respiratoires inférieures	38	24.6	49	32.7	694	33.7	640	30.9
Diseases of the digestive system — Maladies de l'appareil digestif								
Total	21	♦13.6	31	20.7	466	22.6	524	25.3
Gastric and duodenal ulcer — Ulcère de l'estomac et du duodénum	1	♦0.6	3	♦2.0	55	2.7	60	2.9
Diseases of the liver — Maladies du foie	5	♦3.2	2	♦1.3	126	6.1	81	3.9
Diseases of the musculoskeletal system and connective tissue — Maladies du système ostéo-articularie, des muscles et du tissu conjonctif	1	♦0.6	11	♦7.3	55	2.7	139	6.7
Diseases of the genitourinary system — Maladies de l'appareil génito-urinaire								
Total	19	♦12.3	24	♦16.0	276	13.4	355	17.1
Disorders of kidney and ureter — Affections du rein et de l'uretère	10	♦6.5	16	♦10.7	192	9.3	207	10.0
Hyperplasia of prostate — Hyperplasie de la prostate	1	♦2.4	..	..	13	♦2.5	..	..
Pregnancy, childbirth and the puerperium — Grossesse, accouchement et puerpéralité								
Total	..	..	-	-	..	..	2	♦3.3
Pregnancy with abortive outcome — Grossesse se terminant par un avortement	..	..	-	-	..	..	-	-
Other direct obstetric causes — Autres décès maternels directs	..	..	-	-	..	..	2	♦3.3
Indirect obstetric causes — Décès maternels indirects	..	..	-	-	..	..	-	-
Certain conditions originating in the perinatal period — Certaines affections dont l'origine se situe dans la période périnatale	1	♦44.3	2	♦92.7	48	153.0	55	185.4
Congenital malformations, deformations and chromosomal abnormalities — Malformations congénitales et anomalies chromosomiques	4	♦177.1	2	♦92.7	83	264.6	88	296.6
Symptoms, signs and abnormal clinical and laboratory findings, not elsewhere classified — Symptômes, signes et résultats anormaux d'examens cliniques et de laboratoire, non classés ailleurs	10	♦6.5	6	♦4.0	64	3.1	84	4.1
All other diseases — Toutes autres maladies	1	♦0.6	-	-	31	1.5	63	3.0
External causes — Causes externes								
Total	92	59.6	53	35.3	934	45.4	369	17.8
Accidents								
Total	63	40.8	37	24.7	536	26.0	278	13.4
Transport accidents — Accidents de transport	27	♦17.5	12	♦8.0	204	9.9	81	3.9
Falls — Chutes	13	♦8.4	17	♦11.3	165	8.0	130	6.3
Accidental drowning and submersion — Noyade et submersion accidentelles	1	♦0.6	-	-	33	1.6	11	♦0.5
Exposure to smoke, fire and flames — Exposition à la fumée, au feu et aux flammes	-	-	1	♦0.7	25	♦1.2	14	♦0.7
Accidental poisoning by and exposure to noxious substances — Intoxication accidentelle par des substances nocives et exposition à ces substances	3	♦1.9	2	♦1.3	32	1.6	12	♦0.6
Intentional self-harm — Lésions auto-infligées	22	♦14.3	10	♦6.7	335	16.3	66	3.2
Assault — Agresssions	1	♦0.6	-	-	11	♦0.5	3	♦0.1
All other external causes — Toutes autres causes externes	6	♦3.9	6	♦4.0	52	2.5	22	♦1.1

Cause of death — Cause de décès	Ireland - Irlande 2006 (C)				Italy - Italie 2002 (C)			
	Male — Masculin		Female — Féminin		Male — Masculin		Female — Féminin	
	Number Nombre	Rate Taux	Number Nombre	Rate Taux	Number Nombre	Rate Taux	Number Nombre	Rate Taux
TOTAL..........	14 111	666.9	13 368	630.9	279 296	1 009.1	281 094	953.5
Certain infectious and parasitic diseases — Certaines maladies infectieuses et parasitaires								
Total.....	76	3.6	79	3.7	2 145	7.8	2 147	7.3
Intestinal infectious diseases — Maladies infectieuses intestinales............	2	♦0.1	3	♦0.1	24	♦0.1	35	0.1
Tuberculosis — Tuberculose.................	10	♦0.5	10	♦0.5	259	0.9	154	0.5
Tetanus — Tétanos.....	-	-	-	-	7	♦0.0	12	♦0.0
Diphtheria — Diphtérie..........	-	-	-	-	-	-	-	-
Whooping cough — Coqueluche..........	-	-	-	-	-	-	-	-
Meningococcal infection — Infection à méningocoques..................	3	♦0.1	1	♦0.0	9	♦0.0	15	♦0.1
Septicaemia — Septicémie	21	♦1.0	22	♦1.0	571	2.1	687	2.3
Acute poliomyelitis — Poliomyélite aiguë	-	-	-	-	-	-	-	-
Measles — Rougeole.....	-	-	-	-	1	♦0.0	5	♦0.0
Viral hepatitis — Hépatite virale..................	10	♦0.5	5	♦0.2	998	3.6	950	3.2
Human immunodeficiency virus [HIV] disease — Maladies dues au virus de l'immunodéficience humaine (VIH)	-	-	-	-	-	-	-	-
Malaria — Paludisme	-	-	-	-	2	♦0.0	1	♦0.0
Neoplasms — Tumeurs	4 209	198.9	3 760	177.5	93 398	337.5	69 672	236.3
Malignant neoplasms — Tumeurs malignes								
Total.....	4 154	196.3	3 714	175.3	90 041	325.3	66 825	226.7
Malignant neoplasm of lip, oral cavity and pharynx — Tumeur maligne de la lèvre, de la cavité buccale et du pharynx	97	4.6	39	1.8	2 123	7.7	737	2.5
Malignant neoplasm of oesophagus — Tumeur maligne de l'oesophage	197	9.3	115	5.4	1 487	5.4	484	1.6
Malignant neoplasm of stomach — Tumeur maligne de l'estomac........	192	9.1	133	6.3	6 266	22.6	4 686	15.9
Malignant neoplasm of colon, rectosigmoid junction, rectum, anus and anal canal — Tumeur maligne du côlon, de la jonction recto-sigmoïdienne, du rectum, de l'anus et du canal anal..........	558	26.4	396	18.7	9 164	33.1	8 072	27.4
Malignant neoplasm of liver and intrahepatic bile ducts — Tumeur maligne du foie et des voies bilaires intrahépatiques	44	2.1	21	♦1.0	3 601	13.0	1 650	5.6
Malignant neoplasm of pancreas — Tumeur maligne du pancréas	194	9.2	213	10.1	4 093	14.8	4 301	14.6
Malignant neoplasm of trachea, bronchus and lung — Tumeur maligne de la trachée, des bronches et du poumon..................	966	45.7	642	30.3	25 765	93.1	6 528	22.1
Malignant neoplasm of female breast — Tumeur maligne du sein chez la femme..........	..	..	667	...	..	..	11 309	44.3
Malignant neoplasm of cervix uteri — Tumeur maligne du col de l'utérus	..	..	90	...	..	..	373	1.5
Malignant neoplasm of prostate — Tumeur maligne de la prostate	532	...	..	..	7 132	74.3	...	..
Malignant neoplasm of lymphoid, haematopoietic and related tissue — Tumeurs malignes primitives ou présumées primitives des tissus lymphoïde, hématopoïétique et apparentés	402	19.0	285	13.5	6 909	25.0	6 257	21.2
Disorders of the blood and blood-forming organs and certain disorders involving the immune mechanism — Maladies du sang et des organes hématopoïétiques et certains troubles du système immunitaire								
Total.....	44	2.1	41	1.9	1 122	4.1	1 364	4.6
Anaemias — Anémies..................	21	♦1.0	28	♦1.3	705	2.5	1 009	3.4
Endocrine, nutritional and metabolic diseases — Maladies endocriniennes, nutritionnelles et métaboliques								
Total.....	361	17.1	359	16.9	9 057	32.7	12 376	42.0
Diabetes mellitus — Diabète sucré..........	274	12.9	242	11.4	7 135	25.8	10 485	35.6
Malnutrition — Malnutrition..........	1	♦0.0	5	♦0.2	56	0.2	92	0.3
Mental and behavioural disorders — Troubles mentaux et du comportement	265	12.5	323	15.2	3 469	12.5	6 635	22.5
Diseases of the nervous system — Maladies du système nerveux..........	329	15.5	368	17.4	6 067	21.9	8 108	27.5
Diseases of the circulatory system — Maladies de l'appareil circulatoire								
Total.....	4 929	232.9	4 733	223.4	105 726	382.0	131 472	446.0
Acute rheumatic fever and chronic rheumatic heart diseases — Rhumatisme articulaire aigu et cardiopathies rhumatismales chroniques	23	♦1.1	26	♦1.2	508	1.8	1 240	4.2
Hypertensive diseases — Maladies hypertensives..........	151	7.1	214	10.1	7 753	28.0	14 140	48.0
Ischaemic heart disease — Cardiopathie ischémique..........	2 741	129.5	2 119	100.0	39 345	142.2	36 035	122.2
Cerebrovascular disease — Maladie cérébrovasculaire..................	767	36.2	1 136	53.6	26 545	95.9	39 350	133.5

Cause of death — Cause de décès	Ireland - Irlande				Italy - Italie			
	2006 (C)				2002 (C)			
	Male — Masculin		Female — Féminin		Male — Masculin		Female — Féminin	
	Number Nombre	Rate Taux	Number Nombre	Rate Taux	Number Nombre	Rate Taux	Number Nombre	Rate Taux
Diseases of arteries, arterioles and capillaries — Maladies des artères, artérioles et capillaires	328	15.5	262	12.4	5 686	20.5	5 327	18.1
Diseases of the respiratory system — Maladies de l'appareil respiratoire								
Total............	1 845	87.2	2 133	100.7	20 617	74.5	15 324	52.0
Influenza — Grippe	1	♦0.0	-	-	191	0.7	290	1.0
Pneumonia — Pneumopathies....................	778	36.8	1 135	53.6	4 388	15.9	4 683	15.9
Chronic lower respiratory diseases — Maladies chroniques des voies respiratoires inférieures	688	32.5	601	28.4	11 633	42.0	6 648	22.6
Diseases of the digestive system — Maladies de l'appareil digestif								
Total............	516	24.4	495	23.4	12 485	45.1	12 234	41.5
Gastric and duodenal ulcer — Ulcère de l'estomac et du duodénum	60	2.8	57	2.7	718	2.6	817	2.8
Diseases of the liver — Maladies du foie	140	6.6	90	4.2	6 214	22.5	4 419	15.0
Diseases of the musculoskeletal system and connective tissue — Maladies du système ostéo-articularie, des muscles et du tissu conjonctif	56	2.6	132	6.2	489	1.8	1 530	5.2
Diseases of the genitourinary system — Maladies de l'appareil génito-urinaire								
Total............	334	15.8	362	17.1	3 946	14.3	4 178	14.2
Disorders of kidney and ureter — Affections du rein et de l'uretère	212	10.0	201	9.5	2 637	9.5	2 848	9.7
Hyperplasia of prostate — Hyperplasie de la prostate.............	6	...	..	...	179	1.9		
Pregnancy, childbirth and the puerperium — Grossesse, accouchement et puerpéralité								
Total............	..	..	..	-	..	..	17	♦3.2
Pregnancy with abortive outcome — Grossesse se terminant par un avortement	..	..	-	-	..	..	2	♦0.4
Other direct obstetric causes — Autres décès maternels directs	..	..	-	-	..	..	15	♦2.8
Indirect obstetric causes — Décès maternels indirects........................	..	..	-	-	..	..	-	-
Certain conditions originating in the perinatal period — Certaines affections dont l'origine se situe dans la période périnatale	65	196.5	45	144.5	749	270.9	540	206.4
Congenital malformations, deformations and chromosomal abnormalities — Malformations congénitales et anomalies chromosomiques	88	266.0	74	237.5	730	264.0	698	266.7
Symptoms, signs and abnormal clinical and laboratory findings, not elsewhere classified — Symptômes, signes et résultats anormaux d'examens cliniques et de laboratoire, non classés ailleurs	53	2.5	42	2.0	3 052	11.0	3 640	12.3
All other diseases — Toutes autres maladies........................	32	1.5	39	1.8	218	0.8	492	1.7
External causes — Causes externes								
Total............	909	43.0	383	18.1	16 026	57.9	10 667	36.2
Accidents								
Total............	531	25.1	270	12.7	11 943	43.2	9 306	31.6
Transport accidents — Accidents de transport	221	10.4	70	3.3	5 731	20.7	1 574	5.3
Falls — Chutes	146	6.9	142	6.7	4 035	14.6	6 517	22.1
Accidental drowning and submersion — Noyade et submersion accidentelles......	43	2.0	8	♦0.4	349	1.3	91	0.3
Exposure to smoke, fire and flames — Exposition à la fumée, au feu et aux flammes	18	♦0.9	8	♦0.4	144	0.5	131	0.4
Accidental poisoning by and exposure to noxious substances — Intoxication accidentelle par des substances nocives et exposition à ces substances	33	1.6	19	♦0.9	158	0.6	139	0.5
Intentional self-harm — Lésions auto-infligées....................	307	14.5	85	4.0	3 145	11.4	924	3.1
Assault — Agresssions	27	♦1.3	10	♦0.5	401	1.4	159	0.5
All other external causes — Toutes autres causes externes..................	44	2.1	18	♦0.8	537	1.9	278	0.9

Cause of death — Cause de décès	Italy - Italie				Latvia - Lettonie			
	2003 (C)				2005 (+C)			
	Male — Masculin		Female — Féminin		Male — Masculin		Female — Féminin	
	Number Nombre	Rate Taux	Number Nombre	Rate Taux	Number Nombre	Rate Taux	Number Nombre	Rate Taux
TOTAL..........	289 826	1 038.2	299 071	1 007.4	16 608	1 566.6	16 169	1 303.5
Certain infectious and parasitic diseases — Certaines maladies infectieuses et parasitaires								
Total..........	3 910	14.0	3 463	11.7	201	19.0	93	7.5
Intestinal infectious diseases — Maladies infectieuses intestinales...........	67	0.2	81	0.3	-	-	3	♦0.2
Tuberculosis — Tuberculose..........	228	0.8	168	0.6	128	12.1	42	3.4
Tetanus — Tétanos..........	3	♦0.0	19	♦0.1	-	-	-	-
Diphtheria — Diphtérie..........	-	-	-	-	1	♦0.1	1	♦0.1
Whooping cough — Coqueluche..........	-	-	-	-	-	-	-	-
Meningococcal infection — Infection à méningocoques..........	9	♦0.0	15	♦0.1	2	♦0.2	-	-
Septicaemia — Septicémie..........	1 104	4.0	1 386	4.7	22	♦2.1	14	♦1.1
Acute poliomyelitis — Poliomyélite aiguë..........	-	-	-	-	-	-	-	-
Measles — Rougeole..........	2	♦0.0	1	♦0.0	-	-	-	-
Viral hepatitis — Hépatite virale..........	800	2.9	776	2.6	6	♦0.6	8	♦0.6
Human immunodeficiency virus [HIV] disease — Maladies dues au virus de l'immunodéficience humaine (VIH)..........	999	3.6	269	0.9	18	♦1.7	8	♦0.6
Malaria — Paludisme..........	2	♦0.0	2	♦0.0	-	-	-	-
Neoplasms — Tumeurs..........	96 127	344.3	71 017	239.2	3 237	305.3	2 663	214.7
Malignant neoplasms — Tumeurs malignes								
Total..........	91 692	328.4	67 325	226.8	3 207	302.5	2 618	211.1
Malignant neoplasm of lip, oral cavity and pharynx — Tumeur maligne de la lèvre, de la cavité buccale et du pharynx..........	2 033	7.3	713	2.4	122	11.5	29	♦2.3
Malignant neoplasm of oesophagus — Tumeur maligne de l'oesophage..........	1 446	5.2	442	1.5	82	7.7	15	♦1.2
Malignant neoplasm of stomach — Tumeur maligne de l'estomac..........	6 381	22.9	4 643	15.6	318	30.0	228	18.4
Malignant neoplasm of colon, rectosigmoid junction, rectum, anus and anal canal — Tumeur maligne du côlon, de la jonction recto-sigmoïdienne, du rectum, de l'anus et du canal anal..........	9 250	33.1	8 005	27.0	316	29.8	382	30.8
Malignant neoplasm of liver and intrahepatic bile ducts — Tumeur maligne du foie et des voies bilaires intrahépatiques..........	6 372	22.8	3 469	11.7	76	7.2	63	5.1
Malignant neoplasm of pancreas — Tumeur maligne du pancréas..........	4 274	15.3	4 503	15.2	203	19.1	167	13.5
Malignant neoplasm of trachea, bronchus and lung — Tumeur maligne de la trachée, des bronches et du poumon..........	25 833	92.5	6 431	21.7	860	81.1	206	16.6
Malignant neoplasm of female breast — Tumeur maligne du sein chez la femme..........	..	..	11 461	44.6	..	..	400	37.1
Malignant neoplasm of cervix uteri — Tumeur maligne du col de l'utérus..........	..	..	364	1.4	..	..	104	9.7
Malignant neoplasm of prostate — Tumeur maligne de la prostate..........	7 707	79.1	..	..	350	115.4	..	..
Malignant neoplasm of lymphoid, haematopoietic and related tissue — Tumeurs malignes primitives ou présumées primitives des tissus lymphoïde, hématopoïétique et apparentés..........	7 026	25.2	6 522	22.0	180	17.0	183	14.8
Disorders of the blood and blood-forming organs and certain disorders involving the immune mechanism — Maladies du sang et des organes hématopoïétiques et certains troubles du système immunitaire								
Total..........	958	3.4	1 418	4.8	14	♦1.3	19	♦1.5
Anaemias — Anémies..........	603	2.2	999	3.4	3	♦0.3	9	♦0.7
Endocrine, nutritional and metabolic diseases — Maladies endocriniennes, nutritionnelles et métaboliques								
Total..........	9 436	33.8	14 591	49.1	98	9.2	156	12.6
Diabetes mellitus — Diabète sucré..........	7 799	27.9	11 960	40.3	89	8.4	140	11.3
Malnutrition — Malnutrition..........	142	0.5	218	0.7	1	♦0.1	3	♦0.2
Mental and behavioural disorders — Troubles mentaux et du comportement	3 230	11.6	6 072	20.5	69	6.5	46	3.7
Diseases of the nervous system — Maladies du système nerveux..........	8 124	29.1	11 168	37.6	216	20.4	159	12.8
Diseases of the circulatory system — Maladies de l'appareil circulatoire								
Total..........	105 874	379.2	135 884	457.7	8 182	771.8	9 893	797.6
Acute rheumatic fever and chronic rheumatic heart diseases — Rhumatisme articularie aigu et cardiopathies rhumatismales chroniques..........	574	2.1	1 382	4.7	40	3.8	59	4.8
Hypertensive diseases — Maladies hypertensives..........	7 784	27.9	14 541	49.0	147	13.9	267	21.5
Ischaemic heart disease — Cardiopathie ischémique..........	41 458	148.5	40 601	136.8	4 403	415.3	4 565	368.0
Cerebrovascular disease — Maladie cérébrovasculaire..........	27 351	98.0	41 576	140.0	2 216	209.0	3 833	309.0

Cause of death — Cause de décès	Italy - Italie 2003 (C)				Latvia - Lettonie 2005 (+C)			
	Male — Masculin		Female — Féminin		Male — Masculin		Female — Féminin	
	Number Nombre	Rate Taux	Number Nombre	Rate Taux	Number Nombre	Rate Taux	Number Nombre	Rate Taux
Diseases of arteries, arterioles and capillaries — Maladies des artères, artérioles et capillaires	5 612	20.1	5 145	17.3	549	51.8	817	65.9
Diseases of the respiratory system — Maladies de l'appareil respiratoire								
Total	23 017	82.4	17 835	60.1	667	62.9	258	20.8
Influenza — Grippe	343	1.2	620	2.1	-	-	-	-
Pneumonia — Pneumopathies	3 577	12.8	4 338	14.6	380	35.8	141	11.4
Chronic lower respiratory diseases — Maladies chroniques des voies respiratoires inférieures	14 538	52.1	8 787	29.6	242	22.8	97	7.8
Diseases of the digestive system — Maladies de l'appareil digestif								
Total	12 139	43.5	11 869	40.0	573	54.1	509	41.0
Gastric and duodenal ulcer — Ulcère de l'estomac et du duodénum	600	2.1	586	2.0	83	7.8	67	5.4
Diseases of the liver — Maladies du foie	6 546	23.4	4 513	15.2	245	23.1	194	15.6
Diseases of the musculoskeletal system and connective tissue — Maladies du système ostéo-articularie, des muscles et du tissu conjonctif	862	3.1	2 231	7.5	18	♦1.7	39	3.1
Diseases of the genitourinary system — Maladies de l'appareil génito-urinaire								
Total	4 412	15.8	4 812	16.2	179	16.9	193	15.6
Disorders of kidney and ureter — Affections du rein et de l'uretère	3 832	13.7	4 278	14.4	142	13.4	185	14.9
Hyperplasia of prostate — Hyperplasie de la prostate	205	2.1	..	..	29	♦9.6	..	..
Pregnancy, childbirth and the puerperium — Grossesse, accouchement et puerpéralité								
Total	..	..	28	♦5.1	..	..	1	♦4.7
Pregnancy with abortive outcome — Grossesse se terminant par un avortement	..	..	4	♦0.7	..	..	-	-
Other direct obstetric causes — Autres décès maternels directs	..	..	22	♦4.0	..	..	-	-
Indirect obstetric causes — Décès maternels indirects	..	..	2	♦0.4	..	..	1	♦4.7
Certain conditions originating in the perinatal period — Certaines affections dont l'origine se situe dans la période périnatale	652	233.3	536	202.6	42	382.3	37	352.0
Congenital malformations, deformations and chromosomal abnormalities — Malformations congénitales et anomalies chromosomiques	891	318.8	907	342.9	51	464.2	35	333.0
Symptoms, signs and abnormal clinical and laboratory findings, not elsewhere classified — Symptômes, signes et résultats anormaux d'examens cliniques et de laboratoire, non classés ailleurs	4 320	15.5	6 448	21.7	614	57.9	1 260	101.6
All other diseases — Toutes autres maladies	306	1.1	676	2.3	16	♦1.5	23	♦1.9
External causes — Causes externes								
Total	15 568	55.8	10 116	34.1	2 431	229.3	785	63.3
Accidents								
Total	11 535	41.3	8 216	27.7	1 650	155.6	563	45.4
Transport accidents — Accidents de transport	5 380	19.3	1 430	4.8	355	33.5	132	10.6
Falls — Chutes	1 561	5.6	1 219	4.1	175	16.5	78	6.3
Accidental drowning and submersion — Noyade et submersion accidentelles	322	1.2	75	0.3	198	18.7	52	4.2
Exposure to smoke, fire and flames — Exposition à la fumée, au feu et aux flammes	124	0.4	93	0.3	127	12.0	73	5.9
Accidental poisoning by and exposure to noxious substances — Intoxication accidentelle par des substances nocives et exposition à ces substances	148	0.5	96	0.3	315	29.7	88	7.1
Intentional self-harm — Lésions auto-infligées	3 078	11.0	997	3.4	445	42.0	119	9.6
Assault — Agresssions	470	1.7	178	0.6	168	15.8	62	5.0
All other external causes — Toutes autres causes externes	485	1.7	725	2.4	168	15.8	41	3.3

21. Death and death rates by cause and sex: 2002 - 2006
Décès et taux de mortalité par cause et sexe : 2002 - 2006 (continued - suite)

Cause of death — Cause de décès	Latvia - Lettonie 2006 (+C)				Lithuania - Lituanie 2005 (+C)			
	Male — Masculin		Female — Féminin		Male — Masculin		Female — Féminin	
	Number Nombre	Rate Taux	Number Nombre	Rate Taux	Number Nombre	Rate Taux	Number Nombre	Rate Taux
TOTAL..........	**16 668**	**1 581.2**	**16 447**	**1 333.0**	**23 384**	**1 468.5**	**20 415**	**1 120.5**
Certain infectious and parasitic diseases — Certaines maladies infectieuses et parasitaires								
Total.......	203	19.3	92	7.5	391	24.6	117	6.4
Intestinal infectious diseases — Maladies infectieuses intestinales...........	1	♦0.1	-	-	1	♦0.1	1	♦0.1
Tuberculosis — Tuberculose......	137	13.0	38	3.1	303	19.0	64	3.5
Tetanus — Tétanos......	-	-	-	-	-	-	3	♦0.2
Diphtheria — Diphtérie......	3	♦0.3	3	♦0.2	-	-	-	-
Whooping cough — Coqueluche......	-	-	-	-	-	-	-	-
Meningococcal infection — Infection à méningocoques......	6	♦0.6	1	♦0.1	8	♦0.5	2	♦0.1
Septicaemia — Septicémie......	6	♦0.6	15	♦1.2	47	3.0	29	♦1.6
Acute poliomyelitis — Poliomyélite aiguë......	-	-	-	-	-	-	-	-
Measles — Rougeole......	-	-	-	-	-	-	-	-
Viral hepatitis — Hépatite virale......	10	♦0.9	10	♦0.8	10	♦0.6	5	♦0.3
Human immunodeficiency virus [HIV] disease — Maladies dues au virus de l'immunodéficience humaine (VIH)......	19	♦1.8	10	♦0.8	3	♦0.2	-	-
Malaria — Paludisme......	1	♦0.1	-	-	-	-	-	-
Neoplasms — Tumeurs...........	**3 287**	**311.8**	**2 826**	**229.1**	**4 482**	**281.5**	**3 683**	**202.2**
Malignant neoplasms — Tumeurs malignes								
Total.......	3 250	308.3	2 778	225.2	4 433	278.4	3 615	198.4
Malignant neoplasm of lip, oral cavity and pharynx — Tumeur maligne de la lèvre, de la cavité buccale et du pharynx......	109	10.3	27	♦2.2	216	13.6	34	1.9
Malignant neoplasm of oesophagus — Tumeur maligne de l'oesophage......	89	8.4	18	♦1.5	121	7.6	19	♦1.0
Malignant neoplasm of stomach — Tumeur maligne de l'estomac......	329	31.2	256	20.7	431	27.1	337	18.5
Malignant neoplasm of colon, rectosigmoid junction, rectum, anus and anal canal — Tumeur maligne du côlon, de la jonction recto-sigmoïdienne, du rectum, de l'anus et du canal anal......	325	30.8	362	29.3	465	29.2	463	25.4
Malignant neoplasm of liver and intrahepatic bile ducts — Tumeur maligne du foie et des voies bilaires intrahépatiques......	84	8.0	56	4.5	84	5.3	88	4.8
Malignant neoplasm of pancreas — Tumeur maligne du pancréas......	141	13.4	188	15.2	225	14.1	234	12.8
Malignant neoplasm of trachea, bronchus and lung — Tumeur maligne de la trachée, des bronches et du poumon......	943	89.5	212	17.2	1 152	72.3	224	12.3
Malignant neoplasm of female breast — Tumeur maligne du sein chez la femme......	..	..	445	41.4	..	..	582	37.7
Malignant neoplasm of cervix uteri — Tumeur maligne du col de l'utérus......	..	..	109	10.1	..	..	215	13.9
Malignant neoplasm of prostate — Tumeur maligne de la prostate......	393	129.2	..	..	477	112.2	..	..
Malignant neoplasm of lymphoid, haematopoietic and related tissue — Tumeurs malignes primitives ou présumées primitives des tissus lymphoïde, hématopoïétique et apparentés......	189	17.9	182	14.8	248	15.6	273	15.0
Disorders of the blood and blood-forming organs and certain disorders involving the immune mechanism — Maladies du sang et des organes hématopoïétiques et certains troubles du système immunitaire								
Total.......	10	♦0.9	19	♦1.5	9	♦0.6	22	♦1.2
Anaemias — Anémies......	5	♦0.5	12	♦1.0	4	♦0.3	8	♦0.4
Endocrine, nutritional and metabolic diseases — Maladies endocriniennes, nutritionnelles et métaboliques								
Total.......	102	9.7	205	16.6	165	10.4	213	11.7
Diabetes mellitus — Diabète sucré......	90	8.5	186	15.1	143	9.0	194	10.6
Malnutrition — Malnutrition......	-	-	1	♦0.1	2	♦0.1	-	-
Mental and behavioural disorders — Troubles mentaux et du comportement	76	7.2	50	4.1	47	3.0	21	♦1.2
Diseases of the nervous system — Maladies du système nerveux..........	205	19.4	147	11.9	244	15.3	199	10.9
Diseases of the circulatory system — Maladies de l'appareil circulatoire								
Total.......	8 022	761.0	9 707	786.8	10 735	674.1	13 088	718.4
Acute rheumatic fever and chronic rheumatic heart diseases — Rhumatisme articulaire aigu et cardiopathies rhumatismales chroniques......	39	3.7	47	3.8	69	4.3	82	4.5
Hypertensive diseases — Maladies hypertensives......	209	19.8	347	28.1	187	11.7	230	12.6
Ischaemic heart disease — Cardiopathie ischémique......	4 215	399.8	4 556	369.3	6 950	436.4	8 099	444.5
Cerebrovascular disease — Maladie cérébrovasculaire......	2 101	199.3	3 583	290.4	2 010	126.2	3 400	186.6

Cause of death — Cause de décès	Latvia - Lettonie				Lithuania - Lituanie			
	2006 (+C)				2005 (+C)			
	Male — Masculin		Female — Féminin		Male — Masculin		Female — Féminin	
	Number Nombre	Rate Taux	Number Nombre	Rate Taux	Number Nombre	Rate Taux	Number Nombre	Rate Taux
Diseases of arteries, arterioles and capillaries — Maladies des artères, artérioles et capillaires	537	50.9	734	59.5	522	32.8	706	38.8
Diseases of the respiratory system — Maladies de l'appareil respiratoire								
Total	642	60.9	271	22.0	1 223	76.8	513	28.2
Influenza — Grippe	-	-	-	-	2	♦0.1	1	♦0.1
Pneumonia — Pneumopathies	376	35.7	163	13.2	461	28.9	199	10.9
Chronic lower respiratory diseases — Maladies chroniques des voies respiratoires inférieures	220	20.9	89	7.2	681	42.8	284	15.6
Diseases of the digestive system — Maladies de l'appareil digestif								
Total	604	57.3	504	40.8	1 085	68.1	800	43.9
Gastric and duodenal ulcer — Ulcère de l'estomac et du duodénum	73	6.9	52	4.2	115	7.2	107	5.9
Diseases of the liver — Maladies du foie	303	28.7	214	17.3	679	42.6	359	19.7
Diseases of the musculoskeletal system and connective tissue — Maladies du système ostéo-articularie, des muscles et du tissu conjonctif	36	3.4	47	3.8	23	♦1.4	65	3.6
Diseases of the genitourinary system — Maladies de l'appareil génito-urinaire								
Total	200	19.0	173	14.0	160	10.0	150	8.2
Disorders of kidney and ureter — Affections du rein et de l'uretère	158	15.0	172	13.9	126	7.9	140	7.7
Hyperplasia of prostate — Hyperplasie de la prostate	37	12.2	..	..	27	♦6.4	..	..
Pregnancy, childbirth and the puerperium — Grossesse, accouchement et puerpéralité								
Total	..	..	2	♦9.0	..	..	4	♦13.1
Pregnancy with abortive outcome — Grossesse se terminant par un avortement	..	..	-	-	..	..	-	-
Other direct obstetric causes — Autres décès maternels directs	..	..	2	♦9.0	..	..	3	♦9.8
Indirect obstetric causes — Décès maternels indirects	..	..	-	-	..	..	1	♦3.3
Certain conditions originating in the perinatal period — Certaines affections dont l'origine se situe dans la période périnatale	47	415.5	34	310.4	50	320.1	36	241.3
Congenital malformations, deformations and chromosomal abnormalities — Malformations congénitales et anomalies chromosomiques	42	371.3	54	493.1	65	416.1	69	462.5
Symptoms, signs and abnormal clinical and laboratory findings, not elsewhere classified — Symptômes, signes et résultats anormaux d'examens cliniques et de laboratoire, non classés ailleurs	696	66.0	1 510	122.4	374	23.5	183	10.0
All other diseases — Toutes autres maladies	26	♦2.5	36	2.9	17	♦1.1	17	♦0.9
External causes — Causes externes								
Total	2 470	234.3	770	62.4	4 314	270.9	1 235	67.8
Accidents								
Total	1 762	167.1	576	46.7	2 667	167.5	808	44.3
Transport accidents — Accidents de transport	333	31.6	114	9.2	657	41.3	228	12.5
Falls — Chutes	225	21.3	89	7.2	389	24.4	117	6.4
Accidental drowning and submersion — Noyade et submersion accidentelles	192	18.2	45	3.6	310	19.5	80	4.4
Exposure to smoke, fire and flames — Exposition à la fumée, au feu et aux flammes	170	16.1	66	5.3	128	8.0	51	2.8
Accidental poisoning by and exposure to noxious substances — Intoxication accidentelle par des substances nocives et exposition à ces substances	344	32.6	104	8.4	549	34.5	145	8.0
Intentional self-harm — Lésions auto-infligées	407	38.6	80	6.5	1 084	68.1	235	12.9
Assault — Agresssions	159	15.1	59	4.8	225	14.1	89	4.9
All other external causes — Toutes autres causes externes	142	13.5	55	4.5	338	21.2	103	5.7

Cause of death — Cause de décès	Lithuania - Lituanie 2006 (+C)				Luxembourg 2004 (+C)			
	Male — Masculin		Female — Féminin		Male — Masculin		Female — Féminin	
	Number Nombre	Rate Taux	Number Nombre	Rate Taux	Number Nombre	Rate Taux	Number Nombre	Rate Taux
TOTAL	23 809	1 505.2	21 004	1 159.0	1 793	791.8	1 737	749.8
Certain infectious and parasitic diseases — Certaines maladies infectieuses et parasitaires								
Total	365	23.1	149	8.2	39	17.2	35	15.1
Intestinal infectious diseases — Maladies infectieuses intestinales	2	♦0.1	1	♦0.1	-	-	3	♦1.3
Tuberculosis — Tuberculose	293	18.5	75	4.1	-	-	-	-
Tetanus — Tétanos	-	-	2	♦0.1	-	-	-	-
Diphtheria — Diphtérie	-	-	-	-	-	-	-	-
Whooping cough — Coqueluche	-	-	-	-	-	-	-	-
Meningococcal infection — Infection à méningocoques	3	♦0.2	7	♦0.4	-	-	-	-
Septicaemia — Septicémie	40	2.5	38	2.1	14	♦6.2	19	♦8.2
Acute poliomyelitis — Poliomyélite aiguë	-	-	-	-	-	-	-	-
Measles — Rougeole	-	-	-	-	-	-	-	-
Viral hepatitis — Hépatite virale	4	♦0.3	5	♦0.3	4	♦1.8	3	♦1.3
Human immunodeficiency virus [HIV] disease — Maladies dues au virus de l'immunodéficience humaine (VIH)	6	♦0.4	-	-	3	♦1.3	1	♦0.4
Malaria — Paludisme	-	-	-	-	-	-	-	-
Neoplasms — Tumeurs	4 672	295.4	3 595	198.4	543	239.8	388	167.5
Malignant neoplasms — Tumeurs malignes								
Total	4 615	291.8	3 533	194.9	536	236.7	379	163.6
Malignant neoplasm of lip, oral cavity and pharynx — Tumeur maligne de la lèvre, de la cavité buccale et du pharynx	199	12.6	37	2.0	26	♦11.5	6	♦2.6
Malignant neoplasm of oesophagus — Tumeur maligne de l'oesophage	143	9.0	22	♦1.2	23	♦10.2	4	♦1.7
Malignant neoplasm of stomach — Tumeur maligne de l'estomac	456	28.8	284	15.7	24	♦10.6	16	♦6.9
Malignant neoplasm of colon, rectosigmoid junction, rectum, anus and anal canal — Tumeur maligne du côlon, de la jonction recto-sigmoïdienne, du rectum, de l'anus et du canal anal	454	28.7	465	25.7	64	28.3	36	15.5
Malignant neoplasm of liver and intrahepatic bile ducts — Tumeur maligne du foie et des voies bilaires intrahépatiques	89	5.6	64	3.5	19	♦8.4	12	♦5.2
Malignant neoplasm of pancreas — Tumeur maligne du pancréas	234	14.8	215	11.9	35	15.5	28	♦12.1
Malignant neoplasm of trachea, bronchus and lung — Tumeur maligne de la trachée, des bronches et du poumon	1 229	77.7	248	13.7	146	64.5	44	19.0
Malignant neoplasm of female breast — Tumeur maligne du sein chez la femme	..	..	510	33.0	..	..	71	37.3
Malignant neoplasm of cervix uteri — Tumeur maligne du col de l'utérus	..	..	236	15.3	..	..	3	♦1.6
Malignant neoplasm of prostate — Tumeur maligne de la prostate	552	129.2	..	..	38	58.6	..	..
Malignant neoplasm of lymphoid, haematopoietic and related tissue — Tumeurs malignes primitives ou présumées primitives des tissus lymphoïde, hématopoïétique et apparentés	250	15.8	280	15.5	36	15.9	41	17.7
Disorders of the blood and blood-forming organs and certain disorders involving the immune mechanism — Maladies du sang et des organes hématopoïétiques et certains troubles du système immunitaire								
Total	18	♦1.1	17	♦0.9	5	♦2.2	7	♦3.0
Anaemias — Anémies	9	♦0.6	12	♦0.7	1	♦0.4	5	♦2.2
Endocrine, nutritional and metabolic diseases — Maladies endocriniennes, nutritionnelles et métaboliques								
Total	162	10.2	200	11.0	27	♦11.9	48	20.7
Diabetes mellitus — Diabète sucré	150	9.5	180	9.9	18	♦7.9	27	♦11.7
Malnutrition — Malnutrition	-	-	1	♦0.1	3	♦1.3	3	♦1.3
Mental and behavioural disorders — Troubles mentaux et du comportement	53	3.4	25	♦1.4	34	15.0	43	18.6
Diseases of the nervous system — Maladies du système nerveux	325	20.5	242	13.4	42	18.5	63	27.2
Diseases of the circulatory system — Maladies de l'appareil circulatoire								
Total	10 769	680.8	13 552	747.8	619	273.4	754	325.5
Acute rheumatic fever and chronic rheumatic heart diseases — Rhumatisme articularie aigu et cardiopathies rhumatismales chroniques	48	3.0	102	5.6	2	♦0.9	1	♦0.4
Hypertensive diseases — Maladies hypertensives	208	13.1	271	15.0	13	♦5.7	24	♦10.4
Ischaemic heart disease — Cardiopathie ischémique	6 828	431.7	8 198	452.4	259	114.4	185	79.9
Cerebrovascular disease — Maladie cérébrovasculaire	2 155	136.2	3 689	203.6	127	56.1	220	95.0

Cause of death — Cause de décès	Lithuania - Lituanie				Luxembourg			
	2006 (+C)				2004 (+C)			
	Male — Masculin		Female — Féminin		Male — Masculin		Female — Féminin	
	Number Nombre	Rate Taux	Number Nombre	Rate Taux	Number Nombre	Rate Taux	Number Nombre	Rate Taux
Diseases of arteries, arterioles and capillaries — Maladies des artères, artérioles et capillaires	451	28.5	659	36.4	20	♦8.8	37	16.0
Diseases of the respiratory system — Maladies de l'appareil respiratoire								
Total...	1 234	78.0	476	26.3	163	72.0	124	53.5
Influenza — Grippe	2	♦0.1	2	♦0.1	2	♦0.9	-	-
Pneumonia — Pneumopathies.....................	442	27.9	218	12.0	57	25.2	52	22.4
Chronic lower respiratory diseases — Maladies chroniques des voies respiratoires inférieures	716	45.3	231	12.7	78	34.4	40	17.3
Diseases of the digestive system — Maladies de l'appareil digestif								
Total...	1 385	87.6	956	52.8	101	44.6	81	35.0
Gastric and duodenal ulcer — Ulcère de l'estomac et du duodénum	105	6.6	119	6.6	2	♦0.9	5	♦2.2
Diseases of the liver — Maladies du foie	918	58.0	474	26.2	56	24.7	17	♦7.3
Diseases of the musculoskeletal system and connective tissue — Maladies du système ostéo-articularie, des muscles et du tissu conjonctif	32	2.0	69	3.8	3	♦1.3	12	♦5.2
Diseases of the genitourinary system — Maladies de l'appareil génito-urinaire								
Total...	161	10.2	148	8.2	12	♦5.3	24	♦10.4
Disorders of kidney and ureter — Affections du rein et de l'uretère	132	8.3	142	7.8	9	♦4.0	18	♦7.8
Hyperplasia of prostate — Hyperplasie de la prostate......................	18	♦4.2	..	..	1	♦1.5	..	..
Pregnancy, childbirth and the puerperium — Grossesse, accouchement et puerpéralité								
Total...	..	..	-	-	..	..	1	♦18.3
Pregnancy with abortive outcome — Grossesse se terminant par un avortement	..	..	-	-	..	..	-	-
Other direct obstetric causes — Autres décès maternels directs	..	..	-	-	..	..	-	-
Indirect obstetric causes — Décès maternels indirects........................	..	..	-	-	..	..	1	♦18.3
Certain conditions originating in the perinatal period — Certaines affections dont l'origine se situe dans la période périnatale	41	258.2	33	214.5	4	♦141.7	5	♦190.2
Congenital malformations, deformations and chromosomal abnormalities — Malformations congénitales et anomalies chromosomiques	71	447.1	69	448.5	5	♦177.1	3	♦114.1
Symptoms, signs and abnormal clinical and laboratory findings, not elsewhere classified — Symptômes, signes et résultats anormaux d'examens cliniques et de laboratoire, non classés ailleurs	400	25.3	210	11.6	52	23.0	57	24.6
All other diseases — Toutes autres maladies.................	29	♦1.8	15	♦0.8	2	♦0.9	4	♦1.7
External causes — Causes externes								
Total...	4 092	258.7	1 248	68.9	142	62.7	88	38.0
Accidents								
Total...	2 684	169.7	854	47.1	88	38.9	70	30.2
Transport accidents — Accidents de transport	658	41.6	241	13.3	39	17.2	15	♦6.5
Falls — Chutes	417	26.4	138	7.6	15	♦6.6	14	♦6.0
Accidental drowning and submersion — Noyade et submersion accidentelles..................................	262	16.6	73	4.0	3	♦1.3	1	♦0.4
Exposure to smoke, fire and flames — Exposition à la fumée, au feu et aux flammes	128	8.1	42	2.3	1	♦0.4	-	-
Accidental poisoning by and exposure to noxious substances — Intoxication accidentelle par des substances nocives et exposition à ces substances	573	36.2	172	9.5	13	♦5.7	5	♦2.2
Intentional self-harm — Lésions auto-infligées.....................	853	53.9	196	10.8	49	21.6	17	♦7.3
Assault — Agresssions	187	11.8	67	3.7	1	♦0.4	1	♦0.4
All other external causes — Toutes autres causes externes....................	368	23.3	131	7.2	4	♦1.8	-	-

Cause of death — Cause de décès	Luxembourg				Malta - Malte			
	2005 (+C)				2004 (+C)			
	Male — Masculin		Female — Féminin		Male — Masculin		Female — Féminin	
	Number Nombre	Rate Taux	Number Nombre	Rate Taux	Number Nombre	Rate Taux	Number Nombre	Rate Taux
TOTAL	1 735	753.9	1 861	791.8	1 491	749.8	1 508	744.9
Certain infectious and parasitic diseases — Certaines maladies infectieuses et parasitaires								
Total	52	22.6	60	25.5	8	♦4.0	5	♦2.5
Intestinal infectious diseases — Maladies infectieuses intestinales	3	♦1.3	3	♦1.3	-	-	-	-
Tuberculosis — Tuberculose	1	♦0.4	-	-	-	-	-	-
Tetanus — Tétanos	-	-	-	-	-	-	-	-
Diphtheria — Diphtérie	-	-	-	-	-	-	-	-
Whooping cough — Coqueluche	-	-	-	-	-	-	-	-
Meningococcal infection — Infection à méningocoques	-	-	1	♦0.4	1	♦0.5	2	♦1.0
Septicaemia — Septicémie	32	13.9	41	17.4	2	♦1.0	2	♦1.0
Acute poliomyelitis — Poliomyélite aiguë	-	-	-	-	-	-	-	-
Measles — Rougeole	-	-	-	-	-	-	-	-
Viral hepatitis — Hépatite virale	1	♦0.4	2	♦0.9	1	♦0.5	-	-
Human immunodeficiency virus [HIV] disease — Maladies dues au virus de l'immunodéficience humaine (VIH)	-	-	1	♦0.4	2	♦1.0	-	-
Malaria — Paludisme	-	-	-	-	-	-	-	-
Neoplasms — Tumeurs	517	224.7	420	178.7	396	199.1	328	162.0
Malignant neoplasms — Tumeurs malignes								
Total	508	220.7	410	174.4	386	194.1	323	159.5
Malignant neoplasm of lip, oral cavity and pharynx — Tumeur maligne de la lèvre, de la cavité buccale et du pharynx	13	♦5.6	3	♦1.3	9	♦4.5	5	♦2.5
Malignant neoplasm of oesophagus — Tumeur maligne de l'oesophage	21	♦9.1	7	♦3.0	3	♦1.5	2	♦1.0
Malignant neoplasm of stomach — Tumeur maligne de l'estomac	23	♦10.0	14	♦6.0	27	♦13.6	16	♦7.9
Malignant neoplasm of colon, rectosigmoid junction, rectum, anus and anal canal — Tumeur maligne du côlon, de la jonction recto-sigmoïdienne, du rectum, de l'anus et du canal anal	52	22.6	62	26.4	38	19.1	41	20.3
Malignant neoplasm of liver and intrahepatic bile ducts — Tumeur maligne du foie et des voies bilaires intrahépatiques	22	♦9.6	16	♦6.8	9	♦4.5	6	♦3.0
Malignant neoplasm of pancreas — Tumeur maligne du pancréas	27	♦11.7	27	♦11.5	25	♦12.6	24	♦11.9
Malignant neoplasm of trachea, bronchus and lung — Tumeur maligne de la trachée, des bronches et du poumon	144	62.6	62	26.4	107	53.8	16	♦7.9
Malignant neoplasm of female breast — Tumeur maligne du sein chez la femme	..	..	62	32.1	..	..	61	36.4
Malignant neoplasm of cervix uteri — Tumeur maligne du col de l'utérus	..	..	4	♦2.1	..	..	6	♦3.6
Malignant neoplasm of prostate — Tumeur maligne de la prostate	50	75.1	..	..	34	56.2	..	..
Malignant neoplasm of lymphoid, haematopoietic and related tissue — Tumeurs malignes primitives ou présumées primitives des tissus lymphoïde, hématopoïétique et apparentés	43	18.7	31	13.2	37	18.6	29	♦14.3
Disorders of the blood and blood-forming organs and certain disorders involving the immune mechanism — Maladies du sang et des organes hématopoïétiques et certains troubles du système immunitaire								
Total	2	♦0.9	11	♦4.7	-	-	6	♦3.0
Anaemias — Anémies	1	♦0.4	7	♦3.0	-	-	4	♦2.0
Endocrine, nutritional and metabolic diseases — Maladies endocriniennes, nutritionnelles et métaboliques								
Total	32	13.9	39	16.6	58	29.2	72	35.6
Diabetes mellitus — Diabète sucré	20	♦8.7	27	♦11.5	54	27.2	60	29.6
Malnutrition — Malnutrition	2	♦0.9	2	♦0.9	-	-	-	-
Mental and behavioural disorders — Troubles mentaux et du comportement	38	16.5	44	18.7	17	♦8.5	48	23.7
Diseases of the nervous system — Maladies du système nerveux	63	27.4	84	35.7	41	20.6	23	♦11.4
Diseases of the circulatory system — Maladies de l'appareil circulatoire								
Total	596	259.0	805	342.5	589	296.2	666	329.0
Acute rheumatic fever and chronic rheumatic heart diseases — Rhumatisme articularie aigu et cardiopathies rhumatismales chroniques	2	♦0.9	7	♦3.0	2	♦1.0	5	♦2.5
Hypertensive diseases — Maladies hypertensives	15	♦6.5	19	♦8.1	6	♦3.0	16	♦7.9
Ischaemic heart disease — Cardiopathie ischémique	216	93.9	184	78.3	346	174.0	301	148.7
Cerebrovascular disease — Maladie cérébrovasculaire	122	53.0	202	85.9	138	69.4	196	96.8

Cause of death — Cause de décès	Luxembourg				Malta - Malte			
	2005 (+C)				2004 (+C)			
	Male — Masculin		Female — Féminin		Male — Masculin		Female — Féminin	
	Number Nombre	Rate Taux	Number Nombre	Rate Taux	Number Nombre	Rate Taux	Number Nombre	Rate Taux
Diseases of arteries, arterioles and capillaries — Maladies des artères, artérioles et capillaires	29	♦12.6	39	16.6	25	♦12.6	20	♦9.9
Diseases of the respiratory system — Maladies de l'appareil respiratoire								
Total..........	144	62.6	130	55.3	183	92.0	140	69.2
Influenza — Grippe	2	♦0.9	3	♦1.3	1	♦0.5	1	♦0.5
Pneumonia — Pneumopathies	38	16.5	48	20.4	45	22.6	36	17.8
Chronic lower respiratory diseases — Maladies chroniques des voies respiratoires inférieures	75	32.6	46	19.6	84	42.2	23	♦11.4
Diseases of the digestive system — Maladies de l'appareil digestif								
Total..........	66	28.7	86	36.6	60	30.2	69	34.1
Gastric and duodenal ulcer — Ulcère de l'estomac et du duodénum	6	♦2.6	8	♦3.4	2	♦1.0	4	♦2.0
Diseases of the liver — Maladies du foie	41	17.8	24	♦10.2	18	♦9.1	10	♦4.9
Diseases of the musculoskeletal system and connective tissue — Maladies du système ostéo-articularie, des muscles et du tissu conjonctif	1	♦0.4	11	♦4.7	4	♦2.0	13	♦6.4
Diseases of the genitourinary system — Maladies de l'appareil génito-urinaire								
Total..........	18	♦7.8	24	♦10.2	26	♦13.1	16	♦7.9
Disorders of kidney and ureter — Affections du rein et de l'uretère	14	♦6.1	23	♦9.8	21	♦10.6	15	♦7.4
Hyperplasia of prostate — Hyperplasie de la prostate..........	-	-	..	..	1	♦1.7	..	..
Pregnancy, childbirth and the puerperium — Grossesse, accouchement et puerpéralité								
Total..........	..	..	1	♦18.6	..	..	-	-
Pregnancy with abortive outcome — Grossesse se terminant par un avortement	..	..	-	-	..	..	-	-
Other direct obstetric causes — Autres décès maternels directs	..	..	1	♦18.6	..	..	-	-
Indirect obstetric causes — Décès maternels indirects..........	..	..	-	-	..	..	-	-
Certain conditions originating in the perinatal period — Certaines affections dont l'origine se situe dans la période périnatale	4	♦143.7	4	♦154.6	6	♦300.3	5	♦264.7
Congenital malformations, deformations and chromosomal abnormalities — Malformations congénitales et anomalies chromosomiques	3	♦107.8	2	♦77.3	11	♦550.6	15	♦794.1
Symptoms, signs and abnormal clinical and laboratory findings, not elsewhere classified — Symptômes, signes et résultats anormaux d'examens cliniques et de laboratoire, non classés ailleurs	60	26.1	62	26.4	7	♦3.5	8	♦4.0
All other diseases — Toutes autres maladies..........	1	♦0.4	5	♦2.1	18	♦9.1	36	17.8
External causes — Causes externes								
Total..........	138	60.0	73	31.1	67	33.7	58	28.6
Accidents								
Total..........	88	38.2	58	24.7	51	25.6	43	21.2
Transport accidents — Accidents de transport	27	♦11.7	19	♦8.1	13	♦6.5	3	♦1.5
Falls — Chutes	29	♦12.6	15	♦6.4	21	♦10.6	32	15.8
Accidental drowning and submersion — Noyade et submersion accidentelles..........	1	♦0.4	1	♦0.4	1	♦0.5	1	♦0.5
Exposure to smoke, fire and flames — Exposition à la fumée, au feu et aux flammes	-	-	2	♦0.9	1	♦0.5	-	-
Accidental poisoning by and exposure to noxious substances — Intoxication accidentelle par des substances nocives et exposition à ces substances	11	♦4.8	1	♦0.4	5	♦2.5	1	♦0.5
Intentional self-harm — Lésions auto-infligées..........	40	17.4	10	♦4.3	14	♦7.0	10	♦4.9
Assault — Agresssions	5	♦2.2	2	♦0.9	2	♦1.0	4	♦2.0
All other external causes — Toutes autres causes externes..........	5	♦2.2	3	♦1.3	-	-	1	♦0.5

	Malta - Malte				Moldova			
Cause of death — Cause de décès	2005 (+C)				2005 (+U)		2006 (+U)	
	Male — Masculin		Female — Féminin		Male — Masculin	Female — Féminin	Male — Masculin	Female — Féminin
	Number Nombre	Rate Taux	Number Nombre	Rate Taux	Number Nombre	Number Nombre	Number Nombre	Number Nombre
TOTAL	1 576	787.6	1 554	764.0	23 357	21 332	22 620	20 517
Certain infectious and parasitic diseases — Certaines maladies infectieuses et parasitaires								
Total	6	♦3.0	9	♦4.4	643	146	601	139
Intestinal infectious diseases — Maladies infectieuses intestinales	-	-	-	-	6	12	5	6
Tuberculosis — Tuberculose	-	-	1	♦0.5	564	95	520	102
Tetanus — Tétanos	-	-	-	-	-	-	-	-
Diphtheria — Diphtérie	-	-	-	-	-	-	-	-
Whooping cough — Coqueluche	-	-	-	-	-	-	-	-
Meningococcal infection — Infection à méningocoques	-	-	1	♦0.5	8	3	1	3
Septicaemia — Septicémie	1	♦0.5	4	♦2.0	7	1	4	4
Acute poliomyelitis — Poliomyélite aiguë	-	-	-	-	-	-	-	-
Measles — Rougeole	-	-	-	-	-	-	-	1
Viral hepatitis — Hépatite virale	2	♦1.0	1	♦0.5	8	3	6	2
Human immunodeficiency virus [HIV] disease — Maladies dues au virus de l'immunodéficience humaine (VIH)	-	-	1	♦0.5	33	13	43	12
Malaria — Paludisme	-	-	-	-	-	-	-	-
Neoplasms — Tumeurs	399	199.4	319	156.8	2 966	2 273	3 096	2 404
Malignant neoplasms — Tumeurs malignes								
Total	387	193.4	312	153.4	2 942	2 242	3 064	2 374
Malignant neoplasm of lip, oral cavity and pharynx — Tumeur maligne de la lèvre, de la cavité buccale et du pharynx	7	♦3.5	6	♦2.9	231	35	204	35
Malignant neoplasm of oesophagus — Tumeur maligne de l'oesophage	8	♦4.0	5	♦2.5	56	14	69	8
Malignant neoplasm of stomach — Tumeur maligne de l'estomac	23	♦11.5	15	♦7.4	301	224	319	183
Malignant neoplasm of colon, rectosigmoid junction, rectum, anus and anal canal — Tumeur maligne du côlon, de la jonction recto-sigmoïdienne, du rectum, de l'anus et du canal anal	47	23.5	43	21.1	344	302	385	320
Malignant neoplasm of liver and intrahepatic bile ducts — Tumeur maligne du foie et des voies bilaires intrahépatiques	5	♦2.5	4	♦2.0	237	107	254	133
Malignant neoplasm of pancreas — Tumeur maligne du pancréas	17	♦8.5	17	♦8.4	168	130	177	115
Malignant neoplasm of trachea, bronchus and lung — Tumeur maligne de la trachée, des bronches et du poumon	105	52.5	17	♦8.4	659	153	689	160
Malignant neoplasm of female breast — Tumeur maligne du sein chez la femme	..		71	41.7	..	421	..	463
Malignant neoplasm of cervix uteri — Tumeur maligne du col de l'utérus	..		2	♦1.2	..	194	..	213
Malignant neoplasm of prostate — Tumeur maligne de la prostate	44	69.9	..		142	..	131	..
Malignant neoplasm of lymphoid, haematopoietic and related tissue — Tumeurs malignes primitives ou présumées primitives des tissus lymphoïde, hématopoïétique et apparentés	36	18.0	27	♦13.3	167	128	154	135
Disorders of the blood and blood-forming organs and certain disorders involving the immune mechanism — Maladies du sang et des organes hématopoïétiques et certains troubles du système immunitaire								
Total	5	♦2.5	3	♦1.5	6	6	13	15
Anaemias — Anémies	4	♦2.0	1	♦0.5	1	2	4	9
Endocrine, nutritional and metabolic diseases — Maladies endocriniennes, nutritionnelles et métaboliques								
Total	56	28.0	69	33.9	161	241	173	244
Diabetes mellitus — Diabète sucré	53	26.5	60	29.5	147	223	161	228
Malnutrition — Malnutrition	-	-	-	-	4	1	-	4
Mental and behavioural disorders — Troubles mentaux et du comportement	24	♦12.0	46	22.6	153	43	140	41
Diseases of the nervous system — Maladies du système nerveux	46	23.0	46	22.6	279	114	257	108
Diseases of the circulatory system — Maladies de l'appareil circulatoire								
Total	659	329.3	729	358.4	11 280	13 886	10 939	13 131
Acute rheumatic fever and chronic rheumatic heart diseases — Rhumatisme articulaire aigu et cardiopathies rhumatismales chroniques	-	-	5	♦2.5	82	131	75	107
Hypertensive diseases — Maladies hypertensives	11	♦5.5	12	♦5.9	190	286	178	294
Ischaemic heart disease — Cardiopathie ischémique	414	206.9	348	171.1	7 552	9 244	7 245	8 634

	Malta - Malte				Moldova			
	2005 (+C)				2005 (+U)		2006 (+U)	
Cause of death — Cause de décès	Male — Masculin		Female — Féminin		Male — Masculin	Female — Féminin	Male — Masculin	Female — Féminin
	Number Nombre	Rate Taux	Number Nombre	Rate Taux	Number Nombre	Number Nombre	Number Nombre	Number Nombre
Cerebrovascular disease — Maladie cérébrovasculaire........................	130	65.0	196	96.4	3 143	4 031	3 066	3 898
Diseases of arteries, arterioles and capillaries — Maladies des artères, artérioles et capillaires	25	♦12.5	26	♦12.8	105	71	147	78
Diseases of the respiratory system — Maladies de l'appareil respiratoire								
Total.........	189	94.5	116	57.0	1 886	958	1 702	911
Influenza — Grippe	-	-	-	-	1	2	-	-
Pneumonia — Pneumopathies	34	17.0	37	18.2	682	277	650	255
Chronic lower respiratory diseases — Maladies chroniques des voies respiratoires inférieures	97	48.5	22	♦10.8	1 084	652	955	625
Diseases of the digestive system — Maladies de l'appareil digestif								
Total.........	57	28.5	66	32.4	2 367	2 255	2 243	2 150
Gastric and duodenal ulcer — Ulcère de l'estomac et du duodénum	8	♦4.0	8	♦3.9	122	58	133	52
Diseases of the liver — Maladies du foie	23	♦11.5	14	♦6.9	1 733	1 959	1 653	1 850
Diseases of the musculoskeletal system and connective tissue — Maladies du système ostéo-articularie, des muscles et du tissu conjonctif	1	♦0.5	13	♦6.4	12	32	9	21
Diseases of the genitourinary system — Maladies de l'appareil génito-urinaire								
Total.........	18	♦9.0	26	♦12.8	214	183	206	179
Disorders of kidney and ureter — Affections du rein et de l'uretère	13	♦6.5	24	♦11.8	169	166	181	171
Hyperplasia of prostate — Hyperplasie de la prostate.........................	2	♦3.2	..	..	41	..	23	..
Pregnancy, childbirth and the puerperium — Grossesse, accouchement et puerpéralité								
Total.........	..	..	-	-	..	8	..	6
Pregnancy with abortive outcome — Grossesse se terminant par un avortement	..	..	-	-	..	1	..	1
Other direct obstetric causes — Autres décès maternels directs	..	..	-	-	..	5	..	3
Indirect obstetric causes — Décès maternels indirects.........................	..	..	-	-	..	2	..	2
Certain conditions originating in the perinatal period — Certaines affections dont l'origine se situe dans la période périnatale	9	♦453.6	6	♦320.2	92	68	87	61
Congenital malformations, deformations and chromosomal abnormalities — Malformations congénitales et anomalies chromosomiques	8	♦403.2	6	♦320.2	98	110	109	94
Symptoms, signs and abnormal clinical and laboratory findings, not elsewhere classified — Symptômes, signes et résultats anormaux d'examens cliniques et de laboratoire, non classés ailleurs	10	♦5.0	22	♦10.8	181	92	158	98
All other diseases — Toutes autres maladies.........................	17	♦8.5	33	16.2	30	10	19	17
External causes — Causes externes								
Total.........	72	36.0	45	22.1	2 989	907	2 868	898
Accidents								
Total.........	52	26.0	39	19.2	1 962	612	1 835	626
Transport accidents — Accidents de transport	14	♦7.0	4	♦2.0	394	130	385	119
Falls — Chutes	14	♦7.0	29	♦14.3	173	46	138	54
Accidental drowning and submersion — Noyade et submersion accidentelles............................	4	♦2.0	-	-	264	63	235	46
Exposure to smoke, fire and flames — Exposition à la fumée, au feu et aux flammes	2	♦1.0	-	-	114	53	107	72
Accidental poisoning by and exposure to noxious substances — Intoxication accidentelle par des substances nocives et exposition à ces substances	7	♦3.5	2	♦1.0	352	131	300	140
Intentional self-harm — Lésions auto-infligées.........................	16	♦8.0	2	♦1.0	532	99	541	96
Assault — Agresssions	1	♦0.5	1	♦0.5	189	106	184	79
All other external causes — Toutes autres causes externes.................	3	♦1.5	3	♦1.5	306	90	308	97

21. Death and death rates by cause and sex: 2002 - 2006
Décès et taux de mortalité par cause et sexe : 2002 - 2006 (continued - suite)

Netherlands - Pays-Bas

Cause of death — Cause de décès	2005 (+C)				2006 (+C)			
	Male — Masculin		Female — Féminin		Male — Masculin		Female — Féminin	
	Number Nombre	Rate Taux	Number Nombre	Rate Taux	Number Nombre	Rate Taux	Number Nombre	Rate Taux
TOTAL.................	66 362	822.2	70 040	849.2	65 294	807.8	70 078	848.1
Certain infectious and parasitic diseases — Certaines maladies infectieuses et parasitaires								
Total......	849	10.5	981	11.9	892	11.0	1 033	12.5
Intestinal infectious diseases — Maladies infectieuses intestinales............	33	0.4	68	0.8	42	0.5	81	1.0
Tuberculosis — Tuberculose........	21	◆0.3	11	◆0.1	19	◆0.2	12	◆0.1
Tetanus — Tétanos......	-	-	-	-	-	-	-	-
Diphtheria — Diphtérie.......	-	-	-	-	-	-	-	-
Whooping cough — Coqueluche........	-	-	-	-	-	-	1	◆0.0
Meningococcal infection — Infection à méningocoques....................	6	◆0.1	5	◆0.1	3	◆0.0	1	◆0.0
Septicaemia — Septicémie........	412	5.1	457	5.5	452	5.6	471	5.7
Acute poliomyelitis — Poliomyélite aiguë.....	-	-	-	-	-	-	-	-
Measles — Rougeole......	-	-	-	-	-	-	-	-
Viral hepatitis — Hépatite virale........	29	◆0.4	16	◆0.2	44	0.5	15	◆0.2
Human immunodeficiency virus [HIV] disease — Maladies dues au virus de l'immunodéficience humaine (VIH).......	66	0.8	14	◆0.2	37	0.5	11	◆0.1
Malaria — Paludisme.........	1	◆0.0	1	◆0.0	1	◆0.0	-	-
Neoplasms — Tumeurs...........	21 720	269.1	18 653	226.1	21 756	269.2	18 807	227.6
Malignant neoplasms — Tumeurs malignes								
Total........	21 241	263.2	18 105	219.5	21 311	263.7	18 183	220.0
Malignant neoplasm of lip, oral cavity and pharynx — Tumeur maligne de la lèvre, de la cavité buccale et du pharynx...........	342	4.2	196	2.4	379	4.7	175	2.1
Malignant neoplasm of oesophagus — Tumeur maligne de l'oesophage......	1 031	12.8	412	5.0	1 062	13.1	391	4.7
Malignant neoplasm of stomach — Tumeur maligne de l'estomac............	963	11.9	566	6.9	857	10.6	593	7.2
Malignant neoplasm of colon, rectosigmoid junction, rectum, anus and anal canal — Tumeur maligne du côlon, de la jonction recto-sigmoïdienne, du rectum, de l'anus et du canal anal........	2 267	28.1	2 333	28.3	2 435	30.1	2 300	27.8
Malignant neoplasm of liver and intrahepatic bile ducts — Tumeur maligne du foie et des voies bilaires intrahépatiques...........	360	4.5	226	2.7	340	4.2	212	2.6
Malignant neoplasm of pancreas — Tumeur maligne du pancréas............	1 037	12.8	1 139	13.8	998	12.3	1 128	13.7
Malignant neoplasm of trachea, bronchus and lung — Tumeur maligne de la trachée, des bronches et du poumon............	6 359	78.8	3 055	37.0	6 254	77.4	3 172	38.4
Malignant neoplasm of female breast — Tumeur maligne du sein chez la femme..........	..		3 301	....	..	..	3 335	49.1
Malignant neoplasm of cervix uteri — Tumeur maligne du col de l'utérus......	..		235		..	..	214	3.1
Malignant neoplasm of prostate — Tumeur maligne de la prostate.............	2 370	...	..	..	2 394	93.8	..	..
Malignant neoplasm of lymphoid, haematopoietic and related tissue — Tumeurs malignes primitives ou présumées primitives des tissus lymphoïde, hématopoïétique et apparentés...........	1 603	19.9	1 353	16.4	1 604	19.8	1 355	16.4
Disorders of the blood and blood-forming organs and certain disorders involving the immune mechanism — Maladies du sang et des organes hématopoïétiques et certains troubles du système immunitaire								
Total......	189	2.3	318	3.9	188	2.3	286	3.5
Anaemias — Anémies................	130	1.6	249	3.0	118	1.5	229	2.8
Endocrine, nutritional and metabolic diseases — Maladies endocriniennes, nutritionnelles et métaboliques								
Total......	1 847	22.9	2 645	32.1	1 762	21.8	2 487	30.1
Diabetes mellitus — Diabète sucré........................	1 599	19.8	2 160	26.2	1 518	18.8	1 992	24.1
Malnutrition — Malnutrition.........	25	◆0.3	58	0.7	21	◆0.3	62	0.8
Mental and behavioural disorders — Troubles mentaux et du comportement	1 913	23.7	4 523	54.8	2 056	25.4	4 912	59.4
Diseases of the nervous system — Maladies du système nerveux..........	1 585	19.6	1 961	23.8	1 681	20.8	2 159	26.1
Diseases of the circulatory system — Maladies de l'appareil circulatoire								
Total......	20 773	257.4	22 577	273.7	19 850	245.6	21 870	264.7
Acute rheumatic fever and chronic rheumatic heart diseases — Rhumatisme articularie aigu et cardiopathies rhumatismales chroniques...............	4	◆0.0	6	◆0.1	1	◆0.0	7	◆0.1
Hypertensive diseases — Maladies hypertensives..............	367	4.5	537	6.5	362	4.5	541	6.5
Ischaemic heart disease — Cardiopathie ischémique..................	7 631	94.5	5 712	69.3	7 184	88.9	5 307	64.2
Cerebrovascular disease — Maladie cérébrovasculaire....................	4 032	50.0	6 294	76.3	3 891	48.1	5 991	72.5

21. Death and death rates by cause and sex: 2002 - 2006
Décès et taux de mortalité par cause et sexe : 2002 - 2006 (continued - suite)

Netherlands - Pays-Bas

Cause of death — Cause de décès	2005 (+C)				2006 (+C)			
	Male — Masculin		Female — Féminin		Male — Masculin		Female — Féminin	
	Number Nombre	Rate Taux	Number Nombre	Rate Taux	Number Nombre	Rate Taux	Number Nombre	Rate Taux
Diseases of arteries, arterioles and capillaries — Maladies des artères, artérioles et capillaires	2 056	25.5	1 406	17.0	1 956	24.2	1 338	16.2
Diseases of the respiratory system — Maladies de l'appareil respiratoire								
Total............	7 305	90.5	7 010	85.0	7 021	86.9	6 710	81.2
Influenza — Grippe	115	1.4	209	2.5	34	0.4	50	0.6
Pneumonia — Pneumopathies............	2 509	31.1	3 095	37.5	2 487	30.8	3 072	37.2
Chronic lower respiratory diseases — Maladies chroniques des voies respiratoires inférieures	3 724	46.1	2 699	32.7	3 638	45.0	2 654	32.1
Diseases of the digestive system — Maladies de l'appareil digestif								
Total............	2 360	29.2	3 024	36.7	2 338	28.9	3 091	37.4
Gastric and duodenal ulcer — Ulcère de l'estomac et du duodénum	144	1.8	161	2.0	135	1.7	165	2.0
Diseases of the liver — Maladies du foie	602	7.5	397	4.8	564	7.0	391	4.7
Diseases of the musculoskeletal system and connective tissue — Maladies du système ostéo-articularie, des muscles et du tissu conjonctif	252	3.1	546	6.6	263	3.3	629	7.6
Diseases of the genitourinary system — Maladies de l'appareil génito-urinaire								
Total............	1 190	14.7	1 670	20.2	1 258	15.6	1 901	23.0
Disorders of kidney and ureter — Affections du rein et de l'uretère	690	8.5	824	10.0	710	8.8	867	10.5
Hyperplasia of prostate — Hyperplasie de la prostate............	56	...	..	..	58	2.3	..	..
Pregnancy, childbirth and the puerperium — Grossesse, accouchement et puerpéralité								
Total............	..	..	16	♦8.5	..	..	15	♦8.1
Pregnancy with abortive outcome — Grossesse se terminant par un avortement	..	..	-	-	..	..	1	♦0.5
Other direct obstetric causes — Autres décès maternels directs	..	..	15	♦8.0	..	..	10	♦5.4
Indirect obstetric causes — Décès maternels indirects............	..	..	1	♦0.5	..	..	4	♦2.2
Certain conditions originating in the perinatal period — Certaines affections dont l'origine se situe dans la période périnatale	292	303.1	217	237.0	241	253.7	166	184.3
Congenital malformations, deformations and chromosomal abnormalities — Malformations congénitales et anomalies chromosomiques	270	280.3	257	280.7	273	287.4	275	305.3
Symptoms, signs and abnormal clinical and laboratory findings, not elsewhere classified — Symptômes, signes et résultats anormaux d'examens cliniques et de laboratoire, non classés ailleurs	2 625	32.5	3 090	37.5	2 584	32.0	3 139	38.0
All other diseases — Toutes autres maladies............	122	1.5	279	3.4	94	1.2	275	3.3
External causes — Causes externes								
Total............	3 070	38.0	2 273	27.6	3 037	37.6	2 323	28.1
Accidents								
Total............	1 744	21.6	1 536	18.6	1 724	21.3	1 571	19.0
Transport accidents — Accidents de transport	588	7.3	214	2.6	557	6.9	232	2.8
Falls — Chutes	509	6.3	673	8.2	572	7.1	692	8.4
Accidental drowning and submersion — Noyade et submersion accidentelles............	76	0.9	17	♦0.2	67	0.8	21	♦0.3
Exposure to smoke, fire and flames — Exposition à la fumée, au feu et aux flammes	31	0.4	36	0.4	34	0.4	28	♦0.3
Accidental poisoning by and exposure to noxious substances — Intoxication accidentelle par des substances nocives et exposition à ces substances	94	1.2	38	0.5	84	1.0	30	♦0.4
Intentional self-harm — Lésions auto-infligées............	1 073	13.3	499	6.0	1 046	12.9	478	5.8
Assault — Agresssions	117	1.4	57	0.7	79	1.0	49	0.6
All other external causes — Toutes autres causes externes............	136	1.7	181	2.2	188	2.3	225	2.7

Norway - Norvège

Cause of death — Cause de décès	2004 (+C)				2005 (+C)			
	Male — Masculin		Female — Féminin		Male — Masculin		Female — Féminin	
	Number Nombre	Rate Taux	Number Nombre	Rate Taux	Number Nombre	Rate Taux	Number Nombre	Rate Taux
TOTAL....................	20 025	879.6	21 232	917.0	20 065	875.0	21 087	904.9
Certain infectious and parasitic diseases — Certaines maladies infectieuses et parasitaires								
Total....................	263	11.6	327	14.1	380	16.6	413	17.7
Intestinal infectious diseases — Maladies infectieuses intestinales............	35	1.5	60	2.6	59	2.6	87	3.7
Tuberculosis — Tuberculose....................	2	♦0.1	5	♦0.2	6	♦0.3	4	♦0.2
Tetanus — Tétanos....................	-	-	-	-	-	-	-	-
Diphtheria — Diphtérie....................	-	-	-	-	-	-	-	-
Whooping cough — Coqueluche....................	1	♦0.0	-	-	-	-	-	-
Meningococcal infection — Infection à méningocoques....................	1	♦0.0	1	♦0.0	1	♦0.0	2	♦0.1
Septicaemia — Septicémie....................	134	5.9	141	6.1	173	7.5	155	6.7
Acute poliomyelitis — Poliomyélite aiguë....................	-	-	-	-	-	-	-	-
Measles — Rougeole....................	-	-	-	-	-	-	-	-
Viral hepatitis — Hépatite virale....................	10	♦0.4	7	♦0.3	11	♦0.5	3	♦0.1
Human immunodeficiency virus [HIV] disease — Maladies dues au virus de l'immunodéficience humaine (VIH)....................	17	♦0.7	6	♦0.3	18	♦0.8	6	♦0.3
Malaria — Paludisme....................	-	-	1	♦0.0	-	-	-	-
Neoplasms — Tumeurs....................	5 694	250.1	5 044	217.9	5 708	248.9	5 104	219.0
Malignant neoplasms — Tumeurs malignes								
Total....................	5 589	245.5	4 900	211.6	5 598	244.1	4 969	213.2
Malignant neoplasm of lip, oral cavity and pharynx — Tumeur maligne de la lèvre, de la cavité buccale et du pharynx....................	88	3.9	50	2.2	92	4.0	51	2.2
Malignant neoplasm of oesophagus — Tumeur maligne de l'oesophage......	137	6.0	59	2.5	135	5.9	57	2.4
Malignant neoplasm of stomach — Tumeur maligne de l'estomac............	244	10.7	164	7.1	242	10.6	196	8.4
Malignant neoplasm of colon, rectosigmoid junction, rectum, anus and anal canal — Tumeur maligne du côlon, de la jonction recto-sigmoïdienne, du rectum, de l'anus et du canal anal....................	806	35.4	780	33.7	715	31.2	753	32.3
Malignant neoplasm of liver and intrahepatic bile ducts — Tumeur maligne du foie et des voies bilaires intrahépatiques....................	65	2.9	70	3.0	95	4.1	76	3.3
Malignant neoplasm of pancreas — Tumeur maligne du pancréas............	297	13.0	325	14.0	297	13.0	337	14.5
Malignant neoplasm of trachea, bronchus and lung — Tumeur maligne de la trachée, des bronches et du poumon....................	1 174	51.6	740	32.0	1 186	51.7	781	33.5
Malignant neoplasm of female breast — Tumeur maligne du sein chez la femme....................	..	..	694	37.1	..	..	695	36.8
Malignant neoplasm of cervix uteri — Tumeur maligne du col de l'utérus......	..	..	81	4.3	..	..	72	3.8
Malignant neoplasm of prostate — Tumeur maligne de la prostate..........	1 074	154.4	..	..	1 041	147.0	..	..
Malignant neoplasm of lymphoid, haematopoietic and related tissue — Tumeurs malignes primitives ou présumées primitives des tissus lymphoïde, hématopoïétique et apparentés....................	491	21.6	424	18.3	438	19.1	410	17.6
Disorders of the blood and blood-forming organs and certain disorders involving the immune mechanism — Maladies du sang et des organes hématopoïétiques et certains troubles du système immunitaire								
Total....................	49	2.2	74	3.2	51	2.2	59	2.5
Anaemias — Anémies....................	21	♦0.9	50	2.2	30	♦1.3	33	1.4
Endocrine, nutritional and metabolic diseases — Maladies endocriniennes, nutritionnelles et métaboliques								
Total....................	367	16.1	462	20.0	493	21.5	633	27.2
Diabetes mellitus — Diabète sucré....................	293	12.9	328	14.2	383	16.7	412	17.7
Malnutrition Malnutrition....................	-	-	-	-	-	-	-	-
Mental and behavioural disorders — Troubles mentaux et du comportement	468	20.6	820	35.4	570	24.9	989	42.4
Diseases of the nervous system — Maladies du système nerveux..........	608	26.7	738	31.9	539	23.5	756	32.4
Diseases of the circulatory system — Maladies de l'appareil circulatoire								
Total....................	7 293	320.4	8 569	370.1	6 886	300.3	7 651	328.3
Acute rheumatic fever and chronic rheumatic heart diseases — Rhumatisme articularie aigu et cardiopathies rhumatismales chroniques....................	17	♦0.7	49	2.1	13	♦0.6	31	1.3
Hypertensive diseases — Maladies hypertensives....................	159	7.0	220	9.5	157	6.8	219	9.4
Ischaemic heart disease — Cardiopathie ischémique....................	3 557	156.2	3 212	138.7	3 302	144.0	2 769	118.8
Cerebrovascular disease — Maladie cérébrovasculaire....................	1 541	67.7	2 287	98.8	1 507	65.7	2 181	93.6

Norway - Norvège

Cause of death — Cause de décès	2004 (+C)				2005 (+C)			
	Male — Masculin		Female — Féminin		Male — Masculin		Female — Féminin	
	Number Nombre	Rate Taux	Number Nombre	Rate Taux	Number Nombre	Rate Taux	Number Nombre	Rate Taux
Diseases of arteries, arterioles and capillaries — Maladies des artères, artérioles et capillaires	557	24.5	414	17.9	492	21.5	371	15.9
Diseases of the respiratory system — Maladies de l'appareil respiratoire								
Total..............	1 711	75.2	1 783	77.0	2 027	88.4	2 054	88.1
Influenza — Grippe	9	♦0.4	12	♦0.5	21	♦0.9	29	♦1.2
Pneumonia — Pneumopathies............	630	27.7	823	35.5	818	35.7	1 077	46.2
Chronic lower respiratory diseases — Maladies chroniques des voies respiratoires inférieures	904	39.7	798	34.5	997	43.5	799	34.3
Diseases of the digestive system — Maladies de l'appareil digestif								
Total..............	628	27.6	763	33.0	537	23.4	697	29.9
Gastric and duodenal ulcer — Ulcère de l'estomac et du duodénum	101	4.4	133	5.7	87	3.8	136	5.8
Diseases of the liver — Maladies du foie	198	8.7	107	4.6	145	6.3	95	4.1
Diseases of the musculoskeletal system and connective tissue — Maladies du système ostéo-articularie, des muscles et du tissu conjonctif	90	4.0	169	7.3	77	3.4	175	7.5
Diseases of the genitourinary system — Maladies de l'appareil génito-urinaire								
Total...........	350	15.4	389	16.8	413	18.0	446	19.1
Disorders of kidney and ureter — Affections du rein et de l'uretère	248	10.9	240	10.4	266	11.6	244	10.5
Hyperplasia of prostate — Hyperplasie de la prostate............	21	♦3.0	..	..	24	♦3.4	..	..
Pregnancy, childbirth and the puerperium — Grossesse, accouchement et puerpéralité								
Total..............	..	..	-	-	..	..	2	♦3.5
Pregnancy with abortive outcome — Grossesse se terminant par un avortement	..	..	-	-	..	..	-	-
Other direct obstetric causes — Autres décès maternels directs	..	..	-	-	..	..	1	♦1.8
Indirect obstetric causes — Décès maternels indirects............	..	..	-	-	..	..	1	♦1.8
Certain conditions originating in the perinatal period — Certaines affections dont l'origine se situe dans la période périnatale	45	154.2	38	136.9	50	172.1	46	166.0
Congenital malformations, deformations and chromosomal abnormalities — Malformations congénitales et anomalies chromosomiques	85	291.2	77	277.4	71	244.4	57	205.8
Symptoms, signs and abnormal clinical and laboratory findings, not elsewhere classified — Symptômes, signes et résultats anormaux d'examens cliniques et de laboratoire, non classés ailleurs	790	34.7	934	40.3	809	35.3	971	41.7
All other diseases — Toutes autres maladies............	31	1.4	43	1.9	24	♦1.0	54	2.3
External causes — Causes externes								
Total............	1 553	68.2	1 002	43.3	1 430	62.4	980	42.1
Accidents								
Total............	1 136	49.9	798	34.5	1 032	45.0	769	33.0
Transport accidents — Accidents de transport	267	11.7	84	3.6	208	9.1	79	3.4
Falls — Chutes	349	15.3	434	18.7	181	7.9	172	7.4
Accidental drowning and submersion — Noyade et submersion accidentelles............	63	2.8	19	♦0.8	69	3.0	13	♦0.6
Exposure to smoke, fire and flames — Exposition à la fumée, au feu et aux flammes	33	1.4	23	♦1.0	37	1.6	24	♦1.0
Accidental poisoning by and exposure to noxious substances — Intoxication accidentelle par des substances nocives et exposition à ces substances	261	11.5	118	5.1	230	10.0	86	3.7
Intentional self-harm — Lésions auto-infligées............	359	15.8	170	7.3	360	15.7	173	7.4
Assault — Agresssions	25	♦1.1	14	♦0.6	17	♦0.7	12	♦0.5
All other external causes — Toutes autres causes externes	33	1.4	20	♦0.9	21	♦0.9	26	♦1.1

Poland - Pologne

Cause of death — Cause de décès	2005 (C)				2006 (C)			
	Male — Masculin		Female — Féminin		Male — Masculin		Female — Féminin	
	Number Nombre	Rate Taux	Number Nombre	Rate Taux	Number Nombre	Rate Taux	Number Nombre	Rate Taux
TOTAL..........	196 786	1 066.0	171 499	870.5	198 298	1 075.6	171 388	870.2
Certain infectious and parasitic diseases — Certaines maladies infectieuses et parasitaires								
Total......	1 489	8.1	827	4.2	1 459	7.9	886	4.5
Intestinal infectious diseases — Maladies infectieuses intestinales............	15	◆0.1	19	◆0.1	8	◆0.0	18	◆0.1
Tuberculosis — Tuberculose..............	631	3.4	175	0.9	578	3.1	161	0.8
Tetanus — Tétanos...........	2	◆0.0	6	◆0.0	2	◆0.0	3	◆0.0
Diphtheria — Diphtérie............	-	-	-	-	-	-	-	-
Whooping cough — Coqueluche............	-	-	1	◆0.0	-	-	-	-
Meningococcal infection — Infection à méningocoques..............	8	◆0.0	7	◆0.0	8	◆0.0	5	◆0.0
Septicaemia — Septicémie	521	2.8	446	2.3	545	3.0	523	2.7
Acute poliomyelitis — Poliomyélite aiguë	-	-	-	-	-	-	-	-
Measles — Rougeole	-	-	-	-	-	-	-	-
Viral hepatitis — Hépatite virale............	132	0.7	88	0.4	154	0.8	81	0.4
Human immunodeficiency virus [HIV] disease — Maladies dues au virus de l'immunodéficience humaine (VIH)	96	0.5	25	◆0.1	76	0.4	25	◆0.1
Malaria — Paludisme	-	-	-	-	1	◆0.0	-	-
Neoplasms — Tumeurs	52 052	282.0	40 313	204.6	52 990	287.4	40 943	207.9
Malignant neoplasms — Tumeurs malignes								
Total...........	51 051	276.5	39 345	199.7	51 777	280.8	39 855	202.3
Malignant neoplasm of lip, oral cavity and pharynx — Tumeur maligne de la lèvre, de la cavité buccale et du pharynx	1 460	7.9	426	2.2	1 504	8.2	475	2.4
Malignant neoplasm of oesophagus — Tumeur maligne de l'oesophage	1 132	6.1	303	1.5	1 174	6.4	272	1.4
Malignant neoplasm of stomach — Tumeur maligne de l'estomac............	3 562	19.3	1 955	9.9	3 535	19.2	1 978	10.0
Malignant neoplasm of colon, rectosigmoid junction, rectum, anus and anal canal — Tumeur maligne du côlon, de la jonction recto-sigmoïdienne, du rectum, de l'anus et du canal anal............	4 959	26.9	4 500	22.8	5 214	28.3	4 462	22.7
Malignant neoplasm of liver and intrahepatic bile ducts — Tumeur maligne du foie et des voies bilaires intrahépatiques	921	5.0	917	4.7	1 045	5.7	945	4.8
Malignant neoplasm of pancreas — Tumeur maligne du pancréas	2 090	11.3	1 982	10.1	2 079	11.3	2 122	10.8
Malignant neoplasm of trachea, bronchus and lung — Tumeur maligne de la trachée, des bronches et du poumon............	16 562	89.7	4 953	25.1	16 658	90.4	5 117	26.0
Malignant neoplasm of female breast — Tumeur maligne du sein chez la femme............	..	..	5 112	30.7	..	..	5 212	31.2
Malignant neoplasm of cervix uteri — Tumeur maligne du col de l'utérus	..	..	1 796	10.8	..	..	1 824	10.9
Malignant neoplasm of prostate — Tumeur maligne de la prostate	3 592	69.9	..	..	3 681	69.8	..	..
Malignant neoplasm of lymphoid, haematopoietic and related tissue — Tumeurs malignes primitives ou présumées primitives des tissus lymphoïde, hématopoïétique et apparentés	2 933	15.9	2 622	13.3	2 945	16.0	2 682	13.6
Disorders of the blood and blood-forming organs and certain disorders involving the immune mechanism — Maladies du sang et des organes hématopoïétiques et certains troubles du système immunitaire								
Total............	257	1.4	326	1.7	214	1.2	249	1.3
Anaemias — Anémies	142	0.8	202	1.0	115	0.6	158	0.8
Endocrine, nutritional and metabolic diseases — Maladies endocriniennes, nutritionnelles et métaboliques								
Total............	2 542	13.8	3 408	17.3	2 712	14.7	3 774	19.2
Diabetes mellitus — Diabète sucré............	2 334	12.6	3 113	15.8	2 528	13.7	3 486	17.7
Malnutrition — Malnutrition............	27	◆0.1	31	0.2	38	0.2	33	0.2
Mental and behavioural disorders — Troubles mentaux et du comportement	1 516	8.2	295	1.5	1 090	9.2	264	1.3
Diseases of the nervous system — Maladies du système nerveux..........	2 381	12.9	2 454	12.5	2 361	12.8	2 468	12.5
Diseases of the circulatory system — Maladies de l'appareil circulatoire								
Total............	79 255	429.3	88 972	451.6	79 708	432.3	88 824	451.0
Acute rheumatic fever and chronic rheumatic heart diseases — Rhumatisme articularie aigu et cardiopathies rhumatismales chroniques	391	2.1	629	3.2	390	2.1	558	2.8
Hypertensive diseases — Maladies hypertensives............	2 311	12.5	3 267	16.6	2 544	13.8	3 421	17.4
Ischaemic heart disease — Cardiopathie ischémique............	27 016	146.3	22 757	115.5	27 228	147.7	22 801	115.8
Cerebrovascular disease — Maladie cérébrovasculaire............	16 702	90.5	22 310	113.2	16 569	89.9	21 812	110.7

Poland - Pologne

Cause of death — Cause de décès	2005 (C)				2006 (C)			
	Male — Masculin		Female — Féminin		Male — Masculin		Female — Féminin	
	Number Nombre	Rate Taux	Number Nombre	Rate Taux	Number Nombre	Rate Taux	Number Nombre	Rate Taux
Diseases of arteries, arterioles and capillaries — Maladies des artères, artérioles et capillaires	13 518	73.2	20 587	104.5	12 945	70.2	19 832	100.7
Diseases of the respiratory system — Maladies de l'appareil respiratoire								
Total	11 066	59.9	7 481	38.0	11 126	60.3	7 341	37.3
Influenza — Grippe	13	♦0.1	39	0.2	6	♦0.0	8	♦0.0
Pneumonia — Pneumopathies	4 372	23.7	4 332	22.0	4 535	24.6	4 236	21.5
Chronic lower respiratory diseases — Maladies chroniques des voies respiratoires inférieures	5 609	30.4	2 353	11.9	5 529	30.0	2 324	11.8
Diseases of the digestive system — Maladies de l'appareil digestif								
Total	9 558	51.8	6 968	35.4	9 312	50.5	6 979	35.4
Gastric and duodenal ulcer — Ulcère de l'estomac et du duodénum	865	4.7	681	3.5	801	4.3	724	3.7
Diseases of the liver — Maladies du foie	4 709	25.5	1 887	9.6	4 830	26.2	2 013	10.2
Diseases of the musculoskeletal system and connective tissue — Maladies du système ostéo-articularie, des muscles et du tissu conjonctif	137	0.7	419	2.1	110	0.6	390	2.0
Diseases of the genitourinary system — Maladies de l'appareil génito-urinaire								
Total	2 251	12.2	2 288	11.6	2 259	12.3	2 436	12.4
Disorders of kidney and ureter — Affections du rein et de l'uretère	2 127	11.5	2 182	11.1	2 147	11.6	2 326	11.8
Hyperplasia of prostate — Hyperplasie de la prostate	39	0.8	..	..	39	0.7	..	..
Pregnancy, childbirth and the puerperium — Grossesse, accouchement et puerpéralité								
Total	..	..	11	♦3.0	..	..	11	♦2.9
Pregnancy with abortive outcome — Grossesse se terminant par un avortement	..	..	3	♦0.8	..	..	1	♦0.3
Other direct obstetric causes — Autres décès maternels directs	..	..	7	♦1.9	..	..	7	♦1.9
Indirect obstetric causes — Décès maternels indirects	..	..	-	-	..	..	3	♦0.8
Certain conditions originating in the perinatal period — Certaines affections dont l'origine se situe dans la période périnatale	687	366.6	489	276.3	721	374.5	529	291.1
Congenital malformations, deformations and chromosomal abnormalities — Malformations congénitales et anomalies chromosomiques	557	297.2	530	299.4	543	282.1	442	243.2
Symptoms, signs and abnormal clinical and laboratory findings, not elsewhere classified — Symptômes, signes et résultats anormaux d'examens cliniques et de laboratoire, non classés ailleurs	13 807	74.8	10 548	53.5	13 942	75.6	9 755	49.5
All other diseases — Toutes autres maladies	20	♦0.1	18	♦0.1	23	♦0.1	24	♦0.1
External causes — Causes externes								
Total	19 211	104.1	6 152	31.2	19 120	103.7	6 073	30.8
Accidents								
Total	11 434	61.9	4 368	22.2	11 436	62.0	4 322	21.9
Transport accidents — Accidents de transport	4 599	24.9	1 354	6.9	4 289	23.3	1 268	6.4
Falls — Chutes	1 876	10.2	1 772	9.0	1 943	10.5	1 725	8.8
Accidental drowning and submersion — Noyade et submersion accidentelles	830	4.5	181	0.9	849	4.6	182	0.9
Exposure to smoke, fire and flames — Exposition à la fumée, au feu et aux flammes	434	2.4	128	0.6	419	2.3	156	0.8
Accidental poisoning by and exposure to noxious substances — Intoxication accidentelle par des substances nocives et exposition à ces substances	1 722	9.3	330	1.7	1 737	9.4	350	1.8
Intentional self-harm — Lésions auto-infligées	5 136	27.8	907	4.6	4 947	26.8	858	4.4
Assault — Agresssions	413	2.2	145	0.7	407	2.2	162	0.8
All other external causes — Toutes autres causes externes	2 228	12.1	732	3.7	2 330	12.6	731	3.7

Portugal

Cause of death — Cause de décès	2002 (+C)				2003 (+C)			
	Male — Masculin		Female — Féminin		Male — Masculin		Female — Féminin	
	Number Nombre	Rate Taux	Number Nombre	Rate Taux	Number Nombre	Rate Taux	Number Nombre	Rate Taux
TOTAL..........	55 687	1 111.6	51 003	951.8	56 226	1 113.8	52 922	981.3
Certain infectious and parasitic diseases — Certaines maladies infectieuses et parasitaires								
Total....	1 463	29.2	578	10.8	1 553	30.8	812	15.1
Intestinal infectious diseases — Maladies infectieuses intestinales..........	9	♦0.2	12	♦0.2	18	♦0.4	24	♦0.4
Tuberculosis — Tuberculose.....	198	4.0	41	0.8	164	3.2	47	0.9
Tetanus — Tétanos....	1	♦0.0	2	♦0.0	1	♦0.0	4	♦0.1
Diphtheria — Diphtérie........	-	-	-	-	-	-	-	-
Whooping cough — Coqueluche.......	-	-	-	-	-	-	-	-
Meningococcal infection — Infection à méningocoques..........	15	♦0.3	17	♦0.3	6	♦0.1	9	♦0.2
Septicaemia — Septicémie....	204	4.1	224	4.2	319	6.3	400	7.4
Acute poliomyelitis — Poliomyélite aiguë	-	-	-	-	-	-	-	-
Measles — Rougeole.......	-	-	-	-	-	-	-	-
Viral hepatitis — Hépatite virale..........	37	0.7	14	♦0.3	70	1.4	26	♦0.5
Human immunodeficiency virus [HIV] disease — Maladies dues au virus de l'immunodéficience humaine (VIH)	824	16.4	175	3.3	776	15.4	200	3.7
Malaria — Paludisme.......	3	♦0.1	2	♦0.0	6	♦0.1	2	♦0.0
Neoplasms — Tumeurs.......	13 467	268.8	9 321	173.9	13 794	273.2	9 463	175.5
Malignant neoplasms — Tumeurs malignes								
Total....	13 201	263.5	9 072	169.3	13 504	267.5	9 207	170.7
Malignant neoplasm of lip, oral cavity and pharynx — Tumeur maligne de la lèvre, de la cavité buccale et du pharynx	513	10.2	94	1.8	519	10.3	90	1.7
Malignant neoplasm of oesophagus — Tumeur maligne de l'oesophage	449	9.0	94	1.8	426	8.4	97	1.8
Malignant neoplasm of stomach — Tumeur maligne de l'estomac.....	1 577	31.5	947	17.7	1 524	30.2	955	17.7
Malignant neoplasm of colon, rectosigmoid junction, rectum, anus and anal canal — Tumeur maligne du côlon, de la jonction recto-sigmoïdienne, du rectum, de l'anus et du canal anal.....	1 775	35.4	1 356	25.3	1 778	35.2	1 443	26.8
Malignant neoplasm of liver and intrahepatic bile ducts — Tumeur maligne du foie et des voies bilaires intrahépatiques.....	457	9.1	234	4.4	467	9.3	218	4.0
Malignant neoplasm of pancreas — Tumeur maligne du pancréas..........	486	9.7	463	8.6	542	10.7	416	7.7
Malignant neoplasm of trachea, bronchus and lung — Tumeur maligne de la trachée, des bronches et du poumon.....	2 453	49.0	582	10.9	2 583	51.2	578	10.7
Malignant neoplasm of female breast — Tumeur maligne du sein chez la femme.....	..	..	1 550	34.0	..	..	1 556	33.9
Malignant neoplasm of cervix uteri — Tumeur maligne du col de l'utérus......	..	..	220	4.8	..	..	220	4.8
Malignant neoplasm of prostate — Tumeur maligne de la prostate..........	1 701	108.7	..	..	1 705	107.3	..	..
Malignant neoplasm of lymphoid, haematopoietic and related tissue — Tumeurs malignes primitives ou présumées primitives des tissus lymphoïde, hématopoïétique et apparentés	956	19.1	817	15.2	1 000	19.8	857	15.9
Disorders of the blood and blood-forming organs and certain disorders involving the immune mechanism — Maladies du sang et des organes hématopoïétiques et certains troubles du système immunitaire								
Total....	109	2.2	115	2.1	116	2.3	139	2.6
Anaemias — Anémies.....	69	1.4	90	1.7	56	1.1	87	1.6
Endocrine, nutritional and metabolic diseases — Maladies endocriniennes, nutritionnelles et métaboliques								
Total....	2 088	41.7	2 896	54.0	2 230	44.2	3 020	56.0
Diabetes mellitus — Diabète sucré.....	1 841	36.7	2 606	48.6	1 937	38.4	2 614	48.5
Malnutrition — Malnutrition.....	29	♦0.6	46	0.9	35	0.7	51	0.9
Mental and behavioural disorders — Troubles mentaux et du comportement	341	6.8	341	6.4	256	5.1	320	5.9
Diseases of the nervous system — Maladies du système nerveux..........	962	19.2	1 045	19.5	1 133	22.4	1 315	24.4
Diseases of the circulatory system — Maladies de l'appareil circulatoire								
Total....	18 698	373.2	22 303	416.2	18 432	365.1	22 603	419.1
Acute rheumatic fever and chronic rheumatic heart diseases — Rhumatisme articularie aigu et cardiopathies rhumatismales chroniques	61	1.2	157	2.9	74	1.5	156	2.9
Hypertensive diseases — Maladies hypertensives.....	432	8.6	707	13.2	453	9.0	755	14.0
Ischaemic heart disease — Cardiopathie ischémique.....	5 261	105.0	4 272	79.7	5 077	100.6	4 547	84.3
Cerebrovascular disease — Maladie cérébrovasculaire.....	8 438	168.4	11 124	207.6	8 218	162.8	10 895	202.0

Portugal

Cause of death — Cause de décès	2002 (+C)				2003 (+C)			
	Male — Masculin		Female — Féminin		Male — Masculin		Female — Féminin	
	Number Nombre	Rate Taux	Number Nombre	Rate Taux	Number Nombre	Rate Taux	Number Nombre	Rate Taux
Diseases of arteries, arterioles and capillaries — Maladies des artères, artérioles et capillaires	889	17.7	1 189	22.2	960	19.0	1 327	24.6
Diseases of the respiratory system — Maladies de l'appareil respiratoire								
Total.........	5 249	104.8	4 001	74.7	5 330	105.6	4 223	78.3
Influenza — Grippe	33	0.7	30	♦0.6	10	♦0.2	8	♦0.1
Pneumonia — Pneumopathies.........	1 904	38.0	1 634	30.5	2 011	39.8	1 793	33.2
Chronic lower respiratory diseases — Maladies chroniques des voies respiratoires inférieures	1 795	35.8	921	17.2	1 783	35.3	927	17.2
Diseases of the digestive system — Maladies de l'appareil digestif								
Total.........	2 791	55.7	1 788	33.4	2 763	54.7	1 849	34.3
Gastric and duodenal ulcer — Ulcère de l'estomac et du duodénum	187	3.7	185	3.5	177	3.5	155	2.9
Diseases of the liver — Maladies du foie	1 659	33.1	597	11.1	1 596	31.6	613	11.4
Diseases of the musculoskeletal system and connective tissue — Maladies du système ostéo-articularie, des muscles et du tissu conjonctif	92	1.8	170	3.2	105	2.1	193	3.6
Diseases of the genitourinary system — Maladies de l'appareil génito-urinaire								
Total.........	1 112	22.2	978	18.3	1 245	24.7	1 183	21.9
Disorders of kidney and ureter — Affections du rein et de l'uretère	961	19.2	823	15.4	1 067	21.1	985	18.3
Hyperplasia of prostate — Hyperplasie de la prostate.........	21	♦1.3	..	..	18	♦1.1	..	..
Pregnancy, childbirth and the puerperium — Grossesse, accouchement et puerpéralité								
Total.........	..	..	8	♦7.0	..	..	8	♦7.1
Pregnancy with abortive outcome — Grossesse se terminant par un avortement	..	..	2	♦1.7	..	..	1	♦0.9
Other direct obstetric causes — Autres décès maternels directs	..	..	5	♦4.4	..	..	4	♦3.6
Indirect obstetric causes — Décès maternels indirects.........	..	..	1	♦0.9	..	..	2	♦1.8
Certain conditions originating in the perinatal period — Certaines affections dont l'origine se situe dans la période périnatale	177	298.5	152	276.0	127	218.2	115	211.8
Congenital malformations, deformations and chromosomal abnormalities — Malformations congénitales et anomalies chromosomiques	142	239.4	119	216.0	119	204.4	112	206.2
Symptoms, signs and abnormal clinical and laboratory findings, not elsewhere classified — Symptômes, signes et résultats anormaux d'examens cliniques et de laboratoire, non classés ailleurs	4 605	91.9	5 441	101.5	4 968	98.4	5 927	109.9
All other diseases — Toutes autres maladies.........	168	3.4	229	4.3	23	♦0.5	42	0.8
External causes — Causes externes								
Total.........	4 223	84.3	1 518	28.3	4 032	79.9	1 598	29.6
Accidents								
Total.........	2 902	57.9	1 100	20.5	2 747	54.4	1 167	21.6
Transport accidents — Accidents de transport	1 739	34.7	481	9.0	1 561	30.9	436	8.1
Falls — Chutes	401	8.0	223	4.2	447	8.9	411	7.6
Accidental drowning and submersion — Noyade et submersion accidentelles.........	125	2.5	47	0.9	125	2.5	42	0.8
Exposure to smoke, fire and flames — Exposition à la fumée, au feu et aux flammes	46	0.9	31	0.6	57	1.1	51	0.9
Accidental poisoning by and exposure to noxious substances — Intoxication accidentelle par des substances nocives et exposition à ces substances	60	1.2	17	♦0.3	47	0.9	27	♦0.5
Intentional self-harm — Lésions auto-infligées.........	947	18.9	265	4.9	888	17.6	267	5.0
Assault — Agresssions	125	2.5	57	1.1	132	2.6	38	0.7
All other external causes — Toutes autres causes externes.........	249	5.0	96	1.8	265	5.2	126	2.3

Romania - Roumanie

Cause of death — Cause de décès	2005 (+C)				2006 (+C)			
	Male — Masculin		Female — Féminin		Male — Masculin		Female — Féminin	
	Number Nombre	Rate Taux	Number Nombre	Rate Taux	Number Nombre	Rate Taux	Number Nombre	Rate Taux
TOTAL..............	**138 461**	**1 313.2**	**123 640**	**1 115.9**	**136 264**	**1 295.1**	**121 830**	**1 101.2**
Certain infectious and parasitic diseases — Certaines maladies infectieuses et parasitaires								
Total.......	1 925	18.3	664	6.0	1 902	18.1	610	5.5
Intestinal infectious diseases — Maladies infectieuses intestinales...........	47	0.4	39	0.4	40	0.4	37	0.3
Tuberculosis — Tuberculose.................................	1 454	13.8	330	3.0	1 398	13.3	306	2.8
Tetanus — Tétanos............................	3	♦0.0	3	♦0.0	3	♦0.0	2	♦0.0
Diphtheria — Diphtérie..........................	-	-	-	-	-	-	-	-
Whooping cough — Coqueluche....................	-	-	-	-	-	-	-	-
Meningococcal infection — Infection à méningocoques...................	9	♦0.1	6	♦0.1	15	♦0.1	4	♦0.0
Septicaemia — Septicémie...........................	160	1.5	117	1.1	222	2.1	131	1.2
Acute poliomyelitis — Poliomyélite aiguë....................	-	-	-	-	-	-	-	-
Measles — Rougeole...........................	4	♦0.0	5	♦0.0	1	♦0.0	2	♦0.0
Viral hepatitis — Hépatite virale.................................	33	0.3	34	0.3	36	0.3	13	♦0.1
Human immunodeficiency virus [HIV] disease — Maladies dues au virus de l'immunodéficience humaine (VIH).................	142	1.3	89	0.8	125	1.2	80	0.7
Malaria — Paludisme..............................	-	-	1	♦0.0	-	-	-	-
Neoplasms — Tumeurs.................................	**26 292**	**249.4**	**18 614**	**168.0**	**26 597**	**252.8**	**18 854**	**170.4**
Malignant neoplasms — Tumeurs malignes								
Total.......	26 081	247.4	18 491	166.9	26 348	250.4	18 678	168.8
Malignant neoplasm of lip, oral cavity and pharynx — Tumeur maligne de la lèvre, de la cavité buccale et du pharynx	1 517	14.4	228	2.1	1 582	15.0	252	2.3
Malignant neoplasm of oesophagus — Tumeur maligne de l'oesophage......	519	4.9	97	0.9	529	5.0	103	0.9
Malignant neoplasm of stomach — Tumeur maligne de l'estomac............	2 516	23.9	1 215	11.0	2 483	23.6	1 290	11.7
Malignant neoplasm of colon, rectosigmoid junction, rectum, anus and anal canal — Tumeur maligne du côlon, de la jonction recto-sigmoïdienne, du rectum, de l'anus et du canal anal	2 557	24.3	2 100	19.0	2 627	25.0	2 240	20.2
Malignant neoplasm of liver and intrahepatic bile ducts — Tumeur maligne du foie et des voies bilaires intrahépatiques....................	1 507	14.3	869	7.8	1 627	15.5	876	7.9
Malignant neoplasm of pancreas — Tumeur maligne du pancréas............	1 390	13.2	947	8.5	1 397	13.3	1 029	9.3
Malignant neoplasm of trachea, bronchus and lung — Tumeur maligne de la trachée, des bronches et du poumon....................	7 323	69.5	1 712	15.5	7 242	68.8	1 801	16.3
Malignant neoplasm of female breast — Tumeur maligne du sein chez la femme....................	..	..	3 169	33.6	..	..	3 075	32.6
Malignant neoplasm of cervix uteri — Tumeur maligne du col de l'utérus......	..	..	1 793	19.0	..	..	1 839	19.5
Malignant neoplasm of prostate — Tumeur maligne de la prostate............	1 623	52.8	..	..	1 679	53.9	..	..
Malignant neoplasm of lymphoid, haematopoietic and related tissue — Tumeurs malignes primitives ou présumées primitives des tissus lymphoïde, hématopoïétique et apparentés....................	1 247	11.8	1 005	9.1	1 343	12.8	1 049	9.5
Disorders of the blood and blood-forming organs and certain disorders involving the immune mechanism — Maladies du sang et des organes hématopoïétiques et certains troubles du système immunitaire								
Total....................	52	0.5	63	0.6	48	0.5	76	0.7
Anaemias — Anémies....................	31	0.3	36	0.3	27	♦0.3	41	0.4
Endocrine, nutritional and metabolic diseases — Maladies endocriniennes, nutritionnelles et métaboliques								
Total.......	1 018	9.7	1 230	11.1	1 020	9.7	1 203	10.9
Diabetes mellitus — Diabète sucré....................	954	9.0	1 169	10.6	975	9.3	1 144	10.3
Malnutrition — Malnutrition....................	37	0.4	36	0.3	25	♦0.2	31	0.3
Mental and behavioural disorders — Troubles mentaux et du comportement	**540**	**5.2**	**148**	**1.3**	**178**	**1.7**	**70**	**0.6**
Diseases of the nervous system — Maladies du système nerveux..........	**1 055**	**10.0**	**907**	**8.2**	**977**	**9.3**	**882**	**8.0**
Diseases of the circulatory system — Maladies de l'appareil circulatoire								
Total....................	77 216	732.4	85 781	774.2	75 982	722.2	84 344	762.4
Acute rheumatic fever and chronic rheumatic heart diseases — Rhumatisme articularie aigu et cardiopathies rhumatismales chroniques....................	277	2.6	373	3.4	299	2.8	361	3.3
Hypertensive diseases — Maladies hypertensives....................	8 978	85.2	12 740	115.0	9 007	85.6	12 499	113.0
Ischaemic heart disease — Cardiopathie ischémique....................	28 012	265.7	26 633	240.4	28 030	266.4	26 587	240.3
Cerebrovascular disease — Maladie cérébrovasculaire....................	25 249	239.5	30 635	276.5	24 585	233.7	29 956	270.8

Romania - Roumanie

Cause of death — Cause de décès	2005 (+C)				2006 (+C)			
	Male — Masculin		Female — Féminin		Male — Masculin		Female — Féminin	
	Number Nombre	Rate Taux	Number Nombre	Rate Taux	Number Nombre	Rate Taux	Number Nombre	Rate Taux
Diseases of arteries, arterioles and capillaries — Maladies des artères, artérioles et capillaires	6 326	60.0	8 511	76.8	5 948	56.5	7 987	72.2
Diseases of the respiratory system — Maladies de l'appareil respiratoire								
Total	8 310	78.8	5 040	45.5	7 840	74.5	4 833	43.7
Influenza — Grippe	7	♦0.1	6	♦0.1	7	♦0.1	6	♦0.1
Pneumonia — Pneumopathies	3 320	31.5	2 238	20.2	3 148	29.9	2 158	19.5
Chronic lower respiratory diseases — Maladies chroniques des voies respiratoires inférieures	4 090	38.8	2 256	20.4	3 929	37.3	2 113	19.1
Diseases of the digestive system — Maladies de l'appareil digestif								
Total	9 068	86.0	5 645	50.9	8 658	82.3	5 547	50.1
Gastric and duodenal ulcer — Ulcère de l'estomac et du duodénum	412	3.9	182	1.6	383	3.6	224	2.0
Diseases of the liver — Maladies du foie	6 616	62.7	3 867	34.9	6 282	59.7	3 686	33.3
Diseases of the musculoskeletal system and connective tissue — Maladies du système ostéo-articularie, des muscles et du tissu conjonctif	18	♦0.2	34	0.3	8	♦0.1	25	♦0.2
Diseases of the genitourinary system — Maladies de l'appareil génito-urinaire								
Total	1 364	12.9	1 012	9.1	1 343	12.8	1 023	9.2
Disorders of kidney and ureter — Affections du rein et de l'uretère	1 108	10.5	1 007	9.1	1 138	10.8	1 015	9.2
Hyperplasia of prostate — Hyperplasie de la prostate	249	8.1	..	..	195	6.3	..	..
Pregnancy, childbirth and the puerperium — Grossesse, accouchement et puerpéralité								
Total	..	..	37	16.7	..	..	34	15.5
Pregnancy with abortive outcome — Grossesse se terminant par un avortement	..	..	15	♦6.8	..	..	12	♦5.5
Other direct obstetric causes — Autres décès maternels directs	..	..	22	♦10.0	..	..	22	♦10.0
Indirect obstetric causes — Décès maternels indirects	..	..	-	-	..	..	-	-
Certain conditions originating in the perinatal period — Certaines affections dont l'origine se situe dans la période périnatale	761	668.2	490	457.4	671	595.0	484	453.6
Congenital malformations, deformations and chromosomal abnormalities — Malformations congénitales et anomalies chromosomiques	549	482.1	451	421.0	456	404.3	400	374.9
Symptoms, signs and abnormal clinical and laboratory findings, not elsewhere classified — Symptômes, signes et résultats anormaux d'examens cliniques et de laboratoire, non classés ailleurs	439	4.2	258	2.3	575	5.5	317	2.9
All other diseases — Toutes autres maladies	27	♦0.3	43	0.4	18	♦0.2	35	0.3
External causes — Causes externes								
Total	9 818	93.1	3 223	29.1	9 991	95.0	3 093	28.0
Accidents								
Total	7 052	66.9	2 488	22.5	7 172	68.2	2 352	21.3
Transport accidents — Accidents de transport	2 597	24.6	929	8.4	2 607	24.8	878	7.9
Falls — Chutes	1 087	10.3	296	2.7	1 024	9.7	270	2.4
Accidental drowning and submersion — Noyade et submersion accidentelles	885	8.4	272	2.5	867	8.2	257	2.3
Exposure to smoke, fire and flames — Exposition à la fumée, au feu et aux flammes	219	2.1	168	1.5	225	2.1	172	1.6
Accidental poisoning by and exposure to noxious substances — Intoxication accidentelle par des substances nocives et exposition à ces substances	574	5.4	348	3.1	821	7.8	336	3.0
Intentional self-harm — Lésions auto-infligées	2 133	20.2	470	4.2	2 240	21.3	481	4.3
Assault — Agresssions	393	3.7	166	1.5	339	3.2	157	1.4
All other external causes — Toutes autres causes externes	240	2.3	99	0.9	240	2.3	103	0.9

21. Death and death rates by cause and sex: 2002 - 2006
Décès et taux de mortalité par cause et sexe : 2002 - 2006 (continued - suite)

Russian Federation - Fédération de Russie[1]

Cause of death — Cause de décès	2005 (+C)				2006 (+C)			
	Male — Masculin		Female — Féminin		Male — Masculin		Female — Féminin	
	Number Nombre	Rate Taux	Number Nombre	Rate Taux	Number Nombre	Rate Taux	Number Nombre	Rate Taux
TOTAL.................	1 245 035	1 875.5	1 058 900	1 380.0	1 148 561	1 740.1	1 018 142	1 331.2
Certain infectious and parasitic diseases — Certaines maladies infectieuses et parasitaires								
Total.........	30 792	46.4	8 204	10.7	28 041	42.5	7 697	10.1
Intestinal infectious diseases — Maladies infectieuses intestinales...........	355	0.5	295	0.4	230	0.3	248	0.3
Tuberculosis — Tuberculose.............	26 681	40.2	5 539	7.2	23 524	35.6	4 950	6.5
Tetanus — Tétanos........	2	◆0.0	5	◆0.0	3	◆0.0	-	-
Diphtheria — Diphtérie........	11	◆0.0	12	◆0.0	7	◆0.0	8	◆0.0
Whooping cough — Coqueluche........	1	◆0.0	2	◆0.0	1	◆0.0	1	◆0.0
Meningococcal infection — Infection à méningocoques................	250	0.4	215	0.3	210	0.3	185	0.2
Septicaemia — Septicémie........	932	1.4	657	0.9	858	1.3	612	0.8
Acute poliomyelitis — Poliomyélite aiguë...........	-	-	-	-	-	-	-	-
Measles — Rougeole.........	-	-	-	-	-	-	1	◆0.0
Viral hepatitis — Hépatite virale.................	646	1.0	427	0.6	655	1.0	461	0.6
Human immunodeficiency virus [HIV] disease — Maladies dues au virus de l'immunodéficience humaine (VIH)...........	1 166	1.8	363	0.5	1 877	2.8	587	0.8
Malaria — Paludisme............	2	◆0.0	-	-	5	◆0.0	-	-
Neoplasms — Tumeurs............	155 840	234.8	132 075	172.1	153 927	233.2	132 305	173.0
Malignant neoplasms — Tumeurs malignes								
Total.........	154 735	233.1	130 667	170.3	152 828	231.5	130 904	171.2
Malignant neoplasm of lip, oral cavity and pharynx — Tumeur maligne de la lèvre, de la cavité buccale et du pharynx	6 841	10.3	1 477	1.9	6 727	10.2	1 508	2.0
Malignant neoplasm of oesophagus — Tumeur maligne de l'oesophage	5 123	7.7	1 529	2.0	5 037	7.6	1 476	1.9
Malignant neoplasm of stomach — Tumeur maligne de l'estomac............	22 085	33.3	16 344	21.3	21 190	32.1	16 170	21.1
Malignant neoplasm of colon, rectosigmoid junction, rectum, anus and anal canal — Tumeur maligne du côlon, de la jonction recto-sigmoïdienne, du rectum, de l'anus et du canal anal........	16 314	24.6	20 079	26.2	16 547	25.1	20 428	26.7
Malignant neoplasm of liver and intrahepatic bile ducts — Tumeur maligne du foie et des voies bilaires intrahépatiques	4 723	7.1	3 665	4.8	4 495	6.8	3 545	4.6
Malignant neoplasm of pancreas — Tumeur maligne du pancréas	7 157	10.8	6 838	8.9	7 117	10.8	6 999	9.2
Malignant neoplasm of trachea, bronchus and lung — Tumeur maligne de la trachée, des bronches et du poumon	44 432	66.9	8 355	10.9	43 579	66.0	8 323	10.9
Malignant neoplasm of female breast — Tumeur maligne du sein chez la femme.......	..	..	22 547	34.1	..	..	22 409	33.8
Malignant neoplasm of cervix uteri — Tumeur maligne du col de l'utérus	..	..	5 985	9.0	..	..	6 047	9.1
Malignant neoplasm of prostate — Tumeur maligne de la prostate	8 196	49.4	..	..	8 516	50.4	..	..
Malignant neoplasm of lymphoid, haematopoietic and related tissue — Tumeurs malignes primitives ou présumées primitives des tissus lymphoïde, hématopoïétique et apparentés	...	...	...	...	...	...	...	...
Disorders of the blood and blood-forming organs and certain disorders involving the immune mechanism — Maladies du sang et des organes hématopoïétiques et certains troubles du système immunitaire								
Total.........	537	0.8	694	0.9	524	0.8	661	0.9
Anaemias — Anémies.................	281	0.4	438	0.6	266	0.4	432	0.6
Endocrine, nutritional and metabolic diseases — Maladies endocriniennes, nutritionnelles et métaboliques								
Total.........	3 794	5.7	7 989	10.4	3 643	5.5	7 925	10.4
Diabetes mellitus — Diabète sucré.................	3 094	4.7	7 340	9.6	3 036	4.6	7 271	9.5
Malnutrition — Malnutrition.................	252	0.4	135	0.2	204	0.3	120	0.2
Mental and behavioural disorders — Troubles mentaux et du comportement	5 425	8.2	2 539	3.3	4 805	7.3	2 331	3.0
Diseases of the nervous system — Maladies du système nerveux...........	10 519	15.8	5 677	7.4	9 352	14.2	5 492	7.2
Diseases of the circulatory system — Maladies de l'appareil circulatoire								
Total.........	601 379	905.9	698 073	909.8	558 230	845.7	673 952	881.2
Acute rheumatic fever and chronic rheumatic heart diseases — Rhumatisme articulaire aigu et cardiopathies rhumatismales chroniques	2 180	3.3	3 516	4.6	2 092	3.2	3 185	4.2
Hypertensive diseases — Maladies hypertensives.................	11 183	16.8	16 318	21.3	11 186	16.9	17 106	22.4
Ischaemic heart disease — Cardiopathie ischémique.................	312 759	471.1	312 785	407.6	294 620	446.4	313 097	409.4
Cerebrovascular disease — Maladie cérébrovasculaire.................	179 213	270.0	285 944	372.7	165 207	250.3	269 771	352.7

21. Death and death rates by cause and sex: 2002 - 2006
Décès et taux de mortalité par cause et sexe : 2002 - 2006 (continued - suite)

Russian Federation - Fédération de Russie[1]

Cause of death — Cause de décès	2005 (+C)				2006 (+C)			
	Male — Masculin		Female — Féminin		Male — Masculin		Female — Féminin	
	Number Nombre	Rate Taux	Number Nombre	Rate Taux	Number Nombre	Rate Taux	Number Nombre	Rate Taux
Diseases of arteries, arterioles and capillaries — Maladies des artères, artérioles et capillaires	...	...	...	...	...	...	...	...
Diseases of the respiratory system — Maladies de l'appareil respiratoire								
Total	69 131	104.1	25 605	33.4	59 190	89.7	23 571	30.8
Influenza — Grippe	72	0.1	51	0.1	48	0.1	45	0.1
Pneumonia — Pneumopathies	35 091	52.9	11 244	14.7	29 005	43.9	9 965	13.0
Chronic lower respiratory diseases — Maladies chroniques des voies respiratoires inférieures	28 820	43.4	12 493	16.3	25 812	39.1	11 725	15.3
Diseases of the digestive system — Maladies de l'appareil digestif								
Total	54 342	81.9	39 466	51.4	51 400	77.9	38 039	49.7
Gastric and duodenal ulcer — Ulcère de l'estomac et du duodénum	5 434	8.2	2 484	3.2	5 203	7.9	2 658	3.5
Diseases of the liver — Maladies du foie	32 111	48.4	22 999	30.0	30 271	45.9	21 276	27.8
Diseases of the musculoskeletal system and connective tissue — Maladies du système ostéo-articularie, des muscles et du tissu conjonctif	652	1.0	1 290	1.7	676	1.0	1 319	1.7
Diseases of the genitourinary system — Maladies de l'appareil génito-urinaire								
Total	6 019	9.1	5 924	7.7	5 792	8.8	5 674	7.4
Disorders of kidney and ureter — Affections du rein et de l'uretère	...	...	...	...	...	...	...	...
Hyperplasia of prostate — Hyperplasie de la prostate	...	...	...	...	...	...	...	...
Pregnancy, childbirth and the puerperium — Grossesse, accouchement et puerpéralité								
Total	..	..	370	25.4	..	..	352	23.8
Pregnancy with abortive outcome — Grossesse se terminant par un avortement	..	..	83	5.7	..	..	76	5.1
Other direct obstetric causes — Autres décès maternels directs	..	..	225	15.4	..	..	223	15.1
Indirect obstetric causes — Décès maternels indirects	..	..	57	3.9	..	..	50	3.4
Certain conditions originating in the perinatal period — Certaines affections dont l'origine se situe dans la période périnatale	4 351	580.5	2 844	401.8	4 107	539.8	2 872	399.6
Congenital malformations, deformations and chromosomal abnormalities — Malformations congénitales et anomalies chromosomiques	3 511	468.4	2 834	400.4	3 286	431.9	2 582	359.2
Symptoms, signs and abnormal clinical and laboratory findings, not elsewhere classified — Symptômes, signes et résultats anormaux d'examens cliniques et de laboratoire, non classés ailleurs	51 390	77.4	54 589	71.1	45 403	68.8	48 768	63.8
All other diseases — Toutes autres maladies	1 096	1.7	1 069	1.4	969	1.5	1 033	1.4
External causes — Causes externes								
Total	246 257	371.0	69 658	90.8	219 216	332.1	63 569	83.1
Accidents								
Total	...	...	...	...	...	...	...	...
Transport accidents — Accidents de transport	29 353	44.2	10 812	14.1	27 850	42.2	10 391	13.6
Falls — Chutes	9 696	14.6	3 189	4.2	8 439	12.8	2 955	3.9
Accidental drowning and submersion — Noyade et submersion accidentelles	12 050	18.2	2 369	3.1	10 210	15.5	2 002	2.6
Exposure to smoke, fire and flames — Exposition à la fumée, au feu et aux flammes	8 601	13.0	3 442	4.5	8 186	12.4	3 237	4.2
Accidental poisoning by and exposure to noxious substances — Intoxication accidentelle par des substances nocives et exposition à ces substances	49 194	74.1	13 812	18.0	43 038	65.2	12 265	16.0
Intentional self-harm — Lésions auto-infligées	38 574	58.1	7 489	9.8	35 608	53.9	7 247	9.5
Assault — Agresssions	26 787	40.4	8 849	11.5	21 629	32.8	7 215	9.4
All other external causes — Toutes autres causes externes	...	...	...	...	...	...	...	...

21. Death and death rates by cause and sex: 2002 - 2006
Décès et taux de mortalité par cause et sexe : 2002 - 2006 (continued - suite)

	San Marino - Saint-Marin				Serbia - Serbie			
Cause of death — Cause de décès	2002 (+U)		2005 (+U)		2005 (+C)			
	Male — Masculin	Female — Féminin	Male — Masculin	Female — Féminin	Male — Masculin		Female — Féminin	
	Number Nombre	Number Nombre	Number Nombre	Number Nombre	Number Nombre	Rate Taux	Number Nombre	Rate Taux
TOTAL...............	114	89	116	103	54 336	1 501.8	52 435	1 371.7
Certain infectious and parasitic diseases — Certaines maladies infectieuses et parasitaires								
Total.........	-	-	-	-	355	9.8	191	5.0
Intestinal infectious diseases — Maladies infectieuses intestinales...........	-	-	-	-	8	◆0.2	7	◆0.2
Tuberculosis — Tuberculose.............	-	-	-	-	168	4.6	59	1.5
Tetanus — Tétanos.................	...	...	...	...	3	◆0.1	4	◆0.1
Diphtheria — Diphtérie.............	...	...	...	...	-		-	
Whooping cough — Coqueluche.............	...	...	...	...	-		-	
Meningococcal infection — Infection à méningocoques.............	...	...	...	...	3	◆0.1	3	◆0.1
Septicaemia — Septicémie.............	...	...	...	...	92	2.5	77	2.0
Acute poliomyelitis — Poliomyélite aiguë.............	...	...	...	...	-		-	
Measles — Rougeole.............	...	...	...	...	-		-	
Viral hepatitis — Hépatite virale.............	...	...	...	...	24	◆0.7	16	◆0.4
Human immunodeficiency virus [HIV] disease — Maladies dues au virus de l'immunodéficience humaine (VIH).............	...	...	...	...	21	◆0.6	4	◆0.1
Malaria — Paludisme.............	...	...	...	...	1	◆0.0	-	
Neoplasms — Tumeurs.............	47	23	49	37	11 374	314.4	8 742	228.7
Malignant neoplasms — Tumeurs malignes								
Total.........	47	23	49	37	11 169	308.7	8 572	224.2
Malignant neoplasm of lip, oral cavity and pharynx — Tumeur maligne de la lèvre, de la cavité buccale et du pharynx.............	-	-	-	-	334	9.2	106	2.8
Malignant neoplasm of oesophagus — Tumeur maligne de l'oesophage......	...	...	...	...	201	5.6	42	1.1
Malignant neoplasm of stomach — Tumeur maligne de l'estomac.............	7	3	9	5	744	20.6	463	12.1
Malignant neoplasm of colon, rectosigmoid junction, rectum, anus and anal canal — Tumeur maligne du côlon, de la jonction recto-sigmoïdienne, du rectum, de l'anus et du canal anal.............	3	3	6	3	1 407	38.9	1 079	28.2
Malignant neoplasm of liver and intrahepatic bile ducts — Tumeur maligne du foie et des voies bilaires intrahépatiques.............	...	...	...	...	428	11.8	304	8.0
Malignant neoplasm of pancreas — Tumeur maligne du pancréas.............	...	...	...	...	518	14.3	470	12.3
Malignant neoplasm of trachea, bronchus and lung — Tumeur maligne de la trachée, des bronches et du poumon.............	7	2	12	7	3 522	97.3	1 021	26.7
Malignant neoplasm of female breast — Tumeur maligne du sein chez la femme.............		7		3	..	..	1 569	48.3
Malignant neoplasm of cervix uteri — Tumeur maligne du col de l'utérus......	...	...	...	...	..	..	486	14.9
Malignant neoplasm of prostate — Tumeur maligne de la prostate.............	...				827	65.9	..	..
Malignant neoplasm of lymphoid, haematopoietic and related tissue — Tumeurs malignes primitives ou présumées primitives des tissus lymphoïde, hématopoïétique et apparentés.............	3	-	-	3	573	15.8	426	11.1
Disorders of the blood and blood-forming organs and certain disorders involving the immune mechanism — Maladies du sang et des organes hématopoïétiques et certains troubles du système immunitaire								
Total.........	1	-	-	-	68	1.9	89	2.3
Anaemias — Anémies.............	1	-	...	...	35	1.0	56	1.5
Endocrine, nutritional and metabolic diseases — Maladies endocriniennes, nutritionnelles et métaboliques								
Total.........	1	1	1	1	1 111	30.7	1 578	41.3
Diabetes mellitus — Diabète sucré.............	1	1	1	1	1 074	29.7	1 501	39.3
Malnutrition — Malnutrition.............	...	...	...	...	4	◆0.1	5	◆0.1
Mental and behavioural disorders — Troubles mentaux et du comportement	-	-	-	-	487	13.5	264	6.9
Diseases of the nervous system — Maladies du système nerveux...........	-	-	-	-	660	18.2	552	14.4
Diseases of the circulatory system — Maladies de l'appareil circulatoire								
Total.........	37	40	49	50	27 969	773.0	32 715	855.8
Acute rheumatic fever and chronic rheumatic heart diseases — Rhumatisme articularie aigu et cardiopathies rhumatismales chroniques.............	1	-	-	-	35	1.0	55	1.4
Hypertensive diseases — Maladies hypertensives.............	2	-	-	2	1 223	33.8	2 000	52.3
Ischaemic heart disease — Cardiopathie ischémique.............	6	2	6	3	7 610	210.3	6 466	169.1

	San Marino - Saint-Marin				Serbia - Serbie			
	2002 (+U)		2005 (+U)		2005 (+C)			
Cause of death — Cause de décès	Male — Masculin	Female — Féminin	Male — Masculin	Female — Féminin	Male — Masculin		Female — Féminin	
	Number Nombre	Number Nombre	Number Nombre	Number Nombre	Number Nombre	Rate Taux	Number Nombre	Rate Taux
Cerebrovascular disease — Maladie cérébrovasculaire	12	15	12	16	7 752	214.3	9 852	257.7
Diseases of arteries, arterioles and capillaries — Maladies des artères, artérioles et capillaires	-	1	...	...	942	26.0	1 106	28.9
Diseases of the respiratory system — Maladies de l'appareil respiratoire								
Total	3	6	3	1	2 692	74.4	1 564	40.9
Influenza — Grippe	...	...	...	...	1	◆0.0	3	◆0.1
Pneumonia — Pneumopathies	2	4	2	1	357	9.9	282	7.4
Chronic lower respiratory diseases — Maladies chroniques des voies respiratoires inférieures	1	2	1	-	1 884	52.1	958	25.1
Diseases of the digestive system — Maladies de l'appareil digestif								
Total	-	2	-	1	2 055	56.8	1 525	39.9
Gastric and duodenal ulcer — Ulcère de l'estomac et du duodénum	...	...	...	...	323	8.9	248	6.5
Diseases of the liver — Maladies du foie	-	2	-	1	815	22.5	277	7.2
Diseases of the musculoskeletal system and connective tissue — Maladies du système ostéo-articularie, des muscles et du tissu conjonctif	-	-	-	-	39	1.1	99	2.6
Diseases of the genitourinary system — Maladies de l'appareil génito-urinaire								
Total	-	-	-	-	977	27.0	724	18.9
Disorders of kidney and ureter — Affections du rein et de l'uretère	...	...	...	...	817	22.6	708	18.5
Hyperplasia of prostate — Hyperplasie de la prostate	...	..	...	..	137	10.9	..	..
Pregnancy, childbirth and the puerperium — Grossesse, accouchement et puerpéralité								
Total	..	-	..	-	..	..	10	◆13.9
Pregnancy with abortive outcome — Grossesse se terminant par un avortement	..	-	..	-	..	..	-	-
Other direct obstetric causes — Autres décès maternels directs	..	-	..	-	..	..	10	◆13.9
Indirect obstetric causes — Décès maternels indirects	..	-	..	-	..	..	-	-
Certain conditions originating in the perinatal period — Certaines affections dont l'origine se situe dans la période périnatale	1	1	-	-	218	586.7	135	385.5
Congenital malformations, deformations and chromosomal abnormalities — Malformations congénitales et anomalies chromosomiques	-	1	-	-	96	258.4	69	197.0
Symptoms, signs and abnormal clinical and laboratory findings, not elsewhere classified — Symptômes, signes et résultats anormaux d'examens cliniques et de laboratoire, non classés ailleurs	17	13	7	12	3 420	94.5	3 133	82.0
All other diseases — Toutes autres maladies	-	-	-	-	20	◆0.6	31	0.8
External causes — Causes externes								
Total	7	2	7	1	2 795	77.3	1 014	26.5
Accidents								
Total	2	1	6	1	1 320	36.5	397	10.4
Transport accidents — Accidents de transport	2	1	6	1	592	16.4	176	4.6
Falls — Chutes	-	-	-	-	115	3.2	44	1.2
Accidental drowning and submersion — Noyade et submersion accidentelles	...	...	...	...	76	2.1	26	◆0.7
Exposure to smoke, fire and flames — Exposition à la fumée, au feu et aux flammes	-	-	-	-	38	1.1	28	◆0.7
Accidental poisoning by and exposure to noxious substances — Intoxication accidentelle par des substances nocives et exposition à ces substances	-	-	-	-	58	1.6	12	◆0.3
Intentional self-harm — Lésions auto-infligées	5	-	1	-	1 010	27.9	432	11.3
Assault — Agresssions	-	1	-	-	116	3.2	46	1.2
All other external causes — Toutes autres causes externes	-	-	-	-	349	9.6	139	3.6

Cause of death — Cause de décès	Serbia - Serbie 2006 (+C)				Slovakia - Slovaquie 2004 (C)			
	Male — Masculin		Female — Féminin		Male — Masculin		Female — Féminin	
	Number Nombre	Rate Taux	Number Nombre	Rate Taux	Number Nombre	Rate Taux	Number Nombre	Rate Taux
TOTAL	52 325	1 452.0	50 559	1 327.7	27 304	1 045.2	24 548	886.1
Certain infectious and parasitic diseases — Certaines maladies infectieuses et parasitaires								
Total	270	7.5	181	4.8	138	5.3	96	3.5
Intestinal infectious diseases — Maladies infectieuses intestinales	3	♦0.1	6	♦0.2	4	♦0.2	6	♦0.2
Tuberculosis — Tuberculose	126	3.5	59	1.5	39	1.5	12	♦0.4
Tetanus — Tétanos	2	♦0.1	4	♦0.1	-	-	-	-
Diphtheria — Diphtérie	-	-	-	-	-	-	-	-
Whooping cough — Coqueluche	-	-	-	-	-	-	-	-
Meningococcal infection — Infection à méningocoques	4	♦0.1	-	-	1	♦0.0	-	-
Septicaemia — Septicémie	63	1.7	57	1.5	69	2.6	64	2.3
Acute poliomyelitis — Poliomyélite aiguë	-	-	-	-	-	-	-	-
Measles — Rougeole	-	-	-	-	-	-	-	-
Viral hepatitis — Hépatite virale	26	♦0.7	26	♦0.7	7	♦0.3	7	♦0.3
Human immunodeficiency virus [HIV] disease — Maladies dues au virus de l'immunodéficience humaine (VIH)	19	♦0.5	6	♦0.2	2	♦0.1	1	♦0.0
Malaria — Paludisme	-	-	-	-	-	-	-	-
Neoplasms — Tumeurs	11 686	324.3	8 858	232.6	6 812	260.8	4 864	175.6
Malignant neoplasms — Tumeurs malignes								
Total	11 495	319.0	8 722	229.1	6 762	258.9	4 819	174.0
Malignant neoplasm of lip, oral cavity and pharynx — Tumeur maligne de la lèvre, de la cavité buccale et du pharynx	389	10.8	114	3.0	551	21.1	50	1.8
Malignant neoplasm of oesophagus — Tumeur maligne de l'oesophage	188	5.2	58	1.5	219	8.4	32	1.2
Malignant neoplasm of stomach — Tumeur maligne de l'estomac	665	18.5	402	10.6	469	18.0	302	10.9
Malignant neoplasm of colon, rectosigmoid junction, rectum, anus and anal canal — Tumeur maligne du côlon, de la jonction recto-sigmoïdienne, du rectum, de l'anus et du canal anal	1 371	38.0	1 051	27.6	1 050	40.2	730	26.4
Malignant neoplasm of liver and intrahepatic bile ducts — Tumeur maligne du foie et des voies bilaires intrahépatiques	471	13.1	333	8.7	196	7.5	153	5.5
Malignant neoplasm of pancreas — Tumeur maligne du pancréas	520	14.4	390	10.2	301	11.5	254	9.2
Malignant neoplasm of trachea, bronchus and lung — Tumeur maligne de la trachée, des bronches et du poumon	3 713	103.0	1 142	30.0	1 657	63.4	389	14.0
Malignant neoplasm of female breast — Tumeur maligne du sein chez la femme	..	..	1 574	48.5	..	..	795	34.3
Malignant neoplasm of cervix uteri — Tumeur maligne du col de l'utérus	..	..	481	14.8	..	..	164	7.1
Malignant neoplasm of prostate — Tumeur maligne de la prostate	901	71.3	..	..	481	72.4	..	..
Malignant neoplasm of lymphoid, haematopoietic and related tissue — Tumeurs malignes primitives ou présumées primitives des tissus lymphoïde, hématopoïétique et apparentés	579	16.1	496	13.0	403	15.4	338	12.2
Disorders of the blood and blood-forming organs and certain disorders involving the immune mechanism — Maladies du sang et des organes hématopoïétiques et certains troubles du système immunitaire								
Total	86	2.4	82	2.2	32	1.2	33	1.2
Anaemias — Anémies	45	1.2	53	1.4	11	♦0.4	15	♦0.5
Endocrine, nutritional and metabolic diseases — Maladies endocriniennes, nutritionnelles et métaboliques								
Total	1 110	30.8	1 530	40.2	321	12.3	464	16.7
Diabetes mellitus — Diabète sucré	1 068	29.6	1 473	38.7	305	11.7	443	16.0
Malnutrition — Malnutrition	12	♦0.3	4	♦0.1	1	♦0.0	2	♦0.1
Mental and behavioural disorders — Troubles mentaux et du comportement	412	11.4	285	7.5	7	♦0.3	7	♦0.3
Diseases of the nervous system — Maladies du système nerveux	635	17.6	507	13.3	353	13.5	255	9.2
Diseases of the circulatory system — Maladies de l'appareil circulatoire								
Total	27 190	754.5	31 735	833.4	13 042	499.3	15 007	541.7
Acute rheumatic fever and chronic rheumatic heart diseases — Rhumatisme articularie aigu et cardiopathies rhumatismales chroniques	42	1.2	68	1.8	45	1.7	73	2.6
Hypertensive diseases — Maladies hypertensives	1 263	35.0	1 994	52.4	1 355	51.9	1 822	65.8
Ischaemic heart disease — Cardiopathie ischémique	7 382	204.8	6 390	167.8	7 216	276.2	8 040	290.2
Cerebrovascular disease — Maladie cérébrovasculaire	7 557	209.7	9 840	258.4	2 096	80.2	2 650	95.7

Cause of death — Cause de décès	Serbia - Serbie 2006 (+C)				Slovakia - Slovaquie 2004 (C)			
	Male — Masculin		Female — Féminin		Male — Masculin		Female — Féminin	
	Number Nombre	Rate Taux	Number Nombre	Rate Taux	Number Nombre	Rate Taux	Number Nombre	Rate Taux
Diseases of arteries, arterioles and capillaries — Maladies des artères, artérioles et capillaires	848	23.5	1 013	26.6	1 060	40.6	1 101	39.7
Diseases of the respiratory system — Maladies de l'appareil respiratoire								
Total	2 344	65.0	1 417	37.2	1 701	65.1	1 252	45.2
Influenza — Grippe	-	-	1	♦0.0	6	♦0.2	11	♦0.4
Pneumonia — Pneumopathies	321	8.9	268	7.0	885	33.9	761	27.5
Chronic lower respiratory diseases — Maladies chroniques des voies respiratoires inférieures	1 537	42.7	803	21.1	551	21.1	242	8.7
Diseases of the digestive system — Maladies de l'appareil digestif								
Total	1 945	54.0	1 355	35.6	1 590	60.9	1 065	38.4
Gastric and duodenal ulcer — Ulcère de l'estomac et du duodénum	323	9.0	264	6.9	164	6.3	103	3.7
Diseases of the liver — Maladies du foie	796	22.1	233	6.1	964	36.9	467	16.9
Diseases of the musculoskeletal system and connective tissue — Maladies du système ostéo-articulaire, des muscles et du tissu conjonctif	36	1.0	127	3.3	16	♦0.6	32	1.2
Diseases of the genitourinary system — Maladies de l'appareil génito-urinaire								
Total	980	27.2	768	20.2	366	14.0	378	13.6
Disorders of kidney and ureter — Affections du rein et de l'uretère	861	23.9	756	19.9	340	13.0	371	13.4
Hyperplasia of prostate — Hyperplasie de la prostate	93	7.4	..	..	12	♦1.8	..	..
Pregnancy, childbirth and the puerperium — Grossesse, accouchement et puerpéralité								
Total	..	..	9	♦12.7	..	..	3	♦5.6
Pregnancy with abortive outcome — Grossesse se terminant par un avortement	..	..	-	-	..	..	-	-
Other direct obstetric causes — Autres décès maternels directs	..	..	8	♦11.3	..	..	3	♦5.6
Indirect obstetric causes — Décès maternels indirects	..	..	1	♦1.4	..	..	-	-
Certain conditions originating in the perinatal period — Certaines affections dont l'origine se situe dans la période périnatale	194	530.1	130	377.9	93	336.4	75	287.3
Congenital malformations, deformations and chromosomal abnormalities — Malformations congénitales et anomalies chromosomiques	88	240.4	82	238.4	75	271.3	66	252.9
Symptoms, signs and abnormal clinical and laboratory findings, not elsewhere classified — Symptômes, signes et résultats anormaux d'examens cliniques et de laboratoire, non classés ailleurs	2 552	70.8	2 361	62.0	369	14.1	277	10.0
All other diseases — Toutes autres maladies	25	♦0.7	35	0.9	1	♦0.0	-	-
External causes — Causes externes								
Total	2 772	76.9	1 097	28.8	2 388	91.4	674	24.3
Accidents								
Total	1 403	38.9	530	13.9	1 515	58.0	433	15.6
Transport accidents — Accidents de transport	675	18.7	214	5.6	610	23.4	159	5.7
Falls — Chutes	179	5.0	90	2.4	300	11.5	104	3.8
Accidental drowning and submersion — Noyade et submersion accidentelles	83	2.3	21	♦0.6	123	4.7	26	♦0.9
Exposure to smoke, fire and flames — Exposition à la fumée, au feu et aux flammes	43	1.2	30	♦0.8	28	♦1.1	21	♦0.8
Accidental poisoning by and exposure to noxious substances — Intoxication accidentelle par des substances nocives et exposition à ces substances	39	1.1	25	♦0.7	110	4.2	29	♦1.0
Intentional self-harm — Lésions auto-infligées	1 022	28.4	422	11.1	564	21.6	112	4.0
Assault — Agresssions	106	2.9	48	1.3	62	2.4	33	1.2
All other external causes — Toutes autres causes externes	241	6.7	97	2.5	247	9.5	96	3.5

Cause of death — Cause de décès	Slovakia - Slovaquie 2005 (C)				Slovenia - Slovénie 2005 (C)			
	Male — Masculin		Female — Féminin		Male — Masculin		Female — Féminin	
	Number Nombre	Rate Taux	Number Nombre	Rate Taux	Number Nombre	Rate Taux	Number Nombre	Rate Taux
TOTAL	28 151	1 076.6	25 324	913.4	9 413	960.4	9 412	921.8
Certain infectious and parasitic diseases — Certaines maladies infectieuses et parasitaires								
Total	117	4.5	114	4.1	81	8.3	121	11.9
Intestinal infectious diseases — Maladies infectieuses intestinales	5	✦0.2	3	✦0.1	4	✦0.4	2	✦0.2
Tuberculosis — Tuberculose	35	1.3	12	✦0.4	8	✦0.8	9	✦0.9
Tetanus — Tétanos	-	-	-	-	-	-	-	-
Diphtheria — Diphtérie	-	-	-	-	-	-	-	-
Whooping cough — Coqueluche	-	-	-	-	-	-	-	-
Meningococcal infection — Infection à méningocoques	3	✦0.1	1	✦0.0	1	✦0.1	-	-
Septicaemia — Septicémie	61	2.3	80	2.9	46	4.7	92	9.0
Acute poliomyelitis — Poliomyélite aiguë	-	-	-	-	-	-	-	-
Measles — Rougeole	-	-	-	-	-	-	-	-
Viral hepatitis — Hépatite virale	5	✦0.2	9	✦0.3	9	✦0.9	7	✦0.7
Human immunodeficiency virus [HIV] disease — Maladies dues au virus de l'immunodéficience humaine (VIH)	-	-	-	-	1	✦0.1	2	✦0.2
Malaria — Paludisme	-	-	-	-	-	-	-	-
Neoplasms — Tumeurs	6 944	265.6	4 930	177.8	2 839	289.7	2 355	230.6
Malignant neoplasms — Tumeurs malignes								
Total	6 906	264.1	4 888	176.3	2 807	286.4	2 299	225.2
Malignant neoplasm of lip, oral cavity and pharynx — Tumeur maligne de la lèvre, de la cavité buccale et du pharynx	529	20.2	67	2.4	114	11.6	17	✦1.7
Malignant neoplasm of oesophagus — Tumeur maligne de l'oesophage	227	8.7	25	✦0.9	74	7.6	14	✦1.4
Malignant neoplasm of stomach — Tumeur maligne de l'estomac	419	16.0	318	11.5	209	21.3	147	14.4
Malignant neoplasm of colon, rectosigmoid junction, rectum, anus and anal canal — Tumeur maligne du côlon, de la jonction recto-sigmoïdienne, du rectum, de l'anus et du canal anal	1 052	40.2	720	26.0	335	34.2	317	31.0
Malignant neoplasm of liver and Intrahepatic bile ducts — Tumeur maligne du foie et des voies bilaires intrahépatiques	205	7.8	149	5.4	93	9.5	40	3.9
Malignant neoplasm of pancreas — Tumeur maligne du pancréas	352	13.5	315	11.4	106	10.8	154	15.1
Malignant neoplasm of trachea, bronchus and lung — Tumeur maligne de la trachée, des bronches et du poumon	1 715	65.6	374	13.5	805	82.1	274	26.8
Malignant neoplasm of female breast — Tumeur maligne du sein chez la femme	..	..	707	30.3	..	..	389	44.1
Malignant neoplasm of cervix uteri — Tumeur maligne du col de l'utérus	..	..	209	9.0	..	..	39	4.4
Malignant neoplasm of prostate — Tumeur maligne de la prostate	541	79.4	..	..	305	98.7	..	..
Malignant neoplasm of lymphoid, haematopoietic and related tissue — Tumeurs malignes primitives ou présumées primitives des tissus lymphoïde, hématopoïétique et apparentés	371	14.2	370	13.3	168	17.1	163	16.0
Disorders of the blood and blood-forming organs and certain disorders involving the immune mechanism — Maladies du sang et des organes hématopoïétiques et certains troubles du système immunitaire								
Total	30	✦1.1	25	✦0.9	13	✦1.3	18	✦1.8
Anaemias — Anémies	8	✦0.3	12	✦0.4	6	✦0.6	12	✦1.2
Endocrine, nutritional and metabolic diseases — Maladies endocriniennes, nutritionnelles et métaboliques								
Total	330	12.6	435	15.7	219	22.3	318	31.1
Diabetes mellitus — Diabète sucré	310	11.9	412	14.9	210	21.4	309	30.3
Malnutrition — Malnutrition	2	✦0.1	-	-	-	-	-	-
Mental and behavioural disorders — Troubles mentaux et du comportement	0	✦0.3	2	✦0.1	97	9.9	68	6.7
Diseases of the nervous system — Maladies du système nerveux	366	14.0	316	11.4	96	9.8	124	12.1
Diseases of the circulatory system — Maladies de l'appareil circulatoire								
Total	13 434	513.7	15 615	563.2	3 295	336.2	4 353	426.3
Acute rheumatic fever and chronic rheumatic heart diseases — Rhumatisme articulaire aigu et cardiopathies rhumatismales chroniques	41	1.6	62	2.2	13	✦1.3	41	4.0
Hypertensive diseases — Maladies hypertensives	1 401	53.6	1 839	66.3	178	18.2	343	33.6
Ischaemic heart disease — Cardiopathie ischémique	7 064	270.1	8 201	295.8	1 128	115.1	1 010	98.9
Cerebrovascular disease — Maladie cérébrovasculaire	1 946	74.4	2 375	85.7	728	74.3	981	96.1

	Slovakia - Slovaquie				Slovenia - Slovénie			
	2005 (C)				2005 (C)			
Cause of death — Cause de décès	Male — Masculin		Female — Féminin		Male — Masculin		Female — Féminin	
	Number Nombre	Rate Taux	Number Nombre	Rate Taux	Number Nombre	Rate Taux	Number Nombre	Rate Taux
Diseases of arteries, arterioles and capillaries — Maladies des artères, artérioles et capillaires	1 759	67.3	1 948	70.3	204	20.8	294	28.8
Diseases of the respiratory system — Maladies de l'appareil respiratoire								
Total	1 782	68.1	1 327	47.9	758	77.3	641	62.8
Influenza — Grippe	8	♦0.3	11	♦0.4	2	♦0.2	6	♦0.6
Pneumonia — Pneumopathies	953	36.4	857	30.9	341	34.8	371	36.3
Chronic lower respiratory diseases — Maladies chroniques des voies respiratoires inférieures	597	22.8	278	10.0	346	35.3	177	17.3
Diseases of the digestive system — Maladies de l'appareil digestif								
Total	1 666	63.7	1 116	40.3	603	61.5	452	44.3
Gastric and duodenal ulcer — Ulcère de l'estomac et du duodénum	138	5.3	114	4.1	42	4.3	60	5.9
Diseases of the liver — Maladies du foie	1 080	41.3	491	17.7	381	38.9	156	15.3
Diseases of the musculoskeletal system and connective tissue — Maladies du système ostéo-articularie, des muscles et du tissu conjonctif	21	♦0.8	30	♦1.1	8	♦0.8	34	3.3
Diseases of the genitourinary system — Maladies de l'appareil génito-urinaire								
Total	339	13.0	357	12.9	103	10.5	166	16.3
Disorders of kidney and ureter — Affections du rein et de l'uretère	301	11.5	343	12.4	91	9.3	131	12.8
Hyperplasia of prostate — Hyperplasie de la prostate	11	♦1.6	..	..	1	♦0.3	..	..
Pregnancy, childbirth and the puerperium — Grossesse, accouchement et puerpéralité								
Total	..	..	2	♦3.7	..	..	1	♦5.5
Pregnancy with abortive outcome — Grossesse se terminant par un avortement	..	..	-	-	..	..	-	-
Other direct obstetric causes — Autres décès maternels directs	..	..	2	♦3.7	..	..	1	♦5.5
Indirect obstetric causes — Décès maternels indirects	..	..	-	-	..	..	-	-
Certain conditions originating in the perinatal period — Certaines affections dont l'origine se situe dans la période périnatale	91	325.2	71	268.4	27	♦288.6	20	♦227.2
Congenital malformations, deformations and chromosomal abnormalities — Malformations congénitales et anomalies chromosomiques	90	321.7	67	253.3	18	♦192.4	22	♦249.9
Symptoms, signs and abnormal clinical and laboratory findings, not elsewhere classified — Symptômes, signes et résultats anormaux d'examens cliniques et de laboratoire, non classés ailleurs	472	18.1	240	8.7	275	28.1	246	24.1
All other diseases — Toutes autres maladies	4	♦0.2	1	♦0.0	8	♦0.8	11	♦1.1
External causes — Causes externes								
Total	2 456	93.9	676	24.4	973	99.3	462	45.2
Accidents								
Total	1 617	61.8	468	16.9	470	48.0	272	26.6
Transport accidents — Accidents de transport	594	22.7	170	6.1	203	20.7	74	7.2
Falls — Chutes	350	13.4	122	4.4	167	17.0	154	15.1
Accidental drowning and submersion — Noyade et submersion accidentelles	111	4.2	27	♦1.0	13	♦1.3	4	♦0.4
Exposure to smoke, fire and flames — Exposition à la fumée, au feu et aux flammes	27	♦1.0	24	♦0.9	4	♦0.4	5	♦0.5
Accidental poisoning by and exposure to noxious substances — Intoxication accidentelle par des substances nocives et exposition à ces substances	130	5.0	32	1.2	21	♦2.1	5	♦0.5
Intentional self-harm — Lésions auto-infligées	584	22.3	95	3.4	391	39.9	112	11.0
Assault — Agresssions	59	2.3	30	♦1.1	14	♦1.4	9	♦0.9
All other external causes — Toutes autres causes externes	196	7.5	83	3.0	98	10.0	69	6.8

21. Death and death rates by cause and sex: 2002 - 2006
Décès et taux de mortalité par cause et sexe : 2002 - 2006 (continued - suite)

Cause of death — Cause de décès	Slovenia - Slovénie 2006 (C) Male — Masculin Number Nombre	Male — Masculin Rate Taux	Female — Féminin Number Nombre	Female — Féminin Rate Taux	Spain - Espagne 2004 (C) Male — Masculin Number Nombre	Male — Masculin Rate Taux	Female — Féminin Number Nombre	Female — Féminin Rate Taux
TOTAL	9 270	940.3	8 910	871.3	194 928	928.8	177 006	815.5
Certain infectious and parasitic diseases — Certaines maladies infectieuses et parasitaires								
Total	61	6.2	90	8.8	4 080	19.4	3 135	14.4
Intestinal infectious diseases — Maladies infectieuses intestinales	1	♦0.1	3	♦0.3	158	0.8	264	1.2
Tuberculosis — Tuberculose	7	♦0.7	11	♦1.1	233	1.1	101	0.5
Tetanus — Tétanos	-	-	-	-	3	♦0.0	1	♦0.0
Diphtheria — Diphtérie	-	-	-	-	-	-	-	-
Whooping cough — Coqueluche	-	-	-	-	1	♦0.0	1	♦0.0
Meningococcal infection — Infection à méningocoques	-	-	-	-	20	♦0.1	42	0.2
Septicaemia — Septicémie	41	4.2	60	5.9	1 406	6.7	1 611	7.4
Acute poliomyelitis — Poliomyélite aiguë	-	-	-	-	-	-	-	-
Measles — Rougeole	-	-	-	-	-	-	1	♦0.0
Viral hepatitis — Hépatite virale	5	♦0.5	5	♦0.5	587	2.8	527	2.4
Human immunodeficiency virus [HIV] disease — Maladies dues au virus de l'immunodéficience humaine (VIH)	-	-	-	-	1 271	6.1	280	1.3
Malaria — Paludisme	-	-	-	-	4	♦0.0	2	♦0.0
Neoplasms — Tumeurs	2 961	300.3	2 384	233.1	62 937	299.9	37 548	173.0
Malignant neoplasms — Tumeurs malignes								
Total	2 931	297.3	2 342	229.0	61 146	291.3	35 994	165.8
Malignant neoplasm of lip, oral cavity and pharynx — Tumeur maligne de la lèvre, de la cavité buccale et du pharynx	125	12.7	23	♦2.2	1 792	8.5	436	2.0
Malignant neoplasm of oesophagus — Tumeur maligne de l'oesophage	65	6.6	15	♦1.5	1 591	7.6	241	1.1
Malignant neoplasm of stomach — Tumeur maligne de l'estomac	208	21.1	129	12.6	3 611	17.2	2 200	10.1
Malignant neoplasm of colon, rectosigmoid junction, rectum, anus and anal canal — Tumeur maligne du côlon, de la jonction recto-sigmoïdienne, du rectum, de l'anus et du canal anal	381	38.6	308	30.1	7 412	35.3	5 559	25.6
Malignant neoplasm of liver and intrahepatic bile ducts — Tumeur maligne du foie et des voies bilaires intrahépatiques	98	9.9	61	6.0	2 918	13.9	1 517	7.0
Malignant neoplasm of pancreas — Tumeur maligne du pancréas	144	14.6	161	15.7	2 445	11.6	2 104	9.7
Malignant neoplasm of trachea, bronchus and lung — Tumeur maligne de la trachée, des bronches et du poumon	800	81.1	257	25.1	16 651	79.3	2 441	11.2
Malignant neoplasm of female breast — Tumeur maligne du sein chez la femme	..	..	399	45.0	..	..	5 833	31.2
Malignant neoplasm of cervix uteri — Tumeur maligne du col de l'utérus	..	..	62	7.0	..	..	539	2.9
Malignant neoplasm of prostate — Tumeur maligne de la prostate	338	106.5	..	..	5 694	88.5	..	..
Malignant neoplasm of lymphoid, haematopoietic and related tissue — Tumeurs malignes primitives ou présumées primitives des tissus lymphoïde, hématopoïétique et apparentés	188	19.1	197	19.3	3 939	18.8	3 431	15.8
Disorders of the blood and blood-forming organs and certain disorders involving the immune mechanism — Maladies du sang et des organes hématopoïétiques et certains troubles du système immunitaire								
Total	11	♦1.1	10	♦1.0	548	2.6	743	3.4
Anaemias — Anémies	5	♦0.5	3	♦0.3	304	1.4	529	2.4
Endocrine, nutritional and metabolic diseases — Maladies endocriniennes, nutritionnelles et métaboliques								
Total	177	18.0	239	23.4	4 668	22.2	7 250	33.4
Diabetes mellitus — Diabète sucré	164	16.6	227	22.2	3 924	18.7	6 042	27.8
Malnutrition — Malnutrition	-	-	-	-	44	0.2	71	0.3
Mental and behavioural disorders — Troubles mentaux et du comportement	81	8.2	61	6.0	4 066	19.4	7 812	36.0
Diseases of the nervous system — Maladies du système nerveux	109	11.1	114	11.1	5 622	26.8	8 486	39.1
Diseases of the circulatory system — Maladies de l'appareil circulatoire								
Total	3 110	315.5	4 116	402.5	56 359	268.5	67 508	311.0
Acute rheumatic fever and chronic rheumatic heart diseases — Rhumatisme articulaire aigu et cardiopathies rhumatismales chroniques	33	3.3	48	4.7	433	2.1	1 138	5.2
Hypertensive diseases — Maladies hypertensives	210	21.3	402	39.3	1 965	9.4	4 241	19.5
Ischaemic heart disease — Cardiopathie ischémique	1 016	103.1	875	85.6	21 898	104.3	16 942	78.1
Cerebrovascular disease — Maladie cérébrovasculaire	664	67.4	858	83.9	14 201	67.7	20 049	92.4

Cause of death — Cause de décès	Slovenia - Slovénie 2006 (C)				Spain - Espagne 2004 (C)			
	Male — Masculin		Female — Féminin		Male — Masculin		Female — Féminin	
	Number Nombre	Rate Taux	Number Nombre	Rate Taux	Number Nombre	Rate Taux	Number Nombre	Rate Taux
Diseases of arteries, arterioles and capillaries — Maladies des artères, artérioles et capillaires	196	19.9	270	26.4	3 562	17.0	2 894	13.3
Diseases of the respiratory system — Maladies de l'appareil respiratoire								
Total..........	645	65.4	593	58.0	23 182	110.5	15 967	73.6
Influenza — Grippe	-	-	4	♦0.4	28	♦0.1	59	0.3
Pneumonia — Pneumopathies	304	30.8	352	34.4	3 847	18.3	3 509	16.2
Chronic lower respiratory diseases — Maladies chroniques des voies respiratoires inférieures	262	26.6	150	14.7	11 583	55.2	3 934	18.1
Diseases of the digestive system — Maladies de l'appareil digestif								
Total..........	620	62.9	420	41.1	10 444	49.8	8 913	41.1
Gastric and duodenal ulcer — Ulcère de l'estomac et du duodénum	49	5.0	40	3.9	345	1.6	265	1.2
Diseases of the liver — Maladies du foie	414	42.0	171	16.7	4 467	21.3	2 034	9.4
Diseases of the musculoskeletal system and connective tissue — Maladies du système ostéo-articularie, des muscles et du tissu conjonctif	10	♦1.0	36	3.5	1 072	5.1	2 474	11.4
Diseases of the genitourinary system — Maladies de l'appareil génito-urinaire								
Total..........	127	12.9	182	17.8	4 054	19.3	4 480	20.6
Disorders of kidney and ureter — Affections du rein et de l'uretère	117	11.9	150	14.7	3 022	14.4	3 146	14.5
Hyperplasia of prostate — Hyperplasie de la prostate..........	-	-	..	..	100	1.6	..	..
Pregnancy, childbirth and the puerperium — Grossesse, accouchement et puerpéralité								
Total..........	..	..	3	♦15.8	..	..	21	♦4.6
Pregnancy with abortive outcome — Grossesse se terminant par un avortement	..	..	-	-	..	..	2	♦0.4
Other direct obstetric causes — Autres décès maternels directs	..	..	3	♦15.8	..	..	17	♦3.7
Indirect obstetric causes — Décès maternels indirects..........	..	..	-	-	..	..	2	♦0.4
Certain conditions originating in the perinatal period — Certaines affections dont l'origine se situe dans la période périnatale	23	♦235.6	19	♦207.2	574	244.4	428	194.8
Congenital malformations, deformations and chromosomal abnormalities — Malformations congénitales et anomalies chromosomiques	19	♦194.6	15	♦163.6	558	237.6	444	202.1
Symptoms, signs and abnormal clinical and laboratory findings, not elsewhere classified — Symptômes, signes et résultats anormaux d'examens cliniques et de laboratoire, non classés ailleurs	214	21.7	135	13.2	4 589	21.9	5 919	27.3
All other diseases — Toutes autres maladies..........	1	♦0.1	4	♦0.4	338	1.6	671	3.1
External causes — Causes externes								
Total..........	1 101	111.7	489	47.8	11 837	56.4	5 207	24.0
Accidents								
Total..........	575	58.3	314	30.7	8 442	40.2	3 793	17.5
Transport accidents — Accidents de transport	243	24.6	50	4.9	4 087	19.5	1 200	5.5
Falls — Chutes	209	21.2	228	22.3	967	4.6	701	3.2
Accidental drowning and submersion — Noyade et submersion accidentelles..........	18	♦1.8	7	♦0.7	475	2.3	97	0.4
Exposure to smoke, fire and flames — Exposition à la fumée, au feu et aux flammes	4	♦0.4	3	♦0.3	130	0.6	88	0.4
Accidental poisoning by and exposure to noxious substances — Intoxication accidentelle par des substances nocives et exposition à ces substances	20	♦2.0	8	♦0.8	566	2.7	170	0.8
Intentional self-harm — Lésions auto-infligées..........	415	42.1	114	11.1	2 651	12.6	856	3.9
Assault — Agresssions	9	♦0.9	4	♦0.4	374	1.8	211	1.0
All other external causes — Toutes autres causes externes..........	102	10.3	57	5.6	370	1.8	347	1.6

Cause of death — Cause de décès	Spain - Espagne				Sweden - Suède			
	2005 (C)				2004 (C)			
	Male — Masculin		Female — Féminin		Male — Masculin		Female — Féminin	
	Number Nombre	Rate Taux	Number Nombre	Rate Taux	Number Nombre	Rate Taux	Number Nombre	Rate Taux
TOTAL...........	201 769	944.3	185 586	842.4	44 192	991.6	46 887	1 033.4
Certain infectious and parasitic diseases — Certaines maladies infectieuses et parasitaires								
Total...........	4 257	19.9	3 236	14.7	550	12.3	605	13.3
Intestinal infectious diseases — Maladies infectieuses intestinales...........	165	0.8	266	1.2	22	◆0.5	34	0.7
Tuberculosis — Tuberculose...........	249	1.2	100	0.5	6	◆0.1	10	◆0.2
Tetanus — Tétanos...........	-	-	2	◆0.0	-	-	-	-
Diphtheria — Diphtérie...........	-	-	-	-	-	-	-	-
Whooping cough — Coqueluche...........	1	◆0.0	-	-	1	◆0.0	-	-
Meningococcal infection — Infection à méningocoques...........	27	◆0.1	28	◆0.1	2	◆0.0	4	◆0.1
Septicaemia — Septicémie...........	1 674	7.8	1 745	7.9	255	5.7	217	4.8
Acute poliomyelitis — Poliomyélite aiguë...........	-	-	-	-	-	-	-	-
Measles — Rougeole...........	-	-	3	◆0.0	-	-	-	-
Viral hepatitis — Hépatite virale...........	552	2.6	515	2.3	32	0.7	16	◆0.4
Human immunodeficiency virus [HIV] disease — Maladies dues au virus de l'immunodéficience humaine (VIH)...........	1 168	5.5	282	1.3	18	◆0.4	2	◆0.0
Malaria — Paludisme...........	-	-	1	◆0.0	2	◆0.0	1	◆0.0
Neoplasms — Tumeurs...........	62 664	293.3	37 542	170.4	11 680	262.1	10 930	240.9
Malignant neoplasms — Tumeurs malignes								
Total...........	60 842	284.7	35 897	162.9	11 341	254.5	10 521	231.9
Malignant neoplasm of lip, oral cavity and pharynx — Tumeur maligne de la lèvre, de la cavité buccale et du pharynx...........	1 757	8.2	441	2.0	191	4.3	116	2.6
Malignant neoplasm of oesophagus — Tumeur maligne de l'oesophage...........	1 522	7.1	234	1.1	307	6.9	107	2.4
Malignant neoplasm of stomach — Tumeur maligne de l'estomac...........	3 549	16.6	2 132	9.7	476	10.7	357	7.9
Malignant neoplasm of colon, rectosigmoid junction, rectum, anus and anal canal — Tumeur maligne du côlon, de la jonction recto-sigmoïdienne, du rectum, de l'anus et du canal anal...........	7 472	35.0	5 462	24.8	1 257	28.2	1 289	28.4
Malignant neoplasm of liver and intrahepatic bile ducts — Tumeur maligne du foie et des voies bilaires intrahépatiques...........	2 881	13.5	1 465	6.6	407	9.1	237	5.2
Malignant neoplasm of pancreas — Tumeur maligne du pancréas...........	2 420	11.3	2 171	9.9	670	15.0	782	17.2
Malignant neoplasm of trachea, bronchus and lung — Tumeur maligne de la trachée, des bronches et du poumon...........	16 647	77.9	2 471	11.2	1 823	40.9	1 495	33.0
Malignant neoplasm of female breast — Tumeur maligne du sein chez la femme...........	..	..	5 727	30.2			1 572	41.8
Malignant neoplasm of cervix uteri — Tumeur maligne du col de l'utérus...........	..	..	594	3.1			159	4.2
Malignant neoplasm of prostate — Tumeur maligne de la prostate...........	5 512	83.9	..	..	2 549	164.4		
Malignant neoplasm of lymphoid, haematopoietic and related tissue — Tumeurs malignes primitives ou présumées primitives des tissus lymphoïde, hématopoïétique et apparentés...........	3 960	18.5	3 349	15.2	1 075	24.1	893	19.7
Disorders of the blood and blood-forming organs and certain disorders involving the immune mechanism — Maladies du sang et des organes hématopoïétiques et certains troubles du système immunitaire								
Total...........	558	2.6	758	3.4	101	2.3	129	2.8
Anaemias — Anémies...........	326	1.5	540	2.5	57	1.3	85	1.9
Endocrine, nutritional and metabolic diseases — Maladies endocriniennes, nutritionnelles et métaboliques								
Total...........	4 857	22.7	7 564	34.3	1 159	26.0	1 141	25.1
Diabetes mellitus — Diabète sucré...........	4 105	19.2	6 234	28.3	1 000	22.4	953	21.0
Malnutrition — Malnutrition...........	53	0.2	76	0.3	19	◆0.4	32	0.7
Mental and behavioural disorders — Troubles mentaux et du comportement	4 156	19.5	8 383	38.1	1 648	37.0	2 921	64.4
Diseases of the nervous system — Maladies du système nerveux...........	6 162	28.8	9 525	43.2	1 206	27.1	1 529	33.7
Diseases of the circulatory system — Maladies de l'appareil circulatoire								
Total...........	57 742	270.2	69 165	313.9	18 596	417.3	20 457	450.9
Acute rheumatic fever and chronic rheumatic heart diseases — Rhumatisme articulaire aigu et cardiopathies rhumatismales chroniques...........	445	2.1	1 158	5.3	43	1.0	112	2.5
Hypertensive diseases — Maladies hypertensives...........	2 121	9.9	4 540	20.6	371	8.3	650	14.3
Ischaemic heart disease — Cardiopathie ischémique...........	22 188	103.8	17 125	77.7	9 673	217.1	8 298	182.9
Cerebrovascular disease — Maladie cérébrovasculaire...........	14 611	68.4	20 139	91.4	3 696	82.9	5 379	118.6

Spain - Espagne | | | | Sweden - Suède

Cause of death — Cause de décès	2005 (C)				2004 (C)			
	Male — Masculin		Female — Féminin		Male — Masculin		Female — Féminin	
	Number Nombre	Rate Taux	Number Nombre	Rate Taux	Number Nombre	Rate Taux	Number Nombre	Rate Taux
Diseases of arteries, arterioles and capillaries — Maladies des artères, artérioles et capillaires	3 489	16.3	2 890	13.1	1 362	30.6	1 315	29.0
Diseases of the respiratory system — Maladies de l'appareil respiratoire								
Total	27 183	127.2	19 906	90.4	2 845	63.8	2 901	63.9
Influenza — Grippe	182	0.9	361	1.6	50	1.1	58	1.3
Pneumonia — Pneumopathies	4 817	22.5	4 493	20.4	1 013	22.7	1 194	26.3
Chronic lower respiratory diseases — Maladies chroniques des voies respiratoires inférieures	13 090	61.3	4 527	20.5	1 333	29.9	1 301	28.7
Diseases of the digestive system — Maladies de l'appareil digestif								
Total	10 541	49.3	9 083	41.2	1 359	30.5	1 554	34.3
Gastric and duodenal ulcer — Ulcère de l'estomac et du duodénum	344	1.6	274	1.2	167	3.7	224	4.9
Diseases of the liver — Maladies du foie	4 492	21.0	1 991	9.0	441	9.9	267	5.9
Diseases of the musculoskeletal system and connective tissue — Maladies du système ostéo-articularie, des muscles et du tissu conjonctif	1 099	5.1	2 497	11.3	130	2.9	289	6.4
Diseases of the genitourinary system — Maladies de l'appareil génito-urinaire								
Total	4 532	21.2	5 035	22.9	576	12.9	546	12.0
Disorders of kidney and ureter — Affections du rein et de l'uretère	3 367	15.8	3 464	15.7	378	8.5	346	7.6
Hyperplasia of prostate — Hyperplasie de la prostate	105	1.6	..	..	39	2.5	..	..
Pregnancy, childbirth and the puerperium — Grossesse, accouchement et puerpéralité								
Total	..	..	18	♦3.9	..	..	2	♦2.0
Pregnancy with abortive outcome — Grossesse se terminant par un avortement	..	..	-	-	..	..	-	-
Other direct obstetric causes — Autres décès maternels directs	..	..	18	♦3.9	..	..	-	-
Indirect obstetric causes — Décès maternels indirects	..	..	-	-	..	..	1	♦1.0
Certain conditions originating in the perinatal period — Certaines affections dont l'origine se situe dans la période périnatale	552	229.8	390	172.4	67	128.9	68	138.9
Congenital malformations, deformations and chromosomal abnormalities — Malformations congénitales et anomalies chromosomiques	513	213.6	449	198.5	126	242.4	138	281.9
Symptoms, signs and abnormal clinical and laboratory findings, not elsewhere classified — Symptômes, signes et résultats anormaux d'examens cliniques et de laboratoire, non classés ailleurs	4 807	22.5	6 162	28.0	925	20.8	1 644	36.2
All other diseases — Toutes autres maladies	348	1.6	769	3.5	49	1.1	92	2.0
External causes — Causes externes								
Total	11 798	55.2	5 104	23.2	3 175	71.2	1 941	42.8
Accidents								
Total	8 606	40.3	3 869	17.6	1 981	44.5	1 406	31.0
Transport accidents — Accidents de transport	3 876	18.1	1 020	4.6	402	9.0	127	2.8
Falls — Chutes	1 025	4.8	738	3.3	413	9.3	333	7.3
Accidental drowning and submersion — Noyade et submersion accidentelles	403	1.9	91	0.4	80	1.8	18	♦0.4
Exposure to smoke, fire and flames — Exposition à la fumée, au feu et aux flammes	157	0.7	66	0.3	40	0.9	21	♦0.5
Accidental poisoning by and exposure to noxious substances — Intoxication accidentelle par des substances nocives et exposition à ces substances	689	3.2	196	0.9	196	4.4	60	1.3
Intentional self-harm — Lésions auto-infligées	2 570	12.0	829	3.8	833	18.7	321	7.1
Assault — Agresssions	292	1.4	97	0.4	60	1.3	37	0.8
All other external causes — Toutes autres causes externes	330	1.5	309	1.4	301	6.8	177	3.9

Cause of death — Cause de décès	Sweden - Suède 2005 (C) Male — Masculin Number Nombre	Rate Taux	Female — Féminin Number Nombre	Rate Taux	Switzerland - Suisse 2004 (C) Male — Masculin Number Nombre	Rate Taux	Female — Féminin Number Nombre	Rate Taux
TOTAL...	44 828	1 001.4	46 947	1 031.1	28 991	801.9	31 189	826.3
Certain infectious and parasitic diseases — Certaines maladies infectieuses et parasitaires								
Total..............	667	14.9	718	15.8	297	8.2	298	7.9
Intestinal infectious diseases — Maladies infectieuses intestinales...........	45	1.0	68	1.5	10	◦0.3	31	0.8
Tuberculosis — Tuberculose.............................	6	◦0.1	9	◦0.2	9	◦0.2	7	◦0.2
Tetanus — Tétanos................................	-	-	-	-	-	-	1	◦0.0
Diphtheria — Diphtérie............................	-	-	-	-	-	-	-	-
Whooping cough — Coqueluche....................	-	-	-	-	-	-	-	-
Meningococcal infection — Infection à méningocoques	3	◦0.1	1	◦0.0	1	◦0.0	2	◦0.1
Septicaemia — Septicémie........................	295	6.6	258	5.7	86	2.4	82	2.2
Acute poliomyelitis — Poliomyélite aiguë	-	-	-	-	-	-	-	-
Measles — Rougeole............................	1	◦0.0	-	-	-	-	-	-
Viral hepatitis — Hépatite virale....................	46	1.0	21	◦0.5	10	◦0.3	10	◦0.3
Human immunodeficiency virus [HIV] disease — Maladies dues au virus de l'immunodéficience humaine (VIH)	21	◦0.5	10	◦0.2	64	1.8	19	◦0.5
Malaria — Paludisme................................	-	-	1	◦0.0	1	◦0.0	-	-
Neoplasms — Tumeurs	11 846	264.6	10 852	238.3	8 690	240.4	7 237	191.7
Malignant neoplasms — Tumeurs malignes								
Total..............	11 501	256.9	10 366	227.7	8 450	233.7	6 979	184.9
Malignant neoplasm of lip, oral cavity and pharynx — Tumeur maligne de la lèvre, de la cavité buccale et du pharynx	186	4.2	107	2.4	251	6.9	75	2.0
Malignant neoplasm of oesophagus — Tumeur maligne de l'oesophage	288	6.4	102	2.2	277	7.7	86	2.3
Malignant neoplasm of stomach — Tumeur maligne de l'estomac........	470	10.5	284	6.2	311	8.6	219	5.8
Malignant neoplasm of colon, rectosigmoid junction, rectum, anus and anal canal — Tumeur maligne du côlon, de la jonction recto-sigmoïdienne, du rectum, de l'anus et du canal anal	1 319	29.5	1 218	26.8	848	23.5	761	20.2
Malignant neoplasm of liver and intrahepatic bile ducts — Tumeur maligne du foie et des voies bilaires intrahépatiques	377	8.4	233	5.1	374	10.3	176	4.7
Malignant neoplasm of pancreas — Tumeur maligne du pancréas	694	15.5	797	17.5	437	12.1	463	12.3
Malignant neoplasm of trachea, bronchus and lung — Tumeur maligne de la trachée, des bronches et du poumon	1 938	43.3	1 567	34.4	1 935	53.5	860	22.8
Malignant neoplasm of female breast — Tumeur maligne du sein chez la femme..	..	..	1 541	40.7	..	..	1 379	43.3
Malignant neoplasm of cervix uteri — Tumeur maligne du col de l'utérus	..	..	136	3.6	..	..	94	3.0
Malignant neoplasm of prostate — Tumeur maligne de la prostate	2 451	156.4	..	..	1 306	112.7	..	..
Malignant neoplasm of lymphoid, haematopoietic and related tissue — Tumeurs malignes primitives ou présumées primitives des tissus lymphoïde, hématopoïétique et apparentés	1 026	22.9	892	19.6	727	20.1	663	17.6
Disorders of the blood and blood-forming organs and certain disorders involving the immune mechanism — Maladies du sang et des organes hématopoïétiques et certains troubles du système immunitaire								
Total..............	132	2.9	175	3.8	59	1.6	104	2.8
Anaemias — Anémies	89	2.0	129	2.8	20	◦0.6	65	1.7
Endocrine, nutritional and metabolic diseases — Maladies endocriniennes, nutritionnelles et métaboliques								
Total..............	1 136	25.4	1 228	27.0	773	21.4	1 055	28.0
Diabetes mellitus — Diabète sucré....................	963	21.5	1 016	22.3	656	18.1	907	24.0
Malnutrition — Malnutrition........................	22	◦0.5	38	0.8	5	◦0.1	14	◦0.4
Mental and behavioural disorders — Troubles mentaux et du comportement	1 638	36.6	3 035	66.7	997	27.6	1 749	46.3
Diseases of the nervous system — Maladies du système nerveux..........	1 224	27.3	1 590	34.9	1 075	29.7	1 564	41.4
Diseases of the circulatory system — Maladies de l'appareil circulatoire								
Total..............	18 734	418.5	19 885	436.7	9 888	273.5	12 563	332.8
Acute rheumatic fever and chronic rheumatic heart diseases — Rhumatisme articulaire aigu et cardiopathies rhumatismales chroniques	66	1.5	94	2.1	31	0.9	56	1.5
Hypertensive diseases — Maladies hypertensives....................	397	8.9	623	13.7	689	19.1	1 456	38.6
Ischaemic heart disease — Cardiopathie ischémique....................	9 678	216.2	8 031	176.4	4 603	127.3	4 595	121.7
Cerebrovascular disease — Maladie cérébrovasculaire....................	3 555	79.4	4 833	106.1	1 626	45.0	2 457	65.1

	Sweden — Suède				Switzerland - Suisse			
	2005 (C)				2004 (C)			
Cause of death — Cause de décès	Male — Masculin		Female — Féminin		Male — Masculin		Female — Féminin	
	Number Nombre	Rate Taux	Number Nombre	Rate Taux	Number Nombre	Rate Taux	Number Nombre	Rate Taux
Diseases of arteries, arterioles and capillaries — Maladies des artères, artérioles et capillaires	1 272	28.4	1 164	25.6	644	17.8	643	17.0
Diseases of the respiratory system — Maladies de l'appareil respiratoire								
Total	3 023	67.5	3 187	70.0	2 068	57.2	1 780	47.2
Influenza — Grippe	71	1.6	120	2.6	20	♦0.6	48	1.3
Pneumonia — Pneumopathies	1 097	24.5	1 301	28.6	617	17.1	804	21.3
Chronic lower respiratory diseases — Maladies chroniques des voies respiratoires inférieures	1 384	30.9	1 425	31.3	1 088	30.1	648	17.2
Diseases of the digestive system — Maladies de l'appareil digestif								
Total	1 494	33.4	1 404	30.8	1 074	29.7	1 179	31.2
Gastric and duodenal ulcer — Ulcère de l'estomac et du duodénum	214	4.8	151	3.3	53	1.5	93	2.5
Diseases of the liver — Maladies du foie	484	10.8	255	5.6	455	12.6	237	6.3
Diseases of the musculoskeletal system and connective tissue — Maladies du système ostéo-articularie, des muscles et du tissu conjonctif	137	3.1	325	7.1	136	3.8	398	10.5
Diseases of the genitourinary system — Maladies de l'appareil génito-urinaire								
Total	614	13.7	526	11.6	256	7.1	280	7.4
Disorders of kidney and ureter — Affections du rein et de l'uretère	404	9.0	334	7.3	132	3.7	173	4.6
Hyperplasia of prostate — Hyperplasie de la prostate	41	2.6	..	..	37	3.2		
Pregnancy, childbirth and the puerperium — Grossesse, accouchement et puerpéralité								
Total	..	..	6	♦5.9	..	..	4	♦5.5
Pregnancy with abortive outcome — Grossesse se terminant par un avortement	..	..	1	♦1.0	..	..	-	-
Other direct obstetric causes — Autres décès maternels directs	..	..	5	♦4.9	..	..	4	♦5.5
Indirect obstetric causes — Décès maternels indirects	..	..	-	-	..	..	-	-
Certain conditions originating in the perinatal period — Certaines affections dont l'origine se situe dans la période périnatale	66	126.8	48	97.3	91	243.7	71	198.6
Congenital malformations, deformations and chromosomal abnormalities — Malformations congénitales et anomalies chromosomiques	133	255.6	118	239.3	101	270.5	118	330.1
Symptoms, signs and abnormal clinical and laboratory findings, not elsewhere classified — Symptômes, signes et résultats anormaux d'examens cliniques et de laboratoire, non classés ailleurs	1 018	22.7	1 880	41.3	1 312	36.3	1 341	35.5
All other diseases — Toutes autres maladies	41	0.9	87	1.9	27	♦0.7	54	1.4
External causes — Causes externes								
Total	2 925	65.3	1 883	41.4	2 147	59.4	1 394	36.9
Accidents								
Total	1 710	38.2	1 257	27.6	1 174	32.5	892	23.6
Transport accidents — Accidents de transport	366	8.2	126	2.8	401	11.1	112	3.0
Falls — Chutes	407	9.1	381	8.4	507	14.0	630	16.7
Accidental drowning and submersion — Noyade et submersion accidentelles	82	1.8	17	♦0.4	33	0.9	15	♦0.4
Exposure to smoke, fire and flames — Exposition à la fumée, au feu et aux flammes	48	1.1	21	♦0.5	22	♦0.6	14	♦0.4
Accidental poisoning by and exposure to noxious substances — Intoxication accidentelle par des substances nocives et exposition à ces substances	231	5.2	64	1.4	13	♦0.4	7	♦0.2
Intentional self-harm — Lésions auto-infligées	835	18.7	384	8.4	856	23.7	427	11.3
Assault — Agresssions	51	1.1	31	0.7	34	0.9	33	0.9
All other external causes — Toutes autres causes externes	329	7.3	211	4.6	83	2.3	42	1.1

Cause of death — Cause de décès	Switzerland - Suisse 2005 (C)				The Former Yugoslav Rep. of Macedonia - L'ex-République yougoslave de Macédoine 2002 (C)			
	Male — Masculin		Female — Féminin		Male — Masculin		Female — Féminin	
	Number Nombre	Rate Taux	Number Nombre	Rate Taux	Number Nombre	Rate Taux	Number Nombre	Rate Taux
TOTAL..	**29 708**	**816.0**	**31 416**	**827.5**	**9 890**	**970.0**	**8 070**	**791.9**
Certain infectious and parasitic diseases — Certaines maladies infectieuses et parasitaires								
Total......................	281	7.7	293	7.7	83	8.1	54	5.3
Intestinal infectious diseases — Maladies infectieuses intestinales............	13	♦0.4	23	♦0.6	5	♦0.5	9	♦0.9
Tuberculosis — Tuberculose...................................	14	♦0.4	7	♦0.2	50	4.9	21	♦2.1
Tetanus — Tétanos.......................................	-		1	♦0.0	-		1	♦0.1
Diphtheria — Diphtérie....................................	-		-		-		-	
Whooping cough — Coqueluche............................	-		-		-		-	
Meningococcal infection — Infection à méningocoques.......	5	♦0.1	2	♦0.1	-		-	
Septicaemia — Septicémie.................................	78	2.1	90	2.4	9	♦0.9	2	♦0.2
Acute poliomyelitis — Poliomyélite aiguë.................	-		-		-		-	
Measles — Rougeole......................................	-		-		-		-	
Viral hepatitis — Hépatite virale........................	9	♦0.2	9	♦0.2	4	♦0.4	4	♦0.4
Human immunodeficiency virus [HIV] disease — Maladies dues au virus de l'immunodéficience humaine (VIH)	52	1.4	23	♦0.6	-		-	
Malaria — Paludisme.....................................	1	♦0.0			-		-	
Neoplasms — Tumeurs..................................	**8 832**	**242.6**	**7 048**	**185.6**	**1 948**	**191.1**	**1 181**	**115.9**
Malignant neoplasms — Tumeurs malignes								
Total......................	8 612	236.6	6 808	179.3	1 892	185.6	1 153	113.1
Malignant neoplasm of lip, oral cavity and pharynx — Tumeur maligne de la lèvre, de la cavité buccale et du pharynx....................	298	8.2	94	2.5	35	3.4	9	♦0.9
Malignant neoplasm of oesophagus — Tumeur maligne de l'oesophage......	304	8.4	105	2.8	22	♦2.2	4	♦0.4
Malignant neoplasm of stomach — Tumeur maligne de l'estomac............	315	8.7	227	6.0	252	24.7	119	11.7
Malignant neoplasm of colon, rectosigmoid junction, rectum, anus and anal canal — Tumeur maligne du côlon, de la jonction recto-sigmoïdienne, du rectum, de l'anus et du canal anal..........	913	25.1	720	19.0	190	18.6	116	11.4
Malignant neoplasm of liver and intrahepatic bile ducts — Tumeur maligne du foie et des voies bilaires intrahépatiques......	366	10.1	162	4.3	...	...	...	...
Malignant neoplasm of pancreas — Tumeur maligne du pancréas............	442	12.1	514	13.5	83	8.1	53	5.2
Malignant neoplasm of trachea, bronchus and lung — Tumeur maligne de la trachée, des bronches et du poumon......................	2 062	56.6	847	22.3	527	51.7	81	7.9
Malignant neoplasm of female breast — Tumeur maligne du sein chez la femme..........................	..		1 294	40.3	..		252	31.5
Malignant neoplasm of cervix uteri — Tumeur maligne du col de l'utérus......	..		88	2.7	..		46	5.8
Malignant neoplasm of prostate — Tumeur maligne de la prostate............	1 264	107.0	..	..	114	45.7	..	..
Malignant neoplasm of lymphoid, haematopoietic and related tissue — Tumeurs malignes primitives ou présumées primitives des tissus lymphoïde, hématopoïétique et apparentés......................	732	20.1	675	17.8	96	9.4	65	6.4
Disorders of the blood and blood-forming organs and certain disorders involving the immune mechanism — Maladies du sang et des organes hématopoïétiques et certains troubles du système immunitaire								
Total......................	75	2.1	101	2.7	4	♦0.4	4	♦0.4
Anaemias — Anémies.....................................	35	1.0	54	1.4	3	♦0.3	4	♦0.4
Endocrine, nutritional and metabolic diseases — Maladies endocriniennes, nutritionnelles et métaboliques								
Total......................	737	20.2	974	25.7	263	25.8	294	28.9
Diabetes mellitus — Diabète sucré........................	617	16.9	813	21.4	259	25.4	292	28.7
Malnutrition — Malnutrition...............................	5	♦0.1	9	♦0.2	1	♦0.1	-	-
Mental and behavioural disorders — Troubles mentaux et du comportement	**1 104**	**30.3**	**2 041**	**53.8**	**36**	**3.5**	**5**	**♦0.5**
Diseases of the nervous system — Maladies du système nerveux.........	**1 089**	**29.9**	**1 673**	**44.1**	**94**	**9.2**	**57**	**5.6**
Diseases of the circulatory system — Maladies de l'appareil circulatoire								
Total......................	10 320	283.5	12 541	330.3	5 189	508.9	5 047	495.3
Acute rheumatic fever and chronic rheumatic heart diseases — Rhumatisme articularie aigu et cardiopathies rhumatismales chroniques............	35	1.0	72	1.9	20	♦2.0	15	♦1.5
Hypertensive diseases — Maladies hypertensives................	763	21.0	1 574	41.5	171	16.8	206	20.2
Ischaemic heart disease — Cardiopathie ischémique..........	4 821	132.4	4 541	119.6	1 298	127.3	737	72.3
Cerebrovascular disease — Maladie cérébrovasculaire..........	1 635	44.9	2 478	65.3	1 659	162.7	1 831	179.7

	Switzerland - Suisse				The Former Yugoslav Rep. of Macedonia - L ex-République yougoslave de Macédoine			
	2005 (C)				**2002 (C)**			
Cause of death — Cause de décès	Male — Masculin		Female — Féminin		Male — Masculin		Female — Féminin	
	Number Nombre	Rate Taux	Number Nombre	Rate Taux	Number Nombre	Rate Taux	Number Nombre	Rate Taux
Diseases of arteries, arterioles and capillaries — Maladies des artères, artérioles et capillaires	661	18.2	681	17.9	191	18.7	211	20.7
Diseases of the respiratory system — Maladies de l'appareil respiratoire								
Total...........	2 239	61.5	2 032	53.5	341	33.4	251	24.6
Influenza — Grippe.........	37	1.0	92	2.4	-	-	-	-
Pneumonia — Pneumopathies..........	690	19.0	885	23.3	38	3.7	40	3.9
Chronic lower respiratory diseases — Maladies chroniques des voies respiratoires inférieures	1 190	32.7	709	18.7	199	19.5	111	10.9
Diseases of the digestive system — Maladies de l'appareil digestif								
Total...........	1 126	30.9	1 275	33.6	256	25.1	123	12.1
Gastric and duodenal ulcer — Ulcère de l'estomac et du duodénum	73	2.0	97	2.6	32	3.1	18	♦1.8
Diseases of the liver — Maladies du foie	461	12.7	231	6.1	125	12.3	42	4.1
Diseases of the musculoskeletal system and connective tissue — Maladies du système ostéo-articularie, des muscles et du tissu conjonctif	131	3.6	354	9.3	1	♦0.1	-	-
Diseases of the genitourinary system — Maladies de l'appareil génito-urinaire								
Total...........	241	6.6	253	6.7	156	15.3	89	8.7
Disorders of kidney and ureter — Affections du rein et de l'uretère	125	3.4	151	4.0	130	12.7	88	8.6
Hyperplasia of prostate — Hyperplasie de la prostate.......................	29	♦2.5	..	..	26	♦10.4	..	..
Pregnancy, childbirth and the puerperium — Grossesse, accouchement et puerpéralité								
Total...........	..	..	4	♦5.5	..	..	3	♦10.8
Pregnancy with abortive outcome — Grossesse se terminant par un avortement	..	..	-	-	..	..	-	-
Other direct obstetric causes — Autres décès maternels directs	..	..	2	♦2.7	..	..	3	♦10.8
Indirect obstetric causes — Décès maternels indirects.......................	..	..	2	♦2.7	..	..	-	-
Certain conditions originating in the perinatal period — Certaines affections dont l'origine se situe dans la période périnatale	94	250.2	66	186.8	86	600.9	83	617.1
Congenital malformations, deformations and chromosomal abnormalities — Malformations congénitales et anomalies chromosomiques	140	372.6	116	328.3	34	237.6	22	♦163.6
Symptoms, signs and abnormal clinical and laboratory findings, not elsewhere classified — Symptômes, signes et résultats anormaux d'examens cliniques et de laboratoire, non classés ailleurs	1 159	31.8	1 230	32.4	841	82.5	667	65.5
All other diseases — Toutes autres maladies.......................	27	♦0.7	67	1.8	-	-	-	-
External causes — Causes externes								
Total...........	2 113	58.0	1 348	35.5	558	54.7	190	18.6
Accidents								
Total...........	1 122	30.8	878	23.1	400	39.2	130	12.8
Transport accidents — Accidents de transport	301	8.3	97	2.6	114	11.2	32	3.1
Falls — Chutes	508	14.0	592	15.6	28	♦2.7	31	3.0
Accidental drowning and submersion — Noyade et submersion accidentelles.......................	21	♦0.6	14	♦0.4	18	♦1.8	4	♦0.4
Exposure to smoke, fire and flames — Exposition à la fumée, au feu et aux flammes	13	♦0.4	18	♦0.5	5	♦0.5	1	♦0.1
Accidental poisoning by and exposure to noxious substances — Intoxication accidentelle par des substances nocives et exposition à ces substances	17	♦0.5	15	♦0.4	17	♦1.7	7	♦0.7
Intentional self-harm — Lésions auto-infligées...............................	899	24.7	400	10.5	99	9.7	50	4.9
Assault — Agresssions	32	0.9	32	0.8	59	5.8	10	♦1.0
All other external causes — Toutes autres causes externes...................	60	1.6	38	1.0	-	-	-	-

Cause of death — Cause de décès	The Former Yugoslav Rep. of Macedonia - L'ex-République yougoslave de Macédoine 2003 (C)				Ukraine 2004 (C)			
	Male — Masculin		Female — Féminin		Male — Masculin		Female — Féminin	
	Number Nombre	Rate Taux	Number Nombre	Rate Taux	Number Nombre	Rate Taux	Number Nombre	Rate Taux
TOTAL..........	9 832	966.5	8 174	809.7	391 370	1 792.0	369 891	1 454.5
Certain infectious and parasitic diseases — Certaines maladies infectieuses et parasitaires								
Total..........	95	9.3	50	5.0	12 117	55.5	3 019	11.9
Intestinal infectious diseases — Maladies infectieuses intestinales..........	10	◆1.0	7	◆0.7	41	0.2	30	◆0.1
Tuberculosis — Tuberculose..........	60	5.9	18	◆1.8	9 131	41.8	1 656	6.5
Tetanus — Tétanos..........	-	-	-	-	2	◆0.0	8	◆0.0
Diphtheria — Diphtérie..........	-	-	-	-	...	...	...	...
Whooping cough — Coqueluche..........	-	-	-	-	-	-	-	-
Meningococcal infection — Infection à méningocoques..........	1	◆0.1	-	-	60	0.3	56	0.2
Septicaemia — Septicémie..........	11	◆1.1	12	◆1.2	450	2.1	275	1.1
Acute poliomyelitis — Poliomyélite aiguë..........	-	-	-	-	-	-	-	-
Measles — Rougeole..........	-	-	-	-	-	-	-	-
Viral hepatitis — Hépatite virale..........	2	◆0.2	2	◆0.2	...	...	...	...
Human immunodeficiency virus [HIV] disease — Maladies dues au virus de l'immunodéficience humaine (VIH)..........	-	-	-	-	1 884	8.6	721	2.8
Malaria — Paludisme..........	-	-	-	-	2	◆0.0	-	-
Neoplasms — Tumeurs..........	1 971	193.8	1 267	125.5	51 808	237.2	40 310	158.5
Malignant neoplasms — Tumeurs malignes								
Total..........	1 920	188.7	1 227	121.5	51 414	235.4	39 905	156.9
Malignant neoplasm of lip, oral cavity and pharynx — Tumeur maligne de la lèvre, de la cavité buccale et du pharynx..........	36	3.5	10	◆1.0	3 065	14.0	453	1.8
Malignant neoplasm of oesophagus — Tumeur maligne de l'oesophage..........	21	◆2.1	9	◆0.9	1 438	6.6	214	0.8
Malignant neoplasm of stomach — Tumeur maligne de l'estomac..........	233	22.9	123	12.2	6 687	30.6	4 179	16.4
Malignant neoplasm of colon, rectosigmoid junction, rectum, anus and anal canal — Tumeur maligne du côlon, de la jonction recto-sigmoïdienne, du rectum, de l'anus et du canal anal..........	200	19.7	130	12.9	5 822	26.7	5 847	23.0
Malignant neoplasm of liver and intrahepatic bile ducts — Tumeur maligne du foie et des voies bilaires intrahépatiques..........	...	...	...	...	...	...	...	...
Malignant neoplasm of pancreas — Tumeur maligne du pancréas..........	87	8.6	52	5.2	...	...	...	...
Malignant neoplasm of trachea, bronchus and lung — Tumeur maligne de la trachée, des bronches et du poumon..........	555	54.6	86	8.5	13 778	63.1	2 567	10.1
Malignant neoplasm of female breast — Tumeur maligne du sein chez la femme..........	..	..	240	29.8	...	...	7 789	35.5
Malignant neoplasm of cervix uteri — Tumeur maligne du col de l'utérus..........	..	..	44	5.5	...	...	2 297	10.5
Malignant neoplasm of prostate — Tumeur maligne de la prostate..........	113	44.7	...	...	2 917	48.0	...	...
Malignant neoplasm of lymphoid, haematopoietic and related tissue — Tumeurs malignes primitives ou présumées primitives des tissus lymphoïde, hématopoïétique et apparentés..........	97	9.5	65	6.4	2 671	12.2	2 183	8.6
Disorders of the blood and blood-forming organs and certain disorders involving the immune mechanism — Maladies du sang et des organes hématopoïétiques et certains troubles du système immunitaire								
Total..........	5	◆0.5	4	◆0.4	198	0.9	159	0.6
Anaemias — Anémies..........	3	◆0.3	4	◆0.4	86	0.4	82	0.3
Endocrine, nutritional and metabolic diseases — Maladies endocriniennes, nutritionnelles et métaboliques								
Total..........	252	24.8	353	35.0	1 309	6.0	1 834	7.2
Diabetes mellitus — Diabète sucré..........	246	24.2	347	34.4	1 116	5.1	1 609	6.3
Malnutrition — Malnutrition..........	-	-	-	-	...	...	...	...
Mental and behavioural disorders — Troubles mentaux et du comportement	36	3.5	4	◆0.4	2 347	10.7	844	3.3
Diseases of the nervous system — Maladies du système nerveux..........	86	8.5	58	5.7	4 337	19.9	2 042	8.0
Diseases of the circulatory system — Maladies de l'appareil circulatoire								
Total..........	5 130	504.3	5 054	500.6	209 436	958.9	264 310	1 039.3
Acute rheumatic fever and chronic rheumatic heart diseases — Rhumatisme articularie aigu et cardiopathies rhumatismales chroniques..........	18	◆1.8	14	◆1.4	952	4.4	1 307	5.1
Hypertensive diseases — Maladies hypertensives..........	233	22.9	274	27.1	339	1.6	284	1.1
Ischaemic heart disease — Cardiopathie ischémique..........	1 280	125.8	786	77.9	140 755	644.5	170 346	669.8
Cerebrovascular disease — Maladie cérébrovasculaire..........	1 725	169.6	1 864	184.6	41 851	191.6	61 884	243.3

Cause of death — Cause de décès	The Former Yugoslav Rep. of Macedonia - L'ex République yougoslave de Macédoine				Ukraine			
	2003 (C)				2004 (C)			
	Male — Masculin		Female — Féminin		Male — Masculin		Female — Féminin	
	Number Nombre	Rate Taux	Number Nombre	Rate Taux	Number Nombre	Rate Taux	Number Nombre	Rate Taux
Diseases of arteries, arterioles and capillaries — Maladies des artères, artérioles et capillaires	220	21.6	207	20.5	13 563	62.1	24 911	98.0
Diseases of the respiratory system — Maladies de l'appareil respiratoire								
Total	406	39.9	301	29.8	20 715	94.8	7 771	30.6
Influenza — Grippe	1	♦0.1	-	-	4	♦0.0	5	♦0.0
Pneumonia — Pneumopathies	67	6.6	38	3.8	4 820	22.1	1 315	5.2
Chronic lower respiratory diseases — Maladies chroniques des voies respiratoires inférieures	242	23.8	156	15.5	...	...	...	...
Diseases of the digestive system — Maladies de l'appareil digestif								
Total	238	23.4	125	12.4	18 206	83.4	9 877	38.8
Gastric and duodenal ulcer — Ulcère de l'estomac et du duodénum	38	3.7	27	♦2.7	1 197	5.5	489	1.9
Diseases of the liver — Maladies du foie	104	10.2	28	♦2.8	...	...	...	...
Diseases of the musculoskeletal system and connective tissue — Maladies du système ostéo-articularie, des muscles et du tissu conjonctif	1	♦0.1	4	♦0.4	328	1.5	559	2.2
Diseases of the genitourinary system — Maladies de l'appareil génito-urinaire								
Total	178	17.5	108	10.7	2 036	9.3	1 787	7.0
Disorders of kidney and ureter — Affections du rein et de l'uretère	136	13.4	108	10.7	1 449	6.6	1 396	5.5
Hyperplasia of prostate — Hyperplasie de la prostate	42	16.6	..	..	296	4.9	..	..
Pregnancy, childbirth and the puerperium — Grossesse, accouchement et puerpéralité								
Total	..	..	1	♦3.7	..	..	56	13.1
Pregnancy with abortive outcome — Grossesse se terminant par un avortement	..	..	-	-	..	..	8	♦1.9
Other direct obstetric causes — Autres décès maternels directs	..	..	1	♦3.7	..	..	...	...
Indirect obstetric causes — Décès maternels indirects	..	..	-	-	..	..	...	...
Certain conditions originating in the perinatal period — Certaines affections dont l'origine se situe dans la période périnatale	99	712.2	67	511.0	940	427.4	628	302.9
Congenital malformations, deformations and chromosomal abnormalities — Malformations congénitales et anomalies chromosomiques	52	374.1	33	251.7	1 172	532.9	957	461.6
Symptoms, signs and abnormal clinical and laboratory findings, not elsewhere classified — Symptômes, signes et résultats anormaux d'examens cliniques et de laboratoire, non classés ailleurs	793	78.0	595	58.9	9 899	45.3	20 346	80.0
All other diseases — Toutes autres maladies	-	-	1	♦0.1	304	1.4	281	1.1
External causes — Causes externes								
Total	490	48.2	149	14.8	56 218	257.4	15 111	59.4
Accidents								
Total	343	33.7	93	9.2	36 085	165.2	9 784	38.5
Transport accidents — Accidents de transport	108	10.6	21	♦2.1	7 156	32.8	2 271	8.9
Falls — Chutes	28	♦2.8	18	♦1.8	2 676	12.3	735	2.9
Accidental drowning and submersion — Noyade et submersion accidentelles	20	♦2.0	2	♦0.2	3 272	15.0	658	2.6
Exposure to smoke, fire and flames — Exposition à la fumée, au feu et aux flammes	7	♦0.7	3	♦0.3	1 763	8.1	646	2.5
Accidental poisoning by and exposure to noxious substances — Intoxication accidentelle par des substances nocives et exposition à ces substances	15	♦1.5	6	♦0.6	11 995	54.9	3 204	12.6
Intentional self-harm — Lésions auto-infligées	97	9.5	40	4.0	9 394	43.0	1 865	7.3
Assault — Agresssions	50	4.9	16	♦1.6	3 401	15.6	1 588	6.2
All other external causes — Toutes autres causes externes	-	-	-	-	7 338	33.6	1 874	7.4

Cause of death — Cause de décès	Ukraine 2005 (C)				United Kingdom - Royaume-Uni 2005 (+C)			
	Male — Masculin		Female — Féminin		Male — Masculin		Female — Féminin	
	Number Nombre	Rate Taux	Number Nombre	Rate Taux	Number Nombre	Rate Taux	Number Nombre	Rate Taux
TOTAL	403 440	...	378 521	...	277 349	940.3	305 615	994.1
Certain infectious and parasitic diseases — Certaines maladies infectieuses et parasitaires								
Total	13 715	...	3 530	...	3 027	10.3	3 961	12.9
Intestinal infectious diseases — Maladies infectieuses intestinales	43	...	32	...	772	2.6	1 549	5.0
Tuberculosis — Tuberculose	10 009	...	1 887	...	229	0.8	153	0.5
Tetanus — Tétanos	2	...	11	...	-	-	-	-
Diphtheria — Diphtérie	1	...	1	...	-	-	-	-
Whooping cough — Coqueluche	1	...	1	...	2	◆0.0	3	◆0.0
Meningococcal infection — Infection à méningocoques	65	...	52	...	51	0.2	40	0.1
Septicaemia — Septicémie	419	...	253	...	1 256	4.3	1 648	5.4
Acute poliomyelitis — Poliomyélite aiguë	-	...	-	...	-	-	-	-
Measles — Rougeole	-	...	-	...	-	-	-	-
Viral hepatitis — Hépatite virale	71	...	44	...	139	0.5	82	0.3
Human immunodeficiency virus [HIV] disease — Maladies dues au virus de l'immunodéficience humaine (VIH)	2 619	...	1 003	...	179	0.6	63	0.2
Malaria — Paludisme	1	...	-	...	6	◆0.0	4	◆0.0
Neoplasms — Tumeurs	51 743	...	40 106	...	81 451	276.1	75 864	246.8
Malignant neoplasms — Tumeurs malignes								
Total	51 312	...	39 685	...	79 784	270.5	73 950	240.6
Malignant neoplasm of lip, oral cavity and pharynx — Tumeur maligne de la lèvre, de la cavité buccale et du pharynx	2 980	...	439	...	1 317	4.5	687	2.2
Malignant neoplasm of oesophagus — Tumeur maligne de l'oesophage	1 405	...	172	...	4 849	16.4	2 573	8.4
Malignant neoplasm of stomach — Tumeur maligne de l'estomac	6 510	...	4 039	...	3 527	12.0	2 152	7.0
Malignant neoplasm of colon, rectosigmoid junction, rectum, anus and anal canal — Tumeur maligne du côlon, de la jonction recto-sigmoïdienne, du rectum, de l'anus et du canal anal	5 980	...	5 856	...	8 653	29.3	7 464	24.3
Malignant neoplasm of liver and intrahepatic bile ducts — Tumeur maligne du foie et des voies bilaires intrahépatiques	1 051	...	704	...	1 697	5.8	1 165	3.8
Malignant neoplasm of pancreas — Tumeur maligne du pancréas	2 446	...	1 880	...	3 464	11.7	3 791	12.3
Malignant neoplasm of trachea, bronchus and lung — Tumeur maligne de la trachée, des bronches et du poumon	13 400	...	2 415	...	19 475	66.0	14 028	45.6
Malignant neoplasm of female breast — Tumeur maligne du sein chez la femme	..	...	7 873	...	..	...	12 434	48.8
Malignant neoplasm of cervix uteri — Tumeur maligne du col de l'utérus	..	..	2 254	...	..	...	1 064	4.2
Malignant neoplasm of prostate — Tumeur maligne de la prostate	3 016				10 005	106.4		
Malignant neoplasm of lymphoid, haematopoietic and related tissue — Tumeurs malignes primitives ou présumées primitives des tissus lymphoïde, hématopoïétique et apparentés	...		...		6 268	21.2	5 391	17.5
Disorders of the blood and blood-forming organs and certain disorders involving the immune mechanism — Maladies du sang et des organes hématopoïétiques et certains troubles du système immunitaire								
Total	189	...	198	...	503	1.7	749	2.4
Anaemias — Anémies	84	...	111	...	202	0.7	399	1.3
Endocrine, nutritional and metabolic diseases — Maladies endocriniennes, nutritionnelles et métaboliques								
Total	1 427	...	1 975	...	3 918	13.3	4 812	15.7
Diabetes mellitus — Diabète sucré	1 220	...	1 755	...	3 084	10.5	3 537	11.5
Malnutrition — Malnutrition	35	...	19	...	36	0.1	42	0.1
Mental and behavioural disorders — Troubles mentaux et du comportement	2 475	...	915	...	5 885	20.0	11 619	37.8
Diseases of the nervous system — Maladies du système nerveux	4 503	...	2 144	...	7 919	26.8	9 081	29.5
Diseases of the circulatory system — Maladies de l'appareil circulatoire								
Total	217 616	...	271 153	...	99 943	338.8	108 790	353.9
Acute rheumatic fever and chronic rheumatic heart diseases — Rhumatisme articularie aigu et cardiopathies rhumatismales chroniques	894	...	1 048	...	372	1.3	939	3.1
Hypertensive diseases — Maladies hypertensives	354	...	261	...	1 755	5.9	2 429	7.9
Ischaemic heart disease — Cardiopathie ischémique	147 550	...	178 041	...	56 337	191.0	44 876	146.0
Cerebrovascular disease — Maladie cérébrovasculaire	42 686	...	62 297	...	21 899	74.2	35 829	116.5

	Ukraine				United Kingdom - Royaume-Uni			
	2005 (C)				2005 (+C)			
Cause of death — Cause de décès	Male — Masculin		Female — Féminin		Male — Masculin		Female — Féminin	
	Number Nombre	Rate Taux	Number Nombre	Rate Taux	Number Nombre	Rate Taux	Number Nombre	Rate Taux
Diseases of arteries, arterioles and capillaries — Maladies des artères, artérioles et capillaires	...	...	...	...	7 120	24.1	6 142	20.0
Diseases of the respiratory system — Maladies de l'appareil respiratoire								
Total	20 607	...	7 391	...	36 736	124.5	44 662	145.3
Influenza — Grippe	8	...	5	...	24	♦0.1	29	♦0.1
Pneumonia — Pneumopathies	5 056	...	1 279	...	13 558	46.0	21 242	69.1
Chronic lower respiratory diseases — Maladies chroniques des voies respiratoires inférieures	13 391		5 556		15 339	52.0	14 533	47.3
Diseases of the digestive system — Maladies de l'appareil digestif								
Total	20 470	...	11 222	...	13 378	45.4	15 623	50.8
Gastric and duodenal ulcer — Ulcère de l'estomac et du duodénum	1 274	...	519		1 671	5.7	1 870	6.1
Diseases of the liver — Maladies du foie	14 936	...	7 807	...	5 269	17.9	3 112	10.1
Diseases of the musculoskeletal system and connective tissue — Maladies du système ostéo-articularie, des muscles et du tissu conjonctif	297		463		1 418	4.8	3 397	11.1
Diseases of the genitourinary system — Maladies de l'appareil génito-urinaire								
Total	1 965	...	1 627		4 633	15.7	6 951	22.6
Disorders of kidney and ureter — Affections du rein et de l'uretère	...	...	...	...	2 183	7.4	2 588	8.4
Hyperplasia of prostate — Hyperplasie de la prostate	...	...	...	..	172	1.8	..	..
Pregnancy, childbirth and the puerperium — Grossesse, accouchement et puerpéralité								
Total	..	..	75	17.6	..	..	51	7.1
Pregnancy with abortive outcome — Grossesse se terminant par un avortement	..	..	10	♦2.3	..	..	7	♦1.0
Other direct obstetric causes — Autres décès maternels directs	..	..	42	9.9	..	..	32	4.4
Indirect obstetric causes — Décès maternels indirects	..	..	23	♦5.4	..	..	12	♦1.7
Certain conditions originating in the perinatal period — Certaines affections dont l'origine se situe dans la période périnatale	1 068	486.3	724	350.7	1 196	...	833	...
Congenital malformations, deformations and chromosomal abnormalities — Malformations congénitales et anomalies chromosomiques	1 205	548.7	978	473.7	1 094		953	...
Symptoms, signs and abnormal clinical and laboratory findings, not elsewhere classified — Symptômes, signes et résultats anormaux d'examens cliniques et de laboratoire, non classés ailleurs	10 721	...	20 926	...	2 936	10.0	8 984	29.2
All other diseases — Toutes autres maladies	308		271	...	666	2.3	1 321	4.3
External causes — Causes externes								
Total	55 131	...	14 823	...	12 646	42.9	7 964	25.9
Accidents								
Total	...	...	...	...	7 383	25.0	5 885	19.1
Transport accidents — Accidents de transport	7 540	...	2 353	...	2 658	9.0	806	2.6
Falls — Chutes	2 683	...	685	...	1 880	6.4	1 980	6.4
Accidental drowning and submersion — Noyade et submersion accidentelles	3 533		649	...	167	0.6	52	0.2
Exposure to smoke, fire and flames — Exposition à la fumée, au feu et aux flammes	2 031		722		186	0.6	140	0.5
Accidental poisoning by and exposure to noxious substances — Intoxication accidentelle par des substances nocives et exposition à ces substances	11 057	...	3 009	...	733	2.5	325	1.1
Intentional self-harm — Lésions auto-infligées	8 861	...	1 761	...	3 054	10.4	993	3.2
Assault — Agresssions	3 104	...	1 437	...	183	0.6	64	0.2
All other external causes — Toutes autres causes externes	...	...	...	...	2 026	6.9	1 022	3.3

21. Death and death rates by cause and sex: 2002 - 2006
Décès et taux de mortalité par cause et sexe : 2002 - 2006 (continued - suite)

Cause of death — Cause de décès	United Kingdom - Royaume-Uni 2006 (+C)				Australia - Australie 2002 (C)			
	Male — Masculin		Female — Féminin		Male — Masculin		Female — Féminin	
	Number Nombre	Rate Taux	Number Nombre	Rate Taux	Number Nombre	Rate Taux	Number Nombre	Rate Taux
TOTAL.................................	274 201	923.4	298 023	964.7	68 678	703.9	64 369	650.3
Certain infectious and parasitic diseases — Certaines maladies infectieuses et parasitaires								
Total......	3 689	12.4	4 914	15.9	942	9.7	834	8.4
Intestinal infectious diseases — Maladies infectieuses intestinales...........	1 287	4.3	2 507	8.1	24	+0.2	35	0.4
Tuberculosis — Tuberculose.................................	240	0.8	163	0.5	20	+0.2	15	+0.2
Tetanus — Tétanos.................................	-	-	1	+0.0	-	-	-	-
Diphtheria — Diphtérie.................................	-	-	-	-	-	-	-	-
Whooping cough — Coqueluche.................................	1	+0.0	1	+0.0	3	+0.0	1	+0.0
Meningococcal infection — Infection à méningocoques.................	29	+0.1	30	+0.1	30	+0.3	16	+0.2
Septicaemia — Septicémie.................................	1 310	4.4	1 640	5.3	503	5.2	567	5.7
Acute poliomyelitis — Poliomyélite aiguë...................	-	-	1	+0.0	-	-	-	-
Measles — Rougeole.................................	1	+0.0	-	-	-	-	-	-
Viral hepatitis — Hépatite virale...................	154	0.5	76	0.2	35	0.4	20	+0.2
Human immunodeficiency virus [HIV] disease — Maladies dues au virus de l'immunodéficience humaine (VIH)...................	168	0.6	77	0.2	101	1.0	10	+0.1
Malaria — Paludisme.................................	6	+0.0	1	+0.0	-	-	3	+0.0
Neoplasms — Tumeurs.................................	82 469	277.7	75 603	244.7	21 440	219.7	16 829	170.0
Malignant neoplasms — Tumeurs malignes								
Total......	80 737	271.9	73 786	238.8	21 017	215.4	16 441	166.1
Malignant neoplasm of lip, oral cavity and pharynx — Tumeur maligne de la lèvre, de la cavité buccale et du pharynx...................	1 299	4.4	708	2.3	485	5.0	183	1.8
Malignant neoplasm of oesophagus — Tumeur maligne de l'oesophage......	4 869	16.4	2 549	8.3	686	7.0	318	3.2
Malignant neoplasm of stomach — Tumeur maligne de l'estomac......	3 262	11.0	2 006	6.5	772	7.9	447	4.5
Malignant neoplasm of colon, rectosigmoid junction, rectum, anus and anal canal — Tumeur maligne du côlon, de la jonction recto-sigmoïdienne, du rectum, de l'anus et du canal anal...................	8 531	28.7	7 463	24.2	2 414	24.7	2 187	22.1
Malignant neoplasm of liver and intrahepatic bile ducts — Tumeur maligne du foie et des voies bilaires intrahépatiques...................	1 884	6.3	1 199	3.9	548	5.6	301	3.0
Malignant neoplasm of pancreas — Tumeur maligne du pancréas...........	3 620	12.2	3 713	12.0	958	9.8	881	8.9
Malignant neoplasm of trachea, bronchus and lung — Tumeur maligne de la trachée, des bronches et du poumon...................	19 647	66.2	14 579	47.2	4 719	48.4	2 526	25.5
Malignant neoplasm of female breast — Tumeur maligne du sein chez la femme...................	..	..	12 349	48.1	..	..	2 681	33.6
Malignant neoplasm of cervix uteri — Tumeur maligne du col de l'utérus......	..	..	952	3.7	..	..	217	2.7
Malignant neoplasm of prostate — Tumeur maligne de la prostate...........	10 052	105.8	..	..	2 820	103.2	..	..
Malignant neoplasm of lymphoid, haematopoietic and related tissue — Tumeurs malignes primitives ou présumées primitives des tissus lymphoïde, hématopoïétique et apparentés...................	6 482	21.8	5 412	17.5	2 142	22.0	1 657	16.7
Disorders of the blood and blood-forming organs and certain disorders involving the immune mechanism — Maladies du sang et des organes hématopoïétiques et certains troubles du système immunitaire								
Total.................................	507	1.7	655	2.1	184	1.9	253	2.6
Anaemias — Anémies.................................	202	0.7	350	1.1	73	0.7	143	1.4
Endocrine, nutritional and metabolic diseases — Maladies endocriniennes, nutritionnelles et métaboliques								
Total.................................	3 825	12.9	4 653	15.1	2 380	24.4	2 241	22.6
Diabetes mellitus — Diabète sucré...................	3 045	10.3	3 394	11.0	1 765	18.1	1 531	15.5
Malnutrition — Malnutrition.................................	35	0.1	63	0.2	40	0.4	54	0.5
Mental and behavioural disorders — Troubles mentaux et du comportement	5 960	20.1	11 894	38.5	1 243	12.7	1 914	19.3
Diseases of the nervous system — Maladies du système nerveux...........	7 873	26.5	9 219	29.8	2 137	21.9	2 452	24.8
Diseases of the circulatory system — Maladies de l'appareil circulatoire								
Total.................................	95 322	321.0	102 963	333.3	23 875	244.7	26 102	263.7
Acute rheumatic fever and chronic rheumatic heart diseases — Rhumatisme articulaire aigu et cardiopathies rhumatismales chroniques...................	359	1.2	859	2.8	84	0.9	178	1.8
Hypertensive diseases — Maladies hypertensives...................	1 855	6.2	2 664	8.6	465	4.8	892	9.0
Ischaemic heart disease — Cardiopathie ischémique...................	52 804	177.8	41 872	135.5	13 768	141.1	12 116	122.4
Cerebrovascular disease — Maladie cérébrovasculaire...................	21 315	71.8	33 872	109.6	4 957	50.8	7 502	75.8

United Kingdom - Royaume-Uni   Australia Australie

Cause of death — Cause de décès	2006 (+C) Male — Masculin Number Nombre	Rate Taux	2006 (+C) Female — Féminin Number Nombre	Rate Taux	2002 (C) Male — Masculin Number Nombre	Rate Taux	2002 (C) Female — Féminin Number Nombre	Rate Taux
Diseases of arteries, arterioles and capillaries — Maladies des artères, artérioles et capillaires	6 944	23.4	5 805	18.8	1 382	14.2	1 252	12.6
Diseases of the respiratory system — Maladies de l'appareil respiratoire								
Total.........	35 517	119.6	42 292	136.9	6 177	63.3	5 463	55.2
Influenza — Grippe	9	+0.0	11	+0.0	24	+0.2	31	0.3
Pneumonia — Pneumopathies	12 809	43.1	19 305	62.5	1 328	13.6	1 680	17.0
Chronic lower respiratory diseases — Maladies chroniques des voies respiratoires inférieures	14 726	49.6	14 234	46.1	3 568	36.6	2 678	27.1
Diseases of the digestive system — Maladies de l'appareil digestif								
Total.........	13 983	47.1	15 659	50.7	2 225	22.8	2 260	22.8
Gastric and duodenal ulcer — Ulcère de l'estomac et du duodénum	1 715	5.8	1 746	5.7	178	1.8	235	2.4
Diseases of the liver — Maladies du foie	5 486	18.5	3 311	10.7	929	9.5	444	4.5
Diseases of the musculoskeletal system and connective tissue — Maladies du système ostéo-articularie, des muscles et du tissu conjonctif	1 418	4.8	3 254	10.5	348	3.6	665	6.7
Diseases of the genitourinary system — Maladies de l'appareil génito-urinaire								
Total.........	4 997	16.8	7 200	23.3	1 323	13.6	1 654	16.7
Disorders of kidney and ureter — Affections du rein et de l'uretère	2 232	7.5	2 556	8.3	1 050	10.8	1 198	12.1
Hyperplasia of prostate — Hyperplasie de la prostate...........	187	2.0	..	..	48	1.8	..	..
Pregnancy, childbirth and the puerperium — Grossesse, accouchement et puerpéralité								
Total.........	..	..	50	6.7	..	..	13	+5.2
Pregnancy with abortive outcome — Grossesse se terminant par un avortement	..	..	3	+0.4	..	..	-	-
Other direct obstetric causes — Autres décès maternels directs	..	..	36	4.8	..	..	13	+5.2
Indirect obstetric causes — Décès maternels indirects.........	..	..	10	+1.3	..	..	-	-
Certain conditions originating in the perinatal period — Certaines affections dont l'origine se situe dans la période périnatale	1 162	...	878	...	353	274.4	301	246.0
Congenital malformations, deformations and chromosomal abnormalities — Malformations congénitales et anomalies chromosomiques	1 051	...	929	...	302	234.8	276	225.6
Symptoms, signs and abnormal clinical and laboratory findings, not elsewhere classified — Symptômes, signes et résultats anormaux d'examens cliniques et de laboratoire, non classés ailleurs	2 846	9.6	8 599	27.8	368	3.8	363	3.7
All other diseases — Toutes autres maladies.............................	646	2.2	1 344	4.4	125	1.3	219	2.2
External causes — Causes externes								
Total.........	12 936	43.6	7 917	25.6	5 256	53.9	2 530	25.6
Accidents								
Total.........	7 710	26.0	6 014	19.5	3 081	31.6	1 796	18.1
Transport accidents — Accidents de transport	2 678	9.0	844	2.7	1 407	14.4	498	5.0
Falls — Chutes	1 918	6.5	2 067	6.7	326	3.3	301	3.0
Accidental drowning and submersion — Noyade et submersion accidentelles	154	0.5	60	0.2	170	1.7	67	0.7
Exposure to smoke, fire and flames — Exposition à la fumée, au feu et aux flammes	222	0.7	145	0.5	71	0.7	37	0.4
Accidental poisoning by and exposure to noxious substances — Intoxication accidentelle par des substances nocives et exposition à ces substances	902	3.0	379	1.2	369	3.8	192	1.9
Intentional self-harm — Lésions auto-infligées.........................	3 186	10.7	936	3.0	1 813	18.6	506	5.1
Assault — Agresssions	201	0.7	58	0.2	191	2.0	95	1.0
All other external causes — Toutes autres causes externes...................	1 839	6.2	909	2.9	171	1.8	133	1.3

21. Death and death rates by cause and sex: 2002 - 2006
Décès et taux de mortalité par cause et sexe : 2002 - 2006 (continued - suite)

Cause of death — Cause de décès	Australia - Australie 2003 (C)				New Zealand - Nouvelle-Zélande 2003 (+C)			
	Male — Masculin		Female — Féminin		Male — Masculin		Female — Féminin	
	Number Nombre	Rate Taux	Number Nombre	Rate Taux	Number Nombre	Rate Taux	Number Nombre	Rate Taux
TOTAL.....	67 940	687.5	63 844	637.1	14 066	713.5	13 995	686.7
Certain infectious and parasitic diseases — Certaines maladies infectieuses et parasitaires								
Total.....	921	9.3	821	8.2	64	3.2	83	4.1
Intestinal infectious diseases — Maladies infectieuses intestinales.....	20	♦0.2	28	♦0.3	1	♦0.1	9	♦0.4
Tuberculosis — Tuberculose.....	23	♦0.2	21	♦0.2	2	♦0.1	8	♦0.4
Tetanus — Tétanos.....	-	-	-	-	-	-	-	-
Diphtheria — Diphtérie.....	-	-	-	-	-	-	-	-
Whooping cough — Coqueluche.....	-	-	-	-	-	-	-	-
Meningococcal infection — Infection à méningocoques.....	12	♦0.1	12	♦0.1	5	♦0.3	8	♦0.4
Septicaemia — Septicémie.....	512	5.2	554	5.5	11	♦0.6	25	♦1.2
Acute poliomyelitis — Poliomyélite aiguë.....	-	-	-	-	-	-	-	-
Measles — Rougeole.....	-	-	-	-	-	-	-	-
Viral hepatitis — Hépatite virale.....	61	0.6	24	♦0.2	14	♦0.7	7	♦0.3
Human immunodeficiency virus [HIV] disease — Maladies dues au virus de l'immunodéficience humaine (VIH).....	99	1.0	11	♦0.1	8	♦0.4	2	♦0.1
Malaria — Paludisme.....	2	♦0.0	-	-	-	-	-	-
Neoplasms — Tumeurs.....	21 396	216.5	16 870	168.4	4 307	218.5	3 773	185.1
Malignant neoplasms — Tumeurs malignes								
Total.....	20 976	212.3	16 469	164.4	4 233	214.7	3 699	181.5
Malignant neoplasm of lip, oral cavity and pharynx — Tumeur maligne de la lèvre, de la cavité buccale et du pharynx	459	4.6	214	2.1	93	4.7	39	1.9
Malignant neoplasm of oesophagus — Tumeur maligne de l'oesophage.....	767	7.8	363	3.6	129	6.5	75	3.7
Malignant neoplasm of stomach — Tumeur maligne de l'estomac.....	686	6.9	482	4.8	206	10.4	109	5.3
Malignant neoplasm of colon, rectosigmoid junction, rectum, anus and anal canal — Tumeur maligne du côlon, de la jonction recto-sigmoïdienne, du rectum, de l'anus et du canal anal.....	2 410	24.4	2 019	20.1	561	28.5	555	27.2
Malignant neoplasm of liver and intrahepatic bile ducts — Tumeur maligne du foie et des voies bilaires intrahépatiques.....	603	6.1	288	2.9	100	5.1	48	2.4
Malignant neoplasm of pancreas — Tumeur maligne du pancréas.....	941	9.5	940	9.4	153	7.8	153	7.5
Malignant neoplasm of trachea, bronchus and lung — Tumeur maligne de la trachée, des bronches et du poumon.....	4 505	45.6	2 481	24.8	848	43.0	618	30.3
Malignant neoplasm of female breast — Tumeur maligne du sein chez la femme.....	..	..	2 710	33.6	..	..	647	40.2
Malignant neoplasm of cervix uteri — Tumeur maligne du col de l'utérus.....	..	..	239	3.0	..	..	58	3.6
Malignant neoplasm of prostate — Tumeur maligne de la prostate.....	2 834	100.9	...	...	556	105.9	...	...
Malignant neoplasm of lymphoid, haematopoietic and related tissue — Tumeurs malignes primitives ou présumées primitives des tissus lymphoïde, hématopoïétique et apparentés.....	2 059	20.8	1 640	16.4	445	22.6	341	16.7
Disorders of the blood and blood-forming organs and certain disorders involving the immune mechanism — Maladies du sang et des organes hématopoïétiques et certains troubles du système immunitaire								
Total.....	189	1.9	255	2.5	28	♦1.4	41	2.0
Anaemias — Anémies.....	83	0.8	151	1.5	13	♦0.7	21	♦1.0
Endocrine, nutritional and metabolic diseases — Maladies endocriniennes, nutritionnelles et métaboliques								
Total.....	2 483	25.1	2 289	22.8	553	28.1	522	25.6
Diabetes mellitus — Diabète sucré.....	1 827	18.5	1 598	15.9	436	22.1	411	20.2
Malnutrition — Malnutrition.....	35	0.4	50	0.5	2	♦0.1	2	♦0.1
Mental and behavioural disorders — Troubles mentaux et du comportement	1 231	12.5	2 007	20.0	253	12.8	509	25.0
Diseases of the nervous system — Maladies du système nerveux.....	1 900	19.2	2 421	24.2	384	19.5	494	24.2
Diseases of the circulatory system — Maladies de l'appareil circulatoire								
Total.....	23 283	235.6	25 320	252.7	5 224	265.0	5 859	287.5
Acute rheumatic fever and chronic rheumatic heart diseases — Rhumatisme articularie aigu et cardiopathies rhumatismales chroniques.....	95	1.0	189	1.9	46	2.3	102	5.0
Hypertensive diseases — Maladies hypertensives.....	478	4.8	879	8.8	89	4.5	158	7.8
Ischaemic heart disease — Cardiopathie ischémique.....	13 440	136.0	11 855	118.3	3 243	164.5	2 953	144.9
Cerebrovascular disease — Maladie cérébrovasculaire.....	4 848	49.1	7 361	73.5	969	49.2	1 723	84.5

Cause of death — Cause de décès	Australia Australie 2003 (C)				New Zealand Nouvelle-Zélande 2003 (+C)			
	Male — Masculin		Female — Féminin		Male — Masculin		Female — Féminin	
	Number Nombre	Rate Taux	Number Nombre	Rate Taux	Number Nombre	Rate Taux	Number Nombre	Rate Taux
Diseases of arteries, arterioles and capillaries — Maladies des artères, artérioles et capillaires	1 335	13.5	1 197	11.9	256	13.0	205	10.1
Diseases of the respiratory system — Maladies de l'appareil respiratoire								
Total	6 163	62.4	5 665	56.5	1 212	61.5	1 146	56.2
Influenza — Grippe	29	✦0.3	36	0.4	5	✦0.3	7	✦0.3
Pneumonia — Pneumopathies	1 511	15.3	1 985	19.8	148	7.5	251	12.3
Chronic lower respiratory diseases — Maladies chroniques des voies respiratoires inférieures	3 332	33.7	2 593	25.9	969	49.2	830	40.7
Diseases of the digestive system — Maladies de l'appareil digestif								
Total	2 288	23.2	2 206	22.0	320	16.2	385	18.9
Gastric and duodenal ulcer — Ulcère de l'estomac et du duodénum	186	1.9	194	1.9	40	2.0	48	2.4
Diseases of the liver — Maladies du foie	973	9.8	402	4.0	80	4.1	52	2.6
Diseases of the musculoskeletal system and connective tissue — Maladies du système ostéo-articularie, des muscles et du tissu conjonctif	312	3.2	698	7.0	73	3.7	154	7.6
Diseases of the genitourinary system — Maladies de l'appareil génito-urinaire								
Total	1 331	13.5	1 649	16.5	190	9.6	191	9.4
Disorders of kidney and ureter — Affections du rein et de l'uretère	1 065	10.8	1 171	11.7	163	8.3	141	6.9
Hyperplasia of prostate — Hyperplasie de la prostate	38	1.4	..	..	11	✦2.1	..	..
Pregnancy, childbirth and the puerperium — Grossesse, accouchement et puerpéralité								
Total	..	..	8	✦3.2	..	..	4	✦7.1
Pregnancy with abortive outcome — Grossesse se terminant par un avortement	..	..	-	-	..	..	1	✦1.8
Other direct obstetric causes — Autres décès maternels directs	..	..	8	✦3.2	..	..	2	✦3.6
Indirect obstetric causes — Décès maternels indirects	..	..	-	-	..	..	1	✦1.8
Certain conditions originating in the perinatal period — Certaines affections dont l'origine se situe dans la période périnatale	339	262.4	264	216.5	83	288.0	54	197.7
Congenital malformations, deformations and chromosomal abnormalities — Malformations congénitales et anomalies chromosomiques	325	251.6	271	222.2	109	378.2	79	289.2
Symptoms, signs and abnormal clinical and laboratory findings, not elsewhere classified — Symptômes, signes et résultats anormaux d'examens cliniques et de laboratoire, non classés ailleurs	483	4.9	403	4.0	57	2.9	53	2.6
All other diseases — Toutes autres maladies	118	1.2	202	2.0	19	✦1.0	35	1.7
External causes — Causes externes								
Total	5 178	52.4	2 495	24.9	1 190	60.4	613	30.1
Accidents								
Total	3 090	31.3	1 785	17.8	730	37.0	427	21.0
Transport accidents — Accidents de transport	1 295	13.1	473	4.7	411	20.8	171	8.4
Falls — Chutes	386	3.9	331	3.3	157	8.0	180	8.8
Accidental drowning and submersion — Noyade et submersion accidentelles	144	1.5	48	0.5	48	2.4	12	✦0.6
Exposure to smoke, fire and flames — Exposition à la fumée, au feu et aux flammes	63	0.6	31	0.3	7	✦0.4	12	✦0.6
Accidental poisoning by and exposure to noxious substances — Intoxication accidentelle par des substances nocives et exposition à ces substances	452	4.6	216	2.2	25	✦1.3	21	✦1.0
Intentional self-harm — Lésions auto-infligées	1 684	17.0	471	4.7	376	19.1	141	6.9
Assault — Agresssions	175	1.8	82	0.8	38	1.9	18	✦0.9
All other external causes — Toutes autres causes externes	229	2.3	157	1.6	46	2.3	27	✦1.3

New Zealand - Nouvelle-Zélande

Cause of death — Cause de décès	2004 (+C)			
	Male — Masculin		Female — Féminin	
	Number Nombre	Rate Taux	Number Nombre	Rate Taux
TOTAL	14 203	711.0	14 442	699.8
Certain infectious and parasitic diseases — Certaines maladies infectieuses et parasitaires				
Total..................	84	4.2	77	3.7
Intestinal infectious diseases — Maladies infectieuses intestinales..................	3	٠0.2	12	٠0.6
Tuberculosis — Tuberculose..................	9	٠0.5	4	٠0.2
Tetanus — Tétanos..................	-	-	-	-
Diphtheria — Diphtérie..................	-	-	-	-
Whooping cough — Coqueluche..................	1	٠0.1	-	-
Meningococcal infection — Infection à méningocoques..................	6	٠0.3	2	٠0.1
Septicaemia — Septicémie..................	14	٠0.7	31	1.5
Acute poliomyelitis — Poliomyélite aiguë..................	-	-	-	-
Measles — Rougeole..................	-	-	-	-
Viral hepatitis — Hépatite virale..................	15	٠0.8	5	٠0.2
Human immunodeficiency virus [HIV] disease — Maladies dues au virus de l'immunodéficience humaine (VIH)..................	11	٠0.6	4	٠0.2
Malaria — Paludisme..................	-	-	-	-
Neoplasms — Tumeurs	4 283	214.4	3 931	190.5
Malignant neoplasms — Tumeurs malignes				
Total..................	4 174	208.9	3 852	186.7
Malignant neoplasm of lip, oral cavity and pharynx — Tumeur maligne de la lèvre, de la cavité buccale et du pharynx......	66	3.3	35	1.7
Malignant neoplasm of oesophagus — Tumeur maligne de l'oesophage..................	132	6.6	74	3.6
Malignant neoplasm of stomach — Tumeur maligne de l'estomac..................	186	9.3	115	5.6
Malignant neoplasm of colon, rectosigmoid junction, rectum, anus and anal canal — Tumeur maligne du côlon, de la jonction recto-sigmoïdienne, du rectum, de l'anus et du canal anal..................	571	28.6	603	29.2
Malignant neoplasm of liver and intrahepatic bile ducts — Tumeur maligne du foie et des voies bilaires intrahépatiques....	117	5.9	56	2.7
Malignant neoplasm of pancreas — Tumeur maligne du pancréas..................	172	8.6	183	8.9
Malignant neoplasm of trachea, bronchus and lung — Tumeur maligne de la trachée, des bronches et du poumon........	929	46.5	626	30.3
Malignant neoplasm of female breast — Tumeur maligne du sein chez la femme..................	..	..	642	...
Malignant neoplasm of cervix uteri — Tumeur maligne du col de l'utérus..................	..	..	71	...
Malignant neoplasm of prostate — Tumeur maligne de la prostate..................	583	...	..	..
Malignant neoplasm of lymphoid, haematopoietic and related tissue — Tumeurs malignes primitives ou présumées primitives des tissus lymphoïde, hématopoïétique et apparentés..................	371	18.6	380	18.4
Disorders of the blood and blood-forming organs and certain disorders involving the immune mechanism — Maladies du sang et des organes hématopoïétiques et certains troubles du système immunitaire				
Total..................	28	٠1.4	36	1.7
Anaemias — Anémies..................	12	٠0.6	19	٠0.9
Endocrine, nutritional and metabolic diseases — Maladies endocriniennes, nutritionnelles et métaboliques				
Total..................	546	27.3	518	25.1
Diabetes mellitus — Diabète sucré..................	438	21.9	406	19.7
Malnutrition — Malnutrition..................	1	٠0.1	3	٠0.1
Mental and behavioural disorders — Troubles mentaux et du comportement	307	15.4	524	25.4
Diseases of the nervous system — Maladies du système nerveux..................	404	20.2	560	27.1
Diseases of the circulatory system — Maladies de l'appareil circulatoire				
Total..................	5 401	270.4	5 896	285.7
Acute rheumatic fever and chronic rheumatic heart diseases — Rhumatisme articulaire aigu et cardiopathies rhumatismales chroniques..................	48	2.4	75	3.6
Hypertensive diseases — Maladies hypertensives..................	104	5.2	179	8.7
Ischaemic heart disease — Cardiopathie ischémique..................	3 368	168.6	2 949	142.9
Cerebrovascular disease — Maladie cérébrovasculaire..................	1 049	52.5	1 757	85.1
Diseases of arteries, arterioles and capillaries — Maladies des artères, artérioles et capillaires..................	277	13.9	231	11.2
Diseases of the respiratory system — Maladies de l'appareil respiratoire				
Total..................	1 192	59.7	1 274	61.7
Influenza — Grippe..................	8	٠0.4	20	٠1.0
Pneumonia — Pneumopathies..................	157	7.9	279	13.5
Chronic lower respiratory diseases — Maladies chroniques des voies respiratoires inférieures..................	943	47.2	910	44.1
Diseases of the digestive system — Maladies de l'appareil digestif				
Total..................	336	16.8	453	22.0
Gastric and duodenal ulcer — Ulcère de l'estomac et du duodénum..................	37	1.9	46	2.2

New Zealand - Nouvelle-Zélande

Cause of death — Cause de décès	2004 (+C)			
	Male — Masculin		Female — Féminin	
	Number Nombre	Rate Taux	Number Nombre	Rate Taux
Diseases of the liver — Maladies du foie	81	4.1	53	2.6
Diseases of the musculoskeletal system and connective tissue — Maladies du système ostéo-articularie, des muscles et du tissu conjonctif	71	3.6	143	6.9
Diseases of the genitourinary system — Maladies de l'appareil génito-urinaire				
Total	191	9.6	179	8.7
Disorders of kidney and ureter — Affections du rein et de l'uretère	149	7.5	129	6.3
Hyperplasia of prostate — Hyperplasie de la prostate	15	...	..	..
Pregnancy, childbirth and the puerperium — Grossesse, accouchement et puerpéralité				
Total	..	..	4	+6.9
Pregnancy with abortive outcome — Grossesse se terminant par un avortement	..	..	-	-
Other direct obstetric causes — Autres décès maternels directs	..	..	1	+1.7
Indirect obstetric causes — Décès maternels indirects	..	..	3	+5.2
Certain conditions originating in the perinatal period — Certaines affections dont l'origine se situe dans la période périnatale	76	255.5	74	261.2
Congenital malformations, deformations and chromosomal abnormalities — Malformations congénitales et anomalies chromosomiques	86	289.1	93	328.3
Symptoms, signs and abnormal clinical and laboratory findings, not elsewhere classified — Symptômes, signes et résultats anormaux d'examens cliniques et de laboratoire, non classés ailleurs	36	1.8	56	2.7
All other diseases — Toutes autres maladies	27	+1.4	42	2.0
External causes — Causes externes				
Total	1 135	56.8	582	28.2
Accidents				
Total	688	34.4	424	20.5
Transport accidents — Accidents de transport	368	18.4	154	7.5
Falls — Chutes	168	8.4	187	9.1
Accidental drowning and submersion — Noyade et submersion accidentelles	44	2.2	13	+0.6
Exposure to smoke, fire and flames — Exposition à la fumée, au feu et aux flammes	11	+0.6	11	+0.5
Accidental poisoning by and exposure to noxious substances — Intoxication accidentelle par des substances nocives et exposition à ces substances	31	1.6	17	+0.8
Intentional self-harm — Lésions auto-infligées	382	19.1	111	5.4
Assault — Agresssions	34	1.7	13	+0.6
All other external causes — Toutes autres causes externes	31	1.6	34	1.6

-

Italics: data from civil registers that are incomplete or of unknown completeness. — Italiques: données incomplètes ou dont le degré d'exactitude n'est pas connu provenant des registres de l'état civil.

'Code' indicates the source of data, as follows:
C - Civil registration, estimated over 90% complete
U - Civil registration, estimated less than 90% complete
| - Other source, estimated reliable
+ - Data tabulated by date of registration rather than occurence.
... - Information not available

Le 'Code' indique la source des données, comme suit:
C - Registres de l'état civil considérés complèts à 90 p. 100 au moins.
U - Registres de l'état civil qui ne sont pas considérés complèts à 90 p. 100 au moins.
| - Autre source, considérée pas douteuses.
+ - Données exploitées selon la date de l'enregistrement et non la date de l'événement.
... - Information pas disponible.

FOOTNOTES - NOTES

* Provisional. - Données provisoires.

+ Rates based on 30 or fewer deaths. - Taux basés sur 30 décès ou moins.

[1] For 2003 and before, data on cause of death do not include the Chechnya region. Therefore, rates must be used with caution as they are based on the total population, which is assumed to include all regions. - Pour 2003 et avant, les données sur les causes de décès ne comprennent par la région de Chechnya. Par conséquent, les taux doivent être utilisés avec précaution car ils sont basés sur la population totale, qui est supposée inclure toutes les régions.

Table 22

Table 22 presents expectation of life at specified ages for each sex for the latest available year.

Description of variables: Expectation of life, e_x is defined as the average number of years of life remaining to persons reaching age x if they continued to be subject to the mortality conditions of the period indicated in the table.

Male and female expectations are shown separately for selected ages beginning at birth and proceeding with ages 5, 10, 15, 20, 25, 30, 35, 40, 45, 50, 55, 60, 65, 70, 75, 85, 90, 95 and 100 years.

The table shows life expectancy derived from an abridged or full life table as reported by the country or area. If data from both an abridged and a full life table are available, the data derived from an abridged life table are shown.

Data are shown with one decimal regardless of the number of digits provided in the original computation.

Life table computation: From the demographic point of view, a life table is regarded as a theoretical model of a population that is continuously replenished by births and depleted by deaths. The model gives a complete picture of the mortality experience of a population based on the assumption that the theoretical cohort is subject, throughout its existence, to the age-specific mortality rates observed at a particular time. Thus levels of mortality prevailing at the time a life table is constructed are assumed to remain unchanged into the future until all members of the cohort have died.

Reliability of data: The values shown in this table come from official life tables. It is assumed that, if necessary, the basic data (population and deaths classified by age and sex) have been adjusted for deficiencies before their use in constructing the life tables.

Limitations: Expectation-of-life values are subject to the same qualifications as have been set forth for population statistics in general and death statistics in particular, as discussed in sections 3 and 4, respectively, of the Technical Notes. They must be interpreted strictly using the underlying assumption that surviving cohorts are subjected to the same age-specific mortality rates of the period to which the life table refers.

Earlier data: Expectation of life at specified ages for each sex has been shown in previous issues of the *Demographic Yearbook*. Data included in this table update the series covering a period of years as follows:

Issue	Years Covered
Historical Supplement CD, 1997	1948 – 1997
Special Issue on Population Ageing and the Situation of Elderly Persons, 1991	1950 – 1990
Historical Supplement, 1979	1948 – 1977
1948	1896 – 1947

751

Tableau 22

Le tableau 22 présente les espérances de vie à des âges déterminés, pour chaque sexe, qui correspondent à la dernière année pour laquelle on dispose de données.

Description des variables : L'espérance de vie, e_x, se définit comme le nombre moyen d'années restant à vivre aux hommes et aux femmes qui ont atteint l'âge x, à supposer qu'ils continuent de connaître les mêmes conditions de mortalité observées pendant la période sur laquelle porte le tableau.

Les chiffres sont présentés séparément pour chaque sexe à partir de la naissance et pour les âges suivants : 5, 10, 15, 20, 25, 30, 35, 40, 45, 50, 55, 60, 65, 70, 75, 80, 85, 90, 95 et 100 ans.

Dans le tableau figurent les espérances de vie calculées selon les tables de mortalité abrégées ou complètes communiquées par les pays et les zones. Si les données provenant des tables de mortalité abrégées et complètes sont disponibles, les données présentées sont celles dérivées de la table abrégée.

Les données sont arrondies à la première décimale, indépendamment du nombre de décimales qui figurent dans le calcul initial.

Calcul des tables de mortalité : du point de vue démographique, les tables de mortalité sont considérées comme des modèles théoriques représentant une population constamment reconstituée par les naissances et réduite par les décès. Ces modèles donnent un aperçu complet de la mortalité d'une population et reposent sur l'hypothèse que chaque cohorte théoriquement distinguée connaît, pendant toute son existence, le taux de mortalité par âge observé à un moment donné. Les mortalités correspondant à l'époque à laquelle sont calculées les tables de mortalité sont ainsi censées demeurer inchangées dans l'avenir jusqu'au décès de tous les membres de la cohorte.

Fiabilité des donnés : étant donné que les chiffres figurant dans ce tableau proviennent de tables officielles de mortalité, elles sont toutes présumées sûres. En ce qui concerne les chiffres extraits de tables officielles de mortalité, on part du principe que les données de base (effectif de la population et nombre de décès selon l'âge et le sexe) ont été ajustées, en tant que de besoin, avant de servir à l'établissement de la table de mortalité.

Insuffisance des données : les espérances de vie appellent les mêmes réserves que celles qui ont été formulées à propos des statistiques de la population en général et des statistiques de mortalité en particulier (voir les sections 3 et 4 des Notes techniques). Lorsque l'on interprète les données, il ne faut jamais perdre de vue que, par hypothèse, les cohortes de survivants sont soumises, pour chaque âge, aux conditions de mortalité de la période visée par la table de mortalité.

Données publiées antérieurement : les espérances de vie à des âges déterminés pour chaque sexe figuraient déjà dans des éditions antérieures de l'Annuaire démographique. Les données présentées dans le tableau 22 actualisent les données qui portaient sur les périodes suivantes :

Éditions	Années considérées
Supplément historique (CD-ROM), 1997	1948 – 1997
Édition spéciale sur le vieillissement de la population et la situation des personnes âgées, 1991	1950 – 1990
Supplément rétrospectif, 1979	1948 – 1977
1948	1896 – 1947

22. Expectation of life at specified ages for each sex: latest available year, 1997 - 2006
Espérance de vie à un âge donné pour chaque sexe: dernière année disponible, 1997 - 2006

Continent, country or area and date / Continent, pays ou zone et date	Age (in years) - Age (en années)																				
	At birth - A la naissance	5	10	15	20	25	30	35	40	45	50	55	60	65	70	75	80	85	90	95	100
AFRICA - AFRIQUE																					
Algeria - Algérie[1]																					
2000																					
Male - Hommes	72.5	70.6	65.8	61.0	56.3	51.6	46.9	42.2	37.6	33.0	28.5	24.1	19.9	16.1	12.4	9.0	5.9	...	...	...	...
Female - Femmes	74.2	72.1	67.3	62.5	57.7	52.9	48.1	43.3	38.6	34.0	29.5	25.1	20.7	16.6	12.8	9.3	6.1	...	...	...	...
Botswana[2]																					
1999																					
Male - Hommes	65.7	...	...	...	...	...	...	...	...	...	...	...	...	...	...	...	...	...	...	...	...
Female - Femmes	69.0	...	...	...	...	...	...	...	...	...	...	...	...	...	...	...	...	...	...	...	...
Djibouti																					
1998																					
Male - Hommes	49.0	...	...	...	...	...	...	...	...	...	...	...	...	...	...	...	...	...	...	...	...
Female - Femmes	52.0	...	...	...	...	...	...	...	...	...	...	...	...	...	...	...	...	...	...	...	...
Egypt - Égypte																					
2001																					
Male - Hommes	65.6	64.7	59.9	55.1	50.4	45.6	40.9	36.2	31.6	27.2	22.9	18.9	15.4	12.1	9.2	6.8	5.2	4.0	...	...	...
Female - Femmes	67.4	66.8	62.0	57.2	52.3	47.5	42.7	37.9	33.1	28.4	23.9	19.5	15.5	11.7	8.6	5.7	4.0	2.8	...	...	...
2003																					
Male - Hommes	67.9	...	...	...	...	...	...	...	...	...	...	...	...	...	...	...	...	...	...	...	...
Female - Femmes	72.3	...	...	...	...	...	...	...	...	...	...	...	...	...	...	...	...	...	...	...	...
Kenya																					
1989 - 1999																					
Male - Hommes	52.9	54.8	51.1	46.6	42.3	38.3	34.5	21.0	27.7	24.1	21.0	17.7	14.5	11 6	8.9	6.7	5.0	3.8	3.1	2.5	...
Female - Femmes	60.4	63.0	59.0	54.3	49.9	45.9	42.2	38.6	34.8	30.9	27.0	23.1	19.3	15.6	12.2	9.2	6.7	4.8	3.6	2.5	...
Lesotho																					
2001																					
Male - Hommes	48.7	...	...	...	...	...	...	...	...	...	...	...	...	...	...	...	...	...	...	...	...
Female - Femmes	56.3	...	...	...	...	...	...	...	...	...	...	...	...	...	...	...	...	...	...	...	...
Malawi																					
1992 - 1997																					
Male - Hommes	43.5	52.1	49.5	45.7	41.9	38.4	34.8	31.2	27.6	24.0	20.6	17.3	14.1	11.2	8.6	6.3	4.4	...	...	...	...
Female - Femmes	46.8	54.5	52.0	48.2	44.4	40.6	36.9	33.2	29.6	25.9	22.2	18.6	15.1	11.9	9.2	6.8	4.6	...	...	...	...
2003[3]																					
Male - Hommes	43.4	...	...	...	...	...	...	...	...	...	...	...	...	...	...	...	...	...	...	...	...
Female - Femmes	46.0	...	...	...	...	...	...	...	...	...	...	...	...	...	...	...	...	...	...	...	...
Mauritius - Maurice																					
2005																					
Male - Hommes	68.9	65.1	60.2	55.3	50.4	45.7	41.0	36.4	32.0	27.7	23.7	19.8	16.3	13.2	10.4	8.1	6.1	4.2	...	...	...
Female - Femmes	75.6	71.7	66.8	61.8	56.9	52.1	47.2	42.4	37.7	33.0	28.5	24.2	20.2	16.6	13.3	10.3	7.6	5.5	...	...	...
Réunion																					
2003																					
Male - Hommes	71.3	...	...	...	...	...	...	...	...	...	...	...	...	...	...	...	...	...	...	...	...
Female - Femmes	79.8	...	...	...	...	...	...	...	...	...	...	...	...	...	...	...	...	...	...	...	...
Saint Helena ex. dep. - Sainte-Hélène sans dép.																					
1995 - 2004																					
Male - Hommes	71.9	68.3	63.3	...	53.6	...	44.3	...	34.6	...	25.9	...	17.7	...	10.8	...	7.5				
Female - Femmes	79.1	74.4	69.8	...	60.0	...	50.0	...	40.1	...	30.8	...	22.1	...	14.7	...	8.5				
South Africa - Afrique du Sud																					
2004																					
Male - Hommes	49.9	...	...	...	...	...	...	...	...	...	...	...	...	...	...	...	...	...	...	...	...
Female - Femmes	52.9	...	...	...	...	...	...	...	...	...	...	...	...	...	...	...	...	...	...	...	...
Swaziland[4]																					
1997																					
Male - Hommes	58.0	...	...	...	...	...	...	...	...	...	...	...	...	...	...	...	...	...	...	...	...
Female - Femmes	63.0	...	...	...	...	...	...	...	...	...	...	...	...	...	...	...	...	...	...	...	...
Zimbabwe																					
2001 - 2002																					
Male - Hommes	42.7	43.3	39.1	34.7	30.0	25.8	22.6	20.6	20.0	19.3	18.3	16.7	14.8	12.5	9.8	6.8	4.0	...	...	...	...
Female - Femmes	45.9	46.0	41.6	37.0	32.5	28.9	26.7	25.7	25.2	25.0	23.2	20.6	17.7	14.5	11.2	7.6	4.5	...	...	...	...

753

Continent, country or area and date / Continent, pays ou zone et date	At birth - A la naissance	5	10	15	20	25	30	35	40	45	50	55	60	65	70	75	80	85	90	95	100
AMERICA, NORTH - AMÉRIQUE DU NORD																					
Anguilla																					
2000 - 2002																					
Male - Hommes	76.5	72.1	67.1	62.1	57.3	53.1	48.4	43.7	39.4	34.7	30.2	25.4	21.1	16.5	12.7	10.0	8.0	6.9	...	...	...
Female - Femmes	81.1	76.4	71.4	66.4	61.4	57.1	52.7	47.7	42.7	38.3	33.5	28.7	24.0	19.4	15.3	10.8	8.3	7.6	...	...	...
Aruba																					
2000																					
Male - Hommes	70.0	65.4	60.5	55.6	50.9	46.7	42.3	37.7	33.0	28.5	24.2	20.1	16.3	13.1	10.4	8.1	5.7	3.9	4.0	3.2	...
Female - Femmes	76.0	71.9	67.0	62.0	57.2	52.5	47.7	43.0	38.3	33.6	28.9	24.4	20.5	16.7	13.1	10.4	7.5	5.5	4.7	3.6	...
British Virgin Islands - Îles Vierges britanniques																					
2004																					
Male - Hommes	69.9	...	...	...	...	...	...	...	...	...	...	...	...	...	...	...	...	...	...	...	...
Female - Femmes	78.5	...	...	...	...	...	...	...	...	...	...	...	...	...	...	...	...	...	...	...	...
Canada																					
2004																					
Male - Hommes	77.8	73.3	68.3	63.4	58.6	53.8	49.0	44.2	39.5	34.8	30.2	25.8	21.6	17.7	14.1	10.9	8.1	5.9	4.3	...	...
Female - Femmes	82.6	78.0	73.1	68.1	63.2	58.3	53.4	48.5	43.6	38.8	34.2	29.6	25.2	21.0	17.0	13.3	10.0	7.2	5.1	...	...
Cuba																					
2001 - 2003																					
Male - Hommes	75.1	70.8	65.9	61.0	56.2	51.5	46.7	42.0	37.4	32.9	28.5	24.3	20.4	16.7	13.3	10.3	7.7	5.3	...	...	...
Female - Femmes	79.0	74.5	69.6	64.7	59.8	54.9	50.1	45.2	40.5	35.8	31.3	26.9	22.6	18.6	14.9	11.5	8.6	5.8	...	...	...
Dominican Republic - République dominicaine[5]																					
2005																					
Male - Hommes	69.2	66.8	62.0	57.2	52.6	48.3	44.1	39.9	35.7	31.6	27.6	23.7	20.1	16.8	13.9	11.3	...	...	...	...	...
Female - Femmes	75.5	72.6	67.8	62.9	58.1	53.3	48.7	44.2	39.6	35.2	30.9	26.7	22.7	19.0	15.6	12.7	...	...	...	...	...
El Salvador																					
2000 - 2005																					
Male - Hommes	67.7	65.3	60.6	55.8	51.2	46.8	42.5	38.4	34.2	30.2	26.2	22.4	18.7	15.2	12.0	9.1	6.8	...	...	...	...
Female - Femmes	73.7	71.1	66.3	61.5	56.8	52.2	47.6	43.1	38.6	34.2	29.9	25.7	21.7	17.9	14.4	11.1	8.4	...	...	...	...
Greenland - Groenland																					
2002 - 2006																					
Male - Hommes	65.7	62.0	57.1	52.4	48.5	44.9	40.5	36.2	31.8	27.5	23.2	19.0	15.1	11.6	8.9	6.9	5.1	4.1	...	...	...
Female - Femmes	71.0	66.7	61.9	57.2	52.5	48.0	43.2	38.6	33.9	29.3	25.0	20.8	17.1	13.5	10.6	8.2	6.2	4.6	...	...	...
Guadeloupe																					
2002																					
Male - Hommes	74.6	70.2	65.3	60.5	55.7	51.2	46.8	42.2	37.7	33.2	29.0	24.8	20.9	17.3	13.8	10.6	7.9	5.1	2.0	0.5	
Female - Femmes	81.5	77.0	72.1	67.1	62.1	57.3	52.4	47.6	42.9	38.2	33.5	28.8	24.4	20.3	16.4	12.7	9.0	5.7	2.3	0.5	
Guatemala																					
1995 - 2000																					
Male - Hommes	61.4	60.6	56.0	51.2	46.8	42.7	38.8	34.9	31.2	27.4	23.7	20.1	16.8	13.6	10.7	8.2	6.1	...	...	...	...
Female - Femmes	67.2	66.2	62.6	56.9	52.3	47.7	43.3	38.9	34.6	30.4	26.3	22.3	18.6	15.2	12.0	9.2	6.9	...	...	...	...
Jamaica - Jamaïque																					
2003																					
Male - Hommes	71.3	67.8	62.9	58.1	53.5	49.3	45.2	41.1	36.9	32.6	28.4	24.2	20.4	17.0	13.8	11.1	8.7	7.0	5.5	...	...
Female - Femmes	77.1	73.7	68.8	63.9	59.0	54.3	49.7	45.0	40.5	36.0	31.6	27.4	23.3	19.6	16.0	12.9	10.1	7.8	5.8	...	...
Martinique																					
2002																					
Male - Hommes	75.4	71.0	66.0	61.1	56.3	51.7	47.1	42.5	37.9	33.4	28.9	24.7	20.4	16.5	13.0	10.0	7.5	4.8	2.0	0.5	
Female - Femmes	82.2	77.7	72.8	67.9	62.9	58.0	53.0	48.1	43.3	38.6	34.0	29.3	24.8	20.3	16.3	12.3	8.9	5.5	2.3	0.5	
Mexico - Mexique																					
2005																					
Male - Hommes	71.9	68.5	63.6	58.7	53.9	49.3	44.8	40.3	35.9	31.6	27.4	23.5	19.8	16.4	13.4	10.7	8.4	6.4	4.8	3.4	2.5
Female - Femmes	77.4	73.7	68.7	63.8	58.9	54.1	49.2	44.4	39.7	35.1	30.6	26.3	22.2	18.4	14.9	11.8	9.1	6.8	5.0	3.5	2.5
Netherlands Antilles - Antilles néerlandaises																					
2002 - 2004																					
Male - Hommes	70.6	67.5	62.6	57.7	53.1	48.9	44.6	40.1	35.5	31.1	26.9	22.9	19.1	15.7	12.5	9.8	7.5	5.6	4.1	2.9	2.3
Female - Femmes	79.0	75.3	70.3	65.3	60.4	55.5	50.6	45.8	41.0	36.4	31.8	27.5	23.3	19.4	15.8	12.6	9.7	7.3	5.4	4.0	3.1

22. Expectation of life at specified ages for each sex: latest available year, 1997 - 2006
Espérance de vie à un âge donné pour chaque sexe: dernière année disponible, 1997 - 2006 (continued - suite)

Continent, country or area and date / Continent, pays ou zone et date	At birth - A la naissance	5	10	15	20	25	30	35	40	45	50	55	60	65	70	75	80	85	90	95	100
AMERICA, NORTH - AMÉRIQUE DU NORD																					
Nicaragua																					
2000 - 2005																					
Male - Hommes	67.2	65.3	60.6	55.7	51.2	46.8	42.5	38.2	34.0	29.9	25.9	22.1	18.5	15.2	12.1	9.4	6.9	...	...	...	...
Female - Femmes	71.9	69.5	64.8	60.0	55.3	50.6	45.9	41.3	36.8	32.4	28.1	24.0	20.2	16.6	13.3	10.3	7.5	...	...	...	...
Panama[6]																					
2000																					
Male - Hommes	72.2	69.2	64.4	59.5	54.8	50.2	45.7	41.0	36.4	31.9	27.5	23.3	19.3	15.6	12.4	9.5	7.1	...	...	...	...
Female - Femmes	76.8	73.7	68.9	64.0	59.2	54.3	49.5	44.8	40.1	35.4	30.9	26.5	22.2	18.1	14.3	10.9	7.9	...	...	...	...
Puerto Rico - Porto Rico																					
2003 - 2005																					
Male - Hommes	73.7	69.4	64.4	59.5	54.8	50.4	46.0	41.5	37.1	32.8	28.6	24.6	20.8	17.2	13.9	10.9	8.4	6.3	4.6	3.3	2.3
Female - Femmes	80.9	76.6	71.6	66.6	61.7	56.8	52.0	47.2	42.4	37.7	33.1	28.6	24.3	20.2	16.3	12.8	9.6	6.9	4.8	3.2	2.0
Saint Kitts and Nevis - Saint-Kitts-et-Nevis																					
1998																					
Male - Hommes	68.2	65.0	60.1	55.3	50.5	45.8	41.1	36.5	32.7	28.5	24.3	20.6	16.6	13.3	11.0	9.1	6.6	4.7	3.4	2.2	0.4
Female - Femmes	70.7	67.5	62.5	57.6	52.7	48.0	43.4	38.8	34.4	29.8	25.4	21.3	17.6	14.3	11.3	8.9	6.3	4.6	3.3	2.2	0.4
Saint Lucia - Sainte-Lucie																					
2005																					
Male - Hommes	69.9	66.4	61.5	56.6	52.0	47.4	43.1	38.6	34.3	30.1	25.9	21.7	17.0	14.7	11.8	9.0	7.2	5.2	...	...	...
Female - Femmes	75.7	72.2	67.3	62.4	57.5	52.6	47.8	43.2	38.4	33.8	29.2	25.0	20.8	17.2	13.8	1.4	7.7	4.8	...	...	...
Saint Vincent and the Grenadines - Saint Vincent-et-les Grenadines																					
2001																					
Male - Hommes	66.9	63.9	59.2	54.3	49.6	45.1	40.7	36.5	32.3	28.2	24.1	19.9	16.2	12.8	9.7	7.3	4.3	4.1	...	...	...
Female - Femmes	72.9	69.3	64.5	59.5	54.7	49.8	45.2	40.7	36.1	31.7	27.3	23.0	19.0	14.6	10.8	7.3	4.1	3.6	...	...	...
Turks Calcos Islands - Îles Turques et Caïques																					
2001																					
Male - Hommes	79.0	75.3	70.3	65.3	60.3	55.8	50.8	46.0	41.2	37.1	33.0	28.4	24.3	20.8	17.5	12.5	7.5	4.1	...	...	...
Female - Femmes	77.4	72.5	67.5	62.5	57.5	52.9	48.2	43.4	38.6	33.8	29.6	25.0	20.0	17.0	13.2	11.7	10.3	8.8	...	...	...
United States - États-Unis																					
2004																					
Male - Hommes	75.2	70.8	65.9	61.0	56.2	51.6	46.9	42.2	37.6	33.1	28.8	24.7	20.8	17.1	13.7	10.7	8.2	6.1	4.4	3.2	2.3
Female - Femmes	80.4	76.0	71.0	66.1	61.2	56.3	51.5	46.6	41.9	37.2	32.7	28.3	24.0	20.0	16.2	12.8	9.8	7.2	5.2	3.7	2.6
AMERICA, SOUTH - AMÉRIQUE DU SUD																					
Argentina - Argentine																					
2000 - 2001																					
Male - Hommes	70.0	66.6	61.7	56.8	52.1	47.4	42.8	38.2	33.7	29.3	25.0	21.1	17.4	14.1	11.1	8.6	6.5	4.9	3.7	2.9	...
Female - Femmes	77.5	73.9	69.0	64.1	59.2	54.4	49.5	44.7	40.0	35.4	30.9	26.5	22.3	18.4	14.7	11.3	8.4	6.2	4.6	3.5	...
Bolivia - Bolivie																					
1995 - 2000																					
Male - Hommes	59.8	60.8	56.7	52.2	48.0	43.7	39.5	35.3	31.2	27.1	23.2	19.5	15.9	12.7	9.8	7.5	5.9	...	...	...	...
Female - Femmes	63.2	63.8	59.7	55.2	50.8	46.5	42.1	37.8	33.6	29.4	25.3	21.4	17.6	14.0	10.8	8.3	6.5	...	...	...	...
Brazil - Brésil[7]																					
2005																					
Male - Hommes	68.1	65.6	60.8	55.9	51.4	47.1	42.8	38.5	34.3	30.3	26.3	22.6	19.2	16.0	13.1	10.8	8.8	...	...	...	...
Female - Femmes	75.8	72.8	67.9	63.0	58.2	53.4	48.6	43.9	39.3	34.7	30.4	26.2	22.3	18.6	15.2	12.2	9.7	...	...	...	...
Chile - Chili[5]																					
2005																					
Male - Hommes	75.5	71.2	66.3	61.4	56.6	51.9	47.2	42.5	37.9	33.3	28.9	24.7	20.7	17.0	13.7	10.8	8.3	...	...	...	...
Female - Femmes	81.5	77.2	72.2	67.3	62.4	57.5	52.6	47.7	42.9	38.1	33.4	28.9	24.5	20.4	16.5	13.0	9.9	...	...	...	...

22. Expectation of life at specified ages for each sex: latest available year, 1997 - 2006
Espérance de vie à un âge donné pour chaque sexe: dernière année disponible, 1997 - 2006 (continued - suite)

Continent, country or area and date / Continent, pays ou zone et date	At birth - A la naissance	5	10	15	20	25	30	35	40	45	50	55	60	65	70	75	80	85	90	95	100
AMERICA, SOUTH - AMÉRIQUE DU SUD																					
Colombia - Colombie																					
2002 - 2007																					
Male - Hommes	69.6	67.0	62.2	57.3	52.8	48.5	44.2	39.8	35.5	31.1	26.8	22.7	18.8	15.3	12.2	9.6	7.5	...	...	...	...
Female - Femmes	75.7	72.9	68.0	63.2	58.3	53.6	48.8	44.0	39.3	34.7	30.2	25.9	21.8	17.9	14.5	11.5	9.2	...	...	...	...
Ecuador - Équateur[8]																					
2000 - 2005																					
Male - Hommes	71.3	68.8	64.1	59.3	54.8	50.5	46.3	42.1	37.8	33.6	29.6	25.5	21.6	17.9	14.4	11.2	8.1	...	...	...	...
Female - Femmes	77.2	74.2	69.4	64.5	59.8	55.1	50.4	45.7	41.1	36.6	32.2	27.8	23.7	19.7	15.8	12.2	8.8	...	...	...	...
French Guiana - Guyane française																					
2002																					
Male - Hommes	72.5	68.7	63.8	58.9	54.2	49.7	45.0	40.7	36.3	32.1	27.9	23.8	19.8	16.4	12.8	9.7	7.3	4.8	2.0	0.5	...
Female - Femmes	79.2	75.3	70.6	65.7	60.8	55.9	51.1	46.4	41.9	37.1	32.7	28.1	23.8	19.8	15.6	12.1	8.4	4.9	2.3	0.5	...
2003																					
Male - Hommes	71.3	...	...	...	...	...	...	...	...	...	...	...	...	...	...	...	...	...	...	...	...
Female - Femmes	79.7	...	...	...	...	...	...	...	...	...	...	...	...	...	...	...	...	...	...	...	...
Paraguay																					
2000 - 2005																					
Male - Hommes	68.6	...	...	...	...	...	...	...	...	...	...	...	...	...	...	...	...	...	...	...	...
Female - Femmes	73.1	...	...	...	...	...	...	...	...	...	...	...	...	...	...	...	...	...	...	...	...	...
Peru - Pérou[7]																					
1995 - 2000																					
Male - Hommes	65.9	65.9	61.4	56.6	52.0	47.4	42.9	38.5	34.1	29.8	25.7	21.7	18.1	14.7	11.7	9.2	7.0	...	...	...	...
Female - Femmes	70.9	70.2	65.6	60.7	55.9	51.2	46.5	41.9	37.3	32.9	28.5	24.3	20.3	16.5	13.3	10.4	7.8	...	...	...	...
Uruguay																					
2006																					
Male - Hommes	72.1	68.5	63.6	58.7	53.8	49.1	44.4	39.7	35.0	30.5	26.0	21.9	18.1	14.7	11.7	9.0	6.7	4.8	3.4	2.7	...
Female - Femmes	79.5	75.7	70.8	65.8	60.9	56.1	51.2	46.3	41.6	36.8	32.3	27.8	23.6	19.4	15.5	11.9	8.8	6.3	4.4	3.1	...
Venezuela (Bolivarian Republic of) - Venezuela (République bolivarienne du)[7]																					
1995 - 2000																					
Male - Hommes	68.6	66.6	61.8	56.9	52.3	47.8	43.3	38.8	34.3	29.9	25.6	21.6	17.9	14.5	11.4	8.6	5.9	...	...	...	...
Female - Femmes	74.5	72.1	67.2	62.3	57.5	52.6	47.8	43.1	38.4	33.7	29.2	24.9	20.8	16.9	13.3	9.9	6.9	...	...	...	...
2002																					
Male - Hommes	70.8	...	...	...	...	...	...	...	...	...	...	...	...	...	...	...	...	...	...	...	...
Female - Femmes	76.6	...	...	...	...	...	...	...	...	...	...	...	...	...	...	...	...	...	...	...	...	...
ASIA - ASIE																					
Afghanistan																					
2002																					
Male - Hommes	43.0	...	...	...	...	...	...	...	...	...	...	...	...	...	...	...	...	...	...	...	...
Female - Femmes	43.0	...	...	...	...	...	...	...	...	...	...	...	...	...	...	...	...	...	...	...	...
Armenia - Arménie																					
2004																					
Male - Hommes	70.3	66.3	61.4	56.5	51.6	46.8	42.0	37.3	32.7	28.2	24.0	19.9	16.2	13.0	10.3	8.0	5.8	3.7	2.4	1.4	1.4
Female - Femmes	76.4	72.2	67.3	62.3	57.4	52.5	47.6	42.7	37.9	33.2	28.5	24.1	19.7	15.8	12.2	9.1	6.5	4.2	2.3	1.4	0.6
2005																					
Male - Hommes	70.3	...	...	...	...	...	...	...	...	...	...	...	...	...	...	...	...	...	...	...	...
Female - Femmes	76.5	...	...	...	...	...	...	...	...	...	...	...	...	...	...	...	...	...	...	...	...
Azerbaijan - Azerbaïdjan																					
2004																					
Male - Hommes	69.6	66.1	61.3	56.4	51.5	46.8	42.1	37.5	33.0	28.6	24.4	20.4	16.7	13.7	11.2	9.1	7.5	5.5	3.9	2.7	0.9
Female - Femmes	75.2	70.9	66.1	61.2	56.3	51.4	46.6	41.8	37.0	32.3	27.7	23.3	19.0	15.3	11.9	9.1	6.8	4.8	3.2	2.0	0.8
2006																					
Male - Hommes	69.6	...	...	...	...	...	...	...	...	...	...	...	...	...	...	...	...	...	...	...	...
Female - Femmes	75.1	...	...	...	...	...	...	...	...	...	...	...	...	...	...	...	...	...	...	...	...
Bahrain - Bahreïn																					
2001																					
Male - Hommes	73.2	...	64.4	59.5	54.7	49.9	45.2	40.4	35.6	30.9	26.4	22.0	17.8	14.1	11.3	9.5	...	...	...	...	...
Female - Femmes	76.2	...	67.1	62.1	57.2	52.3	47.4	42.5	37.7	32.9	28.2	23.7	19.6	15.9	12.9	10.9	...	...	...	...	...

22. Expectation of life at specified ages for each sex: latest available year, 1997 - 2006
Espérance de vie à un âge donné pour chaque sexe: dernière année disponible, 1997 - 2006 (continued - suite)

Continent, country or area and date — Continent, pays ou zone et date	At birth - A la naissance	5	10	15	20	25	30	35	40	45	50	55	60	65	70	75	80	85	90	95	100
ASIA - ASIE																					
2005																					
Male - Hommes	73.1	...	...	...	...	...	...	...	...	...	...	...	...	...	...	...	...	...	...	...	
Female - Femmes	77.3	...	...	...	...	...	...	...	...	...	...	...	...	...	...	...	...	...	...	...	
Bangladesh																					
2006																					
Male - Hommes	64.7	...	...	...	...	...	...	...	...	...	...	...	...	...	...	...	...	...	...	...	
Female - Femmes	65.9	...	...	...	...	...	...	...	...	...	...	...	...	...	...	...	...	...	...	...	
Bhutan - Bhoutan																					
2005																					
Male - Hommes	65.6	...	...	...	...	...	...	...	...	...	...	...	...	...	...	...	...	...	...	...	
Female - Femmes	66.8	...	...	...	...	...	...	...	...	...	...	...	...	...	...	...	...	...	...	...	
China - Chine[9,10]																					
2000																					
Male - Hommes	69.6	...	...	...	...	...	...	...	...	...	...	...	...	...	...	...	...	...	...	...	
Female - Femmes	73.3	...	...	...	...	...	...	...	...	...	...	...	...	...	...	...	...	...	...	...	
China: Hong Kong SAR - Chine: Hong Kong RAS																					
2005																					
Male - Hommes	78.8	74.0	69.1	64.1	59.2	54.3	49.4	44.6	39.9	35.1	30.5	26.0	21.7	17.7	14.1	10.8	8.1	6.0	4.3	3.1	2.1
Female - Femmes	84.6	79.8	74.8	69.9	64.9	60.0	55.1	50.2	45.3	40.5	35.7	31.0	26.4	21.9	17.7	13.8	10.4	7.6	5.4	3.7	2.6
2006																					
Male - Hommes	79.4	...	...	...	...	...	...	...	...	...	...	...	...	...	...	...	...	...	...	...	
Female - Femmes	85.5	...	...	...	...	...	...	...	...	...	...	...	...	...	...	...	...	...	...	...	
China: Macao SAR - Chine: Macao RAS																					
2002 - 2005																					
Male - Hommes	77.6	73.1	68.2	63.2	58.3	53.5	48.8	44.1	39.4	34.7	30.2	25.7	21.3	17.1	13.2	9.8	7.1	4.7	2.8	1.5	1.3
Female - Femmes	82.3	77.7	72.7	67.8	62.8	57.9	53.0	48.1	43.3	38.5	33.7	28.9	24.2	19.7	15.2	11.2	8.1	5.7	3.7	2.3	2.7
Cyprus - Chypre[11]																					
2004 - 2005																					
Male - Hommes	77.0	72.4	67.5	62.5	57.8	53.0	48.3	43.6	38.8	34.1	29.5	25.0	20.7	16.7	13.1	9.7	6.9	4.8	3.3	2.3	...
Female - Femmes	81.7	77.0	72.1	67.2	62.2	57.3	52.4	47.6	42.7	37.8	33.1	28.3	23.8	19.3	15.2	11.3	8.1	5.6	4.5	3.4	
Georgia - Géorgie																					
2004																					
Male - Hommes	67.8	64.7	59.9	55.0	50.1	45.3	40.6	36.1	31.8	27.5	23.4	19.4	16.0	12.4	9.6	6.7	4.9	2.6	...	...	...
Female - Femmes	74.9	71.9	67.0	62.1	57.1	52.2	47.4	42.6	37.8	33.1	28.5	23.9	19.7	15.5	12.1	8.7	6.1	3.8	...	...	...
2006																					
Male - Hommes	69.8	...	...	...	...	...	...	...	...	...	...	...	...	...	...	...	...	...	...	...	
Female - Femmes	78.5	...	...	...	...	...	...	...	...	...	...	...	...	...	...	...	...	...	...	...	
India - Inde[12]																					
2001 - 2005																					
Male - Hommes	62.3	63.5	59.0	54.3	49.6	45.1	40.6	36.3	31.9	27.7	23.7	19.9	16.4	13.5	10.9	...	...	...	...	...	...
Female - Femmes	63.9	67.0	62.5	57.8	53.3	48.9	44.4	40.0	35.5	31.0	26.7	22.5	18.7	15.3	12.3	...	...	...	...	...	...
Iran (Islamic Republic of) - Iran (République islamique d')																					
2001																					
Male - Hommes	67.6	...	...	...	...	...	...	...	...	...	...	...	...	...	...	...	...	...	...	...	
Female - Femmes	70.4	...	...	...	...	...	...	...	...	...	...	...	...	...	...	...	...	...	...	...	
Iraq																					
1997																					
Male - Hommes	58.0	...	...	...	...	...	...	...	...	...	...	...	...	...	...	...	...	...	...	...	
Female - Femmes	59.0	...	...	...	...	...	...	...	...	...	...	...	...	...	...	...	...	...	...	...	
Israel - Israël[13]																					
2002 - 2006																					
Male - Hommes	78.0	73.5	68.6	63.6	58.7	54.0	49.2	44.4	39.7	35.0	30.4	26.0	21.8	17.9	14.3	11.2	8.6	6.6	...	...	...
Female - Femmes	82.0	77.5	72.5	67.6	62.6	57.7	52.8	47.9	43.0	38.2	33.5	28.9	24.4	20.1	16.0	12.4	9.2	6.7	...	...	...
Japan - Japon[14]																					
2006																					
Male - Hommes	79.0	74.3	69.3	64.4	59.5	54.7	49.8	45.0	40.3	35.6	31.0	26.6	22.4	18.5	14.7	11.3	8.5	6.1	4.3	3.1	2.2
Female - Femmes	85.8	81.1	76.1	71.2	66.2	61.3	56.4	51.5	46.7	41.9	37.1	32.5	27.9	23.4	19.1	15.0	11.3	8.1	5.7	3.9	2.6
Jordan - Jordanie[15]																					
2005																					
Male - Hommes	70.6	...	...	...	...	...	...	...	...	...	...	...	...	...	...	...	...	...	...	...	
Female - Femmes	72.4	...	...	...	...	...	...	...	...	...	...	...	...	...	...	...	...	...	...	...	

22. Expectation of life at specified ages for each sex: latest available year, 1997 - 2006
Espérance de vie à un âge donné pour chaque sexe: dernière année disponible, 1997 - 2006 (continued - suite)

Continent, country or area and date / Continent, pays ou zone et date	At birth - À la naissance	5	10	15	20	25	30	35	40	45	50	55	60	65	70	75	80	85	90	95	100
ASIA - ASIE																					
Kazakhstan																					
2005																					
Male - Hommes	60.3	56.6	51.8	46.9	42.3	38.0	33.9	30.1	26.3	22.6	19.3	16.3	13.5	11.1	9.0	7.3	5.7	4.2	3.1	2.3	1.8
Female - Femmes	71.8	68.0	63.1	58.2	53.4	48.7	44.0	39.5	35.0	30.6	26.3	22.3	18.5	14.9	11.7	8.9	6.5	4.6	3.2	2.2	1.7
Korea (Republic of) - Corée (République de)																					
2006																					
Male - Hommes	75.7	71.2	66.3	61.3	56.4	51.6	46.7	41.9	37.2	32.6	28.2	24.0	19.9	16.1	12.6	9.6	7.1	5.3	4.0	3.2	2.7
Female - Femmes	82.4	77.8	72.8	67.9	63.0	58.0	53.2	48.3	43.4	38.6	33.9	29.2	24.6	20.1	15.9	12.0	8.7	6.2	4.5	3.4	2.8
Kyrgyzstan - Kirghizistan																					
2006																					
Male - Hommes	63.5	61.0	56.1	51.3	46.4	41.8	37.3	33.1	29.0	25.0	21.4	18.0	14.9	12.2	9.8	8.2	7.1	6.2	3.0	6.1	6.1
Female - Femmes	72.1	69.5	64.6	59.7	54.8	50.0	45.3	40.6	36.0	31.5	27.1	23.0	19.2	15.7	12.8	10.2	8.4	7.7	5.2	5.2	1.5
Lao People's Democratic Republic - République démocratique populaire lao[16]																					
2005																					
Male - Hommes	55.0	...	...	...	...	...	...	...	...	...	...	...	...	...	...	...	...	...	...	...	...
Female - Femmes	63.0	...	...	...	...	...	...	...	...	...	...	...	...	...	...	...	...	...	...	...	...
Malaysia - Malaisie																					
2005																					
Male - Hommes	70.6	66.2	...	...	51.9	...	...	...	33.7	...	...	20.8	16.9	...	...	...	...	...	...	...	...
Female - Femmes	76.4	71.9	...	...	57.2	...	...	...	37.9	...	...	24.1	19.8	...	...	...	...	...	...	...	...
Maldives																					
2005																					
Male - Hommes	71.7	68.0	63.2	58.3	53.5	48.6	43.7	38.9	34.1	29.4	24.7	20.2	16.2	12.7	9.1	6.4	...	...	...	...	...
Female - Femmes	72.7	69.0	64.1	59.2	54.3	49.4	44.5	39.6	34.8	30.1	25.3	20.9	16.5	12.8	8.9	6.0	...	...	...	...	...
Mongolia - Mongolie																					
1998 - 2007																					
Male - Hommes	63.1	61.3	56.5	51.6	46.9	42.3	38.0	33.7	29.7	25.9	22.4	19.2	16.1	13.7	12.0	...	...	...	...	...	...
Female - Femmes	70.2	68.9	64.0	59.1	54.2	49.5	44.8	40.2	35.7	31.3	27.2	23.3	19.7	16.7	14.3	...	...	...	...	...	...
Myanmar[17]																					
2005																					
Male - Hommes	62.5	65.2	60.7	56.0	51.2	46.5	41.8	37.1	32.6	28.2	23.9	20.0	16.5	13.4	10.7	8.6	6.8	5.4	...	...	...
Female - Femmes	66.6	68.5	63.9	59.1	54.3	49.5	44.7	40.0	35.4	30.8	26.3	22.1	18.1	14.6	11.5	8.9	6.8	5.2	...	...	...
Nepal - Népal																					
2006																					
Male - Hommes	62.9	...	...	...	...	...	...	...	...	...	...	...	...	...	...	...	...	...	...	...	...
Female - Femmes	63.7	...	...	...	...	...	...	...	...	...	...	...	...	...	...	...	...	...	...	...	...
Occupied Palestinian Territory - Territoire palestinien occupé																					
2001																					
Male - Hommes	70.5	67.5	62.7	57.8	53.1	48.4	43.6	38.9	34.2	29.6	25.2	21.1	17.2	13.8	10.7	8.1	6.1	...	...	...	...
Female - Femmes	73.6	70.3	65.5	60.5	55.7	50.9	46.1	41.3	36.6	32.0	27.5	23.2	19.0	15.2	11.7	8.8	6.4	...	...	...	...
Oman																					
2006																					
Male - Hommes	73.2	...	...	...	...	...	...	...	...	...	...	...	...	...	...	...	...	...	...	...	...
Female - Femmes	75.4	...	...	...	...	...	...	...	...	...	...	...	...	...	...	...	...	...	...	...	...
Pakistan[18,19]																					
2003																					
Male - Hommes	64.7	66.6	61.9	57.1	52.4	47.7	43.1	38.6	34.1	29.7	25.6	21.8	18.5	15.4	11.9	...	...	...	...	...	...
Female - Femmes	65.6	67.2	62.4	57.4	52.6	48.0	43.5	38.9	34.4	30.0	25.7	21.8	18.5	15.4	12.9	...	...	...	...	...	...
Qatar																					
2006																					
Male - Hommes	76.7	72.5	67.6	62.7	58.2	53.8	49.1	44.3	39.6	34.9	30.2	25.6	21.1	16.9	13.6	10.7	8.2	...	...	...	...
Female - Femmes	76.7	72.4	67.5	62.6	57.7	52.8	47.9	42.9	38.0	33.1	28.3	23.6	19.0	15.3	12.0	10.1	9.2	...	...	...	...
Singapore - Singapour																					
2005																					
Male - Hommes	77.9	73.1	68.1	63.2	58.3	53.4	48.5	43.7	38.9	34.2	29.5	25.1	20.9	17.0	13.5	10.4	7.4	4.6	...	...	...
Female - Femmes	81.6	76.8	71.9	66.9	62.0	57.0	52.1	47.2	42.3	37.5	32.7	28.1	23.6	19.3	15.3	11.4	7.9	4.7	...	...	...

22. Expectation of life at specified ages for each sex: latest available year, 1997 - 2006
Espérance de vie à un âge donné pour chaque sexe: dernière année disponible, 1997 - 2006 (continued - suite)

Continent, country or area and date / Continent, pays ou zone et date	At birth - A la naissance	5	10	15	20	25	30	35	40	45	50	55	60	65	70	75	80	85	90	95	100
ASIA - ASIE																					
Turkey - Turquie																					
2006																					
Male - Hommes	69.1	...	...	...	...	...	...	...	...	...	...	...	...	...	...	...	...	...	...	...	...
Female - Femmes	74.0	...	...	...	...	...	...	...	...	...	...	...	...	...	...	...	...	...	...	...	...
Yemen - Yémen																					
2004																					
Male - Hommes	60.2	...	...	...	...	...	...	...	...	...	...	...	...	...	...	...	...	...	...	...	...
Female - Femmes	62.0	...	...	...	...	...	...	...	...	...	...	...	...	...	...	...	...	...	...	...	...
EUROPE																					
Åland Islands - Îles d'Åland[20]																					
2005																					
Male - Hommes	78.8	74.3	69.3	64.7	59.7	54.7	49.7	45.0	40.0	35.8	31.0	26.1	21.5	17.1	13.5	10.6	7.3	6.0	4.5	2.8	0.0
Female - Femmes	81.1	77.2	72.2	67.2	62.2	57.2	52.6	48.0	43.0	38.2	33.9	29.3	24.7	20.6	16.7	13.1	10.2	7.2	4.9	3.1	2.2
Albania - Albanie																					
2000																					
Male - Hommes	72.5	69.5	64.8	59.9	55.1	50.4	45.8	41.1	36.4	31.8	27.3	22.9	18.6	14.8	11.3	8.4	6.0	3.8	...	...	...
Female - Femmes	77.3	74.4	69.5	64.7	59.8	54.9	50.0	45.2	40.3	35.5	30.8	26.1	21.6	17.3	13.2	9.6	6.4	3.8	...	...	...
Austria - Autriche																					
2006																					
Male - Hommes	75.5	72.5	67.6	62.6	57.8	53.0	48.2	43.4	38.6	33.9	29.4	25.1	21.0	17.2	13.6	10.4	7.6	5.3	3.7	2.7	...
Female - Femmes	81.5	78.0	73.0	68.1	63.2	58.2	53.3	48.4	43.5	38.7	34.0	29.4	24.9	20.6	16.4	12.5	9.0	6.2	4.2	3.0	...
Belarus - Bélarus																					
2006																					
Male - Hommes	63.6	59.2	54.2	49.3	44.5	39.9	35.6	31.4	27.4	23.5	20.0	16.7	13.8	11.4	9.3	7.4	5.7	4.3	3.1	2.1	1.4
Female - Femmes	75.5	71.1	66.1	61.2	56.3	51.4	46.6	41.9	37.3	32.7	28.2	24.0	20.0	16.2	12.7	9.5	7.0	5.0	3.5	2.4	1.6
Belgium - Belgique																					
2004																					
Male - Hommes	76.5	71.8	66.9	61.9	57.1	52.4	47.6	42.8	38.1	33.4	29.0	24.7	20.6	16.8	13.2	10.0	7.3	5.1	3.6	2.5	2.1
Female - Femmes	82.4	77.7	72.8	67.8	62.9	57.9	53.0	48.1	43.3	38.5	33.9	29.4	25.0	20.7	16.5	12.6	9.2	6.4	4.4	3.1	2.2
Bosnia and Herzegovina - Bosnie-Herzégovine																					
2003																					
Male - Hommes	71.3	...	...	...	...	...	...	...	...	...	...	...	...	...	...	...	...	...	...	...	...
Female - Femmes	76.7	...	...	...	...	...	...	...	...	...	...	...	...	...	...	...	...	...	...	...	...
Bulgaria - Bulgarie																					
2004 - 2006																					
Male - Hommes	69.1	65.0	60.1	55.2	50.4	45.6	40.9	36.2	31.6	27.3	23.2	19.5	16.1	13.1	10.3	7.8	5.8	4.2	2.9	1.9	0.5
Female - Femmes	76.3	72.1	67.2	62.3	57.4	52.5	47.6	42.8	38.0	33.3	28.8	24.4	20.2	16.1	12.4	9.2	6.5	4.5	3.0	1.8	0.5
Czech Republic - République tchèque																					
2006																					
Male - Hommes	73.4	68.8	63.9	58.9	54.1	49.3	44.5	39.7	35.0	30.4	26.0	22.0	18.2	14.8	11.7	8.8	6.4	4.5	3.0	1.9	1.2
Female - Femmes	79.7	74.9	70.0	65.0	60.1	55.1	50.2	45.3	40.4	35.7	31.0	26.5	22.1	18.0	14.1	10.5	7.4	4.8	3.0	1.7	1.0
Denmark - Danemark[21]																					
2005 - 2006																					
Male - Hommes	75.9	71.3	66.4	61.4	56.5	51.7	46.9	42.1	37.3	32.7	28.2	24.0	19.9	16.2	12.7	9.6	7.1	5.1	3.6	2.4	1.9
Female - Femmes	80.4	75.8	70.8	65.9	60.9	56.0	51.0	46.1	41.3	36.5	31.9	27.4	23.1	19.0	15.2	11.8	8.8	6.3	4.3	2.9	2.1
Estonia - Estonie																					
2005																					
Male - Hommes	67.2	62.7	57.8	52.9	48.1	43.5	39.1	34.5	30.2	26.1	22.3	19.0	15.8	13.1	10.5	8.2	6.3	4.4	...	...	...
Female - Femmes	78.1	73.7	68.8	63.8	58.9	54.1	49.2	44.4	39.6	35.0	30.5	26.2	22.1	18.0	14.2	10.7	7.6	5.2	...	...	...
Finland - Finlande[22]																					
2006																					
Male - Hommes	75.8	71.1	66.1	61.2	56.4	51.7	46.9	42.2	37.5	33.0	28.6	24.4	20.5	16.8	13.3	10.1	7.4	5.2	3.6	2.5	1.4
Female - Femmes	82.8	78.1	73.1	68.2	63.2	58.3	53.4	48.5	43.7	38.9	34.2	29.7	25.2	20.9	16.7	12.8	9.2	6.4	4.3	2.9	1.7
France[23]																					
2005																					
Male - Hommes	76.8	72.2	67.2	62.3	57.4	52.7	47.9	43.1	38.4	33.9	29.6	25.4	21.5	17.7	14.1	10.9	8.0	5.8	4.1	3.3	5.2
Female - Femmes	83.8	79.1	74.2	69.2	64.3	59.4	54.4	49.6	44.7	40.0	35.4	30.8	26.4	22.0	17.8	13.8	10.1	7.1	4.8	3.3	2.9

22. Expectation of life at specified ages for each sex: latest available year, 1997 - 2006
Espérance de vie à un âge donné pour chaque sexe: dernière année disponible, 1997 - 2006 (continued - suite)

Continent, country or area and date / Continent, pays ou zone et date	At birth - A la naissance	5	10	15	20	25	30	35	40	45	50	55	60	65	70	75	80	85	90	95	100
EUROPE																					
Germany - Allemagne																					
2004 - 2006																					
Male - Hommes	76.6	72.0	67.1	62.1	57.2	52.4	47.6	42.8	38.0	33.3	28.9	24.6	20.6	16.8	13.2	10.1	7.5	5.4	3.8	2.7	2.0
Female - Femmes	82.1	77.4	72.5	67.5	62.6	57.6	52.7	47.8	42.9	38.1	33.5	28.9	24.5	20.2	16.0	12.2	8.9	6.2	4.1	2.8	2.1
Gibraltar																					
2001																					
Male - Hommes	78.5	73.5	68.5	63.5	58.5	53.5	...	43.5	...	33.9	...	25.8	...	17.9	...	11.3	...	...	...	...	...
Female - Femmes	83.3	79.5	75.0	70.0	65.0	60.0	...	50.3	...	40.3	...	30.3	...	20.6	...	13.7	...	...	...	...	...
Greece - Grèce																					
2006																					
Male - Hommes	77.1	72.4	67.5	62.5	57.7	53.0	48.3	43.5	38.8	34.2	29.7	25.4	21.3	17.4	13.8	10.6	7.9	5.9	4.5	3.3	2.4
Female - Femmes	82.0	77.3	72.4	67.4	62.5	57.5	52.6	47.7	42.8	38.0	33.3	28.6	24.0	19.6	15.3	11.3	8.1	5.7	4.2	3.1	2.1
Hungary - Hongrie																					
2006																					
Male - Hommes	69.0	64.6	59.6	54.7	49.8	45.0	40.2	35.5	30.9	26.6	22.8	19.4	16.3	13.4	10.7	8.3	6.1	4.2	2.6	1.5	0.6
Female - Femmes	77.4	72.8	67.9	62.9	58.0	53.1	48.1	43.3	38.5	33.8	29.4	25.2	21.1	17.2	13.5	10.1	7.2	4.7	2.8	1.5	0.6
Iceland - Islande																					
2005 - 2006																					
Male - Hommes	79.4	74.7	69.7	64.7	59.9	55.2	50.4	45.5	40.7	35.8	31.1	26.6	22.3	18.3	14.5	11.0	7.8	5.5	3.6	2.1	...
Female - Femmes	83.0	78.2	73.2	68.3	63.4	58.5	53.5	48.6	43.7	38.8	34.1	29.5	25.0	20.6	16.6	12.7	9.4	6.5	4.4	3.1	...
Ireland - Irlande																					
2002																					
Male - Hommes	75.1	70.7	65.7	60.8	56.0	51.3	46.5	41.8	37.0	32.3	27.8	23.4	19.2	15.4	11.9	8.9	6.5	4.6	3.3	2.4	1.7
Female - Femmes	80.3	75.7	70.8	65.8	60.9	56.0	51.1	46.2	41.4	36.6	31.9	27.4	22.9	18.7	14.8	11.2	8.2	5.8	4.1	2.9	2.1
Italy - Italie																					
2004																					
Male - Hommes	77.9	73.3	68.3	63.4	58.6	53.8	49.0	44.2	39.4	34.7	30.1	25.6	21.4	17.4	13.8	10.6	7.8	5.6	4.0	2.8	1.9
Female - Femmes	83.7	79.1	74.1	69.1	64.2	59.3	54.3	49.4	44.6	39.7	35.0	30.4	25.8	21.4	17.2	13.3	9.8	6.9	4.8	3.3	2.2
Latvia - Lettonie																					
2006																					
Male - Hommes	65.9	61.5	56.6	51.7	46.9	42.1	37.6	33.2	29.1	25.3	21.6	18.2	15.0	12.1	9.5	7.2	5.3	3.8	2.6	...	...
Female - Femmes	76.8	72.8	67.9	62.9	58.0	53.2	48.3	43.5	38.8	34.2	29.8	25.5	21.5	17.8	14.4	11.4	8.8	6.7	5.0	...	...
Lithuania - Lituanie																					
2006																					
Male - Hommes	65.3	60.9	56.0	51.1	46.4	41.8	37.4	33.1	28.9	25.1	21.5	18.4	15.5	13.1	10.6	8.4	6.3	4.8	3.5	2.6	1.8
Female - Femmes	77.1	72.7	67.8	62.8	57.9	53.0	48.2	43.5	38.8	34.3	29.9	25.6	21.6	17.7	13.9	10.4	7.4	5.1	3.4	2.3	2.3
Luxembourg																					
2000 - 2002																					
Male - Hommes	74.8	70.4	65.4	60.5	55.7	51.0	46.3	41.6	36.9	32.3	27.8	23.6	19.5	15.8	12.5	9.5	7.0	5.0	3.4	2.1	1.5
Female - Femmes	81.0	76.5	71.5	66.6	61.6	56.7	51.9	47.0	42.2	37.5	32.8	28.2	23.8	19.7	15.8	12.2	9.1	6.5	4.3	2.6	1.5
Malta - Malte																					
2006																					
Male - Hommes	76.8	72.4	67.4	62.5	57.6	52.8	47.9	43.1	38.3	33.6	28.9	24.5	20.2	16.1	12.5	9.4	6.9	...	...	...	...
Female - Femmes	81.2	77.0	72.2	67.3	62.3	57.3	52.3	47.5	42.5	37.7	33.1	28.3	23.8	19.5	15.4	11.7	8.4	...	...	...	...
Moldova																					
2006																					
Male - Hommes	64.6	60.6	55.8	50.9	46.1	41.3	36.7	32.3	28.1	24.2	20.6	17.4	14.4	11.6	9.3	7.3	5.7	4.3	3.2	2.2	...
Female - Femmes	72.2	68.3	63.3	58.4	53.6	48.7	43.8	39.0	34.3	29.8	25.5	21.4	17.6	14.3	11.2	8.6	6.5	4.8	3.5	2.3	...
Netherlands - Pays-Bas																					
2006																					
Male - Hommes	77.4	73.4	68.4	63.5	58.5	53.7	48.8	44.0	39.1	34.4	29.7	25.3	21.0	16.9	13.2	10.0	7.3	5.2	3.6	2.5	...
Female - Femmes	81.7	77.7	72.7	67.7	62.8	57.8	52.9	48.0	43.2	38.4	33.7	29.2	24.8	20.5	16.4	12.6	9.2	6.4	4.3	2.9	...
Norway - Norvège[24]																					
2006																					
Male - Hommes	78.1	73.5	68.5	63.5	58.7	53.9	49.2	44.4	39.6	34.9	30.3	25.8	21.5	17.5	13.8	10.4	7.5	5.3	3.6	2.6	1.9
Female - Femmes	82.7	77.9	73.0	68.0	63.1	58.1	53.2	48.3	43.5	38.7	34.0	29.4	24.9	20.6	16.5	12.6	9.2	6.4	4.2	2.8	2.1
Poland - Pologne																					
2006																					
Male - Hommes	70.4	61.5	56.6	51.8	47.1	42.3	37.6	33.1	28.8	24.8	21.1	17.7	14.5	11.7	9.1	6.9	5.2	...	...	...	...
Female - Femmes	79.0	70.2	65.2	60.3	55.4	50.5	45.6	40.7	36.0	31.5	27.1	22.8	18.8	14.9	11.3	8.3	5.9	...	...	...	...
Portugal																					
2005 - 2006																					
Male - Hommes	75.2	70.5	65.6	60.7	55.9	51.1	46.3	41.7	37.1	32.7	28.4	24.2	20.2	16.3	12.8	9.6	7.0	5.0	...	...	...
Female - Femmes	81.8	77.1	72.1	67.2	62.2	57.3	52.4	47.5	42.7	38.0	33.3	28.7	24.2	19.8	15.6	11.8	8.4	5.8	...	...	...

22. Expectation of life at specified ages for each sex: latest available year, 1997 - 2006
Espérance de vie à un âge donné pour chaque sexe: dernière année disponible, 1997 - 2006 (continued - suite)

Continent, country or area and date / Continent, pays ou zone et date	At birth - A la naissance	5	10	15	20	25	30	35	40	45	50	55	60	65	70	75	80	85	90	95	100
EUROPE																					
Romania - Roumanie																					
2004 - 2006																					
Male - Hommes	68.7	65.2	60.3	55.4	50.6	45.8	41.0	36.3	31.8	27.5	23.6	20.0	16.6	13.5	10.7	8.2	6.1	4.5	3.3	2.4	1.8
Female - Femmes	75.8	72.0	67.1	62.2	57.3	52.4	47.5	42.7	37.9	33.3	28.8	24.4	20.2	16.3	12.6	9.3	6.7	4.7	3.3	2.3	1.6
Russian Federation - Fédération de Russie																					
2006																					
Male - Hommes	60.4	56.3	51.4	46.5	41.8	37.5	33.6	29.8	26.1	22.6	19.4	16.5	13.8	11.4	9.3	7.4	5.9	4.6	3.4	2.8	1.4
Female - Femmes	73.2	69.1	64.2	59.2	54.4	49.7	45.0	40.5	36.0	31.6	27.3	23.2	19.4	15.6	12.2	9.2	6.7	4.7	3.3	2.5	1.8
San Marino - Saint-Marin																					
2000																					
Male - Hommes	77.4	73.0	68.0	63.1	58.5	53.8	49.1	44.3	39.5	34.7	30.1	25.6	21.4	17.2	13.5	10.5	7.7	5.7	3.8	2.3	0.5
Female - Femmes	84.0	79.6	74.6	69.6	64.7	59.7	54.8	49.9	45.0	40.2	35.4	30.7	26.0	21.6	17.1	13.1	9.3	6.3	4.3	2.7	0.5
Serbia - Serbie																					
2006																					
Male - Hommes	70.6	66.2	61.3	56.4	51.5	46.8	42.0	37.3	32.6	28.1	23.8	20.0	16.4	13.3	10.4	7.9	5.9	...	...	...	...
Female - Femmes	75.9	71.4	66.5	61.5	56.6	51.7	46.8	41.9	37.1	32.4	27.9	23.5	19.3	15.3	11.8	8.7	6.2	...	...	...	...
Slovakia - Slovaquie																					
2006																					
Male - Hommes	70.4	66.0	61.1	56.2	51.3	46.5	41.8	37.0	32.4	28.0	23.9	20.1	16.5	13.3	10.5	8.1	6.1	4.5	3.2	2.2	0.8
Female - Femmes	78.2	73.7	68.8	63.8	58.9	53.9	49.0	44.1	39.3	34.5	29.9	25.5	21.2	17.1	13.2	9.8	6.9	4.6	2.9	1.7	0.7
Slovenia - Slovénie																					
2005 - 2006																					
Male - Hommes	74.8	70.2	65.2	60.3	55.4	50.7	46.0	41.2	36.5	32.0	27.7	23.6	19.7	16.1	12.7	9.8	7.4	5.4	3.9	3.1	1.0
Female - Femmes	81.9	77.2	72.3	67.3	62.4	57.5	52.5	47.7	42.8	38.0	33.2	28.7	24.3	20.1	15.9	12.2	8.9	6.3	4.5	3.1	1.0
Spain - Espagne																					
2004 - 2005																					
Male - Hommes	77.0	72.4	67.4	62.5	57.6	52.8	48.0	43.2	38.5	33.9	29.5	25.2	21.1	17.2	13.6	10.4	7.6	5.4	3.7	2.1	0.5
Female - Femmes	83.5	78.8	73.9	68.9	64.0	59.1	54.1	49.2	44.4	39.6	34.8	30.2	25.6	21.1	16.8	12.8	9.3	6.4	4.2	2.3	0.5
Sweden - Suède																					
2006																					
Male - Hommes	78.7	74.0	69.0	64.1	59.2	54.4	49.6	44.7	39.9	35.1	30.5	26.0	21.7	17.6	13.9	10.5	7.6	5.2	3.6	2.5	1.9
Female - Femmes	82.9	78.2	73.2	68.3	63.3	58.4	53.5	48.6	43.7	38.9	34.1	29.5	25.0	20.8	16.6	12.8	9.4	6.5	4.4	3.1	2.2
Switzerland - Suisse																					
2005 - 2006																					
Male - Hommes	78.9	74.3	69.4	64.4	59.6	54.8	49.9	45.1	40.3	35.6	31.0	26.5	22.3	18.2	14.4	11.0	8.0	5.7	4.1	3.1	...
Female - Femmes	83.9	79.3	74.3	69.3	64.4	59.5	54.6	49.7	44.8	40.0	35.3	30.6	26.1	21.7	17.5	13.5	9.9	6.9	4.8	3.5	...
The Former Yugoslav Rep. of Macedonia - L'ex-République yougoslave de Macédoine																					
2005																					
Male - Hommes	71.6	67.7	62.8	57.8	53.0	48.1	43.3	38.5	33.8	29.1	24.8	20.8	17.0	13.5	10.4	7.7	5.5	4.0	2.9	2.4	0.5
Female - Femmes	75.9	72.2	67.3	62.3	57.4	52.5	47.5	42.7	37.8	33.1	28.5	24.0	19.7	15.7	12.0	8.9	6.4	4.7	3.4	2.9	0.5
Ukraine																					
2005 - 2006																					
Male - Hommes	62.4	58.3	53.4	48.5	43.7	39.2	34.9	30.8	27.0	23.4	20.1	17.1	14.3	11.8	9.5	7.5	5.8	4.4	3.1	2.0	0.8
Female - Femmes	74.1	69.9	65.0	60.1	55.2	50.3	45.6	41.0	36.5	32.0	27.7	23.5	19.6	15.8	12.4	9.3	6.8	4.8	3.3	2.1	0.8
United Kingdom - Royaume-Uni[25]																					
2000																					
Male - Hommes	75.3	70.9	65.9	61.0	56.1	51.4	46.6	41.9	37.1	32.5	27.9	23.6	19.5	15.7	12.3	9.4	7.0	5.0	3.7	2.7	2.0
Female - Femmes	80.1	75.6	70.6	65.7	60.8	55.9	51.0	46.1	41.2	36.5	31.8	27.3	23.0	18.8	15.0	11.5	8.6	6.1	4.3	3.0	2.2
OCEANIA - OCÉANIE																					
Australia - Australie																					
2003 - 2005																					
Male - Hommes	78.5	74.0	69.0	64.1	59.2	54.5	49.7	45.0	40.2	35.6	31.0	26.5	22.2	18.1	14.4	11.0	8.2	5.9	4.2	3.2	2.5
Female - Femmes	83.3	78.8	73.8	68.9	63.9	59.0	54.1	49.3	44.4	39.6	34.9	30.3	25.7	21.4	17.2	13.4	9.9	7.1	4.9	3.6	2.8
Guam																					
2004																					
Male - Hommes	75.1	...	...	...	...	...	...	...	...	...	...	...	...	...	...	...	...	...	...	...	...
Female - Femmes	81.3	...	...	...	...	...	...	...	...	...	...	...	...	...	...	...	...	...	...	...	...

22. Expectation of life at specified ages for each sex: latest available year, 1997 - 2006
Espérance de vie à un âge donné pour chaque sexe: dernière année disponible, 1997 - 2006 (continued - suite)

Continent, country or area and date / Continent, pays ou zone et date	At birth - À la naissance	5	10	15	20	25	30	35	40	45	50	55	60	65	70	75	80	85	90	95	100
OCEANIA - OCÉANIE																					
Kiribati 1995 - 2000																					
Male - Hommes	58.2	...	...	...	...	...	...	...	...	...	...	...	...	...	...	...	...	...	...	...	...
Female - Femmes	67.3	...	...	...	...	...	...	...	...	...	...	...	...	...	...	...	...	...	...	...	...
Marshall Islands - Îles Marshall 2004																					
Male - Hommes	67.0	...	...	...	...	...	...	...	...	...	...	...	...	...	...	...	...	...	...	...	...
Female - Femmes	70.6	...	...	...	...	...	...	...	...	...	...	...	...	...	...	...	...	...	...	...	...
Nauru 1997 - 2002																					
Male - Hommes	52.5	...	...	...	...	...	...	...	...	...	...	...	...	...	...	...	...	...	...	...	...
Female - Femmes	58.2	...	...	...	...	...	...	...	...	...	...	...	...	...	...	...	...	...	...	...	...
New Caledonia - Nouvelle-Calédonie 2003																					
Male - Hommes	71.3	67.0	62.1	57.2	52.4	48.0	43.3	38.8	34.2	29.7	25.4	21.2	17.4	13.8	11.0	9.0	7.1	5.1	3.8	9.8	...
Female - Femmes	77.3	72.7	67.8	62.9	58.1	53.3	48.5	43.8	39.0	34.3	29.8	25.4	21.5	17.4	14.3	10.9	8.5	6.4	5.0	2.7	...
New Zealand - Nouvelle-Zélande 2004 - 2006																					
Male - Hommes	77.9	73.4	68.4	63.5	58.8	54.1	49.3	44.5	39.8	35.1	30.6	26.1	21.8	17.8	14.2	10.9	8.1	5.8	4.3	...	...
Female - Femmes	81.9	77.4	72.4	67.5	62.6	57.7	52.8	48.0	43.1	38.4	33.7	29.2	24.7	20.5	16.5	12.8	9.5	6.7	4.6	...	...
Palau - Palaos 2000																					
Male - Hommes	66.6	...	...	...	...	...	...	...	...	...	...	...	...	...	...	...	...	...	...	...	...
Female - Femmes	74.5	...	...	...	...	...	...	...	...	...	...	...	...	...	...	...	...	...	...	...	...
Papua New Guinea - Papouasie-Nouvelle-Guinée 2000																					
Male - Hommes	53.7	54.1	50.2	45.7	41.6	37.7	33.7	29.8	25.9	22.1	18.5	15.0	11.9	9.2	6.9	5.0	3.6	2.6	1.7	0.6	...
Female - Femmes	54.8	54.7	50.8	46.3	42.1	38.1	34.1	30.1	26.2	22.3	18.6	15.2	12.0	9.2	6.8	5.0	3.6	2.5	1.6	0.6	...
Tonga 1998																					
Male - Hommes	69.8	66.5	61.6	56.7	52.0	47.2	42.5	37.8	33.1	28.5	24.1	20.0	16.3	13.0	10.4	7.2	5.5	...	...	...	...
Female - Femmes	71.8	68.3	63.5	58.6	53.7	48.9	44.2	39.4	34.8	30.2	25.8	21.6	17.7	14.1	11.2	7.8	5.9	...	...	...	...
Tuvalu 1997 - 2002																					
Male - Hommes	61.7	59.5	54.8	50.0	45.2	40.6	35.9	32.1	28.0	24.1	20.0	17.1	13.7	10.8	9.0	6.9	5.4	...	...	...	...
Female - Femmes	65.1	62.6	57.7	53.7	50.0	45.3	40.9	36.6	32.2	28.1	23.8	20.3	16.9	13.2	10.6	7.9	6.4	...	...	...	...
Vanuatu 1999																					
Male - Hommes	65.6	...	...	...	...	...	...	...	...	...	...	...	...	...	...	...	...	...	...	...	...
Female - Femmes	69.0	...	...	...	...	...	...	...	...	...	...	...	...	...	...	...	...	...	...	...	...

FOOTNOTES - NOTES

[1] For Algerian population only. - Pour la population algérienne seulement.

[2] Data refer to national projections. - Les données se réfèrent aux projections nationales.

[3] Projections based on the 1998 Malawi Population and Housing Census. - Les projections sont basées sur les résultats du recensement de la population et de l'habitat de Malawi de 1998.

[4] Data for 1997 refer to last twelve months preceding population and housing census of 1997. - Les données pour 1997 se réfèrent au douze mois précédant le recensement de population et de l'habitat de 1997.

[5] Data refer to national projections for 2005 - 2010. - Les données se rapportent aux prévisions nationales pour 2005-2010.

[6] Excluding tribal Indian population. - Non compris les Indiens vivant en tribus.

[7] Excluding Indian jungle population. - Non compris les Indiens de la jungle.

[8] Excluding nomadic Indian tribes. - Non compris les tribus d'Indiens nomades.

[9] Life expectancy in 2000 is calculated by the death data of 2000's Population Census, which modified by the mortality rates from the annual national sample surveys on population changes since 1990 . - L'espérance de vie en 2000 par est calculée en se fondant sur les données relatives aux décès issues du recensement de la population de 2000 modifiées par les taux de mortalité extraits des enquêtés nationales annuelles par sondage concernant l'évolution de la population depuis 1990.

[10] For statistical purposes, the data for China do not include those for the Hong Kong Special Administrative Region (Hong Kong SAR), Macao Special Administrative Region (Macao SAR) and Taiwan province of China. - Pour la présentation des statistiques, les données pour la Chine ne comprennent pas la Région Administrative Spéciale de Hong Kong (Hong Kong RAS), la Région Administrative Spéciale de Macao (Macao RAS) et Taïwan province de Chine.

[11] Data refer to government controlled areas. - Les données se rapportent aux zones contrôlées par le Gouvernement.

[12] Including data for the Indian-held part of Jammu and Kashmir, the final status of which has not yet been determined. - Y compris les données pour la partie du Jammu et du Cachemire occupée par l'Inde dont le statut définitif n'a pas encore été déterminé.

[13] Including data for East Jerusalem and Israeli residents in certain other territories under occupation by Israeli military forces since June 1967. - Y compris les données pour Jérusalem-Est et les résidents israéliens dans certains autres territoires occupés depuis 1967 par les forces armées israéliennes.

[14] Data refer to Japanese nationals in Japan only. - Les données se raportent aux nationaux japonais au Japon seulement.

[15] Excluding data for Jordanian territory under occupation since June 1967 by Israeli military forces. Excluding foreigners, including registered Palestinian refugees. - Non compris les données pour le territoire jordanien occupé depuis juin 1967 par les forces armées israéliennes. Non compris les étrangers, mais y compris les réfugiés de Palestine enregistrés.

[16] Data estimated from population and housing census 2005. - Données dérivées du recensement de population et du logement de 2005.

[17] Data refer to urban areas only. - Données ne concernant que les zones urbaines.

[18] Data based on Pakistan Demographic Survey (PDS 2003) . - Données extraites de l'enquête démographique effectuée par le Pakistan en 2003.

[19] Excluding data for the Pakistan-held part of Jammu and Kashmir, the final status of which has not yet been determined. - Non compris les données concernant la partie du Jammu et Cachemire occupée par le Pakistan dont le statut définitif n'a pas été déterminé.

[20] Also included in Finland. - Comprise aussi dans Finlande.

[21] Excluding Faeroe Islands and Greenland shown separately, if available. - Non compris les Iles Féroé et le Gröenland, qui font l'objet de rubriques distinctes, si disponible.

[22] Including Aland Islands. - Y compris les Îles d'Åland.

[23] Excluding Overseas Departments, namely, French Guiana, Guadeloupe, Martinique and Reunion, shown separately, if available. - Non compris les départements d'outre mer, c'est-à-dire la Guyane française, la Guadeloupe, la Martinique et la Réunion, qui font l'objet de rubriques distinctes, si disponible.

[24] Excluding Svalbard and Jan Mayen Island shown separately, if available. - Non compris Svalbard et Jan Mayen qui font l'objet de rubriques distinctes, si disponible.

[25] Excluding Channel Islands and Isle of Man, shown separately, if available. - Non compris les îles Anglo-Normandes et l'île de Man, qui font l'objet de rubriques distinctes, si disponible.

Table 23

Table 23 presents number of marriages and crude marriage rates by urban/rural residence for every year with available data between 2002 and 2006.

Description of variables: Marriage is defined as the act, ceremony or process by which the legal relationship of husband and wife is constituted. The legality of the union may be established by civil, religious or other means as recognized by the laws of each country. [i]

Marriage statistics in this table, therefore, include both first marriages and remarriages after divorce, widowhood or annulment. They do not, unless otherwise noted, include resumption of marriage ties after legal separation. These statistics refer to the number of marriages performed, and not to the number of persons marrying.

Statistics shown are obtained from civil registers of marriage. Exceptions, such as data from church registers, are identified in footnotes.

The urban/rural classification of marriages is that provided by each country or area; it is presumed to be based on the national census definitions of urban population which have been set forth at the end of the technical notes for table 6.

For certain countries, there is a discrepancy between the total number of marriages shown in this table and those shown in subsequent tables for the same year. Usually this discrepancy arises because the total number of marriages occurring in a given year is revised although the remaining tabulations are not.

Rate computation: Crude marriage rates are the annual number of marriages per 1 000 mid-year population. Rates by urban/rural residence are the annual number of marriages, in the appropriate urban or rural category, per 1 000 corresponding mid-year population. Rates presented in this table have been limited to those for countries or areas having at least a total of 30 marriages in a given year. These rates are calculated by the Statistics Division of the United Nations based on the appropriate reference population (for example: total population, nationals only etc.) if known and available. If the reference population is not known or unavailable the total population is used to calculate the rates. Therefore, if the population that is used to calculate the rates is different from the correct reference population, the rates presented might under- or overstate the true situation in a country or area.

Reliability of data: Each country or area has been asked to indicate the estimated completeness of the number of marriages recorded in its civil register. These national assessments are indicated by the quality codes C and U that appear in the first column of this table.

C indicates that the data are estimated to be virtually complete, that is, representing at least 90 per cent of the marriages occurring each year, while U indicates that data are estimated to be incomplete, that is, representing less than 90 per cent of the marriages occurring each year. The code ... indicates that no information was provided regarding completeness.

Data from civil registers which are reported as incomplete or of unknown completeness (coded U or ...) are considered unreliable. They appear in italics in this table; rates are not computed for these data.

These quality codes apply only to data from civil registers. For more information about the quality of vital statistics data in general, see section 4.2 of the Technical Notes.

Limitations: Statistics on marriages are subject to the same qualifications that have been set forth for vital statistics in general and marriage statistics in particular as discussed in section 4 of the Technical Notes.

The fact that marriage is a legal event, unlike birth and death that are biological events, has implications for international comparability of data. Marriage has been defined, for statistical purposes, in terms of the laws of individual countries or areas. These laws vary throughout the world. In addition, comparability is further limited because some countries or areas compile statistics only for civil marriages although religious marriages may also be legally recognized; in other countries or areas, the only available records are church registers and, therefore, the statistics may not reflect marriages that are civil marriages only.

Because in many countries or areas marriage is a civil legal contract which, to establish its legality, must be celebrated before a civil officer, it follows that for these countries or areas registration would tend to be almost automatic at the time of, or immediately following, the marriage ceremony. This factor should be kept in mind when considering the reliability of data, described above. For this reason the practice of tabulating data by date of registration does not generally pose serious problems of comparability as it does in the case of birth and death statistics.

As indicators of family formation, the statistics on the number of marriages presented in this table are bound to be deficient to the extent that they do not include either customary unions, which are not registered even though they are considered legal and binding under customary law, or consensual unions (also known as extra-legal or de facto unions). In general, lower marriage rates over a period of years are an indication of higher incidence of customary or consensual unions.

In addition, rates are affected also by the quality and limitations of the population estimates that are used in their computation. The problems of under-enumeration or over-enumeration and, to some extent, the differences in definition of total population have been discussed in section 3 of the Technical Notes dealing with population data in general, and specific information pertaining to individual countries or areas is given in the footnotes to table 3.

Strict correspondence between the numerator of the rate and the denominator is not always obtained; for example, marriages among civilian and military segments of the population may be related to civilian population. The effect of this may be to increase the rates, but, in most cases, this effect is negligible.

It should be emphasized that crude marriage rates like crude birth, death and divorce rates, may be seriously affected by the age-sex-marital structure of the population to which they relate. Crude marriage rates do, however, provide a simple measure of the level and changes in marriage.

The comparability of data by urban/rural residence is affected by the national definitions of urban and rural used in tabulating these data. It is assumed, in the absence of specific information to the contrary, that the definitions of urban and rural used in connection with the national population census were also used in the compilation of the vital statistics for each country or area. However, it cannot be excluded that, for a given country or area, different definitions of urban and rural are used for the vital statistics data and the population census data respectively. When known, the definitions of urban in national population censuses are presented at the end of the technical notes for table 6. As discussed in detail in the notes, these definitions vary considerably from one country or area to another.

In addition to problems of comparability, marriage rates classified by urban/rural residence are also subject to certain special types of bias. If, when calculating marriage rates, different definitions of urban are used in connection with the vital events and the population data, and if this results in a net difference between the numerator and denominator of the rate in the population at risk, then the marriage rates would be biased. Urban/rural differentials in marriage rates may also be affected by whether the vital events have been tabulated in terms of place of occurrence or place of usual residence. This problem is discussed in more detail in section 4.1.4.1. of the Technical Notes.

Earlier data: Marriages and crude marriage rates have been shown in each issue of the *Demographic Yearbook*. For more information on specific topics, and years for which data are reported, readers should consult the Historical Index.

NOTES

[i] *Principles and Recommendations for a Vital Statistics System Revision 2*, Sales No. E. 01.XVII.10, United Nations, New York, 2001

Tableau 23

Le tableau 23 présente des données sur les mariages et les taux bruts de nuptialité selon le lieu de résidence (zone urbaine ou rurale) pour les années où l'information est disponible entre 2002 et 2006.

Description des variables : le mariage désigne l'acte, la cérémonie ou la procédure qui établit un rapport légal entre mari et femme. L'union peut être rendue légale par une procédure civile ou religieuse, ou par toute autre procédure, conformément à la législation du pays[1].

Les statistiques de la nuptialité présentées dans ce tableau comprennent donc les premiers mariages et les remariages faisant suite à un divorce, un veuvage ou une annulation. Toutefois, sauf indication contraire, elles ne comprennent pas les unions reconstituées après une séparation légale. Ces statistiques se rapportent au nombre de mariages célébrés, non au nombre de personnes qui se marient.

Les statistiques présentées reposent sur l'enregistrement des mariages par les services de l'état civil. Les exceptions (données provenant des registres des églises, par exemple) font l'objet d'une note à la fin du tableau.

La classification des mariages selon le lieu de résidence (zone urbaine ou rurale) est celle qui a été communiquée par chaque pays ou zone ; on part du principe qu'elle repose sur les définitions de la population urbaine utilisées pour les recensements nationaux telles qu'elles sont reproduites à la fin des notes techniques se rapportant au tableau 6.

Pour quelques pays il y a une discordance entre le nombre total de mariages présenté dans ce tableau et ceux présentés après pour la même année. Habituellement ces différences apparaissent lorsque le nombre total des mariages pour une certaine année a été révisé alors que les autres tabulations ne l'ont pas été.

Calcul des taux : les taux bruts de nuptialité représentent le nombre annuel de mariages pour 1 000 habitants au milieu de l'année. Les taux selon le lieu de résidence (zone urbaine ou rurale) représentent le nombre annuel de mariages, classés selon la catégorie urbaine ou rurale appropriée, pour 1 000 habitants au milieu de l'année. Les taux du tableau 23 ne se rapportent qu'aux pays ou zones où l'on a enregistré un total d'au moins 30 mariages pendant une année donnée. Ces taux sont calculés par la division de statistique des Nations Unies sur la base de la population de référence adéquate (par exemple : population totale, nationaux seulement, etc.) si connue et disponible. Si la population de référence n'est pas connue ou n'est pas disponible, la population totale est utilisée pour calculer les taux. Par conséquent, si la population utilisée pour calculer les taux est différente de la population de référence adéquate, les taux présentés sont susceptibles de sous ou sur estimer la situation réelle d'un pays ou d'un territoire.

Fiabilité des données : il a été demandé à chaque pays ou zone d'indiquer le degré estimatif de complétude des données sur les mariages figurant dans ses registres d'état civil. Ces évaluations nationales sont signalées par les codes de qualité 'C' et 'U' qui apparaissent dans la deuxième colonne du tableau.

La lettre 'C' indique que les données sont jugées à peu près complètes, c'est-à-dire qu'elles représentent au moins 90 p. 100 des mariages survenus chaque année ; la lettre 'U' signale que les données sont jugées incomplètes, c'est-à-dire qu'elles représentent moins de 90 p. 100 des mariages survenus chaque année. Le code '...' indique qu'aucun renseignement n'a été communiqué quant à la complétude des données.

Les données issues des registres de l'état civil qui sont déclarées incomplètes ou dont le degré de complétude n'est pas connu (code 'U' ou '...') sont jugées douteuses. Elles apparaissent en italique dans le tableau et les taux correspondants n'ont pas été calculés.

Les codes de qualité ne s'appliquent qu'aux données provenant des registres de l'état civil. Pour plus de précisions sur la qualité des données reposant sur les statistiques de l'état civil en général, voir la section 4.2 des Notes techniques.

Insuffisance des données : les statistiques relatives aux mariages appellent les mêmes réserves que celles qui ont été formulées à propos des statistiques de l'état civil en général et des statistiques concernant la nuptialité en particulier (voir la section 4 des Notes techniques).

Le fait que le mariage soit un acte juridique, à la différence de la naissance et du décès, qui sont des faits biologiques, a des répercussions sur la comparabilité internationale des données. Aux fins de la statistique, le mariage est défini par la législation de chaque pays ou zone. Cette législation varie d'un pays à l'autre. La comparabilité est limitée en outre du fait que certains pays ou zones ne réunissent des statistiques que pour les mariages civils, bien que les mariages religieux y soient également reconnus par la loi ; dans d'autres, les seuls relevés disponibles sont les registres des églises et, en conséquence, les statistiques peuvent ne pas rendre compte des mariages exclusivement civils.

Étant donné que, dans de nombreux pays ou zones, le mariage est un contrat juridique civil qui, pour être légal, doit être conclu devant un officier d'état civil, il s'ensuit que dans ces pays ou zones l'enregistrement se fait à peu près systématiquement au moment de la cérémonie ou immédiatement après. Il faut tenir compte de cet élément lorsque l'on évalue la fiabilité des données, dont il est question plus haut. C'est pourquoi la pratique consistant à exploiter les données selon la date de l'enregistrement ne pose généralement pas les graves problèmes de comparabilité auxquels on se heurte dans le cas des statistiques concernant les naissances et les décès.

Les statistiques relatives au nombre des mariages présentées dans ce tableau donnent une idée forcément trompeuse de la formation des familles, dans la mesure où elles ne tiennent compte ni des mariages coutumiers, qui ne sont pas enregistrés bien qu'ils soient considérés comme légaux et créateurs d'obligations en vertu du droit coutumier, ni des unions consensuelles (appelées également unions non légalisées ou unions de fait). En général, une diminution du taux de nuptialité pendant un certain nombre d'années indique une augmentation des mariages coutumiers ou des unions consensuelles.

L'exactitude des taux dépend également de la qualité et des insuffisances des estimations de population qui sont utilisées pour leur calcul. Le problème des erreurs par excès ou par défaut commises lors du dénombrement et, dans une certaine mesure, le problème de l'hétérogénéité des définitions de la population totale ont été examinés à la section 3 des Notes techniques relative à la population en général ; des indications concernant les différents pays ou zones sont données en note à la fin du tableau 3.

Il n'a pas toujours été possible d'obtenir une correspondance rigoureuse entre le numérateur et le dénominateur pour le calcul des taux. Par exemple, les mariages parmi la population civile et les militaires sont parfois rapportés à la population civile. Cela peut avoir pour effet d'accroître les taux, mais, dans la plupart des cas, il est probable que la différence sera négligeable.

Il faut souligner que les taux bruts de nuptialité, de même que les taux bruts de natalité, de mortalité et de divortialité, peuvent varier sensiblement selon la structure par âge et par sexe de la population à laquelle ils se rapportent. Les taux bruts de nuptialité offrent néanmoins un moyen simple de mesurer la fréquence et l'évolution des mariages.

La comparabilité des données selon le lieu de résidence (zone urbaine ou rurale) peut être limitée par les définitions nationales des termes « urbain » et « rural » utilisées pour le classement de ces données. En l'absence d'indications contraires, on a supposé que les mêmes définitions avaient servi pour le recensement national de la population et pour l'établissement des statistiques de l'état civil pour chaque pays ou zone. Toutefois, il n'est pas exclu que, pour une zone ou un pays donné, des définitions différentes aient été retenues. Les définitions du terme « urbain » utilisées pour les recensements nationaux de population ont été présentées à la fin des notes techniques du tableau 6 lorsqu'elles étaient connues. Comme on l'a précisé dans les notes techniques relatives au tableau 6, ces définitions varient considérablement d'un pays ou d'une zone à l'autre.

Outre les problèmes de comparabilité, les taux de nuptialité classés selon le lieu de résidence (zone urbaine ou rurale) sont également sujets à des distorsions particulières. Si l'on utilise des définitions différentes du terme « urbain » pour classer les faits d'état civil et les données relatives à la population lors du calcul des taux et qu'il en résulte une différence nette entre le numérateur et le dénominateur pour le taux de la population exposée au risque, les taux de nuptialité s'en trouveront faussés. La différence entre ces taux pour les zones urbaines et rurales pourra aussi être faussée selon que les faits d'état civil auront été classés d'après le lieu où ils se sont produits ou d'après le lieu de résidence habituel. Ce problème est examiné plus en détail à la section 4.1.4.1 des Notes techniques.

Données publiées antérieurement : les différentes éditions de l'Annuaire démographique regroupent des données sur le nombre des mariages. Pour plus de précisions concernant les années et les sujets pour lesquels des données ont été publiées, se reporter à l'index historique.

NOTE

[1] *Principes et recommandations pour un système de statistiques de l'état civil, deuxième révision*, numéro de vente : F.01.XVII.10, publication des Nations Unies, New York, 2003.

23. Marriages and crude marriage rates, by urban/rural residence: 2002 - 2006
Mariages et taux bruts de nuptialité, selon la résidence, urbaine/rurale: 2002 - 2006

Continent, country or area, and urban/rural residence / Continent, pays ou zone et résidence, urbaine/rurale	Co-de[a]	Number - Nombre					Rate - Taux				
		2002	2003	2004	2005	2006	2002	2003	2004	2005	2006
AFRICA - AFRIQUE											
Algeria - Algérie[1]											
Total	...	218 620	240 463	267 633	279 548	295 295	...	...	...	...	...
Egypt - Égypte[2]											
Total	+...	510 517	537 092	550 709	522 751	522 887	...	...	...	...	...
Urban - Urbaine	+...	183 538	185 880	175 361	170 556	168 323	...	...	...	...	...
Rural - Rurale	+...	326 979	351 212	375 348	352 195	354 564	...	...	...	...	...
Libyan Arab Jamahiriya - Jamahiriya arabe libyenne[3]											
Total	U	33 323	...	...	...	...	...	...	...	...	...
Mauritius - Maurice											
Total	+C	10 484	10 812	11 385	11 294	11 471	8.7	8.8	9.2	9.1	9.2
Urban - Urbaine	+C	3 295	3 298	3 422	3 551	3 468	6.4	6.4	6.6	6.8	6.6
Rural - Rurale	+C	7 189	7 514	7 963	7 743	8 003	10.3	10.7	11.2	10.8	11.0
Réunion											
Total	C	3 284	*3 212	*3 269	*3 115	*2 982	4.4	*4.2	*4.3	*4.0	*3.8
Saint Helena ex. dep. - Sainte-Hélène sans dép.											
Total	C	13	20	10	10		...	...	...	...	...
Seychelles											
Total	+C	865	823	905	886	984	10.3	9.9	11.0	10.7	11.6
South Africa - Afrique du Sud											
Total	...	177 202	178 689	176 521	180 657		...	...	...	...	...
AMERICA, NORTH - AMÉRIQUE DU NORD											
Anguilla[4]											
Total	C	53	75	70	89	79	4.4	6.1	5.6	6.5	5.5
Aruba[5]											
Total	C	728	663	606	572	...	7.8	7.0	6.2	5.7	...
Belize											
Total	+C	1 622	...	...	...	...	6.1	...	...	...	...
Bermuda - Bermudes											
Total	C	937	861	868	820	876	14.9	13.7	13.7	12.9	13.7
British Virgin Islands - Îles Vierges britanniques											
Total	C	384	475	426	...	...	18.3	22.3	19.6	...	...
Canada											
Total	C	146 738	147 391	...	...	...	4.7	4.7	...	...	...
Cayman Islands - Îles Caïmanes											
Total	+C	321	344	920	810	...	7.6	7.9	20.8	16.8	...
Costa Rica											
Total	C	23 926	24 448	25 370	25 631	26 575	6.0	6.0	6.1	6.0	6.1
Cuba											
Total	C	56 876	54 739	50 878	51 831	56 377	5.1	4.9	4.5	4.6	5.0
Urban - Urbaine	C	51 728	50 103	46 655	48 335	52 818	6.1	5.9	5.5	5.7	6.2
Rural - Rurale	C	5 148	4 636	4 223	3 496	3 559	1.9	1.7	1.5	1.3	1.3
Dominican Republic - République dominicaine											
Total	+C	36 685	37 225	38 642	39 439	...	4.2	4.2	4.3	4.3	...
El Salvador											
Total	...	25 998	24 972	25 172	24 396	24 441	...	...	...	...	...
Urban - Urbaine	...	22 102	20 836	20 828	20 449	20 659	...	...	...	...	...
Rural - Rurale	...	3 896	4 136	4 344	3 947	3 782	...	...	...	...	...
Guadeloupe											
Total	C	1 809	1 701	1 771	1 727	1 736	4.1	3.9	4.0	3.9	3.8
Guatemala											
Total	C	51 857	51 247	53 860	52 186	57 505	4.3	4.2	4.3	4.1	4.4
Jamaica - Jamaïque											
Total	C	23 070	22 476	21 670	25 937	23 148	8.8	8.6	8.2	9.8	8.7
Martinique											
Total	C	1 524	1 414	1 425	1 453	1 477	3.9	3.6	3.6	3.7	3.7

Continent, country or area, and urban/rural residence / Continent, pays ou zone et résidence, urbaine/rurale	Code[a]	Number - Nombre					Rate - Taux				
		2002	2003	2004	2005	2006	2002	2003	2004	2005	2006
AMERICA, NORTH - AMÉRIQUE DU NORD											
Mexico - Mexique[6]											
Total	+C	616 654	584 142	600 563	595 713	586 978	6.1	5.7	5.8	5.7	5.6
Urban - Urbaine	+C	469 962	436 825	447 840	446 557	445 475	6.2	5.7	5.7	5.6	5.5
Rural - Rurale	+C	134 326	132 873	134 918	132 052	126 157	5.4	5.4	5.5	5.4	5.2
Netherlands Antilles - Antilles néerlandaises[7]											
Total	C	677	748	710	901	1 104	3.9	4.2	3.9	4.9	5.8
Nicaragua											
Total	+C	21 037	21 390	18 679	23 069	...	4.0	4.0	3.5	4.2	...
Panama[8]											
Total	C	9 558	10 310	10 290	*10 512	10 747	3.1	3.3	3.2	*3.3	3.3
Urban - Urbaine	C	...	8 622	...	...	...	...	...	...	...	...
Rural - Rurale	C	...	1 688	...	...	...	...	...	...	...	...
Puerto Rico - Porto Rico											
Total	C	25 645	25 236	23 650	23 511	...	6.6	6.5	6.1	6.0	...
Saint Lucia - Sainte-Lucie											
Total	C	500	540	*459	...	...	3.1	3.4	*2.8	...	...
Saint Vincent and the Grenadines - Saint Vincent-et-les Grenadines											
Total	+C	509	491	526	576	...	4.7	4.7	5.0	5.6	...
Trinidad and Tobago - Trinité-et-Tobago											
Total	C	7 434	...	...	...	...	5.8	...	...	...	...
Turks Caicos Islands - Îles Turques et Caïques											
Total	C	593	491	499	489	...	28.4	19.5	18.1	16.0	...
United States - États-Unis											
Total	C	2 254 000	2 245 000	2 279 000	2 249 000	*2 160 000	7.8	7.7	7.8	7.6	*7.2
AMERICA, SOUTH - AMÉRIQUE DU SUD											
Argentina - Argentine											
Total	C	122 343	129 049	128 212	132 720	134 496	3.3	3.4	3.4	3.4	3.5
Bolivia - Bolivie											
Total	U	34 060	22 570	29 674	21 958	20 810	...	...	...	...	...
Brazil - Brésil[9]											
Total	U	715 166	748 981	806 968	835 846	889 828	...	...	...	...	...
Chile - Chili											
Total	+C	60 971	56 659	53 403	53 842	...	3.9	3.6	3.3	3.3	...
Urban - Urbaine	+C	54 404	51 265	50 181	48 603	...	4.1	3.8	3.6	3.4	...
Rural - Rurale	+C	6 567	5 394	3 222	5 239	...	3.0	2.5	1.5	2.4	...
Ecuador - Équateur[10]											
Total	U	66 208	65 393	63 299	66 612	74 036	...	...	...	...	...
French Guiana - Guyane française											
Total	C	522	524	539	596	629	3.0	2.9	2.9	3.0	3.2
Paraguay											
Total	U	16 100	17 717	17 763	19 826	...	...	...	...	...	...
Suriname											
Total	C	2 005	1 936	1 951	2 013	...	4.2	4.0	4.0	4.0	...
Uruguay											
Total	C	14 073	14 147	13 123	13 075	12 415	4.3	4.3	4.0	4.0	3.7
Venezuela (Bolivarian Republic of) - Venezuela (République bolivarienne du)[9]											
Total	C	73 163	74 562	74 103	86 093	89 772	2.9	2.9	2.8	3.2	3.3

23. Marriages and crude marriage rates, by urban/rural residence: 2002 - 2006
Mariages et taux bruts de nuptialité, selon la résidence, urbaine/rurale: 2002 - 2006 (continued - suite)

Continent, country or area, and urban/rural residence / Continent, pays ou zone et résidence, urbaine/rurale	Code[a]	Number - Nombre					Rate - Taux				
		2002	2003	2004	2005	2006	2002	2003	2004	2005	2006

ASIA - ASIE

Armenia - Arménie											
Total	C	13 682	15 463	16 975	16 624	16 887	4.3	4.8	5.3	5.2	5.2
Urban - Urbaine	C	9 207	10 174	11 164	10 975	11 139	4.5	4.9	5.4	5.3	5.4
Rural - Rurale	C	4 475	5 289	5 811	5 649	5 748	3.9	4.6	5.0	4.9	5.0
Azerbaijan - Azerbaïdjan											
Total	+C	41 661	56 091	62 177	71 643	79 443	5.1	6.8	7.5	8.5	9.4
Urban - Urbaine	+C	22 438	26 935	30 873	...	...	5.4	6.3	7.2	...	...
Rural - Rurale	+C	19 223	29 156	31 304	...	...	4.8	7.3	7.8	...	...
Bahrain - Bahreïn											
Total	...	4 909	5 373	4 929	4 669	4 714	...	...	...	...	...
Brunei Darussalam - Brunéi Darussalam											
Total	...	2 288	2 262	2 027	...	...	...	...	...	...	...
China - Chine[11]											
Total	+C	7 860 000	8 114 000	8 672 000	8 231 000	...	6.1	6.3	6.7	6.3	...
China: Hong Kong SAR - Chine: Hong Kong RAS											
Total	C	32 070	35 439	41 376	43 018	50 328	4.8	5.3	6.1	6.3	7.3
China: Macao SAR - Chine: Macao RAS											
Total	+C	1 209	1 309	1 737	1 734	2 100	2.8	3.0	3.8	3.7	4.2
Cyprus - Chypre[12]											
Total	C	10 284	5 556	5 349	5 881	4 887	14.5	7.7	7.3	7.8	6.3
Urban - Urbaine	C	6 641	9 563[13]	4 275	...	...	...	...	...	...	...
Rural - Rurale	C	3 643	1 247[13]	1 074	...	...	...	...	...	...	...
Georgia - Géorgie											
Total	C	12 535	12 696	14 866	18 012	21 845	2.9	2.9	3.4	4.1	5.0
Urban - Urbaine	C	...	8 161	...	...	...	...	3.6	...	...	...
Rural - Rurale	C	...	4 535	...	...	...	...	2.2	...	...	...
Iran (Islamic Republic of) - Iran (République islamique d')[14]											
Total	C	650 960	681 034	723 976	787 671	778 023	9.9	10.2	10.7	11.5	11.0
Urban - Urbaine	C	513 772	522 160	527 337	558 424	...	11.9	11.9	11.9	12.2	...
Rural - Rurale	C	137 188	158 874	196 639	229 247	...	6.1	7.0	8.4	10.0	...
Iraq											
Total	U	...	...	262 554	...	...	...	...	...	...	...
Israel - Israël[15]											
Total	C	39 718	39 154	39 855	41 024	...	6.0	5.9	5.9	5.9	...
Japan - Japon[16]											
Total	+C	757 331	740 191	720 417	714 265	730 971	6.0	5.9	5.7	5.7	5.8
Urban - Urbaine	+C	629 906	617 978	606 934	627 290	666 236	...	...	...	...	...
Rural - Rurale	+C	127 425	122 213	113 483	86 975	64 735	...	...	...	...	...
Jordan - Jordanie[17]											
Total	+C	46 873	48 784	53 754	56 418	59 335	9.3	9.4	10.2	10.4	10.7
Kazakhstan											
Total	C	98 986	110 414	114 685	123 045	137 204	6.7	7.4	7.6	8.1	9.0
Urban - Urbaine	C	58 529	66 794	69 794	77 074	85 622	6.9	7.9	8.1	8.9	9.8
Rural - Rurale	C	40 457	43 620	44 891	45 971	51 582	6.3	6.8	7.0	7.1	7.9
Korea (Republic of) - Corée (République de)[18]											
Total[19]	+C	306 573	304 932	310 944	316 375	332 752	6.4	6.3	6.4	6.5	6.8
Urban - Urbaine	+C	246 930	243 564	244 654	246 987	262 298	6.5	6.3	6.3	6.3	6.6
Rural - Rurale	+C	53 765	53 145	53 914	55 029	58 383	5.4	5.4	5.5	5.7	6.2
Kuwait - Koweït											
Total	C	11 973	12 246	12 359	12 419	12 584	5.3	5.3	5.2	5.1	...
Kyrgyzstan - Kirghizistan											
Total	C	31 240	34 266	34 542	37 321	43 760	6.3	6.8	6.8	7.3	8.4
Urban - Urbaine	C	9 065	9 953	11 039	11 651	12 372	5.1	5.6	6.1	6.4	6.7
Rural - Rurale	C	22 175	24 313	23 503	25 670	31 388	6.9	7.5	7.2	7.7	9.4
Lebanon - Liban											
Total	C	31 653	30 636	30 014	29 705	29 078	...	...	8.0	...	...
Maldives											
Total	...	2 594	3 088	3 400	4 932	...	...	...	...	...	...
Urban - Urbaine	...	1 121	1 376	1 626	2 123	...	...	...	...	...	...
Rural - Rurale	...	1 473	1 712	1 774	2 809	...	...	...	...	...	...

23. Marriages and crude marriage rates, by urban/rural residence: 2002 - 2006
Mariages et taux bruts de nuptialité, selon la résidence, urbaine/rurale: 2002 - 2006 (continued - suite)

Continent, country or area, and urban/rural residence / Continent, pays ou zone et résidence, urbaine/rurale	Code[a]	Number - Nombre					Rate - Taux				
		2002	2003	2004	2005	2006	2002	2003	2004	2005	2006
ASIA - ASIE											
Mongolia - Mongolie											
Total	C	13 514	14 572	11 242	14 993	48 996[20]	5.5	5.9	4.5	5.9	19.0
Urban - Urbaine	C	7 206	8 374	6 195	8 242	31 529[20]	5.1	5.8	4.2	5.4	20.2
Rural - Rurale	C	6 308	6 198	5 047	6 751	17 467[20]	6.0	5.9	4.9	6.6	17.2
Occupied Palestinian Territory - Territoire palestinien occupé											
Total	C	22 611	26 267	27 634	28 876	28 233	6.7	7.5	7.6	7.7	7.3
Philippines											
Total	U	*583 167*	*593 553*	*582 281*	*518 595*		...	...	...	...	...
Qatar											
Total	C	2 351	2 550	2 649	2 734	3 019	3.4	3.6	3.5	3.4	3.2
Saudi Arabia - Arabie saoudite											
Total	...	*98 343*	*111 063*	*105 066*	*119 294*		...	...	...	...	...
Singapore - Singapour[21]											
Total	+C	23 198	21 962	22 189	22 992	23 706	5.6	5.2	5.2	5.3	5.3
Sri Lanka											
Total	+U	*197 589*	*195 914*	*191 985*	**194 352*		...	...	...	...	...
Syrian Arab Republic - République arabe syrienne[22]											
Total	+U	*174 449*	*174 449*	*194 258*	*201 264*	*205 557*	...	...	...	...	...
Tajikistan - Tadjikistan											
Total	C	32 262	39 143	47 320	52 352	57 278	5.0	6.0	7.1	7.6	8.2
Urban - Urbaine	C	9 721	11 190	...	...	...	5.7	6.4	...	...	...
Rural - Rurale	C	22 541	27 953	...	...	...	4.8	5.8	...	...	...
Turkey - Turquie											
Total	C	510 155[23]	565 468[24]	615 357[24]	641 241[24]	636 121[24]	7.4	8.1	8.6	8.9	8.7
United Arab Emirates - Émirats arabes unis											
Total	...	*11 285*	*12 277*	*12 794*			...	...	...	...	...
Viet Nam											
Total	C	*964 701	...	...	...	...	*12.1	...	...	...	...
Urban - Urbaine	C	*254 281	...	...	...	...	*12.7	...	...	...	...
Rural - Rurale	C	*710 420	...	...	...	...	*11.9	...	...	...	...
Yemen - Yémen											
Total	...	*10 934*	...	...	...	...	...	...	...	...	...
EUROPE											
Åland Islands - Îles d'Åland[25]											
Total	C	90	110	136	112	116	3.4	4.2	5.1	4.2	4.3
Urban - Urbaine	C	42	45	53	51	46	4.0	4.2	5.0	4.7	4.3
Rural - Rurale	C	48	65	83	61	70	3.1	4.1	5.3	3.8	4.4
Albania - Albanie											
Total	C	26 202	27 342	20 949	21 795	21 332	8.5	8.8	6.7	6.9	6.8
Urban - Urbaine	C	12 171	11 785	9 679	...	...	9.0	8.6	6.9	...	...
Rural - Rurale	C	14 031	15 557	11 270	...	...	8.0	9.0	6.5	...	...
Andorra - Andorre											
Total	C	186	197	218	224	296	2.7	2.6	2.8	2.8	3.6
Austria - Autriche[26]											
Total	C	36 570	37 195	38 528	39 153	36 923	4.5	4.6	4.7	4.8	4.5
Belarus - Bélarus											
Total	C	66 652	69 905	60 265	73 333	78 979	6.7	7.1	6.1	7.5	8.1
Urban - Urbaine	C	53 838	57 028	49 001	60 114	64 965	7.7	8.1	6.9	8.5	9.2
Rural - Rurale	C	12 814	12 877	11 264	13 219	14 014	4.4	4.5	4.1	4.9	5.3
Belgium - Belgique[27]											
Total	C	40 434	41 777	43 326	43 182	44 850	3.9	4.0	4.2	4.1	4.3
Bosnia and Herzegovina - Bosnie-Herzégovine											
Total	C	20 122	20 733	22 252	21 698	21 501	5.3	5.4	5.8	5.6	5.6
Bulgaria - Bulgarie[28]											
Total	C	29 218	30 645	31 038	33 501	32 773	3.7	3.9	4.0	4.3	4.3
Urban - Urbaine	C	23 085	24 543	24 857	26 658	26 159	4.2	4.5	4.6	4.9	4.8
Rural - Rurale	C	6 133	6 102	6 181	6 843	6 614	2.6	2.6	2.6	3.0	2.9

Continent, country or area, and urban/rural residence / Continent, pays ou zone et résidence, urbaine/rurale	Code[a]	Number - Nombre					Rate - Taux				
		2002	2003	2004	2005	2006	2002	2003	2004	2005	2006
EUROPE											
Croatia - Croatie											
Total	C	22 806	22 337	22 700	22 138	22 092	5.1	5.0	5.1	5.0	5.0
Urban - Urbaine	C	12 918	12 375	12 713	12 326	12 396	...	...	...	...	...
Rural - Rurale	C	9 888	9 962	9 987	9 812	9 696	...	...	...	...	...
Czech Republic - République tchèque											
Total	C	52 732	48 943	51 447	51 829	52 860	5.2	4.8	5.0	5.1	5.1
Urban - Urbaine	C	40 014	37 134	38 999	39 392	40 010	5.3	4.9	5.2	5.2	5.3
Rural - Rurale	C	12 718	11 809	12 448	12 437	12 850	4.8	4.4	4.6	4.6	4.7
Denmark - Danemark[29]											
Total	C	37 210	35 041	37 711	36 148	36 452	6.9	6.5	7.0	6.7	6.7
Estonia - Estonie											
Total	C	5 853	5 699	6 009	6 121	6 954	4.3	4.2	4.5	4.5	5.2
Urban - Urbaine[6]	C	4 020	3 933	4 183	4 341	4 893	4.3	4.2	4.5	4.7	5.3
Rural - Rurale[6]	C	1 491	1 491	1 582	1 533	1 810	3.6	3.6	3.8	3.7	4.4
Finland - Finlande[30]											
Total	C	26 969	25 815	29 342	29 283	28 236	5.2	5.0	5.6	5.6	5.4
Urban - Urbaine	C	19 398	18 534	20 957	20 961	20 049	6.0	5.7	6.5	6.4	6.0
Rural - Rurale	C	7 571	7 281	8 385	8 322	8 187	3.8	3.7	4.2	4.2	4.2
France[31]											
Total	C	279 087	275 963	271 598	276 303	267 260	4.7	4.6	4.5	4.5	4.4
Urban - Urbaine[32]	C	214 125	210 905	205 239	206 846	196 863	...	...	...	...	...
Rural - Rurale[32]	C	60 099	59 503	60 768	63 658	63 937	...	...	...	...	...
Germany - Allemagne											
Total	C	391 963	382 911	395 992	388 451	373 681	4.8	4.6	4.8	4.7	4.5
Gibraltar											
Total	C	166	179	159	182	161	5.8	6.3	5.5	6.3	5.5
Greece - Grèce											
Total	C	57 872	61 081	51 377	61 043	57 802	5.3	5.5	4.6	5.5	5.2
Urban - Urbaine	C	...	...	...	43 099	40 536	...	...	...	...	...
Rural - Rurale	C	...	...	...	17 944	17 266	...	...	...	...	...
Hungary - Hongrie											
Total	C	46 008	45 398	43 791	44 234	44 528	4.5	4.5	4.3	4.4	4.4
Urban - Urbaine[33]	C	31 207[34]	30 703[34]	29 682	30 759	31 842	4.7	4.7	4.5	4.6	4.7
Rural - Rurale[33]	C	13 912[34]	13 702[34]	12 963	12 471	11 784	3.9	3.8	3.7	3.6	3.5
Iceland - Islande[35]											
Total	C	1 652	1 473	1 515	1 659	1 681	5.7	5.1	5.2	5.6	5.5
Urban - Urbaine	C	1 581	1 400	1 428	1 576	1 610	5.9	5.2	5.3	5.7	5.7
Rural - Rurale	C	71	73	87	83	71	3.3	3.4	4.0	4.0	3.2
Ireland - Irlande											
Total	C	20 556	20 302	20 619	21 355	21 841	5.2	5.1	5.1	5.2	5.2
Isle of Man - Îles de Man											
Total	C	430	413	399	...	...	5.6	5.3	5.1	...	...
Italy - Italie											
Total	C	270 013	264 097	248 969	247 740	243 508	4.7	4.6	4.3	4.2	4.1
Latvia - Lettonie											
Total	C	9 738	9 989	10 370	12 544	14 616	4.2	4.3	4.5	5.5	6.4
Urban - Urbaine	C	7 115	7 373	7 664	9 081	10 563	4.5	4.7	4.9	5.8	6.8
Rural - Rurale	C	2 623	2 616	2 706	3 463	4 053	3.5	3.5	3.6	4.7	5.5
Liechtenstein											
Total	C	175	149	164	187	*151	5.2	4.4	4.8	5.4	*4.3
Lithuania - Lituanie											
Total	C	16 151	16 975	19 130	19 938	21 246	4.7	4.9	5.6	5.8	6.3
Urban - Urbaine	C	11 637	12 066	13 239	14 156	14 598	5.0	5.2	5.8	6.2	6.4
Rural - Rurale	C	4 514	4 909	5 891	5 782	6 648	3.9	4.3	5.1	5.1	5.9
Luxembourg[35]											
Total	C	2 020	2 001	1 999	2 032	1 948	4.5	4.4	4.4	4.4	4.1
Malta - Malte[36]											
Total	C	2 240	2 350	2 402	2 374	2 536	5.8	5.9	6.0	5.9	6.2
Urban - Urbaine	C	...	...	2 210	...	...	...	...	...	...	...
Rural - Rurale	C	...	...	192	...	...	...	...	...	...	...
Moldova											
Total	C	21 685	24 961	25 164	27 187	27 128	6.0	6.9	7.0	7.6	7.6
Urban - Urbaine	C	10 194	11 520	11 160	12 553	13 174	6.9	7.8	7.6	8.5	8.9
Rural - Rurale	C	11 491	13 441	14 004	14 634	13 954	5.4	6.3	6.6	6.9	6.6
Monaco											
Total	C	175	183	171	161	...	...	...	...	...	...

23. Marriages and crude marriage rates, by urban/rural residence: 2002 - 2006
Mariages et taux bruts de nuptialité, selon la résidence, urbaine/rurale: 2002 - 2006 (continued - suite)

Continent, country or area, and urban/rural residence / Continent, pays ou zone et résidence, urbaine/rurale	Code[a]	Number - Nombre					Rate - Taux				
		2002	2003	2004	2005	2006	2002	2003	2004	2005	2006
EUROPE											
Montenegro											
Total.	C	3 794	4 050	3 440	3 291	3 462	6.1	6.5	5.5	5.3	...
Urban - Urbaine	C	...	2 962	2 322	...	...	...	7.7	6.0	...	...
Rural - Rurale	C	...	1 088	1 118	...	...	...	4.6	4.8	...	...
Netherlands - Pays-Bas[37]											
Total.	C	85 808	80 427	73 441	72 263	72 369	5.3	5.0	4.5	4.4	4.4
Urban - Urbaine	C	46 913	45 295	42 102	41 555	41 783	4.5	4.3	3.9	3.9	3.9
Rural - Rurale	C	29 403	26 897	24 698	24 276	24 270	5.2	4.7	4.4	4.4	4.4
Norway - Norvège[38]											
Total.	C	24 069	22 361	22 354	22 392	21 721[39]	5.3	4.9	4.9	4.8	4.7
Poland - Pologne											
Total.	C	191 935	195 446	191 824	206 916	226 181	5.0	5.1	5.0	5.4	5.9
Urban - Urbaine	C	115 816	118 709	116 407	125 630	137 163	4.9	5.0	5.0	5.4	5.9
Rural - Rurale	C	76 119	76 737	75 417	81 286	89 018	5.2	5.2	5.1	5.5	6.0
Portugal											
Total.	C	56 457	53 735	49 178	48 671	47 857	5.4	5.1	4.7	4.6	4.5
Romania - Roumanie											
Total.	C	129 018	133 953	143 304	141 832	146 637	5.9	6.2	6.6	6.6	6.8
Urban - Urbaine	C	76 547	81 483	90 179	92 651	96 605	6.6	7.0	7.6	7.8	8.1
Rural - Rurale	C	52 471	52 470	53 125	49 181	50 032	5.2	5.2	5.4	5.0	5.2
Russian Federation - Fédération de Russie											
Total.	C	1 019 762	1 091 778	979 667	1 066 366	1 113 562	7.0	7.6	6.8	7.5	7.8
San Marino - Saint-Marin											
Total.	C	208	200	207[40]	223[40]	216[40]	7.3	6.9	7.0	7.2	6.9
Serbia - Serbie[41]											
Total.	+C	41 947	41 914	42 030	38 846	39 756	5.6	5.6	5.6	5.2	5.4
Urban - Urbaine	+C	25 703	25 904	26 248	25 168	25 288	6.1	6.1	6.2	5.9	5.9
Rural - Rurale	+C	16 244	16 010	15 782	13 678	14 468	5.0	4.9	4.9	4.3	4.6
Slovakia - Slovaquie											
Total.	C	25 062	26 002	27 885	26 149	25 939	4.7	4.8	5.2	4.9	4.8
Urban - Urbaine	C	14 370	15 068	15 986	15 180	15 022	4.8	5.0	5.3	5.1	5.0
Rural - Rurale	C	10 692	10 934	11 899	10 969	10 917	4.5	4.6	5.0	4.6	4.5
Slovenia - Slovénie											
Total.	C	7 064	6 756	6 558	5 769	6 368	3.5	3.4	3.3	2.9	3.2
Urban - Urbaine	C	3 768	3 624	3 521	2 971	3 357	3.9	3.7	3.6	3.1	3.5
Rural - Rurale	C	3 296	3 132	3 037	2 798	3 011	3.4	3.2	3.1	2.8	3.0
Spain - Espagne											
Total.	C	211 522	212 300	216 149	209 415[42]	211 818[42]	5.1	5.1	5.1	4.8	4.8
Sweden - Suède											
Total.	C	38 012	39 041	43 088	44 381	45 551	4.3	4.4	4.8	4.9	5.0
Switzerland - Suisse											
Total.	C	40 213	40 056	39 460	40 139	39 817	5.5	5.5	5.3	5.4	5.3
Urban - Urbaine	C	31 082	30 901	30 154	30 809	30 649	5.8	5.8	5.6	5.7	5.6
Rural - Rurale	C	9 131	9 155	9 306	9 330	9 168	4.7	4.7	4.7	4.7	4.6
The Former Yugoslav Rep. of Macedonia - L'ex-République yougoslave de Macédoine											
Total.	C	14 522	*14 402	*14 073	14 500	14 908	7.1	*7.1	*6.9	7.1	7.3
Urban - Urbaine	C	7 905	...	...	7 709	7 848	...	...	...	...	...
Rural - Rurale	C	6 617	...	...	6 791	7 060	...	...	...	...	...
Ukraine											
Total.	C	317 228	370 966	278 225	332 143	354 959	6.6	7.8	5.9	7.1	7.6
Urban - Urbaine	C	231 532	277 014	209 369	252 889	270 504	7.2	8.7	...	...	...
Rural - Rurale	C	85 696	93 952	68 856	79 254	84 455	5.4	6.0	...	...	...
United Kingdom - Royaume-Uni[43]											
Total.	C	293 021	306 214	...	...	...	4.9	5.1	...	...	...
OCEANIA - OCÉANIE											
American Samoa - Samoas américaines											
Total.	C	292	285	287	202	171	4.8	4.6	4.5	3.1	2.6

23. Marriages and crude marriage rates, by urban/rural residence: 2002 - 2006
Mariages et taux bruts de nuptialité, selon la résidence, urbaine/rurale: 2002 - 2006 (continued - suite)

Continent, country or area, and urban/rural residence / Continent, pays ou zone et résidence, urbaine/rurale	Code[a]	Number - Nombre					Rate - Taux				
		2002	2003	2004	2005	2006	2002	2003	2004	2005	2006
OCEANIA - OCÉANIE											
Australia - Australie											
Total	+C	105 435	106 394	110 958[44]	109 323	...	5.4	5.3	5.5	5.4	...
Cook Islands - Îles Cook[45]											
Total	+C	604	623	645	755	*707	32.8	33.9	31.8	37.4	*34.0
Fiji - Fidji											
Total	+C	7 584	7 440	7 076	...	...	9.3	9.1	8.6	...	...
French Polynesia - Polynésie française											
Total	C	1 042	1 047	...	...	...	4.3	4.2	...	...	...
Guam											
Total	C	1 288	1 334	...	...	...	8.0	8.0	...	...	...
New Caledonia - Nouvelle-Calédonie											
Total	C	905	873	847	940	927	4.1	3.9	3.7	...	...
Urban - Urbaine	C	621	594	...	...	...	...	...	...	...	...
Rural - Rurale	C	284	279	...	...	...	...	...	...	...	...
New Zealand - Nouvelle-Zélande											
Total	+C	20 690	21 419	21 006	20 470	21 461	5.3	5.3	5.2	5.0	5.1
Niue - Nioué											
Total	C	15	12	14	...	...	...	...	...	...	...
Tonga											
Total	+C	750	697	...	...	...	7.4	6.9	...	...	...

FOOTNOTES - NOTES

Italics: data from civil registers which are incomplete or of unknown completeness. - Italiques: données incomplètes ou dont le degré d'exactitude n'est pas connu, provenant des registres de l'état civil.

* Provisional. - Données provisoires.

[a] 'Code' indicates the source of data, as follows:
C - Civil registration, estimated over 90% complete
U - Civil registration, estimated less than 90% complete
| - Other source, estimated reliable
+ - Data tabulated by date of registration rather than occurence.
... - Information not available

Le 'Code' indique la source des données, comme suit:
C - Registres de l'état civil considérés complets à 90 p. 100 au moins.
U - Registres de l'état civil qui ne sont pas considérés complèts à 90 p. 100 au moins.
| - Autre source, considérée pas douteuses.
+ - Données exploitées selon la date de l'enregistrement et non la date de l'événement.
... - Information pas disponible.

[1] For Algerian population only. - Pour la population algérienne seulement.
[2] Including marriages resumed after 'revocable divorce' (among Moslem population), which approximates legal separation. - Y compris les unions reconstituées après un 'divorce révocable' (parmi la population musulmane), qui est à peu près l'équivalent d'une séparation légale.
[3] Data refer to Libyan nationals only. - Les données se raportent aux nationaux libyens seulement.
[4] Data exclude visitors. - Les données non compris des visiteurs.
[5] For resident population only. - Pour la population résidante seulement.
[6] Urban and rural distribution of marriages and divorces is displayed by place of residence of groom/husband. The difference between 'Total' and the sum of urban and rural is due to the unknown place of residence of grooms/husbands and to grooms/husbands living outside country. - Les mariages et divorces sont classés par rapport à la résidence urbaine/rurale de l'époux. La somme des mariages et divorces par résidence urbaine/rurale est différente du 'total' car elle ne tient pas compte ni des résidences inconnues de l'époux ni des mariages et divorces d'époux vivant à l'étranger.

[7] Number of marriages of which at least one person was resident of the Netherlands Antilles (marital tourism is excluded). - Nombre de couples mariés dont l'un des membres au moins résidait aux Antilles néerlandaises (le tourisme conjugal n'est pas pris en compte).
[8] Excluding tribal Indian population. - Non compris les Indiens vivant en tribus.
[9] Excluding Indian jungle population. - Non compris les Indiens de la jungle.
[10] Excluding nomadic Indian tribes. - Non compris les tribus d'Indiens nomades.
[11] For statistical purposes, the data for China do not include those for the Hong Kong Special Administrative Region (Hong Kong SAR), Macao Special Administrative Region (Macao SAR) and Taiwan province of China. - Pour la présentation des statistiques, les données pour la Chine ne comprennent pas la Région Administrative Spéciale de Hong Kong (Hong Kong RAS), la Région Administrative Spéciale de Macao (Macao RAS) et Taïwan province de Chine.
[12] Data refer to government controlled areas. For resident population only. - Les données se rapportent aux zones contrôlées par le Gouvernement. Pour la population résidante seulement.
[13] Unrevised data. - Les données n'ont pas été révisées.
[14] Data relate to the Iranian Year which begins on 21 March and ends on 20 March of the following year. - Les données concernent l'année iranienne, qui commence le 21 mars et se termine le 20 mars de l'année suivante.
[15] Including data for East Jerusalem and Israeli residents in certain other territories under occupation by Israeli military forces since June 1967. - Y compris les données pour Jérusalem-Est et les résidents israéliens dans certains autres territoires occupés depuis 1967 par les forces armées israéliennes.
[16] Data refer to Japanese nationals in Japan only. - Les données se raportent aux nationaux japonais au Japon seulement.
[17] Excluding data for Jordanian territory under occupation since June 1967 by Israeli military forces. Excluding foreigners, including registered Palestinian refugees. - Non compris les données pour le territoire jordanien occupé depuis juin 1967 par les forces armées israéliennes. Non compris les étrangers, mais y compris les réfugiés de Palestine enregistrés.
[18] Excluding alien armed forces, civilian aliens employed by armed forces, and foreign diplomatic personnel and their dependants. - Non compris les militaires étrangers, les civils étrangers employés par les forces armées ni le personnel diplomatique étranger et les membres de leur famille les accompagnant.
[19] Including Korean marriages abroad. - Y compris les mariages coréens à l'étranger.
[20] Since 2006, the Government of Mongolia has started to implement " Newly married couple" programme that aims to promote marriage. - En 2006, le Gouvernement mongol a lancé le programme intitulé « jeunes mariés » qui vise à promouvoir le mariage.

[21] Figures exclude marriages previously officiated outside Singapore or under religious and customary rites. Registration of Kandyan marriages is complete; registration of Moslem and general marriages is incomplete. - Les figures excluent les mariages célébrés précédemment au dehors de Singapour ou sous les rites religieuse ou accoutumés. Tous les mariages des Kandyens sont enregistrés; l'enregistrement des mariages musulmans et des autres mariages est incomplet.

[22] Excluding nomads. - Non compris les nomades.

[23] Data from Turkish Statistical Institute. Data revised by MERNIS (Central Population Administrative System). - Données de l'Institut turc de statistique. Données révisées par MERNIS (Système central de données démographiques).

[24] Data from MERNIS (Central Population Administrative System). - Données de MERNIS (Système central de données démographiques).

[25] Also included in Finland. - Comprise aussi dans Finlande.

[26] Excluding aliens temporarily in the area. - Non compris les étrangers se trouvant temporairement le territoire.

[27] Including armed forces stationed outside the country, but excluding alien armed forces in the area unless marriage performed by local foreign authority. - Y compris les militaires nationaux hors du pays et les militaires étrangers en garnison sur le territoire, sauf si le mariage a été célébré pour l'autorité locale.

[28] Including Bulgarian nationals outside the country, but excluding foreigners in the country. - Y compris les nationaux bulgares à l'étranger, mais non compris les étrangers sur le territoire.

[29] Excluding Faeroe Islands and Greenland shown separately, if available. - Non compris les Iles Féroé et le Gröenland, qui font l'objet de rubriques distinctes, si disponible.

[30] Only marriages in which the bride was resident in Finland. Including Aland Islands. - Seulement mariages où l'épouse réside en Finlande. Y compris les Îles d'Åland.

[31] Including armed forces stationed outside the country. Excluding Overseas Departments, namely, French Guiana, Guadeloupe, Martinique and Reunion, shown separately, if available. - Y compris les militaires nationaux hors du pays. Non compris les départements d'outre mer, c'est-à-dire la Guyane française, la Guadeloupe, la Martinique et la Réunion, qui font l'objet de rubriques distinctes, si disponible.

[32] Urban/rural figures, excluding nationals outside the country. - Les chiffres urbaine/rurale, non compris les nationaux hors du pays.

[33] Total includes the data of foreigners, persons of unknown residence and homeless, but the categories urban and rural do not. - Total incluant les étrangers, les personnes de résidence inconnue et les sans-abri, ce qui n'est pas le cas pour les catégories urbaines et rurales.

[34] The difference between 'Total' and the sum of 'urban' and 'rural' is due to the cases of unknown place of residence or residence abroad. - La différence entre le 'Total' et la somme des données selon la résidence urbaine/rurale se rapporte à la situation ou on ignore la résidence ou si la résidence est à l'étranger.

[35] Data refer to de jure population. - Les données se raportent a la population de droit.

[36] Rates computed on population including civilian nationals temporarily outside the country. - Les taux sont calculés sur la base d'un chiffre de population qui comprend les civils nationaux temporairement hors du pays.

[37] The difference between 'Total' and the sum of 'urban' and 'rural' is due to the cases of unknown place of residence or residence abroad. Including same sex marriages. Marriages of couples of which at least one partner is recorded in a Dutch municipal register, irrespective of the country where the marriage was performed. - La différence entre le 'Total' et la somme des données selon la résidence urbaine/rurale se rapporte à la situation ou on ignore la résidence ou si la résidence est à l'étranger. Y compris les mariages entre personnes du même sexe. Mariages où un des conjoints au moins est inscrit dans un registre municipal néerlandais, quel que soit le pays où le mariage a été contracté.

[38] Excluding Svalbard and Jan Mayen Island shown separately, if available. For resident population only. - Non compris Svalbard et Jan Mayen qui font l'objet de rubriques distinctes, si disponible. Pour la population résidante seulement.

[39] Only marriages in which the groom was resident in Norway. - Seulement mariages où l'époux réside en Norvège.

[40] Includes civil and religious marriages as well as not specified. - Y compris les mariages civils, religieux ou non précisés.

[41] Without data for Kosovo and Metohia. - Sans les données pour le Kosovo and Metohie.

[42] Including same sex marriages. - Y compris les mariages entre personnes du même sexe.

[43] Excluding Channel Islands and Isle of Man, shown separately, if available. - Non compris les îles Anglo-Normandes et l'île de Man, qui font l'objet de rubriques distinctes, si disponible.

[44] In 2004, marriage registrations were sampled for the states for the states of New South Wales, Victoria, Queensland and South Australia, while the other states and territories were fully enumerated. - En 2004, on a procédé à des enquêtes par échantillonnage concernant les enregistrements de mariages dans les états de New South Wales, Victoria, Queenslands et South Australia et à un dénombrement complet dans les autres états et territoires.

[45] Excluding Niue, shown separately, which is part of Cook Islands, but because of remoteness is administered separately. - Non compris Nioué, qui fait l'objet d'une rubrique distincte et qui fait partie des îles Cook, mais qui, en raison de son éloignement, est administrée séparément.

Table 24

Table 24 presents the marriages cross-classified by age of groom and age of bride for every year with available data between 2002 and 2006.

Description of variables: Marriage is defined as the act, ceremony or process by which the legal relationship of husband and wife is constituted. The legality of the union may be established by civil, religious or other means as recognized by the laws of each country. [i]

Marriage statistics in this table, therefore, include both first marriages and remarriages after divorce, widowhood or annulment. They do not, unless otherwise noted, include resumption of marriage ties after legal separation. These statistics refer to the number of marriages performed, and not to the number of persons marrying.

Age is defined as age at last birthday, that is, the difference between the date of birth and the date of the occurrence of the event, expressed in completed solar years. The age classification generally used in this table is the following: under 20 years, 5-year age groups through 90-94, and 100 years and over. Age classification for the groom is restricted to 5 year age groups until 65+.

In an effort to provide interpretation of these statistics, countries or areas providing data on marriages by age of groom and bride have been requested to specify "the minimum legal age at which marriage can take place with and without parental consent". This information is presented in the table 24-1 below.

Reliability of data: Data from civil registers of marriages that are reported as incomplete (less than 90 per cent completeness) or of unknown completeness are considered unreliable and are set in *italics* rather than in roman type. Table 23 and the technical notes for that table provide more detailed information on the completeness of marriage registration. For more information about the quality of vital statistics data in general, see section 4.2 of the Technical Notes.

Limitations: Statistics on marriages by age of groom and age of bride are subject to the same qualifications as have been set forth for vital statistics in general and marriage statistics in particular as discussed in Section 4 of the Technical Notes.

The fact that marriage is a legal event, unlike birth and death that are biological events, has implications for international comparability of data. Marriage has been defined, for statistical purposes, in terms of the laws of individual countries or areas. These laws vary throughout the world. In addition, comparability is further limited because some countries or areas compile statistics only for civil marriages although religious marriages may also be legally recognized; in other countries or areas, the only available records are church registers and, therefore, the statistics may not reflect to marriages that are civil marriages only.

Because in many countries or areas marriage is a civil legal contract which, to establish its legality, must be celebrated before a civil officer, it follows that for these countries or areas registration would tend to be almost automatic at the time of, or immediately following, the marriage ceremony. This factor should be kept in mind when considering the reliability of data, described above. For this reason the practice of tabulating data by date of registration does not generally pose serious problems of comparability as it does in the case of birth and death statistics.

Because these statistics are classified according to age, they are subject to the limitations with respect to accuracy of age reporting similar to those already discussed in connection with Section 3.1.3 of the Technical Notes. It is probable that biases are less pronounced in marriage statistics, because information is obtained from the persons concerned and since marriage is a legal act, the participants are likely to give correct information. However, in some countries or areas, there appears to be a concentration of marriages at the legal minimum age for marriage and at the age at which valid marriage may be contracted without parental consent, indicating perhaps an overstatement in some cases to comply with the law.

Aside from the possibility of age misreporting, it should be noted that marriage patterns at younger ages, that is, for ages up to 24 years, are influenced to a large extent by laws regarding the minimum age for marriage

Factors that may influence age reporting, particularly at older ages include an inclination to understate the age of the bride in order that it may be equal to or less than that of the groom.

The absence of frequencies in the unknown age group does not necessarily indicate completely accurate reporting and tabulation of the age item. It is sometimes an indication that the unknowns have been eliminated by assigning ages to them before tabulation, or by proportionate distribution after tabulation.

Another age-reporting factor that must be kept in mind in using these data is the variation that may result from calculating age at marriage from year of birth rather than from day, month and year of birth. Information on this factor is given in footnotes when known.

Earlier data: Marriages by age of groom and age of bride have been shown for the latest available year in most issues of the *Demographic Yearbook*. Data cross-classified by age of groom and bride have been presented in previous issues featuring marriage and divorce statistics. For information on the specific topics and the years covered, readers should consult the Historical Index.

24-1 Minimum legal age at which marriage can take place

Country or area	With parental consent		Without parental consent	
	Groom	Bride	Groom	Bride
Africa				
Egypt	18	16	...	...
Mauritius	16	16	18	18
America, North				
Anguilla	...	...	18	18
Bahamas	..		..	..
Bermuda	16	16	18	18
Canada	16	16	16	16
Costa Rica	16	16	18	18
Cuba	14	14	16	16
El Salvador	15	14	15	14
Mexico	16	14	18	18
Panama	16	14	18	18
Puerto Rico	16	14	18	16
America, South				
Brazil	14	12	...	...
Chile	14	12	18	18
Ecuador	14	12	...	...
Uruguay	14	12	18	18
Venezuela	21	18	...	...
Asia				
Armenia	18	17	...	...
Azerbaijan	18	17	...	...
Bahrain	15	...	...	...
China: Hong Kong SAR	16	16	21	21

Country or area	With parental consent		Without parental consent	
	Groom	Bride	Groom	Bride
China: Macao SAR	16	16	18	18
Israel	…	17	…	17
Japan	18	16	20	20
Kazakhstan	16	16	18	17
Korea (Republic of)	18	16	20	20
Kyrgyzstan	18	18	18	18
Occupied Palestinian Territory	15.5	14.5	…	…
Philippines	18-20	18-20	21	21
Singapore	16 (Muslim marriages) 18 (Civil marriages)	16 (Muslim marriages) 18 (Civil marriages)	21 (Muslim marriages) 21 (Civil marriages)	.. (Muslim marriages) 21 (Civil marriage) 18 if person has previously been married
Tajikistan	17	17	16	16
Turkey	15	14	18	18
Uzbekistan	17	17	17	17
Europe				
Albania	18	16	…	…
Austria	18	16	18	16
Belarus	18	18	18	18
Belgium	17	15	18	18
Bosnia and Herzegovina	18	18	18	18
Bulgaria	16	16	18	18
Croatia	16	16	18	18
Czech Republic	16	16	18	18
Denmark	18	15	18	18
Estonia	15	15	18	18
Finland	Under 18 consent of Ministry of Justice necessary	Under 18, consent of Ministry of Justice necessary	18	18
France	16	14	18	18
Hungary	16	16	18	18
Iceland	18	18	18	18
Ireland	…	…	18	18
Italy	16	16	…	…

Country or area	With parental consent		Without parental consent	
	Groom	Bride	Groom	Bride
Latvia	16	16	10	18
Lithuania	15 (by judgment)	15 (by judgment)	18	18
Luxembourg	…	…	18	18
Malta	16	16	18	18
Netherlands	16	16	18	18
Norway	16	16	18	18
Poland	-	16, 17	18	18
Portugal	16	16	18	18
Republic of Moldova	16	14	18	16
Romania	17	16	18	18
Russian Federation	16	16	18	18
Serbia and Montenegro	16	16	18	18
Slovakia	16	16	18	18
Slovenia	15	15	18	18
Spain	…	…	18	18
Sweden	18	18	18	18
Switzerland	…	…	18	18
The Former Yugoslav Rep. of Macedonia	16	16	18	18
Ukraine	14	14	18	17
United Kingdom	16	16	18	18
Oceania				
Australia	16	16	18	16
New Zealand	16	16	16	16

NOTES

[i] *Principles and Recommendations for a Vital Statistics System Revision 2*, Sales No. E. 01.XVII.10, United Nations, New York, 2001

Tableau 24

Le tableau 24 présente des statistiques concernant les mariages classés selon l'âge de l'époux et selon l'âge de l'épouse pour les années où les données sont disponibles entre 2002 et 2006.

Description des variables : le mariage désigne l'acte, la cérémonie ou la procédure qui établit un rapport légal entre mari et femme. L'union peut être rendue légale par une procédure civile ou religieuse, ou par toute autre procédure, conformément à la législation du pays[1].

Les statistiques de la nuptialité présentées dans ce tableau comprennent donc les premiers mariages et les remariages faisant suite à un divorce, un veuvage ou une annulation. Toutefois, sauf indication contraire, elles ne comprennent pas les unions reconstituées après une séparation légale. Ces statistiques se rapportent au nombre de mariages célébrés, non au nombre de personnes qui se marient.

L'âge désigne l'âge au dernier anniversaire, c'est-à-dire la différence entre la date de naissance et la date de l'événement, exprimée en années solaires révolues. Le classement par âge utilisé dans le tableau 24 comprend les groupes suivants : moins de 20 ans, groupes quinquennaux jusqu'à 90-94 ans, 100 ans et plus. Le classement par âge pour l'époux est quinquennal jusqu'à 65 ans.

Dans un effort de fournir l'interprétation de ces statistiques, les pays ou les zones fournissant des données sur les mariages par l'âge de l'épouse et de par l'âge de mari ont été demandés d'indiquer "l'âge légal minimum avec auquel le mariage peut avoir lieu avec et sans consentement parental". Cette information est présentée dans le tableau 24-1 ci-dessous.

Fiabilité des données : les données sur les mariages issues des registres de l'état civil qui sont déclarées incomplètes (degré de complétude inférieur à 90 p. 100) ou dont le degré de complétude n'est pas connu sont jugées douteuses et apparaissent en italique et non en caractères romains. Le tableau 23 et les notes techniques s'y rapportant présentent des renseignements plus détaillés sur le degré de complétude de l'enregistrement des mariages. Pour plus de précisions sur la qualité des données reposant sur les statistiques de l'état civil en général, voir la section 4.2 des notes techniques.

Insuffisance des données : les statistiques des mariages selon l'âge de l'époux et selon l'âge de l'épouse appellent les mêmes réserves que celles formulées à propos des statistiques de l'état civil en général et des statistiques de la nuptialité en particulier (voir la section 4 des Notes techniques).

Le fait que le mariage soit un acte juridique, à la différence de la naissance et du décès, qui sont des faits biologiques, a des répercussions sur la comparabilité internationale des données. Aux fins de la statistique, le mariage est défini par la législation de chaque pays ou zone. Cette législation varie d'un pays à l'autre. La comparabilité est limitée en outre du fait que certains pays et zones ne réunissent des statistiques que pour les mariages civils, bien que les mariages religieux y soient également reconnus par la loi ; dans d'autres, les seuls relevés disponibles sont les registres des églises et, en conséquence, les statistiques peuvent ne pas rendre compte des mariages exclusivement civils.

Le mariage étant, dans de nombreux pays ou zones, un contrat juridique civil qui, pour être légal, doit être conclu devant un officier d'état civil, il s'ensuit que, dans ces pays ou zones, l'enregistrement se fait à peu près systématiquement au moment de la cérémonie ou immédiatement après. Il faut tenir compte de cet élément lorsque l'on évalue la fiabilité des données, dont il est question plus haut. C'est pourquoi la pratique consistant à exploiter les données selon la date de l'enregistrement ne pose généralement pas les graves problèmes de comparabilité auxquels on se heurte dans le cas des statistiques des naissances et des décès.

Étant donné que ces statistiques sont classées selon l'âge, elles appellent les mêmes réserves concernant l'exactitude des déclarations d'âge que celles dont il a déjà été question à la section 3.1.3 des Notes techniques. Il est probable que les statistiques de la nuptialité sont moins faussées par ce genre d'erreur, car les renseignements sont donnés par les intéressés eux-mêmes, et, comme le mariage est un acte juridique, il y a toutes chances que leurs déclarations soient exactes. Toutefois, dans certains pays ou zones, il semble y avoir une concentration de mariages à l'âge minimal légal de nubilité ainsi qu'à l'âge auquel le mariage peut être valablement contracté sans le consentement des parents, ce qui peut indiquer que certains déclarants se vieillissent pour se conformer à la loi.

Outre la possibilité d'erreurs dans les déclarations d'âge, il convient de noter que la législation fixant l'âge minimal de nubilité influe notablement sur les caractéristiques de la nuptialité pour les premiers âges, c'est-à-dire jusqu'à 24 ans.

Parmi les facteurs pouvant exercer une influence sur les déclarations d'âge, en particulier celles qui sont faites par des personnes plus âgées, il faut citer la tendance à diminuer l'âge de l'épouse de façon qu'il soit égal ou inférieur à celui de l'époux.

Si aucun nombre ne figure dans la rangée réservée aux âges inconnus, cela ne signifie pas nécessairement que les déclarations d'âge et l'exploitation des données par âge aient été tout à fait exactes. C'est parfois une indication que l'on a attribué un âge aux personnes d'âge inconnu avant l'exploitation des données ou qu'elles ont été réparties proportionnellement entre les différents groupes après cette opération.

Il importe de ne pas oublier non plus, lorsque l'on utilisera ces données, que l'on calcule parfois l'âge des conjoints au moment du mariage sur la base de l'année de naissance seulement et non d'après la date exacte (jour, mois et année) de naissance. Des renseignements à ce sujet sont donnés en note chaque fois que possible.

Donnés publiées antérieurement : on trouve dans la plupart des éditions de l'*Annuaire démographique* des statistiques concernant les mariages selon l'âge de l'époux et selon l'âge de l'épouse qui ont été établies à partir des données les plus récentes dont on disposait à l'époque. Des données croisant l'âge des épuces ont été présentés dans des éditions antérieurs, plus particulièrement consacrées aux statistiques de la nuptialité et de la divortialité. Pour plus de précisions concernant les années et les sujets pour lesquels des données ont été publiées, se reporter à l'index historique.

24-1 L'âge légal minimum avec auquel le mariage peut avoir lieu

Pays ou zone	Avec consentement parental		Sans consentement parental	
	Epoux	Epouse	Epoux	Epouse
Afrique				
Egypte	18	16	…	…
Maurice	16	16	18	18
Amérique du Nord				
Anguilla	…	…	18	18
Bahamas	..	..	..	..
Bermudes	16	16	18	18
Canada	16	16	16	16
Costa Rica	16	16	18	18
Cuba	14	14	16	16
El Salvador	15	14	15	14
Mexique	16	14	18	18
Panama	16	14	18	18
Porto Rico	16	14	18	16
Amérique du Sud				
Brésil	14	12	…	…
Chili	14	12	18	18
Equateur	14	12	…	…
Uruguay	14	12	18	18

Pays ou zone	Avec consentement parental		Sans consentement parental	
	Epoux	Epouse	Epoux	Epouse
Venezuela	21	18	...	...
Asie				
Arménie	18	17	...	...
Azerbaïdjan	18	17	...	...
Bahreïn	15	...	...	...
Chine: Hong Kong RAS	16	16	21	21
Chine: Macao RAS	16	16	18	18
Israël	...	17	...	17
Japon	18	16	20	20
Kazakhstan	16	16	18	17
Corée (République de)	18	16	20	20
Kirghizistan	18	18	18	18
Territoire palestinien occupé	15.5	14.5	...	...
Philippines	18-20	18-20	21	21
Singapour	16 (mariages musulmans) 18 (mariages civils)	16 (mariages musulmans) 18 (mariages civils)	21 (mariages musulmans) 21 (mariages civils)	.. (mariages musulmans) 21 (mariages civils) 18 si le mariage n'est pas le premier
Tadjikistan	17	17	16	16
Turquie	15	14	18	18
Ouzbékistan	17	17	17	17
Europe				
Albanie	18	16	...	...
Autriche	18	16	18	16
Bélarus	18	18	18	18
Belgique	17	15	18	18
Bosnie-Herzégovine	18	18	18	18
Bulgarie	16	16	18	18
Croatie	16	16	18	18
République tchèque	16	16	18	18
Danemark	18	15	18	18
Estonie	15	15	18	18

Pays ou zone	Avec consentement parental		Sans consentement parental	
	Epoux	Epouse	Epoux	Epouse
Finlande	Agrément du Ministère de la justice requis de moins de 18	Agrément du Ministère de la justice requis de moins de 18	18	18
France	16	14	18	18
Hongrie	16	16	18	18
Islande	18	18	18	18
Irlande	...	...	18	18
Italie	16	16	...	...
Lettonie	16	16	18	18
Lituanie	15 (en vertu d'une décision de justice)	15 (en vertu d'une décision de justice)	18	18
Luxembourg	...	...	18	18
Malte	16	16	18	18
Pays-Bas	16	16	18	18
Norvège	16	16	18	18
Pologne	-	16, 17	18	18
Portugal	16	16	18	18
République de Moldova	16	14	18	16
Roumanie	17	16	18	18
Fédération de Russie	16	16	18	18
Serbie-et-Montenegro	16	16	18	18
Slovaque	16	16	18	18
Slovénie	15	15	18	18
Espagne	...	...	18	18
Suede	18	18	18	18
Suisse	...	...	18	18
L'ex-République yougoslave de Macédoine	16	16	18	18
Ukraine	14	14	18	17
Royaume-Uni	16	16	18	18
Océanie				
Australie	16	16	18	16
Nouvelle-Zélande	16	16	16	16

NOTE

[1] *Principes et recommandations pour un système de statistiques de l'état civil, deuxième révision*, numéro de vente F.01.XVII.10, publication des Nations Unies, New York, 2003.

24. Marriages by age of bridegroom and by age of bride: latest available year, 1997 - 2006
Mariages selon l'âge de l'époux et selon l'âge de l'épouse: dernière année disponible, 1997 - 2006

Continent, country or area, year and age of bride / Continent, pays ou zone, date et âge de l'épouse	Total	15-19	20-24	25-29	30-34	35-39	40-44	45-49	50-54	55-59	60-64	65+	Unknown Inconnu
AFRICA - AFRIQUE													
Egypt - Égypte													
1998[1] (+U)													
Total..................	503 651	15 724[a]	106 970	183 211	110 462	40 594	16 337	11 067	6 152	4 412	3 471	5 112	139
0 - 19..................	63 838	5 374[a]	6 967	32 482	12 733	4 117	1 013	480	226	160	104	119	63
20 - 24..................	141 655	2 484[a]	5 359	71 878	43 050	12 489	3 071	1 547	685	388	311	366	27
25 - 29..................	137 177	5 806[a]	39 168	35 264	38 140	10 821	3 469	2 144	866	594	380	502	23
30 - 34..................	130 581	1 945[a]	54 882	42 091	13 919	8 680	3 772	2 287	1 121	700	523	646	15
35 - 39..................	14 116	50[a]	339	933	1 779	3 286	2 916	2 017	1 019	674	489	611	3
40 - 44..................	7 259	31[a]	150	289	519	755	1 475	1 436	946	615	440	601	2
45 - 49..................	4 424	28[a]	56	158	200	303	421	878	786	577	458	558	1
50 - 54..................	2 044	3[a]	25	43	54	64	120	164	398	400	312	461	-
55 - 59..................	1 029	3[a]	15	30	28	24	23	35	76	214	243	337	1
60 - 64..................	584	-[a]	9	26	20	14	8	14	10	42	152	288	1
65 - 69..................	354	-[a]	-	17	10	14	12	9	9	6	27	250	-
70 - 74..................	241	-[a]	-	-	9	6	9	17	4	13	18	165	...
75 +..................	345	-[a]	-	-	-	21	28	37	5	29	14	208	3
Unknown - Inconnu......	4	-[a]	-	-	1	-	-	2	1	-	-	-	-
Mauritius - Maurice													
2006 (+C)													
Total..................	11 471	136	1 635	4 087	2 410	1 256	833	468	273	182	181[j]	...	10
0 - 14..................	59	3	14	22	5	5	5	1	-	2	2[j]	...	-
15 - 19..................	1 444	87	599	605	124	18	3	3	1	2	1[j]	...	1
20 - 24..................	3 442	35	783	1 852	590	131	29	11	4	2	1[j]	...	4
25 - 29..................	3 106	9	193	1 381	995	354	117	38	11	7	1[j]	...	-
30 - 34..................	1 419	2	32	168	528	375	216	69	13	10	6[j]	...	-
35 - 39..................	830	-	6	32	113	271	238	101	38	16	15[j]	...	-
40 - 44..................	555	-	3	16	42	73	160	133	67	37	24[j]	...	-
45 - 49..................	307	-	3	4	6	17	50	82	82	42	21[j]	...	-
50 - 54..................	161	-	1	1	2	8	10	20	47	43	29[j]	...	-
55 - 59..................	64	-	-	-	1	1	2	4	8	15	33[j]	...	-
60 +..................	67	-	-	1	1	2	1	6	2	6	48[j]	...	-
Unknown - Inconnu......	17	-	1	5	3	1	2	-	-	-	-[j]	...	5
Réunion													
2002 (C)													
Total..................	3 284	16[d]	402	908	761	428	294	192	120	62	101[j]	...	...
15 - 19..................	148	8[d]	77	46	9	6	-	2	-	-	-[j]	...	...
20 - 24..................	823	4[d]	264	370	130	31	10	7	6	1	-[j]	...	...
25 - 29..................	921	4[d]	49	401	323	78	36	20	7	3	-[j]	...	...
30 - 34..................	551	-[d]	7	68	214	152	58	26	15	6	5[j]	...	...
35 - 39..................	372	-[d]	3	18	58	110	109	44	16	8	6[j]	...	...
40 - 44..................	229	-[d]	2	5	21	38	60	46	28	14	15[j]	...	...
45 - 49..................	99	-[d]	-	-	2	10	15	30	23	11	8[j]	...	...
50 - 54..................	65	-[d]	-	-	2	2	5	13	21	5	17[j]	...	...
55 - 59..................	38	-[d]	-	-	2	1	1	3	3	10	18[j]	...	...
60 +..................	38	-[d]	-	-	-	-	-	1	1	4	32[j]	...	...
Seychelles													
2006 (+C)													
Total..................	984	1	64	176	254	213	122	69	38	47[i]	...	...	-
0 - 14..................	-	-	-	-	-	-	-	-	-	-[i]	...	...	-
15 - 19..................	20	1	13	1	2	1	1	-	-	1[i]	...	...	-
20 - 24..................	124	-	36	46	23	13	5	-	1	-[i]	...	...	-
25 - 29..................	272	-	10	100	97	43	11	7	-	4[i]	...	...	-
30 - 34..................	234	-	3	20	101	73	22	10	2	3[i]	...	...	-
35 - 39..................	167	-	1	6	20	61	49	16	11	3[i]	...	...	-
40 - 44..................	88	-	-	2	7	17	27	22	9	4[i]	...	...	-
45 - 49..................	47	-	-	1	4	5	5	12	8	12[i]	...	...	-
50 - 54..................	16	-	1	-	-	-	2	2	6	5[i]	...	...	-
55 +..................	16	-	-	-	-	-	-	-	1	15[i]	...	...	-
Unknown - Inconnu......	-	-	-	-	-	-	-	-	-	-[i]	...	...	-

24. Marriages by age of bridegroom and by age of bride: latest available year, 1997 - 2006
Mariages selon l'âge de l'époux et selon l'âge de l'épouse: dernière année disponible, 1997 - 2006 (continued - suite)

Continent, country or area, year and age of bride / Continent, pays ou zone, date et âge de l'épouse	Total	15-19	20-24	25-29	30-34	35-39	40-44	45-49	50-54	55-59	60-64	65+	Unknown Inconnu
AMERICA, NORTH - AMÉRIQUE DU NORD													
Anguilla[2]													
2005 (C)													
Total....................	89	...	...	...	...	...	...	...	...	...	...	...	...
18 - 23	16	...	...	...	...	...	...	...	...	...	...	...	...
24 - 29	21	...	...	...	...	...	...	...	...	...	...	...	...
30 - 35	27	...	...	...	...	...	...	...	...	...	...	...	...
36 - 41	8	...	...	...	...	...	...	...	...	...	...	...	...
42 - 47	9	...	...	...	...	...	...	...	...	...	...	...	...
48 - 53	3	...	...	...	...	...	...	...	...	...	...	...	...
54 - 58	2	...	...	...	...	...	...	...	...	...	...	...	...
59 - 64	2	...	...	...	...	...	...	...	...	...	...	...	...
65 + ...	1	...	...	...	...	...	...	...	...	...	...	...	...
Aruba[3]													
2005 (C)													
Total....................	572	8	55	102	128	83	58	44	33	36	10	15	...
0 - 14	-	-	-	-	-	-	-	-	-	-	-	-	...
15 - 19	24	1	13	6	4	-	-	-	-	-	-	-	...
20 - 24	99	5	32	29	20	9	3	-	-	-	1	-	...
25 - 29	117	2	7	40	39	14	9	2	2	-	1	1	...
30 - 34	100	-	3	13	41	23	11	7	2	-	-	-	...
35 - 39	87	-	-	10	19	16	20	9	7	4	2	-	...
40 - 44	52	-	-	2	3	13	7	11	6	5	1	4	...
45 - 49	49	-	-	1	2	2	8	9	10	12	1	4	...
50 - 54	31	-	-	1	-	3	-	2	5	14	2	4	...
55 - 59	8	-	-	-	-	1	-	3	1	1	1	1	...
60 - 64	1	-	-	-	-	1	-	-	-	-	-	-	...
65 - 69	3	-	-	-	-	1	-	-	-	-	1	1	...
70 - 74	-	-	-	-	-	-	-	-	-	-	-	-	...
75 + ...	1	-	-	-	-	-	-	1	-	-	-	-	...
Bahamas													
2001 (C)													
Total....................	1 787	11	254	490	406	247	120	97	64	36	51[j]	...	11
15 - 19	82	5	48	20	6	1	1	1	-	-	[j]	...	-
20 - 24	430	5	136	180	80	19	7	1	1	-	1[j]	...	-
25 - 29	474	-	39	201	143	62	16	8	4	1	[j]	...	-
30 - 34	333	-	23	56	107	84	24	20	11	7	1[j]	...	-
35 - 39	197	1	6	19	47	51	32	22	8	6	5[j]	...	-
40 - 44	132	-	-	10	18	21	29	24	16	8	6[j]	...	-
45 - 49	61	-	1	2	5	6	8	16	10	3	10[j]	...	-
50 - 54	41	-	1	2	-	3	1	4	9	6	15[j]	...	-
55 - 59	12	-	-	-	-	-	2	-	3	3	4[j]	...	-
60 + ...	14	-	-	-	-	-	-	1	2	2	9[j]	...	-
Unknown - Inconnu	11	-	-	-	-	-	-	-	-	-	[j]	...	11
Belize													
1998 (+C)													
Total....................	1 374	97	443	332	198	99	62	41	25	21	43[j]	...	13
0 - 14	13	...	...	...	...	...	...	...	...	...	...	...	...
15 - 19	329	...	...	...	...	...	...	...	...	...	...	...	...
20 - 24	434	...	...	...	...	...	...	...	...	...	...	...	...
25 - 29	273	...	...	...	...	...	...	...	...	...	...	...	...
30 - 34	142	...	...	...	...	...	...	...	...	...	...	...	...
35 - 39	64	...	...	...	...	...	...	...	...	...	...	...	...
40 - 44	31	...	...	...	...	...	...	...	...	...	...	...	...
45 - 49	35	...	...	...	...	...	...	...	...	...	...	...	...
50 - 54	13	...	...	...	...	...	...	...	...	...	...	...	...
55 - 59	14	...	...	...	...	...	...	...	...	...	...	...	...
60 + ...	15	...	...	...	...	...	...	...	...	...	...	...	...
Unknown - Inconnu	11	...	...	...	...	...	...	...	...	...	...	...	...
Bermuda - Bermudes													
2003 (C)													
Total....................	861	-[a]	191[k]	...	386[l]	...	162[m]	...	91[n]	...	31[j]	...	...
0 - 19	9	-[a]	7[k]	...	1[l]	...	1[m]	...	-[n]	...	[j]	...	...
20 - 29	256	-[a]	135[k]	...	105[l]	...	14[m]	...	2[n]	...	[j]	...	...
30 - 39	380	-[a]	45[k]	...	246[l]	...	75[m]	...	14[n]	...	[j]	...	...
40 - 49	152	-[a]	4[k]	...	33[l]	...	60[m]	...	49[n]	...	6[j]	...	...

24. Marriages by age of bridegroom and by age of bride: latest available year, 1997 - 2006
Mariages selon l'âge de l'époux et selon l'âge de l'épouse: dernière année disponible, 1997 - 2006 (continued - suite)

Continent, country or area, year and age of bride / Continent, pays ou zone, date et âge de l'épouse	Total	Age of groom âge de l'époux											Unknown Inconnu
		15-19	20-24	25-29	30-34	35-39	40-44	45-49	50-54	55-59	60-64	65+	
AMERICA, NORTH - AMÉRIQUE DU NORD													
Bermuda - Bermudes													
2003													
50 - 59	52	-a	-k	...	1l	...	11m	...	26n	...	14j	...	...
60 +	12	-a	-k	...	-l	...	1m	...	-n	...	11j	...	...
Canada													
2002 (C)													
Total	146 738	919	19 421	43 355	30 788	18 266	11 497	7 711	5 667	3 686	2 101	3 246	81
15 - 19	3 504	544	2 047	644	189	45	24	6	1	1	1	-	2
20 - 24	31 526	324	13 344	13 341	3 313	815	241	82	37	6	5	-	16
25 - 29	45 377	39	3 381	23 768	12 896	3 740	1 064	302	103	41	15	-	19
30 - 34	25 579	9	489	4 529	10 739	6 334	2 367	730	253	80	21	15	13
35 - 39	14 675	2	112	814	2 775	4 970	3 387	1 608	660	225	78	37	7
40 - 44	9 526	-	37	189	644	1 683	2 864	2 190	1 180	506	151	78	4
45 - 49	6 827	1	6	55	170	515	1 169	1 892	1 620	885	329	183	2
50 - 54	4 349	-	4	9	50	122	298	691	1 292	1 027	508	346	2
55 - 59	2 372	-	-	1	7	31	61	167	405	669	520	509	2
60 - 64	1 254	-	-	-	-	3	13	32	86	183	324	610	3
65 - 69	807	-	-	-	-	2	5	5	23	52	113	606	1
70 - 74	481	-	-	-	2	2	1	2	5	3	25	440	1
75 +	431	-	-	-	-	-	-	3	2	7	11	408	-
Unknown - Inconnu	30	-	1	5	3	4	3	1	-	1	-	3	9
Costa Rica													
2006 (C)													
Total	26 575	938	5 937	7 067	4 251	2 536	1 714	1 117	1 990h	...	...	...	1 025
0 - 14	30	8	12	2	4	1	-	1	1h	...	...	...	1
15 - 19	3 548	516	1 761	798	245	104	51	27	17h	...	...	...	29
20 - 24	7 622	259	2 915	2 675	978	409	190	74	86h	...	...	...	36
25 - 29	6 150	75	809	2 574	1 509	605	299	147	116h	...	...	...	16
30 - 34	3 072	35	227	640	919	609	297	162	165h	...	...	...	18
35 - 39	1 829	23	97	193	328	425	338	192	217h	...	...	...	16
40 - 44	1 297	7	46	77	139	217	302	229	270h	...	...	...	10
45 - 49	834	2	16	33	64	78	128	163	341h	...	...	...	9
50 +	1 078	2	14	15	27	55	92	115	750h	...	...	...	6
Unknown - Inconnu	1 115	11	40	60	38	33	17	7	27h	...	...	...	882
Cuba													
2005 (C)													
Total	51 831	1 369	6 989	8 638	9 514	7 873	5 942	3 188	2 549	1 977	1 550	2 151	87
0 - 14	124	34	62	13	9	2	-	-	1	2	-	1	-
15 - 19	5 702	879	2 422	1 250	634	275	110	41	25	25	14	20	5
20 - 24	10 276	323	2 981	3 186	1 992	966	402	145	93	66	49	54	19
25 - 29	8 060	69	840	2 140	2 396	1 347	664	239	136	98	52	72	7
30 - 34	8 122	32	367	1 149	2 333	1 998	1 151	475	263	140	97	111	6
35 - 39	6 527	13	156	497	1 210	1 728	1 437	579	380	235	132	154	4
40 - 44	5 214	8	85	224	555	969	1 285	802	564	321	199	198	4
45 - 49	2 795	4	26	67	197	299	493	501	497	343	191	176	1
50 - 54	1 960	4	17	47	85	155	214	217	344	360	255	261	1
55 - 59	1 331	1	7	27	34	57	98	99	146	250	298	313	1
60 - 64	801	-	10	13	27	42	38	48	62	77	173	311	-
65 - 69	423	-	3	10	17	18	18	22	19	28	53	234	1
70 - 74	210	1	6	2	8	3	7	7	7	16	19	134	-
75 +	225	1	5	8	15	11	19	12	11	15	18	110	-
Unknown - Inconnu	61	-	2	5	2	3	6	1	1	1	-	2	38
Dominican Republic - République dominicaine													
2005 (+C)													
Total	39 439	428	4 762	8 738	7 279	5 364	3 923	2 712	5 181h	...	...	...	1 052
0 - 14	42	5	10	10	3	3	1	1	1h	...	...	...	8
15 - 19	2 281	172	855	620	289	131	83	45	46h	...	...	...	40
20 - 24	8 395	138	2 322	3 141	1 445	631	319	171	196h	...	...	...	32
25 - 29	8 750	66	938	3 095	2 348	1 122	547	292	312h	...	...	...	30
30 - 34	6 813	26	324	1 170	1 938	1 557	872	450	466h	...	...	...	10
35 - 39	4 364	5	125	331	711	1 131	939	522	590h	...	...	...	10
40 - 44	2 910	3	71	146	276	439	656	597	717h	...	...	...	5
45 - 49	1 888	2	33	63	94	166	286	389	840h	...	...	...	15
50 +	2 609	3	28	75	79	125	167	212	1 920h	...	...	...	-
Unknown - Inconnu	1 387	8	56	87	96	59	53	33	93h	...	...	...	902

24. Marriages by age of bridegroom and by age of bride: latest available year, 1997 - 2006
Mariages selon l'âge de l'époux et selon l'âge de l'épouse: dernière année disponible, 1997 - 2006 (continued - suite)

Continent, country or area, year and age of bride / Continent, pays ou zone, date et âge de l'épouse	Total	15-19	20-24	25-29	30-34	35-39	40-44	45-49	50-54	55-59	60-64	65+	Unknown Inconnu
AMERICA, NORTH - AMÉRIQUE DU NORD													
Grenada - Grenade													
2000 (+C)													
Total	616	2	44	132	149	112	70	50	18	14	13	11	1
15 - 19	18	2	8	4	3	1	-	-	-	-	-	-	-
20 - 24	89	-	23	43	15	7	-	1	-	-	-	-	-
25 - 29	163	-	10	60	58	21	10	3	1	-	-	-	-
30 - 34	122	-	2	18	52	33	14	3	-	-	-	-	-
35 - 39	93	-	-	5	13	33	26	14	1	-	1	-	-
40 - 44	58	-	-	2	7	12	15	11	6	4	-	1	-
45 - 49	38	-	1	-	1	3	3	13	8	4	3	2	-
50 - 54	13	-	-	-	-	1	2	3	2	3	1	1	-
55 - 59	9	-	-	-	-	1	-	1	-	3	3	1	-
60 - 64	8	-	-	-	-	-	-	1	-	-	4	3	-
65 +	4	-	-	-	-	-	-	-	-	-	1	3	-
Unknown - Inconnu	1	-	-	-	-	-	-	-	-	-	-	-	1
Guadeloupe													
2003 (C)													
Total	1 701	3	49	320	437	328	197	121	74	63	41	68	-
0 - 14	-	-	-	-	-	-	-	-	-	-	-	-	-
15 - 19	28	1	8	13	4	2	-	-	-	-	-	-	-
20 - 24	226	2	24	116	56	19	5	4	-	-	-	-	-
25 - 29	423	-	14	139	169	74	19	4	1	2	-	1	-
30 - 34	412	-	2	46	159	128	46	18	3	6	2	2	-
35 - 39	238	-	-	4	33	70	60	35	8	7	3	-	-
40 - 44	122	-	-	-	14	19	35	23	18	6	7	-	-
45 - 49	94	-	1	2	-	6	18	22	25	13	5	2	-
50 - 54	61	-	-	-	-	-	4	9	10	18	13	7	-
55 - 59	35	-	-	-	2	1	-	6	6	5	4	11	-
60 - 64	29	-	-	-	-	-	1	-	3	5	4	16	-
65 - 69	11	-	-	-	-	-	-	-	-	-	2	9	-
70 +	22	-	-	-	-	-	-	-	-	1	1	20	-
Guatemala													
2006 (C)													
Total	57 505	8 402	20 560	12 370	5 641	2 937	2 064	1 545	1 102	882	720	1 095	168
0 - 14	1 110	509	466	96	22	4	4	1	3	-	-	-	1
15 - 19	18 790	5 969	9 346	2 616	552	167	57	33	16	6	3	7	5
20 - 24	17 622	1 655	8 529	5 323	1 403	385	162	83	35	22	5	16	3
25 - 29	8 550	217	1 818	3 426	1 924	675	252	107	54	35	19	23	-
30 - 34	3 973	29	282	714	1 317	856	422	163	79	54	29	27	-
35 - 39	2 172	7	57	140	301	611	583	251	105	51	35	30	1
40 - 44	1 522	3	20	42	68	168	401	434	192	94	50	49	1
45 - 49	1 230	2	12	5	32	50	129	354	333	154	88	71	-
50 - 54	842	2	7	5	7	11	36	87	212	235	133	107	-
55 - 59	599	2	-	1	6	4	12	23	44	160	196	151	-
60 - 64	391	-	6	-	3	2	2	8	16	57	111	186	-
65 - 69	238	1	1	-	-	3	-	-	6	9	36	182	-
70 - 74	164	-	2	-	3	1	1	1	5	3	13	135	-
75 +	145	6	14	2	3	-	3	-	2	2	2	111	-
Unknown - Inconnu	157	7	16	5	3	-	2	1	1	-	1	1	120
Jamaica - Jamaïque													
2005 (C)													
Total	25 903	70	2 375	6 224	5 976	4 118	2 893	1 797	1 085	605	325	435	...
0 - 14	-	-	-	-	-	-	-	-	-	-	-	-	...
15 - 19	363	24	184	94	33	16	4	4	-	3	1	-	...
20 - 24	4 379	31	1 457	1 804	668	227	106	46	24	6	5	5	...
25 - 29	7 018	12	484	3 047	2 176	804	313	109	37	20	8	8	...
30 - 34	5 356	2	146	865	2 059	1 298	601	237	72	37	16	23	...
35 - 39	3 549	-	64	282	085	1 007	002	300	140	60	18	22	...
40 - 44	2 448	1	23	85	236	472	705	498	249	97	39	43	...
45 - 49	1 414	-	8	30	79	156	260	336	279	141	63	62	...
50 - 54	761	-	2	12	27	43	84	129	209	129	68	58	...
55 - 59	324	-	2	3	6	9	12	41	61	80	57	53	...
60 - 64	143	-	2	1	3	3	3	5	9	24	30	63	...
65 - 69	85	-	1	1	2	3	3	1	4	6	15	49	...
70 - 74	39	-	1	-	-	-	-	-	1	2	4	31	...
75 +	24	-	1	-	2	-	-	1	-	1	1	18	...

Continent, country or area, year and age of bride / Continent, pays ou zone, date et âge de l'épouse	Total	15-19	20-24	25-29	30-34	35-39	40-44	45-49	50-54	55-59	60-64	65+	Unknown Inconnu
AMERICA, NORTH - AMÉRIQUE DU NORD													
Martinique													
2003 (C)													
Total	1 414	1	46	235	340	273	185	114	83	48	31	58	-
15 - 19	11	1	4	4	1	1	-	-	-	-	-	-	-
20 - 24	144	-	32	63	31	13	5	-	-	-	-	-	-
25 - 29	328	-	7	120	122	53	16	5	1	3	1	-	-
30 - 34	353	-	3	37	147	113	45	5	1	2	-	-	-
35 - 39	203	-	-	8	27	62	61	29	13	1	1	1	-
40 - 44	144	-	-	1	9	23	43	39	15	8	4	2	-
45 - 49	83	-	-	1	1	4	11	21	28	11	2	4	-
50 - 54	60	-	-	-	1	3	4	11	17	9	7	8	-
55 - 59	38	-	-	-	1	1	-	4	6	10	6	10	-
60 - 64	17	-	-	-	-	-	-	-	2	1	8	6	-
65 - 69	17	-	-	-	-	-	-	-	-	3	2	12	-
70 +	16	-	-	1	-	-	-	-	-	-	-	15	-
Unknown - Inconnu	-	-	-	-	-	-	-	-	-	-	-	-	-
Mexico - Mexique													
2006 (+C)													
Total	586 978	66 559	194 375	155 156	79 094	35 032	18 670	11 643	7 464	5 648	5 093	7 663	504
0 - 14	4 014	2 097	1 405	332	102	32	11	4	1	1	4	1	-
15 - 19	148 442	49 221	72 672	19 776	4 828	1 237	386	147	52	35	22	16	16
20 - 24	194 555	13 485	95 820	61 749	17 020	4 299	1 272	511	190	92	43	48	15
25 - 29	122 443	1 438	20 334	58 286	29 591	8 188	2 725	1 006	449	210	112	88	12
30 - 34	55 144	228	3 256	12 180	20 978	10 913	4 271	1 756	770	392	200	188	10
35 - 39	25 056	44	621	2 175	5 064	7 456	4 961	2 388	1 070	626	315	325	10
40 - 44	13 519	11	121	429	1 114	2 133	3 476	2 917	1 516	794	516	490	2
45 - 49	8 545	7	33	108	269	563	1 114	2 077	1 777	1 101	757	737	2
50 - 54	5 547	-	4	20	62	129	308	602	1 159	1 273	1 005	983	2
55 - 59	3 655	-	5	4	15	33	88	159	326	800	1 146	1 075	4
60 - 64	2 389	-	4	3	5	14	26	54	108	214	695	1 265	1
65 - 69	1 529	-	1	3	-	2	9	7	27	72	203	1 204	-
70 - 74	849	1	1	-	1	1	4	4	10	25	56	746	-
75 - 79	367	-	1	-	-	1	1	2	2	7	12	341	-
80 - 84	112	-	-	-	2	-	-	1	1	3	1	104	-
85 - 89	31	-	-	-	-	1	-	-	-	1	-	29	-
90 - 94	6	-	-	-	-	-	-	-	-	-	-	6	-
95 +	15	-	2	-	-	-	-	-	-	-	1	12	-
Unknown - Inconnu	760	27	95	91	43	30	18	8	6	2	5	5	430
Panama													
2005[4]* (C)													
Total	10 512	111	1 485	2 709	2 187	1 307	1 384[m]	...	666[n]	...	631[j]	...	32
0 - 14	15	3	5	5	2	-	-[m]	...	-[n]	...	-[j]	...	-
15 - 19	619	61	281	193	60	23	-[m]	...	-[n]	...	-[j]	...	1
20 - 24	2 377	31	779	924	443	115	75[m]	...	10[n]	...	-[j]	...	-
25 - 29	2 826	11	302	1 144	845	332	134[m]	...	53[n]	...	4[j]	...	1
30 - 34	1 754	5	79	328	588	401	278[m]	...	54[n]	...	21[j]	...	-
35 - 39	1 054	-	22	77	182	288	364[m]	...	84[n]	...	37[j]	...	-
40 - 49	1 071	-	9	30	53	131	455[m]	...	262[n]	...	131[j]	...	-
50 - 59	474	-	-	3	6	10	68[m]	...	171[n]	...	216[j]	...	-
60 - 69	189	-	-	-	-	2	4[m]	...	24[n]	...	159[j]	...	-
70 +	55	-	-	-	-	-	-[m]	...	1[n]	...	54[j]	...	-
Unknown - Inconnu	78	-	8	5	8	5	6[m]	...	7[n]	...	9[j]	...	30
Puerto Rico - Porto Rico													
2005 (C)													
Total	23 511	1 134	5 286	5 945	3 480	2 249	1 553	1 207	864	648	526	619	-
0 - 14	33	20	11	1	1	-	-	-	-	-	-	-	-
15 - 19	2 817	819	1 488	391	76	28	11	2	1	-	-	1	-
20 - 24	6 040	239	2 826	2 130	571	192	58	12	7	3	2	-	-
25 - 29	5 321	46	733	2 494	1 295	472	177	63	29	7	1	4	-
30 - 34	3 148	9	172	690	1 024	667	324	157	58	29	12	6	-
35 - 39	1 906	-	46	176	343	532	387	237	108	41	25	11	-
40 - 44	1 387	1	7	51	123	242	345	279	170	90	55	24	-
45 - 49	1 074	-	3	10	33	78	168	277	218	150	81	56	-
50 - 54	726	-	-	1	11	30	58	117	170	155	97	87	-
55 - 59	496	-	-	-	3	6	21	43	76	114	124	109	-
60 - 64	303	-	-	-	-	1	2	12	18	47	84	139	-

24. Marriages by age of bridegroom and by age of bride: latest available year, 1997 - 2006
Mariages selon l'âge de l'époux et selon l'âge de l'épouse: dernière année disponible, 1997 - 2006 (continued - suite)

Continent, country or area, year and age of bride Continent, pays ou zone, date et âge de l'épouse	Total	Age of groom âge de l'époux											Unknown Inconnu
		15-19	20-24	25-29	30-34	35-39	40-44	45-49	50-54	55-59	60-64	65+	
AMERICA, NORTH - AMÉRIQUE DU NORD													
Puerto Rico - Porto Rico													
2005													
65 - 69	139	-	-	1	-	1	2	5	9	10	32	79	-
70 - 74	77	-	-	-	-	-	-	2	-	2	9	64	-
75 - 79	29	-	-	-	-	-	-	-	-	-	3	26	-
80 - 84	10	-	-	-	-	-	-	1	-	-	-	9	-
85 - 89	5	-	-	-	-	-	-	-	-	-	1	4	-
90 + ...	-	-	-	-	-	-	-	-	-	-	-	-	-
Unknown - Inconnu	-	-	-	-	-	-	-	-	-	-	-	-	-
Saint Kitts and Nevis - Saint-Kitts-et-Nevis													
1998 (C)													
Total	315	3	28	72	62	57	36	21	19	6	2	4	5
15 - 19	5	1	1	2	1	-	-	-	-	-	-	-	-
20 - 24	44	1	16	21	2	2	1	-	1	-	-	-	-
25 - 29	84	-	9	33	23	10	6	3	-	-	-	-	-
30 - 34	76	-	1	14	22	25	8	4	1	1	-	-	-
35 - 39	47	1	-	2	10	14	10	5	2	1	1	-	1
40 - 44	28	-	1	-	2	3	8	6	8	-	-	-	-
45 - 49	13	-	-	-	1	1	3	3	4	1	-	-	-
50 - 54	8	-	-	-	-	1	2	-	2	1	1	1	-
55 - 59	3	-	-	-	-	-	-	-	1	2	-	-	-
60 - 64	-	-	-	-	-	-	-	-	-	-	-	-	-
65 + ...	3	-	-	-	-	-	-	-	-	-	-	3	-
Unknown - Inconnu	4	-	-	-	-	-	-	-	-	-	-	-	4
Saint Lucia - Sainte-Lucie													
2003* (C)													
Total	489	1	31	114	103	95	61	34	18	9	8	15	...
0 - 14	-	-	-	-	-	-	-	-	-	-	-	-	...
15 - 19	8	-	6	2	-	-	-	-	-	-	-	-	...
20 - 24	84	1	17	41	17	7	1	-	-	-	-	-	...
25 - 29	128	-	8	41	47	23	4	3	1	-	1	-	...
30 - 34	102	-	-	23	30	30	11	5	2	1	-	-	...
35 - 39	71	-	-	4	6	26	22	8	5	-	-	-	...
40 - 44	41	-	-	2	1	7	16	10	2	2	1	-	...
45 - 49	23	-	-	1	-	2	3	7	5	2	-	3	...
50 - 54	13	-	-	2	-	-	3	1	2	1	3	1	...
55 - 59	8	-	-	-	-	-	-	-	1	1	2	4	...
60 - 64	4	-	-	-	-	-	-	-	-	1	1	2	...
65 + ...	7	-	-	-	-	-	-	1	-	1	-	5	...
Trinidad and Tobago - Trinité-et-Tobago													
2002 (C)													
Total	7 434	113	1 316	2 147	1 401	969	586	301	258	143	76	124	...
0 - 14	9	-	4	3	1	-	-	-	1	-	-	-	...
15 - 19	769	75	371	211	70	31	7	3	-	-	1	-	...
20 - 24	2 176	35	707	927	338	119	33	9	4	1	1	2	...
25 - 29	1 832	2	183	760	505	253	84	21	15	6	2	1	...
30 - 34	1 063	1	37	185	326	283	139	53	27	8	4	-	...
35 - 39	691	-	10	45	126	190	164	79	52	11	9	5	...
40 - 44	404	-	3	13	28	71	116	70	54	28	10	11	...
45 - 49	228	-	-	2	7	13	27	47	63	32	18	19	...
50 - 54	116	-	-	-	-	6	11	11	23	32	14	19	...
55 - 59	74	-	-	-	-	2	5	6	12	18	13	18	...
60 - 64	28	-	1	-	-	1	-	2	5	4	3	12	...
65 + ...	44	-	-	1	-	-	-	-	2	3	1	37	...
Turks Caicos Islands - Îles Turques et Caïques													
2005 (C)													
Total	489	-	19	88	149	95	69	34	20	6	7	1	1
0 - 14	-	-	-	-	-	-	-	-	-	-	-	-	-
15 - 19	3	-	1	1	1	-	-	-	-	-	-	-	-
20 - 24	40	-	12	18	8	1	1	-	-	-	-	-	-
25 - 29	120	-	4	45	48	14	5	2	1	-	1	-	-
30 - 34	142	-	2	19	69	31	13	5	3	-	-	-	-
35 - 39	103	-	-	5	18	37	28	9	5	1	-	-	-
40 - 44	37	-	-	-	1	9	15	7	2	1	1	1	-

Continent, country or area, year and age of bride / Continent, pays ou zone, date et âge de l'épouse	Total	15-19	20-24	25-29	30-34	35-39	40-44	45-49	50-54	55-59	60-64	65+	Unknown Inconnu
AMERICA, NORTH - AMÉRIQUE DU NORD													
Turks Caicos Islands - Îles Turques et Caïques													
2005													
45 - 49	31	-	-	-	4	3	5	7	7	4	1	-	-
50 - 54	8	-	-	-	-	-	2	2	2	-	2	-	-
55 - 59	3	-	-	-	-	-	-	1	-	-	2	-	-
60 - 64	1	-	-	-	-	-	-	1	-	-	-	-	-
65 +	-	-	-	-	-	-	-	-	-	-	-	-	-
Unknown - Inconnu	1	-	-	-	-	-	-	-	-	-	-	-	1
AMERICA, SOUTH - AMÉRIQUE DU SUD													
Brazil - Brésil[5]													
2006 (U)													
Total	889 828	34 232	233 353	261 850	149 130	79 857	45 937	27 591	17 694	12 846	8 840	17 699	776
0 - 14	636	195	314	79	26	11	4	-	1	-	-	1	-
15 - 19	146 935	21 660	80 003	33 309	8 380	2 364	745	237	100	41	25	61	2
20 - 24	270 813	9 673	109 983	103 991	32 303	9 553	3 205	1 104	469	236	107	180	4
25 - 29	217 410	1 999	33 225	92 125	57 202	20 458	7 203	2 815	1 161	563	277	374	6
30 - 34	110 443	470	7 212	23 934	35 421	23 698	10 798	4 573	2 037	1 063	526	709	2
35 - 39	58 147	139	1 845	6 026	11 138	15 114	11 567	5 785	2 967	1 615	829	1 121	1
40 - 44	34 374	52	503	1 659	3 241	5 820	7 868	6 362	3 738	2 246	1 192	1 692	...
45 - 49	20 826	22	152	486	996	1 981	3 032	4 217	3 572	2 481	1 551	2 334	1
50 - 54	13 054	7	59	125	271	567	1 043	1 658	2 340	2 463	1 727	2 793	1
55 - 59	7 653	2	20	60	84	184	303	573	891	1 413	1 438	2 683	2
60 - 64	4 094	6	12	18	29	59	90	157	270	457	775	2 221	-
65 +	4 666	6	18	31	37	47	77	109	148	268	393	3 530	1
Unknown - Inconnu	777	1	7	7	2	1	2	1	-	-	-	-	756
Chile - Chili													
2005 (+C)													
Total	53 842	1 075	11 486	18 326	11 898	4 775	2 335	1 205	673	542	443	1 084	...
0 - 14	1	-	1	-	-	-	-	-	-	-	-	-	...
15 - 19	4 690	631	2 630	1 042	293	60	23	7	2	2	-	-	...
20 - 24	16 227	369	6 555	6 566	2 091	486	112	27	11	2	-	8	...
25 - 29	16 893	61	1 842	8 347	5 024	1 129	346	90	32	8	3	11	...
30 - 34	8 262	11	372	1 937	3 427	1 634	582	194	49	21	18	17	...
35 - 39	3 340	3	64	353	814	1 034	623	234	106	53	26	30	...
40 - 44	1 600	-	13	65	184	321	388	277	139	81	52	80	...
45 - 49	1 030	-	7	11	47	82	176	235	144	122	86	120	...
50 - 54	629	-	1	4	15	22	58	90	113	108	82	136	...
55 - 59	431	-	1	-	2	6	19	26	46	82	77	172	...
60 - 64	306	-	-	-	1	1	5	19	26	37	67	150	...
65 - 69	196	-	-	-	-	-	1	3	3	13	18	158	...
70 - 74	143	-	-	1	-	-	2	3	-	7	12	118	...
75 +	94	-	-	-	-	-	-	-	2	6	2	84	...
Ecuador - Équateur[6]													
2004 (U)													
Total	63 299	6 442	21 199	15 879	8 408	4 248	2 524	1 585	1 019	655	436	845	29
0 - 14	532	214	228	63	13	6	-	3	1	-	-	-	1
15 - 19	15 666	4 407	7 919	2 464	610	153	49	27	9	1	4	4	4
20 - 24	21 715	1 553	10 147	6 746	2 221	648	241	74	36	14	11	15	4
25 - 29	12 299	211	2 334	5 108	2 913	1 071	375	156	67	30	15	16	1
30 - 34	5 681	32	402	1 128	1 871	1 214	555	259	102	57	27	33	1
35 - 39	2 959	14	89	261	565	769	634	336	148	70	36	36	-
40 - 44	1 737	5	39	64	142	259	452	348	220	104	54	49	-
45 - 49	1 047	3	12	21	52	85	148	249	218	121	55	82	-
50 - 54	677	-	5	12	13	30	45	94	157	147	75	99	-
55 - 59	353	-	2	2	-	8	14	25	47	69	81	105	-
60 - 64	232	-	1	1	1	2	5	7	9	23	48	135	-
65 - 69	170	-	2	1	-	-	3	2	2	17	24	118	-
70 +	182	-	5	2	3	2	-	4	3	2	6	153	1
Unknown - Inconnu	49	3	14	6	4	1	3	1	-	-	-	-	17
2005 (U)													
Total	66 612	6 549[a]	21 650	17 113	8 952	4 720	2 786	1 726	3 080[h]	...	...	...	36
0 - 19	16 487												
20 - 24	22 379	...	...	...	...	...	...	...	...	...	...	...	...

24. Marriages by age of bridegroom and by age of bride: latest available year, 1997 - 2006
Mariages selon l'âge de l'époux et selon l'âge de l'épouse: dernière année disponible, 1997 - 2006 (continued - suite)

Continent, country or area, year and age of bride / Continent, pays ou zone, date et âge de l'épouse	Total	\<Age of groom âge de l'époux\> 15-19	20-24	25-29	30-34	35-39	40-44	45-49	50-54	55-59	60-64	65+	Unknown Inconnu
AMERICA, SOUTH - AMÉRIQUE DU SUD													
Ecuador - Équateur[6]													
2005													
25 - 29	13 407	...	...	...	...	...	...	...	...	...	...	...	...
30 - 34	6 170	...	...	...	...	...	...	...	...	...	...	...	...
35 - 39	3 290	...	...	...	...	...	...	...	...	...	...	...	...
40 - 44	1 965	...	...	...	...	...	...	...	...	...	...	...	...
45 - 49	1 155	...	...	...	...	...	...	...	...	...	...	...	...
50 +	1 692	...	...	...	...	...	...	...	...	...	...	...	...
Unknown - Inconnu	67	...	...	...	...	...	...	...	...	...	...	...	...
French Guiana - Guyane française													
2003 (C)													
Total	524	4	34	100	131	86	54	38	25	29	8	15	...
15 - 19	25	-	9	6	3	4	2	1	-	-	-	-	...
20 - 24	90	3	18	35	21	8	3	1	1	-	-	-	...
25 - 29	128	-	6	40	45	19	7	4	3	3	-	1	...
30 - 34	117	1	1	12	40	25	19	7	6	6	-	-	...
35 - 39	64	-	-	4	13	19	13	7	1	5	1	1	...
40 - 44	30	-	-	-	4	5	7	11	2	-	-	1	...
45 - 49	34	-	-	1	4	5	2	2	7	10	1	2	...
50 - 54	22	-	-	1	1	1	-	4	5	4	4	2	...
55 - 59	7	-	-	1	-	-	1	-	-	1	1	3	...
60 - 64	3	-	-	-	-	-	-	1	-	-	1	1	...
65 - 69	3	-	-	-	-	-	-	-	-	-	-	3	...
70 - 74	1	-	-	-	-	-	-	-	-	-	-	1	...
75 - 79	-	-	-	-	-	-	-	-	-	-	-	-	...
80 +	-	-	-	-	-	-	-	-	-	-	-	-	...
Paraguay													
2005 (U)													
Total	19 826	670	5 831	6 058	3 196	1 699	928	530	326	186	127	262	13
0 - 14	33	5	11	12	2	-	1	2	-	-	-	-	-
15 - 19	4 107	439	2 110	1 105	312	81	32	20	3	3	2	-	-
20 - 24	6 861	185	2 798	2 577	863	281	74	41	17	9	6	10	-
25 - 29	4 312	29	738	1 808	1 078	425	134	57	24	5	4	9	1
30 - 34	2 022	7	113	420	664	471	206	71	37	17	5	9	2
35 - 39	1 013	3	36	91	188	303	227	83	39	18	18	7	-
40 - 44	594	-	12	25	60	90	169	131	49	29	13	16	-
45 - 49	350	1	5	7	13	34	64	81	64	33	20	28	-
50 - 54	208	1	2	7	7	7	19	28	55	33	25	24	-
55 - 59	111	-	2	3	3	3	-	6	22	24	17	30	1
60 - 64	80	-	-	1	2	3	-	4	9	9	10	42	-
65 - 69	52	-	-	-	1	1	1	3	1	3	7	35	-
70 - 74	32	-	-	-	-	-	-	1	2	1	-	28	-
75 +	30	-	1	-	-	-	-	1	3	1	-	24	-
Unknown - Inconnu	21	-	3	2	3	-	1	1	1	1	-	-	9
Suriname													
2002 (C)													
Total	2 005	23	421	542	367	208	142	101	65	136[i]	...	...	...
0 - 14	6	...	...	...	...	...	...	...	...	...	...	...	...
15 - 19	382	...	...	...	...	...	...	...	...	...	...	...	...
20 - 24	596	...	...	...	...	...	...	...	...	...	...	...	...
25 - 29	333	...	...	...	...	...	...	...	...	...	...	...	...
30 - 34	233	...	...	...	...	...	...	...	...	...	...	...	...
35 - 39	187	...	...	...	...	...	...	...	...	...	...	...	...
40 - 44	113	...	...	...	...	...	...	...	...	...	...	...	...
45 - 49	72	...	...	...	...	...	...	...	...	...	...	...	...
50 - 54	36	...	...	...	...	...	...	...	...	...	...	...	...
55 +	47	...	...	...	...	...	...	...	...	...	...	...	...
Uruguay													
2002 (C)													
Total	14 073	453[a]	3 015	4 227	2 292	1 209	1 335[m]	...	1 542[h]	...	...	...	-
0 - 19	1 728	300[a]	978	342	78	15	9[m]	...	6[h]	...	...	...	-
20 - 24	3 618	111[a]	1 434	1 446	423	120	57[m]	...	27[h]	...	...	...	-
25 - 29	3 900	33[a]	468	1 890	930	366	177[m]	...	36[h]	...	...	...	-
30 - 34	1 890	3[a]	93	384	642	363	318[m]	...	87[h]	...	...	...	-
35 - 39	972	-[a]	33	111	141	234	309[m]	...	144[h]	...	...	...	-
40 - 49	1 011	6[a]	9	36	72	105	378[m]	...	405[h]	...	...	...	-

Continent, country or area, year and age of bride / Continent, pays ou zone, date et âge de l'épouse	Total	15-19	20-24	25-29	30-34	35-39	40-44	45-49	50-54	55-59	60-64	65+	Unknown Inconnu
AMERICA, SOUTH - AMÉRIQUE DU SUD													
Uruguay													
2002													
50 +	954	-a	-	18	6	6	87m	...	837h	...	...	...	-
Unknown - Inconnu	-	-a	-	-	-	-	_m	...	_h	...	...	...	-
Venezuela (Bolivarian Republic of) - Venezuela (République bolivarienne du)5													
2006 (C)													
Total	89 772	3 754	21 439	27 154	16 146	8 470	4 849	3 078	1 949	1 113	1 814j	...	...
0 - 14	428	129	199	62	22	5	5	1	1	1	_j	...	...
15 - 19	12 978	2 414	6 426	2 799	871	286	103	40	20	6	13j	...	...
20 - 24	26 296	901	10 531	9 749	3 402	1 074	362	154	60	26	37j	...	...
25 - 29	24 136	200	3 308	10 934	6 126	2 173	764	351	138	63	77j	...	...
30 - 34	11 805	70	686	2 636	3 997	2 438	1 103	482	237	91	64j	...	...
35 - 39	6 150	18	176	692	1 223	1 672	1 133	638	320	155	123j	...	...
40 - 44	3 407	10	70	177	355	561	895	659	384	155	141j	...	...
45 - 49	1 963	7	19	65	100	185	314	464	385	207	217j	...	...
50 - 54	1 196	1	11	25	25	51	118	198	277	204	286j	...	...
55 - 59	654	3	5	4	8	13	32	70	80	140	299j	...	...
60 +	759	1	8	11	17	12	20	21	47	65	557j	...	...
ASIA - ASIE													
Armenia - Arménie													
2006 (C)													
Total	16 887	95	4 372	6 904	3 161	1 112	468	308	147	107	213j	...	...
15 - 19	2 018	70	948	860	125	13	1	-	-	1	_j	...	...
20 - 24	8 980	24	3 177	4 304	1 273	166	27	6	-	3	_j	...	...
25 - 29	3 783	1	224	1 602	1 347	473	105	21	5	3	2j	...	...
30 - 34	1 089	-	17	116	366	322	174	76	12	5	1j	...	...
35 - 39	363	-	1	15	32	105	95	79	27	8	1j	...	...
40 - 44	190	-	2	4	9	17	38	66	31	9	14j	...	...
45 - 49	173	-	3	2	4	12	23	38	34	28	29j	...	...
50 - 54	114	-	-	1	3	3	2	13	29	25	38j	...	...
55 - 59	86	-	-	-	1	1	1	6	8	23	46j	...	...
60 +	91	-	-	-	1	-	2	3	1	2	82j	...	...
Azerbaijan - Azerbaïdjan													
2004 (+C)													
Total	62 177	570a	16 957	25 009	11 732	4 182	1 538	746	429	269	745j	...	...
0 - 17	3 214	89a	1 393	1 341	350	33	3	1	2	-	2j	...	...
18 - 19	10 706	262a	4 432	4 522	1 272	171	34	5	3	-	5j	...	...
20 - 24	29 324	191a	9 633	13 185	5 031	1 072	169	25	5	6	7j	...	...
25 - 29	11 404	18a	1 209	5 013	3 379	1 332	333	79	13	13	15j	...	...
30 - 34	3 681	5a	213	709	1 261	888	382	112	53	13	45j	...	...
35 - 39	1 867	3a	58	186	347	496	369	177	99	37	95j	...	...
40 - 44	1 063	1a	13	40	72	158	203	211	111	72	182j	...	...
45 - 49	539	1a	2	8	11	29	41	113	103	62	169j	...	...
50 - 54	188	-a	1	3	5	1	4	15	33	38	88j	...	...
55 - 59	76	-a	1	1	1	1	-	5	4	21	42j	...	...
60 +	115	-a	2	1	3	1	-	3	3	7	95j	...	...
China: Hong Kong SAR - Chine: Hong Kong RAS													
2005 (C)													
Total	43 018	220b	3 525	9 948	10 834	6 056	4 099	2 978	1 938	1 247	687	1 486	...
16 - 19	935	92b	420	232	107	38	23	11	6	2	1	3	...
20 - 24	8 114	106b	2 188	2 622	1 483	780	467	284	98	48	14	24	...
25 - 29	14 231	16b	648	5 583	4 439	1 636	891	556	232	133	37	60	...
30 - 34	10 208	1b	175	1 222	3 927	2 078	1 130	681	440	261	123	170	...
35 - 39	4 687	1b	57	192	645	1 113	894	630	440	271	157	287	...
40 - 44	2 492	2b	20	59	153	277	482	474	360	224	156	285	...
45 - 49	1 198	1b	14	21	55	94	148	238	233	145	77	172	...
50 - 54	612	1b	2	13	19	27	50	76	102	99	46	177	...

Continent, country or area, year and age of bride / Continent, pays ou zone, date et âge de l'épouse	Total	15-19	20-24	25-29	30-34	35-39	40-44	45-49	50-54	55-59	60-64	65+	Unknown Inconnu
ASIA - ASIE													
China: Hong Kong SAR - Chine: Hong Kong RAS													
2005													
55 - 59	252	-[b]	1	3	5	10	11	21	21	42	43	95	...
60 - 64	113	-[b]	-	-	1	1	3	5	1	10	23	69	...
65 - 69	73	-[b]	-	1	-	1	-	-	2	7	7	55	...
70 - 74	64	-[b]	-	-	-	1	-	1	3	5	2	52	...
75 + ...	39	-[b]	-	-	-	-	-	1	-	-	1	37	...
China: Macao SAR - Chine: Macao RAS													
2006 (+C)													
Total	2 100	27	350	610	537	225	147	87	55	22	11	29	...
0 - 14	-	-	-	-	-	-	-	-	-	-	-	-	
15 - 19	55	8	33	9	3	2	-	-	-	-	-	-	
20 - 24	627	15	262	207	84	27	18	7	5	2	-	-	
25 - 29	719	4	43	325	241	61	20	19	5	-	-	1	
30 - 34	381	-	8	51	175	75	44	11	6	8	3	-	
35 - 39	165	-	2	10	21	45	39	21	15	6	-	6	
40 - 44	87	-	2	6	9	8	22	15	14	3	3	5	
45 - 49	35	-	-	2	2	5	4	10	4	2	1	5	
50 - 54	21	-	-	-	2	2	-	4	6	1	1	5	
55 - 59	4	-	-	-	-	-	-	-	-	-	2	2	
60 - 64	1	-	-	-	-	-	-	-	-	-	-	1	
65 - 69	2	-	-	-	-	-	-	-	-	-	1	1	
70 + ...	3	-	-	-	-	-	-	-	-	-	-	3	
Cyprus - Chypre													
2006[7,8] (C)													
Total	4 887	13	645	1 813	1 117	559	302	151	97	70	41	76	3
15 - 19	131	7	84	31	7	2	-	-	-	-	-	-	-
20 - 24	1 302	4	449	627	145	42	23	7	4	1	-	-	-
25 - 29	1 931	-	83	985	573	178	71	21	10	7	1	2	-
30 - 34	838	2	21	134	319	214	93	29	15	4	2	5	-
35 - 39	313	-	5	24	50	91	60	42	16	7	11	7	-
40 - 44	155	-	3	10	14	23	36	23	18	14	5	9	-
45 - 49	107	-	-	2	6	9	17	24	15	13	8	13	-
50 - 54	54	-	-	-	3	-	1	3	15	14	4	14	-
55 - 59	31	-	-	-	-	-	1	2	4	8	8	8	-
60 - 64	13	-	-	-	-	-	-	-	-	1	2	10	-
65 - 69	6	-	-	-	-	-	-	-	-	1	-	5	-
70 - 74	2	-	-	-	-	-	-	-	-	-	-	2	-
75 - 79	1	-	-	-	-	-	-	-	-	-	-	1	-
80 + ...	-	-	-	-	-	-	-	-	-	-	-	-	-
Unknown - Inconnu	3	-	-	-	-	-	-	-	-	-	-	-	3
Georgia - Géorgie													
2006 (C)													
Total	21 845	886[b]	5 696	6 495	4 039	2 291	1 152	553	288	164	281[j]	...	...
16 - 19	3 700	...	...	...	...	...	...	...	...	...	...	...	...
20 - 24	8 602	...	...	...	...	...	...	...	...	...	...	...	...
25 - 29	4 992	...	...	...	...	...	...	...	...	...	...	...	...
30 - 34	2 302	...	...	...	...	...	...	...	...	...	...	...	...
35 - 39	1 067	...	...	...	...	...	...	...	...	...	...	...	...
40 - 44	508	...	...	...	...	...	...	...	...	...	...	...	...
45 - 49	305	...	...	...	...	...	...	...	...	...	...	...	...
50 - 54	174	...	...	...	...	...	...	...	...	...	...	...	...
55 - 59	83	...	...	...	...	...	...	...	...	...	...	...	...
60 + ...	112	...	...	...	...	...	...	...	...	...	...	...	...
Israel - Israël[9]													
2005 (C)													
Total	41 029	1 361	10 177	16 473	8 074	2 405	979	545	366	254	151	244	...
15 - 19	6 771	1 062	3 576	1 784	309	34	5	-	-	-	-	1	...
20 - 24	14 913	289	6 093	6 572	1 657	218	56	21	3	-	1	3	...
25 - 29	12 773	9	458	7 403	3 918	764	151	47	13	6	2	2	...
30 - 34	4 011	1	39	640	1 957	915	302	100	35	11	6	5	...
35 - 39	1 226	-	7	64	203	412	289	133	66	32	9	11	...
40 - 44	513	-	2	6	26	57	129	135	73	35	18	32	...
45 - 49	357	-	-	1	3	3	38	91	109	63	24	25	...
50 - 54	198	-	-	1	-	1	9	16	56	63	29	23	...

Continent, country or area, year and age of bride / Continent, pays ou zone, date et âge de l'épouse	Total	15-19	20-24	25-29	30-34	35-39	40-44	45-49	50-54	55-59	60-64	65+	Unknown Inconnu
ASIA - ASIE													
Israel - Israël[9]													
2005													
55 - 59	144	-	1	1	-	1	-	1	8	38	45	49	...
60 - 64	51	-	-	-	1	-	-	-	1	5	11	33	...
65 - 69	35	-	-	-	-	-	-	1	2	1	5	26	...
70 - 74	23	-	-	-	-	-	-	-	-	-	1	22	...
75 +	14	-	1	1	-	-	-	-	-	-	-	12	...
Japan - Japon[10]													
2006 (+C)													
Total	627 602	6 638	82 068	215 485	168 378	78 279	32 259	16 313	10 615	9 117	4 301	4 147	2
15 - 19	15 159	4 699	6 988	2 112	766	307	116	65	60	41	4	1	-
20 - 24	124 021	1 679	55 093	42 554	15 374	5 113	1 890	1 034	644	452	134	53	1
25 - 29	250 183	208	16 527	139 393	67 618	17 558	4 846	1 954	1 074	739	187	79	-
30 - 34	145 428	43	2 822	27 015	70 186	31 257	8 575	3 075	1 306	803	232	114	-
35 - 39	54 152	8	528	3 844	12 513	20 157	10 175	3 745	1 691	1 049	308	134	-
40 - 44	17 234	-	81	478	1 614	3 159	5 221	3 392	1 668	1 088	360	173	-
45 - 49	8 118	1	22	63	248	601	1 079	2 266	1 933	1 252	437	216	-
50 - 54	5 239	-	3	17	45	93	268	598	1 600	1 615	623	377	-
55 - 59	4 365	-	-	7	10	25	73	154	514	1 664	1 188	730	-
60 - 64	1 982	-	-	2	4	7	14	23	105	304	642	881	-
65 - 69	1 017	-	-	-	-	-	1	5	17	92	147	755	-
70 - 74	458	-	-	-	-	-	1	-	2	16	29	410	-
75 - 79	183	-	-	-	-	2	-	-	1	2	9	169	-
80 +	56	-	-	-	-	-	-	-	-	-	1	55	-
Unknown - Inconnu	7	-	4	-	-	-	-	2	-	-	-	-	1
Jordan - Jordanie													
1999[11] (+C)													
Total	39 443	1 095	10 920	15 384	6 781	2 378	1 017	621	361	345	231	305	...
0 - 14	36	5	15	13	2	-	-	-	-	-	-	-	...
15 - 19	12 991	865	5 824	4 847	1 096	209	75	44	9	15	4	2	...
20 - 24	15 789	184	4 377	7 316	2 862	692	195	73	39	22	11	17	...
25 - 29	6 517	29	537	2 663	1 938	758	272	156	70	48	24	22	...
30 - 34	2 414	6	110	399	671	495	268	145	98	103	62	55	...
35 - 39	990	6	31	95	152	166	135	130	76	65	66	68	...
40 - 44	414	-	16	31	41	41	49	52	41	49	34	60	...
45 - 49	163	-	7	10	15	10	16	17	18	20	14	36	...
50 +	129	-	3	10	4	7	7	4	10	23	16	45	...
Kazakhstan													
2006 (C)													
Total	137 204	4 380[a]	48 429	45 372	19 497	8 466	4 435	2 586	1 573	1 052	1 414[j]	...	-
0 - 17	1 640	439[a]	938	221	34	5	1	2	-	-	-[j]	...	-
18 - 19	18 425	2 390[a]	11 064	4 180	678	89	15	8	1	-	-[j]	...	-
20 - 24	66 450	1 428[a]	32 097	25 716	5 860	1 025	240	53	18	11	2[j]	...	-
25 - 29	27 519	95[a]	3 757	12 861	7 465	2 339	676	211	64	36	15[j]	...	-
30 - 34	11 413	18[a]	469	1 983	4 368	2 864	1 120	378	128	60	25[j]	...	-
35 - 39	5 039	5[a]	75	333	888	1 692	1 204	521	210	64	47[j]	...	-
40 - 44	2 575	1[a]	20	58	158	346	834	652	284	135	87[j]	...	-
45 - 49	1 756	2[a]	3	14	33	87	268	554	418	242	135[j]	...	-
50 - 54	1 020	-[a]	3	3	7	11	61	165	308	285	177[j]	...	-
55 - 59	618	1[a]	-	1	1	4	15	34	124	176	262[j]	...	-
60 +	743	-[a]	2	1	3	3	1	8	18	43	664[j]	...	-
Unknown - Inconnu	6	1[a]	1	1	2	1	-	-	-	-	-[j]	...	-
Korea (Republic of) - Corée (République de)[12]													
2006 (+C)													
Total	332 752	1 039	15 051	115 521	111 895	40 095	19 512	13 479	7 582	4 429	2 247	1 901	-
0 - 14	15	9	4	1	1	-	-	-	-	-	-	-	-
15 - 19	7 763	778	1 172	919	1 336	2 116	1 020	301	90	17	9	4	-
20 - 24	49 498	219	10 274	22 412	10 119	3 799	1 785	674	144	52	15	5	-
25 - 29	158 852	28	3 262	84 468	60 921	7 433	1 701	691	233	87	19	9	-
30 - 34	62 702	3	281	7 065	35 571	14 912	3 075	1 179	391	170	45	10	-
35 - 39	22 858	1	48	550	3 369	9 367	5 712	2 486	924	290	87	24	-
40 - 44	13 671	1	8	78	477	1 928	4 543	4 103	1 598	648	199	88	-
45 - 49	9 477	-	1	25	88	459	1 385	3 279	2 547	1 117	409	167	-
50 - 54	4 633	-	1	3	11	70	256	668	1 389	1 375	602	258	-
55 - 59	1 809	-	-	-	1	10	32	88	230	556	550	342	-

24. Marriages by age of bridegroom and by age of bride: latest available year, 1997 - 2006
Mariages selon l'âge de l'époux et selon l'âge de l'épouse: dernière année disponible, 1997 - 2006 (continued - suite)

Continent, country or area, year and age of bride / Continent, pays ou zone, date et âge de l'épouse	Total	|<--- Age of groom âge de l'époux											
		15-19	20-24	25-29	30-34	35-39	40-44	45-49	50-54	55-59	60-64	65+	Unknown Inconnu
ASIA - ASIE													
Korea (Republic of) - Corée (République de)[12]													
2006													
60 - 64	877	-	-	-	1	1	3	9	32	98	273	460	-
65 - 69	396	-	-	-	-	-	-	1	4	18	38	335	-
70 - 74	147	-	-	-	-	-	-	-	1	1	145		-
75 + ...	54	-	-	-	-	-	-	-	-	-	-	54	-
Unknown - Inconnu		-	-	-	-	-	-	-	-	-	-	-	-
Kuwait - Koweït													
2006 (C)													
Total....................	12 584	454[a]	3 983	3 485	1 574	788	520	336	187	99	58	57	1 043
0 - 14....................	66	15[a]	37	8	-	-	-	1	-	-	-	-	5
15 - 19	2 855	321[a]	1 556	540	97	29	13	11	3	3	1	-	281
20 - 24	4 943	106[a]	2 036	1 677	482	111	34	35	9	3	4	2	444
25 - 29	2 346	9[a]	212	921	581	251	138	51	20	11	3	2	147
30 - 34	1 002	1[a]	28	174	253	208	132	79	37	13	7	5	65
35 - 39	543	-[a]	10	50	75	112	102	68	38	21	16	8	43
40 - 44	329	-[a]	5	27	39	42	64	46	45	18	11	9	23
45 - 49	151	-[a]	1	12	16	13	16	30	21	16	6	11	9
50 - 54	57	-[a]	-	4	2	4	5	7	9	9	4	9	4
55 - 59	17	-[a]	-	-	2	-	1	1	1	5	2	4	1
60 + ...	12	-[a]	-	-	-	1	-	1	1	-	3	6	
Unknown - Inconnu	263	2[a]	98	72	27	17	15	6	3	-	1	1	21
Kyrgyzstan - Kirghizistan													
2006 (C)													
Total....................	43 760	836	14 390	16 730	6 644	2 540	1 138	607	345	229	81	220	-
0 - 14....................	-	-	-	-	-	-	-	-	-	-	-	-	-
15 - 19	7 611	588	4 473	2 287	245	12	4	1	-	-	-	1	-
20 - 24	22 369	227	9 287	10 461	2 060	274	38	13	4	2	1	2	-
25 - 29	8 142	17	543	3 629	2 952	783	147	42	20	7	2	-	-
30 - 34	2 979	3	73	295	1 221	932	322	83	26	12	5	7	-
35 - 39	1 250	1	8	46	144	453	346	164	44	25	8	11	-
40 - 44	619	-	3	9	20	75	223	145	70	37	9	28	-
45 - 49	370	-	1	1	2	8	39	127	78	63	18	33	-
50 - 54	229	-	1	1	-	3	17	25	85	49	12	36	-
55 - 59	95	-	-	-	-	-	2	7	15	29	14	28	-
60 - 64	26	-	-	-	-	-	-	-	1	5	2	18	-
65 - 69	48	-	-	-	-	-	-	2	-	10	36		-
70 - 74	14	-	-	-	-	-	-	-	-	-	-	14	-
75 + ...	8	-	1	1	-	-	-	-	-	-	-	6	-
Unknown - Inconnu	-												
Mongolia - Mongolie[13]													
2006 (C)													
Total....................	48 996	852[d]	16 392	17 726	8 952	3 352	1 199	352	171[h]	...	...	...	...
18 - 19	2 342	...	...	...	...	...	...	...	...	...	...	...	...
20 - 24	20 792	...	...	...	...	...	...	...	...	...	...	...	...
25 - 29	15 389	...	...	...	...	...	...	...	...	...	...	...	...
30 - 34	6 796	...	...	...	...	...	...	...	...	...	...	...	...
35 - 39	2 578	...	...	...	...	...	...	...	...	...	...	...	...
40 - 44	749	...	...	...	...	...	...	...	...	...	...	...	...
45 - 49	231	...	...	...	...	...	...	...	...	...	...	...	...
50 + ...	119	...	...	...	...	...	...	...	...	...	...	...	...
Occupied Palestinian Territory - Territoire palestinien occupé													
2006 (C)													
Total....................	28 233	2 155	10 934	9 671	2 850	902	509	346	222	179	343[j]		-
0 - 14....................	742	168	420	144	8	1	-	-	-	-	-[j]	...	-
15 - 19	13 971	1 761	7 102	4 314	677	75	21	10	4	2	4[j]	...	-
20 - 24	9 326	205	3 165	4 124	1 361	314	93	31	17	4	12[j]	...	-
25 - 29	2 508	20	213	974	610	317	174	108	46	21	25[j]	...	-
30 - 34	890	1	28	98	158	181	141	100	65	51	67[j]	...	-
35 - 39	453	-	5	13	30	58	102	46	44	59	96[j]	...	-
40 - 44	243	-	-	3	6	12	34	35	36	27	90[j]	...	-
45 - 49	64	-	-	-	-	3	3	11	9	7	31[j]	...	-
50 - 54	22	-	1	-	-	1	1	4	1	7	7[j]	...	-

24. Marriages by age of bridegroom and by age of bride: latest available year, 1997 - 2006
Mariages selon l'âge de l'époux et selon l'âge de l'épouse: dernière année disponible, 1997 - 2006 (continued - suite)

Continent, country or area, year and age of bride / Continent, pays ou zone, date et âge de l'épouse	Total / Total	Age of groom âge de l'époux											Unknown Inconnu
		15-19	20-24	25-29	30-34	35-39	40-44	45-49	50-54	55-59	60-64	65+	

ASIA - ASIE

Occupied Palestinian Territory - Territoire palestinien occupé
2006

55 - 59	5	-	-	1	-	-	-	1	-	1	2ʲ	...	-
60 +	9	-	-	-	-	-	-	-	-	-	9ʲ	...	-
Unknown - Inconnu	-	-	-	-	-	-	-	-	-	-	ʲ	...	-

Philippines
2003 (U)

Total	593 553	19 799ᵃ	185 610	191 627	97 265	43 067	22 826	12 903	20 216ʰ	...	...	...	240
0 - 19	80 045	10 727ᵃ	44 378	18 063	4 769	1 301	437	164	195ʰ	...	...	...	11
20 - 24	235 351	7 972ᵃ	110 699	81 680	24 177	6 512	2 217	968	1 086ʰ	...	...	...	40
25 - 29	152 719	891ᵃ	25 287	72 773	36 304	10 876	3 640	1 483	1 445ʰ	...	...	...	20
30 - 34	63 908	145ᵃ	4 008	15 002	23 766	12 415	4 794	1 911	1 847ʰ	...	...	...	20
35 - 39	28 845	33ᵃ	853	3 115	6 111	8 576	5 676	2 436	2 036ʰ	...	...	...	9
40 - 44	15 000	7ᵃ	209	697	1 550	2 530	4 381	2 976	2 639ʰ	...	...	...	11
45 - 49	8 124	6ᵃ	47	163	389	645	1 246	2 175	3 452ʰ	...	...	...	1
50 +	9 288	12ᵃ	90	101	169	201	426	785	7 498ʰ	...	...	...	6
Unknown - Inconnu	273	6ᵃ	39	33	30	11	9	5	18ʰ	...	...	...	122

2005 (U)

Total	518 595	15 786ᵃ	155 408	175 647	84 140	38 494	19 390	11 559	18 116ʰ	...	...	...	55
0 - 19	69 335	...	...	...	...	...	...	...	...	...	...	...	...
20 - 24	200 210	...	...	...	...	...	...	...	...	...	...	...	...
25 - 29	141 944	...	...	...	...	...	...	...	...	...	...	...	...
30 - 34	55 228	...	...	...	...	...	...	...	...	...	...	...	...
35 - 39	24 969	...	...	...	...	...	...	...	...	...	...	...	...
40 - 44	12 353	...	...	...	...	...	...	...	...	...	...	...	...
45 - 49	6 726	...	...	...	...	...	...	...	...	...	...	...	...
50 +	7 736	...	...	...	...	...	...	...	...	...	...	...	...
Unknown - Inconnu	94	...	...	...	...	...	...	...	...	...	...	...	...

Qatar
2006 (C)

Total	3 019	76	797	1 092	565	211	127	76	43	18	6	8	-
0 - 14	-	-	-	-	-	-	-	-	-	-	-	-	-
15 - 19	460	52	235	137	29	2	2	3	-	-	-	-	-
20 - 24	1 324	21	470	588	183	46	8	4	3	-	-	1	-
25 - 29	710	3	73	300	213	68	27	15	5	4	2	-	-
30 - 34	296	-	15	46	104	58	35	17	12	6	1	2	-
35 - 39	131	-	3	10	27	22	35	23	8	1	1	1	-
40 - 44	55	-	1	5	7	10	12	6	6	3	2	3	-
45 - 49	34	-	-	6	2	4	8	5	6	3	-	-	-
50 - 54	5	-	-	-	-	1	-	3	1	-	-	-	-
55 - 59	1	-	-	-	-	-	-	-	-	-	-	1	-
60 +	3	-	-	-	-	-	-	-	2	1	-	-	-
Unknown - Inconnu	-	-	-	-	-	-	-	-	-	-	-	-	-

Singapore - Singapour¹⁴,¹⁵
2006 (+C)

Total	23 706	125	1 985	8 505	6 327	2 929	1 613	1 064	610	312	236ʲ	...	...
0 - 14	-	-	-	-	-	-	-	-	-	-	ʲ	...	...
15 - 19	636	99	254	119	57	49	32	18	4	4	ʲ	...	...
20 - 24	5 114	24	1 271	2 295	899	340	164	66	33	16	6ʲ	...	...
25 - 29	10 317	1	373	5 316	3 116	881	375	142	81	24	8ʲ	...	...
30 - 34	4 479	1	67	653	1 892	1 019	417	268	103	44	15ʲ	...	...
35 - 39	1 681	-	14	97	282	495	355	256	107	53	22ʲ	...	...
40 - 44	825	-	4	21	65	113	202	181	124	72	43ʲ	...	...
45 - 49	377	-	1	3	9	24	55	98	99	47	41ʲ	...	...
50 - 54	158	-	1	1	4	6	12	28	46	31	29ʲ	...	...
55 - 59	81	-	-	-	2	2	1	6	10	18	42ʲ	...	...
60 +	38	-	-	-	1	-	-	1	3	3	30ʲ	...	...

Sri Lanka
2003 (+U)

Total	195 914	...	61 991	47 776	18 480	7 595	3 589	3 210	...	...	...	...	...
16 - 20	11 664	...	...	...	...	...	...	...	...	...	...	...	...
21 - 24	49 940	...	...	...	...	...	...	...	...	...	...	...	...
25 - 29	68 808	...	...	...	...	...	...	...	...	...	...	...	...
30 - 34	38 981	...	...	...	...	...	...	...	...	...	...	...	...
35 - 39	14 096	...	...	...	...	...	...	...	...	...	...	...	...

Continent, country or area, year and age of bride / Continent, pays ou zone, date et âge de l'épouse	Total	Age of groom âge de l'époux											Unknown Inconnu
		15-19	20-24	25-29	30-34	35-39	40-44	45-49	50-54	55-59	60-64	65+	
ASIA - ASIE													
Sri Lanka													
2003													
40 - 44	6 137	...	...	...	...	...	...	...	...	...	...	...	
45 + ...	6 288	...	...	...	...	...	...	...	...	...	...	...	
Tajikistan - Tadjikistan													
2000 (C)													
Total..................	26 597	2 278	13 733	7 534	1 741	560	293	122	77	60	87	84	28
15 - 19	10 431	2 063	6 757	1 494	93	17	2	3	-	-	1	1	-
20 - 24	12 345	202	6 728	4 658	601	101	28	9	5	-	1	-	12
25 - 29	2 575	12	200	1 292	758	179	85	13	11	7	2	9	7
30 - 34	654	-	25	60	241	175	67	24	17	8	16	20	1
35 - 39	264	-	13	18	30	65	59	25	10	13	16	14	1
40 - 44	122	-	1	5	11	18	32	16	13	9	13	4	-
45 - 49	66	-	-	2	3	3	12	19	9	3	8	7	-
50 - 54	65	-	2	-	2	1	7	11	10	10	14	8	-
55 - 59	16	-	-	-	-	-	1	1	1	4	6	3	-
60 - 64	19	-	-	-	-	1	-	1	-	5	5	6	1
65 - 69	9	-	-	1	-	-	-	-	1	1	4	2	-
70 - 74	11	1	-	-	-	-	-	-	-	-	1	9	-
75 + ...	1	-	-	-	-	-	-	-	-	-	-	1	-
Unknown - Inconnu	19	-	7	4	2	-	-	-	-	-	-	-	6
Turkey - Turquie[16]													
2006 (C)													
Total..................	636 121	18 647[a]	201 822	264 032	85 970	27 202	14 072	7 594	5 543	3 881	2 683	4 675	-
0 - 15..................	-	-[a]	-	-	-	-	-	-	-	-	-	-	-
16 - 19	163 913	12 690[a]	81 024	60 281	8 523	1 025	240	63	33	14	14	6	-
20 - 24	254 430	4 957[a]	98 431	118 999	26 194	4 220	1 046	309	135	63	34	42	-
25 - 29	138 415	837[a]	19 761	72 345	32 916	8 336	2 594	822	411	187	98	108	-
30 - 34	42 278	131[a]	2 187	10 496	14 688	8 208	3 746	1 384	681	343	198	216	-
35 - 39	16 077	24[a]	330	1 510	2 878	4 058	3 596	1 668	937	519	240	317	-
40 - 44	9 455	8[a]	74	326	639	1 166	2 245	1 951	1 278	754	472	542	-
45 - 49	4 870	-[a]	12	65	102	148	481	1 098	1 178	685	445	656	-
50 - 54	3 172	-[a]	3	8	25	29	92	254	716	803	489	753	-
55 - 59	1 760	-[a]	-	1	4	9	27	39	140	406	413	721	-
60 - 64	874	-[a]	-	-	1	1	2	3	24	91	187	565	-
65 - 69	504	-[a]	-	-	-	1	2	2	7	11	74	407	-
70 - 74	230	-[a]	-	-	-	1	-	1	-	3	15	210	-
75 - 79	108	-[a]	-	-	-	-	1	-	2	2	4	99	-
80 - 84	31	-[a]	-	-	-	-	-	-	1	-	-	30	-
85 - 89	2	-[a]	-	-	-	-	-	-	-	-	-	2	-
90 - 94	2	-[a]	-	1	-	-	-	-	-	-	-	1	-
95 + ...	-	-[a]	-	-	-	-	-	-	-	-	-	-	-
Unknown - Inconnu	-	-[a]	-	-	-	-	-	-	-	-	-	-	-
Uzbekistan - Ouzbékistan													
2000 (C)													
Total..................	168 908	8 783[a]	102 113	41 332	8 139	3 369	1 911	1 118	684	454	1 005[j]	...	...
0 - 17..................	9 606	1 762[a]	6 732	1 032	69	8	3	-	-	-	-[j]	...	...
18 - 19	52 422	5 687[a]	38 985	7 320	361	55	7	1	1	2	3[j]	...	...
20 - 24	84 289	1 299[a]	54 562	25 189	2 631	416	144	30	3	5	10[j]	...	...
25 - 29	13 386	34[a]	1 669	7 135	3 129	944	305	103	32	8	27[j]	...	...
30 - 34	4 351	1[a]	147	558	1 659	1 124	467	207	93	32	63[j]	...	...
35 - 39	2 103	-[a]	14	85	238	675	528	257	130	98	78[j]	...	...
40 - 44	1 134	-[a]	1	13	41	122	343	261	152	82	119[j]	...	...
45 - 49	626	-[a]	-	-	9	22	94	193	122	70	116[j]	...	...
50 - 54	440	-[a]	-	-	2	3	17	59	129	91	139[j]	...	...
55 - 59	194	-[a]	-	-	-	-	2	7	18	37	130[j]	...	...
60 + ...	354	-[a]	-	-	-	-	1	-	4	29	320[j]	...	...
Unknown - Inconnu	3	-[a]	3	-	-	-	-	-	-	-	-[j]	...	...

Continent, country or area, year and age of bride / Continent, pays ou zone, date et âge de l'épouse	Total	Age of groom âge de l'époux											
		15-19	20-24	25-29	30-34	35-39	40-44	45-49	50-54	55-59	60-64	65+	Unknown Inconnu
EUROPE													
Albania - Albanie													
2006 (C)													
Total	21 332	237[a]	4 468	9 609	4 522	1 452	531	249	264[h]	...	...	...	...
0 - 19	5 333	...	...	...	...	...	...	...	...	...	...	...	...
20 - 24	10 276	...	...	...	...	...	...	...	...	...	...	...	...
25 - 29	3 749	...	...	...	...	...	...	...	...	...	...	...	...
30 - 34	1 169	...	...	...	...	...	...	...	...	...	...	...	...
35 - 39	466	...	...	...	...	...	...	...	...	...	...	...	...
40 - 44	185	...	...	...	...	...	...	...	...	...	...	...	...
45 - 49	95	...	...	...	...	...	...	...	...	...	...	...	...
50 +	59	...	...	...	...	...	...	...	...	...	...	...	...
Austria - Autriche[17]													
2006 (C)													
Total	36 923	276	3 288	7 943	8 930	6 357	3 867	2 490	1 386	1 079	690	617	-
0 - 14	-	-	-	-	-	-	-	-	-	-	-	-	-
15 - 19	1 058	166	582	217	51	26	7	5	2	1	1	-	-
20 - 24	6 052	80	1 930	2 528	931	383	117	47	23	7	4	2	-
25 - 29	10 220	19	565	4 019	3 704	1 271	392	155	47	31	12	5	-
30 - 34	7 725	7	120	857	3 162	2 276	812	327	93	43	19	9	-
35 - 39	4 746	3	45	199	780	1 664	1 184	514	191	101	46	19	-
40 - 44	3 018	1	24	80	193	525	877	684	323	187	77	47	-
45 - 49	1 981	-	14	31	71	165	349	493	373	263	130	92	-
50 - 54	1 061	-	5	9	29	32	99	200	227	216	150	94	-
55 - 59	601	-	2	2	8	14	20	49	88	173	126	119	-
60 - 64	286	-	-	1	1	-	4	12	14	43	93	118	-
65 - 69	111	-	1	-	-	-	2	3	4	11	23	67	-
70 - 74	35	-	-	-	-	1	2	-	1	1	7	23	-
75 - 79	17	-	-	-	-	-	1	-	-	2	1	13	-
80 - 84	10	-	-	-	-	-	1	1	-	-	-	8	-
85 - 89	2	-	-	-	-	-	-	-	-	-	1	1	-
90 +	-	-	-	-	-	-	-	-	-	-	-	-	-
Unknown - Inconnu	-	-	-	-	-	-	-	-	-	-	-	-	-
Belarus - Bélarus													
2006 (C)													
Total	78 979	2 010[a]	31 270	22 689	8 930	4 673	3 106	2 370	1 604	1 074	1 253[j]	...	...
0 - 17	1 031	252[a]	655	113	9	2	-	-	-	-	-[j]	...	...
18 - 19	8 614	851[a]	5 878	1 609	215	44	10	4	2	1	-[j]	...	...
20 - 24	37 002	780[a]	20 809	12 248	2 361	532	163	65	30	11	3[j]	...	...
25 - 29	15 279	113[a]	3 339	6 757	3 269	1 165	415	140	48	21	12[j]	...	...
30 - 34	6 607	11[a]	485	1 527	2 188	1 394	625	257	79	30	11[j]	...	...
35 - 39	3 417	3[a]	75	350	664	986	765	371	134	57	12[j]	...	...
40 - 44	2 305	-[a]	17	72	173	384	723	550	246	93	47[j]	...	...
45 - 49	1 869	-[a]	7	10	43	129	302	664	437	189	88[j]	...	...
50 - 54	1 335	-[a]	3	1	5	27	79	258	468	334	160[j]	...	...
55 - 59	745	-[a]	-	2	1	8	16	47	130	263	278[j]	...	...
60 +	775	-[a]	2	-	2	2	8	14	30	75	642[j]	...	...
Belgium - Belgique[18]													
2000 (C)													
Total	45 123	217	6 944	16 216	8 374	4 795	2 963	2 138	1 599	831	494	552	...
15 - 19	1 410	106	764	380	111	32	10	5	1	-	-	1	...
20 - 24	13 112	74	4 680	6 434	1 404	347	104	46	14	6	1	2	...
25 - 29	14 485	24	1 244	7 854	3 671	1 097	365	131	73	21	2	3	...
30 - 34	6 169	7	172	1 161	2 195	1 549	615	280	120	52	14	4	...
35 - 39	3 702	5	57	240	674	1 114	760	480	232	96	27	17	...
40 - 44	2 556	1	21	102	224	457	679	515	333	129	60	35	...
45 - 49	1 805	-	3	30	68	150	308	462	406	197	102	79	...
50 - 54	1 065	-	2	13	22	36	101	170	314	196	124	87	...
55 - 59	437	-	1	1	2	9	16	37	75	98	94	104	...
60 - 64	195	-	-	1	3	3	3	10	22	25	50	78	...
65 - 69	106	-	-	-	-	1	2	2	7	8	16	70	...
70 - 74	45	-	-	-	-	-	-	-	2	2	3	38	...
75 +	36	-	-	-	-	-	-	-	-	1	1	34	...

Continent, country or area, year and age of bride / Continent, pays ou zone, date et âge de l'épouse	Total	15-19	20-24	25-29	30-34	35-39	40-44	45-49	50-54	55-59	60-64	65+	Unknown Inconnu
EUROPE													
Bosnia and Herzegovina - Bosnie-Herzégovine													
2006 (C)													
Total	21 501	338	5 256	7 569	3 944	1 806	999	532	363	239	132	318	5
15 - 19	2 982	216	1 708	860	156	22	16	3	1	-	-	-	-
20 - 24	8 215	105	2 988	3 784	1 027	227	58	15	5	2	-	3	1
25 - 29	5 477	13	493	2 554	1 727	486	147	39	9	5	1	2	1
30 - 34	2 223	1	49	299	833	620	283	83	40	9	4	2	-
35 - 39	1 005	1	6	43	153	332	290	106	38	27	5	4	-
40 - 44	589	1	6	13	29	87	142	154	82	39	14	21	1
45 - 49	378	-	-	7	8	20	43	87	85	54	31	43	-
50 - 54	296	-	-	-	1	7	15	32	86	65	33	57	-
55 - 59	139	-	-	2	-	1	4	10	11	27	29	55	-
60 - 64	69	-	-	-	1	-	1	1	3	7	9	47	-
65 - 69	53	-	-	-	1	-	-	-	2	3	2	45	-
70 - 74	27	-	-	-	-	-	-	-	-	-	2	25	-
75 +	14	-	-	-	-	-	-	-	-	-	-	14	-
Unknown - Inconnu	34	1	6	7	8	4	-	2	1	1	2	-	2
Bulgaria - Bulgarie[19]													
2006 (C)													
Total	32 773	314	5 498	12 389	7 854	3 073	1 402	817	580	377	199	270	...
0 - 14	-	-	-	-	-	-	-	-	-	-	-	-	...
15 - 19	2 481	196	1 245	786	201	34	10	4	4	1	-	-	...
20 - 24	11 202	93	3 370	5 427	1 792	354	94	43	14	6	2	1	...
25 - 29	10 933	16	756	5 234	3 592	917	263	100	34	11	8	2	...
30 - 34	4 540	5	97	806	1 880	1 073	411	165	63	26	10	4	...
35 - 39	1 658	2	17	99	314	516	366	181	99	45	14	5	...
40 - 44	795	-	5	22	57	132	188	171	123	54	30	13	...
45 - 49	466	1	1	7	13	33	49	114	114	70	27	37	...
50 - 54	321	-	1	7	3	11	17	33	91	91	34	33	...
55 - 59	193	1	-	-	2	2	3	4	31	55	42	53	...
60 - 64	95	-	-	1	-	-	1	1	5	15	22	50	...
65 - 69	58	-	-	-	-	1	-	1	1	3	8	44	...
70 - 74	22	-	-	-	-	-	-	-	-	-	2	20	...
75 +	9	-	-	-	-	-	-	-	1	-	-	8	...
Croatia - Croatie													
2006 (C)													
Total	22 092	215	4 000	8 492	4 967	1 982	863	536	305	277	126	324	4
0 - 14	-	-	-	-	-	-	-	-	-	-	-	-	-
15 - 19	1 598	142	922	424	87	17	2	3	-	-	-	-	1
20 - 24	7 219	65	2 432	3 463	971	215	40	21	7	5	-	-	-
25 - 29	7 727	6	588	3 977	2 367	581	144	43	11	4	1	4	1
30 - 34	3 011	1	52	547	1 305	726	241	93	30	13	1	2	-
35 - 39	1 046	1	5	71	199	333	233	127	43	22	7	4	1
40 - 44	498	-	-	8	27	79	147	128	58	30	7	14	-
45 - 49	345	-	1	-	6	24	42	79	84	48	23	38	-
50 - 54	262	-	-	-	-	6	10	27	46	76	41	55	1
55 - 59	183	-	-	-	2	-	3	8	18	68	26	58	-
60 - 64	101	-	-	-	-	-	1	5	7	8	15	65	-
65 - 69	49	-	-	-	-	-	-	1	-	-	4	44	-
70 - 74	32	-	-	-	-	-	-	1	1	3	1	26	-
75 - 79	10	-	-	-	-	-	-	-	-	-	-	10	-
80 - 84	4	-	-	-	-	-	-	-	-	-	-	4	-
85 +	-	-	-	-	-	-	-	-	-	-	-	-	-
Unknown - Inconnu	7	-	-	2	3	1	-	-	-	-	-	1	-
Czech Republic - République tchèque													
2006 (C)													
Total	52 860	198	4 819	19 218	14 110	5 341	3 038	1 972	1 716	1 253	648	547	-
0 - 14	-	-	-	-	-	-	-	-	-	-	-	-	-
15 - 19	1 071	67	508	312	124	36	11	7	6	-	-	-	-
20 - 24	11 204	98	2 933	5 534	2 018	416	130	42	21	10	2	-	-
25 - 29	21 472	22	1 084	10 959	6 998	1 579	536	160	92	29	6	7	-
30 - 34	9 632	8	237	1 997	4 070	1 907	839	322	152	67	24	9	-
35 - 39	3 287	2	42	325	630	931	686	372	183	78	29	9	-
40 - 44	2 144	-	12	72	208	334	549	468	303	143	34	21	-
45 - 49	1 496	1	1	14	41	104	191	388	402	241	82	31	-

24. Marriages by age of bridegroom and by age of bride: latest available year, 1997 - 2006
Mariages selon l'âge de l'époux et selon l'âge de l'épouse: dernière année disponible, 1997 - 2006 (continued - suite)

Continent, pays ou zone, date et âge de l'épouse	Total	15-19	20-24	25-29	30-34	35-39	40-44	45-49	50-54	55-59	60-64	65+	Unknown Inconnu
EUROPE													
Czech Republic - République tchèque													
2006													
50 - 54	1 211	-	1	2	14	26	70	149	381	359	140	69	-
55 - 59	779	-	1	1	5	8	20	49	132	240	202	121	-
60 - 64	344	-	-	2	2	-	4	11	39	66	96	124	-
65 - 69	128	-	-	-	-	-	2	2	4	16	25	79	-
70 - 74	50	-	-	-	-	-	-	-	1	4	7	38	-
75 - 79	30	-	-	-	-	-	-	-	-	-	1	29	-
80 - 84	8	-	-	-	-	-	-	1	-	-	-	7	-
85 - 89	3	-	-	-	-	-	-	-	-	-	-	3	-
90 - 94	-	-	-	-	-	-	-	-	-	-	-	-	-
95 - 99	1	-	-	-	-	-	-	1	-	-	-	-	-
100 +	-	-	-	-	-	-	-	-	-	-	-	-	-
Unknown - Inconnu	-	-	-	-	-	-	-	-	-	-	-	-	-
Denmark - Danemark[20]													
2006 (C)													
Total	36 452	72	1 515	7 798	9 267	5 835	3 887	2 517	1 867	1 385	870	604	835
0 - 14	-	-	-	-	-	-	-	-	-	-	-	-	-
15 - 19	352	38	159	57	16	5	3	-	-	-	-	-	74
20 - 24	3 244	13	880	1 490	453	134	43	15	4	4	-	-	208
25 - 29	9 953	4	297	4 688	3 521	896	231	67	16	11	1	3	218
30 - 34	8 378	-	61	1 140	4 011	2 122	652	170	56	20	12	3	131
35 - 39	4 686	-	14	152	863	1 766	1 189	432	124	47	16	7	76
40 - 44	3 146	-	5	38	141	564	1 123	718	317	140	33	13	54
45 - 49	2 112	-	2	9	27	103	355	649	576	244	95	19	33
50 - 54	1 454	-	-	3	3	20	86	243	497	381	162	39	20
55 - 59	899	-	-	-	2	7	24	48	140	337	248	82	11
60 - 64	492	-	-	-	-	1	6	12	30	96	189	153	5
65 - 69	224	-	-	-	-	-	-	5	9	27	54	128	1
70 +	156	-	-	-	-	-	-	-	2	3	12	137	2
Unknown - Inconnu	1 356	17	97	221	230	217	175	158	96	75	48	20	2
Estonia - Estonie													
2006 (C)													
Total	6 954	100	1 250	1 920	1 413	873	485	361	243	155	73	81	-
0 - 14	-	-	-	-	-	-	-	-	-	-	-	-	-
15 - 19	417	64	248	72	23	8	2	-	-	-	-	-	-
20 - 24	1 929	30	767	792	253	54	18	11	3	1	-	-	-
25 - 29	1 879	3	184	812	553	215	79	23	7	2	-	1	-
30 - 34	1 110	2	41	192	416	286	97	52	14	8	2	-	-
35 - 39	632	-	8	40	126	221	125	69	32	9	-	2	-
40 - 44	348	-	1	9	27	62	109	71	39	20	7	3	-
45 - 49	266	1	1	3	10	24	38	89	62	25	8	5	-
50 - 54	190	-	-	-	5	3	15	39	59	40	20	9	-
55 - 59	96	-	-	-	-	-	2	6	17	37	19	15	-
60 - 64	39	-	-	-	-	-	-	1	6	10	10	12	-
65 - 69	26	-	-	-	-	-	-	-	4	3	5	14	-
70 - 74	12	-	-	-	-	-	-	-	-	-	2	10	-
75 - 79	8	-	-	-	-	-	-	-	-	-	-	8	-
80 - 84	1	-	-	-	-	-	-	-	-	-	-	1	-
85 - 89	-	-	-	-	-	-	-	-	-	-	-	-	-
90 - 94	1	-	-	-	-	-	-	-	-	-	-	1	-
95 +	-	-	-	-	-	-	-	-	-	-	-	-	-
Unknown - Inconnu	-	-	-	-	-	-	-	-	-	-	-	-	-
Finland - Finlande[21,22]													
2006 (C)													
Total	28 236	237	2 872	7 636	6 169	3 847	2 659	1 969	1 259	845	437	306	-
0 - 14	-	-	-	-	-	-	-	-	-	-	-	-	-
15 - 19	735	150	419	126	28	6	3	1	-	1	1	-	-
20 - 24	4 626	71	1 865	2 055	450	127	34	14	6	3	-	1	-
25 - 29	8 585	10	460	4 495	2 678	673	186	59	15	8	1	-	-
30 - 34	5 207	3	81	767	2 320	1 373	451	142	47	18	5	-	-
35 - 39	3 105	2	26	126	495	1 153	827	319	130	21	4	2	-
40 - 44	2 164	1	9	46	129	370	769	556	199	70	11	4	-
45 - 49	1 754	-	5	17	49	108	288	623	401	191	60	12	-
50 - 54	959	-	5	3	11	29	78	176	313	227	95	22	-
55 - 59	620	-	1	1	8	6	14	66	114	213	140	57	-

Continent, country or area, year and age of bride / Continent, pays ou zone, date et âge de l'épouse	Total	15-19	20-24	25-29	30-34	35-39	40-44	45-49	50-54	55-59	60-64	65+	Unknown Inconnu
EUROPE													
Finland - Finlande[21,22]													
2006													
60 - 64	288	-	1	-	1	1	7	11	24	72	90	81	-
65 - 69	109	-	-	-	-	1	2	2	4	14	25	61	-
70 - 74	49	-	-	-	-	-	-	-	5	3	4	37	-
75 - 79	25	-	-	-	-	-	-	-	1	4	1	19	-
80 - 84	7	-	-	-	-	-	-	-	-	-	-	7	-
85 - 89	2	-	-	-	-	-	-	-	-	-	-	2	-
90 - 94	1	-	-	-	-	-	-	-	-	-	-	1	-
95 +	-	-	-	-	-	-	-	-	-	-	-	-	-
Unknown - Inconnu	-	-	-	-	-	-	-	-	-	-	-	-	-
France[23,24]													
2006 (C)													
Total	267 260	327	16 896	74 252	65 283	38 447	24 036	16 404	12 662	9 223	4 993	4 737	-
0 - 14	2	-	-	2	-	-	-	-	-	-	-	-	-
15 - 19	2 599	132	1 110	903	331	76	22	11	7	3	2	2	-
20 - 24	39 143	140	11 043	19 816	5 919	1 487	425	177	85	32	13	6	-
25 - 29	85 791	40	3 903	44 549	27 262	6 931	1 963	676	273	115	53	26	-
30 - 34	52 911	11	558	7 014	24 090	13 557	4 651	1 830	720	290	140	50	-
35 - 39	31 234	1	160	1 305	5 576	11 183	7 431	3 204	1 406	642	220	106	-
40 - 44	20 305	2	66	419	1 397	3 581	6 150	4 466	2 419	1 213	395	197	-
45 - 49	14 020	-	39	148	483	1 181	2 295	3 740	3 309	1 725	739	361	-
50 - 54	9 990	-	12	63	165	339	807	1 618	2 871	2 400	1 113	602	-
55 - 59	6 247	-	1	19	43	86	234	513	1 191	1 982	1 257	921	-
60 - 64	2 831	-	1	7	14	18	42	135	288	622	779	925	-
65 - 69	1 192	1	-	2	3	5	13	25	73	142	195	733	-
70 - 74	565	-	2	-	-	1	3	4	16	41	67	431	-
75 - 79	247	-	1	-	-	1	-	4	2	7	16	216	-
80 - 84	126	-	-	3	-	-	-	1	2	6	3	111	-
85 - 89	46	-	-	2	-	-	1	-	-	3	1	39	-
90 - 94	9	-	-	-	-	-	-	-	-	-	-	9	-
95 - 99	2	-	-	-	-	-	-	-	-	-	-	2	-
100 +	-	-	-	-	-	-	-	-	-	-	-	-	-
Unknown - Inconnu	-	-	-	-	-	-	-	-	-	-	-	-	-
Germany - Allemagne													
2006 (C)													
Total	373 681	1 619	29 488	81 922	84 255	66 955	42 094	25 745	16 738	10 902	6 596	7 367	...
0 - 14	-	-	-	-	-	-	-	-	-	-	-	-	...
15 - 19	7 970	863	4 426	1 885	474	186	81	39	8	5	1	2	...
20 - 24	60 028	633	19 063	26 684	8 953	3 064	1 072	338	120	69	20	12	...
25 - 29	104 394	88	4 903	43 470	36 353	13 767	3 929	1 193	385	184	75	47	...
30 - 34	73 214	14	740	7 691	29 823	23 505	7 869	2 298	771	323	118	62	...
35 - 39	48 693	12	202	1 546	6 611	19 006	13 299	5 082	1 809	721	262	143	...
40 - 44	31 597	5	84	421	1 461	5 566	10 645	7 553	3 440	1 502	582	338	...
45 - 49	21 344	3	47	154	419	1 448	3 806	6 397	4 944	2 479	1 033	614	...
50 - 54	13 038	1	17	47	120	330	1 100	2 174	3 761	3 019	1 523	946	...
55 - 59	6 910	-	3	18	30	66	222	546	1 151	1 899	1 583	1 392	...
60 - 64	3 384	-	2	3	7	9	57	88	254	534	994	1 436	...
65 - 69	2 092	-	-	2	4	5	10	29	76	128	331	1 507	...
70 - 74	663	-	1	1	-	2	2	8	13	31	57	548	...
75 +	354	-	-	-	-	1	2	-	6	8	17	320	...
Greece - Grèce													
2006 (C)													
Total	57 802	321	3 385	15 907	18 919	9 982	4 161	2 126	1 080	751	411	757	-
0 - 14	56	26	22	7	-	-	-	-	-	-	-	-	-
15 - 19	1 741	201	787	502	183	43	14	5	3	2	-	-	-
20 - 24	9 506	64	1 874	4 434	2 284	651	121	49	18	5	6	-	-
25 - 29	21 965	20	566	8 733	8 722	2 915	725	172	63	25	12	12	-
30 - 34	14 336	7	111	1 874	6 470	3 911	1 275	463	126	65	20	14	-
35 - 39	5 612	1	19	287	1 049	2 003	1 283	598	227	96	28	21	-
40 - 44	2 092	2	4	60	157	357	560	485	236	132	46	53	-
45 - 49	1 167	-	2	7	40	79	142	269	237	187	90	114	-
50 - 54	662	-	-	2	10	16	34	69	137	140	93	161	-
55 - 59	368	-	-	1	4	4	6	12	28	74	85	154	-
60 - 64	147	-	-	-	-	3	1	1	2	18	20	102	-
65 - 69	92	-	-	-	-	-	-	3	2	6	10	71	-
70 - 74	48	-	-	-	-	-	-	-	1	1	1	45	-

Continent, country or area, year and age of bride / Continent, pays ou zone, date et âge de l'épouse	Total	15-19	20-24	25-29	30-34	35-39	40-44	45-49	50-54	55-59	60-64	65+	Unknown Inconnu
EUROPE													
Greece - Grèce													
2006													
75 - 79	5	-	-	-	-	-	-	-	-	-	-	5	-
80 - 84	4	-	-	-	-	-	-	-	-	-	-	4	-
85 - 89	-	-	-	-	-	-	-	-	-	-	-	-	-
90 - 94	1	-	-	-	-	-	-	-	-	-	-	1	-
95 +	-	-	-	-	-	-	-	-	-	-	-	-	-
Unknown - Inconnu	-	-	-	-	-	-	-	-	-	-	-	-	-
Hungary - Hongrie													
2006 (C)													
Total	44 528	329	4 218	16 382	12 333	4 610	1 902	1 485	1 342	900	522	505	-
0 - 14	-	-	-	-	-	-	-	-	-	-	-	-	-
15 - 19	1 435	213	659	389	126	25	9	8	5	-	-	1	-
20 - 24	9 495	76	2 290	4 857	1 781	354	78	33	18	5	3	-	-
25 - 29	17 661	33	976	8 785	5 944	1 381	326	100	76	20	17	3	-
30 - 34	8 587	7	239	2 025	3 702	1 693	501	269	94	41	10	6	-
35 - 39	2 882	-	47	259	612	840	513	322	186	72	19	12	-
40 - 44	1 312	-	5	44	119	207	284	285	205	100	43	20	-
45 - 49	1 152	-	2	16	32	75	127	283	337	161	79	40	-
50 - 54	1 075	-	-	6	16	26	50	148	321	285	139	84	-
55 - 59	526	-	-	-	1	6	12	31	72	167	129	108	-
60 - 64	242	-	-	1	-	2	1	4	21	35	64	114	-
65 - 69	98	-	-	-	-	-	1	2	4	12	13	66	-
70 - 74	45	-	-	-	-	1	-	-	2	1	5	36	-
75 - 79	13	-	-	-	-	-	-	-	-	-	-	13	-
80 - 84	2	-	-	-	-	-	-	-	1	-	-	1	-
85 - 89	2	-	-	-	-	-	-	-	-	-	1	1	-
90 - 94	1	-	-	-	-	-	-	-	-	1	-	-	-
95 +	-	-	-	-	-	-	-	-	-	-	-	-	-
Unknown - Inconnu	-	-	-	-	-	-	-	-	-	-	-	-	-
Iceland - Islande[25]													
2006 (C)													
Total	1 681	3	75	394	427	284	171	141	74	51	30	27	4
0 - 14	-	-	-	-	-	-	-	-	-	-	-	-	-
15 - 19	11	1	4	4	-	1	-	-	-	-	-	1	-
20 - 24	176	2	43	89	26	10	3	2	-	-	-	-	1
25 - 29	494	-	24	244	156	48	8	8	-	2	1	2	1
30 - 34	392	-	3	44	199	105	28	7	2	2	1	-	1
35 - 39	238	-	-	10	45	82	65	20	8	4	3	-	1
40 - 44	153	-	-	3	1	30	48	46	16	7	1	1	-
45 - 49	106	-	-	-	-	7	16	44	24	10	3	2	-
50 - 54	54	-	-	-	-	1	3	10	17	13	9	1	-
55 - 59	36	-	-	-	-	-	-	4	6	10	9	7	-
60 - 64	10	-	-	-	-	-	-	-	1	3	2	4	-
65 - 69	7	-	-	-	-	-	-	-	-	-	1	6	-
70 - 74	3	-	-	-	-	-	-	-	-	-	-	3	-
75 +	-	-	-	-	-	-	-	-	-	-	-	-	-
Unknown - Inconnu	1	-	1	-	-	-	-	-	-	-	-	-	-
Ireland - Irlande													
2005 (C)													
Total	21 355	116	1 025	6 475	7 903	3 145	1 289	598	358	209	120	112	5
0 - 14	-	-	-	-	-	-	-	-	-	-	-	-	-
15 - 19	246	78	103	43	13	6	2	-	-	-	1	-	-
20 - 24	2 052	31	551	981	372	83	21	9	2	1	1	-	-
25 - 29	8 481	3	293	4 165	3 155	679	138	33	8	5	1	-	1
30 - 34	6 733	3	58	1 093	3 681	1 391	361	98	32	9	2	1	4
35 - 39	2 208	1	14	150	585	785	438	151	64	14	3	3	-
40 - 44	780	-	5	21	67	154	242	145	81	39	20	6	-
45 - 49	404	-	1	13	21	36	68	111	82	44	16	12	-
50 - 54	223	-	-	5	1	8	15	43	65	40	33	13	-
55 - 59	120	-	-	-	1	1	2	6	19	40	28	23	-
60 - 64	58	-	-	-	1	-	-	1	5	17	11	23	-
65 - 69	21	-	-	-	-	-	1	1	-	-	3	16	-
70 - 74	9	-	-	-	-	-	-	-	-	-	-	9	-
75 - 79	5	-	-	-	-	-	-	-	-	-	-	5	-
80 - 84	-	-	-	-	-	-	-	-	-	-	-	-	-
85 - 89	1	-	-	-	-	-	-	-	-	-	-	1	-

Continent, country or area, year and age of bride / Continent, pays ou zone, date et âge de l'épouse	Total	15-19	20-24	25-29	30-34	35-39	40-44	45-49	50-54	55-59	60-64	65+	Unknown Inconnu
EUROPE													
Ireland - Irlande													
2005													
90 - 94	1	-	-	-	-	-	-	-	-	-	1	-	-
95 + ...	-	-	-	-	-	-	-	-	-	-	-	-	-
Unknown - Inconnu	13	-	-	4	6	2	1	-	-	-	-	-	-
Isle of Man - Îles de Man													
1999[26] (C)													
Total..................	403	1	37	99	103	59	30	22	21	12	8	11	...
15 - 19	7	-	1	3	2	1	-	-	-	-	-	-	...
20 - 24	64	19	21	13	8	3	-	-	-	-	-	-	...
25 - 29	119	1	11	52	37	13	2	2	1	-	-	-	...
30 - 34	79	-	4	19	29	16	5	1	3	1	1	-	...
35 - 39	47	-	1	3	17	13	8	1	3	1	-	-	...
40 - 44	34	-	1	1	4	5	6	6	4	4	3	-	...
45 - 49	23	-	-	-	1	3	4	7	3	1	2	2	...
50 - 54	16	-	-	-	-	-	1	4	7	2	2	-	...
55 - 59	5	-	-	-	-	-	1	1	-	2	-	1	...
60 - 64	3	-	-	-	-	-	-	-	-	-	-	3	...
65 - 69	5	-	-	-	-	-	-	-	-	1	-	4	...
70 - 74	1	-	-	-	-	-	-	-	-	-	-	1	...
75 + ...	-	-	-	-	-	-	-	-	-	-	-	-	...
2004 (C)													
Total..................	399	1	34	89	108	52	49	22	16	12	8	8	...
0 - 14.................	-	...	-	...	...	...	...	...	...	...	...	...	...
15 - 19	6	...	...	...	...	...	...	...	...	...	...	...	...
20 - 24	64	...	...	...	...	...	...	...	...	...	...	...	...
25 - 29	95	...	...	...	...	...	...	...	...	...	...	...	...
30 - 34	103	...	...	...	...	...	...	...	...	...	...	...	...
35 - 39	55	...	...	...	...	...	...	...	...	...	...	...	...
40 - 44	28	...	...	...	...	...	...	...	...	...	...	...	...
45 - 49	17	...	...	...	...	...	...	...	...	...	...	...	...
50 - 54	11	...	...	...	...	...	...	...	...	...	...	...	...
55 - 59	10	...	...	...	...	...	...	...	...	...	...	...	...
60 - 64	5	...	...	...	...	...	...	...	...	...	...	...	...
65 - 69	3	...	...	...	...	...	...	...	...	...	...	...	...
70 - 74	2	...	...	...	...	...	...	...	...	...	...	...	...
75 + ...	-	...	...	...	...	...	...	...	...	...	...	...	...
Italy - Italie													
2005 (C)													
Total..................	247 740	700	14 190	67 751	84 903	40 657	17 283	8 266	5 020	3 737	2 168	3 065	-
0 - 14.................	-	-	-	-	-	-	-	-	-	-	-	-	-
15 - 19	5 344	393	2 805	1 533	419	125	35	21	8	2	3	-	-
20 - 24	38 262	236	8 214	19 716	7 495	1 683	501	184	118	65	30	20	-
25 - 29	89 067	43	2 485	36 557	37 915	8 949	1 985	605	243	163	65	57	-
30 - 34	66 522	18	490	8 480	32 777	17 495	4 919	1 410	507	247	96	83	-
35 - 39	26 085	4	107	1 106	5 327	9 914	5 739	2 219	892	438	181	158	-
40 - 44	10 742	3	40	234	774	1 995	3 146	2 185	1 200	649	270	246	-
45 - 49	5 329	2	29	66	126	385	727	1 177	1 128	839	415	435	-
50 - 54	3 082	-	12	37	36	84	178	341	668	740	451	535	-
55 - 59	1 757	1	5	10	17	14	34	89	204	437	379	567	-
60 - 64	841	-	2	6	9	5	10	25	41	120	190	433	-
65 - 69	397	-	1	2	3	1	3	3	8	30	62	284	-
70 - 74	181	-	-	4	2	3	4	3	3	5	18	139	-
75 - 79	92	-	-	-	1	3	-	3	-	2	6	77	-
80 - 84	29	-	-	-	1	-	-	1	-	-	-	27	-
85 - 89	9	-	-	-	1	1	2	-	-	-	2	3	-
90 - 94	1	-	-	-	-	-	-	-	-	-	-	1	-
95 + ...	-	-	-	-	-	-	-	-	-	-	-	-	-
Latvia - Lettonie													
2006 (C)													
Total..................	14 616	156	2 991	4 361	2 772	1 519	879	679	435	330	198	296	-
0 - 14.................	-	-	-	-	-	-	-	-	-	-	-	-	-
15 - 19	674	90	408	133	31	8	2	2	-	-	-	-	-
20 - 24	4 527	53	1 967	1 795	496	147	43	18	6	1	1	-	-
25 - 29	4 074	7	502	1 865	1 123	367	139	42	19	7	3	-	-
30 - 34	2 069	4	74	429	791	463	187	78	19	16	6	2	-
35 - 39	1 137	1	30	109	243	344	193	138	49	22	4	4	-

Continent, country or area, year and age of bride — Continent, pays ou zone, date et âge de l'épouse	Total	15-19	20-24	25-29	30-34	35-39	40-44	45-49	50-54	55-59	60-64	65+	Unknown Inconnu
EUROPE													
Latvia - Lettonie													
2006													
40 - 44	717	-	7	25	62	125	193	169	83	29	15	9	-
45 - 49	505	1	3	4	19	49	87	142	105	59	25	11	-
50 - 54	360	-	-	-	5	15	25	61	100	94	32	28	-
55 - 59	240	-	-	1	-	1	8	25	41	62	54	48	-
60 - 64	125	-	-	-	1	-	1	2	9	24	38	50	-
65 - 69	117	-	-	-	1	-	1	2	4	12	16	81	-
70 - 74	37	-	-	-	-	-	-	-	-	2	2	33	-
75 - 79	24	-	-	-	-	-	-	-	-	1	1	22	-
80 - 84	10	-	-	-	-	-	-	-	-	1	1	8	-
85 +	-	-	-	-	-	-	-	-	-	-	-	-	-
Unknown - Inconnu	-	-	-	-	-	-	-	-	-	-	-	-	-
Liechtenstein													
1997 (C)													
Total	203	...	...	...	...	...	...	...	...	...	...	...	-
0 - 20	10	...	...	...	...	...	...	...	...	...	...	...	-
21 - 25	50	...	...	...	...	...	...	...	...	...	...	...	-
26 - 30	77	...	...	...	...	...	...	...	...	...	...	...	-
31 - 35	31	...	...	...	...	...	...	...	...	...	...	...	-
36 - 40	19	...	...	...	...	...	...	...	...	...	...	...	-
41 - 45	8	...	...	...	...	...	...	...	...	...	...	...	-
46 - 50	6	...	...	...	...	...	...	...	...	...	...	...	-
51 +	2	...	...	...	...	...	...	...	...	...	...	...	-
Unknown - Inconnu	-	...	...	...	...	...	...	...	...	...	...	...	-
2006* (C)													
Total	151	1	14	30	28	27	18	11	7	7	3	5	...
Lithuania - Lituanie													
2006 (C)													
Total	21 246	422	5 503	7 203	3 398	1 740	1 028	721	420	319	207	285	-
0 - 14	2	1	1	-	-	-	-	-	-	-	-	-	-
15 - 19	1 767	253	1 058	376	59	15	3	3	-	-	-	-	-
20 - 24	8 080	147	3 592	3 276	787	188	65	18	1	5	1	-	-
25 - 29	5 830	20	724	2 952	1 430	443	171	54	25	4	5	2	-
30 - 34	2 262	1	102	488	812	515	218	77	31	10	4	4	-
35 - 39	1 187	-	21	82	240	387	248	127	52	22	5	3	-
40 - 44	737	-	5	21	53	139	200	177	71	46	16	9	-
45 - 49	573	-	-	5	14	44	92	183	120	64	33	18	-
50 - 54	334	-	-	3	3	6	26	64	89	77	30	36	-
55 - 59	209	-	-	-	-	3	3	15	22	62	62	42	-
60 - 64	134	-	-	-	-	-	2	3	8	22	39	60	-
65 - 69	75	-	-	-	-	-	-	-	-	6	10	59	-
70 - 74	36	-	-	-	-	-	-	-	-	1	1	34	-
75 +	20	-	-	-	-	-	-	-	1	-	1	18	-
Unknown - Inconnu	-	-	-	-	-	-	-	-	-	-	-	-	-
Luxembourg													
2006 (C)													
Total	1 948	3	109	469	501	359	204	114	95	49	24	21	-
0 - 14	-	-	-	-	-	-	-	-	-	-	-	-	-
15 - 19	18	-	7	5	2	1	1	-	-	-	1	1	-
20 - 24	253	1	62	121	41	13	7	4	3	1	-	-	-
25 - 29	632	-	30	261	224	75	24	10	6	2	-	-	-
30 - 34	447	1	8	57	173	144	43	15	3	3	-	-	-
35 - 39	260	-	1	19	44	85	62	28	13	5	1	2	-
40 - 44	150	-	-	4	12	33	43	29	20	6	3	-	-
45 - 49	88	-	1	2	3	7	17	19	22	11	3	3	-
50 - 54	60	1	-	-	2	1	7	6	23	12	6	2	-
55 - 59	25	-	-	-	-	-	-	2	3	8	8	4	-
60 - 64	12	-	-	-	-	-	-	1	1	1	2	7	-
65 - 69	2	-	-	-	-	-	-	-	-	-	-	2	-
70 - 74	1	-	-	-	-	-	-	-	1	-	-	-	-
75 +	-	-	-	-	-	-	-	-	-	-	-	-	-
Unknown - Inconnu	-	-	-	-	-	-	-	-	-	-	-	-	-
Malta - Malte													
2006 (C)													
Total	2 536	12	309	1 082	604	227	121	68	34	36	19	18	6
15 - 19	58	8	31	16	2	1	-	-	-	-	-	-	-

Continent, country or area, year and age of bride / Continent, pays ou zone, date et âge de l'épouse	Total	15-19	20-24	25-29	30-34	35-39	40-44	45-49	50-54	55-59	60-64	65+	Unknown Inconnu
EUROPE													
Malta - Malte													
2006													
20 - 24	748	4	201	411	110	12	5	3	1	-	1	-	
25 - 29	998	-	64	551	287	72	15	7	1	1	-	-	
30 - 34	382	-	10	90	165	66	33	9	6	2	1	-	
35 - 39	153	-	2	10	34	55	36	12	3	1	-	-	
40 - 44	80	-	-	2	5	15	21	18	7	9	-	3	
45 - 49	48	-	-	1	1	6	5	14	4	10	2	5	
50 - 54	32	-	-	-	-	-	5	5	8	8	5	1	
55 - 59	17	-	-	-	-	-	1	-	3	4	6	3	
60 - 64	9	-	-	-	-	-	-	-	1	1	3	4	
65 +	3	-	-	-	-	-	-	-	-	-	1	2	
Unknown - Inconnu	8	-	1	1	-	-	-	-	-	-	-	-	6
Moldova[27]													
2006 (C)													
Total	20 142	752[a]	9 994	7 047	1 732	390	119	49	21	9	7	22	...
0 - 15	3	1[a]	1	1	-	-	-	-	-	-	-	-	...
16 - 19	4 687	442[a]	3 065	1 036	129	9	2	3	-	1	-	-	...
20 - 24	11 425	280[a]	6 127	4 202	697	94	18	3	1	3	-	-	...
25 - 29	3 210	25[a]	733	1 602	665	147	22	12	3	-	1	-	...
30 - 34	574	3[a]	61	181	197	92	30	7	2	-	1	-	...
35 - 39	134	1[a]	7	21	36	31	29	7	2	-	-	-	...
40 - 44	46	-[a]	-	4	6	13	11	8	4	1	-	-	...
45 - 49	27	-[a]	-	-	2	4	6	9	4	2	-	-	...
50 - 54	10	-[a]	-	-	1	-	-	-	5	2	1	1	...
55 - 59	5	-[a]	-	-	-	-	1	-	-	-	2	2	...
60 - 64	4	-[a]	-	-	-	-	-	-	-	-	2	2	...
65 - 69	4	-[a]	-	-	-	-	-	-	-	-	-	4	...
70 - 74	2	-[a]	-	-	-	-	-	-	-	-	-	2	...
75 +	11	-[a]	-	-	-	-	-	-	-	-	-	11	...
Unknown - Inconnu	-	-[a]	-	-	-	-	-	-	-	-	-	-	...
Montenegro													
2004 (C)													
Total	3 440	36	653	1 161	741	426	171	110	47	30	20	45	-
0 - 14	-	...	...	...	...	...	...	...	...	...	...	...	
15 - 19	456	...	...	...	...	...	...	...	...	...	...	...	
20 - 24	1 202	...	...	...	...	...	...	...	...	...	...	...	
25 - 29	971	...	...	...	...	...	...	...	...	...	...	...	
30 - 34	434	...	...	...	...	...	...	...	...	...	...	...	
35 - 39	179	...	...	...	...	...	...	...	...	...	...	...	
40 - 44	78	...	...	...	...	...	...	...	...	...	...	...	
45 - 49	52	...	...	...	...	...	...	...	...	...	...	...	
50 - 54	33	...	...	...	...	...	...	...	...	...	...	...	
55 - 59	18	...	...	...	...	...	...	...	...	...	...	...	
60 - 64	6	...	...	...	...	...	...	...	...	...	...	...	
65 +	11	...	...	...	...	...	...	...	...	...	...	...	
Unknown - Inconnu	-	...	...	...	...	...	...	...	...	...	...	...	
Netherlands - Pays-Bas[28,29]													
2006 (C)													
Total	71 157	99	4 746	16 151	18 681	12 197	6 911	4 410	3 019	2 144	1 373	1 426	...
15 - 19	766	60	409	211	42	27	11	4	1	1	-	-	...
20 - 24	10 875	34	3 371	5 151	1 573	496	154	58	19	13	3	3	...
25 - 29	21 119	2	773	8 823	8 237	2 316	633	204	74	36	12	9	...
30 - 34	15 692	2	136	1 600	7 049	4 769	1 411	463	152	77	21	12	...
35 - 39	8 944	1	41	273	1 424	3 435	2 301	898	343	139	58	31	...
40 - 44	5 161	-	13	64	271	865	1 661	1 314	555	263	108	47	...
45 - 49	3 422	-	2	20	67	227	558	1 028	843	396	174	107	...
50 - 54	2 361	-	1	6	15	50	144	342	748	632	275	148	...
55 - 59	1 404	-	-	3	2	8	26	73	203	439	402	248	...
60 - 64	741	-	-	-	-	3	6	21	53	112	248	298	...
65 - 69	424	-	-	-	-	1	5	5	24	29	57	303	...
70 - 74	150	-	-	-	-	-	1	-	1	6	12	130	...
75 - 79	64	-	-	-	-	-	-	-	2	...	2	60	...
80 - 84	29	-	-	-	1	-	-	-	1	1	1	25	...
85 - 89	4	-	-	-	-	-	-	-	-	-	-	4	...

Continent, country or area, year and age of bride / Continent, pays ou zone, date et âge de l'épouse	Total / Total	Age of groom âge de l'époux											Unknown Inconnu
		15-19	20-24	25-29	30-34	35-39	40-44	45-49	50-54	55-59	60-64	65+	
EUROPE													
Netherlands - Pays-Bas[28,29]													
2006													
90 - 94	-	-	-	-	-	-	-	-	-	-	-	-	...
95 +	1	-	-	-	-	-	-	-	-	-	-	1	
Norway - Norvège[30,31]													
2006 (C)													
Total	21 721	65	1 297	4 360	5 548	3 836	2 380	1 664	1 132	757	423	259	-
0 - 14	-	-	-	-	-	-	-	-	-	-	-	-	-
15 - 19	399	40	184	87	50	16	12	3	2	4	-	1	-
20 - 24	2 897	23	864	1 152	463	213	106	41	16	13	5	1	-
25 - 29	6 234	2	211	2 535	2 218	752	281	132	61	30	11	1	-
30 - 34	5 116	-	32	506	2 313	1 407	508	202	90	36	17	5	-
35 - 39	2 881	-	6	62	422	1 092	736	332	134	56	29	12	-
40 - 44	1 761	-	-	16	68	281	532	478	240	105	28	13	-
45 - 49	1 082	-	-	-	11	65	165	334	289	145	55	18	-
50 - 54	715	-	-	2	2	9	35	118	228	208	87	26	-
55 - 59	372	-	-	-	-	1	3	21	56	130	114	47	-
60 - 64	162	-	-	-	-	-	2	3	14	23	59	61	-
65 - 69	64	-	-	-	1	-	-	-	2	7	17	37	-
70 - 74	25	-	-	-	-	-	-	-	-	-	1	24	-
75 - 79	9	-	-	-	-	-	-	-	-	-	-	9	-
80 - 84	4	-	-	-	-	-	-	-	-	-	-	4	-
85 +	-	-	-	-	-	-	-	-	-	-	-	-	-
Unknown - Inconnu	-	-	-	-	-	-	-	-	-	-	-	-	-
Poland - Pologne													
2006 (C)													
Total	226 181	2 126	58 890	99 219	35 792	11 135	5 331	3 979	3 162	2 409	1 334	2 804	...
15 - 19	13 478	1 280	8 708	2 892	481	76	19	11	6	2	1	2	...
20 - 24	95 088	769	41 321	43 519	7 786	1 199	307	114	42	15	8	8	...
25 - 29	77 895	68	8 112	47 305	17 358	3 489	968	369	157	54	8	7	...
30 - 34	20 457	8	661	4 893	8 610	3 840	1 415	635	254	92	28	21	...
35 - 39	6 057	1	74	515	1 231	1 829	1 247	663	325	117	36	19	...
40 - 44	3 222	-	9	73	252	465	835	789	451	214	76	58	...
45 - 49	3 203	-	4	15	53	173	398	874	863	505	159	159	...
50 - 54	2 786	-	-	4	15	50	112	388	770	738	339	370	...
55 - 59	1 811	-	1	3	3	8	29	115	220	529	377	526	...
60 - 64	932	-	-	-	1	5	1	12	53	106	200	554	...
65 - 69	706	-	-	-	1	-	-	5	12	27	76	585	...
70 - 74	364	-	-	-	1	1	-	2	3	6	15	336	...
75 - 79	130	-	-	-	-	-	-	1	2	3	6	118	...
80 - 84	41	-	-	-	-	-	-	1	2	1	3	34	...
85 - 89	11	-	-	-	-	-	-	-	2	-	2	7	...
Portugal													
2006 (C)													
Total	47 857	540	8 020	18 222	10 831	4 029	2 057	1 353	900	668	469	768	-
0 - 14	-	-	-	-	-	-	-	-	-	-	-	-	-
15 - 19	2 537	294	1 518	559	114	34	10	6	-	1	1	-	-
20 - 24	12 078	201	4 576	5 528	1 370	274	80	32	12	4	1	-	-
25 - 29	17 746	35	1 566	9 658	4 976	1 023	294	120	41	21	2	10	-
30 - 34	8 084	8	284	2 078	3 437	1 431	496	205	80	36	21	8	-
35 - 39	3 047	1	57	308	722	845	589	285	123	60	30	27	-
40 - 44	1 645	1	12	64	156	296	398	354	186	99	44	35	-
45 - 49	1 038	-	5	18	43	91	139	227	218	140	73	84	-
50 - 54	714	-	1	8	8	24	42	88	167	172	99	105	-
55 - 59	438	-	-	1	4	7	6	26	50	93	104	147	-
60 - 64	242	-	-	-	1	2	2	5	14	29	54	135	-
65 - 69	163	-	1	-	-	2	1	3	8	10	32	106	-
70 - 74	76	-	-	-	-	-	-	2	-	2	3	69	-
75 - 79	32	-	-	-	-	-	-	-	1	1	1	29	-
80 - 84	11	-	-	-	-	-	-	-	-	-	1	10	-
85 - 89	5	-	-	-	-	-	-	-	-	-	2	3	-
90 - 94	1	-	-	-	-	-	-	-	-	-	1	-	-
95 +	-	-	-	-	-	-	-	-	-	-	-	-	-
Unknown - Inconnu	-	-	-	-	-	-	-	-	-	-	-	-	-

24. Marriages by age of bridegroom and by age of bride: latest available year, 1997 - 2006
Mariages selon l'âge de l'époux et selon l'âge de l'épouse: dernière année disponible, 1997 - 2006 (continued - suite)

Continent, country or area, year and age of bride / Continent, pays ou zone, date et âge de l'épouse	Total	Age of groom âge de l'époux											Unknown Inconnu
		15-19	20-24	25-29	30-34	35-39	40-44	45-49	50-54	55-59	60-64	65+	
EUROPE													
Romania - Roumanie													
2006 (C)													
Total	146 637	2 249	28 747	58 111	27 924	13 516	5 173	4 014	2 887	1 801	2 215	-	...
15 - 19	19 966	1 439	9 296	7 083	1 690	337	71	27	14	4	5	-	...
20 - 24	47 912	583	14 770	24 234	6 493	1 342	283	112	52	28	15	-	...
25 - 29	42 322	138	3 914	22 156	11 116	3 619	785	342	161	58	33	-	...
30 - 34	17 361	49	577	3 766	6 427	4 319	1 197	611	252	108	55	-	...
35 - 39	9 299	27	129	738	1 790	3 089	1 702	1 009	494	195	126	-	...
40 - 44	3 309	8	34	86	296	578	709	827	462	202	107	-	...
45 - 49	2 707	3	17	27	76	171	301	751	739	388	234	-	...
50 - 54	1 806	2	5	17	23	40	98	251	512	464	394	-	...
55 - 59	1 014	-	2	2	8	15	25	74	156	269	463	-	...
60 - 64	941	-	3	2	5	6	2	10	45	85	783	-	...
65 +	-	-	-	-	-	-	-	-	-	-	-	-	...
San Marino - Saint-Marin[32]													
2004 (C)													
Total	207	-	9	56	59	30	14	7	3	8	2	2	17
0 - 14	-	-	-	-	-	-	-	-	-	-	-	-	-
15 - 19	-	-	-	-	-	-	-	-	-	-	-	-	-
20 - 24	16	-	4	4	1	-	2	-	-	1	-	-	4
25 - 29	63	-	1	28	20	4	-	1	-	1	-	-	8
30 - 34	37	-	-	3	13	13	4	-	-	-	-	-	4
35 - 39	11	-	-	-	2	2	2	1	-	2	1	-	1
40 - 44	5	-	-	-	1	-	2	-	-	2	-	-	-
45 - 49	4	-	-	-	-	1	1	-	1	1	-	-	-
50 - 54	2	-	-	-	-	-	-	-	1	-	-	1	-
55 - 59	1	-	-	-	-	-	-	-	1	-	-	-	-
60 +	-	-	-	-	-	-	-	-	-	-	-	-	-
Unknown - Inconnu	68	-	4	21	22	10	3	4	1	1	1	1	-
Serbia - Serbie													
2006[33] (+C)													
Total	39 756	430	6 869	13 927	8 968	3 737	1 848	1 143	873	676	352	842	91
0 - 14	-	-	-	-	-	-	-	-	-	-	-	-	-
15 - 19	3 535	263	1 837	1 103	243	59	16	3	6	1	-	1	3
20 - 24	12 422	138	4 068	5 869	1 865	331	88	28	10	5	5	3	12
25 - 29	12 251	20	794	5 819	3 969	1 133	328	109	39	14	7	4	15
30 - 34	5 642	3	114	933	2 431	1 336	507	189	79	27	11	8	4
35 - 39	2 097	-	19	100	325	668	501	267	124	51	14	26	2
40 - 44	1 093	1	5	28	63	123	274	266	156	105	35	33	4
45 - 49	841	-	2	11	15	40	81	175	225	130	60	100	2
50 - 54	703	-	2	6	10	16	28	73	173	193	67	134	1
55 - 59	447	-	1	4	4	6	11	21	38	114	92	154	2
60 - 64	219	-	-	1	2	1	2	2	12	20	42	137	-
65 - 69	156	-	-	-	-	2	-	2	4	6	14	128	-
70 - 74	83	-	1	-	-	-	-	-	1	3	2	76	-
75 +	40	-	-	-	-	-	-	1	2	3	-	34	-
Unknown - Inconnu	227	5	26	53	41	22	12	7	4	4	3	4	46
Slovakia - Slovaquie													
2006 (C)													
Total	25 939	483	4 232	10 303	5 814	2 161	1 134	675	488	297	181	171	...
15 - 19	1 649	325	897	330	67	18	4	5	1	2	-	-	...
20 - 24	8 001	144	2 466	3 890	1 148	237	76	22	9	7	1	1	...
25 - 29	9 858	11	756	5 174	2 832	701	256	84	24	16	4	-	...
30 - 34	3 629	3	96	776	1 461	768	313	117	59	19	11	6	...
35 - 39	1 148	-	12	101	231	316	245	149	56	28	6	4	...
40 - 44	598	-	1	24	54	74	151	145	88	33	19	9	...
45 - 49	422	-	3	5	14	34	65	100	107	57	20	17	...
50 - 54	327	-	1	2	6	9	21	42	105	70	37	28	...
55 - 59	186	-	-	-	1	2	3	11	36	45	56	32	...
60 - 64	65	-	-	-	-	1	-	-	1	11	23	29	...
65 - 69	37	-	-	-	-	-	-	-	2	2	4	29	...
70 - 74	15	-	-	1	-	-	-	-	-	1	-	13	...
75 - 79	2	-	-	-	-	1	-	-	-	-	-	1	...
80 - 84	2	-	-	-	-	-	-	-	-	-	-	2	...
85 +	-	-	-	-	-	-	-	-	-	-	-	-	...

Continent, country or area, year and age of bride / Continent, pays ou zone, date et âge de l'épouse	Total	15-19	20-24	25-29	30-34	35-39	40-44	45-49	50-54	55-59	60-64	65+	Unknown Inconnu
EUROPE													
Slovenia - Slovénie													
2006 (C)													
Total	6 368	39	621	2 199	1 805	745	383	202	139	107	53	75	-
0 - 14	-	-	-	-	-	-	-	-	-	-	-	-	-
15 - 19	184	22	100	45	10	4	1	1	1	-	-	-	-
20 - 24	1 184	11	342	578	204	39	8	1	-	-	1	-	-
25 - 29	2 700	2	146	1 322	941	210	58	14	5	1	1	-	-
30 - 34	1 292	4	26	223	564	295	123	37	13	5	2	-	-
35 - 39	430	-	4	20	74	155	101	37	23	13	2	1	-
40 - 44	217	-	3	9	8	30	56	50	34	15	3	9	-
45 - 49	131	-	-	1	2	5	26	39	28	17	9	4	-
50 - 54	104	-	-	-	1	5	8	18	23	29	12	8	-
55 - 59	69	-	-	1	1	2	1	5	6	22	15	16	-
60 - 64	26	-	-	-	-	-	-	-	4	4	5	13	-
65 - 69	23	-	-	-	-	-	-	-	2	-	3	18	-
70 - 74	6	-	-	-	-	-	1	-	-	-	-	5	-
75 - 79	2	-	-	-	-	-	-	-	-	1	-	1	-
80 +	-	-	-	-	-	-	-	-	-	-	-	-	-
Unknown - Inconnu	-	-	-	-	-	-	-	-	-	-	-	-	-
Spain - Espagne[29]													
2005 (C)													
Total	208 146	534	12 424	74 928	68 597	25 882	10 832	5 856	3 588	2 330	1 450	1 725	-
0 - 14	3	1	1	-	-	-	-	-	-	-	-	1	-
15 - 19	2 460	254	1 183	688	229	76	15	9	4	-	1	1	-
20 - 24	27 386	188	6 907	14 423	4 261	1 023	335	141	57	30	10	11	-
25 - 29	90 353	66	3 463	48 491	30 793	5 412	1 300	450	203	108	40	27	-
30 - 34	53 802	21	644	9 795	28 145	10 874	2 727	968	357	154	73	44	-
35 - 39	17 561	3	134	1 160	4 161	6 394	3 253	1 378	602	286	120	70	-
40 - 44	7 870	-	58	243	757	1 597	2 227	1 468	795	421	187	117	-
45 - 49	4 388	1	24	85	181	374	758	1 059	857	528	297	224	-
50 - 54	2 226	-	7	20	46	106	169	298	510	481	292	297	-
55 - 59	1 084	-	2	16	16	17	34	63	164	227	247	298	-
60 - 64	524	-	1	1	4	7	7	18	24	71	135	256	-
65 - 69	246	-	-	3	2	2	5	3	12	16	31	172	-
70 - 74	140	-	-	-	1	-	1	1	2	6	12	117	-
75 - 79	70	-	-	2	1	-	1	-	-	2	4	60	-
80 - 84	27	-	-	-	-	-	-	-	1	-	1	25	-
85 - 89	6	-	-	1	-	-	-	-	-	-	-	5	-
90 +	-	-	-	-	-	-	-	-	-	-	-	-	-
Unknown - Inconnu	-	-	-	-	-	-	-	-	-	-	-	-	-
Sweden - Suède[34]													
2006 (C)													
Total	41 498	387	3 316	10 355	10 843	6 606	3 904	2 349	1 691	1 109	591	347	...
0 - 14	-	-	-	-	-	-	-	-	-	-	-	-	...
15 - 19	68	38	27	1	2	-	-	-	-	-	-	-	...
20 - 24	1 611	187	1 059	293	54	12	2	3	-	-	-	1	...
25 - 29	7 391	116	1 445	4 487	1 121	171	33	15	2	-	1	-	...
30 - 34	11 446	27	537	4 111	5 398	1 118	217	33	5	-	-	-	...
35 - 39	7 739	13	162	1 018	2 958	2 731	696	140	19	2	-	-	...
40 - 44	4 892	3	45	292	911	1 733	1 439	360	88	17	3	1	...
45 - 49	2 914	1	20	95	263	554	898	748	267	55	11	2	...
50 - 54	2 131	1	11	33	83	193	400	630	558	174	38	10	...
55 - 59	1 638	1	7	17	36	63	152	288	485	441	118	30	...
60 - 64	970	-	1	6	14	21	47	102	207	295	232	45	...
65 - 69	423	-	2	2	2	7	10	26	46	93	134	101	...
70 - 74	154	-	-	-	-	2	7	4	6	22	35	78	...
75 - 79	121	-	-	-	1	1	3	-	8	10	19	79	...
80 +	-	-	-	-	-	-	-	-	-	-	-	-	...
Switzerland - Suisse													
2006 (C)													
Total	39 817	197	3 514	8 993	10 367	6 869	3 791	2 194	1 563	1 135	646	548	...
0 - 14	-	-	-	-	-	-	-	-	-	-	-	-	...
15 - 19	1 042	91	587	255	64	29	8	4	2	2	-	-	...
20 - 24	6 223	77	1 953	2 497	965	370	175	92	46	23	16	9	...
25 - 29	11 783	16	647	4 426	4 093	1 559	557	256	124	70	23	12	...
30 - 34	9 526	4	184	1 275	3 907	2 545	937	342	172	101	40	19	...
35 - 39	5 065	4	66	288	937	1 696	1 122	501	252	107	63	29	...

24. Marriages by age of bridegroom and by age of bride: latest available year, 1997 - 2006
Mariages selon l'âge de l'époux et selon l'âge de l'épouse: dernière année disponible, 1997 - 2006 (continued - suite)

Continent, country or area, year and age of bride / Continent, pays ou zone, date et âge de l'épouse	Total	15-19	20-24	25-29	30-34	35-39	40-44	45-49	50-54	55-59	60-64	65+	Unknown Inconnu
EUROPE													
Switzerland - Suisse													
2006													
40 - 44	2 542	3	39	131	224	438	672	437	304	167	82	45	...
45 - 49	1 587	2	23	65	95	136	216	355	303	224	110	58	...
50 - 54	1 063	-	12	35	48	57	67	143	250	235	133	83	...
55 - 59	560	-	3	17	24	22	26	44	82	150	97	95	...
60 - 64	255	-	-	2	6	15	7	14	22	43	65	81	...
65 - 69	100	-	-	2	2	-	3	2	5	12	16	58	...
70 - 74	43	-	-	-	1	2	1	3	1	1	1	33	...
75 - 79	17	-	-	-	1	-	-	1	-	-	-	15	...
80 - 84	8	-	-	-	-	-	-	-	-	-	-	8	...
85 - 89	3	-	-	-	-	-	-	-	-	-	-	3	...
90 +	-	-	-	-	-	-	-	-	-	-	-	-	...
The Former Yugoslav Rep. of Macedonia - L'ex-République yougoslave de Macédoine													
2006 (C)													
Total	14 908	424	4 216	5 576	2 596	978	483	254	152	72	51	106	...
0 - 14	-	-	-	-	-	-	-	-	-	-	-	-	...
15 - 19	2 568	301	1 522	598	123	19	1	2	1	-	-	1	...
20 - 24	5 935	116	2 350	2 670	654	113	22	5	3	1	-	1	...
25 - 29	3 958	5	312	2 089	1 167	276	75	23	8	1	-	2	...
30 - 34	1 277	1	20	174	546	348	128	40	12	2	2	4	...
35 - 39	546	-	6	25	87	179	148	56	26	13	4	2	...
40 - 44	275	1	2	13	12	31	86	68	35	7	11	9	...
45 - 49	168	-	4	4	4	9	20	47	37	17	11	15	...
50 - 54	92	-	-	2	1	2	2	10	25	18	6	26	...
55 - 59	43	-	-	1	1	-	1	-	3	9	16	12	...
60 - 64	22	-	-	-	1	-	-	-	2	4	1	14	...
65 - 69	10	-	-	-	-	1	-	-	-	-	-	9	...
70 - 74	10	-	-	-	-	-	-	2	-	-	-	8	...
75 +	4	-	-	-	-	-	-	1	-	-	-	3	...
Ukraine													
2006 (C)													
Total	354 959	12 088[a]	134 135	97 860	42 279	21 458	13 819	10 939	7 842	5 595	8 944[j]		...
0 - 15	334	114[a]	195	22	3	-	-	-	-	-	-[j]		...
16 - 19	61 175	7 380[a]	39 690	11 978	1 723	287	72	24	12	7	2[j]		...
20 - 24	153 356	4 113[a]	80 347	51 714	12 853	3 047	829	281	118	31	23[j]		...
25 - 29	63 150	406[a]	11 749	26 726	15 197	5 807	2 068	814	249	95	39[j]		...
30 - 34	27 744	55[a]	1 767	5 787	8 859	6 225	3 041	1 292	471	168	79[j]		...
35 - 39	14 492	18[a]	310	1 279	2 727	3 957	3 194	1 863	736	265	143[j]		...
40 - 44	9 994	1[a]	50	260	684	1 457	2 891	2 578	1 260	549	264[j]		...
45 - 49	8 743	-[a]	17	72	197	542	1 266	2 793	2 194	1 059	603[j]		...
50 - 54	6 291	1[a]	6	10	28	106	359	997	1 975	1 682	1 127[j]		...
55 - 59	4 267	-[a]	2	3	5	22	84	265	665	1 365	1 856[j]		...
60 +	5 413	-[a]	2	9	3	8	15	32	162	374	4 808[j]		...
United Kingdom - Royaume-Uni[35]													
2002 (C)													
Total	293 021	2 023	28 666	74 858	72 592	44 189	25 558	15 910	11 891	8 055	4 324	4 955	-
0 - 14	-	-	-	-	-	-	-	-	-	-	-	-	-
15 - 19	7 505	1 100	3 628	1 771	687	191	77	31	9	7	2	2	-
20 - 24	51 478	659	16 996	21 406	8 351	2 659	909	283	128	54	19	14	-
25 - 29	82 892	167	5 757	37 256	26 710	8 790	2 792	826	351	154	55	34	-
30 - 34	62 279	57	1 525	10 717	26 222	14 924	5 598	1 960	794	335	95	52	-
35 - 39	35 978	27	510	2 725	7 698	11 770	7 452	3 328	1 483	622	252	102	-
40 - 44	21 019	9	169	709	2 178	4 131	5 582	4 120	2 430	1 102	385	198	-
45 - 49	13 232	3	51	205	547	1 245	2 231	3 469	2 927	1 688	556	310	-
50 - 54	8 955	1	13	45	154	366	698	1 439	2 565	2 151	937	586	-
55 - 59	4 903	-	5	14	36	90	182	350	925	1 408	1 076	817	-
60 - 64	2 366	-	-	8	7	13	22	91	210	406	659	950	-
65 - 69	1 251	-	1	2	-	8	9	10	48	97	215	861	-
70 - 74	662	-	1	-	2	2	5	2	12	20	49	569	-
75 - 79	328	-	-	-	-	-	1	-	1	9	17	300	-
80 - 84	128	-	1	-	-	-	-	1	1	1	5	119	-
85 - 89	44	-	-	-	-	-	-	-	1	-	2	41	-

811

Continent, country or area, year and age of bride / Continent, pays ou zone, date et âge de l'épouse	Total	15-19	20-24	25-29	30-34	35-39	40-44	45-49	50-54	55-59	60-64	65+	Unknown Inconnu
EUROPE													
United Kingdom - Royaume-Uni[35]													
2002													
90 - 94	1	-	-	-	-	-	-	-	-	1	-	-	-
Unknown - Inconnu	-	-	-	-	-	-	-	-	-	-	-	-	-
OCEANIA - OCÉANIE													
Australia - Australie													
2005 (+C)													
Total	109 323	327	11 413	30 721	27 577	14 517	8 424	5 666	4 073	3 106	1 653	1 794	...
0 - 14	-	-	-	-	-	-	-	-	-	-	-	-	...
15 - 19	1 590	168	888	386	93	37	7	4	...	...	...	...	...
20 - 24	20 149	132	8 083	8 567	2 440	612	186	76	27	14	8	...	...
25 - 29	34 568	21	2 045	17 325	10 872	3 003	842	272	108	60	11	...	...
30 - 34	23 717	3	313	3 689	10 946	5 628	2 041	681	250	123	36	...	...
35 - 39	11 403	...	57	598	2 604	3 779	2 484	1 127	456	212	57	...	...
40 - 44	6 391	...	...	129	477	1 086	1 850	1 518	774	362	113	...	...
45 - 49	4 549	-	7	17	103	284	723	1 310	1 149	630	225	101	...
50 - 54	3 231	-	-	7	31	74	236	532	908	889	368	186	...
55 - 59	1 869	-	...	3	...	11	42	120	306	597	458	...	...
60 - 64	909	-	-	-	...	3	10	22	74	175	275	...	...
65 - 69	496	-	-	-	-	-	3	...	13	34	79	...	...
70 - 74	241	-	-	-	-	-	-	...	...	6	14	...	...
75 - 79	135	-	-	-	-	-	-	...	...	...	5	...	...
80 - 84	54	-	-	-	-	-	-	-	...	...	...	50	...
85 - 89	21	-	-	-	-	-	-	-	-	...	...	-	...
90 +	-	-	-	-	-	-	-	-	-	-	-	-	...
Unknown - Inconnu	-	-	-	-	-	-	-	-	-	-	-	-	...
Fiji - Fidji													
2004 (+C)													
Total	7 076	125	2 060	2 429	1 113	522	334	217	125	74	40	37	...
0 - 14	-	...	...	...	...	...	...	...	...	...	...	...	...
15 - 19	1 176	...	...	...	...	...	...	...	...	...	...	...	...
20 - 24	2 990	...	...	...	...	...	...	...	...	...	...	...	...
25 - 29	1 438	...	...	...	...	...	...	...	...	...	...	...	...
30 - 34	656	...	...	...	...	...	...	...	...	...	...	...	...
35 - 39	367	...	...	...	...	...	...	...	...	...	...	...	...
40 - 44	204	...	...	...	...	...	...	...	...	...	...	...	...
45 - 49	128	...	...	...	...	...	...	...	...	...	...	...	...
50 - 54	62	...	...	...	...	...	...	...	...	...	...	...	...
55 - 59	35	...	...	...	...	...	...	...	...	...	...	...	...
60 - 64	13	...	...	...	...	...	...	...	...	...	...	...	...
65 +	7	...	...	...	...	...	...	...	...	...	...	...	...
Guam													
2003 (C)													
Total	1 334	41[a]	268	353	240	171	110	55	46	14	36[j]	...	...
0 - 19	96	23[a]	49	18	3	-	3	-	-	-	[j]	...	...
20 - 24	334	14[a]	164	102	34	14	2	3	1	-	[j]	...	...
25 - 29	374	2[a]	36	180	104	24	15	6	4	1	2[j]	...	...
30 - 34	230	1[a]	15	38	69	63	27	6	8	2	1[j]	...	...
35 - 39	140	1[a]	4	12	26	48	32	11	4	1	1[j]	...	...
40 - 44	74	-[a]	-	3	4	13	21	12	13	2	6[j]	...	...
45 - 49	42	-[a]	-	-	-	7	10	10	8	4	3[j]	...	...
50 - 54	23	-[a]	-	-	-	-	-	7	6	3	7[j]	...	...
55 - 59	10	-[a]	-	-	-	-	-	-	2	-	8[j]	...	...
60 - 69	8	-[a]	-	-	-	1	-	-	-	1	6[j]	...	...
70 +	3	-[a]	-	-	-	1	-	-	-	-	2[j]	...	...
New Caledonia - Nouvelle-Calédonie													
2003 (C)													
Total	873	1[a]	65	199	228	139	125[m]	...	85[n]	...	31[j]	...	...
0 - 19	24	-[a]	9	5	8	1	1[m]	...	[n]	...	[j]	...	...
20 - 24	146	1[a]	42	66	22	6	5[m]	...	3[n]	...	1[j]	...	...
25 - 29	255	-[a]	12	95	100	30	15[m]	...	3[n]	...	[j]	...	...

24. Marriages by age of bridegroom and by age of bride: latest available year, 1997 - 2006
Mariages selon l'âge de l'époux et selon l'âge de l'épouse: dernière année disponible, 1997 - 2006 (continued - suite)

Continent, country or area, year and age of bride / Continent, pays ou zone, date et âge de l'épouse	Total	15-19	20-24	25-29	30-34	35-39	40-44	45-49	50-54	55-59	60-64	65+	Unknown Inconnu
OCEANIA - OCÉANIE													
New Caledonia - Nouvelle-Calédonie													
2003													
30 - 34	184	-[a]	2	28	76	45	23[m]	...	10[n]	...	-[j]	...	...
35 - 39	105	-[a]	-	1	18	41	33[m]	...	11[n]	...	1[j]	...	...
40 - 49	109	-[a]	-	4	4	14	44[m]	...	34[n]	...	9[j]	...	...
50 - 59	35	-[a]	-	-	-	2	4[m]	...	19[n]	...	10[j]	...	...
60 +	15	-[a]	-	-	-	-	-[m]	...	5[n]	...	10[j]	...	...
New Zealand - Nouvelle-Zélande													
2006 (+C)													
Total	21 461	191	2 545	5 397	4 655	3 005	1 907	1 335	934	677	380	435	-
15 - 19	521	119	280	89	21	6	4	1	-	-	1	-	-
20 - 24	3 940	61	1 721	1 556	396	140	45	15	2	1	2	1	-
25 - 29	5 811	9	457	2 901	1 692	501	160	54	20	12	4	1	-
30 - 34	4 492	2	69	698	1 961	1 158	399	131	50	12	7	5	-
35 - 39	2 452	-	13	121	457	833	594	267	102	41	20	4	-
40 - 44	1 567	-	2	24	95	269	468	375	203	87	29	15	-
45 - 49	1 191	-	2	8	24	83	179	355	282	158	61	39	-
50 - 54	681	-	-	-	7	13	40	105	194	195	77	50	-
55 - 59	404	-	1	-	2	1	16	24	61	116	108	75	-
60 - 64	203	-	-	-	-	1	1	6	17	45	55	78	-
65 - 69	113	-	-	-	-	-	1	2	3	6	12	89	-
70 - 74	56	-	-	-	-	-	-	-	-	3	3	50	-
75 - 79	30	-	-	-	-	-	-	-	-	1	1	28	-
Unknown - Inconnu	-	-	-	-	-	-	-	-	-	-	-	-	-
Samoa													
2001 (U)													
Total	*821*	*10*	*149*	*223*	*165*	*116*	*60*	*40*	*25*	*9*	*12*	*8*	*4*
15 - 19	*71*	...	...	...	...	...	...	...	...	...	...	...	...
20 - 24	*285*	...	...	...	...	...	...	...	...	...	...	...	...
25 - 29	*177*	...	...	...	...	...	...	...	...	...	...	...	...
30 - 34	*114*	...	...	...	...	...	...	...	...	...	...	...	...
35 - 39	*83*	...	...	...	...	...	...	...	...	...	...	...	...
40 - 44	*39*	...	...	...	...	...	...	...	...	...	...	...	...
45 - 49	*23*	...	...	...	...	...	...	...	...	...	...	...	...
50 - 54	*12*	...	...	...	...	...	...	...	...	...	...	...	...
55 - 59	*11*	...	...	...	...	...	...	...	...	...	...	...	...
60 - 64	*1*	...	...	...	...	...	...	...	...	...	...	...	...
65 - 69	*2*	...	...	...	...	...	...	...	...	...	...	...	...
70 - 74	*-*	...	...	...	...	...	...	...	...	...	...	...	...
75 +	*-*	...	...	...	...	...	...	...	...	...	...	...	...
Unknown - Inconnu	*3*	...	...	...	...	...	...	...	...	...	...	...	...
Tonga													
2000 (+C)													
Total	747	62	257	217	106	36	28	12	29[h]	...	...	...	...
15 - 19	169	...	...	...	...	...	...	...	...	...	...	...	...
20 - 24	278	...	...	...	...	...	...	...	...	...	...	...	...
25 - 29	163	...	...	...	...	...	...	...	...	...	...	...	...
30 - 34	82	...	...	...	...	...	...	...	...	...	...	...	...
35 - 39	27	...	...	...	...	...	...	...	...	...	...	...	...
40 - 44	9	...	...	...	...	...	...	...	...	...	...	...	...
45 - 49	10	...	...	...	...	...	...	...	...	...	...	...	...
50 +	9	...	...	...	...	...	...	...	...	...	...	...	...

FOOTNOTES - NOTES

Italics: data from civil registers which are incomplete or of unknown completeness. - Italiques: données incomplètes ou dont le degré d'exactitude n'est pas connu, provenant des registres de l'état civil.

* Provisional. - Données provisoires.

'Code' indicates the source of data, as follows:

C - Civil registration, estimated over 90% complete

U - Civil registration, estimated less than 90% complete

| - Other source, estimated reliable

+ - Data tabulated by date of registration rather than occurence.

... - Information not available

Le 'Code' indique la source des données, comme suit:

C - Registres de l'état civil considérés complèts à 90 p. 100 au moins.

U - Registres de l'état civil qui ne sont pas considérés complèts à 90 p. 100 au moins.

| - Autre source, considérée pas douteuses.

+ - Données exploitées selon la date de l'enregistrement et non la date de l'événement.

... - Information pas disponible.

a Refers to 0-19 years of age. - Données se raporten au groupe d'âges 0-19.

b Refers to 16-19 years of age. - Données se raporten au groupe d'âges 16-19.

[c] Refers to 17-19 years of age. - Données se raporten au groupe d'âges 17-19.

[d] Refers to 18-19 years of age. - Données se raporten au groupe d'âges 18-19.

[e] Refers to 35+ years of age. - Données se raporten au groupe d'âges 35+.

[f] Refers to 40+ years of age. - Données se raporten au groupe d'âges 40+.

[g] Refers to 45+ years of age. - Données se raporten au groupe d'âges 45+.

[h] Refers to 50+ years of age. - Données se raporten au groupe d'âges 50+.

[i] Refers to 55+ years of age. - Données se raporten au groupe d'âges 55+.

[j] Refers to 60+ years of age. - Données se raporten au groupe d'âges 60+.

[k] Refers to 20-29 years of age. - Données se raporten au groupe d'âges 20-29.

[l] Refers to 30-39 years of age. - Données se raporten au groupe d'âges 30-39.

[m] Refers to 40-49 years of age. - Données se raporten au groupe d'âges 40-49.

[n] Refers to 50-59 years of age. - Données se raporten au groupe d'âges 50-59.

[1] Including marriages resumed after 'revocable divorce' (among Moslem population), which approximates legal separation. - Y compris les unions reconstituées après un 'divorce révocable' (parmi la population musulmane), qui est à peu près l'équivalent d'une séparation légale.

[2] Data exclude visitors. - Les données non compris des visiteurs.

[3] For resident population only. - Pour la population résidante seulement.

[4] Excluding tribal Indian population. - Non compris les Indiens vivant en tribus.

[5] Excluding Indian jungle population. - Non compris les Indiens de la jungle.

[6] Excluding nomadic Indian tribes. - Non compris les tribus d'Indiens nomades.

[7] Figures refer to marriages of residents only. - Chiffres se rapportent exclusivement aux mariages de résidents.

[8] Data refer to government controlled areas. - Les données se rapportent aux zones contrôlées par le Gouvernement.

[9] Including data for East Jerusalem and Israeli residents in certain other territories under occupation by Israeli military forces since June 1967. - Y compris les données pour Jérusalem-Est et les résidents israéliens dans certains autres territoires occupés depuis 1967 par les forces armées israéliennes.

[10] Data refer to Japanese nationals in Japan only; and to grooms and brides married for the first time whose marriages occurred and were registered in the same year. - Les données se raportent aux nationaux japonais au Japon seulement; et aux époux et épouses mariés pour la première fois, dont le mariage a été célébré et enregistré la même année.

[11] Excluding data for Jordanian territory under occupation since June 1967 by Israeli military forces. Excluding foreigners, including registered Palestinian refugees. - Non compris les données pour le territoire jordanien occupé depuis juin 1967 par les forces armées israéliennes. Non compris les étrangers, mais y compris les réfugiés de Palestine enregistrés.

[12] Excluding alien armed forces, civilian aliens employed by armed forces, and foreign diplomatic personnel and their dependants. - Non compris les militaires étrangers, les civils étrangers employés par les forces armées ni le personnel diplomatique étranger et les membres de leur famille les accompagnant.

[13] Since 2006, the Government of Mongolia has started to implement " Newly married couple" programme that aims to promote marriage. - En 2006, le Gouvernement mongol a lancé le programme intitulé « jeunes mariés » qui vise à promouvoir le mariage.

[14] Registration of Kandyan marriages is complete; registration of Moslem and general marriages is incomplete. - Tous les mariages des Kandyens sont enregistrés; l'enregistrement des mariages musulmans et des autres mariages est incomplet.

[15] Figures exclude marriages previously officiated outside Singapore or under religious and customary rites. - Les figures excluent les mariages célébrés précédemment au dehors de Singapour ou sous les rites réligieuse ou accoutumés.

[16] Data from MERNIS (Central Population Administrative System). - Données de MERNIS (Système central de données démographiques).

[17] Excluding aliens temporarily in the area. - Non compris les étrangers se trouvant temporairement le territoire.

[18] Including armed forces stationed outside the country, but excluding alien armed forces in the area unless marriage performed by local foreign authority. - Y compris les militaires nationaux hors du pays et les militaires étrangers en garnison sur le territoire, sauf si le mariage a été célébré pour l'autorité locale.

[19] Including Bulgarian nationals outside the country, but excluding foreigners in the country. - Y compris les nationaux bulgares à l'étranger, mais non compris les étrangers sur le territoire.

[20] Excluding Faeroe Islands and Greenland shown separately, if available. - Non compris les Iles Féroé et le Gröenland, qui font l'objet de rubriques distinctes, si disponible.

[21] Including Aland Islands. - Y compris les Îles d'Åland.

[22] Only marriages in which the bride was resident in Finland. - Seulement mariages où l'épouse réside en Finlande.

[23] Excluding Overseas Departments, namely, French Guiana, Guadeloupe, Martinique and Reunion, shown separately, if available. - Non compris les départements d'outre mer, c'est-à-dire la Guyane française, la Guadeloupe, la Martinique et la Réunion, qui font l'objet de rubriques distinctes, si disponible.

[24] Including armed forces stationed outside the country. - Y compris les militaires nationaux hors du pays.

[25] Data refer to de jure population. - Les données se rapportent à la population de droit.

[26] Unrevised data. - Les données n'ont pas été révisées.

[27] Data refer to first marriages only. - Données se rapportent aux premiers mariages seulement.

[28] Marriages of couples of which at least one partner is recorded in a Dutch municipal register, irrespective of the country where the marriage was performed. - Mariages où un des conjoints au moins est inscrit dans un registre municipal néerlandais, quel que soit le pays où le mariage a été contracté.

[29] Excluding same sex marriages. - À l'exclusion des mariages entre personnes du même sexe.

[30] Excluding Svalbard and Jan Mayen Island shown separately, if available. - Non compris Svalbard et Jan Mayen qui font l'objet de rubriques distinctes, si disponible.

[31] Only marriages in which the groom was resident in Norway. - Seulement mariages où l'époux réside en Norvège.

[32] Includes civil and religious marriages as well as not specified. - Y compris les mariages civils, religieux ou non précisés.

[33] Without data for Kosovo and Metohia. - Sans les données pour le Kosovo and Metohia.

[34] Data only include marriages where both the bride and the groom are registered. - Données ne portant que sur les mariages entre conjoints enregistrés.

[35] Excluding Channel Islands and Isle of Man, shown separately, if available. - Non compris les îles Anglo-Normandes et l'île de Man, qui font l'objet de rubriques distinctes, si disponible.

Table 25

Table 25 presents number of divorces and crude divorce rates for as many years as possible between 2002 and 2006.

Description of variables: Divorce is defined as a final legal dissolution of a marriage, that is, that separation of husband and wife which confers on the parties the right to remarriage under civil, religious and/or other provisions, according to the laws of each country[i].

Unless otherwise noted, divorce statistics exclude legal separations that do not allow remarriage. These statistics refer to the number of divorces granted, and not to the number of persons divorcing.

Divorce statistics are obtained from court records and/or civil registers according to national practice. The actual compilation of these statistics may be the responsibility of the civil registrar, the national statistical office or other government offices.

The urban/rural classification of divorces is that provided by each country or area; it is presumed to be based on the national census definitions of urban population, which have been set forth at the end of the technical notes for table 6.

Rate computation: Crude divorce rates by urban/rural residence are the annual number of divorces per 1 000 mid-year population. Rates presented in this table have been limited to those countries or areas having at least a total of 30 divorces in a given year. These rates are calculated by the Statistics Division of the United Nations based on the appropriate reference population (for example: total population, nationals only etc.) if known and available. If the reference population is not known or unavailable the total population is used to calculate the rates. Therefore, if the population that is used to calculate the rates is different from the correct reference population, the rates presented might under- or overstate the true situation in a country or area.

Reliability of data: Each country or area has been asked to indicate the estimated completeness of the divorces recorded in its civil register. These national assessments are indicated by the quality codes C and U that appear in the first column of this table.

C indicates that the data are estimated to be virtually complete, that is, representing at least 90 per cent of the divorces that occur each year, while U indicates that data are estimated to be incomplete, that is, representing less than 90 per cent of the divorces occurring each year. The code ... indicates that no information was provided regarding completeness.

Data from civil registers that are reported as incomplete or of unknown completeness (coded U or ...) are considered unreliable. They appear in *italics* in this table and the rates were not computed on data so coded. These quality codes apply only to data from civil registers. For more information about the quality of vital statistics data in general, see section 4.2 of the Technical Notes.

Limitations: Statistics on divorces are subject to the same qualifications as have been set forth for vital statistics in general and divorce statistics in particular as discussed in section 4 of the Technical Notes.

Divorce, like marriage, is a legal event, and this has implications for international comparability of data. Divorce has been defined, for statistical purposes, in terms of the laws of individual countries or areas. The laws pertaining to divorce vary considerably from one country or area to another. This variation in the legal provision for divorce also affects the incidence of divorce, which is relatively low in countries or areas where divorce decrees are difficult to obtain.

Since divorces are granted by courts and statistics on divorce refer to the actual divorce decree, effective as of the date of the decree, marked year-to-year fluctuations may reflect court delays and clearances rather than trends in the incidence of divorce. The comparability of divorce statistics may also be affected by tabulation procedures. In some countries or areas annulments and/or legal separations may be included. This practice is more common for countries or areas in which the number of divorces is small. Information on this practice is given in the footnotes when known.

Because the registration of a divorce in many countries or areas is the responsibility solely of the court or the authority which granted it, and since the registration recording such cases is part of the records of the court proceedings, it follows that divorces are likely to be registered soon after the decree is granted. For this reason the practice of tabulating data by date of registration does not generally pose serious problems of comparability as it does in the case of birth and death statistics.

As noted briefly above, the incidence of divorce is affected by the relative ease or difficulty of obtaining a divorce according to the laws of individual countries or areas. The incidence of divorce is also affected by the ability of individuals to meet financial and other costs of the court procedures. Connected with this aspect is the influence of certain religious faiths on the incidence of divorce. For all these reasons, divorce statistics are not strictly comparable as measures of family dissolution by legal means. Furthermore, family dissolution by other than legal means, such as separation, is not measured in statistics for divorce.

For certain countries or areas there is or was no legal provision for divorce in the sense used here, and therefore no data for these countries or areas appear in this table.

In addition, it should be noted that rates are affected also by the quality and limitations of the population estimates that are used in their computation. The problems of under-enumeration or over-enumeration, and to some extent, the differences in definition of total population, have been discussed in section 3 of the Technical Notes dealing with population data in general, and specific information pertaining to individual countries or areas is given in the footnotes to table 3.

As will be seen from the footnotes, strict correspondence between the numerator of the rate and the denominator is not always obtained; for example, divorces among civilian plus military segments of the population may be related to civilian population only. The effect of this may be to increase the rates but, in most cases, the effect is negligible.

As mentioned above, data for some countries or areas may include annulments and/or legal separations. This practice affects the comparability of the crude divorce rates. For example, inclusion of annulments in the numerator of the rates produces a negligible effect on the rates, but inclusion of legal separations may have a measurable effect on the level.

It should be emphasized that crude divorce rates like crude birth, death and marriage rates may be seriously affected by age-sex structure of the populations to which they relate. Like crude marriage rates, they are also affected by the existing distribution of the population by marital status. Nevertheless, crude divorce rates provide a simple measure of the level and changes in divorces.

The comparability of data by urban/rural residence is affected by the national definitions of urban and rural used in tabulating these data. It is assumed, in the absence of specific information to the contrary, that the definitions of urban and rural used in connection with the national population census were also used in the compilation of the vital statistics for each country or area. However, it cannot be excluded that, for a given country or area, different definitions of urban and rural are used for the vital statistics data and the population census data respectively. When known, the definitions of urban in national population censuses are presented at the end of the technical notes for table 6. As discussed in detail in the notes, these definitions vary considerably from one country or area to another.

In addition to problems of comparability, divorce rates classified by urban/rural residence are also subject to certain special types of bias. If, when calculating divorce rates, different definitions of urban are used in connection with the vital events and the population data, and if this results in a net difference between the numerator and denominator of the rate in the population at risk, then the divorce rates would be biased. Urban/rural differentials in divorce rates may also be affected by whether the vital events have been tabulated in terms of place of occurrence or place of usual residence. This problem is discussed in more detail in section 4.1.4.1. of the Technical Notes.

Earlier data: Divorces have been shown in previous issues of the Demographic Yearbook. The earliest data, which were for 1935, appeared in the 1951 issue. For more information on specific topics and years for which data are reported, readers should consult the Historical Index.

NOTES

[i] For definition, please see section 4.1.1 of the Technical Notes.

Tableau 25

Le tableau 25 présente des statistiques concernant les divorces et les taux bruts de divortialité pour le plus grand nombre d'années possible entre 2002 et 2006.

Description des variables : le divorce est la dissolution légale et définitive des liens du mariage, c'est-à-dire la séparation de l'époux et de l'épouse qui confère aux parties le droit de se remarier civilement ou religieusement, ou selon toute autre procédure, conformément à la législation du pays[1].

Sauf indication contraire, les statistiques de la divortialité n'englobent pas les séparations légales qui excluent un remariage. Ces statistiques se rapportent aux jugements de divorce prononcés, non aux personnes divorcées.

Les statistiques de la divortialité proviennent, selon la pratique suivie par chaque pays, des actes des tribunaux et/ou des registres de l'état civil. L'officier d'état civil, les services nationaux de statistique ou d'autres services gouvernementaux peuvent être chargés d'établir ces statistiques.

La classification des divorces selon le lieu de résidence (zone urbaine ou rurale) est celle qui a été communiquée par chaque pays ou zone ; on part du principe qu'elle repose sur les définitions de la population urbaine utilisées pour les recensements nationaux, qui sont reproduites à la fin des notes techniques du tableau 6.

Calcul des taux : les taux bruts de divortialité selon le lieu de résidence (zone urbaine ou rurale) représentent le nombre annuel de divorces enregistrés pour 1 000 habitants au milieu de l'année. Les taux du tableau 25 ne se rapportent qu'aux pays ou zones où l'on a enregistré un total d'au moins 30 divorces pendant une année donnée. Ces taux sont calculés par la division de statistique des Nations Unies sur la base de la population de référence adéquate (par exemple : population totale, nationaux seulement, etc.) si connue et disponible. Si la population de référence n'est pas connue ou n'est pas disponible, la population totale est utilisée pour calculer les taux. Par conséquent, si la population utilisée pour calculer les taux est différente de la population de référence adéquate, les taux présentés sont susceptibles de sous ou sur estimer la situation réelle d'un pays ou d'un territoire.

Fiabilité des données : il a été demandé à chaque pays ou zone d'indiquer le degré estimatif de complétude des données sur les divorces figurant dans ses registres d'état civil. Ces évaluations nationales sont désignées par les codes de qualité 'C' et 'U' qui apparaissent dans la deuxième colonne du tableau.

La lettre 'C' indique que les données sont jugées à peu près complètes, c'est-à-dire qu'elles représentent au moins 90 p. 100 des divorces survenus chaque année ; la lettre 'U' signale que les données sont jugées incomplètes, c'est-à-dire qu'elles représentent moins de 90 p. 100 des divorces survenus chaque année. Le code '...' indique qu'aucun renseignement n'a été communiqué quant à la complétude des données.

Les données issues des registres de l'état civil qui sont déclarées incomplètes ou dont le degré de complétude n'est pas connu (code 'U' ou '...') sont jugées douteuses. Elles apparaissent en italique dans le tableau et les taux correspondants n'ont pas été calculés. Les codes de qualité ne s'appliquent qu'aux données extraites des registres de l'état civil. Pour plus de précisions sur la qualité des données reposant sur les statistiques de l'état civil en général, voir la section 4.2 des notes techniques.

Insuffisance des données : les statistiques des divorces appellent les mêmes réserves que celles formulées à propos des statistiques de l'état civil en général et des statistiques de divortialité en particulier (voir la section 4 des notes techniques).

Le divorce est, comme le mariage, un acte juridique, et ce fait influe sur la comparabilité internationale des données. Aux fins de la statistique, le divorce est défini par la législation de chaque pays ou zone. La législation sur le divorce varie considérablement d'un pays ou d'une zone à l'autre, ce qui influe aussi sur la fréquence des divorces, laquelle est relativement faible dans les pays ou zones où le jugement de divorce est difficile à obtenir.

Du fait que les divorces sont prononcés par les tribunaux et que les statistiques de la divortialité se rapportent aux jugements de divorce proprement dits, qui prennent effet à la date où ces jugements sont rendus, il se peut que des fluctuations annuelles accusées traduisent le rythme plus ou moins rapide auquel les affaires sont jugées plutôt que l'évolution de la fréquence des divorces. Les méthodes d'exploitation des données peuvent aussi influer sur la comparabilité des statistiques de la divortialité. Dans certains pays ou zones, ces statistiques peuvent comprendre les annulations et/ou les séparations légales. C'est notamment le cas dans les pays ou zones où les divorces sont peu nombreux. Lorsqu'ils sont connus, des renseignements à ce propos sont donnés en note à la fin du tableau.

Étant donné que dans de nombreux pays ou zones, le tribunal ou l'autorité qui a prononcé le divorce est seul habilité à enregistrer cet acte, et, comme l'acte d'enregistrement figure alors sur les registres du tribunal, l'enregistrement suit généralement de peu le jugement. C'est pourquoi la pratique consistant à exploiter les données selon la date de l'enregistrement ne pose généralement pas les graves problèmes de comparabilité auxquels on se heurte dans le cas des statistiques des naissances et des décès.

Comme on l'a brièvement mentionné ci-dessus, la fréquence des divorces est fonction notamment de la facilité relative avec laquelle la législation de chaque pays ou zone permet d'obtenir le divorce. Elle dépend également de la capacité des intéressés à supporter les frais de procédure. Il faut aussi citer l'influence de certaines religions sur la fréquence des divorces. Pour toutes ces raisons, les statistiques de divortialité ne sont pas rigoureusement comparables et ne permettent pas de mesurer exactement la fréquence des dissolutions légales des mariages. De plus, elles ne rendent pas compte des cas de dissolution extrajudiciaire du mariage, comme la séparation.

Dans certains pays ou zones, il n'existe ou il n'existait pas de législation sur le divorce selon l'acception retenue aux fins du tableau 25, si bien que l'on ne dispose pas de données les concernant.

De surcroît, il convient de noter que l'exactitude des taux dépend également de la qualité et des insuffisances des estimations de population qui sont utilisées pour leur calcul. Le problème des erreurs par excès ou par défaut commises lors du dénombrement et, dans une certaine mesure, le problème de l'hétérogénéité des définitions de la population totale ont été examinés à la section 3 des notes techniques, relative à la population en général ; des explications concernant les différents pays ou zones sont données en note à la fin du tableau 3.

Comme on le verra dans les notes, il n'a pas toujours été possible d'obtenir une correspondance rigoureuse entre le numérateur et le dénominateur pour le calcul des taux. Par exemple, les divorces parmi la population civile et les militaires sont parfois rapportés à la population civile seulement. Cela peut avoir pour effet d'accroître les taux, mais, dans la plupart des cas, il est probable que la différence sera négligeable.

Comme indiqué plus haut, les données concernant certains pays ou zones peuvent comprendre les annulations et/ou les séparations légales. Cette pratique influe sur la comparabilité des taux bruts de divortialité. Par exemple, l'inclusion des annulations dans le numérateur a une influence négligeable, mais l'inclusion des séparations légales peut avoir un effet appréciable.

Il faut souligner que les taux bruts de divortialité, de même que les taux bruts de natalité, de mortalité et de nuptialité, peuvent varier sensiblement selon la structure par âge et par sexe. Comme les taux bruts de nuptialité, ils peuvent également varier en raison de la répartition de la population selon l'état matrimonial. Les taux bruts de divortialité offrent néanmoins un moyen simple de mesurer la fréquence et l'évolution des divorces.

La comparabilité des données selon le lieu de résidence (zone urbaine ou rurale) peut être limitée par les définitions nationales des termes « urbain » et « rural » utilisées pour la mise en tableaux de ces données. En l'absence d'indications contraires, on a supposé que les mêmes définitions avaient servi pour le recensement national de la population et pour l'établissement des statistiques de l'état civil pour chaque pays ou zone. Toutefois, il n'est pas exclu que, pour une zone ou un pays donné, des définitions différentes aient été retenues. Les définitions du terme « urbain » utilisées pour les recensements nationaux de population ont été présentées à la fin des notes techniques du tableau 6 lorsqu'elles étaient connues. Comme on l'a précisé dans les notes techniques relatives au tableau 6, ces définitions varient considérablement d'un pays ou d'une zone à l'autre.

Outre les problèmes de comparabilité, les taux de divortialité classés selon le lieu de résidence (zone urbaine ou rurale) sont également sujets à des distorsions particulières. Si l'on utilise des définitions différentes du terme « urbain » pour classer les faits d'état civil et les données relatives à la population lors du calcul des taux et qu'il en résulte une différence nette entre le numérateur et le dénominateur pour le taux de la population exposée au risque, les taux de divortialité s'en trouveront faussés. La différence entre ces taux pour les zones urbaines et rurales pourra aussi être faussée selon que les faits d'état civil auront été classés d'après le lieu de l'événement ou d'après le lieu de résidence habituel. Ce problème est examiné plus en détail à la section 4.1.4.1 des notes techniques.

Données publiées antérieurement : des statistiques concernant les divorces ont déjà été présentées dans des éditions antérieures de l'*Annuaire démographique*. Les plus anciennes, qui portaient sur 1935, ont été publiées dans l'édition de 1951. Pour plus de précisions concernant les années et les sujets pour lesquels des données ont été publiées, se reporter à l'index historique.

NOTE

[1] Pour la définition, voir la section 4.1.1 des Notes techniques.

25. Divorces and crude divorce rates by urban/rural residence: 2002 - 2006
Divorces et taux bruts de divortialité selon la résidence, urbaine/rurale: 2002 - 2006

Continent, country or area, and urban/rural residence / Continent, pays ou zone et résidence, urbaine/rurale	Code	Number - Nombre					Rate - Taux				
		2002	2003	2004	2005	2006	2002	2003	2004	2005	2006
AFRICA - AFRIQUE											
Egypt - Égypte[1]											
Total	U	70 069	69 867	64 496	65 047	65 461	...	...	...	...	...
Urban - Urbaine	U	36 098	35 442	31 360	32 791	33 603	...	...	...	...	...
Rural - Rurale	U	33 971	34 425	33 136	32 256	31 858	...	...	...	...	...
Libyan Arab Jamahiriya - Jamahiriya arabe libyenne[2]											
Total	C	1 740	...	...	...	...	0.3	...	...	...	...
Mauritius - Maurice											
Total	+C	1 291	1 190	1 162	1 133	1 379	1.1	1.0	0.9	0.9	1.1
Réunion											
Total	C	940	*844	...	...	...	1.3	*1.1	...	...	...
Saint Helena ex. dep. - Sainte-Hélène sans dép.											
Total	C	13	12	8	...	...	...	...	...	...	...
Seychelles											
Total	+C	112	126	171	140	142	1.3	1.5	2.1	1.7	1.7
South Africa - Afrique du Sud[3]											
Total	...	31 370	31 566	31 768	32 484		...	...	...	...	...
AMERICA, NORTH - AMÉRIQUE DU NORD											
Anguilla											
Total	+C	11	9	19	22		...	...	...	...	...
Aruba											
Total	C	498	480	484	444	...	5.3	5.0	5.0	4.4	...
Belize											
Total	+C	45	...	...	...	...	0.2	...	...	...	...
Bermuda - Bermudes											
Total	C	252	207	185	213	179	4.0	3.3	2.9	3.4	2.8
British Virgin Islands - Îles Vierges britanniques											
Total	C	56	77	60		...	2.7	3.6	2.8	...	...
Canada											
Total	C	70 155	70 828	69 644	...	...	2.2	2.2	2.2	...	...
Cayman Islands - Îles Caïmanes											
Total	+C	...	...	...	145	158	...	...	...	3.0	3.0
Costa Rica											
Total	C	7 786	9 442	9 467	9 887	...	1.9	2.3	2.3	2.3	...
Cuba											
Total	C	35 590	33 851	35 594	34 359	35 837	3.2	3.0	3.2	3.1	3.2
Urban - Urbaine	C	32 966	31 130	33 017	32 251	33 739	3.9	3.7	3.9	3.8	4.0
Rural - Rurale	C	2 624	2 721	2 577	2 108	2 098	1.0	1.0	0.9	0.8	0.8
Dominican Republic - République dominicaine											
Total	+C	12 972	14 618	17 691	16 649	...	1.5	1.6	1.9	1.8	...
El Salvador											
Total	...	4 179	4 121	4 625	4 963	5 576	...	...	...	...	...
Urban - Urbaine	...	4 052	3 993	4 415	4 722	5 369	...	...	...	...	...
Rural - Rurale	...	127	128	210	241	207	...	...	...	...	...
Guatemala											
Total	C	904	967	1 888	2 888	1 917	0.1	0.1	0.2	0.2	0.1
Jamaica - Jamaïque											
Total	C	1 745	1 600	1 739	1 806	1 768	0.7	0.6	0.7	0.7	0.7
Mexico - Mexique											
Total	+C	60 641	64 248	67 575	70 184	72 396	0.6	0.6	0.7	0.7	0.7
Urban - Urbaine[4]	+C	52 589	55 272	58 689	61 926	62 997	0.7	0.7	0.7	0.8	0.8
Rural - Rurale[4]	+C	2 626	2 908	2 907	2 964	3 458	0.1	0.1	0.1	0.1	0.1
Netherlands Antilles - Antilles néerlandaises											
Total	C	510	540	513	534	491	2.9	3.0	2.8	2.9	2.6
Nicaragua											
Total	...	3 051	3 170	2 779	3 916		...	...	...	...	...

25. Divorces and crude divorce rates by urban/rural residence: 2002 - 2006
Divorces et taux bruts de divortialité selon la résidence, urbaine/rurale: 2002 - 2006 (continued - suite)

Continent, country or area, and urban/rural residence / Continent, pays ou zone et résidence, urbaine/rurale	Code[a]	Number - Nombre					Rate - Taux				
		2002	2003	2004	2005	2006	2002	2003	2004	2005	2006
AMERICA, NORTH - AMÉRIQUE DU NORD											
Panama[5]											
Total...................	C	2 313	*2 732	2 652	2 758	2 866	0.8	*0.9	0.8	0.9	0.9
Puerto Rico - Porto Rico											
Total...................	C	14 578	14 225	15 197	15 816	...	3.8	3.7	3.9	4.0	...
Saint Lucia - Sainte-Lucie											
Total...................	C	45	113	*114	...	...	0.3	0.7	*0.7	...	...
Saint Vincent and the Grenadines - Saint Vincent-et-les Grenadines											
Total...................	+C	45	93	85	92	...	0.4	0.9	0.8	0.9	...
Trinidad and Tobago - Trinité-et-Tobago											
Total...................	C	1 565					1.2				
Turks Caicos Islands - Îles Turques et Caïques											
Total...................	C	46	9	16	24	22	2.2	...	...	...	...
AMERICA, SOUTH - AMÉRIQUE DU SUD											
Brazil - Brésil[6]											
Total...................	...	...	135 564	130 527	153 839	164 974	...	...	...	...	...
Chile - Chili[7]											
Total...................	C	...	...	...	...	4 091	...	...	...	...	0.2
Ecuador - Équateur[8]											
Total...................	+...	10 987	10 912	11 251	11 725	13 981	...	...	...	...	...
Suriname											
Total...................	C	797	629	607[9]	724[10]	...	1.7	1.3	1.2	1.5	...
Uruguay											
Total...................	+C	6 761	*14 003	*14 300	...	...	2.0	*4.2	*4.3	...	...
Venezuela (Bolivarian Republic of) - Venezuela (République bolivarienne du)[6]											
Total...................	...	16 627	20 077	21 260	21 451	24 481	...	...	...	...	...
ASIA - ASIE											
Armenia - Arménie											
Total...................	C	1 684	1 820	1 968	2 466	2 797	0.5	0.6	0.6	0.8	0.9
Urban - Urbaine	C	1 456	1 536	1 658	2 019	2 235	0.7	0.7	0.8	1.0	1.1
Rural - Rurale	C	228	284	310	447	562	0.2	0.2	0.3	0.4	0.5
Azerbaijan - Azerbaïdjan											
Total...................	+C	5 738	6 671	6 914	8 895	7 817	0.7	0.8	0.8	1.1	0.9
Urban - Urbaine	+C	4 726	5 555	5 606	...	...	1.1	1.3	1.3	...	...
Rural - Rurale	+C	1 012	1 116	1 308	...	...	0.3	0.3	0.3	...	...
Bahrain - Bahreïn											
Total...................	...	838	923	1 030	1 051	1 130	...	...	...	...	...
Brunei Darussalam - Brunéi Darussalam											
Total...................	...	328	349	392			...	...	...	...	...
Cambodia - Cambodge											
Total...................	...	...	...	158 011	...	...	...	...	...	...	...
Urban - Urbaine	...	...	...	24 778	...	...	...	...	...	...	...
Rural - Rurale	...	...	...	133 233	...	...	...	...	...	...	...
China - Chine[11]											
Total...................	+C	1 177 000	1 330 000	1 665 000	1 785 000	...	0.9	1.0	1.3	1.4	...
China: Hong Kong SAR - Chine: Hong Kong RAS											
Total...................	...	12 943	13 829	15 604	14 873	17 424	...	...	...	...	...
China: Macao SAR - Chine: Macao RAS											
Total...................	C	385	440	475	573	592	0.9	1.0	1.0	1.2	1.2

25. Divorces and crude divorce rates by urban/rural residence: 2002 - 2006
Divorces et taux bruts de divortialité selon la résidence, urbaine/rurale: 2002 - 2006 (continued - suite)

Continent, country or area, and urban/rural residence / Continent, pays ou zone et résidence, urbaine/rurale	Code[a]	Number - Nombre					Rate - Taux				
		2002	2003	2004	2005	2006	2002	2003	2004	2005	2006
ASIA - ASIE											
Cyprus - Chypre[12]											
Total	C	1 320	1 472	1 614	1 514	1 753	1.9	2.0	2.2	2.0	2.3
Urban - Urbaine[4]	C	1 023	1 162	1 293	1 208	1 424	...	...	...	...	...
Rural - Rurale[4]	C	247	267	258	254	268	...	...	...	...	...
Georgia - Géorgie											
Total	C	1 836	1 825	1 793	1 928	2 060	0.4	0.4	0.4	0.4	0.5
Urban - Urbaine	C	...	1 802	...	...	...	...	0.8	...	...	...
Rural - Rurale	C	...	23	...	...	...	...	...	...	...	...
Iran (Islamic Republic of) - Iran (République islamique d')[13]											
Total	C	67 256	72 359	73 882	84 243	94 040	1.0	1.1	1.1	1.2	1.3
Urban - Urbaine	C	61 074	64 213	63 406	70 024	...	1.4	1.5	1.4	1.5	...
Rural - Rurale	C	6 182	8 146	10 476	14 219	...	0.3	0.4	0.4	0.6	...
Israel - Israël[14]											
Total	C	10 939	10 689	11 181	11 030	...	1.7	1.6	1.6	1.6	...
Japan - Japon[15]											
Total	+C	289 836	283 854	270 804	261 917	257 475	2.3	2.2	2.1	2.1	2.0
Urban - Urbaine	+C	238 811	234 304	224 699	227 275	232 234	...	...	...	...	...
Rural - Rurale	+C	51 025	49 550	46 105	34 642	25 241	...	...	...	...	...
Jordan - Jordanie[16]											
Total	+C	9 032	9 022	9 791	10 231	11 431	1.8	1.7	1.9	1.9	2.1
Kazakhstan											
Total	C	31 236	31 717	31 492	32 377	35 834	2.1	2.1	2.1	2.1	2.3
Urban - Urbaine	C	25 563	26 451	26 288	26 973	29 533	3.0	3.1	3.1	3.1	3.4
Rural - Rurale	C	5 673	5 266	5 204	5 404	6 301	0.9	0.8	0.8	0.8	1.0
Korea (Republic of) - Corée (République de)[17]											
Total[18]	+C	145 324	167 096	139 365	128 468	125 032	3.0	3.5	2.9	2.6	2.6
Urban - Urbaine	+C	117 511	135 753	111 582	102 668	99 201	3.1	3.5	2.9	2.6	2.5
Rural - Rurale	+C	25 600	28 921	25 069	23 060	22 578	2.6	2.9	2.6	2.4	2.4
Kuwait - Koweït											
Total	C	3 891	3 998	4 899	4 538	4 239	1.7	1.7	2.0	1.8	...
Kyrgyzstan - Kirghizistan											
Total	C	6 104	5 367	5 311	6 097	6 870	1.2	1.1	1.0	1.2	1.3
Urban - Urbaine	C	3 780	3 280	3 441	3 543	3 947	2.1	1.8	1.9	1.9	2.1
Rural - Rurale	C	2 324	2 087	1 870	2 554	2 923	0.7	0.6	0.6	0.8	0.9
Lebanon - Liban											
Total	+C	4 060	4 328	4 372	4 746	4 388	...	...	1.2	...	...
Maldives											
Total	...	836	1 135	1 161	1 757	...	...	...	...	...	...
Urban - Urbaine	...	431	530	589	935	...	...	...	...	...	...
Rural - Rurale	...	405	605	572	822	...	...	...	...	...	...
Mongolia - Mongolie											
Total	C	688	884	1 098	1 622	1 448	0.3	0.4	0.4	0.6	0.6
Urban - Urbaine	C	583	813	1 032	1 508	1 310	0.4	0.6	0.7	1.0	0.8
Rural - Rurale	C	105	71	66	114	138	0.1	0.1	0.1	0.1	0.1
Occupied Palestinian Territory - Territoire palestinien occupé											
Total	C	3 046	3 909	3 961	4 211	3 756	0.9	1.1	1.1	1.1	1.0
Qatar											
Total	C	732	790	787	643	826	1.1	1.1	1.0	0.8	0.9
Saudi Arabia - Arabie saoudite											
Total	...	20 794	24 435	24 318	24 862		...	...	...	...	...
Singapore - Singapour											
Total	+C	5 538	6 293	6 047	6 569	6 649	1.3	1.5	1.4	1.5	1.5
Syrian Arab Republic - République arabe syrienne[19]											
Total	U	14 314	14 314	17 336	17 821	19 984	...	...	...	...	...
Tajikistan - Tadjikistan											
Total	C	2 283	2 390	2 587	2 885	3 018	0.4	0.4	0.4	0.4	0.4
Urban - Urbaine	C	1 822	1 860	...	...	...	1.1	1.1	...	...	...
Rural - Rurale	C	461	530	...	...	...	0.1	0.1	...	...	...
Turkey - Turquie											
Total	C	95 323[20]	92 637[21]	91 022[21]	95 895[21]	93 489[21]	1.4	1.3	1.3	1.3	1.3

25. Divorces and crude divorce rates by urban/rural residence: 2002 - 2006
Divorces et taux bruts de divortialité selon la résidence, urbaine/rurale: 2002 - 2006 (continued - suite)

Continent, country or area, and urban/rural residence / Continent, pays ou zone et résidence, urbaine/rurale	Code[a]	Number - Nombre					Rate - Taux				
		2002	2003	2004	2005	2006	2002	2003	2004	2005	2006
ASIA - ASIE											
United Arab Emirates - Émirats arabes unis											
Total....................	...	3 390	3 243	3 577	...	...	...	...	...	...	...
Viet Nam											
Total....................	C	*39 829	...	...	...	...	*0.5	...	...	...	...
Urban - Urbaine	C	*14 542	...	...	...	...	*0.7	...	...	...	...
Rural - Rurale	C	*25 287	...	...	...	...	*0.4	...	...	...	...
Yemen - Yémen											
Total....................	...	998	104	...	...	...	...	...	...	...	...
EUROPE											
Åland Islands - Îles d'Åland[22]											
Total....................	C	65	56	53	41	63	2.5	2.1	2.0	1.5	2.3
Urban - Urbaine	C	35	24	25	19	32	3.3	...	...	...	3.0
Rural - Rurale	C	30	32	28	22	31	1.9	2.0	...	...	1.9
Albania - Albanie											
Total....................	C	3 494	3 634	2 968	3 929	4 075	1.1	1.2	0.9	1.3	1.3
Austria - Autriche[23]											
Total....................	C	19 918	19 066	19 590	19 453	20 336	2.5	2.3	2.4	2.4	2.5
Belarus - Bélarus											
Total....................	C	37 386	31 679	29 133	30 531	31 814	3.8	3.2	3.0	3.1	3.3
Urban - Urbaine	C	31 066	26 453	24 597	25 810	26 928	4.4	3.8	3.5	3.7	3.8
Rural - Rurale	C	6 320	5 226	4 536	4 721	4 886	2.2	1.8	1.6	1.7	1.8
Belgium - Belgique[24]											
Total....................	C	30 628	31 355	31 418	30 844	29 183	3.0	3.0	3.0	2.9	2.8
Bosnia and Herzegovina - Bosnie-Herzégovine											
Total....................	C	2 272	1 918	1 523	1 763	1 659	0.6	0.5	0.4	0.5	0.4
Bulgaria - Bulgarie[25]											
Total....................	C	10 197	12 000	14 657	14 663	14 815	1.3	1.5	1.9	1.9	1.9
Urban - Urbaine	C	8 613	9 973	11 803	11 801	12 153	1.6	1.8	2.2	2.2	2.2
Rural - Rurale	C	1 584	2 027	2 854	2 862	2 662	0.7	0.9	1.2	1.2	1.2
Croatia - Croatie											
Total....................	C	4 496	4 934	4 985	4 883	4 651	1.0	1.1	1.1	1.1	1.0
Urban - Urbaine	C	3 241	3 553	3 509	3 533	3 371	...	...	...	...	...
Rural - Rurale	C	1 255	1 381	1 476	1 350	1 280	...	...	...	...	...
Czech Republic - République tchèque											
Total....................	C	31 758	32 824	33 060	31 288	31 415	3.1	3.2	3.2	3.1	3.1
Urban - Urbaine	C	26 070	26 569	26 841	25 233	25 214	3.5	3.5	3.6	3.3	3.3
Rural - Rurale	C	5 688	6 255	6 219	6 055	6 201	2.1	2.3	2.3	2.3	2.3
Denmark - Danemark[26]											
Total....................	C	15 304	15 763	15 774	15 300	14 343	2.8	2.9	2.9	2.8	2.6
Estonia - Estonie											
Total....................	C	4 074	3 973	4 158	4 054	3 811	3.0	2.9	3.1	3.0	2.8
Urban - Urbaine[27]........	C	3 030	2 865	2 997	2 882	2 676	3.2	3.1	3.2	3.1	2.9
Rural - Rurale[27]..........	C	907	970	1 016	1 056	1 058	2.2	2.3	2.5	2.6	2.6
Faeroe Islands - Îles Féroé											
Total....................	C	53	57	48	67	61	1.1	1.2	1.0	1.4	1.3
Finland - Finlande[28]											
Total....................	C	13 336	13 475	13 234	13 383	13 255	2.6	2.6	2.5	2.6	2.5
Urban - Urbaine	C	9 561	9 613	9 344	9 451	9 396	3.0	3.0	2.9	2.9	2.8
Rural - Rurale	C	3 775	3 862	3 890	3 932	3 859	1.9	2.0	2.0	2.0	2.0
France[29]											
Total....................	C	115 861	125 175	131 335	152 020	139 147	1.9	2.1	2.2	2.5	2.3
Germany - Allemagne											
Total....................	C	204 214	213 975	213 691	201 693	190 928	2.5	2.6	2.6	2.4	2.3
Gibraltar											
Total....................	C	150	159	119	97	121	5.3	5.6	4.1	3.4	4.2
Greece - Grèce											
Total....................	C	11 080	12 033	12 307	13 494	...	1.0	1.1	1.1	1.2	...

25. Divorces and crude divorce rates by urban/rural residence: 2002 - 2006
Divorces et taux bruts de divortialité selon la résidence, urbaine/rurale: 2002 - 2006 (continued - suite)

Continent, country or area, and urban/rural residence / Continent, pays ou zone et résidence, urbaine/rurale	Co-dé[d]	Number - Nombre					Rate - Taux				
		2002	2003	2004	2005	2006	2002	2003	2004	2005	2006
EUROPE											
Hungary - Hongrie											
Total	C	25 493	25 040	24 633	24 795	24 866	2.5	2.5	2.4	2.5	2.5
Urban - Urbaine[30]	C	18 528	18 135	17 567	17 685	17 910	2.8	2.8	2.7	2.7	2.7
Rural - Rurale[30]	C	6 797	6 770	6 850	6 863	6 728	1.9	1.9	1.9	2.0	2.0
Iceland - Islande[31]											
Total	C	529	531	560	564	498	1.8	1.8	1.9	1.9	1.6
Urban - Urbaine	C	504	508	524	531[32]	474	1.9	1.9	1.9	1.9	1.7
Rural - Rurale	C	25	23	36	32[32]	24	...	...	1.7	1.5	...
Ireland - Irlande											
Total	C	2 591	2 970	3 347	3 411	3 466	0.7	0.7	0.8	0.8	0.8
Isle of Man - Îles de Man											
Total	+C	402	338	...	...	...	5.2	4.4	...	...	...
Italy - Italie											
Total	C	41 835	43 856	45 097	47 036	...	0.7	0.8	0.8	0.8	...
Latvia - Lettonie											
Total	C	5 952	4 828	5 271	6 341	7 249	2.5	2.1	2.3	2.8	3.2
Urban - Urbaine	C	4 769	3 774	4 117	4 870	5 545	3.0	2.4	2.6	3.1	3.6
Rural - Rurale	C	1 183	1 054	1 154	1 471	1 704	1.6	1.4	1.6	2.0	2.3
Liechtenstein											
Total	C	99	84	101	94	*81	2.9	2.5	2.9	2.7	*2.3
Lithuania - Lituanie											
Total	C	10 579	10 599	10 997	11 097	11 202	3.0	3.1	3.2	3.3	3.3
Urban - Urbaine	C	8 398	8 377	8 106	8 105	7 946	3.6	3.6	3.5	3.6	3.5
Rural - Rurale	C	2 181	2 222	2 891	2 992	3 256	1.9	1.9	2.5	2.6	2.9
Luxembourg											
Total	C	1 092	1 026	1 055	1 046	1 182	2.4	2.3	2.3	2.2	2.5
Moldova											
Total	C	12 698	14 672	14 918	14 521	12 594	3.5	4.1	4.1	4.0	3.5
Urban - Urbaine	C	8 947	10 565	11 015	10 816	9 652	6.0	7.1	7.5	7.3	6.5
Rural - Rurale	C	3 751	4 107	3 903	3 705	2 942	1.8	1.9	1.8	1.7	1.4
Monaco											
Total	C	69	73	82	69	...	...	...	...	...	...
Montenegro											
Total	C	506	494	505	499	470	0.8	0.8	0.8	0.8	...
Urban - Urbaine	C	...	408	422	...	...	...	1.1	1.1	...	...
Rural - Rurale	C	...	86	83	...	...	...	0.4	0.4	...	...
Netherlands - Pays-Bas[33]											
Total	C	33 179	31 479	31 098	31 905	31 734	2.1	1.9	1.9	2.0	1.9
Urban - Urbaine	C	23 582	22 700	21 614	22 312	22 019	2.2	2.2	2.0	2.1	2.0
Rural - Rurale	C	8 999	8 245	8 929	9 074	9 195	1.6	1.5	1.6	1.6	1.7
Norway - Norvège[34]											
Total	C	10 450	10 757	11 045[35]	11 040[35]	10 598[35]	2.3	2.4	2.4	2.4	2.3
Poland - Pologne[36]											
Total	C	45 414	48 632	56 332	67 578	71 912	1.2	1.3	1.5	1.8	1.9
Urban - Urbaine	C	38 254	40 876	45 954	53 611	57 915	1.6	1.7	2.0	2.3	2.5
Rural - Rurale	C	7 072	7 669	10 288	13 846	13 807	0.5	0.5	0.7	0.9	0.9
Portugal											
Total	C	27 960	22 818	23 348	22 853	23 935	2.7	2.2	2.2	2.2	2.3
Romania - Roumanie											
Total	C	31 790	33 073	35 225	33 193	32 672	1.5	1.5	1.6	1.5	1.5
Urban - Urbaine	C	22 675	23 542	25 134	23 709	23 338	2.0	2.0	2.1	2.0	2.0
Rural - Rurale	C	9 115	9 531	10 091	9 484	9 334	0.9	0.9	1.0	1.0	1.0
Russian Federation - Fédération de Russie											
Total	C	853 647	798 824	635 835	604 942	640 837	5.9	5.5	4.4	4.2	4.5
San Marino - Saint-Marin											
Total	+C	45	45	62	61	...	1.6	1.6	2.1	2.0	...
Serbia - Serbie[37]											
Total	+C	9 982	7 938	8 845	7 661	8 204	1.3	1.1	1.2	1.0	1.1
Urban - Urbaine	+C	6 876	5 342	6 032	5 282	5 707	1.6	1.3	1.4	1.2	1.3
Rural - Rurale	+C	3 106	2 596	2 813	2 379	2 497	1.0	0.8	0.9	0.7	0.8
Slovakia - Slovaquie											
Total	C	10 960	10 716	10 889	11 553	12 716	2.0	2.0	2.0	2.1	2.4
Urban - Urbaine	C	7 782	7 720	7 700	8 209	8 926	2.6	2.6	2.6	2.7	3.0
Rural - Rurale	C	3 178	2 996	3 189	3 344	3 790	1.3	1.3	1.3	1.4	1.6

25. Divorces and crude divorce rates by urban/rural residence: 2002 - 2006
Divorces et taux bruts de divortialité selon la résidence, urbaine/rurale: 2002 - 2006 (continued - suite)

Continent, country or area, and urban/rural residence / Continent, pays ou zone et résidence, urbaine/rurale	Code[a]	Number - Nombre					Rate - Taux				
		2002	2003	2004	2005	2006	2002	2003	2004	2005	2006
EUROPE											
Slovenia - Slovénie											
Total	C	2 457	2 461	2 411	2 647	2 334	1.2	1.2	1.2	1.3	1.2
Urban - Urbaine	C	1 533	1 533	1 442	1 623	1 379	1.6	1.6	1.5	1.7	1.4
Rural - Rurale	C	924	928	969	1 024	955	0.9	0.9	1.0	1.0	1.0
Spain - Espagne											
Total	C	41 621	45 448	50 974	72 848	...	1.0	1.1	1.2	1.7	...
Sweden - Suède											
Total	C	21 322	21 130	20 106	20 000	20 295	2.4	2.4	2.2	2.2	2.2
Switzerland - Suisse											
Total	C	16 363	16 799	17 949	21 332	20 981	2.2	2.3	2.4	2.9	2.8
Urban - Urbaine	C	12 968	13 189	14 080	16 811	16 466	2.4	2.5	2.6	3.1	3.0
Rural - Rurale	C	3 395	3 610	3 869	4 521	4 515	1.7	1.8	2.0	2.3	2.3
The Former Yugoslav Rep. of Macedonia - L'ex-République yougoslave de Macédoine											
Total	C	1 310	1 405	1 645	1 552	1 475	0.6	0.7	0.8	0.8	0.7
Urban - Urbaine	C	...	...	...	1 009	...	...	...	...	...	...
Rural - Rurale	C	...	...	...	543	...	...	...	...	...	...
Ukraine											
Total	C	183 538	177 183	173 163	183 455	179 123	3.8	3.7	3.7	3.9	3.8
Urban - Urbaine	C	145 457	138 053	134 372	141 971	138 993	4.5	4.3	...	...	...
Rural - Rurale	C	38 081	39 130	38 791	41 484	40 130	2.4	2.5	...	...	...
United Kingdom - Royaume-Uni[38]											
Total	C	160 528	166 536				2.7	2.8			
OCEANIA - OCÉANIE											
Australia - Australie											
Total	+C	54 004	53 145	52 747	52 399	...	2.7	2.7	2.6	2.6	...
Guam											
Total	C	475	883	...	...	...	2.9	5.3	...	...	...
New Caledonia - Nouvelle-Calédonie[39]											
Total	C	219	246	...	...	...	1.0	1.1	...	...	...
Urban - Urbaine	C	129	139								
Rural - Rurale	C	17	25								
New Zealand - Nouvelle-Zélande											
Total	+C	10 292	10 491	10 609	9 972	10 065	2.6	2.6	2.6	2.4	2.4
Niue - Nioué											
Total	C	-									
Northern Mariana Islands - Îles Mariannes septentrionales[40]											
Total	U	...	401	...	...	...	...	...	...	...	...
Urban - Urbaine	U	...	375								
Rural - Rurale	U	...	26								
Samoa											
Total	U	*44*	*34*	*38*	**44*	...					
Tonga											
Total	+C	109	103	...	...	...	1.1	1.0	...	...	...

FOOTNOTES - NOTES

Italics: data from civil registers which are incomplete or of unknown completeness. - Italiques: données incomplètes ou dont le degré d'exactitude n'est pas connu, provenant des registres de l'état civil.

* Provisional. - Données provisoires.

[a] 'Code' indicates the source of data, as follows:
C - Civil registration, estimated over 90% complete
U - Civil registration, estimated less than 90% complete
| - Other source, estimated reliable
+ - Data tabulated by date of registration rather than occurence.
... - Information not available

Le 'Code' indique la source des données, comme suit:
C - Registres de l'état civil considérés complèts à 90 p. 100 au moins.

U - Registres de l'état civil qui ne sont pas considérés complèts à 90 p. 100 au moins.

| - Autre source, considérée pas douteuses.

+ - Données exploitées selon la date de l'enregistrement et non la date de l'événement.

... - Information pas disponible.

[1] Including 'revocable divorces' (among Moslem population), which approximate legal separations. - Y compris les 'divorces révocables' (parmi la population musulmane), qui sont à peu près l'équivalent des séparations légales.

[2] Data refer to Libyan nationals only. - Les données se raportent aux nationaux libyens seulement.

[3] Including annulments and legal separations. - Y compris les annulations et séparations légales.

[4] The total number includes 'Unknown residence', but the categories urban and rural do not. - Le nombre total inclue 'Résidence inconnue ', mais les catégories Urbain et Rural ne l'incluent pas.

[5] Excluding tribal Indian population. - Non compris les Indiens vivant en tribus.

[6] Excluding Indian jungle population. - Non compris les Indiens de la jungle.

[7] A new divorce law took effect from October 2005. - Une nouvelle loi sur le divorce est entrée en vigueur en octobre 2005.

[8] Excluding nomadic Indian tribes. - Non compris les tribus d'Indiens nomades.

[9] From June 23, 2003 there has been a revision of marriage legislation in the case of annulments. As of 2004 annulmets include with divorce. - Le 23 juin 2003, la législation relative au mariage a été révisée pour les cas d'annulation. À compter de l'année 2004, les annulations comprennent les divorces.

[10] Including annulments. - Y compris les annulations.

[11] For statistical purposes, the data for China do not include those for the Hong Kong Special Administrative Region (Hong Kong SAR), Macao Special Administrative Region (Macao SAR) and Taiwan province of China. - Pour la présentation des statistiques, les données pour la Chine ne comprennent pas la Région Administrative Spéciale de Hong Kong (Hong Kong RAS), la Région Administrative Spéciale de Macao (Macao RAS) et Taïwan province de Chine.

[12] Data refer to government controlled areas. Data according to the place of usual residence of husband. - Les données se rapportent aux zones contrôlées par le Gouvernement. Données correspondant au lieu de résidence habituelle du mari.

[13] Data relate to the Iranian Year which begins on 21 March and ends on 20 March of the following year. - Les données concernent l'année iranienne, qui commence le 21 mars et se termine le 20 mars de l'année suivante.

[14] Including data for East Jerusalem and Israeli residents in certain other territories under occupation by Israeli military forces since June 1967. - Y compris les données pour Jérusalem-Est et les résidents israéliens dans certains autres territoires occupés depuis 1967 par les forces armées israéliennes.

[15] Data refer to Japanese nationals in Japan only. - Les données se raportent aux nationaux japonais au Japon seulement.

[16] Excluding data for Jordanian territory under occupation since June 1967 by Israeli military forces. Excluding foreigners, including registered Palestinian refugees. - Non compris les données pour le territoire jordanien occupé depuis juin 1967 par les forces armées israéliennes. Non compris les étrangers, mais y compris les réfugiés de Palestine enregistrés.

[17] Excluding alien armed forces, civilian aliens employed by armed forces, and foreign diplomatic personnel and their dependants. - Non compris les militaires étrangers, les civils étrangers employés par les forces armées ni le personnel diplomatique étranger et les membres de leur famille les accompagnant.

[18] Including Korean divorces abroad. - Y compris les divorces coréens à l'étranger.

[19] Excluding nomads. - Non compris les nomades.

[20] Data from Turkish Statistical Institute. Data revised by MERNIS (Central Population Administrative System). - Données de l'Institut turc de statistique. Données révisées par MERNIS (Système central de données démographiques).

[21] Data from MERNIS (Central Population Administrative System). - Données de MERNIS (Système central de données démographiques).

[22] Also included in Finland. - Comprise aussi dans Finlande.

[23] Excluding aliens temporarily in the area. - Non compris les étrangers se trouvant temporairement le territoire.

[24] Including divorces among armed forces stationed outside the country and alien armed forces in the area. - Y compris les divorces de militaires nationaux hors du pays et les militaires étrangers en garnison sur le territoire.

[25] Including Bulgarian nationals outside the country, but excluding foreigners in the country. - Y compris les nationaux bulgares à l'étranger, mais non compris les étrangers sur le territoire.

[26] Excluding Faeroe Islands and Greenland shown separately, if available. - Non compris les Iles Féroé et le Gröenland, qui font l'objet de rubriques distinctes, si disponible.

[27] The total number includes 'Unknown residence', but the categories urban and rural do not. Urban and rural distribution of marriages and divorces is displayed by place of residence of groom/husband. The difference between 'Total' and the sum of urban and rural is due to the unknown place of residence of grooms/husbands and to grooms/husbands living outside country. - Le nombre total inclue 'Résidence inconnue ', mais les catégories Urbain et Rural ne l'incluent pas. Les mariages et divorces sont classés par rapport à la résidence urbaine/rurale de l'époux. La somme des mariages et divorces par résidence urbaine/rurale est différente du 'total' car elle ne tient pas compte ni des résidences inconnues de l'époux ni des mariages et divorces d'époux vivant à l'étranger.

[28] Including nationals temporarily outside the country. Including Aland Islands. - Y compris les nationaux se trouvant temporairement hors du pays. Y compris les Îles d'Åland.

[29] Excluding Overseas Departments, namely, French Guiana, Guadeloupe, Martinique and Reunion, shown separately, if available. - Non compris les départements d'outre mer, c'est-à-dire la Guyane française, la Guadeloupe, la Martinique et la Réunion, qui font l'objet de rubriques distinctes, si disponible.

[30] Total includes the data of foreigners, persons of unknown residence and homeless, but the categories urban and rural do not. - Total incluant les étrangers, les personnes de résidence inconnue et les sans-abri, ce qui n'est pas le cas pour les catégories urbaines et rurales.

[31] Data refer to de jure population. - Les données se raportent a la population de droit.

[32] The difference between 'Total' and the sum of 'urban' and 'rural' is due to the cases of unknown place of residence or residence abroad. - La différence entre le 'Total' et la somme des données selon la résidence urbaine/rurale se rapporte à la situation ou on ignore la résidence ou si la résidence est à l'étranger.

[33] For 2004, based on the general office for civil registration. - En 2004, d'après la direction générale du registre de l'etat civil.

[34] Excluding Svalbard and Jan Mayen Island shown separately, if available. - Non compris Svalbard et Jan Mayen qui font l'objet de rubriques distinctes, si disponible.

[35] Data refer to male residents in Norway only. - Ces données ne concernent que les hommes habitant en Norvège.

[36] Data for urban and rural exclude divorces if both persons live aboard. - Les données pour les zones urbaines et rurales excluent le divorce si les deux personnes vivent à l'étranger.

[37] Without data for Kosovo and Metohia. - Sans les données pour le Kosovo and Metohie.

[38] Excluding Channel Islands and Isle of Man, shown separately, if available. - Non compris les îles Anglo-Normandes et l'île de Man, qui font l'objet de rubriques distinctes, si disponible.

[39] Divorces are based on place of residence at marriage not at divorce. - Les divorces sont comptés en fonction du lieu de résidence au mariage, et non pas au divorce.

[40] Data refer to Saipan only. - Saipan seulement.

Annex I: United Nations Annual interpolated mid-year population, estimates 1997 - 2006
Annexe I: Population au milieu de l'année interpolée, estimations 1997 - 2006

Continent and country or area / Continent et pays ou zone	Population estimates (in thousands) - Estimations (en milliers)[1]									
	1997	1998	1999	2000	2001	2002	2003	2004	2005	2006
AFRICA — AFRIQUE										
Algeria - Algérie	29 216	29 646	30 072	30 506	30 954	31 414	31 885	32 366	32 854	33 351
Angola	12 953	13 257	13 578	13 930	14 318	14 737	15 180	15 636	16 095	16 557
Benin - Bénin	6 607	6 804	7 009	7 227	7 460	7 706	7 962	8 224	8 490	8 760
Botswana	1 638	1 671	1 701	1 729	1 753	1 775	1 795	1 815	1 836	1 858
Burkina Faso	10 876	11 192	11 526	11 882	12 262	12 664	13 082	13 507	13 933	14 359
Burundi	6 378	6 447	6 539	6 668	6 839	7 049	7 294	7 566	7 859	8 173
Cameroon - Cameroun	14 774	15 130	15 491	15 861	16 240	16 627	17 019	17 409	17 795	18 175
Cape Verde - Cap-Vert	420	430	440	451	461	472	484	495	507	519
Central African Republic - République centrafricaine ...	3 625	3 709	3 789	3 864	3 933	3 997	4 060	4 123	4 191	4 265
Chad - Tchad	7 633	7 893	8 169	8 465	8 783	9 119	9 465	9 810	10 146	10 468
Comoros - Comores	643	661	680	699	718	738	758	778	798	818
Congo	2 955	3 037	3 120	3 203	3 285	3 367	3 449	3 530	3 610	3 689
Côte d'Ivoire	15 856	16 279	16 679	17 049	17 385	17 691	17 982	18 275	18 585	18 914
Democratic Republic of the Congo - République démocratique du Congo	47 532	48 495	49 517	50 689	52 036	53 537	55 175	56 918	58 741	60 644
Djibouti	663	687	709	730	747	763	777	790	804	819
Egypt - Égypte	62 941	64 119	65 316	66 529	67 757	69 004	70 268	71 550	72 850	74 166
Equatorial Guinea - Guinée équatoriale	401	411	420	431	441	451	462	473	484	496
Eritrea - Érythrée	3 341	3 437	3 553	3 684	3 833	3 999	4 176	4 354	4 527	4 692
Ethiopia - Éthiopie	63 934	65 738	67 552	69 388	71 250	73 134	75 046	76 995	78 986	81 021
Gabon	1 109	1 134	1 158	1 182	1 205	1 228	1 249	1 270	1 291	1 311
Gambia - Gambie	1 247	1 292	1 338	1 384	1 431	1 477	1 524	1 571	1 617	1 663
Ghana	18 790	19 237	19 688	20 148	20 617	21 094	21 575	22 057	22 535	23 008
Guinea - Guinée	7 722	7 889	8 047	8 203	8 359	8 514	8 671	8 833	9 003	9 181
Guinea-Bissau - Guinée-Bissau	1 261	1 295	1 332	1 370	1 412	1 456	1 502	1 549	1 597	1 646
Kenya	28 914	29 678	30 455	31 252	32 071	32 913	33 780	34 675	35 599	36 553
Lesotho	1 788	1 823	1 856	1 886	1 911	1 932	1 950	1 966	1 981	1 995
Liberia - Libéria	2 476	2 698	2 906	3 071	3 181	3 247	3 292	3 348	3 442	3 579
Libyan Arab Jamahiriya - Jamahiriya arabe libyenne	5 030	5 133	5 238	5 346	5 456	5 568	5 683	5 799	5 918	6 039
Madagascar	14 809	15 259	15 719	16 187	16 662	17 145	17 636	18 135	18 643	19 159
Malawi	10 607	10 941	11 288	11 623	11 945	12 260	12 574	12 894	13 226	13 571
Mali	9 211	9 462	9 726	10 004	10 298	10 607	10 930	11 265	11 611	11 968
Mauritania - Mauritanie	2 354	2 422	2 493	2 566	2 642	2 721	2 801	2 882	2 963	3 044
Mauritius - Maurice[2]	1 150	1 162	1 174	1 186	1 197	1 209	1 220	1 231	1 241	1 252
Morocco - Maroc	27 733	28 109	28 475	28 827	29 166	29 495	29 821	30 152	30 495	30 853
Mozambique	16 878	17 311	17 745	18 194	18 660	19 134	19 610	20 078	20 533	20 971
Namibia - Namibie	1 752	1 798	1 841	1 879	1 913	1 942	1 969	1 994	2 020	2 047
Niger	9 981	10 350	10 732	11 124	11 527	11 941	12 367	12 808	13 264	13 737
Nigeria - Nigéria	115 193	118 348	121 542	124 773	128 039	131 336	134 659	138 001	141 356	144 720
Réunion	688	700	712	724	737	749	761	774	785	796
Rwanda	6 363	7 015	7 660	8 176	8 530	8 762	8 912	9 052	9 234	9 464
Saint Helena - Sainte-Hélène[3]	5	6	6	6	6	6	6	6	6	6
Sao Tome and Principe - Sao Tomé-et-Principe	133	135	138	140	143	145	148	150	153	155
Senegal - Sénégal	9 548	9 803	10 065	10 334	10 609	10 891	11 179	11 472	11 770	12 072
Seychelles	78	79	80	81	82	83	84	85	86	86
Sierra Leone	4 216	4 284	4 384	4 521	4 703	4 924	5 163	5 390	5 586	5 743
Somalia - Somalie	6 433	6 622	6 837	7 055	7 272	7 494	7 721	7 954	8 196	8 445
South Africa - Afrique du Sud	43 236	44 009	44 729	45 398	46 017	46 581	47 089	47 541	47 939	48 282
Southern Africa - Afrique méridionale	49 412	50 321	51 167	51 950	52 669	53 319	53 905	54 430	54 900	55 316
Sudan - Soudan	31 044	31 830	32 602	33 349	34 063	34 752	35 436	36 145	36 900	37 707
Swaziland	999	1 020	1 040	1 058	1 075	1 089	1 102	1 114	1 125	1 134
Togo	4 846	5 033	5 221	5 403	5 576	5 744	5 907	6 071	6 239	6 410
Tunisia - Tunisie	9 226	9 341	9 453	9 564	9 672	9 780	9 888	9 996	10 105	10 215
Uganda - Ouganda	22 576	23 252	23 953	24 690	25 467	26 284	27 139	28 028	28 947	29 899
United Republic of Tanzania - République Unie de Tanzanie	31 492	32 254	33 031	33 849	34 712	35 615	36 551	37 508	38 478	39 459
Western Sahara - Sahara occidental	276	286	298	315	337	362	389	416	440	462
Zambia - Zambie	9 742	9 986	10 224	10 451	10 665	10 870	11 069	11 270	11 478	11 696
Zimbabwe	12 195	12 369	12 524	12 656	12 767	12 859	12 941	13 025	13 120	13 228

Annex I: United Nations Annual interpolated mid-year population, estimates 1997 - 2006
Annexe I: Population au milieu de l'année interpolée, estimations 1997 - 2006
(continued — suite)

Continent and country or area Continent et pays ou zone	Population estimates (in thousands) - Estimations (en milliers)[1]									
	1997	1998	1999	2000	2001	2002	2003	2004	2005	2006
AMERICA, NORTH — AMERIQUE DU NORD										
Anguilla	11	11	11	11	11	12	12	12	12	12
Antigua and Barbuda - Antigua-et-Barbuda	72	73	75	77	78	80	81	82	83	84
Aruba	87	88	89	90	93	96	99	101	103	104
Bahamas	290	294	299	303	307	311	315	319	323	327
Barbados - Barbade	283	284	285	286	288	289	290	291	292	293
Belize	226	232	238	245	251	257	263	269	276	282
Bermuda - Bermudes	62	62	63	63	63	63	64	64	64	64
British Virgin Islands - Îles Vierges britanniques	19	20	20	21	21	21	21	22	22	22
Canada	29 859	30 127	30 402	30 689	30 992	31 308	31 632	31 955	32 271	32 577
Cayman Islands - Îles Caïmanes	36	37	39	40	41	43	44	45	46	46
Costa Rica	3 655	3 748	3 840	3 929	4 014	4 097	4 176	4 253	4 327	4 399
Cuba	11 026	11 068	11 107	11 142	11 174	11 203	11 227	11 247	11 260	11 267
Dominica - Dominique	69	69	69	68	68	68	68	68	68	68
Dominican Republic - République dominicaine	8 305	8 452	8 598	8 744	8 890	9 035	9 180	9 325	9 470	9 615
El Salvador	5 862	5 976	6 088	6 195	6 297	6 392	6 485	6 576	6 668	6 762
Greenland - Groenland	56	56	56	56	56	57	57	57	57	58
Grenada - Grenade	99	99	100	100	101	102	104	105	105	106
Guadeloupe	412	415	418	421	425	428	432	435	438	442
Guatemala	10 471	10 714	10 966	11 229	11 505	11 793	12 090	12 397	12 710	13 029
Haiti - Haïti	8 131	8 279	8 427	8 573	8 718	8 861	9 005	9 149	9 296	9 446
Honduras	5 825	5 949	6 072	6 196	6 320	6 446	6 573	6 702	6 834	6 969
Jamaica - Jamaïque	2 529	2 549	2 569	2 589	2 609	2 628	2 647	2 665	2 682	2 699
Martinique	380	382	384	386	388	390	392	394	396	397
Mexico - Mexique	95 204	96 870	98 401	99 735	100 834	101 734	102 525	103 338	104 266	105 342
Montserrat	8	7	6	5	5	5	5	5	6	6
Netherlands Antilles - Antilles néerlandaises	186	184	182	181	180	181	182	184	186	189
Nicaragua	4 855	4 944	5 028	5 108	5 184	5 256	5 325	5 394	5 463	5 532
Panama	2 781	2 837	2 893	2 950	3 006	3 063	3 119	3 175	3 232	3 288
Puerto Rico - Porto Rico	3 756	3 783	3 809	3 834	3 858	3 881	3 903	3 925	3 947	3 969
Saint Kitts and Nevis - Saint-Kitts-et-Nevis	44	45	45	46	47	47	48	49	49	50
Saint Lucia - Sainte-Lucie	149	150	151	153	154	156	158	159	161	163
Saint Pierre and Miquelon - Saint Pierre-et-Miquelon	6	6	6	6	6	6	6	6	6	6
Saint Vincent and the Grenadines - Saint Vincent-et-les Grenadines	114	115	115	116	117	117	118	118	119	120
Trinidad and Tobago - Trinité-et-Tobago	1 284	1 290	1 295	1 301	1 305	1 310	1 315	1 319	1 324	1 328
Turks Caicos Islands - Îles Turques et Caïques	17	17	18	19	20	21	22	24	24	25
United States - États-Unis	276 043	278 961	281 898	284 857	287 837	290 832	293 837	296 844	299 846	302 841
United States Virgin Islands - Îles Vierges américaines	109	109	110	110	111	111	111	111	111	111
AMERICA, SOUTH — AMERIQUE DU SUD										
Argentina - Argentine	35 689	36 102	36 504	36 896	37 274	37 642	38 005	38 372	38 747	39 134
Bolivia - Bolivie	7 813	7 980	8 147	8 317	8 488	8 661	8 835	9 009	9 182	9 354
Brazil - Brésil	166 566	169 087	171 622	174 161	176 702	179 246	181 787	184 318	186 831	189 323
Chile - Chili	14 828	15 029	15 223	15 412	15 596	15 776	15 951	16 124	16 295	16 465
Colombia - Colombie	39 633	40 320	41 004	41 683	42 354	43 019	43 675	44 317	44 946	45 558
Ecuador - Équateur	11 786	11 966	12 139	12 306	12 466	12 621	12 771	12 917	13 061	13 202
Falkland Islands (Malvinas) - Îles Falkland (Malvinas)	3	3	3	3	3	3	3	3	3	3
French Guiana - Guyane française	149	154	160	165	171	176	182	187	192	197
Guyana	738	736	735	734	735	736	738	739	739	739
Paraguay	5 019	5 129	5 239	5 349	5 460	5 571	5 682	5 793	5 904	6 016
Peru - Pérou	24 613	24 973	25 322	25 663	25 995	26 321	26 641	26 959	27 274	27 589
Suriname	424	428	432	436	440	443	447	450	452	455
Uruguay	3 265	3 287	3 305	3 318	3 325	3 326	3 325	3 324	3 326	3 331

Annex I: United Nations Annual interpolated mid-year population, estimates 1997 - 2006
Annexe I: Population au milieu de l'année interpolée, estimations 1997 - 2006
(continued — suite)

Continent and country or area / Continent et pays ou zone	Population estimates (in thousands) - Estimations (en milliers)[1]									
	1997	1998	1999	2000	2001	2002	2003	2004	2005	2006
AMERICA, SOUTH — AMERIQUE DU SUD										
Venezuela (Bolivarian Republic of) - Venezuela (République bolivarienne du)	23 009	23 474	23 938	24 402	24 867	25 331	25 795	26 260	26 726	27 191
ASIA — ASIE										
Afghanistan	19 476	19 837	20 220	20 737	21 414	22 214	23 115	24 076	25 067	26 088
Armenia - Arménie	3 143	3 119	3 100	3 082	3 065	3 050	3 038	3 027	3 018	3 010
Azerbaijan - Azerbaïdjan	7 961	8 030	8 090	8 143	8 189	8 229	8 266	8 306	8 352	8 406
Bahrain - Bahreïn	608	622	636	650	665	680	695	710	725	739
Bangladesh	131 524	134 127	136 757	139 434	142 167	144 943	147 741	150 528	153 281	155 991
Bhutan - Bhoutan	517	529	543	559	574	591	607	623	637	649
Brunei Darussalam - Brunéi Darussalam	310	318	326	333	341	349	358	366	374	382
Cambodia - Cambodge	11 989	12 264	12 526	12 780	13 024	13 259	13 489	13 720	13 956	14 197
China - Chine[4]	1 237 431	1 248 852	1 259 740	1 269 962	1 279 486	1 288 401	1 296 838	1 304 983	1 312 979	1 320 864
China - Hong Kong SAR - Chine - Hong Kong RAS[5]	6 399	6 489	6 577	6 662	6 746	6 826	6 905	6 982	7 057	7 132
China - Macao SAR - Chine - Macao RAS[6]	424	429	435	441	448	454	461	468	473	478
Cyprus - Chypre	753	764	776	786	797	807	817	827	836	846
Timor Leste	833	816	809	819	849	896	954	1 013	1 067	1 114
Georgia - Géorgie	4 887	4 829	4 774	4 720	4 666	4 614	4 564	4 517	4 473	4 433
India - Inde	991 513	1 009 905	1 028 145	1 046 235	1 064 156	1 081 899	1 099 494	1 116 985	1 134 403	1 151 751
Indonesia - Indonésie	203 122	205 970	208 825	211 693	214 575	217 466	220 355	223 225	226 063	228 864
Iran (Islamic Republic of) - Iran (République islamique d')	63 916	64 700	65 435	66 125	66 770	67 383	68 001	68 669	69 421	70 270
Iraq	23 013	23 709	24 392	25 052	25 687	26 301	26 892	27 456	27 996	28 506
Israel - Israël	5 682	5 821	5 954	6 084	6 212	6 335	6 455	6 574	6 692	6 810
Japan - Japon	126 150	126 469	126 765	127 034	127 273	127 483	127 659	127 798	127 897	127 953
Jordan - Jordanie	4 541	4 620	4 700	4 799	4 919	5 055	5 207	5 371	5 544	5 729
Kazakhstan	15 474	15 253	15 072	14 954	14 910	14 933	15 008	15 107	15 211	15 314
Korea (Dem. People's Republic of) - Corée (Rép. populaire dém. de)	22 269	22 518	22 745	22 946	23 122	23 272	23 401	23 514	23 616	23 708
Korea (Republic of) - Corée (République de)	45 786	46 146	46 479	46 780	47 047	47 282	47 490	47 684	47 870	48 050
Kuwait - Koweït	1 839	1 966	2 103	2 228	2 339	2 439	2 531	2 617	2 700	2 779
Kyrgyzstan - Kirghizistan	4 724	4 802	4 878	4 946	5 005	5 057	5 105	5 153	5 204	5 259
Lao People's Democratic Republic - République démocratique populaire lao	4 919	5 025	5 127	5 224	5 316	5 402	5 487	5 574	5 664	5 759
Lebanon - Liban	3 631	3 681	3 726	3 772	3 821	3 869	3 918	3 965	4 011	4 055
Malaysia - Malaisie	21 668	22 214	22 752	23 274	23 775	24 258	24 728	25 191	25 653	26 114
Maldives	259	264	268	273	277	282	286	291	295	300
Mongolia - Mongolie	2 426	2 439	2 454	2 470	2 488	2 509	2 533	2 557	2 581	2 605
Myanmar	44 288	44 850	45 385	45 884	46 343	46 768	47 170	47 565	47 967	48 379
Nepal - Népal	22 767	23 321	23 873	24 419	24 958	25 491	26 021	26 554	27 094	27 641
Oman	2 281	2 329	2 369	2 402	2 427	2 444	2 459	2 479	2 507	2 546
Pakistan	134 395	137 845	141 202	144 360	147 289	150 036	152 680	155 333	158 081	160 943
Philippines	71 579	73 092	74 633	76 213	77 834	79 490	81 172	82 868	84 566	86 264
Qatar	553	569	590	617	649	687	727	764	796	821
Saudi Arabia - Arabie saoudite	19 193	19 718	20 260	20 807	21 357	21 916	22 481	23 047	23 612	24 175
Singapore - Singapour	3 703	3 817	3 923	4 017	4 097	4 164	4 221	4 274	4 327	4 382
Sri Lanka	18 373	18 498	18 611	18 714	18 805	18 887	18 964	19 040	19 121	19 207
Syrian Arab Republic - République arabe syrienne	15 342	15 712	16 099	16 511	16 949	17 411	17 893	18 389	18 894	19 408
Tajikistan - Tadjikistan	5 937	6 018	6 097	6 173	6 246	6 318	6 391	6 467	6 550	6 640
Thailand - Thaïlande	58 830	59 475	60 091	60 666	61 192	61 675	62 127	62 565	63 003	63 444
Turkey - Turquie	64 941	66 039	67 115	68 158	69 164	70 136	71 084	72 025	72 970	73 922
Turkmenistan - Turkménistan	4 334	4 390	4 445	4 502	4 564	4 630	4 698	4 766	4 833	4 899
United Arab Emirates - Émirats arabes unis	2 734	2 900	3 072	3 247	3 424	3 603	3 779	3 947	4 104	4 248
Uzbekistan - Ouzbékistan	23 688	24 034	24 375	24 724	25 083	25 452	25 828	26 209	26 593	26 981
Viet Nam	75 741	76 857	77 964	79 094	80 256	81 440	82 640	83 839	85 029	86 206

Annex I: United Nations Annual interpolated mid-year population, estimates 1997 - 2006
Annexe I: Population au milieu de l'année interpolée, estimations 1997 - 2006
(continued — suite)

Continent and country or area / Continent et pays ou zone	Population estimates (in thousands) - Estimations (en milliers)[1]									
	1997	1998	1999	2000	2001	2002	2003	2004	2005	2006
ASIA — ASIE										
Occupied Palestinian Territory - Territoire palestinien occupé	2 821	2 927	3 036	3 149	3 266	3 387	3 510	3 636	3 762	3 889
Yemen - Yémen	16 635	17 145	17 655	18 182	18 730	19 295	19 877	20 478	21 096	21 732
EUROPE										
Albania - Albanie	3 101	3 088	3 081	3 080	3 085	3 098	3 115	3 134	3 154	3 172
Andorra - Andorre	66	66	66	66	68	69	71	72	73	74
Austria - Autriche	8 088	8 092	8 097	8 111	8 137	8 172	8 212	8 253	8 292	8 327
Belarus - Bélarus	10 198	10 152	10 103	10 052	10 001	9 951	9 899	9 848	9 795	9 742
Belgium - Belgique	10 125	10 143	10 165	10 193	10 229	10 271	10 316	10 360	10 398	10 430
Bosnia and Herzegovina - Bosnie-Herzégovine	3 463	3 575	3 694	3 787	3 846	3 881	3 897	3 905	3 915	3 926
Bulgaria - Bulgarie	8 196	8 127	8 063	8 003	7 946	7 894	7 844	7 795	7 745	7 693
Channel Islands - Îles Anglo-Normandes	145	146	146	147	147	148	148	148	149	149
Croatia - Croatie	4 618	4 572	4 531	4 506	4 498	4 506	4 522	4 540	4 551	4 556
Czech Republic - République tchèque	10 279	10 257	10 237	10 220	10 209	10 202	10 197	10 195	10 192	10 189
Denmark - Danemark	5 271	5 294	5 315	5 335	5 354	5 372	5 388	5 403	5 417	5 430
Estonia - Estonie	1 401	1 389	1 379	1 370	1 363	1 357	1 352	1 348	1 344	1 340
Faeroe Islands - Îles Féroé	44	45	46	46	47	47	48	48	48	49
Finland - Finlande	5 140	5 152	5 164	5 176	5 189	5 203	5 217	5 231	5 246	5 261
France	58 585	58 750	58 943	59 187	59 492	59 849	60 236	60 624	60 991	61 330
Germany - Allemagne	82 070	82 165	82 235	82 309	82 395	82 485	82 568	82 628	82 652	82 641
Gibraltar	27	27	27	27	28	28	28	29	29	29
Greece - Grèce	10 813	10 876	10 929	10 975	11 011	11 038	11 060	11 079	11 100	11 123
Holy See - Saint-Siège[7]	1	1	1	1	1	1	1	1	1	1
Hungary - Hongrie	10 293	10 267	10 240	10 214	10 189	10 164	10 139	10 113	10 086	10 058
Iceland - Islande	273	275	278	281	284	287	290	293	296	298
Ireland - Irlande	3 672	3 709	3 753	3 804	3 862	3 926	3 995	4 068	4 143	4 221
Isle of Man - Îles de Man	74	75	76	77	77	78	78	78	78	78
Italy - Italie	57 441	57 497	57 575	57 692	57 856	58 055	58 271	58 475	58 646	58 779
Latvia - Lettonie	2 435	2 415	2 397	2 379	2 361	2 345	2 330	2 315	2 302	2 289
Liechtenstein	32	32	32	33	33	34	34	34	35	35
Lithuania - Lituanie	3 578	3 551	3 525	3 503	3 483	3 468	3 454	3 440	3 425	3 408
Luxembourg	420	426	432	437	441	445	449	452	457	461
Malta - Malte	383	385	387	389	392	394	397	400	403	405
Monaco	32	32	32	32	32	32	32	32	33	33
Montenegro	648	661	669	670	664	651	635	620	608	601
Moldova - Moldova	4 305	4 255	4 201	4 145	4 089	4 033	3 978	3 925	3 877	3 833
Netherlands - Pays-Bas	15 651	15 743	15 834	15 924	16 014	16 103	16 188	16 264	16 328	16 379
Norway - Norvège	4 409	4 435	4 461	4 489	4 518	4 547	4 578	4 609	4 639	4 669
Poland - Pologne	38 582	38 538	38 485	38 433	38 384	38 338	38 294	38 247	38 196	38 140
Portugal	10 091	10 130	10 176	10 227	10 284	10 346	10 410	10 472	10 528	10 579
Romania - Roumanie	22 450	22 345	22 242	22 138	22 032	21 928	21 826	21 726	21 628	21 532
Russian Federation - Fédération de Russie	148 667	148 339	147 927	147 423	146 828	146 159	145 438	144 696	143 953	143 221
San Marino - Saint-Marin	26	26	27	27	28	28	29	30	30	31
Serbia - Serbie	10 246	10 222	10 180	10 131	10 074	10 011	9 949	9 897	9 863	9 851
Slovakia - Slovaquie	5 382	5 385	5 387	5 388	5 388	5 388	5 387	5 387	5 387	5 388
Slovenia - Slovénie	1 973	1 977	1 980	1 984	1 987	1 991	1 994	1 997	1 999	2 001
Spain - Espagne	39 549	39 663	39 877	40 229	40 742	41 388	42 103	42 795	43 397	43 887
Sweden - Suède	8 855	8 855	8 857	8 868	8 889	8 920	8 957	8 998	9 038	9 078
Switzerland - Suisse	7 197	7 219	7 239	7 263	7 292	7 324	7 358	7 392	7 424	7 455
The Former Yugoslav Rep. of Macedonia - L'ex-République yougoslave de Macédoine	1 983	1 993	2 002	2 009	2 016	2 022	2 026	2 030	2 034	2 036
Ukraine	50 260	49 791	49 313	48 854	48 428	48 027	47 649	47 282	46 918	46 557
United Kingdom - Royaume-Uni	58 280	58 454	58 648	58 868	59 116	59 388	59 676	59 965	60 245	60 512
OCEANIA — OCEANIE										
American Samoa - Samoas américaines	54	55	56	57	58	60	61	63	64	65
Australia - Australie[8]	18 502	18 709	18 920	19 139	19 367	19 604	19 844	20 081	20 310	20 530
Cook Islands - Îles Cook	17	17	16	16	16	15	15	14	14	14

Annex I: United Nations Annual interpolated mid-year population, estimates 1997 - 2006
Annexe I: Population au milieu de l'année interpolée, estimations 1997 - 2006
(continued — suite)

Continent and country or area / Continent et pays ou zone	Population estimates (in thousands) - Estimations (en milliers)[1]									
	1997	1998	1999	2000	2001	2002	2003	2004	2005	2006
OCEANIA — OCEANIE										
Fiji - Fidji	783	790	796	802	807	813	818	823	828	833
French Polynesia - Polynésie française	224	228	232	236	240	244	248	252	256	259
Guam	149	151	153	155	158	160	163	166	169	171
Kiribati	80	81	83	84	86	87	89	90	92	94
Marshall Islands - Îles Marshall	51	52	52	52	53	54	54	56	57	58
Micronesia, Federated States of - Micronésie, États Fédérés de La	108	108	107	107	107	108	109	109	110	111
Nauru	10	10	10	10	10	10	10	10	10	10
New Caledonia - Nouvelle-Calédonie	202	207	211	215	219	223	227	230	234	238
New Zealand - Nouvelle-Zélande	3 750	3 782	3 815	3 854	3 899	3 948	4 000	4 050	4 097	4 140
Niue - Nioué	2	2	2	2	2	2	2	2	2	2
Northern Mariana Islands - Îles Mariannes septentrionales	62	65	67	69	71	74	76	78	80	82
Palau - Palaos	18	18	19	19	20	20	20	20	20	20
Papua New Guinea - Papouasie-Nouvelle-Guinée	4 970	5 105	5 243	5 381	5 520	5 659	5 798	5 935	6 070	6 202
Pitcairn	-	-	-	-	-	-	-	-	-	-
Samoa	172	174	176	177	179	180	181	183	184	185
Solomon Islands - Îles Salomon	383	393	404	415	427	438	449	461	472	484
Tokelau - Tokélaou	1	2	2	2	2	1	1	1	1	1
Tonga	98	98	98	98	98	98	99	99	99	100
Tuvalu	10	10	10	10	10	10	10	10	10	10
Vanuatu	179	182	186	190	194	199	204	210	215	221
Wallis and Futuna Islands - Îles Wallis et Futuna	15	15	15	15	15	15	15	15	15	15

FOOTNOTES - NOTES

[1] For 1996-2005 all data refer to annual interpolated estimates of mid-year population. All estimates are produced by the United Nations, Department of Economic and Social Affairs, Population Division (2007) and published in *World Population Prospects: The 2006 Revision*.CD-ROM Edition - Extended Dataset in Excel and ASCII formats (United Nations publication, Sales No. E.07.XIII.7). — Les données pour 1996-2005 sont des estimations de population au milieu de l'année interpolée. Toutes ces données sont produites par Les Nations Unies, Département des Affaires Sociales et Économiques, Division de Population (2007)et ont été publiées dans *World Population Prospects: The 2006 Revision. CD-ROM Edition - Extended Dataset in Excel and ASCII formats* (United Nations publication, Sales No. E.07.XIII.7).

[2] Including Agalega, Rodrigues and Saint Brandon. — Y compris Agalega, Rodrigues et Saint Brandon.

[3] Including Ascension and Tristan da Cunha. — Y compris Ascension et Tristan da Cunha.

[4] For statistical purposes, the data for China do not include Hong Kong and Macao Special Administrative Regions (SAR) of China. — A des fins statistiques, les données pour la Chine ne comprennent pas les Régions Administratives Spéciales (SAR) de Hong Kong et Macao.

[5] As of 1 July 1997, Hong Kong became a Special Administrative Region (SAR) of China. — A partir du 1 juillet 1997, Hong Kong est devenue une Région Administrative Spéciale (SAR) de la Chine.

[6] As of 20 December 1999, Macao became a Special Administrative Region (SAR) of China. — A partir du 20 décembre 1999, Macao est devenue une Région Administrative Spéciale (SAR) de la Chine.

[7] Refers to the Vatican City State. — Ce rapport à l'état du Vatican.

[8] Including Christmas Island, Cocos (Keeling) Islands and Norfolk Island. — Y compris Christmas Island, Cocos (Keeling) Islands et Norfolk Island.

Annex II: United Nations Medium Variant Population Projections - Vital statistics summary and expectation of life at birth: 2005 - 2010

Annexe II: Projections de la population de variante moyenne de l'ONU - Aperçu des statistiques de l'état civil et espérance de vie à la naissance: 2005 - 2010

Continent, country or area — Continent, pays ou zone	Crude birth rate — Taux bruts de natalité[1]	Crude death rate — Taux bruts de mortalité[1]	Infant mortality rate — Décès d'enfants de moins d'un an[1]	Expectation of life at birth — Espérance de vie à la naissance[1]		Total fertility rate— Indice synthétique de fécondité[1]	Natural increase — Accroissement naturel[1]
				Male — Masculin	Female — Féminin		
AFRICA — AFRIQUE							
Algeria - Algérie	20.8	4.9	31.1	70.9	73.7	2.38	1.59
Angola	47.3	20.5	131.9	41.2	44.3	6.43	2.68
Benin - Bénin	40.2	11.2	98.0	55.6	57.8	5.42	2.90
Botswana	24.9	14.1	46.5	50.5	50.7	2.90	1.07
Burkina Faso	44.0	14.4	104.4	50.7	53.8	6.00	2.97
Burundi	47.1	15.6	99.4	48.1	51.0	6.80	3.15
Cameroon - Cameroun	34.5	14.4	87.5	50.0	50.8	4.31	2.01
Cape Verde - Cap-Vert	28.9	4.7	24.6	68.3	74.5	3.37	2.42
Central African Republic - République centrafricaine	36.1	18.1	96.8	43.3	46.1	4.58	1.80
Chad - Tchad	45.5	15.4	119.2	49.3	52.0	6.20	3.01
Comoros - Comores	33.3	6.5	48.4	63.0	67.4	4.30	2.69
Congo	35.1	11.4	70.3	54.0	56.6	4.49	2.37
Côte d'Ivoire	35.3	15.4	116.9	47.5	49.3	4.46	1.99
Democratic Republic of the Congo - République démocratique du Congo	49.6	18.1	113.5	45.2	47.7	6.70	3.15
Djibouti	28.7	11.3	85.3	53.6	56.0	3.95	1.74
Egypt - Égypte	24.2	5.6	29.3	69.1	73.6	2.89	1.86
Equatorial Guinea - Guinée équatoriale	38.5	14.8	92.3	50.4	52.8	5.36	2.38
Eritrea - Érythrée	39.3	9.2	55.3	55.6	60.3	5.05	3.01
Ethiopia - Éthiopie	38.2	13.0	86.9	51.7	54.3	5.29	2.53
Gabon	25.7	11.7	53.8	56.4	57.1	3.06	1.40
Gambia - Gambie	34.9	10.4	74.2	58.6	60.3	4.70	2.46
Ghana	29.6	9.3	56.6	59.6	60.5	3.84	2.03
Guinea - Guinée	39.8	11.9	102.5	54.4	57.6	5.44	2.79
Guinea-Bissau - Guinée-Bissau	49.6	18.4	112.7	44.9	47.9	7.07	3.11
Kenya	39.2	11.8	64.4	53.0	55.2	4.96	2.75
Lesotho	29.0	19.2	64.6	42.9	42.3	3.37	0.99
Liberia - Libéria	49.6	18.3	132.5	44.8	46.6	6.77	3.13
Libyan Arab Jamahiriya - Jamahiriya arabe libyenne	23.4	4.1	18.0	71.7	76.9	2.72	1.93
Madagascar	36.4	9.7	65.5	57.7	61.3	4.78	2.67
Malawi	40.7	14.8	89.4	48.1	48.4	5.59	2.59
Mali	48.1	14.7	128.5	52.1	56.6	6.52	3.34
Mauritania - Mauritanie	32.5	7.9	63.0	62.4	66.0	4.37	2.46
Mauritius - Maurice[2]	14.9	7.0	14.0	69.5	76.2	1.86	0.78
Morocco - Maroc	20.5	5.8	30.6	69.0	73.4	2.38	1.47
Mozambique	39.5	19.8	95.9	41.7	42.4	5.11	1.97
Namibia - Namibie	25.7	12.4	42.3	52.5	53.1	3.19	1.32
Niger	49.0	13.8	110.8	57.8	56.0	7.19	3.52
Nigeria - Nigéria	39.9	16.8	109.5	46.4	47.3	5.32	2.30
Réunion	18.0	5.3	13.4	72.3	80.5	2.36	1.27
Rwanda	44.5	17.2	112.4	44.6	47.8	5.92	2.73
Sao Tome and Principe - Sao Tomé-et-Principe	32.4	7.5	72.3	63.6	67.4	3.85	2.49
Senegal - Sénégal	35.2	9.0	65.7	61.1	65.1	4.69	2.62
Sierra Leone	46.2	22.1	160.3	41.0	44.2	6.47	2.41
Somalia - Somalie	42.9	16.6	116.3	46.9	49.4	6.04	2.64
South Africa - Afrique du Sud	22.3	17.0	44.8	48.8	49.7	2.64	0.53
Southern Africa - Afrique méridionale	22.9	16.9	46.4	48.5	49.3	2.71	0.60
Sudan - Soudan	31.5	10.1	64.9	57.1	60.1	4.23	2.15
Swaziland	28.5	21.2	71.0	39.8	39.4	3.45	0.73
Togo	36.8	10.1	88.6	56.7	60.1	4.80	2.66
Tunisia - Tunisie	16.7	5.6	19.8	71.9	76.0	1.93	1.12
Uganda - Ouganda	46.6	13.4	76.9	50.8	52.2	6.46	3.32
United Republic of Tanzania - République Unie de Tanzanie	39.0	12.9	72.6	51.4	53.6	5.16	2.62
Western Sahara - Sahara occidental	23.3	5.8	44.2	64.3	68.1	2.70	1.75
Zambia - Zambie	39.3	18.8	92.7	42.1	42.5	5.18	2.04
Zimbabwe	27.9	17.9	58.0	44.1	42.7	3.19	1.00
AMERICA, NORTH — AMERIQUE DU NORD							
Aruba	14.1	7.1	17.0	71.3	77.1	2.04	0.70
Bahamas	16.9	6.1	13.8	70.6	76.3	2.02	1.08

Annex II: United Nations Medium Variant Population Projections - Vital statistics summary and expectation of life at birth: 2005 - 2010

Annexe II: Projections de la population de variante moyenne de l'ONU - Aperçu des statistiques de l'état civil et espérance de vie à la naissance: 2005 - 2010

(continued — suite)

Continent, country or area / Continent, pays ou zone	Crude birth rate — Taux bruts de natalité[1]	Crude death rate — Taux bruts de mortalité[1]	Infant mortality rate — Décès d'enfants de moins d'un an[1]	Expectation of life at birth — Espérance de vie à la naissance[1]		Total fertility rate — Indice synthétique de fécondité[1]	Natural increase — Accroissement naturel[1]
				Male — Masculin	Female — Féminin		
AMERICA, NORTH — AMERIQUE DU NORD							
Barbados - Barbade	11.0	7.0	10.1	74.4	79.8	1.50	0.40
Belize	25.2	3.8	16.4	73.3	79.2	2.94	2.14
Canada	10.3	7.4	4.8	78.3	82.9	1.53	0.29
Costa Rica	17.8	4.1	9.9	76.5	81.2	2.10	1.37
Cuba	10.3	7.6	5.1	76.2	80.4	1.49	0.28
Dominican Republic - République dominicaine	23.5	5.9	29.6	69.3	75.5	2.81	1.75
El Salvador	22.8	5.9	21.5	68.8	74.9	2.68	1.70
Grenada - Grenade	18.0	8.3	33.8	67.0	70.4	2.30	0.97
Guadeloupe	14.8	6.4	6.8	76.0	82.2	2.11	0.84
Guatemala	33.2	5.7	30.1	66.7	73.8	4.15	2.76
Haiti - Haïti	27.9	9.2	48.8	59.1	62.8	3.55	1.87
Honduras	27.9	5.6	28.2	66.9	73.7	3.31	2.23
Jamaica - Jamaïque	19.9	7.1	13.6	70.0	75.2	2.43	1.27
Martinique	12.4	7.6	6.6	76.5	82.3	1.91	0.48
Mexico - Mexique	19.3	4.8	16.7	73.7	78.6	2.21	1.46
Netherlands Antilles - Antilles néerlandaises	12.5	7.9	14.8	71.3	78.8	1.85	0.46
Nicaragua	24.9	4.7	21.5	69.9	76.0	2.76	2.02
Panama	20.8	5.0	18.2	73.0	78.2	2.56	1.58
Puerto Rico - Porto Rico	13.3	7.6	7.2	74.7	82.7	1.83	0.57
Saint Lucia - Sainte-Lucie	19.1	6.6	12.6	71.9	75.6	2.18	1.24
Saint Vincent and the Grenadines - Saint Vincent-et-les Grenadines	20.1	6.8	23.3	69.5	73.8	2.20	1.33
Trinidad and Tobago - Trinité-et-Tobago	14.8	8.1	12.4	67.8	71.8	1.64	0.67
United States - États-Unis	14.0	8.2	6.3	75.6	80.8	2.05	0.58
United States Virgin Islands - Îles Vierges américaines	13.4	6.6	8.6	75.5	83.3	2.15	0.69
AMERICA, SOUTH — AMERIQUE DU SUD							
Argentina - Argentine	17.5	7.7	13.4	71.6	79.1	2.25	0.99
Bolivia - Bolivie	27.3	7.6	45.6	63.4	67.7	3.50	1.98
Brazil - Brésil	19.2	6.3	23.6	68.8	76.1	2.25	1.28
Chile - Chili	15.0	5.4	7.2	75.5	81.5	1.94	0.97
Colombia - Colombie	18.7	5.5	19.1	69.2	76.6	2.22	1.32
Ecuador - Équateur	21.0	5.1	21.1	72.1	78.0	2.58	1.59
French Guiana - Guyane française	23.9	3.7	13.4	72.6	79.9	3.27	2.01
Guyana	17.1	8.4	42.9	64.2	69.9	2.33	0.87
Paraguay	24.8	5.5	32.0	69.7	73.9	3.08	1.93
Peru - Pérou	20.9	6.1	21.2	68.9	74.0	2.51	1.47
Suriname	19.5	6.9	27.7	67.0	73.6	2.42	1.26
Uruguay	15.1	9.2	13.1	72.8	79.9	2.12	0.58
Venezuela (Bolivarian Republic of) - Venezuela (République bolivarienne du)	21.4	5.1	17.0	70.9	76.8	2.55	1.64
ASIA — ASIE							
Afghanistan	48.2	19.9	157.0	43.9	43.8	7.07	2.83
Armenia - Arménie	16.2	7.6	72.3	63.8	71.2	1.82	0.87
Azerbaijan - Azerbaïdjan	17.1	3.2	11.2	74.3	77.5	2.29	1.39
Bahrain - Bahreïn	12.2	7.5	5.9	76.5	81.6	1.61	0.47
Bangladesh	24.8	7.5	52.5	63.2	65.0	2.83	1.73
Bhutan - Bhoutan	18.5	7.2	45.0	64.0	67.5	2.19	1.13
Brunei Darussalam - Brunéi Darussalam ...	26.4	9.0	62.7	57.3	61.9	3.18	1.75
Cambodia - Cambodge	18.7	6.3	26.6	68.7	72.7	2.18	1.24
China - Chine[3]	13.1	7.1	23.0	71.3	74.8	1.73	0.60
China - Hong Kong SAR - Chine - Hong Kong RAS[4]	7.6	5.9	3.7	79.4	85.1	0.97	0.17
China - Macao SAR - Chine - Macao RAS[5]	7.5	4.7	7.0	78.5	82.8	0.91	0.29
Cyprus - Chypre	10.8	11.8	38.7	67.1	74.8	1.41	...
Timor-Leste	18.8	5.1	19.5	72.3	76.2	2.14	1.37
Georgia - Géorgie	31.7	9.1	81.5	57.8	61.5	4.26	2.27
India - Inde	23.0	8.2	55.0	63.2	66.4	2.81	1.48

833

Annex II: United Nations Medium Variant Population Projections - Vital statistics summary and expectation of life at birth: 2005 - 2010

Annexe II: Projections de la population de variante moyenne de l'ONU - Aperçu des statistiques de l'état civil et espérance de vie à la naissance: 2005 - 2010

(continued — suite)

Continent, country or area Continent, pays ou zone	Crude birth rate — Taux bruts de natalité[1]	Crude death rate — Taux bruts de mortalité[1]	Infant mortality rate — Décès d'enfants de moins d'un an[1]	Expectation of life at birth — Espérance de vie à la naissance[1]		Total fertility rate— Indice synthétique de fécondité[1]	Natural increase — Accroissement naturel[1]
				Male — Masculin	Female — Féminin		
ASIA — ASIE							
Indonesia - Indonésie	26.8	7.1	51.4	63.0	65.8	3.21	1.97
Iran (Islamic Republic of) - Iran (République islamique d')	20.3	5.4	30.6	69.4	72.6	2.04	1.49
Iraq	19.7	5.5	4.7	78.6	82.8	2.75	1.42
Israel - Israël	25.9	3.9	19.4	70.8	74.5	3.13	2.20
Japan - Japon	8.3	9.0	3.2	79.0	86.1	1.27	...
Jordan - Jordanie	17.9	1.9	8.1	76.0	79.9	2.18	1.61
Kazakhstan	19.7	10.1	24.1	61.6	72.4	2.31	0.97
Korea (Dem. People's Republic of) - Corée (Rép. populaire dém. de)	13.2	9.9	48.2	65.1	69.3	1.85	0.34
Korea (Republic of) - Corée (République de)	9.3	5.9	4.1	75.0	82.2	1.21	0.35
Kuwait - Koweït	18.2	7.0	22.0	69.9	74.2	2.21	1.11
Kyrgyzstan - Kirghizistan	21.8	8.1	53.1	62.0	69.9	2.48	1.38
Lao People's Democratic Republic - République démocratique populaire lao	20.6	4.5	8.9	72.0	76.7	2.60	1.62
Lebanon - Liban	35.9	3.7	17.5	71.8	75.0	5.09	3.22
Malaysia - Malaisie	18.2	9.7	66.0	59.1	65.3	2.07	0.85
Maldives	23.4	5.7	34.1	67.6	69.5	2.63	1.76
Mongolia - Mongolie	18.4	6.6	39.8	63.9	69.9	1.87	1.18
Myanmar	25.8	4.8	23.1	69.5	73.9	3.23	2.10
Nepal - Népal	28.1	7.7	53.9	63.2	64.2	3.28	2.04
Oman	22.1	2.7	12.3	74.2	77.5	3.00	1.93
Pakistan	15.0	7.2	11.0	68.8	76.2	1.88	0.78
Philippines	8.2	5.3	3.0	78.0	81.9	1.26	0.29
Qatar	16.2	2.4	8.2	75.2	76.4	2.66	1.39
Saudi Arabia - Arabie saoudite	24.9	3.7	18.8	70.9	75.3	3.35	2.12
Singapore - Singapour	14.6	8.5	10.6	66.5	75.0	1.85	0.61
Sri Lanka	27.3	6.4	60.2	64.1	69.4	3.35	2.09
Syrian Arab Republic - République arabe syrienne	26.7	3.4	16.0	72.3	76.1	3.08	2.33
Tajikistan - Tadjikistan	21.8	8.2	74.7	59.0	67.5	2.50	1.36
Thailand - Thaïlande	42.1	8.9	66.7	60.0	61.7	6.53	3.32
Turkey - Turquie	18.4	5.9	27.5	69.4	74.3	2.14	1.25
Turkmenistan - Turkménistan	22.6	6.7	55.0	64.0	70.4	2.49	1.59
United Arab Emirates - Émirats arabes unis	16.2	1.4	8.2	77.2	81.5	2.31	1.48
Uzbekistan - Ouzbékistan	19.7	6.4	27.4	68.0	72.9	2.33	1.32
Viet Nam	23.9	6.0	39.3	67.5	72.0	3.00	1.79
Occupied Palestinian Territory - Territoire palestinien occupé	27.2	7.1	67.5	65.2	65.8	3.52	2.01
Yemen - Yémen	38.3	7.4	58.6	61.1	64.4	5.50	3.09
EUROPE							
Albania - Albanie	16.3	5.9	19.2	73.4	79.7	2.06	1.04
Austria - Autriche	9.2	9.4	4.4	76.9	82.6	1.42	...
Belarus - Bélarus	9.4	14.7	9.4	63.1	75.2	1.20	...
Belgium - Belgique	10.4	10.0	4.2	76.5	82.3	1.65	0.05
Bosnia and Herzegovina - Bosnie-Herzégovine	8.8	9.5	12.0	72.2	77.4	1.23	...
Bulgaria - Bulgarie	8.9	14.8	11.8	69.5	76.7	1.31	...
Channel Islands - Îles Anglo-Normandes	9.4	9.5	5.2	76.6	81.5	1.42	...
Croatia - Croatie	9.0	12.1	6.4	72.3	79.2	1.35	...
Czech Republic - République tchèque	9.2	10.9	3.8	73.4	79.5	1.24	...
Denmark - Danemark	11.2	10.3	4.4	76.0	80.6	1.80	0.09
Estonia - Estonie	10.8	14.3	7.2	65.9	76.8	1.49	...
Finland - Finlande	11.1	9.7	3.7	76.1	82.4	1.83	0.14
France	12.2	8.9	4.2	77.1	84.1	1.89	0.33
Germany - Allemagne	8.2	10.7	4.3	76.5	82.1	1.36	...
Greece - Grèce	9.3	9.9	6.7	77.1	81.9	1.33	...
Hungary - Hongrie	9.3	13.2	6.8	69.2	77.4	1.28	...
Iceland - Islande	14.3	6.2	2.9	80.2	83.3	2.05	0.81
Ireland - Irlande	15.5	7.0	4.9	76.5	81.4	1.96	0.85
Italy - Italie	9.2	10.5	5.0	77.5	83.5	1.38	...

Annex II: United Nations Medium Variant Population Projections - Vital statistics summary and expectation of life at birth: 2005 - 2010

Annexe II: Projections de la population de variante moyenne de l'ONU - Aperçu des statistiques de l'état civil et espérance de vie à la naissance: 2005 - 2010

(continued — suite)

Continent, country or area Continent, pays ou zone	Crude birth rate — Taux bruts de natalité[1]	Crude death rate — Taux bruts de mortalité[1]	Infant mortality rate — Décès d'enfants de moins d'un an[1]	Expectation of life at birth — Espérance de vie à la naissance[1]		Total fertility rate— Indice synthétique de fécondité[1]	Natural increase — Accroissement naturel[1]
				Male — Masculin	Female — Féminin		
EUROPE							
Latvia - Lettonie	9.3	13.6	10.4	67.3	77.7	1.29	...
Lithuania - Lituanie	9.1	12.3	8.5	67.5	78.3	1.26	...
Luxembourg	11.5	8.7	4.5	75.7	81.6	1.66	0.28
Malta - Malte	9.8	8.0	6.5	77.3	81.4	1.37	0.18
Montenegro	13.6	9.6	22.3	72.4	76.8	1.83	0.39
Moldova - Moldova	11.4	12.5	15.8	65.1	72.5	1.40	...
Netherlands - Pays-Bas	11.1	8.6	4.7	77.5	81.9	1.72	0.25
Norway - Norvège	11.9	9.1	3.3	77.8	82.5	1.85	0.28
Poland - Pologne	9.5	10.0	6.7	71.3	79.8	1.23	...
Portugal	10.5	10.6	5.0	75.0	81.2	1.46	...
Romania - Roumanie	9.8	12.4	14.9	69.0	76.1	1.30	...
Russian Federation - Fédération de Russie	10.7	16.2	16.6	59.0	72.6	1.34	...
Serbia - Serbie	12.8	11.6	11.7	71.7	76.3	1.79	0.13
Slovakia - Slovaquie	10.0	10.0	6.9	70.7	78.5	1.25	...
Slovenia - Slovénie	9.0	9.9	4.8	74.1	81.5	1.28	...
Spain - Espagne	10.8	8.8	4.2	77.7	84.2	1.41	0.21
Sweden - Suède	11.3	10.1	3.2	78.7	83.0	1.80	0.12
Switzerland - Suisse	9.2	8.1	4.1	79.0	84.2	1.42	0.11
The Former Yugoslav Rep. of Macedonia - L'ex-République yougoslave de Macédoine	10.9	9.2	14.8	71.8	76.6	1.43	0.17
Ukraine	9.2	16.4	12.8	62.1	73.8	1.22	...
United Kingdom - Royaume-Uni	12.0	9.9	4.8	77.2	81.6	1.82	0.20
OCEANIA — OCEANIE							
Australia - Australie[6]	12.4	7.1	4.4	78.9	83.6	1.79	0.53
Fiji - Fidji	21.1	6.6	19.5	66.6	71.1	2.75	1.45
French Polynesia - Polynésie française	18.3	5.2	8.0	71.7	76.8	2.26	1.31
Guam	18.5	5.5	9.0	73.3	77.9	2.54	1.30
Micronesia, Federated States of - Micronésie, États Fédérés de La	22.0	5.1	24.7	69.9	74.1	2.68	1.68
New Caledonia - Nouvelle-Calédonie	16.4	5.5	6.1	72.8	79.7	2.08	1.08
New Zealand - Nouvelle-Zélande	13.7	7.1	5.0	78.2	82.2	1.99	0.66
Papua New Guinea - Papouasie-Nouvelle-Guinée	29.6	9.6	60.7	54.6	60.4	3.79	2.00
Samoa	24.7	5.4	22.3	68.5	74.9	3.93	1.93
Solomon Islands - Îles Salomon	30.5	7.2	54.5	62.7	64.5	3.87	2.32
Tonga	25.6	5.7	18.6	72.3	74.3	3.83	1.99
Vanuatu	28.8	5.0	28.3	68.3	72.1	3.74	2.37

FOOTNOTES - NOTES

[1] All data are medium variant projections, produced by the United Nations, Department of Economic and Social Affairs, Population Division (2007) and published in *World Population Prospects: The 2006 Revision. CD-ROM Edition - Extended Dataset in Excel and ASCII formats* (United Nations publication, Sales No. E.07.XIII.7). — Toutes ces données sont des projections de la population au milieu de l'année de variante moyenne; elles sont produites par Les Nations Unies, Département des Affaires Sociales et Économiques, ont été publiées dans *World Population Prospects: The 2006 Revision. CD-ROM Edition - Extended Dataset in Excel and ASCII formats* (United Nations publication, Sales No. E.07.XIII.7).

[2] Including Agalega, Rodrigues and Saint Brandon. — Y compris Agalega, Rodrigues et Saint Brandon.

[3] For statistical purposes, the data for China do not include Hong Kong and Macao Special Administrative Regions (SAR) of China. — A des fins statistiques, les données pour la Chine ne comprennent pas les Régions Administratives Spéciales (SAR) de Hong Kong et Macao.

[4] As of 1 July 1997, Hong Kong became a Special Administrative Region (SAR) of China. — A partir du 1 juillet 1997, Hong Kong est devenue une Région Administrative Spéciale (SAR) de la Chine.

[5] As of 20 December 1999, Macao became a Special Administrative Region (SAR) of China. — A partir du 20 décembre 1999, Macao est devenue une Région Administrative Spéciale (SAR) de la Chine.

[6] Including Christmas Island, Cocos (Keeling) Islands and Norfolk Island. — Y compris Christmas Island, Cocos (Keeling) Islands et Norfolk Island.

Subject-matter	Year of issue	Time coverage	Subject-matter	Year of issue	Time coverage
	1993	1989-93		1998-99	Latest
	1994	1990-94		1999CD[iv]	1990-98
	1995	1991-95		2000-2006	Latest
	1996	1992-96	- by age of mother and birth order	1949/50	1936-47
	1997	1993-97		1954	Latest
	1997HS[iii]	1948-97		1959	1949-58
	1998	1994-98		1965	1955-64
	1999	1995-99		1969	1963-68
	1999CD[iv]	1980-99		1975	1966-74
	2000	1996-00		1981	1972-80
	2001	1997-01		1986	1977-85
	2002	1998-02		1999CD[iv]	1990-98
	2003	1999-03	- by age of mother and sex	1965-1968	Latest
	2004	2000-04		1969	1963-68
	2005	2001-05		1970-1974	Latest
	2006	2002-06		1975	1966-74
				1976-1978	Latest
- by age of father	1949/50	1942-49		1978HS[ii]	1948-77
	1954	1936-53		1979-1980	Latest
	1959	1949-58		1981	1972-80
	1965	1955-64		1982-1985	Latest
	1969	1963-68		1986	1977-85
	1975	1966-74		1987-1991	Latest
	1981	1972-80		1992	1983-92
	1999CD[iv]	1990-98		1993-1997	Latest
				1997HS[iii]	1948-96
- by age of mother	1948	1936-47		1998-99	Latest
	1949/50	1936-49		1999CD[iv]	1990-98
	1954	1936-53		2000-2006	Latest
	1955-1956	Latest			
	1958	Latest	- by age of mother and urban/rural residence (see: by urban/rural residence, below)		
	1959	1949-58			
	1960-1964	Latest			
	1965	1955-64			
	1966-1968	Latest	- by birth order	1948	1936-47
	1969	1963-68		1949/50	1936-49
	1970-1974	Latest		1954	1936-53
	1975	1966-74		1955	Latest
	1976-1978	Latest		1959	1949-58
	1978HS[ii]	1948-77		1965	1955-64
	1979-1980	Latest		1969	1963-68
	1981	1972-80		1975	1966-74
	1982-1985	Latest		1981	1972-80
	1986	1977-85		1986	1977-85
	1987-1991	Latest			
	1992	1983-92			
	1993-1997	Latest			
	1997HS[iii] [3]	1948-96			

Subject-matter	Year of issue	Time coverage	Subject-matter	Year of issue	Time coverage
	1976-1980	Latest		1954	1936-53
	1981	1972-80		1959	1949-58
	1982-1985	Latest		1965	1955-64
	1986	1977-85		1969	1963-68
	1987-1991	Latest		1975	1966-74
	1992	1983-92		1981	1972-80
	1993-1997	Latest		1986	1977-85
	1997HS[iii]	1948-96		1999CD[iv]	1990-98
	1998-1999	Latest			
	1999CD[iv]	1990-98	**Birth rates**	1948	1932-47
	2000-2006	Latest		1949/50	1932-49
				1951	1905-30[v]
- illegitimate	1959	1949-58			1930-50
	1965	1955-64		1952	1920-34[v]
	1969	1963-68			1934-51
	1975	1966-74		1953	1920-39[v]
	1981	1972-80			1940-52
	1986	1977-85		1954	1920-39[v]
	1999CD[iv]	1990-98			1939-53
				1955	1920-34[v]
- legitimate	1948	1936-47			1946-54
	1949/50	1936-49		1956	1947-55
	1954	1936-53		1957	1948-56
	1959	1949-58		1958	1948-57
	1965	1955-64		1959	1920-54[v]
	1969	1963-68			1953-58
	1975	1966-74		1960	1950-59
	1981	1972-80		1961	1945-59[v]
	1986	1977-85			1952-61
	1999CD[iv]	1990-98		1962	1945-54[v]
- legitimate, by age of father	1959	1949-58			1952-62
	1965	1955-64		1963	1945-59[v]
	1969	1963-68			1954-63
	1975	1966-74		1964	1960-64
	1981	1972-80		1965	1920-64[v]
	1986	1977-85			1950-65
- legitimate, by age of mother	1954	1936-53		1966	1950-64[v]
	1959	1949-58			1957-66
	1965	1955-64		1967	1963-67
	1969	1963-68		1968	1964-68
	1975	1966-74		1969	1925-69[v]
	1981	1972-80			1954-69
	1986	1977-85		1970	1966-70
- legitimate, by duration of marriage	1948	1936-47		1971	1967-71
	1949/50	1936-49		1972	1968-72
				1973	1969-73
				1974	1970-74
				1975	1956-75
				1976	1972-76
				1977	1973-77

Index
Historical index
(See notes at end of index)

Subject-matter	Year of issue	Time coverage
	1974	1965-73
	1975-1979	Latest
	1978HS[ii]	1948-77
	1980	1971-79
	1981-1984	Latest
	1985	1976-84
	1986-1991	Latest
	1991PA[vii]	1950-1990
	1992	1983-1992
	1993-1995	Latest
	1996	1987-95
	1997	Latest
	1997HS[iii]	1948-96
	1998-2006	Latest
- by age and sex and urban/rural residence	1967	Latest
	1972	Latest
	1974	1965-73
	1975-1979	Latest
	1980	1971-79
	1981-1984	Latest
	1985	1976-84
	1986-1991	Latest
	1991PA[vii]	1950-1990
	1992	1983-1992
	1993-1995	Latest
	1996	1987-95
	1997	Latest
	1997HS[iii]	1948-96
	1998-2006	Latest
- by cause	1951	1947-49
	1952	1947-51[vi]
	1953	1947-52
	1954	1945-53
	1955-1956	Latest
	1957	1952-56
	1958-1960	Latest
	1961	1955-60
	1962-1965	Latest
	1966	1960-65
	1967-1973	Latest
	1974	1965-73
	1975-1979	Latest
	1980	1971-79
	1981-1984	Latest
	1985	1976-84
	1986-1991	Latest
	1991PA[vii]	1960-90
	1992-1995	Latest
	1996	1987-95
	1997-2000	Latest
	2002	1995-02

Subject-matter	Year of issue	Time coverage
	2004	1995-04
	2006	2002-06
- by cause, age and sex	1957	Latest
	1961	Latest
	1991PA[vii]	1960-90
- by cause and sex	1967	Latest
	1974	Latest
	1980	Latest
	1985	Latest
	1996	Latest
	2006	2002-06
- by marital status, age and sex	1961	Latest
	1967	Latest
	1974	Latest
	1980	Latest
	1985	Latest
	1996	Latest
- by occupation, age and sex	1957	Latest
- by occupation and age, males	1961	Latest
	1967	Latest
- by urban/rural residence	1967	Latest
	1968	1964-68
	1969	1965-69
	1970	1966-70
	1971	1967-71
	1972	1968-72
	1973	1969-73
	1974	1965-74
	1975	1971-75
	1976	1972-76
	1977	1973-77
	1978	1974-78
	1979	1975-79
	1980	1971-80
	1981	1977-81
	1982	1978-82
	1983	1979-83
	1984	1980-84
	1985	1976-85
	1986	1982-86
	1987	1983-87
	1988	1984-88
	1989	1985-89
	1990	1986-90
	1991	1987-91
	1992	1983-92
	1993	1989-93

Index
Historical index

Subject-matter	Year of issue	Time coverage	Subject-matter	Year of issue	Time coverage
	1958	1948-57	- by age of mother	1954	1936-53
	1959	1949-58		1959	1949-58
	1960	1950-59		1965	1955-64
	1961	1952-60		1969	1963-68
	1962	1953-61		1975	1966-74
	1963	1953-62		1981	1972-80
	1964	1959-63		1986	1977-85
	1965	1955-64	- by age of mother		
	1966	1947-65	and birth order	1954	Latest
	1967	1962-66		1959	1949-58
	1968	1963-67		1965	3-Latest
	1969	1959-68		1969	1963-68
	1970	1965-69		1975	1966-74
	1971	1966-70		1981	1972-80
	1972	1967-71		1986	1977-85
	1973	1968-72	- by period of		
	1974	1965-73	gestation	1957	1950-56
	1975	1966-74		1959	1949-58
	1976	1971-75		1961	1952-60
	1977	1972-76		1965	5-Latest
	1978	1973-77		1966	1956-65
	1979	1974-78		1967-1968	Latest
	1980	1971-79		1969	1963-68
	1981	1972-80		1974	1965-73
	1982	1977-81		1975	1966-74
	1983	1978-82		1980	1971-79
	1984	1979-83		1981	1972-80
	1985	1975-84		1985	1976-84
	1986	1977-85		1986	1977-85
	1987	1982-86		1996	1987-95
	1988	1983-87			
	1989	1984-88	- by sex	1961	1952-60
	1990	1985-89		1965	5 Latest
	1991	1986-90		1969	1963-68
	1992	1987-91		1975	1966-74
	1993	1988-92		1981	1972-80
	1994	1989-93		1986	1977-85
	1995	1990-94	- by urban/rural		
	1996	1987-95	residence	1971	1966-70
	1997	1992-96		1972	1967-71
	1998	1993-97		1973	1968-72
	1999	1994-98		1974	1965-73
	1999CD[iv]	1990-98		1975	1966-74
	2000	1995-99		1976	1971-75
	2001	1997-01		1977	1972-76
	2002	1998-02		1978	1973-77
	2003	1999-03		1979	1974-78
	2004	2000-04		1980	1971-79
	2005	2001-05		1981	1972 80
	2006	2002-06		1982	1977-81
				1983	1978-82
				1984	1979-83
				1985	1975-84
				1986	1977-85

Subject-matter	Year of issue	Time coverage	Subject-matter	Year of issue	Time coverage
	1987	1982-86	**Foetal Death Ratios**		
	1988	1983-87	- by period of		
	1989	1984-88	gestation	1957	1950-56
	1990	1985-89		1959	1949-58
	1991	1986-90		1961	1952-60
	1992	1987-91		1965	5-Latest
	1993	1988-92		1966	1956-65
	1994	1989-93		1967-1968	Latest
	1995	1990-94		1969	1963-68
	1996	1987-95		1974	1965-73
	1997	1992-96		1975	1966-74
	1998	1993-97		1980	1971-79
	1999	1994-98		1981	1972-80
	1999CD[iv]	1990-98		1985	1976-84
	2000	1995-99		1986	1977-85
	2001	1997-01		1996	1987-95
	2002	1998-02		1999CD[iv]	1990-98
	2003	1999-03			
	2004	2000-04	**Foetal death ratios, late**	1951	1935-50
	2005	2001-05		1952	1935-51
	2006	2002-06		1953	1936-52
- illegitimate	1961	1952-60		1954	1938-53
	1965	5-Latest		1955	1946-54
	1969	1963-68		1956	1947-55
	1975	1966-74		1957	1948-56
	1981	1972-80		1958	1948-57
	1986	1977-85		1959	1920-54[v]
					1953-58
- illegitimate,				1960	1950-59
percent	1961	1952-60		1961	1945-49[v]
	1965	5-Latest			1952-60
	1969	1963-68		1962	1945-54[v]
	1975	1966-74			1952-61
	1981	1972-80		1963	1945-59[v]
	1986	1977-85			1953-62
				1964	1959-63
- legitimate	1959	1949-58		1965	1950-64[v]
	1965	1955-64			1955-64
	1969	1963-68		1966	1950-64[v]
	1975	1966-74			1956-65
	1981	1972-80		1967	1962-66
	1986	1977-85		1968	1963-67
- legitimate by age				1969	1950-64[v]
of mother	1959	1949-58			1959-68
	1965	1955-64		1970	1965-69
	1969	1963-68		1971	1966-70
	1975	1966-74		1972	1967-71
	1981	1972-80		1973	1968-72
	1986	1977-85		1974	1965-73
	1996	1987-95		1975	1966-74

Subject matter	Year of issue	Time coverage	Subject-matter	Year of issue	Time coverage
	1977	1973-77	residence		
	1978	1974-78		1974	1965-73
	1978HS[ii]	1948-78		1975-1979	Latest
	1979	1975-79		1980	1971-79
	1980	1971-80		1981-1984	Latest
	1981	1977-81		1985	1976-84
	1982	1978-82		1986-1991	Latest
	1983	1979-83		1992	1983-92
	1984	1980-84		1993-1995	Latest
	1985	1976-85		1996	1987-95
	1986	1982-86		1997-1999	Latest
	1987	1983-87			
	1988	1984-88	- by month	1967	1962-66
	1989	1985-89		1974	1965-73
	1990	1986-90		1980	1971-79
	1991	1987-91		1985	1976-84
	1992	1983-92			
	1993	1989-93	- by urban/rural residence	1967	Latest
	1994	1990-94		1968	1964-68
	1995	1991-95		1969	1965-69
	1996	1987-96		1970	1966-70
	1997	1993-97		1971	1967-71
	1997HS[iii]	1948-97		1972	1968-72
	1998	1994-98		1973	1969-73
	1999	1995-99		1974	1965-74
	2000	1996-00		1975	1971-75
	2001	1997-01		1976	1972-76
	2002	1998-02		1977	1973-77
	2003	1999-03		1978	1974-78
	2004	2000-04		1979	1975-79
	2005	2001-05		1980	1971-80
	2006	2002-06		1981	1977-81
				1982	1978-82
- by age and sex	1948	1936-47		1983	1979-83
	1951	1936-49		1984	1980-84
	1957	1948-56		1985	1976-85
	1961	1952-60		1986	1982-86
	1962-1965	Latest		1987	1983-87
	1966	1956-65		1988	1984-88
	1967-1973	Latest		1989	1985-89
	1974	1965-73		1990	1986-90
	1975-1979	Latest		1991	1987-91
	1980	1971-79		1992	1983-92
	1981-1984	Latest		1993	1989-93
	1985	1976-84		1994	1990-94
	1986-1991	Latest		1995	1991-95
	1992	1983-92		1996	1987-96
	1993-1995	Latest		1997	1993-97
	1996	1987-95		1998	1994-98
	1997-2004	Latest		1999	1995-99
	2005	1996-05		2000	1996-00
	2006	2002-06		2001	1997-01
				2002	1998-02
- by age and sex and urban/rural	1967-1973	Latest		2003	1999-03
				2004	2000-04

Index
Historical index
(See notes at end of index)

Subject-matter	Year of issue	Time coverage	Subject-matter	Year of issue	Time coverage
	2005	2001-05		1991	1987-91
	2006	2002-06		1992	1983-92
				1993	1989-93
Infant mortality rates	1948	1932-47		1994	1990-94
	1949/50	1932-49		1995	1991-95
	1951	1930-50		1996	1987-96
	1952	1920-34ᵛ		1997	1993-97
		1934-51		1997HSⁱⁱⁱ	1948-97
	1953	1920-39ᵛ		1998	1994-98
		1940-52		1999	1995-99
	1954	1920-39ᵛ		2000	1996-00
		1946-53		2001	1997-01
	1955	1920-34ᵛ		2002	1998-02
		1946-54		2003	1999-03
	1956	1947-55		2004	2000-04
	1957	1948-56		2005	2001-05
	1958	1948-57		2006	2002-06
	1959	1949-58			
	1960	1950-59	- by age and sex	1948	1936-47
	1961	1945-59ᵛ		1951	1936-49
		1952-61		1957	1948-56
	1962	1945-54ᵛ		1961	1952-60
		1952-62		1966	1956-65
	1963	1945-59ᵛ		1967	1962-66
	1963	1954-63		1971-1973	Latest
	1964	1960-64		1974	1965-73
	1965	1961-65		1975-1979	Latest
	1966	1920-64ᵛ		1980	1971-79
		1951-66		1981-1984	Latest
	1967	1963-67		1985	1976-84
	1968	1964-68		1986-1991	Latest
	1969	1965-69		1992	1983-92
	1970	1966-70		1993-1995	Latest
	1971	1967-71		1996	1987-95
	1972	1968-72		1997-2006	Latest
	1973	1969-73	- by age and sex		
	1974	1965-74	and urban/rural		
	1975	1971-75	residence	1971-1973	Latest
	1976	1972-76		1974	1965-73
	1977	1973-77		1975-1979	Latest
	1978	1974-78		1980	1971-79
	1978HSⁱⁱ	1948-78		1981-1984	Latest
	1979	1975-79		1985	1976-84
	1980	1971-80		1986-1991	Latest
	1981	1977-81		1992	1983-92
	1982	1978-82		1993-1995	Latest
	1983	1979-83		1996	1987-95
	1984	1980-84		1997-1999	Latest
	1985	1976-85	- by urban/rural		
	1986	1982-86	residence	1967	Latest
	1987	1983-87		1968	1964-68
	1988	1984-88		1969	1965-69
	1989	1985-89		1970	1966-70
	1990	1986-90		1971	1967-71
				1972	1968-72

857

Subject-matter	Year of issue	Time coverage	Subject-matter	Year of issue	Time coverage
specified ages, by sex				1967	1963-67
	1951	1891-1950		1968	1949-68
	1952	1891-1951[vi]		1969	1965-69
	1953	1891-1952		1970	1966-70
	1954	1891-1953[vi]		1971	1967-71
	1957	1900-56		1972	1968-72
	1961	1940-60		1973	1969-73
	1966	2-Latest		1974	1970-74
	1974	2-Latest		1975	1971-75
	1980	2-Latest		1976	1957-76
	1985	2-Latest		1977	1973-77
	1996	2-Latest		1978	1974-78
- survivors at specified ages, by sex				1979	1975-79
				1980	1976-80
	1948	1891-1945		1981	1977-81
	1951	1891-1950		1982	1963-82
	1952	1891-1951[vi]		1983	1979-83
	1953	1891-1952		1984	1980-84
	1954	1891-1953[vi]		1985	1981-85
	1957	1900-56		1986	1982-86
	1961	1940-60		1987	1983-87
	1966	2-Latest		1988	1984-88
	1974	2-Latest		1989	1985-89
	1980	2-Latest		1990	1971-90
	1985	2-Latest		1991	1987-91
	1996	2-Latest		1992	1988-92
				1993	1989-93
Literacy (see: Population)				1994	1990-94
				1995	1991-95
Localities (see: Population)				1996	1992-96
				1997	1993-97
M				1998	1994-98
				1999	1995-99
Major civil divisions (see: Population)				2000	1996-00
				2001	1997-01
				2002	1998-02
Marriages	1948	1932-47		2003	1999-03
	1949/50	1934-49		2004	2000-04
	1951	1935-50		2005	2001-05
	1952	1936-51		2006	2002-06
	1953	1950-52			
	1954	1946-53	- by age of bride	1948	1936-47
	1955	1946-54		1949/50	1936-49
	1956	1947-55		1958	1948-57
	1957	1948-56		1959-1967	Latest
	1958	1940-57		1968	1958-67
	1959	1949-58		1969-1975	Latest
	1960	1950-59		1976	1966-75
	1961	1952-61		1977-1981	Latest
	1962	1953-62		1982	1972-81
	1963	1954-63		1983-1986	Latest
	1964	1960-64		1987	1975-86
	1965	1956-65		1988-1989	Latest
	1966	1962-66		1990	1980-1989

Index
Historical index
(See notes at end of index)

Subject-matter	Year of issue	Time coverage
	1966	1960-65
	1970	1962-69
	1977	1967-76
	1989	1975-88
by country or area of intended residence	1948	1945-47
	1949/50	1945-48
	1951	1948-50
	1952	1949-51
	1954	1950-53
	1957	1953-56
	1959	1956-58
	1977	1958-76
	1989	1975-88
- immigrants, long term		
by age and sex	1948	1945-47
	1949/50	1946-48
	1951	1948-50
	1952	1949-51
	1954	1950-53
	1957	1953-56
	1959	1955-58
	1962	1958-61
	1966	1960-65
	1970	1962-69
	1977	1967-76
	1989	1975-88
by country or area of last residence	1948	1945-47
	1949/50	1945-48
	1951	1948-50
	1952	1949-51
	1954	1950-53
	1957	1953-56
	1959	1956-58
	1977	1958-76
	1989	1975-88
	1948	1945-47
	1949/50	1945-48
- refugees, by country or area of destination:		
repatriated by the International Refugee Organization	1952	1947-51
resettled by the International Refugee	1952	1947-51

Subject-matter	Year of issue	Time coverage
Organization		
Mortality [see: Death(s), Death rates, infant deaths, infant mortality rates, Foetal death(s), Foetal death ratios, Life tables, Maternal deaths, Maternal mortality rates, Neonatal deaths, Neo-natal mortality rates, Perinatal mortality, Post-neo-natal deaths, Post-neo-natal mortality rates]		
N		
Natality (see: Births and Birthrates)		
Natural increase rates	1958-1978	Latest
	1978HS[ii]	1948-78
	1979-1997	Latest
	1998	1995-98
	1999	1996-99
	2000	1995-00
	2001-2005	2000-05
	2006	2005-10
Neo-natal mortality		
- by sex	1948	1936-47
	1951	1936-50
	1957	1948-56
	1961	1952-60
	1963-1965	Latest
	1966	1961-65
	1967	1962-66
	2000-2004	Latest
- by sex and urban/rural residence	1968-1973	Latest
	1974	1965-73
	1975-1979	Latest
	1980	1971-79
	1981-1984	Latest
	1985	1976-84
	1986-1991	Latest
	1992	1983-92
	1993-1995	Latest
	1996	1987-95
	1997	Latest
	1997HS[iii]	1948-96
	1998-1999	Latest
Neo-natal mortality rates		
- by sex	1948	1936-47
	1951	1936-50

864

Subject-matter	Year of issue	Time coverage	Subject-matter	Year of issue	Time coverage
	1989	1980-88[vi]		1993	1985-93
- by citizenship	1956	1945-55	- by literacy, age and sex (see also: illiteracy, below)	1948	Latest
	1963	1955-63		1955	1945-54
	1964	1955-64[vi]		1963	1955-63
	1971	1962-71		1964	1955-64[vi]
	1973	1965-73[vi]		1971	1962-71
- by citizenship, sex and age	1977	Latest	- by literacy, age and sex and urban/rural residence		
	1983	1974-83			
	1989	Latest		1973	1965-73[vi]
- by ethnic composition and sex				1979	1970-79[vi]
	1956	1945-55		1983	1974-83
	1963	1955-63		1988	1980-88[vi]
	1964	1955-64[vi]		1993	1985-93
	1971	1962-71	- by localities of: 100000+ inhabitants		
	1973	1965-73[vi]		1948	Latest
	1979	1970-79[vi]		1952	Latest
	1983	1974-83		1955	1945-54
	1988	1980-88[vi]		1960	1920-61
	1993	1985-93		1962	1955-62
- by households, number and size (see also: Households)				1963	1955-63[vi]
				1970	1950-70
	1955	1945-54		1971	1962-71
	1962	1955-62		1973	1965-73[vi]
	1963	1955-63[vi]		1979	1970-79[vi]
	1968	Latest		1983	1974-83
	1971	1962-71		1988	1980-88[vi]
	1973	1965-73[vi]		1993	1985-93
	1976	Latest	20000+ inhabitants	1948	Latest
	1982	Latest		1952	Latest
	1987	1975-86		1955	1945-54
	1990	1980-89		1960	1920-61
	1995	1985-95		1962	1955-62
- by language and sex	1956	1945-55		1963	1955-63[vi]
	1963	1955-63		1970	1950-70
	1964	1955-64[vi]		1971	1962-71
	1971	1962-71		1973	1965-73[vi]
	1973	1965-73[vi]		1979	1970-79[vi]
	1979	1970-79[vi]		1983	1974-83
	1983	1974-83		1988	1980-88[vi]
	1988	1980-88[vi]		1993	1985-93
	1993	1985-93	- by locality size-classes and sex		
- by level of education, age and sex				1948	Latest
	1956	1945-55		1952	Latest
	1963	1955-63		1955	1945-54
	1964	1955-64[vi]		1962	1955-62
	1971	1962-71		1963	1955-63[vi]
	1973	1965-73[vi]		1971	1962-71
	1979	1970-79[vi]		1973	1965-73[vi]
	1983	1974-83		1979	1970-79[vi]
	1988	1980-88[vi]		1983	1974-83

Subject-matter	Year of issue	Time coverage	Subject-matter	Year of issue	Time coverage
cities, below)				1964	1955-64
				1972	1962-72
- civil division (see: by major civil divisions, above)			by industry, status and sex and urban/rural residence		
				1973	1965-73[vi]
- density (see: Density)				1979	1970-79[vi]
				1984	1974-84
- Disabled	1991PA[vii]	Latest		1988	1980-88[vi]
- economically active:				1994	1985-94
by age and sex	1945	1945-54	by living arrangements, age, sex and urban/rural residence		
	1956	1945-55			
	1964	1955-64		1987	1975-86
	1972	1962-72		1995	1985-95
by age and sex and urban/rural residence			by occupation, age and sex		
	1973	1965-73[vi]		1956	1945-55
	1979	1970-79[vi]		1964	1955-64
	1984	1974-84		1972	1962-72
	1988	1980-88[vi]	by occupation, age and sex and urban/rural residence		
	1994	1985-94			
by age and sex, per cent	1949/50	1930-48			
	1954	Latest		1973	1965-73[vi]
	1955	1945-54		1979	1970-79[vi]
	1956	1945-55		1984	1974-84
	1964	1955-64		1988	1980-88[vi]
	1972	1962-72		1994	1985-94
by age and sex, per cent and urban/rural residence			by occupation, status and sex		
	1973	1965-73[vi]		1956	1945-55
	1979	1970-79[vi]		1964	1955-64
	1984	1974-84		1972	1962-72
	1988	1980-88[vi]	by occupation, status and sex and urban/rural residence		
	1994	1985-94			
by industry, age and sex	1956	1945-55			
	1964	1955-64		1973	1965-73[vi]
	1972	1962-72		1979	1970-7vi[vi]
by industry, age, sex and urban/rural residence				1984	1974-84
				1988	1980-88[vi]
	1973	1965-74[vi]		1994	1985-94
	1979	1970-79[vi]			
	1984	1974-84	by sex	1948	Latest
	1988	1980-88[vi]		1949/50	1926-48
	1994	1985-94		1955	1945-54
by industry, status and sex				1956	1945-55
	1948	Latest		1960	1920-60
	1949/50	Latest		1963	1955-63
	1955	1945-54		1964	1955-64

Index
Historical index
(See notes at end of index)

Subject-matter	Year of issue	Time coverage
	1967	1960-67
		1963-67
	1968	1960-68
		1963-68
	1969	1960-69
		1963-69
	1970	1963-70
		1965-70
	1971	1963-71
		1965-71
	1972	1963-72
		1965-72
	1973	1965-73
		1970-73
	1974	1965-74
		1970-74
	1975	1965-75
		1970-75
	1976	1965-76
		1970-76
	1977	1965-77
		1970-77
	1978-1979	1970-75
	1980-1983	1975-80
	1984-1986	1980-85
	1987-1992	1985-90
	1993-1997	1990-95
	1998-2000	1995-00
	2001-2005	2000-05
	2006	2005-10
- Homeless by age and sex	1991PA[vii]	Latest
- illiteracy rates by sex	1948	Latest
	1955	1945-54
	1960	1920-60
	1963	1955-63[vi]
	1964	1955-64[vi]
	1970	1950-70
- illiteracy rates by sex and urban/rural residence	1973	1965-73
	1979	1970-79[vi]
	1983	1974-83
	1988	1980-88[vi]
	1993	1985-93
- Illiterate, by sex	1948	Latest
	1955	1945-54
	1960	1920-60
	1963	1955-63
	1964	1955-64
	1970	1950-70
- illiterate, by sex	1948	Latest

Subject-matter	Year of issue	Time coverage
and age		
	1955	1945-54
	1963	1955-63
	1964	1955-64[vi]
	1970	1950-70
- illiterate, by sex and age and urban/rural residence	1973	1965-73
	1979	1970-79[vi]
	1983	1974-83
	1988	1980-88[vi]
	1993	1985-93
- illiterate, by sex and urban/rural residence	1973	1965-73
	1979	1970-79[vi]
	1983	1974-83
	1988	1980-88[vi]
	1993	1985-93
- in collective living quarters and homeless	1991PA[vii]	Latest
- in households (see: by household type, above, also: Households)		
- in localities (see: by localities and by locality size-classes, above)		
- increase rates (see: growth rates, above)		
- literacy rates: by sex (see also: illiteracy rates, above)	1955	1945-54
- literacy rates, by sex and age	1955	1945-54
- literate, by sex and age (see also: illiterate, above)	1948	Latest
	1955	1945-54
	1963	1955-63
	1964	1955-64[vi]
- literate, by sex and age by urban/rural residence	1971	1962-71
	1973	1965-73[vi]
	1979	1970-74[vi]

Subject-matter	Year of issue	Time coverage	Subject-matter	Year of issue	Time coverage
	1971	1962-71		1965	1930-65
	1972	1963-72		1966	1930-66
	1973	1964-73		1967	1930-67
	1974	1965-74		1968	1930-68
	1975	1966-75		1969	1930-69
	1976	1967-76		1970	1950-70
	1977	1968-77		1971	1950-71
	1978	1969-78		1972	1950-72
	1978HS[ii]	1948-78		1973	1950-73
	1979	1970-79		1974	1950-74
	1980	1971-80		1975	1950-75
	1981	1972-81		1976	1950-76
	1982	1973-82		1977	1950-77
	1983	1974-83		1978	1950-78
	1984	1975-84		1979	1950-79
	1985	1976-85		1980	1950-80
	1986	1977-86		1981	1950-81
	1987	1978-87		1982	1950-82
	1988	1979-88		1983	1950-83
	1989	1980-89		1984	1950-84
	1990	1981-90		1985	1950-85
	1991	1982-91		1986	1950-86
	1992	1983-92		1987	1950-87
	1993	1984-93		1988	1950-88
	1994	1985-94		1989	1950-89
	1995	1986-95		1990	1950-90
	1996	1987-96		1991	1950-91
	1997	1988-97		1992	1950-92
	1997HS[iii]	1948-97		1993	1950-93
	1998	1989-98		1994	1950-94
	1999	1990-99		1995	1950-95
	2000	1991-00		1996	1950-96
	2001	1992-01		1997	1950-97
	2002	1993-02		1998-1999	1950-00
	2003	1994-03		2000	1950-00
	2004	1995-04		2001	1950-01
	2005	1996-05		2002	1950-02
	2006	1997-06		2003	1950-03
				2004	1950-04
- of major regions	1949/50	1920-49		2005	1950-05
	1951	1950		2006	1950-06
	1952	1920-51			
	1953	1920-52	- of regions	1949/50	1920-49
	1954	1920-53		1952	1920-51
	1955	1920-54		1953	1920-52
	1956	1920-55		1954	1920-53
	1957	1920-56		1955	1920-54
	1958	1920-57		1956	1920-55
	1959	1920-58		1957	1920-56
	1960	1920-59		1958	1920-57
	1961	1920-60		1959	1920-58
	1962	1920-61		1960	1920-59
	1963	1930-62		1961	1920-60
	1964	1930-63		1962	1920-61

Subject-matter	Year of issue	Time coverage	Subject-matter	Year of issue	Time coverage
numbers	1960	1920-60		1974-1978	Latest
	1970	1950-70		1978HS[ii]	1948-77
percent	1949/50	1926-48		1979-1996	Latest
	1960	1920-60		1979-1997	Latest
	1970	1950-70		1997HS[iii]	1948-96
- urban/rural residence	1968	1964-68		1998-2006	Latest
	1969	1965-69	estimated	1963	Latest
	1970	1950-70		1967	Latest
	1971	1962-71		1970	1950-70
	1972	1968-72		1971-1997	Latest
	1973	1965-73		1997HS[iii]	1948-96
	1974	1966-74		1998-05	Latest
	1975	1967-75	by country or area of birth and sex	1971	1962-71
	1976	1967-76		1973	1965-73[vi]
	1977	1968-77	by country or area of birth and sex and age	1977	Latest
	1978	1969-78			
	1979	1970-79			
	1980	1971-80			
	1981	1972-81	by citizenship and sex	1971	1962-71
	1982	1973-82		1973	1965-73[vi]
	1983	1974-83	by citizenship and sex and age	1977	Latest
	1984	1975-84		1983	1974-83
	1985	1976-85		1989	1980-88
	1986	1977-86			
	1987	1978-87	by ethnic composition and sex	1971	Latest
	1988	1979-88		1973	1965-73[vi]
	1989	1980-89		1979	1970-79[vi]
	1990	1981-90		1983	1974-83
	1991	1982-91		1988	1980-88[vi]
	1992	1983-92		1993	1985-93
	1993	1984-93	by households, number and size (see also: Households)	1968	Latest
	1994	1985-94		1971	1962-71
	1995	1986-95		1973	1965-73[vi]
	1996	1987-96		1976	Latest
	1997	1988-97		1982	Latest
	1998	1989-98		1987	1975-86
	1999	1990-99		1990	1980-89
	2000	1991-00		1995	1985-95
	2001	1992-01	by language and sex	1971	1962-71
	2002	1993-02			
	2003	1994-03		1973	1965-73[vi]
	2004	1995-04		1979	1970-79[vi]
	2005	1996-05		1983	1974-83
	2006	1997-06		1988	1980-88[vi]
				1993	1985-93
by age and sex: enumerated	1963	1955-63	by level of education,	1971	1962-71
	1964	1955-64[vi]			
	1967	Latest			
	1970	1950-70			
	1971	1962-71			
	1972	Latest			
	1973	1965-73			

Subject-matter	Year of issue	Time coverage	Subject-matter	Year of issue	Time coverage
age and sex				1977	1968-77
	1973	1965-73[vi]		1978	1969-78
	1979	1970-79[vi]		1979	1970-79
	1983	1974-83		1980	1971-80
	1988	1980-88[vi]		1981	1972-81
	1993	1985-93		1982	1973-82
by literacy,				1983	1974-83
age and sex	1971	1962-71		1984	1975-84
	1973	1965-73[vi]		1985	1976-85
	1979	1970-79[vi]		1986	1977-86
	1983	1974-83		1987	1978-87
	1988	1980-88[vi]		1988	1979-88
	1993	1985-93		1989	1980-89
by major civil				1990	1981-90
divisions	1971	1962-71		1991	1982-91
	1973	1965-73[vi]		1992	1983-92
	1979	1970-79[vi]		1993	1984-93
	1983	1974-83		1994	1985-94
	1988	1980-88[vi]		1995	1986-95
	1993	1985-93		1996	1987-96
by marital				1997	1988-97
status, age				1998	1989-98
and sex	1971	1962-71		1999	1990-99
	1973	1965-73[vi]		2000	1991-00
by religion and				2001	1992-01
sex	1971	1962-71		2002	1993-02
	1973	1965-73[vi]		2003	1994-03
	1979	1970-79[vi]		2004	1995-04
	1983	1974-83		2005	1996-05
	1988	1980-88[vi]		2006	1997-06
	1993	1985-93			
by school			percent	1948	Latest
attendance,				1952	1900-51
age and sex	1971	1962-71		1955	1945-54
	1973	1965-73[vi]		1960	1920-60
	1979	1970-79[vi]		1962	1955-62
	1983	1974-83		1970	1950-70
	1988	1980-88[vi]		1971	1962-71
	1993	1985-93		1973	1965-73
by sex:				1974	1966-74
				1975	1967-75
numbers	1948	Latest		1976	1967-76
	1952	1900-51		1977	1968-77
	1955	1945-54		1978	1969-78
	1960	1920-60		1979	1970-79
	1962	1955-62		1980	1971-80
	1963	1955-63		1981	1972-81
	1964	1955-64[vi]		1982	1973-82
	1967	Latest		1983	1974-83
	1970	1950-70		1984	1975-84
	1971	1962-71		1985	1976-85
	1972	Latest		1986	1977-86
	1973	1965-73		1987	1978-87
	1974	1966-74		1988	1979-88
	1975	1967-75			
	1976	1967-76			

Subject-matter	Year of issue	Time coverage
	1955	1945-54
	1962	1955-62
	1964	1955-64[vi]
	1971	1962-71
	1973	1965-73[vi]
	1979	1970-79[vi]
	1983	1974-83
	1988	1980-88[vi]
	1993	1985-93
Household characteristics	1955	1945-54
	1962	1955-62
	1963	1955-63[vi]
	1971	1962-71
	1973	1965-73[vi]
	1976	1966-75
	1983	1974-83
	1987	1975-86
	1995	1985-95
Personal characteristics	1955	1945-54
	1962	1955-62
	1971	1962-71
	1973	1965-73[vi]
	1979	1970-79[vi]
	1983	1974-83

Subject-matter	Year of issue	Time coverage
	1988	1980-88[vi]
	1993	1985-93
-Population trends	1960	1920-60
	1970	1950-70

U

Urban/rural births
(see: Births)

Urban/rural deaths
(see: Deaths)

Urban/rural infant deaths
(see: Infant deaths)

Urban/rural population
(see: Population:
urban/rural residence)

**Urban/rural population
by average size of
households** (see:
Households)

APPENDIX

Special text of each Demographic Yearbook:

Divorce:

'Uses of Marriage and Divorce Statistics', 1958.

Marriage:

'Uses of Marriage and Divorce Statistics', 1958.

Households:

'Concepts and definitions of households, householder and institutional population', 1987.

Migration:

'Statistics of International Migration', 1977.

Mortality:

'Recent Mortality Trends', 1951.
'Development of Statistics of Causes of Death', 1951.
'Factors in Declining Mortality', 1957.
'Notes on Methods of Evaluating the Reliability of Conventional Mortality Statistics', 1961.
'Recent Trends of Mortality', 1966.
'Mortality Trends among Elderly Persons', 1991PA[vii].

Natality:

'Graphic Presentation of Trends in Fertility', 1959.
'Recent Trends in Birth Rates', 1965.
'Recent Changes in World Fertility', 1969.

Population

'World Population Trends, 1920-1949', 1949/50.
'Urban Trends and Characteristics', 1952.
'Background to the1950 Censuses of Population', 1955.
'The World Demographic Situation', 1956.
'How Well Do We Know the Present Size and Trend of the World's Population?', 1960.
'Notes on Availability of National Population Census Data and Methods of Estimating their Reliability', 1962.
'Availability and Adequacy of Selected Data Obtained from Population Censuses Taken 1955-1963', 1963.
'Availability of Selected Population Census Statistics: 1955-1964', 1964.
'Statistical Concepts and Definitions of Urban and Rural Population', 1967.
'Statistical Concepts and Definitions of Household', 1968.
'How Well Do We Know the Present Size and Trend of the World's Population?', 1970.
'United Nations Recommendations on Topics to be Investigated in a Population Census
Compared with Country Practice in National Censuses taken 1965-1971', 1971.
'Statistical Definitions of Urban Population and their Use in Applied Demography', 1972.
'Dates of National Population and Housing Census carried out during the decade1965-1974', 1974.
'Dates of National Population and/or Housing Censuses taken or anticipated during the decade 1975-1984', 1979.
'Dates of National Population and/or Housing Censuses taken during the decade1965-1974 and taken or anticipated during the decade 1975-1984', 1983.
'Dates of National Population and/or Housing Censuses taken during the decade1975-1984 and taken or anticipated during the decade 1985-1994', 1988 and 1993.
'Statistics Concerning the Economically Active Population: An Overview', 1984.

'Disability', 1991PA[vii].
'Population Ageing', 1991PA[vii].
'Special Needs for the Study of Population Ageing and Elderly Persons', 1991PA[vii].

General Notes

This cumulative index covers the contents of each of the 52 issues of the Demographic Yearbook. 'Year of issue' stands for the particular issue in which the indicated subject-matter appears. Unless otherwise specified, 'Time coverage' designates the years for which annual statistics are shown in the Demographic Yearbook referred to in 'Year of issue' column. 'Latest' or '2-Latest' indicates that data are for latest available year(s) only.

---

[i] Only titles not available for preceding bibliography.

[ii] Historical Supplement to the 30th DYB published in a separate volume in year 1979.

[iii] Historical Supplement to the 49th DYB published in a separate volume (CD-ROM) in year 2000.

[iv] Supplement to the 51st DYB focusing on natality published in a separate volume (CD-ROM) in year 2002.

[v] Five-year average rates.

[vi] Only data not available for preceding issue.

[vii] Population ageing published in separate volume.

Index
Index historique (suite)
(Voir notes à la fin de l'index)

Index
Index historique (suite)
(Voir notes à la fin de l'index)

Index
Index historique (suite)
(Voir notes à la fin de l'index)

Index
Index historique (suite)
(Voir notes à la fin de l'index)

Sujet	Année de l'édition	Période considérée	Sujet	Année de l'édition	Période considérée
	1961	1945-59 [vi]		1987-1992	1985-90
		1952-61		1993-1997	1990-95
	1962	1945-54 [vi]		1998-2000	1995-00
		1952-62		2001-2005	2000-05
	1963	1945-59 [vi]		2006	2005-10
		1954-63	pour les grandes		
	1964	1960-64	régions (continentales)	1964-1977	Dernière
	1965	1961-65		1978-1979	1970-75
	1966	1920-64 [vi]		1980-1983	1975-80
		1951-66		1984-1986	1980-85
	1967	1963-67		1987-1992	1985-90
	1968	1964-68		1993-1997	1990-95
	1969	1965-69		1998-2000	1995-00
	1970	1966-70		2001-2005	2000-05
	1971	1967-71		2006	2005-10
	1972	1968-72			
	1973	1969-73	pour les régions	1949/50	1947
	1974	1965-74		1956-1977	Dernière
	1975	1971-75		1978-1979	1970-75
	1976	1972-76		1980-1983	1975-80
	1977	1973-77		1984-1986	1980-85
	1978	1974-78		1987-1992	1985-90
	1978SR [i]	1948-78		1993-1997	1990-95
	1979	1975-79		1998-2000	1995-00
	1980	1971-80		2001-2005	2000-05
	1981	1977-81		2006	2005-10
	1982	1978-82			
	1983	1979-83	pour l'ensemble du		
	1984	1980-84	monde	1949/50	1947
	1985	1976-85		1956-1977	Dernière
	1986	1982-86		1978-1979	1970-75
	1987	1983-87		1980-1983	1975-80
	1988	1984-88		1984-1986	1980-85
	1989	1985-89		1987-1992	1985-90
	1990	1986-90		1993-1997	1990-95
	1991	1987-91		1998-2000	1995-00
	1992	1983-92		2001-2005	2000-05
	1993	1989-93		2006	2005-10
	1994	1990-94			
	1995	1991-95	-selon l'âge et le sexe	1948	1935-47
	1996	1987-96		1949/50	1936-49
	1997	1993-97		1951	1936-50
	1997SR [ii]	1948-97		1952	1936-51
	1998	1994-98		1953	1940-52
	1999	1995-99		1954	1946-53
	2000	1996-00		1955-1956	Dernière
	2001	1997-01		1957	1948-56
	2002	1998-02		1961	1952-60
	2003	1999-03		1966	1950-65
	2004	2000-04		1967	Dernière
	2005	2001-05		1972	Dernière
	2006	2002-06		1974	1965-73
				1975-1978	Dernière
-d'enfants de moins d'un an				1978SR [i]	1948-77
(voir: Mortalités infantile)				1979	Dernière
				1980	1971-79
-estimatifs:				1981-1984	Dernière
pour les continents	1949/50	1947		1985	1976-84
	1956-1977	Dernière		1986-1991	Dernière
	1978-1979	1970-75		1991 VP [v]	1950-90
	1980-1983	1975-80		1992	1983-92
	1984-1986	1980-85		1993-1995	Dernière

Index
Index historique (suite)
(Voir notes à la fin de l'index)

Index
Index historique (suite)
(Voir notes à la fin de l'index)

Index
Index historique (suite)
(Voir notes à la fin de l'index)

Index
Index historique (suite)
(Voir notes à la fin de l'index)

Index
Index historique (suite)
(Voir notes à la fin de l'index)

Index
Index historique (suite)
(Voir notes à la fin de l'index)

Index
Index historique (suite)
(Voir notes à la fin de l'index)

Index
Index historique (suite)
(Voir notes à la fin de l'index)

Index
Index historique (suite)
(Voir notes à la fin de l'index)

Index
Index historique (suite)
(Voir notes à la fin de l'index)

Index
Index historique (suite)
(Voir notes à la fin de l'index)

Index
Index historique (suite)
(Voir notes à la fin de l'index)

Index
Index historique (suite)
(Voir notes à la fin de l'index)

Index
Index historique (suite)
(Voir notes à la fin de l'index)

Index
Index historique (suite)
(Voir notes à la fin de l'index)

Sujet	Année de l'édition	Période considérée	Sujet	Année de l'édition	Période considérée
	1978	1974-78		1998-2000	1995-00
	1978SR [i]	1948-78		2001-2005	2000-05
	1979	1975-79		2006	2005-10
	1980	1971-80			
	1981	1977-81	pour l'ensemble du monde		
	1982	1978-82		1949/50	1947
	1983	1979-83		1956-1977	Dernière
	1984	1980-84		1978-1979	1970-75
	1985	1976-85		1980-1983	1975-80
	1986	1982-86		1984-1986	1980-85
	1987	1983-87		1987-1992	1985-90
	1988	1984-88		1993-1997	1990-95
	1989	1985-89		1998-2000	1995-00
	1990	1986-90		2001-2005	2000-05
	1991	1987-91		2006	2005-10
	1992	1983-92			
	1993	1989-93	-selon l'âge et le sexe	1948	1935-47
	1994	1990-94		1949/50	1936-49
	1995	1991-95		1951	1936-50
	1996	1987-96		1952	1936-51
	1997	1993-97		1953	1940-52
	1997SR [ii]	1948-96		1954	1946-53
	1998	1994-98		1955-1956	Dernière
	1999	1995-99		1957	1948-1956
	2000	1996-00		1961	1952-60
	2001	1997-01		1966	1950-65
	2002	1998-02		1978SR [i]	1948-77
	2003	1999-03		1998-2006	Dernière
	2004	2000-04	-selon l'âge et le sexe et la résidence (urbaine/rurale)	1967	Dernière
	2005	2001-05		1972	Dernière
	2006	2002-06		1974	1965-73
-estimatifs:				1975-1978	Dernière
pour les continents	1949/50	1947		1979	Dernière
	1956-1977	Dernière		1980	1971-79
	1978-1979	1970-75		1981-1984	Dernière
	1980-1983	1975-80		1985	1976-84
	1984-1986	1980-85		1986-1991	Dernière
	1987-1992	1985-90		1991 VP [v]	1950-90
	1993-1997	1990-95		1992	1983-92
	1998-2000	1995-00		1993-1995	Dernière
	2001-2005	2000-05		1996	1987-95
	2006	2005-10		1997	Dernière
pour les grandes régions (continentales)				1997SR. [ii]	1948-96
	1964-1977	Dernière		1998-2006	Dernière
	1978-1970	1970-75	-selon la cause	1951	1947-49
	1980-1983	1975-80		1952	1947-51 [iii]
	1984-1986	1980-85		1953	1947-52
	1987-1992	1985-90		1954	1945-53
	1993-1997	1990-95		1955-1956	Dernière
	1998-2000	1995-00		1957	1952-56
	2001-2005	2000-05		1958-1960	Dernière
	2006	2005-10		1961	1955-60
				1962-1965	Dernière
pour les régions	1949/50	1947		1966	1960-65
	1956-1977	Dernière		1967-1973	Dernière
	1978-1979	1970-75		1974	1965-73
	1980-1983	1975-80		1975-1979	Dernière
	1984-1986	1980-85		1980	1971-79
	1987-1992	1985-90		1981-1984	Dernière
	1993-1997	1990-95		1985	1976-84
				1986-1991	Dernière

Index
Index historique (suite)
(Voir notes à la fin de l'index)

Index
Index historique (suite)
(Voir notes à la fin de l'index)

Index
Index historique (suite)
(Voir notes à la fin de l'index)

Index
Index historique (suite)
(Voir notes à la fin de l'index)

Sujet	Année de l'édition	Période considérée
	1975	1966-74
	1981	1972-80
	1986	1977-85
	1999CD [vii]	1990-98
-selon l'âge de la mère	1948	1936-47
	1949/50	1936-49
	1954	1936-53
	1955-1956	Dernière
	1958	Dernière
	1959	1949-58
	1960-1964	Dernière
	1965	1955-64
	1966-1968	Dernière
	1969	1963-68
	1970-1974	Dernière
	1975	1966-74
	1976-1978	Dernière
	1978SR [i]	1948-77
	1979-1980	Dernière
	1981	1972-80
	1982-1985	Dernière
	1986	1977-85
	1987-1991	Dernière
	1992	1983-92
	1993-1997	Dernièro
	1997SR [ii]	1948-96'
	1998-1999	Dernière
	1999CD [vii]	1990-98
	2000-2006	Dernière
-selon l'âge de la mère et le rang de naissance	1949/50	1936-47
	1954	Dernière
	1959	1949-58
	1965	1955-64
	1969	1963-68
	1975	1966-74
	1981	1972-80
	1986	1977-85
	1999CD [vii]	1990-98
-selon l'âge de la mère et la résidence (urbaine/rurale) (voir: selon la résidence (urbaine/rurale), ci-dessous)		
-selon l'âge de la mère et le sexe	1965-1968	Dernière
	1969	1963-68
	1970-1974	Dernière
	1975	1966-74
	1976-1978	Dernière
	1978SR [i]	1948-77
	1979-1980	Dernière
	1981	1972-80
	1982-1985	Dernière
	1986	1977-85
	1987-1991	Dernière
	1992	1983-92
	1993-1997	Dernière
	1997SR [ii]	1948-96
	1998-1999	Dernière

Sujet	Année de l'édition	Période considérée
	1999CD [vii]	1990-98
	2000-2006	Dernière
-selon l'âge du père	1949/50	1942-49
	1954	1936-53
	1959	1949-58
	1965	1955-64
	1969	1963-68
	1975	1966-74
	1981	1972-80
	1986	1977-85
	1999CD [vii]	1990-98
-selon la durée de gestation	1975	Dernière
	1981	1972-80
	1986	1977-85
	1999CD [vii]	1990-98
-selon la durée du mariage (voir: légitimes selon la durée du mariage)		
-selon le mois	2002	1980-02
-selon la profession du père	1965	Dernière
	1969	Dernière
-selon la résidence (urbaine/rurale)	1965	Dernière
	1967	Dernière
	1968	1964-68
	1969	1964-68
	1970	1966-70
	1971	1967-71
	1972	1968-72
	1973	1969-73
	1974	1970-74
	1975	1956-75
	1976	1972-76
	1977	1973-77
	1978	1974-78
	1979	1975-79
	1980	1976-80
	1981	1962-81
	1982	1978-82
	1983	1979-83
	1984	1980-84
	1985	1981-85
	1986	1967-86
	1987	1983-87
	1988	1984-88
	1989	1985-89
	1990	1986-90
	1991	1987-91
	1992	1983-92
	1993	1989-93
	1994	1990-94
	1995	1991-95
	1996	1992-96
	1997	1993-97
	1998	1994-98
	1999	1995-99
	1999CD [vii]	1980-99
	2000	1996-00

Index
Index historique (suite)
(Voir notes à la fin de l'index)

Index
Index historique (suite)
(Voir notes à la fin de l'index)

Sujet	Année de l'édition	Période considérée	Sujet	Année de l'édition	Période considérée
	1971	1967-71		1956-1977	Dernière
	1972	1968-72		1978-1979	1970-75
	1973	1969-73		1980-1983	1975-80
	1974	1970-74		1984-1986	1980-85
	1975	1956-75		1987-1992	1985-90
	1976	1972-76		1993-1997	1990-95
	1977	1973-77		1998-2000	1995-00
	1978	1974-78		2001-2005	2000-05
	1978SR [i]	1948-78		2006	2005-10
	1979	1975-79			
	1980	1976-80	pour le monde	1949/50	1947
	1981	1962-81		1956-1977	Dernière
	1982	1978-82		1978-1979	1970-75
	1983	1979-83		1980-1983	1975-80
	1984	1980-84		1984-1986	1980-85
	1985	1981-85		1987-1992	1985-90
	1986	1967-86		1993-1997	1990-95
	1987	1983-87		1998-2000	1995-00
	1988	1984-88		2001-2005	2000-05
	1989	1985-89		2006	2005-10
	1990	1986-90			
	1991	1987-91	-illégitimes (voir également légitimes)	1959	1949-58
	1992	1983-92	-légitimes	1954	1936-53
	1993	1989-93		1959	1949-58
	1994	1990-94		1965	Dernière
	1995	1991-95		1969	Dernière
	1996	1992-96		1975	Dernière
	1997	1993-97		1981	Dernière
	1997SR [ii]	1948-97		1986	Dernière
	1998	1994-98	-légitimes selon l'âge de la mère	1954	1936-53
	1999	1995-99		1959	1949-58
	1999CD [vii]	1985-99		1965	Dernière
	2000	1996-00		1969	Dernière
	2001	1997-01		1975	Dernière
	2002	1998-02		1981	Dernière
	2003	1999-03		1986	Dernière
	2004	2000-04	-légitimes selon l'âge du père	1959	1949-58
	2005	2001-05		1965	Dernière
	2006	2002-06		1969	Dernière
-estimatifs:				1975	Dernière
pour les continents	1949/50	1947		1981	Dernière
	1956-1977	Dernière		1986	Dernière
	1978-1979	1970-75	-légitimes selon la durée du mariage	1959	1950-57
	1980-1986	1975-80		1965	Dernière
	1987-1992	1985-90		1969	Dernière
	1993-1997	1990-95		1975	Dernière
	1998-2000	1995-00	-selon l'âge de la mère	1948	1936-47
	2001-2005	2000-05		1949/50	1936-49
	2006	2005-10		1951	1936-50
pour les grandes régions	1964-1977	Dernière		1952	1936-50
	1978-1979	1970-75		1953	1936-52
	1980-1983	1975-80		1954	1936-53
	1984-1986	1980-85		1955-1958	Dernière
	1987-1992	1985-90		1959	1949-58
	1993-1997	1990-95		1965	1955-64
	1998-2000	1995-00		1969	1963-68
	2001-2005	2000-05		1975	1966-74
	2006	2005-10		1976-1978	Dernière
pour les régions	1949/50	1947			

Index
Index historique (suite)
(Voir notes à la fin de l'index)

Index
Index historique (suite)
(Voir notes à la fin de l'index)

Index
Index historique (suite)
(Voir notes à la fin de l'index)

Index
Index historique (suite)
(Voir notes à la fin de l'index)

Index
Index historique (suite)
(Voir notes à la fin de l'index)

Index
Index historique (suite)
(Voir notes à la fin de l'index)

Index
Index historique (suite)
(Voir notes à la fin de l'index)

Sujet	Année de l'édition	Période considérée	Sujet	Année de l'édition	Période considérée
	1975	1966-75		1967	1930-67
	1976	1967-76		1968	1930-68
	1977	1968-77		1969	1930-69
	1978	1969-78		1970	1950-70
	1978SR [i]	1948-78		1971	1950-71
	1979	1970-79		1972	1950-72
	1980	1971-80		1973	1950-73
	1981	1972-81		1974	1950-74
	1982	1973-82		1975	1950-75
	1983	1974-83		1976	1950-76
	1984	1975-84		1977	1950-77
	1985	1976-85		1978	1950-78
	1986	1977-86		1979	1950-79
	1987	1978-87		1980	1950-80
	1988	1979-88		1981	1950-81
	1989	1980-89		1982	1950-82
	1990	1981-90		1983	1950-83
	1991	1982-91		1984	1950-84
	1992	1983-92		1985	1950-85
	1993	1984-93		1986	1950-86
	1994	1985-94		1987	1950-87
	1995	1986-95		1988	1950-88
	1996	1987-96		1989	1950-89
	1997	1988-97		1990	1950-90
	1997SR [ii]	1948-97		1991	1950-91
	1998	1989-98		1992	1950-92
	1999	1990-99		1993	1950-93
	2000	1991-00		1994	1950-94
	2001	1992-01		1995	1950-95
	2002	1993-02		1996	1950-96
	2003	1994-03		1997	1950-97
	2004	1995-04		1998-2000	1950-00
	2005	1996-05		2001	1950-01
	2006	1997-06		2002	1950-02
				2003	1950-03
-des principales divisions administratives	1952	Dernière		2004	1950-04
	1955	1945-54		2005	1950-05
	1962	1955-62		2006	1950-06
	1963	1955-63 [iii]	-des villes:		
	1971	1962-71	capitale	1952	Dernière
	1973	1965-73 [iii]		1955	1945-54
	1979	1970-79 [iii]		1957	Dernière
	1983	1974-83		1960	1939-61
	1988	1980-88 [iii]		1962	1955-62
	1993	1985-93		1963	1955-63
-des régions	1949/50	1920-49		1964-1969	Dernière
	1952	1920-51		1970	1950-70
	1953	1920-52		1971	1962-71
	1954	1920-53		1972	Dernière
	1955	1920-54		1973	1965-73
	1956	1920-55		1974-2006	Dernière
	1957	1920-56			
	1958	1920-57	de 100 000 habitants et plus	1952	Dernière
	1959	1920-58		1955	1945-54
	1960	1920-59		1957	Dernière
	1961	1920-60		1960	1939-61
	1962	1920-61		1962	1955-62
	1963	1930-62		1963	1955-63
	1964	1930-63		1964-1969	Dernière
	1965	1930-65		1970	1950-70
	1966	1930-66			

Index
Index historique (suite)
(Voir notes à la fin de l'index)

Index
Index historique (suite)
(Voir notes à la fin de l'index)

Index
Index historique (suite)
(Voir notes à la fin de l'index)

Index
Index historique (suite)
(Voir notes à la fin de l'index)

Index
Index historique (suite)
(Voir notes à la fin de l'index)

Index
Index historique (suite)
(Voir notes à la fin de l'index)

Index
Index historique (suite)
(Voir notes à la fin de l'index)

T

Tables de mortalité (voir: Mortalité, tables de)

Taux (voir: Accroissement intercensitaire de la population; Accroissement naturel; Alphabétisme; Analphabétisme; Annulation; Divortialité; Fécondité Intercensitaire; Mortalité Infantile, Mortalité maternelle; Mortalité néonatale; Mortalité post-néonatale; Mortalité, tables de; Mortalité; Natalité; Nuptialité; Reproduction; taux bruts et nets de)

Taux bruts de reproduction (voir: Reproduction)

Taux nets de reproduction (voir: Reproduction)

Texte spécial (voir liste détaillée dans l'Appendice de cet index)

Index
Index historique (suite)
(Voir notes à la fin de l'index)

Sujet	Année de l'édition	Période considérée	Sujet	Année de l'édition	Période considérée
U			**Urbaine/rurale(naissances)** (voir: Naissances)		
Urbaine/rurale (décès) (voir: Décès)			**Urbaine/rurale(population)** (voir: Population selon la résidence (urbaine/rurale))		
Urbaine/rurale (ménages: dimension moyenne des) (voir: Ménages)			**V**		
Urbaine/rurale (mortalité infantile) (voir: Mortalité infantile)			**Vieillissement** (voir: Population)		
			Villes (voir: Population)		

Index
Index historique (suite)
(Voir notes à la fin de l'index)

APPENDICE

Texte spécial de chaque Annuaire démographique

Divorce:

"Application des statistiques de la nuptialité et de la divortialité", 1958.

Mariage:

"Application des statistiques de la nuptialité et de la divortialité", 1958.

Ménages:

"Concepts et définitions des ménages, du chef de ménage et de la population des collectivités", 1987.

Migration:

"'Statistiques des migrations internationales",1977.

Mortalité:

"Tendances récentes de la mortalité", 1951.
"Développement des statistiques des causes de décès",1951.
"Les facteurs du fléchissement de la mortalité",1957.
"Notes sur les méthodes d'évaluation de la fiabilité des statistiques classiques de la mortalité",1961.
"Mortalité: Tendances récentes",1966.
"Tendances de la mortalité chez les personnes âgées",1991VP [v].

Natalité:

"Présentation graphiques des tendances de la fécondité",1959.

"Taux de natalité: Tendances récentes",1965.

Population:

"Tendances démo-graphiques mondiales,1920-1949",1949/50.
"Mouvements d'urbanisation et ses caractéristiques",1952.
"Les recensements de population de 1950",1955.
"Situation démographique mondiale",1956.
"Ce que nous savons de l'état et de l'évolution de la population mondiale",1960.
"Notes sur les statistiques disponibles des recensements nationaux de population et méthodes d'évaluation de leur exactitude",1962.
"Disponibilité et qualité de certaines données statistiques fondées sur les recensements de population effectués entre 1955 et 1963",1963.
"Disponibilité de certaines statistiques fondées sur les recensements de population: 1955-1964",1964.

"Définitions et concepts statistiques de la population urbaine et de la population rurale",1967.
"Application des statistiques de la nuptialité et de la divortialité",1958.
"Ce que nous savons de l'état et de l'évolution de la population mondiale",1970.
"Recommandations de l'Organisation des Nations Unies quant aux sujets sur lesquels doit porter un recensement de population, en regard de la pratique adoptée par les différents pays dans les recensements nationaux effectués de 1965 à 1971",1971.
"Les définitions statistiques de la population urbaine et leurs usages en démographie appliquée",1972.

"Evolution récente de la fécondité dans le monde",1969.
"Dates des recensements nationaux de la population et de l'habitation effectués au cours de la décennie

Index
Index historique (suite)
(Voir notes à la fin de l'index)

1965-1974", 1974.

"Dates des recensements nationaux de la population et de l'habitation effectués ou prévus, au cours de la décennie 1975-1984",1979.

"Dates des recensements nationaux de la population et/ou de l'habitation effectués au cours de la décennie 1965-1974 et effectués ou prévus au cours de la décennie1975-1984",1983.

"Définitions et concepts statistiques du ménage",1968.

"Dates des recensements nationaux de la population et/ou de l'habitation effectués au cours de la décennie 1975-1984 et effectués ou prévus au cours de la décennie1985-1994", 1988, 1993.

"Statistiques concernant la population active: un aperçu",1984.

"'Etude du vieillissement et de la situation des personnes âgées: Besoins particuliers",1991VP [v].

"Les incapacités", 1991VP [v].

"Le vieillissement", 1991VP [v].

Notes générales

Cet index alphabétique donne la liste des sujets traités dans chacune de 51 éditions de l'Annuaire démographique. La colonne "Année de l'édition" indique l'édition spécifique dans laquelle le sujet a été traité. Sauf indication contraire, la colonne "Période considérée" désigne les années pour lesquelles les statistiques annuelles apparaissant dans l'Annuaire démographique sont indiquées sous la colonne "Année de l'édition". La rubrique "Dernière" ou " 2-Dernières" indique que les données représentent la ou les dernières années disponibles seulement.

---

[i] Le Supplément rétrospectif du 30ème Annuaire Démographique fait l'objet d'un tirage spécial publié en 1979.

[ii] Le Supplément rétrospectif du 49ème Annuaire Démographique fait l'objet d'un tirage spécial (CD-ROM) publié en 2000

[iii] Données non disponibles dans l'édition précédente seulement.

[iv] Titres non disponibles dans la bibliographie précédente seulement.

[v] Taux moyens pour 5 ans.

[vi] Vieillissement de la population.

[vii] Le Supplément du 51 Annuaire Démographique, ayant comme suject la natalité, fait l'objet d'un tirage spécial (CD-ROM) publié en 2002.